D1648936

TO

BY

ON

BY DAY the LORD directs his love,
at night his song is with me—
a prayer to the God of my life.

PSALM 42:8

THE TWO-YEAR

DAILY
READING & PRAYER
BIBLE

New International Version

Zondervan Publishing House
Grand Rapids, Michigan 49530, U.S.A.

Library of Congress Catalog Card Number 97-61396
Published by Zondervan Publishing House
Grand Rapids, Michigan 49530, U.S.A.
http://www.zondervan.com

Printed in the United States of America

98 99 00 01 02 03 04 9 8 7 6 5 4 3 2

RRD

You will be pleased to know that a portion of the purchase price of your new NIV Bible has been provided to International Bible Society to help spread the gospel of Jesus Christ around the world!

Table of Contents

Preface to the NIV

THE NEW INTERNATIONAL VERSION is a completely new translation of the Holy Bible made by over a hundred scholars working directly from the best available Hebrew, Aramaic and Greek texts. It had its beginning in 1965 when, after several years of exploratory study by committees from the Christian Reformed Church and the National Association of Evangelicals, a group of scholars met at Palos Heights, Illinois, and concurred in the need for a new translation of the Bible in contemporary English. This group, though not made up of official church representatives, was transdenominational. Its conclusion was endorsed by a large number of leaders from many denominations who met in Chicago in 1966.

Responsibility for the new version was delegated by the Palos Heights group to a self-governing body of fifteen, the Committee on Bible Translation, composed for the most part of biblical scholars from colleges, universities and seminaries. In 1967 the New York Bible Society (now the International Bible Society) generously undertook the financial sponsorship of the project—a sponsorship that made it possible to enlist the help of many distinguished scholars. The fact that participants from the United States, Great Britain, Canada, Australia and New Zealand worked together gave the project its international scope. That they were from many denominations—including Anglican, Assemblies of God, Baptist, Brethren, Christian Reformed, Church of Christ, Evangelical Free, Lutheran, Mennonite, Methodist, Nazarene, Presbyterian, Wesleyan and other churches—helped to safeguard the translation from sectarian bias.

How it was made helps to give the New International Version its distinctiveness. The translation of each book was assigned to a team of scholars. Next, one of the Intermediate Editorial Committees revised the initial translation, with constant reference to the Hebrew, Aramaic or Greek. Their work then went to one of the General Editorial Committees, which checked it in detail and made another thorough revision. This revision in turn was carefully reviewed by the Committee on Bible Translation, which made further changes and then released the final version for publication. In this way the entire Bible underwent three revisions, during each of which the translation was examined for its faithfulness to the original languages and for its English style.

All this involved many thousands of hours of research and discussion regarding the meaning of the texts and the precise way of putting them into English. It may well be that no other translation has been made by a more thorough process of review and revision from committee to committee than this one.

From the beginning of the project, the Committee on Bible Translation held to certain goals for the New International Version: that it would be an accurate translation and one that would have clarity and literary quality and so prove suitable for public and private reading, teaching, preaching, memorizing and liturgical use. The Committee also sought to preserve some measure of continuity with the long tradition of translating the Scriptures into English.

In working toward these goals, the translators were united in their commitment to the authority and infallibility of the Bible as God's Word in written form. They believe that it contains the divine answer to the deepest needs of humanity, that it sheds unique light on our path in a dark world, and that it sets forth the way to our eternal well-being.

The first concern of the translators has been the accuracy of the translation and its fidelity to the thought of the biblical writers. They have weighed the significance of the lexical and grammatical details of the Hebrew, Aramaic and Greek texts. At the same time, they have striven for more than a word-for-word translation. Because thought patterns and syntax differ from language to language, faithful communication of the meaning of the writers of the Bible demands frequent modifications in sentence structure and constant regard for the contextual meanings of words.

A sensitive feeling for style does not always accompany scholarship. Accordingly the Committee on Bible Translation submitted the developing version to a number of stylistic consultants. Two of them read every book of both Old and New Testaments twice—once before and once after the last major revision—and made invaluable suggestions. Samples of the translation were tested for clarity and ease of reading by various kinds of people—young and old, highly educated and less well educated, ministers and laymen.

Concern for clear and natural English—that the New International Version should be idiomatic but not idiosyncratic, contemporary but not dated—motivated the translators and consultants. At the same time, they tried to reflect the differing styles of the biblical writers. In view of the international use of English, the translators sought to avoid obvious Americanisms on the one hand and obvious Anglicisms on the other. A British edition reflects the comparatively few differences of significant idiom and of spelling.

As for the traditional pronouns "thou," "thee" and "thine" in reference to the Deity, the translators judged that to use these archaisms (along with the old verb forms such as "doest," "wouldest" and "hadst") would violate accuracy in translation. Neither Hebrew, Aramaic nor Greek uses special pronouns for the persons of the Godhead. A present-day translation is not enhanced by forms that in the time of the King James Version were used in everyday speech, whether referring to God or man.

For the Old Testament the standard Hebrew text, the Masoretic Text as published in the latest editions of *Biblia Hebraica,* was used throughout. The Dead Sea Scrolls contain material bearing on an earlier stage of the Hebrew text. They were consulted, as were the Samaritan Pentateuch and the ancient scribal traditions relating to textual changes. Sometimes a variant Hebrew reading in the margin of the Masoretic Text was followed instead of the text itself. Such instances, being variants within the Masoretic tradition, are not specified by footnotes. In rare cases, words in the consonantal text were divided differently from the way they appear in the Masoretic Text. Footnotes indicate this. The translators also consulted the more important early versions—the Septuagint; Aquila, Symmachus and Theodotion; the Vulgate; the Syriac Peshitta; the Targums; and for the Psalms the *Juxta Hebraica* of Jerome. Readings from these versions were occasionally followed where the Masoretic Text seemed doubtful and where accepted principles of textual criticism showed that one or more of these textual witnesses appeared to provide the correct reading. Such instances are footnoted. Sometimes vowel letters and vowel signs did not, in the judgment of the translators, represent the correct vowels for the original consonantal text. Accordingly some words were read with a different set of vowels. These instances are usually not indicated by footnotes.

The Greek text used in translating the New Testament was an eclectic one. No other piece of ancient literature has such an abundance of manuscript witnesses as does the New Testament. Where existing manuscripts differ, the translators made their choice of readings according to accepted principles of New Testament textual criticism. Footnotes call attention to places where there was uncertainty about what the original text was. The best current printed texts of the Greek New Testament were used.

There is a sense in which the work of translation is never wholly finished. This applies to all great literature and uniquely so to the Bible. In 1973 the New Testament in the New International Version was published. Since then, suggestions for corrections and revisions have been received from various sources. The Committee on Bible Translation carefully considered the suggestions and adopted a number of them. These were incorporated in the first printing of the entire Bible in 1978. Additional revisions were made by the Committee on Bible Translation in 1983 and appear in printings after that date.

As in other ancient documents, the precise meaning of the biblical texts is sometimes uncertain. This is more often the case with the Hebrew and Aramaic texts than with the Greek text. Although archaeological and linguistic discoveries in this century aid in understanding difficult passages, some uncertainties remain. The more significant of these have been called to the reader's attention in the footnotes.

In regard to the divine name *YHWH,* commonly referred to as the *Tetragrammaton,* the translators adopted the device used in most English versions of rendering that name as "LORD" in capital letters to distinguish it from *Adonai,* another Hebrew word rendered "Lord," for which small letters are used. Wherever the two names stand together in the Old Testament as a compound name of God, they are rendered "Sovereign LORD."

Because for most readers today the phrases "the LORD of hosts" and "God of hosts" have little meaning, this version renders them "the LORD Almighty" and "God Almighty." These renderings convey the sense of the Hebrew, namely, "he who is sovereign over all the 'hosts' (powers) in heaven and on earth, especially over the 'hosts' (armies) of Israel." For readers unacquainted with Hebrew this does not make clear the distinction between *Sabaoth* ("hosts" or "Almighty") and *Shaddai* (which can also be translated "Almighty"), but the latter occurs infrequently and is always footnoted. When *Adonai* and *YHWH Sabaoth* occur together, they are rendered "the Lord, the LORD Almighty."

As for other proper nouns, the familiar spellings of the King James Version are generally retained. Names traditionally spelled with "ch," except where it is final, are usually spelled in this translation with "k" or "c," since the biblical languages do not have the sound that "ch" frequently indicates in English—for example, in *chant.* For well-known names such as Zechariah, however, the traditional spelling has been retained. Variation in the spelling of names in the original languages has usually not been indicated. Where a person or place has two or more different names in the Hebrew, Aramaic or Greek texts, the more familiar one has generally been used, with footnotes where needed.

To achieve clarity the translators sometimes supplied words not in the original texts but required by the context. If there was uncertainty about such material, it is enclosed in brackets. Also for the sake of clarity or style, nouns, including some proper nouns, are sometimes substituted for pronouns, and vice versa. And though the Hebrew writers often shifted back and forth between first, second and third personal pronouns without change of antecedent, this translation often makes them uniform, in accordance with English style and without the use of footnotes.

Poetical passages are printed as poetry, that is, with indentation of lines and with separate stanzas. These are generally designed to reflect the structure of Hebrew poetry. This poetry is normally characterized by parallelism in balanced lines. Most of the poetry in the Bible is in the Old Testament, and scholars differ regarding the scansion of Hebrew lines. The translators determined the stanza divisions for the most part by analysis of the subject matter. The stanzas therefore serve as poetic paragraphs.

As an aid to the reader, italicized sectional headings are inserted in most of the books. They are not to be regarded as part of the NIV text, are not for oral reading, and are not intended to dictate the interpretation of the sections they head.

The footnotes in this version are of several kinds, most of which need no explanation. Those giving alternative translations begin with "Or" and generally introduce the alternative with the last word preceding it in the text, except when it is a single-word alternative; in poetry quoted in a footnote a slant mark indicates a line division. Footnotes introduced by "Or" do not have uniform significance. In some cases two possible translations were considered to have about equal validity. In other cases, though the translators were convinced that the translation in the text was correct, they judged that another interpretation was possible and of sufficient importance to be represented in a footnote.

In the New Testament, footnotes that refer to uncertainty regarding the original text are introduced by "Some manuscripts" or similar expressions. In the Old Testament, evidence for the reading chosen is given first and evidence for the alternative is added after a semicolon (for example: Septuagint; Hebrew *father*). In such notes the term "Hebrew" refers to the Masoretic Text.

It should be noted that minerals, flora and fauna, architectural details, articles of clothing and jewelry, musical instruments and other articles cannot always be identified with precision. Also measures of capacity in the biblical period are particularly uncertain (see the table of weights and measures following the text).

Like all translations of the Bible, made as they are by imperfect man, this one undoubtedly falls short of its goals. Yet we are grateful to God for the extent to which he has enabled us to realize these goals and for the strength he has given us and our colleagues to complete our task. We offer this version of the Bible to him in whose name and for whose glory it has been made. We pray that it will lead many into a better understanding of the Holy Scriptures and a fuller knowledge of Jesus Christ the incarnate Word, of whom the Scriptures so faithfully testify.

The Committee on Bible Translation

June 1978
(Revised August 1983)

Names of the translators and editors may be secured
from the International Bible Society,
translation sponsors of the New International Version,
1820 Jet Stream Drive, Colorado Springs, Colorado
80921-3696 U.S.A.

Introduction

The Purpose of the *Daily Reading & Prayer Bible*

JUST AS the key to quality relationships with other people is time spent in communication, so the key to a growing relationship with the personal God of heaven and earth is time invested in listening to his Word and speaking to him in prayer. The concept of communicating with God, of speaking directly and openly with him just as we would talk with an intimate friend, is one of the great truths of the spiritual life. As central as these twin disciplines of Scripture and prayer are to our spiritual life, most believers are frustrated by hit-or-miss approaches to both. It is no surprise, then, that most people spend a minimal amount of time in either of these disciplines and fail to develop intimacy with the One for whom they were created. As a result, their time in prayer and the Word can begin to seem shallow or even boring.

The Daily Reading & Prayer Bible is a tool that will guide you through the process of reading Scripture and praying Scripture back to God. It will enable you to think God's thoughts after him and to personalize them in your own thinking and practice. This Bible provides you with a balanced diet of reading and prayer by guiding you each day through both Old and New Testament selections, followed by different types of prayers. Because the prayers in the readings are based on Scripture, you can be assured that they will be pleasing to God. This Bible will encourage you in your walk with God by enhancing the quality and depth of your communication with him.

Most of us want to pray more than we actually do, but we often find that our prayers are sporadic and unsatisfying. One problem with prayer is that it is easy to slip into the extreme of all form and no freedom, or the opposite extreme of all freedom and no form. An extreme form-oriented approach leads to a rote or impersonal practice of prayer, while an extreme freedom focus results in an unbalanced and undisciplined prayer life, which can degenerate into a series of one "gimme" after another. The *Daily Reading & Prayer Bible* was designed to make prayer a more enriching experience by providing both form and freedom in the practice of prayer. The form is Scripture itself, and the freedom is your own thoughts and prayers in response to the truths of Scripture.

The Structure of the *Daily Reading & Prayer Bible*

The *Daily Reading & Prayer Bible* is unique in that it is designed to guide you through the Old Testament every two years and the New Testament each year. Many people find it too difficult to read through the entire Bible every year, but a two-year cycle for the Old Testament is realistic and attainable. On the other hand, reading through the New Testament once each year is reasonably easy to achieve. Thus, this Bible will guide you twice through the New Testament in its 730 days of readings. Another advantage of this design is greater equity between the lengths of the daily Old and New Testament readings.

This Bible provides you with a daily exposure to both the Old Testament and the New Testament.

The daily readings from the Old Testament follow standard canonical order, with these exceptions:

1. Psalm readings appear every seven days. These texts are evenly spaced throughout the Old Testament reading cycle.
2. A chapter of Proverbs appears every three to four weeks throughout the Old Testament portions.
3. The books of 1 and 2 Chronicles have been moved from their usual place after 2 Kings to precede the book of Isaiah. These books furnish a priestly perspective on the history contained in 2 Samuel through 2 Kings, and this move avoids the repetition that would result from the usual Scriptural order. This arrangement also provides the background for the prophetic books, which begin with Isaiah.

The design of the daily New Testament readings distributes the four Gospels through the yearly New Testament cycle for a better mix between gospel and epistle. Matthew is immediately followed by Acts; Mark appears between Romans and 1 Corinthians; Luke appears between Colossians and 1 Thessalonians; and John appears between 2 Peter and 1 John.

The *Daily Reading & Prayer Bible* encourages you to pause and pray after each of these two daily readings. The prayers that appear after each reading are themselves adapted from Scripture; they are designed to lead you through the process of praying Scripture back to God. To create this collection of Biblical prayers and affirmations, I consulted several translations as well as the original language of each passage. The result is essentially my own translation of the passages, which I then adapted into a personalized format so that they could be used in the context of both individual and group prayer. A number of these prayers and affirmations were derived from negative statements and evaluations in the Bible, so I rephrased them into positive statements. In other cases, principles have been derived from the lives of Biblical characters. Each of the prayers and affirmations is followed by a prompt to pause and offer your own thoughts and prayers to the Lord. In this way, there is both form (the Word of the Lord) and freedom (your personal response) in these prayers.

The Scripture prayers after the Old Testament readings are adapted from *Face to Face: Praying the Scriptures for Intimate Worship*. They cycle through seven kinds of prayer followed by the appropriate prompts: Adoration, Confession, Renewal, Petition, Intercession, Affirmation and Thanksgiving.

The prayers after the New Testament readings are adapted from *Face to Face: Praying the Scriptures for Spiritual Growth*. These prayers are in the form of affirmations derived from Scripture. They appear in a cycle of five categories followed by the appropriate prompts: The Attributes of God, The Works of God, My Relationship to God, The Character I Want to Cultivate, and My Relationship to Others. Many of the affirmations are expressed as desires; you will be affirming that these are the things you want to be true of your life. Using this Bible on a regular basis will be a faith-building exercise that will make these affirmations increasingly real in your life.

In addition to the body of the *Daily Reading & Prayer Bible* itself, I have included an additional tool to help you develop a more satisfying prayer life. The set of *Morning Affirmations,* which begins on page xv, is designed to help you renew your mind at the beginning of each day. *Morning Affirmations* will guide you in praying through a Biblical perspective on the fundamental issues of life: Who am I? Where did I come from? Why am I here? Where am I going? As you read and pray through *Morning Affirmations*, you are reviewing God's perspective on your faith, your identity, your purpose and your hope. As with the Scripture prayers after the daily readings in the Bible itself, *Morning Affirmations* is my own translation, adapted and personalized for personal prayer.

How to Use the *Daily Reading & Prayer Bible*

There are two primary approaches to using this Bible. The first is to use it to begin each day with the Lord. In this case, you would go through all four daily elements—Old Testament reading, prayer, New Testament reading, prayer—in the morning. The second approach is to use this Bible both in the morning and in the evening—Old Testament text and prayer in the morning, New Testament text and prayer in the evening. Try both of these approaches and see which works best for you. And although you can tie these daily readings to the calendar, there is no need to do so, particularly if you find yourself falling behind. You can always decide to mark your place with a bookmark and later continue where you left off.

It is essential that you do not merely read the prayers, but actually make them personal. Be sure to use the prayer response prompts following each printed prayer to add your own individual thoughts and prayers to each reading. Because the prayers and affirmations are cyclical, they will assist you in having a balanced diet of prayer every week. While using this Bible, you might even consider starting a journal to record your own thoughts and prayers as they come to mind. You can also use your journal to keep a list of prayers for yourself and others, as well as to note specific answers to prayer.

This Bible has been designed primarily for personal devotional times, but it can also be used profitably with another person or with a group of people. To assist you in personalizing these prayers and affirmations for individual use, they have been put in the singular form whenever possible. When the *Daily Reading & Prayer Bible* is being used by two or more people, simply reword the prayers into plural form as you read them, and pause to pray together rather than individually.

The God of the Bible is infinite, personal and triune. As a communion of three Persons, one of God's purposes in creating us is to display the glory of his being and attributes to intelligent, moral creatures who are capable of responding to him. Our Lord, in summarizing the Law and the Prophets, gave us the essence of this response: "'Love the Lord your God with all your heart and with all your soul and with all your mind.' This is the first and greatest commandment. And the second is like it: 'Love your neighbor as yourself.'" (Matthew 22:37–39).

Another way of summarizing our high and holy calling and purpose as followers of Jesus Christ is this: to love God completely, to love self correctly and to love others compassionately. It is my prayer that as you use this *Daily Reading & Prayer Bible*, you will find yourself growing in your ability to respond to God's boundless love in all of these ways.

Blessings,
Kenneth Boa

Morning Affirmations

SUBMITTING TO GOD

***IN** view of Your mercy, O God, may I present my body as a living sacrifice, holy and pleasing to You, which is my reasonable service. May I not be conformed to the pattern of this world but be transformed by the renewing of my mind, that I may prove that Your will is good and acceptable and perfect. (Romans 12:1–2)*

***I SUBMIT** myself and my life to you, O God.*

ADORATION AND THANKSGIVING

***I WILL** exalt You, my God and King; I will bless Your name for ever and ever. Every day I will bless You, and I will praise Your name for ever and ever. Great are You, Lord, and most worthy of praise; Your greatness is unsearchable. One generation shall praise Your works to another and shall declare Your mighty acts. I will meditate on the glorious splendor of Your majesty and on Your wonderful works. Many shall speak of the might of Your awesome works, and I will proclaim Your great deeds. I will express the memory of Your abundant goodness and joyfully sing of Your righteousness. You, O Lord, are gracious and compassionate, slow to anger, and great in lovingkindness. You are good to all, and Your tender mercies are over all Your works. (Psalm 145:1–9)*

***FOR** who You are and what you have done,*
accept my praise, O Lord.

***BLESSED** are You, O Lord, for You have heard the voice of my prayers. You are my strength and my shield; my heart trusts in You, and I am helped. My heart greatly rejoices, and I will give thanks to You in song. (Psalm 28:6–7)*

***FOR** who You are and for what You have done,*
accept my thanks, O Lord.

EXAMINATION

***SEARCH** me, O God, and know my heart; test me and know my anxious thoughts. See if there is any offensive way in me, and lead me in the way everlasting. (Psalm 139:23–24)*

***HOLY SPIRIT,** search my heart and reveal to me any unconfessed sin you find in me.*

"COME now, let us reason together: Though your sins are like scarlet, they shall be as white as snow; though they are red as crimson, they shall be like wool." (Isaiah 1:18)

LORD, *I thank you for your promise of forgiveness.*

MY IDENTITY IN JESUS CHRIST

I HAVE been crucified with You and it is no longer I who live, but You who live in me; and the life which I now live in the flesh I live by faith in You, the Son of God, who loved me, and delivered Yourself up for me. (Galatians 2:20)

I REJOICE, *Lord Jesus, in the identity I have in You.*

BUT You, O God, demonstrate Your own love for us in that, while we were still sinners, Christ died for us. (Romans 5:8)

I HAVE *forgiveness from the penalty of sin because You died for me.*

IN You, O Christ, I was circumcised with a circumcision made without hands, in the removal of the body of the flesh by Your circumcision, having been buried with You in baptism and raised with You through faith in the working of God, who raised You from the dead. (Colossians 2:11–12)

I HAVE *freedom from the power of sin because I died with You.*

I EAGERLY expect and hope that I will in no way be ashamed, but will have sufficient courage so that now as always You, Jesus Christ, will be exalted in my body, whether by life or by death. For to me, to live in You, Jesus Christ, means everything and to die is gain. (Philippians 1:20–21)

I HAVE *fulfillment for this day because You live in me.*

THANKS be to God, who always leads us in triumph in You and through us spreads everywhere the fragrance of the knowledge of You. (2 Corinthians 2:14)

BY *faith, I will allow You, O Christ, to manifest Your life through me.*

FILLING OF THE SPIRIT

I WAS once darkness, but now I am light in You, O Lord. May I walk as a child of light (for the fruit of the light consists in all goodness and righteousness and truth), learning what is pleasing to You. (Ephesians 5:8) . . . As I walk in You, O Spirit, I will not fulfill the desires of the flesh. For the flesh desires what is contrary to You, and You, Holy Spirit, desire what is contrary to the flesh; for you oppose each other, so that I may not do the things that I wish. But if I am led by You, I am not under the law. (Galatians 5:16) . . . Since I live in You, Spirit, may I also walk in You. (Galatians 5:25)

HOLY SPIRIT, *control me and fill me today.*

FRUIT OF THE SPIRIT

BUT Your fruit, O Holy Spirit, is love, joy, peace, patience, kindness, goodness, faithfulness, gentleness and self-control; against such things there is no law. (Galatians 5:19–23) . . . I want to glorify the Father by bearing much fruit and so prove to be Christ's disciple. (John 15:8)

HOLY SPIRIT, *may your fruit grow in me.*

PURPOSE OF MY LIFE

I WILL seek first Your kingdom and Your righteousness. (Matthew 6:33) . . . I want to love You, O Lord my God, with all my heart, and with all my soul, and with all my mind, and I want to love my neighbor as myself. (Matthew 22:37, 39) . . . Lord, the love we have from You is patient, it is kind, it does not envy; love does not boast, it is not arrogant, it does not behave rudely; it does not seek its own, it is not easily provoked, it keeps no record of wrongs; it does not rejoice in unrighteousness, but rejoices with the truth; it bears all things, believes all things, hopes all things, endures all things. Love never fails. (1 Corinthians 13:4–7)

O LORD, *may your purpose be fulfilled in my life today—to love You completely, to love myself correctly and to love others compassionately.*

I HAVE been called to follow You, Jesus Christ, and to be a fisher of people. (Matthew 4:19) . . . You have called us to go and make disciples of all nations and You are with us always. (Matthew 28:19–20) . . . We will be Your witnesses to the ends of the earth. (Acts 1:8)

I WILL *be a witness to those who do not know You, Jesus, and I will participate in Your Great Commission.*

CIRCUMSTANCES OF THE DAY

O GOD, I know that all things work together for good to those who love You, to those who have been called according to Your purpose. Those You foreknew, You also predestined to be conformed to the likeness of Your Son, that You might be the firstborn among many brothers and sisters. (Romans 8:28–29)

I ACKNOWLEDGE *that You are in control of all things in my life, and that You have my best interests at heart. Because of this I will trust You and commit my day to You, O Lord.*

I WILL trust in You, Lord, with all my heart, and not lean on my own understanding. In all my ways I will acknowledge You, and You will make my paths straight. (Proverbs 3:5–6)

I WILL *obey You today and trust You for all my needs.*

PROTECTION IN SPIRITUAL WARFARE

SINCE I have been raised up with You, O Christ, I will keep seeking the things above, where You are at the right hand of God. I will set my mind on the things above, not on the things that are on earth. (Colossians 3:1–2) . . . I will be anxious for nothing, but in everything by prayer and supplication with thanksgiving I will let my requests be made known to You, O God. And Your peace, which surpasses all comprehension, shall guard my heart and my mind in Christ Jesus. Whatever is true, whatever is honorable, whatever is right, whatever is pure, whatever is lovely, whatever is of good repute, if there is any excellence and anything worthy of praise, I will let my mind dwell on these things. (Philippians 4:6–9)

O LORD, *guard my heart against the temptations of the world and renew my heart and spirit.*

FATHER, I know that my old self was crucified with Christ, so that I am no longer a slave to sin, for he who has died is freed from sin. I will reckon myself as dead to sin, but alive to You in Christ Jesus. I will not present the parts of my body to sin as instruments of unrighteousness, but I will present myself to You, O God, as one alive from the dead, and the parts of my body as instruments of righteousness to You. (Romans 6:6–7, 12–13)

O LORD, *guard my heart against the weaknesses and temptation of the flesh so that I may reckon myself dead to sin.*

AS I submit myself to You, O God, and resist the devil, he will flee from me. (James 4:7) . . . I will be of sober spirit and on the alert. My adversary, the devil, prowls about like a roaring lion, seeking someone to devour. But I will resist him, firm in my faith. (1 Peter 5:8–9) . . . I will take up Your full armor, O God, that I may be able to resist and stand firm. I put on the belt of truth and the breastplate of righteousness; I put on my feet the preparation of the gospel of peace; and I take up the shield of faith with which I will be able to extinguish all the flaming missiles of the evil one. I take the helmet of salvation and the sword of Your Spirit, which is Your Word, O God. With all prayer and petition I will pray at all times in Your Spirit and be on the alert with all perseverance and petition for all the saints. (Ephesians 6:13–18)

***O LORD,** guard my heart against the attacks of the devil and give me the strength to resist him.*

THE COMING OF JESUS CHRIST AND MY FUTURE WITH HIM

YOUR kingdom come, Your will be done. (Matthew 6:10) . . . You have said, "I am coming quickly." Amen. Come, Lord Jesus. (Revelation 22:20) . . . I consider that the sufferings of this present time are not worthy to be compared with the glory that is to be revealed to me. (Romans 8:18) . . . I will not lose heart, but though my outer self is decaying, yet my inner self is being renewed day by day. For momentary, light affliction is producing for me an eternal weight of glory far beyond all comparison, while I look not at the things which are seen, but at the things which are not seen; for the things which are seen are temporal, but the things which are not seen are eternal. (2 Corinthians 4:16–18) . . . My citizenship is in heaven, from which also I eagerly wait for You, my Savior, my Lord Jesus Christ. (Philippians 3:20)

***LORD JESUS,** I eagerly await the day when You will come again.*

YEAR
One

OT **Genesis 1:1–2:3** YEAR 1 DAY 1

The Beginning

1 In the beginning God created the
heavens and the earth. 2Now the
earth was[a] formless and empty, darkness was over the surface of the deep,
and the Spirit of God was hovering
over the waters.

3And God said, "Let there be light," and
there was light. 4God saw that the
light was good, and he separated the
light from the darkness. 5God called
the light "day," and the darkness he
called "night." And there was
evening, and there was morning—
the first day.
6And God said, "Let there be an expanse
between the waters to separate water
from water." 7So God made the expanse and separated the water under
the expanse from the water above it.
And it was so. 8God called the expanse "sky." And there was evening,
and there was morning—the second
day.
9And God said, "Let the water under the
sky be gathered to one place, and let
dry ground appear." And it was so.
10God called the dry ground "land,"
and the gathered waters he called
"seas." And God saw that it was good.
11Then God said, "Let the land produce vegetation: seed-bearing plants
and trees on the land that bear fruit
with seed in it, according to their various kinds." And it was so. 12The land
produced vegetation: plants bearing
seed according to their kinds and
trees bearing fruit with seed in it according to their kinds. And God saw
that it was good. 13And there was
evening, and there was morning—
the third day.
14And God said, "Let there be lights in the
expanse of the sky to separate the day
from the night, and let them serve as
signs to mark seasons and days and
years, 15and let them be lights in the
expanse of the sky to give light on the
earth." And it was so. 16God made
two great lights—the greater light to
govern the day and the lesser light to
govern the night. He also made the
stars. 17God set them in the expanse
of the sky to give light on the earth,
18to govern the day and the night,
and to separate light from darkness.
And God saw that it was good. 19And
there was evening, and there was
morning—the fourth day.
20And God said, "Let the water teem with
living creatures, and let birds fly
above the earth across the expanse of
the sky." 21So God created the great
creatures of the sea and every living
and moving thing with which the water teems, according to their kinds,
and every winged bird according to
its kind. And God saw that it was
good. 22God blessed them and said,
"Be fruitful and increase in number
and fill the water in the seas, and let
the birds increase on the earth."
23And there was evening, and there
was morning—the fifth day.
24And God said, "Let the land produce
living creatures according to their
kinds: livestock, creatures that move
along the ground, and wild animals,
each according to its kind." And it
was so. 25God made the wild animals
according to their kinds, the livestock
according to their kinds, and all the
creatures that move along the ground
according to their kinds. And God
saw that it was good.
26Then God said, "Let us make
man in our image, in our likeness,
and let them rule over the fish of the
sea and the birds of the air, over the
livestock, over all the earth,[b] and over
all the creatures that move along the
ground."

27So God created man in his own
image,

[a] 2 Or possibly *became* [b] 26 Hebrew; Syriac *all the wild animals*

in the image of God he created
him;
male and female he created them.

[28]God blessed them and said to
them, "Be fruitful and increase in
number; fill the earth and subdue it.
Rule over the fish of the sea and the
birds of the air and over every living
creature that moves on the ground."
[29]Then God said, "I give you every
seed-bearing plant on the face of the
whole earth and every tree that has
fruit with seed in it. They will be
yours for food. [30]And to all the beasts
of the earth and all the birds of the
air and all the creatures that move on
the ground—everything that has the
breath of life in it—I give every green
plant for food." And it was so.
[31]God saw all that he had made,
and it was very good. And there was
evening, and there was morning—
the sixth day.

2 Thus the heavens and the earth
were completed in all their vast array.

[2]By the seventh day God had finished
the work he had been doing; so on
the seventh day he rested[c] from all
his work. [3]And God blessed the seventh day and made it holy, because
on it he rested from all the work of
creating that he had done.

[c] 2 Or *ceased*; also in verse 3

PRAYER: ADORATION

O LORD, our Lord, how majestic is Your name in all the earth! You have set Your glory above the heavens! (Psalm 8:1) . . . O Lord of hosts, God of Israel, enthroned between the cherubim, You alone are God over all the kingdoms of the earth. You have made heaven and earth. (Isaiah 37:16)

PAUSE *to express your thoughts of praise and worship.*

NT Matthew 1:1-25

The Genealogy of Jesus

1 A record of the genealogy of Jesus Christ
the son of David, the son of Abraham:

[2]Abraham was the father of Isaac,
Isaac the father of Jacob,
Jacob the father of Judah and his brothers,
[3]Judah the father of Perez and Zerah, whose mother was Tamar,
Perez the father of Hezron,
Hezron the father of Ram,
[4]Ram the father of Amminadab,
Amminadab the father of Nahshon,
Nahshon the father of Salmon,
[5]Salmon the father of Boaz, whose mother was Rahab,
Boaz the father of Obed, whose mother was Ruth,
Obed the father of Jesse,
[6]and Jesse the father of King David.

David was the father of Solomon, whose mother had been Uriah's wife,
[7]Solomon the father of Rehoboam,
Rehoboam the father of Abijah,
Abijah the father of Asa,
[8]Asa the father of Jehoshaphat,
Jehoshaphat the father of Jehoram,
Jehoram the father of Uzziah,
[9]Uzziah the father of Jotham,
Jotham the father of Ahaz,
Ahaz the father of Hezekiah,
[10]Hezekiah the father of Manasseh,
Manasseh the father of Amon,
Amon the father of Josiah,
[11]and Josiah the father of Jeconiah[a] and his brothers at the time of the exile to Babylon.

[12]After the exile to Babylon:
Jeconiah was the father of Shealtiel,
Shealtiel the father of Zerubbabel,
[13]Zerubbabel the father of Abiud,
Abiud the father of Eliakim,
Eliakim the father of Azor,
[14]Azor the father of Zadok,
Zadok the father of Akim,
Akim the father of Eliud,

[a] *11* That is, Jehoiachin; also in verse 12

[15]Eliud the father of Eleazar,
Eleazar the father of Matthan,
Matthan the father of Jacob,
[16]and Jacob the father of Joseph, the
husband of Mary, of whom was
born Jesus, who is called Christ.

[17]Thus there were fourteen generations
in all from Abraham to David, fourteen
from David to the exile to Babylon, and
fourteen from the exile to the Christ.[b]

The Birth of Jesus Christ

[18]This is how the birth of Jesus Christ
came about: His mother Mary was
pledged to be married to Joseph, but before they came together, she was found to
be with child through the Holy Spirit.
[19]Because Joseph her husband was a righteous man and did not want to expose her
to public disgrace, he had in mind to divorce her quietly.
[20]But after he had considered this, an
angel of the Lord appeared to him in a
dream and said, "Joseph son of David, do
not be afraid to take Mary home as your
wife, because what is conceived in her is
from the Holy Spirit. [21]She will give birth
to a son, and you are to give him the
name Jesus,[c] because he will save his people from their sins."
[22]All this took place to fulfill what the
Lord had said through the prophet: [23]"The
virgin will be with child and will give
birth to a son, and they will call him Immanuel"[d]—which means, "God with us."
[24]When Joseph woke up, he did what
the angel of the Lord had commanded
him and took Mary home as his wife.
[25]But he had no union with her until she
gave birth to a son. And he gave him the
name Jesus.

[b] 17 Or *Messiah.* "The Christ" (Greek) and "the Messiah" (Hebrew) both mean "the Anointed One." [c] 21 *Jesus* is the Greek form of *Joshua,* which means *the* LORD *saves.* [d] 23 Isaiah 7:14

PRAYER: THE ATTRIBUTES OF GOD

YOU are my God, and I will give thanks to You; You are my God, and I will exalt You. I will give thanks to You, Lord, for You are good; Your loyal love endures forever. (Psalm 118:28–29)

***PAUSE** to reflect on these affirmations about the person, powers and perfection of God.*

OT **Genesis 2:4–25**

YEAR 1
DAY 2

Adam and Eve

[4]This is the account of the heavens and
the earth when they were created.

When the LORD God made the earth
and the heavens— [5]and no shrub of the
field had yet appeared on the earth[a] and
no plant of the field had yet sprung up,
for the LORD God had not sent rain on the
earth[a] and there was no man to work the
ground, [6]but streams[b] came up from the
earth and watered the whole surface of
the ground— [7]the LORD God formed the
man[c] from the dust of the ground and
breathed into his nostrils the breath of
life, and the man became a living being.
[8]Now the LORD God had planted a garden in the east, in Eden; and there he put
the man he had formed. [9]And the LORD
God made all kinds of trees grow out of
the ground—trees that were pleasing to
the eye and good for food. In the middle
of the garden were the tree of life and the
tree of the knowledge of good and evil.
[10]A river watering the garden flowed
from Eden; from there it was separated
into four headwaters. [11]The name of the
first is the Pishon; it winds through the
entire land of Havilah, where there is
gold. [12](The gold of that land is good; aro-
matic resin[d] and onyx are also there.)
[13]The name of the second river is the Gihon; it winds through the entire land of

[a] 5 Or *land;* also in verse 6 [b] 6 Or *mist* [c] 7 The Hebrew for *man (adam)* sounds like and may be related to the Hebrew for *ground (adamah);* it is also the name *Adam* (see Gen. 2:20). [d] 12 Or *good; pearls*

Cush.[e] 14The name of the third river is the
Tigris; it runs along the east side of Asshur.
And the fourth river is the Euphrates.
15The LORD God took the man and put
him in the Garden of Eden to work it and
take care of it. 16And the LORD God commanded the man, "You are free to eat
from any tree in the garden; 17but you
must not eat from the tree of the knowledge of good and evil, for when you eat
of it you will surely die."
18The LORD God said, "It is not good for
the man to be alone. I will make a helper
suitable for him."
19Now the LORD God had formed out of
the ground all the beasts of the field and
all the birds of the air. He brought them
to the man to see what he would name
them; and whatever the man called each
living creature, that was its name. 20So the
man gave names to all the livestock, the
birds of the air and all the beasts of the
field.

But for Adam[f] no suitable helper was
found. 21So the LORD God caused the man
to fall into a deep sleep; and while he was
sleeping, he took one of the man's ribs[g]
and closed up the place with flesh. 22Then
the LORD God made a woman from the
rib[h] he had taken out of the man, and he
brought her to the man.
23The man said,

"This is now bone of my bones
and flesh of my flesh;
she shall be called 'woman,[i]'
for she was taken out of man."

24For this reason a man will leave his father and mother and be united to his wife,
and they will become one flesh.
25The man and his wife were both
naked, and they felt no shame.

[e] 13 Possibly southeast Mesopotamia [f] 20 Or *the man* [g] 21 Or *took part of the man's side* [h] 22 Or *part* [i] 23 The Hebrew for *woman* sounds like the Hebrew for *man*.

PRAYER: CONFESSION

YOU, Lord, are in Your holy temple; You are on Your heavenly throne. You observe all people; Your eyes examine them.

(Psalm 11:4)

***ASK** the Spirit to search your heart and reveal any areas of unconfessed sin. Acknowledge these to the Lord and thank Him for His forgiveness.*

NT Matthew 2:1–23

The Visit of the Magi

2 After Jesus was born in Bethlehem in Judea, during the time of King Herod,
Magi[a] from the east came to Jerusalem 2and
asked, "Where is the one who has been
born king of the Jews? We saw his star in the
east[b] and have come to worship him."
3When King Herod heard this he was disturbed, and all Jerusalem with him. 4When
he had called together all the people's chief
priests and teachers of the law, he asked
them where the Christ[c] was to be born. 5"In
Bethlehem in Judea," they replied, "for this
is what the prophet has written:

6" 'But you, Bethlehem, in the land of
Judah,
are by no means least among the
rulers of Judah;
for out of you will come a ruler
who will be the shepherd of my
people Israel.'[d]"

7Then Herod called the Magi secretly
and found out from them the exact time
the star had appeared. 8He sent them to
Bethlehem and said, "Go and make a
careful search for the child. As soon as you
find him, report to me, so that I too may
go and worship him."
9After they had heard the king, they
went on their way, and the star they had
seen in the east[e] went ahead of them until it stopped over the place where the
child was. 10When they saw the star, they
were overjoyed. 11On coming to the house,
they saw the child with his mother Mary,
and they bowed down and worshiped

[a] 1 Traditionally *Wise Men* [b] 2 Or *star when it rose* [c] 4 Or *Messiah* [d] 6 Micah 5:2 [e] 9 Or *seen when it rose*

him. Then they opened their treasures and
presented him with gifts of gold and of
incense and of myrrh. 12And having been
warned in a dream not to go back to Herod, they returned to their country by another route.

The Escape to Egypt

13When they had gone, an angel of the
Lord appeared to Joseph in a dream. "Get
up," he said, "take the child and his mother and escape to Egypt. Stay there until I
tell you, for Herod is going to search for
the child to kill him."
14So he got up, took the child and his
mother during the night and left for
Egypt, 15where he stayed until the death of
Herod. And so was fulfilled what the Lord
had said through the prophet: "Out of
Egypt I called my son."[f]
16When Herod realized that he had
been outwitted by the Magi, he was furious, and he gave orders to kill all the boys
in Bethlehem and its vicinity who were
two years old and under, in accordance
with the time he had learned from the
Magi. 17Then what was said through the
prophet Jeremiah was fulfilled:

18 "A voice is heard in Ramah,
weeping and great mourning,
Rachel weeping for her children
and refusing to be comforted,
because they are no more."[g]

The Return to Nazareth

19After Herod died, an angel of the Lord
appeared in a dream to Joseph in Egypt
20and said, "Get up, take the child and his
mother and go to the land of Israel, for
those who were trying to take the child's
life are dead."
21So he got up, took the child and his
mother and went to the land of Israel.
22But when he heard that Archelaus was
reigning in Judea in place of his father
Herod, he was afraid to go there. Having
been warned in a dream, he withdrew to
the district of Galilee, 23and he went and
lived in a town called Nazareth. So was
fulfilled what was said through the prophets: "He will be called a Nazarene."

f 15 Hosea 11:1 *g* 18 Jer. 31:15

PRAYER: THE WORKS OF GOD

WHEN I consider Your heavens, the work of Your fingers, the moon and the stars, which You have set in place, what is man that You are mindful of him, and the son of man that You care for him? You made him a little lower than the heavenly beings and crowned him with glory and honor. You made human beings the rulers over the works of Your hands, and You put everything under their feet. (Psalm 8:3–6)

TAKE *a moment to consider the greatness of God's wonderful works.*

YEAR 1
DAY 3

OT **Genesis 3:1–24**

The Fall of Man

3 Now the serpent was more crafty than
any of the wild animals the LORD God
had made. He said to the woman, "Did
God really say, 'You must not eat from any
tree in the garden'?"
2The woman said to the serpent, "We
may eat fruit from the trees in the garden,
3but God did say, 'You must not eat fruit
from the tree that is in the middle of the
garden, and you must not touch it, or you
will die.' "
4"You will not surely die," the serpent
said to the woman. 5"For God knows that
when you eat of it your eyes will be
opened, and you will be like God, knowing good and evil."
6When the woman saw that the fruit of
the tree was good for food and pleasing to
the eye, and also desirable for gaining wisdom, she took some and ate it. She also

gave some to her husband, who was with
her, and he ate it. 7 Then the eyes of both of
them were opened, and they realized they
were naked; so they sewed fig leaves together and made coverings for themselves.
8 Then the man and his wife heard the
sound of the LORD God as he was walking
in the garden in the cool of the day, and
they hid from the LORD God among the
trees of the garden. 9 But the LORD God
called to the man, "Where are you?"
10 He answered, "I heard you in the garden, and I was afraid because I was naked;
so I hid."
11 And he said, "Who told you that you
were naked? Have you eaten from the tree
that I commanded you not to eat from?"
12 The man said, "The woman you put
here with me—she gave me some fruit
from the tree, and I ate it."
13 Then the LORD God said to the
woman, "What is this you have done?"
The woman said, "The serpent deceived
me, and I ate."
14 So the LORD God said to the serpent,
"Because you have done this,

"Cursed are you above all the
livestock
and all the wild animals!
You will crawl on your belly
and you will eat dust
all the days of your life.
15 And I will put enmity
between you and the woman,
and between your offspring[a] and
hers;
he will crush[b] your head,
and you will strike his heel."

16 To the woman he said,

"I will greatly increase your pains in
childbearing;
with pain you will give birth to
children.
Your desire will be for your husband,
and he will rule over you."

17 To Adam he said, "Because you listened to your wife and ate from the tree
about which I commanded you, 'You
must not eat of it,'

"Cursed is the ground because of you;
through painful toil you will eat of
it
all the days of your life.
18 It will produce thorns and thistles for
you,
and you will eat the plants of the
field.
19 By the sweat of your brow
you will eat your food
until you return to the ground,
since from it you were taken;
for dust you are
and to dust you will return."

20 Adam[c] named his wife Eve,[d] because
she would become the mother of all the
living.
21 The LORD God made garments of skin
for Adam and his wife and clothed them.
22 And the LORD God said, "The man has
now become like one of us, knowing
good and evil. He must not be allowed to
reach out his hand and take also from the
tree of life and eat, and live forever." 23 So
the LORD God banished him from the
Garden of Eden to work the ground from
which he had been taken. 24 After he drove
the man out, he placed on the east side[e]
of the Garden of Eden cherubim and a
flaming sword flashing back and forth to
guard the way to the tree of life.

[a] 15 Or *seed* [b] 15 Or *strike* [c] 20 Or *The man* [d] 20 *Eve* probably means *living.* [e] 24 Or *placed in front*

PRAYER: RENEWAL

O LORD my God, may I fear You, walk in all Your ways, love You, and serve You with all my heart and with all my soul. (Deuteronomy 10:12) . . . Christ Jesus, I have not been made perfect, but I press on to lay hold of that for which You laid hold of me. I do not consider myself yet to have attained it, but one thing I do: forgetting what is behind and stretching forward to what is ahead, I press on toward the goal to win the prize of the upward call of God in You. (Philippians 3:12–14)

__PAUSE__ to add your own prayers for personal renewal.

NT Matthew 3:1-17

John the Baptist Prepares the Way

3 In those days John the Baptist came,
preaching in the Desert of Judea 2and
saying, "Repent, for the kingdom of heav-
en is near." 3This is he who was spoken of
through the prophet Isaiah:

"A voice of one calling in the desert,
'Prepare the way for the Lord,
make straight paths for him.' "[a]

4John's clothes were made of camel's
hair, and he had a leather belt around his
waist. His food was locusts and wild honey. 5People went out to him from Jerusalem and all Judea and the whole region
of the Jordan. 6Confessing their sins, they
were baptized by him in the Jordan River.
7But when he saw many of the Pharisees and Sadducees coming to where he
was baptizing, he said to them: "You
brood of vipers! Who warned you to flee
from the coming wrath? 8Produce fruit in
keeping with repentance. 9And do not
think you can say to yourselves, 'We have
Abraham as our father.' I tell you that out
of these stones God can raise up children
for Abraham. 10The ax is already at the
root of the trees, and every tree that does
not produce good fruit will be cut down
and thrown into the fire.
11"I baptize you with[b] water for repentance. But after me will come one who is
more powerful than I, whose sandals I am
not fit to carry. He will baptize you with
the Holy Spirit and with fire. 12His winnowing fork is in his hand, and he will
clear his threshing floor, gathering his
wheat into the barn and burning up the
chaff with unquenchable fire."

The Baptism of Jesus

13Then Jesus came from Galilee to the
Jordan to be baptized by John. 14But John
tried to deter him, saying, "I need to be
baptized by you, and do you come to me?"
15Jesus replied, "Let it be so now; it is
proper for us to do this to fulfill all righteousness." Then John consented.
16As soon as Jesus was baptized, he
went up out of the water. At that moment
heaven was opened, and he saw the Spirit of God descending like a dove and light-
ing on him. 17And a voice from heaven
said, "This is my Son, whom I love; with
him I am well pleased."

[a] 3 Isaiah 40:3 [b] 11 Or *in*

PRAYER: MY RELATIONSHIP TO GOD

O LORD, bless us and keep us; O Lord, make Your face shine upon us and be gracious to us; O Lord, turn Your face toward us and give us peace. (Numbers 6:24–26) . . . You have loved me, O God, and called me to be a saint; You, O God my Father, and the Lord Jesus Christ have given me grace and peace. (Romans 1:7)

***PAUSE** to thank God for the relationship that you enjoy with Him in Jesus Christ.*

YEAR 1 DAY 4

OT Genesis 4:1-26

Cain and Abel

4 Adam[a] lay with his wife Eve, and she
became pregnant and gave birth to
Cain.[b] She said, "With the help of the
LORD I have brought forth[c] a man." 2Later
she gave birth to his brother Abel.
Now Abel kept flocks, and Cain worked
the soil. 3In the course of time Cain
brought some of the fruits of the soil as
an offering to the LORD. 4But Abel brought
fat portions from some of the firstborn of
his flock. The LORD looked with favor on
Abel and his offering, 5but on Cain and
his offering he did not look with favor. So

[a] 1 Or *The man* [b] 1 *Cain* sounds like the Hebrew for *brought forth* or *acquired.* [c] 1 Or *have acquired*

Cain was very angry, and his face was
downcast.
6Then the LORD said to Cain, "Why are
you angry? Why is your face downcast? 7If
you do what is right, will you not be accepted? But if you do not do what is right,
sin is crouching at your door; it desires to
have you, but you must master it."
8Now Cain said to his brother Abel,
"Let's go out to the field."[d] And while they
were in the field, Cain attacked his brother Abel and killed him.
9Then the LORD said to Cain, "Where is
your brother Abel?"

"I don't know," he replied. "Am I my brother's keeper?"
10The LORD said, "What have you done?
Listen! Your brother's blood cries out to
me from the ground. 11Now you are under a curse and driven from the ground,
which opened its mouth to receive your
brother's blood from your hand. 12When
you work the ground, it will no longer
yield its crops for you. You will be a restless wanderer on the earth."
13Cain said to the LORD, "My punishment is more than I can bear. 14Today you
are driving me from the land, and I will
be hidden from your presence; I will be a
restless wanderer on the earth, and whoever finds me will kill me."
15But the LORD said to him, "Not so[e];
if anyone kills Cain, he will suffer
vengeance seven times over." Then the
LORD put a mark on Cain so that no one
who found him would kill him. 16So Cain
went out from the LORD's presence and
lived in the land of Nod,[f] east of Eden.
17Cain lay with his wife, and she became pregnant and gave birth to Enoch.
Cain was then building a city, and he
named it after his son Enoch. 18To Enoch
was born Irad, and Irad was the father of
Mehujael, and Mehujael was the father of
Methushael, and Methushael was the father of Lamech.
19Lamech married two women, one
named Adah and the other Zillah. 20Adah
gave birth to Jabal; he was the father of
those who live in tents and raise livestock.
21His brother's name was Jubal; he was the
father of all who play the harp and flute.
22Zillah also had a son, Tubal-Cain, who
forged all kinds of tools out of[g] bronze
and iron. Tubal-Cain's sister was Naamah.
23Lamech said to his wives,

"Adah and Zillah, listen to me;
wives of Lamech, hear my words.
I have killed[h] a man for wounding me,
a young man for injuring me.
24If Cain is avenged seven times,
then Lamech seventy-seven times."

25Adam lay with his wife again, and she
gave birth to a son and named him Seth,[i]
saying, "God has granted me another
child in place of Abel, since Cain killed
him." 26Seth also had a son, and he
named him Enosh.

At that time men began to call on[j] the name of the LORD.

[d] 8 Samaritan Pentateuch, Septuagint, Vulgate and Syriac; Masoretic Text does not have *"Let's go out to the field."* [e] 15 Septuagint, Vulgate and Syriac; Hebrew *Very well* [f] 16 *Nod* means *wandering* (see verses 12 and 14). [g] 22 Or *who instructed all who work in* [h] 23 Or *I will kill* [i] 25 *Seth* probably means *granted.* [j] 26 Or *to proclaim*

PRAYER: PETITION

MY body is a temple of Your Holy Spirit, who is in me and whom I have received from You, Lord God. I am not my own, for I was bought at a price; therefore may I glorify You in my body. (1 Corinthians 6:19–20)

***PAUSE** here to petition God for growth in your desire to know and please Jesus Christ. Pray for a greater love and commitment to Him, for the grace to practice His presence and for the grace to glorify Him in your life. Offer prayers regarding your activities for this day and any special concerns you may have.*

NT Matthew 4:1–25

The Temptation of Jesus

4 Then Jesus was led by the Spirit into
the desert to be tempted by the devil.
2 After fasting forty days and forty nights,
he was hungry. 3 The tempter came to him
and said, "If you are the Son of God, tell
these stones to become bread."
4 Jesus answered, "It is written: 'Man
does not live on bread alone, but on every
word that comes from the mouth of
God.'[a]"
5 Then the devil took him to the holy
city and had him stand on the highest
point of the temple. 6 "If you are the Son
of God," he said, "throw yourself down.
For it is written:

" 'He will command his angels
concerning you,
and they will lift you up in their
hands,
so that you will not strike your foot
against a stone.'[b]"

7 Jesus answered him, "It is also written:
'Do not put the Lord your God to the
test.'[c]"
8 Again, the devil took him to a very
high mountain and showed him all the
kingdoms of the world and their splendor. 9 "All this I will give you," he said, "if
you will bow down and worship me."
10 Jesus said to him, "Away from me, Satan! For it is written: 'Worship the Lord
your God, and serve him only.'[d]"
11 Then the devil left him, and angels
came and attended him.

Jesus Begins to Preach

12 When Jesus heard that John had been
put in prison, he returned to Galilee.
13 Leaving Nazareth, he went and lived in
Capernaum, which was by the lake in the
area of Zebulun and Naphtali— 14 to fulfill
what was said through the prophet Isaiah:

15 "Land of Zebulun and land of
Naphtali,
the way to the sea, along the
Jordan,
Galilee of the Gentiles—
16 the people living in darkness
have seen a great light;
on those living in the land of the
shadow of death
a light has dawned."[e]

17 From that time on Jesus began to
preach, "Repent, for the kingdom of heav-
en is near."

The Calling of the First Disciples

18 As Jesus was walking beside the Sea of
Galilee, he saw two brothers, Simon
called Peter and his brother Andrew. They
were casting a net into the lake, for they
were fishermen. 19 "Come, follow me,"
Jesus said, "and I will make you fishers of
men." 20 At once they left their nets and
followed him.
21 Going on from there, he saw two other brothers, James son of Zebedee and his
brother John. They were in a boat with
their father Zebedee, preparing their nets.
Jesus called them, 22 and immediately they
left the boat and their father and followed
him.

Jesus Heals the Sick

23 Jesus went throughout Galilee, teaching in their synagogues, preaching the
good news of the kingdom, and healing
every disease and sickness among the
people. 24 News about him spread all over
Syria, and people brought to him all who
were ill with various diseases, those suffering severe pain, the demon-possessed,
those having seizures, and the paralyzed,
and he healed them. 25 Large crowds from
Galilee, the Decapolis,[f] Jerusalem, Judea
and the region across the Jordan followed
him.

[a] *4* Deut. 8:3 [b] *6* Psalm 91:11,12 [c] *7* Deut. 6:16 [d] *10* Deut. 6:13 [e] *16* Isaiah 9:1,2 [f] *25* That is, the Ten Cities

PRAYER: THE CHARACTER I WANT TO CULTIVATE

LORD, who may dwell in Your tabernacle? Who may live on Your holy mountain? Those who walk uprightly and work righteousness and speak the truth in their hearts; they do not slander with their

tongues or do evil to their neighbor or take up a reproach against their friends; they despise the reprobate but honor those who fear You. They keep their oath even when it hurts, lend their money without interest and do not accept bribes against the innocent. Those who do these things will never be shaken.

(Psalm 15:1–5)

***TAKE** a moment to ask the Lord for the grace to grow in godly character.*

YEAR 1
DAY 5

OT Genesis 5:1–6:22

From Adam to Noah

5 This is the written account of Adam's
line.

When God created man, he made him
in the likeness of God. 2He created them
male and female and blessed them. And
when they were created, he called them
"man.[a]"
3When Adam had lived 130 years, he
had a son in his own likeness, in his own
image; and he named him Seth. 4After Seth
was born, Adam lived 800 years and had
other sons and daughters. 5Altogether,
Adam lived 930 years, and then he died.
6When Seth had lived 105 years, he became the father[b] of Enosh. 7And after he
became the father of Enosh, Seth lived
807 years and had other sons and daughters. 8Altogether, Seth lived 912 years, and
then he died.
9When Enosh had lived 90 years, he became the father of Kenan. 10And after he
became the father of Kenan, Enosh lived
815 years and had other sons and daughters. 11Altogether, Enosh lived 905 years,
and then he died.
12When Kenan had lived 70 years, he
became the father of Mahalalel. 13And after he became the father of Mahalalel, Kenan lived 840 years and had other sons
and daughters. 14Altogether, Kenan lived
910 years, and then he died.
15When Mahalalel had lived 65 years,
he became the father of Jared. 16And after
he became the father of Jared, Mahalalel
lived 830 years and had other sons and
daughters. 17Altogether, Mahalalel lived
895 years, and then he died.
18When Jared had lived 162 years, he
became the father of Enoch. 19And after he
became the father of Enoch, Jared lived
800 years and had other sons and daughters. 20Altogether, Jared lived 962 years,
and then he died.
21When Enoch had lived 65 years, he
became the father of Methuselah. 22And
after he became the father of Methuselah,
Enoch walked with God 300 years and
had other sons and daughters. 23Altogeth-
er, Enoch lived 365 years. 24Enoch walked
with God; then he was no more, because
God took him away.
25When Methuselah had lived 187 years,
he became the father of Lamech. 26And after he became the father of Lamech,
Methuselah lived 782 years and had other
sons and daughters. 27Altogether, Methuselah lived 969 years, and then he died.
28When Lamech had lived 182 years, he
had a son. 29He named him Noah[c] and
said, "He will comfort us in the labor and
painful toil of our hands caused by the
ground the LORD has cursed." 30After
Noah was born, Lamech lived 595 years
and had other sons and daughters. 31Alto-
gether, Lamech lived 777 years, and then
he died.
32After Noah was 500 years old, he became the father of Shem, Ham and Japheth.

The Flood

6 When men began to increase in number on the earth and daughters were
born to them, 2the sons of God saw that
the daughters of men were beautiful, and
they married any of them they chose.
3Then the LORD said, "My Spirit will not
contend with[d] man forever, for he is mortal[e]; his days will be a hundred and twenty years."
4The Nephilim were on the earth in

[a] 2 Hebrew *adam* [b] 6 *Father* may mean *ancestor;* also in verses 7–26. [c] 29 *Noah* sounds like the Hebrew for *comfort.* [d] 3 Or *My spirit will not remain in* [e] 3 Or *corrupt*

those days—and also afterward—when
the sons of God went to the daughters of
men and had children by them. They were
the heroes of old, men of renown.
5The LORD saw how great man's wickedness on the earth had become, and that
every inclination of the thoughts of his
heart was only evil all the time. 6The LORD
was grieved that he had made man on the
earth, and his heart was filled with pain.
7So the LORD said, "I will wipe mankind,
whom I have created, from the face of the
earth—men and animals, and creatures
that move along the ground, and birds of
the air—for I am grieved that I have made
them." 8But Noah found favor in the eyes
of the LORD.

9This is the account of Noah.

Noah was a righteous man, blameless
among the people of his time, and he
walked with God. 10Noah had three sons:
Shem, Ham and Japheth.
11Now the earth was corrupt in God's
sight and was full of violence. 12God saw
how corrupt the earth had become, for all
the people on earth had corrupted their
ways. 13So God said to Noah, "I am going
to put an end to all people, for the earth is
filled with violence because of them. I am
surely going to destroy both them and the
earth. 14So make yourself an ark of cypress[f]
wood; make rooms in it and coat it with
pitch inside and out. 15This is how you are
to build it: The ark is to be 450 feet long,
75 feet wide and 45 feet high.[g] 16Make a
roof for it and finish[h] the ark to within 18
inches[i] of the top. Put a door in the side of
the ark and make lower, middle and upper
decks. 17I am going to bring floodwaters on
the earth to destroy all life under the heavens, every creature that has the breath of
life in it. Everything on earth will perish.
18But I will establish my covenant with
you, and you will enter the ark—you and
your sons and your wife and your sons'
wives with you. 19You are to bring into the
ark two of all living creatures, male and female, to keep them alive with you. 20Two
of every kind of bird, of every kind of animal and of every kind of creature that
moves along the ground will come to you
to be kept alive. 21You are to take every kind
of food that is to be eaten and store it away
as food for you and for them."
22Noah did everything just as God commanded him.

[f]14 The meaning of the Hebrew for this word is uncertain. [g]15 Hebrew *300 cubits long, 50 cubits wide and 30 cubits high* (about 140 meters long, 23 meters wide and 13.5 meters high) [h]16 Or *Make an opening for light by finishing* [i]16 Hebrew *a cubit* (about 0.5 meter)

PRAYER: INTERCESSION

WE must take heed to ourselves and to all the flock of which Your Holy Spirit has made us overseers to shepherd Your church, which You, Jesus, purchased with Your own blood. (Acts 20:28)

***TAKE** a few moments to intercede on behalf of your local church, other churches, evangelism and discipleship ministries, educational ministries and any other special concerns you may have.*

NT Matthew 5:1–20

The Beatitudes

5 Now when he saw the crowds, he went
up on a mountainside and sat down.
His disciples came to him, 2and he began
to teach them, saying:

3"Blessed are the poor in spirit,
for theirs is the kingdom of heaven.
4Blessed are those who mourn,
for they will be comforted.
5Blessed are the meek,
for they will inherit the earth.
6Blessed are those who hunger and
thirst for righteousness,
for they will be filled.
7Blessed are the merciful,
for they will be shown mercy.
8Blessed are the pure in heart,
for they will see God.
9Blessed are the peacemakers,
for they will be called sons of God.

10 Blessed are those who are persecuted
because of righteousness,
for theirs is the kingdom of heaven.

11 "Blessed are you when people insult
you, persecute you and falsely say all
kinds of evil against you because of me.
12 Rejoice and be glad, because great is
your reward in heaven, for in the same
way they persecuted the prophets who
were before you.

Salt and Light

13 "You are the salt of the earth. But if
the salt loses its saltiness, how can it be
made salty again? It is no longer good for
anything, except to be thrown out and
trampled by men.
14 "You are the light of the world. A city
on a hill cannot be hidden. 15 Neither do
people light a lamp and put it under a
bowl. Instead they put it on its stand, and
it gives light to everyone in the house. 16 In
the same way, let your light shine before
men, that they may see your good deeds
and praise your Father in heaven.

The Fulfillment of the Law

17 "Do not think that I have come to
abolish the Law or the Prophets; I have
not come to abolish them but to fulfill
them. 18 I tell you the truth, until heaven
and earth disappear, not the smallest letter, not the least stroke of a pen, will by
any means disappear from the Law until
everything is accomplished. 19 Anyone
who breaks one of the least of these commandments and teaches others to do the
same will be called least in the kingdom
of heaven, but whoever practices and
teaches these commands will be called
great in the kingdom of heaven. 20 For I tell
you that unless your righteousness surpasses that of the Pharisees and the teachers of the law, you will certainly not enter
the kingdom of heaven.

PRAYER: MY RELATIONSHIP TO OTHERS

FRIENDS love at all times; they are born for times of adversity. (Proverbs 17:17) . . . We must be devoted to one another in love, honoring one another above ourselves. (Romans 12:10)

PAUSE *to review your relationships with others and to commit them to the Lord.*

YEAR 1 DAY 6

OT Genesis 7:1–8:22

7 The LORD then said to Noah, "Go into
the ark, you and your whole family, because I have found you righteous in this
generation. 2 Take with you seven[a] of every
kind of clean animal, a male and its mate,
and two of every kind of unclean animal,
a male and its mate, 3 and also seven of
every kind of bird, male and female, to
keep their various kinds alive throughout
the earth. 4 Seven days from now I will
send rain on the earth for forty days and
forty nights, and I will wipe from the face
of the earth every living creature I have
made."
5 And Noah did all that the LORD commanded him.
6 Noah was six hundred years old when
the floodwaters came on the earth. 7 And
Noah and his sons and his wife and his
sons' wives entered the ark to escape the
waters of the flood. 8 Pairs of clean and unclean animals, of birds and of all creatures
that move along the ground, 9 male and female, came to Noah and entered the ark,
as God had commanded Noah. 10 And after the seven days the floodwaters came
on the earth.
11 In the six hundredth year of Noah's life,
on the seventeenth day of the second
month—on that day all the springs of the
great deep burst forth, and the floodgates
of the heavens were opened. 12 And rain fell
on the earth forty days and forty nights.
13 On that very day Noah and his sons,
Shem, Ham and Japheth, together with his

[a] 2 Or *seven pairs;* also in verse 3

wife and the wives of his three sons, entered
the ark. 14They had with them every wild
animal according to its kind, all livestock
according to their kinds, every creature that
moves along the ground according to its
kind and every bird according to its kind,
everything with wings. 15Pairs of all creatures that have the breath of life in them
came to Noah and entered the ark. 16The
animals going in were male and female of
every living thing, as God had commanded Noah. Then the LORD shut him in.

17For forty days the flood kept coming
on the earth, and as the waters increased
they lifted the ark high above the earth.
18The waters rose and increased greatly on
the earth, and the ark floated on the surface of the water. 19They rose greatly on
the earth, and all the high mountains under the entire heavens were covered. 20The
waters rose and covered the mountains to
a depth of more than twenty feet.[b,c]
21Every living thing that moved on the
earth perished—birds, livestock, wild animals, all the creatures that swarm over
the earth, and all mankind. 22Everything
on dry land that had the breath of life in
its nostrils died. 23Every living thing on
the face of the earth was wiped out; men
and animals and the creatures that move
along the ground and the birds of the air
were wiped from the earth. Only Noah
was left, and those with him in the ark.

24The waters flooded the earth for a
hundred and fifty days.

8 But God remembered Noah and all the
wild animals and the livestock that
were with him in the ark, and he sent a
wind over the earth, and the waters receded. 2Now the springs of the deep and
the floodgates of the heavens had been
closed, and the rain had stopped falling
from the sky. 3The water receded steadily
from the earth. At the end of the hundred
and fifty days the water had gone down,
4and on the seventeenth day of the seventh month the ark came to rest on the
mountains of Ararat. 5The waters continued to recede until the tenth month, and
on the first day of the tenth month the
tops of the mountains became visible.

6After forty days Noah opened the window he had made in the ark 7and sent out
a raven, and it kept flying back and forth
until the water had dried up from the
earth. 8Then he sent out a dove to see if
the water had receded from the surface of
the ground. 9But the dove could find no
place to set its feet because there was water over all the surface of the earth; so it
returned to Noah in the ark. He reached
out his hand and took the dove and
brought it back to himself in the ark. 10He
waited seven more days and again sent
out the dove from the ark. 11When the
dove returned to him in the evening, there
in its beak was a freshly plucked olive
leaf! Then Noah knew that the water had
receded from the earth. 12He waited seven
more days and sent the dove out again,
but this time it did not return to him.

13By the first day of the first month of
Noah's six hundred and first year, the water had dried up from the earth. Noah
then removed the covering from the ark
and saw that the surface of the ground
was dry. 14By the twenty-seventh day of
the second month the earth was completely dry.

15Then God said to Noah, 16"Come out
of the ark, you and your wife and your
sons and their wives. 17Bring out every
kind of living creature that is with you—
the birds, the animals, and all the creatures that move along the ground—so
they can multiply on the earth and be
fruitful and increase in number upon it."

18So Noah came out, together with his
sons and his wife and his sons' wives. 19All
the animals and all the creatures that
move along the ground and all the
birds—everything that moves on the
earth—came out of the ark, one kind after another.

20Then Noah built an altar to the LORD
and, taking some of all the clean animals
and clean birds, he sacrificed burnt offerings on it. 21The LORD smelled the pleasing aroma and said in his heart: "Never
again will I curse the ground because of
man, even though[d] every inclination of
his heart is evil from childhood. And never again will I destroy all living creatures,
as I have done.

22"As long as the earth endures,
seedtime and harvest,
cold and heat,
summer and winter,
day and night
will never cease."

[b] 20 Hebrew *fifteen cubits* (about 6.9 meters)
[c] 20 Or *rose more than twenty feet, and the mountains were covered* [d] 21 Or *man, for*

PRAYER: AFFIRMATION

YOUR love, O Christ, compels me, because I am convinced that You are the One who died for all, and therefore all died. And You died for all, that those who live should no longer live for themselves but for the One who died for them and was raised again. (2 Corinthians 5:14–15) . . . You redeemed us from the curse of the law by becoming a curse for us, for it is written: "Cursed is everyone who hangs on a tree." (Galatians 3:13)

***PAUSE** to reflect on these Biblical affirmations.*

NT Matthew 5:21-48

Murder

21 "You have heard that it was said to the
people long ago, 'Do not murder,[a] and
anyone who murders will be subject to
judgment.' 22 But I tell you that anyone who
is angry with his brother[b] will be subject
to judgment. Again, anyone who says to
his brother, 'Raca,[c]' is answerable to the
Sanhedrin. But anyone who says, 'You
fool!' will be in danger of the fire of hell.
23 "Therefore, if you are offering your gift
at the altar and there remember that your
brother has something against you,
24 leave your gift there in front of the altar.
First go and be reconciled to your brother; then come and offer your gift.
25 "Settle matters quickly with your adversary who is taking you to court. Do it
while you are still with him on the way,
or he may hand you over to the judge, and
the judge may hand you over to the officer, and you may be thrown into prison.
26 I tell you the truth, you will not get out
until you have paid the last penny.[d]

Adultery

27 "You have heard that it was said, 'Do
not commit adultery.'[e] 28 But I tell you that
anyone who looks at a woman lustfully has
already committed adultery with her in his
heart. 29 If your right eye causes you to sin,
gouge it out and throw it away. It is better
for you to lose one part of your body than
for your whole body to be thrown into hell.
30 And if your right hand causes you to sin,
cut it off and throw it away. It is better for
you to lose one part of your body than for
your whole body to go into hell.

Divorce

31 "It has been said, 'Anyone who divorces his wife must give her a certificate
of divorce.'[f] 32 But I tell you that anyone
who divorces his wife, except for marital
unfaithfulness, causes her to become an
adulteress, and anyone who marries the
divorced woman commits adultery.

Oaths

33 "Again, you have heard that it was said
to the people long ago, 'Do not break
your oath, but keep the oaths you have
made to the Lord.' 34 But I tell you, Do not
swear at all: either by heaven, for it is
God's throne; 35 or by the earth, for it is his
footstool; or by Jerusalem, for it is the city
of the Great King. 36 And do not swear by
your head, for you cannot make even one
hair white or black. 37 Simply let your 'Yes'
be 'Yes,' and your 'No,' 'No'; anything beyond this comes from the evil one.

An Eye for an Eye

38 "You have heard that it was said, 'Eye
for eye, and tooth for tooth.'[g] 39 But I tell
you, Do not resist an evil person. If someone strikes you on the right cheek, turn to
him the other also. 40 And if someone
wants to sue you and take your tunic, let
him have your cloak as well. 41 If someone
forces you to go one mile, go with him
two miles. 42 Give to the one who asks you,
and do not turn away from the one who
wants to borrow from you.

Love for Enemies

43 "You have heard that it was said, 'Love
your neighbor[h] and hate your enemy.'

[a] 21 Exodus 20:13 [b] 22 Some manuscripts *brother without cause* [c] 22 An Aramaic term of contempt [d] 26 Greek *kodrantes* [e] 27 Exodus 20:14 [f] 31 Deut. 24:1 [g] 38 Exodus 21:24; Lev. 24:20; Deut. 19:21 [h] 43 Lev. 19:18

[44]But I tell you: Love your enemies[i] and
pray for those who persecute you, [45]that
you may be sons of your Father in heaven.
He causes his sun to rise on the evil and
the good, and sends rain on the righteous
and the unrighteous. [46]If you love those
who love you, what reward will you get?
Are not even the tax collectors doing that?
[47]And if you greet only your brothers, what
are you doing more than others? Do not
even pagans do that? [48]Be perfect, therefore, as your heavenly Father is perfect.

[i] 44 Some late manuscripts *enemies, bless those who curse you, do good to those who hate you*

PRAYER: THE ATTRIBUTES OF GOD

YOU, O God, are not a man, that You should lie, or a son of man, that You should change Your mind. Have You spoken and not done it? Have You promised and not fulfilled it? (Numbers 23:19) . . . You who are the Glory of Israel do not lie or change Your mind, for You are not a man, that You should change Your mind. (1 Samuel 15:29)

***PAUSE** to reflect on these affirmations about the person, powers and perfection of God.*

OT **Psalms 1–2** YEAR 1 DAY 7

Psalm 1

[1]Blessed is the man
who does not walk in the counsel of the wicked
or stand in the way of sinners
or sit in the seat of mockers.
[2]But his delight is in the law of the LORD,
and on his law he meditates day and night.
[3]He is like a tree planted by streams of water,
which yields its fruit in season
and whose leaf does not wither.
Whatever he does prospers.

[4]Not so the wicked!
They are like chaff
that the wind blows away.
[5]Therefore the wicked will not stand in the judgment,
nor sinners in the assembly of the righteous.

[6]For the LORD watches over the way of the righteous,
but the way of the wicked will perish.

Psalm 2

[1]Why do the nations conspire[a]
and the peoples plot in vain?
[2]The kings of the earth take their stand
and the rulers gather together
against the LORD
and against his Anointed One.[b]
[3]"Let us break their chains," they say,
"and throw off their fetters."

[4]The One enthroned in heaven laughs;
the Lord scoffs at them.
[5]Then he rebukes them in his anger
and terrifies them in his wrath, saying,
[6]"I have installed my King[c]
on Zion, my holy hill."

[7]I will proclaim the decree of the LORD:

He said to me, "You are my Son[d];
today I have become your Father.[e]
[8]Ask of me,
and I will make the nations your inheritance,
the ends of the earth your possession.
[9]You will rule them with an iron scepter[f];
you will dash them to pieces like pottery."

[a] 1 Hebrew; Septuagint *rage* [b] 2 Or *anointed one* [c] 6 Or *king* [d] 7 Or *son*; also in verse 12 [e] 7 Or *have begotten you* [f] 9 Or *will break them with a rod of iron*

10 Therefore, you kings, be wise;
be warned, you rulers of the earth.
11 Serve the LORD with fear
and rejoice with trembling.
12 Kiss the Son, lest he be angry
and you be destroyed in your way,
for his wrath can flare up in a
moment.
Blessed are all who take refuge in
him.

PRAYER: THANKSGIVING

O LORD, in Your unfailing love You have led the people You have redeemed. In Your strength You have guided them to Your holy dwelling. You have brought them in and planted them on the mountain of Your inheritance—the place, O Lord, You made for Your dwelling; the sanctuary, O Lord, Your hands have established. (Exodus 15:13, 17)

PAUSE *to offer your own expressions of thanksgiving.*

NT Matthew 6:1-15

Giving to the Needy

6 "Be careful not to do your 'acts of righteousness' before men, to be seen by
them. If you do, you will have no reward
from your Father in heaven.
2 "So when you give to the needy, do not
announce it with trumpets, as the hypocrites do in the synagogues and on the
streets, to be honored by men. I tell you the
truth, they have received their reward in
full. 3 But when you give to the needy, do
not let your left hand know what your right
hand is doing, 4 so that your giving may be
in secret. Then your Father, who sees what
is done in secret, will reward you.

Prayer

5 "And when you pray, do not be like the
hypocrites, for they love to pray standing
in the synagogues and on the street corners to be seen by men. I tell you the
truth, they have received their reward in
full. 6 But when you pray, go into your
room, close the door and pray to your Father, who is unseen. Then your Father,
who sees what is done in secret, will reward you. 7 And when you pray, do not
keep on babbling like pagans, for they
think they will be heard because of their
many words. 8 Do not be like them, for
your Father knows what you need before
you ask him.
9 "This, then, is how you should pray:

" 'Our Father in heaven,
hallowed be your name,
10 your kingdom come,
your will be done
on earth as it is in heaven.
11 Give us today our daily bread.
12 Forgive us our debts,
as we also have forgiven our debtors.
13 And lead us not into temptation,
but deliver us from the evil one.[a]'

14 For if you forgive men when they sin
against you, your heavenly Father will also
forgive you. 15 But if you do not forgive
men their sins, your Father will not forgive your sins.

[a] 13 Or *from evil;* some late manuscripts *one, / for yours is the kingdom and the power and the glory forever. Amen.*

PRAYER: THE WORKS OF GOD

WHO is a God like You, who pardons iniquity and forgives the transgression of the remnant of Your inheritance? You do not stay angry forever but delight to show mercy. You will have compassion on Your people; You will tread their iniquities underfoot and hurl all their sins into the depths of the sea. (Micah 7:18–19)

TAKE *a moment to consider the greatness of God's wonderful works.*

God's Covenant With Noah

9 Then God blessed Noah and his sons,
saying to them, "Be fruitful and increase in number and fill the earth. 2The
fear and dread of you will fall upon all the
beasts of the earth and all the birds of the
air, upon every creature that moves along
the ground, and upon all the fish of the
sea; they are given into your hands.
3Everything that lives and moves will be
food for you. Just as I gave you the green
plants, I now give you everything.
4"But you must not eat meat that has its
lifeblood still in it. 5And for your lifeblood I will surely demand an accounting. I will demand an accounting from
every animal. And from each man, too, I
will demand an accounting for the life of
his fellow man.

6"Whoever sheds the blood of man,
by man shall his blood be shed;
for in the image of God
has God made man.

7As for you, be fruitful and increase in
number; multiply on the earth and increase upon it."
8Then God said to Noah and to his
sons with him: 9"I now establish my covenant with you and with your descendants after you 10and with every living
creature that was with you—the birds, the
livestock and all the wild animals, all
those that came out of the ark with you—
every living creature on earth. 11I establish
my covenant with you: Never again will
all life be cut off by the waters of a flood;
never again will there be a flood to destroy the earth."
12And God said, "This is the sign of the
covenant I am making between me and
you and every living creature with you, a
covenant for all generations to come: 13I
have set my rainbow in the clouds, and it
will be the sign of the covenant between
me and the earth. 14Whenever I bring
clouds over the earth and the rainbow appears in the clouds, 15I will remember my
covenant between me and you and all living creatures of every kind. Never again
will the waters become a flood to destroy
all life. 16Whenever the rainbow appears
in the clouds, I will see it and remember
the everlasting covenant between God
and all living creatures of every kind on
the earth."
17So God said to Noah, "This is the sign
of the covenant I have established between me and all life on the earth."

The Sons of Noah

18The sons of Noah who came out of
the ark were Shem, Ham and Japheth.
(Ham was the father of Canaan.) 19These
were the three sons of Noah, and from
them came the people who were scattered
over the earth.
20Noah, a man of the soil, proceeded[a]
to plant a vineyard. 21When he drank
some of its wine, he became drunk and
lay uncovered inside his tent. 22Ham, the
father of Canaan, saw his father's nakedness and told his two brothers outside.
23But Shem and Japheth took a garment
and laid it across their shoulders; then
they walked in backward and covered
their father's nakedness. Their faces were
turned the other way so that they would
not see their father's nakedness.
24When Noah awoke from his wine and
found out what his youngest son had
done to him, 25he said,

"Cursed be Canaan!
The lowest of slaves
will he be to his brothers."

26He also said,

"Blessed be the LORD, the God of
Shem!
May Canaan be the slave of Shem.[b]
27May God extend the territory of
Japheth[c];
may Japheth live in the tents of
Shem,
and may Canaan be his[d] slave."

28After the flood Noah lived 350 years.
29Altogether, Noah lived 950 years, and
then he died.

[a] 20 Or *soil, was the first* [b] 26 Or *be his slave*
[c] 27 *Japheth* sounds like the Hebrew for *extend.*
[d] 27 Or *their*

PRAYER: ADORATION

HOW great are Your works, O Lord! Your thoughts are very deep. Senseless people do not know; fools do not understand that though the wicked spring up like grass and all the evildoers flourish, they will be destroyed forever. But You, O Lord, are exalted forever. (Psalm 92:5–8) . . . You are the Lord, that is Your name. You will not give Your glory to another or Your praise to idols. (Isaiah 42:8)

***PAUSE** to express your thoughts of praise and worship.*

NT Matthew 6:16–34

Fasting

16 "When you fast, do not look somber
as the hypocrites do, for they disfigure
their faces to show men they are fasting. I
tell you the truth, they have received their
reward in full. 17 But when you fast, put oil
on your head and wash your face, 18 so that
it will not be obvious to men that you are
fasting, but only to your Father, who is
unseen; and your Father, who sees what is
done in secret, will reward you.

Treasures in Heaven

19 "Do not store up for yourselves treasures on earth, where moth and rust destroy, and where thieves break in and
steal. 20 But store up for yourselves treasures in heaven, where moth and rust do
not destroy, and where thieves do not
break in and steal. 21 For where your treasure is, there your heart will be also.
22 "The eye is the lamp of the body. If
your eyes are good, your whole body will
be full of light. 23 But if your eyes are bad,
your whole body will be full of darkness.
If then the light within you is darkness,
how great is that darkness!
24 "No one can serve two masters. Either
he will hate the one and love the other, or
he will be devoted to the one and despise
the other. You cannot serve both God and
Money.

Do Not Worry

25 "Therefore I tell you, do not worry
about your life, what you will eat or drink;
or about your body, what you will wear.
Is not life more important than food, and
the body more important than clothes?
26 Look at the birds of the air; they do not
sow or reap or store away in barns, and
yet your heavenly Father feeds them. Are
you not much more valuable than they?
27 Who of you by worrying can add a single hour to his life[a]?
28 "And why do you worry about clothes?
See how the lilies of the field grow. They
do not labor or spin. 29 Yet I tell you that
not even Solomon in all his splendor was
dressed like one of these. 30 If that is how
God clothes the grass of the field, which is
here today and tomorrow is thrown into
the fire, will he not much more clothe you,
O you of little faith? 31 So do not worry,
saying, 'What shall we eat?' or 'What shall
we drink?' or 'What shall we wear?' 32 For
the pagans run after all these things, and
your heavenly Father knows that you need
them. 33 But seek first his kingdom and his
righteousness, and all these things will be
given to you as well. 34 Therefore do not
worry about tomorrow, for tomorrow will
worry about itself. Each day has enough
trouble of its own.

[a] 27 Or *single cubit to his height*

PRAYER: MY RELATIONSHIP TO GOD

YOU lifted me out of the slimy pit, O God, out of the mud and mire; You set my feet on a rock and gave me a firm place to stand. You put a new song in my mouth, a hymn of praise to You, my God. Many will see and fear and put their trust in You, O Lord. (Psalm 40:2–3) . . . I shall know the truth, and the truth shall set me free. Everyone who commits sin is a

slave of sin. And a slave has no permanent place in the family, but a child belongs to it forever. So if You, the Son of God, set me free, I shall be free indeed. (John 8:32, 34–36)

***PAUSE** to thank God for the relationship that you enjoy with Him in Jesus Christ.*

YEAR 1
DAY 9

OT Genesis 10:1-32

The Table of Nations

10 This is the account of Shem, Ham and Japheth, Noah's sons, who themselves had sons after the flood.

The Japhethites

2 The sons[a] of Japheth:
Gomer, Magog, Madai, Javan, Tubal, Meshech and Tiras.
3 The sons of Gomer:
Ashkenaz, Riphath and Togarmah.
4 The sons of Javan:
Elishah, Tarshish, the Kittim and
the Rodanim.[b] 5 (From these the
maritime peoples spread out into their territories by their clans within their nations, each with its own language.)

The Hamites

6 The sons of Ham:
Cush, Mizraim,[c] Put and Canaan.
7 The sons of Cush:
Seba, Havilah, Sabtah, Raamah and Sabteca.
The sons of Raamah:
Sheba and Dedan.

8 Cush was the father[d] of Nimrod, who
grew to be a mighty warrior on the earth.
9 He was a mighty hunter before the LORD;
that is why it is said, "Like Nimrod, a
mighty hunter before the LORD." 10 The
first centers of his kingdom were Babylon, Erech, Akkad and Calneh, in[e] Shinar.[f]
11 From that land he went to Assyria, where
he built Nineveh, Rehoboth Ir,[g] Calah
12 and Resen, which is between Nineveh
and Calah, that is the great city.

13 Mizraim was the father of
the Ludites, Anamites, Lehabites,
Naphtuhites, 14 Pathrusites, Casluhites (from whom the Philistines came) and Caphtorites.

15 Canaan was the father of
Sidon his firstborn,[h] and of the Hittites, 16 Jebusites, Amorites, Girgashites, 17 Hivites, Arkites, Sinites, 18 Arvadites, Zemarites and Hamathites.

Later the Canaanite clans scattered
19 and the borders of Canaan reached from Sidon toward Gerar as far as Gaza, and then toward Sodom, Gomorrah, Admah and Zeboiim, as far as Lasha.
20 These are the sons of Ham by their clans and languages, in their territories and nations.

The Semites

21 Sons were also born to Shem, whose older brother was[i] Japheth; Shem was the ancestor of all the sons of Eber.

22 The sons of Shem:
Elam, Asshur, Arphaxad, Lud and Aram.
23 The sons of Aram:
Uz, Hul, Gether and Meshech.[j]
24 Arphaxad was the father of[k] Shelah,
and Shelah the father of Eber.
25 Two sons were born to Eber:
One was named Peleg,[l] because in his time the earth was divided; his brother was named Joktan.
26 Joktan was the father of
Almodad, Sheleph, Hazarmaveth,

[a] 2 *Sons* may mean *descendants* or *successors* or *nations*; also in verses 3, 4, 6, 7, 20–23, 29 and 31. [b] 4 Some manuscripts of the Masoretic Text and Samaritan Pentateuch (see also Septuagint and 1 Chron. 1:7); most manuscripts of the Masoretic Text *Dodanim* [c] 6 That is, Egypt; also in verse 13 [d] 8 *Father* may mean *ancestor* or *predecessor* or *founder*; also in verses 13, 15, 24 and 26. [e] 10 Or *Erech and Akkad—all of them in* [f] 10 That is, Babylonia [g] 11 Or *Nineveh with its city squares* [h] 15 Or *of the Sidonians, the foremost* [i] 21 Or *Shem, the older brother of* [j] 23 See Septuagint and 1 Chron. 1:17; Hebrew *Mash* [k] 24 Hebrew; Septuagint *father of Cainan, and Cainan was the father of* [l] 25 *Peleg* means *division*.

Jerah, [27]Hadoram, Uzal, Diklah,
[28]Obal, Abimael, Sheba, [29]Ophir,
Havilah and Jobab. All these were
sons of Joktan.

[30]The region where they lived stretched
from Mesha toward Sephar, in the eastern
hill country.

[31]These are the sons of Shem by their
clans and languages, in their territories
and nations.

[32]These are the clans of Noah's sons, according to their lines of descent, within
their nations. From these the nations
spread out over the earth after the flood.

PRAYER: CONFESSION

I WILL endure discipline, for You are treating me as Your child. For what child is not disciplined by its father? If I am without discipline, of which all have become partakers, then I am an illegitimate child and not a true child. Moreover, we have all had human fathers who disciplined us, and we respected them; how much more should I be disciplined by You, the Father of my spirit, and live? (Hebrews 12:7–9)

*(**ASK** the Spirit to search your heart and reveal any areas of unconfessed sin. Acknowledge these to the Lord and thank Him for His forgiveness.)*

NT Matthew 7:1–29

Judging Others

7 "Do not judge, or you too will be
judged. [2]For in the same way you judge
others, you will be judged, and with the
measure you use, it will be measured to
you.
[3]"Why do you look at the speck of saw-
dust in your brother's eye and pay no attention to the plank in your own eye?
[4]How can you say to your brother, 'Let me
take the speck out of your eye,' when all
the time there is a plank in your own eye?
[5]You hypocrite, first take the plank out of
your own eye, and then you will see clearly to remove the speck from your brother's eye.
[6]"Do not give dogs what is sacred; do
not throw your pearls to pigs. If you do,
they may trample them under their feet,
and then turn and tear you to pieces.

Ask, Seek, Knock

[7]"Ask and it will be given to you; seek
and you will find; knock and the door will
be opened to you. [8]For everyone who asks
receives; he who seeks finds; and to him
who knocks, the door will be opened.
[9]"Which of you, if his son asks for
bread, will give him a stone? [10]Or if he
asks for a fish, will give him a snake? [11]If
you, then, though you are evil, know how
to give good gifts to your children, how
much more will your Father in heaven
give good gifts to those who ask him! [12]So
in everything, do to others what you
would have them do to you, for this sums
up the Law and the Prophets.

The Narrow and Wide Gates

[13]"Enter through the narrow gate. For
wide is the gate and broad is the road that
leads to destruction, and many enter
through it. [14]But small is the gate and narrow the road that leads to life, and only a
few find it.

A Tree and Its Fruit

[15]"Watch out for false prophets. They
come to you in sheep's clothing, but inwardly they are ferocious wolves. [16]By
their fruit you will recognize them. Do
people pick grapes from thornbushes, or
figs from thistles? [17]Likewise every good
tree bears good fruit, but a bad tree bears
bad fruit. [18]A good tree cannot bear bad
fruit, and a bad tree cannot bear good
fruit. [19]Every tree that does not bear good
fruit is cut down and thrown into the fire.
[20]Thus, by their fruit you will recognize
them.
[21]"Not everyone who says to me, 'Lord,
Lord,' will enter the kingdom of heaven,
but only he who does the will of my Father
who is in heaven. [22]Many will say to me on

that day, 'Lord, Lord, did we not prophesy
in your name, and in your name drive out
demons and perform many miracles?'
²³Then I will tell them plainly, 'I never
knew you. Away from me, you evildoers!'

The Wise and Foolish Builders

²⁴"Therefore everyone who hears these
words of mine and puts them into practice is like a wise man who built his house
on the rock. ²⁵The rain came down, the
streams rose, and the winds blew and beat
against that house; yet it did not fall, because it had its foundation on the rock.
²⁶But everyone who hears these words of
mine and does not put them into practice
is like a foolish man who built his house
on sand. ²⁷The rain came down, the
streams rose, and the winds blew and beat
against that house, and it fell with a great
crash."

²⁸When Jesus had finished saying these
things, the crowds were amazed at his
teaching, ²⁹because he taught as one who
had authority, and not as their teachers of
the law.

PRAYER: THE CHARACTER I WANT TO CULTIVATE

I WILL not let love and truth leave me; I will bind them around my neck and write them on the tablet of my heart. (Proverbs 3:3) . . . The love we have from You, O Lord, is patient, it is kind, it does not envy; love does not boast, it is not arrogant, it does not behave rudely; it does not seek its own, it is not provoked, it keeps no record of wrongs; it does not rejoice in unrighteousness but rejoices with the truth; it bears all things, believes all things, hopes all things, endures all things. Love never fails. (1 Corinthians 13:4–8)

***TAKE** a moment to ask the Lord for the grace to grow in godly character.*

YEAR 1 DAY 10

OT Genesis 11:1–32

The Tower of Babel

11 Now the whole world had one language and a common speech. ²As men
moved eastward,[a] they found a plain in
Shinar[b] and settled there.
³They said to each other, "Come, let's
make bricks and bake them thoroughly."
They used brick instead of stone, and tar
for mortar. ⁴Then they said, "Come, let us
build ourselves a city, with a tower that
reaches to the heavens, so that we may
make a name for ourselves and not be
scattered over the face of the whole
earth."
⁵But the LORD came down to see the city
and the tower that the men were building.
⁶The LORD said, "If as one people speaking the same language they have begun to
do this, then nothing they plan to do will
be impossible for them. ⁷Come, let us go
down and confuse their language so they
will not understand each other."
⁸So the LORD scattered them from there
over all the earth, and they stopped building the city. ⁹That is why it was called Babel[c]—because there the LORD confused
the language of the whole world. From
there the LORD scattered them over the
face of the whole earth.

From Shem to Abram

¹⁰This is the account of Shem.

Two years after the flood, when Shem
was 100 years old, he became the father[d]
of Arphaxad. ¹¹And after he became the father of Arphaxad, Shem lived 500 years
and had other sons and daughters.
¹²When Arphaxad had lived 35 years, he
became the father of Shelah. ¹³And after
he became the father of Shelah, Arphaxad

[a] 2 Or *from the east;* or *in the east* [b] 2 That is, Babylonia [c] 9 That is, Babylon; *Babel* sounds like the Hebrew for *confused.* [d] 10 *Father* may mean *ancestor;* also in verses 11–25.

lived 403 years and had other sons and daughters.[e]

14 When Shelah had lived 30 years, he became the father of Eber. 15 And after he became the father of Eber, Shelah lived 403 years and had other sons and daughters.

16 When Eber had lived 34 years, he became the father of Peleg. 17 And after he became the father of Peleg, Eber lived 430 years and had other sons and daughters.

18 When Peleg had lived 30 years, he became the father of Reu. 19 And after he became the father of Reu, Peleg lived 209 years and had other sons and daughters.

20 When Reu had lived 32 years, he became the father of Serug. 21 And after he became the father of Serug, Reu lived 207 years and had other sons and daughters.

22 When Serug had lived 30 years, he became the father of Nahor. 23 And after he became the father of Nahor, Serug lived 200 years and had other sons and daughters.

24 When Nahor had lived 29 years, he became the father of Terah. 25 And after he became the father of Terah, Nahor lived 119 years and had other sons and daughters.

26 After Terah had lived 70 years, he became the father of Abram, Nahor and Haran.

27 This is the account of Terah.

Terah became the father of Abram, Nahor and Haran. And Haran became the father of Lot. 28 While his father Terah was still alive, Haran died in Ur of the Chaldeans, in the land of his birth. 29 Abram and Nahor both married. The name of Abram's wife was Sarai, and the name of Nahor's wife was Milcah; she was the daughter of Haran, the father of both Milcah and Iscah. 30 Now Sarai was barren; she had no children.

31 Terah took his son Abram, his grandson Lot son of Haran, and his daughter-in-law Sarai, the wife of his son Abram, and together they set out from Ur of the Chaldeans to go to Canaan. But when they came to Haran, they settled there.

32 Terah lived 205 years, and he died in Haran.

[e] 12,13 Hebrew, Septuagint (see also Luke 3:35, 36 and note at Gen. 10:24) *35 years, he became the father of Cainan. 13And after he became the father of Cainan, Arphaxad lived 430 years and had other sons and daughters, and then he died. When Cainan had lived 130 years, he became the father of Shelah. And after he became the father of Shelah, Cainan lived 330 years and had other sons and daughters*

PRAYER: RENEWAL

O CHRIST, You must increase; I must decrease. (John 3:30) . . . Jesus, You are the true vine, and Your Father is the gardener. He cuts off every branch in You that bears no fruit, while every branch that does bear fruit He prunes, that it may bear more fruit. May I abide in You, and You in me. As the branch cannot bear fruit of itself, unless it abides in the vine, neither can I bear fruit unless I abide in You. (John 15:1–2, 4)

***PAUSE** to add your own prayers for personal renewal.*

NT Matthew 8:1–17

The Man With Leprosy

8 When he came down from the mountainside, large crowds followed him. 2 A man with leprosy[a] came and knelt before him and said, "Lord, if you are willing, you can make me clean."

3 Jesus reached out his hand and touched the man. "I am willing," he said. "Be clean!" Immediately he was cured[b] of his leprosy. 4 Then Jesus said to him, "See that you don't tell anyone. But go, show yourself to the priest and offer the gift Moses commanded, as a testimony to them."

The Faith of the Centurion

5 When Jesus had entered Capernaum, a centurion came to him, asking for help. 6 "Lord," he said, "my servant lies at home paralyzed and in terrible suffering."

[a] 2 The Greek word was used for various diseases affecting the skin—not necessarily leprosy.
[b] 3 Greek *made clean*

7 Jesus said to him, "I will go and heal
him."
8 The centurion replied, "Lord, I do not
deserve to have you come under my roof.
But just say the word, and my servant will
be healed. 9 For I myself am a man under
authority, with soldiers under me. I tell
this one, 'Go,' and he goes; and that one,
'Come,' and he comes. I say to my servant,
'Do this,' and he does it."
10 When Jesus heard this, he was astonished and said to those following him, "I
tell you the truth, I have not found anyone in Israel with such great faith. 11 I say
to you that many will come from the east
and the west, and will take their places at
the feast with Abraham, Isaac and Jacob
in the kingdom of heaven. 12 But the subjects of the kingdom will be thrown outside, into the darkness, where there will
be weeping and gnashing of teeth."
13 Then Jesus said to the centurion, "Go!
It will be done just as you believed it
would." And his servant was healed at
that very hour.

Jesus Heals Many

14 When Jesus came into Peter's house,
he saw Peter's mother-in-law lying in bed
with a fever. 15 He touched her hand and
the fever left her, and she got up and began to wait on him.
16 When evening came, many who were
demon-possessed were brought to him,
and he drove out the spirits with a word
and healed all the sick. 17 This was to fulfill what was spoken through the prophet
Isaiah:

"He took up our infirmities
 and carried our diseases."[c]

[c] 17 Isaiah 53:4

PRAYER: MY RELATIONSHIP TO OTHERS

I WILL give generously to others without a grudging heart. (Deuteronomy 15:10) . . . I will not withhold good from those to whom it is due, when it is within my power to act. (Proverbs 3:27)

***PAUSE** to review your relationships with others and to commit them to the Lord.*

OT Genesis 12:1–13:18

YEAR 1 DAY 11

The Call of Abram

12 The LORD had said to Abram, "Leave your country, your people and your father's household and go to the land I will show you.

2 "I will make you into a great nation
 and I will bless you;
I will make your name great,
 and you will be a blessing.
3 I will bless those who bless you,
 and whoever curses you I will
 curse;
and all peoples on earth
 will be blessed through you."

4 So Abram left, as the LORD had told
him; and Lot went with him. Abram was
seventy-five years old when he set out
from Haran. 5 He took his wife Sarai, his
nephew Lot, all the possessions they had
accumulated and the people they had acquired in Haran, and they set out for the
land of Canaan, and they arrived there.
6 Abram traveled through the land as
far as the site of the great tree of Moreh
at Shechem. At that time the Canaanites
were in the land. 7 The LORD appeared to
Abram and said, "To your offspring[a] I
will give this land." So he built an altar
there to the LORD, who had appeared to
him.
8 From there he went on toward the hills
east of Bethel and pitched his tent, with
Bethel on the west and Ai on the east.
There he built an altar to the LORD and
called on the name of the LORD. 9 Then
Abram set out and continued toward the
Negev.

[a] 7 Or *seed*

Abram in Egypt

10Now there was a famine in the land,
and Abram went down to Egypt to live
there for a while because the famine was
severe. 11As he was about to enter Egypt,
he said to his wife Sarai, "I know what a
beautiful woman you are. 12When the
Egyptians see you, they will say, 'This is
his wife.' Then they will kill me but will
let you live. 13Say you are my sister, so that
I will be treated well for your sake and my
life will be spared because of you."
14When Abram came to Egypt, the
Egyptians saw that she was a very beautiful woman. 15And when Pharaoh's officials saw her, they praised her to Pharaoh,
and she was taken into his palace. 16He
treated Abram well for her sake, and
Abram acquired sheep and cattle, male
and female donkeys, menservants and
maidservants, and camels.
17But the LORD inflicted serious diseases
on Pharaoh and his household because of
Abram's wife Sarai. 18So Pharaoh summoned Abram. "What have you done to
me?" he said. "Why didn't you tell me she
was your wife? 19Why did you say, 'She is my
sister,' so that I took her to be my wife? Now
then, here is your wife. Take her and go!"
20Then Pharaoh gave orders about Abram to
his men, and they sent him on his way, with
his wife and everything he had.

Abram and Lot Separate

13 So Abram went up from Egypt to the
Negev, with his wife and everything he
had, and Lot went with him. 2Abram had
become very wealthy in livestock and in
silver and gold.
3From the Negev he went from place to
place until he came to Bethel, to the place
between Bethel and Ai where his tent had
been earlier 4and where he had first built
an altar. There Abram called on the name
of the LORD.
5Now Lot, who was moving about with
Abram, also had flocks and herds and
tents. 6But the land could not support
them while they stayed together, for their
possessions were so great that they were
not able to stay together. 7And quarreling
arose between Abram's herdsmen and the
herdsmen of Lot. The Canaanites and Perizzites were also living in the land at that
time.
8So Abram said to Lot, "Let's not have
any quarreling between you and me, or
between your herdsmen and mine, for we
are brothers. 9Is not the whole land before
you? Let's part company. If you go to the
left, I'll go to the right; if you go to the
right, I'll go to the left."
10Lot looked up and saw that the whole
plain of the Jordan was well watered, like
the garden of the LORD, like the land of
Egypt, toward Zoar. (This was before the
LORD destroyed Sodom and Gomorrah.)
11So Lot chose for himself the whole plain
of the Jordan and set out toward the east.
The two men parted company: 12Abram
lived in the land of Canaan, while Lot
lived among the cities of the plain and
pitched his tents near Sodom. 13Now the
men of Sodom were wicked and were sinning greatly against the LORD.
14The LORD said to Abram after Lot had
parted from him, "Lift up your eyes from
where you are and look north and south,
east and west. 15All the land that you see
I will give to you and your offspring[b] forever. 16I will make your offspring like the
dust of the earth, so that if anyone could
count the dust, then your offspring could
be counted. 17Go, walk through the length
and breadth of the land, for I am giving it
to you."
18So Abram moved his tents and went to
live near the great trees of Mamre at Hebron, where he built an altar to the LORD.

[b] *15* Or *seed;* also in verse 16

PRAYER: PETITION

MAY I follow Abraham's example of willingness to offer all that I have to You, holding nothing back and trusting in Your character and in Your promises. (Genesis 22:2–12, 16–18)

PAUSE *here to petition God for wisdom. Ask Him to develop your eternal perspective, to renew your mind with truth and to help you develop greater skill in each area of your life. Offer prayers regarding your activities for this day and any special concerns you may have.*

NT Matthew 8:18–34

The Cost of Following Jesus

[18]When Jesus saw the crowd around him, he gave orders to cross to the other side of the lake. [19]Then a teacher of the law came to him and said, "Teacher, I will follow you wherever you go."
[20]Jesus replied, "Foxes have holes and birds of the air have nests, but the Son of Man has no place to lay his head."
[21]Another disciple said to him, "Lord, first let me go and bury my father."
[22]But Jesus told him, "Follow me, and let the dead bury their own dead."

Jesus Calms the Storm

[23]Then he got into the boat and his disciples followed him. [24]Without warning, a furious storm came up on the lake, so that the waves swept over the boat. But Jesus was sleeping. [25]The disciples went and woke him, saying, "Lord, save us! We're going to drown!"
[26]He replied, "You of little faith, why are you so afraid?" Then he got up and rebuked the winds and the waves, and it was completely calm.
[27]The men were amazed and asked, "What kind of man is this? Even the winds and the waves obey him!"

The Healing of Two Demon-possessed Men

[28]When he arrived at the other side in the region of the Gadarenes,[a] two demon-possessed men coming from the tombs met him. They were so violent that no one could pass that way. [29]"What do you want with us, Son of God?" they shouted. "Have you come here to torture us before the appointed time?"
[30]Some distance from them a large herd of pigs was feeding. [31]The demons begged Jesus, "If you drive us out, send us into the herd of pigs."
[32]He said to them, "Go!" So they came out and went into the pigs, and the whole herd rushed down the steep bank into the lake and died in the water. [33]Those tending the pigs ran off, went into the town and reported all this, including what had happened to the demon-possessed men. [34]Then the whole town went out to meet Jesus. And when they saw him, they pleaded with him to leave their region.

[a] *28* Some manuscripts *Gergesenes;* others *Gerasenes*

PRAYER: THE ATTRIBUTES OF GOD

YOU, O Lord my God, You are God of gods and Lord of lords, the great God, mighty and awesome; You show no partiality and accept no bribes. You execute justice for the fatherless and the widow and love aliens, giving them food and clothing. (Deuteronomy 10:17–18) . . . As for You, O God, Your way is perfect; Your word, O Lord, is proven. You are a shield to all who take refuge in You. For who is God besides You? And who is the Rock except You, our God? (Psalm 18:30–31)

PAUSE *to reflect on these affirmations about the person, powers and perfection of God.*

YEAR 1 DAY 12

OT Genesis 14:1–24

Abram Rescues Lot

14 At this time Amraphel king of Shinar,[a] Arioch king of Ellasar, Kedorlaomer king of Elam and Tidal king of Goiim [2]went to war against Bera king of Sodom, Birsha king of Gomorrah, Shinab king of Admah, Shemeber king of Zeboiim, and the king of Bela (that is, Zoar). [3]All these latter kings joined forces in the Valley of

[a] *1* That is, Babylonia; also in verse 9

Siddim (the Salt Sea[b]). 4For twelve years they had been subject to Kedorlaomer, but in the thirteenth year they rebelled.

5In the fourteenth year, Kedorlaomer and the kings allied with him went out and defeated the Rephaites in Ashteroth Karnaim, the Zuzites in Ham, the Emites in Shaveh Kiriathaim 6and the Horites in the hill country of Seir, as far as El Paran near the desert. 7Then they turned back and went to En Mishpat (that is, Kadesh), and they conquered the whole territory of the Amalekites, as well as the Amorites who were living in Hazazon Tamar.

8Then the king of Sodom, the king of Gomorrah, the king of Admah, the king of Zeboiim and the king of Bela (that is, Zoar) marched out and drew up their battle lines in the Valley of Siddim 9against Kedorlaomer king of Elam, Tidal king of Goiim, Amraphel king of Shinar and Arioch king of Ellasar—four kings against five. 10Now the Valley of Siddim was full of tar pits, and when the kings of Sodom and Gomorrah fled, some of the men fell into them and the rest fled to the hills. 11The four kings seized all the goods of Sodom and Gomorrah and all their food; then they went away. 12They also carried off Abram's nephew Lot and his possessions, since he was living in Sodom.

13One who had escaped came and reported this to Abram the Hebrew. Now Abram was living near the great trees of Mamre the Amorite, a brother[c] of Eshcol and Aner, all of whom were allied with Abram. 14When Abram heard that his relative had been taken captive, he called out the 318 trained men born in his household and went in pursuit as far as Dan. 15During the night Abram divided his men to attack them and he routed them, pursuing them as far as Hobah, north of Damascus. 16He recovered all the goods and brought back his relative Lot and his possessions, together with the women and the other people.

17After Abram returned from defeating Kedorlaomer and the kings allied with him, the king of Sodom came out to meet him in the Valley of Shaveh (that is, the King's Valley).

18Then Melchizedek king of Salem[d] brought out bread and wine. He was priest of God Most High, 19and he blessed Abram, saying,

> "Blessed be Abram by God Most High,
> Creator[e] of heaven and earth.
> 20And blessed be[f] God Most High,
> who delivered your enemies into
> your hand."

Then Abram gave him a tenth of everything.

21The king of Sodom said to Abram, "Give me the people and keep the goods for yourself."

22But Abram said to the king of Sodom, "I have raised my hand to the LORD, God Most High, Creator of heaven and earth, and have taken an oath 23that I will accept nothing belonging to you, not even a thread or the thong of a sandal, so that you will never be able to say, 'I made Abram rich.' 24I will accept nothing but what my men have eaten and the share that belongs to the men who went with me—to Aner, Eshcol and Mamre. Let them have their share."

[b] 3 That is, the Dead Sea [c] 13 Or *a relative;* or *an ally* [d] 18 That is, Jerusalem [e] 19 Or *Possessor;* also in verse 22 [f] 20 Or *And praise be to*

PRAYER: INTERCESSION

MAY we rejoice, become complete, be of good comfort, be of one mind, and live in peace; and You, the God of love and peace, will be with us. (2 Corinthians 13:11)

***TAKE** a few moments to intercede on behalf of your immediate family and other relatives. Offer prayers for their spiritual, emotional and physical concerns.*

NT Matthew 9:1–17

Jesus Heals a Paralytic

9 Jesus stepped into a boat, crossed over
and came to his own town. 2Some men
brought to him a paralytic, lying on a
mat. When Jesus saw their faith, he said
to the paralytic, "Take heart, son; your sins
are forgiven."
3At this, some of the teachers of the law
said to themselves, "This fellow is blaspheming!"
4Knowing their thoughts, Jesus said,
"Why do you entertain evil thoughts in
your hearts? 5Which is easier: to say, 'Your
sins are forgiven,' or to say, 'Get up and
walk'? 6But so that you may know that the
Son of Man has authority on earth to forgive sins. . . ." Then he said to the paralytic, "Get up, take your mat and go home."
7And the man got up and went home.
8When the crowd saw this, they were filled
with awe; and they praised God, who had
given such authority to men.

The Calling of Matthew

9As Jesus went on from there, he saw a
man named Matthew sitting at the tax collector's booth. "Follow me," he told him,
and Matthew got up and followed him.
10While Jesus was having dinner at Matthew's house, many tax collectors and "sinners" came and ate with him and his disciples. 11When the Pharisees saw this, they
asked his disciples, "Why does your teacher
eat with tax collectors and 'sinners'?"
12On hearing this, Jesus said, "It is not
the healthy who need a doctor, but the
sick. 13But go and learn what this means:
'I desire mercy, not sacrifice.'[a] For I have
not come to call the righteous, but sinners."

Jesus Questioned About Fasting

14Then John's disciples came and asked
him, "How is it that we and the Pharisees
fast, but your disciples do not fast?"
15Jesus answered, "How can the guests
of the bridegroom mourn while he is with
them? The time will come when the
bridegroom will be taken from them;
then they will fast.
16"No one sews a patch of unshrunk
cloth on an old garment, for the patch
will pull away from the garment, making
the tear worse. 17Neither do men pour
new wine into old wineskins. If they do,
the skins will burst, the wine will run out
and the wineskins will be ruined. No,
they pour new wine into new wineskins,
and both are preserved."

[a] 13 Hosea 6:6

PRAYER: THE WORKS OF GOD

TO us a child is born, to us a son is given, and the government is on Your shoulders. And You are called Wonderful Counselor, Mighty God, Everlasting Father, Prince of Peace. Of the increase of Your government and peace there will be no end. You reign on the throne of David and over his kingdom, establishing and upholding it with justice and righteousness from this time on and forever. Your zeal, O Lord of hosts, will accomplish this. (Isaiah 9:6–7)

***TAKE** a moment to consider the greatness of God's wonderful works.*

YEAR 1 DAY 13

OT Genesis 15:1–16:16

God's Covenant With Abram

15 After this, the word of the LORD came
to Abram in a vision:

"Do not be afraid, Abram.
I am your shield,[a]
your very great reward.[b]"

2But Abram said, "O Sovereign LORD,
what can you give me since I remain

[a] 1 Or *sovereign* [b] 1 Or *shield; / your reward will be very great*

childless and the one who will inherit[c] my estate is Eliezer of Damascus?" 3 And Abram said, "You have given me no children; so a servant in my household will be my heir."

4 Then the word of the LORD came to him: "This man will not be your heir, but a son coming from your own body will be your heir." 5 He took him outside and said, "Look up at the heavens and count the stars—if indeed you can count them." Then he said to him, "So shall your offspring be."

6 Abram believed the LORD, and he credited it to him as righteousness.

7 He also said to him, "I am the LORD, who brought you out of Ur of the Chaldeans to give you this land to take possession of it."

8 But Abram said, "O Sovereign LORD, how can I know that I will gain possession of it?"

9 So the LORD said to him, "Bring me a heifer, a goat and a ram, each three years old, along with a dove and a young pigeon."

10 Abram brought all these to him, cut them in two and arranged the halves opposite each other; the birds, however, he did not cut in half. 11 Then birds of prey came down on the carcasses, but Abram drove them away.

12 As the sun was setting, Abram fell into a deep sleep, and a thick and dreadful darkness came over him. 13 Then the LORD said to him, "Know for certain that your descendants will be strangers in a country not their own, and they will be enslaved and mistreated four hundred years. 14 But I will punish the nation they serve as slaves, and afterward they will come out with great possessions. 15 You, however, will go to your fathers in peace and be buried at a good old age. 16 In the fourth generation your descendants will come back here, for the sin of the Amorites has not yet reached its full measure."

17 When the sun had set and darkness had fallen, a smoking firepot with a blazing torch appeared and passed between the pieces. 18 On that day the LORD made a covenant with Abram and said, "To your descendants I give this land, from the river[d] of Egypt to the great river, the Euphrates— 19 the land of the Kenites, Kenizzites, Kadmonites, 20 Hittites, Perizzites, Rephaites, 21 Amorites, Canaanites, Girgashites and Jebusites."

Hagar and Ishmael

16 Now Sarai, Abram's wife, had borne him no children. But she had an Egyptian maidservant named Hagar; 2 so she said to Abram, "The LORD has kept me from having children. Go, sleep with my maidservant; perhaps I can build a family through her."

Abram agreed to what Sarai said. 3 So after Abram had been living in Canaan ten years, Sarai his wife took her Egyptian maidservant Hagar and gave her to her husband to be his wife. 4 He slept with Hagar, and she conceived.

When she knew she was pregnant, she began to despise her mistress. 5 Then Sarai said to Abram, "You are responsible for the wrong I am suffering. I put my servant in your arms, and now that she knows she is pregnant, she despises me. May the LORD judge between you and me."

6 "Your servant is in your hands," Abram said. "Do with her whatever you think best." Then Sarai mistreated Hagar; so she fled from her.

7 The angel of the LORD found Hagar near a spring in the desert; it was the spring that is beside the road to Shur. 8 And he said, "Hagar, servant of Sarai, where have you come from, and where are you going?"

"I'm running away from my mistress Sarai," she answered.

9 Then the angel of the LORD told her, "Go back to your mistress and submit to her." 10 The angel added, "I will so increase your descendants that they will be too numerous to count."

11 The angel of the LORD also said to her:

"You are now with child
  and you will have a son.
You shall name him Ishmael,[e]
  for the LORD has heard of your misery.
12 He will be a wild donkey of a man;
  his hand will be against everyone
  and everyone's hand against him,
and he will live in hostility
  toward[f] all his brothers."

13 She gave this name to the LORD who spoke to her: "You are the God who sees

[c] 2 The meaning of the Hebrew for this phrase is uncertain. [d] 18 Or *Wadi* [e] 11 *Ishmael* means *God hears.* [f] 12 Or *live to the east / of*

me," for she said, "I have now seen[g] the One who sees me." 14That is why the well was called Beer Lahai Roi[h]; it is still there, between Kadesh and Bered.

15So Hagar bore Abram a son, and Abram gave the name Ishmael to the son she had borne. 16Abram was eighty-six years old when Hagar bore him Ishmael.

[g] 13 Or *seen the back of* [h] 14 *Beer Lahai Roi* means *well of the Living One who sees me.*

PRAYER: AFFIRMATION

THOSE who sow sparingly will also reap sparingly, and those who sow bountifully will also reap bountifully. Each one should give as he has decided in his heart, not reluctantly or under compulsion; for You love a cheerful giver. And You are able to make all grace abound to us, so that always having all sufficiency in everything, we may abound in every good work. As it is written: "He has scattered abroad His gifts to the poor; His righteousness endures forever." Now You, the One who supplies seed to the sower and bread for food, will also supply and increase our seed and will increase the fruits of our righteousness. (2 Corinthians 9:6–10)

PAUSE *to reflect on these Biblical affirmations.*

NT Matthew 9:18–38

A Dead Girl and a Sick Woman

18While he was saying this, a ruler came and knelt before him and said, "My daughter has just died. But come and put your hand on her, and she will live." 19Jesus got up and went with him, and so did his disciples.

20Just then a woman who had been subject to bleeding for twelve years came up behind him and touched the edge of his cloak. 21She said to herself, "If I only touch his cloak, I will be healed."

22Jesus turned and saw her. "Take heart, daughter," he said, "your faith has healed you." And the woman was healed from that moment.

23When Jesus entered the ruler's house and saw the flute players and the noisy crowd, 24he said, "Go away. The girl is not dead but asleep." But they laughed at him. 25After the crowd had been put outside, he went in and took the girl by the hand, and she got up. 26News of this spread through all that region.

Jesus Heals the Blind and Mute

27As Jesus went on from there, two blind men followed him, calling out, "Have mercy on us, Son of David!"

28When he had gone indoors, the blind men came to him, and he asked them, "Do you believe that I am able to do this?"

"Yes, Lord," they replied.

29Then he touched their eyes and said, "According to your faith will it be done to you"; 30and their sight was restored. Jesus warned them sternly, "See that no one knows about this." 31But they went out and spread the news about him all over that region.

32While they were going out, a man who was demon-possessed and could not talk was brought to Jesus. 33And when the demon was driven out, the man who had been mute spoke. The crowd was amazed and said, "Nothing like this has ever been seen in Israel."

34But the Pharisees said, "It is by the prince of demons that he drives out demons."

The Workers Are Few

35Jesus went through all the towns and villages, teaching in their synagogues, preaching the good news of the kingdom and healing every disease and sickness. 36When he saw the crowds, he had compassion on them, because they were harassed and helpless, like sheep without a shepherd. 37Then he said to his disciples, "The harvest is plentiful but the workers are few. 38Ask the Lord of the harvest, therefore, to send out workers into his harvest field."

PRAYER: MY RELATIONSHIP TO GOD

O LORD, You are my rock and my fortress and my deliverer; O God, You are my rock; I will take refuge in You. You are my shield and the horn of my salvation, my stronghold and my refuge—my Savior; You save me from violence; I call on You, Lord; You are worthy of praise, and I am saved from my enemies. **(2 Samuel 22:2–4)**

__PAUSE__ to thank God for the relationship that you enjoy with Him in Jesus Christ.

YEAR 1
DAY 14

OT Psalms 3–4

Psalm 3

A psalm of David. When he fled from his son Absalom.

[1]O LORD, how many are my foes!
How many rise up against me!
[2]Many are saying of me,
"God will not deliver him." *Selah*[a]

[3]But you are a shield around me, O LORD;
you bestow glory on me and lift[b] up my head.
[4]To the LORD I cry aloud,
and he answers me from his holy hill. *Selah*

[5]I lie down and sleep;
I wake again, because the LORD sustains me.
[6]I will not fear the tens of thousands
drawn up against me on every side.

[7]Arise, O LORD!
Deliver me, O my God!
Strike all my enemies on the jaw;
break the teeth of the wicked.

[8]From the LORD comes deliverance.
May your blessing be on your people. *Selah*

Psalm 4

For the director of music. With stringed instruments. A psalm of David.

[1]Answer me when I call to you,
O my righteous God.
Give me relief from my distress;
be merciful to me and hear my prayer.

[2]How long, O men, will you turn my glory into shame[c]?
How long will you love delusions
and seek false gods[d]? *Selah*
[3]Know that the LORD has set apart the godly for himself;
the LORD will hear when I call to him.

[4]In your anger do not sin;
when you are on your beds,
search your hearts and be silent. *Selah*

[5]Offer right sacrifices
and trust in the LORD.

[6]Many are asking, "Who can show us any good?"
Let the light of your face shine upon us, O LORD.
[7]You have filled my heart with greater joy
than when their grain and new wine abound.
[8]I will lie down and sleep in peace,
for you alone, O LORD,
make me dwell in safety.

[a] 2 A word of uncertain meaning, occurring frequently in the Psalms; possibly a musical term [b] 3 Or *LORD, / my Glorious One, who lifts* [c] 2 Or *you dishonor my Glorious One* [d] 2 Or *seek lies*

PRAYER: THANKSGIVING

WE give thanks to You, Lord God Almighty, the One who is and who was, because You have taken Your great power and have begun to reign. (Revelation 11:17) . . . There will no longer be any curse. Your throne and the throne of the Lamb will be in the new Jerusalem, and Your servants will serve You. They will see Your face, and Your name will be on their foreheads. And there will be no night there; they will not need the light of a lamp or the light of the sun, for You, Lord God, will give them light. And they shall reign for ever and ever. (Revelation 22:3–5)

***PAUSE** to offer your own expressions of thanksgiving.*

NT Matthew 10:1–42

Jesus Sends Out the Twelve

10 He called his twelve disciples to him
and gave them authority to drive out
evil[a] spirits and to heal every disease and
sickness.
2 These are the names of the twelve
apostles: first, Simon (who is called Peter)
and his brother Andrew; James son of
Zebedee, and his brother John; 3 Philip
and Bartholomew; Thomas and Matthew
the tax collector; James son of Alphaeus,
and Thaddaeus; 4 Simon the Zealot and Judas Iscariot, who betrayed him.
5 These twelve Jesus sent out with the
following instructions: "Do not go among
the Gentiles or enter any town of the
Samaritans. 6 Go rather to the lost sheep
of Israel. 7 As you go, preach this message:
'The kingdom of heaven is near.' 8 Heal the
sick, raise the dead, cleanse those who
have leprosy,[b] drive out demons. Freely
you have received, freely give. 9 Do not
take along any gold or silver or copper in
your belts; 10 take no bag for the journey,
or extra tunic, or sandals or a staff; for the
worker is worth his keep.
11 "Whatever town or village you enter,
search for some worthy person there and
stay at his house until you leave. 12 As you
enter the home, give it your greeting. 13 If
the home is deserving, let your peace rest
on it; if it is not, let your peace return to
you. 14 If anyone will not welcome you or
listen to your words, shake the dust off
your feet when you leave that home or
town. 15 I tell you the truth, it will be more
bearable for Sodom and Gomorrah on
the day of judgment than for that town.
16 I am sending you out like sheep among
wolves. Therefore be as shrewd as snakes
and as innocent as doves.
17 "Be on your guard against men; they
will hand you over to the local councils
and flog you in their synagogues. 18 On my
account you will be brought before governors and kings as witnesses to them and
to the Gentiles. 19 But when they arrest
you, do not worry about what to say or
how to say it. At that time you will be giv-
en what to say, 20 for it will not be you
speaking, but the Spirit of your Father
speaking through you.
21 "Brother will betray brother to death,
and a father his child; children will rebel
against their parents and have them put
to death. 22 All men will hate you because
of me, but he who stands firm to the end
will be saved. 23 When you are persecuted
in one place, flee to another. I tell you the
truth, you will not finish going through
the cities of Israel before the Son of Man
comes.
24 "A student is not above his teacher,
nor a servant above his master. 25 It is
enough for the student to be like his
teacher, and the servant like his master. If
the head of the house has been called
Beelzebub,[c] how much more the members of his household!
26 "So do not be afraid of them. There is
nothing concealed that will not be disclosed, or hidden that will not be made
known. 27 What I tell you in the dark,
speak in the daylight; what is whispered
in your ear, proclaim from the roofs. 28 Do

[a] 1 Greek *unclean* [b] 8 The Greek word was used for various diseases affecting the skin—not necessarily leprosy. [c] 25 Greek *Beezeboul* or *Beelzeboul*

not be afraid of those who kill the body
but cannot kill the soul. Rather, be afraid
of the One who can destroy both soul and
body in hell. 29Are not two sparrows sold
for a penny[d]? Yet not one of them will fall
to the ground apart from the will of your
Father. 30And even the very hairs of your
head are all numbered. 31So don't be
afraid; you are worth more than many
sparrows.
32"Whoever acknowledges me before
men, I will also acknowledge him before
my Father in heaven. 33But whoever disowns me before men, I will disown him
before my Father in heaven.
34"Do not suppose that I have come to
bring peace to the earth. I did not come
to bring peace, but a sword. 35For I have
come to turn

" 'a man against his father,
a daughter against her mother,
a daughter-in-law against her mother-in-law—
36 a man's enemies will be the members of his own household.'[e]

37"Anyone who loves his father or mother more than me is not worthy of me; anyone who loves his son or daughter more
than me is not worthy of me; 38and anyone who does not take his cross and follow me is not worthy of me. 39Whoever
finds his life will lose it, and whoever loses
his life for my sake will find it.
40"He who receives you receives me, and
he who receives me receives the one who
sent me. 41Anyone who receives a prophet
because he is a prophet will receive a
prophet's reward, and anyone who receives
a righteous man because he is a righteous
man will receive a righteous man's reward.
42And if anyone gives even a cup of cold
water to one of these little ones because he
is my disciple, I tell you the truth, he will
certainly not lose his reward."

[d] 29 Greek *an assarion* [e] 36 Micah 7:6

PRAYER: THE CHARACTER I WANT TO CULTIVATE

TO fear You, Lord, is wisdom; and to depart from evil is understanding. (Job 28:28) . . . To fear You, Lord, is the beginning of wisdom; all who practice Your commandments have good understanding. Your praise endures forever. (Psalm 111:10)

***TAKE** a moment to ask the Lord for the grace to grow in godly character.*

YEAR 1 DAY 15

OT Genesis 17:1–18:33

The Covenant of Circumcision

17 When Abram was ninety-nine years
old, the LORD appeared to him and
said, "I am God Almighty[a]; walk before
me and be blameless. 2I will confirm my
covenant between me and you and will
greatly increase your numbers."
3Abram fell facedown, and God said to
him, 4"As for me, this is my covenant with
you: You will be the father of many nations. 5No longer will you be called
Abram[b]; your name will be Abraham,[c] for
I have made you a father of many nations.
6I will make you very fruitful; I will make
nations of you, and kings will come from
you. 7I will establish my covenant as an
everlasting covenant between me and you
and your descendants after you for the
generations to come, to be your God and
the God of your descendants after you.
8The whole land of Canaan, where you
are now an alien, I will give as an everlasting possession to you and your descendants after you; and I will be their
God."
9Then God said to Abraham, "As for
you, you must keep my covenant, you and
your descendants after you for the generations to come. 10This is my covenant with
you and your descendants after you, the
covenant you are to keep: Every male

[a] 1 Hebrew *El-Shaddai* [b] 5 *Abram* means *exalted father.* [c] 5 *Abraham* means *father of many.*

among you shall be circumcised. 11 You are
to undergo circumcision, and it will be
the sign of the covenant between me and
you. 12 For the generations to come every
male among you who is eight days old
must be circumcised, including those
born in your household or bought with
money from a foreigner—those who are
not your offspring. 13 Whether born in
your household or bought with your
money, they must be circumcised. My
covenant in your flesh is to be an everlasting covenant. 14 Any uncircumcised
male, who has not been circumcised in
the flesh, will be cut off from his people;
he has broken my covenant."
15 God also said to Abraham, "As for Sarai your wife, you are no longer to call her
Sarai; her name will be Sarah. 16 I will bless
her and will surely give you a son by her.
I will bless her so that she will be the
mother of nations; kings of peoples will
come from her."
17 Abraham fell facedown; he laughed
and said to himself, "Will a son be born
to a man a hundred years old? Will Sarah
bear a child at the age of ninety?" 18 And
Abraham said to God, "If only Ishmael
might live under your blessing!"
19 Then God said, "Yes, but your wife
Sarah will bear you a son, and you will
call him Isaac.[d] I will establish my covenant with him as an everlasting covenant
for his descendants after him. 20 And as for
Ishmael, I have heard you: I will surely
bless him; I will make him fruitful and
will greatly increase his numbers. He will
be the father of twelve rulers, and I will
make him into a great nation. 21 But my
covenant I will establish with Isaac,
whom Sarah will bear to you by this time
next year." 22 When he had finished speaking with Abraham, God went up from
him.
23 On that very day Abraham took his
son Ishmael and all those born in his
household or bought with his money,
every male in his household, and circumcised them, as God told him. 24 Abraham
was ninety-nine years old when he was
circumcised, 25 and his son Ishmael was
thirteen; 26 Abraham and his son Ishmael
were both circumcised on that same day.
27 And every male in Abraham's household, including those born in his household or bought from a foreigner, was circumcised with him.

The Three Visitors

18 The LORD appeared to Abraham near
the great trees of Mamre while he was
sitting at the entrance to his tent in the
heat of the day. 2 Abraham looked up and
saw three men standing nearby. When he
saw them, he hurried from the entrance
of his tent to meet them and bowed low
to the ground.
3 He said, "If I have found favor in your
eyes, my lord,[e] do not pass your servant
by. 4 Let a little water be brought, and then
you may all wash your feet and rest under
this tree. 5 Let me get you something to eat,
so you can be refreshed and then go on
your way—now that you have come to
your servant."
"Very well," they answered, "do as you
say."
6 So Abraham hurried into the tent to
Sarah. "Quick," he said, "get three seahs[f]
of fine flour and knead it and bake some
bread."
7 Then he ran to the herd and selected a
choice, tender calf and gave it to a servant,
who hurried to prepare it. 8 He then
brought some curds and milk and the calf
that had been prepared, and set these before them. While they ate, he stood near
them under a tree.
9 "Where is your wife Sarah?" they asked
him.
"There, in the tent," he said.
10 Then the LORD[g] said, "I will surely return to you about this time next year, and
Sarah your wife will have a son."
Now Sarah was listening at the entrance
to the tent, which was behind him. 11 Abraham and Sarah were already old and well
advanced in years, and Sarah was past the
age of childbearing. 12 So Sarah laughed to
herself as she thought, "After I am worn
out and my master[h] is old, will I now have
this pleasure?"
13 Then the LORD said to Abraham, "Why
did Sarah laugh and say, 'Will I really have
a child, now that I am old?' 14 Is anything
too hard for the LORD? I will return to you
at the appointed time next year and Sarah will have a son."
15 Sarah was afraid, so she lied and said,
"I did not laugh."
But he said, "Yes, you did laugh."

[d] 19 *Isaac* means *he laughs.* [e] 3 Or *O Lord*
[f] 6 That is, probably about 20 quarts (about 22 liters) [g] 10 Hebrew *Then he* [h] 12 Or *husband*

Abraham Pleads for Sodom

16When the men got up to leave, they
looked down toward Sodom, and Abraham walked along with them to see them
on their way. 17Then the LORD said, "Shall
I hide from Abraham what I am about to
do? 18Abraham will surely become a great
and powerful nation, and all nations on
earth will be blessed through him. 19For I
have chosen him, so that he will direct his
children and his household after him to
keep the way of the LORD by doing what
is right and just, so that the LORD will
bring about for Abraham what he has
promised him."
20Then the LORD said, "The outcry
against Sodom and Gomorrah is so great
and their sin so grievous 21that I will go
down and see if what they have done is as
bad as the outcry that has reached me. If
not, I will know."
22The men turned away and went toward Sodom, but Abraham remained
standing before the LORD.[i] 23Then Abraham approached him and said: "Will you
sweep away the righteous with the
wicked? 24What if there are fifty righteous
people in the city? Will you really sweep
it away and not spare[j] the place for the
sake of the fifty righteous people in it?
25Far be it from you to do such a thing—
to kill the righteous with the wicked,
treating the righteous and the wicked
alike. Far be it from you! Will not the
Judge[k] of all the earth do right?"
26The LORD said, "If I find fifty righteous
people in the city of Sodom, I will spare
the whole place for their sake."
27Then Abraham spoke up again: "Now
that I have been so bold as to speak to the
Lord, though I am nothing but dust and
ashes, 28what if the number of the righteous is five less than fifty? Will you destroy the whole city because of five people?"
"If I find forty-five there," he said, "I
will not destroy it."
29Once again he spoke to him, "What if
only forty are found there?"
He said, "For the sake of forty, I will not
do it."
30Then he said, "May the Lord not be
angry, but let me speak. What if only thirty can be found there?"
He answered, "I will not do it if I find
thirty there."
31Abraham said, "Now that I have been
so bold as to speak to the Lord, what if
only twenty can be found there?"
He said, "For the sake of twenty, I will
not destroy it."
32Then he said, "May the Lord not be
angry, but let me speak just once more.
What if only ten can be found there?"
He answered, "For the sake of ten, I will
not destroy it."
33When the LORD had finished speaking
with Abraham, he left, and Abraham returned home.

[i] 22 Masoretic Text; an ancient Hebrew scribal tradition *but the LORD remained standing before Abraham* [j] 24 Or *forgive;* also in verse 26 [k] 25 Or *Ruler*

PRAYER: ADORATION

YOU, O Lord Most High, are awesome, the great King over all the earth! You are the King of all the earth, and I will sing Your praise. You reign over the nations; You are seated on Your holy throne. (Psalm 47:2, 7–8) . . . You must be treated as holy by those who come near You, and before all people You will be honored. (Leviticus 10:3)

PAUSE *to express your thoughts of praise and worship.*

NT Matthew 11:1–30

Jesus and John the Baptist

11 After Jesus had finished instructing his
twelve disciples, he went on from there
to teach and preach in the towns of Galilee.[a]
2When John heard in prison what
Christ was doing, he sent his disciples 3to
ask him, "Are you the one who was to
come, or should we expect someone
else?"

[a] 1 Greek *in their towns*

4 Jesus replied, "Go back and report to
John what you hear and see: 5 The blind receive sight, the lame walk, those who have
leprosy[b] are cured, the deaf hear, the dead
are raised, and the good news is preached
to the poor. 6 Blessed is the man who does
not fall away on account of me."
7 As John's disciples were leaving, Jesus
began to speak to the crowd about John:
"What did you go out into the desert to
see? A reed swayed by the wind? 8 If not,
what did you go out to see? A man
dressed in fine clothes? No, those who
wear fine clothes are in kings' palaces.
9 Then what did you go out to see? A
prophet? Yes, I tell you, and more than a
prophet. 10 This is the one about whom it
is written:

" 'I will send my messenger ahead of
you,
who will prepare your way before
you.'[c]

11 I tell you the truth: Among those born
of women there has not risen anyone
greater than John the Baptist; yet he who
is least in the kingdom of heaven is
greater than he. 12 From the days of John
the Baptist until now, the kingdom of
heaven has been forcefully advancing,
and forceful men lay hold of it. 13 For all
the Prophets and the Law prophesied until John. 14 And if you are willing to accept
it, he is the Elijah who was to come. 15 He
who has ears, let him hear.
16 "To what can I compare this generation? They are like children sitting in the
marketplaces and calling out to others:

17 " 'We played the flute for you,
and you did not dance;
we sang a dirge,
and you did not mourn.'

18 For John came neither eating nor drinking, and they say, 'He has a demon.' 19 The
Son of Man came eating and drinking, and
they say, 'Here is a glutton and a drunkard,
a friend of tax collectors and "sinners." '
But wisdom is proved right by her actions."

Woe on Unrepentant Cities

20 Then Jesus began to denounce the cities in which most of his miracles had
been performed, because they did not repent. 21 "Woe to you, Korazin! Woe to you,
Bethsaida! If the miracles that were performed in you had been performed in
Tyre and Sidon, they would have repented long ago in sackcloth and ashes. 22 But
I tell you, it will be more bearable for Tyre
and Sidon on the day of judgment than
for you. 23 And you, Capernaum, will you
be lifted up to the skies? No, you will go
down to the depths.[d] If the miracles that
were performed in you had been performed in Sodom, it would have remained to this day. 24 But I tell you that it
will be more bearable for Sodom on the
day of judgment than for you."

Rest for the Weary

25 At that time Jesus said, "I praise you,
Father, Lord of heaven and earth, because
you have hidden these things from the
wise and learned, and revealed them to
little children. 26 Yes, Father, for this was
your good pleasure.
27 "All things have been committed to
me by my Father. No one knows the Son
except the Father, and no one knows the
Father except the Son and those to whom
the Son chooses to reveal him.
28 "Come to me, all you who are weary
and burdened, and I will give you rest.
29 Take my yoke upon you and learn from
me, for I am gentle and humble in heart,
and you will find rest for your souls. 30 For
my yoke is easy and my burden is light."

[b] *5* The Greek word was used for various diseases affecting the skin—not necessarily leprosy.
[c] *10* Mal. 3:1 [d] *23* Greek *Hades*

PRAYER: MY RELATIONSHIP TO OTHERS

I WILL stay away from foolish people, for I will not find knowledge on their lips. (Proverbs 14:7) . . . I will not make friends with hot-tempered people or associate with those easily angered, lest I learn their ways and set a snare for my soul. (Proverbs 22:24–25)

__PAUSE__ to review your relationships with others and to commit them to the Lord.

YEAR 1 DAY 16

OT Genesis 19:1-38

Sodom and Gomorrah Destroyed

19 The two angels arrived at Sodom in
the evening, and Lot was sitting in the
gateway of the city. When he saw them, he
got up to meet them and bowed down
with his face to the ground. 2 "My lords,"
he said, "please turn aside to your servant's house. You can wash your feet and
spend the night and then go on your way
early in the morning."

"No," they answered, "we will spend
the night in the square."

3 But he insisted so strongly that they
did go with him and entered his house.
He prepared a meal for them, baking
bread without yeast, and they ate. 4 Before
they had gone to bed, all the men from
every part of the city of Sodom—both
young and old—surrounded the house.
5 They called to Lot, "Where are the men
who came to you tonight? Bring them out
to us so that we can have sex with them."

6 Lot went outside to meet them and
shut the door behind him 7 and said, "No,
my friends. Don't do this wicked thing.
8 Look, I have two daughters who have
never slept with a man. Let me bring them
out to you, and you can do what you like
with them. But don't do anything to these
men, for they have come under the protection of my roof."

9 "Get out of our way," they replied. And
they said, "This fellow came here as an
alien, and now he wants to play the
judge! We'll treat you worse than them."
They kept bringing pressure on Lot and
moved forward to break down the door.

10 But the men inside reached out and
pulled Lot back into the house and shut
the door. 11 Then they struck the men who
were at the door of the house, young and
old, with blindness so that they could not
find the door.

12 The two men said to Lot, "Do you
have anyone else here—sons-in-law, sons
or daughters, or anyone else in the city
who belongs to you? Get them out of
here, 13 because we are going to destroy
this place. The outcry to the LORD against
its people is so great that he has sent us to
destroy it."

14 So Lot went out and spoke to his
sons-in-law, who were pledged to marry[a]
his daughters. He said, "Hurry and get out
of this place, because the LORD is about to
destroy the city!" But his sons-in-law
thought he was joking.

15 With the coming of dawn, the angels
urged Lot, saying, "Hurry! Take your wife
and your two daughters who are here, or
you will be swept away when the city is
punished."

16 When he hesitated, the men grasped
his hand and the hands of his wife and of
his two daughters and led them safely out
of the city, for the LORD was merciful to
them. 17 As soon as they had brought them
out, one of them said, "Flee for your lives!
Don't look back, and don't stop anywhere
in the plain! Flee to the mountains or you
will be swept away!"

18 But Lot said to them, "No, my lords,[b]
please! 19 Your[c] servant has found favor in
your[c] eyes, and you[c] have shown great
kindness to me in sparing my life. But I
can't flee to the mountains; this disaster
will overtake me, and I'll die. 20 Look, here
is a town near enough to run to, and it is
small. Let me flee to it—it is very small,
isn't it? Then my life will be spared."

21 He said to him, "Very well, I will grant
this request too; I will not overthrow the
town you speak of. 22 But flee there quickly, because I cannot do anything until you
reach it." (That is why the town was called
Zoar.[d])

23 By the time Lot reached Zoar, the sun
had risen over the land. 24 Then the LORD
rained down burning sulfur on Sodom
and Gomorrah—from the LORD out of the
heavens. 25 Thus he overthrew those cities
and the entire plain, including all those
living in the cities—and also the vegetation in the land. 26 But Lot's wife looked
back, and she became a pillar of salt.

27 Early the next morning Abraham got
up and returned to the place where he
had stood before the LORD. 28 He looked
down toward Sodom and Gomorrah, toward all the land of the plain, and he saw
dense smoke rising from the land, like
smoke from a furnace.

29 So when God destroyed the cities of

[a] 14 Or *were married to* [b] 18 Or *No, Lord;* or *No, my lord* [c] 19 The Hebrew is singular. [d] 22 *Zoar* means *small.*

the plain, he remembered Abraham, and
he brought Lot out of the catastrophe that
overthrew the cities where Lot had lived.

Lot and His Daughters

30Lot and his two daughters left Zoar
and settled in the mountains, for he was
afraid to stay in Zoar. He and his two
daughters lived in a cave. 31One day the
older daughter said to the younger, "Our
father is old, and there is no man around
here to lie with us, as is the custom all
over the earth. 32Let's get our father to
drink wine and then lie with him and preserve our family line through our father."
33That night they got their father to
drink wine, and the older daughter went
in and lay with him. He was not aware of
it when she lay down or when she got up.
34The next day the older daughter said
to the younger, "Last night I lay with my
father. Let's get him to drink wine again
tonight, and you go in and lie with him
so we can preserve our family line
through our father." 35So they got their father to drink wine that night also, and the
younger daughter went and lay with him.
Again he was not aware of it when she lay
down or when she got up.
36So both of Lot's daughters became
pregnant by their father. 37The older
daughter had a son, and she named him
Moab[e]; he is the father of the Moabites of
today. 38The younger daughter also had a
son, and she named him Ben-Ammi[f]; he
is the father of the Ammonites of today.

[e] 37 *Moab* sounds like the Hebrew for *from father.*
[f] 38 *Ben-Ammi* means *son of my people.*

PRAYER: CONFESSION

LORD, I have heard of Your fame, and I stand in awe of Your deeds. O Lord, revive Your works in our day; in our time make them known; in wrath remember mercy. (Habakkuk 3:2)

***ASK** the Spirit to search your heart and reveal any areas of unconfessed sin. Acknowledge these to the Lord and thank Him for His forgiveness.*

NT Matthew 12:1–21

Lord of the Sabbath

12 At that time Jesus went through the
grainfields on the Sabbath. His disciples were hungry and began to pick some
heads of grain and eat them. 2When the
Pharisees saw this, they said to him,
"Look! Your disciples are doing what is
unlawful on the Sabbath."
3He answered, "Haven't you read what
David did when he and his companions
were hungry? 4He entered the house of
God, and he and his companions ate the
consecrated bread—which was not lawful
for them to do, but only for the priests. 5Or
haven't you read in the Law that on the
Sabbath the priests in the temple desecrate
the day and yet are innocent? 6I tell you
that one[a] greater than the temple is here.
7If you had known what these words
mean, 'I desire mercy, not sacrifice,'[b] you
would not have condemned the innocent.
8For the Son of Man is Lord of the Sabbath."
9Going on from that place, he went into
their synagogue, 10and a man with a shriveled hand was there. Looking for a reason
to accuse Jesus, they asked him, "Is it lawful to heal on the Sabbath?"
11He said to them, "If any of you has a
sheep and it falls into a pit on the Sabbath, will you not take hold of it and lift
it out? 12How much more valuable is a
man than a sheep! Therefore it is lawful
to do good on the Sabbath."
13Then he said to the man, "Stretch out
your hand." So he stretched it out and it
was completely restored, just as sound as
the other. 14But the Pharisees went out
and plotted how they might kill Jesus.

God's Chosen Servant

15Aware of this, Jesus withdrew from
that place. Many followed him, and he
healed all their sick, 16warning them not
to tell who he was. 17This was to fulfill

[a] 6 Or *something;* also in verses 41 and 42
[b] 7 Hosea 6:6

what was spoken through the prophet Isaiah:

18 "Here is my servant whom I have
chosen,
the one I love, in whom I delight;
I will put my Spirit on him,
and he will proclaim justice to the
nations.
19 He will not quarrel or cry out;
no one will hear his voice in the
streets.
20 A bruised reed he will not break,
and a smoldering wick he will not
snuff out,
till he leads justice to victory.
21 In his name the nations will put
their hope."[c]

[c] *21* Isaiah 42:1–4

PRAYER: THE ATTRIBUTES OF GOD

O GOD, You revealed Yourself to Moses as "I AM WHO I AM." (Exodus 3:14) . . . Jesus Christ, You are the same yesterday, today and forever. (Hebrews 13:8)

***PAUSE** to reflect on these affirmations about the person, powers and perfection of God.*

YEAR 1 DAY 17

OT Genesis 20:1–18

Abraham and Abimelech

20 Now Abraham moved on from there
into the region of the Negev and
lived between Kadesh and Shur. For a
while he stayed in Gerar, 2and there Abraham said of his wife Sarah, "She is my sister." Then Abimelech king of Gerar sent
for Sarah and took her.
3But God came to Abimelech in a
dream one night and said to him, "You
are as good as dead because of the
woman you have taken; she is a married
woman."
4Now Abimelech had not gone near
her, so he said, "Lord, will you destroy an
innocent nation? 5Did he not say to me,
'She is my sister,' and didn't she also say,
'He is my brother'? I have done this with
a clear conscience and clean hands."
6Then God said to him in the dream,
"Yes, I know you did this with a clear conscience, and so I have kept you from sinning against me. That is why I did not let
you touch her. 7Now return the man's
wife, for he is a prophet, and he will pray
for you and you will live. But if you do not
return her, you may be sure that you and
all yours will die."
8Early the next morning Abimelech
summoned all his officials, and when he
told them all that had happened, they
were very much afraid. 9Then Abimelech
called Abraham in and said, "What have
you done to us? How have I wronged
you that you have brought such great
guilt upon me and my kingdom? You
have done things to me that should not
be done." 10And Abimelech asked Abraham, "What was your reason for doing
this?"
11Abraham replied, "I said to myself,
'There is surely no fear of God in this
place, and they will kill me because of my
wife.' 12Besides, she really is my sister, the
daughter of my father though not of my
mother; and she became my wife. 13And
when God had me wander from my father's household, I said to her, 'This is
how you can show your love to me:
Everywhere we go, say of me, "He is my
brother." ' "
14Then Abimelech brought sheep and
cattle and male and female slaves and
gave them to Abraham, and he returned
Sarah his wife to him. 15And Abimelech
said, "My land is before you; live wherever you like."
16To Sarah he said, "I am giving your
brother a thousand shekels[a] of silver. This
is to cover the offense against you before

[a] *16* That is, about 25 pounds (about 11.5 kilograms)

all who are with you; you are completely
vindicated."
17Then Abraham prayed to God, and
God healed Abimelech, his wife and his
slave girls so they could have children
again, 18for the LORD had closed up every
womb in Abimelech's household because
of Abraham's wife Sarah.

PRAYER: RENEWAL

LORD, may I not turn aside from following You, but serve You with all my heart. May I not turn aside to go after worthless things which do not profit or deliver me, because they are useless. (1 Samuel 12:20–21) . . . O Lord, we know that the works of the flesh are evident; they are immorality, impurity, sensuality, idolatry, sorcery, hatred, discord, jealousy, fits of rage, selfish ambition, dissension, factions, envy, drunkenness, revelry and the like. Those who practice such things will not inherit Your kingdom. But the fruit of the Spirit is love, joy, peace, patience, kindness, goodness, faithfulness, gentleness and self-control; against such things there is no law. (Galatians 5:19–23)

PAUSE *to add your own prayers for personal renewal.*

NT Matthew 12:22–50

Jesus and Beelzebub

22Then they brought him a demon-possessed man who was blind and mute, and
Jesus healed him, so that he could both
talk and see. 23All the people were astonished and said, "Could this be the Son of
David?"
24But when the Pharisees heard this,
they said, "It is only by Beelzebub,[a] the
prince of demons, that this fellow drives
out demons."
25Jesus knew their thoughts and said to
them, "Every kingdom divided against itself will be ruined, and every city or
household divided against itself will not
stand. 26If Satan drives out Satan, he is divided against himself. How then can his
kingdom stand? 27And if I drive out
demons by Beelzebub, by whom do your
people drive them out? So then, they will
be your judges. 28But if I drive out demons
by the Spirit of God, then the kingdom of
God has come upon you.
29"Or again, how can anyone enter a
strong man's house and carry off his possessions unless he first ties up the strong
man? Then he can rob his house.
30"He who is not with me is against me,
and he who does not gather with me scatters. 31And so I tell you, every sin and blasphemy will be forgiven men, but the blasphemy against the Spirit will not be
forgiven. 32Anyone who speaks a word
against the Son of Man will be forgiven,
but anyone who speaks against the Holy
Spirit will not be forgiven, either in this
age or in the age to come.
33"Make a tree good and its fruit will be
good, or make a tree bad and its fruit will
be bad, for a tree is recognized by its fruit.
34You brood of vipers, how can you who
are evil say anything good? For out of the
overflow of the heart the mouth speaks.
35The good man brings good things out of
the good stored up in him, and the evil
man brings evil things out of the evil
stored up in him. 36But I tell you that men
will have to give account on the day of
judgment for every careless word they
have spoken. 37For by your words you will
be acquitted, and by your words you will
be condemned."

The Sign of Jonah

38Then some of the Pharisees and teachers of the law said to him, "Teacher, we
want to see a miraculous sign from you."
39He answered, "A wicked and adulterous generation asks for a miraculous sign!
But none will be given it except the sign
of the prophet Jonah. 40For as Jonah was
three days and three nights in the belly of

[a] 24 Greek *Beezeboul* or *Beelzeboul*; also in verse 27

a huge fish, so the Son of Man will be
three days and three nights in the heart of
the earth. 41The men of Nineveh will stand
up at the judgment with this generation
and condemn it; for they repented at the
preaching of Jonah, and now one[b] greater
than Jonah is here. 42The Queen of the
South will rise at the judgment with this
generation and condemn it; for she came
from the ends of the earth to listen to
Solomon's wisdom, and now one greater
than Solomon is here.
43"When an evil[c] spirit comes out of a
man, it goes through arid places seeking
rest and does not find it. 44Then it says, 'I
will return to the house I left.' When it arrives, it finds the house unoccupied, swept
clean and put in order. 45Then it goes and
takes with it seven other spirits more
wicked than itself, and they go in and live
there. And the final condition of that man
is worse than the first. That is how it will
be with this wicked generation."

Jesus' Mother and Brothers

46While Jesus was still talking to the
crowd, his mother and brothers stood
outside, wanting to speak to him. 47Some-
one told him, "Your mother and brothers
are standing outside, wanting to speak to
you."[d]
48He replied to him, "Who is my mother, and who are my brothers?" 49Pointing
to his disciples, he said, "Here are my
mother and my brothers. 50For whoever
does the will of my Father in heaven is my
brother and sister and mother."

[b] *41* Or *something;* also in verse 42 [c] *43* Greek *unclean* [d] *47* Some manuscripts do not have verse 47.

PRAYER: THE WORKS OF GOD

GOD, You sent Your word to the children of Israel, telling the good news of peace through Jesus Christ, who is Lord of all. Jesus commanded the apostles to preach to the people and to testify that He is the One whom You appointed as judge of the living and the dead. To Him all the prophets witness that, through His name, everyone who believes in Him receives forgiveness of sins. (Acts 10:36, 42–43)

TAKE *a moment to consider the greatness of God's wonderful works.*

YEAR 1 DAY 18

OT Genesis 21:1–22:24

The Birth of Isaac

21 Now the LORD was gracious to Sarah as
he had said, and the LORD did for Sarah what he had promised. 2Sarah became
pregnant and bore a son to Abraham in
his old age, at the very time God had
promised him. 3Abraham gave the name
Isaac[a] to the son Sarah bore him. 4When
his son Isaac was eight days old, Abraham
circumcised him, as God commanded
him. 5Abraham was a hundred years old
when his son Isaac was born to him.
6Sarah said, "God has brought me
laughter, and everyone who hears about
this will laugh with me." 7And she added,
"Who would have said to Abraham that
Sarah would nurse children? Yet I have
borne him a son in his old age."

Hagar and Ishmael Sent Away

8The child grew and was weaned, and
on the day Isaac was weaned Abraham
held a great feast. 9But Sarah saw that the
son whom Hagar the Egyptian had borne
to Abraham was mocking, 10and she said
to Abraham, "Get rid of that slave woman
and her son, for that slave woman's son
will never share in the inheritance with
my son Isaac."
11The matter distressed Abraham greatly because it concerned his son. 12But God
said to him, "Do not be so distressed
about the boy and your maidservant. Listen to whatever Sarah tells you, because it
is through Isaac that your offspring[b] will

[a] *3* *Isaac* means *he laughs.* [b] *12* Or *seed*

be reckoned. 13 I will make the son of the
maidservant into a nation also, because
he is your offspring."
14 Early the next morning Abraham took
some food and a skin of water and gave
them to Hagar. He set them on her shoulders and then sent her off with the boy.
She went on her way and wandered in the
desert of Beersheba.
15 When the water in the skin was gone,
she put the boy under one of the bushes.
16 Then she went off and sat down nearby,
about a bowshot away, for she thought, "I
cannot watch the boy die." And as she sat
there nearby, she[c] began to sob.
17 God heard the boy crying, and the angel of God called to Hagar from heaven
and said to her, "What is the matter, Hagar? Do not be afraid; God has heard the
boy crying as he lies there. 18 Lift the boy
up and take him by the hand, for I will
make him into a great nation."
19 Then God opened her eyes and she
saw a well of water. So she went and filled
the skin with water and gave the boy a
drink.
20 God was with the boy as he grew up.
He lived in the desert and became an
archer. 21 While he was living in the Desert
of Paran, his mother got a wife for him
from Egypt.

The Treaty at Beersheba

22 At that time Abimelech and Phicol the
commander of his forces said to Abraham, "God is with you in everything you
do. 23 Now swear to me here before God
that you will not deal falsely with me or
my children or my descendants. Show to
me and the country where you are living
as an alien the same kindness I have
shown to you."
24 Abraham said, "I swear it."
25 Then Abraham complained to Abimelech about a well of water that Abimelech's
servants had seized. 26 But Abimelech said,
"I don't know who has done this. You did
not tell me, and I heard about it only
today."
27 So Abraham brought sheep and cattle
and gave them to Abimelech, and the two
men made a treaty. 28 Abraham set apart
seven ewe lambs from the flock, 29 and
Abimelech asked Abraham, "What is the
meaning of these seven ewe lambs you
have set apart by themselves?"
30 He replied, "Accept these seven lambs
from my hand as a witness that I dug this
well."
31 So that place was called Beersheba,[d]
because the two men swore an oath there.
32 After the treaty had been made at
Beersheba, Abimelech and Phicol the
commander of his forces returned to the
land of the Philistines. 33 Abraham planted a tamarisk tree in Beersheba, and there
he called upon the name of the LORD, the
Eternal God. 34 And Abraham stayed in the
land of the Philistines for a long time.

Abraham Tested

22 Some time later God tested Abraham.
He said to him, "Abraham!"
"Here I am," he replied.
2 Then God said, "Take your son, your
only son, Isaac, whom you love, and go to
the region of Moriah. Sacrifice him there
as a burnt offering on one of the mountains I will tell you about."
3 Early the next morning Abraham got
up and saddled his donkey. He took with
him two of his servants and his son Isaac.
When he had cut enough wood for the
burnt offering, he set out for the place
God had told him about. 4 On the third
day Abraham looked up and saw the
place in the distance. 5 He said to his servants, "Stay here with the donkey while I
and the boy go over there. We will worship and then we will come back to you."
6 Abraham took the wood for the burnt
offering and placed it on his son Isaac,
and he himself carried the fire and the
knife. As the two of them went on together, 7 Isaac spoke up and said to his father Abraham, "Father?"
"Yes, my son?" Abraham replied.
"The fire and wood are here," Isaac said,
"but where is the lamb for the burnt offering?"
8 Abraham answered, "God himself will
provide the lamb for the burnt offering,
my son." And the two of them went on together.
9 When they reached the place God had
told him about, Abraham built an altar
there and arranged the wood on it. He
bound his son Isaac and laid him on the
altar, on top of the wood. 10 Then he
reached out his hand and took the knife

[c] 16 Hebrew; Septuagint *the child* [d] 31 *Beersheba* can mean *well of seven* or *well of the oath.*

to slay his son. 11But the angel of the LORD
called out to him from heaven, "Abraham! Abraham!"
"Here I am," he replied.
12"Do not lay a hand on the boy," he
said. "Do not do anything to him. Now I
know that you fear God, because you have
not withheld from me your son, your
only son."
13Abraham looked up and there in a
thicket he saw a ram[e] caught by its horns.
He went over and took the ram and sacrificed it as a burnt offering instead of his
son. 14So Abraham called that place The
LORD Will Provide. And to this day it is
said, "On the mountain of the LORD it will
be provided."
15The angel of the LORD called to Abraham from heaven a second time 16and
said, "I swear by myself, declares the LORD,
that because you have done this and have
not withheld your son, your only son, 17I
will surely bless you and make your descendants as numerous as the stars in the
sky and as the sand on the seashore. Your
descendants will take possession of the
cities of their enemies, 18and through your
offspring[f] all nations on earth will be
blessed, because you have obeyed me."
19Then Abraham returned to his servants, and they set off together for Beersheba. And Abraham stayed in Beersheba.

Nahor's Sons

20Some time later Abraham was told,
"Milcah is also a mother; she has borne
sons to your brother Nahor: 21Uz the firstborn, Buz his brother, Kemuel (the father
of Aram), 22Kesed, Hazo, Pildash, Jidlaph
and Bethuel." 23Bethuel became the father
of Rebekah. Milcah bore these eight sons
to Abraham's brother Nahor. 24His concubine, whose name was Reumah, also had
sons: Tebah, Gaham, Tahash and Maacah.

[e] *13* Many manuscripts of the Masoretic Text, Samaritan Pentateuch, Septuagint and Syriac; most manuscripts of the Masoretic Text *a ram behind ⌊him⌋*
[f] *18* Or *seed*

PRAYER: PETITION

WHEN I ask, it will be given to me; when I seek, I will find; when I knock, the door will be opened to me. For everyone who asks receives; everyone who seeks finds; and to everyone who knocks, the door will be opened. (Matthew 7:7–8; Luke 11:9–10)

PAUSE *here to petition God for spiritual insight so that you might have understanding of His Word. Ask for insight into your identity in Jesus Christ: that you might know who you are, what direction your life should take and what His purpose for your life is. Offer prayers regarding your activities for this day and any special concerns you may have.*

NT Matthew 13:1–23

The Parable of the Sower

13 That same day Jesus went out of the
house and sat by the lake. 2Such large
crowds gathered around him that he got
into a boat and sat in it, while all the people stood on the shore. 3Then he told
them many things in parables, saying: "A
farmer went out to sow his seed. 4As he
was scattering the seed, some fell along
the path, and the birds came and ate it up.
5Some fell on rocky places, where it did
not have much soil. It sprang up quickly,
because the soil was shallow. 6But when
the sun came up, the plants were
scorched, and they withered because they
had no root. 7Other seed fell among
thorns, which grew up and choked the
plants. 8Still other seed fell on good soil,
where it produced a crop—a hundred, sixty or thirty times what was sown. 9He who
has ears, let him hear."
10The disciples came to him and asked,
"Why do you speak to the people in parables?"
11He replied, "The knowledge of the secrets of the kingdom of heaven has been
given to you, but not to them. 12Whoev-
er has will be given more, and he will
have an abundance. Whoever does not
have, even what he has will be taken from

him. [13]This is why I speak to them in parables:

"Though seeing, they do not see;
though hearing, they do not hear or understand.

[14]In them is fulfilled the prophecy of Isaiah:

" 'You will be ever hearing but never understanding;
you will be ever seeing but never perceiving.
[15]For this people's heart has become calloused;
they hardly hear with their ears,
and they have closed their eyes.
Otherwise they might see with their eyes,
hear with their ears,
understand with their hearts
and turn, and I would heal them.'[a]

[16]But blessed are your eyes because they see, and your ears because they hear. [17]For I tell you the truth, many prophets and righteous men longed to see what you see but did not see it, and to hear what you hear but did not hear it.

[18]"Listen then to what the parable of the sower means: [19]When anyone hears the message about the kingdom and does not understand it, the evil one comes and snatches away what was sown in his heart. This is the seed sown along the path. [20]The one who received the seed that fell on rocky places is the man who hears the word and at once receives it with joy. [21]But since he has no root, he lasts only a short time. When trouble or persecution comes because of the word, he quickly falls away. [22]The one who received the seed that fell among the thorns is the man who hears the word, but the worries of this life and the deceitfulness of wealth choke it, making it unfruitful. [23]But the one who received the seed that fell on good soil is the man who hears the word and understands it. He produces a crop, yielding a hundred, sixty or thirty times what was sown."

[a] *15* Isaiah 6:9,10

PRAYER: MY RELATIONSHIP TO GOD

O LORD my God, You are one. I want to love You, Lord my God, with all my heart and with all my soul and with all my strength. (Deuteronomy 6:4–5) . . . Those who love their father or mother more than You are not worthy of You; those who love their son or daughter more than You are not worthy of You. (Matthew 10:37)

***PAUSE** to thank God for the relationship that you enjoy with Him in Jesus Christ.*

YEAR 1 DAY 19

OT Genesis 23:1-20

The Death of Sarah

23 Sarah lived to be a hundred and twenty-seven years old. [2]She died at Kiriath Arba (that is, Hebron) in the land of Canaan, and Abraham went to mourn for Sarah and to weep over her.

[3]Then Abraham rose from beside his dead wife and spoke to the Hittites.[a] He said, [4]"I am an alien and a stranger among you. Sell me some property for a burial site here so I can bury my dead."

[5]The Hittites replied to Abraham, [6]"Sir, listen to us. You are a mighty prince among us. Bury your dead in the choicest of our tombs. None of us will refuse you his tomb for burying your dead."

[7]Then Abraham rose and bowed down before the people of the land, the Hittites. [8]He said to them, "If you are willing to let me bury my dead, then listen to me and intercede with Ephron son of Zohar on my behalf [9]so he will sell me the cave of Machpelah, which belongs to him and is at the end of his field. Ask him to sell it

[a] *3* Or *the sons of Heth;* also in verses 5, 7, 10, 16, 18 and 20

to me for the full price as a burial site
among you."
10Ephron the Hittite was sitting among
his people and he replied to Abraham in
the hearing of all the Hittites who had
come to the gate of his city. 11"No, my
lord," he said. "Listen to me; I give[b] you
the field, and I give[b] you the cave that is
in it. I give[b] it to you in the presence of
my people. Bury your dead."
12Again Abraham bowed down before
the people of the land 13and he said to
Ephron in their hearing, "Listen to me, if
you will. I will pay the price of the field.
Accept it from me so I can bury my dead
there."
14Ephron answered Abraham, 15"Listen
to me, my lord; the land is worth four
hundred shekels[c] of silver, but what is that
between me and you? Bury your dead."
16Abraham agreed to Ephron's terms
and weighed out for him the price he
had named in the hearing of the Hittites:
four hundred shekels of silver, according
to the weight current among the merchants.
17So Ephron's field in Machpelah near
Mamre—both the field and the cave in it,
and all the trees within the borders of the
field—was deeded 18to Abraham as his
property in the presence of all the Hittites
who had come to the gate of the city. 19Af-
terward Abraham buried his wife Sarah in
the cave in the field of Machpelah near
Mamre (which is at Hebron) in the land
of Canaan. 20So the field and the cave in
it were deeded to Abraham by the Hittites
as a burial site.

[b] *11* Or *sell* [c] *15* That is, about 10 pounds (about 4.5 kilograms)

PRAYER: INTERCESSION

YOU, Father, are my witness, whom I serve in my spirit in the gospel of Your Son, of how unceasingly I make mention of Your people in my prayers. (Romans 1:9)

***TAKE** a few moments to intercede on behalf of other believers, such as your personal friends, those in ministry and those who are oppressed and in need.*

NT Matthew 13:24-58

The Parable of the Weeds

24Jesus told them another parable: "The
kingdom of heaven is like a man who
sowed good seed in his field. 25But while
everyone was sleeping, his enemy came
and sowed weeds among the wheat, and
went away. 26When the wheat sprouted
and formed heads, then the weeds also
appeared.
27"The owner's servants came to him
and said, 'Sir, didn't you sow good seed in
your field? Where then did the weeds
come from?'
28" 'An enemy did this,' he replied.
"The servants asked him, 'Do you want
us to go and pull them up?'
29" 'No,' he answered, 'because while
you are pulling the weeds, you may root
up the wheat with them. 30Let both grow
together until the harvest. At that time I
will tell the harvesters: First collect the
weeds and tie them in bundles to be
burned; then gather the wheat and bring
it into my barn.' "

The Parables of the Mustard Seed and the Yeast

31He told them another parable: "The
kingdom of heaven is like a mustard seed,
which a man took and planted in his
field. 32Though it is the smallest of all
your seeds, yet when it grows, it is the
largest of garden plants and becomes a
tree, so that the birds of the air come and
perch in its branches."
33He told them still another parable:
"The kingdom of heaven is like yeast that
a woman took and mixed into a large
amount[a] of flour until it worked all
through the dough."
34Jesus spoke all these things to the
crowd in parables; he did not say anything

[a] *33* Greek *three satas* (probably about 1/2 bushel or 22 liters)

to them without using a parable. [35]So was fulfilled what was spoken through the prophet:

> "I will open my mouth in parables,
> I will utter things hidden since the creation of the world."[b]

The Parable of the Weeds Explained

[36]Then he left the crowd and went into the house. His disciples came to him and said, "Explain to us the parable of the weeds in the field."

[37]He answered, "The one who sowed the good seed is the Son of Man. [38]The field is the world, and the good seed stands for the sons of the kingdom. The weeds are the sons of the evil one, [39]and the enemy who sows them is the devil. The harvest is the end of the age, and the harvesters are angels.

[40]"As the weeds are pulled up and burned in the fire, so it will be at the end of the age. [41]The Son of Man will send out his angels, and they will weed out of his kingdom everything that causes sin and all who do evil. [42]They will throw them into the fiery furnace, where there will be weeping and gnashing of teeth. [43]Then the righteous will shine like the sun in the kingdom of their Father. He who has ears, let him hear.

The Parables of the Hidden Treasure and the Pearl

[44]"The kingdom of heaven is like treasure hidden in a field. When a man found it, he hid it again, and then in his joy went and sold all he had and bought that field.

[45]"Again, the kingdom of heaven is like a merchant looking for fine pearls. [46]When he found one of great value, he went away and sold everything he had and bought it.

The Parable of the Net

[47]"Once again, the kingdom of heaven is like a net that was let down into the lake and caught all kinds of fish. [48]When it was full, the fishermen pulled it up on the shore. Then they sat down and collected the good fish in baskets, but threw the bad away. [49]This is how it will be at the end of the age. The angels will come and separate the wicked from the righteous [50]and throw them into the fiery furnace, where there will be weeping and gnashing of teeth.

[51]"Have you understood all these things?" Jesus asked.

"Yes," they replied.

[52]He said to them, "Therefore every teacher of the law who has been instructed about the kingdom of heaven is like the owner of a house who brings out of his storeroom new treasures as well as old."

A Prophet Without Honor

[53]When Jesus had finished these parables, he moved on from there. [54]Coming to his hometown, he began teaching the people in their synagogue, and they were amazed. "Where did this man get this wisdom and these miraculous powers?" they asked. [55]"Isn't this the carpenter's son? Isn't his mother's name Mary, and aren't his brothers James, Joseph, Simon and Judas? [56]Aren't all his sisters with us? Where then did this man get all these things?" [57]And they took offense at him.

But Jesus said to them, "Only in his hometown and in his own house is a prophet without honor."

[58]And he did not do many miracles there because of their lack of faith.

[b] 35 Psalm 78:2

PRAYER: THE CHARACTER I WANT TO CULTIVATE

I WILL not follow the crowd in doing wrong. (Exodus 23:2) . . . There are six things You hate, O Lord, seven that are detestable to You: haughty eyes, a lying tongue, hands that shed innocent blood, a heart that devises wicked plans, feet that run swiftly to evil, a false witness who breathes lies and one who causes strife among brothers and sisters. (Proverbs 6:16–19)

***TAKE** a moment to ask the Lord for the grace to grow in godly character.*

OT **Genesis 24:1-67** YEAR 1 DAY 20

Isaac and Rebekah

24 Abraham was now old and well advanced in years, and the LORD had
blessed him in every way. 2He said to the
chief[a] servant in his household, the one
in charge of all that he had, "Put your
hand under my thigh. 3I want you to
swear by the LORD, the God of heaven and
the God of earth, that you will not get a
wife for my son from the daughters of the
Canaanites, among whom I am living,
4but will go to my country and my own
relatives and get a wife for my son Isaac."
5The servant asked him, "What if the
woman is unwilling to come back with
me to this land? Shall I then take your son
back to the country you came from?"
6"Make sure that you do not take my son
back there," Abraham said. 7"The LORD, the
God of heaven, who brought me out of my
father's household and my native land and
who spoke to me and promised me on
oath, saying, 'To your offspring[b] I will give
this land'—he will send his angel before
you so that you can get a wife for my son
from there. 8If the woman is unwilling to
come back with you, then you will be released from this oath of mine. Only do not
take my son back there." 9So the servant
put his hand under the thigh of his master
Abraham and swore an oath to him concerning this matter.
10Then the servant took ten of his master's camels and left, taking with him all
kinds of good things from his master. He
set out for Aram Naharaim[c] and made his
way to the town of Nahor. 11He had the
camels kneel down near the well outside
the town; it was toward evening, the time
the women go out to draw water.
12Then he prayed, "O LORD, God of my
master Abraham, give me success today,
and show kindness to my master Abraham. 13See, I am standing beside this
spring, and the daughters of the towns-
people are coming out to draw water.
14May it be that when I say to a girl, 'Please
let down your jar that I may have a drink,'
and she says, 'Drink, and I'll water your
camels too'—let her be the one you have
chosen for your servant Isaac. By this I will
know that you have shown kindness to
my master."
15Before he had finished praying, Rebekah came out with her jar on her shoulder. She was the daughter of Bethuel son
of Milcah, who was the wife of Abraham's
brother Nahor. 16The girl was very beautiful, a virgin; no man had ever lain with
her. She went down to the spring, filled
her jar and came up again.
17The servant hurried to meet her and
said, "Please give me a little water from
your jar."
18"Drink, my lord," she said, and quickly lowered the jar to her hands and gave
him a drink.
19After she had given him a drink, she
said, "I'll draw water for your camels too,
until they have finished drinking." 20So
she quickly emptied her jar into the
trough, ran back to the well to draw more
water, and drew enough for all his camels.
21Without saying a word, the man watched
her closely to learn whether or not the
LORD had made his journey successful.
22When the camels had finished drinking, the man took out a gold nose ring
weighing a beka[d] and two gold bracelets
weighing ten shekels.[e] 23Then he asked,
"Whose daughter are you? Please tell me,
is there room in your father's house for us
to spend the night?"
24She answered him, "I am the daughter of Bethuel, the son that Milcah bore to
Nahor." 25And she added, "We have plenty of straw and fodder, as well as room for
you to spend the night."
26Then the man bowed down and worshiped the LORD, 27saying, "Praise be to
the LORD, the God of my master Abraham,
who has not abandoned his kindness and
faithfulness to my master. As for me, the
LORD has led me on the journey to the
house of my master's relatives."
28The girl ran and told her mother's
household about these things. 29Now Rebekah had a brother named Laban, and
he hurried out to the man at the spring.
30As soon as he had seen the nose ring,
and the bracelets on his sister's arms, and
had heard Rebekah tell what the man said

[a] 2 Or *oldest* [b] 7 Or *seed* [c] 10 That is, Northwest Mesopotamia [d] 22 That is, about 1/5 ounce (about 5.5 grams) [e] 22 That is, about 4 ounces (about 110 grams)

to her, he went out to the man and found him standing by the camels near the spring. 31"Come, you who are blessed by the LORD," he said. "Why are you standing out here? I have prepared the house and a place for the camels."

32So the man went to the house, and the camels were unloaded. Straw and fodder were brought for the camels, and water for him and his men to wash their feet. 33Then food was set before him, but he said, "I will not eat until I have told you what I have to say."

"Then tell us," ⌞Laban⌟ said.

34So he said, "I am Abraham's servant. 35The LORD has blessed my master abundantly, and he has become wealthy. He has given him sheep and cattle, silver and gold, menservants and maidservants, and camels and donkeys. 36My master's wife Sarah has borne him a son in her[f] old age, and he has given him everything he owns. 37And my master made me swear an oath, and said, 'You must not get a wife for my son from the daughters of the Canaanites, in whose land I live, 38but go to my father's family and to my own clan, and get a wife for my son.'

39"Then I asked my master, 'What if the woman will not come back with me?'

40"He replied, 'The LORD, before whom I have walked, will send his angel with you and make your journey a success, so that you can get a wife for my son from my own clan and from my father's family. 41Then, when you go to my clan, you will be released from my oath even if they refuse to give her to you—you will be released from my oath.'

42"When I came to the spring today, I said, 'O LORD, God of my master Abraham, if you will, please grant success to the journey on which I have come. 43See, I am standing beside this spring; if a maiden comes out to draw water and I say to her, "Please let me drink a little water from your jar," 44and if she says to me, "Drink, and I'll draw water for your camels too," let her be the one the LORD has chosen for my master's son.'

45"Before I finished praying in my heart, Rebekah came out, with her jar on her shoulder. She went down to the spring and drew water, and I said to her, 'Please give me a drink.'

46"She quickly lowered her jar from her shoulder and said, 'Drink, and I'll water your camels too.' So I drank, and she watered the camels also.

47"I asked her, 'Whose daughter are you?'

"She said, 'The daughter of Bethuel son of Nahor, whom Milcah bore to him.'

"Then I put the ring in her nose and the bracelets on her arms, 48and I bowed down and worshiped the LORD. I praised the LORD, the God of my master Abraham, who had led me on the right road to get the granddaughter of my master's brother for his son. 49Now if you will show kindness and faithfulness to my master, tell me; and if not, tell me, so I may know which way to turn."

50Laban and Bethuel answered, "This is from the LORD; we can say nothing to you one way or the other. 51Here is Rebekah; take her and go, and let her become the wife of your master's son, as the LORD has directed."

52When Abraham's servant heard what they said, he bowed down to the ground before the LORD. 53Then the servant brought out gold and silver jewelry and articles of clothing and gave them to Rebekah; he also gave costly gifts to her brother and to her mother. 54Then he and the men who were with him ate and drank and spent the night there.

When they got up the next morning, he said, "Send me on my way to my master."

55But her brother and her mother replied, "Let the girl remain with us ten days or so; then you[g] may go."

56But he said to them, "Do not detain me, now that the LORD has granted success to my journey. Send me on my way so I may go to my master."

57Then they said, "Let's call the girl and ask her about it." 58So they called Rebekah and asked her, "Will you go with this man?"

"I will go," she said.

59So they sent their sister Rebekah on her way, along with her nurse and Abraham's servant and his men. 60And they blessed Rebekah and said to her,

"Our sister, may you increase
  to thousands upon thousands;
may your offspring possess
  the gates of their enemies."

61Then Rebekah and her maids got

f 36 Or *his*   g 55 Or *she*

ready and mounted their camels and went back with the man. So the servant took Rebekah and left.

62 Now Isaac had come from Beer Lahai Roi, for he was living in the Negev. 63 He went out to the field one evening to meditate,[h] and as he looked up, he saw camels approaching. 64 Rebekah also looked up and saw Isaac. She got down from her camel 65 and asked the servant, "Who is that man in the field coming to meet us?"

"He is my master," the servant answered. So she took her veil and covered herself.

66 Then the servant told Isaac all he had done. 67 Isaac brought her into the tent of his mother Sarah, and he married Rebekah. So she became his wife, and he loved her; and Isaac was comforted after his mother's death.

[h] *63* The meaning of the Hebrew for this word is uncertain.

PRAYER: AFFIRMATION

YOU, Lord, are a jealous God, punishing the children for the sin of the fathers to the third and fourth generation of those who hate You, but showing loving-kindness to a thousand generations of those who love You and keep Your commandments. (Exodus 20:5–6; Deuteronomy 5:9–10)

***PAUSE** to reflect on these Biblical affirmations.*

NT Matthew 14:1-36

John the Baptist Beheaded

14 At that time Herod the tetrarch heard the reports about Jesus, 2 and he said to his attendants, "This is John the Baptist; he has risen from the dead! That is why miraculous powers are at work in him."

3 Now Herod had arrested John and bound him and put him in prison because of Herodias, his brother Philip's wife, 4 for John had been saying to him: "It is not lawful for you to have her." 5 Herod wanted to kill John, but he was afraid of the people, because they considered him a prophet.

6 On Herod's birthday the daughter of Herodias danced for them and pleased Herod so much 7 that he promised with an oath to give her whatever she asked. 8 Prompted by her mother, she said, "Give me here on a platter the head of John the Baptist." 9 The king was distressed, but because of his oaths and his dinner guests, he ordered that her request be granted 10 and had John beheaded in the prison. 11 His head was brought in on a platter and given to the girl, who carried it to her mother. 12 John's disciples came and took his body and buried it. Then they went and told Jesus.

Jesus Feeds the Five Thousand

13 When Jesus heard what had happened, he withdrew by boat privately to a solitary place. Hearing of this, the crowds followed him on foot from the towns. 14 When Jesus landed and saw a large crowd, he had compassion on them and healed their sick.

15 As evening approached, the disciples came to him and said, "This is a remote place, and it's already getting late. Send the crowds away, so they can go to the villages and buy themselves some food."

16 Jesus replied, "They do not need to go away. You give them something to eat."

17 "We have here only five loaves of bread and two fish," they answered.

18 "Bring them here to me," he said. 19 And he directed the people to sit down on the grass. Taking the five loaves and the two fish and looking up to heaven, he gave thanks and broke the loaves. Then he gave them to the disciples, and the disciples gave them to the people. 20 They all ate and were satisfied, and the disciples picked up twelve basketfuls of broken pieces that were left over. 21 The number of those who ate was about five thousand men, besides women and children.

Jesus Walks on the Water

22 Immediately Jesus made the disciples get into the boat and go on ahead of him to the other side, while he dismissed the

crowd. [23]After he had dismissed them, he
went up on a mountainside by himself to
pray. When evening came, he was there
alone, [24]but the boat was already a considerable distance[a] from land, buffeted by
the waves because the wind was against it.
[25]During the fourth watch of the night
Jesus went out to them, walking on the
lake. [26]When the disciples saw him walking on the lake, they were terrified. "It's a
ghost," they said, and cried out in fear.
[27]But Jesus immediately said to them:
"Take courage! It is I. Don't be afraid."
[28]"Lord, if it's you," Peter replied, "tell
me to come to you on the water."
[29]"Come," he said.
Then Peter got down out of the boat,
walked on the water and came toward
Jesus. [30]But when he saw the wind, he was
afraid and, beginning to sink, cried out,
"Lord, save me!"
[31]Immediately Jesus reached out his
hand and caught him. "You of little faith,"
he said, "why did you doubt?"
[32]And when they climbed into the boat,
the wind died down. [33]Then those who
were in the boat worshiped him, saying,
"Truly you are the Son of God."
[34]When they had crossed over, they
landed at Gennesaret. [35]And when the
men of that place recognized Jesus, they
sent word to all the surrounding country.
People brought all their sick to him [36]and
begged him to let the sick just touch the
edge of his cloak, and all who touched
him were healed.

[a] 24 Greek *many stadia*

PRAYER: MY RELATIONSHIP TO OTHERS

FROM the beginning of creation You made us male and female. For this reason a man shall leave his father and mother and shall cleave to his wife, and the two shall become one flesh. So they are no longer two, but one flesh. Therefore what You have joined together, let no one separate. (Matthew 19:4–6; Mark 10:6–9)

__PAUSE__ to review your relationships with others and to commit them to the Lord.

YEAR 1 DAY 21

OT Psalms 5–6

Psalm 5

For the director of music. For flutes.
A psalm of David.

[1]Give ear to my words, O LORD,
consider my sighing.
[2]Listen to my cry for help,
my King and my God,
for to you I pray.
[3]In the morning, O LORD, you hear my voice;
in the morning I lay my requests before you
and wait in expectation.

[4]You are not a God who takes pleasure in evil;
with you the wicked cannot dwell.
[5]The arrogant cannot stand in your presence;
you hate all who do wrong.
[6]You destroy those who tell lies;
bloodthirsty and deceitful men
the LORD abhors.

[7]But I, by your great mercy,
will come into your house;
in reverence will I bow down
toward your holy temple.
[8]Lead me, O LORD, in your righteousness
because of my enemies—
make straight your way before me.

[9]Not a word from their mouth can be trusted;
their heart is filled with destruction.
Their throat is an open grave;
with their tongue they speak deceit.
[10]Declare them guilty, O God!
Let their intrigues be their downfall.

Banish them for their many sins,
for they have rebelled against you.

11 But let all who take refuge in you be glad;
let them ever sing for joy.
Spread your protection over them,
that those who love your name may rejoice in you.
12 For surely, O LORD, you bless the righteous;
you surround them with your favor as with a shield.

Psalm 6

For the director of music. With stringed instruments. According to *sheminith.*[a] A psalm of David.

1 O LORD, do not rebuke me in your anger
or discipline me in your wrath.
2 Be merciful to me, LORD, for I am faint;
O LORD, heal me, for my bones are in agony.
3 My soul is in anguish.
How long, O LORD, how long?

4 Turn, O LORD, and deliver me;
save me because of your unfailing love.
5 No one remembers you when he is dead.
Who praises you from the grave[b]?

6 I am worn out from groaning;
all night long I flood my bed with weeping
and drench my couch with tears.
7 My eyes grow weak with sorrow;
they fail because of all my foes.

8 Away from me, all you who do evil,
for the LORD has heard my weeping.
9 The LORD has heard my cry for mercy;
the LORD accepts my prayer.
10 All my enemies will be ashamed and dismayed;
they will turn back in sudden disgrace.

[a] Title: Probably a musical term [b] 5 Hebrew *Sheol*

PRAYER: THANKSGIVING

I WILL remember Your works, O Lord; surely, I will remember Your wonders of long ago. I will meditate on all Your works and consider all Your mighty deeds. Your way, O God, is holy. What god is so great as You? You are the God who works wonders; You have revealed Your strength among the peoples. You redeemed Your people with Your power, the descendants of Jacob and Joseph. (Psalm 77:11–15)

***PAUSE** to offer your own expressions of thanksgiving.*

NT Matthew 15:1–28

Clean and Unclean

15 Then some Pharisees and teachers of
the law came to Jesus from Jerusalem
and asked, 2 "Why do your disciples break
the tradition of the elders? They don't
wash their hands before they eat!"
3 Jesus replied, "And why do you break
the command of God for the sake of your
tradition? 4 For God said, 'Honor your father and mother'[a] and 'Anyone who
curses his father or mother must be put to
death.'[b] 5 But you say that if a man says to
his father or mother, 'Whatever help you
might otherwise have received from me is
a gift devoted to God,' 6 he is not to 'hon-
or his father[c]' with it. Thus you nullify the
word of God for the sake of your tradition. 7 You hypocrites! Isaiah was right
when he prophesied about you:

8 " 'These people honor me with their lips,
but their hearts are far from me.
9 They worship me in vain;
their teachings are but rules taught by men.'[d]"

10 Jesus called the crowd to him and
said, "Listen and understand. 11 What goes

[a] 4 Exodus 20:12; Deut. 5:16 [b] 4 Exodus 21:17; Lev. 20:9 [c] 6 Some manuscripts *father or his mother* [d] 9 Isaiah 29:13

into a man's mouth does not make him 'unclean,' but what comes out of his mouth, that is what makes him 'unclean.' "

12Then the disciples came to him and asked, "Do you know that the Pharisees were offended when they heard this?"

13He replied, "Every plant that my heavenly Father has not planted will be pulled up by the roots. 14Leave them; they are blind guides.[e] If a blind man leads a blind man, both will fall into a pit."

15Peter said, "Explain the parable to us."

16"Are you still so dull?" Jesus asked them. 17"Don't you see that whatever enters the mouth goes into the stomach and then out of the body? 18But the things that come out of the mouth come from the heart, and these make a man 'unclean.' 19For out of the heart come evil thoughts, murder, adultery, sexual immorality, theft, false testimony, slander. 20These are what make a man 'unclean'; but eating with unwashed hands does not make him 'unclean.' "

The Faith of the Canaanite Woman

21Leaving that place, Jesus withdrew to the region of Tyre and Sidon. 22A Canaanite woman from that vicinity came to him, crying out, "Lord, Son of David, have mercy on me! My daughter is suffering terribly from demon-possession."

23Jesus did not answer a word. So his disciples came to him and urged him, "Send her away, for she keeps crying out after us."

24He answered, "I was sent only to the lost sheep of Israel."

25The woman came and knelt before him. "Lord, help me!" she said.

26He replied, "It is not right to take the children's bread and toss it to their dogs."

27"Yes, Lord," she said, "but even the dogs eat the crumbs that fall from their masters' table."

28Then Jesus answered, "Woman, you have great faith! Your request is granted." And her daughter was healed from that very hour.

[e] 14 Some manuscripts *guides of the blind*

PRAYER: THE ATTRIBUTES OF GOD

I WILL enter Your gates with thanksgiving, O Lord, and Your courts with praise; I will give thanks to You and bless Your name. For You are good and Your loving-kindness endures forever; Your faithfulness continues through all generations. (Psalm 100:4–5) . . . May Your glory endure forever; may You rejoice in Your works. (Psalm 104:31)

PAUSE *to reflect on these affirmations about the person, powers and perfection of God.*

YEAR 1 DAY 22

OT Genesis 25:1-34

The Death of Abraham

25 Abraham took[a] another wife, whose name was Keturah. 2She bore him Zimran, Jokshan, Medan, Midian, Ishbak and Shuah. 3Jokshan was the father of Sheba and Dedan; the descendants of Dedan were the Asshurites, the Letushites and the Leummites. 4The sons of Midian were Ephah, Epher, Hanoch, Abida and Eldaah. All these were descendants of Keturah.

5Abraham left everything he owned to Isaac. 6But while he was still living, he gave gifts to the sons of his concubines and sent them away from his son Isaac to the land of the east.

7Altogether, Abraham lived a hundred and seventy-five years. 8Then Abraham breathed his last and died at a good old age, an old man and full of years; and he was gathered to his people. 9His sons Isaac and Ishmael buried him in the cave of Machpelah near Mamre, in the field of Ephron son of Zohar the Hittite, 10the field Abraham had bought from the Hittites.[b] There Abraham was buried with his

[a] 1 Or *had taken* [b] 10 Or *the sons of Heth*

wife Sarah. 11After Abraham's death, God
blessed his son Isaac, who then lived near
Beer Lahai Roi.

Ishmael's Sons

12This is the account of Abraham's son
Ishmael, whom Sarah's maidservant, Hagar the Egyptian, bore to Abraham.

13These are the names of the sons of Ishmael, listed in the order of their birth: Nebaioth the firstborn of Ishmael, Kedar, Adbeel, Mibsam, 14Mishma, Dumah, Massa,
15Hadad, Tema, Jetur, Naphish and Kedemah. 16These were the sons of Ishmael, and
these are the names of the twelve tribal
rulers according to their settlements and
camps. 17Altogether, Ishmael lived a hundred and thirty-seven years. He breathed his
last and died, and he was gathered to his
people. 18His descendants settled in the
area from Havilah to Shur, near the border
of Egypt, as you go toward Asshur. And they
lived in hostility toward[c] all their brothers.

Jacob and Esau

19This is the account of Abraham's son
Isaac.

Abraham became the father of Isaac,
20and Isaac was forty years old when he
married Rebekah daughter of Bethuel the
Aramean from Paddan Aram[d] and sister
of Laban the Aramean.

21Isaac prayed to the LORD on behalf of
his wife, because she was barren. The
LORD answered his prayer, and his wife Rebekah became pregnant. 22The babies jos-
tled each other within her, and she said,
"Why is this happening to me?" So she
went to inquire of the LORD.

23The LORD said to her,

"Two nations are in your womb,
and two peoples from within you
will be separated;
one people will be stronger than the
other,
and the older will serve the younger."

24When the time came for her to give
birth, there were twin boys in her womb.
25The first to come out was red, and his
whole body was like a hairy garment; so
they named him Esau.[e] 26After this, his
brother came out, with his hand grasping
Esau's heel; so he was named Jacob.[f] Isaac
was sixty years old when Rebekah gave
birth to them.

27The boys grew up, and Esau became a
skillful hunter, a man of the open country, while Jacob was a quiet man, staying
among the tents. 28Isaac, who had a taste
for wild game, loved Esau, but Rebekah
loved Jacob.

29Once when Jacob was cooking some
stew, Esau came in from the open country,
famished. 30He said to Jacob, "Quick, let me
have some of that red stew! I'm famished!"
(That is why he was also called Edom.[g])

31Jacob replied, "First sell me your
birthright."

32"Look, I am about to die," Esau said.
"What good is the birthright to me?"

33But Jacob said, "Swear to me first." So
he swore an oath to him, selling his
birthright to Jacob.

34Then Jacob gave Esau some bread and
some lentil stew. He ate and drank, and
then got up and left.

So Esau despised his birthright.

[c] 18 Or *lived to the east of* [d] 20 That is, Northwest Mesopotamia [e] 25 *Esau* may mean *hairy*; he was also called Edom, which means *red.* [f] 26 *Jacob* means *he grasps the heel* (figuratively, *he deceives*). [g] 30 *Edom* means *red.*

PRAYER: ADORATION

YOU are the God of Abraham and the Fear of Isaac. (Genesis 31:42) . . . You, O Lord, are great and greatly to be praised; You are to be feared above all gods. For all the gods of the nations are idols, but You made the heavens. Splendor and majesty are before You; strength and joy are in Your place. I will ascribe to You glory and strength. I will ascribe to You the glory due Your name and worship You in the beauty of holiness. All the earth trembles before You. The world is firmly established, it will not be moved.

(1 Chronicles 16:25–30)

PAUSE *to express your thoughts of praise and worship.*

NT Matthew 15:29–16:28

Jesus Feeds the Four Thousand

29 Jesus left there and went along the Sea
of Galilee. Then he went up on a mountainside and sat down. 30 Great crowds
came to him, bringing the lame, the
blind, the crippled, the mute and many
others, and laid them at his feet; and he
healed them. 31 The people were amazed
when they saw the mute speaking, the
crippled made well, the lame walking and
the blind seeing. And they praised the
God of Israel.
32 Jesus called his disciples to him and
said, "I have compassion for these people;
they have already been with me three days
and have nothing to eat. I do not want to
send them away hungry, or they may collapse on the way."
33 His disciples answered, "Where could
we get enough bread in this remote place
to feed such a crowd?"
34 "How many loaves do you have?"
Jesus asked.
"Seven," they replied, "and a few small
fish."
35 He told the crowd to sit down on the
ground. 36 Then he took the seven loaves
and the fish, and when he had given
thanks, he broke them and gave them to
the disciples, and they in turn to the people. 37 They all ate and were satisfied. Afterward the disciples picked up seven basketfuls of broken pieces that were left
over. 38 The number of those who ate was
four thousand, besides women and children. 39 After Jesus had sent the crowd
away, he got into the boat and went to the
vicinity of Magadan.

The Demand for a Sign

16 The Pharisees and Sadducees came to
Jesus and tested him by asking him to
show them a sign from heaven.
2 He replied,[a] "When evening comes,
you say, 'It will be fair weather, for the sky
is red,' 3 and in the morning, 'Today it will
be stormy, for the sky is red and overcast.'
You know how to interpret the appearance of the sky, but you cannot interpret
the signs of the times. 4 A wicked and adulterous generation looks for a miraculous
sign, but none will be given it except the
sign of Jonah." Jesus then left them and
went away.

The Yeast of the Pharisees and Sadducees

5 When they went across the lake, the
disciples forgot to take bread. 6 "Be careful," Jesus said to them. "Be on your guard
against the yeast of the Pharisees and Sadducees."
7 They discussed this among themselves
and said, "It is because we didn't bring
any bread."
8 Aware of their discussion, Jesus asked,
"You of little faith, why are you talking
among yourselves about having no bread?
9 Do you still not understand? Don't you
remember the five loaves for the five thousand, and how many basketfuls you gathered? 10 Or the seven loaves for the four
thousand, and how many basketfuls you
gathered? 11 How is it you don't understand that I was not talking to you about
bread? But be on your guard against the
yeast of the Pharisees and Sadducees."
12 Then they understood that he was not
telling them to guard against the yeast
used in bread, but against the teaching of
the Pharisees and Sadducees.

Peter's Confession of Christ

13 When Jesus came to the region of
Caesarea Philippi, he asked his disciples,
"Who do people say the Son of Man is?"
14 They replied, "Some say John the Baptist; others say Elijah; and still others, Jeremiah or one of the prophets."
15 "But what about you?" he asked.
"Who do you say I am?"
16 Simon Peter answered, "You are the
Christ,[b] the Son of the living God."
17 Jesus replied, "Blessed are you, Simon son of Jonah, for this was not revealed to you by man, but by my Father
in heaven. 18 And I tell you that you are
Peter,[c] and on this rock I will build my
church, and the gates of Hades[d] will not
overcome it.[e] 19 I will give you the keys of
the kingdom of heaven; whatever you
bind on earth will be[f] bound in heaven,
and whatever you loose on earth will be[f]
loosed in heaven." 20 Then he warned his

[a] 2 Some early manuscripts do not have the rest of verse 2 and all of verse 3. [b] 16 Or *Messiah;* also in verse 20 [c] 18 *Peter* means *rock.* [d] 18 Or *hell* [e] 18 Or *not prove stronger than it* [f] 19 Or *have been*

disciples not to tell anyone that he was the Christ.

Jesus Predicts His Death

21 From that time on Jesus began to explain to his disciples that he must go to Jerusalem and suffer many things at the hands of the elders, chief priests and teachers of the law, and that he must be killed and on the third day be raised to life.

22 Peter took him aside and began to rebuke him. "Never, Lord!" he said. "This shall never happen to you!"

23 Jesus turned and said to Peter, "Get behind me, Satan! You are a stumbling block to me; you do not have in mind the things of God, but the things of men."

24 Then Jesus said to his disciples, "If anyone would come after me, he must deny himself and take up his cross and follow me. 25 For whoever wants to save his life[g] will lose it, but whoever loses his life for me will find it. 26 What good will it be for a man if he gains the whole world, yet forfeits his soul? Or what can a man give in exchange for his soul? 27 For the Son of Man is going to come in his Father's glory with his angels, and then he will reward each person according to what he has done. 28 I tell you the truth, some who are standing here will not taste death before they see the Son of Man coming in his kingdom."

[g] 25 The Greek word means either *life* or *soul*; also in verse 26.

PRAYER: THE WORKS OF GOD

O GOD, You completed the heavens and the earth in all their vast array. By the seventh day You finished the work that You had done, and You rested on the seventh day from all Your creative work. And You blessed the seventh day and sanctified it, because on it You rested from all the work of creating that You had done. (Genesis 2:1–3) . . . O Lord, God of Israel, enthroned between the cherubim, You alone are God over all the kingdoms of the earth. You have made heaven and earth. (2 Kings 19:15)

TAKE *a moment to consider the greatness of God's wonderful works.*

YEAR 1 DAY 23

OT Genesis 26:1–35

Isaac and Abimelech

26 Now there was a famine in the land—besides the earlier famine of Abraham's time—and Isaac went to Abimelech king of the Philistines in Gerar. 2 The LORD appeared to Isaac and said, "Do not go down to Egypt; live in the land where I tell you to live. 3 Stay in this land for a while, and I will be with you and will bless you. For to you and your descendants I will give all these lands and will confirm the oath I swore to your father Abraham. 4 I will make your descendants as numerous as the stars in the sky and will give them all these lands, and through your offspring[a] all nations on earth will be blessed, 5 because Abraham obeyed me and kept my requirements, my commands, my decrees and my laws." 6 So Isaac stayed in Gerar.

7 When the men of that place asked him about his wife, he said, "She is my sister," because he was afraid to say, "She is my wife." He thought, "The men of this place might kill me on account of Rebekah, because she is beautiful."

8 When Isaac had been there a long time, Abimelech king of the Philistines looked down from a window and saw Isaac caressing his wife Rebekah. 9 So Abimelech summoned Isaac and said, "She is really your wife! Why did you say, 'She is my sister'?"

Isaac answered him, "Because I thought I might lose my life on account of her."

10 Then Abimelech said, "What is this you have done to us? One of the men

[a] 4 Or *seed*

might well have slept with your wife, and
you would have brought guilt upon us."
11 So Abimelech gave orders to all the
people: "Anyone who molests this man or
his wife shall surely be put to death."
12 Isaac planted crops in that land and
the same year reaped a hundredfold, because the LORD blessed him. 13 The man
became rich, and his wealth continued to
grow until he became very wealthy. 14 He
had so many flocks and herds and servants that the Philistines envied him. 15 So
all the wells that his father's servants had
dug in the time of his father Abraham, the
Philistines stopped up, filling them with
earth.
16 Then Abimelech said to Isaac, "Move
away from us; you have become too powerful for us."
17 So Isaac moved away from there and
encamped in the Valley of Gerar and settled there. 18 Isaac reopened the wells that
had been dug in the time of his father
Abraham, which the Philistines had
stopped up after Abraham died, and he
gave them the same names his father had
given them.
19 Isaac's servants dug in the valley and
discovered a well of fresh water there.
20 But the herdsmen of Gerar quarreled
with Isaac's herdsmen and said, "The water is ours!" So he named the well Esek,[b]
because they disputed with him. 21 Then
they dug another well, but they quarreled
over that one also; so he named it Sitnah.[c]
22 He moved on from there and dug another well, and no one quarreled over it.
He named it Rehoboth,[d] saying, "Now the
LORD has given us room and we will flourish in the land."
23 From there he went up to Beersheba.
24 That night the LORD appeared to him
and said, "I am the God of your father
Abraham. Do not be afraid, for I am with
you; I will bless you and will increase the
number of your descendants for the sake
of my servant Abraham."
25 Isaac built an altar there and called on
the name of the LORD. There he pitched
his tent, and there his servants dug a well.
26 Meanwhile, Abimelech had come to
him from Gerar, with Ahuzzath his personal adviser and Phicol the commander
of his forces. 27 Isaac asked them, "Why
have you come to me, since you were hostile to me and sent me away?"
28 They answered, "We saw clearly that
the LORD was with you; so we said, 'There
ought to be a sworn agreement between
us'—between us and you. Let us make a
treaty with you 29 that you will do us no
harm, just as we did not molest you but
always treated you well and sent you away
in peace. And now you are blessed by the
LORD."
30 Isaac then made a feast for them, and
they ate and drank. 31 Early the next morning the men swore an oath to each other.
Then Isaac sent them on their way, and
they left him in peace.
32 That day Isaac's servants came and
told him about the well they had dug.
They said, "We've found water!" 33 He
called it Shibah,[e] and to this day the name
of the town has been Beersheba.[f]
34 When Esau was forty years old, he
married Judith daughter of Beeri the Hittite, and also Basemath daughter of Elon
the Hittite. 35 They were a source of grief to
Isaac and Rebekah.

[b] 20 *Esek* means *dispute.* [c] 21 *Sitnah* means *opposition.* [d] 22 *Rehoboth* means *room.* [e] 33 *Shibah* can mean *oath* or *seven.* [f] 33 *Beersheba* can mean *well of the oath* or *well of seven.*

PRAYER: CONFESSION

SAVE me from bloodguilt, O God, the God of my salvation, and my tongue will sing aloud of Your righteousness. O Lord, open my lips, and my mouth will declare Your praise. For You do not desire sacrifice, or I would bring it; You do not delight in burnt offerings. The sacrifices You desire are a broken spirit; a broken and contrite heart, O God, You will not despise. (Psalm 51:14–17)

__ASK__ the Spirit to search your heart and reveal any areas of unconfessed sin. Acknowledge these to the Lord and thank Him for His forgiveness.

NT Matthew 17:1–27

The Transfiguration

17 After six days Jesus took with him Peter, James and John the brother of
James, and led them up a high mountain
by themselves. 2There he was transfigured
before them. His face shone like the sun,
and his clothes became as white as the
light. 3Just then there appeared before
them Moses and Elijah, talking with Jesus.
4Peter said to Jesus, "Lord, it is good for
us to be here. If you wish, I will put up
three shelters—one for you, one for Moses and one for Elijah."
5While he was still speaking, a bright
cloud enveloped them, and a voice from
the cloud said, "This is my Son, whom I
love; with him I am well pleased. Listen
to him!"
6When the disciples heard this, they fell
facedown to the ground, terrified. 7But
Jesus came and touched them. "Get up,"
he said. "Don't be afraid." 8When they
looked up, they saw no one except Jesus.
9As they were coming down the mountain, Jesus instructed them, "Don't tell
anyone what you have seen, until the Son
of Man has been raised from the dead."
10The disciples asked him, "Why then
do the teachers of the law say that Elijah
must come first?"
11Jesus replied, "To be sure, Elijah
comes and will restore all things. 12But I
tell you, Elijah has already come, and they
did not recognize him, but have done to
him everything they wished. In the same
way the Son of Man is going to suffer at
their hands." 13Then the disciples understood that he was talking to them about
John the Baptist.

The Healing of a Boy With a Demon

14When they came to the crowd, a man
approached Jesus and knelt before him.
15"Lord, have mercy on my son," he said.
"He has seizures and is suffering greatly.
He often falls into the fire or into the water. 16I brought him to your disciples, but
they could not heal him."
17"O unbelieving and perverse generation," Jesus replied, "how long shall I stay
with you? How long shall I put up with
you? Bring the boy here to me." 18Jesus rebuked the demon, and it came out of the
boy, and he was healed from that moment.
19Then the disciples came to Jesus in
private and asked, "Why couldn't we
drive it out?"
20He replied, "Because you have so little faith. I tell you the truth, if you have
faith as small as a mustard seed, you can
say to this mountain, 'Move from here to
there' and it will move. Nothing will be
impossible for you.[a]"
22When they came together in Galilee,
he said to them, "The Son of Man is going to be betrayed into the hands of men.
23They will kill him, and on the third day
he will be raised to life." And the disciples
were filled with grief.

The Temple Tax

24After Jesus and his disciples arrived in
Capernaum, the collectors of the two-
drachma tax came to Peter and asked,
"Doesn't your teacher pay the temple tax[b]?"
25"Yes, he does," he replied.
When Peter came into the house, Jesus
was the first to speak. "What do you think,
Simon?" he asked. "From whom do the
kings of the earth collect duty and taxes—
from their own sons or from others?"
26"From others," Peter answered.
"Then the sons are exempt," Jesus said
to him. 27"But so that we may not offend
them, go to the lake and throw out your
line. Take the first fish you catch; open its
mouth and you will find a four-drachma
coin. Take it and give it to them for my tax
and yours."

[a] 20 Some manuscripts *you.* 21*But this kind does not go out except by prayer and fasting.* [b] 24 Greek *the two drachmas*

PRAYER: MY RELATIONSHIP TO GOD

MAY we glory in Your holy name, O Lord. Let the hearts of those who seek You rejoice. May we seek You and Your strength; may we seek Your face always. May we remember the wonderful works You have done, the miracles and the judgments You have

***pronounced.* (1 Chronicles 16:10–12) *. . . Since I am receiving a kingdom that cannot be shaken, I will be thankful and so worship You, my God, acceptably with reverence and awe, for You are a consuming fire.* (Hebrews 12:28–29)**

PAUSE *to thank God for the relationship that you enjoy with Him in Jesus Christ.*

YEAR 1 DAY 24

OT Genesis 27:1-46

Jacob Gets Isaac's Blessing

27 When Isaac was old and his eyes were
so weak that he could no longer see,
he called for Esau his older son and said
to him, "My son."
"Here I am," he answered.
[2]Isaac said, "I am now an old man and
don't know the day of my death. [3]Now
then, get your weapons—your quiver and
bow—and go out to the open country to
hunt some wild game for me. [4]Prepare me
the kind of tasty food I like and bring it
to me to eat, so that I may give you my
blessing before I die."
[5]Now Rebekah was listening as Isaac
spoke to his son Esau. When Esau left for
the open country to hunt game and bring
it back, [6]Rebekah said to her son Jacob,
"Look, I overheard your father say to your
brother Esau, [7]'Bring me some game and
prepare me some tasty food to eat, so that
I may give you my blessing in the presence
of the LORD before I die.' [8]Now, my son, listen carefully and do what I tell you: [9]Go out
to the flock and bring me two choice young
goats, so I can prepare some tasty food for
your father, just the way he likes it. [10]Then
take it to your father to eat, so that he may
give you his blessing before he dies."
[11]Jacob said to Rebekah his mother,
"But my brother Esau is a hairy man, and
I'm a man with smooth skin. [12]What if my
father touches me? I would appear to be
tricking him and would bring down a
curse on myself rather than a blessing."
[13]His mother said to him, "My son, let
the curse fall on me. Just do what I say; go
and get them for me."
[14]So he went and got them and brought
them to his mother, and she prepared some
tasty food, just the way his father liked it.
[15]Then Rebekah took the best clothes of
Esau her older son, which she had in the
house, and put them on her younger son
Jacob. [16]She also covered his hands and the
smooth part of his neck with the goatskins.
[17]Then she handed to her son Jacob the
tasty food and the bread she had made.
[18]He went to his father and said, "My
father."
"Yes, my son," he answered. "Who
is it?"
[19]Jacob said to his father, "I am Esau
your firstborn. I have done as you told me.
Please sit up and eat some of my game so
that you may give me your blessing."
[20]Isaac asked his son, "How did you
find it so quickly, my son?"
"The LORD your God gave me success,"
he replied.
[21]Then Isaac said to Jacob, "Come near so
I can touch you, my son, to know whether
you really are my son Esau or not."
[22]Jacob went close to his father Isaac,
who touched him and said, "The voice is
the voice of Jacob, but the hands are the
hands of Esau." [23]He did not recognize
him, for his hands were hairy like those
of his brother Esau; so he blessed him.
[24]"Are you really my son Esau?" he asked.
"I am," he replied.
[25]Then he said, "My son, bring me some
of your game to eat, so that I may give you
my blessing."
Jacob brought it to him and he ate; and
he brought some wine and he drank.
[26]Then his father Isaac said to him, "Come
here, my son, and kiss me."
[27]So he went to him and kissed him.
When Isaac caught the smell of his
clothes, he blessed him and said,

"Ah, the smell of my son
is like the smell of a field
that the LORD has blessed.
[28]May God give you of heaven's dew
and of earth's richness—
an abundance of grain and new
wine.

[29] May nations serve you
and peoples bow down to you.
Be lord over your brothers,
and may the sons of your mother
bow down to you.
May those who curse you be cursed
and those who bless you be blessed."

[30] After Isaac finished blessing him and
Jacob had scarcely left his father's presence, his brother Esau came in from hunting. [31] He too prepared some tasty food
and brought it to his father. Then he said
to him, "My father, sit up and eat some of
my game, so that you may give me your
blessing."
[32] His father Isaac asked him, "Who are
you?"
"I am your son," he answered, "your
firstborn, Esau."
[33] Isaac trembled violently and said,
"Who was it, then, that hunted game and
brought it to me? I ate it just before you
came and I blessed him—and indeed he
will be blessed!"
[34] When Esau heard his father's words,
he burst out with a loud and bitter cry and
said to his father, "Bless me—me too, my
father!"
[35] But he said, "Your brother came deceitfully and took your blessing."
[36] Esau said, "Isn't he rightly named Jacob[a]? He has deceived me these two times:
He took my birthright, and now he's tak-
en my blessing!" Then he asked, "Haven't
you reserved any blessing for me?"
[37] Isaac answered Esau, "I have made
him lord over you and have made all his
relatives his servants, and I have sustained
him with grain and new wine. So what
can I possibly do for you, my son?"
[38] Esau said to his father, "Do you have
only one blessing, my father? Bless me
too, my father!" Then Esau wept aloud.
[39] His father Isaac answered him,

"Your dwelling will be
away from the earth's richness,
away from the dew of heaven above.
[40] You will live by the sword
and you will serve your brother.
But when you grow restless,
you will throw his yoke
from off your neck."

Jacob Flees to Laban

[41] Esau held a grudge against Jacob because of the blessing his father had given
him. He said to himself, "The days of
mourning for my father are near; then I
will kill my brother Jacob."
[42] When Rebekah was told what her older son Esau had said, she sent for her
younger son Jacob and said to him, "Your
brother Esau is consoling himself with the
thought of killing you. [43] Now then, my son,
do what I say: Flee at once to my brother
Laban in Haran. [44] Stay with him for a while
until your brother's fury subsides. [45] When
your brother is no longer angry with you
and forgets what you did to him, I'll send
word for you to come back from there. Why
should I lose both of you in one day?"
[46] Then Rebekah said to Isaac, "I'm dis-
gusted with living because of these Hittite
women. If Jacob takes a wife from among
the women of this land, from Hittite
women like these, my life will not be
worth living."

[a] 36 *Jacob* means *he grasps the heel* (figuratively, *he deceives*).

PRAYER: RENEWAL

MAY I remove the places of idolatry from my life, and like Asa, let my heart be fully committed to You all my days. (2 Chronicles 15:17) . . . May I trust in You, Lord, and do good; may I dwell in the land and feed on Your faithfulness. When I delight myself in You, You will give me the desires of my heart. I will commit my way to You and trust in You, and You will bring it to pass. You will bring forth my righteousness like the light, and my justice like the noonday. May I rest in You and wait patiently for You; I will not fret because of those who prosper in their way, because of those who practice evil schemes. (Psalm 37:3–7)

***PAUSE** to add your own prayers for personal renewal.*

NT **Matthew 18:1-35**

The Greatest in the Kingdom of Heaven

18 At that time the disciples came to
Jesus and asked, "Who is the greatest
in the kingdom of heaven?"
2He called a little child and had him
stand among them. 3And he said: "I tell
you the truth, unless you change and become like little children, you will never
enter the kingdom of heaven. 4Therefore,
whoever humbles himself like this child
is the greatest in the kingdom of heaven.
5"And whoever welcomes a little child
like this in my name welcomes me. 6But
if anyone causes one of these little ones
who believe in me to sin, it would be better for him to have a large millstone hung
around his neck and to be drowned in the
depths of the sea.
7"Woe to the world because of the
things that cause people to sin! Such
things must come, but woe to the man
through whom they come! 8If your hand
or your foot causes you to sin, cut it off
and throw it away. It is better for you to
enter life maimed or crippled than to have
two hands or two feet and be thrown into
eternal fire. 9And if your eye causes you to
sin, gouge it out and throw it away. It is
better for you to enter life with one eye
than to have two eyes and be thrown into
the fire of hell.

The Parable of the Lost Sheep

10"See that you do not look down on
one of these little ones. For I tell you that
their angels in heaven always see the face
of my Father in heaven.[a]
12"What do you think? If a man owns
a hundred sheep, and one of them wanders away, will he not leave the ninety-
nine on the hills and go to look for the
one that wandered off? 13And if he finds
it, I tell you the truth, he is happier about
that one sheep than about the ninety-
nine that did not wander off. 14In the
same way your Father in heaven is not
willing that any of these little ones
should be lost.

A Brother Who Sins Against You

15"If your brother sins against you,[b] go
and show him his fault, just between the
two of you. If he listens to you, you have
won your brother over. 16But if he will not
listen, take one or two others along, so
that 'every matter may be established by
the testimony of two or three witnesses.'[c]
17If he refuses to listen to them, tell it to
the church; and if he refuses to listen even
to the church, treat him as you would a
pagan or a tax collector.
18"I tell you the truth, whatever you
bind on earth will be[d] bound in heaven,
and whatever you loose on earth will be[d]
loosed in heaven.
19"Again, I tell you that if two of you on
earth agree about anything you ask for, it
will be done for you by my Father in heav-
en. 20For where two or three come together in my name, there am I with
them."

The Parable of the Unmerciful Servant

21Then Peter came to Jesus and asked,
"Lord, how many times shall I forgive my
brother when he sins against me? Up to
seven times?"
22Jesus answered, "I tell you, not seven
times, but seventy-seven times.[e]
23"Therefore, the kingdom of heaven is
like a king who wanted to settle accounts
with his servants. 24As he began the settlement, a man who owed him ten thousand talents[f] was brought to him. 25Since
he was not able to pay, the master ordered
that he and his wife and his children and
all that he had be sold to repay the debt.
26"The servant fell on his knees before
him. 'Be patient with me,' he begged, 'and
I will pay back everything.' 27The servant's
master took pity on him, canceled the
debt and let him go.
28"But when that servant went out, he
found one of his fellow servants who
owed him a hundred denarii.[g] He grabbed
him and began to choke him. 'Pay back
what you owe me!' he demanded.
29"His fellow servant fell to his knees
and begged him, 'Be patient with me, and
I will pay you back.'
30"But he refused. Instead, he went off
and had the man thrown into prison un-

[a] 10 Some manuscripts *heaven.* [11]*The Son of Man came to save what was lost.* [b] 15 Some manuscripts do not have *against you.* [c] 16 Deut. 19:15 [d] 18 Or *have been* [e] 22 Or *seventy times seven* [f] 24 That is, millions of dollars [g] 28 That is, a few dollars

til he could pay the debt. [31]When the other servants saw what had happened, they
were greatly distressed and went and told
their master everything that had happened.
[32]"Then the master called the servant in.
'You wicked servant,' he said, 'I canceled
all that debt of yours because you begged
me to. [33]Shouldn't you have had mercy on
your fellow servant just as I had on you?'
[34]In anger his master turned him over to
the jailers to be tortured, until he should
pay back all he owed.
[35]"This is how my heavenly Father will
treat each of you unless you forgive your
brother from your heart."

PRAYER: THE CHARACTER I WANT TO CULTIVATE

I WILL put away perversity from my mouth and keep corrupt talk far from my lips. (Proverbs 4:24) . . . I will not let any corrupt word come out of my mouth, but only what is helpful for building others up according to their needs, that it may impart grace to those who hear. (Ephesians 4:29)

***TAKE** a moment to ask the Lord for the grace to grow in godly character.*

YEAR 1 DAY 25

OT Proverbs 1

Prologue: Purpose and Theme

1 The proverbs of Solomon son of David, king of Israel:

[2]for attaining wisdom and discipline;
for understanding words of insight;
[3]for acquiring a disciplined and prudent life,
doing what is right and just and fair;
[4]for giving prudence to the simple,
knowledge and discretion to the young—
[5]let the wise listen and add to their learning,
and let the discerning get guidance—
[6]for understanding proverbs and parables,
the sayings and riddles of the wise.

[7]The fear of the LORD is the beginning of knowledge,
but fools[a] despise wisdom and discipline.

Exhortations to Embrace Wisdom

Warning Against Enticement

[8]Listen, my son, to your father's instruction
and do not forsake your mother's teaching.
[9]They will be a garland to grace your head
and a chain to adorn your neck.

[10]My son, if sinners entice you,
do not give in to them.
[11]If they say, "Come along with us;
let's lie in wait for someone's blood,
let's waylay some harmless soul;
[12]let's swallow them alive, like the grave,[b]
and whole, like those who go down to the pit;
[13]we will get all sorts of valuable things
and fill our houses with plunder;
[14]throw in your lot with us,
and we will share a common purse"—
[15]my son, do not go along with them,
do not set foot on their paths;
[16]for their feet rush into sin,
they are swift to shed blood.
[17]How useless to spread a net
in full view of all the birds!
[18]These men lie in wait for their own blood;
they waylay only themselves!
[19]Such is the end of all who go after ill-gotten gain;

[a] 7 The Hebrew words rendered *fool* in Proverbs, and often elsewhere in the Old Testament, denote one who is morally deficient. [b] 12 Hebrew *Sheol*

it takes away the lives of those who
get it.

Warning Against Rejecting Wisdom

20 Wisdom calls aloud in the street,
she raises her voice in the public
squares;
21 at the head of the noisy streets[c] she
cries out,
in the gateways of the city she
makes her speech:

22 "How long will you simple ones[d] love
your simple ways?
How long will mockers delight in
mockery
and fools hate knowledge?
23 If you had responded to my rebuke,
I would have poured out my heart
to you
and made my thoughts known to
you.
24 But since you rejected me when I
called
and no one gave heed when I
stretched out my hand,
25 since you ignored all my advice
and would not accept my rebuke,
26 I in turn will laugh at your disaster;
I will mock when calamity
overtakes you—
27 when calamity overtakes you like a
storm,
when disaster sweeps over you like
a whirlwind,
when distress and trouble
overwhelm you.

28 "Then they will call to me but I will
not answer;
they will look for me but will not
find me.
29 Since they hated knowledge
and did not choose to fear the
LORD,
30 since they would not accept my advice
and spurned my rebuke,
31 they will eat the fruit of their ways
and be filled with the fruit of their
schemes.
32 For the waywardness of the simple
will kill them,
and the complacency of fools will
destroy them;
33 but whoever listens to me will live in
safety
and be at ease, without fear of
harm."

[c] 21 Hebrew; Septuagint / *on the tops of the walls*
[d] 22 The Hebrew word rendered *simple* in Proverbs generally denotes one without moral direction and inclined to evil.

PRAYER: PETITION

MAY I not pervert justice, show partiality, or accept a bribe, for a bribe blinds the eyes of the wise and perverts the words of the righteous. (Deuteronomy 16:19)

__PAUSE__ here to petition God for growth in love and compassion toward others. Offer prayers for your loved ones, for those who do not know Jesus and for those in need. Offer prayers regarding your activities for this day and any special concerns you may have.

NT Matthew 19:1–15

Divorce

19 When Jesus had finished saying these
things, he left Galilee and went into
the region of Judea to the other side of the
Jordan. 2 Large crowds followed him, and
he healed them there.
3 Some Pharisees came to him to test
him. They asked, "Is it lawful for a man to
divorce his wife for any and every reason?"
4 "Haven't you read," he replied, "that at
the beginning the Creator 'made them
male and female,'[a] 5 and said, 'For this reason a man will leave his father and mother and be united to his wife, and the two
will become one flesh'[b]? 6 So they are no
longer two, but one. Therefore what God
has joined together, let man not separate."
7 "Why then," they asked, "did Moses

[a] 4 Gen. 1:27 [b] 5 Gen. 2:24

command that a man give his wife a certificate of divorce and send her away?"

[8]Jesus replied, "Moses permitted you to divorce your wives because your hearts were hard. But it was not this way from the beginning. [9]I tell you that anyone who divorces his wife, except for marital unfaithfulness, and marries another woman commits adultery."

[10]The disciples said to him, "If this is the situation between a husband and wife, it is better not to marry."

[11]Jesus replied, "Not everyone can accept this word, but only those to whom it has been given. [12]For some are eunuchs because they were born that way; others were made that way by men; and others have renounced marriage[c] because of the kingdom of heaven. The one who can accept this should accept it."

The Little Children and Jesus

[13]Then little children were brought to Jesus for him to place his hands on them and pray for them. But the disciples rebuked those who brought them.

[14]Jesus said, "Let the little children come to me, and do not hinder them, for the kingdom of heaven belongs to such as these." [15]When he had placed his hands on them, he went on from there.

[c] 12 Or *have made themselves eunuchs*

PRAYER: MY RELATIONSHIP TO OTHERS

LIKE Abraham, I should direct my children and my household after me to keep Your way, O Lord, by doing what is right and just. (Genesis 18:19) . . . I will learn to fear You all the days I live on the earth and teach Your words to my children. (Deuteronomy 4:10)

***PAUSE** to review your relationships to others and to commit them to the Lord.*

YEAR 1 DAY 26

OT Genesis 28:1–29:35

28 So Isaac called for Jacob and blessed[a] him and commanded him: "Do not marry a Canaanite woman. [2]Go at once to Paddan Aram,[b] to the house of your mother's father Bethuel. Take a wife for yourself there, from among the daughters of Laban, your mother's brother. [3]May God Almighty[c] bless you and make you fruitful and increase your numbers until you become a community of peoples. [4]May he give you and your descendants the blessing given to Abraham, so that you may take possession of the land where you now live as an alien, the land God gave to Abraham." [5]Then Isaac sent Jacob on his way, and he went to Paddan Aram, to Laban son of Bethuel the Aramean, the brother of Rebekah, who was the mother of Jacob and Esau.

[6]Now Esau learned that Isaac had blessed Jacob and had sent him to Paddan Aram to take a wife from there, and that when he blessed him he commanded him, "Do not marry a Canaanite woman," [7]and that Jacob had obeyed his father and mother and had gone to Paddan Aram. [8]Esau then realized how displeasing the Canaanite women were to his father Isaac; [9]so he went to Ishmael and married Mahalath, the sister of Nebaioth and daughter of Ishmael son of Abraham, in addition to the wives he already had.

Jacob's Dream at Bethel

[10]Jacob left Beersheba and set out for Haran. [11]When he reached a certain place, he stopped for the night because the sun had set. Taking one of the stones there, he put it under his head and lay down to sleep. [12]He had a dream in which he saw a stairway[d] resting on the earth, with its top reaching to heaven, and the angels of God were ascending and descending on it. [13]There above it[e] stood the LORD, and he

[a] 1 Or *greeted* [b] 2 That is, Northwest Mesopotamia; also in verses 5, 6 and 7 [c] 3 Hebrew *El-Shaddai* [d] 12 Or *ladder* [e] 13 Or *There beside him*

said: "I am the LORD, the God of your father Abraham and the God of Isaac. I will
give you and your descendants the land
on which you are lying. 14Your descendants will be like the dust of the earth,
and you will spread out to the west and
to the east, to the north and to the south.
All peoples on earth will be blessed
through you and your offspring. 15I am
with you and will watch over you wherever you go, and I will bring you back to
this land. I will not leave you until I have
done what I have promised you."
16When Jacob awoke from his sleep, he
thought, "Surely the LORD is in this place,
and I was not aware of it." 17He was afraid
and said, "How awesome is this place!
This is none other than the house of God;
this is the gate of heaven."
18Early the next morning Jacob took the
stone he had placed under his head and
set it up as a pillar and poured oil on top
of it. 19He called that place Bethel,[f] though
the city used to be called Luz.
20Then Jacob made a vow, saying, "If
God will be with me and will watch over
me on this journey I am taking and will
give me food to eat and clothes to wear
21so that I return safely to my father's
house, then the LORD[g] will be my God
22and[h] this stone that I have set up as a pillar will be God's house, and of all that you
give me I will give you a tenth."

Jacob Arrives in Paddan Aram

29 Then Jacob continued on his journey
and came to the land of the eastern
peoples. 2There he saw a well in the field,
with three flocks of sheep lying near it because the flocks were watered from that
well. The stone over the mouth of the well
was large. 3When all the flocks were gathered there, the shepherds would roll the
stone away from the well's mouth and water the sheep. Then they would return the
stone to its place over the mouth of the
well.
4Jacob asked the shepherds, "My brothers, where are you from?"
"We're from Haran," they replied.
5He said to them, "Do you know Laban,
Nahor's grandson?"
"Yes, we know him," they answered.
6Then Jacob asked them, "Is he well?"
"Yes, he is," they said, "and here comes
his daughter Rachel with the sheep."
7"Look," he said, "the sun is still high;
it is not time for the flocks to be gathered.
Water the sheep and take them back to
pasture."
8"We can't," they replied, "until all the
flocks are gathered and the stone has been
rolled away from the mouth of the well.
Then we will water the sheep."
9While he was still talking with them,
Rachel came with her father's sheep, for
she was a shepherdess. 10When Jacob saw
Rachel daughter of Laban, his mother's
brother, and Laban's sheep, he went over
and rolled the stone away from the mouth
of the well and watered his uncle's sheep.
11Then Jacob kissed Rachel and began to
weep aloud. 12He had told Rachel that he
was a relative of her father and a son of
Rebekah. So she ran and told her father.
13As soon as Laban heard the news
about Jacob, his sister's son, he hurried to
meet him. He embraced him and kissed
him and brought him to his home, and
there Jacob told him all these things.
14Then Laban said to him, "You are my
own flesh and blood."

Jacob Marries Leah and Rachel

After Jacob had stayed with him for a
whole month, 15Laban said to him, "Just
because you are a relative of mine, should
you work for me for nothing? Tell me
what your wages should be."
16Now Laban had two daughters; the
name of the older was Leah, and the
name of the younger was Rachel. 17Leah
had weak[i] eyes, but Rachel was lovely in
form, and beautiful. 18Jacob was in love
with Rachel and said, "I'll work for you
seven years in return for your younger
daughter Rachel."
19Laban said, "It's better that I give her
to you than to some other man. Stay here
with me." 20So Jacob served seven years to
get Rachel, but they seemed like only a
few days to him because of his love for
her.
21Then Jacob said to Laban, "Give me
my wife. My time is completed, and I
want to lie with her."
22So Laban brought together all the
people of the place and gave a feast. 23But
when evening came, he took his daughter

[f] 19 *Bethel* means *house of God.* [g] 20,21 Or *Since God . . . father's house, the LORD* [h] 21,22 Or *house, and the LORD will be my God, 22then* [i] 17 Or *delicate*

Leah and gave her to Jacob, and Jacob lay
with her. 24And Laban gave his servant girl
Zilpah to his daughter as her maidservant.
25When morning came, there was Leah!
So Jacob said to Laban, "What is this you
have done to me? I served you for Rachel,
didn't I? Why have you deceived me?"
26Laban replied, "It is not our custom
here to give the younger daughter in marriage before the older one. 27Finish this
daughter's bridal week; then we will give
you the younger one also, in return for another seven years of work."
28And Jacob did so. He finished the
week with Leah, and then Laban gave him
his daughter Rachel to be his wife. 29La-
ban gave his servant girl Bilhah to his
daughter Rachel as her maidservant. 30Ja-
cob lay with Rachel also, and he loved Rachel more than Leah. And he worked for
Laban another seven years.

Jacob's Children

31When the LORD saw that Leah was not
loved, he opened her womb, but Rachel
was barren. 32Leah became pregnant and
gave birth to a son. She named him Reuben,[j] for she said, "It is because the LORD
has seen my misery. Surely my husband
will love me now."
33She conceived again, and when she
gave birth to a son she said, "Because the
LORD heard that I am not loved, he gave
me this one too." So she named him Simeon.[k]
34Again she conceived, and when she
gave birth to a son she said, "Now at last
my husband will become attached to me,
because I have borne him three sons." So
he was named Levi.[l]
35She conceived again, and when she
gave birth to a son she said, "This time I
will praise the LORD." So she named him
Judah.[m] Then she stopped having children.

[j] 32 *Reuben* sounds like the Hebrew for *he has seen my misery*; the name means *see, a son*. [k] 33 *Simeon* probably means *one who hears*. [l] 34 *Levi* sounds like and may be derived from the Hebrew for *attached*. [m] 35 *Judah* sounds like and may be derived from the Hebrew for *praise*.

PRAYER: INTERCESSION

WE are the fragrance of Christ to You, O God, among those who are being saved and among those who are perishing; to the one, we are an aroma from death to death; to the other, an aroma from life to life. And who is sufficient for these things? (2 Corinthians 2:15–16)

***TAKE** a few moments to intercede on behalf of friends, relatives, neighbors and coworkers who do not yet know salvation in Jesus Christ.*

NT Matthew 19:16–20:16

The Rich Young Man

16Now a man came up to Jesus and
asked, "Teacher, what good thing must I
do to get eternal life?"
17"Why do you ask me about what is
good?" Jesus replied. "There is only One
who is good. If you want to enter life,
obey the commandments."
18"Which ones?" the man inquired.
Jesus replied, " 'Do not murder, do not
commit adultery, do not steal, do not give
false testimony, 19honor your father and
mother,'[a] and 'love your neighbor as yourself.'[b]"
20"All these I have kept," the young man
said. "What do I still lack?"
21Jesus answered, "If you want to be perfect, go, sell your possessions and give to
the poor, and you will have treasure in
heaven. Then come, follow me."
22When the young man heard this, he
went away sad, because he had great
wealth.
23Then Jesus said to his disciples, "I tell
you the truth, it is hard for a rich man to
enter the kingdom of heaven. 24Again I tell
you, it is easier for a camel to go through
the eye of a needle than for a rich man to
enter the kingdom of God."
25When the disciples heard this, they
were greatly astonished and asked, "Who
then can be saved?"

[a] 19 Exodus 20:12–16; Deut. 5:16–20
[b] 19 Lev. 19:18

26 Jesus looked at them and said, "With
man this is impossible, but with God all
things are possible."
27 Peter answered him, "We have left
everything to follow you! What then will
there be for us?"
28 Jesus said to them, "I tell you the truth,
at the renewal of all things, when the Son
of Man sits on his glorious throne, you who
have followed me will also sit on twelve
thrones, judging the twelve tribes of Israel.
29 And everyone who has left houses or
brothers or sisters or father or mother[c] or
children or fields for my sake will receive a
hundred times as much and will inherit
eternal life. 30 But many who are first will be
last, and many who are last will be first.

The Parable of the Workers in the Vineyard

20 "For the kingdom of heaven is like a
landowner who went out early in the
morning to hire men to work in his vineyard. 2 He agreed to pay them a denarius for
the day and sent them into his vineyard.
3 "About the third hour he went out and
saw others standing in the marketplace
doing nothing. 4 He told them, 'You also
go and work in my vineyard, and I will
pay you whatever is right.' 5 So they went.
"He went out again about the sixth
hour and the ninth hour and did the same
thing. 6 About the eleventh hour he went
out and found still others standing
around. He asked them, 'Why have you
been standing here all day long doing
nothing?'
7 " 'Because no one has hired us,' they
answered.
"He said to them, 'You also go and
work in my vineyard.'
8 "When evening came, the owner of the
vineyard said to his foreman, 'Call the
workers and pay them their wages, beginning with the last ones hired and going
on to the first.'
9 "The workers who were hired about the
eleventh hour came and each received a
denarius. 10 So when those came who were
hired first, they expected to receive more.
But each one of them also received a denarius. 11 When they received it, they began
to grumble against the landowner. 12 'These
men who were hired last worked only one
hour,' they said, 'and you have made them
equal to us who have borne the burden of
the work and the heat of the day.'
13 "But he answered one of them,
'Friend, I am not being unfair to you.
Didn't you agree to work for a denarius?
14 Take your pay and go. I want to give the
man who was hired last the same as I
gave you. 15 Don't I have the right to do
what I want with my own money? Or are
you envious because I am generous?'
16 "So the last will be first, and the first
will be last."

[c] 29 Some manuscripts *mother or wife*

PRAYER: THE ATTRIBUTES OF GOD

WHO is like You, O Lord? Who is like You—majestic in holiness, awesome in praises, working wonders? (Exodus 15:11) . . . You, O Lord, have declared: "My thoughts are not your thoughts, neither are your ways My ways. As the heavens are higher than the earth, so are My ways higher than your ways, and My thoughts than your thoughts." (Isaiah 55:8–9)

***PAUSE** to reflect on these affirmations about the person, powers and perfection of God.*

YEAR 1 DAY 27

OT Genesis 30:1–43

30 When Rachel saw that she was not
bearing Jacob any children, she became jealous of her sister. So she said to
Jacob, "Give me children, or I'll die!"
2 Jacob became angry with her and said,
"Am I in the place of God, who has kept
you from having children?"
3 Then she said, "Here is Bilhah, my

maidservant. Sleep with her so that she
can bear children for me and that through
her I too can build a family."
4 So she gave him her servant Bilhah as a
wife. Jacob slept with her, 5 and she became
pregnant and bore him a son. 6 Then Rachel
said, "God has vindicated me; he has listened to my plea and given me a son." Because of this she named him Dan.[a]
7 Rachel's servant Bilhah conceived
again and bore Jacob a second son. 8 Then
Rachel said, "I have had a great struggle
with my sister, and I have won." So she
named him Naphtali.[b]
9 When Leah saw that she had stopped
having children, she took her maidservant
Zilpah and gave her to Jacob as a wife.
10 Leah's servant Zilpah bore Jacob a son.
11 Then Leah said, "What good fortune!"[c]
So she named him Gad.[d]
12 Leah's servant Zilpah bore Jacob a second son. 13 Then Leah said, "How happy I
am! The women will call me happy." So
she named him Asher.[e]
14 During wheat harvest, Reuben went
out into the fields and found some man-
drake plants, which he brought to his
mother Leah. Rachel said to Leah, "Please
give me some of your son's mandrakes."
15 But she said to her, "Wasn't it enough
that you took away my husband? Will you
take my son's mandrakes too?"
"Very well," Rachel said, "he can sleep
with you tonight in return for your son's
mandrakes."
16 So when Jacob came in from the fields
that evening, Leah went out to meet him.
"You must sleep with me," she said. "I
have hired you with my son's mandrakes." So he slept with her that night.
17 God listened to Leah, and she became
pregnant and bore Jacob a fifth son.
18 Then Leah said, "God has rewarded me
for giving my maidservant to my husband." So she named him Issachar.[f]
19 Leah conceived again and bore Jacob
a sixth son. 20 Then Leah said, "God has
presented me with a precious gift. This
time my husband will treat me with hon-
or, because I have borne him six sons." So
she named him Zebulun.[g]
21 Some time later she gave birth to a
daughter and named her Dinah.
22 Then God remembered Rachel; he listened to her and opened her womb. 23 She
became pregnant and gave birth to a son
and said, "God has taken away my disgrace." 24 She named him Joseph,[h] and
said, "May the LORD add to me another
son."

Jacob's Flocks Increase

25 After Rachel gave birth to Joseph, Jacob said to Laban, "Send me on my way
so I can go back to my own homeland.
26 Give me my wives and children, for
whom I have served you, and I will be on
my way. You know how much work I've
done for you."
27 But Laban said to him, "If I have
found favor in your eyes, please stay. I
have learned by divination that[i] the LORD
has blessed me because of you." 28 He
added, "Name your wages, and I will pay
them."
29 Jacob said to him, "You know how I
have worked for you and how your livestock has fared under my care. 30 The little
you had before I came has increased greatly, and the LORD has blessed you wherever I have been. But now, when may I do
something for my own household?"
31 "What shall I give you?" he asked.
"Don't give me anything," Jacob replied.
"But if you will do this one thing for me,
I will go on tending your flocks and watching over them: 32 Let me go through all
your flocks today and remove from them
every speckled or spotted sheep, every
dark-colored lamb and every spotted or
speckled goat. They will be my wages.
33 And my honesty will testify for me in the
future, whenever you check on the wages
you have paid me. Any goat in my possession that is not speckled or spotted, or any
lamb that is not dark-colored, will be considered stolen."
34 "Agreed," said Laban. "Let it be as you
have said." 35 That same day he removed
all the male goats that were streaked or
spotted, and all the speckled or spotted female goats (all that had white on them)
and all the dark-colored lambs, and he
placed them in the care of his sons. 36 Then
he put a three-day journey between himself and Jacob, while Jacob continued to
tend the rest of Laban's flocks.

[a] 6 *Dan* here means *he has vindicated.* [b] 8 *Naphtali* means *my struggle.* [c] 11 Or *"A troop is coming!"* [d] 11 *Gad* can mean *good fortune* or *a troop.* [e] 13 *Asher* means *happy.* [f] 18 *Issachar* sounds like the Hebrew for *reward.* [g] 20 *Zebulun* probably means *honor.* [h] 24 *Joseph* means *may he add.* [i] 27 Or possibly *have become rich and*

37Jacob, however, took fresh-cut branches from poplar, almond and plane trees and made white stripes on them by peeling the bark and exposing the white inner wood of the branches. 38Then he placed the peeled branches in all the watering troughs, so that they would be directly in front of the flocks when they came to drink. When the flocks were in heat and came to drink, 39they mated in front of the branches. And they bore young that were streaked or speckled or spotted. 40Jacob set apart the young of the flock by themselves, but made the rest face the streaked and dark-colored animals that belonged to Laban. Thus he made separate flocks for himself and did not put them with Laban's animals. 41Whenever the stronger females were in heat, Jacob would place the branches in the troughs in front of the animals so they would mate near the branches, 42but if the animals were weak, he would not place them there. So the weak animals went to Laban and the strong ones to Jacob. 43In this way the man grew exceedingly prosperous and came to own large flocks, and maidservants and menservants, and camels and donkeys.

PRAYER: AFFIRMATION

THERE is no one who has left house or brothers or sisters or mother or father or children or fields for Your sake and the gospel's, who will not receive a hundred times as much in this present age—houses, brothers, sisters, mothers, children and fields, along with persecutions—and in the age to come, eternal life. (Matthew 19:29; Mark 10:29–30) . . . If anyone comes to You and does not hate his father and mother, his wife and children, his brothers and sisters—yes, even his own life—he cannot be Your disciple. And whoever does not carry his cross and follow You cannot be Your disciple. (Luke 14:26–27)

PAUSE *to reflect on these Biblical affirmations.*

NT Matthew 20:17-34

Jesus Again Predicts His Death

17Now as Jesus was going up to Jerusalem, he took the twelve disciples aside and said to them, 18"We are going up to Jerusalem, and the Son of Man will be betrayed to the chief priests and the teachers of the law. They will condemn him to death 19and will turn him over to the Gentiles to be mocked and flogged and crucified. On the third day he will be raised to life!"

A Mother's Request

20Then the mother of Zebedee's sons came to Jesus with her sons and, kneeling down, asked a favor of him.

21"What is it you want?" he asked.

She said, "Grant that one of these two sons of mine may sit at your right and the other at your left in your kingdom."

22"You don't know what you are asking," Jesus said to them. "Can you drink the cup I am going to drink?"

"We can," they answered.

23Jesus said to them, "You will indeed drink from my cup, but to sit at my right or left is not for me to grant. These places belong to those for whom they have been prepared by my Father."

24When the ten heard about this, they were indignant with the two brothers. 25Jesus called them together and said, "You know that the rulers of the Gentiles lord it over them, and their high officials exercise authority over them. 26Not so with you. Instead, whoever wants to become great among you must be your servant, 27and whoever wants to be first must be your slave— 28just as the Son of Man did not come to be served, but to serve, and to give his life as a ransom for many."

Two Blind Men Receive Sight

29As Jesus and his disciples were leaving Jericho, a large crowd followed him. 30Two blind men were sitting by the road-

side, and when they heard that Jesus was
going by, they shouted, "Lord, Son of David, have mercy on us!"
31 The crowd rebuked them and told
them to be quiet, but they shouted all the louder, "Lord, Son of David, have mercy on us!"
32 Jesus stopped and called them. "What do you want me to do for you?" he asked.
33 "Lord," they answered, "we want our sight."
34 Jesus had compassion on them and
touched their eyes. Immediately they received their sight and followed him.

PRAYER: THE WORKS OF GOD

HOW great are Your works, O Lord! Your thoughts are very deep. Senseless people do not know; fools do not understand that though the wicked spring up like grass and all the evildoers flourish, they will be destroyed forever. But You, O Lord, are exalted forever. (Psalm 92:5–7) . . . You, O Lord, are near to all who call upon You, to all who call upon You in truth. You fulfill the desires of those who fear You; You hear their cry and save them. You preserve all who love You, but all the wicked You will destroy. (Psalm 145:18–20)

TAKE *a moment to consider the greatness of God's wonderful works.*

YEAR 1 DAY 28

OT Psalms 7–8

Psalm 7

A *shiggaion*[a] of David, which he sang to the LORD concerning Cush, a Benjamite.

1 O LORD my God, I take refuge in you;
save and deliver me from all who pursue me,
2 or they will tear me like a lion
and rip me to pieces with no one to rescue me.

3 O LORD my God, if I have done this
and there is guilt on my hands—
4 if I have done evil to him who is at peace with me
or without cause have robbed my foe—
5 then let my enemy pursue and overtake me;
let him trample my life to the ground
and make me sleep in the dust. *Selah*

6 Arise, O LORD, in your anger;
rise up against the rage of my enemies.
Awake, my God; decree justice.
7 Let the assembled peoples gather around you.
Rule over them from on high;
8 let the LORD judge the peoples.
Judge me, O LORD, according to my righteousness,
according to my integrity, O Most High.
9 O righteous God,
who searches minds and hearts,
bring to an end the violence of the wicked
and make the righteous secure.

10 My shield[b] is God Most High,
who saves the upright in heart.
11 God is a righteous judge,
a God who expresses his wrath every day.
12 If he does not relent,
he[c] will sharpen his sword;
he will bend and string his bow.
13 He has prepared his deadly weapons;
he makes ready his flaming arrows.

14 He who is pregnant with evil
and conceives trouble gives birth to disillusionment.
15 He who digs a hole and scoops it out
falls into the pit he has made.

[a] Title: Probably a literary or musical term [b] 10 Or *sovereign* [c] 12 Or *If a man does not repent, / God*

16 The trouble he causes recoils on
himself;
his violence comes down on his
own head.

17 I will give thanks to the LORD because
of his righteousness
and will sing praise to the name of
the LORD Most High.

Psalm 8

For the director of music. According to *gittith.*[d] A psalm of David.

1 O LORD, our Lord,
how majestic is your name in all
the earth!

You have set your glory
above the heavens.
2 From the lips of children and infants
you have ordained praise[e]
because of your enemies,
to silence the foe and the avenger.

3 When I consider your heavens,
the work of your fingers,
the moon and the stars,
which you have set in place,
4 what is man that you are mindful of
him,
the son of man that you care for
him?
5 You made him a little lower than the
heavenly beings[f]
and crowned him with glory and
honor.

6 You made him ruler over the works of
your hands;
you put everything under his feet:
7 all flocks and herds,
and the beasts of the field,
8 the birds of the air,
and the fish of the sea,
all that swim the paths of the seas.

9 O LORD, our Lord,
how majestic is your name in all
the earth!

[d] Title: Probably a musical term [e] 2 Or *strength*
[f] 5 Or *than God*

PRAYER: THANKSGIVING

O LORD, You have loved me with an everlasting love; You have drawn me with loving-kindness. (Jeremiah 31:3) . . . You led Your people with cords of human kindness, with bands of love; You lifted the yoke from their neck and bent down to feed them. (Hosea 11:4)

***PAUSE** to offer your own expressions of thanksgiving.*

NT Matthew 21:1-22

The Triumphal Entry

21 As they approached Jerusalem and
came to Bethphage on the Mount of
Olives, Jesus sent two disciples, 2 saying to
them, "Go to the village ahead of you, and
at once you will find a donkey tied there,
with her colt by her. Untie them and bring
them to me. 3 If anyone says anything to
you, tell him that the Lord needs them,
and he will send them right away."
4 This took place to fulfill what was spoken through the prophet:

5 "Say to the Daughter of Zion,
'See, your king comes to you,
gentle and riding on a donkey,
on a colt, the foal of a donkey.' "[a]

6 The disciples went and did as Jesus had
instructed them. 7 They brought the donkey and the colt, placed their cloaks on
them, and Jesus sat on them. 8 A very large
crowd spread their cloaks on the road,
while others cut branches from the trees
and spread them on the road. 9 The crowds
that went ahead of him and those that followed shouted,

"Hosanna[b] to the Son of David!"

"Blessed is he who comes in the name
of the Lord!"[c]

[a] 5 Zech. 9:9 [b] 9 A Hebrew expression meaning "Save!" which became an exclamation of praise; also in verse 15 [c] 9 Psalm 118:26

"Hosanna[d] in the highest!"

10 When Jesus entered Jerusalem, the whole city was stirred and asked, "Who is this?"

11 The crowds answered, "This is Jesus, the prophet from Nazareth in Galilee."

Jesus at the Temple

12 Jesus entered the temple area and drove out all who were buying and selling there. He overturned the tables of the money changers and the benches of those selling doves. 13 "It is written," he said to them, " 'My house will be called a house of prayer,'[e] but you are making it a 'den of robbers.'[f]"

14 The blind and the lame came to him at the temple, and he healed them. 15 But when the chief priests and the teachers of the law saw the wonderful things he did and the children shouting in the temple area, "Hosanna to the Son of David," they were indignant.

16 "Do you hear what these children are saying?" they asked him.

"Yes," replied Jesus, "have you never read,

" 'From the lips of children and
infants
you have ordained praise'[g]?"

17 And he left them and went out of the city to Bethany, where he spent the night.

The Fig Tree Withers

18 Early in the morning, as he was on his way back to the city, he was hungry. 19 Seeing a fig tree by the road, he went up to it but found nothing on it except leaves. Then he said to it, "May you never bear fruit again!" Immediately the tree withered.

20 When the disciples saw this, they were amazed. "How did the fig tree wither so quickly?" they asked.

21 Jesus replied, "I tell you the truth, if you have faith and do not doubt, not only can you do what was done to the fig tree, but also you can say to this mountain, 'Go, throw yourself into the sea,' and it will be done. 22 If you believe, you will receive whatever you ask for in prayer."

[d] *9* A Hebrew expression meaning "Save!" which became an exclamation of praise; also in verse 15
[e] *13* Isaiah 56:7 [f] *13* Jer. 7:11 [g] *16* Psalm 8:2

PRAYER: MY RELATIONSHIP TO GOD

I AM the salt of the earth, but if the salt loses its flavor, how can it be made salty again? It is no longer good for anything, except to be thrown out and trampled underfoot. I am the light of the world. A city set on a hill cannot be hidden. Neither do people light a lamp and put it under a basket, but on a lampstand, and it gives light to all who are in the house. In the same way, I must let my light shine before all people, that they may see my good deeds and praise You, my Father in heaven. (Matthew 5:13–16) . . . We are Your temple, O God, and Your Spirit lives in us. (1 Corinthians 3:16)

***PAUSE** to thank God for the relationship that you enjoy with Him in Jesus Christ.*

YEAR 1
DAY 29

OT Genesis 31:1–55

Jacob Flees From Laban

31 Jacob heard that Laban's sons were saying, "Jacob has taken everything our father owned and has gained all this wealth from what belonged to our father." 2 And Jacob noticed that Laban's attitude toward him was not what it had been.

3 Then the LORD said to Jacob, "Go back to the land of your fathers and to your relatives, and I will be with you."

4 So Jacob sent word to Rachel and Leah
to come out to the fields where his flocks
were. 5 He said to them, "I see that your father's attitude toward me is not what it
was before, but the God of my father has
been with me. 6 You know that I've worked
for your father with all my strength, 7 yet
your father has cheated me by changing
my wages ten times. However, God has
not allowed him to harm me. 8 If he said,
'The speckled ones will be your wages,'
then all the flocks gave birth to speckled
young; and if he said, 'The streaked ones
will be your wages,' then all the flocks
bore streaked young. 9 So God has taken
away your father's livestock and has given
them to me.

10 "In breeding season I once had a
dream in which I looked up and saw that
the male goats mating with the flock were
streaked, speckled or spotted. 11 The angel
of God said to me in the dream, 'Jacob.' I
answered, 'Here I am.' 12 And he said,
'Look up and see that all the male goats
mating with the flock are streaked, speckled or spotted, for I have seen all that Laban has been doing to you. 13 I am the
God of Bethel, where you anointed a pillar and where you made a vow to me.
Now leave this land at once and go back
to your native land.' "

14 Then Rachel and Leah replied, "Do we
still have any share in the inheritance of
our father's estate? 15 Does he not regard
us as foreigners? Not only has he sold us,
but he has used up what was paid for us.
16 Surely all the wealth that God took away
from our father belongs to us and our
children. So do whatever God has told
you."

17 Then Jacob put his children and his
wives on camels, 18 and he drove all his
livestock ahead of him, along with all the
goods he had accumulated in Paddan
Aram,[a] to go to his father Isaac in the land
of Canaan.

19 When Laban had gone to shear his
sheep, Rachel stole her father's household
gods. 20 Moreover, Jacob deceived Laban
the Aramean by not telling him he was
running away. 21 So he fled with all he had,
and crossing the River,[b] he headed for the
hill country of Gilead.

Laban Pursues Jacob

22 On the third day Laban was told that
Jacob had fled. 23 Taking his relatives with
him, he pursued Jacob for seven days and
caught up with him in the hill country of
Gilead. 24 Then God came to Laban the Aramean in a dream at night and said to
him, "Be careful not to say anything to Jacob, either good or bad."

25 Jacob had pitched his tent in the hill
country of Gilead when Laban overtook
him, and Laban and his relatives camped
there too. 26 Then Laban said to Jacob,
"What have you done? You've deceived
me, and you've carried off my daughters
like captives in war. 27 Why did you run off
secretly and deceive me? Why didn't you
tell me, so I could send you away with joy
and singing to the music of tambourines
and harps? 28 You didn't even let me kiss
my grandchildren and my daughters
good-by. You have done a foolish thing.
29 I have the power to harm you; but last
night the God of your father said to me,
'Be careful not to say anything to Jacob,
either good or bad.' 30 Now you have gone
off because you longed to return to your
father's house. But why did you steal my
gods?"

31 Jacob answered Laban, "I was afraid,
because I thought you would take your
daughters away from me by force. 32 But if
you find anyone who has your gods, he
shall not live. In the presence of our relatives, see for yourself whether there is anything of yours here with me; and if so,
take it." Now Jacob did not know that Rachel had stolen the gods.

33 So Laban went into Jacob's tent and
into Leah's tent and into the tent of the
two maidservants, but he found nothing.
After he came out of Leah's tent, he entered Rachel's tent. 34 Now Rachel had tak-
en the household gods and put them inside her camel's saddle and was sitting on
them. Laban searched through everything
in the tent but found nothing.

35 Rachel said to her father, "Don't be
angry, my lord, that I cannot stand up in
your presence; I'm having my period." So
he searched but could not find the household gods.

36 Jacob was angry and took Laban to
task. "What is my crime?" he asked Laban.
"What sin have I committed that you hunt
me down? 37 Now that you have searched

[a] *18* That is, Northwest Mesopotamia [b] *21* That is, the Euphrates

through all my goods, what have you
found that belongs to your household?
Put it here in front of your relatives and
mine, and let them judge between the two
of us.
38"I have been with you for twenty years
now. Your sheep and goats have not mis-
carried, nor have I eaten rams from your
flocks. 39I did not bring you animals torn
by wild beasts; I bore the loss myself. And
you demanded payment from me for
whatever was stolen by day or night.
40This was my situation: The heat consumed me in the daytime and the cold at
night, and sleep fled from my eyes. 41It
was like this for the twenty years I was in
your household. I worked for you fourteen years for your two daughters and six
years for your flocks, and you changed my
wages ten times. 42If the God of my father,
the God of Abraham and the Fear of Isaac,
had not been with me, you would surely
have sent me away empty-handed. But
God has seen my hardship and the toil of
my hands, and last night he rebuked
you."
43Laban answered Jacob, "The women
are my daughters, the children are my
children, and the flocks are my flocks. All
you see is mine. Yet what can I do today
about these daughters of mine, or about
the children they have borne? 44Come
now, let's make a covenant, you and I, and
let it serve as a witness between us."
45So Jacob took a stone and set it up as
a pillar. 46He said to his relatives, "Gather
some stones." So they took stones and
piled them in a heap, and they ate there
by the heap. 47Laban called it Jegar Sahadutha,[c] and Jacob called it Galeed.[d]
48Laban said, "This heap is a witness between you and me today." That is why it
was called Galeed. 49It was also called
Mizpah,[e] because he said, "May the LORD
keep watch between you and me when we
are away from each other. 50If you mistreat
my daughters or if you take any wives besides my daughters, even though no one
is with us, remember that God is a witness
between you and me."
51Laban also said to Jacob, "Here is this
heap, and here is this pillar I have set up
between you and me. 52This heap is a witness, and this pillar is a witness, that I will
not go past this heap to your side to harm
you and that you will not go past this
heap and pillar to my side to harm me.
53May the God of Abraham and the God
of Nahor, the God of their father, judge
between us."
So Jacob took an oath in the name of
the Fear of his father Isaac. 54He offered a
sacrifice there in the hill country and invited his relatives to a meal. After they had
eaten, they spent the night there.
55Early the next morning Laban kissed
his grandchildren and his daughters and
blessed them. Then he left and returned
home.

[c] 47 The Aramaic *Jegar Sahadutha* means *witness heap.* [d] 47 The Hebrew *Galeed* means *witness heap.* [e] 49 *Mizpah* means *watchtower.*

PRAYER: ADORATION

MY soul magnifies You, Lord, and my spirit rejoices in You, my Savior, for You, O Mighty One, have done great things for me, and holy is Your name. Your mercy is on those who fear You, from generation to generation. (Luke 1:46–47, 49–50)

PAUSE *to express your thoughts of praise and worship.*

NT Matthew 21:23–46

The Authority of Jesus Questioned

23Jesus entered the temple courts, and,
while he was teaching, the chief priests
and the elders of the people came to him.
"By what authority are you doing these
things?" they asked. "And who gave you
this authority?"
24Jesus replied, "I will also ask you one
question. If you answer me, I will tell you
by what authority I am doing these things.
25John's baptism—where did it come
from? Was it from heaven, or from men?"
They discussed it among themselves
and said, "If we say, 'From heaven,' he will

ask, 'Then why didn't you believe him?'
26But if we say, 'From men'—we are afraid
of the people, for they all hold that John
was a prophet."
27So they answered Jesus, "We don't
know."
Then he said, "Neither will I tell you
by what authority I am doing these
things.

The Parable of the Two Sons

28"What do you think? There was a man
who had two sons. He went to the first
and said, 'Son, go and work today in the
vineyard.'
29" 'I will not,' he answered, but later he
changed his mind and went.
30"Then the father went to the other son
and said the same thing. He answered, 'I
will, sir,' but he did not go.
31"Which of the two did what his father
wanted?"
"The first," they answered.
Jesus said to them, "I tell you the truth,
the tax collectors and the prostitutes are
entering the kingdom of God ahead of
you. 32For John came to you to show you
the way of righteousness, and you did
not believe him, but the tax collectors
and the prostitutes did. And even after
you saw this, you did not repent and believe him.

The Parable of the Tenants

33"Listen to another parable: There was
a landowner who planted a vineyard. He
put a wall around it, dug a winepress in it
and built a watchtower. Then he rented
the vineyard to some farmers and went
away on a journey. 34When the harvest
time approached, he sent his servants to
the tenants to collect his fruit.
35"The tenants seized his servants; they
beat one, killed another, and stoned a
third. 36Then he sent other servants to
them, more than the first time, and the
tenants treated them the same way. 37Last
of all, he sent his son to them. 'They will
respect my son,' he said.
38"But when the tenants saw the son,
they said to each other, 'This is the heir.
Come, let's kill him and take his inheritance.' 39So they took him and threw him
out of the vineyard and killed him.
40"Therefore, when the owner of the
vineyard comes, what will he do to those
tenants?"
41"He will bring those wretches to a
wretched end," they replied, "and he will
rent the vineyard to other tenants, who
will give him his share of the crop at harvest time."
42Jesus said to them, "Have you never
read in the Scriptures:

" 'The stone the builders rejected
  has become the capstone[a];
the Lord has done this,
  and it is marvelous in our eyes'[b]?

43"Therefore I tell you that the kingdom
of God will be taken away from you and
given to a people who will produce its
fruit. 44He who falls on this stone will be
broken to pieces, but he on whom it falls
will be crushed."[c]
45When the chief priests and the Pharisees heard Jesus' parables, they knew he
was talking about them. 46They looked for
a way to arrest him, but they were afraid
of the crowd because the people held that
he was a prophet.

[a] 42 Or *cornerstone* [b] 42 Psalm 118:22,23
[c] 44 Some manuscripts do not have verse 44.

PRAYER: THE CHARACTER I WANT TO CULTIVATE

WHEN I am blessed with abundance, I will beware lest my heart become proud, and I forget You, O Lord my God, who provides all good things—lest I think that it was my power and the strength of my hand that brought this wealth. (Deuteronomy 8:12–14, 17) . . . If I am proud, I will be destroyed; if I have a haughty spirit, I will fall. (Proverbs 16:18)

__TAKE__ a moment to ask the Lord for the grace to grow in godly character.

YEAR 1 DAY 30

OT Genesis 32:1–33:20

Jacob Prepares to Meet Esau

32 Jacob also went on his way, and the
angels of God met him. 2When Jacob
saw them, he said, "This is the camp of
God!" So he named that place Mahanaim.[a]
3Jacob sent messengers ahead of him to
his brother Esau in the land of Seir, the
country of Edom. 4He instructed them:
"This is what you are to say to my master
Esau: 'Your servant Jacob says, I have been
staying with Laban and have remained
there till now. 5I have cattle and donkeys,
sheep and goats, menservants and maidservants. Now I am sending this message
to my lord, that I may find favor in your
eyes.' "
6When the messengers returned to Jacob, they said, "We went to your brother
Esau, and now he is coming to meet you,
and four hundred men are with him."
7In great fear and distress Jacob divided
the people who were with him into two
groups,[b] and the flocks and herds and
camels as well. 8He thought, "If Esau
comes and attacks one group,[c] the group[c]
that is left may escape."
9Then Jacob prayed, "O God of my father Abraham, God of my father Isaac,
O LORD, who said to me, 'Go back to your
country and your relatives, and I will
make you prosper,' 10I am unworthy of all
the kindness and faithfulness you have
shown your servant. I had only my staff
when I crossed this Jordan, but now I
have become two groups. 11Save me, I
pray, from the hand of my brother Esau,
for I am afraid he will come and attack
me, and also the mothers with their children. 12But you have said, 'I will surely
make you prosper and will make your descendants like the sand of the sea, which
cannot be counted.' "
13He spent the night there, and from
what he had with him he selected a gift
for his brother Esau: 14two hundred female goats and twenty male goats, two
hundred ewes and twenty rams, 15thirty
female camels with their young, forty
cows and ten bulls, and twenty female
donkeys and ten male donkeys. 16He put
them in the care of his servants, each herd
by itself, and said to his servants, "Go
ahead of me, and keep some space between the herds."
17He instructed the one in the lead:
"When my brother Esau meets you and
asks, 'To whom do you belong, and where
are you going, and who owns all these animals in front of you?' 18then you are to
say, 'They belong to your servant Jacob.
They are a gift sent to my lord Esau, and
he is coming behind us.' "
19He also instructed the second, the
third and all the others who followed the
herds: "You are to say the same thing to
Esau when you meet him. 20And be sure
to say, 'Your servant Jacob is coming behind us.' " For he thought, "I will pacify
him with these gifts I am sending on
ahead; later, when I see him, perhaps he
will receive me." 21So Jacob's gifts went on
ahead of him, but he himself spent the
night in the camp.

Jacob Wrestles With God

22That night Jacob got up and took his
two wives, his two maidservants and his
eleven sons and crossed the ford of the
Jabbok. 23After he had sent them across
the stream, he sent over all his possessions. 24So Jacob was left alone, and a man
wrestled with him till daybreak. 25When
the man saw that he could not overpower him, he touched the socket of Jacob's
hip so that his hip was wrenched as he
wrestled with the man. 26Then the man
said, "Let me go, for it is daybreak."
But Jacob replied, "I will not let you go
unless you bless me."
27The man asked him, "What is your
name?"
"Jacob," he answered.
28Then the man said, "Your name will
no longer be Jacob, but Israel,[d] because
you have struggled with God and with
men and have overcome."
29Jacob said, "Please tell me your
name."
But he replied, "Why do you ask my
name?" Then he blessed him there.
30So Jacob called the place Peniel,[e] say-

[a] 2 *Mahanaim* means *two camps.* [b] 7 Or *camps;* also in verse 10 [c] 8 Or *camp* [d] 28 *Israel* means *he struggles with God.* [e] 30 *Peniel* means *face of God.*

ing, "It is because I saw God face to face,
and yet my life was spared."
31 The sun rose above him as he passed
Peniel,[f] and he was limping because of his
hip. 32 Therefore to this day the Israelites
do not eat the tendon attached to the
socket of the hip, because the socket of Jacob's hip was touched near the tendon.

Jacob Meets Esau

33 Jacob looked up and there was Esau,
coming with his four hundred men;
so he divided the children among Leah,
Rachel and the two maidservants. 2 He put
the maidservants and their children in
front, Leah and her children next, and Rachel and Joseph in the rear. 3 He himself
went on ahead and bowed down to the
ground seven times as he approached his
brother.
4 But Esau ran to meet Jacob and embraced him; he threw his arms around his
neck and kissed him. And they wept.
5 Then Esau looked up and saw the
women and children. "Who are these
with you?" he asked.
Jacob answered, "They are the children
God has graciously given your servant."
6 Then the maidservants and their children approached and bowed down.
7 Next, Leah and her children came and
bowed down. Last of all came Joseph and
Rachel, and they too bowed down.
8 Esau asked, "What do you mean by all
these droves I met?"
"To find favor in your eyes, my lord," he
said.
9 But Esau said, "I already have plenty,
my brother. Keep what you have for yourself."
10 "No, please!" said Jacob. "If I have
found favor in your eyes, accept this gift
from me. For to see your face is like seeing the face of God, now that you have received me favorably. 11 Please accept the
present that was brought to you, for God
has been gracious to me and I have all I
need." And because Jacob insisted, Esau
accepted it.
12 Then Esau said, "Let us be on our way;
I'll accompany you."
13 But Jacob said to him, "My lord knows
that the children are tender and that I
must care for the ewes and cows that are
nursing their young. If they are driven
hard just one day, all the animals will die.
14 So let my lord go on ahead of his servant,
while I move along slowly at the pace of
the droves before me and that of the children, until I come to my lord in Seir."
15 Esau said, "Then let me leave some of
my men with you."
"But why do that?" Jacob asked. "Just
let me find favor in the eyes of my lord."
16 So that day Esau started on his way
back to Seir. 17 Jacob, however, went to
Succoth, where he built a place for himself and made shelters for his livestock.
That is why the place is called Succoth.[g]
18 After Jacob came from Paddan Aram,[h]
he arrived safely at the[i] city of Shechem in
Canaan and camped within sight of the
city. 19 For a hundred pieces of silver,[j] he
bought from the sons of Hamor, the father of Shechem, the plot of ground
where he pitched his tent. 20 There he set
up an altar and called it El Elohe Israel[k].

[f] 31 Hebrew *Penuel,* a variant of *Peniel*
[g] 17 *Succoth* means *shelters.* [h] 18 That is, Northwest Mesopotamia [i] 18 Or *arrived at Shalem, a* [j] 19 Hebrew *hundred kesitahs;* a kesitah was a unit of money of unknown weight and value.
[k] 20 *El Elohe Israel* can mean *God, the God of Israel* or *mighty is the God of Israel.*

PRAYER: CONFESSION

YOUR eyes see the way people live, and You see all their steps. There is no darkness or deep shadow where people who do evil can hide. You do not need to examine them further, that they should come before You in judgment.

(Job 34:21–23)

ASK *the Spirit to search your heart and reveal any areas of unconfessed sin. Acknowledge these to the Lord and thank Him for His forgiveness.*

NT Matthew 22:1–22

The Parable of the Wedding Banquet

22 Jesus spoke to them again in parables, saying: 2"The kingdom of heaven is like a king who prepared a wedding banquet for his son. 3He sent his servants to those who had been invited to the banquet to tell them to come, but they refused to come.

4"Then he sent some more servants and said, 'Tell those who have been invited that I have prepared my dinner: My oxen and fattened cattle have been butchered, and everything is ready. Come to the wedding banquet.'

5"But they paid no attention and went off—one to his field, another to his business. 6The rest seized his servants, mistreated them and killed them. 7The king was enraged. He sent his army and destroyed those murderers and burned their city.

8"Then he said to his servants, 'The wedding banquet is ready, but those I invited did not deserve to come. 9Go to the street corners and invite to the banquet anyone you find.' 10So the servants went out into the streets and gathered all the people they could find, both good and bad, and the wedding hall was filled with guests.

11"But when the king came in to see the guests, he noticed a man there who was not wearing wedding clothes. 12'Friend,' he asked, 'how did you get in here without wedding clothes?' The man was speechless.

13"Then the king told the attendants, 'Tie him hand and foot, and throw him outside, into the darkness, where there will be weeping and gnashing of teeth.'

14"For many are invited, but few are chosen."

Paying Taxes to Caesar

15Then the Pharisees went out and laid plans to trap him in his words. 16They sent their disciples to him along with the Herodians. "Teacher," they said, "we know you are a man of integrity and that you teach the way of God in accordance with the truth. You aren't swayed by men, because you pay no attention to who they are. 17Tell us then, what is your opinion? Is it right to pay taxes to Caesar or not?"

18But Jesus, knowing their evil intent, said, "You hypocrites, why are you trying to trap me? 19Show me the coin used for paying the tax." They brought him a denarius, 20and he asked them, "Whose portrait is this? And whose inscription?"

21"Caesar's," they replied.

Then he said to them, "Give to Caesar what is Caesar's, and to God what is God's."

22When they heard this, they were amazed. So they left him and went away.

PRAYER: MY RELATIONSHIP TO OTHERS

LORD Jesus, You prayed these words for the unity of all who would believe in You: "I ask that all of them may be one, Father, just as You are in Me and I am in You, that they also may be in Us, that the world may believe that You sent Me. And the glory which You gave Me I have given to them, that they may be one, just as We are one: I in them, and You in Me, that they may be perfected in unity, that the world may know that You have sent Me and have loved them, even as You have loved Me."

(John 17:21–23)

***PAUSE** to review your relationships with others and to commit them to the Lord.*

YEAR 1 DAY 31

OT Genesis 34:1-31

Dinah and the Shechemites

34 Now Dinah, the daughter Leah had borne to Jacob, went out to visit the women of the land. 2When Shechem son of Hamor the Hivite, the ruler of that area, saw her, he took her and violated her. 3His heart was drawn to Dinah daughter of Jacob, and he loved the girl and spoke tenderly to her. 4And Shechem said to his father Hamor, "Get me this girl as my wife."

5When Jacob heard that his daughter Dinah had been defiled, his sons were in the fields with his livestock; so he kept quiet about it until they came home.

6Then Shechem's father Hamor went out to talk with Jacob. 7Now Jacob's sons had come in from the fields as soon as they heard what had happened. They were filled with grief and fury, because Shechem had done a disgraceful thing in[a] Israel by lying with Jacob's daughter—a thing that should not be done.

8But Hamor said to them, "My son Shechem has his heart set on your daughter. Please give her to him as his wife. 9Intermarry with us; give us your daughters and take our daughters for yourselves. 10You can settle among us; the land is open to you. Live in it, trade[b] in it, and acquire property in it."

11Then Shechem said to Dinah's father and brothers, "Let me find favor in your eyes, and I will give you whatever you ask. 12Make the price for the bride and the gift I am to bring as great as you like, and I'll pay whatever you ask me. Only give me the girl as my wife."

13Because their sister Dinah had been defiled, Jacob's sons replied deceitfully as they spoke to Shechem and his father Hamor. 14They said to them, "We can't do such a thing; we can't give our sister to a man who is not circumcised. That would be a disgrace to us. 15We will give our consent to you on one condition only: that you become like us by circumcising all your males. 16Then we will give you our daughters and take your daughters for ourselves. We'll settle among you and become one people with you. 17But if you will not agree to be circumcised, we'll take our sister[c] and go."

18Their proposal seemed good to Hamor and his son Shechem. 19The young man, who was the most honored of all his father's household, lost no time in doing what they said, because he was delighted with Jacob's daughter. 20So Hamor and his son Shechem went to the gate of their city to speak to their fellow townsmen. 21"These men are friendly toward us," they said. "Let them live in our land and trade in it; the land has plenty of room for them. We can marry their daughters and they can marry ours. 22But the men will consent to live with us as one people only on the condition that our males be circumcised, as they themselves are. 23Won't their livestock, their property and all their other animals become ours? So let us give our consent to them, and they will settle among us."

24All the men who went out of the city gate agreed with Hamor and his son Shechem, and every male in the city was circumcised.

25Three days later, while all of them were still in pain, two of Jacob's sons, Simeon and Levi, Dinah's brothers, took their swords and attacked the unsuspecting city, killing every male. 26They put Hamor and his son Shechem to the sword and took Dinah from Shechem's house and left. 27The sons of Jacob came upon the dead bodies and looted the city where[d] their sister had been defiled. 28They seized their flocks and herds and donkeys and everything else of theirs in the city and out in the fields. 29They carried off all their wealth and all their women and children, taking as plunder everything in the houses.

30Then Jacob said to Simeon and Levi, "You have brought trouble on me by making me a stench to the Canaanites and Perizzites, the people living in this land. We are few in number, and if they join forces against me and attack me, I and my household will be destroyed."

31But they replied, "Should he have treated our sister like a prostitute?"

[a] 7 Or *against* [b] 10 Or *move about freely;* also in verse 21 [c] 17 Hebrew *daughter* [d] 27 Or *because*

PRAYER: RENEWAL

MAY I flee from sexual immorality. All other sins people commit are outside their bodies, but sexually immoral people sin against their own bodies. (1 Corinthians 6:18) . . . May I not set my heart on evil things, or be an idolater or commit sexual immorality. (1 Corinthians 10:6–8)

***PAUSE** to add your own prayers for personal renewal.*

NT Matthew 22:23-46

Marriage at the Resurrection

23 That same day the Sadducees, who say
there is no resurrection, came to him with
a question. 24 "Teacher," they said, "Moses
told us that if a man dies without having
children, his brother must marry the widow and have children for him. 25 Now
there were seven brothers among us. The
first one married and died, and since he
had no children, he left his wife to his
brother. 26 The same thing happened to
the second and third brother, right on
down to the seventh. 27 Finally, the woman
died. 28 Now then, at the resurrection,
whose wife will she be of the seven, since
all of them were married to her?"

29 Jesus replied, "You are in error because
you do not know the Scriptures or the
power of God. 30 At the resurrection people
will neither marry nor be given in marriage; they will be like the angels in heav-
en. 31 But about the resurrection of the
dead—have you not read what God said to
you, 32 'I am the God of Abraham, the God
of Isaac, and the God of Jacob'[a]? He is not
the God of the dead but of the living."

33 When the crowds heard this, they
were astonished at his teaching.

The Greatest Commandment

34 Hearing that Jesus had silenced the
Sadducees, the Pharisees got together.
35 One of them, an expert in the law, tested
him with this question: 36 "Teacher, which
is the greatest commandment in the Law?"

37 Jesus replied: " 'Love the Lord your
God with all your heart and with all your
soul and with all your mind.'[b] 38 This is the
first and greatest commandment. 39 And
the second is like it: 'Love your neighbor
as yourself.'[c] 40 All the Law and the Prophets hang on these two commandments."

Whose Son Is the Christ?

41 While the Pharisees were gathered together, Jesus asked them, 42 "What do you
think about the Christ[d]? Whose son is he?"

"The son of David," they replied.

43 He said to them, "How is it then that
David, speaking by the Spirit, calls him
'Lord'? For he says,

44 " 'The Lord said to my Lord:
"Sit at my right hand
until I put your enemies
under your feet." '[e]

45 If then David calls him 'Lord,' how can
he be his son?" 46 No one could say a word
in reply, and from that day on no one
dared to ask him any more questions.

[a] 32 Exodus 3:6 [b] 37 Deut. 6:5 [c] 39 Lev. 19:18
[d] 42 Or *Messiah* [e] 44 Psalm 110:1

PRAYER: THE ATTRIBUTES OF GOD

I ACKNOWLEDGE this day and take it to my heart that You, Lord, are God in heaven above and on the earth below; there is no other. (Deuteronomy 4:39) . . . You are the Lord, and there is no other; apart from You there is no God. From the rising of the sun to its setting, we know there is none besides You. You are the Lord, and there is no other. (Isaiah 45:5–6)

***PAUSE** to reflect on these affirmations about the person, powers and perfection of God.*

YEAR 1 DAY 32

OT Genesis 35:1–36:43

Jacob Returns to Bethel

35 Then God said to Jacob, "Go up to
Bethel and settle there, and build an
altar there to God, who appeared to you
when you were fleeing from your brother
Esau."
2So Jacob said to his household and to
all who were with him, "Get rid of the foreign gods you have with you, and purify
yourselves and change your clothes. 3Then
come, let us go up to Bethel, where I will
build an altar to God, who answered me
in the day of my distress and who has
been with me wherever I have gone." 4So
they gave Jacob all the foreign gods they
had and the rings in their ears, and Jacob
buried them under the oak at Shechem.
5Then they set out, and the terror of God
fell upon the towns all around them so
that no one pursued them.
6Jacob and all the people with him
came to Luz (that is, Bethel) in the land
of Canaan. 7There he built an altar, and
he called the place El Bethel,[a] because
it was there that God revealed himself
to him when he was fleeing from his
brother.
8Now Deborah, Rebekah's nurse, died
and was buried under the oak below Bethel. So it was named Allon Bacuth.[b]
9After Jacob returned from Paddan
Aram,[c] God appeared to him again and
blessed him. 10God said to him, "Your
name is Jacob,[d] but you will no longer be
called Jacob; your name will be Israel.[e]"
So he named him Israel.
11And God said to him, "I am God
Almighty[f]; be fruitful and increase in
number. A nation and a community of
nations will come from you, and kings
will come from your body. 12The land I
gave to Abraham and Isaac I also give to
you, and I will give this land to your descendants after you." 13Then God went up
from him at the place where he had talked
with him.
14Jacob set up a stone pillar at the place
where God had talked with him, and he
poured out a drink offering on it; he also
poured oil on it. 15Jacob called the place
where God had talked with him Bethel.[g]

The Deaths of Rachel and Isaac

16Then they moved on from Bethel.
While they were still some distance from
Ephrath, Rachel began to give birth and
had great difficulty. 17And as she was having great difficulty in childbirth, the midwife said to her, "Don't be afraid, for you
have another son." 18As she breathed her
last—for she was dying—she named her
son Ben-Oni.[h] But his father named him
Benjamin.[i]
19So Rachel died and was buried on the
way to Ephrath (that is, Bethlehem).
20Over her tomb Jacob set up a pillar, and
to this day that pillar marks Rachel's
tomb.
21Israel moved on again and pitched his
tent beyond Migdal Eder. 22While Israel
was living in that region, Reuben went in
and slept with his father's concubine Bilhah, and Israel heard of it.

Jacob had twelve sons:
23The sons of Leah:
Reuben the firstborn of Jacob,
Simeon, Levi, Judah, Issachar and
Zebulun.
24The sons of Rachel:
Joseph and Benjamin.
25The sons of Rachel's maidservant Bilhah:
Dan and Naphtali.
26The sons of Leah's maidservant Zilpah:
Gad and Asher.
These were the sons of Jacob, who were
born to him in Paddan Aram.

27Jacob came home to his father Isaac
in Mamre, near Kiriath Arba (that is, Hebron), where Abraham and Isaac had
stayed. 28Isaac lived a hundred and eighty
years. 29Then he breathed his last and died
and was gathered to his people, old and
full of years. And his sons Esau and Jacob
buried him.

[a] 7 *El Bethel* means *God of Bethel.* [b] 8 *Allon Bacuth* means *oak of weeping.* [c] 9 That is, Northwest Mesopotamia; also in verse 26 [d] 10 *Jacob* means *he grasps the heel* (figuratively, *he deceives*).
[e] 10 *Israel* means *he struggles with God.*
[f] 11 Hebrew *El-Shaddai* [g] 15 *Bethel* means *house of God.* [h] 18 *Ben-Oni* means *son of my trouble.*
[i] 18 *Benjamin* means *son of my right hand.*

Esau's Descendants

36 This is the account of Esau (that is,
Edom).

2 Esau took his wives from the
women of Canaan: Adah daughter of
Elon the Hittite, and Oholibamah
daughter of Anah and granddaughter
of Zibeon the Hivite— 3 also Basemath daughter of Ishmael and sister
of Nebaioth.
4 Adah bore Eliphaz to Esau, Basemath bore Reuel, 5 and Oholibamah
bore Jeush, Jalam and Korah. These
were the sons of Esau, who were born
to him in Canaan.
6 Esau took his wives and sons and
daughters and all the members of his
household, as well as his livestock
and all his other animals and all the
goods he had acquired in Canaan,
and moved to a land some distance
from his brother Jacob. 7 Their possessions were too great for them to
remain together; the land where they
were staying could not support them
both because of their livestock. 8 So
Esau (that is, Edom) settled in the
hill country of Seir.

9 This is the account of Esau the father
of the Edomites in the hill country of Seir.

10 These are the names of Esau's sons:
Eliphaz, the son of Esau's wife
Adah, and Reuel, the son of Esau's
wife Basemath.
11 The sons of Eliphaz:
Teman, Omar, Zepho, Gatam and
Kenaz.
12 Esau's son Eliphaz also had a concubine named Timna, who bore
him Amalek. These were grandsons of Esau's wife Adah.
13 The sons of Reuel:
Nahath, Zerah, Shammah and
Mizzah. These were grandsons of
Esau's wife Basemath.
14 The sons of Esau's wife Oholibamah
daughter of Anah and granddaughter
of Zibeon, whom she bore to Esau:
Jeush, Jalam and Korah.

15 These were the chiefs among Esau's
descendants:
The sons of Eliphaz the firstborn of
Esau:
Chiefs Teman, Omar, Zepho, Kenaz, 16 Korah,[j] Gatam and Amalek.
These were the chiefs descended
from Eliphaz in Edom; they were
grandsons of Adah.
17 The sons of Esau's son Reuel:
Chiefs Nahath, Zerah, Shammah
and Mizzah. These were the chiefs
descended from Reuel in Edom;
they were grandsons of Esau's wife
Basemath.
18 The sons of Esau's wife Oholibamah:
Chiefs Jeush, Jalam and Korah.
These were the chiefs descended
from Esau's wife Oholibamah
daughter of Anah.
19 These were the sons of Esau (that is,
Edom), and these were their chiefs.

20 These were the sons of Seir the Horite,
who were living in the region:
Lotan, Shobal, Zibeon, Anah, 21 Dishon, Ezer and Dishan. These sons
of Seir in Edom were Horite chiefs.
22 The sons of Lotan:
Hori and Homam.[k] Timna was Lotan's sister.
23 The sons of Shobal:
Alvan, Manahath, Ebal, Shepho
and Onam.
24 The sons of Zibeon:
Aiah and Anah. This is the Anah
who discovered the hot springs[l] in
the desert while he was grazing the
donkeys of his father Zibeon.
25 The children of Anah:
Dishon and Oholibamah daughter
of Anah.
26 The sons of Dishon[m]:
Hemdan, Eshban, Ithran and Keran.
27 The sons of Ezer:
Bilhan, Zaavan and Akan.
28 The sons of Dishan:
Uz and Aran.
29 These were the Horite chiefs:
Lotan, Shobal, Zibeon, Anah, 30 Dishon, Ezer and Dishan. These were
the Horite chiefs, according to
their divisions, in the land of Seir.

[j] *16* Masoretic Text; Samaritan Pentateuch (see also Gen. 36:11 and 1 Chron. 1:36) does not have *Korah.* [k] *22* Hebrew *Hemam,* a variant of *Homam* (see 1 Chron. 1:39) [l] *24* Vulgate; Syriac *discovered water;* the meaning of the Hebrew for this word is uncertain. [m] *26* Hebrew *Dishan,* a variant of *Dishon*

The Rulers of Edom

31 These were the kings who reigned in
Edom before any Israelite king reigned[n]:
32 Bela son of Beor became king of
Edom. His city was named Dinhabah.
33 When Bela died, Jobab son of Zerah
from Bozrah succeeded him as
king.
34 When Jobab died, Husham from the
land of the Temanites succeeded
him as king.
35 When Husham died, Hadad son of
Bedad, who defeated Midian in
the country of Moab, succeeded
him as king. His city was named
Avith.
36 When Hadad died, Samlah from
Masrekah succeeded him as king.
37 When Samlah died, Shaul from Rehoboth
on the river[o] succeeded
him as king.
38 When Shaul died, Baal-Hanan son of
Acbor succeeded him as king.
39 When Baal-Hanan son of Acbor died,
Hadad[p] succeeded him as king. His
city was named Pau, and his wife's
name was Mehetabel daughter of
Matred, the daughter of Me-Zahab.

40 These were the chiefs descended from
Esau, by name, according to their clans
and regions:
Timna, Alvah, Jetheth, 41 Oholibamah,
Elah, Pinon, 42 Kenaz, Teman,
Mibzar, 43 Magdiel and Iram. These
were the chiefs of Edom, according
to their settlements in the land
they occupied.

This was Esau the father of the Edomites.

[n] 31 Or *before an Israelite king reigned over them*
[o] 37 Possibly the Euphrates [p] 39 Many manuscripts of the Masoretic Text, Samaritan Pentateuch and Syriac (see also 1 Chron. 1:50); most manuscripts of the Masoretic Text *Hadar*

PRAYER: PETITION

LET me hear Your unfailing love in the morning, O Lord, for I have put my trust in You. Show me the way I should walk, for to You I lift up my soul. (Psalm 143:8)

***PAUSE** here to petition God to help you be a faithful steward of your time, talents, possessions and relationships. Offer prayers of petition regarding your activities for this day and any special concerns you may have.*

NT Matthew 23:1-39

Seven Woes

23 Then Jesus said to the crowds and to
his disciples: 2 "The teachers of the law
and the Pharisees sit in Moses' seat. 3 So
you must obey them and do everything
they tell you. But do not do what they do,
for they do not practice what they preach.
4 They tie up heavy loads and put them on
men's shoulders, but they themselves are
not willing to lift a finger to move them.
5 "Everything they do is done for men to
see: They make their phylacteries[a] wide
and the tassels on their garments long;
6 they love the place of honor at banquets
and the most important seats in the synagogues;
7 they love to be greeted in the
marketplaces and to have men call them
'Rabbi.'
8 "But you are not to be called 'Rabbi,'
for you have only one Master and you are
all brothers. 9 And do not call anyone on
earth 'father,' for you have one Father, and
he is in heaven. 10 Nor are you to be called
'teacher,' for you have one Teacher, the
Christ.[b] 11 The greatest among you will be
your servant. 12 For whoever exalts himself
will be humbled, and whoever humbles
himself will be exalted.
13 "Woe to you, teachers of the law and
Pharisees, you hypocrites! You shut the
kingdom of heaven in men's faces. You
yourselves do not enter, nor will you let
those enter who are trying to.[c]

[a] 5 That is, boxes containing Scripture verses, worn on forehead and arm [b] 10 Or *Messiah*
[c] 13 Some manuscripts *to.* 14 *Woe to you, teachers of the law and Pharisees, you hypocrites! You devour widows' houses and for a show make lengthy prayers. Therefore you will be punished more severely.*

15 "Woe to you, teachers of the law and Pharisees, you hypocrites! You travel over land and sea to win a single convert, and when he becomes one, you make him twice as much a son of hell as you are.

16 "Woe to you, blind guides! You say, 'If anyone swears by the temple, it means nothing; but if anyone swears by the gold of the temple, he is bound by his oath.' 17 You blind fools! Which is greater: the gold, or the temple that makes the gold sacred? 18 You also say, 'If anyone swears by the altar, it means nothing; but if anyone swears by the gift on it, he is bound by his oath.' 19 You blind men! Which is greater: the gift, or the altar that makes the gift sacred? 20 Therefore, he who swears by the altar swears by it and by everything on it. 21 And he who swears by the temple swears by it and by the one who dwells in it. 22 And he who swears by heaven swears by God's throne and by the one who sits on it.

23 "Woe to you, teachers of the law and Pharisees, you hypocrites! You give a tenth of your spices—mint, dill and cummin. But you have neglected the more important matters of the law—justice, mercy and faithfulness. You should have practiced the latter, without neglecting the former. 24 You blind guides! You strain out a gnat but swallow a camel.

25 "Woe to you, teachers of the law and Pharisees, you hypocrites! You clean the outside of the cup and dish, but inside they are full of greed and self-indulgence. 26 Blind Pharisee! First clean the inside of the cup and dish, and then the outside also will be clean.

27 "Woe to you, teachers of the law and Pharisees, you hypocrites! You are like whitewashed tombs, which look beautiful on the outside but on the inside are full of dead men's bones and everything unclean. 28 In the same way, on the outside you appear to people as righteous but on the inside you are full of hypocrisy and wickedness.

29 "Woe to you, teachers of the law and Pharisees, you hypocrites! You build tombs for the prophets and decorate the graves of the righteous. 30 And you say, 'If we had lived in the days of our forefathers, we would not have taken part with them in shedding the blood of the prophets.' 31 So you testify against yourselves that you are the descendants of those who murdered the prophets. 32 Fill up, then, the measure of the sin of your forefathers!

33 "You snakes! You brood of vipers! How will you escape being condemned to hell? 34 Therefore I am sending you prophets and wise men and teachers. Some of them you will kill and crucify; others you will flog in your synagogues and pursue from town to town. 35 And so upon you will come all the righteous blood that has been shed on earth, from the blood of righteous Abel to the blood of Zechariah son of Berekiah, whom you murdered between the temple and the altar. 36 I tell you the truth, all this will come upon this generation.

37 "O Jerusalem, Jerusalem, you who kill the prophets and stone those sent to you, how often I have longed to gather your children together, as a hen gathers her chicks under her wings, but you were not willing. 38 Look, your house is left to you desolate. 39 For I tell you, you will not see me again until you say, 'Blessed is he who comes in the name of the Lord.'[d]"

[d] 39 Psalm 118:26

PRAYER: THE WORKS OF GOD

LORD, we look forward to the day when Your kingdom will come in all its fullness: The wolf will dwell with the lamb, and the leopard will lie down with the goat, and the calf and the lion and the yearling together, and a little child will lead them. The cow will feed with the bear; their young will lie down together, and the lion will eat straw like the ox. The infant will play near the hole of the cobra, and the young child will put his hand into the viper's hole. They will neither harm nor destroy on all Your holy mountain, for the earth will be full of the knowledge of You, O Lord, as the waters cover the sea. (Isaiah 11:6–9)

***TAKE** a moment to consider the greatness of God's wonderful works.*

OT **Genesis 37:1-36** YEAR 1 DAY 33

Joseph's Dreams

37 Jacob lived in the land where his father had stayed, the land of Canaan.

2This is the account of Jacob.

Joseph, a young man of seventeen, was tending the flocks with his brothers, the sons of Bilhah and the sons of Zilpah, his father's wives, and he brought their father a bad report about them.

3Now Israel loved Joseph more than any of his other sons, because he had been born to him in his old age; and he made a richly ornamented[a] robe for him. 4When his brothers saw that their father loved him more than any of them, they hated him and could not speak a kind word to him.

5Joseph had a dream, and when he told it to his brothers, they hated him all the more. 6He said to them, "Listen to this dream I had: 7We were binding sheaves of grain out in the field when suddenly my sheaf rose and stood upright, while your sheaves gathered around mine and bowed down to it."

8His brothers said to him, "Do you intend to reign over us? Will you actually rule us?" And they hated him all the more because of his dream and what he had said.

9Then he had another dream, and he told it to his brothers. "Listen," he said, "I had another dream, and this time the sun and moon and eleven stars were bowing down to me."

10When he told his father as well as his brothers, his father rebuked him and said, "What is this dream you had? Will your mother and I and your brothers actually come and bow down to the ground before you?" 11His brothers were jealous of him, but his father kept the matter in mind.

Joseph Sold by His Brothers

12Now his brothers had gone to graze their father's flocks near Shechem, 13and Israel said to Joseph, "As you know, your brothers are grazing the flocks near Shechem. Come, I am going to send you to them."

"Very well," he replied.

14So he said to him, "Go and see if all is well with your brothers and with the flocks, and bring word back to me." Then he sent him off from the Valley of Hebron.

When Joseph arrived at Shechem, 15a man found him wandering around in the fields and asked him, "What are you looking for?"

16He replied, "I'm looking for my brothers. Can you tell me where they are grazing their flocks?"

17"They have moved on from here," the man answered. "I heard them say, 'Let's go to Dothan.' "

So Joseph went after his brothers and found them near Dothan. 18But they saw him in the distance, and before he reached them, they plotted to kill him.

19"Here comes that dreamer!" they said to each other. 20"Come now, let's kill him and throw him into one of these cisterns and say that a ferocious animal devoured him. Then we'll see what comes of his dreams."

21When Reuben heard this, he tried to rescue him from their hands. "Let's not take his life," he said. 22"Don't shed any blood. Throw him into this cistern here in the desert, but don't lay a hand on him." Reuben said this to rescue him from them and take him back to his father.

23So when Joseph came to his brothers, they stripped him of his robe—the richly ornamented robe he was wearing— 24and they took him and threw him into the cistern. Now the cistern was empty; there was no water in it.

25As they sat down to eat their meal, they looked up and saw a caravan of Ishmaelites coming from Gilead. Their camels were loaded with spices, balm and myrrh, and they were on their way to take them down to Egypt.

26Judah said to his brothers, "What will we gain if we kill our brother and cover up his blood? 27Come, let's sell him to the Ishmaelites and not lay our hands on him; after all, he is our brother, our own flesh and blood." His brothers agreed.

28So when the Midianite merchants

[a] 3 The meaning of the Hebrew for *richly ornamented* is uncertain; also in verses 23 and 32.

came by, his brothers pulled Joseph up
out of the cistern and sold him for twenty shekels[b] of silver to the Ishmaelites,
who took him to Egypt.
29 When Reuben returned to the cistern
and saw that Joseph was not there, he tore
his clothes. 30 He went back to his brothers and said, "The boy isn't there! Where
can I turn now?"
31 Then they got Joseph's robe, slaughtered a goat and dipped the robe in the
blood. 32 They took the ornamented robe
back to their father and said, "We found
this. Examine it to see whether it is your
son's robe."
33 He recognized it and said, "It is my
son's robe! Some ferocious animal has devoured him. Joseph has surely been torn
to pieces."
34 Then Jacob tore his clothes, put on
sackcloth and mourned for his son many
days. 35 All his sons and daughters came to
comfort him, but he refused to be comforted. "No," he said, "in mourning will I
go down to the grave[c] to my son." So his
father wept for him.
36 Meanwhile, the Midianites[d] sold Joseph in Egypt to Potiphar, one of Pharaoh's officials, the captain of the guard.

[b] *28* That is, about 8 ounces (about 0.2 kilogram) [c] *35* Hebrew *Sheol* [d] *36* Samaritan Pentateuch, Septuagint, Vulgate and Syriac (see also verse 28); Masoretic Text *Medanites*

PRAYER: INTERCESSION

O LORD, may I honor all people, love the community of believers, fear You, and honor the king. (1 Peter 2:17)

***TAKE** a few moments to intercede on behalf of your local, state or provincial, and national governments. Pray for spiritual revival in the nation and offer prayers regarding current events and concerns.*

NT Matthew 24:1–51

Signs of the End of the Age

24 Jesus left the temple and was walking
away when his disciples came up to
him to call his attention to its buildings.
2 "Do you see all these things?" he asked.
"I tell you the truth, not one stone here
will be left on another; every one will be
thrown down."
3 As Jesus was sitting on the Mount of
Olives, the disciples came to him privately. "Tell us," they said, "when will this
happen, and what will be the sign of your
coming and of the end of the age?"
4 Jesus answered: "Watch out that no
one deceives you. 5 For many will come in
my name, claiming, 'I am the Christ,[a]' and
will deceive many. 6 You will hear of wars
and rumors of wars, but see to it that you
are not alarmed. Such things must happen, but the end is still to come. 7 Nation
will rise against nation, and kingdom
against kingdom. There will be famines
and earthquakes in various places. 8 All
these are the beginning of birth pains.
9 "Then you will be handed over to be
persecuted and put to death, and you will
be hated by all nations because of me. 10 At
that time many will turn away from the
faith and will betray and hate each other,
11 and many false prophets will appear and
deceive many people. 12 Because of the increase of wickedness, the love of most will
grow cold, 13 but he who stands firm to the
end will be saved. 14 And this gospel of the
kingdom will be preached in the whole
world as a testimony to all nations, and
then the end will come.
15 "So when you see standing in the holy
place 'the abomination that causes desolation,'[b] spoken of through the prophet
Daniel—let the reader understand—
16 then let those who are in Judea flee to
the mountains. 17 Let no one on the roof
of his house go down to take anything out
of the house. 18 Let no one in the field go
back to get his cloak. 19 How dreadful it
will be in those days for pregnant women
and nursing mothers! 20 Pray that your
flight will not take place in winter or on
the Sabbath. 21 For then there will be great
distress, unequaled from the beginning of
the world until now—and never to be

[a] *5* Or *Messiah*; also in verse 23 [b] *15* Daniel 9:27; 11:31; 12:11

equaled again. 22 If those days had not been cut short, no one would survive, but for the sake of the elect those days will be shortened. 23 At that time if anyone says to you, 'Look, here is the Christ!' or, 'There he is!' do not believe it. 24 For false Christs and false prophets will appear and perform great signs and miracles to deceive even the elect—if that were possible. 25 See, I have told you ahead of time.

26 "So if anyone tells you, 'There he is, out in the desert,' do not go out; or, 'Here he is, in the inner rooms,' do not believe it. 27 For as lightning that comes from the east is visible even in the west, so will be the coming of the Son of Man. 28 Wherever there is a carcass, there the vultures will gather.

29 "Immediately after the distress of those days

" 'the sun will be darkened,
  and the moon will not give its light;
the stars will fall from the sky,
  and the heavenly bodies will be
    shaken.'[c]

30 "At that time the sign of the Son of Man will appear in the sky, and all the nations of the earth will mourn. They will see the Son of Man coming on the clouds of the sky, with power and great glory. 31 And he will send his angels with a loud trumpet call, and they will gather his elect from the four winds, from one end of the heavens to the other.

32 "Now learn this lesson from the fig tree: As soon as its twigs get tender and its leaves come out, you know that summer is near. 33 Even so, when you see all these things, you know that it[d] is near, right at the door. 34 I tell you the truth, this generation[e] will certainly not pass away until all these things have happened. 35 Heaven and earth will pass away, but my words will never pass away.

The Day and Hour Unknown

36 "No one knows about that day or hour, not even the angels in heaven, nor the Son,[f] but only the Father. 37 As it was in the days of Noah, so it will be at the coming of the Son of Man. 38 For in the days before the flood, people were eating and drinking, marrying and giving in marriage, up to the day Noah entered the ark; 39 and they knew nothing about what would happen until the flood came and took them all away. That is how it will be at the coming of the Son of Man. 40 Two men will be in the field; one will be taken and the other left. 41 Two women will be grinding with a hand mill; one will be taken and the other left.

42 "Therefore keep watch, because you do not know on what day your Lord will come. 43 But understand this: If the owner of the house had known at what time of night the thief was coming, he would have kept watch and would not have let his house be broken into. 44 So you also must be ready, because the Son of Man will come at an hour when you do not expect him.

45 "Who then is the faithful and wise servant, whom the master has put in charge of the servants in his household to give them their food at the proper time? 46 It will be good for that servant whose master finds him doing so when he returns. 47 I tell you the truth, he will put him in charge of all his possessions. 48 But suppose that servant is wicked and says to himself, 'My master is staying away a long time,' 49 and he then begins to beat his fellow servants and to eat and drink with drunkards. 50 The master of that servant will come on a day when he does not expect him and at an hour he is not aware of. 51 He will cut him to pieces and assign him a place with the hypocrites, where there will be weeping and gnashing of teeth.

[c] *29* Isaiah 13:10; 34:4 [d] *33* Or *he* [e] *34* Or *race*
[f] *36* Some manuscripts do not have *nor the Son.*

PRAYER: MY RELATIONSHIP TO GOD

O LORD, You are my strength and my shield; my heart trusts in You, and I am helped. My heart greatly rejoices, and I will give thanks to You in song. (Psalm 28:7) . . . I will not let my heart be troubled. I will trust in You, Father, and also in Christ. (John 14:1)

***PAUSE** to thank God for the relationship that you enjoy with Him in Jesus Christ.*

YEAR 1
DAY 34

OT Genesis 38:1-30

Judah and Tamar

38 At that time, Judah left his brothers
and went down to stay with a man of
Adullam named Hirah. 2There Judah met
the daughter of a Canaanite man named
Shua. He married her and lay with her;
3she became pregnant and gave birth to a
son, who was named Er. 4She conceived
again and gave birth to a son and named
him Onan. 5She gave birth to still another son and named him Shelah. It was at
Kezib that she gave birth to him.
6Judah got a wife for Er, his firstborn,
and her name was Tamar. 7But Er, Judah's
firstborn, was wicked in the LORD's sight;
so the LORD put him to death.
8Then Judah said to Onan, "Lie with
your brother's wife and fulfill your duty
to her as a brother-in-law to produce offspring for your brother." 9But Onan
knew that the offspring would not be his;
so whenever he lay with his brother's
wife, he spilled his semen on the ground
to keep from producing offspring for his
brother. 10What he did was wicked in the
LORD's sight; so he put him to death also.
11Judah then said to his daughter-in-law
Tamar, "Live as a widow in your father's
house until my son Shelah grows up." For
he thought, "He may die too, just like his
brothers." So Tamar went to live in her father's house.
12After a long time Judah's wife, the
daughter of Shua, died. When Judah had
recovered from his grief, he went up to
Timnah, to the men who were shearing
his sheep, and his friend Hirah the Adullamite went with him.
13When Tamar was told, "Your father-
in-law is on his way to Timnah to shear
his sheep," 14she took off her widow's
clothes, covered herself with a veil to disguise herself, and then sat down at the entrance to Enaim, which is on the road to
Timnah. For she saw that, though Shelah
had now grown up, she had not been giv-
en to him as his wife.
15When Judah saw her, he thought she
was a prostitute, for she had covered her
face. 16Not realizing that she was his
daughter-in-law, he went over to her by
the roadside and said, "Come now, let me
sleep with you."
"And what will you give me to sleep
with you?" she asked.
17"I'll send you a young goat from my
flock," he said.
"Will you give me something as a
pledge until you send it?" she asked.
18He said, "What pledge should I give
you?"
"Your seal and its cord, and the staff in
your hand," she answered. So he gave
them to her and slept with her, and she
became pregnant by him. 19After she left,
she took off her veil and put on her widow's clothes again.
20Meanwhile Judah sent the young goat
by his friend the Adullamite in order to
get his pledge back from the woman, but
he did not find her. 21He asked the men
who lived there, "Where is the shrine
prostitute who was beside the road at Enaim?"
"There hasn't been any shrine prostitute
here," they said.
22So he went back to Judah and said, "I
didn't find her. Besides, the men who
lived there said, 'There hasn't been any
shrine prostitute here.' "
23Then Judah said, "Let her keep what
she has, or we will become a laughingstock. After all, I did send her this young
goat, but you didn't find her."
24About three months later Judah was
told, "Your daughter-in-law Tamar is
guilty of prostitution, and as a result she
is now pregnant."
Judah said, "Bring her out and have her
burned to death!"
25As she was being brought out, she
sent a message to her father-in-law. "I am
pregnant by the man who owns these,"
she said. And she added, "See if you recognize whose seal and cord and staff these
are."
26Judah recognized them and said, "She
is more righteous than I, since I wouldn't
give her to my son Shelah." And he did
not sleep with her again.
27When the time came for her to give
birth, there were twin boys in her womb.
28As she was giving birth, one of them put
out his hand; so the midwife took a scarlet thread and tied it on his wrist and said,
"This one came out first." 29But when he

drew back his hand, his brother came out,
and she said, "So this is how you have
broken out!" And he was named Perez.[a]
30Then his brother, who had the scarlet
thread on his wrist, came out and he was
given the name Zerah.[b]

[a]29 *Perez* means *breaking out* [b]30 *Zerah* can mean *scarlet* or *brightness*

PRAYER: AFFIRMATION

YOUR Scripture, O Lord, is God-breathed and is useful for teaching, for reproof, for correction and for training in righteousness, that we, Your people, may be thoroughly equipped for every good work. (2 Timothy 3:16–17) . . . We have the prophetic word made more certain, to which I will do well to pay attention, as to a light shining in a dark place, until the day dawns and the morning star rises in my heart. (2 Peter 1:19)

***PAUSE** to reflect on these Biblical affirmations.*

NT Matthew 25:1–46

The Parable of the Ten Virgins

25 "At that time the kingdom of heaven
will be like ten virgins who took their
lamps and went out to meet the bridegroom. 2Five of them were foolish and
five were wise. 3The foolish ones took
their lamps but did not take any oil with
them. 4The wise, however, took oil in jars
along with their lamps. 5The bridegroom
was a long time in coming, and they all
became drowsy and fell asleep.
6"At midnight the cry rang out: 'Here's
the bridegroom! Come out to meet him!'
7"Then all the virgins woke up and
trimmed their lamps. 8The foolish ones
said to the wise, 'Give us some of your oil;
our lamps are going out.'
9" 'No,' they replied, 'there may not be
enough for both us and you. Instead, go
to those who sell oil and buy some for
yourselves.'
10"But while they were on their way to
buy the oil, the bridegroom arrived. The
virgins who were ready went in with him
to the wedding banquet. And the door
was shut.
11"Later the others also came. 'Sir! Sir!'
they said. 'Open the door for us!'
12"But he replied, 'I tell you the truth, I
don't know you.'
13"Therefore keep watch, because you
do not know the day or the hour.

The Parable of the Talents

14"Again, it will be like a man going on
a journey, who called his servants and entrusted his property to them. 15To one he
gave five talents[a] of money, to another
two talents, and to another one talent,
each according to his ability. Then he
went on his journey. 16The man who had
received the five talents went at once and
put his money to work and gained five
more. 17So also, the one with the two talents gained two more. 18But the man who
had received the one talent went off, dug
a hole in the ground and hid his master's
money.
19"After a long time the master of those
servants returned and settled accounts
with them. 20The man who had received
the five talents brought the other five.
'Master,' he said, 'you entrusted me with
five talents. See, I have gained five more.'
21"His master replied, 'Well done, good
and faithful servant! You have been faithful with a few things; I will put you in
charge of many things. Come and share
your master's happiness!'
22"The man with the two talents also
came. 'Master,' he said, 'you entrusted me
with two talents; see, I have gained two
more.'
23"His master replied, 'Well done, good
and faithful servant! You have been faithful with a few things; I will put you in
charge of many things. Come and share
your master's happiness!'
24"Then the man who had received the
one talent came. 'Master,' he said, 'I knew
that you are a hard man, harvesting where

[a]15 A talent was worth more than a thousand dollars.

you have not sown and gathering where
you have not scattered seed. 25So I was
afraid and went out and hid your talent in
the ground. See, here is what belongs to
you.'
26"His master replied, 'You wicked, lazy
servant! So you knew that I harvest where
I have not sown and gather where I have
not scattered seed? 27Well then, you
should have put my money on deposit
with the bankers, so that when I returned
I would have received it back with interest.
28" 'Take the talent from him and give it
to the one who has the ten talents. 29For
everyone who has will be given more, and
he will have an abundance. Whoever does
not have, even what he has will be taken
from him. 30And throw that worthless servant outside, into the darkness, where
there will be weeping and gnashing of
teeth.'

The Sheep and the Goats

31"When the Son of Man comes in his
glory, and all the angels with him, he will
sit on his throne in heavenly glory. 32All
the nations will be gathered before him,
and he will separate the people one from
another as a shepherd separates the sheep
from the goats. 33He will put the sheep on
his right and the goats on his left.
34"Then the King will say to those on
his right, 'Come, you who are blessed by
my Father; take your inheritance, the kingdom prepared for you since the creation
of the world. 35For I was hungry and you
gave me something to eat, I was thirsty
and you gave me something to drink, I
was a stranger and you invited me in, 36I
needed clothes and you clothed me, I was
sick and you looked after me, I was in
prison and you came to visit me.'
37"Then the righteous will answer him,
'Lord, when did we see you hungry and
feed you, or thirsty and give you something to drink? 38When did we see you a
stranger and invite you in, or needing
clothes and clothe you? 39When did we
see you sick or in prison and go to visit
you?'
40"The King will reply, 'I tell you the
truth, whatever you did for one of the
least of these brothers of mine, you did
for me.'
41"Then he will say to those on his left,
'Depart from me, you who are cursed,
into the eternal fire prepared for the devil and his angels. 42For I was hungry and
you gave me nothing to eat, I was thirsty
and you gave me nothing to drink, 43I was
a stranger and you did not invite me in, I
needed clothes and you did not clothe
me, I was sick and in prison and you did
not look after me.'
44"They also will answer, 'Lord, when
did we see you hungry or thirsty or a
stranger or needing clothes or sick or in
prison, and did not help you?'
45"He will reply, 'I tell you the truth,
whatever you did not do for one of the
least of these, you did not do for me.'
46"Then they will go away to eternal
punishment, but the righteous to eternal
life."

PRAYER: THE CHARACTER I WANT TO CULTIVATE

***INSTRUCT** those who are wise, and they will be wiser still; teach those who are righteous, and they will increase in learning. (Proverbs 9:9) . . . If I heed instruction, I am on the path of life, but those who refuse correction go astray. (Proverbs 10:17)*

TAKE *a moment to ask the Lord for the grace to grow in godly character.*

Psalm 9[a]

For the director of music. To ⌊the tune of⌋ "The Death of the Son." A psalm of David.

1 I will praise you, O LORD, with all my
heart;
I will tell of all your wonders.
2 I will be glad and rejoice in you;
I will sing praise to your name,
O Most High.

3 My enemies turn back;
they stumble and perish before you.
4 For you have upheld my right and my
cause;
you have sat on your throne,
judging righteously.
5 You have rebuked the nations and
destroyed the wicked;
you have blotted out their name for
ever and ever.
6 Endless ruin has overtaken the enemy,
you have uprooted their cities;
even the memory of them has
perished.

7 The LORD reigns forever;
he has established his throne for
judgment.
8 He will judge the world in
righteousness;
he will govern the peoples with
justice.
9 The LORD is a refuge for the oppressed,
a stronghold in times of trouble.
10 Those who know your name will trust
in you,
for you, LORD, have never forsaken
those who seek you.

11 Sing praises to the LORD, enthroned in
Zion;
proclaim among the nations what
he has done.
12 For he who avenges blood remembers;
he does not ignore the cry of the
afflicted.

13 O LORD, see how my enemies
persecute me!
Have mercy and lift me up from the
gates of death,
14 that I may declare your praises
in the gates of the Daughter of Zion
and there rejoice in your salvation.
15 The nations have fallen into the pit
they have dug;
their feet are caught in the net they
have hidden.
16 The LORD is known by his justice;
the wicked are ensnared by the
work of their hands.
Higgaion[b] *Selah*

17 The wicked return to the grave,[c]
all the nations that forget God.
18 But the needy will not always be
forgotten,
nor the hope of the afflicted ever
perish.

19 Arise, O LORD, let not man triumph;
let the nations be judged in your
presence.
20 Strike them with terror, O LORD;
let the nations know they are but
men. *Selah*

[a] Psalms 9 and 10 may have been originally a single acrostic poem, the stanzas of which begin with the successive letters of the Hebrew alphabet. In the Septuagint they constitute one psalm. [b] *16* Or *Meditation;* possibly a musical notation [c] *17* Hebrew *Sheol*

PRAYER: THANKSGIVING

YOU, Lord my God, are the faithful God, who keeps Your covenant and Your loving-kindness to a thousand generations of those who love You and keep Your commands. (Deuteronomy 7:9) . . . I will tell of Your loving-kindness, Lord, and praise Your deeds, according to all You have done for us, and Your great goodness toward the house of Israel, which You have bestowed on them according to Your mercies, and according to the multitude of Your loving-kindnesses. (Isaiah 63:7)

PAUSE *to offer your own expressions of thanksgiving.*

NT Matthew 26:1-35

The Plot Against Jesus

26 When Jesus had finished saying all these things, he said to his disciples, 2"As you know, the Passover is two days away—and the Son of Man will be handed over to be crucified."

3Then the chief priests and the elders of the people assembled in the palace of the high priest, whose name was Caiaphas, 4and they plotted to arrest Jesus in some sly way and kill him. 5"But not during the Feast," they said, "or there may be a riot among the people."

Jesus Anointed at Bethany

6While Jesus was in Bethany in the home of a man known as Simon the Leper, 7a woman came to him with an alabaster jar of very expensive perfume, which she poured on his head as he was reclining at the table.

8When the disciples saw this, they were indignant. "Why this waste?" they asked. 9"This perfume could have been sold at a high price and the money given to the poor."

10Aware of this, Jesus said to them, "Why are you bothering this woman? She has done a beautiful thing to me. 11The poor you will always have with you, but you will not always have me. 12When she poured this perfume on my body, she did it to prepare me for burial. 13I tell you the truth, wherever this gospel is preached throughout the world, what she has done will also be told, in memory of her."

Judas Agrees to Betray Jesus

14Then one of the Twelve—the one called Judas Iscariot—went to the chief priests 15and asked, "What are you willing to give me if I hand him over to you?" So they counted out for him thirty silver coins. 16From then on Judas watched for an opportunity to hand him over.

The Lord's Supper

17On the first day of the Feast of Unleavened Bread, the disciples came to Jesus and asked, "Where do you want us to make preparations for you to eat the Passover?"

18He replied, "Go into the city to a certain man and tell him, 'The Teacher says: My appointed time is near. I am going to celebrate the Passover with my disciples at your house.' " 19So the disciples did as Jesus had directed them and prepared the Passover.

20When evening came, Jesus was reclining at the table with the Twelve. 21And while they were eating, he said, "I tell you the truth, one of you will betray me."

22They were very sad and began to say to him one after the other, "Surely not I, Lord?"

23Jesus replied, "The one who has dipped his hand into the bowl with me will betray me. 24The Son of Man will go just as it is written about him. But woe to that man who betrays the Son of Man! It would be better for him if he had not been born."

25Then Judas, the one who would betray him, said, "Surely not I, Rabbi?"

Jesus answered, "Yes, it is you."[a]

26While they were eating, Jesus took bread, gave thanks and broke it, and gave it to his disciples, saying, "Take and eat; this is my body."

27Then he took the cup, gave thanks and offered it to them, saying, "Drink from it, all of you. 28This is my blood of the[b] covenant, which is poured out for many for the forgiveness of sins. 29I tell you, I will not drink of this fruit of the vine from now on until that day when I drink it anew with you in my Father's kingdom."

30When they had sung a hymn, they went out to the Mount of Olives.

Jesus Predicts Peter's Denial

31Then Jesus told them, "This very night you will all fall away on account of me, for it is written:

> " 'I will strike the shepherd,
> and the sheep of the flock will be
> scattered.'[c]

32But after I have risen, I will go ahead of you into Galilee."

33Peter replied, "Even if all fall away on account of you, I never will."

34"I tell you the truth," Jesus answered, "this very night, before the rooster crows, you will disown me three times."

35But Peter declared, "Even if I have to die with you, I will never disown you." And all the other disciples said the same.

[a] *25* Or *"You yourself have said it"* [b] *28* Some manuscripts *the new* [c] *31* Zech. 13:7

PRAYER: MY RELATIONSHIP TO OTHERS

HOW beautiful on the mountains are the feet of those who bring good news, who proclaim Your peace, who bring good tidings, who proclaim Your salvation. (Isaiah 52:7; Nahum 1:15) . . . As I follow You, You will make me a fisher of people. (Matthew 4:19; Mark 1:17)

__PAUSE__ to review your relationships with others and to commit them to the Lord.

YEAR 1
DAY 36

OT Genesis 39:1–40:23

Joseph and Potiphar's Wife

39 Now Joseph had been taken down to
Egypt. Potiphar, an Egyptian who was
one of Pharaoh's officials, the captain of
the guard, bought him from the Ishmaelites who had taken him there.
2The LORD was with Joseph and he
prospered, and he lived in the house of his
Egyptian master. 3When his master saw
that the LORD was with him and that the
LORD gave him success in everything he
did, 4Joseph found favor in his eyes and
became his attendant. Potiphar put him in
charge of his household, and he entrusted
to his care everything he owned. 5From the
time he put him in charge of his household and of all that he owned, the LORD
blessed the household of the Egyptian because of Joseph. The blessing of the LORD
was on everything Potiphar had, both in
the house and in the field. 6So he left in
Joseph's care everything he had; with Joseph in charge, he did not concern himself
with anything except the food he ate.
Now Joseph was well-built and handsome, 7and after a while his master's wife
took notice of Joseph and said, "Come to
bed with me!"
8But he refused. "With me in charge,"
he told her, "my master does not concern
himself with anything in the house; everything he owns he has entrusted to my
care. 9No one is greater in this house than
I am. My master has withheld nothing
from me except you, because you are his
wife. How then could I do such a wicked
thing and sin against God?" 10And though
she spoke to Joseph day after day, he refused to go to bed with her or even be
with her.
11One day he went into the house to attend to his duties, and none of the household servants was inside. 12She caught
him by his cloak and said, "Come to bed
with me!" But he left his cloak in her
hand and ran out of the house.
13When she saw that he had left his
cloak in her hand and had run out of the
house, 14she called her household servants. "Look," she said to them, "this Hebrew has been brought to us to make
sport of us! He came in here to sleep with
me, but I screamed. 15When he heard me
scream for help, he left his cloak beside
me and ran out of the house."
16She kept his cloak beside her until his
master came home. 17Then she told him
this story: "That Hebrew slave you brought
us came to me to make sport of me. 18But
as soon as I screamed for help, he left his
cloak beside me and ran out of the house."
19When his master heard the story his
wife told him, saying, "This is how your
slave treated me," he burned with anger.
20Joseph's master took him and put him
in prison, the place where the king's prisoners were confined.
But while Joseph was there in the
prison, 21the LORD was with him; he
showed him kindness and granted him favor in the eyes of the prison warden. 22So
the warden put Joseph in charge of all
those held in the prison, and he was made
responsible for all that was done there.
23The warden paid no attention to anything under Joseph's care, because the
LORD was with Joseph and gave him success in whatever he did.

The Cupbearer and the Baker

40 Some time later, the cupbearer and
the baker of the king of Egypt of-

fended their master, the king of Egypt.
2Pharaoh was angry with his two officials,
the chief cupbearer and the chief baker,
3and put them in custody in the house of
the captain of the guard, in the same
prison where Joseph was confined. 4The
captain of the guard assigned them to Joseph, and he attended them.

After they had been in custody for some
time, 5each of the two men—the cupbearer and the baker of the king of Egypt,
who were being held in prison—had a
dream the same night, and each dream
had a meaning of its own.

6When Joseph came to them the next
morning, he saw that they were dejected.
7So he asked Pharaoh's officials who were
in custody with him in his master's house,
"Why are your faces so sad today?"

8"We both had dreams," they answered,
"but there is no one to interpret them."

Then Joseph said to them, "Do not interpretations belong to God? Tell me your
dreams."

9So the chief cupbearer told Joseph his
dream. He said to him, "In my dream I
saw a vine in front of me, 10and on the
vine were three branches. As soon as it
budded, it blossomed, and its clusters
ripened into grapes. 11Pharaoh's cup was
in my hand, and I took the grapes,
squeezed them into Pharaoh's cup and
put the cup in his hand."

12"This is what it means," Joseph said to
him. "The three branches are three days.
13Within three days Pharaoh will lift up
your head and restore you to your position, and you will put Pharaoh's cup in
his hand, just as you used to do when you
were his cupbearer. 14But when all goes
well with you, remember me and show
me kindness; mention me to Pharaoh and
get me out of this prison. 15For I was
forcibly carried off from the land of the
Hebrews, and even here I have done nothing to deserve being put in a dungeon."

16When the chief baker saw that Joseph
had given a favorable interpretation, he
said to Joseph, "I too had a dream: On my
head were three baskets of bread.[a] 17In the
top basket were all kinds of baked goods
for Pharaoh, but the birds were eating
them out of the basket on my head."

18"This is what it means," Joseph said.
"The three baskets are three days. 19With-
in three days Pharaoh will lift off your
head and hang you on a tree.[b] And the
birds will eat away your flesh."

20Now the third day was Pharaoh's
birthday, and he gave a feast for all his officials. He lifted up the heads of the chief
cupbearer and the chief baker in the presence of his officials: 21He restored the
chief cupbearer to his position, so that he
once again put the cup into Pharaoh's
hand, 22but he hanged[c] the chief baker,
just as Joseph had said to them in his interpretation.

23The chief cupbearer, however, did not
remember Joseph; he forgot him.

[a] 16 Or *three wicker baskets* [b] 19 Or *and impale you on a pole* [c] 22 Or *impaled*

PRAYER: ADORATION

OH, the depth of the riches of Your wisdom and knowledge! How unsearchable are Your judgments, and Your ways past finding out! For who has known Your mind, O Lord? Or who has been Your counselor? Or who has first given to You, that You should repay him? For from You and through You and to You are all things. To You be the glory forever! Amen. (Romans 11:33–36) . . . Hallelujah! Salvation and glory and power belong to You, our God, because Your judgments are true and righteous. (Revelation 19:1–2)

PAUSE *to express your thoughts of praise and worship.*

NT Matthew 26:36–75

Gethsemane

[36]Then Jesus went with his disciples to a place called Gethsemane, and he said to them, "Sit here while I go over there and pray." [37]He took Peter and the two sons of Zebedee along with him, and he began to be sorrowful and troubled. [38]Then he said to them, "My soul is overwhelmed with sorrow to the point of death. Stay here and keep watch with me."

[39]Going a little farther, he fell with his face to the ground and prayed, "My Father, if it is possible, may this cup be taken from me. Yet not as I will, but as you will."

[40]Then he returned to his disciples and found them sleeping. "Could you men not keep watch with me for one hour?" he asked Peter. [41]"Watch and pray so that you will not fall into temptation. The spirit is willing, but the body is weak."

[42]He went away a second time and prayed, "My Father, if it is not possible for this cup to be taken away unless I drink it, may your will be done."

[43]When he came back, he again found them sleeping, because their eyes were heavy. [44]So he left them and went away once more and prayed the third time, saying the same thing.

[45]Then he returned to the disciples and said to them, "Are you still sleeping and resting? Look, the hour is near, and the Son of Man is betrayed into the hands of sinners. [46]Rise, let us go! Here comes my betrayer!"

Jesus Arrested

[47]While he was still speaking, Judas, one of the Twelve, arrived. With him was a large crowd armed with swords and clubs, sent from the chief priests and the elders of the people. [48]Now the betrayer had arranged a signal with them: "The one I kiss is the man; arrest him." [49]Going at once to Jesus, Judas said, "Greetings, Rabbi!" and kissed him.

[50]Jesus replied, "Friend, do what you came for."[a]

Then the men stepped forward, seized Jesus and arrested him. [51]With that, one of Jesus' companions reached for his sword, drew it out and struck the servant of the high priest, cutting off his ear.

[52]"Put your sword back in its place," Jesus said to him, "for all who draw the sword will die by the sword. [53]Do you think I cannot call on my Father, and he will at once put at my disposal more than twelve legions of angels? [54]But how then would the Scriptures be fulfilled that say it must happen in this way?"

[55]At that time Jesus said to the crowd, "Am I leading a rebellion, that you have come out with swords and clubs to capture me? Every day I sat in the temple courts teaching, and you did not arrest me. [56]But this has all taken place that the writings of the prophets might be fulfilled." Then all the disciples deserted him and fled.

Before the Sanhedrin

[57]Those who had arrested Jesus took him to Caiaphas, the high priest, where the teachers of the law and the elders had assembled. [58]But Peter followed him at a distance, right up to the courtyard of the high priest. He entered and sat down with the guards to see the outcome.

[59]The chief priests and the whole Sanhedrin were looking for false evidence against Jesus so that they could put him to death. [60]But they did not find any, though many false witnesses came forward.

Finally two came forward [61]and declared, "This fellow said, 'I am able to destroy the temple of God and rebuild it in three days.' "

[62]Then the high priest stood up and said to Jesus, "Are you not going to answer? What is this testimony that these men are bringing against you?" [63]But Jesus remained silent.

The high priest said to him, "I charge you under oath by the living God: Tell us if you are the Christ,[b] the Son of God."

[64]"Yes, it is as you say," Jesus replied. "But I say to all of you: In the future you will see the Son of Man sitting at the right hand of the Mighty One and coming on the clouds of heaven."

[65]Then the high priest tore his clothes and said, "He has spoken blasphemy! Why do we need any more witnesses?

[a] 50 Or *"Friend, why have you come?"* [b] 63 Or *Messiah;* also in verse 68

Look, now you have heard the blasphemy. 66 What do you think?"

"He is worthy of death," they answered.

67 Then they spit in his face and struck him with their fists. Others slapped him 68 and said, "Prophesy to us, Christ. Who hit you?"

Peter Disowns Jesus

69 Now Peter was sitting out in the courtyard, and a servant girl came to him. "You also were with Jesus of Galilee," she said.

70 But he denied it before them all. "I don't know what you're talking about," he said.

71 Then he went out to the gateway, where another girl saw him and said to the people there, "This fellow was with Jesus of Nazareth."

72 He denied it again, with an oath: "I don't know the man!"

73 After a little while, those standing there went up to Peter and said, "Surely you are one of them, for your accent gives you away."

74 Then he began to call down curses on himself and he swore to them, "I don't know the man!"

Immediately a rooster crowed. 75 Then Peter remembered the word Jesus had spoken: "Before the rooster crows, you will disown me three times." And he went outside and wept bitterly.

PRAYER: THE ATTRIBUTES OF GOD

YOU are the living God, and there is no god besides You. You put to death and You bring to life, You have wounded and You will heal, and no one can deliver from Your hand. (Deuteronomy 32:39) . . . Lord, the God of our fathers, are You not the God who is in heaven? Are You not the ruler over all the kingdoms of the nations? Power and might are in Your hand, and no one is able to withstand You. (2 Chronicles 20:6)

***PAUSE** to reflect on these affirmations about the person, powers and perfection of God.*

YEAR 1 DAY 37

OT Genesis 41:1-57

Pharaoh's Dreams

41 When two full years had passed, Pharaoh had a dream: He was standing by the Nile, 2 when out of the river there came up seven cows, sleek and fat, and they grazed among the reeds. 3 After them, seven other cows, ugly and gaunt, came up out of the Nile and stood beside those on the riverbank. 4 And the cows that were ugly and gaunt ate up the seven sleek, fat cows. Then Pharaoh woke up.

5 He fell asleep again and had a second dream: Seven heads of grain, healthy and good, were growing on a single stalk. 6 After them, seven other heads of grain sprouted—thin and scorched by the east wind. 7 The thin heads of grain swallowed up the seven healthy, full heads. Then Pharaoh woke up; it had been a dream.

8 In the morning his mind was troubled, so he sent for all the magicians and wise men of Egypt. Pharaoh told them his dreams, but no one could interpret them for him.

9 Then the chief cupbearer said to Pharaoh, "Today I am reminded of my shortcomings. 10 Pharaoh was once angry with his servants, and he imprisoned me and the chief baker in the house of the captain of the guard. 11 Each of us had a dream the same night, and each dream had a meaning of its own. 12 Now a young Hebrew was there with us, a servant of the captain of the guard. We told him our dreams, and he interpreted them for us, giving each man the interpretation of his dream. 13 And things turned out exactly as he interpreted them to us: I was restored to my position, and the other man was hanged.[a]"

[a] 13 Or *impaled*

14 So Pharaoh sent for Joseph, and he was quickly brought from the dungeon. When he had shaved and changed his clothes, he came before Pharaoh.

15 Pharaoh said to Joseph, "I had a dream, and no one can interpret it. But I have heard it said of you that when you hear a dream you can interpret it."

16 "I cannot do it," Joseph replied to Pharaoh, "but God will give Pharaoh the answer he desires."

17 Then Pharaoh said to Joseph, "In my dream I was standing on the bank of the Nile, 18 when out of the river there came up seven cows, fat and sleek, and they grazed among the reeds. 19 After them, seven other cows came up—scrawny and very ugly and lean. I had never seen such ugly cows in all the land of Egypt. 20 The lean, ugly cows ate up the seven fat cows that came up first. 21 But even after they ate them, no one could tell that they had done so; they looked just as ugly as before. Then I woke up.

22 "In my dreams I also saw seven heads of grain, full and good, growing on a single stalk. 23 After them, seven other heads sprouted—withered and thin and scorched by the east wind. 24 The thin heads of grain swallowed up the seven good heads. I told this to the magicians, but none could explain it to me."

25 Then Joseph said to Pharaoh, "The dreams of Pharaoh are one and the same. God has revealed to Pharaoh what he is about to do. 26 The seven good cows are seven years, and the seven good heads of grain are seven years; it is one and the same dream. 27 The seven lean, ugly cows that came up afterward are seven years, and so are the seven worthless heads of grain scorched by the east wind: They are seven years of famine.

28 "It is just as I said to Pharaoh: God has shown Pharaoh what he is about to do. 29 Seven years of great abundance are coming throughout the land of Egypt, 30 but seven years of famine will follow them. Then all the abundance in Egypt will be forgotten, and the famine will ravage the land. 31 The abundance in the land will not be remembered, because the famine that follows it will be so severe. 32 The reason the dream was given to Pharaoh in two forms is that the matter has been firmly decided by God, and God will do it soon.

33 "And now let Pharaoh look for a discerning and wise man and put him in charge of the land of Egypt. 34 Let Pharaoh appoint commissioners over the land to take a fifth of the harvest of Egypt during the seven years of abundance. 35 They should collect all the food of these good years that are coming and store up the grain under the authority of Pharaoh, to be kept in the cities for food. 36 This food should be held in reserve for the country, to be used during the seven years of famine that will come upon Egypt, so that the country may not be ruined by the famine."

37 The plan seemed good to Pharaoh and to all his officials. 38 So Pharaoh asked them, "Can we find anyone like this man, one in whom is the spirit of God[b]?"

39 Then Pharaoh said to Joseph, "Since God has made all this known to you, there is no one so discerning and wise as you. 40 You shall be in charge of my palace, and all my people are to submit to your orders. Only with respect to the throne will I be greater than you."

Joseph in Charge of Egypt

41 So Pharaoh said to Joseph, "I hereby put you in charge of the whole land of Egypt." 42 Then Pharaoh took his signet ring from his finger and put it on Joseph's finger. He dressed him in robes of fine linen and put a gold chain around his neck. 43 He had him ride in a chariot as his second-in-command,[c] and men shouted before him, "Make way[d]!" Thus he put him in charge of the whole land of Egypt.

44 Then Pharaoh said to Joseph, "I am Pharaoh, but without your word no one will lift hand or foot in all Egypt." 45 Pharaoh gave Joseph the name Zaphenath-Paneah and gave him Asenath daughter of Potiphera, priest of On,[e] to be his wife. And Joseph went throughout the land of Egypt.

46 Joseph was thirty years old when he entered the service of Pharaoh king of Egypt. And Joseph went out from Pharaoh's presence and traveled throughout Egypt. 47 During the seven years of abundance the land produced plentifully. 48 Joseph collected all the food produced in

[b] 38 Or *of the gods* [c] 43 Or *in the chariot of his second-in-command;* or *in his second chariot*
[d] 43 Or *Bow down* [e] 45 That is, Heliopolis; also in verse 50

those seven years of abundance in Egypt
and stored it in the cities. In each city he
put the food grown in the fields surrounding it. 49Joseph stored up huge
quantities of grain, like the sand of the
sea; it was so much that he stopped keeping records because it was beyond measure.

50Before the years of famine came, two
sons were born to Joseph by Asenath
daughter of Potiphera, priest of On. 51Jo-
seph named his firstborn Manasseh[f] and
said, "It is because God has made me forget all my trouble and all my father's
household." 52The second son he named
Ephraim[g] and said, "It is because God has
made me fruitful in the land of my suffering."

53The seven years of abundance in
Egypt came to an end, 54and the seven
years of famine began, just as Joseph had
said. There was famine in all the other
lands, but in the whole land of Egypt
there was food. 55When all Egypt began
to feel the famine, the people cried to
Pharaoh for food. Then Pharaoh told all
the Egyptians, "Go to Joseph and do what
he tells you."

56When the famine had spread over the
whole country, Joseph opened the storehouses and sold grain to the Egyptians,
for the famine was severe throughout
Egypt. 57And all the countries came to
Egypt to buy grain from Joseph, because
the famine was severe in all the world.

[f] 51 *Manasseh* sounds like and may be derived from the Hebrew for *forget*. [g] 52 *Ephraim* sounds like the Hebrew for *twice fruitful*.

PRAYER: CONFESSION

YOU, Lord my God, are gracious and compassionate, and You will not turn Your face from me if I return to You.

(2 Chronicles 30:9)

***ASK** the Spirit to search your heart and reveal any areas of unconfessed sin. Acknowledge these to the Lord and thank Him for His forgiveness.*

NT Matthew 27:1-31

Judas Hangs Himself

27 Early in the morning, all the chief
priests and the elders of the people
came to the decision to put Jesus to death.
2They bound him, led him away and
handed him over to Pilate, the governor.

3When Judas, who had betrayed him,
saw that Jesus was condemned, he was
seized with remorse and returned the thirty silver coins to the chief priests and the
elders. 4"I have sinned," he said, "for I
have betrayed innocent blood."

"What is that to us?" they replied.
"That's your responsibility."

5So Judas threw the money into the
temple and left. Then he went away and
hanged himself.

6The chief priests picked up the coins
and said, "It is against the law to put this
into the treasury, since it is blood money."
7So they decided to use the money to buy
the potter's field as a burial place for foreigners. 8That is why it has been called the
Field of Blood to this day. 9Then what was
spoken by Jeremiah the prophet was fulfilled: "They took the thirty silver coins,
the price set on him by the people of Israel, 10and they used them to buy the potter's field, as the Lord commanded me."[a]

Jesus Before Pilate

11Meanwhile Jesus stood before the governor, and the governor asked him, "Are
you the king of the Jews?"

"Yes, it is as you say," Jesus replied.

12When he was accused by the chief
priests and the elders, he gave no answer.
13Then Pilate asked him, "Don't you hear
the testimony they are bringing against
you?" 14But Jesus made no reply, not even
to a single charge—to the great amazement of the governor.

15Now it was the governor's custom at
the Feast to release a prisoner chosen by
the crowd. 16At that time they had a no-
torious prisoner, called Barabbas. 17So
when the crowd had gathered, Pilate

[a] 10 See Zech. 11:12,13; Jer. 19:1–13; 32:6–9.

asked them, "Which one do you want me
to release to you: Barabbas, or Jesus who
is called Christ?" 18 For he knew it was out
of envy that they had handed Jesus over
to him.
19 While Pilate was sitting on the judge's
seat, his wife sent him this message:
"Don't have anything to do with that innocent man, for I have suffered a great
deal today in a dream because of him."
20 But the chief priests and the elders
persuaded the crowd to ask for Barabbas
and to have Jesus executed.
21 "Which of the two do you want me to
release to you?" asked the governor.
"Barabbas," they answered.
22 "What shall I do, then, with Jesus who
is called Christ?" Pilate asked.
They all answered, "Crucify him!"
23 "Why? What crime has he committed?" asked Pilate.
But they shouted all the louder, "Crucify him!"
24 When Pilate saw that he was getting
nowhere, but that instead an uproar was
starting, he took water and washed his
hands in front of the crowd. "I am innocent of this man's blood," he said. "It is
your responsibility!"
25 All the people answered, "Let his
blood be on us and on our children!"
26 Then he released Barabbas to them.
But he had Jesus flogged, and handed him
over to be crucified.

The Soldiers Mock Jesus

27 Then the governor's soldiers took
Jesus into the Praetorium and gathered
the whole company of soldiers around
him. 28 They stripped him and put a scarlet robe on him, 29 and then twisted together a crown of thorns and set it on his
head. They put a staff in his right hand
and knelt in front of him and mocked
him. "Hail, king of the Jews!" they said.
30 They spit on him, and took the staff and
struck him on the head again and again.
31 After they had mocked him, they took
off the robe and put his own clothes on
him. Then they led him away to crucify
him.

PRAYER: THE WORKS OF GOD

O GOD, our Father, You presented Christ as a sacrifice of atonement through faith in His blood. You did this to demonstrate Your righteousness, because in Your mercy, You passed over the sins committed before Jesus died. You did it to demonstrate Your righteousness in the present time, that You might be just and the justifier of those who have faith in Jesus. (Romans 3:25–26)

***TAKE** a moment to consider the greatness of God's wonderful works.*

YEAR 1 DAY 38

OT Genesis 42:1–38

Joseph's Brothers Go to Egypt

42 When Jacob learned that there was
grain in Egypt, he said to his sons,
"Why do you just keep looking at each
other?" 2 He continued, "I have heard that
there is grain in Egypt. Go down there and
buy some for us, so that we may live and
not die."
3 Then ten of Joseph's brothers went
down to buy grain from Egypt. 4 But Jacob
did not send Benjamin, Joseph's brother,
with the others, because he was afraid that
harm might come to him. 5 So Israel's sons
were among those who went to buy grain,
for the famine was in the land of Canaan
also.
6 Now Joseph was the governor of the
land, the one who sold grain to all its people. So when Joseph's brothers arrived,
they bowed down to him with their faces
to the ground. 7 As soon as Joseph saw his
brothers, he recognized them, but he pretended to be a stranger and spoke harshly to them. "Where do you come from?"
he asked.

"From the land of Canaan," they replied, "to buy food."

8 Although Joseph recognized his brothers, they did not recognize him. 9 Then he remembered his dreams about them and said to them, "You are spies! You have come to see where our land is unprotected."

10 "No, my lord," they answered. "Your servants have come to buy food. 11 We are all the sons of one man. Your servants are honest men, not spies."

12 "No!" he said to them. "You have come to see where our land is unprotected."

13 But they replied, "Your servants were twelve brothers, the sons of one man, who lives in the land of Canaan. The youngest is now with our father, and one is no more."

14 Joseph said to them, "It is just as I told you: You are spies! 15 And this is how you will be tested: As surely as Pharaoh lives, you will not leave this place unless your youngest brother comes here. 16 Send one of your number to get your brother; the rest of you will be kept in prison, so that your words may be tested to see if you are telling the truth. If you are not, then as surely as Pharaoh lives, you are spies!" 17 And he put them all in custody for three days.

18 On the third day, Joseph said to them, "Do this and you will live, for I fear God: 19 If you are honest men, let one of your brothers stay here in prison, while the rest of you go and take grain back for your starving households. 20 But you must bring your youngest brother to me, so that your words may be verified and that you may not die." This they proceeded to do.

21 They said to one another, "Surely we are being punished because of our brother. We saw how distressed he was when he pleaded with us for his life, but we would not listen; that's why this distress has come upon us."

22 Reuben replied, "Didn't I tell you not to sin against the boy? But you wouldn't listen! Now we must give an accounting for his blood." 23 They did not realize that Joseph could understand them, since he was using an interpreter.

24 He turned away from them and began to weep, but then turned back and spoke to them again. He had Simeon taken from them and bound before their eyes.

25 Joseph gave orders to fill their bags with grain, to put each man's silver back in his sack, and to give them provisions for their journey. After this was done for them, 26 they loaded their grain on their donkeys and left.

27 At the place where they stopped for the night one of them opened his sack to get feed for his donkey, and he saw his silver in the mouth of his sack. 28 "My silver has been returned," he said to his brothers. "Here it is in my sack."

Their hearts sank and they turned to each other trembling and said, "What is this that God has done to us?"

29 When they came to their father Jacob in the land of Canaan, they told him all that had happened to them. They said, 30 "The man who is lord over the land spoke harshly to us and treated us as though we were spying on the land. 31 But we said to him, 'We are honest men; we are not spies. 32 We were twelve brothers, sons of one father. One is no more, and the youngest is now with our father in Canaan.'

33 "Then the man who is lord over the land said to us, 'This is how I will know whether you are honest men: Leave one of your brothers here with me, and take food for your starving households and go. 34 But bring your youngest brother to me so I will know that you are not spies but honest men. Then I will give your brother back to you, and you can trade[a] in the land.' "

35 As they were emptying their sacks, there in each man's sack was his pouch of silver! When they and their father saw the money pouches, they were frightened. 36 Their father Jacob said to them, "You have deprived me of my children. Joseph is no more and Simeon is no more, and now you want to take Benjamin. Everything is against me!"

37 Then Reuben said to his father, "You may put both of my sons to death if I do not bring him back to you. Entrust him to my care, and I will bring him back."

38 But Jacob said, "My son will not go down there with you; his brother is dead and he is the only one left. If harm comes to him on the journey you are taking, you will bring my gray head down to the grave[b] in sorrow."

[a] 34 Or *move about freely* [b] 38 Hebrew *Sheol*

PRAYER: RENEWAL

LIKE Josiah, may I do what is right in Your sight, Lord. May I walk in the ways of David and not turn aside to the right or to the left. Give me a tender and responsive heart, so that I will humble myself before You when I hear Your word. (2 Chronicles 34:1–2, 27) . . . Jesus, may I walk in Your steps, withdrawing to lonely places and praying to the Father. (Mark 1:35; Luke 5:16)

PAUSE *to add your own prayers for personal renewal.*

NT Matthew 27:32–66

The Crucifixion

32 As they were going out, they met a man from Cyrene, named Simon, and they forced him to carry the cross. 33 They came to a place called Golgotha (which means The Place of the Skull). 34 There they offered Jesus wine to drink, mixed with gall; but after tasting it, he refused to drink it. 35 When they had crucified him, they divided up his clothes by casting lots.[a] 36 And sitting down, they kept watch over him there. 37 Above his head they placed the written charge against him: THIS IS JESUS, THE KING OF THE JEWS. 38 Two robbers were crucified with him, one on his right and one on his left. 39 Those who passed by hurled insults at him, shaking their heads 40 and saying, "You who are going to destroy the temple and build it in three days, save yourself! Come down from the cross, if you are the Son of God!"

41 In the same way the chief priests, the teachers of the law and the elders mocked him. 42 "He saved others," they said, "but he can't save himself! He's the King of Israel! Let him come down now from the cross, and we will believe in him. 43 He trusts in God. Let God rescue him now if he wants him, for he said, 'I am the Son of God.' " 44 In the same way the robbers who were crucified with him also heaped insults on him.

The Death of Jesus

45 From the sixth hour until the ninth hour darkness came over all the land. 46 About the ninth hour Jesus cried out in a loud voice, *"Eloi, Eloi,*[b] *lama sabachthani?"*—which means, "My God, my God, why have you forsaken me?"[c]

47 When some of those standing there heard this, they said, "He's calling Elijah."

48 Immediately one of them ran and got a sponge. He filled it with wine vinegar, put it on a stick, and offered it to Jesus to drink. 49 The rest said, "Now leave him alone. Let's see if Elijah comes to save him."

50 And when Jesus had cried out again in a loud voice, he gave up his spirit.

51 At that moment the curtain of the temple was torn in two from top to bottom. The earth shook and the rocks split. 52 The tombs broke open and the bodies of many holy people who had died were raised to life. 53 They came out of the tombs, and after Jesus' resurrection they went into the holy city and appeared to many people.

54 When the centurion and those with him who were guarding Jesus saw the earthquake and all that had happened, they were terrified, and exclaimed, "Surely he was the Son[d] of God!"

55 Many women were there, watching from a distance. They had followed Jesus from Galilee to care for his needs. 56 Among them were Mary Magdalene, Mary the mother of James and Joses, and the mother of Zebedee's sons.

The Burial of Jesus

57 As evening approached, there came a rich man from Arimathea, named Joseph, who had himself become a disciple of Jesus. 58 Going to Pilate, he asked for Jesus' body, and Pilate ordered that it be given to him. 59 Joseph took the body, wrapped it in a clean linen cloth, 60 and

[a] 35 A few late manuscripts *lots that the word spoken by the prophet might be fulfilled: "They divided my garments among themselves and cast lots for my clothing"* (Psalm 22:18) [b] 46 Some manuscripts *Eli, Eli* [c] 46 Psalm 22:1 [d] 54 Or *a son*

placed it in his own new tomb that he
had cut out of the rock. He rolled a big
stone in front of the entrance to the tomb
and went away. [61]Mary Magdalene and
the other Mary were sitting there opposite the tomb.

The Guard at the Tomb

[62]The next day, the one after Preparation Day, the chief priests and the Pharisees went to Pilate. [63]"Sir," they said, "we
remember that while he was still alive that
deceiver said, 'After three days I will rise
again.' [64]So give the order for the tomb to
be made secure until the third day. Otherwise, his disciples may come and steal
the body and tell the people that he has
been raised from the dead. This last deception will be worse than the first."
[65]"Take a guard," Pilate answered. "Go,
make the tomb as secure as you know
how." [66]So they went and made the tomb
secure by putting a seal on the stone and
posting the guard.

PRAYER: MY RELATIONSHIP TO GOD

BY Your grace, O God, I will not despise my birthright for the things of this world. (Genesis 25:33–34) . . . I will fear You, Lord, and serve You in truth with all my heart, for I consider what great things You have done for me. (1 Samuel 12:24)

***PAUSE** to thank God for the relationship that you enjoy with Him in Jesus Christ.*

OT Genesis 43:1-34

YEAR 1 DAY 39

The Second Journey to Egypt

43 Now the famine was still severe in the
land. [2]So when they had eaten all the
grain they had brought from Egypt, their
father said to them, "Go back and buy us
a little more food."
[3]But Judah said to him, "The man
warned us solemnly, 'You will not see my
face again unless your brother is with you.'
[4]If you will send our brother along with
us, we will go down and buy food for you.
[5]But if you will not send him, we will not
go down, because the man said to us, 'You
will not see my face again unless your
brother is with you.' "
[6]Israel asked, "Why did you bring this
trouble on me by telling the man you had
another brother?"
[7]They replied, "The man questioned us
closely about ourselves and our family. 'Is
your father still living?' he asked us. 'Do
you have another brother?' We simply answered his questions. How were we to
know he would say, 'Bring your brother
down here'?"
[8]Then Judah said to Israel his father,
"Send the boy along with me and we will
go at once, so that we and you and our
children may live and not die. [9]I myself
will guarantee his safety; you can hold me
personally responsible for him. If I do not
bring him back to you and set him here
before you, I will bear the blame before
you all my life. [10]As it is, if we had not delayed, we could have gone and returned
twice."
[11]Then their father Israel said to them,
"If it must be, then do this: Put some of
the best products of the land in your bags
and take them down to the man as a
gift—a little balm and a little honey, some
spices and myrrh, some pistachio nuts
and almonds. [12]Take double the amount
of silver with you, for you must return the
silver that was put back into the mouths
of your sacks. Perhaps it was a mistake.
[13]Take your brother also and go back to
the man at once. [14]And may God
Almighty[a] grant you mercy before the
man so that he will let your other brother and Benjamin come back with you. As
for me, if I am bereaved, I am bereaved."
[15]So the men took the gifts and double

[a] 14 Hebrew *El-Shaddai*

the amount of silver, and Benjamin also. They hurried down to Egypt and presented themselves to Joseph. [16]When Joseph saw Benjamin with them, he said to the steward of his house, "Take these men to my house, slaughter an animal and prepare dinner; they are to eat with me at noon."

[17]The man did as Joseph told him and took the men to Joseph's house. [18]Now the men were frightened when they were taken to his house. They thought, "We were brought here because of the silver that was put back into our sacks the first time. He wants to attack us and overpower us and seize us as slaves and take our donkeys."

[19]So they went up to Joseph's steward and spoke to him at the entrance to the house. [20]"Please, sir," they said, "we came down here the first time to buy food. [21]But at the place where we stopped for the night we opened our sacks and each of us found his silver—the exact weight—in the mouth of his sack. So we have brought it back with us. [22]We have also brought additional silver with us to buy food. We don't know who put our silver in our sacks."

[23]"It's all right," he said. "Don't be afraid. Your God, the God of your father, has given you treasure in your sacks; I received your silver." Then he brought Simeon out to them.

[24]The steward took the men into Joseph's house, gave them water to wash their feet and provided fodder for their donkeys. [25]They prepared their gifts for Joseph's arrival at noon, because they had heard that they were to eat there.

[26]When Joseph came home, they presented to him the gifts they had brought into the house, and they bowed down before him to the ground. [27]He asked them how they were, and then he said, "How is your aged father you told me about? Is he still living?"

[28]They replied, "Your servant our father is still alive and well." And they bowed low to pay him honor.

[29]As he looked about and saw his brother Benjamin, his own mother's son, he asked, "Is this your youngest brother, the one you told me about?" And he said, "God be gracious to you, my son." [30]Deeply moved at the sight of his brother, Joseph hurried out and looked for a place to weep. He went into his private room and wept there.

[31]After he had washed his face, he came out and, controlling himself, said, "Serve the food."

[32]They served him by himself, the brothers by themselves, and the Egyptians who ate with him by themselves, because Egyptians could not eat with Hebrews, for that is detestable to Egyptians. [33]The men had been seated before him in the order of their ages, from the firstborn to the youngest; and they looked at each other in astonishment. [34]When portions were served to them from Joseph's table, Benjamin's portion was five times as much as anyone else's. So they feasted and drank freely with him.

PRAYER: PETITION

MAY my conscience testify that I have conducted myself in the world in the holiness and sincerity that are from You, not in fleshly wisdom but in Your grace, especially in my relationships with others. (2 Corinthians 1:12)

***PAUSE** here to offer prayers of petition regarding your family and your ministry. Ask for help and guidance in sharing Jesus with others and helping others grow in Him. Ask for guidance in your vocation and your avocations. Offer prayers of petition regarding your activities for this day and any special concerns you may have.*

NT Matthew 28:1-20

The Resurrection

28 After the Sabbath, at dawn on the
first day of the week, Mary Magdalene and the other Mary went to look at
the tomb.
2There was a violent earthquake, for an
angel of the Lord came down from heav-
en and, going to the tomb, rolled back the
stone and sat on it. 3His appearance was
like lightning, and his clothes were white
as snow. 4The guards were so afraid of him
that they shook and became like dead
men.
5The angel said to the women, "Do not
be afraid, for I know that you are looking
for Jesus, who was crucified. 6He is not
here; he has risen, just as he said. Come
and see the place where he lay. 7Then go
quickly and tell his disciples: 'He has risen
from the dead and is going ahead of you
into Galilee. There you will see him.' Now
I have told you."
8So the women hurried away from the
tomb, afraid yet filled with joy, and ran to
tell his disciples. 9Suddenly Jesus met
them. "Greetings," he said. They came to
him, clasped his feet and worshiped him.
10Then Jesus said to them, "Do not be
afraid. Go and tell my brothers to go to
Galilee; there they will see me."

The Guards' Report

11While the women were on their way,
some of the guards went into the city and
reported to the chief priests everything
that had happened. 12When the chief
priests had met with the elders and devised a plan, they gave the soldiers a large
sum of money, 13telling them, "You are to
say, 'His disciples came during the night
and stole him away while we were asleep.'
14If this report gets to the governor, we will
satisfy him and keep you out of trouble."
15So the soldiers took the money and did
as they were instructed. And this story has
been widely circulated among the Jews to
this very day.

The Great Commission

16Then the eleven disciples went to Galilee, to the mountain where Jesus had told
them to go. 17When they saw him, they
worshiped him; but some doubted.
18Then Jesus came to them and said, "All
authority in heaven and on earth has been
given to me. 19Therefore go and make disciples of all nations, baptizing them in[a]
the name of the Father and of the Son and
of the Holy Spirit, 20and teaching them to
obey everything I have commanded you.
And surely I am with you always, to the
very end of the age."

[a] *19* Or *into;* see Acts 8:16; 19:5; Romans 6:3; 1 Cor. 1:13; 10:2 and Gal. 3:27.

PRAYER: THE CHARACTER I WANT TO CULTIVATE

I WILL not wear myself out to get rich; I will have the understanding to cease. I will not set my desire on what flies away, for wealth surely sprouts wings and flies into the heavens like an eagle. (Proverbs 23:4–5) . . . I want to learn to be content in whatever circumstances I am. Whether I am abased or in abundance, whether I am filled or hungry, I want to learn the secret of being content in any and every situation. I can do all things through You who strengthen me. (Philippians 4:11–13)

***TAKE** a moment to ask the Lord for the grace to grow in godly character.*

OT Genesis 44:1-34

A Silver Cup in a Sack

44 Now Joseph gave these instructions
to the steward of his house: "Fill the
men's sacks with as much food as they
can carry, and put each man's silver in the
mouth of his sack. 2 Then put my cup, the
silver one, in the mouth of the youngest
one's sack, along with the silver for his
grain." And he did as Joseph said.
3 As morning dawned, the men were sent
on their way with their donkeys. 4 They had
not gone far from the city when Joseph
said to his steward, "Go after those men at
once, and when you catch up with them,
say to them, 'Why have you repaid good
with evil? 5 Isn't this the cup my master
drinks from and also uses for divination?
This is a wicked thing you have done.' "
6 When he caught up with them, he repeated these words to them. 7 But they said
to him, "Why does my lord say such
things? Far be it from your servants to do
anything like that! 8 We even brought back
to you from the land of Canaan the silver
we found inside the mouths of our sacks.
So why would we steal silver or gold from
your master's house? 9 If any of your servants is found to have it, he will die; and
the rest of us will become my lord's slaves."
10 "Very well, then," he said, "let it be as
you say. Whoever is found to have it will
become my slave; the rest of you will be
free from blame."
11 Each of them quickly lowered his sack
to the ground and opened it. 12 Then the
steward proceeded to search, beginning
with the oldest and ending with the
youngest. And the cup was found in Benjamin's sack. 13 At this, they tore their
clothes. Then they all loaded their donkeys and returned to the city.
14 Joseph was still in the house when Judah and his brothers came in, and they
threw themselves to the ground before
him. 15 Joseph said to them, "What is this
you have done? Don't you know that a man
like me can find things out by divination?"
16 "What can we say to my lord?" Judah
replied. "What can we say? How can we
prove our innocence? God has uncovered
your servants' guilt. We are now my lord's
slaves—we ourselves and the one who
was found to have the cup."
17 But Joseph said, "Far be it from me to
do such a thing! Only the man who was
found to have the cup will become my
slave. The rest of you, go back to your father in peace."
18 Then Judah went up to him and said:
"Please, my lord, let your servant speak a
word to my lord. Do not be angry with
your servant, though you are equal to
Pharaoh himself. 19 My lord asked his servants, 'Do you have a father or a brother?'
20 And we answered, 'We have an aged father, and there is a young son born to him
in his old age. His brother is dead, and he
is the only one of his mother's sons left,
and his father loves him.'
21 "Then you said to your servants, 'Bring
him down to me so I can see him for myself.' 22 And we said to my lord, 'The boy
cannot leave his father; if he leaves him,
his father will die.' 23 But you told your servants, 'Unless your youngest brother
comes down with you, you will not see
my face again.' 24 When we went back to
your servant my father, we told him what
my lord had said.
25 "Then our father said, 'Go back and
buy a little more food.' 26 But we said, 'We
cannot go down. Only if our youngest
brother is with us will we go. We cannot
see the man's face unless our youngest
brother is with us.'
27 "Your servant my father said to us,
'You know that my wife bore me two sons.
28 One of them went away from me, and I
said, "He has surely been torn to pieces."
And I have not seen him since. 29 If you
take this one from me too and harm
comes to him, you will bring my gray
head down to the grave[a] in misery.'
30 "So now, if the boy is not with us
when I go back to your servant my father
and if my father, whose life is closely
bound up with the boy's life, 31 sees that
the boy isn't there, he will die. Your servants will bring the gray head of our father down to the grave in sorrow. 32 Your
servant guaranteed the boy's safety to my
father. I said, 'If I do not bring him back
to you, I will bear the blame before you,
my father, all my life!'
33 "Now then, please let your servant re-

[a] 29 Hebrew *Sheol;* also in verse 31

main here as my lord's slave in place of
the boy, and let the boy return with his
brothers. 34How can I go back to my father if the boy is not with me? No! Do not
let me see the misery that would come
upon my father."

PRAYER: INTERCESSION

REMEMBER me, O my God, and do not blot out what I have done in Your name. Remember me, O my God, for good.
(Nehemiah 13:14, 31)

***TAKE** a few moments to intercede on behalf of local, national and world missions. Pray that the Great Commission would be fulfilled and for any special concerns you may have for missions.*

NT Acts 1:1-26

Jesus Taken Up Into Heaven

1 In my former book, Theophilus, I wrote
about all that Jesus began to do and to
teach 2until the day he was taken up to
heaven, after giving instructions through
the Holy Spirit to the apostles he had chosen. 3After his suffering, he showed himself to these men and gave many convinc-
ing proofs that he was alive. He appeared
to them over a period of forty days and
spoke about the kingdom of God. 4On
one occasion, while he was eating with
them, he gave them this command: "Do
not leave Jerusalem, but wait for the gift
my Father promised, which you have
heard me speak about. 5For John baptized
with[a] water, but in a few days you will be
baptized with the Holy Spirit."

6So when they met together, they asked
him, "Lord, are you at this time going to
restore the kingdom to Israel?"

7He said to them: "It is not for you to
know the times or dates the Father has set
by his own authority. 8But you will receive
power when the Holy Spirit comes on
you; and you will be my witnesses in Jerusalem, and in all Judea and Samaria, and
to the ends of the earth."

9After he said this, he was taken up before their very eyes, and a cloud hid him
from their sight.

10They were looking intently up into the
sky as he was going, when suddenly two
men dressed in white stood beside them.
11"Men of Galilee," they said, "why do you
stand here looking into the sky? This
same Jesus, who has been taken from you
into heaven, will come back in the same
way you have seen him go into heaven."

Matthias Chosen to Replace Judas

12Then they returned to Jerusalem from
the hill called the Mount of Olives, a Sabbath day's walk[b] from the city. 13When
they arrived, they went upstairs to the
room where they were staying. Those
present were Peter, John, James and Andrew; Philip and Thomas, Bartholomew
and Matthew; James son of Alphaeus and
Simon the Zealot, and Judas son of James.
14They all joined together constantly in
prayer, along with the women and Mary
the mother of Jesus, and with his brothers.

15In those days Peter stood up among
the believers[c] (a group numbering about
a hundred and twenty) 16and said,
"Brothers, the Scripture had to be fulfilled which the Holy Spirit spoke long
ago through the mouth of David concerning Judas, who served as guide for
those who arrested Jesus— 17he was one
of our number and shared in this ministry."

18(With the reward he got for his
wickedness, Judas bought a field; there he
fell headlong, his body burst open and all
his intestines spilled out. 19Everyone in
Jerusalem heard about this, so they called
that field in their language Akeldama, that
is, Field of Blood.)

20"For," said Peter, "it is written in the
book of Psalms,

" 'May his place be deserted;
let there be no one to dwell in it,'[d]

and,

[a] 5 Or *in* [b] 12 That is, about 3/4 mile (about 1,100 meters) [c] 15 Greek *brothers* [d] 20 Psalm 69:25

" 'May another take his place of
leadership.'[e]

[21]Therefore it is necessary to choose one of the men who have been with us the whole time the Lord Jesus went in and out among us, [22]beginning from John's baptism to the time when Jesus was taken up from us. For one of these must become a witness with us of his resurrection."

[23]So they proposed two men: Joseph called Barsabbas (also known as Justus) and Matthias. [24]Then they prayed, "Lord, you know everyone's heart. Show us which of these two you have chosen [25]to take over this apostolic ministry, which Judas left to go where he belongs." [26]Then they cast lots, and the lot fell to Matthias; so he was added to the eleven apostles.

[e] *20* Psalm 109:8

PRAYER: MY RELATIONSHIP TO OTHERS

I WILL not hate my brother or sister in my heart. (Leviticus 19:17) . . . Hatred stirs up strife, but love covers all transgressions. (Proverbs 10:12)

***PAUSE** to review your relationships with others and to commit them to the Lord.*

YEAR 1
DAY 41

OT Genesis 45:1-28

Joseph Makes Himself Known

45 Then Joseph could no longer control himself before all his attendants, and he cried out, "Have everyone leave my presence!" So there was no one with Joseph when he made himself known to his brothers. [2]And he wept so loudly that the Egyptians heard him, and Pharaoh's household heard about it.

[3]Joseph said to his brothers, "I am Joseph! Is my father still living?" But his brothers were not able to answer him, because they were terrified at his presence.

[4]Then Joseph said to his brothers, "Come close to me." When they had done so, he said, "I am your brother Joseph, the one you sold into Egypt! [5]And now, do not be distressed and do not be angry with yourselves for selling me here, because it was to save lives that God sent me ahead of you. [6]For two years now there has been famine in the land, and for the next five years there will not be plowing and reaping. [7]But God sent me ahead of you to preserve for you a remnant on earth and to save your lives by a great deliverance.[a]

[8]"So then, it was not you who sent me here, but God. He made me father to Pharaoh, lord of his entire household and ruler of all Egypt. [9]Now hurry back to my father and say to him, 'This is what your son Joseph says: God has made me lord of all Egypt. Come down to me; don't delay. [10]You shall live in the region of Goshen and be near me—you, your children and grandchildren, your flocks and herds, and all you have. [11]I will provide for you there, because five years of famine are still to come. Otherwise you and your household and all who belong to you will become destitute.'

[12]"You can see for yourselves, and so can my brother Benjamin, that it is really I who am speaking to you. [13]Tell my father about all the honor accorded me in Egypt and about everything you have seen. And bring my father down here quickly."

[14]Then he threw his arms around his brother Benjamin and wept, and Benjamin embraced him, weeping. [15]And he kissed all his brothers and wept over them. Afterward his brothers talked with him.

[16]When the news reached Pharaoh's palace that Joseph's brothers had come, Pharaoh and all his officials were pleased. [17]Pharaoh said to Joseph, "Tell your

[a] *7* Or *save you as a great band of survivors*

brothers, 'Do this: Load your animals and
return to the land of Canaan, 18and bring
your father and your families back to me.
I will give you the best of the land of
Egypt and you can enjoy the fat of the
land.'

19"You are also directed to tell them,
'Do this: Take some carts from Egypt for
your children and your wives, and get
your father and come. 20Never mind
about your belongings, because the best
of all Egypt will be yours.' "

21So the sons of Israel did this. Joseph
gave them carts, as Pharaoh had commanded, and he also gave them provisions for their journey. 22To each of them
he gave new clothing, but to Benjamin he
gave three hundred shekels[b] of silver and
five sets of clothes. 23And this is what he
sent to his father: ten donkeys loaded
with the best things of Egypt, and ten female donkeys loaded with grain and
bread and other provisions for his journey. 24Then he sent his brothers away, and
as they were leaving he said to them,
"Don't quarrel on the way!"

25So they went up out of Egypt and
came to their father Jacob in the land of
Canaan. 26They told him, "Joseph is still
alive! In fact, he is ruler of all Egypt." Jacob was stunned; he did not believe them.
27But when they told him everything Joseph had said to them, and when he saw
the carts Joseph had sent to carry him
back, the spirit of their father Jacob revived. 28And Israel said, "I'm convinced!
My son Joseph is still alive. I will go and
see him before I die."

[b] 22 That is, about 7 1/2 pounds (about 3.5 kilograms)

PRAYER: AFFIRMATION

THE hour is coming and now is, when true worshipers will worship You, Father, in spirit and truth, for You are seeking such to worship You. You are spirit, and those who worship You must worship in spirit and truth. (John 4:23–24) . . . Jesus, those who obey Your commandments abide in You, and You in them. And this is how I know that You abide in me: by the Spirit whom You have given me. (1 John 3:24)

PAUSE *to reflect on these Biblical affirmations.*

NT Acts 2:1–41

The Holy Spirit Comes at Pentecost

2 When the day of Pentecost came, they
were all together in one place. 2Sud-
denly a sound like the blowing of a violent wind came from heaven and filled
the whole house where they were sitting.
3They saw what seemed to be tongues of
fire that separated and came to rest on
each of them. 4All of them were filled
with the Holy Spirit and began to speak
in other tongues[a] as the Spirit enabled
them.

5Now there were staying in Jerusalem
God-fearing Jews from every nation under heaven. 6When they heard this sound,
a crowd came together in bewilderment,
because each one heard them speaking in
his own language. 7Utterly amazed, they
asked: "Are not all these men who are
speaking Galileans? 8Then how is it that
each of us hears them in his own native
language? 9Parthians, Medes and Elamites; residents of Mesopotamia, Judea and
Cappadocia, Pontus and Asia, 10Phrygia
and Pamphylia, Egypt and the parts of
Libya near Cyrene; visitors from Rome
11(both Jews and converts to Judaism);
Cretans and Arabs—we hear them declaring the wonders of God in our own
tongues!" 12Amazed and perplexed, they
asked one another, "What does this
mean?"

13Some, however, made fun of them
and said, "They have had too much
wine.[b]"

Peter Addresses the Crowd

14Then Peter stood up with the Eleven,

[a] 4 Or *languages;* also in verse 11 [b] 13 Or *sweet wine*

raised his voice and addressed the crowd:
"Fellow Jews and all of you who live in
Jerusalem, let me explain this to you; listen carefully to what I say. 15These men are
not drunk, as you suppose. It's only nine
in the morning! 16No, this is what was
spoken by the prophet Joel:

17" 'In the last days, God says,
I will pour out my Spirit on all
people.
Your sons and daughters will
prophesy,
your young men will see visions,
your old men will dream dreams.
18Even on my servants, both men and
women,
I will pour out my Spirit in those
days,
and they will prophesy.
19I will show wonders in the heaven
above
and signs on the earth below,
blood and fire and billows of
smoke.
20The sun will be turned to darkness
and the moon to blood
before the coming of the great and
glorious day of the Lord.
21And everyone who calls
on the name of the Lord will be
saved.'[c]

22"Men of Israel, listen to this: Jesus of
Nazareth was a man accredited by God to
you by miracles, wonders and signs,
which God did among you through him,
as you yourselves know. 23This man was
handed over to you by God's set purpose
and foreknowledge; and you, with the
help of wicked men,[d] put him to death by
nailing him to the cross. 24But God raised
him from the dead, freeing him from the
agony of death, because it was impossible
for death to keep its hold on him. 25Da-
vid said about him:

" 'I saw the Lord always before me.
Because he is at my right hand,
I will not be shaken.
26Therefore my heart is glad and my
tongue rejoices;
my body also will live in hope,
27because you will not abandon me to
the grave,
nor will you let your Holy One see
decay.
28You have made known to me the
paths of life;
you will fill me with joy in your
presence.'[e]

29"Brothers, I can tell you confidently
that the patriarch David died and was
buried, and his tomb is here to this day.
30But he was a prophet and knew that
God had promised him on oath that he
would place one of his descendants on
his throne. 31Seeing what was ahead, he
spoke of the resurrection of the Christ,[f]
that he was not abandoned to the grave,
nor did his body see decay. 32God has
raised this Jesus to life, and we are all witnesses of the fact. 33Exalted to the right
hand of God, he has received from the Father the promised Holy Spirit and has
poured out what you now see and hear.
34For David did not ascend to heaven,
and yet he said,

" 'The Lord said to my Lord:
"Sit at my right hand
35until I make your enemies
a footstool for your feet." '[g]

36"Therefore let all Israel be assured of
this: God has made this Jesus, whom you
crucified, both Lord and Christ."
37When the people heard this, they were
cut to the heart and said to Peter and the
other apostles, "Brothers, what shall
we do?"
38Peter replied, "Repent and be baptized, every one of you, in the name of
Jesus Christ for the forgiveness of your
sins. And you will receive the gift of the
Holy Spirit. 39The promise is for you and
your children and for all who are far off—
for all whom the Lord our God will call."
40With many other words he warned
them; and he pleaded with them, "Save
yourselves from this corrupt generation."
41Those who accepted his message were
baptized, and about three thousand were
added to their number that day.

[c] *21* Joel 2:28–32 [d] *23* Or *of those not having the law* (that is, Gentiles) [e] *28* Psalm 16:8–11
[f] *31* Or *Messiah.* "The Christ" (Greek) and "the Messiah" (Hebrew) both mean "the Anointed One"; also in verse 36. [g] *35* Psalm 110:1

PRAYER: THE ATTRIBUTES OF GOD

O LORD God, You are compassionate and gracious, slow to anger and abounding in loving-kindness and truth, maintaining love to thousands, and forgiving iniquity, transgression and sin. (Exodus 34:6–7) . . . Lord, You execute righteousness and justice for all who are oppressed. You are compassionate and gracious, slow to anger and abounding in loving-kindness. (Psalm 103:6, 8)

***PAUSE** to reflect on these affirmations about the person, powers and perfection of God.*

YEAR 1 DAY 42

OT Psalm 10

Psalm 10[a]

1 Why, O LORD, do you stand far off?
Why do you hide yourself in times of trouble?

2 In his arrogance the wicked man hunts down the weak,
who are caught in the schemes he devises.
3 He boasts of the cravings of his heart;
he blesses the greedy and reviles the LORD.
4 In his pride the wicked does not seek him;
in all his thoughts there is no room for God.
5 His ways are always prosperous;
he is haughty and your laws are far from him;
he sneers at all his enemies.
6 He says to himself, "Nothing will shake me;
I'll always be happy and never have trouble."
7 His mouth is full of curses and lies and threats;
trouble and evil are under his tongue.
8 He lies in wait near the villages;
from ambush he murders the innocent,
watching in secret for his victims.
9 He lies in wait like a lion in cover;
he lies in wait to catch the helpless;
he catches the helpless and drags them off in his net.
10 His victims are crushed, they collapse;
they fall under his strength.
11 He says to himself, "God has forgotten;
he covers his face and never sees."

12 Arise, LORD! Lift up your hand, O God.
Do not forget the helpless.
13 Why does the wicked man revile God?
Why does he say to himself,
"He won't call me to account"?
14 But you, O God, do see trouble and grief;
you consider it to take it in hand.
The victim commits himself to you;
you are the helper of the fatherless.
15 Break the arm of the wicked and evil man;
call him to account for his wickedness
that would not be found out.

16 The LORD is King for ever and ever;
the nations will perish from his land.
17 You hear, O LORD, the desire of the afflicted;
you encourage them, and you listen to their cry,
18 defending the fatherless and the oppressed,
in order that man, who is of the earth, may terrify no more.

[a] Psalms 9 and 10 may have been originally a single acrostic poem, the stanzas of which begin with the successive letters of the Hebrew alphabet. In the Septuagint they constitute one psalm.

PRAYER: THANKSGIVING

WE know Your grace, Lord Jesus Christ, that though You were rich, yet for our sakes You became poor, that through Your poverty we might become rich. (2 Corinthians 8:9) . . . O God, we thank You for Your indescribable gift! (2 Corinthians 9:15)

PAUSE *to offer your own expressions of thanksgiving.*

NT Acts 2:42–3:26

The Fellowship of the Believers

42They devoted themselves to the apostles' teaching and to the fellowship, to the
breaking of bread and to prayer. 43Every-
one was filled with awe, and many wonders and miraculous signs were done by
the apostles. 44All the believers were together and had everything in common.
45Selling their possessions and goods, they
gave to anyone as he had need. 46Every
day they continued to meet together in
the temple courts. They broke bread in
their homes and ate together with glad
and sincere hearts, 47praising God and enjoying the favor of all the people. And the
Lord added to their number daily those
who were being saved.

Peter Heals the Crippled Beggar

3 One day Peter and John were going up
to the temple at the time of prayer—at
three in the afternoon. 2Now a man crippled from birth was being carried to the
temple gate called Beautiful, where he
was put every day to beg from those going into the temple courts. 3When he saw
Peter and John about to enter, he asked
them for money. 4Peter looked straight at
him, as did John. Then Peter said, "Look
at us!" 5So the man gave them his attention, expecting to get something from
them.

6Then Peter said, "Silver or gold I do
not have, but what I have I give you. In
the name of Jesus Christ of Nazareth,
walk." 7Taking him by the right hand, he
helped him up, and instantly the man's
feet and ankles became strong. 8He
jumped to his feet and began to walk.
Then he went with them into the temple
courts, walking and jumping, and praising God. 9When all the people saw him
walking and praising God, 10they recognized him as the same man who used to
sit begging at the temple gate called Beautiful, and they were filled with wonder
and amazement at what had happened to
him.

Peter Speaks to the Onlookers

11While the beggar held on to Peter and
John, all the people were astonished and
came running to them in the place called
Solomon's Colonnade. 12When Peter saw
this, he said to them: "Men of Israel, why
does this surprise you? Why do you stare
at us as if by our own power or godliness
we had made this man walk? 13The God
of Abraham, Isaac and Jacob, the God of
our fathers, has glorified his servant Jesus.
You handed him over to be killed, and
you disowned him before Pilate, though
he had decided to let him go. 14You disowned the Holy and Righteous One and
asked that a murderer be released to you.
15You killed the author of life, but God
raised him from the dead. We are witnesses of this. 16By faith in the name of
Jesus, this man whom you see and know
was made strong. It is Jesus' name and the
faith that comes through him that has giv-
en this complete healing to him, as you
can all see.

17"Now, brothers, I know that you acted in ignorance, as did your leaders. 18But
this is how God fulfilled what he had
foretold through all the prophets, saying
that his Christ[a] would suffer. 19Repent,
then, and turn to God, so that your sins
may be wiped out, that times of refresh-
ing may come from the Lord, 20and that
he may send the Christ, who has been appointed for you—even Jesus. 21He must
remain in heaven until the time comes for
God to restore everything, as he promised
long ago through his holy prophets. 22For
Moses said, 'The Lord your God will raise

[a] *18* Or *Messiah;* also in verse 20

up for you a prophet like me from among
your own people; you must listen to
everything he tells you. [23]Anyone who
does not listen to him will be completely
cut off from among his people.'[b]
[24]"Indeed, all the prophets from Samuel on, as many as have spoken, have foretold these days. [25]And you are heirs of the
prophets and of the covenant God made
with your fathers. He said to Abraham,
'Through your offspring all peoples on
earth will be blessed.'[c] [26]When God raised
up his servant, he sent him first to you to
bless you by turning each of you from
your wicked ways."

[b] 23 Deut. 18:15,18,19 [c] 25 Gen. 22:18; 26:4

PRAYER: THE WORKS OF GOD

YOU, Lord God, formed man from the dust of the ground and breathed into his nostrils the breath of life, and man became a living being. And out of the ground You made every tree grow that is pleasing to the eye and good for food. In the middle of the garden were the tree of life and the tree of the knowledge of good and evil. Then You took the man and put him in the Garden of Eden to cultivate it and take care of it. (Genesis 2:7, 9, 15) . . . In the day that You, O God, created man and woman, You made them in Your likeness. (Genesis 5:1)

***TAKE** a moment to consider the greatness of God's wonderful works.*

YEAR 1 DAY 43

OT Genesis 46:1-34

Jacob Goes to Egypt

46 So Israel set out with all that was his,
and when he reached Beersheba, he
offered sacrifices to the God of his father
Isaac.
[2]And God spoke to Israel in a vision at
night and said, "Jacob! Jacob!"
"Here I am," he replied.
[3]"I am God, the God of your father," he
said. "Do not be afraid to go down to
Egypt, for I will make you into a great nation there. [4]I will go down to Egypt with
you, and I will surely bring you back
again. And Joseph's own hand will close
your eyes."
[5]Then Jacob left Beersheba, and Israel's
sons took their father Jacob and their children and their wives in the carts that Pharaoh had sent to transport him. [6]They also
took with them their livestock and the
possessions they had acquired in Canaan,
and Jacob and all his offspring went to
Egypt. [7]He took with him to Egypt his
sons and grandsons and his daughters
and granddaughters—all his offspring.
[8]These are the names of the sons of Israel (Jacob and his descendants) who
went to Egypt:

Reuben the firstborn of Jacob.
[9]The sons of Reuben:
Hanoch, Pallu, Hezron and Carmi.
[10]The sons of Simeon:
Jemuel, Jamin, Ohad, Jakin, Zohar
and Shaul the son of a Canaanite
woman.
[11]The sons of Levi:
Gershon, Kohath and Merari.
[12]The sons of Judah:
Er, Onan, Shelah, Perez and Zerah
(but Er and Onan had died in the
land of Canaan).
The sons of Perez:
Hezron and Hamul.
[13]The sons of Issachar:
Tola, Puah,[a] Jashub[b] and Shimron.
[14]The sons of Zebulun:
Sered, Elon and Jahleel.
[15]These were the sons Leah bore to Ja-

[a] 13 Samaritan Pentateuch and Syriac (see also 1 Chron. 7:1); Masoretic Text *Puvah*
[b] 13 Samaritan Pentateuch and some Septuagint manuscripts (see also Num. 26:24 and 1 Chron. 7:1); Masoretic Text *Iob*

cob in Paddan Aram,[c] besides his daughter Dinah. These sons and daughters of
his were thirty-three in all.

16 The sons of Gad:
Zephon,[d] Haggi, Shuni, Ezbon, Eri,
Arodi and Areli.
17 The sons of Asher:
Imnah, Ishvah, Ishvi and Beriah.
Their sister was Serah.
The sons of Beriah:
Heber and Malkiel.
18 These were the children born to Jacob
by Zilpah, whom Laban had given to his
daughter Leah—sixteen in all.

19 The sons of Jacob's wife Rachel:
Joseph and Benjamin. 20 In Egypt,
Manasseh and Ephraim were born
to Joseph by Asenath daughter of
Potiphera, priest of On.[e]
21 The sons of Benjamin:
Bela, Beker, Ashbel, Gera, Naaman,
Ehi, Rosh, Muppim, Huppim and
Ard.
22 These were the sons of Rachel who
were born to Jacob—fourteen in all.

23 The son of Dan:
Hushim.
24 The sons of Naphtali:
Jahziel, Guni, Jezer and Shillem.
25 These were the sons born to Jacob by
Bilhah, whom Laban had given to his
daughter Rachel—seven in all.

26 All those who went to Egypt with Jacob—those who were his direct descendants, not counting his sons' wives—
numbered sixty-six persons. 27 With the
two sons[f] who had been born to Joseph
in Egypt, the members of Jacob's family,
which went to Egypt, were seventy[g] in all.

28 Now Jacob sent Judah ahead of him
to Joseph to get directions to Goshen.
When they arrived in the region of Goshen, 29 Joseph had his chariot made ready
and went to Goshen to meet his father Israel. As soon as Joseph appeared before
him, he threw his arms around his father[h]
and wept for a long time.
30 Israel said to Joseph, "Now I am ready
to die, since I have seen for myself that
you are still alive."
31 Then Joseph said to his brothers and
to his father's household, "I will go up
and speak to Pharaoh and will say to him,
'My brothers and my father's household,
who were living in the land of Canaan,
have come to me. 32 The men are shepherds; they tend livestock, and they have
brought along their flocks and herds and
everything they own.' 33 When Pharaoh
calls you in and asks, 'What is your occupation?' 34 you should answer, 'Your servants have tended livestock from our boy-
hood on, just as our fathers did.' Then you
will be allowed to settle in the region of
Goshen, for all shepherds are detestable
to the Egyptians."

[c] *15* That is, Northwest Mesopotamia
[d] *16* Samaritan Pentateuch and Septuagint (see also Num. 26:15); Masoretic Text *Ziphion*
[e] *20* That is, Heliopolis
[f] *27* Hebrew; Septuagint *the nine children*
[g] *27* Hebrew (see also Exodus 1:5 and footnote); Septuagint (see also Acts 7:14) *seventy-five*
[h] *29* Hebrew *around him*

PRAYER: ADORATION

LORD my God, You are God in the heavens above and in the earth below. (Joshua 2:11) . . . You stretch out the north over empty space; You suspend the earth on nothing. (Job 26:7) . . . You made the Pleiades and Orion and turn deep darkness into morning and darken day into night. You call for the waters of the sea and pour them out over the face of the earth—the Lord is Your name.

(Amos 5:8)

PAUSE *to express your thoughts of praise and worship.*

NT Acts 4:1-22

Peter and John Before the Sanhedrin

4 The priests and the captain of the temple guard and the Sadducees came up
to Peter and John while they were speaking to the people. [2]They were greatly disturbed because the apostles were teaching
the people and proclaiming in Jesus the
resurrection of the dead. [3]They seized Peter and John, and because it was evening,
they put them in jail until the next day.
[4]But many who heard the message believed, and the number of men grew to
about five thousand.
[5]The next day the rulers, elders and
teachers of the law met in Jerusalem. [6]An-
nas the high priest was there, and so were
Caiaphas, John, Alexander and the other
men of the high priest's family. [7]They had
Peter and John brought before them and
began to question them: "By what power
or what name did you do this?"
[8]Then Peter, filled with the Holy Spirit,
said to them: "Rulers and elders of the
people! [9]If we are being called to account
today for an act of kindness shown to a
cripple and are asked how he was healed,
[10]then know this, you and all the people
of Israel: It is by the name of Jesus Christ
of Nazareth, whom you crucified but
whom God raised from the dead, that this
man stands before you healed. [11]He is

" 'the stone you builders rejected,
which has become the capstone.[a,b]

[12]Salvation is found in no one else, for
there is no other name under heaven giv-
en to men by which we must be saved."
[13]When they saw the courage of Peter
and John and realized that they were un-
schooled, ordinary men, they were astonished and they took note that these
men had been with Jesus. [14]But since they
could see the man who had been healed
standing there with them, there was nothing they could say. [15]So they ordered
them to withdraw from the Sanhedrin
and then conferred together. [16]"What are
we going to do with these men?" they
asked. "Everybody living in Jerusalem
knows they have done an outstanding
miracle, and we cannot deny it. [17]But to
stop this thing from spreading any further among the people, we must warn
these men to speak no longer to anyone
in this name."
[18]Then they called them in again and
commanded them not to speak or teach
at all in the name of Jesus. [19]But Peter and
John replied, "Judge for yourselves
whether it is right in God's sight to obey
you rather than God. [20]For we cannot help
speaking about what we have seen and
heard."
[21]After further threats they let them go.
They could not decide how to punish
them, because all the people were praising God for what had happened. [22]For the
man who was miraculously healed was
over forty years old.

[a] 11 Or *cornerstone* [b] 11 Psalm 118:22

PRAYER: MY RELATIONSHIP TO GOD

HAVE You, O Lord, as much delight in burnt offerings and sacrifices as in obedience to Your voice? To obey is better than sacrifice, and to heed is better than the fat of rams. For rebellion is like the sin of divination, and stubbornness is as iniquity and idolatry. (1 Samuel 15:22–23) . . . I desire not only to call You "Lord" but to do what You say. By Your grace I will come to You, hear Your words and put them into practice. Then I will be like one who built a house, who dug down deep and laid the foundation on rock, and when a flood came, the torrent struck that house but could not shake it, because it was well built. (Luke 6:46–48)

***PAUSE** to thank God for the relationship that you enjoy with Him in Jesus Christ.*

YEAR 1 DAY 44

OT **Genesis 47:1-31**

47 Joseph went and told Pharaoh, "My
father and brothers, with their flocks
and herds and everything they own, have
come from the land of Canaan and are
now in Goshen." 2He chose five of his
brothers and presented them before Pharaoh.
3Pharaoh asked the brothers, "What is
your occupation?"
"Your servants are shepherds," they
replied to Pharaoh, "just as our fathers
were." 4They also said to him, "We have
come to live here awhile, because the
famine is severe in Canaan and your servants' flocks have no pasture. So now,
please let your servants settle in Goshen."
5Pharaoh said to Joseph, "Your father
and your brothers have come to you, 6and
the land of Egypt is before you; settle your
father and your brothers in the best part
of the land. Let them live in Goshen. And
if you know of any among them with special ability, put them in charge of my own
livestock."
7Then Joseph brought his father Jacob
in and presented him before Pharaoh. After Jacob blessed[a] Pharaoh, 8Pharaoh
asked him, "How old are you?"
9And Jacob said to Pharaoh, "The years
of my pilgrimage are a hundred and thirty. My years have been few and difficult,
and they do not equal the years of the pilgrimage of my fathers." 10Then Jacob
blessed[b] Pharaoh and went out from his
presence.
11So Joseph settled his father and his
brothers in Egypt and gave them property in the best part of the land, the district
of Rameses, as Pharaoh directed. 12Joseph
also provided his father and his brothers
and all his father's household with food,
according to the number of their children.

Joseph and the Famine

13There was no food, however, in the
whole region because the famine was severe; both Egypt and Canaan wasted away
because of the famine. 14Joseph collected
all the money that was to be found in
Egypt and Canaan in payment for the
grain they were buying, and he brought it
to Pharaoh's palace. 15When the money of
the people of Egypt and Canaan was gone,
all Egypt came to Joseph and said, "Give
us food. Why should we die before your
eyes? Our money is used up."
16"Then bring your livestock," said Joseph. "I will sell you food in exchange for
your livestock, since your money is gone."
17So they brought their livestock to Joseph, and he gave them food in exchange
for their horses, their sheep and goats,
their cattle and donkeys. And he brought
them through that year with food in exchange for all their livestock.
18When that year was over, they came to
him the following year and said, "We cannot hide from our lord the fact that since
our money is gone and our livestock belongs to you, there is nothing left for our
lord except our bodies and our land.
19Why should we perish before your
eyes—we and our land as well? Buy us
and our land in exchange for food, and
we with our land will be in bondage to
Pharaoh. Give us seed so that we may live
and not die, and that the land may not become desolate."
20So Joseph bought all the land in
Egypt for Pharaoh. The Egyptians, one
and all, sold their fields, because the
famine was too severe for them. The land
became Pharaoh's, 21and Joseph reduced
the people to servitude,[c] from one end of
Egypt to the other. 22However, he did not
buy the land of the priests, because they
received a regular allotment from Pharaoh and had food enough from the allotment Pharaoh gave them. That is why
they did not sell their land.
23Joseph said to the people, "Now that
I have bought you and your land today for
Pharaoh, here is seed for you so you can
plant the ground. 24But when the crop
comes in, give a fifth of it to Pharaoh. The
other four-fifths you may keep as seed for
the fields and as food for yourselves and
your households and your children."
25"You have saved our lives," they said.
"May we find favor in the eyes of our lord;
we will be in bondage to Pharaoh."
26So Joseph established it as a law con-

[a] *7* Or *greeted* [b] *10* Or *said farewell to*
[c] *21* Samaritan Pentateuch and Septuagint (see also Vulgate); Masoretic Text *and he moved the people into the cities*

cerning land in Egypt—still in force today—that a fifth of the produce belongs
to Pharaoh. It was only the land of the
priests that did not become Pharaoh's.
27 Now the Israelites settled in Egypt in
the region of Goshen. They acquired
property there and were fruitful and increased greatly in number.
28 Jacob lived in Egypt seventeen years,
and the years of his life were a hundred
and forty-seven. 29 When the time drew
near for Israel to die, he called for his son
Joseph and said to him, "If I have found
favor in your eyes, put your hand under
my thigh and promise that you will show
me kindness and faithfulness. Do not
bury me in Egypt, 30 but when I rest with
my fathers, carry me out of Egypt and
bury me where they are buried."
"I will do as you say," he said.
31 "Swear to me," he said. Then Joseph
swore to him, and Israel worshiped as he
leaned on the top of his staff.[d]

[d] 31 Or *Israel bowed down at the head of his bed*

PRAYER: CONFESSION

MY Lord, let Your power be great, just as You have spoken, saying, "The Lord is slow to anger and abounding in mercy, forgiving iniquity and transgression." (Numbers 14:17–18)

***ASK** the Spirit to search your heart and reveal any areas of unconfessed sin. Acknowledge these to the Lord and thank Him for His forgiveness.*

NT Acts 4:23–37

The Believers' Prayer

23 On their release, Peter and John went
back to their own people and reported all
that the chief priests and elders had said
to them. 24 When they heard this, they
raised their voices together in prayer to
God. "Sovereign Lord," they said, "you
made the heaven and the earth and the
sea, and everything in them. 25 You spoke
by the Holy Spirit through the mouth of
your servant, our father David:

" 'Why do the nations rage
    and the peoples plot in vain?
26 The kings of the earth take their stand
    and the rulers gather together
against the Lord
    and against his Anointed One.[a,b]

27 Indeed Herod and Pontius Pilate met together with the Gentiles and the people[c]
of Israel in this city to conspire against
your holy servant Jesus, whom you
anointed. 28 They did what your power
and will had decided beforehand should
happen. 29 Now, Lord, consider their
threats and enable your servants to speak
your word with great boldness. 30 Stretch
out your hand to heal and perform miraculous signs and wonders through the
name of your holy servant Jesus."
31 After they prayed, the place where
they were meeting was shaken. And they
were all filled with the Holy Spirit and
spoke the word of God boldly.

The Believers Share Their Possessions

32 All the believers were one in heart and
mind. No one claimed that any of his possessions was his own, but they shared
everything they had. 33 With great power
the apostles continued to testify to the resurrection of the Lord Jesus, and much
grace was upon them all. 34 There were no
needy persons among them. For from
time to time those who owned lands or
houses sold them, brought the money
from the sales 35 and put it at the apostles'
feet, and it was distributed to anyone as
he had need.
36 Joseph, a Levite from Cyprus, whom
the apostles called Barnabas (which
means Son of Encouragement), 37 sold a
field he owned and brought the money
and put it at the apostles' feet.

[a] 26 That is, Christ or Messiah [b] 26 Psalm 2:1,2
[c] 27 The Greek is plural.

PRAYER: THE CHARACTER I WANT TO CULTIVATE

***FOOLS** show their annoyance at once, but if I am prudent, I will overlook an insult. (Proverbs 12:16) . . . I will not be quickly provoked in my spirit, for anger rests in the hearts of fools. (Ecclesiastes 7:9)*

***TAKE** a moment to ask the Lord for the grace to grow in godly character.*

YEAR 1
DAY 45

OT Genesis 48:1-22

Manasseh and Ephraim

48 Some time later Joseph was told,
"Your father is ill." So he took his two
sons Manasseh and Ephraim along with
him. 2When Jacob was told, "Your son Joseph has come to you," Israel rallied his
strength and sat up on the bed.
3Jacob said to Joseph, "God Almighty[a]
appeared to me at Luz in the land of Canaan, and there he blessed me 4and said
to me, 'I am going to make you fruitful
and will increase your numbers. I will
make you a community of peoples, and I
will give this land as an everlasting possession to your descendants after you.'
5"Now then, your two sons born to you
in Egypt before I came to you here will be
reckoned as mine; Ephraim and Manasseh will be mine, just as Reuben and Simeon are mine. 6Any children born to you
after them will be yours; in the territory
they inherit they will be reckoned under
the names of their brothers. 7As I was returning from Paddan,[b] to my sorrow Rachel died in the land of Canaan while we
were still on the way, a little distance from
Ephrath. So I buried her there beside the
road to Ephrath" (that is, Bethlehem).
8When Israel saw the sons of Joseph, he
asked, "Who are these?"
9"They are the sons God has given me
here," Joseph said to his father.
Then Israel said, "Bring them to me so
I may bless them."
10Now Israel's eyes were failing because
of old age, and he could hardly see. So Joseph brought his sons close to him, and
his father kissed them and embraced
them.
11Israel said to Joseph, "I never expected to see your face again, and now God
has allowed me to see your children too."
12Then Joseph removed them from Israel's knees and bowed down with his
face to the ground. 13And Joseph took
both of them, Ephraim on his right toward Israel's left hand and Manasseh on
his left toward Israel's right hand, and
brought them close to him. 14But Israel
reached out his right hand and put it on
Ephraim's head, though he was the
younger, and crossing his arms, he put his
left hand on Manasseh's head, even
though Manasseh was the firstborn.
15Then he blessed Joseph and said,

"May the God before whom my
fathers
Abraham and Isaac walked,
the God who has been my shepherd
all my life to this day,
16the Angel who has delivered me from
all harm
—may he bless these boys.
May they be called by my name
and the names of my fathers
Abraham and Isaac,
and may they increase greatly
upon the earth."

17When Joseph saw his father placing
his right hand on Ephraim's head he was
displeased; so he took hold of his father's
hand to move it from Ephraim's head to
Manasseh's head. 18Joseph said to him,
"No, my father, this one is the firstborn;
put your right hand on his head."
19But his father refused and said, "I
know, my son, I know. He too will become a people, and he too will become
great. Nevertheless, his younger brother
will be greater than he, and his descen-

[a] 3 Hebrew *El-Shaddai* [b] 7 That is, Northwest Mesopotamia

dants will become a group of nations."
20 He blessed them that day and said,

"In your[c] name will Israel pronounce
this blessing:
'May God make you like Ephraim
and Manasseh.' "

So he put Ephraim ahead of Manasseh.
21 Then Israel said to Joseph, "I am
about to die, but God will be with you[d]
and take you[d] back to the land of your[d]
fathers. 22 And to you, as one who is over
your brothers, I give the ridge of land[e] I
took from the Amorites with my sword
and my bow."

[c] *20* The Hebrew is singular. [d] *21* The Hebrew is plural. [e] *22* Or *And to you I give one portion more than to your brothers—the portion*

PRAYER: RENEWAL

MAY Your name, Lord Jesus, be magnified in my life. (Acts 19:17) . . . In view of Your mercy, O God, may I present my body as a living sacrifice, holy and pleasing to You, which is my reasonable service. (Romans 12:1)

***PAUSE** to add your own prayers for personal renewal.*

NT Acts 5:1-16

Ananias and Sapphira

5 Now a man named Ananias, together
with his wife Sapphira, also sold a
piece of property. 2 With his wife's full
knowledge he kept back part of the money for himself, but brought the rest and
put it at the apostles' feet.
3 Then Peter said, "Ananias, how is it
that Satan has so filled your heart that you
have lied to the Holy Spirit and have kept
for yourself some of the money you received for the land? 4 Didn't it belong to
you before it was sold? And after it was
sold, wasn't the money at your disposal?
What made you think of doing such a
thing? You have not lied to men but to
God."
5 When Ananias heard this, he fell down
and died. And great fear seized all who
heard what had happened. 6 Then the
young men came forward, wrapped up his
body, and carried him out and buried
him.
7 About three hours later his wife came
in, not knowing what had happened. 8 Peter asked her, "Tell me, is this the price
you and Ananias got for the land?"
"Yes," she said, "that is the price."
9 Peter said to her, "How could you
agree to test the Spirit of the Lord? Look!
The feet of the men who buried your husband are at the door, and they will carry
you out also."
10 At that moment she fell down at his
feet and died. Then the young men came
in and, finding her dead, carried her out
and buried her beside her husband.
11 Great fear seized the whole church and
all who heard about these events.

The Apostles Heal Many

12 The apostles performed many miraculous signs and wonders among the people. And all the believers used to meet together in Solomon's Colonnade. 13 No one
else dared join them, even though they
were highly regarded by the people.
14 Nevertheless, more and more men and
women believed in the Lord and were
added to their number. 15 As a result, people brought the sick into the streets and
laid them on beds and mats so that at
least Peter's shadow might fall on some of
them as he passed by. 16 Crowds gathered
also from the towns around Jerusalem,
bringing their sick and those tormented
by evil[a] spirits, and all of them were
healed.

[a] *16* Greek *unclean*

PRAYER: MY RELATIONSHIP TO OTHERS

I WILL learn to do good, seek justice, remove the oppressor, defend the orphan and plead for the widow. (Isaiah 1:17) . . . This is pure and undefiled religion before You, my God and Father: to visit orphans and widows in their affliction and to keep oneself unspotted from the world. (James 1:27)

***PAUSE** to review your relationships with others and to commit them to the Lord.*

YEAR 1
DAY 46

OT Proverbs 2

Moral Benefits of Wisdom

2 My son, if you accept my words
and store up my commands within you,
2 turning your ear to wisdom
and applying your heart to understanding,
3 and if you call out for insight
and cry aloud for understanding,
4 and if you look for it as for silver
and search for it as for hidden treasure,
5 then you will understand the fear of the LORD
and find the knowledge of God.
6 For the LORD gives wisdom,
and from his mouth come knowledge and understanding.
7 He holds victory in store for the upright,
he is a shield to those whose walk is blameless,
8 for he guards the course of the just
and protects the way of his faithful ones.

9 Then you will understand what is right and just
and fair—every good path.
10 For wisdom will enter your heart,
and knowledge will be pleasant to your soul.
11 Discretion will protect you,
and understanding will guard you.
12 Wisdom will save you from the ways of wicked men,
from men whose words are perverse,
13 who leave the straight paths
to walk in dark ways,
14 who delight in doing wrong
and rejoice in the perverseness of evil,
15 whose paths are crooked
and who are devious in their ways.

16 It will save you also from the adulteress,
from the wayward wife with her seductive words,
17 who has left the partner of her youth
and ignored the covenant she made before God.[a]
18 For her house leads down to death
and her paths to the spirits of the dead.
19 None who go to her return
or attain the paths of life.

20 Thus you will walk in the ways of good men
and keep to the paths of the righteous.
21 For the upright will live in the land,
and the blameless will remain in it;
22 but the wicked will be cut off from the land,
and the unfaithful will be torn from it.

[a] 17 Or *covenant of her God*

PRAYER: PETITION

MAY I do no injustice in judgment, nor show partiality to the poor or favoritism to the great, but judge my neighbor fairly. (Leviticus 19:15)

__PAUSE__ here to petition God for growth in your character and personal discipline, and for physical health and strength. Ask that He empower you for spiritual warfare against the temptations of the world, the flesh and the devil. Offer prayers regarding your activities for this day and any special concerns you may have.

NT Acts 5:17-42

The Apostles Persecuted

17Then the high priest and all his associates, who were members of the party of
the Sadducees, were filled with jealousy.
18They arrested the apostles and put them
in the public jail. 19But during the night
an angel of the Lord opened the doors of
the jail and brought them out. 20"Go,
stand in the temple courts," he said, "and
tell the people the full message of this
new life."

21At daybreak they entered the temple
courts, as they had been told, and began
to teach the people.

When the high priest and his associates arrived, they called together the Sanhedrin—the full assembly of the elders
of Israel—and sent to the jail for the
apostles. 22But on arriving at the jail, the
officers did not find them there. So they
went back and reported, 23"We found the
jail securely locked, with the guards
standing at the doors; but when we
opened them, we found no one inside."
24On hearing this report, the captain of
the temple guard and the chief priests
were puzzled, wondering what would
come of this.

25Then someone came and said, "Look!
The men you put in jail are standing in
the temple courts teaching the people."
26At that, the captain went with his officers and brought the apostles. They did
not use force, because they feared that the
people would stone them.

27Having brought the apostles, they
made them appear before the Sanhedrin
to be questioned by the high priest. 28"We
gave you strict orders not to teach in this
name," he said. "Yet you have filled Jerusalem with your teaching and are determined to make us guilty of this man's
blood."

29Peter and the other apostles replied:
"We must obey God rather than men!
30The God of our fathers raised Jesus from
the dead—whom you had killed by hanging him on a tree. 31God exalted him to
his own right hand as Prince and Savior
that he might give repentance and forgiveness of sins to Israel. 32We are witnesses of these things, and so is the Holy
Spirit, whom God has given to those who
obey him."

33When they heard this, they were furious and wanted to put them to death.
34But a Pharisee named Gamaliel, a
teacher of the law, who was honored by
all the people, stood up in the Sanhedrin
and ordered that the men be put outside
for a little while. 35Then he addressed
them: "Men of Israel, consider carefully
what you intend to do to these men.
36Some time ago Theudas appeared,
claiming to be somebody, and about four
hundred men rallied to him. He was
killed, all his followers were dispersed,
and it all came to nothing. 37After him, Judas the Galilean appeared in the days of
the census and led a band of people in revolt. He too was killed, and all his followers were scattered. 38Therefore, in the
present case I advise you: Leave these men
alone! Let them go! For if their purpose
or activity is of human origin, it will fail.
39But if it is from God, you will not be
able to stop these men; you will only find
yourselves fighting against God."

40His speech persuaded them. They
called the apostles in and had them
flogged. Then they ordered them not to
speak in the name of Jesus, and let
them go.

[41]The apostles left the Sanhedrin, rejoicing because they had been counted
worthy of suffering disgrace for the Name.
[42]Day after day, in the temple courts and
from house to house, they never stopped
teaching and proclaiming the good news
that Jesus is the Christ.[a]

[a] 42 Or *Messiah*

PRAYER: THE ATTRIBUTES OF GOD

GREAT are You, Lord, and most worthy of praise; You are to be feared above all gods. For all the gods of the nations are idols, but You made the heavens. Splendor and majesty are before You; strength and beauty are in Your sanctuary. I will ascribe to You, O Lord, glory and strength. I will ascribe to You the glory due Your name and worship You in the beauty of holiness. (Psalm 96:4–9) . . . Holy, Holy, Holy are You, Lord of hosts; the whole earth is full of Your glory. (Isaiah 6:3)

PAUSE *to reflect on these affirmations about the person, powers and perfection of God.*

YEAR 1 DAY 47

OT Genesis 49:1–28

Jacob Blesses His Sons

49 Then Jacob called for his sons and said: "Gather around so I can tell you what will happen to you in days to come.

[2] "Assemble and listen, sons of Jacob;
listen to your father Israel.

[3] "Reuben, you are my firstborn,
my might, the first sign of my strength,
excelling in honor, excelling in power.
[4] Turbulent as the waters, you will no longer excel,
for you went up onto your father's bed,
onto my couch and defiled it.

[5] "Simeon and Levi are brothers—
their swords[a] are weapons of violence.
[6] Let me not enter their council,
let me not join their assembly,
for they have killed men in their anger
and hamstrung oxen as they pleased.
[7] Cursed be their anger, so fierce,
and their fury, so cruel!
I will scatter them in Jacob
and disperse them in Israel.

[8] "Judah,[b] your brothers will praise you;
your hand will be on the neck of your enemies;
your father's sons will bow down to you.
[9] You are a lion's cub, O Judah;
you return from the prey, my son.
Like a lion he crouches and lies down,
like a lioness—who dares to rouse him?
[10] The scepter will not depart from Judah,
nor the ruler's staff from between his feet,
until he comes to whom it belongs[c]
and the obedience of the nations is his.
[11] He will tether his donkey to a vine,
his colt to the choicest branch;
he will wash his garments in wine,
his robes in the blood of grapes.
[12] His eyes will be darker than wine,
his teeth whiter than milk.[d]

[13] "Zebulun will live by the seashore
and become a haven for ships;
his border will extend toward Sidon.

[a] 5 The meaning of the Hebrew for this word is uncertain. [b] 8 *Judah* sounds like and may be derived from the Hebrew for *praise.* [c] 10 Or *until Shiloh comes;* or *until he comes to whom tribute belongs* [d] 12 Or *will be dull from wine, / his teeth white from milk*

[14] "Issachar is a rawboned[e] donkey
lying down between two
saddlebags.[f]
[15] When he sees how good is his resting
place
and how pleasant is his land,
he will bend his shoulder to the
burden
and submit to forced labor.

[16] "Dan[g] will provide justice for his
people
as one of the tribes of Israel.
[17] Dan will be a serpent by the roadside,
a viper along the path,
that bites the horse's heels
so that its rider tumbles backward.

[18] "I look for your deliverance, O LORD.

[19] "Gad[h] will be attacked by a band of
raiders,
but he will attack them at their
heels.

[20] "Asher's food will be rich;
he will provide delicacies fit for a
king.

[21] "Naphtali is a doe set free
that bears beautiful fawns.[i]

[22] "Joseph is a fruitful vine,
a fruitful vine near a spring,
whose branches climb over a wall.[j]
[23] With bitterness archers attacked him;
they shot at him with hostility.
[24] But his bow remained steady,
his strong arms stayed[k] limber,
because of the hand of the Mighty
One of Jacob,
because of the Shepherd, the Rock
of Israel,
[25] because of your father's God, who
helps you,
because of the Almighty,[l] who
blesses you
with blessings of the heavens above,
blessings of the deep that lies
below,
blessings of the breast and womb.
[26] Your father's blessings are greater
than the blessings of the ancient
mountains,
than[m] the bounty of the age-old
hills.
Let all these rest on the head of
Joseph,
on the brow of the prince among[n]
his brothers.

[27] "Benjamin is a ravenous wolf;
in the morning he devours the prey,
in the evening he divides the
plunder."

[28] All these are the twelve tribes of Israel, and this is what their father said to them when he blessed them, giving each the blessing appropriate to him.

[e] 14 Or *strong* [f] 14 Or *campfires* [g] 16 *Dan* here means *he provides justice.* [h] 19 *Gad* can mean *attack* and *band of raiders.* [i] 21 Or *free; / he utters beautiful words* [j] 22 Or *Joseph is a wild colt, / a wild colt near a spring, / a wild donkey on a terraced hill* [k] 23,24 Or *archers will attack . . . will shoot . . . will remain . . . will stay* [l] 25 Hebrew *Shaddai* [m] 26 Or *of my progenitors, / as great as* [n] 26 Or *the one separated from*

PRAYER: INTERCESSION

O LORD, be gracious to us; we have hoped in You. Be our strength every morning, our salvation in time of distress. (Isaiah 33:2)

***TAKE** a few moments to intercede on behalf of the poor and hungry, the oppressed and persecuted, and those in control of world and national resources. Offer prayers for peace among nations and regarding current events and concerns.*

NT Acts 6:1-15

The Choosing of the Seven

6 In those days when the number of disciples was increasing, the Grecian Jews among them complained against the Hebraic Jews because their widows were being overlooked in the daily distribution of food. [2] So the Twelve gathered all the disciples together and said, "It would not be right for us to neglect the ministry of the

word of God in order to wait on tables.
[3]Brothers, choose seven men from among
you who are known to be full of the Spirit and wisdom. We will turn this responsibility over to them [4]and will give our attention to prayer and the ministry of the
word."
[5]This proposal pleased the whole
group. They chose Stephen, a man full of
faith and of the Holy Spirit; also Philip,
Procorus, Nicanor, Timon, Parmenas, and
Nicolas from Antioch, a convert to Judaism. [6]They presented these men to the
apostles, who prayed and laid their hands
on them.
[7]So the word of God spread. The number of disciples in Jerusalem increased
rapidly, and a large number of priests became obedient to the faith.

Stephen Seized

[8]Now Stephen, a man full of God's
grace and power, did great wonders and
miraculous signs among the people. [9]Op-
position arose, however, from members of
the Synagogue of the Freedmen (as it was
called)—Jews of Cyrene and Alexandria as
well as the provinces of Cilicia and Asia.
These men began to argue with Stephen,
[10]but they could not stand up against his
wisdom or the Spirit by whom he spoke.
[11]Then they secretly persuaded some
men to say, "We have heard Stephen speak
words of blasphemy against Moses and
against God."
[12]So they stirred up the people and the
elders and the teachers of the law. They
seized Stephen and brought him before
the Sanhedrin. [13]They produced false witnesses, who testified, "This fellow never
stops speaking against this holy place and
against the law. [14]For we have heard him
say that this Jesus of Nazareth will destroy
this place and change the customs Moses
handed down to us."
[15]All who were sitting in the Sanhedrin
looked intently at Stephen, and they saw
that his face was like the face of an angel.

PRAYER: THE WORKS OF GOD

O LORD, You uphold all who fall and lift up all who are bowed down. The eyes of all look to You, and You give them their food at the proper time. You open Your hand and satisfy the desire of every living thing. (Psalm 145:14–16) . . . Lord, You are my God; I will exalt You and praise Your name, for You have done wonderful things—things planned long ago in perfect faithfulness. (Isaiah 25:1)

***TAKE** a moment to consider the greatness of God's wonderful works.*

YEAR 1 DAY 48

OT Genesis 49:29–50:26

The Death of Jacob

[29]Then he gave them these instructions:
"I am about to be gathered to my people.
Bury me with my fathers in the cave in the
field of Ephron the Hittite, [30]the cave in
the field of Machpelah, near Mamre in
Canaan, which Abraham bought as a
burial place from Ephron the Hittite,
along with the field. [31]There Abraham and
his wife Sarah were buried, there Isaac
and his wife Rebekah were buried, and
there I buried Leah. [32]The field and the
cave in it were bought from the Hittites.[a]"
[33]When Jacob had finished giving instructions to his sons, he drew his feet up
into the bed, breathed his last and was
gathered to his people.

50 Joseph threw himself upon his father
and wept over him and kissed him.
[2]Then Joseph directed the physicians in
his service to embalm his father Israel. So
the physicians embalmed him, [3]taking a
full forty days, for that was the time required for embalming. And the Egyptians
mourned for him seventy days.
[4]When the days of mourning had
passed, Joseph said to Pharaoh's court, "If

[a] 32 Or *the sons of Heth*

I have found favor in your eyes, speak to
Pharaoh for me. Tell him, 5'My father made
me swear an oath and said, "I am about to
die; bury me in the tomb I dug for myself
in the land of Canaan." Now let me go up
and bury my father; then I will return.' "
6Pharaoh said, "Go up and bury your
father, as he made you swear to do."
7So Joseph went up to bury his father.
All Pharaoh's officials accompanied
him—the dignitaries of his court and all
the dignitaries of Egypt— 8besides all the
members of Joseph's household and his
brothers and those belonging to his father's household. Only their children and
their flocks and herds were left in Goshen.
9Chariots and horsemen[b] also went up
with him. It was a very large company.
10When they reached the threshing floor
of Atad, near the Jordan, they lamented
loudly and bitterly; and there Joseph observed a seven-day period of mourning for
his father. 11When the Canaanites who
lived there saw the mourning at the
threshing floor of Atad, they said, "The
Egyptians are holding a solemn ceremony of mourning." That is why that place
near the Jordan is called Abel Mizraim.[c]
12So Jacob's sons did as he had commanded them: 13They carried him to the
land of Canaan and buried him in the
cave in the field of Machpelah, near Mamre, which Abraham had bought as a burial place from Ephron the Hittite, along
with the field. 14After burying his father,
Joseph returned to Egypt, together with
his brothers and all the others who had
gone with him to bury his father.

Joseph Reassures His Brothers

15When Joseph's brothers saw that their
father was dead, they said, "What if Joseph
holds a grudge against us and pays us back
for all the wrongs we did to him?" 16So they
sent word to Joseph, saying, "Your father
left these instructions before he died: 17'This
is what you are to say to Joseph: I ask you
to forgive your brothers the sins and the
wrongs they committed in treating you so
badly.' Now please forgive the sins of the
servants of the God of your father." When
their message came to him, Joseph wept.
18His brothers then came and threw
themselves down before him. "We are
your slaves," they said.
19But Joseph said to them, "Don't be
afraid. Am I in the place of God? 20You intended to harm me, but God intended it
for good to accomplish what is now being done, the saving of many lives. 21So
then, don't be afraid. I will provide for
you and your children." And he reassured
them and spoke kindly to them.

The Death of Joseph

22Joseph stayed in Egypt, along with all
his father's family. He lived a hundred
and ten years 23and saw the third generation of Ephraim's children. Also the children of Makir son of Manasseh were
placed at birth on Joseph's knees.[d]
24Then Joseph said to his brothers, "I
am about to die. But God will surely come
to your aid and take you up out of this
land to the land he promised on oath to
Abraham, Isaac and Jacob." 25And Joseph
made the sons of Israel swear an oath and
said, "God will surely come to your aid,
and then you must carry my bones up
from this place."
26So Joseph died at the age of a hundred
and ten. And after they embalmed him,
he was placed in a coffin in Egypt.

[b] 9 Or *charioteers* [c] 11 *Abel Mizraim* means *mourning of the Egyptians.* [d] 23 That is, were counted as his

PRAYER: AFFIRMATION

O LORD, I am blessed if I find wisdom and gain understanding, for wisdom's profit is greater than that of silver, and her gain is more than fine gold. She is more precious than jewels, and nothing I desire can compare with her. Long life is in her right hand; in her left hand are riches and honor. Her ways are pleasant ways, and all her paths are peace. She is a tree of life to those who embrace her, and happy are those who hold her fast. (Proverbs 3:13–18)

***PAUSE** to reflect on these Biblical affirmations.*

NT **Acts 7:1-53**

Stephen's Speech to the Sanhedrin

7 Then the high priest asked him, "Are
these charges true?"
2To this he replied: "Brothers and fathers, listen to me! The God of glory appeared to our father Abraham while he
was still in Mesopotamia, before he lived
in Haran. 3'Leave your country and your
people,' God said, 'and go to the land I
will show you.'[a]
4"So he left the land of the Chaldeans
and settled in Haran. After the death of
his father, God sent him to this land
where you are now living. 5He gave him
no inheritance here, not even a foot of
ground. But God promised him that he
and his descendants after him would possess the land, even though at that time
Abraham had no child. 6God spoke to
him in this way: 'Your descendants will be
strangers in a country not their own, and
they will be enslaved and mistreated four
hundred years. 7But I will punish the nation they serve as slaves,' God said, 'and
afterward they will come out of that country and worship me in this place.'[b] 8Then
he gave Abraham the covenant of circumcision. And Abraham became the father of
Isaac and circumcised him eight days after his birth. Later Isaac became the father
of Jacob, and Jacob became the father of
the twelve patriarchs.
9"Because the patriarchs were jealous of
Joseph, they sold him as a slave into
Egypt. But God was with him 10and rescued him from all his troubles. He gave
Joseph wisdom and enabled him to gain
the goodwill of Pharaoh king of Egypt; so
he made him ruler over Egypt and all his
palace.
11"Then a famine struck all Egypt and
Canaan, bringing great suffering, and our
fathers could not find food. 12When Jacob
heard that there was grain in Egypt, he
sent our fathers on their first visit. 13On
their second visit, Joseph told his brothers who he was, and Pharaoh learned
about Joseph's family. 14After this, Joseph
sent for his father Jacob and his whole
family, seventy-five in all. 15Then Jacob
went down to Egypt, where he and our fathers died. 16Their bodies were brought
back to Shechem and placed in the tomb
that Abraham had bought from the sons
of Hamor at Shechem for a certain sum of
money.
17"As the time drew near for God to fulfill his promise to Abraham, the number
of our people in Egypt greatly increased.
18Then another king, who knew nothing
about Joseph, became ruler of Egypt. 19He
dealt treacherously with our people and
oppressed our forefathers by forcing them
to throw out their newborn babies so that
they would die.
20"At that time Moses was born, and he
was no ordinary child.[c] For three months
he was cared for in his father's house.
21When he was placed outside, Pharaoh's
daughter took him and brought him up
as her own son. 22Moses was educated in
all the wisdom of the Egyptians and was
powerful in speech and action.
23"When Moses was forty years old, he
decided to visit his fellow Israelites. 24He
saw one of them being mistreated by an
Egyptian, so he went to his defense and
avenged him by killing the Egyptian.
25Moses thought that his own people
would realize that God was using him to
rescue them, but they did not. 26The next
day Moses came upon two Israelites who
were fighting. He tried to reconcile them
by saying, 'Men, you are brothers; why do
you want to hurt each other?'
27"But the man who was mistreating the
other pushed Moses aside and said, 'Who
made you ruler and judge over us? 28Do
you want to kill me as you killed the Egyptian yesterday?'[d] 29When Moses heard this,
he fled to Midian, where he settled as a
foreigner and had two sons.
30"After forty years had passed, an angel
appeared to Moses in the flames of a
burning bush in the desert near Mount Sinai. 31When he saw this, he was amazed
at the sight. As he went over to look more
closely, he heard the Lord's voice: 32'I am
the God of your fathers, the God of Abraham, Isaac and Jacob.'[e] Moses trembled
with fear and did not dare to look.
33"Then the Lord said to him, 'Take off
your sandals; the place where you are
standing is holy ground. 34I have indeed
seen the oppression of my people in

[a] *3* Gen. 12:1 [b] *7* Gen. 15:13,14 [c] *20* Or *was fair in the sight of God* [d] *28* Exodus 2:14 [e] *32* Exodus 3:6

Egypt. I have heard their groaning and
have come down to set them free. Now
come, I will send you back to Egypt.'[f]
35 "This is the same Moses whom they
had rejected with the words, 'Who made
you ruler and judge?' He was sent to be
their ruler and deliverer by God himself,
through the angel who appeared to him
in the bush. 36 He led them out of Egypt
and did wonders and miraculous signs in
Egypt, at the Red Sea[g] and for forty years
in the desert.
37 "This is that Moses who told the Israelites,
'God will send you a prophet like
me from your own people.'[h] 38 He was in
the assembly in the desert, with the angel
who spoke to him on Mount Sinai, and
with our fathers; and he received living
words to pass on to us.
39 "But our fathers refused to obey him.
Instead, they rejected him and in their
hearts turned back to Egypt. 40 They told
Aaron, 'Make us gods who will go before
us. As for this fellow Moses who led us
out of Egypt—we don't know what has
happened to him!'[i] 41 That was the time
they made an idol in the form of a calf.
They brought sacrifices to it and held a
celebration in honor of what their hands
had made. 42 But God turned away and
gave them over to the worship of the
heavenly bodies. This agrees with what is
written in the book of the prophets:

" 'Did you bring me sacrifices and
offerings
forty years in the desert, O house of
Israel?
43 You have lifted up the shrine of
Molech
and the star of your god Rephan,
the idols you made to worship.
Therefore I will send you into exile'[j]
beyond Babylon.

44 "Our forefathers had the tabernacle of
the Testimony with them in the desert. It
had been made as God directed Moses,
according to the pattern he had seen.
45 Having received the tabernacle, our fathers
under Joshua brought it with them
when they took the land from the nations
God drove out before them. It remained
in the land until the time of David, 46 who
enjoyed God's favor and asked that he
might provide a dwelling place for the
God of Jacob.[k] 47 But it was Solomon who
built the house for him.
48 "However, the Most High does not
live in houses made by men. As the
prophet says:

49 " 'Heaven is my throne,
and the earth is my footstool.
What kind of house will you build for
me?
says the Lord.
Or where will my resting place be?
50 Has not my hand made all these
things?'[l]

51 "You stiff-necked people, with uncircumcised
hearts and ears! You are just like
your fathers: You always resist the Holy
Spirit! 52 Was there ever a prophet your fathers
did not persecute? They even killed
those who predicted the coming of the
Righteous One. And now you have betrayed
and murdered him— 53 you who
have received the law that was put into
effect through angels but have not
obeyed it."

[f] *34* Exodus 3:5,7,8,10 [g] *36* That is, Sea of Reeds [h] *37* Deut. 18:15 [i] *40* Exodus 32:1 [j] *43* Amos 5:25–27 [k] *46* Some early manuscripts *the house of Jacob* [l] *50* Isaiah 66:1,2

PRAYER: MY RELATIONSHIP TO GOD

I KNOW, O my Redeemer, that You live, and that in the end You will stand upon the earth. And after my skin has been destroyed, yet in my flesh I will see You, O God; I myself will see You and behold You with my own eyes and not another. How my heart yearns within me! (Job 19:25–27) . . . I have hope in You, O God, that there will be a resurrection of both the righteous and the wicked. In view of this I strive always to keep my conscience blameless before You and before people. (Acts 24:15–16)

***PAUSE** to thank God for the relationship that you enjoy with Him in Jesus Christ.*

OT Psalms 11–12

YEAR 1 DAY 49

Psalm 11

For the director of music. Of David.

1 In the LORD I take refuge.
How then can you say to me:
"Flee like a bird to your mountain.
2 For look, the wicked bend their bows;
they set their arrows against the strings
to shoot from the shadows
at the upright in heart.
3 When the foundations are being destroyed,
what can the righteous do[a]?"

4 The LORD is in his holy temple;
the LORD is on his heavenly throne.
He observes the sons of men;
his eyes examine them.
5 The LORD examines the righteous,
but the wicked[b] and those who love violence
his soul hates.
6 On the wicked he will rain
fiery coals and burning sulfur;
a scorching wind will be their lot.

7 For the LORD is righteous,
he loves justice;
upright men will see his face.

Psalm 12

For the director of music. According to *sheminith.*[c] A psalm of David.

1 Help, LORD, for the godly are no more;
the faithful have vanished from among men.
2 Everyone lies to his neighbor;
their flattering lips speak with deception.

3 May the LORD cut off all flattering lips
and every boastful tongue
4 that says, "We will triumph with our tongues;
we own our lips[d]—who is our master?"

5 "Because of the oppression of the weak
and the groaning of the needy,
I will now arise," says the LORD.
"I will protect them from those who malign them."
6 And the words of the LORD are flawless,
like silver refined in a furnace of clay,
purified seven times.

7 O LORD, you will keep us safe
and protect us from such people forever.
8 The wicked freely strut about
when what is vile is honored among men.

[a] 3 Or *what is the Righteous One doing* [b] 5 Or *The* LORD, *the Righteous One, examines the wicked, /* [c] Title: Probably a musical term [d] 4 Or */ our lips are our plowshares*

PRAYER: THANKSGIVING

HAS any other people heard Your voice speaking out of the midst of the fire, as the children of Israel have, and lived?

Has any god ever tried to take for himself one nation from the midst of another nation, by trials, by miraculous signs and wonders, by war, by a mighty hand and an outstretched arm, and by great and awesome deeds, like all the things You, Lord God, did for Israel in Egypt before their very eyes? The Israelites were shown these things so that they might know that You are the Lord, God; there is no other besides You. Because You loved their fathers, You chose their descendants after them, and You brought them out of Egypt by Your presence

and Your great power; You drove out from before the Israelites nations greater and mightier than they, to bring them in and to give them their land as an inheritance. (Deuteronomy 4:33–35, 37–38)

***PAUSE** to offer your own expressions of thanksgiving.*

NT Acts 7:54–8:8

The Stoning of Stephen

54When they heard this, they were furious and gnashed their teeth at him. 55But
Stephen, full of the Holy Spirit, looked up
to heaven and saw the glory of God, and
Jesus standing at the right hand of God.
56"Look," he said, "I see heaven open and
the Son of Man standing at the right hand
of God."

57At this they covered their ears and,
yelling at the top of their voices, they all
rushed at him, 58dragged him out of the
city and began to stone him. Meanwhile,
the witnesses laid their clothes at the feet
of a young man named Saul.

59While they were stoning him, Stephen
prayed, "Lord Jesus, receive my spirit."
60Then he fell on his knees and cried out,
"Lord, do not hold this sin against them."
When he had said this, he fell asleep.

8 And Saul was there, giving approval to
his death.

The Church Persecuted and Scattered

On that day a great persecution broke
out against the church at Jerusalem, and all
except the apostles were scattered throughout Judea and Samaria. 2Godly men buried
Stephen and mourned deeply for him.
3But Saul began to destroy the church. Going from house to house, he dragged off
men and women and put them in prison.

Philip in Samaria

4Those who had been scattered
preached the word wherever they went.
5Philip went down to a city in Samaria
and proclaimed the Christ[a] there. 6When
the crowds heard Philip and saw the
miraculous signs he did, they all paid
close attention to what he said. 7With
shrieks, evil[b] spirits came out of many,
and many paralytics and cripples were
healed. 8So there was great joy in that city.

[a] 5 Or *Messiah* [b] 7 Greek *unclean*

PRAYER: THE CHARACTER I WANT TO CULTIVATE

I WILL be strong and courageous; I will not be afraid or discouraged because of my adversaries, for there is a greater power with me than with them, for You, O Lord my God, are with me to help me. (2 Chronicles 32:7–8) . . . I will not be afraid of my adversaries, but I will remember You, Lord, who are great and awesome. (Nehemiah 4:14)

***TAKE** a moment to ask the Lord for the grace to grow in godly character.*

YEAR 1 DAY 50

OT Exodus 1:1–2:25

The Israelites Oppressed

1 These are the names of the sons of Israel who went to Egypt with Jacob, each
with his family: 2Reuben, Simeon, Levi
and Judah; 3Issachar, Zebulun and Benjamin; 4Dan and Naphtali; Gad and Asher.
5The descendants of Jacob numbered seventy[a] in all; Joseph was already in Egypt.

6Now Joseph and all his brothers and
all that generation died, 7but the Israelites
were fruitful and multiplied greatly and
became exceedingly numerous, so that
the land was filled with them.

[a] 5 Masoretic Text (see also Gen. 46:27); Dead Sea Scrolls and Septuagint (see also Acts 7:14 and note at Gen. 46:27) *seventy-five*

8 Then a new king, who did not know
about Joseph, came to power in Egypt.
9 "Look," he said to his people, "the Israelites have become much too numerous
for us. 10 Come, we must deal shrewdly
with them or they will become even more
numerous and, if war breaks out, will join
our enemies, fight against us and leave the
country."
11 So they put slave masters over them to
oppress them with forced labor, and they
built Pithom and Rameses as store cities
for Pharaoh. 12 But the more they were oppressed, the more they multiplied and
spread; so the Egyptians came to dread
the Israelites 13 and worked them ruthlessly. 14 They made their lives bitter with hard
labor in brick and mortar and with all
kinds of work in the fields; in all their
hard labor the Egyptians used them ruthlessly.
15 The king of Egypt said to the Hebrew
midwives, whose names were Shiphrah
and Puah, 16 "When you help the Hebrew
women in childbirth and observe them
on the delivery stool, if it is a boy, kill
him; but if it is a girl, let her live." 17 The
midwives, however, feared God and did
not do what the king of Egypt had told
them to do; they let the boys live. 18 Then
the king of Egypt summoned the midwives and asked them, "Why have you
done this? Why have you let the boys
live?"
19 The midwives answered Pharaoh,
"Hebrew women are not like Egyptian
women; they are vigorous and give birth
before the midwives arrive."
20 So God was kind to the midwives and
the people increased and became even
more numerous. 21 And because the midwives feared God, he gave them families
of their own.
22 Then Pharaoh gave this order to all
his people: "Every boy that is born[b] you
must throw into the Nile, but let every girl
live."

The Birth of Moses

2 Now a man of the house of Levi married a Levite woman, 2 and she became
pregnant and gave birth to a son. When
she saw that he was a fine child, she hid
him for three months. 3 But when she
could hide him no longer, she got a papyrus basket for him and coated it with
tar and pitch. Then she placed the child
in it and put it among the reeds along the
bank of the Nile. 4 His sister stood at a distance to see what would happen to him.
5 Then Pharaoh's daughter went down
to the Nile to bathe, and her attendants
were walking along the river bank. She
saw the basket among the reeds and sent
her slave girl to get it. 6 She opened it and
saw the baby. He was crying, and she felt
sorry for him. "This is one of the Hebrew
babies," she said.
7 Then his sister asked Pharaoh's daughter, "Shall I go and get one of the Hebrew
women to nurse the baby for you?"
8 "Yes, go," she answered. And the girl
went and got the baby's mother. 9 Pharaoh's daughter said to her, "Take this
baby and nurse him for me, and I will pay
you." So the woman took the baby and
nursed him. 10 When the child grew older,
she took him to Pharaoh's daughter and
he became her son. She named him
Moses,[c] saying, "I drew him out of the
water."

Moses Flees to Midian

11 One day, after Moses had grown up,
he went out to where his own people were
and watched them at their hard labor. He
saw an Egyptian beating a Hebrew, one of
his own people. 12 Glancing this way and
that and seeing no one, he killed the
Egyptian and hid him in the sand. 13 The
next day he went out and saw two Hebrews fighting. He asked the one in the
wrong, "Why are you hitting your fellow
Hebrew?"
14 The man said, "Who made you ruler
and judge over us? Are you thinking of
killing me as you killed the Egyptian?"
Then Moses was afraid and thought,
"What I did must have become known."
15 When Pharaoh heard of this, he tried
to kill Moses, but Moses fled from Pharaoh and went to live in Midian, where he
sat down by a well. 16 Now a priest of Midian had seven daughters, and they came
to draw water and fill the troughs to water their father's flock. 17 Some shepherds
came along and drove them away, but
Moses got up and came to their rescue
and watered their flock.

[b] *22* Masoretic Text; Samaritan Pentateuch, Septuagint and Targums *born to the Hebrews*
[c] *10* *Moses* sounds like the Hebrew for *draw out.*

18When the girls returned to Reuel their father, he asked them, "Why have you returned so early today?"

19They answered, "An Egyptian rescued us from the shepherds. He even drew water for us and watered the flock."

20"And where is he?" he asked his daughters. "Why did you leave him? Invite him to have something to eat."

21Moses agreed to stay with the man, who gave his daughter Zipporah to Moses in marriage. 22Zipporah gave birth to a son, and Moses named him Gershom,[d] saying, "I have become an alien in a foreign land."

23During that long period, the king of Egypt died. The Israelites groaned in their slavery and cried out, and their cry for help because of their slavery went up to God. 24God heard their groaning and he remembered his covenant with Abraham, with Isaac and with Jacob. 25So God looked on the Israelites and was concerned about them.

[d] 22 *Gershom* sounds like the Hebrew for *an alien there.*

PRAYER: ADORATION

YOU, the Lord, alone have declared what is to come from the distant past. There is no God apart from You, a righteous God and a Savior; there is none besides You. You are God, and there is no other. (Isaiah 45:21–22) . . . You are my hope, O Lord God; You are my trust from my youth. As for me, I will always have hope; I will praise You more and more. (Psalm 71:5, 14)

***PAUSE** to express your thoughts of praise and worship.*

NT Acts 8:9-40

Simon the Sorcerer

9Now for some time a man named Simon had practiced sorcery in the city and amazed all the people of Samaria. He boasted that he was someone great, 10and all the people, both high and low, gave him their attention and exclaimed, "This man is the divine power known as the Great Power." 11They followed him because he had amazed them for a long time with his magic. 12But when they believed Philip as he preached the good news of the kingdom of God and the name of Jesus Christ, they were baptized, both men and women. 13Simon himself believed and was baptized. And he followed Philip everywhere, astonished by the great signs and miracles he saw.

14When the apostles in Jerusalem heard that Samaria had accepted the word of God, they sent Peter and John to them. 15When they arrived, they prayed for them that they might receive the Holy Spirit, 16because the Holy Spirit had not yet come upon any of them; they had simply been baptized into[a] the name of the Lord Jesus. 17Then Peter and John placed their hands on them, and they received the Holy Spirit.

18When Simon saw that the Spirit was given at the laying on of the apostles' hands, he offered them money 19and said, "Give me also this ability so that everyone on whom I lay my hands may receive the Holy Spirit."

20Peter answered: "May your money perish with you, because you thought you could buy the gift of God with money! 21You have no part or share in this ministry, because your heart is not right before God. 22Repent of this wickedness and pray to the Lord. Perhaps he will forgive you for having such a thought in your heart. 23For I see that you are full of bitterness and captive to sin."

24Then Simon answered, "Pray to the Lord for me so that nothing you have said may happen to me."

25When they had testified and proclaimed the word of the Lord, Peter and John returned to Jerusalem, preaching the gospel in many Samaritan villages.

[a] 16 Or *in*

Philip and the Ethiopian

[26]Now an angel of the Lord said to Philip, "Go south to the road—the desert road—that goes down from Jerusalem to Gaza." [27]So he started out, and on his way he met an Ethiopian[b] eunuch, an important official in charge of all the treasury of Candace, queen of the Ethiopians. This man had gone to Jerusalem to worship, [28]and on his way home was sitting in his chariot reading the book of Isaiah the prophet. [29]The Spirit told Philip, "Go to that chariot and stay near it."

[30]Then Philip ran up to the chariot and heard the man reading Isaiah the prophet. "Do you understand what you are reading?" Philip asked.

[31]"How can I," he said, "unless someone explains it to me?" So he invited Philip to come up and sit with him.

[32]The eunuch was reading this passage of Scripture:

"He was led like a sheep to the
slaughter,
and as a lamb before the shearer is
silent,
so he did not open his mouth.
[33]In his humiliation he was deprived of
justice.
Who can speak of his descendants?
For his life was taken from the
earth."[c]

[34]The eunuch asked Philip, "Tell me, please, who is the prophet talking about, himself or someone else?" [35]Then Philip began with that very passage of Scripture and told him the good news about Jesus.

[36]As they traveled along the road, they came to some water and the eunuch said, "Look, here is water. Why shouldn't I be baptized?"[d] [38]And he gave orders to stop the chariot. Then both Philip and the eunuch went down into the water and Philip baptized him. [39]When they came up out of the water, the Spirit of the Lord suddenly took Philip away, and the eunuch did not see him again, but went on his way rejoicing. [40]Philip, however, appeared at Azotus and traveled about, preaching the gospel in all the towns until he reached Caesarea.

[b] 27 That is, from the upper Nile region
[c] 33 Isaiah 53:7,8 [d] 36 Some late manuscripts *baptized?" [37]Philip said, "If you believe with all your heart, you may." The eunuch answered, "I believe that Jesus Christ is the Son of God."*

PRAYER: MY RELATIONSHIP TO OTHERS

FAR be it from me that I should sin against You, Lord, by ceasing to pray for others. (1 Samuel 12:23). I will do nothing out of selfish ambition or vain conceit, but in humility I will esteem others as more important than myself. I will look not only to my own interests, but also to the interests of others. (Philippians 2:3–4)

PAUSE *to review your relationships with others and to commit them to the Lord.*

OT Exodus 3:1–22 — YEAR 1 DAY 51

Moses and the Burning Bush

3 Now Moses was tending the flock of Jethro his father-in-law, the priest of Midian, and he led the flock to the far side of the desert and came to Horeb, the mountain of God. [2]There the angel of the LORD appeared to him in flames of fire from within a bush. Moses saw that though the bush was on fire it did not burn up. [3]So Moses thought, "I will go over and see this strange sight—why the bush does not burn up."

[4]When the LORD saw that he had gone over to look, God called to him from within the bush, "Moses! Moses!"

And Moses said, "Here I am."

[5]"Do not come any closer," God said. "Take off your sandals, for the place where you are standing is holy ground." [6]Then

he said, "I am the God of your father, the God of Abraham, the God of Isaac and the God of Jacob." At this, Moses hid his face, because he was afraid to look at God.

7The LORD said, "I have indeed seen the misery of my people in Egypt. I have heard them crying out because of their slave drivers, and I am concerned about their suffering. 8So I have come down to rescue them from the hand of the Egyptians and to bring them up out of that land into a good and spacious land, a land flowing with milk and honey—the home of the Canaanites, Hittites, Amorites, Perizzites, Hivites and Jebusites. 9And now the cry of the Israelites has reached me, and I have seen the way the Egyptians are oppressing them. 10So now, go. I am sending you to Pharaoh to bring my people the Israelites out of Egypt."

11But Moses said to God, "Who am I, that I should go to Pharaoh and bring the Israelites out of Egypt?"

12And God said, "I will be with you. And this will be the sign to you that it is I who have sent you: When you have brought the people out of Egypt, you[a] will worship God on this mountain."

13Moses said to God, "Suppose I go to the Israelites and say to them, 'The God of your fathers has sent me to you,' and they ask me, 'What is his name?' Then what shall I tell them?"

14God said to Moses, "I AM WHO I AM.[b] This is what you are to say to the Israelites: 'I AM has sent me to you.' "

15God also said to Moses, "Say to the Israelites, 'The LORD,[c] the God of your fathers—the God of Abraham, the God of Isaac and the God of Jacob—has sent me to you.' This is my name forever, the name by which I am to be remembered from generation to generation.

16"Go, assemble the elders of Israel and say to them, 'The LORD, the God of your fathers—the God of Abraham, Isaac and Jacob—appeared to me and said: I have watched over you and have seen what has been done to you in Egypt. 17And I have promised to bring you up out of your misery in Egypt into the land of the Canaanites, Hittites, Amorites, Perizzites, Hivites and Jebusites—a land flowing with milk and honey.'

18"The elders of Israel will listen to you. Then you and the elders are to go to the king of Egypt and say to him, 'The LORD, the God of the Hebrews, has met with us. Let us take a three-day journey into the desert to offer sacrifices to the LORD our God.' 19But I know that the king of Egypt will not let you go unless a mighty hand compels him. 20So I will stretch out my hand and strike the Egyptians with all the wonders that I will perform among them. After that, he will let you go.

21"And I will make the Egyptians favorably disposed toward this people, so that when you leave you will not go empty-handed. 22Every woman is to ask her neighbor and any woman living in her house for articles of silver and gold and for clothing, which you will put on your sons and daughters. And so you will plunder the Egyptians."

[a] *12* The Hebrew is plural. [b] *14* Or *I WILL BE WHAT I WILL BE* [c] *15* The Hebrew for *LORD* sounds like and may be derived from the Hebrew for *I AM* in verse 14.

PRAYER: CONFESSION

YOU are not a God who takes pleasure in wickedness; evil cannot dwell with You. (Psalm 5:4)

***ASK** the Spirit to search your heart and reveal any areas of unconfessed sin. Acknowledge these to the Lord and thank Him for His forgiveness.*

NT Acts 9:1–19a

Saul's Conversion

9 Meanwhile, Saul was still breathing out murderous threats against the Lord's disciples. He went to the high priest 2and asked him for letters to the synagogues in Damascus, so that if he found any there who belonged to the Way, whether men or women, he might take them as prisoners to Jerusalem. 3As he neared Damascus on his journey, suddenly a light from

heaven flashed around him. 4He fell to
the ground and heard a voice say to him,
"Saul, Saul, why do you persecute me?"
5"Who are you, Lord?" Saul asked.
"I am Jesus, whom you are persecuting," he replied. 6"Now get up and go into
the city, and you will be told what you
must do."
7The men traveling with Saul stood
there speechless; they heard the sound but
did not see anyone. 8Saul got up from
the ground, but when he opened his eyes
he could see nothing. So they led him
by the hand into Damascus. 9For three
days he was blind, and did not eat or
drink anything.
10In Damascus there was a disciple
named Ananias. The Lord called to him in
a vision, "Ananias!"
"Yes, Lord," he answered.
11The Lord told him, "Go to the house
of Judas on Straight Street and ask for a
man from Tarsus named Saul, for he is
praying. 12In a vision he has seen a man
named Ananias come and place his hands
on him to restore his sight."
13"Lord," Ananias answered, "I have
heard many reports about this man and
all the harm he has done to your saints in
Jerusalem. 14And he has come here with
authority from the chief priests to arrest
all who call on your name."
15But the Lord said to Ananias, "Go!
This man is my chosen instrument to carry my name before the Gentiles and their
kings and before the people of Israel. 16I
will show him how much he must suffer
for my name."
17Then Ananias went to the house and
entered it. Placing his hands on Saul, he
said, "Brother Saul, the Lord—Jesus, who
appeared to you on the road as you were
coming here—has sent me so that you may
see again and be filled with the Holy Spirit." 18Immediately, something like scales fell
from Saul's eyes, and he could see again. He
got up and was baptized, 19and after taking
some food, he regained his strength.

PRAYER: THE ATTRIBUTES OF GOD

YOU, O Lord, will guard the feet of Your saints, but the wicked will be silenced in darkness. It is not by strength that one prevails; those who contend with You, Lord, will be shattered. You will thunder against them from heaven; You will judge the ends of the earth. You will give strength to Your king and exalt the horn of Your anointed. (1 Samuel 2:9–10)

You have sworn by Yourself; the word has gone out of Your mouth in righteousness and will not return. Every knee will bow before You, and every tongue will acknowledge You. (Isaiah 45:23)

__PAUSE__ to reflect on these affirmations about the person, powers and perfection of God.

YEAR 1 DAY 52

OT Exodus 4:1–5:23

Signs for Moses

4 Moses answered, "What if they do not
believe me or listen to me and say, 'The
Lord did not appear to you'?"
2Then the Lord said to him, "What is
that in your hand?"
"A staff," he replied.
3The Lord said, "Throw it on the
ground."
Moses threw it on the ground and it became a snake, and he ran from it. 4Then
the Lord said to him, "Reach out your
hand and take it by the tail." So Moses
reached out and took hold of the snake
and it turned back into a staff in his hand.
5"This," said the Lord, "is so that they
may believe that the Lord, the God of
their fathers—the God of Abraham, the
God of Isaac and the God of Jacob—has
appeared to you."
6Then the Lord said, "Put your hand inside your cloak." So Moses put his hand

into his cloak, and when he took it out, it
was leprous,[a] like snow.
7 "Now put it back into your cloak," he
said. So Moses put his hand back into his
cloak, and when he took it out, it was restored, like the rest of his flesh.
8 Then the LORD said, "If they do not believe you or pay attention to the first
miraculous sign, they may believe the second. 9 But if they do not believe these two
signs or listen to you, take some water
from the Nile and pour it on the dry
ground. The water you take from the river will become blood on the ground."
10 Moses said to the LORD, "O Lord, I
have never been eloquent, neither in the
past nor since you have spoken to your
servant. I am slow of speech and tongue."
11 The LORD said to him, "Who gave man
his mouth? Who makes him deaf or
mute? Who gives him sight or makes him
blind? Is it not I, the LORD? 12 Now go; I
will help you speak and will teach you
what to say."
13 But Moses said, "O Lord, please send
someone else to do it."
14 Then the LORD's anger burned against
Moses and he said, "What about your
brother, Aaron the Levite? I know he can
speak well. He is already on his way to
meet you, and his heart will be glad when
he sees you. 15 You shall speak to him and
put words in his mouth; I will help both
of you speak and will teach you what to
do. 16 He will speak to the people for you,
and it will be as if he were your mouth
and as if you were God to him. 17 But take
this staff in your hand so you can perform
miraculous signs with it."

Moses Returns to Egypt

18 Then Moses went back to Jethro his
father-in-law and said to him, "Let me go
back to my own people in Egypt to see if
any of them are still alive."
Jethro said, "Go, and I wish you well."
19 Now the LORD had said to Moses in
Midian, "Go back to Egypt, for all the
men who wanted to kill you are dead."
20 So Moses took his wife and sons, put
them on a donkey and started back to
Egypt. And he took the staff of God in his
hand.
21 The LORD said to Moses, "When you
return to Egypt, see that you perform before Pharaoh all the wonders I have given
you the power to do. But I will harden his
heart so that he will not let the people go.
22 Then say to Pharaoh, 'This is what the
LORD says: Israel is my firstborn son, 23 and
I told you, "Let my son go, so he may worship me." But you refused to let him go;
so I will kill your firstborn son.' "
24 At a lodging place on the way, the
LORD met ⌊Moses⌋[b] and was about to kill
him. 25 But Zipporah took a flint knife, cut
off her son's foreskin and touched
⌊Moses'⌋ feet with it.[c] "Surely you are a
bridegroom of blood to me," she said.
26 So the LORD let him alone. (At that time
she said "bridegroom of blood," referring
to circumcision.)
27 The LORD said to Aaron, "Go into the
desert to meet Moses." So he met Moses
at the mountain of God and kissed him.
28 Then Moses told Aaron everything the
LORD had sent him to say, and also about
all the miraculous signs he had commanded him to perform.
29 Moses and Aaron brought together all
the elders of the Israelites, 30 and Aaron
told them everything the LORD had said to
Moses. He also performed the signs before the people, 31 and they believed. And
when they heard that the LORD was concerned about them and had seen their
misery, they bowed down and worshiped.

Bricks Without Straw

5 Afterward Moses and Aaron went to
Pharaoh and said, "This is what the
LORD, the God of Israel, says: 'Let my people go, so that they may hold a festival to
me in the desert.' "
2 Pharaoh said, "Who is the LORD, that I
should obey him and let Israel go? I do not
know the LORD and I will not let Israel go."
3 Then they said, "The God of the Hebrews has met with us. Now let us take a
three-day journey into the desert to offer
sacrifices to the LORD our God, or he may
strike us with plagues or with the sword."
4 But the king of Egypt said, "Moses and
Aaron, why are you taking the people
away from their labor? Get back to your
work!" 5 Then Pharaoh said, "Look, the
people of the land are now numerous,
and you are stopping them from working."

[a] 6 The Hebrew word was used for various diseases affecting the skin—not necessarily leprosy.
[b] 24 Or ⌊*Moses' son*⌋; Hebrew *him* [c] 25 Or *and drew near ⌊Moses'⌋ feet*

6 That same day Pharaoh gave this order to the slave drivers and foremen in charge of the people: 7 "You are no longer to supply the people with straw for making bricks; let them go and gather their own straw. 8 But require them to make the same number of bricks as before; don't reduce the quota. They are lazy; that is why they are crying out, 'Let us go and sacrifice to our God.' 9 Make the work harder for the men so that they keep working and pay no attention to lies."

10 Then the slave drivers and the foremen went out and said to the people, "This is what Pharaoh says: 'I will not give you any more straw. 11 Go and get your own straw wherever you can find it, but your work will not be reduced at all.' " 12 So the people scattered all over Egypt to gather stubble to use for straw. 13 The slave drivers kept pressing them, saying, "Complete the work required of you for each day, just as when you had straw." 14 The Israelite foremen appointed by Pharaoh's slave drivers were beaten and were asked, "Why didn't you meet your quota of bricks yesterday or today, as before?"

15 Then the Israelite foremen went and appealed to Pharaoh: "Why have you treated your servants this way? 16 Your servants are given no straw, yet we are told, 'Make bricks!' Your servants are being beaten, but the fault is with your own people."

17 Pharaoh said, "Lazy, that's what you are—lazy! That is why you keep saying, 'Let us go and sacrifice to the LORD.' 18 Now get to work. You will not be given any straw, yet you must produce your full quota of bricks."

19 The Israelite foremen realized they were in trouble when they were told, "You are not to reduce the number of bricks required of you for each day." 20 When they left Pharaoh, they found Moses and Aaron waiting to meet them, 21 and they said, "May the LORD look upon you and judge you! You have made us a stench to Pharaoh and his officials and have put a sword in their hand to kill us."

God Promises Deliverance

22 Moses returned to the LORD and said, "O Lord, why have you brought trouble upon this people? Is this why you sent me? 23 Ever since I went to Pharaoh to speak in your name, he has brought trouble upon this people, and you have not rescued your people at all."

PRAYER: RENEWAL

LIKE Enoch, may I walk with You. (Genesis 5:24) . . . Like Noah, may I find favor in Your eyes, O Lord. (Genesis 6:8)

***PAUSE** to add your own prayers for personal renewal.*

NT Acts 9:19b–43

Saul in Damascus and Jerusalem

Saul spent several days with the disciples in Damascus. 20 At once he began to preach in the synagogues that Jesus is the Son of God. 21 All those who heard him were astonished and asked, "Isn't he the man who raised havoc in Jerusalem among those who call on this name? And hasn't he come here to take them as prisoners to the chief priests?" 22 Yet Saul grew more and more powerful and baffled the Jews living in Damascus by proving that Jesus is the Christ.[a]

23 After many days had gone by, the Jews conspired to kill him, 24 but Saul learned of their plan. Day and night they kept close watch on the city gates in order to kill him. 25 But his followers took him by night and lowered him in a basket through an opening in the wall.

26 When he came to Jerusalem, he tried to join the disciples, but they were all afraid of him, not believing that he really was a disciple. 27 But Barnabas took him and brought him to the apostles. He told them how Saul on his journey had seen the Lord and that the Lord had spoken to him, and how in Damascus he had preached fearlessly in the name of Jesus.

[a] 22 Or *Messiah*

28 So Saul stayed with them and moved
about freely in Jerusalem, speaking boldly in the name of the Lord. 29 He talked
and debated with the Grecian Jews, but
they tried to kill him. 30 When the brothers learned of this, they took him down to
Caesarea and sent him off to Tarsus.

31 Then the church throughout Judea,
Galilee and Samaria enjoyed a time of
peace. It was strengthened; and encouraged by the Holy Spirit, it grew in numbers, living in the fear of the Lord.

Aeneas and Dorcas

32 As Peter traveled about the country, he
went to visit the saints in Lydda. 33 There
he found a man named Aeneas, a paralytic who had been bedridden for eight
years. 34 "Aeneas," Peter said to him, "Jesus
Christ heals you. Get up and take care of
your mat." Immediately Aeneas got up.
35 All those who lived in Lydda and Sharon saw him and turned to the Lord.

36 In Joppa there was a disciple named
Tabitha (which, when translated, is Dorcas[b]), who was always doing good and
helping the poor. 37 About that time she
became sick and died, and her body was
washed and placed in an upstairs room.
38 Lydda was near Joppa; so when the disciples heard that Peter was in Lydda, they
sent two men to him and urged him,
"Please come at once!"

39 Peter went with them, and when he
arrived he was taken upstairs to the room.
All the widows stood around him, crying
and showing him the robes and other
clothing that Dorcas had made while she
was still with them.

40 Peter sent them all out of the room;
then he got down on his knees and prayed.
Turning toward the dead woman, he said,
"Tabitha, get up." She opened her eyes, and
seeing Peter she sat up. 41 He took her by the
hand and helped her to her feet. Then he
called the believers and the widows and
presented her to them alive. 42 This became
known all over Joppa, and many people believed in the Lord. 43 Peter stayed in Joppa
for some time with a tanner named Simon.

[b] 36 Both *Tabitha* (Aramaic) and *Dorcas* (Greek) mean *gazelle*.

PRAYER: THE WORKS OF GOD

YOU, Lord God, will swallow up death forever, and You will wipe away the tears from every face; You will remove the reproach of Your people from all the earth, for You, the Lord, have spoken. And it will be said in that day, "Behold, this is our God; we have waited for Him, and He will save us. This is the Lord, we have trusted in Him. Let us rejoice and be glad in His salvation." (Isaiah 25:8–9) . . . You will create new heavens and a new earth, O Sovereign Lord. The former things will not be remembered, nor will they come to mind. (Isaiah 65:17)

***TAKE** a moment to consider the greatness of God's wonderful works.*

YEAR 1 DAY 53

OT Exodus 6:1–27

6 Then the LORD said to Moses, "Now
you will see what I will do to Pharaoh:
Because of my mighty hand he will let
them go; because of my mighty hand he
will drive them out of his country."

2 God also said to Moses, "I am the
LORD. 3 I appeared to Abraham, to Isaac
and to Jacob as God Almighty,[a] but by my
name the LORD[b] I did not make myself
known to them.[c] 4 I also established my
covenant with them to give them the land
of Canaan, where they lived as aliens.
5 Moreover, I have heard the groaning of
the Israelites, whom the Egyptians are en-
slaving, and I have remembered my covenant.

6 "Therefore, say to the Israelites: 'I am

[a] 3 Hebrew *El-Shaddai* [b] 3 See note at Exodus 3:15. [c] 3 Or *Almighty, and by my name the LORD did I not let myself be known to them?*

the LORD, and I will bring you out from
under the yoke of the Egyptians. I will free
you from being slaves to them, and I will
redeem you with an outstretched arm and
with mighty acts of judgment. [7]I will take
you as my own people, and I will be your
God. Then you will know that I am the
LORD your God, who brought you out
from under the yoke of the Egyptians.
[8]And I will bring you to the land I swore
with uplifted hand to give to Abraham, to
Isaac and to Jacob. I will give it to you as
a possession. I am the LORD.' "
[9]Moses reported this to the Israelites,
but they did not listen to him because of
their discouragement and cruel bondage.
[10]Then the LORD said to Moses, [11]"Go,
tell Pharaoh king of Egypt to let the Israelites go out of his country."
[12]But Moses said to the LORD, "If the Israelites will not listen to me, why would
Pharaoh listen to me, since I speak with
faltering lips[d]?"

Family Record of Moses and Aaron

[13]Now the LORD spoke to Moses and
Aaron about the Israelites and Pharaoh
king of Egypt, and he commanded them
to bring the Israelites out of Egypt.

[14]These were the heads of their families[e]:

The sons of Reuben the firstborn son of Israel were Hanoch and Pallu, Hezron and Carmi. These were the clans of Reuben.
[15]The sons of Simeon were Jemuel, Jamin, Ohad, Jakin, Zohar and Shaul the son of a Canaanite woman. These were the clans of Simeon.
[16]These were the names of the sons of Levi according to their records: Gershon, Kohath and Merari. Levi lived 137 years.
[17]The sons of Gershon, by clans, were Libni and Shimei.
[18]The sons of Kohath were Amram, Izhar, Hebron and Uzziel. Kohath lived 133 years.
[19]The sons of Merari were Mahli and Mushi.
These were the clans of Levi according to their records.
[20]Amram married his father's sister Jochebed, who bore him Aaron and Moses. Amram lived 137 years.
[21]The sons of Izhar were Korah, Nepheg and Zicri.
[22]The sons of Uzziel were Mishael, Elzaphan and Sithri.
[23]Aaron married Elisheba, daughter of Amminadab and sister of Nahshon, and she bore him Nadab and Abihu, Eleazar and Ithamar.
[24]The sons of Korah were Assir, Elkanah and Abiasaph. These were the Korahite clans.
[25]Eleazar son of Aaron married one of the daughters of Putiel, and she bore him Phinehas.

These were the heads of the Levite families, clan by clan.

[26]It was this same Aaron and Moses to
whom the LORD said, "Bring the Israelites
out of Egypt by their divisions." [27]They were
the ones who spoke to Pharaoh king of
Egypt about bringing the Israelites out of
Egypt. It was the same Moses and Aaron.

[d] 12 Hebrew *I am uncircumcised of lips;* also in verse 30 [e] 14 The Hebrew for *families* here and in verse 25 refers to units larger than clans.

PRAYER: PETITION

MAY I consider the members of my earthly body as dead to immorality, impurity, passion, evil desires and greed, which is idolatry. Because of these, O God, Your wrath is coming. I used to walk in these ways, in the life I once lived. (Colossians 3:5–7)

PAUSE *here to petition God for growth in your desire to know and please Jesus Christ. Pray for a greater love and commitment to Him, for the grace to practice His presence and for the grace to glorify Him in your life. Offer prayers regarding your activities for this day and any special concerns you may have.*

NT Acts 10:1–23a

Cornelius Calls for Peter

10 At Caesarea there was a man named Cornelius, a centurion in what was known as the Italian Regiment. 2He and all his family were devout and God-fearing; he gave generously to those in need and prayed to God regularly. 3One day at about three in the afternoon he had a vision. He distinctly saw an angel of God, who came to him and said, "Cornelius!"

4Cornelius stared at him in fear. "What is it, Lord?" he asked.

The angel answered, "Your prayers and gifts to the poor have come up as a memorial offering before God. 5Now send men to Joppa to bring back a man named Simon who is called Peter. 6He is staying with Simon the tanner, whose house is by the sea."

7When the angel who spoke to him had gone, Cornelius called two of his servants and a devout soldier who was one of his attendants. 8He told them everything that had happened and sent them to Joppa.

Peter's Vision

9About noon the following day as they were on their journey and approaching the city, Peter went up on the roof to pray. 10He became hungry and wanted something to eat, and while the meal was being prepared, he fell into a trance. 11He saw heaven opened and something like a large sheet being let down to earth by its four corners. 12It contained all kinds of four-footed animals, as well as reptiles of the earth and birds of the air. 13Then a voice told him, "Get up, Peter. Kill and eat."

14"Surely not, Lord!" Peter replied. "I have never eaten anything impure or unclean."

15The voice spoke to him a second time, "Do not call anything impure that God has made clean."

16This happened three times, and immediately the sheet was taken back to heaven.

17While Peter was wondering about the meaning of the vision, the men sent by Cornelius found out where Simon's house was and stopped at the gate. 18They called out, asking if Simon who was known as Peter was staying there.

19While Peter was still thinking about the vision, the Spirit said to him, "Simon, three[a] men are looking for you. 20So get up and go downstairs. Do not hesitate to go with them, for I have sent them."

21Peter went down and said to the men, "I'm the one you're looking for. Why have you come?"

22The men replied, "We have come from Cornelius the centurion. He is a righteous and God-fearing man, who is respected by all the Jewish people. A holy angel told him to have you come to his house so that he could hear what you have to say." 23Then Peter invited the men into the house to be his guests.

[a] 19 One early manuscript *two;* other manuscripts do not have the number.

PRAYER: MY RELATIONSHIP TO GOD

YOU know how I am formed; You remember that I am dust. As for people, their days are like grass; they flourish like flowers of the field. The wind passes over them and they are gone, and their place remembers them no more. But Your loving-kindness, O Lord, is from everlasting to everlasting to those who fear You, and Your righteousness with their children's children, to those who keep Your covenant and remember to obey Your precepts. (Psalm 103:14–18)

PAUSE *to thank God for the relationship that you enjoy with Him in Jesus Christ.*

YEAR 1 DAY 54

OT Exodus 6:28–7:24

Aaron to Speak for Moses

[28]Now when the LORD spoke to Moses
in Egypt, [29]he said to him, "I am the LORD.
Tell Pharaoh king of Egypt everything I
tell you."
[30]But Moses said to the LORD, "Since I
speak with faltering lips, why would Pharaoh listen to me?"
7 Then the LORD said to Moses, "See, I
have made you like God to Pharaoh,
and your brother Aaron will be your
prophet. [2]You are to say everything I command you, and your brother Aaron is to
tell Pharaoh to let the Israelites go out of
his country. [3]But I will harden Pharaoh's
heart, and though I multiply my miraculous signs and wonders in Egypt, [4]he will
not listen to you. Then I will lay my hand
on Egypt and with mighty acts of judgment I will bring out my divisions, my
people the Israelites. [5]And the Egyptians
will know that I am the LORD when I
stretch out my hand against Egypt and
bring the Israelites out of it."
[6]Moses and Aaron did just as the LORD
commanded them. [7]Moses was eighty
years old and Aaron eighty-three when
they spoke to Pharaoh.

Aaron's Staff Becomes a Snake

[8]The LORD said to Moses and Aaron,
[9]"When Pharaoh says to you, 'Perform a
miracle,' then say to Aaron, 'Take your staff
and throw it down before Pharaoh,' and it
will become a snake."
[10]So Moses and Aaron went to Pharaoh
and did just as the LORD commanded.
Aaron threw his staff down in front of
Pharaoh and his officials, and it became
a snake. [11]Pharaoh then summoned wise
men and sorcerers, and the Egyptian magicians also did the same things by their
secret arts: [12]Each one threw down his
staff and it became a snake. But Aaron's
staff swallowed up their staffs. [13]Yet Pharaoh's heart became hard and he would
not listen to them, just as the LORD had
said.

The Plague of Blood

[14]Then the LORD said to Moses, "Pharaoh's heart is unyielding; he refuses to let
the people go. [15]Go to Pharaoh in the
morning as he goes out to the water. Wait
on the bank of the Nile to meet him, and
take in your hand the staff that was
changed into a snake. [16]Then say to him,
'The LORD, the God of the Hebrews, has
sent me to say to you: Let my people go,
so that they may worship me in the desert.
But until now you have not listened.
[17]This is what the LORD says: By this you
will know that I am the LORD: With the
staff that is in my hand I will strike the
water of the Nile, and it will be changed
into blood. [18]The fish in the Nile will die,
and the river will stink; the Egyptians will
not be able to drink its water.' "
[19]The LORD said to Moses, "Tell Aaron,
'Take your staff and stretch out your hand
over the waters of Egypt—over the
streams and canals, over the ponds and
all the reservoirs'—and they will turn to
blood. Blood will be everywhere in Egypt,
even in the wooden buckets and stone
jars."
[20]Moses and Aaron did just as the LORD
had commanded. He raised his staff in
the presence of Pharaoh and his officials
and struck the water of the Nile, and all
the water was changed into blood. [21]The
fish in the Nile died, and the river
smelled so bad that the Egyptians could
not drink its water. Blood was everywhere
in Egypt.
[22]But the Egyptian magicians did the
same things by their secret arts, and Pharaoh's heart became hard; he would not
listen to Moses and Aaron, just as the
LORD had said. [23]Instead, he turned and
went into his palace, and did not take
even this to heart. [24]And all the Egyptians
dug along the Nile to get drinking water,
because they could not drink the water of
the river.

PRAYER: INTERCESSION

***WE** have many parts in one body, but all the parts do not have the same function; in the same way, we who are many are one body in You, Christ Jesus, and individually members of one another. And we have different gifts, according to the grace You have given to us.*

(Romans 12:4–6)

***TAKE** a few moments to intercede on behalf of your local church, other churches, evangelism and discipleship ministries, educational ministries and any other special concerns you may have.*

NT Acts 10:23b–48

Peter at Cornelius' House

The next day Peter started out with them, and some of the brothers from Joppa went along. 24The following day he arrived in Caesarea. Cornelius was expecting them and had called together his relatives and close friends. 25As Peter entered the house, Cornelius met him and fell at his feet in reverence. 26But Peter made him get up. "Stand up," he said, "I am only a man myself."

27Talking with him, Peter went inside and found a large gathering of people. 28He said to them: "You are well aware that it is against our law for a Jew to associate with a Gentile or visit him. But God has shown me that I should not call any man impure or unclean. 29So when I was sent for, I came without raising any objection. May I ask why you sent for me?"

30Cornelius answered: "Four days ago I was in my house praying at this hour, at three in the afternoon. Suddenly a man in shining clothes stood before me 31and said, 'Cornelius, God has heard your prayer and remembered your gifts to the poor. 32Send to Joppa for Simon who is called Peter. He is a guest in the home of Simon the tanner, who lives by the sea.' 33So I sent for you immediately, and it was good of you to come. Now we are all here in the presence of God to listen to everything the Lord has commanded you to tell us."

34Then Peter began to speak: "I now realize how true it is that God does not show favoritism 35but accepts men from every nation who fear him and do what is right. 36You know the message God sent to the people of Israel, telling the good news of peace through Jesus Christ, who is Lord of all. 37You know what has happened throughout Judea, beginning in Galilee after the baptism that John preached— 38how God anointed Jesus of Nazareth with the Holy Spirit and power, and how he went around doing good and healing all who were under the power of the devil, because God was with him.

39"We are witnesses of everything he did in the country of the Jews and in Jerusalem. They killed him by hanging him on a tree, 40but God raised him from the dead on the third day and caused him to be seen. 41He was not seen by all the people, but by witnesses whom God had already chosen—by us who ate and drank with him after he rose from the dead. 42He commanded us to preach to the people and to testify that he is the one whom God appointed as judge of the living and the dead. 43All the prophets testify about him that everyone who believes in him receives forgiveness of sins through his name."

44While Peter was still speaking these words, the Holy Spirit came on all who heard the message. 45The circumcised believers who had come with Peter were astonished that the gift of the Holy Spirit had been poured out even on the Gentiles. 46For they heard them speaking in tongues[a] and praising God.

Then Peter said, 47"Can anyone keep these people from being baptized with water? They have received the Holy Spirit just as we have." 48So he ordered that they be baptized in the name of Jesus Christ. Then they asked Peter to stay with them for a few days.

[a] 46 Or *other languages*

PRAYER: THE CHARACTER I WANT TO CULTIVATE

IF I am afraid of people, fear will trap me. But if I trust in You, O Lord, You will keep me safe. (Proverbs 29:25) . . . Cursed is the one who trusts in people, who depends on human strength and whose heart turns away from You, O Lord. But blessed is the one who trusts in You, whose confidence is in You. (Jeremiah 17:5, 7)

***TAKE** a moment to ask the Lord for the grace to grow in godly character.*

YEAR 1
DAY 55

OT Exodus 7:25–8:32

The Plague of Frogs

25 Seven days passed after the LORD struck
the Nile. 8 1 Then the LORD said to Moses,
"Go to Pharaoh and say to him, 'This
is what the LORD says: Let my people go,
so that they may worship me. 2 If you
refuse to let them go, I will plague your
whole country with frogs. 3 The Nile will
teem with frogs. They will come up into
your palace and your bedroom and onto
your bed, into the houses of your officials
and on your people, and into your ovens
and kneading troughs. 4 The frogs will go
up on you and your people and all your
officials.' "
5 Then the LORD said to Moses, "Tell Aaron, 'Stretch out your hand with your staff
over the streams and canals and ponds,
and make frogs come up on the land of
Egypt.' "
6 So Aaron stretched out his hand over
the waters of Egypt, and the frogs came up
and covered the land. 7 But the magicians
did the same things by their secret arts;
they also made frogs come up on the land
of Egypt.
8 Pharaoh summoned Moses and Aaron
and said, "Pray to the LORD to take the
frogs away from me and my people, and
I will let your people go to offer sacrifices
to the LORD."
9 Moses said to Pharaoh, "I leave to you
the honor of setting the time for me to
pray for you and your officials and your
people that you and your houses may be
rid of the frogs, except for those that remain in the Nile."
10 "Tomorrow," Pharaoh said.
Moses replied, "It will be as you say, so
that you may know there is no one like
the LORD our God. 11 The frogs will leave
you and your houses, your officials and
your people; they will remain only in the
Nile."
12 After Moses and Aaron left Pharaoh,
Moses cried out to the LORD about the
frogs he had brought on Pharaoh. 13 And
the LORD did what Moses asked. The frogs
died in the houses, in the courtyards and
in the fields. 14 They were piled into heaps,
and the land reeked of them. 15 But when
Pharaoh saw that there was relief, he
hardened his heart and would not listen
to Moses and Aaron, just as the LORD had
said.

The Plague of Gnats

16 Then the LORD said to Moses, "Tell
Aaron, 'Stretch out your staff and strike
the dust of the ground,' and throughout
the land of Egypt the dust will become
gnats." 17 They did this, and when Aaron
stretched out his hand with the staff and
struck the dust of the ground, gnats came
upon men and animals. All the dust
throughout the land of Egypt became
gnats. 18 But when the magicians tried to
produce gnats by their secret arts, they
could not. And the gnats were on men
and animals.
19 The magicians said to Pharaoh, "This
is the finger of God." But Pharaoh's heart
was hard and he would not listen, just as
the LORD had said.

The Plague of Flies

20 Then the LORD said to Moses, "Get up
early in the morning and confront Pharaoh as he goes to the water and say to
him, 'This is what the LORD says: Let my
people go, so that they may worship me.
21 If you do not let my people go, I will

send swarms of flies on you and your officials, on your people and into your
houses. The houses of the Egyptians will
be full of flies, and even the ground where
they are.
22 " 'But on that day I will deal differently with the land of Goshen, where my
people live; no swarms of flies will be
there, so that you will know that I, the
LORD, am in this land. 23 I will make a distinction[a] between my people and your
people. This miraculous sign will occur
tomorrow.' "
24 And the LORD did this. Dense swarms
of flies poured into Pharaoh's palace and
into the houses of his officials, and
throughout Egypt the land was ruined by
the flies.
25 Then Pharaoh summoned Moses and
Aaron and said, "Go, sacrifice to your God
here in the land."
26 But Moses said, "That would not be
right. The sacrifices we offer the LORD our
God would be detestable to the Egyptians.
And if we offer sacrifices that are detestable in their eyes, will they not stone
us? 27 We must take a three-day journey
into the desert to offer sacrifices to the
LORD our God, as he commands us."
28 Pharaoh said, "I will let you go to offer sacrifices to the LORD your God in the
desert, but you must not go very far. Now
pray for me."
29 Moses answered, "As soon as I leave
you, I will pray to the LORD, and tomorrow the flies will leave Pharaoh and his
officials and his people. Only be sure that
Pharaoh does not act deceitfully again by
not letting the people go to offer sacrifices
to the LORD."
30 Then Moses left Pharaoh and prayed
to the LORD, 31 and the LORD did what Moses asked: The flies left Pharaoh and his officials and his people; not a fly remained.
32 But this time also Pharaoh hardened his
heart and would not let the people go.

[a] 23 Septuagint and Vulgate; Hebrew *will put a deliverance*

PRAYER: AFFIRMATION

I BELIEVE that it is through Your grace, Lord Jesus, that I am saved. (Acts 15:11) . . . Jesus, I trusted in You when I heard the word of truth, the gospel of my salvation. Having believed, I was sealed in You with the Holy Spirit of promise, who is a deposit guaranteeing my inheritance until the redemption of those who are the Father's possession, to the praise of His glory. (Ephesians 1:13–14)

***PAUSE** to reflect on these Biblical affirmations.*

NT Acts 11:1-30

Peter Explains His Actions

11 The apostles and the brothers throughout Judea heard that the Gentiles also
had received the word of God. 2 So when
Peter went up to Jerusalem, the circumcised believers criticized him 3 and said,
"You went into the house of uncircumcised men and ate with them."
4 Peter began and explained everything
to them precisely as it had happened: 5 "I
was in the city of Joppa praying, and in a
trance I saw a vision. I saw something like
a large sheet being let down from heaven
by its four corners, and it came down to
where I was. 6 I looked into it and saw
four-footed animals of the earth, wild
beasts, reptiles, and birds of the air. 7 Then
I heard a voice telling me, 'Get up, Peter.
Kill and eat.'
8 "I replied, 'Surely not, Lord! Nothing
impure or unclean has ever entered my
mouth.'
9 "The voice spoke from heaven a second time, 'Do not call anything impure
that God has made clean.' 10 This happened three times, and then it was all
pulled up to heaven again.
11 "Right then three men who had been
sent to me from Caesarea stopped at the
house where I was staying. 12 The Spirit
told me to have no hesitation about going with them. These six brothers also
went with me, and we entered the man's

house. [13]He told us how he had seen an
angel appear in his house and say, 'Send
to Joppa for Simon who is called Peter.
[14]He will bring you a message through
which you and all your household will be
saved.'

[15]"As I began to speak, the Holy Spirit
came on them as he had come on us at
the beginning. [16]Then I remembered what
the Lord had said: 'John baptized with[a]
water, but you will be baptized with the
Holy Spirit.' [17]So if God gave them the
same gift as he gave us, who believed in
the Lord Jesus Christ, who was I to think
that I could oppose God?"

[18]When they heard this, they had no
further objections and praised God, saying, "So then, God has granted even the
Gentiles repentance unto life."

The Church in Antioch

[19]Now those who had been scattered by
the persecution in connection with Stephen traveled as far as Phoenicia, Cyprus
and Antioch, telling the message only to
Jews. [20]Some of them, however, men from
Cyprus and Cyrene, went to Antioch and
began to speak to Greeks also, telling
them the good news about the Lord Jesus.
[21]The Lord's hand was with them, and a
great number of people believed and
turned to the Lord.

[22]News of this reached the ears of the
church at Jerusalem, and they sent Barnabas to Antioch. [23]When he arrived and
saw the evidence of the grace of God, he
was glad and encouraged them all to remain true to the Lord with all their hearts.
[24]He was a good man, full of the Holy
Spirit and faith, and a great number of
people were brought to the Lord.

[25]Then Barnabas went to Tarsus to look
for Saul, [26]and when he found him, he
brought him to Antioch. So for a whole
year Barnabas and Saul met with the
church and taught great numbers of people. The disciples were called Christians
first at Antioch.

[27]During this time some prophets came
down from Jerusalem to Antioch. [28]One
of them, named Agabus, stood up and
through the Spirit predicted that a severe
famine would spread over the entire Roman world. (This happened during the
reign of Claudius.) [29]The disciples, each
according to his ability, decided to provide help for the brothers living in Judea.
[30]This they did, sending their gift to the elders by Barnabas and Saul.

[a] 16 Or *in*

PRAYER: MY RELATIONSHIP TO OTHERS

A VIRTUOUS wife is the crown of her husband, but she who causes shame is like decay in his bones. (Proverbs 12:4) . . . Who can find a virtuous wife? She is worth far more than jewels. The heart of her husband trusts in her so that he has no lack of gain. She brings him good, not harm, all the days of her life. (Proverbs 31:10–12)

***PAUSE** to review your relationships with others and to commit them to the Lord.*

YEAR 1 DAY 56

OT Psalms 13–14

Psalm 13

For the director of music. A psalm of David.

[1]How long, O LORD? Will you forget
me forever?
How long will you hide your face
from me?
[2]How long must I wrestle with my
thoughts
and every day have sorrow in my
heart?
How long will my enemy triumph
over me?

[3]Look on me and answer, O LORD my
God.

Give light to my eyes, or I will sleep
in death;
4 my enemy will say, "I have overcome
him,"
and my foes will rejoice when I fall.

5 But I trust in your unfailing love;
my heart rejoices in your salvation.
6 I will sing to the LORD,
for he has been good to me.

Psalm 14

For the director of music. Of David.

1 The fool[a] says in his heart,
"There is no God."
They are corrupt, their deeds are vile;
there is no one who does good.

2 The LORD looks down from heaven
on the sons of men
to see if there are any who
understand,
any who seek God.

3 All have turned aside,
they have together become corrupt;
there is no one who does good,
not even one.

4 Will evildoers never learn—
those who devour my people as
men eat bread
and who do not call on the LORD?
5 There they are, overwhelmed with
dread,
for God is present in the company
of the righteous.
6 You evildoers frustrate the plans of the
poor,
but the LORD is their refuge.

7 Oh, that salvation for Israel would
come out of Zion!
When the LORD restores the fortunes
of his people,
let Jacob rejoice and Israel be glad!

[a] *1* The Hebrew words rendered *fool* in Psalms denote one who is morally deficient.

PRAYER: THANKSGIVING

I WILL sing of Your mercies, Lord, forever; with my mouth I will make Your faithfulness known through all generations. I will declare that Your loving-kindness will be built up forever, that You will establish Your faithfulness in the heavens. And the heavens will praise Your wonders, O Lord, Your faithfulness also in the assembly of the holy ones. For who in the heavens can be compared with You? Who is like You among the children of the mighty? You are greatly feared in the council of the holy ones and more awesome than all who surround You. O Lord God of hosts, who is like You, O mighty Lord? Your faithfulness also surrounds You. (Psalm 89:1–2, 5–8)

PAUSE *to offer your own expressions of thanksgiving.*

NT Acts 12:1–19a

Peter's Miraculous Escape From Prison

12 It was about this time that King Herod
arrested some who belonged to the
church, intending to persecute them. 2 He
had James, the brother of John, put to
death with the sword. 3 When he saw that
this pleased the Jews, he proceeded to
seize Peter also. This happened during the
Feast of Unleavened Bread. 4 After arresting
him, he put him in prison, handing him
over to be guarded by four squads of four
soldiers each. Herod intended to bring
him out for public trial after the Passover.

5 So Peter was kept in prison, but the
church was earnestly praying to God for
him.

6 The night before Herod was to bring
him to trial, Peter was sleeping between
two soldiers, bound with two chains, and
sentries stood guard at the entrance. 7 Suddenly an angel of the Lord appeared and
a light shone in the cell. He struck Peter
on the side and woke him up. "Quick, get
up!" he said, and the chains fell off Peter's
wrists.

8 Then the angel said to him, "Put on

your clothes and sandals." And Peter did so. "Wrap your cloak around you and follow me," the angel told him. [9]Peter followed him out of the prison, but he had no idea that what the angel was doing was really happening; he thought he was seeing a vision. [10]They passed the first and second guards and came to the iron gate leading to the city. It opened for them by itself, and they went through it. When they had walked the length of one street, suddenly the angel left him.

[11]Then Peter came to himself and said, "Now I know without a doubt that the Lord sent his angel and rescued me from Herod's clutches and from everything the Jewish people were anticipating."

[12]When this had dawned on him, he went to the house of Mary the mother of John, also called Mark, where many people had gathered and were praying. [13]Peter knocked at the outer entrance, and a servant girl named Rhoda came to answer the door. [14]When she recognized Peter's voice, she was so overjoyed she ran back without opening it and exclaimed, "Peter is at the door!"

[15]"You're out of your mind," they told her. When she kept insisting that it was so, they said, "It must be his angel."

[16]But Peter kept on knocking, and when they opened the door and saw him, they were astonished. [17]Peter motioned with his hand for them to be quiet and described how the Lord had brought him out of prison. "Tell James and the brothers about this," he said, and then he left for another place.

[18]In the morning, there was no small commotion among the soldiers as to what had become of Peter. [19]After Herod had a thorough search made for him and did not find him, he cross-examined the guards and ordered that they be executed.

PRAYER: THE ATTRIBUTES OF GOD

YOUR loving-kindness, O Lord, reaches to the heavens, Your faithfulness to the skies. Your righteousness is like the mighty mountains; Your judgments are like the great deep. O Lord, You preserve people and beasts. How priceless is Your loving-kindness, O God! Both the high and low among people find refuge in the shadow of Your wings. For with You is the fountain of life; in Your light we see light. (Psalm 36:5–7, 9)

***PAUSE** to reflect on these affirmations about the person, powers and perfection of God.*

OT Exodus 9:1–35

YEAR 1 DAY 57

The Plague on Livestock

9 Then the LORD said to Moses, "Go to Pharaoh and say to him, 'This is what the LORD, the God of the Hebrews, says: "Let my people go, so that they may worship me." [2]If you refuse to let them go and continue to hold them back, [3]the hand of the LORD will bring a terrible plague on your livestock in the field—on your horses and donkeys and camels and on your cattle and sheep and goats. [4]But the LORD will make a distinction between the livestock of Israel and that of Egypt, so that no animal belonging to the Israelites will die.' "

[5]The LORD set a time and said, "Tomorrow the LORD will do this in the land." [6]And the next day the LORD did it: All the livestock of the Egyptians died, but not one animal belonging to the Israelites died. [7]Pharaoh sent men to investigate and found that not even one of the animals of the Israelites had died. Yet his heart was unyielding and he would not let the people go.

The Plague of Boils

[8]Then the LORD said to Moses and Aaron, "Take handfuls of soot from a furnace and have Moses toss it into the air in the

presence of Pharaoh. 9 It will become fine dust over the whole land of Egypt, and festering boils will break out on men and animals throughout the land."

10 So they took soot from a furnace and stood before Pharaoh. Moses tossed it into the air, and festering boils broke out on men and animals. 11 The magicians could not stand before Moses because of the boils that were on them and on all the Egyptians. 12 But the LORD hardened Pharaoh's heart and he would not listen to Moses and Aaron, just as the LORD had said to Moses.

The Plague of Hail

13 Then the LORD said to Moses, "Get up early in the morning, confront Pharaoh and say to him, 'This is what the LORD, the God of the Hebrews, says: Let my people go, so that they may worship me, 14 or this time I will send the full force of my plagues against you and against your officials and your people, so you may know that there is no one like me in all the earth. 15 For by now I could have stretched out my hand and struck you and your people with a plague that would have wiped you off the earth. 16 But I have raised you up[a] for this very purpose, that I might show you my power and that my name might be proclaimed in all the earth. 17 You still set yourself against my people and will not let them go. 18 Therefore, at this time tomorrow I will send the worst hailstorm that has ever fallen on Egypt, from the day it was founded till now. 19 Give an order now to bring your livestock and everything you have in the field to a place of shelter, because the hail will fall on every man and animal that has not been brought in and is still out in the field, and they will die.' "

20 Those officials of Pharaoh who feared the word of the LORD hurried to bring their slaves and their livestock inside. 21 But those who ignored the word of the LORD left their slaves and livestock in the field.

22 Then the LORD said to Moses, "Stretch out your hand toward the sky so that hail will fall all over Egypt—on men and animals and on everything growing in the fields of Egypt." 23 When Moses stretched out his staff toward the sky, the LORD sent thunder and hail, and lightning flashed down to the ground. So the LORD rained hail on the land of Egypt; 24 hail fell and lightning flashed back and forth. It was the worst storm in all the land of Egypt since it had become a nation. 25 Throughout Egypt hail struck everything in the fields—both men and animals; it beat down everything growing in the fields and stripped every tree. 26 The only place it did not hail was the land of Goshen, where the Israelites were.

27 Then Pharaoh summoned Moses and Aaron. "This time I have sinned," he said to them. "The LORD is in the right, and I and my people are in the wrong. 28 Pray to the LORD, for we have had enough thunder and hail. I will let you go; you don't have to stay any longer."

29 Moses replied, "When I have gone out of the city, I will spread out my hands in prayer to the LORD. The thunder will stop and there will be no more hail, so you may know that the earth is the LORD's. 30 But I know that you and your officials still do not fear the LORD God."

31 (The flax and barley were destroyed, since the barley had headed and the flax was in bloom. 32 The wheat and spelt, however, were not destroyed, because they ripen later.)

33 Then Moses left Pharaoh and went out of the city. He spread out his hands toward the LORD; the thunder and hail stopped, and the rain no longer poured down on the land. 34 When Pharaoh saw that the rain and hail and thunder had stopped, he sinned again: He and his officials hardened their hearts. 35 So Pharaoh's heart was hard and he would not let the Israelites go, just as the LORD had said through Moses.

[a] 16 Or *have spared you*

PRAYER: ADORATION

LORD, You have been our dwelling place throughout all generations. Before the mountains were born or You brought forth the earth and the world; from everlasting to everlasting You are God. You

turn people back into dust and say, "Return to dust." For a thousand years in Your sight are like yesterday when it passes by or like a watch in the night. (Psalm 90:1–4) . . . Lord Jesus Christ, You are the same yesterday, today, and forever. (Hebrews 13:8)

PAUSE *to express your thoughts of praise and worship.*

NT Acts 12:19b–13:12

Herod's Death

Then Herod went from Judea to Caesarea and stayed there a while. [20]He had been quarreling with the people of Tyre and Sidon; they now joined together and sought an audience with him. Having secured the support of Blastus, a trusted personal servant of the king, they asked for peace, because they depended on the king's country for their food supply.

[21]On the appointed day Herod, wearing his royal robes, sat on his throne and delivered a public address to the people. [22]They shouted, "This is the voice of a god, not of a man." [23]Immediately, because Herod did not give praise to God, an angel of the Lord struck him down, and he was eaten by worms and died.

[24]But the word of God continued to increase and spread.

[25]When Barnabas and Saul had finished their mission, they returned from[a] Jerusalem, taking with them John, also called Mark.

Barnabas and Saul Sent Off

13 In the church at Antioch there were prophets and teachers: Barnabas, Simeon called Niger, Lucius of Cyrene, Manaen (who had been brought up with Herod the tetrarch) and Saul. [2]While they were worshiping the Lord and fasting, the Holy Spirit said, "Set apart for me Barnabas and Saul for the work to which I have called them." [3]So after they had fasted and prayed, they placed their hands on them and sent them off.

On Cyprus

[4]The two of them, sent on their way by the Holy Spirit, went down to Seleucia and sailed from there to Cyprus. [5]When they arrived at Salamis, they proclaimed the word of God in the Jewish synagogues. John was with them as their helper.

[6]They traveled through the whole island until they came to Paphos. There they met a Jewish sorcerer and false prophet named Bar-Jesus, [7]who was an attendant of the proconsul, Sergius Paulus. The proconsul, an intelligent man, sent for Barnabas and Saul because he wanted to hear the word of God. [8]But Elymas the sorcerer (for that is what his name means) opposed them and tried to turn the proconsul from the faith. [9]Then Saul, who was also called Paul, filled with the Holy Spirit, looked straight at Elymas and said, [10]"You are a child of the devil and an enemy of everything that is right! You are full of all kinds of deceit and trickery. Will you never stop perverting the right ways of the Lord? [11]Now the hand of the Lord is against you. You are going to be blind, and for a time you will be unable to see the light of the sun."

Immediately mist and darkness came over him, and he groped about, seeking someone to lead him by the hand. [12]When the proconsul saw what had happened, he believed, for he was amazed at the teaching about the Lord.

[a] *25* Some manuscripts *to*

PRAYER: THE WORKS OF GOD

YOUR foolishness, O God, is wiser than human wisdom, and Your weakness is stronger than human strength. But You chose the foolish things of the world to shame the wise, and You chose the weak things of the world to shame the strong; the lowly things of this world and

the despised things You have chosen, and the things that are not, to nullify the things that are, so that no one may boast before You.
(1 Corinthians 1:25, 27–29)

TAKE *a moment to consider the greatness of God's wonderful works.*

YEAR 1 DAY 58

OT Exodus 10:1–29

The Plague of Locusts

10 Then the LORD said to Moses, "Go to
Pharaoh, for I have hardened his
heart and the hearts of his officials so that
I may perform these miraculous signs of
mine among them 2 that you may tell your
children and grandchildren how I dealt
harshly with the Egyptians and how I performed my signs among them, and that
you may know that I am the LORD."
3 So Moses and Aaron went to Pharaoh
and said to him, "This is what the LORD,
the God of the Hebrews, says: 'How long
will you refuse to humble yourself before
me? Let my people go, so that they may
worship me. 4 If you refuse to let them go,
I will bring locusts into your country tomorrow. 5 They will cover the face of the
ground so that it cannot be seen. They
will devour what little you have left after
the hail, including every tree that is growing in your fields. 6 They will fill your
houses and those of all your officials and
all the Egyptians—something neither
your fathers nor your forefathers have ever
seen from the day they settled in this land
till now.' " Then Moses turned and left
Pharaoh.
7 Pharaoh's officials said to him, "How
long will this man be a snare to us? Let
the people go, so that they may worship
the LORD their God. Do you not yet realize that Egypt is ruined?"
8 Then Moses and Aaron were brought
back to Pharaoh. "Go, worship the LORD
your God," he said. "But just who will be
going?"
9 Moses answered, "We will go with our
young and old, with our sons and daughters, and with our flocks and herds, because we are to celebrate a festival to the
LORD."
10 Pharaoh said, "The LORD be with
you—if I let you go, along with your
women and children! Clearly you are
bent on evil.[a] 11 No! Have only the men
go; and worship the LORD, since that's
what you have been asking for." Then Moses and Aaron were driven out of Pharaoh's presence.
12 And the LORD said to Moses, "Stretch
out your hand over Egypt so that locusts
will swarm over the land and devour
everything growing in the fields, everything left by the hail."
13 So Moses stretched out his staff over
Egypt, and the LORD made an east wind
blow across the land all that day and all
that night. By morning the wind had
brought the locusts; 14 they invaded all
Egypt and settled down in every area of
the country in great numbers. Never before had there been such a plague of locusts, nor will there ever be again. 15 They
covered all the ground until it was black.
They devoured all that was left after the
hail—everything growing in the fields and
the fruit on the trees. Nothing green remained on tree or plant in all the land of
Egypt.
16 Pharaoh quickly summoned Moses
and Aaron and said, "I have sinned
against the LORD your God and against
you. 17 Now forgive my sin once more and
pray to the LORD your God to take this
deadly plague away from me."
18 Moses then left Pharaoh and prayed
to the LORD. 19 And the LORD changed the
wind to a very strong west wind, which
caught up the locusts and carried them
into the Red Sea.[b] Not a locust was left
anywhere in Egypt. 20 But the LORD hardened Pharaoh's heart, and he would not
let the Israelites go.

The Plague of Darkness

21 Then the LORD said to Moses, "Stretch
out your hand toward the sky so that

[a] 10 Or *Be careful, trouble is in store for you!*
[b] 19 Hebrew *Yam Suph*; that is, Sea of Reeds

darkness will spread over Egypt—darkness that can be felt." 22So Moses stretched out his hand toward the sky, and total darkness covered all Egypt for three days. 23No one could see anyone else or leave his place for three days. Yet all the Israelites had light in the places where they lived.

24Then Pharaoh summoned Moses and said, "Go, worship the LORD. Even your women and children may go with you; only leave your flocks and herds behind."

25But Moses said, "You must allow us to have sacrifices and burnt offerings to present to the LORD our God. 26Our livestock too must go with us; not a hoof is to be left behind. We have to use some of them in worshiping the LORD our God, and until we get there we will not know what we are to use to worship the LORD."

27But the LORD hardened Pharaoh's heart, and he was not willing to let them go. 28Pharaoh said to Moses, "Get out of my sight! Make sure you do not appear before me again! The day you see my face you will die."

29"Just as you say," Moses replied, "I will never appear before you again."

PRAYER: CONFESSION

YOU, O God, fashion the hearts of all and understand all their works. (Psalm 33:15)

***ASK** the Spirit to search your heart and reveal any areas of unconfessed sin. Acknowledge these to the Lord and thank Him for His forgiveness.*

NT Acts 13:13-52

In Pisidian Antioch

13From Paphos, Paul and his companions sailed to Perga in Pamphylia, where John left them to return to Jerusalem. 14From Perga they went on to Pisidian Antioch. On the Sabbath they entered the synagogue and sat down. 15After the reading from the Law and the Prophets, the synagogue rulers sent word to them, saying, "Brothers, if you have a message of encouragement for the people, please speak."

16Standing up, Paul motioned with his hand and said: "Men of Israel and you Gentiles who worship God, listen to me! 17The God of the people of Israel chose our fathers; he made the people prosper during their stay in Egypt, with mighty power he led them out of that country, 18he endured their conduct[a] for about forty years in the desert, 19he overthrew seven nations in Canaan and gave their land to his people as their inheritance. 20All this took about 450 years.

"After this, God gave them judges until the time of Samuel the prophet. 21Then the people asked for a king, and he gave them Saul son of Kish, of the tribe of Benjamin, who ruled forty years. 22After removing Saul, he made David their king. He testified concerning him: 'I have found David son of Jesse a man after my own heart; he will do everything I want him to do.'

23"From this man's descendants God has brought to Israel the Savior Jesus, as he promised. 24Before the coming of Jesus, John preached repentance and baptism to all the people of Israel. 25As John was completing his work, he said: 'Who do you think I am? I am not that one. No, but he is coming after me, whose sandals I am not worthy to untie.'

26"Brothers, children of Abraham, and you God-fearing Gentiles, it is to us that this message of salvation has been sent. 27The people of Jerusalem and their rulers did not recognize Jesus, yet in condemning him they fulfilled the words of the prophets that are read every Sabbath. 28Though they found no proper ground for a death sentence, they asked Pilate to have him executed. 29When they had carried out all that was written about him, they took him down from the tree and laid him in a tomb. 30But God raised him from the dead, 31and for many days he was seen by those who had traveled with him from Galilee to Jerusalem. They are now his witnesses to our people.

32"We tell you the good news: What

[a] 18 Some manuscripts *and cared for them*

God promised our fathers 33he has fulfilled for us, their children, by raising up
Jesus. As it is written in the second Psalm:

" 'You are my Son;
today I have become your Father.[b]'[c]

34The fact that God raised him from the
dead, never to decay, is stated in these
words:

" 'I will give you the holy and sure
blessings promised to David.'[d]

35So it is stated elsewhere:

" 'You will not let your Holy One see
decay.'[e]

36"For when David had served God's
purpose in his own generation, he fell
asleep; he was buried with his fathers and
his body decayed. 37But the one whom
God raised from the dead did not see
decay.

38"Therefore, my brothers, I want you to
know that through Jesus the forgiveness
of sins is proclaimed to you. 39Through
him everyone who believes is justified
from everything you could not be justified
from by the law of Moses. 40Take care that
what the prophets have said does not happen to you:

41" 'Look, you scoffers,
wonder and perish,
for I am going to do something in
your days
that you would never believe,
even if someone told you.'[f]"

42As Paul and Barnabas were leaving the
synagogue, the people invited them to
speak further about these things on the
next Sabbath. 43When the congregation
was dismissed, many of the Jews and devout converts to Judaism followed Paul
and Barnabas, who talked with them and
urged them to continue in the grace of
God.

44On the next Sabbath almost the
whole city gathered to hear the word of
the Lord. 45When the Jews saw the crowds,
they were filled with jealousy and talked
abusively against what Paul was saying.

46Then Paul and Barnabas answered
them boldly: "We had to speak the word
of God to you first. Since you reject it and
do not consider yourselves worthy of eternal life, we now turn to the Gentiles. 47For
this is what the Lord has commanded us:

" 'I have made you[g] a light for the
Gentiles,
that you[g] may bring salvation to the
ends of the earth.'[h]"

48When the Gentiles heard this, they
were glad and honored the word of the
Lord; and all who were appointed for eternal life believed.

49The word of the Lord spread through
the whole region. 50But the Jews incited
the God-fearing women of high standing
and the leading men of the city. They
stirred up persecution against Paul and
Barnabas, and expelled them from their
region. 51So they shook the dust from
their feet in protest against them and
went to Iconium. 52And the disciples
were filled with joy and with the Holy
Spirit.

[b] 33 Or *have begotten you* [c] 33 Psalm 2:7
[d] 34 Isaiah 55:3 [e] 35 Psalm 16:10 [f] 41 Hab. 1:5
[g] 47 The Greek is singular. [h] 47 Isaiah 49:6

PRAYER: MY RELATIONSHIP TO GOD

HAVE mercy on me, O God, have mercy on me, for in You my soul takes refuge. I will take refuge in the shadow of Your wings until destruction passes by. I cry out to You, O God Most High, to You who fulfill Your purpose for me. (Psalm 57:1–2) . . . O Lord God, O Holy One of Israel, in repentance and rest is our salvation; in quietness and trust is our strength. (Isaiah 30:15)

***PAUSE** to thank God for the relationship that you enjoy with Him in Jesus Christ.*

YEAR 1 DAY 59

OT Exodus 11:1–12:51

The Plague on the Firstborn

11 Now the LORD had said to Moses, "I will bring one more plague on Pharaoh and on Egypt. After that, he will let you go from here, and when he does, he will drive you out completely. [2]Tell the people that men and women alike are to ask their neighbors for articles of silver and gold." [3](The LORD made the Egyptians favorably disposed toward the people, and Moses himself was highly regarded in Egypt by Pharaoh's officials and by the people.)

[4]So Moses said, "This is what the LORD says: 'About midnight I will go throughout Egypt. [5]Every firstborn son in Egypt will die, from the firstborn son of Pharaoh, who sits on the throne, to the firstborn son of the slave girl, who is at her hand mill, and all the firstborn of the cattle as well. [6]There will be loud wailing throughout Egypt—worse than there has ever been or ever will be again. [7]But among the Israelites not a dog will bark at any man or animal.' Then you will know that the LORD makes a distinction between Egypt and Israel. [8]All these officials of yours will come to me, bowing down before me and saying, 'Go, you and all the people who follow you!' After that I will leave." Then Moses, hot with anger, left Pharaoh.

[9]The LORD had said to Moses, "Pharaoh will refuse to listen to you—so that my wonders may be multiplied in Egypt." [10]Moses and Aaron performed all these wonders before Pharaoh, but the LORD hardened Pharaoh's heart, and he would not let the Israelites go out of his country.

The Passover

12 The LORD said to Moses and Aaron in Egypt, [2]"This month is to be for you the first month, the first month of your year. [3]Tell the whole community of Israel that on the tenth day of this month each man is to take a lamb[a] for his family, one for each household. [4]If any household is too small for a whole lamb, they must share one with their nearest neighbor, having taken into account the number of people there are. You are to determine the amount of lamb needed in accordance with what each person will eat. [5]The animals you choose must be year-old males without defect, and you may take them from the sheep or the goats. [6]Take care of them until the fourteenth day of the month, when all the people of the community of Israel must slaughter them at twilight. [7]Then they are to take some of the blood and put it on the sides and tops of the doorframes of the houses where they eat the lambs. [8]That same night they are to eat the meat roasted over the fire, along with bitter herbs, and bread made without yeast. [9]Do not eat the meat raw or cooked in water, but roast it over the fire—head, legs and inner parts. [10]Do not leave any of it till morning; if some is left till morning, you must burn it. [11]This is how you are to eat it: with your cloak tucked into your belt, your sandals on your feet and your staff in your hand. Eat it in haste; it is the LORD's Passover.

[12]"On that same night I will pass through Egypt and strike down every firstborn—both men and animals—and I will bring judgment on all the gods of Egypt. I am the LORD. [13]The blood will be a sign for you on the houses where you are; and when I see the blood, I will pass over you. No destructive plague will touch you when I strike Egypt.

[14]"This is a day you are to commemorate; for the generations to come you shall celebrate it as a festival to the LORD—a lasting ordinance. [15]For seven days you are to eat bread made without yeast. On the first day remove the yeast from your houses, for whoever eats anything with yeast in it from the first day through the seventh must be cut off from Israel. [16]On the first day hold a sacred assembly, and another one on the seventh day. Do no work at all on these days, except to prepare food for everyone to eat—that is all you may do.

[17]"Celebrate the Feast of Unleavened Bread, because it was on this very day that I brought your divisions out of Egypt. Celebrate this day as a lasting ordinance for the generations to come. [18]In the first

[a] 3 The Hebrew word can mean *lamb* or *kid*; also in verse 4.

month you are to eat bread made without yeast, from the evening of the fourteenth day until the evening of the twenty-first day. 19For seven days no yeast is to be found in your houses. And whoever eats anything with yeast in it must be cut off from the community of Israel, whether he is an alien or native-born. 20Eat nothing made with yeast. Wherever you live, you must eat unleavened bread."

21Then Moses summoned all the elders of Israel and said to them, "Go at once and select the animals for your families and slaughter the Passover lamb. 22Take a bunch of hyssop, dip it into the blood in the basin and put some of the blood on the top and on both sides of the doorframe. Not one of you shall go out the door of his house until morning. 23When the LORD goes through the land to strike down the Egyptians, he will see the blood on the top and sides of the doorframe and will pass over that doorway, and he will not permit the destroyer to enter your houses and strike you down.

24"Obey these instructions as a lasting ordinance for you and your descendants. 25When you enter the land that the LORD will give you as he promised, observe this ceremony. 26And when your children ask you, 'What does this ceremony mean to you?' 27then tell them, 'It is the Passover sacrifice to the LORD, who passed over the houses of the Israelites in Egypt and spared our homes when he struck down the Egyptians.' " Then the people bowed down and worshiped. 28The Israelites did just what the LORD commanded Moses and Aaron.

29At midnight the LORD struck down all the firstborn in Egypt, from the firstborn of Pharaoh, who sat on the throne, to the firstborn of the prisoner, who was in the dungeon, and the firstborn of all the livestock as well. 30Pharaoh and all his officials and all the Egyptians got up during the night, and there was loud wailing in Egypt, for there was not a house without someone dead.

The Exodus

31During the night Pharaoh summoned Moses and Aaron and said, "Up! Leave my people, you and the Israelites! Go, worship the LORD as you have requested. 32Take your flocks and herds, as you have said, and go. And also bless me."

33The Egyptians urged the people to hurry and leave the country. "For otherwise," they said, "we will all die!" 34So the people took their dough before the yeast was added, and carried it on their shoulders in kneading troughs wrapped in clothing. 35The Israelites did as Moses instructed and asked the Egyptians for articles of silver and gold and for clothing. 36The LORD had made the Egyptians favorably disposed toward the people, and they gave them what they asked for; so they plundered the Egyptians.

37The Israelites journeyed from Rameses to Succoth. There were about six hundred thousand men on foot, besides women and children. 38Many other people went up with them, as well as large droves of livestock, both flocks and herds. 39With the dough they had brought from Egypt, they baked cakes of unleavened bread. The dough was without yeast because they had been driven out of Egypt and did not have time to prepare food for themselves.

40Now the length of time the Israelite people lived in Egypt[b] was 430 years. 41At the end of the 430 years, to the very day, all the LORD's divisions left Egypt. 42Because the LORD kept vigil that night to bring them out of Egypt, on this night all the Israelites are to keep vigil to honor the LORD for the generations to come.

Passover Restrictions

43The LORD said to Moses and Aaron, "These are the regulations for the Passover:

"No foreigner is to eat of it. 44Any slave you have bought may eat of it after you have circumcised him, 45but a temporary resident and a hired worker may not eat of it.

46"It must be eaten inside one house; take none of the meat outside the house. Do not break any of the bones. 47The whole community of Israel must celebrate it.

48"An alien living among you who wants to celebrate the LORD's Passover must have all the males in his household circumcised; then he may take part like

[b] *40* Masoretic Text; Samaritan Pentateuch and Septuagint *Egypt and Canaan*

one born in the land. No uncircumcised male may eat of it. [49]The same law applies to the native-born and to the alien living among you."

[50]All the Israelites did just what the LORD had commanded Moses and Aaron. [51]And on that very day the LORD brought the Israelites out of Egypt by their divisions.

PRAYER: RENEWAL

***H**AS a nation changed its gods that were not gods? But Your people have exchanged their Glory for that which is worthless. By Your grace may I not forsake You, the fountain of living waters, to dig my own cisterns, broken cisterns that can hold no water. (Jeremiah 2:11, 13) . . . As one who shares in the heavenly calling, may I fix my thoughts on You, Jesus, the Apostle and High Priest of my confession. (Hebrews 3:1)*

__PAUSE__ to add your own prayers for personal renewal.

NT Acts 14:1-20

In Iconium

14 At Iconium Paul and Barnabas went as usual into the Jewish synagogue. There they spoke so effectively that a great number of Jews and Gentiles believed. [2]But the Jews who refused to believe stirred up the Gentiles and poisoned their minds against the brothers. [3]So Paul and Barnabas spent considerable time there, speaking boldly for the Lord, who confirmed the message of his grace by enabling them to do miraculous signs and wonders. [4]The people of the city were divided; some sided with the Jews, others with the apostles. [5]There was a plot afoot among the Gentiles and Jews, together with their leaders, to mistreat them and stone them. [6]But they found out about it and fled to the Lycaonian cities of Lystra and Derbe and to the surrounding country, [7]where they continued to preach the good news.

In Lystra and Derbe

[8]In Lystra there sat a man crippled in his feet, who was lame from birth and had never walked. [9]He listened to Paul as he was speaking. Paul looked directly at him, saw that he had faith to be healed [10]and called out, "Stand up on your feet!" At that, the man jumped up and began to walk.

[11]When the crowd saw what Paul had done, they shouted in the Lycaonian language, "The gods have come down to us in human form!" [12]Barnabas they called Zeus, and Paul they called Hermes because he was the chief speaker. [13]The priest of Zeus, whose temple was just outside the city, brought bulls and wreaths to the city gates because he and the crowd wanted to offer sacrifices to them.

[14]But when the apostles Barnabas and Paul heard of this, they tore their clothes and rushed out into the crowd, shouting: [15]"Men, why are you doing this? We too are only men, human like you. We are bringing you good news, telling you to turn from these worthless things to the living God, who made heaven and earth and sea and everything in them. [16]In the past, he let all nations go their own way. [17]Yet he has not left himself without testimony: He has shown kindness by giving you rain from heaven and crops in their seasons; he provides you with plenty of food and fills your hearts with joy." [18]Even with these words, they had difficulty keeping the crowd from sacrificing to them.

[19]Then some Jews came from Antioch and Iconium and won the crowd over. They stoned Paul and dragged him outside the city, thinking he was dead. [20]But after the disciples had gathered around him, he got up and went back into the city. The next day he and Barnabas left for Derbe.

PRAYER: THE CHARACTER I WANT TO CULTIVATE

YOU, O Lord, desire mercy, not sacrifice, and the knowledge of You more than burnt offerings. (Hosea 6:6) . . . Blessed are the merciful, for they shall obtain mercy. (Matthew 5:7)

***TAKE** a moment to ask the Lord for the grace to grow in godly character.*

YEAR 1 DAY 60

OT Exodus 13:1–22

Consecration of the Firstborn

13 The LORD said to Moses, [2]"Consecrate
to me every firstborn male. The first offspring of every womb among the Israelites
belongs to me, whether man or animal."
[3]Then Moses said to the people, "Commemorate this day, the day you came out
of Egypt, out of the land of slavery, because the LORD brought you out of it with
a mighty hand. Eat nothing containing
yeast. [4]Today, in the month of Abib, you
are leaving. [5]When the LORD brings you
into the land of the Canaanites, Hittites,
Amorites, Hivites and Jebusites—the land
he swore to your forefathers to give you,
a land flowing with milk and honey—you
are to observe this ceremony in this
month: [6]For seven days eat bread made
without yeast and on the seventh day
hold a festival to the LORD. [7]Eat unleavened bread during those seven days; nothing with yeast in it is to be seen among
you, nor shall any yeast be seen anywhere
within your borders. [8]On that day tell
your son, 'I do this because of what the
LORD did for me when I came out of
Egypt.' [9]This observance will be for you
like a sign on your hand and a reminder
on your forehead that the law of the LORD
is to be on your lips. For the LORD brought
you out of Egypt with his mighty hand.
[10]You must keep this ordinance at the appointed time year after year.
[11]"After the LORD brings you into the
land of the Canaanites and gives it to you,
as he promised on oath to you and your
forefathers, [12]you are to give over to the
LORD the first offspring of every womb. All
the firstborn males of your livestock belong to the LORD. [13]Redeem with a lamb
every firstborn donkey, but if you do not
redeem it, break its neck. Redeem every
firstborn among your sons.
[14]"In days to come, when your son asks
you, 'What does this mean?' say to him,
'With a mighty hand the LORD brought us
out of Egypt, out of the land of slavery.
[15]When Pharaoh stubbornly refused to let
us go, the LORD killed every firstborn in
Egypt, both man and animal. This is why
I sacrifice to the LORD the first male offspring of every womb and redeem each of
my firstborn sons.' [16]And it will be like a
sign on your hand and a symbol on your
forehead that the LORD brought us out of
Egypt with his mighty hand."

Crossing the Sea

[17]When Pharaoh let the people go, God
did not lead them on the road through
the Philistine country, though that was
shorter. For God said, "If they face war,
they might change their minds and return
to Egypt." [18]So God led the people around
by the desert road toward the Red Sea.[a]
The Israelites went up out of Egypt armed
for battle.
[19]Moses took the bones of Joseph with
him because Joseph had made the sons of
Israel swear an oath. He had said, "God
will surely come to your aid, and then you
must carry my bones up with you from
this place."[b]
[20]After leaving Succoth they camped at
Etham on the edge of the desert. [21]By day
the LORD went ahead of them in a pillar
of cloud to guide them on their way and
by night in a pillar of fire to give them
light, so that they could travel by day or
night. [22]Neither the pillar of cloud by day
nor the pillar of fire by night left its place
in front of the people.

[a] *18* Hebrew *Yam Suph;* that is, Sea of Reeds
[b] *19* See Gen. 50:25.

PRAYER: PETITION

MAY I be strong and courageous and careful to obey Your word; may I not turn from it to the right or to the left, that I may act wisely wherever I go. (Joshua 1:7)

***PAUSE** here to petition God for wisdom. Ask Him to develop your eternal perspective, to renew your mind with truth and to help you develop greater skill in each area of your life. Offer prayers regarding your activities for this day and any special concerns you may have.*

NT Acts 14:21–15:21

The Return to Antioch in Syria

21They preached the good news in that
city and won a large number of disciples.
Then they returned to Lystra, Iconium and
Antioch, 22strengthening the disciples and
encouraging them to remain true to the
faith. "We must go through many hardships to enter the kingdom of God," they
said. 23Paul and Barnabas appointed elders[a] for them in each church and, with
prayer and fasting, committed them to the
Lord, in whom they had put their trust.
24After going through Pisidia, they came
into Pamphylia, 25and when they had
preached the word in Perga, they went
down to Attalia.
26From Attalia they sailed back to Antioch, where they had been committed to
the grace of God for the work they had
now completed. 27On arriving there, they
gathered the church together and reported all that God had done through them
and how he had opened the door of faith
to the Gentiles. 28And they stayed there a
long time with the disciples.

The Council at Jerusalem

15 Some men came down from Judea to
Antioch and were teaching the brothers: "Unless you are circumcised, according to the custom taught by Moses, you
cannot be saved." 2This brought Paul and
Barnabas into sharp dispute and debate
with them. So Paul and Barnabas were appointed, along with some other believers,
to go up to Jerusalem to see the apostles
and elders about this question. 3The
church sent them on their way, and as
they traveled through Phoenicia and
Samaria, they told how the Gentiles had
been converted. This news made all the
brothers very glad. 4When they came to
Jerusalem, they were welcomed by the
church and the apostles and elders, to
whom they reported everything God had
done through them.
5Then some of the believers who belonged to the party of the Pharisees stood
up and said, "The Gentiles must be circumcised and required to obey the law of
Moses."
6The apostles and elders met to consider this question. 7After much discussion,
Peter got up and addressed them: "Brothers, you know that some time ago God
made a choice among you that the Gentiles
might hear from my lips the message of the
gospel and believe. 8God, who knows the
heart, showed that he accepted them by
giving the Holy Spirit to them, just as he
did to us. 9He made no distinction between us and them, for he purified their
hearts by faith. 10Now then, why do you try
to test God by putting on the necks of the
disciples a yoke that neither we nor our fathers have been able to bear? 11No! We believe it is through the grace of our Lord
Jesus that we are saved, just as they are."
12The whole assembly became silent as
they listened to Barnabas and Paul telling
about the miraculous signs and wonders
God had done among the Gentiles
through them. 13When they finished,
James spoke up: "Brothers, listen to me.
14Simon[b] has described to us how God at
first showed his concern by taking from
the Gentiles a people for himself. 15The
words of the prophets are in agreement
with this, as it is written:

16" 'After this I will return
   and rebuild David's fallen tent.
Its ruins I will rebuild,

[a] 23 Or *Barnabas ordained elders;* or *Barnabas had elders elected* [b] 14 Greek *Simeon,* a variant of *Simon;* that is, Peter

and I will restore it,
[17]that the remnant of men may seek the Lord,
and all the Gentiles who bear my name,
says the Lord, who does these things'[c]
[18] that have been known for ages.[d]

[19]"It is my judgment, therefore, that we
should not make it difficult for the Gentiles who are turning to God. [20]Instead we
should write to them, telling them to abstain from food polluted by idols, from
sexual immorality, from the meat of strangled animals and from blood. [21]For Moses has been preached in every city from
the earliest times and is read in the synagogues on every Sabbath."

[c] 17 Amos 9:11,12 [d] 17,18 Some manuscripts *things'— / [18]known to the Lord for ages is his work*

PRAYER: MY RELATIONSHIP TO OTHERS

I WILL honor my father and my mother. (Exodus 20:12; Deuteronomy 5:16) . . . The parents of the righteous will greatly rejoice, and those who beget a wise child will be glad. May my father and mother be glad; may she who gave me birth rejoice. (Proverbs 23:24–25)

***PAUSE** to review your relationships with others and to commit them to the Lord.*

YEAR 1 DAY 61

OT Exodus 14:1-31

14 Then the LORD said to Moses, [2]"Tell
the Israelites to turn back and encamp
near Pi Hahiroth, between Migdol and
the sea. They are to encamp by the sea, directly opposite Baal Zephon. [3]Pharaoh
will think, 'The Israelites are wandering
around the land in confusion, hemmed in
by the desert.' [4]And I will harden Pharaoh's heart, and he will pursue them. But
I will gain glory for myself through Pharaoh and all his army, and the Egyptians
will know that I am the LORD." So the Israelites did this.

[5]When the king of Egypt was told that
the people had fled, Pharaoh and his officials changed their minds about them
and said, "What have we done? We have
let the Israelites go and have lost their services!" [6]So he had his chariot made ready
and took his army with him. [7]He took six
hundred of the best chariots, along with
all the other chariots of Egypt, with officers over all of them. [8]The LORD hardened
the heart of Pharaoh king of Egypt, so that
he pursued the Israelites, who were
marching out boldly. [9]The Egyptians—all
Pharaoh's horses and chariots, horsemen[a]
and troops—pursued the Israelites and
overtook them as they camped by the sea
near Pi Hahiroth, opposite Baal Zephon.

[10]As Pharaoh approached, the Israelites
looked up, and there were the Egyptians,
marching after them. They were terrified
and cried out to the LORD. [11]They said to
Moses, "Was it because there were no
graves in Egypt that you brought us to the
desert to die? What have you done to us
by bringing us out of Egypt? [12]Didn't we
say to you in Egypt, 'Leave us alone; let us
serve the Egyptians'? It would have been
better for us to serve the Egyptians than to
die in the desert!"

[13]Moses answered the people, "Do not
be afraid. Stand firm and you will see the
deliverance the LORD will bring you today.
The Egyptians you see today you will never see again. [14]The LORD will fight for you;
you need only to be still."

[15]Then the LORD said to Moses, "Why
are you crying out to me? Tell the Israelites to move on. [16]Raise your staff and
stretch out your hand over the sea to divide the water so that the Israelites can go
through the sea on dry ground. [17]I will
harden the hearts of the Egyptians so that
they will go in after them. And I will gain
glory through Pharaoh and all his army,

[a] 9 Or *charioteers;* also in verses 17, 18, 23, 26 and 28

through his chariots and his horsemen.
18The Egyptians will know that I am the
LORD when I gain glory through Pharaoh,
his chariots and his horsemen."
19Then the angel of God, who had been
traveling in front of Israel's army, withdrew and went behind them. The pillar of
cloud also moved from in front and stood
behind them, 20coming between the armies of Egypt and Israel. Throughout the
night the cloud brought darkness to the
one side and light to the other side; so
neither went near the other all night long.
21Then Moses stretched out his hand
over the sea, and all that night the LORD
drove the sea back with a strong east wind
and turned it into dry land. The waters
were divided, 22and the Israelites went
through the sea on dry ground, with a
wall of water on their right and on their
left.
23The Egyptians pursued them, and all
Pharaoh's horses and chariots and horsemen followed them into the sea. 24During
the last watch of the night the LORD
looked down from the pillar of fire and
cloud at the Egyptian army and threw it
into confusion. 25He made the wheels of
their chariots come off[b] so that they had
difficulty driving. And the Egyptians said,
"Let's get away from the Israelites! The
LORD is fighting for them against Egypt."
26Then the LORD said to Moses, "Stretch
out your hand over the sea so that the waters may flow back over the Egyptians and
their chariots and horsemen." 27Moses
stretched out his hand over the sea, and
at daybreak the sea went back to its place.
The Egyptians were fleeing toward[c] it, and
the LORD swept them into the sea. 28The
water flowed back and covered the chariots and horsemen—the entire army of
Pharaoh that had followed the Israelites
into the sea. Not one of them survived.
29But the Israelites went through the sea
on dry ground, with a wall of water on
their right and on their left. 30That day the
LORD saved Israel from the hands of the
Egyptians, and Israel saw the Egyptians lying dead on the shore. 31And when the Israelites saw the great power the LORD displayed against the Egyptians, the people
feared the LORD and put their trust in him
and in Moses his servant.

[b] 25 Or *He jammed the wheels of their chariots* (see Samaritan Pentateuch, Septuagint and Syriac)
[c] 27 Or *from*

PRAYER: INTERCESSION

WE should bear with one another in love and make every effort to keep the unity of the Spirit in the bond of peace.
(Ephesians 4:2–3)

TAKE *a few moments to intercede on behalf of your immediate family and other relatives. Offer prayers for their spiritual, emotional and physical concerns.*

NT Acts 15:22–41

The Council's Letter to Gentile Believers

22Then the apostles and elders, with the
whole church, decided to choose some of
their own men and send them to Antioch
with Paul and Barnabas. They chose Judas
(called Barsabbas) and Silas, two men
who were leaders among the brothers.
23With them they sent the following letter:

The apostles and elders, your brothers,

To the Gentile believers in Antioch, Syria and Cilicia:

Greetings.

24We have heard that some went
out from us without our authorization and disturbed you, troubling
your minds by what they said. 25So
we all agreed to choose some men
and send them to you with our dear
friends Barnabas and Paul— 26men
who have risked their lives for the
name of our Lord Jesus Christ.
27Therefore we are sending Judas and
Silas to confirm by word of mouth
what we are writing. 28It seemed good

to the Holy Spirit and to us not to burden you with anything beyond the following requirements: [29]You are to abstain from food sacrificed to idols, from blood, from the meat of strangled animals and from sexual immorality. You will do well to avoid these things.

Farewell.

[30]The men were sent off and went down to Antioch, where they gathered the church together and delivered the letter.
[31]The people read it and were glad for its encouraging message. [32]Judas and Silas, who themselves were prophets, said much to encourage and strengthen the brothers.
[33]After spending some time there, they were sent off by the brothers with the blessing of peace to return to those who had sent them.[a] [35]But Paul and Barnabas remained in Antioch, where they and many others taught and preached the word of the Lord.

Disagreement Between Paul and Barnabas

[36]Some time later Paul said to Barnabas, "Let us go back and visit the brothers in all the towns where we preached the word of the Lord and see how they are doing."
[37]Barnabas wanted to take John, also called Mark, with them, [38]but Paul did not think it wise to take him, because he had deserted them in Pamphylia and had not continued with them in the work. [39]They had such a sharp disagreement that they parted company. Barnabas took Mark and sailed for Cyprus, [40]but Paul chose Silas and left, commended by the brothers to the grace of the Lord. [41]He went through Syria and Cilicia, strengthening the churches.

[a] 33 Some manuscripts *them,* [34]*but Silas decided to remain there*

PRAYER: THE ATTRIBUTES OF GOD

MY soul blesses You, O Lord my God, You are very great; You are clothed with splendor and majesty.

(Psalm 104:1)

***PAUSE** to reflect on these affirmations about the person, powers and perfection of God.*

YEAR 1 DAY 62

OT Exodus 15:1-27

The Song of Moses and Miriam

15 Then Moses and the Israelites sang this song to the LORD:

"I will sing to the LORD,
for he is highly exalted.
The horse and its rider
he has hurled into the sea.
[2]The LORD is my strength and my song;
he has become my salvation.
He is my God, and I will praise him,
my father's God, and I will exalt him.
[3]The LORD is a warrior;
the LORD is his name.
[4]Pharaoh's chariots and his army
he has hurled into the sea.
The best of Pharaoh's officers
are drowned in the Red Sea.[a]
[5]The deep waters have covered them;
they sank to the depths like a stone.
[6]"Your right hand, O LORD,
was majestic in power.
Your right hand, O LORD,
shattered the enemy.
[7]In the greatness of your majesty
you threw down those who opposed you.
You unleashed your burning anger;
it consumed them like stubble.
[8]By the blast of your nostrils
the waters piled up.
The surging waters stood firm like a wall;
the deep waters congealed in the heart of the sea.

[a] 4 Hebrew *Yam Suph*; that is, Sea of Reeds; also in verse 22

[9] "The enemy boasted,
'I will pursue, I will overtake them.
I will divide the spoils;
I will gorge myself on them.
I will draw my sword
and my hand will destroy them.'
[10] But you blew with your breath,
and the sea covered them.
They sank like lead
in the mighty waters.

[11] "Who among the gods is like you,
O LORD?
Who is like you—
majestic in holiness,
awesome in glory,
working wonders?
[12] You stretched out your right hand
and the earth swallowed them.

[13] "In your unfailing love you will lead
the people you have redeemed.
In your strength you will guide them
to your holy dwelling.
[14] The nations will hear and tremble;
anguish will grip the people of
Philistia.
[15] The chiefs of Edom will be terrified,
the leaders of Moab will be seized
with trembling,
the people[b] of Canaan will melt away;
[16] terror and dread will fall upon them.
By the power of your arm
they will be as still as a stone—
until your people pass by, O LORD,
until the people you bought[c] pass
by.
[17] You will bring them in and plant
them
on the mountain of your
inheritance—
the place, O LORD, you made for your
dwelling,
the sanctuary, O Lord, your hands
established.
[18] The LORD will reign
for ever and ever."

[19] When Pharaoh's horses, chariots and
horsemen[d] went into the sea, the LORD
brought the waters of the sea back over
them, but the Israelites walked through
the sea on dry ground. [20] Then Miriam the
prophetess, Aaron's sister, took a tambourine in her hand, and all the women
followed her, with tambourines and dancing. [21] Miriam sang to them:

"Sing to the LORD,
for he is highly exalted.
The horse and its rider
he has hurled into the sea."

The Waters of Marah and Elim

[22] Then Moses led Israel from the Red Sea
and they went into the Desert of Shur. For
three days they traveled in the desert without finding water. [23] When they came to Marah, they could not drink its water because
it was bitter. (That is why the place is called
Marah.[e]) [24] So the people grumbled against
Moses, saying, "What are we to drink?"
[25] Then Moses cried out to the LORD, and
the LORD showed him a piece of wood. He
threw it into the water, and the water became sweet.

There the LORD made a decree and a law
for them, and there he tested them. [26] He
said, "If you listen carefully to the voice of
the LORD your God and do what is right
in his eyes, if you pay attention to his
commands and keep all his decrees, I will
not bring on you any of the diseases I
brought on the Egyptians, for I am the
LORD, who heals you."

[27] Then they came to Elim, where there
were twelve springs and seventy palm trees,
and they camped there near the water.

[b] 15 Or *rulers* [c] 16 Or *created* [d] 19 Or *charioteers*
[e] 23 *Marah* means *bitter.*

PRAYER: AFFIRMATION

NAKED I came from my mother's womb, and naked I will depart. O Lord, You give and You take away; blessed be Your name, O Lord. (Job 1:21) . . . Godliness with contentment is great gain. For I brought nothing into the world, and I can take nothing out of it. But if I have food and clothing, with these I will be content. (1 Timothy 6:6–8)

PAUSE *to reflect on these Biblical affirmations.*

NT **Acts 16:1-40**

Timothy Joins Paul and Silas

16 He came to Derbe and then to Lystra,
where a disciple named Timothy
lived, whose mother was a Jewess and a
believer, but whose father was a Greek.
[2]The brothers at Lystra and Iconium spoke
well of him. [3]Paul wanted to take him
along on the journey, so he circumcised
him because of the Jews who lived in that
area, for they all knew that his father was
a Greek. [4]As they traveled from town to
town, they delivered the decisions
reached by the apostles and elders in Jerusalem for the people to obey. [5]So the
churches were strengthened in the faith
and grew daily in numbers.

Paul's Vision of the Man of Macedonia

[6]Paul and his companions traveled
throughout the region of Phrygia and Galatia, having been kept by the Holy Spirit
from preaching the word in the province
of Asia. [7]When they came to the border of
Mysia, they tried to enter Bithynia, but the
Spirit of Jesus would not allow them to.
[8]So they passed by Mysia and went down
to Troas. [9]During the night Paul had a vision of a man of Macedonia standing and
begging him, "Come over to Macedonia
and help us." [10]After Paul had seen the vision, we got ready at once to leave for
Macedonia, concluding that God had
called us to preach the gospel to them.

Lydia's Conversion in Philippi

[11]From Troas we put out to sea and
sailed straight for Samothrace, and the
next day on to Neapolis. [12]From there we
traveled to Philippi, a Roman colony and
the leading city of that district of Macedonia. And we stayed there several days.

[13]On the Sabbath we went outside the
city gate to the river, where we expected to
find a place of prayer. We sat down and
began to speak to the women who had
gathered there. [14]One of those listening
was a woman named Lydia, a dealer in
purple cloth from the city of Thyatira,
who was a worshiper of God. The Lord
opened her heart to respond to Paul's
message. [15]When she and the members of
her household were baptized, she invited
us to her home. "If you consider me a believer in the Lord," she said, "come and
stay at my house." And she persuaded us.

Paul and Silas in Prison

[16]Once when we were going to the place
of prayer, we were met by a slave girl who
had a spirit by which she predicted the future. She earned a great deal of money for
her owners by fortune-telling. [17]This girl
followed Paul and the rest of us, shouting,
"These men are servants of the Most High
God, who are telling you the way to be
saved." [18]She kept this up for many days.
Finally Paul became so troubled that he
turned around and said to the spirit, "In
the name of Jesus Christ I command you
to come out of her!" At that moment the
spirit left her.

[19]When the owners of the slave girl realized that their hope of making money
was gone, they seized Paul and Silas and
dragged them into the marketplace to face
the authorities. [20]They brought them before the magistrates and said, "These men
are Jews, and are throwing our city into an
uproar [21]by advocating customs unlawful
for us Romans to accept or practice."

[22]The crowd joined in the attack against
Paul and Silas, and the magistrates ordered them to be stripped and beaten.
[23]After they had been severely flogged,
they were thrown into prison, and the jailer was commanded to guard them carefully. [24]Upon receiving such orders, he put
them in the inner cell and fastened their
feet in the stocks.

[25]About midnight Paul and Silas were
praying and singing hymns to God, and
the other prisoners were listening to
them. [26]Suddenly there was such a violent
earthquake that the foundations of the
prison were shaken. At once all the prison
doors flew open, and everybody's chains
came loose. [27]The jailer woke up, and
when he saw the prison doors open, he
drew his sword and was about to kill himself because he thought the prisoners had
escaped. [28]But Paul shouted, "Don't harm
yourself! We are all here!"

[29]The jailer called for lights, rushed in
and fell trembling before Paul and Silas.
[30]He then brought them out and asked,
"Sirs, what must I do to be saved?"

[31]They replied, "Believe in the Lord Jesus,

and you will be saved—you and your
household." [32]Then they spoke the word of
the Lord to him and to all the others in his
house. [33]At that hour of the night the jailer
took them and washed their wounds; then
immediately he and all his family were
baptized. [34]The jailer brought them into his
house and set a meal before them; he was
filled with joy because he had come to believe in God—he and his whole family.

[35]When it was daylight, the magistrates
sent their officers to the jailer with the order: "Release those men." [36]The jailer told
Paul, "The magistrates have ordered that
you and Silas be released. Now you can
leave. Go in peace."

[37]But Paul said to the officers: "They beat us publicly without a trial, even though we are Roman citizens, and threw us into prison. And now do they want to get rid of us quietly? No! Let them come themselves and escort us out."

[38]The officers reported this to the magistrates, and when they heard that Paul
and Silas were Roman citizens, they were
alarmed. [39]They came to appease them
and escorted them from the prison, requesting them to leave the city. [40]After
Paul and Silas came out of the prison,
they went to Lydia's house, where they
met with the brothers and encouraged
them. Then they left.

PRAYER: THE WORKS OF GOD

O LORD, in six days You made the heavens and the earth, the sea, and all that is in them, and rested on the seventh day. Therefore You blessed the Sabbath day and made it holy. (Exodus 20:11) . . . You alone are the Lord. You made the heavens, even the heaven of heavens, and all their starry host, the earth and all that is on it, the seas and all that is in them. You give life to all that is in them, and the host of heaven worships You. (Nehemiah 9:6)

__TAKE__ a moment to consider the greatness of God's wonderful works.

YEAR 1 DAY 63

OT Psalms 15–16

Psalm 15

A psalm of David.

[1]LORD, who may dwell in your
sanctuary?
Who may live on your holy hill?

[2]He whose walk is blameless
and who does what is righteous,
who speaks the truth from his heart
[3] and has no slander on his tongue,
who does his neighbor no wrong
and casts no slur on his fellowman,
[4]who despises a vile man
but honors those who fear the LORD,
who keeps his oath
even when it hurts,
[5]who lends his money without usury
and does not accept a bribe against
the innocent.

He who does these things
will never be shaken.

Psalm 16

A *miktam*[a] of David.

[1]Keep me safe, O God,
for in you I take refuge.

[2]I said to the LORD, "You are my Lord;
apart from you I have no good
thing."
[3]As for the saints who are in the land,
they are the glorious ones in whom
is all my delight.[b]
[4]The sorrows of those will increase
who run after other gods.
I will not pour out their libations of
blood
or take up their names on my lips.

[5]LORD, you have assigned me my
portion and my cup;

[a]Title: Probably a literary or musical term [b]3 Or *As for the pagan priests who are in the land / and the nobles in whom all delight, I said:*

you have made my lot secure.
[6]The boundary lines have fallen for me
in pleasant places;
surely I have a delightful
inheritance.

[7]I will praise the LORD, who counsels
me;
even at night my heart instructs me.
[8]I have set the LORD always before me.
Because he is at my right hand,
I will not be shaken.

[9]Therefore my heart is glad and my
tongue rejoices;
my body also will rest secure,
[10]because you will not abandon me to
the grave,[c]
nor will you let your Holy One[d] see
decay.
[11]You have made[e] known to me the
path of life;
you will fill me with joy in your
presence,
with eternal pleasures at your right
hand.

[c] 10 Hebrew *Sheol* [d] 10 Or *your faithful one*
[e] 11 Or *You will make*

PRAYER: THANKSGIVING

I CALLED to You in my distress, O Lord, and You answered me. From the depths of the grave I called for help, and You heard my voice. (Jonah 2:2) . . . I will exult in You, O Lord; I will rejoice in You, the God of my salvation. You are my strength; You make my feet like the feet of a deer and enable me to go on the heights. (Habakkuk 3:18–19)

***PAUSE** to offer your own expressions of thanksgiving.*

NT Acts 17:1–15

In Thessalonica

17 When they had passed through Amphipolis and Apollonia, they came to
Thessalonica, where there was a Jewish
synagogue. [2]As his custom was, Paul
went into the synagogue, and on three
Sabbath days he reasoned with them
from the Scriptures, [3]explaining and
proving that the Christ[a] had to suffer and
rise from the dead. "This Jesus I am proclaiming to you is the Christ,[a]" he said.
[4]Some of the Jews were persuaded and
joined Paul and Silas, as did a large number of God-fearing Greeks and not a few
prominent women.
[5]But the Jews were jealous; so they
rounded up some bad characters from the
marketplace, formed a mob and started a
riot in the city. They rushed to Jason's house
in search of Paul and Silas in order to bring
them out to the crowd.[b] [6]But when they did
not find them, they dragged Jason and
some other brothers before the city officials, shouting: "These men who have
caused trouble all over the world have now
come here, [7]and Jason has welcomed them
into his house. They are all defying Caesar's
decrees, saying that there is another king,
one called Jesus." [8]When they heard this,
the crowd and the city officials were thrown
into turmoil. [9]Then they made Jason and
the others post bond and let them go.

In Berea

[10]As soon as it was night, the brothers
sent Paul and Silas away to Berea. On arriving there, they went to the Jewish synagogue. [11]Now the Bereans were of more
noble character than the Thessalonians,
for they received the message with great
eagerness and examined the Scriptures
every day to see if what Paul said was true.
[12]Many of the Jews believed, as did also a
number of prominent Greek women and
many Greek men.
[13]When the Jews in Thessalonica
learned that Paul was preaching the word
of God at Berea, they went there too, agitating the crowds and stirring them up.
[14]The brothers immediately sent Paul to
the coast, but Silas and Timothy stayed at
Berea. [15]The men who escorted Paul
brought him to Athens and then left with
instructions for Silas and Timothy to join
him as soon as possible.

[a] 3 Or *Messiah* [b] 5 Or *the assembly of the people*

PRAYER: MY RELATIONSHIP TO GOD

YOU, O Lord, are my shepherd; I shall not be in want. You make me lie down in green pastures; You lead me beside quiet waters; You restore my soul. You guide me in the paths of righteousness for Your name's sake. Even though I walk through the valley of the shadow of death, I will fear no evil, for You are with me. Your rod and Your staff, they comfort me. You prepare a table before me in the presence of my enemies. You anoint my head with oil; my cup overflows. Surely goodness and mercy will follow me all the days of my life, and I will dwell in Your house, O Lord, forever. (Psalm 23:1–6)

__PAUSE__ to thank God for the relationship that you enjoy with Him in Jesus Christ.

YEAR 1
DAY 64

OT Exodus 16:1-36

Manna and Quail

16 The whole Israelite community set out from Elim and came to the Desert of Sin, which is between Elim and Sinai, on the fifteenth day of the second month after they had come out of Egypt. 2In the desert the whole community grumbled against Moses and Aaron. 3The Israelites said to them, "If only we had died by the LORD's hand in Egypt! There we sat around pots of meat and ate all the food we wanted, but you have brought us out into this desert to starve this entire assembly to death."

4Then the LORD said to Moses, "I will rain down bread from heaven for you. The people are to go out each day and gather enough for that day. In this way I will test them and see whether they will follow my instructions. 5On the sixth day they are to prepare what they bring in, and that is to be twice as much as they gather on the other days."

6So Moses and Aaron said to all the Israelites, "In the evening you will know that it was the LORD who brought you out of Egypt, 7and in the morning you will see the glory of the LORD, because he has heard your grumbling against him. Who are we, that you should grumble against us?" 8Moses also said, "You will know that it was the LORD when he gives you meat to eat in the evening and all the bread you want in the morning, because he has heard your grumbling against him. Who are we? You are not grumbling against us, but against the LORD."

9Then Moses told Aaron, "Say to the entire Israelite community, 'Come before the LORD, for he has heard your grumbling.' "

10While Aaron was speaking to the whole Israelite community, they looked toward the desert, and there was the glory of the LORD appearing in the cloud.

11The LORD said to Moses, 12"I have heard the grumbling of the Israelites. Tell them, 'At twilight you will eat meat, and in the morning you will be filled with bread. Then you will know that I am the LORD your God.' "

13That evening quail came and covered the camp, and in the morning there was a layer of dew around the camp. 14When the dew was gone, thin flakes like frost on the ground appeared on the desert floor. 15When the Israelites saw it, they said to each other, "What is it?" For they did not know what it was.

Moses said to them, "It is the bread the LORD has given you to eat. 16This is what the LORD has commanded: 'Each one is to gather as much as he needs. Take an omer[a] for each person you have in your tent.' "

17The Israelites did as they were told; some gathered much, some little. 18And when they measured it by the omer, he who gathered much did not have too much, and he who gathered little did not have too little. Each one gathered as much as he needed.

[a] *16* That is, probably about 2 quarts (about 2 liters); also in verses 18, 32, 33 and 36

19 Then Moses said to them, "No one is
to keep any of it until morning."
20 However, some of them paid no attention to Moses; they kept part of it until morning, but it was full of maggots and
began to smell. So Moses was angry with
them.
21 Each morning everyone gathered as
much as he needed, and when the sun
grew hot, it melted away. 22 On the sixth
day, they gathered twice as much—two
omers[b] for each person—and the leaders
of the community came and reported this
to Moses. 23 He said to them, "This is what
the LORD commanded: 'Tomorrow is to be
a day of rest, a holy Sabbath to the LORD.
So bake what you want to bake and boil
what you want to boil. Save whatever is
left and keep it until morning.' "
24 So they saved it until morning, as Moses commanded, and it did not stink or
get maggots in it. 25 "Eat it today," Moses
said, "because today is a Sabbath to the
LORD. You will not find any of it on the
ground today. 26 Six days you are to gather
it, but on the seventh day, the Sabbath,
there will not be any."
27 Nevertheless, some of the people went
out on the seventh day to gather it, but
they found none. 28 Then the LORD said to
Moses, "How long will you[c] refuse to keep
my commands and my instructions?
29 Bear in mind that the LORD has given
you the Sabbath; that is why on the sixth
day he gives you bread for two days.
Everyone is to stay where he is on the seventh day; no one is to go out." 30 So the
people rested on the seventh day.
31 The people of Israel called the bread
manna.[d] It was white like coriander seed
and tasted like wafers made with honey.
32 Moses said, "This is what the LORD has
commanded: 'Take an omer of manna and
keep it for the generations to come, so they
can see the bread I gave you to eat in the
desert when I brought you out of Egypt.' "
33 So Moses said to Aaron, "Take a jar
and put an omer of manna in it. Then
place it before the LORD to be kept for the
generations to come."
34 As the LORD commanded Moses, Aaron put the manna in front of the Testimony, that it might be kept. 35 The Israelites ate manna forty years, until they came
to a land that was settled; they ate manna
until they reached the border of Canaan.
36 (An omer is one tenth of an ephah.)

[b] 22 That is, probably about 4 quarts (about 4.5 liters) [c] 28 The Hebrew is plural. [d] *31 Manna* means *What is it?* (see verse 15).

PRAYER: ADORATION

I WILL exalt You, my God and King; I will bless Your name for ever and ever. Every day I will bless You, and I will praise Your name for ever and ever. Great are You, Lord, and most worthy of praise; Your greatness is unsearchable. (Psalm 145:1–3) . . . Out of the north You come in golden splendor; with You is awesome majesty. You, the Almighty, are beyond our reach; You are exalted in power, and in Your justice and great righteousness You do not oppress. (Job 37:22–23)

PAUSE *to express your thoughts of praise and worship.*

NT Acts 17:16–34

In Athens

16 While Paul was waiting for them in
Athens, he was greatly distressed to see
that the city was full of idols. 17 So he reasoned in the synagogue with the Jews and
the God-fearing Greeks, as well as in the
marketplace day by day with those who
happened to be there. 18 A group of Epi-
curean and Stoic philosophers began to
dispute with him. Some of them asked,
"What is this babbler trying to say?" Others remarked, "He seems to be advocating
foreign gods." They said this because Paul
was preaching the good news about Jesus
and the resurrection. 19 Then they took
him and brought him to a meeting of the
Areopagus, where they said to him, "May
we know what this new teaching is that

you are presenting? [20]You are bringing some strange ideas to our ears, and we want to know what they mean." [21](All the Athenians and the foreigners who lived there spent their time doing nothing but talking about and listening to the latest ideas.)

[22]Paul then stood up in the meeting of the Areopagus and said: "Men of Athens! I see that in every way you are very religious. [23]For as I walked around and looked carefully at your objects of worship, I even found an altar with this inscription: TO AN UNKNOWN GOD. Now what you worship as something unknown I am going to proclaim to you.

[24]"The God who made the world and everything in it is the Lord of heaven and earth and does not live in temples built by hands. [25]And he is not served by human hands, as if he needed anything, because he himself gives all men life and breath and everything else. [26]From one man he made every nation of men, that they should inhabit the whole earth; and he determined the times set for them and the exact places where they should live. [27]God did this so that men would seek him and perhaps reach out for him and find him, though he is not far from each one of us. [28]'For in him we live and move and have our being.' As some of your own poets have said, 'We are his offspring.'

[29]"Therefore since we are God's offspring, we should not think that the divine being is like gold or silver or stone—an image made by man's design and skill. [30]In the past God overlooked such ignorance, but now he commands all people everywhere to repent. [31]For he has set a day when he will judge the world with justice by the man he has appointed. He has given proof of this to all men by raising him from the dead."

[32]When they heard about the resurrection of the dead, some of them sneered, but others said, "We want to hear you again on this subject." [33]At that, Paul left the Council. [34]A few men became followers of Paul and believed. Among them was Dionysius, a member of the Areopagus, also a woman named Damaris, and a number of others.

PRAYER: THE CHARACTER I WANT TO CULTIVATE

LORD, make me to know my end and what is the measure of my days; let me know how fleeting is my life. (Psalm 39:4) . . . Teach me to number my days, that I may gain a heart of wisdom. (Psalm 90:12)

***TAKE** a moment to ask the Lord for the grace to grow in godly character.*

YEAR 1 DAY 65

OT Exodus 17:1–18:27

Water From the Rock

17 The whole Israelite community set out from the Desert of Sin, traveling from place to place as the LORD commanded. They camped at Rephidim, but there was no water for the people to drink. [2]So they quarreled with Moses and said, "Give us water to drink."

Moses replied, "Why do you quarrel with me? Why do you put the LORD to the test?"

[3]But the people were thirsty for water there, and they grumbled against Moses. They said, "Why did you bring us up out of Egypt to make us and our children and livestock die of thirst?"

[4]Then Moses cried out to the LORD, "What am I to do with these people? They are almost ready to stone me."

[5]The LORD answered Moses, "Walk on ahead of the people. Take with you some of the elders of Israel and take in your hand the staff with which you struck the Nile, and go. [6]I will stand there before you by the rock at Horeb. Strike the rock, and water will come out of it for the people to drink." So Moses did this in the sight of the elders of Israel. [7]And he called the place Massah[a] and Meribah[b] because the Israelites quarreled and because they test-

[a] 7 *Massah* means *testing.* [b] 7 *Meribah* means *quarreling.*

ed the LORD saying, "Is the LORD among us or not?"

The Amalekites Defeated

8The Amalekites came and attacked the Israelites at Rephidim. 9Moses said to Joshua, "Choose some of our men and go out to fight the Amalekites. Tomorrow I will stand on top of the hill with the staff of God in my hands."

10So Joshua fought the Amalekites as Moses had ordered, and Moses, Aaron and Hur went to the top of the hill. 11As long as Moses held up his hands, the Israelites were winning, but whenever he lowered his hands, the Amalekites were winning. 12When Moses' hands grew tired, they took a stone and put it under him and he sat on it. Aaron and Hur held his hands up—one on one side, one on the other—so that his hands remained steady till sunset. 13So Joshua overcame the Amalekite army with the sword.

14Then the LORD said to Moses, "Write this on a scroll as something to be remembered and make sure that Joshua hears it, because I will completely blot out the memory of Amalek from under heaven."

15Moses built an altar and called it The LORD is my Banner. 16He said, "For hands were lifted up to the throne of the LORD. The[c] LORD will be at war against the Amalekites from generation to generation."

Jethro Visits Moses

18 Now Jethro, the priest of Midian and father-in-law of Moses, heard of everything God had done for Moses and for his people Israel, and how the LORD had brought Israel out of Egypt.

2After Moses had sent away his wife Zipporah, his father-in-law Jethro received her 3and her two sons. One son was named Gershom,[d] for Moses said, "I have become an alien in a foreign land"; 4and the other was named Eliezer,[e] for he said, "My father's God was my helper; he saved me from the sword of Pharaoh."

5Jethro, Moses' father-in-law, together with Moses' sons and wife, came to him in the desert, where he was camped near the mountain of God. 6Jethro had sent word to him, "I, your father-in-law Jethro, am coming to you with your wife and her two sons."

7So Moses went out to meet his father-in-law and bowed down and kissed him. They greeted each other and then went into the tent. 8Moses told his father-in-law about everything the LORD had done to Pharaoh and the Egyptians for Israel's sake and about all the hardships they had met along the way and how the LORD had saved them.

9Jethro was delighted to hear about all the good things the LORD had done for Israel in rescuing them from the hand of the Egyptians. 10He said, "Praise be to the LORD, who rescued you from the hand of the Egyptians and of Pharaoh, and who rescued the people from the hand of the Egyptians. 11Now I know that the LORD is greater than all other gods, for he did this to those who had treated Israel arrogantly." 12Then Jethro, Moses' father-in-law, brought a burnt offering and other sacrifices to God, and Aaron came with all the elders of Israel to eat bread with Moses' father-in-law in the presence of God.

13The next day Moses took his seat to serve as judge for the people, and they stood around him from morning till evening. 14When his father-in-law saw all that Moses was doing for the people, he said, "What is this you are doing for the people? Why do you alone sit as judge, while all these people stand around you from morning till evening?"

15Moses answered him, "Because the people come to me to seek God's will. 16Whenever they have a dispute, it is brought to me, and I decide between the parties and inform them of God's decrees and laws."

17Moses' father-in-law replied, "What you are doing is not good. 18You and these people who come to you will only wear yourselves out. The work is too heavy for you; you cannot handle it alone. 19Listen now to me and I will give you some advice, and may God be with you. You must be the people's representative before God and bring their disputes to him. 20Teach them the decrees and laws, and show them the way to live and the duties they are to perform. 21But select capable men from all the people—men who fear God, trustworthy men who hate dishonest gain—and appoint them as officials over

[c] 16 Or *"Because a hand was against the throne of the* LORD, *the* [d] 3 *Gershom* sounds like the Hebrew for *an alien there.* [e] 4 *Eliezer* means *my God is helper.*

thousands, hundreds, fifties and tens.
22Have them serve as judges for the people at all times, but have them bring every
difficult case to you; the simple cases they
can decide themselves. That will make
your load lighter, because they will share
it with you. 23If you do this and God so
commands, you will be able to stand the
strain, and all these people will go home
satisfied."
24Moses listened to his father-in-law
and did everything he said. 25He chose capable men from all Israel and made them
leaders of the people, officials over thousands, hundreds, fifties and tens. 26They
served as judges for the people at all
times. The difficult cases they brought to
Moses, but the simple ones they decided
themselves.
27Then Moses sent his father-in-law on
his way, and Jethro returned to his own
country.

PRAYER: CONFESSION

YOU, O God, will not always strive with us, nor will You harbor Your anger forever; You do not treat us as our sins deserve or repay us according to our iniquities. For as high as the heavens are above the earth, so great is Your love for those who fear You; As far as the east is from the west, so far have You removed our transgressions from us. As a father has compassion on his children, so You have compassion on those who fear You.

(Psalm 103:9–13)

***ASK** the Spirit to search your heart and reveal any areas of unconfessed sin. Acknowledge these to the Lord and thank Him for His forgiveness.*

NT Acts 18:1-28

In Corinth

18 After this, Paul left Athens and went to
Corinth. 2There he met a Jew named
Aquila, a native of Pontus, who had recently come from Italy with his wife Priscilla, because Claudius had ordered all the
Jews to leave Rome. Paul went to see them,
3and because he was a tentmaker as they
were, he stayed and worked with them.
4Every Sabbath he reasoned in the synagogue, trying to persuade Jews and Greeks.
5When Silas and Timothy came from
Macedonia, Paul devoted himself exclusively to preaching, testifying to the Jews
that Jesus was the Christ.[a] 6But when the
Jews opposed Paul and became abusive,
he shook out his clothes in protest and
said to them, "Your blood be on your own
heads! I am clear of my responsibility.
From now on I will go to the Gentiles."
7Then Paul left the synagogue and went
next door to the house of Titius Justus, a
worshiper of God. 8Crispus, the synagogue ruler, and his entire household believed in the Lord; and many of the Corinthians who heard him believed and
were baptized.
9One night the Lord spoke to Paul in a
vision: "Do not be afraid; keep on speaking, do not be silent. 10For I am with you,
and no one is going to attack and harm
you, because I have many people in this
city." 11So Paul stayed for a year and a half,
teaching them the word of God.
12While Gallio was proconsul of Achaia, the Jews made a united attack on Paul
and brought him into court. 13"This
man," they charged, "is persuading the
people to worship God in ways contrary
to the law."
14Just as Paul was about to speak, Gallio said to the Jews, "If you Jews were
making a complaint about some misdemeanor or serious crime, it would be reasonable for me to listen to you. 15But since
it involves questions about words and
names and your own law—settle the matter yourselves. I will not be a judge of such
things." 16So he had them ejected from
the court. 17Then they all turned on Sosthenes the synagogue ruler and beat him
in front of the court. But Gallio showed
no concern whatever.

[a] 5 Or *Messiah;* also in verse 28

Priscilla, Aquila and Apollos

18 Paul stayed on in Corinth for some
time. Then he left the brothers and sailed
for Syria, accompanied by Priscilla and
Aquila. Before he sailed, he had his hair
cut off at Cenchrea because of a vow he
had taken. 19 They arrived at Ephesus,
where Paul left Priscilla and Aquila. He
himself went into the synagogue and reasoned with the Jews. 20 When they asked
him to spend more time with them, he
declined. 21 But as he left, he promised, "I
will come back if it is God's will." Then
he set sail from Ephesus. 22 When he landed at Caesarea, he went up and greeted
the church and then went down to Antioch.

23 After spending some time in Antioch,
Paul set out from there and traveled from
place to place throughout the region of
Galatia and Phrygia, strengthening all the
disciples.

24 Meanwhile a Jew named Apollos, a native of Alexandria, came to Ephesus. He
was a learned man, with a thorough
knowledge of the Scriptures. 25 He had
been instructed in the way of the Lord, and
he spoke with great fervor[b] and taught
about Jesus accurately, though he knew
only the baptism of John. 26 He began to
speak boldly in the synagogue. When
Priscilla and Aquila heard him, they invited him to their home and explained to
him the way of God more adequately.

27 When Apollos wanted to go to Achaia, the brothers encouraged him and
wrote to the disciples there to welcome
him. On arriving, he was a great help to
those who by grace had believed. 28 For he
vigorously refuted the Jews in public debate, proving from the Scriptures that
Jesus was the Christ.

[b] 25 Or *with fervor in the Spirit*

PRAYER: MY RELATIONSHIP TO OTHERS

SINCE we were called into fellowship with You, Lord Jesus Christ, all of us should agree with one another, so that there may be no divisions among us, and that we may be perfectly joined together in the same mind and in the same judgment. (1 Corinthians 1:9–10) . . . There is neither Jew nor Greek, there is neither slave nor free, there is neither male nor female, for we are all one in You, Christ Jesus. (Galatians 3:28)

PAUSE *to review your relationships with others and to commit them to the Lord.*

YEAR 1 DAY 66

OT Exodus 19:1-25

At Mount Sinai

19 In the third month after the Israelites
left Egypt—on the very day—they
came to the Desert of Sinai. 2 After they set
out from Rephidim, they entered the
Desert of Sinai, and Israel camped there
in the desert in front of the mountain.

3 Then Moses went up to God, and the
LORD called to him from the mountain
and said, "This is what you are to say to
the house of Jacob and what you are to
tell the people of Israel: 4 'You yourselves
have seen what I did to Egypt, and how I
carried you on eagles' wings and brought
you to myself. 5 Now if you obey me fully
and keep my covenant, then out of all nations you will be my treasured possession.
Although the whole earth is mine, 6 you[a]
will be for me a kingdom of priests and a
holy nation.' These are the words you are
to speak to the Israelites."

7 So Moses went back and summoned
the elders of the people and set before
them all the words the LORD had commanded him to speak. 8 The people all responded together, "We will do everything
the LORD has said." So Moses brought
their answer back to the LORD.

9 The LORD said to Moses, "I am going

[a] 5,6 Or *possession, for the whole earth is mine.* 6 *You*

to come to you in a dense cloud, so that the people will hear me speaking with you and will always put their trust in you." Then Moses told the LORD what the people had said.

10 And the LORD said to Moses, "Go to the people and consecrate them today and tomorrow. Have them wash their clothes 11 and be ready by the third day, because on that day the LORD will come down on Mount Sinai in the sight of all the people. 12 Put limits for the people around the mountain and tell them, 'Be careful that you do not go up the mountain or touch the foot of it. Whoever touches the mountain shall surely be put to death. 13 He shall surely be stoned or shot with arrows; not a hand is to be laid on him. Whether man or animal, he shall not be permitted to live.' Only when the ram's horn sounds a long blast may they go up to the mountain."

14 After Moses had gone down the mountain to the people, he consecrated them, and they washed their clothes. 15 Then he said to the people, "Prepare yourselves for the third day. Abstain from sexual relations."

16 On the morning of the third day there was thunder and lightning, with a thick cloud over the mountain, and a very loud trumpet blast. Everyone in the camp trembled. 17 Then Moses led the people out of the camp to meet with God, and they stood at the foot of the mountain. 18 Mount Sinai was covered with smoke, because the LORD descended on it in fire. The smoke billowed up from it like smoke from a furnace, the whole mountain[b] trembled violently, 19 and the sound of the trumpet grew louder and louder. Then Moses spoke and the voice of God answered him.[c]

20 The LORD descended to the top of Mount Sinai and called Moses to the top of the mountain. So Moses went up 21 and the LORD said to him, "Go down and warn the people so they do not force their way through to see the LORD and many of them perish. 22 Even the priests, who approach the LORD, must consecrate themselves, or the LORD will break out against them."

23 Moses said to the LORD, "The people cannot come up Mount Sinai, because you yourself warned us, 'Put limits around the mountain and set it apart as holy.' "

24 The LORD replied, "Go down and bring Aaron up with you. But the priests and the people must not force their way through to come up to the LORD, or he will break out against them."

25 So Moses went down to the people and told them.

[b] 18 Most Hebrew manuscripts; a few Hebrew manuscripts and Septuagint *all the people* [c] 19 Or *and God answered him with thunder*

PRAYER: RENEWAL

MAY I have respect for You, Lord, and serve You faithfully. May I do it with all my heart. (2 Chronicles 19:9) . . . May I meditate on Your precepts and consider Your ways. May I delight in Your statutes, and not forget Your word. Deal bountifully with Your servant, that I may live and keep Your word. Open my eyes that I may see wonderful things from Your law. (Psalm 119:15–18)

PAUSE *to add your own prayers for personal renewal.*

NT Acts 19:1–22

Paul in Ephesus

19 While Apollos was at Corinth, Paul took the road through the interior and arrived at Ephesus. There he found some disciples 2 and asked them, "Did you receive the Holy Spirit when[a] you believed?"

They answered, "No, we have not even heard that there is a Holy Spirit."

3 So Paul asked, "Then what baptism did you receive?"

"John's baptism," they replied.

[a] 2 Or *after*

4Paul said, "John's baptism was a baptism of repentance. He told the people to
believe in the one coming after him, that
is, in Jesus." 5On hearing this, they were
baptized into[b] the name of the Lord Jesus.
6When Paul placed his hands on them,
the Holy Spirit came on them, and they
spoke in tongues[c] and prophesied. 7There
were about twelve men in all.
8Paul entered the synagogue and spoke
boldly there for three months, arguing
persuasively about the kingdom of God.
9But some of them became obstinate;
they refused to believe and publicly maligned the Way. So Paul left them. He
took the disciples with him and had discussions daily in the lecture hall of Tyrannus. 10This went on for two years, so
that all the Jews and Greeks who lived in
the province of Asia heard the word of
the Lord.
11God did extraordinary miracles
through Paul, 12so that even handker-
chiefs and aprons that had touched him
were taken to the sick, and their illnesses
were cured and the evil spirits left them.
13Some Jews who went around driving
out evil spirits tried to invoke the name of
the Lord Jesus over those who were demon-possessed. They would say, "In the
name of Jesus, whom Paul preaches, I
command you to come out." 14Seven sons
of Sceva, a Jewish chief priest, were doing
this. 15⌞One day⌟ the evil spirit answered
them, "Jesus I know, and I know about
Paul, but who are you?" 16Then the man
who had the evil spirit jumped on them
and overpowered them all. He gave them
such a beating that they ran out of the
house naked and bleeding.
17When this became known to the Jews
and Greeks living in Ephesus, they were all
seized with fear, and the name of the Lord
Jesus was held in high honor. 18Many of
those who believed now came and openly confessed their evil deeds. 19A number
who had practiced sorcery brought their
scrolls together and burned them publicly.
When they calculated the value of the
scrolls, the total came to fifty thousand
drachmas.[d] 20In this way the word of the
Lord spread widely and grew in power.
21After all this had happened, Paul decided to go to Jerusalem, passing through
Macedonia and Achaia. "After I have been
there," he said, "I must visit Rome also."
22He sent two of his helpers, Timothy and
Erastus, to Macedonia, while he stayed in
the province of Asia a little longer.

[b] 5 Or *in* [c] 6 Or *other languages* [d] 19 A drachma was a silver coin worth about a day's wages.

PRAYER: THE ATTRIBUTES OF GOD

YOU, Lord, do not see as people see. People look at my outward appearance, but You look at my heart. (1 Samuel 16:7) . . . Lord, You have searched me and You know me. You know when I sit down and when I rise up; You understand my thoughts from afar. You scrutinize my path and my lying down and are acquainted with all my ways. Before a word is on my tongue, O Lord, You know it completely. (Psalm 139:1–4)

***PAUSE** to reflect on these affirmations about the person, powers and perfection of God.*

YEAR 1 DAY 67

OT Proverbs 3

Further Benefits of Wisdom

3 My son, do not forget my teaching,
but keep my commands in your
heart,
2 for they will prolong your life many
years
and bring you prosperity.
3 Let love and faithfulness never leave
you;
bind them around your neck,
write them on the tablet of your
heart.

[4]Then you will win favor and a good name
in the sight of God and man.

[5]Trust in the LORD with all your heart
and lean not on your own understanding;
[6]in all your ways acknowledge him,
and he will make your paths straight.[a]

[7]Do not be wise in your own eyes;
fear the LORD and shun evil.
[8]This will bring health to your body
and nourishment to your bones.

[9]Honor the LORD with your wealth,
with the firstfruits of all your crops;
[10]then your barns will be filled to overflowing,
and your vats will brim over with new wine.

[11]My son, do not despise the LORD's discipline
and do not resent his rebuke,
[12]because the LORD disciplines those he loves,
as a father[b] the son he delights in.

[13]Blessed is the man who finds wisdom,
the man who gains understanding,
[14]for she is more profitable than silver
and yields better returns than gold.
[15]She is more precious than rubies;
nothing you desire can compare with her.
[16]Long life is in her right hand;
in her left hand are riches and honor.
[17]Her ways are pleasant ways,
and all her paths are peace.
[18]She is a tree of life to those who embrace her;
those who lay hold of her will be blessed.

[19]By wisdom the LORD laid the earth's foundations,
by understanding he set the heavens in place;
[20]by his knowledge the deeps were divided,
and the clouds let drop the dew.

[21]My son, preserve sound judgment and discernment,
do not let them out of your sight;
[22]they will be life for you,
an ornament to grace your neck.
[23]Then you will go on your way in safety,
and your foot will not stumble;
[24]when you lie down, you will not be afraid;
when you lie down, your sleep will be sweet.
[25]Have no fear of sudden disaster
or of the ruin that overtakes the wicked,
[26]for the LORD will be your confidence
and will keep your foot from being snared.

[27]Do not withhold good from those who deserve it,
when it is in your power to act.
[28]Do not say to your neighbor,
"Come back later; I'll give it tomorrow"—
when you now have it with you.

[29]Do not plot harm against your neighbor,
who lives trustfully near you.
[30]Do not accuse a man for no reason—
when he has done you no harm.

[31]Do not envy a violent man
or choose any of his ways,
[32]for the LORD detests a perverse man
but takes the upright into his confidence.

[33]The LORD's curse is on the house of the wicked,
but he blesses the home of the righteous.
[34]He mocks proud mockers
but gives grace to the humble.
[35]The wise inherit honor,
but fools he holds up to shame.

[a] 6 Or *will direct your paths* [b] 12 Hebrew; Septuagint / *and he punishes*

PRAYER: PETITION

O LORD, may I not enter the path of the wicked or walk in the way of evil people. (Proverbs 4:14)

__PAUSE__ here to petition God for spiritual insight so that you might have understanding of His Word. Ask for insight into your identity in Jesus Christ: that you might know who you are, what direction your life should take and what His purpose for your life is. Offer prayers regarding your activities for this day and any special concerns you may have.

NT Acts 19:23-41

The Riot in Ephesus

[23]About that time there arose a great disturbance about the Way. [24]A silversmith named Demetrius, who made silver shrines of Artemis, brought in no little business for the craftsmen. [25]He called them together, along with the workmen in related trades, and said: "Men, you know we receive a good income from this business. [26]And you see and hear how this fellow Paul has convinced and led astray large numbers of people here in Ephesus and in practically the whole province of Asia. He says that man-made gods are no gods at all. [27]There is danger not only that our trade will lose its good name, but also that the temple of the great goddess Artemis will be discredited, and the goddess herself, who is worshiped throughout the province of Asia and the world, will be robbed of her divine majesty."

[28]When they heard this, they were furious and began shouting: "Great is Artemis of the Ephesians!" [29]Soon the whole city was in an uproar. The people seized Gaius and Aristarchus, Paul's traveling companions from Macedonia, and rushed as one man into the theater. [30]Paul wanted to appear before the crowd, but the disciples would not let him. [31]Even some of the officials of the province, friends of Paul, sent him a message begging him not to venture into the theater.

[32]The assembly was in confusion: Some were shouting one thing, some another. Most of the people did not even know why they were there. [33]The Jews pushed Alexander to the front, and some of the crowd shouted instructions to him. He motioned for silence in order to make a defense before the people. [34]But when they realized he was a Jew, they all shouted in unison for about two hours: "Great is Artemis of the Ephesians!"

[35]The city clerk quieted the crowd and said: "Men of Ephesus, doesn't all the world know that the city of Ephesus is the guardian of the temple of the great Artemis and of her image, which fell from heaven? [36]Therefore, since these facts are undeniable, you ought to be quiet and not do anything rash. [37]You have brought these men here, though they have neither robbed temples nor blasphemed our goddess. [38]If, then, Demetrius and his fellow craftsmen have a grievance against anybody, the courts are open and there are proconsuls. They can press charges. [39]If there is anything further you want to bring up, it must be settled in a legal assembly. [40]As it is, we are in danger of being charged with rioting because of today's events. In that case we would not be able to account for this commotion, since there is no reason for it." [41]After he had said this, he dismissed the assembly.

PRAYER: THE WORKS OF GOD

FATHER, I rejoice that Your Son Jesus has fulfilled Your promises:
A Shoot will come forth from the stump of Jesse;
from his roots a Branch will bear fruit. The Spirit of the Lord will rest on Him—
the Spirit of wisdom and of understanding, the Spirit of counsel and of power,
the Spirit of knowledge and of the fear of the Lord—and He will delight in

the fear of the Lord. He will not judge by what He sees with His eyes, or decide by what He hears with His ears, but with righteousness He will judge the poor and decide with fairness for the meek of the earth. And He will strike the earth with the rod of His mouth; with the breath of His lips He will slay the wicked. Righteousness will be His belt and faithfulness the sash around His waist.
(Isaiah 11:1–5)

TAKE *a moment to consider the greatness of God's wonderful works.*

YEAR 1
DAY 68

OT Exodus 20:1–26

The Ten Commandments

20 And God spoke all these words:

2 "I am the LORD your God, who
brought you out of Egypt, out of
the land of slavery.
3 "You shall have no other gods before[a] me.
4 "You shall not make for yourself an
idol in the form of anything in
heaven above or on the earth beneath or in the waters below.
5 You shall not bow down to
them or worship them; for I, the
LORD your God, am a jealous
God, punishing the children for
the sin of the fathers to the third
and fourth generation of those
who hate me, 6 but showing love
to a thousand ⌊generations⌋ of
those who love me and keep my
commandments.
7 "You shall not misuse the name of
the LORD your God, for the LORD
will not hold anyone guiltless
who misuses his name.
8 "Remember the Sabbath day by keeping it holy. 9 Six days you shall labor and do all your work, 10 but
the seventh day is a Sabbath to
the LORD your God. On it you
shall not do any work, neither
you, nor your son or daughter,
nor your manservant or maidservant, nor your animals, nor
the alien within your gates. 11 For
in six days the LORD made the
heavens and the earth, the sea,
and all that is in them, but he
rested on the seventh day. Therefore the LORD blessed the Sabbath day and made it holy.
12 "Honor your father and your mother, so that you may live long in
the land the LORD your God is
giving you.
13 "You shall not murder.
14 "You shall not commit adultery.
15 "You shall not steal.
16 "You shall not give false testimony
against your neighbor.
17 "You shall not covet your neighbor's
house. You shall not covet your
neighbor's wife, or his manservant or maidservant, his ox or
donkey, or anything that belongs to your neighbor."

18 When the people saw the thunder and
lightning and heard the trumpet and saw
the mountain in smoke, they trembled
with fear. They stayed at a distance 19 and
said to Moses, "Speak to us yourself and
we will listen. But do not have God speak
to us or we will die."
20 Moses said to the people, "Do not be
afraid. God has come to test you, so that
the fear of God will be with you to keep
you from sinning."
21 The people remained at a distance,
while Moses approached the thick darkness where God was.

Idols and Altars

22 Then the LORD said to Moses, "Tell the
Israelites this: 'You have seen for yourselves that I have spoken to you from
heaven: 23 Do not make any gods to be
alongside me; do not make for yourselves
gods of silver or gods of gold.
24 " 'Make an altar of earth for me and
sacrifice on it your burnt offerings and fellowship offerings,[b] your sheep and goats

[a] 3 Or *besides* [b] 24 Traditionally *peace offerings*

and your cattle. Wherever I cause my name to be honored, I will come to you and bless you. 25If you make an altar of stones for me, do not build it with dressed stones, for you will defile it if you use a tool on it. 26And do not go up to my altar on steps, lest your nakedness be exposed on it.'

PRAYER: INTERCESSION

HOLY Spirit, help me in my weakness, for I do not know what I ought to pray for, but You Yourself intercede for me with groans that words cannot express. And He who searches my heart knows Your mind, because You intercede for the saints according to the Father's will.

(Romans 8:26–27)

***TAKE** a few moments to intercede on behalf of other believers, such as your personal friends, those in ministry and those who are oppressed and in need.*

NT Acts 20:1-38

Through Macedonia and Greece

20 When the uproar had ended, Paul sent for the disciples and, after encouraging them, said good-by and set out for Macedonia. 2He traveled through that area, speaking many words of encouragement to the people, and finally arrived in Greece, 3where he stayed three months. Because the Jews made a plot against him just as he was about to sail for Syria, he decided to go back through Macedonia. 4He was accompanied by Sopater son of Pyrrhus from Berea, Aristarchus and Secundus from Thessalonica, Gaius from Derbe, Timothy also, and Tychicus and Trophimus from the province of Asia. 5These men went on ahead and waited for us at Troas. 6But we sailed from Philippi after the Feast of Unleavened Bread, and five days later joined the others at Troas, where we stayed seven days.

Eutychus Raised From the Dead at Troas

7On the first day of the week we came together to break bread. Paul spoke to the people and, because he intended to leave the next day, kept on talking until midnight. 8There were many lamps in the upstairs room where we were meeting. 9Seated in a window was a young man named Eutychus, who was sinking into a deep sleep as Paul talked on and on. When he was sound asleep, he fell to the ground from the third story and was picked up dead. 10Paul went down, threw himself on the young man and put his arms around him. "Don't be alarmed," he said. "He's alive!" 11Then he went upstairs again and broke bread and ate. After talking until daylight, he left. 12The people took the young man home alive and were greatly comforted.

Paul's Farewell to the Ephesian Elders

13We went on ahead to the ship and sailed for Assos, where we were going to take Paul aboard. He had made this arrangement because he was going there on foot. 14When he met us at Assos, we took him aboard and went on to Mitylene. 15The next day we set sail from there and arrived off Kios. The day after that we crossed over to Samos, and on the following day arrived at Miletus. 16Paul had decided to sail past Ephesus to avoid spending time in the province of Asia, for he was in a hurry to reach Jerusalem, if possible, by the day of Pentecost.

17From Miletus, Paul sent to Ephesus for the elders of the church. 18When they arrived, he said to them: "You know how I lived the whole time I was with you, from the first day I came into the province of Asia. 19I served the Lord with great humility and with tears, although I was severely tested by the plots of the Jews. 20You know that I have not hesitated to preach anything that would be helpful to you but have taught you publicly and from house to house. 21I have declared to both Jews and Greeks that they must turn to God in repentance and have faith in our Lord Jesus.

22 "And now, compelled by the Spirit, I
am going to Jerusalem, not knowing what
will happen to me there. 23 I only know
that in every city the Holy Spirit warns me
that prison and hardships are facing me.
24 However, I consider my life worth nothing to me, if only I may finish the race and
complete the task the Lord Jesus has giv-
en me—the task of testifying to the gospel
of God's grace.
25 "Now I know that none of you among
whom I have gone about preaching the
kingdom will ever see me again. 26 Therefore, I declare to you today that I am innocent of the blood of all men. 27 For I
have not hesitated to proclaim to you the
whole will of God. 28 Keep watch over
yourselves and all the flock of which the
Holy Spirit has made you overseers.[a] Be
shepherds of the church of God,[b] which
he bought with his own blood. 29 I know
that after I leave, savage wolves will come
in among you and will not spare the flock.
30 Even from your own number men will
arise and distort the truth in order to draw
away disciples after them. 31 So be on your
guard! Remember that for three years I
never stopped warning each of you night
and day with tears.
32 "Now I commit you to God and to the
word of his grace, which can build you up
and give you an inheritance among all
those who are sanctified. 33 I have not coveted anyone's silver or gold or clothing.
34 You yourselves know that these hands of
mine have supplied my own needs and the
needs of my companions. 35 In everything I
did, I showed you that by this kind of hard
work we must help the weak, remembering the words the Lord Jesus himself said:
'It is more blessed to give than to receive.' "
36 When he had said this, he knelt down
with all of them and prayed. 37 They all
wept as they embraced him and kissed
him. 38 What grieved them most was his
statement that they would never see his
face again. Then they accompanied him
to the ship.

[a] 28 Traditionally *bishops* [b] 28 Many manuscripts *of the Lord*

PRAYER: MY RELATIONSHIP TO GOD

YOU, O Lord my God, want me to fear You, to walk in all Your ways, to love You and to serve You, O Lord my God, with all my heart and with all my soul. (Deuteronomy 10:12) . . . I want to know You, O God, and serve You with a whole heart and with a willing mind; for You search my heart and understand every motive behind my thoughts. (1 Chronicles 28:9)

***PAUSE** to thank God for the relationship that you enjoy with Him in Jesus Christ.*

YEAR 1
DAY 69

OT **Exodus 21:1-36**

21 "These are the laws you are to set before them:

Hebrew Servants

2 "If you buy a Hebrew servant, he is to
serve you for six years. But in the seventh
year, he shall go free, without paying anything. 3 If he comes alone, he is to go free
alone; but if he has a wife when he comes,
she is to go with him. 4 If his master gives
him a wife and she bears him sons or
daughters, the woman and her children
shall belong to her master, and only the
man shall go free.
5 "But if the servant declares, 'I love my
master and my wife and children and do
not want to go free,' 6 then his master must
take him before the judges.[a] He shall take
him to the door or the doorpost and
pierce his ear with an awl. Then he will be
his servant for life.
7 "If a man sells his daughter as a servant, she is not to go free as menservants
do. 8 If she does not please the master who

[a] 6 Or *before God*

has selected her for himself,[b] he must let her be redeemed. He has no right to sell her to foreigners, because he has broken faith with her. 9If he selects her for his son, he must grant her the rights of a daughter. 10If he marries another woman, he must not deprive the first one of her food, clothing and marital rights. 11If he does not provide her with these three things, she is to go free, without any payment of money.

Personal Injuries

12"Anyone who strikes a man and kills him shall surely be put to death. 13However, if he does not do it intentionally, but God lets it happen, he is to flee to a place I will designate. 14But if a man schemes and kills another man deliberately, take him away from my altar and put him to death.

15"Anyone who attacks[c] his father or his mother must be put to death.

16"Anyone who kidnaps another and either sells him or still has him when he is caught must be put to death.

17"Anyone who curses his father or mother must be put to death.

18"If men quarrel and one hits the other with a stone or with his fist[d] and he does not die but is confined to bed, 19the one who struck the blow will not be held responsible if the other gets up and walks around outside with his staff; however, he must pay the injured man for the loss of his time and see that he is completely healed.

20"If a man beats his male or female slave with a rod and the slave dies as a direct result, he must be punished, 21but he is not to be punished if the slave gets up after a day or two, since the slave is his property.

22"If men who are fighting hit a pregnant woman and she gives birth prematurely[e] but there is no serious injury, the offender must be fined whatever the woman's husband demands and the court allows. 23But if there is serious injury, you are to take life for life, 24eye for eye, tooth for tooth, hand for hand, foot for foot, 25burn for burn, wound for wound, bruise for bruise.

26"If a man hits a manservant or maidservant in the eye and destroys it, he must let the servant go free to compensate for the eye. 27And if he knocks out the tooth of a manservant or maidservant, he must let the servant go free to compensate for the tooth.

28"If a bull gores a man or a woman to death, the bull must be stoned to death, and its meat must not be eaten. But the owner of the bull will not be held responsible. 29If, however, the bull has had the habit of goring and the owner has been warned but has not kept it penned up and it kills a man or woman, the bull must be stoned and the owner also must be put to death. 30However, if payment is demanded of him, he may redeem his life by paying whatever is demanded. 31This law also applies if the bull gores a son or daughter. 32If the bull gores a male or female slave, the owner must pay thirty shekels[f] of silver to the master of the slave, and the bull must be stoned.

33"If a man uncovers a pit or digs one and fails to cover it and an ox or a donkey falls into it, 34the owner of the pit must pay for the loss; he must pay its owner, and the dead animal will be his.

35"If a man's bull injures the bull of another and it dies, they are to sell the live one and divide both the money and the dead animal equally. 36However, if it was known that the bull had the habit of goring, yet the owner did not keep it penned up, the owner must pay, animal for animal, and the dead animal will be his.

[b] 8 Or *master so that he does not choose her* [c] 15 Or *kills* [d] 18 Or *with a tool* [e] 22 Or *she has a miscarriage* [f] 32 That is, about 12 ounces (about 0.3 kilogram)

PRAYER: AFFIRMATION

JESUS, You rejoiced in the Holy Spirit and said, "I praise You, Father, Lord of heaven and earth, because You have hidden these things from the wise and learned, and revealed them to little children. Yes, Father, for this was well pleasing in Your sight. All things have been

delivered to Me by You, Father. No one knows the Son except You, and no one knows You except the Son and those to whom the Son chooses to reveal You." (Matthew 11:25–27; Luke 10:21–22)

***PAUSE** to reflect on these Biblical affirmations.*

NT Acts 21:1–36

On to Jerusalem

21 After we had torn ourselves away from them, we put out to sea and sailed straight to Cos. The next day we went to Rhodes and from there to Patara. 2We found a ship crossing over to Phoenicia, went on board and set sail. 3After sighting Cyprus and passing to the south of it, we sailed on to Syria. We landed at Tyre, where our ship was to unload its cargo. 4Finding the disciples there, we stayed with them seven days. Through the Spirit they urged Paul not to go on to Jerusalem. 5But when our time was up, we left and continued on our way. All the disciples and their wives and children accompanied us out of the city, and there on the beach we knelt to pray. 6After saying good-by to each other, we went aboard the ship, and they returned home.

7We continued our voyage from Tyre and landed at Ptolemais, where we greeted the brothers and stayed with them for a day. 8Leaving the next day, we reached Caesarea and stayed at the house of Philip the evangelist, one of the Seven. 9He had four unmarried daughters who prophesied.

10After we had been there a number of days, a prophet named Agabus came down from Judea. 11Coming over to us, he took Paul's belt, tied his own hands and feet with it and said, "The Holy Spirit says, 'In this way the Jews of Jerusalem will bind the owner of this belt and will hand him over to the Gentiles.' "

12When we heard this, we and the people there pleaded with Paul not to go up to Jerusalem. 13Then Paul answered, "Why are you weeping and breaking my heart? I am ready not only to be bound, but also to die in Jerusalem for the name of the Lord Jesus." 14When he would not be dissuaded, we gave up and said, "The Lord's will be done."

15After this, we got ready and went up to Jerusalem. 16Some of the disciples from Caesarea accompanied us and brought us to the home of Mnason, where we were to stay. He was a man from Cyprus and one of the early disciples.

Paul's Arrival at Jerusalem

17When we arrived at Jerusalem, the brothers received us warmly. 18The next day Paul and the rest of us went to see James, and all the elders were present. 19Paul greeted them and reported in detail what God had done among the Gentiles through his ministry.

20When they heard this, they praised God. Then they said to Paul: "You see, brother, how many thousands of Jews have believed, and all of them are zealous for the law. 21They have been informed that you teach all the Jews who live among the Gentiles to turn away from Moses, telling them not to circumcise their children or live according to our customs. 22What shall we do? They will certainly hear that you have come, 23so do what we tell you. There are four men with us who have made a vow. 24Take these men, join in their purification rites and pay their expenses, so that they can have their heads shaved. Then everybody will know there is no truth in these reports about you, but that you yourself are living in obedience to the law. 25As for the Gentile believers, we have written to them our decision that they should abstain from food sacrificed to idols, from blood, from the meat of strangled animals and from sexual immorality."

26The next day Paul took the men and purified himself along with them. Then he went to the temple to give notice of the date when the days of purification would end and the offering would be made for each of them.

Paul Arrested

27When the seven days were nearly over, some Jews from the province of Asia saw Paul at the temple. They stirred up the whole crowd and seized him, 28shouting,

"Men of Israel, help us! This is the man
who teaches all men everywhere against
our people and our law and this place.
And besides, he has brought Greeks into
the temple area and defiled this holy
place." [29](They had previously seen
Trophimus the Ephesian in the city with
Paul and assumed that Paul had brought
him into the temple area.)
[30]The whole city was aroused, and the
people came running from all directions.
Seizing Paul, they dragged him from the
temple, and immediately the gates were
shut. [31]While they were trying to kill him,
news reached the commander of the Roman troops that the whole city of Jerusalem was in an uproar. [32]He at once took
some officers and soldiers and ran down
to the crowd. When the rioters saw the
commander and his soldiers, they
stopped beating Paul.
[33]The commander came up and arrested him and ordered him to be bound
with two chains. Then he asked who he
was and what he had done. [34]Some in the
crowd shouted one thing and some another, and since the commander could
not get at the truth because of the uproar,
he ordered that Paul be taken into the barracks. [35]When Paul reached the steps, the
violence of the mob was so great he had
to be carried by the soldiers. [36]The crowd
that followed kept shouting, "Away with
him!"

PRAYER: THE CHARACTER I WANT TO CULTIVATE

I KNOW, my God, that You test my heart and are pleased with integrity. (1 Chronicles 29:17) . . . May those who hope in You not be ashamed because of me, O Lord God of hosts. May those who seek You not be dishonored because of me, O God of Israel. (Psalm 69:6)

__TAKE__ a moment to ask the Lord for the grace to grow in godly character.

OT Psalm 17

Psalm 17

A prayer of David.

[1]Hear, O LORD, my righteous plea;
listen to my cry.
Give ear to my prayer—
it does not rise from deceitful lips.
[2]May my vindication come from you;
may your eyes see what is right.

[3]Though you probe my heart and
examine me at night,
though you test me, you will find
nothing;
I have resolved that my mouth will
not sin.
[4]As for the deeds of men—
by the word of your lips
I have kept myself
from the ways of the violent.
[5]My steps have held to your paths;
my feet have not slipped.

[6]I call on you, O God, for you will
answer me;
give ear to me and hear my prayer.
[7]Show the wonder of your great love,
you who save by your right hand
those who take refuge in you from
their foes.
[8]Keep me as the apple of your eye;
hide me in the shadow of your
wings
[9]from the wicked who assail me,
from my mortal enemies who
surround me.

[10]They close up their callous hearts,
and their mouths speak with
arrogance.
[11]They have tracked me down, they now
surround me,
with eyes alert, to throw me to the
ground.
[12]They are like a lion hungry for prey,
like a great lion crouching in
cover.

[13]Rise up, O LORD, confront them, bring
them down;

rescue me from the wicked by your
sword.
[14] O LORD, by your hand save me from
such men,
from men of this world whose
reward is in this life.

You still the hunger of those you
cherish;
their sons have plenty,
and they store up wealth for their
children.
[15] And I—in righteousness I will see
your face;
when I awake, I will be satisfied
with seeing your likeness.

PRAYER: THANKSGIVING

AS the Israelites rejoiced, may I also rejoice in You, O God: Rejoice greatly, O daughter of Zion! Shout, O daughter of Jerusalem! Behold, Your King is coming to you; He is just and having salvation, humble and riding on a donkey, on a colt, the foal of a donkey. He will proclaim peace to the nations; His dominion will extend from sea to sea and from the River to the ends of the earth. (Zechariah 9:9–10)

***PAUSE** to offer your own expressions of thanksgiving.*

NT Acts 21:37–22:21

Paul Speaks to the Crowd

[37] As the soldiers were about to take Paul
into the barracks, he asked the commander, "May I say something to you?"
"Do you speak Greek?" he replied.
[38] "Aren't you the Egyptian who started a
revolt and led four thousand terrorists out
into the desert some time ago?"
[39] Paul answered, "I am a Jew, from Tarsus in Cilicia, a citizen of no ordinary city.
Please let me speak to the people."
[40] Having received the commander's
permission, Paul stood on the steps and
motioned to the crowd. When they were
all silent, he said to them in Aramaic[a]:
22 [1] "Brothers and fathers, listen now to
my defense."
[2] When they heard him speak to them
in Aramaic, they became very quiet.
Then Paul said: [3] "I am a Jew, born in
Tarsus of Cilicia, but brought up in this
city. Under Gamaliel I was thoroughly
trained in the law of our fathers and was
just as zealous for God as any of you are
today. [4] I persecuted the followers of this
Way to their death, arresting both men
and women and throwing them into
prison, [5] as also the high priest and all the
Council can testify. I even obtained letters
from them to their brothers in Damascus,
and went there to bring these people as
prisoners to Jerusalem to be punished.
[6] "About noon as I came near Damascus, suddenly a bright light from heaven
flashed around me. [7] I fell to the ground
and heard a voice say to me, 'Saul! Saul!
Why do you persecute me?'
[8] " 'Who are you, Lord?' I asked.
" 'I am Jesus of Nazareth, whom you are
persecuting,' he replied. [9] My companions
saw the light, but they did not understand
the voice of him who was speaking to me.
[10] " 'What shall I do, Lord?' I asked.
" 'Get up,' the Lord said, 'and go into
Damascus. There you will be told all that
you have been assigned to do.' [11] My companions led me by the hand into Damascus, because the brilliance of the light had
blinded me.
[12] "A man named Ananias came to see
me. He was a devout observer of the law
and highly respected by all the Jews living
there. [13] He stood beside me and said,
'Brother Saul, receive your sight!' And at
that very moment I was able to see him.
[14] "Then he said: 'The God of our fathers
has chosen you to know his will and to
see the Righteous One and to hear words
from his mouth. [15] You will be his witness
to all men of what you have seen and
heard. [16] And now what are you waiting
for? Get up, be baptized and wash your
sins away, calling on his name.'

[a] *40* Or possibly *Hebrew;* also in 22:2

[17] "When I returned to Jerusalem and
was praying at the temple, I fell into a
trance [18] and saw the Lord speaking.
'Quick!' he said to me. 'Leave Jerusalem
immediately, because they will not accept
your testimony about me.'
[19] " 'Lord,' I replied, 'these men know
that I went from one synagogue to another to imprison and beat those who believe in you. [20] And when the blood of
your martyr[b] Stephen was shed, I stood
there giving my approval and guarding
the clothes of those who were killing
him.'
[21] "Then the Lord said to me, 'Go; I will
send you far away to the Gentiles.' "

[b] 20 Or *witness*

PRAYER: MY RELATIONSHIP TO OTHERS

If I acknowledge You before others, Lord Jesus, You will also acknowledge me before Your Father in heaven. But if I deny You before others, You will also deny me before Your Father in heaven. (Matthew 10:32–33) . . . I will not be ashamed to testify about You, O Lord, but I will join with others in suffering for the gospel according to Your power, O God. (2 Timothy 1:8)

PAUSE *to review your relationships with others and to commit them to the Lord.*

YEAR 1 DAY 71

OT Exodus 22:1–31

Protection of Property

22 "If a man steals an ox or a sheep and
slaughters it or sells it, he must pay
back five head of cattle for the ox and four
sheep for the sheep.
[2] "If a thief is caught breaking in and is
struck so that he dies, the defender is not
guilty of bloodshed; [3] but if it happens[a] after sunrise, he is guilty of bloodshed.
"A thief must certainly make restitution,
but if he has nothing, he must be sold to
pay for his theft.
[4] "If the stolen animal is found alive in
his possession—whether ox or donkey or
sheep—he must pay back double.
[5] "If a man grazes his livestock in a field
or vineyard and lets them stray and they
graze in another man's field, he must
make restitution from the best of his own
field or vineyard.
[6] "If a fire breaks out and spreads into
thornbushes so that it burns shocks of
grain or standing grain or the whole field,
the one who started the fire must make
restitution.
[7] "If a man gives his neighbor silver or
goods for safekeeping and they are stolen
from the neighbor's house, the thief, if he
is caught, must pay back double. [8] But if
the thief is not found, the owner of the
house must appear before the judges[b] to
determine whether he has laid his hands
on the other man's property. [9] In all cases
of illegal possession of an ox, a donkey, a
sheep, a garment, or any other lost property about which somebody says, 'This is
mine,' both parties are to bring their cases
before the judges. The one whom the
judges declare[c] guilty must pay back double to his neighbor.
[10] "If a man gives a donkey, an ox, a
sheep or any other animal to his neighbor
for safekeeping and it dies or is injured or
is taken away while no one is looking,
[11] the issue between them will be settled by
the taking of an oath before the LORD that
the neighbor did not lay hands on the
other person's property. The owner is to
accept this, and no restitution is required.
[12] But if the animal was stolen from the
neighbor, he must make restitution to the
owner. [13] If it was torn to pieces by a wild
animal, he shall bring in the remains as
evidence and he will not be required to
pay for the torn animal.
[14] "If a man borrows an animal from his

[a] 3 Or *if he strikes him* [b] 8 Or *before God;* also in verse 9 [c] 9 Or *whom God declares*

neighbor and it is injured or dies while
the owner is not present, he must make
restitution. 15 But if the owner is with the
animal, the borrower will not have to pay.
If the animal was hired, the money paid
for the hire covers the loss.

Social Responsibility

16 "If a man seduces a virgin who is not
pledged to be married and sleeps with
her, he must pay the bride-price, and she
shall be his wife. 17 If her father absolutely refuses to give her to him, he must still
pay the bride-price for virgins.
18 "Do not allow a sorceress to live.
19 "Anyone who has sexual relations
with an animal must be put to death.
20 "Whoever sacrifices to any god other
than the LORD must be destroyed.[d]
21 "Do not mistreat an alien or oppress
him, for you were aliens in Egypt.
22 "Do not take advantage of a widow or
an orphan. 23 If you do and they cry out to
me, I will certainly hear their cry. 24 My
anger will be aroused, and I will kill you
with the sword; your wives will become
widows and your children fatherless.
25 "If you lend money to one of my people among you who is needy, do not be
like a moneylender; charge him no interest.[e] 26 If you take your neighbor's cloak as
a pledge, return it to him by sunset, 27 because his cloak is the only covering he has
for his body. What else will he sleep in?
When he cries out to me, I will hear, for I
am compassionate.
28 "Do not blaspheme God[f] or curse the
ruler of your people.
29 "Do not hold back offerings from
your granaries or your vats.[g]
"You must give me the firstborn of your
sons. 30 Do the same with your cattle and
your sheep. Let them stay with their
mothers for seven days, but give them to
me on the eighth day.
31 "You are to be my holy people. So do
not eat the meat of an animal torn by wild
beasts; throw it to the dogs.

[d] 20 The Hebrew term refers to the irrevocable giving over of things or persons to the LORD, often by totally destroying them. [e] 25 Or *excessive interest* [f] 28 Or *Do not revile the judges* [g] 29 The meaning of the Hebrew for this phrase is uncertain.

PRAYER: ADORATION

O LORD, God of Israel, there is no God like You in heaven above or on earth below; You keep Your covenant of mercy with Your servants who walk before You with all their heart. (1 Kings 8:23; 2 Chronicles 6:14) . . . I know that You alone, whose name is the Lord, are the Most High over all the earth. (Psalm 83:18)

PAUSE *to express your thoughts of praise and worship.*

NT Acts 22:22–23:11

Paul the Roman Citizen

22 The crowd listened to Paul until he
said this. Then they raised their voices and
shouted, "Rid the earth of him! He's not
fit to live!"
23 As they were shouting and throwing off
their cloaks and flinging dust into the air,
24 the commander ordered Paul to be taken
into the barracks. He directed that he be
flogged and questioned in order to find out
why the people were shouting at him like
this. 25 As they stretched him out to flog
him, Paul said to the centurion standing
there, "Is it legal for you to flog a Roman
citizen who hasn't even been found guilty?"
26 When the centurion heard this, he
went to the commander and reported it.
"What are you going to do?" he asked.
"This man is a Roman citizen."
27 The commander went to Paul and
asked, "Tell me, are you a Roman citizen?"
"Yes, I am," he answered.
28 Then the commander said, "I had to
pay a big price for my citizenship."
"But I was born a citizen," Paul replied.
29 Those who were about to question
him withdrew immediately. The commander himself was alarmed when he
realized that he had put Paul, a Roman
citizen, in chains.

Before the Sanhedrin

30The next day, since the commander
wanted to find out exactly why Paul was
being accused by the Jews, he released him
and ordered the chief priests and all the
Sanhedrin to assemble. Then he brought
Paul and had him stand before them.

23 Paul looked straight at the Sanhedrin
and said, "My brothers, I have fulfilled
my duty to God in all good conscience to
this day." 2At this the high priest Ananias
ordered those standing near Paul to strike
him on the mouth. 3Then Paul said to
him, "God will strike you, you whitewashed wall! You sit there to judge me according to the law, yet you yourself violate
the law by commanding that I be struck!"

4Those who were standing near Paul
said, "You dare to insult God's high
priest?"

5Paul replied, "Brothers, I did not realize that he was the high priest; for it is
written: 'Do not speak evil about the ruler
of your people.'[a]"

6Then Paul, knowing that some of them
were Sadducees and the others Pharisees,
called out in the Sanhedrin, "My brothers,
I am a Pharisee, the son of a Pharisee. I
stand on trial because of my hope in the
resurrection of the dead." 7When he said
this, a dispute broke out between the
Pharisees and the Sadducees, and the assembly was divided. 8(The Sadducees say
that there is no resurrection, and that
there are neither angels nor spirits, but the
Pharisees acknowledge them all.)

9There was a great uproar, and some of
the teachers of the law who were Pharisees
stood up and argued vigorously. "We find
nothing wrong with this man," they said.
"What if a spirit or an angel has spoken
to him?" 10The dispute became so violent
that the commander was afraid Paul
would be torn to pieces by them. He ordered the troops to go down and take him
away from them by force and bring him
into the barracks.

11The following night the Lord stood
near Paul and said, "Take courage! As you
have testified about me in Jerusalem, so
you must also testify in Rome."

[a]5 Exodus 22:28

PRAYER: THE ATTRIBUTES OF GOD

YOU, O God, are the Rock; Your work is perfect, for all Your ways are just. A God of faithfulness and without injustice, upright and just are You. (Deuteronomy 32:4)

***PAUSE** to reflect on these affirmations about the person, powers and perfection of God.*

YEAR 1
DAY 72

OT Exodus 23:1–24:18

Laws of Justice and Mercy

23 "Do not spread false reports. Do not
help a wicked man by being a malicious witness.

2"Do not follow the crowd in doing
wrong. When you give testimony in a lawsuit, do not pervert justice by siding with
the crowd, 3and do not show favoritism to
a poor man in his lawsuit.

4"If you come across your enemy's ox or
donkey wandering off, be sure to take it
back to him. 5If you see the donkey of
someone who hates you fallen down under its load, do not leave it there; be sure
you help him with it.

6"Do not deny justice to your poor people in their lawsuits. 7Have nothing to do
with a false charge and do not put an innocent or honest person to death, for I
will not acquit the guilty.

8"Do not accept a bribe, for a bribe
blinds those who see and twists the words
of the righteous.

9"Do not oppress an alien; you yourselves know how it feels to be aliens, because you were aliens in Egypt.

Sabbath Laws

[10] "For six years you are to sow your fields and harvest the crops, [11] but during the seventh year let the land lie unplowed and unused. Then the poor among your people may get food from it, and the wild animals may eat what they leave. Do the same with your vineyard and your olive grove.

[12] "Six days do your work, but on the seventh day do not work, so that your ox and your donkey may rest and the slave born in your household, and the alien as well, may be refreshed.

[13] "Be careful to do everything I have said to you. Do not invoke the names of other gods; do not let them be heard on your lips.

The Three Annual Festivals

[14] "Three times a year you are to celebrate a festival to me.

[15] "Celebrate the Feast of Unleavened Bread; for seven days eat bread made without yeast, as I commanded you. Do this at the appointed time in the month of Abib, for in that month you came out of Egypt.

"No one is to appear before me empty-handed.

[16] "Celebrate the Feast of Harvest with the firstfruits of the crops you sow in your field.

"Celebrate the Feast of Ingathering at the end of the year, when you gather in your crops from the field.

[17] "Three times a year all the men are to appear before the Sovereign LORD.

[18] "Do not offer the blood of a sacrifice to me along with anything containing yeast.

"The fat of my festival offerings must not be kept until morning.

[19] "Bring the best of the firstfruits of your soil to the house of the LORD your God.

"Do not cook a young goat in its mother's milk.

God's Angel to Prepare the Way

[20] "See, I am sending an angel ahead of you to guard you along the way and to bring you to the place I have prepared. [21] Pay attention to him and listen to what he says. Do not rebel against him; he will not forgive your rebellion, since my Name is in him. [22] If you listen carefully to what he says and do all that I say, I will be an enemy to your enemies and will oppose those who oppose you. [23] My angel will go ahead of you and bring you into the land of the Amorites, Hittites, Perizzites, Canaanites, Hivites and Jebusites, and I will wipe them out. [24] Do not bow down before their gods or worship them or follow their practices. You must demolish them and break their sacred stones to pieces. [25] Worship the LORD your God, and his blessing will be on your food and water. I will take away sickness from among you, [26] and none will miscarry or be barren in your land. I will give you a full life span.

[27] "I will send my terror ahead of you and throw into confusion every nation you encounter. I will make all your enemies turn their backs and run. [28] I will send the hornet ahead of you to drive the Hivites, Canaanites and Hittites out of your way. [29] But I will not drive them out in a single year, because the land would become desolate and the wild animals too numerous for you. [30] Little by little I will drive them out before you, until you have increased enough to take possession of the land.

[31] "I will establish your borders from the Red Sea[a] to the Sea of the Philistines,[b] and from the desert to the River.[c] I will hand over to you the people who live in the land and you will drive them out before you. [32] Do not make a covenant with them or with their gods. [33] Do not let them live in your land, or they will cause you to sin against me, because the worship of their gods will certainly be a snare to you."

The Covenant Confirmed

24 Then he said to Moses, "Come up to the LORD, you and Aaron, Nadab and Abihu, and seventy of the elders of Israel. You are to worship at a distance, [2] but Moses alone is to approach the LORD; the others must not come near. And the people may not come up with him."

[3] When Moses went and told the people all the LORD's words and laws, they responded with one voice, "Everything the LORD has said we will do." [4] Moses then wrote down everything the LORD had said.

He got up early the next morning and

[a] 31 Hebrew *Yam Suph*; that is, Sea of Reeds
[b] 31 That is, the Mediterranean [c] 31 That is, the Euphrates

built an altar at the foot of the mountain
and set up twelve stone pillars representing the twelve tribes of Israel. 5 Then he
sent young Israelite men, and they offered
burnt offerings and sacrificed young bulls
as fellowship offerings[d] to the LORD. 6 Moses took half of the blood and put it in
bowls, and the other half he sprinkled on
the altar. 7 Then he took the Book of the
Covenant and read it to the people. They
responded, "We will do everything the
LORD has said; we will obey."
8 Moses then took the blood, sprinkled
it on the people and said, "This is the
blood of the covenant that the LORD has
made with you in accordance with all
these words."
9 Moses and Aaron, Nadab and Abihu,
and the seventy elders of Israel went up
10 and saw the God of Israel. Under his feet
was something like a pavement made of
sapphire,[e] clear as the sky itself. 11 But God
did not raise his hand against these leaders of the Israelites; they saw God, and
they ate and drank.
12 The LORD said to Moses, "Come up to
me on the mountain and stay here, and I
will give you the tablets of stone, with the
law and commands I have written for
their instruction."
13 Then Moses set out with Joshua his
aide, and Moses went up on the mountain
of God. 14 He said to the elders, "Wait here
for us until we come back to you. Aaron
and Hur are with you, and anyone involved in a dispute can go to them."
15 When Moses went up on the mountain, the cloud covered it, 16 and the glory
of the LORD settled on Mount Sinai. For
six days the cloud covered the mountain,
and on the seventh day the LORD called to
Moses from within the cloud. 17 To the
Israelites the glory of the LORD looked like
a consuming fire on top of the mountain.
18 Then Moses entered the cloud as he
went on up the mountain. And he stayed
on the mountain forty days and forty
nights.

[d] 5 Traditionally *peace offerings* [e] 10 Or *lapis lazuli*

PRAYER: CONFESSION

A PERSON'S wickedness will punish him; his backsliding will reprove him. I know, therefore, and see that it is evil and bitter to forsake You, O Lord my God, and have no fear of You. (Jeremiah 2:19)

***ASK** the Spirit to search your heart and reveal any areas of unconfessed sin. Acknowledge these to the Lord and thank Him for His forgiveness.*

NT Acts 23:12-35

The Plot to Kill Paul

12 The next morning the Jews formed a
conspiracy and bound themselves with an
oath not to eat or drink until they had
killed Paul. 13 More than forty men were
involved in this plot. 14 They went to the
chief priests and elders and said, "We have
taken a solemn oath not to eat anything
until we have killed Paul. 15 Now then, you
and the Sanhedrin petition the commander to bring him before you on the pretext of wanting more accurate information about his case. We are ready to kill
him before he gets here."
16 But when the son of Paul's sister
heard of this plot, he went into the barracks and told Paul.
17 Then Paul called one of the centurions
and said, "Take this young man to the
commander; he has something to tell
him." 18 So he took him to the commander.
The centurion said, "Paul, the prisoner,
sent for me and asked me to bring this
young man to you because he has something to tell you."
19 The commander took the young man
by the hand, drew him aside and asked,
"What is it you want to tell me?"
20 He said: "The Jews have agreed to ask
you to bring Paul before the Sanhedrin tomorrow on the pretext of wanting more
accurate information about him. 21 Don't
give in to them, because more than forty
of them are waiting in ambush for him.

They have taken an oath not to eat or drink until they have killed him. They are ready now, waiting for your consent to their request."

[22]The commander dismissed the young man and cautioned him, "Don't tell anyone that you have reported this to me."

Paul Transferred to Caesarea

[23]Then he called two of his centurions and ordered them, "Get ready a detachment of two hundred soldiers, seventy horsemen and two hundred spearmen[a] to go to Caesarea at nine tonight. [24]Provide mounts for Paul so that he may be taken safely to Governor Felix."

[25]He wrote a letter as follows:

[26]Claudius Lysias,

To His Excellency, Governor Felix:

Greetings.

[27]This man was seized by the Jews and they were about to kill him, but I came with my troops and rescued him, for I had learned that he is a Roman citizen. [28]I wanted to know why they were accusing him, so I brought him to their Sanhedrin. [29]I found that the accusation had to do with questions about their law, but there was no charge against him that deserved death or imprisonment. [30]When I was informed of a plot to be carried out against the man, I sent him to you at once. I also ordered his accusers to present to you their case against him.

[31]So the soldiers, carrying out their orders, took Paul with them during the night and brought him as far as Antipatris. [32]The next day they let the cavalry go on with him, while they returned to the barracks. [33]When the cavalry arrived in Caesarea, they delivered the letter to the governor and handed Paul over to him. [34]The governor read the letter and asked what province he was from. Learning that he was from Cilicia, [35]he said, "I will hear your case when your accusers get here." Then he ordered that Paul be kept under guard in Herod's palace.

[a] 23 The meaning of the Greek for this word is uncertain.

PRAYER: THE WORKS OF GOD

MULTITUDES who sleep in the dust of the earth will awake, some to everlasting life, others to shame and everlasting contempt. Those who are wise will shine like the brightness of the heavens, and those who lead many to righteousness will be like the stars for ever and ever. (Daniel 12:2–3) . . . An hour is coming when all who are in the graves will hear Your voice, O Son of Man, and will come out—those who have done good will rise to a resurrection of life, and those who have done evil will rise to a resurrection of judgment. (John 5:28–29)

***TAKE** a moment to consider the greatness of God's wonderful works.*

YEAR 1 DAY 73

OT Exodus 25:1-40

Offerings for the Tabernacle

25 The LORD said to Moses, [2]"Tell the Israelites to bring me an offering. You are to receive the offering for me from each man whose heart prompts him to give. [3]These are the offerings you are to receive from them: gold, silver and bronze; [4]blue, purple and scarlet yarn and fine linen; goat hair; [5]ram skins dyed red and hides of sea cows[a]; acacia wood; [6]olive oil for the light; spices for the anointing oil and for the fragrant incense; [7]and onyx stones and other gems

[a] 5 That is, dugongs

to be mounted on the ephod and breastpiece.

8 "Then have them make a sanctuary for me, and I will dwell among them. 9 Make this tabernacle and all its furnishings exactly like the pattern I will show you.

The Ark

10 "Have them make a chest of acacia wood—two and a half cubits long, a cubit and a half wide, and a cubit and a half high.[b] 11 Overlay it with pure gold, both inside and out, and make a gold molding around it. 12 Cast four gold rings for it and fasten them to its four feet, with two rings on one side and two rings on the other. 13 Then make poles of acacia wood and overlay them with gold. 14 Insert the poles into the rings on the sides of the chest to carry it. 15 The poles are to remain in the rings of this ark; they are not to be removed. 16 Then put in the ark the Testimony, which I will give you.

17 "Make an atonement cover[c] of pure gold—two and a half cubits long and a cubit and a half wide.[d] 18 And make two cherubim out of hammered gold at the ends of the cover. 19 Make one cherub on one end and the second cherub on the other; make the cherubim of one piece with the cover, at the two ends. 20 The cherubim are to have their wings spread upward, overshadowing the cover with them. The cherubim are to face each other, looking toward the cover. 21 Place the cover on top of the ark and put in the ark the Testimony, which I will give you. 22 There, above the cover between the two cherubim that are over the ark of the Testimony, I will meet with you and give you all my commands for the Israelites.

The Table

23 "Make a table of acacia wood—two cubits long, a cubit wide and a cubit and a half high.[e] 24 Overlay it with pure gold and make a gold molding around it. 25 Also make around it a rim a handbreadth[f] wide and put a gold molding on the rim. 26 Make four gold rings for the table and fasten them to the four corners, where the four legs are. 27 The rings are to be close to the rim to hold the poles used in carrying the table. 28 Make the poles of acacia wood, overlay them with gold and carry the table with them. 29 And make its plates and dishes of pure gold, as well as its pitchers and bowls for the pouring out of offerings. 30 Put the bread of the Presence on this table to be before me at all times.

The Lampstand

31 "Make a lampstand of pure gold and hammer it out, base and shaft; its flowerlike cups, buds and blossoms shall be of one piece with it. 32 Six branches are to extend from the sides of the lampstand—three on one side and three on the other. 33 Three cups shaped like almond flowers with buds and blossoms are to be on one branch, three on the next branch, and the same for all six branches extending from the lampstand. 34 And on the lampstand there are to be four cups shaped like almond flowers with buds and blossoms. 35 One bud shall be under the first pair of branches extending from the lampstand, a second bud under the second pair, and a third bud under the third pair—six branches in all. 36 The buds and branches shall all be of one piece with the lampstand, hammered out of pure gold.

37 "Then make its seven lamps and set them up on it so that they light the space in front of it. 38 Its wick trimmers and trays are to be of pure gold. 39 A talent[g] of pure gold is to be used for the lampstand and all these accessories. 40 See that you make them according to the pattern shown you on the mountain.

[b] *10* That is, about 3 3/4 feet (about 1.1 meters) long and 2 1/4 feet (about 0.7 meter) wide and high [c] *17* Traditionally *a mercy seat* [d] *17* That is, about 3 3/4 feet (about 1.1 meters) long and 2 1/4 feet (about 0.7 meter) wide [e] *23* That is, about 3 feet (about 0.9 meter) long and 1 1/2 feet (about 0.5 meter) wide and 2 1/4 feet (about 0.7 meter) high [f] *25* That is, about 3 inches (about 8 centimeters) [g] *39* That is, about 75 pounds (about 34 kilograms)

PRAYER: RENEWAL

MAY I be anxious for nothing, but in everything, by prayer and petition with thanksgiving, let my requestsbe known to You, O God. And may Your peace, which transcends all

understanding, guard my heart and my mind in Christ Jesus.
(Philippians 4:6–7) . . . May I prepare my mind for action and be self-controlled,
setting my hope fully on the grace to be given to me at Your revelation,
Christ Jesus. (1 Peter 1:13)

PAUSE *to add your own prayers for personal renewal.*

NT Acts 24:1–27

The Trial Before Felix

24 Five days later the high priest Ananias went down to Caesarea with some
of the elders and a lawyer named Tertullus, and they brought their charges
against Paul before the governor. [2]When
Paul was called in, Tertullus presented his
case before Felix: "We have enjoyed a
long period of peace under you, and your
foresight has brought about reforms in
this nation. [3]Everywhere and in every
way, most excellent Felix, we acknowledge this with profound gratitude. [4]But in
order not to weary you further, I would
request that you be kind enough to hear
us briefly.
[5]"We have found this man to be a troublemaker, stirring up riots among the Jews
all over the world. He is a ringleader of
the Nazarene sect [6]and even tried to desecrate the temple; so we seized him. [8]By[a]
examining him yourself you will be able
to learn the truth about all these charges
we are bringing against him."
[9]The Jews joined in the accusation, as-
serting that these things were true.
[10]When the governor motioned for
him to speak, Paul replied: "I know that
for a number of years you have been a
judge over this nation; so I gladly make
my defense. [11]You can easily verify that
no more than twelve days ago I went up
to Jerusalem to worship. [12]My accusers
did not find me arguing with anyone at
the temple, or stirring up a crowd in the
synagogues or anywhere else in the city.
[13]And they cannot prove to you the
charges they are now making against me.
[14]However, I admit that I worship the
God of our fathers as a follower of the
Way, which they call a sect. I believe
everything that agrees with the Law and
that is written in the Prophets, [15]and I
have the same hope in God as these men,
that there will be a resurrection of both
the righteous and the wicked. [16]So I strive
always to keep my conscience clear before God and man.
[17]"After an absence of several years, I
came to Jerusalem to bring my people
gifts for the poor and to present offerings.
[18]I was ceremonially clean when they
found me in the temple courts doing this.
There was no crowd with me, nor was I involved in any disturbance. [19]But there are
some Jews from the province of Asia, who
ought to be here before you and bring
charges if they have anything against me.
[20]Or these who are here should state what
crime they found in me when I stood before the Sanhedrin— [21]unless it was this
one thing I shouted as I stood in their
presence: 'It is concerning the resurrection
of the dead that I am on trial before you
today.' "
[22]Then Felix, who was well acquainted
with the Way, adjourned the proceedings.
"When Lysias the commander comes," he
said, "I will decide your case." [23]He ordered the centurion to keep Paul under
guard but to give him some freedom and
permit his friends to take care of his
needs.
[24]Several days later Felix came with his
wife Drusilla, who was a Jewess. He sent
for Paul and listened to him as he spoke
about faith in Christ Jesus. [25]As Paul discoursed on righteousness, self-control and
the judgment to come, Felix was afraid
and said, "That's enough for now! You
may leave. When I find it convenient, I
will send for you." [26]At the same time he
was hoping that Paul would offer him a
bribe, so he sent for him frequently and
talked with him.
[27]When two years had passed, Felix was
succeeded by Porcius Festus, but because
Felix wanted to grant a favor to the Jews,
he left Paul in prison.

[a] 6–8 Some manuscripts *him and wanted to judge him according to our law. [7]But the commander, Lysias, came and with the use of much force snatched him from our hands [8]and ordered his accusers to come before you. By*

PRAYER: MY RELATIONSHIP TO GOD

I WILL praise You, O Lord my God, with all my heart, and I will glorify Your name forever. For great is Your love toward me; You have delivered my soul from the depths of the grave. (Psalm 86:12–13)

***PAUSE** to thank God for the relationship that you enjoy with Him in Jesus Christ.*

YEAR 1
DAY 74

OT Exodus 26:1-37

The Tabernacle

26 "Make the tabernacle with ten curtains
of finely twisted linen and blue, purple and scarlet yarn, with cherubim worked
into them by a skilled craftsman. 2All the
curtains are to be the same size—twenty-
eight cubits long and four cubits wide.[a]
3Join five of the curtains together, and do
the same with the other five. 4Make loops
of blue material along the edge of the end
curtain in one set, and do the same with the
end curtain in the other set. 5Make fifty
loops on one curtain and fifty loops on the
end curtain of the other set, with the loops
opposite each other. 6Then make fifty gold
clasps and use them to fasten the curtains
together so that the tabernacle is a unit.
7"Make curtains of goat hair for the tent
over the tabernacle—eleven altogether. 8All
eleven curtains are to be the same size—
thirty cubits long and four cubits wide.[b]
9Join five of the curtains together into one
set and the other six into another set. Fold
the sixth curtain double at the front of the
tent. 10Make fifty loops along the edge of
the end curtain in one set and also along
the edge of the end curtain in the other set.
11Then make fifty bronze clasps and put
them in the loops to fasten the tent together as a unit. 12As for the additional
length of the tent curtains, the half curtain
that is left over is to hang down at the rear
of the tabernacle. 13The tent curtains will
be a cubit[c] longer on both sides; what is
left will hang over the sides of the tabernacle so as to cover it. 14Make for the tent
a covering of ram skins dyed red, and over
that a covering of hides of sea cows.[d]
15"Make upright frames of acacia wood
for the tabernacle. 16Each frame is to be ten
cubits long and a cubit and a half wide,[e]
17with two projections set parallel to each
other. Make all the frames of the tabernacle in this way. 18Make twenty frames for the
south side of the tabernacle 19and make
forty silver bases to go under them—two
bases for each frame, one under each projection. 20For the other side, the north side
of the tabernacle, make twenty frames 21and
forty silver bases—two under each frame.
22Make six frames for the far end, that is, the
west end of the tabernacle, 23and make two
frames for the corners at the far end. 24At
these two corners they must be double
from the bottom all the way to the top, and
fitted into a single ring; both shall be like
that. 25So there will be eight frames and sixteen silver bases—two under each frame.
26"Also make crossbars of acacia wood:
five for the frames on one side of the
tabernacle, 27five for those on the other
side, and five for the frames on the west,
at the far end of the tabernacle. 28The center crossbar is to extend from end to end
at the middle of the frames. 29Overlay the
frames with gold and make gold rings to
hold the crossbars. Also overlay the crossbars with gold.
30"Set up the tabernacle according to
the plan shown you on the mountain.
31"Make a curtain of blue, purple and
scarlet yarn and finely twisted linen, with
cherubim worked into it by a skilled
craftsman. 32Hang it with gold hooks on
four posts of acacia wood overlaid with
gold and standing on four silver bases.
33Hang the curtain from the clasps and
place the ark of the Testimony behind the

[a] *2* That is, about 42 feet (about 12.5 meters) long and 6 feet (about 1.8 meters) wide [b] *8* That is, about 45 feet (about 13.5 meters) long and 6 feet (about 1.8 meters) wide [c] *13* That is, about 1 1/2 feet (about 0.5 meter) [d] *14* That is, dugongs [e] *16* That is, about 15 feet (about 4.5 meters) long and 2 1/4 feet (about 0.7 meter) wide

curtain. The curtain will separate the Holy
Place from the Most Holy Place. 34Put the
atonement cover on the ark of the Testimony in the Most Holy Place. 35Place the
table outside the curtain on the north side
of the tabernacle and put the lampstand
opposite it on the south side.

36"For the entrance to the tent make a
curtain of blue, purple and scarlet yarn
and finely twisted linen—the work of an
embroiderer. 37Make gold hooks for this
curtain and five posts of acacia wood
overlaid with gold. And cast five bronze
bases for them.

PRAYER: PETITION

LORD, may I not be ashamed to testify about You, but join with others in suffering for the gospel according to Your power.
(2 Timothy 1:8)

***PAUSE** here to petition God for growth in love and compassion toward others. Offer prayers for your loved ones, for those who do not know Jesus and for those in need. Offer prayers regarding your activities for this day and any special concerns you may have.*

NT Acts 25:1–22

The Trial Before Festus

25 Three days after arriving in the province, Festus went up from Caesarea to
Jerusalem, 2where the chief priests and
Jewish leaders appeared before him and
presented the charges against Paul. 3They
urgently requested Festus, as a favor to
them, to have Paul transferred to Jerusalem, for they were preparing an ambush
to kill him along the way. 4Festus answered, "Paul is being held at Caesarea,
and I myself am going there soon. 5Let
some of your leaders come with me and
press charges against the man there, if he
has done anything wrong."

6After spending eight or ten days with
them, he went down to Caesarea, and the
next day he convened the court and ordered that Paul be brought before him.
7When Paul appeared, the Jews who had
come down from Jerusalem stood around
him, bringing many serious charges
against him, which they could not prove.

8Then Paul made his defense: "I have
done nothing wrong against the law of
the Jews or against the temple or against
Caesar."

9Festus, wishing to do the Jews a favor,
said to Paul, "Are you willing to go up to
Jerusalem and stand trial before me there
on these charges?"

10Paul answered: "I am now standing
before Caesar's court, where I ought to be
tried. I have not done any wrong to the
Jews, as you yourself know very well. 11If,
however, I am guilty of doing anything
deserving death, I do not refuse to die. But
if the charges brought against me by these
Jews are not true, no one has the right to
hand me over to them. I appeal to Caesar!"

12After Festus had conferred with his
council, he declared: "You have appealed
to Caesar. To Caesar you will go!"

Festus Consults King Agrippa

13A few days later King Agrippa and Bernice arrived at Caesarea to pay their respects to Festus. 14Since they were spending many days there, Festus discussed
Paul's case with the king. He said: "There
is a man here whom Felix left as a prisoner. 15When I went to Jerusalem, the
chief priests and elders of the Jews
brought charges against him and asked
that he be condemned.

16"I told them that it is not the Roman
custom to hand over any man before he
has faced his accusers and has had an opportunity to defend himself against their
charges. 17When they came here with me,
I did not delay the case, but convened the
court the next day and ordered the man
to be brought in. 18When his accusers got
up to speak, they did not charge him
with any of the crimes I had expected.
19Instead, they had some points of dispute with him about their own religion
and about a dead man named Jesus who

Paul claimed was alive. [20]I was at a loss how to investigate such matters; so I asked if he would be willing to go to Jerusalem and stand trial there on these charges. [21]When Paul made his appeal to be held over for the Emperor's decision, I ordered him held until I could send him to Caesar."

[22]Then Agrippa said to Festus, "I would like to hear this man myself."

He replied, "Tomorrow you will hear him."

PRAYER: THE CHARACTER I WANT TO CULTIVATE

I WILL not spread false reports, nor will I help a wicked person by being a malicious witness. (Exodus 23:1) . . . Lying lips are hateful to You, Lord, but You delight in those who deal faithfully. (Proverbs 12:22)

TAKE *a moment to ask the Lord for the grace to grow in godly character.*

YEAR 1
DAY 75

OT Exodus 27:1-21

The Altar of Burnt Offering

27 "Build an altar of acacia wood, three cubits[a] high; it is to be square, five cubits long and five cubits wide.[b] [2]Make a horn at each of the four corners, so that the horns and the altar are of one piece, and overlay the altar with bronze. [3]Make all its utensils of bronze—its pots to remove the ashes, and its shovels, sprinkling bowls, meat forks and firepans. [4]Make a grating for it, a bronze network, and make a bronze ring at each of the four corners of the network. [5]Put it under the ledge of the altar so that it is halfway up the altar. [6]Make poles of acacia wood for the altar and overlay them with bronze. [7]The poles are to be inserted into the rings so they will be on two sides of the altar when it is carried. [8]Make the altar hollow, out of boards. It is to be made just as you were shown on the mountain.

The Courtyard

[9]"Make a courtyard for the tabernacle. The south side shall be a hundred cubits[c] long and is to have curtains of finely twisted linen, [10]with twenty posts and twenty bronze bases and with silver hooks and bands on the posts. [11]The north side shall also be a hundred cubits long and is to have curtains, with twenty posts and twenty bronze bases and with silver hooks and bands on the posts.

[12]"The west end of the courtyard shall be fifty cubits[d] wide and have curtains, with ten posts and ten bases. [13]On the east end, toward the sunrise, the courtyard shall also be fifty cubits wide. [14]Curtains fifteen cubits[e] long are to be on one side of the entrance, with three posts and three bases, [15]and curtains fifteen cubits long are to be on the other side, with three posts and three bases.

[16]"For the entrance to the courtyard, provide a curtain twenty cubits[f] long, of blue, purple and scarlet yarn and finely twisted linen—the work of an embroiderer—with four posts and four bases. [17]All the posts around the courtyard are to have silver bands and hooks, and bronze bases. [18]The courtyard shall be a hundred cubits long and fifty cubits wide,[g] with curtains of finely twisted linen five cubits[h] high, and with bronze bases. [19]All the other articles used in the service of the tabernacle, whatever their function, including all the tent pegs for it and those for the courtyard, are to be of bronze.

Oil for the Lampstand

[20]"Command the Israelites to bring you clear oil of pressed olives for the light so that the lamps may be kept burning. [21]In

[a] *1* That is, about 4 1/2 feet (about 1.3 meters) [b] *1* That is, about 7 1/2 feet (about 2.3 meters) long and wide [c] *9* That is, about 150 feet (about 46 meters); also in verse 11 [d] *12* That is, about 75 feet (about 23 meters); also in verse 13 [e] *14* That is, about 22 1/2 feet (about 6.9 meters); also in verse 15 [f] *16* That is, about 30 feet (about 9 meters) [g] *18* That is, about 150 feet (about 46 meters) long and 75 feet (about 23 meters) wide [h] *18* That is, about 7 1/2 feet (about 2.3 meters)

the Tent of Meeting, outside the curtain that is in front of the Testimony, Aaron and his sons are to keep the lamps burning before the LORD from evening till morning. This is to be a lasting ordinance among the Israelites for the generations to come.

PRAYER: INTERCESSION

THE god of this age has blinded the minds of unbelievers, so that they cannot see the light of the gospel of Your glory, O Christ, You who are the image of God. (2 Corinthians 4:4)

***TAKE** a few moments to intercede on behalf of friends, relatives, neighbors and coworkers who do not yet know salvation in Jesus Christ.*

NT Acts 25:23–26:32

Paul Before Agrippa

23The next day Agrippa and Bernice
came with great pomp and entered the
audience room with the high ranking officers and the leading men of the city. At
the command of Festus, Paul was brought
in. 24Festus said: "King Agrippa, and all
who are present with us, you see this
man! The whole Jewish community has
petitioned me about him in Jerusalem
and here in Caesarea, shouting that he
ought not to live any longer. 25I found he
had done nothing deserving of death, but
because he made his appeal to the Emperor I decided to send him to Rome.
26But I have nothing definite to write to
His Majesty about him. Therefore I have
brought him before all of you, and especially before you, King Agrippa, so that as
a result of this investigation I may have
something to write. 27For I think it is un-
reasonable to send on a prisoner without
specifying the charges against him."

26 Then Agrippa said to Paul, "You have
permission to speak for yourself."

So Paul motioned with his hand and
began his defense: 2"King Agrippa, I consider myself fortunate to stand before you
today as I make my defense against all the
accusations of the Jews, 3and especially so
because you are well acquainted with all
the Jewish customs and controversies.
Therefore, I beg you to listen to me patiently.

4"The Jews all know the way I have lived
ever since I was a child, from the beginning of my life in my own country, and
also in Jerusalem. 5They have known me
for a long time and can testify, if they are
willing, that according to the strictest sect
of our religion, I lived as a Pharisee. 6And
now it is because of my hope in what God
has promised our fathers that I am on trial today. 7This is the promise our twelve
tribes are hoping to see fulfilled as they
earnestly serve God day and night. O king,
it is because of this hope that the Jews are
accusing me. 8Why should any of you
consider it incredible that God raises the
dead?

9"I too was convinced that I ought to do
all that was possible to oppose the name
of Jesus of Nazareth. 10And that is just
what I did in Jerusalem. On the authority
of the chief priests I put many of the saints
in prison, and when they were put to
death, I cast my vote against them. 11Many
a time I went from one synagogue to another to have them punished, and I tried
to force them to blaspheme. In my obses-
sion against them, I even went to foreign
cities to persecute them.

12"On one of these journeys I was going
to Damascus with the authority and commission of the chief priests. 13About noon,
O king, as I was on the road, I saw a light
from heaven, brighter than the sun, blazing around me and my companions. 14We
all fell to the ground, and I heard a voice
saying to me in Aramaic,[a] 'Saul, Saul, why
do you persecute me? It is hard for you to
kick against the goads.'

15"Then I asked, 'Who are you, Lord?'

" 'I am Jesus, whom you are persecuting,' the Lord replied. 16'Now get up and
stand on your feet. I have appeared to you
to appoint you as a servant and as a witness of what you have seen of me and
what I will show you. 17I will rescue you

[a] 14 Or *Hebrew*

from your own people and from the Gentiles. I am sending you to them 18to open their eyes and turn them from darkness to light, and from the power of Satan to God, so that they may receive forgiveness of sins and a place among those who are sanctified by faith in me.'

19"So then, King Agrippa, I was not disobedient to the vision from heaven. 20First to those in Damascus, then to those in Jerusalem and in all Judea, and to the Gentiles also, I preached that they should repent and turn to God and prove their repentance by their deeds. 21That is why the Jews seized me in the temple courts and tried to kill me. 22But I have had God's help to this very day, and so I stand here and testify to small and great alike. I am saying nothing beyond what the prophets and Moses said would happen— 23that the Christ[b] would suffer and, as the first to rise from the dead, would proclaim light to his own people and to the Gentiles."

24At this point Festus interrupted Paul's defense. "You are out of your mind, Paul!" he shouted. "Your great learning is driving you insane."

25"I am not insane, most excellent Festus," Paul replied. "What I am saying is true and reasonable. 26The king is familiar with these things, and I can speak freely to him. I am convinced that none of this has escaped his notice, because it was not done in a corner. 27King Agrippa, do you believe the prophets? I know you do."

28Then Agrippa said to Paul, "Do you think that in such a short time you can persuade me to be a Christian?"

29Paul replied, "Short time or long—I pray God that not only you but all who are listening to me today may become what I am, except for these chains."

30The king rose, and with him the governor and Bernice and those sitting with them. 31They left the room, and while talking with one another, they said, "This man is not doing anything that deserves death or imprisonment."

32Agrippa said to Festus, "This man could have been set free if he had not appealed to Caesar."

[b] 23 Or *Messiah*

PRAYER: MY RELATIONSHIP TO OTHERS

I WILL not take vengeance or bear a grudge against others, but I will love my neighbor as myself. (Leviticus 19:18) . . .
Whatever I want others to do to me, I will also do to them, for this is the Law and the Prophets. (Matthew 7:12)

***PAUSE** to review your relationships with others and to commit them to the Lord.*

YEAR 1
DAY 76

OT Exodus 28:1-43

The Priestly Garments

28 "Have Aaron your brother brought to you from among the Israelites, along with his sons Nadab and Abihu, Eleazar and Ithamar, so they may serve me as priests. 2Make sacred garments for your brother Aaron, to give him dignity and honor. 3Tell all the skilled men to whom I have given wisdom in such matters that they are to make garments for Aaron, for his consecration, so he may serve me as priest. 4These are the garments they are to make: a breastpiece, an ephod, a robe, a woven tunic, a turban and a sash. They are to make these sacred garments for your brother Aaron and his sons, so they may serve me as priests. 5Have them use gold, and blue, purple and scarlet yarn, and fine linen.

The Ephod

6"Make the ephod of gold, and of blue, purple and scarlet yarn, and of finely twisted linen—the work of a skilled craftsman. 7It is to have two shoulder pieces attached to two of its corners, so it can be fastened. 8 Its skillfully woven waistband is to be like it—of one piece with the ephod and made with gold, and with blue, purple and scarlet yarn, and with finely twisted linen.

9 "Take two onyx stones and engrave on them the names of the sons of Israel 10 in the order of their birth—six names on one stone and the remaining six on the other. 11 Engrave the names of the sons of Israel on the two stones the way a gem cutter engraves a seal. Then mount the stones in gold filigree settings 12 and fasten them on the shoulder pieces of the ephod as memorial stones for the sons of Israel. Aaron is to bear the names on his shoulders as a memorial before the LORD. 13 Make gold filigree settings 14 and two braided chains of pure gold, like a rope, and attach the chains to the settings.

The Breastpiece

15 "Fashion a breastpiece for making decisions—the work of a skilled craftsman. Make it like the ephod: of gold, and of blue, purple and scarlet yarn, and of finely twisted linen. 16 It is to be square—a span[a] long and a span wide—and folded double. 17 Then mount four rows of precious stones on it. In the first row there shall be a ruby, a topaz and a beryl; 18 in the second row a turquoise, a sapphire[b] and an emerald; 19 in the third row a jacinth, an agate and an amethyst; 20 in the fourth row a chrysolite, an onyx and a jasper.[c] Mount them in gold filigree settings. 21 There are to be twelve stones, one for each of the names of the sons of Israel, each engraved like a seal with the name of one of the twelve tribes.

22 "For the breastpiece make braided chains of pure gold, like a rope. 23 Make two gold rings for it and fasten them to two corners of the breastpiece. 24 Fasten the two gold chains to the rings at the corners of the breastpiece, 25 and the other ends of the chains to the two settings, attaching them to the shoulder pieces of the ephod at the front. 26 Make two gold rings and attach them to the other two corners of the breastpiece on the inside edge next to the ephod. 27 Make two more gold rings and attach them to the bottom of the shoulder pieces on the front of the ephod, close to the seam just above the waistband of the ephod. 28 The rings of the breastpiece are to be tied to the rings of the ephod with blue cord, connecting it to the waistband, so that the breastpiece will not swing out from the ephod.

29 "Whenever Aaron enters the Holy Place, he will bear the names of the sons of Israel over his heart on the breastpiece of decision as a continuing memorial before the LORD. 30 Also put the Urim and the Thummim in the breastpiece, so they may be over Aaron's heart whenever he enters the presence of the LORD. Thus Aaron will always bear the means of making decisions for the Israelites over his heart before the LORD.

Other Priestly Garments

31 "Make the robe of the ephod entirely of blue cloth, 32 with an opening for the head in its center. There shall be a woven edge like a collar[d] around this opening, so that it will not tear. 33 Make pomegranates of blue, purple and scarlet yarn around the hem of the robe, with gold bells between them. 34 The gold bells and the pomegranates are to alternate around the hem of the robe. 35 Aaron must wear it when he ministers. The sound of the bells will be heard when he enters the Holy Place before the LORD and when he comes out, so that he will not die.

36 "Make a plate of pure gold and engrave on it as on a seal: HOLY TO THE LORD. 37 Fasten a blue cord to it to attach it to the turban; it is to be on the front of the turban. 38 It will be on Aaron's forehead, and he will bear the guilt involved in the sacred gifts the Israelites consecrate, whatever their gifts may be. It will be on Aaron's forehead continually so that they will be acceptable to the LORD.

39 "Weave the tunic of fine linen and make the turban of fine linen. The sash is to be the work of an embroiderer. 40 Make tunics, sashes and headbands for Aaron's sons, to give them dignity and honor. 41 After you put these clothes on your brother Aaron and his sons, anoint and ordain them. Consecrate them so they may serve me as priests.

42 "Make linen undergarments as a cov-

[a] *16* That is, about 9 inches (about 22 centimeters)
[b] *18* Or *lapis lazuli* [c] *20* The precise identification of some of these precious stones is uncertain.
[d] *32* The meaning of the Hebrew for this word is uncertain.

ering for the body, reaching from the
waist to the thigh. 43Aaron and his sons
must wear them whenever they enter the
Tent of Meeting or approach the altar to
minister in the Holy Place, so that they
will not incur guilt and die.
"This is to be a lasting ordinance for
Aaron and his descendants.

PRAYER: AFFIRMATION

LORD Jesus Christ, You have been raised from the dead, the firstfruits of those who have fallen asleep. For since death came through a man, the resurrection of the dead comes also through a Man. For as in Adam all die, so in You all will be made alive. But each in his own order: You, the firstfruits; afterward, those who are Yours at Your coming. Then the end will come, when You deliver the kingdom to God the Father, after You have abolished all rule and all authority and power. For You must reign until You have put all Your enemies under Your feet. The last enemy that will be destroyed is death. (1 Corinthians 15:20–26)

***PAUSE** to reflect on these Biblical affirmations.*

NT Acts 27:1–26

Paul Sails for Rome

27 When it was decided that we would
sail for Italy, Paul and some other
prisoners were handed over to a centurion named Julius, who belonged to the
Imperial Regiment. 2We boarded a ship
from Adramyttium about to sail for ports
along the coast of the province of Asia,
and we put out to sea. Aristarchus, a
Macedonian from Thessalonica, was
with us.
3The next day we landed at Sidon; and
Julius, in kindness to Paul, allowed him
to go to his friends so they might provide
for his needs. 4From there we put out to
sea again and passed to the lee of Cyprus
because the winds were against us. 5When
we had sailed across the open sea off the
coast of Cilicia and Pamphylia, we landed at Myra in Lycia. 6There the centurion
found an Alexandrian ship sailing for Italy and put us on board. 7We made slow
headway for many days and had difficulty arriving off Cnidus. When the wind did
not allow us to hold our course, we sailed
to the lee of Crete, opposite Salmone. 8We
moved along the coast with difficulty and
came to a place called Fair Havens, near
the town of Lasea.
9Much time had been lost, and sailing
had already become dangerous because
by now it was after the Fast.[a] So Paul
warned them, 10"Men, I can see that our
voyage is going to be disastrous and bring
great loss to ship and cargo, and to our
own lives also." 11But the centurion, instead of listening to what Paul said, followed the advice of the pilot and of the
owner of the ship. 12Since the harbor was
unsuitable to winter in, the majority decided that we should sail on, hoping to
reach Phoenix and winter there. This was
a harbor in Crete, facing both southwest
and northwest.

The Storm

13When a gentle south wind began to
blow, they thought they had obtained
what they wanted; so they weighed anchor and sailed along the shore of Crete.
14Before very long, a wind of hurricane
force, called the "northeaster," swept
down from the island. 15The ship was
caught by the storm and could not head
into the wind; so we gave way to it and
were driven along. 16As we passed to the
lee of a small island called Cauda, we
were hardly able to make the lifeboat secure. 17When the men had hoisted it
aboard, they passed ropes under the ship
itself to hold it together. Fearing that they
would run aground on the sandbars of
Syrtis, they lowered the sea anchor and let
the ship be driven along. 18We took such
a violent battering from the storm that the

[a] 9 That is, the Day of Atonement (Yom Kippur)

next day they began to throw the cargo overboard. [19]On the third day, they threw the ship's tackle overboard with their own hands. [20]When neither sun nor stars appeared for many days and the storm continued raging, we finally gave up all hope of being saved.

[21]After the men had gone a long time without food, Paul stood up before them and said: "Men, you should have taken my advice not to sail from Crete; then you would have spared yourselves this damage and loss. [22]But now I urge you to keep up your courage, because not one of you will be lost; only the ship will be destroyed.
[23]Last night an angel of the God whose I am and whom I serve stood beside me [24]and said, 'Do not be afraid, Paul. You must stand trial before Caesar; and God has graciously given you the lives of all who sail with you.' [25]So keep up your courage, men, for I have faith in God that it will happen just as he told me. [26]Nevertheless, we must run aground on some island."

PRAYER: THE ATTRIBUTES OF GOD

LORD, there is no one holy like You; there is no one besides You; nor is there any Rock like You, our God. (1 Samuel 2:2) . . .
You are but one God, Father, from whom all things came and for whom I live; and there is but one Lord Jesus Christ, through whom all things came and through whom I live. (1 Corinthians 8:6)

***PAUSE** to reflect on these affirmations about the person, powers and perfection of God.*

YEAR 1 DAY 77

OT Psalm 18

Psalm 18

For the director of music. Of David the servant of the LORD. He sang to the LORD the words of this song when the LORD delivered him from the hand of all his enemies and from the hand of Saul. He said:

[1]I love you, O LORD, my strength.

[2]The LORD is my rock, my fortress and my deliverer;
my God is my rock, in whom I take refuge.
He is my shield and the horn[a] of my salvation, my stronghold.
[3]I call to the LORD, who is worthy of praise,
and I am saved from my enemies.

[4]The cords of death entangled me;
the torrents of destruction overwhelmed me.
[5]The cords of the grave[b] coiled around me;
the snares of death confronted me.
[6]In my distress I called to the LORD;
I cried to my God for help.
From his temple he heard my voice;
my cry came before him, into his ears.

[7]The earth trembled and quaked,
and the foundations of the mountains shook;
they trembled because he was angry.
[8]Smoke rose from his nostrils;
consuming fire came from his mouth,
burning coals blazed out of it.
[9]He parted the heavens and came down;
dark clouds were under his feet.
[10]He mounted the cherubim and flew;
he soared on the wings of the wind.
[11]He made darkness his covering, his canopy around him—
the dark rain clouds of the sky.
[12]Out of the brightness of his presence clouds advanced,
with hailstones and bolts of lightning.
[13]The LORD thundered from heaven;

[a] 2 *Horn* here symbolizes strength. [b] 5 Hebrew *Sheol*

the voice of the Most High
resounded.[c]
14 He shot his arrows and scattered ⌊the
enemies⌋,
great bolts of lightning and routed
them.
15 The valleys of the sea were exposed
and the foundations of the earth
laid bare
at your rebuke, O LORD,
at the blast of breath from your
nostrils.

16 He reached down from on high and
took hold of me;
he drew me out of deep waters.
17 He rescued me from my powerful
enemy,
from my foes, who were too strong
for me.
18 They confronted me in the day of my
disaster,
but the LORD was my support.
19 He brought me out into a spacious
place;
he rescued me because he delighted
in me.

20 The LORD has dealt with me according
to my righteousness;
according to the cleanness of my
hands he has rewarded me.
21 For I have kept the ways of the LORD;
I have not done evil by turning
from my God.
22 All his laws are before me;
I have not turned away from his
decrees.
23 I have been blameless before him
and have kept myself from sin.
24 The LORD has rewarded me according
to my righteousness,
according to the cleanness of my
hands in his sight.

25 To the faithful you show yourself
faithful,
to the blameless you show yourself
blameless,
26 to the pure you show yourself pure,
but to the crooked you show
yourself shrewd.
27 You save the humble
but bring low those whose eyes are
haughty.
28 You, O LORD, keep my lamp burning;
my God turns my darkness into
light.
29 With your help I can advance against
a troop[d];
with my God I can scale a wall.

30 As for God, his way is perfect;
the word of the LORD is flawless.
He is a shield
for all who take refuge in him.
31 For who is God besides the LORD?
And who is the Rock except our
God?
32 It is God who arms me with strength
and makes my way perfect.
33 He makes my feet like the feet of a
deer;
he enables me to stand on the
heights.
34 He trains my hands for battle;
my arms can bend a bow of bronze.
35 You give me your shield of victory,
and your right hand sustains me;
you stoop down to make me great.
36 You broaden the path beneath me,
so that my ankles do not turn.

37 I pursued my enemies and overtook
them;
I did not turn back till they were
destroyed.
38 I crushed them so that they could not
rise;
they fell beneath my feet.
39 You armed me with strength for
battle;
you made my adversaries bow at my
feet.
40 You made my enemies turn their
backs in flight,
and I destroyed my foes.
41 They cried for help, but there was no
one to save them—
to the LORD, but he did not answer.
42 I beat them as fine as dust borne on
the wind;
I poured them out like mud in the
streets.

43 You have delivered me from the
attacks of the people;
you have made me the head of
nations;
people I did not know are subject
to me.

[c] *13* Some Hebrew manuscripts and Septuagint (see also 2 Samuel 22:14); most Hebrew manuscripts *resounded, / amid hailstones and bolts of lightning*
[d] *29* Or *can run through a barricade*

44 As soon as they hear me, they obey
me;
foreigners cringe before me.
45 They all lose heart;
they come trembling from their
strongholds.

46 The LORD lives! Praise be to my Rock!
Exalted be God my Savior!
47 He is the God who avenges me,
who subdues nations under me,
48 who saves me from my enemies.
You exalted me above my foes;
from violent men you rescued me.
49 Therefore I will praise you among the
nations, O LORD;
I will sing praises to your name.
50 He gives his king great victories;
he shows unfailing kindness to his
anointed,
to David and his descendants
forever.

PRAYER: THANKSGIVING

JESUS, You, the Son of Man, did not come to be served, but to serve, and to give Your life as a ransom for many. (Matthew 20:28) . . . Jesus, we remember that You took bread, gave thanks, and broke it, and gave it to Your disciples, saying, "Take and eat; this is My body." Then You took the cup, gave thanks, and offered it to them, saying, "Drink from it, all of you. This is My blood of the new covenant, which is poured out for many for the forgiveness of sins." (Matthew 26:26–28)

__PAUSE__ to offer your own expressions of thanksgiving.

NT Acts 27:27–28:10

The Shipwreck

27 On the fourteenth night we were still
being driven across the Adriatic[a] Sea,
when about midnight the sailors sensed
they were approaching land. 28 They took
soundings and found that the water was a
hundred and twenty feet[b] deep. A short
time later they took soundings again and
found it was ninety feet[c] deep. 29 Fearing
that we would be dashed against the
rocks, they dropped four anchors from
the stern and prayed for daylight. 30 In an
attempt to escape from the ship, the
sailors let the lifeboat down into the sea,
pretending they were going to lower some
anchors from the bow. 31 Then Paul said to
the centurion and the soldiers, "Unless
these men stay with the ship, you cannot
be saved." 32 So the soldiers cut the ropes
that held the lifeboat and let it fall away.
33 Just before dawn Paul urged them all
to eat. "For the last fourteen days," he said,
"you have been in constant suspense and
have gone without food—you haven't eat-
en anything. 34 Now I urge you to take some
food. You need it to survive. Not one of
you will lose a single hair from his head."
35 After he said this, he took some bread
and gave thanks to God in front of them
all. Then he broke it and began to eat.
36 They were all encouraged and ate some
food themselves. 37 Altogether there were
276 of us on board. 38 When they had eat-
en as much as they wanted, they lightened
the ship by throwing the grain into the sea.
39 When daylight came, they did not recognize the land, but they saw a bay with
a sandy beach, where they decided to run
the ship aground if they could. 40 Cutting
loose the anchors, they left them in the
sea and at the same time untied the ropes
that held the rudders. Then they hoisted
the foresail to the wind and made for the
beach. 41 But the ship struck a sandbar and
ran aground. The bow stuck fast and
would not move, and the stern was broken to pieces by the pounding of the surf.
42 The soldiers planned to kill the prisoners to prevent any of them from swimming
away and escaping. 43 But the centurion
wanted to spare Paul's life and kept them

[a] *27* In ancient times the name referred to an area extending well south of Italy. [b] *28* Greek *twenty orguias* (about 37 meters) [c] *28* Greek *fifteen orguias* (about 27 meters)

from carrying out their plan. He ordered those who could swim to jump overboard first and get to land. [44]The rest were to get there on planks or on pieces of the ship. In this way everyone reached land in safety.

Ashore on Malta

28 Once safely on shore, we found out that the island was called Malta. [2]The islanders showed us unusual kindness. They built a fire and welcomed us all because it was raining and cold. [3]Paul gathered a pile of brushwood and, as he put it on the fire, a viper, driven out by the heat, fastened itself on his hand. [4]When the islanders saw the snake hanging from his hand, they said to each other, "This man must be a murderer; for though he escaped from the sea, Justice has not allowed him to live." [5]But Paul shook the snake off into the fire and suffered no ill effects. [6]The people expected him to swell up or suddenly fall dead, but after waiting a long time and seeing nothing unusual happen to him, they changed their minds and said he was a god.

[7]There was an estate nearby that belonged to Publius, the chief official of the island. He welcomed us to his home and for three days entertained us hospitably. [8]His father was sick in bed, suffering from fever and dysentery. Paul went in to see him and, after prayer, placed his hands on him and healed him. [9]When this had happened, the rest of the sick on the island came and were cured. [10]They honored us in many ways and when we were ready to sail, they furnished us with the supplies we needed.

PRAYER: THE WORKS OF GOD

***GOD** so loved the world that He gave You, Jesus, His only begotten Son, that whoever believes in You should not perish but have eternal life. For God did not send You into the world to condemn the world, but to save the world through You. (John 3:16–17)*

***TAKE** a moment to consider the greatness of God's wonderful works.*

YEAR 1 DAY 78

OT Exodus 29:1–46

Consecration of the Priests

29 "This is what you are to do to consecrate them, so they may serve me as priests: Take a young bull and two rams without defect. [2]And from fine wheat flour, without yeast, make bread, and cakes mixed with oil, and wafers spread with oil. [3]Put them in a basket and present them in it—along with the bull and the two rams. [4]Then bring Aaron and his sons to the entrance to the Tent of Meeting and wash them with water. [5]Take the garments and dress Aaron with the tunic, the robe of the ephod, the ephod itself and the breastpiece. Fasten the ephod on him by its skillfully woven waistband. [6]Put the turban on his head and attach the sacred diadem to the turban. [7]Take the anointing oil and anoint him by pouring it on his head. [8]Bring his sons and dress them in tunics [9]and put headbands on them. Then tie sashes on Aaron and his sons.[a] The priesthood is theirs by a lasting ordinance. In this way you shall ordain Aaron and his sons.

[10]"Bring the bull to the front of the Tent of Meeting, and Aaron and his sons shall lay their hands on its head. [11]Slaughter it in the LORD's presence at the entrance to the Tent of Meeting. [12]Take some of the bull's blood and put it on the horns of the altar with your finger, and pour out the rest of it at the base of the altar. [13]Then take all the fat around the inner parts, the covering of the liver, and both kidneys with the fat on them, and burn them on the altar. [14]But burn the bull's flesh and its hide and its offal outside the camp. It is a sin offering.

[15]"Take one of the rams, and Aaron and his sons shall lay their hands on its head.

[a] 9 Hebrew; Septuagint *on them*

16 Slaughter it and take the blood and
sprinkle it against the altar on all sides.
17 Cut the ram into pieces and wash the inner parts and the legs, putting them with
the head and the other pieces. 18 Then
burn the entire ram on the altar. It is a
burnt offering to the LORD, a pleasing aroma, an offering made to the LORD by fire.

19 "Take the other ram, and Aaron and
his sons shall lay their hands on its head.
20 Slaughter it, take some of its blood and
put it on the lobes of the right ears of Aaron and his sons, on the thumbs of their
right hands, and on the big toes of their
right feet. Then sprinkle blood against the
altar on all sides. 21 And take some of the
blood on the altar and some of the
anointing oil and sprinkle it on Aaron
and his garments and on his sons and
their garments. Then he and his sons and
their garments will be consecrated.

22 "Take from this ram the fat, the fat
tail, the fat around the inner parts, the
covering of the liver, both kidneys with
the fat on them, and the right thigh. (This
is the ram for the ordination.) 23 From the
basket of bread made without yeast,
which is before the LORD, take a loaf, and
a cake made with oil, and a wafer. 24 Put
all these in the hands of Aaron and his
sons and wave them before the LORD as a
wave offering. 25 Then take them from
their hands and burn them on the altar
along with the burnt offering for a pleasing aroma to the LORD, an offering made
to the LORD by fire. 26 After you take the
breast of the ram for Aaron's ordination,
wave it before the LORD as a wave offering,
and it will be your share.

27 "Consecrate those parts of the ordination ram that belong to Aaron and his
sons: the breast that was waved and the
thigh that was presented. 28 This is always
to be the regular share from the Israelites
for Aaron and his sons. It is the contribution the Israelites are to make to the LORD
from their fellowship offerings.[b]

29 "Aaron's sacred garments will belong
to his descendants so that they can be
anointed and ordained in them. 30 The son
who succeeds him as priest and comes to
the Tent of Meeting to minister in the
Holy Place is to wear them seven days.

31 "Take the ram for the ordination and
cook the meat in a sacred place. 32 At the
entrance to the Tent of Meeting, Aaron
and his sons are to eat the meat of the ram
and the bread that is in the basket. 33 They
are to eat these offerings by which atonement was made for their ordination and
consecration. But no one else may eat
them, because they are sacred. 34 And if
any of the meat of the ordination ram or
any bread is left over till morning, burn it
up. It must not be eaten, because it is sacred.

35 "Do for Aaron and his sons everything
I have commanded you, taking seven days
to ordain them. 36 Sacrifice a bull each day
as a sin offering to make atonement. Purify the altar by making atonement for it,
and anoint it to consecrate it. 37 For seven
days make atonement for the altar and
consecrate it. Then the altar will be most
holy, and whatever touches it will be holy.

38 "This is what you are to offer on the
altar regularly each day: two lambs a year
old. 39 Offer one in the morning and the
other at twilight. 40 With the first lamb offer a tenth of an ephah[c] of fine flour
mixed with a quarter of a hin[d] of oil from
pressed olives, and a quarter of a hin of
wine as a drink offering. 41 Sacrifice the
other lamb at twilight with the same grain
offering and its drink offering as in the
morning—a pleasing aroma, an offering
made to the LORD by fire.

42 "For the generations to come this
burnt offering is to be made regularly at
the entrance to the Tent of Meeting before
the LORD. There I will meet you and speak
to you; 43 there also I will meet with the Israelites, and the place will be consecrated
by my glory.

44 "So I will consecrate the Tent of Meeting and the altar and will consecrate Aaron and his sons to serve me as priests.
45 Then I will dwell among the Israelites
and be their God. 46 They will know that I
am the LORD their God, who brought
them out of Egypt so that I might dwell
among them. I am the LORD their God.

[b] *28* Traditionally *peace offerings* [c] *40* That is, probably about 2 quarts (about 2 liters) [d] *40* That is, probably about 1 quart (about 1 liter)

PRAYER: ADORATION

YOURS, O Lord, is the greatness and the power and the glory and the victory and the majesty, for everything in heaven and earth is Yours. Yours, O Lord, is the kingdom, and You are exalted as head over all. Both riches and honor come from You, and You are the ruler of all things. In Your hand are power and might to exalt and to give strength to all. Therefore, my God, I give thanks and praise to Your glorious name. All things come from You, and I can only give You what comes from Your hand.
(1 Chronicles 29:11–14)

PAUSE *to express your thoughts of praise and worship.*

NT Acts 28:11-31

Arrival at Rome

11 After three months we put out to sea in
a ship that had wintered in the island. It
was an Alexandrian ship with the figure-
head of the twin gods Castor and Pollux.
12 We put in at Syracuse and stayed there
three days. 13 From there we set sail and arrived at Rhegium. The next day the south
wind came up, and on the following day
we reached Puteoli. 14 There we found some
brothers who invited us to spend a week
with them. And so we came to Rome. 15 The
brothers there had heard that we were
coming, and they traveled as far as the Forum of Appius and the Three Taverns to
meet us. At the sight of these men Paul
thanked God and was encouraged. 16 When
we got to Rome, Paul was allowed to live
by himself, with a soldier to guard him.

Paul Preaches at Rome Under Guard

17 Three days later he called together the
leaders of the Jews. When they had assembled, Paul said to them: "My brothers,
although I have done nothing against our
people or against the customs of our ancestors, I was arrested in Jerusalem and
handed over to the Romans. 18 They examined me and wanted to release me, because I was not guilty of any crime deserving death. 19 But when the Jews
objected, I was compelled to appeal to
Caesar—not that I had any charge to
bring against my own people. 20 For this
reason I have asked to see you and talk
with you. It is because of the hope of Israel that I am bound with this chain."
21 They replied, "We have not received
any letters from Judea concerning you,
and none of the brothers who have come
from there has reported or said anything
bad about you. 22 But we want to hear what
your views are, for we know that people
everywhere are talking against this sect."
23 They arranged to meet Paul on a certain day, and came in even larger numbers
to the place where he was staying. From
morning till evening he explained and declared to them the kingdom of God and
tried to convince them about Jesus from
the Law of Moses and from the Prophets.
24 Some were convinced by what he said,
but others would not believe. 25 They dis-
agreed among themselves and began to
leave after Paul had made this final statement: "The Holy Spirit spoke the truth to
your forefathers when he said through
Isaiah the prophet:

26 " 'Go to this people and say,
"You will be ever hearing but never
understanding;
you will be ever seeing but never
perceiving."
27 For this people's heart has become
calloused;
they hardly hear with their ears,
and they have closed their eyes.
Otherwise they might see with their
eyes,
hear with their ears,
understand with their hearts
and turn, and I would heal them.'[a]

28 "Therefore I want you to know that
God's salvation has been sent to the Gentiles, and they will listen!"[b]

[a] 27 Isaiah 6:9,10 [b] 28 Some manuscripts *listen!"* [29] *After he said this, the Jews left, arguing vigorously among themselves.*

[30]For two whole years Paul stayed there in his own rented house and welcomed all who came to see him. [31]Boldly and without hindrance he preached the kingdom of God and taught about the Lord Jesus Christ.

PRAYER: MY RELATIONSHIP TO GOD

LORD Jesus, You are in Your Father, and I am in You, and You are in me. (John 14:20) . . . If I have been united with You, O Christ, in the likeness of Your death, I will certainly also be united with You in the likeness of Your resurrection. (Romans 6:5)

PAUSE *to thank God for the relationship that you enjoy with Him in Jesus Christ.*

YEAR 1 DAY 79

OT Exodus 30:1–38

The Altar of Incense

30 "Make an altar of acacia wood for burning incense. [2]It is to be square, a cubit long and a cubit wide, and two cubits high[a]—its horns of one piece with it. [3]Overlay the top and all the sides and the horns with pure gold, and make a gold molding around it. [4]Make two gold rings for the altar below the molding—two on opposite sides—to hold the poles used to carry it. [5]Make the poles of acacia wood and overlay them with gold. [6]Put the altar in front of the curtain that is before the ark of the Testimony—before the atonement cover that is over the Testimony—where I will meet with you.

[7]"Aaron must burn fragrant incense on the altar every morning when he tends the lamps. [8]He must burn incense again when he lights the lamps at twilight so incense will burn regularly before the LORD for the generations to come. [9]Do not offer on this altar any other incense or any burnt offering or grain offering, and do not pour a drink offering on it. [10]Once a year Aaron shall make atonement on its horns. This annual atonement must be made with the blood of the atoning sin offering for the generations to come. It is most holy to the LORD."

Atonement Money

[11]Then the LORD said to Moses, [12]"When you take a census of the Israelites to count them, each one must pay the LORD a ransom for his life at the time he is counted. Then no plague will come on them when you number them. [13]Each one who crosses over to those already counted is to give a half shekel,[b] according to the sanctuary shekel, which weighs twenty gerahs. This half shekel is an offering to the LORD. [14]All who cross over, those twenty years old or more, are to give an offering to the LORD. [15]The rich are not to give more than a half shekel and the poor are not to give less when you make the offering to the LORD to atone for your lives. [16]Receive the atonement money from the Israelites and use it for the service of the Tent of Meeting. It will be a memorial for the Israelites before the LORD, making atonement for your lives."

Basin for Washing

[17]Then the LORD said to Moses, [18]"Make a bronze basin, with its bronze stand, for washing. Place it between the Tent of Meeting and the altar, and put water in it. [19]Aaron and his sons are to wash their hands and feet with water from it. [20]Whenever they enter the Tent of Meeting, they shall wash with water so that they will not die. Also, when they approach the altar to minister by presenting an offering made to the LORD by fire, [21]they shall wash their hands and feet so

[a] *2* That is, about 1 1/2 feet (about 0.5 meter) long and wide and about 3 feet (about 0.9 meter) high
[b] *13* That is, about 1/5 ounce (about 6 grams); also in verse 15

that they will not die. This is to be a lasting ordinance for Aaron and his descendants for the generations to come."

Anointing Oil

22 Then the LORD said to Moses, 23 "Take the following fine spices: 500 shekels[c] of liquid myrrh, half as much (that is, 250 shekels) of fragrant cinnamon, 250 shekels of fragrant cane, 24 500 shekels of cassia—all according to the sanctuary shekel—and a hin[d] of olive oil. 25 Make these into a sacred anointing oil, a fragrant blend, the work of a perfumer. It will be the sacred anointing oil. 26 Then use it to anoint the Tent of Meeting, the ark of the Testimony, 27 the table and all its articles, the lampstand and its accessories, the altar of incense, 28 the altar of burnt offering and all its utensils, and the basin with its stand. 29 You shall consecrate them so they will be most holy, and whatever touches them will be holy.

30 "Anoint Aaron and his sons and consecrate them so they may serve me as priests. 31 Say to the Israelites, 'This is to be my sacred anointing oil for the generations to come. 32 Do not pour it on men's bodies and do not make any oil with the same formula. It is sacred, and you are to consider it sacred. 33 Whoever makes perfume like it and whoever puts it on anyone other than a priest must be cut off from his people.' "

Incense

34 Then the LORD said to Moses, "Take fragrant spices—gum resin, onycha and galbanum—and pure frankincense, all in equal amounts, 35 and make a fragrant blend of incense, the work of a perfumer. It is to be salted and pure and sacred. 36 Grind some of it to powder and place it in front of the Testimony in the Tent of Meeting, where I will meet with you. It shall be most holy to you. 37 Do not make any incense with this formula for yourselves; consider it holy to the LORD. 38 Whoever makes any like it to enjoy its fragrance must be cut off from his people."

[c] 23 That is, about 12 1/2 pounds (about 6 kilograms) [d] 24 That is, probably about 4 quarts (about 4 liters)

PRAYER: CONFESSION

TO fear You, Lord, is to hate evil; wisdom hates pride and arrogance and the evil way and the perverse mouth. (Proverbs 8:13)

***ASK** the Spirit to search your heart and reveal any areas of unconfessed sin. Acknowledge these to the Lord and thank Him for His forgiveness.*

NT Romans 1:1–32

1 Paul, a servant of Christ Jesus, called to be an apostle and set apart for the gospel of God— 2 the gospel he promised beforehand through his prophets in the Holy Scriptures 3 regarding his Son, who as to his human nature was a descendant of David, 4 and who through the Spirit[a] of holiness was declared with power to be the Son of God[b] by his resurrection from the dead: Jesus Christ our Lord. 5 Through him and for his name's sake, we received grace and apostleship to call people from among all the Gentiles to the obedience that comes from faith. 6 And you also are among those who are called to belong to Jesus Christ.

7 To all in Rome who are loved by God and called to be saints:

Grace and peace to you from God our Father and from the Lord Jesus Christ.

Paul's Longing to Visit Rome

8 First, I thank my God through Jesus Christ for all of you, because your faith is being reported all over the world. 9 God, whom I serve with my whole heart in preaching the gospel of his Son, is my witness how constantly I remember you 10 in my prayers at all times; and I pray that now at last by God's will the way may be opened for me to come to you.

11 I long to see you so that I may impart to you some spiritual gift to make you

[a] 4 Or *who as to his spirit* [b] 4 Or *was appointed to be the Son of God with power*

strong— 12that is, that you and I may be mutually encouraged by each other's faith. 13I do not want you to be unaware, brothers, that I planned many times to come to you (but have been prevented from doing so until now) in order that I might have a harvest among you, just as I have had among the other Gentiles.

14I am obligated both to Greeks and non-Greeks, both to the wise and the foolish. 15That is why I am so eager to preach the gospel also to you who are at Rome.

16I am not ashamed of the gospel, because it is the power of God for the salvation of everyone who believes: first for the Jew, then for the Gentile. 17For in the gospel a righteousness from God is revealed, a righteousness that is by faith from first to last,[c] just as it is written: "The righteous will live by faith."[d]

God's Wrath Against Mankind

18The wrath of God is being revealed from heaven against all the godlessness and wickedness of men who suppress the truth by their wickedness, 19since what may be known about God is plain to them, because God has made it plain to them. 20For since the creation of the world God's invisible qualities—his eternal power and divine nature—have been clearly seen, being understood from what has been made, so that men are without excuse.

21For although they knew God, they neither glorified him as God nor gave thanks to him, but their thinking became futile and their foolish hearts were darkened. 22Although they claimed to be wise, they became fools 23and exchanged the glory of the immortal God for images made to look like mortal man and birds and animals and reptiles.

24Therefore God gave them over in the sinful desires of their hearts to sexual impurity for the degrading of their bodies with one another. 25They exchanged the truth of God for a lie, and worshiped and served created things rather than the Creator—who is forever praised. Amen.

26Because of this, God gave them over to shameful lusts. Even their women exchanged natural relations for unnatural ones. 27In the same way the men also abandoned natural relations with women and were inflamed with lust for one another. Men committed indecent acts with other men, and received in themselves the due penalty for their perversion.

28Furthermore, since they did not think it worthwhile to retain the knowledge of God, he gave them over to a depraved mind, to do what ought not to be done. 29They have become filled with every kind of wickedness, evil, greed and depravity. They are full of envy, murder, strife, deceit and malice. They are gossips, 30slanderers, God-haters, insolent, arrogant and boastful; they invent ways of doing evil; they disobey their parents; 31they are senseless, faithless, heartless, ruthless. 32Although they know God's righteous decree that those who do such things deserve death, they not only continue to do these very things but also approve of those who practice them.

[c] 17 Or *is from faith to faith* [d] 17 Hab. 2:4

PRAYER: THE CHARACTER I WANT TO CULTIVATE

WHEN pride comes, then comes dishonor, but with humility comes wisdom. (Proverbs 11:2) . . . The proud will be humbled and the lofty will be brought low; You alone, O Lord, will be exalted. (Isaiah 2:11)

TAKE *a moment to ask the Lord for the grace to grow in godly character.*

OT Exodus 31:1–32:35

Bezalel and Oholiab

31 Then the LORD said to Moses, 2“See, I
have chosen Bezalel son of Uri, the
son of Hur, of the tribe of Judah, 3and I
have filled him with the Spirit of God,
with skill, ability and knowledge in all
kinds of crafts— 4to make artistic designs
for work in gold, silver and bronze, 5to cut
and set stones, to work in wood, and to
engage in all kinds of craftsmanship.
6Moreover, I have appointed Oholiab son
of Ahisamach, of the tribe of Dan, to help
him. Also I have given skill to all the
craftsmen to make everything I have commanded you: 7the Tent of Meeting, the ark
of the Testimony with the atonement cover on it, and all the other furnishings of
the tent— 8the table and its articles, the
pure gold lampstand and all its accessories, the altar of incense, 9the altar of
burnt offering and all its utensils, the
basin with its stand— 10and also the woven garments, both the sacred garments
for Aaron the priest and the garments for
his sons when they serve as priests, 11and
the anointing oil and fragrant incense for
the Holy Place. They are to make them
just as I commanded you.”

The Sabbath

12Then the LORD said to Moses, 13“Say to
the Israelites, ‘You must observe my Sabbaths. This will be a sign between me and
you for the generations to come, so you
may know that I am the LORD, who makes
you holy.[a]
14“ ‘Observe the Sabbath, because it is
holy to you. Anyone who desecrates it
must be put to death; whoever does any
work on that day must be cut off from his
people. 15For six days, work is to be done,
but the seventh day is a Sabbath of rest,
holy to the LORD. Whoever does any work
on the Sabbath day must be put to death.
16The Israelites are to observe the Sabbath,
celebrating it for the generations to come
as a lasting covenant. 17It will be a sign between me and the Israelites forever, for in
six days the LORD made the heavens and
the earth, and on the seventh day he ab-
stained from work and rested.’ ”
18When the LORD finished speaking to
Moses on Mount Sinai, he gave him the
two tablets of the Testimony, the tablets
of stone inscribed by the finger of God.

The Golden Calf

32 When the people saw that Moses was
so long in coming down from the
mountain, they gathered around Aaron
and said, “Come, make us gods[b] who will
go before us. As for this fellow Moses who
brought us up out of Egypt, we don’t
know what has happened to him.”
2Aaron answered them, “Take off the
gold earrings that your wives, your sons
and your daughters are wearing, and bring
them to me.” 3So all the people took off
their earrings and brought them to Aaron.
4He took what they handed him and
made it into an idol cast in the shape of
a calf, fashioning it with a tool. Then they
said, “These are your gods,[c] O Israel, who
brought you up out of Egypt.”
5When Aaron saw this, he built an altar
in front of the calf and announced, “Tomorrow there will be a festival to the
LORD.” 6So the next day the people rose
early and sacrificed burnt offerings and
presented fellowship offerings.[d] Afterward
they sat down to eat and drink and got up
to indulge in revelry.
7Then the LORD said to Moses, “Go
down, because your people, whom you
brought up out of Egypt, have become
corrupt. 8They have been quick to turn
away from what I commanded them and
have made themselves an idol cast in the
shape of a calf. They have bowed down to
it and sacrificed to it and have said, ‘These
are your gods, O Israel, who brought you
up out of Egypt.’
9“I have seen these people,” the LORD
said to Moses, “and they are a stiff-necked
people. 10Now leave me alone so that my
anger may burn against them and that I
may destroy them. Then I will make you
into a great nation.”
11But Moses sought the favor of the LORD
his God. “O LORD,” he said, “why should
your anger burn against your people,

[a] 13 Or *who sanctifies you;* or *who sets you apart as holy* [b] 1 Or *a god;* also in verses 23 and 31
[c] 4 Or *This is your god;* also in verse 8
[d] 6 Traditionally *peace offerings*

whom you brought out of Egypt with great power and a mighty hand? 12Why should the Egyptians say, 'It was with evil intent that he brought them out, to kill them in the mountains and to wipe them off the face of the earth'? Turn from your fierce anger; relent and do not bring disaster on your people. 13Remember your servants Abraham, Isaac and Israel, to whom you swore by your own self: 'I will make your descendants as numerous as the stars in the sky and I will give your descendants all this land I promised them, and it will be their inheritance forever.' " 14Then the LORD relented and did not bring on his people the disaster he had threatened.

15Moses turned and went down the mountain with the two tablets of the Testimony in his hands. They were inscribed on both sides, front and back. 16The tablets were the work of God; the writing was the writing of God, engraved on the tablets.

17When Joshua heard the noise of the people shouting, he said to Moses, "There is the sound of war in the camp."

18Moses replied:

"It is not the sound of victory,
it is not the sound of defeat;
it is the sound of singing that I hear."

19When Moses approached the camp and saw the calf and the dancing, his anger burned and he threw the tablets out of his hands, breaking them to pieces at the foot of the mountain. 20And he took the calf they had made and burned it in the fire; then he ground it to powder, scattered it on the water and made the Israelites drink it.

21He said to Aaron, "What did these people do to you, that you led them into such great sin?"

22"Do not be angry, my lord," Aaron answered. "You know how prone these people are to evil. 23They said to me, 'Make us gods who will go before us. As for this fellow Moses who brought us up out of Egypt, we don't know what has happened to him.' 24So I told them, 'Whoever has any gold jewelry, take it off.' Then they gave me the gold, and I threw it into the fire, and out came this calf!"

25Moses saw that the people were running wild and that Aaron had let them get out of control and so become a laughingstock to their enemies. 26So he stood at the entrance to the camp and said, "Whoever is for the LORD, come to me." And all the Levites rallied to him.

27Then he said to them, "This is what the LORD, the God of Israel, says: 'Each man strap a sword to his side. Go back and forth through the camp from one end to the other, each killing his brother and friend and neighbor.' " 28The Levites did as Moses commanded, and that day about three thousand of the people died. 29Then Moses said, "You have been set apart to the LORD today, for you were against your own sons and brothers, and he has blessed you this day."

30The next day Moses said to the people, "You have committed a great sin. But now I will go up to the LORD; perhaps I can make atonement for your sin."

31So Moses went back to the LORD and said, "Oh, what a great sin these people have committed! They have made themselves gods of gold. 32But now, please forgive their sin—but if not, then blot me out of the book you have written."

33The LORD replied to Moses, "Whoever has sinned against me I will blot out of my book. 34Now go, lead the people to the place I spoke of, and my angel will go before you. However, when the time comes for me to punish, I will punish them for their sin."

35And the LORD struck the people with a plague because of what they did with the calf Aaron had made.

PRAYER: RENEWAL

MAY I not trust in myself or in my own righteousness nor view others with contempt. (Luke 18:9) . . .
May I not be like those who do not make You their strength but trust in the abundance of their wealth and strengthen themselves in their evil desires. (Psalm 52:7)

***PAUSE** to add your own prayers for personal renewal.*

NT Romans 2:1–16

God's Righteous Judgment

2 You, therefore, have no excuse, you who pass judgment on someone else, for at whatever point you judge the other, you are condemning yourself, because you who pass judgment do the same things. [2]Now we know that God's judgment against those who do such things is based on truth. [3]So when you, a mere man, pass judgment on them and yet do the same things, do you think you will escape God's judgment? [4]Or do you show contempt for the riches of his kindness, tolerance and patience, not realizing that God's kindness leads you toward repentance?

[5]But because of your stubbornness and your unrepentant heart, you are storing up wrath against yourself for the day of God's wrath, when his righteous judgment will be revealed. [6]God "will give to each person according to what he has done."[a] [7]To those who by persistence in doing good seek glory, honor and immortality, he will give eternal life. [8]But for those who are self-seeking and who reject the truth and follow evil, there will be wrath and anger. [9]There will be trouble and distress for every human being who does evil: first for the Jew, then for the Gentile; [10]but glory, honor and peace for everyone who does good: first for the Jew, then for the Gentile. [11]For God does not show favoritism.

[12]All who sin apart from the law will also perish apart from the law, and all who sin under the law will be judged by the law. [13]For it is not those who hear the law who are righteous in God's sight, but it is those who obey the law who will be declared righteous. [14](Indeed, when Gentiles, who do not have the law, do by nature things required by the law, they are a law for themselves, even though they do not have the law, [15]since they show that the requirements of the law are written on their hearts, their consciences also bearing witness, and their thoughts now accusing, now even defending them.) [16]This will take place on the day when God will judge men's secrets through Jesus Christ, as my gospel declares.

[a] 6 Psalm 62:12; Prov. 24:12

PRAYER: MY RELATIONSHIP TO OTHERS

Is this not the fast You have chosen: to loose the bonds of wickedness, to undo the cords of the yoke, and to let the oppressed go free and break every yoke? Is it not to share our food with the hungry and to provide the poor wanderer with shelter; when we see the naked, to clothe them, and not to turn away from our own flesh? Then our light will break forth like the dawn, and our healing will quickly appear, and our righteousness will go before us; Your glory, O Lord, will be our rear guard. Then we will call, and You will answer; we will cry, and You will say, "Here I am." If we put away the yoke from our midst, the pointing of the finger and malicious talk, and if we extend our souls to the hungry and satisfy the afflicted soul, then our light will rise in the darkness, and our gloom will become like the noonday. (Isaiah 58:6–10)

PAUSE *to review your relationships with others and to commit them to the Lord.*

YEAR 1 DAY 81

OT Exodus 33:1-23

33 Then the LORD said to Moses, "Leave
this place, you and the people you
brought up out of Egypt, and go up to the
land I promised on oath to Abraham,
Isaac and Jacob, saying, 'I will give it to
your descendants.' [2]I will send an angel
before you and drive out the Canaanites,
Amorites, Hittites, Perizzites, Hivites and
Jebusites. [3]Go up to the land flowing with
milk and honey. But I will not go with
you, because you are a stiff-necked people
and I might destroy you on the way."
[4]When the people heard these distress-
ing words, they began to mourn and no
one put on any ornaments. [5]For the LORD
had said to Moses, "Tell the Israelites, 'You
are a stiff-necked people. If I were to go
with you even for a moment, I might destroy you. Now take off your ornaments
and I will decide what to do with you.' "
[6]So the Israelites stripped off their ornaments at Mount Horeb.

The Tent of Meeting

[7]Now Moses used to take a tent and pitch
it outside the camp some distance away,
calling it the "tent of meeting." Anyone inquiring of the LORD would go to the tent of
meeting outside the camp. [8]And whenever
Moses went out to the tent, all the people
rose and stood at the entrances to their
tents, watching Moses until he entered the
tent. [9]As Moses went into the tent, the pillar of cloud would come down and stay at
the entrance, while the LORD spoke with
Moses. [10]Whenever the people saw the pillar of cloud standing at the entrance to the
tent, they all stood and worshiped, each at
the entrance to his tent. [11]The LORD would
speak to Moses face to face, as a man speaks
with his friend. Then Moses would return
to the camp, but his young aide Joshua son
of Nun did not leave the tent.

Moses and the Glory of the LORD

[12]Moses said to the LORD, "You have
been telling me, 'Lead these people,' but
you have not let me know whom you will
send with me. You have said, 'I know you
by name and you have found favor with
me.' [13]If you are pleased with me, teach me
your ways so I may know you and continue to find favor with you. Remember
that this nation is your people."
[14]The LORD replied, "My Presence will
go with you, and I will give you rest."
[15]Then Moses said to him, "If your Presence does not go with us, do not send us
up from here. [16]How will anyone know
that you are pleased with me and with
your people unless you go with us? What
else will distinguish me and your people
from all the other people on the face of
the earth?"
[17]And the LORD said to Moses, "I will do
the very thing you have asked, because I
am pleased with you and I know you by
name."
[18]Then Moses said, "Now show me your
glory."
[19]And the LORD said, "I will cause all my
goodness to pass in front of you, and I
will proclaim my name, the LORD, in your
presence. I will have mercy on whom I
will have mercy, and I will have compassion on whom I will have compassion.
[20]But," he said, "you cannot see my face,
for no one may see me and live."
[21]Then the LORD said, "There is a place
near me where you may stand on a rock.
[22]When my glory passes by, I will put you
in a cleft in the rock and cover you with
my hand until I have passed by. [23]Then I
will remove my hand and you will see my
back; but my face must not be seen."

PRAYER: PETITION

TURN to me, O Lord, and be gracious to me, for I am lonely and afflicted. The troubles of my heart have multiplied; free me from my distresses. Look on my affliction and my pain and forgive all my sins. (Psalm 25:16–18)

PAUSE *here to petition God to help you be a faithful steward of your time, talents, possessions and relationships. Offer prayers of petition regarding your activities for this day and any special concerns you may have.*

NT Romans 2:17–29

The Jews and the Law

17Now you, if you call yourself a Jew; if
you rely on the law and brag about your
relationship to God; 18if you know his will
and approve of what is superior because
you are instructed by the law; 19if you are
convinced that you are a guide for the
blind, a light for those who are in the
dark, 20an instructor of the foolish, a
teacher of infants, because you have in the
law the embodiment of knowledge and
truth— 21you, then, who teach others, do
you not teach yourself? You who preach
against stealing, do you steal? 22You who
say that people should not commit adultery, do you commit adultery? You who
abhor idols, do you rob temples? 23You
who brag about the law, do you dishonor
God by breaking the law? 24As it is written: "God's name is blasphemed among
the Gentiles because of you."[a]

25Circumcision has value if you observe
the law, but if you break the law, you have
become as though you had not been circumcised. 26If those who are not circumcised keep the law's requirements, will
they not be regarded as though they were
circumcised? 27The one who is not circumcised physically and yet obeys the law
will condemn you who, even though you
have the[b] written code and circumcision,
are a lawbreaker.

28A man is not a Jew if he is only one
outwardly, nor is circumcision merely
outward and physical. 29No, a man is a
Jew if he is one inwardly; and circumcision is circumcision of the heart, by the
Spirit, not by the written code. Such a
man's praise is not from men, but from
God.

[a] 24 Isaiah 52:5; Ezek. 36:22 [b] 27 Or *who, by means of a*

PRAYER: THE ATTRIBUTES OF GOD

O LORD, You will be gracious to whom You will be gracious, and You will have compassion on whom You will have compassion. (Exodus 33:19) . . . Lord Jesus, You are holy and true; You hold the key of David. What You open no one can shut, and what You shut no one can open. (Revelation 3:7)

PAUSE *to reflect on these affirmations about the person, powers and perfection of God.*

OT **Exodus 34:1-35** YEAR 1 DAY 82

The New Stone Tablets

34 The LORD said to Moses, "Chisel out
two stone tablets like the first ones,
and I will write on them the words that
were on the first tablets, which you broke.
2 Be ready in the morning, and then come
up on Mount Sinai. Present yourself to me
there on top of the mountain. 3 No one is
to come with you or be seen anywhere on
the mountain; not even the flocks and
herds may graze in front of the mountain."
4 So Moses chiseled out two stone
tablets like the first ones and went up
Mount Sinai early in the morning, as the
LORD had commanded him; and he carried the two stone tablets in his hands.
5 Then the LORD came down in the cloud
and stood there with him and proclaimed
his name, the LORD. 6 And he passed in
front of Moses, proclaiming, "The LORD,
the LORD, the compassionate and gracious
God, slow to anger, abounding in love
and faithfulness, 7 maintaining love to
thousands, and forgiving wickedness, rebellion and sin. Yet he does not leave the
guilty unpunished; he punishes the children and their children for the sin of the
fathers to the third and fourth generation."
8 Moses bowed to the ground at once
and worshiped. 9 "O Lord, if I have found
favor in your eyes," he said, "then let the
Lord go with us. Although this is a stiff-
necked people, forgive our wickedness
and our sin, and take us as your inheritance."
10 Then the LORD said: "I am making a
covenant with you. Before all your people
I will do wonders never before done in
any nation in all the world. The people
you live among will see how awesome is
the work that I, the LORD, will do for you.
11 Obey what I command you today. I will
drive out before you the Amorites,
Canaanites, Hittites, Perizzites, Hivites
and Jebusites. 12 Be careful not to make a
treaty with those who live in the land
where you are going, or they will be a
snare among you. 13 Break down their altars, smash their sacred stones and cut
down their Asherah poles.[a] 14 Do not worship any other god, for the LORD, whose
name is Jealous, is a jealous God.

15 "Be careful not to make a treaty with
those who live in the land; for when they
prostitute themselves to their gods and
sacrifice to them, they will invite you and
you will eat their sacrifices. 16 And when
you choose some of their daughters as
wives for your sons and those daughters
prostitute themselves to their gods, they
will lead your sons to do the same.
17 "Do not make cast idols.
18 "Celebrate the Feast of Unleavened
Bread. For seven days eat bread made
without yeast, as I commanded you. Do
this at the appointed time in the month
of Abib, for in that month you came out
of Egypt.
19 "The first offspring of every womb belongs to me, including all the firstborn
males of your livestock, whether from
herd or flock. 20 Redeem the firstborn donkey with a lamb, but if you do not redeem
it, break its neck. Redeem all your firstborn sons.
"No one is to appear before me empty-
handed.
21 "Six days you shall labor, but on the
seventh day you shall rest; even during the
plowing season and harvest you must rest.
22 "Celebrate the Feast of Weeks with
the firstfruits of the wheat harvest, and the
Feast of Ingathering at the turn of
the year.[b] 23 Three times a year all your
men are to appear before the Sovereign
LORD, the God of Israel. 24 I will drive out
nations before you and enlarge your territory, and no one will covet your land
when you go up three times each year to
appear before the LORD your God.
25 "Do not offer the blood of a sacrifice
to me along with anything containing
yeast, and do not let any of the sacrifice
from the Passover Feast remain until
morning.
26 "Bring the best of the firstfruits of
your soil to the house of the LORD your
God.
"Do not cook a young goat in its mother's milk."
27 Then the LORD said to Moses, "Write
down these words, for in accordance with
these words I have made a covenant with

[a] *13* That is, symbols of the goddess Asherah
[b] *22* That is, in the fall

you and with Israel." [28]Moses was there
with the LORD forty days and forty nights
without eating bread or drinking water.
And he wrote on the tablets the words of
the covenant—the Ten Commandments.

The Radiant Face of Moses

[29]When Moses came down from Mount
Sinai with the two tablets of the Testimony in his hands, he was not aware that his
face was radiant because he had spoken
with the LORD. [30]When Aaron and all the
Israelites saw Moses, his face was radiant,
and they were afraid to come near him.
[31]But Moses called to them; so Aaron and
all the leaders of the community came
back to him, and he spoke to them. [32]Af-
terward all the Israelites came near him,
and he gave them all the commands the
LORD had given him on Mount Sinai.

[33]When Moses finished speaking to
them, he put a veil over his face. [34]But
whenever he entered the LORD's presence
to speak with him, he removed the veil
until he came out. And when he came out
and told the Israelites what he had been
commanded, [35]they saw that his face was
radiant. Then Moses would put the veil
back over his face until he went in to
speak with the LORD.

PRAYER: INTERCESSION

LORD, may I remind others to be subject to rulers and authorities, to be obedient, to be ready for every good work, to slander no one, to be peaceable and gentle, and to show true humility toward all people. (Titus 3:1–2)

***TAKE** a few moments to intercede on behalf of your local, state or provincial, and national governments. Pray for spiritual revival in the nation and offer prayers regarding current events and concerns.*

NT Romans 3:1–20

God's Faithfulness

3 What advantage, then, is there in being
a Jew, or what value is there in circumcision? [2]Much in every way! First of all,
they have been entrusted with the very
words of God.

[3]What if some did not have faith? Will
their lack of faith nullify God's faithfulness? [4]Not at all! Let God be true, and
every man a liar. As it is written:

> "So that you may be proved right
> when you speak
> and prevail when you judge."[a]

[5]But if our unrighteousness brings out
God's righteousness more clearly, what
shall we say? That God is unjust in bringing his wrath on us? (I am using a human
argument.) [6]Certainly not! If that were so,
how could God judge the world? [7]Some-
one might argue, "If my falsehood enhances God's truthfulness and so increases his glory, why am I still
condemned as a sinner?" [8]Why not say—
as we are being slanderously reported as
saying and as some claim that we say—
"Let us do evil that good may result"?
Their condemnation is deserved.

No One Is Righteous

[9]What shall we conclude then? Are we
any better[b]? Not at all! We have already
made the charge that Jews and Gentiles
alike are all under sin. [10]As it is written:

> "There is no one righteous, not even
> one;
> [11] there is no one who understands,
> no one who seeks God.
> [12] All have turned away,
> they have together become
> worthless;
> there is no one who does good,
> not even one."[c]
> [13] "Their throats are open graves;
> their tongues practice deceit."[d]
> "The poison of vipers is on their
> lips."[e]
> [14] "Their mouths are full of cursing
> and bitterness."[f]

[a] *4* Psalm 51:4 [b] *9* Or *worse* [c] *12* Psalms 14:1–3; 53:1–3; Eccles. 7:20 [d] *13* Psalm 5:9 [e] *13* Psalm 140:3 [f] *14* Psalm 10:7

[15] "Their feet are swift to shed blood;
[16] ruin and misery mark their ways,
[17] and the way of peace they do not know."[g]
[18] "There is no fear of God before their eyes."[h]

[19] Now we know that whatever the law
says, it says to those who are under the law, so that every mouth may be silenced and the whole world held accountable to God.
[20] Therefore no one will be declared righteous in his sight by observing the law; rather, through the law we become conscious of sin.

[g] 17 Isaiah 59:7,8 [h] 18 Psalm 36:1

PRAYER: THE WORKS OF GOD

O GOD, You are the maker of the Bear and Orion, the Pleiades, and the constellations of the south. You do great things that cannot be fathomed and wonderful works that cannot be counted. (Job 9:9–10) . . . The day is Yours, O God; the night also is Yours; You established the sun and moon. It was You who set all the boundaries of the earth; You made both summer and winter. (Psalm 74:16–17)

***TAKE** a moment to consider the greatness of God's wonderful works.*

YEAR 1 DAY 83

OT Exodus 35:1–36:7

Sabbath Regulations

35 Moses assembled the whole Israelite community and said to them, "These are the things the LORD has commanded you to do:
[2] For six days, work is to be done, but the seventh day shall be your holy day, a Sabbath of rest to the LORD. Whoever does any work on it must be put to death.
[3] Do not light a fire in any of your dwellings on the Sabbath day."

Materials for the Tabernacle

[4] Moses said to the whole Israelite community, "This is what the LORD has commanded:
[5] From what you have, take an offering for the LORD. Everyone who is willing is to bring to the LORD an offering of gold, silver and bronze;
[6] blue, purple and scarlet yarn and fine linen; goat hair;
[7] ram skins dyed red and hides of sea cows[a]; acacia wood;
[8] olive oil for the light; spices for the anointing oil and for the fragrant incense;
[9] and onyx stones and other gems to be mounted on the ephod and breastpiece.

[10] "All who are skilled among you are to come and make everything the LORD has commanded:
[11] the tabernacle with its tent and its covering, clasps, frames, crossbars, posts and bases;
[12] the ark with its poles and the atonement cover and the curtain that shields it;
[13] the table with its poles and all its articles and the bread of the Presence;
[14] the lampstand that is for light with its accessories, lamps and oil for the light;
[15] the altar of incense with its poles, the anointing oil and the fragrant incense; the curtain for the doorway at the entrance to the tabernacle;
[16] the altar of burnt offering with its bronze grating, its poles and all its utensils; the bronze basin with its stand;
[17] the curtains of the courtyard with its posts and bases, and the curtain for the entrance to the courtyard;
[18] the tent pegs for the tabernacle and for the courtyard, and their ropes;
[19] the woven garments worn for ministering in the sanctuary—both the sacred garments for Aaron the priest and the garments for his sons when they serve as priests."

[20] Then the whole Israelite community withdrew from Moses' presence,
[21] and everyone who was willing and whose heart moved him came and brought an offering to the LORD for the work on the Tent of Meeting, for all its service, and for the sacred garments.
[22] All who were willing, men and women alike, came and brought gold jewelry of all kinds: brooches, earrings, rings and ornaments. They all presented their gold as a wave offering to the

[a] 7 That is, dugongs; also in verse 23

LORD. 23Everyone who had blue, purple or
scarlet yarn or fine linen, or goat hair, ram
skins dyed red or hides of sea cows
brought them. 24Those presenting an offering of silver or bronze brought it as an
offering to the LORD, and everyone who
had acacia wood for any part of the work
brought it. 25Every skilled woman spun
with her hands and brought what she had
spun—blue, purple or scarlet yarn or fine
linen. 26And all the women who were willing and had the skill spun the goat hair.
27The leaders brought onyx stones and
other gems to be mounted on the ephod
and breastpiece. 28They also brought spices
and olive oil for the light and for the
anointing oil and for the fragrant incense.
29All the Israelite men and women who
were willing brought to the LORD freewill
offerings for all the work the LORD through
Moses had commanded them to do.

Bezalel and Oholiab

30Then Moses said to the Israelites, "See,
the LORD has chosen Bezalel son of Uri,
the son of Hur, of the tribe of Judah, 31and
he has filled him with the Spirit of God,
with skill, ability and knowledge in all
kinds of crafts— 32to make artistic designs
for work in gold, silver and bronze, 33to cut
and set stones, to work in wood and to engage in all kinds of artistic craftsmanship.
34And he has given both him and Oholiab son of Ahisamach, of the tribe of Dan,
the ability to teach others. 35He has filled
them with skill to do all kinds of work as
craftsmen, designers, embroiderers in
blue, purple and scarlet yarn and fine
linen, and weavers—all of them master
36 craftsmen and designers. 1So Bezalel,
Oholiab and every skilled person to
whom the LORD has given skill and ability to know how to carry out all the work
of constructing the sanctuary are to do the
work just as the LORD has commanded."

2Then Moses summoned Bezalel and
Oholiab and every skilled person to
whom the LORD had given ability and
who was willing to come and do the
work. 3They received from Moses all the
offerings the Israelites had brought to carry out the work of constructing the sanctuary. And the people continued to bring
freewill offerings morning after morning.
4So all the skilled craftsmen who were doing all the work on the sanctuary left their
work 5and said to Moses, "The people are
bringing more than enough for doing the
work the LORD commanded to be done."

6Then Moses gave an order and they
sent this word throughout the camp: "No
man or woman is to make anything else
as an offering for the sanctuary." And so
the people were restrained from bringing
more, 7because what they already had was
more than enough to do all the work.

PRAYER: AFFIRMATION

I AM always of good courage and know that as long as I am at home in the body, I am away from You, Lord. For I live by faith, not by sight. I am of good courage and would prefer to be absent from the body and to be at home with You. (2 Corinthians 5:6–8) . . . Now I am Your child, Father, and what I shall be has not yet been revealed. I know that when Christ is revealed, I shall be like Him, for I shall see Him as He is. And everyone who has this hope in Him purifies himself, just as He is pure. (1 John 3:2–3)

PAUSE *to reflect on these Biblical affirmations.*

NT Romans 3:21–31

Righteousness Through Faith

21But now a righteousness from God,
apart from law, has been made known, to
which the Law and the Prophets testify.
22This righteousness from God comes
through faith in Jesus Christ to all who
believe. There is no difference, 23for all
have sinned and fall short of the glory of
God, 24and are justified freely by his grace
through the redemption that came by
Christ Jesus. 25God presented him as a sac-

rifice of atonement,[a] through faith in his
blood. He did this to demonstrate his justice, because in his forbearance he had left
the sins committed beforehand unpunished— [26]he did it to demonstrate his justice at the present time, so as to be just
and the one who justifies those who have
faith in Jesus.
[27]Where, then, is boasting? It is excluded. On what principle? On that of observing the law? No, but on that of faith. [28]For
we maintain that a man is justified by faith
apart from observing the law. [29]Is God the
God of Jews only? Is he not the God of
Gentiles too? Yes, of Gentiles too, [30]since
there is only one God, who will justify the
circumcised by faith and the uncircumcised through that same faith. [31]Do we,
then, nullify the law by this faith? Not at
all! Rather, we uphold the law.

[a] 25 Or *as the one who would turn aside his wrath, taking away sin*

PRAYER: MY RELATIONSHIP TO GOD

I WILL not depend on human strength, but on You, O Lord my God, for help and deliverance. (2 Chronicles 16:7–8, 12) . . .
How great is Your goodness, O Lord, which You have stored up for those who fear You, which You have prepared for those who take refuge in You in the sight of others! (Psalm 31:19)

PAUSE *to thank God for the relationship that you enjoy with Him in Jesus Christ.*

YEAR 1
DAY 84

OT Psalm 19

Psalm 19

For the director of music. A psalm of David.

[1]The heavens declare the glory of God;
the skies proclaim the work of his
hands.
[2]Day after day they pour forth speech;
night after night they display
knowledge.
[3]There is no speech or language
where their voice is not heard.[a]
[4]Their voice[b] goes out into all the earth,
their words to the ends of the world.

In the heavens he has pitched a tent
for the sun,
[5] which is like a bridegroom coming
forth from his pavilion,
like a champion rejoicing to run his
course.
[6]It rises at one end of the heavens
and makes its circuit to the other;
nothing is hidden from its heat.

[7]The law of the LORD is perfect,
reviving the soul.
The statutes of the LORD are trustworthy,
making wise the simple.
[8]The precepts of the LORD are right,
giving joy to the heart.
The commands of the LORD are radiant,
giving light to the eyes.
[9]The fear of the LORD is pure,
enduring forever.
The ordinances of the LORD are sure
and altogether righteous.
[10]They are more precious than gold,
than much pure gold;
they are sweeter than honey,
than honey from the comb.
[11]By them is your servant warned;
in keeping them there is great reward.

[12]Who can discern his errors?
Forgive my hidden faults.
[13]Keep your servant also from willful sins;
may they not rule over me.
Then will I be blameless,
innocent of great transgression.

[14]May the words of my mouth and the
meditation of my heart
be pleasing in your sight,
O LORD, my Rock and my Redeemer.

[a] 3 Or *They have no speech, there are no words; / no sound is heard from them* [b] 4 Septuagint, Jerome and Syriac; Hebrew *line*

PRAYER: THANKSGIVING

PRAISE be to You, the God of Israel, because You have visited us and have redeemed Your people. You have raised up a horn of salvation for us in the house of Your servant David (as You spoke by the mouth of Your holy prophets of long ago), salvation from our enemies and from the hand of all who hate us—to show mercy to our fathers and to remember Your holy covenant, the oath You swore to our father Abraham: to rescue us from the hand of our enemies, and to enable us to serve You without fear in holiness and righteousness before You all our days. (Luke 1:68–75)

PAUSE *to offer your own expressions of thanksgiving.*

NT Romans 4:1–25

Abraham Justified by Faith

4 What then shall we say that Abraham,
our forefather, discovered in this matter? 2If, in fact, Abraham was justified by
works, he had something to boast
about—but not before God. 3What does
the Scripture say? "Abraham believed
God, and it was credited to him as righteousness."[a]

4Now when a man works, his wages are
not credited to him as a gift, but as an
obligation. 5However, to the man who
does not work but trusts God who justifies the wicked, his faith is credited as
righteousness. 6David says the same thing
when he speaks of the blessedness of the
man to whom God credits righteousness
apart from works:

7"Blessed are they
whose transgressions are forgiven,
whose sins are covered.
8Blessed is the man
whose sin the Lord will never count
against him."[b]

9Is this blessedness only for the circumcised, or also for the uncircumcised?
We have been saying that Abraham's faith
was credited to him as righteousness.
10Under what circumstances was it credited? Was it after he was circumcised, or before? It was not after, but before! 11And he
received the sign of circumcision, a seal of
the righteousness that he had by faith
while he was still uncircumcised. So then,
he is the father of all who believe but have
not been circumcised, in order that righteousness might be credited to them.
12And he is also the father of the circumcised who not only are circumcised but
who also walk in the footsteps of the faith
that our father Abraham had before he
was circumcised.

13It was not through law that Abraham
and his offspring received the promise
that he would be heir of the world, but
through the righteousness that comes by
faith. 14For if those who live by law are
heirs, faith has no value and the promise
is worthless, 15because law brings wrath.
And where there is no law there is no
transgression.

16Therefore, the promise comes by faith,
so that it may be by grace and may be
guaranteed to all Abraham's offspring—
not only to those who are of the law but
also to those who are of the faith of Abraham. He is the father of us all. 17As it is
written: "I have made you a father of
many nations."[c] He is our father in the
sight of God, in whom he believed—the
God who gives life to the dead and calls
things that are not as though they were.

18Against all hope, Abraham in hope believed and so became the father of many
nations, just as it had been said to him,
"So shall your offspring be."[d] 19Without
weakening in his faith, he faced the fact
that his body was as good as dead—since
he was about a hundred years old—and
that Sarah's womb was also dead. 20Yet he
did not waver through unbelief regarding
the promise of God, but was strengthened
in his faith and gave glory to God, 21being
fully persuaded that God had power to do
what he had promised. 22This is why "it
was credited to him as righteousness."
23The words "it was credited to him" were

[a] *3* Gen. 15:6; also in verse 22 [b] *8* Psalm 32:1,2 [c] *17* Gen. 17:5 [d] *18* Gen. 15:5

written not for him alone, 24but also for us, to whom God will credit righteousness—for us who believe in him who raised Jesus our Lord from the dead. 25He was delivered over to death for our sins and was raised to life for our justification.

PRAYER: THE CHARACTER I WANT TO CULTIVATE

BEFORE I was afflicted, I went astray, O Lord, but now I keep Your word. It was good for me to be afflicted, so that I might learn Your statutes. (Psalm 119:67, 71) . . . I will not despise Your discipline, O Lord, nor lose heart when You rebuke me, for whom You love You discipline, and You chastise every child whom You receive. (Hebrews 12:5–6)

TAKE *a moment to ask the Lord for the grace to grow in godly character.*

YEAR 1
DAY 85

OT Exodus 36:8–37:29

The Tabernacle

8All the skilled men among the workmen made the tabernacle with ten curtains of finely twisted linen and blue, purple and scarlet yarn, with cherubim worked into them by a skilled craftsman. 9All the curtains were the same size—twenty-eight cubits long and four cubits wide.[a] 10They joined five of the curtains together and did the same with the other five. 11Then they made loops of blue material along the edge of the end curtain in one set, and the same was done with the end curtain in the other set. 12They also made fifty loops on one curtain and fifty loops on the end curtain of the other set, with the loops opposite each other. 13Then they made fifty gold clasps and used them to fasten the two sets of curtains together so that the tabernacle was a unit.

14They made curtains of goat hair for the tent over the tabernacle—eleven altogether. 15All eleven curtains were the same size—thirty cubits long and four cubits wide.[b] 16They joined five of the curtains into one set and the other six into another set. 17Then they made fifty loops along the edge of the end curtain in one set and also along the edge of the end curtain in the other set. 18They made fifty bronze clasps to fasten the tent together as a unit. 19Then they made for the tent a covering of ram skins dyed red, and over that a covering of hides of sea cows.[c]

20They made upright frames of acacia wood for the tabernacle. 21Each frame was ten cubits long and a cubit and a half wide,[d] 22with two projections set parallel to each other. They made all the frames of the tabernacle in this way. 23They made twenty frames for the south side of the tabernacle 24and made forty silver bases to go under them—two bases for each frame, one under each projection. 25For the other side, the north side of the tabernacle, they made twenty frames 26and forty silver bases—two under each frame. 27They made six frames for the far end, that is, the west end of the tabernacle, 28and two frames were made for the corners of the tabernacle at the far end. 29At these two corners the frames were double from the bottom all the way to the top and fitted into a single ring; both were made alike. 30So there were eight frames and sixteen silver bases—two under each frame.

31They also made crossbars of acacia wood: five for the frames on one side of the tabernacle, 32five for those on the other side, and five for the frames on the west, at the far end of the tabernacle. 33They made the center crossbar so that it extended from end to end at the middle of the frames. 34They overlaid the frames with gold and made gold rings to hold the crossbars. They also overlaid the crossbars with gold.

[a] *9* That is, about 42 feet (about 12.5 meters) long and 6 feet (about 1.8 meters) wide [b] *15* That is, about 45 feet (about 13.5 meters) long and 6 feet (about 1.8 meters) wide [c] *19* That is, dugongs [d] *21* That is, about 15 feet (about 4.5 meters) long and 2 1/4 feet (about 0.7 meter) wide

35They made the curtain of blue, purple
and scarlet yarn and finely twisted linen,
with cherubim worked into it by a skilled
craftsman. 36They made four posts of acacia wood for it and overlaid them with
gold. They made gold hooks for them and
cast their four silver bases. 37For the entrance to the tent they made a curtain of
blue, purple and scarlet yarn and finely
twisted linen—the work of an embroiderer; 38and they made five posts with hooks
for them. They overlaid the tops of the
posts and their bands with gold and made
their five bases of bronze.

The Ark

37 Bezalel made the ark of acacia
wood—two and a half cubits long, a
cubit and a half wide, and a cubit and a
half high.[e] 2He overlaid it with pure gold,
both inside and out, and made a gold
molding around it. 3He cast four gold
rings for it and fastened them to its four
feet, with two rings on one side and two
rings on the other. 4Then he made poles
of acacia wood and overlaid them with
gold. 5And he inserted the poles into the
rings on the sides of the ark to carry it.

6He made the atonement cover of pure
gold—two and a half cubits long and a cubit and a half wide.[f] 7Then he made two
cherubim out of hammered gold at the
ends of the cover. 8He made one cherub on
one end and the second cherub on the other; at the two ends he made them of one
piece with the cover. 9The cherubim had
their wings spread upward, overshadowing
the cover with them. The cherubim faced
each other, looking toward the cover.

The Table

10They[g] made the table of acacia
wood—two cubits long, a cubit wide, and
a cubit and a half high.[h] 11Then they overlaid it with pure gold and made a gold
molding around it. 12They also made
around it a rim a handbreadth[i] wide and
put a gold molding on the rim. 13They cast
four gold rings for the table and fastened
them to the four corners, where the four
legs were. 14The rings were put close to the
rim to hold the poles used in carrying the
table. 15The poles for carrying the table
were made of acacia wood and were overlaid with gold. 16And they made from
pure gold the articles for the table—its
plates and dishes and bowls and its pitchers for the pouring out of drink offerings.

The Lampstand

17They made the lampstand of pure
gold and hammered it out, base and shaft;
its flowerlike cups, buds and blossoms
were of one piece with it. 18Six branches
extended from the sides of the lampstand—three on one side and three on the
other. 19Three cups shaped like almond
flowers with buds and blossoms were on
one branch, three on the next branch and
the same for all six branches extending
from the lampstand. 20And on the lampstand were four cups shaped like almond
flowers with buds and blossoms. 21One
bud was under the first pair of branches
extending from the lampstand, a second
bud under the second pair, and a third
bud under the third pair—six branches in
all. 22The buds and the branches were all
of one piece with the lampstand, hammered out of pure gold.

23They made its seven lamps, as well as
its wick trimmers and trays, of pure gold.
24They made the lampstand and all its accessories from one talent[j] of pure gold.

The Altar of Incense

25They made the altar of incense out of
acacia wood. It was square, a cubit long
and a cubit wide, and two cubits high[k]—
its horns of one piece with it. 26They overlaid the top and all the sides and the
horns with pure gold, and made a gold
molding around it. 27They made two gold
rings below the molding—two on opposite sides—to hold the poles used to carry it. 28They made the poles of acacia
wood and overlaid them with gold.

29They also made the sacred anointing
oil and the pure, fragrant incense—the
work of a perfumer.

[e] *1* That is, about 3 3/4 feet (about 1.1 meters) long and 2 1/4 feet (about 0.7 meter) wide and high
[f] *6* That is, about 3 3/4 feet (about 1.1 meters) long and 2 1/4 feet (about 0.7 meter) wide
[g] *10* Or *He;* also in verses 11–29
[h] *10* That is, about 3 feet (about 0.9 meter) long, 1 1/2 feet (about 0.5 meter) wide, and 2 1/4 feet (about 0.7 meter) high
[i] *12* That is, about 3 inches (about 8 centimeters)
[j] *24* That is, about 75 pounds (about 34 kilograms)
[k] *25* That is, about 1 1/2 feet (about 0.5 meter) long and wide, and about 3 feet (about 0.9 meter) high

PRAYER: ADORATION

O LORD, You have searched me and You know me. You know when I sit down and when I rise up; You understand my thoughts from afar. You scrutinize my path and my lying down and are acquainted with all my ways. Before a word is on my tongue, O Lord, You know it completely. You have enclosed me behind and before, and laid Your hand upon me. Such knowledge is too wonderful for me; it is too lofty for me to attain.

(Psalm 139:1–6)

***PAUSE** to express your thoughts of praise and worship.*

NT Romans 5:1–21

Peace and Joy

5 Therefore, since we have been justified
through faith, we[a] have peace with God
through our Lord Jesus Christ, 2through
whom we have gained access by faith into
this grace in which we now stand. And we[a]
rejoice in the hope of the glory of God.
3Not only so, but we[a] also rejoice in our
sufferings, because we know that suffering
produces perseverance; 4perseverance,
character; and character, hope. 5And hope
does not disappoint us, because God has
poured out his love into our hearts by the
Holy Spirit, whom he has given us.
6You see, at just the right time, when we
were still powerless, Christ died for the
ungodly. 7Very rarely will anyone die for a
righteous man, though for a good man
someone might possibly dare to die. 8But
God demonstrates his own love for us in
this: While we were still sinners, Christ
died for us.
9Since we have now been justified by
his blood, how much more shall we be
saved from God's wrath through him!
10For if, when we were God's enemies, we
were reconciled to him through the death
of his Son, how much more, having been
reconciled, shall we be saved through his
life! 11Not only is this so, but we also rejoice in God through our Lord Jesus
Christ, through whom we have now received reconciliation.

Death Through Adam, Life Through Christ

12Therefore, just as sin entered the
world through one man, and death
through sin, and in this way death came
to all men, because all sinned— 13for before the law was given, sin was in the
world. But sin is not taken into account
when there is no law. 14Nevertheless,
death reigned from the time of Adam to
the time of Moses, even over those who
did not sin by breaking a command, as
did Adam, who was a pattern of the one
to come.
15But the gift is not like the trespass. For
if the many died by the trespass of the one
man, how much more did God's grace
and the gift that came by the grace of the
one man, Jesus Christ, overflow to the
many! 16Again, the gift of God is not like
the result of the one man's sin: The judgment followed one sin and brought condemnation, but the gift followed many
trespasses and brought justification. 17For
if, by the trespass of the one man, death
reigned through that one man, how much
more will those who receive God's abundant provision of grace and of the gift of
righteousness reign in life through the
one man, Jesus Christ.
18Consequently, just as the result of one
trespass was condemnation for all men,
so also the result of one act of righteousness was justification that brings life for
all men. 19For just as through the disobedience of the one man the many were
made sinners, so also through the obedience of the one man the many will be
made righteous.
20The law was added so that the trespass
might increase. But where sin increased,
grace increased all the more, 21so that, just
as sin reigned in death, so also grace
might reign through righteousness to
bring eternal life through Jesus Christ our
Lord.

[a] *1* Or *let us*

PRAYER: MY RELATIONSHIP TO OTHERS

WE who are strong ought to bear the weaknesses of those who are not strong and not to please ourselves. Each of us should please our neighbors for their good, to build them up. (Romans 15:1–2) . . . I am not to seek my own good, but rather the good of others. (1 Corinthians 10:24)

***PAUSE** to review your relationships with others and to commit them to the Lord.*

YEAR 1 DAY 86

OT Exodus 38:1-31

The Altar of Burnt Offering

38 They[a] built the altar of burnt offering
of acacia wood, three cubits[b] high; it
was square, five cubits long and five cubits wide.[c] 2They made a horn at each of
the four corners, so that the horns and the
altar were of one piece, and they overlaid
the altar with bronze. 3They made all its
utensils of bronze—its pots, shovels,
sprinkling bowls, meat forks and firepans.
4They made a grating for the altar, a
bronze network, to be under its ledge,
halfway up the altar. 5They cast bronze
rings to hold the poles for the four corners of the bronze grating. 6They made
the poles of acacia wood and overlaid
them with bronze. 7They inserted the
poles into the rings so they would be on
the sides of the altar for carrying it. They
made it hollow, out of boards.

Basin for Washing

8They made the bronze basin and its
bronze stand from the mirrors of the
women who served at the entrance to the
Tent of Meeting.

The Courtyard

9Next they made the courtyard. The
south side was a hundred cubits[d] long
and had curtains of finely twisted linen,
10with twenty posts and twenty bronze
bases, and with silver hooks and bands on
the posts. 11The north side was also a hundred cubits long and had twenty posts
and twenty bronze bases, with silver
hooks and bands on the posts.
12The west end was fifty cubits[e] wide
and had curtains, with ten posts and ten
bases, with silver hooks and bands on the
posts. 13The east end, toward the sunrise,
was also fifty cubits wide. 14Curtains fifteen cubits[f] long were on one side of the
entrance, with three posts and three bases,
15and curtains fifteen cubits long were on
the other side of the entrance to the courtyard, with three posts and three bases.
16All the curtains around the courtyard
were of finely twisted linen. 17The bases
for the posts were bronze. The hooks and
bands on the posts were silver, and their
tops were overlaid with silver; so all the
posts of the courtyard had silver bands.
18The curtain for the entrance to the
courtyard was of blue, purple and scarlet
yarn and finely twisted linen—the work
of an embroiderer. It was twenty cubits[g]
long and, like the curtains of the courtyard, five cubits[h] high, 19with four posts
and four bronze bases. Their hooks and
bands were silver, and their tops were
overlaid with silver. 20All the tent pegs of
the tabernacle and of the surrounding
courtyard were bronze.

The Materials Used

21These are the amounts of the materials used for the tabernacle, the tabernacle
of the Testimony, which were recorded at
Moses' command by the Levites under the
direction of Ithamar son of Aaron, the
priest. 22(Bezalel son of Uri, the son of

[a] *1* Or *He;* also in verses 2–9 [b] *1* That is, about 4 1/2 feet (about 1.3 meters) [c] *1* That is, about 7 1/2 feet (about 2.3 meters) long and wide
[d] *9* That is, about 150 feet (about 46 meters)
[e] *12* That is, about 75 feet (about 23 meters)
[f] *14* That is, about 22 1/2 feet (about 6.9 meters)
[g] *18* That is, about 30 feet (about 9 meters)
[h] *18* That is, about 7 1/2 feet (about 2.3 meters)

Hur, of the tribe of Judah, made everything the LORD commanded Moses; [23]with him was Oholiab son of Ahisamach, of the tribe of Dan—a craftsman and designer, and an embroiderer in blue, purple and scarlet yarn and fine linen.) [24]The total amount of the gold from the wave offering used for all the work on the sanctuary was 29 talents and 730 shekels,[i] according to the sanctuary shekel.

[25]The silver obtained from those of the community who were counted in the census was 100 talents and 1,775 shekels,[j] according to the sanctuary shekel— [26]one beka per person, that is, half a shekel,[k] according to the sanctuary shekel, from everyone who had crossed over to those counted, twenty years old or more, a total of 603,550 men. [27]The 100 talents[l] of silver were used to cast the bases for the sanctuary and for the curtain—100 bases from the 100 talents, one talent for each base. [28]They used the 1,775 shekels[m] to make the hooks for the posts, to overlay the tops of the posts, and to make their bands.

[29]The bronze from the wave offering was 70 talents and 2,400 shekels.[n] [30]They used it to make the bases for the entrance to the Tent of Meeting, the bronze altar with its bronze grating and all its utensils, [31]the bases for the surrounding courtyard and those for its entrance and all the tent pegs for the tabernacle and those for the surrounding courtyard.

[i] *24* The weight of the gold was a little over one ton (about 1 metric ton). [j] *25* The weight of the silver was a little over 3 3/4 tons (about 3.4 metric tons). [k] *26* That is, about 1/5 ounce (about 5.5 grams) [l] *27* That is, about 3 3/4 tons (about 3.4 metric tons) [m] *28* That is, about 45 pounds (about 20 kilograms) [n] *29* The weight of the bronze was about 2 1/2 tons (about 2.4 metric tons).

PRAYER: CONFESSION

***O LORD, be gracious to me; heal my soul, for I have sinned against You.* (Psalm 41:4)**

***ASK** the Spirit to search your heart and reveal any areas of unconfessed sin. Acknowledge these to the Lord and thank Him for His forgiveness.*

NT Romans 6:1-14

Dead to Sin, Alive in Christ

6 What shall we say, then? Shall we go on sinning so that grace may increase? [2]By no means! We died to sin; how can we live in it any longer? [3]Or don't you know that all of us who were baptized into Christ Jesus were baptized into his death? [4]We were therefore buried with him through baptism into death in order that, just as Christ was raised from the dead through the glory of the Father, we too may live a new life.

[5]If we have been united with him like this in his death, we will certainly also be united with him in his resurrection. [6]For we know that our old self was crucified with him so that the body of sin might be done away with,[a] that we should no longer be slaves to sin— [7]because anyone who has died has been freed from sin.

[8]Now if we died with Christ, we believe that we will also live with him. [9]For we know that since Christ was raised from the dead, he cannot die again; death no longer has mastery over him. [10]The death he died, he died to sin once for all; but the life he lives, he lives to God.

[11]In the same way, count yourselves dead to sin but alive to God in Christ Jesus. [12]Therefore do not let sin reign in your mortal body so that you obey its evil desires. [13]Do not offer the parts of your body to sin, as instruments of wickedness, but rather offer yourselves to God, as those who have been brought from death to life; and offer the parts of your body to him as instruments of righteousness. [14]For sin shall not be your master, because you are not under law, but under grace.

[a] *6* Or *be rendered powerless*

PRAYER: THE ATTRIBUTES OF GOD

YOU must be treated as holy by those who come near You, O Lord, and before all people You will be honored. (Leviticus 10:3) . . . You, O Lord of hosts, will be exalted in judgment; and You, the holy God, will show Yourself holy in righteousness. (Isaiah 5:16)

***PAUSE** to reflect on these affirmations about the person, powers and perfection of God.*

YEAR 1
DAY 87

OT Exodus 39:1–40:38

The Priestly Garments

39 From the blue, purple and scarlet
yarn they made woven garments for
ministering in the sanctuary. They also
made sacred garments for Aaron, as the
LORD commanded Moses.

The Ephod

2They[a] made the ephod of gold, and of
blue, purple and scarlet yarn, and of finely twisted linen. 3They hammered out
thin sheets of gold and cut strands to be
worked into the blue, purple and scarlet
yarn and fine linen—the work of a skilled
craftsman. 4They made shoulder pieces
for the ephod, which were attached to two
of its corners, so it could be fastened. 5Its
skillfully woven waistband was like it—of
one piece with the ephod and made with
gold, and with blue, purple and scarlet
yarn, and with finely twisted linen, as the
LORD commanded Moses.

6They mounted the onyx stones in gold
filigree settings and engraved them like a
seal with the names of the sons of Israel.
7Then they fastened them on the shoulder
pieces of the ephod as memorial stones
for the sons of Israel, as the LORD commanded Moses.

The Breastpiece

8They fashioned the breastpiece—the
work of a skilled craftsman. They made it
like the ephod: of gold, and of blue, purple and scarlet yarn, and of finely twisted
linen. 9It was square—a span[b] long and a
span wide—and folded double. 10Then
they mounted four rows of precious
stones on it. In the first row there was a
ruby, a topaz and a beryl; 11in the second
row a turquoise, a sapphire[c] and an emerald; 12in the third row a jacinth, an agate
and an amethyst; 13in the fourth row a
chrysolite, an onyx and a jasper.[d] They
were mounted in gold filigree settings.
14There were twelve stones, one for each
of the names of the sons of Israel, each engraved like a seal with the name of one of
the twelve tribes.

15For the breastpiece they made braided chains of pure gold, like a rope. 16They
made two gold filigree settings and two
gold rings, and fastened the rings to two
of the corners of the breastpiece. 17They
fastened the two gold chains to the rings
at the corners of the breastpiece, 18and the
other ends of the chains to the two settings, attaching them to the shoulder
pieces of the ephod at the front. 19They
made two gold rings and attached them
to the other two corners of the breastpiece
on the inside edge next to the ephod.
20Then they made two more gold rings
and attached them to the bottom of the
shoulder pieces on the front of the ephod,
close to the seam just above the waistband
of the ephod. 21They tied the rings of the
breastpiece to the rings of the ephod with
blue cord, connecting it to the waistband
so that the breastpiece would not swing
out from the ephod—as the LORD commanded Moses.

Other Priestly Garments

22They made the robe of the ephod entirely of blue cloth—the work of a
weaver— 23with an opening in the center

[a] 2 Or *He;* also in verses 7, 8 and 22 [b] 9 That is, about 9 inches (about 22 centimeters) [c] *11* Or *lapis lazuli* [d] *13* The precise identification of some of these precious stones is uncertain.

of the robe like the opening of a collar,[e]
and a band around this opening, so that
it would not tear. 24They made pomegranates of blue, purple and scarlet yarn
and finely twisted linen around the hem
of the robe. 25And they made bells of pure
gold and attached them around the hem
between the pomegranates. 26The bells
and pomegranates alternated around the
hem of the robe to be worn for ministering, as the LORD commanded Moses.
27For Aaron and his sons, they made tunics of fine linen—the work of a weaver—
28and the turban of fine linen, the linen
headbands and the undergarments of
finely twisted linen. 29The sash was of
finely twisted linen and blue, purple and
scarlet yarn—the work of an embroiderer—as the LORD commanded Moses.
30They made the plate, the sacred diadem, out of pure gold and engraved on it,
like an inscription on a seal: HOLY TO THE
LORD. 31Then they fastened a blue cord to
it to attach it to the turban, as the LORD
commanded Moses.

Moses Inspects the Tabernacle

32So all the work on the tabernacle, the
Tent of Meeting, was completed. The Israelites did everything just as the LORD commanded Moses. 33Then they brought the
tabernacle to Moses: the tent and all its
furnishings, its clasps, frames, crossbars,
posts and bases; 34the covering of ram
skins dyed red, the covering of hides of
sea cows[f] and the shielding curtain; 35the
ark of the Testimony with its poles and
the atonement cover; 36the table with all
its articles and the bread of the Presence;
37the pure gold lampstand with its row of
lamps and all its accessories, and the oil
for the light; 38the gold altar, the anointing oil, the fragrant incense, and the curtain for the entrance to the tent; 39the
bronze altar with its bronze grating, its
poles and all its utensils; the basin with
its stand; 40the curtains of the courtyard
with its posts and bases, and the curtain
for the entrance to the courtyard; the
ropes and tent pegs for the courtyard; all
the furnishings for the tabernacle, the Tent
of Meeting; 41and the woven garments
worn for ministering in the sanctuary,
both the sacred garments for Aaron the
priest and the garments for his sons when
serving as priests.
42The Israelites had done all the work
just as the LORD had commanded Moses.
43Moses inspected the work and saw that
they had done it just as the LORD had
commanded. So Moses blessed them.

Setting Up the Tabernacle

40 Then the LORD said to Moses: 2"Set
up the tabernacle, the Tent of Meeting, on the first day of the first month.
3Place the ark of the Testimony in it and
shield the ark with the curtain. 4Bring in
the table and set out what belongs on it.
Then bring in the lampstand and set up
its lamps. 5Place the gold altar of incense
in front of the ark of the Testimony and
put the curtain at the entrance to the
tabernacle.
6"Place the altar of burnt offering in
front of the entrance to the tabernacle, the
Tent of Meeting; 7place the basin between
the Tent of Meeting and the altar and put
water in it. 8Set up the courtyard around
it and put the curtain at the entrance to
the courtyard.
9"Take the anointing oil and anoint the
tabernacle and everything in it; consecrate
it and all its furnishings, and it will be
holy. 10Then anoint the altar of burnt offering and all its utensils; consecrate the
altar, and it will be most holy. 11Anoint the
basin and its stand and consecrate them.
12"Bring Aaron and his sons to the entrance to the Tent of Meeting and wash
them with water. 13Then dress Aaron in
the sacred garments, anoint him and consecrate him so he may serve me as priest.
14Bring his sons and dress them in tunics.
15Anoint them just as you anointed their
father, so they may serve me as priests.
Their anointing will be to a priesthood
that will continue for all generations to
come." 16Moses did everything just as the
LORD commanded him.
17So the tabernacle was set up on the
first day of the first month in the second
year. 18When Moses set up the tabernacle,
he put the bases in place, erected the
frames, inserted the crossbars and set up
the posts. 19Then he spread the tent over
the tabernacle and put the covering over
the tent, as the LORD commanded him.
20He took the Testimony and placed it
in the ark, attached the poles to the ark

[e] *23* The meaning of the Hebrew for this word is uncertain. [f] *34* That is, dugongs

and put the atonement cover over it.
21Then he brought the ark into the tabernacle and hung the shielding curtain and
shielded the ark of the Testimony, as the
LORD commanded him.
22Moses placed the table in the Tent of
Meeting on the north side of the tabernacle outside the curtain 23and set out the
bread on it before the LORD, as the LORD
commanded him.
24He placed the lampstand in the Tent
of Meeting opposite the table on the
south side of the tabernacle 25and set up
the lamps before the LORD, as the LORD
commanded him.
26Moses placed the gold altar in the Tent
of Meeting in front of the curtain 27and
burned fragrant incense on it, as the LORD
commanded him. 28Then he put up the
curtain at the entrance to the tabernacle.
29He set the altar of burnt offering near
the entrance to the tabernacle, the Tent of
Meeting, and offered on it burnt offerings
and grain offerings, as the LORD commanded him.
30He placed the basin between the Tent
of Meeting and the altar and put water in
it for washing, 31and Moses and Aaron
and his sons used it to wash their hands
and feet. 32They washed whenever they
entered the Tent of Meeting or approached the altar, as the LORD commanded Moses.
33Then Moses set up the courtyard
around the tabernacle and altar and put
up the curtain at the entrance to the courtyard. And so Moses finished the work.

The Glory of the LORD

34Then the cloud covered the Tent of
Meeting, and the glory of the LORD filled
the tabernacle. 35Moses could not enter
the Tent of Meeting because the cloud had
settled upon it, and the glory of the LORD
filled the tabernacle.
36In all the travels of the Israelites,
whenever the cloud lifted from above the
tabernacle, they would set out; 37but if the
cloud did not lift, they did not set out—
until the day it lifted. 38So the cloud of the
LORD was over the tabernacle by day, and
fire was in the cloud by night, in the sight
of all the house of Israel during all their
travels.

PRAYER: RENEWAL

MAY I not worry about my life, what I will eat or what I will drink; or about my body, what I will wear. Life is more than food, and the body more than clothes. The birds of the air do not sow or reap or gather into barns, and yet You, my heavenly Father, feed them. Am I not much more valuable than they? Can I add a single hour to my life by worrying? And why do I worry about clothes? I will consider how the lilies of the field grow; they neither labor nor spin, yet not even Solomon in all his splendor was dressed like one of these. But if You so clothe the grass of the field, which is here today and tomorrow is thrown into the fire, will You not much more clothe me? So may I not worry, saying, "What shall I eat?" or "What shall I drink?" or "What shall I wear?" For the pagans run after all these things, and You, my heavenly Father, know that I need them. But may I seek first Your kingdom and Your righteousness, and all these things will be added to me. (Matthew 6:25–33; Luke 12:22–31)

***PAUSE** to add your own prayers for personal renewal.*

NT Romans 6:15–7:6

Slaves to Righteousness

15What then? Shall we sin because we are
not under law but under grace? By no
means! 16Don't you know that when you
offer yourselves to someone to obey him
as slaves, you are slaves to the one whom
you obey—whether you are slaves to sin,
which leads to death, or to obedience,

which leads to righteousness? 17But thanks be to God that, though you used to be slaves to sin, you wholeheartedly obeyed the form of teaching to which you were entrusted. 18You have been set free from sin and have become slaves to righteousness.

19I put this in human terms because you are weak in your natural selves. Just as you used to offer the parts of your body in slavery to impurity and to ever-increasing wickedness, so now offer them in slavery to righteousness leading to holiness. 20When you were slaves to sin, you were free from the control of righteousness. 21What benefit did you reap at that time from the things you are now ashamed of? Those things result in death! 22But now that you have been set free from sin and have become slaves to God, the benefit you reap leads to holiness, and the result is eternal life. 23For the wages of sin is death, but the gift of God is eternal life in[a] Christ Jesus our Lord.

An Illustration From Marriage

7 Do you not know, brothers—for I am speaking to men who know the law—that the law has authority over a man only as long as he lives? 2For example, by law a married woman is bound to her husband as long as he is alive, but if her husband dies, she is released from the law of marriage. 3So then, if she marries another man while her husband is still alive, she is called an adulteress. But if her husband dies, she is released from that law and is not an adulteress, even though she marries another man.

4So, my brothers, you also died to the law through the body of Christ, that you might belong to another, to him who was raised from the dead, in order that we might bear fruit to God. 5For when we were controlled by the sinful nature,[b] the sinful passions aroused by the law were at work in our bodies, so that we bore fruit for death. 6But now, by dying to what once bound us, we have been released from the law so that we serve in the new way of the Spirit, and not in the old way of the written code.

[a] 23 Or *through* [b] 5 Or *the flesh;* also in verse 25

PRAYER: THE WORKS OF GOD

YOUR eyes, O Lord, move to and fro throughout the whole earth to strengthen those whose hearts are fully committed to You. (2 Chronicles 16:9) . . . For those who revere Your name, O Lord Almighty, the sun of righteousness will rise with healing in his wings. And they will go out and leap like calves released from the stall. (Malachi 4:2)

TAKE *a moment to consider the greatness of God's wonderful works.*

YEAR 1 DAY 88

OT Leviticus 1:1–2:16

The Burnt Offering

1 The LORD called to Moses and spoke to him from the Tent of Meeting. He said, 2"Speak to the Israelites and say to them: 'When any of you brings an offering to the LORD, bring as your offering an animal from either the herd or the flock.

3" 'If the offering is a burnt offering from the herd, he is to offer a male without defect. He must present it at the entrance to the Tent of Meeting so that it[a] will be acceptable to the LORD. 4He is to lay his hand on the head of the burnt offering, and it will be accepted on his behalf to make atonement for him. 5He is to slaughter the young bull before the LORD, and then Aaron's sons the priests shall bring the blood and sprinkle it against the altar on all sides at the entrance to the Tent of Meeting. 6He is to skin the burnt offering and cut it into pieces. 7The sons of Aaron the priest are to put fire on the altar and arrange wood on the fire. 8Then Aaron's sons the priests shall arrange the pieces, including the head and the fat, on the burning wood that is on the

[a] 3 Or *he*

altar. 9He is to wash the inner parts and the
legs with water, and the priest is to burn all
of it on the altar. It is a burnt offering, an
offering made by fire, an aroma pleasing to
the LORD.
10" 'If the offering is a burnt offering
from the flock, from either the sheep or
the goats, he is to offer a male without defect. 11He is to slaughter it at the north side
of the altar before the LORD, and Aaron's
sons the priests shall sprinkle its blood
against the altar on all sides. 12He is to cut
it into pieces, and the priest shall arrange
them, including the head and the fat, on
the burning wood that is on the altar. 13He
is to wash the inner parts and the legs
with water, and the priest is to bring all of
it and burn it on the altar. It is a burnt offering, an offering made by fire, an aroma
pleasing to the LORD.
14" 'If the offering to the LORD is a burnt
offering of birds, he is to offer a dove or a
young pigeon. 15The priest shall bring it to
the altar, wring off the head and burn it
on the altar; its blood shall be drained out
on the side of the altar. 16He is to remove
the crop with its contents[b] and throw it to
the east side of the altar, where the ashes
are. 17He shall tear it open by the wings,
not severing it completely, and then the
priest shall burn it on the wood that is on
the fire on the altar. It is a burnt offering,
an offering made by fire, an aroma pleasing to the LORD.

The Grain Offering

2 " 'When someone brings a grain offering to the LORD, his offering is to be of
fine flour. He is to pour oil on it, put incense on it 2and take it to Aaron's sons the
priests. The priest shall take a handful of
the fine flour and oil, together with all the
incense, and burn this as a memorial portion on the altar, an offering made by fire,
an aroma pleasing to the LORD. 3The rest
of the grain offering belongs to Aaron and
his sons; it is a most holy part of the offerings made to the LORD by fire.
4" 'If you bring a grain offering baked in
an oven, it is to consist of fine flour: cakes
made without yeast and mixed with oil, or[c]
wafers made without yeast and spread with
oil. 5If your grain offering is prepared on a
griddle, it is to be made of fine flour mixed
with oil, and without yeast. 6Crumble it
and pour oil on it; it is a grain offering. 7If
your grain offering is cooked in a pan, it is
to be made of fine flour and oil. 8Bring the
grain offering made of these things to the
LORD; present it to the priest, who shall take
it to the altar. 9He shall take out the memorial portion from the grain offering and
burn it on the altar as an offering made by
fire, an aroma pleasing to the LORD. 10The
rest of the grain offering belongs to Aaron
and his sons; it is a most holy part of the
offerings made to the LORD by fire.
11" 'Every grain offering you bring to the
LORD must be made without yeast, for you
are not to burn any yeast or honey in an
offering made to the LORD by fire. 12You
may bring them to the LORD as an offering of the firstfruits, but they are not to be
offered on the altar as a pleasing aroma.
13Season all your grain offerings with salt.
Do not leave the salt of the covenant of
your God out of your grain offerings; add
salt to all your offerings.
14" 'If you bring a grain offering of firstfruits to the LORD, offer crushed heads of
new grain roasted in the fire. 15Put oil and
incense on it; it is a grain offering. 16The
priest shall burn the memorial portion of
the crushed grain and the oil, together
with all the incense, as an offering made
to the LORD by fire.

[b] 16 Or *crop and the feathers;* the meaning of the Hebrew for this word is uncertain. [c] 4 Or *and*

PRAYER: PETITION

MAY I follow Your commands and precepts and be careful to observe them, for this is my wisdom and understanding in the sight of others. (Deuteronomy 4:5–6)

PAUSE *here to offer prayers of petition regarding your family and your ministry. Ask for help and guidance in sharing Jesus with others and helping others grow in Him. Ask for guidance in your vocation and your avocations. Offer prayers of petition regarding your activities for this day and any special concerns you may have.*

NT Romans 7:7-25

Struggling With Sin

[7]What shall we say, then? Is the law sin? Certainly not! Indeed I would not have known what sin was except through the law. For I would not have known what coveting really was if the law had not said, "Do not covet."[a] [8]But sin, seizing the opportunity afforded by the commandment, produced in me every kind of covetous desire. For apart from law, sin is dead. [9]Once I was alive apart from law; but when the commandment came, sin sprang to life and I died. [10]I found that the very commandment that was intended to bring life actually brought death. [11]For sin, seizing the opportunity afforded by the commandment, deceived me, and through the commandment put me to death. [12]So then, the law is holy, and the commandment is holy, righteous and good.

[13]Did that which is good, then, become death to me? By no means! But in order that sin might be recognized as sin, it produced death in me through what was good, so that through the commandment sin might become utterly sinful.

[14]We know that the law is spiritual; but I am unspiritual, sold as a slave to sin. [15]I do not understand what I do. For what I want to do I do not do, but what I hate I do. [16]And if I do what I do not want to do, I agree that the law is good. [17]As it is, it is no longer I myself who do it, but it is sin living in me. [18]I know that nothing good lives in me, that is, in my sinful nature.[b] For I have the desire to do what is good, but I cannot carry it out. [19]For what I do is not the good I want to do; no, the evil I do not want to do—this I keep on doing. [20]Now if I do what I do not want to do, it is no longer I who do it, but it is sin living in me that does it.

[21]So I find this law at work: When I want to do good, evil is right there with me. [22]For in my inner being I delight in God's law; [23]but I see another law at work in the members of my body, waging war against the law of my mind and making me a prisoner of the law of sin at work within my members. [24]What a wretched man I am! Who will rescue me from this body of death? [25]Thanks be to God—through Jesus Christ our Lord!

So then, I myself in my mind am a slave to God's law, but in the sinful nature a slave to the law of sin.

[a] *7* Exodus 20:17; Deut. 5:21 [b] *18* Or *my flesh*

PRAYER: MY RELATIONSHIP TO GOD

I WILL not let Your word depart from my mouth, O Lord, but I will meditate on it day and night, so that I may be careful to do all that is written in it; for then I will be prosperous, and I will act wisely. (Joshua 1:8) . . . I am committed to You, O God, and to the word of Your grace, which is able to build me up and give me an inheritance among all those who are sanctified. (Acts 20:32)

***PAUSE** to thank God for the relationship that you enjoy with Him in Jesus Christ.*

YEAR 1 DAY 89

OT Leviticus 3:1–4:35

The Fellowship Offering

3 " 'If someone's offering is a fellowship offering,[a] and he offers an animal from the herd, whether male or female, he is to present before the LORD an animal without defect. [2]He is to lay his hand on the head of his offering and slaughter it at the entrance to the Tent of Meeting. Then Aaron's sons the priests shall sprinkle the blood against the altar on all sides. [3]From

[a] *1* Traditionally *peace offering;* also in verses 3, 6 and 9

the fellowship offering he is to bring a sacrifice made to the LORD by fire: all the fat that covers the inner parts or is connected to them, 4both kidneys with the fat on them near the loins, and the covering of the liver, which he will remove with the kidneys. 5Then Aaron's sons are to burn it on the altar on top of the burnt offering that is on the burning wood, as an offering made by fire, an aroma pleasing to the LORD.

6" 'If he offers an animal from the flock as a fellowship offering to the LORD, he is to offer a male or female without defect. 7If he offers a lamb, he is to present it before the LORD. 8He is to lay his hand on the head of his offering and slaughter it in front of the Tent of Meeting. Then Aaron's sons shall sprinkle its blood against the altar on all sides. 9From the fellowship offering he is to bring a sacrifice made to the LORD by fire: its fat, the entire fat tail cut off close to the backbone, all the fat that covers the inner parts or is connected to them, 10both kidneys with the fat on them near the loins, and the covering of the liver, which he will remove with the kidneys. 11The priest shall burn them on the altar as food, an offering made to the LORD by fire.

12" 'If his offering is a goat, he is to present it before the LORD. 13He is to lay his hand on its head and slaughter it in front of the Tent of Meeting. Then Aaron's sons shall sprinkle its blood against the altar on all sides. 14From what he offers he is to make this offering to the LORD by fire: all the fat that covers the inner parts or is connected to them, 15both kidneys with the fat on them near the loins, and the covering of the liver, which he will remove with the kidneys. 16The priest shall burn them on the altar as food, an offering made by fire, a pleasing aroma. All the fat is the LORD's.

17" 'This is a lasting ordinance for the generations to come, wherever you live: You must not eat any fat or any blood.' "

The Sin Offering

4 The LORD said to Moses, 2"Say to the Israelites: 'When anyone sins unintentionally and does what is forbidden in any of the LORD's commands—

3" 'If the anointed priest sins, bringing guilt on the people, he must bring to the LORD a young bull without defect as a sin offering for the sin he has committed. 4He is to present the bull at the entrance to the Tent of Meeting before the LORD. He is to lay his hand on its head and slaughter it before the LORD. 5Then the anointed priest shall take some of the bull's blood and carry it into the Tent of Meeting. 6He is to dip his finger into the blood and sprinkle some of it seven times before the LORD, in front of the curtain of the sanctuary. 7The priest shall then put some of the blood on the horns of the altar of fragrant incense that is before the LORD in the Tent of Meeting. The rest of the bull's blood he shall pour out at the base of the altar of burnt offering at the entrance to the Tent of Meeting. 8He shall remove all the fat from the bull of the sin offering—the fat that covers the inner parts or is connected to them, 9both kidneys with the fat on them near the loins, and the covering of the liver, which he will remove with the kidneys— 10just as the fat is removed from the ox[b] sacrificed as a fellowship offering.[c] Then the priest shall burn them on the altar of burnt offering. 11But the hide of the bull and all its flesh, as well as the head and legs, the inner parts and offal— 12that is, all the rest of the bull—he must take outside the camp to a place ceremonially clean, where the ashes are thrown, and burn it in a wood fire on the ash heap.

13" 'If the whole Israelite community sins unintentionally and does what is forbidden in any of the LORD's commands, even though the community is unaware of the matter, they are guilty. 14When they become aware of the sin they committed, the assembly must bring a young bull as a sin offering and present it before the Tent of Meeting. 15The elders of the community are to lay their hands on the bull's head before the LORD, and the bull shall be slaughtered before the LORD. 16Then the anointed priest is to take some of the bull's blood into the Tent of Meeting. 17He shall dip his finger into the blood and sprinkle it before the LORD seven times in front of the curtain. 18He is to put some of the blood on the horns of the altar that is before the LORD in the Tent of Meeting. The rest of the blood he shall pour out at

[b] *10* The Hebrew word can include both male and female. [c] *10* Traditionally *peace offering;* also in verses 26, 31 and 35

the base of the altar of burnt offering at the entrance to the Tent of Meeting. [19]He shall remove all the fat from it and burn it on the altar, [20]and do with this bull just as he did with the bull for the sin offering. In this way the priest will make atonement for them, and they will be forgiven. [21]Then he shall take the bull outside the camp and burn it as he burned the first bull. This is the sin offering for the community.

[22]" 'When a leader sins unintentionally and does what is forbidden in any of the commands of the LORD his God, he is guilty. [23]When he is made aware of the sin he committed, he must bring as his offering a male goat without defect. [24]He is to lay his hand on the goat's head and slaughter it at the place where the burnt offering is slaughtered before the LORD. It is a sin offering. [25]Then the priest shall take some of the blood of the sin offering with his finger and put it on the horns of the altar of burnt offering and pour out the rest of the blood at the base of the altar. [26]He shall burn all the fat on the altar as he burned the fat of the fellowship offering. In this way the priest will make atonement for the man's sin, and he will be forgiven.

[27]" 'If a member of the community sins unintentionally and does what is forbidden in any of the LORD's commands, he is guilty. [28]When he is made aware of the sin he committed, he must bring as his offering for the sin he committed a female goat without defect. [29]He is to lay his hand on the head of the sin offering and slaughter it at the place of the burnt offering. [30]Then the priest is to take some of the blood with his finger and put it on the horns of the altar of burnt offering and pour out the rest of the blood at the base of the altar. [31]He shall remove all the fat, just as the fat is removed from the fellowship offering, and the priest shall burn it on the altar as an aroma pleasing to the LORD. In this way the priest will make atonement for him, and he will be forgiven.

[32]" 'If he brings a lamb as his sin offering, he is to bring a female without defect. [33]He is to lay his hand on its head and slaughter it for a sin offering at the place where the burnt offering is slaughtered. [34]Then the priest shall take some of the blood of the sin offering with his finger and put it on the horns of the altar of burnt offering and pour out the rest of the blood at the base of the altar. [35]He shall remove all the fat, just as the fat is removed from the lamb of the fellowship offering, and the priest shall burn it on the altar on top of the offerings made to the LORD by fire. In this way the priest will make atonement for him for the sin he has committed, and he will be forgiven.

PRAYER: INTERCESSION

BUT let all who take refuge in You be glad; let them ever sing for joy because You defend them. And let those who love Your name be joyful in You. (Psalm 5:11)

***TAKE** a few moments to intercede on behalf of local, national and world missions. Pray that the Great Commission would be fulfilled and for any special concerns you may have for missions.*

NT Romans 8:1-17

Life Through the Spirit

8 Therefore, there is now no condemnation for those who are in Christ Jesus,[a] [2]because through Christ Jesus the law of the Spirit of life set me free from the law of sin and death. [3]For what the law was powerless to do in that it was weakened by the sinful nature,[b] God did by sending his own Son in the likeness of sinful man to be a sin offering.[c] And so he condemned sin in sinful man,[d] [4]in order that the righteous requirements of the law might be fully met in us, who do not live according to the sinful nature but according to the Spirit.

[a] *1* Some later manuscripts *Jesus, who do not live according to the sinful nature but according to the Spirit,*
[b] *3* Or *the flesh;* also in verses 4, 5, 8, 9, 12 and 13
[c] *3* Or *man, for sin*
[d] *3* Or *in the flesh*

5Those who live according to the sinful
nature have their minds set on what that
nature desires; but those who live in accordance with the Spirit have their minds
set on what the Spirit desires. 6The mind
of sinful man[e] is death, but the mind controlled by the Spirit is life and peace; 7the
sinful mind[f] is hostile to God. It does not
submit to God's law, nor can it do so.
8Those controlled by the sinful nature
cannot please God.
9You, however, are controlled not by the
sinful nature but by the Spirit, if the Spirit of God lives in you. And if anyone does
not have the Spirit of Christ, he does not
belong to Christ. 10But if Christ is in you,
your body is dead because of sin, yet your
spirit is alive because of righteousness.
11And if the Spirit of him who raised Jesus
from the dead is living in you, he who
raised Christ from the dead will also give
life to your mortal bodies through his
Spirit, who lives in you.
12Therefore, brothers, we have an obligation—but it is not to the sinful nature,
to live according to it. 13For if you live according to the sinful nature, you will die;
but if by the Spirit you put to death the
misdeeds of the body, you will live, 14be-
cause those who are led by the Spirit of
God are sons of God. 15For you did not receive a spirit that makes you a slave again
to fear, but you received the Spirit of sonship.[g] And by him we cry, *"Abba,*[h] Father."
16The Spirit himself testifies with our spirit that we are God's children. 17Now if we
are children, then we are heirs—heirs of
God and co-heirs with Christ, if indeed
we share in his sufferings in order that we
may also share in his glory.

[e] 6 Or *mind set on the flesh* [f] 7 Or *the mind set on the flesh* [g] 15 Or *adoption* [h] 15 Aramaic for *Father*

PRAYER: THE CHARACTER I WANT TO CULTIVATE

I SHALL not covet my neighbor's house, my neighbor's wife, his manservant or maidservant, his ox or donkey, or anything that belongs to my neighbor. (Exodus 20:17; Deuteronomy 5:21) . . . I will be on my guard against all covetousness, for my life does not consist in the abundance of my possessions. (Luke 12:15)

TAKE *a moment to ask the Lord for the grace to grow in godly character.*

YEAR 1 DAY 90

OT Leviticus 5:1–6:30

5 " 'If a person sins because he does not
speak up when he hears a public charge
to testify regarding something he has seen
or learned about, he will be held responsible.
2" 'Or if a person touches anything ceremonially unclean—whether the carcasses of unclean wild animals or of unclean
livestock or of unclean creatures that
move along the ground—even though he
is unaware of it, he has become unclean
and is guilty.
3" 'Or if he touches human uncleanness—anything that would make him unclean—even though he is unaware of it,
when he learns of it he will be guilty.
4" 'Or if a person thoughtlessly takes an
oath to do anything, whether good or
evil—in any matter one might carelessly
swear about—even though he is unaware
of it, in any case when he learns of it he
will be guilty.
5" 'When anyone is guilty in any of
these ways, he must confess in what way
he has sinned 6and, as a penalty for the
sin he has committed, he must bring to
the LORD a female lamb or goat from the
flock as a sin offering; and the priest shall
make atonement for him for his sin.
7" 'If he cannot afford a lamb, he is to
bring two doves or two young pigeons to
the LORD as a penalty for his sin—one for
a sin offering and the other for a burnt offering. 8He is to bring them to the priest,
who shall first offer the one for the sin offering. He is to wring its head from its
neck, not severing it completely, 9and is to
sprinkle some of the blood of the sin of-

fering against the side of the altar; the rest of the blood must be drained out at the base of the altar. It is a sin offering. 10The priest shall then offer the other as a burnt offering in the prescribed way and make atonement for him for the sin he has committed, and he will be forgiven.

11" 'If, however, he cannot afford two doves or two young pigeons, he is to bring as an offering for his sin a tenth of an ephah[a] of fine flour for a sin offering. He must not put oil or incense on it, because it is a sin offering. 12He is to bring it to the priest, who shall take a handful of it as a memorial portion and burn it on the altar on top of the offerings made to the LORD by fire. It is a sin offering. 13In this way the priest will make atonement for him for any of these sins he has committed, and he will be forgiven. The rest of the offering will belong to the priest, as in the case of the grain offering.' "

The Guilt Offering

14The LORD said to Moses: 15"When a person commits a violation and sins unintentionally in regard to any of the LORD's holy things, he is to bring to the LORD as a penalty a ram from the flock, one without defect and of the proper value in silver, according to the sanctuary shekel.[b] It is a guilt offering. 16He must make restitution for what he has failed to do in regard to the holy things, add a fifth of the value to that and give it all to the priest, who will make atonement for him with the ram as a guilt offering, and he will be forgiven.

17"If a person sins and does what is forbidden in any of the LORD's commands, even though he does not know it, he is guilty and will be held responsible. 18He is to bring to the priest as a guilt offering a ram from the flock, one without defect and of the proper value. In this way the priest will make atonement for him for the wrong he has committed unintentionally, and he will be forgiven. 19It is a guilt offering; he has been guilty of[c] wrongdoing against the LORD."

6 The LORD said to Moses: 2"If anyone sins and is unfaithful to the LORD by deceiving his neighbor about something entrusted to him or left in his care or stolen, or if he cheats him, 3or if he finds lost property and lies about it, or if he swears falsely, or if he commits any such sin that people may do— 4when he thus sins and becomes guilty, he must return what he has stolen or taken by extortion, or what was entrusted to him, or the lost property he found, 5or whatever it was he swore falsely about. He must make restitution in full, add a fifth of the value to it and give it all to the owner on the day he presents his guilt offering. 6And as a penalty he must bring to the priest, that is, to the LORD, his guilt offering, a ram from the flock, one without defect and of the proper value. 7In this way the priest will make atonement for him before the LORD, and he will be forgiven for any of these things he did that made him guilty."

The Burnt Offering

8The LORD said to Moses: 9"Give Aaron and his sons this command: 'These are the regulations for the burnt offering: The burnt offering is to remain on the altar hearth throughout the night, till morning, and the fire must be kept burning on the altar. 10The priest shall then put on his linen clothes, with linen undergarments next to his body, and shall remove the ashes of the burnt offering that the fire has consumed on the altar and place them beside the altar. 11Then he is to take off these clothes and put on others, and carry the ashes outside the camp to a place that is ceremonially clean. 12The fire on the altar must be kept burning; it must not go out. Every morning the priest is to add firewood and arrange the burnt offering on the fire and burn the fat of the fellowship offerings[d] on it. 13The fire must be kept burning on the altar continuously; it must not go out.

The Grain Offering

14" 'These are the regulations for the grain offering: Aaron's sons are to bring it before the LORD, in front of the altar. 15The priest is to take a handful of fine flour and oil, together with all the incense on the grain offering, and burn the memorial portion on the altar as an aroma pleasing to the LORD. 16Aaron and his sons shall eat the rest of it, but it is to be eaten without

[a] *11* That is, probably about 2 quarts (about 2 liters)
[b] *15* That is, about 2/5 ounce (about 11.5 grams)
[c] *19* Or *has made full expiation for his*
[d] *12* Traditionally *peace offerings*

yeast in a holy place; they are to eat it in the courtyard of the Tent of Meeting. [17]It must not be baked with yeast; I have given it as their share of the offerings made to me by fire. Like the sin offering and the guilt offering, it is most holy. [18]Any male descendant of Aaron may eat it. It is his regular share of the offerings made to the LORD by fire for the generations to come. Whatever touches them will become holy.[e]"

[19]The LORD also said to Moses, [20]"This is the offering Aaron and his sons are to bring to the LORD on the day he[f] is anointed: a tenth of an ephah[g] of fine flour as a regular grain offering, half of it in the morning and half in the evening. [21]Prepare it with oil on a griddle; bring it well-mixed and present the grain offering broken[h] in pieces as an aroma pleasing to the LORD. [22]The son who is to succeed him as anointed priest shall prepare it. It is the LORD's regular share and is to be burned completely. [23]Every grain offering of a priest shall be burned completely; it must not be eaten."

The Sin Offering

[24]The LORD said to Moses, [25]"Say to Aaron and his sons: 'These are the regulations for the sin offering: The sin offering is to be slaughtered before the LORD in the place the burnt offering is slaughtered; it is most holy. [26]The priest who offers it shall eat it; it is to be eaten in a holy place, in the courtyard of the Tent of Meeting. [27]Whatever touches any of the flesh will become holy, and if any of the blood is spattered on a garment, you must wash it in a holy place. [28]The clay pot the meat is cooked in must be broken; but if it is cooked in a bronze pot, the pot is to be scoured and rinsed with water. [29]Any male in a priest's family may eat it; it is most holy. [30]But any sin offering whose blood is brought into the Tent of Meeting to make atonement in the Holy Place must not be eaten; it must be burned.

[e] *18* Or *Whoever touches them must be holy;* similarly in verse 27 [f] *20* Or *each* [g] *20* That is, probably about 2 quarts (about 2 liters) [h] *21* The meaning of the Hebrew for this word is uncertain.

PRAYER: AFFIRMATION

TO fear You, Lord, that is wisdom, and to depart from evil is understanding. (Job 28:28) . . . Blessed is everyone who fears You, Lord, and who walks in Your ways. (Psalm 128:1) . . . You take pleasure in those who fear You, O Lord, who put their hope in Your unfailing love. (Psalm 147:11)

***PAUSE** to reflect on these Biblical affirmations.*

NT Romans 8:18–39

Future Glory

[18]I consider that our present sufferings are not worth comparing with the glory that will be revealed in us. [19]The creation waits in eager expectation for the sons of God to be revealed. [20]For the creation was subjected to frustration, not by its own choice, but by the will of the one who subjected it, in hope [21]that[a] the creation itself will be liberated from its bondage to decay and brought into the glorious freedom of the children of God.

[22]We know that the whole creation has been groaning as in the pains of childbirth right up to the present time. [23]Not only so, but we ourselves, who have the firstfruits of the Spirit, groan inwardly as we wait eagerly for our adoption as sons, the redemption of our bodies. [24]For in this hope we were saved. But hope that is seen is no hope at all. Who hopes for what he already has? [25]But if we hope for what we do not yet have, we wait for it patiently.

[26]In the same way, the Spirit helps us in our weakness. We do not know what we ought to pray for, but the Spirit himself intercedes for us with groans that words cannot express. [27]And he who searches our hearts knows the mind of the Spirit, because the Spirit intercedes for the saints in accordance with God's will.

[a] *20,21* Or *subjected it in hope. [21]For*

More Than Conquerors

[28]And we know that in all things God works for the good of those who love him,[b] who[c] have been called according to his purpose. [29]For those God foreknew he also predestined to be conformed to the likeness of his Son, that he might be the firstborn among many brothers. [30]And those he predestined, he also called; those he called, he also justified; those he justified, he also glorified.

[31]What, then, shall we say in response to this? If God is for us, who can be against us? [32]He who did not spare his own Son, but gave him up for us all—how will he not also, along with him, graciously give us all things? [33]Who will bring any charge against those whom God has chosen? It is God who justifies. [34]Who is he that condemns? Christ Jesus, who died—more than that, who was raised to life—is at the right hand of God and is also interceding for us. [35]Who shall separate us from the love of Christ? Shall trouble or hardship or persecution or famine or nakedness or danger or sword? [36]As it is written:

"For your sake we face death all day
long;
we are considered as sheep to be
slaughtered."[d]

[37]No, in all these things we are more than conquerors through him who loved us. [38]For I am convinced that neither death nor life, neither angels nor demons,[e] neither the present nor the future, nor any powers, [39]neither height nor depth, nor anything else in all creation, will be able to separate us from the love of God that is in Christ Jesus our Lord.

[b] 28 Some manuscripts *And we know that all things work together for good to those who love God* [c] 28 Or *works together with those who love him to bring about what is good—with those who* [d] 36 Psalm 44:22 [e] 38 Or *nor heavenly rulers*

PRAYER: MY RELATIONSHIP TO OTHERS

WIVES should submit to their own husbands as to You, O Lord. For the husband is the head of the wife, as You, O Christ, also are the head of the church; and You are the Savior of the body. As the church is subject to You, so wives should be to their husbands in everything. Husbands should love their wives, just as You, O Christ, also loved the church and gave Yourself up for her that You might sanctify and cleanse her by the washing with water through the word, that You might present her to Yourself as a glorious church, without spot or wrinkle or any other blemish, but holy and blameless. So husbands ought to love their own wives as their own bodies. He who loves his own wife loves himself; for no one ever hated his own flesh, but nourishes and cherishes it, just as You also do the church, for we are members of Your body. (Ephesians 5:22–30)

PAUSE *to review your relationships with others and to commit them to the Lord.*

YEAR 1 DAY 91

OT Psalms 20–21

Psalm 20

For the director of music. A psalm of David.

[1]May the LORD answer you when you
are in distress;
may the name of the God of Jacob
protect you.
[2]May he send you help from the
sanctuary
and grant you support from Zion.
[3]May he remember all your sacrifices
and accept your burnt offerings.
Selah
[4]May he give you the desire of your
heart

and make all your plans succeed.
[5]We will shout for joy when you are victorious
and will lift up our banners in the name of our God.
May the LORD grant all your requests.

[6]Now I know that the LORD saves his anointed;
he answers him from his holy heaven
with the saving power of his right hand.
[7]Some trust in chariots and some in horses,
but we trust in the name of the LORD our God.
[8]They are brought to their knees and fall,
but we rise up and stand firm.

[9]O LORD, save the king!
Answer[a] us when we call!

Psalm 21

For the director of music. A psalm of David.

[1]O LORD, the king rejoices in your strength.
How great is his joy in the victories you give!
[2]You have granted him the desire of his heart
and have not withheld the request of his lips. *Selah*
[3]You welcomed him with rich blessings
and placed a crown of pure gold on his head.
[4]He asked you for life, and you gave it to him—
length of days, for ever and ever.
[5]Through the victories you gave, his glory is great;
you have bestowed on him splendor and majesty.
[6]Surely you have granted him eternal blessings
and made him glad with the joy of your presence.
[7]For the king trusts in the LORD;
through the unfailing love of the Most High
he will not be shaken.

[8]Your hand will lay hold on all your enemies;
your right hand will seize your foes.
[9]At the time of your appearing
you will make them like a fiery furnace.
In his wrath the LORD will swallow them up,
and his fire will consume them.
[10]You will destroy their descendants from the earth,
their posterity from mankind.
[11]Though they plot evil against you
and devise wicked schemes, they cannot succeed;
[12]for you will make them turn their backs
when you aim at them with drawn bow.

[13]Be exalted, O LORD, in your strength;
we will sing and praise your might.

[a] 9 Or *save! / O King, answer*

PRAYER: THANKSGIVING

I THANK You, Lord Jesus, for Your promises: "I will see you again and your hearts will rejoice, and no one will take your joy from you. And in that day you will not ask Me any question. I tell you the truth, whatever you ask the Father in My name He will give you. Ask, and you will receive, that your joy may be full." You, Father, love me because I have loved Jesus and have believed that He came forth from You.

(John 16:22–24, 27)

PAUSE *to offer your own expressions of thanksgiving.*

NT Romans 9:1-33

God's Sovereign Choice

9 I speak the truth in Christ—I am not
lying, my conscience confirms it in the
Holy Spirit— 2I have great sorrow and unceasing anguish in my heart. 3For I could
wish that I myself were cursed and cut off
from Christ for the sake of my brothers,
those of my own race, 4the people of Israel. Theirs is the adoption as sons; theirs
the divine glory, the covenants, the receiving of the law, the temple worship and
the promises. 5Theirs are the patriarchs,
and from them is traced the human ancestry of Christ, who is God over all, forever praised![a] Amen.
6It is not as though God's word had
failed. For not all who are descended from
Israel are Israel. 7Nor because they are his
descendants are they all Abraham's children. On the contrary, "It is through Isaac
that your offspring will be reckoned."[b] 8In
other words, it is not the natural children
who are God's children, but it is the children of the promise who are regarded as
Abraham's offspring. 9For this was how the
promise was stated: "At the appointed time
I will return, and Sarah will have a son."[c]
10Not only that, but Rebekah's children
had one and the same father, our father
Isaac. 11Yet, before the twins were born or
had done anything good or bad—in order
that God's purpose in election might
stand: 12not by works but by him who
calls—she was told, "The older will serve
the younger."[d] 13Just as it is written: "Jacob I loved, but Esau I hated."[e]
14What then shall we say? Is God unjust? Not at all! 15For he says to Moses,

> "I will have mercy on whom I have
> mercy,
> and I will have compassion on
> whom I have compassion."[f]

16It does not, therefore, depend on man's
desire or effort, but on God's mercy. 17For
the Scripture says to Pharaoh: "I raised
you up for this very purpose, that I might
display my power in you and that my
name might be proclaimed in all the
earth."[g] 18Therefore God has mercy on
whom he wants to have mercy, and he
hardens whom he wants to harden.
19One of you will say to me: "Then why
does God still blame us? For who resists
his will?" 20But who are you, O man, to
talk back to God? "Shall what is formed
say to him who formed it, 'Why did you
make me like this?' "[h] 21Does not the potter have the right to make out of the same
lump of clay some pottery for noble purposes and some for common use?
22What if God, choosing to show his
wrath and make his power known, bore
with great patience the objects of his
wrath—prepared for destruction? 23What
if he did this to make the riches of his glory known to the objects of his mercy,
whom he prepared in advance for glory—
24even us, whom he also called, not only
from the Jews but also from the Gentiles?
25As he says in Hosea:

> "I will call them 'my people' who are
> not my people;
> and I will call her 'my loved one'
> who is not my loved one,"[i]

26and,

> "It will happen that in the very place
> where it was said to them,
> 'You are not my people,'
> they will be called 'sons of the living
> God.' "[j]

27Isaiah cries out concerning Israel:

> "Though the number of the Israelites
> be like the sand by the sea,
> only the remnant will be saved.
> 28For the Lord will carry out
> his sentence on earth with speed
> and finality."[k]

29It is just as Isaiah said previously:

> "Unless the Lord Almighty
> had left us descendants,
> we would have become like Sodom,
> we would have been like
> Gomorrah."[l]

Israel's Unbelief

30What then shall we say? That the
Gentiles, who did not pursue righteous-

[a] *5* Or *Christ, who is over all. God be forever praised!* Or *Christ. God who is over all be forever praised!*
[b] *7* Gen. 21:12 [c] *9* Gen. 18:10,14
[d] *12* Gen. 25:23 [e] *13* Mal. 1:2,3
[f] *15* Exodus 33:19 [g] *17* Exodus 9:16
[h] *20* Isaiah 29:16; 45:9 [i] *25* Hosea 2:23
[j] *26* Hosea 1:10 [k] *28* Isaiah 10:22,23
[l] *29* Isaiah 1:9

ness, have obtained it, a righteousness that is by faith; [31]but Israel, who pursued a law of righteousness, has not attained it. [32]Why not? Because they pursued it not by faith but as if it were by works. They stumbled over the "stumbling stone." [33]As it is written:

"See, I lay in Zion a stone that causes
men to stumble
and a rock that makes them fall,
and the one who trusts in him will
never be put to shame."[m]

[m] 33 Isaiah 8:14; 28:16

PRAYER: THE ATTRIBUTES OF GOD

YOU, O Son of God, are the radiance of God's glory and the exact representation of His being, upholding all things by Your powerful word. After You cleansed our sins, You sat down at the right hand of the Majesty on high, having become as much superior to angels as the name You have inherited is more excellent than theirs. (Hebrews 1:3–4)

***PAUSE** to reflect on these affirmations about the person, powers and perfection of God.*

YEAR 1 DAY 92

OT Leviticus 7:1-38

The Guilt Offering

7 " 'These are the regulations for the guilt
offering, which is most holy: [2]The guilt
offering is to be slaughtered in the place
where the burnt offering is slaughtered,
and its blood is to be sprinkled against the
altar on all sides. [3]All its fat shall be offered: the fat tail and the fat that covers the
inner parts, [4]both kidneys with the fat on
them near the loins, and the covering of
the liver, which is to be removed with the
kidneys. [5]The priest shall burn them on
the altar as an offering made to the LORD
by fire. It is a guilt offering. [6]Any male in
a priest's family may eat it, but it must be
eaten in a holy place; it is most holy.
[7]" 'The same law applies to both the sin
offering and the guilt offering: They belong to the priest who makes atonement
with them. [8]The priest who offers a burnt
offering for anyone may keep its hide for
himself. [9]Every grain offering baked in an
oven or cooked in a pan or on a griddle
belongs to the priest who offers it, [10]and
every grain offering, whether mixed with
oil or dry, belongs equally to all the sons
of Aaron.

The Fellowship Offering

[11]" 'These are the regulations for the fellowship offering[a] a person may present to
the LORD:

[12]" 'If he offers it as an expression of
thankfulness, then along with this thank
offering he is to offer cakes of bread made
without yeast and mixed with oil, wafers
made without yeast and spread with oil,
and cakes of fine flour well-kneaded and
mixed with oil. [13]Along with his fellowship offering of thanksgiving he is to
present an offering with cakes of bread
made with yeast. [14]He is to bring one of
each kind as an offering, a contribution to
the LORD; it belongs to the priest who
sprinkles the blood of the fellowship offerings. [15]The meat of his fellowship offering of thanksgiving must be eaten on
the day it is offered; he must leave none
of it till morning.
[16]" 'If, however, his offering is the result
of a vow or is a freewill offering, the sacrifice shall be eaten on the day he offers
it, but anything left over may be eaten on
the next day. [17]Any meat of the sacrifice
left over till the third day must be burned
up. [18]If any meat of the fellowship offering is eaten on the third day, it will not be
accepted. It will not be credited to the one
who offered it, for it is impure; the person
who eats any of it will be held responsible.
[19]" 'Meat that touches anything ceremonially unclean must not be eaten; it

[a] 11 Traditionally *peace offering;* also in verses 13–37

must be burned up. As for other meat,
anyone ceremonially clean may eat it.
20But if anyone who is unclean eats any
meat of the fellowship offering belonging
to the LORD, that person must be cut off
from his people. 21If anyone touches
something unclean—whether human uncleanness or an unclean animal or any unclean, detestable thing—and then eats any
of the meat of the fellowship offering belonging to the LORD, that person must be
cut off from his people.' "

Eating Fat and Blood Forbidden

22The LORD said to Moses, 23"Say to the
Israelites: 'Do not eat any of the fat of cattle, sheep or goats. 24The fat of an animal
found dead or torn by wild animals may
be used for any other purpose, but you
must not eat it. 25Anyone who eats the fat
of an animal from which an offering by
fire may be[b] made to the LORD must be cut
off from his people. 26And wherever you
live, you must not eat the blood of any
bird or animal. 27If anyone eats blood,
that person must be cut off from his people.' "

The Priests' Share

28The LORD said to Moses, 29"Say to the
Israelites: 'Anyone who brings a fellowship offering to the LORD is to bring part
of it as his sacrifice to the LORD. 30With his
own hands he is to bring the offering
made to the LORD by fire; he is to bring
the fat, together with the breast, and wave
the breast before the LORD as a wave offering. 31The priest shall burn the fat on
the altar, but the breast belongs to Aaron
and his sons. 32You are to give the right
thigh of your fellowship offerings to the
priest as a contribution. 33The son of Aaron who offers the blood and the fat of the
fellowship offering shall have the right
thigh as his share. 34From the fellowship
offerings of the Israelites, I have taken the
breast that is waved and the thigh that is
presented and have given them to Aaron
the priest and his sons as their regular
share from the Israelites.' "

35This is the portion of the offerings
made to the LORD by fire that were allotted to Aaron and his sons on the day they
were presented to serve the LORD as
priests. 36On the day they were anointed,
the LORD commanded that the Israelites
give this to them as their regular share for
the generations to come.

37These, then, are the regulations for the
burnt offering, the grain offering, the sin
offering, the guilt offering, the ordination
offering and the fellowship offering,
38which the LORD gave Moses on Mount
Sinai on the day he commanded the Israelites to bring their offerings to the LORD,
in the Desert of Sinai.

[b] 25 Or *fire is*

PRAYER: ADORATION

WHERE can I go from Your Spirit? Or where can I flee from Your presence? If I ascend to heaven, You are there; if I make my bed in Sheol, You are there. If I take the wings of the dawn, if I dwell in the depths of the sea, even there Your hand will lead me; Your right hand will lay hold of me. If I say, "Surely the darkness will cover me," even the night will be light around me. The darkness is not dark to You, and the night shines as the day; darkness and light are alike to You. (Psalm 139:7–12)

***PAUSE** to express your thoughts of praise and worship.*

NT Romans 10:1–21

10 Brothers, my heart's desire and
prayer to God for the Israelites is that
they may be saved. 2For I can testify
about them that they are zealous for
God, but their zeal is not based on
knowledge. 3Since they did not know the
righteousness that comes from God and
sought to establish their own, they did
not submit to God's righteousness.
4Christ is the end of the law so that there

may be righteousness for everyone who
believes.
[5]Moses describes in this way the righteousness that is by the law: "The man
who does these things will live by them."[a]
[6]But the righteousness that is by faith says:
"Do not say in your heart, 'Who will ascend into heaven?'[b]" (that is, to bring
Christ down) [7]"or 'Who will descend into
the deep?'[c]" (that is, to bring Christ up
from the dead). [8]But what does it say?
"The word is near you; it is in your mouth
and in your heart,"[d] that is, the word of
faith we are proclaiming: [9]That if you confess with your mouth, "Jesus is Lord," and
believe in your heart that God raised him
from the dead, you will be saved. [10]For it
is with your heart that you believe and are
justified, and it is with your mouth that
you confess and are saved. [11]As the Scripture says, "Anyone who trusts in him will
never be put to shame."[e] [12]For there is no
difference between Jew and Gentile—the
same Lord is Lord of all and richly blesses
all who call on him, [13]for, "Everyone who
calls on the name of the Lord will be
saved."[f]
[14]How, then, can they call on the one
they have not believed in? And how can
they believe in the one of whom they have
not heard? And how can they hear without someone preaching to them? [15]And
how can they preach unless they are sent?
As it is written, "How beautiful are the feet
of those who bring good news!"[g]
[16]But not all the Israelites accepted the
good news. For Isaiah says, "Lord, who
has believed our message?"[h] [17]Conse-
quently, faith comes from hearing the
message, and the message is heard
through the word of Christ. [18]But I ask:
Did they not hear? Of course they did:

"Their voice has gone out into all the
earth,
their words to the ends of the
world."[i]

[19]Again I ask: Did Israel not understand?
First, Moses says,

"I will make you envious by those
who are not a nation;
I will make you angry by a nation
that has no understanding."[j]

[20]And Isaiah boldly says,

"I was found by those who did not
seek me;
I revealed myself to those who did
not ask for me."[k]

[21]But concerning Israel he says,

"All day long I have held out my
hands
to a disobedient and obstinate
people."[l]

[a] *5* Lev. 18:5 [b] *6* Deut. 30:12 [c] *7* Deut. 30:13
[d] *8* Deut. 30:14 [e] *11* Isaiah 28:16 [f] *13* Joel 2:32
[g] *15* Isaiah 52:7 [h] *16* Isaiah 53:1 [i] *18* Psalm 19:4
[j] *19* Deut. 32:21 [k] *20* Isaiah 65:1
[l] *21* Isaiah 65:2

PRAYER: THE WORKS OF GOD

***WHEN** You, O Son of Man, come in Your glory, and all the angels with You, You will sit on Your glorious throne. All the nations will be gathered before You, and You will separate the people one from another as a shepherd separates the sheep from the goats. You will put the sheep on Your right and the goats on Your left. Then You, O King, will say to those on Your right, "Come, you who are blessed by My Father; inherit the kingdom prepared for you since the foundation of the world."*

(Matthew 25:31–34)

***TAKE** a moment to consider the greatness of God's wonderful works.*

YEAR 1 DAY 93

OT Leviticus 8:1-36

The Ordination of Aaron and His Sons

8 The LORD said to Moses, 2"Bring Aaron and his sons, their garments, the anointing oil, the bull for the sin offering, the two rams and the basket containing bread made without yeast, 3and gather the entire assembly at the entrance to the Tent of Meeting." 4Moses did as the LORD commanded him, and the assembly gathered at the entrance to the Tent of Meeting.

5Moses said to the assembly, "This is what the LORD has commanded to be done." 6Then Moses brought Aaron and his sons forward and washed them with water. 7He put the tunic on Aaron, tied the sash around him, clothed him with the robe and put the ephod on him. He also tied the ephod to him by its skillfully woven waistband; so it was fastened on him. 8He placed the breastpiece on him and put the Urim and Thummim in the breastpiece. 9Then he placed the turban on Aaron's head and set the gold plate, the sacred diadem, on the front of it, as the LORD commanded Moses.

10Then Moses took the anointing oil and anointed the tabernacle and everything in it, and so consecrated them. 11He sprinkled some of the oil on the altar seven times, anointing the altar and all its utensils and the basin with its stand, to consecrate them. 12He poured some of the anointing oil on Aaron's head and anointed him to consecrate him. 13Then he brought Aaron's sons forward, put tunics on them, tied sashes around them and put headbands on them, as the LORD commanded Moses.

14He then presented the bull for the sin offering, and Aaron and his sons laid their hands on its head. 15Moses slaughtered the bull and took some of the blood, and with his finger he put it on all the horns of the altar to purify the altar. He poured out the rest of the blood at the base of the altar. So he consecrated it to make atonement for it. 16Moses also took all the fat around the inner parts, the covering of the liver, and both kidneys and their fat, and burned it on the altar. 17But the bull with its hide and its flesh and its offal he burned up outside the camp, as the LORD commanded Moses.

18He then presented the ram for the burnt offering, and Aaron and his sons laid their hands on its head. 19Then Moses slaughtered the ram and sprinkled the blood against the altar on all sides. 20He cut the ram into pieces and burned the head, the pieces and the fat. 21He washed the inner parts and the legs with water and burned the whole ram on the altar as a burnt offering, a pleasing aroma, an offering made to the LORD by fire, as the LORD commanded Moses.

22He then presented the other ram, the ram for the ordination, and Aaron and his sons laid their hands on its head. 23Moses slaughtered the ram and took some of its blood and put it on the lobe of Aaron's right ear, on the thumb of his right hand and on the big toe of his right foot. 24Moses also brought Aaron's sons forward and put some of the blood on the lobes of their right ears, on the thumbs of their right hands and on the big toes of their right feet. Then he sprinkled blood against the altar on all sides. 25He took the fat, the fat tail, all the fat around the inner parts, the covering of the liver, both kidneys and their fat and the right thigh. 26Then from the basket of bread made without yeast, which was before the LORD, he took a cake of bread, and one made with oil, and a wafer; he put these on the fat portions and on the right thigh. 27He put all these in the hands of Aaron and his sons and waved them before the LORD as a wave offering. 28Then Moses took them from their hands and burned them on the altar on top of the burnt offering as an ordination offering, a pleasing aroma, an offering made to the LORD by fire. 29He also took the breast—Moses' share of the ordination ram—and waved it before the LORD as a wave offering, as the LORD commanded Moses.

30Then Moses took some of the anointing oil and some of the blood from the altar and sprinkled them on Aaron and his garments and on his sons and their garments. So he consecrated Aaron and his garments and his sons and their garments.

31Moses then said to Aaron and his sons, "Cook the meat at the entrance to the Tent of Meeting and eat it there with the bread from the basket of ordination offerings, as I commanded, saying,[a] 'Aaron and his

[a] 31 Or *I was commanded:*

sons are to eat it.' 32Then burn up the rest
of the meat and the bread. 33Do not leave
the entrance to the Tent of Meeting for sev-
en days, until the days of your ordination
are completed, for your ordination will
last seven days. 34What has been done today was commanded by the LORD to make
atonement for you. 35You must stay at the
entrance to the Tent of Meeting day and
night for seven days and do what the LORD
requires, so you will not die; for that is
what I have been commanded." 36So Aaron and his sons did everything the LORD
commanded through Moses.

PRAYER: CONFESSION

O GOD, those whom You love, You rebuke and discipline. Therefore may I be zealous and repent. (Revelation 3:19)

__ASK__ the Spirit to search your heart and reveal any areas of unconfessed sin. Acknowledge these to the Lord and thank Him for His forgiveness.

NT Romans 11:1–24

The Remnant of Israel

11 I ask then: Did God reject his people?
By no means! I am an Israelite myself,
a descendant of Abraham, from the tribe
of Benjamin. 2God did not reject his people, whom he foreknew. Don't you know
what the Scripture says in the passage
about Elijah—how he appealed to God
against Israel: 3"Lord, they have killed
your prophets and torn down your altars;
I am the only one left, and they are trying
to kill me"[a]? 4And what was God's answer
to him? "I have reserved for myself seven
thousand who have not bowed the knee
to Baal."[b] 5So too, at the present time
there is a remnant chosen by grace. 6And
if by grace, then it is no longer by works;
if it were, grace would no longer be grace.[c]

7What then? What Israel sought so
earnestly it did not obtain, but the elect
did. The others were hardened, 8as it is
written:

"God gave them a spirit of stupor,
eyes so that they could not see
and ears so that they could not
hear,
to this very day."[d]

9And David says:

"May their table become a snare and a
trap,
a stumbling block and a retribution
for them.
10May their eyes be darkened so they
cannot see,
and their backs be bent forever."[e]

Ingrafted Branches

11Again I ask: Did they stumble so as to
fall beyond recovery? Not at all! Rather,
because of their transgression, salvation
has come to the Gentiles to make Israel
envious. 12But if their transgression
means riches for the world, and their loss
means riches for the Gentiles, how much
greater riches will their fullness bring!

13I am talking to you Gentiles. Inas-
much as I am the apostle to the Gentiles,
I make much of my ministry 14in the hope
that I may somehow arouse my own people to envy and save some of them. 15For
if their rejection is the reconciliation of
the world, what will their acceptance be
but life from the dead? 16If the part of the
dough offered as firstfruits is holy, then
the whole batch is holy; if the root is holy,
so are the branches.

17If some of the branches have been
broken off, and you, though a wild olive
shoot, have been grafted in among the
others and now share in the nourishing
sap from the olive root, 18do not boast
over those branches. If you do, consider
this: You do not support the root, but the
root supports you. 19You will say then,
"Branches were broken off so that I could
be grafted in." 20Granted. But they were
broken off because of unbelief, and you
stand by faith. Do not be arrogant, but
be afraid. 21For if God did not spare the

[a] *3* 1 Kings 19:10,14 [b] *4* 1 Kings 19:18
[c] *6* Some manuscripts *by grace. But if by works, then it is no longer grace; if it were, work would no longer be work.* [d] *8* Deut. 29:4; Isaiah 29:10
[e] *10* Psalm 69:22,23

natural branches, he will not spare you either.
[22]Consider therefore the kindness and sternness of God: sternness to those who fell, but kindness to you, provided that you continue in his kindness. Otherwise, you also will be cut off. [23]And if they do not persist in unbelief, they will be grafted in, for God is able to graft them in again. [24]After all, if you were cut out of an olive tree that is wild by nature, and contrary to nature were grafted into a cultivated olive tree, how much more readily will these, the natural branches, be grafted into their own olive tree!

PRAYER: MY RELATIONSHIP TO GOD

I DO not want to be like the rocky places on which the seed was thrown—like those who hear the word and at once receive it with joy, but since they have no root, last only a short time; when affliction or persecution comes because of the word, they quickly fall away. Nor do I want to be like the soil among the thorns on which seed was sown—like those who hear the word, but the worries of this world, the deceitfulness of riches and pleasures, and the desires for other things come in and choke the word, making it immature and unfruitful. Instead, I want to be like the good soil on which seed was sown—like those who with noble and good hearts hear the word, understand and accept it, and with perseverance bear fruit, yielding thirty, sixty or a hundred times what was sown.
(Matthew 13:20–23; Mark 4:16–20; Luke 8:13–15)

***PAUSE** to thank God for the relationship that you enjoy with Him in Jesus Christ.*

YEAR 1
DAY 94

OT Leviticus 9:1-24

The Priests Begin Their Ministry

9 On the eighth day Moses summoned Aaron and his sons and the elders of Israel. [2]He said to Aaron, "Take a bull calf for your sin offering and a ram for your burnt offering, both without defect, and present them before the LORD. [3]Then say to the Israelites: 'Take a male goat for a sin offering, a calf and a lamb—both a year old and without defect—for a burnt offering, [4]and an ox[a] and a ram for a fellowship offering[b] to sacrifice before the LORD, together with a grain offering mixed with oil. For today the LORD will appear to you.' "

[5]They took the things Moses commanded to the front of the Tent of Meeting, and the entire assembly came near and stood before the LORD. [6]Then Moses said, "This is what the LORD has commanded you to do, so that the glory of the LORD may appear to you."

[7]Moses said to Aaron, "Come to the altar and sacrifice your sin offering and your burnt offering and make atonement for yourself and the people; sacrifice the offering that is for the people and make atonement for them, as the LORD has commanded."

[8]So Aaron came to the altar and slaughtered the calf as a sin offering for himself. [9]His sons brought the blood to him, and he dipped his finger into the blood and put it on the horns of the altar; the rest of the blood he poured out at the base of the altar. [10]On the altar he burned the fat, the kidneys and the covering of the liver from the sin offering, as the LORD commanded Moses; [11]the flesh and the hide he burned up outside the camp.

[12]Then he slaughtered the burnt offering. His sons handed him the blood, and

[a]4 The Hebrew word can include both male and female; also in verses 18 and 19. [b]4 Traditionally *peace offering;* also in verses 18 and 22

he sprinkled it against the altar on all
sides. 13They handed him the burnt offering piece by piece, including the head,
and he burned them on the altar. 14He
washed the inner parts and the legs and
burned them on top of the burnt offering
on the altar.

15Aaron then brought the offering that
was for the people. He took the goat for
the people's sin offering and slaughtered
it and offered it for a sin offering as he did
with the first one.

16He brought the burnt offering and offered it in the prescribed way. 17He also
brought the grain offering, took a handful of it and burned it on the altar in addition to the morning's burnt offering.

18He slaughtered the ox and the ram as
the fellowship offering for the people. His
sons handed him the blood, and he sprinkled it against the altar on all sides. 19But
the fat portions of the ox and the ram—
the fat tail, the layer of fat, the kidneys and
the covering of the liver— 20these they laid
on the breasts, and then Aaron burned the
fat on the altar. 21Aaron waved the breasts
and the right thigh before the LORD as a
wave offering, as Moses commanded.

22Then Aaron lifted his hands toward
the people and blessed them. And having
sacrificed the sin offering, the burnt offering and the fellowship offering, he
stepped down.

23Moses and Aaron then went into the
Tent of Meeting. When they came out,
they blessed the people; and the glory of
the LORD appeared to all the people. 24Fire
came out from the presence of the LORD
and consumed the burnt offering and the
fat portions on the altar. And when all the
people saw it, they shouted for joy and
fell facedown.

PRAYER: RENEWAL

MAY I act in the fear of You, Lord, faithfully and with a loyal heart. (2 Chronicles 19:9) . . . Your foremost commandment is this: "Hear, O Israel; the Lord our God, the Lord is one; and you shall love the Lord your God with all your heart and with all your soul and with all your mind and with all your strength." The second is this: "You shall love your neighbor as yourself." There is no commandment greater than these. To love You with all my heart and with all my understanding and with all my strength and to love my neighbor as myself are more important than all burnt offerings and sacrifices. (Mark 12:29–31, 33)

PAUSE *to add your own prayers for personal renewal.*

NT Romans 11:25–36

All Israel Will Be Saved

25I do not want you to be ignorant of
this mystery, brothers, so that you may
not be conceited: Israel has experienced a
hardening in part until the full number
of the Gentiles has come in. 26And so all
Israel will be saved, as it is written:

"The deliverer will come from Zion;
he will turn godlessness away from
Jacob.
27And this is[a] my covenant with them
when I take away their sins."[b]

28As far as the gospel is concerned, they
are enemies on your account; but as far as
election is concerned, they are loved on
account of the patriarchs, 29for God's gifts
and his call are irrevocable. 30Just as you
who were at one time disobedient to God
have now received mercy as a result of
their disobedience, 31so they too have now
become disobedient in order that they too
may now[c] receive mercy as a result of
God's mercy to you. 32For God has bound
all men over to disobedience so that he
may have mercy on them all.

[a] *27* Or *will be* [b] *27* Isaiah 59:20,21; 27:9; Jer. 31:33,34 [c] *31* Some manuscripts do not have *now.*

Doxology

33 Oh, the depth of the riches of the
wisdom and[d] knowledge of
God!
How unsearchable his judgments,
and his paths beyond tracing out!
34 "Who has known the mind of the
Lord?
Or who has been his counselor?"[e]
35 "Who has ever given to God,
that God should repay him?"[f]
36 For from him and through him and to
him are all things.
To him be the glory forever! Amen.

[d] 33 Or *riches and the wisdom and the*
[e] 34 Isaiah 40:13 [f] 35 Job 41:11

PRAYER: THE CHARACTER I WANT TO CULTIVATE

BLESSED are those who do not walk in the counsel of the wicked or stand in the way of sinners or sit in the seat of scorners. But their delight is in Your law, O Lord, and on Your law they meditate day and night. And they shall be like trees planted by streams of water; they yield fruit in season and their leaves do not wither; whatever they do will prosper. (Psalm 1:1–3)

TAKE *a moment to ask the Lord for the grace to grow in godly character.*

YEAR 1 DAY 95

OT Proverbs 4

Wisdom Is Supreme

4 Listen, my sons, to a father's
instruction;
pay attention and gain
understanding.
2 I give you sound learning,
so do not forsake my teaching.
3 When I was a boy in my father's
house,
still tender, and an only child of my
mother,
4 he taught me and said,
"Lay hold of my words with all your
heart;
keep my commands and you will
live.
5 Get wisdom, get understanding;
do not forget my words or swerve
from them.
6 Do not forsake wisdom, and she will
protect you;
love her, and she will watch over
you.
7 Wisdom is supreme; therefore get
wisdom.
Though it cost all you have,[a] get
understanding.
8 Esteem her, and she will exalt you;
embrace her, and she will honor
you.
9 She will set a garland of grace on your
head
and present you with a crown of
splendor."

10 Listen, my son, accept what I say,
and the years of your life will be
many.
11 I guide you in the way of wisdom
and lead you along straight paths.
12 When you walk, your steps will not be
hampered;
when you run, you will not
stumble.
13 Hold on to instruction, do not let it
go;
guard it well, for it is your life.
14 Do not set foot on the path of the
wicked
or walk in the way of evil men.
15 Avoid it, do not travel on it;
turn from it and go on your way.
16 For they cannot sleep till they do evil;
they are robbed of slumber till they
make someone fall.
17 They eat the bread of wickedness
and drink the wine of violence.

18 The path of the righteous is like the
first gleam of dawn,

[a] 7 Or *Whatever else you get*

shining ever brighter till the full
light of day.
[19] But the way of the wicked is like deep
darkness;
they do not know what makes them
stumble.

[20] My son, pay attention to what I say;
listen closely to my words.
[21] Do not let them out of your sight,
keep them within your heart;
[22] for they are life to those who find
them
and health to a man's whole body.
[23] Above all else, guard your heart,
for it is the wellspring of life.
[24] Put away perversity from your mouth;
keep corrupt talk far from your lips.
[25] Let your eyes look straight ahead,
fix your gaze directly before you.
[26] Make level[b] paths for your feet
and take only ways that are firm.
[27] Do not swerve to the right or the left;
keep your foot from evil.

[b] 26 Or *Consider the*

PRAYER: PETITION

LORD God, may I be strong and courageous, and act. May I not be afraid or discouraged, for You, Lord God, are with me. You will not fail me or forsake me. (1 Chronicles 28:20)

PAUSE *here to petition God for growth in your character and personal discipline, and for physical health and strength. Ask that He empower you for spiritual warfare against the temptations of the world, the flesh and the devil. Offer prayers regarding your activities for this day and any special concerns you may have.*

NT Romans 12:1-8

Living Sacrifices

12 Therefore, I urge you, brothers, in
view of God's mercy, to offer your
bodies as living sacrifices, holy and pleasing to God—this is your spiritual[a] act of
worship. [2] Do not conform any longer to
the pattern of this world, but be transformed by the renewing of your mind.
Then you will be able to test and approve
what God's will is—his good, pleasing
and perfect will.
[3] For by the grace given me I say to every
one of you: Do not think of yourself more
highly than you ought, but rather think of
yourself with sober judgment, in accordance with the measure of faith God has
given you. [4] Just as each of us has one
body with many members, and these
members do not all have the same function, [5] so in Christ we who are many form
one body, and each member belongs to
all the others. [6] We have different gifts, according to the grace given us. If a man's
gift is prophesying, let him use it in proportion to his[b] faith. [7] If it is serving, let
him serve; if it is teaching, let him teach;
[8] if it is encouraging, let him encourage; if
it is contributing to the needs of others,
let him give generously; if it is leadership,
let him govern diligently; if it is showing
mercy, let him do it cheerfully.

[a] 1 Or *reasonable* [b] 6 Or *in agreement with the*

PRAYER: MY RELATIONSHIP TO OTHERS

THOSE who spare the rod hate their children, but those who love their children are careful to discipline them. (Proverbs 13:24) . . . Foolishness is bound up in the hearts of children, but the rod of discipline will drive it far from them. (Proverbs 22:15)

PAUSE *to review your relationships with others and to commit them to the Lord.*

YEAR 1 DAY 96

OT Leviticus 10:1-20

The Death of Nadab and Abihu

10 Aaron's sons Nadab and Abihu took their censers, put fire in them and added incense; and they offered unauthorized fire before the LORD, contrary to his command. 2So fire came out from the presence of the LORD and consumed them, and they died before the LORD. 3Moses then said to Aaron, "This is what the LORD spoke of when he said:

" 'Among those who approach me
I will show myself holy;
in the sight of all the people
I will be honored.' "

Aaron remained silent.

4Moses summoned Mishael and Elzaphan, sons of Aaron's uncle Uzziel, and said to them, "Come here; carry your cousins outside the camp, away from the front of the sanctuary." 5So they came and carried them, still in their tunics, outside the camp, as Moses ordered.

6Then Moses said to Aaron and his sons Eleazar and Ithamar, "Do not let your hair become unkempt,[a] and do not tear your clothes, or you will die and the LORD will be angry with the whole community. But your relatives, all the house of Israel, may mourn for those the LORD has destroyed by fire. 7Do not leave the entrance to the Tent of Meeting or you will die, because the LORD's anointing oil is on you." So they did as Moses said.

8Then the LORD said to Aaron, 9"You and your sons are not to drink wine or other fermented drink whenever you go into the Tent of Meeting, or you will die. This is a lasting ordinance for the generations to come. 10You must distinguish between the holy and the common, between the unclean and the clean, 11and you must teach the Israelites all the decrees the LORD has given them through Moses."

12Moses said to Aaron and his remaining sons, Eleazar and Ithamar, "Take the grain offering left over from the offerings made to the LORD by fire and eat it prepared without yeast beside the altar, for it is most holy. 13Eat it in a holy place, because it is your share and your sons' share of the offerings made to the LORD by fire; for so I have been commanded. 14But you and your sons and your daughters may eat the breast that was waved and the thigh that was presented. Eat them in a ceremonially clean place; they have been given to you and your children as your share of the Israelites' fellowship offerings.[b] 15The thigh that was presented and the breast that was waved must be brought with the fat portions of the offerings made by fire, to be waved before the LORD as a wave offering. This will be the regular share for you and your children, as the LORD has commanded."

16When Moses inquired about the goat of the sin offering and found that it had been burned up, he was angry with Eleazar and Ithamar, Aaron's remaining sons, and asked, 17"Why didn't you eat the sin offering in the sanctuary area? It is most holy; it was given to you to take away the guilt of the community by making atonement for them before the LORD. 18Since its blood was not taken into the Holy Place, you should have eaten the goat in the sanctuary area, as I commanded."

19Aaron replied to Moses, "Today they sacrificed their sin offering and their burnt offering before the LORD, but such things as this have happened to me. Would the LORD have been pleased if I had eaten the sin offering today?" 20When Moses heard this, he was satisfied.

[a] 6 Or *Do not uncover your heads* [b] 14 Traditionally *peace offerings*

PRAYER: INTERCESSION

O LORD, I know that You will maintain the cause of the afflicted and justice for the poor. (Psalm 140:12)

TAKE *a few moments to intercede on behalf of the poor and hungry, the oppressed and persecuted, and those in control of world and national resources. Offer prayers for peace among nations and regarding current events and concerns.*

NT Romans 12:9–21

Love

9 Love must be sincere. Hate what is evil;
cling to what is good. 10 Be devoted to one
another in brotherly love. Honor one another above yourselves. 11 Never be lacking
in zeal, but keep your spiritual fervor,
serving the Lord. 12 Be joyful in hope, patient in affliction, faithful in prayer.
13 Share with God's people who are in
need. Practice hospitality.
14 Bless those who persecute you; bless
and do not curse. 15 Rejoice with those
who rejoice; mourn with those who
mourn. 16 Live in harmony with one another. Do not be proud, but be willing to
associate with people of low position.[a]
Do not be conceited.
17 Do not repay anyone evil for evil. Be
careful to do what is right in the eyes of
everybody. 18 If it is possible, as far as it depends on you, live at peace with everyone.
19 Do not take revenge, my friends, but
leave room for God's wrath, for it is written: "It is mine to avenge; I will repay,"[b]
says the Lord. 20 On the contrary:

"If your enemy is hungry, feed him;
if he is thirsty, give him something to drink.
In doing this, you will heap burning coals on his head."[c]

21 Do not be overcome by evil, but overcome evil with good.

[a] *16* Or *willing to do menial work* [b] *19* Deut. 32:35
[c] *20* Prov. 25:21,22

PRAYER: THE ATTRIBUTES OF GOD

YOU are a jealous and avenging God; You take vengeance and are filled with wrath. You are slow to anger and great in power and will not leave the guilty unpunished. Your way is in the whirlwind and the storm, and clouds are the dust of Your feet. (Nahum 1:2–3) . . . Are You a God nearby, and not a God far away? Who can hide in secret places so that You cannot see them? Do You not fill heaven and earth? (Jeremiah 23:23–24)

PAUSE *to reflect on these affirmations about the person, powers and perfection of God.*

YEAR 1
DAY 97

OT Leviticus 11:1–12:8

Clean and Unclean Food

11 The LORD said to Moses and Aaron,
2 "Say to the Israelites: 'Of all the animals that live on land, these are the ones
you may eat: 3 You may eat any animal
that has a split hoof completely divided
and that chews the cud.
4 " 'There are some that only chew the
cud or only have a split hoof, but you
must not eat them. The camel, though it
chews the cud, does not have a split hoof;

it is ceremonially unclean for you. 5The
coney,[a] though it chews the cud, does not
have a split hoof; it is unclean for you.
6The rabbit, though it chews the cud, does
not have a split hoof; it is unclean for you.
7And the pig, though it has a split hoof
completely divided, does not chew the
cud; it is unclean for you. 8You must not
eat their meat or touch their carcasses;
they are unclean for you.

9" 'Of all the creatures living in the water of the seas and the streams, you may
eat any that have fins and scales. 10But all
creatures in the seas or streams that do
not have fins and scales—whether among
all the swarming things or among all the
other living creatures in the water—you
are to detest. 11And since you are to detest
them, you must not eat their meat and
you must detest their carcasses. 12Any-
thing living in the water that does not
have fins and scales is to be detestable to
you.

13" 'These are the birds you are to detest
and not eat because they are detestable:
the eagle, the vulture, the black vulture,
14the red kite, any kind of black kite, 15any
kind of raven, 16the horned owl, the
screech owl, the gull, any kind of hawk,
17the little owl, the cormorant, the great
owl, 18the white owl, the desert owl, the
osprey, 19the stork, any kind of heron, the
hoopoe and the bat.[b]

20" 'All flying insects that walk on all
fours are to be detestable to you. 21There
are, however, some winged creatures that
walk on all fours that you may eat: those
that have jointed legs for hopping on the
ground. 22Of these you may eat any kind
of locust, katydid, cricket or grasshopper.
23But all other winged creatures that have
four legs you are to detest.

24" 'You will make yourselves unclean
by these; whoever touches their carcasses
will be unclean till evening. 25Whoever
picks up one of their carcasses must wash
his clothes, and he will be unclean till
evening.

26" 'Every animal that has a split hoof
not completely divided or that does not
chew the cud is unclean for you; whoever
touches ⌊the carcass of⌋ any of them will
be unclean. 27Of all the animals that walk
on all fours, those that walk on their paws
are unclean for you; whoever touches
their carcasses will be unclean till evening.
28Anyone who picks up their carcasses
must wash his clothes, and he will be unclean till evening. They are unclean for
you.

29" 'Of the animals that move about on
the ground, these are unclean for you: the
weasel, the rat, any kind of great lizard,
30the gecko, the monitor lizard, the wall
lizard, the skink and the chameleon. 31Of
all those that move along the ground,
these are unclean for you. Whoever
touches them when they are dead will be
unclean till evening. 32When one of them
dies and falls on something, that article,
whatever its use, will be unclean, whether
it is made of wood, cloth, hide or sackcloth. Put it in water; it will be unclean till
evening, and then it will be clean. 33If one
of them falls into a clay pot, everything in
it will be unclean, and you must break the
pot. 34Any food that could be eaten but
has water on it from such a pot is unclean,
and any liquid that could be drunk from
it is unclean. 35Anything that one of their
carcasses falls on becomes unclean; an
oven or cooking pot must be broken up.
They are unclean, and you are to regard
them as unclean. 36A spring, however, or
a cistern for collecting water remains
clean, but anyone who touches one of
these carcasses is unclean. 37If a carcass
falls on any seeds that are to be planted,
they remain clean. 38But if water has been
put on the seed and a carcass falls on it, it
is unclean for you.

39" 'If an animal that you are allowed to
eat dies, anyone who touches the carcass
will be unclean till evening. 40Anyone
who eats some of the carcass must wash
his clothes, and he will be unclean till
evening. Anyone who picks up the carcass
must wash his clothes, and he will be unclean till evening.

41" 'Every creature that moves about on
the ground is detestable; it is not to be eat-
en. 42You are not to eat any creature that
moves about on the ground, whether it
moves on its belly or walks on all fours or
on many feet; it is detestable. 43Do not defile yourselves by any of these creatures.
Do not make yourselves unclean by
means of them or be made unclean by
them. 44I am the LORD your God; consecrate yourselves and be holy, because I am
holy. Do not make yourselves unclean by

[a] *5* That is, the hyrax or rock badger [b] *19* The precise identification of some of the birds, insects and animals in this chapter is uncertain.

any creature that moves about on the
ground. 45 I am the LORD who brought you
up out of Egypt to be your God; therefore
be holy, because I am holy.
46 " 'These are the regulations concerning animals, birds, every living thing that
moves in the water and every creature that
moves about on the ground. 47 You must
distinguish between the unclean and the
clean, between living creatures that may
be eaten and those that may not be eat-
en.' "

Purification After Childbirth

12 The LORD said to Moses, 2 "Say to the
Israelites: 'A woman who becomes
pregnant and gives birth to a son will be
ceremonially unclean for seven days, just
as she is unclean during her monthly period. 3 On the eighth day the boy is to be
circumcised. 4 Then the woman must wait
thirty-three days to be purified from her
bleeding. She must not touch anything sacred or go to the sanctuary until the days
of her purification are over. 5 If she gives
birth to a daughter, for two weeks the
woman will be unclean, as during her period. Then she must wait sixty-six days to
be purified from her bleeding.
6 " 'When the days of her purification
for a son or daughter are over, she is to
bring to the priest at the entrance to the
Tent of Meeting a year-old lamb for a
burnt offering and a young pigeon or a
dove for a sin offering. 7 He shall offer
them before the LORD to make atonement
for her, and then she will be ceremonially clean from her flow of blood.
" 'These are the regulations for the
woman who gives birth to a boy or a girl.
8 If she cannot afford a lamb, she is to
bring two doves or two young pigeons,
one for a burnt offering and the other for
a sin offering. In this way the priest will
make atonement for her, and she will be
clean.' "

PRAYER: AFFIRMATION

O GOD our Father, those You foreknew, You also predestined to be conformed to the likeness of Your Son, that He might be the firstborn among many brothers and sisters. And those You predestined, You also called; those You called, You also justified; those You justified, You also glorified. (Romans 8:29–30)

***PAUSE** to reflect on these Biblical affirmations.*

NT Romans 13:1–14

Submission to the Authorities

13 Everyone must submit himself to the
governing authorities, for there is no
authority except that which God has established. The authorities that exist have
been established by God. 2 Consequently,
he who rebels against the authority is rebelling against what God has instituted,
and those who do so will bring judgment
on themselves. 3 For rulers hold no terror
for those who do right, but for those who
do wrong. Do you want to be free from
fear of the one in authority? Then do what
is right and he will commend you. 4 For he
is God's servant to do you good. But if you
do wrong, be afraid, for he does not bear
the sword for nothing. He is God's servant, an agent of wrath to bring punishment on the wrongdoer. 5 Therefore, it is
necessary to submit to the authorities, not
only because of possible punishment but
also because of conscience.
6 This is also why you pay taxes, for the
authorities are God's servants, who give
their full time to governing. 7 Give everyone what you owe him: If you owe taxes,
pay taxes; if revenue, then revenue; if respect, then respect; if honor, then honor.

Love, for the Day Is Near

8 Let no debt remain outstanding, except the continuing debt to love one another, for he who loves his fellowman has
fulfilled the law. 9 The commandments,
"Do not commit adultery," "Do not mur-

der," "Do not steal," "Do not covet,"[a] and
whatever other commandment there may
be, are summed up in this one rule: "Love
your neighbor as yourself."[b] 10 Love does
no harm to its neighbor. Therefore love is
the fulfillment of the law.
11 And do this, understanding the
present time. The hour has come for you
to wake up from your slumber, because
our salvation is nearer now than when we
first believed. 12 The night is nearly over;
the day is almost here. So let us put aside
the deeds of darkness and put on the armor of light. 13 Let us behave decently, as
in the daytime, not in orgies and drunkenness, not in sexual immorality and debauchery, not in dissension and jealousy.
14 Rather, clothe yourselves with the Lord
Jesus Christ, and do not think about how
to gratify the desires of the sinful nature.[c]

[a] 9 Exodus 20:13–15,17; Deut. 5:17–19,21
[b] 9 Lev. 19:18 [c] 14 Or *the flesh*

PRAYER: THE WORKS OF GOD

AT the right time, when we were helpless, Christ died for the ungodly. For rarely will anyone die for one who is righteous, though perhaps for a good person someone would even dare to die. But You, O God, demonstrate Your own love for us in that while we were still sinners, Christ died for us. (Romans 5:6–8)

***TAKE** a moment to consider the greatness of God's wonderful works.*

YEAR 1 DAY 98

OT Psalm 22

Psalm 22

For the director of music. To ⌞the tune of⌟ "The Doe of the Morning." A psalm of David.

1 My God, my God, why have you
forsaken me?
Why are you so far from saving me,
so far from the words of my
groaning?
2 O my God, I cry out by day, but you
do not answer,
by night, and am not silent.

3 Yet you are enthroned as the Holy
One;
you are the praise of Israel.[a]
4 In you our fathers put their trust;
they trusted and you delivered
them.
5 They cried to you and were saved;
in you they trusted and were not
disappointed.

6 But I am a worm and not a man,
scorned by men and despised by
the people.
7 All who see me mock me;
they hurl insults, shaking their
heads:
8 "He trusts in the LORD;
let the LORD rescue him.
Let him deliver him,
since he delights in him."

9 Yet you brought me out of the womb;
you made me trust in you
even at my mother's breast.
10 From birth I was cast upon you;
from my mother's womb you have
been my God.
11 Do not be far from me,
for trouble is near
and there is no one to help.

12 Many bulls surround me;
strong bulls of Bashan encircle me.
13 Roaring lions tearing their prey
open their mouths wide against me.
14 I am poured out like water,
and all my bones are out of joint.
My heart has turned to wax;
it has melted away within me.
15 My strength is dried up like a
potsherd,
and my tongue sticks to the roof of
my mouth;
you lay me[b] in the dust of death.
16 Dogs have surrounded me;

[a] 3 Or *Yet you are holy, / enthroned on the praises of Israel* [b] 15 Or */ I am laid*

a band of evil men has encircled me,
they have pierced[c] my hands and my feet.
17 I can count all my bones;
people stare and gloat over me.
18 They divide my garments among them
and cast lots for my clothing.

19 But you, O LORD, be not far off;
O my Strength, come quickly to help me.
20 Deliver my life from the sword,
my precious life from the power of the dogs.
21 Rescue me from the mouth of the lions;
save[d] me from the horns of the wild oxen.

22 I will declare your name to my brothers;
in the congregation I will praise you.
23 You who fear the LORD, praise him!
All you descendants of Jacob, honor him!
Revere him, all you descendants of Israel!
24 For he has not despised or disdained
the suffering of the afflicted one;
he has not hidden his face from him
but has listened to his cry for help.

25 From you comes the theme of my praise in the great assembly;
before those who fear you[e] will I fulfill my vows.
26 The poor will eat and be satisfied;
they who seek the LORD will praise him—
may your hearts live forever!
27 All the ends of the earth
will remember and turn to the LORD,
and all the families of the nations
will bow down before him,
28 for dominion belongs to the LORD
and he rules over the nations.

29 All the rich of the earth will feast and worship;
all who go down to the dust will kneel before him—
those who cannot keep themselves alive.
30 Posterity will serve him;
future generations will be told about the Lord.
31 They will proclaim his righteousness
to a people yet unborn—
for he has done it.

[c] 16 Some Hebrew manuscripts, Septuagint and Syriac; most Hebrew manuscripts *like the lion,*
[d] 21 Or *you have heard* [e] 25 Hebrew *him*

PRAYER: THANKSGIVING

O GOD, since I have been justified by Christ's blood, much more shall I be saved from Your wrath through Him. For if, when I was Your enemy, I was reconciled to You through the death of Your Son, much more, having been reconciled, shall I be saved through His life. And not only this, but I also rejoice in You through my Lord Jesus Christ, through whom I have now received reconciliation. (Romans 5:9–11)

PAUSE *to offer your own expressions of thanksgiving.*

NT Romans 14:1-23

The Weak and the Strong

14 Accept him whose faith is weak, without passing judgment on disputable matters. 2One man's faith allows him to eat everything, but another man, whose faith is weak, eats only vegetables. 3The man who eats everything must not look down on him who does not, and the man who does not eat everything must not condemn the man who does, for God has accepted him. 4Who are you to judge someone else's servant? To his own master he stands or falls. And he will stand, for the Lord is able to make him stand.

5One man considers one day more sacred than another; another man considers every day alike. Each one should be fully convinced in his own mind. 6He who re-

gards one day as special, does so to the
Lord. He who eats meat, eats to the Lord,
for he gives thanks to God; and he who
abstains, does so to the Lord and gives
thanks to God. [7]For none of us lives to
himself alone and none of us dies to himself alone. [8]If we live, we live to the Lord;
and if we die, we die to the Lord. So,
whether we live or die, we belong to the
Lord.

[9]For this very reason, Christ died and
returned to life so that he might be the
Lord of both the dead and the living.
[10]You, then, why do you judge your brother? Or why do you look down on your
brother? For we will all stand before God's
judgment seat. [11]It is written:

" 'As surely as I live,' says the Lord,
'every knee will bow before me;
every tongue will confess to God.' "[a]

[12]So then, each of us will give an account
of himself to God.

[13]Therefore let us stop passing judgment on one another. Instead, make up
your mind not to put any stumbling block
or obstacle in your brother's way. [14]As one
who is in the Lord Jesus, I am fully convinced that no food[b] is unclean in itself.
But if anyone regards something as unclean, then for him it is unclean. [15]If your
brother is distressed because of what you
eat, you are no longer acting in love. Do
not by your eating destroy your brother
for whom Christ died. [16]Do not allow
what you consider good to be spoken of
as evil. [17]For the kingdom of God is not a
matter of eating and drinking, but of righteousness, peace and joy in the Holy Spirit, [18]because anyone who serves Christ in
this way is pleasing to God and approved
by men.

[19]Let us therefore make every effort to
do what leads to peace and to mutual edification. [20]Do not destroy the work of
God for the sake of food. All food is clean,
but it is wrong for a man to eat anything
that causes someone else to stumble. [21]It
is better not to eat meat or drink wine or
to do anything else that will cause your
brother to fall.

[22]So whatever you believe about these
things keep between yourself and God.
Blessed is the man who does not condemn himself by what he approves. [23]But
the man who has doubts is condemned if
he eats, because his eating is not from
faith; and everything that does not come
from faith is sin.

[a] *11* Isaiah 45:23 [b] *14* Or *that nothing*

PRAYER: MY RELATIONSHIP TO GOD

YOU have plans for me, O Lord; You have declared that you have plans to prosper me and not to harm me, plans to give me a future and a hope. (Jeremiah 29:11)

***PAUSE** to thank God for the relationship that you enjoy with Him in Jesus Christ.*

YEAR 1 DAY 99

OT Leviticus 13:1-59

Regulations About Infectious Skin Diseases

13 The LORD said to Moses and Aaron,
[2]"When anyone has a swelling or a
rash or a bright spot on his skin that may
become an infectious skin disease,[a] he
must be brought to Aaron the priest or to
one of his sons[b] who is a priest. [3]The
priest is to examine the sore on his skin,
and if the hair in the sore has turned
white and the sore appears to be more
than skin deep,[c] it is an infectious skin
disease. When the priest examines him, he
shall pronounce him ceremonially unclean. [4]If the spot on his skin is white but
does not appear to be more than skin

[a] *2* Traditionally *leprosy*; the Hebrew word was used for various diseases affecting the skin—not necessarily leprosy; also elsewhere in this chapter. [b] *2* Or *descendants* [c] *3* Or *be lower than the rest of the skin*; also elsewhere in this chapter

deep and the hair in it has not turned white, the priest is to put the infected person in isolation for seven days. [5]On the seventh day the priest is to examine him, and if he sees that the sore is unchanged and has not spread in the skin, he is to keep him in isolation another seven days. [6]On the seventh day the priest is to examine him again, and if the sore has faded and has not spread in the skin, the priest shall pronounce him clean; it is only a rash. The man must wash his clothes, and he will be clean. [7]But if the rash does spread in his skin after he has shown himself to the priest to be pronounced clean, he must appear before the priest again. [8]The priest is to examine him, and if the rash has spread in the skin, he shall pronounce him unclean; it is an infectious disease.

[9]"When anyone has an infectious skin disease, he must be brought to the priest. [10]The priest is to examine him, and if there is a white swelling in the skin that has turned the hair white and if there is raw flesh in the swelling, [11]it is a chronic skin disease and the priest shall pronounce him unclean. He is not to put him in isolation, because he is already unclean.

[12]"If the disease breaks out all over his skin and, so far as the priest can see, it covers all the skin of the infected person from head to foot, [13]the priest is to examine him, and if the disease has covered his whole body, he shall pronounce that person clean. Since it has all turned white, he is clean. [14]But whenever raw flesh appears on him, he will be unclean. [15]When the priest sees the raw flesh, he shall pronounce him unclean. The raw flesh is unclean; he has an infectious disease. [16]Should the raw flesh change and turn white, he must go to the priest. [17]The priest is to examine him, and if the sores have turned white, the priest shall pronounce the infected person clean; then he will be clean.

[18]"When someone has a boil on his skin and it heals, [19]and in the place where the boil was, a white swelling or reddish-white spot appears, he must present himself to the priest. [20]The priest is to examine it, and if it appears to be more than skin deep and the hair in it has turned white, the priest shall pronounce him unclean. It is an infectious skin disease that has broken out where the boil was. [21]But if, when the priest examines it, there is no white hair in it and it is not more than skin deep and has faded, then the priest is to put him in isolation for seven days. [22]If it is spreading in the skin, the priest shall pronounce him unclean; it is infectious. [23]But if the spot is unchanged and has not spread, it is only a scar from the boil, and the priest shall pronounce him clean.

[24]"When someone has a burn on his skin and a reddish-white or white spot appears in the raw flesh of the burn, [25]the priest is to examine the spot, and if the hair in it has turned white, and it appears to be more than skin deep, it is an infectious disease that has broken out in the burn. The priest shall pronounce him unclean; it is an infectious skin disease. [26]But if the priest examines it and there is no white hair in the spot and if it is not more than skin deep and has faded, then the priest is to put him in isolation for seven days. [27]On the seventh day the priest is to examine him, and if it is spreading in the skin, the priest shall pronounce him unclean; it is an infectious skin disease. [28]If, however, the spot is unchanged and has not spread in the skin but has faded, it is a swelling from the burn, and the priest shall pronounce him clean; it is only a scar from the burn.

[29]"If a man or woman has a sore on the head or on the chin, [30]the priest is to examine the sore, and if it appears to be more than skin deep and the hair in it is yellow and thin, the priest shall pronounce that person unclean; it is an itch, an infectious disease of the head or chin. [31]But if, when the priest examines this kind of sore, it does not seem to be more than skin deep and there is no black hair in it, then the priest is to put the infected person in isolation for seven days. [32]On the seventh day the priest is to examine the sore, and if the itch has not spread and there is no yellow hair in it and it does not appear to be more than skin deep, [33]he must be shaved except for the diseased area, and the priest is to keep him in isolation another seven days. [34]On the seventh day the priest is to examine the itch, and if it has not spread in the skin and appears to be no more than skin deep, the priest shall pronounce him clean. He must wash his clothes, and he will be clean. [35]But if the itch does spread in the

skin after he is pronounced clean, [36]the priest is to examine him, and if the itch has spread in the skin, the priest does not need to look for yellow hair; the person is unclean. [37]If, however, in his judgment it is unchanged and black hair has grown in it, the itch is healed. He is clean, and the priest shall pronounce him clean.

[38]"When a man or woman has white spots on the skin, [39]the priest is to examine them, and if the spots are dull white, it is a harmless rash that has broken out on the skin; that person is clean.

[40]"When a man has lost his hair and is bald, he is clean. [41]If he has lost his hair from the front of his scalp and has a bald forehead, he is clean. [42]But if he has a reddish-white sore on his bald head or forehead, it is an infectious disease breaking out on his head or forehead. [43]The priest is to examine him, and if the swollen sore on his head or forehead is reddish-white like an infectious skin disease, [44]the man is diseased and is unclean. The priest shall pronounce him unclean because of the sore on his head.

[45]"The person with such an infectious disease must wear torn clothes, let his hair be unkempt,[d] cover the lower part of his face and cry out, 'Unclean! Unclean!' [46]As long as he has the infection he remains unclean. He must live alone; he must live outside the camp.

Regulations About Mildew

[47]"If any clothing is contaminated with mildew—any woolen or linen clothing, [48]any woven or knitted material of linen or wool, any leather or anything made of leather— [49]and if the contamination in the clothing, or leather, or woven or knitted material, or any leather article, is greenish or reddish, it is a spreading mildew and must be shown to the priest. [50]The priest is to examine the mildew and isolate the affected article for seven days. [51]On the seventh day he is to examine it, and if the mildew has spread in the clothing, or the woven or knitted material, or the leather, whatever its use, it is a destructive mildew; the article is unclean. [52]He must burn up the clothing, or the woven or knitted material of wool or linen, or any leather article that has the contamination in it, because the mildew is destructive; the article must be burned up.

[53]"But if, when the priest examines it, the mildew has not spread in the clothing, or the woven or knitted material, or the leather article, [54]he shall order that the contaminated article be washed. Then he is to isolate it for another seven days. [55]After the affected article has been washed, the priest is to examine it, and if the mildew has not changed its appearance, even though it has not spread, it is unclean. Burn it with fire, whether the mildew has affected one side or the other. [56]If, when the priest examines it, the mildew has faded after the article has been washed, he is to tear the contaminated part out of the clothing, or the leather, or the woven or knitted material. [57]But if it reappears in the clothing, or in the woven or knitted material, or in the leather article, it is spreading, and whatever has the mildew must be burned with fire. [58]The clothing, or the woven or knitted material, or any leather article that has been washed and is rid of the mildew, must be washed again, and it will be clean."

[59]These are the regulations concerning contamination by mildew in woolen or linen clothing, woven or knitted material, or any leather article, for pronouncing them clean or unclean.

[d] 45 Or *clothes, uncover his head*

PRAYER: ADORATION

YOU formed my inward parts, O Lord; You wove me together in my mother's womb. I thank You because I am fearfully and wonderfully made; Your works are wonderful, and my soul knows it full well. My frame was not hidden from You when I was made in secret and skillfully wrought in the depths of the earth. Your eyes saw my embryo, and all the days ordained for me were written in Your book before one of them came to be. (Psalm 139:13–16)

PAUSE *to express your thoughts of praise and worship.*

NT Romans 15:1-13

15 We who are strong ought to bear with the failings of the weak and not to please ourselves. [2]Each of us should please his neighbor for his good, to build him up. [3]For even Christ did not please himself but, as it is written: "The insults of those who insult you have fallen on me."[a] [4]For everything that was written in the past was written to teach us, so that through endurance and the encouragement of the Scriptures we might have hope.

[5]May the God who gives endurance and encouragement give you a spirit of unity among yourselves as you follow Christ Jesus, [6]so that with one heart and mouth you may glorify the God and Father of our Lord Jesus Christ.

[7]Accept one another, then, just as Christ accepted you, in order to bring praise to God. [8]For I tell you that Christ has become a servant of the Jews[b] on behalf of God's truth, to confirm the promises made to the patriarchs [9]so that the Gentiles may glorify God for his mercy, as it is written:

"Therefore I will praise you among the Gentiles;
I will sing hymns to your name."[c]

[10]Again, it says,

"Rejoice, O Gentiles, with his people."[d]

[11]And again,

"Praise the Lord, all you Gentiles,
and sing praises to him, all you peoples."[e]

[12]And again, Isaiah says,

"The Root of Jesse will spring up,
one who will arise to rule over the nations;
the Gentiles will hope in him."[f]

[13]May the God of hope fill you with all joy and peace as you trust in him, so that you may overflow with hope by the power of the Holy Spirit.

[a] *3* Psalm 69:9 [b] *8* Greek *circumcision*
[c] *9* 2 Samuel 22:50; Psalm 18:49 [d] *10* Deut. 32:43
[e] *11* Psalm 117:1 [f] *12* Isaiah 11:10

PRAYER: THE CHARACTER I WANT TO CULTIVATE

I WILL be strong and courageous, being careful to obey Your word, O Lord; I will not turn from it to the right or to the left, that I may act wisely wherever I go. (Joshua 1:7) . . . I will take courage and not be afraid, for You, Lord Jesus, are with me. (Mark 6:50)

***TAKE** a moment to ask the Lord for the grace to grow in godly character.*

YEAR 1 DAY 100

OT Leviticus 14:1-57

Cleansing From Infectious Skin Diseases

14 The LORD said to Moses, [2]"These are the regulations for the diseased person at the time of his ceremonial cleansing, when he is brought to the priest: [3]The priest is to go outside the camp and examine him. If the person has been healed of his infectious skin disease,[a] [4]the priest shall order that two live clean birds and some cedar wood, scarlet yarn and hyssop be brought for the one to be cleansed. [5]Then the priest shall order that one of the birds be killed over fresh water in a clay pot. [6]He is then to take the live bird and dip it, together with the cedar wood, the scarlet yarn and the hyssop, into the blood of the bird that was killed over the fresh water. [7]Seven times he shall sprinkle the one to be cleansed of the infectious disease and pronounce him clean. Then

[a] *3* Traditionally *leprosy*; the Hebrew word was used for various diseases affecting the skin—not necessarily leprosy; also elsewhere in this chapter.

he is to release the live bird in the open
fields.
8 "The person to be cleansed must wash
his clothes, shave off all his hair and bathe
with water; then he will be ceremonially
clean. After this he may come into the
camp, but he must stay outside his tent
for seven days. 9 On the seventh day he
must shave off all his hair; he must shave
his head, his beard, his eyebrows and the
rest of his hair. He must wash his clothes
and bathe himself with water, and he will
be clean.
10 "On the eighth day he must bring two
male lambs and one ewe lamb a year old,
each without defect, along with three-
tenths of an ephah[b] of fine flour mixed
with oil for a grain offering, and one log[c]
of oil. 11 The priest who pronounces him
clean shall present both the one to be
cleansed and his offerings before the LORD
at the entrance to the Tent of Meeting.
12 "Then the priest is to take one of the
male lambs and offer it as a guilt offering,
along with the log of oil; he shall wave
them before the LORD as a wave offering.
13 He is to slaughter the lamb in the holy
place where the sin offering and the burnt
offering are slaughtered. Like the sin offering, the guilt offering belongs to the
priest; it is most holy. 14 The priest is to
take some of the blood of the guilt offering and put it on the lobe of the right ear
of the one to be cleansed, on the thumb
of his right hand and on the big toe of his
right foot. 15 The priest shall then take
some of the log of oil, pour it in the palm
of his own left hand, 16 dip his right forefinger into the oil in his palm, and with
his finger sprinkle some of it before the
LORD seven times. 17 The priest is to put
some of the oil remaining in his palm on
the lobe of the right ear of the one to be
cleansed, on the thumb of his right hand
and on the big toe of his right foot, on top
of the blood of the guilt offering. 18 The
rest of the oil in his palm the priest shall
put on the head of the one to be cleansed
and make atonement for him before the
LORD.
19 "Then the priest is to sacrifice the sin
offering and make atonement for the one
to be cleansed from his uncleanness. After that, the priest shall slaughter the
burnt offering 20 and offer it on the altar,
together with the grain offering, and make
atonement for him, and he will be clean.

21 "If, however, he is poor and cannot afford these, he must take one male lamb as
a guilt offering to be waved to make
atonement for him, together with a tenth
of an ephah[d] of fine flour mixed with oil
for a grain offering, a log of oil, 22 and two
doves or two young pigeons, which he can
afford, one for a sin offering and the other for a burnt offering.
23 "On the eighth day he must bring
them for his cleansing to the priest at the
entrance to the Tent of Meeting, before
the LORD. 24 The priest is to take the lamb
for the guilt offering, together with the log
of oil, and wave them before the LORD as
a wave offering. 25 He shall slaughter the
lamb for the guilt offering and take some
of its blood and put it on the lobe of the
right ear of the one to be cleansed, on the
thumb of his right hand and on the big
toe of his right foot. 26 The priest is to pour
some of the oil into the palm of his own
left hand, 27 and with his right forefinger
sprinkle some of the oil from his palm
seven times before the LORD. 28 Some of
the oil in his palm he is to put on the
same places he put the blood of the guilt
offering—on the lobe of the right ear of
the one to be cleansed, on the thumb of
his right hand and on the big toe of his
right foot. 29 The rest of the oil in his palm
the priest shall put on the head of the one
to be cleansed, to make atonement for
him before the LORD. 30 Then he shall sacrifice the doves or the young pigeons,
which the person can afford, 31 one[e] as a
sin offering and the other as a burnt offering, together with the grain offering. In
this way the priest will make atonement
before the LORD on behalf of the one to
be cleansed."
32 These are the regulations for anyone
who has an infectious skin disease and
who cannot afford the regular offerings
for his cleansing.

Cleansing From Mildew

33 The LORD said to Moses and Aaron,
34 "When you enter the land of Canaan,
which I am giving you as your possession,
and I put a spreading mildew in a house

[b] *10* That is, probably about 6 quarts (about 6.5 liters) [c] *10* That is, probably about 2/3 pint (about 0.3 liter); also in verses 12, 15, 21 and 24
[d] *21* That is, probably about 2 quarts (about 2 liters)
[e] *31* Septuagint and Syriac; Hebrew *31 such as the person can afford, one*

in that land, 35the owner of the house must go and tell the priest, 'I have seen something that looks like mildew in my house.' 36The priest is to order the house to be emptied before he goes in to examine the mildew, so that nothing in the house will be pronounced unclean. After this the priest is to go in and inspect the house. 37He is to examine the mildew on the walls, and if it has greenish or reddish depressions that appear to be deeper than the surface of the wall, 38the priest shall go out the doorway of the house and close it up for seven days. 39On the seventh day the priest shall return to inspect the house. If the mildew has spread on the walls, 40he is to order that the contaminated stones be torn out and thrown into an unclean place outside the town. 41He must have all the inside walls of the house scraped and the material that is scraped off dumped into an unclean place outside the town. 42Then they are to take other stones to replace these and take new clay and plaster the house.

43"If the mildew reappears in the house after the stones have been torn out and the house scraped and plastered, 44the priest is to go and examine it and, if the mildew has spread in the house, it is a destructive mildew; the house is unclean. 45It must be torn down—its stones, timbers and all the plaster—and taken out of the town to an unclean place.

46"Anyone who goes into the house while it is closed up will be unclean till evening. 47Anyone who sleeps or eats in the house must wash his clothes.

48"But if the priest comes to examine it and the mildew has not spread after the house has been plastered, he shall pronounce the house clean, because the mildew is gone. 49To purify the house he is to take two birds and some cedar wood, scarlet yarn and hyssop. 50He shall kill one of the birds over fresh water in a clay pot. 51Then he is to take the cedar wood, the hyssop, the scarlet yarn and the live bird, dip them into the blood of the dead bird and the fresh water, and sprinkle the house seven times. 52He shall purify the house with the bird's blood, the fresh water, the live bird, the cedar wood, the hyssop and the scarlet yarn. 53Then he is to release the live bird in the open fields outside the town. In this way he will make atonement for the house, and it will be clean."

54These are the regulations for any infectious skin disease, for an itch, 55for mildew in clothing or in a house, 56and for a swelling, a rash or a bright spot, 57to determine when something is clean or unclean.

These are the regulations for infectious skin diseases and mildew.

PRAYER: CONFESSION

I RETURN to You, Lord my God, for I have stumbled because of my iniquity. I take words with me and return to You, saying, "Take away all iniquity and receive me graciously, that I may offer the fruit of my lips." (Hosea 14:1–2)

***ASK** the Spirit to search your heart and reveal any areas of unconfessed sin. Acknowledge these to the Lord and thank Him for His forgiveness.*

NT Romans 15:14–33

Paul the Minister to the Gentiles

14I myself am convinced, my brothers, that you yourselves are full of goodness, complete in knowledge and competent to instruct one another. 15I have written you quite boldly on some points, as if to remind you of them again, because of the grace God gave me 16to be a minister of Christ Jesus to the Gentiles with the priestly duty of proclaiming the gospel of God, so that the Gentiles might become an offering acceptable to God, sanctified by the Holy Spirit.

17Therefore I glory in Christ Jesus in my service to God. 18I will not venture to speak of anything except what Christ has accomplished through me in leading the Gentiles to obey God by what I have said and done— 19by the power of signs and miracles, through the power of the Spirit.

So from Jerusalem all the way around to
Illyricum, I have fully proclaimed the
gospel of Christ. 20 It has always been my
ambition to preach the gospel where
Christ was not known, so that I would not
be building on someone else's foundation. 21 Rather, as it is written:

"Those who were not told about him
will see,
and those who have not heard will
understand."[a]

22 This is why I have often been hindered
from coming to you.

Paul's Plan to Visit Rome

23 But now that there is no more place
for me to work in these regions, and since
I have been longing for many years to see
you, 24 I plan to do so when I go to Spain.
I hope to visit you while passing through
and to have you assist me on my journey
there, after I have enjoyed your company
for a while. 25 Now, however, I am on my
way to Jerusalem in the service of the
saints there. 26 For Macedonia and Achaia
were pleased to make a contribution for
the poor among the saints in Jerusalem.
27 They were pleased to do it, and indeed
they owe it to them. For if the Gentiles
have shared in the Jews' spiritual blessings, they owe it to the Jews to share with
them their material blessings. 28 So after I
have completed this task and have made
sure that they have received this fruit, I
will go to Spain and visit you on the way.
29 I know that when I come to you, I will
come in the full measure of the blessing
of Christ.

30 I urge you, brothers, by our Lord Jesus
Christ and by the love of the Spirit, to join
me in my struggle by praying to God for
me. 31 Pray that I may be rescued from the
unbelievers in Judea and that my service
in Jerusalem may be acceptable to the
saints there, 32 so that by God's will I may
come to you with joy and together with
you be refreshed. 33 The God of peace be
with you all. Amen.

[a] *21* Isaiah 52:15

PRAYER: MY RELATIONSHIP TO OTHERS

THERE are different kinds of gifts, but the same Spirit. And there are different kinds of service, but the same Lord. And there are different kinds of working, but You are the same God who works all of them in all people. But to each one the manifestation of Your Spirit is given for the common good. (1 Corinthians 12:4–7)

***PAUSE** to review your relationships with others and to commit them to the Lord.*

YEAR 1
DAY 101

OT Leviticus 15:1–33

Discharges Causing Uncleanness

15 The LORD said to Moses and Aaron,
2 "Speak to the Israelites and say to
them: 'When any man has a bodily discharge, the discharge is unclean. 3 Whether
it continues flowing from his body or is
blocked, it will make him unclean. This is
how his discharge will bring about uncleanness:

4 " 'Any bed the man with a discharge
lies on will be unclean, and anything he
sits on will be unclean. 5 Anyone who
touches his bed must wash his clothes
and bathe with water, and he will be unclean till evening. 6 Whoever sits on anything that the man with a discharge sat on
must wash his clothes and bathe with water, and he will be unclean till evening.

7 " 'Whoever touches the man who has
a discharge must wash his clothes and
bathe with water, and he will be unclean
till evening.

8 " 'If the man with the discharge spits
on someone who is clean, that person
must wash his clothes and bathe with water, and he will be unclean till evening.

9 " 'Everything the man sits on when
riding will be unclean, 10 and whoever
touches any of the things that were under
him will be unclean till evening; whoever
picks up those things must wash his
clothes and bathe with water, and he will
be unclean till evening.
11 " 'Anyone the man with a discharge
touches without rinsing his hands with
water must wash his clothes and bathe
with water, and he will be unclean till
evening.
12 " 'A clay pot that the man touches
must be broken, and any wooden article
is to be rinsed with water.
13 " 'When a man is cleansed from his
discharge, he is to count off seven days for
his ceremonial cleansing; he must wash
his clothes and bathe himself with fresh
water, and he will be clean. 14 On the
eighth day he must take two doves or two
young pigeons and come before the LORD
to the entrance to the Tent of Meeting and
give them to the priest. 15 The priest is to
sacrifice them, the one for a sin offering
and the other for a burnt offering. In this
way he will make atonement before the
LORD for the man because of his discharge.
16 " 'When a man has an emission of semen, he must bathe his whole body with
water, and he will be unclean till evening.
17 Any clothing or leather that has semen
on it must be washed with water, and it
will be unclean till evening. 18 When a
man lies with a woman and there is an
emission of semen, both must bathe with
water, and they will be unclean till
evening.
19 " 'When a woman has her regular flow
of blood, the impurity of her monthly period will last seven days, and anyone who
touches her will be unclean till evening.
20 " 'Anything she lies on during her period will be unclean, and anything she sits
on will be unclean. 21 Whoever touches her
bed must wash his clothes and bathe with
water, and he will be unclean till evening.
22 Whoever touches anything she sits on
must wash his clothes and bathe with water, and he will be unclean till evening.
23 Whether it is the bed or anything she
was sitting on, when anyone touches it, he
will be unclean till evening.
24 " 'If a man lies with her and her
monthly flow touches him, he will be unclean for seven days; any bed he lies on
will be unclean.
25 " 'When a woman has a discharge of
blood for many days at a time other than
her monthly period or has a discharge
that continues beyond her period, she will
be unclean as long as she has the discharge, just as in the days of her period.
26 Any bed she lies on while her discharge
continues will be unclean, as is her bed
during her monthly period, and anything
she sits on will be unclean, as during her
period. 27 Whoever touches them will be
unclean; he must wash his clothes and
bathe with water, and he will be unclean
till evening.
28 " 'When she is cleansed from her discharge, she must count off seven days, and
after that she will be ceremonially clean.
29 On the eighth day she must take two
doves or two young pigeons and bring
them to the priest at the entrance to the
Tent of Meeting. 30 The priest is to sacrifice
one for a sin offering and the other for a
burnt offering. In this way he will make
atonement for her before the LORD for the
uncleanness of her discharge.
31 " 'You must keep the Israelites separate from things that make them unclean,
so they will not die in their uncleanness
for defiling my dwelling place,[a] which is
among them.' "
32 These are the regulations for a man
with a discharge, for anyone made unclean by an emission of semen, 33 for a
woman in her monthly period, for a man
or a woman with a discharge, and for a
man who lies with a woman who is ceremonially unclean.

[a] 31 Or *my tabernacle*

PRAYER: RENEWAL

GOD, I pray that You, according to the riches of Your glory, would strengthen me with power through Your Spirit in my inner being, so that Christ may dwell in my heart through faith. And may I, being rooted and grounded in love, be able to comprehend with all the saints

what is the width and length and height and depth of the love of Christ, and to know this love that surpasses knowledge, that I may be filled to the measure of all Your fullness. (Ephesians 3:16–19) . . . May I be strong in the grace that is in You, Christ Jesus. (2 Timothy 2:1)

PAUSE *to add your own prayers for personal renewal.*

NT Romans 16:1–27

Personal Greetings

16 I commend to you our sister Phoebe,
a servant[a] of the church in Cenchrea.
2 I ask you to receive her in the Lord in a
way worthy of the saints and to give her
any help she may need from you, for she
has been a great help to many people, including me.

3 Greet Priscilla[b] and Aquila, my fellow
workers in Christ Jesus. 4 They risked
their lives for me. Not only I but all
the churches of the Gentiles are grateful to them.
5 Greet also the church that meets at their
house.
Greet my dear friend Epenetus, who
was the first convert to Christ in the
province of Asia.
6 Greet Mary, who worked very hard for
you.
7 Greet Andronicus and Junias, my relatives who have been in prison with
me. They are outstanding among the
apostles, and they were in Christ before I was.
8 Greet Ampliatus, whom I love in the
Lord.
9 Greet Urbanus, our fellow worker in
Christ, and my dear friend Stachys.
10 Greet Apelles, tested and approved in
Christ.
Greet those who belong to the household of Aristobulus.
11 Greet Herodion, my relative.
Greet those in the household of Narcissus who are in the Lord.
12 Greet Tryphena and Tryphosa, those
women who work hard in the Lord.
Greet my dear friend Persis, another
woman who has worked very hard in
the Lord.
13 Greet Rufus, chosen in the Lord, and
his mother, who has been a mother
to me, too.
14 Greet Asyncritus, Phlegon, Hermes, Patrobas, Hermas and the brothers with
them.
15 Greet Philologus, Julia, Nereus and his
sister, and Olympas and all the saints
with them.
16 Greet one another with a holy kiss.
All the churches of Christ send greetings.

17 I urge you, brothers, to watch out for
those who cause divisions and put obstacles in your way that are contrary to the
teaching you have learned. Keep away
from them. 18 For such people are not serving our Lord Christ, but their own appetites. By smooth talk and flattery they
deceive the minds of naive people.
19 Everyone has heard about your obedience, so I am full of joy over you; but I
want you to be wise about what is good,
and innocent about what is evil.
20 The God of peace will soon crush Satan under your feet.
The grace of our Lord Jesus be with you.
21 Timothy, my fellow worker, sends his
greetings to you, as do Lucius, Jason and
Sosipater, my relatives.
22 I, Tertius, who wrote down this letter,
greet you in the Lord.
23 Gaius, whose hospitality I and the
whole church here enjoy, sends you his
greetings.
Erastus, who is the city's director of
public works, and our brother Quartus
send you their greetings.[c]
25 Now to him who is able to establish
you by my gospel and the proclamation
of Jesus Christ, according to the revelation
of the mystery hidden for long ages past,
26 but now revealed and made known
through the prophetic writings by the
command of the eternal God, so that all
nations might believe and obey him—
27 to the only wise God be glory forever
through Jesus Christ! Amen.

[a] *1* Or *deaconess* [b] *3* Greek *Prisca,* a variant of *Priscilla* [c] *23* Some manuscripts *their greetings.* *24May the grace of our Lord Jesus Christ be with all of you. Amen.*

PRAYER: THE ATTRIBUTES OF GOD

AS for You, O God, Your way is perfect; Your word, O Lord, is proven. You are a shield for all who take refuge in You. For who are You, O God, besides the Lord? And who is the Rock except You, who are our God? (2 Samuel 22:31–32) . . . Lord, You long to be gracious and rise to show compassion. For You, O Lord, are a God of justice; blessed are all those who wait for You! (Isaiah 30:18)

***PAUSE** to reflect on these affirmations about the person, powers and perfection of God.*

YEAR 1 DAY 102

OT Leviticus 16:1–34

The Day of Atonement

16 The LORD spoke to Moses after the
death of the two sons of Aaron who
died when they approached the LORD. 2The
LORD said to Moses: "Tell your brother Aaron not to come whenever he chooses into
the Most Holy Place behind the curtain in
front of the atonement cover on the ark, or
else he will die, because I appear in the
cloud over the atonement cover.
3"This is how Aaron is to enter the sanctuary area: with a young bull for a sin offering and a ram for a burnt offering. 4He
is to put on the sacred linen tunic, with
linen undergarments next to his body; he
is to tie the linen sash around him and
put on the linen turban. These are sacred
garments; so he must bathe himself with
water before he puts them on. 5From the
Israelite community he is to take two
male goats for a sin offering and a ram for
a burnt offering.
6"Aaron is to offer the bull for his own
sin offering to make atonement for himself and his household. 7Then he is to take
the two goats and present them before the
LORD at the entrance to the Tent of Meeting. 8He is to cast lots for the two goats—
one lot for the LORD and the other for the
scapegoat.[a] 9Aaron shall bring the goat
whose lot falls to the LORD and sacrifice it
for a sin offering. 10But the goat chosen by
lot as the scapegoat shall be presented
alive before the LORD to be used for making atonement by sending it into the
desert as a scapegoat.
11"Aaron shall bring the bull for his own
sin offering to make atonement for himself and his household, and he is to
slaughter the bull for his own sin offering.
12He is to take a censer full of burning
coals from the altar before the LORD and
two handfuls of finely ground fragrant incense and take them behind the curtain.
13He is to put the incense on the fire before the LORD, and the smoke of the incense will conceal the atonement cover
above the Testimony, so that he will not
die. 14He is to take some of the bull's
blood and with his finger sprinkle it on
the front of the atonement cover; then he
shall sprinkle some of it with his finger
seven times before the atonement cover.
15"He shall then slaughter the goat for
the sin offering for the people and take its
blood behind the curtain and do with it as
he did with the bull's blood: He shall
sprinkle it on the atonement cover and in
front of it. 16In this way he will make atonement for the Most Holy Place because of
the uncleanness and rebellion of the Israelites, whatever their sins have been. He is
to do the same for the Tent of Meeting,
which is among them in the midst of their
uncleanness. 17No one is to be in the Tent
of Meeting from the time Aaron goes in to
make atonement in the Most Holy Place
until he comes out, having made atonement for himself, his household and the
whole community of Israel.
18"Then he shall come out to the altar
that is before the LORD and make atonement for it. He shall take some of the
bull's blood and some of the goat's blood
and put it on all the horns of the altar.
19He shall sprinkle some of the blood on

[a] 8 That is, the goat of removal; Hebrew *azazel*; also in verses 10 and 26

it with his finger seven times to cleanse it and to consecrate it from the uncleanness of the Israelites.

20 "When Aaron has finished making atonement for the Most Holy Place, the Tent of Meeting and the altar, he shall bring forward the live goat.
21 He is to lay both hands on the head of the live goat and confess over it all the wickedness and rebellion of the Israelites—all their sins—and put them on the goat's head. He shall send the goat away into the desert in the care of a man appointed for the task.
22 The goat will carry on itself all their sins to a solitary place; and the man shall release it in the desert.

23 "Then Aaron is to go into the Tent of Meeting and take off the linen garments he put on before he entered the Most Holy Place, and he is to leave them there.
24 He shall bathe himself with water in a holy place and put on his regular garments. Then he shall come out and sacrifice the burnt offering for himself and the burnt offering for the people, to make atonement for himself and for the people.
25 He shall also burn the fat of the sin offering on the altar.

26 "The man who releases the goat as a scapegoat must wash his clothes and bathe himself with water; afterward he may come into the camp.
27 The bull and the goat for the sin offerings, whose blood was brought into the Most Holy Place to make atonement, must be taken outside the camp; their hides, flesh and offal are to be burned up.
28 The man who burns them must wash his clothes and bathe himself with water; afterward he may come into the camp.

29 "This is to be a lasting ordinance for you: On the tenth day of the seventh month you must deny yourselves[b] and not do any work—whether native-born or an alien living among you—
30 because on this day atonement will be made for you, to cleanse you. Then, before the LORD, you will be clean from all your sins.
31 It is a sabbath of rest, and you must deny yourselves; it is a lasting ordinance.
32 The priest who is anointed and ordained to succeed his father as high priest is to make atonement. He is to put on the sacred linen garments
33 and make atonement for the Most Holy Place, for the Tent of Meeting and the altar, and for the priests and all the people of the community.

34 "This is to be a lasting ordinance for you: Atonement is to be made once a year for all the sins of the Israelites."

And it was done, as the LORD commanded Moses.

[b] 29 Or *must fast;* also in verse 31

PRAYER: PETITION

I WAS once darkness, but now I am light in You, Lord. May I walk as a child of light (for the fruit of the light consists in all goodness and righteousness and truth), learning what is pleasing to You. (Ephesians 5:8–10)

***PAUSE** here to petition God for growth in your desire to know and please Jesus Christ. Pray for a greater love and commitment to Him, for the grace to practice His presence and for the grace to glorify Him in your life. Offer prayers regarding your activities for this day and any special concerns you may have.*

NT Mark 1:1–39

John the Baptist Prepares the Way

1 The beginning of the gospel about Jesus Christ, the Son of God.[a]

2 It is written in Isaiah the prophet:

"I will send my messenger ahead of you,
who will prepare your way"[b]—
3 "a voice of one calling in the desert,
'Prepare the way for the Lord,
make straight paths for him.' "[c]

4 And so John came, baptizing in the

[a] 1 Some manuscripts do not have *the Son of God.*
[b] 2 Mal. 3:1 [c] 3 Isaiah 40:3

desert region and preaching a baptism of repentance for the forgiveness of sins. 5The whole Judean countryside and all the people of Jerusalem went out to him. Confessing their sins, they were baptized by him in the Jordan River. 6John wore clothing made of camel's hair, with a leather belt around his waist, and he ate locusts and wild honey. 7And this was his message: "After me will come one more powerful than I, the thongs of whose sandals I am not worthy to stoop down and untie. 8I baptize you with[d] water, but he will baptize you with the Holy Spirit."

The Baptism and Temptation of Jesus

9At that time Jesus came from Nazareth in Galilee and was baptized by John in the Jordan. 10As Jesus was coming up out of the water, he saw heaven being torn open and the Spirit descending on him like a dove. 11And a voice came from heaven: "You are my Son, whom I love; with you I am well pleased."

12At once the Spirit sent him out into the desert, 13and he was in the desert forty days, being tempted by Satan. He was with the wild animals, and angels attended him.

The Calling of the First Disciples

14After John was put in prison, Jesus went into Galilee, proclaiming the good news of God. 15"The time has come," he said. "The kingdom of God is near. Repent and believe the good news!"

16As Jesus walked beside the Sea of Galilee, he saw Simon and his brother Andrew casting a net into the lake, for they were fishermen. 17"Come, follow me," Jesus said, "and I will make you fishers of men." 18At once they left their nets and followed him.

19When he had gone a little farther, he saw James son of Zebedee and his brother John in a boat, preparing their nets. 20Without delay he called them, and they left their father Zebedee in the boat with the hired men and followed him.

Jesus Drives Out an Evil Spirit

21They went to Capernaum, and when the Sabbath came, Jesus went into the synagogue and began to teach. 22The people were amazed at his teaching, because he taught them as one who had authority, not as the teachers of the law. 23Just then a man in their synagogue who was possessed by an evil[e] spirit cried out, 24"What do you want with us, Jesus of Nazareth? Have you come to destroy us? I know who you are—the Holy One of God!"

25"Be quiet!" said Jesus sternly. "Come out of him!" 26The evil spirit shook the man violently and came out of him with a shriek.

27The people were all so amazed that they asked each other, "What is this? A new teaching—and with authority! He even gives orders to evil spirits and they obey him." 28News about him spread quickly over the whole region of Galilee.

Jesus Heals Many

29As soon as they left the synagogue, they went with James and John to the home of Simon and Andrew. 30Simon's mother-in-law was in bed with a fever, and they told Jesus about her. 31So he went to her, took her hand and helped her up. The fever left her and she began to wait on them.

32That evening after sunset the people brought to Jesus all the sick and demon-possessed. 33The whole town gathered at the door, 34and Jesus healed many who had various diseases. He also drove out many demons, but he would not let the demons speak because they knew who he was.

Jesus Prays in a Solitary Place

35Very early in the morning, while it was still dark, Jesus got up, left the house and went off to a solitary place, where he prayed. 36Simon and his companions went to look for him, 37and when they found him, they exclaimed: "Everyone is looking for you!"

38Jesus replied, "Let us go somewhere else—to the nearby villages—so I can preach there also. That is why I have come." 39So he traveled throughout Galilee, preaching in their synagogues and driving out demons.

[d] *8* Or *in* [e] *23* Greek *unclean;* also in verses 26 and 27

PRAYER: THE WORKS OF GOD

YOU are the great God, the great King above all gods. In Your hand are the depths of the earth, and the summits of the mountains are Yours also. The sea is Yours, for You made it, and Your hands formed the dry land. You are our God and we are the people of Your pasture and the sheep under Your care. (Psalm 95:3–5, 7)

***TAKE** a moment to consider the greatness of God's wonderful works.*

YEAR 1 DAY 103

OT Leviticus 17:1–18:30

Eating Blood Forbidden

17 The LORD said to Moses, 2"Speak to Aaron and his sons and to all the Israelites
and say to them: 'This is what the LORD has
commanded: 3Any Israelite who sacrifices
an ox,[a] a lamb or a goat in the camp or outside of it 4instead of bringing it to the entrance to the Tent of Meeting to present it
as an offering to the LORD in front of the
tabernacle of the LORD—that man shall be
considered guilty of bloodshed; he has
shed blood and must be cut off from his
people. 5This is so the Israelites will bring
to the LORD the sacrifices they are now making in the open fields. They must bring
them to the priest, that is, to the LORD, at
the entrance to the Tent of Meeting and sacrifice them as fellowship offerings.[b] 6The
priest is to sprinkle the blood against the altar of the LORD at the entrance to the Tent
of Meeting and burn the fat as an aroma
pleasing to the LORD. 7They must no longer
offer any of their sacrifices to the goat idols[c]
to whom they prostitute themselves. This is
to be a lasting ordinance for them and for
the generations to come.'
8"Say to them: 'Any Israelite or any alien
living among them who offers a burnt offering or sacrifice 9and does not bring it
to the entrance to the Tent of Meeting to
sacrifice it to the LORD—that man must be
cut off from his people.
10" 'Any Israelite or any alien living
among them who eats any blood—I will
set my face against that person who eats
blood and will cut him off from his people. 11For the life of a creature is in the
blood, and I have given it to you to make
atonement for yourselves on the altar; it is
the blood that makes atonement for one's
life. 12Therefore I say to the Israelites,
"None of you may eat blood, nor may an
alien living among you eat blood."
13" 'Any Israelite or any alien living
among you who hunts any animal or bird
that may be eaten must drain out the
blood and cover it with earth, 14because
the life of every creature is its blood. That
is why I have said to the Israelites, "You
must not eat the blood of any creature, because the life of every creature is its blood;
anyone who eats it must be cut off."
15" 'Anyone, whether native-born or
alien, who eats anything found dead or
torn by wild animals must wash his
clothes and bathe with water, and he will
be ceremonially unclean till evening; then
he will be clean. 16But if he does not wash
his clothes and bathe himself, he will be
held responsible.' "

Unlawful Sexual Relations

18 The LORD said to Moses, 2"Speak to the
Israelites and say to them: 'I am the
LORD your God. 3You must not do as they
do in Egypt, where you used to live, and
you must not do as they do in the land of
Canaan, where I am bringing you. Do not
follow their practices. 4You must obey my
laws and be careful to follow my decrees.
I am the LORD your God. 5Keep my decrees
and laws, for the man who obeys them
will live by them. I am the LORD.
6" 'No one is to approach any close relative to have sexual relations. I am the LORD.
7" 'Do not dishonor your father by having sexual relations with your mother. She
is your mother; do not have relations with
her.

[a] 3 The Hebrew word can include both male and female. [b] 5 Traditionally *peace offerings* [c] 7 Or *demons*

8" 'Do not have sexual relations with
your father's wife; that would dishonor
your father.
9" 'Do not have sexual relations with
your sister, either your father's daughter or
your mother's daughter, whether she was
born in the same home or elsewhere.
10" 'Do not have sexual relations with
your son's daughter or your daughter's
daughter; that would dishonor you.
11" 'Do not have sexual relations with
the daughter of your father's wife, born to
your father; she is your sister.
12" 'Do not have sexual relations with
your father's sister; she is your father's
close relative.
13" 'Do not have sexual relations with
your mother's sister, because she is your
mother's close relative.
14" 'Do not dishonor your father's
brother by approaching his wife to have
sexual relations; she is your aunt.
15" 'Do not have sexual relations with
your daughter-in-law. She is your son's
wife; do not have relations with her.
16" 'Do not have sexual relations with
your brother's wife; that would dishonor
your brother.
17" 'Do not have sexual relations with
both a woman and her daughter. Do not
have sexual relations with either her son's
daughter or her daughter's daughter; they
are her close relatives. That is wickedness.
18" 'Do not take your wife's sister as a rival wife and have sexual relations with her
while your wife is living.
19" 'Do not approach a woman to have
sexual relations during the uncleanness of
her monthly period.
20" 'Do not have sexual relations with
your neighbor's wife and defile yourself
with her.
21" 'Do not give any of your children to be
sacrificed[d] to Molech, for you must not profane the name of your God. I am the LORD.
22" 'Do not lie with a man as one lies
with a woman; that is detestable.
23" 'Do not have sexual relations with
an animal and defile yourself with it. A
woman must not present herself to an animal to have sexual relations with it; that
is a perversion.
24" 'Do not defile yourselves in any of
these ways, because this is how the nations
that I am going to drive out before you became defiled. 25Even the land was defiled;
so I punished it for its sin, and the land
vomited out its inhabitants. 26But you must
keep my decrees and my laws. The native-
born and the aliens living among you must
not do any of these detestable things, 27for
all these things were done by the people
who lived in the land before you, and the
land became defiled. 28And if you defile the
land, it will vomit you out as it vomited
out the nations that were before you.
29" 'Everyone who does any of these detestable things—such persons must be cut
off from their people. 30Keep my requirements and do not follow any of the detestable customs that were practiced before you came and do not defile yourselves
with them. I am the LORD your God.' "

[d] 21 *Or to be passed through ⌊the fire⌋*

PRAYER: INTERCESSION

O LORD, how good and pleasant it is when brothers and sisters live together in unity! (Psalm 133:1)

***TAKE** a few moments to intercede on behalf of your local church, other churches, evangelism and discipleship ministries, educational ministries and any other special concerns you may have.*

NT Mark 1:40–2:17

A Man With Leprosy

40A man with leprosy[a] came to him and
begged him on his knees, "If you are willing, you can make me clean."
41Filled with compassion, Jesus reached
out his hand and touched the man. "I am
willing," he said. "Be clean!" 42Immediate-
ly the leprosy left him and he was cured.

[a] 40 The Greek word was used for various diseases affecting the skin—not necessarily leprosy.

43 Jesus sent him away at once with a strong warning: 44 "See that you don't tell this to anyone. But go, show yourself to the priest and offer the sacrifices that Moses commanded for your cleansing, as a testimony to them." 45 Instead he went out and began to talk freely, spreading the news. As a result, Jesus could no longer enter a town openly but stayed outside in lonely places. Yet the people still came to him from everywhere.

Jesus Heals a Paralytic

2 A few days later, when Jesus again entered Capernaum, the people heard that he had come home. 2 So many gathered that there was no room left, not even outside the door, and he preached the word to them. 3 Some men came, bringing to him a paralytic, carried by four of them. 4 Since they could not get him to Jesus because of the crowd, they made an opening in the roof above Jesus and, after digging through it, lowered the mat the paralyzed man was lying on. 5 When Jesus saw their faith, he said to the paralytic, "Son, your sins are forgiven."

6 Now some teachers of the law were sitting there, thinking to themselves, 7 "Why does this fellow talk like that? He's blaspheming! Who can forgive sins but God alone?"

8 Immediately Jesus knew in his spirit that this was what they were thinking in their hearts, and he said to them, "Why are you thinking these things? 9 Which is easier: to say to the paralytic, 'Your sins are forgiven,' or to say, 'Get up, take your mat and walk'? 10 But that you may know that the Son of Man has authority on earth to forgive sins . . . ." He said to the paralytic, 11 "I tell you, get up, take your mat and go home." 12 He got up, took his mat and walked out in full view of them all. This amazed everyone and they praised God, saying, "We have never seen anything like this!"

The Calling of Levi

13 Once again Jesus went out beside the lake. A large crowd came to him, and he began to teach them. 14 As he walked along, he saw Levi son of Alphaeus sitting at the tax collector's booth. "Follow me," Jesus told him, and Levi got up and followed him.

15 While Jesus was having dinner at Levi's house, many tax collectors and "sinners" were eating with him and his disciples, for there were many who followed him. 16 When the teachers of the law who were Pharisees saw him eating with the "sinners" and tax collectors, they asked his disciples: "Why does he eat with tax collectors and 'sinners'?"

17 On hearing this, Jesus said to them, "It is not the healthy who need a doctor, but the sick. I have not come to call the righteous, but sinners."

PRAYER: MY RELATIONSHIP TO GOD

YOU have loved me with an everlasting love; You have drawn me with loving-kindness. (Jeremiah 31:3) . . . Who shall separate me from Your love, O Christ? Shall tribulation, or distress, or persecution, or famine, or nakedness, or danger or sword? As it is written: "For Your sake we face death all day long; we are considered as sheep to be slaughtered." Yet in all these things I am more than a conqueror through You who love me. (Romans 8:35–37)

PAUSE *to thank God for the relationship that you enjoy with Him in Jesus Christ.*

YEAR 1 DAY 104

OT Leviticus 19:1-37

Various Laws

19 The LORD said to Moses, 2"Speak to the entire assembly of Israel and say to them: 'Be holy because I, the LORD your God, am holy.

3" 'Each of you must respect his mother and father, and you must observe my Sabbaths. I am the LORD your God.

4" 'Do not turn to idols or make gods of cast metal for yourselves. I am the LORD your God.

5" 'When you sacrifice a fellowship offering[a] to the LORD, sacrifice it in such a way that it will be accepted on your behalf. 6It shall be eaten on the day you sacrifice it or on the next day; anything left over until the third day must be burned up. 7If any of it is eaten on the third day, it is impure and will not be accepted. 8Whoever eats it will be held responsible because he has desecrated what is holy to the LORD; that person must be cut off from his people.

9" 'When you reap the harvest of your land, do not reap to the very edges of your field or gather the gleanings of your harvest. 10Do not go over your vineyard a second time or pick up the grapes that have fallen. Leave them for the poor and the alien. I am the LORD your God.

11" 'Do not steal.

" 'Do not lie.

" 'Do not deceive one another.

12" 'Do not swear falsely by my name and so profane the name of your God. I am the LORD.

13" 'Do not defraud your neighbor or rob him.

" 'Do not hold back the wages of a hired man overnight.

14" 'Do not curse the deaf or put a stumbling block in front of the blind, but fear your God. I am the LORD.

15" 'Do not pervert justice; do not show partiality to the poor or favoritism to the great, but judge your neighbor fairly.

16" 'Do not go about spreading slander among your people.

" 'Do not do anything that endangers your neighbor's life. I am the LORD.

17" 'Do not hate your brother in your heart. Rebuke your neighbor frankly so you will not share in his guilt.

18" 'Do not seek revenge or bear a grudge against one of your people, but love your neighbor as yourself. I am the LORD.

19" 'Keep my decrees.

" 'Do not mate different kinds of animals.

" 'Do not plant your field with two kinds of seed.

" 'Do not wear clothing woven of two kinds of material.

20" 'If a man sleeps with a woman who is a slave girl promised to another man but who has not been ransomed or given her freedom, there must be due punishment. Yet they are not to be put to death, because she had not been freed. 21The man, however, must bring a ram to the entrance to the Tent of Meeting for a guilt offering to the LORD. 22With the ram of the guilt offering the priest is to make atonement for him before the LORD for the sin he has committed, and his sin will be forgiven.

23" 'When you enter the land and plant any kind of fruit tree, regard its fruit as forbidden.[b] For three years you are to consider it forbidden[b]; it must not be eaten. 24In the fourth year all its fruit will be holy, an offering of praise to the LORD. 25But in the fifth year you may eat its fruit. In this way your harvest will be increased. I am the LORD your God.

26" 'Do not eat any meat with the blood still in it.

" 'Do not practice divination or sorcery.

27" 'Do not cut the hair at the sides of your head or clip off the edges of your beard.

28" 'Do not cut your bodies for the dead or put tattoo marks on yourselves. I am the LORD.

29" 'Do not degrade your daughter by making her a prostitute, or the land will turn to prostitution and be filled with wickedness.

30" 'Observe my Sabbaths and have reverence for my sanctuary. I am the LORD.

31" 'Do not turn to mediums or seek out spiritists, for you will be defiled by them. I am the LORD your God.

32" 'Rise in the presence of the aged,

[a] 5 Traditionally *peace offering* [b] 23 Hebrew *uncircumcised*

show respect for the elderly and revere
your God. I am the LORD.
33" 'When an alien lives with you in
your land, do not mistreat him. 34The
alien living with you must be treated as
one of your native-born. Love him as
yourself, for you were aliens in Egypt. I
am the LORD your God.
35" 'Do not use dishonest standards
when measuring length, weight or quantity. 36Use honest scales and honest
weights, an honest ephah[c] and an honest
hin.[d] I am the LORD your God, who
brought you out of Egypt.
37" 'Keep all my decrees and all my laws
and follow them. I am the LORD.' "

[c] 36 An ephah was a dry measure. [d] 36 A hin was a liquid measure.

PRAYER: AFFIRMATION

FATHER, those who are in Christ, Your Son, are new creations; the old things have passed away; behold, they have become new. (2 Corinthians 5:17) . . . The mystery that has been kept hidden for ages and generations is now disclosed to the saints. O God, to them You have chosen to make known among the Gentiles the glorious riches of this mystery, which is Christ in us, the hope of glory. (Colossians 1:26–27)

***PAUSE** to reflect on these Biblical affirmations.*

NT Mark 2:18–3:19

Jesus Questioned About Fasting

18Now John's disciples and the Pharisees were fasting. Some people came and
asked Jesus, "How is it that John's disciples and the disciples of the Pharisees are
fasting, but yours are not?"
19Jesus answered, "How can the guests
of the bridegroom fast while he is with
them? They cannot, so long as they have
him with them. 20But the time will come
when the bridegroom will be taken from
them, and on that day they will fast.
21"No one sews a patch of unshrunk
cloth on an old garment. If he does, the
new piece will pull away from the old,
making the tear worse. 22And no one pours
new wine into old wineskins. If he does,
the wine will burst the skins, and both the
wine and the wineskins will be ruined. No,
he pours new wine into new wineskins."

Lord of the Sabbath

23One Sabbath Jesus was going through
the grainfields, and as his disciples walked
along, they began to pick some heads of
grain. 24The Pharisees said to him, "Look,
why are they doing what is unlawful on
the Sabbath?"
25He answered, "Have you never read
what David did when he and his companions were hungry and in need? 26In
the days of Abiathar the high priest, he entered the house of God and ate the consecrated bread, which is lawful only for
priests to eat. And he also gave some to
his companions."
27Then he said to them, "The Sabbath
was made for man, not man for the Sabbath. 28So the Son of Man is Lord even of
the Sabbath."
3 Another time he went into the synagogue, and a man with a shriveled
hand was there. 2Some of them were looking for a reason to accuse Jesus, so they
watched him closely to see if he would
heal him on the Sabbath. 3Jesus said to
the man with the shriveled hand, "Stand
up in front of everyone."
4Then Jesus asked them, "Which is lawful on the Sabbath: to do good or to do
evil, to save life or to kill?" But they remained silent.
5He looked around at them in anger
and, deeply distressed at their stubborn
hearts, said to the man, "Stretch out your
hand." He stretched it out, and his hand
was completely restored. 6Then the Pharisees went out and began to plot with the
Herodians how they might kill Jesus.

Crowds Follow Jesus

7Jesus withdrew with his disciples to the

lake, and a large crowd from Galilee followed. [8]When they heard all he was doing,
many people came to him from Judea,
Jerusalem, Idumea, and the regions across
the Jordan and around Tyre and Sidon.
[9]Because of the crowd he told his disciples
to have a small boat ready for him, to keep
the people from crowding him. [10]For he
had healed many, so that those with diseases were pushing forward to touch him.
[11]Whenever the evil[a] spirits saw him, they
fell down before him and cried out, "You
are the Son of God." [12]But he gave them
strict orders not to tell who he was.

The Appointing of the Twelve Apostles

[13]Jesus went up on a mountainside and
called to him those he wanted, and they
came to him. [14]He appointed twelve—
designating them apostles[b]—that they
might be with him and that he might
send them out to preach [15]and to have authority to drive out demons. [16]These are
the twelve he appointed: Simon (to
whom he gave the name Peter); [17]James
son of Zebedee and his brother John (to
them he gave the name Boanerges, which
means Sons of Thunder); [18]Andrew, Philip, Bartholomew, Matthew, Thomas,
James son of Alphaeus, Thaddaeus, Simon the Zealot [19]and Judas Iscariot, who
betrayed him.

[a] *11* Greek *unclean;* also in verse 30 [b] *14* Some manuscripts do not have *designating them apostles.*

PRAYER: THE CHARACTER I WANT TO CULTIVATE

SINCE I have been approved by You, O God, to be entrusted with the gospel, I speak not as one who wants to please people but instead so as to please You, the One who tests my heart. I will not seek glory from people. (1 Thessalonians 2:4, 6)

***TAKE** a moment to ask the Lord for the grace to grow in godly character.*

YEAR 1 DAY 105

OT Psalms 23–24

Psalm 23

A psalm of David.

[1]The LORD is my shepherd, I shall not
be in want.
[2] He makes me lie down in green
pastures,
he leads me beside quiet waters,
[3] he restores my soul.
He guides me in paths of righteousness
for his name's sake.
[4]Even though I walk
through the valley of the shadow of
death,[a]
I will fear no evil,
for you are with me;
your rod and your staff,
they comfort me.

[5]You prepare a table before me
in the presence of my enemies.
You anoint my head with oil;
my cup overflows.
[6]Surely goodness and love will follow
me
all the days of my life,
and I will dwell in the house of the
LORD
forever.

Psalm 24

Of David. A psalm.

[1]The earth is the LORD's, and everything
in it,
the world, and all who live in it;
[2]for he founded it upon the seas
and established it upon the waters.

[3]Who may ascend the hill of the LORD?
Who may stand in his holy place?
[4]He who has clean hands and a pure
heart,
who does not lift up his soul to an
idol

[a] *4* Or *through the darkest valley*

or swear by what is false.[b]
5 He will receive blessing from the LORD
and vindication from God his
Savior.
6 Such is the generation of those who
seek him,
who seek your face, O God of
Jacob.[c] *Selah*

7 Lift up your heads, O you gates;
be lifted up, you ancient doors,
that the King of glory may come in.
8 Who is this King of glory?
The LORD strong and mighty,
the LORD mighty in battle.
9 Lift up your heads, O you gates;
lift them up, you ancient doors,
that the King of glory may come in.
10 Who is he, this King of glory?
The LORD Almighty—
he is the King of glory. *Selah*

[b] 4 Or *swear falsely* [c] 6 Two Hebrew manuscripts and Syriac (see also Septuagint); most Hebrew manuscripts *face, Jacob*

PRAYER: THANKSGIVING

YOU are the God who answered me in the day of my distress and have been with me wherever I have gone. (Genesis 35:3) . . . God Almighty, You are my shepherd, the Rock of Israel, who helps me and blesses me with blessings of the heavens above. (Genesis 49:24–25)

PAUSE *to offer your own expressions of thanksgiving.*

NT Mark 3:20–4:20

Jesus and Beelzebub

20 Then Jesus entered a house, and again
a crowd gathered, so that he and his disciples were not even able to eat. 21 When
his family heard about this, they went to
take charge of him, for they said, "He is
out of his mind."
22 And the teachers of the law who came
down from Jerusalem said, "He is possessed by Beelzebub[a]! By the prince of
demons he is driving out demons."
23 So Jesus called them and spoke to them
in parables: "How can Satan drive out Satan? 24 If a kingdom is divided against itself,
that kingdom cannot stand. 25 If a house is
divided against itself, that house cannot
stand. 26 And if Satan opposes himself and
is divided, he cannot stand; his end has
come. 27 In fact, no one can enter a strong
man's house and carry off his possessions
unless he first ties up the strong man. Then
he can rob his house. 28 I tell you the truth,
all the sins and blasphemies of men will be
forgiven them. 29 But whoever blasphemes
against the Holy Spirit will never be forgiv-
en; he is guilty of an eternal sin."
30 He said this because they were saying,
"He has an evil spirit."

Jesus' Mother and Brothers

31 Then Jesus' mother and brothers arrived. Standing outside, they sent someone
in to call him. 32 A crowd was sitting around
him, and they told him, "Your mother and
brothers are outside looking for you."
33 "Who are my mother and my brothers?" he asked.
34 Then he looked at those seated in a
circle around him and said, "Here are my
mother and my brothers! 35 Whoever does
God's will is my brother and sister and
mother."

The Parable of the Sower

4 Again Jesus began to teach by the lake.
The crowd that gathered around him
was so large that he got into a boat and
sat in it out on the lake, while all the people were along the shore at the water's
edge. 2 He taught them many things by
parables, and in his teaching said: 3 "Listen! A farmer went out to sow his seed.
4 As he was scattering the seed, some fell
along the path, and the birds came and
ate it up. 5 Some fell on rocky places,
where it did not have much soil. It sprang
up quickly, because the soil was shallow.
6 But when the sun came up, the plants
were scorched, and they withered because
they had no root. 7 Other seed fell among
thorns, which grew up and choked the

[a] 22 Greek *Beezeboul* or *Beelzeboul*

plants, so that they did not bear grain.
[8]Still other seed fell on good soil. It came
up, grew and produced a crop, multiply-
ing thirty, sixty, or even a hundred times."
[9]Then Jesus said, "He who has ears to
hear, let him hear."
[10]When he was alone, the Twelve and
the others around him asked him about
the parables. [11]He told them, "The secret
of the kingdom of God has been given to
you. But to those on the outside everything is said in parables [12]so that,

" 'they may be ever seeing but never
perceiving,
and ever hearing but never
understanding;
otherwise they might turn and be
forgiven!'[b]"

[13]Then Jesus said to them, "Don't you
understand this parable? How then will
you understand any parable? [14]The farmer
sows the word. [15]Some people are like
seed along the path, where the word is
sown. As soon as they hear it, Satan comes
and takes away the word that was sown in
them. [16]Others, like seed sown on rocky
places, hear the word and at once receive
it with joy. [17]But since they have no root,
they last only a short time. When trouble
or persecution comes because of the
word, they quickly fall away. [18]Still others,
like seed sown among thorns, hear the
word; [19]but the worries of this life, the deceitfulness of wealth and the desires for
other things come in and choke the word,
making it unfruitful. [20]Others, like seed
sown on good soil, hear the word, accept
it, and produce a crop—thirty, sixty or
even a hundred times what was sown."

[b] *12* Isaiah 6:9,10

PRAYER: MY RELATIONSHIP TO OTHERS

YOU have called me to go and proclaim Your kingdom, O God. (Luke 9:60) . . . As the Father has sent You, You also send us, Lord Jesus. (John 20:21)

PAUSE *to review your relationships with others and to commit them to the Lord.*

YEAR 1 DAY 106

OT Leviticus 20:1-27

Punishments for Sin

20 The LORD said to Moses, [2]"Say to the
Israelites: 'Any Israelite or any alien
living in Israel who gives[a] any of his children to Molech must be put to death. The
people of the community are to stone
him. [3]I will set my face against that man
and I will cut him off from his people; for
by giving his children to Molech, he has
defiled my sanctuary and profaned my
holy name. [4]If the people of the community close their eyes when that man gives
one of his children to Molech and they
fail to put him to death, [5]I will set my face
against that man and his family and will
cut off from their people both him and all
who follow him in prostituting themselves to Molech.
[6]" 'I will set my face against the person
who turns to mediums and spiritists to
prostitute himself by following them, and
I will cut him off from his people.
[7]" 'Consecrate yourselves and be holy,
because I am the LORD your God. [8]Keep
my decrees and follow them. I am the
LORD, who makes you holy.[b]
[9]" 'If anyone curses his father or mother, he must be put to death. He has cursed
his father or his mother, and his blood
will be on his own head.
[10]" 'If a man commits adultery with another man's wife—with the wife of his
neighbor—both the adulterer and the
adulteress must be put to death.
[11]" 'If a man sleeps with his father's wife,
he has dishonored his father. Both the man
and the woman must be put to death; their
blood will be on their own heads.

[a] 2 Or *sacrifices;* also in verses 3 and 4 [b] *8* Or *who sanctifies you;* or *who sets you apart as holy*

12" 'If a man sleeps with his daughter-
in-law, both of them must be put to
death. What they have done is a perversion; their blood will be on their own
heads.
13" 'If a man lies with a man as one lies
with a woman, both of them have done
what is detestable. They must be put to
death; their blood will be on their own
heads.
14" 'If a man marries both a woman and
her mother, it is wicked. Both he and they
must be burned in the fire, so that no
wickedness will be among you.
15" 'If a man has sexual relations with
an animal, he must be put to death, and
you must kill the animal.
16" 'If a woman approaches an animal
to have sexual relations with it, kill both
the woman and the animal. They must be
put to death; their blood will be on their
own heads.
17" 'If a man marries his sister, the
daughter of either his father or his mother, and they have sexual relations, it is a
disgrace. They must be cut off before the
eyes of their people. He has dishonored
his sister and will be held responsible.
18" 'If a man lies with a woman during
her monthly period and has sexual relations with her, he has exposed the source
of her flow, and she has also uncovered it.
Both of them must be cut off from their
people.
19" 'Do not have sexual relations with
the sister of either your mother or your father, for that would dishonor a close relative; both of you would be held responsible.
20" 'If a man sleeps with his aunt, he has
dishonored his uncle. They will be held
responsible; they will die childless.
21" 'If a man marries his brother's wife,
it is an act of impurity; he has dishonored
his brother. They will be childless.
22" 'Keep all my decrees and laws and
follow them, so that the land where I am
bringing you to live may not vomit you
out. 23You must not live according to the
customs of the nations I am going to drive
out before you. Because they did all these
things, I abhorred them. 24But I said to
you, "You will possess their land; I will
give it to you as an inheritance, a land
flowing with milk and honey." I am the
LORD your God, who has set you apart
from the nations.
25" 'You must therefore make a distinction between clean and unclean animals
and between unclean and clean birds. Do
not defile yourselves by any animal or
bird or anything that moves along the
ground—those which I have set apart as
unclean for you. 26You are to be holy to
me[c] because I, the LORD, am holy, and I
have set you apart from the nations to be
my own.
27" 'A man or woman who is a medium
or spiritist among you must be put to
death. You are to stone them; their blood
will be on their own heads.' "

[c] 26 Or *be my holy ones*

PRAYER: ADORATION

HOW precious are Your thoughts to me, O God! How vast is the sum of them! If I should count them, they would outnumber the grains of sand. When I awake, I am still with You. (Psalm 139:17–18) . . . To whom can I liken You or count You equal? To whom can I compare You that You may be alike? (Isaiah 46:5)

***PAUSE** to express your thoughts of praise and worship.*

NT Mark 4:21–41

A Lamp on a Stand

21He said to them, "Do you bring in a
lamp to put it under a bowl or a bed? Instead, don't you put it on its stand? 22For
whatever is hidden is meant to be disclosed, and whatever is concealed is
meant to be brought out into the open.
23If anyone has ears to hear, let him hear."
24"Consider carefully what you hear,"
he continued. "With the measure you use,
it will be measured to you—and even

more. 25Whoever has will be given more;
whoever does not have, even what he has
will be taken from him."

The Parable of the Growing Seed

26He also said, "This is what the kingdom of God is like. A man scatters seed
on the ground. 27Night and day, whether
he sleeps or gets up, the seed sprouts and
grows, though he does not know how.
28All by itself the soil produces grain—first
the stalk, then the head, then the full kernel in the head. 29As soon as the grain is
ripe, he puts the sickle to it, because the
harvest has come."

The Parable of the Mustard Seed

30Again he said, "What shall we say the
kingdom of God is like, or what parable
shall we use to describe it? 31It is like a
mustard seed, which is the smallest seed
you plant in the ground. 32Yet when
planted, it grows and becomes the largest
of all garden plants, with such big
branches that the birds of the air can
perch in its shade."
33With many similar parables Jesus
spoke the word to them, as much as they
could understand. 34He did not say anything to them without using a parable.
But when he was alone with his own disciples, he explained everything.

Jesus Calms the Storm

35That day when evening came, he said
to his disciples, "Let us go over to the other side." 36Leaving the crowd behind, they
took him along, just as he was, in the
boat. There were also other boats with
him. 37A furious squall came up, and the
waves broke over the boat, so that it was
nearly swamped. 38Jesus was in the stern,
sleeping on a cushion. The disciples woke
him and said to him, "Teacher, don't you
care if we drown?"
39He got up, rebuked the wind and said
to the waves, "Quiet! Be still!" Then the
wind died down and it was completely
calm.
40He said to his disciples, "Why are you
so afraid? Do you still have no faith?"
41They were terrified and asked each
other, "Who is this? Even the wind and
the waves obey him!"

PRAYER: THE ATTRIBUTES OF GOD

I WILL arise and bless You, Lord, my God; You are from everlasting to everlasting. Blessed be Your glorious name, which is exalted above all blessing and praise! (Nehemiah 9:5) . . . Glory to You, O God, in the highest, and on earth peace to those on whom Your favor rests. (Luke 2:14)

PAUSE *to reflect on these affirmations about the person, powers and perfection of God.*

YEAR 1
DAY 107

OT Leviticus 21:1-24

Rules for Priests

21 The LORD said to Moses, "Speak to the
priests, the sons of Aaron, and say to
them: 'A priest must not make himself ceremonially unclean for any of his people
who die, 2except for a close relative, such
as his mother or father, his son or daughter, his brother, 3or an unmarried sister
who is dependent on him since she has
no husband—for her he may make himself unclean. 4He must not make himself
unclean for people related to him by marriage,[a] and so defile himself.
5" 'Priests must not shave their heads or
shave off the edges of their beards or cut
their bodies. 6They must be holy to their
God and must not profane the name of
their God. Because they present the offerings made to the LORD by fire, the food of
their God, they are to be holy.
7" 'They must not marry women defiled
by prostitution or divorced from their

[a] 4 Or *unclean as a leader among his people*

husbands, because priests are holy to their God. 8 Regard them as holy, because they offer up the food of your God. Consider them holy, because I the LORD am holy—I who make you holy.[b]

9 " 'If a priest's daughter defiles herself by becoming a prostitute, she disgraces her father; she must be burned in the fire.

10 " 'The high priest, the one among his brothers who has had the anointing oil poured on his head and who has been ordained to wear the priestly garments, must not let his hair become unkempt[c] or tear his clothes. 11 He must not enter a place where there is a dead body. He must not make himself unclean, even for his father or mother, 12 nor leave the sanctuary of his God or desecrate it, because he has been dedicated by the anointing oil of his God. I am the LORD.

13 " 'The woman he marries must be a virgin. 14 He must not marry a widow, a divorced woman, or a woman defiled by prostitution, but only a virgin from his own people, 15 so he will not defile his offspring among his people. I am the LORD, who makes him holy.[d]' "

16 The LORD said to Moses, 17 "Say to Aaron: 'For the generations to come none of your descendants who has a defect may come near to offer the food of his God. 18 No man who has any defect may come near: no man who is blind or lame, disfigured or deformed; 19 no man with a crippled foot or hand, 20 or who is hunchbacked or dwarfed, or who has any eye defect, or who has festering or running sores or damaged testicles. 21 No descendant of Aaron the priest who has any defect is to come near to present the offerings made to the LORD by fire. He has a defect; he must not come near to offer the food of his God. 22 He may eat the most holy food of his God, as well as the holy food; 23 yet because of his defect, he must not go near the curtain or approach the altar, and so desecrate my sanctuary. I am the LORD, who makes them holy.[e]' "

24 So Moses told this to Aaron and his sons and to all the Israelites.

[b] 8 Or *who sanctify you*; or *who set you apart as holy* [c] 10 Or *not uncover his head* [d] 15 Or *who sanctifies him*; or *who sets him apart as holy* [e] 23 Or *who sanctifies them*; or *who sets them apart as holy*

PRAYER: CONFESSION

MY trespasses are multiplied before You, and my sins testify against me. For my transgressions are with me, and I know my iniquities: transgressing and lying against You, O Lord, turning my back on You, speaking oppression and revolt, uttering lies my heart has conceived. (Isaiah 59:12–13)

***ASK** the Spirit to search your heart and reveal any areas of unconfessed sin. Acknowledge these to the Lord and thank Him for His forgiveness.*

NT Mark 5:1–20

The Healing of a Demon-possessed Man

5 They went across the lake to the region of the Gerasenes.[a] 2 When Jesus got out of the boat, a man with an evil[b] spirit came from the tombs to meet him. 3 This man lived in the tombs, and no one could bind him any more, not even with a chain. 4 For he had often been chained hand and foot, but he tore the chains apart and broke the irons on his feet. No one was strong enough to subdue him. 5 Night and day among the tombs and in the hills he would cry out and cut himself with stones.

6 When he saw Jesus from a distance, he ran and fell on his knees in front of him. 7 He shouted at the top of his voice, "What do you want with me, Jesus, Son of the Most High God? Swear to God that you won't torture me!" 8 For Jesus had said to him, "Come out of this man, you evil spirit!"

9 Then Jesus asked him, "What is your name?"

"My name is Legion," he replied, "for we

[a] 1 Some manuscripts *Gadarenes*; other manuscripts *Gergesenes* [b] 2 Greek *unclean*; also in verses 8 and 13

are many." [10]And he begged Jesus again
and again not to send them out of the area.
[11]A large herd of pigs was feeding on the
nearby hillside. [12]The demons begged
Jesus, "Send us among the pigs; allow us
to go into them." [13]He gave them permission, and the evil spirits came out and
went into the pigs. The herd, about two
thousand in number, rushed down the
steep bank into the lake and were
drowned.
[14]Those tending the pigs ran off and reported this in the town and countryside,
and the people went out to see what had
happened. [15]When they came to Jesus,
they saw the man who had been possessed by the legion of demons, sitting
there, dressed and in his right mind; and
they were afraid. [16]Those who had seen it
told the people what had happened to the
demon-possessed man—and told about
the pigs as well. [17]Then the people began
to plead with Jesus to leave their region.
[18]As Jesus was getting into the boat, the
man who had been demon-possessed
begged to go with him. [19]Jesus did not let
him, but said, "Go home to your family
and tell them how much the Lord has
done for you, and how he has had mercy
on you." [20]So the man went away and began to tell in the Decapolis[c] how much
Jesus had done for him. And all the people were amazed.

[c] *20* That is, the Ten Cities

PRAYER: THE WORKS OF GOD

AS the earth brings forth its sprouts and as a garden causes that which is sown to spring up, so You, Lord God, will make righteousness and praise spring up before all nations. (Isaiah 61:11)

***TAKE** a moment to consider the greatness of God's wonderful works.*

YEAR 1 DAY 108

OT Leviticus 22:1-33

22 The LORD said to Moses, [2]"Tell Aaron
and his sons to treat with respect the
sacred offerings the Israelites consecrate to
me, so they will not profane my holy
name. I am the LORD.
[3]"Say to them: 'For the generations to
come, if any of your descendants is ceremonially unclean and yet comes near the
sacred offerings that the Israelites consecrate to the LORD, that person must be cut
off from my presence. I am the LORD.
[4]" 'If a descendant of Aaron has an infectious skin disease[a] or a bodily discharge, he may not eat the sacred offerings
until he is cleansed. He will also be unclean if he touches something defiled by
a corpse or by anyone who has an emission of semen, [5]or if he touches any crawling thing that makes him unclean, or any
person who makes him unclean, whatever the uncleanness may be. [6]The one who
touches any such thing will be unclean till
evening. He must not eat any of the sacred
offerings unless he has bathed himself
with water. [7]When the sun goes down, he
will be clean, and after that he may eat the
sacred offerings, for they are his food. [8]He
must not eat anything found dead or torn
by wild animals, and so become unclean
through it. I am the LORD.
[9]" 'The priests are to keep my requirements so that they do not become guilty
and die for treating them with contempt.
I am the LORD, who makes them holy.[b]
[10]" 'No one outside a priest's family
may eat the sacred offering, nor may the
guest of a priest or his hired worker eat it.
[11]But if a priest buys a slave with money,
or if a slave is born in his household, that
slave may eat his food. [12]If a priest's
daughter marries anyone other than a
priest, she may not eat any of the sacred
contributions. [13]But if a priest's daughter
becomes a widow or is divorced, yet has
no children, and she returns to live in her
father's house as in her youth, she may eat

[a] *4* Traditionally *leprosy;* the Hebrew word was used for various diseases affecting the skin—not necessarily leprosy. [b] *9* Or *who sanctifies them;* or *who sets them apart as holy;* also in verse 16

of her father's food. No unauthorized person, however, may eat any of it.

14 " 'If anyone eats a sacred offering by mistake, he must make restitution to the priest for the offering and add a fifth of the value to it. 15 The priests must not desecrate the sacred offerings the Israelites present to the LORD 16 by allowing them to eat the sacred offerings and so bring upon them guilt requiring payment. I am the LORD, who makes them holy.' "

Unacceptable Sacrifices

17 The LORD said to Moses, 18 "Speak to Aaron and his sons and to all the Israelites and say to them: 'If any of you—either an Israelite or an alien living in Israel—presents a gift for a burnt offering to the LORD, either to fulfill a vow or as a freewill offering, 19 you must present a male without defect from the cattle, sheep or goats in order that it may be accepted on your behalf. 20 Do not bring anything with a defect, because it will not be accepted on your behalf. 21 When anyone brings from the herd or flock a fellowship offering[c] to the LORD to fulfill a special vow or as a freewill offering, it must be without defect or blemish to be acceptable. 22 Do not offer to the LORD the blind, the injured or the maimed, or anything with warts or festering or running sores. Do not place any of these on the altar as an offering made to the LORD by fire. 23 You may, however, present as a freewill offering an ox[d] or a sheep that is deformed or stunted, but it will not be accepted in fulfillment of a vow. 24 You must not offer to the LORD an animal whose testicles are bruised, crushed, torn or cut. You must not do this in your own land, 25 and you must not accept such animals from the hand of a foreigner and offer them as the food of your God. They will not be accepted on your behalf, because they are deformed and have defects.' "

26 The LORD said to Moses, 27 "When a calf, a lamb or a goat is born, it is to remain with its mother for seven days. From the eighth day on, it will be acceptable as an offering made to the LORD by fire. 28 Do not slaughter a cow or a sheep and its young on the same day.

29 "When you sacrifice a thank offering to the LORD, sacrifice it in such a way that it will be accepted on your behalf. 30 It must be eaten that same day; leave none of it till morning. I am the LORD.

31 "Keep my commands and follow them. I am the LORD. 32 Do not profane my holy name. I must be acknowledged as holy by the Israelites. I am the LORD, who makes[e] you holy[f] 33 and who brought you out of Egypt to be your God. I am the LORD."

[c] 21 Traditionally *peace offering* [d] 23 The Hebrew word can include both male and female. [e] 32 Or *made* [f] 32 Or *who sanctifies you;* or *who sets you apart as holy*

PRAYER: RENEWAL

MAY I fear You, Lord, and serve You in truth with all my heart, for I consider what great things You have done for me. (1 Samuel 12:24) . . . May I not transgress Your commandments, Lord, for I cannot prosper in disobedience. May I not forsake You. (2 Chronicles 24:20)

***PAUSE** to add your own prayers for personal renewal.*

NT Mark 5:21-43

A Dead Girl and a Sick Woman

21 When Jesus had again crossed over by boat to the other side of the lake, a large crowd gathered around him while he was by the lake. 22 Then one of the synagogue rulers, named Jairus, came there. Seeing Jesus, he fell at his feet 23 and pleaded earnestly with him, "My little daughter is dying. Please come and put your hands on her so that she will be healed and live." 24 So Jesus went with him.

A large crowd followed and pressed around him. 25 And a woman was there who had been subject to bleeding for twelve years. 26 She had suffered a great deal under the care of many doctors and had spent all she had, yet instead of getting better she grew worse. 27When she heard about Jesus, she came up behind him in the crowd and touched his cloak, 28because she thought, "If I just touch his clothes, I will be healed." 29Immediately her bleeding stopped and she felt in her body that she was freed from her suffering.

30At once Jesus realized that power had gone out from him. He turned around in the crowd and asked, "Who touched my clothes?"

31"You see the people crowding against you," his disciples answered, "and yet you can ask, 'Who touched me?' "

32But Jesus kept looking around to see who had done it. 33Then the woman, knowing what had happened to her, came and fell at his feet and, trembling with fear, told him the whole truth. 34He said to her, "Daughter, your faith has healed you. Go in peace and be freed from your suffering."

35While Jesus was still speaking, some men came from the house of Jairus, the synagogue ruler. "Your daughter is dead," they said. "Why bother the teacher any more?"

36Ignoring what they said, Jesus told the synagogue ruler, "Don't be afraid; just believe."

37He did not let anyone follow him except Peter, James and John the brother of James. 38When they came to the home of the synagogue ruler, Jesus saw a commotion, with people crying and wailing loudly. 39He went in and said to them, "Why all this commotion and wailing? The child is not dead but asleep." 40But they laughed at him.

After he put them all out, he took the child's father and mother and the disciples who were with him, and went in where the child was. 41He took her by the hand and said to her, *"Talitha koum!"* (which means, "Little girl, I say to you, get up!"). 42Immediately the girl stood up and walked around (she was twelve years old). At this they were completely astonished. 43He gave strict orders not to let anyone know about this, and told them to give her something to eat.

PRAYER: MY RELATIONSHIP TO GOD

LORD Jesus, all those the Father gives You will come to You, and whoever comes to You, You will never cast out. For You have come down from heaven, not to do Your own will, but the will of Him who sent You. And this is the will of Him who sent You, that You will lose none of all those He has given You, but raise them up at the last day. For Your Father's will is that those who look to You and believe in You may have eternal life, and You will raise them up at the last day. (John 6:37–40)

PAUSE *to thank God for the relationship that you enjoy with Him in Jesus Christ.*

YEAR 1 DAY 109

OT Leviticus 23:1-44

23 The LORD said to Moses, 2"Speak to the Israelites and say to them: 'These are my appointed feasts, the appointed feasts of the LORD, which you are to proclaim as sacred assemblies.

The Sabbath

3" 'There are six days when you may work, but the seventh day is a Sabbath of rest, a day of sacred assembly. You are not to do any work; wherever you live, it is a Sabbath to the LORD.

The Passover and Unleavened Bread

4" 'These are the LORD's appointed feasts, the sacred assemblies you are to proclaim at their appointed times: 5The LORD's Passover begins at twilight on the fourteenth day of the first month. 6On the fifteenth day of that month the LORD's

Feast of Unleavened Bread begins; for seven days you must eat bread made without yeast. [7]On the first day hold a sacred assembly and do no regular work. [8]For seven days present an offering made to the LORD by fire. And on the seventh day hold a sacred assembly and do no regular work.' "

Firstfruits

[9]The LORD said to Moses, [10]"Speak to the Israelites and say to them: 'When you enter the land I am going to give you and you reap its harvest, bring to the priest a sheaf of the first grain you harvest. [11]He is to wave the sheaf before the LORD so it will be accepted on your behalf; the priest is to wave it on the day after the Sabbath. [12]On the day you wave the sheaf, you must sacrifice as a burnt offering to the LORD a lamb a year old without defect, [13]together with its grain offering of two-tenths of an ephah[a] of fine flour mixed with oil—an offering made to the LORD by fire, a pleasing aroma—and its drink offering of a quarter of a hin[b] of wine. [14]You must not eat any bread, or roasted or new grain, until the very day you bring this offering to your God. This is to be a lasting ordinance for the generations to come, wherever you live.

Feast of Weeks

[15]" 'From the day after the Sabbath, the day you brought the sheaf of the wave offering, count off seven full weeks. [16]Count off fifty days up to the day after the seventh Sabbath, and then present an offering of new grain to the LORD. [17]From wherever you live, bring two loaves made of two-tenths of an ephah of fine flour, baked with yeast, as a wave offering of firstfruits to the LORD. [18]Present with this bread seven male lambs, each a year old and without defect, one young bull and two rams. They will be a burnt offering to the LORD, together with their grain offerings and drink offerings—an offering made by fire, an aroma pleasing to the LORD. [19]Then sacrifice one male goat for a sin offering and two lambs, each a year old, for a fellowship offering.[c] [20]The priest is to wave the two lambs before the LORD as a wave offering, together with the bread of the firstfruits. They are a sacred offering to the LORD for the priest. [21]On that same day you are to proclaim a sacred assembly and do no regular work. This is to be a lasting ordinance for the generations to come, wherever you live.

[22]" 'When you reap the harvest of your land, do not reap to the very edges of your field or gather the gleanings of your harvest. Leave them for the poor and the alien. I am the LORD your God.' "

Feast of Trumpets

[23]The LORD said to Moses, [24]"Say to the Israelites: 'On the first day of the seventh month you are to have a day of rest, a sacred assembly commemorated with trumpet blasts. [25]Do no regular work, but present an offering made to the LORD by fire.' "

Day of Atonement

[26]The LORD said to Moses, [27]"The tenth day of this seventh month is the Day of Atonement. Hold a sacred assembly and deny yourselves,[d] and present an offering made to the LORD by fire. [28]Do no work on that day, because it is the Day of Atonement, when atonement is made for you before the LORD your God. [29]Anyone who does not deny himself on that day must be cut off from his people. [30]I will destroy from among his people anyone who does any work on that day. [31]You shall do no work at all. This is to be a lasting ordinance for the generations to come, wherever you live. [32]It is a sabbath of rest for you, and you must deny yourselves. From the evening of the ninth day of the month until the following evening you are to observe your sabbath."

Feast of Tabernacles

[33]The LORD said to Moses, [34]"Say to the Israelites: 'On the fifteenth day of the seventh month the LORD's Feast of Tabernacles begins, and it lasts for seven days. [35]The first day is a sacred assembly; do no regular work. [36]For seven days present offerings made to the LORD by fire, and on the eighth day hold a sacred assembly and present an offering made to the LORD by fire. It is the closing assembly; do no regular work.

[a] *13* That is, probably about 4 quarts (about 4.5 liters); also in verse 17 [b] *13* That is, probably about 1 quart (about 1 liter) [c] *19* Traditionally *peace offering* [d] *27* Or *and fast;* also in verses 29 and 32

37(" 'These are the LORD's appointed
feasts, which you are to proclaim as sacred
assemblies for bringing offerings made to
the LORD by fire—the burnt offerings and
grain offerings, sacrifices and drink offerings required for each day. 38These offerings are in addition to those for the LORD's
Sabbaths and[e] in addition to your gifts
and whatever you have vowed and all the
freewill offerings you give to the LORD.)
39" 'So beginning with the fifteenth day
of the seventh month, after you have gathered the crops of the land, celebrate the
festival to the LORD for seven days; the first
day is a day of rest, and the eighth day
also is a day of rest. 40On the first day you
are to take choice fruit from the trees, and
palm fronds, leafy branches and poplars,
and rejoice before the LORD your God for
seven days. 41Celebrate this as a festival to
the LORD for seven days each year. This is
to be a lasting ordinance for the generations to come; celebrate it in the seventh
month. 42Live in booths for seven days: All
native-born Israelites are to live in booths
43so your descendants will know that I
had the Israelites live in booths when I
brought them out of Egypt. I am the LORD
your God.' "
44So Moses announced to the Israelites
the appointed feasts of the LORD.

[e] 38 Or *These feasts are in addition to the LORD's Sabbaths, and these offerings are*

PRAYER: PETITION

MAY I be worthy of respect, not double-tongued, not addicted to wine, not fond of dishonest gain, but holding the mystery of the faith with a clear conscience. (1 Timothy 3:8–9)

***PAUSE** here to petition God for wisdom. Ask Him to develop your eternal perspective, to renew your mind with truth and to help you develop greater skill in each area of your life. Offer prayers regarding your activities for this day and any special concerns you may have.*

NT Mark 6:1–29

A Prophet Without Honor

6 Jesus left there and went to his hometown, accompanied by his disciples.
2When the Sabbath came, he began to
teach in the synagogue, and many who
heard him were amazed.
"Where did this man get these things?"
they asked. "What's this wisdom that has
been given him, that he even does miracles! 3Isn't this the carpenter? Isn't this
Mary's son and the brother of James, Joseph,[a] Judas and Simon? Aren't his sisters
here with us?" And they took offense at
him.
4Jesus said to them, "Only in his hometown, among his relatives and in his own
house is a prophet without honor." 5He
could not do any miracles there, except
lay his hands on a few sick people and
heal them. 6And he was amazed at their
lack of faith.

Jesus Sends Out the Twelve

Then Jesus went around teaching from
village to village. 7Calling the Twelve to
him, he sent them out two by two and
gave them authority over evil[b] spirits.
8These were his instructions: "Take
nothing for the journey except a staff—no
bread, no bag, no money in your belts.
9Wear sandals but not an extra tunic.
10Whenever you enter a house, stay there
until you leave that town. 11And if any
place will not welcome you or listen to
you, shake the dust off your feet when you
leave, as a testimony against them."
12They went out and preached that people should repent. 13They drove out many
demons and anointed many sick people
with oil and healed them.

John the Baptist Beheaded

14King Herod heard about this, for
Jesus' name had become well known.
Some were saying,[c] "John the Baptist has
been raised from the dead, and that is

[a] 3 Greek *Joses,* a variant of *Joseph* [b] 7 Greek *unclean* [c] 14 Some early manuscripts *He was saying*

why miraculous powers are at work in
him."
15Others said, "He is Elijah."
And still others claimed, "He is a
prophet, like one of the prophets of long
ago."
16But when Herod heard this, he said,
"John, the man I beheaded, has been
raised from the dead!"
17For Herod himself had given orders to
have John arrested, and he had him
bound and put in prison. He did this because of Herodias, his brother Philip's
wife, whom he had married. 18For John
had been saying to Herod, "It is not lawful for you to have your brother's wife."
19So Herodias nursed a grudge against
John and wanted to kill him. But she was
not able to, 20because Herod feared John
and protected him, knowing him to be a
righteous and holy man. When Herod
heard John, he was greatly puzzled[d]; yet
he liked to listen to him.
21Finally the opportune time came. On
his birthday Herod gave a banquet for his
high officials and military commanders
and the leading men of Galilee. 22When
the daughter of Herodias came in and
danced, she pleased Herod and his dinner
guests.
The king said to the girl, "Ask me for
anything you want, and I'll give it to you."
23And he promised her with an oath,
"Whatever you ask I will give you, up to
half my kingdom."
24She went out and said to her mother,
"What shall I ask for?"
"The head of John the Baptist," she answered.
25At once the girl hurried in to the king
with the request: "I want you to give me
right now the head of John the Baptist on
a platter."
26The king was greatly distressed, but
because of his oaths and his dinner
guests, he did not want to refuse her. 27So
he immediately sent an executioner with
orders to bring John's head. The man
went, beheaded John in the prison, 28and
brought back his head on a platter. He
presented it to the girl, and she gave it to
her mother. 29On hearing of this, John's
disciples came and took his body and laid
it in a tomb.

[d] 20 Some early manuscripts *he did many things*

PRAYER: THE CHARACTER I WANT TO CULTIVATE

***WHAT** is desirable in a person is kindness, and it is better to be poor than to be a liar. (Proverbs 19:22) . . . As one of Your chosen people, O God, holy and beloved, I will put on a heart of compassion, kindness, humility, gentleness and patience, bearing with others and forgiving others even as You, Lord, forgave me; and above all these things I will put on love, which is the bond of perfection. (Colossians 3:12–14)*

***TAKE** a moment to ask the Lord for the grace to grow in godly character.*

YEAR 1
DAY 110

OT Leviticus 24:1–23

Oil and Bread Set Before the L*ORD*

24 The LORD said to Moses, 2"Command
the Israelites to bring you clear oil of
pressed olives for the light so that the
lamps may be kept burning continually.
3Outside the curtain of the Testimony in
the Tent of Meeting, Aaron is to tend the
lamps before the LORD from evening till
morning, continually. This is to be a lasting ordinance for the generations to
come. 4The lamps on the pure gold lampstand before the LORD must be tended
continually.
5"Take fine flour and bake twelve loaves
of bread, using two-tenths of an ephah[a]
for each loaf. 6Set them in two rows, six in
each row, on the table of pure gold before
the LORD. 7Along each row put some pure

[a] 5 That is, probably about 4 quarts (about 4.5 liters)

incense as a memorial portion to represent the bread and to be an offering made to the LORD by fire. 8This bread is to be set out before the LORD regularly, Sabbath after Sabbath, on behalf of the Israelites, as a lasting covenant. 9It belongs to Aaron and his sons, who are to eat it in a holy place, because it is a most holy part of their regular share of the offerings made to the LORD by fire."

A Blasphemer Stoned

10Now the son of an Israelite mother and an Egyptian father went out among the Israelites, and a fight broke out in the camp between him and an Israelite. 11The son of the Israelite woman blasphemed the Name with a curse; so they brought him to Moses. (His mother's name was Shelomith, the daughter of Dibri the Danite.) 12They put him in custody until the will of the LORD should be made clear to them.

13Then the LORD said to Moses: 14"Take the blasphemer outside the camp. All those who heard him are to lay their hands on his head, and the entire assembly is to stone him. 15Say to the Israelites: 'If anyone curses his God, he will be held responsible; 16anyone who blasphemes the name of the LORD must be put to death. The entire assembly must stone him. Whether an alien or native-born, when he blasphemes the Name, he must be put to death.

17" 'If anyone takes the life of a human being, he must be put to death. 18Anyone who takes the life of someone's animal must make restitution—life for life. 19If anyone injures his neighbor, whatever he has done must be done to him: 20fracture for fracture, eye for eye, tooth for tooth. As he has injured the other, so he is to be injured. 21Whoever kills an animal must make restitution, but whoever kills a man must be put to death. 22You are to have the same law for the alien and the native-born. I am the LORD your God.' "

23Then Moses spoke to the Israelites, and they took the blasphemer outside the camp and stoned him. The Israelites did as the LORD commanded Moses.

PRAYER: INTERCESSION

FATHER, I pray that Your beloved children may prosper in all things and be in good health, even as their souls prosper.

(3 John 2)

TAKE *a few moments to intercede on behalf of your immediate family and other relatives. Offer prayers for their spiritual, emotional and physical concerns.*

NT Mark 6:30–56

Jesus Feeds the Five Thousand

30The apostles gathered around Jesus and reported to him all they had done and taught. 31Then, because so many people were coming and going that they did not even have a chance to eat, he said to them, "Come with me by yourselves to a quiet place and get some rest."

32So they went away by themselves in a boat to a solitary place. 33But many who saw them leaving recognized them and ran on foot from all the towns and got there ahead of them. 34When Jesus landed and saw a large crowd, he had compassion on them, because they were like sheep without a shepherd. So he began teaching them many things.

35By this time it was late in the day, so his disciples came to him. "This is a remote place," they said, "and it's already very late. 36Send the people away so they can go to the surrounding countryside and villages and buy themselves something to eat."

37But he answered, "You give them something to eat."

They said to him, "That would take eight months of a man's wages[a]! Are we to go and spend that much on bread and give it to them to eat?"

[a] 37 Greek *take two hundred denarii*

38"How many loaves do you have?" he
asked. "Go and see."
When they found out, they said,
"Five—and two fish."
39Then Jesus directed them to have all
the people sit down in groups on the
green grass. 40So they sat down in groups
of hundreds and fifties. 41Taking the five
loaves and the two fish and looking up to
heaven, he gave thanks and broke the
loaves. Then he gave them to his disciples
to set before the people. He also divided
the two fish among them all. 42They all ate
and were satisfied, 43and the disciples
picked up twelve basketfuls of broken
pieces of bread and fish. 44The number of
the men who had eaten was five thousand.

Jesus Walks on the Water

45Immediately Jesus made his disciples
get into the boat and go on ahead of him
to Bethsaida, while he dismissed the
crowd. 46After leaving them, he went up
on a mountainside to pray.
47When evening came, the boat was in
the middle of the lake, and he was alone
on land. 48He saw the disciples straining
at the oars, because the wind was against
them. About the fourth watch of the night
he went out to them, walking on the lake.
He was about to pass by them, 49but when
they saw him walking on the lake, they
thought he was a ghost. They cried out,
50because they all saw him and were terrified.
Immediately he spoke to them and
said, "Take courage! It is I. Don't be
afraid." 51Then he climbed into the boat
with them, and the wind died down. They
were completely amazed, 52for they had
not understood about the loaves; their
hearts were hardened.
53When they had crossed over, they landed at Gennesaret and anchored there. 54As
soon as they got out of the boat, people
recognized Jesus. 55They ran throughout
that whole region and carried the sick on
mats to wherever they heard he was. 56And
wherever he went—into villages, towns or
countryside—they placed the sick in the
marketplaces. They begged him to let them
touch even the edge of his cloak, and all
who touched him were healed.

PRAYER: MY RELATIONSHIP TO OTHERS

I WILL love my enemies and pray for those who persecute me. (Matthew 5:44) . . . I will love my enemies, do good to those who hate me, bless those who curse me, and pray for those who mistreat me. I will do to others as I would have them do to me. (Luke 6:27–28, 31)

PAUSE *to review your relationships with others and to commit them to the Lord.*

YEAR 1 DAY 111

OT Leviticus 25:1–55

The Sabbath Year

25 The LORD said to Moses on Mount Sinai, 2"Speak to the Israelites and say
to them: 'When you enter the land I am
going to give you, the land itself must observe a sabbath to the LORD. 3For six years
sow your fields, and for six years prune
your vineyards and gather their crops.
4But in the seventh year the land is to have
a sabbath of rest, a sabbath to the LORD.
Do not sow your fields or prune your
vineyards. 5Do not reap what grows of itself or harvest the grapes of your untended vines. The land is to have a year of rest.
6Whatever the land yields during the sabbath year will be food for you—for yourself, your manservant and maidservant,
and the hired worker and temporary resident who live among you, 7as well as for
your livestock and the wild animals in
your land. Whatever the land produces
may be eaten.

The Year of Jubilee

8" 'Count off seven sabbaths of years—

seven times seven years—so that the sev-
en sabbaths of years amount to a period
of forty-nine years. 9Then have the trumpet sounded everywhere on the tenth day
of the seventh month; on the Day of
Atonement sound the trumpet throughout your land. 10Consecrate the fiftieth
year and proclaim liberty throughout the
land to all its inhabitants. It shall be a jubilee for you; each one of you is to return
to his family property and each to his own
clan. 11The fiftieth year shall be a jubilee
for you; do not sow and do not reap what
grows of itself or harvest the untended
vines. 12For it is a jubilee and is to be holy
for you; eat only what is taken directly
from the fields.

13" 'In this Year of Jubilee everyone is to
return to his own property.

14" 'If you sell land to one of your countrymen or buy any from him, do not take
advantage of each other. 15You are to buy
from your countryman on the basis of the
number of years since the Jubilee. And he
is to sell to you on the basis of the number of years left for harvesting crops.
16When the years are many, you are to increase the price, and when the years are
few, you are to decrease the price, because
what he is really selling you is the number of crops. 17Do not take advantage of
each other, but fear your God. I am the
LORD your God.

18" 'Follow my decrees and be careful to
obey my laws, and you will live safely in
the land. 19Then the land will yield its
fruit, and you will eat your fill and live
there in safety. 20You may ask, "What will
we eat in the seventh year if we do not
plant or harvest our crops?" 21I will send
you such a blessing in the sixth year that
the land will yield enough for three years.
22While you plant during the eighth year,
you will eat from the old crop and will
continue to eat from it until the harvest of
the ninth year comes in.

23" 'The land must not be sold permanently, because the land is mine and you
are but aliens and my tenants. 24Through-
out the country that you hold as a possession, you must provide for the redemption of the land.

25" 'If one of your countrymen becomes
poor and sells some of his property, his
nearest relative is to come and redeem
what his countryman has sold. 26If, however, a man has no one to redeem it for
him but he himself prospers and acquires
sufficient means to redeem it, 27he is to
determine the value for the years since he
sold it and refund the balance to the man
to whom he sold it; he can then go back
to his own property. 28But if he does not
acquire the means to repay him, what he
sold will remain in the possession of the
buyer until the Year of Jubilee. It will be
returned in the Jubilee, and he can then
go back to his property.

29" 'If a man sells a house in a walled
city, he retains the right of redemption a
full year after its sale. During that time he
may redeem it. 30If it is not redeemed before a full year has passed, the house in
the walled city shall belong permanently
to the buyer and his descendants. It is not
to be returned in the Jubilee. 31But houses
in villages without walls around them are
to be considered as open country. They
can be redeemed, and they are to be returned in the Jubilee.

32" 'The Levites always have the right to
redeem their houses in the Levitical
towns, which they possess. 33So the property of the Levites is redeemable—that is,
a house sold in any town they hold—and
is to be returned in the Jubilee, because
the houses in the towns of the Levites are
their property among the Israelites. 34But
the pastureland belonging to their towns
must not be sold; it is their permanent
possession.

35" 'If one of your countrymen becomes
poor and is unable to support himself
among you, help him as you would an
alien or a temporary resident, so he can
continue to live among you. 36Do not take
interest of any kind[a] from him, but fear
your God, so that your countryman may
continue to live among you. 37You must
not lend him money at interest or sell
him food at a profit. 38I am the LORD your
God, who brought you out of Egypt to
give you the land of Canaan and to be
your God.

39" 'If one of your countrymen becomes
poor among you and sells himself to you,
do not make him work as a slave. 40He is
to be treated as a hired worker or a temporary resident among you; he is to work
for you until the Year of Jubilee. 41Then he
and his children are to be released, and he
will go back to his own clan and to the

[a] 36 Or *take excessive interest;* similarly in verse 37

property of his forefathers. 42Because the
Israelites are my servants, whom I brought
out of Egypt, they must not be sold as
slaves. 43Do not rule over them ruthlessly,
but fear your God.
44" 'Your male and female slaves are to
come from the nations around you; from
them you may buy slaves. 45You may also
buy some of the temporary residents living
among you and members of their clans
born in your country, and they will become
your property. 46You can will them to your
children as inherited property and can
make them slaves for life, but you must not
rule over your fellow Israelites ruthlessly.
47" 'If an alien or a temporary resident
among you becomes rich and one of your
countrymen becomes poor and sells himself to the alien living among you or to a
member of the alien's clan, 48he retains
the right of redemption after he has sold
himself. One of his relatives may redeem
him: 49An uncle or a cousin or any blood
relative in his clan may redeem him. Or if
he prospers, he may redeem himself. 50He
and his buyer are to count the time from
the year he sold himself up to the Year of
Jubilee. The price for his release is to be
based on the rate paid to a hired man for
that number of years. 51If many years remain, he must pay for his redemption a
larger share of the price paid for him. 52If
only a few years remain until the Year of
Jubilee, he is to compute that and pay for
his redemption accordingly. 53He is to be
treated as a man hired from year to year;
you must see to it that his owner does not
rule over him ruthlessly.
54" 'Even if he is not redeemed in any of
these ways, he and his children are to be
released in the Year of Jubilee, 55for the Israelites belong to me as servants. They are
my servants, whom I brought out of
Egypt. I am the LORD your God.

PRAYER: AFFIRMATION

YOU, O Christ, have appeared once for all at the end of the ages to do away with sin by sacrificing Yourself. And as it is appointed for people to die once and after that to face judgment, so You were offered once to bear the sins of many; and You will appear a second time, not to bear sin but to bring salvation to those who eagerly wait for You. (Hebrews 9:26–28) . . . O Jesus, You were chosen before the creation of the world but were revealed in these last times for my sake. Through You I believe in God the Father, who raised You from the dead and glorified You, so that my faith and hope are in Almighty God. (1 Peter 1:20–21)

PAUSE *to reflect on these Biblical affirmations.*

NT Mark 7:1–23

Clean and Unclean

7 The Pharisees and some of the teachers
of the law who had come from Jerusalem gathered around Jesus and 2saw
some of his disciples eating food with
hands that were "unclean," that is, unwashed. 3(The Pharisees and all the Jews
do not eat unless they give their hands a
ceremonial washing, holding to the tradition of the elders. 4When they come from
the marketplace they do not eat unless
they wash. And they observe many other
traditions, such as the washing of cups,
pitchers and kettles.[a])
5So the Pharisees and teachers of the
law asked Jesus, "Why don't your disciples
live according to the tradition of the elders instead of eating their food with 'unclean' hands?"
6He replied, "Isaiah was right when he
prophesied about you hypocrites; as it is
written:

" 'These people honor me with their
lips,
but their hearts are far from me.
7They worship me in vain;
their teachings are but rules taught
by men.'[b]

[a] 4 Some early manuscripts *pitchers, kettles and dining couches* [b] 6,7 Isaiah 29:13

8 You have let go of the commands of God
and are holding on to the traditions of
men."
9 And he said to them: "You have a fine
way of setting aside the commands of
God in order to observe[c] your own traditions! 10 For Moses said, 'Honor your father and your mother,'[d] and, 'Anyone who
curses his father or mother must be put to
death.'[e] 11 But you say that if a man says to
his father or mother: 'Whatever help you
might otherwise have received from me is
Corban' (that is, a gift devoted to God),
12 then you no longer let him do anything
for his father or mother. 13 Thus you nullify the word of God by your tradition that
you have handed down. And you do
many things like that."
14 Again Jesus called the crowd to him
and said, "Listen to me, everyone, and understand this. 15 Nothing outside a man
can make him 'unclean' by going into
him. Rather, it is what comes out of a man
that makes him 'unclean.'[f]"
17 After he had left the crowd and entered the house, his disciples asked him
about this parable. 18 "Are you so dull?" he
asked. "Don't you see that nothing that
enters a man from the outside can make
him 'unclean'? 19 For it doesn't go into his
heart but into his stomach, and then out
of his body." (In saying this, Jesus declared all foods "clean.")
20 He went on: "What comes out of a
man is what makes him 'unclean.' 21 For
from within, out of men's hearts, come
evil thoughts, sexual immorality, theft,
murder, adultery, 22 greed, malice, deceit,
lewdness, envy, slander, arrogance and
folly. 23 All these evils come from inside
and make a man 'unclean.' "

[c] 9 Some manuscripts *set up* [d] *10* Exodus 20:12; Deut. 5:16 [e] *10* Exodus 21:17; Lev. 20:9
[f] *15* Some early manuscripts *'unclean.'* [16] *If anyone has ears to hear, let him hear.*

PRAYER: THE ATTRIBUTES OF GOD

O GOD, will You indeed dwell on earth? Heaven and the highest heaven cannot contain You. (1 Kings 8:27) . . . O God, You sit enthroned above the circle of the earth, and its inhabitants are like grasshoppers. You stretch out the heavens like a curtain and spread them out like a tent to dwell in. You reduce rulers to nothing and make the judges of this world meaningless. (Isaiah 40:22–23)

PAUSE *to reflect on these affirmations about the person, powers and perfection of God.*

OT Psalm 25

YEAR 1
DAY 112

Psalm 25[a]

Of David.

1 To you, O LORD, I lift up my soul;
2 in you I trust, O my God.
Do not let me be put to shame,
nor let my enemies triumph over me.
3 No one whose hope is in you
will ever be put to shame,
but they will be put to shame
who are treacherous without excuse.

4 Show me your ways, O LORD,
teach me your paths;
5 guide me in your truth and teach me,
for you are God my Savior,
and my hope is in you all day long.
6 Remember, O LORD, your great mercy
and love,
for they are from of old.
7 Remember not the sins of my youth
and my rebellious ways;
according to your love remember me,
for you are good, O LORD.

8 Good and upright is the LORD;

[a] This psalm is an acrostic poem, the verses of which begin with the successive letters of the Hebrew alphabet.

therefore he instructs sinners in his ways.
[9] He guides the humble in what is right
and teaches them his way.
[10] All the ways of the LORD are loving and faithful
for those who keep the demands of his covenant.
[11] For the sake of your name, O LORD,
forgive my iniquity, though it is great.
[12] Who, then, is the man that fears the LORD?
He will instruct him in the way chosen for him.
[13] He will spend his days in prosperity,
and his descendants will inherit the land.
[14] The LORD confides in those who fear him;
he makes his covenant known to them.
[15] My eyes are ever on the LORD,
for only he will release my feet from the snare.

[16] Turn to me and be gracious to me,
for I am lonely and afflicted.
[17] The troubles of my heart have multiplied;
free me from my anguish.
[18] Look upon my affliction and my distress
and take away all my sins.
[19] See how my enemies have increased
and how fiercely they hate me!
[20] Guard my life and rescue me;
let me not be put to shame,
for I take refuge in you.
[21] May integrity and uprightness protect me,
because my hope is in you.

[22] Redeem Israel, O God,
from all their troubles!

PRAYER: THANKSGIVING

MY heart rejoices in You, O Lord; my horn is exalted in You. My mouth boasts over my enemies, for I delight in Your salvation. (1 Samuel 2:1) . . . You reached down from on high and took hold of me; You drew me out of deep waters. You delivered me from my strong enemies, from those who hated me, for they were stronger than I. (2 Samuel 22:17–18)

***PAUSE** to offer your own expressions of thanksgiving.*

NT Mark 7:24–8:13

The Faith of a Syrophoenician Woman

[24]Jesus left that place and went to the
vicinity of Tyre.[a] He entered a house and
did not want anyone to know it; yet he
could not keep his presence secret. [25]In
fact, as soon as she heard about him, a woman whose little daughter was possessed by an evil[b] spirit came and fell at his feet.
[26]The woman was a Greek, born in Syrian Phoenicia. She begged Jesus to drive the demon out of her daughter.
[27]"First let the children eat all they want," he told her, "for it is not right to take the children's bread and toss it to their dogs."
[28]"Yes, Lord," she replied, "but even the dogs under the table eat the children's crumbs."
[29]Then he told her, "For such a reply, you may go; the demon has left your daughter."
[30]She went home and found her child lying on the bed, and the demon gone.

The Healing of a Deaf and Mute Man

[31]Then Jesus left the vicinity of Tyre and went through Sidon, down to the Sea of Galilee and into the region of the Decapolis.[c]
[32]There some people brought to him a man who was deaf and could hardly talk, and they begged him to place his hand on the man.
[33]After he took him aside, away from the crowd, Jesus put his fingers into the man's ears. Then he spit and touched the man's tongue.
[34]He looked up to heaven

[a] 24 Many early manuscripts *Tyre and Sidon*
[b] 25 Greek *unclean*
[c] 31 That is, the Ten Cities

and with a deep sigh said to him, *"Ephphatha!"* (which means, "Be opened!"). [35]At this, the man's ears were opened, his tongue was loosened and he began to speak plainly.

[36]Jesus commanded them not to tell anyone. But the more he did so, the more they kept talking about it. [37]People were overwhelmed with amazement. "He has done everything well," they said. "He even makes the deaf hear and the mute speak."

Jesus Feeds the Four Thousand

8 During those days another large crowd gathered. Since they had nothing to eat, Jesus called his disciples to him and said, [2]"I have compassion for these people; they have already been with me three days and have nothing to eat. [3]If I send them home hungry, they will collapse on the way, because some of them have come a long distance."

[4]His disciples answered, "But where in this remote place can anyone get enough bread to feed them?"

[5]"How many loaves do you have?" Jesus asked.

"Seven," they replied.

[6]He told the crowd to sit down on the ground. When he had taken the seven loaves and given thanks, he broke them and gave them to his disciples to set before the people, and they did so. [7]They had a few small fish as well; he gave thanks for them also and told the disciples to distribute them. [8]The people ate and were satisfied. Afterward the disciples picked up seven basketfuls of broken pieces that were left over. [9]About four thousand men were present. And having sent them away, [10]he got into the boat with his disciples and went to the region of Dalmanutha.

[11]The Pharisees came and began to question Jesus. To test him, they asked him for a sign from heaven. [12]He sighed deeply and said, "Why does this generation ask for a miraculous sign? I tell you the truth, no sign will be given to it." [13]Then he left them, got back into the boat and crossed to the other side.

PRAYER: THE WORKS OF GOD

YOU will magnify Yourself and sanctify Yourself, and You will make Yourself known in the sight of many nations, and they will know that You are the Lord. (Ezekiel 38:23) . . . The earth will be filled with the knowledge of Your glory, O Lord, as the waters cover the sea. (Habakkuk 2:14)

***TAKE** a moment to consider the greatness of God's wonderful works.*

YEAR 1 DAY 113

OT Leviticus 26:1-46

Reward for Obedience

26 " 'Do not make idols or set up an image or a sacred stone for yourselves, and do not place a carved stone in your land to bow down before it. I am the LORD your God.

[2]" 'Observe my Sabbaths and have reverence for my sanctuary. I am the LORD.

[3]" 'If you follow my decrees and are careful to obey my commands, [4]I will send you rain in its season, and the ground will yield its crops and the trees of the field their fruit. [5]Your threshing will continue until grape harvest and the grape harvest will continue until planting, and you will eat all the food you want and live in safety in your land.

[6]" 'I will grant peace in the land, and you will lie down and no one will make you afraid. I will remove savage beasts from the land, and the sword will not pass through your country. [7]You will pursue your enemies, and they will fall by the sword before you. [8]Five of you will chase a hundred, and a hundred of you will chase ten thousand, and your enemies will fall by the sword before you.

[9]" 'I will look on you with favor and make you fruitful and increase your num-

bers, and I will keep my covenant with
you. 10You will still be eating last year's
harvest when you will have to move it out
to make room for the new. 11I will put my
dwelling place[a] among you, and I will not
abhor you. 12I will walk among you and
be your God, and you will be my people.
13I am the LORD your God, who brought
you out of Egypt so that you would no
longer be slaves to the Egyptians; I broke
the bars of your yoke and enabled you to
walk with heads held high.

Punishment for Disobedience

14" 'But if you will not listen to me and
carry out all these commands, 15and if you
reject my decrees and abhor my laws and
fail to carry out all my commands and so
violate my covenant, 16then I will do this
to you: I will bring upon you sudden terror, wasting diseases and fever that will
destroy your sight and drain away your
life. You will plant seed in vain, because
your enemies will eat it. 17I will set my
face against you so that you will be defeated by your enemies; those who hate
you will rule over you, and you will flee
even when no one is pursuing you.

18" 'If after all this you will not listen to
me, I will punish you for your sins seven
times over. 19I will break down your stubborn pride and make the sky above you
like iron and the ground beneath you like
bronze. 20Your strength will be spent in
vain, because your soil will not yield its
crops, nor will the trees of the land yield
their fruit.

21" 'If you remain hostile toward me and
refuse to listen to me, I will multiply your
afflictions seven times over, as your sins deserve. 22I will send wild animals against
you, and they will rob you of your children,
destroy your cattle and make you so few in
number that your roads will be deserted.

23" 'If in spite of these things you do not
accept my correction but continue to be
hostile toward me, 24I myself will be hostile toward you and will afflict you for
your sins seven times over. 25And I will
bring the sword upon you to avenge the
breaking of the covenant. When you withdraw into your cities, I will send a plague
among you, and you will be given into enemy hands. 26When I cut off your supply
of bread, ten women will be able to bake
your bread in one oven, and they will dole
out the bread by weight. You will eat, but
you will not be satisfied.

27" 'If in spite of this you still do not listen to me but continue to be hostile toward me, 28then in my anger I will be hostile toward you, and I myself will punish
you for your sins seven times over. 29You
will eat the flesh of your sons and the
flesh of your daughters. 30I will destroy
your high places, cut down your incense
altars and pile your dead bodies on the
lifeless forms of your idols, and I will abhor you. 31I will turn your cities into ruins
and lay waste your sanctuaries, and I will
take no delight in the pleasing aroma of
your offerings. 32I will lay waste the land,
so that your enemies who live there will
be appalled. 33I will scatter you among the
nations and will draw out my sword and
pursue you. Your land will be laid waste,
and your cities will lie in ruins. 34Then the
land will enjoy its sabbath years all the
time that it lies desolate and you are in
the country of your enemies; then the
land will rest and enjoy its sabbaths. 35All
the time that it lies desolate, the land will
have the rest it did not have during the
sabbaths you lived in it.

36" 'As for those of you who are left, I
will make their hearts so fearful in the
lands of their enemies that the sound of
a windblown leaf will put them to flight.
They will run as though fleeing from the
sword, and they will fall, even though no
one is pursuing them. 37They will stumble
over one another as though fleeing from
the sword, even though no one is pursuing them. So you will not be able to stand
before your enemies. 38You will perish
among the nations; the land of your enemies will devour you. 39Those of you who
are left will waste away in the lands of
their enemies because of their sins; also
because of their fathers' sins they will
waste away.

40" 'But if they will confess their sins and
the sins of their fathers—their treachery
against me and their hostility toward me,
41which made me hostile toward them so
that I sent them into the land of their enemies—then when their uncircumcised
hearts are humbled and they pay for their
sin, 42I will remember my covenant with
Jacob and my covenant with Isaac and my
covenant with Abraham, and I will re-

[a] 11 Or *my tabernacle*

member the land. 43 For the land will be deserted by them and will enjoy its sabbaths while it lies desolate without them. They will pay for their sins because they rejected my laws and abhorred my decrees. 44 Yet in spite of this, when they are in the land of their enemies, I will not reject them or abhor them so as to destroy them completely, breaking my covenant with them. I am the LORD their God. 45 But for their sake I will remember the covenant with their ancestors whom I brought out of Egypt in the sight of the nations to be their God. I am the LORD.' "

46 These are the decrees, the laws and the regulations that the LORD established on Mount Sinai between himself and the Israelites through Moses.

PRAYER: ADORATION

YOU are the high and lofty One who inhabits eternity, whose name is holy. You live in a high and holy place but also with the one who is contrite and lowly in spirit. You revive the spirit of the lowly and the hearts of the contrite. (Isaiah 57:15) . . . Like the multitudes who went before Jesus, we also shout: "Hosanna to the Son of David! Blessed is He who comes in the name of the Lord! Hosanna in the highest!" (Matthew 21:9)

***PAUSE** to express your thoughts of praise and worship.*

NT Mark 8:14–38

The Yeast of the Pharisees and Herod

14 The disciples had forgotten to bring bread, except for one loaf they had with them in the boat. 15 "Be careful," Jesus warned them. "Watch out for the yeast of the Pharisees and that of Herod."

16 They discussed this with one another and said, "It is because we have no bread."

17 Aware of their discussion, Jesus asked them: "Why are you talking about having no bread? Do you still not see or understand? Are your hearts hardened? 18 Do you have eyes but fail to see, and ears but fail to hear? And don't you remember? 19 When I broke the five loaves for the five thousand, how many basketfuls of pieces did you pick up?"

"Twelve," they replied.

20 "And when I broke the seven loaves for the four thousand, how many basketfuls of pieces did you pick up?"

They answered, "Seven."

21 He said to them, "Do you still not understand?"

The Healing of a Blind Man at Bethsaida

22 They came to Bethsaida, and some people brought a blind man and begged Jesus to touch him. 23 He took the blind man by the hand and led him outside the village. When he had spit on the man's eyes and put his hands on him, Jesus asked, "Do you see anything?"

24 He looked up and said, "I see people; they look like trees walking around."

25 Once more Jesus put his hands on the man's eyes. Then his eyes were opened, his sight was restored, and he saw everything clearly. 26 Jesus sent him home, saying, "Don't go into the village.[a]"

Peter's Confession of Christ

27 Jesus and his disciples went on to the villages around Caesarea Philippi. On the way he asked them, "Who do people say I am?"

28 They replied, "Some say John the Baptist; others say Elijah; and still others, one of the prophets."

29 "But what about you?" he asked. "Who do you say I am?"

Peter answered, "You are the Christ.[b]"

30 Jesus warned them not to tell anyone about him.

Jesus Predicts His Death

31 He then began to teach them that the Son of Man must suffer many things and

[a] 26 Some manuscripts *Don't go and tell anyone in the village* [b] 29 Or *Messiah.* "The Christ" (Greek) and "the Messiah" (Hebrew) both mean "the Anointed One."

be rejected by the elders, chief priests and teachers of the law, and that he must be killed and after three days rise again. [32]He spoke plainly about this, and Peter took him aside and began to rebuke him.

[33]But when Jesus turned and looked at his disciples, he rebuked Peter. "Get behind me, Satan!" he said. "You do not have in mind the things of God, but the things of men."

[34]Then he called the crowd to him along with his disciples and said: "If anyone would come after me, he must deny himself and take up his cross and follow me. [35]For whoever wants to save his life[c] will lose it, but whoever loses his life for me and for the gospel will save it. [36]What good is it for a man to gain the whole world, yet forfeit his soul? [37]Or what can a man give in exchange for his soul? [38]If anyone is ashamed of me and my words in this adulterous and sinful generation, the Son of Man will be ashamed of him when he comes in his Father's glory with the holy angels."

[c] 35 The Greek word means either *life* or *soul*; also in verse 36.

PRAYER: MY RELATIONSHIP TO GOD

O GOD, You are my refuge and strength, an ever-present help in trouble. Therefore I will not fear, though the earth give way and the mountains slip into the heart of the sea. (Psalm 46:1–2) . . . I will not fear, for You are with me; I will not be dismayed, for You are my God. You will strengthen me and help me; You will uphold me with Your righteous right hand. For You are the Lord my God, You take hold of my right hand and say to me, "Do not fear; I will help you." (Isaiah 41:10, 13)

***PAUSE** to thank God for the relationship that you enjoy with Him in Jesus Christ.*

YEAR 1
DAY 114

OT Leviticus 27:1–34

Redeeming What Is the LORD's

27 The LORD said to Moses, [2]"Speak to the Israelites and say to them: 'If anyone makes a special vow to dedicate persons to the LORD by giving equivalent values, [3]set the value of a male between the ages of twenty and sixty at fifty shekels[a] of silver, according to the sanctuary shekel[b]; [4]and if it is a female, set her value at thirty shekels.[c] [5]If it is a person between the ages of five and twenty, set the value of a male at twenty shekels[d] and of a female at ten shekels.[e] [6]If it is a person between one month and five years, set the value of a male at five shekels[f] of silver and that of a female at three shekels[g] of silver. [7]If it is a person sixty years old or more, set the value of a male at fifteen shekels[h] and of a female at ten shekels. [8]If anyone making the vow is too poor to pay the specified amount, he is to present the person to the priest, who will set the value for him according to what the man making the vow can afford.

[9]" 'If what he vowed is an animal that is acceptable as an offering to the LORD, such an animal given to the LORD becomes holy. [10]He must not exchange it or substitute a good one for a bad one, or a bad one for a good one; if he should substitute one animal for another, both it and the substitute become holy. [11]If what he vowed is a ceremonially unclean animal—one that is not acceptable as an offering to the LORD—the animal must be presented to the priest, [12]who will judge

[a] 3 That is, about 1 1/4 pounds (about 0.6 kilogram); also in verse 16 [b] 3 That is, about 2/5 ounce (about 11.5 grams); also in verse 25 [c] 4 That is, about 12 ounces (about 0.3 kilogram) [d] 5 That is, about 8 ounces (about 0.2 kilogram) [e] 5 That is, about 4 ounces (about 110 grams); also in verse 7 [f] 6 That is, about 2 ounces (about 55 grams) [g] 6 That is, about 1 1/4 ounces (about 35 grams) [h] 7 That is, about 6 ounces (about 170 grams)

its quality as good or bad. Whatever value the priest then sets, that is what it will
be. 13If the owner wishes to redeem the
animal, he must add a fifth to its value.
14" 'If a man dedicates his house as
something holy to the LORD, the priest will
judge its quality as good or bad. Whatever
value the priest then sets, so it will remain.
15If the man who dedicates his house redeems it, he must add a fifth to its value,
and the house will again become his.
16" 'If a man dedicates to the LORD part
of his family land, its value is to be set according to the amount of seed required for
it—fifty shekels of silver to a homer[i] of
barley seed. 17If he dedicates his field during the Year of Jubilee, the value that has
been set remains. 18But if he dedicates his
field after the Jubilee, the priest will determine the value according to the number
of years that remain until the next Year of
Jubilee, and its set value will be reduced.
19If the man who dedicates the field wishes
to redeem it, he must add a fifth to its value, and the field will again become his.
20If, however, he does not redeem the field,
or if he has sold it to someone else, it can
never be redeemed. 21When the field is released in the Jubilee, it will become holy,
like a field devoted to the LORD; it will become the property of the priests.[j]
22" 'If a man dedicates to the LORD a
field he has bought, which is not part of
his family land, 23the priest will determine
its value up to the Year of Jubilee, and the
man must pay its value on that day as
something holy to the LORD. 24In the Year
of Jubilee the field will revert to the person from whom he bought it, the one
whose land it was. 25Every value is to be
set according to the sanctuary shekel,
twenty gerahs to the shekel.
26" 'No one, however, may dedicate the
firstborn of an animal, since the firstborn
already belongs to the LORD; whether an
ox[k] or a sheep, it is the LORD's. 27If it is one
of the unclean animals, he may buy it
back at its set value, adding a fifth of the
value to it. If he does not redeem it, it is
to be sold at its set value.
28" 'But nothing that a man owns and
devotes[l] to the LORD—whether man or animal or family land—may be sold or redeemed; everything so devoted is most
holy to the LORD.
29" 'No person devoted to destruction[m]
may be ransomed; he must be put to death.
30" 'A tithe of everything from the land,
whether grain from the soil or fruit from the
trees, belongs to the LORD; it is holy to the
LORD. 31If a man redeems any of his tithe, he
must add a fifth of the value to it. 32The entire tithe of the herd and flock—every tenth
animal that passes under the shepherd's
rod—will be holy to the LORD. 33He must
not pick out the good from the bad or make
any substitution. If he does make a substitution, both the animal and its substitute
become holy and cannot be redeemed.' "

34These are the commands the LORD gave
Moses on Mount Sinai for the Israelites.

[i] 16 That is, probably about 6 bushels (about 220 liters) [j] 21 Or *priest* [k] 26 The Hebrew word can include both male and female. [l] 28 The Hebrew term refers to the irrevocable giving over of things or persons to the LORD. [m] 29 The Hebrew term refers to the irrevocable giving over of things or persons to the LORD, often by totally destroying them.

PRAYER: CONFESSION

WE have sinned with our fathers; we have committed iniquity and acted wickedly. (Psalm 106:6)

***ASK** the Spirit to search your heart and reveal any areas of unconfessed sin. Acknowledge these to the Lord and thank Him for His forgiveness.*

NT Mark 9:1–32

9 And he said to them, "I tell you the
truth, some who are standing here will
not taste death before they see the kingdom of God come with power."

The Transfiguration

2After six days Jesus took Peter, James
and John with him and led them up a high
mountain, where they were all alone. There

he was transfigured before them. 3His
clothes became dazzling white, whiter than
anyone in the world could bleach them.
4And there appeared before them Elijah
and Moses, who were talking with Jesus.
5Peter said to Jesus, "Rabbi, it is good
for us to be here. Let us put up three shelters—one for you, one for Moses and one
for Elijah." 6(He did not know what to
say, they were so frightened.)
7Then a cloud appeared and enveloped
them, and a voice came from the cloud:
"This is my Son, whom I love. Listen to
him!"
8Suddenly, when they looked around,
they no longer saw anyone with them except Jesus.
9As they were coming down the mountain, Jesus gave them orders not to tell
anyone what they had seen until the Son
of Man had risen from the dead. 10They
kept the matter to themselves, discussing
what "rising from the dead" meant.
11And they asked him, "Why do the
teachers of the law say that Elijah must
come first?"
12Jesus replied, "To be sure, Elijah does
come first, and restores all things. Why
then is it written that the Son of Man
must suffer much and be rejected? 13But I
tell you, Elijah has come, and they have
done to him everything they wished, just
as it is written about him."

The Healing of a Boy With an Evil Spirit

14When they came to the other disciples, they saw a large crowd around them
and the teachers of the law arguing with
them. 15As soon as all the people saw
Jesus, they were overwhelmed with wonder and ran to greet him.
16"What are you arguing with them
about?" he asked.
17A man in the crowd answered,
"Teacher, I brought you my son, who is
possessed by a spirit that has robbed him
of speech. 18Whenever it seizes him, it
throws him to the ground. He foams at
the mouth, gnashes his teeth and becomes rigid. I asked your disciples to drive
out the spirit, but they could not."
19"O unbelieving generation," Jesus
replied, "how long shall I stay with you?
How long shall I put up with you? Bring
the boy to me."
20So they brought him. When the spirit
saw Jesus, it immediately threw the boy
into a convulsion. He fell to the ground
and rolled around, foaming at the mouth.
21Jesus asked the boy's father, "How
long has he been like this?"
"From childhood," he answered. 22"It
has often thrown him into fire or water to
kill him. But if you can do anything, take
pity on us and help us."
23" 'If you can'?" said Jesus. "Everything
is possible for him who believes."
24Immediately the boy's father exclaimed, "I do believe; help me overcome
my unbelief!"
25When Jesus saw that a crowd was running to the scene, he rebuked the evil[a]
spirit. "You deaf and mute spirit," he said,
"I command you, come out of him and
never enter him again."
26The spirit shrieked, convulsed him violently and came out. The boy looked so
much like a corpse that many said, "He's
dead." 27But Jesus took him by the hand
and lifted him to his feet, and he
stood up
28After Jesus had gone indoors, his disciples asked him privately, "Why couldn't
we drive it out?"
29He replied, "This kind can come out
only by prayer.[b]"
30They left that place and passed
through Galilee. Jesus did not want anyone to know where they were, 31because he
was teaching his disciples. He said to
them, "The Son of Man is going to be betrayed into the hands of men. They will
kill him, and after three days he will rise."
32But they did not understand what he
meant and were afraid to ask him about it.

[a] 25 Greek *unclean* [b] 29 Some manuscripts *prayer and fasting*

PRAYER: THE CHARACTER I WANT TO CULTIVATE

TO fear You, O Lord, is the beginning of knowledge, but fools despise wisdom and discipline. (Proverbs 1:7) . . . Lord, You give wisdom; from Your mouth come knowledge and understanding. You store up

sound wisdom for the upright; You are a shield to those who walk in integrity, guarding the paths of the just and protecting the way of Your saints. Then I will understand righteousness and justice and honesty—every good path, for wisdom will enter my heart, and knowledge will be pleasant to my soul. Discretion will protect me, and understanding will guard me. (Proverbs 2:6–11)

***TAKE** a moment to ask the Lord for the grace to grow in godly character.*

YEAR 1 DAY 115

OT Numbers 1:1-54

The Census

1 The LORD spoke to Moses in the Tent of Meeting in the Desert of Sinai on the first day of the second month of the second year after the Israelites came out of Egypt. He said: [2]"Take a census of the whole Israelite community by their clans and families, listing every man by name, one by one. [3]You and Aaron are to number by their divisions all the men in Israel twenty years old or more who are able to serve in the army. [4]One man from each tribe, each the head of his family, is to help you. [5]These are the names of the men who are to assist you:

from Reuben, Elizur son of Shedeur;
[6]from Simeon, Shelumiel son of Zurishaddai;
[7]from Judah, Nahshon son of Amminadab;
[8]from Issachar, Nethanel son of Zuar;
[9]from Zebulun, Eliab son of Helon;
[10]from the sons of Joseph:
from Ephraim, Elishama son of Ammihud;
from Manasseh, Gamaliel son of Pedahzur;
[11]from Benjamin, Abidan son of Gideoni;
[12]from Dan, Ahiezer son of Ammishaddai;
[13]from Asher, Pagiel son of Ocran;
[14]from Gad, Eliasaph son of Deuel;
[15]from Naphtali, Ahira son of Enan."

[16]These were the men appointed from the community, the leaders of their ancestral tribes. They were the heads of the clans of Israel.

[17]Moses and Aaron took these men whose names had been given, [18]and they called the whole community together on the first day of the second month. The people indicated their ancestry by their clans and families, and the men twenty years old or more were listed by name, one by one, [19]as the LORD commanded Moses. And so he counted them in the Desert of Sinai:

[20]From the descendants of Reuben the firstborn son of Israel:
All the men twenty years old or more who were able to serve in the army were listed by name, one by one, according to the records of their clans and families. [21]The number from the tribe of Reuben was 46,500.

[22]From the descendants of Simeon:
All the men twenty years old or more who were able to serve in the army were counted and listed by name, one by one, according to the records of their clans and families. [23]The number from the tribe of Simeon was 59,300.

[24]From the descendants of Gad:
All the men twenty years old or more who were able to serve in the army were listed by name, according to the records of their clans and families. [25]The number from the tribe of Gad was 45,650.

[26]From the descendants of Judah:
All the men twenty years old or more who were able to serve in the army were listed by name, according to the records of their clans and families. [27]The number from the tribe of Judah was 74,600.

[28]From the descendants of Issachar:
All the men twenty years old or more who were able to serve in the army were listed by name, according-

ing to the records of their clans and families. 29The number from the tribe of Issachar was 54,400.

30From the descendants of Zebulun:
All the men twenty years old or more who were able to serve in the army were listed by name, according to the records of their clans and families. 31The number from the tribe of Zebulun was 57,400.

32From the sons of Joseph:
From the descendants of Ephraim:
All the men twenty years old or more who were able to serve in the army were listed by name, according to the records of their clans and families. 33The number from the tribe of Ephraim was 40,500.
34From the descendants of Manasseh:
All the men twenty years old or more who were able to serve in the army were listed by name, according to the records of their clans and families. 35The number from the tribe of Manasseh was 32,200.

36From the descendants of Benjamin:
All the men twenty years old or more who were able to serve in the army were listed by name, according to the records of their clans and families. 37The number from the tribe of Benjamin was 35,400.

38From the descendants of Dan:
All the men twenty years old or more who were able to serve in the army were listed by name, according to the records of their clans and families. 39The number from the tribe of Dan was 62,700.

40From the descendants of Asher:
All the men twenty years old or more who were able to serve in the army were listed by name, according to the records of their clans and families. 41The number from the tribe of Asher was 41,500.

42From the descendants of Naphtali:
All the men twenty years old or more who were able to serve in the army were listed by name, according to the records of their clans and families. 43The number from the tribe of Naphtali was 53,400.

44These were the men counted by Moses and Aaron and the twelve leaders of Israel, each one representing his family.
45All the Israelites twenty years old or more who were able to serve in Israel's army were counted according to their families. 46The total number was 603,550.
47The families of the tribe of Levi, however, were not counted along with the others. 48The LORD had said to Moses:
49"You must not count the tribe of Levi or include them in the census of the other Israelites. 50Instead, appoint the Levites to be in charge of the tabernacle of the Testimony—over all its furnishings and everything belonging to it. They are to carry the tabernacle and all its furnishings; they are to take care of it and encamp around it. 51Whenever the tabernacle is to move, the Levites are to take it down, and whenever the tabernacle is to be set up, the Levites shall do it. Anyone else who goes near it shall be put to death. 52The Israelites are to set up their tents by divisions, each man in his own camp under his own standard. 53The Levites, however, are to set up their tents around the tabernacle of the Testimony so that wrath will not fall on the Israelite community. The Levites are to be responsible for the care of the tabernacle of the Testimony."
54The Israelites did all this just as the LORD commanded Moses.

PRAYER: RENEWAL

YOU are the Lord my God; may I consecrate myself and be holy because You are holy. You are the Lord who brought Your people up out of Egypt to be their God; therefore may I be holy, because You are holy. (Leviticus 11:44–45; 19:2) . . . As an obedient child, may I

not conform myself to the former lusts I had when I lived in ignorance, but as You who called me are holy, so may I be holy in all my conduct, because it is written: "You shall be holy, for I am holy." (1 Peter 1:14–16)

PAUSE *to add your own prayers for personal renewal.*

NT Mark 9:33–10:12

Who Is the Greatest?

33They came to Capernaum. When he was in the house, he asked them, "What were you arguing about on the road?" 34But they kept quiet because on the way they had argued about who was the greatest.

35Sitting down, Jesus called the Twelve and said, "If anyone wants to be first, he must be the very last, and the servant of all."

36He took a little child and had him stand among them. Taking him in his arms, he said to them, 37"Whoever welcomes one of these little children in my name welcomes me; and whoever welcomes me does not welcome me but the one who sent me."

Whoever Is Not Against Us Is for Us

38"Teacher," said John, "we saw a man driving out demons in your name and we told him to stop, because he was not one of us."

39"Do not stop him," Jesus said. "No one who does a miracle in my name can in the next moment say anything bad about me, 40for whoever is not against us is for us. 41I tell you the truth, anyone who gives you a cup of water in my name because you belong to Christ will certainly not lose his reward.

Causing to Sin

42"And if anyone causes one of these little ones who believe in me to sin, it would be better for him to be thrown into the sea with a large millstone tied around his neck. 43If your hand causes you to sin, cut it off. It is better for you to enter life maimed than with two hands to go into hell, where the fire never goes out.[a] 45And if your foot causes you to sin, cut it off. It is better for you to enter life crippled than to have two feet and be thrown into hell.[b] 47And if your eye causes you to sin, pluck it out. It is better for you to enter the kingdom of God with one eye than to have two eyes and be thrown into hell, 48where

" 'their worm does not die,
and the fire is not quenched.'[c]

49Everyone will be salted with fire.

50"Salt is good, but if it loses its saltiness, how can you make it salty again? Have salt in yourselves, and be at peace with each other."

Divorce

10 Jesus then left that place and went into the region of Judea and across the Jordan. Again crowds of people came to him, and as was his custom, he taught them.

2Some Pharisees came and tested him by asking, "Is it lawful for a man to divorce his wife?"

3"What did Moses command you?" he replied.

4They said, "Moses permitted a man to write a certificate of divorce and send her away."

5"It was because your hearts were hard that Moses wrote you this law," Jesus replied. 6"But at the beginning of creation God 'made them male and female.'[d] 7'For this reason a man will leave his father and mother and be united to his wife,[e] 8and the two will become one flesh.'[f] So they are no longer two, but one. 9Therefore what God has joined together, let man not separate."

10When they were in the house again, the disciples asked Jesus about this. 11He answered, "Anyone who divorces his wife and marries another woman commits adultery against her. 12And if she divorces her husband and marries another man, she commits adultery."

[a] 43 Some manuscripts *out,* 44*where* / " *'their worm does not die,* / *and the fire is not quenched.'*
[b] 45 Some manuscripts *hell,* 46*where* / " *'their worm does not die,* / *and the fire is not quenched.'*
[c] 48 Isaiah 66:24 [d] 6 Gen. 1:27 [e] 7 Some early manuscripts do not have *and be united to his wife.*
[f] 8 Gen. 2:24

PRAYER: MY RELATIONSHIP TO OTHERS

AS I give, it will be given to me; a good measure, pressed down, shaken together and running over will be poured into my lap. For with the measure I use, it will be measured back to me. (Luke 6:38)

***PAUSE** to review your relationships with others and to commit them to the Lord.*

YEAR 1 DAY 116

OT Proverbs 5

Warning Against Adultery

5 My son, pay attention to my wisdom,
listen well to my words of insight,
2 that you may maintain discretion
and your lips may preserve knowledge.
3 For the lips of an adulteress drip honey,
and her speech is smoother than oil;
4 but in the end she is bitter as gall,
sharp as a double-edged sword.
5 Her feet go down to death;
her steps lead straight to the grave.[a]
6 She gives no thought to the way of life;
her paths are crooked, but she knows it not.

7 Now then, my sons, listen to me;
do not turn aside from what I say.
8 Keep to a path far from her,
do not go near the door of her house,
9 lest you give your best strength to others
and your years to one who is cruel,
10 lest strangers feast on your wealth
and your toil enrich another man's house.
11 At the end of your life you will groan,
when your flesh and body are spent.
12 You will say, "How I hated discipline!
How my heart spurned correction!
13 I would not obey my teachers
or listen to my instructors.
14 I have come to the brink of utter ruin
in the midst of the whole assembly."

15 Drink water from your own cistern,
running water from your own well.
16 Should your springs overflow in the streets,
your streams of water in the public squares?
17 Let them be yours alone,
never to be shared with strangers.
18 May your fountain be blessed,
and may you rejoice in the wife of your youth.
19 A loving doe, a graceful deer—
may her breasts satisfy you always,
may you ever be captivated by her love.
20 Why be captivated, my son, by an adulteress?
Why embrace the bosom of another man's wife?

21 For a man's ways are in full view of the LORD,
and he examines all his paths.
22 The evil deeds of a wicked man ensnare him;
the cords of his sin hold him fast.
23 He will die for lack of discipline,
led astray by his own great folly.

[a] 5 Hebrew *Sheol*

PRAYER: PETITION

O LORD, I pray, let Your ear be attentive to the prayer of Your servant and to the prayer of Your servants who delight in revering Your name. (Nehemiah 1:11)

***PAUSE** here to petition God for spiritual insight so that you might have understanding of His Word. Ask for insight into your identity in Jesus Christ: that you might know who you are, what direction your life should take and what His purpose for your life is. Offer prayers regarding your activities for this day and any special concerns you may have.*

NT Mark 10:13–52

The Little Children and Jesus

13 People were bringing little children to Jesus to have him touch them, but the disciples rebuked them. 14 When Jesus saw this, he was indignant. He said to them, "Let the little children come to me, and do not hinder them, for the kingdom of God belongs to such as these. 15 I tell you the truth, anyone who will not receive the kingdom of God like a little child will never enter it." 16 And he took the children in his arms, put his hands on them and blessed them.

The Rich Young Man

17 As Jesus started on his way, a man ran up to him and fell on his knees before him. "Good teacher," he asked, "what must I do to inherit eternal life?"

18 "Why do you call me good?" Jesus answered. "No one is good—except God alone. 19 You know the commandments: 'Do not murder, do not commit adultery, do not steal, do not give false testimony, do not defraud, honor your father and mother.'[a]"

20 "Teacher," he declared, "all these I have kept since I was a boy."

21 Jesus looked at him and loved him. "One thing you lack," he said. "Go, sell everything you have and give to the poor, and you will have treasure in heaven. Then come, follow me."

22 At this the man's face fell. He went away sad, because he had great wealth.

23 Jesus looked around and said to his disciples, "How hard it is for the rich to enter the kingdom of God!"

24 The disciples were amazed at his words. But Jesus said again, "Children, how hard it is[b] to enter the kingdom of God! 25 It is easier for a camel to go through the eye of a needle than for a rich man to enter the kingdom of God."

26 The disciples were even more amazed, and said to each other, "Who then can be saved?"

27 Jesus looked at them and said, "With man this is impossible, but not with God; all things are possible with God."

28 Peter said to him, "We have left everything to follow you!"

29 "I tell you the truth," Jesus replied, "no one who has left home or brothers or sisters or mother or father or children or fields for me and the gospel 30 will fail to receive a hundred times as much in this present age (homes, brothers, sisters, mothers, children and fields—and with them, persecutions) and in the age to come, eternal life. 31 But many who are first will be last, and the last first."

Jesus Again Predicts His Death

32 They were on their way up to Jerusalem, with Jesus leading the way, and the disciples were astonished, while those who followed were afraid. Again he took the Twelve aside and told them what was going to happen to him. 33 "We are going up to Jerusalem," he said, "and the Son of Man will be betrayed to the chief priests and teachers of the law. They will condemn him to death and will hand him over to the Gentiles, 34 who will mock him and spit on him, flog him and kill him. Three days later he will rise."

The Request of James and John

35 Then James and John, the sons of Zebedee, came to him. "Teacher," they

[a] *19* Exodus 20:12–16; Deut. 5:16–20 [b] *24* Some manuscripts *is for those who trust in riches*

said, "we want you to do for us whatever
we ask."
36 "What do you want me to do for
you?" he asked.
37 They replied, "Let one of us sit at your
right and the other at your left in your glory."
38 "You don't know what you are asking," Jesus said. "Can you drink the cup I
drink or be baptized with the baptism I
am baptized with?"
39 "We can," they answered.
Jesus said to them, "You will drink the
cup I drink and be baptized with the baptism I am baptized with, 40 but to sit at my
right or left is not for me to grant. These
places belong to those for whom they
have been prepared."
41 When the ten heard about this, they
became indignant with James and John.
42 Jesus called them together and said,
"You know that those who are regarded as
rulers of the Gentiles lord it over them,
and their high officials exercise authority
over them. 43 Not so with you. Instead,
whoever wants to become great among
you must be your servant, 44 and whoever
wants to be first must be slave of all. 45 For
even the Son of Man did not come to be
served, but to serve, and to give his life as
a ransom for many."

Blind Bartimaeus Receives His Sight

46 Then they came to Jericho. As Jesus
and his disciples, together with a large
crowd, were leaving the city, a blind man,
Bartimaeus (that is, the Son of Timaeus),
was sitting by the roadside begging.
47 When he heard that it was Jesus of Nazareth, he began to shout, "Jesus, Son of
David, have mercy on me!"
48 Many rebuked him and told him to
be quiet, but he shouted all the more,
"Son of David, have mercy on me!"
49 Jesus stopped and said, "Call him."
So they called to the blind man, "Cheer
up! On your feet! He's calling you."
50 Throwing his cloak aside, he jumped to
his feet and came to Jesus.
51 "What do you want me to do for
you?" Jesus asked him.
The blind man said, "Rabbi, I want to
see."
52 "Go," said Jesus, "your faith has
healed you." Immediately he received his
sight and followed Jesus along the road.

PRAYER: THE ATTRIBUTES OF GOD

WHERE does wisdom come from? Where does understanding dwell? It is hidden from the eyes of every living thing and concealed from the birds of the air. Destruction and Death say, "Only a rumor of it has reached our ears." You understand its way, O God, and You know its place. For You look to the ends of the earth and see everything under the heavens.

(Job 28:20–24)

PAUSE *to reflect on these affirmations about the person, powers and perfection of God.*

YEAR 1
DAY 117

OT Numbers 2:1–34

The Arrangement of the Tribal Camps

2 The LORD said to Moses and Aaron:
2 "The Israelites are to camp around the
Tent of Meeting some distance from it,
each man under his standard with the
banners of his family."

3 On the east, toward the sunrise,
the divisions of the camp of Judah
are to encamp under their standard.
The leader of the people of Judah is
Nahshon son of Amminadab. 4 His
division numbers 74,600.
5 The tribe of Issachar will camp
next to them. The leader of the people of Issachar is Nethanel son of
Zuar. 6 His division numbers 54,400.
7 The tribe of Zebulun will be next.
The leader of the people of Zebulun

is Eliab son of Helon. [8]His division numbers 57,400.

[9]All the men assigned to the camp of Judah, according to their divisions, number 186,400. They will set out first.

[10]On the south will be the divisions of the camp of Reuben under their standard. The leader of the people of Reuben is Elizur son of Shedeur. [11]His division numbers 46,500.

[12]The tribe of Simeon will camp next to them. The leader of the people of Simeon is Shelumiel son of Zurishaddai. [13]His division numbers 59,300.

[14]The tribe of Gad will be next. The leader of the people of Gad is Eliasaph son of Deuel.[a] [15]His division numbers 45,650.

[16]All the men assigned to the camp of Reuben, according to their divisions, number 151,450. They will set out second.

[17]Then the Tent of Meeting and the camp of the Levites will set out in the middle of the camps. They will set out in the same order as they encamp, each in his own place under his standard.

[18]On the west will be the divisions of the camp of Ephraim under their standard. The leader of the people of Ephraim is Elishama son of Ammihud. [19]His division numbers 40,500.

[20]The tribe of Manasseh will be next to them. The leader of the people of Manasseh is Gamaliel son of Pedahzur. [21]His division numbers 32,200.

[22]The tribe of Benjamin will be next. The leader of the people of Benjamin is Abidan son of Gideoni. [23]His division numbers 35,400.

[24]All the men assigned to the camp of Ephraim, according to their divisions, number 108,100. They will set out third.

[25]On the north will be the divisions of the camp of Dan, under their standard. The leader of the people of Dan is Ahiezer son of Ammishaddai. [26]His division numbers 62,700.

[27]The tribe of Asher will camp next to them. The leader of the people of Asher is Pagiel son of Ocran. [28]His division numbers 41,500.

[29]The tribe of Naphtali will be next. The leader of the people of Naphtali is Ahira son of Enan. [30]His division numbers 53,400.

[31]All the men assigned to the camp of Dan number 157,600. They will set out last, under their standards.

[32]These are the Israelites, counted according to their families. All those in the camps, by their divisions, number 603,550. [33]The Levites, however, were not counted along with the other Israelites, as the LORD commanded Moses.

[34]So the Israelites did everything the LORD commanded Moses; that is the way they encamped under their standards, and that is the way they set out, each with his clan and family.

[a] *14* Many manuscripts of the Masoretic Text, Samaritan Pentateuch and Vulgate (see also Num. 1:14); most manuscripts of the Masoretic Text *Reuel*

PRAYER: INTERCESSION

LORD Jesus, we are encouraged by these words You prayed for all who would believe in You: "I ask that all of them may be one, Father, just as You are in Me and I am in You, that they also may be in Us, that the world may believe that You sent Me. And the glory that You gave Me I have given to them, that they may be one, just as We are one: I in them, and You in Me, that they may be perfected in one, that the world may know that You have sent Me and have loved them, even as You have loved Me."

(John 17:21–23)

TAKE *a few moments to intercede on behalf of other believers, such as your personal friends, those in ministry and those who are oppressed and in need.*

NT Mark 11:1–33

The Triumphal Entry

11 As they approached Jerusalem and
came to Bethphage and Bethany at the
Mount of Olives, Jesus sent two of his disciples, 2saying to them, "Go to the village
ahead of you, and just as you enter it, you
will find a colt tied there, which no one
has ever ridden. Untie it and bring it here.
3If anyone asks you, 'Why are you doing
this?' tell him, 'The Lord needs it and will
send it back here shortly.' "
4They went and found a colt outside in
the street, tied at a doorway. As they untied it, 5some people standing there asked,
"What are you doing, untying that colt?"
6They answered as Jesus had told them to,
and the people let them go. 7When they
brought the colt to Jesus and threw their
cloaks over it, he sat on it. 8Many people
spread their cloaks on the road, while others spread branches they had cut in the
fields. 9Those who went ahead and those
who followed shouted,

"Hosanna![a]"

"Blessed is he who comes in the name
of the Lord!"[b]

10"Blessed is the coming kingdom of
our father David!"

"Hosanna in the highest!"

11Jesus entered Jerusalem and went to
the temple. He looked around at everything, but since it was already late, he
went out to Bethany with the Twelve.

Jesus Clears the Temple

12The next day as they were leaving
Bethany, Jesus was hungry. 13Seeing in the
distance a fig tree in leaf, he went to find
out if it had any fruit. When he reached
it, he found nothing but leaves, because it
was not the season for figs. 14Then he said
to the tree, "May no one ever eat fruit
from you again." And his disciples heard
him say it.
15On reaching Jerusalem, Jesus entered
the temple area and began driving out
those who were buying and selling there.
He overturned the tables of the money
changers and the benches of those selling
doves, 16and would not allow anyone to
carry merchandise through the temple
courts. 17And as he taught them, he said,
"Is it not written:

" 'My house will be called
a house of prayer for all nations'[c]?

But you have made it 'a den of robbers.'[d]"
18The chief priests and the teachers of
the law heard this and began looking for
a way to kill him, for they feared him, because the whole crowd was amazed at his
teaching.
19When evening came, they[e] went out of
the city.

The Withered Fig Tree

20In the morning, as they went along,
they saw the fig tree withered from the
roots. 21Peter remembered and said to
Jesus, "Rabbi, look! The fig tree you
cursed has withered!"
22"Have[f] faith in God," Jesus answered.
23"I tell you the truth, if anyone says to
this mountain, 'Go, throw yourself into
the sea,' and does not doubt in his heart
but believes that what he says will happen, it will be done for him. 24Therefore I
tell you, whatever you ask for in prayer,
believe that you have received it, and it
will be yours. 25And when you stand praying, if you hold anything against anyone,
forgive him, so that your Father in heav-
en may forgive you your sins.[g]"

The Authority of Jesus Questioned

27They arrived again in Jerusalem, and
while Jesus was walking in the temple
courts, the chief priests, the teachers of the
law and the elders came to him. 28"By
what authority are you doing these
things?" they asked. "And who gave you
authority to do this?"
29Jesus replied, "I will ask you one question. Answer me, and I will tell you by
what authority I am doing these things.
30John's baptism—was it from heaven, or
from men? Tell me!"
31They discussed it among themselves
and said, "If we say, 'From heaven,' he will

[a] 9 A Hebrew expression meaning "Save!" which became an exclamation of praise; also in verse 10 [b] 9 Psalm 118:25,26 [c] 17 Isaiah 56:7 [d] 17 Jer. 7:11 [e] 19 Some early manuscripts *he* [f] 22 Some early manuscripts *If you have* [g] 25 Some manuscripts *sins.* [26]*But if you do not forgive, neither will your Father who is in heaven forgive your sins.*

ask, 'Then why didn't you believe him?' [32]But if we say, 'From men' . . . ." (They feared the people, for everyone held that John really was a prophet.)

[33]So they answered Jesus, "We don't know."

Jesus said, "Neither will I tell you by what authority I am doing these things."

PRAYER: THE WORKS OF GOD

THE light has come into the world, but people loved darkness rather than light because their deeds were evil. For those who do evil hate the light and will not come into the light, for fear that their deeds will be exposed. But those who practice the truth come into the light, so that their deeds may be clearly seen as having been done through You, O God.
(John 3:19–21)

TAKE *a moment to consider the greatness of God's wonderful works.*

YEAR 1
DAY 118

OT Numbers 3:1-51

The Levites

3 This is the account of the family of Aaron and Moses at the time the LORD talked with Moses on Mount Sinai.

[2]The names of the sons of Aaron were Nadab the firstborn and Abihu, Eleazar and Ithamar. [3]Those were the names of Aaron's sons, the anointed priests, who were ordained to serve as priests. [4]Nadab and Abihu, however, fell dead before the LORD when they made an offering with unauthorized fire before him in the Desert of Sinai. They had no sons; so only Eleazar and Ithamar served as priests during the lifetime of their father Aaron.

[5]The LORD said to Moses, [6]"Bring the tribe of Levi and present them to Aaron the priest to assist him. [7]They are to perform duties for him and for the whole community at the Tent of Meeting by doing the work of the tabernacle. [8]They are to take care of all the furnishings of the Tent of Meeting, fulfilling the obligations of the Israelites by doing the work of the tabernacle. [9]Give the Levites to Aaron and his sons; they are the Israelites who are to be given wholly to him.[a] [10]Appoint Aaron and his sons to serve as priests; anyone else who approaches the sanctuary must be put to death."

[11]The LORD also said to Moses, [12]"I have taken the Levites from among the Israelites in place of the first male offspring of every Israelite woman. The Levites are mine, [13]for all the firstborn are mine. When I struck down all the firstborn in Egypt, I set apart for myself every firstborn in Israel, whether man or animal. They are to be mine. I am the LORD."

[14]The LORD said to Moses in the Desert of Sinai, [15]"Count the Levites by their families and clans. Count every male a month old or more." [16]So Moses counted them, as he was commanded by the word of the LORD.

[17]These were the names of the sons of Levi:
Gershon, Kohath and Merari.
[18]These were the names of the Gershonite clans:
Libni and Shimei.
[19]The Kohathite clans:
Amram, Izhar, Hebron and Uzziel.
[20]The Merarite clans:
Mahli and Mushi.

These were the Levite clans, according to their families.

[21]To Gershon belonged the clans of the Libnites and Shimeites; these were the Gershonite clans. [22]The number of all the males a month old or more who were counted was 7,500. [23]The Gershonite clans

[a] 9 Most manuscripts of the Masoretic Text; some manuscripts of the Masoretic Text, Samaritan Pentateuch and Septuagint (see also Num. 8:16) *to me*

were to camp on the west, behind the tabernacle. [24]The leader of the families of the Gershonites was Eliasaph son of Lael. [25]At the Tent of Meeting the Gershonites were responsible for the care of the tabernacle and tent, its coverings, the curtain at the entrance to the Tent of Meeting, [26]the curtains of the courtyard, the curtain at the entrance to the courtyard surrounding the tabernacle and altar, and the ropes—and everything related to their use.

[27]To Kohath belonged the clans of the Amramites, Izharites, Hebronites and Uzzielites; these were the Kohathite clans. [28]The number of all the males a month old or more was 8,600.[b] The Kohathites were responsible for the care of the sanctuary. [29]The Kohathite clans were to camp on the south side of the tabernacle. [30]The leader of the families of the Kohathite clans was Elizaphan son of Uzziel. [31]They were responsible for the care of the ark, the table, the lampstand, the altars, the articles of the sanctuary used in ministering, the curtain, and everything related to their use. [32]The chief leader of the Levites was Eleazar son of Aaron, the priest. He was appointed over those who were responsible for the care of the sanctuary.

[33]To Merari belonged the clans of the Mahlites and the Mushites; these were the Merarite clans. [34]The number of all the males a month old or more who were counted was 6,200. [35]The leader of the families of the Merarite clans was Zuriel son of Abihail; they were to camp on the north side of the tabernacle. [36]The Merarites were appointed to take care of the frames of the tabernacle, its crossbars, posts, bases, all its equipment, and everything related to their use, [37]as well as the posts of the surrounding courtyard with their bases, tent pegs and ropes.

[38]Moses and Aaron and his sons were to camp to the east of the tabernacle, toward the sunrise, in front of the Tent of Meeting. They were responsible for the care of the sanctuary on behalf of the Israelites. Anyone else who approached the sanctuary was to be put to death.

[39]The total number of Levites counted at the LORD's command by Moses and Aaron according to their clans, including every male a month old or more, was 22,000.

[40]The LORD said to Moses, "Count all the firstborn Israelite males who are a month old or more and make a list of their names. [41]Take the Levites for me in place of all the firstborn of the Israelites, and the livestock of the Levites in place of all the firstborn of the livestock of the Israelites. I am the LORD."

[42]So Moses counted all the firstborn of the Israelites, as the LORD commanded him. [43]The total number of firstborn males a month old or more, listed by name, was 22,273.

[44]The LORD also said to Moses, [45]"Take the Levites in place of all the firstborn of Israel, and the livestock of the Levites in place of their livestock. The Levites are to be mine. I am the LORD. [46]To redeem the 273 firstborn Israelites who exceed the number of the Levites, [47]collect five shekels[c] for each one, according to the sanctuary shekel, which weighs twenty gerahs. [48]Give the money for the redemption of the additional Israelites to Aaron and his sons."

[49]So Moses collected the redemption money from those who exceeded the number redeemed by the Levites. [50]From the firstborn of the Israelites he collected silver weighing 1,365 shekels,[d] according to the sanctuary shekel. [51]Moses gave the redemption money to Aaron and his sons, as he was commanded by the word of the LORD.

[b] *28* Hebrew; some Septuagint manuscripts *8,300*
[c] *47* That is, about 2 ounces (about 55 grams)
[d] *50* That is, about 35 pounds (about 15.5 kilograms)

PRAYER: AFFIRMATION

BEHOLD, a virgin shall be with child and give birth to a son, and they will call His name Immanuel, which means, "God with us." (Matthew 1:23)

***PAUSE** to reflect on these Biblical affirmations.*

NT Mark 12:1–27

The Parable of the Tenants

12 He then began to speak to them in parables: "A man planted a vineyard. He
put a wall around it, dug a pit for the winepress and built a watchtower. Then he rented the vineyard to some farmers and went
away on a journey. 2At harvest time he sent
a servant to the tenants to collect from
them some of the fruit of the vineyard.
3But they seized him, beat him and sent
him away empty-handed. 4Then he sent
another servant to them; they struck this
man on the head and treated him shamefully. 5He sent still another, and that one
they killed. He sent many others; some of
them they beat, others they killed.

6"He had one left to send, a son, whom
he loved. He sent him last of all, saying,
'They will respect my son.'

7"But the tenants said to one another,
'This is the heir. Come, let's kill him, and
the inheritance will be ours.' 8So they took
him and killed him, and threw him out
of the vineyard.

9"What then will the owner of the vineyard do? He will come and kill those tenants and give the vineyard to others.
10Haven't you read this scripture:

" 'The stone the builders rejected
has become the capstone[a];
11the Lord has done this,
and it is marvelous in our eyes'[b]?"

12Then they looked for a way to arrest
him because they knew he had spoken the
parable against them. But they were afraid
of the crowd; so they left him and went
away.

Paying Taxes to Caesar

13Later they sent some of the Pharisees
and Herodians to Jesus to catch him in
his words. 14They came to him and said,
"Teacher, we know you are a man of integrity. You aren't swayed by men, because you pay no attention to who they
are; but you teach the way of God in accordance with the truth. Is it right to pay
taxes to Caesar or not? 15Should we pay
or shouldn't we?"

But Jesus knew their hypocrisy. "Why
are you trying to trap me?" he asked.
"Bring me a denarius and let me look at
it." 16They brought the coin, and he asked
them, "Whose portrait is this? And whose
inscription?"

"Caesar's," they replied.

17Then Jesus said to them, "Give to Caesar what is Caesar's and to God what is
God's."

And they were amazed at him.

Marriage at the Resurrection

18Then the Sadducees, who say there is
no resurrection, came to him with a question. 19"Teacher," they said, "Moses wrote
for us that if a man's brother dies and
leaves a wife but no children, the man
must marry the widow and have children
for his brother. 20Now there were seven
brothers. The first one married and died
without leaving any children. 21The second
one married the widow, but he also died,
leaving no child. It was the same with the
third. 22In fact, none of the seven left any
children. Last of all, the woman died too.
23At the resurrection[c] whose wife will she
be, since the seven were married to her?"

24Jesus replied, "Are you not in error because you do not know the Scriptures or
the power of God? 25When the dead rise, they
will neither marry nor be given in marriage; they will be like the angels in heav-
en. 26Now about the dead rising—have
you not read in the book of Moses, in the
account of the bush, how God said to
him, 'I am the God of Abraham, the God
of Isaac, and the God of Jacob'[d]? 27He is
not the God of the dead, but of the living.
You are badly mistaken!"

[a] 10 Or *cornerstone* [b] 11 Psalm 118:22,23
[c] 23 Some manuscripts *resurrection, when men rise from the dead,* [d] 26 Exodus 3:6

PRAYER: MY RELATIONSHIP TO GOD

I WANT to love You, Lord my God, obey Your voice, and hold fast to You. For You are my life and the length of my days. (Deuteronomy 30:20) . . . I love You, O Lord, my strength. You are my rock and

my fortress and my deliverer; my God, You are my rock, in whom I take refuge. You are my shield and the horn of my salvation, my stronghold. I call upon You, Lord, for You are worthy of praise, and I am saved from my enemies. (Psalm 18:1–3)

PAUSE *to thank God for the relationship that you enjoy with Him in Jesus Christ.*

YEAR 1
DAY 119

OT Psalm 26

Psalm 26

Of David.

[1]Vindicate me, O LORD,
for I have led a blameless life;
I have trusted in the LORD
without wavering.
[2]Test me, O LORD, and try me,
examine my heart and my mind;
[3]for your love is ever before me,
and I walk continually in your
truth.
[4]I do not sit with deceitful men,
nor do I consort with hypocrites;
[5]I abhor the assembly of evildoers
and refuse to sit with the wicked.
[6]I wash my hands in innocence,
and go about your altar, O LORD,
[7]proclaiming aloud your praise
and telling of all your wonderful
deeds.
[8]I love the house where you live,
O LORD,
the place where your glory dwells.

[9]Do not take away my soul along with
sinners,
my life with bloodthirsty men,
[10]in whose hands are wicked schemes,
whose right hands are full of bribes.
[11]But I lead a blameless life;
redeem me and be merciful to me.

[12]My feet stand on level ground;
in the great assembly I will praise
the LORD.

PRAYER: THANKSGIVING

I CRIED out, and You heard me and saved me out of all my troubles. Your angels encamp around those who fear You and deliver them. (Psalm 34:6–7) . . . I waited patiently for You, Lord, and You turned to me and heard my cry. You lifted me out of the slimy pit, out of the mud and mire; You set my feet on a rock and gave me a firm place to stand. You put a new song in my mouth, a hymn of praise to You, my God. Many will see and fear and put their trust in You. (Psalm 40:1–3)

PAUSE *to offer your own expressions of thanksgiving.*

NT Mark 12:28–44

The Greatest Commandment

[28]One of the teachers of the law came
and heard them debating. Noticing that
Jesus had given them a good answer, he
asked him, "Of all the commandments,
which is the most important?"
[29]"The most important one," answered
Jesus, "is this: 'Hear, O Israel, the Lord our
God, the Lord is one.[a] [30]Love the Lord
your God with all your heart and with all
your soul and with all your mind and
with all your strength.'[b] [31]The second is
this: 'Love your neighbor as yourself.'[c]
There is no commandment greater than
these."
[32]"Well said, teacher," the man replied.

[a] 29 *Or the Lord our God is one Lord* [b] 30 Deut. 6:4,5 [c] 31 Lev. 19:18

"You are right in saying that God is one and there is no other but him. 33To love him with all your heart, with all your understanding and with all your strength, and to love your neighbor as yourself is more important than all burnt offerings and sacrifices."

34When Jesus saw that he had answered wisely, he said to him, "You are not far from the kingdom of God." And from then on no one dared ask him any more questions.

Whose Son Is the Christ?

35While Jesus was teaching in the temple courts, he asked, "How is it that the teachers of the law say that the Christ[d] is the son of David? 36David himself, speaking by the Holy Spirit, declared:

" 'The Lord said to my Lord:
"Sit at my right hand
until I put your enemies
under your feet." '[e]

37David himself calls him 'Lord.' How then can he be his son?"

The large crowd listened to him with delight.

38As he taught, Jesus said, "Watch out for the teachers of the law. They like to walk around in flowing robes and be greeted in the marketplaces, 39and have the most important seats in the synagogues and the places of honor at banquets. 40They devour widows' houses and for a show make lengthy prayers. Such men will be punished most severely."

The Widow's Offering

41Jesus sat down opposite the place where the offerings were put and watched the crowd putting their money into the temple treasury. Many rich people threw in large amounts. 42But a poor widow came and put in two very small copper coins,[f] worth only a fraction of a penny.[g]

43Calling his disciples to him, Jesus said, "I tell you the truth, this poor widow has put more into the treasury than all the others. 44They all gave out of their wealth; but she, out of her poverty, put in everything—all she had to live on."

[d] 35 Or *Messiah* [e] 36 Psalm 110:1 [f] 42 Greek *two lepta* [g] 42 Greek *kodrantes*

PRAYER: THE CHARACTER I WANT TO CULTIVATE

I WILL not steal, nor deal falsely, nor deceive others. (Leviticus 19:11) . . . I will not pervert justice or show partiality. I will not accept a bribe, for a bribe blinds the eyes of the wise and perverts the words of the righteous. (Deuteronomy 16:19)

***TAKE** a moment to ask the Lord for the grace to grow in godly character.*

YEAR 1
DAY 120

OT Numbers 4:1-49

The Kohathites

4 The LORD said to Moses and Aaron: 2"Take a census of the Kohathite branch of the Levites by their clans and families. 3Count all the men from thirty to fifty years of age who come to serve in the work in the Tent of Meeting.

4"This is the work of the Kohathites in the Tent of Meeting: the care of the most holy things. 5When the camp is to move, Aaron and his sons are to go in and take down the shielding curtain and cover the ark of the Testimony with it. 6Then they are to cover this with hides of sea cows,[a] spread a cloth of solid blue over that and put the poles in place.

7"Over the table of the Presence they are to spread a blue cloth and put on it the plates, dishes and bowls, and the jars for drink offerings; the bread that is continually there is to remain on it. 8Over these they are to spread a scarlet cloth, cover that with hides of sea cows and put its poles in place.

9"They are to take a blue cloth and cov-

[a] 6 That is, dugongs; also in verses 8, 10, 11, 12, 14 and 25

er the lampstand that is for light, together with its lamps, its wick trimmers and
trays, and all its jars for the oil used to
supply it. 10Then they are to wrap it and
all its accessories in a covering of hides of
sea cows and put it on a carrying frame.
11"Over the gold altar they are to spread
a blue cloth and cover that with hides of
sea cows and put its poles in place.
12"They are to take all the articles used
for ministering in the sanctuary, wrap
them in a blue cloth, cover that with hides
of sea cows and put them on a carrying
frame.
13"They are to remove the ashes from
the bronze altar and spread a purple cloth
over it. 14Then they are to place on it all
the utensils used for ministering at the altar, including the firepans, meat forks,
shovels and sprinkling bowls. Over it they
are to spread a covering of hides of sea
cows and put its poles in place.
15"After Aaron and his sons have finished covering the holy furnishings and
all the holy articles, and when the camp
is ready to move, the Kohathites are to
come to do the carrying. But they must
not touch the holy things or they will die.
The Kohathites are to carry those things
that are in the Tent of Meeting.
16"Eleazar son of Aaron, the priest, is to
have charge of the oil for the light, the fragrant incense, the regular grain offering
and the anointing oil. He is to be in
charge of the entire tabernacle and everything in it, including its holy furnishings
and articles."
17The LORD said to Moses and Aaron,
18"See that the Kohathite tribal clans are
not cut off from the Levites. 19So that they
may live and not die when they come
near the most holy things, do this for
them: Aaron and his sons are to go into
the sanctuary and assign to each man his
work and what he is to carry. 20But the Kohathites must not go in to look at the holy
things, even for a moment, or they will
die."

The Gershonites

21The LORD said to Moses, 22"Take a census also of the Gershonites by their families and clans. 23Count all the men from
thirty to fifty years of age who come to
serve in the work at the Tent of Meeting.
24"This is the service of the Gershonite
clans as they work and carry burdens:
25They are to carry the curtains of the
tabernacle, the Tent of Meeting, its covering and the outer covering of hides of sea
cows, the curtains for the entrance to the
Tent of Meeting, 26the curtains of the
courtyard surrounding the tabernacle and
altar, the curtain for the entrance, the
ropes and all the equipment used in its
service. The Gershonites are to do all that
needs to be done with these things. 27All
their service, whether carrying or doing
other work, is to be done under the direction of Aaron and his sons. You shall
assign to them as their responsibility all
they are to carry. 28This is the service of the
Gershonite clans at the Tent of Meeting.
Their duties are to be under the direction
of Ithamar son of Aaron, the priest.

The Merarites

29"Count the Merarites by their clans
and families. 30Count all the men from
thirty to fifty years of age who come to
serve in the work at the Tent of Meeting.
31This is their duty as they perform service
at the Tent of Meeting: to carry the frames
of the tabernacle, its crossbars, posts and
bases, 32as well as the posts of the surrounding courtyard with their bases, tent
pegs, ropes, all their equipment and
everything related to their use. Assign to
each man the specific things he is to carry. 33This is the service of the Merarite
clans as they work at the Tent of Meeting
under the direction of Ithamar son of Aaron, the priest."

The Numbering of the Levite Clans

34Moses, Aaron and the leaders of the
community counted the Kohathites by
their clans and families. 35All the men
from thirty to fifty years of age who came
to serve in the work in the Tent of Meeting, 36counted by clans, were 2,750. 37This
was the total of all those in the Kohathite
clans who served in the Tent of Meeting.
Moses and Aaron counted them according
to the LORD's command through Moses.
38The Gershonites were counted by their
clans and families. 39All the men from thirty to fifty years of age who came to serve
in the work at the Tent of Meeting,
40counted by their clans and families, were
2,630. 41This was the total of those in the
Gershonite clans who served at the Tent of

Meeting. Moses and Aaron counted them
according to the LORD's command.
42 The Merarites were counted by their
clans and families. 43 All the men from thirty to fifty years of age who came to serve
in the work at the Tent of Meeting,
44 counted by their clans, were 3,200. 45 This
was the total of those in the Merarite clans.
Moses and Aaron counted them according
to the LORD's command through Moses.
46 So Moses, Aaron and the leaders of Israel counted all the Levites by their clans
and families. 47 All the men from thirty to
fifty years of age who came to do the work
of serving and carrying the Tent of Meeting 48 numbered 8,580. 49 At the LORD's
command through Moses, each was assigned his work and told what to carry.
Thus they were counted, as the LORD
commanded Moses.

PRAYER: ADORATION

BLESSED are You, O Lord, God of Israel our father, forever and ever. Yours, O Lord, is the greatness and the power and the glory and the victory and the majesty, for everything in heaven and earth is Yours. Yours, O Lord, is the kingdom, and You are exalted as head over all. Both riches and honor come from You, and You are the ruler of all things. In Your hand is power and might to exalt and to give strength to all. Therefore, my God, I give You thanks and I praise Your glorious name. (1 Chronicles 29:10–13)

***PAUSE** to express your thoughts of praise and worship.*

NT Mark 13:1–37

Signs of the End of the Age

13 As he was leaving the temple, one of
his disciples said to him, "Look,
Teacher! What massive stones! What magnificent buildings!"
2 "Do you see all these great buildings?"
replied Jesus. "Not one stone here will be
left on another; every one will be thrown
down."
3 As Jesus was sitting on the Mount of
Olives opposite the temple, Peter, James,
John and Andrew asked him privately,
4 "Tell us, when will these things happen?
And what will be the sign that they are all
about to be fulfilled?"
5 Jesus said to them: "Watch out that no
one deceives you. 6 Many will come in my
name, claiming, 'I am he,' and will deceive
many. 7 When you hear of wars and rumors of wars, do not be alarmed. Such
things must happen, but the end is still to
come. 8 Nation will rise against nation,
and kingdom against kingdom. There will
be earthquakes in various places, and
famines. These are the beginning of birth
pains.
9 "You must be on your guard. You will
be handed over to the local councils and
flogged in the synagogues. On account of
me you will stand before governors and
kings as witnesses to them. 10 And the
gospel must first be preached to all nations. 11 Whenever you are arrested and
brought to trial, do not worry beforehand
about what to say. Just say whatever is giv-
en you at the time, for it is not you speaking, but the Holy Spirit.
12 "Brother will betray brother to death,
and a father his child. Children will rebel
against their parents and have them put
to death. 13 All men will hate you because
of me, but he who stands firm to the end
will be saved.
14 "When you see 'the abomination that
causes desolation'[a] standing where it[b]
does not belong—let the reader understand—then let those who are in Judea
flee to the mountains. 15 Let no one on the
roof of his house go down or enter the
house to take anything out. 16 Let no one
in the field go back to get his cloak. 17 How
dreadful it will be in those days for pregnant women and nursing mothers! 18 Pray
that this will not take place in winter,
19 because those will be days of distress unequaled from the beginning, when God
created the world, until now—and never

[a] *14* Daniel 9:27; 11:31; 12:11 [b] *14* Or *he;* also in verse 29

to be equaled again. [20]If the Lord had not
cut short those days, no one would survive. But for the sake of the elect, whom
he has chosen, he has shortened them.
[21]At that time if anyone says to you, 'Look,
here is the Christ[c]!' or, 'Look, there he is!'
do not believe it. [22]For false Christs and
false prophets will appear and perform
signs and miracles to deceive the elect—if
that were possible. [23]So be on your guard;
I have told you everything ahead of time.
[24]"But in those days, following that distress,

" 'the sun will be darkened,
and the moon will not give its light;
[25]the stars will fall from the sky,
and the heavenly bodies will be
shaken.'[d]

[26]"At that time men will see the Son of
Man coming in clouds with great power
and glory. [27]And he will send his angels
and gather his elect from the four winds,
from the ends of the earth to the ends of
the heavens.
[28]"Now learn this lesson from the fig
tree: As soon as its twigs get tender and its
leaves come out, you know that summer
is near. [29]Even so, when you see these
things happening, you know that it is
near, right at the door. [30]I tell you the
truth, this generation[e] will certainly not
pass away until all these things have happened. [31]Heaven and earth will pass away,
but my words will never pass away.

The Day and Hour Unknown

[32]"No one knows about that day or hour,
not even the angels in heaven, nor the Son,
but only the Father. [33]Be on guard! Be
alert[f]! You do not know when that time
will come. [34]It's like a man going away: He
leaves his house and puts his servants in
charge, each with his assigned task, and
tells the one at the door to keep watch.
[35]"Therefore keep watch because you do
not know when the owner of the house
will come back—whether in the evening,
or at midnight, or when the rooster crows,
or at dawn. [36]If he comes suddenly, do not
let him find you sleeping. [37]What I say to
you, I say to everyone: 'Watch!' "

[c] 21 Or *Messiah* [d] 25 Isaiah 13:10; 34:4 [e] 30 Or *race* [f] 33 Some manuscripts *alert and pray*

PRAYER: MY RELATIONSHIP TO OTHERS

STARTING a quarrel is like breaching a dam, so I will stop a quarrel before it breaks out. (Proverbs 17:14) . . . If it is possible, I will live at peace with all people, as far as it depends on me. (Romans 12:18)

***PAUSE** to review your relationships with others and to commit them to the Lord.*

YEAR 1
DAY 121

OT Numbers 5:1–6:27

The Purity of the Camp

5 The LORD said to Moses, [2]"Command
the Israelites to send away from the
camp anyone who has an infectious skin
disease[a] or a discharge of any kind, or
who is ceremonially unclean because of
a dead body. [3]Send away male and female
alike; send them outside the camp so
they will not defile their camp, where I
dwell among them." [4]The Israelites did
this; they sent them outside the camp.
They did just as the LORD had instructed
Moses.

Restitution for Wrongs

[5]The LORD said to Moses, [6]"Say to the
Israelites: 'When a man or woman wrongs
another in any way[b] and so is unfaithful
to the LORD, that person is guilty [7]and
must confess the sin he has committed.
He must make full restitution for his
wrong, add one fifth to it and give it all to
the person he has wronged. [8]But if that

[a] 2 Traditionally *leprosy;* the Hebrew word was used for various diseases affecting the skin—not necessarily leprosy. [b] 6 Or *woman commits any wrong common to mankind*

person has no close relative to whom restitution can be made for the wrong, the restitution belongs to the LORD and must be given to the priest, along with the ram with which atonement is made for him. 9All the sacred contributions the Israelites bring to a priest will belong to him. 10Each man's sacred gifts are his own, but what he gives to the priest will belong to the priest.' "

The Test for an Unfaithful Wife

11Then the LORD said to Moses, 12"Speak to the Israelites and say to them: 'If a man's wife goes astray and is unfaithful to him 13by sleeping with another man, and this is hidden from her husband and her impurity is undetected (since there is no witness against her and she has not been caught in the act), 14and if feelings of jealousy come over her husband and he suspects his wife and she is impure—or if he is jealous and suspects her even though she is not impure— 15then he is to take his wife to the priest. He must also take an offering of a tenth of an ephah[c] of barley flour on her behalf. He must not pour oil on it or put incense on it, because it is a grain offering for jealousy, a reminder offering to draw attention to guilt.

16" 'The priest shall bring her and have her stand before the LORD. 17Then he shall take some holy water in a clay jar and put some dust from the tabernacle floor into the water. 18After the priest has had the woman stand before the LORD, he shall loosen her hair and place in her hands the reminder offering, the grain offering for jealousy, while he himself holds the bitter water that brings a curse. 19Then the priest shall put the woman under oath and say to her, "If no other man has slept with you and you have not gone astray and become impure while married to your husband, may this bitter water that brings a curse not harm you. 20But if you have gone astray while married to your husband and you have defiled yourself by sleeping with a man other than your husband"— 21here the priest is to put the woman under this curse of the oath—"may the LORD cause your people to curse and denounce you when he causes your thigh to waste away and your abdomen to swell.[d] 22May this water that brings a curse enter your body so that your abdomen swells and your thigh wastes away.[e]"

" 'Then the woman is to say, "Amen. So be it."

23" 'The priest is to write these curses on a scroll and then wash them off into the bitter water. 24He shall have the woman drink the bitter water that brings a curse, and this water will enter her and cause bitter suffering. 25The priest is to take from her hands the grain offering for jealousy, wave it before the LORD and bring it to the altar. 26The priest is then to take a handful of the grain offering as a memorial offering and burn it on the altar; after that, he is to have the woman drink the water. 27If she has defiled herself and been unfaithful to her husband, then when she is made to drink the water that brings a curse, it will go into her and cause bitter suffering; her abdomen will swell and her thigh waste away,[f] and she will become accursed among her people. 28If, however, the woman has not defiled herself and is free from impurity, she will be cleared of guilt and will be able to have children.

29" 'This, then, is the law of jealousy when a woman goes astray and defiles herself while married to her husband, 30or when feelings of jealousy come over a man because he suspects his wife. The priest is to have her stand before the LORD and is to apply this entire law to her. 31The husband will be innocent of any wrongdoing, but the woman will bear the consequences of her sin.' "

The Nazirite

6 The LORD said to Moses, 2"Speak to the Israelites and say to them: 'If a man or woman wants to make a special vow, a vow of separation to the LORD as a Nazirite, 3he must abstain from wine and other fermented drink and must not drink vinegar made from wine or from other fermented drink. He must not drink grape juice or eat grapes or raisins. 4As long as he is a Nazirite, he must not eat anything that comes from the grapevine, not even the seeds or skins.

5" 'During the entire period of his vow of separation no razor may be used on his

[c] *15* That is, probably about 2 quarts (about 2 liters)
[d] *21* Or *causes you to have a miscarrying womb and barrenness*
[e] *22* Or *body and cause you to be barren and have a miscarrying womb*
[f] *27* Or *suffering; she will have barrenness and a miscarrying womb*

head. He must be holy until the period of
his separation to the LORD is over; he must
let the hair of his head grow long.
[6]Throughout the period of his separation
to the LORD he must not go near a dead
body. [7]Even if his own father or mother
or brother or sister dies, he must not make
himself ceremonially unclean on account
of them, because the symbol of his separation to God is on his head. [8]Through-
out the period of his separation he is consecrated to the LORD.

[9]" 'If someone dies suddenly in his
presence, thus defiling the hair he has
dedicated, he must shave his head on the
day of his cleansing—the seventh day.
[10]Then on the eighth day he must bring
two doves or two young pigeons to the
priest at the entrance to the Tent of Meeting. [11]The priest is to offer one as a sin offering and the other as a burnt offering to
make atonement for him because he
sinned by being in the presence of the
dead body. That same day he is to consecrate his head. [12]He must dedicate himself
to the LORD for the period of his separation and must bring a year-old male lamb
as a guilt offering. The previous days do
not count, because he became defiled during his separation.

[13]" 'Now this is the law for the Nazirite
when the period of his separation is over.
He is to be brought to the entrance to the
Tent of Meeting. [14]There he is to present
his offerings to the LORD: a year-old male
lamb without defect for a burnt offering,
a year-old ewe lamb without defect for a
sin offering, a ram without defect for a fellowship offering,[g] [15]together with their
grain offerings and drink offerings, and a
basket of bread made without yeast—
cakes made of fine flour mixed with oil,
and wafers spread with oil.

[16]" 'The priest is to present them before
the LORD and make the sin offering and
the burnt offering. [17]He is to present the
basket of unleavened bread and is to sacrifice the ram as a fellowship offering to
the LORD, together with its grain offering
and drink offering.

[18]" 'Then at the entrance to the Tent of
Meeting, the Nazirite must shave off the
hair that he dedicated. He is to take the
hair and put it in the fire that is under
the sacrifice of the fellowship offering.

[19]" 'After the Nazirite has shaved off the
hair of his dedication, the priest is to place
in his hands a boiled shoulder of the ram,
and a cake and a wafer from the basket,
both made without yeast. [20]The priest
shall then wave them before the LORD as
a wave offering; they are holy and belong
to the priest, together with the breast that
was waved and the thigh that was presented. After that, the Nazirite may drink
wine.

[21]" 'This is the law of the Nazirite who
vows his offering to the LORD in accordance with his separation, in addition to
whatever else he can afford. He must fulfill the vow he has made, according to the
law of the Nazirite.' "

The Priestly Blessing

[22]The LORD said to Moses, [23]"Tell Aaron
and his sons, 'This is how you are to bless
the Israelites. Say to them:

[24]" ' "The LORD bless you
and keep you;
[25]the LORD make his face shine upon you
and be gracious to you;
[26]the LORD turn his face toward you
and give you peace." '

[27]"So they will put my name on the Israelites, and I will bless them."

g 14 Traditionally *peace offering;* also in verses 17 and 18

PRAYER: CONFESSION

O LORD, do not rebuke me in Your wrath, and do not chasten me in Your anger. For Your arrows have pierced me deeply, and Your hand has pressed down upon me. There is no health in my body because of Your wrath—no peace in my bones because of my sin. For my iniquities have gone over my head; as a heavy burden, they weigh too much for me. (Psalm 38:1–4)

ASK *the Spirit to search your heart and reveal any areas of unconfessed sin. Acknowledge these to the Lord and thank Him for His forgiveness.*

NT Mark 14:1-42

Jesus Anointed at Bethany

14 Now the Passover and the Feast of Unleavened Bread were only two days
away, and the chief priests and the teachers of the law were looking for some sly
way to arrest Jesus and kill him. 2"But not
during the Feast," they said, "or the people may riot."
3While he was in Bethany, reclining at
the table in the home of a man known as
Simon the Leper, a woman came with an
alabaster jar of very expensive perfume,
made of pure nard. She broke the jar and
poured the perfume on his head.
4Some of those present were saying in-
dignantly to one another, "Why this waste
of perfume? 5It could have been sold for
more than a year's wages[a] and the money
given to the poor." And they rebuked her
harshly.
6"Leave her alone," said Jesus. "Why are
you bothering her? She has done a beautiful thing to me. 7The poor you will always have with you, and you can help
them any time you want. But you will not
always have me. 8She did what she could.
She poured perfume on my body beforehand to prepare for my burial. 9I tell you
the truth, wherever the gospel is preached
throughout the world, what she has done
will also be told, in memory of her."
10Then Judas Iscariot, one of the Twelve,
went to the chief priests to betray Jesus to
them. 11They were delighted to hear this
and promised to give him money. So he
watched for an opportunity to hand him
over.

The Lord's Supper

12On the first day of the Feast of Unleavened Bread, when it was customary to
sacrifice the Passover lamb, Jesus' disciples
asked him, "Where do you want us to go
and make preparations for you to eat the
Passover?"
13So he sent two of his disciples, telling
them, "Go into the city, and a man carrying a jar of water will meet you. Follow
him. 14Say to the owner of the house he
enters, 'The Teacher asks: Where is my
guest room, where I may eat the Passover
with my disciples?' 15He will show you a
large upper room, furnished and ready.
Make preparations for us there."
16The disciples left, went into the city
and found things just as Jesus had told
them. So they prepared the Passover.
17When evening came, Jesus arrived
with the Twelve. 18While they were reclining at the table eating, he said, "I tell you
the truth, one of you will betray me—one
who is eating with me."
19They were saddened, and one by one
they said to him, "Surely not I?"
20"It is one of the Twelve," he replied,
"one who dips bread into the bowl with
me. 21The Son of Man will go just as it is
written about him. But woe to that man
who betrays the Son of Man! It would be
better for him if he had not been born."
22While they were eating, Jesus took
bread, gave thanks and broke it, and gave
it to his disciples, saying, "Take it; this is
my body."
23Then he took the cup, gave thanks and
offered it to them, and they all drank
from it.
24"This is my blood of the[b] covenant,
which is poured out for many," he said to
them. 25"I tell you the truth, I will not
drink again of the fruit of the vine until
that day when I drink it anew in the kingdom of God."
26When they had sung a hymn, they
went out to the Mount of Olives.

Jesus Predicts Peter's Denial

27"You will all fall away," Jesus told
them, "for it is written:

" 'I will strike the shepherd,
  and the sheep will be scattered.'[c]

28But after I have risen, I will go ahead of
you into Galilee."
29Peter declared, "Even if all fall away, I
will not."
30"I tell you the truth," Jesus answered,
"today—yes, tonight—before the rooster
crows twice[d] you yourself will disown me
three times."
31But Peter insisted emphatically, "Even
if I have to die with you, I will never disown you." And all the others said the
same.

[a] 5 Greek *than three hundred denarii* [b] 24 Some manuscripts *the new* [c] 27 Zech. 13:7 [d] 30 Some early manuscripts do not have *twice.*

Gethsemane

[32]They went to a place called Gethsemane, and Jesus said to his disciples, "Sit here while I pray." [33]He took Peter, James and John along with him, and he began to be deeply distressed and troubled. [34]"My soul is overwhelmed with sorrow to the point of death," he said to them. "Stay here and keep watch."

[35]Going a little farther, he fell to the ground and prayed that if possible the hour might pass from him. [36]"*Abba*,[e] Father," he said, "everything is possible for you. Take this cup from me. Yet not what I will, but what you will."

[37]Then he returned to his disciples and found them sleeping. "Simon," he said to Peter, "are you asleep? Could you not keep watch for one hour? [38]Watch and pray so that you will not fall into temptation. The spirit is willing, but the body is weak."

[39]Once more he went away and prayed the same thing. [40]When he came back, he again found them sleeping, because their eyes were heavy. They did not know what to say to him.

[41]Returning the third time, he said to them, "Are you still sleeping and resting? Enough! The hour has come. Look, the Son of Man is betrayed into the hands of sinners. [42]Rise! Let us go! Here comes my betrayer!"

[e] *36* Aramaic for *Father*

PRAYER: THE ATTRIBUTES OF GOD

O GOD, You are exalted beyond our understanding; the number of Your years is unsearchable. (Job 36:26) . . . You are He; You are the first, and You are also the last. (Isaiah 48:12)

***PAUSE** to reflect on these affirmations about the person, powers and perfection of God.*

OT Numbers 7:1-89 — YEAR 1 DAY 122

Offerings at the Dedication of the Tabernacle

7 When Moses finished setting up the tabernacle, he anointed it and consecrated it and all its furnishings. He also anointed and consecrated the altar and all its utensils. [2]Then the leaders of Israel, the heads of families who were the tribal leaders in charge of those who were counted, made offerings. [3]They brought as their gifts before the LORD six covered carts and twelve oxen—an ox from each leader and a cart from every two. These they presented before the tabernacle.

[4]The LORD said to Moses, [5]"Accept these from them, that they may be used in the work at the Tent of Meeting. Give them to the Levites as each man's work requires."

[6]So Moses took the carts and oxen and gave them to the Levites. [7]He gave two carts and four oxen to the Gershonites, as their work required, [8]and he gave four carts and eight oxen to the Merarites, as their work required. They were all under the direction of Ithamar son of Aaron, the priest. [9]But Moses did not give any to the Kohathites, because they were to carry on their shoulders the holy things, for which they were responsible.

[10]When the altar was anointed, the leaders brought their offerings for its dedication and presented them before the altar. [11]For the LORD had said to Moses, "Each day one leader is to bring his offering for the dedication of the altar."

[12]The one who brought his offering on the first day was Nahshon son of Amminadab of the tribe of Judah.

[13]His offering was one silver plate weighing a hundred and thirty shekels,[a] and one silver sprinkling bowl weighing seventy shekels,[b] both

[a] *13* That is, about 3 1/4 pounds (about 1.5 kilograms); also elsewhere in this chapter
[b] *13* That is, about 1 3/4 pounds (about 0.8 kilogram); also elsewhere in this chapter

according to the sanctuary shekel,
each filled with fine flour mixed with
oil as a grain offering; 14 one gold dish
weighing ten shekels,[c] filled with incense; 15 one young bull, one ram and
one male lamb a year old, for a burnt
offering; 16 one male goat for a sin offering; 17 and two oxen, five rams, five
male goats and five male lambs a
year old, to be sacrificed as a fellowship offering.[d] This was the offering
of Nahshon son of Amminadab.

18 On the second day Nethanel son of
Zuar, the leader of Issachar, brought his
offering.

19 The offering he brought was one silver plate weighing a hundred and
thirty shekels, and one silver sprinkling bowl weighing seventy shekels,
both according to the sanctuary
shekel, each filled with fine flour
mixed with oil as a grain offering;
20 one gold dish weighing ten shekels,
filled with incense; 21 one young bull,
one ram and one male lamb a year
old, for a burnt offering; 22 one male
goat for a sin offering; 23 and two
oxen, five rams, five male goats and
five male lambs a year old, to be sacrificed as a fellowship offering. This
was the offering of Nethanel son of
Zuar.

24 On the third day, Eliab son of Helon, the
leader of the people of Zebulun, brought
his offering.

25 His offering was one silver plate
weighing a hundred and thirty
shekels, and one silver sprinkling
bowl weighing seventy shekels, both
according to the sanctuary shekel,
each filled with fine flour mixed with
oil as a grain offering; 26 one gold dish
weighing ten shekels, filled with incense; 27 one young bull, one ram and
one male lamb a year old, for a burnt
offering; 28 one male goat for a sin offering; 29 and two oxen, five rams, five
male goats and five male lambs a
year old, to be sacrificed as a fellowship offering. This was the offering of
Eliab son of Helon.

30 On the fourth day Elizur son of Shedeur, the leader of the people of Reuben,
brought his offering.

31 His offering was one silver plate
weighing a hundred and thirty
shekels, and one silver sprinkling
bowl weighing seventy shekels, both
according to the sanctuary shekel,
each filled with fine flour mixed with
oil as a grain offering; 32 one gold dish
weighing ten shekels, filled with incense; 33 one young bull, one ram and
one male lamb a year old, for a burnt
offering; 34 one male goat for a sin offering; 35 and two oxen, five rams, five
male goats and five male lambs a
year old, to be sacrificed as a fellowship offering. This was the offering of
Elizur son of Shedeur.

36 On the fifth day Shelumiel son of Zurishaddai, the leader of the people of Simeon, brought his offering.

37 His offering was one silver plate
weighing a hundred and thirty
shekels, and one silver sprinkling
bowl weighing seventy shekels, both
according to the sanctuary shekel,
each filled with fine flour mixed with
oil as a grain offering; 38 one gold dish
weighing ten shekels, filled with incense; 39 one young bull, one ram and
one male lamb a year old, for a burnt
offering; 40 one male goat for a sin offering; 41 and two oxen, five rams, five
male goats and five male lambs a
year old, to be sacrificed as a fellowship offering. This was the offering of
Shelumiel son of Zurishaddai.

42 On the sixth day Eliasaph son of Deuel,
the leader of the people of Gad, brought
his offering.

43 His offering was one silver plate
weighing a hundred and thirty
shekels, and one silver sprinkling
bowl weighing seventy shekels, both
according to the sanctuary shekel,
each filled with fine flour mixed with
oil as a grain offering; 44 one gold dish
weighing ten shekels, filled with incense; 45 one young bull, one ram and
one male lamb a year old, for a burnt
offering; 46 one male goat for a sin offering; 47 and two oxen, five rams, five
male goats and five male lambs a
year old, to be sacrificed as a fellowship offering. This was the offering of
Eliasaph son of Deuel.

[c] *14* That is, about 4 ounces (about 110 grams); also elsewhere in this chapter [d] *17* Traditionally *peace offering;* also elsewhere in this chapter

48 On the seventh day Elishama son of Ammihud, the leader of the people of Ephraim, brought his offering.
49 His offering was one silver plate
weighing a hundred and thirty
shekels, and one silver sprinkling
bowl weighing seventy shekels, both
according to the sanctuary shekel,
each filled with fine flour mixed with
oil as a grain offering; 50 one gold dish
weighing ten shekels, filled with incense; 51 one young bull, one ram and
one male lamb a year old, for a burnt
offering; 52 one male goat for a sin offering; 53 and two oxen, five rams, five
male goats and five male lambs a
year old, to be sacrificed as a fellowship offering. This was the offering of
Elishama son of Ammihud.

54 On the eighth day Gamaliel son of Pedahzur, the leader of the people of Manasseh, brought his offering.
55 His offering was one silver plate
weighing a hundred and thirty
shekels, and one silver sprinkling
bowl weighing seventy shekels, both
according to the sanctuary shekel,
each filled with fine flour mixed with
oil as a grain offering; 56 one gold dish
weighing ten shekels, filled with incense; 57 one young bull, one ram and
one male lamb a year old, for a burnt
offering; 58 one male goat for a sin offering; 59 and two oxen, five rams, five
male goats and five male lambs a
year old, to be sacrificed as a fellowship offering. This was the offering of
Gamaliel son of Pedahzur.

60 On the ninth day Abidan son of Gideoni, the leader of the people of Benjamin,
brought his offering.
61 His offering was one silver plate
weighing a hundred and thirty
shekels, and one silver sprinkling
bowl weighing seventy shekels, both
according to the sanctuary shekel,
each filled with fine flour mixed with
oil as a grain offering; 62 one gold dish
weighing ten shekels, filled with incense; 63 one young bull, one ram and
one male lamb a year old, for a burnt
offering; 64 one male goat for a sin offering; 65 and two oxen, five rams, five
male goats and five male lambs a
year old, to be sacrificed as a fellowship offering. This was the offering of
Abidan son of Gideoni.

66 On the tenth day Ahiezer son of Ammishaddai, the leader of the people of
Dan, brought his offering.
67 His offering was one silver plate
weighing a hundred and thirty
shekels, and one silver sprinkling
bowl weighing seventy shekels, both
according to the sanctuary shekel,
each filled with fine flour mixed with
oil as a grain offering; 68 one gold dish
weighing ten shekels, filled with incense; 69 one young bull, one ram and
one male lamb a year old, for a burnt
offering; 70 one male goat for a sin offering; 71 and two oxen, five rams, five
male goats and five male lambs a
year old, to be sacrificed as a fellowship offering. This was the offering of
Ahiezer son of Ammishaddai.

72 On the eleventh day Pagiel son of Ocran, the leader of the people of Asher,
brought his offering.
73 His offering was one silver plate
weighing a hundred and thirty
shekels, and one silver sprinkling
bowl weighing seventy shekels, both
according to the sanctuary shekel,
each filled with fine flour mixed with
oil as a grain offering; 74 one gold dish
weighing ten shekels, filled with incense; 75 one young bull, one ram and
one male lamb a year old, for a burnt
offering; 76 one male goat for a sin offering; 77 and two oxen, five rams, five
male goats and five male lambs a
year old, to be sacrificed as a fellowship offering. This was the offering of
Pagiel son of Ocran.

78 On the twelfth day Ahira son of Enan,
the leader of the people of Naphtali,
brought his offering.
79 His offering was one silver plate
weighing a hundred and thirty
shekels, and one silver sprinkling
bowl weighing seventy shekels, both
according to the sanctuary shekel,
each filled with fine flour mixed with
oil as a grain offering; 80 one gold dish
weighing ten shekels, filled with incense; 81 one young bull, one ram and
one male lamb a year old, for a burnt
offering; 82 one male goat for a sin offering; 83 and two oxen, five rams, five

male goats and five male lambs a
year old, to be sacrificed as a fellowship offering. This was the offering of
Ahira son of Enan.

84 These were the offerings of the Israelite leaders for the dedication of the altar
when it was anointed: twelve silver plates,
twelve silver sprinkling bowls and twelve
gold dishes. 85 Each silver plate weighed a
hundred and thirty shekels, and each
sprinkling bowl seventy shekels. Altogether, the silver dishes weighed two
thousand four hundred shekels,[e] according to the sanctuary shekel. 86 The twelve
gold dishes filled with incense weighed
ten shekels each, according to the sanctuary shekel. Altogether, the gold dishes
weighed a hundred and twenty shekels.[f]
87 The total number of animals for the
burnt offering came to twelve young bulls,
twelve rams and twelve male lambs a year
old, together with their grain offering.
Twelve male goats were used for the sin
offering. 88 The total number of animals
for the sacrifice of the fellowship offering
came to twenty-four oxen, sixty rams, sixty male goats and sixty male lambs a year
old. These were the offerings for the dedication of the altar after it was anointed.
89 When Moses entered the Tent of
Meeting to speak with the LORD, he heard
the voice speaking to him from between
the two cherubim above the atonement
cover on the ark of the Testimony. And he
spoke with him.

[e] *85* That is, about 60 pounds (about 28 kilograms)
[f] *86* That is, about 3 pounds (about 1.4 kilograms)

PRAYER: RENEWAL

AS Your servant, O Christ, and a steward of Your possessions, may I be found faithful. (1 Corinthians 4:1–2) . . . Those who want to get rich fall into temptation and a snare and into many foolish and harmful desires that plunge them into ruin and destruction. For the love of money is a root of all kinds of evil, and some, by longing for it, have wandered from the faith and pierced themselves with many sorrows. But let me flee from these things and pursue righteousness, godliness, faith, love, patience and gentleness. (1 Timothy 6:9–11)

***PAUSE** to add your own prayers for personal renewal.*

NT Mark 14:43–72

Jesus Arrested

43 Just as he was speaking, Judas, one of
the Twelve, appeared. With him was a
crowd armed with swords and clubs, sent
from the chief priests, the teachers of the
law, and the elders.
44 Now the betrayer had arranged a signal with them: "The one I kiss is the man;
arrest him and lead him away under
guard." 45 Going at once to Jesus, Judas
said, "Rabbi!" and kissed him. 46 The men
seized Jesus and arrested him. 47 Then one
of those standing near drew his sword and
struck the servant of the high priest, cutting off his ear.
48 "Am I leading a rebellion," said Jesus,
"that you have come out with swords and
clubs to capture me? 49 Every day I was
with you, teaching in the temple courts,
and you did not arrest me. But the Scriptures must be fulfilled." 50 Then everyone
deserted him and fled.
51 A young man, wearing nothing but a
linen garment, was following Jesus. When
they seized him, 52 he fled naked, leaving
his garment behind.

Before the Sanhedrin

53 They took Jesus to the high priest, and
all the chief priests, elders and teachers of
the law came together. 54 Peter followed
him at a distance, right into the courtyard
of the high priest. There he sat with the
guards and warmed himself at the fire.
55 The chief priests and the whole Sanhedrin were looking for evidence against
Jesus so that they could put him to death,
but they did not find any. 56 Many testified

falsely against him, but their statements did not agree.

57Then some stood up and gave this false testimony against him: 58"We heard him say, 'I will destroy this man-made temple and in three days will build another, not made by man.' " 59Yet even then their testimony did not agree.

60Then the high priest stood up before them and asked Jesus, "Are you not going to answer? What is this testimony that these men are bringing against you?" 61But Jesus remained silent and gave no answer.

Again the high priest asked him, "Are you the Christ,[a] the Son of the Blessed One?"

62"I am," said Jesus. "And you will see the Son of Man sitting at the right hand of the Mighty One and coming on the clouds of heaven."

63The high priest tore his clothes. "Why do we need any more witnesses?" he asked. 64"You have heard the blasphemy. What do you think?"

They all condemned him as worthy of death. 65Then some began to spit at him; they blindfolded him, struck him with their fists, and said, "Prophesy!" And the guards took him and beat him.

Peter Disowns Jesus

66While Peter was below in the courtyard, one of the servant girls of the high priest came by. 67When she saw Peter warming himself, she looked closely at him.

"You also were with that Nazarene, Jesus," she said.

68But he denied it. "I don't know or understand what you're talking about," he said, and went out into the entryway.[b]

69When the servant girl saw him there, she said again to those standing around, "This fellow is one of them." 70Again he denied it.

After a little while, those standing near said to Peter, "Surely you are one of them, for you are a Galilean."

71He began to call down curses on himself, and he swore to them, "I don't know this man you're talking about."

72Immediately the rooster crowed the second time.[c] Then Peter remembered the word Jesus had spoken to him: "Before the rooster crows twice[d] you will disown me three times." And he broke down and wept.

[a] 61 Or *Messiah* [b] 68 Some early manuscripts *entryway and the rooster crowed* [c] 72 Some early manuscripts do not have *the second time.* [d] 72 Some early manuscripts do not have *twice.*

PRAYER: THE WORKS OF GOD

THE earth is Yours, O Lord, and everything in it, the world and all who dwell in it. For You founded it upon the seas and established it upon the waters. (Psalm 24:1–2)

__TAKE__ a moment to consider the greatness of God's wonderful works.

YEAR 1 DAY 123

OT Numbers 8:1–9:23

Setting Up the Lamps

8 The LORD said to Moses, 2"Speak to Aaron and say to him, 'When you set up the seven lamps, they are to light the area in front of the lampstand.' "

3Aaron did so; he set up the lamps so that they faced forward on the lampstand, just as the LORD commanded Moses. 4This is how the lampstand was made: It was made of hammered gold—from its base to its blossoms. The lampstand was made exactly like the pattern the LORD had shown Moses.

The Setting Apart of the Levites

5The LORD said to Moses: 6"Take the Levites from among the other Israelites and make them ceremonially clean. 7To purify them, do this: Sprinkle the water of cleansing on them; then have them shave their whole bodies and wash their clothes, and so purify themselves. 8Have them take a young bull with its grain offering of fine flour mixed with oil; then you are to take a second young bull for a sin offering. 9Bring the Levites to the front of the Tent of Meeting and assemble the whole Israelite community. 10You are to bring the Levites before the LORD, and the Israelites are to lay their hands on them. 11Aaron is to present the Levites before the LORD as a wave offering from the Israelites, so that they may be ready to do the work of the LORD.

12"After the Levites lay their hands on the heads of the bulls, use the one for a sin offering to the LORD and the other for a burnt offering, to make atonement for the Levites. 13Have the Levites stand in front of Aaron and his sons and then present them as a wave offering to the LORD. 14In this way you are to set the Levites apart from the other Israelites, and the Levites will be mine.

15"After you have purified the Levites and presented them as a wave offering, they are to come to do their work at the Tent of Meeting. 16They are the Israelites who are to be given wholly to me. I have taken them as my own in place of the firstborn, the first male offspring from every Israelite woman. 17Every firstborn male in Israel, whether man or animal, is mine. When I struck down all the firstborn in Egypt, I set them apart for myself. 18And I have taken the Levites in place of all the firstborn sons in Israel. 19Of all the Israelites, I have given the Levites as gifts to Aaron and his sons to do the work at the Tent of Meeting on behalf of the Israelites and to make atonement for them so that no plague will strike the Israelites when they go near the sanctuary."

20Moses, Aaron and the whole Israelite community did with the Levites just as the LORD commanded Moses. 21The Levites purified themselves and washed their clothes. Then Aaron presented them as a wave offering before the LORD and made atonement for them to purify them. 22After that, the Levites came to do their work at the Tent of Meeting under the supervision of Aaron and his sons. They did with the Levites just as the LORD commanded Moses.

23The LORD said to Moses, 24"This applies to the Levites: Men twenty-five years old or more shall come to take part in the work at the Tent of Meeting, 25but at the age of fifty, they must retire from their regular service and work no longer. 26They may assist their brothers in performing their duties at the Tent of Meeting, but they themselves must not do the work. This, then, is how you are to assign the responsibilities of the Levites."

The Passover

9 The LORD spoke to Moses in the Desert of Sinai in the first month of the second year after they came out of Egypt. He said, 2"Have the Israelites celebrate the Passover at the appointed time. 3Celebrate it at the appointed time, at twilight on the fourteenth day of this month, in accordance with all its rules and regulations."

4So Moses told the Israelites to celebrate the Passover, 5and they did so in the Desert of Sinai at twilight on the fourteenth day of the first month. The Israelites did everything just as the LORD commanded Moses.

6But some of them could not celebrate the Passover on that day because they were ceremonially unclean on account of a dead body. So they came to Moses and Aaron that same day 7and said to Moses, "We have become unclean because of a dead body, but why should we be kept from presenting the LORD's offering with the other Israelites at the appointed time?"

8Moses answered them, "Wait until I find out what the LORD commands concerning you."

9Then the LORD said to Moses, 10"Tell the Israelites: 'When any of you or your descendants are unclean because of a dead body or are away on a journey, they may still celebrate the LORD's Passover. 11They are to celebrate it on the fourteenth day of the second month at twilight. They are to eat the lamb, together with unleavened bread and bitter herbs. 12They must not leave any of it till morning or break any of its bones. When they celebrate the Passover, they must follow all the regulations. 13But if a man who is ceremonially clean and not on a journey fails to celebrate the Passover, that person must be cut off from his people because he did not present the LORD's offering at the appointed time. That man will bear the consequences of his sin.

14" 'An alien living among you who wants to celebrate the LORD's Passover must do so in accordance with its rules and regulations. You must have the same regulations for the alien and the native-born.' "

The Cloud Above the Tabernacle

15On the day the tabernacle, the Tent of the Testimony, was set up, the cloud covered it. From evening till morning the cloud above the tabernacle looked like fire. [16]That is how it continued to be; the cloud covered it, and at night it looked like fire. [17]Whenever the cloud lifted from above the Tent, the Israelites set out; wherever the cloud settled, the Israelites encamped. [18]At the LORD's command the Israelites set out, and at his command they encamped. As long as the cloud stayed over the tabernacle, they remained in camp. [19]When the cloud remained over the tabernacle a long time, the Israelites obeyed the LORD's order and did not set out. [20]Sometimes the cloud was over the tabernacle only a few days; at the LORD's command they would encamp, and then at his command they would set out. [21]Sometimes the cloud stayed only from evening till morning, and when it lifted in the morning, they set out. Whether by day or by night, whenever the cloud lifted, they set out. [22]Whether the cloud stayed over the tabernacle for two days or a month or a year, the Israelites would remain in camp and not set out; but when it lifted, they would set out. [23]At the LORD's command they encamped, and at the LORD's command they set out. They obeyed the LORD's order, in accordance with his command through Moses.

PRAYER: PETITION

MAY I put away all of these things: anger, wrath, malice, slander and abusive language from my mouth.
(Colossians 3:8)

PAUSE *here to petition God for growth in love and compassion toward others. Offer prayers for your loved ones, for those who do not know Jesus and for those in need. Offer prayers regarding your activities for this day and any special concerns you may have.*

NT Mark 15:1–47

Jesus Before Pilate

15 Very early in the morning, the chief priests, with the elders, the teachers of the law and the whole Sanhedrin, reached a decision. They bound Jesus, led him away and handed him over to Pilate.

[2]"Are you the king of the Jews?" asked Pilate.

"Yes, it is as you say," Jesus replied.

[3]The chief priests accused him of many things. [4]So again Pilate asked him, "Aren't you going to answer? See how many things they are accusing you of."

[5]But Jesus still made no reply, and Pilate was amazed.

[6]Now it was the custom at the Feast to release a prisoner whom the people requested. [7]A man called Barabbas was in prison with the insurrectionists who had committed murder in the uprising. [8]The crowd came up and asked Pilate to do for them what he usually did.

[9]"Do you want me to release to you the king of the Jews?" asked Pilate, [10]knowing it was out of envy that the chief priests had handed Jesus over to him. [11]But the chief priests stirred up the crowd to have Pilate release Barabbas instead.

[12]"What shall I do, then, with the one you call the king of the Jews?" Pilate asked them.

[13]"Crucify him!" they shouted.

[14]"Why? What crime has he committed?" asked Pilate.

But they shouted all the louder, "Crucify him!"

[15]Wanting to satisfy the crowd, Pilate released Barabbas to them. He had Jesus flogged, and handed him over to be crucified.

The Soldiers Mock Jesus

[16]The soldiers led Jesus away into the palace (that is, the Praetorium) and called together the whole company of soldiers. [17]They put a purple robe on him, then twisted together a crown of thorns and set it on him. [18]And they began to call out to him, "Hail, king of the Jews!" [19]Again and again they struck him on the head with a staff and spit on him. Falling on their knees, they paid homage to him. [20]And when they had mocked him, they took off

the purple robe and put his own clothes on him. Then they led him out to crucify him.

The Crucifixion

[21]A certain man from Cyrene, Simon, the father of Alexander and Rufus, was passing by on his way in from the country, and they forced him to carry the cross. [22]They brought Jesus to the place called Golgotha (which means The Place of the Skull). [23]Then they offered him wine mixed with myrrh, but he did not take it. [24]And they crucified him. Dividing up his clothes, they cast lots to see what each would get.

[25]It was the third hour when they crucified him. [26]The written notice of the charge against him read: THE KING OF THE JEWS. [27]They crucified two robbers with him, one on his right and one on his left.[a] [29]Those who passed by hurled insults at him, shaking their heads and saying, "So! You who are going to destroy the temple and build it in three days, [30]come down from the cross and save yourself!"

[31]In the same way the chief priests and the teachers of the law mocked him among themselves. "He saved others," they said, "but he can't save himself! [32]Let this Christ,[b] this King of Israel, come down now from the cross, that we may see and believe." Those crucified with him also heaped insults on him.

The Death of Jesus

[33]At the sixth hour darkness came over the whole land until the ninth hour. [34]And at the ninth hour Jesus cried out in a loud voice, *"Eloi, Eloi, lama sabachthani?"*—which means, "My God, my God, why have you forsaken me?"[c]

[35]When some of those standing near heard this, they said, "Listen, he's calling Elijah."

[36]One man ran, filled a sponge with wine vinegar, put it on a stick, and offered it to Jesus to drink. "Now leave him alone. Let's see if Elijah comes to take him down," he said.

[37]With a loud cry, Jesus breathed his last.

[38]The curtain of the temple was torn in two from top to bottom. [39]And when the centurion, who stood there in front of Jesus, heard his cry and[d] saw how he died, he said, "Surely this man was the Son[e] of God!"

[40]Some women were watching from a distance. Among them were Mary Magdalene, Mary the mother of James the younger and of Joses, and Salome. [41]In Galilee these women had followed him and cared for his needs. Many other women who had come up with him to Jerusalem were also there.

The Burial of Jesus

[42]It was Preparation Day (that is, the day before the Sabbath). So as evening approached, [43]Joseph of Arimathea, a prominent member of the Council, who was himself waiting for the kingdom of God, went boldly to Pilate and asked for Jesus' body. [44]Pilate was surprised to hear that he was already dead. Summoning the centurion, he asked him if Jesus had already died. [45]When he learned from the centurion that it was so, he gave the body to Joseph. [46]So Joseph bought some linen cloth, took down the body, wrapped it in the linen, and placed it in a tomb cut out of rock. Then he rolled a stone against the entrance of the tomb. [47]Mary Magdalene and Mary the mother of Joses saw where he was laid.

[a] 27 Some manuscripts *left,* [28]*and the scripture was fulfilled which says, "He was counted with the lawless ones"* (Isaiah 53:12) [b] 32 Or *Messiah*
[c] 34 Psalm 22:1 [d] 39 Some manuscripts do not have *heard his cry and* [e] 39 Or *a son*

PRAYER: MY RELATIONSHIP TO GOD

I WILL give thanks to You, O Lord, and call upon Your name and make known to others what You have done. I will sing to You, sing praises to You, and tell of all Your wonderful acts. (1 Chronicles 16:8–9) . . . I trust in Your loyal love; my heart rejoices in Your salvation. I will sing to You, O Lord, for You have dealt bountifully with me. (Psalm 13:5–6)

__PAUSE__ to thank God for the relationship that you enjoy with Him in Jesus Christ.

YEAR 1
DAY 124

OT **Numbers 10:1-36**

The Silver Trumpets

10 The LORD said to Moses: 2“Make two
trumpets of hammered silver, and use
them for calling the community together
and for having the camps set out. 3When
both are sounded, the whole community
is to assemble before you at the entrance
to the Tent of Meeting. 4If only one is
sounded, the leaders—the heads of the
clans of Israel—are to assemble before
you. 5When a trumpet blast is sounded,
the tribes camping on the east are to set
out. 6At the sounding of a second blast,
the camps on the south are to set out. The
blast will be the signal for setting out. 7To
gather the assembly, blow the trumpets,
but not with the same signal.

8“The sons of Aaron, the priests, are to
blow the trumpets. This is to be a lasting
ordinance for you and the generations to
come. 9When you go into battle in your
own land against an enemy who is oppressing you, sound a blast on the trumpets. Then you will be remembered by the
LORD your God and rescued from your enemies. 10Also at your times of rejoicing—
your appointed feasts and New Moon festivals—you are to sound the trumpets over
your burnt offerings and fellowship offerings,[a] and they will be a memorial for you
before your God. I am the LORD your God.”

The Israelites Leave Sinai

11On the twentieth day of the second
month of the second year, the cloud lifted from above the tabernacle of the Testimony. 12Then the Israelites set out from
the Desert of Sinai and traveled from
place to place until the cloud came to rest
in the Desert of Paran. 13They set out, this
first time, at the LORD's command through
Moses.

14The divisions of the camp of Judah
went first, under their standard. Nahshon
son of Amminadab was in command.
15Nethanel son of Zuar was over the division of the tribe of Issachar, 16and Eliab
son of Helon was over the division of the
tribe of Zebulun. 17Then the tabernacle
was taken down, and the Gershonites and
Merarites, who carried it, set out.

18The divisions of the camp of Reuben
went next, under their standard. Elizur son
of Shedeur was in command. 19Shelumiel
son of Zurishaddai was over the division
of the tribe of Simeon, 20and Eliasaph son
of Deuel was over the division of the tribe
of Gad. 21Then the Kohathites set out, carrying the holy things. The tabernacle was
to be set up before they arrived.

22The divisions of the camp of Ephraim
went next, under their standard. Elishama
son of Ammihud was in command. 23Ga-
maliel son of Pedahzur was over the division of the tribe of Manasseh, 24and Abidan son of Gideoni was over the division
of the tribe of Benjamin.

25Finally, as the rear guard for all the
units, the divisions of the camp of Dan set
out, under their standard. Ahiezer son of
Ammishaddai was in command. 26Pagiel
son of Ocran was over the division of the
tribe of Asher, 27and Ahira son of Enan
was over the division of the tribe of Naphtali. 28This was the order of march for the
Israelite divisions as they set out.

29Now Moses said to Hobab son of Reuel the Midianite, Moses' father-in-law, “We
are setting out for the place about which
the LORD said, 'I will give it to you.' Come
with us and we will treat you well, for the
LORD has promised good things to Israel.”

30He answered, “No, I will not go; I am
going back to my own land and my own
people.”

31But Moses said, “Please do not leave
us. You know where we should camp in
the desert, and you can be our eyes. 32If
you come with us, we will share with you
whatever good things the LORD gives us.”

33So they set out from the mountain of
the LORD and traveled for three days. The
ark of the covenant of the LORD went before them during those three days to find
them a place to rest. 34The cloud of the
LORD was over them by day when they set
out from the camp.

35Whenever the ark set out, Moses said,

“Rise up, O LORD!
  May your enemies be scattered;
  may your foes flee before you.”

36Whenever it came to rest, he said,

“Return, O LORD,
  to the countless thousands of Israel.”

[a] 10 Traditionally *peace offerings*

PRAYER: INTERCESSION

USE me, O God, to open the eyes of others and to turn them from darkness to light, and from the power of Satan to You, so that they may receive forgiveness of sins and an inheritance among those who have been sanctified by faith in Jesus. (Acts 26:18)

***TAKE** a few moments to intercede on behalf of friends, relatives, neighbors and coworkers who do not yet know salvation in Jesus Christ.*

NT Mark 16:1–20

The Resurrection

16 When the Sabbath was over, Mary Magdalene, Mary the mother of James, and
Salome bought spices so that they might go
to anoint Jesus' body. 2Very early on the first
day of the week, just after sunrise, they were
on their way to the tomb 3and they asked
each other, "Who will roll the stone away
from the entrance of the tomb?"
4But when they looked up, they saw
that the stone, which was very large, had
been rolled away. 5As they entered the
tomb, they saw a young man dressed in a
white robe sitting on the right side, and
they were alarmed.
6"Don't be alarmed," he said. "You are
looking for Jesus the Nazarene, who was
crucified. He has risen! He is not here. See
the place where they laid him. 7But go, tell
his disciples and Peter, 'He is going ahead
of you into Galilee. There you will see
him, just as he told you.' "
8Trembling and bewildered, the women
went out and fled from the tomb. They
said nothing to anyone, because they were
afraid.

[The earliest manuscripts and some other ancient witnesses do not have Mark 16:9–20.]

9When Jesus rose early on the first day
of the week, he appeared first to Mary
Magdalene, out of whom he had driven
seven demons. 10She went and told those
who had been with him and who were
mourning and weeping. 11When they
heard that Jesus was alive and that she
had seen him, they did not believe it.
12Afterward Jesus appeared in a different form to two of them while they were
walking in the country. 13These returned
and reported it to the rest; but they did
not believe them either.
14Later Jesus appeared to the Eleven as
they were eating; he rebuked them for
their lack of faith and their stubborn refusal to believe those who had seen him
after he had risen.
15He said to them, "Go into all the
world and preach the good news to all creation. 16Whoever believes and is baptized
will be saved, but whoever does not believe will be condemned. 17And these signs
will accompany those who believe: In my
name they will drive out demons; they
will speak in new tongues; 18they will pick
up snakes with their hands; and when
they drink deadly poison, it will not hurt
them at all; they will place their hands on
sick people, and they will get well."
19After the Lord Jesus had spoken to
them, he was taken up into heaven and he
sat at the right hand of God. 20Then the
disciples went out and preached everywhere, and the Lord worked with them
and confirmed his word by the signs that
accompanied it.

PRAYER: THE CHARACTER I WANT TO CULTIVATE

IN a multitude of words, transgression does not cease, but those who restrain their lips are wise. (Proverbs 10:19) . . . Fools have no delight in understanding but only in airing their own opinions. (Proverbs 18:2)

***TAKE** a moment to ask the Lord for the grace to grow in godly character.*

YEAR 1 DAY 125

OT **Numbers 11:1-35**

Fire From the L*ORD*

11 Now the people complained about
their hardships in the hearing of the
LORD, and when he heard them his anger
was aroused. Then fire from the LORD
burned among them and consumed some
of the outskirts of the camp. 2When the
people cried out to Moses, he prayed to
the LORD and the fire died down. 3So that
place was called Taberah,[a] because fire
from the LORD had burned among them.

Quail From the L*ORD*

4The rabble with them began to crave
other food, and again the Israelites started wailing and said, "If only we had meat
to eat! 5We remember the fish we ate in
Egypt at no cost—also the cucumbers,
melons, leeks, onions and garlic. 6But
now we have lost our appetite; we never
see anything but this manna!"

7The manna was like coriander seed
and looked like resin. 8The people went
around gathering it, and then ground it in
a handmill or crushed it in a mortar. They
cooked it in a pot or made it into cakes.
And it tasted like something made with
olive oil. 9When the dew settled on the
camp at night, the manna also came
down.

10Moses heard the people of every family wailing, each at the entrance to his
tent. The LORD became exceedingly angry,
and Moses was troubled. 11He asked the
LORD, "Why have you brought this trouble on your servant? What have I done to
displease you that you put the burden of
all these people on me? 12Did I conceive
all these people? Did I give them birth?
Why do you tell me to carry them in my
arms, as a nurse carries an infant, to the
land you promised on oath to their forefathers? 13Where can I get meat for all
these people? They keep wailing to me,
'Give us meat to eat!' 14I cannot carry all
these people by myself; the burden is too
heavy for me. 15If this is how you are going to treat me, put me to death right
now—if I have found favor in your eyes—
and do not let me face my own ruin."

16The LORD said to Moses: "Bring me
seventy of Israel's elders who are known
to you as leaders and officials among the
people. Have them come to the Tent of
Meeting, that they may stand there with
you. 17I will come down and speak with
you there, and I will take of the Spirit that
is on you and put the Spirit on them. They
will help you carry the burden of the people so that you will not have to carry it
alone.

18"Tell the people: 'Consecrate yourselves in preparation for tomorrow, when
you will eat meat. The LORD heard you
when you wailed, "If only we had meat to
eat! We were better off in Egypt!" Now the
LORD will give you meat, and you will eat
it. 19You will not eat it for just one day, or
two days, or five, ten or twenty days, 20but
for a whole month—until it comes out of
your nostrils and you loathe it—because
you have rejected the LORD, who is among
you, and have wailed before him, saying,
"Why did we ever leave Egypt?" ' "

21But Moses said, "Here I am among six
hundred thousand men on foot, and you
say, 'I will give them meat to eat for a
whole month!' 22Would they have enough
if flocks and herds were slaughtered for
them? Would they have enough if all the
fish in the sea were caught for them?"

23The LORD answered Moses, "Is the
LORD's arm too short? You will now see
whether or not what I say will come true
for you."

24So Moses went out and told the people what the LORD had said. He brought
together seventy of their elders and had
them stand around the Tent. 25Then the
LORD came down in the cloud and spoke
with him, and he took of the Spirit that
was on him and put the Spirit on the seventy elders. When the Spirit rested on
them, they prophesied, but they did not
do so again.[b]

26However, two men, whose names
were Eldad and Medad, had remained in
the camp. They were listed among the elders, but did not go out to the Tent. Yet
the Spirit also rested on them, and they
prophesied in the camp. 27A young man
ran and told Moses, "Eldad and Medad
are prophesying in the camp."

[a] 3 *Taberah* means *burning.* [b] 25 Or *prophesied and continued to do so*

28Joshua son of Nun, who had been Moses' aide since youth, spoke up and said, "Moses, my lord, stop them!"

29But Moses replied, "Are you jealous for my sake? I wish that all the LORD's people were prophets and that the LORD would put his Spirit on them!" 30Then Moses and the elders of Israel returned to the camp.

31Now a wind went out from the LORD and drove quail in from the sea. It brought them[c] down all around the camp to about three feet[d] above the ground, as far as a day's walk in any direction. 32All that day and night and all the next day the people went out and gathered quail. No one gathered less than ten homers.[e] Then they spread them out all around the camp. 33But while the meat was still between their teeth and before it could be consumed, the anger of the LORD burned against the people, and he struck them with a severe plague. 34Therefore the place was named Kibroth Hattaavah,[f] because there they buried the people who had craved other food.

35From Kibroth Hattaavah the people traveled to Hazeroth and stayed there.

[c] 31 Or *They flew* [d] 31 Hebrew *two cubits* (about 1 meter) [e] 32 That is, probably about 60 bushels (about 2.2 kiloliters) [f] 34 *Kibroth Hattaavah* means *graves of craving.*

PRAYER: AFFIRMATION

BLESSED are those who persevere under trial, because when they have been approved, they will receive the crown of life that You have promised to those who love You. (James 1:12) . . . I have overcome, O God, because You are in me, and You are greater than he who is in the world. (1 John 4:4)

PAUSE *to reflect on these Biblical affirmations.*

NT 1 Corinthians 1:1-17

1 Paul, called to be an apostle of Christ Jesus by the will of God, and our brother Sosthenes,

2To the church of God in Corinth, to those sanctified in Christ Jesus and called to be holy, together with all those everywhere who call on the name of our Lord Jesus Christ—their Lord and ours:

3Grace and peace to you from God our Father and the Lord Jesus Christ.

Thanksgiving

4I always thank God for you because of his grace given you in Christ Jesus. 5For in him you have been enriched in every way—in all your speaking and in all your knowledge— 6because our testimony about Christ was confirmed in you. 7Therefore you do not lack any spiritual gift as you eagerly wait for our Lord Jesus Christ to be revealed. 8He will keep you strong to the end, so that you will be blameless on the day of our Lord Jesus Christ. 9God, who has called you into fellowship with his Son Jesus Christ our Lord, is faithful.

Divisions in the Church

10I appeal to you, brothers, in the name of our Lord Jesus Christ, that all of you agree with one another so that there may be no divisions among you and that you may be perfectly united in mind and thought. 11My brothers, some from Chloe's household have informed me that there are quarrels among you. 12What I mean is this: One of you says, "I follow Paul"; another, "I follow Apollos"; another, "I follow Cephas[a]"; still another, "I follow Christ."

13Is Christ divided? Was Paul crucified for you? Were you baptized into[b] the name of Paul? 14I am thankful that I did not baptize any of you except Crispus and Gaius, 15so no one can say that you were baptized into my name. 16(Yes, I also baptized the household of Stephanas; beyond that, I don't remember if I baptized anyone else.) 17For Christ did not send me to baptize, but to preach the gospel—not with words of human wisdom, lest the cross of Christ be emptied of its power.

[a] 12 That is, Peter [b] 13 Or *in;* also in verse 15

PRAYER: MY RELATIONSHIP TO OTHERS

LOVE is as strong as death; its jealousy is as cruel as the grave; its flames are a blazing fire from You, O Lord. Many waters cannot quench love, nor can rivers overflow it. If a man were to give all the wealth of his house for love, it would be utterly scorned. (Song of Songs 8:6–7) . . . A husband should not break his promises to the wife of his youth, because she is a companion and a wife by covenant. Lord God of hosts, You seek a godly offspring and hate divorce; therefore we must take heed to our spirit and not break faith. (Malachi 2:14–16)

__PAUSE__ to review your relationships with others and to commit them to the Lord.

YEAR 1 DAY 126

OT Psalm 27

Psalm 27

Of David.

[1]The LORD is my light and my salvation—
whom shall I fear?
The LORD is the stronghold of my life—
of whom shall I be afraid?
[2]When evil men advance against me
to devour my flesh,[a]
when my enemies and my foes attack me,
they will stumble and fall.
[3]Though an army besiege me,
my heart will not fear;
though war break out against me,
even then will I be confident.

[4]One thing I ask of the LORD,
this is what I seek:
that I may dwell in the house of the LORD
all the days of my life,
to gaze upon the beauty of the LORD
and to seek him in his temple.
[5]For in the day of trouble
he will keep me safe in his dwelling;
he will hide me in the shelter of his tabernacle
and set me high upon a rock.
[6]Then my head will be exalted
above the enemies who surround me;
at his tabernacle will I sacrifice with shouts of joy;
I will sing and make music to the LORD.

[7]Hear my voice when I call, O LORD;
be merciful to me and answer me.
[8]My heart says of you, "Seek his[b] face!"
Your face, LORD, I will seek.
[9]Do not hide your face from me,
do not turn your servant away in anger;
you have been my helper.
Do not reject me or forsake me,
O God my Savior.
[10]Though my father and mother forsake me,
the LORD will receive me.
[11]Teach me your way, O LORD;
lead me in a straight path
because of my oppressors.
[12]Do not turn me over to the desire of my foes,
for false witnesses rise up against me,
breathing out violence.

[13]I am still confident of this:
I will see the goodness of the LORD
in the land of the living.
[14]Wait for the LORD;
be strong and take heart
and wait for the LORD.

[a] 2 Or *to slander me* [b] 8 Or *To you, O my heart, he has said, "Seek my*

PRAYER: THANKSGIVING

MY soul blesses You, O Lord; and all that is within me blesses Your holy name. My soul blesses You, O Lord, and I will not forget all Your benefits; You forgive all my iniquities and heal all my diseases; You redeem my life from the pit and crown me with love and compassion; You satisfy my desires with good things, so that my youth is renewed like the eagle's. (Psalm 103:1–5)

***PAUSE** to offer your own expressions of thanksgiving.*

NT 1 Corinthians 1:18–2:5

Christ the Wisdom and Power of God

[18]For the message of the cross is foolishness to those who are perishing, but to us who are being saved it is the power of God. [19]For it is written:

> "I will destroy the wisdom of the wise;
> the intelligence of the intelligent I
> will frustrate."[a]

[20]Where is the wise man? Where is the scholar? Where is the philosopher of this age? Has not God made foolish the wisdom of the world? [21]For since in the wisdom of God the world through its wisdom did not know him, God was pleased through the foolishness of what was preached to save those who believe. [22]Jews demand miraculous signs and Greeks look for wisdom, [23]but we preach Christ crucified: a stumbling block to Jews and foolishness to Gentiles, [24]but to those whom God has called, both Jews and Greeks, Christ the power of God and the wisdom of God. [25]For the foolishness of God is wiser than man's wisdom, and the weakness of God is stronger than man's strength.

[26]Brothers, think of what you were when you were called. Not many of you were wise by human standards; not many were influential; not many were of noble birth. [27]But God chose the foolish things of the world to shame the wise; God chose the weak things of the world to shame the strong. [28]He chose the lowly things of this world and the despised things—and the things that are not—to nullify the things that are, [29]so that no one may boast before him. [30]It is because of him that you are in Christ Jesus, who has become for us wisdom from God—that is, our righteousness, holiness and redemption. [31]Therefore, as it is written: "Let him who boasts boast in the Lord."[b]

2 When I came to you, brothers, I did not come with eloquence or superior wisdom as I proclaimed to you the testimony about God.[c] [2]For I resolved to know nothing while I was with you except Jesus Christ and him crucified. [3]I came to you in weakness and fear, and with much trembling. [4]My message and my preaching were not with wise and persuasive words, but with a demonstration of the Spirit's power, [5]so that your faith might not rest on men's wisdom, but on God's power.

[a] *19* Isaiah 29:14 [b] *31* Jer. 9:24 [c] *1* Some manuscripts *as I proclaimed to you God's mystery*

PRAYER: THE ATTRIBUTES OF GOD

NOTHING is too difficult for You, O Lord. (Genesis 18:14) . . . All things are possible with You, O God. (Matthew 19:26; Mark 10:27)

***PAUSE** to reflect on these affirmations about the person, powers and perfection of God.*

YEAR 1 DAY 127

OT Numbers 12:1–13:33

Miriam and Aaron Oppose Moses

12 Miriam and Aaron began to talk
against Moses because of his Cushite
wife, for he had married a Cushite. 2 "Has
the LORD spoken only through Moses?"
they asked. "Hasn't he also spoken
through us?" And the LORD heard this.
3 (Now Moses was a very humble man,
more humble than anyone else on the
face of the earth.)
4 At once the LORD said to Moses, Aaron
and Miriam, "Come out to the Tent of
Meeting, all three of you." So the three of
them came out. 5 Then the LORD came
down in a pillar of cloud; he stood at the
entrance to the Tent and summoned Aaron and Miriam. When both of them
stepped forward, 6 he said, "Listen to my
words:

"When a prophet of the LORD is
among you,
I reveal myself to him in visions,
I speak to him in dreams.
7 But this is not true of my servant
Moses;
he is faithful in all my house.
8 With him I speak face to face,
clearly and not in riddles;
he sees the form of the LORD.
Why then were you not afraid
to speak against my servant Moses?"

9 The anger of the LORD burned against
them, and he left them.
10 When the cloud lifted from above the
Tent, there stood Miriam—leprous,[a] like
snow. Aaron turned toward her and saw
that she had leprosy; 11 and he said to Moses, "Please, my lord, do not hold against
us the sin we have so foolishly committed. 12 Do not let her be like a stillborn infant coming from its mother's womb with
its flesh half eaten away."
13 So Moses cried out to the LORD,
"O God, please heal her!"
14 The LORD replied to Moses, "If her father had spit in her face, would she not
have been in disgrace for seven days? Confine her outside the camp for seven days;
after that she can be brought back." 15 So
Miriam was confined outside the camp
for seven days, and the people did not
move on till she was brought back.
16 After that, the people left Hazeroth
and encamped in the Desert of Paran.

Exploring Canaan

13 The LORD said to Moses, 2 "Send some
men to explore the land of Canaan,
which I am giving to the Israelites. From
each ancestral tribe send one of its leaders."
3 So at the LORD's command Moses sent
them out from the Desert of Paran. All of
them were leaders of the Israelites. 4 These
are their names:

from the tribe of Reuben, Shammua
son of Zaccur;
5 from the tribe of Simeon, Shaphat
son of Hori;
6 from the tribe of Judah, Caleb son of
Jephunneh;
7 from the tribe of Issachar, Igal son of
Joseph;
8 from the tribe of Ephraim, Hoshea
son of Nun;
9 from the tribe of Benjamin, Palti son
of Raphu;
10 from the tribe of Zebulun, Gaddiel
son of Sodi;
11 from the tribe of Manasseh (a tribe
of Joseph), Gaddi son of Susi;
12 from the tribe of Dan, Ammiel son of
Gemalli;
13 from the tribe of Asher, Sethur son of
Michael;
14 from the tribe of Naphtali, Nahbi
son of Vophsi;
15 from the tribe of Gad, Geuel son of
Maki.

16 These are the names of the men Moses
sent to explore the land. (Moses gave Hoshea son of Nun the name Joshua.)
17 When Moses sent them to explore Canaan, he said, "Go up through the Negev
and on into the hill country. 18 See what
the land is like and whether the people
who live there are strong or weak, few or
many. 19 What kind of land do they live in?
Is it good or bad? What kind of towns do
they live in? Are they unwalled or fortified? 20 How is the soil? Is it fertile or poor?
Are there trees on it or not? Do your best

[a] *10* The Hebrew word was used for various diseases affecting the skin—not necessarily leprosy.

to bring back some of the fruit of the land." (It was the season for the first ripe grapes.)

21 So they went up and explored the land from the Desert of Zin as far as Rehob, toward Lebo[a] Hamath. 22 They went up through the Negev and came to Hebron, where Ahiman, Sheshai and Talmai, the descendants of Anak, lived. (Hebron had been built seven years before Zoan in Egypt.) 23 When they reached the Valley of Eshcol,[b] they cut off a branch bearing a single cluster of grapes. Two of them carried it on a pole between them, along with some pomegranates and figs. 24 That place was called the Valley of Eshcol because of the cluster of grapes the Israelites cut off there. 25 At the end of forty days they returned from exploring the land.

Report on the Exploration

26 They came back to Moses and Aaron and the whole Israelite community at Kadesh in the Desert of Paran. There they reported to them and to the whole assembly and showed them the fruit of the land. 27 They gave Moses this account: "We went into the land to which you sent us, and it does flow with milk and honey! Here is its fruit. 28 But the people who live there are powerful, and the cities are fortified and very large. We even saw descendants of Anak there. 29 The Amalekites live in the Negev; the Hittites, Jebusites and Amorites live in the hill country; and the Canaanites live near the sea and along the Jordan."

30 Then Caleb silenced the people before Moses and said, "We should go up and take possession of the land, for we can certainly do it."

31 But the men who had gone up with him said, "We can't attack those people; they are stronger than we are." 32 And they spread among the Israelites a bad report about the land they had explored. They said, "The land we explored devours those living in it. All the people we saw there are of great size. 33 We saw the Nephilim there (the descendants of Anak come from the Nephilim). We seemed like grasshoppers in our own eyes, and we looked the same to them."

[a] 21 Or *toward the entrance to* [b] 23 *Eshcol* means *cluster;* also in verse 24.

PRAYER: ADORATION

HOW great You are, O Sovereign Lord! There is no one like You, and there is no God besides You, according to all that I have heard with my ears. (2 Samuel 7:22; 1 Chronicles 17:20) . . . You alone are the Lord. You made the heavens, the heaven of heavens, and all their host, the earth and all that is on it, the seas and all that is in them. You give life to all that is in them, and the host of heaven worships You. (Nehemiah 9:6)

PAUSE *to express your thoughts of praise and worship.*

NT 1 Corinthians 2:6–16

Wisdom From the Spirit

6 We do, however, speak a message of wisdom among the mature, but not the wisdom of this age or of the rulers of this age, who are coming to nothing. 7 No, we speak of God's secret wisdom, a wisdom that has been hidden and that God destined for our glory before time began. 8 None of the rulers of this age understood it, for if they had, they would not have crucified the Lord of glory. 9 However, as it is written:

"No eye has seen,
no ear has heard,
no mind has conceived
what God has prepared for those
who love him"[a]—

10 but God has revealed it to us by his Spirit.

The Spirit searches all things, even the deep things of God. 11 For who among men knows the thoughts of a man except the man's spirit within him? In the same way no one knows the thoughts of God except the Spirit of God. 12 We have not

[a] 9 Isaiah 64:4

received the spirit of the world but the Spirit who is from God, that we may understand what God has freely given us. [13]This is what we speak, not in words taught us by human wisdom but in words taught by the Spirit, expressing spiritual truths in spiritual words.[b] [14]The man without the Spirit does not accept the things that come from the Spirit of God, for they are foolishness to him, and he cannot understand them, because they are spiritually discerned. [15]The spiritual man makes judgments about all things, but he himself is not subject to any man's judgment:

[16]"For who has known the mind of the
Lord
that he may instruct him?"[c]

But we have the mind of Christ.

[b] *13* Or *Spirit, interpreting spiritual truths to spiritual men* [c] *16* Isaiah 40:13

PRAYER: THE WORKS OF GOD

O SERVANT of God, people despised and rejected You; You were a man of sorrows, and acquainted with grief. And like one from whom others hide their faces, You were despised, and we did not esteem You. Surely You have borne our infirmities and carried our sorrows; yet we considered You stricken, smitten by God, and afflicted. But You were pierced for our transgressions, You were crushed for our iniquities; the punishment that brought us peace was upon You, and by Your wounds we are healed. All of us like sheep have gone astray, all of us have turned to our own way, and the Lord has laid on You the iniquity of us all. (Isaiah 53:3–6)

***TAKE** a moment to consider the greatness of God's wonderful works.*

YEAR 1 DAY 128

OT Numbers 14:1–45

The People Rebel

14 That night all the people of the community raised their voices and wept aloud. [2]All the Israelites grumbled against Moses and Aaron, and the whole assembly said to them, "If only we had died in Egypt! Or in this desert! [3]Why is the LORD bringing us to this land only to let us fall by the sword? Our wives and children will be taken as plunder. Wouldn't it be better for us to go back to Egypt?" [4]And they said to each other, "We should choose a leader and go back to Egypt."

[5]Then Moses and Aaron fell facedown in front of the whole Israelite assembly gathered there. [6]Joshua son of Nun and Caleb son of Jephunneh, who were among those who had explored the land, tore their clothes [7]and said to the entire Israelite assembly, "The land we passed through and explored is exceedingly good. [8]If the LORD is pleased with us, he will lead us into that land, a land flowing with milk and honey, and will give it to us. [9]Only do not rebel against the LORD. And do not be afraid of the people of the land, because we will swallow them up. Their protection is gone, but the LORD is with us. Do not be afraid of them."

[10]But the whole assembly talked about stoning them. Then the glory of the LORD appeared at the Tent of Meeting to all the Israelites. [11]The LORD said to Moses, "How long will these people treat me with contempt? How long will they refuse to believe in me, in spite of all the miraculous signs I have performed among them? [12]I will strike them down with a plague and destroy them, but I will make you into a nation greater and stronger than they."

[13]Moses said to the LORD, "Then the Egyptians will hear about it! By your power you brought these people up from among them. [14]And they will tell the inhabitants of this land about it. They have already heard that you, O LORD, are with these people and that you, O LORD, have

been seen face to face, that your cloud
stays over them, and that you go before
them in a pillar of cloud by day and a pillar of fire by night. [15]If you put these people to death all at one time, the nations
who have heard this report about you will
say, [16]'The LORD was not able to bring
these people into the land he promised
them on oath; so he slaughtered them in
the desert.'

[17]"Now may the Lord's strength be displayed, just as you have declared: [18]'The
LORD is slow to anger, abounding in love
and forgiving sin and rebellion. Yet he
does not leave the guilty unpunished; he
punishes the children for the sin of the fathers to the third and fourth generation.'
[19]In accordance with your great love, forgive the sin of these people, just as you
have pardoned them from the time they
left Egypt until now."

[20]The LORD replied, "I have forgiven
them, as you asked. [21]Nevertheless, as
surely as I live and as surely as the glory
of the LORD fills the whole earth, [22]not one
of the men who saw my glory and the
miraculous signs I performed in Egypt
and in the desert but who disobeyed me
and tested me ten times— [23]not one of
them will ever see the land I promised on
oath to their forefathers. No one who has
treated me with contempt will ever see it.
[24]But because my servant Caleb has a different spirit and follows me wholeheartedly, I will bring him into the land he
went to, and his descendants will inherit
it. [25]Since the Amalekites and Canaanites
are living in the valleys, turn back tomorrow and set out toward the desert along
the route to the Red Sea.[a]"

[26]The LORD said to Moses and Aaron:
[27]"How long will this wicked community
grumble against me? I have heard the
complaints of these grumbling Israelites.
[28]So tell them, 'As surely as I live, declares
the LORD, I will do to you the very things
I heard you say: [29]In this desert your bodies will fall—every one of you twenty
years old or more who was counted in the
census and who has grumbled against me.
[30]Not one of you will enter the land I
swore with uplifted hand to make your
home, except Caleb son of Jephunneh
and Joshua son of Nun. [31]As for your children that you said would be taken as
plunder, I will bring them in to enjoy the
land you have rejected. [32]But you—your
bodies will fall in this desert. [33]Your children will be shepherds here for forty
years, suffering for your unfaithfulness,
until the last of your bodies lies in the
desert. [34]For forty years—one year for each
of the forty days you explored the land—
you will suffer for your sins and know
what it is like to have me against you.' [35]I,
the LORD, have spoken, and I will surely
do these things to this whole wicked community, which has banded together
against me. They will meet their end in
this desert; here they will die."

[36]So the men Moses had sent to explore
the land, who returned and made the
whole community grumble against him
by spreading a bad report about it—
[37]these men responsible for spreading the
bad report about the land were struck
down and died of a plague before the
LORD. [38]Of the men who went to explore
the land, only Joshua son of Nun and Caleb son of Jephunneh survived.

[39]When Moses reported this to all the
Israelites, they mourned bitterly. [40]Early
the next morning they went up toward the
high hill country. "We have sinned," they
said. "We will go up to the place the LORD
promised."

[41]But Moses said, "Why are you dis-
obeying the LORD's command? This will
not succeed! [42]Do not go up, because the
LORD is not with you. You will be defeated by your enemies, [43]for the Amalekites
and Canaanites will face you there. Because you have turned away from the
LORD, he will not be with you and you
will fall by the sword."

[44]Nevertheless, in their presumption
they went up toward the high hill country, though neither Moses nor the ark of
the LORD's covenant moved from the
camp. [45]Then the Amalekites and Canaanites who lived in that hill country came
down and attacked them and beat them
down all the way to Hormah.

[a] 25 Hebrew *Yam Suph;* that is, Sea of Reeds

PRAYER: CONFESSION

MAY I learn the importance of forgiveness from You, Jesus, who were asked by Peter: "Lord, how often shall my brother sin against me, and I forgive him? Up to seven times?" And You said to him, "I tell you, not seven times, but up to seventy times seven."

(Matthew 18:21–22)

***ASK** the Spirit to search your heart and reveal any areas of unconfessed sin. Acknowledge these to the Lord and thank Him for His forgiveness.*

NT 1 Corinthians 3:1–23

On Divisions in the Church

3 Brothers, I could not address you as
spiritual but as worldly—mere infants
in Christ. 2 I gave you milk, not solid food,
for you were not yet ready for it. Indeed,
you are still not ready. 3 You are still worldly. For since there is jealousy and quarreling among you, are you not worldly? Are
you not acting like mere men? 4 For when
one says, "I follow Paul," and another, "I
follow Apollos," are you not mere men?
5 What, after all, is Apollos? And what is
Paul? Only servants, through whom you
came to believe—as the Lord has assigned
to each his task. 6 I planted the seed, Apollos watered it, but God made it grow. 7 So
neither he who plants nor he who waters
is anything, but only God, who makes
things grow. 8 The man who plants and the
man who waters have one purpose, and
each will be rewarded according to his
own labor. 9 For we are God's fellow workers; you are God's field, God's building.
10 By the grace God has given me, I laid
a foundation as an expert builder, and
someone else is building on it. But each
one should be careful how he builds. 11 For
no one can lay any foundation other than
the one already laid, which is Jesus Christ.
12 If any man builds on this foundation using gold, silver, costly stones, wood, hay or
straw, 13 his work will be shown for what it
is, because the Day will bring it to light. It
will be revealed with fire, and the fire will
test the quality of each man's work. 14 If
what he has built survives, he will receive
his reward. 15 If it is burned up, he will suffer loss; he himself will be saved, but only
as one escaping through the flames.
16 Don't you know that you yourselves
are God's temple and that God's Spirit
lives in you? 17 If anyone destroys God's
temple, God will destroy him; for God's
temple is sacred, and you are that temple.
18 Do not deceive yourselves. If any one
of you thinks he is wise by the standards
of this age, he should become a "fool" so
that he may become wise. 19 For the wisdom of this world is foolishness in God's
sight. As it is written: "He catches the wise
in their craftiness"[a]; 20 and again, "The
Lord knows that the thoughts of the wise
are futile."[b] 21 So then, no more boasting
about men! All things are yours,
22 whether Paul or Apollos or Cephas[c] or
the world or life or death or the present
or the future—all are yours, 23 and you are
of Christ, and Christ is of God.

[a] *19* Job 5:13 [b] *20* Psalm 94:11 [c] *22* That is, Peter

PRAYER: MY RELATIONSHIP TO GOD

THROUGH the law I died to the law so that I might live for God. I have been crucified with You, O Christ, and it is no longer I who live, but You live in me. The life that I now live in the flesh, I live by faith in You, the Son of God, who loved me and gave Yourself for me.

(Galatians 2:19–20)

***PAUSE** to thank God for the relationship that you enjoy with Him in Jesus Christ.*

OT Numbers 15:1-41

Supplementary Offerings

15 The LORD said to Moses, 2"Speak to the Israelites and say to them: 'After you enter the land I am giving you as a home 3and you present to the LORD offerings made by fire, from the herd or the flock, as an aroma pleasing to the LORD—whether burnt offerings or sacrifices, for special vows or freewill offerings or festival offerings— 4then the one who brings his offering shall present to the LORD a grain offering of a tenth of an ephah[a] of fine flour mixed with a quarter of a hin[b] of oil. 5With each lamb for the burnt offering or the sacrifice, prepare a quarter of a hin of wine as a drink offering.

6" 'With a ram prepare a grain offering of two-tenths of an ephah[c] of fine flour mixed with a third of a hin[d] of oil, 7and a third of a hin of wine as a drink offering. Offer it as an aroma pleasing to the LORD.

8" 'When you prepare a young bull as a burnt offering or sacrifice, for a special vow or a fellowship offering[e] to the LORD, 9bring with the bull a grain offering of three-tenths of an ephah[f] of fine flour mixed with half a hin[g] of oil. 10Also bring half a hin of wine as a drink offering. It will be an offering made by fire, an aroma pleasing to the LORD. 11Each bull or ram, each lamb or young goat, is to be prepared in this manner. 12Do this for each one, for as many as you prepare.

13" 'Everyone who is native-born must do these things in this way when he brings an offering made by fire as an aroma pleasing to the LORD. 14For the generations to come, whenever an alien or anyone else living among you presents an offering made by fire as an aroma pleasing to the LORD, he must do exactly as you do. 15The community is to have the same rules for you and for the alien living among you; this is a lasting ordinance for the generations to come. You and the alien shall be the same before the LORD: 16The same laws and regulations will apply both to you and to the alien living among you.' "

17The LORD said to Moses, 18"Speak to the Israelites and say to them: 'When you enter the land to which I am taking you 19and you eat the food of the land, present a portion as an offering to the LORD. 20Present a cake from the first of your ground meal and present it as an offering from the threshing floor. 21Throughout the generations to come you are to give this offering to the LORD from the first of your ground meal.

Offerings for Unintentional Sins

22" 'Now if you unintentionally fail to keep any of these commands the LORD gave Moses— 23any of the LORD's commands to you through him, from the day the LORD gave them and continuing through the generations to come— 24and if this is done unintentionally without the community being aware of it, then the whole community is to offer a young bull for a burnt offering as an aroma pleasing to the LORD, along with its prescribed grain offering and drink offering, and a male goat for a sin offering. 25The priest is to make atonement for the whole Israelite community, and they will be forgiven, for it was not intentional and they have brought to the LORD for their wrong an offering made by fire and a sin offering. 26The whole Israelite community and the aliens living among them will be forgiven, because all the people were involved in the unintentional wrong.

27" 'But if just one person sins unintentionally, he must bring a year-old female goat for a sin offering. 28The priest is to make atonement before the LORD for the one who erred by sinning unintentionally, and when atonement has been made for him, he will be forgiven. 29One and the same law applies to everyone who sins unintentionally, whether he is a native-born Israelite or an alien.

30" 'But anyone who sins defiantly, whether native-born or alien, blasphemes the LORD, and that person must be cut off from his people. 31Because he has de-

[a] *4* That is, probably about 2 quarts (about 2 liters)
[b] *4* That is, probably about 1 quart (about 1 liter); also in verse 5
[c] *6* That is, probably about 4 quarts (about 4.5 liters)
[d] *6* That is, probably about 1 1/4 quarts (about 1.2 liters); also in verse 7
[e] *8* Traditionally *peace offering*
[f] *9* That is, probably about 6 quarts (about 6.5 liters)
[g] *9* That is, probably about 2 quarts (about 2 liters); also in verse 10

spised the LORD's word and broken his
commands, that person must surely be
cut off; his guilt remains on him.' "

The Sabbath-Breaker Put to Death

32While the Israelites were in the desert,
a man was found gathering wood on the
Sabbath day. 33Those who found him gathering wood brought him to Moses and Aaron and the whole assembly, 34and they
kept him in custody, because it was not
clear what should be done to him. 35Then
the LORD said to Moses, "The man must
die. The whole assembly must stone him
outside the camp." 36So the assembly took
him outside the camp and stoned him to
death, as the LORD commanded Moses.

Tassels on Garments

37The LORD said to Moses, 38"Speak to
the Israelites and say to them: 'Throughout the generations to come you are to
make tassels on the corners of your garments, with a blue cord on each tassel.
39You will have these tassels to look at and
so you will remember all the commands
of the LORD, that you may obey them and
not prostitute yourselves by going after
the lusts of your own hearts and eyes.
40Then you will remember to obey all my
commands and will be consecrated to
your God. 41I am the LORD your God, who
brought you out of Egypt to be your God.
I am the LORD your God.' "

PRAYER: RENEWAL

O LORD, may I not be like those who draw near to You with their mouths and honor You with their lips but whose hearts are far from You; their reverence for You is made up only of human rules. (Isaiah 29:13) . . . I desire not only to call You "Lord" but to do what You say. By Your grace I will come to You, hear Your words, and put them into practice. Then I will be like someone who built a house, who dug down deep and laid the foundation on rock; when a flood came, the torrent struck that house but could not shake it, because it was well built. (Luke 6:46–48)

***PAUSE** to add your own prayers for personal renewal.*

NT 1 Corinthians 4:1–21

Apostles of Christ

4 So then, men ought to regard us as servants of Christ and as those entrusted
with the secret things of God. 2Now it is
required that those who have been given
a trust must prove faithful. 3I care very little if I am judged by you or by any human
court; indeed, I do not even judge myself.
4My conscience is clear, but that does not
make me innocent. It is the Lord who
judges me. 5Therefore judge nothing before the appointed time; wait till the Lord
comes. He will bring to light what is hidden in darkness and will expose the motives of men's hearts. At that time each
will receive his praise from God.
6Now, brothers, I have applied these
things to myself and Apollos for your benefit, so that you may learn from us the
meaning of the saying, "Do not go beyond what is written." Then you will not
take pride in one man over against another. 7For who makes you different from
anyone else? What do you have that you
did not receive? And if you did receive it,
why do you boast as though you did not?
8Already you have all you want! Already
you have become rich! You have become
kings—and that without us! How I wish
that you really had become kings so that
we might be kings with you! 9For it seems
to me that God has put us apostles on display at the end of the procession, like men
condemned to die in the arena. We have
been made a spectacle to the whole universe, to angels as well as to men. 10We are
fools for Christ, but you are so wise in
Christ! We are weak, but you are strong!
You are honored, we are dishonored! 11To
this very hour we go hungry and thirsty,
we are in rags, we are brutally treated, we
are homeless. 12We work hard with our

own hands. When we are cursed, we bless; when we are persecuted, we endure it; 13when we are slandered, we answer kindly. Up to this moment we have become the scum of the earth, the refuse of the world.

14I am not writing this to shame you, but to warn you, as my dear children. 15Even though you have ten thousand guardians in Christ, you do not have many fathers, for in Christ Jesus I became your father through the gospel. 16Therefore I urge you to imitate me. 17For this reason I am sending to you Timothy, my son whom I love, who is faithful in the Lord. He will remind you of my way of life in Christ Jesus, which agrees with what I teach everywhere in every church.

18Some of you have become arrogant, as if I were not coming to you. 19But I will come to you very soon, if the Lord is willing, and then I will find out not only how these arrogant people are talking, but what power they have. 20For the kingdom of God is not a matter of talk but of power. 21What do you prefer? Shall I come to you with a whip, or in love and with a gentle spirit?

PRAYER: THE CHARACTER I WANT TO CULTIVATE

O LORD, thank You for the truth You have spoken when You said, "Let not those who are wise boast of wisdom, and let not those who are strong boast of strength, and let not those who are rich boast of riches; but let those who boast boast about this: that they understand and know Me, that I am the Lord, who exercises loving-kindness, justice and righteousness on earth; for in these I delight." (Jeremiah 9:23–24)

TAKE *a moment to ask the Lord for the grace to grow in godly character.*

YEAR 1 DAY 130

OT Numbers 16:1–50

Korah, Dathan and Abiram

16 Korah son of Izhar, the son of Kohath, the son of Levi, and certain Reubenites—Dathan and Abiram, sons of Eliab, and On son of Peleth—became insolent[a] 2and rose up against Moses. With them were 250 Israelite men, well-known community leaders who had been appointed members of the council. 3They came as a group to oppose Moses and Aaron and said to them, "You have gone too far! The whole community is holy, every one of them, and the LORD is with them. Why then do you set yourselves above the LORD's assembly?"

4When Moses heard this, he fell facedown. 5Then he said to Korah and all his followers: "In the morning the LORD will show who belongs to him and who is holy, and he will have that person come near him. The man he chooses he will cause to come near him. 6You, Korah, and all your followers are to do this: Take censers 7and tomorrow put fire and incense in them before the LORD. The man the LORD chooses will be the one who is holy. You Levites have gone too far!"

8Moses also said to Korah, "Now listen, you Levites! 9Isn't it enough for you that the God of Israel has separated you from the rest of the Israelite community and brought you near himself to do the work at the LORD's tabernacle and to stand before the community and minister to them? 10He has brought you and all your fellow Levites near himself, but now you are trying to get the priesthood too. 11It is against the LORD that you and all your followers have banded together. Who is Aaron that you should grumble against him?"

12Then Moses summoned Dathan and Abiram, the sons of Eliab. But they said, "We will not come! 13Isn't it enough that you have brought us up out of a land flowing with milk and honey to kill us in the desert? And now you also want to lord

[a] *1* Or *Peleth—took* ⌊*men*⌋

it over us? 14Moreover, you haven't brought us into a land flowing with milk and honey or given us an inheritance of fields and vineyards. Will you gouge out the eyes of[b] these men? No, we will not come!"

15Then Moses became very angry and said to the LORD, "Do not accept their offering. I have not taken so much as a donkey from them, nor have I wronged any of them."

16Moses said to Korah, "You and all your followers are to appear before the LORD tomorrow—you and they and Aaron. 17Each man is to take his censer and put incense in it—250 censers in all—and present it before the LORD. You and Aaron are to present your censers also." 18So each man took his censer, put fire and incense in it, and stood with Moses and Aaron at the entrance to the Tent of Meeting. 19When Korah had gathered all his followers in opposition to them at the entrance to the Tent of Meeting, the glory of the LORD appeared to the entire assembly. 20The LORD said to Moses and Aaron, 21"Separate yourselves from this assembly so I can put an end to them at once."

22But Moses and Aaron fell facedown and cried out, "O God, God of the spirits of all mankind, will you be angry with the entire assembly when only one man sins?"

23Then the LORD said to Moses, 24"Say to the assembly, 'Move away from the tents of Korah, Dathan and Abiram.' "

25Moses got up and went to Dathan and Abiram, and the elders of Israel followed him. 26He warned the assembly, "Move back from the tents of these wicked men! Do not touch anything belonging to them, or you will be swept away because of all their sins." 27So they moved away from the tents of Korah, Dathan and Abiram. Dathan and Abiram had come out and were standing with their wives, children and little ones at the entrances to their tents.

28Then Moses said, "This is how you will know that the LORD has sent me to do all these things and that it was not my idea: 29If these men die a natural death and experience only what usually happens to men, then the LORD has not sent me. 30But if the LORD brings about something totally new, and the earth opens its mouth and swallows them, with everything that belongs to them, and they go down alive into the grave,[c] then you will know that these men have treated the LORD with contempt."

31As soon as he finished saying all this, the ground under them split apart 32and the earth opened its mouth and swallowed them, with their households and all Korah's men and all their possessions. 33They went down alive into the grave, with everything they owned; the earth closed over them, and they perished and were gone from the community. 34At their cries, all the Israelites around them fled, shouting, "The earth is going to swallow us too!"

35And fire came out from the LORD and consumed the 250 men who were offering the incense.

36The LORD said to Moses, 37"Tell Eleazar son of Aaron, the priest, to take the censers out of the smoldering remains and scatter the coals some distance away, for the censers are holy— 38the censers of the men who sinned at the cost of their lives. Hammer the censers into sheets to overlay the altar, for they were presented before the LORD and have become holy. Let them be a sign to the Israelites."

39So Eleazar the priest collected the bronze censers brought by those who had been burned up, and he had them hammered out to overlay the altar, 40as the LORD directed him through Moses. This was to remind the Israelites that no one except a descendant of Aaron should come to burn incense before the LORD, or he would become like Korah and his followers.

41The next day the whole Israelite community grumbled against Moses and Aaron. "You have killed the LORD's people," they said.

42But when the assembly gathered in opposition to Moses and Aaron and turned toward the Tent of Meeting, suddenly the cloud covered it and the glory of the LORD appeared. 43Then Moses and Aaron went to the front of the Tent of Meeting, 44and the LORD said to Moses, 45"Get away from this assembly so I can put an end to them at once." And they fell facedown.

46Then Moses said to Aaron, "Take your censer and put incense in it, along with fire from the altar, and hurry to the assembly to make atonement for them. Wrath has come

[b] *14* Or *you make slaves of;* or *you deceive*
[c] *30* Hebrew *Sheol;* also in verse 33

out from the LORD; the plague has started." 47 So Aaron did as Moses said, and ran into the midst of the assembly. The plague had already started among the people, but Aaron offered the incense and made atonement for them. 48 He stood between the living and the dead, and the plague stopped. 49 But 14,700 people died from the plague, in addition to those who had died because of Korah. 50 Then Aaron returned to Moses at the entrance to the Tent of Meeting, for the plague had stopped.

PRAYER: PETITION

LORD God, guard my soul and rescue me; let me not be ashamed, for I take refuge in You. May integrity and uprightness protect me, for I wait for You. (Psalm 25:20–21)

PAUSE *here to petition God to help you be a faithful steward of your time, talents, possessions and relationships. Offer prayers of petition regarding your activities for this day and any special concerns you may have.*

NT 1 Corinthians 5:1–13

Expel the Immoral Brother!

5 It is actually reported that there is sexual immorality among you, and of a kind that does not occur even among pagans: A man has his father's wife. 2 And you are proud! Shouldn't you rather have been filled with grief and have put out of your fellowship the man who did this? 3 Even though I am not physically present, I am with you in spirit. And I have already passed judgment on the one who did this, just as if I were present. 4 When you are assembled in the name of our Lord Jesus and I am with you in spirit, and the power of our Lord Jesus is present, 5 hand this man over to Satan, so that the sinful nature[a] may be destroyed and his spirit saved on the day of the Lord.

6 Your boasting is not good. Don't you know that a little yeast works through the whole batch of dough? 7 Get rid of the old yeast that you may be a new batch without yeast—as you really are. For Christ, our Passover lamb, has been sacrificed. 8 Therefore let us keep the Festival, not with the old yeast, the yeast of malice and wickedness, but with bread without yeast, the bread of sincerity and truth.

9 I have written you in my letter not to associate with sexually immoral people— 10 not at all meaning the people of this world who are immoral, or the greedy and swindlers, or idolaters. In that case you would have to leave this world. 11 But now I am writing you that you must not associate with anyone who calls himself a brother but is sexually immoral or greedy, an idolater or a slanderer, a drunkard or a swindler. With such a man do not even eat.

12 What business is it of mine to judge those outside the church? Are you not to judge those inside? 13 God will judge those outside. "Expel the wicked man from among you."[b]

[a] 5 Or *that his body*; or *that the flesh*   [b] 13 Deut. 17:7; 19:19; 21:21; 22:21,24; 24:7

PRAYER: MY RELATIONSHIP TO OTHERS

YOUR commandments will be upon my heart, and I will teach them diligently to my children and talk about them when I sit in my house and when I walk along the way and when I lie down and when I rise up. (Deuteronomy 6:6–7) . . . Wise children heed their parent's instruction, but a scoffer does not listen to rebuke. (Proverbs 13:1)

PAUSE *to review your relationships with others and to commit them to the Lord.*

OT **Numbers 17:1–18:32** YEAR 1 DAY 131

The Budding of Aaron's Staff

17 The LORD said to Moses, 2 "Speak to the Israelites and get twelve staffs from them, one from the leader of each of their ancestral tribes. Write the name of each man on his staff. 3 On the staff of Levi write Aaron's name, for there must be one staff for the head of each ancestral tribe. 4 Place them in the Tent of Meeting in front of the Testimony, where I meet with you. 5 The staff belonging to the man I choose will sprout, and I will rid myself of this constant grumbling against you by the Israelites."

6 So Moses spoke to the Israelites, and their leaders gave him twelve staffs, one for the leader of each of their ancestral tribes, and Aaron's staff was among them. 7 Moses placed the staffs before the LORD in the Tent of the Testimony.

8 The next day Moses entered the Tent of the Testimony and saw that Aaron's staff, which represented the house of Levi, had not only sprouted but had budded, blossomed and produced almonds. 9 Then Moses brought out all the staffs from the LORD's presence to all the Israelites. They looked at them, and each man took his own staff.

10 The LORD said to Moses, "Put back Aaron's staff in front of the Testimony, to be kept as a sign to the rebellious. This will put an end to their grumbling against me, so that they will not die." 11 Moses did just as the LORD commanded him.

12 The Israelites said to Moses, "We will die! We are lost, we are all lost! 13 Anyone who even comes near the tabernacle of the LORD will die. Are we all going to die?"

Duties of Priests and Levites

18 The LORD said to Aaron, "You, your sons and your father's family are to bear the responsibility for offenses against the sanctuary, and you and your sons alone are to bear the responsibility for offenses against the priesthood. 2 Bring your fellow Levites from your ancestral tribe to join you and assist you when you and your sons minister before the Tent of the Testimony. 3 They are to be responsible to you and are to perform all the duties of the Tent, but they must not go near the furnishings of the sanctuary or the altar, or both they and you will die. 4 They are to join you and be responsible for the care of the Tent of Meeting—all the work at the Tent—and no one else may come near where you are.

5 "You are to be responsible for the care of the sanctuary and the altar, so that wrath will not fall on the Israelites again. 6 I myself have selected your fellow Levites from among the Israelites as a gift to you, dedicated to the LORD to do the work at the Tent of Meeting. 7 But only you and your sons may serve as priests in connection with everything at the altar and inside the curtain. I am giving you the service of the priesthood as a gift. Anyone else who comes near the sanctuary must be put to death."

Offerings for Priests and Levites

8 Then the LORD said to Aaron, "I myself have put you in charge of the offerings presented to me; all the holy offerings the Israelites give me I give to you and your sons as your portion and regular share. 9 You are to have the part of the most holy offerings that is kept from the fire. From all the gifts they bring me as most holy offerings, whether grain or sin or guilt offerings, that part belongs to you and your sons. 10 Eat it as something most holy; every male shall eat it. You must regard it as holy.

11 "This also is yours: whatever is set aside from the gifts of all the wave offerings of the Israelites. I give this to you and your sons and daughters as your regular share. Everyone in your household who is ceremonially clean may eat it.

12 "I give you all the finest olive oil and all the finest new wine and grain they give the LORD as the firstfruits of their harvest. 13 All the land's firstfruits that they bring to the LORD will be yours. Everyone in your household who is ceremonially clean may eat it.

14 "Everything in Israel that is devoted[a] to the LORD is yours. 15 The first offspring of every womb, both man and animal,

[a] *14* The Hebrew term refers to the irrevocable giving over of things or persons to the LORD.

that is offered to the LORD is yours. But you must redeem every firstborn son and every firstborn male of unclean animals. 16 When they are a month old, you must redeem them at the redemption price set at five shekels[b] of silver, according to the sanctuary shekel, which weighs twenty gerahs.

17 "But you must not redeem the firstborn of an ox, a sheep or a goat; they are holy. Sprinkle their blood on the altar and burn their fat as an offering made by fire, an aroma pleasing to the LORD. 18 Their meat is to be yours, just as the breast of the wave offering and the right thigh are yours. 19 Whatever is set aside from the holy offerings the Israelites present to the LORD I give to you and your sons and daughters as your regular share. It is an everlasting covenant of salt before the LORD for both you and your offspring."

20 The LORD said to Aaron, "You will have no inheritance in their land, nor will you have any share among them; I am your share and your inheritance among the Israelites.

21 "I give to the Levites all the tithes in Israel as their inheritance in return for the work they do while serving at the Tent of Meeting. 22 From now on the Israelites must not go near the Tent of Meeting, or they will bear the consequences of their sin and will die. 23 It is the Levites who are to do the work at the Tent of Meeting and bear the responsibility for offenses against it. This is a lasting ordinance for the generations to come. They will receive no inheritance among the Israelites. 24 Instead, I give to the Levites as their inheritance the tithes that the Israelites present as an offering to the LORD. That is why I said concerning them: 'They will have no inheritance among the Israelites.' "

25 The LORD said to Moses, 26 "Speak to the Levites and say to them: 'When you receive from the Israelites the tithe I give you as your inheritance, you must present a tenth of that tithe as the LORD's offering. 27 Your offering will be reckoned to you as grain from the threshing floor or juice from the winepress. 28 In this way you also will present an offering to the LORD from all the tithes you receive from the Israelites. From these tithes you must give the LORD's portion to Aaron the priest. 29 You must present as the LORD's portion the best and holiest part of everything given to you.'

30 "Say to the Levites: 'When you present the best part, it will be reckoned to you as the product of the threshing floor or the winepress. 31 You and your households may eat the rest of it anywhere, for it is your wages for your work at the Tent of Meeting. 32 By presenting the best part of it you will not be guilty in this matter; then you will not defile the holy offerings of the Israelites, and you will not die.' "

[b] *16* That is, about 2 ounces (about 55 grams)

PRAYER: INTERCESSION

MAY I submit myself to the governing authorities. For there is no authority except from You, O God, and the authorities that exist have been established by You. Consequently, those who resist authority have opposed Your ordinance, and those who do so will bring judgment on themselves. (Romans 13:1–2)

***TAKE** a few moments to intercede on behalf of your local, state or provincial, and national governments. Pray for spiritual revival in the nation and offer prayers regarding current events and concerns.*

NT 1 Corinthians 6:1–11

Lawsuits Among Believers

6 If any of you has a dispute with another, dare he take it before the ungodly for judgment instead of before the saints? 2 Do you not know that the saints will judge the world? And if you are to judge the world, are you not competent to judge trivial cases? 3 Do you not know that we will judge angels? How much more the things of this life! 4 Therefore, if you

have disputes about such matters, appoint
as judges even men of little account in the
church![a] 5I say this to shame you. Is it
possible that there is nobody among you
wise enough to judge a dispute between
believers? 6But instead, one brother goes
to law against another—and this in front
of unbelievers!

7The very fact that you have lawsuits
among you means you have been completely defeated already. Why not rather
be wronged? Why not rather be cheated?
8Instead, you yourselves cheat and do
wrong, and you do this to your brothers.

9Do you not know that the wicked will
not inherit the kingdom of God? Do not
be deceived: Neither the sexually immoral
nor idolaters nor adulterers nor male
prostitutes nor homosexual offenders
10nor thieves nor the greedy nor drunkards nor slanderers nor swindlers will inherit the kingdom of God. 11And that is
what some of you were. But you were
washed, you were sanctified, you were justified in the name of the Lord Jesus Christ
and by the Spirit of our God.

[a] 4 Or *matters, do you appoint as judges men of little account in the church?*

PRAYER: THE ATTRIBUTES OF GOD

YOU, Lord God, are the faithful God. You keep Your covenant and Your loving-kindness to a thousand generations of those who love You and keep Your commands. (Deuteronomy 7:9) . . . I call this to mind, and therefore I have hope: Your mercies, O Lord, never cease, for Your compassions never fail. They are new every morning; great is Your faithfulness. (Lamentations 3:21–23)

***PAUSE** to reflect on these affirmations about the person, powers and perfection of God.*

YEAR 1 DAY 132

OT Numbers 19:1 22

The Water of Cleansing

19 The LORD said to Moses and Aaron:
2"This is a requirement of the law that
the LORD has commanded: Tell the Israelites to bring you a red heifer without defect or blemish and that has never been
under a yoke. 3Give it to Eleazar the priest;
it is to be taken outside the camp and
slaughtered in his presence. 4Then Eleazar
the priest is to take some of its blood on
his finger and sprinkle it seven times toward the front of the Tent of Meeting.
5While he watches, the heifer is to be
burned—its hide, flesh, blood and offal.
6The priest is to take some cedar wood,
hyssop and scarlet wool and throw them
onto the burning heifer. 7After that, the
priest must wash his clothes and bathe
himself with water. He may then come
into the camp, but he will be ceremonially unclean till evening. 8The man who
burns it must also wash his clothes and
bathe with water, and he too will be unclean till evening.

9"A man who is clean shall gather up
the ashes of the heifer and put them in a
ceremonially clean place outside the
camp. They shall be kept by the Israelite
community for use in the water of cleansing; it is for purification from sin. 10The
man who gathers up the ashes of the
heifer must also wash his clothes, and he
too will be unclean till evening. This will
be a lasting ordinance both for the Israelites and for the aliens living among them.

11"Whoever touches the dead body of
anyone will be unclean for seven days.
12He must purify himself with the water
on the third day and on the seventh day;
then he will be clean. But if he does not
purify himself on the third and seventh
days, he will not be clean. 13Whoever
touches the dead body of anyone and fails
to purify himself defiles the LORD's tabernacle. That person must be cut off from

Israel. Because the water of cleansing has not been sprinkled on him, he is unclean; his uncleanness remains on him.

[14]"This is the law that applies when a person dies in a tent: Anyone who enters the tent and anyone who is in it will be unclean for seven days, [15]and every open container without a lid fastened on it will be unclean.

[16]"Anyone out in the open who touches someone who has been killed with a sword or someone who has died a natural death, or anyone who touches a human bone or a grave, will be unclean for seven days.

[17]"For the unclean person, put some ashes from the burned purification offering into a jar and pour fresh water over them. [18]Then a man who is ceremonially clean is to take some hyssop, dip it in the water and sprinkle the tent and all the furnishings and the people who were there. He must also sprinkle anyone who has touched a human bone or a grave or someone who has been killed or someone who has died a natural death. [19]The man who is clean is to sprinkle the unclean person on the third and seventh days, and on the seventh day he is to purify him. The person being cleansed must wash his clothes and bathe with water, and that evening he will be clean. [20]But if a person who is unclean does not purify himself, he must be cut off from the community, because he has defiled the sanctuary of the LORD. The water of cleansing has not been sprinkled on him, and he is unclean. [21]This is a lasting ordinance for them.

"The man who sprinkles the water of cleansing must also wash his clothes, and anyone who touches the water of cleansing will be unclean till evening. [22]Anything that an unclean person touches becomes unclean, and anyone who touches it becomes unclean till evening."

PRAYER: AFFIRMATION

O GOD, I know that if my earthly house is destroyed, I have a building from You, a house not made with hands, eternal in the heavens. For in this house I groan, longing to be clothed with my heavenly dwelling, because when I am clothed, I will not be found naked. For while I am in this house I groan, being burdened, because I do not want to be unclothed but to be clothed, so that what is mortal may be swallowed up by life. Now You have made me for this very purpose and have given me Your Spirit as a guarantee. (2 Corinthians 5:1–5)

***PAUSE** to reflect on these Biblical affirmations.*

NT 1 Corinthians 6:12–20

Sexual Immorality

[12]"Everything is permissible for me"—but not everything is beneficial. "Everything is permissible for me"—but I will not be mastered by anything. [13]"Food for the stomach and the stomach for food"—but God will destroy them both. The body is not meant for sexual immorality, but for the Lord, and the Lord for the body. [14]By his power God raised the Lord from the dead, and he will raise us also. [15]Do you not know that your bodies are members of Christ himself? Shall I then take the members of Christ and unite them with a prostitute? Never! [16]Do you not know that he who unites himself with a prostitute is one with her in body? For it is said, "The two will become one flesh."[a] [17]But he who unites himself with the Lord is one with him in spirit.

[18]Flee from sexual immorality. All other sins a man commits are outside his body, but he who sins sexually sins against his own body. [19]Do you not know that your body is a temple of the Holy Spirit, who is in you, whom you have received from God? You are not your own; [20]you were bought at a price. Therefore honor God with your body.

[a] *16* Gen. 2:24

PRAYER: THE WORKS OF GOD

O SON of Man, You are going to come in the glory of Your Father with Your angels, and then You will reward people according to their works. (Matthew 16:27) . . . As the lightning comes from the east and flashes to the west, so will be Your coming, O Son of Man. Your sign will appear in the sky, and all the nations of the earth will mourn, and they will see You coming on the clouds of the sky with power and great glory. (Matthew 24:27, 30)

***TAKE** a moment to consider the greatness of God's wonderful works.*

YEAR 1 DAY 133

OT Psalms 28–29

Psalm 28

Of David.

1 To you I call, O LORD my Rock;
do not turn a deaf ear to me.
For if you remain silent,
I will be like those who have gone down to the pit.
2 Hear my cry for mercy
as I call to you for help,
as I lift up my hands
toward your Most Holy Place.

3 Do not drag me away with the wicked,
with those who do evil,
who speak cordially with their neighbors
but harbor malice in their hearts.
4 Repay them for their deeds
and for their evil work;
repay them for what their hands have done
and bring back upon them what they deserve.
5 Since they show no regard for the works of the LORD
and what his hands have done,
he will tear them down
and never build them up again.

6 Praise be to the LORD,
for he has heard my cry for mercy.
7 The LORD is my strength and my shield;
my heart trusts in him, and I am helped.
My heart leaps for joy
and I will give thanks to him in song.

8 The LORD is the strength of his people,
a fortress of salvation for his anointed one.
9 Save your people and bless your inheritance;
be their shepherd and carry them forever.

Psalm 29

A psalm of David.

1 Ascribe to the LORD, O mighty ones,
ascribe to the LORD glory and strength.
2 Ascribe to the LORD the glory due his name;
worship the LORD in the splendor of his[a] holiness.

3 The voice of the LORD is over the waters;
the God of glory thunders,
the LORD thunders over the mighty waters.
4 The voice of the LORD is powerful;
the voice of the LORD is majestic.
5 The voice of the LORD breaks the cedars;
the LORD breaks in pieces the cedars of Lebanon.
6 He makes Lebanon skip like a calf,
Sirion[b] like a young wild ox.
7 The voice of the LORD strikes
with flashes of lightning.
8 The voice of the LORD shakes the desert;

[a] 2 Or *LORD with the splendor of* [b] 6 That is, Mount Hermon

the LORD shakes the Desert of
Kadesh.
[9]The voice of the LORD twists the oaks[c]
and strips the forests bare.
And in his temple all cry, "Glory!"
[10]The LORD sits[d] enthroned over the flood;
the LORD is enthroned as King
forever.
[11]The LORD gives strength to his people;
the LORD blesses his people with
peace.

[c] 9 Or *LORD makes the deer give birth* [d] 10 Or *sat*

PRAYER: THANKSGIVING

O LORD, because You help me, I will not be disgraced. Therefore I have set my face like flint, and I know I will not be put to shame. You vindicate me, O Lord, and are near; who then will contend with me? Surely You will help me; who is he that will condemn me? (Isaiah 50:7–9) . . . Abba Father, I did not receive a spirit of slavery again to fear, but I received the Spirit of adoption by whom I cry to You. The Spirit Himself testifies with my spirit that I am Your child. (Romans 8:15–16)

***PAUSE** to offer your own expressions of thanksgiving.*

NT 1 Corinthians 7:1-40

Marriage

7 Now for the matters you wrote about:
It is good for a man not to marry.[a] [2]But
since there is so much immorality, each
man should have his own wife, and each
woman her own husband. [3]The husband
should fulfill his marital duty to his wife,
and likewise the wife to her husband.
[4]The wife's body does not belong to her
alone but also to her husband. In the
same way, the husband's body does not
belong to him alone but also to his wife.
[5]Do not deprive each other except by mutual consent and for a time, so that you
may devote yourselves to prayer. Then
come together again so that Satan will not
tempt you because of your lack of self-
control. [6]I say this as a concession, not as
a command. [7]I wish that all men were as
I am. But each man has his own gift from
God; one has this gift, another has that.

[8]Now to the unmarried and the widows
I say: It is good for them to stay unmarried, as I am. [9]But if they cannot control
themselves, they should marry, for it is
better to marry than to burn with passion.

[10]To the married I give this command
(not I, but the Lord): A wife must not separate from her husband. [11]But if she does,
she must remain unmarried or else be reconciled to her husband. And a husband
must not divorce his wife.

[12]To the rest I say this (I, not the Lord):
If any brother has a wife who is not a believer and she is willing to live with him,
he must not divorce her. [13]And if a woman
has a husband who is not a believer and
he is willing to live with her, she must not
divorce him. [14]For the unbelieving husband has been sanctified through his wife,
and the unbelieving wife has been sanctified through her believing husband. Otherwise your children would be unclean,
but as it is, they are holy.

[15]But if the unbeliever leaves, let him do
so. A believing man or woman is not
bound in such circumstances; God has
called us to live in peace. [16]How do you
know, wife, whether you will save your
husband? Or, how do you know, husband, whether you will save your wife?

[17]Nevertheless, each one should retain
the place in life that the Lord assigned to
him and to which God has called him.
This is the rule I lay down in all the
churches. [18]Was a man already circumcised when he was called? He should not
become uncircumcised. Was a man uncircumcised when he was called? He should
not be circumcised. [19]Circumcision is
nothing and uncircumcision is nothing.
Keeping God's commands is what counts.
[20]Each one should remain in the situation
which he was in when God called him.

[a] 1 Or *"It is good for a man not to have sexual relations with a woman."*

[21]Were you a slave when you were called?
Don't let it trouble you—although if you
can gain your freedom, do so. [22]For he
who was a slave when he was called by the
Lord is the Lord's freedman; similarly, he
who was a free man when he was called
is Christ's slave. [23]You were bought at a
price; do not become slaves of men.
[24]Brothers, each man, as responsible to
God, should remain in the situation God
called him to.

[25]Now about virgins: I have no command from the Lord, but I give a judgment as one who by the Lord's mercy is
trustworthy. [26]Because of the present crisis, I think that it is good for you to remain as you are. [27]Are you married? Do
not seek a divorce. Are you unmarried?
Do not look for a wife. [28]But if you do
marry, you have not sinned; and if a virgin marries, she has not sinned. But those
who marry will face many troubles in this
life, and I want to spare you this.

[29]What I mean, brothers, is that the
time is short. From now on those who
have wives should live as if they had
none; [30]those who mourn, as if they did
not; those who are happy, as if they were
not; those who buy something, as if it
were not theirs to keep; [31]those who use
the things of the world, as if not engrossed in them. For this world in its
present form is passing away.

[32]I would like you to be free from concern. An unmarried man is concerned
about the Lord's affairs—how he can
please the Lord. [33]But a married man is
concerned about the affairs of this
world—how he can please his wife—
[34]and his interests are divided. An unmarried woman or virgin is concerned about
the Lord's affairs: Her aim is to be devoted to the Lord in both body and spirit. But
a married woman is concerned about the
affairs of this world—how she can please
her husband. [35]I am saying this for your
own good, not to restrict you, but that you
may live in a right way in undivided devotion to the Lord.

[36]If anyone thinks he is acting improperly toward the virgin he is engaged to,
and if she is getting along in years and he
feels he ought to marry, he should do as
he wants. He is not sinning. They should
get married. [37]But the man who has settled
the matter in his own mind, who is under
no compulsion but has control over his
own will, and who has made up his mind
not to marry the virgin—this man also
does the right thing. [38]So then, he who
marries the virgin does right, but he who
does not marry her does even better.[b]

[39]A woman is bound to her husband as
long as he lives. But if her husband dies, she
is free to marry anyone she wishes, but he
must belong to the Lord. [40]In my judgment,
she is happier if she stays as she is—and I
think that I too have the Spirit of God.

[b] 36-38 Or [36]*If anyone thinks he is not treating his daughter properly, and if she is getting along in years, and he feels she ought to marry, he should do as he wants. He is not sinning. He should let her get married.* [37]*But the man who has settled the matter in his own mind, who is under no compulsion but has control over his own will, and who has made up his mind to keep the virgin unmarried—this man also does the right thing.* [38]*So then, he who gives his virgin in marriage does right, but he who does not give her in marriage does even better.*

PRAYER: MY RELATIONSHIP TO GOD

O LORD, You are my light and my salvation; whom shall I fear? You are the strength of my life; of whom shall I be afraid? (Psalm 27:1) . . . When I am afraid, I will trust in You. When I am afraid, I will trust in You whose word I praise. In You I have put my trust. I will not fear; what can mortals do to me? (Psalm 56:3–4)

***PAUSE** to thank God for the relationship that you enjoy with Him in Jesus Christ.*

YEAR 1 DAY 134

OT **Numbers 20:1-29**

Water From the Rock

20 In the first month the whole Israelite
community arrived at the Desert of
Zin, and they stayed at Kadesh. There Miriam died and was buried.
2Now there was no water for the community, and the people gathered in opposition to Moses and Aaron. 3They quarreled with Moses and said, "If only we
had died when our brothers fell dead before the LORD! 4Why did you bring the
LORD's community into this desert, that
we and our livestock should die here?
5Why did you bring us up out of Egypt to
this terrible place? It has no grain or figs,
grapevines or pomegranates. And there is
no water to drink!"
6Moses and Aaron went from the assembly to the entrance to the Tent of
Meeting and fell facedown, and the glory
of the LORD appeared to them. 7The LORD
said to Moses, 8"Take the staff, and you
and your brother Aaron gather the assembly together. Speak to that rock before
their eyes and it will pour out its water.
You will bring water out of the rock for
the community so they and their livestock
can drink."
9So Moses took the staff from the
LORD's presence, just as he commanded
him. 10He and Aaron gathered the assembly together in front of the rock and Moses said to them, "Listen, you rebels, must
we bring you water out of this rock?"
11Then Moses raised his arm and struck
the rock twice with his staff. Water gushed
out, and the community and their livestock drank.
12But the LORD said to Moses and Aaron, "Because you did not trust in me
enough to honor me as holy in the sight
of the Israelites, you will not bring this
community into the land I give them."
13These were the waters of Meribah,[a]
where the Israelites quarreled with the
LORD and where he showed himself holy
among them.

Edom Denies Israel Passage

14Moses sent messengers from Kadesh
to the king of Edom, saying:

"This is what your brother Israel
says: You know about all the hardships that have come upon us. 15Our
forefathers went down into Egypt,
and we lived there many years. The
Egyptians mistreated us and our fathers, 16but when we cried out to the
LORD, he heard our cry and sent an
angel and brought us out of Egypt.
"Now we are here at Kadesh, a
town on the edge of your territory.
17Please let us pass through your
country. We will not go through any
field or vineyard, or drink water from
any well. We will travel along the
king's highway and not turn to the
right or to the left until we have
passed through your territory."

18But Edom answered:

"You may not pass through here; if
you try, we will march out and attack
you with the sword."

19The Israelites replied:

"We will go along the main road,
and if we or our livestock drink any
of your water, we will pay for it. We
only want to pass through on foot—
nothing else."

20Again they answered:

"You may not pass through."

Then Edom came out against them
with a large and powerful army. 21Since
Edom refused to let them go through their
territory, Israel turned away from them.

The Death of Aaron

22The whole Israelite community set
out from Kadesh and came to Mount Hor.
23At Mount Hor, near the border of Edom,
the LORD said to Moses and Aaron, 24"Aaron will be gathered to his people. He will
not enter the land I give the Israelites, because both of you rebelled against my
command at the waters of Meribah. 25Get
Aaron and his son Eleazar and take them
up Mount Hor. 26Remove Aaron's garments and put them on his son Eleazar,
for Aaron will be gathered to his people;
he will die there."

[a] 13 *Meribah* means *quarreling.*

[27]Moses did as the LORD commanded: They went up Mount Hor in the sight of the whole community. [28]Moses removed Aaron's garments and put them on his son Eleazar. And Aaron died there on top of the mountain. Then Moses and Eleazar came down from the mountain, [29]and when the whole community learned that Aaron had died, the entire house of Israel mourned for him thirty days.

PRAYER: ADORATION

WE praise You, Lord! We praise You in Your sanctuary; we praise You in Your mighty heavens. We praise You for Your mighty acts; we praise You according to Your excellent greatness. We praise You with the sound of the trumpet; we praise You with the harp and lyre. We praise You with the timbrel and dancing; we praise You with stringed instruments and flutes. We praise You on the sounding cymbals; we praise You on the resounding cymbals. Let everything that has breath praise You. We praise You, Lord! (Psalm 150:1–6)

***PAUSE** to express your thoughts of praise and worship.*

NT 1 Corinthians 8:1-13

Food Sacrificed to Idols

8 Now about food sacrificed to idols: We know that we all possess knowledge.[a] Knowledge puffs up, but love builds up. [2]The man who thinks he knows something does not yet know as he ought to know. [3]But the man who loves God is known by God.

[4]So then, about eating food sacrificed to idols: We know that an idol is nothing at all in the world and that there is no God but one. [5]For even if there are so-called gods, whether in heaven or on earth (as indeed there are many "gods" and many "lords"), [6]yet for us there is but one God, the Father, from whom all things came and for whom we live; and there is but one Lord, Jesus Christ, through whom all things came and through whom we live.

[7]But not everyone knows this. Some people are still so accustomed to idols that when they eat such food they think of it as having been sacrificed to an idol, and since their conscience is weak, it is defiled. [8]But food does not bring us near to God; we are no worse if we do not eat, and no better if we do.

[9]Be careful, however, that the exercise of your freedom does not become a stumbling block to the weak. [10]For if anyone with a weak conscience sees you who have this knowledge eating in an idol's temple, won't he be emboldened to eat what has been sacrificed to idols? [11]So this weak brother, for whom Christ died, is destroyed by your knowledge. [12]When you sin against your brothers in this way and wound their weak conscience, you sin against Christ. [13]Therefore, if what I eat causes my brother to fall into sin, I will never eat meat again, so that I will not cause him to fall.

[a] 1 Or *"We all possess knowledge," as you say*

PRAYER: THE CHARACTER I WANT TO CULTIVATE

THOSE who listen to a life-giving rebuke, O Lord, will be at home among the wise. Those who refuse instruction despise themselves, but those who heed correction, Lord, gain understanding. (Proverbs 15:31–32) . . . A rebuke, Lord, goes deeper into one who is wise than a hundred lashes into a fool. (Proverbs 17:10)

***TAKE** a moment to ask the Lord for the grace to grow in godly character.*

YEAR 1 DAY 135

OT Numbers 21:1-35

Arad Destroyed

21 When the Canaanite king of Arad, who lived in the Negev, heard that Israel was coming along the road to Atharim, he attacked the Israelites and captured some of them. 2Then Israel made this vow to the LORD: "If you will deliver these people into our hands, we will totally destroy[a] their cities." 3The LORD listened to Israel's plea and gave the Canaanites over to them. They completely destroyed them and their towns; so the place was named Hormah.[b]

The Bronze Snake

4They traveled from Mount Hor along the route to the Red Sea,[c] to go around Edom. But the people grew impatient on the way; 5they spoke against God and against Moses, and said, "Why have you brought us up out of Egypt to die in the desert? There is no bread! There is no water! And we detest this miserable food!"

6Then the LORD sent venomous snakes among them; they bit the people and many Israelites died. 7The people came to Moses and said, "We sinned when we spoke against the LORD and against you. Pray that the LORD will take the snakes away from us." So Moses prayed for the people.

8The LORD said to Moses, "Make a snake and put it up on a pole; anyone who is bitten can look at it and live." 9So Moses made a bronze snake and put it up on a pole. Then when anyone was bitten by a snake and looked at the bronze snake, he lived.

The Journey to Moab

10The Israelites moved on and camped at Oboth. 11Then they set out from Oboth and camped in Iye Abarim, in the desert that faces Moab toward the sunrise. 12From there they moved on and camped in the Zered Valley. 13They set out from there and camped alongside the Arnon, which is in the desert extending into Amorite territory. The Arnon is the border of Moab, between Moab and the Amorites. 14That is why the Book of the Wars of the LORD says:

". . . Waheb in Suphah[d] and the
    ravines,
  the Arnon 15and[e] the slopes of the
    ravines
that lead to the site of Ar
  and lie along the border of Moab."

16From there they continued on to Beer, the well where the LORD said to Moses, "Gather the people together and I will give them water."

17Then Israel sang this song:

"Spring up, O well!
  Sing about it,
18about the well that the princes dug,
  that the nobles of the people sank—
  the nobles with scepters and staffs."

Then they went from the desert to Mattanah, 19from Mattanah to Nahaliel, from Nahaliel to Bamoth, 20and from Bamoth to the valley in Moab where the top of Pisgah overlooks the wasteland.

Defeat of Sihon and Og

21Israel sent messengers to say to Sihon king of the Amorites:

> 22"Let us pass through your country. We will not turn aside into any field or vineyard, or drink water from any well. We will travel along the king's highway until we have passed through your territory."

23But Sihon would not let Israel pass through his territory. He mustered his entire army and marched out into the desert against Israel. When he reached Jahaz, he fought with Israel. 24Israel, however, put him to the sword and took over his land from the Arnon to the Jabbok, but only as far as the Ammonites, because their border was fortified. 25Israel captured all the cities of the Amorites and occupied them, including Heshbon and all its surrounding settlements. 26Heshbon was the city of Sihon king of the Amorites, who had fought against the former king of Moab

[a] 2 The Hebrew term refers to the irrevocable giving over of things or persons to the LORD, often by totally destroying them; also in verse 3.
[b] 3 *Hormah* means *destruction.* [c] 4 Hebrew *Yam Suph*; that is, Sea of Reeds [d] 14 The meaning of the Hebrew for this phrase is uncertain.
[e] 14,15 Or *"I have been given from Suphah and the ravines / of the Arnon* [15]*to*

and had taken from him all his land as far as the Arnon.

[27]That is why the poets say:

"Come to Heshbon and let it be
rebuilt;
let Sihon's city be restored.

[28]"Fire went out from Heshbon,
a blaze from the city of Sihon.
It consumed Ar of Moab,
the citizens of Arnon's heights.
[29]Woe to you, O Moab!
You are destroyed, O people of
Chemosh!
He has given up his sons as fugitives
and his daughters as captives
to Sihon king of the Amorites.

[30]"But we have overthrown them;
Heshbon is destroyed all the way to
Dibon.
We have demolished them as far as
Nophah,
which extends to Medeba."

[31]So Israel settled in the land of the Amorites.

[32]After Moses had sent spies to Jazer, the Israelites captured its surrounding settlements and drove out the Amorites who
were there. [33]Then they turned and went up along the road toward Bashan, and Og king of Bashan and his whole army marched out to meet them in battle at Edrei.

[34]The LORD said to Moses, "Do not be afraid of him, for I have handed him over to you, with his whole army and his land. Do to him what you did to Sihon king of the Amorites, who reigned in Heshbon."

[35]So they struck him down, together with his sons and his whole army, leaving them no survivors. And they took possession of his land.

PRAYER: CONFESSION

HEAL me, O Lord, and I will be healed; save me, and I will be saved, for You are the One I praise. (Jeremiah 17:14)

***ASK** the Spirit to search your heart and reveal any areas of unconfessed sin. Acknowledge these to the Lord and thank Him for His forgiveness.*

NT 1 Corinthians 9:1–27

The Rights of an Apostle

9 Am I not free? Am I not an apostle?
Have I not seen Jesus our Lord? Are you
not the result of my work in the Lord?
[2]Even though I may not be an apostle to
others, surely I am to you! For you are the
seal of my apostleship in the Lord.
[3]This is my defense to those who sit in
judgment on me. [4]Don't we have the right
to food and drink? [5]Don't we have the
right to take a believing wife along with
us, as do the other apostles and the Lord's
brothers and Cephas[a]? [6]Or is it only I and
Barnabas who must work for a living?
[7]Who serves as a soldier at his own expense? Who plants a vineyard and does
not eat of its grapes? Who tends a flock
and does not drink of the milk? [8]Do I say
this merely from a human point of view?
Doesn't the Law say the same thing? [9]For
it is written in the Law of Moses: "Do not
muzzle an ox while it is treading out
the grain."[b] Is it about oxen that God is
concerned? [10]Surely he says this for us,
doesn't he? Yes, this was written for us,
because when the plowman plows and
the thresher threshes, they ought to do so
in the hope of sharing in the harvest. [11]If
we have sown spiritual seed among you,
is it too much if we reap a material harvest from you? [12]If others have this right
of support from you, shouldn't we have
it all the more?

But we did not use this right. On the
contrary, we put up with anything rather
than hinder the gospel of Christ. [13]Don't
you know that those who work in the
temple get their food from the temple,
and those who serve at the altar share in
what is offered on the altar? [14]In the same
way, the Lord has commanded that those
who preach the gospel should receive
their living from the gospel.
[15]But I have not used any of these rights.
And I am not writing this in the hope that

[a] 5 That is, Peter [b] 9 Deut. 25:4

you will do such things for me. I would
rather die than have anyone deprive me of
this boast. [16]Yet when I preach the gospel,
I cannot boast, for I am compelled to
preach. Woe to me if I do not preach the
gospel! [17]If I preach voluntarily, I have a
reward; if not voluntarily, I am simply discharging the trust committed to me.
[18]What then is my reward? Just this: that
in preaching the gospel I may offer it free
of charge, and so not make use of my
rights in preaching it.

[19]Though I am free and belong to no
man, I make myself a slave to everyone, to
win as many as possible. [20]To the Jews I
became like a Jew, to win the Jews. To
those under the law I became like one under the law (though I myself am not under the law), so as to win those under the
law. [21]To those not having the law I became like one not having the law (though
I am not free from God's law but am under Christ's law), so as to win those not
having the law. [22]To the weak I became
weak, to win the weak. I have become all
things to all men so that by all possible
means I might save some. [23]I do all this
for the sake of the gospel, that I may share
in its blessings.

[24]Do you not know that in a race all the
runners run, but only one gets the prize?
Run in such a way as to get the prize.
[25]Everyone who competes in the games
goes into strict training. They do it to get
a crown that will not last; but we do it to
get a crown that will last forever. [26]There-
fore I do not run like a man running aimlessly; I do not fight like a man beating
the air. [27]No, I beat my body and make it
my slave so that after I have preached to
others, I myself will not be disqualified
for the prize.

PRAYER: MY RELATIONSHIP TO OTHERS

LORD, we know that there should be no division in the body, but its members should have concern for each other. If one member suffers, all the members suffer with it; if one member is honored, all the members rejoice with it. Now we are Your body, O Christ, and each one of us is a member of it. (1 Corinthians 12:25–27)

__PAUSE__ to review your relationships with others and to commit them to the Lord.

YEAR 1 DAY 136

OT Numbers 22:1–41

Balak Summons Balaam

22 Then the Israelites traveled to the
plains of Moab and camped along
the Jordan across from Jericho.[a]

[2]Now Balak son of Zippor saw all that
Israel had done to the Amorites, [3]and
Moab was terrified because there were so
many people. Indeed, Moab was filled
with dread because of the Israelites.

[4]The Moabites said to the elders of Midian, "This horde is going to lick up everything around us, as an ox licks up the
grass of the field."

So Balak son of Zippor, who was king
of Moab at that time, [5]sent messengers to
summon Balaam son of Beor, who was at
Pethor, near the River,[b] in his native land.
Balak said:

"A people has come out of Egypt;
they cover the face of the land and
have settled next to me. [6]Now come
and put a curse on these people, because they are too powerful for me.
Perhaps then I will be able to defeat
them and drive them out of the
country. For I know that those you
bless are blessed, and those you curse
are cursed."

[7]The elders of Moab and Midian left,
taking with them the fee for divination.
When they came to Balaam, they told him
what Balak had said.

[8]"Spend the night here," Balaam said to

[a] 1 Hebrew *Jordan of Jericho;* possibly an ancient name for the Jordan River [b] 5 That is, the Euphrates

them, "and I will bring you back the answer the LORD gives me." So the Moabite
princes stayed with him.
[9]God came to Balaam and asked, "Who
are these men with you?"
[10]Balaam said to God, "Balak son of
Zippor, king of Moab, sent me this message: [11]'A people that has come out of
Egypt covers the face of the land. Now
come and put a curse on them for me.
Perhaps then I will be able to fight them
and drive them away.' "
[12]But God said to Balaam, "Do not go
with them. You must not put a curse on
those people, because they are blessed."
[13]The next morning Balaam got up and
said to Balak's princes, "Go back to your
own country, for the LORD has refused to
let me go with you."
[14]So the Moabite princes returned to
Balak and said, "Balaam refused to come
with us."
[15]Then Balak sent other princes, more
numerous and more distinguished than
the first. [16]They came to Balaam and said:

> "This is what Balak son of Zippor
> says: Do not let anything keep you
> from coming to me, [17]because I will
> reward you handsomely and do
> whatever you say. Come and put a
> curse on these people for me."

[18]But Balaam answered them, "Even if
Balak gave me his palace filled with silver
and gold, I could not do anything great or
small to go beyond the command of the
LORD my God. [19]Now stay here tonight as
the others did, and I will find out what
else the LORD will tell me."
[20]That night God came to Balaam and
said, "Since these men have come to summon you, go with them, but do only what
I tell you."

Balaam's Donkey

[21]Balaam got up in the morning, saddled his donkey and went with the princes
of Moab. [22]But God was very angry when
he went, and the angel of the LORD stood
in the road to oppose him. Balaam was
riding on his donkey, and his two servants
were with him. [23]When the donkey saw
the angel of the LORD standing in the road
with a drawn sword in his hand, she
turned off the road into a field. Balaam
beat her to get her back on the road.
[24]Then the angel of the LORD stood in a
narrow path between two vineyards, with
walls on both sides. [25]When the donkey
saw the angel of the LORD, she pressed
close to the wall, crushing Balaam's foot
against it. So he beat her again.
[26]Then the angel of the LORD moved on
ahead and stood in a narrow place where
there was no room to turn, either to the
right or to the left. [27]When the donkey saw
the angel of the LORD, she lay down under Balaam, and he was angry and beat
her with his staff. [28]Then the LORD opened
the donkey's mouth, and she said to Balaam, "What have I done to you to make
you beat me these three times?"
[29]Balaam answered the donkey, "You
have made a fool of me! If I had a sword
in my hand, I would kill you right now."
[30]The donkey said to Balaam, "Am I not
your own donkey, which you have always
ridden, to this day? Have I been in the
habit of doing this to you?"
"No," he said.
[31]Then the LORD opened Balaam's eyes,
and he saw the angel of the LORD standing in the road with his sword drawn. So
he bowed low and fell facedown.
[32]The angel of the LORD asked him,
"Why have you beaten your donkey these
three times? I have come here to oppose
you because your path is a reckless one
before me.[c] [33]The donkey saw me and
turned away from me these three times. If
she had not turned away, I would certainly have killed you by now, but I would
have spared her."
[34]Balaam said to the angel of the LORD,
"I have sinned. I did not realize you were
standing in the road to oppose me. Now
if you are displeased, I will go back."
[35]The angel of the LORD said to Balaam,
"Go with the men, but speak only what I
tell you." So Balaam went with the princes
of Balak.
[36]When Balak heard that Balaam was
coming, he went out to meet him at the
Moabite town on the Arnon border, at the
edge of his territory. [37]Balak said to Balaam, "Did I not send you an urgent summons? Why didn't you come to me? Am I
really not able to reward you?"
[38]"Well, I have come to you now," Balaam replied. "But can I say just anything?

[c] *32* The meaning of the Hebrew for this clause is uncertain.

I must speak only what God puts in my
mouth."
39Then Balaam went with Balak to Kiriath
Huzoth. 40Balak sacrificed cattle and sheep,
and gave some to Balaam and the princes
who were with him. 41The next morning Balak took Balaam up to Bamoth Baal, and
from there he saw part of the people.

PRAYER: RENEWAL

MAY I keep Your commandments, O Lord my God, and walk in Your ways and fear You. May I follow You and fear You; may I keep Your commandments, hear Your voice, serve You and hold fast to You. (Deuteronomy 8:6; 13:4) . . . Since I call on You, Father, who judge each person's work impartially, may I conduct myself in fear during the time of my sojourn on earth. (1 Peter 1:17)

PAUSE *to add your own prayers for personal renewal.*

NT 1 Corinthians 10:1–22

Warnings From Israel's History

10 For I do not want you to be ignorant
of the fact, brothers, that our forefathers were all under the cloud and that
they all passed through the sea. 2They
were all baptized into Moses in the cloud
and in the sea. 3They all ate the same spiritual food 4and drank the same spiritual
drink; for they drank from the spiritual
rock that accompanied them, and that
rock was Christ. 5Nevertheless, God was
not pleased with most of them; their bodies were scattered over the desert.
6Now these things occurred as examples[a] to keep us from setting our hearts on
evil things as they did. 7Do not be idolaters, as some of them were; as it is written: "The people sat down to eat and
drink and got up to indulge in pagan revelry."[b] 8We should not commit sexual immorality, as some of them did—and in
one day twenty-three thousand of them
died. 9We should not test the Lord, as
some of them did—and were killed by
snakes. 10And do not grumble, as some of
them did—and were killed by the destroying angel.
11These things happened to them as examples and were written down as warnings for us, on whom the fulfillment of
the ages has come. 12So, if you think you
are standing firm, be careful that you
don't fall! 13No temptation has seized you
except what is common to man. And God
is faithful; he will not let you be tempted
beyond what you can bear. But when you
are tempted, he will also provide a way
out so that you can stand up under it.

Idol Feasts and the Lord's Supper

14Therefore, my dear friends, flee from
idolatry. 15I speak to sensible people;
judge for yourselves what I say. 16Is not the
cup of thanksgiving for which we give
thanks a participation in the blood of
Christ? And is not the bread that we break
a participation in the body of Christ? 17Be-
cause there is one loaf, we, who are many,
are one body, for we all partake of the one
loaf.
18Consider the people of Israel: Do not
those who eat the sacrifices participate in
the altar? 19Do I mean then that a sacrifice
offered to an idol is anything, or that an
idol is anything? 20No, but the sacrifices
of pagans are offered to demons, not to
God, and I do not want you to be participants with demons. 21You cannot drink
the cup of the Lord and the cup of
demons too; you cannot have a part in
both the Lord's table and the table of
demons. 22Are we trying to arouse the
Lord's jealousy? Are we stronger than he?

[a] 6 Or *types;* also in verse 11 [b] 7 Exodus 32:6

PRAYER: THE ATTRIBUTES OF GOD

I REJOICE in the knowledge that one day, every creature in heaven and on earth and under the earth and on the sea and all that is in them will sing of You, Almighty King: "To Him who sits on the throne and to the Lamb be blessing and honor and glory and power for ever and ever!" (Revelation 5:13)

***PAUSE** to reflect on these affirmations about the person, powers and perfection of God.*

YEAR 1 DAY 137

OT Proverbs 6

Warnings Against Folly

6 My son, if you have put up security
for your neighbor,
if you have struck hands in pledge
for another,
2 if you have been trapped by what you
said,
ensnared by the words of your
mouth,
3 then do this, my son, to free yourself,
since you have fallen into your
neighbor's hands:
Go and humble yourself;
press your plea with your neighbor!
4 Allow no sleep to your eyes,
no slumber to your eyelids.
5 Free yourself, like a gazelle from the
hand of the hunter,
like a bird from the snare of the
fowler.

6 Go to the ant, you sluggard;
consider its ways and be wise!
7 It has no commander,
no overseer or ruler,
8 yet it stores its provisions in summer
and gathers its food at harvest.

9 How long will you lie there, you
sluggard?
When will you get up from your
sleep?
10 A little sleep, a little slumber,
a little folding of the hands to rest—
11 and poverty will come on you like a
bandit
and scarcity like an armed man.[a]

12 A scoundrel and villain,
who goes about with a corrupt
mouth,
13 who winks with his eye,
signals with his feet
and motions with his fingers,
14 who plots evil with deceit in his
heart—
he always stirs up dissension.
15 Therefore disaster will overtake him in
an instant;
he will suddenly be destroyed—
without remedy.

16 There are six things the LORD hates,
seven that are detestable to him:
17 haughty eyes,
a lying tongue,
hands that shed innocent blood,
18 a heart that devises wicked
schemes,
feet that are quick to rush into
evil,
19 a false witness who pours out lies
and a man who stirs up
dissension among brothers.

Warning Against Adultery

20 My son, keep your father's commands
and do not forsake your mother's
teaching.
21 Bind them upon your heart forever;
fasten them around your neck.
22 When you walk, they will guide you;
when you sleep, they will watch
over you;
when you awake, they will speak to
you.
23 For these commands are a lamp,
this teaching is a light,
and the corrections of discipline
are the way to life,

[a] 11 Or *like a vagrant / and scarcity like a beggar*

[24] keeping you from the immoral woman,
from the smooth tongue of the wayward wife.
[25] Do not lust in your heart after her beauty
or let her captivate you with her eyes,
[26] for the prostitute reduces you to a loaf of bread,
and the adulteress preys upon your very life.
[27] Can a man scoop fire into his lap
without his clothes being burned?
[28] Can a man walk on hot coals
without his feet being scorched?
[29] So is he who sleeps with another man's wife;
no one who touches her will go unpunished.
[30] Men do not despise a thief if he steals
to satisfy his hunger when he is starving.
[31] Yet if he is caught, he must pay sevenfold,
though it costs him all the wealth of his house.
[32] But a man who commits adultery lacks judgment;
whoever does so destroys himself.
[33] Blows and disgrace are his lot,
and his shame will never be wiped away;
[34] for jealousy arouses a husband's fury,
and he will show no mercy when he takes revenge.
[35] He will not accept any compensation;
he will refuse the bribe, however great it is.

PRAYER: PETITION

LORD, help me to be careful and watch myself closely, lest I forget the things my eyes have seen or let them depart from my heart as long as I live. May I teach them to my children and to their children after them. (Deuteronomy 4:9)

***PAUSE** here to offer prayers of petition regarding your family and your ministry. Ask for help and guidance in sharing Jesus with others and helping others grow in Him. Ask for guidance in your vocation and your avocations. Offer prayers of petition regarding your activities for this day and any special concerns you may have.*

NT 1 Corinthians 10:23–11:1

The Believer's Freedom

[23] "Everything is permissible"—but not
everything is beneficial. "Everything is
permissible"—but not everything is constructive. [24] Nobody should seek his own
good, but the good of others.
[25] Eat anything sold in the meat market
without raising questions of conscience,
[26] for, "The earth is the Lord's, and everything in it."[a]
[27] If some unbeliever invites you to a
meal and you want to go, eat whatever is
put before you without raising questions
of conscience. [28] But if anyone says to you,
"This has been offered in sacrifice," then
do not eat it, both for the sake of the man
who told you and for conscience' sake[b]—
[29] the other man's conscience, I mean, not
yours. For why should my freedom be
judged by another's conscience? [30] If I take
part in the meal with thankfulness, why
am I denounced because of something I
thank God for?
[31] So whether you eat or drink or whatever you do, do it all for the glory of God.
[32] Do not cause anyone to stumble,
whether Jews, Greeks or the church of
God— [33] even as I try to please everybody
in every way. For I am not seeking my own
good but the good of many, so that they
11 may be saved. [1] Follow my example, as
I follow the example of Christ.

[a] 26 Psalm 24:1 [b] 28 Some manuscripts *conscience' sake, for "the earth is the Lord's and everything in it"*

PRAYER: THE WORKS OF GOD

WE know Your grace, O Lord Jesus Christ, that though You were rich, yet for our sakes You became poor, that we, through Your poverty, might become rich. (2 Corinthians 8:9)

***TAKE** a moment to consider the greatness of God's wonderful works.*

OT Numbers 23:1-30

Balaam's First Oracle

23 Balaam said, "Build me seven altars
here, and prepare seven bulls and sev-
en rams for me." 2Balak did as Balaam
said, and the two of them offered a bull
and a ram on each altar.
3Then Balaam said to Balak, "Stay here
beside your offering while I go aside. Perhaps the LORD will come to meet with me.
Whatever he reveals to me I will tell you."
Then he went off to a barren height.
4God met with him, and Balaam said,
"I have prepared seven altars, and on each
altar I have offered a bull and a ram."
5The LORD put a message in Balaam's
mouth and said, "Go back to Balak and
give him this message."
6So he went back to him and found
him standing beside his offering, with all
the princes of Moab. 7Then Balaam uttered his oracle:

"Balak brought me from Aram,
the king of Moab from the eastern mountains.
'Come,' he said, 'curse Jacob for me;
come, denounce Israel.'
8How can I curse
those whom God has not cursed?
How can I denounce
those whom the LORD has not denounced?
9From the rocky peaks I see them,
from the heights I view them.
I see a people who live apart
and do not consider themselves one of the nations.
10Who can count the dust of Jacob
or number the fourth part of Israel?
Let me die the death of the righteous,
and may my end be like theirs!"

11Balak said to Balaam, "What have you
done to me? I brought you to curse my
enemies, but you have done nothing but
bless them!"
12He answered, "Must I not speak what
the LORD puts in my mouth?"

Balaam's Second Oracle

13Then Balak said to him, "Come with
me to another place where you can see
them; you will see only a part but not all
of them. And from there, curse them for
me." 14So he took him to the field of Zo-
phim on the top of Pisgah, and there he
built seven altars and offered a bull and a
ram on each altar.
15Balaam said to Balak, "Stay here beside your offering while I meet with him
over there."
16The LORD met with Balaam and put a
message in his mouth and said, "Go back
to Balak and give him this message."
17So he went to him and found him
standing beside his offering, with the
princes of Moab. Balak asked him, "What
did the LORD say?"
18Then he uttered his oracle:

"Arise, Balak, and listen;
hear me, son of Zippor.
19God is not a man, that he should lie,
nor a son of man, that he should change his mind.
Does he speak and then not act?
Does he promise and not fulfill?
20I have received a command to bless;
he has blessed, and I cannot change it.

21"No misfortune is seen in Jacob,
no misery observed in Israel.[a]
The LORD their God is with them;
the shout of the King is among them.
22God brought them out of Egypt;

[a] 21 Or *He has not looked on Jacob's offenses / or on the wrongs found in Israel.*

they have the strength of a wild ox.
23 There is no sorcery against Jacob,
no divination against Israel.
It will now be said of Jacob
and of Israel, 'See what God has
done!'
24 The people rise like a lioness;
they rouse themselves like a lion
that does not rest till he devours his
prey
and drinks the blood of his
victims."

25 Then Balak said to Balaam, "Neither
curse them at all nor bless them at all!"
26 Balaam answered, "Did I not tell you
I must do whatever the LORD says?"

Balaam's Third Oracle

27 Then Balak said to Balaam, "Come, let
me take you to another place. Perhaps it
will please God to let you curse them for
me from there." 28 And Balak took Balaam
to the top of Peor, overlooking the wasteland.
29 Balaam said, "Build me seven altars
here, and prepare seven bulls and seven
rams for me." 30 Balak did as Balaam had
said, and offered a bull and a ram on each
altar.

PRAYER: INTERCESSION

O GOD, with all prayer and petition, we should pray always in Your Spirit, and to this end we should be watchful with all perseverance and petition for all the saints. (Ephesians 6:18)

***TAKE** a few moments to intercede on behalf of local, national and world missions. Pray that the Great Commission would be fulfilled and for any special concerns you may have for missions.*

NT 1 Corinthians 11:2-16

Propriety in Worship

2 I praise you for remembering me in
everything and for holding to the teachings,[a] just as I passed them on to you.
3 Now I want you to realize that the
head of every man is Christ, and the head
of the woman is man, and the head of
Christ is God. 4 Every man who prays or
prophesies with his head covered dishonors his head. 5 And every woman who
prays or prophesies with her head uncovered dishonors her head—it is just as
though her head were shaved. 6 If a
woman does not cover her head, she
should have her hair cut off; and if it is a
disgrace for a woman to have her hair cut
or shaved off, she should cover her head.
7 A man ought not to cover his head,[b]
since he is the image and glory of God;
but the woman is the glory of man. 8 For
man did not come from woman, but
woman from man; 9 neither was man created for woman, but woman for man.
10 For this reason, and because of the angels, the woman ought to have a sign of
authority on her head.
11 In the Lord, however, woman is not
independent of man, nor is man independent of woman. 12 For as woman came
from man, so also man is born of woman.
But everything comes from God. 13 Judge
for yourselves: Is it proper for a woman to
pray to God with her head uncovered?
14 Does not the very nature of things teach
you that if a man has long hair, it is a disgrace to him, 15 but that if a woman has
long hair, it is her glory? For long hair is
given to her as a covering. 16 If anyone
wants to be contentious about this, we
have no other practice—nor do the
churches of God.

[a] 2 Or *traditions* [b] 4-7 Or *4Every man who prays or prophesies with long hair dishonors his head. 5And every woman who prays or prophesies with no covering* ⌞*of hair*⌟ *on her head dishonors her head—she is just like one of the "shorn women." 6If a woman has no covering, let her be for now with short hair, but since it is a disgrace for a woman to have her hair shorn or shaved, she should grow it again. 7A man ought not to have long hair*

PRAYER: MY RELATIONSHIP TO GOD

IF I wish to come after You, Jesus Christ, I must deny myself and take up my cross and follow You. For if I want to save my life, I will lose it, but if I lose my life for You and for the gospel, I will find it. For what profit will I have if I gain the whole world, yet forfeit my soul? Or what will I give in exchange for my soul?

(Matthew 16:24–26; Mark 8:34–37; Luke 9:23–25)

***PAUSE** to thank God for the relationship that you enjoy with Him in Jesus Christ.*

YEAR 1 DAY 139

OT Numbers 24:1–25:18

24 Now when Balaam saw that it pleased
the LORD to bless Israel, he did not re-
sort to sorcery as at other times, but turned
his face toward the desert. 2 When Balaam
looked out and saw Israel encamped tribe
by tribe, the Spirit of God came upon him
3 and he uttered his oracle:

"The oracle of Balaam son of Beor,
the oracle of one whose eye sees clearly,
4 the oracle of one who hears the words of God,
who sees a vision from the Almighty,[a]
who falls prostrate, and whose eyes are opened:

5 "How beautiful are your tents, O Jacob,
your dwelling places, O Israel!

6 "Like valleys they spread out,
like gardens beside a river,
like aloes planted by the LORD,
like cedars beside the waters.
7 Water will flow from their buckets;
their seed will have abundant water.

"Their king will be greater than Agag;
their kingdom will be exalted.

8 "God brought them out of Egypt;
they have the strength of a wild ox.
They devour hostile nations
and break their bones in pieces;
with their arrows they pierce them.
9 Like a lion they crouch and lie down,
like a lioness—who dares to rouse them?

"May those who bless you be blessed
and those who curse you be cursed!"

10 Then Balak's anger burned against Balaam. He struck his hands together and
said to him, "I summoned you to curse
my enemies, but you have blessed them
these three times. 11 Now leave at once and
go home! I said I would reward you hand-
somely, but the LORD has kept you from
being rewarded."
12 Balaam answered Balak, "Did I not
tell the messengers you sent me, 13 'Even if
Balak gave me his palace filled with silver
and gold, I could not do anything of my
own accord, good or bad, to go beyond
the command of the LORD—and I must
say only what the LORD says'? 14 Now I am
going back to my people, but come, let
me warn you of what this people will do
to your people in days to come."

Balaam's Fourth Oracle

15 Then he uttered his oracle:

"The oracle of Balaam son of Beor,
the oracle of one whose eye sees clearly,
16 the oracle of one who hears the words of God,
who has knowledge from the Most High,
who sees a vision from the Almighty,
who falls prostrate, and whose eyes are opened:

17 "I see him, but not now;
I behold him, but not near.
A star will come out of Jacob;

[a] 4 Hebrew *Shaddai;* also in verse 16

a scepter will rise out of Israel.
He will crush the foreheads of Moab,
the skulls[b] of[c] all the sons of Sheth.[d]
18 Edom will be conquered;
Seir, his enemy, will be conquered,
but Israel will grow strong.
19 A ruler will come out of Jacob
and destroy the survivors of the city."

Balaam's Final Oracles

20 Then Balaam saw Amalek and uttered
his oracle:

"Amalek was first among the nations,
but he will come to ruin at last."

21 Then he saw the Kenites and uttered
his oracle:

"Your dwelling place is secure,
your nest is set in a rock;
22 yet you Kenites will be destroyed
when Asshur takes you captive."

23 Then he uttered his oracle:

"Ah, who can live when God does
this?[e]
24 Ships will come from the shores of
Kittim;
they will subdue Asshur and Eber,
but they too will come to ruin."

25 Then Balaam got up and returned
home and Balak went his own way.

Moab Seduces Israel

25 While Israel was staying in Shittim,
the men began to indulge in sexual
immorality with Moabite women, 2 who
invited them to the sacrifices to their
gods. The people ate and bowed down before these gods. 3 So Israel joined in worshiping the Baal of Peor. And the LORD's
anger burned against them.
4 The LORD said to Moses, "Take all the
leaders of these people, kill them and expose them in broad daylight before the
LORD, so that the LORD's fierce anger may
turn away from Israel."
5 So Moses said to Israel's judges, "Each
of you must put to death those of your
men who have joined in worshiping the
Baal of Peor."
6 Then an Israelite man brought to his
family a Midianite woman right before
the eyes of Moses and the whole assembly of Israel while they were weeping at
the entrance to the Tent of Meeting.
7 When Phinehas son of Eleazar, the son
of Aaron, the priest, saw this, he left the
assembly, took a spear in his hand 8 and
followed the Israelite into the tent. He
drove the spear through both of them—
through the Israelite and into the
woman's body. Then the plague against
the Israelites was stopped; 9 but those who
died in the plague numbered 24,000.
10 The LORD said to Moses, 11 "Phinehas
son of Eleazar, the son of Aaron, the
priest, has turned my anger away from the
Israelites; for he was as zealous as I am for
my honor among them, so that in my zeal
I did not put an end to them. 12 Therefore
tell him I am making my covenant of
peace with him. 13 He and his descendants
will have a covenant of a lasting priesthood, because he was zealous for the
honor of his God and made atonement
for the Israelites."
14 The name of the Israelite who was
killed with the Midianite woman was
Zimri son of Salu, the leader of a Sime-
onite family. 15 And the name of the Midianite woman who was put to death was
Cozbi daughter of Zur, a tribal chief of a
Midianite family.
16 The LORD said to Moses, 17 "Treat the
Midianites as enemies and kill them, 18 because they treated you as enemies when
they deceived you in the affair of Peor and
their sister Cozbi, the daughter of a Midianite leader, the woman who was killed
when the plague came as a result of Peor."

[b] 17 Samaritan Pentateuch (see also Jer. 48:45); the meaning of the word in the Masoretic Text is uncertain. [c] 17 Or possibly *Moab, / batter* [d] 17 Or *all the noisy boasters* [e] 23 Masoretic Text; with a different word division of the Hebrew *A people will gather from the north.*

PRAYER: AFFIRMATION

THOSE who wish to become great among others must become their servant, and those who wish to be first among them must be their slave. (Matthew 20:26–27; Mark 10:43–44) . . .

Those who exalt themselves will be humbled, and those who humble themselves will be exalted. (Matthew 23:12; Luke 14:11; 18:14)

PAUSE *to reflect on these Biblical affirmations.*

NT 1 Corinthians 11:17–34

The Lord's Supper

17 In the following directives I have no
praise for you, for your meetings do more
harm than good. 18 In the first place, I hear
that when you come together as a church,
there are divisions among you, and to
some extent I believe it. 19 No doubt there
have to be differences among you to show
which of you have God's approval. 20 When
you come together, it is not the Lord's Supper you eat, 21 for as you eat, each of you
goes ahead without waiting for anybody
else. One remains hungry, another gets
drunk. 22 Don't you have homes to eat and
drink in? Or do you despise the church of
God and humiliate those who have nothing? What shall I say to you? Shall I praise
you for this? Certainly not!

23 For I received from the Lord what I also
passed on to you: The Lord Jesus, on the
night he was betrayed, took bread, 24 and
when he had given thanks, he broke it and
said, "This is my body, which is for you; do
this in remembrance of me." 25 In the same
way, after supper he took the cup, saying,
"This cup is the new covenant in my blood;
do this, whenever you drink it, in remembrance of me." 26 For whenever you eat this
bread and drink this cup, you proclaim the
Lord's death until he comes.

27 Therefore, whoever eats the bread or
drinks the cup of the Lord in an unworthy
manner will be guilty of sinning against
the body and blood of the Lord. 28 A man
ought to examine himself before he eats
of the bread and drinks of the cup. 29 For
anyone who eats and drinks without rec-
ognizing the body of the Lord eats and
drinks judgment on himself. 30 That is why
many among you are weak and sick, and
a number of you have fallen asleep. 31 But
if we judged ourselves, we would not come
under judgment. 32 When we are judged by
the Lord, we are being disciplined so that
we will not be condemned with the world.

33 So then, my brothers, when you come
together to eat, wait for each other. 34 If
anyone is hungry, he should eat at home,
so that when you meet together it may not
result in judgment.

And when I come I will give further directions.

PRAYER: THE CHARACTER I WANT TO CULTIVATE

If I love money, O God, I will not be satisfied with money; if I love abundance, I will not be satisfied with its increase. (Ecclesiastes 5:10)

TAKE *a moment to ask the Lord for the grace to grow in godly character.*

YEAR 1 DAY 140

OT Psalm 30

Psalm 30

A psalm. A song. For the dedication of the temple.[a] Of David.

1 I will exalt you, O LORD,
for you lifted me out of the depths
and did not let my enemies gloat
over me.
2 O LORD my God, I called to you for
help
and you healed me.
3 O LORD, you brought me up from the
grave[b];
you spared me from going down
into the pit.

[a] Title: Or *palace* [b] 3 Hebrew *Sheol*

[4]Sing to the LORD, you saints of his;
praise his holy name.
[5]For his anger lasts only a moment,
but his favor lasts a lifetime;
weeping may remain for a night,
but rejoicing comes in the morning.

[6]When I felt secure, I said,
"I will never be shaken."
[7]O LORD, when you favored me,
you made my mountain[c] stand
firm;
but when you hid your face,
I was dismayed.

[8]To you, O LORD, I called;
to the Lord I cried for mercy:
[9]"What gain is there in my
destruction,[d]
in my going down into the pit?
Will the dust praise you?
Will it proclaim your faithfulness?
[10]Hear, O LORD, and be merciful to me;
O LORD, be my help."

[11]You turned my wailing into dancing;
you removed my sackcloth and
clothed me with joy,
[12]that my heart may sing to you and not
be silent.
O LORD my God, I will give you
thanks forever.

[c] 7 Or *hill country* [d] 9 Or *there if I am silenced*

PRAYER: THANKSGIVING

O LORD, the heavens shout for joy! The earth rejoices! The mountains break out into singing! For You have comforted Your people and will have compassion on Your afflicted ones. (Isaiah 49:13) . . . I will greatly rejoice in You, O Lord; my soul will be joyful in You, my God. For You have clothed me with garments of salvation and arrayed me in a robe of righteousness, as a bridegroom decks himself with ornaments, and as a bride adorns herself with her jewels. (Isaiah 61:10)

***PAUSE** to offer your own expressions of thanksgiving.*

NT 1 Corinthians 12:1-31a

Spiritual Gifts

12 Now about spiritual gifts, brothers, I
do not want you to be ignorant. [2]You
know that when you were pagans, somehow or other you were influenced and led
astray to mute idols. [3]Therefore I tell you
that no one who is speaking by the Spirit
of God says, "Jesus be cursed," and no one
can say, "Jesus is Lord," except by the Holy
Spirit.
[4]There are different kinds of gifts, but
the same Spirit. [5]There are different kinds
of service, but the same Lord. [6]There are
different kinds of working, but the same
God works all of them in all men.
[7]Now to each one the manifestation of
the Spirit is given for the common good.
[8]To one there is given through the Spirit
the message of wisdom, to another the
message of knowledge by means of the
same Spirit, [9]to another faith by the same
Spirit, to another gifts of healing by that
one Spirit, [10]to another miraculous powers, to another prophecy, to another distinguishing between spirits, to another
speaking in different kinds of tongues,[a]
and to still another the interpretation of
tongues.[a] [11]All these are the work of one
and the same Spirit, and he gives them to
each one, just as he determines.

One Body, Many Parts

[12]The body is a unit, though it is made
up of many parts; and though all its parts
are many, they form one body. So it is
with Christ. [13]For we were all baptized by[b]
one Spirit into one body—whether Jews
or Greeks, slave or free—and we were all
given the one Spirit to drink.
[14]Now the body is not made up of one
part but of many. [15]If the foot should say,
"Because I am not a hand, I do not belong
to the body," it would not for that reason
cease to be part of the body. [16]And if the

[a] 10 Or *languages;* also in verse 28 [b] 13 Or *with;* or *in*

ear should say, "Because I am not an eye, I do not belong to the body," it would not for that reason cease to be part of the body. [17]If the whole body were an eye, where would the sense of hearing be? If the whole body were an ear, where would the sense of smell be? [18]But in fact God has arranged the parts in the body, every one of them, just as he wanted them to be. [19]If they were all one part, where would the body be? [20]As it is, there are many parts, but one body.

[21]The eye cannot say to the hand, "I don't need you!" And the head cannot say to the feet, "I don't need you!" [22]On the contrary, those parts of the body that seem to be weaker are indispensable, [23]and the parts that we think are less honorable we treat with special honor. And the parts that are unpresentable are treated with special modesty, [24]while our presentable parts need no special treatment. But God has combined the members of the body and has given greater honor to the parts that lacked it, [25]so that there should be no division in the body, but that its parts should have equal concern for each other. [26]If one part suffers, every part suffers with it; if one part is honored, every part rejoices with it.

[27]Now you are the body of Christ, and each one of you is a part of it. [28]And in the church God has appointed first of all apostles, second prophets, third teachers, then workers of miracles, also those having gifts of healing, those able to help others, those with gifts of administration, and those speaking in different kinds of tongues. [29]Are all apostles? Are all prophets? Are all teachers? Do all work miracles? [30]Do all have gifts of healing? Do all speak in tongues[c]? Do all interpret? [31]But eagerly desire[d] the greater gifts.

[c] 30 Or *other languages* [d] 31 Or *But you are eagerly desiring*

PRAYER: MY RELATIONSHIP TO OTHERS

YOU say to me, O Lord, "Behold, lift up your eyes and look at the fields, for they are white for harvest. Even now the reaper draws his wages and gathers fruit for eternal life, that those who sow and those who reap may rejoice together." (John 4:35–36)

PAUSE *to review your relationships with others and to commit them to the Lord.*

OT Numbers 26:1–65 — YEAR 1 DAY 141

The Second Census

26 After the plague the LORD said to Moses and Eleazar son of Aaron, the priest, [2]"Take a census of the whole Israelite community by families—all those twenty years old or more who are able to serve in the army of Israel." [3]So on the plains of Moab by the Jordan across from Jericho,[a] Moses and Eleazar the priest spoke with them and said, [4]"Take a census of the men twenty years old or more, as the LORD commanded Moses."

These were the Israelites who came out of Egypt:

[5]The descendants of Reuben, the firstborn son of Israel, were:

through Hanoch, the Hanochite clan;
through Pallu, the Palluite clan;
[6]through Hezron, the Hezronite clan;
through Carmi, the Carmite clan.

[7]These were the clans of Reuben; those numbered were 43,730.

[8]The son of Pallu was Eliab, [9]and the sons of Eliab were Nemuel, Dathan and Abiram. The same Dathan and Abiram were the community officials who rebelled against Moses and Aaron and were among Korah's followers when they rebelled against the LORD. [10]The earth opened its mouth and swallowed them

[a] 3 Hebrew *Jordan of Jericho;* possibly an ancient name for the Jordan River; also in verse 63

along with Korah, whose followers died when the fire devoured the 250 men. And they served as a warning sign.
11The line of Korah, however, did not die out.

12The descendants of Simeon by their clans were:
through Nemuel, the Nemuelite clan;
through Jamin, the Jaminite clan;
through Jakin, the Jakinite clan;
13through Zerah, the Zerahite clan;
through Shaul, the Shaulite clan.
14These were the clans of Simeon; there were 22,200 men.

15The descendants of Gad by their clans were:
through Zephon, the Zephonite clan;
through Haggi, the Haggite clan;
through Shuni, the Shunite clan;
16through Ozni, the Oznite clan;
through Eri, the Erite clan;
17through Arodi,[b] the Arodite clan;
through Areli, the Arelite clan.
18These were the clans of Gad; those numbered were 40,500.

19Er and Onan were sons of Judah, but they died in Canaan.
20The descendants of Judah by their clans were:
through Shelah, the Shelanite clan;
through Perez, the Perezite clan;
through Zerah, the Zerahite clan.
21The descendants of Perez were:
through Hezron, the Hezronite clan;
through Hamul, the Hamulite clan.
22These were the clans of Judah; those numbered were 76,500.

23The descendants of Issachar by their clans were:
through Tola, the Tolaite clan;
through Puah, the Puite[c] clan;
24through Jashub, the Jashubite clan;
through Shimron, the Shimronite clan.
25These were the clans of Issachar; those numbered were 64,300.

26The descendants of Zebulun by their clans were:
through Sered, the Seredite clan;
through Elon, the Elonite clan;
through Jahleel, the Jahleelite clan.
27These were the clans of Zebulun; those numbered were 60,500.

28The descendants of Joseph by their clans through Manasseh and Ephraim were:

29The descendants of Manasseh:
through Makir, the Makirite clan (Makir was the father of Gilead);
through Gilead, the Gileadite clan.
30These were the descendants of Gilead:
through Iezer, the Iezerite clan;
through Helek, the Helekite clan;
31through Asriel, the Asrielite clan;
through Shechem, the Shechemite clan;
32through Shemida, the Shemidaite clan;
through Hepher, the Hepherite clan.
33(Zelophehad son of Hepher had no sons; he had only daughters, whose names were Mahlah, Noah, Hoglah, Milcah and Tirzah.)
34These were the clans of Manasseh; those numbered were 52,700.

35These were the descendants of Ephraim by their clans:
through Shuthelah, the Shuthelahite clan;
through Beker, the Bekerite clan;
through Tahan, the Tahanite clan.
36These were the descendants of Shuthelah:
through Eran, the Eranite clan.
37These were the clans of Ephraim; those numbered were 32,500.

These were the descendants of Joseph by their clans.

38The descendants of Benjamin by their clans were:
through Bela, the Belaite clan;
through Ashbel, the Ashbelite clan;
through Ahiram, the Ahiramite clan;
39through Shupham,[d] the Shuphamite clan;
through Hupham, the Huphamite clan.
40The descendants of Bela through Ard and Naaman were:

[b] *17* Samaritan Pentateuch and Syriac (see also Gen. 46:16); Masoretic Text *Arod* [c] *23* Samaritan Pentateuch, Septuagint, Vulgate and Syriac (see also 1 Chron. 7:1); Masoretic Text *through Puvah, the Punite* [d] *39* A few manuscripts of the Masoretic Text, Samaritan Pentateuch, Vulgate and Syriac (see also Septuagint); most manuscripts of the Masoretic Text *Shephupham*

through Ard,[e] the Ardite clan;
through Naaman, the Naamite clan.
41 These were the clans of Benjamin; those numbered were 45,600.

42 These were the descendants of Dan by their clans:
through Shuham, the Shuhamite clan.
These were the clans of Dan: 43 All of them were Shuhamite clans; and those numbered were 64,400.

44 The descendants of Asher by their clans were:
through Imnah, the Imnite clan;
through Ishvi, the Ishvite clan;
through Beriah, the Beriite clan;
45 and through the descendants of Beriah:
through Heber, the Heberite clan;
through Malkiel, the Malkielite clan.
46 (Asher had a daughter named Serah.)
47 These were the clans of Asher; those numbered were 53,400.

48 The descendants of Naphtali by their clans were:
through Jahzeel, the Jahzeelite clan;
through Guni, the Gunite clan;
49 through Jezer, the Jezerite clan;
through Shillem, the Shillemite clan.
50 These were the clans of Naphtali; those numbered were 45,400.

51 The total number of the men of Israel was 601,730.

52 The LORD said to Moses, 53 "The land is to be allotted to them as an inheritance based on the number of names. 54 To a
larger group give a larger inheritance, and to a smaller group a smaller one; each is to receive its inheritance according to the number of those listed. 55 Be sure that the land is distributed by lot. What each group inherits will be according to the names for its ancestral tribe. 56 Each inheritance is to be distributed by lot among the larger and smaller groups."

57 These were the Levites who were counted by their clans:
through Gershon, the Gershonite clan;
through Kohath, the Kohathite clan;
through Merari, the Merarite clan.
58 These also were Levite clans:
the Libnite clan,
the Hebronite clan,
the Mahlite clan,
the Mushite clan,
the Korahite clan.
(Kohath was the forefather of Amram; 59 the name of Amram's wife was Jochebed, a descendant of Levi, who was born to the Levites[f] in Egypt. To Amram she bore Aaron, Moses and their sister Miriam. 60 Aaron was the father of Nadab and Abihu, Eleazar and Ithamar. 61 But Nadab and Abihu died when they made an offering before the LORD with unauthorized fire.)

62 All the male Levites a month old or more numbered 23,000. They were not counted along with the other Israelites because they received no inheritance among them.

63 These are the ones counted by Moses and Eleazar the priest when they counted the Israelites on the plains of Moab by the Jordan across from Jericho. 64 Not one of
them was among those counted by Moses and Aaron the priest when they counted the Israelites in the Desert of Sinai. 65 For
the LORD had told those Israelites they would surely die in the desert, and not one of them was left except Caleb son of Jephunneh and Joshua son of Nun.

[e] *40* Samaritan Pentateuch and Vulgate (see also Septuagint); Masoretic Text does not have *through Ard.* [f] *59* Or *Jochebed, a daughter of Levi, who was born to Levi*

PRAYER: ADORATION

O GOD, in the year that King Uzziah died, Isaiah saw You sitting on a throne, high and exalted, and the train of Your robe filled the temple. Above it stood the seraphim; each one had six wings: with two

they covered their faces, with two they covered their feet, and with two they flew. And one cried to the other and said, "Holy, Holy, Holy is the Lord of hosts; the whole earth is full of His glory!" (Isaiah 6:1–3)

PAUSE *to express your thoughts of praise and worship.*

NT 1 Corinthians 13:1b–13:13

Love

And now I will show you the most excellent way.
13 If I speak in the tongues[a] of men and
of angels, but have not love, I am only
a resounding gong or a clanging cymbal.
2 If I have the gift of prophecy and can
fathom all mysteries and all knowledge,
and if I have a faith that can move mountains, but have not love, I am nothing. 3 If
I give all I possess to the poor and surrender my body to the flames,[b] but have
not love, I gain nothing.
4 Love is patient, love is kind. It does not
envy, it does not boast, it is not proud. 5 It
is not rude, it is not self-seeking, it is not
easily angered, it keeps no record of
wrongs. 6 Love does not delight in evil but
rejoices with the truth. 7 It always protects,
always trusts, always hopes, always perseveres.
8 Love never fails. But where there are
prophecies, they will cease; where there are
tongues, they will be stilled; where there is
knowledge, it will pass away. 9 For we know
in part and we prophesy in part, 10 but when
perfection comes, the imperfect disappears.
11 When I was a child, I talked like a child,
I thought like a child, I reasoned like a
child. When I became a man, I put childish ways behind me. 12 Now we see but a
poor reflection as in a mirror; then we shall
see face to face. Now I know in part; then I
shall know fully, even as I am fully known.
13 And now these three remain: faith,
hope and love. But the greatest of these is
love.

[a] 1 Or *languages* [b] 3 Some early manuscripts *body that I may boast*

PRAYER: THE ATTRIBUTES OF GOD

O LORD, You bring death and make alive; You bring down to the grave and raise up. You, Lord, send poverty and wealth; You humble and You exalt. You raise the poor from the dust and lift the needy from the ash heap, to seat them with princes and make them inherit a throne of honor. For the foundations of the earth are Yours, O Lord, and You have set the world upon them. (1 Samuel 2:6–8)

PAUSE *to reflect on these affirmations about the person, powers and perfection of God.*

YEAR 1
DAY 142

OT Numbers 27:1–23

Zelophehad's Daughters

27 The daughters of Zelophehad son of
Hepher, the son of Gilead, the son of
Makir, the son of Manasseh, belonged to
the clans of Manasseh son of Joseph. The
names of the daughters were Mahlah,
Noah, Hoglah, Milcah and Tirzah. They
approached 2 the entrance to the Tent of
Meeting and stood before Moses, Eleazar
the priest, the leaders and the whole assembly, and said, 3 "Our father died in the
desert. He was not among Korah's followers, who banded together against the
LORD, but he died for his own sin and left
no sons. 4 Why should our father's name
disappear from his clan because he had

no son? Give us property among our father's relatives."

5 So Moses brought their case before the LORD 6 and the LORD said to him, 7 "What Zelophehad's daughters are saying is right. You must certainly give them property as an inheritance among their father's relatives and turn their father's inheritance over to them.

8 "Say to the Israelites, 'If a man dies and leaves no son, turn his inheritance over to his daughter. 9 If he has no daughter, give his inheritance to his brothers. 10 If he has no brothers, give his inheritance to his father's brothers. 11 If his father had no brothers, give his inheritance to the nearest relative in his clan, that he may possess it. This is to be a legal requirement for the Israelites, as the LORD commanded Moses.' "

Joshua to Succeed Moses

12 Then the LORD said to Moses, "Go up this mountain in the Abarim range and see the land I have given the Israelites. 13 After you have seen it, you too will be gathered to your people, as your brother Aaron was, 14 for when the community rebelled at the waters in the Desert of Zin, both of you disobeyed my command to honor me as holy before their eyes." (These were the waters of Meribah Kadesh, in the Desert of Zin.)

15 Moses said to the LORD, 16 "May the LORD, the God of the spirits of all mankind, appoint a man over this community 17 to go out and come in before them, one who will lead them out and bring them in, so the LORD's people will not be like sheep without a shepherd."

18 So the LORD said to Moses, "Take Joshua son of Nun, a man in whom is the spirit,[a] and lay your hand on him. 19 Have him stand before Eleazar the priest and the entire assembly and commission him in their presence. 20 Give him some of your authority so the whole Israelite community will obey him. 21 He is to stand before Eleazar the priest, who will obtain decisions for him by inquiring of the Urim before the LORD. At his command he and the entire community of the Israelites will go out, and at his command they will come in."

22 Moses did as the LORD commanded him. He took Joshua and had him stand before Eleazar the priest and the whole assembly. 23 Then he laid his hands on him and commissioned him, as the LORD instructed through Moses.

[a] 18 Or *Spirit*

PRAYER: CONFESSION

YOU, the Lord God, have said, "I, even I, am He who blots out your transgressions for My own sake, and I will not remember your sins." (Isaiah 43:25)

***ASK** the Spirit to search your heart and reveal any areas of unconfessed sin. Acknowledge these to the Lord and thank Him for His forgiveness.*

NT 1 Corinthians 14:1–25

Gifts of Prophecy and Tongues

14 Follow the way of love and eagerly desire spiritual gifts, especially the gift of prophecy. 2 For anyone who speaks in a tongue[a] does not speak to men but to God. Indeed, no one understands him; he utters mysteries with his spirit.[b] 3 But everyone who prophesies speaks to men for their strengthening, encouragement and comfort. 4 He who speaks in a tongue edifies himself, but he who prophesies edifies the church. 5 I would like every one of you to speak in tongues,[c] but I would rather have you prophesy. He who prophesies is greater than one who speaks in tongues,[c] unless he interprets, so that the church may be edified.

6 Now, brothers, if I come to you and speak in tongues, what good will I be to you, unless I bring you some revelation or knowledge or prophecy or word of in-

[a] 2 Or *another language;* also in verses 4, 13, 14, 19, 26 and 27 [b] 2 Or *by the Spirit* [c] 5 Or *other languages;* also in verses 6, 18, 22, 23 and 39

struction? [7]Even in the case of lifeless things that make sounds, such as the flute or harp, how will anyone know what tune is being played unless there is a distinction in the notes? [8]Again, if the trumpet does not sound a clear call, who will get ready for battle? [9]So it is with you. Unless you speak intelligible words with your tongue, how will anyone know what you are saying? You will just be speaking into the air. [10]Undoubtedly there are all sorts of languages in the world, yet none of them is without meaning. [11]If then I do not grasp the meaning of what someone is saying, I am a foreigner to the speaker, and he is a foreigner to me. [12]So it is with you. Since you are eager to have spiritual gifts, try to excel in gifts that build up the church.

[13]For this reason anyone who speaks in a tongue should pray that he may interpret what he says. [14]For if I pray in a tongue, my spirit prays, but my mind is unfruitful. [15]So what shall I do? I will pray with my spirit, but I will also pray with my mind; I will sing with my spirit, but I will also sing with my mind. [16]If you are praising God with your spirit, how can one who finds himself among those who do not understand[d] say "Amen" to your thanksgiving, since he does not know what you are saying? [17]You may be giving thanks well enough, but the other man is not edified.

[18]I thank God that I speak in tongues more than all of you. [19]But in the church I would rather speak five intelligible words to instruct others than ten thousand words in a tongue.

[20]Brothers, stop thinking like children. In regard to evil be infants, but in your thinking be adults. [21]In the Law it is written:

"Through men of strange tongues
  and through the lips of foreigners
I will speak to this people,
  but even then they will not listen to
    me,"[e]
says the Lord.

[22]Tongues, then, are a sign, not for believers but for unbelievers; prophecy, however, is for believers, not for unbelievers. [23]So if the whole church comes together and everyone speaks in tongues, and some who do not understand[f] or some unbelievers come in, will they not say that you are out of your mind? [24]But if an unbeliever or someone who does not understand[g] comes in while everybody is prophesying, he will be convinced by all that he is a sinner and will be judged by all, [25]and the secrets of his heart will be laid bare. So he will fall down and worship God, exclaiming, "God is really among you!"

[d] 16 Or *among the inquirers* [e] 21 Isaiah 28:11,12
[f] 23 Or *some inquirers* [g] 24 Or *or some inquirer*

PRAYER: THE WORKS OF GOD

YOU, O Holy One, have asked, "To whom will you compare Me? Or who is My equal?" We lift our eyes to the heavens and see Who has created them. You bring out the starry host by number and call them each by name. Because of Your great might and the strength of Your power, not one of them is missing. Do we not know? Have we not heard? You are the everlasting God, the Lord, the Creator of the ends of the earth. You do not grow tired or weary. No one can fathom Your understanding. (Isaiah 40:25–26, 28)

***TAKE** a moment to consider the greatness of God's wonderful works.*

YEAR 1 DAY 143

OT Numbers 28:1-31

Daily Offerings

28 The LORD said to Moses, [2]"Give this command to the Israelites and say to them: 'See that you present to me at the appointed time the food for my offerings made by fire, as an aroma pleasing to me.' [3]Say to them: 'This is the offering made by fire that you are to present to the LORD:

two lambs a year old without defect, as a regular burnt offering each day. 4Prepare one lamb in the morning and the other at twilight, 5together with a grain offering of a tenth of an ephah[a] of fine flour mixed with a quarter of a hin[b] of oil from pressed olives. 6This is the regular burnt offering instituted at Mount Sinai as a pleasing aroma, an offering made to the LORD by fire. 7The accompanying drink offering is to be a quarter of a hin of fermented drink with each lamb. Pour out the drink offering to the LORD at the sanctuary. 8Prepare the second lamb at twilight, along with the same kind of grain offering and drink offering that you prepare in the morning. This is an offering made by fire, an aroma pleasing to the LORD.

Sabbath Offerings

9" 'On the Sabbath day, make an offering of two lambs a year old without defect, together with its drink offering and a grain offering of two-tenths of an ephah[c] of fine flour mixed with oil. 10This is the burnt offering for every Sabbath, in addition to the regular burnt offering and its drink offering.

Monthly Offerings

11" 'On the first of every month, present to the LORD a burnt offering of two young bulls, one ram and seven male lambs a year old, all without defect. 12With each bull there is to be a grain offering of three-tenths of an ephah[d] of fine flour mixed with oil; with the ram, a grain offering of two-tenths of an ephah of fine flour mixed with oil; 13and with each lamb, a grain offering of a tenth of an ephah of fine flour mixed with oil. This is for a burnt offering, a pleasing aroma, an offering made to the LORD by fire. 14With each bull there is to be a drink offering of half a hin[e] of wine; with the ram, a third of a hin[f]; and with each lamb, a quarter of a hin. This is the monthly burnt offering to be made at each new moon during the year. 15Besides the regular burnt offering with its drink offering, one male goat is to be presented to the LORD as a sin offering.

The Passover

16" 'On the fourteenth day of the first month the LORD's Passover is to be held. 17On the fifteenth day of this month there is to be a festival; for seven days eat bread made without yeast. 18On the first day hold a sacred assembly and do no regular work. 19Present to the LORD an offering made by fire, a burnt offering of two young bulls, one ram and seven male lambs a year old, all without defect. 20With each bull prepare a grain offering of three-tenths of an ephah of fine flour mixed with oil; with the ram, two-tenths; 21and with each of the seven lambs, one-tenth. 22Include one male goat as a sin offering to make atonement for you. 23Prepare these in addition to the regular morning burnt offering. 24In this way prepare the food for the offering made by fire every day for seven days as an aroma pleasing to the LORD; it is to be prepared in addition to the regular burnt offering and its drink offering. 25On the seventh day hold a sacred assembly and do no regular work.

Feast of Weeks

26" 'On the day of firstfruits, when you present to the LORD an offering of new grain during the Feast of Weeks, hold a sacred assembly and do no regular work. 27Present a burnt offering of two young bulls, one ram and seven male lambs a year old as an aroma pleasing to the LORD. 28With each bull there is to be a grain offering of three-tenths of an ephah of fine flour mixed with oil; with the ram, two-tenths; 29and with each of the seven lambs, one-tenth. 30Include one male goat to make atonement for you. 31Prepare these together with their drink offerings, in addition to the regular burnt offering and its grain offering. Be sure the animals are without defect.

[a] *5* That is, probably about 2 quarts (about 2 liters); also in verses 13, 21 and 29 [b] *5* That is, probably about 1 quart (about 1 liter); also in verses 7 and 14 [c] *9* That is, probably about 4 quarts (about 4.5 liters); also in verses 12, 20 and 28 [d] *12* That is, probably about 6 quarts (about 6.5 liters); also in verses 20 and 28 [e] *14* That is, probably about 2 quarts (about 2 liters) [f] *14* That is, probably about 1 1/4 quarts (about 1.2 liters)

PRAYER: RENEWAL

MAY I not love with words or tongue, but in deed and in truth. By this I will know that I am of the truth and my heart will be assured before You, O God; for if my heart condemns me, You are greater than my heart, and You know all things. If my heart does not condemn me, I have confidence before You and receive from You whatever I ask, because I keep Your commandments and do the things that are pleasing in Your sight. (1 John 3:18–22)

***PAUSE** to add your own prayers for personal renewal.*

NT 1 Corinthians 14:26-40

Orderly Worship

[26]What then shall we say, brothers?
When you come together, everyone has a
hymn, or a word of instruction, a revelation, a tongue or an interpretation. All of
these must be done for the strengthening
of the church. [27]If anyone speaks in a
tongue, two—or at the most three—
should speak, one at a time, and someone
must interpret. [28]If there is no interpreter,
the speaker should keep quiet in the
church and speak to himself and God.

[29]Two or three prophets should speak,
and the others should weigh carefully
what is said. [30]And if a revelation comes
to someone who is sitting down, the first
speaker should stop. [31]For you can all
prophesy in turn so that everyone may be
instructed and encouraged. [32]The spirits of
prophets are subject to the control of
prophets. [33]For God is not a God of disorder but of peace.

As in all the congregations of the saints,
[34]women should remain silent in the
churches. They are not allowed to speak,
but must be in submission, as the Law
says. [35]If they want to inquire about something, they should ask their own husbands at home; for it is disgraceful for a
woman to speak in the church.

[36]Did the word of God originate with
you? Or are you the only people it has
reached? [37]If anybody thinks he is a
prophet or spiritually gifted, let him acknowledge that what I am writing to you
is the Lord's command. [38]If he ignores
this, he himself will be ignored.[a]

[39]Therefore, my brothers, be eager to
prophesy, and do not forbid speaking in
tongues. [40]But everything should be done
in a fitting and orderly way.

[a] 38 Some manuscripts *If he is ignorant of this, let him be ignorant*

PRAYER: MY RELATIONSHIP TO GOD

I WANT to be a doer of Your word, O Lord, and not merely a hearer who deceives myself. For those who hear Your word and do not do it are like people who look at their natural faces in a mirror and, after looking at themselves, go away and immediately forget what kind of people they are. But those who look intently into Your perfect law of freedom and continue in it, who hear and do not forget Your word, Lord. but do it, these will be blessed in what they do. (James 1:22–25)

***PAUSE** to thank God for the relationship that you enjoy with Him in Jesus Christ.*

YEAR 1 DAY 144

OT **Numbers 29:1-40**

Feast of Trumpets

29 " 'On the first day of the seventh month hold a sacred assembly and do no regular work. It is a day for you to sound the trumpets.
[2]As an aroma pleasing to the LORD, prepare a burnt offering of one young bull, one ram and seven male lambs a year old, all without defect.
[3]With the bull prepare a grain offering of three-tenths of an ephah[a] of fine flour mixed with oil; with the ram, two-tenths[b];
[4]and with each of the seven lambs, one-tenth.[c] [5]Include one male goat as a sin offering to make atonement for you. [6]These are in addition to the monthly and daily burnt offerings with their grain offerings and drink offerings as specified. They are offerings made to the LORD by fire—a pleasing aroma.

Day of Atonement

[7]" 'On the tenth day of this seventh month hold a sacred assembly. You must deny yourselves[d] and do no work.
[8]Present as an aroma pleasing to the LORD a burnt offering of one young bull, one ram and seven male lambs a year old, all without defect. [9]With the bull prepare a grain offering of three-tenths of an ephah of fine flour mixed with oil; with the ram, two-tenths; [10]and with each of the seven lambs, one-tenth. [11]Include one male goat as a sin offering, in addition to the sin offering for atonement and the regular burnt offering with its grain offering, and their drink offerings.

Feast of Tabernacles

[12]" 'On the fifteenth day of the seventh month, hold a sacred assembly and do no regular work. Celebrate a festival to the LORD for seven days. [13]Present an offering made by fire as an aroma pleasing to the LORD, a burnt offering of thirteen young bulls, two rams and fourteen male lambs a year old, all without defect. [14]With each of the thirteen bulls prepare a grain offering of three-tenths of an ephah of fine flour mixed with oil; with each of the two rams, two-tenths; [15]and with each of the fourteen lambs, one-tenth. [16]Include one male goat as a sin offering, in addition to the regular burnt offering with its grain offering and drink offering.

[17]" 'On the second day prepare twelve young bulls, two rams and fourteen male lambs a year old, all without defect.
[18]With the bulls, rams and lambs, prepare their grain offerings and drink offerings according to the number specified. [19]Include one male goat as a sin offering, in addition to the regular burnt offering with its grain offering, and their drink offerings.

[20]" 'On the third day prepare eleven bulls, two rams and fourteen male lambs a year old, all without defect. [21]With the bulls, rams and lambs, prepare their grain offerings and drink offerings according to the number specified. [22]Include one male goat as a sin offering, in addition to the regular burnt offering with its grain offering and drink offering.

[23]" 'On the fourth day prepare ten bulls, two rams and fourteen male lambs a year old, all without defect. [24]With the bulls, rams and lambs, prepare their grain offerings and drink offerings according to the number specified. [25]Include one male goat as a sin offering, in addition to the regular burnt offering with its grain offering and drink offering

[26]" 'On the fifth day prepare nine bulls, two rams and fourteen male lambs a year old, all without defect. [27]With the bulls, rams and lambs, prepare their grain offerings and drink offerings according to the number specified. [28]Include one male goat as a sin offering, in addition to the regular burnt offering with its grain offering and drink offering.

[29]" 'On the sixth day prepare eight bulls, two rams and fourteen male lambs a year old, all without defect. [30]With the bulls, rams and lambs, prepare their grain offerings and drink offerings according to the number specified. [31]Include one male goat as a sin offering, in addition to the regular burnt offering with its grain offering and drink offering.

[a] 3 That is, probably about 6 quarts (about 6.5 liters); also in verses 9 and 14 [b] 3 That is, probably about 4 quarts (about 4.5 liters); also in verses 9 and 14 [c] 4 That is, probably about 2 quarts (about 2 liters); also in verses 10 and 15 [d] 7 Or *must fast*

32" 'On the seventh day prepare seven
bulls, two rams and fourteen male lambs
a year old, all without defect. 33With the
bulls, rams and lambs, prepare their grain
offerings and drink offerings according to
the number specified. 34Include one male
goat as a sin offering, in addition to the
regular burnt offering with its grain offering and drink offering.
35" 'On the eighth day hold an assembly and do no regular work. 36Present an
offering made by fire as an aroma pleasing to the LORD, a burnt offering of one
bull, one ram and seven male lambs a
year old, all without defect. 37With the
bull, the ram and the lambs, prepare their
grain offerings and drink offerings according to the number specified. 38In-
clude one male goat as a sin offering, in
addition to the regular burnt offering with
its grain offering and drink offering.
39" 'In addition to what you vow and
your freewill offerings, prepare these for
the LORD at your appointed feasts: your
burnt offerings, grain offerings, drink offerings and fellowship offerings.[e]' "
40Moses told the Israelites all that the
LORD commanded him.

[e] 39 Traditionally *peace offerings*

PRAYER: PETITION

O LORD, may I not say, "Today or tomorrow I will go to this or that city, spend a year there, carry on business, and make a profit." For I do not even know what my life will be tomorrow. I am a vapor that appears for a little while and then vanishes away. Instead, let me say, "If the Lord wills, I will live and do this or that." Otherwise, I boast in my arrogance, and all such boasting is evil. (James 4:13–16)

***PAUSE** here to petition God for growth in your character and personal discipline, and for physical health and strength. Ask that He empower you for spiritual warfare against the temptations of the world, the flesh and the devil. Offer prayers regarding your activities for this day and any special concerns you may have.*

NT 1 Corinthians 15:1–11

The Resurrection of Christ

15 Now, brothers, I want to remind you of
the gospel I preached to you, which you
received and on which you have taken your
stand. 2By this gospel you are saved, if you
hold firmly to the word I preached to you.
Otherwise, you have believed in vain.
3For what I received I passed on to you
as of first importance[a]: that Christ died for
our sins according to the Scriptures, 4that
he was buried, that he was raised on the
third day according to the Scriptures, 5and
that he appeared to Peter,[b] and then to the
Twelve. 6After that, he appeared to more
than five hundred of the brothers at the
same time, most of whom are still living,
though some have fallen asleep. 7Then he
appeared to James, then to all the apostles, 8and last of all he appeared to me
also, as to one abnormally born.
9For I am the least of the apostles and do
not even deserve to be called an apostle, because I persecuted the church of God. 10But
by the grace of God I am what I am, and
his grace to me was not without effect. No,
I worked harder than all of them—yet not
I, but the grace of God that was with me.
11Whether, then, it was I or they, this is what
we preach, and this is what you believed.

[a] 3 Or *you at the first* [b] 5 Greek *Cephas*

PRAYER: THE CHARACTER I WANT TO CULTIVATE

THOSE who are slow to anger, O Lord, are better than the mighty, and those who rule their spirits than those who take a city. (Proverbs 16:32) . . . In my anger, Lord, I will not sin;

I will not let the sun go down while I am still angry,
and I will not give the devil a foothold.
(Ephesians 4:26–27)

TAKE *a moment to ask the Lord for the grace to grow in godly character.*

YEAR 1
DAY 145

OT Numbers 30:1–31:54

Vows

30 Moses said to the heads of the tribes of Israel: "This is what the LORD commands: 2When a man makes a vow to the LORD or takes an oath to obligate himself by a pledge, he must not break his word but must do everything he said.

3"When a young woman still living in her father's house makes a vow to the LORD or obligates herself by a pledge 4and her father hears about her vow or pledge but says nothing to her, then all her vows and every pledge by which she obligated herself will stand. 5But if her father forbids her when he hears about it, none of her vows or the pledges by which she obligated herself will stand; the LORD will release her because her father has forbidden her.

6"If she marries after she makes a vow or after her lips utter a rash promise by which she obligates herself 7and her husband hears about it but says nothing to her, then her vows or the pledges by which she obligated herself will stand. 8But if her husband forbids her when he hears about it, he nullifies the vow that obligates her or the rash promise by which she obligates herself, and the LORD will release her.

9"Any vow or obligation taken by a widow or divorced woman will be binding on her.

10"If a woman living with her husband makes a vow or obligates herself by a pledge under oath 11and her husband hears about it but says nothing to her and does not forbid her, then all her vows or the pledges by which she obligated herself will stand. 12But if her husband nullifies them when he hears about them, then none of the vows or pledges that came from her lips will stand. Her husband has nullified them, and the LORD will release her. 13Her husband may confirm or nullify any vow she makes or any sworn pledge to deny herself. 14But if her husband says nothing to her about it from day to day, then he confirms all her vows or the pledges binding on her. He confirms them by saying nothing to her when he hears about them. 15If, however, he nullifies them some time after he hears about them, then he is responsible for her guilt."

16These are the regulations the LORD gave Moses concerning relationships between a man and his wife, and between a father and his young daughter still living in his house.

Vengeance on the Midianites

31 The LORD said to Moses, 2"Take vengeance on the Midianites for the Israelites. After that, you will be gathered to your people."

3So Moses said to the people, "Arm some of your men to go to war against the Midianites and to carry out the LORD's vengeance on them. 4Send into battle a thousand men from each of the tribes of Israel." 5So twelve thousand men armed for battle, a thousand from each tribe, were supplied from the clans of Israel. 6Moses sent them into battle, a thousand from each tribe, along with Phinehas son of Eleazar, the priest, who took with him articles from the sanctuary and the trumpets for signaling.

7They fought against Midian, as the LORD commanded Moses, and killed every man. 8Among their victims were Evi, Rekem, Zur, Hur and Reba—the five kings of Midian. They also killed Balaam son of Beor with the sword. 9The Israelites captured the Midianite women and children and took all the Midianite herds, flocks and goods as plunder. 10They burned all the towns where the Midianites had settled, as well as all their camps. 11They took all the plunder and spoils, including the

people and animals, [12]and brought the
captives, spoils and plunder to Moses and
Eleazar the priest and the Israelite assembly at their camp on the plains of Moab,
by the Jordan across from Jericho.[a]
[13]Moses, Eleazar the priest and all the
leaders of the community went to meet
them outside the camp. [14]Moses was angry
with the officers of the army—the commanders of thousands and commanders
of hundreds—who returned from the
battle.
[15]"Have you allowed all the women to
live?" he asked them. [16]"They were the
ones who followed Balaam's advice and
were the means of turning the Israelites
away from the LORD in what happened at
Peor, so that a plague struck the LORD's
people. [17]Now kill all the boys. And kill
every woman who has slept with a man,
[18]but save for yourselves every girl who
has never slept with a man.
[19]"All of you who have killed anyone or
touched anyone who was killed must stay
outside the camp seven days. On the third
and seventh days you must purify yourselves and your captives. [20]Purify every
garment as well as everything made of
leather, goat hair or wood."
[21]Then Eleazar the priest said to the soldiers who had gone into battle, "This is
the requirement of the law that the LORD
gave Moses: [22]Gold, silver, bronze, iron,
tin, lead [23]and anything else that can withstand fire must be put through the fire,
and then it will be clean. But it must also
be purified with the water of cleansing.
And whatever cannot withstand fire must
be put through that water. [24]On the seventh day wash your clothes and you will
be clean. Then you may come into the
camp."

Dividing the Spoils

[25]The LORD said to Moses, [26]"You and
Eleazar the priest and the family heads of
the community are to count all the people and animals that were captured. [27]Di-
vide the spoils between the soldiers who
took part in the battle and the rest of the
community. [28]From the soldiers who
fought in the battle, set apart as tribute for
the LORD one out of every five hundred,
whether persons, cattle, donkeys, sheep or
goats. [29]Take this tribute from their half
share and give it to Eleazar the priest as
the LORD's part. [30]From the Israelites' half,
select one out of every fifty, whether persons, cattle, donkeys, sheep, goats or other animals. Give them to the Levites, who
are responsible for the care of the LORD's
tabernacle." [31]So Moses and Eleazar the
priest did as the LORD commanded Moses.
[32]The plunder remaining from the
spoils that the soldiers took was 675,000
sheep, [33]72,000 cattle, [34]61,000 donkeys
[35]and 32,000 women who had never slept
with a man.
[36]The half share of those who fought in
the battle was:

337,500 sheep, [37]of which the tribute
for the LORD was 675;
[38]36,000 cattle, of which the tribute for
the LORD was 72;
[39]30,500 donkeys, of which the tribute
for the LORD was 61;
[40]16,000 people, of which the tribute
for the LORD was 32.

[41]Moses gave the tribute to Eleazar the
priest as the LORD's part, as the LORD commanded Moses.
[42]The half belonging to the Israelites,
which Moses set apart from that of the
fighting men— [43]the community's half—
was 337,500 sheep, [44]36,000 cattle,
[45]30,500 donkeys [46]and 16,000 people.
[47]From the Israelites' half, Moses selected
one out of every fifty persons and animals,
as the LORD commanded him, and gave
them to the Levites, who were responsible
for the care of the LORD's tabernacle.
[48]Then the officers who were over the
units of the army—the commanders of
thousands and commanders of hundreds—went to Moses [49]and said to him,
"Your servants have counted the soldiers
under our command, and not one is missing. [50]So we have brought as an offering
to the LORD the gold articles each of us acquired—armlets, bracelets, signet rings,
earrings and necklaces—to make atonement for ourselves before the LORD."
[51]Moses and Eleazar the priest accepted
from them the gold—all the crafted articles. [52]All the gold from the commanders
of thousands and commanders of hundreds that Moses and Eleazar presented
as a gift to the LORD weighed 16,750
shekels.[b] [53]Each soldier had taken plunder

[a] 12 Hebrew *Jordan of Jericho;* possibly an ancient name for the Jordan River [b] 52 That is, about 420 pounds (about 190 kilograms)

for himself. 54Moses and Eleazar the priest accepted the gold from the commanders of thousands and commanders of hundreds and brought it into the Tent of Meeting as a memorial for the Israelites before the LORD.

PRAYER: INTERCESSION

LORD Jesus, may I remember those in prison as though bound with them, and those who are mistreated, as though suffering with them. (Hebrews 13:3)

***TAKE** a few moments to intercede on behalf of the poor and hungry, the oppressed and persecuted, and those in control of world and national resources. Offer prayers for peace among nations and regarding current events and concerns.*

NT 1 Corinthians 15:12–34

The Resurrection of the Dead

12But if it is preached that Christ has been raised from the dead, how can some of you say that there is no resurrection of the dead? 13If there is no resurrection of the dead, then not even Christ has been raised. 14And if Christ has not been raised, our preaching is useless and so is your faith. 15More than that, we are then found to be false witnesses about God, for we have testified about God that he raised Christ from the dead. But he did not raise him if in fact the dead are not raised. 16For if the dead are not raised, then Christ has not been raised either. 17And if Christ has not been raised, your faith is futile; you are still in your sins. 18Then those also who have fallen asleep in Christ are lost. 19If only for this life we have hope in Christ, we are to be pitied more than all men.

20But Christ has indeed been raised from the dead, the firstfruits of those who have fallen asleep. 21For since death came through a man, the resurrection of the dead comes also through a man. 22For as in Adam all die, so in Christ all will be made alive. 23But each in his own turn: Christ, the firstfruits; then, when he comes, those who belong to him. 24Then the end will come, when he hands over the kingdom to God the Father after he has destroyed all dominion, authority and power. 25For he must reign until he has put all his enemies under his feet. 26The last enemy to be destroyed is death. 27For he "has put everything under his feet."[a] Now when it says that "everything" has been put under him, it is clear that this does not include God himself, who put everything under Christ. 28When he has done this, then the Son himself will be made subject to him who put everything under him, so that God may be all in all.

29Now if there is no resurrection, what will those do who are baptized for the dead? If the dead are not raised at all, why are people baptized for them? 30And as for us, why do we endanger ourselves every hour? 31I die every day—I mean that, brothers—just as surely as I glory over you in Christ Jesus our Lord. 32If I fought wild beasts in Ephesus for merely human reasons, what have I gained? If the dead are not raised,

"Let us eat and drink,
for tomorrow we die."[b]

33Do not be misled: "Bad company corrupts good character." 34Come back to your senses as you ought, and stop sinning; for there are some who are ignorant of God—I say this to your shame.

[a] 27 Psalm 8:6 [b] 32 Isaiah 22:13

PRAYER: MY RELATIONSHIP TO OTHERS

YOUR foremost commandment, O God, is this: "Hear, O Israel; the Lord our God, the Lord is one; and you shall love the Lord your God with all your heart and with all your soul and with all your mind and

with all your strength." The second is this: "You shall love your neighbor as yourself." There is no commandment greater than these, O God. To love You with all my heart and with all my understanding and with all my strength, and to love my neighbor as myself are more important than all burnt offerings and sacrifices. (Mark 12:29–31, 33)

__PAUSE__ to review your relationships with others and to commit them to the Lord.

YEAR 1 DAY 146

OT Numbers 32:1–42

The Transjordan Tribes

32 The Reubenites and Gadites, who had
very large herds and flocks, saw that
the lands of Jazer and Gilead were suitable for livestock. 2So they came to Moses
and Eleazar the priest and to the leaders
of the community, and said, 3"Ataroth,
Dibon, Jazer, Nimrah, Heshbon, Elealeh,
Sebam, Nebo and Beon— 4the land the
LORD subdued before the people of Israel—are suitable for livestock, and your
servants have livestock. 5If we have found
favor in your eyes," they said, "let this
land be given to your servants as our possession. Do not make us cross the Jordan."

6Moses said to the Gadites and Reubenites, "Shall your countrymen go to war
while you sit here? 7Why do you discourage the Israelites from going over into the
land the LORD has given them? 8This is
what your fathers did when I sent them
from Kadesh Barnea to look over the land.
9After they went up to the Valley of Eshcol and viewed the land, they discouraged
the Israelites from entering the land the
LORD had given them. 10The LORD's anger
was aroused that day and he swore this
oath: 11'Because they have not followed
me wholeheartedly, not one of the men
twenty years old or more who came up
out of Egypt will see the land I promised
on oath to Abraham, Isaac and Jacob—
12not one except Caleb son of Jephunneh
the Kenizzite and Joshua son of Nun, for
they followed the LORD wholeheartedly.'
13The LORD's anger burned against Israel
and he made them wander in the desert
forty years, until the whole generation of
those who had done evil in his sight was
gone.

14"And here you are, a brood of sinners,
standing in the place of your fathers and
making the LORD even more angry with Israel. 15If you turn away from following
him, he will again leave all this people in
the desert, and you will be the cause of
their destruction."

16Then they came up to him and said,
"We would like to build pens here for our
livestock and cities for our women and
children. 17But we are ready to arm ourselves and go ahead of the Israelites until
we have brought them to their place.
Meanwhile our women and children will
live in fortified cities, for protection from
the inhabitants of the land. 18We will not
return to our homes until every Israelite
has received his inheritance. 19We will not
receive any inheritance with them on the
other side of the Jordan, because our inheritance has come to us on the east side
of the Jordan."

20Then Moses said to them, "If you will
do this—if you will arm yourselves before
the LORD for battle, 21and if all of you will
go armed over the Jordan before the LORD
until he has driven his enemies out before
him— 22then when the land is subdued
before the LORD, you may return and be
free from your obligation to the LORD and
to Israel. And this land will be your possession before the LORD.

23"But if you fail to do this, you will be
sinning against the LORD; and you may be
sure that your sin will find you out.
24Build cities for your women and children, and pens for your flocks, but do
what you have promised."

25The Gadites and Reubenites said to
Moses, "We your servants will do as our
lord commands. 26Our children and
wives, our flocks and herds will remain
here in the cities of Gilead. 27But your servants, every man armed for battle, will

cross over to fight before the LORD, just as
our lord says."
28 Then Moses gave orders about them
to Eleazar the priest and Joshua son of
Nun and to the family heads of the Israelite tribes. 29 He said to them, "If the Gadites and Reubenites, every man armed for
battle, cross over the Jordan with you before the LORD, then when the land is subdued before you, give them the land of
Gilead as their possession. 30 But if they do
not cross over with you armed, they must
accept their possession with you in Canaan."
31 The Gadites and Reubenites answered,
"Your servants will do what the LORD has
said. 32 We will cross over before the LORD
into Canaan armed, but the property we
inherit will be on this side of the Jordan."
33 Then Moses gave to the Gadites, the
Reubenites and the half-tribe of Manasseh
son of Joseph the kingdom of Sihon king
of the Amorites and the kingdom of Og
king of Bashan—the whole land with its
cities and the territory around them.
34 The Gadites built up Dibon, Ataroth,
Aroer, 35 Atroth Shophan, Jazer, Jogbehah,
36 Beth Nimrah and Beth Haran as fortified
cities, and built pens for their flocks.
37 And the Reubenites rebuilt Heshbon,
Elealeh and Kiriathaim, 38 as well as Nebo
and Baal Meon (these names were
changed) and Sibmah. They gave names
to the cities they rebuilt.
39 The descendants of Makir son of Manasseh went to Gilead, captured it and
drove out the Amorites who were there.
40 So Moses gave Gilead to the Makirites,
the descendants of Manasseh, and they
settled there. 41 Jair, a descendant of Manasseh, captured their settlements and
called them Havvoth Jair.[a] 42 And Nobah
captured Kenath and its surrounding settlements and called it Nobah after himself.

[a] 41 Or *them the settlements of Jair*

PRAYER: AFFIRMATION

O GOD, apart from the law, Your righteousness has been made known, being witnessed by the Law and the Prophets, even Your righteousness through faith in Jesus Christ to all who believe. For there is no difference, for all have sinned and fall short of Your glory, being justified freely by Your grace through the redemption that is in Christ Jesus. (Romans 3:21–24)

***PAUSE** to reflect on these Biblical affirmations.*

NT 1 Corinthians 15:35–58

The Resurrection Body

35 But someone may ask, "How are the
dead raised? With what kind of body will
they come?" 36 How foolish! What you
sow does not come to life unless it dies.
37 When you sow, you do not plant the
body that will be, but just a seed, perhaps
of wheat or of something else. 38 But God
gives it a body as he has determined, and
to each kind of seed he gives its own body.
39 All flesh is not the same: Men have one
kind of flesh, animals have another, birds
another and fish another. 40 There are also
heavenly bodies and there are earthly
bodies; but the splendor of the heavenly
bodies is one kind, and the splendor of
the earthly bodies is another. 41 The sun
has one kind of splendor, the moon another and the stars another; and star dif-
fers from star in splendor.
42 So will it be with the resurrection of
the dead. The body that is sown is perishable, it is raised imperishable; 43 it is
sown in dishonor, it is raised in glory; it
is sown in weakness, it is raised in power;
44 it is sown a natural body, it is raised a
spiritual body.
If there is a natural body, there is also a
spiritual body. 45 So it is written: "The first
man Adam became a living being"[a]; the
last Adam, a life-giving spirit. 46 The spiritual did not come first, but the natural,
and after that the spiritual. 47 The first man
was of the dust of the earth, the second
man from heaven. 48 As was the earthly
man, so are those who are of the earth;

[a] 45 Gen. 2:7

and as is the man from heaven, so also are those who are of heaven. [49]And just as we have borne the likeness of the earthly man, so shall we[b] bear the likeness of the man from heaven.

[50]I declare to you, brothers, that flesh and blood cannot inherit the kingdom of God, nor does the perishable inherit the imperishable. [51]Listen, I tell you a mystery: We will not all sleep, but we will all be changed— [52]in a flash, in the twinkling of an eye, at the last trumpet. For the trumpet will sound, the dead will be raised imperishable, and we will be changed. [53]For the perishable must clothe itself with the imperishable, and the mortal with immortality. [54]When the perishable has been clothed with the imperishable, and the mortal with immortality, then the saying that is written will come true: "Death has been swallowed up in victory."[c]

[55] "Where, O death, is your victory?
Where, O death, is your sting?"[d]

[56]The sting of death is sin, and the power of sin is the law. [57]But thanks be to God! He gives us the victory through our Lord Jesus Christ.

[58]Therefore, my dear brothers, stand firm. Let nothing move you. Always give yourselves fully to the work of the Lord, because you know that your labor in the Lord is not in vain.

[b] *49* Some early manuscripts *so let us*
[c] *54* Isaiah 25:8 [d] *55* Hosea 13:14

PRAYER: THE ATTRIBUTES OF GOD

TO You, O God, belong wisdom and power; counsel and understanding are Yours. (Job 12:13) . . . Hallelujah! Salvation and glory and power belong to You, our God, because Your judgments are true and righteous. (Revelation 19:1–2)

***PAUSE** to reflect on these affirmations about the person, powers and perfection of God.*

YEAR 1 DAY 147

OT Psalm 31

Psalm 31

For the director of music. A psalm of David.

[1]In you, O LORD, I have taken refuge;
let me never be put to shame;
deliver me in your righteousness.
[2]Turn your ear to me,
come quickly to my rescue;
be my rock of refuge,
a strong fortress to save me.
[3]Since you are my rock and my fortress,
for the sake of your name lead and guide me.
[4]Free me from the trap that is set for me,
for you are my refuge.
[5]Into your hands I commit my spirit;
redeem me, O LORD, the God of truth.

[6]I hate those who cling to worthless idols;
I trust in the LORD.
[7]I will be glad and rejoice in your love,
for you saw my affliction
and knew the anguish of my soul.
[8]You have not handed me over to the enemy
but have set my feet in a spacious place.

[9]Be merciful to me, O LORD, for I am in distress;
my eyes grow weak with sorrow,
my soul and my body with grief.
[10]My life is consumed by anguish
and my years by groaning;
my strength fails because of my affliction,[a]
and my bones grow weak.
[11]Because of all my enemies,
I am the utter contempt of my neighbors;

[a] *10* Or *guilt*

I am a dread to my friends—
those who see me on the street flee from me.
12 I am forgotten by them as though I were dead;
I have become like broken pottery.
13 For I hear the slander of many;
there is terror on every side;
they conspire against me
and plot to take my life.

14 But I trust in you, O LORD;
I say, "You are my God."
15 My times are in your hands;
deliver me from my enemies
and from those who pursue me.
16 Let your face shine on your servant;
save me in your unfailing love.
17 Let me not be put to shame, O LORD,
for I have cried out to you;
but let the wicked be put to shame
and lie silent in the grave.[b]
18 Let their lying lips be silenced,
for with pride and contempt
they speak arrogantly against the righteous.

19 How great is your goodness,
which you have stored up for those who fear you,
which you bestow in the sight of men
on those who take refuge in you.
20 In the shelter of your presence you hide them
from the intrigues of men;
in your dwelling you keep them safe
from accusing tongues.

21 Praise be to the LORD,
for he showed his wonderful love to me
when I was in a besieged city.
22 In my alarm I said,
"I am cut off from your sight!"
Yet you heard my cry for mercy
when I called to you for help.

23 Love the LORD, all his saints!
The LORD preserves the faithful,
but the proud he pays back in full.
24 Be strong and take heart,
all you who hope in the LORD.

[b] 17 Hebrew *Sheol*

PRAYER: THANKSGIVING

LORD Jesus, we rejoice that you fulfilled the words of the prophet Isaiah: "The Spirit of the Lord is upon Me, because He has anointed Me to preach good news to the poor. He has sent Me to proclaim freedom for the captives and recovery of sight to the blind, to set free those who are downtrodden, to proclaim the acceptable year of the Lord." (Luke 4:18–19)

***PAUSE** to offer your own expressions of thanksgiving.*

NT 1 Corinthians 16:1–24

The Collection for God's People

16 Now about the collection for God's
people: Do what I told the Galatian
churches to do. 2On the first day of every
week, each one of you should set aside a
sum of money in keeping with his income, saving it up, so that when I come
no collections will have to be made.
3Then, when I arrive, I will give letters of
introduction to the men you approve and
send them with your gift to Jerusalem. 4If
it seems advisable for me to go also, they
will accompany me.

Personal Requests

5After I go through Macedonia, I will
come to you—for I will be going through
Macedonia. 6Perhaps I will stay with you
awhile, or even spend the winter, so that
you can help me on my journey, wherever I go. 7I do not want to see you now and
make only a passing visit; I hope to spend
some time with you, if the Lord permits.
8But I will stay on at Ephesus until Pentecost, 9because a great door for effective
work has opened to me, and there are
many who oppose me.

10If Timothy comes, see to it that he has
nothing to fear while he is with you, for
he is carrying on the work of the Lord, just
as I am. 11No one, then, should refuse to
accept him. Send him on his way in peace

so that he may return to me. I am expecting him along with the brothers.
12 Now about our brother Apollos: I
strongly urged him to go to you with the
brothers. He was quite unwilling to go
now, but he will go when he has the opportunity.
13 Be on your guard; stand firm in the
faith; be men of courage; be strong. 14 Do
everything in love.
15 You know that the household of
Stephanas were the first converts in Achaia, and they have devoted themselves to
the service of the saints. I urge you, brothers, 16 to submit to such as these and to
everyone who joins in the work, and
labors at it. 17 I was glad when Stephanas,
Fortunatus and Achaicus arrived, because
they have supplied what was lacking from
you. 18 For they refreshed my spirit and
yours also. Such men deserve recognition.

Final Greetings

19 The churches in the province of Asia
send you greetings. Aquila and Priscilla[a]
greet you warmly in the Lord, and so does
the church that meets at their house. 20 All
the brothers here send you greetings.
Greet one another with a holy kiss.
21 I, Paul, write this greeting in my own
hand.
22 If anyone does not love the Lord—a
curse be on him. Come, O Lord[b]!
23 The grace of the Lord Jesus be with
you.
24 My love to all of you in Christ Jesus.
Amen.[c]

[a] 19 Greek *Prisca,* a variant of *Priscilla* [b] 22 In Aramaic the expression *Come, O Lord* is *Marana tha.* [c] 24 Some manuscripts do not have *Amen.*

PRAYER: THE WORKS OF GOD

O GOD, You give strength to the weary and increase the power of the weak. Even youths grow tired and weary, and young men stumble and fall; but we who wait for You, O Lord, will renew our strength. We will mount up with wings like eagles; we will run and not grow weary; we will walk and not be faint. (Isaiah 40:29–31)

***TAKE** a moment to consider the greatness of God's wonderful works.*

YEAR 1
DAY 148

OT Numbers 33:1–34:29

Stages in Israel's Journey

33 Here are the stages in the journey of
the Israelites when they came out of
Egypt by divisions under the leadership of
Moses and Aaron. 2 At the LORD's command Moses recorded the stages in their
journey. This is their journey by stages:

3 The Israelites set out from Rameses on the fifteenth day of the first
month, the day after the Passover.
They marched out boldly in full view
of all the Egyptians, 4 who were burying all their firstborn, whom the
LORD had struck down among them;
for the LORD had brought judgment
on their gods.
5 The Israelites left Rameses and
camped at Succoth.
6 They left Succoth and camped at
Etham, on the edge of the desert.
7 They left Etham, turned back to Pi
Hahiroth, to the east of Baal Zephon,
and camped near Migdol.
8 They left Pi Hahiroth[a] and passed
through the sea into the desert, and
when they had traveled for three days
in the Desert of Etham, they camped
at Marah.
9 They left Marah and went to Elim,
where there were twelve springs and
seventy palm trees, and they camped
there.

[a] 8 Many manuscripts of the Masoretic Text, Samaritan Pentateuch and Vulgate; most manuscripts of the Masoretic Text *left from before Hahiroth*

[10]They left Elim and camped by the Red Sea.[b]
[11]They left the Red Sea and camped in the Desert of Sin.
[12]They left the Desert of Sin and camped at Dophkah.
[13]They left Dophkah and camped at Alush.
[14]They left Alush and camped at Rephidim, where there was no water for the people to drink.
[15]They left Rephidim and camped in the Desert of Sinai.
[16]They left the Desert of Sinai and camped at Kibroth Hattaavah.
[17]They left Kibroth Hattaavah and camped at Hazeroth.
[18]They left Hazeroth and camped at Rithmah.
[19]They left Rithmah and camped at Rimmon Perez.
[20]They left Rimmon Perez and camped at Libnah.
[21]They left Libnah and camped at Rissah.
[22]They left Rissah and camped at Kehelathah.
[23]They left Kehelathah and camped at Mount Shepher.
[24]They left Mount Shepher and camped at Haradah.
[25]They left Haradah and camped at Makheloth.
[26]They left Makheloth and camped at Tahath.
[27]They left Tahath and camped at Terah.
[28]They left Terah and camped at Mithcah.
[29]They left Mithcah and camped at Hashmonah.
[30]They left Hashmonah and camped at Moseroth.
[31]They left Moseroth and camped at Bene Jaakan.
[32]They left Bene Jaakan and camped at Hor Haggidgad.
[33]They left Hor Haggidgad and camped at Jotbathah.
[34]They left Jotbathah and camped at Abronah.
[35]They left Abronah and camped at Ezion Geber.
[36]They left Ezion Geber and camped at Kadesh, in the Desert of Zin.
[37]They left Kadesh and camped at Mount Hor, on the border of Edom.
[38]At the LORD's command Aaron the priest went up Mount Hor, where he died on the first day of the fifth month of the fortieth year after the Israelites came out of Egypt.
[39]Aaron was a hundred and twenty-three years old when he died on Mount Hor.
[40]The Canaanite king of Arad, who lived in the Negev of Canaan, heard that the Israelites were coming.
[41]They left Mount Hor and camped at Zalmonah.
[42]They left Zalmonah and camped at Punon.
[43]They left Punon and camped at Oboth.
[44]They left Oboth and camped at Iye Abarim, on the border of Moab.
[45]They left Iyim[c] and camped at Dibon Gad.
[46]They left Dibon Gad and camped at Almon Diblathaim.
[47]They left Almon Diblathaim and camped in the mountains of Abarim, near Nebo.
[48]They left the mountains of Abarim and camped on the plains of Moab by the Jordan across from Jericho.[d]
[49]There on the plains of Moab they camped along the Jordan from Beth Jeshimoth to Abel Shittim.

[50]On the plains of Moab by the Jordan across from Jericho the LORD said to Moses,
[51]"Speak to the Israelites and say to them: 'When you cross the Jordan into Canaan,
[52]drive out all the inhabitants of the land before you. Destroy all their carved images and their cast idols, and demolish all their high places.
[53]Take possession of the land and settle in it, for I have given you the land to possess.
[54]Distribute the land by lot, according to your clans. To a larger group give a larger inheritance, and to a smaller group a smaller one. Whatever falls to them by lot will be theirs. Distribute it according to your ancestral tribes.
[55]" 'But if you do not drive out the inhabitants of the land, those you allow to remain will become barbs in your eyes

[b] *10* Hebrew *Yam Suph*; that is, Sea of Reeds; also in verse 11 [c] *45* That is, Iye Abarim [d] *48* Hebrew *Jordan of Jericho*; possibly an ancient name for the Jordan River; also in verse 50

and thorns in your sides. They will give
you trouble in the land where you will
live. 56And then I will do to you what I
plan to do to them.' "

Boundaries of Canaan

34 The LORD said to Moses, 2"Command
the Israelites and say to them: 'When
you enter Canaan, the land that will be allotted to you as an inheritance will have
these boundaries:

3" 'Your southern side will include some
of the Desert of Zin along the border of
Edom. On the east, your southern boundary will start from the end of the Salt Sea,[e]
4cross south of Scorpion[f] Pass, continue
on to Zin and go south of Kadesh Barnea.
Then it will go to Hazar Addar and over to
Azmon, 5where it will turn, join the Wadi
of Egypt and end at the Sea.[g]
6" 'Your western boundary will be the
coast of the Great Sea. This will be your
boundary on the west.
7" 'For your northern boundary, run a
line from the Great Sea to Mount Hor
8and from Mount Hor to Lebo[h] Hamath.
Then the boundary will go to Zedad, 9con-
tinue to Ziphron and end at Hazar Enan.
This will be your boundary on the north.
10" 'For your eastern boundary, run a
line from Hazar Enan to Shepham. 11The
boundary will go down from Shepham to
Riblah on the east side of Ain and continue along the slopes east of the Sea of
Kinnereth.[i] 12Then the boundary will go
down along the Jordan and end at the Salt
Sea.
" 'This will be your land, with its
boundaries on every side.' "
13Moses commanded the Israelites: "Assign this land by lot as an inheritance. The
LORD has ordered that it be given to the
nine and a half tribes, 14because the families of the tribe of Reuben, the tribe of
Gad and the half-tribe of Manasseh have
received their inheritance. 15These two
and a half tribes have received their inheritance on the east side of the Jordan of
Jericho,[j] toward the sunrise."
16The LORD said to Moses, 17"These are
the names of the men who are to assign
the land for you as an inheritance: Eleazar the priest and Joshua son of Nun.
18And appoint one leader from each tribe
to help assign the land. 19These are their
names:

Caleb son of Jephunneh,
from the tribe of Judah;
20Shemuel son of Ammihud,
from the tribe of Simeon;
21Elidad son of Kislon,
from the tribe of Benjamin;
22Bukki son of Jogli,
the leader from the tribe of Dan;
23Hanniel son of Ephod,
the leader from the tribe of Manasseh son of Joseph;
24Kemuel son of Shiphtan,
the leader from the tribe of Ephraim son of Joseph;
25Elizaphan son of Parnach,
the leader from the tribe of Zebulun;
26Paltiel son of Azzan,
the leader from the tribe of Issachar;
27Ahihud son of Shelomi,
the leader from the tribe of Asher;
28Pedahel son of Ammihud,
the leader from the tribe of Naphtali."

29These are the men the LORD commanded to assign the inheritance to the
Israelites in the land of Canaan.

[e] 3 That is, the Dead Sea; also in verse 12
[f] 4 Hebrew *Akrabbim*
[g] 5 That is, the Mediterranean; also in verses 6 and 7
[h] 8 Or *to the entrance to*
[i] 11 That is, Galilee
[j] 15 *Jordan of Jericho* was possibly an ancient name for the Jordan River.

PRAYER: ADORATION

A GREAT multitude, which no one could number, from all nations and tribes and peoples and languages, will stand before the throne and before the Lamb, clothed with white robes, with palm branches in their hands, and will cry out with a loud voice, "Salvation belongs to You, our God, who sits on the throne, and to the Lamb!"

(Revelation 7:9–10)

PAUSE *to express your thoughts of praise and worship.*

NT 2 Corinthians 1:1–11

1 Paul, an apostle of Christ Jesus by the
will of God, and Timothy our brother,

To the church of God in Corinth, together with all the saints throughout
Achaia:

2Grace and peace to you from God our
Father and the Lord Jesus Christ.

The God of All Comfort

3Praise be to the God and Father of our
Lord Jesus Christ, the Father of compassion and the God of all comfort, 4who
comforts us in all our troubles, so that we
can comfort those in any trouble with the
comfort we ourselves have received from
God. 5For just as the sufferings of Christ
flow over into our lives, so also through
Christ our comfort overflows. 6If we are
distressed, it is for your comfort and salvation; if we are comforted, it is for your
comfort, which produces in you patient
endurance of the same sufferings we suffer. 7And our hope for you is firm, because
we know that just as you share in our sufferings, so also you share in our comfort.
8We do not want you to be uninformed,
brothers, about the hardships we suffered
in the province of Asia. We were under
great pressure, far beyond our ability to
endure, so that we despaired even of life.
9Indeed, in our hearts we felt the sentence
of death. But this happened that we might
not rely on ourselves but on God, who
raises the dead. 10He has delivered us from
such a deadly peril, and he will deliver us.
On him we have set our hope that he will
continue to deliver us, 11as you help us by
your prayers. Then many will give thanks
on our[a] behalf for the gracious favor granted us in answer to the prayers of many.

[a] 11 Many manuscripts *your*

PRAYER: MY RELATIONSHIP TO GOD

WHY is my soul so downcast? Why am I so disturbed deep within my being? I will hope in You, O God, for I will yet praise You for the help of Your presence. O my God, my soul is downcast within me; therefore I will remember You. Why is my soul so downcast? Why am I so disturbed within my being? I will hope in You, my God, for I will yet praise You—the help of my countenance and my God. (Psalm 42:5–6, 11)

PAUSE *to thank God for the relationship that you enjoy with Him in Jesus Christ.*

YEAR 1 DAY 149

OT Numbers 35:1–34

Towns for the Levites

35 On the plains of Moab by the Jordan
across from Jericho,[a] the LORD said to
Moses, 2"Command the Israelites to give
the Levites towns to live in from the inheritance the Israelites will possess. And
give them pasturelands around the towns.
3Then they will have towns to live in and
pasturelands for their cattle, flocks and all
their other livestock.

4"The pasturelands around the towns
that you give the Levites will extend out
fifteen hundred feet[b] from the town wall.
5Outside the town, measure three thousand feet[c] on the east side, three thousand
on the south side, three thousand on the
west and three thousand on the north,
with the town in the center. They will have
this area as pastureland for the towns.

Cities of Refuge

6"Six of the towns you give the Levites

[a] 1 Hebrew *Jordan of Jericho;* possibly an ancient name for the Jordan River [b] 4 Hebrew *a thousand cubits* (about 450 meters) [c] 5 Hebrew *two thousand cubits* (about 900 meters)

will be cities of refuge, to which a person
who has killed someone may flee. In addition, give them forty-two other towns.
7In all you must give the Levites forty-
eight towns, together with their pasturelands. 8The towns you give the Levites
from the land the Israelites possess are to
be given in proportion to the inheritance
of each tribe: Take many towns from a
tribe that has many, but few from one that
has few."
9Then the LORD said to Moses: 10"Speak
to the Israelites and say to them: 'When you
cross the Jordan into Canaan, 11select some
towns to be your cities of refuge, to which
a person who has killed someone accidentally may flee. 12They will be places of
refuge from the avenger, so that a person accused of murder may not die before he
stands trial before the assembly. 13These six
towns you give will be your cities of refuge.
14Give three on this side of the Jordan and
three in Canaan as cities of refuge. 15These
six towns will be a place of refuge for Israelites, aliens and any other people living
among them, so that anyone who has
killed another accidentally can flee there.
16" 'If a man strikes someone with an
iron object so that he dies, he is a murderer; the murderer shall be put to death.
17Or if anyone has a stone in his hand that
could kill, and he strikes someone so that
he dies, he is a murderer; the murderer
shall be put to death. 18Or if anyone has a
wooden object in his hand that could kill,
and he hits someone so that he dies, he is
a murderer; the murderer shall be put to
death. 19The avenger of blood shall put the
murderer to death; when he meets him, he
shall put him to death. 20If anyone with
malice aforethought shoves another or
throws something at him intentionally so
that he dies 21or if in hostility he hits him
with his fist so that he dies, that person
shall be put to death; he is a murderer. The
avenger of blood shall put the murderer to
death when he meets him.
22" 'But if without hostility someone
suddenly shoves another or throws something at him unintentionally 23or, without
seeing him, drops a stone on him that
could kill him, and he dies, then since he
was not his enemy and he did not intend
to harm him, 24the assembly must judge
between him and the avenger of blood according to these regulations. 25The assembly must protect the one accused of murder from the avenger of blood and send
him back to the city of refuge to which he
fled. He must stay there until the death of
the high priest, who was anointed with
the holy oil.
26" 'But if the accused ever goes outside
the limits of the city of refuge to which he
has fled 27and the avenger of blood finds
him outside the city, the avenger of blood
may kill the accused without being guilty
of murder. 28The accused must stay in his
city of refuge until the death of the high
priest; only after the death of the high
priest may he return to his own property.
29" 'These are to be legal requirements
for you throughout the generations to
come, wherever you live.
30" 'Anyone who kills a person is to be
put to death as a murderer only on the
testimony of witnesses. But no one is to
be put to death on the testimony of only
one witness.
31" 'Do not accept a ransom for the life
of a murderer, who deserves to die. He
must surely be put to death.
32" 'Do not accept a ransom for anyone
who has fled to a city of refuge and so allow him to go back and live on his own
land before the death of the high priest.
33" 'Do not pollute the land where you
are. Bloodshed pollutes the land, and
atonement cannot be made for the land
on which blood has been shed, except by
the blood of the one who shed it. 34Do
not defile the land where you live and
where I dwell, for I, the LORD, dwell
among the Israelites.' "

PRAYER: CONFESSION

YOUR eyes are everywhere, O Lord, keeping watch on the evil and the good. (Proverbs 15:3) . . . You, O God, fashion the hearts of all and understand all their works. (Psalm 33:15)

***ASK** the Spirit to search your heart and reveal any areas of unconfessed sin. Acknowledge these to the Lord and thank Him for His forgiveness.*

NT 2 Corinthians 1:12–2:4

Paul's Change of Plans

12 Now this is our boast: Our conscience testifies that we have conducted ourselves in the world, and especially in our relations with you, in the holiness and sincerity that are from God. We have done so not according to worldly wisdom but according to God's grace. 13 For we do not write you anything you cannot read or understand. And I hope that, 14 as you have understood us in part, you will come to understand fully that you can boast of us just as we will boast of you in the day of the Lord Jesus.

15 Because I was confident of this, I planned to visit you first so that you might benefit twice. 16 I planned to visit you on my way to Macedonia and to come back to you from Macedonia, and then to have you send me on my way to Judea. 17 When I planned this, did I do it lightly? Or do I make my plans in a worldly manner so that in the same breath I say, "Yes, yes" and "No, no"?

18 But as surely as God is faithful, our message to you is not "Yes" and "No."
19 For the Son of God, Jesus Christ, who was preached among you by me and Silas[a] and Timothy, was not "Yes" and "No," but in him it has always been "Yes." 20 For no matter how many promises God has made, they are "Yes" in Christ. And so through him the "Amen" is spoken by us to the glory of God. 21 Now it is God who makes both us and you stand firm in Christ. He anointed us, 22 set his seal of ownership on us, and put his Spirit in our hearts as a deposit, guaranteeing what is to come.

23 I call God as my witness that it was in order to spare you that I did not return to Corinth. 24 Not that we lord it over your faith, but we work with you for your joy, because it is by faith you stand firm.

2 1 So I made up my mind that I would not make another painful visit to you.
2 For if I grieve you, who is left to make me glad but you whom I have grieved? 3 I wrote as I did so that when I came I should not be distressed by those who ought to make me rejoice. I had confidence in all of you, that you would all share my joy. 4 For I wrote you out of great distress and anguish of heart and with many tears, not to grieve you but to let you know the depth of my love for you.

[a] 19 Greek *Silvanus,* a variant of *Silas*

PRAYER: THE CHARACTER I WANT TO CULTIVATE

I WILL be strong and courageous and act. I will not be afraid or discouraged, for You, Lord God, are with me. You will not fail me or forsake me. (1 Chronicles 28:20)

***TAKE** a moment to ask the Lord for the grace to grow in godly character.*

YEAR 1 DAY 150

OT Numbers 36:1–13

Inheritance of Zelophehad's Daughters

36 The family heads of the clan of Gilead son of Makir, the son of Manasseh, who were from the clans of the descendants of Joseph, came and spoke before Moses and the leaders, the heads of the Israelite families. 2 They said, "When the LORD commanded my lord to give the land as an inheritance to the Israelites by lot, he ordered you to give the inheritance of our brother Zelophehad to his daughters. 3 Now suppose they marry men from other Israelite tribes; then their inheritance will be taken from our ancestral inheritance and added to that of the tribe they marry into. And so part of the inheritance allotted to us will be taken away. 4 When the Year of Jubilee for the Israelites comes, their inheritance will be added to that of the tribe into which they marry, and their property will be taken from the tribal inheritance of our forefathers."

5Then at the LORD's command Moses
gave this order to the Israelites: "What the
tribe of the descendants of Joseph is saying is right. 6This is what the LORD commands for Zelophehad's daughters: They
may marry anyone they please as long as
they marry within the tribal clan of their
father. 7No inheritance in Israel is to pass
from tribe to tribe, for every Israelite shall
keep the tribal land inherited from his
forefathers. 8Every daughter who inherits
land in any Israelite tribe must marry
someone in her father's tribal clan, so that
every Israelite will possess the inheritance
of his fathers. 9No inheritance may pass
from tribe to tribe, for each Israelite tribe
is to keep the land it inherits."
10So Zelophehad's daughters did as the
LORD commanded Moses. 11Zelophehad's
daughters—Mahlah, Tirzah, Hoglah, Milcah and Noah—married their cousins on
their father's side. 12They married within
the clans of the descendants of Manasseh
son of Joseph, and their inheritance remained in their father's clan and tribe.
13These are the commands and regulations the LORD gave through Moses to the
Israelites on the plains of Moab by the
Jordan across from Jericho.[a]

[a] 13 Hebrew *Jordan of Jericho;* possibly an ancient name for the Jordan River

PRAYER: RENEWAL

LIKE Abraham, may I call upon Your name; You are the Everlasting God. (Genesis 13:4; 21:33) . . . May I rejoice in my tribulations, knowing that tribulation produces perseverance; and perseverance, character; and character, hope. And hope does not disappoint, because Your love, O God, has been poured out into my heart through the Holy Spirit, whom You have given to me. (Romans 5:3–5)

PAUSE *to add your own prayers for personal renewal.*

NT 2 Corinthians 2:5–3:6

Forgiveness for the Sinner

5If anyone has caused grief, he has not
so much grieved me as he has grieved all
of you, to some extent—not to put it too
severely. 6The punishment inflicted on
him by the majority is sufficient for him.
7Now instead, you ought to forgive and
comfort him, so that he will not be overwhelmed by excessive sorrow. 8I urge you,
therefore, to reaffirm your love for him.
9The reason I wrote you was to see if you
would stand the test and be obedient in
everything. 10If you forgive anyone, I also
forgive him. And what I have forgiven—if
there was anything to forgive—I have forgiven in the sight of Christ for your sake,
11in order that Satan might not outwit us.
For we are not unaware of his schemes.

Ministers of the New Covenant

12Now when I went to Troas to preach
the gospel of Christ and found that the
Lord had opened a door for me, 13I still
had no peace of mind, because I did not
find my brother Titus there. So I said good-
by to them and went on to Macedonia.
14But thanks be to God, who always
leads us in triumphal procession in Christ
and through us spreads everywhere the
fragrance of the knowledge of him. 15For
we are to God the aroma of Christ among
those who are being saved and those who
are perishing. 16To the one we are the
smell of death; to the other, the fragrance
of life. And who is equal to such a task?
17Unlike so many, we do not peddle the
word of God for profit. On the contrary,
in Christ we speak before God with sincerity, like men sent from God.
3 Are we beginning to commend ourselves again? Or do we need, like some
people, letters of recommendation to you
or from you? 2You yourselves are our letter, written on our hearts, known and read
by everybody. 3You show that you are a
letter from Christ, the result of our ministry, written not with ink but with the
Spirit of the living God, not on tablets of
stone but on tablets of human hearts.

[4]Such confidence as this is ours through Christ before God. [5]Not that we are competent in ourselves to claim anything for ourselves, but our competence comes from God. [6]He has made us competent as ministers of a new covenant—not of the letter but of the Spirit; for the letter kills, but the Spirit gives life.

PRAYER: MY RELATIONSHIP TO OTHERS

If I am generous, O God, I will prosper; if I water others, I will myself be refreshed. (Proverbs 11:25) . . . Those who are generous, O God, will be blessed, for they share their food with the poor. (Proverbs 22:9)

***PAUSE** to review your relationships with others and to commit them to the Lord.*

YEAR 1 DAY 151

OT Deuteronomy 1:1-46

The Command to Leave Horeb

1 These are the words Moses spoke to all Israel in the desert east of the Jordan—that is, in the Arabah—opposite Suph, between Paran and Tophel, Laban, Hazeroth and Dizahab. [2](It takes eleven days to go from Horeb to Kadesh Barnea by the Mount Seir road.)

[3]In the fortieth year, on the first day of the eleventh month, Moses proclaimed to the Israelites all that the LORD had commanded him concerning them. [4]This was after he had defeated Sihon king of the Amorites, who reigned in Heshbon, and at Edrei had defeated Og king of Bashan, who reigned in Ashtaroth.

[5]East of the Jordan in the territory of Moab, Moses began to expound this law, saying:

[6]The LORD our God said to us at Horeb, "You have stayed long enough at this mountain. [7]Break camp and advance into the hill country of the Amorites; go to all the neighboring peoples in the Arabah, in the mountains, in the western foothills, in the Negev and along the coast, to the land of the Canaanites and to Lebanon, as far as the great river, the Euphrates. [8]See, I have given you this land. Go in and take possession of the land that the LORD swore he would give to your fathers—to Abraham, Isaac and Jacob—and to their descendants after them."

The Appointment of Leaders

[9]At that time I said to you, "You are too heavy a burden for me to carry alone. [10]The LORD your God has increased your numbers so that today you are as many as the stars in the sky. [11]May the LORD, the God of your fathers, increase you a thousand times and bless you as he has promised! [12]But how can I bear your problems and your burdens and your disputes all by myself? [13]Choose some wise, understanding and respected men from each of your tribes, and I will set them over you."

[14]You answered me, "What you propose to do is good."

[15]So I took the leading men of your tribes, wise and respected men, and appointed them to have authority over you—as commanders of thousands, of hundreds, of fifties and of tens and as tribal officials. [16]And I charged your judges at that time: Hear the disputes between your brothers and judge fairly, whether the case is between brother Israelites or between one of them and an alien. [17]Do not show partiality in judging; hear both small and great alike. Do not be afraid of any man, for judgment belongs to God. Bring me any case too hard for you, and I will hear it. [18]And at that time I told you everything you were to do.

Spies Sent Out

[19]Then, as the LORD our God commanded us, we set out from Horeb and went toward the hill country of the Amorites through all that vast and dreadful desert that you have seen, and so we reached Kadesh Barnea. [20]Then I said to you, "You

have reached the hill country of the Amorites, which the LORD our God is giving us.
21 See, the LORD your God has given you the
land. Go up and take possession of it as the
LORD, the God of your fathers, told you. Do
not be afraid; do not be discouraged."
22 Then all of you came to me and said,
"Let us send men ahead to spy out the
land for us and bring back a report about
the route we are to take and the towns we
will come to."
23 The idea seemed good to me; so I selected twelve of you, one man from each
tribe. 24 They left and went up into the hill
country, and came to the Valley of Eshcol
and explored it. 25 Taking with them some
of the fruit of the land, they brought it
down to us and reported, "It is a good
land that the LORD our God is giving us."

Rebellion Against the LORD

26 But you were unwilling to go up; you
rebelled against the command of the
LORD your God. 27 You grumbled in your
tents and said, "The LORD hates us; so he
brought us out of Egypt to deliver us into
the hands of the Amorites to destroy us.
28 Where can we go? Our brothers have
made us lose heart. They say, 'The people
are stronger and taller than we are; the cities are large, with walls up to the sky. We
even saw the Anakites there.' "
29 Then I said to you, "Do not be terrified;
do not be afraid of them. 30 The LORD your
God, who is going before you, will fight for
you, as he did for you in Egypt, before your
very eyes, 31 and in the desert. There you saw
how the LORD your God carried you, as a
father carries his son, all the way you went
until you reached this place."
32 In spite of this, you did not trust in
the LORD your God, 33 who went ahead of
you on your journey, in fire by night and
in a cloud by day, to search out places for
you to camp and to show you the way you
should go.
34 When the LORD heard what you said,
he was angry and solemnly swore: 35 "Not
a man of this evil generation shall see the
good land I swore to give your forefathers,
36 except Caleb son of Jephunneh. He will
see it, and I will give him and his descendants the land he set his feet on, because
he followed the LORD wholeheartedly."
37 Because of you the LORD became angry
with me also and said, "You shall not enter it, either. 38 But your assistant, Joshua
son of Nun, will enter it. Encourage him,
because he will lead Israel to inherit it.
39 And the little ones that you said would
be taken captive, your children who do
not yet know good from bad—they will
enter the land. I will give it to them and
they will take possession of it. 40 But as for
you, turn around and set out toward the
desert along the route to the Red Sea.[a]"
41 Then you replied, "We have sinned
against the LORD. We will go up and fight,
as the LORD our God commanded us." So
every one of you put on his weapons, thinking it easy to go up into the hill country.
42 But the LORD said to me, "Tell them,
'Do not go up and fight, because I will not
be with you. You will be defeated by your
enemies.' "
43 So I told you, but you would not listen. You rebelled against the LORD's command and in your arrogance you marched
up into the hill country. 44 The Amorites
who lived in those hills came out against
you; they chased you like a swarm of bees
and beat you down from Seir all the way
to Hormah. 45 You came back and wept before the LORD, but he paid no attention to
your weeping and turned a deaf ear to
you. 46 And so you stayed in Kadesh many
days—all the time you spent there.

[a] 40 Hebrew *Yam Suph;* that is, Sea of Reeds

PRAYER: PETITION

MAY Your merciful kindness be my comfort, O God, according to Your promise to Your servant.

(Psalm 119:76)

PAUSE *here to petition God for growth in your desire to know and please Jesus Christ. Pray for a greater love and commitment to Him, for the grace to practice His presence and for the grace to glorify Him in your life. Offer prayers regarding your activities for this day and any special concerns you may have.*

NT 2 Corinthians 3:7-18

The Glory of the New Covenant

[7]Now if the ministry that brought
death, which was engraved in letters on
stone, came with glory, so that the Israelites could not look steadily at the face of
Moses because of its glory, fading though
it was, [8]will not the ministry of the Spirit
be even more glorious? [9]If the ministry
that condemns men is glorious, how
much more glorious is the ministry that
brings righteousness! [10]For what was glorious has no glory now in comparison
with the surpassing glory. [11]And if what
was fading away came with glory, how
much greater is the glory of that which
lasts!

[12]Therefore, since we have such a hope,
we are very bold. [13]We are not like Moses,
who would put a veil over his face to keep
the Israelites from gazing at it while the
radiance was fading away. [14]But their
minds were made dull, for to this day the
same veil remains when the old covenant
is read. It has not been removed, because
only in Christ is it taken away. [15]Even to
this day when Moses is read, a veil covers
their hearts. [16]But whenever anyone turns
to the Lord, the veil is taken away. [17]Now
the Lord is the Spirit, and where the Spirit of the Lord is, there is freedom. [18]And
we, who with unveiled faces all reflect[a] the
Lord's glory, are being transformed into
his likeness with ever-increasing glory,
which comes from the Lord, who is the
Spirit.

[a] 18 Or *contemplate*

PRAYER: THE ATTRIBUTES OF GOD

I WILL sing to You, Lord, for You are highly exalted. You, O Lord, are my strength and my song; You have become my salvation. You are my God, and I will praise You, my father's God, and I will exalt You.

(Exodus 15:1–2)

***PAUSE** to reflect on these affirmations about the person, powers and perfection of God.*

YEAR 1 DAY 152

OT Deuteronomy 2:1-37

Wanderings in the Desert

2 Then we turned back and set out toward the desert along the route to the
Red Sea,[a] as the LORD had directed me. For
a long time we made our way around the
hill country of Seir.

[2]Then the LORD said to me, [3]"You have
made your way around this hill country
long enough; now turn north. [4]Give the
people these orders: 'You are about to
pass through the territory of your brothers the descendants of Esau, who live in
Seir. They will be afraid of you, but be very
careful. [5]Do not provoke them to war, for
I will not give you any of their land, not
even enough to put your foot on. I have
given Esau the hill country of Seir as his
own. [6]You are to pay them in silver for the
food you eat and the water you drink.' "

[7]The LORD your God has blessed you in
all the work of your hands. He has
watched over your journey through this
vast desert. These forty years the LORD
your God has been with you, and you
have not lacked anything.

[8]So we went on past our brothers the
descendants of Esau, who live in Seir. We
turned from the Arabah road, which
comes up from Elath and Ezion Geber,
and traveled along the desert road of
Moab.

[9]Then the LORD said to me, "Do not harass the Moabites or provoke them to war,
for I will not give you any part of their
land. I have given Ar to the descendants
of Lot as a possession."

[10](The Emites used to live there—a peo-

[a] 1 Hebrew *Yam Suph*; that is, Sea of Reeds

ple strong and numerous, and as tall as
the Anakites. 11Like the Anakites, they too
were considered Rephaites, but the Moabites called them Emites. 12Horites used
to live in Seir, but the descendants of Esau
drove them out. They destroyed the Horites from before them and settled in their
place, just as Israel did in the land the
LORD gave them as their possession.)
13And the LORD said, "Now get up and
cross the Zered Valley." So we crossed the
valley.
14Thirty-eight years passed from the
time we left Kadesh Barnea until we
crossed the Zered Valley. By then, that entire generation of fighting men had perished from the camp, as the LORD had
sworn to them. 15The LORD's hand was
against them until he had completely
eliminated them from the camp.
16Now when the last of these fighting
men among the people had died, 17the
LORD said to me, 18"Today you are to pass
by the region of Moab at Ar. 19When you
come to the Ammonites, do not harass
them or provoke them to war, for I will
not give you possession of any land belonging to the Ammonites. I have given it
as a possession to the descendants of Lot."
20(That too was considered a land of the
Rephaites, who used to live there; but the
Ammonites called them Zamzummites.
21They were a people strong and numerous, and as tall as the Anakites. The LORD
destroyed them from before the Ammonites, who drove them out and settled
in their place. 22The LORD had done the
same for the descendants of Esau, who
lived in Seir, when he destroyed the Horites from before them. They drove them
out and have lived in their place to this
day. 23And as for the Avvites who lived in
villages as far as Gaza, the Caphtorites
coming out from Caphtor[b] destroyed
them and settled in their place.)

Defeat of Sihon King of Heshbon

24"Set out now and cross the Arnon
Gorge. See, I have given into your hand Sihon the Amorite, king of Heshbon, and
his country. Begin to take possession of it
and engage him in battle. 25This very day
I will begin to put the terror and fear of
you on all the nations under heaven. They
will hear reports of you and will tremble
and be in anguish because of you."
26From the desert of Kedemoth I sent
messengers to Sihon king of Heshbon offering peace and saying, 27"Let us pass
through your country. We will stay on the
main road; we will not turn aside to the
right or to the left. 28Sell us food to eat
and water to drink for their price in silver.
Only let us pass through on foot— 29as
the descendants of Esau, who live in Seir,
and the Moabites, who live in Ar, did for
us—until we cross the Jordan into the
land the LORD our God is giving us." 30But
Sihon king of Heshbon refused to let us
pass through. For the LORD your God had
made his spirit stubborn and his heart obstinate in order to give him into your
hands, as he has now done.
31The LORD said to me, "See, I have begun to deliver Sihon and his country over
to you. Now begin to conquer and possess his land."
32When Sihon and all his army came
out to meet us in battle at Jahaz, 33the
LORD our God delivered him over to us
and we struck him down, together with
his sons and his whole army. 34At that
time we took all his towns and completely destroyed[c] them—men, women and
children. We left no survivors. 35But the
livestock and the plunder from the towns
we had captured we carried off for ourselves. 36From Aroer on the rim of the Arnon Gorge, and from the town in the
gorge, even as far as Gilead, not one town
was too strong for us. The LORD our God
gave us all of them. 37But in accordance
with the command of the LORD our God,
you did not encroach on any of the land
of the Ammonites, neither the land along
the course of the Jabbok nor that around
the towns in the hills.

[b] *23* That is, Crete [c] *34* The Hebrew term refers to the irrevocable giving over of things or persons to the LORD, often by totally destroying them.

PRAYER: INTERCESSION

IS this not the fast You have chosen: to loose the bonds of wickedness, to undo the cords of the yoke, and to let the oppressed go free and break every yoke? Is it not to share our food with the hungry and to

provide the poor wanderer with shelter; when we see the naked, to clothe them, and not to turn away from our own flesh? Then our light will break forth like the dawn, and our healing will quickly appear, and our righteousness will go before us; Your glory, O Lord, will be our rear guard. Then we will call, and You will answer; we will cry, and You will say, "Here I am." If we put away the yoke from our midst, the pointing of the finger and malicious talk, and if we extend our souls to the hungry and satisfy the afflicted soul, then our light will rise in the darkness, and our gloom will become like the noonday. (Isaiah 58:6–10)

***TAKE** a few moments to intercede on behalf of your local church, other churches, evangelism and discipleship ministries, educational ministries and any other special concerns you may have.*

NT 2 Corinthians 4:1–18

Treasures in Jars of Clay

4 Therefore, since through God's mercy we have this ministry, we do not lose heart. 2 Rather, we have renounced secret and shameful ways; we do not use deception, nor do we distort the word of God. On the contrary, by setting forth the truth plainly we commend ourselves to every man's conscience in the sight of God. 3 And even if our gospel is veiled, it is veiled to those who are perishing. 4 The god of this age has blinded the minds of unbelievers, so that they cannot see the light of the gospel of the glory of Christ, who is the image of God. 5 For we do not preach ourselves, but Jesus Christ as Lord, and ourselves as your servants for Jesus' sake. 6 For God, who said, "Let light shine out of darkness,"[a] made his light shine in our hearts to give us the light of the knowledge of the glory of God in the face of Christ.

7 But we have this treasure in jars of clay to show that this all-surpassing power is from God and not from us. 8 We are hard pressed on every side, but not crushed; perplexed, but not in despair; 9 persecuted, but not abandoned; struck down, but not destroyed. 10 We always carry around in our body the death of Jesus, so that the life of Jesus may also be revealed in our body. 11 For we who are alive are always being given over to death for Jesus' sake, so that his life may be revealed in our mortal body. 12 So then, death is at work in us, but life is at work in you.

13 It is written: "I believed; therefore I have spoken."[b] With that same spirit of faith we also believe and therefore speak, 14 because we know that the one who raised the Lord Jesus from the dead will also raise us with Jesus and present us with you in his presence. 15 All this is for your benefit, so that the grace that is reaching more and more people may cause thanksgiving to overflow to the glory of God.

16 Therefore we do not lose heart. Though outwardly we are wasting away, yet inwardly we are being renewed day by day. 17 For our light and momentary troubles are achieving for us an eternal glory that far outweighs them all. 18 So we fix our eyes not on what is seen, but on what is unseen. For what is seen is temporary, but what is unseen is eternal.

[a] *6* Gen. 1:3 [b] *13* Psalm 116:10

PRAYER: THE WORKS OF GOD

I MUST be ready, for You, Jesus, the Son of Man, will come at an hour when I do not expect You. (Matthew 24:44; Luke 12:40) . . . Many will see You, O Son of Man, coming in clouds with great power and glory. And You will send Your angels and gather Your elect from the four winds, from the ends of the earth to the ends of the heavens. We must take heed and be watchful, for we do not know when that time will come. (Mark 13:26–27, 33)

***TAKE** a moment to consider the greatness of God's wonderful works.*

OT **Deuteronomy 3:1–29** YEAR 1 DAY 153

Defeat of Og King of Bashan

3 Next we turned and went up along the road toward Bashan, and Og king of Bashan with his whole army marched out to meet us in battle at Edrei. 2The LORD said to me, "Do not be afraid of him, for I have handed him over to you with his whole army and his land. Do to him what you did to Sihon king of the Amorites, who reigned in Heshbon."

3So the LORD our God also gave into our hands Og king of Bashan and all his army. We struck them down, leaving no survivors. 4At that time we took all his cities. There was not one of the sixty cities that we did not take from them—the whole region of Argob, Og's kingdom in Bashan. 5All these cities were fortified with high walls and with gates and bars, and there were also a great many unwalled villages. 6We completely destroyed[a] them, as we had done with Sihon king of Heshbon, destroying[a] every city—men, women and children. 7But all the livestock and the plunder from their cities we carried off for ourselves.

8So at that time we took from these two kings of the Amorites the territory east of the Jordan, from the Arnon Gorge as far as Mount Hermon. 9(Hermon is called Sirion by the Sidonians; the Amorites call it Senir.) 10We took all the towns on the plateau, and all Gilead, and all Bashan as far as Salecah and Edrei, towns of Og's kingdom in Bashan. 11(Only Og king of Bashan was left of the remnant of the Rephaites. His bed[b] was made of iron and was more than thirteen feet long and six feet wide.[c] It is still in Rabbah of the Ammonites.)

Division of the Land

12Of the land that we took over at that time, I gave the Reubenites and the Gadites the territory north of Aroer by the Arnon Gorge, including half the hill country of Gilead, together with its towns. 13The rest of Gilead and also all of Bashan, the kingdom of Og, I gave to the half tribe of Manasseh. (The whole region of Argob in Bashan used to be known as a land of the Rephaites. 14Jair, a descendant of Manasseh, took the whole region of Argob as far as the border of the Geshurites and the Maacathites; it was named after him, so that to this day Bashan is called Havvoth Jair.[d]) 15And I gave Gilead to Makir. 16But to the Reubenites and the Gadites I gave the territory extending from Gilead down to the Arnon Gorge (the middle of the gorge being the border) and out to the Jabbok River, which is the border of the Ammonites. 17Its western border was the Jordan in the Arabah, from Kinnereth to the Sea of the Arabah (the Salt Sea[e]), below the slopes of Pisgah.

18I commanded you at that time: "The LORD your God has given you this land to take possession of it. But all your able-bodied men, armed for battle, must cross over ahead of your brother Israelites. 19However, your wives, your children and your livestock (I know you have much livestock) may stay in the towns I have given you, 20until the LORD gives rest to your brothers as he has to you, and they too have taken over the land that the LORD your God is giving them, across the Jordan. After that, each of you may go back to the possession I have given you."

Moses Forbidden to Cross the Jordan

21At that time I commanded Joshua: "You have seen with your own eyes all that the LORD your God has done to these two kings. The LORD will do the same to all the kingdoms over there where you are going. 22Do not be afraid of them; the LORD your God himself will fight for you."

23At that time I pleaded with the LORD: 24"O Sovereign LORD, you have begun to show to your servant your greatness and your strong hand. For what god is there in heaven or on earth who can do the deeds and mighty works you do? 25Let me go over and see the good land beyond the Jordan—that fine hill country and Lebanon."

26But because of you the LORD was angry with me and would not listen to me. "That is enough," the LORD said. "Do not

[a] 6 The Hebrew term refers to the irrevocable giving over of things or persons to the LORD, often by totally destroying them. [b] 11 Or *sarcophagus*
[c] 11 Hebrew *nine cubits long and four cubits wide* (about 4 meters long and 1.8 meters wide)
[d] 14 Or *called the settlements of Jair* [e] 17 That is, the Dead Sea

speak to me anymore about this matter.
27Go up to the top of Pisgah and look west
and north and south and east. Look at the
land with your own eyes, since you are
not going to cross this Jordan. 28But commission Joshua, and encourage and
strengthen him, for he will lead this people across and will cause them to inherit
the land that you will see." 29So we stayed
in the valley near Beth Peor.

PRAYER: AFFIRMATION

LORD Jesus Christ, I acknowledge that you suffered for me, leaving me an example that I should follow: For "[You] committed no sin, and no deceit was found in [Your] mouth." When You were reviled, You did not retaliate; when You suffered, You made no threats, but entrusted Yourself to God who judges righteously; and You Yourself bore our sins in Your body on the tree, so that I might die to sins and live for righteousness; by Your wounds I have been healed. For I was like a sheep going astray, but now I have returned to You, the Shepherd and Overseer of my soul. (1 Peter 2:21–25)

***PAUSE** to reflect on these Biblical affirmations.*

NT 2 Corinthians 5:1-21

Our Heavenly Dwelling

5 Now we know that if the earthly tent we
live in is destroyed, we have a building
from God, an eternal house in heaven, not
built by human hands. 2Meanwhile we
groan, longing to be clothed with our
heavenly dwelling, 3because when we are
clothed, we will not be found naked. 4For
while we are in this tent, we groan and are
burdened, because we do not wish to be
unclothed but to be clothed with our
heavenly dwelling, so that what is mortal
may be swallowed up by life. 5Now it is
God who has made us for this very purpose and has given us the Spirit as a deposit, guaranteeing what is to come.

6Therefore we are always confident and
know that as long as we are at home in the
body we are away from the Lord. 7We live
by faith, not by sight. 8We are confident, I
say, and would prefer to be away from the
body and at home with the Lord. 9So we
make it our goal to please him, whether we
are at home in the body or away from it.
10For we must all appear before the judgment seat of Christ, that each one may receive what is due him for the things done
while in the body, whether good or bad.

The Ministry of Reconciliation

11Since, then, we know what it is to fear
the Lord, we try to persuade men. What
we are is plain to God, and I hope it is
also plain to your conscience. 12We are not
trying to commend ourselves to you
again, but are giving you an opportunity
to take pride in us, so that you can answer
those who take pride in what is seen
rather than in what is in the heart. 13If we
are out of our mind, it is for the sake of
God; if we are in our right mind, it is for
you. 14For Christ's love compels us, because we are convinced that one died for
all, and therefore all died. 15And he died
for all, that those who live should no
longer live for themselves but for him
who died for them and was raised again.

16So from now on we regard no one from
a worldly point of view. Though we once
regarded Christ in this way, we do so no
longer. 17Therefore, if anyone is in Christ,
he is a new creation; the old has gone, the
new has come! 18All this is from God, who
reconciled us to himself through Christ and
gave us the ministry of reconciliation: 19that
God was reconciling the world to himself
in Christ, not counting men's sins against
them. And he has committed to us the message of reconciliation. 20We are therefore
Christ's ambassadors, as though God were
making his appeal through us. We implore
you on Christ's behalf: Be reconciled to
God. 21God made him who had no sin to
be sin[a] for us, so that in him we might become the righteousness of God.

[a] 21 Or *be a sin offering*

PRAYER: MY RELATIONSHIP TO GOD

I AM convinced that neither death nor life, nor angels nor principalities, nor things present nor things to come, nor powers, nor height nor depth, nor anything else in all creation, will be able to separate me from Your love, O God, that is in Christ Jesus my Lord. (Romans 8:38–39)

***PAUSE** to thank God for the relationship that you enjoy with Him in Jesus Christ.*

OT Psalm 32

Psalm 32

Of David. A *maskil*.[a]

1 Blessed is he
whose transgressions are forgiven,
whose sins are covered.
2 Blessed is the man
whose sin the LORD does not count against him
and in whose spirit is no deceit.

3 When I kept silent,
my bones wasted away
through my groaning all day long.
4 For day and night
your hand was heavy upon me;
my strength was sapped
as in the heat of summer. *Selah*
5 Then I acknowledged my sin to you
and did not cover up my iniquity.
I said, "I will confess
my transgressions to the LORD"—
and you forgave
the guilt of my sin. *Selah*

6 Therefore let everyone who is godly
pray to you
while you may be found;
surely when the mighty waters rise,
they will not reach him.
7 You are my hiding place;
you will protect me from trouble
and surround me with songs of deliverance. *Selah*

8 I will instruct you and teach you in the way you should go;
I will counsel you and watch over you.
9 Do not be like the horse or the mule,
which have no understanding
but must be controlled by bit and bridle
or they will not come to you.
10 Many are the woes of the wicked,
but the LORD's unfailing love
surrounds the man who trusts in him.

11 Rejoice in the LORD and be glad, you righteous;
sing, all you who are upright in heart!

[a] Title: Probably a literary or musical term

PRAYER: THANKSGIVING

FROM Your fullness, O Christ, we have all received grace upon grace. For the law was given through Moses; grace and truth came through You. Jesus, You are the Lamb of God, who takes away the sin of the world. (John 1:16–17, 29)

***PAUSE** to offer your own expressions of thanksgiving.*

NT 2 Corinthians 6:1-13

6 As God's fellow workers we urge you not to receive God's grace in vain. 2For he says,

> "In the time of my favor I heard you,
> and in the day of salvation I helped you."[a]

I tell you, now is the time of God's favor, now is the day of salvation.

Paul's Hardships

3We put no stumbling block in anyone's path, so that our ministry will not be discredited. 4Rather, as servants of God we commend ourselves in every way: in great endurance; in troubles, hardships and distresses; 5in beatings, imprisonments and riots; in hard work, sleepless nights and hunger; 6in purity, understanding, patience and kindness; in the Holy Spirit and in sincere love; 7in truthful speech and in the power of God; with weapons of righteousness in the right hand and in the left; 8through glory and dishonor, bad report and good report; genuine, yet regarded as impostors; 9known, yet regarded as unknown; dying, and yet we live on; beaten, and yet not killed; 10sorrowful, yet always rejoicing; poor, yet making many rich; having nothing, and yet possessing everything.

11We have spoken freely to you, Corinthians, and opened wide our hearts to you. 12We are not withholding our affection from you, but you are withholding yours from us. 13As a fair exchange—I speak as to my children—open wide your hearts also.

[a] 2 Isaiah 49:8

PRAYER: THE CHARACTER I WANT TO CULTIVATE

I WILL teach my children to fear You, O Lord: Who are they who love life and desire many days that they may see good? They are to keep their tongues from evil and their lips from speaking guile. They are to depart from evil and do good, to seek peace and pursue it. Your eyes, O Lord, are on the righteous, and Your ears are attentive to their cry. (Psalm 34:11–15)

***TAKE** a moment to ask the Lord for the grace to grow in godly character.*

YEAR 1 DAY 155

OT Deuteronomy 4:1-49

Obedience Commanded

4 Hear now, O Israel, the decrees and laws I am about to teach you. Follow them so that you may live and may go in and take possession of the land that the LORD, the God of your fathers, is giving you. 2Do not add to what I command you and do not subtract from it, but keep the commands of the LORD your God that I give you.

3You saw with your own eyes what the LORD did at Baal Peor. The LORD your God destroyed from among you everyone who followed the Baal of Peor, 4but all of you who held fast to the LORD your God are still alive today.

5See, I have taught you decrees and laws as the LORD my God commanded me, so that you may follow them in the land you are entering to take possession of it. 6Observe them carefully, for this will show your wisdom and understanding to the nations, who will hear about all these decrees and say, "Surely this great nation is a wise and understanding people." 7What other nation is so great as to have their gods near them the way the LORD our God is near us whenever we pray to him? 8And what other nation is so great as to have such righteous decrees and laws as this body of laws I am setting before you today?

9Only be careful, and watch yourselves closely so that you do not forget the things your eyes have seen or let them slip from your heart as long as you live. Teach them to your children and to their children after them. 10Remember the day you stood before the LORD your God at Horeb, when he said to me, "Assemble the people before me to hear my words so that they may learn to revere me as long as they live in the land and may teach them to their children." 11You came near and stood at the foot of the mountain while it blazed with fire to the very heavens, with black clouds and deep darkness. 12Then the LORD spoke to you out of the fire. You heard the sound of words but saw no form; there was only a voice. 13He declared to you his covenant, the Ten Commandments, which he commanded you to follow and then wrote them on two stone tablets. 14And the LORD directed me at that time to teach you the decrees and laws you are to follow in the land that you are crossing the Jordan to possess.

Idolatry Forbidden

15You saw no form of any kind the day the LORD spoke to you at Horeb out of the fire. Therefore watch yourselves very carefully, 16so that you do not become corrupt and make for yourselves an idol, an image of any shape, whether formed like a man or a woman, 17or like any animal on earth or any bird that flies in the air, 18or like any creature that moves along the ground or any fish in the waters below. 19And when you look up to the sky and see the sun, the moon and the stars—all the heavenly array—do not be enticed into bowing down to them and worshiping things the LORD your God has apportioned to all the nations under heaven. 20But as for you, the LORD took you and brought you out of the iron-smelting furnace, out of Egypt, to be the people of his inheritance, as you now are.

21The LORD was angry with me because of you, and he solemnly swore that I would not cross the Jordan and enter the good land the LORD your God is giving you as your inheritance. 22I will die in this land; I will not cross the Jordan; but you are about to cross over and take possession of that good land. 23Be careful not to forget the covenant of the LORD your God that he made with you; do not make for yourselves an idol in the form of anything the LORD your God has forbidden. 24For the LORD your God is a consuming fire, a jealous God.

25After you have had children and grandchildren and have lived in the land a long time—if you then become corrupt and make any kind of idol, doing evil in the eyes of the LORD your God and provoking him to anger, 26I call heaven and earth as witnesses against you this day that you will quickly perish from the land that you are crossing the Jordan to possess. You will not live there long but will certainly be destroyed. 27The LORD will scatter you among the peoples, and only a few of you will survive among the nations to which the LORD will drive you. 28There you will worship man-made gods of wood and stone, which cannot see or hear or eat or smell. 29But if from there you seek the LORD your God, you will find him if you look for him with all your heart and with all your soul. 30When you are in distress and all these things have happened to you, then in later days you will return to the LORD your God and obey him. 31For the LORD your God is a merciful God; he will not abandon or destroy you or forget the covenant with your forefathers, which he confirmed to them by oath.

The LORD Is God

32Ask now about the former days, long before your time, from the day God created man on the earth; ask from one end of the heavens to the other. Has anything so great as this ever happened, or has anything like it ever been heard of? 33Has any other people heard the voice of God[a] speaking out of fire, as you have, and lived? 34Has any god ever tried to take for himself one nation out of another nation, by testings, by miraculous signs and wonders, by war, by a mighty hand and an outstretched arm, or by great and awesome deeds, like all the things the LORD your God did for you in Egypt before your very eyes?

35You were shown these things so that you might know that the LORD is God; besides him there is no other. 36From heaven he made you hear his voice to discipline you. On earth he showed you his great fire, and you heard his words from out of the fire. 37Because he loved your

[a] 33 Or *of a god*

forefathers and chose their descendants
after them, he brought you out of Egypt
by his Presence and his great strength, 38 to
drive out before you nations greater and
stronger than you and to bring you into
their land to give it to you for your inheritance, as it is today.
39 Acknowledge and take to heart this
day that the LORD is God in heaven above
and on the earth below. There is no other. 40 Keep his decrees and commands,
which I am giving you today, so that it
may go well with you and your children
after you and that you may live long in the
land the LORD your God gives you for all
time.

Cities of Refuge

41 Then Moses set aside three cities east
of the Jordan, 42 to which anyone who had
killed a person could flee if he had unintentionally killed his neighbor without
malice aforethought. He could flee into
one of these cities and save his life. 43 The
cities were these: Bezer in the desert plateau, for the Reubenites; Ramoth in Gilead, for the Gadites; and Golan in Bashan,
for the Manassites.

Introduction to the Law

44 This is the law Moses set before the Israelites. 45 These are the stipulations, decrees and laws Moses gave them when they
came out of Egypt 46 and were in the valley
near Beth Peor east of the Jordan, in the
land of Sihon king of the Amorites, who
reigned in Heshbon and was defeated by
Moses and the Israelites as they came out
of Egypt. 47 They took possession of his
land and the land of Og king of Bashan,
the two Amorite kings east of the Jordan.
48 This land extended from Aroer on the
rim of the Arnon Gorge to Mount Siyon[b]
(that is, Hermon), 49 and included all the
Arabah east of the Jordan, as far as the Sea
of the Arabah,[c] below the slopes of Pisgah.

[b] *48* Hebrew; Syriac (see also Deut. 3:9) *Sirion*
[c] *49* That is, the Dead Sea

PRAYER: ADORATION

YOU are great and most worthy of praise, O Lord; You are to be feared above all gods. For all the gods of the nations are idols, but You made the heavens. Splendor and majesty are before You; strength and beauty are in Your sanctuary. I will ascribe to You glory and strength. I will ascribe to You the glory due Your name and worship You in the beauty of holiness. (Psalm 96:4–9)

PAUSE *to express your thoughts of praise and worship.*

NT 2 Corinthians 6:14–7:1

Do Not Be Yoked With Unbelievers

14 Do not be yoked together with unbelievers. For what do righteousness and
wickedness have in common? Or what fellowship can light have with darkness?
15 What harmony is there between Christ
and Belial[a]? What does a believer have in
common with an unbeliever? 16 What agreement is there between the temple of God
and idols? For we are the temple of the living God. As God has said: "I will live with
them and walk among them, and I will be
their God, and they will be my people."[b]

17 "Therefore come out from them
and be separate,
says the Lord.
Touch no unclean thing,
and I will receive you."[c]
18 "I will be a Father to you,
and you will be my sons and
daughters,
says the Lord Almighty."[d]

7 Since we have these promises, dear
friends, let us purify ourselves from
everything that contaminates body and
spirit, perfecting holiness out of reverence
for God.

[a] *15* Greek *Beliar,* a variant of *Belial*
[b] *16* Lev. 26:12; Jer. 32:38; Ezek. 37:27
[c] *17* Isaiah 52:11; Ezek. 20:34,41
[d] *18* 2 Samuel 7:14; 7:8

PRAYER: MY RELATIONSHIP TO OTHERS

O GOD, I will not defraud my neighbors or rob them. (Leviticus 19:13) . . . I will not mistreat my neighbors, but I will fear You, God; for You are the Lord my God. (Leviticus 25:17)

__PAUSE__ to review your relationships with others and to commit them to the Lord.

YEAR 1
DAY 156

OT Deuteronomy 5:1–6:25

The Ten Commandments

5 Moses summoned all Israel and said:
Hear, O Israel, the decrees and laws I
declare in your hearing today. Learn them
and be sure to follow them. 2The LORD our
God made a covenant with us at Horeb.
3It was not with our fathers that the LORD
made this covenant, but with us, with all
of us who are alive here today. 4The LORD
spoke to you face to face out of the fire on
the mountain. 5(At that time I stood between the LORD and you to declare to you
the word of the LORD, because you were
afraid of the fire and did not go up the
mountain.) And he said:

6 "I am the LORD your God, who
brought you out of Egypt, out of
the land of slavery.

7 "You shall have no other gods before[a] me.

8 "You shall not make for yourself an
idol in the form of anything in
heaven above or on the earth beneath or in the waters below.
9You shall not bow down to
them or worship them; for I, the
LORD your God, am a jealous
God, punishing the children for
the sin of the fathers to the third
and fourth generation of those
who hate me, 10but showing love
to a thousand ⌊generations⌋ of
those who love me and keep my
commandments.

11 "You shall not misuse the name of
the LORD your God, for the LORD
will not hold anyone guiltless
who misuses his name.

12 "Observe the Sabbath day by keeping
it holy, as the LORD your God has
commanded you. 13Six days you
shall labor and do all your work,
14but the seventh day is a Sabbath to the LORD your God. On
it you shall not do any work,
neither you, nor your son or
daughter, nor your manservant
or maidservant, nor your ox,
your donkey or any of your animals, nor the alien within your
gates, so that your manservant
and maidservant may rest, as
you do. 15Remember that you
were slaves in Egypt and that the
LORD your God brought you out
of there with a mighty hand and
an outstretched arm. Therefore
the LORD your God has commanded you to observe the Sabbath day.

16 "Honor your father and your mother, as the LORD your God has
commanded you, so that you
may live long and that it may go
well with you in the land the
LORD your God is giving you.

17 "You shall not murder.

18 "You shall not commit adultery.

19 "You shall not steal.

20 "You shall not give false testimony
against your neighbor.

21 "You shall not covet your neighbor's
wife. You shall not set your desire on your neighbor's house or
land, his manservant or maidservant, his ox or donkey, or
anything that belongs to your
neighbor."

22These are the commandments the
LORD proclaimed in a loud voice to your
whole assembly there on the mountain
from out of the fire, the cloud and the
deep darkness; and he added nothing

[a] 7 Or *besides*

more. Then he wrote them on two stone tablets and gave them to me.

23When you heard the voice out of the darkness, while the mountain was ablaze with fire, all the leading men of your tribes and your elders came to me. 24And you said, "The LORD our God has shown us his glory and his majesty, and we have heard his voice from the fire. Today we have seen that a man can live even if God speaks with him. 25But now, why should we die? This great fire will consume us, and we will die if we hear the voice of the LORD our God any longer. 26For what mortal man has ever heard the voice of the living God speaking out of fire, as we have, and survived? 27Go near and listen to all that the LORD our God says. Then tell us whatever the LORD our God tells you. We will listen and obey."

28The LORD heard you when you spoke to me and the LORD said to me, "I have heard what this people said to you. Everything they said was good. 29Oh, that their hearts would be inclined to fear me and keep all my commands always, so that it might go well with them and their children forever!

30"Go, tell them to return to their tents. 31But you stay here with me so that I may give you all the commands, decrees and laws you are to teach them to follow in the land I am giving them to possess."

32So be careful to do what the LORD your God has commanded you; do not turn aside to the right or to the left. 33Walk in all the way that the LORD your God has commanded you, so that you may live and prosper and prolong your days in the land that you will possess.

Love the LORD Your God

6 These are the commands, decrees and laws the LORD your God directed me to teach you to observe in the land that you are crossing the Jordan to possess, 2so that you, your children and their children after them may fear the LORD your God as long as you live by keeping all his decrees and commands that I give you, and so that you may enjoy long life. 3Hear, O Israel, and be careful to obey so that it may go well with you and that you may increase greatly in a land flowing with milk and honey, just as the LORD, the God of your fathers, promised you.

4Hear, O Israel: The LORD our God, the LORD is one.[b] 5Love the LORD your God with all your heart and with all your soul and with all your strength. 6These commandments that I give you today are to be upon your hearts. 7Impress them on your children. Talk about them when you sit at home and when you walk along the road, when you lie down and when you get up. 8Tie them as symbols on your hands and bind them on your foreheads. 9Write them on the doorframes of your houses and on your gates.

10When the LORD your God brings you into the land he swore to your fathers, to Abraham, Isaac and Jacob, to give you—a land with large, flourishing cities you did not build, 11houses filled with all kinds of good things you did not provide, wells you did not dig, and vineyards and olive groves you did not plant—then when you eat and are satisfied, 12be careful that you do not forget the LORD, who brought you out of Egypt, out of the land of slavery.

13Fear the LORD your God, serve him only and take your oaths in his name. 14Do not follow other gods, the gods of the peoples around you; 15for the LORD your God, who is among you, is a jealous God and his anger will burn against you, and he will destroy you from the face of the land. 16Do not test the LORD your God as you did at Massah. 17Be sure to keep the commands of the LORD your God and the stipulations and decrees he has given you. 18Do what is right and good in the LORD's sight, so that it may go well with you and you may go in and take over the good land that the LORD promised on oath to your forefathers, 19thrusting out all your enemies before you, as the LORD said.

20In the future, when your son asks you, "What is the meaning of the stipulations, decrees and laws the LORD our God has commanded you?" 21tell him: "We were slaves of Pharaoh in Egypt, but the LORD brought us out of Egypt with a mighty hand. 22Before our eyes the LORD sent miraculous signs and wonders—great and terrible—upon Egypt and Pharaoh and his whole household. 23But he brought us out from there to bring us in and give us the land that he promised on oath to our forefathers. 24The LORD commanded us to obey

[b] 4 Or *The LORD our God is one LORD;* or *The LORD is our God, the LORD is one;* or *The LORD is our God, the LORD alone*

all these decrees and to fear the LORD our God, so that we might always prosper and be kept alive, as is the case today. [25]And if we are careful to obey all this law before the LORD our God, as he has commanded us, that will be our righteousness."

PRAYER: CONFESSION

I CONFESS my iniquity; I am troubled by my sin. O Lord, do not forsake me; O my God, be not far from me! Make haste to help me, O Lord my salvation. (Psalm 38:18, 21–22)

***ASK** the Spirit to search your heart and reveal any areas of unconfessed sin. Acknowledge these to the Lord and thank Him for His forgiveness.*

NT 2 Corinthians 7:2–16

Paul's Joy

[2]Make room for us in your hearts. We have wronged no one, we have corrupted no one, we have exploited no one. [3]I do not say this to condemn you; I have said before that you have such a place in our hearts that we would live or die with you. [4]I have great confidence in you; I take great pride in you. I am greatly encouraged; in all our troubles my joy knows no bounds.

[5]For when we came into Macedonia, this body of ours had no rest, but we were harassed at every turn—conflicts on the outside, fears within. [6]But God, who comforts the downcast, comforted us by the coming of Titus, [7]and not only by his coming but also by the comfort you had given him. He told us about your longing for me, your deep sorrow, your ardent concern for me, so that my joy was greater than ever.

[8]Even if I caused you sorrow by my letter, I do not regret it. Though I did regret it—I see that my letter hurt you, but only for a little while— [9]yet now I am happy, not because you were made sorry, but because your sorrow led you to repentance. For you became sorrowful as God intended and so were not harmed in any way by us. [10]Godly sorrow brings repentance that leads to salvation and leaves no regret, but worldly sorrow brings death. [11]See what this godly sorrow has produced in you: what earnestness, what eagerness to clear yourselves, what indignation, what alarm, what longing, what concern, what readiness to see justice done. At every point you have proved yourselves to be innocent in this matter. [12]So even though I wrote to you, it was not on account of the one who did the wrong or of the injured party, but rather that before God you could see for yourselves how devoted to us you are. [13]By all this we are encouraged.

In addition to our own encouragement, we were especially delighted to see how happy Titus was, because his spirit has been refreshed by all of you. [14]I had boasted to him about you, and you have not embarrassed me. But just as everything we said to you was true, so our boasting about you to Titus has proved to be true as well. [15]And his affection for you is all the greater when he remembers that you were all obedient, receiving him with fear and trembling. [16]I am glad I can have complete confidence in you.

PRAYER: THE ATTRIBUTES OF GOD

BLESSED be Your name, O God, for ever and ever, for wisdom and power belong to You. You change the times and the seasons; You raise up kings and depose them. You give wisdom to the wise and knowledge to those who have understanding. You reveal deep and hidden things; You know what is in the darkness, and light dwells with You. (Daniel 2:20–22)

***PAUSE** to reflect on these affirmations about the person, powers and perfection of God.*

OT **Deuteronomy 7:1–8:20** YEAR 1 DAY 157

Driving Out the Nations

7 When the LORD your God brings you
into the land you are entering to possess and drives out before you many nations—the Hittites, Girgashites, Amorites,
Canaanites, Perizzites, Hivites and Jebusites, seven nations larger and stronger
than you— 2and when the LORD your God
has delivered them over to you and you
have defeated them, then you must destroy them totally.[a] Make no treaty with
them, and show them no mercy. 3Do not
intermarry with them. Do not give your
daughters to their sons or take their
daughters for your sons, 4for they will turn
your sons away from following me to
serve other gods, and the LORD's anger will
burn against you and will quickly destroy
you. 5This is what you are to do to them:
Break down their altars, smash their sacred stones, cut down their Asherah poles[b]
and burn their idols in the fire. 6For you
are a people holy to the LORD your God.
The LORD your God has chosen you out of
all the peoples on the face of the earth to
be his people, his treasured possession.

7The LORD did not set his affection on
you and choose you because you were
more numerous than other peoples, for
you were the fewest of all peoples. 8But it
was because the LORD loved you and kept
the oath he swore to your forefathers that
he brought you out with a mighty hand
and redeemed you from the land of slavery, from the power of Pharaoh king of
Egypt. 9Know therefore that the LORD your
God is God; he is the faithful God, keeping his covenant of love to a thousand
generations of those who love him and
keep his commands. 10But

those who hate him he will repay to
their face by destruction;
he will not be slow to repay to their
face those who hate him.

11Therefore, take care to follow the commands, decrees and laws I give you today.

12If you pay attention to these laws and
are careful to follow them, then the LORD
your God will keep his covenant of love
with you, as he swore to your forefathers.
13He will love you and bless you and increase your numbers. He will bless the
fruit of your womb, the crops of your
land—your grain, new wine and oil—the
calves of your herds and the lambs of your
flocks in the land that he swore to your
forefathers to give you. 14You will be
blessed more than any other people; none
of your men or women will be childless,
nor any of your livestock without young.
15The LORD will keep you free from every
disease. He will not inflict on you the horrible diseases you knew in Egypt, but he
will inflict them on all who hate you.
16You must destroy all the peoples the
LORD your God gives over to you. Do not
look on them with pity and do not serve
their gods, for that will be a snare to you.

17You may say to yourselves, "These nations are stronger than we are. How can
we drive them out?" 18But do not be afraid
of them; remember well what the LORD
your God did to Pharaoh and to all Egypt.
19You saw with your own eyes the great trials, the miraculous signs and wonders, the
mighty hand and outstretched arm, with
which the LORD your God brought you
out. The LORD your God will do the same
to all the peoples you now fear. 20More-
over, the LORD your God will send the hornet among them until even the survivors
who hide from you have perished. 21Do
not be terrified by them, for the LORD your
God, who is among you, is a great and
awesome God. 22The LORD your God will
drive out those nations before you, little
by little. You will not be allowed to elim-
inate them all at once, or the wild animals
will multiply around you. 23But the LORD
your God will deliver them over to you,
throwing them into great confusion until
they are destroyed. 24He will give their
kings into your hand, and you will wipe
out their names from under heaven. No
one will be able to stand up against you;
you will destroy them. 25The images of
their gods you are to burn in the fire. Do
not covet the silver and gold on them, and
do not take it for yourselves, or you will
be ensnared by it, for it is detestable to the
LORD your God. 26Do not bring a de-

[a] *2* The Hebrew term refers to the irrevocable giving over of things or persons to the LORD, often by totally destroying them; also in verse 26. [b] *5* That is, symbols of the goddess Asherah; here and elsewhere in Deuteronomy

testable thing into your house or you, like it, will be set apart for destruction. Utterly abhor and detest it, for it is set apart for destruction.

Do Not Forget the L*ORD*

8 Be careful to follow every command I am giving you today, so that you may live and increase and may enter and possess the land that the LORD promised on oath to your forefathers. 2Remember how the LORD your God led you all the way in the desert these forty years, to humble you and to test you in order to know what was in your heart, whether or not you would keep his commands. 3He humbled you, causing you to hunger and then feeding you with manna, which neither you nor your fathers had known, to teach you that man does not live on bread alone but on every word that comes from the mouth of the LORD. 4Your clothes did not wear out and your feet did not swell during these forty years. 5Know then in your heart that as a man disciplines his son, so the LORD your God disciplines you.

6Observe the commands of the LORD your God, walking in his ways and revering him. 7For the LORD your God is bringing you into a good land—a land with streams and pools of water, with springs flowing in the valleys and hills; 8a land with wheat and barley, vines and fig trees, pomegranates, olive oil and honey; 9a land where bread will not be scarce and you will lack nothing; a land where the rocks are iron and you can dig copper out of the hills.

10When you have eaten and are satisfied, praise the LORD your God for the good land he has given you. 11Be careful that you do not forget the LORD your God, failing to observe his commands, his laws and his decrees that I am giving you this day. 12Otherwise, when you eat and are satisfied, when you build fine houses and settle down, 13and when your herds and flocks grow large and your silver and gold increase and all you have is multiplied, 14then your heart will become proud and you will forget the LORD your God, who brought you out of Egypt, out of the land of slavery. 15He led you through the vast and dreadful desert, that thirsty and waterless land, with its venomous snakes and scorpions. He brought you water out of hard rock. 16He gave you manna to eat in the desert, something your fathers had never known, to humble and to test you so that in the end it might go well with you. 17You may say to yourself, "My power and the strength of my hands have produced this wealth for me." 18But remember the LORD your God, for it is he who gives you the ability to produce wealth, and so confirms his covenant, which he swore to your forefathers, as it is today.

19If you ever forget the LORD your God and follow other gods and worship and bow down to them, I testify against you today that you will surely be destroyed. 20Like the nations the LORD destroyed before you, so you will be destroyed for not obeying the LORD your God.

PRAYER: RENEWAL

MAY I be faithful and fear You, O God. (Nehemiah 7:2) . . . O God, I have this hope in You: that there will be a resurrection of both the righteous and the wicked. In view of this, may I strive always to keep my conscience blameless before You and before all people. (Acts 24:15–16)

***PAUSE** to add your own prayers for personal renewal.*

NT 2 Corinthians 8:1–15

Generosity Encouraged

8 And now, brothers, we want you to know about the grace that God has given the Macedonian churches. 2Out of the most severe trial, their overflowing joy and their extreme poverty welled up in rich generosity. 3For I testify that they gave as much as they were able, and even be-

yond their ability. Entirely on their own,
[4]they urgently pleaded with us for the
privilege of sharing in this service to the
saints. [5]And they did not do as we expected, but they gave themselves first to
the Lord and then to us in keeping with
God's will. [6]So we urged Titus, since he
had earlier made a beginning, to bring
also to completion this act of grace on
your part. [7]But just as you excel in everything—in faith, in speech, in knowledge,
in complete earnestness and in your love
for us[a]—see that you also excel in this
grace of giving.

[8]I am not commanding you, but I want
to test the sincerity of your love by comparing it with the earnestness of others.
[9]For you know the grace of our Lord Jesus
Christ, that though he was rich, yet for
your sakes he became poor, so that you
through his poverty might become rich.

[10]And here is my advice about what is
best for you in this matter: Last year you
were the first not only to give but also to
have the desire to do so. [11]Now finish the
work, so that your eager willingness to do
it may be matched by your completion of
it, according to your means. [12]For if the
willingness is there, the gift is acceptable
according to what one has, not according
to what he does not have.

[13]Our desire is not that others might be
relieved while you are hard pressed, but
that there might be equality. [14]At the
present time your plenty will supply what
they need, so that in turn their plenty will
supply what you need. Then there will be
equality, [15]as it is written: "He who gathered much did not have too much, and he
who gathered little did not have too little."[b]

[a] *7* Some manuscripts *in our love for you*
[b] *15* Exodus 16:18

PRAYER: THE WORKS OF GOD

LORD Jesus, how can I thank You for the suffering You endured for my sake?: During Your trials some began to spit at You and blindfold You and strike You with their fists and say to You, "Prophesy!" And the guards received You with slaps in the face. The soldiers put a purple robe on You, then twisted together a crown of thorns and set it on You. And they began to call out to You, "Hail, king of the Jews!" Again and again they struck You on the head with a staff and spit on You, and bending their knees, they paid mock homage to You. When they crucified You, those who passed by hurled insults at You, wagging their heads and saying, "Ha! You who are going to destroy the temple and build it in three days, save Yourself and come down from the cross!" And at the ninth hour You cried out in a loud voice, "Eloi, Eloi, lama sabachthani?" which means, "My God, My God, why have You forsaken Me?" (Mark 14:65; 15:17–19, 29–30, 34)

***TAKE** a moment to consider the greatness of God's wonderful works.*

YEAR 1 DAY 158

OT Proverbs 7

Warning Against the Adulteress

7 My son, keep my words
and store up my commands within
you.
[2]Keep my commands and you will live;
guard my teachings as the apple of
your eye.
[3]Bind them on your fingers;
write them on the tablet of your
heart.
[4]Say to wisdom, "You are my sister,"
and call understanding your
kinsman;
[5]they will keep you from the
adulteress,
from the wayward wife with her
seductive words.

[6]At the window of my house
I looked out through the lattice.
[7]I saw among the simple,
I noticed among the young men,
a youth who lacked judgment.
[8]He was going down the street near her corner,
walking along in the direction of her house
[9]at twilight, as the day was fading,
as the dark of night set in.

[10]Then out came a woman to meet him,
dressed like a prostitute and with crafty intent.
[11](She is loud and defiant,
her feet never stay at home;
[12]now in the street, now in the squares,
at every corner she lurks.)
[13]She took hold of him and kissed him
and with a brazen face she said:

[14]"I have fellowship offerings[a] at home;
today I fulfilled my vows.
[15]So I came out to meet you;
I looked for you and have found you!
[16]I have covered my bed
with colored linens from Egypt.
[17]I have perfumed my bed
with myrrh, aloes and cinnamon.
[18]Come, let's drink deep of love till morning;
let's enjoy ourselves with love!
[19]My husband is not at home;
he has gone on a long journey.
[20]He took his purse filled with money
and will not be home till full moon."

[21]With persuasive words she led him astray;
she seduced him with her smooth talk.
[22]All at once he followed her
like an ox going to the slaughter,
like a deer[b] stepping into a noose[c]
[23] till an arrow pierces his liver,
like a bird darting into a snare,
little knowing it will cost him his life.

[24]Now then, my sons, listen to me;
pay attention to what I say.
[25]Do not let your heart turn to her ways
or stray into her paths.
[26]Many are the victims she has brought down;
her slain are a mighty throng.
[27]Her house is a highway to the grave,[d]
leading down to the chambers of death.

[a] *14* Traditionally *peace offerings* [b] *22* Syriac (see also Septuagint); Hebrew *fool* [c] *22* The meaning of the Hebrew for this line is uncertain.
[d] *27* Hebrew *Sheol*

PRAYER: PETITION

MAY I not take revenge, but leave room for Your wrath, O God, for You have said, "Vengeance is Mine; I will repay." (Deuteronomy 32:35) . . . May I not be overcome by evil, but overcome evil with good. (Romans 12:21)

***PAUSE** here to petition God for wisdom. Ask Him to develop your eternal perspective, to renew your mind with truth and to help you develop greater skill in each area of your life. Offer prayers regarding your activities for this day and any special concerns you may have.*

NT 2 Corinthians 8:16–9:5

Titus Sent to Corinth

[16]I thank God, who put into the heart of Titus the same concern I have for you.
[17]For Titus not only welcomed our appeal, but he is coming to you with much enthusiasm and on his own initiative. [18]And we are sending along with him the brother who is praised by all the churches for his service to the gospel. [19]What is more, he was chosen by the churches to accompany us as we carry the offering, which we administer in order to honor the Lord himself and to show our eagerness to help. [20]We want to avoid any criticism of the way we administer this liberal gift.
[21]For we are taking pains to do what is

right, not only in the eyes of the Lord but
also in the eyes of men.
22In addition, we are sending with them
our brother who has often proved to us in
many ways that he is zealous, and now
even more so because of his great confidence in you. 23As for Titus, he is my partner and fellow worker among you; as for
our brothers, they are representatives of
the churches and an honor to Christ.
24Therefore show these men the proof of
your love and the reason for our pride in
you, so that the churches can see it.
9 There is no need for me to write to you
about this service to the saints. 2For I
know your eagerness to help, and I have
been boasting about it to the Macedonians, telling them that since last year you
in Achaia were ready to give; and your enthusiasm has stirred most of them to action. 3But I am sending the brothers in order that our boasting about you in this
matter should not prove hollow, but that
you may be ready, as I said you would be.
4For if any Macedonians come with me
and find you unprepared, we—not to say
anything about you—would be ashamed
of having been so confident. 5So I thought
it necessary to urge the brothers to visit
you in advance and finish the arrangements for the generous gift you had
promised. Then it will be ready as a generous gift, not as one grudgingly given.

PRAYER: MY RELATIONSHIP TO GOD

WHO are those that fear You, O Lord? You will instruct them in the way they should choose. (Psalm 25:12) . . . You will instruct me and teach me in the way I should go; You will counsel me and watch over me. (Psalm 32:8)

PAUSE *to thank God for the relationship that you enjoy with Him in Jesus Christ.*

YEAR 1 DAY 159

OT Deuteronomy 9:1–29

Not Because of Israel's Righteousness

9 Hear, O Israel. You are now about to
cross the Jordan to go in and dispossess nations greater and stronger than
you, with large cities that have walls up to
the sky. 2The people are strong and tall—
Anakites! You know about them and have
heard it said: "Who can stand up against
the Anakites?" 3But be assured today that
the LORD your God is the one who goes
across ahead of you like a devouring fire.
He will destroy them; he will subdue
them before you. And you will drive them
out and annihilate them quickly, as the
LORD has promised you.
4After the LORD your God has driven
them out before you, do not say to yourself, "The LORD has brought me here to
take possession of this land because of my
righteousness." No, it is on account of the
wickedness of these nations that the LORD
is going to drive them out before you. 5It
is not because of your righteousness or
your integrity that you are going in to take
possession of their land; but on account
of the wickedness of these nations, the
LORD your God will drive them out before
you, to accomplish what he swore to your
fathers, to Abraham, Isaac and Jacob. 6Un-
derstand, then, that it is not because of
your righteousness that the LORD your
God is giving you this good land to possess, for you are a stiff-necked people.

The Golden Calf

7Remember this and never forget how
you provoked the LORD your God to anger
in the desert. From the day you left Egypt
until you arrived here, you have been rebellious against the LORD. 8At Horeb you
aroused the LORD's wrath so that he was
angry enough to destroy you. 9When I
went up on the mountain to receive the
tablets of stone, the tablets of the covenant that the LORD had made with you,
I stayed on the mountain forty days and

forty nights; I ate no bread and drank no
water. [10]The LORD gave me two stone
tablets inscribed by the finger of God. On
them were all the commandments the
LORD proclaimed to you on the mountain
out of the fire, on the day of the assembly.

[11]At the end of the forty days and forty
nights, the LORD gave me the two stone
tablets, the tablets of the covenant. [12]Then
the LORD told me, "Go down from here at
once, because your people whom you
brought out of Egypt have become corrupt. They have turned away quickly from
what I commanded them and have made
a cast idol for themselves."

[13]And the LORD said to me, "I have seen
this people, and they are a stiff-necked
people indeed! [14]Let me alone, so that I
may destroy them and blot out their
name from under heaven. And I will
make you into a nation stronger and
more numerous than they."

[15]So I turned and went down from the
mountain while it was ablaze with fire.
And the two tablets of the covenant were
in my hands.[a] [16]When I looked, I saw that
you had sinned against the LORD your
God; you had made for yourselves an idol
cast in the shape of a calf. You had turned
aside quickly from the way that the LORD
had commanded you. [17]So I took the two
tablets and threw them out of my hands,
breaking them to pieces before your eyes.

[18]Then once again I fell prostrate before
the LORD for forty days and forty nights; I
ate no bread and drank no water, because
of all the sin you had committed, doing
what was evil in the LORD's sight and so
provoking him to anger. [19]I feared the
anger and wrath of the LORD, for he was
angry enough with you to destroy you.
But again the LORD listened to me. [20]And
the LORD was angry enough with Aaron to
destroy him, but at that time I prayed for
Aaron too. [21]Also I took that sinful thing
of yours, the calf you had made, and
burned it in the fire. Then I crushed it and
ground it to powder as fine as dust and
threw the dust into a stream that flowed
down the mountain.

[22]You also made the LORD angry at Taberah, at Massah and at Kibroth Hattaavah.

[23]And when the LORD sent you out from
Kadesh Barnea, he said, "Go up and take
possession of the land I have given you."
But you rebelled against the command of
the LORD your God. You did not trust him
or obey him. [24]You have been rebellious
against the LORD ever since I have known
you.

[25]I lay prostrate before the LORD those
forty days and forty nights because the
LORD had said he would destroy you. [26]I
prayed to the LORD and said, "O Sovereign
LORD, do not destroy your people, your
own inheritance that you redeemed by
your great power and brought out of Egypt
with a mighty hand. [27]Remember your servants Abraham, Isaac and Jacob. Overlook
the stubbornness of this people, their
wickedness and their sin. [28]Otherwise, the
country from which you brought us will
say, 'Because the LORD was not able to take
them into the land he had promised them,
and because he hated them, he brought
them out to put them to death in the
desert.' [29]But they are your people, your inheritance that you brought out by your
great power and your outstretched arm."

[a] 15 Or *And I had the two tablets of the covenant with me, one in each hand*

PRAYER: INTERCESSION

O LORD my God, may Your commandments be upon my heart, so that I may teach them diligently to my children and talk about them when I sit in my house and when I walk along the way and when I lie down and when I rise up. (Deuteronomy 6:6–7)

***TAKE** a few moments to intercede on behalf of your immediate family and other relatives. Offer prayers for their spiritual, emotional and physical concerns.*

NT 2 Corinthians 9:6-15

Sowing Generously

[6]Remember this: Whoever sows sparingly will also reap sparingly, and whoever sows generously will also reap generously. [7]Each man should give what he has decided in his heart to give, not reluctantly or under compulsion, for God loves a cheerful giver. [8]And God is able to make all grace abound to you, so that in all things at all times, having all that you need, you will abound in every good work. [9]As it is written:

"He has scattered abroad his gifts to
the poor;
his righteousness endures forever."[a]

[10]Now he who supplies seed to the sower and bread for food will also supply and increase your store of seed and will enlarge the harvest of your righteousness. [11]You will be made rich in every way so that you can be generous on every occasion, and through us your generosity will result in thanksgiving to God.

[12]This service that you perform is not only supplying the needs of God's people but is also overflowing in many expressions of thanks to God. [13]Because of the service by which you have proved yourselves, men will praise God for the obedience that accompanies your confession of the gospel of Christ, and for your generosity in sharing with them and with everyone else. [14]And in their prayers for you their hearts will go out to you, because of the surpassing grace God has given you. [15]Thanks be to God for his indescribable gift!

[a] 9 Psalm 112:9

PRAYER: THE CHARACTER I WANT TO CULTIVATE

If we pursue righteousness and love, we will find life, righteousness and honor. (Proverbs 21:21) . . . The goal of the instruction of Your Word, O Lord, is love that comes from a pure heart and a good conscience and a sincere faith. (1 Timothy 1:5)

TAKE *a moment to ask the Lord for the grace to grow in godly character.*

YEAR 1 DAY 160

OT Deuteronomy 10:1–11:32

Tablets Like the First Ones

10 At that time the LORD said to me, "Chisel out two stone tablets like the first ones and come up to me on the mountain. Also make a wooden chest.[a] [2]I will write on the tablets the words that were on the first tablets, which you broke. Then you are to put them in the chest."

[3]So I made the ark out of acacia wood and chiseled out two stone tablets like the first ones, and I went up on the mountain with the two tablets in my hands. [4]The LORD wrote on these tablets what he had written before, the Ten Commandments he had proclaimed to you on the mountain, out of the fire, on the day of the assembly. And the LORD gave them to me. [5]Then I came back down the mountain and put the tablets in the ark I had made, as the LORD commanded me, and they are there now.

[6](The Israelites traveled from the wells of the Jaakanites to Moserah. There Aaron died and was buried, and Eleazar his son succeeded him as priest. [7]From there they traveled to Gudgodah and on to Jotbathah, a land with streams of water. [8]At that time the LORD set apart the tribe of Levi to carry the ark of the covenant of the LORD, to stand before the LORD to minister and to pronounce blessings in his name, as they still do today. [9]That is why the Levites have no share or inheritance among their brothers; the LORD is their inheritance, as the LORD your God told them.)

[10]Now I had stayed on the mountain

[a] 1 That is, an ark

forty days and nights, as I did the first time, and the LORD listened to me at this time also. It was not his will to destroy you. 11"Go," the LORD said to me, "and lead the people on their way, so that they may enter and possess the land that I swore to their fathers to give them."

Fear the LORD

12And now, O Israel, what does the LORD your God ask of you but to fear the LORD your God, to walk in all his ways, to love him, to serve the LORD your God with all your heart and with all your soul, 13and to observe the LORD's commands and decrees that I am giving you today for your own good?

14To the LORD your God belong the heavens, even the highest heavens, the earth and everything in it. 15Yet the LORD set his affection on your forefathers and loved them, and he chose you, their descendants, above all the nations, as it is today. 16Circumcise your hearts, therefore, and do not be stiff-necked any longer. 17For the LORD your God is God of gods and Lord of lords, the great God, mighty and awesome, who shows no partiality and accepts no bribes. 18He defends the cause of the fatherless and the widow, and loves the alien, giving him food and clothing. 19And you are to love those who are aliens, for you yourselves were aliens in Egypt. 20Fear the LORD your God and serve him. Hold fast to him and take your oaths in his name. 21He is your praise; he is your God, who performed for you those great and awesome wonders you saw with your own eyes. 22Your forefathers who went down into Egypt were seventy in all, and now the LORD your God has made you as numerous as the stars in the sky.

Love and Obey the LORD

11 Love the LORD your God and keep his requirements, his decrees, his laws and his commands always. 2Remember today that your children were not the ones who saw and experienced the discipline of the LORD your God: his majesty, his mighty hand, his outstretched arm; 3the signs he performed and the things he did in the heart of Egypt, both to Pharaoh king of Egypt and to his whole country; 4what he did to the Egyptian army, to its horses and chariots, how he overwhelmed them with the waters of the Red Sea[b] as they were pursuing you, and how the LORD brought lasting ruin on them. 5It was not your children who saw what he did for you in the desert until you arrived at this place, 6and what he did to Dathan and Abiram, sons of Eliab the Reubenite, when the earth opened its mouth right in the middle of all Israel and swallowed them up with their households, their tents and every living thing that belonged to them. 7But it was your own eyes that saw all these great things the LORD has done.

8Observe therefore all the commands I am giving you today, so that you may have the strength to go in and take over the land that you are crossing the Jordan to possess, 9and so that you may live long in the land that the LORD swore to your forefathers to give to them and their descendants, a land flowing with milk and honey. 10The land you are entering to take over is not like the land of Egypt, from which you have come, where you planted your seed and irrigated it by foot as in a vegetable garden. 11But the land you are crossing the Jordan to take possession of is a land of mountains and valleys that drinks rain from heaven. 12It is a land the LORD your God cares for; the eyes of the LORD your God are continually on it from the beginning of the year to its end.

13So if you faithfully obey the commands I am giving you today—to love the LORD your God and to serve him with all your heart and with all your soul— 14then I will send rain on your land in its season, both autumn and spring rains, so that you may gather in your grain, new wine and oil. 15I will provide grass in the fields for your cattle, and you will eat and be satisfied.

16Be careful, or you will be enticed to turn away and worship other gods and bow down to them. 17Then the LORD's anger will burn against you, and he will shut the heavens so that it will not rain and the ground will yield no produce, and you will soon perish from the good land the LORD is giving you. 18Fix these words of mine in your hearts and minds; tie them as symbols on your hands and bind them on your foreheads. 19Teach them to your children, talking about them when you sit at home and when you walk along

[b] 4 Hebrew *Yam Suph*; that is, Sea of Reeds

the road, when you lie down and when you get up. [20]Write them on the doorframes of your houses and on your gates, [21]so that your days and the days of your children may be many in the land that the LORD swore to give your forefathers, as many as the days that the heavens are above the earth.

[22]If you carefully observe all these commands I am giving you to follow—to love the LORD your God, to walk in all his ways and to hold fast to him— [23]then the LORD will drive out all these nations before you, and you will dispossess nations larger and stronger than you. [24]Every place where you set your foot will be yours: Your territory will extend from the desert to Lebanon, and from the Euphrates River to the western sea.[c] [25]No man will be able to stand against you. The LORD your God, as he promised you, will put the terror and fear of you on the whole land, wherever you go.

[26]See, I am setting before you today a blessing and a curse— [27]the blessing if you obey the commands of the LORD your God that I am giving you today; [28]the curse if you disobey the commands of the LORD your God and turn from the way that I command you today by following other gods, which you have not known. [29]When the LORD your God has brought you into the land you are entering to possess, you are to proclaim on Mount Gerizim the blessings, and on Mount Ebal the curses. [30]As you know, these mountains are across the Jordan, west of the road,[d] toward the setting sun, near the great trees of Moreh, in the territory of those Canaanites living in the Arabah in the vicinity of Gilgal. [31]You are about to cross the Jordan to enter and take possession of the land the LORD your God is giving you. When you have taken it over and are living there, [32]be sure that you obey all the decrees and laws I am setting before you today.

[c] 24 That is, the Mediterranean [d] 30 Or *Jordan, westward*

PRAYER: AFFIRMATION

JESUS, You are the way and the truth and the life. No one comes to the Father except through You. (John 14:6) . . . Lord Jesus, through You the forgiveness of sins is proclaimed: Through You everyone who believes is justified from all things from which they could not be justified by the law of Moses. (Acts 13:38–39)

***PAUSE** to reflect on these Biblical affirmations.*

NT 2 Corinthians 10:1–18

Paul's Defense of His Ministry

10 By the meekness and gentleness of Christ, I appeal to you—I, Paul, who am "timid" when face to face with you, but "bold" when away! [2]I beg you that when I come I may not have to be as bold as I expect to be toward some people who think that we live by the standards of this world. [3]For though we live in the world, we do not wage war as the world does. [4]The weapons we fight with are not the weapons of the world. On the contrary, they have divine power to demolish strongholds. [5]We demolish arguments and every pretension that sets itself up against the knowledge of God, and we take captive every thought to make it obedient to Christ. [6]And we will be ready to punish every act of disobedience, once your obedience is complete.

[7]You are looking only on the surface of things.[a] If anyone is confident that he belongs to Christ, he should consider again that we belong to Christ just as much as he. [8]For even if I boast somewhat freely about the authority the Lord gave us for building you up rather than pulling you down, I will not be ashamed of it. [9]I do not want to seem to be trying to frighten you with my letters. [10]For some say, "His letters are weighty and forceful, but in person he is unimpressive and his speaking amounts to nothing." [11]Such people

[a] 7 Or *Look at the obvious facts*

should realize that what we are in our letters when we are absent, we will be in our actions when we are present.

[12]We do not dare to classify or compare ourselves with some who commend themselves. When they measure themselves by themselves and compare themselves with themselves, they are not wise.
[13]We, however, will not boast beyond proper limits, but will confine our boasting to the field God has assigned to us, a field that reaches even to you. [14]We are not going too far in our boasting, as would be the case if we had not come to you, for we did get as far as you with the gospel of Christ. [15]Neither do we go beyond our limits by boasting of work done by others.[b] Our hope is that, as your faith continues to grow, our area of activity among you will greatly expand, [16]so that we can preach the gospel in the regions beyond you. For we do not want to boast about work already done in another man's territory. [17]But, "Let him who boasts boast in the Lord."[c] [18]For it is not the one who commends himself who is approved, but the one whom the Lord commends.

[b] 13–15 Or [13]*We, however, will not boast about things that cannot be measured, but we will boast according to the standard of measurement that the God of measure has assigned us—a measurement that relates even to you.* [14] *. . . .* [15]*Neither do we boast about things that cannot be measured in regard to the work done by others.*
[c] 17 Jer. 9:24

PRAYER: MY RELATIONSHIP TO OTHERS

HOUSES and wealth are inherited from fathers, but a prudent wife is from You, Lord. (Proverbs 19:14) . . .
Charm is deceptive, and beauty is fleeting; but a woman who fears You, Lord, shall be praised. (Proverbs 31:30)

PAUSE *to review your relationships with others and to commit them to the Lord.*

YEAR 1 DAY 161

OT Psalm 33

Psalm 33

[1]Sing joyfully to the LORD, you righteous;
it is fitting for the upright to praise him.
[2]Praise the LORD with the harp;
make music to him on the ten-stringed lyre.
[3]Sing to him a new song;
play skillfully, and shout for joy.

[4]For the word of the LORD is right and true;
he is faithful in all he does.
[5]The LORD loves righteousness and justice;
the earth is full of his unfailing love.

[6]By the word of the LORD were the heavens made,
their starry host by the breath of his mouth.
[7]He gathers the waters of the sea into jars[a];
he puts the deep into storehouses.
[8]Let all the earth fear the LORD;
let all the people of the world revere him.
[9]For he spoke, and it came to be;
he commanded, and it stood firm.
[10]The LORD foils the plans of the nations;
he thwarts the purposes of the peoples.
[11]But the plans of the LORD stand firm forever,
the purposes of his heart through all generations.

[12]Blessed is the nation whose God is the LORD,
the people he chose for his inheritance.
[13]From heaven the LORD looks down
and sees all mankind;
[14]from his dwelling place he watches
all who live on earth—

[a] 7 Or *sea as into a heap*

[15]he who forms the hearts of all,
who considers everything they do.
[16]No king is saved by the size of his army;
no warrior escapes by his great
strength.
[17]A horse is a vain hope for deliverance;
despite all its great strength it
cannot save.
[18]But the eyes of the LORD are on those
who fear him,
on those whose hope is in his
unfailing love,
[19]to deliver them from death
and keep them alive in famine.

[20]We wait in hope for the LORD;
he is our help and our shield.
[21]In him our hearts rejoice,
for we trust in his holy name.
[22]May your unfailing love rest upon us,
O LORD,
even as we put our hope in you.

PRAYER: THANKSGIVING

O SERVANT of God, You were oppressed and afflicted, yet You did not open Your mouth; You were led like a lamb to the slaughter, and as a sheep before the shearer is silent, so You did not open Your mouth. By oppression and judgment You were taken away. And who can speak of Your descendants? For You were cut off from the land of the living; You were stricken for the transgression of God's people. You who are God's righteous servant will justify many by Your knowledge, and You will bear their iniquities. Therefore, God will give You a portion among the great, and You will divide the spoils with the strong, because You poured out Your life unto death, and were numbered with the transgressors. For You bore the sin of many, and made intercession for the transgressors. (Isaiah 53:7–8, 11–12)

***PAUSE** to offer your own expressions of thanksgiving.*

NT 2 Corinthians 11:1–15

Paul and the False Apostles

11 I hope you will put up with a little of
my foolishness; but you are already
doing that. [2]I am jealous for you with a
godly jealousy. I promised you to one
husband, to Christ, so that I might
present you as a pure virgin to him. [3]But
I am afraid that just as Eve was deceived
by the serpent's cunning, your minds may
somehow be led astray from your sincere
and pure devotion to Christ. [4]For if someone comes to you and preaches a Jesus
other than the Jesus we preached, or if you
receive a different spirit from the one you
received, or a different gospel from the
one you accepted, you put up with it easily enough. [5]But I do not think I am in the
least inferior to those "super-apostles." [6]I
may not be a trained speaker, but I do
have knowledge. We have made this perfectly clear to you in every way.
[7]Was it a sin for me to lower myself in
order to elevate you by preaching the
gospel of God to you free of charge? [8]I
robbed other churches by receiving support from them so as to serve you. [9]And
when I was with you and needed something, I was not a burden to anyone, for the
brothers who came from Macedonia supplied what I needed. I have kept myself
from being a burden to you in any way,
and will continue to do so. [10]As surely as
the truth of Christ is in me, nobody in the
regions of Achaia will stop this boasting of
mine. [11]Why? Because I do not love you?
God knows I do! [12]And I will keep on doing what I am doing in order to cut the
ground from under those who want an opportunity to be considered equal with us
in the things they boast about.
[13]For such men are false apostles, deceitful workmen, masquerading as apostles of
Christ. [14]And no wonder, for Satan himself
masquerades as an angel of light. [15]It is
not surprising, then, if his servants masquerade as servants of righteousness. Their
end will be what their actions deserve.

PRAYER: THE ATTRIBUTES OF GOD

I KNOW that You are a gracious and compassionate God, slow to anger and abounding in loving-kindness, a God who relents from sending calamity. (Jonah 4:2)

***PAUSE** to reflect on these affirmations about the person, powers and perfection of God.*

YEAR 1 DAY 162

OT Deuteronomy 12:1–32

The One Place of Worship

12 These are the decrees and laws you must be careful to follow in the land that the LORD, the God of your fathers, has given you to possess—as long as you live in the land. 2Destroy completely all the places on the high mountains and on the hills and under every spreading tree where the nations you are dispossessing worship their gods. 3Break down their altars, smash their sacred stones and burn their Asherah poles in the fire; cut down the idols of their gods and wipe out their names from those places.

4You must not worship the LORD your God in their way. 5But you are to seek the place the LORD your God will choose from among all your tribes to put his Name there for his dwelling. To that place you must go; 6there bring your burnt offerings and sacrifices, your tithes and special gifts, what you have vowed to give and your freewill offerings, and the firstborn of your herds and flocks. 7There, in the presence of the LORD your God, you and your families shall eat and shall rejoice in everything you have put your hand to, because the LORD your God has blessed you.

8You are not to do as we do here today, everyone as he sees fit, 9since you have not yet reached the resting place and the inheritance the LORD your God is giving you. 10But you will cross the Jordan and settle in the land the LORD your God is giving you as an inheritance, and he will give you rest from all your enemies around you so that you will live in safety. 11Then to the place the LORD your God will choose as a dwelling for his Name—there you are to bring everything I command you: your burnt offerings and sacrifices, your tithes and special gifts, and all the choice possessions you have vowed to the LORD. 12And there rejoice before the LORD your God, you, your sons and daughters, your menservants and maidservants, and the Levites from your towns, who have no allotment or inheritance of their own. 13Be careful not to sacrifice your burnt offerings anywhere you please. 14Offer them only at the place the LORD will choose in one of your tribes, and there observe everything I command you.

15Nevertheless, you may slaughter your animals in any of your towns and eat as much of the meat as you want, as if it were gazelle or deer, according to the blessing the LORD your God gives you. Both the ceremonially unclean and the clean may eat it. 16But you must not eat the blood; pour it out on the ground like water. 17You must not eat in your own towns the tithe of your grain and new wine and oil, or the firstborn of your herds and flocks, or whatever you have vowed to give, or your freewill offerings or special gifts. 18Instead, you are to eat them in the presence of the LORD your God at the place the LORD your God will choose—you, your sons and daughters, your menservants and maidservants, and the Levites from your towns—and you are to rejoice before the LORD your God in everything you put your hand to. 19Be careful not to neglect the Levites as long as you live in your land.

20When the LORD your God has enlarged your territory as he promised you, and you crave meat and say, "I would like some meat," then you may eat as much of it as you want. 21If the place where the LORD your God chooses to put his Name is too far away from you, you may slaughter animals from the herds and flocks the LORD has given you, as I have commanded you, and in your own towns you may eat as much of them as you want. [22]Eat them as you would gazelle or deer. Both the ceremonially unclean and the clean may eat. [23]But be sure you do not eat the blood, because the blood is the life, and you must not eat the life with the meat. [24]You must not eat the blood; pour it out on the ground like water. [25]Do not eat it, so that it may go well with you and your children after you, because you will be doing what is right in the eyes of the LORD.

[26]But take your consecrated things and whatever you have vowed to give, and go to the place the LORD will choose. [27]Present your burnt offerings on the altar of the LORD your God, both the meat and the blood. The blood of your sacrifices must be poured beside the altar of the LORD your God, but you may eat the meat. [28]Be careful to obey all these regulations I am giving you, so that it may always go well with you and your children after you, because you will be doing what is good and right in the eyes of the LORD your God.

[29]The LORD your God will cut off before you the nations you are about to invade and dispossess. But when you have driven them out and settled in their land, [30]and after they have been destroyed before you, be careful not to be ensnared by inquiring about their gods, saying, "How do these nations serve their gods? We will do the same." [31]You must not worship the LORD your God in their way, because in worshiping their gods, they do all kinds of detestable things the LORD hates. They even burn their sons and daughters in the fire as sacrifices to their gods.

[32]See that you do all I command you; do not add to it or take away from it.

PRAYER: ADORATION

O SON of Man, You will come with the clouds of heaven. In the presence of the Ancient of Days, You will be given dominion and glory and a kingdom, so that people of every nation and language will worship You. Your dominion is an everlasting dominion that will not pass away, and Your kingdom is one that will never be destroyed. (Daniel 7:13–14)

PAUSE *to express your thoughts of praise and worship.*

NT 2 Corinthians 11:16–33

Paul Boasts About His Sufferings

[16]I repeat: Let no one take me for a fool. But if you do, then receive me just as you would a fool, so that I may do a little boasting. [17]In this self-confident boasting I am not talking as the Lord would, but as a fool. [18]Since many are boasting in the way the world does, I too will boast. [19]You gladly put up with fools since you are so wise! [20]In fact, you even put up with anyone who enslaves you or exploits you or takes advantage of you or pushes himself forward or slaps you in the face. [21]To my shame I admit that we were too weak for that!

What anyone else dares to boast about—I am speaking as a fool—I also dare to boast about. [22]Are they Hebrews? So am I. Are they Israelites? So am I. Are they Abraham's descendants? So am I. [23]Are they servants of Christ? (I am out of my mind to talk like this.) I am more. I have worked much harder, been in prison more frequently, been flogged more severely, and been exposed to death again and again. [24]Five times I received from the Jews the forty lashes minus one. [25]Three times I was beaten with rods, once I was stoned, three times I was shipwrecked, I spent a night and a day in the open sea, [26]I have been constantly on the move. I have been in danger from rivers, in danger from bandits, in danger from my own countrymen, in danger from Gentiles; in danger in the city, in danger in the country, in danger at sea; and in danger from false brothers. [27]I have labored and toiled and have often gone without sleep; I have known hunger and thirst and have often gone without food; I have been cold and naked. [28]Besides everything else, I face daily the pressure of my concern for all the churches. [29]Who is weak, and I do not feel weak? Who is led into sin, and I do not inwardly burn?

[30]If I must boast, I will boast of the things that show my weakness. [31]The God and Father of the Lord Jesus, who is to be praised forever, knows that I am not lying. [32]In Damascus the governor under King Aretas had the city of the Damascenes guarded in order to arrest me. [33]But I was lowered in a basket from a window in the wall and slipped through his hands.

PRAYER: THE WORKS OF GOD

EVERY animal of the forest is Yours, and the cattle on a thousand hills, O God. You know every bird in the mountains, and everything that moves in the field is Yours. (Psalm 50:10–11) . . . The heavens are Yours; the earth also is Yours; You founded the world and all its fullness. (Psalm 89:11)

***TAKE** a moment to consider the greatness of God's wonderful works.*

YEAR 1
DAY 163

OT Deuteronomy 13:1–14:29

Worshiping Other Gods

13 If a prophet, or one who foretells by dreams, appears among you and announces to you a miraculous sign or wonder, [2]and if the sign or wonder of which he has spoken takes place, and he says, "Let us follow other gods" (gods you have not known) "and let us worship them," [3]you must not listen to the words of that prophet or dreamer. The LORD your God is testing you to find out whether you love him with all your heart and with all your soul. [4]It is the LORD your God you must follow, and him you must revere. Keep his commands and obey him; serve him and hold fast to him. [5]That prophet or dreamer must be put to death, because he preached rebellion against the LORD your God, who brought you out of Egypt and redeemed you from the land of slavery; he has tried to turn you from the way the LORD your God commanded you to follow. You must purge the evil from among you.

[6]If your very own brother, or your son or daughter, or the wife you love, or your closest friend secretly entices you, saying, "Let us go and worship other gods" (gods that neither you nor your fathers have known, [7]gods of the peoples around you, whether near or far, from one end of the land to the other), [8]do not yield to him or listen to him. Show him no pity. Do not spare him or shield him. [9]You must certainly put him to death. Your hand must be the first in putting him to death, and then the hands of all the people. [10]Stone him to death, because he tried to turn you away from the LORD your God, who brought you out of Egypt, out of the land of slavery. [11]Then all Israel will hear and be afraid, and no one among you will do such an evil thing again.

[12]If you hear it said about one of the towns the LORD your God is giving you to live in [13]that wicked men have arisen among you and have led the people of their town astray, saying, "Let us go and worship other gods" (gods you have not known), [14]then you must inquire, probe and investigate it thoroughly. And if it is true and it has been proved that this detestable thing has been done among you, [15]you must certainly put to the sword all who live in that town. Destroy it completely,[a] both its people and its livestock. [16]Gather all the plunder of the town into the middle of the public square and completely burn the town and all its plunder as a whole burnt offering to the LORD your God. It is to remain a ruin forever, never to be rebuilt. [17]None of those condemned things[a] shall be found in your hands, so that the LORD will turn from his fierce anger; he will show you mercy, have compassion on you, and increase your numbers, as he promised on oath to your

[a] *15,17* The Hebrew term refers to the irrevocable giving over of things or persons to the LORD, often by totally destroying them.

forefathers, 18 because you obey the LORD
your God, keeping all his commands that I
am giving you today and doing what is
right in his eyes.

Clean and Unclean Food

14 You are the children of the LORD your
God. Do not cut yourselves or shave
the front of your heads for the dead, 2 for
you are a people holy to the LORD your
God. Out of all the peoples on the face of
the earth, the LORD has chosen you to be
his treasured possession.
3 Do not eat any detestable thing. 4 These
are the animals you may eat: the ox, the
sheep, the goat, 5 the deer, the gazelle, the
roe deer, the wild goat, the ibex, the antelope and the mountain sheep.[b] 6 You may
eat any animal that has a split hoof divided in two and that chews the cud.
7 However, of those that chew the cud or
that have a split hoof completely divided
you may not eat the camel, the rabbit or
the coney.[c] Although they chew the cud,
they do not have a split hoof; they are ceremonially unclean for you. 8 The pig is
also unclean; although it has a split hoof,
it does not chew the cud. You are not to
eat their meat or touch their carcasses.
9 Of all the creatures living in the water,
you may eat any that has fins and scales.
10 But anything that does not have fins and
scales you may not eat; for you it is unclean.
11 You may eat any clean bird. 12 But these
you may not eat: the eagle, the vulture, the
black vulture, 13 the red kite, the black kite,
any kind of falcon, 14 any kind of raven,
15 the horned owl, the screech owl, the gull,
any kind of hawk, 16 the little owl, the great
owl, the white owl, 17 the desert owl, the
osprey, the cormorant, 18 the stork, any
kind of heron, the hoopoe and the bat.
19 All flying insects that swarm are unclean to you; do not eat them. 20 But any
winged creature that is clean you may eat.
21 Do not eat anything you find already
dead. You may give it to an alien living in
any of your towns, and he may eat it, or
you may sell it to a foreigner. But you are
a people holy to the LORD your God.
Do not cook a young goat in its mother's milk.

Tithes

22 Be sure to set aside a tenth of all that
your fields produce each year. 23 Eat the
tithe of your grain, new wine and oil, and
the firstborn of your herds and flocks in
the presence of the LORD your God at the
place he will choose as a dwelling for his
Name, so that you may learn to revere the
LORD your God always. 24 But if that place
is too distant and you have been blessed
by the LORD your God and cannot carry
your tithe (because the place where the
LORD will choose to put his Name is so far
away), 25 then exchange your tithe for silver, and take the silver with you and go to
the place the LORD your God will choose.
26 Use the silver to buy whatever you like:
cattle, sheep, wine or other fermented
drink, or anything you wish. Then you
and your household shall eat there in the
presence of the LORD your God and rejoice. 27 And do not neglect the Levites living in your towns, for they have no allotment or inheritance of their own.
28 At the end of every three years, bring
all the tithes of that year's produce and
store it in your towns, 29 so that the Levites
(who have no allotment or inheritance of
their own) and the aliens, the fatherless
and the widows who live in your towns
may come and eat and be satisfied, and so
that the LORD your God may bless you in
all the work of your hands.

[b] *5* The precise identification of some of the birds and animals in this chapter is uncertain. [c] *7* That is, the hyrax or rock badger

PRAYER: CONFESSION

WHO may ascend Your holy hill, O Lord? Who may stand in Your holy place? Those who have clean hands and pure hearts, who have not lifted up their souls to idols or sworn by what is false.

(Psalm 24:3–4)

***ASK** the Spirit to search your heart and reveal any areas of unconfessed sin. Acknowledge these to the Lord and thank Him for His forgiveness.*

NT 2 Corinthians 12:1–10

Paul's Vision and His Thorn

12 I must go on boasting. Although there is nothing to be gained, I will go on to visions and revelations from the Lord. 2I know a man in Christ who fourteen years ago was caught up to the third heaven. Whether it was in the body or out of the body I do not know—God knows. 3And I know that this man—whether in the body or apart from the body I do not know, but God knows— 4was caught up to paradise. He heard inexpressible things, things that man is not permitted to tell. 5I will boast about a man like that, but I will not boast about myself, except about my weaknesses. 6Even if I should choose to boast, I would not be a fool, because I would be speaking the truth. But I refrain, so no one will think more of me than is warranted by what I do or say.

7To keep me from becoming conceited because of these surpassingly great revelations, there was given me a thorn in my flesh, a messenger of Satan, to torment me. 8Three times I pleaded with the Lord to take it away from me. 9But he said to me, "My grace is sufficient for you, for my power is made perfect in weakness." Therefore I will boast all the more gladly about my weaknesses, so that Christ's power may rest on me. 10That is why, for Christ's sake, I delight in weaknesses, in insults, in hardships, in persecutions, in difficulties. For when I am weak, then I am strong.

PRAYER: MY RELATIONSHIP TO GOD

JOY in You, my Lord, is my strength. (Nehemiah 8:10) . . . Better is one day in Your courts than a thousand elsewhere, O Lord Almighty. I would rather be a doorkeeper in Your house, my God, than dwell in the tents of the wicked. For You, Lord God, are a sun and shield. You will give grace and glory; no good thing do You withhold from those who walk in integrity. O Lord of hosts, blessed are those who trust in You! (Psalm 84:10–12)

***PAUSE** to thank God for the relationship that you enjoy with Him in Jesus Christ.*

YEAR 1 DAY 164

OT Deuteronomy 15:1–23

The Year for Canceling Debts

15 At the end of every seven years you must cancel debts. 2This is how it is to be done: Every creditor shall cancel the loan he has made to his fellow Israelite. He shall not require payment from his fellow Israelite or brother, because the LORD's time for canceling debts has been proclaimed. 3You may require payment from a foreigner, but you must cancel any debt your brother owes you. 4However, there should be no poor among you, for in the land the LORD your God is giving you to possess as your inheritance, he will richly bless you, 5if only you fully obey the LORD your God and are careful to follow all these commands I am giving you today. 6For the LORD your God will bless you as he has promised, and you will lend to many nations but will borrow from none. You will rule over many nations but none will rule over you.

7If there is a poor man among your brothers in any of the towns of the land that the LORD your God is giving you, do not be hardhearted or tightfisted toward your poor brother. 8Rather be openhanded and freely lend him whatever he needs. 9Be careful not to harbor this wicked thought: "The seventh year, the year for canceling debts, is near," so that you do not show ill will toward your needy brother and give him nothing. He may then appeal to the LORD against you, and you will be found guilty of sin. 10 Give generously to him and do so without a grudging heart; then because of this the LORD your God will bless you in all your work and in everything you put your hand to. 11 There will always be poor people in the land. Therefore I command you to be openhanded toward your brothers and toward the poor and needy in your land.

Freeing Servants

12 If a fellow Hebrew, a man or a woman, sells himself to you and serves you six years, in the seventh year you must let him go free. 13 And when you release him, do not send him away empty-handed. 14 Supply him liberally from your flock, your threshing floor and your winepress. Give to him as the LORD your God has blessed you. 15 Remember that you were slaves in Egypt and the LORD your God redeemed you. That is why I give you this command today.

16 But if your servant says to you, "I do not want to leave you," because he loves you and your family and is well off with you, 17 then take an awl and push it through his ear lobe into the door, and he will become your servant for life. Do the same for your maidservant.

18 Do not consider it a hardship to set your servant free, because his service to you these six years has been worth twice as much as that of a hired hand. And the LORD your God will bless you in everything you do.

The Firstborn Animals

19 Set apart for the LORD your God every firstborn male of your herds and flocks. Do not put the firstborn of your oxen to work, and do not shear the firstborn of your sheep. 20 Each year you and your family are to eat them in the presence of the LORD your God at the place he will choose. 21 If an animal has a defect, is lame or blind, or has any serious flaw, you must not sacrifice it to the LORD your God. 22 You are to eat it in your own towns. Both the ceremonially unclean and the clean may eat it, as if it were gazelle or deer. 23 But you must not eat the blood; pour it out on the ground like water.

PRAYER: RENEWAL

O LORD my God, may You be with me as You were with our fathers; may You never leave me nor forsake me. Incline my heart to You, that I may walk in all Your ways and keep Your commands and Your statutes and Your judgments, which You gave our fathers. May all the peoples of the earth know that You, Lord, are God; there is no other. Let my heart be fully committed to You, the Lord my God, to walk in Your statutes and keep Your commandments, as at this day. (1 Kings 8:57–58, 60–61)

***PAUSE** to add your own prayers for personal renewal.*

NT 2 Corinthians 12:11–21

Paul's Concern for the Corinthians

11 I have made a fool of myself, but you drove me to it. I ought to have been commended by you, for I am not in the least inferior to the "super-apostles," even though I am nothing. 12 The things that mark an apostle—signs, wonders and miracles—were done among you with great perseverance. 13 How were you inferior to the other churches, except that I was never a burden to you? Forgive me this wrong!

14 Now I am ready to visit you for the third time, and I will not be a burden to you, because what I want is not your possessions but you. After all, children should not have to save up for their parents, but parents for their children. 15 So I will very gladly spend for you everything I have and expend myself as well. If I love you more, will you love me less? 16 Be that as it may, I have not been a burden to you. Yet, crafty fellow that I am, I caught you by trickery! 17 Did I exploit you through any of the men I sent you? 18 I urged Titus

to go to you and I sent our brother with him. Titus did not exploit you, did he? Did we not act in the same spirit and follow the same course?

19 Have you been thinking all along that we have been defending ourselves to you? We have been speaking in the sight of God as those in Christ; and everything we do, dear friends, is for your strengthening. 20 For I am afraid that when I come I may not find you as I want you to be, and you may not find me as you want me to be. I fear that there may be quarreling, jealousy, outbursts of anger, factions, slander, gossip, arrogance and disorder. 21 I am afraid that when I come again my God will humble me before you, and I will be grieved over many who have sinned earlier and have not repented of the impurity, sexual sin and debauchery in which they have indulged.

PRAYER: THE CHARACTER I WANT TO CULTIVATE

I WILL receive the words of wisdom and treasure her commands within me, turning my ear to wisdom and applying my heart to understanding. If I cry for discernment and lift up my voice for understanding, if I seek her as silver and search for her as for hidden treasures, then I will understand what it is to fear You, O Lord, and what it is to know You, O God.

(Proverbs 2:1–5)

TAKE *a moment to ask the Lord for the grace to grow in godly character.*

YEAR 1 DAY 165

OT Deuteronomy 16:1–22

Passover

16 Observe the month of Abib and celebrate the Passover of the LORD your God, because in the month of Abib he brought you out of Egypt by night. 2 Sacrifice as the Passover to the LORD your God an animal from your flock or herd at the place the LORD will choose as a dwelling for his Name. 3 Do not eat it with bread made with yeast, but for seven days eat unleavened bread, the bread of affliction, because you left Egypt in haste—so that all the days of your life you may remember the time of your departure from Egypt. 4 Let no yeast be found in your possession in all your land for seven days. Do not let any of the meat you sacrifice on the evening of the first day remain until morning.

5 You must not sacrifice the Passover in any town the LORD your God gives you 6 except in the place he will choose as a dwelling for his Name. There you must sacrifice the Passover in the evening, when the sun goes down, on the anniversary[a] of your departure from Egypt. 7 Roast it and eat it at the place the LORD your God will choose. Then in the morning return to your tents. 8 For six days eat unleavened bread and on the seventh day hold an assembly to the LORD your God and do no work.

Feast of Weeks

9 Count off seven weeks from the time you begin to put the sickle to the standing grain. 10 Then celebrate the Feast of Weeks to the LORD your God by giving a freewill offering in proportion to the blessings the LORD your God has given you. 11 And rejoice before the LORD your God at the place he will choose as a dwelling for his Name—you, your sons and daughters, your menservants and maidservants, the Levites in your towns, and the aliens, the fatherless and the widows living among you. 12 Remember that you were slaves in Egypt, and follow carefully these decrees.

Feast of Tabernacles

13 Celebrate the Feast of Tabernacles for seven days after you have gathered the produce of your threshing floor and your winepress. 14 Be joyful at your Feast—you, your sons and daughters, your menservants and maidservants, and the Levites,

[a] 6 Or *down, at the time of day*

the aliens, the fatherless and the widows who live in your towns. [15]For seven days celebrate the Feast to the LORD your God at the place the LORD will choose. For the LORD your God will bless you in all your harvest and in all the work of your hands, and your joy will be complete.

[16]Three times a year all your men must appear before the LORD your God at the place he will choose: at the Feast of Unleavened Bread, the Feast of Weeks and the Feast of Tabernacles. No man should appear before the LORD empty-handed: [17]Each of you must bring a gift in proportion to the way the LORD your God has blessed you.

Judges

[18]Appoint judges and officials for each of your tribes in every town the LORD your God is giving you, and they shall judge the people fairly. [19]Do not pervert justice or show partiality. Do not accept a bribe, for a bribe blinds the eyes of the wise and twists the words of the righteous. [20]Follow justice and justice alone, so that you may live and possess the land the LORD your God is giving you.

Worshiping Other Gods

[21]Do not set up any wooden Asherah pole[b] beside the altar you build to the LORD your God, [22]and do not erect a sacred stone, for these the LORD your God hates.

[b] 21 Or *Do not plant any tree dedicated to Asherah*

PRAYER: PETITION

LORD, may I learn the divine perspective Joseph had when he said to his brothers, "Do not be grieved or angry with yourselves for selling me here, for God sent me before you to save lives. He sent me ahead of you to preserve for you a remnant on earth and to save your lives by a great deliverance. So it was not you who sent me here, but God." (Genesis 45:5, 7–8)

***PAUSE** here to petition God for spiritual insight so that you might have understanding of His Word. Ask for insight into your identity in Jesus Christ: that you might know who you are, what direction your life should take and what His purpose for your life is. Offer prayers regarding your activities for this day and any special concerns you may have.*

NT 2 Corinthians 13:1–14

Final Warnings

13 This will be my third visit to you. "Every matter must be established by the testimony of two or three witnesses."[a] [2]I already gave you a warning when I was with you the second time. I now repeat it while absent: On my return I will not spare those who sinned earlier or any of the others, [3]since you are demanding proof that Christ is speaking through me. He is not weak in dealing with you, but is powerful among you. [4]For to be sure, he was crucified in weakness, yet he lives by God's power. Likewise, we are weak in him, yet by God's power we will live with him to serve you.

[5]Examine yourselves to see whether you are in the faith; test yourselves. Do you not realize that Christ Jesus is in you—unless, of course, you fail the test? [6]And I trust that you will discover that we have not failed the test. [7]Now we pray to God that you will not do anything wrong. Not that people will see that we have stood the test but that you will do what is right even though we may seem to have failed. [8]For we cannot do anything against the truth, but only for the truth. [9]We are glad whenever we are weak but you are strong; and our prayer is for your perfection. [10]This is why I write these things when I am absent, that when I come I may not have to be harsh in my use of authority—the authority the Lord gave me for building you up, not for tearing you down.

[a] 1 Deut. 19:15

Final Greetings

11Finally, brothers, good-by. Aim for
perfection, listen to my appeal, be of one
mind, live in peace. And the God of love
and peace will be with you.

12Greet one another with a holy kiss.
13All the saints send their greetings.

14May the grace of the Lord Jesus Christ,
and the love of God, and the fellowship
of the Holy Spirit be with you all.

PRAYER: MY RELATIONSHIP TO OTHERS

I WILL discipline my children while there is hope and not be a willing party to their death. (Proverbs 19:18) . . . The rod and reproof impart wisdom, but children left to themselves bring shame to their mother. (Proverbs 29:15)

***PAUSE** to review your relationships with others and to commit them to the Lord.*

YEAR 1
DAY 166

OT Deuteronomy 17:1–18:22

17 Do not sacrifice to the LORD your God
an ox or a sheep that has any defect or
flaw in it, for that would be detestable to
him.

2If a man or woman living among you
in one of the towns the LORD gives you is
found doing evil in the eyes of the LORD
your God in violation of his covenant,
3and contrary to my command has worshiped other gods, bowing down to them
or to the sun or the moon or the stars of
the sky, 4and this has been brought to
your attention, then you must investigate
it thoroughly. If it is true and it has been
proved that this detestable thing has been
done in Israel, 5take the man or woman
who has done this evil deed to your city
gate and stone that person to death. 6On
the testimony of two or three witnesses a
man shall be put to death, but no one
shall be put to death on the testimony of
only one witness. 7The hands of the witnesses must be the first in putting him to
death, and then the hands of all the people. You must purge the evil from among
you.

Law Courts

8If cases come before your courts that are
too difficult for you to judge—whether
bloodshed, lawsuits or assaults—take them
to the place the LORD your God will choose.
9Go to the priests, who are Levites, and to
the judge who is in office at that time. Inquire of them and they will give you the
verdict. 10You must act according to the decisions they give you at the place the LORD
will choose. Be careful to do everything
they direct you to do. 11Act according to the
law they teach you and the decisions they
give you. Do not turn aside from what they
tell you, to the right or to the left. 12The
man who shows contempt for the judge or
for the priest who stands ministering there
to the LORD your God must be put to death.
You must purge the evil from Israel. 13All
the people will hear and be afraid, and will
not be contemptuous again.

The King

14When you enter the land the LORD
your God is giving you and have taken
possession of it and settled in it, and you
say, "Let us set a king over us like all the
nations around us," 15be sure to appoint
over you the king the LORD your God
chooses. He must be from among your
own brothers. Do not place a foreigner
over you, one who is not a brother Israelite. 16The king, moreover, must not acquire great numbers of horses for himself
or make the people return to Egypt to get
more of them, for the LORD has told you,
"You are not to go back that way again."
17He must not take many wives, or his
heart will be led astray. He must not ac-
cumulate large amounts of silver and
gold.

18When he takes the throne of his kingdom, he is to write for himself on a scroll a copy of this law, taken from that of the priests, who are Levites. 19It is to be with him, and he is to read it all the days of his life so that he may learn to revere the LORD his God and follow carefully all the words of this law and these decrees 20and not consider himself better than his brothers and turn from the law to the right or to the left. Then he and his descendants will reign a long time over his kingdom in Israel.

Offerings for Priests and Levites

18 The priests, who are Levites—indeed the whole tribe of Levi—are to have no allotment or inheritance with Israel. They shall live on the offerings made to the LORD by fire, for that is their inheritance. 2They shall have no inheritance among their brothers; the LORD is their inheritance, as he promised them.

3This is the share due the priests from the people who sacrifice a bull or a sheep: the shoulder, the jowls and the inner parts. 4You are to give them the firstfruits of your grain, new wine and oil, and the first wool from the shearing of your sheep, 5for the LORD your God has chosen them and their descendants out of all your tribes to stand and minister in the LORD's name always.

6If a Levite moves from one of your towns anywhere in Israel where he is living, and comes in all earnestness to the place the LORD will choose, 7he may minister in the name of the LORD his God like all his fellow Levites who serve there in the presence of the LORD. 8He is to share equally in their benefits, even though he has received money from the sale of family possessions.

Detestable Practices

9When you enter the land the LORD your God is giving you, do not learn to imitate the detestable ways of the nations there. 10Let no one be found among you who sacrifices his son or daughter in[a] the fire, who practices divination or sorcery, interprets omens, engages in witchcraft, 11or casts spells, or who is a medium or spiritist or who consults the dead. 12Anyone who does these things is detestable to the LORD, and because of these detestable practices the LORD your God will drive out those nations before you. 13You must be blameless before the LORD your God.

The Prophet

14The nations you will dispossess listen to those who practice sorcery or divination. But as for you, the LORD your God has not permitted you to do so. 15The LORD your God will raise up for you a prophet like me from among your own brothers. You must listen to him. 16For this is what you asked of the LORD your God at Horeb on the day of the assembly when you said, "Let us not hear the voice of the LORD our God nor see this great fire anymore, or we will die."

17The LORD said to me: "What they say is good. 18I will raise up for them a prophet like you from among their brothers; I will put my words in his mouth, and he will tell them everything I command him. 19If anyone does not listen to my words that the prophet speaks in my name, I myself will call him to account. 20But a prophet who presumes to speak in my name anything I have not commanded him to say, or a prophet who speaks in the name of other gods, must be put to death."

21You may say to yourselves, "How can we know when a message has not been spoken by the LORD?" 22If what a prophet proclaims in the name of the LORD does not take place or come true, that is a message the LORD has not spoken. That prophet has spoken presumptuously. Do not be afraid of him.

[a] 10 Or *who makes his son or daughter pass through*

PRAYER: INTERCESSION

O LORD, may we be deeply devoted to one another, honoring one another above ourselves. (Romans 12:10)

***TAKE** a few moments to intercede on behalf of other believers, such as your personal friends, those in ministry and those who are oppressed and in need.*

NT Galatians 1:1-10

1 Paul, an apostle—sent not from men
nor by man, but by Jesus Christ and
God the Father, who raised him from the
dead— 2and all the brothers with me,

To the churches in Galatia:

3Grace and peace to you from God our
Father and the Lord Jesus Christ, 4who
gave himself for our sins to rescue us from
the present evil age, according to the will
of our God and Father, 5to whom be glory for ever and ever. Amen.

No Other Gospel

6I am astonished that you are so quickly deserting the one who called you by the
grace of Christ and are turning to a different gospel— 7which is really no gospel
at all. Evidently some people are throwing you into confusion and are trying to
pervert the gospel of Christ. 8But even if
we or an angel from heaven should
preach a gospel other than the one we
preached to you, let him be eternally condemned! 9As we have already said, so now
I say again: If anybody is preaching to you
a gospel other than what you accepted, let
him be eternally condemned!

10Am I now trying to win the approval
of men, or of God? Or am I trying to
please men? If I were still trying to please
men, I would not be a servant of Christ.

PRAYER: THE ATTRIBUTES OF GOD

GREAT are You, Lord, and most worthy of praise in Your city, O God, Your holy mountain. As is Your name, O God, so is Your praise to the ends of the earth; Your right hand is filled with righteousness. (Psalm 48:1, 10) . . . Lord Jesus Christ, You received honor and glory from God the Father when the voice came to You from the Majestic Glory, saying, "This is My beloved Son, with whom I am well pleased." (2 Peter 1:17)

***PAUSE** to reflect on these affirmations about the person, powers and perfection of God.*

YEAR 1 DAY 167

OT Deuteronomy 19:1-21

Cities of Refuge

19 When the LORD your God has destroyed the nations whose land he is
giving you, and when you have driven
them out and settled in their towns and
houses, 2then set aside for yourselves
three cities centrally located in the land
the LORD your God is giving you to possess. 3Build roads to them and divide into
three parts the land the LORD your God is
giving you as an inheritance, so that anyone who kills a man may flee there.

4This is the rule concerning the man
who kills another and flees there to save
his life—one who kills his neighbor unintentionally, without malice aforethought. 5For instance, a man may go into
the forest with his neighbor to cut wood,
and as he swings his ax to fell a tree, the
head may fly off and hit his neighbor and
kill him. That man may flee to one of
these cities and save his life. 6Otherwise,
the avenger of blood might pursue him in
a rage, overtake him if the distance is too
great, and kill him even though he is not
deserving of death, since he did it to his
neighbor without malice aforethought.
7This is why I command you to set aside
for yourselves three cities.

8If the LORD your God enlarges your territory, as he promised on oath to your
forefathers, and gives you the whole land
he promised them, 9because you carefully follow all these laws I command you today—to love the LORD your God and to
walk always in his ways—then you are to
set aside three more cities. 10Do this so
that innocent blood will not be shed in

your land, which the LORD your God is
giving you as your inheritance, and so that
you will not be guilty of bloodshed.
11 But if a man hates his neighbor and
lies in wait for him, assaults and kills him,
and then flees to one of these cities, 12 the
elders of his town shall send for him,
bring him back from the city, and hand
him over to the avenger of blood to die.
13 Show him no pity. You must purge from
Israel the guilt of shedding innocent
blood, so that it may go well with you.
14 Do not move your neighbor's boundary stone set up by your predecessors in
the inheritance you receive in the land the
LORD your God is giving you to possess.

Witnesses

15 One witness is not enough to convict
a man accused of any crime or offense he
may have committed. A matter must be
established by the testimony of two or
three witnesses.
16 If a malicious witness takes the stand
to accuse a man of a crime, 17 the two men
involved in the dispute must stand in the
presence of the LORD before the priests
and the judges who are in office at the
time. 18 The judges must make a thorough
investigation, and if the witness proves to
be a liar, giving false testimony against his
brother, 19 then do to him as he intended
to do to his brother. You must purge the
evil from among you. 20 The rest of the
people will hear of this and be afraid, and
never again will such an evil thing be
done among you. 21 Show no pity: life for
life, eye for eye, tooth for tooth, hand for
hand, foot for foot.

PRAYER: AFFIRMATION

JESUS, You taught that I cannot serve two masters; I will hate the one and love the other, or I will be devoted to the one and despise the other. Therefore, I know I cannot serve both God and wealth. (Matthew 6:24; Luke 16:13) . . . If I am rich in this present world, I should not be arrogant or set my hope on the uncertainty of riches but on You, O God, for You richly provide me with everything for my enjoyment. I should do good, be rich in good works, and be generous and willing to share. In this way, I will lay up treasure for myself as a firm foundation for the future, so that I may lay hold of true life. (1 Timothy 6:17–19)

PAUSE *to reflect on these Biblical affirmations.*

NT Galatians 1:11–24

Paul Called by God

11 I want you to know, brothers, that the
gospel I preached is not something that
man made up. 12 I did not receive it from
any man, nor was I taught it; rather, I received it by revelation from Jesus Christ.
13 For you have heard of my previous way
of life in Judaism, how intensely I persecuted the church of God and tried to destroy it. 14 I was advancing in Judaism beyond many Jews of my own age and was
extremely zealous for the traditions of my
fathers. 15 But when God, who set me apart
from birth[a] and called me by his grace, was
pleased 16 to reveal his Son in me so that I
might preach him among the Gentiles, I
did not consult any man, 17 nor did I go up
to Jerusalem to see those who were apostles before I was, but I went immediately
into Arabia and later returned to Damascus.
18 Then after three years, I went up to
Jerusalem to get acquainted with Peter[b]
and stayed with him fifteen days. 19 I saw
none of the other apostles—only James,
the Lord's brother. 20 I assure you before
God that what I am writing you is no lie.
21 Later I went to Syria and Cilicia. 22 I was
personally unknown to the churches of
Judea that are in Christ. 23 They only heard
the report: "The man who formerly persecuted us is now preaching the faith he
once tried to destroy." 24 And they praised
God because of me.

[a] *15* Or *from my mother's womb* [b] *18* Greek *Cephas*

PRAYER: THE WORKS OF GOD

GOD'S grace was given to us in You, Christ Jesus, before the beginning of time and has now been revealed through Your appearing, O Savior, You who abolished death and brought life and immortality to light through the gospel. (2 Timothy 1:9–10) . . . We see You, Jesus—the One who was made a little lower than the angels—now crowned with glory and honor because You suffered death, so that by the grace of God You might taste death for everyone. In bringing many of us to glory, it was fitting that God, for whom and through whom everything exists, should make You—the author of our salvation—perfect through suffering. (Hebrews 2:9–10)

***TAKE** a moment to consider the greatness of God's wonderful works.*

YEAR 1 DAY 168

OT Psalm 34

Psalm 34[a]

Of David. When he pretended to be insane before Abimelech, who drove him away, and he left.

1 I will extol the LORD at all times;
his praise will always be on my lips.
2 My soul will boast in the LORD;
let the afflicted hear and rejoice.
3 Glorify the LORD with me;
let us exalt his name together.

4 I sought the LORD, and he answered me;
he delivered me from all my fears.
5 Those who look to him are radiant;
their faces are never covered with shame.
6 This poor man called, and the LORD heard him;
he saved him out of all his troubles.
7 The angel of the LORD encamps around those who fear him,
and he delivers them.

8 Taste and see that the LORD is good;
blessed is the man who takes refuge in him.
9 Fear the LORD, you his saints,
for those who fear him lack nothing.
10 The lions may grow weak and hungry,
but those who seek the LORD lack no good thing.

11 Come, my children, listen to me;
I will teach you the fear of the LORD.
12 Whoever of you loves life
and desires to see many good days,
13 keep your tongue from evil
and your lips from speaking lies.
14 Turn from evil and do good;
seek peace and pursue it.

15 The eyes of the LORD are on the righteous
and his ears are attentive to their cry;
16 the face of the LORD is against those who do evil,
to cut off the memory of them from the earth.

17 The righteous cry out, and the LORD hears them;
he delivers them from all their troubles.
18 The LORD is close to the brokenhearted
and saves those who are crushed in spirit.

19 A righteous man may have many troubles,
but the LORD delivers him from them all;
20 he protects all his bones,
not one of them will be broken.

21 Evil will slay the wicked;
the foes of the righteous will be condemned.
22 The LORD redeems his servants;
no one will be condemned who takes refuge in him.

[a] This psalm is an acrostic poem, the verses of which begin with the successive letters of the Hebrew alphabet.

PRAYER: THANKSGIVING

I WILL sing to You, O Lord, and give praise to You, for You have rescued the lives of the needy from the hands of evildoers. (Jeremiah 20:13) . . . You, O Lord, are good, a refuge in times of trouble; You know those who trust in You. (Nahum 1:7)

***PAUSE** to offer your own expressions of thanksgiving.*

NT Galatians 2:1–10

Paul Accepted by the Apostles

2 Fourteen years later I went up again to
Jerusalem, this time with Barnabas. I
took Titus along also. [2]I went in response
to a revelation and set before them the
gospel that I preach among the Gentiles.
But I did this privately to those who
seemed to be leaders, for fear that I was
running or had run my race in vain. [3]Yet
not even Titus, who was with me, was
compelled to be circumcised, even
though he was a Greek. [4]⌊This matter
arose⌋ because some false brothers had in-
filtrated our ranks to spy on the freedom
we have in Christ Jesus and to make us
slaves. [5]We did not give in to them for a
moment, so that the truth of the gospel
might remain with you.
[6]As for those who seemed to be important—whatever they were makes no difference to me; God does not judge by external appearance—those men added nothing to my message. [7]On the contrary, they
saw that I had been entrusted with the task
of preaching the gospel to the Gentiles,[a]
just as Peter had been to the Jews.[b] [8]For
God, who was at work in the ministry of
Peter as an apostle to the Jews, was also at
work in my ministry as an apostle to the
Gentiles. [9]James, Peter[c] and John, those re-
puted to be pillars, gave me and Barnabas
the right hand of fellowship when they
recognized the grace given to me. They
agreed that we should go to the Gentiles,
and they to the Jews. [10]All they asked was
that we should continue to remember the
poor, the very thing I was eager to do.

[a] 7 Greek *uncircumcised* [b] 7 Greek *circumcised;* also in verses 8 and 9 [c] 9 Greek *Cephas;* also in verses 11 and 14

PRAYER: MY RELATIONSHIP TO GOD

I WILL praise You, O Lord, with all my heart; I will tell of all Your wonders. I will be glad and rejoice in You; I will sing praise to Your name, O Most High. (Psalm 9:1–2) . . . The righteous will rejoice in You, O Lord, for praise is becoming to the upright. (Psalm 33:1)

***PAUSE** to thank God for the relationship that you enjoy with Him in Jesus Christ.*

YEAR 1 DAY 169

OT Deuteronomy 20:1–20

Going to War

20 When you go to war against your enemies and see horses and chariots
and an army greater than yours, do not be
afraid of them, because the LORD your
God, who brought you up out of Egypt,
will be with you. [2]When you are about to
go into battle, the priest shall come forward and address the army. [3]He shall say:
"Hear, O Israel, today you are going into
battle against your enemies. Do not be
fainthearted or afraid; do not be terrified
or give way to panic before them. [4]For the
LORD your God is the one who goes with

you to fight for you against your enemies
to give you victory."
5The officers shall say to the army: "Has
anyone built a new house and not dedicated it? Let him go home, or he may die
in battle and someone else may dedicate
it. 6Has anyone planted a vineyard and
not begun to enjoy it? Let him go home,
or he may die in battle and someone else
enjoy it. 7Has anyone become pledged to
a woman and not married her? Let him go
home, or he may die in battle and someone else marry her." 8Then the officers
shall add, "Is any man afraid or fainthearted? Let him go home so that his
brothers will not become disheartened
too." 9When the officers have finished
speaking to the army, they shall appoint
commanders over it.
10When you march up to attack a city,
make its people an offer of peace. 11If they
accept and open their gates, all the people
in it shall be subject to forced labor and
shall work for you. 12If they refuse to make
peace and they engage you in battle, lay
siege to that city. 13When the LORD your
God delivers it into your hand, put to the
sword all the men in it. 14As for the
women, the children, the livestock and
everything else in the city, you may take
these as plunder for yourselves. And you
may use the plunder the LORD your God
gives you from your enemies. 15This is
how you are to treat all the cities that are
at a distance from you and do not belong
to the nations nearby.
16However, in the cities of the nations
the LORD your God is giving you as an inheritance, do not leave alive anything that
breathes. 17Completely destroy[a] them—
the Hittites, Amorites, Canaanites, Perizzites, Hivites and Jebusites—as the LORD
your God has commanded you. 18Other-
wise, they will teach you to follow all the
detestable things they do in worshiping
their gods, and you will sin against the
LORD your God.
19When you lay siege to a city for a long
time, fighting against it to capture it, do
not destroy its trees by putting an ax to
them, because you can eat their fruit. Do
not cut them down. Are the trees of the
field people, that you should besiege
them?[b] 20However, you may cut down
trees that you know are not fruit trees and
use them to build siege works until the
city at war with you falls.

[a] *17* The Hebrew term refers to the irrevocable giving over of things or persons to the LORD, often by totally destroying them. [b] *19* Or *down to use in the siege, for the fruit trees are for the benefit of man.*

PRAYER: ADORATION

YOU, Almighty Creator, asked: "Where were you when I laid the foundations of the earth? Tell Me, if you have understanding. Who determined its measurements? Surely you know! Or who stretched the line across it? On what were its bases sunk, or who laid its cornerstone when the morning stars sang together and all the children of God shouted for joy?" (Job 38:4–7) . . . You revealed Yourself to Moses as "I AM WHO I AM." (Exodus 3:14)

PAUSE *to express your thoughts of praise and worship.*

NT Galatians 2:11–21

Paul Opposes Peter

11When Peter came to Antioch, I opposed him to his face, because he was
clearly in the wrong. 12Before certain men
came from James, he used to eat with the
Gentiles. But when they arrived, he began
to draw back and separate himself from
the Gentiles because he was afraid of
those who belonged to the circumcision
group. 13The other Jews joined him in his
hypocrisy, so that by their hypocrisy even
Barnabas was led astray.
14When I saw that they were not acting
in line with the truth of the gospel, I said
to Peter in front of them all, "You are a
Jew, yet you live like a Gentile and not like
a Jew. How is it, then, that you force Gentiles to follow Jewish customs?

[15]"We who are Jews by birth and not 'Gentile sinners' [16]know that a man is not justified by observing the law, but by faith in Jesus Christ. So we, too, have put our faith in Christ Jesus that we may be justified by faith in Christ and not by observing the law, because by observing the law no one will be justified.

[17]"If, while we seek to be justified in Christ, it becomes evident that we ourselves are sinners, does that mean that Christ promotes sin? Absolutely not! [18]If I rebuild what I destroyed, I prove that I am a lawbreaker. [19]For through the law I died to the law so that I might live for God. [20]I have been crucified with Christ and I no longer live, but Christ lives in me. The life I live in the body, I live by faith in the Son of God, who loved me and gave himself for me. [21]I do not set aside the grace of God, for if righteousness could be gained through the law, Christ died for nothing!"[a]

[a] 21 Some interpreters end the quotation after verse 14.

PRAYER: THE CHARACTER I WANT TO CULTIVATE

I WILL not be dishonest in judgment, in measurement of weight or quantity. I will be honest and just in my business affairs. (Leviticus 19:35–36) . . . The integrity of the upright guides them, but the unfaithful are destroyed by their duplicity. (Proverbs 11:3)

***TAKE** a moment to ask the Lord for the grace to grow in godly character.*

YEAR 1 DAY 170

OT Deuteronomy 21:1–23

Atonement for an Unsolved Murder

21 If a man is found slain, lying in a field in the land the LORD your God is giving you to possess, and it is not known who killed him, [2]your elders and judges shall go out and measure the distance from the body to the neighboring towns. [3]Then the elders of the town nearest the body shall take a heifer that has never been worked and has never worn a yoke [4]and lead her down to a valley that has not been plowed or planted and where there is a flowing stream. There in the valley they are to break the heifer's neck. [5]The priests, the sons of Levi, shall step forward, for the LORD your God has chosen them to minister and to pronounce blessings in the name of the LORD and to decide all cases of dispute and assault. [6]Then all the elders of the town nearest the body shall wash their hands over the heifer whose neck was broken in the valley, [7]and they shall declare: "Our hands did not shed this blood, nor did our eyes see it done. [8]Accept this atonement for your people Israel, whom you have redeemed, O LORD, and do not hold your people guilty of the blood of an innocent man." And the bloodshed will be atoned for. [9]So you will purge from yourselves the guilt of shedding innocent blood, since you have done what is right in the eyes of the LORD.

Marrying a Captive Woman

[10]When you go to war against your enemies and the LORD your God delivers them into your hands and you take captives, [11]if you notice among the captives a beautiful woman and are attracted to her, you may take her as your wife. [12]Bring her into your home and have her shave her head, trim her nails [13]and put aside the clothes she was wearing when captured. After she has lived in your house and mourned her father and mother for a full month, then you may go to her and be her husband and she shall be your wife. [14]If you are not pleased with her, let her go wherever she wishes. You must not sell her or treat her as a slave, since you have dishonored her.

The Right of the Firstborn

[15]If a man has two wives, and he loves

one but not the other, and both bear him sons but the firstborn is the son of the wife he does not love, 16 when he wills his property to his sons, he must not give the rights of the firstborn to the son of the wife he loves in preference to his actual firstborn, the son of the wife he does not love. 17 He must acknowledge the son of his unloved wife as the firstborn by giving him a double share of all he has. That son is the first sign of his father's strength. The right of the firstborn belongs to him.

A Rebellious Son

18 If a man has a stubborn and rebellious son who does not obey his father and mother and will not listen to them when they discipline him, 19 his father and mother shall take hold of him and bring him to the elders at the gate of his town. 20 They shall say to the elders, "This son of ours is stubborn and rebellious. He will not obey us. He is a profligate and a drunkard." 21 Then all the men of his town shall stone him to death. You must purge the evil from among you. All Israel will hear of it and be afraid.

Various Laws

22 If a man guilty of a capital offense is put to death and his body is hung on a tree, 23 you must not leave his body on the tree overnight. Be sure to bury him that same day, because anyone who is hung on a tree is under God's curse. You must not desecrate the land the LORD your God is giving you as an inheritance.

PRAYER: CONFESSION

YOU have been just in all that has happened to me, O God; You have acted faithfully, while I did wrong. (Nehemiah 9:33)

***ASK** the Spirit to search your heart and reveal any areas of unconfessed sin. Acknowledge these to the Lord and thank Him for His forgiveness.*

NT Galatians 3:1–14

Faith or Observance of the Law

3 You foolish Galatians! Who has bewitched you? Before your very eyes Jesus Christ was clearly portrayed as crucified. 2 I would like to learn just one thing from you: Did you receive the Spirit by observing the law, or by believing what you heard? 3 Are you so foolish? After beginning with the Spirit, are you now trying to attain your goal by human effort? 4 Have you suffered so much for nothing—if it really was for nothing? 5 Does God give you his Spirit and work miracles among you because you observe the law, or because you believe what you heard?

6 Consider Abraham: "He believed God, and it was credited to him as righteousness."[a] 7 Understand, then, that those who believe are children of Abraham. 8 The Scripture foresaw that God would justify the Gentiles by faith, and announced the gospel in advance to Abraham: "All nations will be blessed through you."[b] 9 So those who have faith are blessed along with Abraham, the man of faith.

10 All who rely on observing the law are under a curse, for it is written: "Cursed is everyone who does not continue to do everything written in the Book of the Law."[c] 11 Clearly no one is justified before God by the law, because, "The righteous will live by faith."[d] 12 The law is not based on faith; on the contrary, "The man who does these things will live by them."[e] 13 Christ redeemed us from the curse of the law by becoming a curse for us, for it is written: "Cursed is everyone who is hung on a tree."[f] 14 He redeemed us in order that the blessing given to Abraham might come to the Gentiles through Christ Jesus, so that by faith we might receive the promise of the Spirit.

[a] *6* Gen. 15:6 [b] *8* Gen. 12:3; 18:18; 22:18 [c] *10* Deut. 27:26 [d] *11* Hab. 2:4 [e] *12* Lev. 18:5 [f] *13* Deut. 21:23

PRAYER: MY RELATIONSHIP TO OTHERS

O LORD, I will pursue the things that lead to peace and to mutual edification. (Romans 14:19) . . . We should bear with one another in love and make every effort to keep the unity of Your Spirit in the bond of peace. (Ephesians 4:2–3)

***PAUSE** to review your relationships with others and to commit them to the Lord.*

YEAR 1 DAY 171

OT Deuteronomy 22:1-30

22 If you see your brother's ox or sheep
straying, do not ignore it but be sure
to take it back to him. [2]If the brother does
not live near you or if you do not know
who he is, take it home with you and keep
it until he comes looking for it. Then give
it back to him. [3]Do the same if you find
your brother's donkey or his cloak or anything he loses. Do not ignore it.

[4]If you see your brother's donkey or his
ox fallen on the road, do not ignore it. Help him get it to its feet.

[5]A woman must not wear men's clothing, nor a man wear women's clothing, for the LORD your God detests anyone who does this.

[6]If you come across a bird's nest beside
the road, either in a tree or on the ground, and the mother is sitting on the young or on the eggs, do not take the mother with
the young. [7]You may take the young, but
be sure to let the mother go, so that it may go well with you and you may have a long life.

[8]When you build a new house, make a parapet around your roof so that you may not bring the guilt of bloodshed on your house if someone falls from the roof.

[9]Do not plant two kinds of seed in your vineyard; if you do, not only the crops you plant but also the fruit of the vineyard will be defiled.[a]

[10]Do not plow with an ox and a donkey yoked together.

[11]Do not wear clothes of wool and linen woven together.

[12]Make tassels on the four corners of the cloak you wear.

Marriage Violations

[13]If a man takes a wife and, after lying
with her, dislikes her [14]and slanders her
and gives her a bad name, saying, "I married this woman, but when I approached her, I did not find proof of her virginity,"
[15]then the girl's father and mother shall
bring proof that she was a virgin to the
town elders at the gate. [16]The girl's father
will say to the elders, "I gave my daughter in marriage to this man, but he dislikes
her. [17]Now he has slandered her and said,
'I did not find your daughter to be a virgin.' But here is the proof of my daughter's virginity." Then her parents shall display the cloth before the elders of the town,
[18]and the elders shall take the man and
punish him. [19]They shall fine him a hundred shekels of silver[b] and give them to the girl's father, because this man has given an Israelite virgin a bad name. She shall continue to be his wife; he must not divorce her as long as he lives.

[20]If, however, the charge is true and no
proof of the girl's virginity can be found,
[21]she shall be brought to the door of her
father's house and there the men of her town shall stone her to death. She has done a disgraceful thing in Israel by being promiscuous while still in her father's house. You must purge the evil from among you.

[22]If a man is found sleeping with another man's wife, both the man who slept with her and the woman must die. You must purge the evil from Israel.

[23]If a man happens to meet in a town a
virgin pledged to be married and he
sleeps with her, [24]you shall take both of
them to the gate of that town and stone them to death—the girl because she was

[a] 9 Or *be forfeited to the sanctuary* [b] 19 That is, about 2 1/2 pounds (about 1 kilogram)

in a town and did not scream for help, and the man because he violated another man's wife. You must purge the evil from among you.

25 But if out in the country a man happens to meet a girl pledged to be married and rapes her, only the man who has done this shall die. 26 Do nothing to the girl; she has committed no sin deserving death. This case is like that of someone who attacks and murders his neighbor, 27 for the man found the girl out in the country, and though the betrothed girl screamed, there was no one to rescue her.

28 If a man happens to meet a virgin who is not pledged to be married and rapes her and they are discovered, 29 he shall pay the girl's father fifty shekels of silver.[c] He must marry the girl, for he has violated her. He can never divorce her as long as he lives.

30 A man is not to marry his father's wife; he must not dishonor his father's bed.

[c] *29* That is, about 1 1/4 pounds (about 0.6 kilogram)

PRAYER: RENEWAL

JESUS, if I abide in You, and Your words abide in me, I can ask whatever I wish, and it will be done for me. As I ask in Your name, I will receive, that my joy may be full. (John 15:7, 16:24) . . . As I walk in Your Spirit, I will not fulfill the desires of the flesh. For the flesh desires what is contrary to the Spirit, and the Spirit what is contrary to the flesh; for they oppose each other, so that I may not do the things that I wish. But if I am led by Your Spirit, I am not under the law. (Galatians 5:16–18)

PAUSE *to add your own prayers for personal renewal.*

NT Galatians 3:15–4:7

The Law and the Promise

15 Brothers, let me take an example from everyday life. Just as no one can set aside or add to a human covenant that has been duly established, so it is in this case. 16 The promises were spoken to Abraham and to his seed. The Scripture does not say "and to seeds," meaning many people, but "and to your seed,"[a] meaning one person, who is Christ. 17 What I mean is this: The law, introduced 430 years later, does not set aside the covenant previously established by God and thus do away with the promise. 18 For if the inheritance depends on the law, then it no longer depends on a promise; but God in his grace gave it to Abraham through a promise.

19 What, then, was the purpose of the law? It was added because of transgressions until the Seed to whom the promise referred had come. The law was put into effect through angels by a mediator. 20 A mediator, however, does not represent just one party; but God is one.

21 Is the law, therefore, opposed to the promises of God? Absolutely not! For if a law had been given that could impart life, then righteousness would certainly have come by the law. 22 But the Scripture declares that the whole world is a prisoner of sin, so that what was promised, being given through faith in Jesus Christ, might be given to those who believe.

23 Before this faith came, we were held prisoners by the law, locked up until faith should be revealed. 24 So the law was put in charge to lead us to Christ[b] that we might be justified by faith. 25 Now that faith has come, we are no longer under the supervision of the law.

Sons of God

26 You are all sons of God through faith in Christ Jesus, 27 for all of you who were baptized into Christ have clothed yourselves with Christ. 28 There is neither Jew nor Greek, slave nor free, male nor female, for you are all one in Christ Jesus. 29 If you belong to Christ, then you are Abraham's seed, and heirs according to the promise.

4 What I am saying is that as long as the heir is a child, he is no different from

[a] *16* Gen. 12:7; 13:15; 24:7 [b] *24* Or *charge until Christ came*

a slave, although he owns the whole estate. 2He is subject to guardians and trustees until the time set by his father. 3So
also, when we were children, we were in
slavery under the basic principles of the
world. 4But when the time had fully
come, God sent his Son, born of a
woman, born under law, 5to redeem those
under law, that we might receive the full
rights of sons. 6Because you are sons, God
sent the Spirit of his Son into our hearts,
the Spirit who calls out, *"Abba,*[c] Father."
7So you are no longer a slave, but a son;
and since you are a son, God has made
you also an heir.

[c] *6* Aramaic for *Father*

PRAYER: THE ATTRIBUTES OF GOD

YOU are the great, the mighty and the awesome God; You keep Your covenant of loving-kindness. (Nehemiah 9:32) . . .
To whom can I liken You or count Your equal, O Lord? To whom can I compare You that You may be alike? (Isaiah 46:5)

***PAUSE** to reflect on these affirmations about the person, powers and perfection of God.*

YEAR 1
DAY 172

OT Deuteronomy 23:1-25

Exclusion From the Assembly

23 No one who has been emasculated by
crushing or cutting may enter the assembly of the LORD.
2No one born of a forbidden marriage[a]
nor any of his descendants may enter the
assembly of the LORD, even down to the
tenth generation.
3No Ammonite or Moabite or any of
his descendants may enter the assembly
of the LORD, even down to the tenth generation. 4For they did not come to meet
you with bread and water on your way
when you came out of Egypt, and they
hired Balaam son of Beor from Pethor in
Aram Naharaim[b] to pronounce a curse on
you. 5However, the LORD your God would
not listen to Balaam but turned the curse
into a blessing for you, because the LORD
your God loves you. 6Do not seek a treaty
of friendship with them as long as you
live.
7Do not abhor an Edomite, for he is
your brother. Do not abhor an Egyptian,
because you lived as an alien in his country. 8The third generation of children born
to them may enter the assembly of the
LORD.

Uncleanness in the Camp

9When you are encamped against your
enemies, keep away from everything impure. 10If one of your men is unclean because of a nocturnal emission, he is to go
outside the camp and stay there. 11But as
evening approaches he is to wash himself,
and at sunset he may return to the camp.
12Designate a place outside the camp
where you can go to relieve yourself. 13As
part of your equipment have something
to dig with, and when you relieve yourself, dig a hole and cover up your excrement. 14For the LORD your God moves
about in your camp to protect you and to
deliver your enemies to you. Your camp
must be holy, so that he will not see
among you anything indecent and turn
away from you.

Miscellaneous Laws

15If a slave has taken refuge with you,
do not hand him over to his master. 16Let
him live among you wherever he likes and
in whatever town he chooses. Do not oppress him.
17No Israelite man or woman is to become a shrine prostitute. 18You must not
bring the earnings of a female prostitute
or of a male prostitute[c] into the house of
the LORD your God to pay any vow, be-

[a] *2* Or *one of illegitimate birth* [b] *4* That is, Northwest Mesopotamia [c] *18* Hebrew *of a dog*

cause the LORD your God detests them both.

[19]Do not charge your brother interest, whether on money or food or anything else that may earn interest. [20]You may charge a foreigner interest, but not a brother Israelite, so that the LORD your God may bless you in everything you put your hand to in the land you are entering to possess.

[21]If you make a vow to the LORD your God, do not be slow to pay it, for the LORD your God will certainly demand it of you and you will be guilty of sin. [22]But if you refrain from making a vow, you will not be guilty. [23]Whatever your lips utter you must be sure to do, because you made your vow freely to the LORD your God with your own mouth.

[24]If you enter your neighbor's vineyard, you may eat all the grapes you want, but do not put any in your basket. [25]If you enter your neighbor's grainfield, you may pick kernels with your hands, but you must not put a sickle to his standing grain.

PRAYER: PETITION

O LORD, may I be above reproach, temperate, sensible, respectable, hospitable, able to teach, not given to drunkenness, not violent but gentle, not quarrelsome, not a lover of money, one who manages my own family well, and who keeps my children under control with proper respect. Grant me a good reputation with outsiders, so that I will not fall into disgrace and the snare of the devil. (1 Timothy 3:2–4, 7)

__PAUSE__ here to petition God for growth in love and compassion toward others. Offer prayers for your loved ones, for those who do not know Jesus and for those in need. Offer prayers regarding your activities for this day and any special concerns you may have.

NT Galatians 4:8–31

Paul's Concern for the Galatians

[8]Formerly, when you did not know God, you were slaves to those who by nature are not gods. [9]But now that you know God—or rather are known by God—how is it that you are turning back to those weak and miserable principles? Do you wish to be enslaved by them all over again? [10]You are observing special days and months and seasons and years! [11]I fear for you, that somehow I have wasted my efforts on you.

[12]I plead with you, brothers, become like me, for I became like you. You have done me no wrong. [13]As you know, it was because of an illness that I first preached the gospel to you. [14]Even though my illness was a trial to you, you did not treat me with contempt or scorn. Instead, you welcomed me as if I were an angel of God, as if I were Christ Jesus himself. [15]What has happened to all your joy? I can testify that, if you could have done so, you would have torn out your eyes and given them to me. [16]Have I now become your enemy by telling you the truth?

[17]Those people are zealous to win you over, but for no good. What they want is to alienate you ⌞from us⌟, so that you may be zealous for them. [18]It is fine to be zealous, provided the purpose is good, and to be so always and not just when I am with you. [19]My dear children, for whom I am again in the pains of childbirth until Christ is formed in you, [20]how I wish I could be with you now and change my tone, because I am perplexed about you!

Hagar and Sarah

[21]Tell me, you who want to be under the law, are you not aware of what the law says? [22]For it is written that Abraham had two sons, one by the slave woman and the other by the free woman. [23]His son by the slave woman was born in the ordinary way; but his son by the free woman was born as the result of a promise.

[24]These things may be taken figuratively, for the women represent two cov-

enants. One covenant is from Mount Sinai and bears children who are to be
slaves: This is Hagar. 25Now Hagar stands
for Mount Sinai in Arabia and corre-
sponds to the present city of Jerusalem,
because she is in slavery with her children.
26But the Jerusalem that is above is free,
and she is our mother. 27For it is written:

"Be glad, O barren woman,
who bears no children;
break forth and cry aloud,
you who have no labor pains;
because more are the children of the
desolate woman
than of her who has a husband."[a]

28Now you, brothers, like Isaac, are children of promise. 29At that time the son
born in the ordinary way persecuted the
son born by the power of the Spirit. It is
the same now. 30But what does the Scripture say? "Get rid of the slave woman and
her son, for the slave woman's son will
never share in the inheritance with the
free woman's son."[b] 31Therefore, brothers,
we are not children of the slave woman,
but of the free woman.

[a] *27* Isaiah 54:1 [b] *30* Gen. 21:10

PRAYER: THE WORKS OF GOD

***A**N hour is coming, and now is, when the dead will hear Your voice, O Son of God, and those who hear will live. For as the Father has life in Himself, so He has granted You to have life in Yourself, and He has given You authority to execute judgment, because You are the Son of Man. (John 5:25–27) . . . We will all stand before Your judgment seat, O Lord. For You have said, "As I live, every knee will bow before Me, and every tongue will confess to God." So then, we will all give an account to You. (Romans 14:10–12)*

***TAKE** a moment to consider the greatness of God's wonderful works.*

YEAR 1
DAY 173

OT Deuteronomy 24:1–25:19

24 If a man marries a woman who becomes displeasing to him because he
finds something indecent about her, and
he writes her a certificate of divorce, gives
it to her and sends her from his house,
2and if after she leaves his house she becomes the wife of another man, 3and her
second husband dislikes her and writes
her a certificate of divorce, gives it to her
and sends her from his house, or if he dies,
4then her first husband, who divorced her,
is not allowed to marry her again after she
has been defiled. That would be detestable
in the eyes of the LORD. Do not bring sin
upon the land the LORD your God is giving you as an inheritance.

5If a man has recently married, he must
not be sent to war or have any other duty
laid on him. For one year he is to be free
to stay at home and bring happiness to
the wife he has married.

6Do not take a pair of millstones—not
even the upper one—as security for a
debt, because that would be taking a
man's livelihood as security.

7If a man is caught kidnapping one of
his brother Israelites and treats him as a
slave or sells him, the kidnapper must die.
You must purge the evil from among you.

8In cases of leprous[a] diseases be very
careful to do exactly as the priests, who
are Levites, instruct you. You must follow
carefully what I have commanded them.
9Remember what the LORD your God did
to Miriam along the way after you came
out of Egypt.

10When you make a loan of any kind to
your neighbor, do not go into his house to
get what he is offering as a pledge. 11Stay
outside and let the man to whom you are
making the loan bring the pledge out to
you. 12If the man is poor, do not go to
sleep with his pledge in your possession.
13Return his cloak to him by sunset so that

[a] *8* The Hebrew word was used for various diseases affecting the skin—not necessarily leprosy.

he may sleep in it. Then he will thank you, and it will be regarded as a righteous act in the sight of the LORD your God.

[14]Do not take advantage of a hired man who is poor and needy, whether he is a brother Israelite or an alien living in one of your towns. [15]Pay him his wages each day before sunset, because he is poor and is counting on it. Otherwise he may cry to the LORD against you, and you will be guilty of sin.

[16]Fathers shall not be put to death for their children, nor children put to death for their fathers; each is to die for his own sin.

[17]Do not deprive the alien or the fatherless of justice, or take the cloak of the widow as a pledge. [18]Remember that you were slaves in Egypt and the LORD your God redeemed you from there. That is why I command you to do this.

[19]When you are harvesting in your field and you overlook a sheaf, do not go back to get it. Leave it for the alien, the fatherless and the widow, so that the LORD your God may bless you in all the work of your hands. [20]When you beat the olives from your trees, do not go over the branches a second time. Leave what remains for the alien, the fatherless and the widow. [21]When you harvest the grapes in your vineyard, do not go over the vines again. Leave what remains for the alien, the fatherless and the widow. [22]Remember that you were slaves in Egypt. That is why I command you to do this.

25 When men have a dispute, they are to take it to court and the judges will decide the case, acquitting the innocent and condemning the guilty. [2]If the guilty man deserves to be beaten, the judge shall make him lie down and have him flogged in his presence with the number of lashes his crime deserves, [3]but he must not give him more than forty lashes. If he is flogged more than that, your brother will be degraded in your eyes.

[4]Do not muzzle an ox while it is treading out the grain.

[5]If brothers are living together and one of them dies without a son, his widow must not marry outside the family. Her husband's brother shall take her and marry her and fulfill the duty of a brother-in-law to her. [6]The first son she bears shall carry on the name of the dead brother so that his name will not be blotted out from Israel.

[7]However, if a man does not want to marry his brother's wife, she shall go to the elders at the town gate and say, "My husband's brother refuses to carry on his brother's name in Israel. He will not fulfill the duty of a brother-in-law to me." [8]Then the elders of his town shall summon him and talk to him. If he persists in saying, "I do not want to marry her," [9]his brother's widow shall go up to him in the presence of the elders, take off one of his sandals, spit in his face and say, "This is what is done to the man who will not build up his brother's family line." [10]That man's line shall be known in Israel as The Family of the Unsandaled.

[11]If two men are fighting and the wife of one of them comes to rescue her husband from his assailant, and she reaches out and seizes him by his private parts, [12]you shall cut off her hand. Show her no pity.

[13]Do not have two differing weights in your bag—one heavy, one light. [14]Do not have two differing measures in your house—one large, one small. [15]You must have accurate and honest weights and measures, so that you may live long in the land the LORD your God is giving you. [16]For the LORD your God detests anyone who does these things, anyone who deals dishonestly.

[17]Remember what the Amalekites did to you along the way when you came out of Egypt. [18]When you were weary and worn out, they met you on your journey and cut off all who were lagging behind; they had no fear of God. [19]When the LORD your God gives you rest from all the enemies around you in the land he is giving you to possess as an inheritance, you shall blot out the memory of Amalek from under heaven. Do not forget!

PRAYER: INTERCESSION

BECAUSE I know what it means to fear You, Lord, may I seek to persuade other people. (2 Corinthians 5:11)

***TAKE** a few moments to intercede on behalf of friends, relatives, neighbors and coworkers who do not yet know salvation in Jesus Christ.*

NT Galatians 5:1–26

Freedom in Christ

5 It is for freedom that Christ has set us free. Stand firm, then, and do not let yourselves be burdened again by a yoke of slavery.

2 Mark my words! I, Paul, tell you that if you let yourselves be circumcised, Christ will be of no value to you at all. 3 Again I declare to every man who lets himself be circumcised that he is obligated to obey the whole law. 4 You who are trying to be justified by law have been alienated from Christ; you have fallen away from grace. 5 But by faith we eagerly await through the Spirit the righteousness for which we hope. 6 For in Christ Jesus neither circumcision nor uncircumcision has any value. The only thing that counts is faith expressing itself through love.

7 You were running a good race. Who cut in on you and kept you from obeying the truth? 8 That kind of persuasion does not come from the one who calls you. 9 "A little yeast works through the whole batch of dough." 10 I am confident in the Lord that you will take no other view. The one who is throwing you into confusion will pay the penalty, whoever he may be. 11 Brothers, if I am still preaching circumcision, why am I still being persecuted? In that case the offense of the cross has been abolished. 12 As for those agitators, I wish they would go the whole way and emasculate themselves!

13 You, my brothers, were called to be free. But do not use your freedom to indulge the sinful nature[a]; rather, serve one another in love. 14 The entire law is summed up in a single command: "Love your neighbor as yourself."[b] 15 If you keep on biting and devouring each other, watch out or you will be destroyed by each other.

Life by the Spirit

16 So I say, live by the Spirit, and you will not gratify the desires of the sinful nature. 17 For the sinful nature desires what is contrary to the Spirit, and the Spirit what is contrary to the sinful nature. They are in conflict with each other, so that you do not do what you want. 18 But if you are led by the Spirit, you are not under law.

19 The acts of the sinful nature are obvious: sexual immorality, impurity and debauchery; 20 idolatry and witchcraft; hatred, discord, jealousy, fits of rage, selfish ambition, dissensions, factions 21 and envy; drunkenness, orgies, and the like. I warn you, as I did before, that those who live like this will not inherit the kingdom of God.

22 But the fruit of the Spirit is love, joy, peace, patience, kindness, goodness, faithfulness, 23 gentleness and self-control. Against such things there is no law. 24 Those who belong to Christ Jesus have crucified the sinful nature with its passions and desires. 25 Since we live by the Spirit, let us keep in step with the Spirit. 26 Let us not become conceited, provoking and envying each other.

[a] *13* Or *the flesh;* also in verses 16, 17, 19 and 24
[b] *14* Lev. 19:18

PRAYER: MY RELATIONSHIP TO GOD

THERE is now no condemnation for those who are in You, Christ Jesus, because the law of the Spirit of life in You has set us free from the law of sin and death. I did not receive a spirit of slavery again to fear, but I received Your Spirit of adoption by whom I cry, "Abba, Father." The Spirit Himself testifies with my spirit that I am Your child, O God. (Romans 8:1–2, 15–16)

PAUSE *to thank God for the relationship that you enjoy with Him in Jesus Christ.*

YEAR 1
DAY 174

OT Deuteronomy 26:1–27:26

Firstfruits and Tithes

26 When you have entered the land the
LORD your God is giving you as an inheritance and have taken possession of it
and settled in it, [2]take some of the firstfruits of all that you produce from the soil
of the land the LORD your God is giving
you and put them in a basket. Then go to
the place the LORD your God will choose
as a dwelling for his Name [3]and say to the
priest in office at the time, "I declare today
to the LORD your God that I have come to
the land the LORD swore to our forefathers
to give us." [4]The priest shall take the basket from your hands and set it down in
front of the altar of the LORD your God.
[5]Then you shall declare before the LORD
your God: "My father was a wandering Aramean, and he went down into Egypt with
a few people and lived there and became
a great nation, powerful and numerous.
[6]But the Egyptians mistreated us and made
us suffer, putting us to hard labor. [7]Then
we cried out to the LORD, the God of our
fathers, and the LORD heard our voice and
saw our misery, toil and oppression. [8]So
the LORD brought us out of Egypt with a
mighty hand and an outstretched arm,
with great terror and with miraculous
signs and wonders. [9]He brought us to this
place and gave us this land, a land flowing
with milk and honey; [10]and now I bring
the firstfruits of the soil that you, O LORD,
have given me." Place the basket before
the LORD your God and bow down before
him. [11]And you and the Levites and the
aliens among you shall rejoice in all the
good things the LORD your God has given
to you and your household.

[12]When you have finished setting aside
a tenth of all your produce in the third
year, the year of the tithe, you shall give it
to the Levite, the alien, the fatherless and
the widow, so that they may eat in your
towns and be satisfied. [13]Then say to the
LORD your God: "I have removed from my
house the sacred portion and have given
it to the Levite, the alien, the fatherless
and the widow, according to all you commanded. I have not turned aside from
your commands nor have I forgotten any
of them. [14]I have not eaten any of the sacred portion while I was in mourning, nor
have I removed any of it while I was unclean, nor have I offered any of it to the
dead. I have obeyed the LORD my God; I
have done everything you commanded
me. [15]Look down from heaven, your holy
dwelling place, and bless your people Israel and the land you have given us as you
promised on oath to our forefathers, a
land flowing with milk and honey."

Follow the LORD's Commands

[16]The LORD your God commands you
this day to follow these decrees and laws;
carefully observe them with all your heart
and with all your soul. [17]You have declared this day that the LORD is your God
and that you will walk in his ways, that
you will keep his decrees, commands and
laws, and that you will obey him. [18]And
the LORD has declared this day that you
are his people, his treasured possession as
he promised, and that you are to keep all
his commands. [19]He has declared that he
will set you in praise, fame and honor
high above all the nations he has made
and that you will be a people holy to the
LORD your God, as he promised.

The Altar on Mount Ebal

27 Moses and the elders of Israel commanded the people: "Keep all these
commands that I give you today. [2]When
you have crossed the Jordan into the land
the LORD your God is giving you, set up
some large stones and coat them with
plaster. [3]Write on them all the words of
this law when you have crossed over to
enter the land the LORD your God is giving you, a land flowing with milk and
honey, just as the LORD, the God of your
fathers, promised you. [4]And when you
have crossed the Jordan, set up these
stones on Mount Ebal, as I command you
today, and coat them with plaster. [5]Build
there an altar to the LORD your God, an altar of stones. Do not use any iron tool
upon them. [6]Build the altar of the LORD
your God with fieldstones and offer burnt
offerings on it to the LORD your God. [7]Sac-
rifice fellowship offerings[a] there, eating
them and rejoicing in the presence of the

[a] 7 Traditionally *peace offerings*

LORD your God. [8]And you shall write very
clearly all the words of this law on these
stones you have set up."

Curses From Mount Ebal

[9]Then Moses and the priests, who are
Levites, said to all Israel, "Be silent, O Israel, and listen! You have now become the
people of the LORD your God. [10]Obey the
LORD your God and follow his commands
and decrees that I give you today."
[11]On the same day Moses commanded
the people:
[12]When you have crossed the Jordan,
these tribes shall stand on Mount Gerizim
to bless the people: Simeon, Levi, Judah,
Issachar, Joseph and Benjamin. [13]And
these tribes shall stand on Mount Ebal to
pronounce curses: Reuben, Gad, Asher,
Zebulun, Dan and Naphtali.
[14]The Levites shall recite to all the people of Israel in a loud voice:

[15]"Cursed is the man who carves an image or casts an idol—a thing detestable to the LORD, the work of the craftsman's hands—and sets it up in secret."

Then all the people shall say, "Amen!"

[16]"Cursed is the man who dishonors his father or his mother."

Then all the people shall say, "Amen!"

[17]"Cursed is the man who moves his neighbor's boundary stone."

Then all the people shall say, "Amen!"

[18]"Cursed is the man who leads the blind astray on the road."

Then all the people shall say, "Amen!"

[19]"Cursed is the man who withholds justice from the alien, the fatherless or the widow."

Then all the people shall say, "Amen!"

[20]"Cursed is the man who sleeps with his father's wife, for he dishonors his father's bed."

Then all the people shall say, "Amen!"

[21]"Cursed is the man who has sexual relations with any animal."

Then all the people shall say, "Amen!"

[22]"Cursed is the man who sleeps with his sister, the daughter of his father or the daughter of his mother."

Then all the people shall say, "Amen!"

[23]"Cursed is the man who sleeps with his mother-in-law."

Then all the people shall say, "Amen!"

[24]"Cursed is the man who kills his neighbor secretly."

Then all the people shall say, "Amen!"

[25]"Cursed is the man who accepts a bribe to kill an innocent person."

Then all the people shall say, "Amen!"

[26]"Cursed is the man who does not uphold the words of this law by carrying them out."

Then all the people shall say, "Amen!"

PRAYER: AFFIRMATION

LORD, who may dwell in Your tabernacle? Who may live on Your holy mountain? Those who walk uprightly and work righteousness and speak the truth in their hearts; they neither slander with their tongues nor do evil to their neighbors nor take up a reproach against their friends; they despise the reprobate but honor those who fear You. They keep their oath even when it hurts, lend their money without interest, and do not accept bribes against the innocent. Those who do these things will never be shaken. (Psalm 15:1–5)

PAUSE *to reflect on these Biblical affirmations.*

NT Galatians 6:1–18

Doing Good to All

6 Brothers, if someone is caught in a sin,
you who are spiritual should restore
him gently. But watch yourself, or you
also may be tempted. 2Carry each other's
burdens, and in this way you will fulfill
the law of Christ. 3If anyone thinks he is
something when he is nothing, he deceives himself. 4Each one should test his
own actions. Then he can take pride in
himself, without comparing himself to
somebody else, 5for each one should carry his own load.
6Anyone who receives instruction in the
word must share all good things with his
instructor.
7Do not be deceived: God cannot be
mocked. A man reaps what he sows. 8The
one who sows to please his sinful nature,
from that nature[a] will reap destruction;
the one who sows to please the Spirit,
from the Spirit will reap eternal life. 9Let
us not become weary in doing good, for
at the proper time we will reap a harvest
if we do not give up. 10Therefore, as we
have opportunity, let us do good to all
people, especially to those who belong to
the family of believers.

Not Circumcision but a New Creation

11See what large letters I use as I write to
you with my own hand!
12Those who want to make a good im-
pression outwardly are trying to compel
you to be circumcised. The only reason
they do this is to avoid being persecuted
for the cross of Christ. 13Not even those
who are circumcised obey the law, yet they
want you to be circumcised that they may
boast about your flesh. 14May I never boast
except in the cross of our Lord Jesus Christ,
through which[b] the world has been crucified to me, and I to the world. 15Neither
circumcision nor uncircumcision means
anything; what counts is a new creation.
16Peace and mercy to all who follow this
rule, even to the Israel of God.
17Finally, let no one cause me trouble,
for I bear on my body the marks of Jesus.
18The grace of our Lord Jesus Christ be
with your spirit, brothers. Amen.

[a] 8 Or *his flesh, from the flesh* [b] 14 Or *whom*

PRAYER: THE CHARACTER I WANT TO CULTIVATE

A TALEBEARER reveals secrets, but the person who is trustworthy conceals a matter. (Proverbs 11:13) . . . These are the things I shall do: speak the truth to others, judge with truth and justice for peace. I shall not plot evil against my neighbor and not love a false oath; for these things You hate, O Lord. (Zechariah 8:16–17)

***TAKE** a moment to ask the Lord for the grace to grow in godly character.*

YEAR 1 DAY 175

OT Psalm 35

Psalm 35

Of David.

1Contend, O LORD, with those who
contend with me;
fight against those who fight against
me.
2Take up shield and buckler;
arise and come to my aid.
3Brandish spear and javelin[a]
against those who pursue me.
Say to my soul,
"I am your salvation."

4May those who seek my life
be disgraced and put to shame;
may those who plot my ruin
be turned back in dismay.
5May they be like chaff before the
wind,

[a] 3 Or *and block the way*

with the angel of the LORD driving
them away;
6 may their path be dark and slippery,
with the angel of the LORD pursuing
them.
7 Since they hid their net for me
without cause
and without cause dug a pit for me,
8 may ruin overtake them by surprise—
may the net they hid entangle them,
may they fall into the pit, to their
ruin.
9 Then my soul will rejoice in the LORD
and delight in his salvation.
10 My whole being will exclaim,
"Who is like you, O LORD?
You rescue the poor from those too
strong for them,
the poor and needy from those who
rob them."

11 Ruthless witnesses come forward;
they question me on things I know
nothing about.
12 They repay me evil for good
and leave my soul forlorn.
13 Yet when they were ill, I put on
sackcloth
and humbled myself with fasting.
When my prayers returned to me
unanswered,
14 I went about mourning
as though for my friend or brother.
I bowed my head in grief
as though weeping for my mother.
15 But when I stumbled, they gathered in
glee;
attackers gathered against me when
I was unaware.
They slandered me without ceasing.
16 Like the ungodly they maliciously
mocked[b];
they gnashed their teeth at me.
17 O Lord, how long will you look on?
Rescue my life from their ravages,
my precious life from these lions.
18 I will give you thanks in the great
assembly;
among throngs of people I will
praise you.

19 Let not those gloat over me
who are my enemies without cause;
let not those who hate me without
reason
maliciously wink the eye.
20 They do not speak peaceably,
but devise false accusations
against those who live quietly in the
land.
21 They gape at me and say, "Aha! Aha!
With our own eyes we have seen it."

22 O LORD, you have seen this; be not
silent.
Do not be far from me, O Lord.
23 Awake, and rise to my defense!
Contend for me, my God and Lord.
24 Vindicate me in your righteousness,
O LORD my God;
do not let them gloat over me.
25 Do not let them think, "Aha, just what
we wanted!"
or say, "We have swallowed him
up."

26 May all who gloat over my distress
be put to shame and confusion;
may all who exalt themselves over me
be clothed with shame and disgrace.
27 May those who delight in my
vindication
shout for joy and gladness;
may they always say, "The LORD be
exalted,
who delights in the well-being of
his servant."
28 My tongue will speak of your
righteousness
and of your praises all day long.

[b] 16 Septuagint; Hebrew may mean *ungodly circle of mockers.*

PRAYER: THANKSGIVING

O GOD, You completed the heavens and the earth in all their vast array. By the seventh day You finished the work that You had done, and rested on the seventh day from all Your creative work. Lord God, You formed a man from the dust of the ground and breathed into his nostrils the breath of life; and he became a living being. (Genesis 2:1–2, 7)

PAUSE *to offer your own expressions of thanksgiving.*

NT Ephesians 1:1-14

1 Paul, an apostle of Christ Jesus by the will of God,

To the saints in Ephesus,[a] the faithful[b] in Christ Jesus:

2 Grace and peace to you from God our Father and the Lord Jesus Christ.

Spiritual Blessings in Christ

3 Praise be to the God and Father of our Lord Jesus Christ, who has blessed us in the heavenly realms with every spiritual blessing in Christ. 4 For he chose us in him before the creation of the world to be holy and blameless in his sight. In love 5 he[c] predestined us to be adopted as his sons through Jesus Christ, in accordance with his pleasure and will— 6 to the praise of his glorious grace, which he has freely given us in the One he loves. 7 In him we have redemption through his blood, the forgiveness of sins, in accordance with the riches of God's grace 8 that he lavished on us with all wisdom and understanding. 9 And he[d] made known to us the mystery of his will according to his good pleasure, which he purposed in Christ, 10 to be put into effect when the times will have reached their fulfillment—to bring all things in heaven and on earth together under one head, even Christ.

11 In him we were also chosen,[e] having been predestined according to the plan of him who works out everything in conformity with the purpose of his will, 12 in order that we, who were the first to hope in Christ, might be for the praise of his glory. 13 And you also were included in Christ when you heard the word of truth, the gospel of your salvation. Having believed, you were marked in him with a seal, the promised Holy Spirit, 14 who is a deposit guaranteeing our inheritance until the redemption of those who are God's possession—to the praise of his glory.

[a] 1 Some early manuscripts do not have *in Ephesus.*
[b] 1 Or *believers who are*
[c] 4,5 Or *sight in love.* [5]*He*
[d] 8,9 Or *us. With all wisdom and understanding,* [9]*he*
[e] 11 Or *were made heirs*

PRAYER: MY RELATIONSHIP TO OTHERS

YOU have called us to go and make disciples of all nations, baptizing them in the name of the Father and of You, the Son, and of the Holy Spirit, teaching them to observe everything You have commanded us. And surely You are with us always, even to the end of the age.

(Matthew 28:19–20)

***PAUSE** to review your relationships with others and to commit them to the Lord.*

OT Deuteronomy 28:1-68

YEAR 1 DAY 176

Blessings for Obedience

28 If you fully obey the LORD your God and carefully follow all his commands I give you today, the LORD your God will set you high above all the nations on earth. 2 All these blessings will come upon you and accompany you if you obey the LORD your God:

3 You will be blessed in the city and blessed in the country.

4 The fruit of your womb will be blessed, and the crops of your land and the young of your livestock—the calves of your herds and the lambs of your flocks.

5 Your basket and your kneading trough will be blessed.

6 You will be blessed when you come in and blessed when you go out.

7 The LORD will grant that the enemies

who rise up against you will be defeated
before you. They will come at you from
one direction but flee from you in seven.
8The LORD will send a blessing on your
barns and on everything you put your
hand to. The LORD your God will bless
you in the land he is giving you.
9The LORD will establish you as his holy
people, as he promised you on oath, if
you keep the commands of the LORD your
God and walk in his ways. 10Then all the
peoples on earth will see that you are
called by the name of the LORD, and they
will fear you. 11The LORD will grant you
abundant prosperity—in the fruit of your
womb, the young of your livestock and
the crops of your ground—in the land he
swore to your forefathers to give you.
12The LORD will open the heavens, the
storehouse of his bounty, to send rain on
your land in season and to bless all the
work of your hands. You will lend to many
nations but will borrow from none. 13The
LORD will make you the head, not the tail.
If you pay attention to the commands of
the LORD your God that I give you this day
and carefully follow them, you will always
be at the top, never at the bottom. 14Do
not turn aside from any of the commands
I give you today, to the right or to the left,
following other gods and serving them.

Curses for Disobedience

15However, if you do not obey the LORD
your God and do not carefully follow all
his commands and decrees I am giving
you today, all these curses will come upon
you and overtake you:

16You will be cursed in the city and
cursed in the country.
17Your basket and your kneading
trough will be cursed.
18The fruit of your womb will be
cursed, and the crops of your land,
and the calves of your herds and the
lambs of your flocks.
19You will be cursed when you
come in and cursed when you go out.

20The LORD will send on you curses, confusion and rebuke in everything you put
your hand to, until you are destroyed and
come to sudden ruin because of the evil
you have done in forsaking him.[a] 21The
LORD will plague you with diseases until
he has destroyed you from the land you
are entering to possess. 22The LORD will
strike you with wasting disease, with fever
and inflammation, with scorching heat
and drought, with blight and mildew,
which will plague you until you perish.
23The sky over your head will be bronze,
the ground beneath you iron. 24The LORD
will turn the rain of your country into dust
and powder; it will come down from the
skies until you are destroyed.
25The LORD will cause you to be defeated before your enemies. You will come at
them from one direction but flee from
them in seven, and you will become a
thing of horror to all the kingdoms on
earth. 26Your carcasses will be food for all
the birds of the air and the beasts of the
earth, and there will be no one to fright-
en them away. 27The LORD will afflict you
with the boils of Egypt and with tumors,
festering sores and the itch, from which
you cannot be cured. 28The LORD will afflict you with madness, blindness and
confusion of mind. 29At midday you will
grope about like a blind man in the dark.
You will be unsuccessful in everything you
do; day after day you will be oppressed
and robbed, with no one to rescue you.
30You will be pledged to be married to a
woman, but another will take her and rav-
ish her. You will build a house, but you
will not live in it. You will plant a vineyard, but you will not even begin to enjoy
its fruit. 31Your ox will be slaughtered before your eyes, but you will eat none of it.
Your donkey will be forcibly taken from
you and will not be returned. Your sheep
will be given to your enemies, and no one
will rescue them. 32Your sons and daughters will be given to another nation, and
you will wear out your eyes watching for
them day after day, powerless to lift a
hand. 33A people that you do not know
will eat what your land and labor produce,
and you will have nothing but cruel oppression all your days. 34The sights you see
will drive you mad. 35The LORD will afflict
your knees and legs with painful boils that
cannot be cured, spreading from the soles
of your feet to the top of your head.
36The LORD will drive you and the king
you set over you to a nation unknown to
you or your fathers. There you will worship other gods, gods of wood and stone.
37You will become a thing of horror and

[a] 20 Hebrew *me*

an object of scorn and ridicule to all the
nations where the LORD will drive you.
38You will sow much seed in the field
but you will harvest little, because locusts
will devour it. 39You will plant vineyards
and cultivate them but you will not drink
the wine or gather the grapes, because
worms will eat them. 40You will have olive trees throughout your country but you
will not use the oil, because the olives will
drop off. 41You will have sons and daughters but you will not keep them, because
they will go into captivity. 42Swarms of locusts will take over all your trees and the
crops of your land.
43The alien who lives among you will
rise above you higher and higher, but you
will sink lower and lower. 44He will lend
to you, but you will not lend to him. He
will be the head, but you will be the tail.
45All these curses will come upon you.
They will pursue you and overtake you
until you are destroyed, because you did
not obey the LORD your God and observe
the commands and decrees he gave you.
46They will be a sign and a wonder to you
and your descendants forever. 47Because
you did not serve the LORD your God joyfully and gladly in the time of prosperity,
48therefore in hunger and thirst, in nakedness and dire poverty, you will serve the
enemies the LORD sends against you. He
will put an iron yoke on your neck until
he has destroyed you.
49The LORD will bring a nation against
you from far away, from the ends of the
earth, like an eagle swooping down, a nation whose language you will not understand, 50a fierce-looking nation without respect for the old or pity for the young.
51They will devour the young of your livestock and the crops of your land until you
are destroyed. They will leave you no grain,
new wine or oil, nor any calves of your
herds or lambs of your flocks until you are
ruined. 52They will lay siege to all the cities
throughout your land until the high fortified walls in which you trust fall down.
They will besiege all the cities throughout
the land the LORD your God is giving you.
53Because of the suffering that your enemy will inflict on you during the siege,
you will eat the fruit of the womb, the
flesh of the sons and daughters the LORD
your God has given you. 54Even the most
gentle and sensitive man among you will
have no compassion on his own brother
or the wife he loves or his surviving children, 55and he will not give to one of them
any of the flesh of his children that he is
eating. It will be all he has left because of
the suffering your enemy will inflict on
you during the siege of all your cities.
56The most gentle and sensitive woman
among you—so sensitive and gentle that
she would not venture to touch the
ground with the sole of her foot—will be-
grudge the husband she loves and her own
son or daughter 57the afterbirth from her
womb and the children she bears. For she
intends to eat them secretly during the
siege and in the distress that your enemy
will inflict on you in your cities.
58If you do not carefully follow all the
words of this law, which are written in this
book, and do not revere this glorious and
awesome name—the LORD your God—
59the LORD will send fearful plagues on you
and your descendants, harsh and prolonged disasters, and severe and lingering
illnesses. 60He will bring upon you all the
diseases of Egypt that you dreaded, and
they will cling to you. 61The LORD will also
bring on you every kind of sickness and disaster not recorded in this Book of the Law,
until you are destroyed. 62You who were as
numerous as the stars in the sky will be left
but few in number, because you did not
obey the LORD your God. 63Just as it pleased
the LORD to make you prosper and increase
in number, so it will please him to ruin
and destroy you. You will be uprooted
from the land you are entering to possess.
64Then the LORD will scatter you among
all nations, from one end of the earth to the
other. There you will worship other gods—
gods of wood and stone, which neither you
nor your fathers have known. 65Among
those nations you will find no repose, no
resting place for the sole of your foot. There
the LORD will give you an anxious mind,
eyes weary with longing, and a despairing
heart. 66You will live in constant suspense,
filled with dread both night and day, never
sure of your life. 67In the morning you will
say, "If only it were evening!" and in the
evening, "If only it were morning!"—because of the terror that will fill your hearts
and the sights that your eyes will see. 68The
LORD will send you back in ships to Egypt
on a journey I said you should never make
again. There you will offer yourselves for
sale to your enemies as male and female
slaves, but no one will buy you.

PRAYER: ADORATION

YOU are the living God, and there is no god besides You. You put to death and You bring to life, You have wounded and You will heal, and no one can deliver from Your hand. (Deuteronomy 32:39) . . . I will remember the former things, those of long ago; You are God, and there is no other; You are God, and there is none like You. (Isaiah 46:9)

PAUSE *to express your thoughts of praise and worship.*

NT Ephesians 1:15–2:10

Thanksgiving and Prayer

15For this reason, ever since I heard about your faith in the Lord Jesus and your love for all the saints, 16I have not stopped giving thanks for you, remembering you in my prayers. 17I keep asking that the God of our Lord Jesus Christ, the glorious Father, may give you the Spirit[a] of wisdom and revelation, so that you may know him better. 18I pray also that the eyes of your heart may be enlightened in order that you may know the hope to which he has called you, the riches of his glorious inheritance in the saints, 19and his incomparably great power for us who believe. That power is like the working of his mighty strength, 20which he exerted in Christ when he raised him from the dead and seated him at his right hand in the heavenly realms, 21far above all rule and authority, power and dominion, and every title that can be given, not only in the present age but also in the one to come. 22And God placed all things under his feet and appointed him to be head over everything for the church, 23which is his body, the fullness of him who fills everything in every way.

Made Alive in Christ

2 As for you, you were dead in your transgressions and sins, 2in which you used to live when you followed the ways of this world and of the ruler of the kingdom of the air, the spirit who is now at work in those who are disobedient. 3All of us also lived among them at one time, gratifying the cravings of our sinful nature[b] and following its desires and thoughts. Like the rest, we were by nature objects of wrath. 4But because of his great love for us, God, who is rich in mercy, 5made us alive with Christ even when we were dead in transgressions—it is by grace you have been saved. 6And God raised us up with Christ and seated us with him in the heavenly realms in Christ Jesus, 7in order that in the coming ages he might show the incomparable riches of his grace, expressed in his kindness to us in Christ Jesus. 8For it is by grace you have been saved, through faith—and this not from yourselves, it is the gift of God— 9not by works, so that no one can boast. 10For we are God's workmanship, created in Christ Jesus to do good works, which God prepared in advance for us to do.

[a] 17 Or *a spirit* [b] 3 Or *our flesh*

PRAYER: THE ATTRIBUTES OF GOD

I WILL give thanks to You, Lord, for You are good; Your love endures forever. (1 Chronicles 16:34) . . . Loving-kindness and truth meet together; righteousness and peace kiss each other. Truth springs forth from the earth, and righteousness looks down from heaven. (Psalm 85:10–11)

PAUSE *to reflect on these affirmations about the person, powers and perfection of God.*

OT **Deuteronomy 29:1–29**

YEAR 1
DAY 177

Renewal of the Covenant

29 These are the terms of the covenant
the LORD commanded Moses to make
with the Israelites in Moab, in addition to
the covenant he had made with them at
Horeb.
2Moses summoned all the Israelites and
said to them:

Your eyes have seen all that the LORD did
in Egypt to Pharaoh, to all his officials and
to all his land. 3With your own eyes you
saw those great trials, those miraculous
signs and great wonders. 4But to this day
the LORD has not given you a mind that understands or eyes that see or ears that hear.
5During the forty years that I led you
through the desert, your clothes did not
wear out, nor did the sandals on your feet.
6You ate no bread and drank no wine or
other fermented drink. I did this so that you
might know that I am the LORD your God.
7When you reached this place, Sihon
king of Heshbon and Og king of Bashan
came out to fight against us, but we defeated them. 8We took their land and gave
it as an inheritance to the Reubenites, the
Gadites and the half-tribe of Manasseh.
9Carefully follow the terms of this covenant, so that you may prosper in everything you do. 10All of you are standing today in the presence of the LORD your
God—your leaders and chief men, your
elders and officials, and all the other men
of Israel, 11together with your children and
your wives, and the aliens living in your
camps who chop your wood and carry
your water. 12You are standing here in order to enter into a covenant with the LORD
your God, a covenant the LORD is making
with you this day and sealing with an
oath, 13to confirm you this day as his people, that he may be your God as he promised you and as he swore to your fathers,
Abraham, Isaac and Jacob. 14I am making
this covenant, with its oath, not only with
you 15who are standing here with us today
in the presence of the LORD our God but
also with those who are not here today.
16You yourselves know how we lived in
Egypt and how we passed through the
countries on the way here. 17You saw
among them their detestable images and
idols of wood and stone, of silver and
gold. 18Make sure there is no man or
woman, clan or tribe among you today
whose heart turns away from the LORD our
God to go and worship the gods of those
nations; make sure there is no root among
you that produces such bitter poison.
19When such a person hears the words of
this oath, he invokes a blessing on himself
and therefore thinks, "I will be safe, even
though I persist in going my own way."
This will bring disaster on the watered land
as well as the dry.[a] 20The LORD will never be
willing to forgive him; his wrath and zeal
will burn against that man. All the curses
written in this book will fall upon him,
and the LORD will blot out his name from
under heaven. 21The LORD will single him
out from all the tribes of Israel for disaster,
according to all the curses of the covenant
written in this Book of the Law.
22Your children who follow you in later generations and foreigners who come
from distant lands will see the calamities
that have fallen on the land and the diseases with which the LORD has afflicted it.
23The whole land will be a burning waste
of salt and sulfur—nothing planted, nothing sprouting, no vegetation growing on
it. It will be like the destruction of Sodom
and Gomorrah, Admah and Zeboiim,
which the LORD overthrew in fierce anger.
24All the nations will ask: "Why has the
LORD done this to this land? Why this
fierce, burning anger?"
25And the answer will be: "It is because
this people abandoned the covenant of the
LORD, the God of their fathers, the covenant
he made with them when he brought them
out of Egypt. 26They went off and worshiped
other gods and bowed down to them, gods
they did not know, gods he had not given
them. 27Therefore the LORD's anger burned
against this land, so that he brought on it
all the curses written in this book. 28In furious anger and in great wrath the LORD uprooted them from their land and thrust
them into another land, as it is now."
29The secret things belong to the LORD
our God, but the things revealed belong
to us and to our children forever, that we
may follow all the words of this law.

[a] 19 Or *way, in order to add drunkenness to thirst."*

PRAYER: CONFESSION

WHEN I sin against You, Lord, I may be sure that my sin will find me out. (Numbers 32:23)

***ASK** the Spirit to search your heart and reveal any areas of unconfessed sin. Acknowledge these to the Lord and thank Him for His forgiveness.*

NT Ephesians 2:11–22

One in Christ

11 Therefore, remember that formerly
you who are Gentiles by birth and called
"uncircumcised" by those who call themselves "the circumcision" (that done in
the body by the hands of men)— 12 remember that at that time you were separate from Christ, excluded from citizenship in Israel and foreigners to the
covenants of the promise, without hope
and without God in the world. 13 But now
in Christ Jesus you who once were far
away have been brought near through the
blood of Christ.
14 For he himself is our peace, who has
made the two one and has destroyed the
barrier, the dividing wall of hostility, 15 by
abolishing in his flesh the law with its
commandments and regulations. His purpose was to create in himself one new
man out of the two, thus making peace,
16 and in this one body to reconcile both
of them to God through the cross, by
which he put to death their hostility. 17 He
came and preached peace to you who
were far away and peace to those who
were near. 18 For through him we both
have access to the Father by one Spirit.
19 Consequently, you are no longer foreigners and aliens, but fellow citizens
with God's people and members of God's
household, 20 built on the foundation of
the apostles and prophets, with Christ
Jesus himself as the chief cornerstone. 21 In
him the whole building is joined together and rises to become a holy temple in
the Lord. 22 And in him you too are being
built together to become a dwelling in
which God lives by his Spirit.

PRAYER: THE WORKS OF GOD

YOU Jesus, the Son of Man, came to seek and to save that which was lost. (Luke 19:10) . . . You, O Son of Man, did not come to be served, but to serve, and to give Your life as a ransom for many. (Mark 10:45)

***TAKE** a moment to consider the greatness of God's wonderful works.*

OT Deuteronomy 30:1–20

YEAR 1 DAY 178

Prosperity After Turning to the LORD

30 When all these blessings and curses I
have set before you come upon you
and you take them to heart wherever the
LORD your God disperses you among the
nations, 2 and when you and your children
return to the LORD your God and obey
him with all your heart and with all your
soul according to everything I command
you today, 3 then the LORD your God will
restore your fortunes[a] and have compassion on you and gather you again from all
the nations where he scattered you. 4 Even
if you have been banished to the most distant land under the heavens, from there
the LORD your God will gather you and
bring you back. 5 He will bring you to the
land that belonged to your fathers, and
you will take possession of it. He will

[a] 3 Or *will bring you back from captivity*

make you more prosperous and numerous than your fathers. 6The LORD your God will circumcise your hearts and the hearts of your descendants, so that you may love him with all your heart and with all your soul, and live. 7The LORD your God will put all these curses on your enemies who hate and persecute you. 8You will again obey the LORD and follow all his commands I am giving you today. 9Then the LORD your God will make you most prosperous in all the work of your hands and in the fruit of your womb, the young of your livestock and the crops of your land. The LORD will again delight in you and make you prosperous, just as he delighted in your fathers, 10if you obey the LORD your God and keep his commands and decrees that are written in this Book of the Law and turn to the LORD your God with all your heart and with all your soul.

The Offer of Life or Death

11Now what I am commanding you today is not too difficult for you or beyond your reach. 12It is not up in heaven, so that you have to ask, "Who will ascend into heaven to get it and proclaim it to us so we may obey it?" 13Nor is it beyond the sea, so that you have to ask, "Who will cross the sea to get it and proclaim it to us so we may obey it?" 14No, the word is very near you; it is in your mouth and in your heart so you may obey it.

15See, I set before you today life and prosperity, death and destruction. 16For I command you today to love the LORD your God, to walk in his ways, and to keep his commands, decrees and laws; then you will live and increase, and the LORD your God will bless you in the land you are entering to possess.

17But if your heart turns away and you are not obedient, and if you are drawn away to bow down to other gods and worship them, 18I declare to you this day that you will certainly be destroyed. You will not live long in the land you are crossing the Jordan to enter and possess.

19This day I call heaven and earth as witnesses against you that I have set before you life and death, blessings and curses. Now choose life, so that you and your children may live 20and that you may love the LORD your God, listen to his voice, and hold fast to him. For the LORD is your life, and he will give you many years in the land he swore to give to your fathers, Abraham, Isaac and Jacob.

PRAYER: RENEWAL

MAY I not be conformed to the pattern of this world, O God, but be transformed by the renewing of my mind, that I may be able to test and approve that Your will is good and pleasing and perfect. (Romans 12:2)

***PAUSE** to add your own prayers for personal renewal.*

NT Ephesians 3:1–13

Paul the Preacher to the Gentiles

3 For this reason I, Paul, the prisoner of Christ Jesus for the sake of you Gentiles—

2Surely you have heard about the administration of God's grace that was given to me for you, 3that is, the mystery made known to me by revelation, as I have already written briefly. 4In reading this, then, you will be able to understand my insight into the mystery of Christ, 5which was not made known to men in other generations as it has now been revealed by the Spirit to God's holy apostles and prophets. 6This mystery is that through the gospel the Gentiles are heirs together with Israel, members together of one body, and sharers together in the promise in Christ Jesus.

7I became a servant of this gospel by the gift of God's grace given me through the working of his power. 8Although I am less than the least of all God's people, this grace was given me: to preach to the Gentiles the unsearchable riches of Christ, 9and to make plain to everyone the administration of this mystery, which for ages past was kept hidden in God, who created all things. 10His intent was that now, through the church, the manifold wisdom of God should be made known to the rulers and authorities in the heavenly realms, 11according to his eternal purpose which he accomplished in Christ Jesus our Lord. 12In him and through faith in him we may approach God with freedom and confidence. 13I ask you, therefore, not to be discouraged because of my sufferings for you, which are your glory.

PRAYER: MY RELATIONSHIP TO GOD

I WILL trust in You, Lord, with all my heart and lean not on my own understanding; in all my ways I will acknowledge You, and You will make my paths straight. I will not be wise in my own eyes, but I will fear You, Lord, and depart from evil. (Proverbs 3:5–7) . . . Not by might nor by power, but by Your Spirit, O Lord God of hosts. (Zechariah 4:6)

__PAUSE__ to thank God for the relationship that you enjoy with Him in Jesus Christ.

YEAR 1 DAY 179

OT Deuteronomy 31:1–30

Joshua to Succeed Moses

31 Then Moses went out and spoke these words to all Israel: 2"I am now a hundred and twenty years old and I am no longer able to lead you. The LORD has said to me, 'You shall not cross the Jordan.' 3The LORD your God himself will cross over ahead of you. He will destroy these nations before you, and you will take possession of their land. Joshua also will cross over ahead of you, as the LORD said. 4And the LORD will do to them what he did to Sihon and Og, the kings of the Amorites, whom he destroyed along with their land. 5The LORD will deliver them to you, and you must do to them all that I have commanded you. 6Be strong and courageous. Do not be afraid or terrified because of them, for the LORD your God goes with you; he will never leave you nor forsake you."

7Then Moses summoned Joshua and said to him in the presence of all Israel, "Be strong and courageous, for you must go with this people into the land that the LORD swore to their forefathers to give them, and you must divide it among them as their inheritance. 8The LORD himself goes before you and will be with you; he will never leave you nor forsake you. Do not be afraid; do not be discouraged."

The Reading of the Law

9So Moses wrote down this law and gave it to the priests, the sons of Levi, who carried the ark of the covenant of the LORD, and to all the elders of Israel. 10Then Moses commanded them: "At the end of every seven years, in the year for canceling debts, during the Feast of Tabernacles, 11when all Israel comes to appear before the LORD your God at the place he will choose, you shall read this law before them in their hearing. 12Assemble the people—men, women and children, and the aliens living in your towns—so they can listen and learn to fear the LORD your God and follow carefully all the words of this law. 13Their children, who do not know this law, must hear it and learn to fear the LORD your God as long as you live in the land you are crossing the Jordan to possess."

Israel's Rebellion Predicted

14The LORD said to Moses, "Now the day of your death is near. Call Joshua and present yourselves at the Tent of Meeting, where I will commission him." So Moses and Joshua came and presented themselves at the Tent of Meeting.

15Then the LORD appeared at the Tent in a pillar of cloud, and the cloud stood over the entrance to the Tent. 16And the LORD

said to Moses: "You are going to rest with
your fathers, and these people will soon
prostitute themselves to the foreign gods
of the land they are entering. They will
forsake me and break the covenant I made
with them. 17On that day I will become
angry with them and forsake them; I will
hide my face from them, and they will be
destroyed. Many disasters and difficulties
will come upon them, and on that day
they will ask, 'Have not these disasters
come upon us because our God is not
with us?' 18And I will certainly hide my
face on that day because of all their
wickedness in turning to other gods.
19"Now write down for yourselves this
song and teach it to the Israelites and have
them sing it, so that it may be a witness for
me against them. 20When I have brought
them into the land flowing with milk and
honey, the land I promised on oath to their
forefathers, and when they eat their fill and
thrive, they will turn to other gods and
worship them, rejecting me and breaking
my covenant. 21And when many disasters
and difficulties come upon them, this song
will testify against them, because it will not
be forgotten by their descendants. I know
what they are disposed to do, even before
I bring them into the land I promised them
on oath." 22So Moses wrote down this song
that day and taught it to the Israelites.
23The LORD gave this command to Joshua son of Nun: "Be strong and courageous, for you will bring the Israelites into
the land I promised them on oath, and I
myself will be with you."
24After Moses finished writing in a book
the words of this law from beginning to
end, 25he gave this command to the Levites who carried the ark of the covenant
of the LORD: 26"Take this Book of the Law
and place it beside the ark of the covenant
of the LORD your God. There it will remain
as a witness against you. 27For I know how
rebellious and stiff-necked you are. If you
have been rebellious against the LORD
while I am still alive and with you, how
much more will you rebel after I die! 28As-
semble before me all the elders of your
tribes and all your officials, so that I can
speak these words in their hearing and
call heaven and earth to testify against
them. 29For I know that after my death
you are sure to become utterly corrupt
and to turn from the way I have commanded you. In days to come, disaster
will fall upon you because you will do evil
in the sight of the LORD and provoke him
to anger by what your hands have made.

The Song of Moses

30And Moses recited the words of this
song from beginning to end in the hearing of the whole assembly of Israel:

PRAYER: PETITION

WHATEVER I do, may I do it all to Your glory, O God.
(1 Corinthians 10:31)

PAUSE *here to petition God to help you be a faithful steward of your time, talents, possessions and relationships. Offer prayers of petition regarding your activities for this day and any special concerns you may have.*

NT Ephesians 3:14–4:16

A Prayer for the Ephesians

14For this reason I kneel before the Father, 15from whom his whole family[a] in
heaven and on earth derives its name. 16I
pray that out of his glorious riches he may
strengthen you with power through his
Spirit in your inner being, 17so that Christ
may dwell in your hearts through faith.
And I pray that you, being rooted and established in love, 18may have power, together with all the saints, to grasp how wide
and long and high and deep is the love of
Christ, 19and to know this love that surpasses knowledge—that you may be filled
to the measure of all the fullness of God.
20Now to him who is able to do immeasurably more than all we ask or imag-

[a] 15 Or *whom all fatherhood*

ine, according to his power that is at work
within us, [21]to him be glory in the church
and in Christ Jesus throughout all generations, for ever and ever! Amen.

Unity in the Body of Christ

4 As a prisoner for the Lord, then, I urge
you to live a life worthy of the calling
you have received. [2]Be completely humble and gentle; be patient, bearing with
one another in love. [3]Make every effort to
keep the unity of the Spirit through the
bond of peace. [4]There is one body and
one Spirit— just as you were called to one
hope when you were called— [5]one Lord,
one faith, one baptism; [6]one God and Father of all, who is over all and through all
and in all.

[7]But to each one of us grace has been
given as Christ apportioned it. [8]This is
why it[b] says:

"When he ascended on high,
he led captives in his train
and gave gifts to men."[c]

[9](What does "he ascended" mean except
that he also descended to the lower, earthly regions[d]? [10]He who descended is the
very one who ascended higher than all the
heavens, in order to fill the whole universe.) [11]It was he who gave some to be
apostles, some to be prophets, some to be
evangelists, and some to be pastors and
teachers, [12]to prepare God's people for
works of service, so that the body of Christ
may be built up [13]until we all reach unity
in the faith and in the knowledge of the
Son of God and become mature, attaining
to the whole measure of the fullness of
Christ.

[14]Then we will no longer be infants,
tossed back and forth by the waves, and
blown here and there by every wind of
teaching and by the cunning and craftiness of men in their deceitful scheming.
[15]Instead, speaking the truth in love, we
will in all things grow up into him who is
the Head, that is, Christ. [16]From him the
whole body, joined and held together by
every supporting ligament, grows and
builds itself up in love, as each part does
its work.

[b] 8 Or *God* [c] 8 Psalm 68:18 [d] 9 Or *the depths of the earth*

PRAYER: THE CHARACTER I WANT TO CULTIVATE

BEFORE my downfall my heart is haughty, but I must have humility before I have honor. (Proverbs 18:12) . . . Blessed are the poor in spirit, for theirs is the kingdom of heaven. Blessed are those who mourn, for they will be comforted. Blessed are the meek, for they will inherit the earth. (Matthew 5:3–5)

***TAKE** a moment to ask the Lord for the grace to grow in godly character.*

YEAR 1 DAY 180

OT Deuteronomy 32:1–52

32 Listen, O heavens, and I will speak;
hear, O earth, the words of my
mouth.
[2]Let my teaching fall like rain
and my words descend like dew,
like showers on new grass,
like abundant rain on tender plants.

[3]I will proclaim the name of the LORD.
Oh, praise the greatness of our
God!
[4]He is the Rock, his works are perfect,
and all his ways are just.
A faithful God who does no wrong,
upright and just is he.

[5]They have acted corruptly toward him;
to their shame they are no longer
his children,
but a warped and crooked
generation.[a]
[6]Is this the way you repay the LORD,

[a] 5 Or *Corrupt are they and not his children, / a generation warped and twisted to their shame*

O foolish and unwise people?
Is he not your Father, your Creator,[b]
who made you and formed you?

7 Remember the days of old;
consider the generations long past.
Ask your father and he will tell you,
your elders, and they will explain to you.
8 When the Most High gave the nations their inheritance,
when he divided all mankind,
he set up boundaries for the peoples
according to the number of the sons of Israel.[c]
9 For the LORD's portion is his people,
Jacob his allotted inheritance.

10 In a desert land he found him,
in a barren and howling waste.
He shielded him and cared for him;
he guarded him as the apple of his eye,
11 like an eagle that stirs up its nest
and hovers over its young,
that spreads its wings to catch them
and carries them on its pinions.
12 The LORD alone led him;
no foreign god was with him.

13 He made him ride on the heights of the land
and fed him with the fruit of the fields.
He nourished him with honey from the rock,
and with oil from the flinty crag,
14 with curds and milk from herd and flock
and with fattened lambs and goats,
with choice rams of Bashan
and the finest kernels of wheat.
You drank the foaming blood of the grape.

15 Jeshurun[d] grew fat and kicked;
filled with food, he became heavy and sleek.
He abandoned the God who made him
and rejected the Rock his Savior.
16 They made him jealous with their foreign gods
and angered him with their detestable idols.
17 They sacrificed to demons, which are not God—
gods they had not known,
gods that recently appeared,
gods your fathers did not fear.
18 You deserted the Rock, who fathered you;
you forgot the God who gave you birth.

19 The LORD saw this and rejected them
because he was angered by his sons and daughters.
20 "I will hide my face from them," he said,
"and see what their end will be;
for they are a perverse generation,
children who are unfaithful.
21 They made me jealous by what is no god
and angered me with their worthless idols.
I will make them envious by those who are not a people;
I will make them angry by a nation that has no understanding.
22 For a fire has been kindled by my wrath,
one that burns to the realm of death[e] below.
It will devour the earth and its harvests
and set afire the foundations of the mountains.

23 "I will heap calamities upon them
and spend my arrows against them.
24 I will send wasting famine against them,
consuming pestilence and deadly plague;
I will send against them the fangs of wild beasts,
the venom of vipers that glide in the dust.
25 In the street the sword will make them childless;
in their homes terror will reign.
Young men and young women will perish,
infants and gray-haired men.
26 I said I would scatter them
and blot out their memory from mankind,
27 but I dreaded the taunt of the enemy,
lest the adversary misunderstand
and say, 'Our hand has triumphed;
the LORD has not done all this.' "

[b] 6 Or *Father, who bought you* [c] 8 Masoretic Text; Dead Sea Scrolls (see also Septuagint) *sons of God* [d] 15 *Jeshurun* means *the upright one,* that is, Israel. [e] 22 Hebrew *to Sheol*

28 They are a nation without sense,
there is no discernment in them.
29 If only they were wise and would
understand this
and discern what their end will be!
30 How could one man chase a
thousand,
or two put ten thousand to flight,
unless their Rock had sold them,
unless the LORD had given them up?
31 For their rock is not like our Rock,
as even our enemies concede.
32 Their vine comes from the vine of
Sodom
and from the fields of Gomorrah.
Their grapes are filled with poison,
and their clusters with bitterness.
33 Their wine is the venom of serpents,
the deadly poison of cobras.

34 "Have I not kept this in reserve
and sealed it in my vaults?
35 It is mine to avenge; I will repay.
In due time their foot will slip;
their day of disaster is near
and their doom rushes upon them."

36 The LORD will judge his people
and have compassion on his servants
when he sees their strength is gone
and no one is left, slave or free.
37 He will say: "Now where are their
gods,
the rock they took refuge in,
38 the gods who ate the fat of their
sacrifices
and drank the wine of their drink
offerings?
Let them rise up to help you!
Let them give you shelter!

39 "See now that I myself am He!
There is no god besides me.
I put to death and I bring to life,
I have wounded and I will heal,
and no one can deliver out of my
hand.
40 I lift my hand to heaven and declare:
As surely as I live forever,
41 when I sharpen my flashing sword
and my hand grasps it in judgment,
I will take vengeance on my adversaries
and repay those who hate me.
42 I will make my arrows drunk with
blood,
while my sword devours flesh:
the blood of the slain and the captives,
the heads of the enemy leaders."

43 Rejoice, O nations, with his people,[f,g]
for he will avenge the blood of his
servants;
he will take vengeance on his enemies
and make atonement for his land
and people.

44 Moses came with Joshua[h] son of Nun
and spoke all the words of this song in the
hearing of the people. 45 When Moses finished reciting all these words to all Israel,
46 he said to them, "Take to heart all the
words I have solemnly declared to you
this day, so that you may command your
children to obey carefully all the words of
this law. 47 They are not just idle words for
you—they are your life. By them you will
live long in the land you are crossing the
Jordan to possess."

Moses to Die on Mount Nebo

48 On that same day the LORD told Moses, 49 "Go up into the Abarim Range to
Mount Nebo in Moab, across from Jericho,
and view Canaan, the land I am giving the
Israelites as their own possession. 50 There
on the mountain that you have climbed
you will die and be gathered to your people, just as your brother Aaron died on
Mount Hor and was gathered to his people. 51 This is because both of you broke
faith with me in the presence of the Israelites at the waters of Meribah Kadesh in the
Desert of Zin and because you did not uphold my holiness among the Israelites.
52 Therefore, you will see the land only from
a distance; you will not enter the land I am
giving to the people of Israel."

f 43 Or *Make his people rejoice, O nations*
g 43 Masoretic Text; Dead Sea Scrolls (see also Septuagint) *people, / and let all the angels worship him /*
h 44 Hebrew *Hoshea,* a variant of *Joshua*

PRAYER: INTERCESSION

O GOD, may we offer petitions, prayers, intercessions and thanksgiving on behalf of all people, for kings and all those who are in authority, that we may live peaceful and quiet lives in all godliness and reverence. This is good and acceptable in Your sight, God our Savior, for You desire all people to be saved and to come to the knowledge of the truth. (1 Timothy 2:1–4)

***TAKE** a few moments to intercede on behalf of your local, state or provincial, and national governments. Pray for spiritual revival in the nation and offer prayers regarding current events and concerns.*

NT Ephesians 4:17–32

Living as Children of Light

17So I tell you this, and insist on it in
the Lord, that you must no longer live as
the Gentiles do, in the futility of their
thinking. 18They are darkened in their understanding and separated from the life of
God because of the ignorance that is in
them due to the hardening of their hearts.
19Having lost all sensitivity, they have giv-
en themselves over to sensuality so as to
indulge in every kind of impurity, with a
continual lust for more.
20You, however, did not come to know
Christ that way. 21Surely you heard of him
and were taught in him in accordance
with the truth that is in Jesus. 22You were
taught, with regard to your former way of
life, to put off your old self, which is being corrupted by its deceitful desires; 23to
be made new in the attitude of your
minds; 24and to put on the new self, created to be like God in true righteousness
and holiness.
25Therefore each of you must put off
falsehood and speak truthfully to his
neighbor, for we are all members of one
body. 26"In your anger do not sin"[a]: Do
not let the sun go down while you are still
angry, 27and do not give the devil a
foothold. 28He who has been stealing
must steal no longer, but must work, doing something useful with his own hands,
that he may have something to share with
those in need.
29Do not let any unwholesome talk
come out of your mouths, but only what
is helpful for building others up according to their needs, that it may benefit
those who listen. 30And do not grieve the
Holy Spirit of God, with whom you were
sealed for the day of redemption. 31Get rid
of all bitterness, rage and anger, brawling
and slander, along with every form of
malice. 32Be kind and compassionate to
one another, forgiving each other, just as
in Christ God forgave you.

[a] *26* Psalm 4:4

PRAYER: MY RELATIONSHIP TO OTHERS

MAY I learn the importance of forgiveness from You, Lord Jesus, who were asked by Peter: "Lord, how often shall my brother sin against me, and I forgive him? Up to seven times?" You said to him, "I tell you, not seven times, but up to seventy times seven." (Matthew 18:21–22) . . . I will love my enemies, do good to them, and lend to them, expecting nothing in return. Then my reward will be great, and I will be Your child, O Most High; for You are kind to the ungrateful and evil. I will be merciful just as You, Father, are merciful. (Luke 6:35–36)

***PAUSE** to review your relationships with others and to commit them to the Lord.*

YEAR 1 DAY 181

OT Deuteronomy 33:1–29

Moses Blesses the Tribes

33 This is the blessing that Moses the man of God pronounced on the Israelites before his death. 2He said:

"The LORD came from Sinai
and dawned over them from Seir;
he shone forth from Mount Paran.
He came with[a] myriads of holy ones
from the south, from his mountain slopes.[b]
3Surely it is you who love the people;
all the holy ones are in your hand.
At your feet they all bow down,
and from you receive instruction,
4the law that Moses gave us,
the possession of the assembly of Jacob.
5He was king over Jeshurun[c]
when the leaders of the people assembled,
along with the tribes of Israel.

6"Let Reuben live and not die,
nor[d] his men be few."

7And this he said about Judah:

"Hear, O LORD, the cry of Judah;
bring him to his people.
With his own hands he defends his cause.
Oh, be his help against his foes!"

8About Levi he said:

"Your Thummim and Urim belong
to the man you favored.
You tested him at Massah;
you contended with him at the waters of Meribah.
9He said of his father and mother,
'I have no regard for them.'
He did not recognize his brothers
or acknowledge his own children,
but he watched over your word
and guarded your covenant.
10He teaches your precepts to Jacob
and your law to Israel.
He offers incense before you
and whole burnt offerings on your altar.
11Bless all his skills, O LORD,
and be pleased with the work of his hands.
Smite the loins of those who rise up against him;
strike his foes till they rise no more."

12About Benjamin he said:

"Let the beloved of the LORD rest secure in him,
for he shields him all day long,
and the one the LORD loves rests between his shoulders."

13About Joseph he said:

"May the LORD bless his land
with the precious dew from heaven above
and with the deep waters that lie below;
14with the best the sun brings forth
and the finest the moon can yield;
15with the choicest gifts of the ancient mountains
and the fruitfulness of the everlasting hills;
16with the best gifts of the earth and its fullness
and the favor of him who dwelt in the burning bush.
Let all these rest on the head of Joseph,
on the brow of the prince among[e] his brothers.
17In majesty he is like a firstborn bull;
his horns are the horns of a wild ox.
With them he will gore the nations,
even those at the ends of the earth.
Such are the ten thousands of Ephraim;
such are the thousands of Manasseh."

18About Zebulun he said:

"Rejoice, Zebulun, in your going out,
and you, Issachar, in your tents.
19They will summon peoples to the mountain
and there offer sacrifices of righteousness;

[a] 2 Or *from* [b] 2 The meaning of the Hebrew for this phrase is uncertain. [c] 5 *Jeshurun* means *the upright one,* that is, Israel; also in verse 26. [d] 6 Or *but let* [e] 16 Or *of the one separated from*

they will feast on the abundance of
the seas,
on the treasures hidden in the
sand."

20 About Gad he said:

"Blessed is he who enlarges Gad's
domain!
Gad lives there like a lion,
tearing at arm or head.
21 He chose the best land for himself;
the leader's portion was kept for
him.
When the heads of the people
assembled,
he carried out the LORD's righteous
will,
and his judgments concerning
Israel."

22 About Dan he said:

"Dan is a lion's cub,
springing out of Bashan."

23 About Naphtali he said:

"Naphtali is abounding with the favor
of the LORD
and is full of his blessing;
he will inherit southward to the
lake."

24 About Asher he said:

"Most blessed of sons is Asher;
let him be favored by his brothers,
and let him bathe his feet in oil.
25 The bolts of your gates will be iron
and bronze,
and your strength will equal your
days.

26 "There is no one like the God of
Jeshurun,
who rides on the heavens to help
you
and on the clouds in his majesty.
27 The eternal God is your refuge,
and underneath are the everlasting
arms.
He will drive out your enemy before
you,
saying, 'Destroy him!'
28 So Israel will live in safety alone;
Jacob's spring is secure
in a land of grain and new wine,
where the heavens drop dew.
29 Blessed are you, O Israel!
Who is like you,
a people saved by the LORD?
He is your shield and helper
and your glorious sword.
Your enemies will cower before you,
and you will trample down their
high places.[f]"

[f] 29 Or *will tread upon their bodies*

PRAYER: AFFIRMATION

THERE is a time for everything, and a season for every activity under heaven. O God, You have made everything beautiful in its time. You have also set eternity in human hearts; yet they cannot fathom what You have done from beginning to end. (Ecclesiastes 3:1, 11)

***PAUSE** to reflect on these Biblical affirmations.*

NT Ephesians 5:1–21

5 Be imitators of God, therefore, as dearly loved children 2 and live a life of love,
just as Christ loved us and gave himself
up for us as a fragrant offering and sacrifice to God.
3 But among you there must not be even
a hint of sexual immorality, or of any kind
of impurity, or of greed, because these are
improper for God's holy people. 4 Nor
should there be obscenity, foolish talk or
coarse joking, which are out of place, but
rather thanksgiving. 5 For of this you can
be sure: No immoral, impure or greedy
person—such a man is an idolater—has
any inheritance in the kingdom of Christ
and of God.[a] 6 Let no one deceive you with
empty words, for because of such things
God's wrath comes on those who are disobedient. 7 Therefore do not be partners
with them.
8 For you were once darkness, but now
you are light in the Lord. Live as children

[a] 5 Or *kingdom of the Christ and God*

of light [9](for the fruit of the light consists
in all goodness, righteousness and truth)
[10]and find out what pleases the Lord.
[11]Have nothing to do with the fruitless
deeds of darkness, but rather expose
them. [12]For it is shameful even to mention
what the disobedient do in secret. [13]But
everything exposed by the light becomes
visible, [14]for it is light that makes everything visible. This is why it is said:

"Wake up, O sleeper,
rise from the dead,
and Christ will shine on you."

[15]Be very careful, then, how you live—
not as unwise but as wise, [16]making the
most of every opportunity, because the
days are evil. [17]Therefore do not be foolish, but understand what the Lord's will
is. [18]Do not get drunk on wine, which
leads to debauchery. Instead, be filled
with the Spirit. [19]Speak to one another
with psalms, hymns and spiritual songs.
Sing and make music in your heart to the
Lord, [20]always giving thanks to God the
Father for everything, in the name of our
Lord Jesus Christ.

[21]Submit to one another out of reverence for Christ.

PRAYER: THE ATTRIBUTES OF GOD

I WILL be still and know that You are God. You will be exalted among the nations. You will be exalted in the earth. (Psalm 46:10) . . . O God and Father of the Lord Jesus—You are blessed forever. (2 Corinthians 11:31)

***PAUSE** to reflect on these affirmations about the person, powers and perfection of God.*

YEAR 1
DAY 182

OT Psalm 36

Psalm 36

For the director of music. Of David the servant of the LORD.

[1]An oracle is within my heart
concerning the sinfulness of the wicked:[a]
There is no fear of God
before his eyes.
[2]For in his own eyes he flatters himself
too much to detect or hate his sin.
[3]The words of his mouth are wicked and deceitful;
he has ceased to be wise and to do good.
[4]Even on his bed he plots evil;
he commits himself to a sinful course
and does not reject what is wrong.

[5]Your love, O LORD, reaches to the heavens,
your faithfulness to the skies.
[6]Your righteousness is like the mighty mountains,
your justice like the great deep.
O LORD, you preserve both man and beast.
[7]How priceless is your unfailing love!
Both high and low among men
find[b] refuge in the shadow of your wings.
[8]They feast on the abundance of your house;
you give them drink from your river of delights.
[9]For with you is the fountain of life;
in your light we see light.

[10]Continue your love to those who know you,
your righteousness to the upright in heart.
[11]May the foot of the proud not come against me,
nor the hand of the wicked drive me away.
[12]See how the evildoers lie fallen—
thrown down, not able to rise!

[a] 1 Or *heart: / Sin proceeds from the wicked.* [b] 7 Or *love, O God! / Men find;* or *love! / Both heavenly beings and men / find*

PRAYER: THANKSGIVING

O LORD, I do not lose heart; even though my outward self is perishing, yet my inner self is being renewed day by day. For this light affliction, which is momentary, is working for me a far more exceeding and eternal weight of glory. So I do not look at the things that are seen but at the things that are unseen. For the things that are seen are temporary, but the things that are unseen are eternal.

(2 Corinthians 4:16–18)

***PAUSE** to offer your own expressions of thanksgiving.*

NT Ephesians 5:22–6:9

Wives and Husbands

22 Wives, submit to your husbands as to the Lord. 23 For the husband is the head of the wife as Christ is the head of the church, his body, of which he is the Savior. 24 Now as the church submits to Christ, so also wives should submit to their husbands in everything.

25 Husbands, love your wives, just as Christ loved the church and gave himself up for her 26 to make her holy, cleansing[a] her by the washing with water through the word, 27 and to present her to himself as a radiant church, without stain or wrinkle or any other blemish, but holy and blameless. 28 In this same way, husbands ought to love their wives as their own bodies. He who loves his wife loves himself. 29 After all, no one ever hated his own body, but he feeds and cares for it, just as Christ does the church— 30 for we are members of his body. 31 "For this reason a man will leave his father and mother and be united to his wife, and the two will become one flesh."[b] 32 This is a profound mystery—but I am talking about Christ and the church. 33 However, each one of you also must love his wife as he loves himself, and the wife must respect her husband.

Children and Parents

6 Children, obey your parents in the Lord, for this is right. 2 "Honor your father and mother"—which is the first commandment with a promise— 3 "that it may go well with you and that you may enjoy long life on the earth."[c]

4 Fathers, do not exasperate your children; instead, bring them up in the training and instruction of the Lord.

Slaves and Masters

5 Slaves, obey your earthly masters with respect and fear, and with sincerity of heart, just as you would obey Christ. 6 Obey them not only to win their favor when their eye is on you, but like slaves of Christ, doing the will of God from your heart. 7 Serve wholeheartedly, as if you were serving the Lord, not men, 8 because you know that the Lord will reward everyone for whatever good he does, whether he is slave or free.

9 And masters, treat your slaves in the same way. Do not threaten them, since you know that he who is both their Master and yours is in heaven, and there is no favoritism with him.

[a] *26* Or *having cleansed* [b] *31* Gen. 2:24
[c] *3* Deut. 5:16

PRAYER: THE WORKS OF GOD

THROUGH You, O Christ, all things were made, and without You nothing was made that has been made. In You was life, and that life was our light. (John 1:3–4)

***TAKE** a moment to consider the greatness of God's wonderful works.*

YEAR 1 DAY 183

OT **Deuteronomy 34:1-12**

The Death of Moses

34 Then Moses climbed Mount Nebo from the plains of Moab to the top of Pisgah, across from Jericho. There the LORD showed him the whole land—from Gilead to Dan, [2]all of Naphtali, the territory of Ephraim and Manasseh, all the land of Judah as far as the western sea,[a] [3]the Negev and the whole region from the Valley of Jericho, the City of Palms, as far as Zoar. [4]Then the LORD said to him, "This is the land I promised on oath to Abraham, Isaac and Jacob when I said, 'I will give it to your descendants.' I have let you see it with your eyes, but you will not cross over into it."

[5]And Moses the servant of the LORD died there in Moab, as the LORD had said. [6]He buried him[b] in Moab, in the valley opposite Beth Peor, but to this day no one knows where his grave is. [7]Moses was a hundred and twenty years old when he died, yet his eyes were not weak nor his strength gone. [8]The Israelites grieved for Moses in the plains of Moab thirty days, until the time of weeping and mourning was over.

[9]Now Joshua son of Nun was filled with the spirit[c] of wisdom because Moses had laid his hands on him. So the Israelites listened to him and did what the LORD had commanded Moses.

[10]Since then, no prophet has risen in Israel like Moses, whom the LORD knew face to face, [11]who did all those miraculous signs and wonders the LORD sent him to do in Egypt—to Pharaoh and to all his officials and to his whole land. [12]For no one has ever shown the mighty power or performed the awesome deeds that Moses did in the sight of all Israel.

[a] 2 That is, the Mediterranean [b] 6 Or *He was buried* [c] 9 Or *Spirit*

PRAYER: ADORATION

WE praise You, Lord! All Your servants praise You; We praise Your name, O Lord. Blessed be Your name both now and forever. From the rising of the sun to its setting, Your name, O Lord, is to be praised. You are high above all nations, Your glory above the heavens. Who is like You, O Lord our God, the One who is enthroned on high, who humbles Himself to behold the things that are in the heavens and in the earth? (Psalm 113:1–6)

***PAUSE** to express your thoughts of praise and worship.*

NT **Ephesians 6:10-24**

The Armor of God

[10]Finally, be strong in the Lord and in his mighty power. [11]Put on the full armor of God so that you can take your stand against the devil's schemes. [12]For our struggle is not against flesh and blood, but against the rulers, against the authorities, against the powers of this dark world and against the spiritual forces of evil in the heavenly realms. [13]Therefore put on the full armor of God, so that when the day of evil comes, you may be able to stand your ground, and after you have done everything, to stand. [14]Stand firm then, with the belt of truth buckled around your waist, with the breastplate of righteousness in place, [15]and with your feet fitted with the readiness that comes from the gospel of peace. [16]In addition to all this, take up the shield of faith, with which you can extinguish all the flaming arrows of the evil one. [17]Take the helmet of salvation and the sword of the Spirit, which is the word of God. [18]And pray in the Spirit on all occasions with all kinds of prayers and requests. With this in mind, be alert and always keep on praying for all the saints.

[19]Pray also for me, that whenever I open
my mouth, words may be given me so
that I will fearlessly make known the mystery of the gospel, [20]for which I am an
ambassador in chains. Pray that I may declare it fearlessly, as I should.

Final Greetings

[21]Tychicus, the dear brother and faithful
servant in the Lord, will tell you everything, so that you also may know how I
am and what I am doing. [22]I am sending
him to you for this very purpose, that you
may know how we are, and that he may
encourage you.

[23]Peace to the brothers, and love with
faith from God the Father and the Lord
Jesus Christ. [24]Grace to all who love our
Lord Jesus Christ with an undying love.

PRAYER: MY RELATIONSHIP TO GOD

As for me and my household, we will serve You, O Lord. (Joshua 24:15) . . . By Your grace, O Lord, I want to hear You say to me, "Well done, good and faithful servant; you have been faithful with a few things; I will put you in charge of many things. Enter into the joy of your Lord." (Matthew 25:21)

***PAUSE** to thank God for the relationship that you enjoy with Him in Jesus Christ.*

YEAR 1
DAY 184

OT Joshua 1:1-18

The LORD Commands Joshua

1 After the death of Moses the servant of
the LORD, the LORD said to Joshua son
of Nun, Moses' aide: [2]"Moses my servant
is dead. Now then, you and all these people, get ready to cross the Jordan River
into the land I am about to give to them—
to the Israelites. [3]I will give you every
place where you set your foot, as I promised Moses. [4]Your territory will extend
from the desert to Lebanon, and from the
great river, the Euphrates—all the Hittite
country—to the Great Sea[a] on the west.
[5]No one will be able to stand up against
you all the days of your life. As I was with
Moses, so I will be with you; I will never
leave you nor forsake you.

[6]"Be strong and courageous, because
you will lead these people to inherit the
land I swore to their forefathers to give
them. [7]Be strong and very courageous. Be
careful to obey all the law my servant Moses gave you; do not turn from it to the
right or to the left, that you may be successful wherever you go. [8]Do not let this
Book of the Law depart from your mouth;
meditate on it day and night, so that you
may be careful to do everything written in
it. Then you will be prosperous and successful. [9]Have I not commanded you? Be
strong and courageous. Do not be terrified; do not be discouraged, for the LORD
your God will be with you wherever
you go."

[10]So Joshua ordered the officers of the
people: [11]"Go through the camp and tell
the people, 'Get your supplies ready. Three
days from now you will cross the Jordan
here to go in and take possession of the
land the LORD your God is giving you for
your own.' "

[12]But to the Reubenites, the Gadites and
the half-tribe of Manasseh, Joshua said,
[13]"Remember the command that Moses
the servant of the LORD gave you: 'The
LORD your God is giving you rest and has
granted you this land.' [14]Your wives, your
children and your livestock may stay in
the land that Moses gave you east of the
Jordan, but all your fighting men, fully
armed, must cross over ahead of your
brothers. You are to help your brothers
[15]until the LORD gives them rest, as he has
done for you, and until they too have tak-
en possession of the land that the LORD

[a] 4 That is, the Mediterranean

your God is giving them. After that, you may go back and occupy your own land, which Moses the servant of the LORD gave you east of the Jordan toward the sunrise."

[16]Then they answered Joshua, "Whatever you have commanded us we will do, and wherever you send us we will go. [17]Just as we fully obeyed Moses, so we will obey you. Only may the LORD your God be with you as he was with Moses. [18]Whoever rebels against your word and does not obey your words, whatever you may command them, will be put to death. Only be strong and courageous!"

PRAYER: CONFESSION

YOU, the Lord our Redeemer, have said, "For a brief moment I forsook you, but with great compassion I will gather you. In a flood of anger I hid My face from you for a moment, but I will have compassion on you with everlasting kindness." (Isaiah 54:7–8)

***ASK** the Spirit to search your heart and reveal any areas of unconfessed sin. Acknowledge these to the Lord and thank Him for His forgiveness.*

NT Philippians 1:1-11

1 Paul and Timothy, servants of Christ Jesus,

To all the saints in Christ Jesus at Philippi, together with the overseers[a] and deacons:

[2]Grace and peace to you from God our Father and the Lord Jesus Christ.

Thanksgiving and Prayer

[3]I thank my God every time I remember you. [4]In all my prayers for all of you, I always pray with joy [5]because of your partnership in the gospel from the first day until now, [6]being confident of this, that he who began a good work in you will carry it on to completion until the day of Christ Jesus.

[7]It is right for me to feel this way about all of you, since I have you in my heart; for whether I am in chains or defending and confirming the gospel, all of you share in God's grace with me. [8]God can testify how I long for all of you with the affection of Christ Jesus.

[9]And this is my prayer: that your love may abound more and more in knowledge and depth of insight, [10]so that you may be able to discern what is best and may be pure and blameless until the day of Christ, [11]filled with the fruit of righteousness that comes through Jesus Christ—to the glory and praise of God.

[a] *1* Traditionally *bishops*

PRAYER: THE CHARACTER I WANT TO CULTIVATE

THOSE who love instruction love knowledge, but those who hate correction are stupid. (Proverbs 12:1) . . . Pride breeds nothing but strife, but wisdom is found in those who take advice. (Proverbs 13:10)

***TAKE** a moment to ask the Lord for the grace to grow in godly character.*

OT **Joshua 2:1-24** YEAR 1 DAY 185

Rahab and the Spies

2 Then Joshua son of Nun secretly sent
two spies from Shittim. "Go, look over
the land," he said, "especially Jericho." So
they went and entered the house of a
prostitute[a] named Rahab and stayed
there.
2The king of Jericho was told, "Look!
Some of the Israelites have come here
tonight to spy out the land." 3So the king
of Jericho sent this message to Rahab:
"Bring out the men who came to you and
entered your house, because they have
come to spy out the whole land."
4But the woman had taken the two men
and hidden them. She said, "Yes, the men
came to me, but I did not know where
they had come from. 5At dusk, when it
was time to close the city gate, the men
left. I don't know which way they went.
Go after them quickly. You may catch up
with them." 6(But she had taken them up
to the roof and hidden them under the
stalks of flax she had laid out on the roof.)
7So the men set out in pursuit of the spies
on the road that leads to the fords of the
Jordan, and as soon as the pursuers had
gone out, the gate was shut.
8Before the spies lay down for the night,
she went up on the roof 9and said to
them, "I know that the LORD has given
this land to you and that a great fear of
you has fallen on us, so that all who live
in this country are melting in fear because
of you. 10We have heard how the LORD
dried up the water of the Red Sea[b] for you
when you came out of Egypt, and what
you did to Sihon and Og, the two kings
of the Amorites east of the Jordan, whom
you completely destroyed.[c] 11When we
heard of it, our hearts melted and everyone's courage failed because of you, for
the LORD your God is God in heaven
above and on the earth below. 12Now
then, please swear to me by the LORD that
you will show kindness to my family, because I have shown kindness to you. Give
me a sure sign 13that you will spare the
lives of my father and mother, my brothers and sisters, and all who belong to
them, and that you will save us from
death."
14"Our lives for your lives!" the men assured her. "If you don't tell what we are
doing, we will treat you kindly and faithfully when the LORD gives us the land."
15So she let them down by a rope
through the window, for the house she
lived in was part of the city wall. 16Now
she had said to them, "Go to the hills so
the pursuers will not find you. Hide yourselves there three days until they return,
and then go on your way."
17The men said to her, "This oath you
made us swear will not be binding on us
18unless, when we enter the land, you
have tied this scarlet cord in the window
through which you let us down, and unless you have brought your father and
mother, your brothers and all your family into your house. 19If anyone goes outside your house into the street, his blood
will be on his own head; we will not be
responsible. As for anyone who is in the
house with you, his blood will be on our
head if a hand is laid on him. 20But if you
tell what we are doing, we will be released
from the oath you made us swear."
21"Agreed," she replied. "Let it be as you
say." So she sent them away and they departed. And she tied the scarlet cord in the
window.
22When they left, they went into the
hills and stayed there three days, until the
pursuers had searched all along the road
and returned without finding them.
23Then the two men started back. They
went down out of the hills, forded the river and came to Joshua son of Nun and
told him everything that had happened to
them. 24They said to Joshua, "The LORD
has surely given the whole land into our
hands; all the people are melting in fear
because of us."

[a] *1* Or possibly *an innkeeper* [b] *10* Hebrew *Yam Suph*; that is, Sea of Reeds [c] *10* The Hebrew term refers to the irrevocable giving over of things or persons to the LORD, often by totally destroying them.

PRAYER: RENEWAL

LIKE Job, may I be blameless and upright, fearing You, Almighty God, and shunning evil. (Job 1:1) . . . O Lord, may I be careful to lead a blameless life. May I walk in the integrity of my heart in the midst of my house. May I set no wicked thing before my eyes. I hate the deeds of those who fall away; may their deeds not cling to me. (Psalm 101:2–3)

***PAUSE** to add your own prayers for personal renewal.*

NT Philippians 1:12–30

Paul's Chains Advance the Gospel

[12]Now I want you to know, brothers,
that what has happened to me has really
served to advance the gospel. [13]As a result,
it has become clear throughout the whole
palace guard[a] and to everyone else that I
am in chains for Christ. [14]Because of my
chains, most of the brothers in the Lord
have been encouraged to speak the word
of God more courageously and fearlessly.

[15]It is true that some preach Christ out
of envy and rivalry, but others out of
goodwill. [16]The latter do so in love, knowing that I am put here for the defense of
the gospel. [17]The former preach Christ out
of selfish ambition, not sincerely, supposing that they can stir up trouble for me
while I am in chains.[b] [18]But what does it
matter? The important thing is that in
every way, whether from false motives or
true, Christ is preached. And because of
this I rejoice.

Yes, and I will continue to rejoice, [19]for
I know that through your prayers and the
help given by the Spirit of Jesus Christ,
what has happened to me will turn out
for my deliverance.[c] [20]I eagerly expect and
hope that I will in no way be ashamed,
but will have sufficient courage so that
now as always Christ will be exalted in my
body, whether by life or by death. [21]For to
me, to live is Christ and to die is gain. [22]If
I am to go on living in the body, this will
mean fruitful labor for me. Yet what shall
I choose? I do not know! [23]I am torn between the two: I desire to depart and be
with Christ, which is better by far; [24]but it
is more necessary for you that I remain in
the body. [25]Convinced of this, I know that
I will remain, and I will continue with all
of you for your progress and joy in the
faith, [26]so that through my being with you
again your joy in Christ Jesus will overflow on account of me.

[27]Whatever happens, conduct yourselves in a manner worthy of the gospel
of Christ. Then, whether I come and see
you or only hear about you in my absence, I will know that you stand firm in
one spirit, contending as one man for the
faith of the gospel [28]without being frightened in any way by those who oppose
you. This is a sign to them that they will
be destroyed, but that you will be saved—
and that by God. [29]For it has been granted to you on behalf of Christ not only to
believe on him, but also to suffer for him,
[30]since you are going through the same
struggle you saw I had, and now hear that
I still have.

[a] *13* Or *whole palace* [b] *16,17* Some late manuscripts have verses 16 and 17 in reverse order. [c] *19* Or *salvation*

PRAYER: MY RELATIONSHIP TO OTHERS

I WILL contribute to the needs of the saints and practice hospitality. (Romans 12:13) . . . I will not forget to do good and to share with others, for with such sacrifices You, my God, are well pleased. (Hebrews 13:16)

***PAUSE** to review your relationships with others and to commit them to the Lord.*

YEAR 1 DAY 186

OT Proverbs 8

Wisdom's Call

8 Does not wisdom call out?
Does not understanding raise her voice?
2 On the heights along the way,
where the paths meet, she takes her stand;
3 beside the gates leading into the city,
at the entrances, she cries aloud:
4 "To you, O men, I call out;
I raise my voice to all mankind.
5 You who are simple, gain prudence;
you who are foolish, gain understanding.
6 Listen, for I have worthy things to say;
I open my lips to speak what is right.
7 My mouth speaks what is true,
for my lips detest wickedness.
8 All the words of my mouth are just;
none of them is crooked or perverse.
9 To the discerning all of them are right;
they are faultless to those who have knowledge.
10 Choose my instruction instead of silver,
knowledge rather than choice gold,
11 for wisdom is more precious than rubies,
and nothing you desire can compare with her.

12 "I, wisdom, dwell together with prudence;
I possess knowledge and discretion.
13 To fear the LORD is to hate evil;
I hate pride and arrogance,
evil behavior and perverse speech.
14 Counsel and sound judgment are mine;
I have understanding and power.
15 By me kings reign
and rulers make laws that are just;
16 by me princes govern,
and all nobles who rule on earth.[a]
17 I love those who love me,
and those who seek me find me.
18 With me are riches and honor,
enduring wealth and prosperity.
19 My fruit is better than fine gold;
what I yield surpasses choice silver.
20 I walk in the way of righteousness,
along the paths of justice,
21 bestowing wealth on those who love me
and making their treasuries full.

22 "The LORD brought me forth as the first of his works,[b,c]
before his deeds of old;
23 I was appointed[d] from eternity,
from the beginning, before the world began.
24 When there were no oceans, I was given birth,
when there were no springs abounding with water;
25 before the mountains were settled in place,
before the hills, I was given birth,
26 before he made the earth or its fields
or any of the dust of the world.
27 I was there when he set the heavens in place,
when he marked out the horizon on the face of the deep,
28 when he established the clouds above
and fixed securely the fountains of the deep,
29 when he gave the sea its boundary
so the waters would not overstep his command,
and when he marked out the foundations of the earth.
30 Then I was the craftsman at his side.
I was filled with delight day after day,
rejoicing always in his presence,
31 rejoicing in his whole world
and delighting in mankind.

32 "Now then, my sons, listen to me;
blessed are those who keep my ways.
33 Listen to my instruction and be wise;
do not ignore it.
34 Blessed is the man who listens to me,
watching daily at my doors,
waiting at my doorway.
35 For whoever finds me finds life
and receives favor from the LORD.
36 But whoever fails to find me harms himself;
all who hate me love death."

[a] 16 Many Hebrew manuscripts and Septuagint; most Hebrew manuscripts *and nobles—all righteous rulers* [b] 22 Or *way*; or *dominion* [c] 22 Or *The LORD possessed me at the beginning of his work*; or *The LORD brought me forth at the beginning of his work* [d] 23 Or *fashioned*

PRAYER: PETITION

EVEN when I am old and gray, do not forsake me, O God, until I declare Your strength to the next generation, Your power to all who are to come. (Psalm 71:18)

***PAUSE** here to offer prayers of petition regarding your family and your ministry. Ask for help and guidance in sharing Jesus with others and helping others grow in Him. Ask for guidance in your vocation and your avocations. Offer prayers of petition regarding your activities for this day and any special concerns you may have.*

NT Philippians 2:1–18

Imitating Christ's Humility

2 If you have any encouragement from
being united with Christ, if any comfort from his love, if any fellowship with
the Spirit, if any tenderness and compassion, [2]then make my joy complete by being like-minded, having the same love,
being one in spirit and purpose. [3]Do
nothing out of selfish ambition or vain
conceit, but in humility consider others
better than yourselves. [4]Each of you
should look not only to your own interests, but also to the interests of others.
[5]Your attitude should be the same as
that of Christ Jesus:

[6]Who, being in very nature[a] God,
did not consider equality with God
something to be grasped,
[7]but made himself nothing,
taking the very nature[b] of a servant,
being made in human likeness.
[8]And being found in appearance as a
man,
he humbled himself
and became obedient to death—
even death on a cross!
[9]Therefore God exalted him to the
highest place
and gave him the name that is
above every name,
[10]that at the name of Jesus every knee
should bow,
in heaven and on earth and under
the earth,
[11]and every tongue confess that Jesus
Christ is Lord,
to the glory of God the Father.

Shining as Stars

[12]Therefore, my dear friends, as you
have always obeyed—not only in my presence, but now much more in my absence—continue to work out your salvation with fear and trembling, [13]for it is
God who works in you to will and to act
according to his good purpose.
[14]Do everything without complaining or
arguing, [15]so that you may become blameless and pure, children of God without
fault in a crooked and depraved generation, in which you shine like stars in the
universe [16]as you hold out[c] the word of
life—in order that I may boast on the day
of Christ that I did not run or labor for
nothing. [17]But even if I am being poured
out like a drink offering on the sacrifice
and service coming from your faith, I am
glad and rejoice with all of you. [18]So you
too should be glad and rejoice with me.

[a] 6 Or *in the form of* [b] 7 Or *the form* [c] 16 Or *hold on to*

PRAYER: THE ATTRIBUTES OF GOD

YOU, O God, are wise in heart and mighty in strength. Who has resisted You without harm? (Job 9:4) . . . Your eyes, O Lord, are everywhere, keeping watch on the evil and the good. (Proverbs 15:3)

***PAUSE** to reflect on these affirmations about the person, powers and perfection of God.*

OT **Joshua 3:1–4:24** YEAR 1 DAY 187

Crossing the Jordan

3 Early in the morning Joshua and all the Israelites set out from Shittim and went to the Jordan, where they camped before crossing over. 2After three days the officers went throughout the camp, 3giving orders to the people: "When you see the ark of the covenant of the LORD your God, and the priests, who are Levites, carrying it, you are to move out from your positions and follow it. 4Then you will know which way to go, since you have never been this way before. But keep a distance of about a thousand yards[a] between you and the ark; do not go near it."

5Joshua told the people, "Consecrate yourselves, for tomorrow the LORD will do amazing things among you."

6Joshua said to the priests, "Take up the ark of the covenant and pass on ahead of the people." So they took it up and went ahead of them.

7And the LORD said to Joshua, "Today I will begin to exalt you in the eyes of all Israel, so they may know that I am with you as I was with Moses. 8Tell the priests who carry the ark of the covenant: 'When you reach the edge of the Jordan's waters, go and stand in the river.' "

9Joshua said to the Israelites, "Come here and listen to the words of the LORD your God. 10This is how you will know that the living God is among you and that he will certainly drive out before you the Canaanites, Hittites, Hivites, Perizzites, Girgashites, Amorites and Jebusites. 11See, the ark of the covenant of the Lord of all the earth will go into the Jordan ahead of you. 12Now then, choose twelve men from the tribes of Israel, one from each tribe. 13And as soon as the priests who carry the ark of the LORD—the Lord of all the earth—set foot in the Jordan, its waters flowing downstream will be cut off and stand up in a heap."

14So when the people broke camp to cross the Jordan, the priests carrying the ark of the covenant went ahead of them. 15Now the Jordan is at flood stage all during harvest. Yet as soon as the priests who carried the ark reached the Jordan and their feet touched the water's edge, 16the water from upstream stopped flowing. It piled up in a heap a great distance away, at a town called Adam in the vicinity of Zarethan, while the water flowing down to the Sea of the Arabah (the Salt Sea[b]) was completely cut off. So the people crossed over opposite Jericho. 17The priests who carried the ark of the covenant of the LORD stood firm on dry ground in the middle of the Jordan, while all Israel passed by until the whole nation had completed the crossing on dry ground.

4 When the whole nation had finished crossing the Jordan, the LORD said to Joshua, 2"Choose twelve men from among the people, one from each tribe, 3and tell them to take up twelve stones from the middle of the Jordan from right where the priests stood and to carry them over with you and put them down at the place where you stay tonight."

4So Joshua called together the twelve men he had appointed from the Israelites, one from each tribe, 5and said to them, "Go over before the ark of the LORD your God into the middle of the Jordan. Each of you is to take up a stone on his shoulder, according to the number of the tribes of the Israelites, 6to serve as a sign among you. In the future, when your children ask you, 'What do these stones mean?' 7tell them that the flow of the Jordan was cut off before the ark of the covenant of the LORD. When it crossed the Jordan, the waters of the Jordan were cut off. These stones are to be a memorial to the people of Israel forever."

8So the Israelites did as Joshua commanded them. They took twelve stones from the middle of the Jordan, according to the number of the tribes of the Israelites, as the LORD had told Joshua; and they carried them over with them to their camp, where they put them down. 9Joshua set up the twelve stones that had been[c] in the middle of the Jordan at the spot where the priests who carried the ark of the covenant had stood. And they are there to this day.

10Now the priests who carried the ark remained standing in the middle of the

[a] 4 Hebrew *about two thousand cubits* (about 900 meters) [b] 16 That is, the Dead Sea [c] 9 Or *Joshua also set up twelve stones*

Jordan until everything the LORD had commanded Joshua was done by the people, just as Moses had directed Joshua. The people hurried over, 11and as soon as all of them had crossed, the ark of the LORD and the priests came to the other side while the people watched. 12The men of Reuben, Gad and the half-tribe of Manasseh crossed over, armed, in front of the Israelites, as Moses had directed them. 13About forty thousand armed for battle crossed over before the LORD to the plains of Jericho for war.

14That day the LORD exalted Joshua in the sight of all Israel; and they revered him all the days of his life, just as they had revered Moses.

15Then the LORD said to Joshua, 16"Command the priests carrying the ark of the Testimony to come up out of the Jordan."

17So Joshua commanded the priests, "Come up out of the Jordan."

18And the priests came up out of the river carrying the ark of the covenant of the LORD. No sooner had they set their feet on the dry ground than the waters of the Jordan returned to their place and ran at flood stage as before.

19On the tenth day of the first month the people went up from the Jordan and camped at Gilgal on the eastern border of Jericho. 20And Joshua set up at Gilgal the twelve stones they had taken out of the Jordan. 21He said to the Israelites, "In the future when your descendants ask their fathers, 'What do these stones mean?' 22tell them, 'Israel crossed the Jordan on dry ground.' 23For the LORD your God dried up the Jordan before you until you had crossed over. The LORD your God did to the Jordan just what he had done to the Red Sea[d] when he dried it up before us until we had crossed over. 24He did this so that all the peoples of the earth might know that the hand of the LORD is powerful and so that you might always fear the LORD your God."

[d] 23 Hebrew *Yam Suph;* that is, Sea of Reeds

PRAYER: INTERCESSION

O GOD, be gracious to us and bless us, and make Your face shine upon us, that Your way may be known on earth, Your salvation among all nations. (Psalm 67:1–2)

***TAKE** a few moments to intercede on behalf of local, national and world missions. Pray that the Great Commission would be fulfilled and for any special concerns you may have for missions.*

NT Philippians 2:19–3:11

Timothy and Epaphroditus

19I hope in the Lord Jesus to send Timothy to you soon, that I also may be cheered when I receive news about you. 20I have no one else like him, who takes a genuine interest in your welfare. 21For everyone looks out for his own interests, not those of Jesus Christ. 22But you know that Timothy has proved himself, because as a son with his father he has served with me in the work of the gospel. 23I hope, therefore, to send him as soon as I see how things go with me. 24And I am confident in the Lord that I myself will come soon.

25But I think it is necessary to send back to you Epaphroditus, my brother, fellow worker and fellow soldier, who is also your messenger, whom you sent to take care of my needs. 26For he longs for all of you and is distressed because you heard he was ill. 27Indeed he was ill, and almost died. But God had mercy on him, and not on him only but also on me, to spare me sorrow upon sorrow. 28Therefore I am all the more eager to send him, so that when you see him again you may be glad and I may have less anxiety. 29Welcome him in the Lord with great joy, and honor men like him, 30because he almost died for the work of Christ, risking his life to make up for the help you could not give me.

No Confidence in the Flesh

3 Finally, my brothers, rejoice in the
Lord! It is no trouble for me to write
the same things to you again, and it is a
safeguard for you.
2Watch out for those dogs, those men
who do evil, those mutilators of the flesh.
3For it is we who are the circumcision, we
who worship by the Spirit of God, who
glory in Christ Jesus, and who put no confidence in the flesh— 4though I myself
have reasons for such confidence.
If anyone else thinks he has reasons to
put confidence in the flesh, I have more:
5circumcised on the eighth day, of the
people of Israel, of the tribe of Benjamin,
a Hebrew of Hebrews; in regard to the
law, a Pharisee; 6as for zeal, persecuting
the church; as for legalistic righteousness,
faultless.
7But whatever was to my profit I now
consider loss for the sake of Christ. 8What
is more, I consider everything a loss compared to the surpassing greatness of
knowing Christ Jesus my Lord, for whose
sake I have lost all things. I consider them
rubbish, that I may gain Christ 9and be
found in him, not having a righteousness
of my own that comes from the law, but
that which is through faith in Christ—the
righteousness that comes from God and
is by faith. 10I want to know Christ and the
power of his resurrection and the fellowship of sharing in his sufferings, becoming like him in his death, 11and so, somehow, to attain to the resurrection from the
dead.

PRAYER: THE WORKS OF GOD

I HAVE come to Mount Zion, to the heavenly Jerusalem, Your city, O living God. I have come to myriad angels, and to the assembly and church of the firstborn who are enrolled in heaven. I have come to You, the Judge of all people, to the spirits of the righteous made perfect, to Jesus the mediator of a new covenant, and to the sprinkled blood that speaks of better things than the blood of Abel. (Hebrews 12:22–24)

TAKE *a moment to consider the greatness of God's wonderful works.*

YEAR 1 DAY 188

OT Joshua 5:1–6:27

Circumcision at Gilgal

5 Now when all the Amorite kings west
of the Jordan and all the Canaanite
kings along the coast heard how the LORD
had dried up the Jordan before the Israelites until we had crossed over, their hearts
melted and they no longer had the
courage to face the Israelites.
2At that time the LORD said to Joshua,
"Make flint knives and circumcise the Israelites again." 3So Joshua made flint
knives and circumcised the Israelites at
Gibeath Haaraloth.[a]
4Now this is why he did so: All those
who came out of Egypt—all the men of
military age—died in the desert on the
way after leaving Egypt. 5All the people
that came out had been circumcised, but
all the people born in the desert during
the journey from Egypt had not. 6The Israelites had moved about in the desert
forty years until all the men who were of
military age when they left Egypt had
died, since they had not obeyed the LORD.
For the LORD had sworn to them that they
would not see the land that he had
solemnly promised their fathers to give
us, a land flowing with milk and honey.
7So he raised up their sons in their place,
and these were the ones Joshua circumcised. They were still uncircumcised because they had not been circumcised on
the way. 8And after the whole nation had
been circumcised, they remained where
they were in camp until they were healed.
9Then the LORD said to Joshua, "Today
I have rolled away the reproach of Egypt

[a] 3 *Gibeath Haaraloth* means *hill of foreskins.*

from you." So the place has been called Gilgal[b] to this day.

10 On the evening of the fourteenth day of the month, while camped at Gilgal on the plains of Jericho, the Israelites celebrated the Passover. 11 The day after the Passover, that very day, they ate some of the produce of the land: unleavened bread and roasted grain. 12 The manna stopped the day after[c] they ate this food from the land; there was no longer any manna for the Israelites, but that year they ate of the produce of Canaan.

The Fall of Jericho

13 Now when Joshua was near Jericho, he looked up and saw a man standing in front of him with a drawn sword in his hand. Joshua went up to him and asked, "Are you for us or for our enemies?"

14 "Neither," he replied, "but as commander of the army of the LORD I have now come." Then Joshua fell facedown to the ground in reverence, and asked him, "What message does my Lord[d] have for his servant?"

15 The commander of the LORD's army replied, "Take off your sandals, for the place where you are standing is holy." And Joshua did so.

6 Now Jericho was tightly shut up because of the Israelites. No one went out and no one came in.

2 Then the LORD said to Joshua, "See, I have delivered Jericho into your hands, along with its king and its fighting men. 3 March around the city once with all the armed men. Do this for six days. 4 Have seven priests carry trumpets of rams' horns in front of the ark. On the seventh day, march around the city seven times, with the priests blowing the trumpets. 5 When you hear them sound a long blast on the trumpets, have all the people give a loud shout; then the wall of the city will collapse and the people will go up, every man straight in."

6 So Joshua son of Nun called the priests and said to them, "Take up the ark of the covenant of the LORD and have seven priests carry trumpets in front of it." 7 And he ordered the people, "Advance! March around the city, with the armed guard going ahead of the ark of the LORD."

8 When Joshua had spoken to the people, the seven priests carrying the seven trumpets before the LORD went forward, blowing their trumpets, and the ark of the LORD's covenant followed them. 9 The armed guard marched ahead of the priests who blew the trumpets, and the rear guard followed the ark. All this time the trumpets were sounding. 10 But Joshua had commanded the people, "Do not give a war cry, do not raise your voices, do not say a word until the day I tell you to shout. Then shout!" 11 So he had the ark of the LORD carried around the city, circling it once. Then the people returned to camp and spent the night there.

12 Joshua got up early the next morning and the priests took up the ark of the LORD. 13 The seven priests carrying the seven trumpets went forward, marching before the ark of the LORD and blowing the trumpets. The armed men went ahead of them and the rear guard followed the ark of the LORD, while the trumpets kept sounding. 14 So on the second day they marched around the city once and returned to the camp. They did this for six days.

15 On the seventh day, they got up at daybreak and marched around the city seven times in the same manner, except that on that day they circled the city seven times. 16 The seventh time around, when the priests sounded the trumpet blast, Joshua commanded the people, "Shout! For the LORD has given you the city! 17 The city and all that is in it are to be devoted[e] to the LORD. Only Rahab the prostitute[f] and all who are with her in her house shall be spared, because she hid the spies we sent. 18 But keep away from the devoted things, so that you will not bring about your own destruction by taking any of them. Otherwise you will make the camp of Israel liable to destruction and bring trouble on it. 19 All the silver and gold and the articles of bronze and iron are sacred to the LORD and must go into his treasury."

20 When the trumpets sounded, the people shouted, and at the sound of the trumpet, when the people gave a loud shout, the wall collapsed; so every man charged straight in, and they took the city.

[b] 9 *Gilgal* sounds like the Hebrew for *roll.* [c] 12 Or *the day* [d] 14 Or *lord* [e] 17 The Hebrew term refers to the irrevocable giving over of things or persons to the LORD, often by totally destroying them; also in verses 18 and 21. [f] 17 Or possibly *innkeeper;* also in verses 22 and 25

21 They devoted the city to the LORD and
destroyed with the sword every living
thing in it—men and women, young and
old, cattle, sheep and donkeys.
22 Joshua said to the two men who had
spied out the land, "Go into the prostitute's house and bring her out and all
who belong to her, in accordance with
your oath to her." 23 So the young men
who had done the spying went in and
brought out Rahab, her father and mother and brothers and all who belonged to
her. They brought out her entire family
and put them in a place outside the camp
of Israel.
24 Then they burned the whole city and
everything in it, but they put the silver
and gold and the articles of bronze and
iron into the treasury of the LORD's house.
25 But Joshua spared Rahab the prostitute,
with her family and all who belonged to
her, because she hid the men Joshua had
sent as spies to Jericho—and she lives
among the Israelites to this day.
26 At that time Joshua pronounced this
solemn oath: "Cursed before the LORD is
the man who undertakes to rebuild this
city, Jericho:

"At the cost of his firstborn son
  will he lay its foundations;
at the cost of his youngest
  will he set up its gates."

27 So the LORD was with Joshua, and his
fame spread throughout the land.

PRAYER: AFFIRMATION

THE wolf will dwell with the lamb, and the leopard will lie down with the goat, and the calf and the lion and the yearling together, and a little child will lead them. The cow will feed with the bear; their young will lie down together, and the lion will eat straw like the ox. The infant will play near the hole of the cobra, and the young child will put his hand into the viper's hole. They will neither harm nor destroy on all Your holy mountain, for the earth will be full of Your knowledge, O Lord, as the waters cover the sea. (Isaiah 11:6–9)

***PAUSE** to reflect on these Biblical affirmations.*

NT Philippians 3:12–4:1

Pressing on Toward the Goal

12 Not that I have already obtained all
this, or have already been made perfect,
but I press on to take hold of that for
which Christ Jesus took hold of me.
13 Brothers, I do not consider myself yet to
have taken hold of it. But one thing I do:
Forgetting what is behind and straining
toward what is ahead, 14 I press on toward
the goal to win the prize for which God
has called me heavenward in Christ Jesus.
15 All of us who are mature should take
such a view of things. And if on some
point you think differently, that too God
will make clear to you. 16 Only let us live
up to what we have already attained.
17 Join with others in following my example, brothers, and take note of those
who live according to the pattern we gave
you. 18 For, as I have often told you before
and now say again even with tears, many
live as enemies of the cross of Christ.
19 Their destiny is destruction, their god is
their stomach, and their glory is in their
shame. Their mind is on earthly things.
20 But our citizenship is in heaven. And we
eagerly await a Savior from there, the Lord
Jesus Christ, 21 who, by the power that enables him to bring everything under his
control, will transform our lowly bodies
so that they will be like his glorious body.
4 Therefore, my brothers, you whom I
love and long for, my joy and crown,
that is how you should stand firm in the
Lord, dear friends!

PRAYER: MY RELATIONSHIP TO GOD

I WANT to follow Abraham's example of willingness and offer all that I have to You, holding nothing back and trusting in Your character and in Your promises. (Genesis 22:2–11) . . . Like Josiah, I want a tender and responsive heart, so that I will humble myself before You when I hear Your word. (2 Chronicles 34:27)

__PAUSE__ to thank God for the relationship that you enjoy with Him in Jesus Christ.

YEAR 1 DAY 189

OT Psalm 37

Psalm 37[a]

Of David.

1 Do not fret because of evil men
or be envious of those who do wrong;
2 for like the grass they will soon wither,
like green plants they will soon die away.

3 Trust in the LORD and do good;
dwell in the land and enjoy safe pasture.
4 Delight yourself in the LORD
and he will give you the desires of your heart.

5 Commit your way to the LORD;
trust in him and he will do this:
6 He will make your righteousness shine like the dawn,
the justice of your cause like the noonday sun.

7 Be still before the LORD and wait patiently for him;
do not fret when men succeed in their ways,
when they carry out their wicked schemes.

8 Refrain from anger and turn from wrath;
do not fret—it leads only to evil.
9 For evil men will be cut off,
but those who hope in the LORD will inherit the land.

10 A little while, and the wicked will be no more;
though you look for them, they will not be found.
11 But the meek will inherit the land
and enjoy great peace.

12 The wicked plot against the righteous
and gnash their teeth at them;
13 but the Lord laughs at the wicked,
for he knows their day is coming.

14 The wicked draw the sword
and bend the bow
to bring down the poor and needy,
to slay those whose ways are upright.
15 But their swords will pierce their own hearts,
and their bows will be broken.

16 Better the little that the righteous have
than the wealth of many wicked;
17 for the power of the wicked will be broken,
but the LORD upholds the righteous.

18 The days of the blameless are known to the LORD,
and their inheritance will endure forever.
19 In times of disaster they will not wither;
in days of famine they will enjoy plenty.

20 But the wicked will perish:
The LORD's enemies will be like the beauty of the fields,
they will vanish—vanish like smoke.

21 The wicked borrow and do not repay,
but the righteous give generously;

[a] This psalm is an acrostic poem, the stanzas of which begin with the successive letters of the Hebrew alphabet.

[22]those the LORD blesses will inherit the land,
but those he curses will be cut off.

[23]If the LORD delights in a man's way,
he makes his steps firm;
[24]though he stumble, he will not fall,
for the LORD upholds him with his hand.

[25]I was young and now I am old,
yet I have never seen the righteous forsaken
or their children begging bread.
[26]They are always generous and lend freely;
their children will be blessed.

[27]Turn from evil and do good;
then you will dwell in the land forever.
[28]For the LORD loves the just
and will not forsake his faithful ones.
They will be protected forever,
but the offspring of the wicked will be cut off;
[29]the righteous will inherit the land
and dwell in it forever.

[30]The mouth of the righteous man utters wisdom,
and his tongue speaks what is just.
[31]The law of his God is in his heart;
his feet do not slip.

[32]The wicked lie in wait for the righteous,
seeking their very lives;
[33]but the LORD will not leave them in their power
or let them be condemned when brought to trial.

[34]Wait for the LORD
and keep his way.
He will exalt you to inherit the land;
when the wicked are cut off, you will see it.

[35]I have seen a wicked and ruthless man
flourishing like a green tree in its native soil,
[36]but he soon passed away and was no more;
though I looked for him, he could not be found.

[37]Consider the blameless, observe the upright;
there is a future[b] for the man of peace.
[38]But all sinners will be destroyed;
the future[c] of the wicked will be cut off.

[39]The salvation of the righteous comes from the LORD;
he is their stronghold in time of trouble.
[40]The LORD helps them and delivers them;
he delivers them from the wicked and saves them,
because they take refuge in him.

[b] 37 Or *there will be posterity* [c] 38 Or *posterity*

PRAYER: THANKSGIVING

I AM confident of this, that You, the One who began a good work in me, will carry it on to completion until the day of Christ Jesus.
(Philippians 1:6)

***PAUSE** to offer your own expressions of thanksgiving.*

NT Philippians 4:2–23

Exhortations

[2]I plead with Euodia and I plead with
Syntyche to agree with each other in the
Lord. [3]Yes, and I ask you, loyal yokefel-
low,[a] help these women who have contended at my side in the cause of the
gospel, along with Clement and the rest
of my fellow workers, whose names are in
the book of life.
[4]Rejoice in the Lord always. I will say it
again: Rejoice! [5]Let your gentleness be evident to all. The Lord is near. [6]Do not be
anxious about anything, but in every-

[a] 3 Or *loyal Syzygus*

thing, by prayer and petition, with thanksgiving, present your requests to God. 7And
the peace of God, which transcends all
understanding, will guard your hearts and
your minds in Christ Jesus.
8Finally, brothers, whatever is true,
whatever is noble, whatever is right, whatever is pure, whatever is lovely, whatever
is admirable—if anything is excellent or
praiseworthy—think about such things.
9Whatever you have learned or received or
heard from me, or seen in me—put it into
practice. And the God of peace will be
with you.

Thanks for Their Gifts

10I rejoice greatly in the Lord that at last
you have renewed your concern for me.
Indeed, you have been concerned, but
you had no opportunity to show it. 11I am
not saying this because I am in need, for
I have learned to be content whatever the
circumstances. 12I know what it is to be in
need, and I know what it is to have plenty. I have learned the secret of being content in any and every situation, whether
well fed or hungry, whether living in plenty or in want. 13I can do everything
through him who gives me strength.
14Yet it was good of you to share in my
troubles. 15Moreover, as you Philippians
know, in the early days of your acquain-
tance with the gospel, when I set out from
Macedonia, not one church shared with
me in the matter of giving and receiving,
except you only; 16for even when I was in
Thessalonica, you sent me aid again and
again when I was in need. 17Not that I am
looking for a gift, but I am looking for
what may be credited to your account. 18I
have received full payment and even
more; I am amply supplied, now that I
have received from Epaphroditus the gifts
you sent. They are a fragrant offering, an
acceptable sacrifice, pleasing to God.
19And my God will meet all your needs according to his glorious riches in Christ
Jesus.
20To our God and Father be glory for
ever and ever. Amen.

Final Greetings

21Greet all the saints in Christ Jesus. The
brothers who are with me send greetings.
22All the saints send you greetings, especially those who belong to Caesar's household.
23The grace of the Lord Jesus Christ be
with your spirit. Amen.[b]

[b]23 Some manuscripts do not have *Amen.*

PRAYER: THE CHARACTER I WANT TO CULTIVATE

I WILL not lay up for myself treasures on earth, where moth and rust destroy and where thieves break in and steal. But I will lay up for myself treasures in heaven, where moth and rust do not destroy and where thieves do not break in and steal. For where my treasure is, there my heart will be also. (Matthew 6:19–21; Luke 12:34)

***TAKE** a moment to ask the Lord for the grace to grow in godly character.*

YEAR 1 DAY 190

OT Joshua 7:1-26

Achan's Sin

7 But the Israelites acted unfaithfully in
regard to the devoted things[a]; Achan
son of Carmi, the son of Zimri,[b] the son
of Zerah, of the tribe of Judah, took some
of them. So the LORD's anger burned
against Israel.
2Now Joshua sent men from Jericho to
Ai, which is near Beth Aven to the east of
Bethel, and told them, "Go up and spy
out the region." So the men went up and
spied out Ai.
3When they returned to Joshua, they
said, "Not all the people will have to go

[a]1 The Hebrew term refers to the irrevocable giving over of things or persons to the LORD, often by totally destroying them; also in verses 11, 12, 13 and 15. [b]1 See Septuagint and 1 Chron. 2:6; Hebrew *Zabdi;* also in verses 17 and 18.

up against Ai. Send two or three thousand men to take it and do not weary all the people, for only a few men are there." 4So about three thousand men went up; but they were routed by the men of Ai, 5who killed about thirty-six of them. They chased the Israelites from the city gate as far as the stone quarries[c] and struck them down on the slopes. At this the hearts of the people melted and became like water.

6Then Joshua tore his clothes and fell facedown to the ground before the ark of the LORD, remaining there till evening. The elders of Israel did the same, and sprinkled dust on their heads. 7And Joshua said, "Ah, Sovereign LORD, why did you ever bring this people across the Jordan to deliver us into the hands of the Amorites to destroy us? If only we had been content to stay on the other side of the Jordan! 8O Lord, what can I say, now that Israel has been routed by its enemies? 9The Canaanites and the other people of the country will hear about this and they will surround us and wipe out our name from the earth. What then will you do for your own great name?"

10The LORD said to Joshua, "Stand up! What are you doing down on your face? 11Israel has sinned; they have violated my covenant, which I commanded them to keep. They have taken some of the devoted things; they have stolen, they have lied, they have put them with their own possessions. 12That is why the Israelites cannot stand against their enemies; they turn their backs and run because they have been made liable to destruction. I will not be with you anymore unless you destroy whatever among you is devoted to destruction.

13"Go, consecrate the people. Tell them, 'Consecrate yourselves in preparation for tomorrow; for this is what the LORD, the God of Israel, says: That which is devoted is among you, O Israel. You cannot stand against your enemies until you remove it.

14" 'In the morning, present yourselves tribe by tribe. The tribe that the LORD takes shall come forward clan by clan; the clan that the LORD takes shall come forward family by family; and the family that the LORD takes shall come forward man by man. 15He who is caught with the devoted things shall be destroyed by fire, along with all that belongs to him. He has violated the covenant of the LORD and has done a disgraceful thing in Israel!' "

16Early the next morning Joshua had Israel come forward by tribes, and Judah was taken. 17The clans of Judah came forward, and he took the Zerahites. He had the clan of the Zerahites come forward by families, and Zimri was taken. 18Joshua had his family come forward man by man, and Achan son of Carmi, the son of Zimri, the son of Zerah, of the tribe of Judah, was taken.

19Then Joshua said to Achan, "My son, give glory to the LORD,[d] the God of Israel, and give him the praise.[e] Tell me what you have done; do not hide it from me."

20Achan replied, "It is true! I have sinned against the LORD, the God of Israel. This is what I have done: 21When I saw in the plunder a beautiful robe from Babylonia,[f] two hundred shekels[g] of silver and a wedge of gold weighing fifty shekels,[h] I coveted them and took them. They are hidden in the ground inside my tent, with the silver underneath."

22So Joshua sent messengers, and they ran to the tent, and there it was, hidden in his tent, with the silver underneath. 23They took the things from the tent, brought them to Joshua and all the Israelites and spread them out before the LORD.

24Then Joshua, together with all Israel, took Achan son of Zerah, the silver, the robe, the gold wedge, his sons and daughters, his cattle, donkeys and sheep, his tent and all that he had, to the Valley of Achor. 25Joshua said, "Why have you brought this trouble on us? The LORD will bring trouble on you today."

Then all Israel stoned him, and after they had stoned the rest, they burned them. 26Over Achan they heaped up a large pile of rocks, which remains to this day. Then the LORD turned from his fierce anger. Therefore that place has been called the Valley of Achor[i] ever since.

[c] 5 Or *as far as Shebarim* [d] 19 A solemn charge to tell the truth [e] 19 Or *and confess to him* [f] 21 Hebrew *Shinar* [g] 21 That is, about 5 pounds (about 2.3 kilograms) [h] 21 That is, about 1 1/4 pounds (about 0.6 kilogram) [i] 26 *Achor* means *trouble.*

PRAYER: ADORATION

O LORD, You have measured the waters in the hollow of Your hand, and marked off the heavens with the breadth of Your hand. You have calculated the dust of the earth in a measure and weighed the mountains in the balance and the hills in scales. (Isaiah 40:12) . . . You are the Lord, and there is no other; apart from You there is no God. From the rising of the sun to its setting, we know there is none besides You. You are the Lord, and there is no other. (Isaiah 45:5–6)

***PAUSE** to express your thoughts of praise and worship.*

NT Colossians 1:1–14

1 Paul, an apostle of Christ Jesus by the
will of God, and Timothy our brother,

2 To the holy and faithful[a] brothers in
Christ at Colosse:

Grace and peace to you from God our
Father.[b]

Thanksgiving and Prayer

3 We always thank God, the Father of
our Lord Jesus Christ, when we pray for
you, 4 because we have heard of your faith
in Christ Jesus and of the love you have
for all the saints— 5 the faith and love that
spring from the hope that is stored up for
you in heaven and that you have already
heard about in the word of truth, the
gospel 6 that has come to you. All over the
world this gospel is bearing fruit and
growing, just as it has been doing among
you since the day you heard it and understood God's grace in all its truth. 7 You
learned it from Epaphras, our dear fellow
servant, who is a faithful minister of
Christ on our[c] behalf, 8 and who also told
us of your love in the Spirit.

9 For this reason, since the day we heard
about you, we have not stopped praying for
you and asking God to fill you with the
knowledge of his will through all spiritual
wisdom and understanding. 10 And we pray
this in order that you may live a life worthy
of the Lord and may please him in every
way: bearing fruit in every good work,
growing in the knowledge of God, 11 being
strengthened with all power according to
his glorious might so that you may have
great endurance and patience, and joyfully
12 giving thanks to the Father, who has qualified you[d] to share in the inheritance of the
saints in the kingdom of light. 13 For he has
rescued us from the dominion of darkness
and brought us into the kingdom of the
Son he loves, 14 in whom we have redemption,[e] the forgiveness of sins.

[a] *2* Or *believing* [b] *2* Some manuscripts *Father and the Lord Jesus Christ* [c] *7* Some manuscripts *your* [d] *12* Some manuscripts *us* [e] *14* A few late manuscripts *redemption through his blood*

PRAYER: MY RELATIONSHIP TO OTHERS

THE people of this world are more shrewd in dealing with their own kind than are the people of light. I would be wise to use worldly wealth to help others, making friends for myself, so that when it is gone, they may welcome me into Your eternal dwellings. (Luke 16:8–9) . . . What is my hope or joy or crown of rejoicing in Your presence, Lord Jesus, at Your coming? My glory and joy is the people in whose lives I have been privileged to have a ministry. (1 Thessalonians 2:19–20)

***PAUSE** to review your relationships with others and to commit them to the Lord.*

YEAR 1
DAY 191

OT Joshua 8:1-35

Ai Destroyed

8 Then the LORD said to Joshua, "Do not
be afraid; do not be discouraged. Take
the whole army with you, and go up and
attack Ai. For I have delivered into your
hands the king of Ai, his people, his city
and his land. [2]You shall do to Ai and its
king as you did to Jericho and its king, except that you may carry off their plunder
and livestock for yourselves. Set an ambush behind the city."

[3]So Joshua and the whole army moved
out to attack Ai. He chose thirty thousand
of his best fighting men and sent them
out at night [4]with these orders: "Listen
carefully. You are to set an ambush behind the city. Don't go very far from it. All
of you be on the alert. [5]I and all those
with me will advance on the city, and
when the men come out against us, as
they did before, we will flee from them.
[6]They will pursue us until we have lured
them away from the city, for they will say,
'They are running away from us as they
did before.' So when we flee from them,
[7]you are to rise up from ambush and take
the city. The LORD your God will give it
into your hand. [8]When you have taken
the city, set it on fire. Do what the LORD
has commanded. See to it; you have my
orders."

[9]Then Joshua sent them off, and they
went to the place of ambush and lay in
wait between Bethel and Ai, to the west of
Ai—but Joshua spent that night with the
people.

[10]Early the next morning Joshua mustered his men, and he and the leaders of
Israel marched before them to Ai. [11]The
entire force that was with him marched
up and approached the city and arrived in
front of it. They set up camp north of Ai,
with the valley between them and the city.
[12]Joshua had taken about five thousand
men and set them in ambush between
Bethel and Ai, to the west of the city.
[13]They had the soldiers take up their positions—all those in the camp to the
north of the city and the ambush to the
west of it. That night Joshua went into
the valley.

[14]When the king of Ai saw this, he and
all the men of the city hurried out early in
the morning to meet Israel in battle at a
certain place overlooking the Arabah. But
he did not know that an ambush had
been set against him behind the city.
[15]Joshua and all Israel let themselves be
driven back before them, and they fled toward the desert. [16]All the men of Ai were
called to pursue them, and they pursued
Joshua and were lured away from the city.
[17]Not a man remained in Ai or Bethel who
did not go after Israel. They left the city
open and went in pursuit of Israel.

[18]Then the LORD said to Joshua, "Hold
out toward Ai the javelin that is in your
hand, for into your hand I will deliver the
city." So Joshua held out his javelin toward Ai. [19]As soon as he did this, the men
in the ambush rose quickly from their position and rushed forward. They entered
the city and captured it and quickly set it
on fire.

[20]The men of Ai looked back and saw
the smoke of the city rising against the
sky, but they had no chance to escape in
any direction, for the Israelites who had
been fleeing toward the desert had turned
back against their pursuers. [21]For when
Joshua and all Israel saw that the ambush
had taken the city and that smoke was going up from the city, they turned around
and attacked the men of Ai. [22]The men of
the ambush also came out of the city
against them, so that they were caught in
the middle, with Israelites on both sides.
Israel cut them down, leaving them neither survivors nor fugitives. [23]But they
took the king of Ai alive and brought him
to Joshua.

[24]When Israel had finished killing all
the men of Ai in the fields and in the
desert where they had chased them, and
when every one of them had been put to
the sword, all the Israelites returned to Ai
and killed those who were in it. [25]Twelve
thousand men and women fell that day—
all the people of Ai. [26]For Joshua did not
draw back the hand that held out his
javelin until he had destroyed[a] all who
lived in Ai. [27]But Israel did carry off for
themselves the livestock and plunder of

[a] *26* The Hebrew term refers to the irrevocable giving over of things or persons to the LORD, often by totally destroying them.

this city, as the LORD had instructed Joshua.

28 So Joshua burned Ai and made it a permanent heap of ruins, a desolate place to this day. 29 He hung the king of Ai on a tree and left him there until evening. At sunset, Joshua ordered them to take his body from the tree and throw it down at the entrance of the city gate. And they raised a large pile of rocks over it, which remains to this day.

The Covenant Renewed at Mount Ebal

30 Then Joshua built on Mount Ebal an altar to the LORD, the God of Israel, 31 as Moses the servant of the LORD had commanded the Israelites. He built it according to what is written in the Book of the Law of Moses—an altar of uncut stones, on which no iron tool had been used. On it they offered to the LORD burnt offerings and sacrificed fellowship offerings.[b] 32 There, in the presence of the Israelites, Joshua copied on stones the law of Moses, which he had written. 33 All Israel, aliens and citizens alike, with their elders, officials and judges, were standing on both sides of the ark of the covenant of the LORD, facing those who carried it—the priests, who were Levites. Half of the people stood in front of Mount Gerizim and half of them in front of Mount Ebal, as Moses the servant of the LORD had formerly commanded when he gave instructions to bless the people of Israel.

34 Afterward, Joshua read all the words of the law—the blessings and the curses—just as it is written in the Book of the Law. 35 There was not a word of all that Moses had commanded that Joshua did not read to the whole assembly of Israel, including the women and children, and the aliens who lived among them.

[b] *31* Traditionally *peace offerings*

PRAYER: CONFESSION

WHEN my soul was fainting away, I remembered You, Lord, and my prayer went up to You—to Your holy temple. Those who cling to worthless idols forsake Your loving-kindness. But I will sacrifice to You with the voice of thanksgiving. I will fulfill what I have vowed. Salvation is from You alone. (Jonah 2:7–9)

***ASK** the Spirit to search your heart and reveal any areas of unconfessed sin. Acknowledge these to the Lord and thank Him for His forgiveness.*

NT Colossians 1:15–23

The Supremacy of Christ

15 He is the image of the invisible God, the firstborn over all creation. 16 For by him all things were created: things in heaven and on earth, visible and invisible, whether thrones or powers or rulers or authorities; all things were created by him and for him. 17 He is before all things, and in him all things hold together. 18 And he is the head of the body, the church; he is the beginning and the firstborn from among the dead, so that in everything he might have the supremacy. 19 For God was pleased to have all his fullness dwell in him, 20 and through him to reconcile to himself all things, whether things on earth or things in heaven, by making peace through his blood, shed on the cross.

21 Once you were alienated from God and were enemies in your minds because of[a] your evil behavior. 22 But now he has reconciled you by Christ's physical body through death to present you holy in his sight, without blemish and free from accusation— 23 if you continue in your faith, established and firm, not moved from the hope held out in the gospel. This is the gospel that you heard and that has been proclaimed to every creature under heaven, and of which I, Paul, have become a servant.

[a] *21* Or *minds, as shown by*

PRAYER: THE ATTRIBUTES OF GOD

LET me fall into Your hands, O Lord, for Your mercies are very great; but do not let me fall into the hands of people. (1 Chronicles 21:13) . . . You, Lord, are good and ready to forgive and abundant in mercy to all who call upon You. (Psalm 86:5)

***PAUSE** to reflect on these affirmations about the person, powers and perfection of God.*

YEAR 1 DAY 192

OT Joshua 9:1-27

The Gibeonite Deception

9 Now when all the kings west of the Jordan heard about these things—those in the hill country, in the western foothills, and along the entire coast of the Great Sea[a] as far as Lebanon (the kings of the Hittites, Amorites, Canaanites, Perizzites, Hivites and Jebusites)— 2 they came together to make war against Joshua and Israel.

3 However, when the people of Gibeon heard what Joshua had done to Jericho and Ai, 4 they resorted to a ruse: They went as a delegation whose donkeys were loaded[b] with worn-out sacks and old wineskins, cracked and mended. 5 The men put worn and patched sandals on their feet and wore old clothes. All the bread of their food supply was dry and moldy. 6 Then they went to Joshua in the camp at Gilgal and said to him and the men of Israel, "We have come from a distant country; make a treaty with us."

7 The men of Israel said to the Hivites, "But perhaps you live near us. How then can we make a treaty with you?"

8 "We are your servants," they said to Joshua.

But Joshua asked, "Who are you and where do you come from?"

9 They answered: "Your servants have come from a very distant country because of the fame of the LORD your God. For we have heard reports of him: all that he did in Egypt, 10 and all that he did to the two kings of the Amorites east of the Jordan—Sihon king of Heshbon, and Og king of Bashan, who reigned in Ashtaroth. 11 And our elders and all those living in our country said to us, 'Take provisions for your journey; go and meet them and say to them, "We are your servants; make a treaty with us." ' 12 This bread of ours was warm when we packed it at home on the day we left to come to you. But now see how dry and moldy it is. 13 And these wineskins that we filled were new, but see how cracked they are. And our clothes and sandals are worn out by the very long journey."

14 The men of Israel sampled their provisions but did not inquire of the LORD. 15 Then Joshua made a treaty of peace with them to let them live, and the leaders of the assembly ratified it by oath.

16 Three days after they made the treaty with the Gibeonites, the Israelites heard that they were neighbors, living near them. 17 So the Israelites set out and on the third day came to their cities: Gibeon, Kephirah, Beeroth and Kiriath Jearim. 18 But the Israelites did not attack them, because the leaders of the assembly had sworn an oath to them by the LORD, the God of Israel.

The whole assembly grumbled against the leaders, 19 but all the leaders answered, "We have given them our oath by the LORD, the God of Israel, and we cannot touch them now. 20 This is what we will do to them: We will let them live, so that wrath will not fall on us for breaking the oath we swore to them." 21 They continued, "Let them live, but let them be woodcutters and water carriers for the entire community." So the leaders' promise to them was kept.

22 Then Joshua summoned the Gibeon-

[a] *1* That is, the Mediterranean [b] *4* Most Hebrew manuscripts; some Hebrew manuscripts, Vulgate and Syriac (see also Septuagint) *They prepared provisions and loaded their donkeys*

ites and said, "Why did you deceive us by saying, 'We live a long way from you,' while actually you live near us? 23You are now under a curse: You will never cease to serve as woodcutters and water carriers for the house of my God."

24They answered Joshua, "Your servants were clearly told how the LORD your God had commanded his servant Moses to give you the whole land and to wipe out all its inhabitants from before you. So we feared for our lives because of you, and that is why we did this. 25We are now in your hands. Do to us whatever seems good and right to you."

26So Joshua saved them from the Israelites, and they did not kill them. 27That day he made the Gibeonites woodcutters and water carriers for the community and for the altar of the LORD at the place the LORD would choose. And that is what they are to this day.

PRAYER: RENEWAL

FATHER, I am the salt of the earth. But if the salt loses its flavor, how can it be made salty again? It is no longer good for anything, except to be thrown out and trampled underfoot by people. I am the light of the world. A city set on a hill cannot be hidden. Neither do people light a lamp and put it under a basket, but on a lampstand, and it gives light to all who are in the house. In the same way, I must let my light shine before all people, that they may see my good deeds and praise You, my Father in heaven. (Matthew 5:13–16)

__PAUSE__ to add your own prayers for personal renewal.

NT Colossians 1:24–2:5

Paul's Labor for the Church

24Now I rejoice in what was suffered for you, and I fill up in my flesh what is still lacking in regard to Christ's afflictions, for the sake of his body, which is the church. 25I have become its servant by the commission God gave me to present to you the word of God in its fullness— 26the mystery that has been kept hidden for ages and generations, but is now disclosed to the saints. 27To them God has chosen to make known among the Gentiles the glorious riches of this mystery, which is Christ in you, the hope of glory.

28We proclaim him, admonishing and teaching everyone with all wisdom, so that we may present everyone perfect in Christ. 29To this end I labor, struggling with all his energy, which so powerfully works in me.

2 I want you to know how much I am struggling for you and for those at Laodicea, and for all who have not met me personally. 2My purpose is that they may be encouraged in heart and united in love, so that they may have the full riches of complete understanding, in order that they may know the mystery of God, namely, Christ, 3in whom are hidden all the treasures of wisdom and knowledge. 4I tell you this so that no one may deceive you by fine-sounding arguments. 5For though I am absent from you in body, I am present with you in spirit and delight to see how orderly you are and how firm your faith in Christ is.

PRAYER: THE WORKS OF GOD

WE are not to be ignorant about those who fall asleep or grieve like other people, who have no hope. For if we believe that You, Jesus, died and rose again, even so the Father will bring with You those who have fallen asleep in You. According to Your own word, we who are alive and remain until Your coming will not precede those who have fallen asleep. For

You Yourself will come down from heaven, with a loud command, with the voice of the archangel, and with the trumpet of God, and the dead in You will rise first. Then we who are alive and remain will be caught up together with them in the clouds to meet You in the air. And so we will be with You forever.
(1 Thessalonians 4:13–17)

TAKE *a moment to consider the greatness of God's wonderful works.*

YEAR 1
DAY 193

OT Joshua 10:1-43

The Sun Stands Still

10 Now Adoni-Zedek king of Jerusalem heard that Joshua had taken Ai and totally destroyed[a] it, doing to Ai and its king as he had done to Jericho and its king, and that the people of Gibeon had made a treaty of peace with Israel and were living near them. [2]He and his people were very much alarmed at this, because Gibeon was an important city, like one of the royal cities; it was larger than Ai, and all its men were good fighters. [3]So Adoni-Zedek king of Jerusalem appealed to Hoham king of Hebron, Piram king of Jarmuth, Japhia king of Lachish and Debir king of Eglon. [4]"Come up and help me attack Gibeon," he said, "because it has made peace with Joshua and the Israelites."

[5]Then the five kings of the Amorites—the kings of Jerusalem, Hebron, Jarmuth, Lachish and Eglon—joined forces. They moved up with all their troops and took up positions against Gibeon and attacked it.

[6]The Gibeonites then sent word to Joshua in the camp at Gilgal: "Do not abandon your servants. Come up to us quickly and save us! Help us, because all the Amorite kings from the hill country have joined forces against us."

[7]So Joshua marched up from Gilgal with his entire army, including all the best fighting men. [8]The LORD said to Joshua, "Do not be afraid of them; I have given them into your hand. Not one of them will be able to withstand you."

[9]After an all-night march from Gilgal, Joshua took them by surprise. [10]The LORD threw them into confusion before Israel, who defeated them in a great victory at Gibeon. Israel pursued them along the road going up to Beth Horon and cut them down all the way to Azekah and Makkedah. [11]As they fled before Israel on the road down from Beth Horon to Azekah, the LORD hurled large hailstones down on them from the sky, and more of them died from the hailstones than were killed by the swords of the Israelites.

[12]On the day the LORD gave the Amorites over to Israel, Joshua said to the LORD in the presence of Israel:

"O sun, stand still over Gibeon,
O moon, over the Valley of Aijalon."
[13]So the sun stood still,
and the moon stopped,
till the nation avenged itself on[b] its enemies,

as it is written in the Book of Jashar.

The sun stopped in the middle of the sky and delayed going down about a full day. [14]There has never been a day like it before or since, a day when the LORD listened to a man. Surely the LORD was fighting for Israel!

[15]Then Joshua returned with all Israel to the camp at Gilgal.

Five Amorite Kings Killed

[16]Now the five kings had fled and hidden in the cave at Makkedah. [17]When Joshua was told that the five kings had been found hiding in the cave at Makkedah, [18]he said, "Roll large rocks up to the mouth of the cave, and post some men there to guard it. [19]But don't stop! Pursue your enemies, attack them from the rear and don't let them reach their cities, for the LORD your God has given them into your hand."

[20]So Joshua and the Israelites destroyed them completely—almost to a man—but the few who were left reached their fortified

[a] *1* The Hebrew term refers to the irrevocable giving over of things or persons to the LORD, often by totally destroying them; also in verses 28, 35, 37, 39 and 40. [b] *13* Or *nation triumphed over*

cities. 21The whole army then returned safely to Joshua in the camp at Makkedah, and
no one uttered a word against the Israelites.
22Joshua said, "Open the mouth of the
cave and bring those five kings out to me."
23So they brought the five kings out of the
cave—the kings of Jerusalem, Hebron, Jarmuth, Lachish and Eglon. 24When they had
brought these kings to Joshua, he summoned all the men of Israel and said to the
army commanders who had come with
him, "Come here and put your feet on the
necks of these kings." So they came forward and placed their feet on their necks.
25Joshua said to them, "Do not be afraid;
do not be discouraged. Be strong and
courageous. This is what the LORD will do
to all the enemies you are going to fight."
26Then Joshua struck and killed the kings
and hung them on five trees, and they were
left hanging on the trees until evening.
27At sunset Joshua gave the order and
they took them down from the trees and
threw them into the cave where they had
been hiding. At the mouth of the cave
they placed large rocks, which are there to
this day.
28That day Joshua took Makkedah. He
put the city and its king to the sword and
totally destroyed everyone in it. He left no
survivors. And he did to the king of Makkedah as he had done to the king of Jericho.

Southern Cities Conquered

29Then Joshua and all Israel with him
moved on from Makkedah to Libnah and
attacked it. 30The LORD also gave that city
and its king into Israel's hand. The city
and everyone in it Joshua put to the
sword. He left no survivors there. And he
did to its king as he had done to the king
of Jericho.
31Then Joshua and all Israel with him
moved on from Libnah to Lachish; he
took up positions against it and attacked
it. 32The LORD handed Lachish over to Israel, and Joshua took it on the second
day. The city and everyone in it he put to
the sword, just as he had done to Libnah.
33Meanwhile, Horam king of Gezer had
come up to help Lachish, but Joshua defeated him and his army—until no survivors were left.
34Then Joshua and all Israel with him
moved on from Lachish to Eglon; they
took up positions against it and attacked
it. 35They captured it that same day and put
it to the sword and totally destroyed everyone in it, just as they had done to Lachish.
36Then Joshua and all Israel with him
went up from Eglon to Hebron and attacked it. 37They took the city and put it
to the sword, together with its king, its villages and everyone in it. They left no survivors. Just as at Eglon, they totally destroyed it and everyone in it.
38Then Joshua and all Israel with him
turned around and attacked Debir. 39They
took the city, its king and its villages, and
put them to the sword. Everyone in it they
totally destroyed. They left no survivors.
They did to Debir and its king as they had
done to Libnah and its king and to Hebron.
40So Joshua subdued the whole region,
including the hill country, the Negev, the
western foothills and the mountain slopes,
together with all their kings. He left no survivors. He totally destroyed all who
breathed, just as the LORD, the God of Israel, had commanded. 41Joshua subdued
them from Kadesh Barnea to Gaza and
from the whole region of Goshen to Gibeon. 42All these kings and their lands Joshua
conquered in one campaign, because the
LORD, the God of Israel, fought for Israel.
43Then Joshua returned with all Israel to
the camp at Gilgal.

PRAYER: PETITION

MAY I be strong and courageous; may I not be afraid or discouraged, for You, Lord my God, will be with me wherever I go. (Joshua 1:9)

***PAUSE** here to petition God for growth in your character and personal discipline, and for physical health and strength. Ask that He empower you for spiritual warfare against the temptations of the world, the flesh and the devil. Offer prayers regarding your activities for this day and any special concerns you may have.*

NT Colossians 2:6–23

Freedom From Human Regulations Through Life With Christ

6So then, just as you received Christ Jesus as Lord, continue to live in him, 7rooted and built up in him, strengthened in the faith as you were taught, and overflowing with thankfulness.

8See to it that no one takes you captive through hollow and deceptive philosophy, which depends on human tradition and the basic principles of this world rather than on Christ.

9For in Christ all the fullness of the Deity lives in bodily form, 10and you have been given fullness in Christ, who is the head over every power and authority. 11In him you were also circumcised, in the putting off of the sinful nature,[a] not with a circumcision done by the hands of men but with the circumcision done by Christ, 12having been buried with him in baptism and raised with him through your faith in the power of God, who raised him from the dead.

13When you were dead in your sins and in the uncircumcision of your sinful nature,[b] God made you[c] alive with Christ. He forgave us all our sins, 14having canceled the written code, with its regulations, that was against us and that stood opposed to us; he took it away, nailing it to the cross. 15And having disarmed the powers and authorities, he made a public spectacle of them, triumphing over them by the cross.[d]

16Therefore do not let anyone judge you by what you eat or drink, or with regard to a religious festival, a New Moon celebration or a Sabbath day. 17These are a shadow of the things that were to come; the reality, however, is found in Christ. 18Do not let anyone who delights in false humility and the worship of angels disqualify you for the prize. Such a person goes into great detail about what he has seen, and his unspiritual mind puffs him up with idle notions. 19He has lost connection with the Head, from whom the whole body, supported and held together by its ligaments and sinews, grows as God causes it to grow.

20Since you died with Christ to the basic principles of this world, why, as though you still belonged to it, do you submit to its rules: 21"Do not handle! Do not taste! Do not touch!"? 22These are all destined to perish with use, because they are based on human commands and teachings. 23Such regulations indeed have an appearance of wisdom, with their self-imposed worship, their false humility and their harsh treatment of the body, but they lack any value in restraining sensual indulgence.

[a] 11 Or *the flesh* [b] 13 Or *your flesh* [c] 13 Some manuscripts *us* [d] 15 Or *them in him*

PRAYER: MY RELATIONSHIP TO GOD

I AM confident that I will see Your goodness, O Lord, in the land of the living. I will hope in You and be of good courage, and You will strengthen my heart. Yes, I will hope in You, Lord. (Psalm 27:13–14) . . . I wait for You, O Lord; My soul waits, and in Your word I put my hope. I hope in You, O Lord, for with You is unfailing love and abundant redemption. (Psalm 130:5, 7)

***PAUSE** to thank God for the relationship that you enjoy with Him in Jesus Christ.*

Northern Kings Defeated

11 When Jabin king of Hazor heard of
this, he sent word to Jobab king of Madon, to the kings of Shimron and Acshaph, 2and to the northern kings who
were in the mountains, in the Arabah
south of Kinnereth, in the western
foothills and in Naphoth Dor[a] on the
west; 3to the Canaanites in the east and
west; to the Amorites, Hittites, Perizzites
and Jebusites in the hill country; and to
the Hivites below Hermon in the region
of Mizpah. 4They came out with all their
troops and a large number of horses and
chariots—a huge army, as numerous as
the sand on the seashore. 5All these kings
joined forces and made camp together at
the Waters of Merom, to fight against Israel.
6The LORD said to Joshua, "Do not be
afraid of them, because by this time tomorrow I will hand all of them over to Israel, slain. You are to hamstring their
horses and burn their chariots."
7So Joshua and his whole army came
against them suddenly at the Waters of
Merom and attacked them, 8and the LORD
gave them into the hand of Israel. They
defeated them and pursued them all the
way to Greater Sidon, to Misrephoth
Maim, and to the Valley of Mizpah on the
east, until no survivors were left. 9Joshua
did to them as the LORD had directed: He
hamstrung their horses and burned their
chariots.
10At that time Joshua turned back and
captured Hazor and put its king to the
sword. (Hazor had been the head of all
these kingdoms.) 11Everyone in it they put
to the sword. They totally destroyed[b]
them, not sparing anything that breathed,
and he burned up Hazor itself.
12Joshua took all these royal cities and
their kings and put them to the sword. He
totally destroyed them, as Moses the servant of the LORD had commanded. 13Yet
Israel did not burn any of the cities built
on their mounds—except Hazor, which
Joshua burned. 14The Israelites carried off
for themselves all the plunder and livestock of these cities, but all the people
they put to the sword until they completely destroyed them, not sparing anyone that breathed. 15As the LORD commanded his servant Moses, so Moses commanded Joshua, and Joshua did it; he left
nothing undone of all that the LORD commanded Moses.
16So Joshua took this entire land: the
hill country, all the Negev, the whole region of Goshen, the western foothills, the
Arabah and the mountains of Israel with
their foothills, 17from Mount Halak,
which rises toward Seir, to Baal Gad in the
Valley of Lebanon below Mount Hermon.
He captured all their kings and struck
them down, putting them to death.
18Joshua waged war against all these kings
for a long time. 19Except for the Hivites
living in Gibeon, not one city made a
treaty of peace with the Israelites, who
took them all in battle. 20For it was the
LORD himself who hardened their hearts
to wage war against Israel, so that he
might destroy them totally, exterminating
them without mercy, as the LORD had
commanded Moses.
21At that time Joshua went and destroyed the Anakites from the hill country: from Hebron, Debir and Anab, from
all the hill country of Judah, and from all
the hill country of Israel. Joshua totally
destroyed them and their towns. 22No Anakites were left in Israelite territory; only
in Gaza, Gath and Ashdod did any survive. 23So Joshua took the entire land, just
as the LORD had directed Moses, and he
gave it as an inheritance to Israel according to their tribal divisions.
Then the land had rest from war.

List of Defeated Kings

12 These are the kings of the land whom
the Israelites had defeated and whose
territory they took over east of the Jordan,
from the Arnon Gorge to Mount Hermon,
including all the eastern side of the Arabah:

2Sihon king of the Amorites,
who reigned in Heshbon. He ruled
from Aroer on the rim of the Arnon
Gorge—from the middle of the

[a] 2 Or *in the heights of Dor* [b] 11 The Hebrew term refers to the irrevocable giving over of things or persons to the LORD, often by totally destroying them; also in verses 12, 20 and 21.

gorge—to the Jabbok River, which is the border of the Ammonites. This included half of Gilead.
3He also ruled over the eastern Arabah from the Sea of Kinnereth[c] to the Sea of the Arabah (the Salt Sea[d]), to Beth Jeshimoth, and then southward below the slopes of Pisgah.

4And the territory of Og king of Bashan, one of the last of the Rephaites, who reigned in Ashtaroth and Edrei.
5He ruled over Mount Hermon, Salecah, all of Bashan to the border of the people of Geshur and Maacah, and half of Gilead to the border of Sihon king of Heshbon.

6Moses, the servant of the LORD, and the Israelites conquered them. And Moses the servant of the LORD gave their land to the Reubenites, the Gadites and the half-tribe of Manasseh to be their possession.

7These are the kings of the land that Joshua and the Israelites conquered on the west side of the Jordan, from Baal Gad in the Valley of Lebanon to Mount Halak, which rises toward Seir (their lands Joshua gave as an inheritance to the tribes of Israel according to their tribal divisions—
8the hill country, the western foothills, the Arabah, the mountain slopes, the desert and the Negev—the lands of the Hittites, Amorites, Canaanites, Perizzites, Hivites and Jebusites):

9the king of Jericho one
the king of Ai (near Bethel) one
10the king of Jerusalem one
the king of Hebron one
11the king of Jarmuth one
the king of Lachish one
12the king of Eglon one
the king of Gezer one
13the king of Debir one
the king of Geder one
14the king of Hormah one
the king of Arad one
15the king of Libnah one
the king of Adullam one
16the king of Makkedah one
the king of Bethel one
17the king of Tappuah one
the king of Hepher one
18the king of Aphek one
the king of Lasharon one
19the king of Madon one
the king of Hazor one
20the king of Shimron Meron one
the king of Acshaph one
21the king of Taanach one
the king of Megiddo one
22the king of Kedesh one
the king of Jokneam in Carmel one
23the king of Dor (in Naphoth Dor[e]) one
the king of Goyim in Gilgal one
24the king of Tirzah one
thirty-one kings in all.

[c] 3 That is, Galilee [d] 3 That is, the Dead Sea
[e] 23 Or *in the heights of Dor*

PRAYER: INTERCESSION

O LORD, the great and awesome God, You are the One who keeps Your covenant and loving-kindness with those who love You and with those who obey Your commandments. We have sinned and committed iniquity; we have been wicked and have rebelled, even turning away from Your commandments and from Your judgments. To You alone belong mercy and forgiveness, even though we have rebelled against You. We have not obeyed Your voice to walk in Your laws, which You set before us through Your servants the prophets. (Daniel 9:4–5, 9–10)

TAKE *a few moments to intercede on behalf of the poor and hungry, the oppressed and persecuted, and those in control of world and national resources. Offer prayers for peace among nations and regarding current events and concerns.*

NT Colossians 3:1–25

Rules for Holy Living

3 Since, then, you have been raised with Christ, set your hearts on things above, where Christ is seated at the right hand of God. 2 Set your minds on things above, not on earthly things. 3 For you died, and your life is now hidden with Christ in God. 4 When Christ, who is your[a] life, appears, then you also will appear with him in glory.

5 Put to death, therefore, whatever belongs to your earthly nature: sexual immorality, impurity, lust, evil desires and greed, which is idolatry. 6 Because of these, the wrath of God is coming.[b] 7 You used to walk in these ways, in the life you once lived. 8 But now you must rid yourselves of all such things as these: anger, rage, malice, slander, and filthy language from your lips. 9 Do not lie to each other, since you have taken off your old self with its practices 10 and have put on the new self, which is being renewed in knowledge in the image of its Creator. 11 Here there is no Greek or Jew, circumcised or uncircumcised, barbarian, Scythian, slave or free, but Christ is all, and is in all.

12 Therefore, as God's chosen people, holy and dearly loved, clothe yourselves with compassion, kindness, humility, gentleness and patience. 13 Bear with each other and forgive whatever grievances you may have against one another. Forgive as the Lord forgave you. 14 And over all these virtues put on love, which binds them all together in perfect unity.

15 Let the peace of Christ rule in your hearts, since as members of one body you were called to peace. And be thankful. 16 Let the word of Christ dwell in you richly as you teach and admonish one another with all wisdom, and as you sing psalms, hymns and spiritual songs with gratitude in your hearts to God. 17 And whatever you do, whether in word or deed, do it all in the name of the Lord Jesus, giving thanks to God the Father through him.

Rules for Christian Households

18 Wives, submit to your husbands, as is fitting in the Lord.

19 Husbands, love your wives and do not be harsh with them.

20 Children, obey your parents in everything, for this pleases the Lord.

21 Fathers, do not embitter your children, or they will become discouraged.

22 Slaves, obey your earthly masters in everything; and do it, not only when their eye is on you and to win their favor, but with sincerity of heart and reverence for the Lord. 23 Whatever you do, work at it with all your heart, as working for the Lord, not for men, 24 since you know that you will receive an inheritance from the Lord as a reward. It is the Lord Christ you are serving. 25 Anyone who does wrong will be repaid for his wrong, and there is no favoritism.

[a] 4 Some manuscripts *our* [b] 6 Some early manuscripts *coming on those who are disobedient*

PRAYER: THE CHARACTER I WANT TO CULTIVATE

***I WANT** to be above reproach, blameless as Your steward, O God, not self-willed, not quick-tempered, not given to wine, not violent, not fond of dishonest gain, but hospitable, a lover of what is good, sensible, just, holy and self-controlled. (Titus 1:6–8)*

***TAKE** a moment to ask the Lord for the grace to grow in godly character.*

OT **Joshua 13:1-33** YEAR 1 DAY 195

Land Still to Be Taken

13 When Joshua was old and well advanced in years, the LORD said to him,
"You are very old, and there are still very
large areas of land to be taken over.

2 "This is the land that remains: all the
regions of the Philistines and Geshurites: 3 from the Shihor River on the
east of Egypt to the territory of Ekron
on the north, all of it counted as
Canaanite (the territory of the five
Philistine rulers in Gaza, Ashdod,
Ashkelon, Gath and Ekron—that of
the Avvites); 4 from the south, all the
land of the Canaanites, from Arah of
the Sidonians as far as Aphek, the region of the Amorites, 5 the area of the
Gebalites[a]; and all Lebanon to the
east, from Baal Gad below Mount
Hermon to Lebo[b] Hamath.

6 "As for all the inhabitants of the
mountain regions from Lebanon to Misrephoth Maim, that is, all the Sidonians,
I myself will drive them out before the Israelites. Be sure to allocate this land to Israel for an inheritance, as I have instructed you, 7 and divide it as an inheritance
among the nine tribes and half of the
tribe of Manasseh."

Division of the Land East of the Jordan

8 The other half of Manasseh,[c] the Reubenites and the Gadites had received the
inheritance that Moses had given them
east of the Jordan, as he, the servant of the
LORD, had assigned it to them.

9 It extended from Aroer on the rim of
the Arnon Gorge, and from the town
in the middle of the gorge, and included the whole plateau of Medeba
as far as Dibon, 10 and all the towns
of Sihon king of the Amorites, who
ruled in Heshbon, out to the border
of the Ammonites. 11 It also included
Gilead, the territory of the people of
Geshur and Maacah, all of Mount
Hermon and all Bashan as far as Salecah— 12 that is, the whole kingdom
of Og in Bashan, who had reigned in
Ashtaroth and Edrei and had survived as one of the last of the Rephaites. Moses had defeated them and
taken over their land. 13 But the Israelites did not drive out the people of
Geshur and Maacah, so they continue to live among the Israelites to this
day.

14 But to the tribe of Levi he gave no inheritance, since the offerings made by fire
to the LORD, the God of Israel, are their inheritance, as he promised them.

15 This is what Moses had given to the tribe
of Reuben, clan by clan:

16 The territory from Aroer on the rim
of the Arnon Gorge, and from the
town in the middle of the gorge, and
the whole plateau past Medeba 17 to
Heshbon and all its towns on the
plateau, including Dibon, Bamoth
Baal, Beth Baal Meon, 18 Jahaz, Kedemoth, Mephaath, 19 Kiriathaim, Sibmah, Zereth Shahar on the hill in the
valley, 20 Beth Peor, the slopes of Pisgah, and Beth Jeshimoth 21—all the
towns on the plateau and the entire
realm of Sihon king of the Amorites,
who ruled at Heshbon. Moses had
defeated him and the Midianite
chiefs, Evi, Rekem, Zur, Hur and
Reba—princes allied with Sihon—
who lived in that country. 22 In addition to those slain in battle, the Israelites had put to the sword Balaam
son of Beor, who practiced divination. 23 The boundary of the Reubenites was the bank of the Jordan. These
towns and their villages were the inheritance of the Reubenites, clan by
clan.

24 This is what Moses had given to the tribe
of Gad, clan by clan:

25 The territory of Jazer, all the towns
of Gilead and half the Ammonite
country as far as Aroer, near Rabbah;
26 and from Heshbon to Ramath Mizpah and Betonim, and from Mahanaim to the territory of Debir; 27 and
in the valley, Beth Haram, Beth Nimrah, Succoth and Zaphon with the

[a] 5 That is, the area of Byblos [b] 5 Or *to the entrance to* [c] 8 Hebrew *With it* (that is, with the other half of Manasseh)

rest of the realm of Sihon king of Heshbon (the east side of the Jordan, the territory up to the end of the Sea of Kinnereth[d]). 28These towns and their villages were the inheritance of the Gadites, clan by clan.

29This is what Moses had given to the half-tribe of Manasseh, that is, to half the family of the descendants of Manasseh, clan by clan:

30The territory extending from Mahanaim and including all of Bashan, the entire realm of Og king of Bashan—all the settlements of Jair in Bashan, sixty towns, 31half of Gilead, and Ashtaroth and Edrei (the royal cities of Og in Bashan). This was for the descendants of Makir son of Manasseh—for half of the sons of Makir, clan by clan.

32This is the inheritance Moses had given when he was in the plains of Moab across the Jordan east of Jericho. 33But to the tribe of Levi, Moses had given no inheritance; the LORD, the God of Israel, is their inheritance, as he promised them.

[d] 27 That is, Galilee

PRAYER: AFFIRMATION

CURSED are those who trust in people, who depend on flesh for their strength and whose hearts turn away from You, Lord. But blessed are those who trust in You, whose confidence is in You. (Jeremiah 17:5, 7) . . . Jesus, You knew all people, and had no need for anyone's testimony about them, for You knew what was in them. (John 2:24–25)

PAUSE *to reflect on these Biblical affirmations.*

NT Colossians 4:1-18

4 Masters, provide your slaves with what is right and fair, because you know that you also have a Master in heaven.

Further Instructions

2Devote yourselves to prayer, being watchful and thankful. 3And pray for us, too, that God may open a door for our message, so that we may proclaim the mystery of Christ, for which I am in chains. 4Pray that I may proclaim it clearly, as I should. 5Be wise in the way you act toward outsiders; make the most of every opportunity. 6Let your conversation be always full of grace, seasoned with salt, so that you may know how to answer everyone.

Final Greetings

7Tychicus will tell you all the news about me. He is a dear brother, a faithful minister and fellow servant in the Lord. 8I am sending him to you for the express purpose that you may know about our[a] circumstances and that he may encourage your hearts. 9He is coming with Onesimus, our faithful and dear brother, who is one of you. They will tell you everything that is happening here.

10My fellow prisoner Aristarchus sends you his greetings, as does Mark, the cousin of Barnabas. (You have received instructions about him; if he comes to you, welcome him.) 11Jesus, who is called Justus, also sends greetings. These are the only Jews among my fellow workers for the kingdom of God, and they have proved a comfort to me. 12Epaphras, who is one of you and a servant of Christ Jesus, sends greetings. He is always wrestling in prayer for you, that you may stand firm in all the will of God, mature and fully assured. 13I vouch for him that he is working hard for you and for those at Laodicea and Hierapolis. 14Our dear friend Luke, the doctor, and Demas send greetings. 15Give my greetings to the brothers at Laodicea, and to Nympha and the church in her house.

16After this letter has been read to you, see that it is also read in the church of the Laodiceans and that you in turn read the letter from Laodicea.

[a] 8 Some manuscripts *that he may know about your*

[17]Tell Archippus: "See to it that you complete the work you have received in the Lord."

[18]I, Paul, write this greeting in my own hand. Remember my chains. Grace be with you.

PRAYER: MY RELATIONSHIP TO OTHERS

THE husband should fulfill his marital duty to his wife, and likewise the wife to her husband. The wife's body does not belong to her alone, but also to her husband. In the same way, the husband's body does not belong to him alone, but also to his wife. (1 Corinthians 7:3–4) . . . Each husband must love his own wife as he loves himself, and each wife must respect her husband. (Ephesians 5:33)

***PAUSE** to review your relationships with others and to commit them to the Lord.*

YEAR 1 DAY 196

OT Psalm 38

Psalm 38

A psalm of David. A petition.

1 O LORD, do not rebuke me in your anger
or discipline me in your wrath.
2 For your arrows have pierced me,
and your hand has come down upon me.
3 Because of your wrath there is no health in my body;
my bones have no soundness because of my sin.
4 My guilt has overwhelmed me
like a burden too heavy to bear.

5 My wounds fester and are loathsome
because of my sinful folly.
6 I am bowed down and brought very low;
all day long I go about mourning.
7 My back is filled with searing pain;
there is no health in my body.
8 I am feeble and utterly crushed;
I groan in anguish of heart.

9 All my longings lie open before you, O Lord;
my sighing is not hidden from you.
10 My heart pounds, my strength fails me;
even the light has gone from my eyes.
11 My friends and companions avoid me because of my wounds;
my neighbors stay far away.
12 Those who seek my life set their traps,
those who would harm me talk of my ruin;
all day long they plot deception.

13 I am like a deaf man, who cannot hear,
like a mute, who cannot open his mouth;
14 I have become like a man who does not hear,
whose mouth can offer no reply.
15 I wait for you, O LORD;
you will answer, O Lord my God.
16 For I said, "Do not let them gloat
or exalt themselves over me when my foot slips."

17 For I am about to fall,
and my pain is ever with me.
18 I confess my iniquity;
I am troubled by my sin.
19 Many are those who are my vigorous enemies;
those who hate me without reason are numerous.
20 Those who repay my good with evil
slander me when I pursue what is good.

21 O LORD, do not forsake me;
be not far from me, O my God.
22 Come quickly to help me,
O Lord my Savior.

PRAYER: THANKSGIVING

MAY I rejoice in You always, O Lord. (Philippians 4:4) . . . You, O God my Savior, have called me, and Christ Jesus is my hope. (1 Timothy 1:1)

***PAUSE** to offer your own expressions of thanksgiving.*

NT Luke 1:1–56

Introduction

1 Many have undertaken to draw up an account of the things that have been fulfilled[a] among us, 2just as they were handed down to us by those who from the first were eyewitnesses and servants of the word. 3Therefore, since I myself have carefully investigated everything from the beginning, it seemed good also to me to write an orderly account for you, most excellent Theophilus, 4so that you may know the certainty of the things you have been taught.

The Birth of John the Baptist Foretold

5In the time of Herod king of Judea there was a priest named Zechariah, who belonged to the priestly division of Abijah; his wife Elizabeth was also a descendant of Aaron. 6Both of them were upright in the sight of God, observing all the Lord's commandments and regulations blamelessly. 7But they had no children, because Elizabeth was barren; and they were both well along in years.

8Once when Zechariah's division was on duty and he was serving as priest before God, 9he was chosen by lot, according to the custom of the priesthood, to go into the temple of the Lord and burn incense. 10And when the time for the burning of incense came, all the assembled worshipers were praying outside.

11Then an angel of the Lord appeared to him, standing at the right side of the altar of incense. 12When Zechariah saw him, he was startled and was gripped with fear. 13But the angel said to him: "Do not be afraid, Zechariah; your prayer has been heard. Your wife Elizabeth will bear you a son, and you are to give him the name John. 14He will be a joy and delight to you, and many will rejoice because of his birth, 15for he will be great in the sight of the Lord. He is never to take wine or other fermented drink, and he will be filled with the Holy Spirit even from birth.[b] 16Many of the people of Israel will he bring back to the Lord their God. 17And he will go on before the Lord, in the spirit and power of Elijah, to turn the hearts of the fathers to their children and the disobedient to the wisdom of the righteous—to make ready a people prepared for the Lord."

18Zechariah asked the angel, "How can I be sure of this? I am an old man and my wife is well along in years."

19The angel answered, "I am Gabriel. I stand in the presence of God, and I have been sent to speak to you and to tell you this good news. 20And now you will be silent and not able to speak until the day this happens, because you did not believe my words, which will come true at their proper time."

21Meanwhile, the people were waiting for Zechariah and wondering why he stayed so long in the temple. 22When he came out, he could not speak to them. They realized he had seen a vision in the temple, for he kept making signs to them but remained unable to speak.

23When his time of service was completed, he returned home. 24After this his wife Elizabeth became pregnant and for five months remained in seclusion. 25"The Lord has done this for me," she said. "In these days he has shown his favor and taken away my disgrace among the people."

The Birth of Jesus Foretold

26In the sixth month, God sent the angel Gabriel to Nazareth, a town in Galilee, 27to a virgin pledged to be married to a man named Joseph, a descendant of David. The virgin's name was Mary. 28The angel went to her and said, "Greetings, you

[a] *1* Or *been surely believed* [b] *15* Or *from his mother's womb*

who are highly favored! The Lord is with
you."
29 Mary was greatly troubled at his
words and wondered what kind of greeting this might be. 30 But the angel said to
her, "Do not be afraid, Mary, you have
found favor with God. 31 You will be with
child and give birth to a son, and you are
to give him the name Jesus. 32 He will be
great and will be called the Son of the
Most High. The Lord God will give him
the throne of his father David, 33 and he
will reign over the house of Jacob forever;
his kingdom will never end."
34 "How will this be," Mary asked the
angel, "since I am a virgin?"
35 The angel answered, "The Holy Spirit
will come upon you, and the power of the
Most High will overshadow you. So the
holy one to be born will be called[c] the
Son of God. 36 Even Elizabeth your relative
is going to have a child in her old age, and
she who was said to be barren is in her
sixth month. 37 For nothing is impossible
with God."
38 "I am the Lord's servant," Mary answered. "May it be to me as you have
said." Then the angel left her.

Mary Visits Elizabeth

39 At that time Mary got ready and hurried to a town in the hill country of Judea,
40 where she entered Zechariah's home
and greeted Elizabeth. 41 When Elizabeth
heard Mary's greeting, the baby leaped in
her womb, and Elizabeth was filled with
the Holy Spirit. 42 In a loud voice she exclaimed: "Blessed are you among women,
and blessed is the child you will bear!
43 But why am I so favored, that the mother of my Lord should come to me? 44 As
soon as the sound of your greeting
reached my ears, the baby in my womb
leaped for joy. 45 Blessed is she who has believed that what the Lord has said to her
will be accomplished!"

Mary's Song

46 And Mary said:

"My soul glorifies the Lord
47 and my spirit rejoices in God my
Savior,
48 for he has been mindful
of the humble state of his servant.
From now on all generations will call
me blessed,
49 for the Mighty One has done great
things for me—
holy is his name.
50 His mercy extends to those who fear
him,
from generation to generation.
51 He has performed mighty deeds with
his arm;
he has scattered those who are
proud in their inmost thoughts.
52 He has brought down rulers from
their thrones
but has lifted up the humble.
53 He has filled the hungry with good
things
but has sent the rich away empty.
54 He has helped his servant Israel,
remembering to be merciful
55 to Abraham and his descendants
forever,
even as he said to our fathers."

56 Mary stayed with Elizabeth for about
three months and then returned home.

[c] 35 Or *So the child to be born will be called holy,*

PRAYER: THE ATTRIBUTES OF GOD

YOU have chosen me as Your witness and servant so that I may know and believe You and understand that You are the Lord. Before You no god was formed, nor will there be one after You. (Isaiah 43:10) . . . Lord God, You are the Alpha and the Omega, who is, and who was, and who is to come, the Almighty. (Revelation 1:8)

PAUSE *to reflect on these affirmations about the person, powers and perfection of God.*

YEAR 1 DAY 197

OT Joshua 14:1-15

Division of the Land West of the Jordan

14 Now these are the areas the Israelites received as an inheritance in the land of Canaan, which Eleazar the priest, Joshua son of Nun and the heads of the tribal clans of Israel allotted to them. [2]Their inheritances were assigned by lot to the nine-and-a-half tribes, as the LORD had commanded through Moses. [3]Moses had granted the two-and-a-half tribes their inheritance east of the Jordan but had not granted the Levites an inheritance among the rest, [4]for the sons of Joseph had become two tribes—Manasseh and Ephraim. The Levites received no share of the land but only towns to live in, with pasturelands for their flocks and herds. [5]So the Israelites divided the land, just as the LORD had commanded Moses.

Hebron Given to Caleb

[6]Now the men of Judah approached Joshua at Gilgal, and Caleb son of Jephunneh the Kenizzite said to him, "You know what the LORD said to Moses the man of God at Kadesh Barnea about you and me. [7]I was forty years old when Moses the servant of the LORD sent me from Kadesh Barnea to explore the land. And I brought him back a report according to my convictions, [8]but my brothers who went up with me made the hearts of the people melt with fear. I, however, followed the LORD my God wholeheartedly. [9]So on that day Moses swore to me, 'The land on which your feet have walked will be your inheritance and that of your children forever, because you have followed the LORD my God wholeheartedly.'[a]

[10]"Now then, just as the LORD promised, he has kept me alive for forty-five years since the time he said this to Moses, while Israel moved about in the desert. So here I am today, eighty-five years old! [11]I am still as strong today as the day Moses sent me out; I'm just as vigorous to go out to battle now as I was then. [12]Now give me this hill country that the LORD promised me that day. You yourself heard then that the Anakites were there and their cities were large and fortified, but, the LORD helping me, I will drive them out just as he said."

[13]Then Joshua blessed Caleb son of Jephunneh and gave him Hebron as his inheritance. [14]So Hebron has belonged to Caleb son of Jephunneh the Kenizzite ever since, because he followed the LORD, the God of Israel, wholeheartedly. [15](Hebron used to be called Kiriath Arba after Arba, who was the greatest man among the Anakites.)

Then the land had rest from war.

[a] 9 Deut. 1:36

PRAYER: ADORATION

MAY I enter into the adoration John witnessed when he heard the voice of many angels encircling the throne and the living creatures and the elders; and their number was myriads of myriads, and thousands of thousands, saying with a loud voice: "Worthy are You, the Lamb who was slain, to receive power and riches and wisdom and strength and honor and glory and blessing!" (Revelation 5:11–12)

PAUSE *to express your thoughts of praise and worship.*

NT Luke 1:57-80

The Birth of John the Baptist

[57]When it was time for Elizabeth to have her baby, she gave birth to a son. [58]Her neighbors and relatives heard that the Lord had shown her great mercy, and they shared her joy.

[59]On the eighth day they came to circumcise the child, and they were going to

name him after his father Zechariah, 60 but
his mother spoke up and said, "No! He is
to be called John."
61 They said to her, "There is no one
among your relatives who has that name."
62 Then they made signs to his father, to
find out what he would like to name the
child. 63 He asked for a writing tablet, and
to everyone's astonishment he wrote, "His
name is John." 64 Immediately his mouth
was opened and his tongue was loosed,
and he began to speak, praising God.
65 The neighbors were all filled with awe,
and throughout the hill country of Judea
people were talking about all these things.
66 Everyone who heard this wondered
about it, asking, "What then is this child
going to be?" For the Lord's hand was
with him.

Zechariah's Song

67 His father Zechariah was filled with
the Holy Spirit and prophesied:

68 "Praise be to the Lord, the God of
Israel,
because he has come and has
redeemed his people.
69 He has raised up a horn[a] of salvation
for us
in the house of his servant David
70 (as he said through his holy prophets
of long ago),
71 salvation from our enemies
and from the hand of all who hate
us—
72 to show mercy to our fathers
and to remember his holy covenant,
73 the oath he swore to our father
Abraham:
74 to rescue us from the hand of our
enemies,
and to enable us to serve him
without fear
75 in holiness and righteousness
before him all our days.

76 And you, my child, will be called a
prophet of the Most High;
for you will go on before the Lord
to prepare the way for him,
77 to give his people the knowledge of
salvation
through the forgiveness of their
sins,
78 because of the tender mercy of our
God,
by which the rising sun will come
to us from heaven
79 to shine on those living in darkness
and in the shadow of death,
to guide our feet into the path of
peace."

80 And the child grew and became strong
in spirit; and he lived in the desert until
he appeared publicly to Israel.

[a] 69 *Horn* here symbolizes strength.

PRAYER: THE WORKS OF GOD

BLESSED are You, O Lord, God of Israel, because You have visited us and have redeemed Your people. You have raised up a horn of salvation for us in the house of Your servant David (as You spoke by the mouth of Your holy prophets of long ago), salvation from our enemies and from the hand of all who hate us—to show mercy to our fathers and to remember Your holy covenant, the oath You swore to our father Abraham: to rescue us from the hand of our enemies, and to enable us to serve You without fear in holiness and righteousness before You all our days. (Luke 1:68–75) . . . The Scriptures predicted that You, Christ Jesus, would suffer and rise from the dead on the third day, and that repentance and forgiveness of sins would be preached in Your name to all nations, beginning at Jerusalem. (Luke 24:46–47)

***TAKE** a moment to consider the greatness of God's wonderful works.*

YEAR 1
DAY 198

OT **Joshua 15:1-63**

Allotment for Judah

15 The allotment for the tribe of Judah,
clan by clan, extended down to the
territory of Edom, to the Desert of Zin in
the extreme south.

2Their southern boundary started
from the bay at the southern end of
the Salt Sea,[a] 3crossed south of Scorpion[b] Pass, continued on to Zin and
went over to the south of Kadesh Barnea. Then it ran past Hezron up to
Addar and curved around to Karka.
4It then passed along to Azmon and
joined the Wadi of Egypt, ending at
the sea. This is their[c] southern
boundary.

5The eastern boundary is the Salt
Sea as far as the mouth of the Jordan.

The northern boundary started
from the bay of the sea at the mouth
of the Jordan, 6went up to Beth Hoglah and continued north of Beth Arabah to the Stone of Bohan son of
Reuben. 7The boundary then went up
to Debir from the Valley of Achor
and turned north to Gilgal, which
faces the Pass of Adummim south of
the gorge. It continued along to the
waters of En Shemesh and came out
at En Rogel. 8Then it ran up the Valley of Ben Hinnom along the southern slope of the Jebusite city (that is,
Jerusalem). From there it climbed to
the top of the hill west of the Hinnom Valley at the northern end of
the Valley of Rephaim. 9From the
hilltop the boundary headed toward
the spring of the waters of Nephtoah,
came out at the towns of Mount
Ephron and went down toward Baalah (that is, Kiriath Jearim). 10Then it
curved westward from Baalah to
Mount Seir, ran along the northern
slope of Mount Jearim (that is, Kesa-
lon), continued down to Beth Shemesh and crossed to Timnah. 11It
went to the northern slope of Ekron,
turned toward Shikkeron, passed
along to Mount Baalah and reached
Jabneel. The boundary ended at the
sea.

12The western boundary is the
coastline of the Great Sea.[d]
These are the boundaries around the people of Judah by their clans.

13In accordance with the LORD's command to him, Joshua gave to Caleb son of
Jephunneh a portion in Judah—Kiriath
Arba, that is, Hebron. (Arba was the forefather of Anak.) 14From Hebron Caleb
drove out the three Anakites—Sheshai,
Ahiman and Talmai—descendants of
Anak. 15From there he marched against
the people living in Debir (formerly
called Kiriath Sepher). 16And Caleb said,
"I will give my daughter Acsah in marriage
to the man who attacks and captures Kiriath Sepher." 17Othniel son of Kenaz, Caleb's brother, took it; so Caleb gave his
daughter Acsah to him in marriage.

18One day when she came to Othniel,
she urged him[e] to ask her father for a
field. When she got off her donkey, Caleb
asked her, "What can I do for you?"

19She replied, "Do me a special favor.
Since you have given me land in the Negev, give me also springs of water." So Caleb gave her the upper and lower springs.

20This is the inheritance of the tribe of
Judah, clan by clan:

21The southernmost towns of the tribe of
Judah in the Negev toward the boundary
of Edom were:

Kabzeel, Eder, Jagur, 22Kinah, Di-
monah, Adadah, 23Kedesh, Hazor,
Ithnan, 24Ziph, Telem, Bealoth, 25Ha-
zor Hadattah, Kerioth Hezron (that
is, Hazor), 26Amam, Shema, Moladah, 27Hazar Gaddah, Heshmon,
Beth Pelet, 28Hazar Shual, Beersheba,
Biziothiah, 29Baalah, Iim, Ezem, 30El-
tolad, Kesil, Hormah, 31Ziklag, Madmannah, Sansannah, 32Lebaoth, Shil-
him, Ain and Rimmon—a total of
twenty-nine towns and their villages.

33In the western foothills:

Eshtaol, Zorah, Ashnah, 34Zanoah,
En Gannim, Tappuah, Enam, 35Jar-
muth, Adullam, Socoh, Azekah,

[a] *2* That is, the Dead Sea; also in verse 5
[b] *3* Hebrew *Akrabbim*
[c] *4* Hebrew *your*
[d] *12* That is, the Mediterranean; also in verse 47
[e] *18* Hebrew and some Septuagint manuscripts; other Septuagint manuscripts (see also note at Judges 1:14) *Othniel, he urged her*

[36]Shaaraim, Adithaim and Gederah (or Gederothaim)[f]—fourteen towns and their villages.

[37]Zenan, Hadashah, Migdal Gad, [38]Dilean, Mizpah, Joktheel, [39]Lachish, Bozkath, Eglon, [40]Cabbon, Lahmas, Kitlish, [41]Gederoth, Beth Dagon, Naamah and Makkedah—sixteen towns and their villages.

[42]Libnah, Ether, Ashan, [43]Iphtah, Ashnah, Nezib, [44]Keilah, Aczib and Mareshah—nine towns and their villages.

[45]Ekron, with its surrounding settlements and villages; [46]west of Ekron, all that were in the vicinity of Ashdod, together with their villages; [47]Ashdod, its surrounding settlements and villages; and Gaza, its settlements and villages, as far as the Wadi of Egypt and the coastline of the Great Sea.

[48]In the hill country:

Shamir, Jattir, Socoh, [49]Dannah, Kiriath Sannah (that is, Debir), [50]Anab, Eshtemoh, Anim, [51]Goshen, Holon and Giloh—eleven towns and their villages.

[52]Arab, Dumah, Eshan, [53]Janim, Beth Tappuah, Aphekah, [54]Humtah, Kiriath Arba (that is, Hebron) and Zior—nine towns and their villages.

[55]Maon, Carmel, Ziph, Juttah, [56]Jezreel, Jokdeam, Zanoah, [57]Kain, Gibeah and Timnah—ten towns and their villages.

[58]Halhul, Beth Zur, Gedor, [59]Maarath, Beth Anoth and Eltekon—six towns and their villages.

[60]Kiriath Baal (that is, Kiriath Jearim) and Rabbah—two towns and their villages.

[61]In the desert:

Beth Arabah, Middin, Secacah, [62]Nibshan, the City of Salt and En Gedi—six towns and their villages.

[63]Judah could not dislodge the Jebusites, who were living in Jerusalem; to this day the Jebusites live there with the people of Judah.

[f]36 Or *Gederah and Gederothaim*

PRAYER: CONFESSION

O LORD, I will not forget the exhortation that addresses me as Your child: "My child, do not despise the Lord's discipline, nor lose heart when you are rebuked by Him, for whom the Lord loves He disciplines, and He chastises every child whom He receives." (Hebrews 12:5–6)

***ASK** the Spirit to search your heart and reveal any areas of unconfessed sin. Acknowledge these to the Lord and thank Him for His forgiveness.*

NT Luke 2:1-40

The Birth of Jesus

2 In those days Caesar Augustus issued a decree that a census should be taken of the entire Roman world. [2](This was the first census that took place while Quirinius was governor of Syria.) [3]And everyone went to his own town to register.

[4]So Joseph also went up from the town of Nazareth in Galilee to Judea, to Bethlehem the town of David, because he belonged to the house and line of David. [5]He went there to register with Mary, who was pledged to be married to him and was expecting a child. [6]While they were there, the time came for the baby to be born, [7]and she gave birth to her firstborn, a son. She wrapped him in cloths and placed him in a manger, because there was no room for them in the inn.

The Shepherds and the Angels

[8]And there were shepherds living out in the fields nearby, keeping watch over their flocks at night. [9]An angel of the Lord appeared to them, and the glory of the Lord shone around them, and they were terrified. [10]But the angel said to them, "Do not be afraid. I bring you good news of great joy that will be for all the people. [11]Today

in the town of David a Savior has been
born to you; he is Christ[a] the Lord. 12This
will be a sign to you: You will find a baby
wrapped in cloths and lying in a manger."
13Suddenly a great company of the
heavenly host appeared with the angel,
praising God and saying,

14 "Glory to God in the highest,
and on earth peace to men on
whom his favor rests."

15When the angels had left them and
gone into heaven, the shepherds said to
one another, "Let's go to Bethlehem and
see this thing that has happened, which
the Lord has told us about."
16So they hurried off and found Mary
and Joseph, and the baby, who was lying
in the manger. 17When they had seen him,
they spread the word concerning what
had been told them about this child,
18and all who heard it were amazed at
what the shepherds said to them. 19But
Mary treasured up all these things and
pondered them in her heart. 20The shepherds returned, glorifying and praising
God for all the things they had heard and
seen, which were just as they had been
told.

Jesus Presented in the Temple

21On the eighth day, when it was time
to circumcise him, he was named Jesus,
the name the angel had given him before
he had been conceived.
22When the time of their purification according to the Law of Moses had been completed, Joseph and Mary took him to Jerusalem to present him to the Lord 23(as it is
written in the Law of the Lord, "Every firstborn male is to be consecrated to the
Lord"[b]), 24and to offer a sacrifice in keeping
with what is said in the Law of the Lord: "a
pair of doves or two young pigeons."[c]
25Now there was a man in Jerusalem
called Simeon, who was righteous and devout. He was waiting for the consolation
of Israel, and the Holy Spirit was upon
him. 26It had been revealed to him by the
Holy Spirit that he would not die before
he had seen the Lord's Christ. 27Moved by
the Spirit, he went into the temple courts.
When the parents brought in the child
Jesus to do for him what the custom of
the Law required, 28Simeon took him in
his arms and praised God, saying:

29 "Sovereign Lord, as you have
promised,
you now dismiss[d] your servant in
peace.
30 For my eyes have seen your salvation,
31 which you have prepared in the
sight of all people,
32 a light for revelation to the Gentiles
and for glory to your people Israel."

33The child's father and mother marveled at what was said about him. 34Then
Simeon blessed them and said to Mary,
his mother: "This child is destined to
cause the falling and rising of many in Israel, and to be a sign that will be spoken
against, 35so that the thoughts of many
hearts will be revealed. And a sword will
pierce your own soul too."
36There was also a prophetess, Anna,
the daughter of Phanuel, of the tribe of
Asher. She was very old; she had lived
with her husband seven years after her
marriage, 37and then was a widow until
she was eighty-four.[e] She never left the
temple but worshiped night and day, fasting and praying. 38Coming up to them at
that very moment, she gave thanks to God
and spoke about the child to all who were
looking forward to the redemption of
Jerusalem.
39When Joseph and Mary had done
everything required by the Law of the
Lord, they returned to Galilee to their own
town of Nazareth. 40And the child grew
and became strong; he was filled with wisdom, and the grace of God was upon him.

[a] *11* Or *Messiah.* "The Christ" (Greek) and "the Messiah" (Hebrew) both mean "the Anointed One"; also in verse 26. [b] *23* Exodus 13:2,12 [c] *24* Lev. 12:8 [d] *29* Or *promised, / now dismiss* [e] *37* Or *widow for eighty-four years*

PRAYER: MY RELATIONSHIP TO GOD

O GOD, I know that You will keep me strong to the end, so that I will be blameless on the day of our Lord Jesus Christ. You are faithful; through You I was called into fellowship with Your Son, Jesus Christ our

Lord. (1 Corinthians 1:8–9) . . . Thanks be to You, O God, who always lead us in triumph in Christ and through us spread everywhere the fragrance of the knowledge of You. (2 Corinthians 2:14)

***PAUSE** to thank God for the relationship that you enjoy with Him in Jesus Christ.*

OT Joshua 16:1–17:18

YEAR 1
DAY 199

Allotment for Ephraim and Manasseh

16 The allotment for Joseph began
at the Jordan of Jericho,[a] east of
the waters of Jericho, and went up
from there through the desert into
the hill country of Bethel. 2It went on
from Bethel (that is, Luz),[b] crossed
over to the territory of the Arkites in
Ataroth, 3descended westward to the
territory of the Japhletites as far as the
region of Lower Beth Horon and on
to Gezer, ending at the sea.
4So Manasseh and Ephraim, the descendants of Joseph, received their inheritance.

5This was the territory of Ephraim, clan by
clan:
The boundary of their inheritance
went from Ataroth Addar in the east
to Upper Beth Horon 6and continued
to the sea. From Micmethath on the
north it curved eastward to Taanath
Shiloh, passing by it to Janoah on the
east. 7Then it went down from Janoah to Ataroth and Naarah, touched
Jericho and came out at the Jordan.
8From Tappuah the border went west
to the Kanah Ravine and ended at the
sea. This was the inheritance of the
tribe of the Ephraimites, clan by clan.
9It also included all the towns and
their villages that were set aside for
the Ephraimites within the inheritance of the Manassites.
10They did not dislodge the Canaanites
living in Gezer; to this day the Canaanites
live among the people of Ephraim but are
required to do forced labor.

17 This was the allotment for the tribe of
Manasseh as Joseph's firstborn, that is,
for Makir, Manasseh's firstborn. Makir
was the ancestor of the Gileadites, who
had received Gilead and Bashan because
the Makirites were great soldiers. 2So this
allotment was for the rest of the people of
Manasseh—the clans of Abiezer, Helek,
Asriel, Shechem, Hepher and Shemida.
These are the other male descendants of
Manasseh son of Joseph by their clans.
3Now Zelophehad son of Hepher, the
son of Gilead, the son of Makir, the son
of Manasseh, had no sons but only
daughters, whose names were Mahlah,
Noah, Hoglah, Milcah and Tirzah. 4They
went to Eleazar the priest, Joshua son of
Nun, and the leaders and said, "The LORD
commanded Moses to give us an inheritance among our brothers." So Joshua
gave them an inheritance along with the
brothers of their father, according to the
LORD's command. 5Manasseh's share consisted of ten tracts of land besides Gilead
and Bashan east of the Jordan, 6because
the daughters of the tribe of Manasseh received an inheritance among the sons.
The land of Gilead belonged to the rest of
the descendants of Manasseh.
7The territory of Manasseh extended from Asher to Micmethath east of
Shechem. The boundary ran southward from there to include the people living at En Tappuah. 8(Manasseh
had the land of Tappuah, but Tappuah itself, on the boundary of Manasseh, belonged to the Ephraimites.)
9Then the boundary continued south
to the Kanah Ravine. There were
towns belonging to Ephraim lying
among the towns of Manasseh, but
the boundary of Manasseh was the
northern side of the ravine and ended at the sea. 10On the south the land
belonged to Ephraim, on the north
to Manasseh. The territory of Manasseh reached the sea and bordered

[a] 1 *Jordan of Jericho* was possibly an ancient name for the Jordan River. [b] 2 Septuagint; Hebrew *Bethel to Luz*

Asher on the north and Issachar on the east.

[11]Within Issachar and Asher, Manasseh also had Beth Shan, Ibleam and the people of Dor, Endor, Taanach and Megiddo, together with their surrounding settlements (the third in the list is Naphoth[c]).

[12]Yet the Manassites were not able to occupy these towns, for the Canaanites were
determined to live in that region. [13]However, when the Israelites grew stronger, they subjected the Canaanites to forced labor but did not drive them out completely.

[14]The people of Joseph said to Joshua, "Why have you given us only one allotment and one portion for an inheritance? We are a numerous people and the LORD has blessed us abundantly."

[15]"If you are so numerous," Joshua answered, "and if the hill country of Ephraim is too small for you, go up into the forest and clear land for yourselves there in the land of the Perizzites and Rephaites."

[16]The people of Joseph replied, "The hill country is not enough for us, and all the Canaanites who live in the plain have iron chariots, both those in Beth Shan and its settlements and those in the Valley of Jezreel."

[17]But Joshua said to the house of Joseph—to Ephraim and Manasseh—"You are numerous and very powerful. You will
have not only one allotment [18]but the
forested hill country as well. Clear it, and its farthest limits will be yours; though the Canaanites have iron chariots and though they are strong, you can drive them out."

[c] 11 That is, Naphoth Dor

PRAYER: RENEWAL

GIVE me understanding, O Lord, and I will keep Your law and observe it with all my heart. Make me walk in the path of Your commands, for there I find delight. Incline my heart to Your testimonies and not to selfish gain. Turn my eyes away from worthless things, and revive me in Your way. (Psalm 119:34–37)

***PAUSE** to add your own prayers for personal renewal.*

NT Luke 2:41–3:20

The Boy Jesus at the Temple

[41]Every year his parents went to Jerusalem for the Feast of the Passover.
[42]When he was twelve years old, they went up to the Feast, according to the custom.
[43]After the Feast was over, while his parents were returning home, the boy Jesus stayed behind in Jerusalem, but they were
unaware of it. [44]Thinking he was in their company, they traveled on for a day. Then they began looking for him among their
relatives and friends. [45]When they did not find him, they went back to Jerusalem to
look for him. [46]After three days they found him in the temple courts, sitting among the teachers, listening to them and
asking them questions. [47]Everyone who heard him was amazed at his under-
standing and his answers. [48]When his parents saw him, they were astonished. His mother said to him, "Son, why have you treated us like this? Your father and I have been anxiously searching for you."

[49]"Why were you searching for me?" he asked. "Didn't you know I had to be in
my Father's house?" [50]But they did not understand what he was saying to them.

[51]Then he went down to Nazareth with them and was obedient to them. But his mother treasured all these things in her
heart. [52]And Jesus grew in wisdom and stature, and in favor with God and men.

John the Baptist Prepares the Way

3 In the fifteenth year of the reign of Tiberius Caesar—when Pontius Pilate was governor of Judea, Herod tetrarch of Galilee, his brother Philip tetrarch of Iturea and Traconitis, and Lysanias tetrarch
of Abilene— [2]during the high priesthood of Annas and Caiaphas, the word of God came to John son of Zechariah in the
desert. [3]He went into all the country

around the Jordan, preaching a baptism
of repentance for the forgiveness of sins.
4As is written in the book of the words of
Isaiah the prophet:

"A voice of one calling in the desert,
'Prepare the way for the Lord,
make straight paths for him.
5Every valley shall be filled in,
every mountain and hill made low.
The crooked roads shall become
straight,
the rough ways smooth.
6And all mankind will see God's
salvation.' "[a]

7John said to the crowds coming out to
be baptized by him, "You brood of vipers!
Who warned you to flee from the coming
wrath? 8Produce fruit in keeping with repentance. And do not begin to say to yourselves, 'We have Abraham as our father.'
For I tell you that out of these stones God
can raise up children for Abraham. 9The ax
is already at the root of the trees, and every
tree that does not produce good fruit will
be cut down and thrown into the fire."
10"What should we do then?" the crowd
asked.
11John answered, "The man with two tunics should share with him who has
none, and the one who has food should
do the same."
12Tax collectors also came to be baptized. "Teacher," they asked, "what should
we do?"
13"Don't collect any more than you are
required to," he told them.
14Then some soldiers asked him, "And
what should we do?"
He replied, "Don't extort money and
don't accuse people falsely—be content
with your pay."
15The people were waiting expectantly
and were all wondering in their hearts if
John might possibly be the Christ.[b] 16John
answered them all, "I baptize you with[c]
water. But one more powerful than I will
come, the thongs of whose sandals I am
not worthy to untie. He will baptize you
with the Holy Spirit and with fire. 17His
winnowing fork is in his hand to clear his
threshing floor and to gather the wheat
into his barn, but he will burn up the
chaff with unquenchable fire." 18And with
many other words John exhorted the
people and preached the good news to
them.
19But when John rebuked Herod the tetrarch because of Herodias, his brother's
wife, and all the other evil things he had
done, 20Herod added this to them all: He
locked John up in prison.

[a] 6 Isaiah 40:3–5 [b] 15 Or *Messiah* [c] 16 Or *in*

PRAYER: THE CHARACTER I WANT TO CULTIVATE

I WILL fight the good fight of faith and lay hold of the eternal life to which I was called, Father, when I made the good confession in the presence of many witnesses. You are the One who gives life to all things; in Your sight, and in the sight of Your Son, Christ Jesus, who testified the good confession before Pontius Pilate, I want to keep this command without blemish or reproach until the appearing of our Lord Jesus Christ, which You will bring about in Your own time. (1 Timothy 6:12–15)

***TAKE** a moment to ask the Lord for the grace to grow in godly character.*

YEAR 1 DAY 200

OT Joshua 18:1–28

Division of the Rest of the Land

18 The whole assembly of the Israelites
gathered at Shiloh and set up the Tent
of Meeting there. The country was
brought under their control, 2but there
were still seven Israelite tribes who had
not yet received their inheritance.
3So Joshua said to the Israelites: "How
long will you wait before you begin to
take possession of the land that the LORD,

the God of your fathers, has given you?
4Appoint three men from each tribe. I will
send them out to make a survey of the
land and to write a description of it, according to the inheritance of each. Then
they will return to me. 5You are to divide
the land into seven parts. Judah is to remain in its territory on the south and the
house of Joseph in its territory on the
north. 6After you have written descrip-
tions of the seven parts of the land, bring
them here to me and I will cast lots for
you in the presence of the LORD our God.
7The Levites, however, do not get a portion among you, because the priestly service of the LORD is their inheritance. And
Gad, Reuben and the half-tribe of Manasseh have already received their inheritance
on the east side of the Jordan. Moses the
servant of the LORD gave it to them."

8As the men started on their way to map
out the land, Joshua instructed them, "Go
and make a survey of the land and write
a description of it. Then return to me, and
I will cast lots for you here at Shiloh in the
presence of the LORD." 9So the men left
and went through the land. They wrote its
description on a scroll, town by town, in
seven parts, and returned to Joshua in the
camp at Shiloh. 10Joshua then cast lots for
them in Shiloh in the presence of the
LORD, and there he distributed the land to
the Israelites according to their tribal divisions.

Allotment for Benjamin

11The lot came up for the tribe of Benjamin, clan by clan. Their allotted territory
lay between the tribes of Judah and Joseph:

12On the north side their boundary
began at the Jordan, passed the
northern slope of Jericho and headed west into the hill country, coming
out at the desert of Beth Aven. 13From
there it crossed to the south slope of
Luz (that is, Bethel) and went down
to Ataroth Addar on the hill south of
Lower Beth Horon.

14From the hill facing Beth Horon
on the south the boundary turned
south along the western side and
came out at Kiriath Baal (that is, Kiriath Jearim), a town of the people of
Judah. This was the western side.

15The southern side began at the
outskirts of Kiriath Jearim on the
west, and the boundary came out at
the spring of the waters of Nephtoah.
16The boundary went down to the
foot of the hill facing the Valley of
Ben Hinnom, north of the Valley of
Rephaim. It continued down the
Hinnom Valley along the southern
slope of the Jebusite city and so to En
Rogel. 17It then curved north, went to
En Shemesh, continued to Geliloth,
which faces the Pass of Adummim,
and ran down to the Stone of Bohan
son of Reuben. 18It continued to the
northern slope of Beth Arabah[a] and
on down into the Arabah. 19It then
went to the northern slope of Beth
Hoglah and came out at the northern
bay of the Salt Sea,[b] at the mouth of
the Jordan in the south. This was the
southern boundary.

20The Jordan formed the boundary
on the eastern side.

These were the boundaries that marked
out the inheritance of the clans of Benjamin on all sides.

21The tribe of Benjamin, clan by clan, had
the following cities:

Jericho, Beth Hoglah, Emek Keziz,
22Beth Arabah, Zemaraim, Bethel,
23Avvim, Parah, Ophrah, 24Kephar
Ammoni, Ophni and Geba—twelve
towns and their villages.

25Gibeon, Ramah, Beeroth, 26Miz-
pah, Kephirah, Mozah, 27Rekem, Ir-
peel, Taralah, 28Zelah, Haeleph, the
Jebusite city (that is, Jerusalem), Gibeah and Kiriath—fourteen towns and
their villages.

This was the inheritance of Benjamin for
its clans.

[a] 18 Septuagint; Hebrew *slope facing the Arabah*
[b] 19 That is, the Dead Sea

PRAYER: PETITION

LIKE Ezra, I want to set my heart to study Your Word, O God, to obey it and to do it, and to teach it to others. (Ezra 7:10)

***PAUSE** here to petition God for growth in your desire to know and please Jesus Christ. Pray for a greater love and commitment to Him, for the grace to practice His presence and for the grace to glorify Him in your life. Offer prayers regarding your activities for this day and any special concerns you may have.*

NT Luke 3:21–4:12

The Baptism and Genealogy of Jesus

21When all the people were being baptized, Jesus was baptized too. And as he
was praying, heaven was opened 22and the
Holy Spirit descended on him in bodily
form like a dove. And a voice came from
heaven: "You are my Son, whom I love;
with you I am well pleased."
23Now Jesus himself was about thirty
years old when he began his ministry. He
was the son, so it was thought, of Joseph,

the son of Heli, 24the son of Matthat,
the son of Levi, the son of Melki,
the son of Jannai, the son of Joseph,
25the son of Mattathias, the son of Amos,
the son of Nahum, the son of Esli,
the son of Naggai, 26the son of Maath,
the son of Mattathias, the son of Semein,
the son of Josech, the son of Joda,
27the son of Joanan, the son of Rhesa,
the son of Zerubbabel, the son of Shealtiel,
the son of Neri, 28the son of Melki,
the son of Addi, the son of Cosam,
the son of Elmadam, the son of Er,
29the son of Joshua, the son of Eliezer,
the son of Jorim, the son of Matthat,
the son of Levi, 30the son of Simeon,
the son of Judah, the son of Joseph,
the son of Jonam, the son of Eliakim,
31the son of Melea, the son of Menna,
the son of Mattatha, the son of Nathan,
the son of David, 32the son of Jesse,
the son of Obed, the son of Boaz,
the son of Salmon,[a] the son of Nahshon,
33the son of Amminadab, the son of Ram,[b]
the son of Hezron, the son of Perez,
the son of Judah, 34the son of Jacob,
the son of Isaac, the son of Abraham,
the son of Terah, the son of Nahor,
35the son of Serug, the son of Reu,
the son of Peleg, the son of Eber,
the son of Shelah, 36the son of Cainan,
the son of Arphaxad, the son of Shem,
the son of Noah, the son of Lamech,
37the son of Methuselah, the son of Enoch,
the son of Jared, the son of Mahalalel,
the son of Kenan, 38the son of Enosh,
the son of Seth, the son of Adam,
the son of God.

The Temptation of Jesus

4 Jesus, full of the Holy Spirit, returned
from the Jordan and was led by the
Spirit in the desert, 2where for forty days
he was tempted by the devil. He ate nothing during those days, and at the end of
them he was hungry.
3The devil said to him, "If you are the
Son of God, tell this stone to become
bread."
4Jesus answered, "It is written: 'Man
does not live on bread alone.'[c]"
5The devil led him up to a high place
and showed him in an instant all the
kingdoms of the world. 6And he said to
him, "I will give you all their authority
and splendor, for it has been given to me,
and I can give it to anyone I want to. 7So
if you worship me, it will all be yours."
8Jesus answered, "It is written: 'Worship
the Lord your God and serve him only.'[d]"

[a] *32* Some early manuscripts *Sala* [b] *33* Some manuscripts *Amminadab, the son of Admin, the son of Arni;* other manuscripts vary widely. [c] *4* Deut. 8:3 [d] *8* Deut. 6:13

[9]The devil led him to Jerusalem and
had him stand on the highest point of the
temple. "If you are the Son of God," he
said, "throw yourself down from here.
[10]For it is written:

" 'He will command his angels
concerning you
to guard you carefully;
[11]they will lift you up in their hands,
so that you will not strike your foot
against a stone.'[e]"

[12]Jesus answered, "It says: 'Do not put
the Lord your God to the test.'[f]"

[e] 11 Psalm 91:11,12 [f] 12 Deut. 6:16

PRAYER: MY RELATIONSHIP TO OTHERS

CHILDREN should obey their parents as believers in You, O Lord, for this is right. "Honor your father and mother"—which is the first commandment with a promise—"that it may go well with you, and that you may live long on the earth." (Ephesians 6:1–3) . . . Children should obey their parents in everything, for this is well-pleasing to You, Lord. (Colossians 3:20)

__PAUSE__ to review your relationships with others and to commit them to the Lord.

YEAR 1
DAY 201

OT Joshua 19:1–20:9

Allotment for Simeon

19 The second lot came out for the tribe
of Simeon, clan by clan. Their inheritance lay within the territory of Judah. [2]It
included:

Beersheba (or Sheba),[a] Moladah,
[3]Hazar Shual, Balah, Ezem, [4]Eltolad,
Bethul, Hormah, [5]Ziklag, Beth Marcaboth, Hazar Susah, [6]Beth Lebaoth
and Sharuhen—thirteen towns and
their villages;

[7]Ain, Rimmon, Ether and Ashan—
four towns and their villages— [8]and
all the villages around these towns as
far as Baalath Beer (Ramah in the
Negev).

This was the inheritance of the tribe of the
Simeonites, clan by clan. [9]The inheritance
of the Simeonites was taken from the
share of Judah, because Judah's portion
was more than they needed. So the Simeonites received their inheritance within
the territory of Judah.

Allotment for Zebulun

[10]The third lot came up for Zebulun, clan
by clan:

The boundary of their inheritance
went as far as Sarid. [11]Going west it
ran to Maralah, touched Dabbesheth,
and extended to the ravine near Jokneam. [12]It turned east from Sarid toward the sunrise to the territory of
Kisloth Tabor and went on to Daberath and up to Japhia. [13]Then it continued eastward to Gath Hepher and
Eth Kazin; it came out at Rimmon
and turned toward Neah. [14]There the
boundary went around on the north
to Hannathon and ended at the Valley of Iphtah El. [15]Included were Kat-
tath, Nahalal, Shimron, Idalah and
Bethlehem. There were twelve towns
and their villages.

[16]These towns and their villages were the
inheritance of Zebulun, clan by clan.

Allotment for Issachar

[17]The fourth lot came out for Issachar,
clan by clan. [18]Their territory included:

Jezreel, Kesulloth, Shunem,
[19]Hapharaim, Shion, Anaharath,
[20]Rabbith, Kishion, Ebez, [21]Remeth,
En Gannim, En Haddah and Beth
Pazzez. [22]The boundary touched Tabor, Shahazumah and Beth Shemesh,
and ended at the Jordan. There were
sixteen towns and their villages.

[a] 2 Or *Beersheba, Sheba;* 1 Chron. 4:28 does not have *Sheba.*

[23]These towns and their villages were the inheritance of the tribe of Issachar, clan by clan.

Allotment for Asher

[24]The fifth lot came out for the tribe of Asher, clan by clan. [25]Their territory included:

Helkath, Hali, Beten, Acshaph,
[26]Allammelech, Amad and Mishal.
On the west the boundary touched
Carmel and Shihor Libnath. [27]It then
turned east toward Beth Dagon,
touched Zebulun and the Valley of
Iphtah El, and went north to Beth
Emek and Neiel, passing Cabul on
the left. [28]It went to Abdon,[b] Rehob,
Hammon and Kanah, as far as
Greater Sidon. [29]The boundary then
turned back toward Ramah and went
to the fortified city of Tyre, turned toward Hosah and came out at the sea
in the region of Aczib, [30]Ummah,
Aphek and Rehob. There were twenty-two towns and their villages.

[31]These towns and their villages were the inheritance of the tribe of Asher, clan by clan.

Allotment for Naphtali

[32]The sixth lot came out for Naphtali, clan by clan:

[33]Their boundary went from He-
leph and the large tree in Zaanannim, passing Adami Nekeb and Jabneel to Lakkum and ending at the
Jordan. [34]The boundary ran west
through Aznoth Tabor and came out
at Hukkok. It touched Zebulun on
the south, Asher on the west and the
Jordan[c] on the east. [35]The fortified
cities were Ziddim, Zer, Hammath,
Rakkath, Kinnereth, [36]Adamah, Ramah, Hazor, [37]Kedesh, Edrei, En Hazor, [38]Iron, Migdal El, Horem, Beth
Anath and Beth Shemesh. There were
nineteen towns and their villages.

[39]These towns and their villages were the inheritance of the tribe of Naphtali, clan by clan.

Allotment for Dan

[40]The seventh lot came out for the tribe of Dan, clan by clan. [41]The territory of their inheritance included:

Zorah, Eshtaol, Ir Shemesh,
[42]Shaalabbin, Aijalon, Ithlah, [43]Elon,
Timnah, Ekron, [44]Eltekeh, Gibbethon, Baalath, [45]Jehud, Bene Berak,
Gath Rimmon, [46]Me Jarkon and Rak-
kon, with the area facing Joppa.

[47](But the Danites had difficulty taking possession of their territory, so they went up and attacked Leshem, took it, put it to the sword and occupied it. They settled in Leshem and named it Dan after their forefather.)

[48]These towns and their villages were the inheritance of the tribe of Dan, clan by clan.

Allotment for Joshua

[49]When they had finished dividing the land into its allotted portions, the Israelites gave Joshua son of Nun an inheritance among them, [50]as the LORD had commanded. They gave him the town he asked for—Timnath Serah[d] in the hill country of Ephraim. And he built up the town and settled there.

[51]These are the territories that Eleazar the priest, Joshua son of Nun and the heads of the tribal clans of Israel assigned by lot at Shiloh in the presence of the LORD at the entrance to the Tent of Meeting. And so they finished dividing the land.

Cities of Refuge

20 Then the LORD said to Joshua: [2]"Tell the Israelites to designate the cities of refuge, as I instructed you through Moses, [3]so that anyone who kills a person accidentally and unintentionally may flee there and find protection from the avenger of blood.

[4]"When he flees to one of these cities, he is to stand in the entrance of the city gate and state his case before the elders of that city. Then they are to admit him into their city and give him a place to live with them. [5]If the avenger of blood pursues him, they must not surrender the one accused, because he killed his neighbor unintentionally and without malice aforethought. [6]He is to stay in that city until he has stood trial before the assembly and until the death of the high priest who is

[b] *28* Some Hebrew manuscripts (see also Joshua 21:30); most Hebrew manuscripts *Ebron*
[c] *34* Septuagint; Hebrew *west, and Judah, the Jordan,*
[d] *50* Also known as *Timnath Heres* (see Judges 2:9)

serving at that time. Then he may go back to his own home in the town from which he fled."

7 So they set apart Kedesh in Galilee in the hill country of Naphtali, Shechem in the hill country of Ephraim, and Kiriath Arba (that is, Hebron) in the hill country of Judah. 8 On the east side of the Jordan of Jericho[a] they designated Bezer in the desert on the plateau in the tribe of Reuben, Ramoth in Gilead in the tribe of Gad, and Golan in Bashan in the tribe of Manasseh. 9 Any of the Israelites or any alien living among them who killed someone accidentally could flee to these designated cities and not be killed by the avenger of blood prior to standing trial before the assembly.

[a] 8 *Jordan of Jericho* was possibly an ancient name for the Jordan River.

PRAYER: INTERCESSION

SINCE we were called into fellowship with You, Lord Jesus Christ, help us to agree with one another, so that there may be no divisions among us, and that we may be perfectly joined together in the same mind and in the same judgment. (1 Corinthians 1:9–10)

***TAKE** a few moments to intercede on behalf of your local church, other churches, evangelism and discipleship ministries, educational ministries and any other special concerns you may have.*

NT Luke 4:13–44

13 When the devil had finished all this tempting, he left him until an opportune time.

Jesus Rejected at Nazareth

14 Jesus returned to Galilee in the power of the Spirit, and news about him spread through the whole countryside. 15 He taught in their synagogues, and everyone praised him.

16 He went to Nazareth, where he had been brought up, and on the Sabbath day he went into the synagogue, as was his custom. And he stood up to read. 17 The scroll of the prophet Isaiah was handed to him. Unrolling it, he found the place where it is written:

18 "The Spirit of the Lord is on me,
because he has anointed me
to preach good news to the poor.
He has sent me to proclaim freedom
for the prisoners
and recovery of sight for the
blind,
to release the oppressed,
19 to proclaim the year of the Lord's
favor."[a]

20 Then he rolled up the scroll, gave it back to the attendant and sat down. The eyes of everyone in the synagogue were fastened on him, 21 and he began by saying to them, "Today this scripture is fulfilled in your hearing."

22 All spoke well of him and were amazed at the gracious words that came from his lips. "Isn't this Joseph's son?" they asked.

23 Jesus said to them, "Surely you will quote this proverb to me: 'Physician, heal yourself! Do here in your hometown what we have heard that you did in Capernaum.' "

24 "I tell you the truth," he continued, "no prophet is accepted in his hometown. 25 I assure you that there were many widows in Israel in Elijah's time, when the sky was shut for three and a half years and there was a severe famine throughout the land. 26 Yet Elijah was not sent to any of them, but to a widow in Zarephath in the region of Sidon. 27 And there were many in Israel with leprosy[b] in the time of Elisha the prophet, yet not one of them was cleansed—only Naaman the Syrian."

28 All the people in the synagogue were furious when they heard this. 29 They got up, drove him out of the town, and took

[a] 19 Isaiah 61:1,2 [b] 27 The Greek word was used for various diseases affecting the skin—not necessarily leprosy.

him to the brow of the hill on which the town was built, in order to throw him down the cliff. [30]But he walked right through the crowd and went on his way.

Jesus Drives Out an Evil Spirit

[31]Then he went down to Capernaum, a town in Galilee, and on the Sabbath began to teach the people. [32]They were amazed at his teaching, because his message had authority.

[33]In the synagogue there was a man possessed by a demon, an evil[c] spirit. He cried out at the top of his voice, [34]"Ha! What do you want with us, Jesus of Nazareth? Have you come to destroy us? I know who you are—the Holy One of God!"

[35]"Be quiet!" Jesus said sternly. "Come out of him!" Then the demon threw the man down before them all and came out without injuring him.

[36]All the people were amazed and said to each other, "What is this teaching? With authority and power he gives orders to evil spirits and they come out!" [37]And the news about him spread throughout the surrounding area.

Jesus Heals Many

[38]Jesus left the synagogue and went to the home of Simon. Now Simon's mother-in-law was suffering from a high fever, and they asked Jesus to help her. [39]So he bent over her and rebuked the fever, and it left her. She got up at once and began to wait on them.

[40]When the sun was setting, the people brought to Jesus all who had various kinds of sickness, and laying his hands on each one, he healed them. [41]Moreover, demons came out of many people, shouting, "You are the Son of God!" But he rebuked them and would not allow them to speak, because they knew he was the Christ.[d]

[42]At daybreak Jesus went out to a solitary place. The people were looking for him and when they came to where he was, they tried to keep him from leaving them. [43]But he said, "I must preach the good news of the kingdom of God to the other towns also, because that is why I was sent." [44]And he kept on preaching in the synagogues of Judea.[e]

[c] 33 Greek *unclean*; also in verse 36 [d] 41 Or *Messiah* [e] 44 Or *the land of the Jews*; some manuscripts *Galilee*

PRAYER: THE ATTRIBUTES OF GOD

MY days are like a lengthened shadow, and I wither away like grass. But You, O Lord, will endure forever, and the remembrance of Your name to all generations. In the beginning You laid the foundations of the earth, and the heavens are the work of Your hands. They will perish, but You will endure. They will all wear out like a garment; like clothing You will change them, and they will be discarded. But You are the same, and Your years will have no end. (Psalm 102:11–12, 25–27)

PAUSE *to reflect on these affirmations about the person, powers and perfection of God.*

YEAR 1 DAY 202

OT Joshua 21:1-45

Towns for the Levites

21 Now the family heads of the Levites approached Eleazar the priest, Joshua son of Nun, and the heads of the other tribal families of Israel [2]at Shiloh in Canaan and said to them, "The LORD commanded through Moses that you give us towns to live in, with pasturelands for our livestock." [3]So, as the LORD had commanded, the Israelites gave the Levites the following towns and pasturelands out of their own inheritance:

[4]The first lot came out for the Kohathites, clan by clan. The Levites who were descendants of Aaron the priest were allotted thirteen towns from the tribes of Ju-

dah, Simeon and Benjamin. [5]The rest of
Kohath's descendants were allotted ten
towns from the clans of the tribes of
Ephraim, Dan and half of Manasseh.

[6]The descendants of Gershon were allotted thirteen towns from the clans of the
tribes of Issachar, Asher, Naphtali and the
half-tribe of Manasseh in Bashan.

[7]The descendants of Merari, clan by
clan, received twelve towns from the
tribes of Reuben, Gad and Zebulun.

[8]So the Israelites allotted to the Levites
these towns and their pasturelands, as the
LORD had commanded through Moses.

[9]From the tribes of Judah and Simeon
they allotted the following towns by
name [10](these towns were assigned to the
descendants of Aaron who were from the
Kohathite clans of the Levites, because
the first lot fell to them):

[11]They gave them Kiriath Arba (that
is, Hebron), with its surrounding pastureland, in the hill country of Judah.
(Arba was the forefather of Anak.)
[12]But the fields and villages around
the city they had given to Caleb son
of Jephunneh as his possession.

[13]So to the descendants of Aaron
the priest they gave Hebron (a city of
refuge for one accused of murder),
Libnah, [14]Jattir, Eshtemoa, [15]Holon,
Debir, [16]Ain, Juttah and Beth Shemesh, together with their pasturelands—nine towns from these two
tribes.

[17]And from the tribe of Benjamin
they gave them Gibeon, Geba, [18]An-
athoth and Almon, together with
their pasturelands—four towns.

[19]All the towns for the priests, the descendants of Aaron, were thirteen, together
with their pasturelands.

[20]The rest of the Kohathite clans of the Levites were allotted towns from the tribe of
Ephraim:

[21]In the hill country of Ephraim
they were given Shechem (a city of
refuge for one accused of murder)
and Gezer, [22]Kibzaim and Beth Horon, together with their pasturelands—four towns.

[23]Also from the tribe of Dan they
received Eltekeh, Gibbethon, [24]Aija-
lon and Gath Rimmon, together with
their pasturelands—four towns.

[25]From half the tribe of Manasseh
they received Taanach and Gath Rimmon, together with their pasturelands—two towns.

[26]All these ten towns and their pasturelands were given to the rest of the Kohathite clans.

[27]The Levite clans of the Gershonites were
given:

from the half-tribe of Manasseh,
Golan in Bashan (a city of refuge for
one accused of murder) and Be Esh-
tarah, together with their pasturelands—two towns;

[28]from the tribe of Issachar,
Kishion, Daberath, [29]Jarmuth and En
Gannim, together with their pasture-
lands—four towns;

[30]from the tribe of Asher,
Mishal, Abdon, [31]Helkath and Rehob,
together with their pasturelands—
four towns;

[32]from the tribe of Naphtali,
Kedesh in Galilee (a city of refuge for
one accused of murder), Hammoth
Dor and Kartan, together with their
pasturelands—three towns.

[33]All the towns of the Gershonite clans
were thirteen, together with their pasturelands.

[34]The Merarite clans (the rest of the Levites) were given:

from the tribe of Zebulun,
Jokneam, Kartah, [35]Dimnah and Nahalal, together with their pasturelands—four towns;

[36]from the tribe of Reuben,
Bezer, Jahaz, [37]Kedemoth and Mephaath, together with their pasturelands—four towns;

[38]from the tribe of Gad,
Ramoth in Gilead (a city of refuge for
one accused of murder), Mahanaim,
[39]Heshbon and Jazer, together with
their pasturelands—four towns in all.

[40]All the towns allotted to the Merarite
clans, who were the rest of the Levites,
were twelve.

[41]The towns of the Levites in the territory held by the Israelites were forty-eight
in all, together with their pasturelands.
[42]Each of these towns had pasturelands
surrounding it; this was true for all these
towns.

[43]So the LORD gave Israel all the land he
had sworn to give their forefathers, and

they took possession of it and settled there. [44]The LORD gave them rest on every side, just as he had sworn to their forefathers. Not one of their enemies withstood them; the LORD handed all their enemies over to them. [45]Not one of all the LORD's good promises to the house of Israel failed; every one was fulfilled.

PRAYER: AFFIRMATION

O GOD, Your divine power has given me all things that pertain to life and godliness through my knowledge of You who called me by Your own glory and virtue. Through these You have given me Your very great and precious promises, so that through them I may be a partaker of the divine nature, having escaped the corruption that is in the world by lust.

(2 Peter 1:3–4)

PAUSE *to reflect on these Biblical affirmations.*

NT Luke 5:1-26

The Calling of the First Disciples

5 One day as Jesus was standing by the Lake of Gennesaret,[a] with the people crowding around him and listening to the word of God, [2]he saw at the water's edge two boats, left there by the fishermen, who were washing their nets. [3]He got into one of the boats, the one belonging to Simon, and asked him to put out a little from shore. Then he sat down and taught the people from the boat.

[4]When he had finished speaking, he said to Simon, "Put out into deep water, and let down[b] the nets for a catch."

[5]Simon answered, "Master, we've worked hard all night and haven't caught anything. But because you say so, I will let down the nets."

[6]When they had done so, they caught such a large number of fish that their nets began to break. [7]So they signaled their partners in the other boat to come and help them, and they came and filled both boats so full that they began to sink.

[8]When Simon Peter saw this, he fell at Jesus' knees and said, "Go away from me, Lord; I am a sinful man!" [9]For he and all his companions were astonished at the catch of fish they had taken, [10]and so were James and John, the sons of Zebedee, Simon's partners.

Then Jesus said to Simon, "Don't be afraid; from now on you will catch men." [11]So they pulled their boats up on shore, left everything and followed him.

The Man With Leprosy

[12]While Jesus was in one of the towns, a man came along who was covered with leprosy.[c] When he saw Jesus, he fell with his face to the ground and begged him, "Lord, if you are willing, you can make me clean."

[13]Jesus reached out his hand and touched the man. "I am willing," he said. "Be clean!" And immediately the leprosy left him.

[14]Then Jesus ordered him, "Don't tell anyone, but go, show yourself to the priest and offer the sacrifices that Moses commanded for your cleansing, as a testimony to them."

[15]Yet the news about him spread all the more, so that crowds of people came to hear him and to be healed of their sicknesses. [16]But Jesus often withdrew to lonely places and prayed.

Jesus Heals a Paralytic

[17]One day as he was teaching, Pharisees and teachers of the law, who had come from every village of Galilee and from Judea and Jerusalem, were sitting there. And the power of the Lord was present for him to heal the sick. [18]Some men came carrying a paralytic on a mat and tried to take him into the house to lay him before Jesus. [19]When they could not find a way to do this because of the crowd, they went up on the roof and low-

[a] *1* That is, Sea of Galilee [b] *4* The Greek verb is plural. [c] *12* The Greek word was used for various diseases affecting the skin—not necessarily leprosy.

ered him on his mat through the tiles
into the middle of the crowd, right in
front of Jesus.
[20]When Jesus saw their faith, he said,
"Friend, your sins are forgiven."
[21]The Pharisees and the teachers of the
law began thinking to themselves, "Who
is this fellow who speaks blasphemy?
Who can forgive sins but God alone?"
[22]Jesus knew what they were thinking
and asked, "Why are you thinking these
things in your hearts? [23]Which is easier: to
say, 'Your sins are forgiven,' or to say, 'Get
up and walk'? [24]But that you may know
that the Son of Man has authority on
earth to forgive sins. . . ." He said to the
paralyzed man, "I tell you, get up, take
your mat and go home." [25]Immediately
he stood up in front of them, took what
he had been lying on and went home
praising God. [26]Everyone was amazed and
gave praise to God. They were filled with
awe and said, "We have seen remarkable
things today."

PRAYER: THE WORKS OF GOD

WE will not all sleep, but we will all be changed in a moment—in the twinkling of an eye—at the last trumpet. For the trumpet will sound, and the dead will be raised imperishable, and we shall be changed. For this perishable must clothe itself with the imperishable, and this mortal with immortality. (1 Corinthians 15:51–53)

***TAKE** a moment to consider the greatness of God's wonderful works.*

YEAR 1
DAY 203

OT Psalm 39

Psalm 39

For the director of music. For Jeduthun.
A psalm of David.

[1]I said, "I will watch my ways
and keep my tongue from sin;
I will put a muzzle on my mouth
as long as the wicked are in my presence."
[2]But when I was silent and still,
not even saying anything good,
my anguish increased.
[3]My heart grew hot within me,
and as I meditated, the fire burned;
then I spoke with my tongue:

[4]"Show me, O LORD, my life's end
and the number of my days;
let me know how fleeting is my life.
[5]You have made my days a mere handbreadth;
the span of my years is as nothing before you.
Each man's life is but a breath. *Selah*
[6]Man is a mere phantom as he goes to and fro:
He bustles about, but only in vain;
he heaps up wealth, not knowing who will get it.

[7]"But now, Lord, what do I look for?
My hope is in you.
[8]Save me from all my transgressions;
do not make me the scorn of fools.
[9]I was silent; I would not open my mouth,
for you are the one who has done this.
[10]Remove your scourge from me;
I am overcome by the blow of your hand.
[11]You rebuke and discipline men for their sin;
you consume their wealth like a moth—
each man is but a breath. *Selah*

[12]"Hear my prayer, O LORD,
listen to my cry for help;
be not deaf to my weeping.
For I dwell with you as an alien,
a stranger, as all my fathers were.
[13]Look away from me, that I may rejoice again
before I depart and am no more."

PRAYER: THANKSGIVING

SURELY Your hand is not too short to save, O God, nor Your ear too dull to hear. But our iniquities have separated us from You, our God; our sins have hidden Your face from us, so that You will not hear. Yet You saw that there was no one to intervene; so Your own arm worked salvation for You, and Your righteousness sustained You. You put on righteousness as Your breastplate, and the helmet of salvation on Your head; You put on the garments of vengeance and wrapped Yourself in zeal as a cloak. From the west, all people will fear Your name, and from the rising of the sun, they will revere Your glory. For You will come like a flood that Your breath drives along. (Isaiah 59:1–2, 16–19)

***PAUSE** to offer your own expressions of thanksgiving.*

NT Luke 5:27–6:16

The Calling of Levi

27 After this, Jesus went out and saw a tax
collector by the name of Levi sitting at his
tax booth. "Follow me," Jesus said to him,
28 and Levi got up, left everything and followed him.

29 Then Levi held a great banquet for
Jesus at his house, and a large crowd of tax
collectors and others were eating with
them. 30 But the Pharisees and the teachers
of the law who belonged to their sect
complained to his disciples, "Why do you
eat and drink with tax collectors and 'sinners'?"

31 Jesus answered them, "It is not the
healthy who need a doctor, but the sick.
32 I have not come to call the righteous,
but sinners to repentance."

Jesus Questioned About Fasting

33 They said to him, "John's disciples often fast and pray, and so do the disciples
of the Pharisees, but yours go on eating
and drinking."

34 Jesus answered, "Can you make the
guests of the bridegroom fast while he is
with them? 35 But the time will come when
the bridegroom will be taken from them;
in those days they will fast."

36 He told them this parable: "No one
tears a patch from a new garment and
sews it on an old one. If he does, he will
have torn the new garment, and the patch
from the new will not match the old.
37 And no one pours new wine into old
wineskins. If he does, the new wine will
burst the skins, the wine will run out and
the wineskins will be ruined. 38 No, new
wine must be poured into new wineskins.
39 And no one after drinking old wine
wants the new, for he says, 'The old is better.' "

Lord of the Sabbath

6 One Sabbath Jesus was going through
the grainfields, and his disciples began
to pick some heads of grain, rub them in
their hands and eat the kernels. 2 Some of
the Pharisees asked, "Why are you doing
what is unlawful on the Sabbath?"

3 Jesus answered them, "Have you never
read what David did when he and his
companions were hungry? 4 He entered
the house of God, and taking the consecrated bread, he ate what is lawful only
for priests to eat. And he also gave some
to his companions." 5 Then Jesus said to
them, "The Son of Man is Lord of the Sabbath."

6 On another Sabbath he went into the
synagogue and was teaching, and a man
was there whose right hand was shriveled.
7 The Pharisees and the teachers of the law
were looking for a reason to accuse Jesus,
so they watched him closely to see if he
would heal on the Sabbath. 8 But Jesus
knew what they were thinking and said to
the man with the shriveled hand, "Get up
and stand in front of everyone." So he got
up and stood there.

9 Then Jesus said to them, "I ask you,
which is lawful on the Sabbath: to do
good or to do evil, to save life or to destroy it?"

10 He looked around at them all, and
then said to the man, "Stretch out your
hand." He did so, and his hand was com-

pletely restored. [11]But they were furious and began to discuss with one another what they might do to Jesus.

The Twelve Apostles

[12]One of those days Jesus went out to a mountainside to pray, and spent the night praying to God. [13]When morning came, he called his disciples to him and chose twelve of them, whom he also designated apostles: [14]Simon (whom he named Peter), his brother Andrew, James, John, Philip, Bartholomew, [15]Matthew, Thomas, James son of Alphaeus, Simon who was called the Zealot, [16]Judas son of James, and Judas Iscariot, who became a traitor.

PRAYER: MY RELATIONSHIP TO GOD

I GIVE You thanks that to all who receive You, Lord Jesus Christ, and believe in Your name, You give the right to become children of God—children born not of natural descent, nor of human decision or a husband's will, but born of God. (John 1:12–13)

***PAUSE** to thank God for the relationship that you enjoy with Him in Jesus Christ.*

YEAR 1 DAY 204

OT Joshua 22:1-34

Eastern Tribes Return Home

22 Then Joshua summoned the Reubenites, the Gadites and the half-tribe of Manasseh [2]and said to them, "You have done all that Moses the servant of the LORD commanded, and you have obeyed me in everything I commanded. [3]For a long time now—to this very day—you have not deserted your brothers but have carried out the mission the LORD your God gave you. [4]Now that the LORD your God has given your brothers rest as he promised, return to your homes in the land that Moses the servant of the LORD gave you on the other side of the Jordan. [5]But be very careful to keep the commandment and the law that Moses the servant of the LORD gave you: to love the LORD your God, to walk in all his ways, to obey his commands, to hold fast to him and to serve him with all your heart and all your soul."

[6]Then Joshua blessed them and sent them away, and they went to their homes. [7](To the half-tribe of Manasseh Moses had given land in Bashan, and to the other half of the tribe Joshua gave land on the west side of the Jordan with their brothers.) When Joshua sent them home, he blessed them, [8]saying, "Return to your homes with your great wealth—with large herds of livestock, with silver, gold, bronze and iron, and a great quantity of clothing—and divide with your brothers the plunder from your enemies."

[9]So the Reubenites, the Gadites and the half-tribe of Manasseh left the Israelites at Shiloh in Canaan to return to Gilead, their own land, which they had acquired in accordance with the command of the LORD through Moses.

[10]When they came to Geliloth near the Jordan in the land of Canaan, the Reubenites, the Gadites and the half-tribe of Manasseh built an imposing altar there by the Jordan. [11]And when the Israelites heard that they had built the altar on the border of Canaan at Geliloth near the Jordan on the Israelite side, [12]the whole assembly of Israel gathered at Shiloh to go to war against them.

[13]So the Israelites sent Phinehas son of Eleazar, the priest, to the land of Gilead—to Reuben, Gad and the half-tribe of Manasseh. [14]With him they sent ten of the chief men, one for each of the tribes of Israel, each the head of a family division among the Israelite clans.

[15]When they went to Gilead—to Reuben, Gad and the half-tribe of Manasseh—they said to them: [16]"The whole assembly of the LORD says: 'How could you break faith with the God of Israel like

this? How could you turn away from the
LORD and build yourselves an altar in rebellion against him now? 17Was not the
sin of Peor enough for us? Up to this very
day we have not cleansed ourselves from
that sin, even though a plague fell on the
community of the LORD! 18And are you
now turning away from the LORD?

" 'If you rebel against the LORD today, tomorrow he will be angry with the whole
community of Israel. 19If the land you possess is defiled, come over to the LORD's land,
where the LORD's tabernacle stands, and
share the land with us. But do not rebel
against the LORD or against us by building
an altar for yourselves, other than the altar
of the LORD our God. 20When Achan son of
Zerah acted unfaithfully regarding the devoted things,[a] did not wrath come upon the
whole community of Israel? He was not the
only one who died for his sin.' "

21Then Reuben, Gad and the half-tribe
of Manasseh replied to the heads of the
clans of Israel: 22"The Mighty One, God,
the LORD! The Mighty One, God, the
LORD! He knows! And let Israel know! If
this has been in rebellion or disobedience
to the LORD, do not spare us this day. 23If
we have built our own altar to turn away
from the LORD and to offer burnt offerings
and grain offerings, or to sacrifice fellowship offerings[b] on it, may the LORD himself call us to account.

24"No! We did it for fear that some day
your descendants might say to ours, 'What
do you have to do with the LORD, the God
of Israel? 25The LORD has made the Jordan
a boundary between us and you—you
Reubenites and Gadites! You have no
share in the LORD.' So your descendants
might cause ours to stop fearing the LORD.

26"That is why we said, 'Let us get ready
and build an altar—but not for burnt offerings or sacrifices.' 27On the contrary, it
is to be a witness between us and you and
the generations that follow, that we will
worship the LORD at his sanctuary with
our burnt offerings, sacrifices and fellowship offerings. Then in the future your descendants will not be able to say to ours,
'You have no share in the LORD.'

28"And we said, 'If they ever say this to
us, or to our descendants, we will answer:
Look at the replica of the LORD's altar,
which our fathers built, not for burnt offerings and sacrifices, but as a witness between us and you.'

29"Far be it from us to rebel against the
LORD and turn away from him today by
building an altar for burnt offerings, grain
offerings and sacrifices, other than the altar of the LORD our God that stands before
his tabernacle."

30When Phinehas the priest and the
leaders of the community—the heads of
the clans of the Israelites—heard what
Reuben, Gad and Manasseh had to say,
they were pleased. 31And Phinehas son of
Eleazar, the priest, said to Reuben, Gad
and Manasseh, "Today we know that the
LORD is with us, because you have not acted unfaithfully toward the LORD in this
matter. Now you have rescued the Israelites from the LORD's hand."

32Then Phinehas son of Eleazar, the
priest, and the leaders returned to Canaan
from their meeting with the Reubenites
and Gadites in Gilead and reported to the
Israelites. 33They were glad to hear the report and praised God. And they talked no
more about going to war against them to
devastate the country where the Reubenites and the Gadites lived.

34And the Reubenites and the Gadites
gave the altar this name: A Witness Between Us that the LORD is God.

[a] *20* The Hebrew term refers to the irrevocable giving over of things or persons to the LORD, often by totally destroying them. [b] *23* Traditionally *peace offerings;* also in verse 27

PRAYER: ADORATION

MAY I fear You, the Lord my God; may I serve You, hold fast to You, and take my oaths in Your name.
For You are my praise and You are my God, who performed for me these great and awesome wonders, which I have seen with my own eyes.
(Deuteronomy 10:20–21) . . . You are the great, the mighty, and the awesome God, who keeps Your covenant of loving-kindness. (Nehemiah 9:32)

PAUSE *to express your thoughts of praise and worship.*

NT Luke 6:17-49

Blessings and Woes

17 He went down with them and stood
on a level place. A large crowd of his disciples was there and a great number of
people from all over Judea, from Jerusalem, and from the coast of Tyre and Sidon, 18 who had come to hear him and to
be healed of their diseases. Those troubled by evil[a] spirits were cured, 19 and the
people all tried to touch him, because
power was coming from him and healing
them all.
20 Looking at his disciples, he said:

"Blessed are you who are poor,
for yours is the kingdom of God.
21 Blessed are you who hunger now,
for you will be satisfied.
Blessed are you who weep now,
for you will laugh.
22 Blessed are you when men hate you,
when they exclude you and insult
you
and reject your name as evil,
because of the Son of Man.

23 "Rejoice in that day and leap for joy,
because great is your reward in heaven.
For that is how their fathers treated the
prophets.

24 "But woe to you who are rich,
for you have already received your
comfort.
25 Woe to you who are well fed now,
for you will go hungry.
Woe to you who laugh now,
for you will mourn and weep.
26 Woe to you when all men speak well
of you,
for that is how their fathers treated
the false prophets.

Love for Enemies

27 "But I tell you who hear me: Love your
enemies, do good to those who hate you,
28 bless those who curse you, pray for
those who mistreat you. 29 If someone
strikes you on one cheek, turn to him the
other also. If someone takes your cloak,
do not stop him from taking your tunic.
30 Give to everyone who asks you, and if
anyone takes what belongs to you, do not
demand it back. 31 Do to others as you
would have them do to you.

32 "If you love those who love you, what
credit is that to you? Even 'sinners' love
those who love them. 33 And if you do
good to those who are good to you, what
credit is that to you? Even 'sinners' do
that. 34 And if you lend to those from
whom you expect repayment, what credit
is that to you? Even 'sinners' lend to 'sinners,' expecting to be repaid in full. 35 But
love your enemies, do good to them, and
lend to them without expecting to get
anything back. Then your reward will be
great, and you will be sons of the Most
High, because he is kind to the ungrateful
and wicked. 36 Be merciful, just as your Father is merciful.

Judging Others

37 "Do not judge, and you will not be
judged. Do not condemn, and you will
not be condemned. Forgive, and you will
be forgiven. 38 Give, and it will be given to
you. A good measure, pressed down,
shaken together and running over, will be
poured into your lap. For with the measure you use, it will be measured to you."
39 He also told them this parable: "Can
a blind man lead a blind man? Will they
not both fall into a pit? 40 A student is not
above his teacher, but everyone who is fully trained will be like his teacher.
41 "Why do you look at the speck of saw-
dust in your brother's eye and pay no attention to the plank in your own eye?
42 How can you say to your brother, 'Brother, let me take the speck out of your eye,'
when you yourself fail to see the plank in
your own eye? You hypocrite, first take the
plank out of your eye, and then you will
see clearly to remove the speck from your
brother's eye.

A Tree and Its Fruit

43 "No good tree bears bad fruit, nor does
a bad tree bear good fruit. 44 Each tree is recognized by its own fruit. People do not
pick figs from thornbushes, or grapes from
briers. 45 The good man brings good things
out of the good stored up in his heart, and
the evil man brings evil things out of the
evil stored up in his heart. For out of the
overflow of his heart his mouth speaks.

[a] 18 Greek *unclean*

The Wise and Foolish Builders

46 "Why do you call me, 'Lord, Lord,' and
do not do what I say? 47 I will show you
what he is like who comes to me and
hears my words and puts them into practice. 48 He is like a man building a house,
who dug down deep and laid the foundation on rock. When a flood came, the
torrent struck that house but could not
shake it, because it was well built. 49 But
the one who hears my words and does not
put them into practice is like a man who
built a house on the ground without a
foundation. The moment the torrent
struck that house, it collapsed and its destruction was complete."

PRAYER: THE CHARACTER I WANT TO CULTIVATE

WHO may ascend Your hill, O Lord? Who may stand in Your holy place? Those who have clean hands and pure hearts, who have not lifted up their souls to idols or sworn by what is false. (Psalm 24:3–4) . . . The path of the righteous is like the first gleam of dawn, shining ever brighter until the full light of day. But the way of the wicked is like darkness; they do not know what makes them stumble. (Proverbs 4:18–19)

***TAKE** a moment to ask the Lord for the grace to grow in godly character.*

YEAR 1
DAY 205

OT Joshua 23:1-16

Joshua's Farewell to the Leaders

23 After a long time had passed and the
LORD had given Israel rest from all
their enemies around them, Joshua, by
then old and well advanced in years,
2 summoned all Israel—their elders, leaders, judges and officials—and said to
them: "I am old and well advanced in
years. 3 You yourselves have seen everything the LORD your God has done to all
these nations for your sake; it was the
LORD your God who fought for you. 4 Remember how I have allotted as an inheritance for your tribes all the land of the
nations that remain—the nations I conquered—between the Jordan and the
Great Sea[a] in the west. 5 The LORD your
God himself will drive them out of your
way. He will push them out before you,
and you will take possession of their land,
as the LORD your God promised you.
6 "Be very strong; be careful to obey all
that is written in the Book of the Law of
Moses, without turning aside to the right
or to the left. 7 Do not associate with these
nations that remain among you; do not
invoke the names of their gods or swear
by them. You must not serve them or bow
down to them. 8 But you are to hold fast
to the LORD your God, as you have until
now.
9 "The LORD has driven out before you
great and powerful nations; to this day no
one has been able to withstand you.
10 One of you routs a thousand, because
the LORD your God fights for you, just as
he promised. 11 So be very careful to love
the LORD your God.
12 "But if you turn away and ally yourselves with the survivors of these nations
that remain among you and if you intermarry with them and associate with them,
13 then you may be sure that the LORD your
God will no longer drive out these nations
before you. Instead, they will become
snares and traps for you, whips on your
backs and thorns in your eyes, until you
perish from this good land, which the
LORD your God has given you.
14 "Now I am about to go the way of all
the earth. You know with all your heart
and soul that not one of all the good
promises the LORD your God gave you has
failed. Every promise has been fulfilled;
not one has failed. 15 But just as every good
promise of the LORD your God has come
true, so the LORD will bring on you all the
evil he has threatened, until he has de-

[a] 4 That is, the Mediterranean

stroyed you from this good land he has given you. 16If you violate the covenant of the LORD your God, which he commanded you, and go and serve other gods and bow down to them, the LORD's anger will burn against you, and you will quickly perish from the good land he has given you."

PRAYER: CONFESSION

LORD, we confess that from within, out of our hearts, proceed evil thoughts, sexual immorality, thefts, murders, adulteries, greed, wickedness, deceit, lewdness, envy, slander, arrogance and folly. All these evil things come from within our hearts and defile us.

(Mark 7:21–23)

***ASK** the Spirit to search your heart and reveal any areas of unconfessed sin. Acknowledge these to the Lord and thank Him for His forgiveness.*

NT Luke 7:1–35

The Faith of the Centurion

7 When Jesus had finished saying all this in the hearing of the people, he entered Capernaum. 2There a centurion's servant, whom his master valued highly, was sick and about to die. 3The centurion heard of Jesus and sent some elders of the Jews to him, asking him to come and heal his servant. 4When they came to Jesus, they pleaded earnestly with him, "This man deserves to have you do this, 5because he loves our nation and has built our synagogue." 6So Jesus went with them.

He was not far from the house when the centurion sent friends to say to him: "Lord, don't trouble yourself, for I do not deserve to have you come under my roof. 7That is why I did not even consider myself worthy to come to you. But say the word, and my servant will be healed. 8For I myself am a man under authority, with soldiers under me. I tell this one, 'Go,' and he goes; and that one, 'Come,' and he comes. I say to my servant, 'Do this,' and he does it."

9When Jesus heard this, he was amazed at him, and turning to the crowd following him, he said, "I tell you, I have not found such great faith even in Israel." 10Then the men who had been sent returned to the house and found the servant well.

Jesus Raises a Widow's Son

11Soon afterward, Jesus went to a town called Nain, and his disciples and a large crowd went along with him. 12As he approached the town gate, a dead person was being carried out—the only son of his mother, and she was a widow. And a large crowd from the town was with her. 13When the Lord saw her, his heart went out to her and he said, "Don't cry."

14Then he went up and touched the coffin, and those carrying it stood still. He said, "Young man, I say to you, get up!" 15The dead man sat up and began to talk, and Jesus gave him back to his mother.

16They were all filled with awe and praised God. "A great prophet has appeared among us," they said. "God has come to help his people." 17This news about Jesus spread throughout Judea[a] and the surrounding country.

Jesus and John the Baptist

18John's disciples told him about all these things. Calling two of them, 19he sent them to the Lord to ask, "Are you the one who was to come, or should we expect someone else?"

20When the men came to Jesus, they said, "John the Baptist sent us to you to ask, 'Are you the one who was to come, or should we expect someone else?' "

21At that very time Jesus cured many who had diseases, sicknesses and evil spirits, and gave sight to many who were blind. 22So he replied to the messengers, "Go back and report to John what you have seen and heard: The blind receive sight, the lame walk, those who have leprosy[b] are cured, the deaf hear, the dead are

[a] 17 Or *the land of the Jews* [b] 22 The Greek word was used for various diseases affecting the skin—not necessarily leprosy.

raised, and the good news is preached to the poor. [23]Blessed is the man who does not fall away on account of me."

[24]After John's messengers left, Jesus began to speak to the crowd about John: "What did you go out into the desert to see? A reed swayed by the wind? [25]If not, what did you go out to see? A man dressed in fine clothes? No, those who wear expensive clothes and indulge in luxury are in palaces. [26]But what did you go out to see? A prophet? Yes, I tell you, and more than a prophet. [27]This is the one about whom it is written:

" 'I will send my messenger ahead of
you,
who will prepare your way before
you.'[c]

[28]I tell you, among those born of women there is no one greater than John; yet the one who is least in the kingdom of God is greater than he."

[29](All the people, even the tax collectors, when they heard Jesus' words, acknowledged that God's way was right, because they had been baptized by John. [30]But the Pharisees and experts in the law rejected God's purpose for themselves, because they had not been baptized by John.)

[31]"To what, then, can I compare the people of this generation? What are they like? [32]They are like children sitting in the marketplace and calling out to each other:

" 'We played the flute for you,
and you did not dance;
we sang a dirge,
and you did not cry.'

[33]For John the Baptist came neither eating bread nor drinking wine, and you say, 'He has a demon.' [34]The Son of Man came eating and drinking, and you say, 'Here is a glutton and a drunkard, a friend of tax collectors and "sinners." ' [35]But wisdom is proved right by all her children."

[c] 27 Mal. 3:1

PRAYER: MY RELATIONSHIP TO OTHERS

I WANT to speak words of encouragement to other believers. (Acts 20:2) . . . We should encourage one another and build each other up in You, Christ Jesus. (1 Thessalonians 5:11)

***PAUSE** to review your relationships with others and to commit them to the Lord.*

YEAR 1 DAY 206

OT Joshua 24:1-33

The Covenant Renewed at Shechem

24 Then Joshua assembled all the tribes of Israel at Shechem. He summoned the elders, leaders, judges and officials of Israel, and they presented themselves before God.

[2]Joshua said to all the people, "This is what the LORD, the God of Israel, says: 'Long ago your forefathers, including Terah the father of Abraham and Nahor, lived beyond the River[a] and worshiped other gods. [3]But I took your father Abraham from the land beyond the River and led him throughout Canaan and gave him many descendants. I gave him Isaac, [4]and to Isaac I gave Jacob and Esau. I assigned the hill country of Seir to Esau, but Jacob and his sons went down to Egypt.

[5]" 'Then I sent Moses and Aaron, and I afflicted the Egyptians by what I did there, and I brought you out. [6]When I brought your fathers out of Egypt, you came to the sea, and the Egyptians pursued them with chariots and horsemen[b] as far as the Red Sea.[c] [7]But they cried to the LORD for help, and he put darkness between you and the Egyptians; he brought the sea over them and covered them. You saw with your own eyes what I did to the Egyptians. Then you lived in the desert for a long time.

[a] 2 That is, the Euphrates; also in verses 3, 14 and 15 [b] 6 Or *charioteers* [c] 6 Hebrew *Yam Suph*; that is, Sea of Reeds

8" 'I brought you to the land of the Amorites who lived east of the Jordan. They
fought against you, but I gave them into
your hands. I destroyed them from before
you, and you took possession of their
land. 9When Balak son of Zippor, the king
of Moab, prepared to fight against Israel,
he sent for Balaam son of Beor to put a
curse on you. 10But I would not listen to
Balaam, so he blessed you again and
again, and I delivered you out of his hand.
11" 'Then you crossed the Jordan and
came to Jericho. The citizens of Jericho
fought against you, as did also the Amorites, Perizzites, Canaanites, Hittites, Girgashites, Hivites and Jebusites, but I gave
them into your hands. 12I sent the hornet
ahead of you, which drove them out before you—also the two Amorite kings. You
did not do it with your own sword and
bow. 13So I gave you a land on which you
did not toil and cities you did not build;
and you live in them and eat from vineyards and olive groves that you did not
plant.'
14"Now fear the LORD and serve him
with all faithfulness. Throw away the gods
your forefathers worshiped beyond the
River and in Egypt, and serve the LORD.
15But if serving the LORD seems undesir-
able to you, then choose for yourselves
this day whom you will serve, whether the
gods your forefathers served beyond the
River, or the gods of the Amorites, in
whose land you are living. But as for me
and my household, we will serve the
LORD."
16Then the people answered, "Far be it
from us to forsake the LORD to serve other gods! 17It was the LORD our God himself who brought us and our fathers up
out of Egypt, from that land of slavery,
and performed those great signs before
our eyes. He protected us on our entire
journey and among all the nations
through which we traveled. 18And the
LORD drove out before us all the nations,
including the Amorites, who lived in the
land. We too will serve the LORD, because
he is our God."
19Joshua said to the people, "You are
not able to serve the LORD. He is a holy
God; he is a jealous God. He will not forgive your rebellion and your sins. 20If you
forsake the LORD and serve foreign gods,
he will turn and bring disaster on you and
make an end of you, after he has been
good to you."
21But the people said to Joshua, "No!
We will serve the LORD."
22Then Joshua said, "You are witnesses
against yourselves that you have chosen to
serve the LORD."
"Yes, we are witnesses," they replied.
23"Now then," said Joshua, "throw away
the foreign gods that are among you and
yield your hearts to the LORD, the God of
Israel."
24And the people said to Joshua, "We
will serve the LORD our God and obey
him."
25On that day Joshua made a covenant
for the people, and there at Shechem he
drew up for them decrees and laws. 26And
Joshua recorded these things in the Book
of the Law of God. Then he took a large
stone and set it up there under the oak
near the holy place of the LORD.
27"See!" he said to all the people. "This
stone will be a witness against us. It has
heard all the words the LORD has said to
us. It will be a witness against you if you
are untrue to your God."

Buried in the Promised Land

28Then Joshua sent the people away,
each to his own inheritance.
29After these things, Joshua son of Nun,
the servant of the LORD, died at the age of
a hundred and ten. 30And they buried him
in the land of his inheritance, at Timnath
Serah[d] in the hill country of Ephraim,
north of Mount Gaash.
31Israel served the LORD throughout the
lifetime of Joshua and of the elders who
outlived him and who had experienced
everything the LORD had done for Israel.
32And Joseph's bones, which the Israelites had brought up from Egypt, were
buried at Shechem in the tract of land that
Jacob bought for a hundred pieces of silver[e] from the sons of Hamor, the father of
Shechem. This became the inheritance of
Joseph's descendants.
33And Eleazar son of Aaron died and
was buried at Gibeah, which had been allotted to his son Phinehas in the hill
country of Ephraim.

[d] *30* Also known as *Timnath Heres* (see Judges 2:9)
[e] *32* Hebrew *hundred kesitahs;* a kesitah was a unit of money of unknown weight and value.

PRAYER: RENEWAL

O LORD, I will not let sin reign in my mortal body that I should obey its evil desires. Nor will I present the parts of my body to sin as instruments of wickedness, but I will present myself to You, Lord God, as one who is alive from the dead. I will present the parts of my body as instruments of righteousness to You. (Romans 6:12–13) . . . May I put away all filthiness and the overflow of wickedness, and in meekness accept the word planted in me, which is able to save my soul. (James 1:21)

***PAUSE** to add your own prayers for personal renewal.*

NT Luke 7:36–8:15

Jesus Anointed by a Sinful Woman

36 Now one of the Pharisees invited Jesus to have dinner with him, so he went to the Pharisee's house and reclined at the table. 37 When a woman who had lived a sinful life in that town learned that Jesus was eating at the Pharisee's house, she brought an alabaster jar of perfume, 38 and as she stood behind him at his feet weeping, she began to wet his feet with her tears. Then she wiped them with her hair, kissed them and poured perfume on them.

39 When the Pharisee who had invited him saw this, he said to himself, "If this man were a prophet, he would know who is touching him and what kind of woman she is—that she is a sinner."

40 Jesus answered him, "Simon, I have something to tell you."

"Tell me, teacher," he said.

41 "Two men owed money to a certain moneylender. One owed him five hundred denarii,[d] and the other fifty. 42 Neither of them had the money to pay him back, so he canceled the debts of both. Now which of them will love him more?"

43 Simon replied, "I suppose the one who had the bigger debt canceled."

"You have judged correctly," Jesus said.

44 Then he turned toward the woman and said to Simon, "Do you see this woman? I came into your house. You did not give me any water for my feet, but she wet my feet with her tears and wiped them with her hair. 45 You did not give me a kiss, but this woman, from the time I entered, has not stopped kissing my feet. 46 You did not put oil on my head, but she has poured perfume on my feet. 47 Therefore, I tell you, her many sins have been forgiven—for she loved much. But he who has been forgiven little loves little."

48 Then Jesus said to her, "Your sins are forgiven."

49 The other guests began to say among themselves, "Who is this who even forgives sins?"

50 Jesus said to the woman, "Your faith has saved you; go in peace."

The Parable of the Sower

8 After this, Jesus traveled about from one town and village to another, proclaiming the good news of the kingdom of God. The Twelve were with him, 2 and also some women who had been cured of evil spirits and diseases: Mary (called Magdalene) from whom seven demons had come out; 3 Joanna the wife of Cuza, the manager of Herod's household; Susanna; and many others. These women were helping to support them out of their own means.

4 While a large crowd was gathering and people were coming to Jesus from town after town, he told this parable: 5 "A farmer went out to sow his seed. As he was scattering the seed, some fell along the path; it was trampled on, and the birds of the air ate it up. 6 Some fell on rock, and when it came up, the plants withered because they had no moisture. 7 Other seed fell among thorns, which grew up with it and choked the plants. 8 Still other seed fell on good soil. It came up and yielded a crop, a hundred times more than was sown."

When he said this, he called out, "He who has ears to hear, let him hear."

9 His disciples asked him what this par-

[d] *41* A denarius was a coin worth about a day's wages.

able meant. 10He said, "The knowledge of
the secrets of the kingdom of God has
been given to you, but to others I speak in
parables, so that,

" 'though seeing, they may not see;
though hearing, they may not
understand.'[a]

11"This is the meaning of the parable:
The seed is the word of God. 12Those
along the path are the ones who hear, and
then the devil comes and takes away the
word from their hearts, so that they may
not believe and be saved. 13Those on the
rock are the ones who receive the word
with joy when they hear it, but they have
no root. They believe for a while, but in
the time of testing they fall away. 14The
seed that fell among thorns stands for
those who hear, but as they go on their
way they are choked by life's worries,
riches and pleasures, and they do not mature. 15But the seed on good soil stands for
those with a noble and good heart, who
hear the word, retain it, and by persever-
ing produce a crop.

[a] *10* Isaiah 6:9

PRAYER: THE ATTRIBUTES OF GOD

O LORD, You reign forever. You have established Your throne for judgment. You will judge the world in righteousness, and You will govern the peoples with justice. You, O Lord, will also be a refuge for the oppressed, a stronghold in times of trouble. Those who know Your name will trust in You, for You, Lord, have never forsaken those who seek You. (Psalm 9:7–10)

PAUSE *to reflect on these affirmations about the person, powers and perfection of God.*

YEAR 1
DAY 207

OT Proverbs 9

Invitations of Wisdom and of Folly

9 Wisdom has built her house;
she has hewn out its seven pillars.
2She has prepared her meat and mixed
her wine;
she has also set her table.
3She has sent out her maids, and she
calls
from the highest point of the city.
4"Let all who are simple come in
here!"
she says to those who lack
judgment.
5"Come, eat my food
and drink the wine I have mixed.
6Leave your simple ways and you will
live;
walk in the way of understanding.

7"Whoever corrects a mocker invites
insult;
whoever rebukes a wicked man
incurs abuse.
8Do not rebuke a mocker or he will
hate you;
rebuke a wise man and he will love
you.
9Instruct a wise man and he will be
wiser still;
teach a righteous man and he will
add to his learning.

10"The fear of the LORD is the beginning
of wisdom,
and knowledge of the Holy One is
understanding.
11For through me your days will be
many,
and years will be added to your life.
12If you are wise, your wisdom will
reward you;
if you are a mocker, you alone will
suffer."

13The woman Folly is loud;
she is undisciplined and without
knowledge.
14She sits at the door of her house,

on a seat at the highest point of the city,
[15] calling out to those who pass by,
who go straight on their way.
[16] "Let all who are simple come in here!"
she says to those who lack judgment.
[17] "Stolen water is sweet;
food eaten in secret is delicious!"
[18] But little do they know that the dead are there,
that her guests are in the depths of the grave.[a]

[a] 18 Hebrew *Sheol*

PRAYER: PETITION

I CALL on You, O God, for You will answer me; incline Your ear to me and hear my prayer. Show Your wonderful loving-kindness, O Savior of those who take refuge at Your right hand from those who rise up against them. Keep me as the apple of Your eye; hide me in the shadow of Your wings. (Psalm 17:6–8)

PAUSE *here to petition God for wisdom. Ask Him to develop your eternal perspective, to renew your mind with truth and to help you develop greater skill in each area of your life. Offer prayers regarding your activities for this day and any special concerns you may have.*

NT Luke 8:16–39

A Lamp on a Stand

[16] "No one lights a lamp and hides it in a jar or puts it under a bed. Instead, he puts it on a stand, so that those who come in can see the light. [17] For there is nothing hidden that will not be disclosed, and nothing concealed that will not be known or brought out into the open. [18] Therefore consider carefully how you listen. Whoever has will be given more; whoever does not have, even what he thinks he has will be taken from him."

Jesus' Mother and Brothers

[19] Now Jesus' mother and brothers came to see him, but they were not able to get near him because of the crowd. [20] Someone told him, "Your mother and brothers are standing outside, wanting to see you."

[21] He replied, "My mother and brothers are those who hear God's word and put it into practice."

Jesus Calms the Storm

[22] One day Jesus said to his disciples, "Let's go over to the other side of the lake." So they got into a boat and set out. [23] As they sailed, he fell asleep. A squall came down on the lake, so that the boat was being swamped, and they were in great danger.

[24] The disciples went and woke him, saying, "Master, Master, we're going to drown!"

He got up and rebuked the wind and the raging waters; the storm subsided, and all was calm. [25] "Where is your faith?" he asked his disciples.

In fear and amazement they asked one another, "Who is this? He commands even the winds and the water, and they obey him."

The Healing of a Demon-possessed Man

[26] They sailed to the region of the Gerasenes,[a] which is across the lake from Galilee. [27] When Jesus stepped ashore, he was met by a demon-possessed man from the town. For a long time this man had not worn clothes or lived in a house, but had lived in the tombs. [28] When he saw Jesus, he cried out and fell at his feet, shouting at the top of his voice, "What do you want with me, Jesus, Son of the Most High God? I beg you, don't torture me!" [29] For Jesus had commanded the evil[b] spirit to come out of the man. Many times it had seized him, and though he was chained hand and foot and kept under guard, he

[a] 26 Some manuscripts *Gadarenes;* other manuscripts *Gergesenes;* also in verse 37
[b] 29 Greek *unclean*

had broken his chains and had been driven by the demon into solitary places.
[30]Jesus asked him, "What is your name?"
"Legion," he replied, because many demons had gone into him. [31]And they begged him repeatedly not to order them to go into the Abyss.
[32]A large herd of pigs was feeding there on the hillside. The demons begged Jesus to let them go into them, and he gave them permission. [33]When the demons came out of the man, they went into the pigs, and the herd rushed down the steep bank into the lake and was drowned.
[34]When those tending the pigs saw what had happened, they ran off and reported this in the town and countryside, [35]and the people went out to see what had happened. When they came to Jesus, they found the man from whom the demons had gone out, sitting at Jesus' feet, dressed and in his right mind; and they were afraid. [36]Those who had seen it told the people how the demon-possessed man had been cured. [37]Then all the people of the region of the Gerasenes asked Jesus to leave them, because they were overcome with fear. So he got into the boat and left.
[38]The man from whom the demons had gone out begged to go with him, but Jesus sent him away, saying, [39]"Return home and tell how much God has done for you." So the man went away and told all over town how much Jesus had done for him.

PRAYER: THE WORKS OF GOD

YOU died for our sins, O Christ, according to the Scriptures; You were buried, and You were raised on the third day according to the Scriptures. (1 Corinthians 15:3–4) . . . Lord Jesus Christ, You gave Yourself for our sins to rescue us from the present evil age, according to the will of our God and Father, to whom be glory for ever and ever. (Galatians 1:3–5)

***TAKE** a moment to consider the greatness of God's wonderful works.*

YEAR 1 DAY 208

OT Judges 1:1–36

Israel Fights the Remaining Canaanites

1 After the death of Joshua, the Israelites asked the LORD, "Who will be the first to go up and fight for us against the Canaanites?"
[2]The LORD answered, "Judah is to go; I have given the land into their hands."
[3]Then the men of Judah said to the Simeonites their brothers, "Come up with us into the territory allotted to us, to fight against the Canaanites. We in turn will go with you into yours." So the Simeonites went with them.
[4]When Judah attacked, the LORD gave the Canaanites and Perizzites into their hands and they struck down ten thousand men at Bezek. [5]It was there that they found Adoni-Bezek and fought against him, putting to rout the Canaanites and Perizzites. [6]Adoni-Bezek fled, but they chased him and caught him, and cut off his thumbs and big toes.
[7]Then Adoni-Bezek said, "Seventy kings with their thumbs and big toes cut off have picked up scraps under my table. Now God has paid me back for what I did to them." They brought him to Jerusalem, and he died there.
[8]The men of Judah attacked Jerusalem also and took it. They put the city to the sword and set it on fire.
[9]After that, the men of Judah went down to fight against the Canaanites living in the hill country, the Negev and the western foothills. [10]They advanced against the Canaanites living in Hebron (formerly called Kiriath Arba) and defeated Sheshai, Ahiman and Talmai.
[11]From there they advanced against the people living in Debir (formerly called Kiriath Sepher). [12]And Caleb said, "I will

give my daughter Acsah in marriage to the man who attacks and captures Kiriath Sepher." [13]Othniel son of Kenaz, Caleb's younger brother, took it; so Caleb gave his daughter Acsah to him in marriage.

[14]One day when she came to Othniel, she urged him[a] to ask her father for a field. When she got off her donkey, Caleb asked her, "What can I do for you?"

[15]She replied, "Do me a special favor. Since you have given me land in the Negev, give me also springs of water." Then Caleb gave her the upper and lower springs.

[16]The descendants of Moses' father-in-law, the Kenite, went up from the City of Palms[b] with the men of Judah to live among the people of the Desert of Judah in the Negev near Arad.

[17]Then the men of Judah went with the Simeonites their brothers and attacked the Canaanites living in Zephath, and they totally destroyed[c] the city. Therefore it was called Hormah.[d] [18]The men of Judah also took[e] Gaza, Ashkelon and Ekron—each city with its territory.

[19]The LORD was with the men of Judah. They took possession of the hill country, but they were unable to drive the people from the plains, because they had iron chariots. [20]As Moses had promised, Hebron was given to Caleb, who drove from it the three sons of Anak. [21]The Benjamites, however, failed to dislodge the Jebusites, who were living in Jerusalem; to this day the Jebusites live there with the Benjamites.

[22]Now the house of Joseph attacked Bethel, and the LORD was with them. [23]When they sent men to spy out Bethel (formerly called Luz), [24]the spies saw a man coming out of the city and they said to him, "Show us how to get into the city and we will see that you are treated well." [25]So he showed them, and they put the city to the sword but spared the man and his whole family. [26]He then went to the land of the Hittites, where he built a city and called it Luz, which is its name to this day.

[27]But Manasseh did not drive out the people of Beth Shan or Taanach or Dor or Ibleam or Megiddo and their surrounding settlements, for the Canaanites were determined to live in that land. [28]When Israel became strong, they pressed the Canaanites into forced labor but never drove them out completely. [29]Nor did Ephraim drive out the Canaanites living in Gezer, but the Canaanites continued to live there among them. [30]Neither did Zebulun drive out the Canaanites living in Kitron or Nahalol, who remained among them; but they did subject them to forced labor. [31]Nor did Asher drive out those living in Acco or Sidon or Ahlab or Aczib or Helbah or Aphek or Rehob, [32]and because of this the people of Asher lived among the Canaanite inhabitants of the land. [33]Neither did Naphtali drive out those living in Beth Shemesh or Beth Anath; but the Naphtalites too lived among the Canaanite inhabitants of the land, and those living in Beth Shemesh and Beth Anath became forced laborers for them. [34]The Amorites confined the Danites to the hill country, not allowing them to come down into the plain. [35]And the Amorites were determined also to hold out in Mount Heres, Aijalon and Shaalbim, but when the power of the house of Joseph increased, they too were pressed into forced labor. [36]The boundary of the Amorites was from Scorpion[f] Pass to Sela and beyond.

[a] 14 Hebrew; Septuagint and Vulgate *Othniel, he urged her* [b] 16 That is, Jericho [c] 17 The Hebrew term refers to the irrevocable giving over of things or persons to the LORD, often by totally destroying them. [d] 17 *Hormah* means *destruction.*
[e] 18 Hebrew; Septuagint *Judah did not take*
[f] 36 Hebrew *Akrabbim*

PRAYER: INTERCESSION

MAY I not seek my own good, O Lord, but rather the good of others. (1 Corinthians 10:24)

***TAKE** a few moments to intercede on behalf of your immediate family and other relatives. Offer prayers for their spiritual, emotional and physical concerns.*

NT **Luke 8:40–9:17**

A Dead Girl and a Sick Woman

[40]Now when Jesus returned, a crowd
welcomed him, for they were all expecting him. [41]Then a man named Jairus, a
ruler of the synagogue, came and fell at
Jesus' feet, pleading with him to come to
his house [42]because his only daughter, a
girl of about twelve, was dying.
As Jesus was on his way, the crowds almost crushed him. [43]And a woman was
there who had been subject to bleeding
for twelve years,[a] but no one could heal
her. [44]She came up behind him and
touched the edge of his cloak, and immediately her bleeding stopped.
[45]"Who touched me?" Jesus asked.
When they all denied it, Peter said,
"Master, the people are crowding and
pressing against you."
[46]But Jesus said, "Someone touched me;
I know that power has gone out from me."
[47]Then the woman, seeing that she
could not go unnoticed, came trembling
and fell at his feet. In the presence of all
the people, she told why she had touched
him and how she had been instantly
healed. [48]Then he said to her, "Daughter,
your faith has healed you. Go in peace."
[49]While Jesus was still speaking, someone came from the house of Jairus, the synagogue ruler. "Your daughter is dead," he
said. "Don't bother the teacher any more."
[50]Hearing this, Jesus said to Jairus,
"Don't be afraid; just believe, and she will
be healed."
[51]When he arrived at the house of Jairus, he did not let anyone go in with him
except Peter, John and James, and the
child's father and mother. [52]Meanwhile,
all the people were wailing and mourning
for her. "Stop wailing," Jesus said. "She is
not dead but asleep."
[53]They laughed at him, knowing that
she was dead. [54]But he took her by the
hand and said, "My child, get up!" [55]Her
spirit returned, and at once she stood up.
Then Jesus told them to give her something to eat. [56]Her parents were astonished, but he ordered them not to tell anyone what had happened.

Jesus Sends Out the Twelve

9 When Jesus had called the Twelve together, he gave them power and authority to drive out all demons and to cure diseases, [2]and he sent them out to preach the
kingdom of God and to heal the sick. [3]He
told them: "Take nothing for the journey—
no staff, no bag, no bread, no money, no
extra tunic. [4]Whatever house you enter, stay
there until you leave that town. [5]If people
do not welcome you, shake the dust off
your feet when you leave their town, as a
testimony against them." [6]So they set out
and went from village to village, preaching
the gospel and healing people everywhere.
[7]Now Herod the tetrarch heard about all
that was going on. And he was perplexed,
because some were saying that John had
been raised from the dead, [8]others that Elijah had appeared, and still others that one
of the prophets of long ago had come back
to life. [9]But Herod said, "I beheaded John.
Who, then, is this I hear such things
about?" And he tried to see him.

Jesus Feeds the Five Thousand

[10]When the apostles returned, they reported to Jesus what they had done. Then
he took them with him and they withdrew
by themselves to a town called Bethsaida,
[11]but the crowds learned about it and followed him. He welcomed them and spoke
to them about the kingdom of God, and
healed those who needed healing.
[12]Late in the afternoon the Twelve came
to him and said, "Send the crowd away so
they can go to the surrounding villages and
countryside and find food and lodging, because we are in a remote place here."
[13]He replied, "You give them something
to eat."
They answered, "We have only five
loaves of bread and two fish—unless we
go and buy food for all this crowd."
[14](About five thousand men were there.)
But he said to his disciples, "Have them
sit down in groups of about fifty each."
[15]The disciples did so, and everybody sat
down. [16]Taking the five loaves and the two
fish and looking up to heaven, he gave
thanks and broke them. Then he gave
them to the disciples to set before the people. [17]They all ate and were satisfied, and
the disciples picked up twelve basketfuls
of broken pieces that were left over.

[a] 43 Many manuscripts *years, and she had spent all she had on doctors*

PRAYER: MY RELATIONSHIP TO GOD

O MY Father, You know what I need before I ask You. (Matthew 6:8) . . . Holy Spirit, help me in my weakness, for I do not know what I ought to pray for, but You Yourself intercede for me with groans that words cannot express. And He who searches my heart knows Your mind, O Spirit, because You intercede for the saints according to the will of God. (Romans 8:26–27)

PAUSE *to thank God for the relationship that you enjoy with Him in Jesus Christ.*

YEAR 1 DAY 209

OT Judges 2:1–23

The Angel of the LORD at Bokim

2 The angel of the LORD went up from Gilgal to Bokim and said, "I brought you up out of Egypt and led you into the land that I swore to give to your forefathers. I said, 'I will never break my covenant with you, 2and you shall not make a covenant with the people of this land, but you shall break down their altars.' Yet you have disobeyed me. Why have you done this? 3Now therefore I tell you that I will not drive them out before you; they will be ⌊thorns⌋ in your sides and their gods will be a snare to you."

4When the angel of the LORD had spoken these things to all the Israelites, the people wept aloud, 5and they called that place Bokim.[a] There they offered sacrifices to the LORD.

Disobedience and Defeat

6After Joshua had dismissed the Israelites, they went to take possession of the land, each to his own inheritance. 7The people served the LORD throughout the lifetime of Joshua and of the elders who outlived him and who had seen all the great things the LORD had done for Israel.

8Joshua son of Nun, the servant of the LORD, died at the age of a hundred and ten. 9And they buried him in the land of his inheritance, at Timnath Heres[b] in the hill country of Ephraim, north of Mount Gaash.

10After that whole generation had been gathered to their fathers, another generation grew up, who knew neither the LORD nor what he had done for Israel. 11Then the Israelites did evil in the eyes of the LORD and served the Baals. 12They forsook the LORD, the God of their fathers, who had brought them out of Egypt. They followed and worshiped various gods of the peoples around them. They provoked the LORD to anger 13because they forsook him and served Baal and the Ashtoreths. 14In his anger against Israel the LORD handed them over to raiders who plundered them. He sold them to their enemies all around, whom they were no longer able to resist. 15Whenever Israel went out to fight, the hand of the LORD was against them to defeat them, just as he had sworn to them. They were in great distress.

16Then the LORD raised up judges,[c] who saved them out of the hands of these raiders. 17Yet they would not listen to their judges but prostituted themselves to other gods and worshiped them. Unlike their fathers, they quickly turned from the way in which their fathers had walked, the way of obedience to the LORD's commands. 18Whenever the LORD raised up a judge for them, he was with the judge and saved them out of the hands of their enemies as long as the judge lived; for the LORD had compassion on them as they groaned under those who oppressed and afflicted them. 19But when the judge died, the people returned to ways even more corrupt than those of their fathers, following other gods and serving and worshiping them. They refused to give up their evil practices and stubborn ways.

[a] *5 Bokim* means *weepers.* [b] *9* Also known as *Timnath Serah* (see Joshua 19:50 and 24:30)
[c] *16* Or *leaders;* similarly in verses 17–19

20Therefore the LORD was very angry with
Israel and said, "Because this nation has violated the covenant that I laid down for
their forefathers and has not listened to
me, 21I will no longer drive out before them
any of the nations Joshua left when he
died. 22I will use them to test Israel and see
whether they will keep the way of the LORD
and walk in it as their forefathers did."
23The LORD had allowed those nations to
remain; he did not drive them out at once
by giving them into the hands of Joshua.

PRAYER: AFFIRMATION

YOUR day, O Lord, will come like a thief. The heavens will pass away with a roar, and the elements will be destroyed by intense heat, and the earth and its works will be laid bare. Your day, O God, will bring about the destruction of the heavens by fire, and the elements will melt with intense heat. (2 Peter 3:10, 12) . . . There will be a new heaven and a new earth, for the first heaven and the first earth will pass away, and there will no longer be any sea. (Revelation 21:1)

***PAUSE** to reflect on these Biblical affirmations.*

NT Luke 9:18-62

Peter's Confession of Christ

18Once when Jesus was praying in private and his disciples were with him, he
asked them, "Who do the crowds say
I am?"
19They replied, "Some say John the Baptist; others say Elijah; and still others, that
one of the prophets of long ago has come
back to life."
20"But what about you?" he asked.
"Who do you say I am?"
Peter answered, "The Christ[a] of God."
21Jesus strictly warned them not to tell
this to anyone. 22And he said, "The Son of
Man must suffer many things and be rejected by the elders, chief priests and
teachers of the law, and he must be killed
and on the third day be raised to life."
23Then he said to them all: "If anyone
would come after me, he must deny himself and take up his cross daily and follow
me. 24For whoever wants to save his life
will lose it, but whoever loses his life for
me will save it. 25What good is it for a man
to gain the whole world, and yet lose or
forfeit his very self? 26If anyone is
ashamed of me and my words, the Son of
Man will be ashamed of him when he
comes in his glory and in the glory of the
Father and of the holy angels. 27I tell you
the truth, some who are standing here will
not taste death before they see the kingdom of God."

The Transfiguration

28About eight days after Jesus said this,
he took Peter, John and James with him
and went up onto a mountain to pray. 29As
he was praying, the appearance of his face
changed, and his clothes became as bright
as a flash of lightning. 30Two men, Moses
and Elijah, 31appeared in glorious splendor, talking with Jesus. They spoke about
his departure, which he was about to bring
to fulfillment at Jerusalem. 32Peter and his
companions were very sleepy, but when
they became fully awake, they saw his glory and the two men standing with him.
33As the men were leaving Jesus, Peter said
to him, "Master, it is good for us to be
here. Let us put up three shelters—one for
you, one for Moses and one for Elijah."
(He did not know what he was saying.)
34While he was speaking, a cloud appeared and enveloped them, and they
were afraid as they entered the cloud. 35A
voice came from the cloud, saying, "This
is my Son, whom I have chosen; listen to
him." 36When the voice had spoken, they
found that Jesus was alone. The disciples
kept this to themselves, and told no one
at that time what they had seen.

The Healing of a Boy With an Evil Spirit

37The next day, when they came down

[a] 20 Or *Messiah*

from the mountain, a large crowd met him. [38]A man in the crowd called out, "Teacher, I beg you to look at my son, for he is my only child. [39]A spirit seizes him and he suddenly screams; it throws him into convulsions so that he foams at the mouth. It scarcely ever leaves him and is destroying him. [40]I begged your disciples to drive it out, but they could not."

[41]"O unbelieving and perverse generation," Jesus replied, "how long shall I stay with you and put up with you? Bring your son here."

[42]Even while the boy was coming, the demon threw him to the ground in a convulsion. But Jesus rebuked the evil[b] spirit, healed the boy and gave him back to his father. [43]And they were all amazed at the greatness of God.

While everyone was marveling at all that Jesus did, he said to his disciples, [44]"Listen carefully to what I am about to tell you: The Son of Man is going to be betrayed into the hands of men." [45]But they did not understand what this meant. It was hidden from them, so that they did not grasp it, and they were afraid to ask him about it.

Who Will Be the Greatest?

[46]An argument started among the disciples as to which of them would be the greatest. [47]Jesus, knowing their thoughts, took a little child and had him stand beside him. [48]Then he said to them, "Whoever welcomes this little child in my name welcomes me; and whoever welcomes me welcomes the one who sent me. For he who is least among you all—he is the greatest."

[49]"Master," said John, "we saw a man driving out demons in your name and we tried to stop him, because he is not one of us."

[50]"Do not stop him," Jesus said, "for whoever is not against you is for you."

Samaritan Opposition

[51]As the time approached for him to be taken up to heaven, Jesus resolutely set out for Jerusalem. [52]And he sent messengers on ahead, who went into a Samaritan village to get things ready for him; [53]but the people there did not welcome him, because he was heading for Jerusalem. [54]When the disciples James and John saw this, they asked, "Lord, do you want us to call fire down from heaven to destroy them[c]?" [55]But Jesus turned and rebuked them, [56]and[d] they went to another village.

The Cost of Following Jesus

[57]As they were walking along the road, a man said to him, "I will follow you wherever you go."

[58]Jesus replied, "Foxes have holes and birds of the air have nests, but the Son of Man has no place to lay his head."

[59]He said to another man, "Follow me."

But the man replied, "Lord, first let me go and bury my father."

[60]Jesus said to him, "Let the dead bury their own dead, but you go and proclaim the kingdom of God."

[61]Still another said, "I will follow you, Lord; but first let me go back and say good-by to my family."

[62]Jesus replied, "No one who puts his hand to the plow and looks back is fit for service in the kingdom of God."

[b] 42 Greek *unclean* [c] 54 Some manuscripts *them, even as Elijah did* [d] 55,56 Some manuscripts *them. And he said, "You do not know what kind of spirit you are of, for the Son of Man did not come to destroy men's lives, but to save them."* [56]*And*

PRAYER: THE CHARACTER I WANT TO CULTIVATE

SHOW me how to love, O Lord, for if I speak in human language and the language of angels, but have not love, I am only a resounding gong or a clanging cymbal. And if I have the gift of prophecy and understand all mysteries and all knowledge, and if I have all faith so as to remove mountains, but have not love, I am nothing. And if I give all my possessions to the poor, and if I deliver my body to be burned, but have not love, it profits me nothing. (1 Corinthians 13:1–3) . . . I want everything I do to be done in love. (1 Corinthians 16:14)

TAKE *a moment to ask the Lord for the grace to grow in godly character.*

Psalm 40

For the director of music. Of David. A psalm.

1 I waited patiently for the LORD;
he turned to me and heard my cry.
2 He lifted me out of the slimy pit,
out of the mud and mire;
he set my feet on a rock
and gave me a firm place to stand.
3 He put a new song in my mouth,
a hymn of praise to our God.
Many will see and fear
and put their trust in the LORD.

4 Blessed is the man
who makes the LORD his trust,
who does not look to the proud,
to those who turn aside to false
gods.[a]
5 Many, O LORD my God,
are the wonders you have done.
The things you planned for us
no one can recount to you;
were I to speak and tell of them,
they would be too many to declare.

6 Sacrifice and offering you did not
desire,
but my ears you have pierced[b,c];
burnt offerings and sin offerings
you did not require.
7 Then I said, "Here I am, I have
come—
it is written about me in the scroll.[d]
8 I desire to do your will, O my God;
your law is within my heart."

9 I proclaim righteousness in the great
assembly;
I do not seal my lips,
as you know, O LORD.
10 I do not hide your righteousness in
my heart;
I speak of your faithfulness and
salvation.
I do not conceal your love and your
truth
from the great assembly.

11 Do not withhold your mercy from me,
O LORD;
may your love and your truth
always protect me.
12 For troubles without number
surround me;
my sins have overtaken me, and I
cannot see.
They are more than the hairs of my
head,
and my heart fails within me.

13 Be pleased, O LORD, to save me;
O LORD, come quickly to help
me.
14 May all who seek to take my life
be put to shame and confusion;
may all who desire my ruin
be turned back in disgrace.
15 May those who say to me, "Aha!
Aha!"
be appalled at their own shame.
16 But may all who seek you
rejoice and be glad in you;
may those who love your salvation
always say,
"The LORD be exalted!"

17 Yet I am poor and needy;
may the Lord think of me.
You are my help and my deliverer;
O my God, do not delay.

[a] 4 Or *to falsehood* [b] 6 Hebrew; Septuagint *but a body you have prepared for me* (see also Symmachus and Theodotion) [c] 6 Or *opened* [d] 7 Or *come / with the scroll written for me*

PRAYER: THANKSGIVING

LORD, You said, "Let there be lights in the expanse of the heavens to separate the day from the night, and let them serve as signs to mark seasons and days and years, and let them be lights in the expanse of the heavens to give light on the earth"; and it was so. You made two great lights—the greater light to govern the day and the lesser light to govern

the night. You also made the stars; You set them in the expanse of the heavens to give light on the earth, and to govern the day and the night, and to separate the light from the darkness. And You saw that it was good.
(Genesis 1:14–19)

***PAUSE** to offer your own expressions of thanksgiving.*

NT Luke 10:1-42

Jesus Sends Out the Seventy-two

10 After this the Lord appointed seventy-two[a] others and sent them two by
two ahead of him to every town and place
where he was about to go. 2He told them,
"The harvest is plentiful, but the workers
are few. Ask the Lord of the harvest, therefore, to send out workers into his harvest
field. 3Go! I am sending you out like
lambs among wolves. 4Do not take a
purse or bag or sandals; and do not greet
anyone on the road.
5"When you enter a house, first say,
'Peace to this house.' 6If a man of peace is
there, your peace will rest on him; if not,
it will return to you. 7Stay in that house,
eating and drinking whatever they give
you, for the worker deserves his wages. Do
not move around from house to house.
8"When you enter a town and are welcomed, eat what is set before you. 9Heal
the sick who are there and tell them, 'The
kingdom of God is near you.' 10But when
you enter a town and are not welcomed,
go into its streets and say, 11'Even the dust
of your town that sticks to our feet we
wipe off against you. Yet be sure of this:
The kingdom of God is near.' 12I tell you,
it will be more bearable on that day for
Sodom than for that town.
13"Woe to you, Korazin! Woe to you,
Bethsaida! For if the miracles that were
performed in you had been performed in
Tyre and Sidon, they would have repented long ago, sitting in sackcloth and
ashes. 14But it will be more bearable for
Tyre and Sidon at the judgment than for
you. 15And you, Capernaum, will you be
lifted up to the skies? No, you will go
down to the depths.[b]
16"He who listens to you listens to me;
he who rejects you rejects me; but he who
rejects me rejects him who sent me."
17The seventy-two returned with joy and
said, "Lord, even the demons submit to us
in your name."
18He replied, "I saw Satan fall like lightning from heaven. 19I have given you authority to trample on snakes and scorpions and to overcome all the power of the
enemy; nothing will harm you. 20Howev-
er, do not rejoice that the spirits submit to
you, but rejoice that your names are written in heaven."
21At that time Jesus, full of joy through
the Holy Spirit, said, "I praise you, Father,
Lord of heaven and earth, because you
have hidden these things from the wise
and learned, and revealed them to little
children. Yes, Father, for this was your
good pleasure.
22"All things have been committed to
me by my Father. No one knows who the
Son is except the Father, and no one
knows who the Father is except the Son
and those to whom the Son chooses to reveal him."
23Then he turned to his disciples and
said privately, "Blessed are the eyes that
see what you see. 24For I tell you that
many prophets and kings wanted to see
what you see but did not see it, and to
hear what you hear but did not hear it."

The Parable of the Good Samaritan

25On one occasion an expert in the law
stood up to test Jesus. "Teacher," he asked,
"what must I do to inherit eternal life?"
26"What is written in the Law?" he
replied. "How do you read it?"
27He answered: " 'Love the Lord your
God with all your heart and with all your
soul and with all your strength and with
all your mind'[c]; and, 'Love your neighbor
as yourself.'[d]"
28"You have answered correctly," Jesus
replied. "Do this and you will live."
29But he wanted to justify himself, so he
asked Jesus, "And who is my neighbor?"
30In reply Jesus said: "A man was going
down from Jerusalem to Jericho, when he

[a] *1* Some manuscripts *seventy;* also in verse 17
[b] *15* Greek *Hades* [c] *27* Deut. 6:5 [d] *27* Lev. 19:18

fell into the hands of robbers. They
stripped him of his clothes, beat him and
went away, leaving him half dead. [31]A
priest happened to be going down the
same road, and when he saw the man, he
passed by on the other side. [32]So too, a Levite, when he came to the place and saw
him, passed by on the other side. [33]But a
Samaritan, as he traveled, came where the
man was; and when he saw him, he took
pity on him. [34]He went to him and bandaged his wounds, pouring on oil and
wine. Then he put the man on his own
donkey, took him to an inn and took care
of him. [35]The next day he took out two silver coins[e] and gave them to the innkeeper. 'Look after him,' he said, 'and when I
return, I will reimburse you for any extra
expense you may have.'
[36]"Which of these three do you think
was a neighbor to the man who fell into
the hands of robbers?"
[37]The expert in the law replied, "The
one who had mercy on him."
Jesus told him, "Go and do likewise."

At the Home of Martha and Mary

[38]As Jesus and his disciples were on
their way, he came to a village where a
woman named Martha opened her home
to him. [39]She had a sister called Mary,
who sat at the Lord's feet listening to what
he said. [40]But Martha was distracted by all
the preparations that had to be made. She
came to him and asked, "Lord, don't you
care that my sister has left me to do the
work by myself? Tell her to help me!"
[41]"Martha, Martha," the Lord answered,
"you are worried and upset about many
things, [42]but only one thing is needed.[f]
Mary has chosen what is better, and it will
not be taken away from her."

[e] 35 Greek *two denarii* [f] 42 Some manuscripts *but few things are needed—or only one*

PRAYER: MY RELATIONSHIP TO OTHERS

YOU taught us concerning the lost, Lord Jesus, when You said, "What man among you, if he has a hundred sheep and loses one of them, does not leave the ninety-nine in the open country and go after the one that is lost until he finds it? And when he finds it, he lays it on his shoulders, rejoicing. And when he comes into his house, he calls his friends and neighbors together and says to them, 'Rejoice with me, for I have found my sheep which was lost!' I tell you that, in the same way, there will be more joy in heaven over one sinner who repents than over ninety-nine righteous people who need no repentance. There is joy in the presence of the angels of God over one sinner who repents." (Luke 15:4–7, 10) . . . From now on I will regard no one only according to the flesh. (2 Corinthians 5:16)

PAUSE *to review your relationships with others and to commit them to the Lord.*

YEAR 1
DAY 211

OT Judges 3:1-31

3 These are the nations the LORD left to
test all those Israelites who had not experienced any of the wars in Canaan [2](he
did this only to teach warfare to the descendants of the Israelites who had not
had previous battle experience): [3]the five
rulers of the Philistines, all the Canaanites, the Sidonians, and the Hivites living
in the Lebanon mountains from Mount
Baal Hermon to Lebo[a] Hamath. [4]They
were left to test the Israelites to see
whether they would obey the LORD's commands, which he had given their forefathers through Moses.
[5]The Israelites lived among the Canaanites, Hittites, Amorites, Perizzites, Hivites
and Jebusites. [6]They took their daughters

[a] 3 Or *to the entrance to*

in marriage and gave their own daughters to their sons, and served their gods.

Othniel

7The Israelites did evil in the eyes of the LORD; they forgot the LORD their God and served the Baals and the Asherahs. 8The anger of the LORD burned against Israel so that he sold them into the hands of Cushan-Rishathaim king of Aram Naharaim,[b] to whom the Israelites were subject for eight years. 9But when they cried out to the LORD, he raised up for them a deliverer, Othniel son of Kenaz, Caleb's younger brother, who saved them. 10The Spirit of the LORD came upon him, so that he became Israel's judge[c] and went to war. The LORD gave Cushan-Rishathaim king of Aram into the hands of Othniel, who overpowered him. 11So the land had peace for forty years, until Othniel son of Kenaz died.

Ehud

12Once again the Israelites did evil in the eyes of the LORD, and because they did this evil the LORD gave Eglon king of Moab power over Israel. 13Getting the Ammonites and Amalekites to join him, Eglon came and attacked Israel, and they took possession of the City of Palms.[d] 14The Israelites were subject to Eglon king of Moab for eighteen years.

15Again the Israelites cried out to the LORD, and he gave them a deliverer—Ehud, a left-handed man, the son of Gera the Benjamite. The Israelites sent him with tribute to Eglon king of Moab. 16Now Ehud had made a double-edged sword about a foot and a half[e] long, which he strapped to his right thigh under his clothing. 17He presented the tribute to Eglon king of Moab, who was a very fat man. 18After Ehud had presented the tribute, he sent on their way the men who had carried it. 19At the idols[f] near Gilgal he himself turned back and said, "I have a secret message for you, O king."

The king said, "Quiet!" And all his attendants left him.

20Ehud then approached him while he was sitting alone in the upper room of his summer palace[g] and said, "I have a message from God for you." As the king rose from his seat, 21Ehud reached with his left hand, drew the sword from his right thigh and plunged it into the king's belly. 22Even the handle sank in after the blade, which came out his back. Ehud did not pull the sword out, and the fat closed in over it. 23Then Ehud went out to the porch[h]; he shut the doors of the upper room behind him and locked them.

24After he had gone, the servants came and found the doors of the upper room locked. They said, "He must be relieving himself in the inner room of the house." 25They waited to the point of embarrassment, but when he did not open the doors of the room, they took a key and unlocked them. There they saw their lord fallen to the floor, dead.

26While they waited, Ehud got away. He passed by the idols and escaped to Seirah. 27When he arrived there, he blew a trumpet in the hill country of Ephraim, and the Israelites went down with him from the hills, with him leading them.

28"Follow me," he ordered, "for the LORD has given Moab, your enemy, into your hands." So they followed him down and, taking possession of the fords of the Jordan that led to Moab, they allowed no one to cross over. 29At that time they struck down about ten thousand Moabites, all vigorous and strong; not a man escaped. 30That day Moab was made subject to Israel, and the land had peace for eighty years.

Shamgar

31After Ehud came Shamgar son of Anath, who struck down six hundred Philistines with an oxgoad. He too saved Israel.

[b] *8* That is, Northwest Mesopotamia [c] *10* Or *leader* [d] *13* That is, Jericho [e] *16* Hebrew *a cubit* (about 0.5 meter) [f] *19* Or *the stone quarries;* also in verse 26 [g] *20* The meaning of the Hebrew for this phrase is uncertain. [h] *23* The meaning of the Hebrew for this word is uncertain.

PRAYER: ADORATION

YOUR word, O Lord, is upright, and all Your work is done in faithfulness. You love righteousness and justice; the earth is full of Your loving-kindness. (Psalm 33:4–5) . . . One thing

You have spoken, O Lord, two things I have heard: That You, O God, are strong and that You, O Lord, are loving. For You reward each person according to what he has done. (Psalm 62:11–12)

***PAUSE** to express your thoughts of praise and worship.*

NT Luke 11:1-54

Jesus' Teaching on Prayer

11 One day Jesus was praying in a certain
place. When he finished, one of his
disciples said to him, "Lord, teach us to
pray, just as John taught his disciples."
2He said to them, "When you pray, say:

" 'Father,[a]
hallowed be your name,
your kingdom come.[b]
3Give us each day our daily bread.
4Forgive us our sins,
for we also forgive everyone who
sins against us.[c]
And lead us not into temptation.[d]' "

5Then he said to them, "Suppose one of
you has a friend, and he goes to him at
midnight and says, 'Friend, lend me three
loaves of bread, 6because a friend of mine
on a journey has come to me, and I have
nothing to set before him.'
7"Then the one inside answers, 'Don't
bother me. The door is already locked,
and my children are with me in bed. I
can't get up and give you anything.' 8I tell
you, though he will not get up and give
him the bread because he is his friend, yet
because of the man's boldness[e] he will get
up and give him as much as he needs.
9"So I say to you: Ask and it will be giv-
en to you; seek and you will find; knock
and the door will be opened to you. 10For
everyone who asks receives; he who seeks
finds; and to him who knocks, the door
will be opened.
11"Which of you fathers, if your son asks
for[f] a fish, will give him a snake instead?
12Or if he asks for an egg, will give him a
scorpion? 13If you then, though you are
evil, know how to give good gifts to your
children, how much more will your Father in heaven give the Holy Spirit to
those who ask him!"

Jesus and Beelzebub

14Jesus was driving out a demon that
was mute. When the demon left, the man
who had been mute spoke, and the crowd
was amazed. 15But some of them said, "By
Beelzebub,[g] the prince of demons, he is
driving out demons." 16Others tested him
by asking for a sign from heaven.
17Jesus knew their thoughts and said to
them: "Any kingdom divided against itself
will be ruined, and a house divided against
itself will fall. 18If Satan is divided against
himself, how can his kingdom stand? I say
this because you claim that I drive out
demons by Beelzebub. 19Now if I drive out
demons by Beelzebub, by whom do your
followers drive them out? So then, they
will be your judges. 20But if I drive out
demons by the finger of God, then the
kingdom of God has come to you.
21"When a strong man, fully armed,
guards his own house, his possessions are
safe. 22But when someone stronger attacks
and overpowers him, he takes away the armor in which the man trusted and divides
up the spoils.
23"He who is not with me is against me,
and he who does not gather with me, scatters.
24"When an evil[h] spirit comes out of a
man, it goes through arid places seeking
rest and does not find it. Then it says, 'I
will return to the house I left.' 25When it arrives, it finds the house swept clean and
put in order. 26Then it goes and takes sev-
en other spirits more wicked than itself,
and they go in and live there. And the final condition of that man is worse than
the first."
27As Jesus was saying these things, a
woman in the crowd called out, "Blessed
is the mother who gave you birth and
nursed you."
28He replied, "Blessed rather are those
who hear the word of God and obey it."

[a] 2 Some manuscripts *Our Father in heaven* [b] 2 Some manuscripts *come. May your will be done on earth as it is in heaven.* [c] 4 Greek *everyone who is indebted to us* [d] 4 Some manuscripts *temptation but deliver us from the evil one* [e] 8 Or *persistence* [f] 11 Some manuscripts *for bread, will give him a stone; or if he asks for* [g] 15 Greek *Beezeboul* or *Beelzeboul;* also in verses 18 and 19 [h] 24 Greek *unclean*

The Sign of Jonah

29 As the crowds increased, Jesus said, "This is a wicked generation. It asks for a miraculous sign, but none will be given it except the sign of Jonah. 30 For as Jonah was a sign to the Ninevites, so also will the Son of Man be to this generation. 31 The Queen of the South will rise at the judgment with the men of this generation and condemn them; for she came from the ends of the earth to listen to Solomon's wisdom, and now one[i] greater than Solomon is here. 32 The men of Nineveh will stand up at the judgment with this generation and condemn it; for they repented at the preaching of Jonah, and now one greater than Jonah is here.

The Lamp of the Body

33 "No one lights a lamp and puts it in a place where it will be hidden, or under a bowl. Instead he puts it on its stand, so that those who come in may see the light. 34 Your eye is the lamp of your body. When your eyes are good, your whole body also is full of light. But when they are bad, your body also is full of darkness. 35 See to it, then, that the light within you is not darkness. 36 Therefore, if your whole body is full of light, and no part of it dark, it will be completely lighted, as when the light of a lamp shines on you."

Six Woes

37 When Jesus had finished speaking, a Pharisee invited him to eat with him; so he went in and reclined at the table. 38 But the Pharisee, noticing that Jesus did not first wash before the meal, was surprised.

39 Then the Lord said to him, "Now then, you Pharisees clean the outside of the cup and dish, but inside you are full of greed and wickedness. 40 You foolish people! Did not the one who made the outside make the inside also? 41 But give what is inside ⌊the dish⌋[j] to the poor, and everything will be clean for you.

42 "Woe to you Pharisees, because you give God a tenth of your mint, rue and all other kinds of garden herbs, but you neglect justice and the love of God. You should have practiced the latter without leaving the former undone.

43 "Woe to you Pharisees, because you love the most important seats in the synagogues and greetings in the marketplaces.

44 "Woe to you, because you are like unmarked graves, which men walk over without knowing it."

45 One of the experts in the law answered him, "Teacher, when you say these things, you insult us also."

46 Jesus replied, "And you experts in the law, woe to you, because you load people down with burdens they can hardly carry, and you yourselves will not lift one finger to help them.

47 "Woe to you, because you build tombs for the prophets, and it was your forefathers who killed them. 48 So you testify that you approve of what your forefathers did; they killed the prophets, and you build their tombs. 49 Because of this, God in his wisdom said, 'I will send them prophets and apostles, some of whom they will kill and others they will persecute.' 50 Therefore this generation will be held responsible for the blood of all the prophets that has been shed since the beginning of the world, 51 from the blood of Abel to the blood of Zechariah, who was killed between the altar and the sanctuary. Yes, I tell you, this generation will be held responsible for it all.

52 "Woe to you experts in the law, because you have taken away the key to knowledge. You yourselves have not entered, and you have hindered those who were entering."

53 When Jesus left there, the Pharisees and the teachers of the law began to oppose him fiercely and to besiege him with questions, 54 waiting to catch him in something he might say.

[i] 31 Or *something;* also in verse 32 [j] 41 Or *what you have*

PRAYER: THE ATTRIBUTES OF GOD

YOUR righteousness, O God, reaches to the heavens. You who have done great things, O God, who is like You? (Psalm 71:19) . . . You, the Lord, alone have declared what is to come

from the distant past. There is no god apart from You, a righteous God and a Savior. There is none besides You. You are God, and there is no other. (Isaiah 45:21–22)

PAUSE *to reflect on these affirmations about the person, powers and perfection of God.*

YEAR 1 DAY 212

OT Judges 4:1-24

Deborah

4 After Ehud died, the Israelites once again
did evil in the eyes of the LORD. 2So the
LORD sold them into the hands of Jabin, a
king of Canaan, who reigned in Hazor. The
commander of his army was Sisera, who
lived in Harosheth Haggoyim. 3Because he
had nine hundred iron chariots and had
cruelly oppressed the Israelites for twenty
years, they cried to the LORD for help.
4Deborah, a prophetess, the wife of Lap-
pidoth, was leading[a] Israel at that time.
5She held court under the Palm of Deborah between Ramah and Bethel in the hill
country of Ephraim, and the Israelites
came to her to have their disputes decided. 6She sent for Barak son of Abinoam
from Kedesh in Naphtali and said to him,
"The LORD, the God of Israel, commands
you: 'Go, take with you ten thousand men
of Naphtali and Zebulun and lead the way
to Mount Tabor. 7I will lure Sisera, the
commander of Jabin's army, with his chariots and his troops to the Kishon River and
give him into your hands.' "
8Barak said to her, "If you go with me,
I will go; but if you don't go with me, I
won't go."
9"Very well," Deborah said, "I will go
with you. But because of the way you are
going about this,[b] the honor will not be
yours, for the LORD will hand Sisera over to
a woman." So Deborah went with Barak to
Kedesh, 10where he summoned Zebulun
and Naphtali. Ten thousand men followed
him, and Deborah also went with him.
11Now Heber the Kenite had left the other Kenites, the descendants of Hobab, Moses' brother-in-law,[c] and pitched his tent by
the great tree in Zaanannim near Kedesh.
12When they told Sisera that Barak son
of Abinoam had gone up to Mount Tabor,
13Sisera gathered together his nine hundred iron chariots and all the men with
him, from Harosheth Haggoyim to the Kishon River.
14Then Deborah said to Barak, "Go!
This is the day the LORD has given Sisera
into your hands. Has not the LORD gone
ahead of you?" So Barak went down
Mount Tabor, followed by ten thousand
men. 15At Barak's advance, the LORD routed Sisera and all his chariots and army by
the sword, and Sisera abandoned his chariot and fled on foot. 16But Barak pursued
the chariots and army as far as Harosheth
Haggoyim. All the troops of Sisera fell by
the sword; not a man was left.
17Sisera, however, fled on foot to the
tent of Jael, the wife of Heber the Kenite,
because there were friendly relations between Jabin king of Hazor and the clan of
Heber the Kenite.
18Jael went out to meet Sisera and said
to him, "Come, my lord, come right in.
Don't be afraid." So he entered her tent,
and she put a covering over him.
19"I'm thirsty," he said. "Please give me
some water." She opened a skin of milk,
gave him a drink, and covered him up.
20"Stand in the doorway of the tent," he
told her. "If someone comes by and asks
you, 'Is anyone here?' say 'No.' "
21But Jael, Heber's wife, picked up a tent
peg and a hammer and went quietly to
him while he lay fast asleep, exhausted.
She drove the peg through his temple into
the ground, and he died.
22Barak came by in pursuit of Sisera,
and Jael went out to meet him. "Come,"
she said, "I will show you the man you're
looking for." So he went in with her, and
there lay Sisera with the tent peg through
his temple—dead.
23On that day God subdued Jabin, the
Canaanite king, before the Israelites.
24And the hand of the Israelites grew
stronger and stronger against Jabin, the
Canaanite king, until they destroyed him.

[a] 4 Traditionally *judging* [b] 9 Or *But on the expedition you are undertaking* [c] 11 Or *father-in-law*

PRAYER: CONFESSION

WHEN I have sinned against You, and when I have turned back to You and confessed my sin, hear from heaven and forgive my sin and restore me. Teach me the good way in which I should walk. When I sin against You—for there is no one who does not sin—may I return to You with all my heart and with all my soul. (1 Kings 8:33–34, 36, 46, 48)

***ASK** the Spirit to search your heart and reveal any areas of unconfessed sin. Acknowledge these to the Lord and thank Him for His forgiveness.*

NT Luke 12:1-34

Warnings and Encouragements

12 Meanwhile, when a crowd of many thousands had gathered, so that they were trampling on one another, Jesus began to speak first to his disciples, saying: "Be on your guard against the yeast of the Pharisees, which is hypocrisy. 2 There is nothing concealed that will not be disclosed, or hidden that will not be made known. 3 What you have said in the dark will be heard in the daylight, and what you have whispered in the ear in the inner rooms will be proclaimed from the roofs.

4 "I tell you, my friends, do not be afraid of those who kill the body and after that can do no more. 5 But I will show you whom you should fear: Fear him who, after the killing of the body, has power to throw you into hell. Yes, I tell you, fear him. 6 Are not five sparrows sold for two pennies[a]? Yet not one of them is forgotten by God. 7 Indeed, the very hairs of your head are all numbered. Don't be afraid; you are worth more than many sparrows.

8 "I tell you, whoever acknowledges me before men, the Son of Man will also acknowledge him before the angels of God. 9 But he who disowns me before men will be disowned before the angels of God. 10 And everyone who speaks a word against the Son of Man will be forgiven, but anyone who blasphemes against the Holy Spirit will not be forgiven.

11 "When you are brought before synagogues, rulers and authorities, do not worry about how you will defend yourselves or what you will say, 12 for the Holy Spirit will teach you at that time what you should say."

The Parable of the Rich Fool

13 Someone in the crowd said to him, "Teacher, tell my brother to divide the inheritance with me."

14 Jesus replied, "Man, who appointed me a judge or an arbiter between you?" 15 Then he said to them, "Watch out! Be on your guard against all kinds of greed; a man's life does not consist in the abundance of his possessions."

16 And he told them this parable: "The ground of a certain rich man produced a good crop. 17 He thought to himself, 'What shall I do? I have no place to store my crops.'

18 "Then he said, 'This is what I'll do. I will tear down my barns and build bigger ones, and there I will store all my grain and my goods. 19 And I'll say to myself, "You have plenty of good things laid up for many years. Take life easy; eat, drink and be merry." '

20 "But God said to him, 'You fool! This very night your life will be demanded from you. Then who will get what you have prepared for yourself?'

21 "This is how it will be with anyone who stores up things for himself but is not rich toward God."

Do Not Worry

22 Then Jesus said to his disciples: "Therefore I tell you, do not worry about your life, what you will eat; or about your body, what you will wear. 23 Life is more than food, and the body more than clothes. 24 Consider the ravens: They do not sow or reap, they have no storeroom or barn; yet God feeds them. And how much more valuable you are than birds!

[a] 6 Greek *two assaria*

[25]Who of you by worrying can add a single hour to his life[b]? [26]Since you cannot do this very little thing, why do you worry about the rest?

[27]"Consider how the lilies grow. They do not labor or spin. Yet I tell you, not even Solomon in all his splendor was dressed like one of these. [28]If that is how God clothes the grass of the field, which is here today, and tomorrow is thrown into the fire, how much more will he clothe you, O you of little faith! [29]And do not set your heart on what you will eat or drink; do not worry about it. [30]For the pagan world runs after all such things, and your Father knows that you need them. [31]But seek his kingdom, and these things will be given to you as well.

[32]"Do not be afraid, little flock, for your Father has been pleased to give you the kingdom. [33]Sell your possessions and give to the poor. Provide purses for yourselves that will not wear out, a treasure in heaven that will not be exhausted, where no thief comes near and no moth destroys. [34]For where your treasure is, there your heart will be also.

[b] 25 Or *single cubit to his height*

PRAYER: THE WORKS OF GOD

EVERYTHING exposed by the light becomes visible, for it is light that makes everything visible. For this reason it is said, "Awake, you who sleep; arise from the dead, and Christ will shine on you." (Ephesians 5:13–14)

***TAKE** a moment to consider the greatness of God's wonderful works.*

YEAR 1 DAY 213

OT Judges 5:1–31

The Song of Deborah

5 On that day Deborah and Barak son of Abinoam sang this song:

[2]"When the princes in Israel take the lead,
when the people willingly offer themselves—
praise the LORD!

[3]"Hear this, you kings! Listen, you rulers!
I will sing to[a] the LORD, I will sing;
I will make music to[b] the LORD, the God of Israel.

[4]"O LORD, when you went out from Seir,
when you marched from the land of Edom,
the earth shook, the heavens poured,
the clouds poured down water.
[5]The mountains quaked before the LORD, the One of Sinai,
before the LORD, the God of Israel.

[6]"In the days of Shamgar son of Anath,
in the days of Jael, the roads were abandoned;
travelers took to winding paths.
[7]Village life[c] in Israel ceased,
ceased until I,[d] Deborah, arose,
arose a mother in Israel.
[8]When they chose new gods,
war came to the city gates,
and not a shield or spear was seen
among forty thousand in Israel.
[9]My heart is with Israel's princes,
with the willing volunteers among the people.
Praise the LORD!

[10]"You who ride on white donkeys,
sitting on your saddle blankets,
and you who walk along the road,
consider [11]the voice of the singers[e] at the watering places.
They recite the righteous acts of the LORD,
the righteous acts of his warriors[f] in Israel.

[a] 3 Or *of* [b] 3 Or / *with song I will praise* [c] 7 Or *Warriors* [d] 7 Or *you* [e] 11 Or *archers;* the meaning of the Hebrew for this word is uncertain. [f] 11 Or *villagers*

"Then the people of the LORD
went down to the city gates.
12 'Wake up, wake up, Deborah!
Wake up, wake up, break out in song!
Arise, O Barak!
Take captive your captives, O son of Abinoam.'

13 "Then the men who were left
came down to the nobles;
the people of the LORD
came to me with the mighty.
14 Some came from Ephraim, whose roots were in Amalek;
Benjamin was with the people who followed you.
From Makir captains came down,
from Zebulun those who bear a commander's staff.
15 The princes of Issachar were with Deborah;
yes, Issachar was with Barak,
rushing after him into the valley.
In the districts of Reuben
there was much searching of heart.
16 Why did you stay among the campfires[g]
to hear the whistling for the flocks?
In the districts of Reuben
there was much searching of heart.
17 Gilead stayed beyond the Jordan.
And Dan, why did he linger by the ships?
Asher remained on the coast
and stayed in his coves.
18 The people of Zebulun risked their very lives;
so did Naphtali on the heights of the field.

19 "Kings came, they fought;
the kings of Canaan fought
at Taanach by the waters of Megiddo,
but they carried off no silver, no plunder.
20 From the heavens the stars fought,
from their courses they fought against Sisera.
21 The river Kishon swept them away,
the age-old river, the river Kishon.
March on, my soul; be strong!
22 Then thundered the horses' hoofs—
galloping, galloping go his mighty steeds.
23 'Curse Meroz,' said the angel of the LORD.
'Curse its people bitterly,
because they did not come to help the LORD,
to help the LORD against the mighty.'

24 "Most blessed of women be Jael,
the wife of Heber the Kenite,
most blessed of tent-dwelling women.
25 He asked for water, and she gave him milk;
in a bowl fit for nobles she brought him curdled milk.
26 Her hand reached for the tent peg,
her right hand for the workman's hammer.
She struck Sisera, she crushed his head,
she shattered and pierced his temple.
27 At her feet he sank,
he fell; there he lay.
At her feet he sank, he fell;
where he sank, there he fell—dead.

28 "Through the window peered Sisera's mother;
behind the lattice she cried out,
'Why is his chariot so long in coming?
Why is the clatter of his chariots delayed?'
29 The wisest of her ladies answer her;
indeed, she keeps saying to herself,
30 'Are they not finding and dividing the spoils:
a girl or two for each man,
colorful garments as plunder for Sisera,
colorful garments embroidered,
highly embroidered garments for my neck—
all this as plunder?'

31 "So may all your enemies perish, O LORD!
But may they who love you be like the sun
when it rises in its strength."

Then the land had peace forty years.

[g] 16 Or *saddlebags*

PRAYER: RENEWAL

LIKE Noah, may I be a righteous person, blameless among the people of my time, and one who walks with You. (Genesis 6:9) . . . Like Moses, may I do all that You command me. (Exodus 39:42; 40:16)

***PAUSE** to add your own prayers for personal renewal.*

NT Luke 12:35–59

Watchfulness

[35] "Be dressed ready for service and keep your lamps burning, [36] like men waiting for their master to return from a wedding banquet, so that when he comes and knocks they can immediately open the door for him. [37] It will be good for those servants whose master finds them watching when he comes. I tell you the truth, he will dress himself to serve, will have them recline at the table and will come and wait on them. [38] It will be good for those servants whose master finds them ready, even if he comes in the second or third watch of the night. [39] But understand this: If the owner of the house had known at what hour the thief was coming, he would not have let his house be broken into. [40] You also must be ready, because the Son of Man will come at an hour when you do not expect him."

[41] Peter asked, "Lord, are you telling this parable to us, or to everyone?"

[42] The Lord answered, "Who then is the faithful and wise manager, whom the master puts in charge of his servants to give them their food allowance at the proper time? [43] It will be good for that servant whom the master finds doing so when he returns. [44] I tell you the truth, he will put him in charge of all his possessions. [45] But suppose the servant says to himself, 'My master is taking a long time in coming,' and he then begins to beat the menservants and maidservants and to eat and drink and get drunk. [46] The master of that servant will come on a day when he does not expect him and at an hour he is not aware of. He will cut him to pieces and assign him a place with the unbelievers.

[47] "That servant who knows his master's will and does not get ready or does not do what his master wants will be beaten with many blows. [48] But the one who does not know and does things deserving punishment will be beaten with few blows. From everyone who has been given much, much will be demanded; and from the one who has been entrusted with much, much more will be asked.

Not Peace but Division

[49] "I have come to bring fire on the earth, and how I wish it were already kindled! [50] But I have a baptism to undergo, and how distressed I am until it is completed! [51] Do you think I came to bring peace on earth? No, I tell you, but division. [52] From now on there will be five in one family divided against each other, three against two and two against three. [53] They will be divided, father against son and son against father, mother against daughter and daughter against mother, mother-in-law against daughter-in-law and daughter-in-law against mother-in-law."

Interpreting the Times

[54] He said to the crowd: "When you see a cloud rising in the west, immediately you say, 'It's going to rain,' and it does. [55] And when the south wind blows, you say, 'It's going to be hot,' and it is. [56] Hypocrites! You know how to interpret the appearance of the earth and the sky. How is it that you don't know how to interpret this present time?

[57] "Why don't you judge for yourselves what is right? [58] As you are going with your adversary to the magistrate, try hard to be reconciled to him on the way, or he may drag you off to the judge, and the judge turn you over to the officer, and the officer throw you into prison. [59] I tell you, you will not get out until you have paid the last penny.[a]"

[a] 59 Greek *lepton*

PRAYER: MY RELATIONSHIP TO GOD

***FATHER in heaven, hallowed be Your name. Your kingdom come; Your will be done on earth as it is in heaven.* (Matthew 6:9–10) . . . *Though I have not seen You, Jesus, I love You; and though I do not see You now, I believe in You; I rejoice with joy inexpressible and full of glory, for I am receiving the end of my faith, the salvation of my soul.* (1 Peter 1:8–9)**

***PAUSE** to thank God for the relationship that you enjoy with Him in Jesus Christ.*

YEAR 1
DAY 214

OT Judges 6:1–40

Gideon

6 Again the Israelites did evil in the eyes
of the LORD, and for seven years he gave
them into the hands of the Midianites.
2 Because the power of Midian was so oppressive, the Israelites prepared shelters
for themselves in mountain clefts, caves
and strongholds. 3 Whenever the Israelites
planted their crops, the Midianites,
Amalekites and other eastern peoples invaded the country. 4 They camped on the
land and ruined the crops all the way to
Gaza and did not spare a living thing for
Israel, neither sheep nor cattle nor donkeys. 5 They came up with their livestock
and their tents like swarms of locusts. It
was impossible to count the men and
their camels; they invaded the land to ravage it. 6 Midian so impoverished the Israelites that they cried out to the LORD for
help.

7 When the Israelites cried to the LORD
because of Midian, 8 he sent them a
prophet, who said, "This is what the LORD,
the God of Israel, says: I brought you up
out of Egypt, out of the land of slavery. 9 I
snatched you from the power of Egypt
and from the hand of all your oppressors.
I drove them from before you and gave
you their land. 10 I said to you, 'I am the
LORD your God; do not worship the gods
of the Amorites, in whose land you live.'
But you have not listened to me."

11 The angel of the LORD came and sat
down under the oak in Ophrah that belonged to Joash the Abiezrite, where his
son Gideon was threshing wheat in a
winepress to keep it from the Midianites.
12 When the angel of the LORD appeared to
Gideon, he said, "The LORD is with you,
mighty warrior."

13 "But sir," Gideon replied, "if the LORD
is with us, why has all this happened to
us? Where are all his wonders that our fathers told us about when they said, 'Did
not the LORD bring us up out of Egypt?'
But now the LORD has abandoned us and
put us into the hand of Midian."

14 The LORD turned to him and said, "Go
in the strength you have and save Israel
out of Midian's hand. Am I not sending
you?"

15 "But Lord,[a]" Gideon asked, "how can
I save Israel? My clan is the weakest in Manasseh, and I am the least in my family."

16 The LORD answered, "I will be with
you, and you will strike down all the Midianites together."

17 Gideon replied, "If now I have found
favor in your eyes, give me a sign that it is
really you talking to me. 18 Please do not
go away until I come back and bring my
offering and set it before you."

And the LORD said, "I will wait until you
return."

19 Gideon went in, prepared a young
goat, and from an ephah[b] of flour he
made bread without yeast. Putting the
meat in a basket and its broth in a pot, he
brought them out and offered them to
him under the oak.

20 The angel of God said to him, "Take
the meat and the unleavened bread, place
them on this rock, and pour out the
broth." And Gideon did so. 21 With the tip
of the staff that was in his hand, the an-

[a] *15* Or *sir* [b] *19* That is, probably about 3/5 bushel (about 22 liters)

gel of the LORD touched the meat and the
unleavened bread. Fire flared from the
rock, consuming the meat and the bread.
And the angel of the LORD disappeared.
22When Gideon realized that it was the
angel of the LORD, he exclaimed, "Ah, Sovereign LORD! I have seen the angel of the
LORD face to face!"

23But the LORD said to him, "Peace! Do
not be afraid. You are not going to die."

24So Gideon built an altar to the LORD
there and called it The LORD is Peace. To
this day it stands in Ophrah of the
Abiezrites.

25That same night the LORD said to him,
"Take the second bull from your father's
herd, the one seven years old.[c] Tear down
your father's altar to Baal and cut down
the Asherah pole[d] beside it. 26Then build
a proper kind of[e] altar to the LORD your
God on the top of this height. Using the
wood of the Asherah pole that you cut
down, offer the second[f] bull as a burnt offering."

27So Gideon took ten of his servants
and did as the LORD told him. But because
he was afraid of his family and the men
of the town, he did it at night rather than
in the daytime.

28In the morning when the men of the
town got up, there was Baal's altar, demolished, with the Asherah pole beside it
cut down and the second bull sacrificed
on the newly built altar!

29They asked each other, "Who did
this?"

When they carefully investigated, they
were told, "Gideon son of Joash did it."

30The men of the town demanded of Joash, "Bring out your son. He must die, because he has broken down Baal's altar and
cut down the Asherah pole beside it."

31But Joash replied to the hostile crowd
around him, "Are you going to plead
Baal's cause? Are you trying to save him?
Whoever fights for him shall be put to
death by morning! If Baal really is a god,
he can defend himself when someone
breaks down his altar." 32So that day they
called Gideon "Jerub-Baal,[g]" saying, "Let
Baal contend with him," because he broke
down Baal's altar.

33Now all the Midianites, Amalekites
and other eastern peoples joined forces
and crossed over the Jordan and camped
in the Valley of Jezreel. 34Then the Spirit
of the LORD came upon Gideon, and he
blew a trumpet, summoning the
Abiezrites to follow him. 35He sent messengers throughout Manasseh, calling
them to arms, and also into Asher, Zebulun and Naphtali, so that they too went
up to meet them.

36Gideon said to God, "If you will save
Israel by my hand as you have promised— 37look, I will place a wool fleece on
the threshing floor. If there is dew only on
the fleece and all the ground is dry, then
I will know that you will save Israel by my
hand, as you said." 38And that is what
happened. Gideon rose early the next day;
he squeezed the fleece and wrung out the
dew—a bowlful of water.

39Then Gideon said to God, "Do not be
angry with me. Let me make just one more
request. Allow me one more test with the
fleece. This time make the fleece dry and
the ground covered with dew." 40That
night God did so. Only the fleece was dry;
all the ground was covered with dew.

[c] 25 Or *Take a full-grown, mature bull from your father's herd* [d] 25 That is, a symbol of the goddess Asherah; here and elsewhere in Judges [e] 26 Or *build with layers of stone an* [f] 26 Or *full-grown*; also in verse 28 [g] 32 *Jerub-Baal* means *let Baal contend.*

PRAYER: PETITION

O LORD, be not far off; O my Strength, come quickly to help me.
(Psalm 22:19)

PAUSE *here to petition God for spiritual insight so that you might have understanding of His Word. Ask for insight into your identity in Jesus Christ: that you might know who you are, what direction your life should take and what His purpose for your life is. Offer prayers regarding your activities for this day and any special concerns you may have.*

NT Luke 13:1-35

Repent or Perish

13 Now there were some present at that time who told Jesus about the Galileans whose blood Pilate had mixed with their sacrifices. 2 Jesus answered, "Do you think that these Galileans were worse sinners than all the other Galileans because they suffered this way? 3 I tell you, no! But unless you repent, you too will all perish. 4 Or those eighteen who died when the tower in Siloam fell on them—do you think they were more guilty than all the others living in Jerusalem? 5 I tell you, no! But unless you repent, you too will all perish."

6 Then he told this parable: "A man had a fig tree, planted in his vineyard, and he went to look for fruit on it, but did not find any. 7 So he said to the man who took care of the vineyard, 'For three years now I've been coming to look for fruit on this fig tree and haven't found any. Cut it down! Why should it use up the soil?'

8 " 'Sir,' the man replied, 'leave it alone for one more year, and I'll dig around it and fertilize it. 9 If it bears fruit next year, fine! If not, then cut it down.' "

A Crippled Woman Healed on the Sabbath

10 On a Sabbath Jesus was teaching in one of the synagogues, 11 and a woman was there who had been crippled by a spirit for eighteen years. She was bent over and could not straighten up at all. 12 When Jesus saw her, he called her forward and said to her, "Woman, you are set free from your infirmity." 13 Then he put his hands on her, and immediately she straightened up and praised God.

14 Indignant because Jesus had healed on the Sabbath, the synagogue ruler said to the people, "There are six days for work. So come and be healed on those days, not on the Sabbath."

15 The Lord answered him, "You hypocrites! Doesn't each of you on the Sabbath untie his ox or donkey from the stall and lead it out to give it water? 16 Then should not this woman, a daughter of Abraham, whom Satan has kept bound for eighteen long years, be set free on the Sabbath day from what bound her?"

17 When he said this, all his opponents were humiliated, but the people were delighted with all the wonderful things he was doing.

The Parables of the Mustard Seed and the Yeast

18 Then Jesus asked, "What is the kingdom of God like? What shall I compare it to? 19 It is like a mustard seed, which a man took and planted in his garden. It grew and became a tree, and the birds of the air perched in its branches."

20 Again he asked, "What shall I compare the kingdom of God to? 21 It is like yeast that a woman took and mixed into a large amount[a] of flour until it worked all through the dough."

The Narrow Door

22 Then Jesus went through the towns and villages, teaching as he made his way to Jerusalem. 23 Someone asked him, "Lord, are only a few people going to be saved?"

He said to them, 24 "Make every effort to enter through the narrow door, because many, I tell you, will try to enter and will not be able to. 25 Once the owner of the house gets up and closes the door, you will stand outside knocking and pleading, 'Sir, open the door for us.'

"But he will answer, 'I don't know you or where you come from.'

26 "Then you will say, 'We ate and drank with you, and you taught in our streets.'

27 "But he will reply, 'I don't know you or where you come from. Away from me, all you evildoers!'

28 "There will be weeping there, and gnashing of teeth, when you see Abraham, Isaac and Jacob and all the prophets in the kingdom of God, but you yourselves thrown out. 29 People will come from east and west and north and south, and will take their places at the feast in the kingdom of God. 30 Indeed there are those who are last who will be first, and first who will be last."

Jesus' Sorrow for Jerusalem

31 At that time some Pharisees came to

[a] *21* Greek *three satas* (probably about 1/2 bushel or 22 liters)

Jesus and said to him, "Leave this place
and go somewhere else. Herod wants to
kill you."
32He replied, "Go tell that fox, 'I will
drive out demons and heal people today
and tomorrow, and on the third day I will
reach my goal.' 33In any case, I must keep
going today and tomorrow and the next
day—for surely no prophet can die outside Jerusalem!
34"O Jerusalem, Jerusalem, you who kill
the prophets and stone those sent to you,
how often I have longed to gather your
children together, as a hen gathers her
chicks under her wings, but you were not
willing! 35Look, your house is left to you
desolate. I tell you, you will not see me
again until you say, 'Blessed is he who
comes in the name of the Lord.'[b]"

[b] 35 Psalm 118:26

PRAYER: THE CHARACTER I WANT TO CULTIVATE

***WISDOM** is foremost; therefore I will get wisdom, and though it cost all I have, I will get understanding. I will esteem her, and she will exalt me; I will embrace her, and she will honor me. (Proverbs 4:7–8) . . . Blessed are those who listen to wisdom, watching daily at her gates, waiting at her doorposts. For whoever finds wisdom finds life and obtains favor from You, Lord. But those who fail to find her injure their own souls; all who hate her love death. (Proverbs 8:34–36)*

***TAKE** a moment to ask the Lord for the grace to grow in godly character.*

YEAR 1 DAY 215

OT Judges 7:1-25

Gideon Defeats the Midianites

7 Early in the morning, Jerub-Baal (that
is, Gideon) and all his men camped at
the spring of Harod. The camp of Midian
was north of them in the valley near the
hill of Moreh. 2The LORD said to Gideon,
"You have too many men for me to deliver Midian into their hands. In order that
Israel may not boast against me that her
own strength has saved her, 3announce
now to the people, 'Anyone who trembles
with fear may turn back and leave Mount
Gilead.' " So twenty-two thousand men
left, while ten thousand remained.
4But the LORD said to Gideon, "There
are still too many men. Take them down
to the water, and I will sift them for you
there. If I say, 'This one shall go with you,'
he shall go; but if I say, 'This one shall not
go with you,' he shall not go."
5So Gideon took the men down to the
water. There the LORD told him, "Separate
those who lap the water with their
tongues like a dog from those who kneel
down to drink." 6Three hundred men
lapped with their hands to their mouths.
All the rest got down on their knees to
drink.
7The LORD said to Gideon, "With the
three hundred men that lapped I will save
you and give the Midianites into your
hands. Let all the other men go, each to
his own place." 8So Gideon sent the rest
of the Israelites to their tents but kept the
three hundred, who took over the provisions and trumpets of the others.
Now the camp of Midian lay below him
in the valley. 9During that night the LORD
said to Gideon, "Get up, go down against
the camp, because I am going to give it
into your hands. 10If you are afraid to attack, go down to the camp with your servant Purah 11and listen to what they are
saying. Afterward, you will be encouraged
to attack the camp." So he and Purah his
servant went down to the outposts of the
camp. 12The Midianites, the Amalekites
and all the other eastern peoples had settled in the valley, thick as locusts. Their
camels could no more be counted than
the sand on the seashore.
13Gideon arrived just as a man was
telling a friend his dream. "I had a

dream," he was saying. "A round loaf of
barley bread came tumbling into the Midianite camp. It struck the tent with such
force that the tent overturned and collapsed."
14His friend responded, "This can be
nothing other than the sword of Gideon
son of Joash, the Israelite. God has given
the Midianites and the whole camp into
his hands."
15When Gideon heard the dream and its
interpretation, he worshiped God. He returned to the camp of Israel and called out,
"Get up! The LORD has given the Midianite camp into your hands." 16Dividing the
three hundred men into three companies,
he placed trumpets and empty jars in the
hands of all of them, with torches inside.
17"Watch me," he told them. "Follow
my lead. When I get to the edge of the
camp, do exactly as I do. 18When I and all
who are with me blow our trumpets, then
from all around the camp blow yours and
shout, 'For the LORD and for Gideon.' "
19Gideon and the hundred men with
him reached the edge of the camp at the
beginning of the middle watch, just after
they had changed the guard. They blew
their trumpets and broke the jars that
were in their hands. 20The three companies blew the trumpets and smashed the
jars. Grasping the torches in their left
hands and holding in their right hands
the trumpets they were to blow, they
shouted, "A sword for the LORD and for
Gideon!" 21While each man held his position around the camp, all the Midianites
ran, crying out as they fled.
22When the three hundred trumpets
sounded, the LORD caused the men
throughout the camp to turn on each other with their swords. The army fled to Beth
Shittah toward Zererah as far as the border of Abel Meholah near Tabbath. 23Isra-
elites from Naphtali, Asher and all Manasseh were called out, and they pursued
the Midianites. 24Gideon sent messengers
throughout the hill country of Ephraim,
saying, "Come down against the Midianites and seize the waters of the Jordan
ahead of them as far as Beth Barah."
So all the men of Ephraim were called
out and they took the waters of the Jordan as far as Beth Barah. 25They also captured two of the Midianite leaders, Oreb
and Zeeb. They killed Oreb at the rock of
Oreb, and Zeeb at the winepress of Zeeb.
They pursued the Midianites and brought
the heads of Oreb and Zeeb to Gideon,
who was by the Jordan.

PRAYER: INTERCESSION

LORD, help us to bear one another's burdens and so fulfill the law of Christ. (Galatians 6:2)

TAKE *a few moments to intercede on behalf of other believers, such as your personal friends, those in ministry and those who are oppressed and in need.*

NT Luke 14:1-35

Jesus at a Pharisee's House

14 One Sabbath, when Jesus went to eat
in the house of a prominent Pharisee,
he was being carefully watched. 2There in
front of him was a man suffering from
dropsy. 3Jesus asked the Pharisees and experts in the law, "Is it lawful to heal on the
Sabbath or not?" 4But they remained
silent. So taking hold of the man, he
healed him and sent him away.
5Then he asked them, "If one of you has
a son[a] or an ox that falls into a well on
the Sabbath day, will you not immediately pull him out?" 6And they had nothing
to say.
7When he noticed how the guests picked
the places of honor at the table, he told
them this parable: 8"When someone invites you to a wedding feast, do not take
the place of honor, for a person more distinguished than you may have been invited. 9If so, the host who invited both of you
will come and say to you, 'Give this man
your seat.' Then, humiliated, you will have
to take the least important place. 10But

[a] 5 Some manuscripts *donkey*

when you are invited, take the lowest place,
so that when your host comes, he will say
to you, 'Friend, move up to a better place.'
Then you will be honored in the presence
of all your fellow guests. 11 For everyone
who exalts himself will be humbled, and
he who humbles himself will be exalted."
12 Then Jesus said to his host, "When
you give a luncheon or dinner, do not invite your friends, your brothers or relatives, or your rich neighbors; if you do,
they may invite you back and so you will
be repaid. 13 But when you give a banquet,
invite the poor, the crippled, the lame, the
blind, 14 and you will be blessed. Although
they cannot repay you, you will be repaid
at the resurrection of the righteous."

The Parable of the Great Banquet

15 When one of those at the table with
him heard this, he said to Jesus, "Blessed
is the man who will eat at the feast in the
kingdom of God."
16 Jesus replied: "A certain man was
preparing a great banquet and invited
many guests. 17 At the time of the banquet
he sent his servant to tell those who had
been invited, 'Come, for everything is now
ready.'
18 "But they all alike began to make excuses. The first said, 'I have just bought a
field, and I must go and see it. Please excuse me.'
19 "Another said, 'I have just bought five
yoke of oxen, and I'm on my way to try
them out. Please excuse me.'
20 "Still another said, 'I just got married,
so I can't come.'
21 "The servant came back and reported
this to his master. Then the owner of the
house became angry and ordered his servant, 'Go out quickly into the streets and
alleys of the town and bring in the poor,
the crippled, the blind and the lame.'
22 " 'Sir,' the servant said, 'what you ordered has been done, but there is still
room.'
23 "Then the master told his servant, 'Go
out to the roads and country lanes and
make them come in, so that my house
will be full. 24 I tell you, not one of those
men who were invited will get a taste of
my banquet.' "

The Cost of Being a Disciple

25 Large crowds were traveling with
Jesus, and turning to them he said: 26 "If
anyone comes to me and does not hate
his father and mother, his wife and children, his brothers and sisters—yes, even
his own life—he cannot be my disciple.
27 And anyone who does not carry his cross
and follow me cannot be my disciple.
28 "Suppose one of you wants to build a
tower. Will he not first sit down and estimate the cost to see if he has enough
money to complete it? 29 For if he lays the
foundation and is not able to finish it,
everyone who sees it will ridicule him,
30 saying, 'This fellow began to build and
was not able to finish.'
31 "Or suppose a king is about to go to
war against another king. Will he not first
sit down and consider whether he is able
with ten thousand men to oppose the one
coming against him with twenty thousand? 32 If he is not able, he will send a delegation while the other is still a long way
off and will ask for terms of peace. 33 In the
same way, any of you who does not give
up everything he has cannot be my disciple.
34 "Salt is good, but if it loses its saltiness, how can it be made salty again? 35 It
is fit neither for the soil nor for the manure pile; it is thrown out.
"He who has ears to hear, let him hear."

PRAYER: MY RELATIONSHIP TO OTHERS

O LORD, You have given us a new commandment: to love one another. Even as You have loved us, so we must love one another. By this all people will know that we are Your disciples, if we have love for one another. (John 13:34) . . . This is Your commandment, that we love one another as You have loved us. (John 15:12)

***PAUSE** to review your relationships with others and to commit them to the Lord.*

OT Judges 8:1-35

YEAR 1 DAY 216

Zebah and Zalmunna

8 Now the Ephraimites asked Gideon, "Why have you treated us like this? Why didn't you call us when you went to fight Midian?" And they criticized him sharply.

[2]But he answered them, "What have I accomplished compared to you? Aren't the gleanings of Ephraim's grapes better than the full grape harvest of Abiezer? [3]God gave Oreb and Zeeb, the Midianite leaders, into your hands. What was I able to do compared to you?" At this, their resentment against him subsided.

[4]Gideon and his three hundred men, exhausted yet keeping up the pursuit, came to the Jordan and crossed it. [5]He said to the men of Succoth, "Give my troops some bread; they are worn out, and I am still pursuing Zebah and Zalmunna, the kings of Midian."

[6]But the officials of Succoth said, "Do you already have the hands of Zebah and Zalmunna in your possession? Why should we give bread to your troops?"

[7]Then Gideon replied, "Just for that, when the LORD has given Zebah and Zalmunna into my hand, I will tear your flesh with desert thorns and briers."

[8]From there he went up to Peniel[a] and made the same request of them, but they answered as the men of Succoth had. [9]So he said to the men of Peniel, "When I return in triumph, I will tear down this tower."

[10]Now Zebah and Zalmunna were in Karkor with a force of about fifteen thousand men, all that were left of the armies of the eastern peoples; a hundred and twenty thousand swordsmen had fallen. [11]Gideon went up by the route of the nomads east of Nobah and Jogbehah and fell upon the unsuspecting army. [12]Zebah and Zalmunna, the two kings of Midian, fled, but he pursued them and captured them, routing their entire army.

[13]Gideon son of Joash then returned from the battle by the Pass of Heres. [14]He caught a young man of Succoth and questioned him, and the young man wrote down for him the names of the seventy-seven officials of Succoth, the elders of the town. [15]Then Gideon came and said to the men of Succoth, "Here are Zebah and Zalmunna, about whom you taunted me by saying, 'Do you already have the hands of Zebah and Zalmunna in your possession? Why should we give bread to your exhausted men?' " [16]He took the elders of the town and taught the men of Succoth a lesson by punishing them with desert thorns and briers. [17]He also pulled down the tower of Peniel and killed the men of the town.

[18]Then he asked Zebah and Zalmunna, "What kind of men did you kill at Tabor?"

"Men like you," they answered, "each one with the bearing of a prince."

[19]Gideon replied, "Those were my brothers, the sons of my own mother. As surely as the LORD lives, if you had spared their lives, I would not kill you." [20]Turning to Jether, his oldest son, he said, "Kill them!" But Jether did not draw his sword, because he was only a boy and was afraid.

[21]Zebah and Zalmunna said, "Come, do it yourself. 'As is the man, so is his strength.' " So Gideon stepped forward and killed them, and took the ornaments off their camels' necks.

Gideon's Ephod

[22]The Israelites said to Gideon, "Rule over us—you, your son and your grandson—because you have saved us out of the hand of Midian."

[23]But Gideon told them, "I will not rule over you, nor will my son rule over you. The LORD will rule over you." [24]And he said, "I do have one request, that each of you give me an earring from your share of the plunder." (It was the custom of the Ishmaelites to wear gold earrings.)

[25]They answered, "We'll be glad to give them." So they spread out a garment, and each man threw a ring from his plunder onto it. [26]The weight of the gold rings he asked for came to seventeen hundred shekels,[b] not counting the ornaments, the pendants and the purple garments worn by the kings of Midian or the chains that were on their camels' necks. [27]Gideon made the gold into an ephod, which he

[a] 8 Hebrew *Penuel,* a variant of *Peniel;* also in verses 9 and 17 [b] 26 That is, about 43 pounds (about 19.5 kilograms)

placed in Ophrah, his town. All Israel
prostituted themselves by worshiping it
there, and it became a snare to Gideon
and his family.

Gideon's Death

[28]Thus Midian was subdued before the
Israelites and did not raise its head again.
During Gideon's lifetime, the land enjoyed peace forty years.
[29]Jerub-Baal son of Joash went back
home to live. [30]He had seventy sons of his
own, for he had many wives. [31]His concubine, who lived in Shechem, also bore
him a son, whom he named Abimelech.
[32]Gideon son of Joash died at a good old
age and was buried in the tomb of his father Joash in Ophrah of the Abiezrites.
[33]No sooner had Gideon died than the
Israelites again prostituted themselves to
the Baals. They set up Baal-Berith as their
god and [34]did not remember the LORD
their God, who had rescued them from
the hands of all their enemies on every
side. [35]They also failed to show kindness
to the family of Jerub-Baal (that is, Gideon) for all the good things he had done
for them.

PRAYER: AFFIRMATION

YOU are my lamp, O Lord; You turn my darkness into light. With Your help I can advance against a troop; with You I can leap over a wall. (2 Samuel 22:29–30) . . . You know the way that I take; when You have tested me, I shall come forth as gold. My feet have held fast to Your steps; I have kept to Your way without turning aside. (Job 23:10–11)

PAUSE *to reflect on these Biblical affirmations.*

NT Luke 15:1–32

The Parable of the Lost Sheep

15 Now the tax collectors and "sinners"
were all gathering around to hear him.
[2]But the Pharisees and the teachers of the
law muttered, "This man welcomes sinners and eats with them."
[3]Then Jesus told them this parable:
[4]"Suppose one of you has a hundred
sheep and loses one of them. Does he not
leave the ninety-nine in the open country
and go after the lost sheep until he finds
it? [5]And when he finds it, he joyfully puts
it on his shoulders [6]and goes home. Then
he calls his friends and neighbors together and says, 'Rejoice with me; I have found
my lost sheep.' [7]I tell you that in the same
way there will be more rejoicing in heav-
en over one sinner who repents than over
ninety-nine righteous persons who do not
need to repent.

The Parable of the Lost Coin

[8]"Or suppose a woman has ten silver
coins[a] and loses one. Does she not light a
lamp, sweep the house and search carefully until she finds it? [9]And when she
finds it, she calls her friends and neighbors together and says, 'Rejoice with me;
I have found my lost coin.' [10]In the same
way, I tell you, there is rejoicing in the
presence of the angels of God over one
sinner who repents."

The Parable of the Lost Son

[11]Jesus continued: "There was a man
who had two sons. [12]The younger one said
to his father, 'Father, give me my share of
the estate.' So he divided his property between them.
[13]"Not long after that, the younger son
got together all he had, set off for a distant country and there squandered his
wealth in wild living. [14]After he had spent
everything, there was a severe famine in
that whole country, and he began to be in
need. [15]So he went and hired himself out
to a citizen of that country, who sent him
to his fields to feed pigs. [16]He longed to
fill his stomach with the pods that the
pigs were eating, but no one gave him
anything.
[17]"When he came to his senses, he said,

[a] *8* Greek *ten drachmas,* each worth about a day's wages

'How many of my father's hired men have
food to spare, and here I am starving to
death! 18 I will set out and go back to my
father and say to him: Father, I have
sinned against heaven and against you. 19 I
am no longer worthy to be called your
son; make me like one of your hired men.'
20 So he got up and went to his father.

"But while he was still a long way off,
his father saw him and was filled with
compassion for him; he ran to his son,
threw his arms around him and kissed
him.

21 "The son said to him, 'Father, I have
sinned against heaven and against you. I
am no longer worthy to be called your
son.[b]'

22 "But the father said to his servants,
'Quick! Bring the best robe and put it on
him. Put a ring on his finger and sandals
on his feet. 23 Bring the fattened calf and
kill it. Let's have a feast and celebrate.
24 For this son of mine was dead and is
alive again; he was lost and is found.' So
they began to celebrate.

25 "Meanwhile, the older son was in the
field. When he came near the house, he
heard music and dancing. 26 So he called
one of the servants and asked him what
was going on. 27 'Your brother has come,'
he replied, 'and your father has killed the
fattened calf because he has him back safe
and sound.'

28 "The older brother became angry and
refused to go in. So his father went out
and pleaded with him. 29 But he answered
his father, 'Look! All these years I've been
slaving for you and never disobeyed your
orders. Yet you never gave me even a
young goat so I could celebrate with my
friends. 30 But when this son of yours who
has squandered your property with prostitutes comes home, you kill the fattened
calf for him!'

31 " 'My son,' the father said, 'you are always with me, and everything I have is
yours. 32 But we had to celebrate and be
glad, because this brother of yours was
dead and is alive again; he was lost and is
found.' "

[b] 21 Some early manuscripts *son. Make me like one of your hired men.*

PRAYER: THE ATTRIBUTES OF GOD

YOU know me, O Lord; You see me and test my thoughts about You.
(Jeremiah 12:3)

PAUSE *to reflect on these affirmations about the person, powers and perfection of God.*

YEAR 1 DAY 217

OT Psalm 41

Psalm 41

For the director of music. A psalm of David.

1 Blessed is he who has regard for the
weak;
the LORD delivers him in times of
trouble.
2 The LORD will protect him and
preserve his life;
he will bless him in the land
and not surrender him to the desire
of his foes.
3 The LORD will sustain him on his
sickbed
and restore him from his bed of
illness.

4 I said, "O LORD, have mercy on me;
heal me, for I have sinned against
you."
5 My enemies say of me in malice,
"When will he die and his name
perish?"
6 Whenever one comes to see me,
he speaks falsely, while his heart
gathers slander;
then he goes out and spreads it
abroad.

7 All my enemies whisper together
against me;

they imagine the worst for me,
saying,
8 "A vile disease has beset him;
he will never get up from the place
where he lies."
9 Even my close friend, whom I trusted,
he who shared my bread,
has lifted up his heel against me.

10 But you, O LORD, have mercy on me;
raise me up, that I may repay them.
11 I know that you are pleased with me,
for my enemy does not triumph
over me.
12 In my integrity you uphold me
and set me in your presence forever.

13 Praise be to the LORD, the God of
Israel,
from everlasting to everlasting.
Amen and Amen.

PRAYER: THANKSGIVING

IN the beginning, O God, You created the heavens and the earth. When the earth was formless and empty, and darkness was over the surface of the deep, Your Spirit hovered over the face of the waters. And You said, "Let there be light," and there was light. Then You said, "Let there be an expanse in the midst of the waters, and let it separate the waters from the waters." So You made the expanse and separated the waters under the expanse from the waters above it, and it was so. Then You said, "Let the waters under the heavens be gathered into one place, and let dry ground appear"; and it was so. And You saw that it was good. (Genesis 1:1–10)

***PAUSE** to offer your own expressions of thanksgiving.*

NT Luke 16:1–31

The Parable of the Shrewd Manager

16 Jesus told his disciples: "There was a
rich man whose manager was accused
of wasting his possessions. 2So he called
him in and asked him, 'What is this I hear
about you? Give an account of your management, because you cannot be manager any longer.'
3 "The manager said to himself, 'What
shall I do now? My master is taking away
my job. I'm not strong enough to dig, and
I'm ashamed to beg— 4I know what I'll do
so that, when I lose my job here, people
will welcome me into their houses.'
5 "So he called in each one of his master's debtors. He asked the first, 'How
much do you owe my master?'
6 " 'Eight hundred gallons[a] of olive oil,'
he replied.
"The manager told him, 'Take your bill,
sit down quickly, and make it four hundred.'
7 "Then he asked the second, 'And how
much do you owe?'
" 'A thousand bushels[b] of wheat,' he
replied.
"He told him, 'Take your bill and make
it eight hundred.'
8 "The master commended the dishonest manager because he had acted shrewdly. For the people of this world are more
shrewd in dealing with their own kind
than are the people of the light. 9I tell you,
use worldly wealth to gain friends for
yourselves, so that when it is gone, you
will be welcomed into eternal dwellings.
10 "Whoever can be trusted with very little can also be trusted with much, and
whoever is dishonest with very little will
also be dishonest with much. 11So if you
have not been trustworthy in handling
worldly wealth, who will trust you with
true riches? 12And if you have not been
trustworthy with someone else's property,
who will give you property of your own?
13 "No servant can serve two masters. Either he will hate the one and love the other, or he will be devoted to the one and
despise the other. You cannot serve both
God and Money."

[a] 6 Greek *one hundred batous* (probably about 3 kiloliters) [b] 7 Greek *one hundred korous* (probably about 35 kiloliters)

14 The Pharisees, who loved money, heard all this and were sneering at Jesus. 15 He said to them, "You are the ones who justify yourselves in the eyes of men, but God knows your hearts. What is highly valued among men is detestable in God's sight.

Additional Teachings

16 "The Law and the Prophets were proclaimed until John. Since that time, the good news of the kingdom of God is being preached, and everyone is forcing his way into it. 17 It is easier for heaven and earth to disappear than for the least stroke of a pen to drop out of the Law.

18 "Anyone who divorces his wife and marries another woman commits adultery, and the man who marries a divorced woman commits adultery.

The Rich Man and Lazarus

19 "There was a rich man who was dressed in purple and fine linen and lived in luxury every day. 20 At his gate was laid a beggar named Lazarus, covered with sores 21 and longing to eat what fell from the rich man's table. Even the dogs came and licked his sores.

22 "The time came when the beggar died and the angels carried him to Abraham's side. The rich man also died and was buried. 23 In hell,[c] where he was in torment, he looked up and saw Abraham far away, with Lazarus by his side. 24 So he called to him, 'Father Abraham, have pity on me and send Lazarus to dip the tip of his finger in water and cool my tongue, because I am in agony in this fire.'

25 "But Abraham replied, 'Son, remember that in your lifetime you received your good things, while Lazarus received bad things, but now he is comforted here and you are in agony. 26 And besides all this, between us and you a great chasm has been fixed, so that those who want to go from here to you cannot, nor can anyone cross over from there to us.'

27 "He answered, 'Then I beg you, father, send Lazarus to my father's house, 28 for I have five brothers. Let him warn them, so that they will not also come to this place of torment.'

29 "Abraham replied, 'They have Moses and the Prophets; let them listen to them.'

30 " 'No, father Abraham,' he said, 'but if someone from the dead goes to them, they will repent.'

31 "He said to him, 'If they do not listen to Moses and the Prophets, they will not be convinced even if someone rises from the dead.' "

[c] 23 Greek *Hades*

PRAYER: THE WORKS OF GOD

SURELY Your hand is not too short to save, O God, nor Your ear too dull to hear. But our iniquities have separated us from You, our God; our sins have hidden Your face from us, so that You will not hear. Yet You saw that there was no one to intervene; so Your own arm worked salvation for You, and Your righteousness sustained You. You put on righteousness as Your breastplate, and the helmet of salvation on Your head; You put on the garments of vengeance and wrapped Yourself in zeal as a cloak. From the west, all people will fear Your name, and from the rising of the sun, they will revere Your glory. For You will come like a flood that Your breath drives along. (Isaiah 59:1–2, 16–19) . . . You led Your people with cords of human kindness, O Lord, with bands of love; You lifted the yoke from their neck and bent down to feed them. (Hosea 11:4)

***TAKE** a moment to consider the greatness of God's wonderful works.*

OT Judges 9:1–57

Abimelech

9 Abimelech son of Jerub-Baal went to his mother's brothers in Shechem and said to them and to all his mother's clan, 2"Ask all the citizens of Shechem, 'Which is better for you: to have all seventy of Jerub-Baal's sons rule over you, or just one man?' Remember, I am your flesh and blood."

3When the brothers repeated all this to the citizens of Shechem, they were inclined to follow Abimelech, for they said, "He is our brother." 4They gave him seventy shekels[a] of silver from the temple of Baal-Berith, and Abimelech used it to hire reckless adventurers, who became his followers. 5He went to his father's home in Ophrah and on one stone murdered his seventy brothers, the sons of Jerub-Baal. But Jotham, the youngest son of Jerub-Baal, escaped by hiding. 6Then all the citizens of Shechem and Beth Millo gathered beside the great tree at the pillar in Shechem to crown Abimelech king.

7When Jotham was told about this, he climbed up on the top of Mount Gerizim and shouted to them, "Listen to me, citizens of Shechem, so that God may listen to you. 8One day the trees went out to anoint a king for themselves. They said to the olive tree, 'Be our king.'

9"But the olive tree answered, 'Should I give up my oil, by which both gods and men are honored, to hold sway over the trees?'

10"Next, the trees said to the fig tree, 'Come and be our king.'

11"But the fig tree replied, 'Should I give up my fruit, so good and sweet, to hold sway over the trees?'

12"Then the trees said to the vine, 'Come and be our king.'

13"But the vine answered, 'Should I give up my wine, which cheers both gods and men, to hold sway over the trees?'

14"Finally all the trees said to the thornbush, 'Come and be our king.'

15"The thornbush said to the trees, 'If you really want to anoint me king over you, come and take refuge in my shade; but if not, then let fire come out of the thornbush and consume the cedars of Lebanon!'

16"Now if you have acted honorably and in good faith when you made Abimelech king, and if you have been fair to Jerub-Baal and his family, and if you have treated him as he deserves— 17and to think that my father fought for you, risked his life to rescue you from the hand of Midian 18(but today you have revolted against my father's family, murdered his seventy sons on a single stone, and made Abimelech, the son of his slave girl, king over the citizens of Shechem because he is your brother)— 19if then you have acted honorably and in good faith toward Jerub-Baal and his family today, may Abimelech be your joy, and may you be his, too! 20But if you have not, let fire come out from Abimelech and consume you, citizens of Shechem and Beth Millo, and let fire come out from you, citizens of Shechem and Beth Millo, and consume Abimelech!"

21Then Jotham fled, escaping to Beer, and he lived there because he was afraid of his brother Abimelech.

22After Abimelech had governed Israel three years, 23God sent an evil spirit between Abimelech and the citizens of Shechem, who acted treacherously against Abimelech. 24God did this in order that the crime against Jerub-Baal's seventy sons, the shedding of their blood, might be avenged on their brother Abimelech and on the citizens of Shechem, who had helped him murder his brothers. 25In opposition to him these citizens of Shechem set men on the hilltops to ambush and rob everyone who passed by, and this was reported to Abimelech.

26Now Gaal son of Ebed moved with his brothers into Shechem, and its citizens put their confidence in him. 27After they had gone out into the fields and gathered the grapes and trodden them, they held a festival in the temple of their god. While they were eating and drinking, they cursed Abimelech. 28Then Gaal son of Ebed said, "Who is Abimelech, and who is Shechem, that we should be subject to him? Isn't he Jerub-Baal's son, and isn't Zebul his deputy? Serve the men of Hamor, She-

[a] 4 That is, about 1 3/4 pounds (about 0.8 kilogram)

chem's father! Why should we serve
Abimelech? 29If only this people were under my command! Then I would get rid
of him. I would say to Abimelech, 'Call
out your whole army!' "[b]
30When Zebul the governor of the city
heard what Gaal son of Ebed said, he was
very angry. 31Under cover he sent messengers to Abimelech, saying, "Gaal son of
Ebed and his brothers have come to Shechem and are stirring up the city against
you. 32Now then, during the night you
and your men should come and lie in
wait in the fields. 33In the morning at sunrise, advance against the city. When Gaal
and his men come out against you, do
whatever your hand finds to do."
34So Abimelech and all his troops set
out by night and took up concealed positions near Shechem in four companies.
35Now Gaal son of Ebed had gone out and
was standing at the entrance to the city
gate just as Abimelech and his soldiers
came out from their hiding place.
36When Gaal saw them, he said to Zebul, "Look, people are coming down from
the tops of the mountains!"
Zebul replied, "You mistake the shadows of the mountains for men."
37But Gaal spoke up again: "Look, people are coming down from the center of
the land, and a company is coming from
the direction of the soothsayers' tree."
38Then Zebul said to him, "Where is
your big talk now, you who said, 'Who is
Abimelech that we should be subject to
him?' Aren't these the men you ridiculed?
Go out and fight them!"
39So Gaal led out[c] the citizens of Shechem and fought Abimelech. 40Abimelech
chased him, and many fell wounded in
the flight—all the way to the entrance to
the gate. 41Abimelech stayed in Arumah,
and Zebul drove Gaal and his brothers
out of Shechem.
42The next day the people of Shechem
went out to the fields, and this was reported to Abimelech. 43So he took his
men, divided them into three companies
and set an ambush in the fields. When he
saw the people coming out of the city, he
rose to attack them. 44Abimelech and the
companies with him rushed forward to a
position at the entrance to the city gate.
Then two companies rushed upon those
in the fields and struck them down. 45All
that day Abimelech pressed his attack
against the city until he had captured it
and killed its people. Then he destroyed
the city and scattered salt over it.
46On hearing this, the citizens in the
tower of Shechem went into the stronghold of the temple of El-Berith. 47When
Abimelech heard that they had assembled
there, 48he and all his men went up Mount
Zalmon. He took an ax and cut off some
branches, which he lifted to his shoulders.
He ordered the men with him, "Quick!
Do what you have seen me do!" 49So all
the men cut branches and followed Abimelech. They piled them against the stronghold and set it on fire over the people inside. So all the people in the tower of
Shechem, about a thousand men and
women, also died.
50Next Abimelech went to Thebez and
besieged it and captured it. 51Inside the city,
however, was a strong tower, to which all
the men and women—all the people of the
city—fled. They locked themselves in and
climbed up on the tower roof. 52Abimelech
went to the tower and stormed it. But as he
approached the entrance to the tower to set
it on fire, 53a woman dropped an upper
millstone on his head and cracked his skull.
54Hurriedly he called to his armor-bearer, "Draw your sword and kill me, so that
they can't say, 'A woman killed him.' " So
his servant ran him through, and he died.
55When the Israelites saw that Abimelech
was dead, they went home.
56Thus God repaid the wickedness that
Abimelech had done to his father by murdering his seventy brothers. 57God also
made the men of Shechem pay for all
their wickedness. The curse of Jotham son
of Jerub-Baal came on them.

[b] 29 Septuagint; Hebrew *him." Then he said to Abimelech, "Call out your whole army!"* [c] 39 Or *Gaal went out in the sight of*

PRAYER: ADORATION

O LORD, You cover Yourself in light as with a garment; You stretch out the heavens like a tent curtain and lay the beams of Your upper chambers in the waters. You make the clouds Your chariot and walk

on the wings of the wind. You make the winds Your messengers, flames of fire Your servants. You set the earth on its foundations so that it can never be moved. You covered it with the deep as with a garment; the waters stood above the mountains. At Your rebuke the waters fled; at the sound of Your thunder they hurried away. They flowed over the mountains and went down into the valleys, to the place You assigned for them. You set a boundary they cannot cross, that they will not return to cover the earth. O Lord, how manifold are Your works! In wisdom You made them all; the earth is full of Your possessions. (Psalm 104:2–9, 24)

***PAUSE** to express your thoughts of praise and worship.*

NT Luke 17:1–37

Sin, Faith, Duty

17 Jesus said to his disciples: "Things that cause people to sin are bound to come, but woe to that person through whom they come. [2]It would be better for him to be thrown into the sea with a millstone tied around his neck than for him to cause one of these little ones to sin. [3]So watch yourselves.

"If your brother sins, rebuke him, and if he repents, forgive him. [4]If he sins against you seven times in a day, and seven times comes back to you and says, 'I repent,' forgive him."

[5]The apostles said to the Lord, "Increase our faith!"

[6]He replied, "If you have faith as small as a mustard seed, you can say to this mulberry tree, 'Be uprooted and planted in the sea,' and it will obey you.

[7]"Suppose one of you had a servant plowing or looking after the sheep. Would he say to the servant when he comes in from the field, 'Come along now and sit down to eat'? [8]Would he not rather say, 'Prepare my supper, get yourself ready and wait on me while I eat and drink; after that you may eat and drink'? [9]Would he thank the servant because he did what he was told to do? [10]So you also, when you have done everything you were told to do, should say, 'We are unworthy servants; we have only done our duty.' "

Ten Healed of Leprosy

[11]Now on his way to Jerusalem, Jesus traveled along the border between Samaria and Galilee. [12]As he was going into a village, ten men who had leprosy[a] met him. They stood at a distance [13]and called out in a loud voice, "Jesus, Master, have pity on us!"

[14]When he saw them, he said, "Go, show yourselves to the priests." And as they went, they were cleansed.

[15]One of them, when he saw he was healed, came back, praising God in a loud voice. [16]He threw himself at Jesus' feet and thanked him—and he was a Samaritan.

[17]Jesus asked, "Were not all ten cleansed? Where are the other nine? [18]Was no one found to return and give praise to God except this foreigner?" [19]Then he said to him, "Rise and go; your faith has made you well."

The Coming of the Kingdom of God

[20]Once, having been asked by the Pharisees when the kingdom of God would come, Jesus replied, "The kingdom of God does not come with your careful observation, [21]nor will people say, 'Here it is,' or 'There it is,' because the kingdom of God is within[b] you."

[22]Then he said to his disciples, "The time is coming when you will long to see one of the days of the Son of Man, but you will not see it. [23]Men will tell you, 'There he is!' or 'Here he is!' Do not go running off after them. [24]For the Son of Man in his day[c] will be like the lightning, which flashes and lights up the sky from one end to the other. [25]But first he must suffer many things and be rejected by this generation.

[26]"Just as it was in the days of Noah, so also will it be in the days of the Son of

[a] 12 The Greek word was used for various diseases affecting the skin—not necessarily leprosy.
[b] 21 Or *among*
[c] 24 Some manuscripts do not have *in his day.*

Man. [27]People were eating, drinking, marrying and being given in marriage up to the day Noah entered the ark. Then the flood came and destroyed them all.

[28]"It was the same in the days of Lot. People were eating and drinking, buying and selling, planting and building. [29]But the day Lot left Sodom, fire and sulfur rained down from heaven and destroyed them all.

[30]"It will be just like this on the day the Son of Man is revealed. [31]On that day no one who is on the roof of his house, with his goods inside, should go down to get them. Likewise, no one in the field should go back for anything. [32]Remember Lot's wife! [33]Whoever tries to keep his life will lose it, and whoever loses his life will preserve it. [34]I tell you, on that night two people will be in one bed; one will be taken and the other left. [35]Two women will be grinding grain together; one will be taken and the other left.[d]"

[37]"Where, Lord?" they asked.

He replied, "Where there is a dead body, there the vultures will gather."

[d] 35 Some manuscripts *left.* [36]*Two men will be in the field; one will be taken and the other left.*

PRAYER: MY RELATIONSHIP TO GOD

I WILL sing of Your strength, yes, I will sing of Your mercy in the morning, for You have been my stronghold, my refuge in times of trouble. To You, O my Strength, I will sing praises, for You are my fortress, my loving God. (Psalm 59:16–17)

***PAUSE** to thank God for the relationship that you enjoy with Him in Jesus Christ.*

YEAR 1 DAY 219

OT Judges 10:1–11:40

Tola

10 After the time of Abimelech a man of Issachar, Tola son of Puah, the son of Dodo, rose to save Israel. He lived in Shamir, in the hill country of Ephraim. [2]He led[a] Israel twenty-three years; then he died, and was buried in Shamir.

Jair

[3]He was followed by Jair of Gilead, who led Israel twenty-two years. [4]He had thirty sons, who rode thirty donkeys. They controlled thirty towns in Gilead, which to this day are called Havvoth Jair.[b] [5]When Jair died, he was buried in Kamon.

Jephthah

[6]Again the Israelites did evil in the eyes of the LORD. They served the Baals and the Ashtoreths, and the gods of Aram, the gods of Sidon, the gods of Moab, the gods of the Ammonites and the gods of the Philistines. And because the Israelites forsook the LORD and no longer served him, [7]he became angry with them. He sold them into the hands of the Philistines and the Ammonites, [8]who that year shattered and crushed them. For eighteen years they oppressed all the Israelites on the east side of the Jordan in Gilead, the land of the Amorites. [9]The Ammonites also crossed the Jordan to fight against Judah, Benjamin and the house of Ephraim; and Israel was in great distress. [10]Then the Israelites cried out to the LORD, "We have sinned against you, forsaking our God and serving the Baals."

[11]The LORD replied, "When the Egyptians, the Amorites, the Ammonites, the Philistines, [12]the Sidonians, the Amalekites and the Maonites[c] oppressed you and you cried to me for help, did I not save you from their hands? [13]But you have forsaken me and served other gods, so I will no longer save you. [14]Go and cry out to the gods you have chosen. Let them save you when you are in trouble!"

[15]But the Israelites said to the LORD, "We

[a] 2 Traditionally *judged;* also in verse 3 [b] 4 Or *called the settlements of Jair* [c] 12 Hebrew; some Septuagint manuscripts *Midianites*

have sinned. Do with us whatever you
think best, but please rescue us now."
16Then they got rid of the foreign gods
among them and served the LORD. And he
could bear Israel's misery no longer.
17When the Ammonites were called to
arms and camped in Gilead, the Israelites
assembled and camped at Mizpah. 18The
leaders of the people of Gilead said to
each other, "Whoever will launch the attack against the Ammonites will be the
head of all those living in Gilead."
11 Jephthah the Gileadite was a mighty
warrior. His father was Gilead; his
mother was a prostitute. 2Gilead's wife
also bore him sons, and when they were
grown up, they drove Jephthah away. "You
are not going to get any inheritance in our
family," they said, "because you are the
son of another woman." 3So Jephthah
fled from his brothers and settled in the
land of Tob, where a group of adventurers
gathered around him and followed him.
4Some time later, when the Ammonites
made war on Israel, 5the elders of Gilead
went to get Jephthah from the land of
Tob. 6"Come," they said, "be our commander, so we can fight the Ammonites."
7Jephthah said to them, "Didn't you
hate me and drive me from my father's
house? Why do you come to me now,
when you're in trouble?"
8The elders of Gilead said to him, "Nevertheless, we are turning to you now;
come with us to fight the Ammonites, and
you will be our head over all who live in
Gilead."
9Jephthah answered, "Suppose you take
me back to fight the Ammonites and the
LORD gives them to me—will I really be
your head?"
10The elders of Gilead replied, "The
LORD is our witness; we will certainly do
as you say." 11So Jephthah went with the
elders of Gilead, and the people made
him head and commander over them.
And he repeated all his words before the
LORD in Mizpah.
12Then Jephthah sent messengers to the
Ammonite king with the question: "What
do you have against us that you have attacked our country?"
13The king of the Ammonites answered
Jephthah's messengers, "When Israel
came up out of Egypt, they took away my
land from the Arnon to the Jabbok, all the
way to the Jordan. Now give it back peaceably."
14Jephthah sent back messengers to the
Ammonite king, 15saying:

"This is what Jephthah says: Israel did
not take the land of Moab or the land
of the Ammonites. 16But when they
came up out of Egypt, Israel went
through the desert to the Red Sea[d]
and on to Kadesh. 17Then Israel sent
messengers to the king of Edom, saying, 'Give us permission to go
through your country,' but the king of
Edom would not listen. They sent
also to the king of Moab, and he refused. So Israel stayed at Kadesh.
18"Next they traveled through the
desert, skirted the lands of Edom and
Moab, passed along the eastern side
of the country of Moab, and camped
on the other side of the Arnon. They
did not enter the territory of Moab,
for the Arnon was its border.
19"Then Israel sent messengers to
Sihon king of the Amorites, who
ruled in Heshbon, and said to him,
'Let us pass through your country to
our own place.' 20Sihon, however, did
not trust Israel[e] to pass through his
territory. He mustered all his men
and encamped at Jahaz and fought
with Israel.
21"Then the LORD, the God of Israel, gave Sihon and all his men into Israel's hands, and they defeated them.
Israel took over all the land of the
Amorites who lived in that country,
22capturing all of it from the Arnon
to the Jabbok and from the desert to
the Jordan.
23"Now since the LORD, the God of
Israel, has driven the Amorites out
before his people Israel, what right
have you to take it over? 24Will you
not take what your god Chemosh
gives you? Likewise, whatever the
LORD our God has given us, we will
possess. 25Are you better than Balak
son of Zippor, king of Moab? Did he
ever quarrel with Israel or fight with
them? 26For three hundred years Israel occupied Heshbon, Aroer, the surrounding settlements and all the

[d] *16* Hebrew *Yam Suph*; that is, Sea of Reeds
[e] *20* Or *however, would not make an agreement for Israel*

towns along the Arnon. Why didn't
you retake them during that time? 27I
have not wronged you, but you are
doing me wrong by waging war
against me. Let the LORD, the Judge,[f]
decide the dispute this day between
the Israelites and the Ammonites."

28The king of Ammon, however, paid no
attention to the message Jephthah sent
him.
29Then the Spirit of the LORD came
upon Jephthah. He crossed Gilead and
Manasseh, passed through Mizpah of Gilead, and from there he advanced against
the Ammonites. 30And Jephthah made a
vow to the LORD: "If you give the Ammonites into my hands, 31whatever comes
out of the door of my house to meet me
when I return in triumph from the Ammonites will be the LORD's, and I will sacrifice it as a burnt offering."
32Then Jephthah went over to fight the
Ammonites, and the LORD gave them into
his hands. 33He devastated twenty towns
from Aroer to the vicinity of Minnith, as
far as Abel Keramim. Thus Israel subdued
Ammon.
34When Jephthah returned to his home
in Mizpah, who should come out to meet
him but his daughter, dancing to the
sound of tambourines! She was an only
child. Except for her he had neither son
nor daughter. 35When he saw her, he tore
his clothes and cried, "Oh! My daughter!
You have made me miserable and
wretched, because I have made a vow to
the LORD that I cannot break."
36"My father," she replied, "you have
given your word to the LORD. Do to me
just as you promised, now that the LORD
has avenged you of your enemies, the Ammonites. 37But grant me this one request,"
she said. "Give me two months to roam
the hills and weep with my friends, because I will never marry."
38"You may go," he said. And he let her
go for two months. She and the girls went
into the hills and wept because she would
never marry. 39After the two months, she
returned to her father and he did to her as
he had vowed. And she was a virgin.
From this comes the Israelite custom
40that each year the young women of Israel go out for four days to commemorate
the daughter of Jephthah the Gileadite.

f 27 Or *Ruler*

PRAYER: CONFESSION

YOU are wise in heart and mighty in strength, O God. Who has resisted You without harm? (Job 9:4)

***ASK** the Spirit to search your heart and reveal any areas of unconfessed sin. Acknowledge these to the Lord and thank Him for His forgiveness.*

NT Luke 18:1-17

The Parable of the Persistent Widow

18 Then Jesus told his disciples a parable
to show them that they should always
pray and not give up. 2He said: "In a certain town there was a judge who neither
feared God nor cared about men. 3And
there was a widow in that town who kept
coming to him with the plea, 'Grant me
justice against my adversary.'
4"For some time he refused. But finally
he said to himself, 'Even though I don't
fear God or care about men, 5yet because
this widow keeps bothering me, I will see
that she gets justice, so that she won't
eventually wear me out with her coming!' "
6And the Lord said, "Listen to what the
unjust judge says. 7And will not God bring
about justice for his chosen ones, who cry
out to him day and night? Will he keep
putting them off? 8I tell you, he will see
that they get justice, and quickly. However, when the Son of Man comes, will he
find faith on the earth?"

The Parable of the Pharisee and the Tax Collector

9To some who were confident of their
own righteousness and looked down on
everybody else, Jesus told this parable:
10"Two men went up to the temple to pray,
one a Pharisee and the other a tax collector.

[11]The Pharisee stood up and prayed about[a] himself: 'God, I thank you that I am not like other men—robbers, evildoers, adulterers—or even like this tax collector. [12]I fast twice a week and give a tenth of all I get.'

[13]"But the tax collector stood at a distance. He would not even look up to heaven, but beat his breast and said, 'God, have mercy on me, a sinner.'

[14]"I tell you that this man, rather than the other, went home justified before God. For everyone who exalts himself will be humbled, and he who humbles himself will be exalted."

The Little Children and Jesus

[15]People were also bringing babies to Jesus to have him touch them. When the disciples saw this, they rebuked them. [16]But Jesus called the children to him and said, "Let the little children come to me, and do not hinder them, for the kingdom of God belongs to such as these. [17]I tell you the truth, anyone who will not receive the kingdom of God like a little child will never enter it."

[a] *11* Or *to*

PRAYER: THE CHARACTER I WANT TO CULTIVATE

I WILL have accurate and honest standards in my business practices. (Deuteronomy 25:15) . . . Those who walk in integrity walk securely, but those who pervert their ways will be found out. (Proverbs 10:9)

***TAKE** a moment to ask the Lord for the grace to grow in godly character.*

YEAR 1 DAY 220

OT Judges 12:1–13:25

Jephthah and Ephraim

12 The men of Ephraim called out their forces, crossed over to Zaphon and said to Jephthah, "Why did you go to fight the Ammonites without calling us to go with you? We're going to burn down your house over your head."

[2]Jephthah answered, "I and my people were engaged in a great struggle with the Ammonites, and although I called, you didn't save me out of their hands. [3]When I saw that you wouldn't help, I took my life in my hands and crossed over to fight the Ammonites, and the LORD gave me the victory over them. Now why have you come up today to fight me?"

[4]Jephthah then called together the men of Gilead and fought against Ephraim. The Gileadites struck them down because the Ephraimites had said, "You Gileadites are renegades from Ephraim and Manasseh." [5]The Gileadites captured the fords of the Jordan leading to Ephraim, and whenever a survivor of Ephraim said, "Let me cross over," the men of Gilead asked him, "Are you an Ephraimite?" If he replied, "No," [6]they said, "All right, say 'Shibboleth.'" If he said, "Sibboleth," because he could not pronounce the word correctly, they seized him and killed him at the fords of the Jordan. Forty two thousand Ephraimites were killed at that time.

[7]Jephthah led[a] Israel six years. Then Jephthah the Gileadite died, and was buried in a town in Gilead.

Ibzan, Elon and Abdon

[8]After him, Ibzan of Bethlehem led Israel. [9]He had thirty sons and thirty daughters. He gave his daughters away in marriage to those outside his clan, and for his sons he brought in thirty young women as wives from outside his clan. Ibzan led Israel seven years. [10]Then Ibzan died, and was buried in Bethlehem.

[11]After him, Elon the Zebulunite led Israel ten years. [12]Then Elon died, and was buried in Aijalon in the land of Zebulun.

[13]After him, Abdon son of Hillel, from Pirathon, led Israel. [14]He had forty sons and thirty grandsons, who rode on seventy donkeys. He led Israel eight years.

[a] *7* Traditionally *judged;* also in verses 8–14

15 Then Abdon son of Hillel died, and was buried at Pirathon in Ephraim, in the hill country of the Amalekites.

The Birth of Samson

13 Again the Israelites did evil in the eyes of the LORD, so the LORD delivered them into the hands of the Philistines for forty years.

2 A certain man of Zorah, named Manoah, from the clan of the Danites, had a wife who was sterile and remained childless. 3 The angel of the LORD appeared to her and said, "You are sterile and childless, but you are going to conceive and have a son. 4 Now see to it that you drink no wine or other fermented drink and that you do not eat anything unclean, 5 because you will conceive and give birth to a son. No razor may be used on his head, because the boy is to be a Nazirite, set apart to God from birth, and he will begin the deliverance of Israel from the hands of the Philistines."

6 Then the woman went to her husband and told him, "A man of God came to me. He looked like an angel of God, very awesome. I didn't ask him where he came from, and he didn't tell me his name. 7 But he said to me, 'You will conceive and give birth to a son. Now then, drink no wine or other fermented drink and do not eat anything unclean, because the boy will be a Nazirite of God from birth until the day of his death.' "

8 Then Manoah prayed to the LORD: "O Lord, I beg you, let the man of God you sent to us come again to teach us how to bring up the boy who is to be born."

9 God heard Manoah, and the angel of God came again to the woman while she was out in the field; but her husband Manoah was not with her. 10 The woman hurried to tell her husband, "He's here! The man who appeared to me the other day!"

11 Manoah got up and followed his wife. When he came to the man, he said, "Are you the one who talked to my wife?"

"I am," he said.

12 So Manoah asked him, "When your words are fulfilled, what is to be the rule for the boy's life and work?"

13 The angel of the LORD answered, "Your wife must do all that I have told her. 14 She must not eat anything that comes from the grapevine, nor drink any wine or other fermented drink nor eat anything unclean. She must do everything I have commanded her."

15 Manoah said to the angel of the LORD, "We would like you to stay until we prepare a young goat for you."

16 The angel of the LORD replied, "Even though you detain me, I will not eat any of your food. But if you prepare a burnt offering, offer it to the LORD." (Manoah did not realize that it was the angel of the LORD.)

17 Then Manoah inquired of the angel of the LORD, "What is your name, so that we may honor you when your word comes true?"

18 He replied, "Why do you ask my name? It is beyond understanding.[a]" 19 Then Manoah took a young goat, together with the grain offering, and sacrificed it on a rock to the LORD. And the LORD did an amazing thing while Manoah and his wife watched: 20 As the flame blazed up from the altar toward heaven, the angel of the LORD ascended in the flame. Seeing this, Manoah and his wife fell with their faces to the ground. 21 When the angel of the LORD did not show himself again to Manoah and his wife, Manoah realized that it was the angel of the LORD.

22 "We are doomed to die!" he said to his wife. "We have seen God!"

23 But his wife answered, "If the LORD had meant to kill us, he would not have accepted a burnt offering and grain offering from our hands, nor shown us all these things or now told us this."

24 The woman gave birth to a boy and named him Samson. He grew and the LORD blessed him, 25 and the Spirit of the LORD began to stir him while he was in Mahaneh Dan, between Zorah and Eshtaol.

[a] 18 Or *is wonderful*

PRAYER: RENEWAL

EXAMINE me, O Lord, and try me; purify my mind and my heart; for Your loving-kindness is ever before me, and I walk in Your truth. (Psalm 26:2–3) . . . May I sow righteousness, reap the fruit of

unfailing love, and break up my fallow ground; for it is time to seek You, O Lord, until You come and rain righteousness on me. (Hosea 10:12)

***PAUSE** to add your own prayers for personal renewal.*

NT Luke 18:18-43

The Rich Ruler

[18]A certain ruler asked him, "Good
teacher, what must I do to inherit eternal
life?"
[19]"Why do you call me good?" Jesus answered. "No one is good—except God
alone. [20]You know the commandments:
'Do not commit adultery, do not murder,
do not steal, do not give false testimony,
honor your father and mother.'[a]"
[21]"All these I have kept since I was a
boy," he said.
[22]When Jesus heard this, he said to him,
"You still lack one thing. Sell everything
you have and give to the poor, and you
will have treasure in heaven. Then come,
follow me."
[23]When he heard this, he became very
sad, because he was a man of great wealth.
[24]Jesus looked at him and said, "How
hard it is for the rich to enter the kingdom
of God! [25]Indeed, it is easier for a camel
to go through the eye of a needle than for
a rich man to enter the kingdom of God."
[26]Those who heard this asked, "Who
then can be saved?"
[27]Jesus replied, "What is impossible
with men is possible with God."
[28]Peter said to him, "We have left all we
had to follow you!"
[29]"I tell you the truth," Jesus said to
them, "no one who has left home or wife
or brothers or parents or children for the
sake of the kingdom of God [30]will fail to
receive many times as much in this age
and, in the age to come, eternal life."

Jesus Again Predicts His Death

[31]Jesus took the Twelve aside and told
them, "We are going up to Jerusalem, and
everything that is written by the prophets
about the Son of Man will be fulfilled.
[32]He will be handed over to the Gentiles.
They will mock him, insult him, spit on
him, flog him and kill him. [33]On the third
day he will rise again."
[34]The disciples did not understand any
of this. Its meaning was hidden from
them, and they did not know what he was
talking about.

A Blind Beggar Receives His Sight

[35]As Jesus approached Jericho, a blind
man was sitting by the roadside begging.
[36]When he heard the crowd going by, he
asked what was happening. [37]They told
him, "Jesus of Nazareth is passing by."
[38]He called out, "Jesus, Son of David,
have mercy on me!"
[39]Those who led the way rebuked him
and told him to be quiet, but he shouted
all the more, "Son of David, have mercy
on me!"
[40]Jesus stopped and ordered the man to
be brought to him. When he came near,
Jesus asked him, [41]"What do you want me
to do for you?"
"Lord, I want to see," he replied.
[42]Jesus said to him, "Receive your sight;
your faith has healed you." [43]Immediate-
ly he received his sight and followed Jesus,
praising God. When all the people saw it,
they also praised God.

[a] *20* Exodus 20:12-16; Deut. 5:16-20

PRAYER: MY RELATIONSHIP TO OTHERS

THOSE who oppress the poor reproach You, our Maker, but whoever is kind to the needy honors You. (Proverbs 14:31) . . . Those who are kind to the poor lend to You, Lord, and You will reward them for what they have done. (Proverbs 19:17)

***PAUSE** to review your relationships with others and to commit them to the Lord.*

OT Judges 14:1–15:20 YEAR 1 DAY 221

Samson's Marriage

14 Samson went down to Timnah and
saw there a young Philistine woman.
2When he returned, he said to his father
and mother, "I have seen a Philistine
woman in Timnah; now get her for me as
my wife."
3His father and mother replied, "Isn't
there an acceptable woman among your
relatives or among all our people? Must
you go to the uncircumcised Philistines to
get a wife?"
But Samson said to his father, "Get her
for me. She's the right one for me." 4(His
parents did not know that this was from
the LORD, who was seeking an occasion to
confront the Philistines; for at that time
they were ruling over Israel.) 5Samson
went down to Timnah together with his
father and mother. As they approached
the vineyards of Timnah, suddenly a
young lion came roaring toward him.
6The Spirit of the LORD came upon him in
power so that he tore the lion apart with
his bare hands as he might have torn a
young goat. But he told neither his father
nor his mother what he had done. 7Then
he went down and talked with the
woman, and he liked her.
8Some time later, when he went back to
marry her, he turned aside to look at the
lion's carcass. In it was a swarm of bees
and some honey, 9which he scooped out
with his hands and ate as he went along.
When he rejoined his parents, he gave
them some, and they too ate it. But he did
not tell them that he had taken the honey from the lion's carcass.
10Now his father went down to see the
woman. And Samson made a feast there,
as was customary for bridegrooms.
11When he appeared, he was given thirty
companions.
12"Let me tell you a riddle," Samson
said to them. "If you can give me the answer within the seven days of the feast, I
will give you thirty linen garments and
thirty sets of clothes. 13If you can't tell me
the answer, you must give me thirty linen
garments and thirty sets of clothes."
"Tell us your riddle," they said. "Let's
hear it."
14He replied,

"Out of the eater, something to eat;
out of the strong, something sweet."

For three days they could not give the answer.
15On the fourth[a] day, they said to Samson's wife, "Coax your husband into explaining the riddle for us, or we will burn
you and your father's household to death.
Did you invite us here to rob us?"
16Then Samson's wife threw herself on
him, sobbing, "You hate me! You don't
really love me. You've given my people a
riddle, but you haven't told me the answer."
"I haven't even explained it to my father
or mother," he replied, "so why should I
explain it to you?" 17She cried the whole
seven days of the feast. So on the seventh
day he finally told her, because she continued to press him. She in turn explained
the riddle to her people.
18Before sunset on the seventh day the
men of the town said to him,

"What is sweeter than honey?
What is stronger than a lion?"

Samson said to them,

"If you had not plowed with my
heifer,
you would not have solved my
riddle."

19Then the Spirit of the LORD came
upon him in power. He went down to
Ashkelon, struck down thirty of their
men, stripped them of their belongings
and gave their clothes to those who had
explained the riddle. Burning with anger,
he went up to his father's house. 20And
Samson's wife was given to the friend who
had attended him at his wedding.

Samson's Vengeance on the Philistines

15 Later on, at the time of wheat harvest,
Samson took a young goat and went
to visit his wife. He said, "I'm going to my
wife's room." But her father would not let
him go in.
2"I was so sure you thoroughly hated
her," he said, "that I gave her to your

[a] 15 Some Septuagint manuscripts and Syriac; Hebrew *seventh*

friend. Isn't her younger sister more attractive? Take her instead."
3 Samson said to them, "This time I have
a right to get even with the Philistines; I
will really harm them." 4 So he went out
and caught three hundred foxes and tied
them tail to tail in pairs. He then fastened
a torch to every pair of tails, 5 lit the
torches and let the foxes loose in the
standing grain of the Philistines. He
burned up the shocks and standing grain,
together with the vineyards and olive
groves.
6 When the Philistines asked, "Who did
this?" they were told, "Samson, the Tim-
nite's son-in-law, because his wife was giv-
en to his friend."
So the Philistines went up and burned
her and her father to death. 7 Samson said
to them, "Since you've acted like this, I
won't stop until I get my revenge on
you." 8 He attacked them viciously and
slaughtered many of them. Then he went
down and stayed in a cave in the rock of
Etam.
9 The Philistines went up and camped in
Judah, spreading out near Lehi. 10 The men
of Judah asked, "Why have you come to
fight us?"
"We have come to take Samson prisoner," they answered, "to do to him as he
did to us."
11 Then three thousand men from Judah
went down to the cave in the rock of Etam
and said to Samson, "Don't you realize
that the Philistines are rulers over us?
What have you done to us?"
He answered, "I merely did to them
what they did to me."
12 They said to him, "We've come to tie
you up and hand you over to the Philistines."
Samson said, "Swear to me that you
won't kill me yourselves."
13 "Agreed," they answered. "We will
only tie you up and hand you over to
them. We will not kill you." So they
bound him with two new ropes and led
him up from the rock. 14 As he approached
Lehi, the Philistines came toward him
shouting. The Spirit of the LORD came
upon him in power. The ropes on his
arms became like charred flax, and the
bindings dropped from his hands. 15 Finding a fresh jawbone of a donkey, he
grabbed it and struck down a thousand
men.
16 Then Samson said,

"With a donkey's jawbone
I have made donkeys of them.[a]
With a donkey's jawbone
I have killed a thousand men."

17 When he finished speaking, he threw
away the jawbone; and the place was
called Ramath Lehi.[b]
18 Because he was very thirsty, he cried
out to the LORD, "You have given your servant this great victory. Must I now die of
thirst and fall into the hands of the uncircumcised?" 19 Then God opened up the
hollow place in Lehi, and water came out
of it. When Samson drank, his strength returned and he revived. So the spring was
called En Hakkore,[c] and it is still there in
Lehi.
20 Samson led[d] Israel for twenty years in
the days of the Philistines.

[a] 16 Or *made a heap or two;* the Hebrew for *donkey* sounds like the Hebrew for *heap.* [b] 17 *Ramath Lehi* means *jawbone hill.* [c] 19 *En Hakkore* means *caller's spring.* [d] 20 Traditionally *judged*

PRAYER: PETITION

O LORD, hear my prayer; listen to the voice of my supplications. In the day of my trouble I will call upon You, for You will answer me. You are great and do wondrous deeds; You alone are God. (Psalm 86:6–7, 10)

PAUSE *here to petition God for growth in love and compassion toward others. Offer prayers for your loved ones, for those who do not know Jesus and for those in need. Offer prayers regarding your activities for this day and any special concerns you may have.*

NT Luke 19:1-27

Zacchaeus the Tax Collector

19 Jesus entered Jericho and was passing
through. 2A man was there by the
name of Zacchaeus; he was a chief tax collector and was wealthy. 3He wanted to see
who Jesus was, but being a short man he
could not, because of the crowd. 4So he
ran ahead and climbed a sycamore-fig tree
to see him, since Jesus was coming that
way.
5When Jesus reached the spot, he
looked up and said to him, "Zacchaeus,
come down immediately. I must stay at
your house today." 6So he came down at
once and welcomed him gladly.
7All the people saw this and began to
mutter, "He has gone to be the guest of a
'sinner.' "
8But Zacchaeus stood up and said to the
Lord, "Look, Lord! Here and now I give
half of my possessions to the poor, and if
I have cheated anybody out of anything, I
will pay back four times the amount."
9Jesus said to him, "Today salvation has
come to this house, because this man,
too, is a son of Abraham. 10For the Son of
Man came to seek and to save what was
lost."

The Parable of the Ten Minas

11While they were listening to this, he
went on to tell them a parable, because he
was near Jerusalem and the people
thought that the kingdom of God was going to appear at once. 12He said: "A man
of noble birth went to a distant country
to have himself appointed king and then
to return. 13So he called ten of his servants
and gave them ten minas.[a] 'Put this money to work,' he said, 'until I come back.'
14"But his subjects hated him and sent
a delegation after him to say, 'We don't
want this man to be our king.'
15"He was made king, however, and returned home. Then he sent for the servants
to whom he had given the money, in order
to find out what they had gained with it.
16"The first one came and said, 'Sir, your
mina has earned ten more.'
17" 'Well done, my good servant!' his
master replied. 'Because you have been
trustworthy in a very small matter, take
charge of ten cities.'
18"The second came and said, 'Sir, your
mina has earned five more.'
19"His master answered, 'You take
charge of five cities.'
20"Then another servant came and said,
'Sir, here is your mina; I have kept it laid
away in a piece of cloth. 21I was afraid of
you, because you are a hard man. You take
out what you did not put in and reap
what you did not sow.'
22"His master replied, 'I will judge you
by your own words, you wicked servant!
You knew, did you, that I am a hard man,
taking out what I did not put in, and reaping what I did not sow? 23Why then didn't
you put my money on deposit, so that
when I came back, I could have collected
it with interest?'
24"Then he said to those standing by,
'Take his mina away from him and give it
to the one who has ten minas.'
25" 'Sir,' they said, 'he already has ten!'
26"He replied, 'I tell you that to everyone who has, more will be given, but as
for the one who has nothing, even what
he has will be taken away. 27But those enemies of mine who did not want me to be
king over them—bring them here and kill
them in front of me.' "

[a] *13* A mina was about three months' wages.

PRAYER: THE ATTRIBUTES OF GOD

YOUR law, O Lord, is perfect, restoring the soul. Your testimony, O Lord, is sure, making wise the simple. Your precepts, O Lord, are right, rejoicing the heart. Your commandment, O Lord, is pure, enlightening the eyes. The fear of You, O Lord, is clean, enduring forever. Your judgments, O Lord, are true and altogether righteous. They are more desirable than gold, than much pure gold. They are sweeter than honey, than

honey from the comb. Moreover, by them is Your servant warned—in keeping them there is great reward. (Psalm 19:7–11) . . . The sum of Your words is truth, and all of Your righteous judgments are eternal. (Psalm 119:160)

***PAUSE** to reflect on these affirmations about the person, powers and perfection of God.*

YEAR 1
DAY 222

OT Judges 16:1-31

Samson and Delilah

16 One day Samson went to Gaza, where
he saw a prostitute. He went in to
spend the night with her. [2]The people of
Gaza were told, "Samson is here!" So they
surrounded the place and lay in wait for
him all night at the city gate. They made
no move during the night, saying, "At
dawn we'll kill him."
[3]But Samson lay there only until the
middle of the night. Then he got up and
took hold of the doors of the city gate, together with the two posts, and tore them
loose, bar and all. He lifted them to his
shoulders and carried them to the top of
the hill that faces Hebron.
[4]Some time later, he fell in love with a
woman in the Valley of Sorek whose
name was Delilah. [5]The rulers of the Philistines went to her and said, "See if you
can lure him into showing you the secret
of his great strength and how we can overpower him so we may tie him up and subdue him. Each one of us will give you
eleven hundred shekels[a] of silver."
[6]So Delilah said to Samson, "Tell me
the secret of your great strength and how
you can be tied up and subdued."
[7]Samson answered her, "If anyone ties
me with seven fresh thongs[b] that have not
been dried, I'll become as weak as any
other man."
[8]Then the rulers of the Philistines
brought her seven fresh thongs that had
not been dried, and she tied him with
them. [9]With men hidden in the room, she
called to him, "Samson, the Philistines
are upon you!" But he snapped the
thongs as easily as a piece of string snaps
when it comes close to a flame. So the secret of his strength was not discovered.
[10]Then Delilah said to Samson, "You
have made a fool of me; you lied to me.
Come now, tell me how you can be tied."
[11]He said, "If anyone ties me securely
with new ropes that have never been used,
I'll become as weak as any other man."
[12]So Delilah took new ropes and tied
him with them. Then, with men hidden
in the room, she called to him, "Samson,
the Philistines are upon you!" But he
snapped the ropes off his arms as if they
were threads.
[13]Delilah then said to Samson, "Until
now, you have been making a fool of me
and lying to me. Tell me how you can be
tied."
He replied, "If you weave the seven
braids of my head into the fabric ⌊on the
loom⌋ and tighten it with the pin, I'll become as weak as any other man." So while
he was sleeping, Delilah took the seven
braids of his head, wove them into the
fabric [14]and[c] tightened it with the pin.
Again she called to him, "Samson, the
Philistines are upon you!" He awoke from
his sleep and pulled up the pin and the
loom, with the fabric.
[15]Then she said to him, "How can you
say, 'I love you,' when you won't confide
in me? This is the third time you have
made a fool of me and haven't told me
the secret of your great strength." [16]With
such nagging she prodded him day after
day until he was tired to death.
[17]So he told her everything. "No razor
has ever been used on my head," he said,
"because I have been a Nazirite set apart
to God since birth. If my head were
shaved, my strength would leave me, and

[a] 5 That is, about 28 pounds (about 13 kilograms)
[b] 7 Or *bowstrings*; also in verses 8 and 9
[c] 13,14 Some Septuagint manuscripts; Hebrew *"⌊I can⌋ if you weave the seven braids of my head into the fabric ⌊on the loom⌋." [14]So she*

I would become as weak as any other
man."
18When Delilah saw that he had told
her everything, she sent word to the rulers
of the Philistines, "Come back once more;
he has told me everything." So the rulers
of the Philistines returned with the silver
in their hands. 19Having put him to sleep
on her lap, she called a man to shave off
the seven braids of his hair, and so began
to subdue him.[d] And his strength left him.
20Then she called, "Samson, the Philistines are upon you!"

He awoke from his sleep and thought,
"I'll go out as before and shake myself
free." But he did not know that the LORD
had left him.
21Then the Philistines seized him,
gouged out his eyes and took him down
to Gaza. Binding him with bronze shackles, they set him to grinding in the prison.
22But the hair on his head began to grow
again after it had been shaved.

The Death of Samson

23Now the rulers of the Philistines assembled to offer a great sacrifice to Dagon
their god and to celebrate, saying, "Our
god has delivered Samson, our enemy,
into our hands."
24When the people saw him, they
praised their god, saying,

"Our god has delivered our enemy
into our hands,
the one who laid waste our land
and multiplied our slain."

25While they were in high spirits, they
shouted, "Bring out Samson to entertain
us." So they called Samson out of the
prison, and he performed for them.

When they stood him among the pillars, 26Samson said to the servant who
held his hand, "Put me where I can feel
the pillars that support the temple, so that
I may lean against them." 27Now the temple was crowded with men and women;
all the rulers of the Philistines were there,
and on the roof were about three thousand men and women watching Samson
perform. 28Then Samson prayed to the
LORD, "O Sovereign LORD, remember me.
O God, please strengthen me just once
more, and let me with one blow get revenge on the Philistines for my two eyes."
29Then Samson reached toward the two
central pillars on which the temple stood.
Bracing himself against them, his right
hand on the one and his left hand on the
other, 30Samson said, "Let me die with the
Philistines!" Then he pushed with all his
might, and down came the temple on the
rulers and all the people in it. Thus he
killed many more when he died than
while he lived.
31Then his brothers and his father's
whole family went down to get him. They
brought him back and buried him between Zorah and Eshtaol in the tomb of
Manoah his father. He had led[e] Israel
twenty years.

[d] 19 Hebrew; some Septuagint manuscripts *and he began to weaken* [e] 31 Traditionally *judged*

PRAYER: INTERCESSION

MAY I sanctify You, O Christ, as Lord in my heart; may I always be ready to give an answer to everyone who asks me, to give the reason for the hope that is in me, but with gentleness and respect. (1 Peter 3:15)

***TAKE** a few moments to intercede on behalf of friends, relatives, neighbors and coworkers who do not yet know salvation in Jesus Christ.*

NT Luke 19:28–20:8

The Triumphal Entry

28After Jesus had said this, he went on
ahead, going up to Jerusalem. 29As he approached Bethphage and Bethany at the
hill called the Mount of Olives, he sent
two of his disciples, saying to them, 30"Go
to the village ahead of you, and as you enter it, you will find a colt tied there, which
no one has ever ridden. Untie it and bring
it here. 31If anyone asks you, 'Why are you
untying it?' tell him, 'The Lord needs it.' "

32 Those who were sent ahead went and
found it just as he had told them. 33 As
they were untying the colt, its owners
asked them, "Why are you untying the
colt?"
34 They replied, "The Lord needs it."
35 They brought it to Jesus, threw their
cloaks on the colt and put Jesus on it. 36 As
he went along, people spread their cloaks
on the road.
37 When he came near the place where
the road goes down the Mount of Olives,
the whole crowd of disciples began joyfully to praise God in loud voices for all
the miracles they had seen:

38 "Blessed is the king who comes in the
name of the Lord!"[a]

"Peace in heaven and glory in the
highest!"

39 Some of the Pharisees in the crowd
said to Jesus, "Teacher, rebuke your disciples!"
40 "I tell you," he replied, "if they keep
quiet, the stones will cry out."
41 As he approached Jerusalem and saw
the city, he wept over it 42 and said, "If you,
even you, had only known on this day
what would bring you peace—but now it
is hidden from your eyes. 43 The days will
come upon you when your enemies will
build an embankment against you and
encircle you and hem you in on every
side. 44 They will dash you to the ground,
you and the children within your walls.
They will not leave one stone on another,
because you did not recognize the time of
God's coming to you."

Jesus at the Temple

45 Then he entered the temple area and
began driving out those who were selling.
46 "It is written," he said to them, " 'My
house will be a house of prayer'[b]; but you
have made it 'a den of robbers.'[c]"
47 Every day he was teaching at the temple. But the chief priests, the teachers of
the law and the leaders among the people
were trying to kill him. 48 Yet they could
not find any way to do it, because all the
people hung on his words.

The Authority of Jesus Questioned

20 One day as he was teaching the people in the temple courts and preaching the gospel, the chief priests and the
teachers of the law, together with the elders, came up to him. 2 "Tell us by what
authority you are doing these things,"
they said. "Who gave you this authority?"
3 He replied, "I will also ask you a question. Tell me, 4 John's baptism—was it
from heaven, or from men?"
5 They discussed it among themselves
and said, "If we say, 'From heaven,' he will
ask, 'Why didn't you believe him?' 6 But if
we say, 'From men,' all the people will
stone us, because they are persuaded that
John was a prophet."
7 So they answered, "We don't know
where it was from."
8 Jesus said, "Neither will I tell you by
what authority I am doing these things."

[a] *38* Psalm 118:26 [b] *46* Isaiah 56:7
[c] *46* Jer. 7:11

PRAYER: THE WORKS OF GOD

WE know, O Lord, that You are God. It is You who made us. We are Your people and the sheep of Your pasture. (Psalm 100:3) . . . O God, You have made everything beautiful in its time. You have also set eternity in our hearts; yet we cannot fathom what You have done from beginning to end. (Ecclesiastes 3:11)

TAKE a moment to consider the greatness of God's wonderful works.

YEAR 1
DAY 223

OT **Judges 17:1–18:31**

Micah's Idols

17 Now a man named Micah from the hill country of Ephraim 2said to his mother, "The eleven hundred shekels[a] of silver that were taken from you and about which I heard you utter a curse—I have that silver with me; I took it."

Then his mother said, "The LORD bless you, my son!"

3When he returned the eleven hundred shekels of silver to his mother, she said, "I solemnly consecrate my silver to the LORD for my son to make a carved image and a cast idol. I will give it back to you."

4So he returned the silver to his mother, and she took two hundred shekels[b] of silver and gave them to a silversmith, who made them into the image and the idol. And they were put in Micah's house.

5Now this man Micah had a shrine, and he made an ephod and some idols and installed one of his sons as his priest. 6In those days Israel had no king; everyone did as he saw fit.

7A young Levite from Bethlehem in Judah, who had been living within the clan of Judah, 8left that town in search of some other place to stay. On his way[c] he came to Micah's house in the hill country of Ephraim.

9Micah asked him, "Where are you from?"

"I'm a Levite from Bethlehem in Judah," he said, "and I'm looking for a place to stay."

10Then Micah said to him, "Live with me and be my father and priest, and I'll give you ten shekels[d] of silver a year, your clothes and your food." 11So the Levite agreed to live with him, and the young man was to him like one of his sons. 12Then Micah installed the Levite, and the young man became his priest and lived in his house. 13And Micah said, "Now I know that the LORD will be good to me, since this Levite has become my priest."

Danites Settle in Laish

18 In those days Israel had no king. And in those days the tribe of the Danites was seeking a place of their own where they might settle, because they had not yet come into an inheritance among the tribes of Israel. 2So the Danites sent five warriors from Zorah and Eshtaol to spy out the land and explore it. These men represented all their clans. They told them, "Go, explore the land."

The men entered the hill country of Ephraim and came to the house of Micah, where they spent the night. 3When they were near Micah's house, they recognized the voice of the young Levite; so they turned in there and asked him, "Who brought you here? What are you doing in this place? Why are you here?"

4He told them what Micah had done for him, and said, "He has hired me and I am his priest."

5Then they said to him, "Please inquire of God to learn whether our journey will be successful."

6The priest answered them, "Go in peace. Your journey has the LORD's approval."

7So the five men left and came to Laish, where they saw that the people were living in safety, like the Sidonians, unsuspecting and secure. And since their land lacked nothing, they were prosperous.[e] Also, they lived a long way from the Sidonians and had no relationship with anyone else.[f]

8When they returned to Zorah and Eshtaol, their brothers asked them, "How did you find things?"

9They answered, "Come on, let's attack them! We have seen that the land is very good. Aren't you going to do something? Don't hesitate to go there and take it over. 10When you get there, you will find an unsuspecting people and a spacious land that God has put into your hands, a land that lacks nothing whatever."

11Then six hundred men from the clan of the Danites, armed for battle, set out from Zorah and Eshtaol. 12On their way they set up camp near Kiriath Jearim in Judah. This is why the place west of Kiriath

[a] 2 That is, about 28 pounds (about 13 kilograms)
[b] 4 That is, about 5 pounds (about 2.3 kilograms)
[c] 8 Or *To carry on his profession*
[d] 10 That is, about 4 ounces (about 110 grams)
[e] 7 The meaning of the Hebrew for this clause is uncertain.
[f] 7 Hebrew; some Septuagint manuscripts *with the Arameans*

Jearim is called Mahaneh Dan[g] to this day.
13 From there they went on to the hill
country of Ephraim and came to Micah's
house.
14 Then the five men who had spied out
the land of Laish said to their brothers,
"Do you know that one of these houses
has an ephod, other household gods, a
carved image and a cast idol? Now you
know what to do." 15 So they turned in
there and went to the house of the young
Levite at Micah's place and greeted him.
16 The six hundred Danites, armed for battle, stood at the entrance to the gate. 17 The
five men who had spied out the land went
inside and took the carved image, the
ephod, the other household gods and the
cast idol while the priest and the six hundred armed men stood at the entrance to
the gate.
18 When these men went into Micah's
house and took the carved image, the
ephod, the other household gods and the
cast idol, the priest said to them, "What
are you doing?"
19 They answered him, "Be quiet! Don't
say a word. Come with us, and be our father and priest. Isn't it better that you
serve a tribe and clan in Israel as priest
rather than just one man's household?"
20 Then the priest was glad. He took the
ephod, the other household gods and the
carved image and went along with the
people. 21 Putting their little children, their
livestock and their possessions in front of
them, they turned away and left.
22 When they had gone some distance
from Micah's house, the men who lived
near Micah were called together and overtook the Danites. 23 As they shouted after
them, the Danites turned and said to Micah, "What's the matter with you that you
called out your men to fight?"
24 He replied, "You took the gods I
made, and my priest, and went away.
What else do I have? How can you ask,
'What's the matter with you?' "
25 The Danites answered, "Don't argue
with us, or some hot-tempered men will
attack you, and you and your family will
lose your lives." 26 So the Danites went
their way, and Micah, seeing that they
were too strong for him, turned around
and went back home.
27 Then they took what Micah had
made, and his priest, and went on to Laish, against a peaceful and unsuspecting
people. They attacked them with the
sword and burned down their city. 28 There
was no one to rescue them because they
lived a long way from Sidon and had no
relationship with anyone else. The city
was in a valley near Beth Rehob.
The Danites rebuilt the city and settled
there. 29 They named it Dan after their
forefather Dan, who was born to Israel—
though the city used to be called Laish.
30 There the Danites set up for themselves
the idols, and Jonathan son of Gershom,
the son of Moses,[h] and his sons were
priests for the tribe of Dan until the time
of the captivity of the land. 31 They continued to use the idols Micah had made,
all the time the house of God was in Shiloh.

[g] 12 *Mahaneh Dan* means *Dan's camp.* [h] 30 An ancient Hebrew scribal tradition, some Septuagint manuscripts and Vulgate; Masoretic Text *Manasseh*

PRAYER: AFFIRMATION

Sin shall not be my master, because I am not under law, but under grace. I have been set free from sin and have become a slave of righteousness. (Romans 6:14, 18) . . . Jesus, You have taught us that those who have Your commandments and obey them are the ones who love You; and those who love You will be loved by Your Father, and You will love them and manifest Yourself to them. (John 14:21)

***PAUSE** to reflect on these Biblical affirmations.*

NT Luke 20:9–47

The Parable of the Tenants

9He went on to tell the people this parable: "A man planted a vineyard, rented it
to some farmers and went away for a long
time. 10At harvest time he sent a servant to
the tenants so they would give him some
of the fruit of the vineyard. But the tenants beat him and sent him away empty-
handed. 11He sent another servant, but
that one also they beat and treated shamefully and sent away empty-handed. 12He
sent still a third, and they wounded him
and threw him out.

13"Then the owner of the vineyard said,
'What shall I do? I will send my son,
whom I love; perhaps they will respect
him.'

14"But when the tenants saw him, they
talked the matter over. 'This is the heir,'
they said. 'Let's kill him, and the inheritance will be ours.' 15So they threw him
out of the vineyard and killed him.

"What then will the owner of the vineyard do to them? 16He will come and kill
those tenants and give the vineyard to
others."

When the people heard this, they said,
"May this never be!"

17Jesus looked directly at them and
asked, "Then what is the meaning of that
which is written:

" 'The stone the builders rejected
has become the capstone'[a][b]?

18Everyone who falls on that stone will be
broken to pieces, but he on whom it falls
will be crushed."

19The teachers of the law and the chief
priests looked for a way to arrest him immediately, because they knew he had spoken this parable against them. But they
were afraid of the people.

Paying Taxes to Caesar

20Keeping a close watch on him, they
sent spies, who pretended to be honest.
They hoped to catch Jesus in something
he said so that they might hand him over
to the power and authority of the governor. 21So the spies questioned him:
"Teacher, we know that you speak and
teach what is right, and that you do not
show partiality but teach the way of God
in accordance with the truth. 22Is it right
for us to pay taxes to Caesar or not?"

23He saw through their duplicity and
said to them, 24"Show me a denarius.
Whose portrait and inscription are on it?"

25"Caesar's," they replied.

He said to them, "Then give to Caesar
what is Caesar's, and to God what is
God's."

26They were unable to trap him in what
he had said there in public. And astonished by his answer, they became silent.

The Resurrection and Marriage

27Some of the Sadducees, who say there
is no resurrection, came to Jesus with a
question. 28"Teacher," they said, "Moses
wrote for us that if a man's brother dies
and leaves a wife but no children, the man
must marry the widow and have children
for his brother. 29Now there were seven
brothers. The first one married a woman
and died childless. 30The second 31and
then the third married her, and in the
same way the seven died, leaving no children. 32Finally, the woman died too.
33Now then, at the resurrection whose
wife will she be, since the seven were married to her?"

34Jesus replied, "The people of this age
marry and are given in marriage. 35But
those who are considered worthy of taking part in that age and in the resurrection
from the dead will neither marry nor be
given in marriage, 36and they can no
longer die; for they are like the angels.
They are God's children, since they are
children of the resurrection. 37But in the
account of the bush, even Moses showed
that the dead rise, for he calls the Lord 'the
God of Abraham, and the God of Isaac,
and the God of Jacob.'[c] 38He is not the
God of the dead, but of the living, for to
him all are alive."

39Some of the teachers of the law responded, "Well said, teacher!" 40And no
one dared to ask him any more questions.

Whose Son Is the Christ?

41Then Jesus said to them, "How is it
that they say the Christ[d] is the Son of Da-

[a] 17 Or *cornerstone* [b] 17 Psalm 118:22
[c] 37 Exodus 3:6 [d] 41 Or *Messiah*

vid? 42 David himself declares in the Book of Psalms:

" 'The Lord said to my Lord:
"Sit at my right hand
43 until I make your enemies
a footstool for your feet." '[e]

44 David calls him 'Lord.' How then can he be his son?"

45 While all the people were listening, Jesus said to his disciples, 46 "Beware of the teachers of the law. They like to walk around in flowing robes and love to be greeted in the marketplaces and have the most important seats in the synagogues and the places of honor at banquets. 47 They devour widows' houses and for a show make lengthy prayers. Such men will be punished most severely."

[e] 43 Psalm 110:1

PRAYER: MY RELATIONSHIP TO GOD

IT is because of You, O God, that I am in Christ Jesus, who has become for me wisdom from You—that is, my righteousness, sanctification and redemption. (1 Corinthians 1:30) . . . You, O God, raised me up with Christ Jesus and seated me with You in the heavenly realms in Him, in order that, in the coming ages, You might show the surpassing riches of Your grace in kindness toward me in Christ Jesus. (Ephesians 2:6–7)

PAUSE *to thank God for the relationship that you enjoy with Him in Jesus Christ.*

YEAR 1 DAY 224

OT Psalms 42–43

Psalm 42[a]

For the director of music. A *maskil*[b] of the Sons of Korah.

1 As the deer pants for streams of water,
so my soul pants for you, O God.
2 My soul thirsts for God, for the living God.
When can I go and meet with God?
3 My tears have been my food
day and night,
while men say to me all day long,
"Where is your God?"
4 These things I remember
as I pour out my soul:
how I used to go with the multitude,
leading the procession to the house of God,
with shouts of joy and thanksgiving
among the festive throng.

5 Why are you downcast, O my soul?
Why so disturbed within me?
Put your hope in God,
for I will yet praise him,
my Savior and 6 my God.
My[c] soul is downcast within me;
therefore I will remember you
from the land of the Jordan,
the heights of Hermon—from Mount Mizar.
7 Deep calls to deep
in the roar of your waterfalls;
all your waves and breakers
have swept over me.

8 By day the LORD directs his love,
at night his song is with me—
a prayer to the God of my life.

9 I say to God my Rock,
"Why have you forgotten me?
Why must I go about mourning,
oppressed by the enemy?"
10 My bones suffer mortal agony
as my foes taunt me,
saying to me all day long,
"Where is your God?"

[a] In many Hebrew manuscripts Psalms 42 and 43 constitute one psalm. [b] Title: Probably a literary or musical term [c] *5,6* A few Hebrew manuscripts, Septuagint and Syriac; most Hebrew manuscripts *praise him for his saving help. / 6 O my God, my*

[11] Why are you downcast, O my soul?
Why so disturbed within me?
Put your hope in God,
for I will yet praise him,
my Savior and my God.

Psalm 43[d]

[1] Vindicate me, O God,
and plead my cause against an
ungodly nation;
rescue me from deceitful and
wicked men.
[2] You are God my stronghold.
Why have you rejected me?
Why must I go about mourning,
oppressed by the enemy?
[3] Send forth your light and your truth,
let them guide me;
let them bring me to your holy
mountain,
to the place where you dwell.
[4] Then will I go to the altar of God,
to God, my joy and my delight.
I will praise you with the harp,
O God, my God.

[5] Why are you downcast, O my soul?
Why so disturbed within me?
Put your hope in God,
for I will yet praise him,
my Savior and my God.

[d] In many Hebrew manuscripts Psalms 42 and 43 constitute one psalm.

PRAYER: THANKSGIVING

LORD, You said, "Let Us make people in Our image, in Our likeness, and let them rule over the fish of the sea and the birds of the air and over the livestock and over all the earth and over all the creatures that creep on the earth." So You created people in Your own image; male and female You created them. Then You blessed them and said to them, "Be fruitful and multiply; fill the earth and subdue it; and rule over the fish of the sea and the birds of the air and over every living creature that moves on the earth." Then You said, "Behold, I have given you every seed-bearing plant on the face of the whole earth and every tree that has fruit with seed in it; they will be yours for food. And to all the beasts of the earth and all the birds of the air and all the creatures that move on the ground, in which there is life, I have given every green plant for food"; and it was so. You saw all that You had made, and it was very good. (Genesis 1:26–31)

***PAUSE** to offer your own expressions of thanksgiving.*

NT Luke 21:1–38

The Widow's Offering

21 As he looked up, Jesus saw the rich
putting their gifts into the temple treasury. [2] He also saw a poor widow put in
two very small copper coins.[a] [3] "I tell you
the truth," he said, "this poor widow has
put in more than all the others. [4] All these
people gave their gifts out of their wealth;
but she out of her poverty put in all she
had to live on."

Signs of the End of the Age

[5] Some of his disciples were remarking
about how the temple was adorned with
beautiful stones and with gifts dedicated
to God. But Jesus said, [6] "As for what you
see here, the time will come when not one
stone will be left on another; every one of
them will be thrown down."
[7] "Teacher," they asked, "when will these
things happen? And what will be the sign
that they are about to take place?"
[8] He replied: "Watch out that you are
not deceived. For many will come in my
name, claiming, 'I am he,' and, 'The time

[a] 2 Greek *two lepta*

is near.' Do not follow them. 9 When you hear of wars and revolutions, do not be frightened. These things must happen first, but the end will not come right away."

10 Then he said to them: "Nation will rise against nation, and kingdom against kingdom. 11 There will be great earthquakes, famines and pestilences in various places, and fearful events and great signs from heaven.

12 "But before all this, they will lay hands on you and persecute you. They will deliver you to synagogues and prisons, and you will be brought before kings and governors, and all on account of my name. 13 This will result in your being witnesses to them. 14 But make up your mind not to worry beforehand how you will defend yourselves. 15 For I will give you words and wisdom that none of your adversaries will be able to resist or contradict. 16 You will be betrayed even by parents, brothers, relatives and friends, and they will put some of you to death. 17 All men will hate you because of me. 18 But not a hair of your head will perish. 19 By standing firm you will gain life.

20 "When you see Jerusalem being surrounded by armies, you will know that its desolation is near. 21 Then let those who are in Judea flee to the mountains, let those in the city get out, and let those in the country not enter the city. 22 For this is the time of punishment in fulfillment of all that has been written. 23 How dreadful it will be in those days for pregnant women and nursing mothers! There will be great distress in the land and wrath against this people. 24 They will fall by the sword and will be taken as prisoners to all the nations. Jerusalem will be trampled on by the Gentiles until the times of the Gentiles are fulfilled.

25 "There will be signs in the sun, moon and stars. On the earth, nations will be in anguish and perplexity at the roaring and tossing of the sea. 26 Men will faint from terror, apprehensive of what is coming on the world, for the heavenly bodies will be shaken. 27 At that time they will see the Son of Man coming in a cloud with power and great glory. 28 When these things begin to take place, stand up and lift up your heads, because your redemption is drawing near."

29 He told them this parable: "Look at the fig tree and all the trees. 30 When they sprout leaves, you can see for yourselves and know that summer is near. 31 Even so, when you see these things happening, you know that the kingdom of God is near.

32 "I tell you the truth, this generation[b] will certainly not pass away until all these things have happened. 33 Heaven and earth will pass away, but my words will never pass away.

34 "Be careful, or your hearts will be weighed down with dissipation, drunkenness and the anxieties of life, and that day will close on you unexpectedly like a trap. 35 For it will come upon all those who live on the face of the whole earth. 36 Be always on the watch, and pray that you may be able to escape all that is about to happen, and that you may be able to stand before the Son of Man."

37 Each day Jesus was teaching at the temple, and each evening he went out to spend the night on the hill called the Mount of Olives, 38 and all the people came early in the morning to hear him at the temple.

[b] 32 Or *race*

PRAYER: THE CHARACTER I WANT TO CULTIVATE

RECKLESS words pierce like a sword, but the tongue of the wise brings healing. (Proverbs 12:18) . . . Do you see those who are hasty in their words? There is more hope for fools than for them. (Proverbs 29:20)

TAKE *a moment to ask the Lord for the grace to grow in godly character.*

OT **Judges 19:1-30** YEAR 1 DAY 225

A Levite and His Concubine

19 In those days Israel had no king. Now a Levite who lived in a remote area in the hill country of Ephraim took a concubine from Bethlehem in Judah. 2But she was unfaithful to him. She left him and went back to her father's house in Bethlehem, Judah. After she had been there four months, 3her husband went to her to persuade her to return. He had with him his servant and two donkeys. She took him into her father's house, and when her father saw him, he gladly welcomed him. 4His father-in-law, the girl's father, prevailed upon him to stay; so he remained with him three days, eating and drinking, and sleeping there.

5On the fourth day they got up early and he prepared to leave, but the girl's father said to his son-in-law, "Refresh yourself with something to eat; then you can go." 6So the two of them sat down to eat and drink together. Afterward the girl's father said, "Please stay tonight and enjoy yourself." 7And when the man got up to go, his father-in-law persuaded him, so he stayed there that night. 8On the morning of the fifth day, when he rose to go, the girl's father said, "Refresh yourself. Wait till afternoon!" So the two of them ate together.

9Then when the man, with his concubine and his servant, got up to leave, his father-in-law, the girl's father, said, "Now look, it's almost evening. Spend the night here; the day is nearly over. Stay and enjoy yourself. Early tomorrow morning you can get up and be on your way home." 10But, unwilling to stay another night, the man left and went toward Jebus (that is, Jerusalem), with his two saddled donkeys and his concubine.

11When they were near Jebus and the day was almost gone, the servant said to his master, "Come, let's stop at this city of the Jebusites and spend the night."

12His master replied, "No. We won't go into an alien city, whose people are not Israelites. We will go on to Gibeah." 13He added, "Come, let's try to reach Gibeah or Ramah and spend the night in one of those places." 14So they went on, and the sun set as they neared Gibeah in Benjamin. 15There they stopped to spend the night. They went and sat in the city square, but no one took them into his home for the night.

16That evening an old man from the hill country of Ephraim, who was living in Gibeah (the men of the place were Benjamites), came in from his work in the fields. 17When he looked and saw the traveler in the city square, the old man asked, "Where are you going? Where did you come from?"

18He answered, "We are on our way from Bethlehem in Judah to a remote area in the hill country of Ephraim where I live. I have been to Bethlehem in Judah and now I am going to the house of the LORD. No one has taken me into his house. 19We have both straw and fodder for our donkeys and bread and wine for ourselves your servants—me, your maidservant, and the young man with us. We don't need anything."

20"You are welcome at my house," the old man said. "Let me supply whatever you need. Only don't spend the night in the square." 21So he took him into his house and fed his donkeys. After they had washed their feet, they had something to eat and drink.

22While they were enjoying themselves, some of the wicked men of the city surrounded the house. Pounding on the door, they shouted to the old man who owned the house, "Bring out the man who came to your house so we can have sex with him."

23The owner of the house went outside and said to them, "No, my friends, don't be so vile. Since this man is my guest, don't do this disgraceful thing. 24Look, here is my virgin daughter, and his concubine. I will bring them out to you now, and you can use them and do to them whatever you wish. But to this man, don't do such a disgraceful thing."

25But the men would not listen to him. So the man took his concubine and sent her outside to them, and they raped her and abused her throughout the night, and at dawn they let her go. 26At daybreak the woman went back to the house where her master was staying, fell down at the door and lay there until daylight.

[27]When her master got up in the morning and opened the door of the house and stepped out to continue on his way, there lay his concubine, fallen in the doorway of the house, with her hands on the threshold. [28]He said to her, "Get up; let's go." But there was no answer. Then the man put her on his donkey and set out for home.

[29]When he reached home, he took a knife and cut up his concubine, limb by limb, into twelve parts and sent them into all the areas of Israel. [30]Everyone who saw it said, "Such a thing has never been seen or done, not since the day the Israelites came up out of Egypt. Think about it! Consider it! Tell us what to do!"

PRAYER: ADORATION

AS the deer pants for the water brooks, so my soul pants for You, O God. My soul thirsts for You, the living God. When shall I come and appear before You? (Psalm 42:1–2) . . . My soul yearns for You in the night; my spirit within me diligently seeks You. When Your judgments come upon the earth, the inhabitants of the world learn righteousness. (Isaiah 26:9)

__PAUSE__ to express your thoughts of praise and worship.

NT Luke 22:1–38

Judas Agrees to Betray Jesus

22 Now the Feast of Unleavened Bread,
called the Passover, was approaching,
[2]and the chief priests and the teachers of
the law were looking for some way to get
rid of Jesus, for they were afraid of the
people. [3]Then Satan entered Judas, called
Iscariot, one of the Twelve. [4]And Judas
went to the chief priests and the officers
of the temple guard and discussed with
them how he might betray Jesus. [5]They
were delighted and agreed to give him
money. [6]He consented, and watched for
an opportunity to hand Jesus over to
them when no crowd was present.

The Last Supper

[7]Then came the day of Unleavened
Bread on which the Passover lamb had to
be sacrificed. [8]Jesus sent Peter and John,
saying, "Go and make preparations for us
to eat the Passover."

[9]"Where do you want us to prepare for
it?" they asked.

[10]He replied, "As you enter the city, a man
carrying a jar of water will meet you. Follow him to the house that he enters, [11]and
say to the owner of the house, 'The Teacher
asks: Where is the guest room, where I may
eat the Passover with my disciples?' [12]He
will show you a large upper room, all furnished. Make preparations there."

[13]They left and found things just as
Jesus had told them. So they prepared the
Passover.

[14]When the hour came, Jesus and his
apostles reclined at the table. [15]And he
said to them, "I have eagerly desired to eat
this Passover with you before I suffer.
[16]For I tell you, I will not eat it again until it finds fulfillment in the kingdom of
God."

[17]After taking the cup, he gave thanks
and said, "Take this and divide it among
you. [18]For I tell you I will not drink again
of the fruit of the vine until the kingdom
of God comes."

[19]And he took bread, gave thanks and
broke it, and gave it to them, saying, "This
is my body given for you; do this in remembrance of me."

[20]In the same way, after the supper he
took the cup, saying, "This cup is the new
covenant in my blood, which is poured
out for you. [21]But the hand of him who is
going to betray me is with mine on the
table. [22]The Son of Man will go as it has
been decreed, but woe to that man who
betrays him." [23]They began to question
among themselves which of them it might
be who would do this.

[24]Also a dispute arose among them as to
which of them was considered to be greatest. [25]Jesus said to them, "The kings of the
Gentiles lord it over them; and those who

exercise authority over them call themselves Benefactors. 26 But you are not to be like that. Instead, the greatest among you should be like the youngest, and the one who rules like the one who serves. 27 For who is greater, the one who is at the table or the one who serves? Is it not the one who is at the table? But I am among you as one who serves. 28 You are those who have stood by me in my trials. 29 And I confer on you a kingdom, just as my Father conferred one on me, 30 so that you may eat and drink at my table in my kingdom and sit on thrones, judging the twelve tribes of Israel.

31 "Simon, Simon, Satan has asked to sift you[a] as wheat. 32 But I have prayed for you, Simon, that your faith may not fail. And when you have turned back, strengthen your brothers."

33 But he replied, "Lord, I am ready to go with you to prison and to death."

34 Jesus answered, "I tell you, Peter, before the rooster crows today, you will deny three times that you know me."

35 Then Jesus asked them, "When I sent you without purse, bag or sandals, did you lack anything?"

"Nothing," they answered.

36 He said to them, "But now if you have a purse, take it, and also a bag; and if you don't have a sword, sell your cloak and buy one. 37 It is written: 'And he was numbered with the transgressors'[b]; and I tell you that this must be fulfilled in me. Yes, what is written about me is reaching its fulfillment."

38 The disciples said, "See, Lord, here are two swords."

"That is enough," he replied.

[a] *31* The Greek is plural. [b] *37* Isaiah 53:12

PRAYER: MY RELATIONSHIP TO OTHERS

I WILL do no injustice in judgment, nor show partiality to the poor or favoritism to the great, but I will judge my neighbor fairly. (Leviticus 19:15) . . . In my faith in You, my glorious Lord Jesus Christ, I will not show partiality to some people above others. (James 2:1)

PAUSE *to review your relationships with others and to commit them to the Lord.*

YEAR 1 DAY 226

OT Judges 20:1–48

Israelites Fight the Benjamites

20 Then all the Israelites from Dan to Beersheba and from the land of Gilead came out as one man and assembled before the LORD in Mizpah. 2 The leaders of all the people of the tribes of Israel took their places in the assembly of the people of God, four hundred thousand soldiers armed with swords. 3 (The Benjamites heard that the Israelites had gone up to Mizpah.) Then the Israelites said, "Tell us how this awful thing happened."

4 So the Levite, the husband of the murdered woman, said, "I and my concubine came to Gibeah in Benjamin to spend the night. 5 During the night the men of Gibeah came after me and surrounded the house, intending to kill me. They raped my concubine, and she died. 6 I took my concubine, cut her into pieces and sent one piece to each region of Israel's inheritance, because they committed this lewd and disgraceful act in Israel. 7 Now, all you Israelites, speak up and give your verdict."

8 All the people rose as one man, saying, "None of us will go home. No, not one of us will return to his house. 9 But now this is what we'll do to Gibeah: We'll go up against it as the lot directs. 10 We'll take ten men out of every hundred from all the tribes of Israel, and a hundred from a thousand, and a thousand from ten thousand, to get provisions for the army. Then, when the army arrives at Gibeah[a] in Benjamin, it can give them what they deserve for all this vileness done in Israel." 11 So all

[a] *10* One Hebrew manuscript; most Hebrew manuscripts *Geba,* a variant of *Gibeah*

the men of Israel got together and united as one man against the city.

12The tribes of Israel sent men throughout the tribe of Benjamin, saying, "What about this awful crime that was committed among you? 13Now surrender those wicked men of Gibeah so that we may put them to death and purge the evil from Israel."

But the Benjamites would not listen to their fellow Israelites. 14From their towns they came together at Gibeah to fight against the Israelites. 15At once the Benjamites mobilized twenty-six thousand swordsmen from their towns, in addition to seven hundred chosen men from those living in Gibeah. 16Among all these soldiers there were seven hundred chosen men who were left-handed, each of whom could sling a stone at a hair and not miss.

17Israel, apart from Benjamin, mustered four hundred thousand swordsmen, all of them fighting men.

18The Israelites went up to Bethel[b] and inquired of God. They said, "Who of us shall go first to fight against the Benjamites?"

The LORD replied, "Judah shall go first."

19The next morning the Israelites got up and pitched camp near Gibeah. 20The men of Israel went out to fight the Benjamites and took up battle positions against them at Gibeah. 21The Benjamites came out of Gibeah and cut down twenty-two thousand Israelites on the battlefield that day. 22But the men of Israel encouraged one another and again took up their positions where they had stationed themselves the first day. 23The Israelites went up and wept before the LORD until evening, and they inquired of the LORD. They said, "Shall we go up again to battle against the Benjamites, our brothers?"

The LORD answered, "Go up against them."

24Then the Israelites drew near to Benjamin the second day. 25This time, when the Benjamites came out from Gibeah to oppose them, they cut down another eighteen thousand Israelites, all of them armed with swords.

26Then the Israelites, all the people, went up to Bethel, and there they sat weeping before the LORD. They fasted that day until evening and presented burnt offerings and fellowship offerings[c] to the LORD. 27And the Israelites inquired of the LORD. (In those days the ark of the covenant of God was there, 28with Phinehas son of Eleazar, the son of Aaron, ministering before it.) They asked, "Shall we go up again to battle with Benjamin our brother, or not?"

The LORD responded, "Go, for tomorrow I will give them into your hands."

29Then Israel set an ambush around Gibeah. 30They went up against the Benjamites on the third day and took up positions against Gibeah as they had done before. 31The Benjamites came out to meet them and were drawn away from the city. They began to inflict casualties on the Israelites as before, so that about thirty men fell in the open field and on the roads—the one leading to Bethel and the other to Gibeah.

32While the Benjamites were saying, "We are defeating them as before," the Israelites were saying, "Let's retreat and draw them away from the city to the roads."

33All the men of Israel moved from their places and took up positions at Baal Tamar, and the Israelite ambush charged out of its place on the west[d] of Gibeah.[e] 34Then ten thousand of Israel's finest men made a frontal attack on Gibeah. The fighting was so heavy that the Benjamites did not realize how near disaster was. 35The LORD defeated Benjamin before Israel, and on that day the Israelites struck down 25,100 Benjamites, all armed with swords. 36Then the Benjamites saw that they were beaten.

Now the men of Israel had given way before Benjamin, because they relied on the ambush they had set near Gibeah. 37The men who had been in ambush made a sudden dash into Gibeah, spread out and put the whole city to the sword. 38The men of Israel had arranged with the ambush that they should send up a great cloud of smoke from the city, 39and then the men of Israel would turn in the battle.

The Benjamites had begun to inflict casualties on the men of Israel (about thirty), and they said, "We are defeating them

[b] *18* Or *to the house of God;* also in verse 26
[c] *26* Traditionally *peace offerings*
[d] *33* Some Septuagint manuscripts and Vulgate; the meaning of the Hebrew for this word is uncertain.
[e] *33* Hebrew *Geba,* a variant of *Gibeah*

as in the first battle." [40]But when the column of smoke began to rise from the city,
the Benjamites turned and saw the smoke
of the whole city going up into the sky.
[41]Then the men of Israel turned on them,
and the men of Benjamin were terrified,
because they realized that disaster had
come upon them. [42]So they fled before
the Israelites in the direction of the desert,
but they could not escape the battle. And
the men of Israel who came out of the
towns cut them down there. [43]They surrounded the Benjamites, chased them and
easily[f] overran them in the vicinity of Gibeah on the east. [44]Eighteen thousand Benjamites fell, all of them valiant fighters.
[45]As they turned and fled toward the
desert to the rock of Rimmon, the Israelites cut down five thousand men along
the roads. They kept pressing after the
Benjamites as far as Gidom and struck
down two thousand more.
[46]On that day twenty-five thousand
Benjamite swordsmen fell, all of them
valiant fighters. [47]But six hundred men
turned and fled into the desert to the rock
of Rimmon, where they stayed four
months. [48]The men of Israel went back to
Benjamin and put all the towns to the
sword, including the animals and everything else they found. All the towns they
came across they set on fire.

[f] 43 The meaning of the Hebrew for this word is uncertain.

PRAYER: CONFESSION

YOU are the righteous God, who searches hearts and secret thoughts. (Psalm 7:9) . . . Your lamp, O Lord, searches my spirit; It searches the inward depths of my being. (Proverbs 20:27)

***ASK** the Spirit to search your heart and reveal any areas of unconfessed sin. Acknowledge these to the Lord and thank Him for His forgiveness.*

NT Luke 22:39–71

Jesus Prays on the Mount of Olives

[39]Jesus went out as usual to the Mount
of Olives, and his disciples followed him.
[40]On reaching the place, he said to them,
"Pray that you will not fall into temptation." [41]He withdrew about a stone's
throw beyond them, knelt down and
prayed, [42]"Father, if you are willing, take
this cup from me; yet not my will, but
yours be done." [43]An angel from heaven
appeared to him and strengthened him.
[44]And being in anguish, he prayed more
earnestly, and his sweat was like drops of
blood falling to the ground.[a]
[45]When he rose from prayer and went
back to the disciples, he found them
asleep, exhausted from sorrow. [46]"Why are
you sleeping?" he asked them. "Get up
and pray so that you will not fall into
temptation."

Jesus Arrested

[47]While he was still speaking a crowd
came up, and the man who was called Judas, one of the Twelve, was leading them.
He approached Jesus to kiss him, [48]but
Jesus asked him, "Judas, are you betraying
the Son of Man with a kiss?"
[49]When Jesus' followers saw what was
going to happen, they said, "Lord, should
we strike with our swords?" [50]And one of
them struck the servant of the high priest,
cutting off his right ear.
[51]But Jesus answered, "No more of
this!" And he touched the man's ear and
healed him.
[52]Then Jesus said to the chief priests, the
officers of the temple guard, and the elders, who had come for him, "Am I leading a rebellion, that you have come with
swords and clubs? [53]Every day I was with
you in the temple courts, and you did not
lay a hand on me. But this is your hour—
when darkness reigns."

Peter Disowns Jesus

[54]Then seizing him, they led him away
and took him into the house of the high
priest. Peter followed at a distance. [55]But
when they had kindled a fire in the mid-

[a] 44 Some early manuscripts do not have verses 43 and 44.

dle of the courtyard and had sat down together, Peter sat down with them. 56A servant girl saw him seated there in the firelight. She looked closely at him and said,
"This man was with him."
57But he denied it. "Woman, I don't
know him," he said.
58A little later someone else saw him
and said, "You also are one of them."
"Man, I am not!" Peter replied.
59About an hour later another asserted,
"Certainly this fellow was with him, for
he is a Galilean."
60Peter replied, "Man, I don't know
what you're talking about!" Just as he was
speaking, the rooster crowed. 61The Lord
turned and looked straight at Peter. Then
Peter remembered the word the Lord had
spoken to him: "Before the rooster crows
today, you will disown me three times."
62And he went outside and wept bitterly.

The Guards Mock Jesus

63The men who were guarding Jesus began mocking and beating him. 64They
blindfolded him and demanded, "Prophesy! Who hit you?" 65And they said many
other insulting things to him.

Jesus Before Pilate and Herod

66At daybreak the council of the elders
of the people, both the chief priests and
teachers of the law, met together, and
Jesus was led before them. 67"If you are
the Christ,[b]" they said, "tell us."
Jesus answered, "If I tell you, you will
not believe me, 68and if I asked you, you
would not answer. 69But from now on, the
Son of Man will be seated at the right
hand of the mighty God."
70They all asked, "Are you then the Son
of God?"
He replied, "You are right in saying
I am."
71Then they said, "Why do we need any
more testimony? We have heard it from
his own lips."

[b] 67 Or *Messiah*

PRAYER: THE ATTRIBUTES OF GOD

YOU, O Lord, are the true God; You are the living God and the everlasting King. At Your wrath the earth trembles, and the nations cannot endure Your indignation. (Jeremiah 10:10) . . . You, Lord Jesus, are the first and the last and the Living One; You were dead, and behold, You are alive forevermore and hold the keys of death and of Hades. (Revelation 1:17–18)

***PAUSE** to reflect on these affirmations about the person, powers and perfection of God.*

YEAR 1 DAY 227

OT Judges 21:1-25

Wives for the Benjamites

21 The men of Israel had taken an oath
at Mizpah: "Not one of us will give his
daughter in marriage to a Benjamite."
2The people went to Bethel,[a] where they
sat before God until evening, raising their
voices and weeping bitterly. 3"O LORD, the
God of Israel," they cried, "why has this
happened to Israel? Why should one tribe
be missing from Israel today?"
4Early the next day the people built an
altar and presented burnt offerings and
fellowship offerings.[b]
5Then the Israelites asked, "Who from
all the tribes of Israel has failed to assemble before the LORD?" For they had taken
a solemn oath that anyone who failed to
assemble before the LORD at Mizpah
should certainly be put to death.
6Now the Israelites grieved for their
brothers, the Benjamites. "Today one tribe
is cut off from Israel," they said. 7"How
can we provide wives for those who are
left, since we have taken an oath by the

[a] 2 Or *to the house of God* [b] 4 Traditionally *peace offerings*

LORD not to give them any of our daughters in marriage?" 8Then they asked, "Which one of the tribes of Israel failed to assemble before the LORD at Mizpah?" They discovered that no one from Jabesh Gilead had come to the camp for the assembly. 9For when they counted the people, they found that none of the people of Jabesh Gilead were there.

10So the assembly sent twelve thousand fighting men with instructions to go to Jabesh Gilead and put to the sword those living there, including the women and children. 11"This is what you are to do," they said. "Kill every male and every woman who is not a virgin." 12They found among the people living in Jabesh Gilead four hundred young women who had never slept with a man, and they took them to the camp at Shiloh in Canaan.

13Then the whole assembly sent an offer of peace to the Benjamites at the rock of Rimmon. 14So the Benjamites returned at that time and were given the women of Jabesh Gilead who had been spared. But there were not enough for all of them.

15The people grieved for Benjamin, because the LORD had made a gap in the tribes of Israel. 16And the elders of the assembly said, "With the women of Benjamin destroyed, how shall we provide wives for the men who are left? 17The Benjamite survivors must have heirs," they said, "so that a tribe of Israel will not be wiped out. 18We can't give them our daughters as wives, since we Israelites have taken this oath: 'Cursed be anyone who gives a wife to a Benjamite.' 19But look, there is the annual festival of the LORD in Shiloh, to the north of Bethel, and east of the road that goes from Bethel to Shechem, and to the south of Lebonah."

20So they instructed the Benjamites, saying, "Go and hide in the vineyards 21and watch. When the girls of Shiloh come out to join in the dancing, then rush from the vineyards and each of you seize a wife from the girls of Shiloh and go to the land of Benjamin. 22When their fathers or brothers complain to us, we will say to them, 'Do us a kindness by helping them, because we did not get wives for them during the war, and you are innocent, since you did not give your daughters to them.' "

23So that is what the Benjamites did. While the girls were dancing, each man caught one and carried her off to be his wife. Then they returned to their inheritance and rebuilt the towns and settled in them.

24At that time the Israelites left that place and went home to their tribes and clans, each to his own inheritance.

25In those days Israel had no king; everyone did as he saw fit.

PRAYER: RENEWAL

MAY I be diligent to add to my faith, virtue; and to virtue, knowledge; and to knowledge, self-control; and to self-control, perseverance; and to perseverance, godliness; and to godliness, kindness; and to kindness, love. For if these qualities are mine in increasing measure, they will keep me from being barren and unfruitful in the full knowledge of You, my Lord Jesus Christ. (2 Peter 1:5–8)

__PAUSE__ to add your own prayers for personal renewal.

NT Luke 23:1–43

23 Then the whole assembly rose and led him off to Pilate. 2And they began to accuse him, saying, "We have found this man subverting our nation. He opposes payment of taxes to Caesar and claims to be Christ,[a] a king."

3So Pilate asked Jesus, "Are you the king of the Jews?"

"Yes, it is as you say," Jesus replied.

4Then Pilate announced to the chief priests and the crowd, "I find no basis for a charge against this man."

5But they insisted, "He stirs up the people all over Judea[b] by his teaching. He

[a] 2 Or *Messiah;* also in verses 35 and 39 [b] 5 Or *over the land of the Jews*

started in Galilee and has come all the
way here."
6On hearing this, Pilate asked if the
man was a Galilean. 7When he learned
that Jesus was under Herod's jurisdiction,
he sent him to Herod, who was also in
Jerusalem at that time.
8When Herod saw Jesus, he was greatly
pleased, because for a long time he had
been wanting to see him. From what he
had heard about him, he hoped to see
him perform some miracle. 9He plied him
with many questions, but Jesus gave him
no answer. 10The chief priests and the
teachers of the law were standing there,
vehemently accusing him. 11Then Herod
and his soldiers ridiculed and mocked
him. Dressing him in an elegant robe,
they sent him back to Pilate. 12That day
Herod and Pilate became friends—before
this they had been enemies.
13Pilate called together the chief priests,
the rulers and the people, 14and said to
them, "You brought me this man as one
who was inciting the people to rebellion.
I have examined him in your presence
and have found no basis for your charges
against him. 15Neither has Herod, for he
sent him back to us; as you can see, he has
done nothing to deserve death. 16There-
fore, I will punish him and then release
him.[c]"
18With one voice they cried out, "Away
with this man! Release Barabbas to us!"
19(Barabbas had been thrown into prison
for an insurrection in the city, and for
murder.)
20Wanting to release Jesus, Pilate appealed to them again. 21But they kept
shouting, "Crucify him! Crucify him!"
22For the third time he spoke to them:
"Why? What crime has this man committed? I have found in him no grounds for
the death penalty. Therefore I will have
him punished and then release him."
23But with loud shouts they insistently
demanded that he be crucified, and their
shouts prevailed. 24So Pilate decided to
grant their demand. 25He released the
man who had been thrown into prison
for insurrection and murder, the one they
asked for, and surrendered Jesus to their
will.

The Crucifixion

26As they led him away, they seized Simon from Cyrene, who was on his way in
from the country, and put the cross on
him and made him carry it behind Jesus.
27A large number of people followed him,
including women who mourned and
wailed for him. 28Jesus turned and said to
them, "Daughters of Jerusalem, do not
weep for me; weep for yourselves and for
your children. 29For the time will come
when you will say, 'Blessed are the barren
women, the wombs that never bore and
the breasts that never nursed!' 30Then

" 'they will say to the mountains, "Fall
on us!"
and to the hills, "Cover us!" '[d]

31For if men do these things when the tree
is green, what will happen when it is dry?"
32Two other men, both criminals, were
also led out with him to be executed.
33When they came to the place called the
Skull, there they crucified him, along with
the criminals—one on his right, the other on his left. 34Jesus said, "Father, forgive
them, for they do not know what they are
doing."[e] And they divided up his clothes
by casting lots.
35The people stood watching, and the
rulers even sneered at him. They said, "He
saved others; let him save himself if he is
the Christ of God, the Chosen One."
36The soldiers also came up and
mocked him. They offered him wine vinegar 37and said, "If you are the king of the
Jews, save yourself."
38There was a written notice above him,
which read: THIS IS THE KING OF THE JEWS.
39One of the criminals who hung there
hurled insults at him: "Aren't you the
Christ? Save yourself and us!"
40But the other criminal rebuked him.
"Don't you fear God," he said, "since you
are under the same sentence? 41We are
punished justly, for we are getting what
our deeds deserve. But this man has done
nothing wrong."
42Then he said, "Jesus, remember me
when you come into your kingdom.[f]"
43Jesus answered him, "I tell you the
truth, today you will be with me in paradise."

[c] 16 Some manuscripts *him." 17Now he was obliged to release one man to them at the Feast.* [d] 30 Hosea 10:8 [e] 34 Some early manuscripts do not have this sentence. [f] 42 Some manuscripts *come with your kingly power*

PRAYER: THE WORKS OF GOD

YOUR power, O God, toward us who believe is power according to the working of Your mighty strength, which You exerted in Christ when You raised Him from the dead and seated Him at Your right hand in the heavenly realms, far above all rule and authority, power and dominion, and every title that can be given, not only in the present age but also in the one to come. (Ephesians 1:19–21)

***TAKE** a moment to consider the greatness of God's wonderful works.*

OT Proverbs 10 — YEAR 1 DAY 228

Proverbs of Solomon

10 The proverbs of Solomon:

A wise son brings joy to his father,
but a foolish son grief to his mother.

2 Ill-gotten treasures are of no value,
but righteousness delivers from death.

3 The LORD does not let the righteous go hungry
but he thwarts the craving of the wicked.

4 Lazy hands make a man poor,
but diligent hands bring wealth.

5 He who gathers crops in summer is a wise son,
but he who sleeps during harvest is a disgraceful son.

6 Blessings crown the head of the righteous,
but violence overwhelms the mouth of the wicked.[a]

7 The memory of the righteous will be a blessing,
but the name of the wicked will rot.

8 The wise in heart accept commands,
but a chattering fool comes to ruin.

9 The man of integrity walks securely,
but he who takes crooked paths will be found out.

10 He who winks maliciously causes grief,
and a chattering fool comes to ruin.

11 The mouth of the righteous is a fountain of life,
but violence overwhelms the mouth of the wicked.

12 Hatred stirs up dissension,
but love covers over all wrongs.

13 Wisdom is found on the lips of the discerning,
but a rod is for the back of him who lacks judgment.

14 Wise men store up knowledge,
but the mouth of a fool invites ruin.

15 The wealth of the rich is their fortified city,
but poverty is the ruin of the poor.

16 The wages of the righteous bring them life,
but the income of the wicked brings them punishment.

17 He who heeds discipline shows the way to life,
but whoever ignores correction leads others astray.

18 He who conceals his hatred has lying lips,
and whoever spreads slander is a fool.

19 When words are many, sin is not absent,
but he who holds his tongue is wise.

20 The tongue of the righteous is choice silver,

[a] 6 Or *but the mouth of the wicked conceals violence;* also in verse 11

but the heart of the wicked is of
little value.

[21]The lips of the righteous nourish
many,
but fools die for lack of judgment.

[22]The blessing of the LORD brings
wealth,
and he adds no trouble to it.

[23]A fool finds pleasure in evil conduct,
but a man of understanding
delights in wisdom.

[24]What the wicked dreads will overtake
him;
what the righteous desire will be
granted.

[25]When the storm has swept by, the
wicked are gone,
but the righteous stand firm forever.

[26]As vinegar to the teeth and smoke to
the eyes,
so is a sluggard to those who send
him.

[27]The fear of the LORD adds length to
life,
but the years of the wicked are cut
short.

[28]The prospect of the righteous is joy,
but the hopes of the wicked come
to nothing.

[29]The way of the LORD is a refuge for the
righteous,
but it is the ruin of those who do
evil.

[30]The righteous will never be uprooted,
but the wicked will not remain in
the land.

[31]The mouth of the righteous brings
forth wisdom,
but a perverse tongue will be cut
out.

[32]The lips of the righteous know what is
fitting,
but the mouth of the wicked only
what is perverse.

PRAYER: PETITION

MAY I discipline myself to godliness. For physical exercise profits a little, but godliness is profitable for all things, since it holds promise for both the present life and the life to come.
(1 Timothy 4:7–8)

PAUSE *here to petition God to help you be a faithful steward of your time, talents, possessions and relationships. Offer prayers of petition regarding your activities for this day and any special concerns you may have.*

NT Luke 23:44–24:12

Jesus' Death

[44]It was now about the sixth hour, and
darkness came over the whole land until
the ninth hour, [45]for the sun stopped
shining. And the curtain of the temple
was torn in two. [46]Jesus called out with a
loud voice, "Father, into your hands I
commit my spirit." When he had said
this, he breathed his last.
[47]The centurion, seeing what had happened, praised God and said, "Surely this
was a righteous man." [48]When all the people who had gathered to witness this sight
saw what took place, they beat their
breasts and went away. [49]But all those who
knew him, including the women who had
followed him from Galilee, stood at a distance, watching these things.

Jesus' Burial

[50]Now there was a man named Joseph,
a member of the Council, a good and upright man, [51]who had not consented to
their decision and action. He came from
the Judean town of Arimathea and he was
waiting for the kingdom of God. [52]Going
to Pilate, he asked for Jesus' body. [53]Then
he took it down, wrapped it in linen cloth
and placed it in a tomb cut in the rock,
one in which no one had yet been laid.

54It was Preparation Day, and the Sabbath
was about to begin.
55The women who had come with Jesus
from Galilee followed Joseph and saw the
tomb and how his body was laid in it.
56Then they went home and prepared
spices and perfumes. But they rested on
the Sabbath in obedience to the commandment.

The Resurrection

24 On the first day of the week, very early in the morning, the women took
the spices they had prepared and went to
the tomb. 2They found the stone rolled
away from the tomb, 3but when they entered, they did not find the body of the
Lord Jesus. 4While they were wondering
about this, suddenly two men in clothes
that gleamed like lightning stood beside
them. 5In their fright the women bowed
down with their faces to the ground, but
the men said to them, "Why do you look
for the living among the dead? 6He is not
here; he has risen! Remember how he told
you, while he was still with you in Galilee: 7'The Son of Man must be delivered
into the hands of sinful men, be crucified
and on the third day be raised again.' "
8Then they remembered his words.
9When they came back from the tomb,
they told all these things to the Eleven and
to all the others. 10It was Mary Magdalene,
Joanna, Mary the mother of James, and
the others with them who told this to the
apostles. 11But they did not believe the
women, because their words seemed to
them like nonsense. 12Peter, however, got
up and ran to the tomb. Bending over, he
saw the strips of linen lying by themselves,
and he went away, wondering to himself
what had happened.

PRAYER: MY RELATIONSHIP TO GOD

O JESUS, peace You leave with me; Your peace You give to me. You do not give to me as the world gives. I will not let my heart be troubled nor let it be fearful. (John 14:27) . . . It is in You, Lord Jesus, that I have peace. In this world I will have tribulation, but I will be of good cheer, because You have overcome the world. (John 16:33)

***PAUSE** to thank God for the relationship that you enjoy with Him in Jesus Christ.*

OT Ruth 1:1–2:23

YEAR 1 DAY 229

Naomi and Ruth

1 In the days when the judges ruled,[a]
there was a famine in the land, and a
man from Bethlehem in Judah, together
with his wife and two sons, went to live
for a while in the country of Moab. 2The
man's name was Elimelech, his wife's
name Naomi, and the names of his two
sons were Mahlon and Kilion. They were
Ephrathites from Bethlehem, Judah. And
they went to Moab and lived there.
3Now Elimelech, Naomi's husband,
died, and she was left with her two sons.
4They married Moabite women, one
named Orpah and the other Ruth. After
they had lived there about ten years, 5both
Mahlon and Kilion also died, and Naomi
was left without her two sons and her husband.
6When she heard in Moab that the
LORD had come to the aid of his people
by providing food for them, Naomi and
her daughters-in-law prepared to return
home from there. 7With her two daughters-in-law she left the place where she
had been living and set out on the road
that would take them back to the land of
Judah.
8Then Naomi said to her two daughters-in-law, "Go back, each of you, to your
mother's home. May the LORD show kindness to you, as you have shown to your
dead and to me. 9May the LORD grant that

[a] 1 Traditionally *judged*

each of you will find rest in the home of
another husband."
Then she kissed them and they wept
aloud 10and said to her, "We will go back
with you to your people."
11But Naomi said, "Return home, my
daughters. Why would you come with
me? Am I going to have any more sons,
who could become your husbands? 12Re-
turn home, my daughters; I am too old to
have another husband. Even if I thought
there was still hope for me—even if I had
a husband tonight and then gave birth to
sons— 13would you wait until they grew
up? Would you remain unmarried for
them? No, my daughters. It is more bitter
for me than for you, because the LORD's
hand has gone out against me!"
14At this they wept again. Then Orpah
kissed her mother-in-law good-by, but
Ruth clung to her.
15"Look," said Naomi, "your sister-in-
law is going back to her people and her
gods. Go back with her."
16But Ruth replied, "Don't urge me to
leave you or to turn back from you. Where
you go I will go, and where you stay I will
stay. Your people will be my people and
your God my God. 17Where you die I will
die, and there I will be buried. May the
LORD deal with me, be it ever so severely,
if anything but death separates you and
me." 18When Naomi realized that Ruth
was determined to go with her, she
stopped urging her.
19So the two women went on until they
came to Bethlehem. When they arrived in
Bethlehem, the whole town was stirred
because of them, and the women exclaimed, "Can this be Naomi?"
20"Don't call me Naomi,[b]" she told
them. "Call me Mara,[c] because the
Almighty[d] has made my life very bitter. 21I
went away full, but the LORD has brought
me back empty. Why call me Naomi? The
LORD has afflicted[e] me; the Almighty has
brought misfortune upon me."
22So Naomi returned from Moab accompanied by Ruth the Moabitess, her
daughter-in-law, arriving in Bethlehem as
the barley harvest was beginning.

Ruth Meets Boaz

2 Now Naomi had a relative on her husband's side, from the clan of Elimelech,
a man of standing, whose name was Boaz.
2And Ruth the Moabitess said to Naomi, "Let me go to the fields and pick up
the leftover grain behind anyone in whose
eyes I find favor."
Naomi said to her, "Go ahead, my
daughter." 3So she went out and began to
glean in the fields behind the harvesters.
As it turned out, she found herself working in a field belonging to Boaz, who was
from the clan of Elimelech.
4Just then Boaz arrived from Bethlehem
and greeted the harvesters, "The LORD be
with you!"
"The LORD bless you!" they called back.
5Boaz asked the foreman of his harvesters, "Whose young woman is that?"
6The foreman replied, "She is the Moabitess who came back from Moab with
Naomi. 7She said, 'Please let me glean and
gather among the sheaves behind the harvesters.' She went into the field and has
worked steadily from morning till now,
except for a short rest in the shelter."
8So Boaz said to Ruth, "My daughter,
listen to me. Don't go and glean in another field and don't go away from here.
Stay here with my servant girls. 9Watch the
field where the men are harvesting, and
follow along after the girls. I have told the
men not to touch you. And whenever you
are thirsty, go and get a drink from the water jars the men have filled."
10At this, she bowed down with her face
to the ground. She exclaimed, "Why have
I found such favor in your eyes that you
notice me—a foreigner?"
11Boaz replied, "I've been told all about
what you have done for your mother-in-
law since the death of your husband—
how you left your father and mother and
your homeland and came to live with a
people you did not know before. 12May
the LORD repay you for what you have
done. May you be richly rewarded by the
LORD, the God of Israel, under whose
wings you have come to take refuge."
13"May I continue to find favor in your
eyes, my lord," she said. "You have given
me comfort and have spoken kindly to
your servant—though I do not have the
standing of one of your servant girls."
14At mealtime Boaz said to her, "Come
over here. Have some bread and dip it in
the wine vinegar."

[b] 20 *Naomi* means *pleasant;* also in verse 21.
[c] 20 *Mara* means *bitter.* [d] 20 Hebrew *Shaddai;* also in verse 21 [e] 21 Or *has testified against*

When she sat down with the harvesters,
he offered her some roasted grain. She ate
all she wanted and had some left over.
[15]As she got up to glean, Boaz gave orders
to his men, "Even if she gathers among
the sheaves, don't embarrass her. [16]Rather,
pull out some stalks for her from the bundles and leave them for her to pick up,
and don't rebuke her."
[17]So Ruth gleaned in the field until
evening. Then she threshed the barley she
had gathered, and it amounted to about
an ephah.[f] [18]She carried it back to town,
and her mother-in-law saw how much she
had gathered. Ruth also brought out and
gave her what she had left over after she
had eaten enough.
[19]Her mother-in-law asked her, "Where
did you glean today? Where did you
work? Blessed be the man who took notice of you!"
Then Ruth told her mother-in-law
about the one at whose place she had
been working. "The name of the man I
worked with today is Boaz," she said.
[20]"The LORD bless him!" Naomi said to
her daughter-in-law. "He has not stopped
showing his kindness to the living and the
dead." She added, "That man is our close
relative; he is one of our kinsman-re-
deemers."
[21]Then Ruth the Moabitess said, "He
even said to me, 'Stay with my workers
until they finish harvesting all my grain.' "
[22]Naomi said to Ruth her daughter-in-
law, "It will be good for you, my daughter, to go with his girls, because in someone else's field you might be harmed."
[23]So Ruth stayed close to the servant
girls of Boaz to glean until the barley and
wheat harvests were finished. And she
lived with her mother-in-law.

[f] 17 That is, probably about 3/5 bushel (about 22 liters)

PRAYER: INTERCESSION

MAY I give to all what they are due: taxes to whom taxes are due, custom to whom custom, respect to whom respect, honor to whom honor. (Romans 13:7)

***TAKE** a few moments to intercede on behalf of your local, state or provincial, and national governments. Pray for spiritual revival in the nation and offer prayers regarding current events and concerns.*

NT Luke 24:13–53

On the Road to Emmaus

[13]Now that same day two of them were
going to a village called Emmaus, about
seven miles[a] from Jerusalem. [14]They were
talking with each other about everything
that had happened. [15]As they talked and
discussed these things with each other,
Jesus himself came up and walked along
with them; [16]but they were kept from rec-
ognizing him.
[17]He asked them, "What are you discussing together as you walk along?"
They stood still, their faces downcast.
[18]One of them, named Cleopas, asked
him, "Are you only a visitor to Jerusalem
and do not know the things that have
happened there in these days?"
[19]"What things?" he asked.
"About Jesus of Nazareth," they replied.
"He was a prophet, powerful in word and
deed before God and all the people. [20]The
chief priests and our rulers handed him
over to be sentenced to death, and they crucified him; [21]but we had hoped that he was
the one who was going to redeem Israel.
And what is more, it is the third day since
all this took place. [22]In addition, some of
our women amazed us. They went to the
tomb early this morning [23]but didn't find
his body. They came and told us that they
had seen a vision of angels, who said he
was alive. [24]Then some of our companions
went to the tomb and found it just as the
women had said, but him they did not see."
[25]He said to them, "How foolish you
are, and how slow of heart to believe all
that the prophets have spoken! [26]Did not
the Christ[b] have to suffer these things and

[a] 13 Greek *sixty stadia* (about 11 kilometers)
[b] 26 Or *Messiah;* also in verse 46

then enter his glory?" 27And beginning
with Moses and all the Prophets, he explained to them what was said in all the
Scriptures concerning himself.
28As they approached the village to
which they were going, Jesus acted as if he
were going farther. 29But they urged him
strongly, "Stay with us, for it is nearly
evening; the day is almost over." So he
went in to stay with them.
30When he was at the table with them,
he took bread, gave thanks, broke it and
began to give it to them. 31Then their eyes
were opened and they recognized him,
and he disappeared from their sight.
32They asked each other, "Were not our
hearts burning within us while he talked
with us on the road and opened the Scriptures to us?"
33They got up and returned at once to
Jerusalem. There they found the Eleven
and those with them, assembled together
34and saying, "It is true! The Lord has risen
and has appeared to Simon." 35Then the
two told what had happened on the way,
and how Jesus was recognized by them
when he broke the bread.

Jesus Appears to the Disciples

36While they were still talking about
this, Jesus himself stood among them and
said to them, "Peace be with you."
37They were startled and frightened,
thinking they saw a ghost. 38He said to
them, "Why are you troubled, and why do
doubts rise in your minds? 39Look at my
hands and my feet. It is I myself! Touch
me and see; a ghost does not have flesh
and bones, as you see I have."
40When he had said this, he showed
them his hands and feet. 41And while they
still did not believe it because of joy and
amazement, he asked them, "Do you have
anything here to eat?" 42They gave him a
piece of broiled fish, 43and he took it and
ate it in their presence.
44He said to them, "This is what I told
you while I was still with you: Everything
must be fulfilled that is written about me
in the Law of Moses, the Prophets and the
Psalms."
45Then he opened their minds so they
could understand the Scriptures. 46He told
them, "This is what is written: The Christ
will suffer and rise from the dead on the
third day, 47and repentance and forgiveness of sins will be preached in his name
to all nations, beginning at Jerusalem.
48You are witnesses of these things. 49I am
going to send you what my Father has
promised; but stay in the city until you
have been clothed with power from on
high."

The Ascension

50When he had led them out to the
vicinity of Bethany, he lifted up his hands
and blessed them. 51While he was blessing
them, he left them and was taken up into
heaven. 52Then they worshiped him and
returned to Jerusalem with great joy.
53And they stayed continually at the temple, praising God.

PRAYER: THE CHARACTER I WANT TO CULTIVATE

I WILL not boast about tomorrow, for I do not know what that day may bring. (Proverbs 27:1) . . . I should not say, "Today or tomorrow I will go to this or that city, spend a year there, carry on business, and make a profit." For I do not even know what my life will be tomorrow. I am a vapor that appears for a little while and then vanishes away. Instead I ought to say, "If the Lord wills, I will live and do this or that." Otherwise, I boast in my arrogance, and all such boasting is evil. (James 4:13–16)

TAKE *a moment to ask the Lord for the grace to grow in godly character.*

OT **Ruth 3:1–4:22**

YEAR 1 DAY 230

Ruth and Boaz at the Threshing Floor

3 One day Naomi her mother-in-law said to her, "My daughter, should I not try to find a home[a] for you, where you will be well provided for? [2]Is not Boaz, with whose servant girls you have been, a kinsman of ours? Tonight he will be winnowing barley on the threshing floor. [3]Wash and perfume yourself, and put on your best clothes. Then go down to the threshing floor, but don't let him know you are there until he has finished eating and drinking. [4]When he lies down, note the place where he is lying. Then go and uncover his feet and lie down. He will tell you what to do."

[5]"I will do whatever you say," Ruth answered. [6]So she went down to the threshing floor and did everything her mother-in-law told her to do.

[7]When Boaz had finished eating and drinking and was in good spirits, he went over to lie down at the far end of the grain pile. Ruth approached quietly, uncovered his feet and lay down. [8]In the middle of the night something startled the man, and he turned and discovered a woman lying at his feet.

[9]"Who are you?" he asked.

"I am your servant Ruth," she said. "Spread the corner of your garment over me, since you are a kinsman-redeemer."

[10]"The LORD bless you, my daughter," he replied. "This kindness is greater than that which you showed earlier: You have not run after the younger men, whether rich or poor. [11]And now, my daughter, don't be afraid. I will do for you all you ask. All my fellow townsmen know that you are a woman of noble character. [12]Although it is true that I am near of kin, there is a kinsman-redeemer nearer than I. [13]Stay here for the night, and in the morning if he wants to redeem, good; let him redeem. But if he is not willing, as surely as the LORD lives I will do it. Lie here until morning."

[14]So she lay at his feet until morning, but got up before anyone could be recognized; and he said, "Don't let it be known that a woman came to the threshing floor."

[15]He also said, "Bring me the shawl you are wearing and hold it out." When she did so, he poured into it six measures of barley and put it on her. Then he[b] went back to town.

[16]When Ruth came to her mother-in-law, Naomi asked, "How did it go, my daughter?"

Then she told her everything Boaz had done for her [17]and added, "He gave me these six measures of barley, saying, 'Don't go back to your mother-in-law empty-handed.' "

[18]Then Naomi said, "Wait, my daughter, until you find out what happens. For the man will not rest until the matter is settled today."

Boaz Marries Ruth

4 Meanwhile Boaz went up to the town gate and sat there. When the kinsman-redeemer he had mentioned came along, Boaz said, "Come over here, my friend, and sit down." So he went over and sat down.

[2]Boaz took ten of the elders of the town and said, "Sit here," and they did so. [3]Then he said to the kinsman-redeemer, "Naomi, who has come back from Moab, is selling the piece of land that belonged to our brother Elimelech. [4]I thought I should bring the matter to your attention and suggest that you buy it in the presence of these seated here and in the presence of the elders of my people. If you will redeem it, do so. But if you[c] will not, tell me, so I will know. For no one has the right to do it except you, and I am next in line."

"I will redeem it," he said.

[5]Then Boaz said, "On the day you buy the land from Naomi and from Ruth the Moabitess, you acquire[d] the dead man's widow, in order to maintain the name of the dead with his property."

[6]At this, the kinsman-redeemer said, "Then I cannot redeem it because I might endanger my own estate. You redeem it yourself. I cannot do it."

[a] *1* Hebrew *find rest* (see Ruth 1:9) [b] *15* Most Hebrew manuscripts; many Hebrew manuscripts, Vulgate and Syriac *she* [c] *4* Many Hebrew manuscripts, Septuagint, Vulgate and Syriac; most Hebrew manuscripts *he* [d] *5* Hebrew; Vulgate and Syriac *Naomi, you acquire Ruth the Moabitess,*

7(Now in earlier times in Israel, for the
redemption and transfer of property to become final, one party took off his sandal
and gave it to the other. This was the
method of legalizing transactions in Israel.)
8So the kinsman-redeemer said to Boaz,
"Buy it yourself." And he removed his sandal.
9Then Boaz announced to the elders
and all the people, "Today you are witnesses that I have bought from Naomi all
the property of Elimelech, Kilion and
Mahlon. 10I have also acquired Ruth the
Moabitess, Mahlon's widow, as my wife,
in order to maintain the name of the dead
with his property, so that his name will
not disappear from among his family or
from the town records. Today you are witnesses!"
11Then the elders and all those at the
gate said, "We are witnesses. May the LORD
make the woman who is coming into
your home like Rachel and Leah, who together built up the house of Israel. May
you have standing in Ephrathah and be
famous in Bethlehem. 12Through the offspring the LORD gives you by this young
woman, may your family be like that of
Perez, whom Tamar bore to Judah."

The Genealogy of David

13So Boaz took Ruth and she became
his wife. Then he went to her, and the
LORD enabled her to conceive, and she
gave birth to a son. 14The women said to
Naomi: "Praise be to the LORD, who this
day has not left you without a kinsman-
redeemer. May he become famous
throughout Israel! 15He will renew your
life and sustain you in your old age. For
your daughter-in-law, who loves you and
who is better to you than seven sons, has
given him birth."
16Then Naomi took the child, laid him
in her lap and cared for him. 17The
women living there said, "Naomi has a
son." And they named him Obed. He was
the father of Jesse, the father of David.
18This, then, is the family line of Perez:

Perez was the father of Hezron,
19 Hezron the father of Ram,
Ram the father of Amminadab,
20 Amminadab the father of Nahshon,
Nahshon the father of Salmon,[e]
21 Salmon the father of Boaz,
Boaz the father of Obed,
22 Obed the father of Jesse,
and Jesse the father of David.

[e] *20* A few Hebrew manuscripts, some Septuagint manuscripts and Vulgate (see also verse 21 and Septuagint of 1 Chron. 2:11); most Hebrew manuscripts *Salma*

PRAYER: AFFIRMATION

THOSE who pursue righteousness and love find life, righteousness and honor. (Proverbs 21:21) . . . Those who heed instruction prosper, and blessed are those who trust in You, O Lord. (Proverbs 16:20)

PAUSE *to reflect on these Biblical affirmations.*

NT 1 Thessalonians 1:1–10

1 Paul, Silas[a] and Timothy,

To the church of the Thessalonians in
God the Father and the Lord Jesus Christ:

Grace and peace to you.[b]

Thanksgiving for the Thessalonians' Faith

2We always thank God for all of you,
mentioning you in our prayers. 3We continually remember before our God and
Father your work produced by faith, your
labor prompted by love, and your endurance inspired by hope in our Lord
Jesus Christ.
4For we know, brothers loved by God,
that he has chosen you, 5because our
gospel came to you not simply with
words, but also with power, with the Holy
Spirit and with deep conviction. You know
how we lived among you for your sake.
6You became imitators of us and of the
Lord; in spite of severe suffering, you wel-

[a] *1* Greek *Silvanus,* a variant of *Silas*

comed the message with the joy given by
the Holy Spirit. 7And so you became a
model to all the believers in Macedonia
and Achaia. 8The Lord's message rang out
from you not only in Macedonia and
Achaia—your faith in God has become
known everywhere. Therefore we do not
need to say anything about it, 9for they
themselves report what kind of reception
you gave us. They tell how you turned to
God from idols to serve the living and true
God, 10and to wait for his Son from heav-
en, whom he raised from the dead—Jesus,
who rescues us from the coming wrath.

[b] 1 Some early manuscripts *you from God our Father and the Lord Jesus Christ*

PRAYER: MY RELATIONSHIP TO OTHERS

WIVES should be submissive to their own husbands, so that if any of them do not believe the word, they may be won without a word by the behavior of their wives, when they see their purity and reverence. Husbands should be considerate as they live with their wives and treat them with respect as the weaker vessel and as co-heirs of the grace of life. (1 Peter 3:1–2, 7)

PAUSE *to review your relationships with others and to commit them to the Lord.*

YEAR 1
DAY 231

OT Psalm 44

Psalm 44

For the director of music. Of the Sons of Korah. A *maskil*.[a]

1We have heard with our ears, O God;
our fathers have told us
what you did in their days,
in days long ago.
2With your hand you drove out the nations
and planted our fathers;
you crushed the peoples
and made our fathers flourish.
3It was not by their sword that they won the land,
nor did their arm bring them victory;
it was your right hand, your arm,
and the light of your face, for you loved them.

4You are my King and my God,
who decrees[b] victories for Jacob.
5Through you we push back our enemies;
through your name we trample our foes.
6I do not trust in my bow,
my sword does not bring me victory;
7but you give us victory over our enemies,
you put our adversaries to shame.
8In God we make our boast all day long,
and we will praise your name forever. *Selah*

9But now you have rejected and humbled us;
you no longer go out with our armies.
10You made us retreat before the enemy,
and our adversaries have plundered us.
11You gave us up to be devoured like sheep
and have scattered us among the nations.
12You sold your people for a pittance,
gaining nothing from their sale.

13You have made us a reproach to our neighbors,
the scorn and derision of those around us.
14You have made us a byword among the nations;

[a] Title: Probably a literary or musical term
[b] 4 Septuagint, Aquila and Syriac; Hebrew *King, O God; / command*

the peoples shake their heads at us.
15 My disgrace is before me all day long,
and my face is covered with shame
16 at the taunts of those who reproach and revile me,
because of the enemy, who is bent on revenge.

17 All this happened to us,
though we had not forgotten you
or been false to your covenant.
18 Our hearts had not turned back;
our feet had not strayed from your path.
19 But you crushed us and made us a haunt for jackals
and covered us over with deep darkness.

20 If we had forgotten the name of our God
or spread out our hands to a foreign god,
21 would not God have discovered it,
since he knows the secrets of the heart?
22 Yet for your sake we face death all day long;
we are considered as sheep to be slaughtered.

23 Awake, O Lord! Why do you sleep?
Rouse yourself! Do not reject us forever.
24 Why do you hide your face
and forget our misery and oppression?

25 We are brought down to the dust;
our bodies cling to the ground.
26 Rise up and help us;
redeem us because of your unfailing love.

PRAYER: THANKSGIVING

YOU are the Lord our God, who brought Your people out of Egypt, out of the land of slavery. (Exodus 20:2) . . . Was it not You who dried up the sea, the waters of the great deep; who made the depths of the sea a road so that the redeemed might cross over? (Isaiah 51:10)

***PAUSE** to offer your own expressions of thanksgiving.*

NT 1 Thessalonians 2:1–16

Paul's Ministry in Thessalonica

2 You know, brothers, that our visit to
you was not a failure. 2We had previously suffered and been insulted in Philippi, as you know, but with the help of
our God we dared to tell you his gospel in
spite of strong opposition. 3For the appeal
we make does not spring from error or
impure motives, nor are we trying to trick
you. 4On the contrary, we speak as men
approved by God to be entrusted with the
gospel. We are not trying to please men
but God, who tests our hearts. 5You know
we never used flattery, nor did we put on
a mask to cover up greed—God is our witness. 6We were not looking for praise from
men, not from you or anyone else.
As apostles of Christ we could have
been a burden to you, 7but we were gentle among you, like a mother caring for
her little children. 8We loved you so much
that we were delighted to share with you
not only the gospel of God but our lives
as well, because you had become so dear
to us. 9Surely you remember, brothers, our
toil and hardship; we worked night and
day in order not to be a burden to anyone
while we preached the gospel of God to
you.

10You are witnesses, and so is God, of
how holy, righteous and blameless we
were among you who believed. 11For you
know that we dealt with each of you as a
father deals with his own children, 12en-
couraging, comforting and urging you to
live lives worthy of God, who calls you
into his kingdom and glory.

13And we also thank God continually
because, when you received the word of
God, which you heard from us, you accepted it not as the word of men, but as
it actually is, the word of God, which is at
work in you who believe. 14For you, brothers, became imitators of God's churches in

Judea, which are in Christ Jesus: You suffered from your own countrymen the same things those churches suffered from the Jews, [15]who killed the Lord Jesus and the prophets and also drove us out. They displease God and are hostile to all men [16]in their effort to keep us from speaking to the Gentiles so that they may be saved. In this way they always heap up their sins to the limit. The wrath of God has come upon them at last.[a]

[a] 16 Or *them fully*

PRAYER: THE ATTRIBUTES OF GOD

I KNOW that You can do all things and that no purpose of Yours can be thwarted. (Job 42:2) . . . From the rising of the sun to its setting, Your name, O Lord, is to be praised. You are high above all nations, Your glory is above the heavens. Who is like You, O Lord our God, the One who is enthroned on high, You who humble Yourself to behold the things that are in the heavens and in the earth? (Psalm 113:3–6)

PAUSE *to reflect on these affirmations about the person, powers and perfection of God.*

OT 1 Samuel 1:1–28

YEAR 1 DAY 232

The Birth of Samuel

1 There was a certain man from Ramathaim, a Zuphite[a] from the hill country of Ephraim, whose name was Elkanah son of Jeroham, the son of Elihu, the son of Tohu, the son of Zuph, an Ephraimite.
[2]He had two wives; one was called Hannah and the other Peninnah. Peninnah had children, but Hannah had none.
[3]Year after year this man went up from his town to worship and sacrifice to the LORD Almighty at Shiloh, where Hophni and Phinehas, the two sons of Eli, were priests of the LORD. [4]Whenever the day came for Elkanah to sacrifice, he would give portions of the meat to his wife Peninnah and to all her sons and daughters.
[5]But to Hannah he gave a double portion because he loved her, and the LORD had closed her womb. [6]And because the LORD had closed her womb, her rival kept provoking her in order to irritate her. [7]This went on year after year. Whenever Hannah went up to the house of the LORD, her rival provoked her till she wept and would not eat. [8]Elkanah her husband would say to her, "Hannah, why are you weeping? Why don't you eat? Why are you downhearted? Don't I mean more to you than ten sons?"
[9]Once when they had finished eating and drinking in Shiloh, Hannah stood up. Now Eli the priest was sitting on a chair by the doorpost of the LORD's temple.[b] [10]In bitterness of soul Hannah wept much and prayed to the LORD. [11]And she made a vow, saying, "O LORD Almighty, if you will only look upon your servant's misery and remember me, and not forget your servant but give her a son, then I will give him to the LORD for all the days of his life, and no razor will ever be used on his head."
[12]As she kept on praying to the LORD, Eli observed her mouth. [13]Hannah was praying in her heart, and her lips were moving but her voice was not heard. Eli thought she was drunk [14]and said to her, "How long will you keep on getting drunk? Get rid of your wine."
[15]"Not so, my lord," Hannah replied, "I am a woman who is deeply troubled. I have not been drinking wine or beer; I was pouring out my soul to the LORD. [16]Do not take your servant for a wicked woman; I have been praying here out of my great anguish and grief."
[17]Eli answered, "Go in peace, and may the God of Israel grant you what you have asked of him."
[18]She said, "May your servant find favor

[a] 1 Or *from Ramathaim Zuphim* [b] 9 That is, tabernacle

in your eyes." Then she went her way and ate something, and her face was no longer downcast.
[19]Early the next morning they arose and worshiped before the LORD and then went back to their home at Ramah. Elkanah lay with Hannah his wife, and the LORD remembered her. [20]So in the course of time Hannah conceived and gave birth to a son. She named him Samuel,[c] saying, "Because I asked the LORD for him."

Hannah Dedicates Samuel

[21]When the man Elkanah went up with all his family to offer the annual sacrifice
to the LORD and to fulfill his vow, [22]Hannah did not go. She said to her husband, "After the boy is weaned, I will take him and present him before the LORD, and he will live there always."
[23]"Do what seems best to you," Elkanah her husband told her. "Stay here until you have weaned him; only may the LORD make good his[d] word." So the woman stayed at home and nursed her son until she had weaned him.
[24]After he was weaned, she took the boy with her, young as he was, along with a three-year-old bull,[e] an ephah[f] of flour and a skin of wine, and brought him to
the house of the LORD at Shiloh. [25]When they had slaughtered the bull, they
brought the boy to Eli, [26]and she said to him, "As surely as you live, my lord, I am the woman who stood here beside you
praying to the LORD. [27]I prayed for this child, and the LORD has granted me what
I asked of him. [28]So now I give him to the LORD. For his whole life he will be given over to the LORD." And he worshiped the LORD there.

[c] 20 *Samuel* sounds like the Hebrew for *heard of God.*
[d] 23 Masoretic Text; Dead Sea Scrolls, Septuagint and Syriac *your*
[e] 24 Dead Sea Scrolls, Septuagint and Syriac; Masoretic Text *with three bulls*
[f] 24 That is, probably about 3/5 bushel (about 22 liters)

PRAYER: ADORATION

NOT to us, O Lord, not to us, but to Your name be glory, because of Your loving-kindness and truth. (Psalm 115:1) . . .
We give praise to You, Lord! For it is good to sing praises to You, our God, because praise is pleasant and beautiful. (Psalm 147:1)

PAUSE *to express your thoughts of praise and worship.*

NT 1 Thessalonians 2:17–3:5

Paul's Longing to See the Thessalonians

[17]But, brothers, when we were torn away from you for a short time (in person, not in thought), out of our intense longing we made every effort to see you.
[18]For we wanted to come to you—certainly I, Paul, did, again and again—but Satan stopped us. [19]For what is our hope, our joy, or the crown in which we will glory in the presence of our Lord Jesus when he comes? Is it not you? [20]Indeed, you are our glory and joy.
3 So when we could stand it no longer, we thought it best to be left by ourselves in Athens. [2]We sent Timothy, who is our brother and God's fellow worker[a] in spreading the gospel of Christ, to strengthen and encourage you in your faith, [3]so that no one would be unsettled by these trials. You know quite well that we were destined for them. [4]In fact, when we were with you, we kept telling you that we would be persecuted. And it turned out that way, as you well know.
[5]For this reason, when I could stand it no longer, I sent to find out about your faith. I was afraid that in some way the tempter might have tempted you and our efforts might have been useless.

[a] 2 Some manuscripts *brother and fellow worker;* other manuscripts *brother and God's servant*

PRAYER: THE WORKS OF GOD

IN the resurrection of the dead, the body that is sown is perishable, but it is raised imperishable; it is sown in dishonor, but it is raised in glory; it is sown in weakness, but it is raised in power; it is sown a natural body, but it is raised a spiritual body. If there is a natural body, there is also a spiritual body. The first man was of the dust of the earth; You, Jesus Christ, the second Man, are from heaven. As was the earthly man, so are those who are of the earth; and as You, the Man from heaven are, so also are those who are of heaven. And just as we have borne the image of the earthly man, so shall we bear Your likeness—You who are the heavenly Man. (1 Corinthians 15:42–44, 47–49)

TAKE *a moment to consider the greatness of God's wonderful works.*

YEAR 1
DAY 233

OT 1 Samuel 2:1-36

Hannah's Prayer

2 Then Hannah prayed and said:

"My heart rejoices in the LORD;
in the LORD my horn[a] is lifted high.
My mouth boasts over my enemies,
for I delight in your deliverance.

2 "There is no one holy[b] like the LORD;
there is no one besides you;
there is no Rock like our God.

3 "Do not keep talking so proudly
or let your mouth speak such arrogance,
for the LORD is a God who knows,
and by him deeds are weighed.

4 "The bows of the warriors are broken,
but those who stumbled are armed with strength.
5 Those who were full hire themselves out for food,
but those who were hungry hunger no more.
She who was barren has borne seven children,
but she who has had many sons pines away.

6 "The LORD brings death and makes alive;
he brings down to the grave[c] and raises up.
7 The LORD sends poverty and wealth;
he humbles and he exalts.
8 He raises the poor from the dust
and lifts the needy from the ash heap;
he seats them with princes
and has them inherit a throne of honor.

"For the foundations of the earth are the LORD's;
upon them he has set the world.
9 He will guard the feet of his saints,
but the wicked will be silenced in darkness.

"It is not by strength that one prevails;
10 those who oppose the LORD will be shattered.
He will thunder against them from heaven;
the LORD will judge the ends of the earth.

"He will give strength to his king
and exalt the horn of his anointed."

11 Then Elkanah went home to Ramah, but the boy ministered before the LORD under Eli the priest.

Eli's Wicked Sons

12 Eli's sons were wicked men; they had
no regard for the LORD. 13 Now it was the
practice of the priests with the people that
whenever anyone offered a sacrifice and
while the meat was being boiled, the servant of the priest would come with a

[a] 1 *Horn* here symbolizes strength; also in verse 10.
[b] 2 Or *no Holy One* [c] 6 Hebrew *Sheol*

three-pronged fork in his hand. 14He would plunge it into the pan or kettle or caldron or pot, and the priest would take for himself whatever the fork brought up. This is how they treated all the Israelites who came to Shiloh. 15But even before the fat was burned, the servant of the priest would come and say to the man who was sacrificing, "Give the priest some meat to roast; he won't accept boiled meat from you, but only raw."

16If the man said to him, "Let the fat be burned up first, and then take whatever you want," the servant would then answer, "No, hand it over now; if you don't, I'll take it by force."

17This sin of the young men was very great in the LORD's sight, for they[d] were treating the LORD's offering with contempt.

18But Samuel was ministering before the LORD—a boy wearing a linen ephod. 19Each year his mother made him a little robe and took it to him when she went up with her husband to offer the annual sacrifice. 20Eli would bless Elkanah and his wife, saying, "May the LORD give you children by this woman to take the place of the one she prayed for and gave to the LORD." Then they would go home. 21And the LORD was gracious to Hannah; she conceived and gave birth to three sons and two daughters. Meanwhile, the boy Samuel grew up in the presence of the LORD.

22Now Eli, who was very old, heard about everything his sons were doing to all Israel and how they slept with the women who served at the entrance to the Tent of Meeting. 23So he said to them, "Why do you do such things? I hear from all the people about these wicked deeds of yours. 24No, my sons; it is not a good report that I hear spreading among the LORD's people. 25If a man sins against another man, God[e] may mediate for him; but if a man sins against the LORD, who will intercede for him?" His sons, however, did not listen to their father's rebuke, for it was the LORD's will to put them to death.

26And the boy Samuel continued to grow in stature and in favor with the LORD and with men.

Prophecy Against the House of Eli

27Now a man of God came to Eli and said to him, "This is what the LORD says: 'Did I not clearly reveal myself to your father's house when they were in Egypt under Pharaoh? 28I chose your father out of all the tribes of Israel to be my priest, to go up to my altar, to burn incense, and to wear an ephod in my presence. I also gave your father's house all the offerings made with fire by the Israelites. 29Why do you[f] scorn my sacrifice and offering that I prescribed for my dwelling? Why do you honor your sons more than me by fattening yourselves on the choice parts of every offering made by my people Israel?'

30"Therefore the LORD, the God of Israel, declares: 'I promised that your house and your father's house would minister before me forever.' But now the LORD declares: 'Far be it from me! Those who honor me I will honor, but those who despise me will be disdained. 31The time is coming when I will cut short your strength and the strength of your father's house, so that there will not be an old man in your family line 32and you will see distress in my dwelling. Although good will be done to Israel, in your family line there will never be an old man. 33Every one of you that I do not cut off from my altar will be spared only to blind your eyes with tears and to grieve your heart, and all your descendants will die in the prime of life.

34" 'And what happens to your two sons, Hophni and Phinehas, will be a sign to you—they will both die on the same day. 35I will raise up for myself a faithful priest, who will do according to what is in my heart and mind. I will firmly establish his house, and he will minister before my anointed one always. 36Then everyone left in your family line will come and bow down before him for a piece of silver and a crust of bread and plead, "Appoint me to some priestly office so I can have food to eat." ' "

[d] 17 Or *men* [e] 25 Or *the judges* [f] 29 The Hebrew is plural.

PRAYER: CONFESSION

YOU have set our iniquities before You, Lord, our secret sins in the light of Your presence. (Psalm 90:8)

ASK the Spirit to search your heart and reveal any areas of unconfessed sin. Acknowledge these to the Lord and thank Him for His forgiveness.

NT 1 Thessalonians 3:6–13

Timothy's Encouraging Report

6But Timothy has just now come to us from you and has brought good news about your faith and love. He has told us that you always have pleasant memories of us and that you long to see us, just as we also long to see you. 7Therefore, brothers, in all our distress and persecution we were encouraged about you because of your faith. 8For now we really live, since you are standing firm in the Lord. 9How can we thank God enough for you in return for all the joy we have in the presence of our God because of you? 10Night and day we pray most earnestly that we may see you again and supply what is lacking in your faith.

11Now may our God and Father himself and our Lord Jesus clear the way for us to come to you. 12May the Lord make your love increase and overflow for each other and for everyone else, just as ours does for you. 13May he strengthen your hearts so that you will be blameless and holy in the presence of our God and Father when our Lord Jesus comes with all his holy ones.

PRAYER: MY RELATIONSHIP TO GOD

THOSE who do not take their cross and follow after You, O Jesus, are not worthy of You. Those who find their lives will lose them, and those who lose their lives for Your sake will find them. (Matthew 10:38–39) . . . Those who wish to become great among others must become their servant, and those who wish to be first among others must be their slave. (Matthew 20:26–27; Mark 10:43–44)

***PAUSE** to thank God for the relationship that you enjoy with Him in Jesus Christ.*

YEAR 1
DAY 234

OT 1 Samuel 3:1–4:22

The LORD Calls Samuel

3 The boy Samuel ministered before the LORD under Eli. In those days the word of the LORD was rare; there were not many visions.

2One night Eli, whose eyes were becoming so weak that he could barely see, was lying down in his usual place. 3The lamp of God had not yet gone out, and Samuel was lying down in the temple[a] of the LORD, where the ark of God was. 4Then the LORD called Samuel.

Samuel answered, "Here I am." 5And he ran to Eli and said, "Here I am; you called me."

But Eli said, "I did not call; go back and lie down." So he went and lay down.

6Again the LORD called, "Samuel!" And Samuel got up and went to Eli and said, "Here I am; you called me."

"My son," Eli said, "I did not call; go back and lie down."

7Now Samuel did not yet know the LORD: The word of the LORD had not yet been revealed to him.

[a] 3 That is, tabernacle

8The LORD called Samuel a third time, and Samuel got up and went to Eli and said, "Here I am; you called me."

Then Eli realized that the LORD was calling the boy. 9So Eli told Samuel, "Go and lie down, and if he calls you, say, 'Speak, LORD, for your servant is listening.' " So Samuel went and lay down in his place.

10The LORD came and stood there, calling as at the other times, "Samuel! Samuel!"

Then Samuel said, "Speak, for your servant is listening."

11And the LORD said to Samuel: "See, I am about to do something in Israel that will make the ears of everyone who hears of it tingle. 12At that time I will carry out against Eli everything I spoke against his family—from beginning to end. 13For I told him that I would judge his family forever because of the sin he knew about; his sons made themselves contemptible,[b] and he failed to restrain them. 14Therefore, I swore to the house of Eli, 'The guilt of Eli's house will never be atoned for by sacrifice or offering.' "

15Samuel lay down until morning and then opened the doors of the house of the LORD. He was afraid to tell Eli the vision, 16but Eli called him and said, "Samuel, my son."

Samuel answered, "Here I am."

17"What was it he said to you?" Eli asked. "Do not hide it from me. May God deal with you, be it ever so severely, if you hide from me anything he told you." 18So Samuel told him everything, hiding nothing from him. Then Eli said, "He is the LORD; let him do what is good in his eyes."

19The LORD was with Samuel as he grew up, and he let none of his words fall to the ground. 20And all Israel from Dan to Beersheba recognized that Samuel was attested as a prophet of the LORD. 21The LORD continued to appear at Shiloh, and there he revealed himself to Samuel through his word.

4 And Samuel's word came to all Israel.

The Philistines Capture the Ark

Now the Israelites went out to fight against the Philistines. The Israelites camped at Ebenezer, and the Philistines at Aphek. 2The Philistines deployed their forces to meet Israel, and as the battle spread, Israel was defeated by the Philistines, who killed about four thousand of them on the battlefield. 3When the soldiers returned to camp, the elders of Israel asked, "Why did the LORD bring defeat upon us today before the Philistines? Let us bring the ark of the LORD's covenant from Shiloh, so that it[c] may go with us and save us from the hand of our enemies."

4So the people sent men to Shiloh, and they brought back the ark of the covenant of the LORD Almighty, who is enthroned between the cherubim. And Eli's two sons, Hophni and Phinehas, were there with the ark of the covenant of God.

5When the ark of the LORD's covenant came into the camp, all Israel raised such a great shout that the ground shook. 6Hearing the uproar, the Philistines asked, "What's all this shouting in the Hebrew camp?"

When they learned that the ark of the LORD had come into the camp, 7the Philistines were afraid. "A god has come into the camp," they said. "We're in trouble! Nothing like this has happened before. 8Woe to us! Who will deliver us from the hand of these mighty gods? They are the gods who struck the Egyptians with all kinds of plagues in the desert. 9Be strong, Philistines! Be men, or you will be subject to the Hebrews, as they have been to you. Be men, and fight!"

10So the Philistines fought, and the Israelites were defeated and every man fled to his tent. The slaughter was very great; Israel lost thirty thousand foot soldiers. 11The ark of God was captured, and Eli's two sons, Hophni and Phinehas, died.

Death of Eli

12That same day a Benjamite ran from the battle line and went to Shiloh, his clothes torn and dust on his head. 13When he arrived, there was Eli sitting on his chair by the side of the road, watching, because his heart feared for the ark of God. When the man entered the town and told what had happened, the whole town sent up a cry.

14Eli heard the outcry and asked, "What is the meaning of this uproar?"

[b] 13 Masoretic Text; an ancient Hebrew scribal tradition and Septuagint *sons blasphemed God*
[c] 3 Or *he*

The man hurried over to Eli, [15]who was ninety-eight years old and whose eyes were set so that he could not see. [16]He told Eli, "I have just come from the battle line; I fled from it this very day."

Eli asked, "What happened, my son?"

[17]The man who brought the news replied, "Israel fled before the Philistines, and the army has suffered heavy losses. Also your two sons, Hophni and Phinehas, are dead, and the ark of God has been captured."

[18]When he mentioned the ark of God, Eli fell backward off his chair by the side of the gate. His neck was broken and he died, for he was an old man and heavy. He had led[d] Israel forty years.

[19]His daughter-in-law, the wife of Phinehas, was pregnant and near the time of delivery. When she heard the news that the ark of God had been captured and that her father-in-law and her husband were dead, she went into labor and gave birth, but was overcome by her labor pains. [20]As she was dying, the women attending her said, "Don't despair; you have given birth to a son." But she did not respond or pay any attention.

[21]She named the boy Ichabod,[e] saying, "The glory has departed from Israel"—because of the capture of the ark of God and the deaths of her father-in-law and her husband. [22]She said, "The glory has departed from Israel, for the ark of God has been captured."

[d] 18 Traditionally *judged* [e] 21 *Ichabod* means *no glory.*

PRAYER: RENEWAL

MAY I fight the good fight of faith and lay hold of the eternal life to which I was called, Father, when I made the good confession in the presence of many witnesses. You are the One who gives life to all things; in Your sight, and in the sight of Your Son, Christ Jesus, who testified the good confession before Pontius Pilate, may I keep this command without blemish or reproach until the appearing of my Lord Jesus Christ, which You will bring about in Your own time. (1 Timothy 6:12–15) . . . O God, may I be diligent to present myself to You as one approved, a worker who does not need to be ashamed and who correctly handles the word of truth. (2 Timothy 2:15)

PAUSE *to add your own prayers for personal renewal.*

NT 1 Thessalonians 4:1–12

Living to Please God

4 Finally, brothers, we instructed you how to live in order to please God, as in fact you are living. Now we ask you and urge you in the Lord Jesus to do this more and more. [2]For you know what instructions we gave you by the authority of the Lord Jesus.

[3]It is God's will that you should be sanctified: that you should avoid sexual immorality; [4]that each of you should learn to control his own body[a] in a way that is holy and honorable, [5]not in passionate lust like the heathen, who do not know God; [6]and that in this matter no one should wrong his brother or take advantage of him. The Lord will punish men for all such sins, as we have already told you and warned you. [7]For God did not call us to be impure, but to live a holy life. [8]Therefore, he who rejects this instruction does not reject man but God, who gives you his Holy Spirit.

[9]Now about brotherly love we do not need to write to you, for you yourselves have been taught by God to love each other. [10]And in fact, you do love all the brothers throughout Macedonia. Yet we urge you, brothers, to do so more and more.

[a] 4 Or *learn to live with his own wife;* or *learn to acquire a wife*

11 Make it your ambition to lead a quiet life, to mind your own business and to work with your hands, just as we told you, 12 so that your daily life may win the respect of outsiders and so that you will not be dependent on anybody.

PRAYER: THE CHARACTER I WANT TO CULTIVATE

YOUR commandment is a lamp, O Lord; Your teaching is a light, and Your reproofs of discipline are the way to life. (Proverbs 6:23) . . . All Scripture is God-breathed and is useful for teaching, for reproof, for correction and for training in righteousness, that we Your people may be thoroughly equipped for every good work. (2 Timothy 3:16–17)

__TAKE__ a moment to ask the Lord for the grace to grow in godly character.

YEAR 1 DAY 235

OT 1 Samuel 5:1–6:21

The Ark in Ashdod and Ekron

5 After the Philistines had captured the ark of God, they took it from Ebenezer to Ashdod. 2 Then they carried the ark into Dagon's temple and set it beside Dagon. 3 When the people of Ashdod rose early the next day, there was Dagon, fallen on his face on the ground before the ark of the LORD! They took Dagon and put him back in his place. 4 But the following morning when they rose, there was Dagon, fallen on his face on the ground before the ark of the LORD! His head and hands had been broken off and were lying on the threshold; only his body remained. 5 That is why to this day neither the priests of Dagon nor any others who enter Dagon's temple at Ashdod step on the threshold.

6 The LORD's hand was heavy upon the people of Ashdod and its vicinity; he brought devastation upon them and afflicted them with tumors.[a] 7 When the men of Ashdod saw what was happening, they said, "The ark of the god of Israel must not stay here with us, because his hand is heavy upon us and upon Dagon our god." 8 So they called together all the rulers of the Philistines and asked them, "What shall we do with the ark of the god of Israel?"

They answered, "Have the ark of the god of Israel moved to Gath." So they moved the ark of the God of Israel.

9 But after they had moved it, the LORD's hand was against that city, throwing it into a great panic. He afflicted the people of the city, both young and old, with an outbreak of tumors.[b] 10 So they sent the ark of God to Ekron.

As the ark of God was entering Ekron, the people of Ekron cried out, "They have brought the ark of the god of Israel around to us to kill us and our people." 11 So they called together all the rulers of the Philistines and said, "Send the ark of the god of Israel away; let it go back to its own place, or it[c] will kill us and our people." For death had filled the city with panic; God's hand was very heavy upon it. 12 Those who did not die were afflicted with tumors, and the outcry of the city went up to heaven.

The Ark Returned to Israel

6 When the ark of the LORD had been in Philistine territory seven months, 2 the Philistines called for the priests and the diviners and said, "What shall we do with the ark of the LORD? Tell us how we should send it back to its place."

3 They answered, "If you return the ark of the god of Israel, do not send it away empty, but by all means send a guilt offering to him. Then you will be healed, and you will know why his hand has not been lifted from you."

4 The Philistines asked, "What guilt offering should we send to him?"

[a] 6 Hebrew; Septuagint and Vulgate *tumors. And rats appeared in their land, and death and destruction were throughout the city* [b] 9 Or *with tumors in the groin* (see Septuagint) [c] 11 Or *he*

They replied, "Five gold tumors and five
gold rats, according to the number of the
Philistine rulers, because the same plague
has struck both you and your rulers.
5Make models of the tumors and of the
rats that are destroying the country, and
pay honor to Israel's god. Perhaps he will
lift his hand from you and your gods and
your land. 6Why do you harden your
hearts as the Egyptians and Pharaoh did?
When he[d] treated them harshly, did they
not send the Israelites out so they could
go on their way?

7"Now then, get a new cart ready, with
two cows that have calved and have never been yoked. Hitch the cows to the cart,
but take their calves away and pen them
up. 8Take the ark of the LORD and put it
on the cart, and in a chest beside it put the
gold objects you are sending back to him
as a guilt offering. Send it on its way, 9but
keep watching it. If it goes up to its own
territory, toward Beth Shemesh, then the
LORD has brought this great disaster on us.
But if it does not, then we will know that
it was not his hand that struck us and that
it happened to us by chance."

10So they did this. They took two such
cows and hitched them to the cart and
penned up their calves. 11They placed the
ark of the LORD on the cart and along with
it the chest containing the gold rats and
the models of the tumors. 12Then the cows
went straight up toward Beth Shemesh,
keeping on the road and lowing all the
way; they did not turn to the right or to
the left. The rulers of the Philistines followed them as far as the border of Beth
Shemesh.

13Now the people of Beth Shemesh
were harvesting their wheat in the valley,
and when they looked up and saw the ark,
they rejoiced at the sight. 14The cart came
to the field of Joshua of Beth Shemesh,
and there it stopped beside a large rock.
The people chopped up the wood of the
cart and sacrificed the cows as a burnt offering to the LORD. 15The Levites took
down the ark of the LORD, together with
the chest containing the gold objects, and
placed them on the large rock. On that
day the people of Beth Shemesh offered
burnt offerings and made sacrifices to the
LORD. 16The five rulers of the Philistines
saw all this and then returned that same
day to Ekron.

17These are the gold tumors the Philistines sent as a guilt offering to the LORD—
one each for Ashdod, Gaza, Ashkelon,
Gath and Ekron. 18And the number of the
gold rats was according to the number of
Philistine towns belonging to the five
rulers—the fortified towns with their
country villages. The large rock, on which[e]
they set the ark of the LORD, is a witness
to this day in the field of Joshua of Beth
Shemesh.

19But God struck down some of the
men of Beth Shemesh, putting seventy[f] of
them to death because they had looked
into the ark of the LORD. The people
mourned because of the heavy blow the
LORD had dealt them, 20and the men of
Beth Shemesh asked, "Who can stand in
the presence of the LORD, this holy God?
To whom will the ark go up from here?"

21Then they sent messengers to the people of Kiriath Jearim, saying, "The Philistines have returned the ark of the LORD.
Come down and take it up to your place."

[d] *6* That is, God [e] *18* A few Hebrew manuscripts (see also Septuagint); most Hebrew manuscripts *villages as far as Greater Abel, where* [f] *19* A few Hebrew manuscripts; most Hebrew manuscripts and Septuagint *50,070*

PRAYER: PETITION

MAY You, O Sovereign Lord, deal well with me for Your name's sake; because of the goodness of Your mercy, deliver me. (Psalm 109:21)

***PAUSE** here to offer prayers of petition regarding your family and your ministry. Ask for help and guidance in sharing Jesus with others and helping others grow in Him. Ask for guidance in your vocation and your avocations. Offer prayers of petition regarding your activities for this day and any special concerns you may have.*

NT 1 Thessalonians 4:13–5:11

The Coming of the Lord

[13]Brothers, we do not want you to be ignorant about those who fall asleep, or to grieve like the rest of men, who have no hope. [14]We believe that Jesus died and rose again and so we believe that God will bring with Jesus those who have fallen asleep in him. [15]According to the Lord's own word, we tell you that we who are still alive, who are left till the coming of the Lord, will certainly not precede those who have fallen asleep. [16]For the Lord himself will come down from heaven, with a loud command, with the voice of the archangel and with the trumpet call of God, and the dead in Christ will rise first. [17]After that, we who are still alive and are left will be caught up together with them in the clouds to meet the Lord in the air. And so we will be with the Lord forever. [18]Therefore encourage each other with these words.

5 Now, brothers, about times and dates we do not need to write to you, [2]for you know very well that the day of the Lord will come like a thief in the night. [3]While people are saying, "Peace and safety," destruction will come on them suddenly, as labor pains on a pregnant woman, and they will not escape.

[4]But you, brothers, are not in darkness so that this day should surprise you like a thief. [5]You are all sons of the light and sons of the day. We do not belong to the night or to the darkness. [6]So then, let us not be like others, who are asleep, but let us be alert and self-controlled. [7]For those who sleep, sleep at night, and those who get drunk, get drunk at night. [8]But since we belong to the day, let us be self-controlled, putting on faith and love as a breastplate, and the hope of salvation as a helmet. [9]For God did not appoint us to suffer wrath but to receive salvation through our Lord Jesus Christ. [10]He died for us so that, whether we are awake or asleep, we may live together with him. [11]Therefore encourage one another and build each other up, just as in fact you are doing.

PRAYER: MY RELATIONSHIP TO OTHERS

I WILL train up my children in the way they should go; even when they are old they will not depart from it. (Proverbs 22:6) . . I will correct my children, and they will give me rest; they will bring delight to my soul. (Proverbs 29:17)

***PAUSE** to review your relationships with others and to commit them to the Lord.*

OT 1 Samuel 7:1–8:22

YEAR 1 DAY 236

7 [1]So the men of Kiriath Jearim came and took up the ark of the LORD. They took it to Abinadab's house on the hill and consecrated Eleazar his son to guard the ark of the LORD.

Samuel Subdues the Philistines at Mizpah

[2]It was a long time, twenty years in all, that the ark remained at Kiriath Jearim, and all the people of Israel mourned and sought after the LORD. [3]And Samuel said to the whole house of Israel, "If you are returning to the LORD with all your hearts, then rid yourselves of the foreign gods and the Ashtoreths and commit yourselves to the LORD and serve him only, and he will deliver you out of the hand of the Philistines." [4]So the Israelites put away their Baals and Ashtoreths, and served the LORD only.

[5]Then Samuel said, "Assemble all Israel at Mizpah and I will intercede with the LORD for you." [6]When they had assembled at Mizpah, they drew water and poured it out before the LORD. On that day they

fasted and there they confessed, "We have
sinned against the LORD." And Samuel
was leader[a] of Israel at Mizpah.
7When the Philistines heard that Israel
had assembled at Mizpah, the rulers of the
Philistines came up to attack them. And
when the Israelites heard of it, they were
afraid because of the Philistines. 8They
said to Samuel, "Do not stop crying out to
the LORD our God for us, that he may rescue us from the hand of the Philistines."
9Then Samuel took a suckling lamb and
offered it up as a whole burnt offering to
the LORD. He cried out to the LORD on Israel's behalf, and the LORD answered him.
10While Samuel was sacrificing the
burnt offering, the Philistines drew near
to engage Israel in battle. But that day the
LORD thundered with loud thunder
against the Philistines and threw them
into such a panic that they were routed
before the Israelites. 11The men of Israel
rushed out of Mizpah and pursued the
Philistines, slaughtering them along the
way to a point below Beth Car.
12Then Samuel took a stone and set it
up between Mizpah and Shen. He named
it Ebenezer,[b] saying, "Thus far has the
LORD helped us." 13So the Philistines were
subdued and did not invade Israelite territory again.
Throughout Samuel's lifetime, the hand
of the LORD was against the Philistines.
14The towns from Ekron to Gath that the
Philistines had captured from Israel were
restored to her, and Israel delivered the
neighboring territory from the power of
the Philistines. And there was peace between Israel and the Amorites.
15Samuel continued as judge over Israel
all the days of his life. 16From year to year
he went on a circuit from Bethel to Gilgal
to Mizpah, judging Israel in all those places.
17But he always went back to Ramah, where
his home was, and there he also judged Israel. And he built an altar there to the LORD.

Israel Asks for a King

8 When Samuel grew old, he appointed
his sons as judges for Israel. 2The name
of his firstborn was Joel and the name of
his second was Abijah, and they served at
Beersheba. 3But his sons did not walk in his
ways. They turned aside after dishonest gain
and accepted bribes and perverted justice.
4So all the elders of Israel gathered together and came to Samuel at Ramah.
5They said to him, "You are old, and your
sons do not walk in your ways; now appoint a king to lead[c] us, such as all the
other nations have."
6But when they said, "Give us a king to
lead us," this displeased Samuel; so he
prayed to the LORD. 7And the LORD told
him: "Listen to all that the people are saying to you; it is not you they have rejected, but they have rejected me as their
king. 8As they have done from the day I
brought them up out of Egypt until this
day, forsaking me and serving other gods,
so they are doing to you. 9Now listen to
them; but warn them solemnly and let
them know what the king who will reign
over them will do."
10Samuel told all the words of the LORD
to the people who were asking him for a
king. 11He said, "This is what the king who
will reign over you will do: He will take
your sons and make them serve with his
chariots and horses, and they will run in
front of his chariots. 12Some he will assign
to be commanders of thousands and commanders of fifties, and others to plow his
ground and reap his harvest, and still others to make weapons of war and equipment
for his chariots. 13He will take your daughters to be perfumers and cooks and bakers.
14He will take the best of your fields and
vineyards and olive groves and give them to
his attendants. 15He will take a tenth of your
grain and of your vintage and give it to his
officials and attendants. 16Your menservants
and maidservants and the best of your cattle[d] and donkeys he will take for his own
use. 17He will take a tenth of your flocks,
and you yourselves will become his slaves.
18When that day comes, you will cry out for
relief from the king you have chosen, and
the LORD will not answer you in that day."
19But the people refused to listen to
Samuel. "No!" they said. "We want a king
over us. 20Then we will be like all the other nations, with a king to lead us and to
go out before us and fight our battles."
21When Samuel heard all that the people said, he repeated it before the LORD.
22The LORD answered, "Listen to them and
give them a king."
Then Samuel said to the men of Israel,
"Everyone go back to his town."

[a] 6 Traditionally *judge* [b] 12 *Ebenezer* means *stone of help.* [c] 5 Traditionally *judge;* also in verses 6 and 20 [d] 16 Septuagint; Hebrew *young men*

PRAYER: INTERCESSION

THIS is pure and undefiled religion before You, my God and Father: to visit orphans and widows in their affliction and to keep myself unspotted from the world. (James 1:27)

***TAKE** a few moments to intercede on behalf of local, national and world missions. Pray that the Great Commission would be fulfilled and for any special concerns you may have for missions.*

NT 1 Thessalonians 5:12–28

Final Instructions

[12]Now we ask you, brothers, to respect
those who work hard among you, who
are over you in the Lord and who admonish you. [13]Hold them in the highest
regard in love because of their work. Live
in peace with each other. [14]And we urge
you, brothers, warn those who are idle,
encourage the timid, help the weak, be
patient with everyone. [15]Make sure that
nobody pays back wrong for wrong, but
always try to be kind to each other and to
everyone else.
[16]Be joyful always; [17]pray continually;
[18]give thanks in all circumstances, for this
is God's will for you in Christ Jesus.
[19]Do not put out the Spirit's fire; [20]do
not treat prophecies with contempt. [21]Test
everything. Hold on to the good. [22]Avoid
every kind of evil.
[23]May God himself, the God of peace,
sanctify you through and through. May
your whole spirit, soul and body be kept
blameless at the coming of our Lord Jesus
Christ. [24]The one who calls you is faithful
and he will do it.

[25]Brothers, pray for us. [26]Greet all the
brothers with a holy kiss. [27]I charge you
before the Lord to have this letter read to
all the brothers.
[28]The grace of our Lord Jesus Christ be
with you.

PRAYER: THE ATTRIBUTES OF GOD

O LORD, God of heaven, You are the great and awesome God, keeping Your covenant of loyal love with those who love You and obey Your commands. (Nehemiah 1:5) . . . Great and marvelous are Your works, Lord God Almighty! Righteous and true are Your ways, King of the nations! Who will not fear You, O Lord, and glorify Your name? For You alone are holy. All nations will come and worship before You, for Your righteous acts have been revealed. (Revelation 15:3–4)

***PAUSE** to reflect on these affirmations about the person, powers and perfection of God.*

YEAR 1
DAY 237

OT 1 Samuel 9:1–27

Samuel Anoints Saul

9 There was a Benjamite, a man of standing, whose name was Kish son of Abiel, the son of Zeror, the son of Becorath,
the son of Aphiah of Benjamin. [2]He had
a son named Saul, an impressive young
man without equal among the Israelites—
a head taller than any of the others.
[3]Now the donkeys belonging to Saul's
father Kish were lost, and Kish said to his
son Saul, "Take one of the servants with
you and go and look for the donkeys." [4]So

he passed through the hill country of Ephraim and through the area around Shalisha, but they did not find them. They went on into the district of Shaalim, but the donkeys were not there. Then he passed through the territory of Benjamin, but they did not find them.

5When they reached the district of Zuph, Saul said to the servant who was with him, "Come, let's go back, or my father will stop thinking about the donkeys and start worrying about us."

6But the servant replied, "Look, in this town there is a man of God; he is highly respected, and everything he says comes true. Let's go there now. Perhaps he will tell us what way to take."

7Saul said to his servant, "If we go, what can we give the man? The food in our sacks is gone. We have no gift to take to the man of God. What do we have?"

8The servant answered him again. "Look," he said, "I have a quarter of a shekel[a] of silver. I will give it to the man of God so that he will tell us what way to take." 9(Formerly in Israel, if a man went to inquire of God, he would say, "Come, let us go to the seer," because the prophet of today used to be called a seer.)

10"Good," Saul said to his servant. "Come, let's go." So they set out for the town where the man of God was.

11As they were going up the hill to the town, they met some girls coming out to draw water, and they asked them, "Is the seer here?"

12"He is," they answered. "He's ahead of you. Hurry now; he has just come to our town today, for the people have a sacrifice at the high place. 13As soon as you enter the town, you will find him before he goes up to the high place to eat. The people will not begin eating until he comes, because he must bless the sacrifice; afterward, those who are invited will eat. Go up now; you should find him about this time."

14They went up to the town, and as they were entering it, there was Samuel, coming toward them on his way up to the high place.

15Now the day before Saul came, the LORD had revealed this to Samuel: 16"About this time tomorrow I will send you a man from the land of Benjamin. Anoint him leader over my people Israel; he will deliver my people from the hand of the Philistines. I have looked upon my people, for their cry has reached me."

17When Samuel caught sight of Saul, the LORD said to him, "This is the man I spoke to you about; he will govern my people."

18Saul approached Samuel in the gateway and asked, "Would you please tell me where the seer's house is?"

19"I am the seer," Samuel replied. "Go up ahead of me to the high place, for today you are to eat with me, and in the morning I will let you go and will tell you all that is in your heart. 20As for the donkeys you lost three days ago, do not worry about them; they have been found. And to whom is all the desire of Israel turned, if not to you and all your father's family?"

21Saul answered, "But am I not a Benjamite, from the smallest tribe of Israel, and is not my clan the least of all the clans of the tribe of Benjamin? Why do you say such a thing to me?"

22Then Samuel brought Saul and his servant into the hall and seated them at the head of those who were invited—about thirty in number. 23Samuel said to the cook, "Bring the piece of meat I gave you, the one I told you to lay aside."

24So the cook took up the leg with what was on it and set it in front of Saul. Samuel said, "Here is what has been kept for you. Eat, because it was set aside for you for this occasion, from the time I said, 'I have invited guests.' " And Saul dined with Samuel that day.

25After they came down from the high place to the town, Samuel talked with Saul on the roof of his house. 26They rose about daybreak and Samuel called to Saul on the roof, "Get ready, and I will send you on your way." When Saul got ready, he and Samuel went outside together. 27As they were going down to the edge of the town, Samuel said to Saul, "Tell the servant to go on ahead of us"—and the servant did so—"but you stay here awhile, so that I may give you a message from God."

[a] 8 That is, about 1/10 ounce (about 3 grams)

PRAYER: AFFIRMATION

NO one can see Your kingdom, O God, without being born again; no one can enter into Your kingdom without being born of water and Your Spirit. That which is born of the flesh is flesh, and that which is born of the Spirit is spirit. The wind blows wherever it pleases, and we hear its sound, but we cannot tell where it comes from, or where it is going. So it is with everyone born of the Spirit.

(John 3:3, 5–6, 8)

***PAUSE** to reflect on these Biblical affirmations.*

NT 2 Thessalonians 1:1–12

1 Paul, Silas[a] and Timothy,

To the church of the Thessalonians in
God our Father and the Lord Jesus Christ:

2Grace and peace to you from God the
Father and the Lord Jesus Christ.

Thanksgiving and Prayer

3We ought always to thank God for you,
brothers, and rightly so, because your
faith is growing more and more, and the
love every one of you has for each other
is increasing. 4Therefore, among God's
churches we boast about your perseverance and faith in all the persecutions and
trials you are enduring.
5All this is evidence that God's judgment is right, and as a result you will be
counted worthy of the kingdom of God,
for which you are suffering. 6God is just:
He will pay back trouble to those who
trouble you 7and give relief to you who
are troubled, and to us as well. This will
happen when the Lord Jesus is revealed
from heaven in blazing fire with his powerful angels. 8He will punish those who
do not know God and do not obey the
gospel of our Lord Jesus. 9They will be
punished with everlasting destruction and
shut out from the presence of the Lord
and from the majesty of his power 10on
the day he comes to be glorified in his
holy people and to be marveled at among
all those who have believed. This includes
you, because you believed our testimony
to you.
11With this in mind, we constantly pray
for you, that our God may count you worthy of his calling, and that by his power
he may fulfill every good purpose of yours
and every act prompted by your faith.
12We pray this so that the name of our
Lord Jesus may be glorified in you, and
you in him, according to the grace of our
God and the Lord Jesus Christ.[b]

[a] 1 Greek *Silvanus,* a variant of *Silas* [b] 12 Or *God and Lord, Jesus Christ*

PRAYER: THE WORKS OF GOD

JOHN was called Your prophet, O Most High; for he went on before You to prepare the way for You, and to give Your people the knowledge of salvation through the forgiveness of their sins because of Your tender mercy, O God, with which the sunrise from on high came from heaven to shine on those living in darkness and in the shadow of death, to guide their feet into the path of peace. (Luke 1:76–79) . . . Jesus, You are the Lamb of God, who takes away the sin of the world.

(John 1:29)

***TAKE** a moment to consider the greatness of God's wonderful works.*

YEAR 1 DAY 238

OT Psalm 45

Psalm 45

For the director of music. To ⌊the tune of⌋ "Lilies." Of the Sons of Korah. A *maskil.*[a] A wedding song.

[1] My heart is stirred by a noble theme
as I recite my verses for the king;
my tongue is the pen of a skillful
writer.

[2] You are the most excellent of men
and your lips have been anointed
with grace,
since God has blessed you forever.
[3] Gird your sword upon your side,
O mighty one;
clothe yourself with splendor and
majesty.
[4] In your majesty ride forth victoriously
in behalf of truth, humility and
righteousness;
let your right hand display awesome
deeds.
[5] Let your sharp arrows pierce the hearts
of the king's enemies;
let the nations fall beneath your
feet.
[6] Your throne, O God, will last for ever
and ever;
a scepter of justice will be the
scepter of your kingdom.
[7] You love righteousness and hate
wickedness;
therefore God, your God, has set
you above your companions
by anointing you with the oil of joy.
[8] All your robes are fragrant with myrrh
and aloes and cassia;
from palaces adorned with ivory
the music of the strings makes you
glad.
[9] Daughters of kings are among your
honored women;
at your right hand is the royal bride
in gold of Ophir.

[10] Listen, O daughter, consider and give
ear:
Forget your people and your father's
house.
[11] The king is enthralled by your beauty;
honor him, for he is your lord.
[12] The Daughter of Tyre will come with a
gift,[b]
men of wealth will seek your favor.

[13] All glorious is the princess within ⌊her
chamber⌋;
her gown is interwoven with gold.
[14] In embroidered garments she is led to
the king;
her virgin companions follow her
and are brought to you.
[15] They are led in with joy and gladness;
they enter the palace of the king.

[16] Your sons will take the place of your
fathers;
you will make them princes
throughout the land.
[17] I will perpetuate your memory
through all generations;
therefore the nations will praise you
for ever and ever.

[a] Title: Probably a literary or musical term [b] 12 Or *A Tyrian robe is among the gifts*

PRAYER: THANKSGIVING

I WILL give thanks to You, O Lord, and call upon Your name, and make known to others what You have done. I will sing to You, sing praises to You, and tell of all Your wonderful acts. (1 Chronicles 16:8–9) . . . O Lord, I know that You have set apart the godly for Yourself; You hear when I call to You. (Psalm 4:3)

PAUSE *to offer your own expressions of thanksgiving.*

NT 2 Thessalonians 2:1–12

The Man of Lawlessness

2 Concerning the coming of our Lord
Jesus Christ and our being gathered to
him, we ask you, brothers, 2not to become
easily unsettled or alarmed by some
prophecy, report or letter supposed to
have come from us, saying that the day of
the Lord has already come. 3Don't let anyone deceive you in any way, for ⌊that day
will not come⌋ until the rebellion occurs
and the man of lawlessness[a] is revealed,
the man doomed to destruction. 4He will
oppose and will exalt himself over everything that is called God or is worshiped,
so that he sets himself up in God's temple, proclaiming himself to be God.
5Don't you remember that when I was
with you I used to tell you these things?
6And now you know what is holding him
back, so that he may be revealed at the
proper time. 7For the secret power of lawlessness is already at work; but the one
who now holds it back will continue to
do so till he is taken out of the way. 8And
then the lawless one will be revealed,
whom the Lord Jesus will overthrow with
the breath of his mouth and destroy by
the splendor of his coming. 9The coming
of the lawless one will be in accordance
with the work of Satan displayed in all
kinds of counterfeit miracles, signs and
wonders, 10and in every sort of evil that
deceives those who are perishing. They
perish because they refused to love the
truth and so be saved. 11For this reason
God sends them a powerful delusion so
that they will believe the lie 12and so that
all will be condemned who have not believed the truth but have delighted in
wickedness.

[a] 3 Some manuscripts *sin*

PRAYER: MY RELATIONSHIP TO GOD

YOUR grace, Lord Jesus Christ, and the love of God, and the fellowship of the Holy Spirit are with me. (2 Corinthians 13:14) . . .
In You, O Christ, I have obtained an inheritance, having been predestined according to the plan of Him who works all things according to the counsel of His will, that I who have trusted in You should be to the praise of His glory. (Ephesians 1:11–12)

***PAUSE** to thank God for the relationship that you enjoy with Him in Jesus Christ.*

YEAR 1 DAY 239

OT 1 Samuel 10:1–27

10 Then Samuel took a flask of oil and
poured it on Saul's head and kissed
him, saying, "Has not the LORD anointed
you leader over his inheritance?[a] 2When
you leave me today, you will meet two
men near Rachel's tomb, at Zelzah on the
border of Benjamin. They will say to you,
'The donkeys you set out to look for have
been found. And now your father has
stopped thinking about them and is worried about you. He is asking, "What shall
I do about my son?" '
3"Then you will go on from there until
you reach the great tree of Tabor. Three
men going up to God at Bethel will meet
you there. One will be carrying three
young goats, another three loaves of
bread, and another a skin of wine. 4They
will greet you and offer you two loaves of
bread, which you will accept from them.
5"After that you will go to Gibeah of
God, where there is a Philistine outpost.
As you approach the town, you will meet

[a] 1 Hebrew; Septuagint and Vulgate *over his people Israel? You will reign over the* LORD*'s people and save them from the power of their enemies round about. And this will be a sign to you that the* LORD *has anointed you leader over his inheritance:*

a procession of prophets coming down
from the high place with lyres, tambourines, flutes and harps being played
before them, and they will be prophesying. 6The Spirit of the LORD will come
upon you in power, and you will prophesy with them; and you will be changed
into a different person. 7Once these signs
are fulfilled, do whatever your hand finds
to do, for God is with you.
8"Go down ahead of me to Gilgal. I will
surely come down to you to sacrifice
burnt offerings and fellowship offerings,[b]
but you must wait seven days until I come
to you and tell you what you are to do."

Saul Made King

9As Saul turned to leave Samuel, God
changed Saul's heart, and all these signs
were fulfilled that day. 10When they arrived
at Gibeah, a procession of prophets met
him; the Spirit of God came upon him in
power, and he joined in their prophesying.
11When all those who had formerly known
him saw him prophesying with the prophets, they asked each other, "What is this
that has happened to the son of Kish? Is
Saul also among the prophets?"
12A man who lived there answered,
"And who is their father?" So it became a
saying: "Is Saul also among the prophets?" 13After Saul stopped prophesying, he
went to the high place.
14Now Saul's uncle asked him and his
servant, "Where have you been?"
"Looking for the donkeys," he said.
"But when we saw they were not to be
found, we went to Samuel."
15Saul's uncle said, "Tell me what Samuel said to you."
16Saul replied, "He assured us that the
donkeys had been found." But he did not
tell his uncle what Samuel had said about
the kingship.
17Samuel summoned the people of Israel to the LORD at Mizpah 18and said to
them, "This is what the LORD, the God of
Israel, says: 'I brought Israel up out of
Egypt, and I delivered you from the power of Egypt and all the kingdoms that oppressed you.' 19But you have now rejected
your God, who saves you out of all your
calamities and distresses. And you have
said, 'No, set a king over us.' So now
present yourselves before the LORD by
your tribes and clans."
20When Samuel brought all the tribes of
Israel near, the tribe of Benjamin was chosen. 21Then he brought forward the tribe
of Benjamin, clan by clan, and Matri's
clan was chosen. Finally Saul son of Kish
was chosen. But when they looked for
him, he was not to be found. 22So they inquired further of the LORD, "Has the man
come here yet?"
And the LORD said, "Yes, he has hidden
himself among the baggage."
23They ran and brought him out, and as
he stood among the people he was a head
taller than any of the others. 24Samuel said
to all the people, "Do you see the man the
LORD has chosen? There is no one like
him among all the people."
Then the people shouted, "Long live
the king!"
25Samuel explained to the people the
regulations of the kingship. He wrote
them down on a scroll and deposited it
before the LORD. Then Samuel dismissed
the people, each to his own home.
26Saul also went to his home in Gibeah, accompanied by valiant men whose
hearts God had touched. 27But some troublemakers said, "How can this fellow save
us?" They despised him and brought him
no gifts. But Saul kept silent.

[b] 8 Traditionally *peace offerings*

PRAYER: ADORATION

WHO has understood what is in Your mind, O Lord, or instructed You as Your counselor? Whom did You consult to enlighten You, and who taught You the path of justice? Who taught You knowledge or showed You the way of understanding? Surely the nations are like a drop in a bucket and are regarded as dust on the scales; You weigh the islands as though they were fine dust. Before You all the nations are as nothing; You

regard them as less than nothing and worthless. To whom, then, will I compare You? Or what likeness will I compare with You? (Isaiah 40:13–15, 17–18)

PAUSE *to express your thoughts of praise and worship.*

NT 2 Thessalonians 2:13–3:5

Stand Firm

[13]But we ought always to thank God for you, brothers loved by the Lord, because from the beginning God chose you[a] to be saved through the sanctifying work of the Spirit and through belief in the truth.
[14]He called you to this through our gospel, that you might share in the glory of our Lord Jesus Christ.
[15]So then, brothers, stand firm and hold to the teachings[b] we passed on to you, whether by word of mouth or by letter.

[16]May our Lord Jesus Christ himself and God our Father, who loved us and by his grace gave us eternal encouragement and good hope,
[17]encourage your hearts and strengthen you in every good deed and word.

Request for Prayer

3 Finally, brothers, pray for us that the message of the Lord may spread rapidly and be honored, just as it was with you.
[2]And pray that we may be delivered from wicked and evil men, for not everyone has faith.
[3]But the Lord is faithful, and he will strengthen and protect you from the evil one.
[4]We have confidence in the Lord that you are doing and will continue to do the things we command.
[5]May the Lord direct your hearts into God's love and Christ's perseverance.

[a] 13 Some manuscripts *because God chose you as his firstfruits* [b] 15 Or *traditions*

PRAYER: THE CHARACTER I WANT TO CULTIVATE

I CANNOT serve two masters; for either I will hate the one and love the other, or I will be devoted to the one and despise the other. I cannot serve both You, O God, and wealth. (Matthew 6:24; Luke 16:13) . . . I will not love the world or the things in the world. If I love the world, Your love, O Father, is not in me. For all that is in the world—the lust of the flesh, the lust of the eyes and the pride of life—is not of You but of the world. And the world and its lusts are passing away, but the one who does Your will, O God, abides forever. (1 John 2:15–17)

TAKE *a moment to ask the Lord for the grace to grow in godly character.*

YEAR 1 DAY 240

OT 1 Samuel 11:1–15

Saul Rescues the City of Jabesh

11 Nahash the Ammonite went up and besieged Jabesh Gilead. And all the men of Jabesh said to him, "Make a treaty with us, and we will be subject to you."

[2]But Nahash the Ammonite replied, "I will make a treaty with you only on the condition that I gouge out the right eye of every one of you and so bring disgrace on all Israel."

[3]The elders of Jabesh said to him, "Give us seven days so we can send messengers throughout Israel; if no one comes to rescue us, we will surrender to you."

[4]When the messengers came to Gibeah of Saul and reported these terms to the people, they all wept aloud.
[5]Just then

Saul was returning from the fields, behind his oxen, and he asked, "What is wrong with the people? Why are they weeping?" Then they repeated to him what the men of Jabesh had said.

6When Saul heard their words, the Spirit of God came upon him in power, and he burned with anger. 7He took a pair of oxen, cut them into pieces, and sent the pieces by messengers throughout Israel, proclaiming, "This is what will be done to the oxen of anyone who does not follow Saul and Samuel." Then the terror of the LORD fell on the people, and they turned out as one man. 8When Saul mustered them at Bezek, the men of Israel numbered three hundred thousand and the men of Judah thirty thousand.

9They told the messengers who had come, "Say to the men of Jabesh Gilead, 'By the time the sun is hot tomorrow, you will be delivered.' " When the messengers went and reported this to the men of Jabesh, they were elated. 10They said to the Ammonites, "Tomorrow we will surrender to you, and you can do to us whatever seems good to you."

11The next day Saul separated his men into three divisions; during the last watch of the night they broke into the camp of the Ammonites and slaughtered them until the heat of the day. Those who survived were scattered, so that no two of them were left together.

Saul Confirmed as King

12The people then said to Samuel, "Who was it that asked, 'Shall Saul reign over us?' Bring these men to us and we will put them to death."

13But Saul said, "No one shall be put to death today, for this day the LORD has rescued Israel."

14Then Samuel said to the people, "Come, let us go to Gilgal and there reaffirm the kingship." 15So all the people went to Gilgal and confirmed Saul as king in the presence of the LORD. There they sacrificed fellowship offerings[a] before the LORD, and Saul and all the Israelites held a great celebration.

[a] 15 Traditionally *peace offerings*

PRAYER: CONFESSION

WHO among us fears You, O Lord, and obeys the word of Your Servant? Let those who walk in darkness and have no light trust in Your name, O Lord, and rely upon You. (Isaiah 50:10)

***ASK** the Spirit to search your heart and reveal any areas of unconfessed sin. Acknowledge these to the Lord and thank Him for His forgiveness.*

NT 2 Thessalonians 3:6–18

Warning Against Idleness

6In the name of the Lord Jesus Christ, we command you, brothers, to keep away from every brother who is idle and does not live according to the teaching[a] you received from us. 7For you yourselves know how you ought to follow our example. We were not idle when we were with you, 8nor did we eat anyone's food without paying for it. On the contrary, we worked night and day, laboring and toiling so that we would not be a burden to any of you. 9We did this, not because we do not have the right to such help, but in order to make ourselves a model for you to follow. 10For even when we were with you, we gave you this rule: "If a man will not work, he shall not eat."

11We hear that some among you are idle. They are not busy; they are busybodies. 12Such people we command and urge in the Lord Jesus Christ to settle down and earn the bread they eat. 13And as for you, brothers, never tire of doing what is right.

14If anyone does not obey our instruction in this letter, take special note of him. Do not associate with him, in order that he may feel ashamed. 15Yet do not regard him as an enemy, but warn him as a brother.

[a] 6 Or *tradition*

Final Greetings

[16]Now may the Lord of peace himself give you peace at all times and in every way. The Lord be with all of you.

[17]I, Paul, write this greeting in my own hand, which is the distinguishing mark in all my letters. This is how I write.

[18]The grace of our Lord Jesus Christ be with you all.

PRAYER: MY RELATIONSHIP TO OTHERS

IN Christ Jesus, Your whole building, O God, is joined together and growing into a holy temple in You, in whom we also are being built together into Your dwelling in the Spirit. (Ephesians 2:21–22) . . . Grace has been given to each one of us according to the measure of Your gift, Christ Jesus. And You gave some to be apostles, some to be prophets, some to be evangelists, and some to be pastors and teachers, to equip the saints for the work of ministry so that Your body will be built up. (Ephesians 4:7, 11–12)

***PAUSE** to review your relationships with others and to commit them to the Lord.*

YEAR 1 DAY 241

OT I Samuel 12:1–25

Samuel's Farewell Speech

12 Samuel said to all Israel, "I have listened to everything you said to me and have set a king over you. [2]Now you have a king as your leader. As for me, I am old and gray, and my sons are here with you. I have been your leader from my youth until this day. [3]Here I stand. Testify against me in the presence of the LORD and his anointed. Whose ox have I taken? Whose donkey have I taken? Whom have I cheated? Whom have I oppressed? From whose hand have I accepted a bribe to make me shut my eyes? If I have done any of these, I will make it right."

[4]"You have not cheated or oppressed us," they replied. "You have not taken anything from anyone's hand."

[5]Samuel said to them, "The LORD is witness against you, and also his anointed is witness this day, that you have not found anything in my hand."

"He is witness," they said.

[6]Then Samuel said to the people, "It is the LORD who appointed Moses and Aaron and brought your forefathers up out of Egypt. [7]Now then, stand here, because I am going to confront you with evidence before the LORD as to all the righteous acts performed by the LORD for you and your fathers.

[8]"After Jacob entered Egypt, they cried to the LORD for help, and the LORD sent Moses and Aaron, who brought your forefathers out of Egypt and settled them in this place.

[9]"But they forgot the LORD their God; so he sold them into the hand of Sisera, the commander of the army of Hazor, and into the hands of the Philistines and the king of Moab, who fought against them. [10]They cried out to the LORD and said, 'We have sinned; we have forsaken the LORD and served the Baals and the Ashtoreths. But now deliver us from the hands of our enemies, and we will serve you.' [11]Then the LORD sent Jerub-Baal,[a] Barak,[b] Jephthah and Samuel,[c] and he delivered you from the hands of your enemies on every side, so that you lived securely.

[12]"But when you saw that Nahash king of the Ammonites was moving against you, you said to me, 'No, we want a king to rule over us'—even though the LORD your God was your king. [13]Now here is the king you have chosen, the one you asked for; see, the LORD has set a king over you. [14]If you fear the LORD and serve and obey him and do not rebel against his com-

[a] *11* Also called *Gideon* [b] *11* Some Septuagint manuscripts and Syriac; Hebrew *Bedan*
[c] *11* Hebrew; some Septuagint manuscripts and Syriac *Samson*

mands, and if both you and the king who reigns over you follow the LORD your God—good! [15]But if you do not obey the LORD, and if you rebel against his commands, his hand will be against you, as it was against your fathers.

[16]"Now then, stand still and see this great thing the LORD is about to do before your eyes! [17]Is it not wheat harvest now? I will call upon the LORD to send thunder and rain. And you will realize what an evil thing you did in the eyes of the LORD when you asked for a king."

[18]Then Samuel called upon the LORD, and that same day the LORD sent thunder and rain. So all the people stood in awe of the LORD and of Samuel.

[19]The people all said to Samuel, "Pray to the LORD your God for your servants so that we will not die, for we have added to all our other sins the evil of asking for a king."

[20]"Do not be afraid," Samuel replied. "You have done all this evil; yet do not turn away from the LORD, but serve the LORD with all your heart. [21]Do not turn away after useless idols. They can do you no good, nor can they rescue you, because they are useless. [22]For the sake of his great name the LORD will not reject his people, because the LORD was pleased to make you his own. [23]As for me, far be it from me that I should sin against the LORD by failing to pray for you. And I will teach you the way that is good and right. [24]But be sure to fear the LORD and serve him faithfully with all your heart; consider what great things he has done for you. [25]Yet if you persist in doing evil, both you and your king will be swept away."

PRAYER: RENEWAL

BY Your grace, I want to observe Your judgments and keep Your statutes, to walk in them; You are the Lord my God. May I keep Your statutes and Your judgments, for the one who obeys them will live by them. You are the Lord. (Leviticus 18:4–5) . . . May I fear You, O Lord, and serve and obey You and not rebel against Your commands. (1 Samuel 12:14)

PAUSE *to add your own prayers for personal renewal.*

NT 1 Timothy 1:1–11

Paul, an apostle of Christ Jesus by the command of God our Savior and of Christ Jesus our hope,

[2]To Timothy my true son in the faith:

Grace, mercy and peace from God the Father and Christ Jesus our Lord.

Warning Against False Teachers of the Law

[3]As I urged you when I went into Macedonia, stay there in Ephesus so that you may command certain men not to teach false doctrines any longer [4]nor to devote themselves to myths and endless genealogies. These promote controversies rather than God's work—which is by faith. [5]The goal of this command is love, which comes from a pure heart and a good conscience and a sincere faith. [6]Some have wandered away from these and turned to meaningless talk. [7]They want to be teachers of the law, but they do not know what they are talking about or what they so confidently affirm.

[8]We know that the law is good if one uses it properly. [9]We also know that law[a] is made not for the righteous but for lawbreakers and rebels, the ungodly and sinful, the unholy and irreligious; for those who kill their fathers or mothers, for murderers, [10]for adulterers and perverts, for slave traders and liars and perjurers—and for whatever else is contrary to the sound doctrine [11]that conforms to the glorious gospel of the blessed God, which he entrusted to me.

[a] 9 Or *that the law*

PRAYER: THE ATTRIBUTES OF GOD

I WILL regard You as holy, Lord of hosts. You shall be my fear, and You shall be my dread. (Isaiah 8:13) . . . You, O Lord, are in Your holy temple; let all the earth be silent before You. (Habakkuk 2:20)

__PAUSE__ to reflect on these affirmations about the person, powers and perfection of God.

YEAR 1
DAY 242

OT 1 Samuel 13:1–22

Samuel Rebukes Saul

13 Saul was ⌞thirty⌟[a] years old when he
became king, and he reigned over Israel ⌞forty-⌟[b] two years.
2 Saul[c] chose three thousand men from
Israel; two thousand were with him at
Micmash and in the hill country of Bethel, and a thousand were with Jonathan at
Gibeah in Benjamin. The rest of the men
he sent back to their homes.
3 Jonathan attacked the Philistine outpost at Geba, and the Philistines heard
about it. Then Saul had the trumpet
blown throughout the land and said, "Let
the Hebrews hear!" 4 So all Israel heard the
news: "Saul has attacked the Philistine
outpost, and now Israel has become a
stench to the Philistines." And the people
were summoned to join Saul at Gilgal.
5 The Philistines assembled to fight Israel, with three thousand[d] chariots, six
thousand charioteers, and soldiers as numerous as the sand on the seashore. They
went up and camped at Micmash, east of
Beth Aven. 6 When the men of Israel saw
that their situation was critical and that
their army was hard pressed, they hid in
caves and thickets, among the rocks, and
in pits and cisterns. 7 Some Hebrews even
crossed the Jordan to the land of Gad and
Gilead.
Saul remained at Gilgal, and all the
troops with him were quaking with fear.
8 He waited seven days, the time set by
Samuel; but Samuel did not come to Gilgal, and Saul's men began to scatter. 9 So
he said, "Bring me the burnt offering and
the fellowship offerings.[e]" And Saul offered up the burnt offering. 10 Just as he
finished making the offering, Samuel arrived, and Saul went out to greet him.
11 "What have you done?" asked Samuel.
Saul replied, "When I saw that the men
were scattering, and that you did not
come at the set time, and that the Philistines were assembling at Micmash, 12 I
thought, 'Now the Philistines will come
down against me at Gilgal, and I have not
sought the LORD's favor.' So I felt compelled to offer the burnt offering."
13 "You acted foolishly," Samuel said.
"You have not kept the command the LORD
your God gave you; if you had, he would
have established your kingdom over Israel
for all time. 14 But now your kingdom will
not endure; the LORD has sought out a man
after his own heart and appointed him
leader of his people, because you have not
kept the LORD's command."
15 Then Samuel left Gilgal[f] and went up
to Gibeah in Benjamin, and Saul counted
the men who were with him. They numbered about six hundred.

Israel Without Weapons

16 Saul and his son Jonathan and the
men with them were staying in Gibeah[g]
in Benjamin, while the Philistines
camped at Micmash. 17 Raiding parties
went out from the Philistine camp in
three detachments. One turned toward
Ophrah in the vicinity of Shual, 18 another toward Beth Horon, and the third toward the borderland overlooking the
Valley of Zeboim facing the desert.

[a] *1* A few late manuscripts of the Septuagint; Hebrew does not have *thirty.* [b] *1* See the round number in Acts 13:21; Hebrew does not have *forty-.* [c] *1,2* Or *and when he had reigned over Israel two years, 2he* [d] *5* Some Septuagint manuscripts and Syriac; Hebrew *thirty thousand* [e] *9* Traditionally *peace offerings* [f] *15* Hebrew; Septuagint *Gilgal and went his way; the rest of the people went after Saul to meet the army, and they went out of Gilgal* [g] *16* Two Hebrew manuscripts; most Hebrew manuscripts *Geba,* a variant of *Gibeah*

19 Not a blacksmith could be found in
the whole land of Israel, because the Philistines had said, "Otherwise the Hebrews
will make swords or spears!" 20 So all Israel went down to the Philistines to have
their plowshares, mattocks, axes and sick-
les[h] sharpened. 21 The price was two thirds
of a shekel[i] for sharpening plowshares
and mattocks, and a third of a shekel[j] for
sharpening forks and axes and for re-
pointing goads.
22 So on the day of the battle not a soldier with Saul and Jonathan had a sword
or spear in his hand; only Saul and his
son Jonathan had them.

[h] 20 Septuagint; Hebrew *plowshares* [i] 21 Hebrew *pim*; that is, about 1/4 ounce (about 8 grams) [j] 21 That is, about 1/8 ounce (about 4 grams)

PRAYER: PETITION

MAY I not imitate what is evil but what is good. The one who does good is of You, O God; the one who does evil has not seen You. (3 John 11)

***PAUSE** here to petition God for growth in your character and personal discipline, and for physical health and strength. Ask that He empower you for spiritual warfare against the temptations of the world, the flesh and the devil. Offer prayers regarding your activities for this day and any special concerns you may have.*

NT 1 Timothy 1:12–20

The Lord's Grace to Paul

12 I thank Christ Jesus our Lord, who has
given me strength, that he considered me
faithful, appointing me to his service.
13 Even though I was once a blasphemer
and a persecutor and a violent man, I was
shown mercy because I acted in ignorance
and unbelief. 14 The grace of our Lord was
poured out on me abundantly, along with
the faith and love that are in Christ Jesus.
15 Here is a trustworthy saying that deserves full acceptance: Christ Jesus came
into the world to save sinners—of whom
I am the worst. 16 But for that very reason
I was shown mercy so that in me, the
worst of sinners, Christ Jesus might display his unlimited patience as an example
for those who would believe on him and
receive eternal life. 17 Now to the King
eternal, immortal, invisible, the only God,
be honor and glory for ever and ever.
Amen.
18 Timothy, my son, I give you this instruction in keeping with the prophecies
once made about you, so that by following them you may fight the good fight,
19 holding on to faith and a good conscience. Some have rejected these and so
have shipwrecked their faith. 20 Among
them are Hymenaeus and Alexander,
whom I have handed over to Satan to be
taught not to blaspheme.

PRAYER: THE WORKS OF GOD

IT is You, O Lord, who measured the waters in the hollow of Your hand. You marked off the heavens with the breadth of Your hand. You have calculated the dust of the earth in a measure, and weighed the mountains in the balance and the hills in scales. (Isaiah 40:12) . . . It is You, Lord God, who created the heavens and stretched them out, who spread out the earth and all that grows on it. You give breath to its people, and spirit to those who walk on it. (Isaiah 42:5)

***TAKE** a moment to consider the greatness of God's wonderful works.*

Jonathan Attacks the Philistines

23 Now a detachment of Philistines
had gone out to the pass at Micmash.
14 1 One day Jonathan son of Saul said to
the young man bearing his armor,
"Come, let's go over to the Philistine outpost on the other side." But he did not tell
his father.
2 Saul was staying on the outskirts of
Gibeah under a pomegranate tree in Migron. With him were about six hundred
men, 3 among whom was Ahijah, who was
wearing an ephod. He was a son of Ichabod's brother Ahitub son of Phinehas, the
son of Eli, the LORD's priest in Shiloh. No
one was aware that Jonathan had left.
4 On each side of the pass that Jonathan
intended to cross to reach the Philistine
outpost was a cliff; one was called Bozez,
and the other Seneh. 5 One cliff stood to
the north toward Micmash, the other to
the south toward Geba.
6 Jonathan said to his young armor-
bearer, "Come, let's go over to the outpost
of those uncircumcised fellows. Perhaps
the LORD will act in our behalf. Nothing
can hinder the LORD from saving, whether
by many or by few."
7 "Do all that you have in mind," his armor-bearer said. "Go ahead; I am with
you heart and soul."
8 Jonathan said, "Come, then; we will
cross over toward the men and let them
see us. 9 If they say to us, 'Wait there until
we come to you,' we will stay where we are
and not go up to them. 10 But if they say,
'Come up to us,' we will climb up, because
that will be our sign that the LORD has giv-
en them into our hands."
11 So both of them showed themselves
to the Philistine outpost. "Look!" said the
Philistines. "The Hebrews are crawling out
of the holes they were hiding in." 12 The
men of the outpost shouted to Jonathan
and his armor-bearer, "Come up to us and
we'll teach you a lesson."
So Jonathan said to his armor-bearer,
"Climb up after me; the LORD has given
them into the hand of Israel."
13 Jonathan climbed up, using his hands
and feet, with his armor-bearer right behind him. The Philistines fell before Jonathan, and his armor-bearer followed and
killed behind him. 14 In that first attack
Jonathan and his armor-bearer killed
some twenty men in an area of about half
an acre.[a]

Israel Routs the Philistines

15 Then panic struck the whole army—
those in the camp and field, and those in
the outposts and raiding parties—and the
ground shook. It was a panic sent by
God.[b]
16 Saul's lookouts at Gibeah in Benjamin
saw the army melting away in all directions. 17 Then Saul said to the men who
were with him, "Muster the forces and see
who has left us." When they did, it was
Jonathan and his armor-bearer who were
not there.
18 Saul said to Ahijah, "Bring the ark of
God." (At that time it was with the Israelites.)[c] 19 While Saul was talking to the
priest, the tumult in the Philistine camp
increased more and more. So Saul said to
the priest, "Withdraw your hand."
20 Then Saul and all his men assembled
and went to the battle. They found the
Philistines in total confusion, striking
each other with their swords. 21 Those Hebrews who had previously been with the
Philistines and had gone up with them to
their camp went over to the Israelites who
were with Saul and Jonathan. 22 When all
the Israelites who had hidden in the hill
country of Ephraim heard that the Philistines were on the run, they joined the battle in hot pursuit. 23 So the LORD rescued
Israel that day, and the battle moved on
beyond Beth Aven.

Jonathan Eats Honey

24 Now the men of Israel were in distress
that day, because Saul had bound the people under an oath, saying, "Cursed be any
man who eats food before evening comes,
before I have avenged myself on my enemies!" So none of the troops tasted food.
25 The entire army[d] entered the woods,
and there was honey on the ground.

[a] 14 Hebrew *half a yoke;* a "yoke" was the land plowed by a yoke of oxen in one day. [b] 15 Or *a terrible panic* [c] 18 Hebrew; Septuagint *"Bring the ephod." (At that time he wore the ephod before the Israelites.)* [d] 25 Or *Now all the people of the land*

26When they went into the woods, they saw
the honey oozing out, yet no one put his
hand to his mouth, because they feared the
oath. 27But Jonathan had not heard that his
father had bound the people with the oath,
so he reached out the end of the staff that
was in his hand and dipped it into the
honeycomb. He raised his hand to his
mouth, and his eyes brightened.[e] 28Then
one of the soldiers told him, "Your father
bound the army under a strict oath, saying,
'Cursed be any man who eats food today!'
That is why the men are faint."
29Jonathan said, "My father has made
trouble for the country. See how my eyes
brightened[f] when I tasted a little of this
honey. 30How much better it would have
been if the men had eaten today some of
the plunder they took from their enemies.
Would not the slaughter of the Philistines
have been even greater?"
31That day, after the Israelites had struck
down the Philistines from Micmash to
Aijalon, they were exhausted. 32They
pounced on the plunder and, taking
sheep, cattle and calves, they butchered
them on the ground and ate them, together with the blood. 33Then someone
said to Saul, "Look, the men are sinning
against the LORD by eating meat that has
blood in it."
"You have broken faith," he said. "Roll
a large stone over here at once." 34Then he
said, "Go out among the men and tell
them, 'Each of you bring me your cattle
and sheep, and slaughter them here and
eat them. Do not sin against the LORD by
eating meat with blood still in it.' "
So everyone brought his ox that night
and slaughtered it there. 35Then Saul built
an altar to the LORD; it was the first time
he had done this.
36Saul said, "Let us go down after the
Philistines by night and plunder them till
dawn, and let us not leave one of them
alive."
"Do whatever seems best to you," they
replied.
But the priest said, "Let us inquire of
God here."
37So Saul asked God, "Shall I go down
after the Philistines? Will you give them
into Israel's hand?" But God did not answer him that day.
38Saul therefore said, "Come here, all
you who are leaders of the army, and let
us find out what sin has been committed
today. 39As surely as the LORD who rescues
Israel lives, even if it lies with my son Jonathan, he must die." But not one of the
men said a word.
40Saul then said to all the Israelites,
"You stand over there; I and Jonathan my
son will stand over here."
"Do what seems best to you," the men
replied.
41Then Saul prayed to the LORD, the God
of Israel, "Give me the right answer."[g] And
Jonathan and Saul were taken by lot, and
the men were cleared. 42Saul said, "Cast
the lot between me and Jonathan my
son." And Jonathan was taken.
43Then Saul said to Jonathan, "Tell me
what you have done."
So Jonathan told him, "I merely tasted
a little honey with the end of my staff.
And now must I die?"
44Saul said, "May God deal with me, be
it ever so severely, if you do not die, Jonathan."
45But the men said to Saul, "Should Jonathan die—he who has brought about this
great deliverance in Israel? Never! As surely as the LORD lives, not a hair of his head
will fall to the ground, for he did this today with God's help." So the men rescued
Jonathan, and he was not put to death.
46Then Saul stopped pursuing the Philistines, and they withdrew to their own
land.
47After Saul had assumed rule over Israel, he fought against their enemies on
every side: Moab, the Ammonites, Edom,
the kings[h] of Zobah, and the Philistines.
Wherever he turned, he inflicted punishment on them.[i] 48He fought valiantly and
defeated the Amalekites, delivering Israel
from the hands of those who had plundered them.

Saul's Family

49Saul's sons were Jonathan, Ishvi and
Malki-Shua. The name of his older daughter was Merab, and that of the younger
was Michal. 50His wife's name was Ahinoam daughter of Ahimaaz. The name of

[e] 27 Or *his strength was renewed* [f] 29 Or *my strength was renewed* [g] 41 Hebrew; Septuagint *"Why have you not answered your servant today? If the fault is in me or my son Jonathan, respond with Urim, but if the men of Israel are at fault, respond with Thummim."* [h] 47 Masoretic Text; Dead Sea Scrolls and Septuagint *king* [i] 47 Hebrew; Septuagint *he was victorious*

the commander of Saul's army was Abner son of Ner, and Ner was Saul's uncle.
[51]Saul's father Kish and Abner's father Ner were sons of Abiel.

[52]All the days of Saul there was bitter war with the Philistines, and whenever Saul saw a mighty or brave man, he took him into his service.

PRAYER: INTERCESSION

LORD, there is no one besides You to help the powerless against the mighty. Help us, O Lord our God, for we rest in You. O Lord, You are our God; do not let people prevail against You. (2 Chronicles 14:11)

***TAKE** a few moments to intercede on behalf of the poor and hungry, the oppressed and persecuted, and those in control of world and national resources. Offer prayers for peace among nations and regarding current events and concerns.*

NT 1 Timothy 2:1–15

Instructions on Worship

2 I urge, then, first of all, that requests, prayers, intercession and thanksgiving be made for everyone— [2]for kings and all those in authority, that we may live peaceful and quiet lives in all godliness and holiness. [3]This is good, and pleases God our Savior, [4]who wants all men to be saved and to come to a knowledge of the truth.
[5]For there is one God and one mediator between God and men, the man Christ Jesus, [6]who gave himself as a ransom for all men—the testimony given in its proper time. [7]And for this purpose I was appointed a herald and an apostle—I am telling the truth, I am not lying—and a teacher of the true faith to the Gentiles.
[8]I want men everywhere to lift up holy hands in prayer, without anger or disputing.
[9]I also want women to dress modestly, with decency and propriety, not with braided hair or gold or pearls or expensive clothes, [10]but with good deeds, appropriate for women who profess to worship God.
[11]A woman should learn in quietness and full submission. [12]I do not permit a woman to teach or to have authority over a man; she must be silent. [13]For Adam was formed first, then Eve. [14]And Adam was not the one deceived; it was the woman who was deceived and became a sinner.
[15]But women[a] will be saved[b] through childbearing—if they continue in faith, love and holiness with propriety.

[a] 15 Greek *she* [b] 15 Or *restored*

PRAYER: MY RELATIONSHIP TO GOD

MY soul waits in hope for You, Lord; You are my help and my shield. My heart rejoices in You, because I trust in Your holy name. (Psalm 33:20–21) . . . Since I am Your child, O God, I am Your heir, and a joint heir with Christ, if indeed I share in His sufferings in order that I may also share in His glory. For I consider that the sufferings of this present time are not worth comparing with the glory that will be revealed to me. (Romans 8:17–18)

***PAUSE** to thank God for the relationship that you enjoy with Him in Jesus Christ.*

OT 1 Samuel 15:1-35 YEAR 1 DAY 244

The LORD *Rejects Saul as King*

15 Samuel said to Saul, "I am the one the
LORD sent to anoint you king over his
people Israel; so listen now to the message from the LORD. 2 This is what the LORD
Almighty says: 'I will punish the Amalekites for what they did to Israel when
they waylaid them as they came up from
Egypt. 3 Now go, attack the Amalekites and
totally destroy[a] everything that belongs to
them. Do not spare them; put to death
men and women, children and infants,
cattle and sheep, camels and donkeys.' "
4 So Saul summoned the men and mustered them at Telaim—two hundred thousand foot soldiers and ten thousand men
from Judah. 5 Saul went to the city of Amalek and set an ambush in the ravine.
6 Then he said to the Kenites, "Go away,
leave the Amalekites so that I do not destroy you along with them; for you
showed kindness to all the Israelites when
they came up out of Egypt." So the Kenites moved away from the Amalekites.
7 Then Saul attacked the Amalekites all
the way from Havilah to Shur, to the east
of Egypt. 8 He took Agag king of the
Amalekites alive, and all his people he totally destroyed with the sword. 9 But Saul
and the army spared Agag and the best of
the sheep and cattle, the fat calves[b] and
lambs—everything that was good. These
they were unwilling to destroy completely, but everything that was despised and
weak they totally destroyed.
10 Then the word of the LORD came to
Samuel: 11 "I am grieved that I have made
Saul king, because he has turned away
from me and has not carried out my instructions." Samuel was troubled, and he
cried out to the LORD all that night.
12 Early in the morning Samuel got up
and went to meet Saul, but he was told,
"Saul has gone to Carmel. There he has set
up a monument in his own honor and
has turned and gone on down to Gilgal."
13 When Samuel reached him, Saul said,
"The LORD bless you! I have carried out
the LORD's instructions."
14 But Samuel said, "What then is this
bleating of sheep in my ears? What is this
lowing of cattle that I hear?"
15 Saul answered, "The soldiers brought
them from the Amalekites; they spared
the best of the sheep and cattle to sacrifice to the LORD your God, but we totally
destroyed the rest."
16 "Stop!" Samuel said to Saul. "Let me
tell you what the LORD said to me last
night."
"Tell me," Saul replied.
17 Samuel said, "Although you were
once small in your own eyes, did you not
become the head of the tribes of Israel?
The LORD anointed you king over Israel.
18 And he sent you on a mission, saying,
'Go and completely destroy those wicked
people, the Amalekites; make war on
them until you have wiped them out.'
19 Why did you not obey the LORD? Why
did you pounce on the plunder and do
evil in the eyes of the LORD?"
20 "But I did obey the LORD," Saul said.
"I went on the mission the LORD assigned
me. I completely destroyed the Amalekites
and brought back Agag their king. 21 The
soldiers took sheep and cattle from the
plunder, the best of what was devoted to
God, in order to sacrifice them to the
LORD your God at Gilgal."
22 But Samuel replied:

"Does the LORD delight in burnt
offerings and sacrifices
as much as in obeying the voice of
the LORD?
To obey is better than sacrifice,
and to heed is better than the fat of
rams.
23 For rebellion is like the sin of
divination,
and arrogance like the evil of
idolatry.
Because you have rejected the word of
the LORD,
he has rejected you as king."

24 Then Saul said to Samuel, "I have
sinned. I violated the LORD's command
and your instructions. I was afraid of the
people and so I gave in to them. 25 Now I

[a] 3 The Hebrew term refers to the irrevocable giving over of things or persons to the LORD, often by totally destroying them; also in verses 8, 9, 15, 18, 20 and 21. [b] 9 Or *the grown bulls;* the meaning of the Hebrew for this phrase is uncertain.

beg you, forgive my sin and come back
with me, so that I may worship the LORD."
26But Samuel said to him, "I will not go
back with you. You have rejected the word
of the LORD, and the LORD has rejected you
as king over Israel!"
27As Samuel turned to leave, Saul
caught hold of the hem of his robe, and
it tore. 28Samuel said to him, "The LORD
has torn the kingdom of Israel from you
today and has given it to one of your
neighbors—to one better than you. 29He
who is the Glory of Israel does not lie or
change his mind; for he is not a man, that
he should change his mind."
30Saul replied, "I have sinned. But
please honor me before the elders of my
people and before Israel; come back with
me, so that I may worship the LORD your
God." 31So Samuel went back with Saul,
and Saul worshiped the LORD.
32Then Samuel said, "Bring me Agag
king of the Amalekites."
Agag came to him confidently,[c] thinking, "Surely the bitterness of death is
past."
33But Samuel said,

"As your sword has made women
childless,
so will your mother be childless
among women."

And Samuel put Agag to death before the
LORD at Gilgal.
34Then Samuel left for Ramah, but Saul
went up to his home in Gibeah of Saul.
35Until the day Samuel died, he did not
go to see Saul again, though Samuel
mourned for him. And the LORD was
grieved that he had made Saul king over
Israel.

[c] 32 Or *him trembling, yet*

PRAYER: AFFIRMATION

YOU will keep in perfect peace those who commit themselves to be faithful to You, because they trust in You. (Isaiah 26:3) . . . I will seek You, Lord, while You may be found and call upon You while You are near. (Isaiah 55:6)

***PAUSE** to reflect on these Biblical affirmations.*

NT 1 Timothy 3:1-16

Overseers and Deacons

3 Here is a trustworthy saying: If anyone
sets his heart on being an overseer,[a] he
desires a noble task. 2Now the overseer
must be above reproach, the husband of
but one wife, temperate, self-controlled,
respectable, hospitable, able to teach, 3not
given to drunkenness, not violent but gentle, not quarrelsome, not a lover of money. 4He must manage his own family well
and see that his children obey him with
proper respect. 5(If anyone does not know
how to manage his own family, how can
he take care of God's church?) 6He must
not be a recent convert, or he may become
conceited and fall under the same judgment as the devil. 7He must also have a
good reputation with outsiders, so that he
will not fall into disgrace and into the
devil's trap.
8Deacons, likewise, are to be men worthy of respect, sincere, not indulging in
much wine, and not pursuing dishonest
gain. 9They must keep hold of the deep
truths of the faith with a clear conscience.
10They must first be tested; and then if
there is nothing against them, let them
serve as deacons.
11In the same way, their wives[b] are to be
women worthy of respect, not malicious
talkers but temperate and trustworthy in
everything.
12A deacon must be the husband of but
one wife and must manage his children
and his household well. 13Those who have
served well gain an excellent standing and
great assurance in their faith in Christ
Jesus.
14Although I hope to come to you soon,
I am writing you these instructions so
that, 15if I am delayed, you will know how
people ought to conduct themselves in

[a] 1 Traditionally *bishop;* also in verse 2 [b] 11 Or *way, deaconesses*

God's household, which is the church of
the living God, the pillar and foundation
of the truth. 16Beyond all question, the
mystery of godliness is great:

He[c] appeared in a body,[d]
was vindicated by the Spirit,
was seen by angels,
was preached among the nations,
was believed on in the world,
was taken up in glory.

[c] 16 Some manuscripts *God* [d] 16 Or *in the flesh*

PRAYER: THE CHARACTER I WANT TO CULTIVATE

SINCE I belong to the day, I will be self-controlled, putting on faith and love as a breastplate and the hope of salvation as a helmet. (1 Thessalonians 5:8) . . . I will prepare my mind for action and be self-controlled, setting my hope fully on the grace to be given to me at Your revelation, Christ Jesus. (1 Peter 1:13)

TAKE *a moment to ask the Lord for the grace to grow in godly character.*

YEAR 1 DAY 245

OT Psalms 46–47

Psalm 46

For the director of music. Of the Sons of Korah. According to *alamoth*.[a] A song.

1God is our refuge and strength,
an ever-present help in trouble.
2Therefore we will not fear, though the earth give way
and the mountains fall into the heart of the sea,
3though its waters roar and foam
and the mountains quake with their surging. *Selah*

4There is a river whose streams make glad the city of God,
the holy place where the Most High dwells.
5God is within her, she will not fall;
God will help her at break of day.
6Nations are in uproar, kingdoms fall;
he lifts his voice, the earth melts.

7The LORD Almighty is with us;
the God of Jacob is our fortress. *Selah*

8Come and see the works of the LORD,
the desolations he has brought on the earth.
9He makes wars cease to the ends of the earth;
he breaks the bow and shatters the spear,
he burns the shields[b] with fire.
10"Be still, and know that I am God;
I will be exalted among the nations,
I will be exalted in the earth."

11The LORD Almighty is with us;
the God of Jacob is our fortress. *Selah*

Psalm 47

For the director of music. Of the Sons of Korah. A psalm.

1Clap your hands, all you nations;
shout to God with cries of joy.
2How awesome is the LORD Most High,
the great King over all the earth!
3He subdued nations under us,
peoples under our feet.
4He chose our inheritance for us,
the pride of Jacob, whom he loved. *Selah*

5God has ascended amid shouts of joy,
the LORD amid the sounding of trumpets.
6Sing praises to God, sing praises;
sing praises to our King, sing praises.

7For God is the King of all the earth;
sing to him a psalm[c] of praise.

[a] Title: Probably a musical term [b] 9 Or *chariots*
[c] 7 Or *a maskil* (probably a literary or musical term)

8 God reigns over the nations;
God is seated on his holy throne.
9 The nobles of the nations assemble
as the people of the God of
Abraham,
for the kings[d] of the earth belong to
God;
he is greatly exalted.

[d] 9 Or *shields*

PRAYER: THANKSGIVING

I WILL give thanks to You, O Lord, because of Your righteousness, and I will sing praise to Your name, Lord Most High. (Psalm 7:17)
. . . You are my light and my salvation, O Lord; whom shall I fear? You are the strength of my life; of whom shall I be afraid? (Psalm 27:1)

***PAUSE** to offer your own expressions of thanksgiving.*

NT 1 Timothy 4:1-16

Instructions to Timothy

4 The Spirit clearly says that in later times
some will abandon the faith and follow deceiving spirits and things taught by
demons. 2 Such teachings come through
hypocritical liars, whose consciences have
been seared as with a hot iron. 3 They forbid people to marry and order them to
abstain from certain foods, which God
created to be received with thanksgiving
by those who believe and who know the
truth. 4 For everything God created is
good, and nothing is to be rejected if it is
received with thanksgiving, 5 because it is
consecrated by the word of God and
prayer.
6 If you point these things out to the
brothers, you will be a good minister of
Christ Jesus, brought up in the truths of
the faith and of the good teaching that
you have followed. 7 Have nothing to do
with godless myths and old wives' tales;
rather, train yourself to be godly. 8 For
physical training is of some value, but
godliness has value for all things, holding
promise for both the present life and the
life to come.
9 This is a trustworthy saying that deserves full acceptance 10 (and for this we labor and strive), that we have put our hope
in the living God, who is the Savior of all
men, and especially of those who believe.
11 Command and teach these things.
12 Don't let anyone look down on you because you are young, but set an example
for the believers in speech, in life, in love,
in faith and in purity. 13 Until I come, devote yourself to the public reading of
Scripture, to preaching and to teaching.
14 Do not neglect your gift, which was giv-
en you through a prophetic message when
the body of elders laid their hands on you.
15 Be diligent in these matters; give yourself wholly to them, so that everyone may
see your progress. 16 Watch your life and
doctrine closely. Persevere in them, because if you do, you will save both yourself and your hearers.

PRAYER: MY RELATIONSHIP TO OTHERS

I WILL seek to walk in wisdom toward outsiders, making the most of every opportunity. My speech is always to be graceful, seasoned with salt, so that I may know how to answer each person. (Colossians 4:5–6)

***PAUSE** to review your relationships with others and to commit them to the Lord.*

YEAR 1 DAY 246

OT 1 Samuel 16:1-23

Samuel Anoints David

16 The LORD said to Samuel, "How long will you mourn for Saul, since I have rejected him as king over Israel? Fill your horn with oil and be on your way; I am sending you to Jesse of Bethlehem. I have chosen one of his sons to be king."

[2]But Samuel said, "How can I go? Saul will hear about it and kill me."

The LORD said, "Take a heifer with you and say, 'I have come to sacrifice to the LORD.' [3]Invite Jesse to the sacrifice, and I will show you what to do. You are to anoint for me the one I indicate."

[4]Samuel did what the LORD said. When he arrived at Bethlehem, the elders of the town trembled when they met him. They asked, "Do you come in peace?"

[5]Samuel replied, "Yes, in peace; I have come to sacrifice to the LORD. Consecrate yourselves and come to the sacrifice with me." Then he consecrated Jesse and his sons and invited them to the sacrifice.

[6]When they arrived, Samuel saw Eliab and thought, "Surely the LORD's anointed stands here before the LORD."

[7]But the LORD said to Samuel, "Do not consider his appearance or his height, for I have rejected him. The LORD does not look at the things man looks at. Man looks at the outward appearance, but the LORD looks at the heart."

[8]Then Jesse called Abinadab and had him pass in front of Samuel. But Samuel said, "The LORD has not chosen this one either." [9]Jesse then had Shammah pass by, but Samuel said, "Nor has the LORD chosen this one." [10]Jesse had seven of his sons pass before Samuel, but Samuel said to him, "The LORD has not chosen these." [11]So he asked Jesse, "Are these all the sons you have?"

"There is still the youngest," Jesse answered, "but he is tending the sheep."

Samuel said, "Send for him; we will not sit down[a] until he arrives."

[12]So he sent and had him brought in. He was ruddy, with a fine appearance and handsome features.

Then the LORD said, "Rise and anoint him; he is the one."

[13]So Samuel took the horn of oil and anointed him in the presence of his brothers, and from that day on the Spirit of the LORD came upon David in power. Samuel then went to Ramah.

David in Saul's Service

[14]Now the Spirit of the LORD had departed from Saul, and an evil[b] spirit from the LORD tormented him.

[15]Saul's attendants said to him, "See, an evil spirit from God is tormenting you. [16]Let our lord command his servants here to search for someone who can play the harp. He will play when the evil spirit from God comes upon you, and you will feel better."

[17]So Saul said to his attendants, "Find someone who plays well and bring him to me."

[18]One of the servants answered, "I have seen a son of Jesse of Bethlehem who knows how to play the harp. He is a brave man and a warrior. He speaks well and is a fine-looking man. And the LORD is with him."

[19]Then Saul sent messengers to Jesse and said, "Send me your son David, who is with the sheep." [20]So Jesse took a donkey loaded with bread, a skin of wine and a young goat and sent them with his son David to Saul.

[21]David came to Saul and entered his service. Saul liked him very much, and David became one of his armor-bearers. [22]Then Saul sent word to Jesse, saying, "Allow David to remain in my service, for I am pleased with him."

[23]Whenever the spirit from God came upon Saul, David would take his harp and play. Then relief would come to Saul; he would feel better, and the evil spirit would leave him.

[a] *11* Some Septuagint manuscripts; Hebrew *not gather around* [b] *14* Or *injurious;* also in verses 15, 16 and 23

PRAYER: ADORATION

YOU are the true God; You are the living God and the everlasting King. At Your wrath, the earth trembles, and the nations cannot endure Your indignation. (Jeremiah 10:10) . . . How great are Your signs, O God, and how mighty are Your wonders! Your kingdom is an eternal kingdom; Your dominion endures from generation to generation. (Daniel 4:3)

PAUSE *to express your thoughts of praise and worship.*

NT 1 Timothy 5:1–25

Advice About Widows, Elders and Slaves

5 Do not rebuke an older man harshly,
but exhort him as if he were your father. Treat younger men as brothers, 2old-
er women as mothers, and younger
women as sisters, with absolute purity.
3Give proper recognition to those widows who are really in need. 4But if a widow has children or grandchildren, these
should learn first of all to put their religion into practice by caring for their own
family and so repaying their parents and
grandparents, for this is pleasing to God.
5The widow who is really in need and left
all alone puts her hope in God and continues night and day to pray and to ask
God for help. 6But the widow who lives
for pleasure is dead even while she lives.
7Give the people these instructions, too,
so that no one may be open to blame. 8If
anyone does not provide for his relatives,
and especially for his immediate family,
he has denied the faith and is worse than
an unbeliever.
9No widow may be put on the list of
widows unless she is over sixty, has been
faithful to her husband,[a] 10and is well
known for her good deeds, such as bringing up children, showing hospitality,
washing the feet of the saints, helping
those in trouble and devoting herself to
all kinds of good deeds.
11As for younger widows, do not put
them on such a list. For when their sensual desires overcome their dedication to
Christ, they want to marry. 12Thus they
bring judgment on themselves, because
they have broken their first pledge. 13Be-
sides, they get into the habit of being idle
and going about from house to house.
And not only do they become idlers, but
also gossips and busybodies, saying things
they ought not to. 14So I counsel younger
widows to marry, to have children, to
manage their homes and to give the enemy no opportunity for slander. 15Some
have in fact already turned away to follow
Satan.
16If any woman who is a believer has
widows in her family, she should help
them and not let the church be burdened
with them, so that the church can help
those widows who are really in need.
17The elders who direct the affairs of the
church well are worthy of double honor,
especially those whose work is preaching
and teaching. 18For the Scripture says, "Do
not muzzle the ox while it is treading out
the grain,"[b] and "The worker deserves his
wages."[c] 19Do not entertain an accusation
against an elder unless it is brought by
two or three witnesses. 20Those who sin
are to be rebuked publicly, so that the others may take warning.
21I charge you, in the sight of God and
Christ Jesus and the elect angels, to keep
these instructions without partiality, and
to do nothing out of favoritism.
22Do not be hasty in the laying on of
hands, and do not share in the sins of others. Keep yourself pure.
23Stop drinking only water, and use a
little wine because of your stomach and
your frequent illnesses.
24The sins of some men are obvious,
reaching the place of judgment ahead of
them; the sins of others trail behind them.
25In the same way, good deeds are obvious, and even those that are not cannot
be hidden.

[a] *9* Or *has had but one husband* [b] *18* Deut. 25:4
[c] *18* Luke 10:7

PRAYER: THE ATTRIBUTES OF GOD

I WILL ascribe to You glory and strength, O Lord. I will ascribe to You the glory due Your name and worship You, Lord, in the beauty of holiness. (Psalm 29:1–2) . . . You reign, O Lord; You are clothed with majesty; You are robed in majesty and armed with strength. Indeed, the world is firmly established; it cannot be moved. Your throne is established from of old; You are from everlasting. Your testimonies stand firm; holiness adorns Your house, O Lord, forever. (Psalm 93:1–2, 5)

***PAUSE** to reflect on these affirmations about the person, powers and perfection of God.*

YEAR 1 DAY 247

OT 1 Samuel 17:1–58

David and Goliath

17 Now the Philistines gathered their forces for war and assembled at Socoh in Judah. They pitched camp at Ephes Dammim, between Socoh and Azekah.
[2]Saul and the Israelites assembled and camped in the Valley of Elah and drew up their battle line to meet the Philistines.
[3]The Philistines occupied one hill and the Israelites another, with the valley between them.
[4]A champion named Goliath, who was from Gath, came out of the Philistine camp. He was over nine feet[a] tall. [5]He had a bronze helmet on his head and wore a coat of scale armor of bronze weighing five thousand shekels[b]; [6]on his legs he wore bronze greaves, and a bronze javelin was slung on his back. [7]His spear shaft was like a weaver's rod, and its iron point weighed six hundred shekels.[c] His shield bearer went ahead of him.
[8]Goliath stood and shouted to the ranks of Israel, "Why do you come out and line up for battle? Am I not a Philistine, and are you not the servants of Saul? Choose a man and have him come down to me. [9]If he is able to fight and kill me, we will become your subjects; but if I overcome him and kill him, you will become our subjects and serve us." [10]Then the Philistine said, "This day I defy the ranks of Israel! Give me a man and let us fight each other." [11]On hearing the Philistine's words, Saul and all the Israelites were dismayed and terrified.
[12]Now David was the son of an Ephrathite named Jesse, who was from Bethlehem in Judah. Jesse had eight sons, and in Saul's time he was old and well advanced in years. [13]Jesse's three oldest sons had followed Saul to the war: The firstborn was Eliab; the second, Abinadab; and the third, Shammah. [14]David was the youngest. The three oldest followed Saul, [15]but David went back and forth from Saul to tend his father's sheep at Bethlehem.
[16]For forty days the Philistine came forward every morning and evening and took his stand.
[17]Now Jesse said to his son David, "Take this ephah[d] of roasted grain and these ten loaves of bread for your brothers and hurry to their camp. [18]Take along these ten cheeses to the commander of their unit.[e] See how your brothers are and bring back some assurance[f] from them. [19]They are with Saul and all the men of Israel in the Valley of Elah, fighting against the Philistines."
[20]Early in the morning David left the flock with a shepherd, loaded up and set out, as Jesse had directed. He reached the camp as the army was going out to its battle positions, shouting the war cry. [21]Israel and the Philistines were drawing up their lines facing each other. [22]David left his things with the keeper of supplies, ran

[a] 4 Hebrew *was six cubits and a span* (about 3 meters) [b] 5 That is, about 125 pounds (about 57 kilograms) [c] 7 That is, about 15 pounds (about 7 kilograms) [d] 17 That is, probably about 3/5 bushel (about 22 liters) [e] 18 Hebrew *thousand* [f] 18 Or *some token*; or *some pledge of spoils*

to the battle lines and greeted his brothers. 23 As he was talking with them, Goliath, the Philistine champion from Gath, stepped out from his lines and shouted his usual defiance, and David heard it. 24 When the Israelites saw the man, they all ran from him in great fear.

25 Now the Israelites had been saying, "Do you see how this man keeps coming out? He comes out to defy Israel. The king will give great wealth to the man who kills him. He will also give him his daughter in marriage and will exempt his father's family from taxes in Israel."

26 David asked the men standing near him, "What will be done for the man who kills this Philistine and removes this disgrace from Israel? Who is this uncircumcised Philistine that he should defy the armies of the living God?"

27 They repeated to him what they had been saying and told him, "This is what will be done for the man who kills him."

28 When Eliab, David's oldest brother, heard him speaking with the men, he burned with anger at him and asked, "Why have you come down here? And with whom did you leave those few sheep in the desert? I know how conceited you are and how wicked your heart is; you came down only to watch the battle."

29 "Now what have I done?" said David. "Can't I even speak?" 30 He then turned away to someone else and brought up the same matter, and the men answered him as before. 31 What David said was overheard and reported to Saul, and Saul sent for him.

32 David said to Saul, "Let no one lose heart on account of this Philistine; your servant will go and fight him."

33 Saul replied, "You are not able to go out against this Philistine and fight him; you are only a boy, and he has been a fighting man from his youth."

34 But David said to Saul, "Your servant has been keeping his father's sheep. When a lion or a bear came and carried off a sheep from the flock, 35 I went after it, struck it and rescued the sheep from its mouth. When it turned on me, I seized it by its hair, struck it and killed it. 36 Your servant has killed both the lion and the bear; this uncircumcised Philistine will be like one of them, because he has defied the armies of the living God. 37 The LORD who delivered me from the paw of the lion and the paw of the bear will deliver me from the hand of this Philistine."

Saul said to David, "Go, and the LORD be with you."

38 Then Saul dressed David in his own tunic. He put a coat of armor on him and a bronze helmet on his head. 39 David fastened on his sword over the tunic and tried walking around, because he was not used to them.

"I cannot go in these," he said to Saul, "because I am not used to them." So he took them off. 40 Then he took his staff in his hand, chose five smooth stones from the stream, put them in the pouch of his shepherd's bag and, with his sling in his hand, approached the Philistine.

41 Meanwhile, the Philistine, with his shield bearer in front of him, kept coming closer to David. 42 He looked David over and saw that he was only a boy, ruddy and handsome, and he despised him. 43 He said to David, "Am I a dog, that you come at me with sticks?" And the Philistine cursed David by his gods. 44 "Come here," he said, "and I'll give your flesh to the birds of the air and the beasts of the field!"

45 David said to the Philistine, "You come against me with sword and spear and javelin, but I come against you in the name of the LORD Almighty, the God of the armies of Israel, whom you have defied. 46 This day the LORD will hand you over to me, and I'll strike you down and cut off your head. Today I will give the carcasses of the Philistine army to the birds of the air and the beasts of the earth, and the whole world will know that there is a God in Israel. 47 All those gathered here will know that it is not by sword or spear that the LORD saves; for the battle is the LORD's, and he will give all of you into our hands."

48 As the Philistine moved closer to attack him, David ran quickly toward the battle line to meet him. 49 Reaching into his bag and taking out a stone, he slung it and struck the Philistine on the forehead. The stone sank into his forehead, and he fell facedown on the ground.

50 So David triumphed over the Philistine with a sling and a stone; without a sword in his hand he struck down the Philistine and killed him.

51 David ran and stood over him. He took hold of the Philistine's sword and

drew it from the scabbard. After he killed him, he cut off his head with the sword.

When the Philistines saw that their hero was dead, they turned and ran. 52 Then the men of Israel and Judah surged forward with a shout and pursued the Philistines to the entrance of Gath[g] and to the gates of Ekron. Their dead were strewn along the Shaaraim road to Gath and Ekron. 53 When the Israelites returned from chasing the Philistines, they plundered their camp. 54 David took the Philistine's head and brought it to Jerusalem, and he put the Philistine's weapons in his own tent.

55 As Saul watched David going out to meet the Philistine, he said to Abner, commander of the army, "Abner, whose son is that young man?"

Abner replied, "As surely as you live, O king, I don't know."

56 The king said, "Find out whose son this young man is."

57 As soon as David returned from killing the Philistine, Abner took him and brought him before Saul, with David still holding the Philistine's head.

58 "Whose son are you, young man?" Saul asked him.

David said, "I am the son of your servant Jesse of Bethlehem."

[g] 52 Some Septuagint manuscripts; Hebrew *a valley*

PRAYER: CONFESSION

O LORD, May I produce fruit in keeping with repentance. (Matthew 3:8)

ASK *the Spirit to search your heart and reveal any areas of unconfessed sin. Acknowledge these to the Lord and thank Him for His forgiveness.*

NT 1 Timothy 6:1–10

6 All who are under the yoke of slavery should consider their masters worthy of full respect, so that God's name and our teaching may not be slandered. 2 Those who have believing masters are not to show less respect for them because they are brothers. Instead, they are to serve them even better, because those who benefit from their service are believers, and dear to them. These are the things you are to teach and urge on them.

Love of Money

3 If anyone teaches false doctrines and does not agree to the sound instruction of our Lord Jesus Christ and to godly teaching, 4 he is conceited and understands nothing. He has an unhealthy interest in controversies and quarrels about words that result in envy, strife, malicious talk, evil suspicions 5 and constant friction between men of corrupt mind, who have been robbed of the truth and who think that godliness is a means to financial gain.

6 But godliness with contentment is great gain. 7 For we brought nothing into the world, and we can take nothing out of it. 8 But if we have food and clothing, we will be content with that. 9 People who want to get rich fall into temptation and a trap and into many foolish and harmful desires that plunge men into ruin and destruction. 10 For the love of money is a root of all kinds of evil. Some people, eager for money, have wandered from the faith and pierced themselves with many griefs.

PRAYER: THE WORKS OF GOD

JESUS, You are the stone that was rejected by the builders, but that has become the chief cornerstone. Salvation is found in no one else, for there is no other name under heaven given to us by which we can be saved. (Acts 4:11–12)

TAKE *a moment to consider the greatness of God's wonderful works.*

OT 1 Samuel 18:1–19:24

YEAR 1 DAY 248

Saul's Jealousy of David

18 After David had finished talking with
Saul, Jonathan became one in spirit
with David, and he loved him as himself.
2 From that day Saul kept David with him
and did not let him return to his father's
house. 3 And Jonathan made a covenant
with David because he loved him as himself. 4 Jonathan took off the robe he was
wearing and gave it to David, along with
his tunic, and even his sword, his bow
and his belt.
5 Whatever Saul sent him to do, David
did it so successfully[a] that Saul gave him
a high rank in the army. This pleased all
the people, and Saul's officers as well.
6 When the men were returning home
after David had killed the Philistine, the
women came out from all the towns of Israel to meet King Saul with singing and
dancing, with joyful songs and with tambourines and lutes. 7 As they danced, they
sang:

"Saul has slain his thousands,
and David his tens of thousands."

8 Saul was very angry; this refrain galled
him. "They have credited David with tens
of thousands," he thought, "but me with
only thousands. What more can he get
but the kingdom?" 9 And from that time
on Saul kept a jealous eye on David.
10 The next day an evil[b] spirit from God
came forcefully upon Saul. He was prophesying in his house, while David was playing the harp, as he usually did. Saul had
a spear in his hand 11 and he hurled it, saying to himself, "I'll pin David to the wall."
But David eluded him twice.
12 Saul was afraid of David, because the
LORD was with David but had left Saul.
13 So he sent David away from him and
gave him command over a thousand men,
and David led the troops in their campaigns. 14 In everything he did he had great
success,[c] because the LORD was with him.
15 When Saul saw how successful[d] he was,
he was afraid of him. 16 But all Israel and
Judah loved David, because he led them
in their campaigns.
17 Saul said to David, "Here is my older
daughter Merab. I will give her to you in
marriage; only serve me bravely and fight
the battles of the LORD." For Saul said to
himself, "I will not raise a hand against
him. Let the Philistines do that!"
18 But David said to Saul, "Who am I,
and what is my family or my father's clan
in Israel, that I should become the king's
son-in-law?" 19 So[e] when the time came for
Merab, Saul's daughter, to be given to David, she was given in marriage to Adriel of
Meholah.
20 Now Saul's daughter Michal was in
love with David, and when they told Saul
about it, he was pleased. 21 "I will give her
to him," he thought, "so that she may be
a snare to him and so that the hand of the
Philistines may be against him." So Saul
said to David, "Now you have a second
opportunity to become my son-in-law."
22 Then Saul ordered his attendants:
"Speak to David privately and say, 'Look,
the king is pleased with you, and his attendants all like you; now become his
son-in-law.' "
23 They repeated these words to David.
But David said, "Do you think it is a small
matter to become the king's son-in-law?
I'm only a poor man and little known."
24 When Saul's servants told him what
David had said, 25 Saul replied, "Say to David, 'The king wants no other price for the
bride than a hundred Philistine foreskins,
to take revenge on his enemies.' " Saul's
plan was to have David fall by the hands
of the Philistines.
26 When the attendants told David these
things, he was pleased to become the
king's son-in-law. So before the allotted
time elapsed, 27 David and his men went
out and killed two hundred Philistines.
He brought their foreskins and presented
the full number to the king so that he
might become the king's son-in-law. Then
Saul gave him his daughter Michal in marriage.
28 When Saul realized that the LORD was
with David and that his daughter Michal
loved David, 29 Saul became still more
afraid of him, and he remained his enemy the rest of his days.
30 The Philistine commanders continued to go out to battle, and as often as

[a] 5 Or *wisely* [b] 10 Or *injurious* [c] 14 Or *he was very wise* [d] 15 Or *wise* [e] 19 Or *However,*

they did, David met with more success[f] than the rest of Saul's officers, and his name became well known.

Saul Tries to Kill David

19 Saul told his son Jonathan and all the attendants to kill David. But Jonathan was very fond of David 2and warned him, "My father Saul is looking for a chance to kill you. Be on your guard tomorrow morning; go into hiding and stay there. 3I will go out and stand with my father in the field where you are. I'll speak to him about you and will tell you what I find out."

4Jonathan spoke well of David to Saul his father and said to him, "Let not the king do wrong to his servant David; he has not wronged you, and what he has done has benefited you greatly. 5He took his life in his hands when he killed the Philistine. The LORD won a great victory for all Israel, and you saw it and were glad. Why then would you do wrong to an innocent man like David by killing him for no reason?"

6Saul listened to Jonathan and took this oath: "As surely as the LORD lives, David will not be put to death."

7So Jonathan called David and told him the whole conversation. He brought him to Saul, and David was with Saul as before.

8Once more war broke out, and David went out and fought the Philistines. He struck them with such force that they fled before him.

9But an evil[g] spirit from the LORD came upon Saul as he was sitting in his house with his spear in his hand. While David was playing the harp, 10Saul tried to pin him to the wall with his spear, but David eluded him as Saul drove the spear into the wall. That night David made good his escape.

11Saul sent men to David's house to watch it and to kill him in the morning. But Michal, David's wife, warned him, "If you don't run for your life tonight, tomorrow you'll be killed." 12So Michal let David down through a window, and he fled and escaped. 13Then Michal took an idol[h] and laid it on the bed, covering it with a garment and putting some goats' hair at the head.

14When Saul sent the men to capture David, Michal said, "He is ill."

15Then Saul sent the men back to see David and told them, "Bring him up to me in his bed so that I may kill him." 16But when the men entered, there was the idol in the bed, and at the head was some goats' hair.

17Saul said to Michal, "Why did you deceive me like this and send my enemy away so that he escaped?"

Michal told him, "He said to me, 'Let me get away. Why should I kill you?' "

18When David had fled and made his escape, he went to Samuel at Ramah and told him all that Saul had done to him. Then he and Samuel went to Naioth and stayed there. 19Word came to Saul: "David is in Naioth at Ramah"; 20so he sent men to capture him. But when they saw a group of prophets prophesying, with Samuel standing there as their leader, the Spirit of God came upon Saul's men and they also prophesied. 21Saul was told about it, and he sent more men, and they prophesied too. Saul sent men a third time, and they also prophesied. 22Finally, he himself left for Ramah and went to the great cistern at Secu. And he asked, "Where are Samuel and David?"

"Over in Naioth at Ramah," they said.

23So Saul went to Naioth at Ramah. But the Spirit of God came even upon him, and he walked along prophesying until he came to Naioth. 24He stripped off his robes and also prophesied in Samuel's presence. He lay that way all that day and night. This is why people say, "Is Saul also among the prophets?"

[f] *30* Or *David acted more wisely* [g] *9* Or *injurious*
[h] *13* Hebrew *teraphim;* also in verse 16

PRAYER: RENEWAL

TEACH me to number my days, O Lord, that I may gain a heart of wisdom. (Psalm 90:12) . . . May I let my eyes look straight ahead and fix my gaze straight before me. May I ponder the path of my

feet so that all my ways will be established. May I not turn to the right or to the left but keep my foot from evil.
(Proverbs 4:25–27)

***PAUSE** to add your own prayers for personal renewal.*

NT 1 Timothy 6:11–21

Paul's Charge to Timothy

[11]But you, man of God, flee from all this, and pursue righteousness, godliness, faith, love, endurance and gentleness. [12]Fight the good fight of the faith. Take hold of the eternal life to which you were called when you made your good confession in the presence of many witnesses. [13]In the sight of God, who gives life to everything, and of Christ Jesus, who while testifying before Pontius Pilate made the good confession, I charge you [14]to keep this command without spot or blame until the appearing of our Lord Jesus Christ, [15]which God will bring about in his own time—God, the blessed and only Ruler, the King of kings and Lord of lords, [16]who alone is immortal and who lives in unapproachable light, whom no one has seen or can see. To him be honor and might forever. Amen.

[17]Command those who are rich in this present world not to be arrogant nor to put their hope in wealth, which is so uncertain, but to put their hope in God, who richly provides us with everything for our enjoyment. [18]Command them to do good, to be rich in good deeds, and to be generous and willing to share. [19]In this way they will lay up treasure for themselves as a firm foundation for the coming age, so that they may take hold of the life that is truly life.

[20]Timothy, guard what has been entrusted to your care. Turn away from godless chatter and the opposing ideas of what is falsely called knowledge, [21]which some have professed and in so doing have wandered from the faith.

Grace be with you.

PRAYER: MY RELATIONSHIP TO GOD

YOU have declared to us, O Lord, "Even now, return to Me with all your heart, with fasting and weeping and mourning." So we will rend our hearts and not our garments. We will return to You, O Lord our God, for You are gracious and compassionate, slow to anger and abounding in loving-kindness, and You relent from sending calamity. (Joel 2:12–13)

***PAUSE** to thank God for the relationship that you enjoy with Him in Jesus Christ.*

YEAR 1
DAY 249

OT Proverbs 11

11 The LORD abhors dishonest scales,
but accurate weights are his delight.

[2]When pride comes, then comes disgrace,
but with humility comes wisdom.

[3]The integrity of the upright guides them,
but the unfaithful are destroyed by their duplicity.

[4]Wealth is worthless in the day of wrath,
but righteousness delivers from death.

[5]The righteousness of the blameless makes a straight way for them,
but the wicked are brought down by their own wickedness.

[6]The righteousness of the upright delivers them,

but the unfaithful are trapped by evil desires.

7 When a wicked man dies, his hope perishes;
all he expected from his power comes to nothing.

8 The righteous man is rescued from trouble,
and it comes on the wicked instead.

9 With his mouth the godless destroys his neighbor,
but through knowledge the righteous escape.

10 When the righteous prosper, the city rejoices;
when the wicked perish, there are shouts of joy.

11 Through the blessing of the upright a city is exalted,
but by the mouth of the wicked it is destroyed.

12 A man who lacks judgment derides his neighbor,
but a man of understanding holds his tongue.

13 A gossip betrays a confidence,
but a trustworthy man keeps a secret.

14 For lack of guidance a nation falls,
but many advisers make victory sure.

15 He who puts up security for another will surely suffer,
but whoever refuses to strike hands in pledge is safe.

16 A kindhearted woman gains respect,
but ruthless men gain only wealth.

17 A kind man benefits himself,
but a cruel man brings trouble on himself.

18 The wicked man earns deceptive wages,
but he who sows righteousness reaps a sure reward.

19 The truly righteous man attains life,
but he who pursues evil goes to his death.

20 The LORD detests men of perverse heart
but he delights in those whose ways are blameless.

21 Be sure of this: The wicked will not go unpunished,
but those who are righteous will go free.

22 Like a gold ring in a pig's snout
is a beautiful woman who shows no discretion.

23 The desire of the righteous ends only in good,
but the hope of the wicked only in wrath.

24 One man gives freely, yet gains even more;
another withholds unduly, but comes to poverty.

25 A generous man will prosper;
he who refreshes others will himself be refreshed.

26 People curse the man who hoards grain,
but blessing crowns him who is willing to sell.

27 He who seeks good finds goodwill,
but evil comes to him who searches for it.

28 Whoever trusts in his riches will fall,
but the righteous will thrive like a green leaf.

29 He who brings trouble on his family will inherit only wind,
and the fool will be servant to the wise.

30 The fruit of the righteous is a tree of life,
and he who wins souls is wise.

31 If the righteous receive their due on earth,
how much more the ungodly and the sinner!

PRAYER: PETITION

HEAR my prayer, O Lord, give ear to my supplications! Answer me in Your faithfulness and righteousness. (Psalm 143:1)

***PAUSE** here to petition God for growth in your desire to know and please Jesus Christ. Pray for a greater love and commitment to Him, for the grace to practice His presence and for the grace to glorify Him in your life. Offer prayers regarding your activities for this day and any special concerns you may have.*

NT 2 Timothy 1:1-18

I Paul, an apostle of Christ Jesus by the will of God, according to the promise of life that is in Christ Jesus,

[2]To Timothy, my dear son:

Grace, mercy and peace from God the Father and Christ Jesus our Lord.

Encouragement to Be Faithful

[3]I thank God, whom I serve, as my forefathers did, with a clear conscience, as night and day I constantly remember you in my prayers. [4]Recalling your tears, I long to see you, so that I may be filled with joy. [5]I have been reminded of your sincere faith, which first lived in your grandmother Lois and in your mother Eunice and, I am persuaded, now lives in you also. [6]For this reason I remind you to fan into flame the gift of God, which is in you through the laying on of my hands. [7]For God did not give us a spirit of timidity, but a spirit of power, of love and of self-discipline.

[8]So do not be ashamed to testify about our Lord, or ashamed of me his prisoner. But join with me in suffering for the gospel, by the power of God, [9]who has saved us and called us to a holy life—not because of anything we have done but because of his own purpose and grace. This grace was given us in Christ Jesus before the beginning of time, [10]but it has now been revealed through the appearing of our Savior, Christ Jesus, who has destroyed death and has brought life and immortality to light through the gospel. [11]And of this gospel I was appointed a herald and an apostle and a teacher. [12]That is why I am suffering as I am. Yet I am not ashamed, because I know whom I have believed, and am convinced that he is able to guard what I have entrusted to him for that day.

[13]What you heard from me, keep as the pattern of sound teaching, with faith and love in Christ Jesus. [14]Guard the good deposit that was entrusted to you—guard it with the help of the Holy Spirit who lives in us.

[15]You know that everyone in the province of Asia has deserted me, including Phygelus and Hermogenes.

[16]May the Lord show mercy to the household of Onesiphorus, because he often refreshed me and was not ashamed of my chains. [17]On the contrary, when he was in Rome, he searched hard for me until he found me. [18]May the Lord grant that he will find mercy from the Lord on that day! You know very well in how many ways he helped me in Ephesus.

PRAYER: THE CHARACTER I WANT TO CULTIVATE

THANKS be to You, O God, the One who gives me the victory through our Lord Jesus Christ. Therefore I will be steadfast, immovable, abounding in Your work, Lord, knowing that my labor in You is not in vain. (1 Corinthians 15:57–58) . . . May our Lord Jesus Christ Himself and You, God our Father, who have loved us and have given us eternal consolation and good hope by grace, comfort our hearts and strengthen us in every good work and word. (2 Thessalonians 2:16–17)

***TAKE** a moment to ask the Lord for the grace to grow in godly character.*

YEAR 1 DAY 250

OT 1 Samuel 20:1-42

David and Jonathan

20 Then David fled from Naioth at Ramah and went to Jonathan and
asked, "What have I done? What is my
crime? How have I wronged your father,
that he is trying to take my life?"
2 "Never!" Jonathan replied. "You are
not going to die! Look, my father doesn't
do anything, great or small, without con-
fiding in me. Why would he hide this
from me? It's not so!"
3 But David took an oath and said,
"Your father knows very well that I have
found favor in your eyes, and he has said
to himself, 'Jonathan must not know this
or he will be grieved.' Yet as surely as the
LORD lives and as you live, there is only a
step between me and death."
4 Jonathan said to David, "Whatever you
want me to do, I'll do for you."
5 So David said, "Look, tomorrow is the
New Moon festival, and I am supposed to
dine with the king; but let me go and hide
in the field until the evening of the day after tomorrow. 6 If your father misses me at
all, tell him, 'David earnestly asked my
permission to hurry to Bethlehem, his
hometown, because an annual sacrifice is
being made there for his whole clan.' 7 If
he says, 'Very well,' then your servant is
safe. But if he loses his temper, you can be
sure that he is determined to harm me.
8 As for you, show kindness to your servant, for you have brought him into a covenant with you before the LORD. If I am
guilty, then kill me yourself! Why hand
me over to your father?"
9 "Never!" Jonathan said. "If I had the
least inkling that my father was determined to harm you, wouldn't I tell you?"
10 David asked, "Who will tell me if your
father answers you harshly?"
11 "Come," Jonathan said, "let's go out
into the field." So they went there together.
12 Then Jonathan said to David: "By the
LORD, the God of Israel, I will surely
sound out my father by this time the day
after tomorrow! If he is favorably disposed toward you, will I not send you
word and let you know? 13 But if my father
is inclined to harm you, may the LORD
deal with me, be it ever so severely, if I do
not let you know and send you away safely. May the LORD be with you as he has
been with my father. 14 But show me unfailing kindness like that of the LORD as
long as I live, so that I may not be killed,
15 and do not ever cut off your kindness
from my family—not even when the LORD
has cut off every one of David's enemies
from the face of the earth."
16 So Jonathan made a covenant with
the house of David, saying, "May the LORD
call David's enemies to account." 17 And
Jonathan had David reaffirm his oath out
of love for him, because he loved him as
he loved himself.
18 Then Jonathan said to David: "Tomorrow is the New Moon festival. You
will be missed, because your seat will be
empty. 19 The day after tomorrow, toward
evening, go to the place where you hid
when this trouble began, and wait by the
stone Ezel. 20 I will shoot three arrows to
the side of it, as though I were shooting
at a target. 21 Then I will send a boy and
say, 'Go, find the arrows.' If I say to him,
'Look, the arrows are on this side of you;
bring them here,' then come, because, as
surely as the LORD lives, you are safe; there
is no danger. 22 But if I say to the boy,
'Look, the arrows are beyond you,' then
you must go, because the LORD has sent
you away. 23 And about the matter you and
I discussed—remember, the LORD is witness between you and me forever."
24 So David hid in the field, and when
the New Moon festival came, the king sat
down to eat. 25 He sat in his customary
place by the wall, opposite Jonathan,[a] and
Abner sat next to Saul, but David's place
was empty. 26 Saul said nothing that day,
for he thought, "Something must have
happened to David to make him ceremonially unclean—surely he is unclean."
27 But the next day, the second day of the
month, David's place was empty again.
Then Saul said to his son Jonathan, "Why
hasn't the son of Jesse come to the meal,
either yesterday or today?"
28 Jonathan answered, "David earnestly
asked me for permission to go to Bethlehem. 29 He said, 'Let me go, because our
family is observing a sacrifice in the town

[a] 25 Septuagint; Hebrew *wall. Jonathan arose*

and my brother has ordered me to be there. If I have found favor in your eyes, let me get away to see my brothers.' That is why he has not come to the king's table."

30Saul's anger flared up at Jonathan and he said to him, "You son of a perverse and rebellious woman! Don't I know that you have sided with the son of Jesse to your own shame and to the shame of the mother who bore you? 31As long as the son of Jesse lives on this earth, neither you nor your kingdom will be established. Now send and bring him to me, for he must die!"

32"Why should he be put to death? What has he done?" Jonathan asked his father. 33But Saul hurled his spear at him to kill him. Then Jonathan knew that his father intended to kill David.

34Jonathan got up from the table in fierce anger; on that second day of the month he did not eat, because he was grieved at his father's shameful treatment of David.

35In the morning Jonathan went out to the field for his meeting with David. He had a small boy with him, 36and he said to the boy, "Run and find the arrows I shoot." As the boy ran, he shot an arrow beyond him. 37When the boy came to the place where Jonathan's arrow had fallen, Jonathan called out after him, "Isn't the arrow beyond you?" 38Then he shouted, "Hurry! Go quickly! Don't stop!" The boy picked up the arrow and returned to his master. 39(The boy knew nothing of all this; only Jonathan and David knew.) 40Then Jonathan gave his weapons to the boy and said, "Go, carry them back to town."

41After the boy had gone, David got up from the south side ⌊of the stone⌋ and bowed down before Jonathan three times, with his face to the ground. Then they kissed each other and wept together—but David wept the most.

42Jonathan said to David, "Go in peace, for we have sworn friendship with each other in the name of the LORD, saying, 'The LORD is witness between you and me, and between your descendants and my descendants forever.' " Then David left, and Jonathan went back to the town.

PRAYER: INTERCESSION

O LORD, we acknowledge that there are different kinds of gifts, but they are given by the same Spirit. And there are different kinds of service, but the same Lord. And there are different kinds of working, but You are the same God who works all of them in all people. But to each one the manifestation of the Spirit is given for the common good. (1 Corinthians 12:4–7)

TAKE *a few moments to intercede on behalf of your local church, other churches, evangelism and discipleship ministries, educational ministries and any other special concerns you may have.*

NT 2 Timothy 2:1–13

2 You then, my son, be strong in the grace that is in Christ Jesus. 2And the things you have heard me say in the presence of many witnesses entrust to reliable men who will also be qualified to teach others. 3Endure hardship with us like a good soldier of Christ Jesus. 4No one serving as a soldier gets involved in civilian affairs—he wants to please his commanding officer. 5Similarly, if anyone competes as an athlete, he does not receive the victor's crown unless he competes according to the rules. 6The hardworking farmer should be the first to receive a share of the crops. 7Reflect on what I am saying, for the Lord will give you insight into all this.

8Remember Jesus Christ, raised from the dead, descended from David. This is my gospel, 9for which I am suffering even to the point of being chained like a criminal. But God's word is not chained. 10Therefore I endure everything for the sake of the elect, that they too may obtain the salvation that is in Christ Jesus, with eternal glory.

11Here is a trustworthy saying:

If we died with him,
 we will also live with him;
12 if we endure,
 we will also reign with him.
If we disown him,
 he will also disown us;
13 if we are faithless,
 he will remain faithful,
 for he cannot disown
 himself.

PRAYER: MY RELATIONSHIP TO OTHERS

IN obedience to the truth I will purify my soul for a sincere love of my brothers and sisters and love others fervently from the heart. (1 Peter 1:22) . . . This is the message we heard from the beginning: that we should love one another. We know that we have passed out of death into life, because we love our brothers and sisters. The one who does not love abides in death. By this we know love, that You, O Jesus Christ, laid down Your life for us, and we ought to lay down our lives for our brothers and sisters.

(1 John 3:11, 14, 16)

__PAUSE__ to review your relationships with others and to commit them to the Lord.

YEAR 1
DAY 251

OT 1 Samuel 21:1–15

David at Nob

21 David went to Nob, to Ahimelech the
priest. Ahimelech trembled when he
met him, and asked, "Why are you alone?
Why is no one with you?"
2 David answered Ahimelech the priest,
"The king charged me with a certain matter and said to me, 'No one is to know
anything about your mission and your instructions.' As for my men, I have told
them to meet me at a certain place. 3 Now
then, what do you have on hand? Give me
five loaves of bread, or whatever you can
find."
4 But the priest answered David, "I don't
have any ordinary bread on hand; however, there is some consecrated bread
here—provided the men have kept themselves from women."
5 David replied, "Indeed women have
been kept from us, as usual whenever[a] I
set out. The men's things[b] are holy even
on missions that are not holy. How much
more so today!" 6 So the priest gave him
the consecrated bread, since there was no
bread there except the bread of the Presence that had been removed from before
the LORD and replaced by hot bread on
the day it was taken away.
7 Now one of Saul's servants was there
that day, detained before the LORD; he was
Doeg the Edomite, Saul's head shepherd.
8 David asked Ahimelech, "Don't you
have a spear or a sword here? I haven't
brought my sword or any other weapon,
because the king's business was urgent."
9 The priest replied, "The sword of Goliath the Philistine, whom you killed in the
Valley of Elah, is here; it is wrapped in a
cloth behind the ephod. If you want it, take
it; there is no sword here but that one."
David said, "There is none like it; give
it to me."

David at Gath

10 That day David fled from Saul and
went to Achish king of Gath. 11 But the servants of Achish said to him, "Isn't this David, the king of the land? Isn't he the one
they sing about in their dances:

" 'Saul has slain his thousands,
 and David his tens of thousands'?"

12 David took these words to heart and
was very much afraid of Achish king of
Gath. 13 So he pretended to be insane in
their presence; and while he was in their
hands he acted like a madman, making

[a] 5 Or *from us in the past few days since* [b] 5 Or *bodies*

marks on the doors of the gate and letting saliva run down his beard.
[14]Achish said to his servants, "Look at the man! He is insane! Why bring him to me? [15]Am I so short of madmen that you have to bring this fellow here to carry on like this in front of me? Must this man come into my house?"

PRAYER: AFFIRMATION

NO one can lay a foundation other than the one already laid; You are the foundation, O Jesus Christ. (1 Corinthians 3:11) . . . It is by faith that I stand firm. (2 Corinthians 1:24)

***PAUSE** to reflect on these Biblical affirmations.*

NT 2 Timothy 2:14-26

A Workman Approved by God

[14]Keep reminding them of these things.
Warn them before God against quarreling
about words; it is of no value, and only
ruins those who listen. [15]Do your best to
present yourself to God as one approved,
a workman who does not need to be
ashamed and who correctly handles the
word of truth. [16]Avoid godless chatter, because those who indulge in it will become
more and more ungodly. [17]Their teaching
will spread like gangrene. Among them
are Hymenaeus and Philetus, [18]who have
wandered away from the truth. They say
that the resurrection has already taken
place, and they destroy the faith of some.
[19]Nevertheless, God's solid foundation
stands firm, sealed with this inscription:
"The Lord knows those who are his,"[a]
and, "Everyone who confesses the name
of the Lord must turn away from wickedness."
[20]In a large house there are articles not
only of gold and silver, but also of wood
and clay; some are for noble purposes and
some for ignoble. [21]If a man cleanses himself from the latter, he will be an instrument for noble purposes, made holy, useful to the Master and prepared to do any
good work.
[22]Flee the evil desires of youth, and pursue righteousness, faith, love and peace,
along with those who call on the Lord out
of a pure heart. [23]Don't have anything to
do with foolish and stupid arguments, because you know they produce quarrels.
[24]And the Lord's servant must not quarrel;
instead, he must be kind to everyone, able
to teach, not resentful. [25]Those who oppose him he must gently instruct, in the
hope that God will grant them repentance
leading them to a knowledge of the truth,
[26]and that they will come to their senses
and escape from the trap of the devil, who
has taken them captive to do his will.

[a] *19* Num. 16:5 (see Septuagint)

PRAYER: THE ATTRIBUTES OF GOD

ONE thing You have spoken; two things I have heard: That You, O God, are strong and that You, O Lord, are loving. For You reward us according to what we have done. (Psalm 62:11–12) . . . You, O Lord, are our judge, You are our lawgiver, You are our king; it is You who will save us. (Isaiah 33:22)

***PAUSE** to reflect on these affirmations about the person, powers and perfection of God.*

OT Psalms 48–49

YEAR 1 DAY 252

Psalm 48

A song. A psalm of the Sons of Korah.

1 Great is the LORD, and most worthy of praise,
in the city of our God, his holy mountain.
2 It is beautiful in its loftiness,
the joy of the whole earth.
Like the utmost heights of Zaphon[a] is Mount Zion,
the[b] city of the Great King.
3 God is in her citadels;
he has shown himself to be her fortress.

4 When the kings joined forces,
when they advanced together,
5 they saw ⌊her⌋ and were astounded;
they fled in terror.
6 Trembling seized them there,
pain like that of a woman in labor.
7 You destroyed them like ships of Tarshish
shattered by an east wind.

8 As we have heard,
so have we seen
in the city of the LORD Almighty,
in the city of our God:
God makes her secure forever. *Selah*

9 Within your temple, O God,
we meditate on your unfailing love.
10 Like your name, O God,
your praise reaches to the ends of the earth;
your right hand is filled with righteousness.
11 Mount Zion rejoices,
the villages of Judah are glad
because of your judgments.

12 Walk about Zion, go around her,
count her towers,
13 consider well her ramparts,
view her citadels,
that you may tell of them to the next generation.
14 For this God is our God for ever and ever;
he will be our guide even to the end.

Psalm 49

For the director of music. Of the Sons of Korah. A psalm.

1 Hear this, all you peoples;
listen, all who live in this world,
2 both low and high,
rich and poor alike:
3 My mouth will speak words of wisdom;
the utterance from my heart will give understanding.
4 I will turn my ear to a proverb;
with the harp I will expound my riddle:

5 Why should I fear when evil days come,
when wicked deceivers surround me—
6 those who trust in their wealth
and boast of their great riches?
7 No man can redeem the life of another
or give to God a ransom for him—
8 the ransom for a life is costly,
no payment is ever enough—
9 that he should live on forever
and not see decay.

10 For all can see that wise men die;
the foolish and the senseless alike perish
and leave their wealth to others.
11 Their tombs will remain their houses[c] forever,
their dwellings for endless generations,
though they had[d] named lands after themselves.

12 But man, despite his riches, does not endure;
he is[e] like the beasts that perish.

13 This is the fate of those who trust in themselves,
and of their followers, who approve their sayings. *Selah*

[a] 2 *Zaphon* can refer to a sacred mountain or the direction north. [b] 2 Or *earth, / Mount Zion, on the northern side / of the* [c] 11 Septuagint and Syriac; Hebrew *In their thoughts their houses will remain* [d] 11 Or / *for they have* [e] 12 Hebrew; Septuagint and Syriac read verse 12 the same as verse 20.

[14]Like sheep they are destined for the
grave,[f]
and death will feed on them.
The upright will rule over them in the
morning;
their forms will decay in the grave,[f]
far from their princely mansions.
[15]But God will redeem my life[g] from the
grave;
he will surely take me to himself.
Selah

[16]Do not be overawed when a man
grows rich,
when the splendor of his house
increases;
[17]for he will take nothing with him
when he dies,
his splendor will not descend with
him.
[18]Though while he lived he counted
himself blessed—
and men praise you when you
prosper—
[19]he will join the generation of his
fathers,
who will never see the light ⌊of life⌋.

[20]A man who has riches without
understanding
is like the beasts that perish.

[f]14 Hebrew *Sheol;* also in verse 15 [g]15 Or *soul*

PRAYER: THANKSGIVING

O LORD my God, many are the wonders You have done, and Your thoughts toward us no one can recount to You; were I to speak and tell of them, they would be too many to declare. (Psalm 40:5) . . . I will praise You forever for what You have done; I will hope in Your name, for it is good. I will praise You in the presence of Your saints. (Psalm 52:9)

***PAUSE** to offer your own expressions of thanksgiving.*

NT 2 Timothy 3:1-9

Godlessness in the Last Days

3 But mark this: There will be terrible
times in the last days. [2]People will be
lovers of themselves, lovers of money,
boastful, proud, abusive, disobedient to
their parents, ungrateful, unholy, [3]without
love, unforgiving, slanderous, without
self-control, brutal, not lovers of the good,
[4]treacherous, rash, conceited, lovers of
pleasure rather than lovers of God— [5]hav-
ing a form of godliness but denying its
power. Have nothing to do with them.
[6]They are the kind who worm their way
into homes and gain control over weak-
willed women, who are loaded down
with sins and are swayed by all kinds of
evil desires, [7]always learning but never
able to acknowledge the truth. [8]Just as
Jannes and Jambres opposed Moses, so
also these men oppose the truth—men of
depraved minds, who, as far as the faith is
concerned, are rejected. [9]But they will not
get very far because, as in the case of those
men, their folly will be clear to everyone.

PRAYER: THE WORKS OF GOD

YOU, Lord Jesus, are coming quickly. Your reward is with You, and You will give to everyone according to what they have done. You are the Alpha and the Omega, the First and the Last, the Beginning and the End. Yes, You are coming quickly. Amen. Come, Lord Jesus. (Revelation 22:12–13, 20)

***TAKE** a moment to consider the greatness of God's wonderful works.*

OT **1 Samuel 22:1-23**

David at Adullam and Mizpah

22 David left Gath and escaped to the cave of Adullam. When his brothers and his father's household heard about it, they went down to him there. 2All those who were in distress or in debt or discontented gathered around him, and he became their leader. About four hundred men were with him.

3From there David went to Mizpah in Moab and said to the king of Moab, "Would you let my father and mother come and stay with you until I learn what God will do for me?" 4So he left them with the king of Moab, and they stayed with him as long as David was in the stronghold.

5But the prophet Gad said to David, "Do not stay in the stronghold. Go into the land of Judah." So David left and went to the forest of Hereth.

Saul Kills the Priests of Nob

6Now Saul heard that David and his men had been discovered. And Saul, spear in hand, was seated under the tamarisk tree on the hill at Gibeah, with all his officials standing around him. 7Saul said to them, "Listen, men of Benjamin! Will the son of Jesse give all of you fields and vineyards? Will he make all of you commanders of thousands and commanders of hundreds? 8Is that why you have all conspired against me? No one tells me when my son makes a covenant with the son of Jesse. None of you is concerned about me or tells me that my son has incited my servant to lie in wait for me, as he does today."

9But Doeg the Edomite, who was standing with Saul's officials, said, "I saw the son of Jesse come to Ahimelech son of Ahitub at Nob. 10Ahimelech inquired of the LORD for him; he also gave him provisions and the sword of Goliath the Philistine."

11Then the king sent for the priest Ahimelech son of Ahitub and his father's whole family, who were the priests at Nob, and they all came to the king. 12Saul said, "Listen now, son of Ahitub."

"Yes, my lord," he answered.

13Saul said to him, "Why have you conspired against me, you and the son of Jesse, giving him bread and a sword and inquiring of God for him, so that he has rebelled against me and lies in wait for me, as he does today?"

14Ahimelech answered the king, "Who of all your servants is as loyal as David, the king's son-in-law, captain of your bodyguard and highly respected in your household? 15Was that day the first time I inquired of God for him? Of course not! Let not the king accuse your servant or any of his father's family, for your servant knows nothing at all about this whole affair."

16But the king said, "You will surely die, Ahimelech, you and your father's whole family."

17Then the king ordered the guards at his side: "Turn and kill the priests of the LORD, because they too have sided with David. They knew he was fleeing, yet they did not tell me."

But the king's officials were not willing to raise a hand to strike the priests of the LORD.

18The king then ordered Doeg, "You turn and strike down the priests." So Doeg the Edomite turned and struck them down. That day he killed eighty-five men who wore the linen ephod. 19He also put to the sword Nob, the town of the priests, with its men and women, its children and infants, and its cattle, donkeys and sheep.

20But Abiathar, a son of Ahimelech son of Ahitub, escaped and fled to join David. 21He told David that Saul had killed the priests of the LORD. 22Then David said to Abiathar: "That day, when Doeg the Edomite was there, I knew he would be sure to tell Saul. I am responsible for the death of your father's whole family. 23Stay with me; don't be afraid; the man who is seeking your life is seeking mine also. You will be safe with me."

PRAYER: ADORATION

YOU, O Holy One, have asked, "To whom will you compare Me? Or who is My equal?" We lift our eyes to the heavens and see Who has created them. You bring out the starry host by number and call them each by name. Because of Your great might and the strength of Your power, not one of them is missing. Do we not know? Have we not heard? You are the everlasting God, the Lord, the Creator of the ends of the earth. You do not grow tired or weary. No one can fathom Your understanding. (Isaiah 40:25–26, 28)

PAUSE *to express your thoughts of praise and worship.*

NT 2 Timothy 3:10–4:8

Paul's Charge to Timothy

10You, however, know all about my
teaching, my way of life, my purpose,
faith, patience, love, endurance, 11persecu-
tions, sufferings—what kinds of things
happened to me in Antioch, Iconium and
Lystra, the persecutions I endured. Yet the
Lord rescued me from all of them. 12In
fact, everyone who wants to live a godly
life in Christ Jesus will be persecuted,
13while evil men and impostors will go
from bad to worse, deceiving and being
deceived. 14But as for you, continue in
what you have learned and have become
convinced of, because you know those
from whom you learned it, 15and how
from infancy you have known the holy
Scriptures, which are able to make you
wise for salvation through faith in Christ
Jesus. 16All Scripture is God-breathed and
is useful for teaching, rebuking, correcting
and training in righteousness, 17so that
the man of God may be thoroughly
equipped for every good work.

4 In the presence of God and of Christ
Jesus, who will judge the living and the
dead, and in view of his appearing and his
kingdom, I give you this charge: 2Preach
the Word; be prepared in season and out
of season; correct, rebuke and encourage—with great patience and careful instruction. 3For the time will come when
men will not put up with sound doctrine.
Instead, to suit their own desires, they will
gather around them a great number of
teachers to say what their itching ears
want to hear. 4They will turn their ears
away from the truth and turn aside to
myths. 5But you, keep your head in all sit-
uations, endure hardship, do the work of
an evangelist, discharge all the duties of
your ministry.

6For I am already being poured out like
a drink offering, and the time has come
for my departure. 7I have fought the good
fight, I have finished the race, I have kept
the faith. 8Now there is in store for me
the crown of righteousness, which the
Lord, the righteous Judge, will award to
me on that day—and not only to me, but
also to all who have longed for his appearing.

PRAYER: MY RELATIONSHIP TO GOD

NO temptation has overtaken me except what is common to all people. And You, O God, are faithful; You will not let me be tempted beyond what I am able, but with the temptation You will also provide a way out, so that I may be able to endure it. (1 Corinthians 10:13) . . . You, O Lord, are faithful; You will strengthen me and protect me from the evil one. (2 Thessalonians 3:3)

PAUSE *to thank God for the relationship that you enjoy with Him in Jesus Christ.*

OT **1 Samuel 23:1-29** YEAR 1 DAY 254

David Saves Keilah

23 When David was told, "Look, the Philistines are fighting against Keilah and are looting the threshing floors," 2he inquired of the LORD, saying, "Shall I go and attack these Philistines?"

The LORD answered him, "Go, attack the Philistines and save Keilah."

3But David's men said to him, "Here in Judah we are afraid. How much more, then, if we go to Keilah against the Philistine forces!"

4Once again David inquired of the LORD, and the LORD answered him, "Go down to Keilah, for I am going to give the Philistines into your hand." 5So David and his men went to Keilah, fought the Philistines and carried off their livestock. He inflicted heavy losses on the Philistines and saved the people of Keilah. 6(Now Abiathar son of Ahimelech had brought the ephod down with him when he fled to David at Keilah.)

Saul Pursues David

7Saul was told that David had gone to Keilah, and he said, "God has handed him over to me, for David has imprisoned himself by entering a town with gates and bars." 8And Saul called up all his forces for battle, to go down to Keilah to besiege David and his men.

9When David learned that Saul was plotting against him, he said to Abiathar the priest, "Bring the ephod." 10David said, "O LORD, God of Israel, your servant has heard definitely that Saul plans to come to Keilah and destroy the town on account of me. 11Will the citizens of Keilah surrender me to him? Will Saul come down, as your servant has heard? O LORD, God of Israel, tell your servant."

And the LORD said, "He will."

12Again David asked, "Will the citizens of Keilah surrender me and my men to Saul?"

And the LORD said, "They will."

13So David and his men, about six hundred in number, left Keilah and kept moving from place to place. When Saul was told that David had escaped from Keilah, he did not go there.

14David stayed in the desert strongholds and in the hills of the Desert of Ziph. Day after day Saul searched for him, but God did not give David into his hands.

15While David was at Horesh in the Desert of Ziph, he learned that Saul had come out to take his life. 16And Saul's son Jonathan went to David at Horesh and helped him find strength in God. 17"Don't be afraid," he said. "My father Saul will not lay a hand on you. You will be king over Israel, and I will be second to you. Even my father Saul knows this." 18The two of them made a covenant before the LORD. Then Jonathan went home, but David remained at Horesh.

19The Ziphites went up to Saul at Gibeah and said, "Is not David hiding among us in the strongholds at Horesh, on the hill of Hakilah, south of Jeshimon? 20Now, O king, come down whenever it pleases you to do so, and we will be responsible for handing him over to the king."

21Saul replied, "The LORD bless you for your concern for me. 22Go and make further preparation. Find out where David usually goes and who has seen him there. They tell me he is very crafty. 23Find out about all the hiding places he uses and come back to me with definite information.[a] Then I will go with you; if he is in the area, I will track him down among all the clans of Judah."

24So they set out and went to Ziph ahead of Saul. Now David and his men were in the Desert of Maon, in the Arabah south of Jeshimon. 25Saul and his men began the search, and when David was told about it, he went down to the rock and stayed in the Desert of Maon. When Saul heard this, he went into the Desert of Maon in pursuit of David.

26Saul was going along one side of the mountain, and David and his men were on the other side, hurrying to get away from Saul. As Saul and his forces were closing in on David and his men to capture them, 27a messenger came to Saul, saying, "Come quickly! The Philistines are raiding the land." 28Then Saul broke off his pursuit of David and went to meet the Philistines. That is why they call this place Sela Hammahlekoth.[b] 29And David went up from there and lived in the strongholds of En Gedi.

[a] 23 Or *me at Nacon* [b] 28 *Sela Hammahlekoth* means *rock of parting.*

PRAYER: CONFESSION

WHY should we complain, O Lord, when punished for our sins? Let us search out and examine our ways, and let us return to You. (Lamentations 3:39–40)

***ASK** the Spirit to search your heart and reveal any areas of unconfessed sin. Acknowledge these to the Lord and thank Him for His forgiveness.*

NT 2 Timothy 4:9–22

Personal Remarks

9Do your best to come to me quickly,
10for Demas, because he loved this world,
has deserted me and has gone to Thessalonica. Crescens has gone to Galatia, and
Titus to Dalmatia. 11Only Luke is with me.
Get Mark and bring him with you, because he is helpful to me in my ministry.
12I sent Tychicus to Ephesus. 13When you
come, bring the cloak that I left with Car-
pus at Troas, and my scrolls, especially the
parchments.
14Alexander the metalworker did me a
great deal of harm. The Lord will repay
him for what he has done. 15You too
should be on your guard against him, because he strongly opposed our message.
16At my first defense, no one came to
my support, but everyone deserted me.
May it not be held against them. 17But the
Lord stood at my side and gave me
strength, so that through me the message
might be fully proclaimed and all the
Gentiles might hear it. And I was delivered from the lion's mouth. 18The Lord
will rescue me from every evil attack and
will bring me safely to his heavenly kingdom. To him be glory for ever and ever.
Amen.

Final Greetings

19Greet Priscilla[a] and Aquila and the
household of Onesiphorus. 20Erastus
stayed in Corinth, and I left Trophimus
sick in Miletus. 21Do your best to get here
before winter. Eubulus greets you, and so
do Pudens, Linus, Claudia and all the
brothers.
22The Lord be with your spirit. Grace be
with you.

[a] 19 Greek *Prisca,* a variant of *Priscilla*

PRAYER: THE CHARACTER I WANT TO CULTIVATE

DIRECT my footsteps according to Your word, O Lord, and let no iniquity have dominion over me. (Psalm 119:133) . . . The hour has come for me to wake up from sleep, for my salvation is nearer now than when I first believed. The night is nearly over; the day is almost here. Therefore I will cast off the works of darkness and put on the armor of light. (Romans 13:11–12)

***TAKE** a moment to ask the Lord for the grace to grow in godly character.*

YEAR 1
DAY 255

OT 1 Samuel 24:1–22

David Spares Saul's Life

24 After Saul returned from pursuing the
Philistines, he was told, "David is in
the Desert of En Gedi." 2So Saul took
three thousand chosen men from all Israel and set out to look for David and his
men near the Crags of the Wild Goats.
3He came to the sheep pens along the
way; a cave was there, and Saul went in to
relieve himself. David and his men were

far back in the cave. [4]The men said, "This
is the day the LORD spoke of when he
said[a] to you, 'I will give your enemy into
your hands for you to deal with as you
wish.' " Then David crept up unnoticed
and cut off a corner of Saul's robe.
[5]Afterward, David was conscience-
stricken for having cut off a corner of his
robe. [6]He said to his men, "The LORD forbid that I should do such a thing to my
master, the LORD's anointed, or lift my
hand against him; for he is the anointed
of the LORD." [7]With these words David rebuked his men and did not allow them to
attack Saul. And Saul left the cave and
went his way.
[8]Then David went out of the cave and
called out to Saul, "My lord the king!"
When Saul looked behind him, David
bowed down and prostrated himself with
his face to the ground. [9]He said to Saul,
"Why do you listen when men say, 'David
is bent on harming you'? [10]This day you
have seen with your own eyes how the
LORD delivered you into my hands in the
cave. Some urged me to kill you, but I
spared you; I said, 'I will not lift my hand
against my master, because he is the
LORD's anointed.' [11]See, my father, look at
this piece of your robe in my hand! I cut
off the corner of your robe but did not kill
you. Now understand and recognize that
I am not guilty of wrongdoing or rebellion. I have not wronged you, but you are
hunting me down to take my life. [12]May
the LORD judge between you and me. And
may the LORD avenge the wrongs you have
done to me, but my hand will not touch
you. [13]As the old saying goes, 'From evildoers come evil deeds,' so my hand will
not touch you.
[14]"Against whom has the king of Israel
come out? Whom are you pursuing? A
dead dog? A flea? [15]May the LORD be our
judge and decide between us. May he consider my cause and uphold it; may he vindicate me by delivering me from your
hand."
[16]When David finished saying this, Saul
asked, "Is that your voice, David my son?"
And he wept aloud. [17]"You are more righteous than I," he said. "You have treated
me well, but I have treated you badly.
[18]You have just now told me of the good
you did to me; the LORD delivered me into
your hands, but you did not kill me.
[19]When a man finds his enemy, does he
let him get away unharmed? May the
LORD reward you well for the way you
treated me today. [20]I know that you will
surely be king and that the kingdom of Israel will be established in your hands.
[21]Now swear to me by the LORD that you
will not cut off my descendants or wipe
out my name from my father's family."
[22]So David gave his oath to Saul. Then
Saul returned home, but David and his
men went up to the stronghold.

[a] 4 Or *"Today the LORD is saying*

PRAYER: RENEWAL

MAY I apply my heart to instruction and my ears to words of knowledge. (Proverbs 23:12) . . . May I watch and pray so that I will not fall into temptation; my spirit is willing, but my flesh is weak. (Matthew 26:41)

__PAUSE__ to add your own prayers for personal renewal.

NT Titus 1:1–16

1 Paul, a servant of God and an apostle of
Jesus Christ for the faith of God's elect
and the knowledge of the truth that leads
to godliness— [2]a faith and knowledge
resting on the hope of eternal life, which
God, who does not lie, promised before
the beginning of time, [3]and at his appointed season he brought his word to
light through the preaching entrusted to
me by the command of God our Savior,

[4]To Titus, my true son in our common
faith:

Grace and peace from God the Father
and Christ Jesus our Savior.

Titus's Task on Crete

5The reason I left you in Crete was that
you might straighten out what was left unfinished and appoint[a] elders in every
town, as I directed you. 6An elder must be
blameless, the husband of but one wife, a
man whose children believe and are not
open to the charge of being wild and disobedient. 7Since an overseer[b] is entrusted
with God's work, he must be blameless—
not overbearing, not quick-tempered, not
given to drunkenness, not violent, not
pursuing dishonest gain. 8Rather he must
be hospitable, one who loves what is
good, who is self-controlled, upright, holy
and disciplined. 9He must hold firmly to
the trustworthy message as it has been
taught, so that he can encourage others by
sound doctrine and refute those who oppose it.
10For there are many rebellious people,
mere talkers and deceivers, especially
those of the circumcision group. 11They
must be silenced, because they are ruining whole households by teaching things
they ought not to teach—and that for the
sake of dishonest gain. 12Even one of their
own prophets has said, "Cretans are always liars, evil brutes, lazy gluttons."
13This testimony is true. Therefore, rebuke
them sharply, so that they will be sound
in the faith 14and will pay no attention to
Jewish myths or to the commands of
those who reject the truth. 15To the pure,
all things are pure, but to those who are
corrupted and do not believe, nothing is
pure. In fact, both their minds and consciences are corrupted. 16They claim to
know God, but by their actions they deny
him. They are detestable, disobedient and
unfit for doing anything good.

[a] 5 Or *ordain* [b] 7 Traditionally *bishop*

PRAYER: MY RELATIONSHIP TO OTHERS

I WILL remember those in prison as though bound with them, and those who are mistreated, as though suffering with them. (Hebrews 13:3) . . . This is pure and undefiled religion before You, my God and Father: to visit orphans and widows in their affliction and to keep oneself unspotted from the world. (James 1:27)

***PAUSE** to review your relationships with others and to commit them to the Lord.*

OT 1 Samuel 25:1-44 — YEAR 1 DAY 256

David, Nabal and Abigail

25 Now Samuel died, and all Israel assembled and mourned for him; and
they buried him at his home in Ramah.
Then David moved down into the
Desert of Maon.[a] 2A certain man in Maon,
who had property there at Carmel, was
very wealthy. He had a thousand goats
and three thousand sheep, which he was
shearing in Carmel. 3His name was Nabal
and his wife's name was Abigail. She was
an intelligent and beautiful woman, but
her husband, a Calebite, was surly and
mean in his dealings.
4While David was in the desert, he
heard that Nabal was shearing sheep. 5So
he sent ten young men and said to them,
"Go up to Nabal at Carmel and greet him
in my name. 6Say to him: 'Long life to
you! Good health to you and your household! And good health to all that is yours!
7" 'Now I hear that it is sheep-shearing
time. When your shepherds were with us,
we did not mistreat them, and the whole
time they were at Carmel nothing of theirs
was missing. 8Ask your own servants and
they will tell you. Therefore be favorable
toward my young men, since we come at
a festive time. Please give your servants
and your son David whatever you can
find for them.' "
9When David's men arrived, they gave

[a] 1 Some Septuagint manuscripts; Hebrew *Paran*

Nabal this message in David's name. Then
they waited.
10 Nabal answered David's servants,
"Who is this David? Who is this son of
Jesse? Many servants are breaking away
from their masters these days. 11 Why
should I take my bread and water, and the
meat I have slaughtered for my shearers,
and give it to men coming from who
knows where?"
12 David's men turned around and went
back. When they arrived, they reported
every word. 13 David said to his men, "Put
on your swords!" So they put on their
swords, and David put on his. About four
hundred men went up with David, while
two hundred stayed with the supplies.
14 One of the servants told Nabal's wife
Abigail: "David sent messengers from the
desert to give our master his greetings, but
he hurled insults at them. 15 Yet these men
were very good to us. They did not mistreat us, and the whole time we were out
in the fields near them nothing was missing. 16 Night and day they were a wall
around us all the time we were herding
our sheep near them. 17 Now think it over
and see what you can do, because disaster is hanging over our master and his
whole household. He is such a wicked
man that no one can talk to him."
18 Abigail lost no time. She took two hundred loaves of bread, two skins of wine, five
dressed sheep, five seahs[b] of roasted grain,
a hundred cakes of raisins and two hundred cakes of pressed figs, and loaded them
on donkeys. 19 Then she told her servants,
"Go on ahead; I'll follow you." But she did
not tell her husband Nabal.
20 As she came riding her donkey into a
mountain ravine, there were David and his
men descending toward her, and she met
them. 21 David had just said, "It's been useless—all my watching over this fellow's
property in the desert so that nothing of
his was missing. He has paid me back evil
for good. 22 May God deal with David,[c] be
it ever so severely, if by morning I leave
alive one male of all who belong to him!"
23 When Abigail saw David, she quickly
got off her donkey and bowed down before David with her face to the ground.
24 She fell at his feet and said: "My lord, let
the blame be on me alone. Please let your
servant speak to you; hear what your servant has to say. 25 May my lord pay no attention to that wicked man Nabal. He is
just like his name—his name is Fool, and
folly goes with him. But as for me, your servant, I did not see the men my master sent.
26 "Now since the LORD has kept you, my
master, from bloodshed and from avenging
yourself with your own hands, as surely as
the LORD lives and as you live, may your enemies and all who intend to harm my master be like Nabal. 27 And let this gift, which
your servant has brought to my master, be
given to the men who follow you. 28 Please
forgive your servant's offense, for the LORD
will certainly make a lasting dynasty for my
master, because he fights the LORD's battles.
Let no wrongdoing be found in you as long
as you live. 29 Even though someone is pursuing you to take your life, the life of my
master will be bound securely in the bun-
dle of the living by the LORD your God. But
the lives of your enemies he will hurl away
as from the pocket of a sling. 30 When the
LORD has done for my master every good
thing he promised concerning him and has
appointed him leader over Israel, 31 my master will not have on his conscience the staggering burden of needless bloodshed or of
having avenged himself. And when the
LORD has brought my master success, remember your servant."
32 David said to Abigail, "Praise be to the
LORD, the God of Israel, who has sent you
today to meet me. 33 May you be blessed for
your good judgment and for keeping me
from bloodshed this day and from avenging myself with my own hands. 34 Otherwise, as surely as the LORD, the God of Israel, lives, who has kept me from harming
you, if you had not come quickly to meet
me, not one male belonging to Nabal
would have been left alive by daybreak."
35 Then David accepted from her hand
what she had brought him and said, "Go
home in peace. I have heard your words
and granted your request."
36 When Abigail went to Nabal, he was
in the house holding a banquet like that
of a king. He was in high spirits and very
drunk. So she told him nothing until daybreak. 37 Then in the morning, when Nabal was sober, his wife told him all these
things, and his heart failed him and he became like a stone. 38 About ten days later,
the LORD struck Nabal and he died.
39 When David heard that Nabal was

[b] *18* That is, probably about a bushel (about 37 liters)   [c] *22* Some Septuagint manuscripts; Hebrew *with David's enemies*

dead, he said, "Praise be to the LORD, who has upheld my cause against Nabal for treating me with contempt. He has kept his servant from doing wrong and has brought Nabal's wrongdoing down on his own head."

Then David sent word to Abigail, asking her to become his wife. [40]His servants went to Carmel and said to Abigail, "David has sent us to you to take you to become his wife."

[41]She bowed down with her face to the ground and said, "Here is your maidservant, ready to serve you and wash the feet of my master's servants." [42]Abigail quickly got on a donkey and, attended by her five maids, went with David's messengers and became his wife. [43]David had also married Ahinoam of Jezreel, and they both were his wives. [44]But Saul had given his daughter Michal, David's wife, to Paltiel[d] son of Laish, who was from Gallim.

[d] 44 Hebrew *Palti,* a variant of *Paltiel*

PRAYER: PETITION

MAY I keep Your statutes and Your commandments and be careful to do as You, O Lord my God, have commanded me; may I not turn aside to the right or to the left.

(Deuteronomy 4:40; 5:32)

***PAUSE** here to petition God for wisdom. Ask Him to develop your eternal perspective, to renew your mind with truth and to help you develop greater skill in each area of your life. Offer prayers regarding your activities for this day and any special concerns you may have.*

NT Titus 2:1-10

What Must Be Taught to Various Groups

2 You must teach what is in accord with sound doctrine. [2]Teach the older men to be temperate, worthy of respect, self-controlled, and sound in faith, in love and in endurance.

[3]Likewise, teach the older women to be reverent in the way they live, not to be slanderers or addicted to much wine, but to teach what is good. [4]Then they can train the younger women to love their husbands and children, [5]to be self-controlled and pure, to be busy at home, to be kind, and to be subject to their husbands, so that no one will malign the word of God.

[6]Similarly, encourage the young men to be self-controlled. [7]In everything set them an example by doing what is good. In your teaching show integrity, seriousness [8]and soundness of speech that cannot be condemned, so that those who oppose you may be ashamed because they have nothing bad to say about us.

[9]Teach slaves to be subject to their masters in everything, to try to please them, not to talk back to them, [10]and not to steal from them, but to show that they can be fully trusted, so that in every way they will make the teaching about God our Savior attractive.

PRAYER: THE ATTRIBUTES OF GOD

IN the beginning was the Word, and the Word was with You, O God, and the Word was You. The Word was in the beginning with You. The Word became flesh and dwelt among us. We have seen His glory, the glory of Your only begotten, O Father, full of grace and truth.

(John 1:1–2, 14)

***PAUSE** to reflect on these affirmations about the person, powers and perfection of God.*

YEAR 1 DAY 257

OT 1 Samuel 26:1-25

David Again Spares Saul's Life

26 The Ziphites went to Saul at Gibeah
and said, "Is not David hiding on the
hill of Hakilah, which faces Jeshimon?"
2So Saul went down to the Desert of
Ziph, with his three thousand chosen
men of Israel, to search there for David.
3Saul made his camp beside the road on
the hill of Hakilah facing Jeshimon, but
David stayed in the desert. When he saw
that Saul had followed him there, 4he sent
out scouts and learned that Saul had definitely arrived.[a]
5Then David set out and went to the
place where Saul had camped. He saw
where Saul and Abner son of Ner, the
commander of the army, had lain down.
Saul was lying inside the camp, with the
army encamped around him.
6David then asked Ahimelech the Hittite and Abishai son of Zeruiah, Joab's
brother, "Who will go down into the
camp with me to Saul?"
"I'll go with you," said Abishai.
7So David and Abishai went to the army
by night, and there was Saul, lying asleep
inside the camp with his spear stuck in
the ground near his head. Abner and the
soldiers were lying around him.
8Abishai said to David, "Today God has
delivered your enemy into your hands.
Now let me pin him to the ground with
one thrust of my spear; I won't strike him
twice."
9But David said to Abishai, "Don't destroy him! Who can lay a hand on the
LORD's anointed and be guiltless? 10As
surely as the LORD lives," he said, "the
LORD himself will strike him; either his
time will come and he will die, or he will
go into battle and perish. 11But the LORD
forbid that I should lay a hand on the
LORD's anointed. Now get the spear and
water jug that are near his head, and
let's go."
12So David took the spear and water jug
near Saul's head, and they left. No one
saw or knew about it, nor did anyone
wake up. They were all sleeping, because
the LORD had put them into a deep sleep.
13Then David crossed over to the other
side and stood on top of the hill some distance away; there was a wide space between them. 14He called out to the army
and to Abner son of Ner, "Aren't you going to answer me, Abner?"
Abner replied, "Who are you who calls
to the king?"
15David said, "You're a man, aren't you?
And who is like you in Israel? Why didn't
you guard your lord the king? Someone
came to destroy your lord the king.
16What you have done is not good. As
surely as the LORD lives, you and your men
deserve to die, because you did not guard
your master, the LORD's anointed. Look
around you. Where are the king's spear
and water jug that were near his head?"
17Saul recognized David's voice and
said, "Is that your voice, David my son?"
David replied, "Yes it is, my lord the
king." 18And he added, "Why is my lord
pursuing his servant? What have I done,
and what wrong am I guilty of? 19Now let
my lord the king listen to his servant's
words. If the LORD has incited you against
me, then may he accept an offering. If, however, men have done it, may they be cursed
before the LORD! They have now driven me
from my share in the LORD's inheritance
and have said, 'Go, serve other gods.' 20Now
do not let my blood fall to the ground far
from the presence of the LORD. The king of
Israel has come out to look for a flea—as
one hunts a partridge in the mountains."
21Then Saul said, "I have sinned. Come
back, David my son. Because you considered my life precious today, I will not try
to harm you again. Surely I have acted like
a fool and have erred greatly."
22"Here is the king's spear," David answered. "Let one of your young men come
over and get it. 23The LORD rewards every
man for his righteousness and faithfulness. The LORD delivered you into my
hands today, but I would not lay a hand
on the LORD's anointed. 24As surely as I
valued your life today, so may the LORD
value my life and deliver me from all trouble."
25Then Saul said to David, "May you be
blessed, my son David; you will do great
things and surely triumph."
So David went on his way, and Saul returned home.

[a] 4 Or *had come to Nacon*

PRAYER: INTERCESSION

If I speak in the languages of humans and of angels, but have not love, I am only a resounding gong or a clanging cymbal. And if I have the gift of prophecy and understand all mysteries and all knowledge, and if I have all faith so as to remove mountains, but have not love, I am nothing. And if I give all my possessions to the poor, and if I deliver my body to be burned, but have not love, it profits me nothing. (1 Corinthians 13:1–3)

TAKE *a few moments to intercede on behalf of your immediate family and other relatives. Offer prayers for their spiritual, emotional and physical concerns.*

NT Titus 2:11–3:8

11 For the grace of God that brings salvation has appeared to all men. 12 It
teaches us to say "No" to ungodliness and
worldly passions, and to live self-controlled, upright and godly lives in this
present age, 13 while we wait for the
blessed hope—the glorious appearing of
our great God and Savior, Jesus Christ,
14 who gave himself for us to redeem us
from all wickedness and to purify for himself a people that are his very own, eager
to do what is good.

15 These, then, are the things you
should teach. Encourage and rebuke with
all authority. Do not let anyone despise
you.

Doing What Is Good

3 Remind the people to be subject to
rulers and authorities, to be obedient,
to be ready to do whatever is good, 2 to
slander no one, to be peaceable and considerate, and to show true humility toward all men.

3 At one time we too were foolish, disobedient, deceived and enslaved by all
kinds of passions and pleasures. We lived
in malice and envy, being hated and hating one another. 4 But when the kindness
and love of God our Savior appeared, 5 he
saved us, not because of righteous things
we had done, but because of his mercy.
He saved us through the washing of rebirth and renewal by the Holy Spirit,
6 whom he poured out on us generously
through Jesus Christ our Savior, 7 so that,
having been justified by his grace, we
might become heirs having the hope of
eternal life. 8 This is a trustworthy saying.
And I want you to stress these things, so
that those who have trusted in God may
be careful to devote themselves to doing
what is good. These things are excellent
and profitable for everyone.

PRAYER: THE WORKS OF GOD

YOU, O God, will impute righteousness to us who believe in You who raised Jesus our Lord from the dead. Jesus was delivered over to death because of our sins and was raised in order to make us right with You. (Romans 4:24–25) . . . If many died because of the sin of the one man, Adam, how much more did Your grace, O God, and the gift that came by the grace of the one Man, Jesus Christ, abound to the many? And the result of Your gift, O God, is not like the result of the one man's sin, for judgment followed one sin and brought condemnation, but Your gift followed many sins and brought justification. (Romans 5:15–16)

TAKE *a moment to consider the greatness of God's wonderful works.*

YEAR 1
DAY 258

OT 1 Samuel 27:1–28:25

David Among the Philistines

27 But David thought to himself, "One
of these days I will be destroyed by
the hand of Saul. The best thing I can do
is to escape to the land of the Philistines.
Then Saul will give up searching for me
anywhere in Israel, and I will slip out of
his hand."
2 So David and the six hundred men
with him left and went over to Achish son
of Maoch king of Gath. 3 David and his
men settled in Gath with Achish. Each
man had his family with him, and David
had his two wives: Ahinoam of Jezreel and
Abigail of Carmel, the widow of Nabal.
4 When Saul was told that David had fled
to Gath, he no longer searched for him.
5 Then David said to Achish, "If I have
found favor in your eyes, let a place be assigned to me in one of the country towns,
that I may live there. Why should your servant live in the royal city with you?"
6 So on that day Achish gave him Ziklag,
and it has belonged to the kings of Judah
ever since. 7 David lived in Philistine territory a year and four months.
8 Now David and his men went up and
raided the Geshurites, the Girzites and the
Amalekites. (From ancient times these
peoples had lived in the land extending to
Shur and Egypt.) 9 Whenever David attacked an area, he did not leave a man or
woman alive, but took sheep and cattle,
donkeys and camels, and clothes. Then he
returned to Achish.
10 When Achish asked, "Where did you
go raiding today?" David would say,
"Against the Negev of Judah" or "Against
the Negev of Jerahmeel" or "Against the
Negev of the Kenites." 11 He did not leave
a man or woman alive to be brought to
Gath, for he thought, "They might inform
on us and say, 'This is what David did.' "
And such was his practice as long as he
lived in Philistine territory. 12 Achish trusted David and said to himself, "He has become so odious to his people, the Israelites, that he will be my servant forever."

Saul and the Witch of Endor

28 In those days the Philistines gathered
their forces to fight against Israel.
Achish said to David, "You must understand that you and your men will accompany me in the army."
2 David said, "Then you will see for
yourself what your servant can do."
Achish replied, "Very well, I will make
you my bodyguard for life."
3 Now Samuel was dead, and all Israel
had mourned for him and buried him in
his own town of Ramah. Saul had expelled the mediums and spiritists from
the land.
4 The Philistines assembled and came
and set up camp at Shunem, while Saul
gathered all the Israelites and set up camp
at Gilboa. 5 When Saul saw the Philistine
army, he was afraid; terror filled his heart.
6 He inquired of the LORD, but the LORD
did not answer him by dreams or Urim or
prophets. 7 Saul then said to his attendants, "Find me a woman who is a medium, so I may go and inquire of her."
"There is one in Endor," they said.
8 So Saul disguised himself, putting on
other clothes, and at night he and two
men went to the woman. "Consult a spirit for me," he said, "and bring up for me
the one I name."
9 But the woman said to him, "Surely
you know what Saul has done. He has cut
off the mediums and spiritists from the
land. Why have you set a trap for my life
to bring about my death?"
10 Saul swore to her by the LORD, "As
surely as the LORD lives, you will not be
punished for this."
11 Then the woman asked, "Whom shall
I bring up for you?"
"Bring up Samuel," he said.
12 When the woman saw Samuel, she
cried out at the top of her voice and said
to Saul, "Why have you deceived me? You
are Saul!"
13 The king said to her, "Don't be afraid.
What do you see?"
The woman said, "I see a spirit[a] coming
up out of the ground."
14 "What does he look like?" he asked.
"An old man wearing a robe is coming
up," she said.
Then Saul knew it was Samuel, and he

[a] 13 Or *see spirits;* or *see gods*

bowed down and prostrated himself with
his face to the ground.
15 Samuel said to Saul, "Why have you
disturbed me by bringing me up?"
"I am in great distress," Saul said. "The
Philistines are fighting against me, and
God has turned away from me. He no
longer answers me, either by prophets or
by dreams. So I have called on you to tell
me what to do."
16 Samuel said, "Why do you consult me,
now that the LORD has turned away from
you and become your enemy? 17 The LORD
has done what he predicted through me.
The LORD has torn the kingdom out of
your hands and given it to one of your
neighbors—to David. 18 Because you did
not obey the LORD or carry out his fierce
wrath against the Amalekites, the LORD has
done this to you today. 19 The LORD will
hand over both Israel and you to the Philistines, and tomorrow you and your sons
will be with me. The LORD will also hand
over the army of Israel to the Philistines."
20 Immediately Saul fell full length on
the ground, filled with fear because of
Samuel's words. His strength was gone,
for he had eaten nothing all that day and
night.
21 When the woman came to Saul and
saw that he was greatly shaken, she said,
"Look, your maidservant has obeyed you.
I took my life in my hands and did what
you told me to do. 22 Now please listen to
your servant and let me give you some
food so you may eat and have the strength
to go on your way."
23 He refused and said, "I will not eat."
But his men joined the woman in urging him, and he listened to them. He got
up from the ground and sat on the couch.
24 The woman had a fattened calf at the
house, which she butchered at once. She
took some flour, kneaded it and baked
bread without yeast. 25 Then she set it before Saul and his men, and they ate. That
same night they got up and left.

PRAYER: AFFIRMATION

I AM no longer a stranger and alien, but a fellow citizen with Your people and a member of Your household, O God, that was built on the foundation of the apostles and prophets, with Christ Jesus Himself as the chief cornerstone. (Ephesians 2:19–20) . . . I have been called, having been loved by You, God my Father, and kept by Jesus Christ. (Jude 1)

PAUSE *to reflect on these Biblical affirmations.*

NT Titus 3:9–15

9 But avoid foolish controversies and genealogies and arguments and quarrels
about the law, because these are unprofitable and useless. 10 Warn a divisive person once, and then warn him a second
time. After that, have nothing to do with
him. 11 You may be sure that such a man
is warped and sinful; he is self-con-
demned.

Final Remarks

12 As soon as I send Artemas or Tychicus
to you, do your best to come to me at Ni-
copolis, because I have decided to winter
there. 13 Do everything you can to help Ze-
nas the lawyer and Apollos on their way
and see that they have everything they
need. 14 Our people must learn to devote
themselves to doing what is good, in order that they may provide for daily neces-
sities and not live unproductive lives.
15 Everyone with me sends you greetings. Greet those who love us in the faith.
Grace be with you all.

PRAYER: MY RELATIONSHIP TO GOD

AS the deer pants for the water brooks, so my soul pants for You, O God. My soul thirsts for You, for the living God. When shall I come and appear before You? (Psalm 42:1–2) . . .

God, You are my God. Earnestly I seek You; my soul thirsts for You. My body longs for You in a dry and weary land where there is no water. (Psalm 63:1)

***PAUSE** to thank God for the relationship that you enjoy with Him in Jesus Christ.*

OT Psalm 50 **YEAR 1 DAY 259**

Psalm 50

A psalm of Asaph.

1 The Mighty One, God, the LORD,
speaks and summons the earth
from the rising of the sun to the place where it sets.
2 From Zion, perfect in beauty,
God shines forth.
3 Our God comes and will not be silent;
a fire devours before him,
and around him a tempest rages.
4 He summons the heavens above,
and the earth, that he may judge his people:
5 "Gather to me my consecrated ones,
who made a covenant with me by sacrifice."
6 And the heavens proclaim his righteousness,
for God himself is judge. *Selah*

7 "Hear, O my people, and I will speak,
O Israel, and I will testify against you:
I am God, your God.
8 I do not rebuke you for your sacrifices
or your burnt offerings, which are ever before me.
9 I have no need of a bull from your stall
or of goats from your pens,
10 for every animal of the forest is mine,
and the cattle on a thousand hills.
11 I know every bird in the mountains,
and the creatures of the field are mine.
12 If I were hungry I would not tell you,
for the world is mine, and all that is in it.
13 Do I eat the flesh of bulls
or drink the blood of goats?
14 Sacrifice thank offerings to God,
fulfill your vows to the Most High,
15 and call upon me in the day of trouble;
I will deliver you, and you will honor me."

16 But to the wicked, God says:

"What right have you to recite my laws
or take my covenant on your lips?
17 You hate my instruction
and cast my words behind you.
18 When you see a thief, you join with him;
you throw in your lot with adulterers.
19 You use your mouth for evil
and harness your tongue to deceit.
20 You speak continually against your brother
and slander your own mother's son.
21 These things you have done and I kept silent;
you thought I was altogether[a] like you.
But I will rebuke you
and accuse you to your face.

22 "Consider this, you who forget God,
or I will tear you to pieces, with none to rescue:
23 He who sacrifices thank offerings honors me,
and he prepares the way
so that I may show him[b] the salvation of God."

[a] 21 Or *thought the 'I AM' was* [b] 23 Or *and to him who considers his way / I will show*

PRAYER: THANKSGIVING

YOU answer us with awesome deeds of righteousness, O God of our salvation, You who are the hope of all the ends of the earth and of the farthest seas; You formed the mountains by Your strength, having armed Yourself with power; and You stilled the roaring of the seas, the roaring of their waves, and the tumult of the peoples. (Psalm 65:5–7)

***PAUSE** to offer your own expressions of thanksgiving.*

NT Philemon 1–25

1Paul, a prisoner of Christ Jesus, and Timothy our brother,

To Philemon our dear friend and fellow worker, 2to Apphia our sister, to Archippus our fellow soldier and to the church that meets in your home:

3Grace to you and peace from God our Father and the Lord Jesus Christ.

Thanksgiving and Prayer

4I always thank my God as I remember you in my prayers, 5because I hear about your faith in the Lord Jesus and your love for all the saints. 6I pray that you may be active in sharing your faith, so that you will have a full understanding of every good thing we have in Christ. 7Your love has given me great joy and encouragement, because you, brother, have refreshed the hearts of the saints.

Paul's Plea for Onesimus

8Therefore, although in Christ I could be bold and order you to do what you ought to do, 9yet I appeal to you on the basis of love. I then, as Paul—an old man and now also a prisoner of Christ Jesus— 10I appeal to you for my son Onesimus,[a] who became my son while I was in chains. 11Formerly he was useless to you, but now he has become useful both to you and to me.

12I am sending him—who is my very heart—back to you. 13I would have liked to keep him with me so that he could take your place in helping me while I am in chains for the gospel. 14But I did not want to do anything without your consent, so that any favor you do will be spontaneous and not forced. 15Perhaps the reason he was separated from you for a little while was that you might have him back for good— 16no longer as a slave, but better than a slave, as a dear brother. He is very dear to me but even dearer to you, both as a man and as a brother in the Lord.

17So if you consider me a partner, welcome him as you would welcome me. 18If he has done you any wrong or owes you anything, charge it to me. 19I, Paul, am writing this with my own hand. I will pay it back—not to mention that you owe me your very self. 20I do wish, brother, that I may have some benefit from you in the Lord; refresh my heart in Christ. 21Confident of your obedience, I write to you, knowing that you will do even more than I ask.

22And one thing more: Prepare a guest room for me, because I hope to be restored to you in answer to your prayers.

23Epaphras, my fellow prisoner in Christ Jesus, sends you greetings. 24And so do Mark, Aristarchus, Demas and Luke, my fellow workers.

25The grace of the Lord Jesus Christ be with your spirit.

[a] *10 Onesimus* means *useful.*

PRAYER: THE CHARACTER I WANT TO CULTIVATE

I WANT to abound in faith, in speech, in knowledge, in all diligence, in love and in the grace of giving. (2 Corinthians 8:7) . . . I want to abound in love and faith toward You, Lord Jesus, and toward all the saints. (Philemon 5)

***TAKE** a moment to ask the Lord for the grace to grow in godly character.*

YEAR 1 DAY 260

OT **1 Samuel 29:1–30:31**

Achish Sends David Back to Ziklag

29 The Philistines gathered all their
forces at Aphek, and Israel camped by
the spring in Jezreel. 2As the Philistine
rulers marched with their units of hundreds and thousands, David and his men
were marching at the rear with Achish.
3The commanders of the Philistines
asked, "What about these Hebrews?"

Achish replied, "Is this not David, who
was an officer of Saul king of Israel? He
has already been with me for over a year,
and from the day he left Saul until now, I
have found no fault in him."

4But the Philistine commanders were
angry with him and said, "Send the man
back, that he may return to the place you
assigned him. He must not go with us
into battle, or he will turn against us during the fighting. How better could he regain his master's favor than by taking the
heads of our own men? 5Isn't this the David they sang about in their dances:

" 'Saul has slain his thousands,
and David his tens of thousands'?"

6So Achish called David and said to
him, "As surely as the LORD lives, you have
been reliable, and I would be pleased to
have you serve with me in the army. From
the day you came to me until now, I have
found no fault in you, but the rulers don't
approve of you. 7Turn back and go in
peace; do nothing to displease the Philistine rulers."

8"But what have I done?" asked David.
"What have you found against your servant from the day I came to you until
now? Why can't I go and fight against the
enemies of my lord the king?"

9Achish answered, "I know that you
have been as pleasing in my eyes as an angel of God; nevertheless, the Philistine
commanders have said, 'He must not go
up with us into battle.' 10Now get up early, along with your master's servants who
have come with you, and leave in the
morning as soon as it is light."

11So David and his men got up early in
the morning to go back to the land of the
Philistines, and the Philistines went up to
Jezreel.

David Destroys the Amalekites

30 David and his men reached Ziklag on
the third day. Now the Amalekites
had raided the Negev and Ziklag. They
had attacked Ziklag and burned it, 2and
had taken captive the women and all who
were in it, both young and old. They
killed none of them, but carried them off
as they went on their way.

3When David and his men came to Ziklag, they found it destroyed by fire and
their wives and sons and daughters taken
captive. 4So David and his men wept
aloud until they had no strength left to
weep. 5David's two wives had been captured—Ahinoam of Jezreel and Abigail,
the widow of Nabal of Carmel. 6David
was greatly distressed because the men
were talking of stoning him; each one was
bitter in spirit because of his sons and
daughters. But David found strength in
the LORD his God.

7Then David said to Abiathar the priest,
the son of Ahimelech, "Bring me the
ephod." Abiathar brought it to him, 8and
David inquired of the LORD, "Shall I pursue this raiding party? Will I overtake
them?"

"Pursue them," he answered. "You will
certainly overtake them and succeed in
the rescue."

9David and the six hundred men with
him came to the Besor Ravine, where
some stayed behind, 10for two hundred
men were too exhausted to cross the
ravine. But David and four hundred men
continued the pursuit.

11They found an Egyptian in a field and
brought him to David. They gave him water to drink and food to eat— 12part of a
cake of pressed figs and two cakes of
raisins. He ate and was revived, for he had
not eaten any food or drunk any water for
three days and three nights.

13David asked him, "To whom do you
belong, and where do you come from?"

He said, "I am an Egyptian, the slave of
an Amalekite. My master abandoned me
when I became ill three days ago. 14We
raided the Negev of the Kerethites and the
territory belonging to Judah and the Negev of Caleb. And we burned Ziklag."

15 David asked him, "Can you lead me down to this raiding party?"

He answered, "Swear to me before God that you will not kill me or hand me over to my master, and I will take you down to them."

16 He led David down, and there they were, scattered over the countryside, eating, drinking and reveling because of the great amount of plunder they had taken from the land of the Philistines and from Judah. 17 David fought them from dusk until the evening of the next day, and none of them got away, except four hundred young men who rode off on camels and fled. 18 David recovered everything the Amalekites had taken, including his two wives. 19 Nothing was missing: young or old, boy or girl, plunder or anything else they had taken. David brought everything back. 20 He took all the flocks and herds, and his men drove them ahead of the other livestock, saying, "This is David's plunder."

21 Then David came to the two hundred men who had been too exhausted to follow him and who were left behind at the Besor Ravine. They came out to meet David and the people with him. As David and his men approached, he greeted them. 22 But all the evil men and troublemakers among David's followers said, "Because they did not go out with us, we will not share with them the plunder we recovered. However, each man may take his wife and children and go."

23 David replied, "No, my brothers, you must not do that with what the LORD has given us. He has protected us and handed over to us the forces that came against us. 24 Who will listen to what you say? The share of the man who stayed with the supplies is to be the same as that of him who went down to the battle. All will share alike." 25 David made this a statute and ordinance for Israel from that day to this.

26 When David arrived in Ziklag, he sent some of the plunder to the elders of Judah, who were his friends, saying, "Here is a present for you from the plunder of the LORD's enemies."

27 He sent it to those who were in Bethel, Ramoth Negev and Jattir; 28 to those in Aroer, Siphmoth, Eshtemoa 29 and Racal; to those in the towns of the Jerahmeelites and the Kenites; 30 to those in Hormah, Bor Ashan, Athach 31 and Hebron; and to those in all the other places where David and his men had roamed.

PRAYER: ADORATION

WE confess that in the beginning was the Word, and the Word was with You, O God, and the Word was You. The Word was in the beginning with You. (John 1:1–2) . . . You are but one God, the Father from whom all things came and for whom I live; and there is but one Lord Jesus Christ, through whom all things came and through whom I live. (1 Corinthians 8:6)

__PAUSE__ to express your thoughts of praise and worship.

NT Hebrews 1:1-14

The Son Superior to Angels

1 In the past God spoke to our forefathers through the prophets at many times and in various ways, 2 but in these last days he has spoken to us by his Son, whom he appointed heir of all things, and through whom he made the universe. 3 The Son is the radiance of God's glory and the exact representation of his being, sustaining all things by his powerful word. After he had provided purification for sins, he sat down at the right hand of the Majesty in heaven. 4 So he became as much superior to the angels as the name he has inherited is superior to theirs.

5 For to which of the angels did God ever say,

> "You are my Son;
> today I have become your Father[a]"[b]?

Or again,

> "I will be his Father,

[a] 5 Or *have begotten you* [b] 5 Psalm 2:7

and he will be my Son"[c]?

[6]And again, when God brings his firstborn into the world, he says,

"Let all God's angels worship him."[d]

[7]In speaking of the angels he says,

"He makes his angels winds,
his servants flames of fire."[e]

[8]But about the Son he says,

"Your throne, O God, will last for ever
and ever,
and righteousness will be the
scepter of your kingdom.
[9]You have loved righteousness and
hated wickedness;
therefore God, your God, has set
you above your companions
by anointing you with the oil of
joy."[f]

[10]He also says,

"In the beginning, O Lord, you laid
the foundations of the earth,
and the heavens are the work of
your hands.
[11]They will perish, but you remain;
they will all wear out like a
garment.
[12]You will roll them up like a robe;
like a garment they will be changed.
But you remain the same,
and your years will never end."[g]

[13]To which of the angels did God ever say,

"Sit at my right hand
until I make your enemies
a footstool for your feet"[h]?

[14]Are not all angels ministering spirits sent to serve those who will inherit salvation?

[c] 5 2 Samuel 7:14; 1 Chron. 17:13
[d] 6 Deut. 32:43 (see Dead Sea Scrolls and Septuagint) [e] 7 Psalm 104:4 [f] 9 Psalm 45:6,7
[g] 12 Psalm 102:25–27 [h] 13 Psalm 110:1

PRAYER: MY RELATIONSHIP TO OTHERS

I WILL trust in You enough to honor You, O Lord, as holy in the sight of others. (Numbers 20:12) . . . As iron sharpens iron, so one person sharpens another. (Proverbs 27:17)

__PAUSE__ to review your relationships with others and to commit them to the Lord.

OT 1 Samuel 31:1–13

Saul Takes His Life

31 Now the Philistines fought against Israel; the Israelites fled before them, and
many fell slain on Mount Gilboa. [2]The Philistines pressed hard after Saul and his sons,
and they killed his sons Jonathan, Abinadab
and Malki-Shua. [3]The fighting grew fierce
around Saul, and when the archers overtook
him, they wounded him critically.
[4]Saul said to his armor-bearer, "Draw
your sword and run me through, or these
uncircumcised fellows will come and run
me through and abuse me."
But his armor-bearer was terrified and
would not do it; so Saul took his own
sword and fell on it. [5]When the armor-bearer saw that Saul was dead, he too fell on his
sword and died with him. [6]So Saul and his
three sons and his armor-bearer and all his
men died together that same day.
[7]When the Israelites along the valley
and those across the Jordan saw that the
Israelite army had fled and that Saul and
his sons had died, they abandoned their
towns and fled. And the Philistines came
and occupied them.
[8]The next day, when the Philistines came
to strip the dead, they found Saul and his
three sons fallen on Mount Gilboa. [9]They
cut off his head and stripped off his armor,
and they sent messengers throughout the
land of the Philistines to proclaim the
news in the temple of their idols and
among their people. [10]They put his armor
in the temple of the Ashtoreths and fastened his body to the wall of Beth Shan.

11When the people of Jabesh Gilead
heard of what the Philistines had done to
Saul, 12all their valiant men journeyed
through the night to Beth Shan. They took
down the bodies of Saul and his sons
from the wall of Beth Shan and went to
Jabesh, where they burned them. 13Then
they took their bones and buried them
under a tamarisk tree at Jabesh, and they
fasted seven days.

PRAYER: CONFESSION

***I KNOW** that You are a gracious and compassionate God, slow to anger and abounding in loving-kindness; You are a God who relents from sending calamity. (Jonah 4:2)*

***ASK** the Spirit to search your heart and reveal any areas of unconfessed sin. Acknowledge these to the Lord and thank Him for His forgiveness.*

NT Hebrews 2:1-18

Warning to Pay Attention

2 We must pay more careful attention,
therefore, to what we have heard, so that
we do not drift away. 2For if the message
spoken by angels was binding, and every violation and disobedience received its just
punishment, 3how shall we escape if we ignore such a great salvation? This salvation,
which was first announced by the Lord, was
confirmed to us by those who heard him.
4God also testified to it by signs, wonders
and various miracles, and gifts of the Holy
Spirit distributed according to his will.

Jesus Made Like His Brothers

5It is not to angels that he has subjected the world to come, about which we are
speaking. 6But there is a place where
someone has testified:

"What is man that you are mindful of
him,
the son of man that you care for
him?
7You made him a little[a] lower than the
angels;
you crowned him with glory and
honor
8 and put everything under his feet."[b]

In putting everything under him, God left
nothing that is not subject to him. Yet at
present we do not see everything subject
to him. 9But we see Jesus, who was made
a little lower than the angels, now
crowned with glory and honor because he
suffered death, so that by the grace of God
he might taste death for everyone.
10In bringing many sons to glory, it was
fitting that God, for whom and through
whom everything exists, should make the
author of their salvation perfect through
suffering. 11Both the one who makes men
holy and those who are made holy are of
the same family. So Jesus is not ashamed
to call them brothers. 12He says,

"I will declare your name to my
brothers;
in the presence of the congregation
I will sing your praises."[c]

13And again,

"I will put my trust in him."[d]

And again he says,

"Here am I, and the children God has
given me."[e]

14Since the children have flesh and
blood, he too shared in their humanity so
that by his death he might destroy him
who holds the power of death—that is,
the devil— 15and free those who all their
lives were held in slavery by their fear of
death. 16For surely it is not angels he
helps, but Abraham's descendants. 17For
this reason he had to be made like his
brothers in every way, in order that he
might become a merciful and faithful
high priest in service to God, and that he
might make atonement for[f] the sins of the
people. 18Because he himself suffered
when he was tempted, he is able to help
those who are being tempted.

[a] 7 Or *him for a little while;* also in verse 9
[b] 8 Psalm 8:4-6 [c] 12 Psalm 22:22
[d] 13 Isaiah 8:17 [e] 13 Isaiah 8:18 [f] 17 Or *and that he might turn aside God's wrath, taking away*

PRAYER: THE ATTRIBUTES OF GOD

ALL Your works will praise you, O Lord, and Your saints will bless You. They will speak of the glory of Your kingdom and talk of Your power, so that all people may know of Your mighty acts and the glorious majesty of Your kingdom. Your kingdom is an everlasting kingdom, and Your dominion endures through all generations. (Psalm 145:10–13) . . . In Your majesty, O Lord, You dwell in the likeness of a throne of sapphire above the expanse that is over the cherubim. (Ezekiel 10:1)

PAUSE *to reflect on these affirmations about the person, powers and perfection of God.*

YEAR 1 DAY 262

OT 2 Samuel 1:1–27

David Hears of Saul's Death

1 After the death of Saul, David returned
from defeating the Amalekites and
stayed in Ziklag two days. 2On the third
day a man arrived from Saul's camp, with
his clothes torn and with dust on his
head. When he came to David, he fell to
the ground to pay him honor.
3"Where have you come from?" David
asked him.
He answered, "I have escaped from the
Israelite camp."
4"What happened?" David asked.
"Tell me."
He said, "The men fled from the battle.
Many of them fell and died. And Saul and
his son Jonathan are dead."
5Then David said to the young man
who brought him the report, "How do
you know that Saul and his son Jonathan
are dead?"
6"I happened to be on Mount Gilboa,"
the young man said, "and there was Saul,
leaning on his spear, with the chariots and
riders almost upon him. 7When he turned
around and saw me, he called out to me,
and I said, 'What can I do?'
8"He asked me, 'Who are you?'
" 'An Amalekite,' I answered.
9"Then he said to me, 'Stand over me
and kill me! I am in the throes of death,
but I'm still alive.'
10"So I stood over him and killed him, because I knew that after he had fallen he
could not survive. And I took the crown that
was on his head and the band on his arm
and have brought them here to my lord."
11Then David and all the men with him
took hold of their clothes and tore them.
12They mourned and wept and fasted till
evening for Saul and his son Jonathan,
and for the army of the LORD and the
house of Israel, because they had fallen by
the sword.
13David said to the young man who
brought him the report, "Where are you
from?"
"I am the son of an alien, an Amalekite," he answered.
14David asked him, "Why were you not
afraid to lift your hand to destroy the
LORD's anointed?"
15Then David called one of his men and
said, "Go, strike him down!" So he struck
him down, and he died. 16For David had
said to him, "Your blood be on your own
head. Your own mouth testified against
you when you said, 'I killed the LORD's
anointed.' "

David's Lament for Saul and Jonathan

17David took up this lament concerning
Saul and his son Jonathan, 18and ordered
that the men of Judah be taught this
lament of the bow (it is written in the
Book of Jashar):

19"Your glory, O Israel, lies slain on
your heights.
How the mighty have fallen!

20"Tell it not in Gath,
proclaim it not in the streets of
Ashkelon,
lest the daughters of the Philistines be
glad,

lest the daughters of the
uncircumcised rejoice.

21 "O mountains of Gilboa,
may you have neither dew nor rain,
nor fields that yield offerings ⌞of grain⌟.
For there the shield of the mighty was defiled,
the shield of Saul—no longer rubbed with oil.
22 From the blood of the slain,
from the flesh of the mighty,
the bow of Jonathan did not turn back,
the sword of Saul did not return unsatisfied.

23 "Saul and Jonathan—
in life they were loved and gracious,
and in death they were not parted.
They were swifter than eagles,
they were stronger than lions.

24 "O daughters of Israel,
weep for Saul,
who clothed you in scarlet and finery,
who adorned your garments with ornaments of gold.

25 "How the mighty have fallen in battle!
Jonathan lies slain on your heights.
26 I grieve for you, Jonathan my brother;
you were very dear to me.
Your love for me was wonderful,
more wonderful than that of women.

27 "How the mighty have fallen!
The weapons of war have perished!"

PRAYER: RENEWAL

MAY I not be like the rocky places on which seed was thrown—like those who hear the word and at once receive it with joy, but since they have no root, last only a short time; when affliction or persecution comes because of the word, they quickly fall away. And may I not be like soil among the thorns—like those who hear the word, but the worries of this world, the deceitfulness of riches and pleasures, and the desires for other things come in and choke the word, making it immature and unfruitful. Instead, may I be like the good soil on which seed was sown, like those who with noble and good hearts hear the word, understand and accept it, and with perseverance bear fruit, yielding thirty, sixty or a hundred times what was sown. (Matthew 13:20–23; Mark 4:16–20; Luke 8:13–15)

***PAUSE** to add your own prayers for personal renewal.*

NT Hebrews 3:1-19

Jesus Greater Than Moses

3 Therefore, holy brothers, who share in
the heavenly calling, fix your thoughts
on Jesus, the apostle and high priest
whom we confess. 2 He was faithful to the
one who appointed him, just as Moses
was faithful in all God's house. 3 Jesus has
been found worthy of greater honor than
Moses, just as the builder of a house has
greater honor than the house itself. 4 For
every house is built by someone, but God
is the builder of everything. 5 Moses was
faithful as a servant in all God's house,
testifying to what would be said in the future. 6 But Christ is faithful as a son over
God's house. And we are his house, if we hold on to our courage and the hope of which we boast.

Warning Against Unbelief

7 So, as the Holy Spirit says:

"Today, if you hear his voice,
8 do not harden your hearts
as you did in the rebellion,
during the time of testing in the desert,
9 where your fathers tested and tried me
and for forty years saw what I did.

[10]That is why I was angry with that generation,
and I said, 'Their hearts are always going astray,
and they have not known my ways.'
[11]So I declared on oath in my anger,
'They shall never enter my rest.' "[a]

[12]See to it, brothers, that none of you
has a sinful, unbelieving heart that turns
away from the living God. [13]But encourage one another daily, as long as it is
called Today, so that none of you may be
hardened by sin's deceitfulness. [14]We have
come to share in Christ if we hold firmly
till the end the confidence we had at first.
[15]As has just been said:

"Today, if you hear his voice,
do not harden your hearts
as you did in the rebellion."[b]

[16]Who were they who heard and rebelled? Were they not all those Moses led
out of Egypt? [17]And with whom was he
angry for forty years? Was it not with
those who sinned, whose bodies fell in
the desert? [18]And to whom did God swear
that they would never enter his rest if not
to those who disobeyed[c]? [19]So we see that
they were not able to enter, because of
their unbelief.

[a] *11* Psalm 95:7–11 [b] *15* Psalm 95:7,8 [c] *18* Or *disbelieved*

PRAYER: THE WORKS OF GOD

BY wisdom, O Lord, You founded the earth; by understanding You established the heavens; by Your knowledge the deeps were divided, and the clouds drop down the dew. (Proverbs 3:19–20) . . . You made the earth and created people upon it. Your own hands stretched out the heavens, and You ordered their starry hosts. (Isaiah 45:12)

***TAKE** a moment to consider the greatness of God's wonderful works.*

YEAR 1 DAY 263

OT 2 Samuel 2:1–32

David Anointed King Over Judah

2 In the course of time, David inquired
of the LORD. "Shall I go up to one of the
towns of Judah?" he asked.

The LORD said, "Go up."

David asked, "Where shall I go?"

"To Hebron," the LORD answered.

[2]So David went up there with his two
wives, Ahinoam of Jezreel and Abigail, the
widow of Nabal of Carmel. [3]David also
took the men who were with him, each
with his family, and they settled in Hebron and its towns. [4]Then the men of Judah came to Hebron and there they
anointed David king over the house of
Judah.

When David was told that it was the
men of Jabesh Gilead who had buried
Saul, [5]he sent messengers to the men of
Jabesh Gilead to say to them, "The LORD
bless you for showing this kindness to
Saul your master by burying him. [6]May
the LORD now show you kindness and
faithfulness, and I too will show you the
same favor because you have done this.
[7]Now then, be strong and brave, for Saul
your master is dead, and the house of Judah has anointed me king over them."

War Between the Houses of David and Saul

[8]Meanwhile, Abner son of Ner, the
commander of Saul's army, had taken Ish-
Bosheth son of Saul and brought him
over to Mahanaim. [9]He made him king
over Gilead, Ashuri[a] and Jezreel, and also
over Ephraim, Benjamin and all Israel.

[10]Ish-Bosheth son of Saul was forty
years old when he became king over Israel, and he reigned two years. The house of
Judah, however, followed David. [11]The

[a] *9* Or *Asher*

length of time David was king in Hebron
over the house of Judah was seven years
and six months.
12 Abner son of Ner, together with the
men of Ish-Bosheth son of Saul, left Mahanaim and went to Gibeon. 13 Joab son
of Zeruiah and David's men went out and
met them at the pool of Gibeon. One
group sat down on one side of the pool
and one group on the other side.
14 Then Abner said to Joab, "Let's have
some of the young men get up and fight
hand to hand in front of us."
"All right, let them do it," Joab said.
15 So they stood up and were counted
off—twelve men for Benjamin and Ish-
Bosheth son of Saul, and twelve for David. 16 Then each man grabbed his opponent by the head and thrust his dagger
into his opponent's side, and they fell
down together. So that place in Gibeon
was called Helkath Hazzurim.[b]
17 The battle that day was very fierce, and
Abner and the men of Israel were defeated by David's men.
18 The three sons of Zeruiah were there:
Joab, Abishai and Asahel. Now Asahel was
as fleet-footed as a wild gazelle. 19 He
chased Abner, turning neither to the right
nor to the left as he pursued him. 20 Abner
looked behind him and asked, "Is that
you, Asahel?"
"It is," he answered.
21 Then Abner said to him, "Turn aside
to the right or to the left; take on one of
the young men and strip him of his
weapons." But Asahel would not stop
chasing him.
22 Again Abner warned Asahel, "Stop
chasing me! Why should I strike you
down? How could I look your brother
Joab in the face?"
23 But Asahel refused to give up the pursuit; so Abner thrust the butt of his spear
into Asahel's stomach, and the spear came
out through his back. He fell there and
died on the spot. And every man stopped
when he came to the place where Asahel
had fallen and died.
24 But Joab and Abishai pursued Abner,
and as the sun was setting, they came to
the hill of Ammah, near Giah on the way
to the wasteland of Gibeon. 25 Then the
men of Benjamin rallied behind Abner.
They formed themselves into a group and
took their stand on top of a hill.
26 Abner called out to Joab, "Must the
sword devour forever? Don't you realize
that this will end in bitterness? How long
before you order your men to stop pursuing their brothers?"
27 Joab answered, "As surely as God
lives, if you had not spoken, the men
would have continued the pursuit of their
brothers until morning.[c]"
28 So Joab blew the trumpet, and all the
men came to a halt; they no longer pursued Israel, nor did they fight anymore.
29 All that night Abner and his men
marched through the Arabah. They
crossed the Jordan, continued through the
whole Bithron[d] and came to Mahanaim.
30 Then Joab returned from pursuing
Abner and assembled all his men. Besides
Asahel, nineteen of David's men were
found missing. 31 But David's men had
killed three hundred and sixty Benjamites
who were with Abner. 32 They took Asahel
and buried him in his father's tomb at
Bethlehem. Then Joab and his men
marched all night and arrived at Hebron
by daybreak.

[b] 16 *Helkath Hazzurim* means *field of daggers* or *field of hostilities.* [c] 27 Or *spoken this morning, the men would not have taken up the pursuit of their brothers;* or *spoken, the men would have given up the pursuit of their brothers by morning* [d] 29 Or *morning;* or *ravine;* the meaning of the Hebrew for this word is uncertain.

PRAYER: PETITION

If we die, will we live again? All the days of my hard service I will wait for my renewal to come. (Job 14:14)

***PAUSE** here to petition God for spiritual insight so that you might have understanding of His Word. Ask for insight into your identity in Jesus Christ: that you might know who you are, what direction your life should take and what His purpose for your life is. Offer prayers regarding your activities for this day and any special concerns you may have.*

NT Hebrews 4:1-13

A Sabbath-Rest for the People of God

4 Therefore, since the promise of entering his rest still stands, let us be careful
that none of you be found to have fallen
short of it. [2]For we also have had the
gospel preached to us, just as they did; but
the message they heard was of no value to
them, because those who heard did not
combine it with faith.[a] [3]Now we who
have believed enter that rest, just as God
has said,

> "So I declared on oath in my anger,
> 'They shall never enter my rest.' "[b]

And yet his work has been finished since
the creation of the world. [4]For somewhere
he has spoken about the seventh day in
these words: "And on the seventh day God
rested from all his work."[c] [5]And again in
the passage above he says, "They shall
never enter my rest."

[6]It still remains that some will enter
that rest, and those who formerly had the
gospel preached to them did not go in,
because of their disobedience. [7]Therefore
God again set a certain day, calling it Today, when a long time later he spoke
through David, as was said before:

> "Today, if you hear his voice,
> do not harden your hearts."[d]

[8]For if Joshua had given them rest, God
would not have spoken later about another day. [9]There remains, then, a Sabbath-rest for the people of God; [10]for anyone who enters God's rest also rests from
his own work, just as God did from his.
[11]Let us, therefore, make every effort to enter that rest, so that no one will fall by following their example of disobedience.

[12]For the word of God is living and active. Sharper than any double-edged
sword, it penetrates even to dividing soul
and spirit, joints and marrow; it judges
the thoughts and attitudes of the heart.
[13]Nothing in all creation is hidden from
God's sight. Everything is uncovered and
laid bare before the eyes of him to whom
we must give account.

[a] 2 Many manuscripts *because they did not share in the faith of those who obeyed* [b] 3 Psalm 95:11; also in verse 5 [c] 4 Gen. 2:2 [d] 7 Psalm 95:7,8

PRAYER: MY RELATIONSHIP TO GOD

WE should be filled with the Spirit, speaking to one another with psalms, hymns and spiritual songs; singing and making music in our hearts to You, always giving thanks to You, Father, for everything, in the name of our Lord Jesus Christ. (Ephesians 5:18–20) . . . O God, I will rejoice always, pray without ceasing, and give thanks in all circumstances, for this is Your will for us in Christ Jesus. (1 Thessalonians 5:16–18)

PAUSE *to thank God for the relationship that you enjoy with Him in Jesus Christ.*

YEAR 1 DAY 264

OT 2 Samuel 3:1-39

3 The war between the house of Saul and
the house of David lasted a long time.
David grew stronger and stronger, while the
house of Saul grew weaker and weaker.

[2]Sons were born to David in Hebron:
His firstborn was Amnon the son
of Ahinoam of Jezreel;
[3]his second, Kileab the son of Abigail the widow of Nabal of Carmel;
the third, Absalom the son of Maacah daughter of Talmai king of
Geshur;
[4]the fourth, Adonijah the son of
Haggith;
the fifth, Shephatiah the son of
Abital;
[5]and the sixth, Ithream the son of
David's wife Eglah.

These were born to David in Hebron.

Abner Goes Over to David

6 During the war between the house of
Saul and the house of David, Abner had
been strengthening his own position in
the house of Saul. 7 Now Saul had had a
concubine named Rizpah daughter of
Aiah. And Ish-Bosheth said to Abner,
"Why did you sleep with my father's concubine?"
8 Abner was very angry because of what
Ish-Bosheth said and he answered, "Am I
a dog's head—on Judah's side? This very
day I am loyal to the house of your father
Saul and to his family and friends. I
haven't handed you over to David. Yet
now you accuse me of an offense involving this woman! 9 May God deal with Abner, be it ever so severely, if I do not do
for David what the LORD promised him
on oath 10 and transfer the kingdom from
the house of Saul and establish David's
throne over Israel and Judah from Dan to
Beersheba." 11 Ish-Bosheth did not dare to
say another word to Abner, because he
was afraid of him.
12 Then Abner sent messengers on his
behalf to say to David, "Whose land is it?
Make an agreement with me, and I will
help you bring all Israel over to you."
13 "Good," said David. "I will make an
agreement with you. But I demand one
thing of you: Do not come into my presence unless you bring Michal daughter of
Saul when you come to see me." 14 Then
David sent messengers to Ish-Bosheth son
of Saul, demanding, "Give me my wife
Michal, whom I betrothed to myself for
the price of a hundred Philistine foreskins."
15 So Ish-Bosheth gave orders and had
her taken away from her husband Paltiel
son of Laish. 16 Her husband, however,
went with her, weeping behind her all the
way to Bahurim. Then Abner said to him,
"Go back home!" So he went back.
17 Abner conferred with the elders of Israel and said, "For some time you have
wanted to make David your king. 18 Now
do it! For the LORD promised David, 'By
my servant David I will rescue my people
Israel from the hand of the Philistines and
from the hand of all their enemies.' "
19 Abner also spoke to the Benjamites in
person. Then he went to Hebron to tell
David everything that Israel and the
whole house of Benjamin wanted to do.
20 When Abner, who had twenty men with
him, came to David at Hebron, David prepared a feast for him and his men. 21 Then
Abner said to David, "Let me go at once
and assemble all Israel for my lord the
king, so that they may make a compact
with you, and that you may rule over all
that your heart desires." So David sent Abner away, and he went in peace.

Joab Murders Abner

22 Just then David's men and Joab returned from a raid and brought with them
a great deal of plunder. But Abner was no
longer with David in Hebron, because
David had sent him away, and he had
gone in peace. 23 When Joab and all the
soldiers with him arrived, he was told that
Abner son of Ner had come to the king
and that the king had sent him away and
that he had gone in peace.
24 So Joab went to the king and said,
"What have you done? Look, Abner came
to you. Why did you let him go? Now he
is gone! 25 You know Abner son of Ner; he
came to deceive you and observe your
movements and find out everything you
are doing."
26 Joab then left David and sent messengers after Abner, and they brought him
back from the well of Sirah. But David did
not know it. 27 Now when Abner returned
to Hebron, Joab took him aside into the
gateway, as though to speak with him privately. And there, to avenge the blood of
his brother Asahel, Joab stabbed him in
the stomach, and he died.
28 Later, when David heard about this,
he said, "I and my kingdom are forever innocent before the LORD concerning the
blood of Abner son of Ner. 29 May his
blood fall upon the head of Joab and
upon all his father's house! May Joab's
house never be without someone who has
a running sore or leprosy[a] or who leans
on a crutch or who falls by the sword or
who lacks food."
30 (Joab and his brother Abishai murdered Abner because he had killed their
brother Asahel in the battle at Gibeon.)
31 Then David said to Joab and all the

[a] *29* The Hebrew word was used for various diseases affecting the skin—not necessarily leprosy.

people with him, "Tear your clothes and put on sackcloth and walk in mourning in front of Abner." King David himself walked behind the bier. 32They buried Abner in Hebron, and the king wept aloud at Abner's tomb. All the people wept also.

33The king sang this lament for Abner:

> "Should Abner have died as the
> lawless die?
> 34 Your hands were not bound,
> your feet were not fettered.
> You fell as one falls before wicked
> men."

And all the people wept over him again.

35Then they all came and urged David to eat something while it was still day; but David took an oath, saying, "May God deal with me, be it ever so severely, if I taste bread or anything else before the sun sets!"

36All the people took note and were pleased; indeed, everything the king did pleased them. 37So on that day all the people and all Israel knew that the king had no part in the murder of Abner son of Ner.

38Then the king said to his men, "Do you not realize that a prince and a great man has fallen in Israel this day? 39And today, though I am the anointed king, I am weak, and these sons of Zeruiah are too strong for me. May the LORD repay the evildoer according to his evil deeds!"

PRAYER: INTERCESSION

ALL of us have become like those who are unclean, and all our righteous acts are like filthy rags; we all shrivel up like leaves, and our iniquities, like the wind, sweep us away. But now, O Lord, You are our Father. We are the clay, You are the potter; we are all the work of Your hand. (Isaiah 64:6, 8)

***TAKE** a few moments to intercede on behalf of other believers, such as your personal friends, those in ministry and those who are oppressed and in need.*

NT Hebrews 4:14–5:10

Jesus the Great High Priest

14Therefore, since we have a great high priest who has gone through the heavens,[a] Jesus the Son of God, let us hold firmly to the faith we profess. 15For we do not have a high priest who is unable to sympathize with our weaknesses, but we have one who has been tempted in every way, just as we are—yet was without sin. 16Let us then approach the throne of grace with confidence, so that we may receive mercy and find grace to help us in our time of need.

5 Every high priest is selected from among men and is appointed to represent them in matters related to God, to offer gifts and sacrifices for sins. 2He is able to deal gently with those who are ignorant and are going astray, since he himself is subject to weakness. 3This is why he has to offer sacrifices for his own sins, as well as for the sins of the people.

4No one takes this honor upon himself; he must be called by God, just as Aaron was. 5So Christ also did not take upon himself the glory of becoming a high priest. But God said to him,

> "You are my Son;
> today I have become your Father."[b][c]

6And he says in another place,

> "You are a priest forever,
> in the order of Melchizedek."[d]

7During the days of Jesus' life on earth, he offered up prayers and petitions with loud cries and tears to the one who could save him from death, and he was heard because of his reverent submission. 8Although he was a son, he learned obedience from what he suffered 9and, once made perfect, he became the source of eternal salvation for all who obey him 10and was designated by God to be high priest in the order of Melchizedek.

[a] 14 Or *gone into heaven* [b] 5 Or *have begotten you* [c] 5 Psalm 2:7 [d] 6 Psalm 110:4

PRAYER: THE CHARACTER I WANT TO CULTIVATE

BLESSED are those who find wisdom, and those who gain understanding, for wisdom's profit is greater than that of silver, and her gain is more than fine gold. She is more precious than jewels, and nothing I desire can compare with her. Long life is in her right hand; in her left hand are riches and honor. Her ways are pleasant ways, and all her paths are peace. She is a tree of life to those who embrace her, and happy are those who hold her fast. (Proverbs 3:13–18) . . . Those who get wisdom love their own soul; those who keep understanding will find good. (Proverbs 19:8)

***TAKE** a moment to ask the Lord for the grace to grow in godly character.*

YEAR 1 DAY 265

OT 2 Samuel 4:1–5:25

Ish-Bosheth Murdered

4 When Ish-Bosheth son of Saul heard
that Abner had died in Hebron, he lost
courage, and all Israel became alarmed.
2Now Saul's son had two men who were
leaders of raiding bands. One was named
Baanah and the other Recab; they were
sons of Rimmon the Beerothite from the
tribe of Benjamin—Beeroth is considered
part of Benjamin, 3because the people of
Beeroth fled to Gittaim and have lived
there as aliens to this day.
4(Jonathan son of Saul had a son who
was lame in both feet. He was five years
old when the news about Saul and Jonathan came from Jezreel. His nurse picked
him up and fled, but as she hurried to
leave, he fell and became crippled. His
name was Mephibosheth.)
5Now Recab and Baanah, the sons of
Rimmon the Beerothite, set out for the
house of Ish-Bosheth, and they arrived
there in the heat of the day while he was
taking his noonday rest. 6They went into
the inner part of the house as if to get
some wheat, and they stabbed him in the
stomach. Then Recab and his brother Baanah slipped away.
7They had gone into the house while he
was lying on the bed in his bedroom. After they stabbed and killed him, they cut
off his head. Taking it with them, they
traveled all night by way of the Arabah.
8They brought the head of Ish-Bosheth to
David at Hebron and said to the king,
"Here is the head of Ish-Bosheth son of
Saul, your enemy, who tried to take your
life. This day the LORD has avenged my
lord the king against Saul and his offspring."
9David answered Recab and his brother Baanah, the sons of Rimmon the
Beerothite, "As surely as the LORD lives,
who has delivered me out of all trouble,
10when a man told me, 'Saul is dead,' and
thought he was bringing good news, I
seized him and put him to death in Ziklag. That was the reward I gave him for his
news! 11How much more—when wicked
men have killed an innocent man in his
own house and on his own bed—should
I not now demand his blood from your
hand and rid the earth of you!"
12So David gave an order to his men,
and they killed them. They cut off their
hands and feet and hung the bodies by
the pool in Hebron. But they took the
head of Ish-Bosheth and buried it in Abner's tomb at Hebron.

David Becomes King Over Israel

5 All the tribes of Israel came to David at
Hebron and said, "We are your own
flesh and blood. 2In the past, while Saul
was king over us, you were the one who
led Israel on their military campaigns.
And the LORD said to you, 'You will shepherd my people Israel, and you will become their ruler.' "
3When all the elders of Israel had come
to King David at Hebron, the king made
a compact with them at Hebron before

the LORD, and they anointed David king over Israel.

4David was thirty years old when he became king, and he reigned forty years. 5In Hebron he reigned over Judah seven years and six months, and in Jerusalem he reigned over all Israel and Judah thirty-three years.

David Conquers Jerusalem

6The king and his men marched to Jerusalem to attack the Jebusites, who lived there. The Jebusites said to David, "You will not get in here; even the blind and the lame can ward you off." They thought, "David cannot get in here." 7Nevertheless, David captured the fortress of Zion, the City of David.

8On that day, David said, "Anyone who conquers the Jebusites will have to use the water shaft[a] to reach those 'lame and blind' who are David's enemies.[b]" That is why they say, "The 'blind and lame' will not enter the palace."

9David then took up residence in the fortress and called it the City of David. He built up the area around it, from the supporting terraces[c] inward. 10And he became more and more powerful, because the LORD God Almighty was with him.

11Now Hiram king of Tyre sent messengers to David, along with cedar logs and carpenters and stonemasons, and they built a palace for David. 12And David knew that the LORD had established him as king over Israel and had exalted his kingdom for the sake of his people Israel.

13After he left Hebron, David took more concubines and wives in Jerusalem, and more sons and daughters were born to him. 14These are the names of the children born to him there: Shammua, Shobab, Nathan, Solomon, 15Ibhar, Elishua, Nepheg, Japhia, 16Elishama, Eliada and Eliphelet.

David Defeats the Philistines

17When the Philistines heard that David had been anointed king over Israel, they went up in full force to search for him, but David heard about it and went down to the stronghold. 18Now the Philistines had come and spread out in the Valley of Rephaim; 19so David inquired of the LORD, "Shall I go and attack the Philistines? Will you hand them over to me?"

The LORD answered him, "Go, for I will surely hand the Philistines over to you."

20So David went to Baal Perazim, and there he defeated them. He said, "As waters break out, the LORD has broken out against my enemies before me." So that place was called Baal Perazim.[d] 21The Philistines abandoned their idols there, and David and his men carried them off.

22Once more the Philistines came up and spread out in the Valley of Rephaim; 23so David inquired of the LORD, and he answered, "Do not go straight up, but circle around behind them and attack them in front of the balsam trees. 24As soon as you hear the sound of marching in the tops of the balsam trees, move quickly, because that will mean the LORD has gone out in front of you to strike the Philistine army." 25So David did as the LORD commanded him, and he struck down the Philistines all the way from Gibeon[e] to Gezer.

[a] 8 Or *use scaling hooks* [b] 8 Or *are hated by David* [c] 9 Or *the Millo* [d] 20 *Baal Perazim* means *the lord who breaks out.* [e] 25 Septuagint (see also 1 Chron. 14:16); Hebrew *Geba*

PRAYER: AFFIRMATION

LIKE Abram, when I believe in Your promises, O God, You will credit it to me as righteousness. (Genesis 15:5–6) . . . Whatever things were written in the past were written for our learning, so that through endurance and the encouragement of the Scriptures we might have hope. (Romans 15:4) . . . Like Abraham, I am waiting for a city that You have planned and built, O God. (Hebrews 11:10)

PAUSE *to reflect on these Biblical affirmations.*

NT Hebrews 5:11–6:12

Warning Against Falling Away

11We have much to say about this, but
it is hard to explain because you are slow
to learn. 12In fact, though by this time you
ought to be teachers, you need someone
to teach you the elementary truths of
God's word all over again. You need milk,
not solid food! 13Anyone who lives on
milk, being still an infant, is not acquainted with the teaching about righteousness. 14But solid food is for the mature, who by constant use have trained
themselves to distinguish good from evil.
6 Therefore let us leave the elementary
teachings about Christ and go on to maturity, not laying again the foundation of
repentance from acts that lead to death,[a]
and of faith in God, 2instruction about
baptisms, the laying on of hands, the resurrection of the dead, and eternal judgment. 3And God permitting, we will do so.
4It is impossible for those who have once
been enlightened, who have tasted the
heavenly gift, who have shared in the Holy
Spirit, 5who have tasted the goodness of the
word of God and the powers of the coming
age, 6if they fall away, to be brought back to
repentance, because[b] to their loss they are
crucifying the Son of God all over again and
subjecting him to public disgrace.
7Land that drinks in the rain often
falling on it and that produces a crop useful to those for whom it is farmed receives
the blessing of God. 8But land that produces thorns and thistles is worthless and
is in danger of being cursed. In the end it
will be burned.
9Even though we speak like this, dear
friends, we are confident of better things in
your case—things that accompany salvation. 10God is not unjust; he will not forget
your work and the love you have shown
him as you have helped his people and
continue to help them. 11We want each of
you to show this same diligence to the very
end, in order to make your hope sure. 12We
do not want you to become lazy, but to imitate those who through faith and patience
inherit what has been promised.

[a] 1 Or *from useless rituals* [b] 6 Or *repentance while*

PRAYER: MY RELATIONSHIP TO OTHERS

LORD Jesus Christ, as Your body may we all be built up until we reach unity in the faith and in the knowledge of You, the Son of God, so that we will become mature and attain to the whole measure of Your fullness. Then we will no longer be infants, being blown and carried by every wind of doctrine and by the cunning and craftiness of people who scheme deceitfully. Instead we will speak the truth in love; we will grow up in every way in You, our Head. (Ephesians 4:13–15)

***PAUSE** to review your relationships with others and to commit them to the Lord.*

YEAR 1 DAY 266

OT Psalm 51

Psalm 51

For the director of music. A psalm of David. When the prophet Nathan came to him after David had committed adultery with Bathsheba.

1Have mercy on me, O God,
according to your unfailing love;
according to your great compassion
blot out my transgressions.
2Wash away all my iniquity
and cleanse me from my sin.

3For I know my transgressions,
and my sin is always before me.
4Against you, you only, have I sinned
and done what is evil in your sight,
so that you are proved right when you speak
and justified when you judge.
5Surely I was sinful at birth,

sinful from the time my mother
conceived me.
6 Surely you desire truth in the inner
parts[a];
you teach[b] me wisdom in the
inmost place.

7 Cleanse me with hyssop, and I will be
clean;
wash me, and I will be whiter than
snow.
8 Let me hear joy and gladness;
let the bones you have crushed
rejoice.
9 Hide your face from my sins
and blot out all my iniquity.

10 Create in me a pure heart, O God,
and renew a steadfast spirit within
me.
11 Do not cast me from your presence
or take your Holy Spirit from me.
12 Restore to me the joy of your salvation
and grant me a willing spirit, to
sustain me.

13 Then I will teach transgressors your
ways,
and sinners will turn back to you.
14 Save me from bloodguilt, O God,
the God who saves me,
and my tongue will sing of your
righteousness.
15 O Lord, open my lips,
and my mouth will declare your
praise.
16 You do not delight in sacrifice, or I
would bring it;
you do not take pleasure in burnt
offerings.
17 The sacrifices of God are[c] a broken
spirit;
a broken and contrite heart,
O God, you will not despise.

18 In your good pleasure make Zion
prosper;
build up the walls of Jerusalem.
19 Then there will be righteous sacrifices,
whole burnt offerings to delight
you;
then bulls will be offered on your
altar.

[a] 6 The meaning of the Hebrew for this phrase is uncertain. [b] 6 Or *you desired . . .; / you taught* [c] 17 Or *My sacrifice, O God, is*

PRAYER: THANKSGIVING

I WILL praise You, O Lord my God, with all my heart, and I will glorify Your name forever. For great is Your love toward me, and You have delivered my soul from the depths of the grave. (Psalm 86:12–13) . . . All who are righteous rejoice in You, O Lord, and give thanks at the remembrance of Your holy name. (Psalm 97:12)

***PAUSE** to offer your own expressions of thanksgiving.*

NT Hebrews 6:13–7:10

The Certainty of God's Promise

13 When God made his promise to Abraham, since there was no one greater for him to swear by, he swore by himself,
14 saying, "I will surely bless you and give you many descendants."[a]
15 And so after waiting patiently, Abraham received what was promised.
16 Men swear by someone greater than themselves, and the oath confirms what is said and puts an end to all argument.
17 Because God wanted to make the unchanging nature of his purpose very clear to the heirs of what was promised, he confirmed it with an oath.
18 God did this so that, by two unchangeable things in which it is impossible for God to lie, we who have fled to take hold of the hope offered to us may be greatly encouraged.
19 We have this hope as an anchor for the soul, firm and secure. It enters the inner sanctuary behind the curtain,
20 where Jesus, who went before us, has entered on our behalf. He has become a high priest forever, in the order of Melchizedek.

[a] 14 Gen. 22:17

Melchizedek the Priest

7 This Melchizedek was king of Salem and priest of God Most High. He met Abraham returning from the defeat of the kings and blessed him, 2and Abraham gave him a tenth of everything. First, his name means "king of righteousness"; then also, "king of Salem" means "king of peace." 3Without father or mother, without genealogy, without beginning of days or end of life, like the Son of God he remains a priest forever.

4Just think how great he was: Even the patriarch Abraham gave him a tenth of the plunder! 5Now the law requires the descendants of Levi who become priests to collect a tenth from the people—that is, their brothers—even though their brothers are descended from Abraham. 6This man, however, did not trace his descent from Levi, yet he collected a tenth from Abraham and blessed him who had the promises. 7And without doubt the lesser person is blessed by the greater. 8In the one case, the tenth is collected by men who die; but in the other case, by him who is declared to be living. 9One might even say that Levi, who collects the tenth, paid the tenth through Abraham, 10because when Melchizedek met Abraham, Levi was still in the body of his ancestor.

PRAYER: THE ATTRIBUTES OF GOD

YOU, O Lord, are a compassionate and gracious God, slow to anger and abounding in loving-kindness and truth. (Psalm 86:15) . . . Great are Your works, O Lord; they are pondered by all who delight in them. Splendid and majestic is Your work, and Your righteousness endures forever. You have caused Your wonderful acts to be remembered; You, Lord, are gracious and compassionate. (Psalm 111:2–4)

PAUSE *to reflect on these affirmations about the person, powers and perfection of God.*

OT 2 Samuel 6:1–7:29 — YEAR 1 DAY 267

The Ark Brought to Jerusalem

6 David again brought together out of Israel chosen men, thirty thousand in all. 2He and all his men set out from Baalah of Judah[a] to bring up from there the ark of God, which is called by the Name,[b] the name of the LORD Almighty, who is enthroned between the cherubim that are on the ark. 3They set the ark of God on a new cart and brought it from the house of Abinadab, which was on the hill. Uzzah and Ahio, sons of Abinadab, were guiding the new cart 4with the ark of God on it,[c] and Ahio was walking in front of it. 5David and the whole house of Israel were celebrating with all their might before the LORD, with songs[d] and with harps, lyres, tambourines, sistrums and cymbals.

6When they came to the threshing floor of Nacon, Uzzah reached out and took hold of the ark of God, because the oxen stumbled. 7The LORD's anger burned against Uzzah because of his irreverent act; therefore God struck him down and he died there beside the ark of God.

8Then David was angry because the LORD's wrath had broken out against Uzzah, and to this day that place is called Perez Uzzah.[e]

9David was afraid of the LORD that day and said, "How can the ark of the LORD ever come to me?" 10He was not willing to take the ark of the LORD to be with him in the City of David. Instead, he took it aside to the house of Obed-Edom the Gittite. 11The ark of the LORD remained in the

[a] 2 That is, Kiriath Jearim; Hebrew *Baale Judah,* a variant of *Baalah of Judah* [b] 2 Hebrew; Septuagint and Vulgate do not have *the Name.* [c] 3,4 Dead Sea Scrolls and some Septuagint manuscripts; Masoretic Text *cart 4and they brought it with the ark of God from the house of Abinadab, which was on the hill* [d] 5 See Dead Sea Scrolls, Septuagint and 1 Chronicles 13:8; Masoretic Text *celebrating before the LORD with all kinds of instruments made of pine.* [e] 8 *Perez Uzzah* means *outbreak against Uzzah.*

house of Obed-Edom the Gittite for three
months, and the LORD blessed him and
his entire household.
12Now King David was told, "The LORD
has blessed the household of Obed-Edom
and everything he has, because of the ark
of God." So David went down and
brought up the ark of God from the house
of Obed-Edom to the City of David with
rejoicing. 13When those who were carrying the ark of the LORD had taken six steps,
he sacrificed a bull and a fattened calf.
14David, wearing a linen ephod, danced
before the LORD with all his might, 15while
he and the entire house of Israel brought
up the ark of the LORD with shouts and
the sound of trumpets.
16As the ark of the LORD was entering the
City of David, Michal daughter of Saul
watched from a window. And when she
saw King David leaping and dancing before
the LORD, she despised him in her heart.
17They brought the ark of the LORD and
set it in its place inside the tent that David
had pitched for it, and David sacrificed
burnt offerings and fellowship offerings[f]
before the LORD. 18After he had finished
sacrificing the burnt offerings and fellowship offerings, he blessed the people in the
name of the LORD Almighty. 19Then he
gave a loaf of bread, a cake of dates and a
cake of raisins to each person in the whole
crowd of Israelites, both men and women.
And all the people went to their homes.
20When David returned home to bless
his household, Michal daughter of Saul
came out to meet him and said, "How the
king of Israel has distinguished himself
today, disrobing in the sight of the slave
girls of his servants as any vulgar fellow
would!"
21David said to Michal, "It was before
the LORD, who chose me rather than your
father or anyone from his house when he
appointed me ruler over the LORD's people Israel—I will celebrate before the
LORD. 22I will become even more undig-
nified than this, and I will be humiliated
in my own eyes. But by these slave girls
you spoke of, I will be held in honor."
23And Michal daughter of Saul had no
children to the day of her death.

God's Promise to David

7 After the king was settled in his palace
and the LORD had given him rest from
all his enemies around him, 2he said to
Nathan the prophet, "Here I am, living in
a palace of cedar, while the ark of God remains in a tent."
3Nathan replied to the king, "Whatever
you have in mind, go ahead and do it, for
the LORD is with you."
4That night the word of the LORD came
to Nathan, saying:

5"Go and tell my servant David,
'This is what the LORD says: Are you
the one to build me a house to dwell
in? 6I have not dwelt in a house from
the day I brought the Israelites up out
of Egypt to this day. I have been moving from place to place with a tent as
my dwelling. 7Wherever I have
moved with all the Israelites, did I
ever say to any of their rulers whom
I commanded to shepherd my people Israel, "Why have you not built
me a house of cedar?" '
8"Now then, tell my servant David,
'This is what the LORD Almighty says:
I took you from the pasture and from
following the flock to be ruler over
my people Israel. 9I have been with
you wherever you have gone, and I
have cut off all your enemies from
before you. Now I will make your
name great, like the names of the
greatest men of the earth. 10And I will
provide a place for my people Israel
and will plant them so that they can
have a home of their own and no
longer be disturbed. Wicked people
will not oppress them anymore, as
they did at the beginning 11and have
done ever since the time I appointed
leaders[g] over my people Israel. I will
also give you rest from all your enemies.
" 'The LORD declares to you that the
LORD himself will establish a house
for you: 12When your days are over
and you rest with your fathers, I will
raise up your offspring to succeed
you, who will come from your own
body, and I will establish his kingdom. 13He is the one who will build
a house for my Name, and I will establish the throne of his kingdom
forever. 14I will be his father, and he
will be my son. When he does wrong,

[f] 17 Traditionally *peace offerings;* also in verse 18
[g] 11 Traditionally *judges*

I will punish him with the rod of
men, with floggings inflicted by men.
15 But my love will never be taken
away from him, as I took it away
from Saul, whom I removed from before you.
16 Your house and your kingdom will endure forever before me[h];
your throne will be established forever.' "

17 Nathan reported to David all the
words of this entire revelation.

David's Prayer

18 Then King David went in and sat before the LORD, and he said:

"Who am I, O Sovereign LORD, and
what is my family, that you have
brought me this far?
19 And as if this
were not enough in your sight,
O Sovereign LORD, you have also spoken about the future of the house of
your servant. Is this your usual way of
dealing with man, O Sovereign LORD?
20 "What more can David say to
you? For you know your servant,
O Sovereign LORD.
21 For the sake of
your word and according to your
will, you have done this great thing
and made it known to your servant.
22 "How great you are, O Sovereign
LORD! There is no one like you, and
there is no God but you, as we have
heard with our own ears.
23 And who
is like your people Israel—the one
nation on earth that God went out to
redeem as a people for himself, and
to make a name for himself, and to
perform great and awesome wonders
by driving out nations and their gods
from before your people, whom you
redeemed from Egypt?[i]
24 You have established your people Israel as your
very own forever, and you, O LORD,
have become their God.
25 "And now, LORD God, keep forever the promise you have made concerning your servant and his house.
Do as you promised,
26 so that your
name will be great forever. Then men
will say, 'The LORD Almighty is God
over Israel!' And the house of your
servant David will be established before you.
27 "O LORD Almighty, God of Israel,
you have revealed this to your servant, saying, 'I will build a house for
you.' So your servant has found
courage to offer you this prayer.
28 O
Sovereign LORD, you are God! Your
words are trustworthy, and you have
promised these good things to your
servant.
29 Now be pleased to bless the
house of your servant, that it may
continue forever in your sight; for
you, O Sovereign LORD, have spoken,
and with your blessing the house of
your servant will be blessed forever."

[h] 16 Some Hebrew manuscripts and Septuagint; most Hebrew manuscripts *you* [i] 23 See Septuagint and 1 Chron. 17:21; Hebrew *wonders for your land and before your people, whom you redeemed from Egypt, from the nations and their gods.*

PRAYER: ADORATION

YOU, O God, bind the cluster of the Pleiades and loose the cords of Orion. You, O God, bring forth the constellations in their seasons and guide the Bear with its cubs. You know the ordinances of the heavens And set their dominion over the earth. (Job 38:31–33) . . . I know that You can do all things and that no purpose of Yours can be thwarted. (Job 42:2)

***PAUSE** to express your thoughts of praise and worship.*

NT Hebrews 7:11–28

Jesus Like Melchizedek

11 If perfection could have been attained through the Levitical priesthood (for on the basis of it the law was given to the people), why was there still need for another priest to come—one in the order of Melchizedek, not in the order of Aaron?
12 For when there is a change of the priesthood, there must also be a change of the law.
13 He of whom these things are said

belonged to a different tribe, and no one from that tribe has ever served at the altar. [14]For it is clear that our Lord descended from Judah, and in regard to that tribe Moses said nothing about priests. [15]And what we have said is even more clear if another priest like Melchizedek appears, [16]one who has become a priest not on the basis of a regulation as to his ancestry but on the basis of the power of an indestructible life. [17]For it is declared:

"You are a priest forever,
in the order of Melchizedek."[a]

[18]The former regulation is set aside because it was weak and useless [19](for the law made nothing perfect), and a better hope is introduced, by which we draw near to God.

[20]And it was not without an oath! Others became priests without any oath, [21]but he became a priest with an oath when God said to him:

"The Lord has sworn
and will not change his mind:
'You are a priest forever.' "[a]

[22]Because of this oath, Jesus has become the guarantee of a better covenant.

[23]Now there have been many of those priests, since death prevented them from continuing in office; [24]but because Jesus lives forever, he has a permanent priesthood. [25]Therefore he is able to save completely[b] those who come to God through him, because he always lives to intercede for them.

[26]Such a high priest meets our need—one who is holy, blameless, pure, set apart from sinners, exalted above the heavens. [27]Unlike the other high priests, he does not need to offer sacrifices day after day, first for his own sins, and then for the sins of the people. He sacrificed for their sins once for all when he offered himself. [28]For the law appoints as high priests men who are weak; but the oath, which came after the law, appointed the Son, who has been made perfect forever.

[a] *17,21* Psalm 110:4 [b] *25* Or *forever*

PRAYER: THE WORKS OF GOD

MY attitude should be the same as Yours, Christ Jesus; though You are in Your very nature God, You did not consider equality with God something to be grasped, but emptied Yourself, becoming like a servant and being made in human form. And appearing as a human being, You humbled Yourself and became obedient to death, even death on a cross. (Philippians 2:5–8)

***TAKE** a moment to consider the greatness of God's wonderful works.*

YEAR 1 DAY 268

OT 2 Samuel 8:1–9:13

David's Victories

8 In the course of time, David defeated the Philistines and subdued them, and he took Metheg Ammah from the control of the Philistines.

[2]David also defeated the Moabites. He made them lie down on the ground and measured them off with a length of cord. Every two lengths of them were put to death, and the third length was allowed to live. So the Moabites became subject to David and brought tribute.

[3]Moreover, David fought Hadadezer son of Rehob, king of Zobah, when he went to restore his control along the Euphrates River. [4]David captured a thousand of his chariots, seven thousand charioteers[a] and twenty thousand foot soldiers. He hamstrung all but a hundred of the chariot horses.

[5]When the Arameans of Damascus came to help Hadadezer king of Zobah, David struck down twenty-two thousand

[a] *4* Septuagint (see also Dead Sea Scrolls and 1 Chron. 18:4); Masoretic Text *captured seventeen hundred of his charioteers*

of them. 6He put garrisons in the Aramean kingdom of Damascus, and the Arameans became subject to him and
brought tribute. The LORD gave David victory wherever he went.
7David took the gold shields that belonged to the officers of Hadadezer and
brought them to Jerusalem. 8From Tebah[b]
and Berothai, towns that belonged to
Hadadezer, King David took a great quantity of bronze.
9When Tou[c] king of Hamath heard that
David had defeated the entire army of
Hadadezer, 10he sent his son Joram[d] to
King David to greet him and congratulate
him on his victory in battle over Hadadezer, who had been at war with Tou. Joram brought with him articles of silver
and gold and bronze.
11King David dedicated these articles to
the LORD, as he had done with the silver
and gold from all the nations he had subdued: 12Edom[e] and Moab, the Ammonites
and the Philistines, and Amalek. He also
dedicated the plunder taken from Hadadezer son of Rehob, king of Zobah.
13And David became famous after he returned from striking down eighteen thousand Edomites[f] in the Valley of Salt.
14He put garrisons throughout Edom,
and all the Edomites became subject to
David. The LORD gave David victory wherever he went.

David's Officials

15David reigned over all Israel, doing
what was just and right for all his people.
16Joab son of Zeruiah was over the army;
Jehoshaphat son of Ahilud was recorder;
17Zadok son of Ahitub and Ahimelech son
of Abiathar were priests; Seraiah was secretary; 18Benaiah son of Jehoiada was over
the Kerethites and Pelethites; and David's
sons were royal advisers.[g]

David and Mephibosheth

9 David asked, "Is there anyone still left
of the house of Saul to whom I can
show kindness for Jonathan's sake?"
2Now there was a servant of Saul's
household named Ziba. They called him
to appear before David, and the king said
to him, "Are you Ziba?"
"Your servant," he replied.
3The king asked, "Is there no one still
left of the house of Saul to whom I can
show God's kindness?"
Ziba answered the king, "There is still a
son of Jonathan; he is crippled in both
feet."
4"Where is he?" the king asked.
Ziba answered, "He is at the house of
Makir son of Ammiel in Lo Debar."
5So King David had him brought from
Lo Debar, from the house of Makir son of
Ammiel.
6When Mephibosheth son of Jonathan,
the son of Saul, came to David, he bowed
down to pay him honor.
David said, "Mephibosheth!"
"Your servant," he replied.
7"Don't be afraid," David said to him,
"for I will surely show you kindness for
the sake of your father Jonathan. I will restore to you all the land that belonged to
your grandfather Saul, and you will always eat at my table."
8Mephibosheth bowed down and said,
"What is your servant, that you should notice a dead dog like me?"
9Then the king summoned Ziba, Saul's
servant, and said to him, "I have given
your master's grandson everything that
belonged to Saul and his family. 10You
and your sons and your servants are to
farm the land for him and bring in the
crops, so that your master's grandson may
be provided for. And Mephibosheth,
grandson of your master, will always eat
at my table." (Now Ziba had fifteen sons
and twenty servants.)
11Then Ziba said to the king, "Your servant will do whatever my lord the king
commands his servant to do." So Mephibosheth ate at David's[h] table like one
of the king's sons.
12Mephibosheth had a young son
named Mica, and all the members of
Ziba's household were servants of Mephibosheth. 13And Mephibosheth lived in
Jerusalem, because he always ate at the
king's table, and he was crippled in both
feet.

[b] 8 See some Septuagint manuscripts (see also 1 Chron. 18:8); Hebrew *Betah.* [c] 9 Hebrew *Toi,* a variant of *Tou;* also in verse 10 [d] 10 A variant of *Hadoram* [e] 12 Some Hebrew manuscripts, Septuagint and Syriac (see also 1 Chron. 18:11); most Hebrew manuscripts *Aram* [f] 13 A few Hebrew manuscripts, Septuagint and Syriac (see also 1 Chron. 18:12); most Hebrew manuscripts *Aram* (that is, Arameans) [g] 18 Or *were priests* [h] 11 Septuagint; Hebrew *my*

PRAYER: CONFESSION

I KNOW, O Lord, that my life is not my own; it is not for me to direct my steps. O Lord, correct me, but with justice—not in Your anger, lest You reduce me to nothing. (Jeremiah 10:23–24)

***ASK** the Spirit to search your heart and reveal any areas of unconfessed sin. Acknowledge these to the Lord and thank Him for His forgiveness.*

NT Hebrews 8:1–13

The High Priest of a New Covenant

8 The point of what we are saying is this: We do have such a high priest, who sat down at the right hand of the throne of the Majesty in heaven, 2and who serves in the sanctuary, the true tabernacle set up by the Lord, not by man.

3Every high priest is appointed to offer both gifts and sacrifices, and so it was necessary for this one also to have something to offer. 4If he were on earth, he would not be a priest, for there are already men who offer the gifts prescribed by the law.
5They serve at a sanctuary that is a copy and shadow of what is in heaven. This is why Moses was warned when he was about to build the tabernacle: "See to it that you make everything according to the pattern shown you on the mountain."[a]
6But the ministry Jesus has received is as superior to theirs as the covenant of which he is mediator is superior to the old one, and it is founded on better promises.
7For if there had been nothing wrong with that first covenant, no place would have been sought for another. 8But God found fault with the people and said[b]:

"The time is coming, declares the Lord,
when I will make a new covenant
with the house of Israel
and with the house of Judah.
9It will not be like the covenant
I made with their forefathers
when I took them by the hand
to lead them out of Egypt,
because they did not remain faithful
to my covenant,
and I turned away from them,
declares the Lord.
10This is the covenant I will make with
the house of Israel
after that time, declares the Lord.
I will put my laws in their minds
and write them on their hearts.
I will be their God,
and they will be my people.
11No longer will a man teach his
neighbor,
or a man his brother, saying, 'Know
the Lord,'
because they will all know me,
from the least of them to the
greatest.
12For I will forgive their wickedness
and will remember their sins no
more."[c]

13By calling this covenant "new," he has made the first one obsolete; and what is obsolete and aging will soon disappear.

[a] 5 Exodus 25:40 [b] 8 Some manuscripts may be translated *fault and said to the people.*
[c] 12 Jer. 31:31–34

PRAYER: MY RELATIONSHIP TO GOD

ALL of us who were baptized into You, Christ Jesus, were baptized into Your death. We are therefore buried with You through baptism into death, in order that, just as You were raised from the dead through the glory of the Father, so we too may walk in newness of life. (Romans 6:3–4) . . . Those who are in You, O Christ, are new creations; the old things have passed away; behold, they have become new. (2 Corinthians 5:17)

***PAUSE** to thank God for the relationship that you enjoy with Him in Jesus Christ.*

OT 2 Samuel 10:1-19

YEAR 1 DAY 269

David Defeats the Ammonites

10 In the course of time, the king of the Ammonites died, and his son Hanun succeeded him as king. 2David thought, "I will show kindness to Hanun son of Nahash, just as his father showed kindness to me." So David sent a delegation to express his sympathy to Hanun concerning his father.

When David's men came to the land of the Ammonites, 3the Ammonite nobles said to Hanun their lord, "Do you think David is honoring your father by sending men to you to express sympathy? Hasn't David sent them to you to explore the city and spy it out and overthrow it?" 4So Hanun seized David's men, shaved off half of each man's beard, cut off their garments in the middle at the buttocks, and sent them away.

5When David was told about this, he sent messengers to meet the men, for they were greatly humiliated. The king said, "Stay at Jericho till your beards have grown, and then come back."

6When the Ammonites realized that they had become a stench in David's nostrils, they hired twenty thousand Aramean foot soldiers from Beth Rehob and Zobah, as well as the king of Maacah with a thousand men, and also twelve thousand men from Tob.

7On hearing this, David sent Joab out with the entire army of fighting men. 8The Ammonites came out and drew up in battle formation at the entrance to their city gate, while the Arameans of Zobah and Rehob and the men of Tob and Maacah were by themselves in the open country.

9Joab saw that there were battle lines in front of him and behind him; so he selected some of the best troops in Israel and deployed them against the Arameans. 10He put the rest of the men under the command of Abishai his brother and deployed them against the Ammonites. 11Joab said, "If the Arameans are too strong for me, then you are to come to my rescue; but if the Ammonites are too strong for you, then I will come to rescue you. 12Be strong and let us fight bravely for our people and the cities of our God. The LORD will do what is good in his sight."

13Then Joab and the troops with him advanced to fight the Arameans, and they fled before him. 14When the Ammonites saw that the Arameans were fleeing, they fled before Abishai and went inside the city. So Joab returned from fighting the Ammonites and came to Jerusalem.

15After the Arameans saw that they had been routed by Israel, they regrouped. 16Hadadezer had Arameans brought from beyond the River[a]; they went to Helam, with Shobach the commander of Hadadezer's army leading them.

17When David was told of this, he gathered all Israel, crossed the Jordan and went to Helam. The Arameans formed their battle lines to meet David and fought against him. 18But they fled before Israel, and David killed seven hundred of their charioteers and forty thousand of their foot soldiers.[b] He also struck down Shobach the commander of their army, and he died there. 19When all the kings who were vassals of Hadadezer saw that they had been defeated by Israel, they made peace with the Israelites and became subject to them.

So the Arameans were afraid to help the Ammonites anymore.

[a] *16* That is, the Euphrates [b] *18* Some Septuagint manuscripts (see also 1 Chron. 19:18); Hebrew *horsemen*

PRAYER: RENEWAL

MAY I receive the words of wisdom and treasure her commands within me, turning my ear to wisdom and applying my heart to understanding. If I cry for discernment and lift up my voice for understanding, if I seek her as silver and search for her as for hidden treasures, then I will understand what it is to fear You and what it

is to know You. Then I will understand righteousness and justice and honesty—every good path. For wisdom will enter my heart, and knowledge will be pleasant to my soul. Discretion will protect me, and understanding will guard me. (Proverbs 2:1–5, 9–11)

***PAUSE** to add your own prayers for personal renewal.*

NT Hebrews 9:1-10

Worship in the Earthly Tabernacle

9 Now the first covenant had regulations for worship and also an earthly sanctuary. [2]A tabernacle was set up. In its first room were the lampstand, the table and the consecrated bread; this was called the Holy Place. [3]Behind the second curtain was a room called the Most Holy Place, [4]which had the golden altar of incense and the gold-covered ark of the covenant. This ark contained the gold jar of manna, Aaron's staff that had budded, and the stone tablets of the covenant. [5]Above the ark were the cherubim of the Glory, overshadowing the atonement cover.[a] But we cannot discuss these things in detail now.

[6]When everything had been arranged like this, the priests entered regularly into the outer room to carry on their ministry. [7]But only the high priest entered the inner room, and that only once a year, and never without blood, which he offered for himself and for the sins the people had committed in ignorance. [8]The Holy Spirit was showing by this that the way into the Most Holy Place had not yet been disclosed as long as the first tabernacle was still standing. [9]This is an illustration for the present time, indicating that the gifts and sacrifices being offered were not able to clear the conscience of the worshiper. [10]They are only a matter of food and drink and various ceremonial washings—external regulations applying until the time of the new order.

[a] 5 Traditionally *the mercy seat*

PRAYER: THE CHARACTER I WANT TO CULTIVATE

I WILL have respect for You, Lord, and serve You faithfully. May I do it with all my heart, for with You, Lord my God, there is no injustice or partiality or bribery. (2 Chronicles 19:7) . . . Whoever is faithful with very little is also faithful with much, and whoever is dishonest with very little will also be dishonest with much. If I am not faithful in handling worldly wealth, who will trust me with true riches? And if I am not faithful with someone else's property, who will give me property of my own? (Luke 16:10–12)

***TAKE** a moment to ask the Lord for the grace to grow in godly character.*

OT 2 Samuel 11:1-27

David and Bathsheba

11 In the spring, at the time when kings go off to war, David sent Joab out with the king's men and the whole Israelite army. They destroyed the Ammonites and besieged Rabbah. But David remained in Jerusalem.

[2]One evening David got up from his bed and walked around on the roof of the palace. From the roof he saw a woman bathing. The woman was very beautiful, [3]and David sent someone to find out about her. The man said, "Isn't this Bathsheba, the daughter of Eliam and the wife of Uriah the Hittite?" [4]Then David sent messengers to get her. She came to him, and he slept with her. (She had purified herself from her uncleanness.)

Then[a] she went back home. 5The woman conceived and sent word to David, saying, "I am pregnant."

6So David sent this word to Joab: "Send me Uriah the Hittite." And Joab sent him to David. 7When Uriah came to him, David asked him how Joab was, how the soldiers were and how the war was going. 8Then David said to Uriah, "Go down to your house and wash your feet." So Uriah left the palace, and a gift from the king was sent after him. 9But Uriah slept at the entrance to the palace with all his master's servants and did not go down to his house.

10When David was told, "Uriah did not go home," he asked him, "Haven't you just come from a distance? Why didn't you go home?"

11Uriah said to David, "The ark and Israel and Judah are staying in tents, and my master Joab and my lord's men are camped in the open fields. How could I go to my house to eat and drink and lie with my wife? As surely as you live, I will not do such a thing!"

12Then David said to him, "Stay here one more day, and tomorrow I will send you back." So Uriah remained in Jerusalem that day and the next. 13At David's invitation, he ate and drank with him, and David made him drunk. But in the evening Uriah went out to sleep on his mat among his master's servants; he did not go home.

14In the morning David wrote a letter to Joab and sent it with Uriah. 15In it he wrote, "Put Uriah in the front line where the fighting is fiercest. Then withdraw from him so he will be struck down and die."

16So while Joab had the city under siege, he put Uriah at a place where he knew the strongest defenders were. 17When the men of the city came out and fought against Joab, some of the men in David's army fell; moreover, Uriah the Hittite died.

18Joab sent David a full account of the battle. 19He instructed the messenger: "When you have finished giving the king this account of the battle, 20the king's anger may flare up, and he may ask you, 'Why did you get so close to the city to fight? Didn't you know they would shoot arrows from the wall? 21Who killed Abimelech son of Jerub-Besheth[b]? Didn't a woman throw an upper millstone on him from the wall, so that he died in Thebez? Why did you get so close to the wall?' If he asks you this, then say to him, 'Also, your servant Uriah the Hittite is dead.' "

22The messenger set out, and when he arrived he told David everything Joab had sent him to say. 23The messenger said to David, "The men overpowered us and came out against us in the open, but we drove them back to the entrance to the city gate. 24Then the archers shot arrows at your servants from the wall, and some of the king's men died. Moreover, your servant Uriah the Hittite is dead."

25David told the messenger, "Say this to Joab: 'Don't let this upset you; the sword devours one as well as another. Press the attack against the city and destroy it.' Say this to encourage Joab."

26When Uriah's wife heard that her husband was dead, she mourned for him. 27After the time of mourning was over, David had her brought to his house, and she became his wife and bore him a son. But the thing David had done displeased the LORD.

[a] 4 Or *with her. When she purified herself from her uncleanness,* [b] 21 Also known as *Jerub-Baal* (that is, Gideon)

PRAYER: PETITION

HEAR, O Lord, and be merciful to me; O Lord, be my helper. You turned my mourning into dancing; You removed my sackcloth and clothed me with gladness, that my heart may sing praise to You and not be silent. O Lord my God, I will give thanks to You forever. (Psalm 30:10–12)

***PAUSE** here to petition God for growth in love and compassion toward others. Offer prayers for your loved ones, for those who do not know Jesus and for those in need. Offer prayers regarding your activities for this day and any special concerns you may have.*

NT Hebrews 9:11–28

The Blood of Christ

11 When Christ came as high priest of the good things that are already here,[a] he went through the greater and more perfect tabernacle that is not man-made, that is to say, not a part of this creation. 12 He did not enter by means of the blood of goats and calves; but he entered the Most Holy Place once for all by his own blood, having obtained eternal redemption. 13 The blood of goats and bulls and the ashes of a heifer sprinkled on those who are ceremonially unclean sanctify them so that they are outwardly clean. 14 How much more, then, will the blood of Christ, who through the eternal Spirit offered himself unblemished to God, cleanse our consciences from acts that lead to death,[b] so that we may serve the living God!

15 For this reason Christ is the mediator of a new covenant, that those who are called may receive the promised eternal inheritance—now that he has died as a ransom to set them free from the sins committed under the first covenant.

16 In the case of a will,[c] it is necessary to prove the death of the one who made it, 17 because a will is in force only when somebody has died; it never takes effect while the one who made it is living. 18 This is why even the first covenant was not put into effect without blood. 19 When Moses had proclaimed every commandment of the law to all the people, he took the blood of calves, together with water, scarlet wool and branches of hyssop, and sprinkled the scroll and all the people. 20 He said, "This is the blood of the covenant, which God has commanded you to keep."[d] 21 In the same way, he sprinkled with the blood both the tabernacle and everything used in its ceremonies. 22 In fact, the law requires that nearly everything be cleansed with blood, and without the shedding of blood there is no forgiveness.

23 It was necessary, then, for the copies of the heavenly things to be purified with these sacrifices, but the heavenly things themselves with better sacrifices than these. 24 For Christ did not enter a man-made sanctuary that was only a copy of the true one; he entered heaven itself, now to appear for us in God's presence. 25 Nor did he enter heaven to offer himself again and again, the way the high priest enters the Most Holy Place every year with blood that is not his own. 26 Then Christ would have had to suffer many times since the creation of the world. But now he has appeared once for all at the end of the ages to do away with sin by the sacrifice of himself. 27 Just as man is destined to die once, and after that to face judgment, 28 so Christ was sacrificed once to take away the sins of many people; and he will appear a second time, not to bear sin, but to bring salvation to those who are waiting for him.

[a] 11 Some early manuscripts *are to come* [b] 14 Or *from useless rituals* [c] 16 Same Greek word as *covenant;* also in verse 17 [d] 20 Exodus 24:8

PRAYER: MY RELATIONSHIP TO OTHERS

WE are the fragrance of Christ to You, O God, among those who are being saved and among those who are perishing;
to the one, we are an aroma from death to death; to the other, an aroma from life to life. And who is sufficient for these things? (2 Corinthians 2:15–16) . . .
I pray that I may share my faith effectively through the knowledge of every good thing I have in You, Christ Jesus.
(Philemon 6)

PAUSE *to review your relationships with others and to commit them to the Lord.*

YEAR 1 DAY 271

OT 2 Samuel 12:1-31

Nathan Rebukes David

12 The LORD sent Nathan to David. When he came to him, he said, "There were two men in a certain town, one rich and the other poor. 2The rich man had a very large number of sheep and cattle, 3but the poor man had nothing except one little ewe lamb he had bought. He raised it, and it grew up with him and his children. It shared his food, drank from his cup and even slept in his arms. It was like a daughter to him.

4"Now a traveler came to the rich man, but the rich man refrained from taking one of his own sheep or cattle to prepare a meal for the traveler who had come to him. Instead, he took the ewe lamb that belonged to the poor man and prepared it for the one who had come to him."

5David burned with anger against the man and said to Nathan, "As surely as the LORD lives, the man who did this deserves to die! 6He must pay for that lamb four times over, because he did such a thing and had no pity."

7Then Nathan said to David, "You are the man! This is what the LORD, the God of Israel, says: 'I anointed you king over Israel, and I delivered you from the hand of Saul. 8I gave your master's house to you, and your master's wives into your arms. I gave you the house of Israel and Judah. And if all this had been too little, I would have given you even more. 9Why did you despise the word of the LORD by doing what is evil in his eyes? You struck down Uriah the Hittite with the sword and took his wife to be your own. You killed him with the sword of the Ammonites. 10Now, therefore, the sword will never depart from your house, because you despised me and took the wife of Uriah the Hittite to be your own.'

11"This is what the LORD says: 'Out of your own household I am going to bring calamity upon you. Before your very eyes I will take your wives and give them to one who is close to you, and he will lie with your wives in broad daylight. 12You did it in secret, but I will do this thing in broad daylight before all Israel.' "

13Then David said to Nathan, "I have sinned against the LORD."

Nathan replied, "The LORD has taken away your sin. You are not going to die. 14But because by doing this you have made the enemies of the LORD show utter contempt,[a] the son born to you will die."

15After Nathan had gone home, the LORD struck the child that Uriah's wife had borne to David, and he became ill. 16David pleaded with God for the child. He fasted and went into his house and spent the nights lying on the ground. 17The elders of his household stood beside him to get him up from the ground, but he refused, and he would not eat any food with them.

18On the seventh day the child died. David's servants were afraid to tell him that the child was dead, for they thought, "While the child was still living, we spoke to David but he would not listen to us. How can we tell him the child is dead? He may do something desperate."

19David noticed that his servants were whispering among themselves and he realized the child was dead. "Is the child dead?" he asked.

"Yes," they replied, "he is dead."

20Then David got up from the ground. After he had washed, put on lotions and changed his clothes, he went into the house of the LORD and worshiped. Then he went to his own house, and at his request they served him food, and he ate.

21His servants asked him, "Why are you acting this way? While the child was alive, you fasted and wept, but now that the child is dead, you get up and eat!"

22He answered, "While the child was still alive, I fasted and wept. I thought, 'Who knows? The LORD may be gracious to me and let the child live.' 23But now that he is dead, why should I fast? Can I bring him back again? I will go to him, but he will not return to me."

24Then David comforted his wife Bathsheba, and he went to her and lay with her. She gave birth to a son, and they named him Solomon. The LORD loved him; 25and because the LORD loved him, he sent word through Nathan the prophet to name him Jedidiah.[b]

[a] *14* Masoretic Text; an ancient Hebrew scribal tradition *this you have shown utter contempt for the* LORD [b] *25 Jedidiah* means *loved by the* LORD.

[26]Meanwhile Joab fought against Rabbah of the Ammonites and captured the
royal citadel. [27]Joab then sent messengers
to David, saying, "I have fought against
Rabbah and taken its water supply. [28]Now
muster the rest of the troops and besiege
the city and capture it. Otherwise I will take
the city, and it will be named after me."
[29]So David mustered the entire army and
went to Rabbah, and attacked and captured it. [30]He took the crown from the head
of their king[c]—its weight was a talent[d] of
gold, and it was set with precious stones—
and it was placed on David's head. He took
a great quantity of plunder from the city
[31]and brought out the people who were
there, consigning them to labor with saws
and with iron picks and axes, and he made
them work at brickmaking.[e] He did this to
all the Ammonite towns. Then David and
his entire army returned to Jerusalem.

[c] *30* Or *of Milcom* (that is, Molech) [d] *30* That is, about 75 pounds (about 34 kilograms) [e] *31* The meaning of the Hebrew for this clause is uncertain.

PRAYER: INTERCESSION

THE harvest is plentiful, but the workers are few. Therefore, I will pray that You, the Lord of the harvest, will send out workers into Your harvest. (Matthew 9:37–38; Luke 10:2)

***TAKE** a few moments to intercede on behalf of friends, relatives, neighbors and coworkers who do not yet know salvation in Jesus Christ.*

NT Hebrews 10:1–18

Christ's Sacrifice Once for All

10 The law is only a shadow of the good
things that are coming—not the realities themselves. For this reason it can
never, by the same sacrifices repeated endlessly year after year, make perfect those
who draw near to worship. [2]If it could,
would they not have stopped being offered? For the worshipers would have
been cleansed once for all, and would no
longer have felt guilty for their sins. [3]But
those sacrifices are an annual reminder of
sins, [4]because it is impossible for the
blood of bulls and goats to take away sins.
[5]Therefore, when Christ came into the
world, he said:

"Sacrifice and offering you did not
desire,
but a body you prepared for me;
[6]with burnt offerings and sin offerings
you were not pleased.
[7]Then I said, 'Here I am—it is written
about me in the scroll—
I have come to do your will,
O God.' "[a]

[8]First he said, "Sacrifices and offerings,
burnt offerings and sin offerings you did
not desire, nor were you pleased with them"
(although the law required them to be
made). [9]Then he said, "Here I am, I have
come to do your will." He sets aside the first
to establish the second. [10]And by that will,
we have been made holy through the sacrifice of the body of Jesus Christ once for all.
[11]Day after day every priest stands and
performs his religious duties; again and
again he offers the same sacrifices, which
can never take away sins. [12]But when this
priest had offered for all time one sacrifice for sins, he sat down at the right hand
of God. [13]Since that time he waits for his
enemies to be made his footstool, [14]be-
cause by one sacrifice he has made perfect
forever those who are being made holy.
[15]The Holy Spirit also testifies to us
about this. First he says:

[16]"This is the covenant I will make with
them
after that time, says the Lord.
I will put my laws in their hearts,
and I will write them on their
minds."[b]

[17]Then he adds:

"Their sins and lawless acts
I will remember no more."[c]

[18]And where these have been forgiven,
there is no longer any sacrifice for sin.

[a] *7* Psalm 40:6–8 (see Septuagint) [b] *16* Jer. 31:33 [c] *17* Jer. 31:34

PRAYER: THE ATTRIBUTES OF GOD

JESUS is Your beloved Son, O God, in whom You are well pleased. (Matthew 3:17; Mark 1:11; Luke 3:22) . . . No one has ever seen You, O God, but God the One and Only who is at your side, Father; He has made You known. (John 1:18)

***PAUSE** to reflect on these affirmations about the person, powers and perfection of God.*

YEAR 1 DAY 272

OT 2 Samuel 13:1-39

Amnon and Tamar

13 In the course of time, Amnon son of
David fell in love with Tamar, the
beautiful sister of Absalom son of David.
[2]Amnon became frustrated to the point
of illness on account of his sister Tamar,
for she was a virgin, and it seemed impossible for him to do anything to her.
[3]Now Amnon had a friend named Jonadab son of Shimeah, David's brother.
Jonadab was a very shrewd man. [4]He
asked Amnon, "Why do you, the king's
son, look so haggard morning after morning? Won't you tell me?"

Amnon said to him, "I'm in love with Tamar, my brother Absalom's sister."
[5]"Go to bed and pretend to be ill," Jonadab said. "When your father comes to see you, say to him, 'I would like my sister Tamar to come and give me something to eat. Let her prepare the food in my sight so I may watch her and then eat it from her hand.' "
[6]So Amnon lay down and pretended to
be ill. When the king came to see him, Amnon said to him, "I would like my sister Tamar to come and make some special bread in my sight, so I may eat from her hand."
[7]David sent word to Tamar at the palace:
"Go to the house of your brother Amnon
and prepare some food for him." [8]So Tamar
went to the house of her brother Amnon,
who was lying down. She took some dough,
kneaded it, made the bread in his sight and
baked it. [9]Then she took the pan and served
him the bread, but he refused to eat.

"Send everyone out of here," Amnon
said. So everyone left him. [10]Then Amnon
said to Tamar, "Bring the food here into
my bedroom so I may eat from your
hand." And Tamar took the bread she had
prepared and brought it to her brother
Amnon in his bedroom. [11]But when she
took it to him to eat, he grabbed her and
said, "Come to bed with me, my sister."
[12]"Don't, my brother!" she said to him.
"Don't force me. Such a thing should not
be done in Israel! Don't do this wicked
thing. [13]What about me? Where could I get
rid of my disgrace? And what about you?
You would be like one of the wicked fools
in Israel. Please speak to the king; he will
not keep me from being married to you."
[14]But he refused to listen to her, and since
he was stronger than she, he raped her.
[15]Then Amnon hated her with intense
hatred. In fact, he hated her more than he
had loved her. Amnon said to her, "Get up
and get out!"
[16]"No!" she said to him. "Sending me
away would be a greater wrong than what
you have already done to me."

But he refused to listen to her. [17]He
called his personal servant and said, "Get
this woman out of here and bolt the door
after her." [18]So his servant put her out and
bolted the door after her. She was wearing
a richly ornamented[a] robe, for this was the
kind of garment the virgin daughters of the
king wore. [19]Tamar put ashes on her head
and tore the ornamented[b] robe she was
wearing. She put her hand on her head and
went away, weeping aloud as she went.
[20]Her brother Absalom said to her, "Has
that Amnon, your brother, been with you?
Be quiet now, my sister; he is your brother. Don't take this thing to heart." And Tamar lived in her brother Absalom's house, a desolate woman.

[a] *18* The meaning of the Hebrew for this phrase is uncertain. [b] *19* The meaning of the Hebrew for this word is uncertain.

21When King David heard all this, he
was furious. 22Absalom never said a word
to Amnon, either good or bad; he hated
Amnon because he had disgraced his sister Tamar.

Absalom Kills Amnon

23Two years later, when Absalom's
sheepshearers were at Baal Hazor near the
border of Ephraim, he invited all the
king's sons to come there. 24Absalom went
to the king and said, "Your servant has
had shearers come. Will the king and his
officials please join me?"
25"No, my son," the king replied. "All of
us should not go; we would only be a burden to you." Although Absalom urged
him, he still refused to go, but gave him
his blessing.
26Then Absalom said, "If not, please let
my brother Amnon come with us."
The king asked him, "Why should he go
with you?" 27But Absalom urged him, so
he sent with him Amnon and the rest of
the king's sons.
28Absalom ordered his men, "Listen!
When Amnon is in high spirits from
drinking wine and I say to you, 'Strike
Amnon down,' then kill him. Don't be
afraid. Have not I given you this order? Be
strong and brave." 29So Absalom's men
did to Amnon what Absalom had ordered. Then all the king's sons got up,
mounted their mules and fled.
30While they were on their way, the report came to David: "Absalom has struck
down all the king's sons; not one of them
is left." 31The king stood up, tore his clothes
and lay down on the ground; and all his
servants stood by with their clothes torn.
32But Jonadab son of Shimeah, David's
brother, said, "My lord should not think
that they killed all the princes; only Amnon is dead. This has been Absalom's expressed intention ever since the day Amnon raped his sister Tamar. 33My lord the
king should not be concerned about the
report that all the king's sons are dead.
Only Amnon is dead."
34Meanwhile, Absalom had fled.
Now the man standing watch looked
up and saw many people on the road west
of him, coming down the side of the hill.
The watchman went and told the king, "I
see men in the direction of Horonaim, on
the side of the hill."[c]
35Jonadab said to the king, "See, the
king's sons are here; it has happened just
as your servant said."
36As he finished speaking, the king's
sons came in, wailing loudly. The king,
too, and all his servants wept very bitterly.
37Absalom fled and went to Talmai son
of Ammihud, the king of Geshur. But King
David mourned for his son every day.
38After Absalom fled and went to Geshur, he stayed there three years. 39And the
spirit of the king[d] longed to go to Absalom, for he was consoled concerning Amnon's death.

[c] 34 Septuagint; Hebrew does not have this sentence. [d] 39 Dead Sea Scrolls and some Septuagint manuscripts; Masoretic Text *But* ⌊*the spirit of*⌋ *David the king*

PRAYER: AFFIRMATION

YOU are my hiding place and my shield, O Lord; I have put my hope in Your word. (Psalm 119:114) . . . Every word You speak is flawless, O God; You are a shield to those who take refuge in You. (Proverbs 30:5)

***PAUSE** to reflect on these Biblical affirmations.*

NT Hebrews 10:19–39

A Call to Persevere

19Therefore, brothers, since we have confidence to enter the Most Holy Place by the
blood of Jesus, 20by a new and living way
opened for us through the curtain, that is,
his body, 21and since we have a great priest
over the house of God, 22let us draw near
to God with a sincere heart in full assurance of faith, having our hearts sprinkled
to cleanse us from a guilty conscience and
having our bodies washed with pure water.
23Let us hold unswervingly to the hope we

profess, for he who promised is faithful.
24And let us consider how we may spur one
another on toward love and good deeds.
25Let us not give up meeting together, as
some are in the habit of doing, but let us
encourage one another—and all the more
as you see the Day approaching.
26If we deliberately keep on sinning after we have received the knowledge of the
truth, no sacrifice for sins is left, 27but only
a fearful expectation of judgment and of
raging fire that will consume the enemies
of God. 28Anyone who rejected the law of
Moses died without mercy on the testimony of two or three witnesses. 29How
much more severely do you think a man
deserves to be punished who has trampled
the Son of God under foot, who has treated as an unholy thing the blood of the
covenant that sanctified him, and who has
insulted the Spirit of grace? 30For we know
him who said, "It is mine to avenge; I will
repay,"[a] and again, "The Lord will judge
his people."[b] 31It is a dreadful thing to fall
into the hands of the living God.
32Remember those earlier days after you
had received the light, when you stood
your ground in a great contest in the face
of suffering. 33Sometimes you were publicly exposed to insult and persecution; at
other times you stood side by side with
those who were so treated. 34You sympa-
thized with those in prison and joyfully
accepted the confiscation of your property, because you knew that you yourselves
had better and lasting possessions.
35So do not throw away your confidence;
it will be richly rewarded. 36You need to
persevere so that when you have done the
will of God, you will receive what he has
promised. 37For in just a very little while,

"He who is coming will come and
will not delay.
38 But my righteous one[c] will live by
faith.
And if he shrinks back,
I will not be pleased with him."[d]

39But we are not of those who shrink back
and are destroyed, but of those who believe and are saved.

[a] *30* Deut. 32:35 [b] *30* Deut. 32:36; Psalm 135:14
[c] *38* One early manuscript *But the righteous*
[d] *38* Hab. 2:3,4

PRAYER: THE WORKS OF GOD

GOD highly exalted You, Christ Jesus, and gave You the name that is above every name, that at Your name, Jesus, every knee should bow, in heaven and on earth and under the earth, and every tongue should confess that You are Lord, to the glory of God the Father. (Philippians 2:9–11) . . . Jesus Christ, You are coming with the clouds, and every eye will see You, even those who pierced You; and all the peoples of the earth will mourn because of You. Even so, Amen. (Revelation 1:7)

TAKE *a moment to consider the greatness of God's wonderful works.*

OT Psalms 52–53 — YEAR 1 DAY 273

Psalm 52

For the director of music. A *maskil*[a] of David. When Doeg the Edomite had gone to Saul and told him: "David has gone to the house of Ahimelech."

1Why do you boast of evil, you mighty
man?
Why do you boast all day long,
you who are a disgrace in the eyes
of God?
2Your tongue plots destruction;
it is like a sharpened razor,
you who practice deceit.
3You love evil rather than good,
falsehood rather than speaking the
truth. *Selah*
4You love every harmful word,
O you deceitful tongue!

[a] Title: Probably a literary or musical term

5 Surely God will bring you down to
 everlasting ruin:
 He will snatch you up and tear you
 from your tent;
 he will uproot you from the land of
 the living. *Selah*
6 The righteous will see and fear;
 they will laugh at him, saying,
7 "Here now is the man
 who did not make God his
 stronghold
 but trusted in his great wealth
 and grew strong by destroying
 others!"

8 But I am like an olive tree
 flourishing in the house of God;
 I trust in God's unfailing love
 for ever and ever.
9 I will praise you forever for what you
 have done;
 in your name I will hope, for your
 name is good.
 I will praise you in the presence of
 your saints.

Psalm 53

For the director of music. According to *mahalath.*[b] A *maskil*[c] of David.

1 The fool says in his heart,
 "There is no God."
 They are corrupt, and their ways are
 vile;
 there is no one who does good.

2 God looks down from heaven
 on the sons of men
 to see if there are any who
 understand,
 any who seek God.
3 Everyone has turned away,
 they have together become
 corrupt;
 there is no one who does good,
 not even one.

4 Will the evildoers never learn—
 those who devour my people as
 men eat bread
 and who do not call on God?
5 There they were, overwhelmed with
 dread,
 where there was nothing to
 dread.
 God scattered the bones of those who
 attacked you;
 you put them to shame, for God
 despised them.

6 Oh, that salvation for Israel would
 come out of Zion!
 When God restores the fortunes of
 his people,
 let Jacob rejoice and Israel be glad!

[b] Title: Probably a musical term [c] Title: Probably a literary or musical term

PRAYER: THANKSGIVING

ALL the kings of the earth will give thanks to You, O Lord, when they hear the words of Your mouth. Yes, they sing of Your ways, O Lord, for Your glory is great. Though You reign on high, yet You look upon the lowly, but the proud You know from afar. (Psalm 138:4–6)

***PAUSE** to offer your own expressions of thanksgiving.*

NT Hebrews 11:1–19

By Faith

11 Now faith is being sure of what we
hope for and certain of what we do
not see. 2 This is what the ancients were
commended for.
3 By faith we understand that the universe was formed at God's command, so
that what is seen was not made out of
what was visible.
4 By faith Abel offered God a better sacrifice than Cain did. By faith he was commended as a righteous man, when God
spoke well of his offerings. And by faith
he still speaks, even though he is dead.
5 By faith Enoch was taken from this life,
so that he did not experience death; he
could not be found, because God had tak-
en him away. For before he was taken, he

was commended as one who pleased
God. [6]And without faith it is impossible
to please God, because anyone who
comes to him must believe that he exists
and that he rewards those who earnestly
seek him.

[7]By faith Noah, when warned about
things not yet seen, in holy fear built an
ark to save his family. By his faith he condemned the world and became heir of the
righteousness that comes by faith.

[8]By faith Abraham, when called to go
to a place he would later receive as his inheritance, obeyed and went, even though
he did not know where he was going. [9]By
faith he made his home in the promised
land like a stranger in a foreign country;
he lived in tents, as did Isaac and Jacob,
who were heirs with him of the same
promise. [10]For he was looking forward to
the city with foundations, whose architect
and builder is God.

[11]By faith Abraham, even though he was
past age—and Sarah herself was barren—
was enabled to become a father because
he[a] considered him faithful who had
made the promise. [12]And so from this one
man, and he as good as dead, came descendants as numerous as the stars in the
sky and as countless as the sand on the
seashore.

[13]All these people were still living by
faith when they died. They did not receive
the things promised; they only saw them
and welcomed them from a distance. And
they admitted that they were aliens and
strangers on earth. [14]People who say such
things show that they are looking for a
country of their own. [15]If they had been
thinking of the country they had left, they
would have had opportunity to return.
[16]Instead, they were longing for a better
country—a heavenly one. Therefore God
is not ashamed to be called their God, for
he has prepared a city for them.

[17]By faith Abraham, when God tested
him, offered Isaac as a sacrifice. He who
had received the promises was about to
sacrifice his one and only son, [18]even
though God had said to him, "It is
through Isaac that your offspring[b] will be
reckoned."[c] [19]Abraham reasoned that God
could raise the dead, and figuratively
speaking, he did receive Isaac back from
death.

[a] *11* Or *By faith even Sarah, who was past age, was enabled to bear children because she* [b] *18* Greek *seed* [c] *18* Gen. 21:12

PRAYER: MY RELATIONSHIP TO GOD

YOU are the true vine, Jesus, and Your Father is the gardener. He cuts off every branch in You that bears no fruit, while every branch that does bear fruit He prunes, that it may bear more fruit. I will abide in You, and You will abide in me. As the branch cannot bear fruit of itself, unless it abides in the vine, neither can I bear fruit, unless I abide in You.

(John 15:1–2, 4)

PAUSE *to thank God for the relationship that you enjoy with Him in Jesus Christ.*

YEAR 1 DAY 274

OT 2 Samuel 14:1–33

Absalom Returns to Jerusalem

14 Joab son of Zeruiah knew that the king's
heart longed for Absalom. [2]So Joab sent
someone to Tekoa and had a wise woman
brought from there. He said to her, "Pretend
you are in mourning. Dress in mourning
clothes, and don't use any cosmetic lotions.
Act like a woman who has spent many days
grieving for the dead. [3]Then go to the king
and speak these words to him." And Joab
put the words in her mouth.

[4]When the woman from Tekoa went[a] to
the king, she fell with her face to the
ground to pay him honor, and she said,
"Help me, O king!"

[a] *4* Many Hebrew manuscripts, Septuagint, Vulgate and Syriac; most Hebrew manuscripts *spoke*

5 The king asked her, "What is troubling
you?"
She said, "I am indeed a widow; my
husband is dead. 6 I your servant had two
sons. They got into a fight with each other in the field, and no one was there to
separate them. One struck the other and
killed him. 7 Now the whole clan has risen
up against your servant; they say, 'Hand
over the one who struck his brother
down, so that we may put him to death
for the life of his brother whom he killed;
then we will get rid of the heir as well.'
They would put out the only burning coal
I have left, leaving my husband neither
name nor descendant on the face of the
earth."
8 The king said to the woman, "Go home,
and I will issue an order in your behalf."
9 But the woman from Tekoa said to
him, "My lord the king, let the blame rest
on me and on my father's family, and let
the king and his throne be without guilt."
10 The king replied, "If anyone says anything to you, bring him to me, and he will
not bother you again."
11 She said, "Then let the king invoke the
LORD his God to prevent the avenger of
blood from adding to the destruction, so
that my son will not be destroyed."
"As surely as the LORD lives," he said,
"not one hair of your son's head will fall
to the ground."
12 Then the woman said, "Let your servant speak a word to my lord the king."
"Speak," he replied.
13 The woman said, "Why then have you
devised a thing like this against the people of God? When the king says this, does
he not convict himself, for the king has
not brought back his banished son? 14 Like
water spilled on the ground, which cannot be recovered, so we must die. But God
does not take away life; instead, he devises
ways so that a banished person may not
remain estranged from him.
15 "And now I have come to say this to
my lord the king because the people have
made me afraid. Your servant thought, 'I
will speak to the king; perhaps he will do
what his servant asks. 16 Perhaps the king
will agree to deliver his servant from the
hand of the man who is trying to cut off
both me and my son from the inheritance
God gave us.'
17 "And now your servant says, 'May the
word of my lord the king bring me rest,
for my lord the king is like an angel of
God in discerning good and evil. May the
LORD your God be with you.' "
18 Then the king said to the woman, "Do
not keep from me the answer to what I
am going to ask you."
"Let my lord the king speak," the
woman said.
19 The king asked, "Isn't the hand of
Joab with you in all this?"
The woman answered, "As surely as you
live, my lord the king, no one can turn to
the right or to the left from anything my
lord the king says. Yes, it was your servant
Joab who instructed me to do this and
who put all these words into the mouth
of your servant. 20 Your servant Joab did
this to change the present situation. My
lord has wisdom like that of an angel of
God—he knows everything that happens
in the land."
21 The king said to Joab, "Very well, I will
do it. Go, bring back the young man Absalom."
22 Joab fell with his face to the ground
to pay him honor, and he blessed the
king. Joab said, "Today your servant
knows that he has found favor in your
eyes, my lord the king, because the king
has granted his servant's request."
23 Then Joab went to Geshur and
brought Absalom back to Jerusalem. 24 But
the king said, "He must go to his own
house; he must not see my face." So Absalom went to his own house and did not
see the face of the king.
25 In all Israel there was not a man so
highly praised for his handsome appearance as Absalom. From the top of his head
to the sole of his foot there was no blemish in him. 26 Whenever he cut the hair of
his head—he used to cut his hair from time
to time when it became too heavy for
him—he would weigh it, and its weight was
two hundred shekels[b] by the royal standard.
27 Three sons and a daughter were born
to Absalom. The daughter's name was Tamar, and she became a beautiful woman.
28 Absalom lived two years in Jerusalem
without seeing the king's face. 29 Then Absalom sent for Joab in order to send him to
the king, but Joab refused to come to him.
So he sent a second time, but he refused to
come. 30 Then he said to his servants, "Look,
Joab's field is next to mine, and he has bar-

[b] *26* That is, about 5 pounds (about 2.3 kilograms)

ley there. Go and set it on fire." So Absalom's servants set the field on fire.
31Then Joab did go to Absalom's house
and he said to him, "Why have your servants set my field on fire?"
32Absalom said to Joab, "Look, I sent
word to you and said, 'Come here so I can
send you to the king to ask, "Why have I
come from Geshur? It would be better for
me if I were still there!" ' Now then, I
want to see the king's face, and if I am
guilty of anything, let him put me to
death."
33So Joab went to the king and told him
this. Then the king summoned Absalom,
and he came in and bowed down with his
face to the ground before the king. And
the king kissed Absalom.

PRAYER: ADORATION

THE earth is Yours, O Lord, and everything in it, the world and all who dwell in it. For You founded it upon the seas and established it upon the waters. (Psalm 24:1–2) . . . You sit enthroned above the circle of the earth, O God, and its inhabitants are like grasshoppers. You stretch out the heavens like a curtain and spread them out like a tent to dwell in. You reduce rulers to nothing and make the judges of this world meaningless. (Isaiah 40:22–23)

PAUSE *to express your thoughts of praise and worship.*

NT Hebrews 11:20-40

20By faith Isaac blessed Jacob and Esau
in regard to their future.
21By faith Jacob, when he was dying,
blessed each of Joseph's sons, and worshiped as he leaned on the top of his staff.
22By faith Joseph, when his end was
near, spoke about the exodus of the Israelites from Egypt and gave instructions
about his bones.
23By faith Moses' parents hid him for
three months after he was born, because
they saw he was no ordinary child, and
they were not afraid of the king's edict.
24By faith Moses, when he had grown up,
refused to be known as the son of Pharaoh's daughter. 25He chose to be mistreated along with the people of God rather
than to enjoy the pleasures of sin for a short
time. 26He regarded disgrace for the sake of
Christ as of greater value than the treasures
of Egypt, because he was looking ahead to
his reward. 27By faith he left Egypt, not fearing the king's anger; he persevered because
he saw him who is invisible. 28By faith he
kept the Passover and the sprinkling of
blood, so that the destroyer of the firstborn
would not touch the firstborn of Israel.
29By faith the people passed through
the Red Sea[a] as on dry land; but when the
Egyptians tried to do so, they were
drowned.
30By faith the walls of Jericho fell, after
the people had marched around them for
seven days.
31By faith the prostitute Rahab, because
she welcomed the spies, was not killed
with those who were disobedient.[b]
32And what more shall I say? I do not
have time to tell about Gideon, Barak,
Samson, Jephthah, David, Samuel and
the prophets, 33who through faith conquered kingdoms, administered justice,
and gained what was promised; who
shut the mouths of lions, 34quenched the
fury of the flames, and escaped the edge
of the sword; whose weakness was
turned to strength; and who became
powerful in battle and routed foreign armies. 35Women received back their dead,
raised to life again. Others were tortured
and refused to be released, so that they
might gain a better resurrection. 36Some
faced jeers and flogging, while still others were chained and put in prison.
37They were stoned[c]; they were sawed in
two; they were put to death by the sword.
They went about in sheepskins and
goatskins, destitute, persecuted and mistreated— 38the world was not worthy of

[a] 29 That is, Sea of Reeds [b] 31 Or *unbelieving*
[c] 37 Some early manuscripts *stoned; they were put to the test;*

them. They wandered in deserts and mountains, and in caves and holes in the ground.
[39]These were all commended for their faith, yet none of them received what had been promised. [40]God had planned something better for us so that only together with us would they be made perfect.

PRAYER: THE CHARACTER I WANT TO CULTIVATE

THOSE who are simple believe everything, but prudent people consider their steps. (Proverbs 14:15) . . . Prudent people see evil and hide themselves, but the simple keep going and suffer for it. (Proverbs 22:3; 27:12)

***TAKE** a moment to ask the Lord for the grace to grow in godly character.*

YEAR 1
DAY 275

OT 2 Samuel 15:1–37

Absalom's Conspiracy

15 In the course of time, Absalom provided himself with a chariot and
horses and with fifty men to run ahead of
him. [2]He would get up early and stand by
the side of the road leading to the city
gate. Whenever anyone came with a complaint to be placed before the king for a
decision, Absalom would call out to him,
"What town are you from?" He would answer, "Your servant is from one of the
tribes of Israel." [3]Then Absalom would
say to him, "Look, your claims are valid
and proper, but there is no representative
of the king to hear you." [4]And Absalom
would add, "If only I were appointed
judge in the land! Then everyone who has
a complaint or case could come to me
and I would see that he gets justice."
[5]Also, whenever anyone approached
him to bow down before him, Absalom
would reach out his hand, take hold of
him and kiss him. [6]Absalom behaved in
this way toward all the Israelites who
came to the king asking for justice, and so
he stole the hearts of the men of Israel.
[7]At the end of four[a] years, Absalom said
to the king, "Let me go to Hebron and fulfill a vow I made to the LORD. [8]While your
servant was living at Geshur in Aram, I
made this vow: 'If the LORD takes me back
to Jerusalem, I will worship the LORD in
Hebron.[b]' "
[9]The king said to him, "Go in peace."
So he went to Hebron.
[10]Then Absalom sent secret messengers
throughout the tribes of Israel to say, "As
soon as you hear the sound of the trumpets, then say, 'Absalom is king in Hebron.' " [11]Two hundred men from Jerusalem had accompanied Absalom. They
had been invited as guests and went quite
innocently, knowing nothing about the
matter. [12]While Absalom was offering sacrifices, he also sent for Ahithophel the Gilonite, David's counselor, to come from
Giloh, his hometown. And so the conspiracy gained strength, and Absalom's
following kept on increasing.

David Flees

[13]A messenger came and told David,
"The hearts of the men of Israel are with
Absalom."
[14]Then David said to all his officials
who were with him in Jerusalem, "Come!
We must flee, or none of us will escape
from Absalom. We must leave immediately, or he will move quickly to overtake
us and bring ruin upon us and put the city
to the sword."
[15]The king's officials answered him,
"Your servants are ready to do whatever
our lord the king chooses."
[16]The king set out, with his entire
household following him; but he left ten
concubines to take care of the palace. [17]So
the king set out, with all the people following him, and they halted at a place
some distance away. [18]All his men

[a] 7 Some Septuagint manuscripts, Syriac and Josephus; Hebrew *forty* [b] 8 Some Septuagint manuscripts; Hebrew does not have *in Hebron.*

marched past him, along with all the Kerethites and Pelethites; and all the six hundred Gittites who had accompanied him
from Gath marched before the king.
[19]The king said to Ittai the Gittite, "Why
should you come along with us? Go back
and stay with King Absalom. You are a
foreigner, an exile from your homeland.
[20]You came only yesterday. And today
shall I make you wander about with us,
when I do not know where I am going?
Go back, and take your countrymen. May
kindness and faithfulness be with you."
[21]But Ittai replied to the king, "As surely as the LORD lives, and as my lord the
king lives, wherever my lord the king may
be, whether it means life or death, there
will your servant be."
[22]David said to Ittai, "Go ahead, march
on." So Ittai the Gittite marched on with
all his men and the families that were
with him.
[23]The whole countryside wept aloud as
all the people passed by. The king also
crossed the Kidron Valley, and all the people moved on toward the desert.
[24]Zadok was there, too, and all the Levites who were with him were carrying the
ark of the covenant of God. They set down
the ark of God, and Abiathar offered sacrifices[c] until all the people had finished
leaving the city.
[25]Then the king said to Zadok, "Take the
ark of God back into the city. If I find favor in the LORD's eyes, he will bring me
back and let me see it and his dwelling
place again. [26]But if he says, 'I am not
pleased with you,' then I am ready; let him
do to me whatever seems good to him."
[27]The king also said to Zadok the priest,
"Aren't you a seer? Go back to the city in
peace, with your son Ahimaaz and Jonathan son of Abiathar. You and Abiathar
take your two sons with you. [28]I will wait
at the fords in the desert until word comes
from you to inform me." [29]So Zadok and
Abiathar took the ark of God back to Jerusalem and stayed there.
[30]But David continued up the Mount of
Olives, weeping as he went; his head was
covered and he was barefoot. All the people with him covered their heads too and
were weeping as they went up. [31]Now David had been told, "Ahithophel is among
the conspirators with Absalom." So David
prayed, "O LORD, turn Ahithophel's counsel into foolishness."
[32]When David arrived at the summit,
where people used to worship God, Hushai the Arkite was there to meet him, his
robe torn and dust on his head. [33]David
said to him, "If you go with me, you will
be a burden to me. [34]But if you return to
the city and say to Absalom, 'I will be your
servant, O king; I was your father's servant
in the past, but now I will be your servant,'
then you can help me by frustrating
Ahithophel's advice. [35]Won't the priests
Zadok and Abiathar be there with you?
Tell them anything you hear in the king's
palace. [36]Their two sons, Ahimaaz son of
Zadok and Jonathan son of Abiathar, are
there with them. Send them to me with
anything you hear."
[37]So David's friend Hushai arrived at
Jerusalem as Absalom was entering the city.

[c] 24 Or *Abiathar went up*

PRAYER: CONFESSION

***THE refining pot is for silver and the furnace for gold, but You, O Lord, test the heart.* (Proverbs 17:3)**

***ASK** the Spirit to search your heart and reveal any areas of unconfessed sin. Acknowledge these to the Lord and thank Him for His forgiveness.*

NT Hebrews 12:1-13

God Disciplines His Sons

12 Therefore, since we are surrounded by
such a great cloud of witnesses, let us
throw off everything that hinders and the
sin that so easily entangles, and let us run
with perseverance the race marked out for
us. [2]Let us fix our eyes on Jesus, the author and perfecter of our faith, who for
the joy set before him endured the cross,
scorning its shame, and sat down at the
right hand of the throne of God. [3]Con-

sider him who endured such opposition from sinful men, so that you will not grow weary and lose heart.

4In your struggle against sin, you have not yet resisted to the point of shedding your blood. 5And you have forgotten that word of encouragement that addresses you as sons:

"My son, do not make light of the
Lord's discipline,
and do not lose heart when he
rebukes you,
6because the Lord disciplines those he
loves,
and he punishes everyone he
accepts as a son."[a]

7Endure hardship as discipline; God is treating you as sons. For what son is not disciplined by his father? 8If you are not disciplined (and everyone undergoes discipline), then you are illegitimate children and not true sons. 9Moreover, we have all had human fathers who disciplined us and we respected them for it. How much more should we submit to the Father of our spirits and live! 10Our fathers disciplined us for a little while as they thought best; but God disciplines us for our good, that we may share in his holiness. 11No discipline seems pleasant at the time, but painful. Later on, however, it produces a harvest of righteousness and peace for those who have been trained by it.

12Therefore, strengthen your feeble arms and weak knees. 13"Make level paths for your feet,"[b] so that the lame may not be disabled, but rather healed.

[a] *6* Prov. 3:11,12 [b] *13* Prov. 4:26

PRAYER: MY RELATIONSHIP TO OTHERS

I WILL bless those who persecute me; I will bless and not curse. (Romans 12:14) . . . I will bear with others and forgive whatever complaints I have against them; I will forgive just as You, Lord, forgave me. (Colossians 3:13)

***PAUSE** to review your relationships with others and to commit them to the Lord.*

YEAR 1 DAY 276

OT 2 Samuel 16:1–17:29

David and Ziba

16 When David had gone a short distance beyond the summit, there was Ziba, the steward of Mephibosheth, waiting to meet him. He had a string of donkeys saddled and loaded with two hundred loaves of bread, a hundred cakes of raisins, a hundred cakes of figs and a skin of wine.

2The king asked Ziba, "Why have you brought these?"

Ziba answered, "The donkeys are for the king's household to ride on, the bread and fruit are for the men to eat, and the wine is to refresh those who become exhausted in the desert."

3The king then asked, "Where is your master's grandson?"

Ziba said to him, "He is staying in Jerusalem, because he thinks, 'Today the house of Israel will give me back my grandfather's kingdom.' "

4Then the king said to Ziba, "All that belonged to Mephibosheth is now yours."

"I humbly bow," Ziba said. "May I find favor in your eyes, my lord the king."

Shimei Curses David

5As King David approached Bahurim, a man from the same clan as Saul's family came out from there. His name was Shimei son of Gera, and he cursed as he came out. 6He pelted David and all the king's officials with stones, though all the troops and the special guard were on David's right and left. 7As he cursed, Shimei said, "Get out, get out, you man of blood, you scoundrel! 8The LORD has repaid you for all the blood you shed in the household

of Saul, in whose place you have reigned.
The LORD has handed the kingdom over
to your son Absalom. You have come to
ruin because you are a man of blood!"
9 Then Abishai son of Zeruiah said to
the king, "Why should this dead dog curse
my lord the king? Let me go over and cut
off his head."
10 But the king said, "What do you and
I have in common, you sons of Zeruiah?
If he is cursing because the LORD said to
him, 'Curse David,' who can ask, 'Why do
you do this?' "
11 David then said to Abishai and all his
officials, "My son, who is of my own flesh,
is trying to take my life. How much more,
then, this Benjamite! Leave him alone; let
him curse, for the LORD has told him to.
12 It may be that the LORD will see my distress and repay me with good for the cursing I am receiving today."
13 So David and his men continued
along the road while Shimei was going
along the hillside opposite him, cursing
as he went and throwing stones at him
and showering him with dirt. 14 The king
and all the people with him arrived at
their destination exhausted. And there he
refreshed himself.

The Advice of Hushai and Ahithophel

15 Meanwhile, Absalom and all the men
of Israel came to Jerusalem, and
Ahithophel was with him. 16 Then Hushai
the Arkite, David's friend, went to Absalom and said to him, "Long live the king!
Long live the king!"
17 Absalom asked Hushai, "Is this the
love you show your friend? Why didn't
you go with your friend?"
18 Hushai said to Absalom, "No, the one
chosen by the LORD, by these people, and
by all the men of Israel—his I will be, and
I will remain with him. 19 Furthermore,
whom should I serve? Should I not serve
the son? Just as I served your father, so I
will serve you."
20 Absalom said to Ahithophel, "Give us
your advice. What should we do?"
21 Ahithophel answered, "Lie with your
father's concubines whom he left to take
care of the palace. Then all Israel will hear
that you have made yourself a stench in
your father's nostrils, and the hands of
everyone with you will be strengthened."
22 So they pitched a tent for Absalom on
the roof, and he lay with his father's concubines in the sight of all Israel.
23 Now in those days the advice Ahithophel gave was like that of one who in-
quires of God. That was how both David
and Absalom regarded all of Ahithophel's
advice.

17 Ahithophel said to Absalom, "I would[a]
choose twelve thousand men and set
out tonight in pursuit of David. 2 I would[b]
attack him while he is weary and weak. I
would[b] strike him with terror, and then all
the people with him will flee. I would[b]
strike down only the king 3 and bring all
the people back to you. The death of the
man you seek will mean the return of all;
all the people will be unharmed." 4 This
plan seemed good to Absalom and to all
the elders of Israel.
5 But Absalom said, "Summon also Hushai the Arkite, so we can hear what he
has to say." 6 When Hushai came to him,
Absalom said, "Ahithophel has given this
advice. Should we do what he says? If not,
give us your opinion."
7 Hushai replied to Absalom, "The advice Ahithophel has given is not good this
time. 8 You know your father and his men;
they are fighters, and as fierce as a wild
bear robbed of her cubs. Besides, your father is an experienced fighter; he will not
spend the night with the troops. 9 Even
now, he is hidden in a cave or some other place. If he should attack your troops
first,[c] whoever hears about it will say,
'There has been a slaughter among the
troops who follow Absalom.' 10 Then even
the bravest soldier, whose heart is like the
heart of a lion, will melt with fear, for all
Israel knows that your father is a fighter
and that those with him are brave.
11 "So I advise you: Let all Israel, from
Dan to Beersheba—as numerous as the
sand on the seashore—be gathered to
you, with you yourself leading them into
battle. 12 Then we will attack him wherever he may be found, and we will fall on
him as dew settles on the ground. Neither
he nor any of his men will be left alive.
13 If he withdraws into a city, then all Israel will bring ropes to that city, and we will
drag it down to the valley until not even
a piece of it can be found."
14 Absalom and all the men of Israel

[a] 1 Or *Let me* [b] 2 Or *will* [c] 9 Or *When some of the men fall at the first attack*

said, "The advice of Hushai the Arkite is better than that of Ahithophel." For the LORD had determined to frustrate the good advice of Ahithophel in order to bring disaster on Absalom.

15 Hushai told Zadok and Abiathar, the priests, "Ahithophel has advised Absalom and the elders of Israel to do such and such, but I have advised them to do so and so. 16 Now send a message immediately and tell David, 'Do not spend the night at the fords in the desert; cross over without fail, or the king and all the people with him will be swallowed up.' "

17 Jonathan and Ahimaaz were staying at En Rogel. A servant girl was to go and inform them, and they were to go and tell King David, for they could not risk being seen entering the city. 18 But a young man saw them and told Absalom. So the two of them left quickly and went to the house of a man in Bahurim. He had a well in his courtyard, and they climbed down into it. 19 His wife took a covering and spread it out over the opening of the well and scattered grain over it. No one knew anything about it.

20 When Absalom's men came to the woman at the house, they asked, "Where are Ahimaaz and Jonathan?"

The woman answered them, "They crossed over the brook."[d] The men searched but found no one, so they returned to Jerusalem.

21 After the men had gone, the two climbed out of the well and went to inform King David. They said to him, "Set out and cross the river at once; Ahithophel has advised such and such against you." 22 So David and all the people with him set out and crossed the Jordan. By daybreak, no one was left who had not crossed the Jordan.

23 When Ahithophel saw that his advice had not been followed, he saddled his donkey and set out for his house in his hometown. He put his house in order and then hanged himself. So he died and was buried in his father's tomb.

24 David went to Mahanaim, and Absalom crossed the Jordan with all the men of Israel. 25 Absalom had appointed Amasa over the army in place of Joab. Amasa was the son of a man named Jether,[e] an Israelite[f] who had married Abigail,[g] the daughter of Nahash and sister of Zeruiah the mother of Joab. 26 The Israelites and Absalom camped in the land of Gilead.

27 When David came to Mahanaim, Shobi son of Nahash from Rabbah of the Ammonites, and Makir son of Ammiel from Lo Debar, and Barzillai the Gileadite from Rogelim 28 brought bedding and bowls and articles of pottery. They also brought wheat and barley, flour and roasted grain, beans and lentils,[h] 29 honey and curds, sheep, and cheese from cows' milk for David and his people to eat. For they said, "The people have become hungry and tired and thirsty in the desert."

[d] 20 Or *"They passed by the sheep pen toward the water."* [e] 25 Hebrew *Ithra*, a variant of *Jether* [f] 25 Hebrew and some Septuagint manuscripts; other Septuagint manuscripts (see also 1 Chron. 2:17) *Ishmaelite* or *Jezreelite* [g] 25 Hebrew *Abigal*, a variant of *Abigail* [h] 28 Most Septuagint manuscripts and Syriac; Hebrew *lentils, and roasted grain*

PRAYER: RENEWAL

May I know You, O Lord, and serve You with my whole heart and with a willing mind; for You search all hearts and understand every motive behind the thoughts. (1 Chronicles 28:9) . . . May I imitate You, O God, as a beloved child, and walk in love, just as Christ loved me and gave Himself up for me as a fragrant offering and sacrifice to You. (Ephesians 5:1–2)

__PAUSE__ to add your own prayers for personal renewal.

NT Hebrews 12:14–29

Warning Against Refusing God

14Make every effort to live in peace with all men and to be holy; without holiness no one will see the Lord. 15See to it that no one misses the grace of God and that no bitter root grows up to cause trouble and defile many. 16See that no one is sexually immoral, or is godless like Esau, who for a single meal sold his inheritance rights as the oldest son. 17Afterward, as you know, when he wanted to inherit this blessing, he was rejected. He could bring about no change of mind, though he sought the blessing with tears.

18You have not come to a mountain that can be touched and that is burning with fire; to darkness, gloom and storm; 19to a trumpet blast or to such a voice speaking words that those who heard it begged that no further word be spoken to them, 20because they could not bear what was commanded: "If even an animal touches the mountain, it must be stoned."[a] 21The sight was so terrifying that Moses said, "I am trembling with fear."[b]

22But you have come to Mount Zion, to the heavenly Jerusalem, the city of the living God. You have come to thousands upon thousands of angels in joyful assembly, 23to the church of the firstborn, whose names are written in heaven. You have come to God, the judge of all men, to the spirits of righteous men made perfect, 24to Jesus the mediator of a new covenant, and to the sprinkled blood that speaks a better word than the blood of Abel.

25See to it that you do not refuse him who speaks. If they did not escape when they refused him who warned them on earth, how much less will we, if we turn away from him who warns us from heaven? 26At that time his voice shook the earth, but now he has promised, "Once more I will shake not only the earth but also the heavens."[c] 27The words "once more" indicate the removing of what can be shaken—that is, created things—so that what cannot be shaken may remain.

28Therefore, since we are receiving a kingdom that cannot be shaken, let us be thankful, and so worship God acceptably with reverence and awe, 29for our "God is a consuming fire."[d]

[a] *20* Exodus 19:12,13 [b] *21* Deut. 9:19
[c] *26* Haggai 2:6 [d] *29* Deut. 4:24

PRAYER: THE ATTRIBUTES OF GOD

WHO has understood what is in Your mind, O Lord, or instructed You as Your counselor? Whom did You consult to enlighten You, and who taught You the path of justice? Who taught You knowledge or showed You the way of understanding? Surely the nations are like a drop in a bucket; they are regarded as dust on the scales; You weigh the islands as though they were fine dust. Before You all the nations are as nothing; You regard them as less than nothing and worthless. To whom, then, will I compare You, O God? Or what likeness will I compare with You? (Isaiah 40:13–15, 17–18)

__PAUSE__ to reflect on these affirmations about the person, powers and perfection of God.

OT Proverbs 12

YEAR 1 DAY 277

12 Whoever loves discipline loves
knowledge,
but he who hates correction is
stupid.

2A good man obtains favor from the
LORD,
but the LORD condemns a crafty
man.

[3]A man cannot be established through wickedness,
but the righteous cannot be uprooted.

[4]A wife of noble character is her husband's crown,
but a disgraceful wife is like decay in his bones.

[5]The plans of the righteous are just,
but the advice of the wicked is deceitful.

[6]The words of the wicked lie in wait for blood,
but the speech of the upright rescues them.

[7]Wicked men are overthrown and are no more,
but the house of the righteous stands firm.

[8]A man is praised according to his wisdom,
but men with warped minds are despised.

[9]Better to be a nobody and yet have a servant
than pretend to be somebody and have no food.

[10]A righteous man cares for the needs of his animal,
but the kindest acts of the wicked are cruel.

[11]He who works his land will have abundant food,
but he who chases fantasies lacks judgment.

[12]The wicked desire the plunder of evil men,
but the root of the righteous flourishes.

[13]An evil man is trapped by his sinful talk,
but a righteous man escapes trouble.

[14]From the fruit of his lips a man is filled with good things
as surely as the work of his hands rewards him.

[15]The way of a fool seems right to him,
but a wise man listens to advice.

[16]A fool shows his annoyance at once,
but a prudent man overlooks an insult.

[17]A truthful witness gives honest testimony,
but a false witness tells lies.

[18]Reckless words pierce like a sword,
but the tongue of the wise brings healing.

[19]Truthful lips endure forever,
but a lying tongue lasts only a moment.

[20]There is deceit in the hearts of those who plot evil,
but joy for those who promote peace.

[21]No harm befalls the righteous,
but the wicked have their fill of trouble.

[22]The LORD detests lying lips,
but he delights in men who are truthful.

[23]A prudent man keeps his knowledge to himself,
but the heart of fools blurts out folly.

[24]Diligent hands will rule,
but laziness ends in slave labor.

[25]An anxious heart weighs a man down,
but a kind word cheers him up.

[26]A righteous man is cautious in friendship,[a]
but the way of the wicked leads them astray.

[27]The lazy man does not roast[b] his game,
but the diligent man prizes his possessions.

[28]In the way of righteousness there is life;
along that path is immortality.

[a] 26 Or *man is a guide to his neighbor* [b] 27 The meaning of the Hebrew for this word is uncertain.

PRAYER: PETITION

***MAY I not love the world or the things in the world. If I love the world, Your love, O Father, is not in me. For all that is in the world—the lust of the flesh, the lust of the eyes, and the pride of life—is not of You, Father, but of the world. And the world and its lusts are passing away, but the one who does Your will abides forever.** (1 John 2:15–17)*

***PAUSE** here to petition God to help you be a faithful steward of your time, talents, possessions and relationships. Offer prayers of petition regarding your activities for this day and any special concerns you may have.*

NT Hebrews 13:1–25

Concluding Exhortations

13 Keep on loving each other as brothers. 2Do not forget to entertain strangers, for by so doing some people have entertained angels without knowing it. 3Remember those in prison as if you were their fellow prisoners, and those who are mistreated as if you yourselves were suffering.

4Marriage should be honored by all, and the marriage bed kept pure, for God will judge the adulterer and all the sexually immoral. 5Keep your lives free from the love of money and be content with what you have, because God has said,

"Never will I leave you;
never will I forsake you."[a]

6So we say with confidence,

"The Lord is my helper; I will not be afraid.
What can man do to me?"[b]

7Remember your leaders, who spoke the word of God to you. Consider the outcome of their way of life and imitate their faith. 8Jesus Christ is the same yesterday and today and forever.

9Do not be carried away by all kinds of strange teachings. It is good for our hearts to be strengthened by grace, not by ceremonial foods, which are of no value to those who eat them. 10We have an altar from which those who minister at the tabernacle have no right to eat.

11The high priest carries the blood of animals into the Most Holy Place as a sin offering, but the bodies are burned outside the camp. 12And so Jesus also suffered outside the city gate to make the people holy through his own blood. 13Let us, then, go to him outside the camp, bearing the disgrace he bore. 14For here we do not have an enduring city, but we are looking for the city that is to come.

15Through Jesus, therefore, let us continually offer to God a sacrifice of praise—the fruit of lips that confess his name. 16And do not forget to do good and to share with others, for with such sacrifices God is pleased.

17Obey your leaders and submit to their authority. They keep watch over you as men who must give an account. Obey them so that their work will be a joy, not a burden, for that would be of no advantage to you.

18Pray for us. We are sure that we have a clear conscience and desire to live honorably in every way. 19I particularly urge you to pray so that I may be restored to you soon.

20May the God of peace, who through the blood of the eternal covenant brought back from the dead our Lord Jesus, that great Shepherd of the sheep, 21equip you with everything good for doing his will, and may he work in us what is pleasing to him, through Jesus Christ, to whom be glory for ever and ever. Amen.

22Brothers, I urge you to bear with my word of exhortation, for I have written you only a short letter.

23I want you to know that our brother Timothy has been released. If he arrives soon, I will come with him to see you.

24Greet all your leaders and all God's people. Those from Italy send you their greetings.

25Grace be with you all.

[a] 5 Deut. 31:6 [b] 6 Psalm 118:6,7

PRAYER: THE WORKS OF GOD

WHAT the law was powerless to do, in that it was weakened through the flesh, You did, O God, by sending Your own Son in the likeness of sinful flesh, on account of sin; You condemned sin in the flesh, in order that the requirement of the law might be fully met in us, who do not walk according to the flesh, but according to Your Spirit. (Romans 8:3–4)

__TAKE__ a moment to consider the greatness of God's wonderful works.

YEAR 1 DAY 278

OT 2 Samuel 18:1–33

Absalom's Death

18 David mustered the men who were
with him and appointed over them
commanders of thousands and commanders of hundreds. 2David sent the
troops out—a third under the command
of Joab, a third under Joab's brother
Abishai son of Zeruiah, and a third under
Ittai the Gittite. The king told the troops,
"I myself will surely march out with you."
3But the men said, "You must not go
out; if we are forced to flee, they won't
care about us. Even if half of us die, they
won't care; but you are worth ten thousand of us.[a] It would be better now for
you to give us support from the city."
4The king answered, "I will do whatever seems best to you."
So the king stood beside the gate while
all the men marched out in units of hundreds and of thousands. 5The king commanded Joab, Abishai and Ittai, "Be gentle with the young man Absalom for my
sake." And all the troops heard the king
giving orders concerning Absalom to each
of the commanders.
6The army marched into the field to fight
Israel, and the battle took place in the forest of Ephraim. 7There the army of Israel
was defeated by David's men, and the casualties that day were great—twenty thousand men. 8The battle spread out over the
whole countryside, and the forest claimed
more lives that day than the sword.
9Now Absalom happened to meet David's men. He was riding his mule, and as
the mule went under the thick branches
of a large oak, Absalom's head got caught
in the tree. He was left hanging in midair,
while the mule he was riding kept on going.
10When one of the men saw this, he told
Joab, "I just saw Absalom hanging in an
oak tree."
11Joab said to the man who had told
him this, "What! You saw him? Why
didn't you strike him to the ground right
there? Then I would have had to give you
ten shekels[b] of silver and a warrior's belt."
12But the man replied, "Even if a thousand shekels[c] were weighed out into my
hands, I would not lift my hand against
the king's son. In our hearing the king
commanded you and Abishai and Ittai,
'Protect the young man Absalom for my
sake.[d]' 13And if I had put my life in jeopardy[e]—and nothing is hidden from the
king—you would have kept your distance
from me."
14Joab said, "I'm not going to wait like
this for you." So he took three javelins in
his hand and plunged them into Absalom's heart while Absalom was still alive
in the oak tree. 15And ten of Joab's armor-
bearers surrounded Absalom, struck him
and killed him.
16Then Joab sounded the trumpet, and
the troops stopped pursuing Israel, for
Joab halted them. 17They took Absalom,
threw him into a big pit in the forest and
piled up a large heap of rocks over him.
Meanwhile, all the Israelites fled to their
homes.
18During his lifetime Absalom had tak-

[a] 3 Two Hebrew manuscripts, some Septuagint manuscripts and Vulgate; most Hebrew manuscripts *care; for now there are ten thousand like us* [b] *11* That is, about 4 ounces (about 115 grams) [c] *12* That is, about 25 pounds (about 11 kilograms) [d] *12* A few Hebrew manuscripts, Septuagint, Vulgate and Syriac; most Hebrew manuscripts may be translated *Absalom, whoever you may be.* [e] *13* Or *Otherwise, if I had acted treacherously toward him*

en a pillar and erected it in the King's Valley as a monument to himself, for he
thought, "I have no son to carry on the
memory of my name." He named the pillar after himself, and it is called Absalom's
Monument to this day.

David Mourns

19 Now Ahimaaz son of Zadok said, "Let
me run and take the news to the king that
the LORD has delivered him from the hand
of his enemies."
20 "You are not the one to take the news
today," Joab told him. "You may take the
news another time, but you must not do
so today, because the king's son is dead."
21 Then Joab said to a Cushite, "Go, tell
the king what you have seen." The Cushite bowed down before Joab and ran off.
22 Ahimaaz son of Zadok again said to
Joab, "Come what may, please let me run
behind the Cushite."
But Joab replied, "My son, why do you
want to go? You don't have any news that
will bring you a reward."
23 He said, "Come what may, I want to
run."
So Joab said, "Run!" Then Ahimaaz ran
by way of the plain[f] and outran the Cushite.
24 While David was sitting between the
inner and outer gates, the watchman went
up to the roof of the gateway by the wall.
As he looked out, he saw a man running
alone. 25 The watchman called out to the
king and reported it.
The king said, "If he is alone, he must
have good news." And the man came closer and closer.
26 Then the watchman saw another man
running, and he called down to the gatekeeper, "Look, another man running
alone!"
The king said, "He must be bringing
good news, too."
27 The watchman said, "It seems to me
that the first one runs like Ahimaaz son of
Zadok."
"He's a good man," the king said. "He
comes with good news."
28 Then Ahimaaz called out to the king,
"All is well!" He bowed down before the
king with his face to the ground and said,
"Praise be to the LORD your God! He has
delivered up the men who lifted their
hands against my lord the king."
29 The king asked, "Is the young man
Absalom safe?"
Ahimaaz answered, "I saw great confusion just as Joab was about to send the
king's servant and me, your servant, but I
don't know what it was."
30 The king said, "Stand aside and wait
here." So he stepped aside and stood
there.
31 Then the Cushite arrived and said,
"My lord the king, hear the good news!
The LORD has delivered you today from all
who rose up against you."
32 The king asked the Cushite, "Is the
young man Absalom safe?"
The Cushite replied, "May the enemies
of my lord the king and all who rise up to
harm you be like that young man."
33 The king was shaken. He went up to
the room over the gateway and wept. As
he went, he said: "O my son Absalom! My
son, my son Absalom! If only I had died
instead of you—O Absalom, my son, my
son!"

f23 That is, the plain of the Jordan

PRAYER: INTERCESSION

YOU, O Lord, have said, "If My people, who are called by My name, will humble themselves and pray and seek My face and turn from their wicked ways, then I will hear from heaven and will forgive their sin and heal their land." (2 Chronicles 7:14)

TAKE *a few moments to intercede on behalf of your local, state or provincial, and national governments. Pray for spiritual revival in the nation and offer prayers regarding current events and concerns.*

NT James 1:1-18

1 James, a servant of God and of the Lord
Jesus Christ,

To the twelve tribes scattered among the
nations:

Greetings.

Trials and Temptations

2Consider it pure joy, my brothers,
whenever you face trials of many kinds,
3because you know that the testing of
your faith develops perseverance. 4Perse-
verance must finish its work so that you
may be mature and complete, not lacking
anything. 5If any of you lacks wisdom, he
should ask God, who gives generously to
all without finding fault, and it will be
given to him. 6But when he asks, he must
believe and not doubt, because he who
doubts is like a wave of the sea, blown
and tossed by the wind. 7That man should
not think he will receive anything from
the Lord; 8he is a double-minded man,
unstable in all he does.
9The brother in humble circumstances
ought to take pride in his high position.
10But the one who is rich should take
pride in his low position, because he will
pass away like a wild flower. 11For the sun
rises with scorching heat and withers the
plant; its blossom falls and its beauty is
destroyed. In the same way, the rich man
will fade away even while he goes about
his business.
12Blessed is the man who perseveres under trial, because when he has stood the
test, he will receive the crown of life that
God has promised to those who love him.
13When tempted, no one should say,
"God is tempting me." For God cannot be
tempted by evil, nor does he tempt anyone; 14but each one is tempted when, by
his own evil desire, he is dragged away
and enticed. 15Then, after desire has conceived, it gives birth to sin; and sin, when
it is full-grown, gives birth to death.
16Don't be deceived, my dear brothers.
17Every good and perfect gift is from
above, coming down from the Father of
the heavenly lights, who does not change
like shifting shadows. 18He chose to give
us birth through the word of truth, that
we might be a kind of firstfruits of all he
created.

PRAYER: MY RELATIONSHIP TO GOD

YOU must increase, O Christ; I must decrease. (John 3:30) . . . Lord Jesus, I thank you for Your word of truth, that unless a grain of wheat falls to the ground and dies, it remains alone. But if it dies, it bears much fruit. Those who love their lives will lose them, and those who hate their lives in this world will keep them for eternal life. (John 12:24–25)

***PAUSE** to thank God for the relationship that you enjoy with Him in Jesus Christ.*

YEAR 1 DAY 279

OT 2 Samuel 19:1-43

19 Joab was told, "The king is weeping
and mourning for Absalom." 2And for
the whole army the victory that day was
turned into mourning, because on that
day the troops heard it said, "The king is
grieving for his son." 3The men stole into
the city that day as men steal in who are
ashamed when they flee from battle. 4The
king covered his face and cried aloud,
"O my son Absalom! O Absalom, my son,
my son!"
5Then Joab went into the house to the
king and said, "Today you have humiliated all your men, who have just saved your
life and the lives of your sons and daughters and the lives of your wives and concubines. 6You love those who hate you
and hate those who love you. You have

made it clear today that the commanders
and their men mean nothing to you. I see
that you would be pleased if Absalom
were alive today and all of us were dead.
[7]Now go out and encourage your men. I
swear by the LORD that if you don't go out,
not a man will be left with you by nightfall. This will be worse for you than all the
calamities that have come upon you from
your youth till now."

[8]So the king got up and took his seat in
the gateway. When the men were told,
"The king is sitting in the gateway," they
all came before him.

David Returns to Jerusalem

Meanwhile, the Israelites had fled to
their homes. [9]Throughout the tribes of Israel, the people were all arguing with each
other, saying, "The king delivered us from
the hand of our enemies; he is the one
who rescued us from the hand of the Philistines. But now he has fled the country
because of Absalom; [10]and Absalom,
whom we anointed to rule over us, has
died in battle. So why do you say nothing
about bringing the king back?"

[11]King David sent this message to Zadok
and Abiathar, the priests: "Ask the elders
of Judah, 'Why should you be the last to
bring the king back to his palace, since
what is being said throughout Israel has
reached the king at his quarters? [12]You are
my brothers, my own flesh and blood. So
why should you be the last to bring back
the king?' [13]And say to Amasa, 'Are you
not my own flesh and blood? May God
deal with me, be it ever so severely, if from
now on you are not the commander of
my army in place of Joab.' "

[14]He won over the hearts of all the men
of Judah as though they were one man.
They sent word to the king, "Return, you
and all your men." [15]Then the king returned and went as far as the Jordan.

Now the men of Judah had come to
Gilgal to go out and meet the king and
bring him across the Jordan. [16]Shimei son
of Gera, the Benjamite from Bahurim,
hurried down with the men of Judah to
meet King David. [17]With him were a thousand Benjamites, along with Ziba, the
steward of Saul's household, and his fifteen sons and twenty servants. They
rushed to the Jordan, where the king was.
[18]They crossed at the ford to take the
king's household over and to do whatever he wished.

When Shimei son of Gera crossed the
Jordan, he fell prostrate before the king
[19]and said to him, "May my lord not hold
me guilty. Do not remember how your
servant did wrong on the day my lord the
king left Jerusalem. May the king put it
out of his mind. [20]For I your servant know
that I have sinned, but today I have come
here as the first of the whole house of Joseph to come down and meet my lord the
king."

[21]Then Abishai son of Zeruiah said,
"Shouldn't Shimei be put to death for
this? He cursed the LORD's anointed."

[22]David replied, "What do you and I
have in common, you sons of Zeruiah?
This day you have become my adversaries! Should anyone be put to death in
Israel today? Do I not know that today I
am king over Israel?" [23]So the king said to
Shimei, "You shall not die." And the king
promised him on oath.

[24]Mephibosheth, Saul's grandson, also
went down to meet the king. He had not
taken care of his feet or trimmed his mus-
tache or washed his clothes from the day
the king left until the day he returned
safely. [25]When he came from Jerusalem to
meet the king, the king asked him, "Why
didn't you go with me, Mephibosheth?"

[26]He said, "My lord the king, since I
your servant am lame, I said, 'I will have
my donkey saddled and will ride on it, so
I can go with the king.' But Ziba my servant betrayed me. [27]And he has slandered
your servant to my lord the king. My lord
the king is like an angel of God; so do
whatever pleases you. [28]All my grandfather's descendants deserved nothing but
death from my lord the king, but you gave
your servant a place among those who eat
at your table. So what right do I have to
make any more appeals to the king?"

[29]The king said to him, "Why say more?
I order you and Ziba to divide the fields."

[30]Mephibosheth said to the king, "Let
him take everything, now that my lord the
king has arrived home safely."

[31]Barzillai the Gileadite also came down
from Rogelim to cross the Jordan with the
king and to send him on his way from
there. [32]Now Barzillai was a very old man,
eighty years of age. He had provided for
the king during his stay in Mahanaim, for
he was a very wealthy man. [33]The king

said to Barzillai, "Cross over with me and
stay with me in Jerusalem, and I will provide for you."
34But Barzillai answered the king, "How
many more years will I live, that I should
go up to Jerusalem with the king? 35I am
now eighty years old. Can I tell the difference between what is good and what is not?
Can your servant taste what he eats and
drinks? Can I still hear the voices of men
and women singers? Why should your servant be an added burden to my lord the
king? 36Your servant will cross over the Jordan with the king for a short distance, but
why should the king reward me in this way?
37Let your servant return, that I may die in
my own town near the tomb of my father
and mother. But here is your servant Kimham. Let him cross over with my lord the
king. Do for him whatever pleases you."
38The king said, "Kimham shall cross
over with me, and I will do for him whatever pleases you. And anything you desire
from me I will do for you."
39So all the people crossed the Jordan,
and then the king crossed over. The king
kissed Barzillai and gave him his blessing,
and Barzillai returned to his home.
40When the king crossed over to Gilgal,
Kimham crossed with him. All the troops
of Judah and half the troops of Israel had
taken the king over.
41Soon all the men of Israel were coming to the king and saying to him, "Why
did our brothers, the men of Judah, steal
the king away and bring him and his
household across the Jordan, together
with all his men?"
42All the men of Judah answered the
men of Israel, "We did this because the
king is closely related to us. Why are you
angry about it? Have we eaten any of the
king's provisions? Have we taken anything
for ourselves?"
43Then the men of Israel answered the
men of Judah, "We have ten shares in the
king; and besides, we have a greater claim
on David than you have. So why do you
treat us with contempt? Were we not the
first to speak of bringing back our king?"
But the men of Judah responded even
more harshly than the men of Israel.

PRAYER: AFFIRMATION

CLEARLY no one is justified before You, O God, by the law, for, "The righteous will live by faith." Lord Jesus Christ, before faith in You came, we were guarded by the law, confined until the faith was later revealed. So the law has become our tutor to lead us to You, that we might be justified by faith. Now that faith has come, we are no longer under a tutor.

(Galatians 3:11, 23–25)

***PAUSE** to reflect on these Biblical affirmations.*

NT James 1:19–27

Listening and Doing

19My dear brothers, take note of this:
Everyone should be quick to listen, slow
to speak and slow to become angry, 20for
man's anger does not bring about the
righteous life that God desires. 21There-
fore, get rid of all moral filth and the evil
that is so prevalent and humbly accept the
word planted in you, which can save you.
22Do not merely listen to the word, and
so deceive yourselves. Do what it says.
23Anyone who listens to the word but
does not do what it says is like a man who
looks at his face in a mirror 24and, after
looking at himself, goes away and immediately forgets what he looks like. 25But
the man who looks intently into the perfect law that gives freedom, and continues
to do this, not forgetting what he has
heard, but doing it—he will be blessed in
what he does.
26If anyone considers himself religious
and yet does not keep a tight rein on his
tongue, he deceives himself and his religion is worthless. 27Religion that God our
Father accepts as pure and faultless is this:
to look after orphans and widows in their
distress and to keep oneself from being
polluted by the world.

PRAYER: THE CHARACTER I WANT TO CULTIVATE

SHOULD I seek great things for myself? I will seek them not. (Jeremiah 45:5) . . . Those who exalt themselves will be humbled, and those who humble themselves will be exalted. (Matthew 23:12; Luke 14:11; 18:14)

***TAKE** a moment to ask the Lord for the grace to grow in godly character.*

YEAR 1
DAY 280

OT Psalms 54–55

Psalm 54

For the director of music. With stringed instruments. A *maskil*[a] of David. When the Ziphites had gone to Saul and said, "Is not David hiding among us?"

1 Save me, O God, by your name;
vindicate me by your might.
2 Hear my prayer, O God;
listen to the words of my mouth.

3 Strangers are attacking me;
ruthless men seek my life—
men without regard for God. *Selah*

4 Surely God is my help;
the Lord is the one who sustains me.

5 Let evil recoil on those who slander me;
in your faithfulness destroy them.

6 I will sacrifice a freewill offering to you;
I will praise your name, O LORD,
for it is good.
7 For he has delivered me from all my troubles,
and my eyes have looked in triumph on my foes.

Psalm 55

For the director of music. With stringed instruments. A *maskil*[a] of David.

1 Listen to my prayer, O God,
do not ignore my plea;
2 hear me and answer me.
My thoughts trouble me and I am distraught
3 at the voice of the enemy,
at the stares of the wicked;
for they bring down suffering upon me
and revile me in their anger.

4 My heart is in anguish within me;
the terrors of death assail me.
5 Fear and trembling have beset me;
horror has overwhelmed me.
6 I said, "Oh, that I had the wings of a dove!
I would fly away and be at rest—
7 I would flee far away
and stay in the desert; *Selah*
8 I would hurry to my place of shelter,
far from the tempest and storm."

9 Confuse the wicked, O Lord,
confound their speech,
for I see violence and strife in the city.
10 Day and night they prowl about on its walls;
malice and abuse are within it.
11 Destructive forces are at work in the city;
threats and lies never leave its streets.

12 If an enemy were insulting me,
I could endure it;
if a foe were raising himself against me,
I could hide from him.
13 But it is you, a man like myself,
my companion, my close friend,
14 with whom I once enjoyed sweet fellowship
as we walked with the throng at the house of God.

15 Let death take my enemies by surprise;
let them go down alive to the grave,[b]

[a] Title: Probably a literary or musical term
[b] *15* Hebrew *Sheol*

for evil finds lodging among
them.

[16]But I call to God,
and the LORD saves me.
[17]Evening, morning and noon
I cry out in distress,
and he hears my voice.
[18]He ransoms me unharmed
from the battle waged against me,
even though many oppose me.
[19]God, who is enthroned forever,
will hear them and afflict them—
Selah
men who never change their ways
and have no fear of God.
[20]My companion attacks his friends;
he violates his covenant.
[21]His speech is smooth as butter,
yet war is in his heart;
his words are more soothing than
oil,
yet they are drawn swords.

[22]Cast your cares on the LORD
and he will sustain you;
he will never let the righteous fall.
[23]But you, O God, will bring down the
wicked
into the pit of corruption;
bloodthirsty and deceitful men
will not live out half their days.

But as for me, I trust in you.

PRAYER: THANKSGIVING

YOU uphold all who fall, O Lord, and lift up all who are bowed down. The eyes of all look to You, and You give them their food at the proper time. You open Your hand and satisfy the desire of every living thing. (Psalm 145:14–16)

PAUSE *to offer your own expressions of thanksgiving.*

NT James 2:1-13

Favoritism Forbidden

2 My brothers, as believers in our glorious Lord Jesus Christ, don't show favoritism. [2]Suppose a man comes into
your meeting wearing a gold ring and fine
clothes, and a poor man in shabby clothes
also comes in. [3]If you show special attention to the man wearing fine clothes and
say, "Here's a good seat for you," but say
to the poor man, "You stand there" or "Sit
on the floor by my feet," [4]have you not
discriminated among yourselves and become judges with evil thoughts?

[5]Listen, my dear brothers: Has not God
chosen those who are poor in the eyes of
the world to be rich in faith and to inherit the kingdom he promised those who
love him? [6]But you have insulted the
poor. Is it not the rich who are exploiting
you? Are they not the ones who are dragging you into court? [7]Are they not the
ones who are slandering the noble name
of him to whom you belong?

[8]If you really keep the royal law found
in Scripture, "Love your neighbor as yourself,"[a] you are doing right. [9]But if you show
favoritism, you sin and are convicted by
the law as lawbreakers. [10]For whoever keeps
the whole law and yet stumbles at just one
point is guilty of breaking all of it. [11]For he
who said, "Do not commit adultery,"[b] also
said, "Do not murder."[c] If you do not
commit adultery but do commit murder,
you have become a lawbreaker.

[12]Speak and act as those who are going
to be judged by the law that gives freedom, [13]because judgment without mercy
will be shown to anyone who has not
been merciful. Mercy triumphs over judgment!

[a] *8* Lev. 19:18 [b] *11* Exodus 20:14; Deut. 5:18
[c] *11* Exodus 20:13; Deut. 5:17

PRAYER: MY RELATIONSHIP TO OTHERS

I WILL submit myself to the governing authorities. For there is no authority except from You, O God, and the authorities that exist have been established by You. Consequently, those who resist authority have opposed Your ordinance, O God, and those who do so will bring judgment on themselves. (Romans 13:1–2)

***PAUSE** to review your relationships with others and to commit them to the Lord.*

YEAR 1
DAY 281

OT **2 Samuel 20:1–21:22**

Sheba Rebels Against David

20 Now a troublemaker named Sheba son of Bicri, a Benjamite, happened to be there. He sounded the trumpet and shouted,

"We have no share in David,
no part in Jesse's son!
Every man to his tent, O Israel!"

[2]So all the men of Israel deserted David to follow Sheba son of Bicri. But the men of Judah stayed by their king all the way from the Jordan to Jerusalem.

[3]When David returned to his palace in Jerusalem, he took the ten concubines he had left to take care of the palace and put them in a house under guard. He provided for them, but did not lie with them. They were kept in confinement till the day of their death, living as widows.

[4]Then the king said to Amasa, "Summon the men of Judah to come to me within three days, and be here yourself."
[5]But when Amasa went to summon Judah, he took longer than the time the king had set for him.

[6]David said to Abishai, "Now Sheba son of Bicri will do us more harm than Absalom did. Take your master's men and pursue him, or he will find fortified cities and escape from us."
[7]So Joab's men and the Kerethites and Pelethites and all the mighty warriors went out under the command of Abishai. They marched out from Jerusalem to pursue Sheba son of Bicri.

[8]While they were at the great rock in Gibeon, Amasa came to meet them. Joab was wearing his military tunic, and strapped over it at his waist was a belt with a dagger in its sheath. As he stepped forward, it dropped out of its sheath.

[9]Joab said to Amasa, "How are you, my brother?" Then Joab took Amasa by the beard with his right hand to kiss him.
[10]Amasa was not on his guard against the dagger in Joab's hand, and Joab plunged it into his belly, and his intestines spilled out on the ground. Without being stabbed again, Amasa died. Then Joab and his brother Abishai pursued Sheba son of Bicri.

[11]One of Joab's men stood beside Amasa and said, "Whoever favors Joab, and whoever is for David, let him follow
Joab!" [12]Amasa lay wallowing in his blood in the middle of the road, and the man saw that all the troops came to a halt there. When he realized that everyone who came up to Amasa stopped, he dragged him from the road into a field
and threw a garment over him. [13]After Amasa had been removed from the road, all the men went on with Joab to pursue Sheba son of Bicri.

[14]Sheba passed through all the tribes of Israel to Abel Beth Maacah[a] and through the entire region of the Berites, who gathered together and followed him.
[15]All the troops with Joab came and besieged Sheba in Abel Beth Maacah. They built a siege ramp up to the city, and it stood against the outer fortifications. While they were battering the wall to bring it down,
[16]a wise woman called from the city, "Listen! Listen! Tell Joab to come here so I can speak to him."
[17]He went toward her, and she asked, "Are you Joab?"

"I am," he answered.

[a] 14 Or *Abel, even Beth Maacah;* also in verse 15

She said, "Listen to what your servant
has to say."
"I'm listening," he said.
18She continued, "Long ago they used to
say, 'Get your answer at Abel,' and that settled it. 19We are the peaceful and faithful in
Israel. You are trying to destroy a city that
is a mother in Israel. Why do you want to
swallow up the LORD's inheritance?"
20"Far be it from me!" Joab replied, "Far
be it from me to swallow up or destroy!
21That is not the case. A man named Sheba son of Bicri, from the hill country of
Ephraim, has lifted up his hand against
the king, against David. Hand over this
one man, and I'll withdraw from the city."
The woman said to Joab, "His head will
be thrown to you from the wall."
22Then the woman went to all the people with her wise advice, and they cut off
the head of Sheba son of Bicri and threw
it to Joab. So he sounded the trumpet,
and his men dispersed from the city, each
returning to his home. And Joab went
back to the king in Jerusalem.
23Joab was over Israel's entire army; Benaiah son of Jehoiada was over the Kerethites and Pelethites; 24Adoniram[b] was in
charge of forced labor; Jehoshaphat son of
Ahilud was recorder; 25Sheva was secretary; Zadok and Abiathar were priests;
26and Ira the Jairite was David's priest.

The Gibeonites Avenged

21 During the reign of David, there was
a famine for three successive years; so
David sought the face of the LORD. The
LORD said, "It is on account of Saul and
his blood-stained house; it is because he
put the Gibeonites to death."
2The king summoned the Gibeonites
and spoke to them. (Now the Gibeonites
were not a part of Israel but were survivors
of the Amorites; the Israelites had sworn
to ⌊spare⌋ them, but Saul in his zeal for Israel and Judah had tried to annihilate
them.) 3David asked the Gibeonites,
"What shall I do for you? How shall I
make amends so that you will bless the
LORD's inheritance?"
4The Gibeonites answered him, "We
have no right to demand silver or gold
from Saul or his family, nor do we have
the right to put anyone in Israel to death."
"What do you want me to do for you?"
David asked.
5They answered the king, "As for the
man who destroyed us and plotted
against us so that we have been decimat-
ed and have no place anywhere in Israel,
6let seven of his male descendants be giv-
en to us to be killed and exposed before
the LORD at Gibeah of Saul—the LORD's
chosen one."
So the king said, "I will give them to
you."
7The king spared Mephibosheth son of
Jonathan, the son of Saul, because of the
oath before the LORD between David and
Jonathan son of Saul. 8But the king took
Armoni and Mephibosheth, the two sons
of Aiah's daughter Rizpah, whom she had
borne to Saul, together with the five sons
of Saul's daughter Merab,[c] whom she had
borne to Adriel son of Barzillai the Meho-
lathite. 9He handed them over to the
Gibeonites, who killed and exposed them
on a hill before the LORD. All seven of
them fell together; they were put to death
during the first days of the harvest, just as
the barley harvest was beginning.
10Rizpah daughter of Aiah took sackcloth and spread it out for herself on a
rock. From the beginning of the harvest
till the rain poured down from the heavens on the bodies, she did not let the
birds of the air touch them by day or the
wild animals by night. 11When David was
told what Aiah's daughter Rizpah, Saul's
concubine, had done, 12he went and took
the bones of Saul and his son Jonathan
from the citizens of Jabesh Gilead. (They
had taken them secretly from the public
square at Beth Shan, where the Philistines
had hung them after they struck Saul
down on Gilboa.) 13David brought the
bones of Saul and his son Jonathan from
there, and the bones of those who had
been killed and exposed were gathered up.
14They buried the bones of Saul and his
son Jonathan in the tomb of Saul's father
Kish, at Zela in Benjamin, and did everything the king commanded. After that,
God answered prayer in behalf of the
land.

[b] *24* Some Septuagint manuscripts (see also 1 Kings 4:6 and 5:14); Hebrew *Adoram* [c] *8* Two Hebrew manuscripts, some Septuagint manuscripts and Syriac (see also 1 Samuel 18:19); most Hebrew and Septuagint manuscripts *Michal*

Wars Against the Philistines

15 Once again there was a battle between the Philistines and Israel. David went down with his men to fight against the Philistines, and he became exhausted. 16 And Ishbi-Benob, one of the descendants of Rapha, whose bronze spearhead weighed three hundred shekels[d] and who was armed with a new ⌊sword⌋, said he would kill David. 17 But Abishai son of Zeruiah came to David's rescue; he struck the Philistine down and killed him. Then David's men swore to him, saying, "Never again will you go out with us to battle, so that the lamp of Israel will not be extinguished."

18 In the course of time, there was another battle with the Philistines, at Gob. At that time Sibbecai the Hushathite killed Saph, one of the descendants of Rapha.

19 In another battle with the Philistines at Gob, Elhanan son of Jaare-Oregim[e] the Bethlehemite killed Goliath[f] the Gittite, who had a spear with a shaft like a weaver's rod.

20 In still another battle, which took place at Gath, there was a huge man with six fingers on each hand and six toes on each foot—twenty-four in all. He also was descended from Rapha. 21 When he taunted Israel, Jonathan son of Shimeah, David's brother, killed him.

22 These four were descendants of Rapha in Gath, and they fell at the hands of David and his men.

[d] 16 That is, about 7 1/2 pounds (about 3.5 kilograms) [e] 19 Or *son of Jair the weaver* [f] 19 Hebrew and Septuagint; 1 Chron. 20:5 *son of Jair killed Lahmi the brother of Goliath*

PRAYER: ADORATION

You are He; You are the first, and You are also the last. (Isaiah 48:12) . . . O God, the Son is the radiance of Your glory and the exact representation of Your being, upholding all things by His powerful word. After He cleansed our sins, He sat down at Your right hand, having become as much superior to angels as the name He has inherited is more excellent than theirs. (Hebrews 1:3–4)

PAUSE *to express your thoughts of praise and worship.*

NT James 2:14–26

Faith and Deeds

14 What good is it, my brothers, if a man claims to have faith but has no deeds? Can such faith save him? 15 Suppose a brother or sister is without clothes and daily food. 16 If one of you says to him, "Go, I wish you well; keep warm and well fed," but does nothing about his physical needs, what good is it? 17 In the same way, faith by itself, if it is not accompanied by action, is dead.

18 But someone will say, "You have faith; I have deeds."

Show me your faith without deeds, and I will show you my faith by what I do. 19 You believe that there is one God. Good! Even the demons believe that—and shudder.

20 You foolish man, do you want evidence that faith without deeds is useless[a]? 21 Was not our ancestor Abraham considered righteous for what he did when he offered his son Isaac on the altar? 22 You see that his faith and his actions were working together, and his faith was made complete by what he did. 23 And the scripture was fulfilled that says, "Abraham believed God, and it was credited to him as righteousness,"[b] and he was called God's friend. 24 You see that a person is justified by what he does and not by faith alone.

25 In the same way, was not even Rahab the prostitute considered righteous for what she did when she gave lodging to the spies and sent them off in a different direction? 26 As the body without the spirit is dead, so faith without deeds is dead.

[a] 20 Some early manuscripts *dead* [b] 23 Gen. 15:6

PRAYER: THE ATTRIBUTES OF GOD

BE exalted, O God, above the heavens; let Your glory be over all the earth. For Your mercy reaches to the heavens, and Your faithfulness reaches to the clouds. (Psalm 57:5, 10) . . . Your word is settled in heaven forever, O Lord. Your faithfulness continues through all generations. You established the earth, and it stands. Your laws continue to this day according to Your purposes, for all things serve You. (Psalm 119:89–91)

***PAUSE** to reflect on these affirmations about the person, powers and perfection of God.*

YEAR 1
DAY 282

OT 2 Samuel 22:1–51

David's Song of Praise

22 David sang to the LORD the words of
this song when the LORD delivered
him from the hand of all his enemies and
from the hand of Saul. 2He said:

"The LORD is my rock, my fortress and my deliverer;
3 my God is my rock, in whom I take refuge,
my shield and the horn[a] of my salvation.
He is my stronghold, my refuge and my savior—
from violent men you save me.
4 I call to the LORD, who is worthy of praise,
and I am saved from my enemies.

5 "The waves of death swirled about me;
the torrents of destruction overwhelmed me.
6 The cords of the grave[b] coiled around me;
the snares of death confronted me.
7 In my distress I called to the LORD;
I called out to my God.
From his temple he heard my voice;
my cry came to his ears.

8 "The earth trembled and quaked,
the foundations of the heavens[c] shook;
they trembled because he was angry.
9 Smoke rose from his nostrils;
consuming fire came from his mouth,
burning coals blazed out of it.
10 He parted the heavens and came down;
dark clouds were under his feet.
11 He mounted the cherubim and flew;
he soared[d] on the wings of the wind.
12 He made darkness his canopy around him—
the dark[e] rain clouds of the sky.
13 Out of the brightness of his presence
bolts of lightning blazed forth.
14 The LORD thundered from heaven;
the voice of the Most High resounded.
15 He shot arrows and scattered ⌞the enemies⌟,
bolts of lightning and routed them.
16 The valleys of the sea were exposed
and the foundations of the earth laid bare
at the rebuke of the LORD,
at the blast of breath from his nostrils.

17 "He reached down from on high and took hold of me;
he drew me out of deep waters.
18 He rescued me from my powerful enemy,
from my foes, who were too strong for me.
19 They confronted me in the day of my disaster,
but the LORD was my support.
20 He brought me out into a spacious place;

[a] 3 *Horn* here symbolizes strength. [b] 6 Hebrew *Sheol* [c] 8 Hebrew; Vulgate and Syriac (see also Psalm 18:7) *mountains* [d] 11 Many Hebrew manuscripts (see also Psalm 18:10); most Hebrew manuscripts *appeared* [e] 12 Septuagint and Vulgate (see also Psalm 18:11); Hebrew *massed*

he rescued me because he delighted
in me.

21 "The LORD has dealt with me
according to my righteousness;
according to the cleanness of my
hands he has rewarded me.
22 For I have kept the ways of the LORD;
I have not done evil by turning
from my God.
23 All his laws are before me;
I have not turned away from his
decrees.
24 I have been blameless before him
and have kept myself from sin.
25 The LORD has rewarded me according
to my righteousness,
according to my cleanness[f] in his
sight.

26 "To the faithful you show yourself
faithful,
to the blameless you show yourself
blameless,
27 to the pure you show yourself pure,
but to the crooked you show
yourself shrewd.
28 You save the humble,
but your eyes are on the haughty to
bring them low.
29 You are my lamp, O LORD;
the LORD turns my darkness into
light.
30 With your help I can advance against
a troop[g];
with my God I can scale a wall.

31 "As for God, his way is perfect;
the word of the LORD is flawless.
He is a shield
for all who take refuge in him.
32 For who is God besides the LORD?
And who is the Rock except our
God?
33 It is God who arms me with strength[h]
and makes my way perfect.
34 He makes my feet like the feet of a
deer;
he enables me to stand on the
heights.
35 He trains my hands for battle;
my arms can bend a bow of bronze.
36 You give me your shield of victory;
you stoop down to make me great.
37 You broaden the path beneath me,
so that my ankles do not turn.
38 "I pursued my enemies and crushed
them;
I did not turn back till they were
destroyed.
39 I crushed them completely, and they
could not rise;
they fell beneath my feet.
40 You armed me with strength for
battle;
you made my adversaries bow at my
feet.
41 You made my enemies turn their
backs in flight,
and I destroyed my foes.
42 They cried for help, but there was no
one to save them—
to the LORD, but he did not answer.
43 I beat them as fine as the dust of the
earth;
I pounded and trampled them like
mud in the streets.

44 "You have delivered me from the
attacks of my people;
you have preserved me as the head
of nations.
People I did not know are subject to
me,
45 and foreigners come cringing to me;
as soon as they hear me, they obey
me.
46 They all lose heart;
they come trembling[i] from their
strongholds.

47 "The LORD lives! Praise be to my Rock!
Exalted be God, the Rock, my
Savior!
48 He is the God who avenges me,
who puts the nations under me,
49 who sets me free from my enemies.
You exalted me above my foes;
from violent men you rescued me.
50 Therefore I will praise you, O LORD,
among the nations;
I will sing praises to your name.
51 He gives his king great victories;
he shows unfailing kindness to his
anointed,
to David and his descendants
forever."

[f] 25 Hebrew; Septuagint and Vulgate (see also Psalm 18:24) *to the cleanness of my hands* [g] 30 Or *can run through a barricade* [h] 33 Dead Sea Scrolls, some Septuagint manuscripts, Vulgate and Syriac (see also Psalm 18:32); Masoretic Text *who is my strong refuge* [i] 46 Some Septuagint manuscripts and Vulgate (see also Psalm 18:45); Masoretic Text *they arm themselves.*

PRAYER: CONFESSION

ALL my ways are before Your eyes, O Lord, and You examine all my paths. (Proverbs 5:21)

***ASK** the Spirit to search your heart and reveal any areas of unconfessed sin. Acknowledge these to the Lord and thank Him for His forgiveness.*

NT James 3:1-18

Taming the Tongue

3 Not many of you should presume to be
teachers, my brothers, because you
know that we who teach will be judged
more strictly. 2We all stumble in many
ways. If anyone is never at fault in what
he says, he is a perfect man, able to keep
his whole body in check.

3When we put bits into the mouths of
horses to make them obey us, we can turn
the whole animal. 4Or take ships as an example. Although they are so large and are
driven by strong winds, they are steered
by a very small rudder wherever the pilot
wants to go. 5Likewise the tongue is a
small part of the body, but it makes great
boasts. Consider what a great forest is set
on fire by a small spark. 6The tongue also
is a fire, a world of evil among the parts
of the body. It corrupts the whole person,
sets the whole course of his life on fire,
and is itself set on fire by hell.

7All kinds of animals, birds, reptiles and
creatures of the sea are being tamed and
have been tamed by man, 8but no man
can tame the tongue. It is a restless evil,
full of deadly poison.

9With the tongue we praise our Lord
and Father, and with it we curse men, who
have been made in God's likeness. 10Out
of the same mouth come praise and cursing. My brothers, this should not be.
11Can both fresh water and salt[a] water
flow from the same spring? 12My brothers,
can a fig tree bear olives, or a grapevine
bear figs? Neither can a salt spring produce fresh water.

Two Kinds of Wisdom

13Who is wise and understanding
among you? Let him show it by his good
life, by deeds done in the humility that
comes from wisdom. 14But if you harbor
bitter envy and selfish ambition in your
hearts, do not boast about it or deny the
truth. 15Such "wisdom" does not come
down from heaven but is earthly, unspiritual, of the devil. 16For where you have
envy and selfish ambition, there you find
disorder and every evil practice.

17But the wisdom that comes from
heaven is first of all pure; then peace-loving, considerate, submissive, full of mercy and good fruit, impartial and sincere.
18Peacemakers who sow in peace raise a
harvest of righteousness.

[a] *11* Greek *bitter* (see also verse 14)

PRAYER: THE WORKS OF GOD

YOU are the Lord who created the heavens; You are God. You fashioned and made the earth and established it; You did not create it to be empty but formed it to be inhabited. You are the Lord, and there is no other. (Isaiah 45:18) . .·. You made the earth by Your power, O God; You established the world by Your wisdom and stretched out the heavens by Your understanding. (Jeremiah 10:12)

***TAKE** a moment to consider the greatness of God's wonderful works.*

OT 2 Samuel 23:1-39 YEAR 1 DAY 283

The Last Words of David

23 These are the last words of David:

"The oracle of David son of Jesse,
the oracle of the man exalted by the
Most High,
the man anointed by the God of
Jacob,
Israel's singer of songs[a]:

2 "The Spirit of the LORD spoke through
me;
his word was on my tongue.
3 The God of Israel spoke,
the Rock of Israel said to me:
'When one rules over men in
righteousness,
when he rules in the fear of God,
4 he is like the light of morning at
sunrise
on a cloudless morning,
like the brightness after rain
that brings the grass from the earth.'

5 "Is not my house right with God?
Has he not made with me an
everlasting covenant,
arranged and secured in every part?
Will he not bring to fruition my
salvation
and grant me my every desire?
6 But evil men are all to be cast aside
like thorns,
which are not gathered with the
hand.
7 Whoever touches thorns
uses a tool of iron or the shaft of a
spear;
they are burned up where they lie."

David's Mighty Men

8 These are the names of David's mighty
men:
Josheb-Basshebeth,[b] a Tahkemonite,[c]
was chief of the Three; he raised his spear
against eight hundred men, whom he
killed[d] in one encounter.
9 Next to him was Eleazar son of Dodai
the Ahohite. As one of the three mighty
men, he was with David when they taunted the Philistines gathered ⌊at Pas Dam-
mim⌋[e] for battle. Then the men of Israel
retreated, 10 but he stood his ground and
struck down the Philistines till his hand
grew tired and froze to the sword. The
LORD brought about a great victory that
day. The troops returned to Eleazar, but
only to strip the dead.
11 Next to him was Shammah son of
Agee the Hararite. When the Philistines
banded together at a place where there
was a field full of lentils, Israel's troops
fled from them. 12 But Shammah took his
stand in the middle of the field. He defended it and struck the Philistines down,
and the LORD brought about a great victory.
13 During harvest time, three of the thirty chief men came down to David at the
cave of Adullam, while a band of Philistines was encamped in the Valley of Rephaim. 14 At that time David was in the
stronghold, and the Philistine garrison
was at Bethlehem. 15 David longed for water and said, "Oh, that someone would
get me a drink of water from the well near
the gate of Bethlehem!" 16 So the three
mighty men broke through the Philistine
lines, drew water from the well near the
gate of Bethlehem and carried it back to
David. But he refused to drink it; instead,
he poured it out before the LORD. 17 "Far
be it from me, O LORD, to do this!" he
said. "Is it not the blood of men who went
at the risk of their lives?" And David
would not drink it.
Such were the exploits of the three
mighty men.
18 Abishai the brother of Joab son of
Zeruiah was chief of the Three.[f] He raised
his spear against three hundred men,
whom he killed, and so he became as famous as the Three. 19 Was he not held in
greater honor than the Three? He became
their commander, even though he was not
included among them.
20 Benaiah son of Jehoiada was a valiant

[a] 1 Or *Israel's beloved singer* [b] 8 Hebrew; some Septuagint manuscripts suggest *Ish-Bosheth,* that is, *Esh-Baal* (see also 1 Chron. 11:11 *Jashobeam*). [c] 8 Probably a variant of *Hacmonite* (see 1 Chron. 11:11) [d] 8 Some Septuagint manuscripts (see also 1 Chron. 11:11); Hebrew and other Septuagint manuscripts *Three; it was Adino the Eznite who killed eight hundred men* [e] 9 See 1 Chron. 11:13; Hebrew *gathered there.* [f] 18 Most Hebrew manuscripts (see also 1 Chron. 11:20); two Hebrew manuscripts and Syriac *Thirty*

fighter from Kabzeel, who performed
great exploits. He struck down two of
Moab's best men. He also went down into
a pit on a snowy day and killed a lion.
21 And he struck down a huge Egyptian. Although the Egyptian had a spear in his
hand, Benaiah went against him with a
club. He snatched the spear from the
Egyptian's hand and killed him with his
own spear. 22 Such were the exploits of Benaiah son of Jehoiada; he too was as famous as the three mighty men. 23 He was
held in greater honor than any of the Thirty, but he was not included among the
Three. And David put him in charge of his
bodyguard.

24 Among the Thirty were:
Asahel the brother of Joab,
Elhanan son of Dodo from Bethlehem,
25 Shammah the Harodite,
Elika the Harodite,
26 Helez the Paltite,
Ira son of Ikkesh from Tekoa,
27 Abiezer from Anathoth,
Mebunnai[g] the Hushathite,
28 Zalmon the Ahohite,
Maharai the Netophathite,
29 Heled[h] son of Baanah the Netophathite,
Ithai son of Ribai from Gibeah in Benjamin,
30 Benaiah the Pirathonite,
Hiddai[i] from the ravines of Gaash,
31 Abi-Albon the Arbathite,
Azmaveth the Barhumite,
32 Eliahba the Shaalbonite,
the sons of Jashen,
Jonathan 33 son of[j] Shammah the Hararite,
Ahiam son of Sharar[k] the Hararite,
34 Eliphelet son of Ahasbai the Maacathite,
Eliam son of Ahithophel the Gilonite,
35 Hezro the Carmelite,
Paarai the Arbite,
36 Igal son of Nathan from Zobah,
the son of Hagri,[l]
37 Zelek the Ammonite,
Naharai the Beerothite, the armor-bearer of Joab son of Zeruiah,
38 Ira the Ithrite,
Gareb the Ithrite
39 and Uriah the Hittite.
There were thirty-seven in all.

[g] *27* Hebrew; some Septuagint manuscripts (see also 1 Chron. 11:29) *Sibbecai* [h] *29* Some Hebrew manuscripts and Vulgate (see also 1 Chron. 11:30); most Hebrew manuscripts *Heleb* [i] *30* Hebrew; some Septuagint manuscripts (see also 1 Chron. 11:32) *Hurai* [j] *33* Some Septuagint manuscripts (see also 1 Chron. 11:34); Hebrew does not have *son of.* [k] *33* Hebrew; some Septuagint manuscripts (see also 1 Chron. 11:35) *Sacar* [l] *36* Some Septuagint manuscripts (see also 1 Chron. 11:38); Hebrew *Haggadi*

PRAYER: RENEWAL

SINCE I live in You, Holy Spirit, may I also walk in You. (Galatians 5:25) . . . Father, may You fill me with the knowledge of Your will through all spiritual wisdom and understanding, so that I may live a life worthy of You and please You in every way, bearing fruit in every good work and growing in Your grace, strengthened with all power according to Your glorious might, so that I may have great endurance and patience with joy. (Colossians 1:9–11)

PAUSE *to add your own prayers for personal renewal.*

NT James 4:1-17

Submit Yourselves to God

4 What causes fights and quarrels among
you? Don't they come from your desires that battle within you? 2 You want
something but don't get it. You kill and
covet, but you cannot have what you
want. You quarrel and fight. You do not
have, because you do not ask God. 3 When
you ask, you do not receive, because you
ask with wrong motives, that you may
spend what you get on your pleasures.
4 You adulterous people, don't you

know that friendship with the world is hatred toward God? Anyone who chooses to be a friend of the world becomes an enemy of God. [5]Or do you think Scripture says without reason that the spirit he caused to live in us envies intensely?[a] [6]But he gives us more grace. That is why Scripture says:

"God opposes the proud
but gives grace to the humble."[b]

[7]Submit yourselves, then, to God. Resist the devil, and he will flee from you. [8]Come near to God and he will come near to you. Wash your hands, you sinners, and purify your hearts, you double-minded. [9]Grieve, mourn and wail. Change your laughter to mourning and your joy to gloom. [10]Humble yourselves before the Lord, and he will lift you up.

[11]Brothers, do not slander one another. Anyone who speaks against his brother or judges him speaks against the law and judges it. When you judge the law, you are not keeping it, but sitting in judgment on it. [12]There is only one Lawgiver and Judge, the one who is able to save and destroy. But you—who are you to judge your neighbor?

Boasting About Tomorrow

[13]Now listen, you who say, "Today or tomorrow we will go to this or that city, spend a year there, carry on business and make money." [14]Why, you do not even know what will happen tomorrow. What is your life? You are a mist that appears for a little while and then vanishes. [15]Instead, you ought to say, "If it is the Lord's will, we will live and do this or that." [16]As it is, you boast and brag. All such boasting is evil. [17]Anyone, then, who knows the good he ought to do and doesn't do it, sins.

[a] 5 Or *that God jealously longs for the spirit that he made to live in us;* or *that the Spirit he caused to live in us longs jealously* [b] 6 Prov. 3:34

PRAYER: MY RELATIONSHIP TO GOD

BY this is Your Father glorified, Lord Jesus: that I bear much fruit, showing myself to be Your disciple. (John 15:8) . . . Just as I presented the members of my body as slaves to impurity and to ever-increasing lawlessness, so I now present my members as slaves to righteousness, leading to holiness. (Romans 6:19)

PAUSE *to thank God for the relationship that you enjoy with Him in Jesus Christ.*

YEAR 1 DAY 284

OT 2 Samuel 24:1-25

David Counts the Fighting Men

24 Again the anger of the LORD burned against Israel, and he incited David against them, saying, "Go and take a census of Israel and Judah."

[2]So the king said to Joab and the army commanders[a] with him, "Go throughout the tribes of Israel from Dan to Beersheba and enroll the fighting men, so that I may know how many there are."

[3]But Joab replied to the king, "May the LORD your God multiply the troops a hundred times over, and may the eyes of my lord the king see it. But why does my lord the king want to do such a thing?"

[4]The king's word, however, overruled Joab and the army commanders; so they left the presence of the king to enroll the fighting men of Israel.

[5]After crossing the Jordan, they camped near Aroer, south of the town in the gorge, and then went through Gad and on to Jazer. [6]They went to Gilead and the region of Tahtim Hodshi, and on to Dan Jaan and around toward Sidon. [7]Then they went toward the fortress of Tyre and all the towns of the Hivites and Canaanites.

[a] 2 Septuagint (see also verse 4 and 1 Chron. 21:2); Hebrew *Joab the army commander*

Finally, they went on to Beersheba in the
Negev of Judah.
8After they had gone through the entire
land, they came back to Jerusalem at the
end of nine months and twenty days.
9Joab reported the number of the fighting men to the king: In Israel there were
eight hundred thousand able-bodied men
who could handle a sword, and in Judah
five hundred thousand.
10David was conscience-stricken after he
had counted the fighting men, and he
said to the LORD, "I have sinned greatly in
what I have done. Now, O LORD, I beg
you, take away the guilt of your servant. I
have done a very foolish thing."
11Before David got up the next morning,
the word of the LORD had come to Gad
the prophet, David's seer: 12"Go and tell
David, 'This is what the LORD says: I am
giving you three options. Choose one of
them for me to carry out against you.' "
13So Gad went to David and said to
him, "Shall there come upon you three[b]
years of famine in your land? Or three
months of fleeing from your enemies
while they pursue you? Or three days of
plague in your land? Now then, think it
over and decide how I should answer the
one who sent me."
14David said to Gad, "I am in deep distress. Let us fall into the hands of the
LORD, for his mercy is great; but do not let
me fall into the hands of men."
15So the LORD sent a plague on Israel
from that morning until the end of the
time designated, and seventy thousand of
the people from Dan to Beersheba died.
16When the angel stretched out his hand
to destroy Jerusalem, the LORD was grieved
because of the calamity and said to the
angel who was afflicting the people,
"Enough! Withdraw your hand." The angel of the LORD was then at the threshing
floor of Araunah the Jebusite.
17When David saw the angel who was
striking down the people, he said to the
LORD, "I am the one who has sinned and
done wrong. These are but sheep. What
have they done? Let your hand fall upon
me and my family."

David Builds an Altar

18On that day Gad went to David and
said to him, "Go up and build an altar to
the LORD on the threshing floor of Araunah the Jebusite." 19So David went up, as
the LORD had commanded through Gad.
20When Araunah looked and saw the king
and his men coming toward him, he went
out and bowed down before the king with
his face to the ground.
21Araunah said, "Why has my lord the
king come to his servant?"
"To buy your threshing floor," David
answered, "so I can build an altar to the
LORD, that the plague on the people may
be stopped."
22Araunah said to David, "Let my lord
the king take whatever pleases him and
offer it up. Here are oxen for the burnt offering, and here are threshing sledges and
ox yokes for the wood. 23O king, Araunah
gives all this to the king." Araunah also
said to him, "May the LORD your God accept you."
24But the king replied to Araunah, "No,
I insist on paying you for it. I will not sacrifice to the LORD my God burnt offerings
that cost me nothing."
So David bought the threshing floor
and the oxen and paid fifty shekels[c] of silver for them. 25David built an altar to the
LORD there and sacrificed burnt offerings
and fellowship offerings.[d] Then the LORD
answered prayer in behalf of the land, and
the plague on Israel was stopped.

[b] *13* Septuagint (see also 1 Chron. 21:12); Hebrew *seven* [c] *24* That is, about 1 1/4 pounds (about 0.6 kilogram) [d] *25* Traditionally *peace offerings*

PRAYER: PETITION

I CRY out to You, O Lord, and say, "You are my refuge, my portion in the land of the living." (Psalm 142:5)

***PAUSE** here to offer prayers of petition regarding your family and your ministry. Ask for help and guidance in sharing Jesus with others and helping others grow in Him. Ask for guidance in your vocation and your avocations. Offer prayers of petition regarding your activities for this day and any special concerns you may have.*

NT James 5:1-20

Warning to Rich Oppressors

5 Now listen, you rich people, weep and wail because of the misery that is coming upon you. [2]Your wealth has rotted, and moths have eaten your clothes. [3]Your gold and silver are corroded. Their corrosion will testify against you and eat your flesh like fire. You have hoarded wealth in the last days. [4]Look! The wages you failed to pay the workmen who mowed your fields are crying out against you. The cries of the harvesters have reached the ears of the Lord Almighty. [5]You have lived on earth in luxury and self-indulgence. You have fattened yourselves in the day of slaughter.[a] [6]You have condemned and murdered innocent men, who were not opposing you.

Patience in Suffering

[7]Be patient, then, brothers, until the Lord's coming. See how the farmer waits for the land to yield its valuable crop and how patient he is for the autumn and spring rains. [8]You too, be patient and stand firm, because the Lord's coming is near. [9]Don't grumble against each other, brothers, or you will be judged. The Judge is standing at the door!

[10]Brothers, as an example of patience in the face of suffering, take the prophets who spoke in the name of the Lord. [11]As you know, we consider blessed those who have persevered. You have heard of Job's perseverance and have seen what the Lord finally brought about. The Lord is full of compassion and mercy.

[12]Above all, my brothers, do not swear—not by heaven or by earth or by anything else. Let your "Yes" be yes, and your "No," no, or you will be condemned.

The Prayer of Faith

[13]Is any one of you in trouble? He should pray. Is anyone happy? Let him sing songs of praise. [14]Is any one of you sick? He should call the elders of the church to pray over him and anoint him with oil in the name of the Lord. [15]And the prayer offered in faith will make the sick person well; the Lord will raise him up. If he has sinned, he will be forgiven. [16]Therefore confess your sins to each other and pray for each other so that you may be healed. The prayer of a righteous man is powerful and effective.

[17]Elijah was a man just like us. He prayed earnestly that it would not rain, and it did not rain on the land for three and a half years. [18]Again he prayed, and the heavens gave rain, and the earth produced its crops.

[19]My brothers, if one of you should wander from the truth and someone should bring him back, [20]remember this: Whoever turns a sinner from the error of his way will save him from death and cover over a multitude of sins.

[a] 5 Or *yourselves as in a day of feasting*

PRAYER: THE CHARACTER I WANT TO CULTIVATE

If I am foolish, my ways will seem right in my own eyes, but if I am wise, I will listen to counsel. (Proverbs 12:15) . . . I will listen to counsel and accept instruction, that I may be wise in my latter days. (Proverbs 19:20)

***TAKE** a moment to ask the Lord for the grace to grow in godly character.*

YEAR 1 DAY 285

OT 1 Kings 1:1-53

Adonijah Sets Himself Up as King

1 When King David was old and well advanced in years, he could not keep warm even when they put covers over him. [2]So his servants said to him, "Let us look for a young virgin to attend the king and take care of him. She can lie beside him so that our lord the king may keep warm."

3 Then they searched throughout Israel for a beautiful girl and found Abishag, a Shunammite, and brought her to the king. 4 The girl was very beautiful; she took care of the king and waited on him, but the king had no intimate relations with her.

5 Now Adonijah, whose mother was Haggith, put himself forward and said, "I will be king." So he got chariots and horses[a] ready, with fifty men to run ahead of him. 6 (His father had never interfered with him by asking, "Why do you behave as you do?" He was also very handsome and was born next after Absalom.)

7 Adonijah conferred with Joab son of Zeruiah and with Abiathar the priest, and they gave him their support. 8 But Zadok the priest, Benaiah son of Jehoiada, Nathan the prophet, Shimei and Rei[b] and David's special guard did not join Adonijah.

9 Adonijah then sacrificed sheep, cattle and fattened calves at the Stone of Zoheleth near En Rogel. He invited all his brothers, the king's sons, and all the men of Judah who were royal officials, 10 but he did not invite Nathan the prophet or Benaiah or the special guard or his brother Solomon.

11 Then Nathan asked Bathsheba, Solomon's mother, "Have you not heard that Adonijah, the son of Haggith, has become king without our lord David's knowing it? 12 Now then, let me advise you how you can save your own life and the life of your son Solomon. 13 Go in to King David and say to him, 'My lord the king, did you not swear to me your servant: "Surely Solomon your son shall be king after me, and he will sit on my throne"? Why then has Adonijah become king?' 14 While you are still there talking to the king, I will come in and confirm what you have said."

15 So Bathsheba went to see the aged king in his room, where Abishag the Shunammite was attending him. 16 Bathsheba bowed low and knelt before the king.

"What is it you want?" the king asked.

17 She said to him, "My lord, you yourself swore to me your servant by the LORD your God: 'Solomon your son shall be king after me, and he will sit on my throne.' 18 But now Adonijah has become king, and you, my lord the king, do not know about it. 19 He has sacrificed great numbers of cattle, fattened calves, and sheep, and has invited all the king's sons, Abiathar the priest and Joab the commander of the army, but he has not invited Solomon your servant. 20 My lord the king, the eyes of all Israel are on you, to learn from you who will sit on the throne of my lord the king after him. 21 Otherwise, as soon as my lord the king is laid to rest with his fathers, I and my son Solomon will be treated as criminals."

22 While she was still speaking with the king, Nathan the prophet arrived. 23 And they told the king, "Nathan the prophet is here." So he went before the king and bowed with his face to the ground.

24 Nathan said, "Have you, my lord the king, declared that Adonijah shall be king after you, and that he will sit on your throne? 25 Today he has gone down and sacrificed great numbers of cattle, fattened calves, and sheep. He has invited all the king's sons, the commanders of the army and Abiathar the priest. Right now they are eating and drinking with him and saying, 'Long live King Adonijah!' 26 But me your servant, and Zadok the priest, and Benaiah son of Jehoiada, and your servant Solomon he did not invite. 27 Is this something my lord the king has done without letting his servants know who should sit on the throne of my lord the king after him?"

David Makes Solomon King

28 Then King David said, "Call in Bathsheba." So she came into the king's presence and stood before him.

29 The king then took an oath: "As surely as the LORD lives, who has delivered me out of every trouble, 30 I will surely carry out today what I swore to you by the LORD, the God of Israel: Solomon your son shall be king after me, and he will sit on my throne in my place."

31 Then Bathsheba bowed low with her face to the ground and, kneeling before the king, said, "May my lord King David live forever!"

32 King David said, "Call in Zadok the priest, Nathan the prophet and Benaiah son of Jehoiada." When they came before the king, 33 he said to them: "Take your lord's servants with you and set Solomon my son on my own mule and take him down to Gihon. 34 There have Zadok the priest and Nathan the prophet anoint him king over Israel. Blow the trumpet and shout, 'Long live King Solomon!' 35 Then you are to go up with him, and he is to

[a] 5 Or *charioteers* [b] 8 Or *and his friends*

come and sit on my throne and reign in my place. I have appointed him ruler over Israel and Judah."

[36]Benaiah son of Jehoiada answered the king, "Amen! May the LORD, the God of my lord the king, so declare it. [37]As the LORD was with my lord the king, so may he be with Solomon to make his throne even greater than the throne of my lord King David!"

[38]So Zadok the priest, Nathan the prophet, Benaiah son of Jehoiada, the Kerethites and the Pelethites went down and put Solomon on King David's mule and escorted him to Gihon. [39]Zadok the priest took the horn of oil from the sacred tent and anointed Solomon. Then they sounded the trumpet and all the people shouted, "Long live King Solomon!" [40]And all the people went up after him, playing flutes and rejoicing greatly, so that the ground shook with the sound.

[41]Adonijah and all the guests who were with him heard it as they were finishing their feast. On hearing the sound of the trumpet, Joab asked, "What's the meaning of all the noise in the city?"

[42]Even as he was speaking, Jonathan son of Abiathar the priest arrived. Adonijah said, "Come in. A worthy man like you must be bringing good news."

[43]"Not at all!" Jonathan answered. "Our lord King David has made Solomon king. [44]The king has sent with him Zadok the priest, Nathan the prophet, Benaiah son of Jehoiada, the Kerethites and the Pelethites, and they have put him on the king's mule, [45]and Zadok the priest and Nathan the prophet have anointed him king at Gihon. From there they have gone up cheering, and the city resounds with it. That's the noise you hear. [46]Moreover, Solomon has taken his seat on the royal throne. [47]Also, the royal officials have come to congratulate our lord King David, saying, 'May your God make Solomon's name more famous than yours and his throne greater than yours!' And the king bowed in worship on his bed [48]and said, 'Praise be to the LORD, the God of Israel, who has allowed my eyes to see a successor on my throne today.' "

[49]At this, all Adonijah's guests rose in alarm and dispersed. [50]But Adonijah, in fear of Solomon, went and took hold of the horns of the altar. [51]Then Solomon was told, "Adonijah is afraid of King Solomon and is clinging to the horns of the altar. He says, 'Let King Solomon swear to me today that he will not put his servant to death with the sword.' "

[52]Solomon replied, "If he shows himself to be a worthy man, not a hair of his head will fall to the ground; but if evil is found in him, he will die." [53]Then King Solomon sent men, and they brought him down from the altar. And Adonijah came and bowed down to King Solomon, and Solomon said, "Go to your home."

PRAYER: INTERCESSION

AS You, Father, sent Your Son into the world, Your Son also has sent us into the world. And He has prayed for those who will believe in Him through our message. (John 17:18, 20)

***TAKE** a few moments to intercede on behalf of local, national and world missions. Pray that the Great Commission would be fulfilled and for any special concerns you may have for missions.*

NT 1 Peter 1:1-12

1 Peter, an apostle of Jesus Christ,

To God's elect, strangers in the world, scattered throughout Pontus, Galatia, Cappadocia, Asia and Bithynia, [2]who have been chosen according to the foreknowledge of God the Father, through the sanctifying work of the Spirit, for obedience to Jesus Christ and sprinkling by his blood:

Grace and peace be yours in abundance.

Praise to God for a Living Hope

[3]Praise be to the God and Father of our Lord Jesus Christ! In his great mercy he has given us new birth into a living hope through the resurrection of Jesus Christ from the dead, [4]and into an inheritance

that can never perish, spoil or fade—kept in heaven for you, [5]who through faith are shielded by God's power until the coming of the salvation that is ready to be revealed in the last time. [6]In this you greatly rejoice, though now for a little while you may have had to suffer grief in all kinds of trials. [7]These have come so that your faith—of greater worth than gold, which perishes even though refined by fire—may be proved genuine and may result in praise, glory and honor when Jesus Christ is revealed. [8]Though you have not seen him, you love him; and even though you do not see him now, you believe in him and are filled with an inexpressible and glorious joy, [9]for you are receiving the goal of your faith, the salvation of your souls.

[10]Concerning this salvation, the prophets, who spoke of the grace that was to come to you, searched intently and with the greatest care, [11]trying to find out the time and circumstances to which the Spirit of Christ in them was pointing when he predicted the sufferings of Christ and the glories that would follow. [12]It was revealed to them that they were not serving themselves but you, when they spoke of the things that have now been told you by those who have preached the gospel to you by the Holy Spirit sent from heaven. Even angels long to look into these things.

PRAYER: MY RELATIONSHIP TO OTHERS

WE are always to thank You, God, for other believers, mentioning them in our prayers. (1 Thessalonians 1:2) . . .

We should ask for one another's prayers. (1 Thessalonians 5:25)

***PAUSE** to review your relationships with others and to commit them to the Lord.*

YEAR 1 DAY 286

OT **1 Kings 2:1-46**

David's Charge to Solomon

2 When the time drew near for David to die, he gave a charge to Solomon his son.

[2]"I am about to go the way of all the earth," he said. "So be strong, show yourself a man, [3]and observe what the LORD your God requires: Walk in his ways, and keep his decrees and commands, his laws and requirements, as written in the Law of Moses, so that you may prosper in all you do and wherever you go, [4]and that the LORD may keep his promise to me: 'If your descendants watch how they live, and if they walk faithfully before me with all their heart and soul, you will never fail to have a man on the throne of Israel.'

[5]"Now you yourself know what Joab son of Zeruiah did to me—what he did to the two commanders of Israel's armies, Abner son of Ner and Amasa son of Jether. He killed them, shedding their blood in peacetime as if in battle, and with that blood stained the belt around his waist and the sandals on his feet. [6]Deal with him according to your wisdom, but do not let his gray head go down to the grave[a] in peace.

[7]"But show kindness to the sons of Barzillai of Gilead and let them be among those who eat at your table. They stood by me when I fled from your brother Absalom.

[8]"And remember, you have with you Shimei son of Gera, the Benjamite from Bahurim, who called down bitter curses on me the day I went to Mahanaim. When he came down to meet me at the Jordan, I swore to him by the LORD: 'I will not put you to death by the sword.' [9]But now, do not consider him innocent. You are a man of wisdom; you will know what to do to him. Bring his gray head down to the grave in blood."

[10]Then David rested with his fathers and was buried in the City of David. [11]He had reigned forty years over Israel—seven

[a] 6 Hebrew *Sheol*; also in verse 9

years in Hebron and thirty-three in Jerusalem. 12So Solomon sat on the throne of
his father David, and his rule was firmly
established.

Solomon's Throne Established

13Now Adonijah, the son of Haggith,
went to Bathsheba, Solomon's mother.
Bathsheba asked him, "Do you come
peacefully?"

He answered, "Yes, peacefully." 14Then
he added, "I have something to say to
you."

"You may say it," she replied.

15"As you know," he said, "the kingdom
was mine. All Israel looked to me as their
king. But things changed, and the kingdom has gone to my brother; for it has
come to him from the LORD. 16Now I have
one request to make of you. Do not
refuse me."

"You may make it," she said.

17So he continued, "Please ask King
Solomon—he will not refuse you—to give
me Abishag the Shunammite as my wife."

18"Very well," Bathsheba replied, "I will
speak to the king for you."

19When Bathsheba went to King Solomon to speak to him for Adonijah, the
king stood up to meet her, bowed down
to her and sat down on his throne. He had
a throne brought for the king's mother,
and she sat down at his right hand.

20"I have one small request to make of
you," she said. "Do not refuse me."

The king replied, "Make it, my mother;
I will not refuse you."

21So she said, "Let Abishag the Shunammite be given in marriage to your
brother Adonijah."

22King Solomon answered his mother,
"Why do you request Abishag the Shunammite for Adonijah? You might as well
request the kingdom for him—after all,
he is my older brother—yes, for him and
for Abiathar the priest and Joab son of
Zeruiah!"

23Then King Solomon swore by the
LORD: "May God deal with me, be it ever
so severely, if Adonijah does not pay with
his life for this request! 24And now, as
surely as the LORD lives—he who has established me securely on the throne of my
father David and has founded a dynasty
for me as he promised—Adonijah shall be
put to death today!" 25So King Solomon
gave orders to Benaiah son of Jehoiada,
and he struck down Adonijah and he
died.

26To Abiathar the priest the king said,
"Go back to your fields in Anathoth. You
deserve to die, but I will not put you to
death now, because you carried the ark of
the Sovereign LORD before my father David and shared all my father's hardships."
27So Solomon removed Abiathar from the
priesthood of the LORD, fulfilling the word
the LORD had spoken at Shiloh about the
house of Eli.

28When the news reached Joab, who
had conspired with Adonijah though not
with Absalom, he fled to the tent of the
LORD and took hold of the horns of the
altar. 29King Solomon was told that Joab
had fled to the tent of the LORD and was
beside the altar. Then Solomon ordered
Benaiah son of Jehoiada, "Go, strike him
down!"

30So Benaiah entered the tent of the
LORD and said to Joab, "The king says,
'Come out!' "

But he answered, "No, I will die here."

Benaiah reported to the king, "This is
how Joab answered me."

31Then the king commanded Benaiah,
"Do as he says. Strike him down and bury
him, and so clear me and my father's
house of the guilt of the innocent blood
that Joab shed. 32The LORD will repay him
for the blood he shed, because without
the knowledge of my father David he attacked two men and killed them with the
sword. Both of them—Abner son of Ner,
commander of Israel's army, and Amasa
son of Jether, commander of Judah's
army—were better men and more upright
than he. 33May the guilt of their blood rest
on the head of Joab and his descendants
forever. But on David and his descendants, his house and his throne, may there
be the LORD's peace forever."

34So Benaiah son of Jehoiada went up
and struck down Joab and killed him, and
he was buried on his own land[b] in the
desert. 35The king put Benaiah son of Jehoiada over the army in Joab's position
and replaced Abiathar with Zadok the
priest.

36Then the king sent for Shimei and said
to him, "Build yourself a house in Jerusalem and live there, but do not go any-

[b] 34 Or *buried in his tomb*

where else. 37The day you leave and cross
the Kidron Valley, you can be sure you will
die; your blood will be on your own head."
38Shimei answered the king, "What you
say is good. Your servant will do as my
lord the king has said." And Shimei stayed
in Jerusalem for a long time.
39But three years later, two of Shimei's
slaves ran off to Achish son of Maacah,
king of Gath, and Shimei was told, "Your
slaves are in Gath." 40At this, he saddled
his donkey and went to Achish at Gath in
search of his slaves. So Shimei went away
and brought the slaves back from Gath.
41When Solomon was told that Shimei
had gone from Jerusalem to Gath and had
returned, 42the king summoned Shimei and
said to him, "Did I not make you swear by
the LORD and warn you, 'On the day you
leave to go anywhere else, you can be sure
you will die'? At that time you said to me,
'What you say is good. I will obey.' 43Why
then did you not keep your oath to the
LORD and obey the command I gave you?"
44The king also said to Shimei, "You
know in your heart all the wrong you did
to my father David. Now the LORD will repay you for your wrongdoing. 45But King
Solomon will be blessed, and David's
throne will remain secure before the LORD
forever."
46Then the king gave the order to Benaiah son of Jehoiada, and he went out and
struck Shimei down and killed him.
The kingdom was now firmly established in Solomon's hands.

PRAYER: AFFIRMATION

LIKE Jesus, dear Father, my food is to do Your will and to accomplish Your work. (John 4:34) . . . This is love: that I walk in obedience to Your commandments, O God. And this is the commandment that I have heard from the beginning: I should walk in love. (2 John 6)

***PAUSE** to reflect on these Biblical affirmations.*

NT 1 Peter 1:13–2:3

Be Holy

13Therefore, prepare your minds for action; be self-controlled; set your hope fully on the grace to be given you when Jesus
Christ is revealed. 14As obedient children,
do not conform to the evil desires you
had when you lived in ignorance. 15But
just as he who called you is holy, so be
holy in all you do; 16for it is written: "Be
holy, because I am holy."[a]
17Since you call on a Father who judges
each man's work impartially, live your
lives as strangers here in reverent fear.
18For you know that it was not with perishable things such as silver or gold that
you were redeemed from the empty way
of life handed down to you from your
forefathers, 19but with the precious blood
of Christ, a lamb without blemish or defect. 20He was chosen before the creation
of the world, but was revealed in these last
times for your sake. 21Through him you
believe in God, who raised him from the
dead and glorified him, and so your faith
and hope are in God.
22Now that you have purified yourselves
by obeying the truth so that you have sincere love for your brothers, love one another deeply, from the heart.[b] 23For you
have been born again, not of perishable
seed, but of imperishable, through the living and enduring word of God. 24For,

"All men are like grass,
and all their glory is like the flowers
of the field;
the grass withers and the flowers fall,
25 but the word of the Lord stands
forever."[c]

And this is the word that was preached to
you.

2 Therefore, rid yourselves of all malice
and all deceit, hypocrisy, envy, and
slander of every kind. 2Like newborn babies, crave pure spiritual milk, so that by
it you may grow up in your salvation,
3now that you have tasted that the Lord is
good.

[a] *16* Lev. 11:44,45; 19:2; 20:7
[b] *22* Some early manuscripts *from a pure heart*
[c] *25* Isaiah 40:6-8

PRAYER: THE ATTRIBUTES OF GOD

O SOVEREIGN Lord, You are God! Your words are true, and You have promised good things to Your servant. (2 Samuel 7:28) . . . You, O Lord, are the Spirit, and where the Spirit of the Lord is, there is freedom. (2 Corinthians 3:17)

***PAUSE** to reflect on these affirmations about the person, powers and perfection of God.*

YEAR 1
DAY 287

OT **Psalms 56–57**

Psalm 56

For the director of music. To ⌊the tune of⌋ "A Dove on Distant Oaks." Of David. A *miktam*.[a] When the Philistines had seized him in Gath.

1 Be merciful to me, O God, for men
hotly pursue me;
all day long they press their attack.
2 My slanderers pursue me all day long;
many are attacking me in their pride.

3 When I am afraid,
I will trust in you.
4 In God, whose word I praise,
in God I trust; I will not be afraid.
What can mortal man do to me?

5 All day long they twist my words;
they are always plotting to harm
me.
6 They conspire, they lurk,
they watch my steps,
eager to take my life.

7 On no account let them escape;
in your anger, O God, bring down
the nations.
8 Record my lament;
list my tears on your scroll[b]—
are they not in your record?

9 Then my enemies will turn back
when I call for help.
By this I will know that God is for
me.
10 In God, whose word I praise,
in the LORD, whose word I praise—
11 in God I trust; I will not be afraid.
What can man do to me?

12 I am under vows to you, O God;
I will present my thank offerings to
you.
13 For you have delivered me[c] from
death
and my feet from stumbling,
that I may walk before God
in the light of life.[d]

Psalm 57

For the director of music. ⌊To the tune of⌋ "Do Not Destroy." Of David. A *miktam*.[a] When he had fled from Saul into the cave.

1 Have mercy on me, O God, have
mercy on me,
for in you my soul takes refuge.
I will take refuge in the shadow of
your wings
until the disaster has passed.

2 I cry out to God Most High,
to God, who fulfills ⌊his purpose⌋
for me.
3 He sends from heaven and saves me,
rebuking those who hotly pursue
me; *Selah*
God sends his love and his
faithfulness.

4 I am in the midst of lions;
I lie among ravenous beasts—
men whose teeth are spears and
arrows,
whose tongues are sharp swords.

5 Be exalted, O God, above the heavens;
let your glory be over all the earth.

6 They spread a net for my feet—
I was bowed down in distress.
They dug a pit in my path—

[a] Title: Probably a literary or musical term [b] 8 Or *I put my tears in your wineskin* [c] 13 Or *my soul* [d] 13 Or *the land of the living*

but they have fallen into it
themselves. *Selah*

7 My heart is steadfast, O God,
my heart is steadfast;
I will sing and make music.
8 Awake, my soul!
Awake, harp and lyre!
I will awaken the dawn.

9 I will praise you, O Lord, among the
nations;
I will sing of you among the peoples.
10 For great is your love, reaching to the
heavens;
your faithfulness reaches to the skies.

11 Be exalted, O God, above the heavens;
let your glory be over all the earth.

PRAYER: THANKSGIVING

FATHER, we look for the time when the Holy City, the new Jerusalem, will come down out of heaven, prepared as a bride adorned for her husband. A loud voice from the throne will say, "Behold, God makes His home with people, and He will dwell with them, and they will be His people, and God Himself will be with them and be their God, and He will wipe every tear from their eyes. There will be no more death or mourning or crying or pain, for the first things have passed away." You, the One who is seated on the throne, will say, "Behold, I make all things new." (Revelation 21:2–5)

***PAUSE** to offer your own expressions of thanksgiving.*

NT 1 Peter 2:4-12

The Living Stone and a Chosen People

4 As you come to him, the living
Stone—rejected by men but chosen by
God and precious to him— 5 you also, like
living stones, are being built into a spiritual house to be a holy priesthood, offering spiritual sacrifices acceptable to God
through Jesus Christ. 6 For in Scripture it
says:

"See, I lay a stone in Zion,
a chosen and precious cornerstone,
and the one who trusts in him
will never be put to shame."[a]

7 Now to you who believe, this stone is
precious. But to those who do not believe,

"The stone the builders rejected
has become the capstone,[b]"[c]

8 and,

"A stone that causes men to stumble
and a rock that makes them fall."[d]

They stumble because they disobey the
message—which is also what they were
destined for.

9 But you are a chosen people, a royal
priesthood, a holy nation, a people belonging to God, that you may declare the
praises of him who called you out of darkness into his wonderful light. 10 Once you
were not a people, but now you are the
people of God; once you had not received
mercy, but now you have received mercy.

11 Dear friends, I urge you, as aliens and
strangers in the world, to abstain from
sinful desires, which war against your
soul. 12 Live such good lives among the pagans that, though they accuse you of doing wrong, they may see your good deeds
and glorify God on the day he visits us.

[a] 6 Isaiah 28:16 [b] 7 Or *cornerstone* [c] 7 Psalm 118:22 [d] 8 Isaiah 8:14

PRAYER: THE WORKS OF GOD

LORD, thank You for Your promise to us: "I will put My law within you and write it on your hearts. I will be your God, and you will be My people. No longer will you teach your neighbor, nor will you

teach a friend, saying, 'Know the Lord,' because You shall all know Me, from the least of you to the greatest. For I will forgive your iniquity and will remember your sins no more." (Jeremiah 31:33–34)

TAKE *a moment to consider the greatness of God's wonderful works.*

YEAR 1
DAY 288

OT 1 Kings 3:1–4:34

Solomon Asks for Wisdom

3 Solomon made an alliance with Pharaoh king of Egypt and married his
daughter. He brought her to the City of
David until he finished building his
palace and the temple of the LORD, and
the wall around Jerusalem. 2The people,
however, were still sacrificing at the high
places, because a temple had not yet been
built for the Name of the LORD. 3Solomon
showed his love for the LORD by walking
according to the statutes of his father David, except that he offered sacrifices and
burned incense on the high places.
4The king went to Gibeon to offer sacrifices, for that was the most important
high place, and Solomon offered a thousand burnt offerings on that altar. 5At Gibeon the LORD appeared to Solomon during the night in a dream, and God said,
"Ask for whatever you want me to give
you."
6Solomon answered, "You have shown
great kindness to your servant, my father
David, because he was faithful to you and
righteous and upright in heart. You have
continued this great kindness to him and
have given him a son to sit on his throne
this very day.
7"Now, O LORD my God, you have
made your servant king in place of my father David. But I am only a little child and
do not know how to carry out my duties.
8Your servant is here among the people
you have chosen, a great people, too numerous to count or number. 9So give your
servant a discerning heart to govern your
people and to distinguish between right
and wrong. For who is able to govern this
great people of yours?"
10The Lord was pleased that Solomon
had asked for this. 11So God said to him,
"Since you have asked for this and not for
long life or wealth for yourself, nor have
asked for the death of your enemies but
for discernment in administering justice,
12I will do what you have asked. I will give
you a wise and discerning heart, so that
there will never have been anyone like
you, nor will there ever be. 13Moreover, I
will give you what you have not asked
for—both riches and honor—so that in
your lifetime you will have no equal
among kings. 14And if you walk in my
ways and obey my statutes and commands as David your father did, I will give
you a long life." 15Then Solomon awoke—
and he realized it had been a dream.
He returned to Jerusalem, stood before
the ark of the Lord's covenant and sacrificed burnt offerings and fellowship offerings.[a] Then he gave a feast for all his
court.

A Wise Ruling

16Now two prostitutes came to the king
and stood before him. 17One of them
said, "My lord, this woman and I live in
the same house. I had a baby while she
was there with me. 18The third day after
my child was born, this woman also had
a baby. We were alone; there was no one
in the house but the two of us.
19"During the night this woman's son
died because she lay on him. 20So she got
up in the middle of the night and took my
son from my side while I your servant was
asleep. She put him by her breast and put
her dead son by my breast. 21The next
morning, I got up to nurse my son—and
he was dead! But when I looked at him
closely in the morning light, I saw that it
wasn't the son I had borne."
22The other woman said, "No! The living one is my son; the dead one is yours."
But the first one insisted, "No! The
dead one is yours; the living one is mine."
And so they argued before the king.
23The king said, "This one says, 'My son

[a] 15 Traditionally *peace offerings*

is alive and your son is dead,' while that
one says, 'No! Your son is dead and mine
is alive.' "
24Then the king said, "Bring me a
sword." So they brought a sword for the
king. 25He then gave an order: "Cut the
living child in two and give half to one
and half to the other."
26The woman whose son was alive was
filled with compassion for her son and
said to the king, "Please, my lord, give her
the living baby! Don't kill him!"
But the other said, "Neither I nor you
shall have him. Cut him in two!"
27Then the king gave his ruling: "Give
the living baby to the first woman. Do not
kill him; she is his mother."
28When all Israel heard the verdict the
king had given, they held the king in awe,
because they saw that he had wisdom
from God to administer justice.

Solomon's Officials and Governors

4 So King Solomon ruled over all Israel.
2And these were his chief officials:

Azariah son of Zadok—the priest;
3Elihoreph and Ahijah, sons of Shisha—secretaries;
Jehoshaphat son of Ahilud—recorder;
4Benaiah son of Jehoiada—commander in chief;
Zadok and Abiathar—priests;
5Azariah son of Nathan—in charge of the district officers;
Zabud son of Nathan—a priest and personal adviser to the king;
6Ahishar—in charge of the palace;
Adoniram son of Abda—in charge of forced labor.

7Solomon also had twelve district governors over all Israel, who supplied provisions for the king and the royal household. Each one had to provide supplies
for one month in the year. 8These are their
names:

Ben-Hur—in the hill country of Ephraim;
9Ben-Deker—in Makaz, Shaalbim, Beth Shemesh and Elon Bethhanan;
10Ben-Hesed—in Arubboth (Socoh and all the land of Hepher were his);
11Ben-Abinadab—in Naphoth Dor[b] (he was married to Taphath daughter of Solomon);
12Baana son of Ahilud—in Taanach and Megiddo, and in all of Beth Shan next to Zarethan below Jezreel, from Beth Shan to Abel Meholah across to Jokmeam;
13Ben-Geber—in Ramoth Gilead (the settlements of Jair son of Manasseh in Gilead were his, as well as the district of Argob in Bashan and its sixty large walled cities with bronze gate bars);
14Ahinadab son of Iddo—in Mahanaim;
15Ahimaaz—in Naphtali (he had married Basemath daughter of Solomon);
16Baana son of Hushai—in Asher and in Aloth;
17Jehoshaphat son of Paruah—in Issachar;
18Shimei son of Ela—in Benjamin;
19Geber son of Uri—in Gilead (the country of Sihon king of the Amorites and the country of Og king of Bashan). He was the only governor over the district.

Solomon's Daily Provisions

20The people of Judah and Israel were
as numerous as the sand on the seashore;
they ate, they drank and they were happy.
21And Solomon ruled over all the kingdoms from the River[c] to the land of the
Philistines, as far as the border of Egypt.
These countries brought tribute and were
Solomon's subjects all his life.
22Solomon's daily provisions were thirty cors[d] of fine flour and sixty cors[e] of
meal, 23ten head of stall-fed cattle, twenty
of pasture-fed cattle and a hundred sheep
and goats, as well as deer, gazelles, roe-
bucks and choice fowl. 24For he ruled over
all the kingdoms west of the River, from
Tiphsah to Gaza, and had peace on all
sides. 25During Solomon's lifetime Judah
and Israel, from Dan to Beersheba, lived
in safety, each man under his own vine
and fig tree.
26Solomon had four[f] thousand stalls for

[b] *11* Or *in the heights of Dor* [c] *21* That is, the Euphrates; also in verse 24 [d] *22* That is, probably about 185 bushels (about 6.6 kiloliters) [e] *22* That is, probably about 375 bushels (about 13.2 kiloliters) [f] *26* Some Septuagint manuscripts (see also 2 Chron. 9:25); Hebrew *forty*

chariot horses, and twelve thousand
horses.[g]
27The district officers, each in his
month, supplied provisions for King Solomon and all who came to the king's table.
They saw to it that nothing was lacking.
28They also brought to the proper place
their quotas of barley and straw for the
chariot horses and the other horses.

Solomon's Wisdom

29God gave Solomon wisdom and very
great insight, and a breadth of understanding as measureless as the sand on
the seashore. 30Solomon's wisdom was
greater than the wisdom of all the men of
the East, and greater than all the wisdom
of Egypt. 31He was wiser than any other
man, including Ethan the Ezrahite—wiser than Heman, Calcol and Darda, the
sons of Mahol. And his fame spread to all
the surrounding nations. 32He spoke three
thousand proverbs and his songs numbered a thousand and five. 33He described
plant life, from the cedar of Lebanon to
the hyssop that grows out of walls. He
also taught about animals and birds, reptiles and fish. 34Men of all nations came
to listen to Solomon's wisdom, sent by all
the kings of the world, who had heard of
his wisdom.

[g] 26 Or *charioteers*

PRAYER: ADORATION

YOUR testimonies, which You have commanded, are righteous and trustworthy. Your righteousness is everlasting, and Your law is truth. (Psalm 119:138, 142) . . . My heart is steadfast, O God; I will sing praises with all my soul. Awake, harp and lyre! I will awaken the dawn. I will praise You, O Lord, among the peoples; I will sing of You among the nations. Your merciful love is higher than the heavens, and Your truth reaches to the skies. (Psalm 108:1–4)

***PAUSE** to express your thoughts of praise and worship.*

NT 1 Peter 2:13–25

Submission to Rulers and Masters

13Submit yourselves for the Lord's sake
to every authority instituted among men:
whether to the king, as the supreme authority, 14or to governors, who are sent by
him to punish those who do wrong and
to commend those who do right. 15For it
is God's will that by doing good you
should silence the ignorant talk of foolish
men. 16Live as free men, but do not use
your freedom as a cover-up for evil; live as
servants of God. 17Show proper respect to
everyone: Love the brotherhood of believers, fear God, honor the king.
18Slaves, submit yourselves to your masters with all respect, not only to those who
are good and considerate, but also to those
who are harsh. 19For it is commendable if
a man bears up under the pain of unjust
suffering because he is conscious of God.
20But how is it to your credit if you receive
a beating for doing wrong and endure it?
But if you suffer for doing good and you
endure it, this is commendable before
God. 21To this you were called, because
Christ suffered for you, leaving you an example, that you should follow in his steps.

22 "He committed no sin,
and no deceit was found in his
mouth."[a]

23When they hurled their insults at him,
he did not retaliate; when he suffered, he
made no threats. Instead, he entrusted
himself to him who judges justly. 24He
himself bore our sins in his body on the
tree, so that we might die to sins and live
for righteousness; by his wounds you have
been healed. 25For you were like sheep going astray, but now you have returned to
the Shepherd and Overseer of your souls.

[a] 22 Isaiah 53:9

PRAYER: MY RELATIONSHIP TO GOD

HAVING the firstfruits of Your Spirit, O Lord, I groan inwardly as I wait eagerly for my adoption, the redemption of my body. For in hope I have been saved, but hope that I can see is not hope; for who hopes for what is already there? But if I hope for what I do not yet have, I eagerly wait for it with patience. (Romans 8:23–25) . . . God of hope, You will fill me with all joy and peace as I trust in You, so that I may overflow with hope by the power of Your Holy Spirit. (Romans 15:13)

***PAUSE** to thank God for the relationship that you enjoy with Him in Jesus Christ.*

YEAR 1
DAY 289

OT 1 Kings 5:1–6:38

Preparations for Building the Temple

5 When Hiram king of Tyre heard that
Solomon had been anointed king to
succeed his father David, he sent his envoys to Solomon, because he had always
been on friendly terms with David. [2]Solo-
mon sent back this message to Hiram:

[3]"You know that because of the
wars waged against my father David
from all sides, he could not build a
temple for the Name of the LORD his
God until the LORD put his enemies
under his feet. [4]But now the LORD my
God has given me rest on every side,
and there is no adversary or disaster.
[5]I intend, therefore, to build a temple
for the Name of the LORD my God, as
the LORD told my father David, when
he said, 'Your son whom I will put on
the throne in your place will build
the temple for my Name.'
[6]"So give orders that cedars of Lebanon be cut for me. My men will
work with yours, and I will pay you
for your men whatever wages you set.
You know that we have no one so
skilled in felling timber as the Sidonians."

[7]When Hiram heard Solomon's message, he was greatly pleased and said,
"Praise be to the LORD today, for he has
given David a wise son to rule over this
great nation."
[8]So Hiram sent word to Solomon:

"I have received the message you
sent me and will do all you want in
providing the cedar and pine logs.
[9]My men will haul them down from
Lebanon to the sea, and I will float
them in rafts by sea to the place you
specify. There I will separate them
and you can take them away. And
you are to grant my wish by providing food for my royal household."

[10]In this way Hiram kept Solomon supplied with all the cedar and pine logs he
wanted, [11]and Solomon gave Hiram twenty thousand cors[a] of wheat as food for his
household, in addition to twenty thousand baths[b,c] of pressed olive oil. Solomon continued to do this for Hiram year
after year. [12]The LORD gave Solomon wisdom, just as he had promised him. There
were peaceful relations between Hiram
and Solomon, and the two of them made
a treaty.
[13]King Solomon conscripted laborers
from all Israel—thirty thousand men.
[14]He sent them off to Lebanon in shifts of
ten thousand a month, so that they spent
one month in Lebanon and two months
at home. Adoniram was in charge of the
forced labor. [15]Solomon had seventy
thousand carriers and eighty thousand
stonecutters in the hills, [16]as well as thirty-three hundred[d] foremen who super-
vised the project and directed the workmen. [17]At the king's command they

[a] *11* That is, probably about 125,000 bushels (about 4,400 kiloliters) [b] *11* Septuagint (see also 2 Chron. 2:10); Hebrew *twenty cors* [c] *11* That is, about 115,000 gallons (about 440 kiloliters)
[d] *16* Hebrew; some Septuagint manuscripts (see also 2 Chron. 2:2, 18) *thirty-six hundred*

removed from the quarry large blocks of
quality stone to provide a foundation of
dressed stone for the temple. 18The craftsmen of Solomon and Hiram and the men
of Gebal[e] cut and prepared the timber and
stone for the building of the temple.

Solomon Builds the Temple

6 In the four hundred and eightieth[f] year
after the Israelites had come out of
Egypt, in the fourth year of Solomon's
reign over Israel, in the month of Ziv, the
second month, he began to build the temple of the LORD.

2The temple that King Solomon built
for the LORD was sixty cubits long, twenty
wide and thirty high.[g] 3The portico at the
front of the main hall of the temple extended the width of the temple, that is
twenty cubits,[h] and projected ten cubits[i]
from the front of the temple. 4He made
narrow clerestory windows in the temple.
5Against the walls of the main hall and
inner sanctuary he built a structure
around the building, in which there were
side rooms. 6The lowest floor was five cubits[j] wide, the middle floor six cubits[k] and
the third floor seven.[l] He made offset
ledges around the outside of the temple
so that nothing would be inserted into the
temple walls.

7In building the temple, only blocks
dressed at the quarry were used, and no
hammer, chisel or any other iron tool was
heard at the temple site while it was being built.

8The entrance to the lowest[m] floor was
on the south side of the temple; a stairway led up to the middle level and from
there to the third. 9So he built the temple
and completed it, roofing it with beams
and cedar planks. 10And he built the side
rooms all along the temple. The height of
each was five cubits, and they were attached to the temple by beams of cedar.

11The word of the LORD came to Solomon: 12"As for this temple you are building, if you follow my decrees, carry out my
regulations and keep all my commands
and obey them, I will fulfill through you
the promise I gave to David your father.
13And I will live among the Israelites and
will not abandon my people Israel."

14So Solomon built the temple and
completed it. 15He lined its interior walls
with cedar boards, paneling them from
the floor of the temple to the ceiling, and
covered the floor of the temple with
planks of pine. 16He partitioned off twenty cubits[h] at the rear of the temple with
cedar boards from floor to ceiling to form
within the temple an inner sanctuary, the
Most Holy Place. 17The main hall in front
of this room was forty cubits[n] long. 18The
inside of the temple was cedar, carved
with gourds and open flowers. Everything
was cedar; no stone was to be seen.

19He prepared the inner sanctuary within the temple to set the ark of the covenant of the LORD there. 20The inner sanctuary was twenty cubits long, twenty wide
and twenty high.[o] He overlaid the inside
with pure gold, and he also overlaid the
altar of cedar. 21Solomon covered the inside of the temple with pure gold, and he
extended gold chains across the front of
the inner sanctuary, which was overlaid
with gold. 22So he overlaid the whole interior with gold. He also overlaid with
gold the altar that belonged to the inner
sanctuary.

23In the inner sanctuary he made a pair
of cherubim of olive wood, each ten cubits[i] high. 24One wing of the first cherub
was five cubits long, and the other wing
five cubits—ten cubits from wing tip to
wing tip. 25The second cherub also measured ten cubits, for the two cherubim
were identical in size and shape. 26The
height of each cherub was ten cubits. 27He
placed the cherubim inside the innermost
room of the temple, with their wings
spread out. The wing of one cherub
touched one wall, while the wing of the
other touched the other wall, and their
wings touched each other in the middle
of the room. 28He overlaid the cherubim
with gold.

29On the walls all around the temple, in
both the inner and outer rooms, he carved
cherubim, palm trees and open flowers.
30He also covered the floors of both the

[e] *18* That is, Byblos [f] *1* Hebrew; Septuagint *four hundred and fortieth* [g] *2* That is, about 90 feet (about 27 meters) long and 30 feet (about 9 meters) wide and 45 feet (about 13.5 meters) high
[h] *3,16* That is, about 30 feet (about 9 meters)
[i] *3,23* That is, about 15 feet (about 4.5 meters)
[j] *6* That is, about 7 1/2 feet (about 2.3 meters); also in verses 10 and 24 [k] *6* That is, about 9 feet (about 2.7 meters) [l] *6* That is, about 10 1/2 feet (about 3.1 meters) [m] *8* Septuagint; Hebrew *middle*
[n] *17* That is, about 60 feet (about 18 meters)
[o] *20* That is, about 30 feet (about 9 meters) long, wide and high

inner and outer rooms of the temple with
gold.
[31]For the entrance of the inner sanctuary he made doors of olive wood with
five-sided jambs. [32]And on the two olive
wood doors he carved cherubim, palm
trees and open flowers, and overlaid the
cherubim and palm trees with beaten
gold. [33]In the same way he made four-sid-
ed jambs of olive wood for the entrance
to the main hall. [34]He also made two pine
doors, each having two leaves that turned
in sockets. [35]He carved cherubim, palm
trees and open flowers on them and overlaid them with gold hammered evenly
over the carvings.
[36]And he built the inner courtyard of
three courses of dressed stone and one
course of trimmed cedar beams.
[37]The foundation of the temple of the
LORD was laid in the fourth year, in the
month of Ziv. [38]In the eleventh year in the
month of Bul, the eighth month, the temple was finished in all its details according to its specifications. He had spent sev-
en years building it.

PRAYER: CONFESSION

BLESSED is the one You discipline, O Lord, the one You teach from Your word. (Psalm 94:12)

***ASK** the Spirit to search your heart and reveal any areas of unconfessed sin. Acknowledge these to the Lord and thank Him for His forgiveness.*

NT 1 Peter 3:1–22

Wives and Husbands

3 Wives, in the same way be submissive
to your husbands so that, if any of
them do not believe the word, they may
be won over without words by the behavior of their wives, [2]when they see the purity and reverence of your lives. [3]Your
beauty should not come from outward
adornment, such as braided hair and the
wearing of gold jewelry and fine clothes.
[4]Instead, it should be that of your inner
self, the unfading beauty of a gentle and
quiet spirit, which is of great worth in
God's sight. [5]For this is the way the holy
women of the past who put their hope in
God used to make themselves beautiful.
They were submissive to their own husbands, [6]like Sarah, who obeyed Abraham
and called him her master. You are her
daughters if you do what is right and do
not give way to fear.
[7]Husbands, in the same way be considerate as you live with your wives, and treat
them with respect as the weaker partner
and as heirs with you of the gracious gift
of life, so that nothing will hinder your
prayers.

Suffering for Doing Good

[8]Finally, all of you, live in harmony
with one another; be sympathetic, love as
brothers, be compassionate and humble.
[9]Do not repay evil with evil or insult with
insult, but with blessing, because to this
you were called so that you may inherit a
blessing. [10]For,

"Whoever would love life
and see good days
must keep his tongue from evil
and his lips from deceitful speech.
[11]He must turn from evil and do good;
he must seek peace and pursue it.
[12]For the eyes of the Lord are on the
righteous
and his ears are attentive to their
prayer,
but the face of the Lord is against
those who do evil."[a]

[13]Who is going to harm you if you are
eager to do good? [14]But even if you should
suffer for what is right, you are blessed.
"Do not fear what they fear[b]; do not be
frightened."[c] [15]But in your hearts set apart
Christ as Lord. Always be prepared to give
an answer to everyone who asks you to
give the reason for the hope that you have.
But do this with gentleness and respect,
[16]keeping a clear conscience, so that those
who speak maliciously against your good
behavior in Christ may be ashamed of

[a] *12* Psalm 34:12–16 [b] *14* Or *not fear their threats* [c] *14* Isaiah 8:12

their slander. [17]It is better, if it is God's will, to suffer for doing good than for doing evil. [18]For Christ died for sins once for all, the righteous for the unrighteous, to bring you to God. He was put to death in the body but made alive by the Spirit, [19]through whom[d] also he went and preached to the spirits in prison [20]who disobeyed long ago when God waited patiently in the days of Noah while the ark was being built. In it only a few people, eight in all, were saved through water, [21]and this water symbolizes baptism that now saves you also—not the removal of dirt from the body but the pledge[e] of a good conscience toward God. It saves you by the resurrection of Jesus Christ, [22]who has gone into heaven and is at God's right hand—with angels, authorities and powers in submission to him.

[d] *18,19* Or *alive in the spirit, [19]through which*
[e] *21* Or *response*

PRAYER: THE CHARACTER I WANT TO CULTIVATE

MAY I be more concerned about the things of God than human things. (Mark 8:33) . . . I will keep my life free from the love of money and be content with what I have, for You have said, "I will never leave you, nor will I forsake you." (Hebrews 13:5)

***TAKE** a moment to ask the Lord for the grace to grow in godly character.*

YEAR 1 DAY 290

OT 1 Kings 7:1-51

Solomon Builds His Palace

7 It took Solomon thirteen years, however, to complete the construction of his palace. [2]He built the Palace of the Forest of Lebanon a hundred cubits long, fifty wide and thirty high,[a] with four rows of cedar columns supporting trimmed cedar beams. [3]It was roofed with cedar above the beams that rested on the columns—forty-five beams, fifteen to a row. [4]Its windows were placed high in sets of three, facing each other. [5]All the doorways had rectangular frames; they were in the front part in sets of three, facing each other.[b]

[6]He made a colonnade fifty cubits long and thirty wide.[c] In front of it was a portico, and in front of that were pillars and an overhanging roof.

[7]He built the throne hall, the Hall of Justice, where he was to judge, and he covered it with cedar from floor to ceiling.[d] [8]And the palace in which he was to live, set farther back, was similar in design. Solomon also made a palace like this hall for Pharaoh's daughter, whom he had married.

[9]All these structures, from the outside to the great courtyard and from foundation to eaves, were made of blocks of high-grade stone cut to size and trimmed with a saw on their inner and outer faces. [10]The foundations were laid with large stones of good quality, some measuring ten cubits[e] and some eight.[f] [11]Above were high-grade stones, cut to size, and cedar beams. [12]The great courtyard was surrounded by a wall of three courses of dressed stone and one course of trimmed cedar beams, as was the inner courtyard of the temple of the LORD with its portico.

The Temple's Furnishings

[13]King Solomon sent to Tyre and brought Huram,[g] [14]whose mother was a widow from the tribe of Naphtali and whose father was a man of Tyre and a craftsman in bronze. Huram was highly skilled and experienced in all kinds of bronze work. He came to King Solomon and did all the work assigned to him.

[15]He cast two bronze pillars, each eigh-

[a] *2* That is, about 150 feet (about 46 meters) long, 75 feet (about 23 meters) wide and 45 feet (about 13.5 meters) high [b] *5* The meaning of the Hebrew for this verse is uncertain. [c] *6* That is, about 75 feet (about 23 meters) long and 45 feet (about 13.5 meters) wide [d] *7* Vulgate and Syriac; Hebrew *floor* [e] *10* That is, about 15 feet (about 4.5 meters) [f] *10* That is, about 12 feet (about 3.6 meters) [g] *13* Hebrew *Hiram,* a variant of *Huram;* also in verses 40 and 45

teen cubits high and twelve cubits
around,[h] by line. 16He also made two capitals of cast bronze to set on the tops of
the pillars; each capital was five cubits[i]
high. 17A network of interwoven chains
festooned the capitals on top of the pillars, seven for each capital. 18He made
pomegranates in two rows[j] encircling
each network to decorate the capitals on
top of the pillars.[k] He did the same for
each capital. 19The capitals on top of the
pillars in the portico were in the shape of
lilies, four cubits[l] high. 20On the capitals
of both pillars, above the bowl-shaped
part next to the network, were the two
hundred pomegranates in rows all
around. 21He erected the pillars at the portico of the temple. The pillar to the south
he named Jakin[m] and the one to the north
Boaz.[n] 22The capitals on top were in the
shape of lilies. And so the work on the pillars was completed.

23He made the Sea of cast metal, circular in shape, measuring ten cubits[o] from
rim to rim and five cubits high. It took a
line of thirty cubits[p] to measure around it.
24Below the rim, gourds encircled it—ten
to a cubit. The gourds were cast in two
rows in one piece with the Sea.

25The Sea stood on twelve bulls, three
facing north, three facing west, three facing south and three facing east. The Sea
rested on top of them, and their hindquarters were toward the center. 26It was a
handbreadth[q] in thickness, and its rim
was like the rim of a cup, like a lily blossom. It held two thousand baths.[r]

27He also made ten movable stands of
bronze; each was four cubits long, four
wide and three high.[s] 28This is how the
stands were made: They had side panels
attached to uprights. 29On the panels between the uprights were lions, bulls and
cherubim—and on the uprights as well.
Above and below the lions and bulls were
wreaths of hammered work. 30Each stand
had four bronze wheels with bronze axles, and each had a basin resting on four
supports, cast with wreaths on each side.
31On the inside of the stand there was an
opening that had a circular frame one cubit[t] deep. This opening was round, and
with its basework it measured a cubit and
a half.[u] Around its opening there was engraving. The panels of the stands were
square, not round. 32The four wheels were
under the panels, and the axles of the
wheels were attached to the stand. The di-
ameter of each wheel was a cubit and a
half. 33The wheels were made like chariot
wheels; the axles, rims, spokes and hubs
were all of cast metal.

34Each stand had four handles, one on
each corner, projecting from the stand.
35At the top of the stand there was a circular band half a cubit[v] deep. The supports and panels were attached to the top
of the stand. 36He engraved cherubim, lions and palm trees on the surfaces of the
supports and on the panels, in every available space, with wreaths all around. 37This
is the way he made the ten stands. They
were all cast in the same molds and were
identical in size and shape.

38He then made ten bronze basins, each
holding forty baths[w] and measuring four
cubits across, one basin to go on each of
the ten stands. 39He placed five of the
stands on the south side of the temple
and five on the north. He placed the Sea
on the south side, at the southeast corner
of the temple. 40He also made the basins
and shovels and sprinkling bowls.

So Huram finished all the work he had
undertaken for King Solomon in the temple of the LORD:

41the two pillars;
the two bowl-shaped capitals on top
of the pillars;
the two sets of network decorating
the two bowl-shaped capitals on
top of the pillars;
42the four hundred pomegranates for
the two sets of network (two rows
of pomegranates for each network,

[h] *15* That is, about 27 feet (about 8.1 meters) high and 18 feet (about 5.4 meters) around [i] *16* That is, about 7 1/2 feet (about 2.3 meters); also in verse 23 [j] *18* Two Hebrew manuscripts and Septuagint; most Hebrew manuscripts *made the pillars, and there were two rows* [k] *18* Many Hebrew manuscripts and Syriac; most Hebrew manuscripts *pomegranates*
[l] *19* That is, about 6 feet (about 1.8 meters); also in verse 38 [m] *21* *Jakin* probably means *he establishes.*
[n] *21* *Boaz* probably means *in him is strength.*
[o] *23* That is, about 15 feet (about 4.5 meters)
[p] *23* That is, about 45 feet (about 13.5 meters)
[q] *26* That is, about 3 inches (about 8 centimeters)
[r] *26* That is, probably about 11,500 gallons (about 44 kiloliters); the Septuagint does not have this sentence. [s] *27* That is, about 6 feet (about 1.8 meters) long and wide and about 4 1/2 feet (about 1.3 meters) high [t] *31* That is, about 1 1/2 feet (about 0.5 meter) [u] *31* That is, about 2 1/4 feet (about 0.7 meter); also in verse 32 [v] *35* That is, about 3/4 foot (about 0.2 meter) [w] *38* That is, about 230 gallons (about 880 liters)

decorating the bowl-shaped capitals on top of the pillars);
43 the ten stands with their ten basins;
44 the Sea and the twelve bulls under it;
45 the pots, shovels and sprinkling bowls.

All these objects that Huram made for
King Solomon for the temple of the LORD
were of burnished bronze. 46 The king had
them cast in clay molds in the plain of the
Jordan between Succoth and Zarethan.
47 Solomon left all these things un-
weighed, because there were so many; the
weight of the bronze was not determined.
48 Solomon also made all the furnishings that were in the LORD's temple:

the golden altar;
the golden table on which was the
bread of the Presence;
49 the lampstands of pure gold (five on
the right and five on the left, in
front of the inner sanctuary);
the gold floral work and lamps and
tongs;
50 the pure gold basins, wick trimmers,
sprinkling bowls, dishes and
censers;
and the gold sockets for the doors of
the innermost room, the Most
Holy Place, and also for the doors
of the main hall of the temple.

51 When all the work King Solomon had
done for the temple of the LORD was finished, he brought in the things his father
David had dedicated—the silver and gold
and the furnishings—and he placed them
in the treasuries of the LORD's temple.

PRAYER: RENEWAL

YOU are God Almighty; may I walk before You and be blameless. (Genesis 17:1) . . . May I love my enemies, do good to them and lend to them, expecting nothing in return. Then my reward will be great and I will be Your child, O Most High; for You are kind to the ungrateful and evil. May I be merciful just as You are merciful. (Luke 6:35–36)

__PAUSE__ to add your own prayers for personal renewal.

NT 1 Peter 4:1–19

Living for God

4 Therefore, since Christ suffered in his
body, arm yourselves also with the same
attitude, because he who has suffered in
his body is done with sin. 2 As a result, he
does not live the rest of his earthly life for
evil human desires, but rather for the will
of God. 3 For you have spent enough time
in the past doing what pagans choose to
do—living in debauchery, lust, drunkenness, orgies, carousing and detestable idolatry. 4 They think it strange that you do not
plunge with them into the same flood of
dissipation, and they heap abuse on you.
5 But they will have to give account to him
who is ready to judge the living and the
dead. 6 For this is the reason the gospel was
preached even to those who are now dead,
so that they might be judged according to
men in regard to the body, but live according to God in regard to the spirit.
7 The end of all things is near. Therefore
be clear minded and self-controlled so
that you can pray. 8 Above all, love each
other deeply, because love covers over a
multitude of sins. 9 Offer hospitality to
one another without grumbling. 10 Each
one should use whatever gift he has received to serve others, faithfully administering God's grace in its various forms. 11 If
anyone speaks, he should do it as one
speaking the very words of God. If anyone
serves, he should do it with the strength
God provides, so that in all things God
may be praised through Jesus Christ. To
him be the glory and the power for ever
and ever. Amen.

Suffering for Being a Christian

12 Dear friends, do not be surprised at
the painful trial you are suffering, as
though something strange were happening to you. 13 But rejoice that you participate in the sufferings of Christ, so that you
may be overjoyed when his glory is revealed. 14 If you are insulted because of the

name of Christ, you are blessed, for the Spirit of glory and of God rests on you. [15]If you suffer, it should not be as a murderer or thief or any other kind of criminal, or even as a meddler. [16]However, if you suffer as a Christian, do not be ashamed, but praise God that you bear that name. [17]For it is time for judgment to begin with the family of God; and if it begins with us, what will the outcome be for those who do not obey the gospel of God? [18]And,

"If it is hard for the righteous to be saved,
what will become of the ungodly and the sinner?"[a]

[19]So then, those who suffer according to God's will should commit themselves to their faithful Creator and continue to do good.

[a] *18* Prov. 11:31

PRAYER: MY RELATIONSHIP TO OTHERS

I PRAY that words may be given to me, that I may open my mouth boldly to make known the mystery of the gospel. (Ephesians 6:19) . . . I pray that You, O God, may open to me a door for the word, so that I may speak the mystery of Christ and proclaim it clearly, as I ought. (Colossians 4:3–4)

PAUSE *to review your relationships with others and to commit them to the Lord.*

YEAR 1 DAY 291

OT 1 Kings 8:1–66

The Ark Brought to the Temple

8 Then King Solomon summoned into
his presence at Jerusalem the elders of
Israel, all the heads of the tribes and the
chiefs of the Israelite families, to bring up
the ark of the LORD's covenant from Zion,
the City of David. [2]All the men of Israel
came together to King Solomon at the
time of the festival in the month of Ethanim, the seventh month.
[3]When all the elders of Israel had ar-
rived, the priests took up the ark, [4]and
they brought up the ark of the LORD and
the Tent of Meeting and all the sacred furnishings in it. The priests and Levites carried them up, [5]and King Solomon and the
entire assembly of Israel that had gathered
about him were before the ark, sacrificing
so many sheep and cattle that they could
not be recorded or counted.
[6]The priests then brought the ark of the
LORD's covenant to its place in the inner
sanctuary of the temple, the Most Holy
Place, and put it beneath the wings of the
cherubim. [7]The cherubim spread their
wings over the place of the ark and overshadowed the ark and its carrying poles.
[8]These poles were so long that their ends
could be seen from the Holy Place in
front of the inner sanctuary, but not from
outside the Holy Place; and they are still
there today. [9]There was nothing in the ark
except the two stone tablets that Moses
had placed in it at Horeb, where the LORD
made a covenant with the Israelites after
they came out of Egypt.
[10]When the priests withdrew from the
Holy Place, the cloud filled the temple of
the LORD. [11]And the priests could not perform their service because of the cloud,
for the glory of the LORD filled his temple.
[12]Then Solomon said, "The LORD has
said that he would dwell in a dark cloud;
[13]I have indeed built a magnificent temple
for you, a place for you to dwell forever."
[14]While the whole assembly of Israel
was standing there, the king turned
around and blessed them. [15]Then he said:

"Praise be to the LORD, the God of Israel, who with his own hand has fulfilled what he promised with his own mouth to my father David. For
he said, [16]'Since the day I brought my
people Israel out of Egypt, I have not
chosen a city in any tribe of Israel to

have a temple built for my Name to
be there, but I have chosen David to
rule my people Israel.'
17 "My father David had it in his
heart to build a temple for the Name
of the LORD, the God of Israel. 18 But
the LORD said to my father David, 'Because it was in your heart to build a
temple for my Name, you did well to
have this in your heart. 19 Nevertheless,
you are not the one to build the temple, but your son, who is your own
flesh and blood—he is the one who
will build the temple for my Name.'
20 "The LORD has kept the promise
he made: I have succeeded David my
father and now I sit on the throne of
Israel, just as the LORD promised, and
I have built the temple for the Name
of the LORD, the God of Israel. 21 I
have provided a place there for the
ark, in which is the covenant of the
LORD that he made with our fathers
when he brought them out of Egypt."

Solomon's Prayer of Dedication

22 Then Solomon stood before the altar
of the LORD in front of the whole assembly of Israel, spread out his hands toward
heaven 23 and said:

"O LORD, God of Israel, there is no
God like you in heaven above or on
earth below—you who keep your
covenant of love with your servants
who continue wholeheartedly in
your way. 24 You have kept your promise to your servant David my father;
with your mouth you have promised
and with your hand you have fulfilled it—as it is today.
25 "Now LORD, God of Israel, keep for
your servant David my father the
promises you made to him when you
said, 'You shall never fail to have a man
to sit before me on the throne of Israel, if only your sons are careful in all
they do to walk before me as you have
done.' 26 And now, O God of Israel, let
your word that you promised your servant David my father come true.
27 "But will God really dwell on
earth? The heavens, even the highest
heaven, cannot contain you. How
much less this temple I have built! 28 Yet
give attention to your servant's prayer
and his plea for mercy, O LORD my
God. Hear the cry and the prayer that
your servant is praying in your presence this day. 29 May your eyes be open
toward this temple night and day, this
place of which you said, 'My Name
shall be there,' so that you will hear the
prayer your servant prays toward this
place. 30 Hear the supplication of your
servant and of your people Israel when
they pray toward this place. Hear from
heaven, your dwelling place, and when
you hear, forgive.
31 "When a man wrongs his neighbor
and is required to take an oath and he
comes and swears the oath before your
altar in this temple, 32 then hear from
heaven and act. Judge between your
servants, condemning the guilty and
bringing down on his own head what
he has done. Declare the innocent not
guilty, and so establish his innocence.
33 "When your people Israel have
been defeated by an enemy because
they have sinned against you, and
when they turn back to you and confess your name, praying and making
supplication to you in this temple,
34 then hear from heaven and forgive
the sin of your people Israel and
bring them back to the land you gave
to their fathers.
35 "When the heavens are shut up
and there is no rain because your people have sinned against you, and when
they pray toward this place and confess your name and turn from their sin
because you have afflicted them,
36 then hear from heaven and forgive
the sin of your servants, your people
Israel. Teach them the right way to live,
and send rain on the land you gave
your people for an inheritance.
37 "When famine or plague comes
to the land, or blight or mildew, locusts or grasshoppers, or when an enemy besieges them in any of their cities, whatever disaster or disease may
come, 38 and when a prayer or plea is
made by any of your people Israel—
each one aware of the afflictions of
his own heart, and spreading out his
hands toward this temple— 39 then
hear from heaven, your dwelling
place. Forgive and act; deal with each
man according to all he does, since
you know his heart (for you alone
know the hearts of all men), 40 so that

they will fear you all the time they
live in the land you gave our fathers.
41 "As for the foreigner who does not
belong to your people Israel but has
come from a distant land because of
your name— 42 for men will hear of
your great name and your mighty
hand and your outstretched arm—
when he comes and prays toward this
temple, 43 then hear from heaven, your
dwelling place, and do whatever the
foreigner asks of you, so that all the
peoples of the earth may know your
name and fear you, as do your own
people Israel, and may know that this
house I have built bears your Name.
44 "When your people go to war
against their enemies, wherever you
send them, and when they pray to
the LORD toward the city you have
chosen and the temple I have built
for your Name, 45 then hear from
heaven their prayer and their plea,
and uphold their cause.
46 "When they sin against you—for
there is no one who does not sin—and
you become angry with them and give
them over to the enemy, who takes
them captive to his own land, far away
or near; 47 and if they have a change of
heart in the land where they are held
captive, and repent and plead with you
in the land of their conquerors and
say, 'We have sinned, we have done
wrong, we have acted wickedly'; 48 and
if they turn back to you with all their
heart and soul in the land of their enemies who took them captive, and
pray to you toward the land you gave
their fathers, toward the city you have
chosen and the temple I have built for
your Name; 49 then from heaven, your
dwelling place, hear their prayer and
their plea, and uphold their cause.
50 And forgive your people, who have
sinned against you; forgive all the offenses they have committed against
you, and cause their conquerors to
show them mercy; 51 for they are your
people and your inheritance, whom
you brought out of Egypt, out of that
iron-smelting furnace.
52 "May your eyes be open to your
servant's plea and to the plea of your
people Israel, and may you listen to
them whenever they cry out to you.
53 For you singled them out from all
the nations of the world to be your
own inheritance, just as you declared
through your servant Moses when
you, O Sovereign LORD, brought our
fathers out of Egypt."

54 When Solomon had finished all these
prayers and supplications to the LORD, he
rose from before the altar of the LORD,
where he had been kneeling with his
hands spread out toward heaven. 55 He
stood and blessed the whole assembly of
Israel in a loud voice, saying:

56 "Praise be to the LORD, who has
given rest to his people Israel just as he
promised. Not one word has failed of
all the good promises he gave through
his servant Moses. 57 May the LORD our
God be with us as he was with our fathers; may he never leave us nor forsake us. 58 May he turn our hearts to
him, to walk in all his ways and to
keep the commands, decrees and regulations he gave our fathers. 59 And
may these words of mine, which I have
prayed before the LORD, be near to the
LORD our God day and night, that he
may uphold the cause of his servant
and the cause of his people Israel according to each day's need, 60 so that all
the peoples of the earth may know
that the LORD is God and that there is
no other. 61 But your hearts must be fully committed to the LORD our God, to
live by his decrees and obey his commands, as at this time."

The Dedication of the Temple

62 Then the king and all Israel with him
offered sacrifices before the LORD. 63 Solomon offered a sacrifice of fellowship offerings[a] to the LORD: twenty-two thousand
cattle and a hundred and twenty thousand
sheep and goats. So the king and all the Israelites dedicated the temple of the LORD.
64 On that same day the king consecrated
the middle part of the courtyard in front of
the temple of the LORD, and there he offered
burnt offerings, grain offerings and the fat
of the fellowship offerings, because the
bronze altar before the LORD was too small
to hold the burnt offerings, the grain offerings and the fat of the fellowship offerings.
65 So Solomon observed the festival at
that time, and all Israel with him—a vast

[a] 63 Traditionally *peace offerings;* also in verse 64

assembly, people from Lebo[b] Hamath to
the Wadi of Egypt. They celebrated it before the LORD our God for seven days and
seven days more, fourteen days in all.
66 On the following day he sent the people
away. They blessed the king and then went
home, joyful and glad in heart for all the
good things the LORD had done for his
servant David and his people Israel.

[b] 65 Or *from the entrance to*

PRAYER: PETITION

MAY I not be dishonest in judgment, O Lord, in measurement of weight or quantity. May I be honest and just in my business affairs. (Leviticus 19:35–36)

***PAUSE** here to petition God for growth in your character and personal discipline, and for physical health and strength. Ask that He empower you for spiritual warfare against the temptations of the world, the flesh and the devil. Offer prayers regarding your activities for this day and any special concerns you may have.*

NT 1 Peter 5:1-14

To Elders and Young Men

5 To the elders among you, I appeal as a
fellow elder, a witness of Christ's sufferings and one who also will share in the
glory to be revealed: 2 Be shepherds of
God's flock that is under your care, serving as overseers—not because you must,
but because you are willing, as God wants
you to be; not greedy for money, but eager to serve; 3 not lording it over those entrusted to you, but being examples to the
flock. 4 And when the Chief Shepherd appears, you will receive the crown of glory
that will never fade away.
5 Young men, in the same way be submissive to those who are older. All of you,
clothe yourselves with humility toward
one another, because,

"God opposes the proud
but gives grace to the humble."[a]

6 Humble yourselves, therefore, under
God's mighty hand, that he may lift you
up in due time. 7 Cast all your anxiety on
him because he cares for you.
8 Be self-controlled and alert. Your enemy the devil prowls around like a roaring
lion looking for someone to devour. 9 Resist him, standing firm in the faith, because you know that your brothers
throughout the world are undergoing the
same kind of sufferings.
10 And the God of all grace, who called
you to his eternal glory in Christ, after you
have suffered a little while, will himself restore you and make you strong, firm and
steadfast. 11 To him be the power for ever
and ever. Amen.

Final Greetings

12 With the help of Silas,[b] whom I regard
as a faithful brother, I have written to you
briefly, encouraging you and testifying
that this is the true grace of God. Stand
fast in it.
13 She who is in Babylon, chosen together with you, sends you her greetings,
and so does my son Mark. 14 Greet one another with a kiss of love.
Peace to all of you who are in Christ.

[a] 5 Prov. 3:34 [b] 12 Greek *Silvanus,* a variant of *Silas*

PRAYER: THE ATTRIBUTES OF GOD

YOU are the righteous God, who searches my heart and secret thoughts. (Psalm 7:9) . . . What I do may seem right to me, but You, Lord, know what I am thinking. (Proverbs 21:2)

***PAUSE** to reflect on these affirmations about the person, powers and perfection of God.*

YEAR 1 DAY 292

OT **1 Kings 9:1–10:29**

The LORD Appears to Solomon

9 When Solomon had finished building the temple of the LORD and the royal palace, and had achieved all he had desired to do, 2 the LORD appeared to him a second time, as he had appeared to him at Gibeon. 3 The LORD said to him:

> "I have heard the prayer and plea you have made before me; I have consecrated this temple, which you have built, by putting my Name there forever. My eyes and my heart will always be there.
>
> 4 "As for you, if you walk before me in integrity of heart and uprightness, as David your father did, and do all I command and observe my decrees and laws, 5 I will establish your royal throne over Israel forever, as I promised David your father when I said, 'You shall never fail to have a man on the throne of Israel.'
>
> 6 "But if you[a] or your sons turn away from me and do not observe the commands and decrees I have given you[a] and go off to serve other gods and worship them, 7 then I will cut off Israel from the land I have given them and will reject this temple I have consecrated for my Name. Israel will then become a byword and an object of ridicule among all peoples. 8 And though this temple is now imposing, all who pass by will be appalled and will scoff and say, 'Why has the LORD done such a thing to this land and to this temple?' 9 People will answer, 'Because they have forsaken the LORD their God, who brought their fathers out of Egypt, and have embraced other gods, worshiping and serving them—that is why the LORD brought all this disaster on them.' "

Solomon's Other Activities

10 At the end of twenty years, during which Solomon built these two buildings—the temple of the LORD and the royal palace— 11 King Solomon gave twenty towns in Galilee to Hiram king of Tyre, because Hiram had supplied him with all the cedar and pine and gold he wanted. 12 But when Hiram went from Tyre to see the towns that Solomon had given him, he was not pleased with them. 13 "What kind of towns are these you have given me, my brother?" he asked. And he called them the Land of Cabul,[b] a name they have to this day. 14 Now Hiram had sent to the king 120 talents[c] of gold.

15 Here is the account of the forced labor King Solomon conscripted to build the LORD's temple, his own palace, the supporting terraces,[d] the wall of Jerusalem, and Hazor, Megiddo and Gezer. 16 (Pharaoh king of Egypt had attacked and captured Gezer. He had set it on fire. He killed its Canaanite inhabitants and then gave it as a wedding gift to his daughter, Solomon's wife. 17 And Solomon rebuilt Gezer.) He built up Lower Beth Horon, 18 Baalath, and Tadmor[e] in the desert, within his land, 19 as well as all his store cities and the towns for his chariots and for his horses[f]—whatever he desired to build in Jerusalem, in Lebanon and throughout all the territory he ruled.

20 All the people left from the Amorites, Hittites, Perizzites, Hivites and Jebusites (these peoples were not Israelites), 21 that is, their descendants remaining in the land, whom the Israelites could not exterminate[g]—these Solomon conscripted for his slave labor force, as it is to this day. 22 But Solomon did not make slaves of any of the Israelites; they were his fighting men, his government officials, his officers, his captains, and the commanders of his chariots and charioteers. 23 They were also the chief officials in charge of Solomon's projects—550 officials supervising the men who did the work.

24 After Pharaoh's daughter had come up from the City of David to the palace Solomon had built for her, he constructed the supporting terraces.

25 Three times a year Solomon sacrificed burnt offerings and fellowship offerings[h]

[a] *6* The Hebrew is plural. [b] *13* *Cabul* sounds like the Hebrew for *good-for-nothing.* [c] *14* That is, about 4 1/2 tons (about 4 metric tons) [d] *15* Or *the Millo;* also in verse 24 [e] *18* The Hebrew may also be read *Tamar.* [f] *19* Or *charioteers* [g] *21* The Hebrew term refers to the irrevocable giving over of things or persons to the LORD, often by totally destroying them. [h] *25* Traditionally *peace offerings*

on the altar he had built for the LORD,
burning incense before the LORD along
with them, and so fulfilled the temple
obligations.
26 King Solomon also built ships at Ezion Geber, which is near Elath in Edom,
on the shore of the Red Sea.[i] 27 And Hiram
sent his men—sailors who knew the sea—
to serve in the fleet with Solomon's men.
28 They sailed to Ophir and brought back
420 talents[j] of gold, which they delivered
to King Solomon.

The Queen of Sheba Visits Solomon

10 When the queen of Sheba heard
about the fame of Solomon and his
relation to the name of the LORD, she came
to test him with hard questions. 2 Arriving
at Jerusalem with a very great caravan—
with camels carrying spices, large quantities of gold, and precious stones—she
came to Solomon and talked with him
about all that she had on her mind. 3 Solomon answered all her questions; nothing
was too hard for the king to explain to her.
4 When the queen of Sheba saw all the wisdom of Solomon and the palace he had
built, 5 the food on his table, the seating of
his officials, the attending servants in their
robes, his cupbearers, and the burnt offerings he made at[k] the temple of the LORD,
she was overwhelmed.
6 She said to the king, "The report I heard
in my own country about your achievements and your wisdom is true. 7 But I did
not believe these things until I came and
saw with my own eyes. Indeed, not even
half was told me; in wisdom and wealth
you have far exceeded the report I heard.
8 How happy your men must be! How happy your officials, who continually stand before you and hear your wisdom! 9 Praise be
to the LORD your God, who has delighted
in you and placed you on the throne of Israel. Because of the LORD's eternal love for
Israel, he has made you king, to maintain
justice and righteousness."
10 And she gave the king 120 talents[l] of
gold, large quantities of spices, and precious stones. Never again were so many
spices brought in as those the queen of
Sheba gave to King Solomon.
11 (Hiram's ships brought gold from
Ophir; and from there they brought great
cargoes of almugwood[m] and precious
stones. 12 The king used the almugwood to
make supports for the temple of the LORD
and for the royal palace, and to make
harps and lyres for the musicians. So
much almugwood has never been imported or seen since that day.)
13 King Solomon gave the queen of Sheba all she desired and asked for, besides
what he had given her out of his royal
bounty. Then she left and returned with
her retinue to her own country.

Solomon's Splendor

14 The weight of the gold that Solomon
received yearly was 666 talents,[n] 15 not including the revenues from merchants and
traders and from all the Arabian kings and
the governors of the land.
16 King Solomon made two hundred large
shields of hammered gold; six hundred bekas[o] of gold went into each shield. 17 He also
made three hundred small shields of hammered gold, with three minas[p] of gold in
each shield. The king put them in the
Palace of the Forest of Lebanon.
18 Then the king made a great throne inlaid with ivory and overlaid with fine gold.
19 The throne had six steps, and its back
had a rounded top. On both sides of the
seat were armrests, with a lion standing
beside each of them. 20 Twelve lions stood
on the six steps, one at either end of each
step. Nothing like it had ever been made
for any other kingdom. 21 All King Solomon's goblets were gold, and all the
household articles in the Palace of the Forest of Lebanon were pure gold. Nothing
was made of silver, because silver was considered of little value in Solomon's days.
22 The king had a fleet of trading ships[q] at
sea along with the ships of Hiram. Once
every three years it returned, carrying gold,
silver and ivory, and apes and baboons.
23 King Solomon was greater in riches
and wisdom than all the other kings of
the earth. 24 The whole world sought audience with Solomon to hear the wisdom
God had put in his heart. 25 Year after year,
everyone who came brought a gift—arti-

[i] 26 Hebrew *Yam Suph*; that is, Sea of Reeds
[j] 28 That is, about 16 tons (about 14.5 metric tons)
[k] 5 Or *the ascent by which he went up to*
[l] 10 That is, about 4 1/2 tons (about 4 metric tons)
[m] 11 Probably a variant of *algumwood*; also in verse 12
[n] 14 That is, about 25 tons (about 23 metric tons)
[o] 16 That is, about 7 1/2 pounds (about 3.5 kilograms)
[p] 17 That is, about 3 3/4 pounds (about 1.7 kilograms)
[q] 22 Hebrew *of ships of Tarshish*

cles of silver and gold, robes, weapons and spices, and horses and mules.

26 Solomon accumulated chariots and horses; he had fourteen hundred chariots and twelve thousand horses,[r] which he kept in the chariot cities and also with him in Jerusalem. 27 The king made silver as common in Jerusalem as stones, and cedar as plentiful as sycamore-fig trees in the foothills. 28 Solomon's horses were imported from Egypt[s] and from Kue[t]—the royal merchants purchased them from Kue. 29 They imported a chariot from Egypt for six hundred shekels[u] of silver, and a horse for a hundred and fifty.[v] They also exported them to all the kings of the Hittites and of the Arameans.

[r] 26 Or *charioteers* [s] 28 Or possibly *Muzur*, a region in Cilicia; also in verse 29 [t] 28 Probably *Cilicia* [u] 29 That is, about 15 pounds (about 7 kilograms) [v] 29 That is, about 3 3/4 pounds (about 1.7 kilograms)

PRAYER: INTERCESSION

O LORD, we will seek to defend the weak and the fatherless and do justice to the afflicted and destitute. May we rescue the poor and needy and deliver them from the hand of the wicked. (Psalm 82:3–4)

***TAKE** a few moments to intercede on behalf of the poor and hungry, the oppressed and persecuted, and those in control of world and national resources. Offer prayers for peace among nations and regarding current events and concerns.*

NT 2 Peter 1:1–11

1 Simon Peter, a servant and apostle of Jesus Christ,

To those who through the righteousness of our God and Savior Jesus Christ have received a faith as precious as ours:

2 Grace and peace be yours in abundance through the knowledge of God and of Jesus our Lord.

Making One's Calling and Election Sure

3 His divine power has given us everything we need for life and godliness through our knowledge of him who called us by his own glory and goodness. 4 Through these he has given us his very great and precious promises, so that through them you may participate in the divine nature and escape the corruption in the world caused by evil desires.

5 For this very reason, make every effort to add to your faith goodness; and to goodness, knowledge; 6 and to knowledge, self-control; and to self-control, perseverance; and to perseverance, godliness; 7 and to godliness, brotherly kindness; and to brotherly kindness, love. 8 For if you possess these qualities in increasing measure, they will keep you from being ineffective and unproductive in your knowledge of our Lord Jesus Christ. 9 But if anyone does not have them, he is nearsighted and blind, and has forgotten that he has been cleansed from his past sins.

10 Therefore, my brothers, be all the more eager to make your calling and election sure. For if you do these things, you will never fall, 11 and you will receive a rich welcome into the eternal kingdom of our Lord and Savior Jesus Christ.

PRAYER: THE WORKS OF GOD

WE praise You, O Jesus, our Messiah, for the vision we have from John: He saw heaven opened, and there before him was a white horse. You are its rider, called Faithful and True; and in righteousness You judge and make war. Your eyes are like a flame of fire, and

on Your head are many crowns. You have a name written on You that no one knows except Yourself. You are clothed in a robe dipped in blood, and Your name is the Word of God. The armies of heaven, riding on white horses and dressed in fine linen, white and clean, are following You. Out of Your mouth goes a sharp sword with which You will strike down the nations; You will rule them with a rod of iron. You tread the winepress of the fury of the wrath of God Almighty. And on Your robe and on Your thigh You have a name written: ***KING OF KINGS AND LORD OF LORDS.* (Revelation 19:11–16)**

***TAKE** a moment to consider the greatness of God's wonderful works.*

YEAR 1 DAY 293

OT 1 Kings 11:1–43

Solomon's Wives

11 King Solomon, however, loved many
foreign women besides Pharaoh's
daughter—Moabites, Ammonites, Edomites, Sidonians and Hittites. 2They were
from nations about which the LORD had
told the Israelites, "You must not intermarry with them, because they will surely
turn your hearts after their gods." Nevertheless, Solomon held fast to them in love.
3He had seven hundred wives of royal
birth and three hundred concubines, and
his wives led him astray. 4As Solomon
grew old, his wives turned his heart after
other gods, and his heart was not fully devoted to the LORD his God, as the heart of
David his father had been. 5He followed
Ashtoreth the goddess of the Sidonians,
and Molech[a] the detestable god of the Ammonites. 6So Solomon did evil in the eyes
of the LORD; he did not follow the LORD
completely, as David his father had done.
7On a hill east of Jerusalem, Solomon
built a high place for Chemosh the detestable god of Moab, and for Molech the
detestable god of the Ammonites. 8He did
the same for all his foreign wives, who
burned incense and offered sacrifices to
their gods.
9The LORD became angry with Solomon
because his heart had turned away from
the LORD, the God of Israel, who had appeared to him twice. 10Although he had
forbidden Solomon to follow other gods,
Solomon did not keep the LORD's command. 11So the LORD said to Solomon,
"Since this is your attitude and you have
not kept my covenant and my decrees,
which I commanded you, I will most certainly tear the kingdom away from you
and give it to one of your subordinates.
12Nevertheless, for the sake of David your
father, I will not do it during your lifetime.
I will tear it out of the hand of your son.
13Yet I will not tear the whole kingdom
from him, but will give him one tribe for
the sake of David my servant and for the
sake of Jerusalem, which I have chosen."

Solomon's Adversaries

14Then the LORD raised up against Solomon an adversary, Hadad the Edomite,
from the royal line of Edom. 15Earlier when
David was fighting with Edom, Joab the
commander of the army, who had gone up
to bury the dead, had struck down all the
men in Edom. 16Joab and all the Israelites
stayed there for six months, until they had
destroyed all the men in Edom. 17But Hadad, still only a boy, fled to Egypt with
some Edomite officials who had served his
father. 18They set out from Midian and went
to Paran. Then taking men from Paran with
them, they went to Egypt, to Pharaoh king
of Egypt, who gave Hadad a house and
land and provided him with food.
19Pharaoh was so pleased with Hadad
that he gave him a sister of his own wife,
Queen Tahpenes, in marriage. 20The sister
of Tahpenes bore him a son named Genubath, whom Tahpenes brought up in
the royal palace. There Genubath lived
with Pharaoh's own children.
21While he was in Egypt, Hadad heard
that David rested with his fathers and that
Joab the commander of the army was also
dead. Then Hadad said to Pharaoh, "Let me
go, that I may return to my own country."
22"What have you lacked here that you

[a] 5 Hebrew *Milcom;* also in verse 33

want to go back to your own country?" Pharaoh asked.

"Nothing," Hadad replied, "but do let me go!"

23 And God raised up against Solomon another adversary, Rezon son of Eliada, who had fled from his master, Hadadezer king of Zobah. 24 He gathered men around him and became the leader of a band of rebels when David destroyed the forces[b] ⌊of Zobah⌋; the rebels went to Damascus, where they settled and took control. 25 Rezon was Israel's adversary as long as Solomon lived, adding to the trouble caused by Hadad. So Rezon ruled in Aram and was hostile toward Israel.

Jeroboam Rebels Against Solomon

26 Also, Jeroboam son of Nebat rebelled against the king. He was one of Solomon's officials, an Ephraimite from Zeredah, and his mother was a widow named Zeruah.

27 Here is the account of how he rebelled against the king: Solomon had built the supporting terraces[c] and had filled in the gap in the wall of the city of David his father. 28 Now Jeroboam was a man of standing, and when Solomon saw how well the young man did his work, he put him in charge of the whole labor force of the house of Joseph.

29 About that time Jeroboam was going out of Jerusalem, and Ahijah the prophet of Shiloh met him on the way, wearing a new cloak. The two of them were alone out in the country, 30 and Ahijah took hold of the new cloak he was wearing and tore it into twelve pieces. 31 Then he said to Jeroboam, "Take ten pieces for yourself, for this is what the LORD, the God of Israel, says: 'See, I am going to tear the kingdom out of Solomon's hand and give you ten tribes. 32 But for the sake of my servant David and the city of Jerusalem, which I have chosen out of all the tribes of Israel, he will have one tribe. 33 I will do this because they have[d] forsaken me and worshiped Ashtoreth the goddess of the Sidonians, Chemosh the god of the Moabites, and Molech the god of the Ammonites, and have not walked in my ways, nor done what is right in my eyes, nor kept my statutes and laws as David, Solomon's father, did.

34 " 'But I will not take the whole kingdom out of Solomon's hand; I have made him ruler all the days of his life for the sake of David my servant, whom I chose and who observed my commands and statutes. 35 I will take the kingdom from his son's hands and give you ten tribes. 36 I will give one tribe to his son so that David my servant may always have a lamp before me in Jerusalem, the city where I chose to put my Name. 37 However, as for you, I will take you, and you will rule over all that your heart desires; you will be king over Israel. 38 If you do whatever I command you and walk in my ways and do what is right in my eyes by keeping my statutes and commands, as David my servant did, I will be with you. I will build you a dynasty as enduring as the one I built for David and will give Israel to you. 39 I will humble David's descendants because of this, but not forever.' "

40 Solomon tried to kill Jeroboam, but Jeroboam fled to Egypt, to Shishak the king, and stayed there until Solomon's death.

Solomon's Death

41 As for the other events of Solomon's reign—all he did and the wisdom he displayed—are they not written in the book of the annals of Solomon? 42 Solomon reigned in Jerusalem over all Israel forty years. 43 Then he rested with his fathers and was buried in the city of David his father. And Rehoboam his son succeeded him as king.

[b] 24 Hebrew *destroyed them* [c] 27 Or *the Millo*
[d] 33 Hebrew; Septuagint, Vulgate and Syriac *because he has*

PRAYER: AFFIRMATION

I AM not trying to win the approval of other people; I want to win Your approval, Lord. If I were still trying to please people, I would not be a servant of Christ. (Galatians 1:10) . . . If I am afraid of people, fear will trap me. But if I trust in You, O Lord, You will keep me safe. (Proverbs 29:25)

***PAUSE** to reflect on these Biblical affirmations.*

NT 2 Peter 1:12–21

Prophecy of Scripture

[12]So I will always remind you of these
things, even though you know them and
are firmly established in the truth you now
have. [13]I think it is right to refresh your
memory as long as I live in the tent of this
body, [14]because I know that I will soon put
it aside, as our Lord Jesus Christ has made
clear to me. [15]And I will make every effort
to see that after my departure you will always be able to remember these things.

[16]We did not follow cleverly invented
stories when we told you about the power and coming of our Lord Jesus Christ,
but we were eyewitnesses of his majesty.
[17]For he received honor and glory from
God the Father when the voice came to
him from the Majestic Glory, saying, "This
is my Son, whom I love; with him I am
well pleased."[a] [18]We ourselves heard this
voice that came from heaven when we
were with him on the sacred mountain.

[19]And we have the word of the prophets made more certain, and you will do
well to pay attention to it, as to a light
shining in a dark place, until the day
dawns and the morning star rises in your
hearts. [20]Above all, you must understand
that no prophecy of Scripture came about
by the prophet's own interpretation. [21]For
prophecy never had its origin in the will
of man, but men spoke from God as they
were carried along by the Holy Spirit.

[a] *17* Matt. 17:5; Mark 9:7; Luke 9:35

PRAYER: MY RELATIONSHIP TO GOD

O GOD, You chose me in Christ, before the foundation of the world, to be holy and blameless in Your sight. In love You predestined me to be adopted as Your child through Jesus Christ, according to the good pleasure of Your will, to the praise of the glory of Your grace, which You bestowed upon me in the One You love. (Ephesians 1:4–6)

***PAUSE** to thank God for the relationship that you enjoy with Him in Jesus Christ.*

OT Psalm 58

YEAR 1 DAY 294

Psalm 58

For the director of music. ⌊To the tune of⌋ "Do Not Destroy." Of David. A *miktam*.[a]

[1]Do you rulers indeed speak justly?
Do you judge uprightly among men?
[2]No, in your heart you devise injustice,
and your hands mete out violence
on the earth.
[3]Even from birth the wicked go astray;
from the womb they are wayward
and speak lies.
[4]Their venom is like the venom of a
snake,
like that of a cobra that has stopped
its ears,
[5]that will not heed the tune of the
charmer,
however skillful the enchanter may
be.

[6]Break the teeth in their mouths,
O God;
tear out, O LORD, the fangs of the
lions!
[7]Let them vanish like water that flows
away;
when they draw the bow, let their
arrows be blunted.
[8]Like a slug melting away as it moves
along,
like a stillborn child, may they not
see the sun.

[9]Before your pots can feel ⌊the heat of⌋
the thorns—

[a] Title: Probably a literary or musical term

whether they be green or dry—the
wicked will be swept away.[b]
10The righteous will be glad when they
are avenged,
when they bathe their feet in the
blood of the wicked.
11Then men will say,
"Surely the righteous still are
rewarded;
surely there is a God who judges
the earth."

[b] 9 The meaning of the Hebrew for this verse is uncertain.

PRAYER: THANKSGIVING

SINCE Your children have partaken of flesh and blood, You also, O Christ, shared in their humanity so that by Your death You might destroy him who holds the power of death—the devil—and free those who all their lives were held in slavery by their fear of death. We thank You, Jesus Christ, that You were made like Your brothers and sisters in every way, in order that You might become a merciful and faithful high priest in things pertaining to God, to make propitiation for our sins. Because You Yourself suffered when You were tempted, You are able to help those of us who are being tempted. (Hebrews 2:14–15, 17–18)

***PAUSE** to offer your own expressions of thanksgiving.*

NT 2 Peter 2:1-22

False Teachers and Their Destruction

2 But there were also false prophets
among the people, just as there will be
false teachers among you. They will secretly introduce destructive heresies, even
denying the sovereign Lord who bought
them—bringing swift destruction on
themselves. 2Many will follow their
shameful ways and will bring the way of
truth into disrepute. 3In their greed these
teachers will exploit you with stories they
have made up. Their condemnation has
long been hanging over them, and their
destruction has not been sleeping.
4For if God did not spare angels when
they sinned, but sent them to hell,[a]
putting them into gloomy dungeons[b] to
be held for judgment; 5if he did not spare
the ancient world when he brought the
flood on its ungodly people, but protected Noah, a preacher of righteousness, and
seven others; 6if he condemned the cities
of Sodom and Gomorrah by burning
them to ashes, and made them an example of what is going to happen to the ungodly; 7and if he rescued Lot, a righteous
man, who was distressed by the filthy lives
of lawless men 8(for that righteous man,
living among them day after day, was tormented in his righteous soul by the lawless deeds he saw and heard)— 9if this is
so, then the Lord knows how to rescue
godly men from trials and to hold the unrighteous for the day of judgment, while
continuing their punishment.[c] 10This is especially true of those who follow the corrupt desire of the sinful nature[d] and despise authority.
Bold and arrogant, these men are not
afraid to slander celestial beings; 11yet even
angels, although they are stronger and
more powerful, do not bring slanderous accusations against such beings in the presence of the Lord. 12But these men blaspheme in matters they do not understand.
They are like brute beasts, creatures of instinct, born only to be caught and destroyed, and like beasts they too will perish.
13They will be paid back with harm for
the harm they have done. Their idea of
pleasure is to carouse in broad daylight.
They are blots and blemishes, reveling in
their pleasures while they feast with you.[e]
14With eyes full of adultery, they never
stop sinning; they seduce the unstable;
they are experts in greed—an accursed

[a] 4 Greek *Tartarus* [b] 4 Some manuscripts *into chains of darkness* [c] 9 Or *unrighteous for punishment until the day of judgment* [d] 10 Or *the flesh* [e] 13 Some manuscripts *in their love feasts*

brood! 15They have left the straight way
and wandered off to follow the way of Balaam son of Beor, who loved the wages of
wickedness. 16But he was rebuked for his
wrongdoing by a donkey—a beast without speech—who spoke with a man's
voice and restrained the prophet's madness.
17These men are springs without water
and mists driven by a storm. Blackest
darkness is reserved for them. 18For they
mouth empty, boastful words and, by appealing to the lustful desires of sinful human nature, they entice people who are
just escaping from those who live in error.
19They promise them freedom, while they
themselves are slaves of depravity—for a
man is a slave to whatever has mastered
him. 20If they have escaped the corruption
of the world by knowing our Lord and
Savior Jesus Christ and are again entangled in it and overcome, they are worse off
at the end than they were at the beginning. 21It would have been better for them
not to have known the way of righteousness, than to have known it and then to
turn their backs on the sacred command
that was passed on to them. 22Of them the
proverbs are true: "A dog returns to its
vomit,"[f] and, "A sow that is washed goes
back to her wallowing in the mud."

[f] 22 Prov. 26:11

PRAYER: THE CHARACTER I WANT TO CULTIVATE

***I WANT** to be worthy of respect, not double-tongued, not addicted to wine, not fond of dishonest gain, but holding the mystery of the faith with a clear conscience. (1 Timothy 3:8–9) . . . Your grace, O God, has appeared, bringing salvation to all people, teaching us to deny ungodliness and worldly passions and to live sensibly, righteously and in a godly manner in the present age. (Titus 2:11–12)*

***TAKE** a moment to ask the Lord for the grace to grow in godly character.*

YEAR 1 DAY 295

OT 1 Kings 12:1–33

Israel Rebels Against Rehoboam

12 Rehoboam went to Shechem, for all
the Israelites had gone there to make
him king. 2When Jeroboam son of Nebat
heard this (he was still in Egypt, where he
had fled from King Solomon), he returned from[a] Egypt. 3So they sent for Jeroboam, and he and the whole assembly
of Israel went to Rehoboam and said to
him: 4"Your father put a heavy yoke on us,
but now lighten the harsh labor and the
heavy yoke he put on us, and we will serve
you."
5Rehoboam answered, "Go away for
three days and then come back to me." So
the people went away.
6Then King Rehoboam consulted the elders who had served his father Solomon
during his lifetime. "How would you advise me to answer these people?" he
asked.
7They replied, "If today you will be a
servant to these people and serve them
and give them a favorable answer, they
will always be your servants."
8But Rehoboam rejected the advice the
elders gave him and consulted the young
men who had grown up with him and
were serving him. 9He asked them, "What
is your advice? How should we answer
these people who say to me, 'Lighten the
yoke your father put on us'?"
10The young men who had grown up
with him replied, "Tell these people who
have said to you, 'Your father put a heavy
yoke on us, but make our yoke lighter'—
tell them, 'My little finger is thicker than
my father's waist. 11My father laid on you
a heavy yoke; I will make it even heavier.
My father scourged you with whips; I will
scourge you with scorpions.' "
12Three days later Jeroboam and all the
people returned to Rehoboam, as the king

[a] 2 Or *he remained in*

had said, "Come back to me in three
days." 13The king answered the people
harshly. Rejecting the advice given him by
the elders, 14he followed the advice of the
young men and said, "My father made
your yoke heavy; I will make it even heavier. My father scourged you with whips; I
will scourge you with scorpions." 15So the
king did not listen to the people, for this
turn of events was from the LORD, to fulfill the word the LORD had spoken to Jeroboam son of Nebat through Ahijah the
Shilonite.
16When all Israel saw that the king refused to listen to them, they answered the
king:

"What share do we have in David,
what part in Jesse's son?
To your tents, O Israel!
Look after your own house,
O David!"

So the Israelites went home. 17But as for
the Israelites who were living in the towns
of Judah, Rehoboam still ruled over them.
18King Rehoboam sent out Adoniram,[b]
who was in charge of forced labor, but all
Israel stoned him to death. King Rehoboam, however, managed to get into his
chariot and escape to Jerusalem. 19So Israel has been in rebellion against the
house of David to this day.
20When all the Israelites heard that Jeroboam had returned, they sent and called
him to the assembly and made him king
over all Israel. Only the tribe of Judah remained loyal to the house of David.
21When Rehoboam arrived in Jerusalem, he mustered the whole house of
Judah and the tribe of Benjamin—a hundred and eighty thousand fighting men—
to make war against the house of Israel
and to regain the kingdom for Rehoboam
son of Solomon.
22But this word of God came to Shemaiah the man of God: 23"Say to Rehoboam son of Solomon king of Judah, to
the whole house of Judah and Benjamin,
and to the rest of the people, 24'This is
what the LORD says: Do not go up to fight
against your brothers, the Israelites. Go
home, every one of you, for this is my doing.' " So they obeyed the word of the
LORD and went home again, as the LORD
had ordered.

Golden Calves at Bethel and Dan

25Then Jeroboam fortified Shechem in
the hill country of Ephraim and lived
there. From there he went out and built
up Peniel.[c]
26Jeroboam thought to himself, "The
kingdom will now likely revert to the
house of David. 27If these people go up to
offer sacrifices at the temple of the LORD
in Jerusalem, they will again give their allegiance to their lord, Rehoboam king of
Judah. They will kill me and return to
King Rehoboam."
28After seeking advice, the king made two
golden calves. He said to the people, "It is
too much for you to go up to Jerusalem.
Here are your gods, O Israel, who brought
you up out of Egypt." 29One he set up in
Bethel, and the other in Dan. 30And this
thing became a sin; the people went even
as far as Dan to worship the one there.
31Jeroboam built shrines on high places
and appointed priests from all sorts of
people, even though they were not Levites. 32He instituted a festival on the fifteenth day of the eighth month, like the
festival held in Judah, and offered sacrifices on the altar. This he did in Bethel,
sacrificing to the calves he had made. And
at Bethel he also installed priests at the
high places he had made. 33On the fifteenth day of the eighth month, a month
of his own choosing, he offered sacrifices
on the altar he had built at Bethel. So he
instituted the festival for the Israelites and
went up to the altar to make offerings.

[b] *18* Some Septuagint manuscripts and Syriac (see also 1 Kings 4:6 and 5:14); Hebrew *Adoram*
[c] *25* Hebrew *Penuel,* a variant of *Peniel*

PRAYER: ADORATION

***GREAT are You, Lord, and most worthy of praise in Your city, Your holy
mountain. We have meditated on Your unfailing love,
O God, in the midst of Your temple. As is Your name, O God, so is Your
praise to the ends of the earth;***

Your right hand is filled with righteousness. (Psalm 48:1, 9–10) . . . We come, we worship and we bow down, we kneel before You, the Lord our Maker. (Psalm 95:6)

PAUSE *to express your thoughts of praise and worship.*

NT 2 Peter 3:1–18

The Day of the Lord

3 Dear friends, this is now my second letter to you. I have written both of them as reminders to stimulate you to wholesome thinking. 2 I want you to recall the words spoken in the past by the holy prophets and the command given by our Lord and Savior through your apostles.

3 First of all, you must understand that in the last days scoffers will come, scoffing and following their own evil desires. 4 They will say, "Where is this 'coming' he promised? Ever since our fathers died, everything goes on as it has since the beginning of creation." 5 But they deliberately forget that long ago by God's word the heavens existed and the earth was formed out of water and by water. 6 By these waters also the world of that time was deluged and destroyed. 7 By the same word the present heavens and earth are reserved for fire, being kept for the day of judgment and destruction of ungodly men.

8 But do not forget this one thing, dear friends: With the Lord a day is like a thousand years, and a thousand years are like a day. 9 The Lord is not slow in keeping his promise, as some understand slowness. He is patient with you, not wanting anyone to perish, but everyone to come to repentance.

10 But the day of the Lord will come like a thief. The heavens will disappear with a roar; the elements will be destroyed by fire, and the earth and everything in it will be laid bare.[a]

11 Since everything will be destroyed in this way, what kind of people ought you to be? You ought to live holy and godly lives 12 as you look forward to the day of God and speed its coming.[b] That day will bring about the destruction of the heavens by fire, and the elements will melt in the heat. 13 But in keeping with his promise we are looking forward to a new heaven and a new earth, the home of righteousness.

14 So then, dear friends, since you are looking forward to this, make every effort to be found spotless, blameless and at peace with him. 15 Bear in mind that our Lord's patience means salvation, just as our dear brother Paul also wrote you with the wisdom that God gave him. 16 He writes the same way in all his letters, speaking in them of these matters. His letters contain some things that are hard to understand, which ignorant and unstable people distort, as they do the other Scriptures, to their own destruction.

17 Therefore, dear friends, since you already know this, be on your guard so that you may not be carried away by the error of lawless men and fall from your secure position. 18 But grow in the grace and knowledge of our Lord and Savior Jesus Christ. To him be glory both now and forever! Amen.

[a] *10* Some manuscripts *be burned up* [b] *12* Or *as you wait eagerly for the day of God to come*

PRAYER: MY RELATIONSHIP TO OTHERS

ABOVE all, I will love others fervently, because love covers a multitude of sins. (1 Peter 4:8) . . . In this is love, not that we loved You, O God, but that You loved us and sent Your Son to be the propitiation for our sins. Since You so loved us, we also ought to love one another. No one has ever seen You; but if we love one another, You abide in us, and Your love is perfected in us. (1 John 4:10–12)

PAUSE *to review your relationships with others and to commit them to the Lord.*

YEAR 1 DAY 296

OT 1 Kings 13:1–34

The Man of God From Judah

13 By the word of the LORD a man of God came from Judah to Bethel, as Jeroboam was standing by the altar to make an offering. 2He cried out against the altar by the word of the LORD: "O altar, altar! This is what the LORD says: 'A son named Josiah will be born to the house of David. On you he will sacrifice the priests of the high places who now make offerings here, and human bones will be burned on you.' " 3That same day the man of God gave a sign: "This is the sign the LORD has declared: The altar will be split apart and the ashes on it will be poured out."

4When King Jeroboam heard what the man of God cried out against the altar at Bethel, he stretched out his hand from the altar and said, "Seize him!" But the hand he stretched out toward the man shriveled up, so that he could not pull it back. 5Also, the altar was split apart and its ashes poured out according to the sign given by the man of God by the word of the LORD.

6Then the king said to the man of God, "Intercede with the LORD your God and pray for me that my hand may be restored." So the man of God interceded with the LORD, and the king's hand was restored and became as it was before.

7The king said to the man of God, "Come home with me and have something to eat, and I will give you a gift."

8But the man of God answered the king, "Even if you were to give me half your possessions, I would not go with you, nor would I eat bread or drink water here. 9For I was commanded by the word of the LORD: 'You must not eat bread or drink water or return by the way you came.' " 10So he took another road and did not return by the way he had come to Bethel.

11Now there was a certain old prophet living in Bethel, whose sons came and told him all that the man of God had done there that day. They also told their father what he had said to the king. 12Their father asked them, "Which way did he go?" And his sons showed him which road the man of God from Judah had taken. 13So he said to his sons, "Saddle the donkey for me." And when they had saddled the donkey for him, he mounted it 14and rode after the man of God. He found him sitting under an oak tree and asked, "Are you the man of God who came from Judah?"

"I am," he replied.

15So the prophet said to him, "Come home with me and eat."

16The man of God said, "I cannot turn back and go with you, nor can I eat bread or drink water with you in this place. 17I have been told by the word of the LORD: 'You must not eat bread or drink water there or return by the way you came.' "

18The old prophet answered, "I too am a prophet, as you are. And an angel said to me by the word of the LORD: 'Bring him back with you to your house so that he may eat bread and drink water.' " (But he was lying to him.) 19So the man of God returned with him and ate and drank in his house.

20While they were sitting at the table, the word of the LORD came to the old prophet who had brought him back. 21He cried out to the man of God who had come from Judah, "This is what the LORD says: 'You have defied the word of the LORD and have not kept the command the LORD your God gave you. 22You came back and ate bread and drank water in the place where he told you not to eat or drink. Therefore your body will not be buried in the tomb of your fathers.' "

23When the man of God had finished eating and drinking, the prophet who had brought him back saddled his donkey for him. 24As he went on his way, a lion met him on the road and killed him, and his body was thrown down on the road, with both the donkey and the lion standing beside it. 25Some people who passed by saw the body thrown down there, with the lion standing beside the body, and they went and reported it in the city where the old prophet lived.

26When the prophet who had brought him back from his journey heard of it, he said, "It is the man of God who defied the word of the LORD. The LORD has given him over to the lion, which has mauled him

and killed him, as the word of the LORD
had warned him."
27 The prophet said to his sons, "Saddle
the donkey for me," and they did so.
28 Then he went out and found the body
thrown down on the road, with the donkey and the lion standing beside it. The
lion had neither eaten the body nor
mauled the donkey. 29 So the prophet
picked up the body of the man of God,
laid it on the donkey, and brought it back
to his own city to mourn for him and
bury him. 30 Then he laid the body in his
own tomb, and they mourned over him
and said, "Oh, my brother!"
31 After burying him, he said to his sons,
"When I die, bury me in the grave where
the man of God is buried; lay my bones
beside his bones. 32 For the message he declared by the word of the LORD against the
altar in Bethel and against all the shrines
on the high places in the towns of
Samaria will certainly come true."
33 Even after this, Jeroboam did not
change his evil ways, but once more appointed priests for the high places from
all sorts of people. Anyone who wanted to
become a priest he consecrated for the
high places. 34 This was the sin of the
house of Jeroboam that led to its downfall and to its destruction from the face of
the earth.

PRAYER: CONFESSION

O LORD, how can I discern my errors? Cleanse me from hidden faults. Keep Your servant also from presumptuous sins; let them not rule over me. Then will I be blameless, and innocent of great transgression.
(Psalm 19:12–13)

***ASK** the Spirit to search your heart and reveal any areas of unconfessed sin. Acknowledge these to the Lord and thank Him for His forgiveness.*

NT John 1:1–42

The Word Became Flesh

1 In the beginning was the Word, and the
Word was with God, and the Word was
God. 2 He was with God in the beginning.
3 Through him all things were made;
without him nothing was made that has
been made. 4 In him was life, and that life
was the light of men. 5 The light shines in
the darkness, but the darkness has not understood[a] it.
6 There came a man who was sent from
God; his name was John. 7 He came as a
witness to testify concerning that light, so
that through him all men might believe.
8 He himself was not the light; he came
only as a witness to the light. 9 The true
light that gives light to every man was
coming into the world.[b]
10 He was in the world, and though the
world was made through him, the world
did not recognize him. 11 He came to that
which was his own, but his own did not
receive him. 12 Yet to all who received him,
to those who believed in his name, he
gave the right to become children of
God— 13 children born not of natural descent,[c] nor of human decision or a husband's will, but born of God.
14 The Word became flesh and made his
dwelling among us. We have seen his glory, the glory of the One and Only,[d] who
came from the Father, full of grace and
truth.
15 John testifies concerning him. He
cries out, saying, "This was he of whom I
said, 'He who comes after me has surpassed me because he was before me.' "
16 From the fullness of his grace we have
all received one blessing after another.
17 For the law was given through Moses;
grace and truth came through Jesus
Christ. 18 No one has ever seen God, but
God the One and Only,[d,e] who is at the
Father's side, has made him known.

John the Baptist Denies Being the Christ

19 Now this was John's testimony when
the Jews of Jerusalem sent priests and Le-

[a] 5 Or *darkness, and the darkness has not overcome*
[b] 9 Or *This was the true light that gives light to every man who comes into the world*
[c] 13 Greek *of bloods*
[d] 14,18 Or *the Only Begotten*
[e] 18 Some manuscripts *but the only* (or *only begotten*) *Son*

vites to ask him who he was. 20He did not fail to confess, but confessed freely, "I am not the Christ.[f]"

21They asked him, "Then who are you? Are you Elijah?"

He said, "I am not."

"Are you the Prophet?"

He answered, "No."

22Finally they said, "Who are you? Give us an answer to take back to those who sent us. What do you say about yourself?"

23John replied in the words of Isaiah the prophet, "I am the voice of one calling in the desert, 'Make straight the way for the Lord.' "[g]

24Now some Pharisees who had been sent 25questioned him, "Why then do you baptize if you are not the Christ, nor Elijah, nor the Prophet?"

26"I baptize with[h] water," John replied, "but among you stands one you do not know. 27He is the one who comes after me, the thongs of whose sandals I am not worthy to untie."

28This all happened at Bethany on the other side of the Jordan, where John was baptizing.

Jesus the Lamb of God

29The next day John saw Jesus coming toward him and said, "Look, the Lamb of God, who takes away the sin of the world! 30This is the one I meant when I said, 'A man who comes after me has surpassed me because he was before me.' 31I myself did not know him, but the reason I came baptizing with water was that he might be revealed to Israel."

32Then John gave this testimony: "I saw the Spirit come down from heaven as a dove and remain on him. 33I would not have known him, except that the one who sent me to baptize with water told me, 'The man on whom you see the Spirit come down and remain is he who will baptize with the Holy Spirit.' 34I have seen and I testify that this is the Son of God."

Jesus' First Disciples

35The next day John was there again with two of his disciples. 36When he saw Jesus passing by, he said, "Look, the Lamb of God!"

37When the two disciples heard him say this, they followed Jesus. 38Turning around, Jesus saw them following and asked, "What do you want?"

They said, "Rabbi" (which means Teacher), "where are you staying?"

39"Come," he replied, "and you will see."

So they went and saw where he was staying, and spent that day with him. It was about the tenth hour.

40Andrew, Simon Peter's brother, was one of the two who heard what John had said and who had followed Jesus. 41The first thing Andrew did was to find his brother Simon and tell him, "We have found the Messiah" (that is, the Christ). 42And he brought him to Jesus.

Jesus looked at him and said, "You are Simon son of John. You will be called Cephas" (which, when translated, is Peter[i]).

[f] 20 Or *Messiah.* "The Christ" (Greek) and "the Messiah" (Hebrew) both mean "the Anointed One"; also in verse 25. [g] 23 Isaiah 40:3 [h] 26 Or *in;* also in verses 31 and 33 [i] 42 Both *Cephas* (Aramaic) and *Peter* (Greek) mean *rock.*

PRAYER: THE ATTRIBUTES OF GOD

YOU, O Lord, are righteous; You love righteousness; the upright will see Your face. (Psalm 11:7) . . . Your eyes are too pure to look at evil; You cannot look on wickedness, my holy God. (Habakkuk 1:13)

PAUSE *to reflect on these affirmations about the person, powers and perfection of God.*

Ahijah's Prophecy Against Jeroboam

14 At that time Abijah son of Jeroboam
became ill, [2]and Jeroboam said to his
wife, "Go, disguise yourself, so you won't
be recognized as the wife of Jeroboam.
Then go to Shiloh. Ahijah the prophet is
there—the one who told me I would be
king over this people. [3]Take ten loaves of
bread with you, some cakes and a jar of
honey, and go to him. He will tell you
what will happen to the boy." [4]So Jeroboam's wife did what he said and went to
Ahijah's house in Shiloh.

Now Ahijah could not see; his sight was
gone because of his age. [5]But the LORD
had told Ahijah, "Jeroboam's wife is coming to ask you about her son, for he is ill,
and you are to give her such and such an
answer. When she arrives, she will pretend
to be someone else."

[6]So when Ahijah heard the sound of
her footsteps at the door, he said, "Come
in, wife of Jeroboam. Why this pretense?
I have been sent to you with bad news.
[7]Go, tell Jeroboam that this is what the
LORD, the God of Israel, says: 'I raised you
up from among the people and made you
a leader over my people Israel. [8]I tore the
kingdom away from the house of David
and gave it to you, but you have not been
like my servant David, who kept my commands and followed me with all his heart,
doing only what was right in my eyes.
[9]You have done more evil than all who
lived before you. You have made for yourself other gods, idols made of metal; you
have provoked me to anger and thrust me
behind your back.

[10]" 'Because of this, I am going to bring
disaster on the house of Jeroboam. I will
cut off from Jeroboam every last male in
Israel—slave or free. I will burn up the
house of Jeroboam as one burns dung,
until it is all gone. [11]Dogs will eat those
belonging to Jeroboam who die in the
city, and the birds of the air will feed on
those who die in the country. The LORD
has spoken!'

[12]"As for you, go back home. When you
set foot in your city, the boy will die. [13]All
Israel will mourn for him and bury him.
He is the only one belonging to Jeroboam who will be buried, because he is the
only one in the house of Jeroboam in
whom the LORD, the God of Israel, has
found anything good.

[14]"The LORD will raise up for himself a
king over Israel who will cut off the family of Jeroboam. This is the day! What?
Yes, even now.[a] [15]And the LORD will strike
Israel, so that it will be like a reed swaying in the water. He will uproot Israel
from this good land that he gave to their
forefathers and scatter them beyond the
River,[b] because they provoked the LORD to
anger by making Asherah poles.[c] [16]And he
will give Israel up because of the sins Jeroboam has committed and has caused Israel to commit."

[17]Then Jeroboam's wife got up and left
and went to Tirzah. As soon as she
stepped over the threshold of the house,
the boy died. [18]They buried him, and all
Israel mourned for him, as the LORD had
said through his servant the prophet Ahijah.

[19]The other events of Jeroboam's reign,
his wars and how he ruled, are written in
the book of the annals of the kings of Israel. [20]He reigned for twenty-two years
and then rested with his fathers. And Nadab his son succeeded him as king.

Rehoboam King of Judah

[21]Rehoboam son of Solomon was king
in Judah. He was forty-one years old when
he became king, and he reigned seventeen
years in Jerusalem, the city the LORD had
chosen out of all the tribes of Israel in
which to put his Name. His mother's name
was Naamah; she was an Ammonite.

[22]Judah did evil in the eyes of the LORD.
By the sins they committed they stirred up
his jealous anger more than their fathers
had done. [23]They also set up for themselves high places, sacred stones and Asherah poles on every high hill and under
every spreading tree. [24]There were even
male shrine prostitutes in the land; the
people engaged in all the detestable practices of the nations the LORD had driven
out before the Israelites.

[a] *14* The meaning of the Hebrew for this sentence is uncertain. [b] *15* That is, the Euphrates [c] *15* That is, symbols of the goddess Asherah; here and elsewhere in 1 Kings

25 In the fifth year of King Rehoboam,
Shishak king of Egypt attacked Jerusalem.
26 He carried off the treasures of the temple
of the LORD and the treasures of the royal
palace. He took everything, including all
the gold shields Solomon had made. 27 So
King Rehoboam made bronze shields to
replace them and assigned these to the
commanders of the guard on duty at the
entrance to the royal palace. 28 Whenever
the king went to the LORD's temple, the
guards bore the shields, and afterward
they returned them to the guardroom.

29 As for the other events of Rehoboam's
reign, and all he did, are they not written
in the book of the annals of the kings of
Judah? 30 There was continual warfare between Rehoboam and Jeroboam. 31 And
Rehoboam rested with his fathers and was
buried with them in the City of David. His
mother's name was Naamah; she was an
Ammonite. And Abijah[d] his son succeeded him as king.

[d] *31* Some Hebrew manuscripts and Septuagint (see also 2 Chron. 12:16); most Hebrew manuscripts *Abijam*

PRAYER: RENEWAL

LORD, may my life show that love is patient, love is kind, it does not envy; love does not boast, it is not arrogant, it does not behave rudely; it does not seek its own, it is not provoked, it keeps no record of wrongs; it does not rejoice in unrighteousness but rejoices with the truth; it bears all things, believes all things, hopes all things, endures all things. Love never fails. (1 Corinthians 13:4–8) . . . May my love abound more and more in full knowledge and depth of insight, so that I may be able to approve the things that are excellent, in order to be sincere and blameless until the day of Christ—having been filled with the fruit of righteousness that comes through Jesus Christ, to Your glory and praise, O God. (Philippians 1:9–11)

***PAUSE** to add your own prayers for personal renewal.*

NT John 1:43–2:11

Jesus Calls Philip and Nathanael

43 The next day Jesus decided to leave for
Galilee. Finding Philip, he said to him,
"Follow me."
44 Philip, like Andrew and Peter, was
from the town of Bethsaida. 45 Philip
found Nathanael and told him, "We have
found the one Moses wrote about in the
Law, and about whom the prophets also
wrote—Jesus of Nazareth, the son of Joseph."
46 "Nazareth! Can anything good come
from there?" Nathanael asked.
"Come and see," said Philip.
47 When Jesus saw Nathanael approaching, he said of him, "Here is a true Israelite, in whom there is nothing false."
48 "How do you know me?" Nathanael
asked.
Jesus answered, "I saw you while you
were still under the fig tree before Philip
called you."
49 Then Nathanael declared, "Rabbi, you
are the Son of God; you are the King of Israel."
50 Jesus said, "You believe[a] because I told
you I saw you under the fig tree. You shall
see greater things than that." 51 He then
added, "I tell you[b] the truth, you[b] shall see
heaven open, and the angels of God ascending and descending on the Son of
Man."

Jesus Changes Water to Wine

2 On the third day a wedding took place
at Cana in Galilee. Jesus' mother was
there, 2 and Jesus and his disciples had
also been invited to the wedding. 3 When
the wine was gone, Jesus' mother said to
him, "They have no more wine."
4 "Dear woman, why do you involve
me?" Jesus replied. "My time has not yet
come."

[a] *50* Or *Do you believe . . . ?* [b] *51* The Greek is plural.

5 His mother said to the servants, "Do
whatever he tells you."
6 Nearby stood six stone water jars, the
kind used by the Jews for ceremonial
washing, each holding from twenty to
thirty gallons.[c]
7 Jesus said to the servants, "Fill the jars
with water"; so they filled them to the
brim.
8 Then he told them, "Now draw some
out and take it to the master of the banquet."
They did so, 9 and the master of the banquet tasted the water that had been turned
into wine. He did not realize where it had
come from, though the servants who had
drawn the water knew. Then he called the
bridegroom aside 10 and said, "Everyone
brings out the choice wine first and then
the cheaper wine after the guests have had
too much to drink; but you have saved the
best till now."
11 This, the first of his miraculous signs,
Jesus performed at Cana in Galilee. He
thus revealed his glory, and his disciples
put their faith in him.

[c] 6 Greek *two to three metretes* (probably about 75 to 115 liters)

PRAYER: THE WORKS OF GOD

In Your Father's house are many dwellings, Lord Jesus; if it were not so, You would have told us. You went there to prepare a place for us. And as You went to prepare a place for us, You will come again and receive us to Yourself, that we also may be where You are. (John 14:2–3)

***TAKE** a moment to consider the greatness of God's wonderful works.*

YEAR 1 DAY 298

OT Proverbs 13

13 A wise son heeds his father's
instruction,
but a mocker does not listen to
rebuke.

2 From the fruit of his lips a man enjoys
good things,
but the unfaithful have a craving for
violence.

3 He who guards his lips guards his life,
but he who speaks rashly will come
to ruin.

4 The sluggard craves and gets nothing,
but the desires of the diligent are
fully satisfied.

5 The righteous hate what is false,
but the wicked bring shame and
disgrace.

6 Righteousness guards the man of
integrity,
but wickedness overthrows the
sinner.

7 One man pretends to be rich, yet has
nothing;
another pretends to be poor, yet has
great wealth.

8 A man's riches may ransom his life,
but a poor man hears no threat.

9 The light of the righteous shines
brightly,
but the lamp of the wicked is
snuffed out.

10 Pride only breeds quarrels,
but wisdom is found in those who
take advice.

11 Dishonest money dwindles away,
but he who gathers money little by
little makes it grow.

12 Hope deferred makes the heart sick,
but a longing fulfilled is a tree of
life.

13 He who scorns instruction will pay
for it,
but he who respects a command is
rewarded.

14 The teaching of the wise is a fountain
of life,

turning a man from the snares of
death.

[15] Good understanding wins favor,
but the way of the unfaithful is
hard.[a]

[16] Every prudent man acts out of
knowledge,
but a fool exposes his folly.

[17] A wicked messenger falls into trouble,
but a trustworthy envoy brings
healing.

[18] He who ignores discipline comes to
poverty and shame,
but whoever heeds correction is
honored.

[19] A longing fulfilled is sweet to the soul,
but fools detest turning from evil.

[20] He who walks with the wise grows
wise,
but a companion of fools suffers
harm.

[21] Misfortune pursues the sinner,
but prosperity is the reward of the
righteous.

[22] A good man leaves an inheritance for
his children's children,
but a sinner's wealth is stored up
for the righteous.

[23] A poor man's field may produce
abundant food,
but injustice sweeps it away.

[24] He who spares the rod hates his son,
but he who loves him is careful to
discipline him.

[25] The righteous eat to their hearts'
content,
but the stomach of the wicked goes
hungry.

[a] 15 Or *unfaithful does not endure*

PRAYER: PETITION

SINCE I died with You, Jesus, to the basic principles of this world, may I not submit to the world's regulations as though I still belonged to it. (Colossians 2:20)

***PAUSE** here to petition God for growth in your desire to know and please Jesus Christ. Pray for a greater love and commitment to Him, for the grace to practice His presence and for the grace to glorify Him in your life. Offer prayers regarding your activities for this day and any special concerns you may have.*

NT John 2:12–3:21

Jesus Clears the Temple

[12]After this he went down to Capernaum with his mother and brothers and
his disciples. There they stayed for a few
days.
[13]When it was almost time for the Jewish Passover, Jesus went up to Jerusalem.
[14]In the temple courts he found men selling cattle, sheep and doves, and others sitting at tables exchanging money. [15]So he
made a whip out of cords, and drove all
from the temple area, both sheep and cattle; he scattered the coins of the money
changers and overturned their tables. [16]To
those who sold doves he said, "Get these
out of here! How dare you turn my Father's house into a market!"
[17]His disciples remembered that it is
written: "Zeal for your house will consume me."[a]
[18]Then the Jews demanded of him,
"What miraculous sign can you show us
to prove your authority to do all this?"
[19]Jesus answered them, "Destroy this
temple, and I will raise it again in three
days."
[20]The Jews replied, "It has taken forty-
six years to build this temple, and you are
going to raise it in three days?" [21]But the
temple he had spoken of was his body.
[22]After he was raised from the dead, his
disciples recalled what he had said. Then

[a] 17 Psalm 69:9

they believed the Scripture and the words
that Jesus had spoken.
23Now while he was in Jerusalem at the
Passover Feast, many people saw the
miraculous signs he was doing and believed in his name.[b] 24But Jesus would not
entrust himself to them, for he knew all
men. 25He did not need man's testimony
about man, for he knew what was in a
man.

Jesus Teaches Nicodemus

3 Now there was a man of the Pharisees
named Nicodemus, a member of the
Jewish ruling council. 2He came to Jesus
at night and said, "Rabbi, we know you
are a teacher who has come from God. For
no one could perform the miraculous
signs you are doing if God were not with
him."
3In reply Jesus declared, "I tell you the
truth, no one can see the kingdom of God
unless he is born again.[c]"
4"How can a man be born when he is
old?" Nicodemus asked. "Surely he cannot enter a second time into his mother's
womb to be born!"
5Jesus answered, "I tell you the truth, no
one can enter the kingdom of God unless
he is born of water and the Spirit. 6Flesh
gives birth to flesh, but the Spirit[d] gives
birth to spirit. 7You should not be surprised at my saying, 'You[e] must be born
again.' 8The wind blows wherever it
pleases. You hear its sound, but you cannot tell where it comes from or where it
is going. So it is with everyone born of the
Spirit."
9"How can this be?" Nicodemus asked.
10"You are Israel's teacher," said Jesus,
"and do you not understand these things?
11I tell you the truth, we speak of what we
know, and we testify to what we have
seen, but still you people do not accept
our testimony. 12I have spoken to you of
earthly things and you do not believe;
how then will you believe if I speak of
heavenly things? 13No one has ever gone
into heaven except the one who came
from heaven—the Son of Man.[f] 14Just as
Moses lifted up the snake in the desert, so
the Son of Man must be lifted up, 15that
everyone who believes in him may have
eternal life.[g]
16"For God so loved the world that he
gave his one and only Son,[h] that whoever believes in him shall not perish but
have eternal life. 17For God did not send
his Son into the world to condemn the
world, but to save the world through him.
18Whoever believes in him is not condemned, but whoever does not believe
stands condemned already because he has
not believed in the name of God's one
and only Son.[i] 19This is the verdict: Light
has come into the world, but men loved
darkness instead of light because their
deeds were evil. 20Everyone who does evil
hates the light, and will not come into the
light for fear that his deeds will be exposed. 21But whoever lives by the truth
comes into the light, so that it may be
seen plainly that what he has done has
been done through God."[j]

[b] 23 Or *and believed in him* [c] 3 Or *born from above;* also in verse 7 [d] 6 Or *but spirit* [e] 7 The Greek is plural. [f] 13 Some manuscripts *Man, who is in heaven* [g] 15 Or *believes may have eternal life in him* [h] 16 Or *his only begotten Son* [i] 18 Or *God's only begotten Son* [j] 21 Some interpreters end the quotation after verse 15.

PRAYER: MY RELATIONSHIP TO GOD

YOU, O God, will not always strive with us, nor will You harbor Your anger forever. You do not treat us as our sins deserve or repay us according to our iniquities. For as high as the heavens are above the earth, so great is Your love for those who fear You; as far as the east is from the west, so far have You removed our transgressions from us. As a father has compassion on his children, so You, O Lord, have compassion on us who fear You. (Psalm 103:9–13)

***PAUSE** to thank God for the relationship that you enjoy with Him in Jesus Christ.*

YEAR 1
DAY 299

OT 1 Kings 15:1–34

Abijah King of Judah

15 In the eighteenth year of the reign of
Jeroboam son of Nebat, Abijah[a] became king of Judah, [2]and he reigned in
Jerusalem three years. His mother's name
was Maacah daughter of Abishalom.[b]
[3]He committed all the sins his father
had done before him; his heart was not
fully devoted to the LORD his God, as the
heart of David his forefather had been.
[4]Nevertheless, for David's sake the LORD
his God gave him a lamp in Jerusalem by
raising up a son to succeed him and by
making Jerusalem strong. [5]For David had
done what was right in the eyes of the
LORD and had not failed to keep any of
the LORD's commands all the days of his
life—except in the case of Uriah the Hittite.
[6]There was war between Rehoboam[c]
and Jeroboam throughout ⌞Abijah's⌟ lifetime. [7]As for the other events of Abijah's
reign, and all he did, are they not written
in the book of the annals of the kings of
Judah? There was war between Abijah and
Jeroboam. [8]And Abijah rested with his fathers and was buried in the City of David.
And Asa his son succeeded him as king.

Asa King of Judah

[9]In the twentieth year of Jeroboam king
of Israel, Asa became king of Judah, [10]and
he reigned in Jerusalem forty-one years.
His grandmother's name was Maacah
daughter of Abishalom.
[11]Asa did what was right in the eyes of
the LORD, as his father David had done.
[12]He expelled the male shrine prostitutes
from the land and got rid of all the idols
his fathers had made. [13]He even deposed
his grandmother Maacah from her position as queen mother, because she had
made a repulsive Asherah pole. Asa cut
the pole down and burned it in the Kidron Valley. [14]Although he did not remove
the high places, Asa's heart was fully committed to the LORD all his life. [15]He
brought into the temple of the LORD the
silver and gold and the articles that he and
his father had dedicated.
[16]There was war between Asa and Baasha king of Israel throughout their reigns.
[17]Baasha king of Israel went up against Judah and fortified Ramah to prevent anyone from leaving or entering the territory
of Asa king of Judah.
[18]Asa then took all the silver and gold
that was left in the treasuries of the LORD's
temple and of his own palace. He entrusted it to his officials and sent them to
Ben-Hadad son of Tabrimmon, the son of
Hezion, the king of Aram, who was ruling
in Damascus. [19]"Let there be a treaty between me and you," he said, "as there was
between my father and your father. See, I
am sending you a gift of silver and gold.
Now break your treaty with Baasha king
of Israel so he will withdraw from me."
[20]Ben-Hadad agreed with King Asa and
sent the commanders of his forces against
the towns of Israel. He conquered Ijon,
Dan, Abel Beth Maacah and all Kinnereth
in addition to Naphtali. [21]When Baasha
heard this, he stopped building Ramah
and withdrew to Tirzah. [22]Then King Asa
issued an order to all Judah—no one was
exempt—and they carried away from Ramah the stones and timber Baasha had
been using there. With them King Asa
built up Geba in Benjamin, and also Mizpah.
[23]As for all the other events of Asa's
reign, all his achievements, all he did and
the cities he built, are they not written in
the book of the annals of the kings of Judah? In his old age, however, his feet became diseased. [24]Then Asa rested with his
fathers and was buried with them in the
city of his father David. And Jehoshaphat
his son succeeded him as king.

Nadab King of Israel

[25]Nadab son of Jeroboam became king
of Israel in the second year of Asa king of
Judah, and he reigned over Israel two
years. [26]He did evil in the eyes of the LORD,
walking in the ways of his father and in
his sin, which he had caused Israel to
commit.

[a] 1 Some Hebrew manuscripts and Septuagint (see also 2 Chron. 12:16); most Hebrew manuscripts *Abijam;* also in verses 7 and 8 [b] 2 A variant of *Absalom;* also in verse 10 [c] 6 Most Hebrew manuscripts; some Hebrew manuscripts and Syriac *Abijam* (that is, Abijah)

[27]Baasha son of Ahijah of the house of
Issachar plotted against him, and he
struck him down at Gibbethon, a Philistine town, while Nadab and all Israel were
besieging it. [28]Baasha killed Nadab in the
third year of Asa king of Judah and succeeded him as king.
[29]As soon as he began to reign, he killed
Jeroboam's whole family. He did not leave
Jeroboam anyone that breathed, but destroyed them all, according to the word of
the LORD given through his servant Ahijah
the Shilonite— [30]because of the sins Jeroboam had committed and had caused Israel to commit, and because he provoked
the LORD, the God of Israel, to anger.
[31]As for the other events of Nadab's
reign, and all he did, are they not written
in the book of the annals of the kings of
Israel? [32]There was war between Asa and
Baasha king of Israel throughout their
reigns.

Baasha King of Israel

[33]In the third year of Asa king of Judah,
Baasha son of Ahijah became king of all
Israel in Tirzah, and he reigned twenty-
four years. [34]He did evil in the eyes of the
LORD, walking in the ways of Jeroboam
and in his sin, which he had caused Israel to commit.

PRAYER: INTERCESSION

LORD, we know that there should be no division in the body, but its members should have concern for each other. If one member suffers, all the members suffer with it; if one member is honored, all the members rejoice with it. Now we are Your body, Jesus, and each one of us is a member of it. (1 Corinthians 12:25–27)

***TAKE** a few moments to intercede on behalf of your local church, other churches, evangelism and discipleship ministries, educational ministries and any other special concerns you may have.*

NT John 3:22–4:26

John the Baptist's Testimony About Jesus

[22]After this, Jesus and his disciples went
out into the Judean countryside, where he
spent some time with them, and baptized.
[23]Now John also was baptizing at Aenon
near Salim, because there was plenty of
water, and people were constantly coming
to be baptized. [24](This was before John
was put in prison.) [25]An argument developed between some of John's disciples
and a certain Jew[a] over the matter of ceremonial washing. [26]They came to John and
said to him, "Rabbi, that man who was
with you on the other side of the Jordan—
the one you testified about—well, he is
baptizing, and everyone is going to him."
[27]To this John replied, "A man can receive only what is given him from heaven.
[28]You yourselves can testify that I said, 'I am
not the Christ[b] but am sent ahead of him.'
[29]The bride belongs to the bridegroom. The
friend who attends the bridegroom waits
and listens for him, and is full of joy when
he hears the bridegroom's voice. That joy
is mine, and it is now complete. [30]He must
become greater; I must become less.
[31]"The one who comes from above is
above all; the one who is from the earth
belongs to the earth, and speaks as one
from the earth. The one who comes from
heaven is above all. [32]He testifies to what
he has seen and heard, but no one accepts
his testimony. [33]The man who has accepted it has certified that God is truthful.
[34]For the one whom God has sent speaks
the words of God, for God[c] gives the Spirit without limit. [35]The Father loves the Son
and has placed everything in his hands.
[36]Whoever believes in the Son has eternal
life, but whoever rejects the Son will not
see life, for God's wrath remains on him."[d]

Jesus Talks With a Samaritan Woman

4 The Pharisees heard that Jesus was
gaining and baptizing more disciples

[a] 25 Some manuscripts *and certain Jews* [b] 28 Or *Messiah* [c] 34 Greek *he* [d] 36 Some interpreters end the quotation after verse 30.

than John, [2]although in fact it was not Jesus who baptized, but his disciples. [3]When the Lord learned of this, he left Judea and went back once more to Galilee.

[4]Now he had to go through Samaria. [5]So he came to a town in Samaria called Sychar, near the plot of ground Jacob had given to his son Joseph. [6]Jacob's well was there, and Jesus, tired as he was from the journey, sat down by the well. It was about the sixth hour.

[7]When a Samaritan woman came to draw water, Jesus said to her, "Will you give me a drink?" [8](His disciples had gone into the town to buy food.)

[9]The Samaritan woman said to him, "You are a Jew and I am a Samaritan woman. How can you ask me for a drink?" (For Jews do not associate with Samaritans.[e])

[10]Jesus answered her, "If you knew the gift of God and who it is that asks you for a drink, you would have asked him and he would have given you living water."

[11]"Sir," the woman said, "you have nothing to draw with and the well is deep. Where can you get this living water? [12]Are you greater than our father Jacob, who gave us the well and drank from it himself, as did also his sons and his flocks and herds?"

[13]Jesus answered, "Everyone who drinks this water will be thirsty again, [14]but whoever drinks the water I give him will never thirst. Indeed, the water I give him will become in him a spring of water welling up to eternal life."

[15]The woman said to him, "Sir, give me this water so that I won't get thirsty and have to keep coming here to draw water."

[16]He told her, "Go, call your husband and come back."

[17]"I have no husband," she replied.

Jesus said to her, "You are right when you say you have no husband. [18]The fact is, you have had five husbands, and the man you now have is not your husband. What you have just said is quite true."

[19]"Sir," the woman said, "I can see that you are a prophet. [20]Our fathers worshiped on this mountain, but you Jews claim that the place where we must worship is in Jerusalem."

[21]Jesus declared, "Believe me, woman, a time is coming when you will worship the Father neither on this mountain nor in Jerusalem. [22]You Samaritans worship what you do not know; we worship what we do know, for salvation is from the Jews. [23]Yet a time is coming and has now come when the true worshipers will worship the Father in spirit and truth, for they are the kind of worshipers the Father seeks. [24]God is spirit, and his worshipers must worship in spirit and in truth."

[25]The woman said, "I know that Messiah" (called Christ) "is coming. When he comes, he will explain everything to us."

[26]Then Jesus declared, "I who speak to you am he."

[e] 9 Or *do not use dishes Samaritans have used*

PRAYER: THE CHARACTER I WANT TO CULTIVATE

I WILL be on my guard; I will stand firm in the faith, act with courage and be strong. (1 Corinthians 16:13) . . . I will be self-controlled in all things, endure hardship, do the work of an evangelist and fulfill my ministry. (2 Timothy 4:5)

TAKE *a moment to ask the Lord for the grace to grow in godly character.*

YEAR 1 DAY 300

OT 1 Kings 16:1–17:24

16 Then the word of the LORD came to Jehu son of Hanani against Baasha: [2]"I lifted you up from the dust and made you leader of my people Israel, but you walked in the ways of Jeroboam and caused my people Israel to sin and to provoke me to anger by their sins. [3]So I am about to consume Baasha and his house, and I will make your house like that of Jeroboam son of Nebat. [4]Dogs will eat

those belonging to Baasha who die in the
city, and the birds of the air will feed on
those who die in the country."
5 As for the other events of Baasha's
reign, what he did and his achievements,
are they not written in the book of the annals of the kings of Israel? 6 Baasha rested
with his fathers and was buried in Tirzah.
And Elah his son succeeded him as king.
7 Moreover, the word of the LORD came
through the prophet Jehu son of Hanani
to Baasha and his house, because of all
the evil he had done in the eyes of the
LORD, provoking him to anger by the
things he did, and becoming like the
house of Jeroboam—and also because he
destroyed it.

Elah King of Israel

8 In the twenty-sixth year of Asa king of
Judah, Elah son of Baasha became king of
Israel, and he reigned in Tirzah two years.
9 Zimri, one of his officials, who had
command of half his chariots, plotted
against him. Elah was in Tirzah at the time,
getting drunk in the home of Arza, the man
in charge of the palace at Tirzah. 10 Zimri
came in, struck him down and killed him
in the twenty-seventh year of Asa king of Judah. Then he succeeded him as king.
11 As soon as he began to reign and was
seated on the throne, he killed off Baasha's whole family. He did not spare a single male, whether relative or friend. 12 So
Zimri destroyed the whole family of Baasha, in accordance with the word of the
LORD spoken against Baasha through the
prophet Jehu— 13 because of all the sins
Baasha and his son Elah had committed
and had caused Israel to commit, so that
they provoked the LORD, the God of Israel, to anger by their worthless idols.
14 As for the other events of Elah's reign,
and all he did, are they not written in the
book of the annals of the kings of Israel?

Zimri King of Israel

15 In the twenty-seventh year of Asa king
of Judah, Zimri reigned in Tirzah seven
days. The army was encamped near Gibbethon, a Philistine town. 16 When the Israelites in the camp heard that Zimri had
plotted against the king and murdered
him, they proclaimed Omri, the commander of the army, king over Israel that
very day there in the camp. 17 Then Omri
and all the Israelites with him withdrew
from Gibbethon and laid siege to Tirzah.
18 When Zimri saw that the city was taken,
he went into the citadel of the royal palace
and set the palace on fire around him. So
he died, 19 because of the sins he had committed, doing evil in the eyes of the LORD
and walking in the ways of Jeroboam and
in the sin he had committed and had
caused Israel to commit.
20 As for the other events of Zimri's
reign, and the rebellion he carried out, are
they not written in the book of the annals
of the kings of Israel?

Omri King of Israel

21 Then the people of Israel were split
into two factions; half supported Tibni
son of Ginath for king, and the other half
supported Omri. 22 But Omri's followers
proved stronger than those of Tibni son
of Ginath. So Tibni died and Omri became king.
23 In the thirty-first year of Asa king of
Judah, Omri became king of Israel, and he
reigned twelve years, six of them in Tirzah.
24 He bought the hill of Samaria from Shemer for two talents[a] of silver and built a
city on the hill, calling it Samaria, after
Shemer, the name of the former owner of
the hill.
25 But Omri did evil in the eyes of the
LORD and sinned more than all those before him. 26 He walked in all the ways of
Jeroboam son of Nebat and in his sin,
which he had caused Israel to commit, so
that they provoked the LORD, the God of
Israel, to anger by their worthless idols.
27 As for the other events of Omri's
reign, what he did and the things he
achieved, are they not written in the book
of the annals of the kings of Israel? 28 Omri
rested with his fathers and was buried in
Samaria. And Ahab his son succeeded
him as king.

Ahab Becomes King of Israel

29 In the thirty-eighth year of Asa king of
Judah, Ahab son of Omri became king of
Israel, and he reigned in Samaria over Israel twenty-two years. 30 Ahab son of Omri
did more evil in the eyes of the LORD than
any of those before him. 31 He not only
considered it trivial to commit the sins of

[a] 24 That is, about 150 pounds (about 70 kilograms)

Jeroboam son of Nebat, but he also married Jezebel daughter of Ethbaal king of
the Sidonians, and began to serve Baal
and worship him. 32He set up an altar for
Baal in the temple of Baal that he built in
Samaria. 33Ahab also made an Asherah
pole and did more to provoke the LORD,
the God of Israel, to anger than did all the
kings of Israel before him.
34In Ahab's time, Hiel of Bethel rebuilt
Jericho. He laid its foundations at the cost
of his firstborn son Abiram, and he set up
its gates at the cost of his youngest son Segub, in accordance with the word of the
LORD spoken by Joshua son of Nun.

Elijah Fed by Ravens

17 Now Elijah the Tishbite, from Tishbe[b]
in Gilead, said to Ahab, "As the LORD,
the God of Israel, lives, whom I serve,
there will be neither dew nor rain in the
next few years except at my word."
2Then the word of the LORD came to Elijah: 3"Leave here, turn eastward and hide
in the Kerith Ravine, east of the Jordan.
4You will drink from the brook, and I have
ordered the ravens to feed you there."
5So he did what the LORD had told him.
He went to the Kerith Ravine, east of the
Jordan, and stayed there. 6The ravens
brought him bread and meat in the morning and bread and meat in the evening,
and he drank from the brook.

The Widow at Zarephath

7Some time later the brook dried up because there had been no rain in the land.
8Then the word of the LORD came to him:
9"Go at once to Zarephath of Sidon and
stay there. I have commanded a widow in
that place to supply you with food." 10So
he went to Zarephath. When he came to
the town gate, a widow was there gathering sticks. He called to her and asked,
"Would you bring me a little water in a jar
so I may have a drink?" 11As she was going to get it, he called, "And bring me,
please, a piece of bread."
12"As surely as the LORD your God lives,"
she replied, "I don't have any bread—only
a handful of flour in a jar and a little oil
in a jug. I am gathering a few sticks to take
home and make a meal for myself and my
son, that we may eat it—and die."
13Elijah said to her, "Don't be afraid. Go
home and do as you have said. But first
make a small cake of bread for me from
what you have and bring it to me, and
then make something for yourself and
your son. 14For this is what the LORD, the
God of Israel, says: 'The jar of flour will
not be used up and the jug of oil will not
run dry until the day the LORD gives rain
on the land.'"
15She went away and did as Elijah had
told her. So there was food every day for
Elijah and for the woman and her family.
16For the jar of flour was not used up and
the jug of oil did not run dry, in keeping
with the word of the LORD spoken by Elijah.
17Some time later the son of the woman
who owned the house became ill. He
grew worse and worse, and finally
stopped breathing. 18She said to Elijah,
"What do you have against me, man of
God? Did you come to remind me of my
sin and kill my son?"
19"Give me your son," Elijah replied. He
took him from her arms, carried him to
the upper room where he was staying, and
laid him on his bed. 20Then he cried out
to the LORD, "O LORD my God, have you
brought tragedy also upon this widow I
am staying with, by causing her son to
die?" 21Then he stretched himself out on
the boy three times and cried to the LORD,
"O LORD my God, let this boy's life return
to him!"
22The LORD heard Elijah's cry, and the
boy's life returned to him, and he lived.
23Elijah picked up the child and carried
him down from the room into the house.
He gave him to his mother and said,
"Look, your son is alive!"
24Then the woman said to Elijah, "Now
I know that you are a man of God and
that the word of the LORD from your
mouth is the truth."

[b] 1 Or *Tishbite, of the settlers*

PRAYER: AFFIRMATION

I AM not competent in myself to claim anything for myself, but my competence comes from You, O God. You have made me competent as a minister of a new covenant, not of the letter, but of Your Spirit;

for the letter kills, but Your Spirit gives life. (2 Corinthians 3:5–6) . . . It is because of You, Father, that I am in Christ Jesus, who has become for me wisdom from You—that is, my righteousness, sanctification and redemption. (1 Corinthians 1:30)

***PAUSE** to reflect on these Biblical affirmations.*

NT John 4:27–54

The Disciples Rejoin Jesus

27 Just then his disciples returned and were surprised to find him talking with a woman. But no one asked, "What do you want?" or "Why are you talking with her?"

28 Then, leaving her water jar, the woman went back to the town and said to the people, 29 "Come, see a man who told me everything I ever did. Could this be the Christ[a]?" 30 They came out of the town and made their way toward him.

31 Meanwhile his disciples urged him, "Rabbi, eat something."

32 But he said to them, "I have food to eat that you know nothing about."

33 Then his disciples said to each other, "Could someone have brought him food?"

34 "My food," said Jesus, "is to do the will of him who sent me and to finish his work. 35 Do you not say, 'Four months more and then the harvest'? I tell you, open your eyes and look at the fields! They are ripe for harvest. 36 Even now the reaper draws his wages, even now he harvests the crop for eternal life, so that the sower and the reaper may be glad together. 37 Thus the saying 'One sows and another reaps' is true. 38 I sent you to reap what you have not worked for. Others have done the hard work, and you have reaped the benefits of their labor."

Many Samaritans Believe

39 Many of the Samaritans from that town believed in him because of the woman's testimony, "He told me everything I ever did." 40 So when the Samaritans came to him, they urged him to stay with them, and he stayed two days. 41 And because of his words many more became believers.

42 They said to the woman, "We no longer believe just because of what you said; now we have heard for ourselves, and we know that this man really is the Savior of the world."

Jesus Heals the Official's Son

43 After the two days he left for Galilee. 44 (Now Jesus himself had pointed out that a prophet has no honor in his own country.) 45 When he arrived in Galilee, the Galileans welcomed him. They had seen all that he had done in Jerusalem at the Passover Feast, for they also had been there.

46 Once more he visited Cana in Galilee, where he had turned the water into wine. And there was a certain royal official whose son lay sick at Capernaum. 47 When this man heard that Jesus had arrived in Galilee from Judea, he went to him and begged him to come and heal his son, who was close to death.

48 "Unless you people see miraculous signs and wonders," Jesus told him, "you will never believe."

49 The royal official said, "Sir, come down before my child dies."

50 Jesus replied, "You may go. Your son will live."

The man took Jesus at his word and departed. 51 While he was still on the way, his servants met him with the news that his boy was living. 52 When he inquired as to the time when his son got better, they said to him, "The fever left him yesterday at the seventh hour."

53 Then the father realized that this was the exact time at which Jesus had said to him, "Your son will live." So he and all his household believed.

54 This was the second miraculous sign that Jesus performed, having come from Judea to Galilee.

[a] 29 Or *Messiah*

PRAYER: MY RELATIONSHIP TO OTHERS

MAY I obey those who are in authority over me with fear and trembling and with sincerity of heart, as I would obey Christ, not with external service as one who wants to please people, but as a slave of Christ, doing Your will, O God, from my heart. With good will may I serve as if I were serving you, O Lord, and not people, knowing that I will receive back from You whatever good I do. (Ephesians 6:5–8) . . . I will treat subordinates with respect, not threatening them, knowing that You, O Lord, are both their Master and mine and that You are in heaven, and there is no partiality with You.

(Ephesians 6:9)

PAUSE *to review your relationships with others and to commit them to the Lord.*

YEAR 1 DAY 301

OT Psalm 59

Psalm 59

For the director of music. ⌞To the tune of⌟ "Do Not Destroy." Of David. A *miktam*.[a] When Saul had sent men to watch David's house in order to kill him.

1 Deliver me from my enemies,
O God;
protect me from those who rise up
against me.
2 Deliver me from evildoers
and save me from bloodthirsty
men.

3 See how they lie in wait for me!
Fierce men conspire against me
for no offense or sin of mine,
O LORD.
4 I have done no wrong, yet they are
ready to attack me.
Arise to help me; look on my
plight!
5 O LORD God Almighty, the God of
Israel,
rouse yourself to punish all the
nations;
show no mercy to wicked traitors.
Selah

6 They return at evening,
snarling like dogs,
and prowl about the city.
7 See what they spew from their
mouths—
they spew out swords from their
lips,
and they say, "Who can hear us?"
8 But you, O LORD, laugh at them;
you scoff at all those nations.

9 O my Strength, I watch for you;
you, O God, are my fortress, 10 my
loving God.

God will go before me
and will let me gloat over those
who slander me.
11 But do not kill them, O Lord our
shield,[b]
or my people will forget.
In your might make them wander
about,
and bring them down.
12 For the sins of their mouths,
for the words of their lips,
let them be caught in their pride.
For the curses and lies they utter,
13 consume them in wrath,
consume them till they are no
more.
Then it will be known to the ends of
the earth
that God rules over Jacob. *Selah*

14 They return at evening,
snarling like dogs,
and prowl about the city.
15 They wander about for food

[a] Title: Probably a literary or musical term [b] *11* Or *sovereign*

and howl if not satisfied.
16 But I will sing of your strength,
in the morning I will sing of your love;
for you are my fortress,
my refuge in times of trouble.

17 O my Strength, I sing praise to you;
you, O God, are my fortress, my loving God.

PRAYER: THANKSGIVING

IT is in You, Lord Jesus, that I have peace. In this world I will have tribulation, but I will be of good cheer, because You have overcome the world. (John 16:33) . . . I have been set apart for Your gospel, O God—I am among those who are called to belong to Jesus Christ. (Romans 1:1, 6)

***PAUSE** to offer your own expressions of thanksgiving.*

NT John 5:1-30

The Healing at the Pool

5 Some time later, Jesus went up to Jerusalem for a feast of the Jews. 2 Now
there is in Jerusalem near the Sheep Gate
a pool, which in Aramaic is called Bethesda[a] and which is surrounded by five
covered colonnades. 3 Here a great number of disabled people used to lie—the
blind, the lame, the paralyzed.[b] 5 One who
was there had been an invalid for thirty-
eight years. 6 When Jesus saw him lying
there and learned that he had been in this
condition for a long time, he asked him,
"Do you want to get well?"

7 "Sir," the invalid replied, "I have no
one to help me into the pool when the water is stirred. While I am trying to get in,
someone else goes down ahead of me."

8 Then Jesus said to him, "Get up! Pick up
your mat and walk." 9 At once the man was
cured; he picked up his mat and walked.

The day on which this took place was a
Sabbath, 10 and so the Jews said to the man
who had been healed, "It is the Sabbath;
the law forbids you to carry your mat."

11 But he replied, "The man who made
me well said to me, 'Pick up your mat and
walk.' "

12 So they asked him, "Who is this fellow who told you to pick it up and walk?"

13 The man who was healed had no idea
who it was, for Jesus had slipped away
into the crowd that was there.

14 Later Jesus found him at the temple
and said to him, "See, you are well again.
Stop sinning or something worse may
happen to you." 15 The man went away
and told the Jews that it was Jesus who
had made him well.

Life Through the Son

16 So, because Jesus was doing these
things on the Sabbath, the Jews persecuted him. 17 Jesus said to them, "My Father
is always at his work to this very day, and
I, too, am working." 18 For this reason the
Jews tried all the harder to kill him; not
only was he breaking the Sabbath, but he
was even calling God his own Father,
making himself equal with God.

19 Jesus gave them this answer: "I tell
you the truth, the Son can do nothing by
himself; he can do only what he sees his
Father doing, because whatever the Father
does the Son also does. 20 For the Father
loves the Son and shows him all he does.
Yes, to your amazement he will show him
even greater things than these. 21 For just as
the Father raises the dead and gives them
life, even so the Son gives life to whom he
is pleased to give it. 22 Moreover, the Father
judges no one, but has entrusted all judgment to the Son, 23 that all may honor the
Son just as they honor the Father. He who
does not honor the Son does not honor
the Father, who sent him.

24 "I tell you the truth, whoever hears my
word and believes him who sent me has

[a] 2 Some manuscripts *Bethzatha;* other manuscripts *Bethsaida* [b] 3 Some less important manuscripts *paralyzed—and they waited for the moving of the waters. 4 From time to time an angel of the Lord would come down and stir up the waters. The first one into the pool after each such disturbance would be cured of whatever disease he had.*

eternal life and will not be condemned; he has crossed over from death to life. [25]I tell you the truth, a time is coming and has now come when the dead will hear the voice of the Son of God and those who hear will live. [26]For as the Father has life in himself, so he has granted the Son to have life in himself. [27]And he has given him authority to judge because he is the Son of Man.

[28]"Do not be amazed at this, for a time is coming when all who are in their graves will hear his voice [29]and come out—those who have done good will rise to live, and those who have done evil will rise to be condemned. [30]By myself I can do nothing; I judge only as I hear, and my judgment is just, for I seek not to please myself but him who sent me.

PRAYER: THE ATTRIBUTES OF GOD

I WILL proclaim Your name, O Lord, and praise Your greatness, O my God. (Deuteronomy 32:3) . . . Your name is the Lord: I know that You alone are the Most High over all the earth. (Psalm 83:18)

PAUSE *to reflect on these affirmations about the person, powers and perfection of God.*

YEAR 1 DAY 302

OT I Kings 18:1-46

Elijah and Obadiah

18 After a long time, in the third year, the word of the LORD came to Elijah: "Go and present yourself to Ahab, and I will send rain on the land." [2]So Elijah went to present himself to Ahab.

Now the famine was severe in Samaria, [3]and Ahab had summoned Obadiah, who was in charge of his palace. (Obadiah was a devout believer in the LORD. [4]While Jezebel was killing off the LORD's prophets, Obadiah had taken a hundred prophets and hidden them in two caves, fifty in each, and had supplied them with food and water.) [5]Ahab had said to Obadiah, "Go through the land to all the springs and valleys. Maybe we can find some grass to keep the horses and mules alive so we will not have to kill any of our animals." [6]So they divided the land they were to cover, Ahab going in one direction and Obadiah in another.

[7]As Obadiah was walking along, Elijah met him. Obadiah recognized him, bowed down to the ground, and said, "Is it really you, my lord Elijah?"

[8]"Yes," he replied. "Go tell your master, 'Elijah is here.' "

[9]"What have I done wrong," asked Obadiah, "that you are handing your servant over to Ahab to be put to death? [10]As surely as the LORD your God lives, there is not a nation or kingdom where my master has not sent someone to look for you. And whenever a nation or kingdom claimed you were not there, he made them swear they could not find you. [11]But now you tell me to go to my master and say, 'Elijah is here.' [12]I don't know where the Spirit of the LORD may carry you when I leave you. If I go and tell Ahab and he doesn't find you, he will kill me. Yet I your servant have worshiped the LORD since my youth. [13]Haven't you heard, my lord, what I did while Jezebel was killing the prophets of the LORD? I hid a hundred of the LORD's prophets in two caves, fifty in each, and supplied them with food and water. [14]And now you tell me to go to my master and say, 'Elijah is here.' He will kill me!"

[15]Elijah said, "As the LORD Almighty lives, whom I serve, I will surely present myself to Ahab today."

Elijah on Mount Carmel

[16]So Obadiah went to meet Ahab and told him, and Ahab went to meet Elijah. [17]When he saw Elijah, he said to him, "Is that you, you troubler of Israel?"

[18]"I have not made trouble for Israel," Elijah replied. "But you and your father's family have. You have abandoned the LORD's commands and have followed the Baals. [19]Now summon the people from all

over Israel to meet me on Mount Carmel.
And bring the four hundred and fifty
prophets of Baal and the four hundred
prophets of Asherah, who eat at Jezebel's
table."
[20]So Ahab sent word throughout all Israel and assembled the prophets on Mount
Carmel. [21]Elijah went before the people and
said, "How long will you waver between
two opinions? If the LORD is God, follow
him; but if Baal is God, follow him."
But the people said nothing.
[22]Then Elijah said to them, "I am the
only one of the LORD's prophets left, but
Baal has four hundred and fifty prophets.
[23]Get two bulls for us. Let them choose
one for themselves, and let them cut it into
pieces and put it on the wood but not set
fire to it. I will prepare the other bull and
put it on the wood but not set fire to it.
[24]Then you call on the name of your god,
and I will call on the name of the LORD.
The god who answers by fire—he is God."
Then all the people said, "What you say
is good."
[25]Elijah said to the prophets of Baal,
"Choose one of the bulls and prepare it
first, since there are so many of you. Call
on the name of your god, but do not light
the fire." [26]So they took the bull given
them and prepared it.
Then they called on the name of Baal
from morning till noon. "O Baal, answer
us!" they shouted. But there was no response; no one answered. And they
danced around the altar they had made.
[27]At noon Elijah began to taunt them.
"Shout louder!" he said. "Surely he is a
god! Perhaps he is deep in thought, or
busy, or traveling. Maybe he is sleeping
and must be awakened." [28]So they shouted louder and slashed themselves with
swords and spears, as was their custom,
until their blood flowed. [29]Midday passed,
and they continued their frantic prophesying until the time for the evening sacrifice. But there was no response, no one
answered, no one paid attention.
[30]Then Elijah said to all the people,
"Come here to me." They came to him, and
he repaired the altar of the LORD, which was
in ruins. [31]Elijah took twelve stones, one for
each of the tribes descended from Jacob, to
whom the word of the LORD had come, saying, "Your name shall be Israel." [32]With the
stones he built an altar in the name of the
LORD, and he dug a trench around it large
enough to hold two seahs[a] of seed. [33]He
arranged the wood, cut the bull into pieces
and laid it on the wood. Then he said to
them, "Fill four large jars with water and
pour it on the offering and on the wood."
[34]"Do it again," he said, and they did it
again.
"Do it a third time," he ordered, and they
did it the third time. [35]The water ran down
around the altar and even filled the trench.
[36]At the time of sacrifice, the prophet
Elijah stepped forward and prayed:
"O LORD, God of Abraham, Isaac and Israel, let it be known today that you are
God in Israel and that I am your servant
and have done all these things at your
command. [37]Answer me, O LORD, answer
me, so these people will know that you,
O LORD, are God, and that you are turning their hearts back again."
[38]Then the fire of the LORD fell and
burned up the sacrifice, the wood, the
stones and the soil, and also licked up the
water in the trench.
[39]When all the people saw this, they fell
prostrate and cried, "The LORD—he is
God! The LORD—he is God!"
[40]Then Elijah commanded them, "Seize
the prophets of Baal. Don't let anyone get
away!" They seized them, and Elijah had
them brought down to the Kishon Valley
and slaughtered there.
[41]And Elijah said to Ahab, "Go, eat and
drink, for there is the sound of a heavy
rain." [42]So Ahab went off to eat and drink,
but Elijah climbed to the top of Carmel,
bent down to the ground and put his face
between his knees.
[43]"Go and look toward the sea," he told
his servant. And he went up and looked.
"There is nothing there," he said.
Seven times Elijah said, "Go back."
[44]The seventh time the servant reported,
"A cloud as small as a man's hand is rising from the sea."
So Elijah said, "Go and tell Ahab, 'Hitch
up your chariot and go down before the
rain stops you.' "
[45]Meanwhile, the sky grew black with
clouds, the wind rose, a heavy rain came
on and Ahab rode off to Jezreel. [46]The
power of the LORD came upon Elijah and,
tucking his cloak into his belt, he ran
ahead of Ahab all the way to Jezreel.

[a] 32 That is, probably about 13 quarts (about 15 liters)

PRAYER: ADORATION

LORD God of hosts—You who touch the earth and it melts, and all who live in it mourn; You who build Your staircase in the heavens and set its foundation on the earth; You who call for the waters of the sea and pour them out over the face of the earth—the Lord is Your name. (Amos 9:5–6) . . . All flesh is silent before You, O Lord, for You are aroused from Your holy dwelling place. (Zechariah 2:13)

***PAUSE** to express your thoughts of praise and worship.*

NT John 5:31–47

Testimonies About Jesus

31 "If I testify about myself, my testimony is not valid. 32 There is another who testifies in my favor, and I know that his testimony about me is valid.

33 "You have sent to John and he has testified to the truth. 34 Not that I accept human testimony; but I mention it that you may be saved. 35 John was a lamp that burned and gave light, and you chose for a time to enjoy his light.

36 "I have testimony weightier than that of John. For the very work that the Father has given me to finish, and which I am doing, testifies that the Father has sent me. 37 And the Father who sent me has himself testified concerning me. You have never heard his voice nor seen his form, 38 nor does his word dwell in you, for you do not believe the one he sent. 39 You diligently study[a] the Scriptures because you think that by them you possess eternal life. These are the Scriptures that testify about me, 40 yet you refuse to come to me to have life.

41 "I do not accept praise from men, 42 but I know you. I know that you do not have the love of God in your hearts. 43 I have come in my Father's name, and you do not accept me; but if someone else comes in his own name, you will accept him. 44 How can you believe if you accept praise from one another, yet make no effort to obtain the praise that comes from the only God[b]?

45 "But do not think I will accuse you before the Father. Your accuser is Moses, on whom your hopes are set. 46 If you believed Moses, you would believe me, for he wrote about me. 47 But since you do not believe what he wrote, how are you going to believe what I say?"

[a] *39* Or *Study diligently* (the imperative)
[b] *44* Some early manuscripts *the Only One*

PRAYER: THE WORKS OF GOD

GOD, You made the world and everything in it. You are Lord of heaven and earth; You do not dwell in temples built by hands. You are not served by human hands, as though You needed anything, since You Yourself give life and breath and everything else to all people. (Acts 17:24–25)

***TAKE** a moment to consider the greatness of God's wonderful works.*

YEAR 1 DAY 303

OT 1 Kings 19:1–21

Elijah Flees to Horeb

19 Now Ahab told Jezebel everything Elijah had done and how he had killed all the prophets with the sword. 2 So Jezebel sent a messenger to Elijah to say, "May the gods deal with me, be it ever so severely, if by this time tomorrow I do not make your life like that of one of them."

[3]Elijah was afraid[a] and ran for his life.
When he came to Beersheba in Judah, he
left his servant there, [4]while he himself
went a day's journey into the desert. He
came to a broom tree, sat down under it
and prayed that he might die. "I have had
enough, LORD," he said. "Take my life; I
am no better than my ancestors." [5]Then
he lay down under the tree and fell asleep.
All at once an angel touched him and
said, "Get up and eat." [6]He looked
around, and there by his head was a cake
of bread baked over hot coals, and a jar of
water. He ate and drank and then lay
down again.
[7]The angel of the LORD came back a second time and touched him and said, "Get
up and eat, for the journey is too much
for you." [8]So he got up and ate and drank.
Strengthened by that food, he traveled
forty days and forty nights until he
reached Horeb, the mountain of God.
[9]There he went into a cave and spent the
night.

The LORD Appears to Elijah

And the word of the LORD came to him:
"What are you doing here, Elijah?"
[10]He replied, "I have been very zealous
for the LORD God Almighty. The Israelites
have rejected your covenant, broken
down your altars, and put your prophets
to death with the sword. I am the only
one left, and now they are trying to kill
me too."
[11]The LORD said, "Go out and stand on
the mountain in the presence of the LORD,
for the LORD is about to pass by."
Then a great and powerful wind tore
the mountains apart and shattered the
rocks before the LORD, but the LORD was
not in the wind. After the wind there was
an earthquake, but the LORD was not in
the earthquake. [12]After the earthquake
came a fire, but the LORD was not in the
fire. And after the fire came a gentle whisper. [13]When Elijah heard it, he pulled his
cloak over his face and went out and
stood at the mouth of the cave.
Then a voice said to him, "What are you
doing here, Elijah?"
[14]He replied, "I have been very zealous
for the LORD God Almighty. The Israelites
have rejected your covenant, broken
down your altars, and put your prophets
to death with the sword. I am the only
one left, and now they are trying to kill
me too."
[15]The LORD said to him, "Go back the
way you came, and go to the Desert of Damascus. When you get there, anoint Hazael king over Aram. [16]Also, anoint Jehu
son of Nimshi king over Israel, and anoint
Elisha son of Shaphat from Abel Meholah
to succeed you as prophet. [17]Jehu will put
to death any who escape the sword of
Hazael, and Elisha will put to death any
who escape the sword of Jehu. [18]Yet I reserve seven thousand in Israel—all whose
knees have not bowed down to Baal and
all whose mouths have not kissed him."

The Call of Elisha

[19]So Elijah went from there and found
Elisha son of Shaphat. He was plowing
with twelve yoke of oxen, and he himself
was driving the twelfth pair. Elijah went
up to him and threw his cloak around
him. [20]Elisha then left his oxen and ran after Elijah. "Let me kiss my father and
mother good-by," he said, "and then I will
come with you."
"Go back," Elijah replied. "What have I
done to you?"
[21]So Elisha left him and went back. He
took his yoke of oxen and slaughtered
them. He burned the plowing equipment
to cook the meat and gave it to the people, and they ate. Then he set out to follow Elijah and became his attendant.

[a] 3 Or *Elijah saw*

PRAYER: CONFESSION

HAVE mercy on me, O God, according to Your loyal love; according to the greatness of Your compassion blot out my transgressions. Wash me completely from my iniquity and cleanse me from my sin. For I know my transgressions, and my sin is ever before me. Against You,

You only, have I sinned and done what is evil in Your sight, so that You are justified when You speak and blameless when You judge.
(Psalm 51:1–4)

__ASK__ the Spirit to search your heart and reveal any areas of unconfessed sin. Acknowledge these to the Lord and thank Him for His forgiveness.

NT John 6:1-24

Jesus Feeds the Five Thousand

6 Some time after this, Jesus crossed to the far shore of the Sea of Galilee (that is, the Sea of Tiberias), 2 and a great crowd of people followed him because they saw the miraculous signs he had performed on the sick. 3 Then Jesus went up on a mountainside and sat down with his disciples. 4 The Jewish Passover Feast was near.

5 When Jesus looked up and saw a great crowd coming toward him, he said to Philip, "Where shall we buy bread for these people to eat?" 6 He asked this only to test him, for he already had in mind what he was going to do.

7 Philip answered him, "Eight months' wages[a] would not buy enough bread for each one to have a bite!"

8 Another of his disciples, Andrew, Simon Peter's brother, spoke up, 9 "Here is a boy with five small barley loaves and two small fish, but how far will they go among so many?"

10 Jesus said, "Have the people sit down." There was plenty of grass in that place, and the men sat down, about five thousand of them. 11 Jesus then took the loaves, gave thanks, and distributed to those who were seated as much as they wanted. He did the same with the fish.

12 When they had all had enough to eat, he said to his disciples, "Gather the pieces that are left over. Let nothing be wasted." 13 So they gathered them and filled twelve baskets with the pieces of the five barley loaves left over by those who had eaten.

14 After the people saw the miraculous sign that Jesus did, they began to say, "Surely this is the Prophet who is to come into the world." 15 Jesus, knowing that they intended to come and make him king by force, withdrew again to a mountain by himself.

Jesus Walks on the Water

16 When evening came, his disciples went down to the lake, 17 where they got into a boat and set off across the lake for Capernaum. By now it was dark, and Jesus had not yet joined them. 18 A strong wind was blowing and the waters grew rough. 19 When they had rowed three or three and a half miles,[b] they saw Jesus approaching the boat, walking on the water; and they were terrified. 20 But he said to them, "It is I; don't be afraid." 21 Then they were willing to take him into the boat, and immediately the boat reached the shore where they were heading.

22 The next day the crowd that had stayed on the opposite shore of the lake realized that only one boat had been there, and that Jesus had not entered it with his disciples, but that they had gone away alone. 23 Then some boats from Tiberias landed near the place where the people had eaten the bread after the Lord had given thanks. 24 Once the crowd realized that neither Jesus nor his disciples were there, they got into the boats and went to Capernaum in search of Jesus.

[a] 7 Greek *two hundred denarii* [b] 19 Greek *rowed twenty-five or thirty stadia* (about 5 or 6 kilometers)

PRAYER: MY RELATIONSHIP TO GOD

I WILL lie down in peace and sleep, for You alone, O Lord, make me dwell in safety. (Psalm 4:8) . . . May You, O God of peace— who through the blood of the eternal covenant brought back from the dead our Lord Jesus, our great Shepherd of the sheep—equip me with every good thing

***to do Your will, and may You work in me what is pleasing in Your sight, through Jesus Christ, to whom be glory for ever and ever.* (Hebrews 13:20–21)**

***PAUSE** to thank God for the relationship that you enjoy with Him in Jesus Christ.*

YEAR 1 DAY 304

OT 1 Kings 20:1–43

Ben-Hadad Attacks Samaria

20 Now Ben-Hadad king of Aram mustered his entire army. Accompanied
by thirty-two kings with their horses and
chariots, he went up and besieged Samaria
and attacked it. 2He sent messengers into
the city to Ahab king of Israel, saying,
"This is what Ben-Hadad says: 3'Your silver
and gold are mine, and the best of your
wives and children are mine.' "
4The king of Israel answered, "Just as
you say, my lord the king. I and all I have
are yours."
5The messengers came again and said,
"This is what Ben-Hadad says: 'I sent to
demand your silver and gold, your wives
and your children. 6But about this time
tomorrow I am going to send my officials
to search your palace and the houses of
your officials. They will seize everything
you value and carry it away.' "
7The king of Israel summoned all the elders of the land and said to them, "See
how this man is looking for trouble!
When he sent for my wives and my children, my silver and my gold, I did not
refuse him."
8The elders and the people all answered, "Don't listen to him or agree to
his demands."
9So he replied to Ben-Hadad's messengers, "Tell my lord the king, 'Your servant
will do all you demanded the first time,
but this demand I cannot meet.' " They left
and took the answer back to Ben-Hadad.
10Then Ben-Hadad sent another message to Ahab: "May the gods deal with me,
be it ever so severely, if enough dust remains in Samaria to give each of my men
a handful."
11The king of Israel answered, "Tell him:
'One who puts on his armor should not
boast like one who takes it off.' "
12Ben-Hadad heard this message while
he and the kings were drinking in their
tents,[a] and he ordered his men: "Prepare
to attack." So they prepared to attack the
city.

Ahab Defeats Ben-Hadad

13Meanwhile a prophet came to Ahab
king of Israel and announced, "This is what
the LORD says: 'Do you see this vast army?
I will give it into your hand today, and then
you will know that I am the LORD.' "
14"But who will do this?" asked Ahab.
The prophet replied, "This is what the
LORD says: 'The young officers of the provincial commanders will do it.' "
"And who will start the battle?" he
asked.
The prophet answered, "You will."
15So Ahab summoned the young officers of the provincial commanders, 232
men. Then he assembled the rest of the Israelites, 7,000 in all. 16They set out at
noon while Ben-Hadad and the 32 kings
allied with him were in their tents getting
drunk. 17The young officers of the provincial commanders went out first.
Now Ben-Hadad had dispatched
scouts, who reported, "Men are advancing
from Samaria."
18He said, "If they have come out for
peace, take them alive; if they have come
out for war, take them alive."
19The young officers of the provincial
commanders marched out of the city with
the army behind them 20and each one
struck down his opponent. At that, the Arameans fled, with the Israelites in pursuit.
But Ben-Hadad king of Aram escaped on
horseback with some of his horsemen.
21The king of Israel advanced and over-

[a] 12 Or *in Succoth;* also in verse 16

powered the horses and chariots and inflicted heavy losses on the Arameans.
22 Afterward, the prophet came to the
king of Israel and said, "Strengthen your
position and see what must be done, because next spring the king of Aram will attack you again."
23 Meanwhile, the officials of the king of
Aram advised him, "Their gods are gods
of the hills. That is why they were too
strong for us. But if we fight them on the
plains, surely we will be stronger than
they. 24 Do this: Remove all the kings from
their commands and replace them with
other officers. 25 You must also raise an
army like the one you lost—horse for
horse and chariot for chariot—so we can
fight Israel on the plains. Then surely we
will be stronger than they." He agreed
with them and acted accordingly.
26 The next spring Ben-Hadad mustered
the Arameans and went up to Aphek to
fight against Israel. 27 When the Israelites
were also mustered and given provisions,
they marched out to meet them. The Israelites camped opposite them like two
small flocks of goats, while the Arameans
covered the countryside.
28 The man of God came up and told the
king of Israel, "This is what the LORD says:
'Because the Arameans think the LORD is
a god of the hills and not a god of the valleys, I will deliver this vast army into your
hands, and you will know that I am the
LORD.' "
29 For seven days they camped opposite
each other, and on the seventh day the
battle was joined. The Israelites inflicted a
hundred thousand casualties on the Aramean foot soldiers in one day. 30 The rest
of them escaped to the city of Aphek,
where the wall collapsed on twenty-seven
thousand of them. And Ben-Hadad fled to
the city and hid in an inner room.
31 His officials said to him, "Look, we
have heard that the kings of the house of
Israel are merciful. Let us go to the king of
Israel with sackcloth around our waists
and ropes around our heads. Perhaps he
will spare your life."
32 Wearing sackcloth around their waists
and ropes around their heads, they went
to the king of Israel and said, "Your servant Ben-Hadad says: 'Please let me live.' "
The king answered, "Is he still alive? He
is my brother."
33 The men took this as a good sign and
were quick to pick up his word. "Yes, your
brother Ben-Hadad!" they said.
"Go and get him," the king said. When
Ben-Hadad came out, Ahab had him
come up into his chariot.
34 "I will return the cities my father took
from your father," Ben-Hadad offered.
"You may set up your own market areas
in Damascus, as my father did in
Samaria."
⌊Ahab said,⌋ "On the basis of a treaty I
will set you free." So he made a treaty with
him, and let him go.

A Prophet Condemns Ahab

35 By the word of the LORD one of the
sons of the prophets said to his companion, "Strike me with your weapon," but
the man refused.
36 So the prophet said, "Because you
have not obeyed the LORD, as soon as you
leave me a lion will kill you." And after
the man went away, a lion found him and
killed him.
37 The prophet found another man and
said, "Strike me, please." So the man
struck him and wounded him. 38 Then the
prophet went and stood by the road waiting for the king. He disguised himself
with his headband down over his eyes.
39 As the king passed by, the prophet called
out to him, "Your servant went into the
thick of the battle, and someone came to
me with a captive and said, 'Guard this
man. If he is missing, it will be your life
for his life, or you must pay a talent[b] of
silver.' 40 While your servant was busy here
and there, the man disappeared."
"That is your sentence," the king of Israel said. "You have pronounced it yourself."
41 Then the prophet quickly removed the
headband from his eyes, and the king of
Israel recognized him as one of the prophets. 42 He said to the king, "This is what the
LORD says: 'You have set free a man I had
determined should die.[c] Therefore it is
your life for his life, your people for his
people.' " 43 Sullen and angry, the king of
Israel went to his palace in Samaria.

[b] *39* That is, about 75 pounds (about 34 kilograms)
[c] *42* The Hebrew term refers to the irrevocable giving over of things or persons to the LORD, often by totally destroying them.

PRAYER: RENEWAL

MAY I not work for the food that perishes, but for the food that endures to eternal life, which the Son of Man gives me, for You, Father, have set Your seal on Him. (John 6:27)

***PAUSE** to add your own prayers for personal renewal.*

NT John 6:25–59

Jesus the Bread of Life

25 When they found him on the other side of the lake, they asked him, "Rabbi, when did you get here?"

26 Jesus answered, "I tell you the truth, you are looking for me, not because you saw miraculous signs but because you ate the loaves and had your fill. 27 Do not work for food that spoils, but for food that endures to eternal life, which the Son of Man will give you. On him God the Father has placed his seal of approval."

28 Then they asked him, "What must we do to do the works God requires?"

29 Jesus answered, "The work of God is this: to believe in the one he has sent."

30 So they asked him, "What miraculous sign then will you give that we may see it and believe you? What will you do? 31 Our forefathers ate the manna in the desert; as it is written: 'He gave them bread from heaven to eat.'[a]"

32 Jesus said to them, "I tell you the truth, it is not Moses who has given you the bread from heaven, but it is my Father who gives you the true bread from heaven. 33 For the bread of God is he who comes down from heaven and gives life to the world."

34 "Sir," they said, "from now on give us this bread."

35 Then Jesus declared, "I am the bread of life. He who comes to me will never go hungry, and he who believes in me will never be thirsty. 36 But as I told you, you have seen me and still you do not believe. 37 All that the Father gives me will come to me, and whoever comes to me I will never drive away. 38 For I have come down from heaven not to do my will but to do the will of him who sent me. 39 And this is the will of him who sent me, that I shall lose none of all that he has given me, but raise them up at the last day. 40 For my Father's will is that everyone who looks to the Son and believes in him shall have eternal life, and I will raise him up at the last day."

41 At this the Jews began to grumble about him because he said, "I am the bread that came down from heaven." 42 They said, "Is this not Jesus, the son of Joseph, whose father and mother we know? How can he now say, 'I came down from heaven'?"

43 "Stop grumbling among yourselves," Jesus answered. 44 "No one can come to me unless the Father who sent me draws him, and I will raise him up at the last day. 45 It is written in the Prophets: 'They will all be taught by God.'[b] Everyone who listens to the Father and learns from him comes to me. 46 No one has seen the Father except the one who is from God; only he has seen the Father. 47 I tell you the truth, he who believes has everlasting life. 48 I am the bread of life. 49 Your forefathers ate the manna in the desert, yet they died. 50 But here is the bread that comes down from heaven, which a man may eat and not die. 51 I am the living bread that came down from heaven. If anyone eats of this bread, he will live forever. This bread is my flesh, which I will give for the life of the world."

52 Then the Jews began to argue sharply among themselves, "How can this man give us his flesh to eat?"

53 Jesus said to them, "I tell you the truth, unless you eat the flesh of the Son of Man and drink his blood, you have no life in you. 54 Whoever eats my flesh and drinks my blood has eternal life, and I will raise him up at the last day. 55 For my flesh is real food and my blood is real drink. 56 Whoever eats my flesh and drinks my blood remains in me, and I in him. 57 Just as the living Father sent me and I live because of the Father, so the one who feeds

[a] *31* Exodus 16:4; Neh. 9:15; Psalm 78:24,25
[b] *45* Isaiah 54:13

on me will live because of me. [58]This is the
bread that came down from heaven. Your
forefathers ate manna and died, but he
who feeds on this bread will live forever."
[59]He said this while teaching in the synagogue in Capernaum.

PRAYER: THE CHARACTER I WANT TO CULTIVATE

YOU have shown me what is good, O Lord. And what do You require of me but to act justly and to love mercy and to walk humbly with You, my God? (Micah 6:8) . . . I will seek Your interests, Christ Jesus, rather than my own. (Philippians 2:21)

TAKE *a moment to ask the Lord for the grace to grow in godly character.*

YEAR 1
DAY 305

OT 1 Kings 21:1–29

Naboth's Vineyard

21 Some time later there was an incident
involving a vineyard belonging to Naboth the Jezreelite. The vineyard was in
Jezreel, close to the palace of Ahab king
of Samaria. [2]Ahab said to Naboth, "Let
me have your vineyard to use for a vegetable garden, since it is close to my
palace. In exchange I will give you a better vineyard or, if you prefer, I will pay you
whatever it is worth."
[3]But Naboth replied, "The LORD forbid
that I should give you the inheritance of
my fathers."
[4]So Ahab went home, sullen and angry
because Naboth the Jezreelite had said, "I
will not give you the inheritance of my fathers." He lay on his bed sulking and refused to eat.
[5]His wife Jezebel came in and asked
him, "Why are you so sullen? Why won't
you eat?"
[6]He answered her, "Because I said to
Naboth the Jezreelite, 'Sell me your vineyard; or if you prefer, I will give you another vineyard in its place.' But he said, 'I
will not give you my vineyard.' "
[7]Jezebel his wife said, "Is this how you
act as king over Israel? Get up and eat!
Cheer up. I'll get you the vineyard of Naboth the Jezreelite."
[8]So she wrote letters in Ahab's name,
placed his seal on them, and sent them to
the elders and nobles who lived in Naboth's city with him. [9]In those letters she
wrote:

"Proclaim a day of fasting and seat
Naboth in a prominent place among
the people. [10]But seat two scoundrels
opposite him and have them testify
that he has cursed both God and the
king. Then take him out and stone
him to death."

[11]So the elders and nobles who lived in
Naboth's city did as Jezebel directed in the
letters she had written to them. [12]They proclaimed a fast and seated Naboth in a
prominent place among the people. [13]Then
two scoundrels came and sat opposite him
and brought charges against Naboth before the people, saying, "Naboth has
cursed both God and the king." So they
took him outside the city and stoned him
to death. [14]Then they sent word to Jezebel:
"Naboth has been stoned and is dead."
[15]As soon as Jezebel heard that Naboth
had been stoned to death, she said to
Ahab, "Get up and take possession of the
vineyard of Naboth the Jezreelite that he
refused to sell you. He is no longer alive,
but dead." [16]When Ahab heard that Naboth was dead, he got up and went down
to take possession of Naboth's vineyard.
[17]Then the word of the LORD came to
Elijah the Tishbite: [18]"Go down to meet
Ahab king of Israel, who rules in Samaria.
He is now in Naboth's vineyard, where he
has gone to take possession of it. [19]Say to
him, 'This is what the LORD says: Have you
not murdered a man and seized his property?' Then say to him, 'This is what the
LORD says: In the place where dogs licked
up Naboth's blood, dogs will lick up your
blood—yes, yours!' "

20 Ahab said to Elijah, "So you have found me, my enemy!"

"I have found you," he answered, "because you have sold yourself to do evil in the eyes of the LORD. 21 'I am going to bring disaster on you. I will consume your descendants and cut off from Ahab every last male in Israel—slave or free. 22 I will make your house like that of Jeroboam son of Nebat and that of Baasha son of Ahijah, because you have provoked me to anger and have caused Israel to sin.'

23 "And also concerning Jezebel the LORD says: 'Dogs will devour Jezebel by the wall of[a] Jezreel.'

24 "Dogs will eat those belonging to Ahab who die in the city, and the birds of the air will feed on those who die in the country."

25 (There was never a man like Ahab, who sold himself to do evil in the eyes of the LORD, urged on by Jezebel his wife. 26 He behaved in the vilest manner by going after idols, like the Amorites the LORD drove out before Israel.)

27 When Ahab heard these words, he tore his clothes, put on sackcloth and fasted. He lay in sackcloth and went around meekly.

28 Then the word of the LORD came to Elijah the Tishbite: 29 "Have you noticed how Ahab has humbled himself before me? Because he has humbled himself, I will not bring this disaster in his day, but I will bring it on his house in the days of his son."

[a] 23 Most Hebrew manuscripts; a few Hebrew manuscripts, Vulgate and Syriac (see also 2 Kings 9:26) *the plot of ground at*

PRAYER: PETITION

RISE up, O Lord! May Your enemies be scattered, and may those who hate You flee before You. (Numbers 10:35)

***PAUSE** here to petition God for wisdom. Ask Him to develop your eternal perspective, to renew your mind with truth and to help you develop greater skill in each area of your life. Offer prayers regarding your activities for this day and any special concerns you may have.*

NT John 6:60–7:24

Many Disciples Desert Jesus

60 On hearing it, many of his disciples said, "This is a hard teaching. Who can accept it?"

61 Aware that his disciples were grumbling about this, Jesus said to them, "Does this offend you? 62 What if you see the Son of Man ascend to where he was before! 63 The Spirit gives life; the flesh counts for nothing. The words I have spoken to you are spirit[a] and they are life. 64 Yet there are some of you who do not believe." For Jesus had known from the beginning which of them did not believe and who would betray him. 65 He went on to say, "This is why I told you that no one can come to me unless the Father has enabled him."

66 From this time many of his disciples turned back and no longer followed him.

67 "You do not want to leave too, do you?" Jesus asked the Twelve.

68 Simon Peter answered him, "Lord, to whom shall we go? You have the words of eternal life. 69 We believe and know that you are the Holy One of God."

70 Then Jesus replied, "Have I not chosen you, the Twelve? Yet one of you is a devil!" 71 (He meant Judas, the son of Simon Iscariot, who, though one of the Twelve, was later to betray him.)

Jesus Goes to the Feast of Tabernacles

7 After this, Jesus went around in Galilee, purposely staying away from Judea because the Jews there were waiting to take his life. 2 But when the Jewish Feast of Tabernacles was near, 3 Jesus' brothers said to him, "You ought to leave here and go to Judea, so that your disciples may see the miracles you do. 4 No one who wants to become a public figure acts in secret. Since you are doing these things, show

[a] 63 Or *Spirit*

yourself to the world." [5]For even his own
brothers did not believe in him.
[6]Therefore Jesus told them, "The right
time for me has not yet come; for you any
time is right. [7]The world cannot hate you,
but it hates me because I testify that what
it does is evil. [8]You go to the Feast. I am
not yet[b] going up to this Feast, because for
me the right time has not yet come."
[9]Having said this, he stayed in Galilee.
[10]However, after his brothers had left for
the Feast, he went also, not publicly, but
in secret. [11]Now at the Feast the Jews were
watching for him and asking, "Where is
that man?"
[12]Among the crowds there was widespread whispering about him. Some said,
"He is a good man."

Others replied, "No, he deceives the
people." [13]But no one would say anything
publicly about him for fear of the Jews.

Jesus Teaches at the Feast

[14]Not until halfway through the Feast
did Jesus go up to the temple courts and
begin to teach. [15]The Jews were amazed
and asked, "How did this man get such
learning without having studied?"
[16]Jesus answered, "My teaching is not
my own. It comes from him who sent me.
[17]If anyone chooses to do God's will, he
will find out whether my teaching comes
from God or whether I speak on my own.
[18]He who speaks on his own does so to
gain honor for himself, but he who works
for the honor of the one who sent him is
a man of truth; there is nothing false
about him. [19]Has not Moses given you the
law? Yet not one of you keeps the law.
Why are you trying to kill me?"
[20]"You are demon-possessed," the
crowd answered. "Who is trying to kill
you?"
[21]Jesus said to them, "I did one miracle,
and you are all astonished. [22]Yet, because
Moses gave you circumcision (though actually it did not come from Moses, but
from the patriarchs), you circumcise a
child on the Sabbath. [23]Now if a child can
be circumcised on the Sabbath so that the
law of Moses may not be broken, why are
you angry with me for healing the whole
man on the Sabbath? [24]Stop judging by
mere appearances, and make a right judgment."

[b] 8 Some early manuscripts do not have *yet.*

PRAYER: MY RELATIONSHIP TO OTHERS

YOU are the Head, O Christ, and under Your control the whole body is being joined and held together by every supporting ligament, even as each individual part works effectively, so that the body grows and edifies itself in love. (Ephesians 4:16)

***PAUSE** to review your relationships with others and to commit them to the Lord.*

OT 1 Kings 22:1-53 — YEAR 1 DAY 306

Micaiah Prophesies Against Ahab

22 For three years there was no war between Aram and Israel. [2]But in the
third year Jehoshaphat king of Judah went
down to see the king of Israel. [3]The king
of Israel had said to his officials, "Don't
you know that Ramoth Gilead belongs to
us and yet we are doing nothing to retake
it from the king of Aram?"
[4]So he asked Jehoshaphat, "Will you go
with me to fight against Ramoth Gilead?"

Jehoshaphat replied to the king of Israel, "I am as you are, my people as your
people, my horses as your horses." [5]But Jehoshaphat also said to the king of Israel,
"First seek the counsel of the LORD."
[6]So the king of Israel brought together
the prophets—about four hundred
men—and asked them, "Shall I go to war
against Ramoth Gilead, or shall I refrain?"

"Go," they answered, "for the Lord will
give it into the king's hand."

[7]But Jehoshaphat asked, "Is there not a
prophet of the LORD here whom we can
inquire of?"
[8]The king of Israel answered Jehoshaphat, "There is still one man through
whom we can inquire of the LORD, but I
hate him because he never prophesies
anything good about me, but always bad.
He is Micaiah son of Imlah."
"The king should not say that," Jehoshaphat replied.
[9]So the king of Israel called one of his
officials and said, "Bring Micaiah son of
Imlah at once."
[10]Dressed in their royal robes, the king
of Israel and Jehoshaphat king of Judah
were sitting on their thrones at the threshing floor by the entrance of the gate of
Samaria, with all the prophets prophesying before them. [11]Now Zedekiah son of
Kenaanah had made iron horns and he
declared, "This is what the LORD says:
'With these you will gore the Arameans
until they are destroyed.' "
[12]All the other prophets were prophesying the same thing. "Attack Ramoth Gilead and be victorious," they said, "for the
LORD will give it into the king's hand."
[13]The messenger who had gone to summon Micaiah said to him, "Look, as one
man the other prophets are predicting
success for the king. Let your word agree
with theirs, and speak favorably."
[14]But Micaiah said, "As surely as the
LORD lives, I can tell him only what the
LORD tells me."
[15]When he arrived, the king asked him,
"Micaiah, shall we go to war against Ramoth Gilead, or shall I refrain?"
"Attack and be victorious," he answered, "for the LORD will give it into the
king's hand."
[16]The king said to him, "How many
times must I make you swear to tell me
nothing but the truth in the name of the
LORD?"
[17]Then Micaiah answered, "I saw all Israel scattered on the hills like sheep without a shepherd, and the LORD said, 'These
people have no master. Let each one go
home in peace.' "
[18]The king of Israel said to Jehoshaphat,
"Didn't I tell you that he never prophesies
anything good about me, but only bad?"
[19]Micaiah continued, "Therefore hear
the word of the LORD: I saw the LORD sitting on his throne with all the host of
heaven standing around him on his right
and on his left. [20]And the LORD said, 'Who
will entice Ahab into attacking Ramoth
Gilead and going to his death there?'
"One suggested this, and another that.
[21]Finally, a spirit came forward, stood before the LORD and said, 'I will entice him.'
[22]" 'By what means?' the LORD asked.
" 'I will go out and be a lying spirit in
the mouths of all his prophets,' he said.
" 'You will succeed in enticing him,' said
the LORD. 'Go and do it.'
[23]"So now the LORD has put a lying spirit in the mouths of all these prophets of
yours. The LORD has decreed disaster for
you."
[24]Then Zedekiah son of Kenaanah went
up and slapped Micaiah in the face.
"Which way did the spirit from[a] the LORD
go when he went from me to speak to
you?" he asked.
[25]Micaiah replied, "You will find out on
the day you go to hide in an inner room."
[26]The king of Israel then ordered, "Take
Micaiah and send him back to Amon the
ruler of the city and to Joash the king's
son [27]and say, 'This is what the king says:
Put this fellow in prison and give him
nothing but bread and water until I return
safely.' "
[28]Micaiah declared, "If you ever return
safely, the LORD has not spoken through
me." Then he added, "Mark my words, all
you people!"

Ahab Killed at Ramoth Gilead

[29]So the king of Israel and Jehoshaphat
king of Judah went up to Ramoth Gilead.
[30]The king of Israel said to Jehoshaphat,
"I will enter the battle in disguise, but you
wear your royal robes." So the king of Israel disguised himself and went into battle.
[31]Now the king of Aram had ordered his
thirty-two chariot commanders, "Do not
fight with anyone, small or great, except
the king of Israel." [32]When the chariot
commanders saw Jehoshaphat, they
thought, "Surely this is the king of Israel."
So they turned to attack him, but when Jehoshaphat cried out, [33]the chariot commanders saw that he was not the king of
Israel and stopped pursuing him.
[34]But someone drew his bow at random
and hit the king of Israel between the sec-

[a] 24 Or *Spirit of*

tions of his armor. The king told his chariot driver, "Wheel around and get me out
of the fighting. I've been wounded." 35All
day long the battle raged, and the king
was propped up in his chariot facing the
Arameans. The blood from his wound ran
onto the floor of the chariot, and that
evening he died. 36As the sun was setting,
a cry spread through the army: "Every
man to his town; everyone to his land!"
37So the king died and was brought to
Samaria, and they buried him there.
38They washed the chariot at a pool in
Samaria (where the prostitutes bathed),[b]
and the dogs licked up his blood, as the
word of the LORD had declared.
39As for the other events of Ahab's reign,
including all he did, the palace he built
and inlaid with ivory, and the cities he fortified, are they not written in the book of
the annals of the kings of Israel? 40Ahab
rested with his fathers. And Ahaziah his
son succeeded him as king.

Jehoshaphat King of Judah

41Jehoshaphat son of Asa became king
of Judah in the fourth year of Ahab king
of Israel. 42Jehoshaphat was thirty-five
years old when he became king, and he
reigned in Jerusalem twenty-five years. His
mother's name was Azubah daughter of
Shilhi. 43In everything he walked in the
ways of his father Asa and did not stray
from them; he did what was right in the
eyes of the LORD. The high places, however, were not removed, and the people continued to offer sacrifices and burn incense
there. 44Jehoshaphat was also at peace
with the king of Israel.
45As for the other events of Jehoshaphat's reign, the things he achieved and
his military exploits, are they not written
in the book of the annals of the kings of
Judah? 46He rid the land of the rest of the
male shrine prostitutes who remained
there even after the reign of his father Asa.
47There was then no king in Edom; a
deputy ruled.
48Now Jehoshaphat built a fleet of trading ships[c] to go to Ophir for gold, but they
never set sail—they were wrecked at Ezion
Geber. 49At that time Ahaziah son of Ahab
said to Jehoshaphat, "Let my men sail with
your men," but Jehoshaphat refused.
50Then Jehoshaphat rested with his fathers and was buried with them in the city
of David his father. And Jehoram his son
succeeded him.

Ahaziah King of Israel

51Ahaziah son of Ahab became king of
Israel in Samaria in the seventeenth year
of Jehoshaphat king of Judah, and he
reigned over Israel two years. 52He did evil
in the eyes of the LORD, because he
walked in the ways of his father and
mother and in the ways of Jeroboam son
of Nebat, who caused Israel to sin. 53He
served and worshiped Baal and provoked
the LORD, the God of Israel, to anger, just
as his father had done.

[b] 38 Or *Samaria and cleaned the weapons*
[c] 48 Hebrew *of ships of Tarshish*

PRAYER: INTERCESSION

MAY we keep Your feast, O Christ our Passover, not with old leaven, or with the leaven of malice and wickedness, but with the unleavened bread of sincerity and truth. (1 Corinthians 5:7–8)

***TAKE** a few moments to intercede on behalf of your immediate family and other relatives. Offer prayers for their spiritual, emotional and physical concerns.*

NT John 7:25–52

Is Jesus the Christ?

25At that point some of the people of
Jerusalem began to ask, "Isn't this the
man they are trying to kill? 26Here he is,
speaking publicly, and they are not saying
a word to him. Have the authorities really concluded that he is the Christ[a]? 27But

[a] 26 Or *Messiah;* also in verses 27, 31, 41 and 42

we know where this man is from; when the Christ comes, no one will know where he is from."

[28]Then Jesus, still teaching in the temple courts, cried out, "Yes, you know me, and you know where I am from. I am not here on my own, but he who sent me is true. You do not know him, [29]but I know him because I am from him and he sent me."

[30]At this they tried to seize him, but no one laid a hand on him, because his time had not yet come. [31]Still, many in the crowd put their faith in him. They said, "When the Christ comes, will he do more miraculous signs than this man?"

[32]The Pharisees heard the crowd whispering such things about him. Then the chief priests and the Pharisees sent temple guards to arrest him.

[33]Jesus said, "I am with you for only a short time, and then I go to the one who sent me. [34]You will look for me, but you will not find me; and where I am, you cannot come."

[35]The Jews said to one another, "Where does this man intend to go that we cannot find him? Will he go where our people live scattered among the Greeks, and teach the Greeks? [36]What did he mean when he said, 'You will look for me, but you will not find me,' and 'Where I am, you cannot come'?"

[37]On the last and greatest day of the Feast, Jesus stood and said in a loud voice, "If anyone is thirsty, let him come to me and drink. [38]Whoever believes in me, as[a] the Scripture has said, streams of living water will flow from within him." [39]By this he meant the Spirit, whom those who believed in him were later to receive. Up to that time the Spirit had not been given, since Jesus had not yet been glorified.

[40]On hearing his words, some of the people said, "Surely this man is the Prophet."

[41]Others said, "He is the Christ."

Still others asked, "How can the Christ come from Galilee? [42]Does not the Scripture say that the Christ will come from David's family[c] and from Bethlehem, the town where David lived?" [43]Thus the people were divided because of Jesus. [44]Some wanted to seize him, but no one laid a hand on him.

Unbelief of the Jewish Leaders

[45]Finally the temple guards went back to the chief priests and Pharisees, who asked them, "Why didn't you bring him in?"

[46]"No one ever spoke the way this man does," the guards declared.

[47]"You mean he has deceived you also?" the Pharisees retorted. [48]"Has any of the rulers or of the Pharisees believed in him? [49]No! But this mob that knows nothing of the law—there is a curse on them."

[50]Nicodemus, who had gone to Jesus earlier and who was one of their own number, asked, [51]"Does our law condemn anyone without first hearing him to find out what he is doing?"

[52]They replied, "Are you from Galilee, too? Look into it, and you will find that a prophet[d] does not come out of Galilee."

[b] 37,38 Or / *If anyone is thirsty, let him come to me. / And let him drink,* [38]*who believes in me.* / As
[c] 42 Greek *seed* [d] 52 Two early manuscripts *the Prophet*

PRAYER: THE ATTRIBUTES OF GOD

ALL people are like grass, and all their glory is like the flower of the field. The grass withers and the flower fades, because Your breath, O Lord, blows on it. Surely the people are like grass. The grass withers and the flower fades, but Your word, O God, stands forever. (Isaiah 40:6–8) . . . How great are Your signs, O God, and how mighty are Your wonders! Your kingdom is an eternal kingdom; Your dominion endures from generation to generation. (Daniel 4:3)

PAUSE *to reflect on these affirmations about the person, powers and perfection of God.*

OT 2 Kings 1:1–2:25

YEAR 1 DAY 307

The LORD'*s Judgment on Ahaziah*

1 After Ahab's death, Moab rebelled
against Israel. 2 Now Ahaziah had fallen
through the lattice of his upper room in
Samaria and injured himself. So he sent
messengers, saying to them, "Go and consult Baal-Zebub, the god of Ekron, to see
if I will recover from this injury."
3 But the angel of the LORD said to Elijah the Tishbite, "Go up and meet the
messengers of the king of Samaria and ask
them, 'Is it because there is no God in Israel that you are going off to consult Baal-
Zebub, the god of Ekron?' 4 Therefore this
is what the LORD says: 'You will not leave
the bed you are lying on. You will certainly die!' " So Elijah went.
5 When the messengers returned to the
king, he asked them, "Why have you
come back?"
6 "A man came to meet us," they replied.
"And he said to us, 'Go back to the king
who sent you and tell him, "This is what
the LORD says: Is it because there is no
God in Israel that you are sending men to
consult Baal-Zebub, the god of Ekron?
Therefore you will not leave the bed you
are lying on. You will certainly die!" ' "
7 The king asked them, "What kind of
man was it who came to meet you and
told you this?"
8 They replied, "He was a man with a
garment of hair and with a leather belt
around his waist."
The king said, "That was Elijah the Tishbite."
9 Then he sent to Elijah a captain with
his company of fifty men. The captain
went up to Elijah, who was sitting on the
top of a hill, and said to him, "Man of
God, the king says, 'Come down!' "
10 Elijah answered the captain, "If I am
a man of God, may fire come down from
heaven and consume you and your fifty
men!" Then fire fell from heaven and consumed the captain and his men.
11 At this the king sent to Elijah another
captain with his fifty men. The captain
said to him, "Man of God, this is what the
king says, 'Come down at once!' "
12 "If I am a man of God," Elijah replied,
"may fire come down from heaven and
consume you and your fifty men!" Then
the fire of God fell from heaven and consumed him and his fifty men.
13 So the king sent a third captain with
his fifty men. This third captain went up
and fell on his knees before Elijah. "Man
of God," he begged, "please have respect
for my life and the lives of these fifty men,
your servants! 14 See, fire has fallen from
heaven and consumed the first two captains and all their men. But now have respect for my life!"
15 The angel of the LORD said to Elijah,
"Go down with him; do not be afraid of
him." So Elijah got up and went down
with him to the king.
16 He told the king, "This is what the
LORD says: Is it because there is no God in
Israel for you to consult that you have sent
messengers to consult Baal-Zebub, the
god of Ekron? Because you have done
this, you will never leave the bed you are
lying on. You will certainly die!" 17 So he
died, according to the word of the LORD
that Elijah had spoken.
Because Ahaziah had no son, Joram[a]
succeeded him as king in the second year
of Jehoram son of Jehoshaphat king of Judah. 18 As for all the other events of Ahaziah's reign, and what he did, are they not
written in the book of the annals of the
kings of Israel?

Elijah Taken Up to Heaven

2 When the LORD was about to take Elijah up to heaven in a whirlwind, Elijah
and Elisha were on their way from Gilgal.
2 Elijah said to Elisha, "Stay here; the LORD
has sent me to Bethel."
But Elisha said, "As surely as the LORD
lives and as you live, I will not leave you."
So they went down to Bethel.
3 The company of the prophets at Bethel came out to Elisha and asked, "Do you
know that the LORD is going to take your
master from you today?"
"Yes, I know," Elisha replied, "but do
not speak of it."
4 Then Elijah said to him, "Stay here, Elisha; the LORD has sent me to Jericho."
And he replied, "As surely as the LORD

[a] 17 Hebrew *Jehoram,* a variant of *Joram*

lives and as you live, I will not leave you."
So they went to Jericho.
[5]The company of the prophets at Jericho went up to Elisha and asked him, "Do you know that the LORD is going to take your master from you today?"

"Yes, I know," he replied, "but do not speak of it."
[6]Then Elijah said to him, "Stay here; the LORD has sent me to the Jordan."

And he replied, "As surely as the LORD lives and as you live, I will not leave you." So the two of them walked on.
[7]Fifty men of the company of the prophets went and stood at a distance, facing the place where Elijah and Elisha
had stopped at the Jordan. [8]Elijah took his cloak, rolled it up and struck the water with it. The water divided to the right and to the left, and the two of them crossed over on dry ground.
[9]When they had crossed, Elijah said to Elisha, "Tell me, what can I do for you before I am taken from you?"

"Let me inherit a double portion of your spirit," Elisha replied.
[10]"You have asked a difficult thing," Elijah said, "yet if you see me when I am taken from you, it will be yours—otherwise not."
[11]As they were walking along and talking together, suddenly a chariot of fire and horses of fire appeared and separated the two of them, and Elijah went up to
heaven in a whirlwind. [12]Elisha saw this and cried out, "My father! My father! The chariots and horsemen of Israel!" And Elisha saw him no more. Then he took hold of his own clothes and tore them apart.
[13]He picked up the cloak that had fallen from Elijah and went back and stood
on the bank of the Jordan. [14]Then he took the cloak that had fallen from him and struck the water with it. "Where now is the LORD, the God of Elijah?" he asked. When he struck the water, it divided to the right and to the left, and he crossed over.
[15]The company of the prophets from Jericho, who were watching, said, "The spirit of Elijah is resting on Elisha." And they went to meet him and bowed to the
ground before him. [16]"Look," they said, "we your servants have fifty able men. Let them go and look for your master. Perhaps the Spirit of the LORD has picked him up and set him down on some mountain or in some valley."

"No," Elisha replied, "do not send them."
[17]But they persisted until he was too ashamed to refuse. So he said, "Send them." And they sent fifty men, who searched for three days but did not find
him. [18]When they returned to Elisha, who was staying in Jericho, he said to them, "Didn't I tell you not to go?"

Healing of the Water

[19]The men of the city said to Elisha, "Look, our lord, this town is well situated, as you can see, but the water is bad and the land is unproductive."
[20]"Bring me a new bowl," he said, "and put salt in it." So they brought it to him.
[21]Then he went out to the spring and threw the salt into it, saying, "This is what the LORD says: 'I have healed this water. Never again will it cause death or make
the land unproductive.' " [22]And the water has remained wholesome to this day, according to the word Elisha had spoken.

Elisha Is Jeered

[23]From there Elisha went up to Bethel. As he was walking along the road, some youths came out of the town and jeered at him. "Go on up, you baldhead!" they
said. "Go on up, you baldhead!" [24]He turned around, looked at them and called down a curse on them in the name of the LORD. Then two bears came out of the woods and mauled forty-two of the
youths. [25]And he went on to Mount Carmel and from there returned to Samaria.

PRAYER: AFFIRMATION

THOSE who are without your Spirit do not accept the things of Your Spirit, which are foolishness to them, and they cannot understand them, for such things are spiritually discerned. "For who has known Your mind, O Lord, that they may instruct You?" But we have the mind

of Christ. (1 Corinthians 2:14, 16) . . . Now I see dimly, as in a mirror, but then I shall see face to face. Now I know in part, but then I shall know fully, even as I am fully known. (1 Corinthians 13:12)

***PAUSE** to reflect on these Biblical affirmations.*

NT John 7:53–8:30

[The earliest manuscripts and many other ancient witnesses do not have John 7:53–8:11.]

53 Then each went to his own home.

8 But Jesus went to the Mount of Olives. 2 At dawn he appeared again in the temple courts, where all the people gathered around him, and he sat down to teach them. 3 The teachers of the law and the Pharisees brought in a woman caught in adultery. They made her stand before the group 4 and said to Jesus, "Teacher, this woman was caught in the act of adultery. 5 In the Law Moses commanded us to stone such women. Now what do you say?" 6 They were using this question as a trap, in order to have a basis for accusing him.

But Jesus bent down and started to write on the ground with his finger. 7 When they kept on questioning him, he straightened up and said to them, "If any one of you is without sin, let him be the first to throw a stone at her." 8 Again he stooped down and wrote on the ground.

9 At this, those who heard began to go away one at a time, the older ones first, until only Jesus was left, with the woman still standing there. 10 Jesus straightened up and asked her, "Woman, where are they? Has no one condemned you?"

11 "No one, sir," she said.

"Then neither do I condemn you," Jesus declared. "Go now and leave your life of sin."

The Validity of Jesus' Testimony

12 When Jesus spoke again to the people, he said, "I am the light of the world. Whoever follows me will never walk in darkness, but will have the light of life."

13 The Pharisees challenged him, "Here you are, appearing as your own witness; your testimony is not valid."

14 Jesus answered, "Even if I testify on my own behalf, my testimony is valid, for I know where I came from and where I am going. But you have no idea where I come from or where I am going. 15 You judge by human standards; I pass judgment on no one. 16 But if I do judge, my decisions are right, because I am not alone. I stand with the Father, who sent me. 17 In your own Law it is written that the testimony of two men is valid. 18 I am one who testifies for myself; my other witness is the Father, who sent me."

19 Then they asked him, "Where is your father?"

"You do not know me or my Father," Jesus replied. "If you knew me, you would know my Father also." 20 He spoke these words while teaching in the temple area near the place where the offerings were put. Yet no one seized him, because his time had not yet come.

21 Once more Jesus said to them, "I am going away, and you will look for me, and you will die in your sin. Where I go, you cannot come."

22 This made the Jews ask, "Will he kill himself? Is that why he says, 'Where I go, you cannot come'?"

23 But he continued, "You are from below; I am from above. You are of this world; I am not of this world. 24 I told you that you would die in your sins; if you do not believe that I am ⌊the one I claim to be⌋,[a] you will indeed die in your sins."

25 "Who are you?" they asked.

"Just what I have been claiming all along," Jesus replied. 26 "I have much to say in judgment of you. But he who sent me is reliable, and what I have heard from him I tell the world."

27 They did not understand that he was telling them about his Father. 28 So Jesus said, "When you have lifted up the Son of Man, then you will know that I am ⌊the one I claim to be⌋ and that I do nothing on my own but speak just what the Father has taught me. 29 The one who sent me is with me; he has not left me alone, for I always do what pleases him." 30 Even as he spoke, many put their faith in him.

[a] *24* Or *I am he;* also in verse 28

PRAYER: THE WORKS OF GOD

YOU are the good Shepherd, Lord Jesus; You lay down Your life for the sheep. You are the good Shepherd; You know Your sheep and Your sheep know You—just as the Father knows You and You know the Father—and You lay down Your life for the sheep. (John 10:11, 14–15) . . . Greater love has no one than this, that he lay down his life for his friends. (John 15:13)

***TAKE** a moment to consider the greatness of God's wonderful works.*

YEAR 1 DAY 308

OT Psalm 60

Psalm 60

For the director of music. To ⌞the tune of⌟ "The Lily of the Covenant." A *miktam*[a] of David. For teaching. When he fought Aram Naharaim[b] and Aram Zobah,[c] and when Joab returned and struck down twelve thousand Edomites in the Valley of Salt.

1 You have rejected us, O God, and burst forth upon us;
you have been angry—now restore us!
2 You have shaken the land and torn it open;
mend its fractures, for it is quaking.
3 You have shown your people desperate times;
you have given us wine that makes us stagger.

4 But for those who fear you, you have raised a banner
to be unfurled against the bow. *Selah*

5 Save us and help us with your right hand,
that those you love may be delivered.
6 God has spoken from his sanctuary:
"In triumph I will parcel out Shechem
and measure off the Valley of Succoth.
7 Gilead is mine, and Manasseh is mine;
Ephraim is my helmet,
Judah my scepter.
8 Moab is my washbasin,
upon Edom I toss my sandal;
over Philistia I shout in triumph."

9 Who will bring me to the fortified city?
Who will lead me to Edom?
10 Is it not you, O God, you who have rejected us
and no longer go out with our armies?
11 Give us aid against the enemy,
for the help of man is worthless.
12 With God we will gain the victory,
and he will trample down our enemies.

[a] Title: Probably a literary or musical term [b] Title: That is, Arameans of Northwest Mesopotamia [c] Title: That is, Arameans of central Syria

PRAYER: THANKSGIVING

YOU, O God, will keep me strong to the end, so that I will be blameless on the day of our Lord Jesus Christ. You are faithful; You have called me into fellowship with Your Son, Jesus Christ, our Lord. (1 Corinthians 1:8–9) . . . No eye has seen, no ear has heard, no mind has conceived, O God, what You have prepared for those who love You. (1 Corinthians 2:9)

***PAUSE** to offer your own expressions of thanksgiving.*

NT John 8:31–59

The Children of Abraham

31To the Jews who had believed him,
Jesus said, "If you hold to my teaching,
you are really my disciples. 32Then you
will know the truth, and the truth will set
you free."

33They answered him, "We are Abraham's descendants[a] and have never been
slaves of anyone. How can you say that we
shall be set free?"

34Jesus replied, "I tell you the truth,
everyone who sins is a slave to sin. 35Now
a slave has no permanent place in the
family, but a son belongs to it forever. 36So
if the Son sets you free, you will be free
indeed. 37I know you are Abraham's descendants. Yet you are ready to kill me, because you have no room for my word. 38I
am telling you what I have seen in the Father's presence, and you do what you have
heard from your father.[b]"

39"Abraham is our father," they answered.

"If you were Abraham's children," said
Jesus, "then you would[c] do the things
Abraham did. 40As it is, you are determined to kill me, a man who has told you
the truth that I heard from God. Abraham
did not do such things. 41You are doing
the things your own father does."

"We are not illegitimate children," they
protested. "The only Father we have is
God himself."

The Children of the Devil

42Jesus said to them, "If God were your
Father, you would love me, for I came from
God and now am here. I have not come on
my own; but he sent me. 43Why is my language not clear to you? Because you are unable to hear what I say. 44You belong to
your father, the devil, and you want to carry out your father's desire. He was a murderer from the beginning, not holding to
the truth, for there is no truth in him.
When he lies, he speaks his native language, for he is a liar and the father of lies.
45Yet because I tell the truth, you do not believe me! 46Can any of you prove me guilty
of sin? If I am telling the truth, why don't
you believe me? 47He who belongs to God
hears what God says. The reason you do
not hear is that you do not belong to God."

The Claims of Jesus About Himself

48The Jews answered him, "Aren't we
right in saying that you are a Samaritan
and demon-possessed?"

49"I am not possessed by a demon," said
Jesus, "but I honor my Father and you dishonor me. 50I am not seeking glory for myself; but there is one who seeks it, and he
is the judge. 51I tell you the truth, if anyone
keeps my word, he will never see death."

52At this the Jews exclaimed, "Now we
know that you are demon-possessed! Abraham died and so did the prophets, yet you
say that if anyone keeps your word, he will
never taste death. 53Are you greater than our
father Abraham? He died, and so did the
prophets. Who do you think you are?"

54Jesus replied, "If I glorify myself, my
glory means nothing. My Father, whom
you claim as your God, is the one who
glorifies me. 55Though you do not know
him, I know him. If I said I did not, I
would be a liar like you, but I do know
him and keep his word. 56Your father
Abraham rejoiced at the thought of seeing
my day; he saw it and was glad."

57"You are not yet fifty years old," the
Jews said to him, "and you have seen
Abraham!"

58"I tell you the truth," Jesus answered,
"before Abraham was born, I am!" 59At
this, they picked up stones to stone him,
but Jesus hid himself, slipping away from
the temple grounds.

[a] 33 Greek *seed;* also in verse 37 [b] 38 Or *presence. Therefore do what you have heard from the Father.* [c] 39 Some early manuscripts *"If you are Abraham's children," said Jesus, "then*

PRAYER: MY RELATIONSHIP TO GOD

WHOM have I in heaven but You? And there is nothing on earth I desire besides You. My flesh and my heart may fail, but You, O God, are the strength of my heart and my portion forever. Those who are far from You will perish; You have cut off all who are unfaithful to You.

But as for me, it is good to be near You. I have made You my refuge,
Lord God, that I may tell of all Your works.
(Psalm 73:25–28)

PAUSE *to thank God for the relationship that you enjoy with Him in Jesus Christ.*

YEAR 1
DAY 309

OT 2 Kings 3:1–27

Moab Revolts

3 Joram[a] son of Ahab became king of Israel in Samaria in the eighteenth year of
Jehoshaphat king of Judah, and he reigned
twelve years. 2He did evil in the eyes of the
LORD, but not as his father and mother had
done. He got rid of the sacred stone of Baal
that his father had made. 3Nevertheless he
clung to the sins of Jeroboam son of Nebat, which he had caused Israel to commit;
he did not turn away from them.

4Now Mesha king of Moab raised
sheep, and he had to supply the king of
Israel with a hundred thousand lambs
and with the wool of a hundred thousand
rams. 5But after Ahab died, the king of
Moab rebelled against the king of Israel.
6So at that time King Joram set out from
Samaria and mobilized all Israel. 7He also
sent this message to Jehoshaphat king of
Judah: "The king of Moab has rebelled
against me. Will you go with me to fight
against Moab?"

"I will go with you," he replied. "I am
as you are, my people as your people, my
horses as your horses."

8"By what route shall we attack?" he
asked.

"Through the Desert of Edom," he answered.

9So the king of Israel set out with the
king of Judah and the king of Edom. After a roundabout march of seven days, the
army had no more water for themselves
or for the animals with them.

10"What!" exclaimed the king of Israel.
"Has the LORD called us three kings together only to hand us over to Moab?"

11But Jehoshaphat asked, "Is there no
prophet of the LORD here, that we may inquire of the LORD through him?"

An officer of the king of Israel answered,
"Elisha son of Shaphat is here. He used to
pour water on the hands of Elijah.[b]"

12Jehoshaphat said, "The word of the
LORD is with him." So the king of Israel
and Jehoshaphat and the king of Edom
went down to him.

13Elisha said to the king of Israel, "What
do we have to do with each other? Go to
the prophets of your father and the
prophets of your mother."

"No," the king of Israel answered, "because it was the LORD who called us three
kings together to hand us over to Moab."

14Elisha said, "As surely as the LORD
Almighty lives, whom I serve, if I did not
have respect for the presence of Jehoshaphat king of Judah, I would not look at
you or even notice you. 15But now bring
me a harpist."

While the harpist was playing, the hand
of the LORD came upon Elisha 16and he
said, "This is what the LORD says: Make
this valley full of ditches. 17For this is what
the LORD says: You will see neither wind
nor rain, yet this valley will be filled with
water, and you, your cattle and your other animals will drink. 18This is an easy
thing in the eyes of the LORD; he will also
hand Moab over to you. 19You will overthrow every fortified city and every major
town. You will cut down every good tree,
stop up all the springs, and ruin every
good field with stones."

20The next morning, about the time for
offering the sacrifice, there it was—water
flowing from the direction of Edom! And
the land was filled with water.

21Now all the Moabites had heard that
the kings had come to fight against them;
so every man, young and old, who could
bear arms was called up and stationed on
the border. 22When they got up early in
the morning, the sun was shining on the
water. To the Moabites across the way, the
water looked red—like blood. 23"That's

[a] *1* Hebrew *Jehoram,* a variant of *Joram;* also in verse 6
[b] *11* That is, he was Elijah's personal servant.

blood!" they said. "Those kings must have fought and slaughtered each other. Now to the plunder, Moab!"

24But when the Moabites came to the
camp of Israel, the Israelites rose up and
fought them until they fled. And the Israelites invaded the land and slaughtered
the Moabites. 25They destroyed the towns,
and each man threw a stone on every
good field until it was covered. They
stopped up all the springs and cut down
every good tree. Only Kir Hareseth was
left with its stones in place, but men
armed with slings surrounded it and attacked it as well.

26When the king of Moab saw that the
battle had gone against him, he took with
him seven hundred swordsmen to break
through to the king of Edom, but they
failed. 27Then he took his firstborn son,
who was to succeed him as king, and offered him as a sacrifice on the city wall.
The fury against Israel was great; they
withdrew and returned to their own land.

PRAYER: ADORATION

O LORD, You reign; You are clothed with majesty; You are robed in majesty and are armed with strength. Indeed, the world is firmly established; it cannot be moved. Your throne is established from of old; You are from everlasting. Your testimonies stand firm; holiness adorns Your house, O Lord, forever. (Psalm 93:1–2, 5) . . . My soul blesses You, O Lord my God, You are very great; You are clothed with splendor and majesty. (Psalm 104:1)

PAUSE *to express your thoughts of praise and worship.*

NT John 9:1–41

Jesus Heals a Man Born Blind

9 As he went along, he saw a man blind
from birth. 2His disciples asked him,
"Rabbi, who sinned, this man or his parents, that he was born blind?"

3"Neither this man nor his parents
sinned," said Jesus, "but this happened so
that the work of God might be displayed in
his life. 4As long as it is day, we must do the
work of him who sent me. Night is coming,
when no one can work. 5While I am in the
world, I am the light of the world."

6Having said this, he spit on the
ground, made some mud with the saliva,
and put it on the man's eyes. 7"Go," he
told him, "wash in the Pool of Siloam"
(this word means Sent). So the man went
and washed, and came home seeing.

8His neighbors and those who had formerly seen him begging asked, "Isn't this
the same man who used to sit and beg?"
9Some claimed that he was.

Others said, "No, he only looks like him."

But he himself insisted, "I am the man."

10"How then were your eyes opened?"
they demanded.

11He replied, "The man they call Jesus
made some mud and put it on my eyes.
He told me to go to Siloam and wash. So
I went and washed, and then I could see."

12"Where is this man?" they asked him.

"I don't know," he said.

The Pharisees Investigate the Healing

13They brought to the Pharisees the
man who had been blind. 14Now the day
on which Jesus had made the mud and
opened the man's eyes was a Sabbath.
15Therefore the Pharisees also asked him
how he had received his sight. "He put
mud on my eyes," the man replied, "and
I washed, and now I see."

16Some of the Pharisees said, "This man
is not from God, for he does not keep the
Sabbath."

But others asked, "How can a sinner do such miraculous signs?" So they were divided.

17Finally they turned again to the blind
man, "What have you to say about him?
It was your eyes he opened."

The man replied, "He is a prophet."

18The Jews still did not believe that he
had been blind and had received his sight

until they sent for the man's parents. [19]"Is this your son?" they asked. "Is this the one you say was born blind? How is it that now he can see?"

[20]"We know he is our son," the parents answered, "and we know he was born blind. [21]But how he can see now, or who opened his eyes, we don't know. Ask him. He is of age; he will speak for himself." [22]His parents said this because they were afraid of the Jews, for already the Jews had decided that anyone who acknowledged that Jesus was the Christ[a] would be put out of the synagogue. [23]That was why his parents said, "He is of age; ask him."

[24]A second time they summoned the man who had been blind. "Give glory to God,[b]" they said. "We know this man is a sinner."

[25]He replied, "Whether he is a sinner or not, I don't know. One thing I do know. I was blind but now I see!"

[26]Then they asked him, "What did he do to you? How did he open your eyes?"

[27]He answered, "I have told you already and you did not listen. Why do you want to hear it again? Do you want to become his disciples, too?"

[28]Then they hurled insults at him and said, "You are this fellow's disciple! We are disciples of Moses! [29]We know that God spoke to Moses, but as for this fellow, we don't even know where he comes from."

[30]The man answered, "Now that is remarkable! You don't know where he comes from, yet he opened my eyes. [31]We know that God does not listen to sinners. He listens to the godly man who does his will. [32]Nobody has ever heard of opening the eyes of a man born blind. [33]If this man were not from God, he could do nothing."

[34]To this they replied, "You were steeped in sin at birth; how dare you lecture us!" And they threw him out.

Spiritual Blindness

[35]Jesus heard that they had thrown him out, and when he found him, he said, "Do you believe in the Son of Man?"

[36]"Who is he, sir?" the man asked. "Tell me so that I may believe in him."

[37]Jesus said, "You have now seen him; in fact, he is the one speaking with you."

[38]Then the man said, "Lord, I believe," and he worshiped him.

[39]Jesus said, "For judgment I have come into this world, so that the blind will see and those who see will become blind."

[40]Some Pharisees who were with him heard him say this and asked, "What? Are we blind too?"

[41]Jesus said, "If you were blind, you would not be guilty of sin; but now that you claim you can see, your guilt remains.

[a] 22 Or *Messiah* [b] 24 A solemn charge to tell the truth (see Joshua 7:19)

PRAYER: THE CHARACTER I WANT TO CULTIVATE

I WILL imitate You, O God, as Your beloved child, and I will walk in love, just as Christ loved me and gave Himself up for me as a fragrant offering and sacrifice to You. (Ephesians 5:1–2) . . . This is love: that I walk in obedience to Your commandments, O God. And this is the commandment I have heard from the beginning: I should walk in love. (2 John 6)

***TAKE** a moment to ask the Lord for the grace to grow in godly character.*

YEAR 1 DAY 310

OT 2 Kings 4:1–44

The Widow's Oil

4 The wife of a man from the company of the prophets cried out to Elisha, "Your servant my husband is dead, and you know that he revered the LORD. But now his creditor is coming to take my two boys as his slaves."

[2]Elisha replied to her, "How can I help you? Tell me, what do you have in your house?"

"Your servant has nothing there at all,"
she said, "except a little oil."
3 Elisha said, "Go around and ask all
your neighbors for empty jars. Don't ask
for just a few. 4 Then go inside and shut
the door behind you and your sons. Pour
oil into all the jars, and as each is filled,
put it to one side."
5 She left him and afterward shut the
door behind her and her sons. They
brought the jars to her and she kept pouring. 6 When all the jars were full, she said
to her son, "Bring me another one."
But he replied, "There is not a jar left."
Then the oil stopped flowing.
7 She went and told the man of God,
and he said, "Go, sell the oil and pay your
debts. You and your sons can live on what
is left."

The Shunammite's Son Restored to Life

8 One day Elisha went to Shunem. And
a well-to-do woman was there, who urged
him to stay for a meal. So whenever he
came by, he stopped there to eat. 9 She said
to her husband, "I know that this man
who often comes our way is a holy man
of God. 10 Let's make a small room on the
roof and put in it a bed and a table, a chair
and a lamp for him. Then he can stay
there whenever he comes to us."
11 One day when Elisha came, he went
up to his room and lay down there. 12 He
said to his servant Gehazi, "Call the Shunammite." So he called her, and she stood
before him. 13 Elisha said to him, "Tell her,
'You have gone to all this trouble for us.
Now what can be done for you? Can we
speak on your behalf to the king or the
commander of the army?' "
She replied, "I have a home among my
own people."
14 "What can be done for her?" Elisha
asked.
Gehazi said, "Well, she has no son and
her husband is old."
15 Then Elisha said, "Call her." So he
called her, and she stood in the doorway.
16 "About this time next year," Elisha said,
"you will hold a son in your arms."
"No, my lord," she objected. "Don't
mislead your servant, O man of God!"
17 But the woman became pregnant, and
the next year about that same time she
gave birth to a son, just as Elisha had told
her.
18 The child grew, and one day he went
out to his father, who was with the
reapers. 19 "My head! My head!" he said to
his father.
His father told a servant, "Carry him to
his mother." 20 After the servant had lifted
him up and carried him to his mother, the
boy sat on her lap until noon, and then
he died. 21 She went up and laid him on
the bed of the man of God, then shut the
door and went out.
22 She called her husband and said,
"Please send me one of the servants and
a donkey so I can go to the man of God
quickly and return."
23 "Why go to him today?" he asked. "It's
not the New Moon or the Sabbath."
"It's all right," she said.
24 She saddled the donkey and said to
her servant, "Lead on; don't slow down
for me unless I tell you." 25 So she set out
and came to the man of God at Mount
Carmel.
When he saw her in the distance, the
man of God said to his servant Gehazi,
"Look! There's the Shunammite! 26 Run to
meet her and ask her, 'Are you all right? Is
your husband all right? Is your child all
right?' "
"Everything is all right," she said.
27 When she reached the man of God at
the mountain, she took hold of his feet.
Gehazi came over to push her away, but
the man of God said, "Leave her alone!
She is in bitter distress, but the LORD has
hidden it from me and has not told me
why."
28 "Did I ask you for a son, my lord?"
she said. "Didn't I tell you, 'Don't raise my
hopes'?"
29 Elisha said to Gehazi, "Tuck your
cloak into your belt, take my staff in your
hand and run. If you meet anyone, do not
greet him, and if anyone greets you, do
not answer. Lay my staff on the boy's
face."
30 But the child's mother said, "As surely as the LORD lives and as you live, I will
not leave you." So he got up and followed
her.
31 Gehazi went on ahead and laid the
staff on the boy's face, but there was no
sound or response. So Gehazi went back
to meet Elisha and told him, "The boy has
not awakened."
32 When Elisha reached the house, there
was the boy lying dead on his couch. 33 He

went in, shut the door on the two of them
and prayed to the LORD. 34Then he got on
the bed and lay upon the boy, mouth to
mouth, eyes to eyes, hands to hands. As
he stretched himself out upon him, the
boy's body grew warm. 35Elisha turned
away and walked back and forth in the
room and then got on the bed and
stretched out upon him once more. The
boy sneezed seven times and opened his
eyes.
36Elisha summoned Gehazi and said,
"Call the Shunammite." And he did.
When she came, he said, "Take your son."
37She came in, fell at his feet and bowed
to the ground. Then she took her son and
went out.

Death in the Pot

38Elisha returned to Gilgal and there
was a famine in that region. While the
company of the prophets was meeting
with him, he said to his servant, "Put on
the large pot and cook some stew for
these men."
39One of them went out into the fields
to gather herbs and found a wild vine. He
gathered some of its gourds and filled the
fold of his cloak. When he returned, he
cut them up into the pot of stew, though
no one knew what they were. 40The stew
was poured out for the men, but as they
began to eat it, they cried out, "O man of
God, there is death in the pot!" And they
could not eat it.
41Elisha said, "Get some flour." He put
it into the pot and said, "Serve it to the
people to eat." And there was nothing
harmful in the pot.

Feeding of a Hundred

42A man came from Baal Shalishah,
bringing the man of God twenty loaves of
barley bread baked from the first ripe
grain, along with some heads of new grain.
"Give it to the people to eat," Elisha said.
43"How can I set this before a hundred
men?" his servant asked.
But Elisha answered, "Give it to the
people to eat. For this is what the LORD
says: 'They will eat and have some left
over.' " 44Then he set it before them, and
they ate and had some left over, according to the word of the LORD.

PRAYER: CONFESSION

O GOD, if I claim to be without sin, I deceive myself and the truth is not in me. If I confess my sins, You are faithful and just and will forgive me my sins and purify me from all unrighteousness. If I claim I have not sinned, I make You out to be a liar and Your word is not in me. (1 John 1:8–10)

***ASK** the Spirit to search your heart and reveal any areas of unconfessed sin. Acknowledge these to the Lord and thank Him for His forgiveness.*

NT John 10:1–42

The Shepherd and His Flock

10 "I tell you the truth, the man who
does not enter the sheep pen by the
gate, but climbs in by some other way, is
a thief and a robber. 2The man who enters
by the gate is the shepherd of his sheep.
3The watchman opens the gate for him,
and the sheep listen to his voice. He calls
his own sheep by name and leads them
out. 4When he has brought out all his
own, he goes on ahead of them, and his
sheep follow him because they know
his voice. 5But they will never follow a
stranger; in fact, they will run away from
him because they do not recognize a
stranger's voice." 6Jesus used this figure of
speech, but they did not understand what
he was telling them.
7Therefore Jesus said again, "I tell you
the truth, I am the gate for the sheep. 8All
who ever came before me were thieves
and robbers, but the sheep did not listen
to them. 9I am the gate; whoever enters
through me will be saved.[a] He will come
in and go out, and find pasture. 10The thief
comes only to steal and kill and destroy;
I have come that they may have life, and
have it to the full.
11"I am the good shepherd. The good

[a] 9 Or *kept safe*

shepherd lays down his life for the sheep.
[12]The hired hand is not the shepherd who
owns the sheep. So when he sees the wolf
coming, he abandons the sheep and runs
away. Then the wolf attacks the flock and
scatters it. [13]The man runs away because
he is a hired hand and cares nothing for
the sheep.

[14]"I am the good shepherd; I know my
sheep and my sheep know me— [15]just as
the Father knows me and I know the Father—and I lay down my life for the sheep.
[16]I have other sheep that are not of this
sheep pen. I must bring them also. They
too will listen to my voice, and there shall
be one flock and one shepherd. [17]The reason my Father loves me is that I lay down
my life—only to take it up again. [18]No one
takes it from me, but I lay it down of my
own accord. I have authority to lay it down
and authority to take it up again. This
command I received from my Father."

[19]At these words the Jews were again divided. [20]Many of them said, "He is demon-possessed and raving mad. Why listen to him?"

[21]But others said, "These are not the sayings of a man possessed by a demon. Can
a demon open the eyes of the blind?"

The Unbelief of the Jews

[22]Then came the Feast of Dedication[b] at
Jerusalem. It was winter, [23]and Jesus was
in the temple area walking in Solomon's
Colonnade. [24]The Jews gathered around
him, saying, "How long will you keep us
in suspense? If you are the Christ,[c] tell us
plainly."

[25]Jesus answered, "I did tell you, but you
do not believe. The miracles I do in my Father's name speak for me, [26]but you do not
believe because you are not my sheep. [27]My
sheep listen to my voice; I know them, and
they follow me. [28]I give them eternal life,
and they shall never perish; no one can
snatch them out of my hand. [29]My Father,
who has given them to me, is greater than
all[d]; no one can snatch them out of my Father's hand. [30]I and the Father are one."

[31]Again the Jews picked up stones to
stone him, [32]but Jesus said to them, "I
have shown you many great miracles from
the Father. For which of these do you
stone me?"

[33]"We are not stoning you for any of
these," replied the Jews, "but for blasphemy, because you, a mere man, claim to be
God."

[34]Jesus answered them, "Is it not written in your Law, 'I have said you are
gods'[e]? [35]If he called them 'gods,' to whom
the word of God came—and the Scripture
cannot be broken— [36]what about the one
whom the Father set apart as his very own
and sent into the world? Why then do you
accuse me of blasphemy because I said, 'I
am God's Son'? [37]Do not believe me unless I do what my Father does. [38]But if I do
it, even though you do not believe me, believe the miracles, that you may know and
understand that the Father is in me, and I
in the Father." [39]Again they tried to seize
him, but he escaped their grasp.

[40]Then Jesus went back across the Jordan to the place where John had been
baptizing in the early days. Here he stayed
[41]and many people came to him. They
said, "Though John never performed a
miraculous sign, all that John said about
this man was true." [42]And in that place
many believed in Jesus.

[b] 22 That is, Hanukkah [c] 24 Or *Messiah*
[d] 29 Many early manuscripts *What my Father has given me is greater than all* [e] 34 Psalm 82:6

PRAYER: MY RELATIONSHIP TO OTHERS

ALL things are from You, O God, who reconciled us to Yourself through Christ and gave us the ministry of reconciliation: namely, that You were reconciling the world to Yourself in Christ, not counting our trespasses against us. And You have committed to us the message of reconciliation. Therefore we are ambassadors for Christ, as though You, O God, were appealing to others through us—we implore them on Christ's behalf to be reconciled to You. (2 Corinthians 5:18–20)

PAUSE *to review your relationships with others and to commit them to the Lord.*

YEAR 1 DAY 311

OT 2 Kings 5:1-27

Naaman Healed of Leprosy

5 Now Naaman was commander of the
army of the king of Aram. He was a
great man in the sight of his master and
highly regarded, because through him the
LORD had given victory to Aram. He was a
valiant soldier, but he had leprosy.[a]
2 Now bands from Aram had gone out
and had taken captive a young girl from
Israel, and she served Naaman's wife. 3 She
said to her mistress, "If only my master
would see the prophet who is in Samaria!
He would cure him of his leprosy."
4 Naaman went to his master and told
him what the girl from Israel had said.
5 "By all means, go," the king of Aram
replied. "I will send a letter to the king of
Israel." So Naaman left, taking with him
ten talents[b] of silver, six thousand shekels[c]
of gold and ten sets of clothing. 6 The letter that he took to the king of Israel read:
"With this letter I am sending my servant
Naaman to you so that you may cure him
of his leprosy."
7 As soon as the king of Israel read the
letter, he tore his robes and said, "Am I
God? Can I kill and bring back to life?
Why does this fellow send someone to me
to be cured of his leprosy? See how he is
trying to pick a quarrel with me!"
8 When Elisha the man of God heard
that the king of Israel had torn his robes,
he sent him this message: "Why have you
torn your robes? Have the man come to
me and he will know that there is a
prophet in Israel." 9 So Naaman went with
his horses and chariots and stopped at the
door of Elisha's house. 10 Elisha sent a messenger to say to him, "Go, wash yourself
seven times in the Jordan, and your flesh
will be restored and you will be cleansed."
11 But Naaman went away angry and
said, "I thought that he would surely
come out to me and stand and call on the
name of the LORD his God, wave his hand
over the spot and cure me of my leprosy.
12 Are not Abana and Pharpar, the rivers of
Damascus, better than any of the waters
of Israel? Couldn't I wash in them and be
cleansed?" So he turned and went off in a
rage.
13 Naaman's servants went to him and
said, "My father, if the prophet had told
you to do some great thing, would you
not have done it? How much more, then,
when he tells you, 'Wash and be
cleansed'!" 14 So he went down and
dipped himself in the Jordan seven times,
as the man of God had told him, and his
flesh was restored and became clean like
that of a young boy.
15 Then Naaman and all his attendants
went back to the man of God. He stood
before him and said, "Now I know that
there is no God in all the world except in
Israel. Please accept now a gift from your
servant."
16 The prophet answered, "As surely as
the LORD lives, whom I serve, I will not accept a thing." And even though Naaman
urged him, he refused.
17 "If you will not," said Naaman,
"please let me, your servant, be given as
much earth as a pair of mules can carry,
for your servant will never again make
burnt offerings and sacrifices to any other god but the LORD. 18 But may the LORD
forgive your servant for this one thing:
When my master enters the temple of
Rimmon to bow down and he is leaning
on my arm and I bow there also—when I
bow down in the temple of Rimmon, may
the LORD forgive your servant for this."
19 "Go in peace," Elisha said.
After Naaman had traveled some distance, 20 Gehazi, the servant of Elisha the
man of God, said to himself, "My master
was too easy on Naaman, this Aramean,
by not accepting from him what he
brought. As surely as the LORD lives, I will
run after him and get something from
him."
21 So Gehazi hurried after Naaman.
When Naaman saw him running toward
him, he got down from the chariot to
meet him. "Is everything all right?" he
asked.
22 "Everything is all right," Gehazi answered. "My master sent me to say, 'Two
young men from the company of the
prophets have just come to me from the
hill country of Ephraim. Please give them

[a] *1* The Hebrew word was used for various diseases affecting the skin—not necessarily leprosy; also in verses 3, 6, 7, 11 and 27. [b] *5* That is, about 750 pounds (about 340 kilograms) [c] *5* That is, about 150 pounds (about 70 kilograms)

a talent[d] of silver and two sets of clothing.' "
23 "By all means, take two talents," said
Naaman. He urged Gehazi to accept
them, and then tied up the two talents of
silver in two bags, with two sets of clothing. He gave them to two of his servants,
and they carried them ahead of Gehazi.
24 When Gehazi came to the hill, he took
the things from the servants and put them
away in the house. He sent the men away
and they left. 25 Then he went in and stood
before his master Elisha.
"Where have you been, Gehazi?" Elisha
asked.
"Your servant didn't go anywhere," Gehazi answered.
26 But Elisha said to him, "Was not my
spirit with you when the man got down
from his chariot to meet you? Is this the
time to take money, or to accept clothes,
olive groves, vineyards, flocks, herds, or
menservants and maidservants? 27 Naaman's leprosy will cling to you and to
your descendants forever." Then Gehazi
went from Elisha's presence and he was
leprous, as white as snow.

[d] 22 That is, about 75 pounds (about 34 kilograms)

PRAYER: RENEWAL

TEACH me to do Your will, for You are my God; may Your good Spirit lead me on level ground. (Psalm 143:10) . . . May I listen to counsel and accept instruction, that I may be wise in my latter days. (Proverbs 19:20)

PAUSE *to add your own prayers for personal renewal.*

NT John 11:1-44

The Death of Lazarus

11 Now a man named Lazarus was sick.
He was from Bethany, the village of
Mary and her sister Martha. 2 This Mary,
whose brother Lazarus now lay sick, was
the same one who poured perfume on the
Lord and wiped his feet with her hair. 3 So
the sisters sent word to Jesus, "Lord, the
one you love is sick."
4 When he heard this, Jesus said, "This
sickness will not end in death. No, it is for
God's glory so that God's Son may be glorified through it." 5 Jesus loved Martha and
her sister and Lazarus. 6 Yet when he heard
that Lazarus was sick, he stayed where he
was two more days.
7 Then he said to his disciples, "Let us go
back to Judea."
8 "But Rabbi," they said, "a short while
ago the Jews tried to stone you, and yet
you are going back there?"
9 Jesus answered, "Are there not twelve
hours of daylight? A man who walks by
day will not stumble, for he sees by this
world's light. 10 It is when he walks by
night that he stumbles, for he has no
light."
11 After he had said this, he went on to
tell them, "Our friend Lazarus has fallen
asleep; but I am going there to wake
him up."
12 His disciples replied, "Lord, if he
sleeps, he will get better." 13 Jesus had been
speaking of his death, but his disciples
thought he meant natural sleep.
14 So then he told them plainly, "Lazarus is dead, 15 and for your sake I am glad
I was not there, so that you may believe.
But let us go to him."
16 Then Thomas (called Didymus) said
to the rest of the disciples, "Let us also go,
that we may die with him."

Jesus Comforts the Sisters

17 On his arrival, Jesus found that Lazarus had already been in the tomb for four
days. 18 Bethany was less than two miles[a]
from Jerusalem, 19 and many Jews had
come to Martha and Mary to comfort
them in the loss of their brother. 20 When
Martha heard that Jesus was coming, she
went out to meet him, but Mary stayed at
home.
21 "Lord," Martha said to Jesus, "if you
had been here, my brother would not

[a] 18 Greek *fifteen stadia* (about 3 kilometers)

have died. 22But I know that even now
God will give you whatever you ask."
23Jesus said to her, "Your brother will
rise again."
24Martha answered, "I know he will rise
again in the resurrection at the last day."
25Jesus said to her, "I am the resurrection and the life. He who believes in me
will live, even though he dies; 26and whoever lives and believes in me will never
die. Do you believe this?"
27"Yes, Lord," she told him, "I believe
that you are the Christ,[b] the Son of God,
who was to come into the world."
28And after she had said this, she went
back and called her sister Mary aside. "The
Teacher is here," she said, "and is asking
for you." 29When Mary heard this, she got
up quickly and went to him. 30Now Jesus
had not yet entered the village, but was
still at the place where Martha had met
him. 31When the Jews who had been with
Mary in the house, comforting her, noticed how quickly she got up and went
out, they followed her, supposing she was
going to the tomb to mourn there.
32When Mary reached the place where
Jesus was and saw him, she fell at his feet
and said, "Lord, if you had been here, my
brother would not have died."
33When Jesus saw her weeping, and the
Jews who had come along with her also
weeping, he was deeply moved in spirit
and troubled. 34"Where have you laid
him?" he asked.
"Come and see, Lord," they replied.
35Jesus wept.
36Then the Jews said, "See how he loved
him!"
37But some of them said, "Could not he
who opened the eyes of the blind man
have kept this man from dying?"

Jesus Raises Lazarus From the Dead

38Jesus, once more deeply moved, came
to the tomb. It was a cave with a stone laid
across the entrance. 39"Take away the
stone," he said.
"But, Lord," said Martha, the sister of
the dead man, "by this time there is a bad
odor, for he has been there four days."
40Then Jesus said, "Did I not tell you
that if you believed, you would see the
glory of God?"
41So they took away the stone. Then
Jesus looked up and said, "Father, I thank
you that you have heard me. 42I knew that
you always hear me, but I said this for the
benefit of the people standing here, that
they may believe that you sent me."
43When he had said this, Jesus called in
a loud voice, "Lazarus, come out!" 44The
dead man came out, his hands and feet
wrapped with strips of linen, and a cloth
around his face.
Jesus said to them, "Take off the grave
clothes and let him go."

[b] 27 Or *Messiah*

PRAYER: THE ATTRIBUTES OF GOD

I WILL sing of Your mercies forever, O Lord. With my mouth I will make Your faithfulness known through all generations. I will declare that Your loving-kindness will be built up forever, that You will establish Your faithfulness in the heavens. The heavens will praise Your wonders, O Lord, and Your faithfulness in the assembly of the holy ones. For who in the heavens can be compared with You, Lord? Who is like You among the children of the mighty? You, O God, are greatly feared in the council of the holy ones and You are more awesome than all who surround You. O Lord God of hosts, who is like You? O mighty Lord, Your faithfulness surrounds You.

(Psalm 89:1–2, 5–8)

***PAUSE** to reflect on these affirmations about the person, powers and perfection of God.*

OT **2 Kings 6:1–7:20** YEAR 1 DAY 312

An Axhead Floats

6 The company of the prophets said to
Elisha, "Look, the place where we meet
with you is too small for us. [2]Let us go to
the Jordan, where each of us can get a
pole; and let us build a place there for us
to live."

And he said, "Go."

[3]Then one of them said, "Won't you
please come with your servants?"

"I will," Elisha replied. [4]And he went
with them.

They went to the Jordan and began to
cut down trees. [5]As one of them was cutting down a tree, the iron axhead fell into
the water. "Oh, my lord," he cried out, "it
was borrowed!"

[6]The man of God asked, "Where did it
fall?" When he showed him the place, Elisha cut a stick and threw it there, and
made the iron float. [7]"Lift it out," he said.
Then the man reached out his hand and
took it.

Elisha Traps Blinded Arameans

[8]Now the king of Aram was at war with
Israel. After conferring with his officers, he
said, "I will set up my camp in such and
such a place."

[9]The man of God sent word to the king
of Israel: "Beware of passing that place,
because the Arameans are going down
there." [10]So the king of Israel checked on
the place indicated by the man of God.
Time and again Elisha warned the king, so
that he was on his guard in such places.

[11]This enraged the king of Aram. He
summoned his officers and demanded of
them, "Will you not tell me which of us
is on the side of the king of Israel?"

[12]"None of us, my lord the king," said
one of his officers, "but Elisha, the prophet who is in Israel, tells the king of Israel
the very words you speak in your bedroom."

[13]"Go, find out where he is," the king
ordered, "so I can send men and capture
him." The report came back: "He is in Dothan." [14]Then he sent horses and chariots
and a strong force there. They went by
night and surrounded the city.

[15]When the servant of the man of God
got up and went out early the next morning, an army with horses and chariots had
surrounded the city. "Oh, my lord, what
shall we do?" the servant asked.

[16]"Don't be afraid," the prophet answered. "Those who are with us are more
than those who are with them."

[17]And Elisha prayed, "O LORD, open his
eyes so he may see." Then the LORD
opened the servant's eyes, and he looked
and saw the hills full of horses and chariots of fire all around Elisha.

[18]As the enemy came down toward him,
Elisha prayed to the LORD, "Strike these
people with blindness." So he struck them
with blindness, as Elisha had asked.

[19]Elisha told them, "This is not the road
and this is not the city. Follow me, and I
will lead you to the man you are looking
for." And he led them to Samaria.

[20]After they entered the city, Elisha said,
"LORD, open the eyes of these men so they
can see." Then the LORD opened their eyes
and they looked, and there they were, inside Samaria.

[21]When the king of Israel saw them, he
asked Elisha, "Shall I kill them, my father?
Shall I kill them?"

[22]"Do not kill them," he answered.
"Would you kill men you have captured
with your own sword or bow? Set food
and water before them so that they may
eat and drink and then go back to their
master." [23]So he prepared a great feast for
them, and after they had finished eating
and drinking, he sent them away, and they
returned to their master. So the bands
from Aram stopped raiding Israel's territory.

Famine in Besieged Samaria

[24]Some time later, Ben-Hadad king of
Aram mobilized his entire army and
marched up and laid siege to Samaria.
[25]There was a great famine in the city; the
siege lasted so long that a donkey's head
sold for eighty shekels[a] of silver, and a
quarter of a cab[b] of seed pods[c] for five
shekels.[d]

[a] 25 That is, about 2 pounds (about 1 kilogram)
[b] 25 That is, probably about 1/2 pint (about 0.3 liter)
[c] 25 Or *of dove's dung*
[d] 25 That is, about 2 ounces (about 55 grams)

26 As the king of Israel was passing by on
the wall, a woman cried to him, "Help
me, my lord the king!"
27 The king replied, "If the LORD does
not help you, where can I get help for
you? From the threshing floor? From the
winepress?" 28 Then he asked her, "What's
the matter?"
She answered, "This woman said to me,
'Give up your son so we may eat him today, and tomorrow we'll eat my son.' 29 So
we cooked my son and ate him. The next
day I said to her, 'Give up your son so we
may eat him,' but she had hidden him."
30 When the king heard the woman's
words, he tore his robes. As he went along
the wall, the people looked, and there,
underneath, he had sackcloth on his
body. 31 He said, "May God deal with me,
be it ever so severely, if the head of Elisha
son of Shaphat remains on his shoulders
today!"
32 Now Elisha was sitting in his house,
and the elders were sitting with him. The
king sent a messenger ahead, but before
he arrived, Elisha said to the elders,
"Don't you see how this murderer is sending someone to cut off my head? Look,
when the messenger comes, shut the door
and hold it shut against him. Is not the
sound of his master's footsteps behind
him?"
33 While he was still talking to them, the
messenger came down to him. And ⌞the
king⌟ said, "This disaster is from the LORD.
Why should I wait for the LORD any
longer?"
7 Elisha said, "Hear the word of the
LORD. This is what the LORD says: About
this time tomorrow, a seah[e] of flour will
sell for a shekel[f] and two seahs[g] of barley
for a shekel at the gate of Samaria."
2 The officer on whose arm the king was
leaning said to the man of God, "Look,
even if the LORD should open the floodgates of the heavens, could this happen?"
"You will see it with your own eyes,"
answered Elisha, "but you will not eat any
of it!"

The Siege Lifted

3 Now there were four men with leprosy[h] at the entrance of the city gate. They
said to each other, "Why stay here until
we die? 4 If we say, 'We'll go into the city'—
the famine is there, and we will die. And
if we stay here, we will die. So let's go over
to the camp of the Arameans and surrender. If they spare us, we live; if they kill us,
then we die."
5 At dusk they got up and went to the
camp of the Arameans. When they
reached the edge of the camp, not a man
was there, 6 for the Lord had caused the Arameans to hear the sound of chariots and
horses and a great army, so that they said
to one another, "Look, the king of Israel
has hired the Hittite and Egyptian kings
to attack us!" 7 So they got up and fled in
the dusk and abandoned their tents and
their horses and donkeys. They left the
camp as it was and ran for their lives.
8 The men who had leprosy reached the
edge of the camp and entered one of the
tents. They ate and drank, and carried
away silver, gold and clothes, and went off
and hid them. They returned and entered
another tent and took some things from
it and hid them also.
9 Then they said to each other, "We're
not doing right. This is a day of good news
and we are keeping it to ourselves. If we
wait until daylight, punishment will overtake us. Let's go at once and report this to
the royal palace."
10 So they went and called out to the city
gatekeepers and told them, "We went into
the Aramean camp and not a man was
there—not a sound of anyone—only teth-
ered horses and donkeys, and the tents
left just as they were." 11 The gatekeepers
shouted the news, and it was reported
within the palace.
12 The king got up in the night and said
to his officers, "I will tell you what the Arameans have done to us. They know we
are starving; so they have left the camp to
hide in the countryside, thinking, 'They
will surely come out, and then we will
take them alive and get into the city.' "
13 One of his officers answered, "Have
some men take five of the horses that are
left in the city. Their plight will be like that
of all the Israelites left here—yes, they will
only be like all these Israelites who are

[e] *1* That is, probably about 7 quarts (about 7.3 liters); also in verses 16 and 18 [f] *1* That is, about 2/5 ounce (about 11 grams); also in verses 16 and 18 [g] *1* That is, probably about 13 quarts (about 15 liters); also in verses 16 and 18 [h] *3* The Hebrew word is used for various diseases affecting the skin—not necessarily leprosy; also in verse 8.

doomed. So let us send them to find out what happened."

[14]So they selected two chariots with their horses, and the king sent them after the Aramean army. He commanded the drivers, "Go and find out what has happened." [15]They followed them as far as the Jordan, and they found the whole road strewn with the clothing and equipment the Arameans had thrown away in their headlong flight. So the messengers returned and reported to the king. [16]Then the people went out and plundered the camp of the Arameans. So a seah of flour sold for a shekel, and two seahs of barley sold for a shekel, as the LORD had said.

[17]Now the king had put the officer on whose arm he leaned in charge of the gate, and the people trampled him in the gateway, and he died, just as the man of God had foretold when the king came down to his house. [18]It happened as the man of God had said to the king: "About this time tomorrow, a seah of flour will sell for a shekel and two seahs of barley for a shekel at the gate of Samaria."

[19]The officer had said to the man of God, "Look, even if the LORD should open the floodgates of the heavens, could this happen?" The man of God had replied, "You will see it with your own eyes, but you will not eat any of it!" [20]And that is exactly what happened to him, for the people trampled him in the gateway, and he died.

PRAYER: PETITION

MAY I be strong and courageous; may I not be afraid or discouraged because of my adversaries; there is a greater power with me than with them, for You, Lord my God, are with me to help me. (2 Chronicles 32:7–8)

***PAUSE** here to petition God for spiritual insight so that you might have understanding of His Word. Ask for insight into your identity in Jesus Christ: that you might know who you are, what direction your life should take and what His purpose for your life is. Offer prayers regarding your activities for this day and any special concerns you may have.*

NT John 11:45–12:11

The Plot to Kill Jesus

[45]Therefore many of the Jews who had come to visit Mary, and had seen what Jesus did, put their faith in him. [46]But some of them went to the Pharisees and told them what Jesus had done. [47]Then the chief priests and the Pharisees called a meeting of the Sanhedrin.

"What are we accomplishing?" they asked. "Here is this man performing many miraculous signs. [48]If we let him go on like this, everyone will believe in him, and then the Romans will come and take away both our place[a] and our nation."

[49]Then one of them, named Caiaphas, who was high priest that year, spoke up, "You know nothing at all! [50]You do not realize that it is better for you that one man die for the people than that the whole nation perish."

[51]He did not say this on his own, but as high priest that year he prophesied that Jesus would die for the Jewish nation, [52]and not only for that nation but also for the scattered children of God, to bring them together and make them one. [53]So from that day on they plotted to take his life.

[54]Therefore Jesus no longer moved about publicly among the Jews. Instead he withdrew to a region near the desert, to a village called Ephraim, where he stayed with his disciples.

[55]When it was almost time for the Jewish Passover, many went up from the country to Jerusalem for their ceremonial cleansing before the Passover. [56]They kept looking for Jesus, and as they stood in the temple area they asked one another, "What do you think? Isn't he coming to the Feast at all?" [57]But the chief priests and Pharisees had given orders that if anyone found out where Jesus was, he should report it so that they might arrest him.

[a] 48 Or *temple*

Jesus Anointed at Bethany

12 Six days before the Passover, Jesus arrived at Bethany, where Lazarus lived,
whom Jesus had raised from the dead.
2Here a dinner was given in Jesus' honor.
Martha served, while Lazarus was among
those reclining at the table with him.
3Then Mary took about a pint[b] of pure
nard, an expensive perfume; she poured it
on Jesus' feet and wiped his feet with her
hair. And the house was filled with the fragrance of the perfume.
4But one of his disciples, Judas Iscariot,
who was later to betray him, objected,
5"Why wasn't this perfume sold and the
money given to the poor? It was worth a
year's wages.[c]" 6He did not say this because he cared about the poor but because
he was a thief; as keeper of the money
bag, he used to help himself to what was
put into it.
7"Leave her alone," Jesus replied. "⌊It
was intended⌋ that she should save this
perfume for the day of my burial. 8You
will always have the poor among you, but
you will not always have me."
9Meanwhile a large crowd of Jews
found out that Jesus was there and came,
not only because of him but also to see
Lazarus, whom he had raised from the
dead. 10So the chief priests made plans to
kill Lazarus as well, 11for on account of
him many of the Jews were going over to
Jesus and putting their faith in him.

[b] 3 Greek *a litra* (probably about 0.5 liter)
[c] 5 Greek *three hundred denarii*

PRAYER: THE WORKS OF GOD

NOTHING is hidden that will not be revealed, and nothing is secret that will not be known and come out into the open. (Luke 8:17) . . . If I am ashamed of You and Your words, Jesus, then You, O Son of Man, will be ashamed of me when You come in Your glory and in the glory of Your Father and with the holy angels. (Luke 9:26)

***TAKE** a moment to consider the greatness of God's wonderful works.*

YEAR 1 DAY 313

OT 2 Kings 8:1–29

The Shunammite's Land Restored

8 Now Elisha had said to the woman
whose son he had restored to life, "Go
away with your family and stay for a while
wherever you can, because the LORD has
decreed a famine in the land that will last
seven years." 2The woman proceeded to
do as the man of God said. She and her
family went away and stayed in the land
of the Philistines seven years.
3At the end of the seven years she came
back from the land of the Philistines and
went to the king to beg for her house and
land. 4The king was talking to Gehazi, the
servant of the man of God, and had said,
"Tell me about all the great things Elisha
has done." 5Just as Gehazi was telling the
king how Elisha had restored the dead to
life, the woman whose son Elisha had
brought back to life came to beg the king
for her house and land.
Gehazi said, "This is the woman, my
lord the king, and this is her son whom
Elisha restored to life." 6The king asked
the woman about it, and she told him.
Then he assigned an official to her case
and said to him, "Give back everything
that belonged to her, including all the income from her land from the day she left
the country until now."

Hazael Murders Ben-Hadad

7Elisha went to Damascus, and Ben-Hadad king of Aram was ill. When the king
was told, "The man of God has come all
the way up here," 8he said to Hazael,
"Take a gift with you and go to meet the
man of God. Consult the LORD through
him; ask him, 'Will I recover from this illness?' "
9Hazael went to meet Elisha, taking
with him as a gift forty camel-loads of all

the finest wares of Damascus. He went in and stood before him, and said, "Your son Ben-Hadad king of Aram has sent me to ask, 'Will I recover from this illness?' "

10 Elisha answered, "Go and say to him, 'You will certainly recover'; but[a] the LORD has revealed to me that he will in fact die." 11 He stared at him with a fixed gaze until Hazael felt ashamed. Then the man of God began to weep.

12 "Why is my lord weeping?" asked Hazael.

"Because I know the harm you will do to the Israelites," he answered. "You will set fire to their fortified places, kill their young men with the sword, dash their little children to the ground, and rip open their pregnant women."

13 Hazael said, "How could your servant, a mere dog, accomplish such a feat?"

"The LORD has shown me that you will become king of Aram," answered Elisha.

14 Then Hazael left Elisha and returned to his master. When Ben-Hadad asked, "What did Elisha say to you?" Hazael replied, "He told me that you would certainly recover." 15 But the next day he took a thick cloth, soaked it in water and spread it over the king's face, so that he died. Then Hazael succeeded him as king.

Jehoram King of Judah

16 In the fifth year of Joram son of Ahab king of Israel, when Jehoshaphat was king of Judah, Jehoram son of Jehoshaphat began his reign as king of Judah. 17 He was thirty-two years old when he became king, and he reigned in Jerusalem eight years. 18 He walked in the ways of the kings of Israel, as the house of Ahab had done, for he married a daughter of Ahab. He did evil in the eyes of the LORD. 19 Nevertheless, for the sake of his servant David, the LORD was not willing to destroy Judah. He had promised to maintain a lamp for David and his descendants forever.

20 In the time of Jehoram, Edom rebelled against Judah and set up its own king. 21 So Jehoram[b] went to Zair with all his chariots. The Edomites surrounded him and his chariot commanders, but he rose up and broke through by night; his army, however, fled back home. 22 To this day Edom has been in rebellion against Judah. Libnah revolted at the same time.

23 As for the other events of Jehoram's reign, and all he did, are they not written in the book of the annals of the kings of Judah? 24 Jehoram rested with his fathers and was buried with them in the City of David. And Ahaziah his son succeeded him as king.

Ahaziah King of Judah

25 In the twelfth year of Joram son of Ahab king of Israel, Ahaziah son of Jehoram king of Judah began to reign. 26 Ahaziah was twenty-two years old when he became king, and he reigned in Jerusalem one year. His mother's name was Athaliah, a granddaughter of Omri king of Israel. 27 He walked in the ways of the house of Ahab and did evil in the eyes of the LORD, as the house of Ahab had done, for he was related by marriage to Ahab's family.

28 Ahaziah went with Joram son of Ahab to war against Hazael king of Aram at Ramoth Gilead. The Arameans wounded Joram; 29 so King Joram returned to Jezreel to recover from the wounds the Arameans had inflicted on him at Ramoth[c] in his battle with Hazael king of Aram.

Then Ahaziah son of Jehoram king of Judah went down to Jezreel to see Joram son of Ahab, because he had been wounded.

[a] *10* The Hebrew may also be read *Go and say, 'You will certainly not recover,' for.* [b] *21* Hebrew *Joram,* a variant of *Jehoram;* also in verses 23 and 24
[c] *29* Hebrew *Ramah,* a variant of *Ramoth*

PRAYER: INTERCESSION

I WAS called to freedom, but may I not use my freedom to indulge the flesh; but through love let me serve others. For the whole law is summed up in these words: "You shall love your neighbor as yourself." (Galatians 5:13–14)

__TAKE__ a few moments to intercede on behalf of other believers, such as your personal friends, those in ministry and those who are oppressed and in need.

NT John 12:12–36

The Triumphal Entry

12 The next day the great crowd that had
come for the Feast heard that Jesus was on
his way to Jerusalem. 13 They took palm
branches and went out to meet him,
shouting,

"Hosanna![a]"

"Blessed is he who comes in the name
of the Lord!"[b]

"Blessed is the King of Israel!"

14 Jesus found a young donkey and sat
upon it, as it is written,

15 "Do not be afraid, O Daughter of
Zion;
see, your king is coming,
seated on a donkey's colt."[c]

16 At first his disciples did not understand all this. Only after Jesus was glorified did they realize that these things had
been written about him and that they had
done these things to him.
17 Now the crowd that was with him
when he called Lazarus from the tomb
and raised him from the dead continued
to spread the word. 18 Many people, because they had heard that he had given
this miraculous sign, went out to meet
him. 19 So the Pharisees said to one another, "See, this is getting us nowhere.
Look how the whole world has gone after
him!"

Jesus Predicts His Death

20 Now there were some Greeks among
those who went up to worship at the
Feast. 21 They came to Philip, who was
from Bethsaida in Galilee, with a request.
"Sir," they said, "we would like to see
Jesus." 22 Philip went to tell Andrew; Andrew and Philip in turn told Jesus.
23 Jesus replied, "The hour has come for
the Son of Man to be glorified. 24 I tell you
the truth, unless a kernel of wheat falls to
the ground and dies, it remains only a
single seed. But if it dies, it produces
many seeds. 25 The man who loves his life
will lose it, while the man who hates his
life in this world will keep it for eternal
life. 26 Whoever serves me must follow me;
and where I am, my servant also will be.
My Father will honor the one who
serves me.
27 "Now my heart is troubled, and what
shall I say? 'Father, save me from this
hour'? No, it was for this very reason I
came to this hour. 28 Father, glorify your
name!"
Then a voice came from heaven, "I have
glorified it, and will glorify it again." 29 The
crowd that was there and heard it said it
had thundered; others said an angel had
spoken to him.
30 Jesus said, "This voice was for your
benefit, not mine. 31 Now is the time for
judgment on this world; now the prince
of this world will be driven out. 32 But I,
when I am lifted up from the earth, will
draw all men to myself." 33 He said this to
show the kind of death he was going to
die.
34 The crowd spoke up, "We have heard
from the Law that the Christ[d] will remain
forever, so how can you say, 'The Son of
Man must be lifted up'? Who is this 'Son
of Man'?"
35 Then Jesus told them, "You are going
to have the light just a little while longer.
Walk while you have the light, before
darkness overtakes you. The man who
walks in the dark does not know where
he is going. 36 Put your trust in the light
while you have it, so that you may become sons of light." When he had finished speaking, Jesus left and hid himself
from them.

[a] *13* A Hebrew expression meaning "Save!" which became an exclamation of praise [b] *13* Psalm 118:25, 26 [c] *15* Zech. 9:9 [d] *34* Or *Messiah*

PRAYER: MY RELATIONSHIP TO GOD

BLESSED are those who have learned to acclaim You, who walk in the light of Your presence, O Lord. We rejoice in Your name all day long; we exalt in Your righteousness. (Psalm 89:15–16) . . .

***Through Jesus, I will continually offer to You, O God, a sacrifice of praise—the fruit of lips that give thanks to Your name.* (Hebrews 13:15)**

***PAUSE** to thank God for the relationship that you enjoy with Him in Jesus Christ.*

YEAR 1 DAY 314

OT 2 Kings 9:1-37

Jehu Anointed King of Israel

9 The prophet Elisha summoned a man from the company of the prophets and said to him, "Tuck your cloak into your belt, take this flask of oil with you and go to Ramoth Gilead. [2]When you get there, look for Jehu son of Jehoshaphat, the son of Nimshi. Go to him, get him away from his companions and take him into an inner room. [3]Then take the flask and pour the oil on his head and declare, 'This is what the LORD says: I anoint you king over Israel.' Then open the door and run; don't delay!"

[4]So the young man, the prophet, went to Ramoth Gilead. [5]When he arrived, he found the army officers sitting together. "I have a message for you, commander," he said.

"For which of us?" asked Jehu.

"For you, commander," he replied.

[6]Jehu got up and went into the house. Then the prophet poured the oil on Jehu's head and declared, "This is what the LORD, the God of Israel, says: 'I anoint you king over the LORD's people Israel. [7]You are to destroy the house of Ahab your master, and I will avenge the blood of my servants the prophets and the blood of all the LORD's servants shed by Jezebel. [8]The whole house of Ahab will perish. I will cut off from Ahab every last male in Israel—slave or free. [9]I will make the house of Ahab like the house of Jeroboam son of Nebat and like the house of Baasha son of Ahijah. [10]As for Jezebel, dogs will devour her on the plot of ground at Jezreel, and no one will bury her.' " Then he opened the door and ran.

[11]When Jehu went out to his fellow officers, one of them asked him, "Is everything all right? Why did this madman come to you?"

"You know the man and the sort of things he says," Jehu replied.

[12]"That's not true!" they said. "Tell us."

Jehu said, "Here is what he told me: 'This is what the LORD says: I anoint you king over Israel.' "

[13]They hurried and took their cloaks and spread them under him on the bare steps. Then they blew the trumpet and shouted, "Jehu is king!"

Jehu Kills Joram and Ahaziah

[14]So Jehu son of Jehoshaphat, the son of Nimshi, conspired against Joram. (Now Joram and all Israel had been defending Ramoth Gilead against Hazael king of Aram, [15]but King Joram[a] had returned to Jezreel to recover from the wounds the Arameans had inflicted on him in the battle with Hazael king of Aram.) Jehu said, "If this is the way you feel, don't let anyone slip out of the city to go and tell the news in Jezreel." [16]Then he got into his chariot and rode to Jezreel, because Joram was resting there and Ahaziah king of Judah had gone down to see him.

[17]When the lookout standing on the tower in Jezreel saw Jehu's troops approaching, he called out, "I see some troops coming."

"Get a horseman," Joram ordered. "Send him to meet them and ask, 'Do you come in peace?' "

[18]The horseman rode off to meet Jehu and said, "This is what the king says: 'Do you come in peace?' "

"What do you have to do with peace?" Jehu replied. "Fall in behind me."

The lookout reported, "The messenger has reached them, but he isn't coming back."

[19]So the king sent out a second horseman. When he came to them he said, "This is what the king says: 'Do you come in peace?' "

Jehu replied, "What do you have to do with peace? Fall in behind me."

[a] *15* Hebrew *Jehoram,* a variant of *Joram;* also in verses 17 and 21–24

20The lookout reported, "He has reached them, but he isn't coming back either. The driving is like that of Jehu son of Nimshi—he drives like a madman."

21"Hitch up my chariot," Joram ordered. And when it was hitched up, Joram king of Israel and Ahaziah king of Judah rode out, each in his own chariot, to meet Jehu. They met him at the plot of ground that had belonged to Naboth the Jezreelite. 22When Joram saw Jehu he asked, "Have you come in peace, Jehu?"

"How can there be peace," Jehu replied, "as long as all the idolatry and witchcraft of your mother Jezebel abound?"

23Joram turned about and fled, calling out to Ahaziah, "Treachery, Ahaziah!"

24Then Jehu drew his bow and shot Joram between the shoulders. The arrow pierced his heart and he slumped down in his chariot. 25Jehu said to Bidkar, his chariot officer, "Pick him up and throw him on the field that belonged to Naboth the Jezreelite. Remember how you and I were riding together in chariots behind Ahab his father when the LORD made this prophecy about him: 26'Yesterday I saw the blood of Naboth and the blood of his sons, declares the LORD, and I will surely make you pay for it on this plot of ground, declares the LORD.'[b] Now then, pick him up and throw him on that plot, in accordance with the word of the LORD."

27When Ahaziah king of Judah saw what had happened, he fled up the road to Beth Haggan.[c] Jehu chased him, shouting, "Kill him too!" They wounded him in his chariot on the way up to Gur near Ibleam, but he escaped to Megiddo and died there. 28His servants took him by chariot to Jerusalem and buried him with his fathers in his tomb in the City of David. 29(In the eleventh year of Joram son of Ahab, Ahaziah had become king of Judah.)

Jezebel Killed

30Then Jehu went to Jezreel. When Jezebel heard about it, she painted her eyes, arranged her hair and looked out of a window. 31As Jehu entered the gate, she asked, "Have you come in peace, Zimri, you murderer of your master?"[d]

32He looked up at the window and called out, "Who is on my side? Who?" Two or three eunuchs looked down at him. 33"Throw her down!" Jehu said. So they threw her down, and some of her blood spattered the wall and the horses as they trampled her underfoot.

34Jehu went in and ate and drank. "Take care of that cursed woman," he said, "and bury her, for she was a king's daughter." 35But when they went out to bury her, they found nothing except her skull, her feet and her hands. 36They went back and told Jehu, who said, "This is the word of the LORD that he spoke through his servant Elijah the Tishbite: On the plot of ground at Jezreel dogs will devour Jezebel's flesh.[e] 37Jezebel's body will be like refuse on the ground in the plot at Jezreel, so that no one will be able to say, 'This is Jezebel.' "

[b] 26 See 1 Kings 21:19. [c] 27 Or *fled by way of the garden house* [d] 31 Or *"Did Zimri have peace, who murdered his master?"* [e] 36 See 1 Kings 21:23.

PRAYER: AFFIRMATION

WHO will bring a charge against those whom You have chosen, O God? You are the One who justifies. Who is he who condemns? It is Christ Jesus who died, who was furthermore raised to life, who is at Your right hand, O God, and is also interceding for me. (Romans 8:33–34)

***PAUSE** to reflect on these Biblical affirmations.*

NT John 12:37–13:17

The Jews Continue in Their Unbelief

37Even after Jesus had done all these miraculous signs in their presence, they still would not believe in him. 38This was to fulfill the word of Isaiah the prophet:

"Lord, who has believed our message
and to whom has the arm of the
Lord been revealed?"[a]

[a] 38 Isaiah 53:1

39 For this reason they could not believe, because, as Isaiah says elsewhere:

40 "He has blinded their eyes
  and deadened their hearts,
so they can neither see with their eyes,
  nor understand with their hearts,
  nor turn—and I would heal them."[b]

41 Isaiah said this because he saw Jesus' glory and spoke about him.

42 Yet at the same time many even among the leaders believed in him. But because of the Pharisees they would not confess their faith for fear they would be put out of the synagogue; 43 for they loved praise from men more than praise from God.

44 Then Jesus cried out, "When a man believes in me, he does not believe in me only, but in the one who sent me. 45 When he looks at me, he sees the one who sent me. 46 I have come into the world as a light, so that no one who believes in me should stay in darkness.

47 "As for the person who hears my words but does not keep them, I do not judge him. For I did not come to judge the world, but to save it. 48 There is a judge for the one who rejects me and does not accept my words; that very word which I spoke will condemn him at the last day. 49 For I did not speak of my own accord, but the Father who sent me commanded me what to say and how to say it. 50 I know that his command leads to eternal life. So whatever I say is just what the Father has told me to say."

Jesus Washes His Disciples' Feet

13 It was just before the Passover Feast. Jesus knew that the time had come for him to leave this world and go to the Father. Having loved his own who were in the world, he now showed them the full extent of his love.[c]

2 The evening meal was being served, and the devil had already prompted Judas Iscariot, son of Simon, to betray Jesus. 3 Jesus knew that the Father had put all things under his power, and that he had come from God and was returning to God; 4 so he got up from the meal, took off his outer clothing, and wrapped a towel around his waist. 5 After that, he poured water into a basin and began to wash his disciples' feet, drying them with the towel that was wrapped around him.

6 He came to Simon Peter, who said to him, "Lord, are you going to wash my feet?"

7 Jesus replied, "You do not realize now what I am doing, but later you will understand."

8 "No," said Peter, "you shall never wash my feet."

Jesus answered, "Unless I wash you, you have no part with me."

9 "Then, Lord," Simon Peter replied, "not just my feet but my hands and my head as well!"

10 Jesus answered, "A person who has had a bath needs only to wash his feet; his whole body is clean. And you are clean, though not every one of you." 11 For he knew who was going to betray him, and that was why he said not every one was clean.

12 When he had finished washing their feet, he put on his clothes and returned to his place. "Do you understand what I have done for you?" he asked them. 13 "You call me 'Teacher' and 'Lord,' and rightly so, for that is what I am. 14 Now that I, your Lord and Teacher, have washed your feet, you also should wash one another's feet. 15 I have set you an example that you should do as I have done for you. 16 I tell you the truth, no servant is greater than his master, nor is a messenger greater than the one who sent him. 17 Now that you know these things, you will be blessed if you do them.

[b] *40* Isaiah 6:10 [c] *1* Or *he loved them to the last*

PRAYER: THE CHARACTER I WANT TO CULTIVATE

WISDOM is better than jewels, and all desirable things cannot be compared with her. Wisdom dwells together with prudence and finds knowledge and discretion. (Proverbs 8:11–12) . . . The wisdom that comes from above is first pure, then peaceable, gentle, submissive, full of mercy and good fruits, without partiality and hypocrisy. And the fruit of righteousness is sown in peace by those who make peace. (James 3:17–18)

TAKE *a moment to ask the Lord for the grace to grow in godly character.*

YEAR 1 DAY 315

OT Psalms 61–62

Psalm 61

For the director of music. With stringed instruments. Of David.

[1]Hear my cry, O God;
listen to my prayer.

[2]From the ends of the earth I call to you,
I call as my heart grows faint;
lead me to the rock that is higher than I.
[3]For you have been my refuge,
a strong tower against the foe.

[4]I long to dwell in your tent forever
and take refuge in the shelter of your wings. *Selah*
[5]For you have heard my vows, O God;
you have given me the heritage of those who fear your name.

[6]Increase the days of the king's life,
his years for many generations.
[7]May he be enthroned in God's presence forever;
appoint your love and faithfulness to protect him.

[8]Then will I ever sing praise to your name
and fulfill my vows day after day.

Psalm 62

For the director of music. For Jeduthun. A psalm of David.

[1]My soul finds rest in God alone;
my salvation comes from him.
[2]He alone is my rock and my salvation;
he is my fortress, I will never be shaken.

[3]How long will you assault a man?
Would all of you throw him down—
this leaning wall, this tottering fence?
[4]They fully intend to topple him
from his lofty place;
they take delight in lies.
With their mouths they bless,
but in their hearts they curse. *Selah*

[5]Find rest, O my soul, in God alone;
my hope comes from him.
[6]He alone is my rock and my salvation;
he is my fortress, I will not be shaken.
[7]My salvation and my honor depend on God[a];
he is my mighty rock, my refuge.
[8]Trust in him at all times, O people;
pour out your hearts to him,
for God is our refuge. *Selah*

[9]Lowborn men are but a breath,
the highborn are but a lie;
if weighed on a balance, they are nothing;
together they are only a breath.
[10]Do not trust in extortion
or take pride in stolen goods;
though your riches increase,
do not set your heart on them.

[11]One thing God has spoken,
two things have I heard:
that you, O God, are strong,
[12] and that you, O Lord, are loving.
Surely you will reward each person
according to what he has done.

[a] 7 Or / *God Most High is my salvation and my honor*

PRAYER: THANKSGIVING

YOU are close to the brokenhearted, Lord, and save those who are crushed in spirit. Many are the afflictions of the righteous, but You deliver the righteous out of them all. (Psalm 34:18–19) . . . You are my refuge and strength, O God, an ever-present help in trouble. Therefore I will not fear, though the earth changes and the mountains slip into the heart of the sea. (Psalm 46:1–2)

PAUSE *to offer your own expressions of thanksgiving.*

NT John 13:18-38

Jesus Predicts His Betrayal

18 “I am not referring to all of you; I
know those I have chosen. But this is to
fulfill the scripture: ‘He who shares my
bread has lifted up his heel against me.’[a]
19 “I am telling you now before it happens, so that when it does happen you
will believe that I am He. 20 I tell you the
truth, whoever accepts anyone I send accepts me; and whoever accepts me accepts
the one who sent me.”
21 After he had said this, Jesus was troubled in spirit and testified, “I tell you the
truth, one of you is going to betray me.”
22 His disciples stared at one another, at
a loss to know which of them he meant.
23 One of them, the disciple whom Jesus
loved, was reclining next to him. 24 Simon
Peter motioned to this disciple and said,
“Ask him which one he means.”
25 Leaning back against Jesus, he asked
him, “Lord, who is it?”
26 Jesus answered, “It is the one to whom
I will give this piece of bread when I have
dipped it in the dish.” Then, dipping the
piece of bread, he gave it to Judas Iscariot,
son of Simon. 27 As soon as Judas took the
bread, Satan entered into him.
“What you are about to do, do quickly,” Jesus told him, 28 but no one at the
meal understood why Jesus said this to
him. 29 Since Judas had charge of the money, some thought Jesus was telling him to
buy what was needed for the Feast, or to
give something to the poor. 30 As soon as
Judas had taken the bread, he went out.
And it was night.

Jesus Predicts Peter's Denial

31 When he was gone, Jesus said, “Now
is the Son of Man glorified and God is
glorified in him. 32 If God is glorified in
him,[b] God will glorify the Son in himself,
and will glorify him at once.
33 “My children, I will be with you only
a little longer. You will look for me, and
just as I told the Jews, so I tell you now:
Where I am going, you cannot come.
34 “A new command I give you: Love one
another. As I have loved you, so you must
love one another. 35 By this all men will
know that you are my disciples, if you
love one another.”
36 Simon Peter asked him, “Lord, where
are you going?”
Jesus replied, “Where I am going, you
cannot follow now, but you will follow
later.”
37 Peter asked, “Lord, why can't I follow
you now? I will lay down my life for you.”
38 Then Jesus answered, “Will you really
lay down your life for me? I tell you the
truth, before the rooster crows, you will
disown me three times!

[a] *18* Psalm 41:9 [b] *32* Many early manuscripts do not have *If God is glorified in him.*

PRAYER: MY RELATIONSHIP TO OTHERS

I WILL not judge my brothers and sisters or regard them with contempt. Instead of judging them, I will resolve not to put a stumbling block or obstacle in their way. (Romans 14:10, 13) . . . I will accept others just as You, O Jesus Christ, accepted me to the glory of God. (Romans 15:7)

PAUSE *to review your relationships with others and to commit them to the Lord.*

YEAR 1 DAY 316

OT 2 Kings 10:1-36

Ahab's Family Killed

10 Now there were in Samaria seventy
sons of the house of Ahab. So Jehu
wrote letters and sent them to Samaria: to
the officials of Jezreel,[a] to the elders and
to the guardians of Ahab's children. He

[a] *1* Hebrew; some Septuagint manuscripts and Vulgate *of the city*

said, 2"As soon as this letter reaches you,
since your master's sons are with you and
you have chariots and horses, a fortified
city and weapons, 3choose the best and
most worthy of your master's sons and set
him on his father's throne. Then fight for
your master's house."
4But they were terrified and said, "If two
kings could not resist him, how can we?"
5So the palace administrator, the city
governor, the elders and the guardians
sent this message to Jehu: "We are your
servants and we will do anything you say.
We will not appoint anyone as king; you
do whatever you think best."
6Then Jehu wrote them a second letter,
saying, "If you are on my side and will
obey me, take the heads of your master's
sons and come to me in Jezreel by this
time tomorrow."
Now the royal princes, seventy of them,
were with the leading men of the city,
who were rearing them. 7When the letter
arrived, these men took the princes and
slaughtered all seventy of them. They put
their heads in baskets and sent them to
Jehu in Jezreel. 8When the messenger arrived, he told Jehu, "They have brought
the heads of the princes."
Then Jehu ordered, "Put them in two
piles at the entrance of the city gate until
morning."
9The next morning Jehu went out. He
stood before all the people and said, "You
are innocent. It was I who conspired
against my master and killed him, but
who killed all these? 10Know then, that
not a word the LORD has spoken against
the house of Ahab will fail. The LORD has
done what he promised through his servant Elijah." 11So Jehu killed everyone in
Jezreel who remained of the house of
Ahab, as well as all his chief men, his
close friends and his priests, leaving him
no survivor.
12Jehu then set out and went toward
Samaria. At Beth Eked of the Shepherds,
13he met some relatives of Ahaziah king of
Judah and asked, "Who are you?"
They said, "We are relatives of Ahaziah,
and we have come down to greet the families of the king and of the queen mother."
14"Take them alive!" he ordered. So they
took them alive and slaughtered them by
the well of Beth Eked—forty-two men. He
left no survivor.
15After he left there, he came upon Jehonadab son of Recab, who was on his
way to meet him. Jehu greeted him and
said, "Are you in accord with me, as I am
with you?"
"I am," Jehonadab answered.
"If so," said Jehu, "give me your hand."
So he did, and Jehu helped him up into
the chariot. 16Jehu said, "Come with me
and see my zeal for the LORD." Then he
had him ride along in his chariot.
17When Jehu came to Samaria, he killed
all who were left there of Ahab's family;
he destroyed them, according to the word
of the LORD spoken to Elijah.

Ministers of Baal Killed

18Then Jehu brought all the people together and said to them, "Ahab served
Baal a little; Jehu will serve him much.
19Now summon all the prophets of Baal,
all his ministers and all his priests. See
that no one is missing, because I am going to hold a great sacrifice for Baal. Anyone who fails to come will no longer live."
But Jehu was acting deceptively in order
to destroy the ministers of Baal.
20Jehu said, "Call an assembly in hon-
or of Baal." So they proclaimed it. 21Then
he sent word throughout Israel, and all
the ministers of Baal came; not one stayed
away. They crowded into the temple of
Baal until it was full from one end to the
other. 22And Jehu said to the keeper of the
wardrobe, "Bring robes for all the ministers of Baal." So he brought out robes for
them.
23Then Jehu and Jehonadab son of Recab went into the temple of Baal. Jehu
said to the ministers of Baal, "Look
around and see that no servants of the
LORD are here with you—only ministers of
Baal." 24So they went in to make sacrifices
and burnt offerings. Now Jehu had posted eighty men outside with this warning:
"If one of you lets any of the men I am
placing in your hands escape, it will be
your life for his life."
25As soon as Jehu had finished making
the burnt offering, he ordered the guards
and officers: "Go in and kill them; let no
one escape." So they cut them down with
the sword. The guards and officers threw
the bodies out and then entered the inner
shrine of the temple of Baal. 26They
brought the sacred stone out of the tem-

ple of Baal and burned it. [27]They demolished the sacred stone of Baal and tore down the temple of Baal, and people have used it for a latrine to this day.

[28]So Jehu destroyed Baal worship in Israel. [29]However, he did not turn away from the sins of Jeroboam son of Nebat, which he had caused Israel to commit—the worship of the golden calves at Bethel and Dan.

[30]The LORD said to Jehu, "Because you have done well in accomplishing what is right in my eyes and have done to the house of Ahab all I had in mind to do, your descendants will sit on the throne of Israel to the fourth generation." [31]Yet Jehu was not careful to keep the law of the LORD, the God of Israel, with all his heart. He did not turn away from the sins of Jeroboam, which he had caused Israel to commit.

[32]In those days the LORD began to reduce the size of Israel. Hazael overpowered the Israelites throughout their territory [33]east of the Jordan in all the land of Gilead (the region of Gad, Reuben and Manasseh), from Aroer by the Arnon Gorge through Gilead to Bashan.

[34]As for the other events of Jehu's reign, all he did, and all his achievements, are they not written in the book of the annals of the kings of Israel?

[35]Jehu rested with his fathers and was buried in Samaria. And Jehoahaz his son succeeded him as king. [36]The time that Jehu reigned over Israel in Samaria was twenty-eight years.

PRAYER: ADORATION

THE works of Your hands, O Lord, are truth and justice; all Your precepts are trustworthy. They stand firm for ever and ever, done in faithfulness and uprightness. You sent redemption to Your people; You have ordained Your covenant forever; holy and awesome is Your name. (Psalm 111:7–9)

***PAUSE** to express your thoughts of praise and worship.*

NT John 14:1–31

Jesus Comforts His Disciples

14 "Do not let your hearts be troubled. Trust in God[a]; trust also in me. [2]In my Father's house are many rooms; if it were not so, I would have told you. I am going there to prepare a place for you. [3]And if I go and prepare a place for you, I will come back and take you to be with me that you also may be where I am. [4]You know the way to the place where I am going."

Jesus the Way to the Father

[5]Thomas said to him, "Lord, we don't know where you are going, so how can we know the way?"

[6]Jesus answered, "I am the way and the truth and the life. No one comes to the Father except through me. [7]If you really knew me, you would know[b] my Father as well. From now on, you do know him and have seen him."

[8]Philip said, "Lord, show us the Father and that will be enough for us."

[9]Jesus answered: "Don't you know me, Philip, even after I have been among you such a long time? Anyone who has seen me has seen the Father. How can you say, 'Show us the Father'? [10]Don't you believe that I am in the Father, and that the Father is in me? The words I say to you are not just my own. Rather, it is the Father, living in me, who is doing his work. [11]Believe me when I say that I am in the Father and the Father is in me; or at least believe on the evidence of the miracles themselves. [12]I tell you the truth, anyone who has faith in me will do what I have been doing. He will do even greater things than these, because I am going to the Father. [13]And I will do whatever you ask in my name, so that the Son may bring glo-

[a] 1 Or *You trust in God* [b] 7 Some early manuscripts *If you really have known me, you will know*

ry to the Father. 14You may ask me for anything in my name, and I will do it.

Jesus Promises the Holy Spirit

15"If you love me, you will obey what I command. 16And I will ask the Father, and he will give you another Counselor to be with you forever— 17the Spirit of truth. The world cannot accept him, because it neither sees him nor knows him. But you know him, for he lives with you and will be[c] in you. 18I will not leave you as orphans; I will come to you. 19Before long, the world will not see me anymore, but you will see me. Because I live, you also will live. 20On that day you will realize that I am in my Father, and you are in me, and I am in you. 21Whoever has my commands and obeys them, he is the one who loves me. He who loves me will be loved by my Father, and I too will love him and show myself to him."

22Then Judas (not Judas Iscariot) said, "But, Lord, why do you intend to show yourself to us and not to the world?"

23Jesus replied, "If anyone loves me, he will obey my teaching. My Father will love him, and we will come to him and make our home with him. 24He who does not love me will not obey my teaching. These words you hear are not my own; they belong to the Father who sent me.

25"All this I have spoken while still with you. 26But the Counselor, the Holy Spirit, whom the Father will send in my name, will teach you all things and will remind you of everything I have said to you. 27Peace I leave with you; my peace I give you. I do not give to you as the world gives. Do not let your hearts be troubled and do not be afraid.

28"You heard me say, 'I am going away and I am coming back to you.' If you loved me, you would be glad that I am going to the Father, for the Father is greater than I. 29I have told you now before it happens, so that when it does happen you will believe. 30I will not speak with you much longer, for the prince of this world is coming. He has no hold on me, 31but the world must learn that I love the Father and that I do exactly what my Father has commanded me.

"Come now; let us leave.

[c] 17 Some early manuscripts *and is*

PRAYER: THE ATTRIBUTES OF GOD

YOU live, O Lord! Blessed are You, my Rock! You are exalted, O God, Rock of my salvation! (2 Samuel 22:47) . . . I will trust in You forever, for in You, Yahweh, the Lord, I have an everlasting Rock. (Isaiah 26:4)

***PAUSE** to reflect on these affirmations about the person, powers and perfection of God.*

YEAR 1 DAY 317

OT 2 Kings 11:1–12:21

Athaliah and Joash

11 When Athaliah the mother of Ahaziah saw that her son was dead, she proceeded to destroy the whole royal family. 2But Jehosheba, the daughter of King Jehoram[a] and sister of Ahaziah, took Joash son of Ahaziah and stole him away from among the royal princes, who were about to be murdered. She put him and his nurse in a bedroom to hide him from Athaliah; so he was not killed. 3He remained hidden with his nurse at the temple of the LORD for six years while Athaliah ruled the land.

4In the seventh year Jehoiada sent for the commanders of units of a hundred, the Carites and the guards and had them brought to him at the temple of the LORD. He made a covenant with them and put them under oath at the temple of the LORD. Then he showed them the king's son. 5He commanded them, saying, "This is what you are to do: You who are in the

[a] 2 Hebrew *Joram,* a variant of *Jehoram*

three companies that are going on duty
on the Sabbath—a third of you guarding
the royal palace, 6a third at the Sur Gate,
and a third at the gate behind the guard,
who take turns guarding the temple—
7and you who are in the other two companies that normally go off Sabbath duty
are all to guard the temple for the king.
8Station yourselves around the king, each
man with his weapon in his hand. Anyone who approaches your ranks[b] must be
put to death. Stay close to the king wherever he goes."

9The commanders of units of a hundred did just as Jehoiada the priest ordered. Each one took his men—those
who were going on duty on the Sabbath
and those who were going off duty—and
came to Jehoiada the priest. 10Then he
gave the commanders the spears and
shields that had belonged to King David
and that were in the temple of the LORD.
11The guards, each with his weapon in his
hand, stationed themselves around the
king—near the altar and the temple, from
the south side to the north side of the
temple.

12Jehoiada brought out the king's son
and put the crown on him; he presented
him with a copy of the covenant and proclaimed him king. They anointed him,
and the people clapped their hands and
shouted, "Long live the king!"

13When Athaliah heard the noise made
by the guards and the people, she went to
the people at the temple of the LORD.
14She looked and there was the king,
standing by the pillar, as the custom was.
The officers and the trumpeters were beside the king, and all the people of the
land were rejoicing and blowing trumpets. Then Athaliah tore her robes and
called out, "Treason! Treason!"

15Jehoiada the priest ordered the commanders of units of a hundred, who were
in charge of the troops: "Bring her out between the ranks[c] and put to the sword
anyone who follows her." For the priest
had said, "She must not be put to death
in the temple of the LORD." 16So they
seized her as she reached the place where
the horses enter the palace grounds, and
there she was put to death.

17Jehoiada then made a covenant between the LORD and the king and people
that they would be the LORD's people. He
also made a covenant between the king
and the people. 18All the people of the
land went to the temple of Baal and tore
it down. They smashed the altars and
idols to pieces and killed Mattan the
priest of Baal in front of the altars.

Then Jehoiada the priest posted guards
at the temple of the LORD. 19He took with
him the commanders of hundreds, the
Carites, the guards and all the people of
the land, and together they brought the
king down from the temple of the LORD
and went into the palace, entering by way
of the gate of the guards. The king then
took his place on the royal throne, 20and
all the people of the land rejoiced. And
the city was quiet, because Athaliah had
been slain with the sword at the palace.

21Joash[d] was seven years old when he
began to reign.

Joash Repairs the Temple

12 In the seventh year of Jehu, Joash[e] became king, and he reigned in Jerusalem forty years. His mother's name was
Zibiah; she was from Beersheba. 2Joash
did what was right in the eyes of the LORD
all the years Jehoiada the priest instructed
him. 3The high places, however, were not
removed; the people continued to offer
sacrifices and burn incense there.

4Joash said to the priests, "Collect all
the money that is brought as sacred offerings to the temple of the LORD—the money collected in the census, the money received from personal vows and the money
brought voluntarily to the temple. 5Let
every priest receive the money from one
of the treasurers, and let it be used to repair whatever damage is found in the temple."

6But by the twenty-third year of King Joash the priests still had not repaired the
temple. 7Therefore King Joash summoned
Jehoiada the priest and the other priests
and asked them, "Why aren't you repairing the damage done to the temple? Take
no more money from your treasurers, but
hand it over for repairing the temple."
8The priests agreed that they would not
collect any more money from the people
and that they would not repair the temple
themselves.

9Jehoiada the priest took a chest and

[b] *8* Or *approaches the precincts* [c] *15* Or *out from the precincts* [d] *21* Hebrew *Jehoash,* a variant of *Joash*
[e] *1* Hebrew *Jehoash,* a variant of *Joash;* also in verses 2, 4, 6, 7 and 18

bored a hole in its lid. He placed it beside the altar, on the right side as one enters the temple of the LORD. The priests who guarded the entrance put into the chest all the money that was brought to the temple of the LORD. 10Whenever they saw that there was a large amount of money in the chest, the royal secretary and the high priest came, counted the money that had been brought into the temple of the LORD and put it into bags. 11When the amount had been determined, they gave the money to the men appointed to supervise the work on the temple. With it they paid those who worked on the temple of the LORD—the carpenters and builders, 12the masons and stonecutters. They purchased timber and dressed stone for the repair of the temple of the LORD, and met all the other expenses of restoring the temple.

13The money brought into the temple was not spent for making silver basins, wick trimmers, sprinkling bowls, trumpets or any other articles of gold or silver for the temple of the LORD; 14it was paid to the workmen, who used it to repair the temple. 15They did not require an accounting from those to whom they gave the money to pay the workers, because they acted with complete honesty. 16The money from the guilt offerings and sin offerings was not brought into the temple of the LORD; it belonged to the priests.

17About this time Hazael king of Aram went up and attacked Gath and captured it. Then he turned to attack Jerusalem. 18But Joash king of Judah took all the sacred objects dedicated by his fathers—Jehoshaphat, Jehoram and Ahaziah, the kings of Judah—and the gifts he himself had dedicated and all the gold found in the treasuries of the temple of the LORD and of the royal palace, and he sent them to Hazael king of Aram, who then withdrew from Jerusalem.

19As for the other events of the reign of Joash, and all he did, are they not written in the book of the annals of the kings of Judah? 20His officials conspired against him and assassinated him at Beth Millo, on the road down to Silla. 21The officials who murdered him were Jozabad son of Shimeath and Jehozabad son of Shomer. He died and was buried with his fathers in the City of David. And Amaziah his son succeeded him as king.

PRAYER: CONFESSION

NO temptation has overtaken me except what is common to all people. You are faithful; You will not let me be tempted beyond what I am able, but with the temptation, You will also provide a way out, so that I may be able to endure it. (1 Corinthians 10:13)

__ASK__ the Spirit to search your heart and reveal any areas of unconfessed sin. Acknowledge these to the Lord and thank Him for His forgiveness.

NT John 15:1–16:4

The Vine and the Branches

15 "I am the true vine, and my Father is the gardener. 2He cuts off every branch in me that bears no fruit, while every branch that does bear fruit he prunes[a] so that it will be even more fruitful. 3You are already clean because of the word I have spoken to you. 4Remain in me, and I will remain in you. No branch can bear fruit by itself; it must remain in the vine. Neither can you bear fruit unless you remain in me.

5"I am the vine; you are the branches. If a man remains in me and I in him, he will bear much fruit; apart from me you can do nothing. 6If anyone does not remain in me, he is like a branch that is thrown away and withers; such branches are picked up, thrown into the fire and burned. 7If you remain in me and my words remain in you, ask whatever you wish, and it will be given you. 8This is to my Father's glory, that you bear much fruit, showing yourselves to be my disciples.

9"As the Father has loved me, so have I loved you. Now remain in my love. 10If

[a] 2 The Greek for *prunes* also means *cleans*.

you obey my commands, you will remain in my love, just as I have obeyed my Father's commands and remain in his love. 11 I have told you this so that my joy may be in you and that your joy may be complete. 12 My command is this: Love each other as I have loved you. 13 Greater love has no one than this, that he lay down his life for his friends. 14 You are my friends if you do what I command. 15 I no longer call you servants, because a servant does not know his master's business. Instead, I have called you friends, for everything that I learned from my Father I have made known to you. 16 You did not choose me, but I chose you and appointed you to go and bear fruit—fruit that will last. Then the Father will give you whatever you ask in my name. 17 This is my command: Love each other.

The World Hates the Disciples

18 "If the world hates you, keep in mind that it hated me first. 19 If you belonged to the world, it would love you as its own. As it is, you do not belong to the world, but I have chosen you out of the world. That is why the world hates you. 20 Remember the words I spoke to you: 'No servant is greater than his master.'[b] If they persecuted me, they will persecute you also. If they obeyed my teaching, they will obey yours also. 21 They will treat you this way because of my name, for they do not know the One who sent me. 22 If I had not come and spoken to them, they would not be guilty of sin. Now, however, they have no excuse for their sin. 23 He who hates me hates my Father as well. 24 If I had not done among them what no one else did, they would not be guilty of sin. But now they have seen these miracles, and yet they have hated both me and my Father. 25 But this is to fulfill what is written in their Law: 'They hated me without reason.'[c]

26 "When the Counselor comes, whom I will send to you from the Father, the Spirit of truth who goes out from the Father, he will testify about me. 27 And you also must testify, for you have been with me from the beginning.

16 "All this I have told you so that you will not go astray. 2 They will put you out of the synagogue; in fact, a time is coming when anyone who kills you will think he is offering a service to God. 3 They will do such things because they have not known the Father or me. 4 I have told you this, so that when the time comes you will remember that I warned you. I did not tell you this at first because I was with you.

[b] *20* John 13:16 [c] *25* Psalms 35:19; 69:4

PRAYER: THE WORKS OF GOD

THE wages of sin is death, but Your gift, O God, is eternal life in Christ Jesus our Lord. (Romans 6:23) . . . Since the children God has given You, Jesus, have bodies made of flesh and blood, You shared in their humanity so that by Your death You might destroy him who holds the power of death—that is, the devil—and free those who all their lives were held in slavery by their fear of death. (Hebrews 2:14–15)

***TAKE** a moment to consider the greatness of God's wonderful works.*

YEAR 1 DAY 318

OT 2 Kings 13:1–25

Jehoahaz King of Israel

13 In the twenty-third year of Joash son of Ahaziah king of Judah, Jehoahaz son of Jehu became king of Israel in Samaria, and he reigned seventeen years. 2 He did evil in the eyes of the LORD by following the sins of Jeroboam son of Nebat, which he had caused Israel to commit, and he did not turn away from them. 3 So the LORD's anger burned against Israel, and for a long time he kept them under the power of Hazael king of Aram and Ben-Hadad his son.

4 Then Jehoahaz sought the LORD's favor,

and the LORD listened to him, for he saw
how severely the king of Aram was oppressing Israel. 5The LORD provided a deliverer for Israel, and they escaped from
the power of Aram. So the Israelites lived
in their own homes as they had before.
6But they did not turn away from the sins
of the house of Jeroboam, which he had
caused Israel to commit; they continued
in them. Also, the Asherah pole[a] remained standing in Samaria.
7Nothing had been left of the army of
Jehoahaz except fifty horsemen, ten chariots and ten thousand foot soldiers, for
the king of Aram had destroyed the rest
and made them like the dust at threshing
time.
8As for the other events of the reign of
Jehoahaz, all he did and his achievements, are they not written in the book of
the annals of the kings of Israel? 9Jehoa-
haz rested with his fathers and was buried
in Samaria. And Jehoash[b] his son succeeded him as king.

Jehoash King of Israel

10In the thirty-seventh year of Joash
king of Judah, Jehoash son of Jehoahaz
became king of Israel in Samaria, and he
reigned sixteen years. 11He did evil in the
eyes of the LORD and did not turn away
from any of the sins of Jeroboam son of
Nebat, which he had caused Israel to
commit; he continued in them.
12As for the other events of the reign of
Jehoash, all he did and his achievements,
including his war against Amaziah king of
Judah, are they not written in the book of
the annals of the kings of Israel? 13Jehoash
rested with his fathers, and Jeroboam succeeded him on the throne. Jehoash was
buried in Samaria with the kings of Israel.
14Now Elisha was suffering from the illness from which he died. Jehoash king of
Israel went down to see him and wept over
him. "My father! My father!" he cried.
"The chariots and horsemen of Israel!"
15Elisha said, "Get a bow and some arrows," and he did so. 16"Take the bow in
your hands," he said to the king of Israel.
When he had taken it, Elisha put his
hands on the king's hands.
17"Open the east window," he said, and
he opened it. "Shoot!" Elisha said, and he
shot. "The LORD's arrow of victory, the arrow of victory over Aram!" Elisha declared. "You will completely destroy the
Arameans at Aphek."
18Then he said, "Take the arrows," and
the king took them. Elisha told him,
"Strike the ground." He struck it three
times and stopped. 19The man of God was
angry with him and said, "You should
have struck the ground five or six times;
then you would have defeated Aram and
completely destroyed it. But now you will
defeat it only three times."
20Elisha died and was buried.
Now Moabite raiders used to enter the
country every spring. 21Once while some
Israelites were burying a man, suddenly
they saw a band of raiders; so they threw
the man's body into Elisha's tomb. When
the body touched Elisha's bones, the man
came to life and stood up on his feet.
22Hazael king of Aram oppressed Israel
throughout the reign of Jehoahaz. 23But
the LORD was gracious to them and had
compassion and showed concern for
them because of his covenant with Abraham, Isaac and Jacob. To this day he has
been unwilling to destroy them or banish
them from his presence.
24Hazael king of Aram died, and Ben-
Hadad his son succeeded him as king.
25Then Jehoash son of Jehoahaz recap-
tured from Ben-Hadad son of Hazael the
towns he had taken in battle from his father Jehoahaz. Three times Jehoash defeated him, and so he recovered the Israelite towns.

[a] 6 That is, a symbol of the goddess Asherah; here and elsewhere in 2 Kings [b] 9 Hebrew *Joash*, a variant of *Jehoash*; also in verses 12–14 and 25

PRAYER: RENEWAL

MAY I have no other gods before You. May I not make for myself an idol in any form. May I not take Your name, O Lord my God, in vain, for You will not hold anyone guiltless who misuses Your name. (Exodus 20:3, 4, 7; Deuteronomy 5:7, 8, 11)

PAUSE *to add your own prayers for personal renewal.*

NT John 16:5–33

The Work of the Holy Spirit

[5] "Now I am going to him who sent me, yet none of you asks me, 'Where are you going?' [6] Because I have said these things, you are filled with grief. [7] But I tell you the truth: It is for your good that I am going away. Unless I go away, the Counselor will not come to you; but if I go, I will send him to you. [8] When he comes, he will convict the world of guilt[a] in regard to sin and righteousness and judgment: [9] in regard to sin, because men do not believe in me; [10] in regard to righteousness, because I am going to the Father, where you can see me no longer; [11] and in regard to judgment, because the prince of this world now stands condemned.

[12] "I have much more to say to you, more than you can now bear. [13] But when he, the Spirit of truth, comes, he will guide you into all truth. He will not speak on his own; he will speak only what he hears, and he will tell you what is yet to come. [14] He will bring glory to me by taking from what is mine and making it known to you. [15] All that belongs to the Father is mine. That is why I said the Spirit will take from what is mine and make it known to you.

[16] "In a little while you will see me no more, and then after a little while you will see me."

The Disciples' Grief Will Turn to Joy

[17] Some of his disciples said to one another, "What does he mean by saying, 'In a little while you will see me no more, and then after a little while you will see me,' and 'Because I am going to the Father'?" [18] They kept asking, "What does he mean by 'a little while'? We don't understand what he is saying."

[19] Jesus saw that they wanted to ask him about this, so he said to them, "Are you asking one another what I meant when I said, 'In a little while you will see me no more, and then after a little while you will see me'? [20] I tell you the truth, you will weep and mourn while the world rejoices. You will grieve, but your grief will turn to joy. [21] A woman giving birth to a child has pain because her time has come; but when her baby is born she forgets the anguish because of her joy that a child is born into the world. [22] So with you: Now is your time of grief, but I will see you again and you will rejoice, and no one will take away your joy. [23] In that day you will no longer ask me anything. I tell you the truth, my Father will give you whatever you ask in my name. [24] Until now you have not asked for anything in my name. Ask and you will receive, and your joy will be complete.

[25] "Though I have been speaking figuratively, a time is coming when I will no longer use this kind of language but will tell you plainly about my Father. [26] In that day you will ask in my name. I am not saying that I will ask the Father on your behalf. [27] No, the Father himself loves you because you have loved me and have believed that I came from God. [28] I came from the Father and entered the world; now I am leaving the world and going back to the Father."

[29] Then Jesus' disciples said, "Now you are speaking clearly and without figures of speech. [30] Now we can see that you know all things and that you do not even need to have anyone ask you questions. This makes us believe that you came from God."

[31] "You believe at last!"[b] Jesus answered. [32] "But a time is coming, and has come, when you will be scattered, each to his own home. You will leave me all alone. Yet I am not alone, for my Father is with me.

[33] "I have told you these things, so that in me you may have peace. In this world you will have trouble. But take heart! I have overcome the world."

[a] 8 Or *will expose the guilt of the world* [b] 31 Or *"Do you now believe?"*

PRAYER: MY RELATIONSHIP TO GOD

WITH regard to my former way of life, I am to put off my old self, which is being corrupted by its deceitful desires, and be renewed in the spirit of my mind; I am to put on the

new self, which was created according to You, O God, in righteousness and true holiness. (Ephesians 4:22–24)

PAUSE *to thank God for the relationship that you enjoy with Him in Jesus Christ.*

YEAR 1 DAY 319

OT Proverbs 14

14 The wise woman builds her house,
but with her own hands the foolish one tears hers down.

2 He whose walk is upright fears the LORD,
but he whose ways are devious despises him.

3 A fool's talk brings a rod to his back,
but the lips of the wise protect them.

4 Where there are no oxen, the manger is empty,
but from the strength of an ox comes an abundant harvest.

5 A truthful witness does not deceive,
but a false witness pours out lies.

6 The mocker seeks wisdom and finds none,
but knowledge comes easily to the discerning.

7 Stay away from a foolish man,
for you will not find knowledge on his lips.

8 The wisdom of the prudent is to give thought to their ways,
but the folly of fools is deception.

9 Fools mock at making amends for sin,
but goodwill is found among the upright.

10 Each heart knows its own bitterness,
and no one else can share its joy.

11 The house of the wicked will be destroyed,
but the tent of the upright will flourish.

12 There is a way that seems right to a man,
but in the end it leads to death.

13 Even in laughter the heart may ache,
and joy may end in grief.

14 The faithless will be fully repaid for their ways,
and the good man rewarded for his.

15 A simple man believes anything,
but a prudent man gives thought to his steps.

16 A wise man fears the LORD and shuns evil,
but a fool is hotheaded and reckless.

17 A quick-tempered man does foolish things,
and a crafty man is hated.

18 The simple inherit folly,
but the prudent are crowned with knowledge.

19 Evil men will bow down in the presence of the good,
and the wicked at the gates of the righteous.

20 The poor are shunned even by their neighbors,
but the rich have many friends.

21 He who despises his neighbor sins,
but blessed is he who is kind to the needy.

22 Do not those who plot evil go astray?
But those who plan what is good find[a] love and faithfulness.

23 All hard work brings a profit,
but mere talk leads only to poverty.

24 The wealth of the wise is their crown,
but the folly of fools yields folly.

25 A truthful witness saves lives,
but a false witness is deceitful.

26 He who fears the LORD has a secure fortress,

[a] 22 Or *show*

and for his children it will be a
refuge.

27 The fear of the LORD is a fountain of
life,
turning a man from the snares of
death.

28 A large population is a king's glory,
but without subjects a prince is
ruined.

29 A patient man has great understanding,
but a quick-tempered man displays
folly.

30 A heart at peace gives life to the body,
but envy rots the bones.

31 He who oppresses the poor shows
contempt for their Maker,
but whoever is kind to the needy
honors God.

32 When calamity comes, the wicked are
brought down,
but even in death the righteous
have a refuge.

33 Wisdom reposes in the heart of the
discerning
and even among fools she lets
herself be known.[b]

34 Righteousness exalts a nation,
but sin is a disgrace to any people.

35 A king delights in a wise servant,
but a shameful servant incurs his
wrath.

[b] 33 Hebrew; Septuagint and Syriac / *but in the heart of fools she is not known*

PRAYER: PETITION

HEAR, O Lord, my voice when I call; be merciful to me and answer me. My heart said of You, "Seek His face!" Your face, Lord, I will seek. (Psalm 27:7–8)

***PAUSE** here to petition God for growth in love and compassion toward others. Offer prayers for your loved ones, for those who do not know Jesus and for those in need. Offer prayers regarding your activities for this day and any special concerns you may have.*

NT John 17:1–26

Jesus Prays for Himself

17 After Jesus said this, he looked toward
heaven and prayed:

"Father, the time has come. Glorify
your Son, that your Son may glorify
you. 2 For you granted him authority
over all people that he might give eternal life to all those you have given
him. 3 Now this is eternal life: that they
may know you, the only true God,
and Jesus Christ, whom you have sent.
4 I have brought you glory on earth by
completing the work you gave me to
do. 5 And now, Father, glorify me in
your presence with the glory I had
with you before the world began.

Jesus Prays for His Disciples

6 "I have revealed you[a] to those
whom you gave me out of the world.
They were yours; you gave them to me
and they have obeyed your word.
7 Now they know that everything you
have given me comes from you. 8 For I
gave them the words you gave me and
they accepted them. They knew with
certainty that I came from you, and
they believed that you sent me. 9 I pray
for them. I am not praying for the
world, but for those you have given
me, for they are yours. 10 All I have is
yours, and all you have is mine. And
glory has come to me through them.
11 I will remain in the world no longer,
but they are still in the world, and I am
coming to you. Holy Father, protect
them by the power of your name—the
name you gave me—so that they may
be one as we are one. 12 While I was
with them, I protected them and kept
them safe by that name you gave me.
None has been lost except the one

[a] 6 Greek *your name;* also in verse 26

doomed to destruction so that Scripture would be fulfilled.
[13]"I am coming to you now, but I say these things while I am still in the world, so that they may have the full measure of my joy within them. [14]I have given them your word and the world has hated them, for they are not of the world any more than I am of the world. [15]My prayer is not that you take them out of the world but that you protect them from the evil one. [16]They are not of the world, even as I am not of it. [17]Sanctify[b] them by the truth; your word is truth. [18]As you sent me into the world, I have sent them into the world. [19]For them I sanctify myself, that they too may be truly sanctified.

Jesus Prays for All Believers

[20]"My prayer is not for them alone. I pray also for those who will believe in me through their message, [21]that all of them may be one, Father, just as you are in me and I am in you. May they also be in us so that the world may believe that you have sent me. [22]I have given them the glory that you gave me, that they may be one as we are one: [23]I in them and you in me. May they be brought to complete unity to let the world know that you sent me and have loved them even as you have loved me.
[24]"Father, I want those you have given me to be with me where I am, and to see my glory, the glory you have given me because you loved me before the creation of the world.
[25]"Righteous Father, though the world does not know you, I know you, and they know that you have sent me. [26]I have made you known to them, and will continue to make you known in order that the love you have for me may be in them and that I myself may be in them."

[b] 17 Greek *hagiazo (set apart for sacred use* or *make holy)*; also in verse 19

PRAYER: THE CHARACTER I WANT TO CULTIVATE

TO fear You, Lord, is to hate evil; wisdom hates pride and arrogance and the evil way and the perverse mouth. (Proverbs 8:13) . . . I will walk properly, as in the daytime, not in partying and drunkenness, not in sexual immorality and evil conduct, not in dissension and jealousy. Instead I will put on You, Lord Jesus Christ, like clothing, rather than thinking about how to satisfy my fleshly lusts. (Romans 13:13–14)

***TAKE** a moment to ask the Lord for the grace to grow in godly character.*

OT **2 Kings 14:1–29** YEAR 1 DAY 320

Amaziah King of Judah

14 In the second year of Jehoash[a] son of Jehoahaz king of Israel, Amaziah son of Joash king of Judah began to reign. [2]He was twenty-five years old when he became king, and he reigned in Jerusalem twenty-nine years. His mother's name was Jehoaddin; she was from Jerusalem. [3]He did what was right in the eyes of the LORD, but not as his father David had done. In everything he followed the example of his father Joash. [4]The high places, however, were not removed; the people continued to offer sacrifices and burn incense there.
[5]After the kingdom was firmly in his grasp, he executed the officials who had murdered his father the king. [6]Yet he did not put the sons of the assassins to death, in accordance with what is written in the Book of the Law of Moses where the LORD commanded: "Fathers shall not be put to death for their children, nor children put to death for their fathers; each is to die for his own sins."[b]
[7]He was the one who defeated ten thousand Edomites in the Valley of Salt

[a] 1 Hebrew *Joash,* a variant of *Jehoash;* also in verses 13, 23 and 27 [b] 6 Deut. 24:16

and captured Sela in battle, calling it Joktheel, the name it has to this day.
8Then Amaziah sent messengers to Jehoash son of Jehoahaz, the son of Jehu,
king of Israel, with the challenge: "Come,
meet me face to face."
9But Jehoash king of Israel replied to Amaziah king of Judah: "A thistle in Lebanon
sent a message to a cedar in Lebanon, 'Give
your daughter to my son in marriage.' Then
a wild beast in Lebanon came along and
trampled the thistle underfoot. 10You have
indeed defeated Edom and now you are arrogant. Glory in your victory, but stay at
home! Why ask for trouble and cause your
own downfall and that of Judah also?"
11Amaziah, however, would not listen, so
Jehoash king of Israel attacked. He and
Amaziah king of Judah faced each other at
Beth Shemesh in Judah. 12Judah was routed by Israel, and every man fled to his
home. 13Jehoash king of Israel captured
Amaziah king of Judah, the son of Joash,
the son of Ahaziah, at Beth Shemesh. Then
Jehoash went to Jerusalem and broke
down the wall of Jerusalem from the
Ephraim Gate to the Corner Gate—a section about six hundred feet long.[c] 14He
took all the gold and silver and all the articles found in the temple of the LORD and
in the treasuries of the royal palace. He also
took hostages and returned to Samaria.
15As for the other events of the reign of
Jehoash, what he did and his achievements,
including his war against Amaziah king of
Judah, are they not written in the book of
the annals of the kings of Israel? 16Jehoash
rested with his fathers and was buried in
Samaria with the kings of Israel. And Jeroboam his son succeeded him as king.
17Amaziah son of Joash king of Judah
lived for fifteen years after the death of Jehoash son of Jehoahaz king of Israel. 18As
for the other events of Amaziah's reign,
are they not written in the book of the annals of the kings of Judah?
19They conspired against him in Jerusalem, and he fled to Lachish, but they
sent men after him to Lachish and killed
him there. 20He was brought back by
horse and was buried in Jerusalem with
his fathers, in the City of David.
21Then all the people of Judah took Azariah,[d] who was sixteen years old, and
made him king in place of his father Amaziah. 22He was the one who rebuilt Elath
and restored it to Judah after Amaziah
rested with his fathers.

Jeroboam II King of Israel

23In the fifteenth year of Amaziah son of
Joash king of Judah, Jeroboam son of Jehoash king of Israel became king in Samaria,
and he reigned forty-one years. 24He did evil
in the eyes of the LORD and did not turn
away from any of the sins of Jeroboam son
of Nebat, which he had caused Israel to
commit. 25He was the one who restored the
boundaries of Israel from Lebo[e] Hamath to
the Sea of the Arabah,[f] in accordance with
the word of the LORD, the God of Israel, spoken through his servant Jonah son of Amittai, the prophet from Gath Hepher.
26The LORD had seen how bitterly everyone in Israel, whether slave or free, was
suffering; there was no one to help them.
27And since the LORD had not said he
would blot out the name of Israel from
under heaven, he saved them by the hand
of Jeroboam son of Jehoash.
28As for the other events of Jeroboam's
reign, all he did, and his military achievements, including how he recovered for Israel both Damascus and Hamath, which
had belonged to Yaudi,[g] are they not written in the book of the annals of the kings
of Israel? 29Jeroboam rested with his fathers, the kings of Israel. And Zechariah
his son succeeded him as king.

[c] 13 Hebrew *four hundred cubits* (about 180 meters) [d] 21 Also called *Uzziah* [e] 25 Or *from the entrance to* [f] 25 That is, the Dead Sea [g] 28 Or *Judah*

PRAYER: INTERCESSION

ALL things are for our benefit, so that the grace that is reaching more and more people may cause thanksgiving to abound to Your glory, O God. (2 Corinthians 4:15)

***TAKE** a few moments to intercede on behalf of friends, relatives, neighbors and coworkers who do not yet know salvation in Jesus Christ.*

NT John 18:1-27

Jesus Arrested

18 When he had finished praying, Jesus
left with his disciples and crossed the
Kidron Valley. On the other side there was
an olive grove, and he and his disciples
went into it.
2 Now Judas, who betrayed him, knew
the place, because Jesus had often met
there with his disciples. 3 So Judas came to
the grove, guiding a detachment of soldiers and some officials from the chief
priests and Pharisees. They were carrying
torches, lanterns and weapons.
4 Jesus, knowing all that was going to
happen to him, went out and asked them,
"Who is it you want?"
5 "Jesus of Nazareth," they replied.
"I am he," Jesus said. (And Judas the
traitor was standing there with them.)
6 When Jesus said, "I am he," they drew
back and fell to the ground.
7 Again he asked them, "Who is it you
want?"
And they said, "Jesus of Nazareth."
8 "I told you that I am he," Jesus answered. "If you are looking for me, then let
these men go." 9 This happened so that the
words he had spoken would be fulfilled: "I
have not lost one of those you gave me."[a]
10 Then Simon Peter, who had a sword,
drew it and struck the high priest's servant, cutting off his right ear. (The servant's name was Malchus.)
11 Jesus commanded Peter, "Put your
sword away! Shall I not drink the cup the
Father has given me?"

Jesus Taken to Annas

12 Then the detachment of soldiers with
its commander and the Jewish officials arrested Jesus. They bound him 13 and
brought him first to Annas, who was the
father-in-law of Caiaphas, the high priest
that year. 14 Caiaphas was the one who had
advised the Jews that it would be good if
one man died for the people.

Peter's First Denial

15 Simon Peter and another disciple
were following Jesus. Because this disciple
was known to the high priest, he went
with Jesus into the high priest's courtyard,
16 but Peter had to wait outside at the door.
The other disciple, who was known to the
high priest, came back, spoke to the girl
on duty there and brought Peter in.
17 "You are not one of his disciples, are
you?" the girl at the door asked Peter.
He replied, "I am not."
18 It was cold, and the servants and officials stood around a fire they had made
to keep warm. Peter also was standing
with them, warming himself.

The High Priest Questions Jesus

19 Meanwhile, the high priest questioned Jesus about his disciples and his
teaching.
20 "I have spoken openly to the world,"
Jesus replied. "I always taught in synagogues or at the temple, where all the Jews
come together. I said nothing in secret.
21 Why question me? Ask those who heard
me. Surely they know what I said."
22 When Jesus said this, one of the officials nearby struck him in the face. "Is this
the way you answer the high priest?" he
demanded.
23 "If I said something wrong," Jesus
replied, "testify as to what is wrong. But if
I spoke the truth, why did you strike me?"
24 Then Annas sent him, still bound, to Caiaphas the high priest.[b]

Peter's Second and Third Denials

25 As Simon Peter stood warming himself, he was asked, "You are not one of his
disciples, are you?"
He denied it, saying, "I am not."
26 One of the high priest's servants, a relative of the man whose ear Peter had cut
off, challenged him, "Didn't I see you
with him in the olive grove?" 27 Again Peter denied it, and at that moment a rooster began to crow.

[a] 9 John 6:39 [b] 24 Or *(Now Annas had sent him, still bound, to Caiaphas the high priest.)*

PRAYER: MY RELATIONSHIP TO OTHERS

I WILL not become conceited, provoking and envying others. (Galatians 5:26) . . . I will do all things without complaining or arguing, so that I may become blameless and pure—Your child, O God, without fault in the midst of a crooked and perverse generation, among whom I shine as a light in the world, holding out the word of life. (Philippians 2:14–16)

***PAUSE** to review your relationships with others and to commit them to the Lord.*

OT 2 Kings 15:1–38

YEAR 1 DAY 321

Azariah King of Judah

15 In the twenty-seventh year of Jeroboam king of Israel, Azariah son of Amaziah king of Judah began to reign. 2 He was sixteen years old when he became king, and he reigned in Jerusalem fifty-two years. His mother's name was Jecoliah; she was from Jerusalem. 3 He did what was right in the eyes of the LORD, just as his father Amaziah had done. 4 The high places, however, were not removed; the people continued to offer sacrifices and burn incense there.

5 The LORD afflicted the king with leprosy[a] until the day he died, and he lived in a separate house.[b] Jotham the king's son had charge of the palace and governed the people of the land.

6 As for the other events of Azariah's reign, and all he did, are they not written in the book of the annals of the kings of Judah? 7 Azariah rested with his fathers and was buried near them in the City of David. And Jotham his son succeeded him as king.

Zechariah King of Israel

8 In the thirty-eighth year of Azariah king of Judah, Zechariah son of Jeroboam became king of Israel in Samaria, and he reigned six months. 9 He did evil in the eyes of the LORD, as his fathers had done. He did not turn away from the sins of Jeroboam son of Nebat, which he had caused Israel to commit.

10 Shallum son of Jabesh conspired against Zechariah. He attacked him in front of the people,[c] assassinated him and succeeded him as king. 11 The other events of Zechariah's reign are written in the book of the annals of the kings of Israel. 12 So the word of the LORD spoken to Jehu was fulfilled: "Your descendants will sit on the throne of Israel to the fourth generation."[d]

Shallum King of Israel

13 Shallum son of Jabesh became king in the thirty-ninth year of Uzziah king of Judah, and he reigned in Samaria one month. 14 Then Menahem son of Gadi went from Tirzah up to Samaria. He attacked Shallum son of Jabesh in Samaria, assassinated him and succeeded him as king.

15 The other events of Shallum's reign, and the conspiracy he led, are written in the book of the annals of the kings of Israel.

16 At that time Menahem, starting out from Tirzah, attacked Tiphsah and everyone in the city and its vicinity, because they refused to open their gates. He sacked Tiphsah and ripped open all the pregnant women.

Menahem King of Israel

17 In the thirty-ninth year of Azariah king of Judah, Menahem son of Gadi became king of Israel, and he reigned in Samaria ten years. 18 He did evil in the eyes of the LORD. During his entire reign he did

[a] *5* The Hebrew word was used for various diseases affecting the skin—not necessarily leprosy. [b] *5* Or *in a house where he was relieved of responsibility*
[c] *10* Hebrew; some Septuagint manuscripts *in Ibleam*
[d] *12* 2 Kings 10:30

not turn away from the sins of Jeroboam son of Nebat, which he had caused Israel to commit.

19 Then Pul[e] king of Assyria invaded the land, and Menahem gave him a thousand talents[f] of silver to gain his support and strengthen his own hold on the kingdom. 20 Menahem exacted this money from Israel. Every wealthy man had to contribute fifty shekels[g] of silver to be given to the king of Assyria. So the king of Assyria withdrew and stayed in the land no longer.

21 As for the other events of Menahem's reign, and all he did, are they not written in the book of the annals of the kings of Israel? 22 Menahem rested with his fathers. And Pekahiah his son succeeded him as king.

Pekahiah King of Israel

23 In the fiftieth year of Azariah king of Judah, Pekahiah son of Menahem became king of Israel in Samaria, and he reigned two years. 24 Pekahiah did evil in the eyes of the LORD. He did not turn away from the sins of Jeroboam son of Nebat, which he had caused Israel to commit. 25 One of his chief officers, Pekah son of Remaliah, conspired against him. Taking fifty men of Gilead with him, he assassinated Pekahiah, along with Argob and Arieh, in the citadel of the royal palace at Samaria. So Pekah killed Pekahiah and succeeded him as king.

26 The other events of Pekahiah's reign, and all he did, are written in the book of the annals of the kings of Israel.

Pekah King of Israel

27 In the fifty-second year of Azariah king of Judah, Pekah son of Remaliah became king of Israel in Samaria, and he reigned twenty years. 28 He did evil in the eyes of the LORD. He did not turn away from the sins of Jeroboam son of Nebat, which he had caused Israel to commit.

29 In the time of Pekah king of Israel, Tiglath-Pileser king of Assyria came and took Ijon, Abel Beth Maacah, Janoah, Kedesh and Hazor. He took Gilead and Galilee, including all the land of Naphtali, and deported the people to Assyria. 30 Then Hoshea son of Elah conspired against Pekah son of Remaliah. He attacked and assassinated him, and then succeeded him as king in the twentieth year of Jotham son of Uzziah.

31 As for the other events of Pekah's reign, and all he did, are they not written in the book of the annals of the kings of Israel?

Jotham King of Judah

32 In the second year of Pekah son of Remaliah king of Israel, Jotham son of Uzziah king of Judah began to reign. 33 He was twenty-five years old when he became king, and he reigned in Jerusalem sixteen years. His mother's name was Jerusha daughter of Zadok. 34 He did what was right in the eyes of the LORD, just as his father Uzziah had done. 35 The high places, however, were not removed; the people continued to offer sacrifices and burn incense there. Jotham rebuilt the Upper Gate of the temple of the LORD.

36 As for the other events of Jotham's reign, and what he did, are they not written in the book of the annals of the kings of Judah? 37 (In those days the LORD began to send Rezin king of Aram and Pekah son of Remaliah against Judah.) 38 Jotham rested with his fathers and was buried with them in the City of David, the city of his father. And Ahaz his son succeeded him as king.

[e] 19 Also called *Tiglath-Pileser* [f] 19 That is, about 37 tons (about 34 metric tons) [g] 20 That is, about 1 1/4 pounds (about 0.6 kilogram)

PRAYER: AFFIRMATION

IS the law opposed to Your promises, O God? Certainly not! For if a law had been given that could impart life, then righteousness would indeed have been by the law. But the Scripture has declared all to be under sin, so that the promise by faith in Jesus Christ might be given to those who believe. (Galatians 3:21–22)

PAUSE *to reflect on these Biblical affirmations.*

NT John 18:28–19:16a

Jesus Before Pilate

28Then the Jews led Jesus from Caiaphas
to the palace of the Roman governor. By
now it was early morning, and to avoid
ceremonial uncleanness the Jews did not
enter the palace; they wanted to be able
to eat the Passover. 29So Pilate came out
to them and asked, "What charges are you
bringing against this man?"
30"If he were not a criminal," they
replied, "we would not have handed him
over to you."
31Pilate said, "Take him yourselves and
judge him by your own law."
"But we have no right to execute anyone," the Jews objected. 32This happened
so that the words Jesus had spoken indicating the kind of death he was going to
die would be fulfilled.
33Pilate then went back inside the
palace, summoned Jesus and asked him,
"Are you the king of the Jews?"
34"Is that your own idea," Jesus asked,
"or did others talk to you about me?"
35"Am I a Jew?" Pilate replied. "It was
your people and your chief priests who
handed you over to me. What is it you
have done?"
36Jesus said, "My kingdom is not of this
world. If it were, my servants would fight
to prevent my arrest by the Jews. But now
my kingdom is from another place."
37"You are a king, then!" said Pilate.
Jesus answered, "You are right in saying
I am a king. In fact, for this reason I was
born, and for this I came into the world,
to testify to the truth. Everyone on the
side of truth listens to me."
38"What is truth?" Pilate asked. With
this he went out again to the Jews and
said, "I find no basis for a charge against
him. 39But it is your custom for me to release to you one prisoner at the time of
the Passover. Do you want me to release
'the king of the Jews'?"
40They shouted back, "No, not him!
Give us Barabbas!" Now Barabbas had
taken part in a rebellion.

Jesus Sentenced to be Crucified

19 Then Pilate took Jesus and had him
flogged. 2The soldiers twisted together a crown of thorns and put it on his
head. They clothed him in a purple robe
3and went up to him again and again, saying, "Hail, king of the Jews!" And they
struck him in the face.
4Once more Pilate came out and said to
the Jews, "Look, I am bringing him out to
you to let you know that I find no basis
for a charge against him." 5When Jesus
came out wearing the crown of thorns and
the purple robe, Pilate said to them, "Here
is the man!"
6As soon as the chief priests and their
officials saw him, they shouted, "Crucify!
Crucify!"
But Pilate answered, "You take him and
crucify him. As for me, I find no basis for
a charge against him."
7The Jews insisted, "We have a law, and
according to that law he must die, because
he claimed to be the Son of God."
8When Pilate heard this, he was even
more afraid, 9and he went back inside the
palace. "Where do you come from?" he
asked Jesus, but Jesus gave him no answer.
10"Do you refuse to speak to me?" Pilate
said. "Don't you realize I have power either to free you or to crucify you?"
11Jesus answered, "You would have no
power over me if it were not given to you
from above. Therefore the one who handed me over to you is guilty of a greater
sin."
12From then on, Pilate tried to set Jesus
free, but the Jews kept shouting, "If you
let this man go, you are no friend of Caesar. Anyone who claims to be a king opposes Caesar."
13When Pilate heard this, he brought
Jesus out and sat down on the judge's seat
at a place known as the Stone Pavement
(which in Aramaic is Gabbatha). 14It was
the day of Preparation of Passover Week,
about the sixth hour.
"Here is your king," Pilate said to the
Jews.
15But they shouted, "Take him away!
Take him away! Crucify him!"
"Shall I crucify your king?" Pilate asked.
"We have no king but Caesar," the chief
priests answered.
16Finally Pilate handed him over to
them to be crucified.

PRAYER: THE ATTRIBUTES OF GOD

YOU, Almighty God, are beyond our reach; You are exalted in power and in Your justice and great righteousness, You do not oppress. (Job 37:23) . . . Great are You, Lord, and mighty in power; Your understanding is infinite. (Psalm 147:5)

***PAUSE** to reflect on these affirmations about the person, powers and perfection of God.*

OT Psalms 63–64

Psalm 63

A psalm of David. When he was in the Desert of Judah.

1 O God, you are my God,
earnestly I seek you;
my soul thirsts for you,
my body longs for you,
in a dry and weary land
where there is no water.

2 I have seen you in the sanctuary
and beheld your power and your glory.
3 Because your love is better than life,
my lips will glorify you.
4 I will praise you as long as I live,
and in your name I will lift up my hands.
5 My soul will be satisfied as with the richest of foods;
with singing lips my mouth will praise you.

6 On my bed I remember you;
I think of you through the watches of the night.
7 Because you are my help,
I sing in the shadow of your wings.
8 My soul clings to you;
your right hand upholds me.

9 They who seek my life will be destroyed;
they will go down to the depths of the earth.
10 They will be given over to the sword
and become food for jackals.

11 But the king will rejoice in God;
all who swear by God's name will praise him,
while the mouths of liars will be silenced.

Psalm 64

For the director of music. A psalm of David.

1 Hear me, O God, as I voice my complaint;
protect my life from the threat of the enemy.
2 Hide me from the conspiracy of the wicked,
from that noisy crowd of evildoers.

3 They sharpen their tongues like swords
and aim their words like deadly arrows.
4 They shoot from ambush at the innocent man;
they shoot at him suddenly, without fear.

5 They encourage each other in evil plans,
they talk about hiding their snares;
they say, "Who will see them[a]?"
6 They plot injustice and say,
"We have devised a perfect plan!"
Surely the mind and heart of man are cunning.

7 But God will shoot them with arrows;
suddenly they will be struck down.
8 He will turn their own tongues against them
and bring them to ruin;
all who see them will shake their heads in scorn.

9 All mankind will fear;
they will proclaim the works of God
and ponder what he has done.
10 Let the righteous rejoice in the LORD
and take refuge in him;
let all the upright in heart praise him!

[a] 5 Or *us*

PRAYER: THANKSGIVING

WE give thanks to You, O God, we give thanks, for Your name is near; we tell of Your wonderful works. (Psalm 75:1) . . . Loving-kindness and truth meet together; righteousness and peace kiss each other. Truth springs forth from the earth, and righteousness looks down from heaven. (Psalm 85:10–11)

***PAUSE** to offer your own expressions of thanksgiving.*

NT John 19:16b–42

The Crucifixion

So the soldiers took charge of Jesus. [17]Carrying his own cross, he went out to the place of the Skull (which in Aramaic is called Golgotha). [18]Here they crucified him, and with him two others—one on each side and Jesus in the middle.

[19]Pilate had a notice prepared and fastened to the cross. It read: JESUS OF NAZARETH, THE KING OF THE JEWS. [20]Many of the Jews read this sign, for the place where Jesus was crucified was near the city, and the sign was written in Aramaic, Latin and Greek. [21]The chief priests of the Jews protested to Pilate, "Do not write 'The King of the Jews,' but that this man claimed to be king of the Jews."

[22]Pilate answered, "What I have written, I have written."

[23]When the soldiers crucified Jesus, they took his clothes, dividing them into four shares, one for each of them, with the undergarment remaining. This garment was seamless, woven in one piece from top to bottom.

[24]"Let's not tear it," they said to one another. "Let's decide by lot who will get it."

This happened that the scripture might be fulfilled which said,

"They divided my garments among
them
and cast lots for my clothing."[a]

So this is what the soldiers did.

[25]Near the cross of Jesus stood his mother, his mother's sister, Mary the wife of Clopas, and Mary Magdalene. [26]When Jesus saw his mother there, and the disciple whom he loved standing nearby, he said to his mother, "Dear woman, here is your son," [27]and to the disciple, "Here is your mother." From that time on, this disciple took her into his home.

The Death of Jesus

[28]Later, knowing that all was now completed, and so that the Scripture would be fulfilled, Jesus said, "I am thirsty." [29]A jar of wine vinegar was there, so they soaked a sponge in it, put the sponge on a stalk of the hyssop plant, and lifted it to Jesus' lips. [30]When he had received the drink, Jesus said, "It is finished." With that, he bowed his head and gave up his spirit.

[31]Now it was the day of Preparation, and the next day was to be a special Sabbath. Because the Jews did not want the bodies left on the crosses during the Sabbath, they asked Pilate to have the legs broken and the bodies taken down. [32]The soldiers therefore came and broke the legs of the first man who had been crucified with Jesus, and then those of the other. [33]But when they came to Jesus and found that he was already dead, they did not break his legs. [34]Instead, one of the soldiers pierced Jesus' side with a spear, bringing a sudden flow of blood and water. [35]The man who saw it has given testimony, and his testimony is true. He knows that he tells the truth, and he testifies so that you also may believe. [36]These things happened so that the scripture would be fulfilled: "Not one of his bones will be broken,"[b] [37]and, as another scripture says, "They will look on the one they have pierced."[c]

The Burial of Jesus

[38]Later, Joseph of Arimathea asked Pilate for the body of Jesus. Now Joseph was a disciple of Jesus, but secretly because he feared the Jews. With Pilate's permission, he came and took the body away. [39]He was accompanied by Nicodemus, the man

[a] *24* Psalm 22:18 [b] *36* Exodus 12:46; Num. 9:12; Psalm 34:20 [c] *37* Zech. 12:10

who earlier had visited Jesus at night. Nicodemus brought a mixture of myrrh and aloes, about seventy-five pounds.[d] 40Taking Jesus' body, the two of them wrapped it, with the spices, in strips of linen. This was in accordance with Jewish burial customs. 41At the place where Jesus was crucified, there was a garden, and in the garden a new tomb, in which no one had ever been laid. 42Because it was the Jewish day of Preparation and since the tomb was nearby, they laid Jesus there.

[d] 39 Greek *a hundred litrai* (about 34 kilograms)

PRAYER: THE WORKS OF GOD

LORD, You appoint the number of the stars and call them each by name. (Psalm 147:4) . . . You, O Lord, give the sun for light by day and decree the moon and stars for light by night; You stir up the sea so that its waves roar—the Lord of hosts is Your name. (Jeremiah 31:35)

***TAKE** a moment to consider the greatness of God's wonderful works.*

YEAR 1
DAY 323

OT 2 Kings 16:1–17:41

Ahaz King of Judah

16 In the seventeenth year of Pekah son of Remaliah, Ahaz son of Jotham king of Judah began to reign. 2Ahaz was twenty years old when he became king, and he reigned in Jerusalem sixteen years. Unlike David his father, he did not do what was right in the eyes of the LORD his God. 3He walked in the ways of the kings of Israel and even sacrificed his son in[a] the fire, following the detestable ways of the nations the LORD had driven out before the Israelites. 4He offered sacrifices and burned incense at the high places, on the hilltops and under every spreading tree.

5Then Rezin king of Aram and Pekah son of Remaliah king of Israel marched up to fight against Jerusalem and besieged Ahaz, but they could not overpower him. 6At that time, Rezin king of Aram recovered Elath for Aram by driving out the men of Judah. Edomites then moved into Elath and have lived there to this day.

7Ahaz sent messengers to say to Tiglath-Pileser king of Assyria, "I am your servant and vassal. Come up and save me out of the hand of the king of Aram and of the king of Israel, who are attacking me." 8And Ahaz took the silver and gold found in the temple of the LORD and in the treasuries of the royal palace and sent it as a gift to the king of Assyria. 9The king of Assyria complied by attacking Damascus and capturing it. He deported its inhabitants to Kir and put Rezin to death.

10Then King Ahaz went to Damascus to meet Tiglath-Pileser king of Assyria. He saw an altar in Damascus and sent to Uriah the priest a sketch of the altar, with detailed plans for its construction. 11So Uriah the priest built an altar in accordance with all the plans that King Ahaz had sent from Damascus and finished it before King Ahaz returned. 12When the king came back from Damascus and saw the altar, he approached it and presented offerings[b] on it. 13He offered up his burnt offering and grain offering, poured out his drink offering, and sprinkled the blood of his fellowship offerings[c] on the altar. 14The bronze altar that stood before the LORD he brought from the front of the temple—from between the new altar and the temple of the LORD—and put it on the north side of the new altar.

15King Ahaz then gave these orders to Uriah the priest: "On the large new altar, offer the morning burnt offering and the evening grain offering, the king's burnt offering and his grain offering, and the burnt offering of all the people of the land, and their grain offering and their drink offering. Sprinkle on the altar all the blood of the burnt offerings and sacrifices. But I will use the bronze altar for

[a] 3 Or *even made his son pass through* [b] 12 Or *and went up* [c] 13 Traditionally *peace offerings*

seeking guidance." 16And Uriah the priest
did just as King Ahaz had ordered.
17King Ahaz took away the side panels
and removed the basins from the movable
stands. He removed the Sea from the
bronze bulls that supported it and set it
on a stone base. 18He took away the Sabbath canopy[d] that had been built at the
temple and removed the royal entryway
outside the temple of the LORD, in defer-
ence to the king of Assyria.
19As for the other events of the reign of
Ahaz, and what he did, are they not written in the book of the annals of the kings
of Judah? 20Ahaz rested with his fathers
and was buried with them in the City of
David. And Hezekiah his son succeeded
him as king.

Hoshea Last King of Israel

17 In the twelfth year of Ahaz king of Judah, Hoshea son of Elah became king
of Israel in Samaria, and he reigned nine
years. 2He did evil in the eyes of the LORD,
but not like the kings of Israel who preceded him.
3Shalmaneser king of Assyria came up
to attack Hoshea, who had been Shalmaneser's vassal and had paid him tribute. 4But the king of Assyria discovered
that Hoshea was a traitor, for he had sent
envoys to So[e] king of Egypt, and he no
longer paid tribute to the king of Assyria,
as he had done year by year. Therefore
Shalmaneser seized him and put him in
prison. 5The king of Assyria invaded the
entire land, marched against Samaria and
laid siege to it for three years. 6In the
ninth year of Hoshea, the king of Assyria
captured Samaria and deported the Israelites to Assyria. He settled them in Halah, in Gozan on the Habor River and in
the towns of the Medes.

Israel Exiled Because of Sin

7All this took place because the Israelites had sinned against the LORD their
God, who had brought them up out of
Egypt from under the power of Pharaoh
king of Egypt. They worshiped other gods
8and followed the practices of the nations
the LORD had driven out before them, as
well as the practices that the kings of Israel had introduced. 9The Israelites secretly did things against the LORD their God
that were not right. From watchtower to
fortified city they built themselves high
places in all their towns. 10They set up sacred stones and Asherah poles on every
high hill and under every spreading tree.
11At every high place they burned incense,
as the nations whom the LORD had driven
out before them had done. They did
wicked things that provoked the LORD to
anger. 12They worshiped idols, though the
LORD had said, "You shall not do this."[f]
13The LORD warned Israel and Judah
through all his prophets and seers: "Turn
from your evil ways. Observe my commands and decrees, in accordance with
the entire Law that I commanded your fathers to obey and that I delivered to you
through my servants the prophets."
14But they would not listen and were as
stiff-necked as their fathers, who did not
trust in the LORD their God. 15They rejected his decrees and the covenant he had
made with their fathers and the warnings
he had given them. They followed worthless idols and themselves became worthless. They imitated the nations around
them although the LORD had ordered
them, "Do not do as they do," and they
did the things the LORD had forbidden
them to do.
16They forsook all the commands of the
LORD their God and made for themselves
two idols cast in the shape of calves, and
an Asherah pole. They bowed down to all
the starry hosts, and they worshiped Baal.
17They sacrificed their sons and daughters
in[g] the fire. They practiced divination and
sorcery and sold themselves to do evil in
the eyes of the LORD, provoking him to
anger.
18So the LORD was very angry with Israel and removed them from his presence.
Only the tribe of Judah was left, 19and
even Judah did not keep the commands
of the LORD their God. They followed the
practices Israel had introduced. 20There-
fore the LORD rejected all the people of Israel; he afflicted them and gave them into
the hands of plunderers, until he thrust
them from his presence.
21When he tore Israel away from the
house of David, they made Jeroboam son
of Nebat their king. Jeroboam enticed Israel away from following the LORD and

[d] 18 Or *the dais of his throne* (see Septuagint)
[e] 4 Or *to Sais, to the; So* is possibly an abbreviation for *Osorkon.* [f] 12 Exodus 20:4, 5 [g] 17 Or *They made their sons and daughters pass through*

caused them to commit a great sin. [22]The
Israelites persisted in all the sins of Jeroboam and did not turn away from them
[23]until the LORD removed them from his
presence, as he had warned through all
his servants the prophets. So the people
of Israel were taken from their homeland
into exile in Assyria, and they are still
there.

Samaria Resettled

[24]The king of Assyria brought people
from Babylon, Cuthah, Avva, Hamath and
Sepharvaim and settled them in the towns
of Samaria to replace the Israelites. They
took over Samaria and lived in its towns.
[25]When they first lived there, they did not
worship the LORD; so he sent lions among
them and they killed some of the people.
[26]It was reported to the king of Assyria:
"The people you deported and resettled in
the towns of Samaria do not know what
the god of that country requires. He has
sent lions among them, which are killing
them off, because the people do not know
what he requires."

[27]Then the king of Assyria gave this order: "Have one of the priests you took
captive from Samaria go back to live there
and teach the people what the god of the
land requires." [28]So one of the priests who
had been exiled from Samaria came to
live in Bethel and taught them how to
worship the LORD.

[29]Nevertheless, each national group
made its own gods in the several towns
where they settled, and set them up in the
shrines the people of Samaria had made
at the high places. [30]The men from Babylon made Succoth Benoth, the men from
Cuthah made Nergal, and the men from
Hamath made Ashima; [31]the Avvites made
Nibhaz and Tartak, and the Sepharvites
burned their children in the fire as sacrifices to Adrammelech and Anammelech,
the gods of Sepharvaim. [32]They worshiped
the LORD, but they also appointed all sorts
of their own people to officiate for them
as priests in the shrines at the high places.
[33]They worshiped the LORD, but they also
served their own gods in accordance with
the customs of the nations from which
they had been brought.

[34]To this day they persist in their former
practices. They neither worship the LORD
nor adhere to the decrees and ordinances,
the laws and commands that the LORD gave
the descendants of Jacob, whom he named
Israel. [35]When the LORD made a covenant
with the Israelites, he commanded them:
"Do not worship any other gods or bow
down to them, serve them or sacrifice to
them. [36]But the LORD, who brought you up
out of Egypt with mighty power and outstretched arm, is the one you must worship.
To him you shall bow down and to him offer sacrifices. [37]You must always be careful
to keep the decrees and ordinances, the
laws and commands he wrote for you. Do
not worship other gods. [38]Do not forget the
covenant I have made with you, and do not
worship other gods. [39]Rather, worship the
LORD your God; it is he who will deliver you
from the hand of all your enemies."

[40]They would not listen, however, but
persisted in their former practices. [41]Even
while these people were worshiping the
LORD, they were serving their idols. To this
day their children and grandchildren continue to do as their fathers did.

PRAYER: ADORATION

YOU, O Most High, are sovereign over the kingdoms of all people and give them to whomever You wish and set over them the lowliest of people. I will bless You, O Most High, and praise and honor You, the One who lives forever. Your dominion is an eternal dominion, and Your kingdom endures from generation to generation. You regard all the inhabitants of the earth as nothing, and do as You please with the host of heaven and the inhabitants of the earth. No one can hold back Your hand or say to You: "What have You done?" I praise, exalt, and honor You, the King of heaven, for all Your works are true, and all Your ways are just, and You are able to humble those who walk in pride. (Daniel 4:17, 34–35, 37)

PAUSE *to express your thoughts of praise and worship.*

NT John 20:1-31

The Empty Tomb

20 Early on the first day of the week, while it was still dark, Mary Magdalene went to the tomb and saw that the stone had been removed from the entrance. 2So she came running to Simon Peter and the other disciple, the one Jesus loved, and said, "They have taken the Lord out of the tomb, and we don't know where they have put him!"

3So Peter and the other disciple started for the tomb. 4Both were running, but the other disciple outran Peter and reached the tomb first. 5He bent over and looked in at the strips of linen lying there but did not go in. 6Then Simon Peter, who was behind him, arrived and went into the tomb. He saw the strips of linen lying there, 7as well as the burial cloth that had been around Jesus' head. The cloth was folded up by itself, separate from the linen. 8Finally the other disciple, who had reached the tomb first, also went inside. He saw and believed. 9(They still did not understand from Scripture that Jesus had to rise from the dead.)

Jesus Appears to Mary Magdalene

10Then the disciples went back to their homes, 11but Mary stood outside the tomb crying. As she wept, she bent over to look into the tomb 12and saw two angels in white, seated where Jesus' body had been, one at the head and the other at the foot.

13They asked her, "Woman, why are you crying?"

"They have taken my Lord away," she said, "and I don't know where they have put him." 14At this, she turned around and saw Jesus standing there, but she did not realize that it was Jesus.

15"Woman," he said, "why are you crying? Who is it you are looking for?"

Thinking he was the gardener, she said, "Sir, if you have carried him away, tell me where you have put him, and I will get him."

16Jesus said to her, "Mary."

She turned toward him and cried out in Aramaic, "Rabboni!" (which means Teacher).

17Jesus said, "Do not hold on to me, for I have not yet returned to the Father. Go instead to my brothers and tell them, 'I am returning to my Father and your Father, to my God and your God.' "

18Mary Magdalene went to the disciples with the news: "I have seen the Lord!" And she told them that he had said these things to her.

Jesus Appears to His Disciples

19On the evening of that first day of the week, when the disciples were together, with the doors locked for fear of the Jews, Jesus came and stood among them and said, "Peace be with you!" 20After he said this, he showed them his hands and side. The disciples were overjoyed when they saw the Lord.

21Again Jesus said, "Peace be with you! As the Father has sent me, I am sending you." 22And with that he breathed on them and said, "Receive the Holy Spirit. 23If you forgive anyone his sins, they are forgiven; if you do not forgive them, they are not forgiven."

Jesus Appears to Thomas

24Now Thomas (called Didymus), one of the Twelve, was not with the disciples when Jesus came. 25So the other disciples told him, "We have seen the Lord!"

But he said to them, "Unless I see the nail marks in his hands and put my finger where the nails were, and put my hand into his side, I will not believe it."

26A week later his disciples were in the house again, and Thomas was with them. Though the doors were locked, Jesus came and stood among them and said, "Peace be with you!" 27Then he said to Thomas, "Put your finger here; see my hands. Reach out your hand and put it into my side. Stop doubting and believe."

28Thomas said to him, "My Lord and my God!"

29Then Jesus told him, "Because you have seen me, you have believed; blessed are those who have not seen and yet have believed."

30Jesus did many other miraculous signs in the presence of his disciples, which are not recorded in this book. 31But these are written that you may[a] believe that Jesus is the Christ, the Son of God, and that by believing you may have life in his name.

[a] *31* Some manuscripts *may continue to*

PRAYER: MY RELATIONSHIP TO GOD

I AM always confident and know that as long as I am at home in the body, I am away from You, Lord. For I live by faith, not by sight. I am of good courage and would prefer to be absent from the body and to be at home with You. (2 Corinthians 5:6–8) . . . Faith is the certainty of things hoped for and the conviction of things not seen. (Hebrews 11:1)

***PAUSE** to thank God for the relationship that you enjoy with Him in Jesus Christ.*

OT 2 Kings 18:1–37 — YEAR 1 DAY 324

Hezekiah King of Judah

18 In the third year of Hoshea son of Elah king of Israel, Hezekiah son of Ahaz king of Judah began to reign. 2He was twenty-five years old when he became king, and he reigned in Jerusalem twenty-nine years. His mother's name was Abijah[a] daughter of Zechariah. 3He did what was right in the eyes of the LORD, just as his father David had done. 4He removed the high places, smashed the sacred stones and cut down the Asherah poles. He broke into pieces the bronze snake Moses had made, for up to that time the Israelites had been burning incense to it. (It was called[b] Nehushtan.[c])

5Hezekiah trusted in the LORD, the God of Israel. There was no one like him among all the kings of Judah, either before him or after him. 6He held fast to the LORD and did not cease to follow him; he kept the commands the LORD had given Moses. 7And the LORD was with him; he was successful in whatever he undertook. He rebelled against the king of Assyria and did not serve him. 8From watchtower to fortified city, he defeated the Philistines, as far as Gaza and its territory.

9In King Hezekiah's fourth year, which was the seventh year of Hoshea son of Elah king of Israel, Shalmaneser king of Assyria marched against Samaria and laid siege to it. 10At the end of three years the Assyrians took it. So Samaria was captured in Hezekiah's sixth year, which was the ninth year of Hoshea king of Israel. 11The king of Assyria deported Israel to Assyria and settled them in Halah, in Gozan on the Habor River and in towns of the Medes. 12This happened because they had not obeyed the LORD their God, but had violated his covenant—all that Moses the servant of the LORD commanded. They neither listened to the commands nor carried them out.

13In the fourteenth year of King Hezekiah's reign, Sennacherib king of Assyria attacked all the fortified cities of Judah and captured them. 14So Hezekiah king of Judah sent this message to the king of Assyria at Lachish: "I have done wrong. Withdraw from me, and I will pay whatever you demand of me." The king of Assyria exacted from Hezekiah king of Judah three hundred talents[d] of silver and thirty talents[e] of gold. 15So Hezekiah gave him all the silver that was found in the temple of the LORD and in the treasuries of the royal palace.

16At this time Hezekiah king of Judah stripped off the gold with which he had covered the doors and doorposts of the temple of the LORD, and gave it to the king of Assyria.

Sennacherib Threatens Jerusalem

17The king of Assyria sent his supreme commander, his chief officer and his field commander with a large army, from Lachish to King Hezekiah at Jerusalem. They came up to Jerusalem and stopped at the aqueduct of the Upper Pool, on the road to the Washerman's Field. 18They called for the king; and Eliakim son of Hilkiah the palace administrator, Shebna the sec-

[a] 2 Hebrew *Abi,* a variant of *Abijah* [b] 4 Or *He called it* [c] 4 *Nehushtan* sounds like the Hebrew for *bronze* and *snake* and *unclean thing.* [d] 14 That is, about 11 tons (about 10 metric tons) [e] 14 That is, about 1 ton (about 1 metric ton)

retary, and Joah son of Asaph the recorder
went out to them.
19 The field commander said to them,
"Tell Hezekiah:

" 'This is what the great king, the
king of Assyria, says: On what are you
basing this confidence of yours?
20 You say you have strategy and military strength—but you speak only
empty words. On whom are you depending, that you rebel against me?
21 Look now, you are depending on
Egypt, that splintered reed of a staff,
which pierces a man's hand and
wounds him if he leans on it! Such is
Pharaoh king of Egypt to all who depend on him. 22 And if you say to me,
"We are depending on the LORD our
God"—isn't he the one whose high
places and altars Hezekiah removed,
saying to Judah and Jerusalem, "You
must worship before this altar in
Jerusalem"?

23 " 'Come now, make a bargain
with my master, the king of Assyria: I
will give you two thousand horses—
if you can put riders on them! 24 How
can you repulse one officer of the
least of my master's officials, even
though you are depending on Egypt
for chariots and horsemen[f]? 25 Furthermore, have I come to attack and
destroy this place without word from
the LORD? The LORD himself told me
to march against this country and destroy it.' "

26 Then Eliakim son of Hilkiah, and
Shebna and Joah said to the field commander, "Please speak to your servants in
Aramaic, since we understand it. Don't
speak to us in Hebrew in the hearing of
the people on the wall."
27 But the commander replied, "Was it
only to your master and you that my master sent me to say these things, and not to
the men sitting on the wall—who, like
you, will have to eat their own filth and
drink their own urine?"
28 Then the commander stood and
called out in Hebrew: "Hear the word of
the great king, the king of Assyria! 29 This
is what the king says: Do not let Hezekiah deceive you. He cannot deliver you
from my hand. 30 Do not let Hezekiah persuade you to trust in the LORD when he
says, 'The LORD will surely deliver us; this
city will not be given into the hand of the
king of Assyria.'
31 "Do not listen to Hezekiah. This is
what the king of Assyria says: Make peace
with me and come out to me. Then every
one of you will eat from his own vine and
fig tree and drink water from his own cistern, 32 until I come and take you to a land
like your own, a land of grain and new
wine, a land of bread and vineyards, a
land of olive trees and honey. Choose life
and not death!
"Do not listen to Hezekiah, for he is
misleading you when he says, 'The LORD
will deliver us.' 33 Has the god of any nation ever delivered his land from the hand
of the king of Assyria? 34 Where are the
gods of Hamath and Arpad? Where are
the gods of Sepharvaim, Hena and Ivvah?
Have they rescued Samaria from my
hand? 35 Who of all the gods of these
countries has been able to save his land
from me? How then can the LORD deliver
Jerusalem from my hand?"
36 But the people remained silent and
said nothing in reply, because the king
had commanded, "Do not answer him."
37 Then Eliakim son of Hilkiah the palace
administrator, Shebna the secretary and
Joah son of Asaph the recorder went to
Hezekiah, with their clothes torn, and told
him what the field commander had said.

[f] 24 Or *charioteers*

PRAYER: CONFESSION

YOU, Lord God, declared this assurance to Jeremiah: "I will cleanse them from all of the sin they have committed against Me, and I will forgive all of the sin they committed when they turned away from Me." (Jeremiah 33:8)

***ASK** the Spirit to search your heart and reveal any areas of unconfessed sin. Acknowledge these to the Lord and thank Him for His forgiveness.*

NT John 21:1-25

Jesus and the Miraculous Catch of Fish

21 Afterward Jesus appeared again to his disciples, by the Sea of Tiberias.[a] It happened this way: 2Simon Peter, Thomas (called Didymus), Nathanael from Cana in Galilee, the sons of Zebedee, and two other disciples were together. 3"I'm going out to fish," Simon Peter told them, and they said, "We'll go with you." So they went out and got into the boat, but that night they caught nothing.

4Early in the morning, Jesus stood on the shore, but the disciples did not realize that it was Jesus.

5He called out to them, "Friends, haven't you any fish?"

"No," they answered.

6He said, "Throw your net on the right side of the boat and you will find some." When they did, they were unable to haul the net in because of the large number of fish.

7Then the disciple whom Jesus loved said to Peter, "It is the Lord!" As soon as Simon Peter heard him say, "It is the Lord," he wrapped his outer garment around him (for he had taken it off) and jumped into the water. 8The other disciples followed in the boat, towing the net full of fish, for they were not far from shore, about a hundred yards.[b] 9When they landed, they saw a fire of burning coals there with fish on it, and some bread.

10Jesus said to them, "Bring some of the fish you have just caught."

11Simon Peter climbed aboard and dragged the net ashore. It was full of large fish, 153, but even with so many the net was not torn. 12Jesus said to them, "Come and have breakfast." None of the disciples dared ask him, "Who are you?" They knew it was the Lord. 13Jesus came, took the bread and gave it to them, and did the same with the fish. 14This was now the third time Jesus appeared to his disciples after he was raised from the dead.

Jesus Reinstates Peter

15When they had finished eating, Jesus said to Simon Peter, "Simon son of John, do you truly love me more than these?"

"Yes, Lord," he said, "you know that I love you."

Jesus said, "Feed my lambs."

16Again Jesus said, "Simon son of John, do you truly love me?"

He answered, "Yes, Lord, you know that I love you."

Jesus said, "Take care of my sheep."

17The third time he said to him, "Simon son of John, do you love me?"

Peter was hurt because Jesus asked him the third time, "Do you love me?" He said, "Lord, you know all things; you know that I love you."

Jesus said, "Feed my sheep. 18I tell you the truth, when you were younger you dressed yourself and went where you wanted; but when you are old you will stretch out your hands, and someone else will dress you and lead you where you do not want to go." 19Jesus said this to indicate the kind of death by which Peter would glorify God. Then he said to him, "Follow me!"

20Peter turned and saw that the disciple whom Jesus loved was following them. (This was the one who had leaned back against Jesus at the supper and had said, "Lord, who is going to betray you?") 21When Peter saw him, he asked, "Lord, what about him?"

22Jesus answered, "If I want him to remain alive until I return, what is that to you? You must follow me." 23Because of this, the rumor spread among the brothers that this disciple would not die. But Jesus did not say that he would not die; he only said, "If I want him to remain alive until I return, what is that to you?"

24This is the disciple who testifies to these things and who wrote them down. We know that his testimony is true.

25Jesus did many other things as well. If every one of them were written down, I suppose that even the whole world would not have room for the books that would be written.

[a] *1* That is, Sea of Galilee [b] *8* Greek *about two hundred cubits* (about 90 meters)

PRAYER: THE CHARACTER I WANT TO CULTIVATE

A GENTLE answer turns away wrath, but a harsh word stirs up anger. The tongue of the wise uses knowledge rightly, but the mouth of the fool pours out folly. (Proverbs 15:1–2) . . . I will put away all of these things: anger, wrath, malice, slander and abusive language from my mouth. (Colossians 3:8)

***TAKE** a moment to ask the Lord for the grace to grow in godly character.*

YEAR 1 DAY 325

OT 2 Kings 19:1-37

Jerusalem's Deliverance Foretold

19 When King Hezekiah heard this, he tore his clothes and put on sackcloth and went into the temple of the LORD. 2 He sent Eliakim the palace administrator, Shebna the secretary and the leading priests, all wearing sackcloth, to the prophet Isaiah son of Amoz. 3 They told him, "This is what Hezekiah says: This day is a day of distress and rebuke and disgrace, as when children come to the point of birth and there is no strength to deliver them. 4 It may be that the LORD your God will hear all the words of the field commander, whom his master, the king of Assyria, has sent to ridicule the living God, and that he will rebuke him for the words the LORD your God has heard. Therefore pray for the remnant that still survives."

5 When King Hezekiah's officials came to Isaiah, 6 Isaiah said to them, "Tell your master, 'This is what the LORD says: Do not be afraid of what you have heard—those words with which the underlings of the king of Assyria have blasphemed me. 7 Listen! I am going to put such a spirit in him that when he hears a certain report, he will return to his own country, and there I will have him cut down with the sword.' "

8 When the field commander heard that the king of Assyria had left Lachish, he withdrew and found the king fighting against Libnah.

9 Now Sennacherib received a report that Tirhakah, the Cushite[a] king ⌞of Egypt⌟, was marching out to fight against him. So he again sent messengers to Hezekiah with this word: 10 "Say to Hezekiah king of Judah: Do not let the god you depend on deceive you when he says, 'Jerusalem will not be handed over to the king of Assyria.' 11 Surely you have heard what the kings of Assyria have done to all the countries, destroying them completely. And will you be delivered? 12 Did the gods of the nations that were destroyed by my forefathers deliver them: the gods of Gozan, Haran, Rezeph and the people of Eden who were in Tel Assar? 13 Where is the king of Hamath, the king of Arpad, the king of the city of Sepharvaim, or of Hena or Ivvah?"

Hezekiah's Prayer

14 Hezekiah received the letter from the messengers and read it. Then he went up to the temple of the LORD and spread it out before the LORD. 15 And Hezekiah prayed to the LORD: "O LORD, God of Israel, enthroned between the cherubim, you alone are God over all the kingdoms of the earth. You have made heaven and earth. 16 Give ear, O LORD, and hear; open your eyes, O LORD, and see; listen to the words Sennacherib has sent to insult the living God.

17 "It is true, O LORD, that the Assyrian kings have laid waste these nations and their lands. 18 They have thrown their gods into the fire and destroyed them, for they were not gods but only wood and stone, fashioned by men's hands. 19 Now, O LORD our God, deliver us from his hand, so that all kingdoms on earth may know that you alone, O LORD, are God."

Isaiah Prophesies Sennacherib's Fall

20 Then Isaiah son of Amoz sent a message to Hezekiah: "This is what the LORD, the God of Israel, says: I have heard your prayer concerning Sennacherib king of Assyria. 21 This is the word that the LORD has spoken against him:

[a] 9 That is, from the upper Nile region

" 'The Virgin Daughter of Zion
despises you and mocks you.
The Daughter of Jerusalem
tosses her head as you flee.
22 Who is it you have insulted and
blasphemed?
Against whom have you raised your
voice
and lifted your eyes in pride?
Against the Holy One of Israel!
23 By your messengers
you have heaped insults on the Lord.
And you have said,
"With my many chariots
I have ascended the heights of the
mountains,
the utmost heights of Lebanon.
I have cut down its tallest cedars,
the choicest of its pines.
I have reached its remotest parts,
the finest of its forests.
24 I have dug wells in foreign lands
and drunk the water there.
With the soles of my feet
I have dried up all the streams of
Egypt."

25 " 'Have you not heard?
Long ago I ordained it.
In days of old I planned it;
now I have brought it to pass,
that you have turned fortified cities
into piles of stone.
26 Their people, drained of power,
are dismayed and put to shame.
They are like plants in the field,
like tender green shoots,
like grass sprouting on the roof,
scorched before it grows up.

27 " 'But I know where you stay
and when you come and go
and how you rage against me.
28 Because you rage against me
and your insolence has reached my
ears,
I will put my hook in your nose
and my bit in your mouth,
and I will make you return
by the way you came.'

29 "This will be the sign for you, O Hezekiah:

"This year you will eat what grows by
itself,
and the second year what springs
from that.
But in the third year sow and reap,
plant vineyards and eat their fruit.
30 Once more a remnant of the house of
Judah
will take root below and bear fruit
above.
31 For out of Jerusalem will come a
remnant,
and out of Mount Zion a band of
survivors.

The zeal of the LORD Almighty will accomplish this.

32 "Therefore this is what the LORD says
concerning the king of Assyria:

"He will not enter this city
or shoot an arrow here.
He will not come before it with shield
or build a siege ramp against it.
33 By the way that he came he will
return;
he will not enter this city,
declares the LORD.
34 I will defend this city and save it,
for my sake and for the sake of
David my servant."

35 That night the angel of the LORD went
out and put to death a hundred and
eighty-five thousand men in the Assyrian
camp. When the people got up the next
morning—there were all the dead bodies!
36 So Sennacherib king of Assyria broke
camp and withdrew. He returned to Nineveh and stayed there.
37 One day, while he was worshiping in
the temple of his god Nisroch, his sons
Adrammelech and Sharezer cut him down
with the sword, and they escaped to the
land of Ararat. And Esarhaddon his son
succeeded him as king.

PRAYER: RENEWAL

MAY I honor my father and my mother. May I not murder. May I not commit adultery.
(Exodus 20:12–14; Deuteronomy 5:16–18)

PAUSE *to add your own prayers for personal renewal.*

NT 1 John 1:1-10

The Word of Life

1 That which was from the beginning, which we have heard, which we have seen with our eyes, which we have looked at and our hands have touched—this we proclaim concerning the Word of life.
2The life appeared; we have seen it and testify to it, and we proclaim to you the eternal life, which was with the Father and has appeared to us. 3We proclaim to you what we have seen and heard, so that you also may have fellowship with us. And our fellowship is with the Father and with his Son, Jesus Christ. 4We write this to make our[a] joy complete.

Walking in the Light

5This is the message we have heard from him and declare to you: God is light; in him there is no darkness at all.
6If we claim to have fellowship with him yet walk in the darkness, we lie and do not live by the truth. 7But if we walk in the light, as he is in the light, we have fellowship with one another, and the blood of Jesus, his Son, purifies us from all[b] sin.
8If we claim to be without sin, we deceive ourselves and the truth is not in us.
9If we confess our sins, he is faithful and just and will forgive us our sins and purify us from all unrighteousness. 10If we claim we have not sinned, we make him out to be a liar and his word has no place in our lives.

[a] 4 Some manuscripts *your* [b] 7 Or *every*

PRAYER: MY RELATIONSHIP TO OTHERS

WE should bear one another's burdens and so fulfill Your law, O Christ. (Galatians 6:2) . . . We should submit to one another out of reverence for You, O Christ. (Ephesians 5:21)

PAUSE *to review your relationships with others and to commit them to the Lord.*

YEAR 1 DAY 326

OT 2 Kings 20:1–21:26

Hezekiah's Illness

20 In those days Hezekiah became ill and was at the point of death. The prophet Isaiah son of Amoz went to him and said, "This is what the LORD says: Put your house in order, because you are going to die; you will not recover."
2Hezekiah turned his face to the wall and prayed to the LORD, 3"Remember, O LORD, how I have walked before you faithfully and with wholehearted devotion and have done what is good in your eyes." And Hezekiah wept bitterly.
4Before Isaiah had left the middle court, the word of the LORD came to him: 5"Go back and tell Hezekiah, the leader of my people, 'This is what the LORD, the God of your father David, says: I have heard your prayer and seen your tears; I will heal you. On the third day from now you will go up to the temple of the LORD. 6I will add fifteen years to your life. And I will deliver you and this city from the hand of the king of Assyria. I will defend this city for my sake and for the sake of my servant David.' "
7Then Isaiah said, "Prepare a poultice of figs." They did so and applied it to the boil, and he recovered.
8Hezekiah had asked Isaiah, "What will be the sign that the LORD will heal me and that I will go up to the temple of the LORD on the third day from now?"
9Isaiah answered, "This is the LORD's sign to you that the LORD will do what he has promised: Shall the shadow go forward ten steps, or shall it go back ten steps?"
10"It is a simple matter for the shadow to go forward ten steps," said Hezekiah. "Rather, have it go back ten steps."

11 Then the prophet Isaiah called upon the LORD, and the LORD made the shadow go back the ten steps it had gone down on the stairway of Ahaz.

Envoys From Babylon

12 At that time Merodach-Baladan son of Baladan king of Babylon sent Hezekiah letters and a gift, because he had heard of Hezekiah's illness. 13 Hezekiah received the messengers and showed them all that was in his storehouses—the silver, the gold, the spices and the fine oil—his armory and everything found among his treasures. There was nothing in his palace or in all his kingdom that Hezekiah did not show them.

14 Then Isaiah the prophet went to King Hezekiah and asked, "What did those men say, and where did they come from?"

"From a distant land," Hezekiah replied. "They came from Babylon."

15 The prophet asked, "What did they see in your palace?"

"They saw everything in my palace," Hezekiah said. "There is nothing among my treasures that I did not show them."

16 Then Isaiah said to Hezekiah, "Hear the word of the LORD: 17 The time will surely come when everything in your palace, and all that your fathers have stored up until this day, will be carried off to Babylon. Nothing will be left, says the LORD. 18 And some of your descendants, your own flesh and blood, that will be born to you, will be taken away, and they will become eunuchs in the palace of the king of Babylon."

19 "The word of the LORD you have spoken is good," Hezekiah replied. For he thought, "Will there not be peace and security in my lifetime?"

20 As for the other events of Hezekiah's reign, all his achievements and how he made the pool and the tunnel by which he brought water into the city, are they not written in the book of the annals of the kings of Judah? 21 Hezekiah rested with his fathers. And Manasseh his son succeeded him as king.

Manasseh King of Judah

21 Manasseh was twelve years old when he became king, and he reigned in Jerusalem fifty-five years. His mother's name was Hephzibah. 2 He did evil in the eyes of the LORD, following the detestable practices of the nations the LORD had driven out before the Israelites. 3 He rebuilt the high places his father Hezekiah had destroyed; he also erected altars to Baal and made an Asherah pole, as Ahab king of Israel had done. He bowed down to all the starry hosts and worshiped them. 4 He built altars in the temple of the LORD, of which the LORD had said, "In Jerusalem I will put my Name." 5 In both courts of the temple of the LORD, he built altars to all the starry hosts. 6 He sacrificed his own son in[a] the fire, practiced sorcery and divination, and consulted mediums and spiritists. He did much evil in the eyes of the LORD, provoking him to anger.

7 He took the carved Asherah pole he had made and put it in the temple, of which the LORD had said to David and to his son Solomon, "In this temple and in Jerusalem, which I have chosen out of all the tribes of Israel, I will put my Name forever. 8 I will not again make the feet of the Israelites wander from the land I gave their forefathers, if only they will be careful to do everything I commanded them and will keep the whole Law that my servant Moses gave them." 9 But the people did not listen. Manasseh led them astray, so that they did more evil than the nations the LORD had destroyed before the Israelites.

10 The LORD said through his servants the prophets: 11 "Manasseh king of Judah has committed these detestable sins. He has done more evil than the Amorites who preceded him and has led Judah into sin with his idols. 12 Therefore this is what the LORD, the God of Israel, says: I am going to bring such disaster on Jerusalem and Judah that the ears of everyone who hears of it will tingle. 13 I will stretch out over Jerusalem the measuring line used against Samaria and the plumb line used against the house of Ahab. I will wipe out Jerusalem as one wipes a dish, wiping it and turning it upside down. 14 I will forsake the remnant of my inheritance and hand them over to their enemies. They will be looted and plundered by all their foes, 15 because they have done evil in my eyes and have provoked me to anger from the day their forefathers came out of Egypt until this day."

[a] 6 Or *He made his own son pass through*

[16]Moreover, Manasseh also shed so much innocent blood that he filled Jerusalem from end to end—besides the sin that he had caused Judah to commit, so that they did evil in the eyes of the LORD.

[17]As for the other events of Manasseh's reign, and all he did, including the sin he committed, are they not written in the book of the annals of the kings of Judah? [18]Manasseh rested with his fathers and was buried in his palace garden, the garden of Uzza. And Amon his son succeeded him as king.

Amon King of Judah

[19]Amon was twenty-two years old when he became king, and he reigned in Jerusalem two years. His mother's name was Meshullemeth daughter of Haruz; she was from Jotbah. [20]He did evil in the eyes of the LORD, as his father Manasseh had done. [21]He walked in all the ways of his father; he worshiped the idols his father had worshiped, and bowed down to them. [22]He forsook the LORD, the God of his fathers, and did not walk in the way of the LORD.

[23]Amon's officials conspired against him and assassinated the king in his palace. [24]Then the people of the land killed all who had plotted against King Amon, and they made Josiah his son king in his place.

[25]As for the other events of Amon's reign, and what he did, are they not written in the book of the annals of the kings of Judah? [26]He was buried in his grave in the garden of Uzza. And Josiah his son succeeded him as king.

PRAYER: PETITION

IN You, O Lord, I have taken refuge; let me never be put to shame. In Your righteousness deliver me and rescue me; turn Your ear to me and save me. Be my rock of refuge, to which I can always go; You have given the commandment to save me, for You are my rock and my fortress. (Psalm 71:1–3)

__PAUSE__ here to petition God to help you be a faithful steward of your time, talents, possessions and relationships. Offer prayers of petition regarding your activities for this day and any special concerns you may have.

NT 1 John 2:1–14

2 My dear children, I write this to you so that you will not sin. But if anybody does sin, we have one who speaks to the Father in our defense—Jesus Christ, the Righteous One. [2]He is the atoning sacrifice for our sins, and not only for ours but also for[a] the sins of the whole world.

[3]We know that we have come to know him if we obey his commands. [4]The man who says, "I know him," but does not do what he commands is a liar, and the truth is not in him. [5]But if anyone obeys his word, God's love[b] is truly made complete in him. This is how we know we are in him: [6]Whoever claims to live in him must walk as Jesus did.

[7]Dear friends, I am not writing you a new command but an old one, which you have had since the beginning. This old command is the message you have heard. [8]Yet I am writing you a new command; its truth is seen in him and you, because the darkness is passing and the true light is already shining.

[9]Anyone who claims to be in the light but hates his brother is still in the darkness. [10]Whoever loves his brother lives in the light, and there is nothing in him[c] to make him stumble. [11]But whoever hates his brother is in the darkness and walks around in the darkness; he does not know where he is going, because the darkness has blinded him.

[12]I write to you, dear children,
because your sins have been
forgiven on account of his
name.

[a] 2 Or *He is the one who turns aside God's wrath, taking away our sins, and not only ours but also*
[b] 5 Or *word, love for God*
[c] 10 Or *it*

[13]I write to you, fathers,
because you have known him who
is from the beginning.
I write to you, young men,
because you have overcome the evil
one.
I write to you, dear children,
because you have known the Father.

[14]I write to you, fathers,
because you have known him who
is from the beginning.
I write to you, young men,
because you are strong,
and the word of God lives in you,
and you have overcome the evil
one.

PRAYER: THE ATTRIBUTES OF GOD

IT is good to give thanks to You, Lord, to sing praises to Your name, O Most High, to declare Your loving-kindness in the morning and Your faithfulness at night. (Psalm 92:1–2) . . . How precious are Your thoughts to me, O God! How vast is the sum of them! If I should count them, they would outnumber the grains of sand. When I awake, I am still with You. (Psalm 139:17–18)

PAUSE *to reflect on these affirmations about the person, powers and perfection of God.*

OT 2 Kings 22:1–20

The Book of the Law Found

22 Josiah was eight years old when he
became king, and he reigned in Jerusalem thirty-one years. His mother's name
was Jedidah daughter of Adaiah; she was
from Bozkath. [2]He did what was right in
the eyes of the LORD and walked in all the
ways of his father David, not turning aside
to the right or to the left.
[3]In the eighteenth year of his reign,
King Josiah sent the secretary, Shaphan
son of Azaliah, the son of Meshullam, to
the temple of the LORD. He said: [4]"Go up
to Hilkiah the high priest and have him
get ready the money that has been
brought into the temple of the LORD,
which the doorkeepers have collected
from the people. [5]Have them entrust it to
the men appointed to supervise the work
on the temple. And have these men pay
the workers who repair the temple of the
LORD— [6]the carpenters, the builders and
the masons. Also have them purchase timber and dressed stone to repair the temple. [7]But they need not account for the
money entrusted to them, because they
are acting faithfully."
[8]Hilkiah the high priest said to Shaphan the secretary, "I have found the
Book of the Law in the temple of the
LORD." He gave it to Shaphan, who read
it. [9]Then Shaphan the secretary went to
the king and reported to him: "Your officials have paid out the money that was in
the temple of the LORD and have entrusted it to the workers and supervisors at the
temple." [10]Then Shaphan the secretary informed the king, "Hilkiah the priest has
given me a book." And Shaphan read
from it in the presence of the king.
[11]When the king heard the words of the
Book of the Law, he tore his robes. [12]He
gave these orders to Hilkiah the priest,
Ahikam son of Shaphan, Acbor son of Micaiah, Shaphan the secretary and Asaiah
the king's attendant: [13]"Go and inquire of
the LORD for me and for the people and
for all Judah about what is written in this
book that has been found. Great is the
LORD's anger that burns against us because
our fathers have not obeyed the words of
this book; they have not acted in accordance with all that is written there concerning us."
[14]Hilkiah the priest, Ahikam, Acbor,
Shaphan and Asaiah went to speak to the
prophetess Huldah, who was the wife of
Shallum son of Tikvah, the son of Harhas,

keeper of the wardrobe. She lived in Jerusalem, in the Second District.
[15]She said to them, "This is what the LORD, the God of Israel, says: Tell the man who sent you to me, [16]'This is what the LORD says: I am going to bring disaster on this place and its people, according to everything written in the book the king of Judah has read. [17]Because they have forsaken me and burned incense to other gods and provoked me to anger by all the idols their hands have made,[a] my anger will burn against this place and will not be quenched.' [18]Tell the king of Judah, who sent you to inquire of the LORD, 'This is what the LORD, the God of Israel, says concerning the words you heard: [19]Because your heart was responsive and you humbled yourself before the LORD when you heard what I have spoken against this place and its people, that they would become accursed and laid waste, and because you tore your robes and wept in my presence, I have heard you, declares the LORD. [20]Therefore I will gather you to your fathers, and you will be buried in peace. Your eyes will not see all the disaster I am going to bring on this place.' "

So they took her answer back to the king.

[a] 17 Or *by everything they have done*

PRAYER: INTERCESSION

O LORD God of Israel, You are righteous, for we are left this day as a remnant. Here we are before You in our guilt, though no one can stand in Your presence because of it. (Ezra 9:15)

TAKE *a few moments to intercede on behalf of your local, state or provincial, and national governments. Pray for spiritual revival in the nation and offer prayers regarding current events and concerns.*

NT 1 John 2:15–27

Do Not Love the World

[15]Do not love the world or anything in the world. If anyone loves the world, the love of the Father is not in him. [16]For everything in the world—the cravings of sinful man, the lust of his eyes and the boasting of what he has and does—comes not from the Father but from the world. [17]The world and its desires pass away, but the man who does the will of God lives forever.

Warning Against Antichrists

[18]Dear children, this is the last hour; and as you have heard that the antichrist is coming, even now many antichrists have come. This is how we know it is the last hour. [19]They went out from us, but they did not really belong to us. For if they had belonged to us, they would have remained with us; but their going showed that none of them belonged to us.

[20]But you have an anointing from the Holy One, and all of you know the truth.[a] [21]I do not write to you because you do not know the truth, but because you do know it and because no lie comes from the truth. [22]Who is the liar? It is the man who denies that Jesus is the Christ. Such a man is the antichrist—he denies the Father and the Son. [23]No one who denies the Son has the Father; whoever acknowledges the Son has the Father also.

[24]See that what you have heard from the beginning remains in you. If it does, you also will remain in the Son and in the Father. [25]And this is what he promised us—even eternal life.

[26]I am writing these things to you about those who are trying to lead you astray. [27]As for you, the anointing you received from him remains in you, and you do not need anyone to teach you. But as his anointing teaches you about all things and as that anointing is real, not counterfeit—just as it has taught you, remain in him.

[a] 20 Some manuscripts *and you know all things*

PRAYER: THE WORKS OF GOD

O SON of Man, You went up to Jerusalem where You were delivered to the chief priests and to the scribes. They condemned You to death and handed You over to the Gentiles, who mocked You and spat upon You, scourged You and killed You. But on the third day You rose again. (Mark 10:33–34) . . . After Your resurrection, Jesus, You said to the two disciples on the road to Emmaus, "Did not the Christ have to suffer these things and then enter His glory?" And beginning with Moses and all the Prophets, You explained to them what was said in all the Scriptures concerning Yourself. Later You appeared to Your disciples and said to them, "These are the words I spoke to you while I was still with you, that everything must be fulfilled that is written about Me in the Law of Moses, the Prophets and the Psalms." (Luke 24:26–27, 44)

***TAKE** a moment to consider the greatness of God's wonderful works.*

YEAR 1
DAY 328

OT 2 Kings 23:1–37

Josiah Renews the Covenant

23 Then the king called together all the
elders of Judah and Jerusalem. [2]He
went up to the temple of the LORD with the
men of Judah, the people of Jerusalem, the
priests and the prophets—all the people
from the least to the greatest. He read in
their hearing all the words of the Book of
the Covenant, which had been found in
the temple of the LORD. [3]The king stood by
the pillar and renewed the covenant in the
presence of the LORD—to follow the LORD
and keep his commands, regulations and
decrees with all his heart and all his soul,
thus confirming the words of the covenant
written in this book. Then all the people
pledged themselves to the covenant.
[4]The king ordered Hilkiah the high
priest, the priests next in rank and the
doorkeepers to remove from the temple
of the LORD all the articles made for Baal
and Asherah and all the starry hosts. He
burned them outside Jerusalem in the
fields of the Kidron Valley and took the
ashes to Bethel. [5]He did away with the pagan priests appointed by the kings of Judah to burn incense on the high places of
the towns of Judah and on those around
Jerusalem—those who burned incense to
Baal, to the sun and moon, to the constellations and to all the starry hosts. [6]He
took the Asherah pole from the temple of
the LORD to the Kidron Valley outside
Jerusalem and burned it there. He ground
it to powder and scattered the dust over
the graves of the common people. [7]He
also tore down the quarters of the male
shrine prostitutes, which were in the temple of the LORD and where women did
weaving for Asherah.
[8]Josiah brought all the priests from the
towns of Judah and desecrated the high
places, from Geba to Beersheba, where
the priests had burned incense. He broke
down the shrines[a] at the gates—at the entrance to the Gate of Joshua, the city governor, which is on the left of the city gate.
[9]Although the priests of the high places
did not serve at the altar of the LORD in
Jerusalem, they ate unleavened bread with
their fellow priests.
[10]He desecrated Topheth, which was in
the Valley of Ben Hinnom, so no one
could use it to sacrifice his son or daughter in[b] the fire to Molech. [11]He removed
from the entrance to the temple of the
LORD the horses that the kings of Judah
had dedicated to the sun. They were in the
court near the room of an official named
Nathan-Melech. Josiah then burned the
chariots dedicated to the sun.
[12]He pulled down the altars the kings of
Judah had erected on the roof near the
upper room of Ahaz, and the altars Manasseh had built in the two courts of the

[a] 8 Or *high places* [b] 10 Or *to make his son or daughter pass through*

temple of the LORD. He removed them
from there, smashed them to pieces and
threw the rubble into the Kidron Valley.
13 The king also desecrated the high places
that were east of Jerusalem on the south
of the Hill of Corruption—the ones Solomon king of Israel had built for Ashtoreth
the vile goddess of the Sidonians, for Chemosh the vile god of Moab, and for Molech[c] the detestable god of the people of
Ammon. 14 Josiah smashed the sacred
stones and cut down the Asherah poles
and covered the sites with human bones.
15 Even the altar at Bethel, the high place
made by Jeroboam son of Nebat, who
had caused Israel to sin—even that altar
and high place he demolished. He burned
the high place and ground it to powder,
and burned the Asherah pole also. 16 Then
Josiah looked around, and when he saw
the tombs that were there on the hillside,
he had the bones removed from them and
burned on the altar to defile it, in accordance with the word of the LORD proclaimed by the man of God who foretold
these things.
17 The king asked, "What is that tomb-
stone I see?"

The men of the city said, "It marks the
tomb of the man of God who came from
Judah and pronounced against the altar of
Bethel the very things you have done to it."
18 "Leave it alone," he said. "Don't let
anyone disturb his bones." So they spared
his bones and those of the prophet who
had come from Samaria.
19 Just as he had done at Bethel, Josiah
removed and defiled all the shrines at the
high places that the kings of Israel had
built in the towns of Samaria that had provoked the LORD to anger. 20 Josiah slaughtered all the priests of those high places on
the altars and burned human bones on
them. Then he went back to Jerusalem.
21 The king gave this order to all the people: "Celebrate the Passover to the LORD
your God, as it is written in this Book of
the Covenant." 22 Not since the days of the
judges who led Israel, nor throughout the
days of the kings of Israel and the kings of
Judah, had any such Passover been observed. 23 But in the eighteenth year of
King Josiah, this Passover was celebrated
to the LORD in Jerusalem.
24 Furthermore, Josiah got rid of the mediums and spiritists, the household gods,
the idols and all the other detestable
things seen in Judah and Jerusalem. This
he did to fulfill the requirements of the
law written in the book that Hilkiah the
priest had discovered in the temple of the
LORD. 25 Neither before nor after Josiah
was there a king like him who turned to
the LORD as he did—with all his heart and
with all his soul and with all his strength,
in accordance with all the Law of Moses.
26 Nevertheless, the LORD did not turn
away from the heat of his fierce anger,
which burned against Judah because of all
that Manasseh had done to provoke him
to anger. 27 So the LORD said, "I will remove Judah also from my presence as I removed Israel, and I will reject Jerusalem,
the city I chose, and this temple, about
which I said, 'There shall my Name be.'[d]"
28 As for the other events of Josiah's reign,
and all he did, are they not written in the
book of the annals of the kings of Judah?
29 While Josiah was king, Pharaoh Neco
king of Egypt went up to the Euphrates
River to help the king of Assyria. King Josiah marched out to meet him in battle,
but Neco faced him and killed him at Megiddo. 30 Josiah's servants brought his
body in a chariot from Megiddo to Jerusalem and buried him in his own tomb.
And the people of the land took Jehoahaz
son of Josiah and anointed him and made
him king in place of his father.

Jehoahaz King of Judah

31 Jehoahaz was twenty-three years old
when he became king, and he reigned in
Jerusalem three months. His mother's
name was Hamutal daughter of Jeremiah;
she was from Libnah. 32 He did evil in the
eyes of the LORD, just as his fathers had
done. 33 Pharaoh Neco put him in chains at
Riblah in the land of Hamath[e] so that he
might not reign in Jerusalem, and he imposed on Judah a levy of a hundred talents[f]
of silver and a talent[g] of gold. 34 Pharaoh
Neco made Eliakim son of Josiah king in
place of his father Josiah and changed Eliakim's name to Jehoiakim. But he took Jehoahaz and carried him off to Egypt, and
there he died. 35 Jehoiakim paid Pharaoh
Neco the silver and gold he demanded. In
order to do so, he taxed the land and ex-

[c] 13 Hebrew *Milcom* [d] 27 1 Kings 8:29
[e] 33 Hebrew; Septuagint (see also 2 Chron. 36:3) *Neco at Riblah in Hamath removed him* [f] 33 That is, about 3 3/4 tons (about 3.4 metric tons)
[g] 33 That is, about 75 pounds (about 34 kilograms)

acted the silver and gold from the people of the land according to their assessments.

Jehoiakim King of Judah

[36]Jehoiakim was twenty-five years old when he became king, and he reigned in Jerusalem eleven years. His mother's name was Zebidah daughter of Pedaiah; she was from Rumah. [37]And he did evil in the eyes of the LORD, just as his fathers had done.

PRAYER: AFFIRMATION

IF I would love life and see good days, I must keep my tongue from evil and my lips from speaking guile. I must turn from evil and do good; I must seek peace and pursue it. For Your eyes, O Lord, are on the righteous, and Your ears attend to their prayer, but Your face is against those who do evil. (1 Peter 3:10–12)

***PAUSE** to reflect on these Biblical affirmations.*

NT 1 John 2:28–3:10

Children of God

[28]And now, dear children, continue in him, so that when he appears we may be confident and unashamed before him at his coming.

[29]If you know that he is righteous, you know that everyone who does what is right has been born of him.

3 How great is the love the Father has lavished on us, that we should be called children of God! And that is what we are! The reason the world does not know us is that it did not know him. [2]Dear friends, now we are children of God, and what we will be has not yet been made known. But we know that when he appears,[a] we shall be like him, for we shall see him as he is. [3]Everyone who has this hope in him purifies himself, just as he is pure.

[4]Everyone who sins breaks the law; in fact, sin is lawlessness. [5]But you know that he appeared so that he might take away our sins. And in him is no sin. [6]No one who lives in him keeps on sinning. No one who continues to sin has either seen him or known him.

[7]Dear children, do not let anyone lead you astray. He who does what is right is righteous, just as he is righteous. [8]He who does what is sinful is of the devil, because the devil has been sinning from the beginning. The reason the Son of God appeared was to destroy the devil's work. [9]No one who is born of God will continue to sin, because God's seed remains in him; he cannot go on sinning, because he has been born of God. [10]This is how we know who the children of God are and who the children of the devil are: Anyone who does not do what is right is not a child of God; nor is anyone who does not love his brother.

[a] 2 Or *when it is made known*

PRAYER: MY RELATIONSHIP TO GOD

I WILL not let sin reign in my mortal body that I should obey its lusts. Nor will I present the parts of my body to sin as instruments of wickedness, but I will present myself to You, my God, as one who is alive from the dead. I will present my body to You as an instrument of righteousness. (Romans 6:12–13) . . . In view of Your mercy, O God, I present my body as a living sacrifice, holy and pleasing to You, which is my reasonable service. (Romans 12:1)

***PAUSE** to thank God for the relationship that you enjoy with Him in Jesus Christ.*

YEAR 1 DAY 329

OT Psalm 65

Psalm 65

For the director of music. A psalm of David. A song.

[1]Praise awaits[a] you, O God, in Zion;
to you our vows will be fulfilled.
[2]O you who hear prayer,
to you all men will come.
[3]When we were overwhelmed by sins,
you forgave[b] our transgressions.
[4]Blessed are those you choose
and bring near to live in your courts!
We are filled with the good things of your house,
of your holy temple.

[5]You answer us with awesome deeds of righteousness,
O God our Savior,
the hope of all the ends of the earth
and of the farthest seas,
[6]who formed the mountains by your power,
having armed yourself with strength,
[7]who stilled the roaring of the seas,
the roaring of their waves,
and the turmoil of the nations.
[8]Those living far away fear your wonders;
where morning dawns and evening fades
you call forth songs of joy.

[9]You care for the land and water it;
you enrich it abundantly.
The streams of God are filled with water
to provide the people with grain,
for so you have ordained it.[c]
[10]You drench its furrows
and level its ridges;
you soften it with showers
and bless its crops.
[11]You crown the year with your bounty,
and your carts overflow with abundance.
[12]The grasslands of the desert overflow;
the hills are clothed with gladness.
[13]The meadows are covered with flocks
and the valleys are mantled with grain;
they shout for joy and sing.

[a] 1 Or *befits;* the meaning of the Hebrew for this word is uncertain. [b] 3 Or *made atonement for* [c] 9 Or *for that is how you prepare the land*

PRAYER: THANKSGIVING

I WILL give thanks to You, O Lord, for You are good; Your lovingkindness endures forever. I will give thanks to You, Lord, for Your unfailing love and Your wonderful acts to Your people, for You satisfy the thirsty soul and fill the hungry soul with good things. (Psalm 107:1, 8–9)

PAUSE *to offer your own expressions of thanksgiving.*

NT 1 John 3:11–4:6

Love One Another

[11]This is the message you heard from
the beginning: We should love one another. [12]Do not be like Cain, who belonged to the evil one and murdered his
brother. And why did he murder him? Because his own actions were evil and his
brother's were righteous. [13]Do not be surprised, my brothers, if the world hates
you. [14]We know that we have passed from
death to life, because we love our brothers. Anyone who does not love remains in
death. [15]Anyone who hates his brother is
a murderer, and you know that no murderer has eternal life in him.

[16]This is how we know what love is:
Jesus Christ laid down his life for us. And
we ought to lay down our lives for our
brothers. [17]If anyone has material possessions and sees his brother in need but has
no pity on him, how can the love of God
be in him? [18]Dear children, let us not love

with words or tongue but with actions
and in truth. [19]This then is how we know
that we belong to the truth, and how we
set our hearts at rest in his presence
[20]whenever our hearts condemn us. For
God is greater than our hearts, and he
knows everything.
[21]Dear friends, if our hearts do not condemn us, we have confidence before God
[22]and receive from him anything we ask,
because we obey his commands and do
what pleases him. [23]And this is his command: to believe in the name of his Son,
Jesus Christ, and to love one another as
he commanded us. [24]Those who obey his
commands live in him, and he in them.
And this is how we know that he lives in
us: We know it by the Spirit he gave us.

Test the Spirits

4 Dear friends, do not believe every spirit, but test the spirits to see whether
they are from God, because many false
prophets have gone out into the world.
[2]This is how you can recognize the Spirit
of God: Every spirit that acknowledges
that Jesus Christ has come in the flesh is
from God, [3]but every spirit that does not
acknowledge Jesus is not from God. This
is the spirit of the antichrist, which you
have heard is coming and even now is already in the world.
[4]You, dear children, are from God and
have overcome them, because the one
who is in you is greater than the one who
is in the world. [5]They are from the world
and therefore speak from the viewpoint of
the world, and the world listens to them.
[6]We are from God, and whoever knows
God listens to us; but whoever is not from
God does not listen to us. This is how we
recognize the Spirit[a] of truth and the spirit of falsehood.

[a] 6 Or *spirit*

PRAYER: THE CHARACTER I WANT TO CULTIVATE

THE one You esteem is humble and contrite of spirit and trembles at Your word. (Isaiah 66:2) . . . Who makes me different from anyone else? And what do I have that I did not receive? And if I did receive it, why should I boast as though I had not received it? (1 Corinthians 4:7)

***TAKE** a moment to ask the Lord for the grace to grow in godly character.*

OT 2 Kings 24:1–20

YEAR 1 DAY 330

24 During Jehoiakim's reign, Nebuchadnezzar king of Babylon invaded the
land, and Jehoiakim became his vassal for
three years. But then he changed his mind
and rebelled against Nebuchadnezzar.
[2]The LORD sent Babylonian,[a] Aramean,
Moabite and Ammonite raiders against
him. He sent them to destroy Judah, in accordance with the word of the LORD proclaimed by his servants the prophets.
[3]Surely these things happened to Judah
according to the LORD's command, in order to remove them from his presence because of the sins of Manasseh and all he
had done, [4]including the shedding of innocent blood. For he had filled Jerusalem
with innocent blood, and the LORD was
not willing to forgive.
[5]As for the other events of Jehoiakim's
reign, and all he did, are they not written
in the book of the annals of the kings of
Judah? [6]Jehoiakim rested with his fathers.
And Jehoiachin his son succeeded him as
king.
[7]The king of Egypt did not march out
from his own country again, because the
king of Babylon had taken all his territory, from the Wadi of Egypt to the Euphrates River.

Jehoiachin King of Judah

[8]Jehoiachin was eighteen years old
when he became king, and he reigned in
Jerusalem three months. His mother's
name was Nehushta daughter of Elna-

[a] 2 Or *Chaldean*

than; she was from Jerusalem. [9]He did evil in the eyes of the LORD, just as his father had done.

[10]At that time the officers of Nebuchadnezzar king of Babylon advanced on Jerusalem and laid siege to it, [11]and Nebuchadnezzar himself came up to the city while his officers were besieging it. [12]Jehoiachin king of Judah, his mother, his attendants, his nobles and his officials all surrendered to him.

In the eighth year of the reign of the king of Babylon, he took Jehoiachin prisoner. [13]As the LORD had declared, Nebuchadnezzar removed all the treasures from the temple of the LORD and from the royal palace, and took away all the gold articles that Solomon king of Israel had made for the temple of the LORD. [14]He carried into exile all Jerusalem: all the officers and fighting men, and all the craftsmen and artisans—a total of ten thousand. Only the poorest people of the land were left.

[15]Nebuchadnezzar took Jehoiachin captive to Babylon. He also took from Jerusalem to Babylon the king's mother, his wives, his officials and the leading men of the land. [16]The king of Babylon also deported to Babylon the entire force of seven thousand fighting men, strong and fit for war, and a thousand craftsmen and artisans. [17]He made Mattaniah, Jehoiachin's uncle, king in his place and changed his name to Zedekiah.

Zedekiah King of Judah

[18]Zedekiah was twenty-one years old when he became king, and he reigned in Jerusalem eleven years. His mother's name was Hamutal daughter of Jeremiah; she was from Libnah. [19]He did evil in the eyes of the LORD, just as Jehoiakim had done. [20]It was because of the LORD's anger that all this happened to Jerusalem and Judah, and in the end he thrust them from his presence.

The Fall of Jerusalem

Now Zedekiah rebelled against the king of Babylon.

PRAYER: ADORATION

LORD Jesus, You are holy and true: You hold the key of David. What You open no one can shut, and what You shut no one can open. (Revelation 3:7)

PAUSE *to express your thoughts of praise and worship.*

NT 1 John 4:7–21

God's Love and Ours

[7]Dear friends, let us love one another, for love comes from God. Everyone who loves has been born of God and knows God. [8]Whoever does not love does not know God, because God is love. [9]This is how God showed his love among us: He sent his one and only Son[a] into the world that we might live through him. [10]This is love: not that we loved God, but that he loved us and sent his Son as an atoning sacrifice for[b] our sins. [11]Dear friends, since God so loved us, we also ought to love one another. [12]No one has ever seen God; but if we love one another, God lives in us and his love is made complete in us.

[13]We know that we live in him and he in us, because he has given us of his Spirit. [14]And we have seen and testify that the Father has sent his Son to be the Savior of the world. [15]If anyone acknowledges that Jesus is the Son of God, God lives in him and he in God. [16]And so we know and rely on the love God has for us.

God is love. Whoever lives in love lives in God, and God in him. [17]In this way, love is made complete among us so that we will have confidence on the day of judgment, because in this world we are like him. [18]There is no fear in love. But perfect love drives out fear, because fear has to do with punishment. The one who fears is not made perfect in love.

[a] 9 Or *his only begotten Son* [b] 10 Or *as the one who would turn aside his wrath, taking away*

19We love because he first loved us. 20If
anyone says, "I love God," yet hates his
brother, he is a liar. For anyone who does
not love his brother, whom he has seen,
cannot love God, whom he has not seen.
21And he has given us this command:
Whoever loves God must also love his
brother.

PRAYER: MY RELATIONSHIP TO OTHERS

MY love must be sincere. I will hate what is evil and cling to what is good. (Romans 12:9) . . . I will rejoice with those who rejoice and weep with those who weep. (Romans 12:15)

***PAUSE** to review your relationships with others and to commit them to the Lord.*

YEAR 1 DAY 331

OT 2 Kings 25:1-30

25 So in the ninth year of Zedekiah's
reign, on the tenth day of the tenth
month, Nebuchadnezzar king of Babylon
marched against Jerusalem with his whole
army. He encamped outside the city and
built siege works all around it. 2The city
was kept under siege until the eleventh
year of King Zedekiah. 3By the ninth day
of the ⌞fourth⌟[a] month the famine in the
city had become so severe that there was
no food for the people to eat. 4Then the
city wall was broken through, and the
whole army fled at night through the gate
between the two walls near the king's garden, though the Babylonians[b] were surrounding the city. They fled toward the Arabah,[c] 5but the Babylonian[d] army pursued
the king and overtook him in the plains
of Jericho. All his soldiers were separated
from him and scattered, 6and he was captured. He was taken to the king of Babylon at Riblah, where sentence was pronounced on him. 7They killed the sons of
Zedekiah before his eyes. Then they put
out his eyes, bound him with bronze
shackles and took him to Babylon.
8On the seventh day of the fifth month,
in the nineteenth year of Nebuchadnezzar
king of Babylon, Nebuzaradan commander of the imperial guard, an official of
the king of Babylon, came to Jerusalem.
9He set fire to the temple of the LORD, the
royal palace and all the houses of Jerusalem. Every important building he
burned down. 10The whole Babylonian
army, under the commander of the imperial guard, broke down the walls around
Jerusalem. 11Nebuzaradan the commander of the guard carried into exile the people who remained in the city, along with
the rest of the populace and those who
had gone over to the king of Babylon.
12But the commander left behind some of
the poorest people of the land to work the
vineyards and fields.
13The Babylonians broke up the bronze
pillars, the movable stands and the bronze
Sea that were at the temple of the LORD
and they carried the bronze to Babylon.
14They also took away the pots, shovels,
wick trimmers, dishes and all the bronze
articles used in the temple service. 15The
commander of the imperial guard took
away the censers and sprinkling bowls—
all that were made of pure gold or silver.
16The bronze from the two pillars, the
Sea and the movable stands, which Solomon had made for the temple of the
LORD, was more than could be weighed.
17Each pillar was twenty-seven feet[e] high.
The bronze capital on top of one pillar
was four and a half feet[f] high and was decorated with a network and pomegranates
of bronze all around. The other pillar,
with its network, was similar.
18The commander of the guard took as
prisoners Seraiah the chief priest, Zephaniah the priest next in rank and the three
doorkeepers. 19Of those still in the city, he
took the officer in charge of the fighting

[a] 3 See Jer. 52:6. [b] 4 Or *Chaldeans;* also in verses 13, 25 and 26 [c] 4 Or *the Jordan Valley* [d] 5 Or *Chaldean;* also in verses 10 and 24 [e] 17 Hebrew *eighteen cubits* (about 8.1 meters) [f] 17 Hebrew *three cubits* (about 1.3 meters)

men and five royal advisers. He also took the secretary who was chief officer in charge of conscripting the people of the land and sixty of his men who were found in the city. [20]Nebuzaradan the commander took them all and brought them to the king of Babylon at Riblah. [21]There at Riblah, in the land of Hamath, the king had them executed.

So Judah went into captivity, away from her land.

[22]Nebuchadnezzar king of Babylon appointed Gedaliah son of Ahikam, the son of Shaphan, to be over the people he had left behind in Judah. [23]When all the army officers and their men heard that the king of Babylon had appointed Gedaliah as governor, they came to Gedaliah at Mizpah—Ishmael son of Nethaniah, Johanan son of Kareah, Seraiah son of Tanhumeth the Netophathite, Jaazaniah the son of the Maacathite, and their men. [24]Gedaliah took an oath to reassure them and their men. "Do not be afraid of the Babylonian officials," he said. "Settle down in the land and serve the king of Babylon, and it will go well with you."

[25]In the seventh month, however, Ishmael son of Nethaniah, the son of Elishama, who was of royal blood, came with ten men and assassinated Gedaliah and also the men of Judah and the Babylonians who were with him at Mizpah. [26]At this, all the people from the least to the greatest, together with the army officers, fled to Egypt for fear of the Babylonians.

Jehoiachin Released

[27]In the thirty-seventh year of the exile of Jehoiachin king of Judah, in the year Evil-Merodach[g] became king of Babylon, he released Jehoiachin from prison on the twenty-seventh day of the twelfth month. [28]He spoke kindly to him and gave him a seat of honor higher than those of the other kings who were with him in Babylon. [29]So Jehoiachin put aside his prison clothes and for the rest of his life ate regularly at the king's table. [30]Day by day the king gave Jehoiachin a regular allowance as long as he lived.

[g] 27 Also called *Amel-Marduk*

PRAYER: CONFESSION

LET the wicked forsake their ways and the unrighteous their thoughts; let them return to You, our Lord, and You will have mercy on them, and to You, our God, for You will abundantly pardon. (Isaiah 55:7)

***ASK** the Spirit to search your heart and reveal any areas of unconfessed sin. Acknowledge these to the Lord and thank Him for His forgiveness.*

NT 1 John 5:1-21

Faith in the Son of God

5 Everyone who believes that Jesus is the Christ is born of God, and everyone who loves the father loves his child as well. [2]This is how we know that we love the children of God: by loving God and carrying out his commands. [3]This is love for God: to obey his commands. And his commands are not burdensome, [4]for everyone born of God overcomes the world. This is the victory that has overcome the world, even our faith. [5]Who is it that overcomes the world? Only he who believes that Jesus is the Son of God.

[6]This is the one who came by water and blood—Jesus Christ. He did not come by water only, but by water and blood. And it is the Spirit who testifies, because the Spirit is the truth. [7]For there are three that testify: [8]the[a] Spirit, the water and the blood; and the three are in agreement. [9]We accept man's testimony, but God's testimony is greater because it is the testimony of God, which he has given about his Son. [10]Anyone who believes in the Son of God has this testimony in his heart. Anyone who does not believe God has made him out to be a liar, because he has not believed the testimony God has given about his Son.

[a] 7,8 Late manuscripts of the Vulgate *testify in heaven: the Father, the Word and the Holy Spirit, and these three are one. [8]And there are three that testify on earth: the* (not found in any Greek manuscript before the sixteenth century)

[11]And this is the testimony: God has given
us eternal life, and this life is in his Son.
[12]He who has the Son has life; he who does
not have the Son of God does not have life.

Concluding Remarks

[13]I write these things to you who believe
in the name of the Son of God so that you
may know that you have eternal life. [14]This
is the confidence we have in approaching
God: that if we ask anything according to
his will, he hears us. [15]And if we know that
he hears us—whatever we ask—we know
that we have what we asked of him.
[16]If anyone sees his brother commit a
sin that does not lead to death, he should
pray and God will give him life. I refer to
those whose sin does not lead to death.
There is a sin that leads to death. I am not
saying that he should pray about that.
[17]All wrongdoing is sin, and there is sin
that does not lead to death.
[18]We know that anyone born of God does
not continue to sin; the one who was born
of God keeps him safe, and the evil one cannot harm him. [19]We know that we are children of God, and that the whole world is
under the control of the evil one. [20]We know
also that the Son of God has come and has
given us understanding, so that we may
know him who is true. And we are in him
who is true—even in his Son Jesus Christ.
He is the true God and eternal life.
[21]Dear children, keep yourselves from
idols.

PRAYER: THE ATTRIBUTES OF GOD

JESUS, You are the Christ, the Son of the living God. (Matthew 16:16) . . . Jesus, You are the way and the truth and the life. No one comes to the Father except through You. (John 14:6)

***PAUSE** to reflect on these affirmations about the person, powers and perfection of God.*

YEAR 1
DAY 332

OT **Ezra 1:1–2:70**

Cyrus Helps the Exiles to Return

1 In the first year of Cyrus king of Persia,
in order to fulfill the word of the LORD
spoken by Jeremiah, the LORD moved the
heart of Cyrus king of Persia to make a
proclamation throughout his realm and
to put it in writing:

[2]"This is what Cyrus king of Persia
says:
" 'The LORD, the God of heaven,
has given me all the kingdoms of the
earth and he has appointed me to
build a temple for him at Jerusalem
in Judah. [3]Anyone of his people
among you—may his God be with
him, and let him go up to Jerusalem
in Judah and build the temple of the
LORD, the God of Israel, the God who
is in Jerusalem. [4]And the people of
any place where survivors may now
be living are to provide him with silver and gold, with goods and livestock, and with freewill offerings for
the temple of God in Jerusalem.' "

[5]Then the family heads of Judah and
Benjamin, and the priests and Levites—
everyone whose heart God had moved—
prepared to go up and build the house of
the LORD in Jerusalem. [6]All their neighbors
assisted them with articles of silver and
gold, with goods and livestock, and with
valuable gifts, in addition to all the freewill
offerings. [7]Moreover, King Cyrus brought
out the articles belonging to the temple of
the LORD, which Nebuchadnezzar had carried away from Jerusalem and had placed
in the temple of his god.[a] [8]Cyrus king of
Persia had them brought by Mithredath
the treasurer, who counted them out to
Sheshbazzar the prince of Judah.
[9]This was the inventory:

gold dishes	30
silver dishes	1,000

[a] 7 Or *gods*

silver pans[b]	29
10 gold bowls	30
matching silver bowls	410
other articles	1,000

11 In all, there were 5,400 articles of gold and of silver. Sheshbazzar brought all these along when the exiles came up from Babylon to Jerusalem.

The List of the Exiles Who Returned

2 Now these are the people of the province who came up from the captivity of the exiles, whom Nebuchadnezzar king of Babylon had taken captive to Babylon (they returned to Jerusalem and Judah, each to his own town,
2 in company with Zerubbabel, Jeshua, Nehemiah, Seraiah, Reelaiah, Mordecai, Bilshan, Mispar, Bigvai, Rehum and Baanah):

The list of the men of the people of Israel:

3 the descendants of Parosh	2,172
4 of Shephatiah	372
5 of Arah	775
6 of Pahath-Moab (through the line of Jeshua and Joab)	2,812
7 of Elam	1,254
8 of Zattu	945
9 of Zaccai	760
10 of Bani	642
11 of Bebai	623
12 of Azgad	1,222
13 of Adonikam	666
14 of Bigvai	2,056
15 of Adin	454
16 of Ater (through Hezekiah)	98
17 of Bezai	323
18 of Jorah	112
19 of Hashum	223
20 of Gibbar	95

21 the men of Bethlehem	123
22 of Netophah	56
23 of Anathoth	128
24 of Azmaveth	42
25 of Kiriath Jearim,[c] Kephirah and Beeroth	743
26 of Ramah and Geba	621
27 of Micmash	122
28 of Bethel and Ai	223
29 of Nebo	52
30 of Magbish	156
31 of the other Elam	1,254
32 of Harim	320
33 of Lod, Hadid and Ono	725
34 of Jericho	345
35 of Senaah	3,630

36 The priests:

the descendants of Jedaiah (through the family of Jeshua)	973
37 of Immer	1,052
38 of Pashhur	1,247
39 of Harim	1,017

40 The Levites:

the descendants of Jeshua and Kadmiel (through the line of Hodaviah)	74

41 The singers:

the descendants of Asaph	128

42 The gatekeepers of the temple:

the descendants of Shallum, Ater, Talmon, Akkub, Hatita and Shobai	139

43 The temple servants:

the descendants of
Ziha, Hasupha, Tabbaoth,
44 Keros, Siaha, Padon,
45 Lebanah, Hagabah, Akkub,
46 Hagab, Shalmai, Hanan,
47 Giddel, Gahar, Reaiah,
48 Rezin, Nekoda, Gazzam,
49 Uzza, Paseah, Besai,
50 Asnah, Meunim, Nephussim,
51 Bakbuk, Hakupha, Harhur,
52 Bazluth, Mehida, Harsha,
53 Barkos, Sisera, Temah,
54 Neziah and Hatipha

55 The descendants of the servants of Solomon:

the descendants of
Sotai, Hassophereth, Peruda,
56 Jaala, Darkon, Giddel,
57 Shephatiah, Hattil,
Pokereth-Hazzebaim and Ami

58 The temple servants and the descendants of the servants of Solomon	392

59 The following came up from the
towns of Tel Melah, Tel Harsha, Ke-
rub, Addon and Immer, but they

[b] 9 The meaning of the Hebrew for this word is uncertain. [c] 25 See Septuagint (see also Neh. 7:29); Hebrew *Kiriath Arim.*

could not show that their families were descended from Israel:

[60]The descendants of
Delaiah, Tobiah and
Nekoda 652

[61]And from among the priests:

The descendants of
Hobaiah, Hakkoz and Barzillai
(a man who had married a
daughter of Barzillai the Gileadite and was called by that name).

[62]These searched for their family records, but they could not find them and so were excluded from the priesthood as unclean. [63]The governor ordered them not to eat any of the most sacred food until there was a priest ministering with the Urim and Thummim.

[64]The whole company numbered 42,360, [65]besides their 7,337 menservants and maidservants; and they also had 200 men and women singers. [66]They had 736 horses, 245 mules, [67]435 camels and 6,720 donkeys.

[68]When they arrived at the house of the LORD in Jerusalem, some of the heads of the families gave freewill offerings toward the rebuilding of the house of God on its site. [69]According to their ability they gave to the treasury for this work 61,000 drachmas[d] of gold, 5,000 minas[e] of silver and 100 priestly garments.

[70]The priests, the Levites, the singers, the gatekeepers and the temple servants settled in their own towns, along with some of the other people, and the rest of the Israelites settled in their towns.

[d] 69 That is, about 1,100 pounds (about 500 kilograms) [e] 69 That is, about 3 tons (about 2.9 metric tons)

PRAYER: RENEWAL

MAY I not steal. May I not bear false witness against my neighbor. May I not covet my neighbor's house, my neighbor's wife, his manservant or maidservant, his ox or donkey, or anything that belongs to my neighbor. (Exodus 20:15–17; Deuteronomy 5:19–21)

***PAUSE** to add your own prayers for personal renewal.*

NT 2 John 1–13

[1]The elder,

To the chosen lady and her children, whom I love in the truth—and not I only, but also all who know the truth— [2]because of the truth, which lives in us and will be with us forever:

[3]Grace, mercy and peace from God the Father and from Jesus Christ, the Father's Son, will be with us in truth and love.

[4]It has given me great joy to find some of your children walking in the truth, just as the Father commanded us. [5]And now, dear lady, I am not writing you a new command but one we have had from the beginning. I ask that we love one another. [6]And this is love: that we walk in obedience to his commands. As you have heard from the beginning, his command is that you walk in love.

[7]Many deceivers, who do not acknowledge Jesus Christ as coming in the flesh, have gone out into the world. Any such person is the deceiver and the antichrist. [8]Watch out that you do not lose what you have worked for, but that you may be rewarded fully. [9]Anyone who runs ahead and does not continue in the teaching of Christ does not have God; whoever continues in the teaching has both the Father and the Son. [10]If anyone comes to you and does not bring this teaching, do not take him into your house or welcome him. [11]Anyone who welcomes him shares in his wicked work.

[12]I have much to write to you, but I do not want to use paper and ink. Instead, I hope to visit you and talk with you face to face, so that our joy may be complete.

[13]The children of your chosen sister send their greetings.

PRAYER: THE WORKS OF GOD

LORD Jesus, You are the Alpha and the Omega, the Beginning and the End. To anyone who is thirsty, You will give to drink without cost from the spring of the water of life. Those who overcome will inherit all this, and You will be their God and they will be Your children. (Revelation 21:6–7)

***TAKE** a moment to consider the greatness of God's wonderful works.*

OT Ezra 3:1–4:24 **YEAR 1 DAY 333**

Rebuilding the Altar

3 When the seventh month came and the
Israelites had settled in their towns, the
people assembled as one man in Jerusalem. [2]Then Jeshua son of Jozadak and his
fellow priests and Zerubbabel son of
Shealtiel and his associates began to build
the altar of the God of Israel to sacrifice
burnt offerings on it, in accordance with
what is written in the Law of Moses the
man of God. [3]Despite their fear of the peoples around them, they built the altar on
its foundation and sacrificed burnt offerings on it to the LORD, both the morning
and evening sacrifices. [4]Then in accordance
with what is written, they celebrated the
Feast of Tabernacles with the required
number of burnt offerings prescribed for
each day. [5]After that, they presented the
regular burnt offerings, the New Moon sacrifices and the sacrifices for all the appointed sacred feasts of the LORD, as well
as those brought as freewill offerings to the
LORD. [6]On the first day of the seventh
month they began to offer burnt offerings
to the LORD, though the foundation of the
LORD's temple had not yet been laid.

Rebuilding the Temple

[7]Then they gave money to the masons
and carpenters, and gave food and drink
and oil to the people of Sidon and Tyre,
so that they would bring cedar logs by sea
from Lebanon to Joppa, as authorized by
Cyrus king of Persia.
[8]In the second month of the second
year after their arrival at the house of God
in Jerusalem, Zerubbabel son of Shealtiel,
Jeshua son of Jozadak and the rest of their
brothers (the priests and the Levites and
all who had returned from the captivity to
Jerusalem) began the work, appointing
Levites twenty years of age and older to
supervise the building of the house of the
LORD. [9]Jeshua and his sons and brothers
and Kadmiel and his sons (descendants of
Hodaviah[a]) and the sons of Henadad and
their sons and brothers—all Levites—
joined together in supervising those working on the house of God.
[10]When the builders laid the foundation of the temple of the LORD, the priests
in their vestments and with trumpets, and
the Levites (the sons of Asaph) with cymbals, took their places to praise the LORD,
as prescribed by David king of Israel.
[11]With praise and thanksgiving they sang
to the LORD:

"He is good;
his love to Israel endures forever."

And all the people gave a great shout of
praise to the LORD, because the foundation of the house of the LORD was laid.
[12]But many of the older priests and Levites
and family heads, who had seen the former temple, wept aloud when they saw
the foundation of this temple being laid,
while many others shouted for joy. [13]No
one could distinguish the sound of the
shouts of joy from the sound of weeping,
because the people made so much noise.
And the sound was heard far away.

Opposition to the Rebuilding

4 When the enemies of Judah and Benjamin heard that the exiles were building a temple for the LORD, the God of Israel, [2]they came to Zerubbabel and to the
heads of the families and said, "Let us
help you build because, like you, we seek

[a] 9 Hebrew *Yehudah,* probably a variant of *Hodaviah*

your God and have been sacrificing to
him since the time of Esarhaddon king of
Assyria, who brought us here."
3 But Zerubbabel, Jeshua and the rest of
the heads of the families of Israel answered,
"You have no part with us in building a
temple to our God. We alone will build it
for the LORD, the God of Israel, as King Cyrus, the king of Persia, commanded us."
4 Then the peoples around them set out
to discourage the people of Judah and
make them afraid to go on building.[b]
5 They hired counselors to work against
them and frustrate their plans during the
entire reign of Cyrus king of Persia and
down to the reign of Darius king of Persia.

Later Opposition Under Xerxes and Artaxerxes

6 At the beginning of the reign of Xerxes,[c] they lodged an accusation against the
people of Judah and Jerusalem.
7 And in the days of Artaxerxes king of
Persia, Bishlam, Mithredath, Tabeel and
the rest of his associates wrote a letter to
Artaxerxes. The letter was written in Aramaic script and in the Aramaic language.[d,e]
8 Rehum the commanding officer and
Shimshai the secretary wrote a letter
against Jerusalem to Artaxerxes the king as
follows:

9 Rehum the commanding officer and
Shimshai the secretary, together with
the rest of their associates—the
judges and officials over the men
from Tripolis, Persia,[f] Erech and Babylon, the Elamites of Susa, 10 and the
other people whom the great and
honorable Ashurbanipal[g] deported
and settled in the city of Samaria and
elsewhere in Trans-Euphrates.

11 (This is a copy of the letter they sent
him.)

To King Artaxerxes,

From your servants, the men of
Trans-Euphrates:

12 The king should know that the
Jews who came up to us from you
have gone to Jerusalem and are rebuilding that rebellious and wicked
city. They are restoring the walls and
repairing the foundations.
13 Furthermore, the king should
know that if this city is built and its
walls are restored, no more taxes,
tribute or duty will be paid, and the
royal revenues will suffer. 14 Now
since we are under obligation to the
palace and it is not proper for us to
see the king dishonored, we are sending this message to inform the king,
15 so that a search may be made in the
archives of your predecessors. In
these records you will find that this
city is a rebellious city, troublesome
to kings and provinces, a place of rebellion from ancient times. That is
why this city was destroyed. 16 We inform the king that if this city is built
and its walls are restored, you will be
left with nothing in Trans-Euphrates.

17 The king sent this reply:

To Rehum the commanding officer,
Shimshai the secretary and the rest of
their associates living in Samaria and
elsewhere in Trans-Euphrates:

Greetings.

18 The letter you sent us has been read
and translated in my presence. 19 I issued an order and a search was made,
and it was found that this city has a
long history of revolt against kings and
has been a place of rebellion and sedi-
tion. 20 Jerusalem has had powerful
kings ruling over the whole of Trans-
Euphrates, and taxes, tribute and duty
were paid to them. 21 Now issue an order to these men to stop work, so that
this city will not be rebuilt until I so order. 22 Be careful not to neglect this matter. Why let this threat grow, to the
detriment of the royal interests?

23 As soon as the copy of the letter of King
Artaxerxes was read to Rehum and Shimshai the secretary and their associates, they
went immediately to the Jews in Jerusalem
and compelled them by force to stop.

24 Thus the work on the house of God in
Jerusalem came to a standstill until the
second year of the reign of Darius king of
Persia.

[b] 4 Or *and troubled them as they built* [c] 6 Hebrew *Ahasuerus,* a variant of Xerxes' Persian name [d] 7 Or *written in Aramaic and translated* [e] 7 The text of Ezra 4:8—6:18 is in Aramaic. [f] 9 Or *officials, magistrates and governors over the men from* [g] 10 Aramaic *Osnappar,* a variant of *Ashurbanipal*

PRAYER: PETITION

OUT of the depths I call to You, O Lord. O Lord, hear my voice and let Your ears be attentive to the voice of my supplications. (Psalm 130:1–2)

PAUSE *here to offer prayers of petition regarding your family and your ministry. Ask for help and guidance in sharing Jesus with others and helping others grow in Him. Ask for guidance in your vocation and your avocations. Offer prayers of petition regarding your activities for this day and any special concerns you may have.*

NT 3 John 1–14

1The elder,

To my dear friend Gaius, whom I love in the truth.

2Dear friend, I pray that you may enjoy good health and that all may go well with you, even as your soul is getting along well.
3It gave me great joy to have some brothers come and tell about your faithfulness to the truth and how you continue to walk in the truth. 4I have no greater joy than to hear that my children are walking in the truth.
5Dear friend, you are faithful in what you are doing for the brothers, even though they are strangers to you. 6They have told the church about your love. You will do well to send them on their way in a manner worthy of God. 7It was for the sake of the Name that they went out, receiving no help from the pagans. 8We ought therefore to show hospitality to such men so that we may work together for the truth.

9I wrote to the church, but Diotrephes, who loves to be first, will have nothing to do with us. 10So if I come, I will call attention to what he is doing, gossiping maliciously about us. Not satisfied with that, he refuses to welcome the brothers. He also stops those who want to do so and puts them out of the church.
11Dear friend, do not imitate what is evil but what is good. Anyone who does what is good is from God. Anyone who does what is evil has not seen God.
12Demetrius is well spoken of by everyone—and even by the truth itself. We also speak well of him, and you know that our testimony is true.
13I have much to write you, but I do not want to do so with pen and ink. 14I hope to see you soon, and we will talk face to face.

Peace to you. The friends here send their greetings. Greet the friends there by name.

PRAYER: MY RELATIONSHIP TO GOD

I WILL incline my ear and come to You; I will hear You, that my soul may live. (Isaiah 55:3) . . . Everyone who hears Your words, Lord Jesus, and does them is like a wise man who built his house on the rock. (Matthew 7:24)

PAUSE *to thank God for the relationship that you enjoy with Him in Jesus Christ.*

YEAR 1 DAY 334

OT Ezra 5:1–17

Tattenai's Letter to Darius

5 Now Haggai the prophet and Zechariah the prophet, a descendant of Iddo, prophesied to the Jews in Judah and Jerusalem in the name of the God of Israel, who was over them. 2Then Zerubbabel son of Shealtiel and Jeshua son of Jozadak set to work to rebuild the house of

God in Jerusalem. And the prophets of
God were with them, helping them.
[3]At that time Tattenai, governor of
Trans-Euphrates, and Shethar-Bozenai
and their associates went to them and
asked, "Who authorized you to rebuild
this temple and restore this structure?"
[4]They also asked, "What are the names of
the men constructing this building?"[a]
[5]But the eye of their God was watching
over the elders of the Jews, and they were
not stopped until a report could go to Darius and his written reply be received.
[6]This is a copy of the letter that Tattenai,
governor of Trans-Euphrates, and Shethar-
Bozenai and their associates, the officials
of Trans-Euphrates, sent to King Darius.
[7]The report they sent him read as follows:

To King Darius:

Cordial greetings.

[8]The king should know that we
went to the district of Judah, to the
temple of the great God. The people
are building it with large stones and
placing the timbers in the walls. The
work is being carried on with diligence and is making rapid progress
under their direction.
[9]We questioned the elders and
asked them, "Who authorized you to
rebuild this temple and restore this
structure?" [10]We also asked them
their names, so that we could write
down the names of their leaders for
your information.
[11]This is the answer they gave us:

"We are the servants of the God of
heaven and earth, and we are rebuilding the temple that was built
many years ago, one that a great king
of Israel built and finished. [12]But because our fathers angered the God of
heaven, he handed them over to Nebuchadnezzar the Chaldean, king of
Babylon, who destroyed this temple
and deported the people to Babylon.
[13]"However, in the first year of Cyrus king of Babylon, King Cyrus issued a decree to rebuild this house of
God. [14]He even removed from the
temple[b] of Babylon the gold and silver articles of the house of God,
which Nebuchadnezzar had taken
from the temple in Jerusalem and
brought to the temple[b] in Babylon.
"Then King Cyrus gave them to a
man named Sheshbazzar, whom he
had appointed governor, [15]and he
told him, 'Take these articles and go
and deposit them in the temple in
Jerusalem. And rebuild the house of
God on its site.' [16]So this Sheshbazzar
came and laid the foundations of the
house of God in Jerusalem. From that
day to the present it has been under
construction but is not yet finished."

[17]Now if it pleases the king, let a
search be made in the royal archives of
Babylon to see if King Cyrus did in fact
issue a decree to rebuild this house of
God in Jerusalem. Then let the king
send us his decision in this matter.

[a] 4 See Septuagint; Aramaic [4]*We told them the names of the men constructing this building.* [b] 14 Or *palace*

PRAYER: INTERCESSION

HOLY Spirit, You convict the world concerning sin and righteousness and judgment. (John 16:8) . . . Knowing the fear of You, Lord, I will seek to persuade others. (2 Corinthians 5:11)

***TAKE** a few moments to intercede on behalf of local, national and world missions. Pray that the Great Commission would be fulfilled and for any special concerns you may have for missions.*

NT Jude 1-25

1Jude, a servant of Jesus Christ and a
brother of James,

To those who have been called, who are
loved by God the Father and kept by[a]
Jesus Christ:

2Mercy, peace and love be yours in
abundance.

The Sin and Doom of Godless Men

3Dear friends, although I was very eager
to write to you about the salvation we
share, I felt I had to write and urge you to
contend for the faith that was once for all
entrusted to the saints. 4For certain men
whose condemnation was written about[b]
long ago have secretly slipped in among
you. They are godless men, who change
the grace of our God into a license for immorality and deny Jesus Christ our only
Sovereign and Lord.
5Though you already know all this, I
want to remind you that the Lord[c] delivered his people out of Egypt, but later destroyed those who did not believe. 6And
the angels who did not keep their positions of authority but abandoned their
own home—these he has kept in darkness, bound with everlasting chains for
judgment on the great Day. 7In a similar
way, Sodom and Gomorrah and the surrounding towns gave themselves up to
sexual immorality and perversion. They
serve as an example of those who suffer
the punishment of eternal fire.
8In the very same way, these dreamers
pollute their own bodies, reject authority
and slander celestial beings. 9But even the
archangel Michael, when he was disputing with the devil about the body of Moses, did not dare to bring a slanderous accusation against him, but said, "The Lord
rebuke you!" 10Yet these men speak abusively against whatever they do not understand; and what things they do understand by instinct, like unreasoning
animals—these are the very things that
destroy them.
11Woe to them! They have taken the way
of Cain; they have rushed for profit into
Balaam's error; they have been destroyed
in Korah's rebellion.
12These men are blemishes at your love
feasts, eating with you without the slight-
est qualm—shepherds who feed only
themselves. They are clouds without rain,
blown along by the wind; autumn trees,
without fruit and uprooted—twice dead.
13They are wild waves of the sea, foaming
up their shame; wandering stars, for
whom blackest darkness has been reserved forever.
14Enoch, the seventh from Adam,
prophesied about these men: "See, the
Lord is coming with thousands upon
thousands of his holy ones 15to judge
everyone, and to convict all the ungodly
of all the ungodly acts they have done in
the ungodly way, and of all the harsh
words ungodly sinners have spoken
against him." 16These men are grumblers
and faultfinders; they follow their own
evil desires; they boast about themselves
and flatter others for their own advantage.

A Call to Persevere

17But, dear friends, remember what the
apostles of our Lord Jesus Christ foretold.
18They said to you, "In the last times there
will be scoffers who will follow their own
ungodly desires." 19These are the men
who divide you, who follow mere natural instincts and do not have the Spirit.
20But you, dear friends, build yourselves
up in your most holy faith and pray in the
Holy Spirit. 21Keep yourselves in God's
love as you wait for the mercy of our Lord
Jesus Christ to bring you to eternal life.
22Be merciful to those who doubt;
23snatch others from the fire and save
them; to others show mercy, mixed with
fear—hating even the clothing stained by
corrupted flesh.

Doxology

24To him who is able to keep you from
falling and to present you before his glorious presence without fault and with
great joy— 25to the only God our Savior
be glory, majesty, power and authority,
through Jesus Christ our Lord, before all
ages, now and forevermore! Amen.

[a] 1 Or *for;* or *in* [b] 4 Or *men who were marked out for condemnation* [c] 5 Some early manuscripts *Jesus*

PRAYER: THE CHARACTER I WANT TO CULTIVATE

I WILL endure discipline, for You, O God, are treating me as Your child. For what child is not disciplined by its father? If I am without discipline, (and all of us undergo discipline), then I am an illegitimate child and not a true child. Moreover, we have all had human fathers who disciplined us, and we respected them; how much more should I be disciplined by You, the Father of my spirit, and live? Our fathers disciplined us for a little while as they thought best; but You, O God, discipline us for our good, that we may share in Your holiness. No discipline seems pleasant at the time, but painful; later on, however, it produces the peaceable fruit of righteousness in those who have been trained by it. (Hebrews 12:7–11)

***TAKE** a moment to ask the Lord for the grace to grow in godly character.*

YEAR 1
DAY 335

OT Ezra 6:1–22

The Decree of Darius

6 King Darius then issued an order, and they searched in the archives stored in the treasury at Babylon. [2]A scroll was found in the citadel of Ecbatana in the province of Media, and this was written on it:

Memorandum:

[3]In the first year of King Cyrus, the king issued a decree concerning the temple of God in Jerusalem:

Let the temple be rebuilt as a place to present sacrifices, and let its foundations be laid. It is to be ninety feet[a] high and ninety feet wide, [4]with three courses of large stones and one of timbers. The costs are to be paid by the royal treasury. [5]Also, the gold and silver articles of the house of God, which Nebuchadnezzar took from the temple in Jerusalem and brought to Babylon, are to be returned to their places in the temple in Jerusalem; they are to be deposited in the house of God.

[6]Now then, Tattenai, governor of Trans-Euphrates, and Shethar-Bozenai and you, their fellow officials of that province, stay away from there. [7]Do not interfere with the work on this temple of God. Let the governor of the Jews and the Jewish elders rebuild this house of God on its site.

[8]Moreover, I hereby decree what you are to do for these elders of the Jews in the construction of this house of God:

The expenses of these men are to be fully paid out of the royal treasury, from the revenues of Trans-Euphrates, so that the work will not stop. [9]Whatever is needed—young bulls, rams, male lambs for burnt offerings to the God of heaven, and wheat, salt, wine and oil, as requested by the priests in Jerusalem—must be given them daily without fail, [10]so that they may offer sacrifices pleasing to the God of heaven and pray for the well-being of the king and his sons.

[11]Furthermore, I decree that if anyone changes this edict, a beam is to be pulled from his house and he is to be lifted up and impaled on it. And for this crime his house is to be made a pile of rubble. [12]May God, who has caused his Name to dwell there, overthrow any king or people who lifts a hand to change this decree or to destroy this temple in Jerusalem.

I Darius have decreed it. Let it be carried out with diligence.

Completion and Dedication of the Temple

[13]Then, because of the decree King Darius had sent, Tattenai, governor of Trans-

[a] 3 Aramaic *sixty cubits* (about 27 meters)

Euphrates, and Shethar-Bozenai and their
associates carried it out with diligence.
[14]So the elders of the Jews continued to
build and prosper under the preaching of
Haggai the prophet and Zechariah, a descendant of Iddo. They finished building
the temple according to the command of
the God of Israel and the decrees of Cyrus, Darius and Artaxerxes, kings of Persia.
[15]The temple was completed on the third
day of the month Adar, in the sixth year
of the reign of King Darius.

[16]Then the people of Israel—the priests,
the Levites and the rest of the exiles—celebrated the dedication of the house of God
with joy. [17]For the dedication of this house
of God they offered a hundred bulls, two
hundred rams, four hundred male lambs
and, as a sin offering for all Israel, twelve
male goats, one for each of the tribes of Israel. [18]And they installed the priests in their
divisions and the Levites in their groups for
the service of God at Jerusalem, according
to what is written in the Book of Moses.

The Passover

[19]On the fourteenth day of the first
month, the exiles celebrated the Passover.
[20]The priests and Levites had purified
themselves and were all ceremonially
clean. The Levites slaughtered the
Passover lamb for all the exiles, for their
brothers the priests and for themselves.
[21]So the Israelites who had returned from
the exile ate it, together with all who had
separated themselves from the unclean
practices of their Gentile neighbors in order to seek the LORD, the God of Israel.
[22]For seven days they celebrated with joy
the Feast of Unleavened Bread, because
the LORD had filled them with joy by
changing the attitude of the king of Assyria, so that he assisted them in the work
on the house of God, the God of Israel.

PRAYER: AFFIRMATION

THOSE who are wise and understanding will show it by their good conduct and works done in the humility that comes from wisdom. If I harbor bitter envy and selfish ambition in my heart, I should not boast and lie against the truth. This kind of wisdom does not come down from above, but is earthly, natural, demonic. For where there is envy and selfish ambition, there is disorder and every evil practice. The wisdom that comes from above is first pure, then peaceable, gentle, submissive, full of mercy and good fruits, without partiality and hypocrisy. And the fruit of righteousness is sown in peace by those who make peace. (James 3:13–18)

***PAUSE** to reflect on these Biblical affirmations.*

NT Revelation 1:1-8

Prologue

1 The revelation of Jesus Christ, which
God gave him to show his servants what
must soon take place. He made it known
by sending his angel to his servant John,
[2]who testifies to everything he saw—that
is, the word of God and the testimony of
Jesus Christ. [3]Blessed is the one who reads
the words of this prophecy, and blessed are
those who hear it and take to heart what is
written in it, because the time is near.

Greetings and Doxology

[4]John,

To the seven churches in the province
of Asia:

Grace and peace to you from him who
is, and who was, and who is to come, and
from the seven spirits[a] before his throne,
[5]and from Jesus Christ, who is the faithful witness, the firstborn from the dead,
and the ruler of the kings of the earth.

To him who loves us and has freed us
from our sins by his blood, [6]and has
made us to be a kingdom and priests to

[a] 4 Or *the sevenfold Spirit*

serve his God and Father—to him be glory and power for ever and ever! Amen.

7 Look, he is coming with the clouds,
and every eye will see him,
even those who pierced him;
and all the peoples of the earth will
mourn because of him.
So shall it be! Amen.

8 "I am the Alpha and the Omega," says
the Lord God, "who is, and who was, and
who is to come, the Almighty."

PRAYER: MY RELATIONSHIP TO OTHERS

I WILL not repay anyone evil for evil, but I will seek to do what is right in the sight of all people. (Romans 12:17) . . . I will not repay evil for evil to anyone, but I will pursue what is good for others. (1 Thessalonians 5:15)

***PAUSE** to review your relationships with others and to commit them to the Lord.*

YEAR 1 DAY 336

OT **Psalms 66–67**

Psalm 66

For the director of music. A song. A psalm.

1 Shout with joy to God, all the earth!
2 Sing the glory of his name;
make his praise glorious!
3 Say to God, "How awesome are your deeds!
So great is your power
that your enemies cringe before you.
4 All the earth bows down to you;
they sing praise to you,
they sing praise to your name." *Selah*

5 Come and see what God has done,
how awesome his works in man's behalf!
6 He turned the sea into dry land,
they passed through the waters on foot—
come, let us rejoice in him.
7 He rules forever by his power,
his eyes watch the nations—
let not the rebellious rise up against him. *Selah*

8 Praise our God, O peoples,
let the sound of his praise be heard;
9 he has preserved our lives
and kept our feet from slipping.
10 For you, O God, tested us;
you refined us like silver.
11 You brought us into prison
and laid burdens on our backs.
12 You let men ride over our heads;
we went through fire and water,
but you brought us to a place of abundance.

13 I will come to your temple with burnt offerings
and fulfill my vows to you—
14 vows my lips promised and my mouth spoke
when I was in trouble.
15 I will sacrifice fat animals to you
and an offering of rams;
I will offer bulls and goats. *Selah*

16 Come and listen, all you who fear God;
let me tell you what he has done for me.
17 I cried out to him with my mouth;
his praise was on my tongue.
18 If I had cherished sin in my heart,
the Lord would not have listened;
19 but God has surely listened
and heard my voice in prayer.
20 Praise be to God,
who has not rejected my prayer
or withheld his love from me!

Psalm 67

For the director of music. With stringed instruments. A psalm. A song.

1 May God be gracious to us and bless us

and make his face shine upon us,
Selah
2 that your ways may be known on earth,
your salvation among all nations.

3 May the peoples praise you, O God;
may all the peoples praise you.
4 May the nations be glad and sing for joy,
for you rule the peoples justly
and guide the nations of the earth.
Selah
5 May the peoples praise you, O God;
may all the peoples praise you.

6 Then the land will yield its harvest,
and God, our God, will bless us.
7 God will bless us,
and all the ends of the earth will fear him.

PRAYER: THANKSGIVING

I GIVE thanks for the word of Your angels to the shepherds: "Do not be afraid. I bring you good news of great joy that will be for all the people. For today in the city of David a Savior has been born to you, who is Christ the Lord." (Luke 2:10–11) . . . You, Jesus, the Son of Man, came to seek and to save that which was lost. (Luke 19:10)

***PAUSE** to offer your own expressions of thanksgiving.*

NT Revelation 1:9-20

One Like a Son of Man

9 I, John, your brother and companion
in the suffering and kingdom and patient
endurance that are ours in Jesus, was on
the island of Patmos because of the word
of God and the testimony of Jesus. 10 On
the Lord's Day I was in the Spirit, and I
heard behind me a loud voice like a trumpet, 11 which said: "Write on a scroll what
you see and send it to the seven churches:
to Ephesus, Smyrna, Pergamum, Thyatira,
Sardis, Philadelphia and Laodicea."
12 I turned around to see the voice that
was speaking to me. And when I turned I
saw seven golden lampstands, 13 and
among the lampstands was someone "like
a son of man,"[a] dressed in a robe reaching down to his feet and with a golden
sash around his chest. 14 His head and hair
were white like wool, as white as snow,
and his eyes were like blazing fire. 15 His
feet were like bronze glowing in a furnace,
and his voice was like the sound of rushing waters. 16 In his right hand he held sev-
en stars, and out of his mouth came a
sharp double-edged sword. His face was
like the sun shining in all its brilliance.
17 When I saw him, I fell at his feet as
though dead. Then he placed his right
hand on me and said: "Do not be afraid.
I am the First and the Last. 18 I am the Living One; I was dead, and behold I am
alive for ever and ever! And I hold the
keys of death and Hades.
19 "Write, therefore, what you have seen,
what is now and what will take place later.
20 The mystery of the seven stars that you
saw in my right hand and of the seven gold-
en lampstands is this: The seven stars are
the angels[b] of the seven churches, and the
seven lampstands are the seven churches.

[a] *13* Daniel 7:13 [b] *20* Or *messengers*

PRAYER: THE ATTRIBUTES OF GOD

YOU are in Your holy temple, O Lord; You are on Your heavenly throne. You observe all people; Your eyes examine them. (Psalm 11:4) . . . The heart is deceitful above all things and incurably sick. Who can understand it? Lord, You search human hearts

and test people's minds to reward them according to their ways,
according to the fruit of their deeds.
(Jeremiah 17:9–10)

PAUSE *to reflect on these affirmations about the person, powers and perfection of God.*

YEAR 1
DAY 337

OT Ezra 7:1–28

Ezra Comes to Jerusalem

7 After these things, during the reign of Artaxerxes king of Persia, Ezra son of Seraiah, the son of Azariah, the son of Hilkiah,
[2]the son of Shallum, the son of Zadok, the
son of Ahitub, [3]the son of Amariah, the
son of Azariah, the son of Meraioth, [4]the
son of Zerahiah, the son of Uzzi, the son
of Bukki, [5]the son of Abishua, the son of
Phinehas, the son of Eleazar, the son of
Aaron the chief priest— [6]this Ezra came up
from Babylon. He was a teacher well versed
in the Law of Moses, which the LORD, the
God of Israel, had given. The king had
granted him everything he asked, for the
hand of the LORD his God was on him.
[7]Some of the Israelites, including priests,
Levites, singers, gatekeepers and temple
servants, also came up to Jerusalem in the
seventh year of King Artaxerxes.
[8]Ezra arrived in Jerusalem in the fifth
month of the seventh year of the king. [9]He
had begun his journey from Babylon on
the first day of the first month, and he arrived in Jerusalem on the first day of the
fifth month, for the gracious hand of his
God was on him. [10]For Ezra had devoted
himself to the study and observance of the
Law of the LORD, and to teaching its decrees and laws in Israel.

King Artaxerxes' Letter to Ezra

[11]This is a copy of the letter King Artaxerxes had given to Ezra the priest and
teacher, a man learned in matters concerning the commands and decrees of the
LORD for Israel:

[12][a]Artaxerxes, king of kings,

To Ezra the priest, a teacher of the
Law of the God of heaven:

Greetings.

[13]Now I decree that any of the Israelites in my kingdom, including
priests and Levites, who wish to go to
Jerusalem with you, may go. [14]You are
sent by the king and his seven advisers
to inquire about Judah and Jerusalem
with regard to the Law of your God,
which is in your hand. [15]Moreover, you
are to take with you the silver and gold
that the king and his advisers have
freely given to the God of Israel, whose
dwelling is in Jerusalem, [16]together
with all the silver and gold you may
obtain from the province of Babylon,
as well as the freewill offerings of the
people and priests for the temple of
their God in Jerusalem. [17]With this
money be sure to buy bulls, rams and
male lambs, together with their grain
offerings and drink offerings, and sacrifice them on the altar of the temple
of your God in Jerusalem.
[18]You and your brother Jews may
then do whatever seems best with the
rest of the silver and gold, in accordance with the will of your God.
[19]Deliver to the God of Jerusalem all
the articles entrusted to you for worship in the temple of your God.
[20]And anything else needed for the
temple of your God that you may
have occasion to supply, you may
provide from the royal treasury.
[21]Now I, King Artaxerxes, order all
the treasurers of Trans-Euphrates to
provide with diligence whatever Ezra
the priest, a teacher of the Law of the
God of heaven, may ask of you—
[22]up to a hundred talents[b] of silver, a
hundred cors[c] of wheat, a hundred
baths[d] of wine, a hundred baths[d] of

[a] *12* The text of Ezra 7:12–26 is in Aramaic.
[b] *22* That is, about 3 3/4 tons (about 3.4 metric tons) [c] *22* That is, probably about 600 bushels (about 22 kiloliters) [d] *22* That is, probably about 600 gallons (about 2.2 kiloliters)

olive oil, and salt without limit. 23Whatever the God of heaven has prescribed, let it be done with diligence for the temple of the God of heaven. Why should there be wrath against the realm of the king and of his sons? 24You are also to know that you have no authority to impose taxes, tribute or duty on any of the priests, Levites, singers, gatekeepers, temple servants or other workers at this house of God.

25And you, Ezra, in accordance with the wisdom of your God, which you possess, appoint magistrates and judges to administer justice to all the people of Trans-Euphrates—all who know the laws of your God. And you are to teach any who do not know them. 26Whoever does not obey the law of your God and the law of the king must surely be punished by death, banishment, confiscation of property, or imprisonment.

27Praise be to the LORD, the God of our fathers, who has put it into the king's heart to bring honor to the house of the LORD in Jerusalem in this way 28and who has extended his good favor to me before the king and his advisers and all the king's powerful officials. Because the hand of the LORD my God was on me, I took courage and gathered leading men from Israel to go up with me.

PRAYER: ADORATION

WE praise You, Lord! We give thanks to You, for You are good; for Your loving mercy endures forever. Who can express Your mighty acts, O Lord, or fully declare Your praise? (Psalm 106:1–2) . . . You endowed the heart with wisdom and gave understanding to the mind. (Job 38:36)

PAUSE *to express your thoughts of praise and worship.*

NT Revelation 2:1–11

To the Church in Ephesus

2 "To the angel[a] of the church in Ephesus write:

These are the words of him who holds the seven stars in his right hand and walks among the seven golden lampstands: 2I know your deeds, your hard work and your perseverance. I know that you cannot tolerate wicked men, that you have tested those who claim to be apostles but are not, and have found them false. 3You have persevered and have endured hardships for my name, and have not grown weary.

4Yet I hold this against you: You have forsaken your first love. 5Remember the height from which you have fallen! Repent and do the things you did at first. If you do not repent, I will come to you and remove your lampstand from its place. 6But you have this in your favor: You hate the practices of the Nicolaitans, which I also hate.

7He who has an ear, let him hear what the Spirit says to the churches. To him who overcomes, I will give the right to eat from the tree of life, which is in the paradise of God.

To the Church in Smyrna

8"To the angel of the church in Smyrna write:

These are the words of him who is the First and the Last, who died and came to life again. 9I know your afflictions and your poverty—yet you are rich! I know the slander of those who say they are Jews and are not, but are a synagogue of Satan. 10Do not be afraid of what you are about to suffer. I tell you, the devil will put some of you in prison to test you, and you will suffer persecution for ten days. Be faithful, even to the

[a] *1* Or *messenger;* also in verses 8, 12 and 18

point of death, and I will give you the crown of life.
[11]He who has an ear, let him hear what the Spirit says to the churches. He who overcomes will not be hurt at all by the second death.

PRAYER: THE WORKS OF GOD

TRIUNE God, we rejoice in the unity we have in You, in which there is one body and one Spirit, just as we were called in one hope of our calling—one Lord, one faith, one baptism, one God and Father of all—who is over all and through all and in all. (Ephesians 4:4–6) . . . I give honor and praise to You, O Christ, for You are the head of the body, the church; You are the beginning and the firstborn from among the dead, so that in everything You might have supremacy. (Colossians 1:18)

***TAKE** a moment to consider the greatness of God's wonderful works.*

YEAR 1 DAY 338

OT Ezra 8:1-36

List of the Family Heads Returning With Ezra

8 These are the family heads and those registered with them who came up with me from Babylon during the reign of King Artaxerxes:

[2]of the descendants of Phinehas, Gershom;
of the descendants of Ithamar, Daniel;
of the descendants of David, Hattush
[3]of the descendants of Shecaniah;

of the descendants of Parosh, Zechariah, and with him were registered 150 men;
[4]of the descendants of Pahath-Moab, Eliehoenai son of Zerahiah, and with him 200 men;
[5]of the descendants of Zattu,[a] Shecaniah son of Jahaziel, and with him 300 men;
[6]of the descendants of Adin, Ebed son of Jonathan, and with him 50 men;
[7]of the descendants of Elam, Jeshaiah son of Athaliah, and with him 70 men;
[8]of the descendants of Shephatiah, Zebadiah son of Michael, and with him 80 men;
[9]of the descendants of Joab, Obadiah son of Jehiel, and with him 218 men;
[10]of the descendants of Bani,[b] Shelomith son of Josiphiah, and with him 160 men;
[11]of the descendants of Bebai, Zechariah son of Bebai, and with him 28 men;
[12]of the descendants of Azgad, Johanan son of Hakkatan, and with him 110 men;
[13]of the descendants of Adonikam, the last ones, whose names were Eliphelet, Jeuel and Shemaiah, and with them 60 men;
[14]of the descendants of Bigvai, Uthai and Zaccur, and with them 70 men.

The Return to Jerusalem

[15]I assembled them at the canal that flows
toward Ahava, and we camped there three
days. When I checked among the people
and the priests, I found no Levites there. [16]So
I summoned Eliezer, Ariel, Shemaiah, Elnathan, Jarib, Elnathan, Nathan, Zechariah
and Meshullam, who were leaders, and Joiarib and Elnathan, who were men of learning, [17]and I sent them to Iddo, the leader in
Casiphia. I told them what to say to Iddo
and his kinsmen, the temple servants in Casiphia, so that they might bring attendants
to us for the house of our God. [18]Because
the gracious hand of our God was on us,
they brought us Sherebiah, a capable man,
from the descendants of Mahli son of Levi,

[a] *5* Some Septuagint manuscripts (also 1 Esdras 8:32); Hebrew does not have *Zattu.* [b] *10* Some Septuagint manuscripts (also 1 Esdras 8:36); Hebrew does not have *Bani.*

the son of Israel, and Sherebiah's sons and brothers, 18 men; 19 and Hashabiah, together with Jeshaiah from the descendants of Merari, and his brothers and nephews, 20 men. 20 They also brought 220 of the temple servants—a body that David and the officials had established to assist the Levites. All were registered by name.

21 There, by the Ahava Canal, I proclaimed a fast, so that we might humble ourselves before our God and ask him for a safe journey for us and our children, with all our possessions. 22 I was ashamed to ask the king for soldiers and horsemen to protect us from enemies on the road, because we had told the king, "The gracious hand of our God is on everyone who looks to him, but his great anger is against all who forsake him." 23 So we fasted and petitioned our God about this, and he answered our prayer.

24 Then I set apart twelve of the leading priests, together with Sherebiah, Hashabiah and ten of their brothers, 25 and I weighed out to them the offering of silver and gold and the articles that the king, his advisers, his officials and all Israel present there had donated for the house of our God. 26 I weighed out to them 650 talents[c] of silver, silver articles weighing 100 talents,[d] 100 talents[d] of gold, 27 20 bowls of gold valued at 1,000 darics,[e] and two fine articles of polished bronze, as precious as gold.

28 I said to them, "You as well as these articles are consecrated to the LORD. The silver and gold are a freewill offering to the LORD, the God of your fathers. 29 Guard them carefully until you weigh them out in the chambers of the house of the LORD in Jerusalem before the leading priests and the Levites and the family heads of Israel." 30 Then the priests and Levites received the silver and gold and sacred articles that had been weighed out to be taken to the house of our God in Jerusalem.

31 On the twelfth day of the first month we set out from the Ahava Canal to go to Jerusalem. The hand of our God was on us, and he protected us from enemies and bandits along the way. 32 So we arrived in Jerusalem, where we rested three days.

33 On the fourth day, in the house of our God, we weighed out the silver and gold and the sacred articles into the hands of Meremoth son of Uriah, the priest. Eleazar son of Phinehas was with him, and so were the Levites Jozabad son of Jeshua and Noadiah son of Binnui. 34 Everything was accounted for by number and weight, and the entire weight was recorded at that time.

35 Then the exiles who had returned from captivity sacrificed burnt offerings to the God of Israel: twelve bulls for all Israel, ninety-six rams, seventy-seven male lambs and, as a sin offering, twelve male goats. All this was a burnt offering to the LORD. 36 They also delivered the king's orders to the royal satraps and to the governors of Trans-Euphrates, who then gave assistance to the people and to the house of God.

[c] *26* That is, about 25 tons (about 22 metric tons)
[d] *26* That is, about 3 3/4 tons (about 3.4 metric tons)
[e] *27* That is, about 19 pounds (about 8.5 kilograms)

PRAYER: CONFESSION

SEARCH me, O God, and know my heart; try me and know my anxious thoughts. See if there is any wicked way in me, and lead me in the way everlasting. (Psalm 139:23–24)

***ASK** the Spirit to search your heart and reveal any areas of unconfessed sin. Acknowledge these to the Lord and thank Him for His forgiveness.*

NT Revelation 2:12-17

To the Church in Pergamum

12 "To the angel of the church in Pergamum write:

These are the words of him who has the sharp, double-edged sword. 13 I know where you live—where Satan has his throne. Yet you remain true to my name. You did not renounce your faith in me, even in the days of Antipas, my faithful witness, who was put to death in your city—where Satan lives.

[14]Nevertheless, I have a few things against you: You have people there who hold to the teaching of Balaam, who taught Balak to entice the Israelites to sin by eating food sacrificed to idols and by committing sexual immorality. [15]Likewise you also have those who hold to the teaching of the Nicolaitans. [16]Repent therefore! Otherwise, I will soon come to you and will fight against them with the sword of my mouth.

[17]He who has an ear, let him hear what the Spirit says to the churches. To him who overcomes, I will give some of the hidden manna. I will also give him a white stone with a new name written on it, known only to him who receives it.

PRAYER: MY RELATIONSHIP TO GOD

NO eye has seen, no ear has heard, no mind has conceived, O God, what You have prepared for those who love You. (1 Corinthians 2:9) . . . Now I see dimly, as in a mirror, but then I shall see face to face. Now I know in part, but then I shall know fully, even as I am fully known. (1 Corinthians 13:12)

***PAUSE** to thank God for the relationship that you enjoy with Him in Jesus Christ.*

YEAR 1 DAY 339

OT Ezra 9:1-15

Ezra's Prayer About Intermarriage

9 After these things had been done, the leaders came to me and said, "The people of Israel, including the priests and the Levites, have not kept themselves separate from the neighboring peoples with their detestable practices, like those of the Canaanites, Hittites, Perizzites, Jebusites, Ammonites, Moabites, Egyptians and Amorites. [2]They have taken some of their daughters as wives for themselves and their sons, and have mingled the holy race with the peoples around them. And the leaders and officials have led the way in this unfaithfulness."

[3]When I heard this, I tore my tunic and cloak, pulled hair from my head and beard and sat down appalled. [4]Then everyone who trembled at the words of the God of Israel gathered around me because of this unfaithfulness of the exiles. And I sat there appalled until the evening sacrifice.

[5]Then, at the evening sacrifice, I rose from my self-abasement, with my tunic and cloak torn, and fell on my knees with my hands spread out to the LORD my God [6]and prayed:

"O my God, I am too ashamed and disgraced to lift up my face to you, my God, because our sins are higher than our heads and our guilt has reached to the heavens. [7]From the days of our forefathers until now, our guilt has been great. Because of our sins, we and our kings and our priests have been subjected to the sword and captivity, to pillage and humiliation at the hand of foreign kings, as it is today.

[8]"But now, for a brief moment, the LORD our God has been gracious in leaving us a remnant and giving us a firm place in his sanctuary, and so our God gives light to our eyes and a little relief in our bondage. [9]Though we are slaves, our God has not deserted us in our bondage. He has shown us kindness in the sight of the kings of Persia: He has granted us new life to rebuild the house of our God and repair its ruins, and he has given us a wall of protection in Judah and Jerusalem.

[10]"But now, O our God, what can we say after this? For we have disre-

garded the commands [11]you gave through your servants the prophets when you said: 'The land you are entering to possess is a land polluted by the corruption of its peoples. By their detestable practices they have filled it with their impurity from one end to the other. [12]Therefore, do not give your daughters in marriage to their sons or take their daughters for your sons. Do not seek a treaty of friendship with them at any time, that you may be strong and eat the good things of the land and leave it to your children as an everlasting inheritance.'

[13]"What has happened to us is a result of our evil deeds and our great guilt, and yet, our God, you have punished us less than our sins have deserved and have given us a remnant like this. [14]Shall we again break your commands and intermarry with the peoples who commit such detestable practices? Would you not be angry enough with us to destroy us, leaving us no remnant or survivor? [15]O LORD, God of Israel, you are righteous! We are left this day as a remnant. Here we are before you in our guilt, though because of it not one of us can stand in your presence."

PRAYER: RENEWAL

LORD, may these Beatitudes become a reality in my life: Blessed are the poor in spirit, for theirs is the kingdom of heaven. Blessed are those who mourn, for they will be comforted. Blessed are the meek, for they will inherit the earth. Blessed are those who hunger and thirst for righteousness, for they shall be satisfied. Blessed are the merciful, for they shall obtain mercy. (Matthew 5:3–7)

***PAUSE** to add your own prayers for personal renewal.*

NT Revelation 2:18–29

To the Church in Thyatira

[18]"To the angel of the church in Thyatira write:

These are the words of the Son of God, whose eyes are like blazing fire and whose feet are like burnished bronze. [19]I know your deeds, your love and faith, your service and perseverance, and that you are now doing more than you did at first.

[20]Nevertheless, I have this against you: You tolerate that woman Jezebel, who calls herself a prophetess. By her teaching she misleads my servants into sexual immorality and the eating of food sacrificed to idols. [21]I have given her time to repent of her immorality, but she is unwilling. [22]So I will cast her on a bed of suffering, and I will make those who commit adultery with her suffer intensely, unless they repent of her ways. [23]I will strike her children dead. Then all the churches will know that I am he who searches hearts and minds, and I will repay each of you according to your deeds. [24]Now I say to the rest of you in Thyatira, to you who do not hold to her teaching and have not learned Satan's so-called deep secrets (I will not impose any other burden on you): [25]Only hold on to what you have until I come.

[26]To him who overcomes and does my will to the end, I will give authority over the nations—

[27]'He will rule them with an iron
scepter;
he will dash them to pieces
like pottery'[a]—

just as I have received authority from my Father. [28]I will also give him the morning star. [29]He who has an ear, let him hear what the Spirit says to the churches.

[a] 27 Psalm 2:9

PRAYER: THE CHARACTER I WANT TO CULTIVATE

I WILL not worry about tomorrow, for tomorrow will worry about itself. Each day has enough trouble of its own. (Matthew 6:34) . . . I will not be worried and troubled about many things, for only one thing is needed. Like Mary, I want to choose what is better, that which will not be taken away from me. (Luke 10:41–42)

***TAKE** a moment to ask the Lord for the grace to grow in godly character.*

OT Proverbs 15

15 A gentle answer turns away wrath,
but a harsh word stirs up anger.

2 The tongue of the wise commends knowledge,
but the mouth of the fool gushes folly.

3 The eyes of the LORD are everywhere,
keeping watch on the wicked and the good.

4 The tongue that brings healing is a tree of life,
but a deceitful tongue crushes the spirit.

5 A fool spurns his father's discipline,
but whoever heeds correction shows prudence.

6 The house of the righteous contains great treasure,
but the income of the wicked brings them trouble.

7 The lips of the wise spread knowledge;
not so the hearts of fools.

8 The LORD detests the sacrifice of the wicked,
but the prayer of the upright pleases him.

9 The LORD detests the way of the wicked
but he loves those who pursue righteousness.

10 Stern discipline awaits him who leaves the path;
he who hates correction will die.

11 Death and Destruction[a] lie open before the LORD—
how much more the hearts of men!

12 A mocker resents correction;
he will not consult the wise.

13 A happy heart makes the face cheerful,
but heartache crushes the spirit.

14 The discerning heart seeks knowledge,
but the mouth of a fool feeds on folly.

15 All the days of the oppressed are wretched,
but the cheerful heart has a continual feast.

16 Better a little with the fear of the LORD
than great wealth with turmoil.

17 Better a meal of vegetables where there is love
than a fattened calf with hatred.

18 A hot-tempered man stirs up dissension,
but a patient man calms a quarrel.

19 The way of the sluggard is blocked with thorns,
but the path of the upright is a highway.

20 A wise son brings joy to his father,
but a foolish man despises his mother.

21 Folly delights a man who lacks judgment,
but a man of understanding keeps a straight course.

22 Plans fail for lack of counsel,
but with many advisers they succeed.

23 A man finds joy in giving an apt reply—

[a] 11 Hebrew *Sheol and Abaddon*

and how good is a timely word!

24 The path of life leads upward for the wise
to keep him from going down to the grave.[b]

25 The LORD tears down the proud man's house
but he keeps the widow's boundaries intact.

26 The LORD detests the thoughts of the wicked,
but those of the pure are pleasing to him.

27 A greedy man brings trouble to his family,
but he who hates bribes will live.

28 The heart of the righteous weighs its answers,
but the mouth of the wicked gushes evil.

29 The LORD is far from the wicked
but he hears the prayer of the righteous.

30 A cheerful look brings joy to the heart,
and good news gives health to the bones.

31 He who listens to a life-giving rebuke
will be at home among the wise.

32 He who ignores discipline despises himself,
but whoever heeds correction gains understanding.

33 The fear of the LORD teaches a man wisdom,[c]
and humility comes before honor.

[b] 24 Hebrew *Sheol* [c] 33 Or *Wisdom teaches the fear of the LORD*

PRAYER: PETITION

MAY I not wear myself out to get rich; give me the understanding to cease. May I not set my desire on what flies away, for wealth surely sprouts wings and flies into the heavens like an eagle. (Proverbs 23:4–5)

***PAUSE** here to petition God for growth in your character and personal discipline, and for physical health and strength. Ask that He empower you for spiritual warfare against the temptations of the world, the flesh and the devil. Offer prayers regarding your activities for this day and any special concerns you may have.*

NT Revelation 3:1–13

To the Church in Sardis

3 "To the angel[a] of the church in Sardis write:

These are the words of him who
holds the seven spirits[b] of God and
the seven stars. I know your deeds;
you have a reputation of being alive,
but you are dead. 2 Wake up! Strength-
en what remains and is about to die,
for I have not found your deeds complete in the sight of my God. 3 Remember, therefore, what you have received and heard; obey it, and repent.
But if you do not wake up, I will come
like a thief, and you will not know at
what time I will come to you.

4 Yet you have a few people in Sardis who have not soiled their clothes.
They will walk with me, dressed in
white, for they are worthy. 5 He who
overcomes will, like them, be dressed
in white. I will never blot out his
name from the book of life, but will
acknowledge his name before my Father and his angels. 6 He who has an
ear, let him hear what the Spirit says
to the churches.

To the Church in Philadelphia

7 "To the angel of the church in Philadelphia write:

[a] 1 Or *messenger;* also in verses 7 and 14 [b] 1 Or *the sevenfold Spirit*

These are the words of him who is holy and true, who holds the key of David. What he opens no one can shut, and what he shuts no one can open. 8I know your deeds. See, I have placed before you an open door that no one can shut. I know that you have little strength, yet you have kept my word and have not denied my name. 9I will make those who are of the synagogue of Satan, who claim to be Jews though they are not, but are liars—I will make them come and fall down at your feet and acknowledge that I have loved you. 10Since you have kept my command to endure patiently, I will also keep you from the hour of trial that is going to come upon the whole world to test those who live on the earth.

11I am coming soon. Hold on to what you have, so that no one will take your crown. 12Him who overcomes I will make a pillar in the temple of my God. Never again will he leave it. I will write on him the name of my God and the name of the city of my God, the new Jerusalem, which is coming down out of heaven from my God; and I will also write on him my new name. 13He who has an ear, let him hear what the Spirit says to the churches.

PRAYER: MY RELATIONSHIP TO OTHERS

WE must encourage one another daily, as long as it is still called "Today," lest any of us be hardened by sin's deceitfulness. (Hebrews 3:13) . . . We should consider how to stir up one another to love and to do good works. (Hebrews 10:24)

***PAUSE** to review your relationships with others and to commit them to the Lord.*

YEAR 1 DAY 341

OT Ezra 10:1-44

The People's Confession of Sin

10 While Ezra was praying and confessing, weeping and throwing himself down before the house of God, a large crowd of Israelites—men, women and children—gathered around him. They too wept bitterly. 2Then Shecaniah son of Jehiel, one of the descendants of Elam, said to Ezra, "We have been unfaithful to our God by marrying foreign women from the peoples around us. But in spite of this, there is still hope for Israel. 3Now let us make a covenant before our God to send away all these women and their children, in accordance with the counsel of my lord and of those who fear the commands of our God. Let it be done according to the Law. 4Rise up; this matter is in your hands. We will support you, so take courage and do it."

5So Ezra rose up and put the leading priests and Levites and all Israel under oath to do what had been suggested. And they took the oath. 6Then Ezra withdrew from before the house of God and went to the room of Jehohanan son of Eliashib. While he was there, he ate no food and drank no water, because he continued to mourn over the unfaithfulness of the exiles.

7A proclamation was then issued throughout Judah and Jerusalem for all the exiles to assemble in Jerusalem. 8Anyone who failed to appear within three days would forfeit all his property, in accordance with the decision of the officials and elders, and would himself be expelled from the assembly of the exiles.

9Within the three days, all the men of Judah and Benjamin had gathered in Jerusalem. And on the twentieth day of the ninth month, all the people were sitting in the square before the house of God, greatly distressed by the occasion and because of the rain. 10Then Ezra the priest stood up and said to them, "You have

been unfaithful; you have married foreign
women, adding to Israel's guilt. [11]Now
make confession to the LORD, the God of
your fathers, and do his will. Separate
yourselves from the peoples around you
and from your foreign wives."

[12]The whole assembly responded with
a loud voice: "You are right! We must do
as you say. [13]But there are many people
here and it is the rainy season; so we cannot stand outside. Besides, this matter
cannot be taken care of in a day or two,
because we have sinned greatly in this
thing. [14]Let our officials act for the whole
assembly. Then let everyone in our towns
who has married a foreign woman come
at a set time, along with the elders and
judges of each town, until the fierce anger
of our God in this matter is turned away
from us." [15]Only Jonathan son of Asahel
and Jahzeiah son of Tikvah, supported by
Meshullam and Shabbethai the Levite,
opposed this.

[16]So the exiles did as was proposed.
Ezra the priest selected men who were
family heads, one from each family division, and all of them designated by name.
On the first day of the tenth month they
sat down to investigate the cases, [17]and by
the first day of the first month they finished dealing with all the men who had
married foreign women.

Those Guilty of Intermarriage

[18]Among the descendants of the priests, the following had married foreign women:

From the descendants of Jeshua son of Jozadak, and his brothers: Maaseiah, Eliezer, Jarib and Gedaliah.
[19](They all gave their hands in pledge to put away their wives, and for their guilt they each presented a ram from the flock as a guilt offering.)

[20]From the descendants of Immer: Hanani and Zebadiah.

[21]From the descendants of Harim: Maaseiah, Elijah, Shemaiah, Jehiel and Uzziah.

[22]From the descendants of Pashhur: Elioenai, Maaseiah, Ishmael, Nethanel, Jozabad and Elasah.

[23]Among the Levites:

Jozabad, Shimei, Kelaiah (that is, Kelita), Pethahiah, Judah and Eliezer.

[24]From the singers: Eliashib.

From the gatekeepers: Shallum, Telem and Uri.

[25]And among the other Israelites:

From the descendants of Parosh: Ramiah, Izziah, Malkijah, Mijamin, Eleazar, Malkijah and Benaiah.

[26]From the descendants of Elam: Mattaniah, Zechariah, Jehiel, Abdi, Jeremoth and Elijah.

[27]From the descendants of Zattu: Elioenai, Eliashib, Mattaniah, Jeremoth, Zabad and Aziza.

[28]From the descendants of Bebai: Jehohanan, Hananiah, Zabbai and Athlai.

[29]From the descendants of Bani: Meshullam, Malluch, Adaiah, Jashub, Sheal and Jeremoth.

[30]From the descendants of Pahath-Moab: Adna, Kelal, Benaiah, Maaseiah, Mattaniah, Bezalel, Binnui and Manasseh.

[31]From the descendants of Harim: Eliezer, Ishijah, Malkijah, Shemaiah, Shimeon,
[32]Benjamin, Malluch and Shemariah.

[33]From the descendants of Hashum: Mattenai, Mattattah, Zabad, Eliphelet, Jeremai, Manasseh and Shimei.

[34]From the descendants of Bani: Maadai, Amram, Uel,
[35]Benaiah, Bedeiah, Keluhi,
[36]Vaniah, Meremoth, Eliashib,
[37]Mattaniah, Mattenai and Jaasu.

[38]From the descendants of Binnui:[a] Shimei,
[39]Shelemiah, Nathan, Adaiah,
[40]Macnadebai, Shashai, Sharai,
[41]Azarel, Shelemiah, Shemariah,
[42]Shallum, Amariah and Joseph.

[43]From the descendants of Nebo: Jeiel, Mattithiah, Zabad, Zebina, Jaddai, Joel and Benaiah.

[44]All these had married foreign women, and some of them had children by these wives.[b]

[a] 37,38 See Septuagint (also 1 Esdras 9:34); Hebrew *Jaasu* [38]*and Bani and Binnui,* [b] 44 Or *and they sent them away with their children*

PRAYER: INTERCESSION

MAY I learn to do good, seek justice, remove the oppressor, defend the orphan, and plead for the widow.
(Isaiah 1:17)

***TAKE** a few moments to intercede on behalf of the poor and hungry, the oppressed and persecuted, and those in control of world and national resources. Offer prayers for peace among nations and regarding current events and concerns.*

NT Revelation 3:14–22

To the Church in Laodicea

14 "To the angel of the church in Laodicea write:

These are the words of the Amen,
the faithful and true witness, the
ruler of God's creation. 15 I know your
deeds, that you are neither cold nor
hot. I wish you were either one or the
other! 16 So, because you are lukewarm—neither hot nor cold—I am
about to spit you out of my mouth.
17 You say, 'I am rich; I have acquired
wealth and do not need a thing.' But
you do not realize that you are
wretched, pitiful, poor, blind and
naked. 18 I counsel you to buy from
me gold refined in the fire, so you
can become rich; and white clothes
to wear, so you can cover your
shameful nakedness; and salve to put
on your eyes, so you can see.
19 Those whom I love I rebuke and
discipline. So be earnest, and repent.
20 Here I am! I stand at the door and
knock. If anyone hears my voice and
opens the door, I will come in and
eat with him, and he with me.
21 To him who overcomes, I will
give the right to sit with me on my
throne, just as I overcame and sat
down with my Father on his throne.
22 He who has an ear, let him hear
what the Spirit says to the churches."

PRAYER: THE ATTRIBUTES OF GOD

I WILL give thanks to You, O Lord, because of Your righteousness. I will sing praise to Your name, O Lord Most High. (Psalm 7:17) . . .
My soul magnifies You, O Lord, and my spirit rejoices in You, God my Savior, for You, Mighty One, have done great things for me, and holy is Your name. Your mercy is on those who fear You, from generation to generation. (Luke 1:46–47, 49–50)

***PAUSE** to reflect on these affirmations about the person, powers and perfection of God.*

YEAR 1 DAY 342

OT Nehemiah 1:1–2:20

Nehemiah's Prayer

1 The words of Nehemiah son of Hacaliah:

In the month of Kislev in the twentieth
year, while I was in the citadel of Susa,
2 Hanani, one of my brothers, came from
Judah with some other men, and I questioned them about the Jewish remnant
that survived the exile, and also about
Jerusalem.
3 They said to me, "Those who survived
the exile and are back in the province are
in great trouble and disgrace. The wall of
Jerusalem is broken down, and its gates
have been burned with fire."

[4]When I heard these things, I sat down and wept. For some days I mourned and fasted and prayed before the God of heaven. [5]Then I said:

"O LORD, God of heaven, the great and awesome God, who keeps his covenant of love with those who love him and obey his commands, [6]let your ear be attentive and your eyes open to hear the prayer your servant is praying before you day and night for your servants, the people of Israel. I confess the sins we Israelites, including myself and my father's house, have committed against you. [7]We have acted very wickedly toward you. We have not obeyed the commands, decrees and laws you gave your servant Moses.

[8]"Remember the instruction you gave your servant Moses, saying, 'If you are unfaithful, I will scatter you among the nations, [9]but if you return to me and obey my commands, then even if your exiled people are at the farthest horizon, I will gather them from there and bring them to the place I have chosen as a dwelling for my Name.'

[10]"They are your servants and your people, whom you redeemed by your great strength and your mighty hand. [11]O Lord, let your ear be attentive to the prayer of this your servant and to the prayer of your servants who delight in revering your name. Give your servant success today by granting him favor in the presence of this man."

I was cupbearer to the king.

Artaxerxes Sends Nehemiah to Jerusalem

2 In the month of Nisan in the twentieth year of King Artaxerxes, when wine was brought for him, I took the wine and gave it to the king. I had not been sad in his presence before; [2]so the king asked me, "Why does your face look so sad when you are not ill? This can be nothing but sadness of heart."

I was very much afraid, [3]but I said to the king, "May the king live forever! Why should my face not look sad when the city where my fathers are buried lies in ruins, and its gates have been destroyed by fire?"

[4]The king said to me, "What is it you want?"

Then I prayed to the God of heaven, [5]and I answered the king, "If it pleases the king and if your servant has found favor in his sight, let him send me to the city in Judah where my fathers are buried so that I can rebuild it."

[6]Then the king, with the queen sitting beside him, asked me, "How long will your journey take, and when will you get back?" It pleased the king to send me; so I set a time.

[7]I also said to him, "If it pleases the king, may I have letters to the governors of Trans-Euphrates, so that they will provide me safe-conduct until I arrive in Judah? [8]And may I have a letter to Asaph, keeper of the king's forest, so he will give me timber to make beams for the gates of the citadel by the temple and for the city wall and for the residence I will occupy?" And because the gracious hand of my God was upon me, the king granted my requests. [9]So I went to the governors of Trans-Euphrates and gave them the king's letters. The king had also sent army officers and cavalry with me.

[10]When Sanballat the Horonite and Tobiah the Ammonite official heard about this, they were very much disturbed that someone had come to promote the welfare of the Israelites.

Nehemiah Inspects Jerusalem's Walls

[11]I went to Jerusalem, and after staying there three days [12]I set out during the night with a few men. I had not told anyone what my God had put in my heart to do for Jerusalem. There were no mounts with me except the one I was riding on.

[13]By night I went out through the Valley Gate toward the Jackal[a] Well and the Dung Gate, examining the walls of Jerusalem, which had been broken down, and its gates, which had been destroyed by fire. [14]Then I moved on toward the Fountain Gate and the King's Pool, but there was not enough room for my mount to get through; [15]so I went up the valley by night, examining the wall. Finally, I turned back and reentered through the Valley Gate. [16]The officials did not know where I had gone or what I was doing, because as yet I had said nothing to the Jews

[a] 13 Or *Serpent* or *Fig*

or the priests or nobles or officials or any
others who would be doing the work.
17Then I said to them, "You see the trouble we are in: Jerusalem lies in ruins, and
its gates have been burned with fire.
Come, let us rebuild the wall of Jerusalem, and we will no longer be in disgrace." 18I also told them about the gracious hand of my God upon me and what
the king had said to me.
They replied, "Let us start rebuilding."
So they began this good work.
19But when Sanballat the Horonite, Tobiah the Ammonite official and Geshem
the Arab heard about it, they mocked and
ridiculed us. "What is this you are doing?"
they asked. "Are you rebelling against the
king?"
20I answered them by saying, "The God
of heaven will give us success. We his servants will start rebuilding, but as for you,
you have no share in Jerusalem or any
claim or historic right to it."

PRAYER: AFFIRMATION

LORD Jesus, those who love You will keep Your word; and Your Father will love them, and You and Your Father will come to them and make Your home with them. (John 14:23) . . . If I serve You, I must follow You; and where You are, I also will be. If I serve You, the Father will honor me. (John 12:26)

***PAUSE** to reflect on these Biblical affirmations.*

NT Revelation 4:1-11

The Throne in Heaven

4 After this I looked, and there before me
was a door standing open in heaven.
And the voice I had first heard speaking to
me like a trumpet said, "Come up here,
and I will show you what must take place
after this." 2At once I was in the Spirit, and
there before me was a throne in heaven
with someone sitting on it. 3And the one
who sat there had the appearance of jasper
and carnelian. A rainbow, resembling an
emerald, encircled the throne. 4Surround-
ing the throne were twenty-four other
thrones, and seated on them were twenty-
four elders. They were dressed in white
and had crowns of gold on their heads.
5From the throne came flashes of lightning, rumblings and peals of thunder. Before the throne, seven lamps were blazing.
These are the seven spirits[a] of God. 6Also
before the throne there was what looked
like a sea of glass, clear as crystal.
In the center, around the throne, were
four living creatures, and they were covered with eyes, in front and in back. 7The
first living creature was like a lion, the second was like an ox, the third had a face
like a man, the fourth was like a flying eagle. 8Each of the four living creatures had
six wings and was covered with eyes all
around, even under his wings. Day and
night they never stop saying:

"Holy, holy, holy
is the Lord God Almighty,
who was, and is, and is to come."

9Whenever the living creatures give glory,
honor and thanks to him who sits on the
throne and who lives for ever and ever,
10the twenty-four elders fall down before
him who sits on the throne, and worship
him who lives for ever and ever. They lay
their crowns before the throne and say:

11 "You are worthy, our Lord and God,
to receive glory and honor and
power,
for you created all things,
and by your will they were created
and have their being."

[a] 5 Or *the sevenfold Spirit*

PRAYER: THE WORKS OF GOD

YOUR hand, O Lord, laid the foundations of the earth, and Your right hand spread out the heavens; when You summon them, they all stand up together. (Isaiah 48:13) . . . Heaven is Your throne, O Lord, and the earth is Your footstool. Your hand made all these things, and so they came into being. (Isaiah 66:1–2)

***TAKE** a moment to consider the greatness of God's wonderful works.*

YEAR 1 DAY 343

OT Psalm 68

Psalm 68

For the director of music. Of David. A psalm. A song.

1 May God arise, may his enemies be
scattered;
may his foes flee before him.
2 As smoke is blown away by the wind,
may you blow them away;
as wax melts before the fire,
may the wicked perish before God.
3 But may the righteous be glad
and rejoice before God;
may they be happy and joyful.

4 Sing to God, sing praise to his name,
extol him who rides on the clouds[a]—
his name is the LORD—
and rejoice before him.
5 A father to the fatherless, a defender
of widows,
is God in his holy dwelling.
6 God sets the lonely in families,[b]
he leads forth the prisoners with
singing;
but the rebellious live in a sun-
scorched land.

7 When you went out before your
people, O God,
when you marched through the
wasteland, *Selah*
8 the earth shook,
the heavens poured down rain,
before God, the One of Sinai,
before God, the God of Israel.
9 You gave abundant showers, O God;
you refreshed your weary
inheritance.
10 Your people settled in it,
and from your bounty, O God, you
provided for the poor.

11 The Lord announced the word,
and great was the company of those
who proclaimed it:
12 "Kings and armies flee in haste;
in the camps men divide the
plunder.
13 Even while you sleep among the
campfires,[c]
the wings of ⌞my⌟ dove are sheathed
with silver,
its feathers with shining gold."
14 When the Almighty[d] scattered the
kings in the land,
it was like snow fallen on Zalmon.

15 The mountains of Bashan are majestic
mountains;
rugged are the mountains of
Bashan.
16 Why gaze in envy, O rugged
mountains,
at the mountain where God chooses
to reign,
where the LORD himself will dwell
forever?
17 The chariots of God are tens of
thousands
and thousands of thousands;
the Lord ⌞has come⌟ from Sinai into
his sanctuary.
18 When you ascended on high,
you led captives in your train;
you received gifts from men,
even from[e] the rebellious—

[a] 4 Or / *prepare the way for him who rides through the deserts* [b] 6 Or *the desolate in a homeland*
[c] 13 Or *saddlebags* [d] 14 Hebrew *Shaddai*
[e] 18 Or *gifts for men, / even*

that you,[f] O LORD God, might dwell
there.

[19]Praise be to the Lord, to God our
Savior,
who daily bears our burdens. *Selah*
[20]Our God is a God who saves;
from the Sovereign LORD comes
escape from death.

[21]Surely God will crush the heads of his
enemies,
the hairy crowns of those who go
on in their sins.
[22]The Lord says, "I will bring them from
Bashan;
I will bring them from the depths
of the sea,
[23]that you may plunge your feet in the
blood of your foes,
while the tongues of your dogs have
their share."

[24]Your procession has come into view,
O God,
the procession of my God and King
into the sanctuary.
[25]In front are the singers, after them the
musicians;
with them are the maidens playing
tambourines.
[26]Praise God in the great congregation;
praise the LORD in the assembly of
Israel.
[27]There is the little tribe of Benjamin,
leading them,
there the great throng of Judah's
princes,
and there the princes of Zebulun
and of Naphtali.

[28]Summon your power, O God[g];
show us your strength, O God, as
you have done before.
[29]Because of your temple at Jerusalem
kings will bring you gifts.
[30]Rebuke the beast among the reeds,
the herd of bulls among the calves
of the nations.
Humbled, may it bring bars of silver.
Scatter the nations who delight in
war.
[31]Envoys will come from Egypt;
Cush[h] will submit herself to God.

[32]Sing to God, O kingdoms of the earth,
sing praise to the Lord, *Selah*
[33]to him who rides the ancient skies
above,
who thunders with mighty voice.
[34]Proclaim the power of God,
whose majesty is over Israel,
whose power is in the skies.
[35]You are awesome, O God, in your
sanctuary;
the God of Israel gives power and
strength to his people.

Praise be to God!

[f]*18* Or *they* [g]*28* Many Hebrew manuscripts, Septuagint and Syriac; most Hebrew manuscripts *Your God has summoned power for you* [h]*31* That is, the upper Nile region

PRAYER: THANKSGIVING

BLESSED is the one You choose and bring near to live in Your courts. I will be satisfied with the goodness of Your house, of Your holy temple. (Psalm 65:4) . . . The one who rests in Your shadow, O Most High God, will be kept safe by You, O Mighty One. I will say of You, "You are my refuge and my fortress, O Lord; You are God, in whom I trust." (Psalm 91:1–2)

PAUSE *to offer your own expressions of thanksgiving.*

NT Revelation 5:1–14

The Scroll and the Lamb

5 Then I saw in the right hand of him
who sat on the throne a scroll with
writing on both sides and sealed with sev-
en seals. [2]And I saw a mighty angel proclaiming in a loud voice, "Who is worthy
to break the seals and open the scroll?"
[3]But no one in heaven or on earth or under the earth could open the scroll or even
look inside it. [4]I wept and wept because
no one was found who was worthy to
open the scroll or look inside. [5]Then one
of the elders said to me, "Do not weep!
See, the Lion of the tribe of Judah, the

Root of David, has triumphed. He is able
to open the scroll and its seven seals."
6Then I saw a Lamb, looking as if it had
been slain, standing in the center of the
throne, encircled by the four living creatures and the elders. He had seven horns
and seven eyes, which are the seven spirits[a] of God sent out into all the earth. 7He
came and took the scroll from the right
hand of him who sat on the throne. 8And
when he had taken it, the four living creatures and the twenty-four elders fell down
before the Lamb. Each one had a harp and
they were holding golden bowls full of incense, which are the prayers of the saints.
9And they sang a new song:

"You are worthy to take the scroll
and to open its seals,
because you were slain,
and with your blood you purchased
men for God
from every tribe and language and
people and nation.
10You have made them to be a kingdom
and priests to serve our God,
and they will reign on the earth."

11Then I looked and heard the voice of
many angels, numbering thousands upon
thousands, and ten thousand times ten
thousand. They encircled the throne and
the living creatures and the elders. 12In a
loud voice they sang:

"Worthy is the Lamb, who was slain,
to receive power and wealth and
wisdom and strength
and honor and glory and praise!"

13Then I heard every creature in heaven
and on earth and under the earth and on
the sea, and all that is in them, singing:

"To him who sits on the throne and
to the Lamb
be praise and honor and glory and
power,
for ever and ever!"

14The four living creatures said, "Amen,"
and the elders fell down and worshiped.

[a] 6 Or *the sevenfold Spirit*

PRAYER: MY RELATIONSHIP TO GOD

I BELIEVE, Lord Jesus, that it is through Your grace that I am saved. (Acts 15:11) . . . By grace I have been saved through faith, and this not of myself; it is Your gift to me, O God, and not of works, so that I cannot boast. (Ephesians 2:8–9)

PAUSE *to thank God for the relationship that you enjoy with Him in Jesus Christ.*

YEAR 1 DAY 344

OT Nehemiah 3:1–32

Builders of the Wall

3 Eliashib the high priest and his fellow
priests went to work and rebuilt the
Sheep Gate. They dedicated it and set its
doors in place, building as far as the Tower of the Hundred, which they dedicated,
and as far as the Tower of Hananel. 2The
men of Jericho built the adjoining section, and Zaccur son of Imri built next to
them.

3The Fish Gate was rebuilt by the sons
of Hassenaah. They laid its beams and put
its doors and bolts and bars in place.
4Meremoth son of Uriah, the son of Hakkoz, repaired the next section. Next to
him Meshullam son of Berekiah, the son
of Meshezabel, made repairs, and next to
him Zadok son of Baana also made repairs. 5The next section was repaired by
the men of Tekoa, but their nobles would
not put their shoulders to the work under
their supervisors.[a]

6The Jeshanah[b] Gate was repaired by
Joiada son of Paseah and Meshullam son
of Besodeiah. They laid its beams and put
its doors and bolts and bars in place.
7Next to them, repairs were made by men

[a] 5 Or *their Lord* or *the governor* [b] 6 Or *Old*

from Gibeon and Mizpah—Melatiah of Gibeon and Jadon of Meronoth—places under the authority of the governor of Trans-Euphrates. 8Uzziel son of Harhaiah, one of the goldsmiths, repaired the next section; and Hananiah, one of the perfume-makers, made repairs next to that. They restored[c] Jerusalem as far as the Broad Wall. 9Rephaiah son of Hur, ruler of a half-district of Jerusalem, repaired the next section. 10Adjoining this, Jedaiah son of Harumaph made repairs opposite his house, and Hattush son of Hashabneiah made repairs next to him. 11Malkijah son of Harim and Hasshub son of Pahath-Moab repaired another section and the Tower of the Ovens. 12Shallum son of Hallohesh, ruler of a half-district of Jerusalem, repaired the next section with the help of his daughters.

13The Valley Gate was repaired by Hanun and the residents of Zanoah. They rebuilt it and put its doors and bolts and bars in place. They also repaired five hundred yards[d] of the wall as far as the Dung Gate.

14The Dung Gate was repaired by Malkijah son of Recab, ruler of the district of Beth Hakkerem. He rebuilt it and put its doors and bolts and bars in place.

15The Fountain Gate was repaired by Shallun son of Col-Hozeh, ruler of the district of Mizpah. He rebuilt it, roofing it over and putting its doors and bolts and bars in place. He also repaired the wall of the Pool of Siloam,[e] by the King's Garden, as far as the steps going down from the City of David. 16Beyond him, Nehemiah son of Azbuk, ruler of a half-district of Beth Zur, made repairs up to a point opposite the tombs[f] of David, as far as the artificial pool and the House of the Heroes.

17Next to him, the repairs were made by the Levites under Rehum son of Bani. Beside him, Hashabiah, ruler of half the district of Keilah, carried out repairs for his district. 18Next to him, the repairs were made by their countrymen under Binnui[g] son of Henadad, ruler of the other half-district of Keilah. 19Next to him, Ezer son of Jeshua, ruler of Mizpah, repaired another section, from a point facing the ascent to the armory as far as the angle. 20Next to him, Baruch son of Zabbai zealously repaired another section, from the angle to the entrance of the house of Eliashib the high priest. 21Next to him, Meremoth son of Uriah, the son of Hakkoz, repaired another section, from the entrance of Eliashib's house to the end of it.

22The repairs next to him were made by the priests from the surrounding region. 23Beyond them, Benjamin and Hasshub made repairs in front of their house; and next to them, Azariah son of Maaseiah, the son of Ananiah, made repairs beside his house. 24Next to him, Binnui son of Henadad repaired another section, from Azariah's house to the angle and the corner, 25and Palal son of Uzai worked opposite the angle and the tower projecting from the upper palace near the court of the guard. Next to him, Pedaiah son of Parosh 26and the temple servants living on the hill of Ophel made repairs up to a point opposite the Water Gate toward the east and the projecting tower. 27Next to them, the men of Tekoa repaired another section, from the great projecting tower to the wall of Ophel.

28Above the Horse Gate, the priests made repairs, each in front of his own house. 29Next to them, Zadok son of Immer made repairs opposite his house. Next to him, Shemaiah son of Shecaniah, the guard at the East Gate, made repairs. 30Next to him, Hananiah son of Shelemiah, and Hanun, the sixth son of Zalaph, repaired another section. Next to them, Meshullam son of Berekiah made repairs opposite his living quarters. 31Next to him, Malkijah, one of the goldsmiths, made repairs as far as the house of the temple servants and the merchants, opposite the Inspection Gate, and as far as the room above the corner; 32and between the room above the corner and the Sheep Gate the goldsmiths and merchants made repairs.

[c] 8 Or *They left out part of* [d] 13 Hebrew *a thousand cubits* (about 450 meters) [e] 15 Hebrew *Shelah,* a variant of *Shiloah,* that is, Siloam [f] 16 Hebrew; Septuagint, some Vulgate manuscripts and Syriac *tomb* [g] 18 Two Hebrew manuscripts and Syriac (see also Septuagint and verse 24); most Hebrew manuscripts *Bavvai*

PRAYER: ADORATION

O LORD, we worship You and Your Son Jesus, for You have made Him our Messiah and King: His throne is Your very throne, O God. His kingdom will last for ever and ever. He will rule by treating everyone fairly. He loves what is right and hates what is evil. So You have placed Him above His companions. You have filled Him with joy by pouring the sacred oil on His head. (Psalm 45:6–7)

***PAUSE** to express your thoughts of praise and worship.*

NT Revelation 6:1–17

The Seals

6 I watched as the Lamb opened the first
of the seven seals. Then I heard one of
the four living creatures say in a voice like
thunder, "Come!" 2I looked, and there before me was a white horse! Its rider held a
bow, and he was given a crown, and he
rode out as a conqueror bent on conquest.
3When the Lamb opened the second
seal, I heard the second living creature say,
"Come!" 4Then another horse came out,
a fiery red one. Its rider was given power
to take peace from the earth and to make
men slay each other. To him was given a
large sword.
5When the Lamb opened the third seal,
I heard the third living creature say,
"Come!" I looked, and there before me
was a black horse! Its rider was holding a
pair of scales in his hand. 6Then I heard
what sounded like a voice among the four
living creatures, saying, "A quart[a] of wheat
for a day's wages,[b] and three quarts of barley for a day's wages,[b] and do not damage
the oil and the wine!"
7When the Lamb opened the fourth
seal, I heard the voice of the fourth living
creature say, "Come!" 8I looked, and there
before me was a pale horse! Its rider was
named Death, and Hades was following
close behind him. They were given power
over a fourth of the earth to kill by sword,
famine and plague, and by the wild beasts
of the earth.
9When he opened the fifth seal, I saw
under the altar the souls of those who had
been slain because of the word of God
and the testimony they had maintained.
10They called out in a loud voice, "How
long, Sovereign Lord, holy and true, until
you judge the inhabitants of the earth and
avenge our blood?" 11Then each of them
was given a white robe, and they were told
to wait a little longer, until the number of
their fellow servants and brothers who
were to be killed as they had been was
completed.
12I watched as he opened the sixth seal.
There was a great earthquake. The sun
turned black like sackcloth made of goat
hair, the whole moon turned blood red,
13and the stars in the sky fell to earth, as
late figs drop from a fig tree when shaken
by a strong wind. 14The sky receded like a
scroll, rolling up, and every mountain and
island was removed from its place.
15Then the kings of the earth, the
princes, the generals, the rich, the mighty,
and every slave and every free man hid in
caves and among the rocks of the mountains. 16They called to the mountains and
the rocks, "Fall on us and hide us from the
face of him who sits on the throne and
from the wrath of the Lamb! 17For the
great day of their wrath has come, and
who can stand?"

[a] 6 Greek *a choinix* (probably about a liter)
[b] 6 Greek *a denarius*

PRAYER: THE CHARACTER I WANT TO CULTIVATE

YOUR word is a lamp to my feet and a light to my path. I have inclined my heart to perform Your statutes to the very end. (Psalm 119:105, 112) . . . We are all children of the light and children of the day.

We do not belong to the night or to the darkness. So then, let us not be like others who are asleep, but instead be alert and self-controlled.
(1 Thessalonians 5:5–6)

TAKE *a moment to ask the Lord for the grace to grow in godly character.*

YEAR 1
DAY 345

OT Nehemiah 4:1–5:19

Opposition to the Rebuilding

4 When Sanballat heard that we were rebuilding the wall, he became angry and was greatly incensed. He ridiculed the Jews, 2and in the presence of his associates and the army of Samaria, he said, "What are those feeble Jews doing? Will they restore their wall? Will they offer sacrifices? Will they finish in a day? Can they bring the stones back to life from those heaps of rubble—burned as they are?"

3Tobiah the Ammonite, who was at his side, said, "What they are building—if even a fox climbed up on it, he would break down their wall of stones!"

4Hear us, O our God, for we are despised. Turn their insults back on their own heads. Give them over as plunder in a land of captivity. 5Do not cover up their guilt or blot out their sins from your sight, for they have thrown insults in the face of[a] the builders.

6So we rebuilt the wall till all of it reached half its height, for the people worked with all their heart.

7But when Sanballat, Tobiah, the Arabs, the Ammonites and the men of Ashdod heard that the repairs to Jerusalem's walls had gone ahead and that the gaps were being closed, they were very angry. 8They all plotted together to come and fight against Jerusalem and stir up trouble against it. 9But we prayed to our God and posted a guard day and night to meet this threat.

10Meanwhile, the people in Judah said, "The strength of the laborers is giving out, and there is so much rubble that we cannot rebuild the wall."

11Also our enemies said, "Before they know it or see us, we will be right there among them and will kill them and put an end to the work."

12Then the Jews who lived near them came and told us ten times over, "Wherever you turn, they will attack us."

13Therefore I stationed some of the people behind the lowest points of the wall at the exposed places, posting them by families, with their swords, spears and bows. 14After I looked things over, I stood up and said to the nobles, the officials and the rest of the people, "Don't be afraid of them. Remember the Lord, who is great and awesome, and fight for your brothers, your sons and your daughters, your wives and your homes."

15When our enemies heard that we were aware of their plot and that God had frustrated it, we all returned to the wall, each to his own work.

16From that day on, half of my men did the work, while the other half were equipped with spears, shields, bows and armor. The officers posted themselves behind all the people of Judah 17who were building the wall. Those who carried materials did their work with one hand and held a weapon in the other, 18and each of the builders wore his sword at his side as he worked. But the man who sounded the trumpet stayed with me.

19Then I said to the nobles, the officials and the rest of the people, "The work is extensive and spread out, and we are widely separated from each other along the wall. 20Wherever you hear the sound of the trumpet, join us there. Our God will fight for us!"

21So we continued the work with half the men holding spears, from the first light of dawn till the stars came out. 22At that time I also said to the people, "Have every man and his helper stay inside Jerusalem at night, so they can serve us as guards by night and workmen by day." 23Neither I nor my brothers nor my men nor the guards with me took off our clothes; each had his weapon, even when he went for water.[b]

[a] 5 Or *have provoked you to anger before* [b] 23 The meaning of the Hebrew for this clause is uncertain.

Nehemiah Helps the Poor

5 Now the men and their wives raised a
great outcry against their Jewish brothers. 2 Some were saying, "We and our sons
and daughters are numerous; in order for
us to eat and stay alive, we must get
grain."
3 Others were saying, "We are mortgag-
ing our fields, our vineyards and our
homes to get grain during the famine."
4 Still others were saying, "We have had
to borrow money to pay the king's tax on
our fields and vineyards. 5 Although we are
of the same flesh and blood as our countrymen and though our sons are as good
as theirs, yet we have to subject our sons
and daughters to slavery. Some of our
daughters have already been enslaved, but
we are powerless, because our fields and
our vineyards belong to others."
6 When I heard their outcry and these
charges, I was very angry. 7 I pondered
them in my mind and then accused the
nobles and officials. I told them, "You are
exacting usury from your own countrymen!" So I called together a large meeting
to deal with them 8 and said: "As far as
possible, we have bought back our Jewish
brothers who were sold to the Gentiles.
Now you are selling your brothers, only
for them to be sold back to us!" They kept
quiet, because they could find nothing to
say.
9 So I continued, "What you are doing is
not right. Shouldn't you walk in the fear
of our God to avoid the reproach of our
Gentile enemies? 10 I and my brothers and
my men are also lending the people money and grain. But let the exacting of usury
stop! 11 Give back to them immediately
their fields, vineyards, olive groves and
houses, and also the usury you are charging them—the hundredth part of the
money, grain, new wine and oil."
12 "We will give it back," they said. "And
we will not demand anything more from
them. We will do as you say."
Then I summoned the priests and made
the nobles and officials take an oath to do
what they had promised. 13 I also shook
out the folds of my robe and said, "In this
way may God shake out of his house and
possessions every man who does not keep
this promise. So may such a man be shak-
en out and emptied!"
At this the whole assembly said,
"Amen," and praised the LORD. And the
people did as they had promised.
14 Moreover, from the twentieth year of
King Artaxerxes, when I was appointed to
be their governor in the land of Judah, until his thirty-second year—twelve years—
neither I nor my brothers ate the food allotted to the governor. 15 But the earlier
governors—those preceding me—placed
a heavy burden on the people and took
forty shekels[c] of silver from them in addition to food and wine. Their assistants
also lorded it over the people. But out of
reverence for God I did not act like that.
16 Instead, I devoted myself to the work on
this wall. All my men were assembled
there for the work; we[d] did not acquire
any land.
17 Furthermore, a hundred and fifty Jews
and officials ate at my table, as well as
those who came to us from the surrounding nations. 18 Each day one ox, six
choice sheep and some poultry were prepared for me, and every ten days an abundant supply of wine of all kinds. In spite
of all this, I never demanded the food allotted to the governor, because the demands were heavy on these people.
19 Remember me with favor, O my God,
for all I have done for these people.

[c] *15* That is, about 1 pound (about 0.5 kilogram)
[d] *16* Most Hebrew manuscripts; some Hebrew manuscripts, Septuagint, Vulgate and Syriac *I*

PRAYER: CONFESSION

CREATE in me a clean heart, O God, and renew a steadfast spirit within me. Do not cast me from Your presence or take Your Holy Spirit from me. Restore to me the joy of Your salvation and uphold me with a willing spirit. Then I will teach transgressors Your ways, and sinners will be converted to You. (Psalm 51:10–13)

ASK *the Spirit to search your heart and reveal any areas of unconfessed sin. Acknowledge these to the Lord and thank Him for His forgiveness.*

NT Revelation 7:1-8

144,000 Sealed

7 After this I saw four angels standing at
the four corners of the earth, holding
back the four winds of the earth to prevent any wind from blowing on the land
or on the sea or on any tree. 2Then I saw
another angel coming up from the east,
having the seal of the living God. He
called out in a loud voice to the four angels who had been given power to harm
the land and the sea: 3"Do not harm the
land or the sea or the trees until we put a
seal on the foreheads of the servants of
our God." 4Then I heard the number of
those who were sealed: 144,000 from all
the tribes of Israel.

5From the tribe of Judah 12,000 were
sealed,
from the tribe of Reuben 12,000,
from the tribe of Gad 12,000,
6from the tribe of Asher 12,000,
from the tribe of Naphtali 12,000,
from the tribe of Manasseh 12,000,
7from the tribe of Simeon 12,000,
from the tribe of Levi 12,000,
from the tribe of Issachar 12,000,
8from the tribe of Zebulun 12,000,
from the tribe of Joseph 12,000,
from the tribe of Benjamin 12,000.

PRAYER: MY RELATIONSHIP TO OTHERS

I WILL accept those whose faith is weak, without passing judgment on their opinions. Who am I to judge another's servant? Whether or not they stand or fall is their own master's concern. And they will stand, for You, O Lord, are able to make them stand. (Romans 14:1, 4) . . . Knowledge puffs up, but love builds up. (1 Corinthians 8:1)

***PAUSE** to review your relationships with others and to commit them to the Lord.*

YEAR 1 DAY 346

OT Nehemiah 6:1–7:73a

Further Opposition to the Rebuilding

6 When word came to Sanballat, Tobiah,
Geshem the Arab and the rest of our
enemies that I had rebuilt the wall and
not a gap was left in it—though up to that
time I had not set the doors in the gates—
2Sanballat and Geshem sent me this message: "Come, let us meet together in one
of the villages[a] on the plain of Ono."

But they were scheming to harm me; 3so
I sent messengers to them with this reply:
"I am carrying on a great project and cannot go down. Why should the work stop
while I leave it and go down to you?" 4Four
times they sent me the same message, and
each time I gave them the same answer.

5Then, the fifth time, Sanballat sent his
aide to me with the same message, and in
his hand was an unsealed letter 6in which
was written:

"It is reported among the nations—and Geshem[b] says it is true—
that you and the Jews are plotting to
revolt, and therefore you are building
the wall. Moreover, according to
these reports you are about to become their king 7and have even appointed prophets to make this
proclamation about you in Jerusalem: 'There is a king in Judah!'
Now this report will get back to the
king; so come, let us confer together."

8I sent him this reply: "Nothing like
what you are saying is happening; you are
just making it up out of your head."

9They were all trying to frighten us, thinking, "Their hands will get too weak for the
work, and it will not be completed."

⌞But I prayed,⌟ "Now strengthen my
hands."

[a] 2 Or *in Kephirim* [b] 6 Hebrew *Gashmu,* a variant of *Geshem*

10 One day I went to the house of Shemaiah son of Delaiah, the son of
Mehetabel, who was shut in at his home.
He said, "Let us meet in the house of God,
inside the temple, and let us close the
temple doors, because men are coming to
kill you—by night they are coming to kill
you."
11 But I said, "Should a man like me run
away? Or should one like me go into the
temple to save his life? I will not go!" 12 I
realized that God had not sent him, but
that he had prophesied against me because Tobiah and Sanballat had hired
him. 13 He had been hired to intimidate
me so that I would commit a sin by doing this, and then they would give me a
bad name to discredit me.

14 Remember Tobiah and Sanballat,
O my God, because of what they have
done; remember also the prophetess Noadiah and the rest of the prophets who
have been trying to intimidate me.

The Completion of the Wall

15 So the wall was completed on the
twenty-fifth of Elul, in fifty-two days.
16 When all our enemies heard about this,
all the surrounding nations were afraid
and lost their self-confidence, because
they realized that this work had been
done with the help of our God.
17 Also, in those days the nobles of Judah were sending many letters to Tobiah,
and replies from Tobiah kept coming to
them. 18 For many in Judah were under
oath to him, since he was son-in-law to
Shecaniah son of Arah, and his son Jehohanan had married the daughter of Meshullam son of Berekiah. 19 Moreover, they
kept reporting to me his good deeds and
then telling him what I said. And Tobiah
sent letters to intimidate me.

7 After the wall had been rebuilt and I
had set the doors in place, the gatekeepers and the singers and the Levites
were appointed. 2 I put in charge of Jerusalem my brother Hanani, along with[c]
Hananiah the commander of the citadel,
because he was a man of integrity and
feared God more than most men do. 3 I
said to them, "The gates of Jerusalem are
not to be opened until the sun is hot.
While the gatekeepers are still on duty,
have them shut the doors and bar them.
Also appoint residents of Jerusalem as
guards, some at their posts and some near
their own houses."

The List of the Exiles Who Returned

4 Now the city was large and spacious,
but there were few people in it, and the
houses had not yet been rebuilt. 5 So my
God put it into my heart to assemble the
nobles, the officials and the common
people for registration by families. I
found the genealogical record of those
who had been the first to return. This is
what I found written there:

6 These are the people of the province who came up from the captivity
of the exiles whom Nebuchadnezzar
king of Babylon had taken captive
(they returned to Jerusalem and Judah, each to his own town, 7 in company with Zerubbabel, Jeshua, Nehemiah, Azariah, Raamiah, Nahamani,
Mordecai, Bilshan, Mispereth, Bigvai,
Nehum and Baanah):

The list of the men of Israel:

8 the descendants of Parosh	2,172
9 of Shephatiah	372
10 of Arah	652
11 of Pahath-Moab (through the line of Jeshua and Joab)	2,818
12 of Elam	1,254
13 of Zattu	845
14 of Zaccai	760
15 of Binnui	648
16 of Bebai	628
17 of Azgad	2,322
18 of Adonikam	667
19 of Bigvai	2,067
20 of Adin	655
21 of Ater (through Hezekiah)	98
22 of Hashum	328
23 of Bezai	324
24 of Hariph	112
25 of Gibeon	95
26 the men of Bethlehem and Netophah	188
27 of Anathoth	128
28 of Beth Azmaveth	42
29 of Kiriath Jearim, Kephirah and Beeroth	743
30 of Ramah and Geba	621
31 of Micmash	122
32 of Bethel and Ai	123

c 2 Or *Hanani, that is,*

[33] of the other Nebo 52
[34] of the other Elam 1,254
[35] of Harim 320
[36] of Jericho 345
[37] of Lod, Hadid and Ono 721
[38] of Senaah 3,930

[39] The priests:

the descendants of Jedaiah (through the family of Jeshua) 973
[40] of Immer 1,052
[41] of Pashhur 1,247
[42] of Harim 1,017

[43] The Levites:

the descendants of Jeshua (through Kadmiel through the line of Hodaviah) 74

[44] The singers:

the descendants of Asaph 148

[45] The gatekeepers:

the descendants of Shallum, Ater, Talmon, Akkub, Hatita and Shobai 138

[46] The temple servants:

the descendants of
Ziha, Hasupha, Tabbaoth,
[47] Keros, Sia, Padon,
[48] Lebana, Hagaba, Shalmai,
[49] Hanan, Giddel, Gahar,
[50] Reaiah, Rezin, Nekoda,
[51] Gazzam, Uzza, Paseah,
[52] Besai, Meunim, Nephussim,
[53] Bakbuk, Hakupha, Harhur,
[54] Bazluth, Mehida, Harsha,
[55] Barkos, Sisera, Temah,
[56] Neziah and Hatipha

[57] The descendants of the servants of Solomon:

the descendants of
Sotai, Sophereth, Perida,
[58] Jaala, Darkon, Giddel,
[59] Shephatiah, Hattil,
Pokereth-Hazzebaim and Amon

[60] The temple servants and the descendants of the servants of Solomon 392

[61] The following came up from the
towns of Tel Melah, Tel Harsha, Ke-
rub, Addon and Immer, but they
could not show that their families
were descended from Israel:

[62] the descendants of Delaiah, Tobiah and Nekoda 642

[63] And from among the priests:

the descendants of Hobaiah, Hakkoz and Barzillai (a man who had married a daughter of Barzillai the Gileadite and was called by that name).

[64] These searched for their family
records, but they could not find them
and so were excluded from the priesthood as unclean.
[65] The governor,
therefore, ordered them not to eat
any of the most sacred food until
there should be a priest ministering
with the Urim and Thummim.

[66] The whole company numbered
42,360,
[67] besides their 7,337 menservants and maidservants; and they also
had 245 men and women singers.
[68] There were 736 horses, 245 mules,[d]
[69] 435 camels and 6,720 donkeys.

[70] Some of the heads of the families
contributed to the work. The governor gave to the treasury 1,000 drachmas[e] of gold, 50 bowls and 530 garments for priests.
[71] Some of the heads
of the families gave to the treasury for
the work 20,000 drachmas[f] of gold
and 2,200 minas[g] of silver.
[72] The to-
tal given by the rest of the people was
20,000 drachmas of gold, 2,000 minas[h] of silver and 67 garments for
priests.

[73] The priests, the Levites, the gatekeepers, the singers and the temple
servants, along with certain of the
people and the rest of the Israelites,
settled in their own towns.

[d] *68* Some Hebrew manuscripts (see also Ezra 2:66); most Hebrew manuscripts do not have this verse.
[e] *70* That is, about 19 pounds (about 8.5 kilograms)
[f] *71* That is, about 375 pounds (about 170 kilograms); also in verse 72
[g] *71* That is, about 1 1/3 tons (about 1.2 metric tons)
[h] *72* That is, about 1 1/4 tons (about 1.1 metric tons)

PRAYER: RENEWAL

LORD, may the Beatitudes You taught become a reality in my life: "Blessed are the pure in heart, for they shall see God. Blessed are the peacemakers, for they shall be called children of God. Blessed are those who are persecuted for the sake of righteousness, for theirs is the kingdom of heaven. Blessed are you when people insult you, persecute you, and falsely say all kinds of evil against you because of Me. Rejoice and be glad, because great is your reward in heaven, for in the same way they persecuted the prophets who were before you." (Matthew 5:8–12)

***PAUSE** to add your own prayers for personal renewal.*

NT Revelation 7:9-17

The Great Multitude in White Robes

[9]After this I looked and there before me
was a great multitude that no one could
count, from every nation, tribe, people
and language, standing before the throne
and in front of the Lamb. They were wearing white robes and were holding palm
branches in their hands. [10]And they cried
out in a loud voice:

"Salvation belongs to our God,
who sits on the throne,
and to the Lamb."

[11]All the angels were standing around the
throne and around the elders and the four
living creatures. They fell down on their
faces before the throne and worshiped
God, [12]saying:

"Amen!
Praise and glory
and wisdom and thanks and honor
and power and strength
be to our God for ever and ever.
Amen!"

[13]Then one of the elders asked me,
"These in white robes—who are they, and
where did they come from?"

[14]I answered, "Sir, you know."

And he said, "These are they who have
come out of the great tribulation; they
have washed their robes and made them
white in the blood of the Lamb. [15]There-
fore,

"they are before the throne of God
and serve him day and night in his temple;
and he who sits on the throne will
spread his tent over them.
[16]Never again will they hunger;
never again will they thirst.
The sun will not beat upon them,
nor any scorching heat.
[17]For the Lamb at the center of the
throne will be their shepherd;
he will lead them to springs of
living water.
And God will wipe away every tear
from their eyes."

PRAYER: THE ATTRIBUTES OF GOD

BEFORE Abraham was born, You always existed, Jesus Christ. (John 8:58) . . . In You, O Christ, all the fullness of the Godhead lives in bodily form. (Colossians 2:9)

***PAUSE** to reflect on these affirmations about the person, powers and perfection of God.*

Ezra Reads the Law

When the seventh month came and
the Israelites had settled in their towns,
8 1all the people assembled as one man
in the square before the Water Gate.
They told Ezra the scribe to bring out the
Book of the Law of Moses, which the LORD
had commanded for Israel.
2So on the first day of the seventh
month Ezra the priest brought the Law before the assembly, which was made up of
men and women and all who were able
to understand. 3He read it aloud from
daybreak till noon as he faced the square
before the Water Gate in the presence of
the men, women and others who could
understand. And all the people listened
attentively to the Book of the Law.
4Ezra the scribe stood on a high wood-
en platform built for the occasion. Beside
him on his right stood Mattithiah, Shema,
Anaiah, Uriah, Hilkiah and Maaseiah;
and on his left were Pedaiah, Mishael,
Malkijah, Hashum, Hashbaddanah,
Zechariah and Meshullam.
5Ezra opened the book. All the people
could see him because he was standing
above them; and as he opened it, the people all stood up. 6Ezra praised the LORD, the
great God; and all the people lifted their
hands and responded, "Amen! Amen!"
Then they bowed down and worshiped the
LORD with their faces to the ground.
7The Levites—Jeshua, Bani, Sherebiah,
Jamin, Akkub, Shabbethai, Hodiah, Maaseiah, Kelita, Azariah, Jozabad, Hanan
and Pelaiah—instructed the people in the
Law while the people were standing there.
8They read from the Book of the Law of
God, making it clear[a] and giving the
meaning so that the people could understand what was being read.
9Then Nehemiah the governor, Ezra the
priest and scribe, and the Levites who
were instructing the people said to them
all, "This day is sacred to the LORD your
God. Do not mourn or weep." For all the
people had been weeping as they listened
to the words of the Law.
10Nehemiah said, "Go and enjoy choice
food and sweet drinks, and send some to
those who have nothing prepared. This
day is sacred to our Lord. Do not grieve,
for the joy of the LORD is your strength."
11The Levites calmed all the people, saying, "Be still, for this is a sacred day. Do
not grieve."
12Then all the people went away to eat
and drink, to send portions of food and
to celebrate with great joy, because they
now understood the words that had been
made known to them.
13On the second day of the month, the
heads of all the families, along with the
priests and the Levites, gathered around
Ezra the scribe to give attention to the
words of the Law. 14They found written in
the Law, which the LORD had commanded through Moses, that the Israelites were
to live in booths during the feast of the
seventh month 15and that they should
proclaim this word and spread it throughout their towns and in Jerusalem: "Go out
into the hill country and bring back
branches from olive and wild olive trees,
and from myrtles, palms and shade trees,
to make booths"—as it is written.[b]
16So the people went out and brought
back branches and built themselves
booths on their own roofs, in their courtyards, in the courts of the house of God
and in the square by the Water Gate and
the one by the Gate of Ephraim. 17The
whole company that had returned from
exile built booths and lived in them. From
the days of Joshua son of Nun until that
day, the Israelites had not celebrated it
like this. And their joy was very great.
18Day after day, from the first day to the
last, Ezra read from the Book of the Law of
God. They celebrated the feast for seven
days, and on the eighth day, in accordance
with the regulation, there was an assembly.

[a] 8 Or *God, translating it* [b] 15 See Lev. 23:37–40.

PRAYER: PETITION

I CALLED on Your name, O Lord, from the depths of the pit. You have heard my voice: "Do not hide Your ear from my cry for relief, from my cry for help." You drew near when I called on You,

and You said, "Do not fear!" O Lord, You pleaded the cause of my soul; You redeemed my life. (Lamentations 3:55–58)

***PAUSE** here to petition God for growth in your desire to know and please Jesus Christ. Pray for a greater love and commitment to Him, for the grace to practice His presence and for the grace to glorify Him in your life. Offer prayers regarding your activities for this day and any special concerns you may have.*

NT Revelation 8:1–13

The Seventh Seal and the Golden Censer

8 When he opened the seventh seal, there was silence in heaven for about half an hour.
2And I saw the seven angels who stand before God, and to them were given seven trumpets.
3Another angel, who had a golden censer, came and stood at the altar. He was given much incense to offer, with the prayers of all the saints, on the golden altar before the throne.
4The smoke of the incense, together with the prayers of the saints, went up before God from the angel's hand.
5Then the angel took the censer, filled it with fire from the altar, and hurled it on the earth; and there came peals of thunder, rumblings, flashes of lightning and an earthquake.

The Trumpets

6Then the seven angels who had the seven trumpets prepared to sound them.
7The first angel sounded his trumpet, and there came hail and fire mixed with blood, and it was hurled down upon the earth. A third of the earth was burned up, a third of the trees were burned up, and all the green grass was burned up.
8The second angel sounded his trumpet, and something like a huge mountain, all ablaze, was thrown into the sea. A third of the sea turned into blood,
9a third of the living creatures in the sea died, and a third of the ships were destroyed.
10The third angel sounded his trumpet, and a great star, blazing like a torch, fell from the sky on a third of the rivers and on the springs of water—
11the name of the star is Wormwood.[a] A third of the waters turned bitter, and many people died from the waters that had become bitter.
12The fourth angel sounded his trumpet, and a third of the sun was struck, a third of the moon, and a third of the stars, so that a third of them turned dark. A third of the day was without light, and also a third of the night.
13As I watched, I heard an eagle that was flying in midair call out in a loud voice: "Woe! Woe! Woe to the inhabitants of the earth, because of the trumpet blasts about to be sounded by the other three angels!"

[a] *11* That is, Bitterness

PRAYER: THE WORKS OF GOD

LORD Jesus, I thank You for the marvelous promise of Your resurrection when You said, "Destroy this temple, and I will raise it again in three days." But You were speaking of the temple of Your body. After You were raised from the dead, Your disciples remembered that You had said this to them, and they believed the Scripture and the words that You had spoken. (John 2:19, 21–22)

***TAKE** a moment to consider the greatness of God's wonderful works.*

OT **Nehemiah 9:1-38**

YEAR 1 DAY 348

The Israelites Confess Their Sins

9 On the twenty-fourth day of the same
month, the Israelites gathered together, fasting and wearing sackcloth and having dust on their heads. 2 Those of Israelite descent had separated themselves from
all foreigners. They stood in their places
and confessed their sins and the wickedness of their fathers. 3 They stood where
they were and read from the Book of the
Law of the LORD their God for a quarter of
the day, and spent another quarter in confession and in worshiping the LORD their
God. 4 Standing on the stairs were the Levites—Jeshua, Bani, Kadmiel, Shebaniah,
Bunni, Sherebiah, Bani and Kenani—who
called with loud voices to the LORD their
God. 5 And the Levites—Jeshua, Kadmiel,
Bani, Hashabneiah, Sherebiah, Hodiah,
Shebaniah and Pethahiah—said: "Stand
up and praise the LORD your God, who is
from everlasting to everlasting.[a]"

"Blessed be your glorious name,
and may it be exalted above all blessing and praise. 6 You alone are the
LORD. You made the heavens, even
the highest heavens, and all their
starry host, the earth and all that is
on it, the seas and all that is in them.
You give life to everything, and the
multitudes of heaven worship you.

7 "You are the LORD God, who
chose Abram and brought him out of
Ur of the Chaldeans and named him
Abraham. 8 You found his heart faithful to you, and you made a covenant
with him to give to his descendants
the land of the Canaanites, Hittites,
Amorites, Perizzites, Jebusites and
Girgashites. You have kept your
promise because you are righteous.

9 "You saw the suffering of our forefathers in Egypt; you heard their cry
at the Red Sea.[b] 10 You sent miraculous
signs and wonders against Pharaoh,
against all his officials and all the
people of his land, for you knew how
arrogantly the Egyptians treated
them. You made a name for yourself,
which remains to this day. 11 You divided the sea before them, so that
they passed through it on dry ground,
but you hurled their pursuers into the
depths, like a stone into mighty waters. 12 By day you led them with a pillar of cloud, and by night with a pillar of fire to give them light on the
way they were to take.

13 "You came down on Mount Sinai; you spoke to them from heaven.
You gave them regulations and laws
that are just and right, and decrees
and commands that are good. 14 You
made known to them your holy Sabbath and gave them commands, decrees and laws through your servant
Moses. 15 In their hunger you gave
them bread from heaven and in their
thirst you brought them water from
the rock; you told them to go in and
take possession of the land you had
sworn with uplifted hand to give
them.

16 "But they, our forefathers, became arrogant and stiff-necked, and
did not obey your commands. 17 They
refused to listen and failed to remember the miracles you performed
among them. They became stiff-
necked and in their rebellion appointed a leader in order to return to
their slavery. But you are a forgiving
God, gracious and compassionate,
slow to anger and abounding in love.
Therefore you did not desert them,
18 even when they cast for themselves
an image of a calf and said, 'This is
your god, who brought you up out of
Egypt,' or when they committed awful blasphemies.

19 "Because of your great compassion you did not abandon them in
the desert. By day the pillar of cloud
did not cease to guide them on their
path, nor the pillar of fire by night to
shine on the way they were to take.
20 You gave your good Spirit to instruct them. You did not withhold
your manna from their mouths, and
you gave them water for their thirst.
21 For forty years you sustained them
in the desert; they lacked nothing,

[a] 5 Or *God for ever and ever* [b] 9 Hebrew *Yam Suph*; that is, Sea of Reeds

their clothes did not wear out nor did
their feet become swollen.
22 "You gave them kingdoms and
nations, allotting to them even the
remotest frontiers. They took over the
country of Sihon[c] king of Heshbon
and the country of Og king of Bashan. 23 You made their sons as numerous as the stars in the sky, and
you brought them into the land that
you told their fathers to enter and
possess. 24 Their sons went in and
took possession of the land. You subdued before them the Canaanites,
who lived in the land; you handed
the Canaanites over to them, along
with their kings and the peoples of
the land, to deal with them as they
pleased. 25 They captured fortified cities and fertile land; they took possession of houses filled with all kinds
of good things, wells already dug,
vineyards, olive groves and fruit trees
in abundance. They ate to the full
and were well-nourished; they rev-
eled in your great goodness.
26 "But they were disobedient and
rebelled against you; they put your
law behind their backs. They killed
your prophets, who had admonished
them in order to turn them back to
you; they committed awful blasphemies. 27 So you handed them over to
their enemies, who oppressed them.
But when they were oppressed they
cried out to you. From heaven you
heard them, and in your great compassion you gave them deliverers,
who rescued them from the hand of
their enemies.
28 "But as soon as they were at rest,
they again did what was evil in your
sight. Then you abandoned them to
the hand of their enemies so that
they ruled over them. And when they
cried out to you again, you heard
from heaven, and in your compassion you delivered them time after
time.
29 "You warned them to return to
your law, but they became arrogant
and disobeyed your commands. They
sinned against your ordinances, by
which a man will live if he obeys
them. Stubbornly they turned their
backs on you, became stiff-necked
and refused to listen. 30 For many
years you were patient with them. By
your Spirit you admonished them
through your prophets. Yet they paid
no attention, so you handed them
over to the neighboring peoples.
31 But in your great mercy you did not
put an end to them or abandon
them, for you are a gracious and
merciful God.
32 "Now therefore, O our God, the
great, mighty and awesome God,
who keeps his covenant of love, do
not let all this hardship seem trifling
in your eyes—the hardship that has
come upon us, upon our kings and
leaders, upon our priests and prophets, upon our fathers and all your
people, from the days of the kings of
Assyria until today. 33 In all that has
happened to us, you have been just;
you have acted faithfully, while we
did wrong. 34 Our kings, our leaders,
our priests and our fathers did not
follow your law; they did not pay attention to your commands or the
warnings you gave them. 35 Even
while they were in their kingdom, enjoying your great goodness to them
in the spacious and fertile land you
gave them, they did not serve you or
turn from their evil ways.
36 "But see, we are slaves today,
slaves in the land you gave our forefathers so they could eat its fruit and
the other good things it produces.
37 Because of our sins, its abundant
harvest goes to the kings you have
placed over us. They rule over our
bodies and our cattle as they please.
We are in great distress.

The Agreement of the People

38 "In view of all this, we are making a
binding agreement, putting it in writing,
and our leaders, our Levites and our
priests are affixing their seals to it."

[c] *22* One Hebrew manuscript and Septuagint; most Hebrew manuscripts *Sihon, that is, the country of the*

PRAYER: INTERCESSION

WE were all baptized by one Spirit into one body—whether Jews or Greeks, slave or free—and we were all given the one Spirit to drink. (1 Corinthians 12:13)

***TAKE** a few moments to intercede on behalf of your local church, other churches, evangelism and discipleship ministries, educational ministries and any other special concerns you may have.*

NT Revelation 9:1-21

9 The fifth angel sounded his trumpet,
and I saw a star that had fallen from the
sky to the earth. The star was given the key
to the shaft of the Abyss. 2When he opened
the Abyss, smoke rose from it like the
smoke from a gigantic furnace. The sun and
sky were darkened by the smoke from the
Abyss. 3And out of the smoke locusts came
down upon the earth and were given power like that of scorpions of the earth. 4They
were told not to harm the grass of the earth
or any plant or tree, but only those people
who did not have the seal of God on their
foreheads. 5They were not given power to
kill them, but only to torture them for five
months. And the agony they suffered was
like that of the sting of a scorpion when it
strikes a man. 6During those days men will
seek death, but will not find it; they will
long to die, but death will elude them.

7The locusts looked like horses prepared for battle. On their heads they wore
something like crowns of gold, and their
faces resembled human faces. 8Their hair
was like women's hair, and their teeth
were like lions' teeth. 9They had breastplates like breastplates of iron, and the
sound of their wings was like the thun-
dering of many horses and chariots rushing into battle. 10They had tails and stings
like scorpions, and in their tails they had
power to torment people for five months.
11They had as king over them the angel of
the Abyss, whose name in Hebrew is
Abaddon, and in Greek, Apollyon.[a]

12The first woe is past; two other woes
are yet to come.

13The sixth angel sounded his trumpet,
and I heard a voice coming from the
horns[b] of the golden altar that is before
God. 14It said to the sixth angel who had
the trumpet, "Release the four angels who
are bound at the great river Euphrates."
15And the four angels who had been kept
ready for this very hour and day and
month and year were released to kill a
third of mankind. 16The number of the
mounted troops was two hundred million. I heard their number.

17The horses and riders I saw in my vision looked like this: Their breastplates
were fiery red, dark blue, and yellow as sulfur. The heads of the horses resembled the
heads of lions, and out of their mouths
came fire, smoke and sulfur. 18A third of
mankind was killed by the three plagues
of fire, smoke and sulfur that came out of
their mouths. 19The power of the horses
was in their mouths and in their tails; for
their tails were like snakes, having heads
with which they inflict injury.

20The rest of mankind that were not
killed by these plagues still did not repent
of the work of their hands; they did not
stop worshiping demons, and idols of gold,
silver, bronze, stone and wood—idols that
cannot see or hear or walk. 21Nor did they
repent of their murders, their magic arts,
their sexual immorality or their thefts.

[a] 11 *Abaddon* and *Apollyon* mean *Destroyer.*
[b] 13 That is, projections

PRAYER: MY RELATIONSHIP TO GOD

IF we drink ordinary water, we will be thirsty again; but if we drink the water You give, O Jesus, we will never thirst. Indeed, the water You give becomes in us a spring of water welling up to eternal life. (John 4:13–14) . . .

I believe the promise of God, that because I hear Your word, Jesus, and believe Him who sent You, I have eternal life and will not come into judgment—I have passed over from death to life. (John 5:24)

***PAUSE** to thank God for the relationship that you enjoy with Him in Jesus Christ.*

YEAR 1 DAY 349

OT Nehemiah 10:1–39

10 Those who sealed it were:

Nehemiah the governor, the son of Hacaliah.

Zedekiah, [2]Seraiah, Azariah, Jeremiah,
[3]Pashhur, Amariah, Malkijah,
[4]Hattush, Shebaniah, Malluch,
[5]Harim, Meremoth, Obadiah,
[6]Daniel, Ginnethon, Baruch,
[7]Meshullam, Abijah, Mijamin,
[8]Maaziah, Bilgai and Shemaiah.
These were the priests.

[9]The Levites:

Jeshua son of Azaniah, Binnui of the sons of Henadad, Kadmiel,
[10]and their associates: Shebaniah,
Hodiah, Kelita, Pelaiah, Hanan,
[11]Mica, Rehob, Hashabiah,
[12]Zaccur, Sherebiah, Shebaniah,
[13]Hodiah, Bani and Beninu.

[14]The leaders of the people:

Parosh, Pahath-Moab, Elam, Zattu, Bani,
[15]Bunni, Azgad, Bebai,
[16]Adonijah, Bigvai, Adin,
[17]Ater, Hezekiah, Azzur,
[18]Hodiah, Hashum, Bezai,
[19]Hariph, Anathoth, Nebai,
[20]Magpiash, Meshullam, Hezir,
[21]Meshezabel, Zadok, Jaddua,
[22]Pelatiah, Hanan, Anaiah,
[23]Hoshea, Hananiah, Hasshub,
[24]Hallohesh, Pilha, Shobek,
[25]Rehum, Hashabnah, Maaseiah,
[26]Ahiah, Hanan, Anan,
[27]Malluch, Harim and Baanah.

[28]"The rest of the people—priests,
Levites, gatekeepers, singers, temple
servants and all who separated themselves from the neighboring peoples
for the sake of the Law of God, together with their wives and all their
sons and daughters who are able to
understand— [29]all these now join
their brothers the nobles, and bind
themselves with a curse and an oath
to follow the Law of God given
through Moses the servant of God
and to obey carefully all the commands, regulations and decrees of
the LORD our Lord.

[30]"We promise not to give our
daughters in marriage to the peoples
around us or take their daughters for
our sons.

[31]"When the neighboring peoples
bring merchandise or grain to sell on
the Sabbath, we will not buy from
them on the Sabbath or on any holy
day. Every seventh year we will forgo
working the land and will cancel all
debts.

[32]"We assume the responsibility for
carrying out the commands to give a
third of a shekel[a] each year for the
service of the house of our God: [33]for
the bread set out on the table; for the
regular grain offerings and burnt offerings; for the offerings on the Sabbaths, New Moon festivals and appointed feasts; for the holy offerings;
for sin offerings to make atonement
for Israel; and for all the duties of the
house of our God.

[34]"We—the priests, the Levites and
the people—have cast lots to determine when each of our families is to
bring to the house of our God at set
times each year a contribution of
wood to burn on the altar of the LORD
our God, as it is written in the Law.

[35]"We also assume responsibility
for bringing to the house of the LORD

[a] 32 That is, about 1/8 ounce (about 4 grams)

each year the firstfruits of our crops and of every fruit tree.

[36]"As it is also written in the Law, we will bring the firstborn of our sons and of our cattle, of our herds and of our flocks to the house of our God, to the priests ministering there.

[37]"Moreover, we will bring to the storerooms of the house of our God, to the priests, the first of our ground meal, of our ⌊grain⌋ offerings, of the fruit of all our trees and of our new wine and oil. And we will bring a tithe of our crops to the Levites, for it is the Levites who collect the tithes in all the towns where we work. [38]A priest descended from Aaron is to accompany the Levites when they receive the tithes, and the Levites are to bring a tenth of the tithes up to the house of our God, to the storerooms of the treasury. [39]The people of Israel, including the Levites, are to bring their contributions of grain, new wine and oil to the storerooms where the articles for the sanctuary are kept and where the ministering priests, the gatekeepers and the singers stay.

"We will not neglect the house of our God."

PRAYER: AFFIRMATION

TO fear You, O Lord, is the beginning of knowledge, but fools despise wisdom and discipline. (Proverbs 1:7) . . . To fear You, O Lord, is a fountain of life, turning one away from the snares of death. (Proverbs 14:27)

***PAUSE** to reflect on these Biblical affirmations.*

NT Revelation 10:1-11

The Angel and the Little Scroll

10 Then I saw another mighty angel coming down from heaven. He was robed in a cloud, with a rainbow above his head; his face was like the sun, and his legs were like fiery pillars. [2]He was holding a little scroll, which lay open in his hand. He planted his right foot on the sea and his left foot on the land, [3]and he gave a loud shout like the roar of a lion. When he shouted, the voices of the seven thunders spoke. [4]And when the seven thunders spoke, I was about to write; but I heard a voice from heaven say, "Seal up what the seven thunders have said and do not write it down."

[5]Then the angel I had seen standing on the sea and on the land raised his right hand to heaven. [6]And he swore by him who lives for ever and ever, who created the heavens and all that is in them, the earth and all that is in it, and the sea and all that is in it, and said, "There will be no more delay! [7]But in the days when the seventh angel is about to sound his trumpet, the mystery of God will be accomplished, just as he announced to his servants the prophets."

[8]Then the voice that I had heard from heaven spoke to me once more: "Go, take the scroll that lies open in the hand of the angel who is standing on the sea and on the land."

[9]So I went to the angel and asked him to give me the little scroll. He said to me, "Take it and eat it. It will turn your stomach sour, but in your mouth it will be as sweet as honey." [10]I took the little scroll from the angel's hand and ate it. It tasted as sweet as honey in my mouth, but when I had eaten it, my stomach turned sour. [11]Then I was told, "You must prophesy again about many peoples, nations, languages and kings."

PRAYER: THE CHARACTER I WANT TO CULTIVATE

ESTABLISH our hearts as blameless and holy in Your presence, O God and Father, at the coming of our Lord Jesus with all His saints. (1 Thessalonians 3:13) . . . I desire to be diligent so that I can have full

assurance of hope to the end. I do not want to become sluggish but to imitate those who through faith and patience inherit what has been promised. (Hebrews 6:11–12)

***TAKE** a moment to ask the Lord for the grace to grow in godly character.*

OT **Psalm 69** YEAR 1 DAY 350

Psalm 69

For the director of music. To ⌊the tune of⌋ "Lilies." Of David.

1 Save me, O God,
for the waters have come up to my neck.
2 I sink in the miry depths,
where there is no foothold.
I have come into the deep waters;
the floods engulf me.
3 I am worn out calling for help;
my throat is parched.
My eyes fail,
looking for my God.
4 Those who hate me without reason
outnumber the hairs of my head;
many are my enemies without cause,
those who seek to destroy me.
I am forced to restore
what I did not steal.

5 You know my folly, O God;
my guilt is not hidden from you.

6 May those who hope in you
not be disgraced because of me,
O Lord, the LORD Almighty;
may those who seek you
not be put to shame because of me,
O God of Israel.
7 For I endure scorn for your sake,
and shame covers my face.
8 I am a stranger to my brothers,
an alien to my own mother's sons;
9 for zeal for your house consumes me,
and the insults of those who insult you fall on me.
10 When I weep and fast,
I must endure scorn;
11 when I put on sackcloth,
people make sport of me.
12 Those who sit at the gate mock me,
and I am the song of the drunkards.

13 But I pray to you, O LORD,
in the time of your favor;
in your great love, O God,
answer me with your sure salvation.
14 Rescue me from the mire,
do not let me sink;
deliver me from those who hate me,
from the deep waters.
15 Do not let the floodwaters engulf me
or the depths swallow me up
or the pit close its mouth over me.
16 Answer me, O LORD, out of the goodness of your love;
in your great mercy turn to me.
17 Do not hide your face from your servant;
answer me quickly, for I am in trouble.
18 Come near and rescue me;
redeem me because of my foes.

19 You know how I am scorned,
disgraced and shamed;
all my enemies are before you.
20 Scorn has broken my heart
and has left me helpless;
I looked for sympathy, but there was none,
for comforters, but I found none.
21 They put gall in my food
and gave me vinegar for my thirst.

22 May the table set before them become a snare;
may it become retribution and[a] a trap.
23 May their eyes be darkened so they cannot see,
and their backs be bent forever.
24 Pour out your wrath on them;
let your fierce anger overtake them.
25 May their place be deserted;
let there be no one to dwell in their tents.
26 For they persecute those you wound
and talk about the pain of those you hurt.

[a] 22 Or *snare / and their fellowship become*

[27]Charge them with crime upon crime;
do not let them share in your salvation.
[28]May they be blotted out of the book of life
and not be listed with the righteous.

[29]I am in pain and distress;
may your salvation, O God, protect me.

[30]I will praise God's name in song
and glorify him with thanksgiving.
[31]This will please the LORD more than an ox,
more than a bull with its horns and hoofs.
[32]The poor will see and be glad—
you who seek God, may your hearts live!
[33]The LORD hears the needy
and does not despise his captive people.

[34]Let heaven and earth praise him,
the seas and all that move in them,
[35]for God will save Zion
and rebuild the cities of Judah.
Then people will settle there and possess it;
[36]the children of his servants will inherit it,
and those who love his name will dwell there.

PRAYER: THANKSGIVING

***SURELY** the righteous will give thanks to Your name; the upright will dwell in Your presence. (Psalm 140:13) . . . O Lord, You are near to all who call upon You, to all who call upon You in truth. You fulfill the desire of those who fear You; You hear their cry and save them. You preserve all who love You, but all the wicked You will destroy. (Psalm 145:18–20)*

***PAUSE** to offer your own expressions of thanksgiving.*

NT Revelation 11:1-14

The Two Witnesses

11 I was given a reed like a measuring rod
and was told, "Go and measure the temple of God and the altar, and count the worshipers there. [2]But exclude the outer court;
do not measure it, because it has been giv-
en to the Gentiles. They will trample on the
holy city for 42 months. [3]And I will give
power to my two witnesses, and they will
prophesy for 1,260 days, clothed in sackcloth." [4]These are the two olive trees and the
two lampstands that stand before the Lord
of the earth. [5]If anyone tries to harm them,
fire comes from their mouths and devours
their enemies. This is how anyone who
wants to harm them must die. [6]These men
have power to shut up the sky so that it will
not rain during the time they are prophesying; and they have power to turn the waters
into blood and to strike the earth with every
kind of plague as often as they want.
[7]Now when they have finished their testimony, the beast that comes up from the
Abyss will attack them, and overpower
and kill them. [8]Their bodies will lie in the
street of the great city, which is figuratively called Sodom and Egypt, where also
their Lord was crucified. [9]For three and a
half days men from every people, tribe,
language and nation will gaze on their
bodies and refuse them burial. [10]The inhabitants of the earth will gloat over them
and will celebrate by sending each other
gifts, because these two prophets had tormented those who live on the earth.
[11]But after the three and a half days a
breath of life from God entered them, and
they stood on their feet, and terror struck
those who saw them. [12]Then they heard a
loud voice from heaven saying to them,
"Come up here." And they went up to
heaven in a cloud, while their enemies
looked on.
[13]At that very hour there was a severe
earthquake and a tenth of the city collapsed. Seven thousand people were
killed in the earthquake, and the survivors
were terrified and gave glory to the God
of heaven.
[14]The second woe has passed; the third
woe is coming soon.

PRAYER: MY RELATIONSHIP TO OTHERS

IF I am righteous, I will be cautious about the friends I choose, but the ways of the wicked will lead me astray. (Proverbs 12:26) . . . I will not give cause for offense in anything, so that my ministry will not be discredited. (2 Corinthians 6:3)

***PAUSE** to review your relationships with others and to commit them to the Lord.*

YEAR 1
DAY 351

OT Nehemiah 11:1-36

The New Residents of Jerusalem

11 Now the leaders of the people settled in
Jerusalem, and the rest of the people
cast lots to bring one out of every ten to
live in Jerusalem, the holy city, while the
remaining nine were to stay in their own
towns. 2The people commended all the
men who volunteered to live in Jerusalem.
3These are the provincial leaders who
settled in Jerusalem (now some Israelites,
priests, Levites, temple servants and descendants of Solomon's servants lived in
the towns of Judah, each on his own
property in the various towns, 4while other people from both Judah and Benjamin
lived in Jerusalem):

From the descendants of Judah:

Athaiah son of Uzziah, the son of
Zechariah, the son of Amariah, the
son of Shephatiah, the son of Mahalalel, a descendant of Perez; 5and Maaseiah son of Baruch, the son of Col-
Hozeh, the son of Hazaiah, the son
of Adaiah, the son of Joiarib, the son
of Zechariah, a descendant of Shelah.
6The descendants of Perez who lived
in Jerusalem totaled 468 able men.

7From the descendants of Benjamin:

Sallu son of Meshullam, the son of
Joed, the son of Pedaiah, the son of
Kolaiah, the son of Maaseiah, the son
of Ithiel, the son of Jeshaiah, 8and his
followers, Gabbai and Sallai—928
men. 9Joel son of Zicri was their chief
officer, and Judah son of Hassenuah
was over the Second District of the city.

10From the priests:

Jedaiah; the son of Joiarib; Jakin; 11Se-
raiah son of Hilkiah, the son of Meshullam, the son of Zadok, the son of
Meraioth, the son of Ahitub, supervi-
sor in the house of God, 12and their
associates, who carried on work for
the temple—822 men; Adaiah son of
Jeroham, the son of Pelaliah, the son
of Amzi, the son of Zechariah, the
son of Pashhur, the son of Malkijah,
13and his associates, who were heads
of families—242 men; Amashsai son
of Azarel, the son of Ahzai, the son of
Meshillemoth, the son of Immer,
14and his[a] associates, who were able
men—128. Their chief officer was
Zabdiel son of Haggedolim.

15From the Levites:

Shemaiah son of Hasshub, the son of
Azrikam, the son of Hashabiah, the
son of Bunni; 16Shabbethai and Jozabad, two of the heads of the Levites,
who had charge of the outside work
of the house of God; 17Mattaniah son
of Mica, the son of Zabdi, the son of
Asaph, the director who led in
thanksgiving and prayer; Bakbukiah,
second among his associates; and
Abda son of Shammua, the son of
Galal, the son of Jeduthun. 18The Levites in the holy city totaled 284.

19The gatekeepers:

Akkub, Talmon and their associates,
who kept watch at the gates—172
men.

20The rest of the Israelites, with the
priests and Levites, were in all the towns
of Judah, each on his ancestral property.

[a] 14 Most Septuagint manuscripts; Hebrew *their*

21 The temple servants lived on the hill
of Ophel, and Ziha and Gishpa were in
charge of them.
22 The chief officer of the Levites in Jerusalem was Uzzi son of Bani, the son of
Hashabiah, the son of Mattaniah, the son
of Mica. Uzzi was one of Asaph's descendants, who were the singers responsible
for the service of the house of God. 23 The
singers were under the king's orders,
which regulated their daily activity.
24 Pethahiah son of Meshezabel, one of
the descendants of Zerah son of Judah,
was the king's agent in all affairs relating
to the people.
25 As for the villages with their fields,
some of the people of Judah lived in Kiriath Arba and its surrounding settlements, in Dibon and its settlements, in
Jekabzeel and its villages, 26 in Jeshua, in
Moladah, in Beth Pelet, 27 in Hazar Shual,
in Beersheba and its settlements, 28 in Ziklag, in Meconah and its settlements, 29 in
En Rimmon, in Zorah, in Jarmuth, 30 Zanoah, Adullam and their villages, in Lachish and its fields, and in Azekah and its
settlements. So they were living all the
way from Beersheba to the Valley of Hinnom.
31 The descendants of the Benjamites
from Geba lived in Micmash, Aija, Bethel
and its settlements, 32 in Anathoth, Nob
and Ananiah, 33 in Hazor, Ramah and Gittaim, 34 in Hadid, Zeboim and Neballat,
35 in Lod and Ono, and in the Valley of the
Craftsmen.
36 Some of the divisions of the Levites of
Judah settled in Benjamin.

PRAYER: ADORATION

I WILL regard You as holy, Lord of hosts; You shall be my fear, and You shall be my dread. (Isaiah 8:13) . . . You are the stability of our times, a wealth of salvation, wisdom and knowledge. Fearing You, O Lord, is the key to this treasure. (Isaiah 33:6)

***PAUSE** to express your thoughts of praise and worship.*

NT Revelation 11:15–19

The Seventh Trumpet

15 The seventh angel sounded his trumpet, and there were loud voices in heaven,
which said:

"The kingdom of the world has
become the kingdom of our
Lord and of his Christ,
and he will reign for ever and ever."

16 And the twenty-four elders, who were
seated on their thrones before God, fell on
their faces and worshiped God, 17 saying:

"We give thanks to you, Lord God
Almighty,
the One who is and who was,
because you have taken your great
power
and have begun to reign.
18 The nations were angry;
and your wrath has come.
The time has come for judging the
dead,
and for rewarding your servants the
prophets
and your saints and those who
reverence your name,
both small and great—
and for destroying those who destroy
the earth."

19 Then God's temple in heaven was
opened, and within his temple was seen the
ark of his covenant. And there came flashes
of lightning, rumblings, peals of thunder,
an earthquake and a great hailstorm.

PRAYER: THE ATTRIBUTES OF GOD

TO You, Lord my God, belong the heavens, even the highest heavens, the earth and everything in it. (Deuteronomy 10:14) . . . There is none like You, O Lord; You are great, and Your name is mighty in power.

Who should not revere You, O King of the nations? It is Your rightful due. For among all the wise of the nations and in all their kingdoms, there is no one like You. (Jeremiah 10:6–7)

***PAUSE** to reflect on these affirmations about the person, powers and perfection of God.*

YEAR 1 DAY 352

OT Nehemiah 12:1-47

Priests and Levites

12 These were the priests and Levites who
returned with Zerubbabel son of
Shealtiel and with Jeshua:
Seraiah, Jeremiah, Ezra,
2 Amariah, Malluch, Hattush,
3 Shecaniah, Rehum, Meremoth,
4 Iddo, Ginnethon,[a] Abijah,
5 Mijamin,[b] Moadiah, Bilgah,
6 Shemaiah, Joiarib, Jedaiah,
7 Sallu, Amok, Hilkiah and Jedaiah.
These were the leaders of the priests and
their associates in the days of Jeshua.
8 The Levites were Jeshua, Binnui, Kadmiel, Sherebiah, Judah, and also Mattaniah, who, together with his associates, was
in charge of the songs of thanksgiving.
9 Bakbukiah and Unni, their associates,
stood opposite them in the services.
10 Jeshua was the father of Joiakim, Joiakim the father of Eliashib, Eliashib the
father of Joiada, 11 Joiada the father of Jonathan, and Jonathan the father of Jaddua.
12 In the days of Joiakim, these were the
heads of the priestly families:
of Seraiah's family, Meraiah;
of Jeremiah's, Hananiah;
13 of Ezra's, Meshullam;
of Amariah's, Jehohanan;
14 of Malluch's, Jonathan;
of Shecaniah's,[c] Joseph;
15 of Harim's, Adna;
of Meremoth's,[d] Helkai;
16 of Iddo's, Zechariah;
of Ginnethon's, Meshullam;
17 of Abijah's, Zicri;
of Miniamin's and of Moadiah's, Piltai;
18 of Bilgah's, Shammua;
of Shemaiah's, Jehonathan;
19 of Joiarib's, Mattenai;
of Jedaiah's, Uzzi;
20 of Sallu's, Kallai;
of Amok's, Eber;
21 of Hilkiah's, Hashabiah;
of Jedaiah's, Nethanel.
22 The family heads of the Levites in the
days of Eliashib, Joiada, Johanan and Jaddua, as well as those of the priests, were
recorded in the reign of Darius the Persian. 23 The family heads among the descendants of Levi up to the time of Johanan son of Eliashib were recorded in the
book of the annals. 24 And the leaders of
the Levites were Hashabiah, Sherebiah,
Jeshua son of Kadmiel, and their associates, who stood opposite them to give
praise and thanksgiving, one section responding to the other, as prescribed by
David the man of God.
25 Mattaniah, Bakbukiah, Obadiah, Meshullam, Talmon and Akkub were gatekeepers who guarded the storerooms at
the gates. 26 They served in the days of Joiakim son of Jeshua, the son of Jozadak,
and in the days of Nehemiah the governor and of Ezra the priest and scribe.

Dedication of the Wall of Jerusalem

27 At the dedication of the wall of Jerusalem, the Levites were sought out from
where they lived and were brought to
Jerusalem to celebrate joyfully the dedication with songs of thanksgiving and
with the music of cymbals, harps and
lyres. 28 The singers also were brought together from the region around Jerusalem—from the villages of the Netophathites, 29 from Beth Gilgal, and from the
area of Geba and Azmaveth, for the
singers had built villages for themselves
around Jerusalem. 30 When the priests and

[a] *4* Many Hebrew manuscripts and Vulgate (see also Neh. 12:16); most Hebrew manuscripts *Ginnethoi* [b] *5* A variant of *Miniamin* [c] *14* Very many Hebrew manuscripts, some Septuagint manuscripts and Syriac (see also Neh. 12:3); most Hebrew manuscripts *Shebaniah's* [d] *15* Some Septuagint manuscripts (see also Neh. 12:3); Hebrew *Meraioth's*

Levites had purified themselves ceremonially, they purified the people, the gates and the wall.

[31]I had the leaders of Judah go up on top[e] of the wall. I also assigned two large choirs to give thanks. One was to proceed on top[f] of the wall to the right, toward the Dung Gate. [32]Hoshaiah and half the leaders of Judah followed them, [33]along with Azariah, Ezra, Meshullam, [34]Judah, Benjamin, Shemaiah, Jeremiah, [35]as well as some priests with trumpets, and also Zechariah son of Jonathan, the son of Shemaiah, the son of Mattaniah, the son of Micaiah, the son of Zaccur, the son of Asaph, [36]and his associates—Shemaiah, Azarel, Milalai, Gilalai, Maai, Nethanel, Judah and Hanani—with musical instruments ⌊prescribed by⌋ David the man of God. Ezra the scribe led the procession. [37]At the Fountain Gate they continued directly up the steps of the City of David on the ascent to the wall and passed above the house of David to the Water Gate on the east.

[38]The second choir proceeded in the opposite direction. I followed them on top[g] of the wall, together with half the people—past the Tower of the Ovens to the Broad Wall, [39]over the Gate of Ephraim, the Jeshanah[h] Gate, the Fish Gate, the Tower of Hananel and the Tower of the Hundred, as far as the Sheep Gate. At the Gate of the Guard they stopped.

[40]The two choirs that gave thanks then took their places in the house of God; so did I, together with half the officials, [41]as well as the priests—Eliakim, Maaseiah, Miniamin, Micaiah, Elioenai, Zechariah and Hananiah with their trumpets— [42]and also Maaseiah, Shemaiah, Eleazar, Uzzi, Jehohanan, Malkijah, Elam and Ezer. The choirs sang under the direction of Jezrahiah. [43]And on that day they offered great sacrifices, rejoicing because God had given them great joy. The women and children also rejoiced. The sound of rejoicing in Jerusalem could be heard far away.

[44]At that time men were appointed to be in charge of the storerooms for the contributions, firstfruits and tithes. From the fields around the towns they were to bring into the storerooms the portions required by the Law for the priests and the Levites, for Judah was pleased with the ministering priests and Levites. [45]They performed the service of their God and the service of purification, as did also the singers and gatekeepers, according to the commands of David and his son Solomon. [46]For long ago, in the days of David and Asaph, there had been directors for the singers and for the songs of praise and thanksgiving to God. [47]So in the days of Zerubbabel and of Nehemiah, all Israel contributed the daily portions for the singers and gatekeepers. They also set aside the portion for the other Levites, and the Levites set aside the portion for the descendants of Aaron.

[e] 31 Or *go alongside* [f] 31 Or *proceed alongside* [g] 38 Or *them alongside* [h] 39 Or *Old*

PRAYER: CONFESSION

I WILL sing praises to You, O Lord, and give thanks at the remembrance of Your holy name. For Your anger lasts only a moment, but Your favor is for a lifetime; weeping may endure for a night, but joy comes in the morning. (Psalm 30:4–5)

***ASK** the Spirit to search your heart and reveal any areas of unconfessed sin. Acknowledge these to the Lord and thank Him for His forgiveness.*

NT Revelation 12:1–13:1a

The Woman and the Dragon

12 A great and wondrous sign appeared in heaven: a woman clothed with the sun, with the moon under her feet and a crown of twelve stars on her head. [2]She was pregnant and cried out in pain as she was about to give birth. [3]Then another sign appeared in heaven: an enormous red dragon with seven heads and ten horns and seven crowns on his heads. [4]His tail swept a third of the stars out of the sky and flung them to the earth. The dragon stood in front of the woman who was about to give birth, so that he might devour her child the moment it was born. [5]She gave birth to a son, a male child, who will rule all the nations with an iron scepter. And her child was snatched up to God and to his throne. [6]The woman fled into the desert to a place prepared for her by God, where she might be taken care of for 1,260 days.

[7]And there was war in heaven. Michael and his angels fought against the dragon, and the dragon and his angels fought back. [8]But he was not strong enough, and they lost their place in heaven. [9]The great dragon was hurled down—that ancient serpent called the devil, or Satan, who leads the whole world astray. He was hurled to the earth, and his angels with him.

[10]Then I heard a loud voice in heaven say:

"Now have come the salvation and
the power and the kingdom of our God,
and the authority of his Christ.
For the accuser of our brothers,
who accuses them before our God day and night,
has been hurled down.
[11]They overcame him
by the blood of the Lamb
and by the word of their testimony;
they did not love their lives so much
as to shrink from death.
[12]Therefore rejoice, you heavens
and you who dwell in them!
But woe to the earth and the sea,
because the devil has gone down to you!
He is filled with fury,
because he knows that his time is short."

[13]When the dragon saw that he had been hurled to the earth, he pursued the woman who had given birth to the male child. [14]The woman was given the two wings of a great eagle, so that she might fly to the place prepared for her in the desert, where she would be taken care of for a time, times and half a time, out of the serpent's reach. [15]Then from his mouth the serpent spewed water like a river, to overtake the woman and sweep her away with the torrent. [16]But the earth helped the woman by opening its mouth and swallowing the river that the dragon had spewed out of his mouth. [17]Then the dragon was enraged at the woman and went off to make war against the rest of her offspring—those who obey God's commandments and hold to the testimony of Jesus. **13** [1]And the dragon[a] stood on the shore of the sea.

[a] *1* Some late manuscripts *And I*

PRAYER: THE WORKS OF GOD

WE rejoice, O Lord, that there will no longer be any curse. Your throne, O God, and the throne of the Lamb will be in the new Jerusalem, and Your servants will serve You. They will see Your face, and Your name will be on their foreheads. And there will be no night there; they will not need the light of a lamp or the light of the sun, for You, Lord God, will give them light. And they shall reign for ever and ever. (Revelation 22:3–5)

TAKE *a moment to consider the greatness of God's wonderful works.*

YEAR 1 DAY 353

OT Nehemiah 13:1–31

Nehemiah's Final Reforms

13 On that day the Book of Moses was read aloud in the hearing of the people and there it was found written that no Ammonite or Moabite should ever be admitted into the assembly of God, [2]because they had not met the Israelites with food and water but had hired Balaam to call a curse down on them. (Our God, however, turned the curse into a blessing.) [3]When

the people heard this law, they excluded
from Israel all who were of foreign descent.
4Before this, Eliashib the priest had been
put in charge of the storerooms of the
house of our God. He was closely associated with Tobiah, 5and he had provided
him with a large room formerly used to
store the grain offerings and incense and
temple articles, and also the tithes of grain,
new wine and oil prescribed for the Levites, singers and gatekeepers, as well as
the contributions for the priests.
6But while all this was going on, I was
not in Jerusalem, for in the thirty-second
year of Artaxerxes king of Babylon I had
returned to the king. Some time later I
asked his permission 7and came back to
Jerusalem. Here I learned about the evil
thing Eliashib had done in providing Tobiah a room in the courts of the house of
God. 8I was greatly displeased and threw
all Tobiah's household goods out of the
room. 9I gave orders to purify the rooms,
and then I put back into them the equipment of the house of God, with the grain
offerings and the incense.
10I also learned that the portions assigned to the Levites had not been given to
them, and that all the Levites and singers
responsible for the service had gone back
to their own fields. 11So I rebuked the officials and asked them, "Why is the house of
God neglected?" Then I called them together and stationed them at their posts.
12All Judah brought the tithes of grain,
new wine and oil into the storerooms. 13I
put Shelemiah the priest, Zadok the
scribe, and a Levite named Pedaiah in
charge of the storerooms and made Hanan son of Zaccur, the son of Mattaniah,
their assistant, because these men were
considered trustworthy. They were made
responsible for distributing the supplies
to their brothers.

14Remember me for this, O my God,
and do not blot out what I have so faithfully done for the house of my God and
its services.

15In those days I saw men in Judah
treading winepresses on the Sabbath and
bringing in grain and loading it on donkeys, together with wine, grapes, figs and
all other kinds of loads. And they were
bringing all this into Jerusalem on the
Sabbath. Therefore I warned them against
selling food on that day. 16Men from Tyre
who lived in Jerusalem were bringing in
fish and all kinds of merchandise and selling them in Jerusalem on the Sabbath to
the people of Judah. 17I rebuked the nobles of Judah and said to them, "What is
this wicked thing you are doing—desecrating the Sabbath day? 18Didn't your
forefathers do the same things, so that our
God brought all this calamity upon us
and upon this city? Now you are stirring
up more wrath against Israel by desecrating the Sabbath."
19When evening shadows fell on the
gates of Jerusalem before the Sabbath, I ordered the doors to be shut and not opened
until the Sabbath was over. I stationed
some of my own men at the gates so that
no load could be brought in on the Sabbath day. 20Once or twice the merchants
and sellers of all kinds of goods spent the
night outside Jerusalem. 21But I warned
them and said, "Why do you spend the
night by the wall? If you do this again, I
will lay hands on you." From that time on
they no longer came on the Sabbath.
22Then I commanded the Levites to purify
themselves and go and guard the gates in
order to keep the Sabbath day holy.

Remember me for this also, O my God,
and show mercy to me according to your
great love.

23Moreover, in those days I saw men of
Judah who had married women from Ashdod, Ammon and Moab. 24Half of their
children spoke the language of Ashdod or
the language of one of the other peoples,
and did not know how to speak the language of Judah. 25I rebuked them and
called curses down on them. I beat some
of the men and pulled out their hair. I
made them take an oath in God's name
and said: "You are not to give your daughters in marriage to their sons, nor are you
to take their daughters in marriage for your
sons or for yourselves. 26Was it not because
of marriages like these that Solomon king
of Israel sinned? Among the many nations
there was no king like him. He was loved
by his God, and God made him king over
all Israel, but even he was led into sin by
foreign women. 27Must we hear now that
you too are doing all this terrible wickedness and are being unfaithful to our God
by marrying foreign women?"
28One of the sons of Joiada son of Eliashib the high priest was son-in-law to San-

ballat the Horonite. And I drove him away
from me.

29 Remember them, O my God, because
they defiled the priestly office and the covenant of the priesthood and of the Levites.
30 So I purified the priests and the Levites of everything foreign, and assigned
them duties, each to his own task. 31 I
also made provision for contributions of
wood at designated times, and for the
firstfruits.

Remember me with favor, O my God.

PRAYER: RENEWAL

MAY I be righteous before You, O God, walking blamelessly in all Your commandments and ordinances. (Luke 1:6) . . . May I love my enemies, do good to those who hate me, bless those who curse me, and pray for those who mistreat me. May I do to others as I would have them do to me. (Luke 6:27–28, 31)

PAUSE *to add your own prayers for personal renewal.*

NT Revelation 13:1b–10

The Beast out of the Sea

And I saw a beast coming out of the sea.
He had ten horns and seven heads, with
ten crowns on his horns, and on each head
a blasphemous name. 2 The beast I saw resembled a leopard, but had feet like those
of a bear and a mouth like that of a lion.
The dragon gave the beast his power and
his throne and great authority. 3 One of the
heads of the beast seemed to have had a fatal wound, but the fatal wound had been
healed. The whole world was astonished
and followed the beast. 4 Men worshiped
the dragon because he had given authority to the beast, and they also worshiped the
beast and asked, "Who is like the beast?
Who can make war against him?"

5 The beast was given a mouth to utter
proud words and blasphemies and to exercise his authority for forty-two months.
6 He opened his mouth to blaspheme God,
and to slander his name and his dwelling
place and those who live in heaven. 7 He
was given power to make war against the
saints and to conquer them. And he was
given authority over every tribe, people,
language and nation. 8 All inhabitants of
the earth will worship the beast—all
whose names have not been written in the
book of life belonging to the Lamb that
was slain from the creation of the world.[a]
9 He who has an ear, let him hear.

10 If anyone is to go into captivity,
into captivity he will go.
If anyone is to be killed[b] with the
sword,
with the sword he will be killed.

This calls for patient endurance and faithfulness on the part of the saints.

[a] 8 Or *written from the creation of the world in the book of life belonging to the Lamb that was slain*
[b] 10 Some manuscripts *anyone kills*

PRAYER: MY RELATIONSHIP TO GOD

I LIFT up my eyes to the hills—where does my help come from? My help comes from You, O Lord, who made heaven and earth. You will not allow my foot to slip; You who watch over me will not slumber. You are my keeper; You, Lord, are my shade at my right hand. The sun will not harm me by day, nor the moon by night. You will keep me from all evil; You will preserve my soul. You will watch over my coming and going from this time forth and forever. (Psalm 121:1–3, 5–8)

PAUSE *to thank God for the relationship that you enjoy with Him in Jesus Christ.*

OT Esther 1:1-22

YEAR 1 DAY 354

Queen Vashti Deposed

1 This is what happened during the time
of Xerxes,[a] the Xerxes who ruled over
127 provinces stretching from India to
Cush[b]: [2]At that time King Xerxes reigned
from his royal throne in the citadel of
Susa, [3]and in the third year of his reign he
gave a banquet for all his nobles and officials. The military leaders of Persia and
Media, the princes, and the nobles of the
provinces were present.
[4]For a full 180 days he displayed the
vast wealth of his kingdom and the splendor and glory of his majesty. [5]When these
days were over, the king gave a banquet,
lasting seven days, in the enclosed garden
of the king's palace, for all the people
from the least to the greatest, who were in
the citadel of Susa. [6]The garden had hang-
ings of white and blue linen, fastened
with cords of white linen and purple material to silver rings on marble pillars.
There were couches of gold and silver on
a mosaic pavement of porphyry, marble,
mother-of-pearl and other costly stones.
[7]Wine was served in goblets of gold, each
one different from the other, and the royal wine was abundant, in keeping with the
king's liberality. [8]By the king's command
each guest was allowed to drink in his
own way, for the king instructed all the
wine stewards to serve each man what he
wished.
[9]Queen Vashti also gave a banquet for
the women in the royal palace of King
Xerxes.
[10]On the seventh day, when King Xerxes
was in high spirits from wine, he commanded the seven eunuchs who served
him—Mehuman, Biztha, Harbona, Big-
tha, Abagtha, Zethar and Carcas— [11]to
bring before him Queen Vashti, wearing
her royal crown, in order to display her
beauty to the people and nobles, for she
was lovely to look at. [12]But when the attendants delivered the king's command,
Queen Vashti refused to come. Then the
king became furious and burned with
anger.
[13]Since it was customary for the king to
consult experts in matters of law and justice, he spoke with the wise men who understood the times [14]and were closest to
the king—Carshena, Shethar, Admatha,
Tarshish, Meres, Marsena and Memucan,
the seven nobles of Persia and Media who
had special access to the king and were
highest in the kingdom.
[15]"According to law, what must be done
to Queen Vashti?" he asked. "She has not
obeyed the command of King Xerxes that
the eunuchs have taken to her."
[16]Then Memucan replied in the presence of the king and the nobles, "Queen
Vashti has done wrong, not only against
the king but also against all the nobles
and the peoples of all the provinces of
King Xerxes. [17]For the queen's conduct
will become known to all the women, and
so they will despise their husbands and
say, 'King Xerxes commanded Queen
Vashti to be brought before him, but she
would not come.' [18]This very day the Persian and Median women of the nobility
who have heard about the queen's conduct will respond to all the king's nobles
in the same way. There will be no end of
disrespect and discord.
[19]"Therefore, if it pleases the king, let
him issue a royal decree and let it be written in the laws of Persia and Media, which
cannot be repealed, that Vashti is never
again to enter the presence of King Xerxes.
Also let the king give her royal position to
someone else who is better than she.
[20]Then when the king's edict is proclaimed throughout all his vast realm, all
the women will respect their husbands,
from the least to the greatest."
[21]The king and his nobles were pleased
with this advice, so the king did as Memucan proposed. [22]He sent dispatches to
all parts of the kingdom, to each province
in its own script and to each people in its
own language, proclaiming in each people's tongue that every man should be
ruler over his own household.

[a] *1* Hebrew *Ahasuerus,* a variant of Xerxes' Persian name; here and throughout Esther [b] *1* That is, the upper Nile region

PRAYER: PETITION

I LOOK to You for my daily bread, to forgive me my debts as I also have forgiven my debtors. Do not lead me into temptation, but deliver me from the evil one. For Yours is the kingdom and the power and the glory forever.

(Matthew 6:11–13)

__PAUSE__ here to petition God for wisdom. Ask Him to develop your eternal perspective, to renew your mind with truth and to help you develop greater skill in each area of your life. Offer prayers regarding your activities for this day and any special concerns you may have.

NT Revelation 13:11–14:5

The Beast out of the Earth

11 Then I saw another beast, coming out
of the earth. He had two horns like a
lamb, but he spoke like a dragon. 12 He exercised all the authority of the first beast
on his behalf, and made the earth and its
inhabitants worship the first beast, whose
fatal wound had been healed. 13 And he
performed great and miraculous signs,
even causing fire to come down from
heaven to earth in full view of men. 14 Because of the signs he was given power to
do on behalf of the first beast, he deceived
the inhabitants of the earth. He ordered
them to set up an image in honor of the
beast who was wounded by the sword and
yet lived. 15 He was given power to give
breath to the image of the first beast, so
that it could speak and cause all who refused to worship the image to be killed.
16 He also forced everyone, small and
great, rich and poor, free and slave, to receive a mark on his right hand or on his
forehead, 17 so that no one could buy or
sell unless he had the mark, which is the
name of the beast or the number of his
name.

18 This calls for wisdom. If anyone has
insight, let him calculate the number of
the beast, for it is man's number. His
number is 666.

The Lamb and the 144,000

14 Then I looked, and there before me
was the Lamb, standing on Mount
Zion, and with him 144,000 who had his
name and his Father's name written on
their foreheads. 2 And I heard a sound
from heaven like the roar of rushing waters and like a loud peal of thunder. The
sound I heard was like that of harpists
playing their harps. 3 And they sang a new
song before the throne and before the
four living creatures and the elders. No
one could learn the song except the
144,000 who had been redeemed from
the earth. 4 These are those who did not
defile themselves with women, for they
kept themselves pure. They follow the
Lamb wherever he goes. They were purchased from among men and offered as
firstfruits to God and the Lamb. 5 No lie
was found in their mouths; they are
blameless.

PRAYER: THE CHARACTER I WANT TO CULTIVATE

I WILL commit my works to You, O Lord, and my plans will be established. (Proverbs 16:3) . . . I want my conscience to testify that I have conducted myself in the world in the holiness and sincerity that are from You, not in fleshly wisdom but in Your grace, O God, especially in my relationships with others.

(2 Corinthians 1:12)

__TAKE__ a moment to ask the Lord for the grace to grow in godly character.

OT Esther 2:1-23 — YEAR 1 DAY 355

Esther Made Queen

2 Later when the anger of King Xerxes had subsided, he remembered Vashti and what she had done and what he had decreed about her. 2Then the king's personal attendants proposed, "Let a search be made for beautiful young virgins for the king. 3Let the king appoint commissioners in every province of his realm to bring all these beautiful girls into the harem at the citadel of Susa. Let them be placed under the care of Hegai, the king's eunuch, who is in charge of the women; and let beauty treatments be given to them. 4Then let the girl who pleases the king be queen instead of Vashti." This advice appealed to the king, and he followed it.

5Now there was in the citadel of Susa a Jew of the tribe of Benjamin, named Mordecai son of Jair, the son of Shimei, the son of Kish, 6who had been carried into exile from Jerusalem by Nebuchadnezzar king of Babylon, among those taken captive with Jehoiachin[a] king of Judah. 7Mordecai had a cousin named Hadassah, whom he had brought up because she had neither father nor mother. This girl, who was also known as Esther, was lovely in form and features, and Mordecai had taken her as his own daughter when her father and mother died.

8When the king's order and edict had been proclaimed, many girls were brought to the citadel of Susa and put under the care of Hegai. Esther also was taken to the king's palace and entrusted to Hegai, who had charge of the harem. 9The girl pleased him and won his favor. Immediately he provided her with her beauty treatments and special food. He assigned to her seven maids selected from the king's palace and moved her and her maids into the best place in the harem.

10Esther had not revealed her nationality and family background, because Mordecai had forbidden her to do so. 11Every day he walked back and forth near the courtyard of the harem to find out how Esther was and what was happening to her.

12Before a girl's turn came to go in to King Xerxes, she had to complete twelve months of beauty treatments prescribed for the women, six months with oil of myrrh and six with perfumes and cosmetics. 13And this is how she would go to the king: Anything she wanted was given her to take with her from the harem to the king's palace. 14In the evening she would go there and in the morning return to another part of the harem to the care of Shaashgaz, the king's eunuch who was in charge of the concubines. She would not return to the king unless he was pleased with her and summoned her by name.

15When the turn came for Esther (the girl Mordecai had adopted, the daughter of his uncle Abihail) to go to the king, she asked for nothing other than what Hegai, the king's eunuch who was in charge of the harem, suggested. And Esther won the favor of everyone who saw her. 16She was taken to King Xerxes in the royal residence in the tenth month, the month of Tebeth, in the seventh year of his reign.

17Now the king was attracted to Esther more than to any of the other women, and she won his favor and approval more than any of the other virgins. So he set a royal crown on her head and made her queen instead of Vashti. 18And the king gave a great banquet, Esther's banquet, for all his nobles and officials. He proclaimed a holiday throughout the provinces and distributed gifts with royal liberality.

Mordecai Uncovers a Conspiracy

19When the virgins were assembled a second time, Mordecai was sitting at the king's gate. 20But Esther had kept secret her family background and nationality just as Mordecai had told her to do, for she continued to follow Mordecai's instructions as she had done when he was bringing her up.

21During the time Mordecai was sitting at the king's gate, Bigthana[b] and Teresh, two of the king's officers who guarded the doorway, became angry and conspired to assassinate King Xerxes. 22But Mordecai found out about the plot and told Queen Esther, who in turn reported it to the

[a] 6 Hebrew *Jeconiah,* a variant of *Jehoiachin*
[b] 21 Hebrew *Bigthan,* a variant of *Bigthana*

king, giving credit to Mordecai. 23And when the report was investigated and found to be true, the two officials were hanged on a gallows.[c] All this was recorded in the book of the annals in the presence of the king.

[c] *23* Or *were hung* (or *impaled*) *on poles;* similarly elsewhere in Esther

PRAYER: INTERCESSION

OH, that we would always have such a heart to fear You and keep all Your commandments, so that it might be well with us and with our children forever! (Deuteronomy 5:29)

TAKE *a few moments to intercede on behalf of your immediate family and other relatives. Offer prayers for their spiritual, emotional and physical concerns.*

NT Revelation 14:6–20

The Three Angels

6Then I saw another angel flying in midair, and he had the eternal gospel to proclaim to those who live on the earth—to every nation, tribe, language and people. 7He said in a loud voice, "Fear God and give him glory, because the hour of his judgment has come. Worship him who made the heavens, the earth, the sea and the springs of water."

8A second angel followed and said, "Fallen! Fallen is Babylon the Great, which made all the nations drink the maddening wine of her adulteries."

9A third angel followed them and said in a loud voice: "If anyone worships the beast and his image and receives his mark on the forehead or on the hand, 10he, too, will drink of the wine of God's fury, which has been poured full strength into the cup of his wrath. He will be tormented with burning sulfur in the presence of the holy angels and of the Lamb. 11And the smoke of their torment rises for ever and ever. There is no rest day or night for those who worship the beast and his image, or for anyone who receives the mark of his name." 12This calls for patient endurance on the part of the saints who obey God's commandments and remain faithful to Jesus.

13Then I heard a voice from heaven say, "Write: Blessed are the dead who die in the Lord from now on."

"Yes," says the Spirit, "they will rest from their labor, for their deeds will follow them."

The Harvest of the Earth

14I looked, and there before me was a white cloud, and seated on the cloud was one "like a son of man"[a] with a crown of gold on his head and a sharp sickle in his hand. 15Then another angel came out of the temple and called in a loud voice to him who was sitting on the cloud, "Take your sickle and reap, because the time to reap has come, for the harvest of the earth is ripe." 16So he who was seated on the cloud swung his sickle over the earth, and the earth was harvested.

17Another angel came out of the temple in heaven, and he too had a sharp sickle. 18Still another angel, who had charge of the fire, came from the altar and called in a loud voice to him who had the sharp sickle, "Take your sharp sickle and gather the clusters of grapes from the earth's vine, because its grapes are ripe." 19The angel swung his sickle on the earth, gathered its grapes and threw them into the great winepress of God's wrath. 20They were trampled in the winepress outside the city, and blood flowed out of the press, rising as high as the horses' bridles for a distance of 1,600 stadia.[b]

[a] *14* Daniel 7:13 [b] *20* That is, about 180 miles (about 300 kilometers)

PRAYER: MY RELATIONSHIP TO OTHERS

If someone is caught in a trespass, we who are spiritual should restore that person in a spirit of gentleness, taking care lest we ourselves should be tempted. (Galatians 6:1)

PAUSE *to review your relationships with others and to commit them to the Lord.*

YEAR 1
DAY 356

OT Esther 3:1-15

Haman's Plot to Destroy the Jews

3 After these events, King Xerxes honored
Haman son of Hammedatha, the Agagite, elevating him and giving him a seat
of honor higher than that of all the other
nobles. 2 All the royal officials at the king's
gate knelt down and paid honor to Haman, for the king had commanded this
concerning him. But Mordecai would not
kneel down or pay him honor.
3 Then the royal officials at the king's
gate asked Mordecai, "Why do you disobey the king's command?" 4 Day after
day they spoke to him but he refused to
comply. Therefore they told Haman about
it to see whether Mordecai's behavior
would be tolerated, for he had told them
he was a Jew.
5 When Haman saw that Mordecai
would not kneel down or pay him honor,
he was enraged. 6 Yet having learned who
Mordecai's people were, he scorned the
idea of killing only Mordecai. Instead Haman looked for a way to destroy all Mordecai's people, the Jews, throughout the
whole kingdom of Xerxes.
7 In the twelfth year of King Xerxes, in
the first month, the month of Nisan, they
cast the *pur* (that is, the lot) in the presence of Haman to select a day and month.
And the lot fell on[a] the twelfth month, the
month of Adar.
8 Then Haman said to King Xerxes,
"There is a certain people dispersed and
scattered among the peoples in all the
provinces of your kingdom whose customs are different from those of all other
people and who do not obey the king's
laws; it is not in the king's best interest to
tolerate them. 9 If it pleases the king, let a
decree be issued to destroy them, and I
will put ten thousand talents[b] of silver
into the royal treasury for the men who
carry out this business."
10 So the king took his signet ring from
his finger and gave it to Haman son of
Hammedatha, the Agagite, the enemy of
the Jews. 11 "Keep the money," the king
said to Haman, "and do with the people
as you please."
12 Then on the thirteenth day of the first
month the royal secretaries were summoned. They wrote out in the script of
each province and in the language of each
people all Haman's orders to the king's satraps, the governors of the various
provinces and the nobles of the various
peoples. These were written in the name
of King Xerxes himself and sealed with his
own ring. 13 Dispatches were sent by couriers to all the king's provinces with the order to destroy, kill and annihilate all the
Jews—young and old, women and little
children—on a single day, the thirteenth
day of the twelfth month, the month of
Adar, and to plunder their goods. 14 A copy
of the text of the edict was to be issued as
law in every province and made known to
the people of every nationality so they
would be ready for that day.
15 Spurred on by the king's command,
the couriers went out, and the edict was
issued in the citadel of Susa. The king and
Haman sat down to drink, but the city of
Susa was bewildered.

[a] 7 Septuagint; Hebrew does not have *And the lot fell on.* [b] 9 That is, about 375 tons (about 345 metric tons)

PRAYER: AFFIRMATION

I KNOW that whatever You do, O God, will remain forever; nothing can be added to it and nothing taken from it. You do it so that people will revere You. (Ecclesiastes 3:14) . . . You, O God, will bring every work into judgment, including every hidden thing, whether it is good or evil. (Ecclesiastes 12:14)

***PAUSE** to reflect on these Biblical affirmations.*

NT Revelation 15:1-8

Seven Angels With Seven Plagues

15 I saw in heaven another great and
marvelous sign: seven angels with the
seven last plagues—last, because with
them God's wrath is completed. [2]And I
saw what looked like a sea of glass mixed
with fire and, standing beside the sea,
those who had been victorious over the
beast and his image and over the number
of his name. They held harps given them
by God [3]and sang the song of Moses the
servant of God and the song of the Lamb:

"Great and marvelous are your deeds,
Lord God Almighty.
Just and true are your ways,
King of the ages.
[4]Who will not fear you, O Lord,
and bring glory to your name?
For you alone are holy.
All nations will come
and worship before you,
for your righteous acts have been
revealed."

[5]After this I looked and in heaven the
temple, that is, the tabernacle of the Testimony, was opened. [6]Out of the temple
came the seven angels with the seven
plagues. They were dressed in clean, shining linen and wore golden sashes around
their chests. [7]Then one of the four living
creatures gave to the seven angels seven
golden bowls filled with the wrath of God,
who lives for ever and ever. [8]And the temple was filled with smoke from the glory of
God and from his power, and no one could
enter the temple until the seven plagues of
the seven angels were completed.

PRAYER: THE ATTRIBUTES OF GOD

RIGHTEOUSNESS and justice are the foundation of Your throne; loving-kindness and truth go before You. (Psalm 89:14)

***PAUSE** to reflect on these affirmations about the person, powers and perfection of God.*

OT Psalms 70–71

Psalm 70

For the director of music. Of David.
A petition.

[1]Hasten, O God, to save me;
O LORD, come quickly to help me.
[2]May those who seek my life
be put to shame and confusion;
may all who desire my ruin
be turned back in disgrace.
[3]May those who say to me, "Aha!
Aha!"
turn back because of their shame.
[4]But may all who seek you
rejoice and be glad in you;
may those who love your salvation
always say,

"Let God be exalted!"

[5] Yet I am poor and needy;
come quickly to me, O God.
You are my help and my deliverer;
O LORD, do not delay.

Psalm 71

[1] In you, O LORD, I have taken refuge;
let me never be put to shame.
[2] Rescue me and deliver me in your righteousness;
turn your ear to me and save me.
[3] Be my rock of refuge,
to which I can always go;
give the command to save me,
for you are my rock and my fortress.
[4] Deliver me, O my God, from the hand of the wicked,
from the grasp of evil and cruel men.

[5] For you have been my hope,
O Sovereign LORD,
my confidence since my youth.
[6] From birth I have relied on you;
you brought me forth from my mother's womb.
I will ever praise you.
[7] I have become like a portent to many,
but you are my strong refuge.
[8] My mouth is filled with your praise,
declaring your splendor all day long.

[9] Do not cast me away when I am old;
do not forsake me when my strength is gone.
[10] For my enemies speak against me;
those who wait to kill me conspire together.
[11] They say, "God has forsaken him;
pursue him and seize him,
for no one will rescue him."
[12] Be not far from me, O God;
come quickly, O my God, to help me.
[13] May my accusers perish in shame;
may those who want to harm me
be covered with scorn and disgrace.
[14] But as for me, I will always have hope;
I will praise you more and more.
[15] My mouth will tell of your righteousness,
of your salvation all day long,
though I know not its measure.
[16] I will come and proclaim your mighty acts, O Sovereign LORD;
I will proclaim your righteousness, yours alone.
[17] Since my youth, O God, you have taught me,
and to this day I declare your marvelous deeds.
[18] Even when I am old and gray,
do not forsake me, O God,
till I declare your power to the next generation,
your might to all who are to come.

[19] Your righteousness reaches to the skies, O God,
you who have done great things.
Who, O God, is like you?
[20] Though you have made me see troubles, many and bitter,
you will restore my life again;
from the depths of the earth
you will again bring me up.
[21] You will increase my honor
and comfort me once again.

[22] I will praise you with the harp
for your faithfulness, O my God;
I will sing praise to you with the lyre,
O Holy One of Israel.
[23] My lips will shout for joy
when I sing praise to you—
I, whom you have redeemed.
[24] My tongue will tell of your righteous acts
all day long,
for those who wanted to harm me
have been put to shame and confusion.

PRAYER: THANKSGIVING

BECAUSE I love You, You will deliver me; You will protect me, for I acknowledge Your name. I will call upon You, and You will answer me; You will be with me in trouble, You will deliver me and honor me. With long life You will satisfy me and show me Your salvation. (Psalm 91:14–16)

__PAUSE__ to offer your own expressions of thanksgiving.

NT Revelation 16:1–21

The Seven Bowls of God's Wrath

16 Then I heard a loud voice from the
temple saying to the seven angels,
"Go, pour out the seven bowls of God's
wrath on the earth."
2 The first angel went and poured out
his bowl on the land, and ugly and
painful sores broke out on the people
who had the mark of the beast and worshiped his image.
3 The second angel poured out his bowl
on the sea, and it turned into blood like
that of a dead man, and every living thing
in the sea died.
4 The third angel poured out his bowl
on the rivers and springs of water, and
they became blood. 5 Then I heard the angel in charge of the waters say:

"You are just in these judgments,
you who are and who were, the
Holy One,
because you have so judged;
6 for they have shed the blood of your
saints and prophets,
and you have given them blood to
drink as they deserve."

7 And I heard the altar respond:

"Yes, Lord God Almighty,
true and just are your judgments."

8 The fourth angel poured out his bowl
on the sun, and the sun was given power
to scorch people with fire. 9 They were
seared by the intense heat and they cursed
the name of God, who had control over
these plagues, but they refused to repent
and glorify him.
10 The fifth angel poured out his bowl
on the throne of the beast, and his kingdom was plunged into darkness. Men
gnawed their tongues in agony 11 and
cursed the God of heaven because of their
pains and their sores, but they refused to
repent of what they had done.
12 The sixth angel poured out his bowl
on the great river Euphrates, and its water
was dried up to prepare the way for the
kings from the East. 13 Then I saw three
evil[a] spirits that looked like frogs; they
came out of the mouth of the dragon, out
of the mouth of the beast and out of the
mouth of the false prophet. 14 They are
spirits of demons performing miraculous
signs, and they go out to the kings of the
whole world, to gather them for the battle on the great day of God Almighty.
15 "Behold, I come like a thief! Blessed
is he who stays awake and keeps his
clothes with him, so that he may not go
naked and be shamefully exposed."
16 Then they gathered the kings together
to the place that in Hebrew is called Armageddon.
17 The seventh angel poured out his
bowl into the air, and out of the temple
came a loud voice from the throne, saying, "It is done!" 18 Then there came
flashes of lightning, rumblings, peals of
thunder and a severe earthquake. No
earthquake like it has ever occurred since
man has been on earth, so tremendous
was the quake. 19 The great city split into
three parts, and the cities of the nations
collapsed. God remembered Babylon the
Great and gave her the cup filled with the
wine of the fury of his wrath. 20 Every island fled away and the mountains could
not be found. 21 From the sky huge hailstones of about a hundred pounds each
fell upon men. And they cursed God on
account of the plague of hail, because the
plague was so terrible.

[a] *13* Greek *unclean*

PRAYER: THE WORKS OF GOD

LORD Jesus, You are the resurrection and the life. Those who believe in You will live, even though they die, and those who live and believe in You will never die. (John 11:25–26) . . . Everything You have created, O God, eagerly waits in expectation of the time when Your children will appear in their full and final glory. (Romans 8:19)

***TAKE** a moment to consider the greatness of God's wonderful works.*

YEAR 1 DAY 358

OT Esther 4:1–17

Mordecai Persuades Esther to Help

4 When Mordecai learned of all that had
been done, he tore his clothes, put on
sackcloth and ashes, and went out into
the city, wailing loudly and bitterly. 2But
he went only as far as the king's gate, because no one clothed in sackcloth was allowed to enter it. 3In every province to
which the edict and order of the king
came, there was great mourning among
the Jews, with fasting, weeping and wailing. Many lay in sackcloth and ashes.
4When Esther's maids and eunuchs
came and told her about Mordecai, she
was in great distress. She sent clothes for
him to put on instead of his sackcloth,
but he would not accept them. 5Then Esther summoned Hathach, one of the
king's eunuchs assigned to attend her, and
ordered him to find out what was troubling Mordecai and why.
6So Hathach went out to Mordecai in
the open square of the city in front of the
king's gate. 7Mordecai told him everything
that had happened to him, including the
exact amount of money Haman had
promised to pay into the royal treasury for
the destruction of the Jews. 8He also gave
him a copy of the text of the edict for their
annihilation, which had been published
in Susa, to show to Esther and explain it
to her, and he told him to urge her to go
into the king's presence to beg for mercy
and plead with him for her people.
9Hathach went back and reported to Esther what Mordecai had said. 10Then she
instructed him to say to Mordecai, 11"All
the king's officials and the people of the
royal provinces know that for any man or
woman who approaches the king in the
inner court without being summoned the
king has but one law: that he be put to
death. The only exception to this is for the
king to extend the gold scepter to him and
spare his life. But thirty days have passed
since I was called to go to the king."
12When Esther's words were reported to
Mordecai, 13he sent back this answer: "Do
not think that because you are in the
king's house you alone of all the Jews will
escape. 14For if you remain silent at this
time, relief and deliverance for the Jews
will arise from another place, but you and
your father's family will perish. And who
knows but that you have come to royal
position for such a time as this?"
15Then Esther sent this reply to Mordecai: 16"Go, gather together all the Jews who
are in Susa, and fast for me. Do not eat or
drink for three days, night or day. I and my
maids will fast as you do. When this is
done, I will go to the king, even though it
is against the law. And if I perish, I perish."
17So Mordecai went away and carried
out all of Esther's instructions.

PRAYER: ADORATION

O LORD, You made the earth by Your power; You established the world by Your wisdom and stretched out the heavens by Your understanding. (Jeremiah 10:12; 51:15) . . . You give the sun for light by day, O Lord, and decree the moon and stars for light by night; You stir up the sea so that its waves roar; the Lord of hosts is Your name. (Jeremiah 31:35)

***PAUSE** to express your thoughts of praise and worship.*

NT Revelation 17:1–18

The Woman on the Beast

17 One of the seven angels who had the
seven bowls came and said to me,
"Come, I will show you the punishment
of the great prostitute, who sits on many
waters. 2With her the kings of the earth
committed adultery and the inhabitants
of the earth were intoxicated with the
wine of her adulteries."
3Then the angel carried me away in the
Spirit into a desert. There I saw a woman

sitting on a scarlet beast that was covered
with blasphemous names and had seven
heads and ten horns. [4]The woman was
dressed in purple and scarlet, and was glittering with gold, precious stones and
pearls. She held a golden cup in her hand,
filled with abominable things and the
filth of her adulteries. [5]This title was written on her forehead:

MYSTERY
BABYLON THE GREAT
THE MOTHER OF PROSTITUTES
AND OF THE ABOMINATIONS OF THE EARTH.

[6]I saw that the woman was drunk with the
blood of the saints, the blood of those
who bore testimony to Jesus.

When I saw her, I was greatly astonished. [7]Then the angel said to me: "Why
are you astonished? I will explain to you
the mystery of the woman and of the
beast she rides, which has the seven heads
and ten horns. [8]The beast, which you saw,
once was, now is not, and will come up
out of the Abyss and go to his destruction.
The inhabitants of the earth whose names
have not been written in the book of life
from the creation of the world will be astonished when they see the beast, because
he once was, now is not, and yet will
come.

[9]"This calls for a mind with wisdom.
The seven heads are seven hills on which
the woman sits. [10]They are also seven
kings. Five have fallen, one is, the other
has not yet come; but when he does come,
he must remain for a little while. [11]The
beast who once was, and now is not, is an
eighth king. He belongs to the seven and
is going to his destruction.

[12]"The ten horns you saw are ten kings
who have not yet received a kingdom, but
who for one hour will receive authority as
kings along with the beast. [13]They have
one purpose and will give their power and
authority to the beast. [14]They will make
war against the Lamb, but the Lamb will
overcome them because he is Lord of
lords and King of kings—and with him
will be his called, chosen and faithful followers."

[15]Then the angel said to me, "The waters you saw, where the prostitute sits, are
peoples, multitudes, nations and languages. [16]The beast and the ten horns you
saw will hate the prostitute. They will
bring her to ruin and leave her naked;
they will eat her flesh and burn her with
fire. [17]For God has put it into their hearts
to accomplish his purpose by agreeing to
give the beast their power to rule, until
God's words are fulfilled. [18]The woman
you saw is the great city that rules over the
kings of the earth."

PRAYER: MY RELATIONSHIP TO GOD

AS the Father has loved You, Jesus, You also have loved me. I must abide in Your love. If I keep Your commandments, I will abide in Your love, just as You kept Your Father's commandments and abide in His love. You have told me this so that Your joy may be in me and that my joy may be full. (John 15:9–11)

PAUSE *to thank God for the relationship that you enjoy with Him in Jesus Christ.*

YEAR 1
DAY 359

OT Esther 5:1-14

Esther's Request to the King

5 On the third day Esther put on her royal robes and stood in the inner court of
the palace, in front of the king's hall. The
king was sitting on his royal throne in the
hall, facing the entrance. [2]When he saw
Queen Esther standing in the court, he
was pleased with her and held out to her
the gold scepter that was in his hand. So
Esther approached and touched the tip of
the scepter.

[3]Then the king asked, "What is it,
Queen Esther? What is your request? Even

up to half the kingdom, it will be given
you."
[4] "If it pleases the king," replied Esther,
"let the king, together with Haman, come
today to a banquet I have prepared for
him."
[5] "Bring Haman at once," the king said,
"so that we may do what Esther asks."
So the king and Haman went to the
banquet Esther had prepared. [6] As they
were drinking wine, the king again asked
Esther, "Now what is your petition? It will
be given you. And what is your request?
Even up to half the kingdom, it will be
granted."
[7] Esther replied, "My petition and my request is this: [8] If the king regards me with
favor and if it pleases the king to grant my
petition and fulfill my request, let the king
and Haman come tomorrow to the banquet I will prepare for them. Then I will
answer the king's question."

Haman's Rage Against Mordecai

[9] Haman went out that day happy and
in high spirits. But when he saw Mordecai at the king's gate and observed that he
neither rose nor showed fear in his presence, he was filled with rage against Mordecai. [10] Nevertheless, Haman restrained
himself and went home.
Calling together his friends and Zeresh,
his wife, [11] Haman boasted to them about
his vast wealth, his many sons, and all the
ways the king had honored him and how
he had elevated him above the other nobles and officials. [12] "And that's not all,"
Haman added. "I'm the only person
Queen Esther invited to accompany the
king to the banquet she gave. And she has
invited me along with the king tomorrow.
[13] But all this gives me no satisfaction as
long as I see that Jew Mordecai sitting at
the king's gate."
[14] His wife Zeresh and all his friends
said to him, "Have a gallows built, seventy-five feet[a] high, and ask the king in the
morning to have Mordecai hanged on it.
Then go with the king to the dinner and
be happy." This suggestion delighted Haman, and he had the gallows built.

[a] 14 Hebrew *fifty cubits* (about 23 meters)

PRAYER: CONFESSION

O LORD, God of heaven, You are the great and awesome God, keeping Your covenant of loyal love with those who love You and obey Your commands. Let Your ear be attentive and Your eyes open so that You may hear the prayer Your servant is praying before You day and night. I confess the sins I have committed against You. (Nehemiah 1:5–6)

ASK *the Spirit to search your heart and reveal any areas of unconfessed sin. Acknowledge these to the Lord and thank Him for His forgiveness.*

NT Revelation 18:1–10

The Fall of Babylon

18 After this I saw another angel coming
down from heaven. He had great authority, and the earth was illuminated by
his splendor. [2] With a mighty voice he
shouted:

"Fallen! Fallen is Babylon the Great!
She has become a home for demons
and a haunt for every evil[a] spirit,
a haunt for every unclean and
detestable bird.
[3] For all the nations have drunk
the maddening wine of her
adulteries.
The kings of the earth committed
adultery with her,
and the merchants of the earth grew
rich from her excessive luxuries."

[4] Then I heard another voice from heav-
en say:

"Come out of her, my people,
so that you will not share in her
sins,
so that you will not receive any of
her plagues;
[5] for her sins are piled up to heaven,

[a] 2 Greek *unclean*

and God has remembered her
crimes.
6 Give back to her as she has given;
pay her back double for what she
has done.
Mix her a double portion from her
own cup.
7 Give her as much torture and grief
as the glory and luxury she gave
herself.
In her heart she boasts,
'I sit as queen; I am not a widow,
and I will never mourn.'
8 Therefore in one day her plagues will
overtake her:
death, mourning and famine.
She will be consumed by fire,
for mighty is the Lord God who
judges her.

9 "When the kings of the earth who
committed adultery with her and shared
her luxury see the smoke of her burning,
they will weep and mourn over her. 10 Terrified at her torment, they will stand far
off and cry:

" 'Woe! Woe, O great city,
O Babylon, city of power!
In one hour your doom has come!'

PRAYER: THE CHARACTER I WANT TO CULTIVATE

I WILL not love with words or tongue but will strive to love in deed and in truth. By this I will know that I am of the truth and my heart will be assured before You; for if my heart condemns me, You, O God, are greater than my heart, and You know all things. If my heart does not condemn me, I have confidence before You and receive from You whatever I ask, because I keep Your commandments and do the things that are pleasing in Your sight. (1 John 3:18–22)

TAKE *a moment to ask the Lord for the grace to grow in godly character.*

YEAR 1 DAY 360

OT Esther 6:1-14

Mordecai Honored

6 That night the king could not sleep; so
he ordered the book of the chronicles,
the record of his reign, to be brought in
and read to him. 2 It was found recorded
there that Mordecai had exposed Bigthana and Teresh, two of the king's officers
who guarded the doorway, who had conspired to assassinate King Xerxes.
3 "What honor and recognition has
Mordecai received for this?" the king
asked.

"Nothing has been done for him," his
attendants answered.
4 The king said, "Who is in the court?"
Now Haman had just entered the outer
court of the palace to speak to the king
about hanging Mordecai on the gallows
he had erected for him.
5 His attendants answered, "Haman is
standing in the court."

"Bring him in," the king ordered.
6 When Haman entered, the king asked
him, "What should be done for the man
the king delights to honor?"

Now Haman thought to himself, "Who
is there that the king would rather honor
than me?" 7 So he answered the king, "For
the man the king delights to honor, 8 have
them bring a royal robe the king has worn
and a horse the king has ridden, one with
a royal crest placed on its head. 9 Then let
the robe and horse be entrusted to one of
the king's most noble princes. Let them
robe the man the king delights to honor,
and lead him on the horse through the
city streets, proclaiming before him, 'This
is what is done for the man the king delights to honor!' "
10 "Go at once," the king commanded
Haman. "Get the robe and the horse and
do just as you have suggested for Mordecai
the Jew, who sits at the king's gate. Do not
neglect anything you have recommended."
11 So Haman got the robe and the horse.

He robed Mordecai, and led him on
horseback through the city streets, proclaiming before him, "This is what is done
for the man the king delights to honor!"
12 Afterward Mordecai returned to the
king's gate. But Haman rushed home,
with his head covered in grief, 13 and told
Zeresh his wife and all his friends everything that had happened to him.

His advisers and his wife Zeresh said
to him, "Since Mordecai, before whom
your downfall has started, is of Jewish
origin, you cannot stand against him—
you will surely come to ruin!" 14 While
they were still talking with him, the
king's eunuchs arrived and hurried Haman away to the banquet Esther had
prepared.

PRAYER: RENEWAL

***THOSE** who live according to the flesh set their minds on the things of the flesh; but those who live according to Your Spirit, O God, set their minds on the things of the Spirit. The mind of the flesh is death, but the mind of Your Spirit is life and peace. (Romans 8:5–6)*

***PAUSE** to add your own prayers for personal renewal.*

NT Revelation 18:11–24

11 "The merchants of the earth will weep
and mourn over her because no one buys
their cargoes any more— 12 cargoes of
gold, silver, precious stones and pearls;
fine linen, purple, silk and scarlet cloth;
every sort of citron wood, and articles of
every kind made of ivory, costly wood,
bronze, iron and marble; 13 cargoes of cinnamon and spice, of incense, myrrh and
frankincense, of wine and olive oil, of fine
flour and wheat; cattle and sheep; horses
and carriages; and bodies and souls of
men.
14 "They will say, 'The fruit you longed
for is gone from you. All your riches and
splendor have vanished, never to be recovered.' 15 The merchants who sold these
things and gained their wealth from her
will stand far off, terrified at her torment.
They will weep and mourn 16 and cry out:

" 'Woe! Woe, O great city,
dressed in fine linen, purple and
scarlet,
and glittering with gold, precious
stones and pearls!
17 In one hour such great wealth has
been brought to ruin!'

"Every sea captain, and all who travel
by ship, the sailors, and all who earn their
living from the sea, will stand far off.
18 When they see the smoke of her burning, they will exclaim, 'Was there ever a
city like this great city?' 19 They will throw
dust on their heads, and with weeping
and mourning cry out:

" 'Woe! Woe, O great city,
where all who had ships on the sea
became rich through her wealth!
In one hour she has been brought to
ruin!
20 Rejoice over her, O heaven!
Rejoice, saints and apostles and
prophets!
God has judged her for the way she
treated you.' "

21 Then a mighty angel picked up a boul-
der the size of a large millstone and threw
it into the sea, and said:

"With such violence
the great city of Babylon will be
thrown down,
never to be found again.
22 The music of harpists and musicians,
flute players and trumpeters,
will never be heard in you again.
No workman of any trade
will ever be found in you again.
The sound of a millstone
will never be heard in you again.
23 The light of a lamp
will never shine in you again.
The voice of bridegroom and bride
will never be heard in you again.

Your merchants were the world's great
men.
By your magic spell all the nations
were led astray.
24In her was found the blood of
prophets and of the saints,
and of all who have been killed on
the earth."

PRAYER: MY RELATIONSHIP TO OTHERS

CONCERNING love among believers: You have taught us, O God, to love each other, and we are to love each other more and more.
(1 Thessalonians 4:9–10)

PAUSE *to review your relationships with others and to commit them to the Lord.*

OT Esther 7:1–8:17

YEAR 1 DAY 361

Haman Hanged

7 So the king and Haman went to dine
with Queen Esther, 2and as they were
drinking wine on that second day, the
king again asked, "Queen Esther, what is
your petition? It will be given you. What
is your request? Even up to half the kingdom, it will be granted."
3Then Queen Esther answered, "If I
have found favor with you, O king, and if
it pleases your majesty, grant me my life—
this is my petition. And spare my people—this is my request. 4For I and my
people have been sold for destruction and
slaughter and annihilation. If we had
merely been sold as male and female
slaves, I would have kept quiet, because
no such distress would justify disturbing
the king.[a]"
5King Xerxes asked Queen Esther, "Who
is he? Where is the man who has dared to
do such a thing?"
6Esther said, "The adversary and enemy
is this vile Haman."
Then Haman was terrified before the
king and queen. 7The king got up in a
rage, left his wine and went out into the
palace garden. But Haman, realizing that
the king had already decided his fate,
stayed behind to beg Queen Esther for his
life.
8Just as the king returned from the
palace garden to the banquet hall, Haman
was falling on the couch where Esther was
reclining.
The king exclaimed, "Will he even molest the queen while she is with me in the
house?"
As soon as the word left the king's
mouth, they covered Haman's face. 9Then
Harbona, one of the eunuchs attending
the king, said, "A gallows seventy-five feet[b]
high stands by Haman's house. He had it
made for Mordecai, who spoke up to help
the king."
The king said, "Hang him on it!" 10So
they hanged Haman on the gallows he
had prepared for Mordecai. Then the
king's fury subsided.

The King's Edict in Behalf of the Jews

8 That same day King Xerxes gave Queen
Esther the estate of Haman, the enemy
of the Jews. And Mordecai came into the
presence of the king, for Esther had told
how he was related to her. 2The king took
off his signet ring, which he had re-
claimed from Haman, and presented it to
Mordecai. And Esther appointed him over
Haman's estate.
3Esther again pleaded with the king,
falling at his feet and weeping. She begged
him to put an end to the evil plan of Haman the Agagite, which he had devised
against the Jews. 4Then the king extended
the gold scepter to Esther and she arose
and stood before him.
5"If it pleases the king," she said, "and
if he regards me with favor and thinks it
the right thing to do, and if he is pleased

[a] 4 Or *quiet, but the compensation our adversary offers cannot be compared with the loss the king would suffer*
[b] 9 Hebrew *fifty cubits* (about 23 meters)

with me, let an order be written overrul-
ing the dispatches that Haman son of
Hammedatha, the Agagite, devised and
wrote to destroy the Jews in all the king's
provinces. 6For how can I bear to see disaster fall on my people? How can I bear
to see the destruction of my family?"
7King Xerxes replied to Queen Esther
and to Mordecai the Jew, "Because Haman attacked the Jews, I have given his estate to Esther, and they have hanged him
on the gallows. 8Now write another decree
in the king's name in behalf of the Jews as
seems best to you, and seal it with the
king's signet ring—for no document written in the king's name and sealed with his
ring can be revoked."
9At once the royal secretaries were summoned—on the twenty-third day of the
third month, the month of Sivan. They
wrote out all Mordecai's orders to the
Jews, and to the satraps, governors and
nobles of the 127 provinces stretching
from India to Cush.[c] These orders were
written in the script of each province and
the language of each people and also to
the Jews in their own script and language.
10Mordecai wrote in the name of King Xerxes, sealed the dispatches with the king's
signet ring, and sent them by mounted
couriers, who rode fast horses especially
bred for the king.
11The king's edict granted the Jews in
every city the right to assemble and protect themselves; to destroy, kill and annihilate any armed force of any nationality
or province that might attack them and
their women and children; and to plunder the property of their enemies. 12The
day appointed for the Jews to do this in
all the provinces of King Xerxes was the
thirteenth day of the twelfth month, the
month of Adar. 13A copy of the text of the
edict was to be issued as law in every province and made known to the people of
every nationality so that the Jews would
be ready on that day to avenge themselves
on their enemies.
14The couriers, riding the royal horses,
raced out, spurred on by the king's command. And the edict was also issued in
the citadel of Susa.
15Mordecai left the king's presence wearing royal garments of blue and white, a
large crown of gold and a purple robe of
fine linen. And the city of Susa held a joy-
ous celebration. 16For the Jews it was a time
of happiness and joy, gladness and honor.
17In every province and in every city, wherever the edict of the king went, there was
joy and gladness among the Jews, with
feasting and celebrating. And many people
of other nationalities became Jews because
fear of the Jews had seized them.

[c] 9 That is, the upper Nile region

PRAYER: PETITION

O LORD, may I watch carefully how I walk, not as unwise but as wise, making the most of every opportunity, because the days are evil. May I not be foolish, but understand what Your will is, O Lord. (Ephesians 5:15–17)

***PAUSE** here to petition God for spiritual insight so that you might have understanding of His Word. Ask for insight into your identity in Jesus Christ: that you might know who you are, what direction your life should take and what His purpose for your life is. Offer prayers regarding your activities for this day and any special concerns you may have.*

NT Revelation 19:1–10

Hallelujah!

19 After this I heard what sounded like
the roar of a great multitude in heav-
en shouting:

"Hallelujah!
Salvation and glory and power belong
to our God,
2 for true and just are his
judgments.
He has condemned the great
prostitute

who corrupted the earth by her
adulteries.
He has avenged on her the blood of
his servants."

[3]And again they shouted:

"Hallelujah!
The smoke from her goes up for ever
and ever."

[4]The twenty-four elders and the four living creatures fell down and worshiped God, who was seated on the throne. And they cried:

"Amen, Hallelujah!"

[5]Then a voice came from the throne, saying:

"Praise our God,
all you his servants,
you who fear him,
both small and great!"

[6]Then I heard what sounded like a great multitude, like the roar of rushing waters and like loud peals of thunder, shouting:

"Hallelujah!
For our Lord God Almighty reigns.
[7]Let us rejoice and be glad
and give him glory!
For the wedding of the Lamb has come,
and his bride has made herself
ready.
[8]Fine linen, bright and clean,
was given her to wear."

(Fine linen stands for the righteous acts of the saints.)

[9]Then the angel said to me, "Write: 'Blessed are those who are invited to the wedding supper of the Lamb!' " And he added, "These are the true words of God."
[10]At this I fell at his feet to worship him. But he said to me, "Do not do it! I am a fellow servant with you and with your brothers who hold to the testimony of Jesus. Worship God! For the testimony of Jesus is the spirit of prophecy."

PRAYER: THE ATTRIBUTES OF GOD

LORD Jesus Christ, Your works have proved that the Father is in You, and that You are in the Father. (John 10:38) . . . You knew, Jesus, that the Father had given all things into Your hands and that You had come from God and were returning to God. (John 13:3)

***PAUSE** to reflect on these affirmations about the person, powers and perfection of God.*

YEAR 1 DAY 362

OT Esther 9:1–10:3

Triumph of the Jews

9 On the thirteenth day of the twelfth
month, the month of Adar, the edict
commanded by the king was to be carried
out. On this day the enemies of the Jews
had hoped to overpower them, but now
the tables were turned and the Jews got the
upper hand over those who hated them.
[2]The Jews assembled in their cities in all
the provinces of King Xerxes to attack those
seeking their destruction. No one could
stand against them, because the people of
all the other nationalities were afraid of
them. [3]And all the nobles of the provinces,
the satraps, the governors and the king's
administrators helped the Jews, because
fear of Mordecai had seized them. [4]Mor-
decai was prominent in the palace; his reputation spread throughout the provinces,
and he became more and more powerful.
[5]The Jews struck down all their enemies
with the sword, killing and destroying
them, and they did what they pleased to
those who hated them. [6]In the citadel of
Susa, the Jews killed and destroyed five
hundred men. [7]They also killed Parshan-
datha, Dalphon, Aspatha, [8]Poratha, Ada-
lia, Aridatha, [9]Parmashta, Arisai, Aridai
and Vaizatha, [10]the ten sons of Haman
son of Hammedatha, the enemy of the
Jews. But they did not lay their hands on
the plunder.

11 The number of those slain in the citadel
of Susa was reported to the king that same
day. 12 The king said to Queen Esther, "The
Jews have killed and destroyed five hundred
men and the ten sons of Haman in the
citadel of Susa. What have they done in the
rest of the king's provinces? Now what is
your petition? It will be given you. What is
your request? It will also be granted."
13 "If it pleases the king," Esther answered,
"give the Jews in Susa permission to carry
out this day's edict tomorrow also, and let
Haman's ten sons be hanged on gallows."
14 So the king commanded that this be
done. An edict was issued in Susa, and they
hanged the ten sons of Haman. 15 The Jews
in Susa came together on the fourteenth
day of the month of Adar, and they put to
death in Susa three hundred men, but they
did not lay their hands on the plunder.
16 Meanwhile, the remainder of the Jews
who were in the king's provinces also assembled to protect themselves and get relief from their enemies. They killed seventy-five thousand of them but did not
lay their hands on the plunder. 17 This happened on the thirteenth day of the month
of Adar, and on the fourteenth they rested and made it a day of feasting and joy.

Purim Celebrated

18 The Jews in Susa, however, had assembled on the thirteenth and fourteenth,
and then on the fifteenth they rested and
made it a day of feasting and joy.
19 That is why rural Jews—those living in
villages—observe the fourteenth of the
month of Adar as a day of joy and feasting,
a day for giving presents to each other.
20 Mordecai recorded these events, and
he sent letters to all the Jews throughout
the provinces of King Xerxes, near and far,
21 to have them celebrate annually the fourteenth and fifteenth days of the month of
Adar 22 as the time when the Jews got relief
from their enemies, and as the month
when their sorrow was turned into joy and
their mourning into a day of celebration.
He wrote them to observe the days as days
of feasting and joy and giving presents of
food to one another and gifts to the poor.
23 So the Jews agreed to continue the celebration they had begun, doing what Mordecai had written to them. 24 For Haman
son of Hammedatha, the Agagite, the enemy of all the Jews, had plotted against the
Jews to destroy them and had cast the *pur*
(that is, the lot) for their ruin and destruction. 25 But when the plot came to the
king's attention,[a] he issued written orders
that the evil scheme Haman had devised
against the Jews should come back onto
his own head, and that he and his sons
should be hanged on the gallows.
26 (Therefore these days were called Purim,
from the word *pur*.) Because of everything
written in this letter and because of what
they had seen and what had happened to
them, 27 the Jews took it upon themselves
to establish the custom that they and their
descendants and all who join them should
without fail observe these two days every
year, in the way prescribed and at the time
appointed. 28 These days should be remembered and observed in every generation by every family, and in every province
and in every city. And these days of Purim
should never cease to be celebrated by the
Jews, nor should the memory of them die
out among their descendants.
29 So Queen Esther, daughter of Abihail,
along with Mordecai the Jew, wrote with
full authority to confirm this second letter concerning Purim. 30 And Mordecai
sent letters to all the Jews in the 127
provinces of the kingdom of Xerxes—
words of goodwill and assurance— 31 to
establish these days of Purim at their designated times, as Mordecai the Jew and
Queen Esther had decreed for them, and
as they had established for themselves
and their descendants in regard to their
times of fasting and lamentation. 32 Esther's decree confirmed these regulations
about Purim, and it was written down in
the records.

The Greatness of Mordecai

10 King Xerxes imposed tribute throughout the empire, to its distant shores.
2 And all his acts of power and might, together with a full account of the greatness
of Mordecai to which the king had raised
him, are they not written in the book of
the annals of the kings of Media and Persia? 3 Mordecai the Jew was second in rank
to King Xerxes, preeminent among the
Jews, and held in high esteem by his many
fellow Jews, because he worked for the
good of his people and spoke up for the
welfare of all the Jews.

[a] 25 Or *when Esther came before the king*

PRAYER: INTERCESSION

MAY we always thank You, O God, for other believers and pray that their faith would grow more and more, and that their love for each other would increase. (2 Thessalonians 1:3)

***TAKE** a few moments to intercede on behalf of other believers, such as your personal friends, those in ministry and those who are oppressed and in need.*

NT Revelation 19:11–20:6

The Rider on the White Horse

[11]I saw heaven standing open and there
before me was a white horse, whose rider
is called Faithful and True. With justice he
judges and makes war. [12]His eyes are like
blazing fire, and on his head are many
crowns. He has a name written on him
that no one knows but he himself. [13]He is
dressed in a robe dipped in blood, and his
name is the Word of God. [14]The armies of
heaven were following him, riding on
white horses and dressed in fine linen,
white and clean. [15]Out of his mouth
comes a sharp sword with which to strike
down the nations. "He will rule them
with an iron scepter."[a] He treads the winepress of the fury of the wrath of God
Almighty. [16]On his robe and on his thigh
he has this name written:

KING OF KINGS AND LORD OF LORDS.

[17]And I saw an angel standing in the
sun, who cried in a loud voice to all the
birds flying in midair, "Come, gather together for the great supper of God, [18]so
that you may eat the flesh of kings, generals, and mighty men, of horses and their
riders, and the flesh of all people, free and
slave, small and great."

[19]Then I saw the beast and the kings of
the earth and their armies gathered together to make war against the rider on the
horse and his army. [20]But the beast was captured, and with him the false prophet who
had performed the miraculous signs on his
behalf. With these signs he had deluded
those who had received the mark of the
beast and worshiped his image. The two of
them were thrown alive into the fiery lake
of burning sulfur. [21]The rest of them were
killed with the sword that came out of the
mouth of the rider on the horse, and all the
birds gorged themselves on their flesh.

The Thousand Years

20 And I saw an angel coming down out
of heaven, having the key to the
Abyss and holding in his hand a great
chain. [2]He seized the dragon, that ancient
serpent, who is the devil, or Satan, and
bound him for a thousand years. [3]He
threw him into the Abyss, and locked and
sealed it over him, to keep him from deceiving the nations anymore until the
thousand years were ended. After that, he
must be set free for a short time.

[4]I saw thrones on which were seated
those who had been given authority to
judge. And I saw the souls of those who
had been beheaded because of their testimony for Jesus and because of the word of
God. They had not worshiped the beast or
his image and had not received his mark
on their foreheads or their hands. They
came to life and reigned with Christ a
thousand years. [5](The rest of the dead did
not come to life until the thousand years
were ended.) This is the first resurrection.
[6]Blessed and holy are those who have part
in the first resurrection. The second death
has no power over them, but they will be
priests of God and of Christ and will reign
with him for a thousand years.

[a] *15* Psalm 2:9

PRAYER: THE WORKS OF GOD

SINCE the creation of the world, Your invisible attributes, O God—Your eternal power and divine nature— have been clearly seen, revealed in what You have made, so that people are without excuse. (Romans 1:20)

***TAKE** a moment to consider the greatness of God's wonderful works.*

YEAR 1
DAY 363

OT Job 1:1–22

Prologue

1 In the land of Uz there lived a man
whose name was Job. This man was
blameless and upright; he feared God and
shunned evil. 2 He had seven sons and
three daughters, 3 and he owned seven
thousand sheep, three thousand camels,
five hundred yoke of oxen and five hundred donkeys, and had a large number of
servants. He was the greatest man among
all the people of the East.
4 His sons used to take turns holding
feasts in their homes, and they would invite their three sisters to eat and drink
with them. 5 When a period of feasting
had run its course, Job would send and
have them purified. Early in the morning
he would sacrifice a burnt offering for
each of them, thinking, "Perhaps my children have sinned and cursed God in their
hearts." This was Job's regular custom.

Job's First Test

6 One day the angels[a] came to present
themselves before the LORD, and Satan[b]
also came with them. 7 The LORD said to
Satan, "Where have you come from?"
Satan answered the LORD, "From roaming through the earth and going back and
forth in it."
8 Then the LORD said to Satan, "Have
you considered my servant Job? There is
no one on earth like him; he is blameless
and upright, a man who fears God and
shuns evil."
9 "Does Job fear God for nothing?" Satan replied. 10 "Have you not put a hedge
around him and his household and everything he has? You have blessed the work
of his hands, so that his flocks and herds
are spread throughout the land. 11 But
stretch out your hand and strike everything he has, and he will surely curse you
to your face."
12 The LORD said to Satan, "Very well,
then, everything he has is in your hands,
but on the man himself do not lay a finger."
Then Satan went out from the presence
of the LORD.
13 One day when Job's sons and daughters were feasting and drinking wine at the
oldest brother's house, 14 a messenger
came to Job and said, "The oxen were
plowing and the donkeys were grazing
nearby, 15 and the Sabeans attacked and
carried them off. They put the servants to
the sword, and I am the only one who has
escaped to tell you!"
16 While he was still speaking, another
messenger came and said, "The fire of
God fell from the sky and burned up the
sheep and the servants, and I am the only
one who has escaped to tell you!"
17 While he was still speaking, another
messenger came and said, "The Chaldeans
formed three raiding parties and swept
down on your camels and carried them off.
They put the servants to the sword, and I am
the only one who has escaped to tell you!"
18 While he was still speaking, yet another messenger came and said, "Your
sons and daughters were feasting and
drinking wine at the oldest brother's
house, 19 when suddenly a mighty wind
swept in from the desert and struck the
four corners of the house. It collapsed on
them and they are dead, and I am the
only one who has escaped to tell you!"
20 At this, Job got up and tore his robe
and shaved his head. Then he fell to the
ground in worship 21 and said:

[a] 6 Hebrew *the sons of God* [b] 6 *Satan* means *accuser.*

"Naked I came from my mother's
womb,
and naked I will depart.[c]
The LORD gave and the LORD has taken
away;
may the name of the LORD be
praised."

[22]In all this, Job did not sin by charging God with wrongdoing.

[c] 21 Or *will return there*

PRAYER: AFFIRMATION

HEAVEN and earth will pass away, but Your words, Lord Jesus, will never pass away. (Matthew 24:35; Luke 21:33)

***PAUSE** to reflect on this Biblical affirmation.*

NT Revelation 20:7-15

Satan's Doom

[7]When the thousand years are over, Satan will be released from his prison [8]and
will go out to deceive the nations in the
four corners of the earth—Gog and Magog—to gather them for battle. In number they are like the sand on the
seashore. [9]They marched across the
breadth of the earth and surrounded the
camp of God's people, the city he loves.
But fire came down from heaven and devoured them. [10]And the devil, who deceived them, was thrown into the lake of
burning sulfur, where the beast and the
false prophet had been thrown. They will
be tormented day and night for ever and
ever.

The Dead Are Judged

[11]Then I saw a great white throne and
him who was seated on it. Earth and sky
fled from his presence, and there was no
place for them. [12]And I saw the dead, great
and small, standing before the throne, and
books were opened. Another book was
opened, which is the book of life. The dead
were judged according to what they had
done as recorded in the books. [13]The sea
gave up the dead that were in it, and death
and Hades gave up the dead that were in
them, and each person was judged according to what he had done. [14]Then death and
Hades were thrown into the lake of fire. The
lake of fire is the second death. [15]If anyone's
name was not found written in the book of
life, he was thrown into the lake of fire.

PRAYER: MY RELATIONSHIP TO GOD

I WILL sing to You, Lord, as long as I live; I will sing praise to You my God, while I have my being. May my meditation be pleasing to You; I will be glad in You, Lord. (Psalm 104:33–34)

***PAUSE** to thank God for the relationship that you enjoy with Him in Jesus Christ.*

YEAR 1 DAY 364

OT Psalm 72

Psalm 72

Of Solomon.

[1]Endow the king with your justice,
O God,
the royal son with your righteousness.
[2]He will[a] judge your people in
righteousness,
your afflicted ones with justice.
[3]The mountains will bring prosperity
to the people,

[a] 2 Or *May he;* similarly in verses 3–11 and 17

the hills the fruit of righteousness.
[4] He will defend the afflicted among the people
and save the children of the needy;
he will crush the oppressor.

[5] He will endure[b] as long as the sun,
as long as the moon, through all generations.
[6] He will be like rain falling on a mown field,
like showers watering the earth.
[7] In his days the righteous will flourish;
prosperity will abound till the moon is no more.

[8] He will rule from sea to sea
and from the River[c] to the ends of the earth.[d]
[9] The desert tribes will bow before him
and his enemies will lick the dust.
[10] The kings of Tarshish and of distant shores
will bring tribute to him;
the kings of Sheba and Seba
will present him gifts.
[11] All kings will bow down to him
and all nations will serve him.

[12] For he will deliver the needy who cry out,
the afflicted who have no one to help.
[13] He will take pity on the weak and the needy
and save the needy from death.
[14] He will rescue them from oppression and violence,
for precious is their blood in his sight.

[15] Long may he live!
May gold from Sheba be given him.
May people ever pray for him
and bless him all day long.
[16] Let grain abound throughout the land;
on the tops of the hills may it sway.
Let its fruit flourish like Lebanon;
let it thrive like the grass of the field.
[17] May his name endure forever;
may it continue as long as the sun.

All nations will be blessed through him,
and they will call him blessed.

[18] Praise be to the LORD God, the God of Israel,
who alone does marvelous deeds.
[19] Praise be to his glorious name forever;
may the whole earth be filled with his glory.
Amen and Amen.

[20] This concludes the prayers of David son of Jesse.

[b] 5 Septuagint; Hebrew *You will be feared* [c] 8 That is, the Euphrates [d] 8 Or *the end of the land*

PRAYER: THANKSGIVING

SURELY You are my salvation, O God; I will trust and not be afraid. For You are my strength and my song, and You have become my salvation. (Isaiah 12:2)

***PAUSE** to offer your own expressions of thanksgiving.*

NT Revelation 21:1–27

The New Jerusalem

21 Then I saw a new heaven and a new
earth, for the first heaven and the first
earth had passed away, and there was no
longer any sea. [2]I saw the Holy City, the
new Jerusalem, coming down out of heav-
en from God, prepared as a bride beauti-
fully dressed for her husband. [3]And I
heard a loud voice from the throne saying, "Now the dwelling of God is with
men, and he will live with them. They will
be his people, and God himself will be
with them and be their God. [4]He will
wipe every tear from their eyes. There will
be no more death or mourning or crying
or pain, for the old order of things has
passed away."
[5]He who was seated on the throne said,
"I am making everything new!" Then he
said, "Write this down, for these words are
trustworthy and true."
[6]He said to me: "It is done. I am the Al-

pha and the Omega, the Beginning and the End. To him who is thirsty I will give to drink without cost from the spring of the water of life. 7 He who overcomes will inherit all this, and I will be his God and he will be my son. 8 But the cowardly, the unbelieving, the vile, the murderers, the sexually immoral, those who practice magic arts, the idolaters and all liars—their place will be in the fiery lake of burning sulfur. This is the second death."

9 One of the seven angels who had the seven bowls full of the seven last plagues came and said to me, "Come, I will show you the bride, the wife of the Lamb." 10 And he carried me away in the Spirit to a mountain great and high, and showed me the Holy City, Jerusalem, coming down out of heaven from God. 11 It shone with the glory of God, and its brilliance was like that of a very precious jewel, like a jasper, clear as crystal. 12 It had a great, high wall with twelve gates, and with twelve angels at the gates. On the gates were written the names of the twelve tribes of Israel. 13 There were three gates on the east, three on the north, three on the south and three on the west. 14 The wall of the city had twelve foundations, and on them were the names of the twelve apostles of the Lamb.

15 The angel who talked with me had a measuring rod of gold to measure the city, its gates and its walls. 16 The city was laid out like a square, as long as it was wide. He measured the city with the rod and found it to be 12,000 stadia[a] in length, and as wide and high as it is long. 17 He measured its wall and it was 144 cubits[b] thick,[c] by man's measurement, which the angel was using. 18 The wall was made of jasper, and the city of pure gold, as pure as glass. 19 The foundations of the city walls were decorated with every kind of precious stone. The first foundation was jasper, the second sapphire, the third chalcedony, the fourth emerald, 20 the fifth sardonyx, the sixth carnelian, the seventh chrysolite, the eighth beryl, the ninth topaz, the tenth chrysoprase, the eleventh jacinth, and the twelfth amethyst.[d] 21 The twelve gates were twelve pearls, each gate made of a single pearl. The great street of the city was of pure gold, like transparent glass.

22 I did not see a temple in the city, because the Lord God Almighty and the Lamb are its temple. 23 The city does not need the sun or the moon to shine on it, for the glory of God gives it light, and the Lamb is its lamp. 24 The nations will walk by its light, and the kings of the earth will bring their splendor into it. 25 On no day will its gates ever be shut, for there will be no night there. 26 The glory and honor of the nations will be brought into it. 27 Nothing impure will ever enter it, nor will anyone who does what is shameful or deceitful, but only those whose names are written in the Lamb's book of life.

[a] *16* That is, about 1,400 miles (about 2,200 kilometers) [b] *17* That is, about 200 feet (about 65 meters) [c] *17* Or *high* [d] *20* The precise identification of some of these precious stones is uncertain.

PRAYER: THE CHARACTER I WANT TO CULTIVATE

WHATEVER is true, whatever is noble, whatever is right, whatever is pure, whatever is lovely, whatever is of good report—if anything is excellent or praiseworthy—I will think about such things. The things I have learned and received and heard and seen in those who walk with You, Christ Jesus, I will practice, and You, the God of peace, will be with me. (Philippians 4:8–9)

TAKE *a moment to ask the Lord for the grace to grow in godly character.*

YEAR 1
DAY 365

OT Job 2:1-13

Job's Second Test

2 On another day the angels[a] came to
present themselves before the LORD,
and Satan also came with them to present
himself before him. 2And the LORD said to
Satan, "Where have you come from?"
Satan answered the LORD, "From roaming through the earth and going back and
forth in it."
3Then the LORD said to Satan, "Have
you considered my servant Job? There is
no one on earth like him; he is blameless
and upright, a man who fears God and
shuns evil. And he still maintains his integrity, though you incited me against
him to ruin him without any reason."
4"Skin for skin!" Satan replied. "A man
will give all he has for his own life. 5But
stretch out your hand and strike his flesh
and bones, and he will surely curse you to
your face."
6The LORD said to Satan, "Very well,
then, he is in your hands; but you must
spare his life."
7So Satan went out from the presence
of the LORD and afflicted Job with painful
sores from the soles of his feet to the top
of his head. 8Then Job took a piece of
broken pottery and scraped himself with
it as he sat among the ashes.
9His wife said to him, "Are you still
holding on to your integrity? Curse God
and die!"
10He replied, "You are talking like a
foolish[b] woman. Shall we accept good
from God, and not trouble?"
In all this, Job did not sin in what he
said.

Job's Three Friends

11When Job's three friends, Eliphaz the
Temanite, Bildad the Shuhite and Zophar
the Naamathite, heard about all the troubles that had come upon him, they set out
from their homes and met together by
agreement to go and sympathize with him
and comfort him. 12When they saw him
from a distance, they could hardly recognize him; they began to weep aloud, and
they tore their robes and sprinkled dust on
their heads. 13Then they sat on the ground
with him for seven days and seven nights.
No one said a word to him, because they
saw how great his suffering was.

[a] *1* Hebrew *the sons of God* [b] *10* The Hebrew word rendered *foolish* denotes moral deficiency.

PRAYER: ADORATION

O LORD, the God of our fathers, are You not the God who is in heaven? Are You not the ruler over all the kingdoms of the nations? Power and might are in Your hand, and no one is able to withstand You.

(2 Chronicles 20:6)

***PAUSE** to express your thoughts of praise and worship.*

NT Revelation 22:1-21

The River of Life

22 Then the angel showed me the river
of the water of life, as clear as crystal,
flowing from the throne of God and of
the Lamb 2down the middle of the great
street of the city. On each side of the river stood the tree of life, bearing twelve
crops of fruit, yielding its fruit every
month. And the leaves of the tree are for
the healing of the nations. 3No longer will
there be any curse. The throne of God and
of the Lamb will be in the city, and his servants will serve him. 4They will see his
face, and his name will be on their foreheads. 5There will be no more night. They
will not need the light of a lamp or the
light of the sun, for the Lord God will give
them light. And they will reign for ever
and ever.
6The angel said to me, "These words are
trustworthy and true. The Lord, the God
of the spirits of the prophets, sent his an-

gel to show his servants the things that
must soon take place."

Jesus Is Coming

7 "Behold, I am coming soon! Blessed is
he who keeps the words of the prophecy
in this book."

8 I, John, am the one who heard and saw
these things. And when I had heard and
seen them, I fell down to worship at the
feet of the angel who had been showing
them to me. 9 But he said to me, "Do not
do it! I am a fellow servant with you and
with your brothers the prophets and of all
who keep the words of this book. Worship God!"
10 Then he told me, "Do not seal up the
words of the prophecy of this book, because the time is near. 11 Let him who does
wrong continue to do wrong; let him who
is vile continue to be vile; let him who
does right continue to do right; and let
him who is holy continue to be holy."

12 "Behold, I am coming soon! My reward is with me, and I will give to everyone according to what he has done. 13 I am
the Alpha and the Omega, the First and
the Last, the Beginning and the End.
14 "Blessed are those who wash their
robes, that they may have the right to the
tree of life and may go through the gates
into the city. 15 Outside are the dogs, those
who practice magic arts, the sexually immoral, the murderers, the idolaters and
everyone who loves and practices falsehood.
16 "I, Jesus, have sent my angel to give
you[a] this testimony for the churches. I am
the Root and the Offspring of David, and
the bright Morning Star."

17 The Spirit and the bride say, "Come!"
And let him who hears say, "Come!"
Whoever is thirsty, let him come; and
whoever wishes, let him take the free gift
of the water of life.

18 I warn everyone who hears the words
of the prophecy of this book: If anyone
adds anything to them, God will add to
him the plagues described in this book.
19 And if anyone takes words away from
this book of prophecy, God will take away
from him his share in the tree of life and
in the holy city, which are described in this
book.
20 He who testifies to these things says,
"Yes, I am coming soon."
Amen. Come, Lord Jesus.
21 The grace of the Lord Jesus be with
God's people. Amen.

[a] *16* The Greek is plural.

PRAYER: MY RELATIONSHIP TO OTHERS

I WILL avoid foolish and ignorant disputes, knowing that they produce quarrels. As Your servant, O Lord, I must not quarrel but be gentle toward all, able to teach, and patient. (2 Timothy 2:23–24) . . . I will not return evil for evil or insult for insult, but I will give blessing instead, because to this You called me, Lord, that I may inherit a blessing.

(1 Peter 3:9)

PAUSE *to review your relationships with others and to commit them to the Lord.*

YEAR
TWO

YEAR 2 DAY 1

OT Job 3:1-26

Job Speaks

3 After this, Job opened his mouth and cursed the day of his birth. 2 He said:

3 "May the day of my birth perish,
and the night it was said, 'A boy is born!'
4 That day—may it turn to darkness;
may God above not care about it;
may no light shine upon it.
5 May darkness and deep shadow[a]
claim it once more;
may a cloud settle over it;
may blackness overwhelm its light.
6 That night—may thick darkness seize it;
may it not be included among the days of the year
nor be entered in any of the months.
7 May that night be barren;
may no shout of joy be heard in it.
8 May those who curse days[b] curse that day,
those who are ready to rouse Leviathan.
9 May its morning stars become dark;
may it wait for daylight in vain
and not see the first rays of dawn,
10 for it did not shut the doors of the womb on me
to hide trouble from my eyes.

11 "Why did I not perish at birth,
and die as I came from the womb?
12 Why were there knees to receive me
and breasts that I might be nursed?
13 For now I would be lying down in peace;
I would be asleep and at rest
14 with kings and counselors of the earth,
who built for themselves places now lying in ruins,
15 with rulers who had gold,
who filled their houses with silver.
16 Or why was I not hidden in the ground like a stillborn child,
like an infant who never saw the light of day?
17 There the wicked cease from turmoil,
and there the weary are at rest.
18 Captives also enjoy their ease;
they no longer hear the slave driver's shout.
19 The small and the great are there,
and the slave is freed from his master.

20 "Why is light given to those in misery,
and life to the bitter of soul,
21 to those who long for death that does not come,
who search for it more than for hidden treasure,
22 who are filled with gladness
and rejoice when they reach the grave?
23 Why is life given to a man
whose way is hidden,
whom God has hedged in?
24 For sighing comes to me instead of food;
my groans pour out like water.
25 What I feared has come upon me;
what I dreaded has happened to me.
26 I have no peace, no quietness;
I have no rest, but only turmoil."

[a] 5 Or *and the shadow of death* [b] 8 Or *the sea*

PRAYER: CONFESSION

HAVE You as much delight in burnt offerings and sacrifices, O Lord, as in obedience to Your voice? To obey is better than sacrifice, and to heed is better than the fat of rams. For rebellion is like the sin of divination, and stubbornness is as iniquity and idolatry. (1 Samuel 15:22–23)

***ASK** the Spirit to search your heart and reveal any areas of unconfessed sin. Acknowledge these to the Lord and thank Him for His forgiveness.*

NT Matthew 1:1–25

The Genealogy of Jesus

1 A record of the genealogy of Jesus Christ the son of David, the son of Abraham:

2 Abraham was the father of Isaac,
Isaac the father of Jacob,
Jacob the father of Judah and his brothers,
3 Judah the father of Perez and Zerah, whose mother was Tamar,
Perez the father of Hezron,
Hezron the father of Ram,
4 Ram the father of Amminadab,
Amminadab the father of Nahshon,
Nahshon the father of Salmon,
5 Salmon the father of Boaz, whose mother was Rahab,
Boaz the father of Obed, whose mother was Ruth,
Obed the father of Jesse,
6 and Jesse the father of King David.

David was the father of Solomon, whose mother had been Uriah's wife,
7 Solomon the father of Rehoboam,
Rehoboam the father of Abijah,
Abijah the father of Asa,
8 Asa the father of Jehoshaphat,
Jehoshaphat the father of Jehoram,
Jehoram the father of Uzziah,
9 Uzziah the father of Jotham,
Jotham the father of Ahaz,
Ahaz the father of Hezekiah,
10 Hezekiah the father of Manasseh,
Manasseh the father of Amon,
Amon the father of Josiah,
11 and Josiah the father of Jeconiah[a] and his brothers at the time of the exile to Babylon.

12 After the exile to Babylon:
Jeconiah was the father of Shealtiel,
Shealtiel the father of Zerubbabel,
13 Zerubbabel the father of Abiud,
Abiud the father of Eliakim,
Eliakim the father of Azor,
14 Azor the father of Zadok,
Zadok the father of Akim,
Akim the father of Eliud,
15 Eliud the father of Eleazar,
Eleazar the father of Matthan,
Matthan the father of Jacob,
16 and Jacob the father of Joseph, the husband of Mary, of whom was born Jesus, who is called Christ.

17 Thus there were fourteen generations in all from Abraham to David, fourteen from David to the exile to Babylon, and fourteen from the exile to the Christ.[b]

The Birth of Jesus Christ

18 This is how the birth of Jesus Christ
came about: His mother Mary was
pledged to be married to Joseph, but before they came together, she was found to
be with child through the Holy Spirit.
19 Because Joseph her husband was a righteous man and did not want to expose her
to public disgrace, he had in mind to divorce her quietly.
20 But after he had considered this, an
angel of the Lord appeared to him in a
dream and said, "Joseph son of David, do
not be afraid to take Mary home as your
wife, because what is conceived in her is
from the Holy Spirit. 21 She will give birth
to a son, and you are to give him the
name Jesus,[c] because he will save his people from their sins."
22 All this took place to fulfill what the
Lord had said through the prophet: 23 "The
virgin will be with child and will give
birth to a son, and they will call him Immanuel"[d]—which means, "God with us."
24 When Joseph woke up, he did what
the angel of the Lord had commanded
him and took Mary home as his wife.
25 But he had no union with her until she
gave birth to a son. And he gave him the
name Jesus.

[a] *11* That is, Jehoiachin; also in verse 12 [b] *17* Or *Messiah.* "The Christ" (Greek) and "the Messiah" (Hebrew) both mean "the Anointed One." [c] *21* *Jesus* is the Greek form of *Joshua,* which means *the* LORD *saves.* [d] *23* Isaiah 7:14

PRAYER: THE ATTRIBUTES OF GOD

YOU fashion the hearts of all and understand all their works, O God. (Psalm 33:15) . . . Death and Destruction lie open before You, Lord; how much more do human hearts! (Proverbs 15:11)

***PAUSE** to reflect on these affirmations about the person, powers and perfection of God.*

YEAR 2
DAY 2

OT Job 4:1–5:27

Eliphaz

4 Then Eliphaz the Temanite replied:

2 "If someone ventures a word with
you, will you be impatient?
But who can keep from speaking?
3 Think how you have instructed many,
how you have strengthened feeble
hands.
4 Your words have supported those who
stumbled;
you have strengthened faltering
knees.
5 But now trouble comes to you, and
you are discouraged;
it strikes you, and you are
dismayed.
6 Should not your piety be your
confidence
and your blameless ways your
hope?

7 "Consider now: Who, being innocent,
has ever perished?
Where were the upright ever
destroyed?
8 As I have observed, those who plow
evil
and those who sow trouble reap it.
9 At the breath of God they are
destroyed;
at the blast of his anger they perish.
10 The lions may roar and growl,
yet the teeth of the great lions are
broken.
11 The lion perishes for lack of prey,
and the cubs of the lioness are
scattered.

12 "A word was secretly brought to me,
my ears caught a whisper of it.
13 Amid disquieting dreams in the night,
when deep sleep falls on men,
14 fear and trembling seized me
and made all my bones shake.
15 A spirit glided past my face,
and the hair on my body stood on
end.
16 It stopped,
but I could not tell what it was.
A form stood before my eyes,
and I heard a hushed voice:
17 'Can a mortal be more righteous than
God?
Can a man be more pure than his
Maker?
18 If God places no trust in his servants,
if he charges his angels with error,
19 how much more those who live in
houses of clay,
whose foundations are in the dust,
who are crushed more readily than
a moth!
20 Between dawn and dusk they are
broken to pieces;
unnoticed, they perish forever.
21 Are not the cords of their tent pulled
up,
so that they die without wisdom?'[a]

5 "Call if you will, but who will answer
you?
To which of the holy ones will you
turn?
2 Resentment kills a fool,
and envy slays the simple.
3 I myself have seen a fool taking root,
but suddenly his house was cursed.
4 His children are far from safety,
crushed in court without a defender.
5 The hungry consume his harvest,
taking it even from among thorns,
and the thirsty pant after his wealth.

[a] *21* Some interpreters end the quotation after verse 17.

[6] For hardship does not spring from the soil,
nor does trouble sprout from the ground.
[7] Yet man is born to trouble
as surely as sparks fly upward.

[8] "But if it were I, I would appeal to God;
I would lay my cause before him.
[9] He performs wonders that cannot be fathomed,
miracles that cannot be counted.
[10] He bestows rain on the earth;
he sends water upon the countryside.
[11] The lowly he sets on high,
and those who mourn are lifted to safety.
[12] He thwarts the plans of the crafty,
so that their hands achieve no success.
[13] He catches the wise in their craftiness,
and the schemes of the wily are swept away.
[14] Darkness comes upon them in the daytime;
at noon they grope as in the night.
[15] He saves the needy from the sword in their mouth;
he saves them from the clutches of the powerful.
[16] So the poor have hope,
and injustice shuts its mouth.

[17] "Blessed is the man whom God corrects;
so do not despise the discipline of the Almighty.[b]
[18] For he wounds, but he also binds up;
he injures, but his hands also heal.
[19] From six calamities he will rescue you;
in seven no harm will befall you.
[20] In famine he will ransom you from death,
and in battle from the stroke of the sword.
[21] You will be protected from the lash of the tongue,
and need not fear when destruction comes.
[22] You will laugh at destruction and famine,
and need not fear the beasts of the earth.
[23] For you will have a covenant with the stones of the field,
and the wild animals will be at peace with you.
[24] You will know that your tent is secure;
you will take stock of your property and find nothing missing.
[25] You will know that your children will be many,
and your descendants like the grass of the earth.
[26] You will come to the grave in full vigor,
like sheaves gathered in season.

[27] "We have examined this, and it is true.
So hear it and apply it to yourself."

[b] 17 Hebrew *Shaddai*; here and throughout Job

PRAYER: RENEWAL

MAY I put away all bitterness and anger and wrath and shouting and slander, along with all malice. And may I be kind and compassionate to others, forgiving them just as You, O God, in Christ also forgave me. (Ephesians 4:31–32)

***PAUSE** to add your own prayers for personal renewal.*

NT Matthew 2:1–23

The Visit of the Magi

2 After Jesus was born in Bethlehem in Judea, during the time of King Herod, Magi[a] from the east came to Jerusalem [2] and asked, "Where is the one who has been born king of the Jews? We saw his star in the east[b] and have come to worship him."

[3] When King Herod heard this he was disturbed, and all Jerusalem with him.
[4] When he had called together all the people's chief priests and teachers of the law, he asked them where the Christ[c] was to be

[a] 1 Traditionally *Wise Men* [b] 2 Or *star when it rose*
[c] 4 Or *Messiah*

born. [5]"In Bethlehem in Judea," they
replied, "for this is what the prophet has
written:

[6] " 'But you, Bethlehem, in the land of
Judah,
are by no means least among the
rulers of Judah;
for out of you will come a ruler
who will be the shepherd of my
people Israel.'[d]"

[7]Then Herod called the Magi secretly
and found out from them the exact time
the star had appeared. [8]He sent them to
Bethlehem and said, "Go and make a
careful search for the child. As soon as you
find him, report to me, so that I too may
go and worship him."
[9]After they had heard the king, they
went on their way, and the star they had
seen in the east[e] went ahead of them until it stopped over the place where the
child was. [10]When they saw the star, they
were overjoyed. [11]On coming to the
house, they saw the child with his mother Mary, and they bowed down and worshiped him. Then they opened their treasures and presented him with gifts of gold
and of incense and of myrrh. [12]And having been warned in a dream not to go
back to Herod, they returned to their
country by another route.

The Escape to Egypt

[13]When they had gone, an angel of the
Lord appeared to Joseph in a dream. "Get
up," he said, "take the child and his mother and escape to Egypt. Stay there until I
tell you, for Herod is going to search for
the child to kill him."
[14]So he got up, took the child and his
mother during the night and left for
Egypt, [15]where he stayed until the death of
Herod. And so was fulfilled what the Lord
had said through the prophet: "Out of
Egypt I called my son."[f]
[16]When Herod realized that he had
been outwitted by the Magi, he was furious, and he gave orders to kill all the boys
in Bethlehem and its vicinity who were
two years old and under, in accordance
with the time he had learned from the
Magi. [17]Then what was said through the
prophet Jeremiah was fulfilled:

[18] "A voice is heard in Ramah,
weeping and great mourning,
Rachel weeping for her children
and refusing to be comforted,
because they are no more."[g]

The Return to Nazareth

[19]After Herod died, an angel of the Lord
appeared in a dream to Joseph in Egypt
[20]and said, "Get up, take the child and his
mother and go to the land of Israel, for
those who were trying to take the child's
life are dead."
[21]So he got up, took the child and his
mother and went to the land of Israel.
[22]But when he heard that Archelaus was
reigning in Judea in place of his father
Herod, he was afraid to go there. Having
been warned in a dream, he withdrew to
the district of Galilee, [23]and he went and
lived in a town called Nazareth. So was
fulfilled what was said through the prophets: "He will be called a Nazarene."

[d] *6* Micah 5:2 [e] *9* Or *seen when it rose*
[f] *15* Hosea 11:1 [g] *18* Jer. 31:15

PRAYER: THE WORKS OF GOD

WE can come to You, Lord Jesus Christ, for to all of us who are weary and burdened, You will give rest. We can take up Your yoke and learn from You, for You are gentle and humble in heart, and we will find rest for our souls. For Your yoke is easy, and Your burden is light. (Matthew 11:28–30)

TAKE *a moment to consider the greatness of God's wonderful works.*

YEAR 2 DAY 3

OT Job 6:1-30

Job

6 Then Job replied:

2 "If only my anguish could be weighed
and all my misery be placed on the scales!
3 It would surely outweigh the sand of the seas—
no wonder my words have been impetuous.
4 The arrows of the Almighty are in me,
my spirit drinks in their poison;
God's terrors are marshaled against me.
5 Does a wild donkey bray when it has grass,
or an ox bellow when it has fodder?
6 Is tasteless food eaten without salt,
or is there flavor in the white of an egg[a]?
7 I refuse to touch it;
such food makes me ill.

8 "Oh, that I might have my request,
that God would grant what I hope for,
9 that God would be willing to crush me,
to let loose his hand and cut me off!
10 Then I would still have this consolation—
my joy in unrelenting pain—
that I had not denied the words of the Holy One.

11 "What strength do I have, that I should still hope?
What prospects, that I should be patient?
12 Do I have the strength of stone?
Is my flesh bronze?
13 Do I have any power to help myself,
now that success has been driven from me?

14 "A despairing man should have the devotion of his friends,
even though he forsakes the fear of the Almighty.
15 But my brothers are as undependable as intermittent streams,
as the streams that overflow
16 when darkened by thawing ice
and swollen with melting snow,
17 but that cease to flow in the dry season,
and in the heat vanish from their channels.
18 Caravans turn aside from their routes;
they go up into the wasteland and perish.
19 The caravans of Tema look for water,
the traveling merchants of Sheba look in hope.
20 They are distressed, because they had been confident;
they arrive there, only to be disappointed.
21 Now you too have proved to be of no help;
you see something dreadful and are afraid.
22 Have I ever said, 'Give something on my behalf,
pay a ransom for me from your wealth,
23 deliver me from the hand of the enemy,
ransom me from the clutches of the ruthless'?

24 "Teach me, and I will be quiet;
show me where I have been wrong.
25 How painful are honest words!
But what do your arguments prove?
26 Do you mean to correct what I say,
and treat the words of a despairing man as wind?
27 You would even cast lots for the fatherless
and barter away your friend.

28 "But now be so kind as to look at me.
Would I lie to your face?
29 Relent, do not be unjust;
reconsider, for my integrity is at stake.[b]
30 Is there any wickedness on my lips?
Can my mouth not discern malice?

[a] 6 The meaning of the Hebrew for this phrase is uncertain. [b] 29 Or *my righteousness still stands*

PRAYER: PETITION

AS one of Your chosen people, holy and beloved, may I put on a heart of compassion, kindness, humility, gentleness and patience, bearing with others and forgiving others even as You, Lord, forgave me; and above all these things may I put on love, which is the bond of perfection. (Colossians 3:12–14)

***PAUSE** here to petition God for growth in love and compassion toward others. Offer prayers for your loved ones, for those who do not know Jesus and for those in need. Offer prayers regarding your activities for this day and any special concerns you may have.*

NT Matthew 3:1–17

John the Baptist Prepares the Way

3 In those days John the Baptist came,
preaching in the Desert of Judea 2and
saying, "Repent, for the kingdom of heav-
en is near." 3This is he who was spoken of
through the prophet Isaiah:

"A voice of one calling in the desert,
'Prepare the way for the Lord,
make straight paths for him.' "[a]

4John's clothes were made of camel's
hair, and he had a leather belt around his
waist. His food was locusts and wild honey. 5People went out to him from Jerusalem and all Judea and the whole region
of the Jordan. 6Confessing their sins, they
were baptized by him in the Jordan River.
7But when he saw many of the Pharisees and Sadducees coming to where he
was baptizing, he said to them: "You
brood of vipers! Who warned you to flee
from the coming wrath? 8Produce fruit in
keeping with repentance. 9And do not
think you can say to yourselves, 'We have
Abraham as our father.' I tell you that out
of these stones God can raise up children
for Abraham. 10The ax is already at the
root of the trees, and every tree that does
not produce good fruit will be cut down
and thrown into the fire.
11"I baptize you with[b] water for repentance. But after me will come one who is
more powerful than I, whose sandals I am
not fit to carry. He will baptize you with
the Holy Spirit and with fire. 12His winnowing fork is in his hand, and he will
clear his threshing floor, gathering his
wheat into the barn and burning up the
chaff with unquenchable fire."

The Baptism of Jesus

13Then Jesus came from Galilee to the
Jordan to be baptized by John. 14But John
tried to deter him, saying, "I need to be
baptized by you, and do you come to me?"
15Jesus replied, "Let it be so now; it is
proper for us to do this to fulfill all righteousness." Then John consented.
16As soon as Jesus was baptized, he
went up out of the water. At that moment
heaven was opened, and he saw the Spirit of God descending like a dove and light-
ing on him. 17And a voice from heaven
said, "This is my Son, whom I love; with
him I am well pleased."

[a] 3 Isaiah 40:3 [b] 11 Or *in*

PRAYER: MY RELATIONSHIP TO GOD

JESUS, You have asked the Father, and He has given me another Comforter to be with me forever, even the Spirit of truth, whom the world cannot receive, because it neither sees Him nor knows Him. But I know Him, for He lives in me. (John 14:16–17)

***PAUSE** to thank God for the relationship that you enjoy with Him in Jesus Christ.*

YEAR 2 DAY 4

OT Proverbs 16

16 To man belong the plans of the heart,
but from the LORD comes the reply of the tongue.

2 All a man's ways seem innocent to him,
but motives are weighed by the LORD.

3 Commit to the LORD whatever you do,
and your plans will succeed.

4 The LORD works out everything for his own ends—
even the wicked for a day of disaster.

5 The LORD detests all the proud of heart.
Be sure of this: They will not go unpunished.

6 Through love and faithfulness sin is atoned for;
through the fear of the LORD a man avoids evil.

7 When a man's ways are pleasing to the LORD,
he makes even his enemies live at peace with him.

8 Better a little with righteousness
than much gain with injustice.

9 In his heart a man plans his course,
but the LORD determines his steps.

10 The lips of a king speak as an oracle,
and his mouth should not betray justice.

11 Honest scales and balances are from the LORD;
all the weights in the bag are of his making.

12 Kings detest wrongdoing,
for a throne is established through righteousness.

13 Kings take pleasure in honest lips;
they value a man who speaks the truth.

14 A king's wrath is a messenger of death,
but a wise man will appease it.

15 When a king's face brightens, it means life;
his favor is like a rain cloud in spring.

16 How much better to get wisdom than gold,
to choose understanding rather than silver!

17 The highway of the upright avoids evil;
he who guards his way guards his life.

18 Pride goes before destruction,
a haughty spirit before a fall.

19 Better to be lowly in spirit and among the oppressed
than to share plunder with the proud.

20 Whoever gives heed to instruction prospers,
and blessed is he who trusts in the LORD.

21 The wise in heart are called discerning,
and pleasant words promote instruction.[a]

22 Understanding is a fountain of life to those who have it,
but folly brings punishment to fools.

23 A wise man's heart guides his mouth,
and his lips promote instruction.[b]

24 Pleasant words are a honeycomb,
sweet to the soul and healing to the bones.

25 There is a way that seems right to a man,
but in the end it leads to death.

26 The laborer's appetite works for him;
his hunger drives him on.

27 A scoundrel plots evil,
and his speech is like a scorching fire.

28 A perverse man stirs up dissension,
and a gossip separates close friends.

29 A violent man entices his neighbor

[a] *21* Or *words make a man persuasive* [b] *23* Or *mouth / and makes his lips persuasive*

and leads him down a path that is
not good.
[30] He who winks with his eye is plotting
perversity;
he who purses his lips is bent on
evil.
[31] Gray hair is a crown of splendor;
it is attained by a righteous life.
[32] Better a patient man than a warrior,
a man who controls his temper
than one who takes a city.
[33] The lot is cast into the lap,
but its every decision is from the
LORD.

PRAYER: INTERCESSION

JESUS, You say to us: "Behold . . . lift up your eyes and look at the fields, for they are white for harvest. Even now the reaper draws his wages, and gathers fruit for eternal life, that those who sow and those who reap may rejoice together." (John 4:35–36)

***TAKE** a few moments to intercede on behalf of friends, relatives, neighbors and coworkers who do not yet know salvation in Jesus Christ.*

NT Matthew 4:1-25

The Temptation of Jesus

4 Then Jesus was led by the Spirit into
the desert to be tempted by the devil.
[2]After fasting forty days and forty nights,
he was hungry. [3]The tempter came to him
and said, "If you are the Son of God, tell
these stones to become bread."
[4]Jesus answered, "It is written: 'Man does
not live on bread alone, but on every word
that comes from the mouth of God.'[a]"
[5]Then the devil took him to the holy
city and had him stand on the highest
point of the temple. [6]"If you are the Son
of God," he said, "throw yourself down.
For it is written:

" 'He will command his angels
concerning you,
and they will lift you up in their
hands,
so that you will not strike your foot
against a stone.'[b]"

[7]Jesus answered him, "It is also written:
'Do not put the Lord your God to the test.'[c]"
[8]Again, the devil took him to a very
high mountain and showed him all the
kingdoms of the world and their splendor. [9]"All this I will give you," he said, "if
you will bow down and worship me."
[10]Jesus said to him, "Away from me, Satan! For it is written: 'Worship the Lord
your God, and serve him only.'[d]"
[11]Then the devil left him, and angels
came and attended him.

Jesus Begins to Preach

[12]When Jesus heard that John had been
put in prison, he returned to Galilee.
[13]Leaving Nazareth, he went and lived in
Capernaum, which was by the lake in the
area of Zebulun and Naphtali— [14]to fulfill
what was said through the prophet Isaiah:

[15] "Land of Zebulun and land of
Naphtali,
the way to the sea, along the
Jordan,
Galilee of the Gentiles—
[16] the people living in darkness
have seen a great light;
on those living in the land of the
shadow of death
a light has dawned."[e]

[17]From that time on Jesus began to
preach, "Repent, for the kingdom of heav-
en is near."

The Calling of the First Disciples

[18]As Jesus was walking beside the Sea of
Galilee, he saw two brothers, Simon called
Peter and his brother Andrew. They were
casting a net into the lake, for they were
fishermen. [19]"Come, follow me," Jesus said,
"and I will make you fishers of men." [20]At
once they left their nets and followed him.
[21]Going on from there, he saw two other
brothers, James son of Zebedee and his

[a] *4* Deut. 8:3 [b] *6* Psalm 91:11,12 [c] *7* Deut. 6:16
[d] *10* Deut. 6:13 [e] *16* Isaiah 9:1,2

brother John. They were in a boat with their
father Zebedee, preparing their nets. Jesus
called them, [22]and immediately they left
the boat and their father and followed him.

Jesus Heals the Sick

[23]Jesus went throughout Galilee, teaching
in their synagogues, preaching the good
news of the kingdom, and healing every
disease and sickness among the people.
[24]News about him spread all over Syria, and
people brought to him all who were ill with
various diseases, those suffering severe
pain, the demon-possessed, those having
seizures, and the paralyzed, and he healed
them. [25]Large crowds from Galilee, the Decapolis,[f] Jerusalem, Judea and the region
across the Jordan followed him.

[f] 25 That is, the Ten Cities

PRAYER: THE CHARACTER I WANT TO CULTIVATE

I WILL not show partiality in judgment; I will hear both small and great alike. I will not be afraid of anyone, for judgment belongs to God. (Deuteronomy 1:17)

***TAKE** a moment to ask the Lord for the grace to grow in godly character.*

YEAR 2 DAY 5

OT Job 7:1–21

7 "Does not man have hard service on earth?
Are not his days like those of a hired man?
2 Like a slave longing for the evening shadows,
or a hired man waiting eagerly for his wages,
3 so I have been allotted months of futility,
and nights of misery have been assigned to me.
4 When I lie down I think, 'How long before I get up?'
The night drags on, and I toss till dawn.
5 My body is clothed with worms and scabs,
my skin is broken and festering.

6 "My days are swifter than a weaver's shuttle,
and they come to an end without hope.
7 Remember, O God, that my life is but a breath;
my eyes will never see happiness again.
8 The eye that now sees me will see me no longer;
you will look for me, but I will be no more.
9 As a cloud vanishes and is gone,
so he who goes down to the grave[a] does not return.
10 He will never come to his house again;
his place will know him no more.

11 "Therefore I will not keep silent;
I will speak out in the anguish of my spirit,
I will complain in the bitterness of my soul.
12 Am I the sea, or the monster of the deep,
that you put me under guard?
13 When I think my bed will comfort me
and my couch will ease my complaint,
14 even then you frighten me with dreams
and terrify me with visions,
15 so that I prefer strangling and death,
rather than this body of mine.
16 I despise my life; I would not live forever.
Let me alone; my days have no meaning.
17 "What is man that you make so much of him,
that you give him so much attention,
18 that you examine him every morning
and test him every moment?
19 Will you never look away from me,

[a] 9 Hebrew *Sheol*

or let me alone even for an instant?
[20]If I have sinned, what have I done to
you,
O watcher of men?
Why have you made me your target?
Have I become a burden to you?[b]
[21]Why do you not pardon my offenses
and forgive my sins?
For I will soon lie down in the dust;
you will search for me, but I will be
no more."

[b] *20* A few manuscripts of the Masoretic Text, an ancient Hebrew scribal tradition and Septuagint; most manuscripts of the Masoretic Text *I have become a burden to myself.*

PRAYER: AFFIRMATION

WHOEVER is faithful with very little is also faithful with much, and whoever is dishonest with very little will also be dishonest with much. If I am not faithful in handling worldly wealth, who will trust me with true riches? And if I am not faithful with someone else's property, who will give me property of my own? (Luke 16:10–12)

***PAUSE** to reflect on these Biblical affirmations.*

NT Matthew 5:1-20

The Beatitudes

5 Now when he saw the crowds, he went
up on a mountainside and sat down.
His disciples came to him, [2]and he began
to teach them, saying:

[3]"Blessed are the poor in spirit,
for theirs is the kingdom of heaven.
[4]Blessed are those who mourn,
for they will be comforted.
[5]Blessed are the meek,
for they will inherit the earth.
[6]Blessed are those who hunger and
thirst for righteousness,
for they will be filled.
[7]Blessed are the merciful,
for they will be shown mercy.
[8]Blessed are the pure in heart,
for they will see God.
[9]Blessed are the peacemakers,
for they will be called sons of God.
[10]Blessed are those who are persecuted
because of righteousness,
for theirs is the kingdom of heaven.

[11]"Blessed are you when people insult
you, persecute you and falsely say all
kinds of evil against you because of me.
[12]Rejoice and be glad, because great is
your reward in heaven, for in the same
way they persecuted the prophets who
were before you.

Salt and Light

[13]"You are the salt of the earth. But if
the salt loses its saltiness, how can it be
made salty again? It is no longer good for
anything, except to be thrown out and
trampled by men.
[14]"You are the light of the world. A city
on a hill cannot be hidden. [15]Neither do
people light a lamp and put it under a
bowl. Instead they put it on its stand,
and it gives light to everyone in the
house. [16]In the same way, let your light
shine before men, that they may see your
good deeds and praise your Father in
heaven.

The Fulfillment of the Law

[17]"Do not think that I have come to
abolish the Law or the Prophets; I have
not come to abolish them but to fulfill
them. [18]I tell you the truth, until heaven
and earth disappear, not the smallest letter, not the least stroke of a pen, will by
any means disappear from the Law until
everything is accomplished. [19]Anyone
who breaks one of the least of these commandments and teaches others to do the
same will be called least in the kingdom
of heaven, but whoever practices and
teaches these commands will be called
great in the kingdom of heaven. [20]For I tell
you that unless your righteousness surpasses that of the Pharisees and the teachers of the law, you will certainly not enter
the kingdom of heaven.

PRAYER: MY RELATIONSHIP TO OTHERS

AS we have opportunity, we should do good to all people, especially to those who belong to the family of faith.
(Galatians 6:10)

***PAUSE** to review your relationships with others and to commit them to the Lord.*

YEAR 2
DAY 6

OT Job 8:1–22

Bildad

8 Then Bildad the Shuhite replied:

2 "How long will you say such things?
Your words are a blustering wind.
3 Does God pervert justice?
Does the Almighty pervert what is right?
4 When your children sinned against him,
he gave them over to the penalty of their sin.
5 But if you will look to God
and plead with the Almighty,
6 if you are pure and upright,
even now he will rouse himself on your behalf
and restore you to your rightful place.
7 Your beginnings will seem humble,
so prosperous will your future be.

8 "Ask the former generations
and find out what their fathers learned,
9 for we were born only yesterday and know nothing,
and our days on earth are but a shadow.
10 Will they not instruct you and tell you?
Will they not bring forth words from their understanding?
11 Can papyrus grow tall where there is no marsh?
Can reeds thrive without water?
12 While still growing and uncut,
they wither more quickly than grass.
13 Such is the destiny of all who forget God;
so perishes the hope of the godless.
14 What he trusts in is fragile[a];
what he relies on is a spider's web.
15 He leans on his web, but it gives way;
he clings to it, but it does not hold.
16 He is like a well-watered plant in the sunshine,
spreading its shoots over the garden;
17 it entwines its roots around a pile of rocks
and looks for a place among the stones.
18 But when it is torn from its spot,
that place disowns it and says, 'I never saw you.'
19 Surely its life withers away,
and[b] from the soil other plants grow.

20 "Surely God does not reject a blameless man
or strengthen the hands of evildoers.
21 He will yet fill your mouth with laughter
and your lips with shouts of joy.
22 Your enemies will be clothed in shame,
and the tents of the wicked will be no more."

[a] *14* The meaning of the Hebrew for this word is uncertain. [b] *19* Or *Surely all the joy it has / is that*

PRAYER: THANKSGIVING

YOU, O Lord, have performed mighty deeds with Your arm; You have scattered those who are proud in the thoughts of their hearts. You have brought down rulers from their thrones and have lifted up the humble. (Luke 1:51–52)

***PAUSE** to offer your own expressions of thanksgiving.*

NT Matthew 5:21-48

Murder

21 "You have heard that it was said to the people long ago, 'Do not murder,[a] and anyone who murders will be subject to judgment.' 22 But I tell you that anyone who is angry with his brother[b] will be subject to judgment. Again, anyone who says to his brother, 'Raca,[c]' is answerable to the Sanhedrin. But anyone who says, 'You fool!' will be in danger of the fire of hell.

23 "Therefore, if you are offering your gift at the altar and there remember that your brother has something against you, 24 leave your gift there in front of the altar. First go and be reconciled to your brother; then come and offer your gift.

25 "Settle matters quickly with your adversary who is taking you to court. Do it while you are still with him on the way, or he may hand you over to the judge, and the judge may hand you over to the officer, and you may be thrown into prison. 26 I tell you the truth, you will not get out until you have paid the last penny.[d]

Adultery

27 "You have heard that it was said, 'Do not commit adultery.'[e] 28 But I tell you that anyone who looks at a woman lustfully has already committed adultery with her in his heart. 29 If your right eye causes you to sin, gouge it out and throw it away. It is better for you to lose one part of your body than for your whole body to be thrown into hell. 30 And if your right hand causes you to sin, cut it off and throw it away. It is better for you to lose one part of your body than for your whole body to go into hell.

Divorce

31 "It has been said, 'Anyone who divorces his wife must give her a certificate of divorce.'[f] 32 But I tell you that anyone who divorces his wife, except for marital unfaithfulness, causes her to become an adulteress, and anyone who marries the divorced woman commits adultery.

Oaths

33 "Again, you have heard that it was said to the people long ago, 'Do not break your oath, but keep the oaths you have made to the Lord.' 34 But I tell you, Do not swear at all: either by heaven, for it is God's throne; 35 or by the earth, for it is his footstool; or by Jerusalem, for it is the city of the Great King. 36 And do not swear by your head, for you cannot make even one hair white or black. 37 Simply let your 'Yes' be 'Yes,' and your 'No,' 'No'; anything beyond this comes from the evil one.

An Eye for an Eye

38 "You have heard that it was said, 'Eye for eye, and tooth for tooth.'[g] 39 But I tell you, Do not resist an evil person. If someone strikes you on the right cheek, turn to him the other also. 40 And if someone wants to sue you and take your tunic, let him have your cloak as well. 41 If someone forces you to go one mile, go with him two miles. 42 Give to the one who asks you, and do not turn away from the one who wants to borrow from you.

Love for Enemies

43 "You have heard that it was said, 'Love your neighbor[h] and hate your enemy.' 44 But I tell you: Love your enemies[i] and pray for those who persecute you, 45 that you may be sons of your Father in heaven. He causes his sun to rise on the evil and the good, and sends rain on the righteous and the unrighteous. 46 If you love those who love you, what reward will you get? Are not even the tax collectors doing that? 47 And if you greet only your brothers, what are you doing more than others? Do not even pagans do that? 48 Be perfect, therefore, as your heavenly Father is perfect.

[a] *21* Exodus 20:13 [b] *22* Some manuscripts *brother without cause* [c] *22* An Aramaic term of contempt [d] *26* Greek *kodrantes* [e] *27* Exodus 20:14 [f] *31* Deut. 24:1 [g] *38* Exodus 21:24; Lev. 24:20; Deut. 19:21 [h] *43* Lev. 19:18 [i] *44* Some late manuscripts *enemies, bless those who curse you, do good to those who hate you*

PRAYER: THE ATTRIBUTES OF GOD

***YOU, O Lord, are upright; You are my Rock, and there is no unrighteousness in You. (Psalm 92:15) . . .
Lord of hosts, You judge righteously and test my heart and mind. To You I have committed my cause. (Jeremiah 11:20)***

***PAUSE** to reflect on these affirmations about the person, powers and perfection of God.*

YEAR 2 DAY 7

OT Psalm 73

Psalm 73

A psalm of Asaph.

[1]Surely God is good to Israel,
to those who are pure in heart.

[2]But as for me, my feet had almost
slipped;
I had nearly lost my foothold.
[3]For I envied the arrogant
when I saw the prosperity of the
wicked.

[4]They have no struggles;
their bodies are healthy and
strong.[a]
[5]They are free from the burdens
common to man;
they are not plagued by human ills.
[6]Therefore pride is their necklace;
they clothe themselves with
violence.
[7]From their callous hearts comes
iniquity[b];
the evil conceits of their minds
know no limits.
[8]They scoff, and speak with malice;
in their arrogance they threaten
oppression.
[9]Their mouths lay claim to heaven,
and their tongues take possession of
the earth.
[10]Therefore their people turn to them
and drink up waters in
abundance.[c]
[11]They say, "How can God know?
Does the Most High have
knowledge?"

[12]This is what the wicked are like—
always carefree, they increase in
wealth.

[13]Surely in vain have I kept my heart
pure;
in vain have I washed my hands in
innocence.
[14]All day long I have been plagued;
I have been punished every
morning.

[15]If I had said, "I will speak thus,"
I would have betrayed your
children.
[16]When I tried to understand all this,
it was oppressive to me
[17]till I entered the sanctuary of God;
then I understood their final
destiny.

[18]Surely you place them on slippery
ground;
you cast them down to ruin.
[19]How suddenly are they destroyed,
completely swept away by terrors!
[20]As a dream when one awakes,
so when you arise, O Lord,
you will despise them as
fantasies.

[21]When my heart was grieved
and my spirit embittered,
[22]I was senseless and ignorant;
I was a brute beast before you.

[23]Yet I am always with you;
you hold me by my right hand.
[24]You guide me with your counsel,
and afterward you will take me into
glory.
[25]Whom have I in heaven but you?

[a] *4* With a different word division of the Hebrew; Masoretic Text *struggles at their death; / their bodies are healthy* [b] *7* Syriac (see also Septuagint); Hebrew *Their eyes bulge with fat* [c] *10* The meaning of the Hebrew for this verse is uncertain.

And earth has nothing I desire
besides you.
26 My flesh and my heart may fail,
but God is the strength of my heart
and my portion forever.

27 Those who are far from you will
perish;
you destroy all who are unfaithful
to you.
28 But as for me, it is good to be near
God.
I have made the Sovereign LORD my
refuge;
I will tell of all your deeds.

PRAYER: ADORATION

WALKING in the way of Your laws, O Lord, I wait for You; Your name and Your memory are the desire of my soul.
(Isaiah 26:8)

PAUSE *to express your thoughts of praise and worship.*

NT Matthew 6:1-15

Giving to the Needy

6 "Be careful not to do your 'acts of righteousness' before men, to be seen by them. If you do, you will have no reward from your Father in heaven.
2 "So when you give to the needy, do not announce it with trumpets, as the hypocrites do in the synagogues and on the streets, to be honored by men. I tell you the truth, they have received their reward
in full. 3 But when you give to the needy,
do not let your left hand know what your
right hand is doing, 4 so that your giving
may be in secret. Then your Father, who sees what is done in secret, will reward you.

Prayer

5 "And when you pray, do not be like the hypocrites, for they love to pray standing in the synagogues and on the street corners to be seen by men. I tell you the truth, they have received their reward in
full. 6 But when you pray, go into your
room, close the door and pray to your Father, who is unseen. Then your Father, who sees what is done in secret, will reward you. 7 And when you pray, do not
keep on babbling like pagans, for they think they will be heard because of their
many words. 8 Do not be like them, for
your Father knows what you need before you ask him.
9 "This, then, is how you should pray:

" 'Our Father in heaven,
hallowed be your name,
10 your kingdom come,
your will be done
on earth as it is in heaven.
11 Give us today our daily bread.
12 Forgive us our debts,
as we also have forgiven our
debtors.
13 And lead us not into temptation,
but deliver us from the evil one.[a]'

14 For if you forgive men when they sin against you, your heavenly Father will also
forgive you. 15 But if you do not forgive
men their sins, your Father will not forgive your sins.

[a] 13 Or *from evil;* some late manuscripts *one, / for yours is the kingdom and the power and the glory forever. Amen.*

PRAYER: THE WORKS OF GOD

BLESSED are those who die in You, Lord, from now on. They will rest from their labor, for their works will follow them.
(Revelation 14:13)

TAKE *a moment to consider the greatness of God's wonderful works.*

YEAR 2 DAY 8

OT Job 9:1-35

Job

9 Then Job replied:

[2] "Indeed, I know that this is true.
But how can a mortal be righteous before God?
[3] Though one wished to dispute with him,
he could not answer him one time out of a thousand.
[4] His wisdom is profound, his power is vast.
Who has resisted him and come out unscathed?
[5] He moves mountains without their knowing it
and overturns them in his anger.
[6] He shakes the earth from its place
and makes its pillars tremble.
[7] He speaks to the sun and it does not shine;
he seals off the light of the stars.
[8] He alone stretches out the heavens
and treads on the waves of the sea.
[9] He is the Maker of the Bear and Orion,
the Pleiades and the constellations of the south.
[10] He performs wonders that cannot be fathomed,
miracles that cannot be counted.
[11] When he passes me, I cannot see him;
when he goes by, I cannot perceive him.
[12] If he snatches away, who can stop him?
Who can say to him, 'What are you doing?'
[13] God does not restrain his anger;
even the cohorts of Rahab cowered at his feet.

[14] "How then can I dispute with him?
How can I find words to argue with him?
[15] Though I were innocent, I could not answer him;
I could only plead with my Judge for mercy.
[16] Even if I summoned him and he responded,
I do not believe he would give me a hearing.
[17] He would crush me with a storm
and multiply my wounds for no reason.
[18] He would not let me regain my breath
but would overwhelm me with misery.
[19] If it is a matter of strength, he is mighty!
And if it is a matter of justice, who will summon him[a]?
[20] Even if I were innocent, my mouth would condemn me;
if I were blameless, it would pronounce me guilty.

[21] "Although I am blameless,
I have no concern for myself;
I despise my own life.
[22] It is all the same; that is why I say,
'He destroys both the blameless and the wicked.'
[23] When a scourge brings sudden death,
he mocks the despair of the innocent.
[24] When a land falls into the hands of the wicked,
he blindfolds its judges.
If it is not he, then who is it?

[25] "My days are swifter than a runner;
they fly away without a glimpse of joy.
[26] They skim past like boats of papyrus,
like eagles swooping down on their prey.
[27] If I say, 'I will forget my complaint,
I will change my expression, and smile,'
[28] I still dread all my sufferings,
for I know you will not hold me innocent.
[29] Since I am already found guilty,
why should I struggle in vain?
[30] Even if I washed myself with soap[b]
and my hands with washing soda,
[31] you would plunge me into a slime pit
so that even my clothes would detest me.

[32] "He is not a man like me that I might answer him,
that we might confront each other in court.
[33] If only there were someone to arbitrate between us,

[a] *19* See Septuagint; Hebrew *me.* [b] *30* Or *snow*

to lay his hand upon us both,
[34] someone to remove God's rod from me,
so that his terror would frighten me
no more.
[35] Then I would speak up without fear of
him,
but as it now stands with me, I
cannot.

PRAYER: CONFESSION

WOE to me, for I am undone because I have unclean lips, I live among a people of unclean lips, and my eyes have seen You, the King, the Lord of hosts! (Isaiah 6:5)

***ASK** the Spirit to search your heart and reveal any areas of unconfessed sin. Acknowledge these to the Lord and thank Him for His forgiveness.*

NT Matthew 6:16–34

Fasting

[16] "When you fast, do not look somber
as the hypocrites do, for they disfigure
their faces to show men they are fasting. I
tell you the truth, they have received their
reward in full. [17] But when you fast, put oil
on your head and wash your face, [18] so that
it will not be obvious to men that you are
fasting, but only to your Father, who is
unseen; and your Father, who sees what is
done in secret, will reward you.

Treasures in Heaven

[19] "Do not store up for yourselves treasures on earth, where moth and rust destroy, and where thieves break in and
steal. [20] But store up for yourselves treasures in heaven, where moth and rust do
not destroy, and where thieves do not
break in and steal. [21] For where your treasure is, there your heart will be also.
[22] "The eye is the lamp of the body. If
your eyes are good, your whole body will
be full of light. [23] But if your eyes are bad,
your whole body will be full of darkness.
If then the light within you is darkness,
how great is that darkness!
[24] "No one can serve two masters. Either
he will hate the one and love the other, or
he will be devoted to the one and despise
the other. You cannot serve both God and
Money.

Do Not Worry

[25] "Therefore I tell you, do not worry
about your life, what you will eat or drink;
or about your body, what you will wear.
Is not life more important than food, and
the body more important than clothes?
[26] Look at the birds of the air; they do not
sow or reap or store away in barns, and
yet your heavenly Father feeds them. Are
you not much more valuable than they?
[27] Who of you by worrying can add a single hour to his life[a]?
[28] "And why do you worry about clothes?
See how the lilies of the field grow. They
do not labor or spin. [29] Yet I tell you that
not even Solomon in all his splendor was
dressed like one of these. [30] If that is how
God clothes the grass of the field, which is
here today and tomorrow is thrown into
the fire, will he not much more clothe you,
O you of little faith? [31] So do not worry,
saying, 'What shall we eat?' or 'What shall
we drink?' or 'What shall we wear?' [32] For
the pagans run after all these things, and
your heavenly Father knows that you need
them. [33] But seek first his kingdom and his
righteousness, and all these things will be
given to you as well. [34] Therefore do not
worry about tomorrow, for tomorrow will
worry about itself. Each day has enough
trouble of its own.

[a] 27 Or *single cubit to his height*

PRAYER: MY RELATIONSHIP TO GOD

YOUR grace is sufficient for me, for Your power is made perfect in weakness. Therefore I will boast all the more gladly in my weaknesses, that Your power, O Christ, may rest upon me. Therefore I can

be content in weaknesses, in insults, in hardships, in persecutions and in difficulties, for Your sake. For when I am weak, then I am strong. (2 Corinthians 12:9–10)

PAUSE *to thank God for the relationship that you enjoy with Him in Jesus Christ.*

OT Job 10:1–11:20

YEAR 2 DAY 9

10 "I loathe my very life;
therefore I will give free rein to my complaint
and speak out in the bitterness of my soul.
2 I will say to God: Do not condemn me,
but tell me what charges you have against me.
3 Does it please you to oppress me,
to spurn the work of your hands,
while you smile on the schemes of the wicked?
4 Do you have eyes of flesh?
Do you see as a mortal sees?
5 Are your days like those of a mortal
or your years like those of a man,
6 that you must search out my faults
and probe after my sin—
7 though you know that I am not guilty
and that no one can rescue me from your hand?

8 "Your hands shaped me and made me.
Will you now turn and destroy me?
9 Remember that you molded me like clay.
Will you now turn me to dust again?
10 Did you not pour me out like milk
and curdle me like cheese,
11 clothe me with skin and flesh
and knit me together with bones and sinews?
12 You gave me life and showed me kindness,
and in your providence watched over my spirit.

13 "But this is what you concealed in your heart,
and I know that this was in your mind:
14 If I sinned, you would be watching me
and would not let my offense go unpunished.
15 If I am guilty—woe to me!
Even if I am innocent, I cannot lift my head,
for I am full of shame
and drowned in[a] my affliction.
16 If I hold my head high, you stalk me like a lion
and again display your awesome power against me.
17 You bring new witnesses against me
and increase your anger toward me;
your forces come against me wave upon wave.

18 "Why then did you bring me out of the womb?
I wish I had died before any eye saw me.
19 If only I had never come into being,
or had been carried straight from the womb to the grave!
20 Are not my few days almost over?
Turn away from me so I can have a moment's joy
21 before I go to the place of no return,
to the land of gloom and deep shadow,[b]
22 to the land of deepest night,
of deep shadow and disorder,
where even the light is like darkness."

Zophar

11 Then Zophar the Naamathite replied:

2 "Are all these words to go unanswered?
Is this talker to be vindicated?
3 Will your idle talk reduce men to silence?

[a] 15 Or *and aware of* [b] 21 Or *and the shadow of death;* also in verse 22

Will no one rebuke you when you
mock?
4 You say to God, 'My beliefs are
flawless
and I am pure in your sight.'
5 Oh, how I wish that God would
speak,
that he would open his lips against
you
6 and disclose to you the secrets of
wisdom,
for true wisdom has two sides.
Know this: God has even forgotten
some of your sin.

7 "Can you fathom the mysteries of
God?
Can you probe the limits of the
Almighty?
8 They are higher than the heavens—
what can you do?
They are deeper than the depths of
the grave[c]—what can you know?
9 Their measure is longer than the earth
and wider than the sea.

10 "If he comes along and confines you
in prison
and convenes a court, who can
oppose him?
11 Surely he recognizes deceitful men;
and when he sees evil, does he not
take note?
12 But a witless man can no more
become wise
than a wild donkey's colt can be
born a man.[d]

13 "Yet if you devote your heart to him
and stretch out your hands to him,
14 if you put away the sin that is in your
hand
and allow no evil to dwell in your
tent,
15 then you will lift up your face without
shame;
you will stand firm and without
fear.
16 You will surely forget your trouble,
recalling it only as waters gone by.
17 Life will be brighter than noonday,
and darkness will become like
morning.
18 You will be secure, because there is
hope;
you will look about you and take
your rest in safety.
19 You will lie down, with no one to
make you afraid,
and many will court your favor.
20 But the eyes of the wicked will fail,
and escape will elude them;
their hope will become a dying gasp."

[c] 8 Hebrew *than Sheol* [d] 12 Or *wild donkey can be born tame*

PRAYER: RENEWAL

MAY I consecrate myself and be holy, because You are the Lord my God. May I keep Your statutes and practice them, for You are the Lord who sanctifies me. (Leviticus 20:7–8)

PAUSE *to add your own prayers for personal renewal.*

NT Matthew 7:1–29

Judging Others

7 "Do not judge, or you too will be
judged. 2 For in the same way you judge
others, you will be judged, and with the
measure you use, it will be measured to
you.
3 "Why do you look at the speck of saw-
dust in your brother's eye and pay no attention to the plank in your own eye?
4 How can you say to your brother, 'Let me
take the speck out of your eye,' when all the
time there is a plank in your own eye? 5 You
hypocrite, first take the plank out of your
own eye, and then you will see clearly to
remove the speck from your brother's eye.
6 "Do not give dogs what is sacred; do
not throw your pearls to pigs. If you do,
they may trample them under their feet,
and then turn and tear you to pieces.

Ask, Seek, Knock

7 "Ask and it will be given to you; seek
and you will find; knock and the door will
be opened to you. 8 For everyone who asks

receives; he who seeks finds; and to him
who knocks, the door will be opened.
9 "Which of you, if his son asks for
bread, will give him a stone? 10 Or if he
asks for a fish, will give him a snake? 11 If
you, then, though you are evil, know how
to give good gifts to your children, how
much more will your Father in heaven
give good gifts to those who ask him! 12 So
in everything, do to others what you
would have them do to you, for this sums
up the Law and the Prophets.

The Narrow and Wide Gates

13 "Enter through the narrow gate. For
wide is the gate and broad is the road that
leads to destruction, and many enter
through it. 14 But small is the gate and narrow the road that leads to life, and only a
few find it.

A Tree and Its Fruit

15 "Watch out for false prophets. They
come to you in sheep's clothing, but inwardly they are ferocious wolves. 16 By their
fruit you will recognize them. Do people
pick grapes from thornbushes, or figs from
thistles? 17 Likewise every good tree bears
good fruit, but a bad tree bears bad fruit.
18 A good tree cannot bear bad fruit, and a
bad tree cannot bear good fruit. 19 Every
tree that does not bear good fruit is cut
down and thrown into the fire. 20 Thus, by
their fruit you will recognize them.
21 "Not everyone who says to me, 'Lord,
Lord,' will enter the kingdom of heaven,
but only he who does the will of my Father
who is in heaven. 22 Many will say to me on
that day, 'Lord, Lord, did we not prophesy
in your name, and in your name drive out
demons and perform many miracles?'
23 Then I will tell them plainly, 'I never
knew you. Away from me, you evildoers!'

The Wise and Foolish Builders

24 "Therefore everyone who hears these
words of mine and puts them into practice
is like a wise man who built his house on
the rock. 25 The rain came down, the streams
rose, and the winds blew and beat against
that house; yet it did not fall, because it had
its foundation on the rock. 26 But everyone
who hears these words of mine and does
not put them into practice is like a foolish
man who built his house on sand. 27 The
rain came down, the streams rose, and the
winds blew and beat against that house,
and it fell with a great crash."

28 When Jesus had finished saying these
things, the crowds were amazed at his teaching, 29 because he taught as one who had authority, and not as their teachers of the law.

PRAYER: THE CHARACTER I WANT TO CULTIVATE

BETTER is open rebuke than love that is concealed. Faithful are the wounds of a friend, but the kisses of an enemy are deceitful. (Proverbs 27:5–6)

***TAKE** a moment to ask the Lord for the grace to grow in godly character.*

OT Job 12:1–25 — **YEAR 2 DAY 10**

Job

12 Then Job replied:

2 "Doubtless you are the people,
and wisdom will die with you!
3 But I have a mind as well as you;
I am not inferior to you.
Who does not know all these things?

4 "I have become a laughingstock to my
friends,
though I called upon God and he
answered—
a mere laughingstock, though
righteous and blameless!
5 Men at ease have contempt for
misfortune
as the fate of those whose feet are
slipping.
6 The tents of marauders are
undisturbed,

and those who provoke God are
secure—
those who carry their god in their
hands.[a]

7 "But ask the animals, and they will
teach you,
or the birds of the air, and they will
tell you;
8 or speak to the earth, and it will teach
you,
or let the fish of the sea inform you.
9 Which of all these does not know
that the hand of the LORD has done
this?
10 In his hand is the life of every creature
and the breath of all mankind.
11 Does not the ear test words
as the tongue tastes food?
12 Is not wisdom found among the aged?
Does not long life bring
understanding?

13 "To God belong wisdom and power;
counsel and understanding are his.
14 What he tears down cannot be rebuilt;
the man he imprisons cannot be
released.
15 If he holds back the waters, there is
drought;
if he lets them loose, they devastate
the land.
16 To him belong strength and victory;
both deceived and deceiver are his.
17 He leads counselors away stripped
and makes fools of judges.
18 He takes off the shackles put on by
kings
and ties a loincloth[b] around their
waist.
19 He leads priests away stripped
and overthrows men long established.
20 He silences the lips of trusted advisers
and takes away the discernment of
elders.
21 He pours contempt on nobles
and disarms the mighty.
22 He reveals the deep things of darkness
and brings deep shadows into the
light.
23 He makes nations great, and destroys
them;
he enlarges nations, and disperses
them.
24 He deprives the leaders of the earth of
their reason;
he sends them wandering through a
trackless waste.
25 They grope in darkness with no light;
he makes them stagger like
drunkards.

[a] 6 Or *secure / in what God's hand brings them*
[b] 18 Or *shackles of kings / and ties a belt*

PRAYER: PETITION

MAY I examine all things, hold fast to the good, and abstain from every form of evil. (1 Thessalonians 5:21–22)

PAUSE *here to petition God to help you be a faithful steward of your time, talents, possessions and relationships. Offer prayers of petition regarding your activities for this day and any special concerns you may have.*

NT Matthew 8:1–17

The Man With Leprosy

8 When he came down from the mountainside, large crowds followed him. 2 A
man with leprosy[a] came and knelt before
him and said, "Lord, if you are willing,
you can make me clean."
3 Jesus reached out his hand and
touched the man. "I am willing," he said.
"Be clean!" Immediately he was cured[b] of
his leprosy. 4 Then Jesus said to him, "See
that you don't tell anyone. But go, show
yourself to the priest and offer the gift Moses commanded, as a testimony to them."

The Faith of the Centurion

5 When Jesus had entered Capernaum, a
centurion came to him, asking for help.
6 "Lord," he said, "my servant lies at home
paralyzed and in terrible suffering."

[a] 2 The Greek word was used for various diseases affecting the skin—not necessarily leprosy.
[b] 3 Greek *made clean*

[7]Jesus said to him, "I will go and heal
him."
[8]The centurion replied, "Lord, I do not
deserve to have you come under my roof.
But just say the word, and my servant will
be healed. [9]For I myself am a man under
authority, with soldiers under me. I tell
this one, 'Go,' and he goes; and that one,
'Come,' and he comes. I say to my servant,
'Do this,' and he does it."
[10]When Jesus heard this, he was astonished and said to those following him, "I
tell you the truth, I have not found anyone in Israel with such great faith. [11]I say
to you that many will come from the east
and the west, and will take their places at
the feast with Abraham, Isaac and Jacob
in the kingdom of heaven. [12]But the subjects of the kingdom will be thrown outside, into the darkness, where there will
be weeping and gnashing of teeth."
[13]Then Jesus said to the centurion, "Go!
It will be done just as you believed it
would." And his servant was healed at
that very hour.

Jesus Heals Many

[14]When Jesus came into Peter's house,
he saw Peter's mother-in-law lying in bed
with a fever. [15]He touched her hand and
the fever left her, and she got up and began to wait on him.
[16]When evening came, many who were
demon-possessed were brought to him, and
he drove out the spirits with a word and
healed all the sick. [17]This was to fulfill what
was spoken through the prophet Isaiah:

> "He took up our infirmities
> and carried our diseases."[c]

[c] 17 Isaiah 53:4

PRAYER: MY RELATIONSHIP TO OTHERS

I WILL not slander other believers. Those who slander their brother or sister or judge their brother or sister slander the law and judge the law. When I judge the law, I am not a doer of the law, but a judge. You are the only Lawgiver and Judge, O God, the One who is able to save and to destroy. Who am I to judge my neighbor? (James 4:11–12)

__PAUSE__ to review your relationships with others and to commit them to the Lord.

YEAR 2 DAY 11

OT Job 13:1–14:22

13 "My eyes have seen all this,
my ears have heard and understood
it.
[2]What you know, I also know;
I am not inferior to you.
[3]But I desire to speak to the Almighty
and to argue my case with God.
[4]You, however, smear me with lies;
you are worthless physicians, all of
you!
[5]If only you would be altogether silent!
For you, that would be wisdom.
[6]Hear now my argument;
listen to the plea of my lips.
[7]Will you speak wickedly on God's
behalf?
Will you speak deceitfully for him?
[8]Will you show him partiality?
Will you argue the case for God?
[9]Would it turn out well if he examined
you?
Could you deceive him as you
might deceive men?
[10]He would surely rebuke you
if you secretly showed partiality.
[11]Would not his splendor terrify you?
Would not the dread of him fall on
you?
[12]Your maxims are proverbs of ashes;
your defenses are defenses of clay.

[13]"Keep silent and let me speak;
then let come to me what may.
[14]Why do I put myself in jeopardy
and take my life in my hands?
[15]Though he slay me, yet will I hope in
him;

I will surely[a] defend my ways to his face.
16 Indeed, this will turn out for my deliverance,
for no godless man would dare come before him!
17 Listen carefully to my words;
let your ears take in what I say.
18 Now that I have prepared my case,
I know I will be vindicated.
19 Can anyone bring charges against me?
If so, I will be silent and die.

20 "Only grant me these two things, O God,
and then I will not hide from you:
21 Withdraw your hand far from me,
and stop frightening me with your terrors.
22 Then summon me and I will answer,
or let me speak, and you reply.
23 How many wrongs and sins have I committed?
Show me my offense and my sin.
24 Why do you hide your face
and consider me your enemy?
25 Will you torment a windblown leaf?
Will you chase after dry chaff?
26 For you write down bitter things against me
and make me inherit the sins of my youth.
27 You fasten my feet in shackles;
you keep close watch on all my paths
by putting marks on the soles of my feet.

28 "So man wastes away like something rotten,
like a garment eaten by moths.

14 "Man born of woman
is of few days and full of trouble.
2 He springs up like a flower and withers away;
like a fleeting shadow, he does not endure.
3 Do you fix your eye on such a one?
Will you bring him[b] before you for judgment?
4 Who can bring what is pure from the impure?
No one!
5 Man's days are determined;
you have decreed the number of his months
and have set limits he cannot exceed.
6 So look away from him and let him alone,
till he has put in his time like a hired man.

7 "At least there is hope for a tree:
If it is cut down, it will sprout again,
and its new shoots will not fail.
8 Its roots may grow old in the ground
and its stump die in the soil,
9 yet at the scent of water it will bud
and put forth shoots like a plant.
10 But man dies and is laid low;
he breathes his last and is no more.
11 As water disappears from the sea
or a riverbed becomes parched and dry,
12 so man lies down and does not rise;
till the heavens are no more, men will not awake
or be roused from their sleep.

13 "If only you would hide me in the grave[c]
and conceal me till your anger has passed!
If only you would set me a time
and then remember me!
14 If a man dies, will he live again?
All the days of my hard service
I will wait for my renewal[d] to come.
15 You will call and I will answer you;
you will long for the creature your hands have made.
16 Surely then you will count my steps
but not keep track of my sin.
17 My offenses will be sealed up in a bag;
you will cover over my sin.

18 "But as a mountain erodes and crumbles
and as a rock is moved from its place,
19 as water wears away stones
and torrents wash away the soil,
so you destroy man's hope.
20 You overpower him once for all, and he is gone;
you change his countenance and send him away.
21 If his sons are honored, he does not know it;
if they are brought low, he does not see it.
22 He feels but the pain of his own body
and mourns only for himself."

[a] 15 Or *He will surely slay me; I have no hope — / yet I will* [b] 3 Septuagint, Vulgate and Syriac; Hebrew *me* [c] 13 Hebrew *Sheol* [d] 14 Or *release*

PRAYER: INTERCESSION

O LORD, God of our fathers Abraham, Isaac and Israel, keep this desire in the hearts of Your people forever, and keep their hearts loyal to You. (1 Chronicles 29:18)

***TAKE** a few moments to intercede on behalf of your local, state or provincial, and national governments. Pray for spiritual revival in the nation and offer prayers regarding current events and concerns.*

NT Matthew 8:18–34

The Cost of Following Jesus

18When Jesus saw the crowd around
him, he gave orders to cross to the other
side of the lake. 19Then a teacher of the
law came to him and said, "Teacher, I will
follow you wherever you go."
20Jesus replied, "Foxes have holes and
birds of the air have nests, but the Son of
Man has no place to lay his head."
21Another disciple said to him, "Lord,
first let me go and bury my father."
22But Jesus told him, "Follow me, and
let the dead bury their own dead."

Jesus Calms the Storm

23Then he got into the boat and his disciples followed him. 24Without warning, a
furious storm came up on the lake, so that
the waves swept over the boat. But Jesus
was sleeping. 25The disciples went and
woke him, saying, "Lord, save us! We're
going to drown!"
26He replied, "You of little faith, why are
you so afraid?" Then he got up and rebuked the winds and the waves, and it was
completely calm.
27The men were amazed and asked,
"What kind of man is this? Even the
winds and the waves obey him!"

The Healing of Two Demon-possessed Men

28When he arrived at the other side in
the region of the Gadarenes,[a] two demon-
possessed men coming from the tombs
met him. They were so violent that no one
could pass that way. 29"What do you want
with us, Son of God?" they shouted.
"Have you come here to torture us before
the appointed time?"
30Some distance from them a large herd
of pigs was feeding. 31The demons begged
Jesus, "If you drive us out, send us into the
herd of pigs."
32He said to them, "Go!" So they came
out and went into the pigs, and the whole
herd rushed down the steep bank into the
lake and died in the water. 33Those tending the pigs ran off, went into the town
and reported all this, including what had
happened to the demon-possessed men.
34Then the whole town went out to meet
Jesus. And when they saw him, they
pleaded with him to leave their region.

[a] 28 Some manuscripts *Gergesenes;* others *Gerasenes*

PRAYER: THE ATTRIBUTES OF GOD

JESUS, You are in the Father, and the Father is in You. You spoke the words of Your Father and did the works of Your Father who dwells in You. You claimed to be in the Father and the Father in You, and You proved it through Your works. (John 14:10–11)

***PAUSE** to reflect on these affirmations about the person, powers and perfection of God.*

YEAR 2 DAY 12

OT Job 15:1-35

Eliphaz

15 Then Eliphaz the Temanite replied:

2 "Would a wise man answer with
empty notions
or fill his belly with the hot east
wind?
3 Would he argue with useless words,
with speeches that have no value?
4 But you even undermine piety
and hinder devotion to God.
5 Your sin prompts your mouth;
you adopt the tongue of the crafty.
6 Your own mouth condemns you, not
mine;
your own lips testify against you.

7 "Are you the first man ever born?
Were you brought forth before the
hills?
8 Do you listen in on God's council?
Do you limit wisdom to yourself?
9 What do you know that we do not
know?
What insights do you have that we
do not have?
10 The gray-haired and the aged are on
our side,
men even older than your father.
11 Are God's consolations not enough
for you,
words spoken gently to you?
12 Why has your heart carried you away,
and why do your eyes flash,
13 so that you vent your rage against God
and pour out such words from your
mouth?

14 "What is man, that he could be pure,
or one born of woman, that he
could be righteous?
15 If God places no trust in his holy ones,
if even the heavens are not pure in
his eyes,
16 how much less man, who is vile and
corrupt,
who drinks up evil like water!

17 "Listen to me and I will explain to you;
let me tell you what I have seen,
18 what wise men have declared,
hiding nothing received from their
fathers
19 (to whom alone the land was given
when no alien passed among them):
20 All his days the wicked man suffers
torment,
the ruthless through all the years
stored up for him.
21 Terrifying sounds fill his ears;
when all seems well, marauders
attack him.
22 He despairs of escaping the darkness;
he is marked for the sword.
23 He wanders about—food for vultures[a];
he knows the day of darkness is at
hand.
24 Distress and anguish fill him with
terror;
they overwhelm him, like a king
poised to attack,
25 because he shakes his fist at God
and vaunts himself against the
Almighty,
26 defiantly charging against him
with a thick, strong shield.

27 "Though his face is covered with fat
and his waist bulges with flesh,
28 he will inhabit ruined towns
and houses where no one lives,
houses crumbling to rubble.
29 He will no longer be rich and his
wealth will not endure,
nor will his possessions spread over
the land.
30 He will not escape the darkness;
a flame will wither his shoots,
and the breath of God's mouth will
carry him away.
31 Let him not deceive himself by
trusting what is worthless,
for he will get nothing in return.
32 Before his time he will be paid in full,
and his branches will not flourish.
33 He will be like a vine stripped of its
unripe grapes,
like an olive tree shedding its
blossoms.
34 For the company of the godless will
be barren,
and fire will consume the tents of
those who love bribes.
35 They conceive trouble and give birth
to evil;
their womb fashions deceit."

[a] 23 Or *about, looking for food*

PRAYER: AFFIRMATION

WHERE is the wise person? Where is the scholar? Where is the disputer of this age? O God, have You not made foolish the wisdom of the world? But to those whom You have called, both Jews and Greeks, Christ is Your power and Your wisdom. (1 Corinthians 1:20, 24) . . . If I think I am somebody when I am nobody, I am fooling myself. (Galatians 6:3)

***PAUSE** to reflect on these Biblical affirmations.*

NT Matthew 9:1–17

Jesus Heals a Paralytic

9 Jesus stepped into a boat, crossed over
and came to his own town. 2Some men
brought to him a paralytic, lying on a
mat. When Jesus saw their faith, he said
to the paralytic, "Take heart, son; your sins
are forgiven."
3At this, some of the teachers of the law
said to themselves, "This fellow is blaspheming!"
4Knowing their thoughts, Jesus said,
"Why do you entertain evil thoughts in
your hearts? 5Which is easier: to say, 'Your
sins are forgiven,' or to say, 'Get up and
walk'? 6But so that you may know that the
Son of Man has authority on earth to forgive sins. . . ." Then he said to the paralytic, "Get up, take your mat and go
home." 7And the man got up and went
home. 8When the crowd saw this, they
were filled with awe; and they praised
God, who had given such authority to
men.

The Calling of Matthew

9As Jesus went on from there, he saw a
man named Matthew sitting at the tax collector's booth. "Follow me," he told him,
and Matthew got up and followed him.
10While Jesus was having dinner at Matthew's house, many tax collectors and
"sinners" came and ate with him and his
disciples. 11When the Pharisees saw this,
they asked his disciples, "Why does your
teacher eat with tax collectors and 'sinners'?"
12On hearing this, Jesus said, "It is not
the healthy who need a doctor, but the
sick. 13But go and learn what this means:
'I desire mercy, not sacrifice.'[a] For I have
not come to call the righteous, but sinners."

Jesus Questioned About Fasting

14Then John's disciples came and asked
him, "How is it that we and the Pharisees
fast, but your disciples do not fast?"
15Jesus answered, "How can the guests
of the bridegroom mourn while he is with
them? The time will come when the
bridegroom will be taken from them;
then they will fast.
16"No one sews a patch of unshrunk
cloth on an old garment, for the patch
will pull away from the garment, making
the tear worse. 17Neither do men pour
new wine into old wineskins. If they do,
the skins will burst, the wine will run out
and the wineskins will be ruined. No,
they pour new wine into new wineskins,
and both are preserved."

[a] *13* Hosea 6:6

PRAYER: THE WORKS OF GOD

YOU are able to do immeasurably more than all that we ask or think, O God, according to Your power that is at work within us. To You be glory in the church and in Christ Jesus throughout all generations, for ever and ever. (Ephesians 3:20–21)

***TAKE** a moment to consider the greatness of God's wonderful works.*

OT Job 16:1–17:16 YEAR 2 DAY 13

Job

16 Then Job replied:

2 "I have heard many things like these;
miserable comforters are you all!
3 Will your long-winded speeches never end?
What ails you that you keep on arguing?
4 I also could speak like you,
if you were in my place;
I could make fine speeches against you
and shake my head at you.
5 But my mouth would encourage you;
comfort from my lips would bring you relief.

6 "Yet if I speak, my pain is not relieved;
and if I refrain, it does not go away.
7 Surely, O God, you have worn me out;
you have devastated my entire household.
8 You have bound me—and it has become a witness;
my gauntness rises up and testifies against me.
9 God assails me and tears me in his anger
and gnashes his teeth at me;
my opponent fastens on me his piercing eyes.
10 Men open their mouths to jeer at me;
they strike my cheek in scorn
and unite together against me.
11 God has turned me over to evil men
and thrown me into the clutches of the wicked.
12 All was well with me, but he shattered me;
he seized me by the neck and crushed me.
He has made me his target;
13 his archers surround me.
Without pity, he pierces my kidneys
and spills my gall on the ground.
14 Again and again he bursts upon me;
he rushes at me like a warrior.

15 "I have sewed sackcloth over my skin
and buried my brow in the dust.
16 My face is red with weeping,
deep shadows ring my eyes;
17 yet my hands have been free of violence
and my prayer is pure.

18 "O earth, do not cover my blood;
may my cry never be laid to rest!
19 Even now my witness is in heaven;
my advocate is on high.
20 My intercessor is my friend[a]
as my eyes pour out tears to God;
21 on behalf of a man he pleads with God
as a man pleads for his friend.

22 "Only a few years will pass
before I go on the journey of no return.

17 1 My spirit is broken,
my days are cut short,
the grave awaits me.
2 Surely mockers surround me;
my eyes must dwell on their hostility.

3 "Give me, O God, the pledge you demand.
Who else will put up security for me?
4 You have closed their minds to understanding;
therefore you will not let them triumph.
5 If a man denounces his friends for reward,
the eyes of his children will fail.

6 "God has made me a byword to everyone,
a man in whose face people spit.
7 My eyes have grown dim with grief;
my whole frame is but a shadow.
8 Upright men are appalled at this;
the innocent are aroused against the ungodly.
9 Nevertheless, the righteous will hold to their ways,
and those with clean hands will grow stronger.

10 "But come on, all of you, try again!
I will not find a wise man among you.
11 My days have passed, my plans are shattered,
and so are the desires of my heart.
12 These men turn night into day;
in the face of darkness they say,
'Light is near.'

[a] 20 Or *My friends treat me with scorn*

13 If the only home I hope for is the
grave,[b]
if I spread out my bed in darkness,
14 if I say to corruption, 'You are my
father,'
and to the worm, 'My mother' or
'My sister,'
15 where then is my hope?
Who can see any hope for me?
16 Will it go down to the gates of death[b]?
Will we descend together into the
dust?"

[b] 13,16 Hebrew *Sheol*

PRAYER: THANKSGIVING

JESUS, we give thanks that You expressed Your concern for the lost when You said, "What man among you, if he has a hundred sheep and loses one of them, does not leave the ninety-nine in the open country and go after the one that is lost until he finds it? And when he finds it, he lays it on his shoulders, rejoicing. And when he comes into his house, he calls his friends and neighbors together and says to them, 'Rejoice with me, for I have found my sheep which was lost!' I tell you that, in the same way, there will be more joy in heaven over one sinner who repents than over ninety-nine righteous people who need no repentance. There is joy in the presence of the angels of God over one sinner who repents." (Luke 15:4–7, 10)

PAUSE *to offer your own expressions of thanksgiving.*

NT Matthew 9:18–38

A Dead Girl and a Sick Woman

18 While he was saying this, a ruler came
and knelt before him and said, "My
daughter has just died. But come and put
your hand on her, and she will live."
19 Jesus got up and went with him, and so
did his disciples.
20 Just then a woman who had been subject to bleeding for twelve years came up
behind him and touched the edge of his
cloak. 21 She said to herself, "If I only
touch his cloak, I will be healed."
22 Jesus turned and saw her. "Take heart,
daughter," he said, "your faith has healed
you." And the woman was healed from
that moment.
23 When Jesus entered the ruler's house
and saw the flute players and the noisy
crowd, 24 he said, "Go away. The girl is not
dead but asleep." But they laughed at
him. 25 After the crowd had been put outside, he went in and took the girl by the
hand, and she got up. 26 News of this
spread through all that region.

Jesus Heals the Blind and Mute

27 As Jesus went on from there, two
blind men followed him, calling out,
"Have mercy on us, Son of David!"
28 When he had gone indoors, the blind
men came to him, and he asked them,
"Do you believe that I am able to do
this?"
"Yes, Lord," they replied.
29 Then he touched their eyes and said,
"According to your faith will it be done to
you"; 30 and their sight was restored. Jesus
warned them sternly, "See that no one
knows about this." 31 But they went out
and spread the news about him all over
that region.
32 While they were going out, a man
who was demon-possessed and could not
talk was brought to Jesus. 33 And when the
demon was driven out, the man who had
been mute spoke. The crowd was amazed
and said, "Nothing like this has ever been
seen in Israel."
34 But the Pharisees said, "It is by the
prince of demons that he drives out
demons."

The Workers Are Few

35 Jesus went through all the towns and
villages, teaching in their synagogues,
preaching the good news of the kingdom
and healing every disease and sickness.
36 When he saw the crowds, he had com-

passion on them, because they were harassed and helpless, like sheep without a
shepherd. [37]Then he said to his disciples,
"The harvest is plentiful but the workers are
few. [38]Ask the Lord of the harvest, therefore,
to send out workers into his harvest field."

PRAYER: MY RELATIONSHIP TO GOD

THE greatest among us should be like the youngest, and the one who rules like the one who serves. For who is greater, the one who is at the table or the one who serves? Is it not the one who is at the table? But You, Jesus, came among us as the One who serves. (Luke 22:26–27)

***PAUSE** to thank God for the relationship that you enjoy with Him in Jesus Christ.*

YEAR 2 DAY 14

OT Psalm 74

Psalm 74

A *maskil*[a] of Asaph.

[1]Why have you rejected us forever,
O God?
Why does your anger smolder
against the sheep of your
pasture?
[2]Remember the people you purchased
of old,
the tribe of your inheritance, whom
you redeemed—
Mount Zion, where you dwelt.
[3]Turn your steps toward these
everlasting ruins,
all this destruction the enemy has
brought on the sanctuary.

[4]Your foes roared in the place where
you met with us;
they set up their standards as signs.
[5]They behaved like men wielding axes
to cut through a thicket of trees.
[6]They smashed all the carved paneling
with their axes and hatchets.
[7]They burned your sanctuary to the
ground;
they defiled the dwelling place of
your Name.
[8]They said in their hearts, "We will
crush them completely!"
They burned every place where God
was worshiped in the land.
[9]We are given no miraculous signs;
no prophets are left,
and none of us knows how long
this will be.
[10]How long will the enemy mock you,
O God?
Will the foe revile your name
forever?
[11]Why do you hold back your hand,
your right hand?
Take it from the folds of your
garment and destroy them!

[12]But you, O God, are my king from of
old;
you bring salvation upon the earth.
[13]It was you who split open the sea by
your power;
you broke the heads of the monster
in the waters.
[14]It was you who crushed the heads of
Leviathan
and gave him as food to the
creatures of the desert.
[15]It was you who opened up springs
and streams;
you dried up the ever flowing rivers.
[16]The day is yours, and yours also the
night;
you established the sun and moon.
[17]It was you who set all the boundaries
of the earth;
you made both summer and winter.

[18]Remember how the enemy has
mocked you, O LORD,
how foolish people have reviled
your name.
[19]Do not hand over the life of your
dove to wild beasts;

[a]Title: Probably a literary or musical term

do not forget the lives of your
afflicted people forever.
20 Have regard for your covenant,
because haunts of violence fill the
dark places of the land.
21 Do not let the oppressed retreat in
disgrace;
may the poor and needy praise your
name.
22 Rise up, O God, and defend your
cause;
remember how fools mock you all
day long.
23 Do not ignore the clamor of your
adversaries,
the uproar of your enemies, which
rises continually.

PRAYER: ADORATION

YOU, O Lord, have declared: "My thoughts are not your thoughts, neither are your ways My ways. As the heavens are higher than the earth, so are My ways higher than your ways, and My thoughts than your thoughts." (Isaiah 55:8–9)

***PAUSE** to express your thoughts of praise and worship.*

NT Matthew 10:1–42

Jesus Sends Out the Twelve

10 He called his twelve disciples to him
and gave them authority to drive out
evil[a] spirits and to heal every disease and
sickness.
2 These are the names of the twelve
apostles: first, Simon (who is called Peter)
and his brother Andrew; James son of
Zebedee, and his brother John; 3 Philip
and Bartholomew; Thomas and Matthew
the tax collector; James son of Alphaeus,
and Thaddaeus; 4 Simon the Zealot and Judas Iscariot, who betrayed him.
5 These twelve Jesus sent out with the following instructions: "Do not go among the
Gentiles or enter any town of the Samaritans. 6 Go rather to the lost sheep of Israel.
7 As you go, preach this message: 'The kingdom of heaven is near.' 8 Heal the sick, raise
the dead, cleanse those who have leprosy,[b]
drive out demons. Freely you have received,
freely give. 9 Do not take along any gold or
silver or copper in your belts; 10 take no bag
for the journey, or extra tunic, or sandals or
a staff; for the worker is worth his keep.
11 "Whatever town or village you enter,
search for some worthy person there and
stay at his house until you leave. 12 As you
enter the home, give it your greeting. 13 If
the home is deserving, let your peace rest
on it; if it is not, let your peace return to
you. 14 If anyone will not welcome you or
listen to your words, shake the dust off
your feet when you leave that home or
town. 15 I tell you the truth, it will be more
bearable for Sodom and Gomorrah on
the day of judgment than for that town.
16 I am sending you out like sheep among
wolves. Therefore be as shrewd as snakes
and as innocent as doves.
17 "Be on your guard against men; they
will hand you over to the local councils and
flog you in their synagogues. 18 On my account you will be brought before governors
and kings as witnesses to them and to the
Gentiles. 19 But when they arrest you, do not
worry about what to say or how to say it.
At that time you will be given what to say,
20 for it will not be you speaking, but the
Spirit of your Father speaking through you.
21 "Brother will betray brother to death,
and a father his child; children will rebel
against their parents and have them put to
death. 22 All men will hate you because of
me, but he who stands firm to the end will
be saved. 23 When you are persecuted in one
place, flee to another. I tell you the truth,
you will not finish going through the cities of Israel before the Son of Man comes.
24 "A student is not above his teacher, nor
a servant above his master. 25 It is enough for
the student to be like his teacher, and the
servant like his master. If the head of the
house has been called Beelzebub,[c] how
much more the members of his household!

[a] *1* Greek *unclean* [b] *8* The Greek word was used for various diseases affecting the skin—not necessarily leprosy. [c] *25* Greek *Beezeboul* or *Beelzeboul*

[26]"So do not be afraid of them. There is
nothing concealed that will not be disclosed, or hidden that will not be made
known. [27]What I tell you in the dark,
speak in the daylight; what is whispered
in your ear, proclaim from the roofs. [28]Do
not be afraid of those who kill the body
but cannot kill the soul. Rather, be afraid
of the One who can destroy both soul and
body in hell. [29]Are not two sparrows sold
for a penny[d]? Yet not one of them will fall
to the ground apart from the will of your
Father. [30]And even the very hairs of your
head are all numbered. [31]So don't be
afraid; you are worth more than many
sparrows.
[32]"Whoever acknowledges me before
men, I will also acknowledge him before
my Father in heaven. [33]But whoever disowns me before men, I will disown him
before my Father in heaven.
[34]"Do not suppose that I have come to
bring peace to the earth. I did not come
to bring peace, but a sword. [35]For I have
come to turn

" 'a man against his father,
a daughter against her mother,
a daughter-in-law against her mother-in-law—
36 a man's enemies will be the members of his own household.'[e]

[37]"Anyone who loves his father or
mother more than me is not worthy of
me; anyone who loves his son or daughter more than me is not worthy of me;
[38]and anyone who does not take his cross
and follow me is not worthy of me.
[39]Whoever finds his life will lose it, and
whoever loses his life for my sake will
find it.
[40]"He who receives you receives me, and
he who receives me receives the one who
sent me. [41]Anyone who receives a prophet
because he is a prophet will receive a
prophet's reward, and anyone who receives
a righteous man because he is a righteous
man will receive a righteous man's reward.
[42]And if anyone gives even a cup of cold
water to one of these little ones because he
is my disciple, I tell you the truth, he will
certainly not lose his reward."

[d] 29 Greek *an assarion* [e] 36 Micah 7:6

PRAYER: THE CHARACTER I WANT TO CULTIVATE

I WILL not trust in myself or in my own righteousness, nor will I view others with contempt. (Luke 18:9) . . . I will be of the same mind with others; I will not be haughty in mind or wise in my own estimation, but I will associate with the humble. (Romans 12:16)

***TAKE** a moment to ask the Lord for the grace to grow in godly character.*

YEAR 2 DAY 15

OT Job 18:1–19:29

Bildad

18 Then Bildad the Shuhite replied:

[2]"When will you end these speeches?
Be sensible, and then we can talk.
[3]Why are we regarded as cattle
and considered stupid in your sight?
[4]You who tear yourself to pieces in your anger,
is the earth to be abandoned for your sake?
Or must the rocks be moved from their place?

[5]"The lamp of the wicked is snuffed out;
the flame of his fire stops burning.
[6]The light in his tent becomes dark;
the lamp beside him goes out.
[7]The vigor of his step is weakened;
his own schemes throw him down.
[8]His feet thrust him into a net
and he wanders into its mesh.
[9]A trap seizes him by the heel;
a snare holds him fast.
[10]A noose is hidden for him on the ground;

a trap lies in his path.
11 Terrors startle him on every side
and dog his every step.
12 Calamity is hungry for him;
disaster is ready for him when he falls.
13 It eats away parts of his skin;
death's firstborn devours his limbs.
14 He is torn from the security of his tent
and marched off to the king of terrors.
15 Fire resides[a] in his tent;
burning sulfur is scattered over his dwelling.
16 His roots dry up below
and his branches wither above.
17 The memory of him perishes from the earth;
he has no name in the land.
18 He is driven from light into darkness
and is banished from the world.
19 He has no offspring or descendants among his people,
no survivor where once he lived.
20 Men of the west are appalled at his fate;
men of the east are seized with horror.
21 Surely such is the dwelling of an evil man;
such is the place of one who knows not God."

Job

19 Then Job replied:

2 "How long will you torment me
and crush me with words?
3 Ten times now you have reproached me;
shamelessly you attack me.
4 If it is true that I have gone astray,
my error remains my concern alone.
5 If indeed you would exalt yourselves above me
and use my humiliation against me,
6 then know that God has wronged me
and drawn his net around me.

7 "Though I cry, 'I've been wronged!' I get no response;
though I call for help, there is no justice.
8 He has blocked my way so I cannot pass;
he has shrouded my paths in darkness.
9 He has stripped me of my honor
and removed the crown from my head.
10 He tears me down on every side till I am gone;
he uproots my hope like a tree.
11 His anger burns against me;
he counts me among his enemies.
12 His troops advance in force;
they build a siege ramp against me
and encamp around my tent.

13 "He has alienated my brothers from me;
my acquaintances are completely estranged from me.
14 My kinsmen have gone away;
my friends have forgotten me.
15 My guests and my maidservants count me a stranger;
they look upon me as an alien.
16 I summon my servant, but he does not answer,
though I beg him with my own mouth.
17 My breath is offensive to my wife;
I am loathsome to my own brothers.
18 Even the little boys scorn me;
when I appear, they ridicule me.
19 All my intimate friends detest me;
those I love have turned against me.
20 I am nothing but skin and bones;
I have escaped with only the skin of my teeth.[b]

21 "Have pity on me, my friends, have pity,
for the hand of God has struck me.
22 Why do you pursue me as God does?
Will you never get enough of my flesh?

23 "Oh, that my words were recorded,
that they were written on a scroll,
24 that they were inscribed with an iron tool on[c] lead,
or engraved in rock forever!
25 I know that my Redeemer[d] lives,
and that in the end he will stand upon the earth.[e]
26 And after my skin has been destroyed,
yet[f] in[g] my flesh I will see God;
27 I myself will see him

[a] 15 Or *Nothing he had remains* [b] 20 Or *only my gums* [c] 24 Or *and* [d] 25 Or *defender* [e] 25 Or *upon my grave* [f] 26 Or *And after I awake, / though this ⌊body⌋ has been destroyed, / then* [g] 26 Or */ apart from*

with my own eyes—I, and not another.
How my heart yearns within me!

28 "If you say, 'How we will hound him, since the root of the trouble lies in him,[h]'
29 you should fear the sword yourselves;
for wrath will bring punishment by the sword,
and then you will know that there is judgment.[i]"

[h] 28 Many Hebrew manuscripts, Septuagint and Vulgate; most Hebrew manuscripts *me*
[i] 29 Or / *that you may come to know the Almighty*

PRAYER: CONFESSION

THE heart is deceitful above all things and incurably sick. Who can understand it? You, Lord, search people's hearts and test people's minds to reward them according to their ways, according to the fruit of their deeds. (Jeremiah 17:9–10)

***ASK** the Spirit to search your heart and reveal any areas of unconfessed sin. Acknowledge these to the Lord and thank Him for His forgiveness.*

NT Matthew 11:1-30

Jesus and John the Baptist

11 After Jesus had finished instructing his
twelve disciples, he went on from there
to teach and preach in the towns of Galilee.[a]
2 When John heard in prison what
Christ was doing, he sent his disciples 3 to
ask him, "Are you the one who was to
come, or should we expect someone
else?"
4 Jesus replied, "Go back and report to
John what you hear and see: 5 The blind receive sight, the lame walk, those who have
leprosy[b] are cured, the deaf hear, the dead
are raised, and the good news is preached
to the poor. 6 Blessed is the man who does
not fall away on account of me."
7 As John's disciples were leaving, Jesus
began to speak to the crowd about John:
"What did you go out into the desert to
see? A reed swayed by the wind? 8 If not,
what did you go out to see? A man dressed
in fine clothes? No, those who wear fine
clothes are in kings' palaces. 9 Then what
did you go out to see? A prophet? Yes, I tell
you, and more than a prophet. 10 This is the
one about whom it is written:

" 'I will send my messenger ahead of you,
who will prepare your way before you.'[c]

11 I tell you the truth: Among those born
of women there has not risen anyone
greater than John the Baptist; yet he who
is least in the kingdom of heaven is
greater than he. 12 From the days of John
the Baptist until now, the kingdom of
heaven has been forcefully advancing,
and forceful men lay hold of it. 13 For all
the Prophets and the Law prophesied until John. 14 And if you are willing to accept
it, he is the Elijah who was to come. 15 He
who has ears, let him hear.
16 "To what can I compare this generation? They are like children sitting in the
marketplaces and calling out to others:

17 " 'We played the flute for you,
and you did not dance;
we sang a dirge,
and you did not mourn.'

18 For John came neither eating nor drinking, and they say, 'He has a demon.' 19 The
Son of Man came eating and drinking,
and they say, 'Here is a glutton and a
drunkard, a friend of tax collectors and
"sinners." ' But wisdom is proved right by
her actions."

Woe on Unrepentant Cities

20 Then Jesus began to denounce the cities in which most of his miracles had been
performed, because they did not repent.
21 "Woe to you, Korazin! Woe to you, Bethsaida! If the miracles that were performed

[a] 1 Greek *in their towns* [b] 5 The Greek word was used for various diseases affecting the skin—not necessarily leprosy. [c] 10 Mal. 3:1

in you had been performed in Tyre and Sidon, they would have repented long ago in
sackcloth and ashes. 22But I tell you, it will
be more bearable for Tyre and Sidon on the
day of judgment than for you. 23And you,
Capernaum, will you be lifted up to the
skies? No, you will go down to the depths.[d]
If the miracles that were performed in you
had been performed in Sodom, it would
have remained to this day. 24But I tell you
that it will be more bearable for Sodom on
the day of judgment than for you."

Rest for the Weary

25At that time Jesus said, "I praise you,
Father, Lord of heaven and earth, because
you have hidden these things from the
wise and learned, and revealed them to
little children. 26Yes, Father, for this was
your good pleasure.

27"All things have been committed to
me by my Father. No one knows the Son
except the Father, and no one knows the
Father except the Son and those to whom
the Son chooses to reveal him.

28"Come to me, all you who are weary
and burdened, and I will give you rest.
29Take my yoke upon you and learn from
me, for I am gentle and humble in heart,
and you will find rest for your souls. 30For
my yoke is easy and my burden is light."

[d] 23 Greek *Hades*

PRAYER: MY RELATIONSHIP TO OTHERS

WE should love one another, for love is from You, O God, and everyone who loves has been born of You and knows You. Whoever does not love does not know You, for You, O God, are love. (1 John 4:7–8)

***PAUSE** to review your relationships with others and to commit them to the Lord.*

YEAR 2 DAY 16

OT Job 20:1–29

Zophar

20 Then Zophar the Naamathite replied:

2"My troubled thoughts prompt me to answer
because I am greatly disturbed.
3I hear a rebuke that dishonors me,
and my understanding inspires me to reply.

4"Surely you know how it has been from of old,
ever since man[a] was placed on the earth,
5that the mirth of the wicked is brief,
the joy of the godless lasts but a moment.
6Though his pride reaches to the heavens
and his head touches the clouds,
7he will perish forever, like his own dung;
those who have seen him will say, 'Where is he?'
8Like a dream he flies away, no more to be found,
banished like a vision of the night.
9The eye that saw him will not see him again;
his place will look on him no more.
10His children must make amends to the poor;
his own hands must give back his wealth.
11The youthful vigor that fills his bones
will lie with him in the dust.

12"Though evil is sweet in his mouth
and he hides it under his tongue,
13though he cannot bear to let it go
and keeps it in his mouth,
14yet his food will turn sour in his stomach;
it will become the venom of serpents within him.
15He will spit out the riches he swallowed;

[a] 4 Or *Adam*

God will make his stomach vomit
them up.
16 He will suck the poison of serpents;
the fangs of an adder will kill him.
17 He will not enjoy the streams,
the rivers flowing with honey and
cream.
18 What he toiled for he must give back
uneaten;
he will not enjoy the profit from his
trading.
19 For he has oppressed the poor and left
them destitute;
he has seized houses he did not
build.

20 "Surely he will have no respite from
his craving;
he cannot save himself by his
treasure.
21 Nothing is left for him to devour;
his prosperity will not endure.
22 In the midst of his plenty, distress will
overtake him;
the full force of misery will come
upon him.
23 When he has filled his belly,
God will vent his burning anger
against him
and rain down his blows upon him.
24 Though he flees from an iron weapon,
a bronze-tipped arrow pierces him.
25 He pulls it out of his back,
the gleaming point out of his liver.
Terrors will come over him;
26 total darkness lies in wait for his
treasures.
A fire unfanned will consume him
and devour what is left in his tent.
27 The heavens will expose his guilt;
the earth will rise up against him.
28 A flood will carry off his house,
rushing waters[b] on the day of God's
wrath.
29 Such is the fate God allots the wicked,
the heritage appointed for them by
God."

[b] 28 Or *The possessions in his house will be carried off, / washed away*

PRAYER: RENEWAL

MAY I not profane Your holy name, but acknowledge You as holy before others. You are the Lord who sanctifies me. (Leviticus 22:32) . . . You, the Lord my God, are one Lord. May I love You with all my heart and with all my soul and with all my strength. (Deuteronomy 6:4–5)

***PAUSE** to add your own prayers for personal renewal.*

NT Matthew 12:1–21

Lord of the Sabbath

12 At that time Jesus went through the
grainfields on the Sabbath. His disciples were hungry and began to pick some
heads of grain and eat them. 2 When the
Pharisees saw this, they said to him,
"Look! Your disciples are doing what is
unlawful on the Sabbath."
3 He answered, "Haven't you read what
David did when he and his companions
were hungry? 4 He entered the house of
God, and he and his companions ate the
consecrated bread—which was not lawful
for them to do, but only for the priests.
5 Or haven't you read in the Law that on
the Sabbath the priests in the temple desecrate the day and yet are innocent? 6 I tell
you that one[a] greater than the temple is
here. 7 If you had known what these words
mean, 'I desire mercy, not sacrifice,'[b] you
would not have condemned the innocent.
8 For the Son of Man is Lord of the Sabbath."
9 Going on from that place, he went into
their synagogue, 10 and a man with a shriveled hand was there. Looking for a reason
to accuse Jesus, they asked him, "Is it lawful to heal on the Sabbath?"
11 He said to them, "If any of you has a
sheep and it falls into a pit on the Sab-

[a] 6 Or *something;* also in verses 41 and 42
[b] 7 Hosea 6:6

bath, will you not take hold of it and lift
it out? [12]How much more valuable is a
man than a sheep! Therefore it is lawful
to do good on the Sabbath."
[13]Then he said to the man, "Stretch out
your hand." So he stretched it out and it
was completely restored, just as sound as
the other. [14]But the Pharisees went out
and plotted how they might kill Jesus.

God's Chosen Servant

[15]Aware of this, Jesus withdrew from
that place. Many followed him, and he
healed all their sick, [16]warning them not
to tell who he was. [17]This was to fulfill
what was spoken through the prophet Isaiah:

[18] "Here is my servant whom I have chosen,
the one I love, in whom I delight;
I will put my Spirit on him,
and he will proclaim justice to the nations.
[19] He will not quarrel or cry out;
no one will hear his voice in the streets.
[20] A bruised reed he will not break,
and a smoldering wick he will not snuff out,
till he leads justice to victory.
[21] In his name the nations will put their hope."[c]

[c] *21* Isaiah 42:1-4

PRAYER: THE ATTRIBUTES OF GOD

SURELY as You, O Lord of hosts, have thought, so it will be, and as You have purposed, so it will stand. For You, Lord of hosts, have purposed, and who can annul it? Your hand is stretched out, and who can turn it back? (Isaiah 14:24, 27)

***PAUSE** to reflect on these affirmations about the person, powers and perfection of God.*

YEAR 2 DAY 17

OT **Job 21:1-34**

Job

21

Then Job replied:

[2] "Listen carefully to my words;
let this be the consolation you give me.
[3] Bear with me while I speak,
and after I have spoken, mock on.

[4] "Is my complaint directed to man?
Why should I not be impatient?
[5] Look at me and be astonished;
clap your hand over your mouth.
[6] When I think about this, I am terrified;
trembling seizes my body.
[7] Why do the wicked live on,
growing old and increasing in power?
[8] They see their children established around them,
their offspring before their eyes.
[9] Their homes are safe and free from fear;
the rod of God is not upon them.
[10] Their bulls never fail to breed;
their cows calve and do not miscarry.
[11] They send forth their children as a flock;
their little ones dance about.
[12] They sing to the music of tambourine and harp;
they make merry to the sound of the flute.
[13] They spend their years in prosperity
and go down to the grave[a] in peace.[b]
[14] Yet they say to God, 'Leave us alone!
We have no desire to know your ways.
[15] Who is the Almighty, that we should serve him?
What would we gain by praying to him?'
[16] But their prosperity is not in their own hands,

[a] *13* Hebrew *Sheol* [b] *13* Or *in an instant*

so I stand aloof from the counsel of
the wicked.

17 "Yet how often is the lamp of the
wicked snuffed out?
How often does calamity come
upon them,
the fate God allots in his anger?
18 How often are they like straw before
the wind,
like chaff swept away by a gale?
19 ⌊It is said,⌋ 'God stores up a man's
punishment for his sons.'
Let him repay the man himself, so
that he will know it!
20 Let his own eyes see his destruction;
let him drink of the wrath of the
Almighty.[c]
21 For what does he care about the
family he leaves behind
when his allotted months come to
an end?

22 "Can anyone teach knowledge to God,
since he judges even the highest?
23 One man dies in full vigor,
completely secure and at ease,
24 his body[d] well nourished,
his bones rich with marrow.
25 Another man dies in bitterness of soul,
never having enjoyed anything good.
26 Side by side they lie in the dust,
and worms cover them both.
27 "I know full well what you are thinking,
the schemes by which you would
wrong me.
28 You say, 'Where now is the great man's
house,
the tents where wicked men lived?'
29 Have you never questioned those who
travel?
Have you paid no regard to their
accounts—
30 that the evil man is spared from the
day of calamity,
that he is delivered from[e] the day of
wrath?
31 Who denounces his conduct to his face?
Who repays him for what he has
done?
32 He is carried to the grave,
and watch is kept over his tomb.
33 The soil in the valley is sweet to him;
all men follow after him,
and a countless throng goes[f] before
him.

34 "So how can you console me with
your nonsense?
Nothing is left of your answers but
falsehood!"

[c] *17-20* Verses 17 and 18 may be taken as exclamations and 19 and 20 as declarations. [d] *24* The meaning of the Hebrew for this word is uncertain. [e] *30* Or *man is reserved for the day of calamity, / that he is brought forth to* [f] *33* Or / *as a countless throng went*

PRAYER: PETITION

MAY I fight the good fight, finish the race, and keep the faith, so that there will be laid up for me the crown of righteousness, which You, Lord, the righteous Judge, will award to me on that day; and not only to me, but also to all who have longed for Christ's appearing.

(2 Timothy 4:7–8)

PAUSE *here to offer prayers of petition regarding your family and your ministry. Ask for help and guidance in sharing Jesus with others and helping others grow in Him. Ask for guidance in your vocation and your avocations. Offer prayers of petition regarding your activities for this day and any special concerns you may have.*

NT Matthew 12:22-50

Jesus and Beelzebub

22 Then they brought him a demon-possessed man who was blind and mute, and
Jesus healed him, so that he could both
talk and see. 23 All the people were astonished and said, "Could this be the Son of
David?"
24 But when the Pharisees heard this,
they said, "It is only by Beelzebub,[a] the

[a] *24* Greek *Beezeboul* or *Beelzeboul;* also in verse 27

prince of demons, that this fellow drives
out demons."
25 Jesus knew their thoughts and said to
them, "Every kingdom divided against itself will be ruined, and every city or
household divided against itself will not
stand. 26 If Satan drives out Satan, he is divided against himself. How then can his
kingdom stand? 27 And if I drive out
demons by Beelzebub, by whom do your
people drive them out? So then, they will
be your judges. 28 But if I drive out demons
by the Spirit of God, then the kingdom of
God has come upon you.
29 "Or again, how can anyone enter a
strong man's house and carry off his possessions unless he first ties up the strong
man? Then he can rob his house.
30 "He who is not with me is against me,
and he who does not gather with me scatters. 31 And so I tell you, every sin and blasphemy will be forgiven men, but the
blasphemy against the Spirit will not be
forgiven. 32 Anyone who speaks a word
against the Son of Man will be forgiven,
but anyone who speaks against the Holy
Spirit will not be forgiven, either in this
age or in the age to come.
33 "Make a tree good and its fruit will be
good, or make a tree bad and its fruit will
be bad, for a tree is recognized by its fruit.
34 You brood of vipers, how can you who
are evil say anything good? For out of the
overflow of the heart the mouth speaks.
35 The good man brings good things out of
the good stored up in him, and the evil
man brings evil things out of the evil
stored up in him. 36 But I tell you that men
will have to give account on the day of
judgment for every careless word they
have spoken. 37 For by your words you will
be acquitted, and by your words you will
be condemned."

The Sign of Jonah

38 Then some of the Pharisees and
teachers of the law said to him, "Teacher,
we want to see a miraculous sign from
you."
39 He answered, "A wicked and adulterous generation asks for a miraculous sign!
But none will be given it except the sign
of the prophet Jonah. 40 For as Jonah was
three days and three nights in the belly of
a huge fish, so the Son of Man will be
three days and three nights in the heart of
the earth. 41 The men of Nineveh will stand
up at the judgment with this generation
and condemn it; for they repented at the
preaching of Jonah, and now one[b] greater
than Jonah is here. 42 The Queen of the
South will rise at the judgment with this
generation and condemn it; for she came
from the ends of the earth to listen to
Solomon's wisdom, and now one greater
than Solomon is here.
43 "When an evil[c] spirit comes out of a
man, it goes through arid places seeking
rest and does not find it. 44 Then it says, 'I
will return to the house I left.' When it arrives, it finds the house unoccupied, swept
clean and put in order. 45 Then it goes and
takes with it seven other spirits more
wicked than itself, and they go in and live
there. And the final condition of that man
is worse than the first. That is how it will
be with this wicked generation."

Jesus' Mother and Brothers

46 While Jesus was still talking to the
crowd, his mother and brothers stood
outside, wanting to speak to him. 47 Someone told him, "Your mother and brothers
are standing outside, wanting to speak to
you."[d]
48 He replied to him, "Who is my mother, and who are my brothers?" 49 Pointing
to his disciples, he said, "Here are my
mother and my brothers. 50 For whoever
does the will of my Father in heaven is my
brother and sister and mother."

[b] *41* Or *something;* also in verse 42 [c] *43* Greek *unclean* [d] *47* Some manuscripts do not have verse 47.

PRAYER: THE WORKS OF GOD

YOU, Lord God, give life to the dead and call into being things that do not exist. (Romans 4:17) . . . The whole family in heaven and on earth derives its name from You, the God and Father of our Lord Jesus Christ. (Ephesians 3:15)

***TAKE** a moment to consider the greatness of God's wonderful works.*

YEAR 2 DAY 18

OT Job 22:1-30

Eliphaz

22 Then Eliphaz the Temanite replied:

2 "Can a man be of benefit to God?
Can even a wise man benefit him?
3 What pleasure would it give the Almighty if you were righteous?
What would he gain if your ways were blameless?

4 "Is it for your piety that he rebukes you
and brings charges against you?
5 Is not your wickedness great?
Are not your sins endless?
6 You demanded security from your brothers for no reason;
you stripped men of their clothing, leaving them naked.
7 You gave no water to the weary
and you withheld food from the hungry,
8 though you were a powerful man, owning land—
an honored man, living on it.
9 And you sent widows away empty-handed
and broke the strength of the fatherless.
10 That is why snares are all around you,
why sudden peril terrifies you,
11 why it is so dark you cannot see,
and why a flood of water covers you.

12 "Is not God in the heights of heaven?
And see how lofty are the highest stars!
13 Yet you say, 'What does God know?
Does he judge through such darkness?
14 Thick clouds veil him, so he does not see us
as he goes about in the vaulted heavens.'
15 Will you keep to the old path
that evil men have trod?
16 They were carried off before their time,
their foundations washed away by a flood.
17 They said to God, 'Leave us alone!
What can the Almighty do to us?'
18 Yet it was he who filled their houses with good things,
so I stand aloof from the counsel of the wicked.

19 "The righteous see their ruin and rejoice;
the innocent mock them, saying,
20 'Surely our foes are destroyed,
and fire devours their wealth.'

21 "Submit to God and be at peace with him;
in this way prosperity will come to you.
22 Accept instruction from his mouth
and lay up his words in your heart.
23 If you return to the Almighty, you will be restored:
If you remove wickedness far from your tent
24 and assign your nuggets to the dust,
your gold of Ophir to the rocks in the ravines,
25 then the Almighty will be your gold,
the choicest silver for you.
26 Surely then you will find delight in the Almighty
and will lift up your face to God.
27 You will pray to him, and he will hear you,
and you will fulfill your vows.
28 What you decide on will be done,
and light will shine on your ways.
29 When men are brought low and you say, 'Lift them up!'
then he will save the downcast.
30 He will deliver even one who is not innocent,
who will be delivered through the cleanness of your hands."

PRAYER: INTERCESSION

YOU, Lord Jesus, told the apostles, "You will receive power when the Holy Spirit comes upon you; and you will be My witnesses in Jerusalem, and in all Judea and Samaria, and to the ends of the earth." (Acts 1:8)

***TAKE** a few moments to intercede on behalf of local, national and world missions. Pray that the Great Commission would be fulfilled, and pray for any special concerns you may have for missions.*

NT Matthew 13:1-23

The Parable of the Sower

13 That same day Jesus went out of the
house and sat by the lake. 2Such large
crowds gathered around him that he got
into a boat and sat in it, while all the people stood on the shore. 3Then he told them
many things in parables, saying: "A farmer
went out to sow his seed. 4As he was scattering the seed, some fell along the path,
and the birds came and ate it up. 5Some
fell on rocky places, where it did not have
much soil. It sprang up quickly, because
the soil was shallow. 6But when the sun
came up, the plants were scorched, and
they withered because they had no root.
7Other seed fell among thorns, which grew
up and choked the plants. 8Still other seed
fell on good soil, where it produced a
crop—a hundred, sixty or thirty times what
was sown. 9He who has ears, let him hear."
10The disciples came to him and asked,
"Why do you speak to the people in parables?"
11He replied, "The knowledge of the secrets of the kingdom of heaven has been
given to you, but not to them. 12Whoever
has will be given more, and he will have
an abundance. Whoever does not have,
even what he has will be taken from him.
13This is why I speak to them in parables:

"Though seeing, they do not see;
though hearing, they do not hear or
understand.

14In them is fulfilled the prophecy of Isaiah:

" 'You will be ever hearing but never
understanding;
you will be ever seeing but never
perceiving.
15For this people's heart has become
calloused;
they hardly hear with their ears,
and they have closed their eyes.
Otherwise they might see with their
eyes,
hear with their ears,
understand with their hearts
and turn, and I would heal them.'[a]

16But blessed are your eyes because they
see, and your ears because they hear. 17For
I tell you the truth, many prophets and
righteous men longed to see what you see
but did not see it, and to hear what you
hear but did not hear it.
18"Listen then to what the parable of
the sower means: 19When anyone hears
the message about the kingdom and does
not understand it, the evil one comes and
snatches away what was sown in his
heart. This is the seed sown along the
path. 20The one who received the seed
that fell on rocky places is the man who
hears the word and at once receives it
with joy. 21But since he has no root, he
lasts only a short time. When trouble or
persecution comes because of the word,
he quickly falls away. 22The one who received the seed that fell among the thorns
is the man who hears the word, but the
worries of this life and the deceitfulness
of wealth choke it, making it unfruitful.
23But the one who received the seed that
fell on good soil is the man who hears
the word and understands it. He produces a crop, yielding a hundred, sixty or
thirty times what was sown."

[a] *15* Isaiah 6:9,10

PRAYER: MY RELATIONSHIP TO GOD

I WILL not lose heart; even though my outward self is perishing, yet my inner self is being renewed day by day. For this light affliction, which is momentary, is working for me a far more exceeding and eternal weight of glory. So I do not look at the things that are seen but at the things that are unseen. For the things that are seen are temporary, but the things that are unseen are eternal. (2 Corinthians 4:16–18)

***PAUSE** to thank God for the relationship that you enjoy with Him in Jesus Christ.*

YEAR 2 DAY 19

OT Job 23:1–24:25

Job

23 Then Job replied:

²"Even today my complaint is bitter;
his hand[a] is heavy in spite of[b] my groaning.
³If only I knew where to find him;
if only I could go to his dwelling!
⁴I would state my case before him
and fill my mouth with arguments.
⁵I would find out what he would answer me,
and consider what he would say.
⁶Would he oppose me with great power?
No, he would not press charges against me.
⁷There an upright man could present his case before him,
and I would be delivered forever from my judge.

⁸"But if I go to the east, he is not there;
if I go to the west, I do not find him.
⁹When he is at work in the north, I do not see him;
when he turns to the south, I catch no glimpse of him.
¹⁰But he knows the way that I take;
when he has tested me, I will come forth as gold.
¹¹My feet have closely followed his steps;
I have kept to his way without turning aside.
¹²I have not departed from the commands of his lips;
I have treasured the words of his mouth more than my daily bread.

¹³"But he stands alone, and who can oppose him?
He does whatever he pleases.
¹⁴He carries out his decree against me,
and many such plans he still has in store.
¹⁵That is why I am terrified before him;
when I think of all this, I fear him.
¹⁶God has made my heart faint;
the Almighty has terrified me.
¹⁷Yet I am not silenced by the darkness,
by the thick darkness that covers my face.

24 "Why does the Almighty not set times for judgment?
Why must those who know him look in vain for such days?
²Men move boundary stones;
they pasture flocks they have stolen.
³They drive away the orphan's donkey
and take the widow's ox in pledge.
⁴They thrust the needy from the path
and force all the poor of the land into hiding.
⁵Like wild donkeys in the desert,
the poor go about their labor of foraging food;
the wasteland provides food for their children.
⁶They gather fodder in the fields
and glean in the vineyards of the wicked.
⁷Lacking clothes, they spend the night naked;
they have nothing to cover themselves in the cold.

[a] 2 Septuagint and Syriac; Hebrew *I the hand on me*
[b] 2 Or *heavy on me in*

[8]They are drenched by mountain rains
and hug the rocks for lack of shelter.
[9]The fatherless child is snatched from
the breast;
the infant of the poor is seized for a
debt.
[10]Lacking clothes, they go about naked;
they carry the sheaves, but still go
hungry.
[11]They crush olives among the terraces[c];
they tread the winepresses, yet
suffer thirst.
[12]The groans of the dying rise from the
city,
and the souls of the wounded cry
out for help.
But God charges no one with
wrongdoing.

[13]"There are those who rebel against the
light,
who do not know its ways
or stay in its paths.
[14]When daylight is gone, the murderer
rises up
and kills the poor and needy;
in the night he steals forth like a
thief.
[15]The eye of the adulterer watches for
dusk;
he thinks, 'No eye will see me,'
and he keeps his face concealed.
[16]In the dark, men break into houses,
but by day they shut themselves in;
they want nothing to do with the
light.
[17]For all of them, deep darkness is their
morning[d];
they make friends with the terrors
of darkness.[e]

[18]"Yet they are foam on the surface of
the water;
their portion of the land is cursed,
so that no one goes to the
vineyards.
[19]As heat and drought snatch away the
melted snow,
so the grave[f] snatches away those
who have sinned.
[20]The womb forgets them,
the worm feasts on them;
evil men are no longer remembered
but are broken like a tree.
[21]They prey on the barren and childless
woman,
and to the widow show no kindness.
[22]But God drags away the mighty by his
power;
though they become established,
they have no assurance of life.
[23]He may let them rest in a feeling of
security,
but his eyes are on their ways.
[24]For a little while they are exalted, and
then they are gone;
they are brought low and gathered
up like all others;
they are cut off like heads of grain.

[25]"If this is not so, who can prove me
false
and reduce my words to nothing?"

[c] 11 Or *olives between the millstones;* the meaning of the Hebrew for this word is uncertain. [d] 17 Or *them, their morning is like the shadow of death* [e] 17 Or *of the shadow of death* [f] 19 Hebrew *Sheol*

PRAYER: AFFIRMATION

YOU have called the humble of the earth to seek You, O Lord, and those who have upheld Your justice to seek righteousness and humility. (Zephaniah 2:3)

***PAUSE** to reflect on these Biblical affirmations.*

NT Matthew 13:24-58

The Parable of the Weeds

[24]Jesus told them another parable: "The
kingdom of heaven is like a man who
sowed good seed in his field. [25]But while
everyone was sleeping, his enemy came
and sowed weeds among the wheat, and
went away. [26]When the wheat sprouted
and formed heads, then the weeds also
appeared.
[27]"The owner's servants came to him
and said, 'Sir, didn't you sow good seed in
your field? Where then did the weeds
come from?'
[28]" 'An enemy did this,' he replied.

"The servants asked him, 'Do you want
us to go and pull them up?'
29 " 'No,' he answered, 'because while you
are pulling the weeds, you may root up the
wheat with them. 30 Let both grow together
until the harvest. At that time I will tell the
harvesters: First collect the weeds and tie
them in bundles to be burned; then gather the wheat and bring it into my barn.' "

The Parables of the Mustard Seed and the Yeast

31 He told them another parable: "The
kingdom of heaven is like a mustard seed,
which a man took and planted in his
field. 32 Though it is the smallest of all
your seeds, yet when it grows, it is the
largest of garden plants and becomes a
tree, so that the birds of the air come and
perch in its branches."
33 He told them still another parable:
"The kingdom of heaven is like yeast that
a woman took and mixed into a large
amount[a] of flour until it worked all
through the dough."
34 Jesus spoke all these things to the
crowd in parables; he did not say anything
to them without using a parable. 35 So was
fulfilled what was spoken through the
prophet:

"I will open my mouth in parables,
I will utter things hidden since the
creation of the world."[b]

The Parable of the Weeds Explained

36 Then he left the crowd and went into
the house. His disciples came to him and
said, "Explain to us the parable of the
weeds in the field."
37 He answered, "The one who sowed
the good seed is the Son of Man. 38 The
field is the world, and the good seed
stands for the sons of the kingdom. The
weeds are the sons of the evil one, 39 and
the enemy who sows them is the devil.
The harvest is the end of the age, and the
harvesters are angels.
40 "As the weeds are pulled up and
burned in the fire, so it will be at the end
of the age. 41 The Son of Man will send out
his angels, and they will weed out of his
kingdom everything that causes sin and
all who do evil. 42 They will throw them
into the fiery furnace, where there will be
weeping and gnashing of teeth. 43 Then the
righteous will shine like the sun in the
kingdom of their Father. He who has ears,
let him hear.

The Parables of the Hidden Treasure and the Pearl

44 "The kingdom of heaven is like treasure hidden in a field. When a man found
it, he hid it again, and then in his joy went
and sold all he had and bought that field.
45 "Again, the kingdom of heaven is like
a merchant looking for fine pearls.
46 When he found one of great value, he
went away and sold everything he had
and bought it.

The Parable of the Net

47 "Once again, the kingdom of heaven
is like a net that was let down into the lake
and caught all kinds of fish. 48 When it was
full, the fishermen pulled it up on the
shore. Then they sat down and collected
the good fish in baskets, but threw the bad
away. 49 This is how it will be at the end of
the age. The angels will come and separate
the wicked from the righteous 50 and throw
them into the fiery furnace, where there
will be weeping and gnashing of teeth.
51 "Have you understood all these
things?" Jesus asked.
"Yes," they replied.
52 He said to them, "Therefore every
teacher of the law who has been instructed about the kingdom of heaven is like the
owner of a house who brings out of his
storeroom new treasures as well as old."

A Prophet Without Honor

53 When Jesus had finished these parables, he moved on from there. 54 Coming
to his hometown, he began teaching the
people in their synagogue, and they were
amazed. "Where did this man get this wisdom and these miraculous powers?" they
asked. 55 "Isn't this the carpenter's son?
Isn't his mother's name Mary, and aren't
his brothers James, Joseph, Simon and
Judas? 56 Aren't all his sisters with us?
Where then did this man get all these
things?" 57 And they took offense at him.
But Jesus said to them, "Only in his
hometown and in his own house is a
prophet without honor."
58 And he did not do many miracles
there because of their lack of faith.

[a] 33 Greek *three satas* (probably about 1/2 bushel or 22 liters) [b] 35 Psalm 78:2

PRAYER: THE CHARACTER I WANT TO CULTIVATE

I WILL be anxious for nothing, but in everything, by prayer and petition with thanksgiving, I will let my requests be known to You. And Your peace, O God, which transcends all understanding, will guard my heart and my mind in Christ Jesus. (Philippians 4:6–7)

***TAKE** a moment to ask the Lord for the grace to grow in godly character.*

YEAR 2 DAY 20

OT Job 25:1–26:14

Bildad

25 Then Bildad the Shuhite replied:

2 "Dominion and awe belong to God;
he establishes order in the heights of heaven.
3 Can his forces be numbered?
Upon whom does his light not rise?
4 How then can a man be righteous before God?
How can one born of woman be pure?
5 If even the moon is not bright
and the stars are not pure in his eyes,
6 how much less man, who is but a maggot—
a son of man, who is only a worm!"

Job

26 Then Job replied:

2 "How you have helped the powerless!
How you have saved the arm that is feeble!
3 What advice you have offered to one without wisdom!
And what great insight you have displayed!
4 Who has helped you utter these words?
And whose spirit spoke from your mouth?
5 "The dead are in deep anguish,
those beneath the waters and all that live in them.
6 Death[a] is naked before God;
Destruction[b] lies uncovered.
7 He spreads out the northern ⌞skies⌟ over empty space;
he suspends the earth over nothing.
8 He wraps up the waters in his clouds,
yet the clouds do not burst under their weight.
9 He covers the face of the full moon,
spreading his clouds over it.
10 He marks out the horizon on the face of the waters
for a boundary between light and darkness.
11 The pillars of the heavens quake,
aghast at his rebuke.
12 By his power he churned up the sea;
by his wisdom he cut Rahab to pieces.
13 By his breath the skies became fair;
his hand pierced the gliding serpent.
14 And these are but the outer fringe of his works;
how faint the whisper we hear of him!
Who then can understand the thunder of his power?"

[a] 6 Hebrew *Sheol* [b] 6 Hebrew *Abaddon*

PRAYER: THANKSGIVING

YOU sent Your word to the children of Israel, O God, telling the good news of peace through Jesus Christ, who is Lord of all. Jesus commanded the apostles to preach to the people and to testify that He is the One whom You appointed as judge of the living and the dead. To Him all the prophets witness that through His name, everyone who believes in Him receives forgiveness of sins. (Acts 10:36, 42–43)

***PAUSE** to offer your own expressions of thanksgiving.*

NT Matthew 14:1-36

John the Baptist Beheaded

14 At that time Herod the tetrarch heard
the reports about Jesus, 2and he said
to his attendants, "This is John the Baptist; he has risen from the dead! That is
why miraculous powers are at work in
him."
3Now Herod had arrested John and
bound him and put him in prison because of Herodias, his brother Philip's
wife, 4for John had been saying to him: "It
is not lawful for you to have her." 5Herod
wanted to kill John, but he was afraid of
the people, because they considered him
a prophet.
6On Herod's birthday the daughter of
Herodias danced for them and pleased
Herod so much 7that he promised with an
oath to give her whatever she asked.
8Prompted by her mother, she said, "Give
me here on a platter the head of John the
Baptist." 9The king was distressed, but because of his oaths and his dinner guests,
he ordered that her request be granted
10and had John beheaded in the prison.
11His head was brought in on a platter and
given to the girl, who carried it to her
mother. 12John's disciples came and took
his body and buried it. Then they went
and told Jesus.

Jesus Feeds the Five Thousand

13When Jesus heard what had happened, he withdrew by boat privately to a
solitary place. Hearing of this, the crowds
followed him on foot from the towns.
14When Jesus landed and saw a large
crowd, he had compassion on them and
healed their sick.
15As evening approached, the disciples
came to him and said, "This is a remote
place, and it's already getting late. Send
the crowds away, so they can go to the villages and buy themselves some food."
16Jesus replied, "They do not need to go
away. You give them something to eat."
17"We have here only five loaves of
bread and two fish," they answered.
18"Bring them here to me," he said.
19And he directed the people to sit down
on the grass. Taking the five loaves and the
two fish and looking up to heaven, he
gave thanks and broke the loaves. Then he
gave them to the disciples, and the disciples gave them to the people. 20They all
ate and were satisfied, and the disciples
picked up twelve basketfuls of broken
pieces that were left over. 21The number of
those who ate was about five thousand
men, besides women and children.

Jesus Walks on the Water

22Immediately Jesus made the disciples
get into the boat and go on ahead of him
to the other side, while he dismissed the
crowd. 23After he had dismissed them, he
went up on a mountainside by himself to
pray. When evening came, he was there
alone, 24but the boat was already a considerable distance[a] from land, buffeted by
the waves because the wind was against it.
25During the fourth watch of the night
Jesus went out to them, walking on the
lake. 26When the disciples saw him walking on the lake, they were terrified. "It's a
ghost," they said, and cried out in fear.
27But Jesus immediately said to them:
"Take courage! It is I. Don't be afraid."
28"Lord, if it's you," Peter replied, "tell
me to come to you on the water."
29"Come," he said.
Then Peter got down out of the boat,
walked on the water and came toward
Jesus. 30But when he saw the wind, he was
afraid and, beginning to sink, cried out,
"Lord, save me!"
31Immediately Jesus reached out his
hand and caught him. "You of little faith,"
he said, "why did you doubt?"
32And when they climbed into the boat,
the wind died down. 33Then those who
were in the boat worshiped him, saying,
"Truly you are the Son of God."
34When they had crossed over, they
landed at Gennesaret. 35And when the
men of that place recognized Jesus, they
sent word to all the surrounding country.
People brought all their sick to him 36and
begged him to let the sick just touch the
edge of his cloak, and all who touched
him were healed.

[a] 24 Greek *many stadia*

PRAYER: MY RELATIONSHIP TO OTHERS

I WILL give to all what they are due: taxes to whom taxes are due, custom to whom custom, respect to whom respect, honor to whom honor. (Romans 13:7) . . . I will honor all people, love the community of believers, fear You, O God, and honor the king. (1 Peter 2:17)

***PAUSE** to review your relationships with others and to commit them to the Lord.*

YEAR 2 DAY 21

OT Psalms 75–76

Psalm 75

For the director of music. ⌞To the tune of⌟ "Do Not Destroy." A psalm of Asaph. A song.

1 We give thanks to you, O God,
we give thanks, for your Name is near;
men tell of your wonderful deeds.

2 You say, "I choose the appointed time;
it is I who judge uprightly.
3 When the earth and all its people quake,
it is I who hold its pillars firm. *Selah*
4 To the arrogant I say, 'Boast no more,'
and to the wicked, 'Do not lift up
your horns.
5 Do not lift your horns against heaven;
do not speak with outstretched
neck.' "

6 No one from the east or the west
or from the desert can exalt a man.
7 But it is God who judges:
He brings one down, he exalts
another.
8 In the hand of the LORD is a cup
full of foaming wine mixed with
spices;
he pours it out, and all the wicked of
the earth
drink it down to its very dregs.

9 As for me, I will declare this forever;
I will sing praise to the God of Jacob.
10 I will cut off the horns of all the wicked,
but the horns of the righteous will
be lifted up.

Psalm 76

For the director of music. With stringed instruments. A psalm of Asaph. A song.

1 In Judah God is known;
his name is great in Israel.
2 His tent is in Salem,
his dwelling place in Zion.
3 There he broke the flashing arrows,
the shields and the swords, the
weapons of war. *Selah*

4 You are resplendent with light,
more majestic than mountains rich
with game.
5 Valiant men lie plundered,
they sleep their last sleep;
not one of the warriors
can lift his hands.
6 At your rebuke, O God of Jacob,
both horse and chariot lie still.
7 You alone are to be feared.
Who can stand before you when
you are angry?
8 From heaven you pronounced
judgment,
and the land feared and was
quiet—
9 when you, O God, rose up to judge,
to save all the afflicted of the land.
Selah
10 Surely your wrath against men brings
you praise,
and the survivors of your wrath are
restrained.[a]

11 Make vows to the LORD your God and
fulfill them;
let all the neighboring lands
bring gifts to the One to be
feared.
12 He breaks the spirit of rulers;
he is feared by the kings of the
earth.

[a] 10 Or *Surely the wrath of men brings you praise, / and with the remainder of wrath you arm yourself*

PRAYER: ADORATION

THRONES were set in place, and You, O Ancient of Days, took Your seat. Your clothing was as white as snow, and the hair of Your head was like pure wool. Your throne was ablaze with flames, and its wheels were a burning fire. A river of fire was flowing and coming out from before You. A thousand thousands attended You; ten thousand times ten thousand stood before You. The court was seated, and the books were opened.

(Daniel 7:9–10)

***PAUSE** to express your thoughts of praise and worship.*

NT Matthew 15:1–28

Clean and Unclean

15 Then some Pharisees and teachers of
the law came to Jesus from Jerusalem
and asked, 2 "Why do your disciples break
the tradition of the elders? They don't
wash their hands before they eat!"
3 Jesus replied, "And why do you break
the command of God for the sake of your
tradition? 4 For God said, 'Honor your father and mother'[a] and 'Anyone who
curses his father or mother must be put to
death.'[b] 5 But you say that if a man says to
his father or mother, 'Whatever help you
might otherwise have received from me is
a gift devoted to God,' 6 he is not to 'hon-
or his father[c]' with it. Thus you nullify the
word of God for the sake of your tradition. 7 You hypocrites! Isaiah was right
when he prophesied about you:

8 " 'These people honor me with their
lips,
but their hearts are far from me.
9 They worship me in vain;
their teachings are but rules taught
by men.'[d]"

10 Jesus called the crowd to him and
said, "Listen and understand. 11 What goes
into a man's mouth does not make him
'unclean,' but what comes out of his
mouth, that is what makes him 'unclean.' "
12 Then the disciples came to him and
asked, "Do you know that the Pharisees
were offended when they heard this?"
13 He replied, "Every plant that my heavenly Father has not planted will be pulled
up by the roots. 14 Leave them; they are
blind guides.[e] If a blind man leads a blind
man, both will fall into a pit."
15 Peter said, "Explain the parable to us."
16 "Are you still so dull?" Jesus asked
them. 17 "Don't you see that whatever enters the mouth goes into the stomach and
then out of the body? 18 But the things that
come out of the mouth come from the
heart, and these make a man 'unclean.'
19 For out of the heart come evil thoughts,
murder, adultery, sexual immorality, theft,
false testimony, slander. 20 These are what
make a man 'unclean'; but eating with unwashed hands does not make him 'unclean.' "

The Faith of the Canaanite Woman

21 Leaving that place, Jesus withdrew to
the region of Tyre and Sidon. 22 A Canaanite woman from that vicinity came to
him, crying out, "Lord, Son of David, have
mercy on me! My daughter is suffering
terribly from demon-possession."
23 Jesus did not answer a word. So his
disciples came to him and urged him,
"Send her away, for she keeps crying out
after us."
24 He answered, "I was sent only to the
lost sheep of Israel."
25 The woman came and knelt before
him. "Lord, help me!" she said.
26 He replied, "It is not right to take the
children's bread and toss it to their dogs."
27 "Yes, Lord," she said, "but even the
dogs eat the crumbs that fall from their
masters' table."
28 Then Jesus answered, "Woman, you
have great faith! Your request is granted."
And her daughter was healed from that
very hour.

[a] 4 Exodus 20:12; Deut. 5:16 [b] 4 Exodus 21:17; Lev. 20:9 [c] 6 Some manuscripts *father or his mother* [d] 9 Isaiah 29:13 [e] 14 Some manuscripts *guides of the blind*

PRAYER: THE ATTRIBUTES OF GOD

O LORD, You are not slow concerning Your promise, as some count slowness, but are patient with us, not wanting anyone to perish, but for all to come to repentance. (2 Peter 3:9)

***PAUSE** to reflect on these affirmations about the person, powers and perfection of God.*

YEAR 2
DAY 22

OT Job 27:1-23

27 And Job continued his discourse:

2 "As surely as God lives, who has denied me justice,
the Almighty, who has made me taste bitterness of soul,
3 as long as I have life within me,
the breath of God in my nostrils,
4 my lips will not speak wickedness,
and my tongue will utter no deceit.
5 I will never admit you are in the right;
till I die, I will not deny my integrity.
6 I will maintain my righteousness and never let go of it;
my conscience will not reproach me as long as I live.

7 "May my enemies be like the wicked,
my adversaries like the unjust!
8 For what hope has the godless when he is cut off,
when God takes away his life?
9 Does God listen to his cry
when distress comes upon him?
10 Will he find delight in the Almighty?
Will he call upon God at all times?

11 "I will teach you about the power of God;
the ways of the Almighty I will not conceal.
12 You have all seen this yourselves.
Why then this meaningless talk?

13 "Here is the fate God allots to the wicked,
the heritage a ruthless man receives from the Almighty:
14 However many his children, their fate is the sword;
his offspring will never have enough to eat.
15 The plague will bury those who survive him,
and their widows will not weep for them.
16 Though he heaps up silver like dust
and clothes like piles of clay,
17 what he lays up the righteous will wear,
and the innocent will divide his silver.
18 The house he builds is like a moth's cocoon,
like a hut made by a watchman.
19 He lies down wealthy, but will do so no more;
when he opens his eyes, all is gone.
20 Terrors overtake him like a flood;
a tempest snatches him away in the night.
21 The east wind carries him off, and he is gone;
it sweeps him out of his place.
22 It hurls itself against him without mercy
as he flees headlong from its power.
23 It claps its hands in derision
and hisses him out of his place.

PRAYER: CONFESSION

YOU, O Lord, have declared, "Even now return to Me with all your heart, with fasting and weeping and mourning. So rend your heart and not your garments." We will return to You, O Lord our God,

for You are gracious and compassionate, slow to anger and abounding in loving-kindness, and You relent from sending calamity.
(Joel 2:12–13)

***ASK** the Spirit to search your heart and reveal any areas of unconfessed sin. Acknowledge these to the Lord and thank Him for His forgiveness.*

NT Matthew 15:29–16:28

Jesus Feeds the Four Thousand

[29]Jesus left there and went along the Sea of Galilee. Then he went up on a mountainside and sat down. [30]Great crowds came to him, bringing the lame, the blind, the crippled, the mute and many others, and laid them at his feet; and he healed them. [31]The people were amazed when they saw the mute speaking, the crippled made well, the lame walking and the blind seeing. And they praised the God of Israel.

[32]Jesus called his disciples to him and said, "I have compassion for these people; they have already been with me three days and have nothing to eat. I do not want to send them away hungry, or they may collapse on the way."

[33]His disciples answered, "Where could we get enough bread in this remote place to feed such a crowd?"

[34]"How many loaves do you have?" Jesus asked.

"Seven," they replied, "and a few small fish."

[35]He told the crowd to sit down on the ground. [36]Then he took the seven loaves and the fish, and when he had given thanks, he broke them and gave them to the disciples, and they in turn to the people. [37]They all ate and were satisfied. Afterward the disciples picked up seven basketfuls of broken pieces that were left over. [38]The number of those who ate was four thousand, besides women and children. [39]After Jesus had sent the crowd away, he got into the boat and went to the vicinity of Magadan.

The Demand for a Sign

16 The Pharisees and Sadducees came to Jesus and tested him by asking him to show them a sign from heaven.

[2]He replied,[a] "When evening comes, you say, 'It will be fair weather, for the sky is red,' [3]and in the morning, 'Today it will be stormy, for the sky is red and overcast.' You know how to interpret the appearance of the sky, but you cannot interpret the signs of the times. [4]A wicked and adulterous generation looks for a miraculous sign, but none will be given it except the sign of Jonah." Jesus then left them and went away.

The Yeast of the Pharisees and Sadducees

[5]When they went across the lake, the disciples forgot to take bread. [6]"Be careful," Jesus said to them. "Be on your guard against the yeast of the Pharisees and Sadducees."

[7]They discussed this among themselves and said, "It is because we didn't bring any bread."

[8]Aware of their discussion, Jesus asked, "You of little faith, why are you talking among yourselves about having no bread? [9]Do you still not understand? Don't you remember the five loaves for the five thousand, and how many basketfuls you gathered? [10]Or the seven loaves for the four thousand, and how many basketfuls you gathered? [11]How is it you don't understand that I was not talking to you about bread? But be on your guard against the yeast of the Pharisees and Sadducees." [12]Then they understood that he was not telling them to guard against the yeast used in bread, but against the teaching of the Pharisees and Sadducees.

Peter's Confession of Christ

[13]When Jesus came to the region of Caesarea Philippi, he asked his disciples, "Who do people say the Son of Man is?"

[14]They replied, "Some say John the Baptist; others say Elijah; and still others, Jeremiah or one of the prophets."

[15]"But what about you?" he asked. "Who do you say I am?"

[a] 2 Some early manuscripts do not have the rest of verse 2 and all of verse 3.

16 Simon Peter answered, "You are the
Christ,[b] the Son of the living God."
17 Jesus replied, "Blessed are you, Simon
son of Jonah, for this was not revealed to
you by man, but by my Father in heaven.
18 And I tell you that you are Peter,[c] and on
this rock I will build my church, and the
gates of Hades[d] will not overcome it.[e] 19 I
will give you the keys of the kingdom of
heaven; whatever you bind on earth will
be[f] bound in heaven, and whatever you
loose on earth will be[f] loosed in heaven."
20 Then he warned his disciples not to tell
anyone that he was the Christ.

Jesus Predicts His Death

21 From that time on Jesus began to explain to his disciples that he must go to
Jerusalem and suffer many things at the
hands of the elders, chief priests and teachers of the law, and that he must be killed
and on the third day be raised to life.
22 Peter took him aside and began to rebuke him. "Never, Lord!" he said. "This
shall never happen to you!"
23 Jesus turned and said to Peter, "Get
behind me, Satan! You are a stumbling
block to me; you do not have in mind the
things of God, but the things of men."
24 Then Jesus said to his disciples, "If
anyone would come after me, he must
deny himself and take up his cross and
follow me. 25 For whoever wants to save
his life[g] will lose it, but whoever loses his
life for me will find it. 26 What good will it
be for a man if he gains the whole world,
yet forfeits his soul? Or what can a man
give in exchange for his soul? 27 For the
Son of Man is going to come in his Father's glory with his angels, and then he
will reward each person according to what
he has done. 28 I tell you the truth, some
who are standing here will not taste death
before they see the Son of Man coming in
his kingdom."

[b] 16 Or *Messiah*; also in verse 20 [c] 18 *Peter* means *rock.* [d] 18 Or *hell* [e] 18 Or *not prove stronger than it* [f] 19 Or *have been* [g] 25 The Greek word means either *life* or *soul*; also in verse 26.

PRAYER: THE WORKS OF GOD

YOU, Lord God, take no pleasure in the death of the wicked but are pleased when the wicked turn from their ways and live. (Ezekiel 18:23; 33:11) . . . Jesus, You said, "It is not the healthy who need a physician, but those who are sick." You did not come to call the righteous, but sinners. (Matthew 9:12–13)

TAKE *a moment to consider the greatness of God's wonderful works.*

OT **Job 28:1–28** YEAR 2 DAY 23

28 "There is a mine for silver
and a place where gold is refined.
2 Iron is taken from the earth,
and copper is smelted from ore.
3 Man puts an end to the darkness;
he searches the farthest recesses
for ore in the blackest darkness.
4 Far from where people dwell he cuts a shaft,
in places forgotten by the foot of man;
far from men he dangles and sways.
5 The earth, from which food comes,
is transformed below as by fire;
6 sapphires[a] come from its rocks,
and its dust contains nuggets of gold.
7 No bird of prey knows that hidden path,
no falcon's eye has seen it.
8 Proud beasts do not set foot on it,
and no lion prowls there.
9 Man's hand assaults the flinty rock
and lays bare the roots of the mountains.
10 He tunnels through the rock;
his eyes see all its treasures.

[a] 6 Or *lapis lazuli*; also in verse 16

[11]He searches[b] the sources of the rivers
and brings hidden things to light.

[12]"But where can wisdom be found?
Where does understanding dwell?
[13]Man does not comprehend its worth;
it cannot be found in the land of the living.
[14]The deep says, 'It is not in me';
the sea says, 'It is not with me.'
[15]It cannot be bought with the finest gold,
nor can its price be weighed in silver.
[16]It cannot be bought with the gold of Ophir,
with precious onyx or sapphires.
[17]Neither gold nor crystal can compare with it,
nor can it be had for jewels of gold.
[18]Coral and jasper are not worthy of mention;
the price of wisdom is beyond rubies.
[19]The topaz of Cush cannot compare with it;
it cannot be bought with pure gold.

[20]"Where then does wisdom come from?
Where does understanding dwell?
[21]It is hidden from the eyes of every living thing,
concealed even from the birds of the air.
[22]Destruction[c] and Death say,
'Only a rumor of it has reached our ears.'
[23]God understands the way to it
and he alone knows where it dwells,
[24]for he views the ends of the earth
and sees everything under the heavens.
[25]When he established the force of the wind
and measured out the waters,
[26]when he made a decree for the rain
and a path for the thunderstorm,
[27]then he looked at wisdom and appraised it;
he confirmed it and tested it.
[28]And he said to man,
'The fear of the Lord—that is wisdom,
and to shun evil is understanding.' "

[b] 11 Septuagint, Aquila and Vulgate; Hebrew *He dams up* [c] 22 Hebrew *Abaddon*

PRAYER: RENEWAL

MAY I not let Your Word depart from my mouth, but meditate on it day and night, so that I may be careful to do all that is written in it; for then I will be prosperous, and I will act wisely.
(Joshua 1:8)

***PAUSE** to add your own prayers for personal renewal.*

NT Matthew 17:1–27

The Transfiguration

17 After six days Jesus took with him Peter, James and John the brother of
James, and led them up a high mountain
by themselves. [2]There he was transfigured
before them. His face shone like the sun,
and his clothes became as white as the
light. [3]Just then there appeared before
them Moses and Elijah, talking with Jesus.
[4]Peter said to Jesus, "Lord, it is good for
us to be here. If you wish, I will put up
three shelters—one for you, one for Moses and one for Elijah."
[5]While he was still speaking, a bright
cloud enveloped them, and a voice from
the cloud said, "This is my Son, whom I
love; with him I am well pleased. Listen
to him!"
[6]When the disciples heard this, they fell
facedown to the ground, terrified. [7]But
Jesus came and touched them. "Get up,"
he said. "Don't be afraid." [8]When they
looked up, they saw no one except Jesus.
[9]As they were coming down the mountain, Jesus instructed them, "Don't tell
anyone what you have seen, until the Son
of Man has been raised from the dead."
[10]The disciples asked him, "Why then

do the teachers of the law say that Elijah
must come first?"
11 Jesus replied, "To be sure, Elijah
comes and will restore all things. 12 But I
tell you, Elijah has already come, and they
did not recognize him, but have done to
him everything they wished. In the same
way the Son of Man is going to suffer at
their hands." 13 Then the disciples understood that he was talking to them about
John the Baptist.

The Healing of a Boy With a Demon

14 When they came to the crowd, a man
approached Jesus and knelt before him.
15 "Lord, have mercy on my son," he said.
"He has seizures and is suffering greatly.
He often falls into the fire or into the water. 16 I brought him to your disciples, but
they could not heal him."
17 "O unbelieving and perverse generation," Jesus replied, "how long shall I stay
with you? How long shall I put up with
you? Bring the boy here to me." 18 Jesus rebuked the demon, and it came out of the
boy, and he was healed from that moment.
19 Then the disciples came to Jesus in
private and asked, "Why couldn't we drive
it out?"
20 He replied, "Because you have so little faith. I tell you the truth, if you have
faith as small as a mustard seed, you can
say to this mountain, 'Move from here to
there' and it will move. Nothing will be
impossible for you.[a]"
22 When they came together in Galilee,
he said to them, "The Son of Man is going to be betrayed into the hands of men.
23 They will kill him, and on the third day
he will be raised to life." And the disciples
were filled with grief.

The Temple Tax

24 After Jesus and his disciples arrived in
Capernaum, the collectors of the two-
drachma tax came to Peter and asked,
"Doesn't your teacher pay the temple
tax[b]?"
25 "Yes, he does," he replied.
When Peter came into the house, Jesus
was the first to speak. "What do you think,
Simon?" he asked. "From whom do the
kings of the earth collect duty and taxes—
from their own sons or from others?"
26 "From others," Peter answered.
"Then the sons are exempt," Jesus said
to him. 27 "But so that we may not offend
them, go to the lake and throw out your
line. Take the first fish you catch; open its
mouth and you will find a four-drachma
coin. Take it and give it to them for my tax
and yours."

[a] 20 Some manuscripts *you.* [21] *But this kind does not go out except by prayer and fasting.* [b] 24 Greek *the two drachmas*

PRAYER: MY RELATIONSHIP TO GOD

I AM confident of this, that You, the One who began a good work in me, will carry it on to completion until Your day, Christ Jesus. (Philippians 1:6) . . . In Your great grace, O God, You called me to Your eternal glory in Christ. After I have suffered a little while, You Yourself will perfect, confirm, strengthen and establish me. (1 Peter 5:10)

PAUSE *to thank God for the relationship that you enjoy with Him in Jesus Christ.*

YEAR 2 DAY 24

OT Job 29:1–25

29 Job continued his discourse:

2 "How I long for the months gone by,
for the days when God watched
over me,
3 when his lamp shone upon my head
and by his light I walked through
darkness!
4 Oh, for the days when I was in my
prime,
when God's intimate friendship
blessed my house,

[5] when the Almighty was still with me
and my children were around me,
[6] when my path was drenched with cream
and the rock poured out for me streams of olive oil.

[7] "When I went to the gate of the city
and took my seat in the public square,
[8] the young men saw me and stepped aside
and the old men rose to their feet;
[9] the chief men refrained from speaking
and covered their mouths with their hands;
[10] the voices of the nobles were hushed,
and their tongues stuck to the roof of their mouths.
[11] Whoever heard me spoke well of me,
and those who saw me commended me,
[12] because I rescued the poor who cried for help,
and the fatherless who had none to assist him.
[13] The man who was dying blessed me;
I made the widow's heart sing.
[14] I put on righteousness as my clothing;
justice was my robe and my turban.
[15] I was eyes to the blind
and feet to the lame.
[16] I was a father to the needy;
I took up the case of the stranger.
[17] I broke the fangs of the wicked
and snatched the victims from their teeth.

[18] "I thought, 'I will die in my own house,
my days as numerous as the grains of sand.
[19] My roots will reach to the water,
and the dew will lie all night on my branches.
[20] My glory will remain fresh in me,
the bow ever new in my hand.'

[21] "Men listened to me expectantly,
waiting in silence for my counsel.
[22] After I had spoken, they spoke no more;
my words fell gently on their ears.
[23] They waited for me as for showers
and drank in my words as the spring rain.
[24] When I smiled at them, they scarcely believed it;
the light of my face was precious to them.[a]
[25] I chose the way for them and sat as their chief;
I dwelt as a king among his troops;
I was like one who comforts mourners.

[a] *24* The meaning of the Hebrew for this clause is uncertain.

PRAYER: PETITION

BY Your grace, O God, I want to live to the end in faith, knowing that I will not receive the promises on earth; I see them and welcome them from a distance. I confess that I am a stranger and a pilgrim on the earth. I long for a better country, a heavenly one. In this way, You will not be ashamed to be called my God, for You have prepared a city for me. Like Moses, may I esteem reproach for the sake of Christ as of greater value than the treasures of this world, because I am looking to the reward.

(Hebrews 11:13, 16, 26)

PAUSE *here to petition God for growth in your character and personal discipline, and for physical health and strength. Ask that He empower you for spiritual warfare against the temptations of the world, the flesh and the devil. Offer prayers regarding your activities for this day and any special concerns you may have.*

NT Matthew 18:1-35

The Greatest in the Kingdom of Heaven

18 At that time the disciples came to
Jesus and asked, "Who is the greatest
in the kingdom of heaven?"
2 He called a little child and had him
stand among them. 3 And he said: "I tell
you the truth, unless you change and become like little children, you will never
enter the kingdom of heaven. 4 Therefore,
whoever humbles himself like this child
is the greatest in the kingdom of heaven.
5 "And whoever welcomes a little child
like this in my name welcomes me. 6 But
if anyone causes one of these little ones
who believe in me to sin, it would be better for him to have a large millstone hung
around his neck and to be drowned in the
depths of the sea.
7 "Woe to the world because of the
things that cause people to sin! Such
things must come, but woe to the man
through whom they come! 8 If your hand
or your foot causes you to sin, cut it off
and throw it away. It is better for you to
enter life maimed or crippled than to have
two hands or two feet and be thrown into
eternal fire. 9 And if your eye causes you to
sin, gouge it out and throw it away. It is
better for you to enter life with one eye
than to have two eyes and be thrown into
the fire of hell.

The Parable of the Lost Sheep

10 "See that you do not look down on
one of these little ones. For I tell you that
their angels in heaven always see the face
of my Father in heaven.[a]
12 "What do you think? If a man owns a
hundred sheep, and one of them wanders
away, will he not leave the ninety-nine on
the hills and go to look for the one that
wandered off? 13 And if he finds it, I tell
you the truth, he is happier about that
one sheep than about the ninety-nine that
did not wander off. 14 In the same way
your Father in heaven is not willing that
any of these little ones should be lost.

A Brother Who Sins Against You

15 "If your brother sins against you,[b] go
and show him his fault, just between the
two of you. If he listens to you, you have
won your brother over. 16 But if he will not
listen, take one or two others along, so
that 'every matter may be established by
the testimony of two or three witnesses.'[c]
17 If he refuses to listen to them, tell it to
the church; and if he refuses to listen even
to the church, treat him as you would a
pagan or a tax collector.
18 "I tell you the truth, whatever you
bind on earth will be[d] bound in heaven,
and whatever you loose on earth will be[d]
loosed in heaven.
19 "Again, I tell you that if two of you on
earth agree about anything you ask for,
it will be done for you by my Father in
heaven. 20 For where two or three come
together in my name, there am I with
them."

The Parable of the Unmerciful Servant

21 Then Peter came to Jesus and asked,
"Lord, how many times shall I forgive my
brother when he sins against me? Up to
seven times?"
22 Jesus answered, "I tell you, not seven
times, but seventy-seven times.[e]
23 "Therefore, the kingdom of heaven is
like a king who wanted to settle accounts
with his servants. 24 As he began the settlement, a man who owed him ten thousand talents[f] was brought to him. 25 Since
he was not able to pay, the master ordered
that he and his wife and his children and
all that he had be sold to repay the debt.
26 "The servant fell on his knees before
him. 'Be patient with me,' he begged, 'and
I will pay back everything.' 27 The servant's
master took pity on him, canceled the
debt and let him go.
28 "But when that servant went out, he
found one of his fellow servants who
owed him a hundred denarii.[g] He grabbed
him and began to choke him. 'Pay back
what you owe me!' he demanded.
29 "His fellow servant fell to his knees
and begged him, 'Be patient with me, and
I will pay you back.'
30 "But he refused. Instead, he went off
and had the man thrown into prison until
he could pay the debt. 31 When the other

[a] 10 Some manuscripts *heaven.* 11 *The Son of Man came to save what was lost.* [b] 15 Some manuscripts do not have *against you.* [c] 16 Deut. 19:15 [d] 18 Or *have been* [e] 22 Or *seventy times seven* [f] 24 That is, millions of dollars [g] 28 That is, a few dollars

servants saw what had happened, they
were greatly distressed and went and told
their master everything that had happened.
32 "Then the master called the servant in.
'You wicked servant,' he said, 'I canceled
all that debt of yours because you begged
me to. 33 Shouldn't you have had mercy on
your fellow servant just as I had on you?'
34 In anger his master turned him over to
the jailers to be tortured, until he should
pay back all he owed.
35 "This is how my heavenly Father will
treat each of you unless you forgive your
brother from your heart."

PRAYER: THE CHARACTER I WANT TO CULTIVATE

If I am hot-tempered, I will stir up dissension, but if I am slow to anger, I will calm a quarrel. (Proverbs 15:18) . . . We should be quick to hear, slow to speak and slow to anger, for our anger does not produce Your righteousness, O God. (James 1:19–20)

__TAKE__ a moment to ask the Lord for the grace to grow in godly character.

YEAR 2 DAY 25

OT Proverbs 17

17 Better a dry crust with peace and quiet
than a house full of feasting,[a] with strife.

2 A wise servant will rule over a disgraceful son,
and will share the inheritance as one of the brothers.

3 The crucible for silver and the furnace for gold,
but the LORD tests the heart.

4 A wicked man listens to evil lips;
a liar pays attention to a malicious tongue.

5 He who mocks the poor shows contempt for their Maker;
whoever gloats over disaster will not go unpunished.

6 Children's children are a crown to the aged,
and parents are the pride of their children.

7 Arrogant[b] lips are unsuited to a fool—
how much worse lying lips to a ruler!

8 A bribe is a charm to the one who gives it;
wherever he turns, he succeeds.

9 He who covers over an offense promotes love,
but whoever repeats the matter separates close friends.

10 A rebuke impresses a man of discernment
more than a hundred lashes a fool.

11 An evil man is bent only on rebellion;
a merciless official will be sent against him.

12 Better to meet a bear robbed of her cubs
than a fool in his folly.

13 If a man pays back evil for good,
evil will never leave his house.

14 Starting a quarrel is like breaching a dam;
so drop the matter before a dispute breaks out.

15 Acquitting the guilty and condemning the innocent—
the LORD detests them both.

16 Of what use is money in the hand of a fool,
since he has no desire to get wisdom?

17 A friend loves at all times,
and a brother is born for adversity.

18 A man lacking in judgment strikes hands in pledge

[a] 1 Hebrew *sacrifices* [b] 7 Or *Eloquent*

and puts up security for his
neighbor.

[19] He who loves a quarrel loves sin;
he who builds a high gate invites
destruction.

[20] A man of perverse heart does not
prosper;
he whose tongue is deceitful falls
into trouble.

[21] To have a fool for a son brings grief;
there is no joy for the father of a
fool.

[22] A cheerful heart is good medicine,
but a crushed spirit dries up the
bones.

[23] A wicked man accepts a bribe in secret
to pervert the course of justice.

[24] A discerning man keeps wisdom in
view,
but a fool's eyes wander to the ends
of the earth.

[25] A foolish son brings grief to his father
and bitterness to the one who bore
him.

[26] It is not good to punish an innocent
man,
or to flog officials for their integrity.

[27] A man of knowledge uses words with
restraint,
and a man of understanding is
even-tempered.

[28] Even a fool is thought wise if he keeps
silent,
and discerning if he holds his
tongue.

PRAYER: INTERCESSION

HEAR from heaven, Your dwelling place, and forgive us and deal with each of us according to what we do, since You know our hearts (for You alone know people's hearts). (2 Chronicles 6:30)

***TAKE** a few moments to intercede on behalf of the poor and hungry, the oppressed and persecuted, and those in control of world and national resources. Offer prayers for peace among nations and regarding current events and concerns.*

NT Matthew 19:1–15

Divorce

19 When Jesus had finished saying these
things, he left Galilee and went into
the region of Judea to the other side of the
Jordan. [2]Large crowds followed him, and
he healed them there.
[3]Some Pharisees came to him to test
him. They asked, "Is it lawful for a man to
divorce his wife for any and every reason?"
[4]"Haven't you read," he replied, "that at
the beginning the Creator 'made them
male and female,'[a] [5]and said, 'For this reason a man will leave his father and mother and be united to his wife, and the two
will become one flesh'[b]? [6]So they are no
longer two, but one. Therefore what God
has joined together, let man not separate."
[7]"Why then," they asked, "did Moses
command that a man give his wife a certificate of divorce and send her away?"
[8]Jesus replied, "Moses permitted you to
divorce your wives because your hearts
were hard. But it was not this way from
the beginning. [9]I tell you that anyone who
divorces his wife, except for marital unfaithfulness, and marries another woman
commits adultery."
[10]The disciples said to him, "If this is
the situation between a husband and
wife, it is better not to marry."
[11]Jesus replied, "Not everyone can accept this word, but only those to whom it
has been given. [12]For some are eunuchs
because they were born that way; others
were made that way by men; and others
have renounced marriage[c] because of the
kingdom of heaven. The one who can accept this should accept it."

[a] 4 Gen. 1:27 [b] 5 Gen. 2:24 [c] 12 Or *have made themselves eunuchs*

The Little Children and Jesus

[13]Then little children were brought to
Jesus for him to place his hands on them
and pray for them. But the disciples rebuked those who brought them.
[14]Jesus said, "Let the little children
come to me, and do not hinder them, for
the kingdom of heaven belongs to such as
these." [15]When he had placed his hands
on them, he went on from there.

PRAYER: MY RELATIONSHIP TO OTHERS

I WILL not provoke my children to anger but bring them up in Your discipline and instruction, O Lord. (Ephesians 6:4) . . . I will not provoke my children, or they will become discouraged. (Colossians 3:21)

***PAUSE** to review your relationships with others and to commit them to the Lord.*

YEAR 2 DAY 26

OT Job 30:1–31

30 "But now they mock me,
men younger than I,
whose fathers I would have disdained
to put with my sheep dogs.
[2]Of what use was the strength of their hands to me,
since their vigor had gone from them?
[3]Haggard from want and hunger,
they roamed[a] the parched land
in desolate wastelands at night.
[4]In the brush they gathered salt herbs,
and their food[b] was the root of the broom tree.
[5]They were banished from their fellow men,
shouted at as if they were thieves.
[6]They were forced to live in the dry stream beds,
among the rocks and in holes in the ground.
[7]They brayed among the bushes
and huddled in the undergrowth.
[8]A base and nameless brood,
they were driven out of the land.

[9]"And now their sons mock me in song;
I have become a byword among them.
[10]They detest me and keep their distance;
they do not hesitate to spit in my face.
[11]Now that God has unstrung my bow
and afflicted me,
they throw off restraint in my presence.
[12]On my right the tribe[c] attacks;
they lay snares for my feet,
they build their siege ramps against me.
[13]They break up my road;
they succeed in destroying me—
without anyone's helping them.[d]
[14]They advance as through a gaping breach;
amid the ruins they come rolling in.
[15]Terrors overwhelm me;
my dignity is driven away as by the wind,
my safety vanishes like a cloud.

[16]"And now my life ebbs away;
days of suffering grip me.
[17]Night pierces my bones;
my gnawing pains never rest.
[18]In his great power ⌞God⌟ becomes like clothing to me[e];
he binds me like the neck of my garment.
[19]He throws me into the mud,
and I am reduced to dust and ashes.

[20]"I cry out to you, O God, but you do not answer;
I stand up, but you merely look at me.
[21]You turn on me ruthlessly;

[a] 3 Or *gnawed* [b] 4 Or *fuel* [c] 12 The meaning of the Hebrew for this word is uncertain. [d] 13 Or *me. / 'No one can help him,' ⌞they say⌟.* [e] 18 Hebrew; Septuagint *⌞God⌟ grasps my clothing*

with the might of your hand you
attack me.
[22] You snatch me up and drive me
before the wind;
you toss me about in the storm.
[23] I know you will bring me down to
death,
to the place appointed for all the
living.

[24] "Surely no one lays a hand on a
broken man
when he cries for help in his
distress.
[25] Have I not wept for those in trouble?
Has not my soul grieved for the
poor?
[26] Yet when I hoped for good, evil came;
when I looked for light, then came
darkness.
[27] The churning inside me never stops;
days of suffering confront me.
[28] I go about blackened, but not by the
sun;
I stand up in the assembly and cry
for help.
[29] I have become a brother of jackals,
a companion of owls.
[30] My skin grows black and peels;
my body burns with fever.
[31] My harp is tuned to mourning,
and my flute to the sound of
wailing.

PRAYER: AFFIRMATION

ALL authority in heaven and on earth has been given to You, Jesus Christ, who are the Son of God. (Matthew 28:18)

. . . Lord Jesus Christ, you are coming with the clouds, and every eye will see You, even those who pierced You; and all the peoples of the earth will mourn because of You. Even so, Amen. (Revelation 1:7)

PAUSE *to reflect on these Biblical affirmations.*

NT Matthew 19:16–20:16

The Rich Young Man

[16] Now a man came up to Jesus and
asked, "Teacher, what good thing must I
do to get eternal life?"
[17] "Why do you ask me about what is
good?" Jesus replied. "There is only One
who is good. If you want to enter life,
obey the commandments."
[18] "Which ones?" the man inquired.
Jesus replied, " 'Do not murder, do not
commit adultery, do not steal, do not give
false testimony, [19] honor your father and
mother,'[a] and 'love your neighbor as yourself.'[b]"
[20] "All these I have kept," the young man
said. "What do I still lack?"
[21] Jesus answered, "If you want to be perfect, go, sell your possessions and give to
the poor, and you will have treasure in
heaven. Then come, follow me."
[22] When the young man heard this, he
went away sad, because he had great
wealth.
[23] Then Jesus said to his disciples, "I tell
you the truth, it is hard for a rich man to
enter the kingdom of heaven. [24] Again I tell
you, it is easier for a camel to go through
the eye of a needle than for a rich man to
enter the kingdom of God."
[25] When the disciples heard this, they
were greatly astonished and asked, "Who
then can be saved?"
[26] Jesus looked at them and said, "With
man this is impossible, but with God all
things are possible."
[27] Peter answered him, "We have left
everything to follow you! What then will
there be for us?"
[28] Jesus said to them, "I tell you the
truth, at the renewal of all things, when
the Son of Man sits on his glorious
throne, you who have followed me will
also sit on twelve thrones, judging the
twelve tribes of Israel. [29] And everyone
who has left houses or brothers or sisters
or father or mother[c] or children or fields
for my sake will receive a hundred times
as much and will inherit eternal life. [30] But

[a] *19* Exodus 20:12–16; Deut. 5:16–20
[b] *19* Lev. 19:18
[c] *29* Some manuscripts *mother or wife*

many who are first will be last, and many
who are last will be first.

The Parable of the Workers in the Vineyard

20 "For the kingdom of heaven is like a
landowner who went out early in the
morning to hire men to work in his vineyard. 2He agreed to pay them a denarius
for the day and sent them into his vineyard.
3"About the third hour he went out and
saw others standing in the marketplace
doing nothing. 4He told them, 'You also
go and work in my vineyard, and I will
pay you whatever is right.' 5So they went.
"He went out again about the sixth
hour and the ninth hour and did the same
thing. 6About the eleventh hour he went
out and found still others standing
around. He asked them, 'Why have you
been standing here all day long doing
nothing?'
7" 'Because no one has hired us,' they
answered.
"He said to them, 'You also go and
work in my vineyard.'
8"When evening came, the owner of the
vineyard said to his foreman, 'Call the
workers and pay them their wages, beginning with the last ones hired and going
on to the first.'
9"The workers who were hired about
the eleventh hour came and each received
a denarius. 10So when those came who
were hired first, they expected to receive
more. But each one of them also received
a denarius. 11When they received it, they
began to grumble against the landowner.
12'These men who were hired last worked
only one hour,' they said, 'and you have
made them equal to us who have borne
the burden of the work and the heat of the
day.'
13"But he answered one of them,
'Friend, I am not being unfair to you.
Didn't you agree to work for a denarius?
14Take your pay and go. I want to give the
man who was hired last the same as I gave
you. 15Don't I have the right to do what I
want with my own money? Or are you envious because I am generous?'
16"So the last will be first, and the first
will be last."

PRAYER: THE ATTRIBUTES OF GOD

JESUS, You are the Christ, the Son of God, who came into the world. (John 11:27) . . . Anyone who has seen You, Jesus, has seen the Father. (John 14:9)

***PAUSE** to reflect on these affirmations about the person, powers and perfection of God.*

YEAR 2 DAY 27

OT **Job 31:1-40**

31 "I made a covenant with my eyes
not to look lustfully at a girl.
2For what is man's lot from God above,
his heritage from the Almighty on
high?
3Is it not ruin for the wicked,
disaster for those who do wrong?
4Does he not see my ways
and count my every step?

5"If I have walked in falsehood
or my foot has hurried after
deceit—
6let God weigh me in honest scales
and he will know that I am
blameless—
7if my steps have turned from the path,
if my heart has been led by my eyes,
or if my hands have been defiled,
8then may others eat what I have sown,
and may my crops be uprooted.

9"If my heart has been enticed by a
woman,
or if I have lurked at my neighbor's
door,
10then may my wife grind another
man's grain,

and may other men sleep with her.
11 For that would have been shameful,
a sin to be judged.
12 It is a fire that burns to Destruction[a];
it would have uprooted my harvest.

13 "If I have denied justice to my
menservants and maidservants
when they had a grievance against
me,
14 what will I do when God confronts
me?
What will I answer when called to
account?
15 Did not he who made me in the
womb make them?
Did not the same one form us both
within our mothers?

16 "If I have denied the desires of the
poor
or let the eyes of the widow grow
weary,
17 if I have kept my bread to myself,
not sharing it with the fatherless—
18 but from my youth I reared him as
would a father,
and from my birth I guided the
widow—
19 if I have seen anyone perishing for
lack of clothing,
or a needy man without a garment,
20 and his heart did not bless me
for warming him with the fleece
from my sheep,
21 if I have raised my hand against the
fatherless,
knowing that I had influence in
court,
22 then let my arm fall from the
shoulder,
let it be broken off at the joint.
23 For I dreaded destruction from God,
and for fear of his splendor I could
not do such things.

24 "If I have put my trust in gold
or said to pure gold, 'You are my
security,'
25 if I have rejoiced over my great wealth,
the fortune my hands had gained,
26 if I have regarded the sun in its
radiance
or the moon moving in splendor,
27 so that my heart was secretly enticed
and my hand offered them a kiss of
homage,
28 then these also would be sins to be
judged,
for I would have been unfaithful to
God on high.

29 "If I have rejoiced at my enemy's
misfortune
or gloated over the trouble that
came to him—
30 I have not allowed my mouth to sin
by invoking a curse against his
life—
31 if the men of my household have
never said,
'Who has not had his fill of Job's
meat?'—
32 but no stranger had to spend the
night in the street,
for my door was always open to the
traveler—
33 if I have concealed my sin as men do,[b]
by hiding my guilt in my heart
34 because I so feared the crowd
and so dreaded the contempt of the
clans
that I kept silent and would not go
outside

35 ("Oh, that I had someone to hear me!
I sign now my defense—let the
Almighty answer me;
let my accuser put his indictment in
writing.
36 Surely I would wear it on my
shoulder,
I would put it on like a crown.
37 I would give him an account of my
every step;
like a prince I would approach
him.)—

38 "if my land cries out against me
and all its furrows are wet with
tears,
39 if I have devoured its yield without
payment
or broken the spirit of its tenants,
40 then let briers come up instead of
wheat
and weeds instead of barley."

The words of Job are ended.

[a] 12 Hebrew *Abaddon* [b] 33 Or *as Adam did*

PRAYER: THANKSGIVING

THE salvation of the righteous comes from You, Lord; You are their stronghold in time of trouble. You help them and deliver them; You deliver them from the wicked and save them, because they take refuge in You. (Psalm 37:39–40)

***PAUSE** to offer your own expressions of thanksgiving.*

NT Matthew 20:17-34

Jesus Again Predicts His Death

17 Now as Jesus was going up to Jerusalem, he took the twelve disciples aside
and said to them, 18 "We are going up to
Jerusalem, and the Son of Man will be betrayed to the chief priests and the teachers of the law. They will condemn him to
death 19 and will turn him over to the Gentiles to be mocked and flogged and crucified. On the third day he will be raised to
life!"

A Mother's Request

20 Then the mother of Zebedee's sons
came to Jesus with her sons and, kneeling
down, asked a favor of him.
21 "What is it you want?" he asked.
She said, "Grant that one of these two
sons of mine may sit at your right and the
other at your left in your kingdom."
22 "You don't know what you are asking," Jesus said to them. "Can you drink
the cup I am going to drink?"
"We can," they answered.
23 Jesus said to them, "You will indeed
drink from my cup, but to sit at my right
or left is not for me to grant. These places
belong to those for whom they have been
prepared by my Father."
24 When the ten heard about this, they
were indignant with the two brothers.
25 Jesus called them together and said,
"You know that the rulers of the Gentiles
lord it over them, and their high officials
exercise authority over them. 26 Not so
with you. Instead, whoever wants to become great among you must be your servant, 27 and whoever wants to be first must
be your slave— 28 just as the Son of Man
did not come to be served, but to serve,
and to give his life as a ransom for many."

Two Blind Men Receive Sight

29 As Jesus and his disciples were leaving
Jericho, a large crowd followed him.
30 Two blind men were sitting by the roadside, and when they heard that Jesus was
going by, they shouted, "Lord, Son of David, have mercy on us!"
31 The crowd rebuked them and told
them to be quiet, but they shouted all the
louder, "Lord, Son of David, have mercy
on us!"
32 Jesus stopped and called them. "What
do you want me to do for you?" he asked.
33 "Lord," they answered, "we want our
sight."
34 Jesus had compassion on them and
touched their eyes. Immediately they received their sight and followed him.

PRAYER: THE WORKS OF GOD

JESUS Christ, You are the faithful witness, the firstborn from the dead, and the ruler of the kings of the earth. To You—who love us and have freed us from our sins by Your blood and have made us to be a kingdom and priests to serve Your God and Father—be glory and power for ever and ever. (Revelation 1:5–6)

***TAKE** a moment to consider the greatness of God's wonderful works.*

YEAR 2 DAY 28

OT Psalm 77

Psalm 77

For the director of music. For Jeduthun. Of Asaph. A psalm.

[1] I cried out to God for help;
I cried out to God to hear me.
[2] When I was in distress, I sought the Lord;
at night I stretched out untiring hands
and my soul refused to be comforted.

[3] I remembered you, O God, and I groaned;
I mused, and my spirit grew faint. *Selah*
[4] You kept my eyes from closing;
I was too troubled to speak.
[5] I thought about the former days,
the years of long ago;
[6] I remembered my songs in the night.
My heart mused and my spirit inquired:

[7] "Will the Lord reject forever?
Will he never show his favor again?
[8] Has his unfailing love vanished forever?
Has his promise failed for all time?
[9] Has God forgotten to be merciful?
Has he in anger withheld his compassion?" *Selah*

[10] Then I thought, "To this I will appeal:
the years of the right hand of the Most High."
[11] I will remember the deeds of the LORD;
yes, I will remember your miracles of long ago.
[12] I will meditate on all your works
and consider all your mighty deeds.

[13] Your ways, O God, are holy.
What god is so great as our God?
[14] You are the God who performs miracles;
you display your power among the peoples.
[15] With your mighty arm you redeemed your people,
the descendants of Jacob and Joseph. *Selah*

[16] The waters saw you, O God,
the waters saw you and writhed;
the very depths were convulsed.
[17] The clouds poured down water,
the skies resounded with thunder;
your arrows flashed back and forth.
[18] Your thunder was heard in the whirlwind,
your lightning lit up the world;
the earth trembled and quaked.
[19] Your path led through the sea,
your way through the mighty waters,
though your footprints were not seen.

[20] You led your people like a flock
by the hand of Moses and Aaron.

PRAYER: ADORATION

BEHOLD, You who form the mountains and create the wind, and reveal Your thoughts to people; You turn dawn to darkness, and tread the high places of the earth—the Lord God of hosts is Your name. (Amos 4:13)

PAUSE *to express your thoughts of praise and worship.*

NT Matthew 21:1–22

The Triumphal Entry

21 As they approached Jerusalem and
came to Bethphage on the Mount of
Olives, Jesus sent two disciples, [2]saying to
them, "Go to the village ahead of you,
and at once you will find a donkey tied
there, with her colt by her. Untie them
and bring them to me. [3]If anyone says
anything to you, tell him that the Lord

needs them, and he will send them right
away."
4 This took place to fulfill what was spoken through the prophet:

5 "Say to the Daughter of Zion,
'See, your king comes to you,
gentle and riding on a donkey,
on a colt, the foal of a donkey.' "[a]

6 The disciples went and did as Jesus had
instructed them. 7 They brought the donkey and the colt, placed their cloaks on
them, and Jesus sat on them. 8 A very large
crowd spread their cloaks on the road,
while others cut branches from the trees
and spread them on the road. 9 The crowds
that went ahead of him and those that followed shouted,

"Hosanna[b] to the Son of David!"

"Blessed is he who comes in the name
of the Lord!"[c]

"Hosanna[b] in the highest!"

10 When Jesus entered Jerusalem, the
whole city was stirred and asked, "Who is
this?"
11 The crowds answered, "This is Jesus,
the prophet from Nazareth in Galilee."

Jesus at the Temple

12 Jesus entered the temple area and
drove out all who were buying and selling
there. He overturned the tables of the
money changers and the benches of those
selling doves. 13 "It is written," he said to
them, " 'My house will be called a house
of prayer,'[d] but you are making it a 'den of
robbers.'[e]"

14 The blind and the lame came to him
at the temple, and he healed them. 15 But
when the chief priests and the teachers of
the law saw the wonderful things he did
and the children shouting in the temple
area, "Hosanna to the Son of David," they
were indignant.
16 "Do you hear what these children are
saying?" they asked him.
"Yes," replied Jesus, "have you never
read,

" 'From the lips of children and
infants
you have ordained praise'[f]?"

17 And he left them and went out of the
city to Bethany, where he spent the night.

The Fig Tree Withers

18 Early in the morning, as he was on his
way back to the city, he was hungry. 19 Seeing a fig tree by the road, he went up to it
but found nothing on it except leaves.
Then he said to it, "May you never bear
fruit again!" Immediately the tree withered.
20 When the disciples saw this, they were
amazed. "How did the fig tree wither so
quickly?" they asked.
21 Jesus replied, "I tell you the truth, if
you have faith and do not doubt, not only
can you do what was done to the fig tree,
but also you can say to this mountain,
'Go, throw yourself into the sea,' and it
will be done. 22 If you believe, you will receive whatever you ask for in prayer."

[a] *5* Zech. 9:9 [b] *9* A Hebrew expression meaning "Save!" which became an exclamation of praise; also in verse 15 [c] *9* Psalm 118:26 [d] *13* Isaiah 56:7 [e] *13* Jer. 7:11 [f] *16* Psalm 8:2

PRAYER: MY RELATIONSHIP TO GOD

JESUS, You are the door; whoever enters through You will be saved and will come in and go out and find pasture. The thief comes only to steal and kill and destroy; You have come that we may have life and have it abundantly. (John 10:9–10)

***PAUSE** to thank God for the relationship that you enjoy with Him in Jesus Christ.*

YEAR 2 DAY 29

OT Job 32:1-22

Elihu

32 So these three men stopped answering Job, because he was righteous in
his own eyes. 2 But Elihu son of Barakel
the Buzite, of the family of Ram, became
very angry with Job for justifying himself
rather than God. 3 He was also angry with
the three friends, because they had found
no way to refute Job, and yet had condemned him.[a] 4 Now Elihu had waited before speaking to Job because they were
older than he. 5 But when he saw that the
three men had nothing more to say, his
anger was aroused.

6 So Elihu son of Barakel the Buzite said:

"I am young in years,
and you are old;
that is why I was fearful,
not daring to tell you what I know.
7 I thought, 'Age should speak;
advanced years should teach
wisdom.'
8 But it is the spirit[b] in a man,
the breath of the Almighty, that
gives him understanding.
9 It is not only the old[c] who are wise,
not only the aged who understand
what is right.

10 "Therefore I say: Listen to me;
I too will tell you what I know.
11 I waited while you spoke,
I listened to your reasoning;
while you were searching for words,
12 I gave you my full attention.
But not one of you has proved Job
wrong;
none of you has answered his
arguments.
13 Do not say, 'We have found wisdom;
let God refute him, not man.'
14 But Job has not marshaled his words
against me,
and I will not answer him with your
arguments.

15 "They are dismayed and have no more
to say;
words have failed them.
16 Must I wait, now that they are silent,
now that they stand there with no
reply?
17 I too will have my say;
I too will tell what I know.
18 For I am full of words,
and the spirit within me compels
me;
19 inside I am like bottled-up wine,
like new wineskins ready to burst.
20 I must speak and find relief;
I must open my lips and reply.
21 I will show partiality to no one,
nor will I flatter any man;
22 for if I were skilled in flattery,
my Maker would soon take me
away.

[a] 3 Masoretic Text; an ancient Hebrew scribal tradition *Job, and so had condemned God* [b] 8 Or *Spirit;* also in verse 18 [c] 9 Or *many;* or *great*

PRAYER: CONFESSION

OUR fathers disciplined us for a little while as they thought best, but You, O God, discipline us for our good, that we may share in Your holiness. No discipline seems pleasant at the time, but painful; later on, however, it produces the peaceable fruit of righteousness for those who have been trained by it. Therefore, let us strengthen our hands that are weary and our feeble knees, and make straight paths for our feet, so that what is lame may not be disabled, but rather healed.

(Hebrews 12:10–13)

***ASK** the Spirit to search your heart and reveal any areas of unconfessed sin. Acknowledge these to the Lord and thank Him for His forgiveness.*

NT Matthew 21:23-46

The Authority of Jesus Questioned

23 Jesus entered the temple courts, and,
while he was teaching, the chief priests
and the elders of the people came to him.
"By what authority are you doing these
things?" they asked. "And who gave you
this authority?"
24 Jesus replied, "I will also ask you one
question. If you answer me, I will tell you
by what authority I am doing these things.
25 John's baptism—where did it come
from? Was it from heaven, or from men?"
They discussed it among themselves
and said, "If we say, 'From heaven,' he will
ask, 'Then why didn't you believe him?'
26 But if we say, 'From men'—we are afraid
of the people, for they all hold that John
was a prophet."
27 So they answered Jesus, "We don't
know."
Then he said, "Neither will I tell you by
what authority I am doing these things.

The Parable of the Two Sons

28 "What do you think? There was a man
who had two sons. He went to the first
and said, 'Son, go and work today in the
vineyard.'
29 " 'I will not,' he answered, but later he
changed his mind and went.
30 "Then the father went to the other son
and said the same thing. He answered, 'I
will, sir,' but he did not go.
31 "Which of the two did what his father
wanted?"
"The first," they answered.
Jesus said to them, "I tell you the truth,
the tax collectors and the prostitutes are
entering the kingdom of God ahead of
you. 32 For John came to you to show you
the way of righteousness, and you did not
believe him, but the tax collectors and the
prostitutes did. And even after you saw
this, you did not repent and believe him.

The Parable of the Tenants

33 "Listen to another parable: There was
a landowner who planted a vineyard. He
put a wall around it, dug a winepress in it
and built a watchtower. Then he rented
the vineyard to some farmers and went
away on a journey. 34 When the harvest
time approached, he sent his servants to
the tenants to collect his fruit.
35 "The tenants seized his servants; they
beat one, killed another, and stoned a
third. 36 Then he sent other servants to
them, more than the first time, and the
tenants treated them the same way. 37 Last
of all, he sent his son to them. 'They will
respect my son,' he said.
38 "But when the tenants saw the son,
they said to each other, 'This is the heir.
Come, let's kill him and take his inheritance.' 39 So they took him and threw him
out of the vineyard and killed him.
40 "Therefore, when the owner of the
vineyard comes, what will he do to those
tenants?"
41 "He will bring those wretches to a
wretched end," they replied, "and he will
rent the vineyard to other tenants, who
will give him his share of the crop at harvest time."
42 Jesus said to them, "Have you never
read in the Scriptures:

" 'The stone the builders rejected
has become the capstone[a];
the Lord has done this,
and it is marvelous in our eyes'[b]?

43 "Therefore I tell you that the kingdom
of God will be taken away from you and
given to a people who will produce its
fruit. 44 He who falls on this stone will be
broken to pieces, but he on whom it falls
will be crushed."[c]
45 When the chief priests and the Pharisees heard Jesus' parables, they knew he
was talking about them. 46 They looked for
a way to arrest him, but they were afraid
of the crowd because the people held that
he was a prophet.

[a] 42 Or *cornerstone* [b] 42 Psalm 118:22,23
[c] 44 Some manuscripts do not have verse 44.

PRAYER: THE CHARACTER I WANT TO CULTIVATE

SINCE I have a great cloud of witnesses surrounding me, I want to lay aside every impediment and the sin that so easily entangles, and run with endurance the race that is set before me, fixing my eyes

on You, Jesus, the author and perfecter of my faith, who for the joy set before You endured the cross, despising the shame, and sat down at the right hand of the throne of God. I will consider You, who endured such hostility from sinners, so that I will not grow weary and lose heart. (Hebrews 12:1–3)

TAKE *a moment to ask the Lord for the grace to grow in godly character.*

YEAR 2 DAY 30

OT Job 33:1-33

33 "But now, Job, listen to my words;
pay attention to everything I say.
2 I am about to open my mouth;
my words are on the tip of my tongue.
3 My words come from an upright heart;
my lips sincerely speak what I know.
4 The Spirit of God has made me;
the breath of the Almighty gives me life.
5 Answer me then, if you can;
prepare yourself and confront me.
6 I am just like you before God;
I too have been taken from clay.
7 No fear of me should alarm you,
nor should my hand be heavy upon you.

8 "But you have said in my hearing—
I heard the very words—
9 'I am pure and without sin;
I am clean and free from guilt.
10 Yet God has found fault with me;
he considers me his enemy.
11 He fastens my feet in shackles;
he keeps close watch on all my paths.'

12 "But I tell you, in this you are not right,
for God is greater than man.
13 Why do you complain to him
that he answers none of man's words[a]?
14 For God does speak—now one way, now another—
though man may not perceive it.
15 In a dream, in a vision of the night,
when deep sleep falls on men
as they slumber in their beds,
16 he may speak in their ears
and terrify them with warnings,
17 to turn man from wrongdoing
and keep him from pride,
18 to preserve his soul from the pit,[b]
his life from perishing by the sword.[c]
19 Or a man may be chastened on a bed of pain
with constant distress in his bones,
20 so that his very being finds food repulsive
and his soul loathes the choicest meal.
21 His flesh wastes away to nothing,
and his bones, once hidden, now stick out.
22 His soul draws near to the pit,[d]
and his life to the messengers of death.[e]

23 "Yet if there is an angel on his side
as a mediator, one out of a thousand,
to tell a man what is right for him,
24 to be gracious to him and say,
'Spare him from going down to the pit[f];
I have found a ransom for him'—
25 then his flesh is renewed like a child's;
it is restored as in the days of his youth.
26 He prays to God and finds favor with him,
he sees God's face and shouts for joy;
he is restored by God to his righteous state.
27 Then he comes to men and says,
'I sinned, and perverted what was right,
but I did not get what I deserved.
28 He redeemed my soul from going down to the pit,[g]
and I will live to enjoy the light.'

[a] 13 Or *that he does not answer for any of his actions*
[b] 18 Or *preserve him from the grave*
[c] 18 Or *from crossing the River*
[d] 22 Or *He draws near to the grave*
[e] 22 Or *to the dead*
[f] 24 Or *grave*
[g] 28 Or *redeemed me from going down to the grave*

[29] "God does all these things to a
man—
twice, even three times—
[30] to turn back his soul from the pit,[h]
that the light of life may shine on
him.

[31] "Pay attention, Job, and listen to me;
be silent, and I will speak.
[32] If you have anything to say, answer
me;
speak up, for I want you to be
cleared.
[33] But if not, then listen to me;
be silent, and I will teach you
wisdom."

[h] 30 Or *turn him back from the grave*

PRAYER: RENEWAL

MAY I be very careful to love You, O Lord my God, to walk in all Your ways, to obey Your commands, to hold fast to You, and to serve You with all my heart and all my soul. (Joshua 22:5)

***PAUSE** to add your own prayers for personal renewal.*

NT Matthew 22:1–22

The Parable of the Wedding Banquet

22 Jesus spoke to them again in parables,
saying: [2] "The kingdom of heaven is
like a king who prepared a wedding banquet for his son. [3] He sent his servants to
those who had been invited to the banquet to tell them to come, but they refused to come.
[4] "Then he sent some more servants and
said, 'Tell those who have been invited
that I have prepared my dinner: My oxen
and fattened cattle have been butchered,
and everything is ready. Come to the wedding banquet.'
[5] "But they paid no attention and went
off—one to his field, another to his business. [6] The rest seized his servants, mistreated them and killed them. [7] The king
was enraged. He sent his army and destroyed those murderers and burned their
city.
[8] "Then he said to his servants, 'The
wedding banquet is ready, but those I invited did not deserve to come. [9] Go to the
street corners and invite to the banquet
anyone you find.' [10] So the servants went
out into the streets and gathered all the
people they could find, both good and
bad, and the wedding hall was filled with
guests.
[11] "But when the king came in to see the
guests, he noticed a man there who was
not wearing wedding clothes. [12] 'Friend,' he
asked, 'how did you get in here without
wedding clothes?' The man was speechless.
[13] "Then the king told the attendants,
'Tie him hand and foot, and throw him
outside, into the darkness, where there
will be weeping and gnashing of teeth.'
[14] "For many are invited, but few are
chosen."

Paying Taxes to Caesar

[15] Then the Pharisees went out and laid
plans to trap him in his words. [16] They sent
their disciples to him along with the
Herodians. "Teacher," they said, "we
know you are a man of integrity and that
you teach the way of God in accordance
with the truth. You aren't swayed by men,
because you pay no attention to who they
are. [17] Tell us then, what is your opinion?
Is it right to pay taxes to Caesar or not?"
[18] But Jesus, knowing their evil intent,
said, "You hypocrites, why are you trying
to trap me? [19] Show me the coin used for
paying the tax." They brought him a denarius, [20] and he asked them, "Whose portrait is this? And whose inscription?"
[21] "Caesar's," they replied.
Then he said to them, "Give to Caesar
what is Caesar's, and to God what is
God's."
[22] When they heard this, they were
amazed. So they left him and went away.

PRAYER: MY RELATIONSHIP TO OTHERS

WE always pray for other believers, that You, our God, may count them worthy of Your calling and fulfill with power every desire for goodness and every work of faith. We ask that Your name, O Lord Jesus, may be glorified in others, and they in You, according to the grace of our God. (2 Thessalonians 1:11–12)

***PAUSE** to review your relationships with others and to commit them to the Lord.*

YEAR 2 DAY 31

OT Job 34:1–35:16

34 Then Elihu said:

2 "Hear my words, you wise men;
listen to me, you men of learning.
3 For the ear tests words
as the tongue tastes food.
4 Let us discern for ourselves what is right;
let us learn together what is good.

5 "Job says, 'I am innocent,
but God denies me justice.
6 Although I am right,
I am considered a liar;
although I am guiltless,
his arrow inflicts an incurable wound.'
7 What man is like Job,
who drinks scorn like water?
8 He keeps company with evildoers;
he associates with wicked men.
9 For he says, 'It profits a man nothing
when he tries to please God.'

10 "So listen to me, you men of understanding.
Far be it from God to do evil,
from the Almighty to do wrong.
11 He repays a man for what he has done;
he brings upon him what his conduct deserves.
12 It is unthinkable that God would do wrong,
that the Almighty would pervert justice.
13 Who appointed him over the earth?
Who put him in charge of the whole world?
14 If it were his intention
and he withdrew his spirit[a] and breath,
15 all mankind would perish together
and man would return to the dust.

16 "If you have understanding, hear this;
listen to what I say.
17 Can he who hates justice govern?
Will you condemn the just and mighty One?
18 Is he not the One who says to kings,
'You are worthless,'
and to nobles, 'You are wicked,'
19 who shows no partiality to princes
and does not favor the rich over the poor,
for they are all the work of his hands?
20 They die in an instant, in the middle of the night;
the people are shaken and they pass away;
the mighty are removed without human hand.

21 "His eyes are on the ways of men;
he sees their every step.
22 There is no dark place, no deep shadow,
where evildoers can hide.
23 God has no need to examine men further,
that they should come before him for judgment.
24 Without inquiry he shatters the mighty
and sets up others in their place.
25 Because he takes note of their deeds,
he overthrows them in the night
and they are crushed.

[a] 14 Or *Spirit*

[26] He punishes them for their
wickedness
where everyone can see them,
[27] because they turned from following
him
and had no regard for any of his
ways.
[28] They caused the cry of the poor to
come before him,
so that he heard the cry of the needy.
[29] But if he remains silent, who can
condemn him?
If he hides his face, who can see
him?
Yet he is over man and nation alike,
30 to keep a godless man from ruling,
from laying snares for the people.

[31] "Suppose a man says to God,
'I am guilty but will offend no more.
[32] Teach me what I cannot see;
if I have done wrong, I will not do
so again.'
[33] Should God then reward you on your
terms,
when you refuse to repent?
You must decide, not I;
so tell me what you know.

[34] "Men of understanding declare,
wise men who hear me say to me,
[35] 'Job speaks without knowledge;
his words lack insight.'
[36] Oh, that Job might be tested to the
utmost
for answering like a wicked man!
[37] To his sin he adds rebellion;
scornfully he claps his hands
among us
and multiplies his words against
God."

35 Then Elihu said:

[2] "Do you think this is just?
You say, 'I will be cleared by God.[b]'
[3] Yet you ask him, 'What profit is it to
me,[c]
and what do I gain by not sinning?'

[4] "I would like to reply to you
and to your friends with you.
[5] Look up at the heavens and see;
gaze at the clouds so high above you.
[6] If you sin, how does that affect him?
If your sins are many, what does
that do to him?
[7] If you are righteous, what do you give
to him,
or what does he receive from your
hand?
[8] Your wickedness affects only a man
like yourself,
and your righteousness only the
sons of men.

[9] "Men cry out under a load of
oppression;
they plead for relief from the arm of
the powerful.
[10] But no one says, 'Where is God my
Maker,
who gives songs in the night,
[11] who teaches more to us than to[d] the
beasts of the earth
and makes us wiser than[e] the birds
of the air?'
[12] He does not answer when men cry out
because of the arrogance of the
wicked.
[13] Indeed, God does not listen to their
empty plea;
the Almighty pays no attention to it.
[14] How much less, then, will he listen
when you say that you do not see
him,
that your case is before him
and you must wait for him,
[15] and further, that his anger never
punishes
and he does not take the least
notice of wickedness.[f]
[16] So Job opens his mouth with empty
talk;
without knowledge he multiplies
words."

[b] 2 Or *My righteousness is more than God's* [c] 3 Or *you* [d] 11 Or *teaches us by* [e] 11 Or *us wise by* [f] 15 Symmachus, Theodotion and Vulgate; the meaning of the Hebrew for this word is uncertain.

PRAYER: PETITION

MAY I submit myself for Your sake, O Lord, to every human authority, whether to a king as being supreme, or to governors sent by him to punish evildoers and to praise

those who do right; for it is Your will that by doing good I may silence the ignorance of foolish people.
(1 Peter 2:13–15)

PAUSE *here to petition God for growth in your desire to know and please Jesus Christ. Pray for a greater love and commitment to Him, for the grace to practice His presence and for the grace to glorify Him in your life. Offer prayers regarding your activities for this day and any special concerns you may have.*

NT Matthew 22:23–46

Marriage at the Resurrection

23 That same day the Sadducees, who say there is no resurrection, came to him with a question. 24 "Teacher," they said, "Moses told us that if a man dies without having children, his brother must marry the widow and have children for him. 25 Now there were seven brothers among us. The first one married and died, and since he had no children, he left his wife to his brother. 26 The same thing happened to the second and third brother, right on down to the seventh. 27 Finally, the woman died. 28 Now then, at the resurrection, whose wife will she be of the seven, since all of them were married to her?"

29 Jesus replied, "You are in error because you do not know the Scriptures or the power of God. 30 At the resurrection people will neither marry nor be given in marriage; they will be like the angels in heaven. 31 But about the resurrection of the dead—have you not read what God said to you, 32 'I am the God of Abraham, the God of Isaac, and the God of Jacob'[a]? He is not the God of the dead but of the living."

33 When the crowds heard this, they were astonished at his teaching.

The Greatest Commandment

34 Hearing that Jesus had silenced the Sadducees, the Pharisees got together. 35 One of them, an expert in the law, tested him with this question: 36 "Teacher, which is the greatest commandment in the Law?"

37 Jesus replied: " 'Love the Lord your God with all your heart and with all your soul and with all your mind.'[b] 38 This is the first and greatest commandment. 39 And the second is like it: 'Love your neighbor as yourself.'[c] 40 All the Law and the Prophets hang on these two commandments."

Whose Son Is the Christ?

41 While the Pharisees were gathered together, Jesus asked them, 42 "What do you think about the Christ[d]? Whose son is he?"

"The son of David," they replied.

43 He said to them, "How is it then that David, speaking by the Spirit, calls him 'Lord'? For he says,

44 " 'The Lord said to my Lord:
"Sit at my right hand
until I put your enemies
under your feet." '[e]

45 If then David calls him 'Lord,' how can he be his son?" 46 No one could say a word in reply, and from that day on no one dared to ask him any more questions.

[a] 32 Exodus 3:6 [b] 37 Deut. 6:5 [c] 39 Lev. 19:18
[d] 42 Or *Messiah* [e] 44 Psalm 110:1

PRAYER: THE ATTRIBUTES OF GOD

THOUGH You are on high, Lord, You look upon the lowly, but the proud You know from afar. (Psalm 138:6) . . . I know, O Lord, that my life is not my own; it is not for me to direct my steps. (Jeremiah 10:23)

PAUSE *to reflect on these affirmations about the person, powers and perfection of God.*

YEAR 2 DAY 32

OT Job 36:1–37:24

36 Elihu continued:

[2] "Bear with me a little longer and I will show you
that there is more to be said in God's behalf.
[3] I get my knowledge from afar;
I will ascribe justice to my Maker.
[4] Be assured that my words are not false;
one perfect in knowledge is with you.

[5] "God is mighty, but does not despise men;
he is mighty, and firm in his purpose.
[6] He does not keep the wicked alive
but gives the afflicted their rights.
[7] He does not take his eyes off the righteous;
he enthrones them with kings
and exalts them forever.
[8] But if men are bound in chains,
held fast by cords of affliction,
[9] he tells them what they have done—
that they have sinned arrogantly.
[10] He makes them listen to correction
and commands them to repent of their evil.
[11] If they obey and serve him,
they will spend the rest of their days in prosperity
and their years in contentment.
[12] But if they do not listen,
they will perish by the sword[a]
and die without knowledge.

[13] "The godless in heart harbor resentment;
even when he fetters them, they do not cry for help.
[14] They die in their youth,
among male prostitutes of the shrines.
[15] But those who suffer he delivers in their suffering;
he speaks to them in their affliction.

[16] "He is wooing you from the jaws of distress
to a spacious place free from restriction,
to the comfort of your table laden with choice food.
[17] But now you are laden with the judgment due the wicked;
judgment and justice have taken hold of you.
[18] Be careful that no one entices you by riches;
do not let a large bribe turn you aside.
[19] Would your wealth
or even all your mighty efforts
sustain you so you would not be in distress?
[20] Do not long for the night,
to drag people away from their homes.[b]
[21] Beware of turning to evil,
which you seem to prefer to affliction.

[22] "God is exalted in his power.
Who is a teacher like him?
[23] Who has prescribed his ways for him,
or said to him, 'You have done wrong'?
[24] Remember to extol his work,
which men have praised in song.
[25] All mankind has seen it;
men gaze on it from afar.
[26] How great is God—beyond our understanding!
The number of his years is past finding out.

[27] "He draws up the drops of water,
which distill as rain to the streams[c];
[28] the clouds pour down their moisture
and abundant showers fall on mankind.
[29] Who can understand how he spreads out the clouds,
how he thunders from his pavilion?
[30] See how he scatters his lightning about him,
bathing the depths of the sea.
[31] This is the way he governs[d] the nations
and provides food in abundance.
[32] He fills his hands with lightning
and commands it to strike its mark.
[33] His thunder announces the coming storm;

[a] 12 Or *will cross the River* [b] 20 The meaning of the Hebrew for verses 18–20 is uncertain. [c] 27 Or *distill from the mist as rain* [d] 31 Or *nourishes*

even the cattle make known its
approach.[e]

37 "At this my heart pounds
and leaps from its place.
2 Listen! Listen to the roar of his voice,
to the rumbling that comes from
his mouth.
3 He unleashes his lightning beneath
the whole heaven
and sends it to the ends of the
earth.
4 After that comes the sound of his roar;
he thunders with his majestic voice.
When his voice resounds,
he holds nothing back.
5 God's voice thunders in marvelous
ways;
he does great things beyond our
understanding.
6 He says to the snow, 'Fall on the
earth,'
and to the rain shower, 'Be a mighty
downpour.'
7 So that all men he has made may
know his work,
he stops every man from his labor.[f]
8 The animals take cover;
they remain in their dens.
9 The tempest comes out from its
chamber,
the cold from the driving winds.
10 The breath of God produces ice,
and the broad waters become frozen.
11 He loads the clouds with moisture;
he scatters his lightning through
them.
12 At his direction they swirl around
over the face of the whole earth
to do whatever he commands them.
13 He brings the clouds to punish men,
or to water his earth[g] and show his
love.
14 "Listen to this, Job;
stop and consider God's wonders.
15 Do you know how God controls the
clouds
and makes his lightning flash?
16 Do you know how the clouds hang
poised,
those wonders of him who is
perfect in knowledge?
17 You who swelter in your clothes
when the land lies hushed under
the south wind,
18 can you join him in spreading out the
skies,
hard as a mirror of cast bronze?

19 "Tell us what we should say to him;
we cannot draw up our case because
of our darkness.
20 Should he be told that I want to
speak?
Would any man ask to be
swallowed up?
21 Now no one can look at the sun,
bright as it is in the skies
after the wind has swept them
clean.
22 Out of the north he comes in golden
splendor;
God comes in awesome majesty.
23 The Almighty is beyond our reach and
exalted in power;
in his justice and great
righteousness, he does not
oppress.
24 Therefore, men revere him,
for does he not have regard for all
the wise in heart?[h]"

[e] 33 Or *announces his coming— / the One zealous against evil* [f] 7 Or / *he fills all men with fear by his power* [g] 13 Or *to favor them* [h] 24 Or *for he does not have regard for any who think they are wise.*

PRAYER: INTERCESSION

O LORD, we should be filled with Your Spirit, speaking to one another with psalms, hymns and spiritual songs; singing and making music in our hearts to You, always giving thanks to You for everything, God our Father, in the name of our Lord Jesus Christ. (Ephesians 5:18–20)

***TAKE** a few moments to intercede on behalf of your local church, other churches, evangelism and discipleship ministries, educational ministries and any other special concerns you may have.*

NT Matthew 23:1-39

Seven Woes

23 Then Jesus said to the crowds and to his disciples: 2 "The teachers of the law and the Pharisees sit in Moses' seat. 3 So you must obey them and do everything they tell you. But do not do what they do, for they do not practice what they preach. 4 They tie up heavy loads and put them on men's shoulders, but they themselves are not willing to lift a finger to move them.

5 "Everything they do is done for men to see: They make their phylacteries[a] wide and the tassels on their garments long; 6 they love the place of honor at banquets and the most important seats in the synagogues; 7 they love to be greeted in the marketplaces and to have men call them 'Rabbi.'

8 "But you are not to be called 'Rabbi,' for you have only one Master and you are all brothers. 9 And do not call anyone on earth 'father,' for you have one Father, and he is in heaven. 10 Nor are you to be called 'teacher,' for you have one Teacher, the Christ.[b] 11 The greatest among you will be your servant. 12 For whoever exalts himself will be humbled, and whoever humbles himself will be exalted.

13 "Woe to you, teachers of the law and Pharisees, you hypocrites! You shut the kingdom of heaven in men's faces. You yourselves do not enter, nor will you let those enter who are trying to.[c]

15 "Woe to you, teachers of the law and Pharisees, you hypocrites! You travel over land and sea to win a single convert, and when he becomes one, you make him twice as much a son of hell as you are.

16 "Woe to you, blind guides! You say, 'If anyone swears by the temple, it means nothing; but if anyone swears by the gold of the temple, he is bound by his oath.' 17 You blind fools! Which is greater: the gold, or the temple that makes the gold sacred? 18 You also say, 'If anyone swears by the altar, it means nothing; but if anyone swears by the gift on it, he is bound by his oath.' 19 You blind men! Which is greater: the gift, or the altar that makes the gift sacred? 20 Therefore, he who swears by the altar swears by it and by everything on it. 21 And he who swears by the temple swears by it and by the one who dwells in it. 22 And he who swears by heaven swears by God's throne and by the one who sits on it.

23 "Woe to you, teachers of the law and Pharisees, you hypocrites! You give a tenth of your spices—mint, dill and cummin. But you have neglected the more important matters of the law—justice, mercy and faithfulness. You should have practiced the latter, without neglecting the former. 24 You blind guides! You strain out a gnat but swallow a camel.

25 "Woe to you, teachers of the law and Pharisees, you hypocrites! You clean the outside of the cup and dish, but inside they are full of greed and self-indulgence. 26 Blind Pharisee! First clean the inside of the cup and dish, and then the outside also will be clean.

27 "Woe to you, teachers of the law and Pharisees, you hypocrites! You are like whitewashed tombs, which look beautiful on the outside but on the inside are full of dead men's bones and everything unclean. 28 In the same way, on the outside you appear to people as righteous but on the inside you are full of hypocrisy and wickedness.

29 "Woe to you, teachers of the law and Pharisees, you hypocrites! You build tombs for the prophets and decorate the graves of the righteous. 30 And you say, 'If we had lived in the days of our forefathers, we would not have taken part with them in shedding the blood of the prophets.' 31 So you testify against yourselves that you are the descendants of those who murdered the prophets. 32 Fill up, then, the measure of the sin of your forefathers!

33 "You snakes! You brood of vipers! How will you escape being condemned to hell? 34 Therefore I am sending you prophets and wise men and teachers. Some of them you will kill and crucify; others you will flog in your synagogues and pursue from town to town. 35 And so upon you will come all the righteous blood that has been shed on earth, from the blood of righteous Abel to the blood of Zechariah son of Berekiah, whom you murdered be-

[a] 5 That is, boxes containing Scripture verses, worn on forehead and arm [b] 10 Or *Messiah*
[c] 13 Some manuscripts *to.* [14] *Woe to you, teachers of the law and Pharisees, you hypocrites! You devour widows' houses and for a show make lengthy prayers. Therefore you will be punished more severely.*

tween the temple and the altar. 36 I tell you
the truth, all this will come upon this generation.
37 "O Jerusalem, Jerusalem, you who kill
the prophets and stone those sent to you,
how often I have longed to gather your
children together, as a hen gathers her
chicks under her wings, but you were not
willing. 38 Look, your house is left to you
desolate. 39 For I tell you, you will not see
me again until you say, 'Blessed is he who
comes in the name of the Lord.'[d]"

[d] 39 Psalm 118:26

PRAYER: THE WORKS OF GOD

JESUS Christ, You are the image of the invisible God, the firstborn over all creation. For by You all things were created that are in heaven and on earth, visible and invisible, whether thrones or dominions or rulers or authorities; all things were created by You and for You. And You are before all things, and in You all things hold together.
(Colossians 1:15–17)

***TAKE** a moment to consider the greatness of God's wonderful works.*

YEAR 2 DAY 33

OT Job 38:1–41

The L*ORD* *Speaks*

38 Then the LORD answered Job out of the storm. He said:

2 "Who is this that darkens my counsel
with words without knowledge?
3 Brace yourself like a man;
I will question you,
and you shall answer me.

4 "Where were you when I laid the earth's foundation?
Tell me, if you understand.
5 Who marked off its dimensions? Surely you know!
Who stretched a measuring line across it?
6 On what were its footings set,
or who laid its cornerstone—
7 while the morning stars sang together
and all the angels[a] shouted for joy?

8 "Who shut up the sea behind doors
when it burst forth from the womb,
9 when I made the clouds its garment
and wrapped it in thick darkness,
10 when I fixed limits for it
and set its doors and bars in place,
11 when I said, 'This far you may come and no farther;
here is where your proud waves halt'?

12 "Have you ever given orders to the morning,
or shown the dawn its place,
13 that it might take the earth by the edges
and shake the wicked out of it?
14 The earth takes shape like clay under a seal;
its features stand out like those of a garment.
15 The wicked are denied their light,
and their upraised arm is broken.

16 "Have you journeyed to the springs of the sea
or walked in the recesses of the deep?
17 Have the gates of death been shown to you?
Have you seen the gates of the shadow of death[b]?
18 Have you comprehended the vast expanses of the earth?
Tell me, if you know all this.

19 "What is the way to the abode of light?
And where does darkness reside?
20 Can you take them to their places?
Do you know the paths to their dwellings?

[a] 7 Hebrew *the sons of God* [b] 17 Or *gates of deep shadows*

[21] Surely you know, for you were already
born!
You have lived so many years!

[22] "Have you entered the storehouses of
the snow
or seen the storehouses of the hail,
[23] which I reserve for times of trouble,
for days of war and battle?
[24] What is the way to the place where
the lightning is dispersed,
or the place where the east winds
are scattered over the earth?
[25] Who cuts a channel for the torrents of
rain,
and a path for the thunderstorm,
[26] to water a land where no man lives,
a desert with no one in it,
[27] to satisfy a desolate wasteland
and make it sprout with grass?
[28] Does the rain have a father?
Who fathers the drops of dew?
[29] From whose womb comes the ice?
Who gives birth to the frost from
the heavens
[30] when the waters become hard as
stone,
when the surface of the deep is
frozen?

[31] "Can you bind the beautiful[c] Pleiades?
Can you loose the cords of Orion?
[32] Can you bring forth the constellations
in their seasons[d]
or lead out the Bear[e] with its cubs?
[33] Do you know the laws of the heavens?
Can you set up ⌊God's[f]⌋ dominion
over the earth?

[34] "Can you raise your voice to the
clouds
and cover yourself with a flood of
water?
[35] Do you send the lightning bolts on
their way?
Do they report to you, 'Here we
are'?
[36] Who endowed the heart[g] with wisdom
or gave understanding to the
mind[g]?
[37] Who has the wisdom to count the
clouds?
Who can tip over the water jars of
the heavens
[38] when the dust becomes hard
and the clods of earth stick
together?

[39] "Do you hunt the prey for the lioness
and satisfy the hunger of the lions
[40] when they crouch in their dens
or lie in wait in a thicket?
[41] Who provides food for the raven
when its young cry out to God
and wander about for lack of food?

[c] 31 Or *the twinkling;* or *the chains of the* [d] 32 Or *the morning star in its season* [e] 32 Or *out Leo* [f] 33 Or *his;* or *their* [g] 36 The meaning of the Hebrew for this word is uncertain.

PRAYER: AFFIRMATION

LORD Jesus, You have said that unless I am converted and become like a little child, I will never enter the kingdom of heaven. Therefore, those who humble themselves like children are the greatest in the kingdom of heaven. (Matthew 18:3–4)

PAUSE *to reflect on these Biblical affirmations.*

NT Matthew 24:1–51

Signs of the End of the Age

24 Jesus left the temple and was walking
away when his disciples came up to
him to call his attention to its buildings.
[2] "Do you see all these things?" he asked.
"I tell you the truth, not one stone here
will be left on another; every one will be
thrown down."
[3] As Jesus was sitting on the Mount of
Olives, the disciples came to him privately. "Tell us," they said, "when will this
happen, and what will be the sign of your
coming and of the end of the age?"
[4] Jesus answered: "Watch out that no
one deceives you. [5] For many will come in
my name, claiming, 'I am the Christ,[a]' and
will deceive many. [6] You will hear of wars

[a] 5 Or *Messiah;* also in verse 23

and rumors of wars, but see to it that you
are not alarmed. Such things must happen, but the end is still to come. 7 Nation
will rise against nation, and kingdom
against kingdom. There will be famines
and earthquakes in various places. 8 All
these are the beginning of birth pains.

9 "Then you will be handed over to be
persecuted and put to death, and you will
be hated by all nations because of me. 10 At
that time many will turn away from the
faith and will betray and hate each other,
11 and many false prophets will appear and
deceive many people. 12 Because of the increase of wickedness, the love of most will
grow cold, 13 but he who stands firm to the
end will be saved. 14 And this gospel of the
kingdom will be preached in the whole
world as a testimony to all nations, and
then the end will come.

15 "So when you see standing in the holy
place 'the abomination that causes desolation,'[b] spoken of through the prophet
Daniel—let the reader understand—
16 then let those who are in Judea flee to
the mountains. 17 Let no one on the roof
of his house go down to take anything out
of the house. 18 Let no one in the field go
back to get his cloak. 19 How dreadful it
will be in those days for pregnant women
and nursing mothers! 20 Pray that your
flight will not take place in winter or on
the Sabbath. 21 For then there will be great
distress, unequaled from the beginning of
the world until now—and never to be
equaled again. 22 If those days had not
been cut short, no one would survive, but
for the sake of the elect those days will be
shortened. 23 At that time if anyone says to
you, 'Look, here is the Christ!' or, 'There
he is!' do not believe it. 24 For false Christs
and false prophets will appear and perform great signs and miracles to deceive
even the elect—if that were possible. 25 See,
I have told you ahead of time.

26 "So if anyone tells you, 'There he is,
out in the desert,' do not go out; or, 'Here
he is, in the inner rooms,' do not believe
it. 27 For as lightning that comes from the
east is visible even in the west, so will be
the coming of the Son of Man. 28 Wherever there is a carcass, there the vultures will
gather.

29 "Immediately after the distress of
those days

" 'the sun will be darkened,
and the moon will not give its light;
the stars will fall from the sky,
and the heavenly bodies will be
shaken.'[c]

30 "At that time the sign of the Son of
Man will appear in the sky, and all the nations of the earth will mourn. They will
see the Son of Man coming on the clouds
of the sky, with power and great glory.
31 And he will send his angels with a loud
trumpet call, and they will gather his elect
from the four winds, from one end of the
heavens to the other.

32 "Now learn this lesson from the fig
tree: As soon as its twigs get tender and its
leaves come out, you know that summer
is near. 33 Even so, when you see all these
things, you know that it[d] is near, right at
the door. 34 I tell you the truth, this generation[e] will certainly not pass away until all
these things have happened. 35 Heaven
and earth will pass away, but my words
will never pass away.

The Day and Hour Unknown

36 "No one knows about that day or
hour, not even the angels in heaven, nor
the Son,[f] but only the Father. 37 As it was
in the days of Noah, so it will be at the
coming of the Son of Man. 38 For in the
days before the flood, people were eating
and drinking, marrying and giving in marriage, up to the day Noah entered the ark;
39 and they knew nothing about what
would happen until the flood came and
took them all away. That is how it will be
at the coming of the Son of Man. 40 Two
men will be in the field; one will be tak-
en and the other left. 41 Two women will
be grinding with a hand mill; one will be
taken and the other left.

42 "Therefore keep watch, because you
do not know on what day your Lord will
come. 43 But understand this: If the owner
of the house had known at what time of
night the thief was coming, he would
have kept watch and would not have let
his house be broken into. 44 So you also
must be ready, because the Son of Man
will come at an hour when you do not expect him.

45 "Who then is the faithful and wise servant, whom the master has put in charge

[b] *15* Daniel 9:27; 11:31; 12:11 [c] *29* Isaiah 13:10; 34:4 [d] *33* Or *he* [e] *34* Or *race* [f] *36* Some manuscripts do not have *nor the Son.*

of the servants in his household to give
them their food at the proper time? [46]It will
be good for that servant whose master
finds him doing so when he returns. [47]I tell
you the truth, he will put him in charge of
all his possessions. [48]But suppose that servant is wicked and says to himself, 'My
master is staying away a long time,' [49]and
he then begins to beat his fellow servants
and to eat and drink with drunkards. [50]The
master of that servant will come on a day
when he does not expect him and at an
hour he is not aware of. [51]He will cut him
to pieces and assign him a place with the
hypocrites, where there will be weeping
and gnashing of teeth.

PRAYER: MY RELATIONSHIP TO GOD

If You, O God, are for me, who can be against me? You who did not spare Your own Son, but delivered Him up for us all, how will You not also, with Him, freely give us all things? (Romans 8:31–32)

***PAUSE** to thank God for the relationship that you enjoy with Him in Jesus Christ.*

YEAR 2 DAY 34

OT Job 39:1–30

39 "Do you know when the mountain
goats give birth?
Do you watch when the doe bears
her fawn?
2 Do you count the months till they
bear?
Do you know the time they give
birth?
3 They crouch down and bring forth
their young;
their labor pains are ended.
4 Their young thrive and grow strong in
the wilds;
they leave and do not return.

5 "Who let the wild donkey go free?
Who untied his ropes?
6 I gave him the wasteland as his home,
the salt flats as his habitat.
7 He laughs at the commotion in the
town;
he does not hear a driver's shout.
8 He ranges the hills for his pasture
and searches for any green thing.

9 "Will the wild ox consent to serve
you?
Will he stay by your manger at
night?
10 Can you hold him to the furrow with
a harness?
Will he till the valleys behind you?
11 Will you rely on him for his great
strength?
Will you leave your heavy work to
him?
12 Can you trust him to bring in your
grain
and gather it to your threshing floor?

13 "The wings of the ostrich flap joyfully,
but they cannot compare with the
pinions and feathers of the
stork.
14 She lays her eggs on the ground
and lets them warm in the sand,
15 unmindful that a foot may crush them,
that some wild animal may trample
them.
16 She treats her young harshly, as if they
were not hers;
she cares not that her labor was in
vain,
17 for God did not endow her with
wisdom
or give her a share of good sense.
18 Yet when she spreads her feathers to
run,
she laughs at horse and rider.

19 "Do you give the horse his strength
or clothe his neck with a flowing
mane?
20 Do you make him leap like a locust,
striking terror with his proud
snorting?
21 He paws fiercely, rejoicing in his
strength,

and charges into the fray.
[22]He laughs at fear, afraid of nothing;
he does not shy away from the sword.
[23]The quiver rattles against his side,
along with the flashing spear and lance.
[24]In frenzied excitement he eats up the ground;
he cannot stand still when the trumpet sounds.
[25]At the blast of the trumpet he snorts, 'Aha!'
He catches the scent of battle from afar,
the shout of commanders and the battle cry.

[26]"Does the hawk take flight by your wisdom
and spread his wings toward the south?
[27]Does the eagle soar at your command
and build his nest on high?
[28]He dwells on a cliff and stays there at night;
a rocky crag is his stronghold.
[29]From there he seeks out his food;
his eyes detect it from afar.
[30]His young ones feast on blood,
and where the slain are, there is he."

PRAYER: THANKSGIVING

WE praise You, Lord; day by day You bear our burdens, O God of our salvation. You, our God, are the God of salvation, and to You belongs escape from death. (Psalm 68:19–20)

***PAUSE** to offer your own expressions of thanksgiving.*

NT Matthew 25:1–46

The Parable of the Ten Virgins

25 "At that time the kingdom of heaven
will be like ten virgins who took their
lamps and went out to meet the bridegroom. [2]Five of them were foolish and
five were wise. [3]The foolish ones took
their lamps but did not take any oil with
them. [4]The wise, however, took oil in jars
along with their lamps. [5]The bridegroom
was a long time in coming, and they all
became drowsy and fell asleep.
[6]"At midnight the cry rang out: 'Here's
the bridegroom! Come out to meet him!'
[7]"Then all the virgins woke up and
trimmed their lamps. [8]The foolish ones
said to the wise, 'Give us some of your oil;
our lamps are going out.'
[9]" 'No,' they replied, 'there may not be
enough for both us and you. Instead, go
to those who sell oil and buy some for
yourselves.'
[10]"But while they were on their way to
buy the oil, the bridegroom arrived. The
virgins who were ready went in with him
to the wedding banquet. And the door
was shut.
[11]"Later the others also came. 'Sir! Sir!'
they said. 'Open the door for us!'
[12]"But he replied, 'I tell you the truth, I
don't know you.'
[13]"Therefore keep watch, because you
do not know the day or the hour.

The Parable of the Talents

[14]"Again, it will be like a man going on
a journey, who called his servants and entrusted his property to them. [15]To one he
gave five talents[a] of money, to another
two talents, and to another one talent,
each according to his ability. Then he
went on his journey. [16]The man who had
received the five talents went at once and
put his money to work and gained five
more. [17]So also, the one with the two talents gained two more. [18]But the man who
had received the one talent went off, dug
a hole in the ground and hid his master's
money.
[19]"After a long time the master of those
servants returned and settled accounts
with them. [20]The man who had received
the five talents brought the other five.
'Master,' he said, 'you entrusted me with
five talents. See, I have gained five more.'

[a] *15* A talent was worth more than a thousand dollars.

21 "His master replied, 'Well done, good
and faithful servant! You have been faithful with a few things; I will put you in
charge of many things. Come and share
your master's happiness!'
22 "The man with the two talents also
came. 'Master,' he said, 'you entrusted me
with two talents; see, I have gained two
more.'
23 "His master replied, 'Well done, good
and faithful servant! You have been faithful with a few things; I will put you in
charge of many things. Come and share
your master's happiness!'
24 "Then the man who had received the
one talent came. 'Master,' he said, 'I knew
that you are a hard man, harvesting where
you have not sown and gathering where
you have not scattered seed. 25 So I was
afraid and went out and hid your talent in
the ground. See, here is what belongs to
you.'
26 "His master replied, 'You wicked, lazy
servant! So you knew that I harvest where
I have not sown and gather where I have
not scattered seed? 27 Well then, you
should have put my money on deposit
with the bankers, so that when I returned
I would have received it back with interest.
28 " 'Take the talent from him and give it
to the one who has the ten talents. 29 For
everyone who has will be given more, and
he will have an abundance. Whoever does
not have, even what he has will be taken
from him. 30 And throw that worthless servant outside, into the darkness, where
there will be weeping and gnashing of
teeth.'

The Sheep and the Goats

31 "When the Son of Man comes in his
glory, and all the angels with him, he will
sit on his throne in heavenly glory. 32 All
the nations will be gathered before him,
and he will separate the people one from
another as a shepherd separates the sheep
from the goats. 33 He will put the sheep on
his right and the goats on his left.
34 "Then the King will say to those on
his right, 'Come, you who are blessed by
my Father; take your inheritance, the kingdom prepared for you since the creation
of the world. 35 For I was hungry and you
gave me something to eat, I was thirsty
and you gave me something to drink, I
was a stranger and you invited me in, 36 I
needed clothes and you clothed me, I was
sick and you looked after me, I was in
prison and you came to visit me.'
37 "Then the righteous will answer him,
'Lord, when did we see you hungry and
feed you, or thirsty and give you something to drink? 38 When did we see you a
stranger and invite you in, or needing
clothes and clothe you? 39 When did we
see you sick or in prison and go to visit
you?'
40 "The King will reply, 'I tell you the
truth, whatever you did for one of the
least of these brothers of mine, you did
for me.'
41 "Then he will say to those on his left,
'Depart from me, you who are cursed,
into the eternal fire prepared for the devil and his angels. 42 For I was hungry and
you gave me nothing to eat, I was thirsty
and you gave me nothing to drink, 43 I was
a stranger and you did not invite me in, I
needed clothes and you did not clothe
me, I was sick and in prison and you did
not look after me.'
44 "They also will answer, 'Lord, when
did we see you hungry or thirsty or a
stranger or needing clothes or sick or in
prison, and did not help you?'
45 "He will reply, 'I tell you the truth,
whatever you did not do for one of the
least of these, you did not do for me.'
46 "Then they will go away to eternal
punishment, but the righteous to eternal
life."

PRAYER: THE CHARACTER I WANT TO CULTIVATE

YOUR kingdom, O God, is not a matter of eating and drinking, but of righteousness and peace and joy in Your Holy Spirit.

(Romans 14:17)

***TAKE** a moment to ask the Lord for the grace to grow in godly character.*

Psalm 78

A *maskil*[a] of Asaph.

1 O my people, hear my teaching;
listen to the words of my mouth.
2 I will open my mouth in parables,
I will utter hidden things, things
from of old—
3 what we have heard and known,
what our fathers have told us.
4 We will not hide them from their
children;
we will tell the next generation
the praiseworthy deeds of the LORD,
his power, and the wonders he has
done.
5 He decreed statutes for Jacob
and established the law in Israel,
which he commanded our forefathers
to teach their children,
6 so the next generation would know
them,
even the children yet to be born,
and they in turn would tell their
children.
7 Then they would put their trust in
God
and would not forget his deeds
but would keep his commands.
8 They would not be like their
forefathers—
a stubborn and rebellious
generation,
whose hearts were not loyal to God,
whose spirits were not faithful to
him.

9 The men of Ephraim, though armed
with bows,
turned back on the day of battle;
10 they did not keep God's covenant
and refused to live by his law.
11 They forgot what he had done,
the wonders he had shown them.
12 He did miracles in the sight of their
fathers
in the land of Egypt, in the region
of Zoan.
13 He divided the sea and led them
through;
he made the water stand firm like a
wall.
14 He guided them with the cloud by day
and with light from the fire all
night.
15 He split the rocks in the desert
and gave them water as abundant as
the seas;
16 he brought streams out of a rocky crag
and made water flow down like
rivers.

17 But they continued to sin against him,
rebelling in the desert against the
Most High.
18 They willfully put God to the test
by demanding the food they craved.
19 They spoke against God, saying,
"Can God spread a table in the
desert?
20 When he struck the rock, water
gushed out,
and streams flowed abundantly.
But can he also give us food?
Can he supply meat for his
people?"
21 When the LORD heard them, he was
very angry;
his fire broke out against Jacob,
and his wrath rose against Israel,
22 for they did not believe in God
or trust in his deliverance.
23 Yet he gave a command to the skies
above
and opened the doors of the
heavens;
24 he rained down manna for the people
to eat,
he gave them the grain of heaven.
25 Men ate the bread of angels;
he sent them all the food they
could eat.
26 He let loose the east wind from the
heavens
and led forth the south wind by his
power.
27 He rained meat down on them like
dust,
flying birds like sand on the
seashore.
28 He made them come down inside
their camp,
all around their tents.
29 They ate till they had more than
enough,

[a] Title: Probably a literary or musical term

for he had given them what they craved.
30 But before they turned from the food they craved,
even while it was still in their mouths,
31 God's anger rose against them;
he put to death the sturdiest among them,
cutting down the young men of Israel.

32 In spite of all this, they kept on sinning;
in spite of his wonders, they did not believe.
33 So he ended their days in futility
and their years in terror.
34 Whenever God slew them, they would seek him;
they eagerly turned to him again.
35 They remembered that God was their Rock,
that God Most High was their Redeemer.
36 But then they would flatter him with their mouths,
lying to him with their tongues;
37 their hearts were not loyal to him,
they were not faithful to his covenant.
38 Yet he was merciful;
he forgave their iniquities
and did not destroy them.
Time after time he restrained his anger
and did not stir up his full wrath.
39 He remembered that they were but flesh,
a passing breeze that does not return.

40 How often they rebelled against him in the desert
and grieved him in the wasteland!
41 Again and again they put God to the test;
they vexed the Holy One of Israel.
42 They did not remember his power—
the day he redeemed them from the oppressor,
43 the day he displayed his miraculous signs in Egypt,
his wonders in the region of Zoan.
44 He turned their rivers to blood;
they could not drink from their streams.
45 He sent swarms of flies that devoured them,
and frogs that devastated them.
46 He gave their crops to the grasshopper,
their produce to the locust.
47 He destroyed their vines with hail
and their sycamore-figs with sleet.
48 He gave over their cattle to the hail,
their livestock to bolts of lightning.
49 He unleashed against them his hot anger,
his wrath, indignation and hostility—
a band of destroying angels.
50 He prepared a path for his anger;
he did not spare them from death
but gave them over to the plague.
51 He struck down all the firstborn of Egypt,
the firstfruits of manhood in the tents of Ham.
52 But he brought his people out like a flock;
he led them like sheep through the desert.
53 He guided them safely, so they were unafraid;
but the sea engulfed their enemies.
54 Thus he brought them to the border of his holy land,
to the hill country his right hand had taken.
55 He drove out nations before them
and allotted their lands to them as an inheritance;
he settled the tribes of Israel in their homes.

56 But they put God to the test
and rebelled against the Most High;
they did not keep his statutes.
57 Like their fathers they were disloyal and faithless,
as unreliable as a faulty bow.
58 They angered him with their high places;
they aroused his jealousy with their idols.
59 When God heard them, he was very angry;
he rejected Israel completely.
60 He abandoned the tabernacle of Shiloh,
the tent he had set up among men.
61 He sent ⌞the ark of⌟ his might into captivity,
his splendor into the hands of the enemy.

62 He gave his people over to the sword;
he was very angry with his
inheritance.
63 Fire consumed their young men,
and their maidens had no wedding
songs;
64 their priests were put to the sword,
and their widows could not weep.

65 Then the Lord awoke as from sleep,
as a man wakes from the stupor of
wine.
66 He beat back his enemies;
he put them to everlasting shame.
67 Then he rejected the tents of Joseph,
he did not choose the tribe of
Ephraim;
68 but he chose the tribe of Judah,
Mount Zion, which he loved.
69 He built his sanctuary like the heights,
like the earth that he established
forever.
70 He chose David his servant
and took him from the sheep pens;
71 from tending the sheep he brought
him
to be the shepherd of his people
Jacob,
of Israel his inheritance.
72 And David shepherded them with
integrity of heart;
with skillful hands he led them.

PRAYER: ADORATION

HEAVEN is Your throne, O Lord, and the earth is Your footstool. Your hand made all these things, and so they came into being. (Isaiah 66:1–2)

***PAUSE** to express your thoughts of praise and worship.*

NT Matthew 26:1-35

The Plot Against Jesus

26 When Jesus had finished saying all
these things, he said to his disciples,
2 "As you know, the Passover is two days
away—and the Son of Man will be handed over to be crucified."
3 Then the chief priests and the elders of
the people assembled in the palace of the
high priest, whose name was Caiaphas,
4 and they plotted to arrest Jesus in some
sly way and kill him. 5 "But not during the
Feast," they said, "or there may be a riot
among the people."

Jesus Anointed at Bethany

6 While Jesus was in Bethany in the
home of a man known as Simon the Leper, 7 a woman came to him with an alabaster jar of very expensive perfume,
which she poured on his head as he was
reclining at the table.
8 When the disciples saw this, they were
indignant. "Why this waste?" they asked.
9 "This perfume could have been sold at a
high price and the money given to the
poor."
10 Aware of this, Jesus said to them,
"Why are you bothering this woman? She
has done a beautiful thing to me. 11 The
poor you will always have with you, but
you will not always have me. 12 When she
poured this perfume on my body, she did
it to prepare me for burial. 13 I tell you the
truth, wherever this gospel is preached
throughout the world, what she has done
will also be told, in memory of her."

Judas Agrees to Betray Jesus

14 Then one of the Twelve—the one
called Judas Iscariot—went to the chief
priests 15 and asked, "What are you willing
to give me if I hand him over to you?" So
they counted out for him thirty silver
coins. 16 From then on Judas watched for
an opportunity to hand him over.

The Lord's Supper

17 On the first day of the Feast of Unleavened Bread, the disciples came to
Jesus and asked, "Where do you want us
to make preparations for you to eat the
Passover?"
18 He replied, "Go into the city to a certain man and tell him, 'The Teacher says:
My appointed time is near. I am going to

celebrate the Passover with my disciples at
your house.' " [19]So the disciples did as
Jesus had directed them and prepared the
Passover.

[20]When evening came, Jesus was reclining at the table with the Twelve. [21]And
while they were eating, he said, "I tell you
the truth, one of you will betray me."

[22]They were very sad and began to say
to him one after the other, "Surely not I,
Lord?"

[23]Jesus replied, "The one who has
dipped his hand into the bowl with me
will betray me. [24]The Son of Man will go
just as it is written about him. But woe to
that man who betrays the Son of Man! It
would be better for him if he had not
been born."

[25]Then Judas, the one who would betray
him, said, "Surely not I, Rabbi?"

Jesus answered, "Yes, it is you."[a]

[26]While they were eating, Jesus took
bread, gave thanks and broke it, and gave
it to his disciples, saying, "Take and eat;
this is my body."

[27]Then he took the cup, gave thanks and
offered it to them, saying, "Drink from it,
all of you. [28]This is my blood of the[b] covenant, which is poured out for many for
the forgiveness of sins. [29]I tell you, I will
not drink of this fruit of the vine from
now on until that day when I drink it
anew with you in my Father's kingdom."

[30]When they had sung a hymn, they
went out to the Mount of Olives.

Jesus Predicts Peter's Denial

[31]Then Jesus told them, "This very night
you will all fall away on account of me,
for it is written:

" 'I will strike the shepherd,
and the sheep of the flock will be
scattered.'[c]

[32]But after I have risen, I will go ahead of
you into Galilee."

[33]Peter replied, "Even if all fall away on
account of you, I never will."

[34]"I tell you the truth," Jesus answered,
"this very night, before the rooster crows,
you will disown me three times."

[35]But Peter declared, "Even if I have to
die with you, I will never disown you."
And all the other disciples said the same.

[a] 25 Or *"You yourself have said it"* [b] 28 Some manuscripts *the new* [c] 31 Zech. 13:7

PRAYER: MY RELATIONSHIP TO OTHERS

O LORD, may You make me increase and abound in my love for believers and for unbelievers. (1 Thessalonians 3:12) . . . Those who love their brothers and sisters abide in the light, and there is no cause for stumbling in them. But those who hate their brothers and sisters are in the darkness and walk in the darkness and do not know where they are going, because the darkness has blinded their eyes. (1 John 2:10–11)

***PAUSE** to review your relationships with others and to commit them to the Lord.*

YEAR 2
DAY 36

OT Job 40:1-24

40 The LORD said to Job:

[2]"Will the one who contends with the
Almighty correct him?
Let him who accuses God answer
him!"

[3]Then Job answered the LORD:

[4]"I am unworthy—how can I reply to
you?
I put my hand over my mouth.
[5]I spoke once, but I have no answer—
twice, but I will say no more."

[6]Then the LORD spoke to Job out of the
storm:

[7]"Brace yourself like a man;
I will question you,
and you shall answer me.

[8] "Would you discredit my justice?
Would you condemn me to justify yourself?
[9] Do you have an arm like God's,
and can your voice thunder like his?
[10] Then adorn yourself with glory and splendor,
and clothe yourself in honor and majesty.
[11] Unleash the fury of your wrath,
look at every proud man and bring him low,
[12] look at every proud man and humble him,
crush the wicked where they stand.
[13] Bury them all in the dust together;
shroud their faces in the grave.
[14] Then I myself will admit to you
that your own right hand can save you.

[15] "Look at the behemoth,[a]
which I made along with you
and which feeds on grass like an ox.
[16] What strength he has in his loins,
what power in the muscles of his belly!
[17] His tail[b] sways like a cedar;
the sinews of his thighs are close-knit.
[18] His bones are tubes of bronze,
his limbs like rods of iron.
[19] He ranks first among the works of God,
yet his Maker can approach him with his sword.
[20] The hills bring him their produce,
and all the wild animals play nearby.
[21] Under the lotus plants he lies,
hidden among the reeds in the marsh.
[22] The lotuses conceal him in their shadow;
the poplars by the stream surround him.
[23] When the river rages, he is not alarmed;
he is secure, though the Jordan should surge against his mouth.
[24] Can anyone capture him by the eyes,[c]
or trap him and pierce his nose?

[a] *15* Possibly the hippopotamus or the elephant
[b] *17* Possibly trunk [c] *24* Or *by a water hole*

PRAYER: CONFESSION

SURELY You desire truth in the inner parts, and in the hidden part You make me know wisdom. (Psalm 51:6)

***ASK** the Spirit to search your heart and reveal any areas of unconfessed sin. Acknowledge these to the Lord and thank Him for His forgiveness.*

NT Matthew 26:36-75

Gethsemane

[36]Then Jesus went with his disciples to
a place called Gethsemane, and he said to
them, "Sit here while I go over there and
pray." [37]He took Peter and the two sons of
Zebedee along with him, and he began to
be sorrowful and troubled. [38]Then he said
to them, "My soul is overwhelmed with
sorrow to the point of death. Stay here
and keep watch with me."
[39]Going a little farther, he fell with his
face to the ground and prayed, "My Father, if it is possible, may this cup be tak-
en from me. Yet not as I will, but as you
will."
[40]Then he returned to his disciples and
found them sleeping. "Could you men
not keep watch with me for one hour?" he
asked Peter. [41]"Watch and pray so that you
will not fall into temptation. The spirit is
willing, but the body is weak."
[42]He went away a second time and
prayed, "My Father, if it is not possible for
this cup to be taken away unless I drink
it, may your will be done."
[43]When he came back, he again found
them sleeping, because their eyes were
heavy. [44]So he left them and went away
once more and prayed the third time, saying the same thing.
[45]Then he returned to the disciples and
said to them, "Are you still sleeping and
resting? Look, the hour is near, and the
Son of Man is betrayed into the hands of

sinners. 46Rise, let us go! Here comes my
betrayer!"

Jesus Arrested

47While he was still speaking, Judas, one
of the Twelve, arrived. With him was a
large crowd armed with swords and clubs,
sent from the chief priests and the elders
of the people. 48Now the betrayer had
arranged a signal with them: "The one I
kiss is the man; arrest him." 49Going at
once to Jesus, Judas said, "Greetings, Rabbi!" and kissed him.

50Jesus replied, "Friend, do what you
came for."[a]

Then the men stepped forward, seized
Jesus and arrested him. 51With that, one of
Jesus' companions reached for his sword,
drew it out and struck the servant of the
high priest, cutting off his ear.

52"Put your sword back in its place,"
Jesus said to him, "for all who draw the
sword will die by the sword. 53Do you
think I cannot call on my Father, and he
will at once put at my disposal more than
twelve legions of angels? 54But how then
would the Scriptures be fulfilled that say
it must happen in this way?"

55At that time Jesus said to the crowd,
"Am I leading a rebellion, that you have
come out with swords and clubs to capture me? Every day I sat in the temple
courts teaching, and you did not arrest
me. 56But this has all taken place that the
writings of the prophets might be fulfilled." Then all the disciples deserted him
and fled.

Before the Sanhedrin

57Those who had arrested Jesus took
him to Caiaphas, the high priest, where
the teachers of the law and the elders had
assembled. 58But Peter followed him at a
distance, right up to the courtyard of the
high priest. He entered and sat down with
the guards to see the outcome.

59The chief priests and the whole Sanhedrin were looking for false evidence
against Jesus so that they could put him
to death. 60But they did not find any,
though many false witnesses came forward.

Finally two came forward 61and declared, "This fellow said, 'I am able to destroy the temple of God and rebuild it in
three days.' "

62Then the high priest stood up and
said to Jesus, "Are you not going to answer? What is this testimony that these
men are bringing against you?" 63But Jesus
remained silent.

The high priest said to him, "I charge
you under oath by the living God: Tell us
if you are the Christ,[b] the Son of God."

64"Yes, it is as you say," Jesus replied.
"But I say to all of you: In the future you
will see the Son of Man sitting at the right
hand of the Mighty One and coming on
the clouds of heaven."

65Then the high priest tore his clothes
and said, "He has spoken blasphemy!
Why do we need any more witnesses?
Look, now you have heard the blasphemy.
66What do you think?"

"He is worthy of death," they answered.

67Then they spit in his face and struck
him with their fists. Others slapped him
68and said, "Prophesy to us, Christ. Who
hit you?"

Peter Disowns Jesus

69Now Peter was sitting out in the courtyard, and a servant girl came to him. "You
also were with Jesus of Galilee," she said.

70But he denied it before them all. "I
don't know what you're talking about," he
said.

71Then he went out to the gateway,
where another girl saw him and said to
the people there, "This fellow was with
Jesus of Nazareth."

72He denied it again, with an oath: "I
don't know the man!"

73After a little while, those standing
there went up to Peter and said, "Surely
you are one of them, for your accent gives
you away."

74Then he began to call down curses on
himself and he swore to them, "I don't
know the man!"

Immediately a rooster crowed. 75Then
Peter remembered the word Jesus had
spoken: "Before the rooster crows, you
will disown me three times." And he went
outside and wept bitterly.

[a] 50 Or *"Friend, why have you come?"* [b] 63 Or *Messiah;* also in verse 68

PRAYER: THE ATTRIBUTES OF GOD

I WILL express the memory of Your abundant goodness and joyfully sing of Your righteousness. You, O Lord, are gracious and compassionate, slow to anger and great in loving-kindness. You are good to all, and Your tender mercies are over all Your works. (Psalm 145:7–9) . . . Blessed are You, the God and Father of our Lord Jesus Christ, the Father of mercies and the God of all comfort. (2 Corinthians 1:3)

__PAUSE__ to reflect on these affirmations about the person, powers and perfection of God.

YEAR 2
DAY 37

OT Job 41:1-34

41 "Can you pull in the leviathan[a] with
a fishhook
or tie down his tongue with a rope?
2 Can you put a cord through his nose
or pierce his jaw with a hook?
3 Will he keep begging you for mercy?
Will he speak to you with gentle
words?
4 Will he make an agreement with you
for you to take him as your slave for
life?
5 Can you make a pet of him like a bird
or put him on a leash for your girls?
6 Will traders barter for him?
Will they divide him up among the
merchants?
7 Can you fill his hide with harpoons
or his head with fishing spears?
8 If you lay a hand on him,
you will remember the struggle and
never do it again!
9 Any hope of subduing him is false;
the mere sight of him is
overpowering.
10 No one is fierce enough to rouse him.
Who then is able to stand against
me?
11 Who has a claim against me that I
must pay?
Everything under heaven belongs to
me.

12 "I will not fail to speak of his limbs,
his strength and his graceful form.
13 Who can strip off his outer coat?
Who would approach him with a
bridle?
14 Who dares open the doors of his
mouth,
ringed about with his fearsome
teeth?
15 His back has[b] rows of shields
tightly sealed together;
16 each is so close to the next
that no air can pass between.
17 They are joined fast to one another;
they cling together and cannot be
parted.
18 His snorting throws out flashes of light;
his eyes are like the rays of dawn.
19 Firebrands stream from his mouth;
sparks of fire shoot out.
20 Smoke pours from his nostrils
as from a boiling pot over a fire of
reeds.
21 His breath sets coals ablaze,
and flames dart from his mouth.
22 Strength resides in his neck;
dismay goes before him.
23 The folds of his flesh are tightly joined;
they are firm and immovable.
24 His chest is hard as rock,
hard as a lower millstone.
25 When he rises up, the mighty are
terrified;
they retreat before his thrashing.
26 The sword that reaches him has no
effect,
nor does the spear or the dart or the
javelin.
27 Iron he treats like straw
and bronze like rotten wood.
28 Arrows do not make him flee;
slingstones are like chaff to him.
29 A club seems to him but a piece of
straw;

[a] *1* Possibly the crocodile [b] *15* Or *His pride is his*

he laughs at the rattling of the
lance.
30 His undersides are jagged potsherds,
leaving a trail in the mud like a
threshing sledge.
31 He makes the depths churn like a
boiling caldron
and stirs up the sea like a pot of
ointment.
32 Behind him he leaves a glistening
wake;
one would think the deep had
white hair.
33 Nothing on earth is his equal—
a creature without fear.
34 He looks down on all that are
haughty;
he is king over all that are proud."

PRAYER: RENEWAL

LIKE Josiah, may I do what is right in Your sight, O Lord, and walk in all the ways of David, not turning aside to the right or to the left. May I turn to You with all my heart and with all my soul and with all my might, in accordance with all of Your Word. (2 Kings 22:2; 23:25) . . . May I speak the truth to others and judge with truth and justice. May I not plot evil against my neighbor nor love a false oath; for all these things You hate, O Lord. (Zechariah 8:16–17)

***PAUSE** to add your own prayers for personal renewal.*

NT Matthew 27:1–31

Judas Hangs Himself

27 Early in the morning, all the chief
priests and the elders of the people
came to the decision to put Jesus to death.
2 They bound him, led him away and
handed him over to Pilate, the governor.
3 When Judas, who had betrayed him,
saw that Jesus was condemned, he was
seized with remorse and returned the thirty silver coins to the chief priests and the
elders. 4 "I have sinned," he said, "for I
have betrayed innocent blood."
"What is that to us?" they replied.
"That's your responsibility."
5 So Judas threw the money into the
temple and left. Then he went away and
hanged himself.
6 The chief priests picked up the coins
and said, "It is against the law to put this
into the treasury, since it is blood money."
7 So they decided to use the money to buy
the potter's field as a burial place for foreigners. 8 That is why it has been called the
Field of Blood to this day. 9 Then what was
spoken by Jeremiah the prophet was fulfilled: "They took the thirty silver coins,
the price set on him by the people of Israel, 10 and they used them to buy the potter's field, as the Lord commanded me."[a]

Jesus Before Pilate

11 Meanwhile Jesus stood before the governor, and the governor asked him, "Are
you the king of the Jews?"
"Yes, it is as you say," Jesus replied.
12 When he was accused by the chief
priests and the elders, he gave no answer.
13 Then Pilate asked him, "Don't you hear
the testimony they are bringing against
you?" 14 But Jesus made no reply, not even
to a single charge—to the great amazement of the governor.
15 Now it was the governor's custom at
the Feast to release a prisoner chosen by
the crowd. 16 At that time they had a noto-
rious prisoner, called Barabbas. 17 So when
the crowd had gathered, Pilate asked them,
"Which one do you want me to release to
you: Barabbas, or Jesus who is called
Christ?" 18 For he knew it was out of envy
that they had handed Jesus over to him.
19 While Pilate was sitting on the judge's
seat, his wife sent him this message:
"Don't have anything to do with that innocent man, for I have suffered a great
deal today in a dream because of him."
20 But the chief priests and the elders
persuaded the crowd to ask for Barabbas
and to have Jesus executed.

[a] *10* See Zech. 11:12,13; Jer. 19:1–13; 32:6–9.

[21] "Which of the two do you want me to
release to you?" asked the governor.
"Barabbas," they answered.
[22] "What shall I do, then, with Jesus who
is called Christ?" Pilate asked.
They all answered, "Crucify him!"
[23] "Why? What crime has he committed?" asked Pilate.
But they shouted all the louder, "Crucify him!"
[24] When Pilate saw that he was getting
nowhere, but that instead an uproar was
starting, he took water and washed his
hands in front of the crowd. "I am innocent of this man's blood," he said. "It is
your responsibility!"
[25] All the people answered, "Let his
blood be on us and on our children!"
[26] Then he released Barabbas to them.
But he had Jesus flogged, and handed him
over to be crucified.

The Soldiers Mock Jesus

[27] Then the governor's soldiers took
Jesus into the Praetorium and gathered
the whole company of soldiers around
him. [28] They stripped him and put a scarlet robe on him, [29] and then twisted together a crown of thorns and set it on his
head. They put a staff in his right hand
and knelt in front of him and mocked
him. "Hail, king of the Jews!" they said.
[30] They spit on him, and took the staff and
struck him on the head again and again.
[31] After they had mocked him, they took
off the robe and put his own clothes on
him. Then they led him away to crucify
him.

PRAYER: THE WORKS OF GOD

LORD, You save the humble but bring low those whose eyes are haughty. (Psalm 18:27) . . . Lord, You guide the humble in what is right and teach the humble Your way. (Psalm 25:9)

***TAKE** a moment to consider the greatness of God's wonderful works.*

YEAR 2 DAY 38

OT Job 42:1–17

Job

42 Then Job replied to the LORD:

[2] "I know that you can do all things;
no plan of yours can be thwarted.
[3] ⌊You asked,⌋ 'Who is this that obscures
my counsel without knowledge?'
Surely I spoke of things I did not
understand,
things too wonderful for me to
know.

[4] ⌊"You said,⌋ 'Listen now, and I will
speak;
I will question you,
and you shall answer me.'
[5] My ears had heard of you
but now my eyes have seen you.
[6] Therefore I despise myself
and repent in dust and ashes."

Epilogue

[7] After the LORD had said these things to
Job, he said to Eliphaz the Temanite, "I
am angry with you and your two friends,
because you have not spoken of me what
is right, as my servant Job has. [8] So now
take seven bulls and seven rams and go to
my servant Job and sacrifice a burnt offering for yourselves. My servant Job will
pray for you, and I will accept his prayer
and not deal with you according to your
folly. You have not spoken of me what is
right, as my servant Job has." [9] So Eliphaz
the Temanite, Bildad the Shuhite and Zophar the Naamathite did what the LORD
told them; and the LORD accepted Job's
prayer.
[10] After Job had prayed for his friends,
the LORD made him prosperous again and
gave him twice as much as he had before.
[11] All his brothers and sisters and everyone
who had known him before came and ate
with him in his house. They comforted
and consoled him over all the trouble the
LORD had brought upon him, and each

one gave him a piece of silver[a] and a gold ring.

12 The LORD blessed the latter part of Job's life more than the first. He had fourteen thousand sheep, six thousand camels, a thousand yoke of oxen and a thousand donkeys. 13 And he also had seven sons and three daughters. 14 The first daughter he named Jemimah, the second Keziah and the third Keren-Happuch. 15 Nowhere in all the land were there found women as beautiful as Job's daughters, and their father granted them an inheritance along with their brothers.

16 After this, Job lived a hundred and forty years; he saw his children and their children to the fourth generation. 17 And so he died, old and full of years.

[a] 11 Hebrew *him a kesitah;* a kesitah was a unit of money of unknown weight and value.

PRAYER: PETITION

MAY I not be afraid of my adversaries, but remember You, the One who is great and awesome. (Nehemiah 4:14)

***PAUSE** here to petition God for wisdom. Ask Him to develop your eternal perspective, to renew your mind with truth and to help you develop greater skill in each area of your life. Offer prayers regarding your activities for this day and any special concerns you may have.*

NT Matthew 27:32-66

The Crucifixion

32 As they were going out, they met a man from Cyrene, named Simon, and they forced him to carry the cross. 33 They came to a place called Golgotha (which means The Place of the Skull). 34 There they offered Jesus wine to drink, mixed with gall; but after tasting it, he refused to drink it. 35 When they had crucified him, they divided up his clothes by casting lots.[a] 36 And sitting down, they kept watch over him there. 37 Above his head they placed the written charge against him: THIS IS JESUS, THE KING OF THE JEWS. 38 Two robbers were crucified with him, one on his right and one on his left. 39 Those who passed by hurled insults at him, shaking their heads 40 and saying, "You who are going to destroy the temple and build it in three days, save yourself! Come down from the cross, if you are the Son of God!"

41 In the same way the chief priests, the teachers of the law and the elders mocked him. 42 "He saved others," they said, "but he can't save himself! He's the King of Israel! Let him come down now from the cross, and we will believe in him. 43 He trusts in God. Let God rescue him now if he wants him, for he said, 'I am the Son of God.' " 44 In the same way the robbers who were crucified with him also heaped insults on him.

The Death of Jesus

45 From the sixth hour until the ninth hour darkness came over all the land. 46 About the ninth hour Jesus cried out in a loud voice, *"Eloi, Eloi,*[b] *lama sabachthani?"*—which means, "My God, my God, why have you forsaken me?"[c]

47 When some of those standing there heard this, they said, "He's calling Elijah."

48 Immediately one of them ran and got a sponge. He filled it with wine vinegar, put it on a stick, and offered it to Jesus to drink. 49 The rest said, "Now leave him alone. Let's see if Elijah comes to save him."

50 And when Jesus had cried out again in a loud voice, he gave up his spirit.

51 At that moment the curtain of the temple was torn in two from top to bottom. The earth shook and the rocks split. 52 The tombs broke open and the bodies of many holy people who had died were raised to life. 53 They came out of the tombs, and after Jesus' resurrection they went into the holy city and appeared to many people.

54 When the centurion and those with him who were guarding Jesus saw the

[a] 35 A few late manuscripts *lots that the word spoken by the prophet might be fulfilled: "They divided my garments among themselves and cast lots for my clothing"* (Psalm 22:18) [b] 46 Some manuscripts *Eli, Eli* [c] 46 Psalm 22:1

earthquake and all that had happened,
they were terrified, and exclaimed, "Surely he was the Son[d] of God!"
55 Many women were there, watching
from a distance. They had followed Jesus
from Galilee to care for his needs.
56 Among them were Mary Magdalene,
Mary the mother of James and Joses, and
the mother of Zebedee's sons.

The Burial of Jesus

57 As evening approached, there came a
rich man from Arimathea, named Joseph,
who had himself become a disciple of
Jesus. 58 Going to Pilate, he asked for Jesus'
body, and Pilate ordered that it be given
to him. 59 Joseph took the body, wrapped
it in a clean linen cloth, 60 and placed it in
his own new tomb that he had cut out of
the rock. He rolled a big stone in front of
the entrance to the tomb and went away.
61 Mary Magdalene and the other Mary
were sitting there opposite the tomb.

The Guard at the Tomb

62 The next day, the one after Preparation Day, the chief priests and the Pharisees went to Pilate. 63 "Sir," they said, "we
remember that while he was still alive that
deceiver said, 'After three days I will rise
again.' 64 So give the order for the tomb to
be made secure until the third day. Otherwise, his disciples may come and steal
the body and tell the people that he has
been raised from the dead. This last deception will be worse than the first."
65 "Take a guard," Pilate answered. "Go,
make the tomb as secure as you know
how." 66 So they went and made the tomb
secure by putting a seal on the stone and
posting the guard.

[d] 54 Or *a son*

PRAYER: MY RELATIONSHIP TO GOD

I HAVE set You always before me, O Lord; because You are at my right hand, I will not be shaken. Therefore my heart is glad, and my glory rejoices; my body also will rest in hope. You will make known to me the path of life; in Your presence is fullness of joy; in Your right hand are pleasures forever. (Psalm 16:8–9, 11)

PAUSE *to thank God for the relationship that you enjoy with Him in Jesus Christ.*

YEAR 2
DAY 39

OT Ecclesiastes 1:1–2:26

Everything Is Meaningless

1 The words of the Teacher,[a] son of David, king in Jerusalem:

2 "Meaningless! Meaningless!"
  says the Teacher.
"Utterly meaningless!
  Everything is meaningless."

3 What does man gain from all his
    labor
  at which he toils under the sun?
4 Generations come and generations go,
  but the earth remains forever.
5 The sun rises and the sun sets,
  and hurries back to where it rises.
6 The wind blows to the south
  and turns to the north;
round and round it goes,
  ever returning on its course.
7 All streams flow into the sea,
  yet the sea is never full.
To the place the streams come from,
  there they return again.
8 All things are wearisome,
  more than one can say.
The eye never has enough of seeing,
  nor the ear its fill of hearing.
9 What has been will be again,
  what has been done will be done
    again;
  there is nothing new under the sun.
10 Is there anything of which one can
    say,

[a] 1 Or *leader of the assembly;* also in verses 2 and 12

"Look! This is something new"?
It was here already, long ago;
it was here before our time.
11 There is no remembrance of men of old,
and even those who are yet to come
will not be remembered
by those who follow.

Wisdom Is Meaningless

12 I, the Teacher, was king over Israel in
Jerusalem. 13 I devoted myself to study and
to explore by wisdom all that is done under heaven. What a heavy burden God has
laid on men! 14 I have seen all the things
that are done under the sun; all of them
are meaningless, a chasing after the wind.

15 What is twisted cannot be straightened;
what is lacking cannot be counted.

16 I thought to myself, "Look, I have
grown and increased in wisdom more
than anyone who has ruled over Jerusalem before me; I have experienced
much of wisdom and knowledge." 17 Then
I applied myself to the understanding of
wisdom, and also of madness and folly,
but I learned that this, too, is a chasing after the wind.

18 For with much wisdom comes much sorrow;
the more knowledge, the more grief.

Pleasures Are Meaningless

2 I thought in my heart, "Come now, I
will test you with pleasure to find out
what is good." But that also proved to be
meaningless. 2 "Laughter," I said, "is foolish. And what does pleasure accomplish?"
3 I tried cheering myself with wine, and
embracing folly—my mind still guiding
me with wisdom. I wanted to see what
was worthwhile for men to do under
heaven during the few days of their lives.
4 I undertook great projects: I built
houses for myself and planted vineyards.
5 I made gardens and parks and planted all
kinds of fruit trees in them. 6 I made reservoirs to water groves of flourishing trees.
7 I bought male and female slaves and had
other slaves who were born in my house.
I also owned more herds and flocks than
anyone in Jerusalem before me. 8 I
amassed silver and gold for myself, and
the treasure of kings and provinces. I acquired men and women singers, and a
harem[b] as well—the delights of the heart
of man. 9 I became greater by far than anyone in Jerusalem before me. In all this my
wisdom stayed with me.

10 I denied myself nothing my eyes desired;
I refused my heart no pleasure.
My heart took delight in all my work,
and this was the reward for all my labor.
11 Yet when I surveyed all that my hands had done
and what I had toiled to achieve,
everything was meaningless, a chasing after the wind;
nothing was gained under the sun.

Wisdom and Folly Are Meaningless

12 Then I turned my thoughts to consider wisdom,
and also madness and folly.
What more can the king's successor do
than what has already been done?
13 I saw that wisdom is better than folly,
just as light is better than darkness.
14 The wise man has eyes in his head,
while the fool walks in the darkness;
but I came to realize
that the same fate overtakes them both.

15 Then I thought in my heart,

"The fate of the fool will overtake me also.
What then do I gain by being wise?"
I said in my heart,
"This too is meaningless."
16 For the wise man, like the fool, will not be long remembered;
in days to come both will be forgotten.
Like the fool, the wise man too must die!

Toil Is Meaningless

17 So I hated life, because the work that
is done under the sun was grievous to me.
All of it is meaningless, a chasing after the
wind. 18 I hated all the things I had toiled
for under the sun, because I must leave
them to the one who comes after me.
19 And who knows whether he will be a

[b] 8 The meaning of the Hebrew for this phrase is uncertain.

wise man or a fool? Yet he will have control over all the work into which I have
poured my effort and skill under the sun.
This too is meaningless. 20So my heart began to despair over all my toilsome labor
under the sun. 21For a man may do his
work with wisdom, knowledge and skill,
and then he must leave all he owns to
someone who has not worked for it. This
too is meaningless and a great misfortune.
22What does a man get for all the toil and
anxious striving with which he labors under the sun? 23All his days his work is pain
and grief; even at night his mind does not
rest. This too is meaningless.
24A man can do nothing better than to
eat and drink and find satisfaction in his
work. This too, I see, is from the hand of
God, 25for without him, who can eat or
find enjoyment? 26To the man who
pleases him, God gives wisdom, knowledge and happiness, but to the sinner he
gives the task of gathering and storing up
wealth to hand it over to the one who
pleases God. This too is meaningless, a
chasing after the wind.

PRAYER: INTERCESSION

MAY I do nothing out of selfish ambition or vain conceit, but in humility may I esteem others as more important than myself. Let me look not only to my own interests, but also to the interests of others. (Philippians 2:3–4)

__TAKE__ a few moments to intercede on behalf of your immediate family and other relatives. Offer prayers for their spiritual, emotional and physical concerns.

NT Matthew 28:1-20

The Resurrection

28 After the Sabbath, at dawn on the
first day of the week, Mary Magdalene and the other Mary went to look at
the tomb.
2There was a violent earthquake, for an
angel of the Lord came down from heav-
en and, going to the tomb, rolled back the
stone and sat on it. 3His appearance was
like lightning, and his clothes were white
as snow. 4The guards were so afraid of him
that they shook and became like dead
men.
5The angel said to the women, "Do not
be afraid, for I know that you are looking
for Jesus, who was crucified. 6He is not
here; he has risen, just as he said. Come
and see the place where he lay. 7Then go
quickly and tell his disciples: 'He has risen
from the dead and is going ahead of you
into Galilee. There you will see him.' Now
I have told you."
8So the women hurried away from the
tomb, afraid yet filled with joy, and ran to
tell his disciples. 9Suddenly Jesus met
them. "Greetings," he said. They came to
him, clasped his feet and worshiped him.
10Then Jesus said to them, "Do not be
afraid. Go and tell my brothers to go to
Galilee; there they will see me."

The Guards' Report

11While the women were on their way,
some of the guards went into the city and
reported to the chief priests everything
that had happened. 12When the chief
priests had met with the elders and devised a plan, they gave the soldiers a large
sum of money, 13telling them, "You are to
say, 'His disciples came during the night
and stole him away while we were asleep.'
14If this report gets to the governor, we will
satisfy him and keep you out of trouble."
15So the soldiers took the money and did
as they were instructed. And this story has
been widely circulated among the Jews to
this very day.

The Great Commission

16Then the eleven disciples went to Galilee, to the mountain where Jesus had told
them to go. 17When they saw him, they
worshiped him; but some doubted.
18Then Jesus came to them and said, "All
authority in heaven and on earth has been
given to me. 19Therefore go and make dis-

ciples of all nations, baptizing them in[a]
the name of the Father and of the Son and
of the Holy Spirit, 20 and teaching them to
obey everything I have commanded you.
And surely I am with you always, to the
very end of the age."

[a] 19 Or *into;* see Acts 8:16; 19:5; Romans 6:3; 1 Cor. 1:13; 10:2 and Gal. 3:27.

PRAYER: THE CHARACTER I WANT TO CULTIVATE

THE waywardness of the simple will kill them, and the complacency of fools will destroy them; but if I listen to wisdom, I will live securely and be at ease from the fear of evil. (Proverbs 1:32–33) . . . If I trust in my own heart, I am foolish, but if I walk in wisdom, I will be delivered. (Proverbs 28:26)

__TAKE__ a moment to ask the Lord for the grace to grow in godly character.

YEAR 2
DAY 40

OT Ecclesiastes 3:1–22

A Time for Everything

3 There is a time for everything,
and a season for every activity
under heaven:

2 a time to be born and a time to die,
a time to plant and a time to
uproot,
3 a time to kill and a time to heal,
a time to tear down and a time to
build,
4 a time to weep and a time to laugh,
a time to mourn and a time to
dance,
5 a time to scatter stones and a time
to gather them,
a time to embrace and a time to
refrain,
6 a time to search and a time to give
up,
a time to keep and a time to throw
away,
7 a time to tear and a time to mend,
a time to be silent and a time to
speak,
8 a time to love and a time to hate,
a time for war and a time for peace.

9 What does the worker gain from his
toil? 10 I have seen the burden God has laid
on men. 11 He has made everything beautiful in its time. He has also set eternity in
the hearts of men; yet they cannot fathom
what God has done from beginning to
end. 12 I know that there is nothing better
for men than to be happy and do good
while they live. 13 That everyone may eat
and drink, and find satisfaction in all his
toil—this is the gift of God. 14 I know that
everything God does will endure forever;
nothing can be added to it and nothing
taken from it. God does it so that men
will revere him.

15 Whatever is has already been,
and what will be has been before;
and God will call the past to
account.[a]

16 And I saw something else under the
sun:

In the place of judgment—wickedness
was there,
in the place of justice—wickedness
was there.

17 I thought in my heart,

"God will bring to judgment
both the righteous and the wicked,
for there will be a time for every
activity,
a time for every deed."

18 I also thought, "As for men, God tests
them so that they may see that they are
like the animals. 19 Man's fate is like that
of the animals; the same fate awaits them
both: As one dies, so dies the other. All
have the same breath[b]; man has no advantage over the animal. Everything is
meaningless. 20 All go to the same place;

[a] 15 Or *God calls back the past* [b] 19 Or *spirit*

all come from dust, and to dust all return.
21 Who knows if the spirit of man rises upward and if the spirit of the animal[c] goes
down into the earth?"
22 So I saw that there is nothing better
for a man than to enjoy his work, because
that is his lot. For who can bring him to
see what will happen after him?

[c] 21 Or *Who knows the spirit of man, which rises upward, or the spirit of the animal, which*

PRAYER: AFFIRMATION

YOU, Jesus, will be great and will be called the Son of the Most High. The Lord God will give You the throne of Your father David, and You will reign over the house of Jacob forever, and Your kingdom will never end. (Luke 1:32–33) . . . The heavens will vanish like smoke; the earth will wear out like a garment, and its inhabitants will die in the same way. But Your salvation will last forever, and Your righteousness will never fail. (Isaiah 51:6)

PAUSE *to reflect on these Biblical affirmations.*

NT Acts 1:1-26

Jesus Taken Up Into Heaven

1 In my former book, Theophilus, I wrote
about all that Jesus began to do and to
teach 2 until the day he was taken up to
heaven, after giving instructions through
the Holy Spirit to the apostles he had chosen. 3 After his suffering, he showed himself to these men and gave many convinc-
ing proofs that he was alive. He appeared
to them over a period of forty days and
spoke about the kingdom of God. 4 On
one occasion, while he was eating with
them, he gave them this command: "Do
not leave Jerusalem, but wait for the gift
my Father promised, which you have
heard me speak about. 5 For John baptized
with[a] water, but in a few days you will be
baptized with the Holy Spirit."
6 So when they met together, they asked
him, "Lord, are you at this time going to
restore the kingdom to Israel?"
7 He said to them: "It is not for you to
know the times or dates the Father has set
by his own authority. 8 But you will receive
power when the Holy Spirit comes on
you; and you will be my witnesses in Jerusalem, and in all Judea and Samaria, and
to the ends of the earth."
9 After he said this, he was taken up before their very eyes, and a cloud hid him
from their sight.
10 They were looking intently up into the
sky as he was going, when suddenly two
men dressed in white stood beside them.
11 "Men of Galilee," they said, "why do you
stand here looking into the sky? This
same Jesus, who has been taken from you
into heaven, will come back in the same
way you have seen him go into heaven."

Matthias Chosen to Replace Judas

12 Then they returned to Jerusalem from
the hill called the Mount of Olives, a Sabbath day's walk[b] from the city. 13 When
they arrived, they went upstairs to the
room where they were staying. Those
present were Peter, John, James and Andrew; Philip and Thomas, Bartholomew
and Matthew; James son of Alphaeus and
Simon the Zealot, and Judas son of James.
14 They all joined together constantly in
prayer, along with the women and Mary
the mother of Jesus, and with his brothers.
15 In those days Peter stood up among
the believers[c] (a group numbering about
a hundred and twenty) 16 and said, "Brothers, the Scripture had to be fulfilled which
the Holy Spirit spoke long ago through
the mouth of David concerning Judas,
who served as guide for those who arrested Jesus— 17 he was one of our number
and shared in this ministry."
18 (With the reward he got for his
wickedness, Judas bought a field; there he
fell headlong, his body burst open and all
his intestines spilled out. 19 Everyone in

[a] 5 Or *in* [b] 12 That is, about 3/4 mile (about 1,100 meters) [c] 15 Greek *brothers*

Jerusalem heard about this, so they called
that field in their language Akeldama, that
is, Field of Blood.)
20 "For," said Peter, "it is written in the
book of Psalms,

" 'May his place be deserted;
let there be no one to dwell in it,'[d]

and,

" 'May another take his place of
leadership.'[e]

21 Therefore it is necessary to choose one
of the men who have been with us the
whole time the Lord Jesus went in and out
among us, 22 beginning from John's baptism to the time when Jesus was taken up
from us. For one of these must become a
witness with us of his resurrection."
23 So they proposed two men: Joseph
called Barsabbas (also known as Justus)
and Matthias. 24 Then they prayed, "Lord,
you know everyone's heart. Show us
which of these two you have chosen 25 to
take over this apostolic ministry, which
Judas left to go where he belongs." 26 Then
they cast lots, and the lot fell to Matthias;
so he was added to the eleven apostles.

[d] 20 Psalm 69:25 [e] 20 Psalm 109:8

PRAYER: MY RELATIONSHIP TO OTHERS

AN anxious heart weighs one down, but a good word makes a person glad. (Proverbs 12:25) . . . God, You comfort us in all our afflictions, so that we can comfort those in any affliction with the comfort we ourselves have received from You. (2 Corinthians 1:4)

PAUSE *to review your relationships with others and to commit them to the Lord.*

YEAR 2 DAY 41

OT Ecclesiastes 4:1-16

Oppression, Toil, Friendlessness

4 Again I looked and saw all the oppression that was taking place under the
sun:

I saw the tears of the oppressed—
and they have no comforter;
power was on the side of their
oppressors—
and they have no comforter.
2 And I declared that the dead,
who had already died,
are happier than the living,
who are still alive.
3 But better than both
is he who has not yet been,
who has not seen the evil
that is done under the sun.

4 And I saw that all labor and all
achievement spring from man's envy of
his neighbor. This too is meaningless, a
chasing after the wind.

5 The fool folds his hands
and ruins himself.
6 Better one handful with tranquillity
than two handfuls with toil
and chasing after the wind.

7 Again I saw something meaningless
under the sun:

8 There was a man all alone;
he had neither son nor brother.
There was no end to his toil,
yet his eyes were not content with
his wealth.
"For whom am I toiling," he asked,
"and why am I depriving myself of
enjoyment?"
This too is meaningless—
a miserable business!

9 Two are better than one,
because they have a good return for
their work:
10 If one falls down,
his friend can help him up.
But pity the man who falls
and has no one to help him up!
11 Also, if two lie down together, they
will keep warm.

But how can one keep warm alone?
[12]Though one may be overpowered,
two can defend themselves.
A cord of three strands is not quickly
broken.

Advancement Is Meaningless

[13]Better a poor but wise youth than an
old but foolish king who no longer knows
how to take warning. [14]The youth may
have come from prison to the kingship, or
he may have been born in poverty within
his kingdom. [15]I saw that all who lived
and walked under the sun followed the
youth, the king's successor. [16]There was no
end to all the people who were before
them. But those who came later were not
pleased with the successor. This too is
meaningless, a chasing after the wind.

PRAYER: THANKSGIVING

LET those who love You, O Lord, hate evil. You preserve the souls of Your saints and deliver them from the hand of the wicked. Light is sown for the righteous and gladness for the upright in heart.
(Psalm 97:10–11)

PAUSE *to offer your own expressions of thanksgiving.*

NT Acts 2:1–41

The Holy Spirit Comes at Pentecost

2 When the day of Pentecost came, they
were all together in one place. [2]Sud-
denly a sound like the blowing of a violent wind came from heaven and filled
the whole house where they were sitting.
[3]They saw what seemed to be tongues of
fire that separated and came to rest on
each of them. [4]All of them were filled with
the Holy Spirit and began to speak in other tongues[a] as the Spirit enabled them.
[5]Now there were staying in Jerusalem
God-fearing Jews from every nation under
heaven. [6]When they heard this sound, a
crowd came together in bewilderment,
because each one heard them speaking in
his own language. [7]Utterly amazed, they
asked: "Are not all these men who are
speaking Galileans? [8]Then how is it that
each of us hears them in his own native
language? [9]Parthians, Medes and Elamites; residents of Mesopotamia, Judea and
Cappadocia, Pontus and Asia, [10]Phrygia
and Pamphylia, Egypt and the parts of
Libya near Cyrene; visitors from Rome
[11](both Jews and converts to Judaism);
Cretans and Arabs—we hear them declaring the wonders of God in our own
tongues!" [12]Amazed and perplexed, they
asked one another, "What does this
mean?"
[13]Some, however, made fun of them
and said, "They have had too much
wine.[b]"

Peter Addresses the Crowd

[14]Then Peter stood up with the Eleven,
raised his voice and addressed the crowd:
"Fellow Jews and all of you who live in
Jerusalem, let me explain this to you; listen carefully to what I say. [15]These men are
not drunk, as you suppose. It's only nine
in the morning! [16]No, this is what was
spoken by the prophet Joel:

[17]" 'In the last days, God says,
I will pour out my Spirit on all
people.
Your sons and daughters will
prophesy,
your young men will see visions,
your old men will dream dreams.
[18]Even on my servants, both men and
women,
I will pour out my Spirit in those
days,
and they will prophesy.
[19]I will show wonders in the heaven
above
and signs on the earth below,
blood and fire and billows of
smoke.
[20]The sun will be turned to darkness
and the moon to blood

[a] 4 Or *languages;* also in verse 11 [b] *13* Or *sweet wine*

before the coming of the great and
glorious day of the Lord.
21 And everyone who calls
on the name of the Lord will be
saved.'[c]

22 "Men of Israel, listen to this: Jesus of
Nazareth was a man accredited by God to
you by miracles, wonders and signs,
which God did among you through him,
as you yourselves know. 23 This man was
handed over to you by God's set purpose
and foreknowledge; and you, with the
help of wicked men,[d] put him to death by
nailing him to the cross. 24 But God raised
him from the dead, freeing him from the
agony of death, because it was impossible
for death to keep its hold on him. 25 David said about him:

" 'I saw the Lord always before me.
Because he is at my right hand,
I will not be shaken.
26 Therefore my heart is glad and my
tongue rejoices;
my body also will live in hope,
27 because you will not abandon me to
the grave,
nor will you let your Holy One see
decay.
28 You have made known to me the
paths of life;
you will fill me with joy in your
presence.'[e]

29 "Brothers, I can tell you confidently
that the patriarch David died and was
buried, and his tomb is here to this day.
30 But he was a prophet and knew that God
had promised him on oath that he would
place one of his descendants on his
throne. 31 Seeing what was ahead, he spoke
of the resurrection of the Christ,[f] that he
was not abandoned to the grave, nor did
his body see decay. 32 God has raised this
Jesus to life, and we are all witnesses of
the fact. 33 Exalted to the right hand of
God, he has received from the Father the
promised Holy Spirit and has poured out
what you now see and hear. 34 For David
did not ascend to heaven, and yet he said,

" 'The Lord said to my Lord:
"Sit at my right hand
35 until I make your enemies
a footstool for your feet." '[g]

36 "Therefore let all Israel be assured of
this: God has made this Jesus, whom you
crucified, both Lord and Christ."
37 When the people heard this, they were
cut to the heart and said to Peter and the
other apostles, "Brothers, what shall
we do?"
38 Peter replied, "Repent and be baptized, every one of you, in the name of
Jesus Christ for the forgiveness of your
sins. And you will receive the gift of the
Holy Spirit. 39 The promise is for you and
your children and for all who are far off—
for all whom the Lord our God will call."
40 With many other words he warned
them; and he pleaded with them, "Save
yourselves from this corrupt generation."
41 Those who accepted his message were
baptized, and about three thousand were
added to their number that day.

[c] 21 Joel 2:28–32 [d] 23 Or *of those not having the law* (that is, Gentiles) [e] 28 Psalm 16:8–11
[f] 31 Or *Messiah.* "The Christ" (Greek) and "the Messiah" (Hebrew) both mean "the Anointed One"; also in verse 36. [g] 35 Psalm 110:1

PRAYER: THE ATTRIBUTES OF GOD

IN my heart I plan my way, but You, O Lord, determine my steps. (Proverbs 16:9) . . . Many are the plans in my heart, but it is Your counsel, O Lord, that will stand. (Proverbs 19:21)

PAUSE *to reflect on these affirmations about the person, powers and perfection of God.*

YEAR 2 DAY 42

OT Psalm 79

Psalm 79

A psalm of Asaph.

1 O God, the nations have invaded your inheritance;
they have defiled your holy temple,
they have reduced Jerusalem to rubble.
2 They have given the dead bodies of your servants
as food to the birds of the air,
the flesh of your saints to the beasts of the earth.
3 They have poured out blood like water
all around Jerusalem,
and there is no one to bury the dead.
4 We are objects of reproach to our neighbors,
of scorn and derision to those around us.

5 How long, O LORD? Will you be angry forever?
How long will your jealousy burn like fire?
6 Pour out your wrath on the nations
that do not acknowledge you,
on the kingdoms
that do not call on your name;
7 for they have devoured Jacob
and destroyed his homeland.
8 Do not hold against us the sins of the fathers;
may your mercy come quickly to meet us,
for we are in desperate need.

9 Help us, O God our Savior,
for the glory of your name;
deliver us and forgive our sins
for your name's sake.
10 Why should the nations say,
"Where is their God?"
Before our eyes, make known among the nations
that you avenge the outpoured blood of your servants.
11 May the groans of the prisoners come before you;
by the strength of your arm
preserve those condemned to die.

12 Pay back into the laps of our neighbors seven times
the reproach they have hurled at you, O Lord.
13 Then we your people, the sheep of your pasture,
will praise you forever;
from generation to generation
we will recount your praise.

PRAYER: ADORATION

WE praise You, the God and Father of our Lord Jesus Christ, for You have blessed us with every spiritual blessing in the heavenly realms in Christ. (Ephesians 1:3) . . . Lord Jesus Christ, You gave Yourself for our sins to rescue us from the present evil age, according to the will of our God and Father, to whom be glory for ever and ever. (Galatians 1:4–5)

PAUSE *to express your thoughts of praise and worship.*

NT Acts 2:42–3:26

The Fellowship of the Believers

42 They devoted themselves to the apostles' teaching and to the fellowship, to the
breaking of bread and to prayer. 43 Everyone was filled with awe, and many wonders and miraculous signs were done by
the apostles. 44 All the believers were together and had everything in common.
45 Selling their possessions and goods, they
gave to anyone as he had need. 46 Every
day they continued to meet together in
the temple courts. They broke bread in
their homes and ate together with glad
and sincere hearts, 47 praising God and en-

joying the favor of all the people. And the
Lord added to their number daily those
who were being saved.

Peter Heals the Crippled Beggar

3 One day Peter and John were going up
to the temple at the time of prayer—at
three in the afternoon. 2Now a man crippled from birth was being carried to the
temple gate called Beautiful, where he was
put every day to beg from those going into
the temple courts. 3When he saw Peter
and John about to enter, he asked them
for money. 4Peter looked straight at him,
as did John. Then Peter said, "Look at us!"
5So the man gave them his attention, expecting to get something from them.
6Then Peter said, "Silver or gold I do not
have, but what I have I give you. In the
name of Jesus Christ of Nazareth, walk."
7Taking him by the right hand, he helped
him up, and instantly the man's feet and
ankles became strong. 8He jumped to his
feet and began to walk. Then he went with
them into the temple courts, walking and
jumping, and praising God. 9When all the
people saw him walking and praising
God, 10they recognized him as the same
man who used to sit begging at the temple gate called Beautiful, and they were
filled with wonder and amazement at
what had happened to him.

Peter Speaks to the Onlookers

11While the beggar held on to Peter and
John, all the people were astonished and
came running to them in the place called
Solomon's Colonnade. 12When Peter saw
this, he said to them: "Men of Israel, why
does this surprise you? Why do you stare
at us as if by our own power or godliness
we had made this man walk? 13The God
of Abraham, Isaac and Jacob, the God of
our fathers, has glorified his servant Jesus.
You handed him over to be killed, and
you disowned him before Pilate, though
he had decided to let him go. 14You disowned the Holy and Righteous One and
asked that a murderer be released to you.
15You killed the author of life, but God
raised him from the dead. We are witnesses of this. 16By faith in the name of
Jesus, this man whom you see and know
was made strong. It is Jesus' name and the
faith that comes through him that has giv-
en this complete healing to him, as you
can all see.
17"Now, brothers, I know that you acted in ignorance, as did your leaders. 18But
this is how God fulfilled what he had
foretold through all the prophets, saying
that his Christ[a] would suffer. 19Repent,
then, and turn to God, so that your sins
may be wiped out, that times of refresh-
ing may come from the Lord, 20and that
he may send the Christ, who has been appointed for you—even Jesus. 21He must
remain in heaven until the time comes for
God to restore everything, as he promised
long ago through his holy prophets. 22For
Moses said, 'The Lord your God will raise
up for you a prophet like me from among
your own people; you must listen to
everything he tells you. 23Anyone who
does not listen to him will be completely
cut off from among his people.'[b]
24"Indeed, all the prophets from Samuel on, as many as have spoken, have foretold these days. 25And you are heirs of the
prophets and of the covenant God made
with your fathers. He said to Abraham,
'Through your offspring all peoples on
earth will be blessed.'[c] 26When God raised
up his servant, he sent him first to you to
bless you by turning each of you from
your wicked ways."

[a] 18 Or *Messiah*; also in verse 20 [b] 23 Deut. 18:15,18,19 [c] 25 Gen. 22:18; 26:4

PRAYER: THE WORKS OF GOD

IN the past, O God, You spoke to our fathers through the prophets at many times and in various ways, but in these last days You have spoken to us by Your Son, whom You appointed heir of all things, and through whom You made the universe. (Hebrews 1:1–2) . . . By faith I understand that the universe was formed by Your word, O God, so that what is seen was not made out of things which are visible. (Hebrews 11:3)

TAKE *a moment to consider the greatness of God's wonderful works.*

OT **Ecclesiastes 5:1–6:12**

YEAR 2 DAY 43

Stand in Awe of God

5 Guard your steps when you go to the
house of God. Go near to listen rather
than to offer the sacrifice of fools, who do
not know that they do wrong.

2 Do not be quick with your mouth,
do not be hasty in your heart
to utter anything before God.
God is in heaven
and you are on earth,
so let your words be few.
3 As a dream comes when there are
many cares,
so the speech of a fool when there
are many words.

4 When you make a vow to God, do not
delay in fulfilling it. He has no pleasure
in fools; fulfill your vow. 5 It is better not
to vow than to make a vow and not fulfill
it. 6 Do not let your mouth lead you into
sin. And do not protest to the ⌞temple⌟
messenger, "My vow was a mistake." Why
should God be angry at what you say and
destroy the work of your hands? 7 Much
dreaming and many words are meaningless. Therefore stand in awe of God.

Riches Are Meaningless

8 If you see the poor oppressed in a district, and justice and rights denied, do not
be surprised at such things; for one official is eyed by a higher one, and over them
both are others higher still. 9 The increase
from the land is taken by all; the king
himself profits from the fields.

10 Whoever loves money never has
money enough;
whoever loves wealth is never
satisfied with his income.
This too is meaningless.

11 As goods increase,
so do those who consume them.
And what benefit are they to the
owner
except to feast his eyes on them?

12 The sleep of a laborer is sweet,
whether he eats little or much,
but the abundance of a rich man
permits him no sleep.

13 I have seen a grievous evil under the
sun:

wealth hoarded to the harm of its
owner,
14 or wealth lost through some
misfortune,
so that when he has a son
there is nothing left for him.
15 Naked a man comes from his
mother's womb,
and as he comes, so he departs.
He takes nothing from his labor
that he can carry in his hand.

16 This too is a grievous evil:

As a man comes, so he departs,
and what does he gain,
since he toils for the wind?
17 All his days he eats in darkness,
with great frustration, affliction and
anger.

18 Then I realized that it is good and
proper for a man to eat and drink, and to
find satisfaction in his toilsome labor under the sun during the few days of life
God has given him—for this is his lot.
19 Moreover, when God gives any man
wealth and possessions, and enables him
to enjoy them, to accept his lot and be
happy in his work—this is a gift of God.
20 He seldom reflects on the days of his life,
because God keeps him occupied with
gladness of heart.

6 I have seen another evil under the sun,
and it weighs heavily on men: 2 God
gives a man wealth, possessions and hon-
or, so that he lacks nothing his heart
desires, but God does not enable him to
enjoy them, and a stranger enjoys them
instead. This is meaningless, a grievous evil.
3 A man may have a hundred children
and live many years; yet no matter how
long he lives, if he cannot enjoy his prosperity and does not receive proper burial,
I say that a stillborn child is better off than
he. 4 It comes without meaning, it departs
in darkness, and in darkness its name is
shrouded. 5 Though it never saw the sun or
knew anything, it has more rest than does
that man— 6 even if he lives a thousand
years twice over but fails to enjoy his prosperity. Do not all go to the same place?

7 All man's efforts are for his mouth,
yet his appetite is never satisfied.
8 What advantage has a wise man
over a fool?
What does a poor man gain
by knowing how to conduct himself
before others?
9 Better what the eye sees
than the roving of the appetite.
This too is meaningless,
a chasing after the wind.

10 Whatever exists has already been
named,
and what man is has been
known;
no man can contend
with one who is stronger than he.
11 The more the words,
the less the meaning,
and how does that profit anyone?

12 For who knows what is good for a
man in life, during the few and meaningless days he passes through like a shadow?
Who can tell him what will happen under
the sun after he is gone?

PRAYER: CONFESSION

BLESSED is the one whose transgression is forgiven, whose sin is covered. Blessed is the one to whom You, O Lord, do not impute iniquity and in whose spirit is no deceit. When I kept silent, my bones wasted away through my groaning all day long. For day and night Your hand was heavy upon me; my strength was sapped as in the heat of summer. I acknowledged my sin to You and did not hide my iniquity. I said, "I will confess my transgressions to the Lord," and You forgave the guilt of my sin.

(Psalm 32:1–5)

ASK *the Spirit to search your heart and reveal any areas of unconfessed sin. Acknowledge these to the Lord and thank Him for His forgiveness.*

NT Acts 4:1–22

Peter and John Before the Sanhedrin

4 The priests and the captain of the temple guard and the Sadducees came up
to Peter and John while they were speaking to the people. 2 They were greatly disturbed because the apostles were teaching
the people and proclaiming in Jesus the
resurrection of the dead. 3 They seized Peter and John, and because it was evening,
they put them in jail until the next day.
4 But many who heard the message believed, and the number of men grew to
about five thousand.
5 The next day the rulers, elders and
teachers of the law met in Jerusalem. 6 Annas the high priest was there, and so were
Caiaphas, John, Alexander and the other
men of the high priest's family. 7 They had
Peter and John brought before them and
began to question them: "By what power
or what name did you do this?"
8 Then Peter, filled with the Holy Spirit,
said to them: "Rulers and elders of the
people! 9 If we are being called to account
today for an act of kindness shown to a
cripple and are asked how he was healed,
10 then know this, you and all the people
of Israel: It is by the name of Jesus Christ
of Nazareth, whom you crucified but
whom God raised from the dead, that this
man stands before you healed. 11 He is

" 'the stone you builders rejected,
which has become the capstone.[a][b]

12 Salvation is found in no one else, for
there is no other name under heaven giv-
en to men by which we must be saved."
13 When they saw the courage of Peter
and John and realized that they were un-
schooled, ordinary men, they were astonished and they took note that these men
had been with Jesus. 14 But since they
could see the man who had been healed
standing there with them, there was nothing they could say. 15 So they ordered them
to withdraw from the Sanhedrin and then
conferred together. 16 "What are we going

[a] 11 Or *cornerstone* [b] 11 Psalm 118:22

to do with these men?" they asked. "Everybody living in Jerusalem knows they have done an outstanding miracle, and we cannot deny it.
[17]But to stop this thing from spreading any further among the people, we must warn these men to speak no longer to anyone in this name."
[18]Then they called them in again and commanded them not to speak or teach at all in the name of Jesus.
[19]But Peter and John replied, "Judge for yourselves whether it is right in God's sight to obey you rather than God.
[20]For we cannot help speaking about what we have seen and heard."
[21]After further threats they let them go. They could not decide how to punish them, because all the people were praising God for what had happened.
[22]For the man who was miraculously healed was over forty years old.

PRAYER: MY RELATIONSHIP TO GOD

TO me, to live is You, O Christ, and to die is gain. (Philippians 1:21) . . . Whatever was gain to me I now consider loss for Your sake, O Christ. What is more, I consider all things loss compared to the surpassing greatness of knowing You as my Lord; for Your sake I suffer the loss of all things and consider them rubbish, that I may gain You and be found in You, not having a righteousness of my own that comes from the law, but that which is through faith in You—the righteousness that comes from God on the basis of faith. (Philippians 3:7–9)

***PAUSE** to thank God for the relationship that you enjoy with Him in Jesus Christ.*

OT Ecclesiastes 7:1–29

YEAR 2 DAY 44

Wisdom

7 A good name is better than fine perfume,
and the day of death better than the day of birth.
[2]It is better to go to a house of mourning
than to go to a house of feasting,
for death is the destiny of every man;
the living should take this to heart.
[3]Sorrow is better than laughter,
because a sad face is good for the heart.
[4]The heart of the wise is in the house of mourning,
but the heart of fools is in the house of pleasure.
[5]It is better to heed a wise man's rebuke
than to listen to the song of fools.
[6]Like the crackling of thorns under the pot,
so is the laughter of fools.
This too is meaningless.

[7]Extortion turns a wise man into a fool,
and a bribe corrupts the heart.

[8]The end of a matter is better than its beginning,
and patience is better than pride.
[9]Do not be quickly provoked in your spirit,
for anger resides in the lap of fools.

[10]Do not say, "Why were the old days better than these?"
For it is not wise to ask such questions.

[11]Wisdom, like an inheritance, is a good thing
and benefits those who see the sun.
[12]Wisdom is a shelter
as money is a shelter,
but the advantage of knowledge is this:
that wisdom preserves the life of its possessor.

[13]Consider what God has done:

Who can straighten
what he has made crooked?

[14]When times are good, be happy;
but when times are bad, consider:
God has made the one
as well as the other.
Therefore, a man cannot discover
anything about his future.

[15]In this meaningless life of mine I have seen both of these:

a righteous man perishing in his righteousness,
and a wicked man living long in his wickedness.
[16]Do not be overrighteous,
neither be overwise—
why destroy yourself?
[17]Do not be overwicked,
and do not be a fool—
why die before your time?
[18]It is good to grasp the one
and not let go of the other.
The man who fears God will avoid all ⌞extremes⌟.[a]

[19]Wisdom makes one wise man more powerful
than ten rulers in a city.

[20]There is not a righteous man on earth
who does what is right and never sins.

[21]Do not pay attention to every word people say,
or you may hear your servant cursing you—
[22]for you know in your heart
that many times you yourself have cursed others.

[23]All this I tested by wisdom and I said,

"I am determined to be wise"—
but this was beyond me.
[24]Whatever wisdom may be,
it is far off and most profound—
who can discover it?
[25]So I turned my mind to understand,
to investigate and to search out
wisdom and the scheme of things
and to understand the stupidity of wickedness
and the madness of folly.

[26]I find more bitter than death
the woman who is a snare,
whose heart is a trap
and whose hands are chains.
The man who pleases God will escape her,
but the sinner she will ensnare.

[27]"Look," says the Teacher,[b] "this is what I have discovered:

"Adding one thing to another to discover the scheme of things—
[28] while I was still searching
but not finding—
I found one ⌞upright⌟ man among a thousand,
but not one ⌞upright⌟ woman among them all.
[29]This only have I found:
God made mankind upright,
but men have gone in search of many schemes."

[a] 18 Or *will follow them both* [b] 27 Or *leader of the assembly*

PRAYER: RENEWAL

MAY I take heed not to practice my righteousness before people, to be seen by them. Otherwise, I will have no reward from You, my Father in heaven. (Matthew 6:1)

***PAUSE** to add your own prayers for personal renewal.*

NT Acts 4:23-37

The Believers' Prayer

[23]On their release, Peter and John went back to their own people and reported all that the chief priests and elders had said to them. [24]When they heard this, they raised their voices together in prayer to God. "Sovereign Lord," they said, "you made the heaven and the earth and the sea, and everything in them. [25]You spoke by the Holy Spirit through the mouth of your servant, our father David:

" 'Why do the nations rage

and the peoples plot in vain?
[26]The kings of the earth take their stand
and the rulers gather together
against the Lord
and against his Anointed One.[a][b]

[27]Indeed Herod and Pontius Pilate met together with the Gentiles and the people[c]
of Israel in this city to conspire against
your holy servant Jesus, whom you
anointed. [28]They did what your power
and will had decided beforehand should
happen. [29]Now, Lord, consider their
threats and enable your servants to speak
your word with great boldness. [30]Stretch
out your hand to heal and perform miraculous signs and wonders through the
name of your holy servant Jesus."

[31]After they prayed, the place where
they were meeting was shaken. And they
were all filled with the Holy Spirit and
spoke the word of God boldly.

The Believers Share Their Possessions

[32]All the believers were one in heart and
mind. No one claimed that any of his possessions was his own, but they shared
everything they had. [33]With great power
the apostles continued to testify to the resurrection of the Lord Jesus, and much
grace was upon them all. [34]There were no
needy persons among them. For from
time to time those who owned lands or
houses sold them, brought the money
from the sales [35]and put it at the apostles'
feet, and it was distributed to anyone as
he had need.

[36]Joseph, a Levite from Cyprus, whom
the apostles called Barnabas (which
means Son of Encouragement), [37]sold a
field he owned and brought the money
and put it at the apostles' feet.

[a] *26* That is, Christ or Messiah [b] *26* Psalm 2:1,2
[c] *27* The Greek is plural.

PRAYER: THE CHARACTER I WANT TO CULTIVATE

I WILL flee from sexual immorality. All other sins people commit are outside their bodies, but sexually immoral people sin against their own bodies. (1 Corinthians 6:18) . . . I will consider the parts of my earthly body as dead to immorality, impurity, passion, evil desires and greed, which is idolatry. Because of these, O God, Your wrath is coming. I used to walk in these ways in the life I once lived. (Colossians 3:5–7)

***TAKE** a moment to ask the Lord for the grace to grow in godly character.*

YEAR 2 DAY 45

OT Ecclesiastes 8:1–17

8 Who is like the wise man?
Who knows the explanation of
things?
Wisdom brightens a man's face
and changes its hard appearance.

Obey the King

[2]Obey the king's command, I say, because you took an oath before God. [3]Do
not be in a hurry to leave the king's presence. Do not stand up for a bad cause, for
he will do whatever he pleases. [4]Since a
king's word is supreme, who can say to
him, "What are you doing?"

[5]Whoever obeys his command will
come to no harm,
and the wise heart will know the
proper time and procedure.
[6]For there is a proper time and
procedure for every matter,
though a man's misery weighs
heavily upon him.

[7]Since no man knows the future,
who can tell him what is to come?
[8]No man has power over the wind to
contain it[a];
so no one has power over the day of
his death.
As no one is discharged in time of war,
so wickedness will not release those
who practice it.

[a] *8* Or *over his spirit to retain it*

9All this I saw, as I applied my mind to
everything done under the sun. There is a
time when a man lords it over others to
his own[b] hurt. 10Then too, I saw the
wicked buried—those who used to come
and go from the holy place and receive
praise[c] in the city where they did this. This
too is meaningless.
11When the sentence for a crime is not
quickly carried out, the hearts of the people are filled with schemes to do wrong.
12Although a wicked man commits a hundred crimes and still lives a long time, I
know that it will go better with God-fearing men, who are reverent before God.
13Yet because the wicked do not fear God,
it will not go well with them, and their
days will not lengthen like a shadow.
14There is something else meaningless
that occurs on earth: righteous men who
get what the wicked deserve, and wicked
men who get what the righteous deserve.
This too, I say, is meaningless. 15So I commend the enjoyment of life, because
nothing is better for a man under the sun
than to eat and drink and be glad. Then
joy will accompany him in his work all
the days of the life God has given him under the sun.
16When I applied my mind to know
wisdom and to observe man's labor on
earth—his eyes not seeing sleep day or
night— 17then I saw all that God has
done. No one can comprehend what goes
on under the sun. Despite all his efforts
to search it out, man cannot discover its
meaning. Even if a wise man claims he
knows, he cannot really comprehend it.

[b] *9* Or *to their* [c] *10* Some Hebrew manuscripts and Septuagint (Aquila); most Hebrew manuscripts *and are forgotten*

PRAYER: PETITION

In You, O Lord, I have taken refuge; let me never be ashamed; deliver me in Your righteousness. Since You are my rock and my fortress, for Your name's sake lead me and guide me. Into Your hands I commit my spirit; redeem me, O Lord God of truth. (Psalm 31:1, 3, 5)

PAUSE *here to petition God for spiritual insight so that you might have understanding of His Word. Ask for insight into your identity in Jesus Christ: that you might know who you are, what direction your life should take and what His purpose for your life is. Offer prayers regarding your activities for this day and any special concerns you may have.*

NT Acts 5:1-16

Ananias and Sapphira

5 Now a man named Ananias, together
with his wife Sapphira, also sold a
piece of property. 2With his wife's full
knowledge he kept back part of the money for himself, but brought the rest and
put it at the apostles' feet.
3Then Peter said, "Ananias, how is it
that Satan has so filled your heart that you
have lied to the Holy Spirit and have kept
for yourself some of the money you received for the land? 4Didn't it belong to
you before it was sold? And after it was
sold, wasn't the money at your disposal?
What made you think of doing such a
thing? You have not lied to men but to
God."
5When Ananias heard this, he fell down
and died. And great fear seized all who
heard what had happened. 6Then the
young men came forward, wrapped up his
body, and carried him out and buried
him.
7About three hours later his wife came
in, not knowing what had happened. 8Pe-
ter asked her, "Tell me, is this the price
you and Ananias got for the land?"
"Yes," she said, "that is the price."
9Peter said to her, "How could you
agree to test the Spirit of the Lord? Look!
The feet of the men who buried your husband are at the door, and they will carry
you out also."
10At that moment she fell down at his
feet and died. Then the young men came
in and, finding her dead, carried her out
and buried her beside her husband.

[11]Great fear seized the whole church and
all who heard about these events.

The Apostles Heal Many

[12]The apostles performed many miraculous signs and wonders among the people. And all the believers used to meet
together in Solomon's Colonnade. [13]No
one else dared join them, even though
they were highly regarded by the people.
[14]Nevertheless, more and more men and
women believed in the Lord and were
added to their number. [15]As a result, people brought the sick into the streets and
laid them on beds and mats so that at
least Peter's shadow might fall on some of
them as he passed by. [16]Crowds gathered
also from the towns around Jerusalem,
bringing their sick and those tormented
by evil[a] spirits, and all of them were
healed.

[a] 16 Greek *unclean*

PRAYER: MY RELATIONSHIP TO OTHERS

IF we have any encouragement from being united with You, O Christ, if any comfort from Your love, if any fellowship of the Spirit, if any affection and compassion, we should also be like-minded, having the same love, being one in spirit and one in purpose. (Philippians 2:1–2) . . . We should all be of one mind and be sympathetic, loving as brothers and sisters, compassionate and humble. (1 Peter 3:8)

PAUSE *to review your relationships with others and to commit them to the Lord.*

YEAR 2 DAY 46

OT Proverbs 18

18 An unfriendly man pursues selfish ends;
he defies all sound judgment.

[2]A fool finds no pleasure in understanding
but delights in airing his own opinions.

[3]When wickedness comes, so does contempt,
and with shame comes disgrace.

[4]The words of a man's mouth are deep waters,
but the fountain of wisdom is a bubbling brook.

[5]It is not good to be partial to the wicked
or to deprive the innocent of justice.

[6]A fool's lips bring him strife,
and his mouth invites a beating.

[7]A fool's mouth is his undoing,
and his lips are a snare to his soul.

[8]The words of a gossip are like choice morsels;
they go down to a man's inmost parts.

[9]One who is slack in his work
is brother to one who destroys.

[10]The name of the LORD is a strong tower;
the righteous run to it and are safe.

[11]The wealth of the rich is their fortified city;
they imagine it an unscalable wall.

[12]Before his downfall a man's heart is proud,
but humility comes before honor.

[13]He who answers before listening—
that is his folly and his shame.

[14]A man's spirit sustains him in sickness,
but a crushed spirit who can bear?

[15]The heart of the discerning acquires knowledge;
the ears of the wise seek it out.

[16]A gift opens the way for the giver

and ushers him into the presence of
the great.

17 The first to present his case seems
right,
till another comes forward and
questions him.

18 Casting the lot settles disputes
and keeps strong opponents apart.

19 An offended brother is more
unyielding than a fortified city,
and disputes are like the barred
gates of a citadel.

20 From the fruit of his mouth a man's
stomach is filled;
with the harvest from his lips he is
satisfied.

21 The tongue has the power of life and
death,
and those who love it will eat its
fruit.

22 He who finds a wife finds what is good
and receives favor from the LORD.

23 A poor man pleads for mercy,
but a rich man answers harshly.

24 A man of many companions may
come to ruin,
but there is a friend who sticks
closer than a brother.

PRAYER: INTERCESSION

JESUS, You have given us a new commandment: to love one another. Even as You have loved us, so we must love one another. By this all people will know that we are Your disciples, if we have love for one another. (John 13:34)

***TAKE** a few moments to intercede on behalf of other believers, such as your personal friends, those in ministry and those who are oppressed and in need.*

NT Acts 5:17-42

The Apostles Persecuted

17 Then the high priest and all his associates, who were members of the party of
the Sadducees, were filled with jealousy.
18 They arrested the apostles and put them
in the public jail. 19 But during the night
an angel of the Lord opened the doors of
the jail and brought them out. 20 "Go,
stand in the temple courts," he said, "and
tell the people the full message of this
new life."

21 At daybreak they entered the temple
courts, as they had been told, and began
to teach the people.

When the high priest and his associates
arrived, they called together the Sanhedrin—the full assembly of the elders of
Israel—and sent to the jail for the apostles. 22 But on arriving at the jail, the officers did not find them there. So they went
back and reported, 23 "We found the jail
securely locked, with the guards standing
at the doors; but when we opened them,
we found no one inside." 24 On hearing
this report, the captain of the temple
guard and the chief priests were puzzled,
wondering what would come of this.

25 Then someone came and said, "Look!
The men you put in jail are standing in
the temple courts teaching the people."
26 At that, the captain went with his officers and brought the apostles. They did
not use force, because they feared that the
people would stone them.

27 Having brought the apostles, they
made them appear before the Sanhedrin
to be questioned by the high priest. 28 "We
gave you strict orders not to teach in this
name," he said. "Yet you have filled Jerusalem with your teaching and are determined to make us guilty of this man's
blood."

29 Peter and the other apostles replied:
"We must obey God rather than men!
30 The God of our fathers raised Jesus from
the dead—whom you had killed by hanging him on a tree. 31 God exalted him to
his own right hand as Prince and Savior
that he might give repentance and forgiveness of sins to Israel. 32 We are wit-

nesses of these things, and so is the Holy
Spirit, whom God has given to those who
obey him."
33When they heard this, they were furious and wanted to put them to death.
34But a Pharisee named Gamaliel, a
teacher of the law, who was honored by
all the people, stood up in the Sanhedrin
and ordered that the men be put outside
for a little while. 35Then he addressed
them: "Men of Israel, consider carefully
what you intend to do to these men.
36Some time ago Theudas appeared,
claiming to be somebody, and about four
hundred men rallied to him. He was
killed, all his followers were dispersed,
and it all came to nothing. 37After him, Judas the Galilean appeared in the days of
the census and led a band of people in revolt. He too was killed, and all his followers were scattered. 38Therefore, in the
present case I advise you: Leave these men
alone! Let them go! For if their purpose
or activity is of human origin, it will fail.
39But if it is from God, you will not be
able to stop these men; you will only find
yourselves fighting against God."
40His speech persuaded them. They
called the apostles in and had them
flogged. Then they ordered them not to
speak in the name of Jesus, and let
them go.
41The apostles left the Sanhedrin, rejoicing because they had been counted
worthy of suffering disgrace for the Name.
42Day after day, in the temple courts and
from house to house, they never stopped
teaching and proclaiming the good news
that Jesus is the Christ.[a]

[a] 42 Or *Messiah*

PRAYER: THE ATTRIBUTES OF GOD

YOUR merciful love is higher than the heavens, O Lord, and Your truth reaches to the skies. (Psalm 108:4) . . . I will give thanks to You, the God of heaven, for Your merciful love endures forever. (Psalm 136:26)

PAUSE *to reflect on these affirmations about the person, powers and perfection of God.*

OT Ecclesiastes 9:1–18 YEAR 2 DAY 47

A Common Destiny for All

9 So I reflected on all this and concluded
that the righteous and the wise and
what they do are in God's hands, but no
man knows whether love or hate awaits
him. 2All share a common destiny—the
righteous and the wicked, the good and
the bad,[a] the clean and the unclean, those
who offer sacrifices and those who do not.

As it is with the good man,
so with the sinner;
as it is with those who take oaths,
so with those who are afraid to take
them.

3This is the evil in everything that happens under the sun: The same destiny
overtakes all. The hearts of men, moreover, are full of evil and there is madness
in their hearts while they live, and afterward they join the dead. 4Anyone who is
among the living has hope[b]—even a live
dog is better off than a dead lion!

5For the living know that they will die,
but the dead know nothing;
they have no further reward,
and even the memory of them is
forgotten.
6Their love, their hate
and their jealousy have long since
vanished;
never again will they have a part
in anything that happens under the
sun.

7Go, eat your food with gladness, and

[a] 2 Septuagint (Aquila), Vulgate and Syriac; Hebrew does not have *and the bad.* [b] 4 Or *What then is to be chosen? With all who live, there is hope*

drink your wine with a joyful heart, for it
is now that God favors what you do. 8Al-
ways be clothed in white, and always
anoint your head with oil. 9Enjoy life with
your wife, whom you love, all the days of
this meaningless life that God has given
you under the sun— all your meaningless
days. For this is your lot in life and in your
toilsome labor under the sun. 10Whatever
your hand finds to do, do it with all your
might, for in the grave,[c] where you are going, there is neither working nor planning
nor knowledge nor wisdom.

11I have seen something else under the
sun:

The race is not to the swift
  or the battle to the strong,
nor does food come to the wise
  or wealth to the brilliant
  or favor to the learned;
but time and chance happen to them
    all.

12Moreover, no man knows when his
hour will come:

As fish are caught in a cruel net,
  or birds are taken in a snare,
so men are trapped by evil times
  that fall unexpectedly upon them.

Wisdom Better Than Folly

13I also saw under the sun this example
of wisdom that greatly impressed me:
14There was once a small city with only a
few people in it. And a powerful king
came against it, surrounded it and built
huge siegeworks against it. 15Now there
lived in that city a man poor but wise, and
he saved the city by his wisdom. But nobody remembered that poor man. 16So I
said, "Wisdom is better than strength."
But the poor man's wisdom is despised,
and his words are no longer heeded.

17The quiet words of the wise are more
    to be heeded
  than the shouts of a ruler of fools.
18Wisdom is better than weapons of war,
  but one sinner destroys much good.

[c] *10* Hebrew *Sheol*

PRAYER: AFFIRMATION

MULTITUDES who sleep in the dust of the earth will awake, some to everlasting life, others to shame and everlasting contempt. Those who are wise will shine like the brightness of the heavens, and those who lead many to righteousness will be like the stars for ever and ever. (Daniel 12:2–3) . . . An hour is coming when all who are in the graves will hear Your voice, O Son of Man, and will come out— those who have done good will rise to a resurrection of life, and those who have done evil will rise to a resurrection of judgment. (John 5:28–29)

PAUSE *to reflect on these Biblical affirmations.*

NT Acts 6:1–15

The Choosing of the Seven

6 In those days when the number of disciples was increasing, the Grecian Jews
among them complained against the Hebraic Jews because their widows were being overlooked in the daily distribution of
food. 2So the Twelve gathered all the disciples together and said, "It would not be
right for us to neglect the ministry of the
word of God in order to wait on tables.
3Brothers, choose seven men from among
you who are known to be full of the Spirit and wisdom. We will turn this responsibility over to them 4and will give our attention to prayer and the ministry of the
word."

5This proposal pleased the whole
group. They chose Stephen, a man full of
faith and of the Holy Spirit; also Philip,
Procorus, Nicanor, Timon, Parmenas, and
Nicolas from Antioch, a convert to Judaism. 6They presented these men to the
apostles, who prayed and laid their hands
on them.

7So the word of God spread. The number of disciples in Jerusalem increased

rapidly, and a large number of priests became obedient to the faith.

Stephen Seized

8Now Stephen, a man full of God's
grace and power, did great wonders and
miraculous signs among the people. 9Op-
position arose, however, from members of
the Synagogue of the Freedmen (as it was
called)—Jews of Cyrene and Alexandria as
well as the provinces of Cilicia and Asia.
These men began to argue with Stephen,
10but they could not stand up against his
wisdom or the Spirit by whom he spoke.
11Then they secretly persuaded some
men to say, "We have heard Stephen speak
words of blasphemy against Moses and
against God."
12So they stirred up the people and the
elders and the teachers of the law. They
seized Stephen and brought him before
the Sanhedrin. 13They produced false witnesses, who testified, "This fellow never
stops speaking against this holy place and
against the law. 14For we have heard him
say that this Jesus of Nazareth will destroy
this place and change the customs Moses
handed down to us."
15All who were sitting in the Sanhedrin
looked intently at Stephen, and they saw
that his face was like the face of an angel.

PRAYER: THE WORKS OF GOD

***I PRAISE** You, Father, Lord of heaven and earth, because You have hidden these things from the wise and learned, and revealed them to little children. Yes, Father, for this was well pleasing in Your sight. You have delivered all things to Your Son Jesus. No one knows the Son except You, Father, and no one knows You except the Son and those to whom the Son chooses to reveal You. (Matthew 11:25–27; Luke 10:21–22)*

***TAKE** a moment to consider the greatness of God's wonderful works.*

OT Ecclesiastes 10:1–20

YEAR 2 DAY 48

10 As dead flies give perfume a bad
smell,
so a little folly outweighs wisdom
and honor.
2The heart of the wise inclines to the
right,
but the heart of the fool to the left.
3Even as he walks along the road,
the fool lacks sense
and shows everyone how stupid he
is.
4If a ruler's anger rises against you,
do not leave your post;
calmness can lay great errors to rest.

5There is an evil I have seen under the
sun,
the sort of error that arises from a
ruler:
6Fools are put in many high positions,
while the rich occupy the low ones.
7I have seen slaves on horseback,
while princes go on foot like slaves.

8Whoever digs a pit may fall into it;
whoever breaks through a wall may
be bitten by a snake.
9Whoever quarries stones may be
injured by them;
whoever splits logs may be
endangered by them.

10If the ax is dull
and its edge unsharpened,
more strength is needed
but skill will bring success.

11If a snake bites before it is charmed,
there is no profit for the charmer.

12Words from a wise man's mouth are
gracious,
but a fool is consumed by his own
lips.
13At the beginning his words are folly;
at the end they are wicked
madness—
14 and the fool multiplies words.

No one knows what is coming—
who can tell him what will happen
after him?

[15] A fool's work wearies him;
he does not know the way to town.

[16] Woe to you, O land whose king was a
servant[a]
and whose princes feast in the
morning.
[17] Blessed are you, O land whose king is
of noble birth
and whose princes eat at a proper
time—
for strength and not for
drunkenness.

[18] If a man is lazy, the rafters sag;
if his hands are idle, the house
leaks.

[19] A feast is made for laughter,
and wine makes life merry,
but money is the answer for
everything.

[20] Do not revile the king even in your
thoughts,
or curse the rich in your bedroom,
because a bird of the air may carry
your words,
and a bird on the wing may report
what you say.

[a] 16 Or *king is a child*

PRAYER: THANKSGIVING

WE give thanks to You, Lord, and call upon Your name; we make Your deeds known among the nations. We sing to You, sing praises to You; we tell of all Your wonders. We glory in Your holy name; let the hearts of those who seek You, O Lord, rejoice. (Psalm 105:1–3)

***PAUSE** to offer your own expressions of thanksgiving.*

NT Acts 7:1–53

Stephen's Speech to the Sanhedrin

7 Then the high priest asked him, "Are
these charges true?"
[2] To this he replied: "Brothers and fathers, listen to me! The God of glory appeared to our father Abraham while he
was still in Mesopotamia, before he lived
in Haran. [3] 'Leave your country and your
people,' God said, 'and go to the land I
will show you.'[a]
[4] "So he left the land of the Chaldeans
and settled in Haran. After the death of
his father, God sent him to this land
where you are now living. [5] He gave him
no inheritance here, not even a foot of
ground. But God promised him that he
and his descendants after him would possess the land, even though at that time
Abraham had no child. [6] God spoke to
him in this way: 'Your descendants will be
strangers in a country not their own, and
they will be enslaved and mistreated four
hundred years. [7] But I will punish the nation they serve as slaves,' God said, 'and
afterward they will come out of that country and worship me in this place.'[b] [8] Then
he gave Abraham the covenant of circumcision. And Abraham became the father of
Isaac and circumcised him eight days after his birth. Later Isaac became the father
of Jacob, and Jacob became the father of
the twelve patriarchs.
[9] "Because the patriarchs were jealous of
Joseph, they sold him as a slave into
Egypt. But God was with him [10] and rescued him from all his troubles. He gave
Joseph wisdom and enabled him to gain
the goodwill of Pharaoh king of Egypt; so
he made him ruler over Egypt and all his
palace.
[11] "Then a famine struck all Egypt and
Canaan, bringing great suffering, and our
fathers could not find food. [12] When Jacob
heard that there was grain in Egypt, he
sent our fathers on their first visit. [13] On
their second visit, Joseph told his brothers who he was, and Pharaoh learned
about Joseph's family. [14] After this, Joseph
sent for his father Jacob and his whole
family, seventy-five in all. [15] Then Jacob
went down to Egypt, where he and our fathers died. [16] Their bodies were brought
back to Shechem and placed in the tomb

[a] 3 Gen. 12:1 [b] 7 Gen. 15:13,14

that Abraham had bought from the sons of Hamor at Shechem for a certain sum of money.

[17]"As the time drew near for God to fulfill his promise to Abraham, the number of our people in Egypt greatly increased. [18]Then another king, who knew nothing about Joseph, became ruler of Egypt. [19]He dealt treacherously with our people and oppressed our forefathers by forcing them to throw out their newborn babies so that they would die.

[20]"At that time Moses was born, and he was no ordinary child.[c] For three months he was cared for in his father's house. [21]When he was placed outside, Pharaoh's daughter took him and brought him up as her own son. [22]Moses was educated in all the wisdom of the Egyptians and was powerful in speech and action.

[23]"When Moses was forty years old, he decided to visit his fellow Israelites. [24]He saw one of them being mistreated by an Egyptian, so he went to his defense and avenged him by killing the Egyptian. [25]Moses thought that his own people would realize that God was using him to rescue them, but they did not. [26]The next day Moses came upon two Israelites who were fighting. He tried to reconcile them by saying, 'Men, you are brothers; why do you want to hurt each other?'

[27]"But the man who was mistreating the other pushed Moses aside and said, 'Who made you ruler and judge over us? [28]Do you want to kill me as you killed the Egyptian yesterday?'[d] [29]When Moses heard this, he fled to Midian, where he settled as a foreigner and had two sons.

[30]"After forty years had passed, an angel appeared to Moses in the flames of a burning bush in the desert near Mount Sinai. [31]When he saw this, he was amazed at the sight. As he went over to look more closely, he heard the Lord's voice: [32]'I am the God of your fathers, the God of Abraham, Isaac and Jacob.'[e] Moses trembled with fear and did not dare to look.

[33]"Then the Lord said to him, 'Take off your sandals; the place where you are standing is holy ground. [34]I have indeed seen the oppression of my people in Egypt. I have heard their groaning and have come down to set them free. Now come, I will send you back to Egypt.'[f]

[35]"This is the same Moses whom they had rejected with the words, 'Who made you ruler and judge?' He was sent to be their ruler and deliverer by God himself, through the angel who appeared to him in the bush. [36]He led them out of Egypt and did wonders and miraculous signs in Egypt, at the Red Sea[g] and for forty years in the desert.

[37]"This is that Moses who told the Israelites, 'God will send you a prophet like me from your own people.'[h] [38]He was in the assembly in the desert, with the angel who spoke to him on Mount Sinai, and with our fathers; and he received living words to pass on to us.

[39]"But our fathers refused to obey him. Instead, they rejected him and in their hearts turned back to Egypt. [40]They told Aaron, 'Make us gods who will go before us. As for this fellow Moses who led us out of Egypt—we don't know what has happened to him!'[i] [41]That was the time they made an idol in the form of a calf. They brought sacrifices to it and held a celebration in honor of what their hands had made. [42]But God turned away and gave them over to the worship of the heavenly bodies. This agrees with what is written in the book of the prophets:

" 'Did you bring me sacrifices and
offerings
forty years in the desert, O house of
Israel?
[43]You have lifted up the shrine of Molech
and the star of your god Rephan,
the idols you made to worship.
Therefore I will send you into exile'[j]
beyond Babylon.

[44]"Our forefathers had the tabernacle of the Testimony with them in the desert. It had been made as God directed Moses, according to the pattern he had seen. [45]Having received the tabernacle, our fathers under Joshua brought it with them when they took the land from the nations God drove out before them. It remained in the land until the time of David, [46]who enjoyed God's favor and asked that he might provide a dwelling place for the God of Jacob.[k] [47]But it was Solomon who built the house for him.

[48]"However, the Most High does not live in houses made by men. As the prophet says:

[c] *20* Or *was fair in the sight of God* [d] *28* Exodus 2:14 [e] *32* Exodus 3:6 [f] *34* Exodus 3:5,7,8,10 [g] *36* That is, Sea of Reeds [h] *37* Deut. 18:15

[49] " 'Heaven is my throne,
and the earth is my footstool.
What kind of house will you build for me?
says the Lord.
Or where will my resting place be?
[50] Has not my hand made all these things?'[l]

[51] "You stiff-necked people, with uncircumcised hearts and ears! You are just like
your fathers: You always resist the Holy
Spirit! [52] Was there ever a prophet your fathers did not persecute? They even killed
those who predicted the coming of the
Righteous One. And now you have betrayed and murdered him— [53] you who
have received the law that was put into
effect through angels but have not
obeyed it."

[i] *40* Exodus 32:1 [j] *43* Amos 5:25–27
[k] *46* Some early manuscripts *the house of Jacob*
[l] *50* Isaiah 66:1,2

PRAYER: MY RELATIONSHIP TO GOD

JESUS, I believe that You are the Christ, the Son of God, and that by believing I have life in Your name. (John 20:31) . . . If I confess You with my mouth, Lord Jesus, and believe in my heart that God raised You from the dead, I will be saved. For it is with my heart that I believe unto righteousness, and it is with my mouth that I confess unto salvation. As the Scripture says, "Whoever trusts in Him will not be put to shame." (Romans 10:9–11)

PAUSE *to thank God for the relationship that you enjoy with Him in Jesus Christ.*

YEAR 2 DAY 49

OT **Psalm 80**

Psalm 80

For the director of music. To ⌞the tune of⌟ "The Lilies of the Covenant." Of Asaph. A psalm.

[1] Hear us, O Shepherd of Israel,
you who lead Joseph like a flock;
you who sit enthroned between the cherubim, shine forth
[2] before Ephraim, Benjamin and Manasseh.
Awaken your might;
come and save us.

[3] Restore us, O God;
make your face shine upon us,
that we may be saved.

[4] O LORD God Almighty,
how long will your anger smolder
against the prayers of your people?
[5] You have fed them with the bread of tears;
you have made them drink tears by the bowlful.
[6] You have made us a source of contention to our neighbors,
and our enemies mock us.

[7] Restore us, O God Almighty;
make your face shine upon us,
that we may be saved.

[8] You brought a vine out of Egypt;
you drove out the nations and planted it.
[9] You cleared the ground for it,
and it took root and filled the land.
[10] The mountains were covered with its shade,
the mighty cedars with its branches.
[11] It sent out its boughs to the Sea,[a]
its shoots as far as the River.[b]

[12] Why have you broken down its walls
so that all who pass by pick its grapes?
[13] Boars from the forest ravage it
and the creatures of the field feed on it.

[a] *11* Probably the Mediterranean [b] *11* That is, the Euphrates

[14] Return to us, O God Almighty!
Look down from heaven and see!
Watch over this vine,
[15] the root your right hand has planted,
the son[c] you have raised up for yourself.

[16] Your vine is cut down, it is burned with fire;
at your rebuke your people perish.
[17] Let your hand rest on the man at your right hand,
the son of man you have raised up for yourself.
[18] Then we will not turn away from you;
revive us, and we will call on your name.

[19] Restore us, O LORD God Almighty;
make your face shine upon us,
that we may be saved.

[c] 15 Or *branch*

PRAYER: ADORATION

HOW lovely are Your dwellings, O Lord of hosts! My soul longs and even faints for Your courts; my heart and my flesh cry out for You, the living God. (Psalm 84:1–2) . . . Your righteousness, O God, reaches to the heavens; You have done great things. O God, who is like You? (Psalm 71:19)

PAUSE *to express your thoughts of praise and worship.*

NT Acts 7:54–8:8

The Stoning of Stephen

[54]When they heard this, they were furious
and gnashed their teeth at him. [55]But Stephen, full of the Holy Spirit, looked up to
heaven and saw the glory of God, and Jesus
standing at the right hand of God. [56]"Look,"
he said, "I see heaven open and the Son of
Man standing at the right hand of God."
[57]At this they covered their ears and,
yelling at the top of their voices, they all
rushed at him, [58]dragged him out of the
city and began to stone him. Meanwhile,
the witnesses laid their clothes at the feet
of a young man named Saul.
[59]While they were stoning him, Stephen
prayed, "Lord Jesus, receive my spirit."
[60]Then he fell on his knees and cried out,
"Lord, do not hold this sin against them."
When he had said this, he fell asleep.
8 And Saul was there, giving approval to
his death.

The Church Persecuted and Scattered

On that day a great persecution broke
out against the church at Jerusalem, and all
except the apostles were scattered throughout Judea and Samaria. [2]Godly men buried
Stephen and mourned deeply for him.
[3]But Saul began to destroy the church. Going from house to house, he dragged off
men and women and put them in prison.

Philip in Samaria

[4]Those who had been scattered
preached the word wherever they went.
[5]Philip went down to a city in Samaria
and proclaimed the Christ[a] there. [6]When
the crowds heard Philip and saw the
miraculous signs he did, they all paid
close attention to what he said. [7]With
shrieks, evil[b] spirits came out of many,
and many paralytics and cripples were
healed. [8]So there was great joy in that city.

[a] 5 Or *Messiah* [b] 7 Greek *unclean*

PRAYER: THE CHARACTER I WANT TO CULTIVATE

LET those who think they stand take heed lest they fall. (1 Corinthians 10:12) . . . I do not dare to classify or compare myself with other people, for it is unwise to measure or compare myself with others. I will not boast beyond proper limits but within the

sphere of Your gospel, O Christ. "Let those who boast, boast in the Lord." For it is not those who commend themselves who are approved, but those whom You commend, Lord. (2 Corinthians 10:12–14, 17–18)

TAKE *a moment to ask the Lord for the grace to grow in godly character.*

YEAR 2
DAY 50

OT Ecclesiastes 11:1-10

Bread Upon the Waters

11 Cast your bread upon the waters,
for after many days you will find it again.
2 Give portions to seven, yes to eight,
for you do not know what disaster may come upon the land.

3 If clouds are full of water,
they pour rain upon the earth.
Whether a tree falls to the south or to the north,
in the place where it falls, there will it lie.
4 Whoever watches the wind will not plant;
whoever looks at the clouds will not reap.

5 As you do not know the path of the wind,
or how the body is formed[a] in a mother's womb,
so you cannot understand the work of God,
the Maker of all things.

6 Sow your seed in the morning,
and at evening let not your hands be idle,
for you do not know which will succeed,
whether this or that,
or whether both will do equally well.

Remember Your Creator While Young

7 Light is sweet,
and it pleases the eyes to see the sun.
8 However many years a man may live,
let him enjoy them all.
But let him remember the days of darkness,
for they will be many.
Everything to come is meaningless.

9 Be happy, young man, while you are young,
and let your heart give you joy in the days of your youth.
Follow the ways of your heart
and whatever your eyes see,
but know that for all these things
God will bring you to judgment.
10 So then, banish anxiety from your heart
and cast off the troubles of your body,
for youth and vigor are meaningless.

[a] 5 Or *know how life* (or *the spirit*) / *enters the body being formed*

PRAYER: CONFESSION

DO You, O God, not see my ways and count all my steps? (Job 31:4)

ASK *the Spirit to search your heart and reveal any areas of unconfessed sin. Acknowledge these to the Lord and thank Him for His forgiveness.*

NT Acts 8:9-40

Simon the Sorcerer

9 Now for some time a man named Simon had practiced sorcery in the city and
amazed all the people of Samaria. He
boasted that he was someone great, 10 and
all the people, both high and low, gave
him their attention and exclaimed, "This
man is the divine power known as the

Great Power." 11They followed him because he had amazed them for a long time with his magic. 12But when they believed Philip as he preached the good news of the kingdom of God and the name of Jesus Christ, they were baptized, both men and women. 13Simon himself believed and was baptized. And he followed Philip everywhere, astonished by the great signs and miracles he saw.

14When the apostles in Jerusalem heard that Samaria had accepted the word of God, they sent Peter and John to them. 15When they arrived, they prayed for them that they might receive the Holy Spirit, 16because the Holy Spirit had not yet come upon any of them; they had simply been baptized into[a] the name of the Lord Jesus. 17Then Peter and John placed their hands on them, and they received the Holy Spirit.

18When Simon saw that the Spirit was given at the laying on of the apostles' hands, he offered them money 19and said, "Give me also this ability so that everyone on whom I lay my hands may receive the Holy Spirit."

20Peter answered: "May your money perish with you, because you thought you could buy the gift of God with money! 21You have no part or share in this ministry, because your heart is not right before God. 22Repent of this wickedness and pray to the Lord. Perhaps he will forgive you for having such a thought in your heart. 23For I see that you are full of bitterness and captive to sin."

24Then Simon answered, "Pray to the Lord for me so that nothing you have said may happen to me."

25When they had testified and proclaimed the word of the Lord, Peter and John returned to Jerusalem, preaching the gospel in many Samaritan villages.

Philip and the Ethiopian

26Now an angel of the Lord said to Philip, "Go south to the road—the desert road—that goes down from Jerusalem to Gaza." 27So he started out, and on his way he met an Ethiopian[b] eunuch, an important official in charge of all the treasury of Candace, queen of the Ethiopians. This man had gone to Jerusalem to worship, 28and on his way home was sitting in his chariot reading the book of Isaiah the prophet. 29The Spirit told Philip, "Go to that chariot and stay near it."

30Then Philip ran up to the chariot and heard the man reading Isaiah the prophet. "Do you understand what you are reading?" Philip asked.

31"How can I," he said, "unless someone explains it to me?" So he invited Philip to come up and sit with him.

32The eunuch was reading this passage of Scripture:

"He was led like a sheep to the slaughter,
  and as a lamb before the shearer is silent,
  so he did not open his mouth.
33In his humiliation he was deprived of justice.
  Who can speak of his descendants?
  For his life was taken from the earth."[c]

34The eunuch asked Philip, "Tell me, please, who is the prophet talking about, himself or someone else?" 35Then Philip began with that very passage of Scripture and told him the good news about Jesus.

36As they traveled along the road, they came to some water and the eunuch said, "Look, here is water. Why shouldn't I be baptized?"[d] 38And he gave orders to stop the chariot. Then both Philip and the eunuch went down into the water and Philip baptized him. 39When they came up out of the water, the Spirit of the Lord suddenly took Philip away, and the eunuch did not see him again, but went on his way rejoicing. 40Philip, however, appeared at Azotus and traveled about, preaching the gospel in all the towns until he reached Caesarea.

[a] *16* Or *in* [b] *27* That is, from the upper Nile region [c] *33* Isaiah 53:7,8 [d] *36* Some late manuscripts *baptized?" 37Philip said, "If you believe with all your heart, you may." The eunuch answered, "I believe that Jesus Christ is the Son of God."*

PRAYER: MY RELATIONSHIP TO OTHERS

I WILL remind others to be subject to rulers and authorities, to be obedient, to be ready for every good work, to slander no one, to be peaceable and gentle, and to show true humility toward all

people. (Titus 3:1–2) . . . Young men should be submissive to those who are older, and all of us should clothe ourselves with humility toward one another, for You, O God, "oppose the proud but give grace to the humble." (1 Peter 5:5)

***PAUSE** to review your relationships with others and to commit them to the Lord.*

YEAR 2
DAY 51

OT Ecclesiastes 12:1-14

12 Remember your Creator
in the days of your youth,
before the days of trouble come
and the years approach when you will say,
"I find no pleasure in them"—
2 before the sun and the light
and the moon and the stars grow dark,
and the clouds return after the rain;
3 when the keepers of the house tremble,
and the strong men stoop,
when the grinders cease because they are few,
and those looking through the windows grow dim;
4 when the doors to the street are closed
and the sound of grinding fades;
when men rise up at the sound of birds,
but all their songs grow faint;
5 when men are afraid of heights
and of dangers in the streets;
when the almond tree blossoms
and the grasshopper drags himself along
and desire no longer is stirred.
Then man goes to his eternal home
and mourners go about the streets.

6 Remember him—before the silver cord is severed,
or the golden bowl is broken;
before the pitcher is shattered at the spring,
or the wheel broken at the well,
7 and the dust returns to the ground it came from,
and the spirit returns to God who gave it.

8 "Meaningless! Meaningless!" says the Teacher.[a]
"Everything is meaningless!"

The Conclusion of the Matter

9 Not only was the Teacher wise, but
also he imparted knowledge to the people. He pondered and searched out and
set in order many proverbs. 10 The Teacher
searched to find just the right words, and
what he wrote was upright and true.
11 The words of the wise are like goads,
their collected sayings like firmly embed-
ded nails—given by one Shepherd. 12 Be
warned, my son, of anything in addition
to them.
Of making many books there is no end, and much study wearies the body.

13 Now all has been heard;
here is the conclusion of the matter:
Fear God and keep his commandments,
for this is the whole ⌞duty⌟ of man.
14 For God will bring every deed into judgment,
including every hidden thing,
whether it is good or evil.

[a] 8 Or *the leader of the assembly;* also in verses 9 and 10

PRAYER: RENEWAL

THE hour has come for me to wake up from sleep, for my salvation is nearer now than when I first believed. The night is nearly over; the day is almost here. Therefore may I cast off the works of darkness and put on the armor of light. (Romans 13:11–12)

***PAUSE** to add your own prayers for personal renewal.*

NT Acts 9:1–19a

Saul's Conversion

9 Meanwhile, Saul was still breathing out murderous threats against the Lord's disciples. He went to the high priest 2and asked him for letters to the synagogues in Damascus, so that if he found any there who belonged to the Way, whether men or women, he might take them as prisoners to Jerusalem. 3As he neared Damascus on his journey, suddenly a light from heaven flashed around him. 4He fell to the ground and heard a voice say to him, "Saul, Saul, why do you persecute me?"

5"Who are you, Lord?" Saul asked.

"I am Jesus, whom you are persecuting," he replied. 6"Now get up and go into the city, and you will be told what you must do."

7The men traveling with Saul stood there speechless; they heard the sound but did not see anyone. 8Saul got up from the ground, but when he opened his eyes he could see nothing. So they led him by the hand into Damascus. 9For three days he was blind, and did not eat or drink anything.

10In Damascus there was a disciple named Ananias. The Lord called to him in a vision, "Ananias!"

"Yes, Lord," he answered.

11The Lord told him, "Go to the house of Judas on Straight Street and ask for a man from Tarsus named Saul, for he is praying. 12In a vision he has seen a man named Ananias come and place his hands on him to restore his sight."

13"Lord," Ananias answered, "I have heard many reports about this man and all the harm he has done to your saints in Jerusalem. 14And he has come here with authority from the chief priests to arrest all who call on your name."

15But the Lord said to Ananias, "Go! This man is my chosen instrument to carry my name before the Gentiles and their kings and before the people of Israel. 16I will show him how much he must suffer for my name."

17Then Ananias went to the house and entered it. Placing his hands on Saul, he said, "Brother Saul, the Lord—Jesus, who appeared to you on the road as you were coming here—has sent me so that you may see again and be filled with the Holy Spirit." 18Immediately, something like scales fell from Saul's eyes, and he could see again. He got up and was baptized, 19and after taking some food, he regained his strength.

PRAYER: THE ATTRIBUTES OF GOD

AH, Lord God! You have made the heavens and the earth by Your great power and outstretched arm. Nothing is too difficult for You. You are the great and mighty God; Your name is the Lord of hosts. You are great in counsel and mighty in deed, and Your eyes see everything that we do; You reward us according to our ways and according to the fruit of our deeds. (Jeremiah 32:17–19)

PAUSE *to reflect on these affirmations about the person, powers and perfection of God.*

YEAR 2 DAY 52

OT Song of Songs 1:1–2:17

1 Solomon's Song of Songs.

Beloved[a]

2Let him kiss me with the kisses of his
mouth—
for your love is more delightful
than wine.

3Pleasing is the fragrance of your
perfumes;

[a] Primarily on the basis of the gender of the Hebrew pronouns used, male and female speakers are indicated in the margins by the captions *Lover* and *Beloved* respectively. The words of others are marked *Friends*. In some instances the divisions and their captions are debatable.

your name is like perfume poured
out.
No wonder the maidens love you!
[4]Take me away with you—let us hurry!
Let the king bring me into his
chambers.

Friends

We rejoice and delight in you[b];
we will praise your love more than
wine.

Beloved

How right they are to adore you!

[5]Dark am I, yet lovely,
O daughters of Jerusalem,
dark like the tents of Kedar,
like the tent curtains of Solomon.[c]
[6]Do not stare at me because I am dark,
because I am darkened by the sun.
My mother's sons were angry with me
and made me take care of the
vineyards;
my own vineyard I have neglected.
[7]Tell me, you whom I love, where you
graze your flock
and where you rest your sheep at
midday.
Why should I be like a veiled woman
beside the flocks of your friends?

Friends

[8]If you do not know, most beautiful of
women,
follow the tracks of the sheep
and graze your young goats
by the tents of the shepherds.

Lover

[9]I liken you, my darling, to a mare
harnessed to one of the chariots of
Pharaoh.
[10]Your cheeks are beautiful with
earrings,
your neck with strings of jewels.
[11]We will make you earrings of gold,
studded with silver.

Beloved

[12]While the king was at his table,
my perfume spread its fragrance.
[13]My lover is to me a sachet of myrrh
resting between my breasts.
[14]My lover is to me a cluster of henna
blossoms
from the vineyards of En Gedi.

Lover

[15]How beautiful you are, my darling!
Oh, how beautiful!
Your eyes are doves.

Beloved

[16]How handsome you are, my lover!
Oh, how charming!
And our bed is verdant.

Lover

[17]The beams of our house are cedars;
our rafters are firs.

Beloved[d]

2 I am a rose[e] of Sharon,
a lily of the valleys.

Lover

[2]Like a lily among thorns
is my darling among the maidens.

Beloved

[3]Like an apple tree among the trees of
the forest
is my lover among the young men.
I delight to sit in his shade,
and his fruit is sweet to my taste.
[4]He has taken me to the banquet hall,
and his banner over me is love.
[5]Strengthen me with raisins,
refresh me with apples,
for I am faint with love.
[6]His left arm is under my head,
and his right arm embraces me.
[7]Daughters of Jerusalem, I charge you
by the gazelles and by the does of
the field:
Do not arouse or awaken love
until it so desires.

[8]Listen! My lover!
Look! Here he comes,
leaping across the mountains,
bounding over the hills.
[9]My lover is like a gazelle or a young
stag.
Look! There he stands behind our
wall,
gazing through the windows,
peering through the lattice.

[b] *4* The Hebrew is masculine singular. [c] *5* Or *Salma* [d] *1* Or *Lover* [e] *1* Possibly a member of the crocus family

[10] My lover spoke and said to me,
"Arise, my darling,
my beautiful one, and come with me.
[11] See! The winter is past;
the rains are over and gone.
[12] Flowers appear on the earth;
the season of singing has come,
the cooing of doves
is heard in our land.
[13] The fig tree forms its early fruit;
the blossoming vines spread their fragrance.
Arise, come, my darling;
my beautiful one, come with me."

Lover

[14] My dove in the clefts of the rock,
in the hiding places on the mountainside,
show me your face,
let me hear your voice;
for your voice is sweet,
and your face is lovely.
[15] Catch for us the foxes,
the little foxes
that ruin the vineyards,
our vineyards that are in bloom.

Beloved

[16] My lover is mine and I am his;
he browses among the lilies.
[17] Until the day breaks
and the shadows flee,
turn, my lover,
and be like a gazelle
or like a young stag
on the rugged hills.[f]

[f] 17 Or *the hills of Bether*

PRAYER: PETITION

JUST as I received You as Lord, Christ Jesus, so let me walk in You, rooted and built up in You, and established in the faith as I was taught, and abounding in thanksgiving. (Colossians 2:6–7)

***PAUSE** here to petition God for growth in love and compassion toward others. Offer prayers for your loved ones, for those who do not know Jesus and for those in need. Offer prayers regarding your activities for this day and any special concerns you may have.*

NT Acts 9:19b–43

Saul in Damascus and Jerusalem

Saul spent several days with the disciples in Damascus. [20]At once he began to
preach in the synagogues that Jesus is the
Son of God. [21]All those who heard him
were astonished and asked, "Isn't he the
man who raised havoc in Jerusalem
among those who call on this name? And
hasn't he come here to take them as prisoners to the chief priests?" [22]Yet Saul grew
more and more powerful and baffled the
Jews living in Damascus by proving that
Jesus is the Christ.[a]

[23]After many days had gone by, the Jews
conspired to kill him, [24]but Saul learned
of their plan. Day and night they kept
close watch on the city gates in order to
kill him. [25]But his followers took him by
night and lowered him in a basket
through an opening in the wall.

[26]When he came to Jerusalem, he tried
to join the disciples, but they were all
afraid of him, not believing that he really
was a disciple. [27]But Barnabas took him
and brought him to the apostles. He told
them how Saul on his journey had seen
the Lord and that the Lord had spoken to
him, and how in Damascus he had
preached fearlessly in the name of Jesus.
[28]So Saul stayed with them and moved
about freely in Jerusalem, speaking boldly in the name of the Lord. [29]He talked
and debated with the Grecian Jews, but
they tried to kill him. [30]When the brothers learned of this, they took him down to
Caesarea and sent him off to Tarsus.

[31]Then the church throughout Judea,
Galilee and Samaria enjoyed a time of
peace. It was strengthened; and encouraged by the Holy Spirit, it grew in numbers, living in the fear of the Lord.

[a] 22 Or *Messiah*

Aeneas and Dorcas

32 As Peter traveled about the country, he went to visit the saints in Lydda. 33 There he found a man named Aeneas, a paralytic who had been bedridden for eight years. 34 "Aeneas," Peter said to him, "Jesus Christ heals you. Get up and take care of your mat." Immediately Aeneas got up. 35 All those who lived in Lydda and Sharon saw him and turned to the Lord.

36 In Joppa there was a disciple named Tabitha (which, when translated, is Dorcas[b]), who was always doing good and helping the poor. 37 About that time she became sick and died, and her body was washed and placed in an upstairs room. 38 Lydda was near Joppa; so when the disciples heard that Peter was in Lydda, they sent two men to him and urged him, "Please come at once!"

39 Peter went with them, and when he arrived he was taken upstairs to the room. All the widows stood around him, crying and showing him the robes and other clothing that Dorcas had made while she was still with them.

40 Peter sent them all out of the room; then he got down on his knees and prayed. Turning toward the dead woman, he said, "Tabitha, get up." She opened her eyes, and seeing Peter she sat up. 41 He took her by the hand and helped her to her feet. Then he called the believers and the widows and presented her to them alive. 42 This became known all over Joppa, and many people believed in the Lord. 43 Peter stayed in Joppa for some time with a tanner named Simon.

[b] 36 Both *Tabitha* (Aramaic) and *Dorcas* (Greek) mean *gazelle*.

PRAYER: THE WORKS OF GOD

BY Your word, O God, the heavens existed long ago and the earth was formed out of water and by water. By these waters also the world of that time was deluged and destroyed. And by Your word the present heavens and earth are reserved for fire, being kept for the day of judgment and the destruction of the ungodly. (2 Peter 3:5–7)

***TAKE** a moment to consider the greatness of God's wonderful works.*

YEAR 2 DAY 53

OT Song of Songs 3:1–4:16

3 All night long on my bed
I looked for the one my heart loves;
I looked for him but did not find him.
2 I will get up now and go about the city,
through its streets and squares;
I will search for the one my heart loves.
So I looked for him but did not find him.
3 The watchmen found me
as they made their rounds in the city.
"Have you seen the one my heart loves?"
4 Scarcely had I passed them
when I found the one my heart loves.
I held him and would not let him go
till I had brought him to my mother's house,
to the room of the one who conceived me.
5 Daughters of Jerusalem, I charge you
by the gazelles and by the does of the field:
Do not arouse or awaken love
until it so desires.

6 Who is this coming up from the desert
like a column of smoke,
perfumed with myrrh and incense
made from all the spices of the merchant?
7 Look! It is Solomon's carriage,
escorted by sixty warriors,
the noblest of Israel,
8 all of them wearing the sword,
all experienced in battle,
each with his sword at his side,
prepared for the terrors of the night.

[9] King Solomon made for himself the
carriage;
he made it of wood from Lebanon.
[10] Its posts he made of silver,
its base of gold.
Its seat was upholstered with purple,
its interior lovingly inlaid
by[a] the daughters of Jerusalem.
[11] Come out, you daughters of Zion,
and look at King Solomon wearing
the crown,
the crown with which his mother
crowned him
on the day of his wedding,
the day his heart rejoiced.

Lover

4 How beautiful you are, my darling!
Oh, how beautiful!
Your eyes behind your veil are doves.
Your hair is like a flock of goats
descending from Mount Gilead.
[2] Your teeth are like a flock of sheep
just shorn,
coming up from the washing.
Each has its twin;
not one of them is alone.
[3] Your lips are like a scarlet ribbon;
your mouth is lovely.
Your temples behind your veil
are like the halves of a pomegranate.
[4] Your neck is like the tower of David,
built with elegance[b];
on it hang a thousand shields,
all of them shields of warriors.
[5] Your two breasts are like two fawns,
like twin fawns of a gazelle
that browse among the lilies.
[6] Until the day breaks
and the shadows flee,
I will go to the mountain of myrrh
and to the hill of incense.
[7] All beautiful you are, my darling;
there is no flaw in you.

[8] Come with me from Lebanon, my
bride,
come with me from Lebanon.
Descend from the crest of Amana,
from the top of Senir, the summit
of Hermon,
from the lions' dens
and the mountain haunts of the
leopards.
[9] You have stolen my heart, my sister,
my bride;
you have stolen my heart
with one glance of your eyes,
with one jewel of your necklace.
[10] How delightful is your love, my sister,
my bride!
How much more pleasing is your
love than wine,
and the fragrance of your perfume
than any spice!
[11] Your lips drop sweetness as the
honeycomb, my bride;
milk and honey are under your
tongue.
The fragrance of your garments is
like that of Lebanon.
[12] You are a garden locked up, my sister,
my bride;
you are a spring enclosed, a sealed
fountain.
[13] Your plants are an orchard of
pomegranates
with choice fruits,
with henna and nard,
[14] nard and saffron,
calamus and cinnamon,
with every kind of incense tree,
with myrrh and aloes
and all the finest spices.
[15] You are[c] a garden fountain,
a well of flowing water
streaming down from Lebanon.

Beloved

[16] Awake, north wind,
and come, south wind!
Blow on my garden,
that its fragrance may spread
abroad.
Let my lover come into his garden
and taste its choice fruits.

[a] *10* Or *its inlaid interior a gift of love / from* [b] *4* The meaning of the Hebrew for this word is uncertain. [c] *15* Or *I am* (spoken by the *Beloved*)

PRAYER: INTERCESSION

ALL things are from You, O God, who reconciled us to Yourself through Christ and gave us the ministry of reconciliation: namely, that You were reconciling the world to Yourself in Christ,

not counting people's trespasses against them. And You have committed to us the message of reconciliation. Therefore we are ambassadors for Christ, as though You were appealing through us, as we implore others on Christ's behalf to be reconciled to You. (2 Corinthians 5:18–20)

***TAKE** a few moments to intercede on behalf of friends, relatives, neighbors and coworkers who do not yet know salvation in Jesus Christ.*

NT Acts 10:1–23a

Cornelius Calls for Peter

10 At Caesarea there was a man named Cornelius, a centurion in what was known as the Italian Regiment. 2He and all his family were devout and God-fearing; he gave generously to those in need and prayed to God regularly. 3One day at about three in the afternoon he had a vision. He distinctly saw an angel of God, who came to him and said, "Cornelius!"

4Cornelius stared at him in fear. "What is it, Lord?" he asked.

The angel answered, "Your prayers and gifts to the poor have come up as a memorial offering before God. 5Now send men to Joppa to bring back a man named Simon who is called Peter. 6He is staying with Simon the tanner, whose house is by the sea."

7When the angel who spoke to him had gone, Cornelius called two of his servants and a devout soldier who was one of his attendants. 8He told them everything that had happened and sent them to Joppa.

Peter's Vision

9About noon the following day as they were on their journey and approaching the city, Peter went up on the roof to pray. 10He became hungry and wanted something to eat, and while the meal was being prepared, he fell into a trance. 11He saw heaven opened and something like a large sheet being let down to earth by its four corners. 12It contained all kinds of four-footed animals, as well as reptiles of the earth and birds of the air. 13Then a voice told him, "Get up, Peter. Kill and eat."

14"Surely not, Lord!" Peter replied. "I have never eaten anything impure or unclean."

15The voice spoke to him a second time, "Do not call anything impure that God has made clean."

16This happened three times, and immediately the sheet was taken back to heaven.

17While Peter was wondering about the meaning of the vision, the men sent by Cornelius found out where Simon's house was and stopped at the gate. 18They called out, asking if Simon who was known as Peter was staying there.

19While Peter was still thinking about the vision, the Spirit said to him, "Simon, three[a] men are looking for you. 20So get up and go downstairs. Do not hesitate to go with them, for I have sent them."

21Peter went down and said to the men, "I'm the one you're looking for. Why have you come?"

22The men replied, "We have come from Cornelius the centurion. He is a righteous and God-fearing man, who is respected by all the Jewish people. A holy angel told him to have you come to his house so that he could hear what you have to say." 23Then Peter invited the men into the house to be his guests.

[a] 19 One early manuscript *two;* other manuscripts do not have the number.

PRAYER: MY RELATIONSHIP TO GOD

FROM everyone who has been given much, much will be required, and from the one who has been entrusted with much, much more will be asked. (Luke 12:48) . . . As Your servant, O Christ, and a steward of Your possessions, may I be found faithful. (1 Corinthians 4:1–2)

***PAUSE** to thank God for the relationship that you enjoy with Him in Jesus Christ.*

YEAR 2
DAY 54

OT Song of Songs 5:1-16

Lover

5 I have come into my garden, my sister, my bride;
I have gathered my myrrh with my spice.
I have eaten my honeycomb and my honey;
I have drunk my wine and my milk.

Friends

Eat, O friends, and drink;
drink your fill, O lovers.

Beloved

2 I slept but my heart was awake.
Listen! My lover is knocking:
"Open to me, my sister, my darling,
my dove, my flawless one.
My head is drenched with dew,
my hair with the dampness of the night."
3 I have taken off my robe—
must I put it on again?
I have washed my feet—
must I soil them again?
4 My lover thrust his hand through the latch-opening;
my heart began to pound for him.
5 I arose to open for my lover,
and my hands dripped with myrrh,
my fingers with flowing myrrh,
on the handles of the lock.
6 I opened for my lover,
but my lover had left; he was gone.
My heart sank at his departure.[a]
I looked for him but did not find him.
I called him but he did not answer.
7 The watchmen found me
as they made their rounds in the city.
They beat me, they bruised me;
they took away my cloak,
those watchmen of the walls!
8 O daughters of Jerusalem, I charge you—
if you find my lover,
what will you tell him?
Tell him I am faint with love.

Friends

9 How is your beloved better than others,
most beautiful of women?
How is your beloved better than others,
that you charge us so?

Beloved

10 My lover is radiant and ruddy,
outstanding among ten thousand.
11 His head is purest gold;
his hair is wavy
and black as a raven.
12 His eyes are like doves
by the water streams,
washed in milk,
mounted like jewels.
13 His cheeks are like beds of spice
yielding perfume.
His lips are like lilies
dripping with myrrh.
14 His arms are rods of gold
set with chrysolite.
His body is like polished ivory
decorated with sapphires.[b]
15 His legs are pillars of marble
set on bases of pure gold.
His appearance is like Lebanon,
choice as its cedars.
16 His mouth is sweetness itself;
he is altogether lovely.
This is my lover, this my friend,
O daughters of Jerusalem.

[a] 6 Or *heart had gone out to him when he spoke*
[b] 14 Or *lapis lazuli*

PRAYER: AFFIRMATION

YOU, Christ Jesus, are not weak in dealing with us, but You are powerful among us. For though You were crucified in weakness, yet You live by the power of God. Likewise, we are weak in You, yet by the power of God we will live with You to serve others. (2 Corinthians 13:3–4)

***PAUSE** to reflect on these Biblical affirmations.*

NT Acts 10:23b–48

Peter at Cornelius' House

The next day Peter started out with them, and some of the brothers from Joppa went along. 24 The following day he arrived in Caesarea. Cornelius was expecting them and had called together his relatives and close friends. 25 As Peter entered the house, Cornelius met him and fell at his feet in reverence. 26 But Peter made him get up. "Stand up," he said, "I am only a man myself."

27 Talking with him, Peter went inside and found a large gathering of people. 28 He said to them: "You are well aware that it is against our law for a Jew to associate with a Gentile or visit him. But God has shown me that I should not call any man impure or unclean. 29 So when I was sent for, I came without raising any objection. May I ask why you sent for me?"

30 Cornelius answered: "Four days ago I was in my house praying at this hour, at three in the afternoon. Suddenly a man in shining clothes stood before me 31 and said, 'Cornelius, God has heard your prayer and remembered your gifts to the poor. 32 Send to Joppa for Simon who is called Peter. He is a guest in the home of Simon the tanner, who lives by the sea.' 33 So I sent for you immediately, and it was good of you to come. Now we are all here in the presence of God to listen to everything the Lord has commanded you to tell us."

34 Then Peter began to speak: "I now realize how true it is that God does not show favoritism 35 but accepts men from every nation who fear him and do what is right. 36 You know the message God sent to the people of Israel, telling the good news of peace through Jesus Christ, who is Lord of all. 37 You know what has happened throughout Judea, beginning in Galilee after the baptism that John preached— 38 how God anointed Jesus of Nazareth with the Holy Spirit and power, and how he went around doing good and healing all who were under the power of the devil, because God was with him.

39 "We are witnesses of everything he did in the country of the Jews and in Jerusalem. They killed him by hanging him on a tree, 40 but God raised him from the dead on the third day and caused him to be seen. 41 He was not seen by all the people, but by witnesses whom God had already chosen—by us who ate and drank with him after he rose from the dead. 42 He commanded us to preach to the people and to testify that he is the one whom God appointed as judge of the living and the dead. 43 All the prophets testify about him that everyone who believes in him receives forgiveness of sins through his name."

44 While Peter was still speaking these words, the Holy Spirit came on all who heard the message. 45 The circumcised believers who had come with Peter were astonished that the gift of the Holy Spirit had been poured out even on the Gentiles. 46 For they heard them speaking in tongues[a] and praising God.

Then Peter said, 47 "Can anyone keep these people from being baptized with water? They have received the Holy Spirit just as we have." 48 So he ordered that they be baptized in the name of Jesus Christ. Then they asked Peter to stay with them for a few days.

[a] 46 Or *other languages*

PRAYER: THE CHARACTER I WANT TO CULTIVATE

I WILL covet no one's money or possessions. (Acts 20:33) . . . Godliness with contentment is great gain. For I brought nothing into the world, and I can take nothing out of it. But if I have food and clothing, with these I will be content.

(1 Timothy 6:6–8)

***TAKE** a moment to ask the Lord for the grace to grow in godly character.*

YEAR 2 DAY 55

OT Song of Songs 6:1-13

Friends

6 Where has your lover gone,
most beautiful of women?
Which way did your lover turn,
that we may look for him with you?

Beloved

2 My lover has gone down to his garden,
to the beds of spices,
to browse in the gardens
and to gather lilies.
3 I am my lover's and my lover is mine;
he browses among the lilies.

Lover

4 You are beautiful, my darling, as Tirzah,
lovely as Jerusalem,
majestic as troops with banners.
5 Turn your eyes from me;
they overwhelm me.
Your hair is like a flock of goats
descending from Gilead.
6 Your teeth are like a flock of sheep
coming up from the washing.
Each has its twin,
not one of them is alone.
7 Your temples behind your veil
are like the halves of a pomegranate.
8 Sixty queens there may be,
and eighty concubines,
and virgins beyond number;
9 but my dove, my perfect one, is unique,
the only daughter of her mother,
the favorite of the one who bore her.
The maidens saw her and called her blessed;
the queens and concubines praised her.

Friends

10 Who is this that appears like the dawn,
fair as the moon, bright as the sun,
majestic as the stars in procession?

Lover

11 I went down to the grove of nut trees
to look at the new growth in the valley,
to see if the vines had budded
or the pomegranates were in bloom.
12 Before I realized it,
my desire set me among the royal chariots of my people.[a]

Friends

13 Come back, come back,
O Shulammite;
come back, come back, that we may gaze on you!

Lover

Why would you gaze on the Shulammite
as on the dance of Mahanaim?

[a] 12 Or *among the chariots of Amminadab;* or *among the chariots of the people of the prince*

PRAYER: THANKSGIVING

I PRAISE You, O Lord! I will thank You with all my heart in the council of the upright and in the assembly. Great are Your works, O Lord; they are pondered by all who delight in them. Splendid and majestic is Your work, and Your righteousness endures forever. You have caused Your wonderful acts to be remembered; You, O Lord, are gracious and compassionate. (Psalm 111:1–4)

PAUSE *to offer your own expressions of thanksgiving.*

NT Acts 11:1-30

Peter Explains His Actions

11 The apostles and the brothers throughout Judea heard that the Gentiles also had received the word of God. 2So when Peter went up to Jerusalem, the circumcised believers criticized him 3and said, "You went into the house of uncircumcised men and ate with them."

4Peter began and explained everything to them precisely as it had happened: 5"I was in the city of Joppa praying, and in a trance I saw a vision. I saw something like a large sheet being let down from heaven by its four corners, and it came down to where I was. 6I looked into it and saw four-footed animals of the earth, wild beasts, reptiles, and birds of the air. 7Then I heard a voice telling me, 'Get up, Peter. Kill and eat.'

8"I replied, 'Surely not, Lord! Nothing impure or unclean has ever entered my mouth.'

9"The voice spoke from heaven a second time, 'Do not call anything impure that God has made clean.' 10This happened three times, and then it was all pulled up to heaven again.

11"Right then three men who had been sent to me from Caesarea stopped at the house where I was staying. 12The Spirit told me to have no hesitation about going with them. These six brothers also went with me, and we entered the man's house. 13He told us how he had seen an angel appear in his house and say, 'Send to Joppa for Simon who is called Peter. 14He will bring you a message through which you and all your household will be saved.'

15"As I began to speak, the Holy Spirit came on them as he had come on us at the beginning. 16Then I remembered what the Lord had said: 'John baptized with[a] water, but you will be baptized with the Holy Spirit.' 17So if God gave them the same gift as he gave us, who believed in the Lord Jesus Christ, who was I to think that I could oppose God?"

18When they heard this, they had no further objections and praised God, saying, "So then, God has granted even the Gentiles repentance unto life."

The Church in Antioch

19Now those who had been scattered by the persecution in connection with Stephen traveled as far as Phoenicia, Cyprus and Antioch, telling the message only to Jews. 20Some of them, however, men from Cyprus and Cyrene, went to Antioch and began to speak to Greeks also, telling them the good news about the Lord Jesus. 21The Lord's hand was with them, and a great number of people believed and turned to the Lord.

22News of this reached the ears of the church at Jerusalem, and they sent Barnabas to Antioch. 23When he arrived and saw the evidence of the grace of God, he was glad and encouraged them all to remain true to the Lord with all their hearts. 24He was a good man, full of the Holy Spirit and faith, and a great number of people were brought to the Lord.

25Then Barnabas went to Tarsus to look for Saul, 26and when he found him, he brought him to Antioch. So for a whole year Barnabas and Saul met with the church and taught great numbers of people. The disciples were called Christians first at Antioch.

27During this time some prophets came down from Jerusalem to Antioch. 28One of them, named Agabus, stood up and through the Spirit predicted that a severe famine would spread over the entire Roman world. (This happened during the reign of Claudius.) 29The disciples, each according to his ability, decided to provide help for the brothers living in Judea. 30This they did, sending their gift to the elders by Barnabas and Saul.

[a] 16 Or *in*

PRAYER: MY RELATIONSHIP TO OTHERS

I WILL remember those who led me, who spoke Your word, O God, to me. I will consider the outcome of their way of life and imitate their faith. I will obey those who lead me and submit to them,

for they keep watch over my soul as those who must give an account. I will obey them, so that they may do this with joy and not with grief, for this would be unprofitable for me. (Hebrews 13:7, 17)

***PAUSE** to review your relationships with others and to commit them to the Lord.*

YEAR 2 DAY 56

OT Psalms 81–82

Psalm 81

For the director of music. According to *gittith*.[a] Of Asaph.

1 Sing for joy to God our strength;
shout aloud to the God of Jacob!
2 Begin the music, strike the tambourine,
play the melodious harp and lyre.

3 Sound the ram's horn at the New Moon,
and when the moon is full, on the day of our Feast;
4 this is a decree for Israel,
an ordinance of the God of Jacob.
5 He established it as a statute for Joseph
when he went out against Egypt,
where we heard a language we did not understand.[b]

6 He says, "I removed the burden from their shoulders;
their hands were set free from the basket.
7 In your distress you called and I rescued you,
I answered you out of a thundercloud;
I tested you at the waters of Meribah. *Selah*

8 "Hear, O my people, and I will warn you—
if you would but listen to me, O Israel!
9 You shall have no foreign god among you;
you shall not bow down to an alien god.
10 I am the LORD your God,
who brought you up out of Egypt.
Open wide your mouth and I will fill it.

11 "But my people would not listen to me;
Israel would not submit to me.
12 So I gave them over to their stubborn hearts
to follow their own devices.

13 "If my people would but listen to me,
if Israel would follow my ways,
14 how quickly would I subdue their enemies
and turn my hand against their foes!
15 Those who hate the LORD would cringe before him,
and their punishment would last forever.
16 But you would be fed with the finest of wheat;
with honey from the rock I would satisfy you."

Psalm 82

A psalm of Asaph.

1 God presides in the great assembly;
he gives judgment among the "gods":

2 "How long will you[c] defend the unjust
and show partiality to the wicked? *Selah*
3 Defend the cause of the weak and fatherless;
maintain the rights of the poor and oppressed.
4 Rescue the weak and needy;
deliver them from the hand of the wicked.

5 "They know nothing, they understand nothing.
They walk about in darkness;
all the foundations of the earth are shaken.

[a] Title: Probably a musical term [b] 5 Or / *and we heard a voice we had not known* [c] 2 The Hebrew is plural.

⁶"I said, 'You are "gods";
you are all sons of the Most High.'
⁷But you will die like mere men;
you will fall like every other ruler."
⁸Rise up, O God, judge the earth,
for all the nations are your inheritance.

PRAYER: ADORATION

YOU are my shield, my very great reward. (Genesis 15:1) . . . As for You, O God, Your way is perfect; Your Word is proven. You are a shield to all who take refuge in You. For who is God besides You? And who is the Rock except You, our God? (Psalm 18:30–31)

***PAUSE** to express your thoughts of praise and worship.*

NT Acts 12:1–19a

Peter's Miraculous Escape From Prison

12 It was about this time that King Herod
arrested some who belonged to the
church, intending to persecute them. ²He
had James, the brother of John, put to
death with the sword. ³When he saw that
this pleased the Jews, he proceeded to
seize Peter also. This happened during the
Feast of Unleavened Bread. ⁴After arresting
him, he put him in prison, handing him
over to be guarded by four squads of four
soldiers each. Herod intended to bring
him out for public trial after the Passover.
⁵So Peter was kept in prison, but the
church was earnestly praying to God for
him.
⁶The night before Herod was to bring
him to trial, Peter was sleeping between
two soldiers, bound with two chains, and
sentries stood guard at the entrance. ⁷Sud-
denly an angel of the Lord appeared and
a light shone in the cell. He struck Peter
on the side and woke him up. "Quick, get
up!" he said, and the chains fell off Peter's
wrists.
⁸Then the angel said to him, "Put on
your clothes and sandals." And Peter did
so. "Wrap your cloak around you and follow me," the angel told him. ⁹Peter followed him out of the prison, but he had
no idea that what the angel was doing was
really happening; he thought he was seeing a vision. ¹⁰They passed the first and
second guards and came to the iron gate
leading to the city. It opened for them by
itself, and they went through it. When
they had walked the length of one street,
suddenly the angel left him.
¹¹Then Peter came to himself and said,
"Now I know without a doubt that the
Lord sent his angel and rescued me from
Herod's clutches and from everything the
Jewish people were anticipating."
¹²When this had dawned on him, he
went to the house of Mary the mother of
John, also called Mark, where many people had gathered and were praying. ¹³Pe-
ter knocked at the outer entrance, and a
servant girl named Rhoda came to answer
the door. ¹⁴When she recognized Peter's
voice, she was so overjoyed she ran back
without opening it and exclaimed, "Peter
is at the door!"
¹⁵"You're out of your mind," they told
her. When she kept insisting that it was so,
they said, "It must be his angel."
¹⁶But Peter kept on knocking, and when
they opened the door and saw him, they
were astonished. ¹⁷Peter motioned with
his hand for them to be quiet and described how the Lord had brought him
out of prison. "Tell James and the brothers about this," he said, and then he left
for another place.
¹⁸In the morning, there was no small
commotion among the soldiers as to
what had become of Peter. ¹⁹After Herod
had a thorough search made for him and
did not find him, he cross-examined the
guards and ordered that they be executed.

PRAYER: THE ATTRIBUTES OF GOD

O LORD of hosts, You are wonderful in counsel and great in wisdom. (Isaiah 28:29) . . . In You, O Christ, are hidden all the treasures of wisdom and knowledge. (Colossians 2:3)

PAUSE *to reflect on these affirmations about the person, powers and perfection of God.*

YEAR 2 DAY 57

OT Song of Songs 7:1-13

7 How beautiful your sandaled feet,
O prince's daughter!
Your graceful legs are like jewels,
the work of a craftsman's hands.
2 Your navel is a rounded goblet
that never lacks blended wine.
Your waist is a mound of wheat
encircled by lilies.
3 Your breasts are like two fawns,
twins of a gazelle.
4 Your neck is like an ivory tower.
Your eyes are the pools of Heshbon
by the gate of Bath Rabbim.
Your nose is like the tower of Lebanon
looking toward Damascus.
5 Your head crowns you like Mount
Carmel.
Your hair is like royal tapestry;
the king is held captive by its
tresses.
6 How beautiful you are and how
pleasing,
O love, with your delights!
7 Your stature is like that of the palm,
and your breasts like clusters of
fruit.
8 I said, "I will climb the palm tree;
I will take hold of its fruit."
May your breasts be like the clusters
of the vine,
the fragrance of your breath like
apples,
9 and your mouth like the best wine.

Beloved

May the wine go straight to my lover,
flowing gently over lips and teeth.[a]
10 I belong to my lover,
and his desire is for me.
11 Come, my lover, let us go to the
countryside,
let us spend the night in the villages.[b]
12 Let us go early to the vineyards
to see if the vines have budded,
if their blossoms have opened,
and if the pomegranates are in
bloom—
there I will give you my love.
13 The mandrakes send out their
fragrance,
and at our door is every delicacy,
both new and old,
that I have stored up for you, my
lover.

[a] 9 Septuagint, Aquila, Vulgate and Syriac; Hebrew *lips of sleepers* [b] 11 Or *henna bushes*

PRAYER: CONFESSION

REMEMBER, O Lord, Your compassions and Your mercies, for they are from of old. Do not remember the sins of my youth or my transgressions; according to Your loyal love remember me for the sake of Your goodness, O Lord. (Psalm 25:6–7)

ASK *the Spirit to search your heart and reveal any areas of unconfessed sin. Acknowledge these to the Lord and thank Him for His forgiveness.*

NT Acts 12:19b–13:12

Herod's Death

Then Herod went from Judea to Caesarea and stayed there a while. [20]He had been quarreling with the people of Tyre and Sidon; they now joined together and sought an audience with him. Having secured the support of Blastus, a trusted personal servant of the king, they asked for peace, because they depended on the king's country for their food supply.

[21]On the appointed day Herod, wearing his royal robes, sat on his throne and delivered a public address to the people. [22]They shouted, "This is the voice of a god, not of a man." [23]Immediately, because Herod did not give praise to God, an angel of the Lord struck him down, and he was eaten by worms and died.

[24]But the word of God continued to increase and spread.

[25]When Barnabas and Saul had finished their mission, they returned from[a] Jerusalem, taking with them John, also called Mark.

Barnabas and Saul Sent Off

13 In the church at Antioch there were prophets and teachers: Barnabas, Simeon called Niger, Lucius of Cyrene, Manaen (who had been brought up with Herod the tetrarch) and Saul. [2]While they were worshiping the Lord and fasting, the Holy Spirit said, "Set apart for me Barnabas and Saul for the work to which I have called them." [3]So after they had fasted and prayed, they placed their hands on them and sent them off.

On Cyprus

[4]The two of them, sent on their way by the Holy Spirit, went down to Seleucia and sailed from there to Cyprus. [5]When they arrived at Salamis, they proclaimed the word of God in the Jewish synagogues. John was with them as their helper.

[6]They traveled through the whole island until they came to Paphos. There they met a Jewish sorcerer and false prophet named Bar-Jesus, [7]who was an attendant of the proconsul, Sergius Paulus. The proconsul, an intelligent man, sent for Barnabas and Saul because he wanted to hear the word of God. [8]But Elymas the sorcerer (for that is what his name means) opposed them and tried to turn the proconsul from the faith. [9]Then Saul, who was also called Paul, filled with the Holy Spirit, looked straight at Elymas and said, [10]"You are a child of the devil and an enemy of everything that is right! You are full of all kinds of deceit and trickery. Will you never stop perverting the right ways of the Lord? [11]Now the hand of the Lord is against you. You are going to be blind, and for a time you will be unable to see the light of the sun."

Immediately mist and darkness came over him, and he groped about, seeking someone to lead him by the hand. [12]When the proconsul saw what had happened, he believed, for he was amazed at the teaching about the Lord.

[a] 25 Some manuscripts *to*

PRAYER: THE WORKS OF GOD

O LORD, if we your people, who are called by Your name, will humble ourselves and pray and seek Your face and turn from our wicked ways, then You will hear from heaven and will forgive our sin and heal our land. (2 Chronicles 7:14) . . . Blessed is the nation whose God You are, O Lord, the people whom You have chosen for Your inheritance. (Psalm 33:12)

***TAKE** a moment to consider the greatness of God's wonderful works.*

YEAR 2 DAY 58

OT Song of Songs 8:1–14

8 If only you were to me like a brother,
who was nursed at my mother's breasts!
Then, if I found you outside,
I would kiss you,
and no one would despise me.
2 I would lead you
and bring you to my mother's house—
she who has taught me.
I would give you spiced wine to drink,
the nectar of my pomegranates.
3 His left arm is under my head
and his right arm embraces me.
4 Daughters of Jerusalem, I charge you:
Do not arouse or awaken love
until it so desires.

Friends

5 Who is this coming up from the desert
leaning on her lover?

Beloved

Under the apple tree I roused you;
there your mother conceived you,
there she who was in labor gave you birth.
6 Place me like a seal over your heart,
like a seal on your arm;
for love is as strong as death,
its jealousy[a] unyielding as the grave.[b]
It burns like blazing fire,
like a mighty flame.[c]
7 Many waters cannot quench love;
rivers cannot wash it away.
If one were to give
all the wealth of his house for love,
it[d] would be utterly scorned.

Friends

8 We have a young sister,
and her breasts are not yet grown.
What shall we do for our sister
for the day she is spoken for?
9 If she is a wall,
we will build towers of silver on her.
If she is a door,
we will enclose her with panels of cedar.

Beloved

10 I am a wall,
and my breasts are like towers.
Thus I have become in his eyes
like one bringing contentment.
11 Solomon had a vineyard in Baal Hamon;
he let out his vineyard to tenants.
Each was to bring for its fruit
a thousand shekels[e] of silver.
12 But my own vineyard is mine to give;
the thousand shekels are for you, O Solomon,
and two hundred[f] are for those who tend its fruit.

Lover

13 You who dwell in the gardens
with friends in attendance,
let me hear your voice!

Beloved

14 Come away, my lover,
and be like a gazelle
or like a young stag
on the spice-laden mountains.

[a] 6 Or *ardor* [b] 6 Hebrew *Sheol* [c] 6 Or / *like the very flame of the* LORD [d] 7 Or *he* [e] 11 That is, about 25 pounds (about 11.5 kilograms); also in verse 12 [f] 12 That is, about 5 pounds (about 2.3 kilograms)

PRAYER: RENEWAL

I DO not want even a hint of immorality, or any impurity or greed in my life, as these are improper for a saint. Nor will I give myself to obscenity, foolish talk or coarse joking, which are not fitting, but rather I will give myself to thanksgiving. (Ephesians 5:3–4)

***PAUSE** to add your own prayers for personal renewal.*

NT Acts 13:13–52

In Pisidian Antioch

13From Paphos, Paul and his companions sailed to Perga in Pamphylia, where
John left them to return to Jerusalem.
14From Perga they went on to Pisidian Antioch. On the Sabbath they entered the
synagogue and sat down. 15After the reading from the Law and the Prophets, the
synagogue rulers sent word to them, saying, "Brothers, if you have a message of encouragement for the people, please speak."
16Standing up, Paul motioned with his
hand and said: "Men of Israel and you
Gentiles who worship God, listen to me!
17The God of the people of Israel chose
our fathers; he made the people prosper
during their stay in Egypt, with mighty
power he led them out of that country,
18he endured their conduct[a] for about
forty years in the desert, 19he overthrew
seven nations in Canaan and gave their
land to his people as their inheritance.
20All this took about 450 years.

"After this, God gave them judges until
the time of Samuel the prophet. 21Then
the people asked for a king, and he gave
them Saul son of Kish, of the tribe of Benjamin, who ruled forty years. 22After removing Saul, he made David their king.
He testified concerning him: 'I have found
David son of Jesse a man after my own
heart; he will do everything I want him
to do.'

23"From this man's descendants God
has brought to Israel the Savior Jesus, as
he promised. 24Before the coming of Jesus,
John preached repentance and baptism to
all the people of Israel. 25As John was
completing his work, he said: 'Who do
you think I am? I am not that one. No,
but he is coming after me, whose sandals
I am not worthy to untie.'

26"Brothers, children of Abraham, and
you God-fearing Gentiles, it is to us that
this message of salvation has been sent.
27The people of Jerusalem and their rulers
did not recognize Jesus, yet in condemning him they fulfilled the words of the
prophets that are read every Sabbath.
28Though they found no proper ground
for a death sentence, they asked Pilate to
have him executed. 29When they had carried out all that was written about him,
they took him down from the tree and
laid him in a tomb. 30But God raised him
from the dead, 31and for many days he
was seen by those who had traveled with
him from Galilee to Jerusalem. They are
now his witnesses to our people.

32"We tell you the good news: What
God promised our fathers 33he has ful-
filled for us, their children, by raising up
Jesus. As it is written in the second Psalm:

" 'You are my Son;
today I have become your Father.'[b][c]

34The fact that God raised him from the
dead, never to decay, is stated in these
words:

" 'I will give you the holy and sure
blessings promised to David.'[d]

35So it is stated elsewhere:

" 'You will not let your Holy One see
decay.'[e]

36"For when David had served God's purpose in his own generation, he fell asleep;
he was buried with his fathers and his body
decayed. 37But the one whom God raised
from the dead did not see decay.

38"Therefore, my brothers, I want you to
know that through Jesus the forgiveness
of sins is proclaimed to you. 39Through
him everyone who believes is justified
from everything you could not be justified
from by the law of Moses. 40Take care that
what the prophets have said does not happen to you:

41" 'Look, you scoffers,
wonder and perish,
for I am going to do something in
your days
that you would never believe,
even if someone told you.'[f]"

42As Paul and Barnabas were leaving the
synagogue, the people invited them to
speak further about these things on the
next Sabbath. 43When the congregation
was dismissed, many of the Jews and devout converts to Judaism followed Paul
and Barnabas, who talked with them and
urged them to continue in the grace of
God.

[a] 18 Some manuscripts *and cared for them* [b] 33 Or *have begotten you* [c] 33 Psalm 2:7 [d] 34 Isaiah 55:3 [e] 35 Psalm 16:10 [f] 41 Hab. 1:5

[44]On the next Sabbath almost the
whole city gathered to hear the word of
the Lord. [45]When the Jews saw the crowds,
they were filled with jealousy and talked
abusively against what Paul was saying.
[46]Then Paul and Barnabas answered
them boldly: "We had to speak the word
of God to you first. Since you reject it and
do not consider yourselves worthy of eternal life, we now turn to the Gentiles. [47]For
this is what the Lord has commanded us:

" 'I have made you[g] a light for the
Gentiles,
that you[g] may bring salvation to the
ends of the earth.'[h]"

[48]When the Gentiles heard this, they
were glad and honored the word of the
Lord; and all who were appointed for eternal life believed.
[49]The word of the Lord spread through
the whole region. [50]But the Jews incited
the God-fearing women of high standing
and the leading men of the city. They
stirred up persecution against Paul and
Barnabas, and expelled them from their
region. [51]So they shook the dust from
their feet in protest against them and went
to Iconium. [52]And the disciples were filled
with joy and with the Holy Spirit.

[g]47 The Greek is singular. [h]47 Isaiah 49:6

PRAYER: MY RELATIONSHIP TO GOD

I KNOW that if my earthly house is destroyed, I have a building from You, O God, eternal in the heavens, a house not made with hands. For in this house I groan, longing to be clothed with my heavenly dwelling, because when I am clothed, I will not be found naked. While I am in this house, I groan, being burdened, because I do not want to be unclothed but to be clothed, so that what is mortal may be swallowed up by life. Now it is You, O God, who have made me for this very purpose and have given me Your Spirit as a guarantee. (2 Corinthians 5:1–5)

PAUSE *to thank God for the relationship that you enjoy with Him in Jesus Christ.*

OT 1 Chronicles 1:1–2:55

YEAR 2 DAY 59

Historical Records From Adam to Abraham

To Noah's Sons

1 Adam, Seth, Enosh, [2]Kenan, Mahalalel,
Jared, [3]Enoch, Methuselah, Lamech,
Noah.

[4]The sons of Noah:[a]
Shem, Ham and Japheth.

The Japhethites

[5]The sons[b] of Japheth:
Gomer, Magog, Madai, Javan, Tubal, Meshech and Tiras.
[6]The sons of Gomer:
Ashkenaz, Riphath[c] and Togarmah.
[7]The sons of Javan:
Elishah, Tarshish, the Kittim and
the Rodanim.

The Hamites

[8]The sons of Ham:
Cush, Mizraim,[d] Put and Canaan.
[9]The sons of Cush:
Seba, Havilah, Sabta, Raamah and
Sabteca.
The sons of Raamah:
Sheba and Dedan.
[10]Cush was the father[e] of

[a]4 Septuagint; Hebrew does not have *The sons of Noah:* [b]5 *Sons* may mean *descendants* or *successors* or *nations;* also in verses 6–10, 17 and 20. [c]6 Many Hebrew manuscripts and Vulgate (see also Septuagint and Gen. 10:3); most Hebrew manuscripts *Diphath* [d]8 That is, Egypt; also in verse 11 [e]10 *Father* may mean *ancestor* or *predecessor* or *founder;* also in verses 11, 13, 18 and 20.

Nimrod, who grew to be a mighty warrior on earth.
[11] Mizraim was the father of
the Ludites, Anamites, Lehabites,
Naphtuhites, [12] Pathrusites, Caslu-
hites (from whom the Philistines came) and Caphtorites.
[13] Canaan was the father of
Sidon his firstborn,[f] and of the Hittites, [14] Jebusites, Amorites, Girgashites, [15] Hivites, Arkites, Sinites,
[16] Arvadites, Zemarites and Hamathites.

The Semites

[17] The sons of Shem:
Elam, Asshur, Arphaxad, Lud and Aram.
The sons of Aram[g]:
Uz, Hul, Gether and Meshech.
[18] Arphaxad was the father of Shelah, and Shelah the father of Eber.
[19] Two sons were born to Eber:
One was named Peleg,[h] because in his time the earth was divided; his brother was named Joktan.
[20] Joktan was the father of
Almodad, Sheleph, Hazarmaveth,
Jerah, [21] Hadoram, Uzal, Diklah,
[22] Obal,[i] Abimael, Sheba, [23] Ophir,
Havilah and Jobab. All these were sons of Joktan.

[24] Shem, Arphaxad,[j] Shelah,
[25] Eber, Peleg, Reu,
[26] Serug, Nahor, Terah
[27] and Abram (that is, Abraham).

The Family of Abraham

[28] The sons of Abraham:
Isaac and Ishmael.

Descendants of Hagar

[29] These were their descendants:
Nebaioth the firstborn of Ishmael,
Kedar, Adbeel, Mibsam, [30] Mishma,
Dumah, Massa, Hadad, Tema, [31] Je-
tur, Naphish and Kedemah. These were the sons of Ishmael.

Descendants of Keturah

[32] The sons born to Keturah, Abraham's concubine:
Zimran, Jokshan, Medan, Midian, Ishbak and Shuah.
The sons of Jokshan:
Sheba and Dedan.
[33] The sons of Midian:
Ephah, Epher, Hanoch, Abida and Eldaah.
All these were descendants of Keturah.

Descendants of Sarah

[34] Abraham was the father of Isaac.
The sons of Isaac:
Esau and Israel.

Esau's Sons

[35] The sons of Esau:
Eliphaz, Reuel, Jeush, Jalam and Korah.
[36] The sons of Eliphaz:
Teman, Omar, Zepho,[k] Gatam and Kenaz;
by Timna: Amalek.[l]
[37] The sons of Reuel:
Nahath, Zerah, Shammah and Mizzah.

The People of Seir in Edom

[38] The sons of Seir:
Lotan, Shobal, Zibeon, Anah, Dishon, Ezer and Dishan.
[39] The sons of Lotan:
Hori and Homam. Timna was Lotan's sister.
[40] The sons of Shobal:
Alvan,[m] Manahath, Ebal, Shepho and Onam.
The sons of Zibeon:
Aiah and Anah.
[41] The son of Anah:
Dishon.
The sons of Dishon:
Hemdan,[n] Eshban, Ithran and Keran.

[f] 13 Or *of the Sidonians, the foremost* [g] 17 One Hebrew manuscript and some Septuagint manuscripts (see also Gen. 10:23); most Hebrew manuscripts do not have this line. [h] 19 *Peleg* means *division.* [i] 22 Some Hebrew manuscripts and Syriac (see also Gen. 10:28); most Hebrew manuscripts *Ebal* [j] 24 Hebrew; some Septuagint manuscripts *Arphaxad, Cainan* (see also note at Gen. 11:10) [k] 36 Many Hebrew manuscripts, some Septuagint manuscripts and Syriac (see also Gen. 36:11); most Hebrew manuscripts *Zephi* [l] 36 Some Septuagint manuscripts (see also Gen. 36:12); Hebrew *Gatam, Kenaz, Timna and Amalek* [m] 40 Many Hebrew manuscripts and some Septuagint manuscripts (see also Gen. 36:23); most Hebrew manuscripts *Alian* [n] 41 Many Hebrew manuscripts and some Septuagint manuscripts (see also Gen. 36:26); most Hebrew manuscripts *Hamran*

[42]The sons of Ezer:
Bilhan, Zaavan and Akan.[o]
The sons of Dishan[p]:
Uz and Aran.

The Rulers of Edom

[43]These were the kings who reigned in Edom before any Israelite king reigned[q]:
Bela son of Beor, whose city was named Dinhabah.
[44]When Bela died, Jobab son of Zerah from Bozrah succeeded him as king.
[45]When Jobab died, Husham from the land of the Temanites succeeded him as king.
[46]When Husham died, Hadad son of Bedad, who defeated Midian in the country of Moab, succeeded him as king. His city was named Avith.
[47]When Hadad died, Samlah from Masrekah succeeded him as king.
[48]When Samlah died, Shaul from Rehoboth on the river[r] succeeded him as king.
[49]When Shaul died, Baal-Hanan son of Acbor succeeded him as king.
[50]When Baal-Hanan died, Hadad succeeded him as king. His city was named Pau,[s] and his wife's name was Mehetabel daughter of Matred, the daughter of Me-Zahab.
[51]Hadad also died.

The chiefs of Edom were:
Timna, Alvah, Jetheth, [52]Oholibamah, Elah, Pinon, [53]Kenaz, Teman, Mibzar, [54]Magdiel and Iram. These were the chiefs of Edom.

Israel's Sons

2 These were the sons of Israel:
Reuben, Simeon, Levi, Judah, Issachar, Zebulun, [2]Dan, Joseph, Benjamin, Naphtali, Gad and Asher.

Judah

To Hezron's Sons

[3]The sons of Judah:
Er, Onan and Shelah. These three were born to him by a Canaanite woman, the daughter of Shua. Er, Judah's firstborn, was wicked in the LORD's sight; so the LORD put
him to death. [4]Tamar, Judah's daughter-in-law, bore him Perez and Zerah. Judah had five sons in all.

[5]The sons of Perez:
Hezron and Hamul.
[6]The sons of Zerah:
Zimri, Ethan, Heman, Calcol and Darda[t]—five in all.
[7]The son of Carmi:
Achar,[u] who brought trouble on Israel by violating the ban on taking devoted things.[v]
[8]The son of Ethan:
Azariah.
[9]The sons born to Hezron were:
Jerahmeel, Ram and Caleb.[w]

From Ram Son of Hezron

[10]Ram was the father of
Amminadab, and Amminadab the father of Nahshon, the leader of
the people of Judah. [11]Nahshon was the father of Salmon,[x] Salmon
the father of Boaz, [12]Boaz the father of Obed and Obed the father of Jesse.
[13]Jesse was the father of
Eliab his firstborn; the second son was Abinadab, the third Shimea,
[14]the fourth Nethanel, the fifth
Raddai, [15]the sixth Ozem and the
seventh David. [16]Their sisters were Zeruiah and Abigail. Zeruiah's three sons were Abishai, Joab and
Asahel. [17]Abigail was the mother of Amasa, whose father was Jether the Ishmaelite.

Caleb Son of Hezron

[18]Caleb son of Hezron had children by his wife Azubah (and by Jerioth). These were her sons: Jesher, Sho-

[o] 42 Many Hebrew and Septuagint manuscripts (see also Gen. 36:27); most Hebrew manuscripts *Zaavan, Jaakan* [p] 42 Hebrew *Dishon,* a variant of *Dishan* [q] 43 Or *before an Israelite king reigned over them* [r] 48 Possibly the Euphrates [s] 50 Many Hebrew manuscripts, some Septuagint manuscripts, Vulgate and Syriac (see also Gen. 36:39); most Hebrew manuscripts *Pai* [t] 6 Many Hebrew manuscripts, some Septuagint manuscripts and Syriac (see also 1 Kings 4:31); most Hebrew manuscripts *Dara* [u] 7 *Achar* means *trouble; Achar* is called *Achan* in Joshua. [v] 7 The Hebrew term refers to the irrevocable giving over of things or persons to the LORD, often by totally destroying them. [w] 9 Hebrew *Kelubai,* a variant of *Caleb* [x] 11 Septuagint (see also Ruth 4:21); Hebrew *Salma*

bab and Ardon. [19]When Azubah
died, Caleb married Ephrath, who
bore him Hur. [20]Hur was the father
of Uri, and Uri the father of Bezalel.
21 Later, Hezron lay with the daughter of Makir the father of Gilead (he had married her when he was sixty years old), and she bore him Segub. [22]Segub was the father of Jair,
who controlled twenty-three towns
in Gilead. [23](But Geshur and Aram
captured Havvoth Jair,[y] as well as Kenath with its surrounding settlements—sixty towns.) All these were descendants of Makir the father of Gilead.

24 After Hezron died in Caleb Ephrathah, Abijah the wife of Hezron bore him Ashhur the father[z] of Tekoa.

Jerahmeel Son of Hezron

25 The sons of Jerahmeel the firstborn of Hezron:
Ram his firstborn, Bunah, Oren,
Ozem and[a] Ahijah. [26]Jerahmeel
had another wife, whose name was Atarah; she was the mother of Onam.
27 The sons of Ram the firstborn of Jerahmeel:
Maaz, Jamin and Eker.
28 The sons of Onam:
Shammai and Jada.
The sons of Shammai:
Nadab and Abishur.
29 Abishur's wife was named Abihail, who bore him Ahban and Molid.
30 The sons of Nadab:
Seled and Appaim. Seled died without children.
31 The son of Appaim:
Ishi, who was the father of Sheshan.
Sheshan was the father of Ahlai.
32 The sons of Jada, Shammai's brother:
Jether and Jonathan. Jether died without children.
33 The sons of Jonathan:
Peleth and Zaza.
These were the descendants of Jerahmeel.
34 Sheshan had no sons—only daughters.
He had an Egyptian servant named
Jarha. [35]Sheshan gave his daughter
in marriage to his servant Jarha, and she bore him Attai.
36 Attai was the father of Nathan,
Nathan the father of Zabad,
37 Zabad the father of Ephlal,
Ephlal the father of Obed,
38 Obed the father of Jehu,
Jehu the father of Azariah,
39 Azariah the father of Helez,
Helez the father of Eleasah,
40 Eleasah the father of Sismai,
Sismai the father of Shallum,
41 Shallum the father of Jekamiah,
and Jekamiah the father of Elishama.

The Clans of Caleb

42 The sons of Caleb the brother of Jerahmeel:
Mesha his firstborn, who was the father of Ziph, and his son Mareshah,[b] who was the father of Hebron.
43 The sons of Hebron:
Korah, Tappuah, Rekem and Shema. [44]Shema was the father of Raham, and Raham the father of Jorkeam. Rekem was the father of
Shammai. [45]The son of Shammai
was Maon, and Maon was the father of Beth Zur.
46 Caleb's concubine Ephah was the mother of Haran, Moza and Gazez. Haran was the father of Gazez.
47 The sons of Jahdai:
Regem, Jotham, Geshan, Pelet, Ephah and Shaaph.
48 Caleb's concubine Maacah was the mother of Sheber and Tirhanah.
[49]She also gave birth to Shaaph the
father of Madmannah and to Sheva the father of Macbenah and Gibea.
Caleb's daughter was Acsah. [50]These
were the descendants of Caleb.

The sons of Hur the firstborn of Ephrathah:
Shobal the father of Kiriath Jearim,
[51]Salma the father of Bethlehem,
and Hareph the father of Beth Gader.

[y] 23 Or *captured the settlements of Jair* [z] 24 *Father* may mean *civic leader* or *military leader*; also in verses 42, 45, 49–52 and possibly elsewhere.
[a] 25 Or *Oren and Ozem, by* [b] 42 The meaning of the Hebrew for this phrase is uncertain.

52 The descendants of Shobal the father
of Kiriath Jearim were:
Haroeh, half the Manahathites,
53 and the clans of Kiriath Jearim: the
Ithrites, Puthites, Shumathites and
Mishraites. From these descended
the Zorathites and Eshtaolites.
54 The descendants of Salma:
Bethlehem, the Netophathites, Atroth Beth Joab, half the Manahathites, the Zorites, 55 and the
clans of scribes[c] who lived at Jabez:
the Tirathites, Shimeathites and
Sucathites. These are the Kenites
who came from Hammath, the father of the house of Recab.[d]

[c] 55 Or *of the Sopherites* [d] 55 Or *father of Beth Recab*

PRAYER: PETITION

ANSWER me, O Lord, for Your loving-kindness is good; in the abundance of Your mercies, turn to me.
(Psalm 69:16)

***PAUSE** here to petition God to help you be a faithful steward of your time, talents, possessions and relationships. Offer prayers of petition regarding your activities for this day and any special concerns you may have.*

NT Acts 14:1-20

In Iconium

14 At Iconium Paul and Barnabas went as
usual into the Jewish synagogue. There
they spoke so effectively that a great number of Jews and Gentiles believed. 2 But the
Jews who refused to believe stirred up the
Gentiles and poisoned their minds against
the brothers. 3 So Paul and Barnabas spent
considerable time there, speaking boldly
for the Lord, who confirmed the message
of his grace by enabling them to do miraculous signs and wonders. 4 The people of
the city were divided; some sided with the
Jews, others with the apostles. 5 There was
a plot afoot among the Gentiles and Jews,
together with their leaders, to mistreat
them and stone them. 6 But they found out
about it and fled to the Lycaonian cities of
Lystra and Derbe and to the surrounding
country, 7 where they continued to preach
the good news.

In Lystra and Derbe

8 In Lystra there sat a man crippled in his
feet, who was lame from birth and had
never walked. 9 He listened to Paul as he
was speaking. Paul looked directly at him,
saw that he had faith to be healed 10 and
called out, "Stand up on your feet!" At that,
the man jumped up and began to walk.
11 When the crowd saw what Paul had
done, they shouted in the Lycaonian language, "The gods have come down to us
in human form!" 12 Barnabas they called
Zeus, and Paul they called Hermes because he was the chief speaker. 13 The
priest of Zeus, whose temple was just outside the city, brought bulls and wreaths to
the city gates because he and the crowd
wanted to offer sacrifices to them.
14 But when the apostles Barnabas and
Paul heard of this, they tore their clothes
and rushed out into the crowd, shouting:
15 "Men, why are you doing this? We too
are only men, human like you. We are
bringing you good news, telling you to
turn from these worthless things to the
living God, who made heaven and earth
and sea and everything in them. 16 In the
past, he let all nations go their own way.
17 Yet he has not left himself without testimony: He has shown kindness by giving
you rain from heaven and crops in their
seasons; he provides you with plenty of
food and fills your hearts with joy." 18 Even
with these words, they had difficulty keeping the crowd from sacrificing to them.
19 Then some Jews came from Antioch
and Iconium and won the crowd over.
They stoned Paul and dragged him outside
the city, thinking he was dead. 20 But after
the disciples had gathered around him, he
got up and went back into the city. The
next day he and Barnabas left for Derbe.

PRAYER: THE CHARACTER I WANT TO CULTIVATE

LORD, may I obey Your instruction to watch and pray so that I will not fall into temptation; the spirit is willing, but the flesh is weak. (Matthew 26:41) . . . I will devote myself to prayer, being watchful and thankful. (Colossians 4:2)

***TAKE** a moment to ask the Lord for the grace to grow in godly character.*

YEAR 2 DAY 60

OT 1 Chronicles 3:1–4:43

The Sons of David

3 These were the sons of David born to him in Hebron:
The firstborn was Amnon the son of Ahinoam of Jezreel;
the second, Daniel the son of Abigail of Carmel;
2 the third, Absalom the son of Maacah daughter of Talmai king of Geshur;
the fourth, Adonijah the son of Haggith;
3 the fifth, Shephatiah the son of Abital;
and the sixth, Ithream, by his wife Eglah.
4 These six were born to David in Hebron, where he reigned seven years and six months.
David reigned in Jerusalem thirty-three years,
5 and these were the children born to him there:
Shammua,[a] Shobab, Nathan and Solomon. These four were by Bathsheba[b] daughter of Ammiel.
6 There were also Ibhar, Elishua,[c]
Eliphelet, 7 Nogah, Nepheg, Japhia,
8 Elishama, Eliada and Eliphelet—
nine in all. 9 All these were the sons of David, besides his sons by his concubines. And Tamar was their sister.

The Kings of Judah

10 Solomon's son was Rehoboam,
Abijah his son,
Asa his son,
Jehoshaphat his son,
11 Jehoram[d] his son,
Ahaziah his son,
Joash his son,
12 Amaziah his son,
Azariah his son,
Jotham his son,
13 Ahaz his son,
Hezekiah his son,
Manasseh his son,
14 Amon his son,
Josiah his son.
15 The sons of Josiah:
Johanan the firstborn,
Jehoiakim the second son,
Zedekiah the third,
Shallum the fourth.
16 The successors of Jehoiakim:
Jehoiachin[e] his son,
and Zedekiah.

The Royal Line After the Exile

17 The descendants of Jehoiachin the captive:
Shealtiel his son,
18 Malkiram, Pedaiah, Shenazzar, Jekamiah, Hoshama and Nedabiah.
19 The sons of Pedaiah:
Zerubbabel and Shimei.
The sons of Zerubbabel:
Meshullam and Hananiah.
Shelomith was their sister.
20 There were also five others:
Hashubah, Ohel, Berekiah, Hasadiah and Jushab-Hesed.
21 The descendants of Hananiah:
Pelatiah and Jeshaiah, and the

[a] 5 Hebrew *Shimea,* a variant of *Shammua*
[b] 5 One Hebrew manuscript and Vulgate (see also Septuagint and 2 Samuel 11:3); most Hebrew manuscripts *Bathshua*
[c] 6 Two Hebrew manuscripts (see also 2 Samuel 5:15 and 1 Chron. 14:5); most Hebrew manuscripts *Elishama*
[d] 11 Hebrew *Joram,* a variant of *Jehoram*
[e] 16 Hebrew *Jeconiah,* a variant of *Jehoiachin;* also in verse 17

sons of Rephaiah, of Arnan, of Obadiah and of Shecaniah.
22 The descendants of Shecaniah:
Shemaiah and his sons:
Hattush, Igal, Bariah, Neariah and Shaphat—six in all.
23 The sons of Neariah:
Elioenai, Hizkiah and Azrikam—three in all.
24 The sons of Elioenai:
Hodaviah, Eliashib, Pelaiah, Akkub, Johanan, Delaiah and Anani—seven in all.

Other Clans of Judah

4 The descendants of Judah:
Perez, Hezron, Carmi, Hur and Shobal.
2 Reaiah son of Shobal was the father of Jahath, and Jahath the father of Ahumai and Lahad. These were the clans of the Zorathites.
3 These were the sons[f] of Etam:
Jezreel, Ishma and Idbash. Their sister was named Hazzelelponi.
4 Penuel was the father of Gedor, and Ezer the father of Hushah.
These were the descendants of Hur, the firstborn of Ephrathah and father[g] of Bethlehem.
5 Ashhur the father of Tekoa had two wives, Helah and Naarah.
6 Naarah bore him Ahuzzam, Hepher, Temeni and Haahashtari. These were the descendants of Naarah.
7 The sons of Helah:
Zereth, Zohar, Ethnan,
8 and Koz, who was the father of Anub and Hazzobebah and of the clans of Aharhel son of Harum.

9 Jabez was more honorable than his
brothers. His mother had named him Jabez,[h] saying, "I gave birth to him in pain."
10 Jabez cried out to the God of Israel, "Oh,
that you would bless me and enlarge my
territory! Let your hand be with me, and
keep me from harm so that I will be free
from pain." And God granted his request.

11 Kelub, Shuhah's brother, was the father of Mehir, who was the father of Eshton.
12 Eshton was the father of Beth Rapha, Paseah and Tehinnah the father of Ir Nahash.[i] These were the men of Recah.

13 The sons of Kenaz:
Othniel and Seraiah.
The sons of Othniel:
Hathath and Meonothai.[j]
14 Meonothai was the father of Ophrah.
Seraiah was the father of Joab, the father of Ge Harashim.[k] It was called this because its people were craftsmen.
15 The sons of Caleb son of Jephunneh:
Iru, Elah and Naam.
The son of Elah:
Kenaz.
16 The sons of Jehallelel:
Ziph, Ziphah, Tiria and Asarel.
17 The sons of Ezrah:
Jether, Mered, Epher and Jalon. One of Mered's wives gave birth to Miriam, Shammai and Ishbah the father of Eshtemoa.
18 (His Judean wife gave birth to Jered the father of Gedor, Heber the father of Soco, and Jekuthiel the father of Zanoah.) These were the children of Pharaoh's daughter Bithiah, whom Mered had married.
19 The sons of Hodiah's wife, the sister of Naham:
the father of Keilah the Garmite, and Eshtemoa the Maacathite.
20 The sons of Shimon:
Amnon, Rinnah, Ben-Hanan and Tilon.
The descendants of Ishi:
Zoheth and Ben-Zoheth.
21 The sons of Shelah son of Judah:
Er the father of Lecah, Laadah the father of Mareshah and the clans of the linen workers at Beth Ashbea,
22 Jokim, the men of Cozeba, and Joash and Saraph, who ruled in Moab and Jashubi Lehem. (These records are from ancient times.)
23 They were the potters who lived at Netaim and Gederah; they stayed there and worked for the king.

Simeon

24 The descendants of Simeon:

[f] 3 Some Septuagint manuscripts (see also Vulgate); Hebrew *father* [g] 4 *Father* may mean *civic leader* or *military leader;* also in verses 12, 14, 17, 18 and possibly elsewhere. [h] 9 *Jabez* sounds like the Hebrew for *pain.* [i] 12 Or *of the city of Nahash* [j] 13 Some Septuagint manuscripts and Vulgate; Hebrew does not have *and Meonothai.* [k] 14 *Ge Harashim* means *valley of craftsmen.*

Nemuel, Jamin, Jarib, Zerah and
Shaul;
25 Shallum was Shaul's son, Mibsam
his son and Mishma his son.
26 The descendants of Mishma:
Hammuel his son, Zaccur his son
and Shimei his son.

27 Shimei had sixteen sons and six
daughters, but his brothers did not have
many children; so their entire clan did not
become as numerous as the people of Judah. 28 They lived in Beersheba, Moladah,
Hazar Shual, 29 Bilhah, Ezem, Tolad, 30 Bethuel, Hormah, Ziklag, 31 Beth Marcaboth,
Hazar Susim, Beth Biri and Shaaraim.
These were their towns until the reign of
David. 32 Their surrounding villages were
Etam, Ain, Rimmon, Token and Ashan—
five towns— 33 and all the villages around
these towns as far as Baalath.[l] These were
their settlements. And they kept a genealogical record.

34 Meshobab, Jamlech, Joshah son of
Amaziah, 35 Joel, Jehu son of Joshi-
biah, the son of Seraiah, the son of
Asiel, 36 also Elioenai, Jaakobah,
Jeshohaiah, Asaiah, Adiel, Jesimiel,
Benaiah, 37 and Ziza son of Shiphi,
the son of Allon, the son of Jedaiah,
the son of Shimri, the son of Shemaiah.

38 The men listed above by name were
leaders of their clans. Their families increased greatly, 39 and they went to the outskirts of Gedor to the east of the valley in
search of pasture for their flocks. 40 They
found rich, good pasture, and the land
was spacious, peaceful and quiet. Some
Hamites had lived there formerly.

41 The men whose names were listed
came in the days of Hezekiah king of Judah. They attacked the Hamites in their
dwellings and also the Meunites who
were there and completely destroyed[m]
them, as is evident to this day. Then they
settled in their place, because there was
pasture for their flocks. 42 And five hundred of these Simeonites, led by Pelatiah,
Neariah, Rephaiah and Uzziel, the sons of
Ishi, invaded the hill country of Seir.
43 They killed the remaining Amalekites
who had escaped, and they have lived
there to this day.

[l] *33* Some Septuagint manuscripts (see also Joshua 19:8); Hebrew *Baal* [m] *41* The Hebrew term refers to the irrevocable giving over of things or persons to the LORD, often by totally destroying them.

PRAYER: INTERCESSION

YOU, the God of Israel, spoke; You, the Rock of Israel, said to David: "He who rules over men in righteousness, who rules in the fear of God, is like the light of morning when the sun rises, a morning without clouds, or like the tender grass springing out of the earth through the sunshine after rain." (2 Samuel 23:3–4)

***TAKE** a few moments to intercede on behalf of your local, state or provincial, and national governments. Pray for spiritual revival in the nation and offer prayers regarding current events and concerns.*

NT Acts 14:21–15:21

The Return to Antioch in Syria

21 They preached the good news in that
city and won a large number of disciples.
Then they returned to Lystra, Iconium and
Antioch, 22 strengthening the disciples and
encouraging them to remain true to the
faith. "We must go through many hardships to enter the kingdom of God," they
said. 23 Paul and Barnabas appointed elders[a] for them in each church and, with
prayer and fasting, committed them to the
Lord, in whom they had put their trust.
24 After going through Pisidia, they came
into Pamphylia, 25 and when they had
preached the word in Perga, they went
down to Attalia.

26 From Attalia they sailed back to Antioch, where they had been committed to
the grace of God for the work they had

[a] *23* Or *Barnabas ordained elders;* or *Barnabas had elders elected*

now completed. 27 On arriving there, they
gathered the church together and reported all that God had done through them
and how he had opened the door of faith
to the Gentiles. 28 And they stayed there a
long time with the disciples.

The Council at Jerusalem

15 Some men came down from Judea to
Antioch and were teaching the brothers: "Unless you are circumcised, according to the custom taught by Moses, you
cannot be saved." 2 This brought Paul and
Barnabas into sharp dispute and debate
with them. So Paul and Barnabas were appointed, along with some other believers,
to go up to Jerusalem to see the apostles
and elders about this question. 3 The
church sent them on their way, and as
they traveled through Phoenicia and
Samaria, they told how the Gentiles had
been converted. This news made all the
brothers very glad. 4 When they came to
Jerusalem, they were welcomed by the
church and the apostles and elders, to
whom they reported everything God had
done through them.

5 Then some of the believers who belonged to the party of the Pharisees stood
up and said, "The Gentiles must be circumcised and required to obey the law of
Moses."

6 The apostles and elders met to consider this question. 7 After much discussion,
Peter got up and addressed them: "Brothers, you know that some time ago God
made a choice among you that the Gentiles might hear from my lips the message
of the gospel and believe. 8 God, who
knows the heart, showed that he accepted
them by giving the Holy Spirit to them,
just as he did to us. 9 He made no distinction between us and them, for he purified
their hearts by faith. 10 Now then, why do
you try to test God by putting on the
necks of the disciples a yoke that neither
we nor our fathers have been able to bear?
11 No! We believe it is through the grace of
our Lord Jesus that we are saved, just as
they are."

12 The whole assembly became silent as
they listened to Barnabas and Paul telling
about the miraculous signs and wonders
God had done among the Gentiles
through them. 13 When they finished,
James spoke up: "Brothers, listen to me.
14 Simon[b] has described to us how God at
first showed his concern by taking from
the Gentiles a people for himself. 15 The
words of the prophets are in agreement
with this, as it is written:

16 " 'After this I will return
and rebuild David's fallen tent.
Its ruins I will rebuild,
and I will restore it,
17 that the remnant of men may seek the
Lord,
and all the Gentiles who bear my
name,
says the Lord, who does these things'[c]
18 that have been known for ages.[d]

19 "It is my judgment, therefore, that we
should not make it difficult for the Gentiles who are turning to God. 20 Instead we
should write to them, telling them to abstain from food polluted by idols, from
sexual immorality, from the meat of strangled animals and from blood. 21 For Moses has been preached in every city from
the earliest times and is read in the synagogues on every Sabbath."

[b] 14 Greek *Simeon,* a variant of *Simon;* that is, Peter
[c] 17 Amos 9:11,12 [d] 17,18 Some manuscripts
things'— / [18]known to the Lord for ages is his work

PRAYER: MY RELATIONSHIP TO OTHERS

I WILL provide those who serve under me with what is just and fair,
knowing that I also have a Master in heaven.
(Colossians 4:1)

PAUSE *to review your relationships with others and to commit them to the Lord.*

Reuben

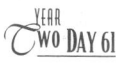

5 The sons of Reuben the firstborn of Israel (he was the firstborn, but when he defiled his father's marriage bed, his rights as firstborn were given to the sons of Joseph son of Israel; so he could not be listed in the genealogical record in accordance with his birthright,
2 and though Judah was the strongest of his brothers and a ruler came from him, the rights of the firstborn belonged to Joseph)—
3 the sons of Reuben the firstborn of Israel:
Hanoch, Pallu, Hezron and Carmi.
4 The descendants of Joel:
Shemaiah his son, Gog his son,
Shimei his son,
5 Micah his son,
Reaiah his son, Baal his son,
6 and Beerah his son, whom Tiglath-Pileser[a] king of Assyria took into exile. Beerah was a leader of the Reubenites.
7 Their relatives by clans, listed according to their genealogical records:
Jeiel the chief, Zechariah,
8 and Bela son of Azaz, the son of Shema, the son of Joel. They settled in the area from Aroer to Nebo and Baal Meon.
9 To the east they occupied the land up to the edge of the desert that extends to the Euphrates River, because their livestock had increased in Gilead.
10 During Saul's reign they waged war against the Hagrites, who were defeated at their hands; they occupied the dwellings of the Hagrites throughout the entire region east of Gilead.

Gad

11 The Gadites lived next to them in Bashan, as far as Salecah:
12 Joel was the chief, Shapham the second, then Janai and Shaphat, in Bashan.
13 Their relatives, by families, were:
Michael, Meshullam, Sheba, Jorai, Jacan, Zia and Eber—seven in all.
14 These were the sons of Abihail son of Huri, the son of Jaroah, the son of Gilead, the son of Michael, the son of Jeshishai, the son of Jahdo, the son of Buz.
15 Ahi son of Abdiel, the son of Guni, was head of their family.
16 The Gadites lived in Gilead, in Bashan and its outlying villages, and on all the pasturelands of Sharon as far as they extended.
17 All these were entered in the genealogical records during the reigns of Jotham king of Judah and Jeroboam king of Israel.

18 The Reubenites, the Gadites and the half-tribe of Manasseh had 44,760 men ready for military service—able-bodied men who could handle shield and sword, who could use a bow, and who were trained for battle.
19 They waged war against the Hagrites, Jetur, Naphish and Nodab.
20 They were helped in fighting them, and God handed the Hagrites and all their allies over to them, because they cried out to him during the battle. He answered their prayers, because they trusted in him.
21 They seized the livestock of the Hagrites—fifty thousand camels, two hundred fifty thousand sheep and two thousand donkeys. They also took one hundred thousand people captive,
22 and many others fell slain, because the battle was God's. And they occupied the land until the exile.

The Half-Tribe of Manasseh

23 The people of the half-tribe of Manasseh were numerous; they settled in the land from Bashan to Baal Hermon, that is, to Senir (Mount Hermon).
24 These were the heads of their families: Epher, Ishi, Eliel, Azriel, Jeremiah, Hodaviah and Jahdiel. They were brave warriors, famous men, and heads of their families.
25 But they were unfaithful to the God of their fathers and prostituted themselves to the gods of the peoples of the land, whom God had destroyed before them.
26 So the God of Israel stirred up the spirit of Pul king of Assyria (that is, Tiglath-Pileser king of Assyria), who took the Reubenites, the Gadites and the half tribe of Manasseh into exile. He took them to Halah, Habor, Hara and the river of Gozan, where they are to this day.

[a] 6 Hebrew *Tilgath-Pilneser,* a variant of *Tiglath-Pileser;* also in verse 26

PRAYER: AFFIRMATION

THOSE who belong to You, Christ Jesus, have crucified the flesh with its passions and desires. (Galatians 5:24) . . . I have put off the old self with its practices and have put on the new self, which is being renewed in full knowledge according to Your image, O my Creator. (Colossians 3:9–10)

__PAUSE__ to reflect on these Biblical affirmations.

NT Acts 15:22-41

The Council's Letter to Gentile Believers

22Then the apostles and elders, with the
whole church, decided to choose some of
their own men and send them to Antioch
with Paul and Barnabas. They chose Judas
(called Barsabbas) and Silas, two men
who were leaders among the brothers.
23With them they sent the following letter:

The apostles and elders, your brothers,

To the Gentile believers in Antioch, Syria and Cilicia:

Greetings.

24We have heard that some went
out from us without our authorization and disturbed you, troubling
your minds by what they said. 25So
we all agreed to choose some men
and send them to you with our dear
friends Barnabas and Paul— 26men
who have risked their lives for the
name of our Lord Jesus Christ.
27Therefore we are sending Judas and
Silas to confirm by word of mouth
what we are writing. 28It seemed good
to the Holy Spirit and to us not to
burden you with anything beyond
the following requirements: 29You are
to abstain from food sacrificed to
idols, from blood, from the meat of
strangled animals and from sexual
immorality. You will do well to avoid
these things.

Farewell.

30The men were sent off and went down
to Antioch, where they gathered the
church together and delivered the letter.
31The people read it and were glad for its
encouraging message. 32Judas and Silas,
who themselves were prophets, said much
to encourage and strengthen the brothers.
33After spending some time there, they
were sent off by the brothers with the
blessing of peace to return to those who
had sent them.[a] 35But Paul and Barnabas
remained in Antioch, where they and
many others taught and preached the
word of the Lord.

Disagreement Between Paul and Barnabas

36Some time later Paul said to Barnabas,
"Let us go back and visit the brothers in
all the towns where we preached the word
of the Lord and see how they are doing."
37Barnabas wanted to take John, also
called Mark, with them, 38but Paul did not
think it wise to take him, because he had
deserted them in Pamphylia and had not
continued with them in the work. 39They
had such a sharp disagreement that they
parted company. Barnabas took Mark and
sailed for Cyprus, 40but Paul chose Silas
and left, commended by the brothers to
the grace of the Lord. 41He went through
Syria and Cilicia, strengthening the
churches.

[a] 33 Some manuscripts *them,* [34]*but Silas decided to remain there*

PRAYER: THE ATTRIBUTES OF GOD

O MOST High, You are sovereign over the kingdoms on earth and give them to whomever You wish and set over them the lowliest of people. I will bless You, Most High, and praise and honor You who live

forever. Your dominion is an eternal dominion, and Your kingdom endures from generation to generation. You regard all the inhabitants of the earth as nothing and do as You please with the host of heaven and the inhabitants of the earth. No one can hold back Your hand or say to You: "What have You done?" I praise, exalt and honor You, King of heaven, for all Your works are true, and all Your ways are just, and You are able to humble those who walk in pride.

(Daniel 4:17, 34–35, 37)

***PAUSE** to reflect on these affirmations about the person, powers and perfection of God.*

YEAR 2
DAY 62

OT 1 Chronicles 6:1–81

Levi

6 The sons of Levi:
Gershon, Kohath and Merari.
2 The sons of Kohath:
Amram, Izhar, Hebron and Uzziel.
3 The children of Amram:
Aaron, Moses and Miriam.
The sons of Aaron:
Nadab, Abihu, Eleazar and Ithamar.
4 Eleazar was the father of Phinehas,
Phinehas the father of Abishua,
5 Abishua the father of Bukki,
Bukki the father of Uzzi,
6 Uzzi the father of Zerahiah,
Zerahiah the father of Meraioth,
7 Meraioth the father of Amariah,
Amariah the father of Ahitub,
8 Ahitub the father of Zadok,
Zadok the father of Ahimaaz,
9 Ahimaaz the father of Azariah,
Azariah the father of Johanan,
10 Johanan the father of Azariah (it was he who served as priest in the temple Solomon built in Jerusalem),
11 Azariah the father of Amariah,
Amariah the father of Ahitub,
12 Ahitub the father of Zadok,
Zadok the father of Shallum,
13 Shallum the father of Hilkiah,
Hilkiah the father of Azariah,
14 Azariah the father of Seraiah,
and Seraiah the father of Jehozadak.
15 Jehozadak was deported when the LORD sent Judah and Jerusalem into exile by the hand of Nebuchadnezzar.

16 The sons of Levi:
Gershon,[a] Kohath and Merari.
17 These are the names of the sons of Gershon:
Libni and Shimei.
18 The sons of Kohath:
Amram, Izhar, Hebron and Uzziel.
19 The sons of Merari:
Mahli and Mushi.
These are the clans of the Levites listed according to their fathers:
20 Of Gershon:
Libni his son, Jehath his son,
Zimmah his son, 21 Joah his son,
Iddo his son, Zerah his son
and Jeatherai his son.
22 The descendants of Kohath:
Amminadab his son, Korah his son,
Assir his son, 23 Elkanah his son,
Ebiasaph his son, Assir his son,
24 Tahath his son, Uriel his son,
Uzziah his son and Shaul his son.
25 The descendants of Elkanah:
Amasai, Ahimoth,
26 Elkanah his son,[b] Zophai his son,
Nahath his son, 27 Eliab his son,
Jeroham his son, Elkanah his son
and Samuel his son.[c]
28 The sons of Samuel:
Joel[d] the firstborn

[a] *16* Hebrew *Gershom,* a variant of *Gershon;* also in verses 17, 20, 43, 62 and 71 [b] *26* Some Hebrew manuscripts, Septuagint and Syriac; most Hebrew manuscripts *Ahimoth* [26]*and Elkanah. The sons of Elkanah:* [c] *27* Some Septuagint manuscripts (see also 1 Samuel 1:19,20 and 1 Chron. 6:33,34); Hebrew does not have *and Samuel his son.*
[d] *28* Some Septuagint manuscripts and Syriac (see also 1 Samuel 8:2 and 1 Chron. 6:33); Hebrew does not have *Joel.*

and Abijah the second son.
29 The descendants of Merari:
Mahli, Libni his son,
Shimei his son, Uzzah his son,
30 Shimea his son, Haggiah his son
and Asaiah his son.

The Temple Musicians

31 These are the men David put in charge of the music in the house of the LORD after the ark came to rest there. 32 They ministered with music before the tabernacle, the Tent of Meeting, until Solomon built the temple of the LORD in Jerusalem. They performed their duties according to the regulations laid down for them.

33 Here are the men who served, together with their sons:
From the Kohathites:
Heman, the musician,
the son of Joel, the son of Samuel,
34 the son of Elkanah, the son of Jeroham,
the son of Eliel, the son of Toah,
35 the son of Zuph, the son of Elkanah,
the son of Mahath, the son of Amasai,
36 the son of Elkanah, the son of Joel,
the son of Azariah, the son of Zephaniah,
37 the son of Tahath, the son of Assir,
the son of Ebiasaph, the son of Korah,
38 the son of Izhar, the son of Kohath,
the son of Levi, the son of Israel;
39 and Heman's associate Asaph, who served at his right hand:
Asaph son of Berekiah, the son of Shimea,
40 the son of Michael, the son of Baaseiah,[e]
the son of Malkijah, 41 the son of Ethni,
the son of Zerah, the son of Adaiah,
42 the son of Ethan, the son of Zimmah,
the son of Shimei, 43 the son of Jahath,
the son of Gershon, the son of Levi;
44 and from their associates, the Merarites, at his left hand:
Ethan son of Kishi, the son of Abdi,
the son of Malluch, 45 the son of Hashabiah,
the son of Amaziah, the son of Hilkiah,
46 the son of Amzi, the son of Bani,
the son of Shemer, 47 the son of Mahli,
the son of Mushi, the son of Merari,
the son of Levi.

48 Their fellow Levites were assigned to all the other duties of the tabernacle, the house of God. 49 But Aaron and his descendants were the ones who presented offerings on the altar of burnt offering and on the altar of incense in connection with all that was done in the Most Holy Place, making atonement for Israel, in accordance with all that Moses the servant of God had commanded.

50 These were the descendants of Aaron:
Eleazar his son, Phinehas his son,
Abishua his son, 51 Bukki his son,
Uzzi his son, Zerahiah his son,
52 Meraioth his son, Amariah his son,
Ahitub his son, 53 Zadok his son
and Ahimaaz his son.

54 These were the locations of their settlements allotted as their territory (they were assigned to the descendants of Aaron who were from the Kohathite clan, because the first lot was for them):

55 They were given Hebron in Judah with its surrounding pasturelands.
56 But the fields and villages around the city were given to Caleb son of Jephunneh.

57 So the descendants of Aaron were given Hebron (a city of refuge), and Libnah,[f] Jattir, Eshtemoa, 58 Hilen,
Debir, 59 Ashan, Juttah[g] and Beth Shemesh, together with their pasturelands. 60 And from the tribe of Benjamin they were given Gibeon,[h] Geba, Alemeth and Anathoth, together with their pasturelands.

These towns, which were distributed among the Kohathite clans, were thirteen in all.

[e] *40* Most Hebrew manuscripts; some Hebrew manuscripts, one Septuagint manuscript and Syriac *Maaseiah* [f] *57* See Joshua 21:13; Hebrew *given the cities of refuge: Hebron, Libnah.* [g] *59* Syriac (see also Septuagint and Joshua 21:16); Hebrew does not have *Juttah.* [h] *60* See Joshua 21:17; Hebrew does not have *Gibeon.*

61The rest of Kohath's descendants were
allotted ten towns from the clans of half
the tribe of Manasseh.
62The descendants of Gershon, clan by
clan, were allotted thirteen towns from
the tribes of Issachar, Asher and Naphtali, and from the part of the tribe of Manasseh that is in Bashan.
63The descendants of Merari, clan by
clan, were allotted twelve towns from the
tribes of Reuben, Gad and Zebulun.
64So the Israelites gave the Levites these
towns and their pasturelands. 65From the
tribes of Judah, Simeon and Benjamin
they allotted the previously named towns.
66Some of the Kohathite clans were giv-
en as their territory towns from the tribe
of Ephraim.
67In the hill country of Ephraim
they were given Shechem (a city of
refuge), and Gezer,[i] 68Jokmeam, Beth
Horon, 69Aijalon and Gath Rimmon,
together with their pasturelands.
70And from half the tribe of Manasseh the Israelites gave Aner and
Bileam, together with their pasturelands, to the rest of the Kohathite
clans.

71The Gershonites received the following:
From the clan of the half-tribe of Manasseh
they received Golan in Bashan and
also Ashtaroth, together with their
pasturelands;
72from the tribe of Issachar
they received Kedesh, Daberath,
73Ramoth and Anem, together with
their pasturelands;
74from the tribe of Asher
they received Mashal, Abdon,
75Hukok and Rehob, together with
their pasturelands;
76and from the tribe of Naphtali
they received Kedesh in Galilee,
Hammon and Kiriathaim, together with their pasturelands.

77The Merarites (the rest of the Levites)
received the following:
From the tribe of Zebulun
they received Jokneam, Kartah,[j]
Rimmono and Tabor, together
with their pasturelands;
78from the tribe of Reuben across the
Jordan east of Jericho
they received Bezer in the desert,
Jahzah, 79Kedemoth and Mephaath,
together with their pasturelands;
80and from the tribe of Gad
they received Ramoth in Gilead,
Mahanaim, 81Heshbon and Jazer,
together with their pasturelands.

[i] 67 See Joshua 21:21; Hebrew *given the cities of refuge: Shechem, Gezer.* [j] 77 See Septuagint and Joshua 21:34; Hebrew does not have *Jokneam, Kartah.*

PRAYER: THANKSGIVING

I LOVE You, Lord, because You heard my voice and my supplications. Because You turned Your ear to me, I will call on You as long as I live. (Psalm 116:1–2) . . . I will give thanks to You, the God of heaven, for Your merciful love endures forever. (Psalm 136:26)

PAUSE *to offer your own expressions of thanksgiving.*

NT Acts 16:1–40

Timothy Joins Paul and Silas

16 He came to Derbe and then to Lystra,
where a disciple named Timothy lived,
whose mother was a Jewess and a believer,
but whose father was a Greek. 2The brothers at Lystra and Iconium spoke well of
him. 3Paul wanted to take him along on the
journey, so he circumcised him because of
the Jews who lived in that area, for they all
knew that his father was a Greek. 4As they
traveled from town to town, they delivered
the decisions reached by the apostles and
elders in Jerusalem for the people to obey.
5So the churches were strengthened in the
faith and grew daily in numbers.

Paul's Vision of the Man of Macedonia

6Paul and his companions traveled
throughout the region of Phrygia and Ga-

latia, having been kept by the Holy Spirit
from preaching the word in the province
of Asia. 7When they came to the border of
Mysia, they tried to enter Bithynia, but the
Spirit of Jesus would not allow them to.
8So they passed by Mysia and went down
to Troas. 9During the night Paul had a vision of a man of Macedonia standing and
begging him, "Come over to Macedonia
and help us." 10After Paul had seen the vision, we got ready at once to leave for
Macedonia, concluding that God had
called us to preach the gospel to them.

Lydia's Conversion in Philippi

11From Troas we put out to sea and
sailed straight for Samothrace, and the
next day on to Neapolis. 12From there we
traveled to Philippi, a Roman colony and
the leading city of that district of Macedonia. And we stayed there several days.
13On the Sabbath we went outside the
city gate to the river, where we expected to
find a place of prayer. We sat down and
began to speak to the women who had
gathered there. 14One of those listening
was a woman named Lydia, a dealer in
purple cloth from the city of Thyatira,
who was a worshiper of God. The Lord
opened her heart to respond to Paul's
message. 15When she and the members of
her household were baptized, she invited
us to her home. "If you consider me a believer in the Lord," she said, "come and
stay at my house." And she persuaded us.

Paul and Silas in Prison

16Once when we were going to the place
of prayer, we were met by a slave girl who
had a spirit by which she predicted the future. She earned a great deal of money for
her owners by fortune-telling. 17This girl
followed Paul and the rest of us, shouting,
"These men are servants of the Most High
God, who are telling you the way to be
saved." 18She kept this up for many days.
Finally Paul became so troubled that he
turned around and said to the spirit, "In
the name of Jesus Christ I command you
to come out of her!" At that moment the
spirit left her.
19When the owners of the slave girl realized that their hope of making money
was gone, they seized Paul and Silas and
dragged them into the marketplace to face
the authorities. 20They brought them before the magistrates and said, "These men
are Jews, and are throwing our city into an
uproar 21by advocating customs unlawful
for us Romans to accept or practice."
22The crowd joined in the attack against
Paul and Silas, and the magistrates ordered
them to be stripped and beaten. 23After they
had been severely flogged, they were
thrown into prison, and the jailer was commanded to guard them carefully. 24Upon receiving such orders, he put them in the inner cell and fastened their feet in the stocks.
25About midnight Paul and Silas were
praying and singing hymns to God, and
the other prisoners were listening to
them. 26Suddenly there was such a violent
earthquake that the foundations of the
prison were shaken. At once all the prison
doors flew open, and everybody's chains
came loose. 27The jailer woke up, and
when he saw the prison doors open, he
drew his sword and was about to kill himself because he thought the prisoners had
escaped. 28But Paul shouted, "Don't harm
yourself! We are all here!"
29The jailer called for lights, rushed in
and fell trembling before Paul and Silas.
30He then brought them out and asked,
"Sirs, what must I do to be saved?"
31They replied, "Believe in the Lord
Jesus, and you will be saved—you and
your household." 32Then they spoke the
word of the Lord to him and to all the
others in his house. 33At that hour of the
night the jailer took them and washed
their wounds; then immediately he and
all his family were baptized. 34The jailer
brought them into his house and set a
meal before them; he was filled with joy
because he had come to believe in God—
he and his whole family.
35When it was daylight, the magistrates
sent their officers to the jailer with the order: "Release those men." 36The jailer told
Paul, "The magistrates have ordered that
you and Silas be released. Now you can
leave. Go in peace."
37But Paul said to the officers: "They
beat us publicly without a trial, even
though we are Roman citizens, and threw
us into prison. And now do they want to
get rid of us quietly? No! Let them come
themselves and escort us out."
38The officers reported this to the magistrates, and when they heard that Paul
and Silas were Roman citizens, they were
alarmed. 39They came to appease them

and escorted them from the prison, requesting them to leave the city. [40]After Paul and Silas came out of the prison, they went to Lydia's house, where they met with the brothers and encouraged them. Then they left.

PRAYER: THE WORKS OF GOD

***JESUS**, You who come from above are above all; he who is from the earth belongs to the earth and speaks as one from the earth. You who come from heaven are above all. You, whom God has sent, speak the words of God, for You give the Spirit without limit. (John 3:31, 34) . . . The Father judges no one, but has given all judgment to You, Jesus, His Son, that all may honor You just as they honor the Father. Those who do not honor You do not honor the Father who sent You. (John 5:22–23)*

***TAKE** a moment to consider the greatness of God's wonderful works.*

YEAR 2
DAY 63

OT **Psalm 83**

Psalm 83

A song. A psalm of Asaph.

1 O God, do not keep silent;
be not quiet, O God, be not still.
2 See how your enemies are astir,
how your foes rear their heads.
3 With cunning they conspire against your people;
they plot against those you cherish.
4 "Come," they say, "let us destroy them as a nation,
that the name of Israel be remembered no more."

5 With one mind they plot together;
they form an alliance against you—
6 the tents of Edom and the Ishmaelites,
of Moab and the Hagrites,
7 Gebal,[a] Ammon and Amalek,
Philistia, with the people of Tyre.
8 Even Assyria has joined them
to lend strength to the descendants of Lot. *Selah*

9 Do to them as you did to Midian,
as you did to Sisera and Jabin at the river Kishon,
10 who perished at Endor
and became like refuse on the ground.
11 Make their nobles like Oreb and Zeeb,
all their princes like Zebah and Zalmunna,
12 who said, "Let us take possession
of the pasturelands of God."

13 Make them like tumbleweed, O my God,
like chaff before the wind.
14 As fire consumes the forest
or a flame sets the mountains ablaze,
15 so pursue them with your tempest
and terrify them with your storm.
16 Cover their faces with shame
so that men will seek your name, O LORD.

17 May they ever be ashamed and dismayed;
may they perish in disgrace.
18 Let them know that you, whose name is the LORD—
that you alone are the Most High
over all the earth.

[a] 7 That is, Byblos

PRAYER: ADORATION

***WHO** gave You authority over the earth, O God? Who put You in charge of the whole world? If You set Your heart on it and withdrew Your spirit and Your breath, all flesh would perish together*

and people would return to dust. (Job 34:13–15) . . . Every animal of the forest is Yours, and the cattle on a thousand hills. You know every bird in the mountains, and everything that moves in the field is Yours. (Psalm 50:10–11)

PAUSE *to express your thoughts of praise and worship.*

NT Acts 17:1–15

In Thessalonica

17 When they had passed through Amphipolis and Apollonia, they came to Thessalonica, where there was a Jewish synagogue. 2 As his custom was, Paul went into the synagogue, and on three Sabbath days he reasoned with them from the Scriptures, 3 explaining and proving that the Christ[a] had to suffer and rise from the dead. "This Jesus I am proclaiming to you is the Christ,[a]" he said. 4 Some of the Jews were persuaded and joined Paul and Silas, as did a large number of God-fearing Greeks and not a few prominent women.

5 But the Jews were jealous; so they rounded up some bad characters from the marketplace, formed a mob and started a riot in the city. They rushed to Jason's house in search of Paul and Silas in order to bring them out to the crowd.[b] 6 But when they did not find them, they dragged Jason and some other brothers before the city officials, shouting: "These men who have caused trouble all over the world have now come here, 7 and Jason has welcomed them into his house. They are all defying Caesar's decrees, saying that there is another king, one called Jesus." 8 When they heard this, the crowd and the city officials were thrown into turmoil. 9 Then they made Jason and the others post bond and let them go.

In Berea

10 As soon as it was night, the brothers sent Paul and Silas away to Berea. On arriving there, they went to the Jewish synagogue. 11 Now the Bereans were of more noble character than the Thessalonians, for they received the message with great eagerness and examined the Scriptures every day to see if what Paul said was true. 12 Many of the Jews believed, as did also a number of prominent Greek women and many Greek men.

13 When the Jews in Thessalonica learned that Paul was preaching the word of God at Berea, they went there too, agitating the crowds and stirring them up. 14 The brothers immediately sent Paul to the coast, but Silas and Timothy stayed at Berea. 15 The men who escorted Paul brought him to Athens and then left with instructions for Silas and Timothy to join him as soon as possible.

[a] 3 Or *Messiah*   [b] 5 Or *the assembly of the people*

PRAYER: MY RELATIONSHIP TO GOD

YOUR grace, O Lord, was poured out on me abundantly, along with the faith and love that are in Christ Jesus. (1 Timothy 1:14) . . . O God, You have saved me and called me with a holy calling, not according to my works but according to Your own purpose and grace. (2 Timothy 1:9)

PAUSE *to thank God for the relationship that you enjoy with Him in Jesus Christ.*

Issachar

7 The sons of Issachar:
Tola, Puah, Jashub and Shimron—four in all.
2 The sons of Tola:
Uzzi, Rephaiah, Jeriel, Jahmai, Ibsam and Samuel—heads of their families. During the reign of David, the descendants of Tola listed as fighting men in their genealogy numbered 22,600.
3 The son of Uzzi:
Izrahiah.
The sons of Izrahiah:
Michael, Obadiah, Joel and Isshiah. All five of them were chiefs.
4 According to their family genealogy, they had 36,000 men ready for battle, for they had many wives and children.
5 The relatives who were fighting men belonging to all the clans of Issachar, as listed in their genealogy, were 87,000 in all.

Benjamin

6 Three sons of Benjamin:
Bela, Beker and Jediael.
7 The sons of Bela:
Ezbon, Uzzi, Uzziel, Jerimoth and Iri, heads of families—five in all. Their genealogical record listed 22,034 fighting men.
8 The sons of Beker:
Zemirah, Joash, Eliezer, Elioenai, Omri, Jeremoth, Abijah, Anathoth and Alemeth. All these were the
sons of Beker. 9 Their genealogical
record listed the heads of families and 20,200 fighting men.
10 The son of Jediael:
Bilhan.
The sons of Bilhan:
Jeush, Benjamin, Ehud, Kenaanah, Zethan, Tarshish and Ahishahar.
11 All these sons of Jediael were
heads of families. There were 17,200 fighting men ready to go out to war.
12 The Shuppites and Huppites were the descendants of Ir, and the Hushites the descendants of Aher.

Naphtali

13 The sons of Naphtali:
Jahziel, Guni, Jezer and Shillem[a]—the descendants of Bilhah.

Manasseh

14 The descendants of Manasseh:
Asriel was his descendant through his Aramean concubine. She gave birth to Makir the father of Gilead.
15 Makir took a wife from among the
Huppites and Shuppites. His sister's name was Maacah.
Another descendant was named Zelophehad, who had only daughters.
16 Makir's wife Maacah gave birth to
a son and named him Peresh. His brother was named Sheresh, and his sons were Ulam and Rakem.
17 The son of Ulam:
Bedan.
These were the sons of Gilead son of
Makir, the son of Manasseh. 18 His
sister Hammoleketh gave birth to Ishhod, Abiezer and Mahlah.
19 The sons of Shemida were:
Ahian, Shechem, Likhi and Aniam.

Ephraim

20 The descendants of Ephraim:
Shuthelah, Bered his son,
Tahath his son, Eleadah his son,
Tahath his son, 21 Zabad his son
and Shuthelah his son.
Ezer and Elead were killed by the native-born men of Gath, when they went down to seize their livestock.
22 Their father Ephraim mourned for
them many days, and his relatives came to comfort him. 23 Then he lay
with his wife again, and she became pregnant and gave birth to a son. He named him Beriah,[b] because there had been misfortune in his family.
24 His daughter was Sheerah, who
built Lower and Upper Beth Horon as well as Uzzen Sheerah.

[a] *13* Some Hebrew and Septuagint manuscripts (see also Gen. 46:24 and Num. 26:49); most Hebrew manuscripts *Shallum* [b] *23 Beriah* sounds like the Hebrew for *misfortune*.

25 Rephah was his son, Resheph his
son,[c]
Telah his son, Tahan his son,
26 Ladan his son, Ammihud his son,
Elishama his son, 27 Nun his son
and Joshua his son.
28 Their lands and settlements included
Bethel and its surrounding villages, Naa-
ran to the east, Gezer and its villages to
the west, and Shechem and its villages all
the way to Ayyah and its villages. 29 Along
the borders of Manasseh were Beth Shan,
Taanach, Megiddo and Dor, together with
their villages. The descendants of Joseph
son of Israel lived in these towns.

Asher

30 The sons of Asher:
Imnah, Ishvah, Ishvi and Beriah.
Their sister was Serah.
31 The sons of Beriah:
Heber and Malkiel, who was the
father of Birzaith.
32 Heber was the father of Japhlet, Shomer and Hotham and of their sister Shua.
33 The sons of Japhlet:
Pasach, Bimhal and Ashvath.
These were Japhlet's sons.
34 The sons of Shomer:
Ahi, Rohgah,[d] Hubbah and Aram.
35 The sons of his brother Helem:
Zophah, Imna, Shelesh and Amal.
36 The sons of Zophah:
Suah, Harnepher, Shual, Beri, Im-
rah, 37 Bezer, Hod, Shamma, Shil-
shah, Ithran[e] and Beera.
38 The sons of Jether:
Jephunneh, Pispah and Ara.
39 The sons of Ulla:
Arah, Hanniel and Rizia.
40 All these were descendants of Asher—
heads of families, choice men, brave warriors and outstanding leaders. The number of men ready for battle, as listed in
their genealogy, was 26,000.

[c] 25 Some Septuagint manuscripts; Hebrew does not have *his son.* [d] 34 Or *of his brother Shomer: Rohgah* [e] 37 Possibly a variant of *Jether*

PRAYER: CONFESSION

WHAT I do may seem right to me, but You, Lord, know what I am thinking. (Proverbs 21:2)

***ASK** the Spirit to search your heart and reveal any areas of unconfessed sin. Acknowledge these to the Lord and thank Him for His forgiveness.*

NT Acts 17:16–34

In Athens

16 While Paul was waiting for them in
Athens, he was greatly distressed to see
that the city was full of idols. 17 So he reasoned in the synagogue with the Jews and
the God-fearing Greeks, as well as in the
marketplace day by day with those who
happened to be there. 18 A group of Epi-
curean and Stoic philosophers began to
dispute with him. Some of them asked,
"What is this babbler trying to say?" Others remarked, "He seems to be advocating
foreign gods." They said this because Paul
was preaching the good news about Jesus
and the resurrection. 19 Then they took
him and brought him to a meeting of the
Areopagus, where they said to him, "May
we know what this new teaching is that
you are presenting? 20 You are bringing
some strange ideas to our ears, and we
want to know what they mean." 21 (All the
Athenians and the foreigners who lived
there spent their time doing nothing but
talking about and listening to the latest
ideas.)
22 Paul then stood up in the meeting of
the Areopagus and said: "Men of Athens!
I see that in every way you are very religious. 23 For as I walked around and
looked carefully at your objects of worship, I even found an altar with this inscription: TO AN UNKNOWN GOD. Now what
you worship as something unknown I am
going to proclaim to you.
24 "The God who made the world and
everything in it is the Lord of heaven and
earth and does not live in temples built by
hands. 25 And he is not served by human
hands, as if he needed anything, because

he himself gives all men life and breath
and everything else. 26 From one man he
made every nation of men, that they
should inhabit the whole earth; and he determined the times set for them and the exact places where they should live. 27 God
did this so that men would seek him and
perhaps reach out for him and find him,
though he is not far from each one of us.
28 'For in him we live and move and have
our being.' As some of your own poets
have said, 'We are his offspring.'

29 "Therefore since we are God's offspring, we should not think that the divine being is like gold or silver or stone—
an image made by man's design and skill.
30 In the past God overlooked such ignorance, but now he commands all people
everywhere to repent. 31 For he has set a
day when he will judge the world with
justice by the man he has appointed. He
has given proof of this to all men by raising him from the dead."

32 When they heard about the resurrection of the dead, some of them sneered,
but others said, "We want to hear you
again on this subject." 33 At that, Paul left
the Council. 34 A few men became followers of Paul and believed. Among them
was Dionysius, a member of the Areopagus, also a woman named Damaris, and a
number of others.

PRAYER: THE CHARACTER I WANT TO CULTIVATE

I WILL consider it all joy whenever I fall into various trials, knowing that the testing of my faith produces endurance. And I will let endurance finish its work, so that I may be mature and complete, lacking in nothing. I am blessed when I persevere under trial, because when I have been approved, I will receive the crown of life that You, O God, have promised to those who love You. (James 1:2–4, 12)

TAKE *a moment to ask the Lord for the grace to grow in godly character.*

YEAR 2 DAY 65

OT 1 Chronicles 8:1-40

The Genealogy of Saul the Benjamite

8 Benjamin was the father of Bela his
firstborn,
Ashbel the second son, Aharah the
third,
2 Nohah the fourth and Rapha the
fifth.
3 The sons of Bela were:
Addar, Gera, Abihud,[a] 4 Abishua,
Naaman, Ahoah, 5 Gera, Shephu-
phan and Huram.
6 These were the descendants of Ehud,
who were heads of families of
those living in Geba and were deported to Manahath:
7 Naaman, Ahijah, and Gera, who
deported them and who was the
father of Uzza and Ahihud.
8 Sons were born to Shaharaim in
Moab after he had divorced his
wives Hushim and Baara. 9 By his
wife Hodesh he had Jobab, Zibia,
Mesha, Malcam, 10 Jeuz, Sakia and
Mirmah. These were his sons,
heads of families. 11 By Hushim he
had Abitub and Elpaal.
12 The sons of Elpaal:
Eber, Misham, Shemed (who built
Ono and Lod with its surrounding
villages), 13 and Beriah and Shema,
who were heads of families of
those living in Aijalon and who
drove out the inhabitants of Gath.
14 Ahio, Shashak, Jeremoth, 15 Zebadiah,
Arad, Eder, 16 Michael, Ishpah and
Joha were the sons of Beriah.
17 Zebadiah, Meshullam, Hizki, Heber,
18 Ishmerai, Izliah and Jobab were
the sons of Elpaal.
19 Jakim, Zicri, Zabdi, 20 Elienai, Zillethai, Eliel, 21 Adaiah, Beraiah and
Shimrath were the sons of Shimei.
22 Ishpan, Eber, Eliel, 23 Abdon, Zicri,

[a] 3 Or *Gera the father of Ehud*

Hanan, [24]Hananiah, Elam, Anthothijah, [25]Iphdeiah and Penuel were the sons of Shashak.
[26]Shamsherai, Shehariah, Athaliah, [27]Jaareshiah, Elijah and Zicri were the sons of Jeroham.
[28]All these were heads of families, chiefs as listed in their genealogy, and they lived in Jerusalem.

[29]Jeiel[b] the father[c] of Gibeon lived in Gibeon.
His wife's name was Maacah, [30]and his firstborn son was Abdon, followed by Zur, Kish, Baal, Ner,[d] Nadab, [31]Gedor, Ahio, Zeker [32]and Mikloth, who was the father of Shimeah. They too lived near their relatives in Jerusalem.
[33]Ner was the father of Kish, Kish the father of Saul, and Saul the father of Jonathan, Malki-Shua, Abinadab and Esh-Baal.[e]
[34]The son of Jonathan:
Merib-Baal,[f] who was the father of Micah.
[35]The sons of Micah:
Pithon, Melech, Tarea and Ahaz.
[36]Ahaz was the father of Jehoaddah, Jehoaddah was the father of Alemeth, Azmaveth and Zimri, and Zimri was the father of Moza.
[37]Moza was the father of Binea; Raphah was his son, Eleasah his son and Azel his son.
[38]Azel had six sons, and these were their names:
Azrikam, Bokeru, Ishmael, Sheariah, Obadiah and Hanan. All these were the sons of Azel.
[39]The sons of his brother Eshek:
Ulam his firstborn, Jeush the second son and Eliphelet the third.
[40]The sons of Ulam were brave warriors who could handle the bow. They had many sons and grandsons—150 in all.
All these were the descendants of Benjamin.

[b] 29 Some Septuagint manuscripts (see also 1 Chron. 9:35); Hebrew does not have *Jeiel.*
[c] 29 *Father* may mean *civic leader* or *military leader.*
[d] 30 Some Septuagint manuscripts (see also 1 Chron. 9:36); Hebrew does not have *Ner.*
[e] 33 Also known as *Ish-Bosheth*
[f] 34 Also known as *Mephibosheth*

PRAYER: RENEWAL

MAY I be holy to You, for You, the Lord, are holy, and You have set me apart to be Your own. (Leviticus 20:26) . . .
May I learn to fear You all the days I live on the earth and teach Your words to my children. (Deuteronomy 4:10)

***PAUSE** to add your own prayers for personal renewal.*

NT Acts 18:1–28

In Corinth

18 After this, Paul left Athens and went to Corinth. [2]There he met a Jew named Aquila, a native of Pontus, who had recently come from Italy with his wife Priscilla, because Claudius had ordered all the Jews to leave Rome. Paul went to see them, [3]and because he was a tentmaker as they were, he stayed and worked with them. [4]Every Sabbath he reasoned in the synagogue, trying to persuade Jews and Greeks.

[5]When Silas and Timothy came from Macedonia, Paul devoted himself exclusively to preaching, testifying to the Jews that Jesus was the Christ.[a] [6]But when the Jews opposed Paul and became abusive, he shook out his clothes in protest and said to them, "Your blood be on your own heads! I am clear of my responsibility. From now on I will go to the Gentiles."

[7]Then Paul left the synagogue and went next door to the house of Titius Justus, a worshiper of God. [8]Crispus, the synagogue ruler, and his entire household believed in the Lord; and many of the Corinthians who heard him believed and were baptized.

[9]One night the Lord spoke to Paul in a

[a] 5 Or *Messiah;* also in verse 28

vision: "Do not be afraid; keep on speaking, do not be silent. 10For I am with you,
and no one is going to attack and harm
you, because I have many people in this
city." 11So Paul stayed for a year and a half,
teaching them the word of God.

12While Gallio was proconsul of Achaia,
the Jews made a united attack on Paul and
brought him into court. 13"This man,"
they charged, "is persuading the people to
worship God in ways contrary to the law."

14Just as Paul was about to speak, Gallio
said to the Jews, "If you Jews were making
a complaint about some misdemeanor or
serious crime, it would be reasonable for
me to listen to you. 15But since it involves
questions about words and names and
your own law—settle the matter yourselves.
I will not be a judge of such things." 16So
he had them ejected from the court. 17Then
they all turned on Sosthenes the synagogue
ruler and beat him in front of the court. But
Gallio showed no concern whatever.

Priscilla, Aquila and Apollos

18Paul stayed on in Corinth for some
time. Then he left the brothers and sailed
for Syria, accompanied by Priscilla and
Aquila. Before he sailed, he had his hair
cut off at Cenchrea because of a vow he
had taken. 19They arrived at Ephesus,
where Paul left Priscilla and Aquila. He
himself went into the synagogue and reasoned with the Jews. 20When they asked
him to spend more time with them, he declined. 21But as he left, he promised, "I will
come back if it is God's will." Then he set
sail from Ephesus. 22When he landed at
Caesarea, he went up and greeted the
church and then went down to Antioch.

23After spending some time in Antioch,
Paul set out from there and traveled from
place to place throughout the region of
Galatia and Phrygia, strengthening all the
disciples.

24Meanwhile a Jew named Apollos, a native of Alexandria, came to Ephesus. He
was a learned man, with a thorough
knowledge of the Scriptures. 25He had
been instructed in the way of the Lord, and
he spoke with great fervor[b] and taught
about Jesus accurately, though he knew
only the baptism of John. 26He began to
speak boldly in the synagogue. When
Priscilla and Aquila heard him, they invited him to their home and explained to
him the way of God more adequately.

27When Apollos wanted to go to Achaia, the brothers encouraged him and
wrote to the disciples there to welcome
him. On arriving, he was a great help to
those who by grace had believed. 28For he
vigorously refuted the Jews in public debate, proving from the Scriptures that
Jesus was the Christ.

[b] 25 Or *with fervor in the Spirit*

PRAYER: MY RELATIONSHIP TO OTHERS

WE are to put off falsehood and speak truthfully to our neighbors, for we are members of one another. (Ephesians 4:25) . . .
We thank You, O God, for other believers, and we pray that their faith would grow more and more, and that their love for each other would increase. (2 Thessalonians 1:3)

***PAUSE** to review your relationships with others and to commit them to the Lord.*

YEAR 2 DAY 66

OT 1 Chronicles 9:1–10:14

9 All Israel was listed in the genealogies
recorded in the book of the kings of Israel.

The People in Jerusalem

The people of Judah were taken captive
to Babylon because of their unfaithfulness. 2Now the first to resettle on their
own property in their own towns were
some Israelites, priests, Levites and temple servants.

3Those from Judah, from Benjamin,

and from Ephraim and Manasseh who
lived in Jerusalem were:
4 Uthai son of Ammihud, the son of
Omri, the son of Imri, the son
of Bani, a descendant of Perez son
of Judah.
5 Of the Shilonites:
Asaiah the firstborn and his sons.
6 Of the Zerahites:
Jeuel.
The people from Judah numbered
690.
7 Of the Benjamites:
Sallu son of Meshullam, the son of
Hodaviah, the son of Hassenuah;
8 Ibneiah son of Jeroham; Elah son
of Uzzi, the son of Micri; and Meshullam son of Shephatiah, the
son of Reuel, the son of Ibnijah.
9 The people from Benjamin, as listed in their genealogy, numbered
956. All these men were heads of
their families.
10 Of the priests:
Jedaiah; Jehoiarib; Jakin;
11 Azariah son of Hilkiah, the son of
Meshullam, the son of Zadok, the
son of Meraioth, the son of Ahitub,
the official in charge of the house
of God;
12 Adaiah son of Jeroham, the son of
Pashhur, the son of Malkijah; and
Maasai son of Adiel, the son of Jah-
zerah, the son of Meshullam, the
son of Meshillemith, the son of
Immer.
13 The priests, who were heads of
families, numbered 1,760. They
were able men, responsible for
ministering in the house of God.
14 Of the Levites:
Shemaiah son of Hasshub, the son
of Azrikam, the son of Hashabiah,
a Merarite; 15 Bakbakkar, Heresh,
Galal and Mattaniah son of Mica,
the son of Zicri, the son of Asaph;
16 Obadiah son of Shemaiah, the
son of Galal, the son of Jeduthun;
and Berekiah son of Asa, the son of
Elkanah, who lived in the villages
of the Netophathites.
17 The gatekeepers:
Shallum, Akkub, Talmon, Ahiman
and their brothers, Shallum their
chief 18 being stationed at the King's
Gate on the east, up to the present
time. These were the gatekeepers
belonging to the camp of the Levites. 19 Shallum son of Kore, the
son of Ebiasaph, the son of Korah,
and his fellow gatekeepers from his
family (the Korahites) were responsible for guarding the thresholds of the Tent[a] just as their fathers
had been responsible for guarding
the entrance to the dwelling of the
LORD. 20 In earlier times Phinehas
son of Eleazar was in charge of the
gatekeepers, and the LORD was with
him. 21 Zechariah son of Meshelemiah was the gatekeeper at the entrance to the Tent of Meeting.

22 Altogether, those chosen to be gatekeepers at the thresholds numbered 212.
They were registered by genealogy in their
villages. The gatekeepers had been assigned to their positions of trust by David
and Samuel the seer. 23 They and their descendants were in charge of guarding the
gates of the house of the LORD—the house
called the Tent. 24 The gatekeepers were on
the four sides: east, west, north and south.
25 Their brothers in their villages had to
come from time to time and share their
duties for seven-day periods. 26 But the four
principal gatekeepers, who were Levites,
were entrusted with the responsibility for
the rooms and treasuries in the house of
God. 27 They would spend the night stationed around the house of God, because
they had to guard it; and they had charge
of the key for opening it each morning.

28 Some of them were in charge of the articles used in the temple service; they
counted them when they were brought in
and when they were taken out. 29 Others
were assigned to take care of the furnishings and all the other articles of the sanctuary, as well as the flour and wine, and the
oil, incense and spices. 30 But some of the
priests took care of mixing the spices. 31 A
Levite named Mattithiah, the firstborn son
of Shallum the Korahite, was entrusted with
the responsibility for baking the offering
bread. 32 Some of their Kohathite brothers
were in charge of preparing for every Sabbath the bread set out on the table.

33 Those who were musicians, heads of
Levite families, stayed in the rooms of the
temple and were exempt from other duties because they were responsible for the
work day and night.

[a] *19* That is, the temple; also in verses 21 and 23

34 All these were heads of Levite families,
chiefs as listed in their genealogy, and
they lived in Jerusalem.

The Genealogy of Saul

35 Jeiel the father[b] of Gibeon lived in
Gibeon.
His wife's name was Maacah, 36 and
his firstborn son was Abdon, followed by Zur, Kish, Baal, Ner, Nadab, 37 Gedor, Ahio, Zechariah and
Mikloth. 38 Mikloth was the father
of Shimeam. They too lived near
their relatives in Jerusalem.
39 Ner was the father of Kish, Kish the
father of Saul, and Saul the father
of Jonathan, Malki-Shua, Abinadab and Esh-Baal.[c]
40 The son of Jonathan:
Merib-Baal,[d] who was the father of
Micah.
41 The sons of Micah:
Pithon, Melech, Tahrea and Ahaz.[e]
42 Ahaz was the father of Jadah, Jadah[f]
was the father of Alemeth, Azmaveth and Zimri, and Zimri was the
father of Moza. 43 Moza was the father of Binea; Rephaiah was his son,
Eleasah his son and Azel his son.
44 Azel had six sons, and these were
their names:
Azrikam, Bokeru, Ishmael, Sheariah, Obadiah and Hanan. These
were the sons of Azel.

Saul Takes His Life

10 Now the Philistines fought against Israel; the Israelites fled before them,
and many fell slain on Mount Gilboa.
2 The Philistines pressed hard after Saul
and his sons, and they killed his sons Jonathan, Abinadab and Malki-Shua. 3 The
fighting grew fierce around Saul, and
when the archers overtook him, they
wounded him.
4 Saul said to his armor-bearer, "Draw
your sword and run me through, or these
uncircumcised fellows will come and
abuse me."
But his armor-bearer was terrified and
would not do it; so Saul took his own
sword and fell on it. 5 When the armor-
bearer saw that Saul was dead, he too fell
on his sword and died. 6 So Saul and his
three sons died, and all his house died together.
7 When all the Israelites in the valley saw
that the army had fled and that Saul and
his sons had died, they abandoned their
towns and fled. And the Philistines came
and occupied them.
8 The next day, when the Philistines
came to strip the dead, they found Saul
and his sons fallen on Mount Gilboa.
9 They stripped him and took his head and
his armor, and sent messengers throughout the land of the Philistines to proclaim
the news among their idols and their people. 10 They put his armor in the temple of
their gods and hung up his head in the
temple of Dagon.
11 When all the inhabitants of Jabesh
Gilead heard of everything the Philistines
had done to Saul, 12 all their valiant men
went and took the bodies of Saul and his
sons and brought them to Jabesh. Then
they buried their bones under the great
tree in Jabesh, and they fasted seven days.
13 Saul died because he was unfaithful to
the LORD; he did not keep the word of the
LORD and even consulted a medium for
guidance, 14 and did not inquire of the LORD.
So the LORD put him to death and turned
the kingdom over to David son of Jesse.

[b] 35 *Father* may mean *civic leader* or *military leader.* [c] 39 Also known as *Ish-Bosheth* [d] 40 Also known as *Mephibosheth* [e] 41 Vulgate and Syriac (see also Septuagint and 1 Chron. 8:35); Hebrew does not have *and Ahaz.* [f] 42 Some Hebrew manuscripts and Septuagint (see also 1 Chron. 8:36); most Hebrew manuscripts *Jarah, Jarah*

PRAYER: PETITION

I HAVE sought You with my whole heart; do not let me stray from Your commands. (Psalm 119:10)

PAUSE *here to offer prayers of petition regarding your family and your ministry. Ask for help and guidance in sharing Jesus with others and helping others grow in Him. Ask for guidance in your vocation and your avocations. Offer prayers of petition regarding your activities for this day and any special concerns you may have.*

NT Acts 19:1–22

Paul in Ephesus

19 While Apollos was at Corinth, Paul
took the road through the interior
and arrived at Ephesus. There he found
some disciples 2 and asked them, "Did you
receive the Holy Spirit when[a] you believed?"
They answered, "No, we have not even
heard that there is a Holy Spirit."
3 So Paul asked, "Then what baptism
did you receive?"
"John's baptism," they replied.
4 Paul said, "John's baptism was a baptism of repentance. He told the people to
believe in the one coming after him, that
is, in Jesus." 5 On hearing this, they were
baptized into[b] the name of the Lord Jesus.
6 When Paul placed his hands on them,
the Holy Spirit came on them, and they
spoke in tongues[c] and prophesied. 7 There
were about twelve men in all.
8 Paul entered the synagogue and spoke
boldly there for three months, arguing
persuasively about the kingdom of God.
9 But some of them became obstinate; they
refused to believe and publicly maligned
the Way. So Paul left them. He took the
disciples with him and had discussions
daily in the lecture hall of Tyrannus. 10 This
went on for two years, so that all the Jews
and Greeks who lived in the province of
Asia heard the word of the Lord.
11 God did extraordinary miracles
through Paul, 12 so that even handker-
chiefs and aprons that had touched him
were taken to the sick, and their illnesses
were cured and the evil spirits left them.
13 Some Jews who went around driving
out evil spirits tried to invoke the name of
the Lord Jesus over those who were demon-possessed. They would say, "In the
name of Jesus, whom Paul preaches, I
command you to come out." 14 Seven sons
of Sceva, a Jewish chief priest, were doing
this. 15 ⌞One day⌟ the evil spirit answered
them, "Jesus I know, and I know about
Paul, but who are you?" 16 Then the man
who had the evil spirit jumped on them
and overpowered them all. He gave them
such a beating that they ran out of the
house naked and bleeding.
17 When this became known to the Jews
and Greeks living in Ephesus, they were
all seized with fear, and the name of the
Lord Jesus was held in high honor. 18 Many
of those who believed now came and
openly confessed their evil deeds. 19 A
number who had practiced sorcery
brought their scrolls together and burned
them publicly. When they calculated the
value of the scrolls, the total came to fifty
thousand drachmas.[d] 20 In this way the
word of the Lord spread widely and grew
in power.
21 After all this had happened, Paul decided to go to Jerusalem, passing through
Macedonia and Achaia. "After I have been
there," he said, "I must visit Rome also."
22 He sent two of his helpers, Timothy and
Erastus, to Macedonia, while he stayed in
the province of Asia a little longer.

[a] 2 Or *after* [b] 5 Or *in* [c] 6 Or *other languages*
[d] 19 A drachma was a silver coin worth about a day's wages.

PRAYER: THE ATTRIBUTES OF GOD

O LORD, You are good, a refuge in times of trouble; You know those who trust in You. (Nahum 1:7) . . . You, O God, are light; in You there is no darkness at all. (1 John 1:5)

PAUSE *to reflect on these affirmations about the person, powers and perfection of God.*

OT Proverbs 19

19 Better a poor man whose walk is blameless
than a fool whose lips are perverse.

2 It is not good to have zeal without knowledge,
nor to be hasty and miss the way.

3 A man's own folly ruins his life,
yet his heart rages against the LORD.

4 Wealth brings many friends,
but a poor man's friend deserts him.

5 A false witness will not go unpunished,
and he who pours out lies will not go free.

6 Many curry favor with a ruler,
and everyone is the friend of a man who gives gifts.

7 A poor man is shunned by all his relatives—
how much more do his friends avoid him!
Though he pursues them with pleading,
they are nowhere to be found.[a]

8 He who gets wisdom loves his own soul;
he who cherishes understanding prospers.

9 A false witness will not go unpunished,
and he who pours out lies will perish.

10 It is not fitting for a fool to live in luxury—
how much worse for a slave to rule over princes!

11 A man's wisdom gives him patience;
it is to his glory to overlook an offense.

12 A king's rage is like the roar of a lion,
but his favor is like dew on the grass.

13 A foolish son is his father's ruin,
and a quarrelsome wife is like a constant dripping.

14 Houses and wealth are inherited from parents,
but a prudent wife is from the LORD.

15 Laziness brings on deep sleep,
and the shiftless man goes hungry.

16 He who obeys instructions guards his life,
but he who is contemptuous of his ways will die.

17 He who is kind to the poor lends to the LORD,
and he will reward him for what he has done.

18 Discipline your son, for in that there is hope;
do not be a willing party to his death.

19 A hot-tempered man must pay the penalty;
if you rescue him, you will have to do it again.

20 Listen to advice and accept instruction,
and in the end you will be wise.

21 Many are the plans in a man's heart,
but it is the LORD's purpose that prevails.

22 What a man desires is unfailing love[b];
better to be poor than a liar.

23 The fear of the LORD leads to life:
Then one rests content, untouched by trouble.

24 The sluggard buries his hand in the dish;
he will not even bring it back to his mouth!

25 Flog a mocker, and the simple will learn prudence;
rebuke a discerning man, and he will gain knowledge.

26 He who robs his father and drives out his mother
is a son who brings shame and disgrace.

27 Stop listening to instruction, my son,
and you will stray from the words of knowledge.

28 A corrupt witness mocks at justice,
and the mouth of the wicked gulps down evil.

29 Penalties are prepared for mockers,
and beatings for the backs of fools.

[a] 7 The meaning of the Hebrew for this sentence is uncertain. [b] 22 Or *A man's greed is his shame*

PRAYER: INTERCESSION

JESUS, You have called us to go and make disciples of all nations, baptizing them in the name of the Father and of the Son and of the Holy Spirit, teaching them to observe everything You have commanded us. And surely You are with us always, even to the end of the age. (Matthew 28:19–20)

***TAKE** a few moments to intercede on behalf of local, national and world missions. Pray that the Great Commission would be fulfilled and for any special concerns you may have for missions.*

NT Acts 19:23-41

The Riot in Ephesus

23 About that time there arose a great disturbance about the Way. 24 A silversmith
named Demetrius, who made silver shrines
of Artemis, brought in no little business for
the craftsmen. 25 He called them together,
along with the workmen in related trades,
and said: "Men, you know we receive a good
income from this business. 26 And you see
and hear how this fellow Paul has convinced and led astray large numbers of people here in Ephesus and in practically the
whole province of Asia. He says that man-
made gods are no gods at all. 27 There is danger not only that our trade will lose its good
name, but also that the temple of the great
goddess Artemis will be discredited, and the
goddess herself, who is worshiped throughout the province of Asia and the world, will
be robbed of her divine majesty."

28 When they heard this, they were furious and began shouting: "Great is Artemis
of the Ephesians!" 29 Soon the whole city
was in an uproar. The people seized Gaius and Aristarchus, Paul's traveling companions from Macedonia, and rushed as
one man into the theater. 30 Paul wanted
to appear before the crowd, but the disciples would not let him. 31 Even some of
the officials of the province, friends of
Paul, sent him a message begging him not
to venture into the theater.

32 The assembly was in confusion: Some
were shouting one thing, some another.
Most of the people did not even know
why they were there. 33 The Jews pushed
Alexander to the front, and some of the
crowd shouted instructions to him. He
motioned for silence in order to make a
defense before the people. 34 But when
they realized he was a Jew, they all shouted in unison for about two hours: "Great
is Artemis of the Ephesians!"

35 The city clerk quieted the crowd and
said: "Men of Ephesus, doesn't all the world
know that the city of Ephesus is the
guardian of the temple of the great Artemis
and of her image, which fell from heaven?
36 Therefore, since these facts are undeniable,
you ought to be quiet and not do anything
rash. 37 You have brought these men here,
though they have neither robbed temples
nor blasphemed our goddess. 38 If, then,
Demetrius and his fellow craftsmen have a
grievance against anybody, the courts are
open and there are proconsuls. They can
press charges. 39 If there is anything further
you want to bring up, it must be settled in
a legal assembly. 40 As it is, we are in danger
of being charged with rioting because of today's events. In that case we would not be
able to account for this commotion, since
there is no reason for it." 41 After he had said
this, he dismissed the assembly.

PRAYER: THE WORKS OF GOD

LORD, grant to us the power of the Spirit that you promised the apostles when You told them, "You will receive power when the Holy Spirit comes upon you; and you will be My witnesses in Jerusalem, and in all Judea and Samaria, and to the ends of the earth." (Acts 1:8)

***TAKE** a moment to consider the greatness of God's wonderful works.*

OT 1 Chronicles 11:1-47 — YEAR 2 DAY 68

David Becomes King Over Israel

11 All Israel came together to David at Hebron and said, "We are your own flesh and blood. 2In the past, even while Saul was king, you were the one who led Israel on their military campaigns. And the LORD your God said to you, 'You will shepherd my people Israel, and you will become their ruler.' "

3When all the elders of Israel had come to King David at Hebron, he made a compact with them at Hebron before the LORD, and they anointed David king over Israel, as the LORD had promised through Samuel.

David Conquers Jerusalem

4David and all the Israelites marched to Jerusalem (that is, Jebus). The Jebusites who lived there 5said to David, "You will not get in here." Nevertheless, David captured the fortress of Zion, the City of David.

6David had said, "Whoever leads the attack on the Jebusites will become commander-in-chief." Joab son of Zeruiah went up first, and so he received the command.

7David then took up residence in the fortress, and so it was called the City of David. 8He built up the city around it, from the supporting terraces[a] to the surrounding wall, while Joab restored the rest of the city. 9And David became more and more powerful, because the LORD Almighty was with him.

David's Mighty Men

10These were the chiefs of David's mighty men—they, together with all Israel, gave his kingship strong support to extend it over the whole land, as the LORD had promised— 11this is the list of David's mighty men:

Jashobeam,[b] a Hacmonite, was chief of the officers[c]; he raised his spear against three hundred men, whom he killed in one encounter.

12Next to him was Eleazar son of Dodai the Ahohite, one of the three mighty men. 13He was with David at Pas Dammim when the Philistines gathered there for battle. At a place where there was a field full of barley, the troops fled from the Philistines. 14But they took their stand in the middle of the field. They defended it and struck the Philistines down, and the LORD brought about a great victory.

15Three of the thirty chiefs came down to David to the rock at the cave of Adullam, while a band of Philistines was encamped in the Valley of Rephaim. 16At that time David was in the stronghold, and the Philistine garrison was at Bethlehem. 17David longed for water and said, "Oh, that someone would get me a drink of water from the well near the gate of Bethlehem!" 18So the Three broke through the Philistine lines, drew water from the well near the gate of Bethlehem and carried it back to David. But he refused to drink it; instead, he poured it out before the LORD. 19"God forbid that I should do this!" he said. "Should I drink the blood of these men who went at the risk of their lives?" Because they risked their lives to bring it back, David would not drink it.

Such were the exploits of the three mighty men.

20Abishai the brother of Joab was chief of the Three. He raised his spear against three hundred men, whom he killed, and so he became as famous as the Three. 21He was doubly honored above the Three and became their commander, even though he was not included among them.

22Benaiah son of Jehoiada was a valiant fighter from Kabzeel, who performed great exploits. He struck down two of Moab's best men. He also went down into a pit on a snowy day and killed a lion. 23And he struck down an Egyptian who was seven and a half feet[d] tall. Although the Egyptian had a spear like a weaver's rod in his hand, Benaiah went against him with a club. He snatched the spear from the Egyptian's hand and killed him with his own spear. 24Such were the exploits of Benaiah son of Jehoiada; he too was as famous as the three mighty men.

[a] 8 Or *the Millo* [b] 11 Possibly a variant of *Jashob-Baal* [c] 11 Or *Thirty*; some Septuagint manuscripts *Three* (see also 2 Samuel 23:8) [d] 23 Hebrew *five cubits* (about 2.3 meters)

[25]He was held in greater honor than any of the Thirty, but he was not included among the Three. And David put him in charge of his bodyguard.

[26]The mighty men were:
Asahel the brother of Joab,
Elhanan son of Dodo from Bethlehem,
[27]Shammoth the Harorite,
Helez the Pelonite,
[28]Ira son of Ikkesh from Tekoa,
Abiezer from Anathoth,
[29]Sibbecai the Hushathite,
Ilai the Ahohite,
[30]Maharai the Netophathite,
Heled son of Baanah the Netophathite,
[31]Ithai son of Ribai from Gibeah in Benjamin,
Benaiah the Pirathonite,
[32]Hurai from the ravines of Gaash,
Abiel the Arbathite,
[33]Azmaveth the Baharumite,
Eliahba the Shaalbonite,
[34]the sons of Hashem the Gizonite,
Jonathan son of Shagee the Hararite,
[35]Ahiam son of Sacar the Hararite,
Eliphal son of Ur,
[36]Hepher the Mekerathite,
Ahijah the Pelonite,
[37]Hezro the Carmelite,
Naarai son of Ezbai,
[38]Joel the brother of Nathan,
Mibhar son of Hagri,
[39]Zelek the Ammonite,
Naharai the Berothite, the armor-bearer of Joab son of Zeruiah,
[40]Ira the Ithrite,
Gareb the Ithrite,
[41]Uriah the Hittite,
Zabad son of Ahlai,
[42]Adina son of Shiza the Reubenite, who was chief of the Reubenites, and the thirty with him,
[43]Hanan son of Maacah,
Joshaphat the Mithnite,
[44]Uzzia the Ashterathite,
Shama and Jeiel the sons of Hotham the Aroerite,
[45]Jediael son of Shimri,
his brother Joha the Tizite,
[46]Eliel the Mahavite,
Jeribai and Joshaviah the sons of Elnaam,
Ithmah the Moabite,
[47]Eliel, Obed and Jaasiel the Mezobaite.

PRAYER: AFFIRMATION

WHEN I seek You, Lord my God, I will find You if I seek with all my heart and with all my soul. (Deuteronomy 4:29) . . .
You are the Lord who made the earth, the Lord who formed it to establish it—the Lord is Your name and You promised this: "Call to Me, and I will answer you and tell you great and unsearchable things you do not know." (Jeremiah 33:2–3)

PAUSE *to reflect on these Biblical affirmations.*

NT Acts 20:1–38

Through Macedonia and Greece

20 When the uproar had ended, Paul
sent for the disciples and, after encouraging them, said good-by and set out
for Macedonia. [2]He traveled through that
area, speaking many words of encouragement to the people, and finally arrived in
Greece, [3]where he stayed three months.
Because the Jews made a plot against him
just as he was about to sail for Syria, he
decided to go back through Macedonia.
[4]He was accompanied by Sopater son of
Pyrrhus from Berea, Aristarchus and Secundus from Thessalonica, Gaius from
Derbe, Timothy also, and Tychicus and
Trophimus from the province of Asia.
[5]These men went on ahead and waited for
us at Troas. [6]But we sailed from Philippi
after the Feast of Unleavened Bread, and
five days later joined the others at Troas,
where we stayed seven days.

Eutychus Raised From the Dead at Troas

[7]On the first day of the week we came

together to break bread. Paul spoke to the
people and, because he intended to leave
the next day, kept on talking until midnight. 8There were many lamps in the upstairs room where we were meeting. 9Seat-
ed in a window was a young man named
Eutychus, who was sinking into a deep
sleep as Paul talked on and on. When he
was sound asleep, he fell to the ground
from the third story and was picked up
dead. 10Paul went down, threw himself on
the young man and put his arms around
him. "Don't be alarmed," he said. "He's
alive!" 11Then he went upstairs again and
broke bread and ate. After talking until
daylight, he left. 12The people took the
young man home alive and were greatly
comforted.

Paul's Farewell to the Ephesian Elders

13We went on ahead to the ship and
sailed for Assos, where we were going to
take Paul aboard. He had made this
arrangement because he was going there
on foot. 14When he met us at Assos, we
took him aboard and went on to Mitylene. 15The next day we set sail from there
and arrived off Kios. The day after that we
crossed over to Samos, and on the following day arrived at Miletus. 16Paul had
decided to sail past Ephesus to avoid
spending time in the province of Asia, for
he was in a hurry to reach Jerusalem, if
possible, by the day of Pentecost.

17From Miletus, Paul sent to Ephesus for
the elders of the church. 18When they arrived, he said to them: "You know how I
lived the whole time I was with you, from
the first day I came into the province of
Asia. 19I served the Lord with great humility and with tears, although I was severely
tested by the plots of the Jews. 20You know
that I have not hesitated to preach anything
that would be helpful to you but have
taught you publicly and from house to
house. 21I have declared to both Jews and
Greeks that they must turn to God in repentance and have faith in our Lord Jesus.

22"And now, compelled by the Spirit, I
am going to Jerusalem, not knowing what
will happen to me there. 23I only know
that in every city the Holy Spirit warns me
that prison and hardships are facing me.
24However, I consider my life worth nothing to me, if only I may finish the race and
complete the task the Lord Jesus has giv-
en me—the task of testifying to the gospel
of God's grace.

25"Now I know that none of you among
whom I have gone about preaching the
kingdom will ever see me again. 26There-
fore, I declare to you today that I am innocent of the blood of all men. 27For I
have not hesitated to proclaim to you the
whole will of God. 28Keep watch over
yourselves and all the flock of which the
Holy Spirit has made you overseers.[a] Be
shepherds of the church of God,[b] which
he bought with his own blood. 29I know
that after I leave, savage wolves will come
in among you and will not spare the flock.
30Even from your own number men will
arise and distort the truth in order to draw
away disciples after them. 31So be on your
guard! Remember that for three years I
never stopped warning each of you night
and day with tears.

32"Now I commit you to God and to the
word of his grace, which can build you up
and give you an inheritance among all
those who are sanctified. 33I have not coveted anyone's silver or gold or clothing.
34You yourselves know that these hands of
mine have supplied my own needs and the
needs of my companions. 35In everything I
did, I showed you that by this kind of hard
work we must help the weak, remembering the words the Lord Jesus himself said:
'It is more blessed to give than to receive.' "

36When he had said this, he knelt down
with all of them and prayed. 37They all
wept as they embraced him and kissed
him. 38What grieved them most was his
statement that they would never see his
face again. Then they accompanied him
to the ship.

[a] 28 Traditionally *bishops* [b] 28 Many manuscripts *of the Lord*

PRAYER: MY RELATIONSHIP TO GOD

SINCE I have been justified by Christ's blood, how much more shall I be saved from Your wrath, O God, through Him. For if, when I was Your enemy, I was reconciled to You through the death of Your Son,

how much more, having been reconciled, shall I be saved through His life. And not only this, but I also rejoice in You through my Lord Jesus Christ, through whom I have now received the reconciliation. (Romans 5:9–11)

PAUSE *to thank God for the relationship that you enjoy with Him in Jesus Christ.*

YEAR 2 DAY 69

OT 1 Chronicles 12:1–40

Warriors Join David

12 These were the men who came to David at Ziklag, while he was banished from the presence of Saul son of Kish (they were among the warriors who helped him in battle; 2they were armed with bows and were able to shoot arrows or to sling stones right-handed or left-handed; they were kinsmen of Saul from the tribe of Benjamin):

3Ahiezer their chief and Joash the sons of Shemaah the Gibeathite; Jeziel and Pelet the sons of Azmaveth; Beracah, Jehu the Anathothite, 4and Ishmaiah the Gibeonite, a mighty man among the Thirty, who was a leader of the Thirty; Jeremiah, Jahaziel, Johanan, Jozabad the Gederathite, 5Eluzai, Jerimoth, Bealiah, Shemariah and Shephatiah the Haruphite; 6Elkanah, Isshiah, Azarel, Joezer and Jashobeam the Korahites; 7and Joelah and Zebadiah the sons of Jeroham from Gedor.

8Some Gadites defected to David at his stronghold in the desert. They were brave warriors, ready for battle and able to handle the shield and spear. Their faces were the faces of lions, and they were as swift as gazelles in the mountains.

9Ezer was the chief,
Obadiah the second in command, Eliab the third,
10Mishmannah the fourth, Jeremiah the fifth,
11Attai the sixth, Eliel the seventh,
12Johanan the eighth, Elzabad the ninth,
13Jeremiah the tenth and Macbannai the eleventh.

14These Gadites were army commanders; the least was a match for a hundred, and the greatest for a thousand. 15It was they who crossed the Jordan in the first month when it was overflowing all its banks, and they put to flight everyone living in the valleys, to the east and to the west.

16Other Benjamites and some men from Judah also came to David in his stronghold. 17David went out to meet them and said to them, "If you have come to me in peace, to help me, I am ready to have you unite with me. But if you have come to betray me to my enemies when my hands are free from violence, may the God of our fathers see it and judge you."

18Then the Spirit came upon Amasai, chief of the Thirty, and he said:

"We are yours, O David!
We are with you, O son of Jesse!
Success, success to you,
and success to those who help you,
for your God will help you."

So David received them and made them leaders of his raiding bands.

19Some of the men of Manasseh defected to David when he went with the Philistines to fight against Saul. (He and his men did not help the Philistines because, after consultation, their rulers sent him away. They said, "It will cost us our heads if he deserts to his master Saul.") 20When David went to Ziklag, these were the men of Manasseh who defected to him: Adnah, Jozabad, Jediael, Michael, Jozabad, Elihu and Zillethai, leaders of units of a thousand in Manasseh. 21They helped David against raiding bands, for all of them were brave warriors, and they were commanders in his army. 22Day after day men came to help David, until he had a great army, like the army of God.[a]

Others Join David at Hebron

23These are the numbers of the men

[a] 22 Or *a great and mighty army*

armed for battle who came to David at
Hebron to turn Saul's kingdom over to
him, as the LORD had said:

24 men of Judah, carrying shield and
spear—6,800 armed for battle;
25 men of Simeon, warriors ready for
battle—7,100;
26 men of Levi—4,600, 27 including Jehoiada, leader of the family of Aaron, with 3,700 men, 28 and Zadok,
a brave young warrior, with 22 officers from his family;
29 men of Benjamin, Saul's kinsmen—
3,000, most of whom had remained loyal to Saul's house until
then;
30 men of Ephraim, brave warriors, famous in their own clans—20,800;
31 men of half the tribe of Manasseh,
designated by name to come and
make David king—18,000;
32 men of Issachar, who understood the
times and knew what Israel should
do—200 chiefs, with all their relatives under their command;
33 men of Zebulun, experienced soldiers prepared for battle with every
type of weapon, to help David
with undivided loyalty—50,000;
34 men of Naphtali—1,000 officers, together with 37,000 men carrying
shields and spears;
35 men of Dan, ready for battle—
28,600;
36 men of Asher, experienced soldiers
prepared for battle—40,000;
37 and from east of the Jordan, men of
Reuben, Gad and the half-tribe of
Manasseh, armed with every type
of weapon—120,000.

38 All these were fighting men who volunteered to serve in the ranks. They came
to Hebron fully determined to make David
king over all Israel. All the rest of the Israelites were also of one mind to make David king. 39 The men spent three days there
with David, eating and drinking, for their
families had supplied provisions for them.
40 Also, their neighbors from as far away as
Issachar, Zebulun and Naphtali came
bringing food on donkeys, camels, mules
and oxen. There were plentiful supplies of
flour, fig cakes, raisin cakes, wine, oil, cattle
and sheep, for there was joy in Israel.

PRAYER: THANKSGIVING

YOU are my God, and I will give thanks to You; You are my God, and I will exalt You. I will give thanks to You, Lord, for You are good; Your loyal love endures forever. (Psalm 118:28–29)

***PAUSE** to offer your own expressions of thanksgiving.*

NT Acts 21:1–36

On to Jerusalem

21 After we had torn ourselves away from
them, we put out to sea and sailed
straight to Cos. The next day we went to
Rhodes and from there to Patara. 2 We
found a ship crossing over to Phoenicia,
went on board and set sail. 3 After sighting
Cyprus and passing to the south of it, we
sailed on to Syria. We landed at Tyre,
where our ship was to unload its cargo.
4 Finding the disciples there, we stayed
with them seven days. Through the Spirit
they urged Paul not to go on to Jerusalem.
5 But when our time was up, we left and
continued on our way. All the disciples
and their wives and children accompanied us out of the city, and there on the
beach we knelt to pray. 6 After saying good-
by to each other, we went aboard the ship,
and they returned home.

7 We continued our voyage from Tyre and
landed at Ptolemais, where we greeted the
brothers and stayed with them for a day.
8 Leaving the next day, we reached Caesarea
and stayed at the house of Philip the evangelist, one of the Seven. 9 He had four unmarried daughters who prophesied.

10 After we had been there a number of
days, a prophet named Agabus came
down from Judea. 11 Coming over to us, he
took Paul's belt, tied his own hands and
feet with it and said, "The Holy Spirit says,
'In this way the Jews of Jerusalem will
bind the owner of this belt and will hand
him over to the Gentiles.' "

[12]When we heard this, we and the people there pleaded with Paul not to go up to Jerusalem. [13]Then Paul answered, "Why are you weeping and breaking my heart? I am ready not only to be bound, but also to die in Jerusalem for the name of the Lord Jesus." [14]When he would not be dissuaded, we gave up and said, "The Lord's will be done."

[15]After this, we got ready and went up to Jerusalem. [16]Some of the disciples from Caesarea accompanied us and brought us to the home of Mnason, where we were to stay. He was a man from Cyprus and one of the early disciples.

Paul's Arrival at Jerusalem

[17]When we arrived at Jerusalem, the brothers received us warmly. [18]The next day Paul and the rest of us went to see James, and all the elders were present. [19]Paul greeted them and reported in detail what God had done among the Gentiles through his ministry.

[20]When they heard this, they praised God. Then they said to Paul: "You see, brother, how many thousands of Jews have believed, and all of them are zealous for the law. [21]They have been informed that you teach all the Jews who live among the Gentiles to turn away from Moses, telling them not to circumcise their children or live according to our customs. [22]What shall we do? They will certainly hear that you have come, [23]so do what we tell you. There are four men with us who have made a vow. [24]Take these men, join in their purification rites and pay their expenses, so that they can have their heads shaved. Then everybody will know there is no truth in these reports about you, but that you yourself are living in obedience to the law. [25]As for the Gentile believers, we have written to them our decision that they should abstain from food sacrificed to idols, from blood, from the meat of strangled animals and from sexual immorality."

[26]The next day Paul took the men and purified himself along with them. Then he went to the temple to give notice of the date when the days of purification would end and the offering would be made for each of them.

Paul Arrested

[27]When the seven days were nearly over, some Jews from the province of Asia saw Paul at the temple. They stirred up the whole crowd and seized him, [28]shouting, "Men of Israel, help us! This is the man who teaches all men everywhere against our people and our law and this place. And besides, he has brought Greeks into the temple area and defiled this holy place." [29](They had previously seen Trophimus the Ephesian in the city with Paul and assumed that Paul had brought him into the temple area.)

[30]The whole city was aroused, and the people came running from all directions. Seizing Paul, they dragged him from the temple, and immediately the gates were shut. [31]While they were trying to kill him, news reached the commander of the Roman troops that the whole city of Jerusalem was in an uproar. [32]He at once took some officers and soldiers and ran down to the crowd. When the rioters saw the commander and his soldiers, they stopped beating Paul.

[33]The commander came up and arrested him and ordered him to be bound with two chains. Then he asked who he was and what he had done. [34]Some in the crowd shouted one thing and some another, and since the commander could not get at the truth because of the uproar, he ordered that Paul be taken into the barracks. [35]When Paul reached the steps, the violence of the mob was so great he had to be carried by the soldiers. [36]The crowd that followed kept shouting, "Away with him!"

PRAYER: THE CHARACTER I WANT TO CULTIVATE

I WILL not seek to justify myself in other people's eyes; You, O God, know my heart, and what is highly esteemed among people is detestable in Your sight. (Luke 16:15) . . . I will not love praise from people more than praise from You, O God. (John 12:43)

***TAKE** a moment to ask the Lord for the grace to grow in godly character.*

Psalm 84

For the director of music. According to *gittith*.[a] Of the Sons of Korah. A psalm.

[1] How lovely is your dwelling place,
O LORD Almighty!
[2] My soul yearns, even faints,
for the courts of the LORD;
my heart and my flesh cry out
for the living God.

[3] Even the sparrow has found a home,
and the swallow a nest for herself,
where she may have her young—
a place near your altar,
O LORD Almighty, my King and my God.
[4] Blessed are those who dwell in your house;
they are ever praising you. *Selah*

[5] Blessed are those whose strength is in you,
who have set their hearts on pilgrimage.
[6] As they pass through the Valley of Baca,
they make it a place of springs;
the autumn rains also cover it with pools.[b]
[7] They go from strength to strength,
till each appears before God in Zion.

[8] Hear my prayer, O LORD God Almighty;
listen to me, O God of Jacob. *Selah*
[9] Look upon our shield,[c] O God;
look with favor on your anointed one.

[10] Better is one day in your courts
than a thousand elsewhere;
I would rather be a doorkeeper in the house of my God
than dwell in the tents of the wicked.
[11] For the LORD God is a sun and shield;
the LORD bestows favor and honor;
no good thing does he withhold
from those whose walk is blameless.

[12] O LORD Almighty,
blessed is the man who trusts in you.

Psalm 85

For the director of music. Of the Sons of Korah. A psalm.

[1] You showed favor to your land,
O LORD;
you restored the fortunes of Jacob.
[2] You forgave the iniquity of your people
and covered all their sins. *Selah*
[3] You set aside all your wrath
and turned from your fierce anger.

[4] Restore us again, O God our Savior,
and put away your displeasure toward us.
[5] Will you be angry with us forever?
Will you prolong your anger through all generations?
[6] Will you not revive us again,
that your people may rejoice in you?
[7] Show us your unfailing love, O LORD,
and grant us your salvation.

[8] I will listen to what God the LORD will say;
he promises peace to his people, his saints—
but let them not return to folly.
[9] Surely his salvation is near those who fear him,
that his glory may dwell in our land.

[10] Love and faithfulness meet together;
righteousness and peace kiss each other.
[11] Faithfulness springs forth from the earth,
and righteousness looks down from heaven.
[12] The LORD will indeed give what is good,
and our land will yield its harvest.
[13] Righteousness goes before him
and prepares the way for his steps.

[a] Title: Probably a musical term [b] 6 Or *blessings*
[c] 9 Or *sovereign*

PRAYER: ADORATION

I WILL bless You, Lord, at all times; Your praise will always be in my mouth. My soul will make its boast in You, Lord; the humble will hear and be glad. May all Your people magnify You with me, and let us exalt Your name together. (Psalm 34:1–3)

PAUSE *to express your thoughts of praise and worship.*

NT Acts 21:37–22:21

Paul Speaks to the Crowd

37 As the soldiers were about to take Paul
into the barracks, he asked the commander, "May I say something to you?"
"Do you speak Greek?" he replied.
38 "Aren't you the Egyptian who started a
revolt and led four thousand terrorists out
into the desert some time ago?"
39 Paul answered, "I am a Jew, from Tarsus in Cilicia, a citizen of no ordinary city.
Please let me speak to the people."
40 Having received the commander's
permission, Paul stood on the steps and
motioned to the crowd. When they were
all silent, he said to them in Aramaic[a]:
22 1 "Brothers and fathers, listen now to
my defense."
2 When they heard him speak to them
in Aramaic, they became very quiet.
Then Paul said: 3 "I am a Jew, born in
Tarsus of Cilicia, but brought up in this
city. Under Gamaliel I was thoroughly
trained in the law of our fathers and was
just as zealous for God as any of you are
today. 4 I persecuted the followers of this
Way to their death, arresting both men
and women and throwing them into
prison, 5 as also the high priest and all the
Council can testify. I even obtained letters
from them to their brothers in Damascus,
and went there to bring these people as
prisoners to Jerusalem to be punished.
6 "About noon as I came near Damascus, suddenly a bright light from heaven
flashed around me. 7 I fell to the ground
and heard a voice say to me, 'Saul! Saul!
Why do you persecute me?'
8 " 'Who are you, Lord?' I asked.
" 'I am Jesus of Nazareth, whom you
are persecuting,' he replied. 9 My companions saw the light, but they did not understand the voice of him who was speaking to me.
10 " 'What shall I do, Lord?' I asked.
" 'Get up,' the Lord said, 'and go into
Damascus. There you will be told all that
you have been assigned to do.' 11 My companions led me by the hand into Damascus, because the brilliance of the light had
blinded me.
12 "A man named Ananias came to see
me. He was a devout observer of the law
and highly respected by all the Jews living
there. 13 He stood beside me and said,
'Brother Saul, receive your sight!' And at
that very moment I was able to see him.
14 "Then he said: 'The God of our fathers
has chosen you to know his will and to
see the Righteous One and to hear words
from his mouth. 15 You will be his witness
to all men of what you have seen and
heard. 16 And now what are you waiting
for? Get up, be baptized and wash your
sins away, calling on his name.'
17 "When I returned to Jerusalem and
was praying at the temple, I fell into a
trance 18 and saw the Lord speaking.
'Quick!' he said to me. 'Leave Jerusalem
immediately, because they will not accept
your testimony about me.'
19 " 'Lord,' I replied, 'these men know
that I went from one synagogue to another to imprison and beat those who believe in you. 20 And when the blood of
your martyr[b] Stephen was shed, I stood
there giving my approval and guarding
the clothes of those who were killing him.'
21 "Then the Lord said to me, 'Go; I will
send you far away to the Gentiles.' "

[a] *40* Or possibly *Hebrew;* also in 22:2 [b] *20* Or *witness*

PRAYER: MY RELATIONSHIP TO OTHERS

I SHALL seek to keep Your commandments, O God: "You shall love the Lord your God with all your heart and with all your soul and with all your mind." This is the first and greatest commandment. And the second is like it: "You shall love your neighbor as yourself." All the Law and the Prophets hang on these two commandments.

(Matthew 22:37–40)

***PAUSE** to review your relationships with others and to commit them to the Lord.*

YEAR 2
DAY 71

OT 1 Chronicles 13:1–14:17

Bringing Back the Ark

13 David conferred with each of his officers, the commanders of thousands and commanders of hundreds. 2 He then said to the whole assembly of Israel, "If it seems good to you and if it is the will of the LORD our God, let us send word far and wide to the rest of our brothers throughout the territories of Israel, and also to the priests and Levites who are with them in their towns and pasturelands, to come and join us. 3 Let us bring the ark of our God back to us, for we did not inquire of[a] it[b] during the reign of Saul." 4 The whole assembly agreed to do this, because it seemed right to all the people.

5 So David assembled all the Israelites, from the Shihor River in Egypt to Lebo[c] Hamath, to bring the ark of God from Kiriath Jearim. 6 David and all the Israelites with him went to Baalah of Judah (Kiriath Jearim) to bring up from there the ark of God the LORD, who is enthroned between the cherubim—the ark that is called by the Name.

7 They moved the ark of God from Abinadab's house on a new cart, with Uzzah and Ahio guiding it. 8 David and all the Israelites were celebrating with all their might before God, with songs and with harps, lyres, tambourines, cymbals and trumpets.

9 When they came to the threshing floor of Kidon, Uzzah reached out his hand to steady the ark, because the oxen stumbled. 10 The LORD's anger burned against Uzzah, and he struck him down because he had put his hand on the ark. So he died there before God.

11 Then David was angry because the LORD's wrath had broken out against Uzzah, and to this day that place is called Perez Uzzah.[d]

12 David was afraid of God that day and asked, "How can I ever bring the ark of God to me?" 13 He did not take the ark to be with him in the City of David. Instead, he took it aside to the house of Obed-Edom the Gittite. 14 The ark of God remained with the family of Obed-Edom in his house for three months, and the LORD blessed his household and everything he had.

David's House and Family

14 Now Hiram king of Tyre sent messengers to David, along with cedar logs, stonemasons and carpenters to build a palace for him. 2 And David knew that the LORD had established him as king over Israel and that his kingdom had been highly exalted for the sake of his people Israel.

3 In Jerusalem David took more wives and became the father of more sons and daughters. 4 These are the names of the children born to him there: Shammua, Shobab, Nathan, Solomon, 5 Ibhar, Elishua, Elpelet, 6 Nogah, Nepheg, Japhia, 7 Elishama, Beeliada[e] and Eliphelet.

David Defeats the Philistines

8 When the Philistines heard that David had been anointed king over all Israel, they went up in full force to search for

[a] 3 Or *we neglected* [b] 3 Or *him* [c] 5 Or *to the entrance to* [d] 11 *Perez Uzzah* means *outbreak against Uzzah.* [e] 7 A variant of *Eliada*

him, but David heard about it and went out to meet them. 9Now the Philistines had come and raided the Valley of Rephaim; 10so David inquired of God: "Shall I go and attack the Philistines? Will you hand them over to me?"

The LORD answered him, "Go, I will hand them over to you."

11So David and his men went up to Baal Perazim, and there he defeated them. He said, "As waters break out, God has broken out against my enemies by my hand." So that place was called Baal Perazim.[f] 12The Philistines had abandoned their gods there, and David gave orders to burn them in the fire.

13Once more the Philistines raided the valley; 14so David inquired of God again, and God answered him, "Do not go straight up, but circle around them and attack them in front of the balsam trees. 15As soon as you hear the sound of marching in the tops of the balsam trees, move out to battle, because that will mean God has gone out in front of you to strike the Philistine army." 16So David did as God commanded him, and they struck down the Philistine army, all the way from Gibeon to Gezer.

17So David's fame spread throughout every land, and the LORD made all the nations fear him.

f 11 *Baal Perazim* means *the lord who breaks out.*

PRAYER: CONFESSION

YOU, O Lord, have said, "Come now, let us reason together. Though your sins are like scarlet, they shall be as white as snow; though they are red as crimson, they shall be like wool." (Isaiah 1:18)

__ASK__ the Spirit to search your heart and reveal any areas of unconfessed sin. Acknowledge these to the Lord and thank Him for His forgiveness.

NT Acts 22:22–23:11

Paul the Roman Citizen

22The crowd listened to Paul until he said this. Then they raised their voices and shouted, "Rid the earth of him! He's not fit to live!"

23As they were shouting and throwing off their cloaks and flinging dust into the air, 24the commander ordered Paul to be taken into the barracks. He directed that he be flogged and questioned in order to find out why the people were shouting at him like this. 25As they stretched him out to flog him, Paul said to the centurion standing there, "Is it legal for you to flog a Roman citizen who hasn't even been found guilty?"

26When the centurion heard this, he went to the commander and reported it. "What are you going to do?" he asked. "This man is a Roman citizen."

27The commander went to Paul and asked, "Tell me, are you a Roman citizen?"

"Yes, I am," he answered.

28Then the commander said, "I had to pay a big price for my citizenship."

"But I was born a citizen," Paul replied.

29Those who were about to question him withdrew immediately. The commander himself was alarmed when he realized that he had put Paul, a Roman citizen, in chains.

Before the Sanhedrin

30The next day, since the commander wanted to find out exactly why Paul was being accused by the Jews, he released him and ordered the chief priests and all the Sanhedrin to assemble. Then he brought Paul and had him stand before them.

23 Paul looked straight at the Sanhedrin and said, "My brothers, I have fulfilled my duty to God in all good conscience to this day." 2At this the high priest Ananias ordered those standing near Paul to strike him on the mouth. 3Then Paul said to him, "God will strike you, you whitewashed wall! You sit there to judge me according to the law, yet you yourself violate the law by commanding that I be struck!"

4Those who were standing near Paul said, "You dare to insult God's high priest?"

[5]Paul replied, "Brothers, I did not realize that he was the high priest; for it is
written: 'Do not speak evil about the ruler
of your people.'[a]"
[6]Then Paul, knowing that some of them
were Sadducees and the others Pharisees,
called out in the Sanhedrin, "My brothers,
I am a Pharisee, the son of a Pharisee. I
stand on trial because of my hope in the
resurrection of the dead." [7]When he said
this, a dispute broke out between the
Pharisees and the Sadducees, and the assembly was divided. [8](The Sadducees say
that there is no resurrection, and that
there are neither angels nor spirits, but the
Pharisees acknowledge them all.)
[9]There was a great uproar, and some of
the teachers of the law who were Pharisees
stood up and argued vigorously. "We find
nothing wrong with this man," they said.
"What if a spirit or an angel has spoken
to him?" [10]The dispute became so violent
that the commander was afraid Paul
would be torn to pieces by them. He ordered the troops to go down and take him
away from them by force and bring him
into the barracks.
[11]The following night the Lord stood
near Paul and said, "Take courage! As you
have testified about me in Jerusalem, so
you must also testify in Rome."

[a] 5 Exodus 22:28

PRAYER: THE ATTRIBUTES OF GOD

YOU declare the end from the beginning, and from ancient times what is still to come, saying, "My purpose will stand, and I will do all My pleasure." (Isaiah 46:10) . . . The word that goes forth from Your mouth, O Lord, will not return to You empty but will accomplish what You desire and achieve the purpose for which You sent it. (Isaiah 55:11)

PAUSE *to reflect on these affirmations about the person, powers and perfection of God.*

YEAR 2 DAY 72

OT 1 Chronicles 15:1–29

The Ark Brought to Jerusalem

15 After David had constructed buildings
for himself in the City of David, he
prepared a place for the ark of God and
pitched a tent for it. [2]Then David said,
"No one but the Levites may carry the ark
of God, because the LORD chose them to
carry the ark of the LORD and to minister
before him forever."
[3]David assembled all Israel in Jerusalem to bring up the ark of the LORD to
the place he had prepared for it. [4]He
called together the descendants of Aaron
and the Levites:
[5]From the descendants of Kohath,
Uriel the leader and 120 relatives;
[6]from the descendants of Merari,
Asaiah the leader and 220 relatives;
[7]from the descendants of Gershon,[a]
Joel the leader and 130 relatives;
[8]from the descendants of Elizaphan,
Shemaiah the leader and 200 relatives;
[9]from the descendants of Hebron,
Eliel the leader and 80 relatives;
[10]from the descendants of Uzziel,
Amminadab the leader and 112
relatives.
[11]Then David summoned Zadok and
Abiathar the priests, and Uriel, Asaiah,
Joel, Shemaiah, Eliel and Amminadab the
Levites. [12]He said to them, "You are the
heads of the Levitical families; you and
your fellow Levites are to consecrate yourselves and bring up the ark of the LORD,
the God of Israel, to the place I have prepared for it. [13]It was because you, the Levites, did not bring it up the first time that
the LORD our God broke out in anger
against us. We did not inquire of him
about how to do it in the prescribed way."
[14]So the priests and Levites consecrated

[a] 7 Hebrew *Gershom,* a variant of *Gershon*

themselves in order to bring up the ark of
the LORD, the God of Israel. 15And the Levites carried the ark of God with the poles
on their shoulders, as Moses had commanded in accordance with the word of
the LORD.

16David told the leaders of the Levites
to appoint their brothers as singers to sing
joyful songs, accompanied by musical instruments: lyres, harps and cymbals.

17So the Levites appointed Heman son
of Joel; from his brothers, Asaph son of
Berekiah; and from their brothers the
Merarites, Ethan son of Kushaiah; 18and
with them their brothers next in rank:
Zechariah,[b] Jaaziel, Shemiramoth, Jehiel,
Unni, Eliab, Benaiah, Maaseiah, Mattithiah, Eliphelehu, Mikneiah, Obed-Edom
and Jeiel,[c] the gatekeepers.

19The musicians Heman, Asaph and
Ethan were to sound the bronze cymbals;
20Zechariah, Aziel, Shemiramoth, Jehiel,
Unni, Eliab, Maaseiah and Benaiah were
to play the lyres according to *alamoth*,[d]
21and Mattithiah, Eliphelehu, Mikneiah,
Obed-Edom, Jeiel and Azaziah were to
play the harps, directing according to
sheminith.[d] 22Kenaniah the head Levite
was in charge of the singing; that was his
responsibility because he was skillful at it.

23Berekiah and Elkanah were to be
doorkeepers for the ark. 24Shebaniah,
Joshaphat, Nethanel, Amasai, Zechariah,
Benaiah and Eliezer the priests were to
blow trumpets before the ark of God.
Obed-Edom and Jehiah were also to be
doorkeepers for the ark.

25So David and the elders of Israel and
the commanders of units of a thousand
went to bring up the ark of the covenant
of the LORD from the house of Obed-
Edom, with rejoicing. 26Because God had
helped the Levites who were carrying the
ark of the covenant of the LORD, seven
bulls and seven rams were sacrificed.
27Now David was clothed in a robe of fine
linen, as were all the Levites who were carrying the ark, and as were the singers, and
Kenaniah, who was in charge of the
singing of the choirs. David also wore a
linen ephod. 28So all Israel brought up the
ark of the covenant of the LORD with
shouts, with the sounding of rams' horns
and trumpets, and of cymbals, and the
playing of lyres and harps.

29As the ark of the covenant of the LORD
was entering the City of David, Michal
daughter of Saul watched from a window.
And when she saw King David dancing and
celebrating, she despised him in her heart.

[b] *18* Three Hebrew manuscripts and most Septuagint manuscripts (see also verse 20 and 1 Chron. 16:5); most Hebrew manuscripts *Zechariah son and* or *Zechariah, Ben and* [c] *18* Hebrew; Septuagint (see also verse 21) *Jeiel and Azaziah* [d] *20,21* Probably a musical term

PRAYER: RENEWAL

O LORD, may I be strong in You and in Your mighty power as I put on Your full armor, so that I will be able to stand against the schemes of the devil. (Ephesians 6:10–11) . . . Since I belong to the day, may I be self-controlled, putting on faith and love as a breastplate, and the hope of salvation as a helmet. (1 Thessalonians 5:8)

***PAUSE** to add your own prayers for personal renewal.*

NT Acts 23:12-35

The Plot to Kill Paul

12The next morning the Jews formed a
conspiracy and bound themselves with an
oath not to eat or drink until they had
killed Paul. 13More than forty men were
involved in this plot. 14They went to the
chief priests and elders and said, "We have
taken a solemn oath not to eat anything
until we have killed Paul. 15Now then, you
and the Sanhedrin petition the commander to bring him before you on the pretext of wanting more accurate information about his case. We are ready to kill
him before he gets here."

16But when the son of Paul's sister
heard of this plot, he went into the barracks and told Paul.

17Then Paul called one of the centurions

and said, "Take this young man to the commander; he has something to tell him." 18So he took him to the commander.

The centurion said, "Paul, the prisoner, sent for me and asked me to bring this young man to you because he has something to tell you."

19The commander took the young man by the hand, drew him aside and asked, "What is it you want to tell me?"

20He said: "The Jews have agreed to ask you to bring Paul before the Sanhedrin tomorrow on the pretext of wanting more accurate information about him. 21Don't give in to them, because more than forty of them are waiting in ambush for him. They have taken an oath not to eat or drink until they have killed him. They are ready now, waiting for your consent to their request."

22The commander dismissed the young man and cautioned him, "Don't tell anyone that you have reported this to me."

Paul Transferred to Caesarea

23Then he called two of his centurions and ordered them, "Get ready a detachment of two hundred soldiers, seventy horsemen and two hundred spearmen[a] to go to Caesarea at nine tonight. 24Provide mounts for Paul so that he may be taken safely to Governor Felix."

25He wrote a letter as follows:

26Claudius Lysias,

To His Excellency, Governor Felix:

Greetings.

27This man was seized by the Jews and they were about to kill him, but I came with my troops and rescued him, for I had learned that he is a Roman citizen. 28I wanted to know why they were accusing him, so I brought him to their Sanhedrin. 29I found that the accusation had to do with questions about their law, but there was no charge against him that deserved death or imprisonment. 30When I was informed of a plot to be carried out against the man, I sent him to you at once. I also ordered his accusers to present to you their case against him.

31So the soldiers, carrying out their orders, took Paul with them during the night and brought him as far as Antipatris. 32The next day they let the cavalry go on with him, while they returned to the barracks. 33When the cavalry arrived in Caesarea, they delivered the letter to the governor and handed Paul over to him. 34The governor read the letter and asked what province he was from. Learning that he was from Cilicia, 35he said, "I will hear your case when your accusers get here." Then he ordered that Paul be kept under guard in Herod's palace.

[a] *23* The meaning of the Greek for this word is uncertain.

PRAYER: THE WORKS OF GOD

THE law was added that the transgression might increase. But where sin increased, grace abounded all the more, so that just as sin reigned in death, so also grace might reign through righteousness to bring eternal life through You, Jesus Christ our Lord. (Romans 5:20–21) . . . O Christ, You have completed the law so that there may be righteousness to everyone who believes. (Romans 10:4)

***TAKE** a moment to consider the greatness of God's wonderful works.*

YEAR 2 DAY 73

OT 1 Chronicles 16:1–43

16 They brought the ark of God and set it inside the tent that David had pitched for it, and they presented burnt offerings and fellowship offerings[a] before God. 2After David had finished sacrificing the burnt offerings and fellowship offerings, he blessed the people in the name of the LORD. 3Then he gave a loaf of bread, a

[a] *1* Traditionally *peace offerings;* also in verse 2

cake of dates and a cake of raisins to each Israelite man and woman.
[4]He appointed some of the Levites to minister before the ark of the LORD, to make petition, to give thanks, and to praise the LORD, the God of Israel: [5]Asaph was the chief, Zechariah second, then Jeiel, Shemiramoth, Jehiel, Mattithiah, Eliab, Benaiah, Obed-Edom and Jeiel. They were to play the lyres and harps, Asaph was to sound the cymbals, [6]and Benaiah and Jahaziel the priests were to blow the trumpets regularly before the ark of the covenant of God.

David's Psalm of Thanks

[7]That day David first committed to Asaph and his associates this psalm of thanks to the LORD:

[8]Give thanks to the LORD, call on his name;
make known among the nations what he has done.
[9]Sing to him, sing praise to him;
tell of all his wonderful acts.
[10]Glory in his holy name;
let the hearts of those who seek the LORD rejoice.
[11]Look to the LORD and his strength;
seek his face always.
[12]Remember the wonders he has done,
his miracles, and the judgments he pronounced,
[13]O descendants of Israel his servant,
O sons of Jacob, his chosen ones.

[14]He is the LORD our God;
his judgments are in all the earth.
[15]He remembers[b] his covenant forever,
the word he commanded, for a thousand generations,
[16]the covenant he made with Abraham,
the oath he swore to Isaac.
[17]He confirmed it to Jacob as a decree,
to Israel as an everlasting covenant:
[18]"To you I will give the land of Canaan
as the portion you will inherit."

[19]When they were but few in number,
few indeed, and strangers in it,
[20]they[c] wandered from nation to nation,
from one kingdom to another.
[21]He allowed no man to oppress them;
for their sake he rebuked kings:
[22]"Do not touch my anointed ones;
do my prophets no harm."

[23]Sing to the LORD, all the earth;
proclaim his salvation day after day.
[24]Declare his glory among the nations,
his marvelous deeds among all peoples.
[25]For great is the LORD and most worthy of praise;
he is to be feared above all gods.
[26]For all the gods of the nations are idols,
but the LORD made the heavens.
[27]Splendor and majesty are before him;
strength and joy in his dwelling place.
[28]Ascribe to the LORD, O families of nations,
ascribe to the LORD glory and strength,
[29]ascribe to the LORD the glory due his name.
Bring an offering and come before him;
worship the LORD in the splendor of his[d] holiness.
[30]Tremble before him, all the earth!
The world is firmly established; it cannot be moved.
[31]Let the heavens rejoice, let the earth be glad;
let them say among the nations,
"The LORD reigns!"
[32]Let the sea resound, and all that is in it;
let the fields be jubilant, and everything in them!
[33]Then the trees of the forest will sing,
they will sing for joy before the LORD,
for he comes to judge the earth.

[34]Give thanks to the LORD, for he is good;
his love endures forever.
[35]Cry out, "Save us, O God our Savior;
gather us and deliver us from the nations,
that we may give thanks to your holy name,
that we may glory in your praise."
[36]Praise be to the LORD, the God of Israel,
from everlasting to everlasting.

[b] *15* Some Septuagint manuscripts (see also Psalm 105:8); Hebrew *Remember* [c] *18–20* One Hebrew manuscript, Septuagint and Vulgate (see also Psalm 105:12); most Hebrew manuscripts *inherit, /* [19]*though you are but few in number, / few indeed, and strangers in it." /* [20]*They* [d] *29* Or *LORD with the splendor of*

Then all the people said "Amen" and
"Praise the LORD."

37 David left Asaph and his associates
before the ark of the covenant of the LORD
to minister there regularly, according to
each day's requirements. 38 He also left
Obed-Edom and his sixty-eight associates
to minister with them. Obed-Edom son of
Jeduthun, and also Hosah, were gatekeepers.
39 David left Zadok the priest and his fellow priests before the tabernacle of the
LORD at the high place in Gibeon 40 to
present burnt offerings to the LORD on the
altar of burnt offering regularly, morning
and evening, in accordance with everything written in the Law of the LORD,
which he had given Israel. 41 With them
were Heman and Jeduthun and the rest of
those chosen and designated by name to
give thanks to the LORD, "for his love endures forever." 42 Heman and Jeduthun
were responsible for the sounding of the
trumpets and cymbals and for the playing
of the other instruments for sacred song.
The sons of Jeduthun were stationed at
the gate.
43 Then all the people left, each for his
own home, and David returned home to
bless his family.

PRAYER: PETITION

O LORD, I cry to You; hasten to me. Hear my voice when I cry to You. Let my prayer be set before You like incense, and the lifting up of my hands like the evening sacrifice. (Psalm 141:1–2)

PAUSE *here to petition God for growth in your character and personal discipline, and for physical health and strength. Ask that He empower you for spiritual warfare against the temptations of the world, the flesh and the devil. Offer prayers regarding your activities for this day and any special concerns you may have.*

NT Acts 24:1–27

The Trial Before Felix

24 Five days later the high priest Ananias went down to Caesarea with some
of the elders and a lawyer named Tertullus, and they brought their charges
against Paul before the governor. 2 When
Paul was called in, Tertullus presented his
case before Felix: "We have enjoyed a
long period of peace under you, and your
foresight has brought about reforms in
this nation. 3 Everywhere and in every
way, most excellent Felix, we acknowledge this with profound gratitude. 4 But in
order not to weary you further, I would
request that you be kind enough to hear
us briefly.
5 "We have found this man to be a troublemaker, stirring up riots among the Jews
all over the world. He is a ringleader of
the Nazarene sect 6 and even tried to desecrate the temple; so we seized him. 8 By[a]
examining him yourself you will be able
to learn the truth about all these charges
we are bringing against him."
9 The Jews joined in the accusation, as-
serting that these things were true.
10 When the governor motioned for him
to speak, Paul replied: "I know that for a
number of years you have been a judge
over this nation; so I gladly make my defense. 11 You can easily verify that no more
than twelve days ago I went up to Jerusalem to worship. 12 My accusers did not
find me arguing with anyone at the temple, or stirring up a crowd in the synagogues or anywhere else in the city. 13 And
they cannot prove to you the charges they
are now making against me. 14 However, I
admit that I worship the God of our fathers as a follower of the Way, which they
call a sect. I believe everything that agrees
with the Law and that is written in the
Prophets, 15 and I have the same hope in
God as these men, that there will be a resurrection of both the righteous and the

[a] 6–8 Some manuscripts *him and wanted to judge him according to our law. 7 But the commander, Lysias, came and with the use of much force snatched him from our hands 8 and ordered his accusers to come before you. By*

wicked. 16So I strive always to keep my conscience clear before God and man.

17"After an absence of several years, I came to Jerusalem to bring my people gifts for the poor and to present offerings. 18I was ceremonially clean when they found me in the temple courts doing this. There was no crowd with me, nor was I involved in any disturbance. 19But there are some Jews from the province of Asia, who ought to be here before you and bring charges if they have anything against me. 20Or these who are here should state what crime they found in me when I stood before the Sanhedrin— 21unless it was this one thing I shouted as I stood in their presence: 'It is concerning the resurrection of the dead that I am on trial before you today.' "

22Then Felix, who was well acquainted with the Way, adjourned the proceedings. "When Lysias the commander comes," he said, "I will decide your case." 23He ordered the centurion to keep Paul under guard but to give him some freedom and permit his friends to take care of his needs.

24Several days later Felix came with his wife Drusilla, who was a Jewess. He sent for Paul and listened to him as he spoke about faith in Christ Jesus. 25As Paul discoursed on righteousness, self-control and the judgment to come, Felix was afraid and said, "That's enough for now! You may leave. When I find it convenient, I will send for you." 26At the same time he was hoping that Paul would offer him a bribe, so he sent for him frequently and talked with him.

27When two years had passed, Felix was succeeded by Porcius Festus, but because Felix wanted to grant a favor to the Jews, he left Paul in prison.

PRAYER: MY RELATIONSHIP TO GOD

GOD my Savior, when Your kindness and love appeared, You saved me, not by works of righteousness that I had done, but according to Your mercy. You saved me through the washing of regeneration and renewal by Your Holy Spirit, whom You poured out on me abundantly through Jesus Christ my Savior, so that having been justified by Your grace, I might become Your heir, having the hope of eternal life. (Titus 3:4–7)

***PAUSE** to thank God for the relationship that you enjoy with Him in Jesus Christ.*

OT I Chronicles 17:1-27

YEAR 2 DAY 74

God's Promise to David

17 After David was settled in his palace, he said to Nathan the prophet, "Here I am, living in a palace of cedar, while the ark of the covenant of the LORD is under a tent."

2Nathan replied to David, "Whatever you have in mind, do it, for God is with you."

3That night the word of God came to Nathan, saying:

4"Go and tell my servant David, 'This is what the LORD says: You are not the one to build me a house to dwell in. 5I have not dwelt in a house from the day I brought Israel up out of Egypt to this day. I have moved from one tent site to another, from one dwelling place to another. 6Wherever I have moved with all the Israelites, did I ever say to any of their leaders[a] whom I commanded to shepherd my people, "Why have you not built me a house of cedar?" '

7"Now then, tell my servant David, 'This is what the LORD Almighty says: I took you from the pasture and from following the flock, to be ruler over my people Israel. 8I have been with you wherever you have gone, and I have cut off all your enemies from

[a] 6 Traditionally *judges;* also in verse 10

before you. Now I will make your
name like the names of the greatest
men of the earth. [9]And I will provide
a place for my people Israel and will
plant them so that they can have a
home of their own and no longer be
disturbed. Wicked people will not
oppress them anymore, as they did at
the beginning [10]and have done ever
since the time I appointed leaders
over my people Israel. I will also subdue all your enemies.

" 'I declare to you that the LORD
will build a house for you: [11]When
your days are over and you go to be
with your fathers, I will raise up your
offspring to succeed you, one of your
own sons, and I will establish his
kingdom. [12]He is the one who will
build a house for me, and I will establish his throne forever. [13]I will be
his father, and he will be my son. I
will never take my love away from
him, as I took it away from your predecessor. [14]I will set him over my
house and my kingdom forever; his
throne will be established forever.' "

[15]Nathan reported to David all the
words of this entire revelation.

David's Prayer

[16]Then King David went in and sat before the LORD, and he said:

"Who am I, O LORD God, and what
is my family, that you have brought
me this far? [17]And as if this were not
enough in your sight, O God, you
have spoken about the future of the
house of your servant. You have
looked on me as though I were the
most exalted of men, O LORD God.

[18]"What more can David say to you
for honoring your servant? For you
know your servant, [19]O LORD. For the
sake of your servant and according to
your will, you have done this great
thing and made known all these
great promises.

[20]"There is no one like you,
O LORD, and there is no God but you,
as we have heard with our own ears.
[21]And who is like your people Israel—the one nation on earth whose
God went out to redeem a people for
himself, and to make a name for
yourself, and to perform great and
awesome wonders by driving out nations from before your people,
whom you redeemed from Egypt?
[22]You made your people Israel your
very own forever, and you, O LORD,
have become their God.

[23]"And now, LORD, let the promise
you have made concerning your servant and his house be established
forever. Do as you promised, [24]so that
it will be established and that your
name will be great forever. Then men
will say, 'The LORD Almighty, the God
over Israel, is Israel's God!' And the
house of your servant David will be
established before you.

[25]"You, my God, have revealed to
your servant that you will build a
house for him. So your servant has
found courage to pray to you.
[26]O LORD, you are God! You have
promised these good things to your
servant. [27]Now you have been pleased
to bless the house of your servant,
that it may continue forever in your
sight; for you, O LORD, have blessed
it, and it will be blessed forever."

PRAYER: INTERCESSION

RESTORE us again, O God of our salvation, and put away Your anger toward us. Will You be angry with us forever? Will You prolong Your anger to all generations? Will You not revive us again, that Your people may rejoice in You? Show us Your loving-kindness, O Lord, and grant us Your salvation. (Psalm 85:4–7)

TAKE *a few moments to intercede on behalf of the poor and hungry, the oppressed and persecuted, and those in control of world and national resources. Offer prayers for peace among nations and regarding current events and concerns.*

NT Acts 25:1-22

The Trial Before Festus

25 Three days after arriving in the province, Festus went up from Caesarea to
Jerusalem, [2]where the chief priests and
Jewish leaders appeared before him and
presented the charges against Paul. [3]They
urgently requested Festus, as a favor to
them, to have Paul transferred to Jerusalem, for they were preparing an ambush
to kill him along the way. [4]Festus answered, "Paul is being held at Caesarea,
and I myself am going there soon. [5]Let
some of your leaders come with me and
press charges against the man there, if he
has done anything wrong."
[6]After spending eight or ten days with
them, he went down to Caesarea, and the
next day he convened the court and ordered that Paul be brought before him.
[7]When Paul appeared, the Jews who had
come down from Jerusalem stood around
him, bringing many serious charges
against him, which they could not prove.
[8]Then Paul made his defense: "I have
done nothing wrong against the law of
the Jews or against the temple or against
Caesar."
[9]Festus, wishing to do the Jews a favor,
said to Paul, "Are you willing to go up to
Jerusalem and stand trial before me there
on these charges?"
[10]Paul answered: "I am now standing
before Caesar's court, where I ought to be
tried. I have not done any wrong to the
Jews, as you yourself know very well. [11]If,
however, I am guilty of doing anything
deserving death, I do not refuse to die. But
if the charges brought against me by these
Jews are not true, no one has the right to
hand me over to them. I appeal to Caesar!"
[12]After Festus had conferred with his
council, he declared: "You have appealed
to Caesar. To Caesar you will go!"

Festus Consults King Agrippa

[13]A few days later King Agrippa and Bernice arrived at Caesarea to pay their respects to Festus. [14]Since they were spending many days there, Festus discussed
Paul's case with the king. He said: "There
is a man here whom Felix left as a prisoner. [15]When I went to Jerusalem, the
chief priests and elders of the Jews
brought charges against him and asked
that he be condemned.
[16]"I told them that it is not the Roman
custom to hand over any man before he
has faced his accusers and has had an opportunity to defend himself against their
charges. [17]When they came here with me,
I did not delay the case, but convened the
court the next day and ordered the man
to be brought in. [18]When his accusers got
up to speak, they did not charge him
with any of the crimes I had expected.
[19]Instead, they had some points of dispute with him about their own religion
and about a dead man named Jesus who
Paul claimed was alive. [20]I was at a loss
how to investigate such matters; so I
asked if he would be willing to go to
Jerusalem and stand trial there on these
charges. [21]When Paul made his appeal to
be held over for the Emperor's decision,
I ordered him held until I could send
him to Caesar."
[22]Then Agrippa said to Festus, "I would
like to hear this man myself."
He replied, "Tomorrow you will hear
him."

PRAYER: THE CHARACTER I WANT TO CULTIVATE

THERE is a way that seems right to me, but its end is the way of death. (Proverbs 14:12) . . . I will examine all things, hold fast to the good and abstain from every form of evil. (1 Thessalonians 5:21–22)

__TAKE__ a moment to ask the Lord for the grace to grow in godly character.

YEAR 2 DAY 75

OT **1 Chronicles 18:1–19:19**

David's Victories

18 In the course of time, David defeated
the Philistines and subdued them,
and he took Gath and its surrounding villages from the control of the Philistines.
2 David also defeated the Moabites, and
they became subject to him and brought
tribute.
3 Moreover, David fought Hadadezer
king of Zobah, as far as Hamath, when he
went to establish his control along the Euphrates River. 4 David captured a thousand
of his chariots, seven thousand charioteers and twenty thousand foot soldiers.
He hamstrung all but a hundred of the
chariot horses.
5 When the Arameans of Damascus
came to help Hadadezer king of Zobah,
David struck down twenty-two thousand
of them. 6 He put garrisons in the Aramean kingdom of Damascus, and the Arameans became subject to him and
brought tribute. The LORD gave David victory everywhere he went.
7 David took the gold shields carried by
the officers of Hadadezer and brought
them to Jerusalem. 8 From Tebah[a] and
Cun, towns that belonged to Hadadezer,
David took a great quantity of bronze,
which Solomon used to make the bronze
Sea, the pillars and various bronze articles.
9 When Tou king of Hamath heard that
David had defeated the entire army of
Hadadezer king of Zobah, 10 he sent his
son Hadoram to King David to greet him
and congratulate him on his victory in
battle over Hadadezer, who had been at
war with Tou. Hadoram brought all kinds
of articles of gold and silver and bronze.
11 King David dedicated these articles to
the LORD, as he had done with the silver
and gold he had taken from all these nations: Edom and Moab, the Ammonites
and the Philistines, and Amalek.
12 Abishai son of Zeruiah struck down
eighteen thousand Edomites in the Valley
of Salt. 13 He put garrisons in Edom, and
all the Edomites became subject to David.
The LORD gave David victory everywhere
he went.

David's Officials

14 David reigned over all Israel, doing
what was just and right for all his people.
15 Joab son of Zeruiah was over the army;
Jehoshaphat son of Ahilud was recorder;
16 Zadok son of Ahitub and Ahimelech[b] son
of Abiathar were priests; Shavsha was secretary; 17 Benaiah son of Jehoiada was over
the Kerethites and Pelethites; and David's
sons were chief officials at the king's side.

The Battle Against the Ammonites

19 In the course of time, Nahash king of
the Ammonites died, and his son succeeded him as king. 2 David thought, "I
will show kindness to Hanun son of Nahash, because his father showed kindness
to me." So David sent a delegation to express his sympathy to Hanun concerning
his father.
When David's men came to Hanun in
the land of the Ammonites to express
sympathy to him, 3 the Ammonite nobles
said to Hanun, "Do you think David is
honoring your father by sending men to
you to express sympathy? Haven't his men
come to you to explore and spy out the
country and overthrow it?" 4 So Hanun
seized David's men, shaved them, cut off
their garments in the middle at the buttocks, and sent them away.
5 When someone came and told David
about the men, he sent messengers to meet
them, for they were greatly humiliated. The
king said, "Stay at Jericho till your beards
have grown, and then come back."
6 When the Ammonites realized that they
had become a stench in David's nostrils,
Hanun and the Ammonites sent a thousand talents[c] of silver to hire chariots and
charioteers from Aram Naharaim,[d] Aram
Maacah and Zobah. 7 They hired thirty-two
thousand chariots and charioteers, as well
as the king of Maacah with his troops, who
came and camped near Medeba, while the
Ammonites were mustered from their
towns and moved out for battle.
8 On hearing this, David sent Joab out

[a] 8 Hebrew *Tibhath,* a variant of *Tebah* [b] 16 Some Hebrew manuscripts, Vulgate and Syriac (see also 2 Samuel 8:17); most Hebrew manuscripts *Abimelech* [c] 6 That is, about 37 tons (about 34 metric tons) [d] 6 That is, Northwest Mesopotamia

with the entire army of fighting men. [9]The
Ammonites came out and drew up in battle formation at the entrance to their city,
while the kings who had come were by
themselves in the open country.
[10]Joab saw that there were battle lines in
front of him and behind him; so he selected some of the best troops in Israel
and deployed them against the Arameans.
[11]He put the rest of the men under the
command of Abishai his brother, and
they were deployed against the Ammonites. [12]Joab said, "If the Arameans are
too strong for me, then you are to rescue
me; but if the Ammonites are too strong
for you, then I will rescue you. [13]Be strong
and let us fight bravely for our people and
the cities of our God. The LORD will do
what is good in his sight."
[14]Then Joab and the troops with him
advanced to fight the Arameans, and they
fled before him. [15]When the Ammonites
saw that the Arameans were fleeing, they
too fled before his brother Abishai and
went inside the city. So Joab went back to
Jerusalem.
[16]After the Arameans saw that they had
been routed by Israel, they sent messengers
and had Arameans brought from beyond
the River,[e] with Shophach the commander
of Hadadezer's army leading them.
[17]When David was told of this, he gathered all Israel and crossed the Jordan; he
advanced against them and formed his battle lines opposite them. David formed his
lines to meet the Arameans in battle, and
they fought against him. [18]But they fled before Israel, and David killed seven thousand of their charioteers and forty thousand of their foot soldiers. He also killed
Shophach the commander of their army.
[19]When the vassals of Hadadezer saw
that they had been defeated by Israel, they
made peace with David and became subject to him.
So the Arameans were not willing to
help the Ammonites anymore.

[e] *16* That is, the Euphrates

PRAYER: AFFIRMATION

YOU, O Lord, will guard the feet of Your saints, but the wicked will be silenced in darkness. It is not by strength that one prevails; those who contend with You will be shattered. You will thunder against them from heaven; You will judge the ends of the earth. You will give strength to Your king and exalt the horn of Your anointed. (1 Samuel 2:9–10)

__PAUSE__ to reflect on these Biblical affirmations.

NT Acts 25:23–26:32

Paul Before Agrippa

[23]The next day Agrippa and Bernice
came with great pomp and entered the
audience room with the high ranking officers and the leading men of the city. At
the command of Festus, Paul was brought
in. [24]Festus said: "King Agrippa, and all
who are present with us, you see this
man! The whole Jewish community has
petitioned me about him in Jerusalem
and here in Caesarea, shouting that he
ought not to live any longer. [25]I found he
had done nothing deserving of death, but
because he made his appeal to the Emperor I decided to send him to Rome.
[26]But I have nothing definite to write to
His Majesty about him. Therefore I have
brought him before all of you, and especially before you, King Agrippa, so that as
a result of this investigation I may have
something to write. [27]For I think it is un-
reasonable to send on a prisoner without
specifying the charges against him."
26 Then Agrippa said to Paul, "You have
permission to speak for yourself."
So Paul motioned with his hand and began his defense: [2]"King Agrippa, I consider
myself fortunate to stand before you today
as I make my defense against all the accusations of the Jews, [3]and especially so because you are well acquainted with all the
Jewish customs and controversies. Therefore, I beg you to listen to me patiently.
[4]"The Jews all know the way I have lived
ever since I was a child, from the beginning

of my life in my own country, and also in
Jerusalem. 5They have known me for a
long time and can testify, if they are willing, that according to the strictest sect of
our religion, I lived as a Pharisee. 6And
now it is because of my hope in what God
has promised our fathers that I am on trial today. 7This is the promise our twelve
tribes are hoping to see fulfilled as they
earnestly serve God day and night. O king,
it is because of this hope that the Jews are
accusing me. 8Why should any of you consider it incredible that God raises the dead?
9"I too was convinced that I ought to do
all that was possible to oppose the name
of Jesus of Nazareth. 10And that is just
what I did in Jerusalem. On the authority
of the chief priests I put many of the saints
in prison, and when they were put to
death, I cast my vote against them. 11Many
a time I went from one synagogue to another to have them punished, and I tried
to force them to blaspheme. In my obses-
sion against them, I even went to foreign
cities to persecute them.
12"On one of these journeys I was going
to Damascus with the authority and commission of the chief priests. 13About noon,
O king, as I was on the road, I saw a light
from heaven, brighter than the sun, blazing around me and my companions. 14We
all fell to the ground, and I heard a voice
saying to me in Aramaic,[a] 'Saul, Saul, why
do you persecute me? It is hard for you to
kick against the goads.'
15"Then I asked, 'Who are you, Lord?'
" 'I am Jesus, whom you are persecuting,' the Lord replied. 16'Now get up and
stand on your feet. I have appeared to you
to appoint you as a servant and as a witness of what you have seen of me and
what I will show you. 17I will rescue you
from your own people and from the Gentiles. I am sending you to them 18to open
their eyes and turn them from darkness to
light, and from the power of Satan to
God, so that they may receive forgiveness
of sins and a place among those who are
sanctified by faith in me.'
19"So then, King Agrippa, I was not disobedient to the vision from heaven. 20First
to those in Damascus, then to those in
Jerusalem and in all Judea, and to the
Gentiles also, I preached that they should
repent and turn to God and prove their repentance by their deeds. 21That is why the
Jews seized me in the temple courts and
tried to kill me. 22But I have had God's
help to this very day, and so I stand here
and testify to small and great alike. I am
saying nothing beyond what the prophets
and Moses said would happen— 23that the
Christ[b] would suffer and, as the first to rise
from the dead, would proclaim light to his
own people and to the Gentiles."
24At this point Festus interrupted Paul's
defense. "You are out of your mind, Paul!"
he shouted. "Your great learning is driving
you insane."
25"I am not insane, most excellent Festus," Paul replied. "What I am saying is
true and reasonable. 26The king is familiar
with these things, and I can speak freely
to him. I am convinced that none of this
has escaped his notice, because it was not
done in a corner. 27King Agrippa, do you
believe the prophets? I know you do."
28Then Agrippa said to Paul, "Do you
think that in such a short time you can
persuade me to be a Christian?"
29Paul replied, "Short time or long—I
pray God that not only you but all who
are listening to me today may become
what I am, except for these chains."
30The king rose, and with him the governor and Bernice and those sitting with
them. 31They left the room, and while
talking with one another, they said, "This
man is not doing anything that deserves
death or imprisonment."
32Agrippa said to Festus, "This man
could have been set free if he had not appealed to Caesar."

[a] 14 Or *Hebrew* [b] 23 Or *Messiah*

PRAYER: MY RELATIONSHIP TO OTHERS

I WILL be hospitable to others without grumbling. As each of us has received a gift, we should use it to serve others, as good stewards of Your manifold grace, O God. (1 Peter 4:9–10)

***PAUSE** to review your relationships with others and to commit them to the Lord.*

YEAR 2 DAY 76

OT **1 Chronicles 20:1–21:30**

The Capture of Rabbah

20 In the spring, at the time when kings
go off to war, Joab led out the armed
forces. He laid waste the land of the Ammonites and went to Rabbah and besieged it, but David remained in Jerusalem. Joab attacked Rabbah and left it in
ruins. 2 David took the crown from the
head of their king[a]—its weight was found
to be a talent[b] of gold, and it was set with
precious stones—and it was placed on
David's head. He took a great quantity of
plunder from the city 3 and brought out
the people who were there, consigning
them to labor with saws and with iron
picks and axes. David did this to all the
Ammonite towns. Then David and his entire army returned to Jerusalem.

War With the Philistines

4 In the course of time, war broke out
with the Philistines, at Gezer. At that time
Sibbecai the Hushathite killed Sippai, one
of the descendants of the Rephaites, and
the Philistines were subjugated.
5 In another battle with the Philistines,
Elhanan son of Jair killed Lahmi the
brother of Goliath the Gittite, who had a
spear with a shaft like a weaver's rod.
6 In still another battle, which took
place at Gath, there was a huge man with
six fingers on each hand and six toes on
each foot—twenty-four in all. He also was
descended from Rapha. 7 When he taunted Israel, Jonathan son of Shimea, David's
brother, killed him.
8 These were descendants of Rapha in
Gath, and they fell at the hands of David
and his men.

David Numbers the Fighting Men

21 Satan rose up against Israel and incited
David to take a census of Israel. 2 So David said to Joab and the commanders of the
troops, "Go and count the Israelites from
Beersheba to Dan. Then report back to me
so that I may know how many there are."
3 But Joab replied, "May the LORD multiply his troops a hundred times over. My
lord the king, are they not all my lord's
subjects? Why does my lord want to do
this? Why should he bring guilt on Israel?"
4 The king's word, however, overruled
Joab; so Joab left and went throughout Israel and then came back to Jerusalem.
5 Joab reported the number of the fighting
men to David: In all Israel there were one
million one hundred thousand men who
could handle a sword, including four
hundred and seventy thousand in Judah.
6 But Joab did not include Levi and Benjamin in the numbering, because the
king's command was repulsive to him.
7 This command was also evil in the sight
of God; so he punished Israel.
8 Then David said to God, "I have
sinned greatly by doing this. Now, I beg
you, take away the guilt of your servant. I
have done a very foolish thing."
9 The LORD said to Gad, David's seer,
10 "Go and tell David, 'This is what the
LORD says: I am giving you three options.
Choose one of them for me to carry out
against you.' "
11 So Gad went to David and said to
him, "This is what the LORD says: 'Take
your choice: 12 three years of famine, three
months of being swept away[c] before your
enemies, with their swords overtaking
you, or three days of the sword of the
LORD—days of plague in the land, with
the angel of the LORD ravaging every part
of Israel.' Now then, decide how I should
answer the one who sent me."
13 David said to Gad, "I am in deep distress. Let me fall into the hands of the
LORD, for his mercy is very great; but do
not let me fall into the hands of men."
14 So the LORD sent a plague on Israel,
and seventy thousand men of Israel fell
dead. 15 And God sent an angel to destroy
Jerusalem. But as the angel was doing so,
the LORD saw it and was grieved because
of the calamity and said to the angel who
was destroying the people, "Enough!
Withdraw your hand." The angel of the
LORD was then standing at the threshing
floor of Araunah[d] the Jebusite.
16 David looked up and saw the angel of
the LORD standing between heaven and
earth, with a drawn sword in his hand ex-

[a] 2 Or *of Milcom,* that is, Molech [b] 2 That is, about 75 pounds (about 34 kilograms)
[c] 12 Hebrew; Septuagint and Vulgate (see also 2 Samuel 24:13) *of fleeing* [d] 15 Hebrew *Ornan,* a variant of *Araunah;* also in verses 18–28

tended over Jerusalem. Then David and the elders, clothed in sackcloth, fell facedown.

[17]David said to God, "Was it not I who ordered the fighting men to be counted? I am the one who has sinned and done wrong. These are but sheep. What have they done? O LORD my God, let your hand fall upon me and my family, but do not let this plague remain on your people."

[18]Then the angel of the LORD ordered Gad to tell David to go up and build an altar to the LORD on the threshing floor of Araunah the Jebusite. [19]So David went up in obedience to the word that Gad had spoken in the name of the LORD.

[20]While Araunah was threshing wheat, he turned and saw the angel; his four sons who were with him hid themselves. [21]Then David approached, and when Araunah looked and saw him, he left the threshing floor and bowed down before David with his face to the ground.

[22]David said to him, "Let me have the site of your threshing floor so I can build an altar to the LORD, that the plague on the people may be stopped. Sell it to me at the full price."

[23]Araunah said to David, "Take it! Let my lord the king do whatever pleases him. Look, I will give the oxen for the burnt offerings, the threshing sledges for the wood, and the wheat for the grain offering. I will give all this."

[24]But King David replied to Araunah, "No, I insist on paying the full price. I will not take for the LORD what is yours, or sacrifice a burnt offering that costs me nothing."

[25]So David paid Araunah six hundred shekels[e] of gold for the site. [26]David built an altar to the LORD there and sacrificed burnt offerings and fellowship offerings.[f] He called on the LORD, and the LORD answered him with fire from heaven on the altar of burnt offering.

[27]Then the LORD spoke to the angel, and he put his sword back into its sheath. [28]At that time, when David saw that the LORD had answered him on the threshing floor of Araunah the Jebusite, he offered sacrifices there. [29]The tabernacle of the LORD, which Moses had made in the desert, and the altar of burnt offering were at that time on the high place at Gibeon. [30]But David could not go before it to inquire of God, because he was afraid of the sword of the angel of the LORD.

[e] *25* That is, about 15 pounds (about 7 kilograms)
[f] *26* Traditionally *peace offerings*

PRAYER: THANKSGIVING

IN the day that You created Your people, You made them in Your likeness. You created them male and female and blessed them in the day they were created. (Genesis 5:1–2) . . . It was You, Lord, who created the heavens and stretched them out, who spread out the earth and all that grows on it; You give breath to its people, and spirit to those who walk on it. (Isaiah 42:5)

PAUSE *to offer your own expressions of thanksgiving.*

NT Acts 27:1–26

Paul Sails for Rome

27 When it was decided that we would sail for Italy, Paul and some other prisoners were handed over to a centurion named Julius, who belonged to the Imperial Regiment. [2]We boarded a ship from Adramyttium about to sail for ports along the coast of the province of Asia, and we put out to sea. Aristarchus, a Macedonian from Thessalonica, was with us.

[3]The next day we landed at Sidon; and Julius, in kindness to Paul, allowed him to go to his friends so they might provide for his needs. [4]From there we put out to sea again and passed to the lee of Cyprus because the winds were against us. [5]When we had sailed across the open sea off the coast of Cilicia and Pamphylia, we landed at Myra in Lycia. [6]There the centurion found an Alexandrian ship sailing for Italy and put us on board. [7]We made slow headway for many days and had difficulty arriving off

Cnidus. When the wind did not allow us to
hold our course, we sailed to the lee of
Crete, opposite Salmone. 8We moved along
the coast with difficulty and came to a place
called Fair Havens, near the town of Lasea.
9Much time had been lost, and sailing
had already become dangerous because by
now it was after the Fast.[a] So Paul warned
them, 10"Men, I can see that our voyage is
going to be disastrous and bring great loss
to ship and cargo, and to our own lives
also." 11But the centurion, instead of listening to what Paul said, followed the advice
of the pilot and of the owner of the ship.
12Since the harbor was unsuitable to winter
in, the majority decided that we should sail
on, hoping to reach Phoenix and winter
there. This was a harbor in Crete, facing
both southwest and northwest.

The Storm

13When a gentle south wind began to
blow, they thought they had obtained
what they wanted; so they weighed anchor
and sailed along the shore of Crete. 14Be-
fore very long, a wind of hurricane force,
called the "northeaster," swept down from
the island. 15The ship was caught by the
storm and could not head into the wind;
so we gave way to it and were driven along.
16As we passed to the lee of a small island
called Cauda, we were hardly able to make
the lifeboat secure. 17When the men had
hoisted it aboard, they passed ropes under
the ship itself to hold it together. Fearing
that they would run aground on the sandbars of Syrtis, they lowered the sea anchor
and let the ship be driven along. 18We took
such a violent battering from the storm
that the next day they began to throw the
cargo overboard. 19On the third day, they
threw the ship's tackle overboard with
their own hands. 20When neither sun nor
stars appeared for many days and the
storm continued raging, we finally gave up
all hope of being saved.
21After the men had gone a long time
without food, Paul stood up before them
and said: "Men, you should have taken my
advice not to sail from Crete; then you
would have spared yourselves this damage
and loss. 22But now I urge you to keep up
your courage, because not one of you will
be lost; only the ship will be destroyed.
23Last night an angel of the God whose I am
and whom I serve stood beside me 24and
said, 'Do not be afraid, Paul. You must
stand trial before Caesar; and God has graciously given you the lives of all who sail
with you.' 25So keep up your courage, men,
for I have faith in God that it will happen
just as he told me. 26Nevertheless, we must
run aground on some island."

[a] 9 That is, the Day of Atonement (Yom Kippur)

PRAYER: THE ATTRIBUTES OF GOD

O SON of Man, You will come with the clouds of heaven. In the presence of the Ancient of Days, You will be given dominion and glory and a kingdom, so that people of every nation and language will worship You. Your dominion is an everlasting dominion that will not pass away, and Your kingdom is one that will never be destroyed. (Daniel 7:13–14)

***PAUSE** to reflect on these affirmations about the person, powers and perfection of God.*

YEAR 2
DAY 77

OT Psalms 86–87

Psalm 86

A prayer of David.

1Hear, O LORD, and answer me,
for I am poor and needy.
2Guard my life, for I am devoted to you.
You are my God; save your servant
who trusts in you.
3Have mercy on me, O Lord,
for I call to you all day long.
4Bring joy to your servant,
for to you, O Lord,
I lift up my soul.

[5]You are forgiving and good, O Lord,
abounding in love to all who call to you.
[6]Hear my prayer, O LORD;
listen to my cry for mercy.
[7]In the day of my trouble I will call to you,
for you will answer me.

[8]Among the gods there is none like you, O Lord;
no deeds can compare with yours.
[9]All the nations you have made
will come and worship before you, O Lord;
they will bring glory to your name.
[10]For you are great and do marvelous deeds;
you alone are God.

[11]Teach me your way, O LORD,
and I will walk in your truth;
give me an undivided heart,
that I may fear your name.
[12]I will praise you, O Lord my God, with all my heart;
I will glorify your name forever.
[13]For great is your love toward me;
you have delivered me from the depths of the grave.[a]

[14]The arrogant are attacking me, O God;
a band of ruthless men seeks my life—
men without regard for you.
[15]But you, O Lord, are a compassionate and gracious God,
slow to anger, abounding in love and faithfulness.
[16]Turn to me and have mercy on me;
grant your strength to your servant
and save the son of your maidservant.[b]
[17]Give me a sign of your goodness,
that my enemies may see it and be put to shame,
for you, O LORD, have helped me and comforted me.

Psalm 87

Of the Sons of Korah. A psalm. A song.

[1]He has set his foundation on the holy mountain;
[2] the LORD loves the gates of Zion
more than all the dwellings of Jacob.
[3]Glorious things are said of you,
O city of God: *Selah*
[4]"I will record Rahab[c] and Babylon
among those who acknowledge me—
Philistia too, and Tyre, along with Cush[d]—
and will say, 'This[e] one was born in Zion.' "

[5]Indeed, of Zion it will be said,
"This one and that one were born in her,
and the Most High himself will establish her."
[6]The LORD will write in the register of the peoples:
"This one was born in Zion." *Selah*
[7]As they make music they will sing,
"All my fountains are in you."

[a] 13 Hebrew *Sheol* [b] 16 Or *save your faithful son* [c] 4 A poetic name for Egypt [d] 4 That is, the upper Nile region [e] 4 Or *"O Rahab and Babylon, / Philistia, Tyre and Cush, / I will record concerning those who acknowledge me: / 'This*

PRAYER: ADORATION

LIKE the roar of rushing waters and like loud peals of thunder, a great multitude will shout, "Hallelujah! For You reign, Lord God Almighty. Let us rejoice and be glad and give You glory! For the marriage of the Lamb has come, and His bride has made herself ready." Blessed are those who are invited to the marriage supper of the Lamb.

(Revelation 19:6–7, 9)

PAUSE *to express your thoughts of praise and worship.*

NT Acts 27:27–28:10

The Shipwreck

27 On the fourteenth night we were still being driven across the Adriatic[a] Sea, when about midnight the sailors sensed they were approaching land. 28 They took soundings and found that the water was a hundred and twenty feet[b] deep. A short time later they took soundings again and found it was ninety feet[c] deep. 29 Fearing that we would be dashed against the rocks, they dropped four anchors from the stern and prayed for daylight. 30 In an attempt to escape from the ship, the sailors let the lifeboat down into the sea, pretending they were going to lower some anchors from the bow. 31 Then Paul said to the centurion and the soldiers, "Unless these men stay with the ship, you cannot be saved." 32 So the soldiers cut the ropes that held the lifeboat and let it fall away.

33 Just before dawn Paul urged them all to eat. "For the last fourteen days," he said, "you have been in constant suspense and have gone without food—you haven't eaten anything. 34 Now I urge you to take some food. You need it to survive. Not one of you will lose a single hair from his head." 35 After he said this, he took some bread and gave thanks to God in front of them all. Then he broke it and began to eat. 36 They were all encouraged and ate some food themselves. 37 Altogether there were 276 of us on board. 38 When they had eaten as much as they wanted, they lightened the ship by throwing the grain into the sea.

39 When daylight came, they did not recognize the land, but they saw a bay with a sandy beach, where they decided to run the ship aground if they could. 40 Cutting loose the anchors, they left them in the sea and at the same time untied the ropes that held the rudders. Then they hoisted the foresail to the wind and made for the beach. 41 But the ship struck a sandbar and ran aground. The bow stuck fast and would not move, and the stern was broken to pieces by the pounding of the surf.

42 The soldiers planned to kill the prisoners to prevent any of them from swimming away and escaping. 43 But the centurion wanted to spare Paul's life and kept them from carrying out their plan. He ordered those who could swim to jump overboard first and get to land. 44 The rest were to get there on planks or on pieces of the ship. In this way everyone reached land in safety.

Ashore on Malta

28 Once safely on shore, we found out that the island was called Malta. 2 The islanders showed us unusual kindness. They built a fire and welcomed us all because it was raining and cold. 3 Paul gathered a pile of brushwood and, as he put it on the fire, a viper, driven out by the heat, fastened itself on his hand. 4 When the islanders saw the snake hanging from his hand, they said to each other, "This man must be a murderer; for though he escaped from the sea, Justice has not allowed him to live." 5 But Paul shook the snake off into the fire and suffered no ill effects. 6 The people expected him to swell up or suddenly fall dead, but after waiting a long time and seeing nothing unusual happen to him, they changed their minds and said he was a god.

7 There was an estate nearby that belonged to Publius, the chief official of the island. He welcomed us to his home and for three days entertained us hospitably. 8 His father was sick in bed, suffering from fever and dysentery. Paul went in to see him and, after prayer, placed his hands on him and healed him. 9 When this had happened, the rest of the sick on the island came and were cured. 10 They honored us in many ways and when we were ready to sail, they furnished us with the supplies we needed.

[a] *27* In ancient times the name referred to an area extending well south of Italy. [b] *28* Greek *twenty orguias* (about 37 meters) [c] *28* Greek *fifteen orguias* (about 27 meters)

PRAYER: THE WORKS OF GOD

FAITH comes from hearing, and hearing by Your word, O Christ. (Romans 10:17) . . . The faith of Your chosen people, O God, and the knowledge of the truth that leads to godliness, is faith and

knowledge resting in the hope of eternal life. It is an eternal life that You promised before the beginning of time—and You do not lie. At the appointed time You manifested Your word through the preaching entrusted to the apostles by Your command, O God our Savior. (Titus 1:1–3)

TAKE *a moment to consider the greatness of God's wonderful works.*

YEAR 2
DAY 78

OT 1 Chronicles 22:1–19

22 Then David said, "The house of the
LORD God is to be here, and also the
altar of burnt offering for Israel."

Preparations for the Temple

[2]So David gave orders to assemble the
aliens living in Israel, and from among
them he appointed stonecutters to prepare dressed stone for building the house
of God. [3]He provided a large amount of
iron to make nails for the doors of the
gateways and for the fittings, and more
bronze than could be weighed. [4]He also
provided more cedar logs than could be
counted, for the Sidonians and Tyrians
had brought large numbers of them to
David.
[5]David said, "My son Solomon is young
and inexperienced, and the house to be
built for the LORD should be of great mag-
nificence and fame and splendor in the
sight of all the nations. Therefore I will
make preparations for it." So David made
extensive preparations before his death.
[6]Then he called for his son Solomon and
charged him to build a house for the LORD,
the God of Israel. [7]David said to Solomon:
"My son, I had it in my heart to build a
house for the Name of the LORD my God.
[8]But this word of the LORD came to me:
'You have shed much blood and have
fought many wars. You are not to build a
house for my Name, because you have
shed much blood on the earth in my sight.
[9]But you will have a son who will be a man
of peace and rest, and I will give him rest
from all his enemies on every side. His
name will be Solomon,[a] and I will grant Israel peace and quiet during his reign. [10]He
is the one who will build a house for my
Name. He will be my son, and I will be his
father. And I will establish the throne of his
kingdom over Israel forever.'
[11]"Now, my son, the LORD be with you,
and may you have success and build the
house of the LORD your God, as he said
you would. [12]May the LORD give you discretion and understanding when he puts
you in command over Israel, so that you
may keep the law of the LORD your God.
[13]Then you will have success if you are
careful to observe the decrees and laws
that the LORD gave Moses for Israel. Be
strong and courageous. Do not be afraid
or discouraged.
[14]"I have taken great pains to provide
for the temple of the LORD a hundred
thousand talents[b] of gold, a million talents[c] of silver, quantities of bronze and
iron too great to be weighed, and wood
and stone. And you may add to them.
[15]You have many workmen: stonecutters,
masons and carpenters, as well as men
skilled in every kind of work [16]in gold and
silver, bronze and iron—craftsmen beyond number. Now begin the work, and
the LORD be with you."
[17]Then David ordered all the leaders of
Israel to help his son Solomon. [18]He said
to them, "Is not the LORD your God with
you? And has he not granted you rest on
every side? For he has handed the inhabitants of the land over to me, and the land
is subject to the LORD and to his people.
[19]Now devote your heart and soul to seeking the LORD your God. Begin to build the
sanctuary of the LORD God, so that you
may bring the ark of the covenant of the
LORD and the sacred articles belonging to
God into the temple that will be built for
the Name of the LORD."

[a] *9 Solomon* sounds like and may be derived from the Hebrew for *peace.* [b] *14* That is, about 3,750 tons (about 3,450 metric tons) [c] *14* That is, about 37,500 tons (about 34,500 metric tons)

PRAYER: CONFESSION

WE will return to You, O Lord. For You have torn us, but You will heal us; You have injured us, but You will bind up our wounds. After two days You will revive us; on the third day You will raise us up, that we may live before You. (Hosea 6:1–2)

***ASK** the Spirit to search your heart and reveal any areas of unconfessed sin. Acknowledge these to the Lord and thank Him for His forgiveness.*

NT Acts 28:11-31

Arrival at Rome

11After three months we put out to sea
in a ship that had wintered in the island.
It was an Alexandrian ship with the fig-
urehead of the twin gods Castor and Pollux. 12We put in at Syracuse and stayed
there three days. 13From there we set sail
and arrived at Rhegium. The next day the
south wind came up, and on the following day we reached Puteoli. 14There we
found some brothers who invited us to
spend a week with them. And so we came
to Rome. 15The brothers there had heard
that we were coming, and they traveled as
far as the Forum of Appius and the Three
Taverns to meet us. At the sight of these
men Paul thanked God and was encouraged. 16When we got to Rome, Paul was
allowed to live by himself, with a soldier
to guard him.

Paul Preaches at Rome Under Guard

17Three days later he called together the
leaders of the Jews. When they had assembled, Paul said to them: "My brothers,
although I have done nothing against our
people or against the customs of our ancestors, I was arrested in Jerusalem and
handed over to the Romans. 18They examined me and wanted to release me, because I was not guilty of any crime deserving death. 19But when the Jews
objected, I was compelled to appeal to
Caesar—not that I had any charge to
bring against my own people. 20For this
reason I have asked to see you and talk
with you. It is because of the hope of Israel that I am bound with this chain."
21They replied, "We have not received
any letters from Judea concerning you,
and none of the brothers who have come
from there has reported or said anything
bad about you. 22But we want to hear
what your views are, for we know that
people everywhere are talking against this
sect."
23They arranged to meet Paul on a certain day, and came in even larger numbers
to the place where he was staying. From
morning till evening he explained and declared to them the kingdom of God and
tried to convince them about Jesus from
the Law of Moses and from the Prophets.
24Some were convinced by what he said,
but others would not believe. 25They dis-
agreed among themselves and began to
leave after Paul had made this final statement: "The Holy Spirit spoke the truth to
your forefathers when he said through
Isaiah the prophet:

26" 'Go to this people and say,
"You will be ever hearing but never
understanding;
you will be ever seeing but never
perceiving."
27For this people's heart has become
calloused;
they hardly hear with their ears,
and they have closed their eyes.
Otherwise they might see with their
eyes,
hear with their ears,
understand with their hearts
and turn, and I would heal them.'[a]

28"Therefore I want you to know that
God's salvation has been sent to the Gentiles, and they will listen!"[b]
30For two whole years Paul stayed there
in his own rented house and welcomed
all who came to see him. 31Boldly and
without hindrance he preached the kingdom of God and taught about the Lord
Jesus Christ.

[a] 27 Isaiah 6:9,10 [b] 28 Some manuscripts *listen!" 29After he said this, the Jews left, arguing vigorously among themselves.*

PRAYER: MY RELATIONSHIP TO GOD

ONCE I was alienated from You, O God, and was an enemy in my mind because of my evil works. But now You have reconciled me, by Christ's fleshly body through death, to present me holy and blameless in Your sight and free from reproach. (Colossians 1:21–22)

***PAUSE** to thank God for the relationship that you enjoy with Him in Jesus Christ.*

YEAR 2
DAY 79

OT 1 Chronicles 23:1–32

The Levites

23 When David was old and full of years,
he made his son Solomon king over
Israel.
2He also gathered together all the leaders of Israel, as well as the priests and Levites. 3The Levites thirty years old or more
were counted, and the total number of
men was thirty-eight thousand. 4David
said, "Of these, twenty-four thousand are
to supervise the work of the temple of the
LORD and six thousand are to be officials
and judges. 5Four thousand are to be gatekeepers and four thousand are to praise
the LORD with the musical instruments I
have provided for that purpose."
6David divided the Levites into groups
corresponding to the sons of Levi: Gershon, Kohath and Merari.

Gershonites

7Belonging to the Gershonites:
Ladan and Shimei.
8The sons of Ladan:
Jehiel the first, Zetham and Joel—three in all.
9The sons of Shimei:
Shelomoth, Haziel and Haran—three in all.
These were the heads of the families of Ladan.
10And the sons of Shimei:
Jahath, Ziza,[a] Jeush and Beriah.
These were the sons of Shimei—four in all.
11Jahath was the first and Ziza the second, but Jeush and Beriah did not have many sons; so they were counted as one family with one assignment.

Kohathites

12The sons of Kohath:
Amram, Izhar, Hebron and Uzziel—four in all.
13The sons of Amram:
Aaron and Moses.
Aaron was set apart, he and his descendants forever, to consecrate the
most holy things, to offer sacrifices
before the LORD, to minister before
him and to pronounce blessings in
his name forever.
14The sons of
Moses the man of God were counted as part of the tribe of Levi.
15The sons of Moses:
Gershom and Eliezer.
16The descendants of Gershom:
Shubael was the first.
17The descendants of Eliezer:
Rehabiah was the first.
Eliezer had no other sons, but the sons of Rehabiah were very numerous.
18The sons of Izhar:
Shelomith was the first.
19The sons of Hebron:
Jeriah the first, Amariah the second, Jahaziel the third and Jekameam the fourth.
20The sons of Uzziel:
Micah the first and Isshiah the second.

Merarites

21The sons of Merari:
Mahli and Mushi.
The sons of Mahli:
Eleazar and Kish.

[a] *10* One Hebrew manuscript, Septuagint and Vulgate (see also verse 11); most Hebrew manuscripts *Zina*

22 Eleazar died without having sons:
he had only daughters. Their
cousins, the sons of Kish, married
them.
23 The sons of Mushi:
Mahli, Eder and Jerimoth—three
in all.

24 These were the descendants of Levi by
their families—the heads of families as
they were registered under their names
and counted individually, that is, the
workers twenty years old or more who
served in the temple of the LORD. 25 For David had said, "Since the LORD, the God of
Israel, has granted rest to his people and
has come to dwell in Jerusalem forever,
26 the Levites no longer need to carry the
tabernacle or any of the articles used in its
service." 27 According to the last instructions of David, the Levites were counted
from those twenty years old or more.
28 The duty of the Levites was to help
Aaron's descendants in the service of the
temple of the LORD: to be in charge of the
courtyards, the side rooms, the purification of all sacred things and the perfor-
mance of other duties at the house of
God. 29 They were in charge of the bread
set out on the table, the flour for the grain
offerings, the unleavened wafers, the baking and the mixing, and all measurements
of quantity and size. 30 They were also to
stand every morning to thank and praise
the LORD. They were to do the same in the
evening 31 and whenever burnt offerings
were presented to the LORD on Sabbaths
and at New Moon festivals and at appointed feasts. They were to serve before
the LORD regularly in the proper number
and in the way prescribed for them.
32 And so the Levites carried out their responsibilities for the Tent of Meeting, for
the Holy Place and, under their brothers
the descendants of Aaron, for the service
of the temple of the LORD.

PRAYER: RENEWAL

O GOD, may I rejoice always, pray without ceasing, and give thanks in all circumstances, for this is Your will for me in Christ Jesus.

(1 Thessalonians 5:16–18)

__PAUSE__ to add your own prayers for personal renewal.

NT Romans 1:1–32

1 Paul, a servant of Christ Jesus, called to
be an apostle and set apart for the
gospel of God— 2 the gospel he promised
beforehand through his prophets in the
Holy Scriptures 3 regarding his Son, who
as to his human nature was a descendant
of David, 4 and who through the Spirit[a] of
holiness was declared with power to be
the Son of God[b] by his resurrection from
the dead: Jesus Christ our Lord. 5 Through
him and for his name's sake, we received
grace and apostleship to call people from
among all the Gentiles to the obedience
that comes from faith. 6 And you also are
among those who are called to belong to
Jesus Christ.

7 To all in Rome who are loved by God
and called to be saints:

Grace and peace to you from God our
Father and from the Lord Jesus Christ.

Paul's Longing to Visit Rome

8 First, I thank my God through Jesus
Christ for all of you, because your faith is
being reported all over the world. 9 God,
whom I serve with my whole heart in
preaching the gospel of his Son, is my witness how constantly I remember you 10 in
my prayers at all times; and I pray that
now at last by God's will the way may be
opened for me to come to you.
11 I long to see you so that I may impart
to you some spiritual gift to make you
strong— 12 that is, that you and I may be
mutually encouraged by each other's
faith. 13 I do not want you to be unaware,
brothers, that I planned many times to
come to you (but have been prevented
from doing so until now) in order that I

[a] 4 Or *who as to his spirit* [b] 4 Or *was appointed to be the Son of God with power*

might have a harvest among you, just as I
have had among the other Gentiles.
14I am obligated both to Greeks and
non-Greeks, both to the wise and the foolish. 15That is why I am so eager to preach
the gospel also to you who are at Rome.
16I am not ashamed of the gospel, because it is the power of God for the salvation of everyone who believes: first for the
Jew, then for the Gentile. 17For in the
gospel a righteousness from God is revealed, a righteousness that is by faith
from first to last,[c] just as it is written: "The
righteous will live by faith."[d]

God's Wrath Against Mankind

18The wrath of God is being revealed
from heaven against all the godlessness
and wickedness of men who suppress the
truth by their wickedness, 19since what may
be known about God is plain to them, because God has made it plain to them. 20For
since the creation of the world God's invisible qualities—his eternal power and divine nature—have been clearly seen, being
understood from what has been made, so
that men are without excuse.
21For although they knew God, they
neither glorified him as God nor gave
thanks to him, but their thinking became
futile and their foolish hearts were darkened. 22Although they claimed to be wise,
they became fools 23and exchanged the
glory of the immortal God for images
made to look like mortal man and birds
and animals and reptiles.
24Therefore God gave them over in the
sinful desires of their hearts to sexual impurity for the degrading of their bodies
with one another. 25They exchanged the
truth of God for a lie, and worshiped and
served created things rather than the Creator—who is forever praised. Amen.
26Because of this, God gave them over
to shameful lusts. Even their women exchanged natural relations for unnatural
ones. 27In the same way the men also
abandoned natural relations with women
and were inflamed with lust for one another. Men committed indecent acts with
other men, and received in themselves the
due penalty for their perversion.
28Furthermore, since they did not think it
worthwhile to retain the knowledge of God,
he gave them over to a depraved mind, to
do what ought not to be done. 29They have
become filled with every kind of wickedness, evil, greed and depravity. They are full
of envy, murder, strife, deceit and malice.
They are gossips, 30slanderers, God-haters,
insolent, arrogant and boastful; they invent
ways of doing evil; they disobey their parents; 31they are senseless, faithless, heartless,
ruthless. 32Although they know God's righteous decree that those who do such things
deserve death, they not only continue to do
these very things but also approve of those
who practice them.

[c] 17 Or *is from faith to faith* [d] 17 Hab. 2:4

PRAYER: THE CHARACTER I WANT TO CULTIVATE

I WILL not set my heart on evil things or be an idolater or commit sexual immorality. (1 Corinthians 10:6–8) . . . This is Your will, O God, that I be sanctified, that I abstain from immorality and learn to control my own body in holiness and honor. For You did not call me to be impure, but to live a holy life. (1 Thessalonians 4:3–4, 7)

TAKE *a moment to ask the Lord for the grace to grow in godly character.*

YEAR 2 DAY 80

OT 1 Chronicles 24:1–31

The Divisions of Priests

24 These were the divisions of the sons
of Aaron:
The sons of Aaron were Nadab, Abihu,
Eleazar and Ithamar. 2But Nadab and Abihu died before their father did, and they
had no sons; so Eleazar and Ithamar
served as the priests. 3With the help of Zadok a descendant of Eleazar and Ahim-

elech a descendant of Ithamar, David separated them into divisions for their appointed order of ministering. [4]A larger
number of leaders were found among Eleazar's descendants than among Ithamar's, and they were divided accordingly:
sixteen heads of families from Eleazar's
descendants and eight heads of families
from Ithamar's descendants. [5]They divided them impartially by drawing lots, for
there were officials of the sanctuary and
officials of God among the descendants of
both Eleazar and Ithamar.

[6]The scribe Shemaiah son of Nethanel,
a Levite, recorded their names in the presence of the king and of the officials: Zadok the priest, Ahimelech son of Abiathar
and the heads of families of the priests
and of the Levites—one family being tak-
en from Eleazar and then one from Ithamar.

[7]The first lot fell to Jehoiarib,
the second to Jedaiah,
[8]the third to Harim,
the fourth to Seorim,
[9]the fifth to Malkijah,
the sixth to Mijamin,
[10]the seventh to Hakkoz,
the eighth to Abijah,
[11]the ninth to Jeshua,
the tenth to Shecaniah,
[12]the eleventh to Eliashib,
the twelfth to Jakim,
[13]the thirteenth to Huppah,
the fourteenth to Jeshebeab,
[14]the fifteenth to Bilgah,
the sixteenth to Immer,
[15]the seventeenth to Hezir,
the eighteenth to Happizzez,
[16]the nineteenth to Pethahiah,
the twentieth to Jehezkel,
[17]the twenty-first to Jakin,
the twenty-second to Gamul,
[18]the twenty-third to Delaiah
and the twenty-fourth to Maaziah.

[19]This was their appointed order of
ministering when they entered the temple
of the LORD, according to the regulations
prescribed for them by their forefather
Aaron, as the LORD, the God of Israel, had
commanded him.

The Rest of the Levites

[20]As for the rest of the descendants of Levi:
from the sons of Amram: Shubael;
from the sons of Shubael: Jehdeiah.
[21]As for Rehabiah, from his sons:
Isshiah was the first.
[22]From the Izharites: Shelomoth;
from the sons of Shelomoth: Jahath.
[23]The sons of Hebron: Jeriah the first,[a]
Amariah the second, Jahaziel the
third and Jekameam the fourth.
[24]The son of Uzziel: Micah;
from the sons of Micah: Shamir.
[25]The brother of Micah: Isshiah;
from the sons of Isshiah: Zechariah.
[26]The sons of Merari: Mahli and Mushi.
The son of Jaaziah: Beno.
[27]The sons of Merari:
from Jaaziah: Beno, Shoham, Zaccur and Ibri.
[28]From Mahli: Eleazar, who had no
sons.
[29]From Kish: the son of Kish:
Jerahmeel.
[30]And the sons of Mushi: Mahli, Eder
and Jerimoth.

These were the Levites, according to
their families. [31]They also cast lots, just as
their brothers the descendants of Aaron
did, in the presence of King David and of
Zadok, Ahimelech, and the heads of families of the priests and of the Levites. The
families of the oldest brother were treated the same as those of the youngest.

[a] *23* Two Hebrew manuscripts and some Septuagint manuscripts (see also 1 Chron. 23:19); most Hebrew manuscripts *The sons of Jeriah:*

PRAYER: PETITION

HEAR my cry, O God, and listen to my prayer. From the ends of the earth I call to You when my heart grows faint; lead me to the rock that is higher than I. You have been a shelter for me and a

strong tower against the enemy. I will dwell in Your tent forever and take refuge in the shelter of Your wings.
(Psalm 61:1–4)

***PAUSE** here to petition God for growth in your desire to know and please Jesus Christ. Pray for a greater love and commitment to Him, for the grace to practice His presence and for the grace to glorify Him in your life. Offer prayers regarding your activities for this day and any special concerns you may have.*

NT Romans 2:1–16

God's Righteous Judgment

2 You, therefore, have no excuse, you
who pass judgment on someone else,
for at whatever point you judge the other,
you are condemning yourself, because
you who pass judgment do the same
things. 2 Now we know that God's judgment against those who do such things is
based on truth. 3 So when you, a mere
man, pass judgment on them and yet do
the same things, do you think you will escape God's judgment? 4 Or do you show
contempt for the riches of his kindness,
tolerance and patience, not realizing that
God's kindness leads you toward repentance?
5 But because of your stubbornness and
your unrepentant heart, you are storing
up wrath against yourself for the day of
God's wrath, when his righteous judgment will be revealed. 6 God "will give to
each person according to what he has
done."[a] 7 To those who by persistence in
doing good seek glory, honor and immortality, he will give eternal life. 8 But for
those who are self-seeking and who reject
the truth and follow evil, there will be
wrath and anger. 9 There will be trouble
and distress for every human being who
does evil: first for the Jew, then for the
Gentile; 10 but glory, honor and peace for
everyone who does good: first for the Jew,
then for the Gentile. 11 For God does not
show favoritism.
12 All who sin apart from the law will
also perish apart from the law, and all
who sin under the law will be judged by
the law. 13 For it is not those who hear the
law who are righteous in God's sight, but
it is those who obey the law who will be
declared righteous. 14 (Indeed, when Gentiles, who do not have the law, do by nature things required by the law, they are a
law for themselves, even though they do
not have the law, 15 since they show that
the requirements of the law are written on
their hearts, their consciences also bearing
witness, and their thoughts now accusing,
now even defending them.) 16 This will
take place on the day when God will
judge men's secrets through Jesus Christ,
as my gospel declares.

[a] 6 Psalm 62:12; Prov. 24:12

PRAYER: MY RELATIONSHIP TO OTHERS

I WILL not bring charges against others without cause, when they have done me no harm. (Proverbs 3:30) . . . I will not take revenge but leave room for Your wrath, O God, for You have said, "Vengeance is Mine; I will repay." I will not be overcome by evil, but overcome evil with good.
(Romans 12:19, 21)

***PAUSE** to review your relationships with others and to commit them to the Lord.*

YEAR 2 DAY 81

OT 1 Chronicles 25:1-31

The Singers

25 David, together with the commanders of the army, set apart some of the sons of Asaph, Heman and Jeduthun for the ministry of prophesying, accompanied by harps, lyres and cymbals. Here is the list of the men who performed this service:

2From the sons of Asaph:
Zaccur, Joseph, Nethaniah and Asarelah. The sons of Asaph were under the supervision of Asaph, who prophesied under the king's supervision.
3As for Jeduthun, from his sons:
Gedaliah, Zeri, Jeshaiah, Shimei,[a] Hashabiah and Mattithiah, six in all, under the supervision of their father Jeduthun, who prophesied, using the harp in thanking and praising the LORD.
4As for Heman, from his sons:
Bukkiah, Mattaniah, Uzziel, Shubael and Jerimoth; Hananiah, Hanani, Eliathah, Giddalti and Romamti-Ezer; Joshbekashah, Mallothi, Hothir and Mahazioth. 5All these were sons of Heman the king's seer. They were given him through the promises of God to exalt him.[b] God gave Heman fourteen sons and three daughters.

6All these men were under the supervision of their fathers for the music of the temple of the LORD, with cymbals, lyres and harps, for the ministry at the house of God. Asaph, Jeduthun and Heman were under the supervision of the king.
7Along with their relatives—all of them trained and skilled in music for the LORD—they numbered 288.
8Young and old alike, teacher as well as student, cast lots for their duties.

9The first lot, which was for Asaph, fell to Joseph,
his sons and relatives,[c] 12[d]
the second to Gedaliah,
he and his relatives and sons, 12
10the third to Zaccur,
his sons and relatives, 12
11the fourth to Izri,[e]
his sons and relatives, 12
12the fifth to Nethaniah,
his sons and relatives, 12
13the sixth to Bukkiah,
his sons and relatives, 12
14the seventh to Jesarelah,[f]
his sons and relatives, 12
15the eighth to Jeshaiah,
his sons and relatives, 12
16the ninth to Mattaniah,
his sons and relatives, 12
17the tenth to Shimei,
his sons and relatives, 12
18the eleventh to Azarel,[g]
his sons and relatives, 12
19the twelfth to Hashabiah,
his sons and relatives, 12
20the thirteenth to Shubael,
his sons and relatives, 12
21the fourteenth to Mattithiah,
his sons and relatives, 12
22the fifteenth to Jerimoth,
his sons and relatives, 12
23the sixteenth to Hananiah,
his sons and relatives, 12
24the seventeenth to Joshbekashah,
his sons and relatives, 12
25the eighteenth to Hanani,
his sons and relatives, 12
26the nineteenth to Mallothi,
his sons and relatives, 12
27the twentieth to Eliathah,
his sons and relatives, 12
28the twenty-first to Hothir,
his sons and relatives, 12
29the twenty-second to Giddalti,
his sons and relatives, 12
30the twenty-third to Mahazioth,
his sons and relatives, 12
31the twenty-fourth to Romamti-Ezer,
his sons and relatives, 12

[a] 3 One Hebrew manuscript and some Septuagint manuscripts (see also verse 17); most Hebrew manuscripts do not have *Shimei.* [b] 5 Hebrew *exalt the horn* [c] 9 See Septuagint; Hebrew does not have *his sons and relatives.* [d] 9 See the total in verse 7; Hebrew does not have *twelve.*
[e] 11 A variant of *Zeri* [f] 14 A variant of *Asarelah*
[g] 18 A variant of *Uzziel*

PRAYER: INTERCESSION

TRIUNE God, we rejoice in the unity we have in You, in which there is one body and one Spirit, just as we were called in one hope of our calling; one Lord, one faith, one baptism, one God and Father of all, who is over all and through all and in all. (Ephesians 4:4–6)

***TAKE** a few moments to intercede on behalf of your local church, other churches, evangelism and discipleship ministries, educational ministries and any other special concerns you may have.*

NT Romans 2:17–29

The Jews and the Law

[17]Now you, if you call yourself a Jew; if
you rely on the law and brag about your
relationship to God; [18]if you know his will
and approve of what is superior because
you are instructed by the law; [19]if you are
convinced that you are a guide for the
blind, a light for those who are in the
dark, [20]an instructor of the foolish, a
teacher of infants, because you have in the
law the embodiment of knowledge and
truth— [21]you, then, who teach others, do
you not teach yourself? You who preach
against stealing, do you steal? [22]You who
say that people should not commit adultery, do you commit adultery? You who
abhor idols, do you rob temples? [23]You
who brag about the law, do you dishonor
God by breaking the law? [24]As it is written: "God's name is blasphemed among
the Gentiles because of you."[a]

[25]Circumcision has value if you observe
the law, but if you break the law, you have
become as though you had not been circumcised. [26]If those who are not circumcised keep the law's requirements, will
they not be regarded as though they were
circumcised? [27]The one who is not circumcised physically and yet obeys the law
will condemn you who, even though you
have the[b] written code and circumcision,
are a lawbreaker.

[28]A man is not a Jew if he is only one
outwardly, nor is circumcision merely
outward and physical. [29]No, a man is a
Jew if he is one inwardly; and circumcision is circumcision of the heart, by the
Spirit, not by the written code. Such a
man's praise is not from men, but from
God.

[a] *24* Isaiah 52:5; Ezek. 36:22 [b] *27* Or *who, by means of a*

PRAYER: THE ATTRIBUTES OF GOD

YOUR word, O God, is living and active and sharper than any double-edged sword, piercing even to the dividing of soul and spirit and of joints and marrow; it judges the thoughts and attitudes of the heart. And there is no creature hidden from Your sight, but everything is uncovered and laid bare before Your eyes— You to whom we must give account. (Hebrews 4:12–13)

***PAUSE** to reflect on these affirmations about the person, powers and perfection of God.*

OT 1 Chronicles 26:1-32

YEAR 2 DAY 82

The Gatekeepers

26 The divisions of the gatekeepers:

From the Korahites: Meshelemiah son
of Kore, one of the sons of Asaph.
2 Meshelemiah had sons:
Zechariah the firstborn,
Jediael the second,
Zebadiah the third,
Jathniel the fourth,
3 Elam the fifth,
Jehohanan the sixth
and Eliehoenai the seventh.
4 Obed-Edom also had sons:
Shemaiah the firstborn,
Jehozabad the second,
Joah the third,
Sacar the fourth,
Nethanel the fifth,
5 Ammiel the sixth,
Issachar the seventh
and Peullethai the eighth.
(For God had blessed Obed-Edom.)

6 His son Shemaiah also had sons,
who were leaders in their father's
family because they were very capable men. 7 The sons of Shemaiah: Othni, Rephael, Obed and Elzabad; his relatives Elihu and
Semakiah were also able men. 8 All
these were descendants of Obed-
Edom; they and their sons and
their relatives were capable men
with the strength to do the work—
descendants of Obed-Edom, 62 in
all.
9 Meshelemiah had sons and relatives,
who were able men—18 in all.

10 Hosah the Merarite had sons: Shimri the first (although he was not
the firstborn, his father had appointed him the first), 11 Hilkiah
the second, Tabaliah the third and
Zechariah the fourth. The sons and
relatives of Hosah were 13 in all.

12 These divisions of the gatekeepers,
through their chief men, had duties for
ministering in the temple of the LORD, just
as their relatives had. 13 Lots were cast for
each gate, according to their families,
young and old alike.
14 The lot for the East Gate fell to
Shelemiah.[a] Then lots were cast for his
son Zechariah, a wise counselor, and the
lot for the North Gate fell to him. 15 The
lot for the South Gate fell to Obed-Edom,
and the lot for the storehouse fell to his
sons. 16 The lots for the West Gate and the
Shalleketh Gate on the upper road fell to
Shuppim and Hosah.
Guard was alongside of guard: 17 There
were six Levites a day on the east, four a
day on the north, four a day on the south
and two at a time at the storehouse. 18 As
for the court to the west, there were four
at the road and two at the court itself.
19 These were the divisions of the gatekeepers who were descendants of Korah
and Merari.

The Treasurers and Other Officials

20 Their fellow Levites were[b] in charge of
the treasuries of the house of God and the
treasuries for the dedicated things.
21 The descendants of Ladan, who were
Gershonites through Ladan and who were
heads of families belonging to Ladan the
Gershonite, were Jehieli, 22 the sons of Jehieli, Zetham and his brother Joel. They
were in charge of the treasuries of the temple of the LORD.
23 From the Amramites, the Izharites,
the Hebronites and the Uzzielites:

24 Shubael, a descendant of Gershom
son of Moses, was the officer in
charge of the treasuries. 25 His relatives through Eliezer: Rehabiah his
son, Jeshaiah his son, Joram his
son, Zicri his son and Shelomith
his son. 26 Shelomith and his relatives were in charge of all the treasuries for the things dedicated by
King David, by the heads of families who were the commanders of
thousands and commanders of
hundreds, and by the other army
commanders. 27 Some of the plunder taken in battle they dedicated
for the repair of the temple of the
LORD. 28 And everything dedicated
by Samuel the seer and by Saul son
of Kish, Abner son of Ner and Joab

[a] 14 A variant of *Meshelemiah* [b] 20 Septuagint; Hebrew *As for the Levites, Ahijah was*

son of Zeruiah, and all the other dedicated things were in the care of Shelomith and his relatives.
29 From the Izharites: Kenaniah and his sons were assigned duties away from the temple, as officials and judges over Israel.
30 From the Hebronites: Hashabiah and his relatives—seventeen hundred able men—were responsible in Israel west of the Jordan for all the work of the LORD and for the king's
service. 31 As for the Hebronites, Jeriah was their chief according to the genealogical records of their families. In the fortieth year of David's reign a search was made in the records, and capable men among the Hebronites were found at Jazer
in Gilead. 32 Jeriah had twenty-seven hundred relatives, who were able men and heads of families, and King David put them in charge of the Reubenites, the Gadites and the half-tribe of Manasseh for every matter pertaining to God and for the affairs of the king.

PRAYER: AFFIRMATION

YOU who are the Glory of Israel do not lie or change Your mind, for You are not a man, that You should change Your mind. (1 Samuel 15:29) . . . Your counsel stands firm forever, O Lord, the plans of Your heart through all generations. (Psalm 33:11)

***PAUSE** to reflect on these Biblical affirmations.*

NT Romans 3:1–20

God's Faithfulness

3 What advantage, then, is there in being a Jew, or what value is there in circumcision? 2 Much in every way! First of all, they have been entrusted with the very words of God.
3 What if some did not have faith? Will their lack of faith nullify God's faithfulness? 4 Not at all! Let God be true, and every man a liar. As it is written:

"So that you may be proved right
when you speak
and prevail when you judge."[a]

5 But if our unrighteousness brings out God's righteousness more clearly, what shall we say? That God is unjust in bringing his wrath on us? (I am using a human
argument.) 6 Certainly not! If that were so, how could God judge the world? 7 Some-
one might argue, "If my falsehood enhances God's truthfulness and so increases his glory, why am I still condemned as a
sinner?" 8 Why not say—as we are being slanderously reported as saying and as some claim that we say—"Let us do evil that good may result"? Their condemnation is deserved.

No One Is Righteous

9 What shall we conclude then? Are we any better[b]? Not at all! We have already made the charge that Jews and Gentiles
alike are all under sin. 10 As it is written:

"There is no one righteous, not even
one;
11 there is no one who understands,
no one who seeks God.
12 All have turned away,
they have together become
worthless;
there is no one who does good,
not even one."[c]
13 "Their throats are open graves;
their tongues practice deceit."[d]
"The poison of vipers is on their
lips."[e]
14 "Their mouths are full of cursing
and bitterness."[f]
15 "Their feet are swift to shed blood;
16 ruin and misery mark their ways,
17 and the way of peace they do not
know."[g]

[a] *4* Psalm 51:4 [b] *9* Or *worse* [c] *12* Psalms 14:1–3; 53:1–3; Eccles. 7:20 [d] *13* Psalm 5:9 [e] *13* Psalm 140:3 [f] *14* Psalm 10:7 [g] *17* Isaiah 59:7,8

[18] "There is no fear of God before
their eyes."[h]

[19]Now we know that whatever the law says, it says to those who are under the law, so that every mouth may be silenced and the whole world held accountable to God. [20]Therefore no one will be declared righteous in his sight by observing the law; rather, through the law we become conscious of sin.

[h] 18 Psalm 36:1

PRAYER: THE WORKS OF GOD

JESUS, You meet our needs as our high priest: You are holy, blameless, undefiled, set apart from sinners and exalted above the heavens. Unlike the other high priests, You do not need to offer sacrifices day after day, first for Your own sins, and then for the sins of the people, for You did this once for all when You offered up Yourself. (Hebrews 7:26–27)

***TAKE** a moment to consider the greatness of God's wonderful works.*

YEAR 2 DAY 83

OT 1 Chronicles 27:1–34

Army Divisions

27 This is the list of the Israelites—heads of families, commanders of thousands and commanders of hundreds, and their officers, who served the king in all that concerned the army divisions that were on duty month by month throughout the year. Each division consisted of 24,000 men.

[2]In charge of the first division, for the first month, was Jashobeam son of Zabdiel. There were 24,000 men in his division. [3]He was a descendant of Perez and chief of all the army officers for the first month.
[4]In charge of the division for the second month was Dodai the Ahohite; Mikloth was the leader of his division. There were 24,000 men in his division.
[5]The third army commander, for the third month, was Benaiah son of Jehoiada the priest. He was chief and there were 24,000 men in his division. [6]This was the Benaiah who was a mighty man among the Thirty and was over the Thirty. His son Ammizabad was in charge of his division.
[7]The fourth, for the fourth month, was Asahel the brother of Joab; his son Zebadiah was his successor. There were 24,000 men in his division.
[8]The fifth, for the fifth month, was the commander Shamhuth the Izrahite. There were 24,000 men in his division.
[9]The sixth, for the sixth month, was Ira the son of Ikkesh the Tekoite. There were 24,000 men in his division.
[10]The seventh, for the seventh month, was Helez the Pelonite, an Ephraimite. There were 24,000 men in his division.
[11]The eighth, for the eighth month, was Sibbecai the Hushathite, a Zerahite. There were 24,000 men in his division.
[12]The ninth, for the ninth month, was Abiezer the Anathothite, a Benjamite. There were 24,000 men in his division.
[13]The tenth, for the tenth month, was Maharai the Netophathite, a Zerahite. There were 24,000 men in his division.
[14]The eleventh, for the eleventh month, was Benaiah the Pirathonite, an Ephraimite. There were 24,000 men in his division.
[15]The twelfth, for the twelfth month, was Heldai the Netophathite, from the family of Othniel. There were 24,000 men in his division.

Officers of the Tribes

[16]The officers over the tribes of Israel:

over the Reubenites: Eliezer son of Zicri;
over the Simeonites: Shephatiah son of Maacah;
17 over Levi: Hashabiah son of Kemuel;
over Aaron: Zadok;
18 over Judah: Elihu, a brother of David;
over Issachar: Omri son of Michael;
19 over Zebulun: Ishmaiah son of Obadiah;
over Naphtali: Jerimoth son of Azriel;
20 over the Ephraimites: Hoshea son of Azaziah;
over half the tribe of Manasseh: Joel son of Pedaiah;
21 over the half-tribe of Manasseh in Gilead: Iddo son of Zechariah;
over Benjamin: Jaasiel son of Abner;
22 over Dan: Azarel son of Jeroham.

These were the officers over the tribes of Israel.

23 David did not take the number of the
men twenty years old or less, because the
LORD had promised to make Israel as numerous as the stars in the sky. 24 Joab son
of Zeruiah began to count the men but
did not finish. Wrath came on Israel on
account of this numbering, and the number was not entered in the book[a] of the
annals of King David.

The King's Overseers

25 Azmaveth son of Adiel was in charge
of the royal storehouses.
Jonathan son of Uzziah was in charge
of the storehouses in the outlying districts, in the towns, the villages and the
watchtowers.
26 Ezri son of Kelub was in charge of the
field workers who farmed the land.
27 Shimei the Ramathite was in charge of
the vineyards.
Zabdi the Shiphmite was in charge of the
produce of the vineyards for the wine vats.
28 Baal-Hanan the Gederite was in
charge of the olive and sycamore-fig trees
in the western foothills.
Joash was in charge of the supplies of
olive oil.
29 Shitrai the Sharonite was in charge of
the herds grazing in Sharon.
Shaphat son of Adlai was in charge of
the herds in the valleys.
30 Obil the Ishmaelite was in charge of
the camels.
Jehdeiah the Meronothite was in charge
of the donkeys.
31 Jaziz the Hagrite was in charge of the
flocks.
All these were the officials in charge of
King David's property.

32 Jonathan, David's uncle, was a counselor, a man of insight and a scribe. Jehiel son of Hacmoni took care of the king's
sons.
33 Ahithophel was the king's counselor.
Hushai the Arkite was the king's friend.
34 Ahithophel was succeeded by Jehoiada
son of Benaiah and by Abiathar.
Joab was the commander of the royal
army.

[a] 24 Septuagint; Hebrew *number*

PRAYER: THANKSGIVING

YOU, O Lord, are a merciful God; You will not forsake us or destroy us or forget the covenant with our forefathers, which You swore to them. (Deuteronomy 4:31) . . . You, O Lord, are a shield around me; You bestow glory on me and lift up my head. (Psalm 3:3)

***PAUSE** to offer your own expressions of thanksgiving.*

NT Romans 3:21-31

Righteousness Through Faith

21 But now a righteousness from God,
apart from law, has been made known, to
which the Law and the Prophets testify.
22 This righteousness from God comes
through faith in Jesus Christ to all who
believe. There is no difference, 23 for all
have sinned and fall short of the glory of
God, 24 and are justified freely by his grace
through the redemption that came by

Christ Jesus. 25God presented him as a sacrifice of atonement,[a] through faith in his
blood. He did this to demonstrate his justice, because in his forbearance he had left
the sins committed beforehand unpunished— 26he did it to demonstrate his justice at the present time, so as to be just
and the one who justifies those who have
faith in Jesus.
27Where, then, is boasting? It is excluded. On what principle? On that of observing the law? No, but on that of faith. 28For
we maintain that a man is justified by faith
apart from observing the law. 29Is God the
God of Jews only? Is he not the God of
Gentiles too? Yes, of Gentiles too, 30since
there is only one God, who will justify the
circumcised by faith and the uncircumcised through that same faith. 31Do we,
then, nullify the law by this faith? Not at
all! Rather, we uphold the law.

[a] 25 Or *as the one who would turn aside his wrath, taking away sin*

PRAYER: MY RELATIONSHIP TO GOD

O FATHER, You have qualified me to share in the inheritance of the saints in the kingdom of light. For You have rescued me from the dominion of darkness and brought me into the kingdom of Your beloved Son, in whom I have redemption, the forgiveness of sins. (Colossians 1:12–14)

***PAUSE** to thank God for the relationship that you enjoy with Him in Jesus Christ.*

YEAR 2 DAY 84

OT Psalm 88

Psalm 88

A song. A psalm of the Sons of Korah. For the director of music. According to *mahalath leannoth.*[a] A *maskil*[b] of Heman the Ezrahite.

1 O LORD, the God who saves me,
day and night I cry out before you.
2 May my prayer come before you;
turn your ear to my cry.

3 For my soul is full of trouble
and my life draws near the grave.[c]
4 I am counted among those who go
down to the pit;
I am like a man without strength.
5 I am set apart with the dead,
like the slain who lie in the grave,
whom you remember no more,
who are cut off from your care.

6 You have put me in the lowest pit,
in the darkest depths.
7 Your wrath lies heavily upon me;
you have overwhelmed me with all
your waves. *Selah*
8 You have taken from me my closest
friends
and have made me repulsive to them.
I am confined and cannot escape;
9 my eyes are dim with grief.

I call to you, O LORD, every day;
I spread out my hands to you.
10 Do you show your wonders to the
dead?
Do those who are dead rise up and
praise you? *Selah*
11 Is your love declared in the grave,
your faithfulness in Destruction[d]?
12 Are your wonders known in the place
of darkness,
or your righteous deeds in the land
of oblivion?

13 But I cry to you for help, O LORD;
in the morning my prayer comes
before you.
14 Why, O LORD, do you reject me
and hide your face from me?

15 From my youth I have been afflicted
and close to death;
I have suffered your terrors and am
in despair.

[a] Title: Possibly a tune, "The Suffering of Affliction"
[b] Title: Probably a literary or musical term
[c] 3 Hebrew *Sheol* [d] 11 Hebrew *Abaddon*

16 Your wrath has swept over me;
your terrors have destroyed me.
17 All day long they surround me like a
flood;
they have completely engulfed me.
18 You have taken my companions and
loved ones from me;
the darkness is my closest friend.

PRAYER: ADORATION

LORD, I know that You are great, and that You are above all gods. You do what pleases You, in the heavens and on the earth, in the seas and all their depths. (Psalm 135:5–6)

***PAUSE** to express your thoughts of praise and worship.*

NT Romans 4:1-25

Abraham Justified by Faith

4 What then shall we say that Abraham,
our forefather, discovered in this matter? 2 If, in fact, Abraham was justified by
works, he had something to boast
about—but not before God. 3 What does
the Scripture say? "Abraham believed
God, and it was credited to him as righteousness."[a]
4 Now when a man works, his wages are
not credited to him as a gift, but as an
obligation. 5 However, to the man who
does not work but trusts God who justifies the wicked, his faith is credited as
righteousness. 6 David says the same thing
when he speaks of the blessedness of the
man to whom God credits righteousness
apart from works:

7 "Blessed are they
whose transgressions are forgiven,
whose sins are covered.
8 Blessed is the man
whose sin the Lord will never count
against him."[b]

9 Is this blessedness only for the circumcised, or also for the uncircumcised?
We have been saying that Abraham's faith
was credited to him as righteousness.
10 Under what circumstances was it credited? Was it after he was circumcised, or before? It was not after, but before! 11 And he
received the sign of circumcision, a seal of
the righteousness that he had by faith
while he was still uncircumcised. So then,
he is the father of all who believe but have
not been circumcised, in order that righteousness might be credited to them.
12 And he is also the father of the circumcised who not only are circumcised but
who also walk in the footsteps of the faith
that our father Abraham had before he
was circumcised.
13 It was not through law that Abraham
and his offspring received the promise
that he would be heir of the world, but
through the righteousness that comes by
faith. 14 For if those who live by law are
heirs, faith has no value and the promise
is worthless, 15 because law brings wrath.
And where there is no law there is no
transgression.
16 Therefore, the promise comes by faith,
so that it may be by grace and may be
guaranteed to all Abraham's offspring—
not only to those who are of the law but
also to those who are of the faith of Abraham. He is the father of us all. 17 As it is
written: "I have made you a father of
many nations."[c] He is our father in the
sight of God, in whom he believed—the
God who gives life to the dead and calls
things that are not as though they were.
18 Against all hope, Abraham in hope believed and so became the father of many
nations, just as it had been said to him,
"So shall your offspring be."[d] 19 Without
weakening in his faith, he faced the fact
that his body was as good as dead—since
he was about a hundred years old—and
that Sarah's womb was also dead. 20 Yet he
did not waver through unbelief regarding
the promise of God, but was strengthened
in his faith and gave glory to God, 21 being
fully persuaded that God had power to do
what he had promised. 22 This is why "it
was credited to him as righteousness."
23 The words "it was credited to him" were

[a] *3* Gen. 15:6; also in verse 22 [b] *8* Psalm 32:1,2
[c] *17* Gen. 17:5 [d] *18* Gen. 15:5

written not for him alone, 24 but also for us, to whom God will credit righteousness—for us who believe in him who raised Jesus our Lord from the dead. 25 He was delivered over to death for our sins and was raised to life for our justification.

PRAYER: THE CHARACTER I WANT TO CULTIVATE

I WILL submit myself to You, O God, and resist the devil, and he will flee from me. I will humble myself before You, Lord, and You will exalt me. (James 4:7, 10)

***TAKE** a moment to ask the Lord for the grace to grow in godly character.*

YEAR 2 DAY 85

OT 1 Chronicles 28:1–21

David's Plans for the Temple

28 David summoned all the officials of Israel to assemble at Jerusalem: the officers over the tribes, the commanders of the divisions in the service of the king, the commanders of thousands and commanders of hundreds, and the officials in charge of all the property and livestock belonging to the king and his sons, together with the palace officials, the mighty men and all the brave warriors.

2 King David rose to his feet and said: "Listen to me, my brothers and my people. I had it in my heart to build a house as a place of rest for the ark of the covenant of the LORD, for the footstool of our God, and I made plans to build it. 3 But God said to me, 'You are not to build a house for my Name, because you are a warrior and have shed blood.'

4 "Yet the LORD, the God of Israel, chose me from my whole family to be king over Israel forever. He chose Judah as leader, and from the house of Judah he chose my family, and from my father's sons he was pleased to make me king over all Israel. 5 Of all my sons—and the LORD has given me many—he has chosen my son Solomon to sit on the throne of the kingdom of the LORD over Israel. 6 He said to me: 'Solomon your son is the one who will build my house and my courts, for I have chosen him to be my son, and I will be his father. 7 I will establish his kingdom forever if he is unswerving in carrying out my commands and laws, as is being done at this time.'

8 "So now I charge you in the sight of all Israel and of the assembly of the LORD, and in the hearing of our God: Be careful to follow all the commands of the LORD your God, that you may possess this good land and pass it on as an inheritance to your descendants forever.

9 "And you, my son Solomon, acknowledge the God of your father, and serve him with wholehearted devotion and with a willing mind, for the LORD searches every heart and understands every motive behind the thoughts. If you seek him, he will be found by you; but if you forsake him, he will reject you forever. 10 Consider now, for the LORD has chosen you to build a temple as a sanctuary. Be strong and do the work."

11 Then David gave his son Solomon the plans for the portico of the temple, its buildings, its storerooms, its upper parts, its inner rooms and the place of atonement. 12 He gave him the plans of all that the Spirit had put in his mind for the courts of the temple of the LORD and all the surrounding rooms, for the treasuries of the temple of God and for the treasuries for the dedicated things. 13 He gave him instructions for the divisions of the priests and Levites, and for all the work of serving in the temple of the LORD, as well as for all the articles to be used in its service. 14 He designated the weight of gold for all the gold articles to be used in various kinds of service, and the weight of silver for all the silver articles to be used in various kinds of service: 15 the weight of gold for the gold lampstands and their lamps, with the weight for each lampstand and its lamps; and the weight of silver for each silver lampstand and its lamps, according

to the use of each lampstand; [16]the weight
of gold for each table for consecrated
bread; the weight of silver for the silver tables; [17]the weight of pure gold for the
forks, sprinkling bowls and pitchers; the
weight of gold for each gold dish; the
weight of silver for each silver dish; [18]and
the weight of the refined gold for the altar of incense. He also gave him the plan
for the chariot, that is, the cherubim of
gold that spread their wings and shelter
the ark of the covenant of the LORD.
[19]"All this," David said, "I have in writing from the hand of the LORD upon me,
and he gave me understanding in all the
details of the plan."
[20]David also said to Solomon his son,
"Be strong and courageous, and do the
work. Do not be afraid or discouraged, for
the LORD God, my God, is with you. He
will not fail you or forsake you until all
the work for the service of the temple of
the LORD is finished. [21]The divisions of the
priests and Levites are ready for all the
work on the temple of God, and every willing man skilled in any craft will help you
in all the work. The officials and all the
people will obey your every command."

PRAYER: CONFESSION

IF I say that I have fellowship with You, O Christ, and yet walk in the darkness, I lie and do not practice the truth. But if I walk in the light, as You are in the light, I have fellowship with others, and Your blood, O Jesus, purifies me from all sin. (1 John 1:6–7)

***ASK** the Spirit to search your heart and reveal any areas of unconfessed sin. Acknowledge these to the Lord and thank Him for His forgiveness.*

NT Romans 5:1–21

Peace and Joy

5 Therefore, since we have been justified
through faith, we[a] have peace with God
through our Lord Jesus Christ, [2]through
whom we have gained access by faith into
this grace in which we now stand. And
we[a] rejoice in the hope of the glory of
God. [3]Not only so, but we[a] also rejoice in
our sufferings, because we know that suffering produces perseverance; [4]persever-
ance, character; and character, hope. [5]And
hope does not disappoint us, because
God has poured out his love into our
hearts by the Holy Spirit, whom he has
given us.
[6]You see, at just the right time, when we
were still powerless, Christ died for the
ungodly. [7]Very rarely will anyone die for a
righteous man, though for a good man
someone might possibly dare to die. [8]But
God demonstrates his own love for us in
this: While we were still sinners, Christ
died for us.
[9]Since we have now been justified by
his blood, how much more shall we be
saved from God's wrath through him!
[10]For if, when we were God's enemies, we
were reconciled to him through the death
of his Son, how much more, having been
reconciled, shall we be saved through his
life! [11]Not only is this so, but we also rejoice in God through our Lord Jesus
Christ, through whom we have now re
ceived reconciliation.

Death Through Adam, Life Through Christ

[12]Therefore, just as sin entered the
world through one man, and death
through sin, and in this way death came
to all men, because all sinned— [13]for before the law was given, sin was in the
world. But sin is not taken into account
when there is no law. [14]Nevertheless,
death reigned from the time of Adam to
the time of Moses, even over those who
did not sin by breaking a command, as
did Adam, who was a pattern of the one
to come.
[15]But the gift is not like the trespass. For
if the many died by the trespass of the one
man, how much more did God's grace
and the gift that came by the grace of the
one man, Jesus Christ, overflow to the
many! [16]Again, the gift of God is not like

[a] 1,2,3 Or *let us*

the result of the one man's sin: The judgment followed one sin and brought condemnation, but the gift followed many trespasses and brought justification. [17]For if, by the trespass of the one man, death reigned through that one man, how much more will those who receive God's abundant provision of grace and of the gift of righteousness reign in life through the one man, Jesus Christ.

[18]Consequently, just as the result of one trespass was condemnation for all men, so also the result of one act of righteousness was justification that brings life for all men. [19]For just as through the disobedience of the one man the many were made sinners, so also through the obedience of the one man the many will be made righteous.

[20]The law was added so that the trespass might increase. But where sin increased, grace increased all the more, [21]so that, just as sin reigned in death, so also grace might reign through righteousness to bring eternal life through Jesus Christ our Lord.

PRAYER: MY RELATIONSHIP TO OTHERS

WIVES should submit to their husbands, as is fitting in You, O Lord. Husbands should love their wives and not be bitter toward them. (Colossians 3:18–19)

***PAUSE** to review your relationships with others and to commit them to the Lord.*

YEAR 2
DAY 86

OT 1 Chronicles 29:1–30

Gifts for Building the Temple

29 Then King David said to the whole assembly: "My son Solomon, the one whom God has chosen, is young and inexperienced. The task is great, because this palatial structure is not for man but for the LORD God. [2]With all my resources I have provided for the temple of my God—gold for the gold work, silver for the silver, bronze for the bronze, iron for the iron and wood for the wood, as well as onyx for the settings, turquoise,[a] stones of various colors, and all kinds of fine stone and marble—all of these in large quantities. [3]Besides, in my devotion to the temple of my God I now give my personal treasures of gold and silver for the temple of my God, over and above everything I have provided for this holy temple: [4]three thousand talents[b] of gold (gold of Ophir) and seven thousand talents[c] of refined silver, for the overlaying of the walls of the buildings, [5]for the gold work and the silver work, and for all the work to be done by the craftsmen. Now, who is willing to consecrate himself today to the LORD?"

[6]Then the leaders of families, the officers of the tribes of Israel, the commanders of thousands and commanders of hundreds, and the officials in charge of the king's work gave willingly. [7]They gave toward the work on the temple of God five thousand talents[d] and ten thousand darics[e] of gold, ten thousand talents[f] of silver, eighteen thousand talents[g] of bronze and a hundred thousand talents[h] of iron. [8]Any who had precious stones gave them to the treasury of the temple of the LORD in the custody of Jehiel the Gershonite. [9]The people rejoiced at the willing response of their leaders, for they had given freely and wholeheartedly to the LORD. David the king also rejoiced greatly.

David's Prayer

[10]David praised the LORD in the presence of the whole assembly, saying,

"Praise be to you, O LORD,

[a] *2* The meaning of the Hebrew for this word is uncertain. [b] *4* That is, about 110 tons (about 100 metric tons) [c] *4* That is, about 260 tons (about 240 metric tons) [d] *7* That is, about 190 tons (about 170 metric tons) [e] *7* That is, about 185 pounds (about 84 kilograms) [f] *7* That is, about 375 tons (about 345 metric tons) [g] *7* That is, about 675 tons (about 610 metric tons) [h] *7* That is, about 3,750 tons (about 3,450 metric tons)

God of our father Israel,
from everlasting to everlasting.
11 Yours, O LORD, is the greatness and
the power
and the glory and the majesty and
the splendor,
for everything in heaven and earth
is yours.
Yours, O LORD, is the kingdom;
you are exalted as head over all.
12 Wealth and honor come from you;
you are the ruler of all things.
In your hands are strength and power
to exalt and give strength to all.
13 Now, our God, we give you thanks,
and praise your glorious name.

14 "But who am I, and who are my people, that we should be able to give as generously as this? Everything comes from
you, and we have given you only what
comes from your hand. 15 We are aliens
and strangers in your sight, as were all our
forefathers. Our days on earth are like a
shadow, without hope. 16 O LORD our God,
as for all this abundance that we have provided for building you a temple for your
Holy Name, it comes from your hand,
and all of it belongs to you. 17 I know, my
God, that you test the heart and are
pleased with integrity. All these things
have I given willingly and with honest intent. And now I have seen with joy how
willingly your people who are here have
given to you. 18 O LORD, God of our fathers
Abraham, Isaac and Israel, keep this desire in the hearts of your people forever,
and keep their hearts loyal to you. 19 And
give my son Solomon the wholehearted
devotion to keep your commands, requirements and decrees and to do everything to build the palatial structure for
which I have provided."
20 Then David said to the whole assembly, "Praise the LORD your God." So they
all praised the LORD, the God of their fathers; they bowed low and fell prostrate
before the LORD and the king.

Solomon Acknowledged as King

21 The next day they made sacrifices to
the LORD and presented burnt offerings to
him: a thousand bulls, a thousand rams
and a thousand male lambs, together with
their drink offerings, and other sacrifices
in abundance for all Israel. 22 They ate and
drank with great joy in the presence of the
LORD that day.
Then they acknowledged Solomon son
of David as king a second time, anointing
him before the LORD to be ruler and Zadok
to be priest. 23 So Solomon sat on the throne
of the LORD as king in place of his father
David. He prospered and all Israel obeyed
him. 24 All the officers and mighty men, as
well as all of King David's sons, pledged
their submission to King Solomon.
25 The LORD highly exalted Solomon in
the sight of all Israel and bestowed on
him royal splendor such as no king over
Israel ever had before.

The Death of David

26 David son of Jesse was king over all Israel. 27 He ruled over Israel forty years—
seven in Hebron and thirty-three in Jerusalem. 28 He died at a good old age, having
enjoyed long life, wealth and honor. His
son Solomon succeeded him as king.
29 As for the events of King David's reign,
from beginning to end, they are written in
the records of Samuel the seer, the records
of Nathan the prophet and the records of
Gad the seer, 30 together with the details of
his reign and power, and the circumstances that surrounded him and Israel
and the kingdoms of all the other lands.

PRAYER: RENEWAL

MAY I be a doer of the word and not merely a hearer who deceives myself. For if I am a hearer of the word and not a doer, I am like those who look at their natural faces in a mirror, and after looking at themselves, go away, and immediately forget what kind of people they are. But if I look intently into the perfect law of freedom and continue in it and I am not a forgetful hearer but a doer of the word, I will be blessed in what I do. (James 1:22–25)

__PAUSE__ to add your own prayers for personal renewal.

NT Romans 6:1-14

Dead to Sin, Alive in Christ

6 What shall we say, then? Shall we go on sinning so that grace may increase? [2]By no means! We died to sin; how can we live in it any longer? [3]Or don't you know that all of us who were baptized into Christ Jesus were baptized into his death? [4]We were therefore buried with him through baptism into death in order that, just as Christ was raised from the dead through the glory of the Father, we too may live a new life.

[5]If we have been united with him like this in his death, we will certainly also be united with him in his resurrection. [6]For we know that our old self was crucified with him so that the body of sin might be done away with,[a] that we should no longer be slaves to sin— [7]because anyone who has died has been freed from sin.

[8]Now if we died with Christ, we believe that we will also live with him. [9]For we know that since Christ was raised from the dead, he cannot die again; death no longer has mastery over him. [10]The death he died, he died to sin once for all; but the life he lives, he lives to God.

[11]In the same way, count yourselves dead to sin but alive to God in Christ Jesus. [12]Therefore do not let sin reign in your mortal body so that you obey its evil desires. [13]Do not offer the parts of your body to sin, as instruments of wickedness, but rather offer yourselves to God, as those who have been brought from death to life; and offer the parts of your body to him as instruments of righteousness. [14]For sin shall not be your master, because you are not under law, but under grace.

[a] 6 Or *be rendered powerless*

PRAYER: THE ATTRIBUTES OF GOD

TO You—the King eternal, immortal, invisible, the only God—be honor and glory for ever and ever. (1 Timothy 1:17)

***PAUSE** to reflect on these affirmations about the person, powers and perfection of God.*

YEAR 2 DAY 87

OT 2 Chronicles 1:1–2:18

Solomon Asks for Wisdom

1 Solomon son of David established himself firmly over his kingdom, for the LORD his God was with him and made him exceedingly great.

[2]Then Solomon spoke to all Israel—to the commanders of thousands and commanders of hundreds, to the judges and to all the leaders in Israel, the heads of families— [3]and Solomon and the whole assembly went to the high place at Gibeon, for God's Tent of Meeting was there, which Moses the LORD's servant had made in the desert. [4]Now David had brought up the ark of God from Kiriath Jearim to the place he had prepared for it, because he had pitched a tent for it in Jerusalem. [5]But the bronze altar that Bezalel son of Uri, the son of Hur, had made was in Gibeon in front of the tabernacle of the LORD; so Solomon and the assembly inquired of him there. [6]Solomon went up to the bronze altar before the LORD in the Tent of Meeting and offered a thousand burnt offerings on it.

[7]That night God appeared to Solomon and said to him, "Ask for whatever you want me to give you."

[8]Solomon answered God, "You have shown great kindness to David my father and have made me king in his place. [9]Now, LORD God, let your promise to my father David be confirmed, for you have made me king over a people who are as numerous as the dust of the earth. [10]Give me wisdom and knowledge, that I may lead this people, for who is able to govern this great people of yours?"

[11]God said to Solomon, "Since this is

your heart's desire and you have not asked
for wealth, riches or honor, nor for the
death of your enemies, and since you have
not asked for a long life but for wisdom
and knowledge to govern my people over
whom I have made you king, 12therefore
wisdom and knowledge will be given you.
And I will also give you wealth, riches and
honor, such as no king who was before you
ever had and none after you will have."
13Then Solomon went to Jerusalem
from the high place at Gibeon, from before the Tent of Meeting. And he reigned
over Israel.
14Solomon accumulated chariots and
horses; he had fourteen hundred chariots
and twelve thousand horses,[a] which he
kept in the chariot cities and also with
him in Jerusalem. 15The king made silver
and gold as common in Jerusalem as
stones, and cedar as plentiful as sycamore-
fig trees in the foothills. 16Solomon's
horses were imported from Egypt[b] and
from Kue[c]—the royal merchants purchased them from Kue. 17They imported a
chariot from Egypt for six hundred
shekels[d] of silver, and a horse for a hundred and fifty.[e] They also exported them
to all the kings of the Hittites and of the
Arameans.

Preparations for Building the Temple

2 Solomon gave orders to build a temple
for the Name of the LORD and a royal
palace for himself. 2He conscripted seventy thousand men as carriers and eighty
thousand as stonecutters in the hills and
thirty-six hundred as foremen over them.
3Solomon sent this message to Hiram[f]
king of Tyre:

"Send me cedar logs as you did for
my father David when you sent him
cedar to build a palace to live in.
4Now I am about to build a temple
for the Name of the LORD my God
and to dedicate it to him for burning
fragrant incense before him, for setting out the consecrated bread regularly, and for making burnt offerings
every morning and evening and on
Sabbaths and New Moons and at the
appointed feasts of the LORD our
God. This is a lasting ordinance for
Israel.
5"The temple I am going to build
will be great, because our God is
greater than all other gods. 6But who
is able to build a temple for him, since
the heavens, even the highest heavens,
cannot contain him? Who then am I
to build a temple for him, except as a
place to burn sacrifices before him?
7"Send me, therefore, a man skilled
to work in gold and silver, bronze
and iron, and in purple, crimson and
blue yarn, and experienced in the art
of engraving, to work in Judah and
Jerusalem with my skilled craftsmen,
whom my father David provided.
8"Send me also cedar, pine and al-
gum[g] logs from Lebanon, for I know
that your men are skilled in cutting
timber there. My men will work with
yours 9to provide me with plenty of
lumber, because the temple I build
must be large and magnificent. 10I
will give your servants, the woods-
men who cut the timber, twenty
thousand cors[h] of ground wheat,
twenty thousand cors of barley, twenty thousand baths[i] of wine and twenty thousand baths of olive oil."

11Hiram king of Tyre replied by letter to
Solomon:

"Because the LORD loves his people, he has made you their king."

12And Hiram added:

"Praise be to the LORD, the God of
Israel, who made heaven and earth!
He has given King David a wise son,
endowed with intelligence and discernment, who will build a temple
for the LORD and a palace for himself.
13"I am sending you Huram-Abi, a
man of great skill, 14whose mother
was from Dan and whose father was
from Tyre. He is trained to work in
gold and silver, bronze and iron,
stone and wood, and with purple
and blue and crimson yarn and fine
linen. He is experienced in all kinds
of engraving and can execute any de-

[a] *14* Or *charioteers* [b] *16* Or possibly *Muzur,* a region in Cilicia; also in verse 17 [c] *16* Probably Cilicia [d] *17* That is, about 15 pounds (about 7 kilograms) [e] *17* That is, about 3 3/4 pounds (about 1.7 kilograms) [f] *3* Hebrew *Huram,* a variant of *Hiram;* also in verses 11 and 12
[g] *8* Probably a variant of *almug;* possibly juniper
[h] *10* That is, probably about 125,000 bushels (about 4,400 kiloliters) [i] *10* That is, probably about 115,000 gallons (about 440 kiloliters)

sign given to him. He will work with your craftsmen and with those of my lord, David your father.

15 "Now let my lord send his servants the wheat and barley and the olive oil and wine he promised, 16 and we will cut all the logs from Lebanon that you need and will float them in rafts by sea down to Joppa. You can then take them up to Jerusalem."

17 Solomon took a census of all the aliens who were in Israel, after the census his father David had taken; and they were found to be 153,600. 18 He assigned 70,000 of them to be carriers and 80,000 to be stonecutters in the hills, with 3,600 foremen over them to keep the people working.

PRAYER: PETITION

MAY I not say when I am tempted, "I am being tempted by God"; for You, O God, cannot be tempted by evil, nor do You tempt anyone. But each one of us is tempted when we are drawn away and enticed by our own lust. Then, after lust has conceived, it gives birth to sin; and sin, when it is full-grown, gives birth to death. (James 1:13–15)

***PAUSE** here to petition God for wisdom. Ask Him to develop your eternal perspective, to renew your mind with truth and to help you develop greater skill in each area of your life. Offer prayers regarding your activities for this day and any special concerns you may have.*

NT Romans 6:15–7:6

Slaves to Righteousness

15 What then? Shall we sin because we are not under law but under grace? By no means! 16 Don't you know that when you offer yourselves to someone to obey him as slaves, you are slaves to the one whom you obey—whether you are slaves to sin, which leads to death, or to obedience, which leads to righteousness? 17 But thanks be to God that, though you used to be slaves to sin, you wholeheartedly obeyed the form of teaching to which you were entrusted. 18 You have been set free from sin and have become slaves to righteousness.

19 I put this in human terms because you are weak in your natural selves. Just as you used to offer the parts of your body in slavery to impurity and to ever-increasing wickedness, so now offer them in slavery to righteousness leading to holiness. 20 When you were slaves to sin, you were free from the control of righteousness. 21 What benefit did you reap at that time from the things you are now ashamed of? Those things result in death! 22 But now that you have been set free from sin and have become slaves to God, the benefit you reap leads to holiness, and the result is eternal life. 23 For the wages of sin is death, but the gift of God is eternal life in[a] Christ Jesus our Lord.

An Illustration From Marriage

7 Do you not know, brothers—for I am speaking to men who know the law—that the law has authority over a man only as long as he lives? 2 For example, by law a married woman is bound to her husband as long as he is alive, but if her husband dies, she is released from the law of marriage. 3 So then, if she marries another man while her husband is still alive, she is called an adulteress. But if her husband dies, she is released from that law and is not an adulteress, even though she marries another man.

4 So, my brothers, you also died to the law through the body of Christ, that you might belong to another, to him who was raised from the dead, in order that we might bear fruit to God. 5 For when we were controlled by the sinful nature,[b] the sinful passions aroused by the law were at work in our bodies, so that we bore fruit for death. 6 But now, by dying to what once bound us, we have been released from the law so that we serve in the new way of the Spirit, and not in the old way of the written code.

[a] 23 Or *through* [b] 5 Or *the flesh;* also in verse 25

PRAYER: THE WORKS OF GOD

O GOD, You were pleased to have all Your fullness dwell in Christ and through Him to reconcile all things to Yourself, whether things on earth or things in heaven, having made peace through the blood of His cross. (Colossians 1:19–20)

__TAKE__ a moment to consider the greatness of God's wonderful works.

YEAR 2 DAY 88

OT 2 Chronicles 3:1–4:22

Solomon Builds the Temple

3 Then Solomon began to build the temple of the LORD in Jerusalem on Mount Moriah, where the LORD had appeared to his father David. It was on the threshing floor of Araunah[a] the Jebusite, the place provided by David. 2He began building on the second day of the second month in the fourth year of his reign.

3The foundation Solomon laid for building the temple of God was sixty cubits long and twenty cubits wide[b] (using the cubit of the old standard). 4The portico at the front of the temple was twenty cubits[c] long across the width of the building and twenty cubits[d] high.

He overlaid the inside with pure gold. 5He paneled the main hall with pine and covered it with fine gold and decorated it with palm tree and chain designs. 6He adorned the temple with precious stones. And the gold he used was gold of Parvaim. 7He overlaid the ceiling beams, doorframes, walls and doors of the temple with gold, and he carved cherubim on the walls.

8He built the Most Holy Place, its length corresponding to the width of the temple—twenty cubits long and twenty cubits wide. He overlaid the inside with six hundred talents[e] of fine gold. 9The gold nails weighed fifty shekels.[f] He also overlaid the upper parts with gold.

10In the Most Holy Place he made a pair of sculptured cherubim and overlaid them with gold. 11The total wingspan of the cherubim was twenty cubits. One wing of the first cherub was five cubits[g] long and touched the temple wall, while its other wing, also five cubits long, touched the wing of the other cherub. 12Similarly one wing of the second cherub was five cubits long and touched the other temple wall, and its other wing, also five cubits long, touched the wing of the first cherub. 13The wings of these cherubim extended twenty cubits. They stood on their feet, facing the main hall.[h]

14He made the curtain of blue, purple and crimson yarn and fine linen, with cherubim worked into it.

15In the front of the temple he made two pillars, which ⌞together⌟ were thirty-five cubits[i] long, each with a capital on top measuring five cubits. 16He made interwoven chains[j] and put them on top of the pillars. He also made a hundred pomegranates and attached them to the chains. 17He erected the pillars in the front of the temple, one to the south and one to the north. The one to the south he named Jakin[k] and the one to the north Boaz.[l]

The Temple's Furnishings

4 He made a bronze altar twenty cubits long, twenty cubits wide and ten cubits high.[m] 2He made the Sea of cast metal, circular in shape, measuring ten cubits from rim to rim and five cubits[n] high. It took a line of thirty cubits[o] to measure around it. 3Below the rim, figures of bulls encircled

[a] *1* Hebrew *Ornan,* a variant of *Araunah* [b] *3* That is, about 90 feet (about 27 meters) long and 30 feet (about 9 meters) wide [c] *4* That is, about 30 feet (about 9 meters); also in verses 8, 11 and 13 [d] *4* Some Septuagint and Syriac manuscripts; Hebrew *and a hundred and twenty* [e] *8* That is, about 23 tons (about 21 metric tons) [f] *9* That is, about 1 1/4 pounds (about 0.6 kilogram) [g] *11* That is, about 7 1/2 feet (about 2.3 meters); also in verse 15 [h] *13* Or *facing inward* [i] *15* That is, about 52 feet (about 16 meters) [j] *16* Or possibly *made chains in the inner sanctuary;* the meaning of the Hebrew for this phrase is uncertain. [k] *17* *Jakin* probably means *he establishes.* [l] *17* *Boaz* probably means *in him is strength.* [m] *1* That is, about 30 feet (about 9 meters) long and wide, and about 15 feet (about 4.5 meters) high [n] *2* That is, about 7 1/2 feet (about 2.3 meters) [o] *2* That is, about 45 feet (about 13.5 meters)

it—ten to a cubit.[p] The bulls were cast in two rows in one piece with the Sea.

[4]The Sea stood on twelve bulls, three facing north, three facing west, three facing south and three facing east. The Sea rested on top of them, and their hindquarters were toward the center. [5]It was a handbreadth[q] in thickness, and its rim was like the rim of a cup, like a lily blossom. It held three thousand baths.[r]

[6]He then made ten basins for washing and placed five on the south side and five on the north. In them the things to be used for the burnt offerings were rinsed, but the Sea was to be used by the priests for washing.

[7]He made ten gold lampstands according to the specifications for them and placed them in the temple, five on the south side and five on the north.

[8]He made ten tables and placed them in the temple, five on the south side and five on the north. He also made a hundred gold sprinkling bowls.

[9]He made the courtyard of the priests, and the large court and the doors for the court, and overlaid the doors with bronze.
[10]He placed the Sea on the south side, at the southeast corner.

[11]He also made the pots and shovels and sprinkling bowls.

So Huram finished the work he had undertaken for King Solomon in the temple of God:

[12]the two pillars;
the two bowl-shaped capitals on top of the pillars;
the two sets of network decorating the two bowl-shaped capitals on top of the pillars;
[13]the four hundred pomegranates for the two sets of network (two rows of pomegranates for each network, decorating the bowl-shaped capitals on top of the pillars);
[14]the stands with their basins;
[15]the Sea and the twelve bulls under it;
[16]the pots, shovels, meat forks and all related articles.

All the objects that Huram-Abi made for King Solomon for the temple of the LORD were of polished bronze. [17]The king had them cast in clay molds in the plain of the Jordan between Succoth and Zarethan.[s] [18]All these things that Solomon made amounted to so much that the weight of the bronze was not determined.

[19]Solomon also made all the furnishings that were in God's temple:

the golden altar;
the tables on which was the bread of the Presence;
[20]the lampstands of pure gold with their lamps, to burn in front of the inner sanctuary as prescribed;
[21]the gold floral work and lamps and tongs (they were solid gold);
[22]the pure gold wick trimmers, sprinkling bowls, dishes and censers; and the gold doors of the temple: the inner doors to the Most Holy Place and the doors of the main hall.

[p] 3 That is, about 1 1/2 feet (about 0.5 meter)
[q] 5 That is, about 3 inches (about 8 centimeters)
[r] 5 That is, about 17,500 gallons (about 66 kiloliters)
[s] 17 Hebrew *Zeredatha,* a variant of *Zarethan*

PRAYER: INTERCESSION

***FAR** be it from me that I should sin against You, O Lord, by ceasing to pray for others. (1 Samuel 12:23)*

***TAKE** a few moments to intercede on behalf of your immediate family and other relatives. Offer prayers for their spiritual, emotional and physical concerns.*

NT Romans 7:7-25

Struggling With Sin

[7]What shall we say, then? Is the law sin? Certainly not! Indeed I would not have known what sin was except through the law. For I would not have known what coveting really was if the law had not said, "Do not covet."[a] [8]But sin, seizing the op-

[a] 7 Exodus 20:17; Deut. 5:21

portunity afforded by the commandment,
produced in me every kind of covetous
desire. For apart from law, sin is dead.
9Once I was alive apart from law; but
when the commandment came, sin
sprang to life and I died. 10I found that the
very commandment that was intended
to bring life actually brought death. 11For
sin, seizing the opportunity afforded by
the commandment, deceived me, and
through the commandment put me to
death. 12So then, the law is holy, and the
commandment is holy, righteous and
good.

13Did that which is good, then, become
death to me? By no means! But in order
that sin might be recognized as sin, it produced death in me through what was
good, so that through the commandment
sin might become utterly sinful.

14We know that the law is spiritual; but
I am unspiritual, sold as a slave to sin. 15I
do not understand what I do. For what I
want to do I do not do, but what I hate
I do. 16And if I do what I do not want to
do, I agree that the law is good. 17As it is,
it is no longer I myself who do it, but it is
sin living in me. 18I know that nothing
good lives in me, that is, in my sinful nature.[b] For I have the desire to do what is
good, but I cannot carry it out. 19For what
I do is not the good I want to do; no, the
evil I do not want to do—this I keep on
doing. 20Now if I do what I do not want
to do, it is no longer I who do it, but it is
sin living in me that does it.

21So I find this law at work: When I
want to do good, evil is right there with
me. 22For in my inner being I delight in
God's law; 23but I see another law at work
in the members of my body, waging war
against the law of my mind and making
me a prisoner of the law of sin at work
within my members. 24What a wretched
man I am! Who will rescue me from this
body of death? 25Thanks be to God—
through Jesus Christ our Lord!

So then, I myself in my mind am a slave
to God's law, but in the sinful nature a
slave to the law of sin.

[b] *18* Or *my flesh*

PRAYER: MY RELATIONSHIP TO GOD

WHEN I was dead in my trespasses and in the uncircumcision of my flesh, You made me alive with Christ, O God. You forgave me all my trespasses, having canceled the written code, with its regulations, that was against me and was contrary to me; You took it away, nailing it to the cross. And having disarmed the powers and authorities, You made a public spectacle of them, triumphing over them by the cross.

(Colossians 2:13–15)

PAUSE *to thank God for the relationship that you enjoy with Him in Jesus Christ.*

YEAR 2
DAY 89

OT 2 Chronicles 5:1-14

5 When all the work Solomon had done
for the temple of the LORD was finished,
he brought in the things his father David
had dedicated—the silver and gold and all
the furnishings—and he placed them in
the treasuries of God's temple.

The Ark Brought to the Temple

2Then Solomon summoned to Jeru-
salem the elders of Israel, all the heads of
the tribes and the chiefs of the Israelite
families, to bring up the ark of the LORD's
covenant from Zion, the City of David.
3And all the men of Israel came together
to the king at the time of the festival in
the seventh month.

4When all the elders of Israel had arrived, the Levites took up the ark, 5and
they brought up the ark and the Tent of
Meeting and all the sacred furnishings in
it. The priests, who were Levites, carried

them up; 6and King Solomon and the entire assembly of Israel that had gathered
about him were before the ark, sacrificing
so many sheep and cattle that they could
not be recorded or counted.

7The priests then brought the ark of the
LORD's covenant to its place in the inner
sanctuary of the temple, the Most Holy
Place, and put it beneath the wings of the
cherubim. 8The cherubim spread their
wings over the place of the ark and covered the ark and its carrying poles. 9These
poles were so long that their ends, extending from the ark, could be seen from
in front of the inner sanctuary, but not
from outside the Holy Place; and they are
still there today. 10There was nothing in
the ark except the two tablets that Moses
had placed in it at Horeb, where the LORD
made a covenant with the Israelites after
they came out of Egypt.

11The priests then withdrew from the
Holy Place. All the priests who were there
had consecrated themselves, regardless of
their divisions. 12All the Levites who were
musicians—Asaph, Heman, Jeduthun and
their sons and relatives—stood on the east
side of the altar, dressed in fine linen and
playing cymbals, harps and lyres. They
were accompanied by 120 priests sounding trumpets. 13The trumpeters and
singers joined in unison, as with one
voice, to give praise and thanks to the
LORD. Accompanied by trumpets, cymbals
and other instruments, they raised their
voices in praise to the LORD and sang:

"He is good;
his love endures forever."

Then the temple of the LORD was filled
with a cloud, 14and the priests could not
perform their service because of the cloud,
for the glory of the LORD filled the temple
of God.

PRAYER: AFFIRMATION

It is for my good that You, Jesus, returned to the Father, because You have sent the Counselor, the Holy Spirit, to me.

Jesus, You told Your disciples, "The Spirit will glorify Me by taking from what is Mine and making it known to you. All that belongs to the Father is Mine. That is why I said that He will take from what is Mine and make it known to you." (John 16:7, 14–15)

PAUSE *to reflect on these Biblical affirmations.*

NT Romans 8:1-17

Life Through the Spirit

8 Therefore, there is now no condemnation for those who are in Christ Jesus,[a]
2because through Christ Jesus the law of
the Spirit of life set me free from the law
of sin and death. 3For what the law was
powerless to do in that it was weakened
by the sinful nature,[b] God did by sending
his own Son in the likeness of sinful man
to be a sin offering.[c] And so he condemned sin in sinful man,[d] 4in order that
the righteous requirements of the law
might be fully met in us, who do not live
according to the sinful nature but according to the Spirit.

5Those who live according to the sinful
nature have their minds set on what that
nature desires; but those who live in accordance with the Spirit have their minds
set on what the Spirit desires. 6The mind
of sinful man[e] is death, but the mind controlled by the Spirit is life and peace; 7the
sinful mind[f] is hostile to God. It does not
submit to God's law, nor can it do so.
8Those controlled by the sinful nature
cannot please God.

9You, however, are controlled not by the
sinful nature but by the Spirit, if the Spirit of God lives in you. And if anyone does
not have the Spirit of Christ, he does not
belong to Christ. 10But if Christ is in you,
your body is dead because of sin, yet your

[a] 1 Some later manuscripts *Jesus, who do not live according to the sinful nature but according to the Spirit,* [b] 3 Or *the flesh;* also in verses 4, 5, 8, 9, 12 and 13 [c] 3 Or *man, for sin* [d] 3 Or *in the flesh* [e] 6 Or *mind set on the flesh* [f] 7 Or *the mind set on the flesh*

spirit is alive because of righteousness. 11And if the Spirit of him who raised Jesus from the dead is living in you, he who raised Christ from the dead will also give life to your mortal bodies through his Spirit, who lives in you.

12Therefore, brothers, we have an obligation—but it is not to the sinful nature, to live according to it. 13For if you live according to the sinful nature, you will die; but if by the Spirit you put to death the misdeeds of the body, you will live, 14because those who are led by the Spirit of God are sons of God. 15For you did not receive a spirit that makes you a slave again to fear, but you received the Spirit of sonship.[g] And by him we cry, *"Abba,*[h] Father." 16The Spirit himself testifies with our spirit that we are God's children. 17Now if we are children, then we are heirs—heirs of God and co-heirs with Christ, if indeed we share in his sufferings in order that we may also share in his glory.

[g] 15 Or *adoption* [h] 15 Aramaic for *Father*

PRAYER: THE CHARACTER I WANT TO CULTIVATE

I WILL be self-controlled and alert; my adversary the devil prowls around like a roaring lion looking for someone to devour. But I will resist him, standing firm in the faith, knowing that my brothers and sisters throughout the world are undergoing the same kind of sufferings. (1 Peter 5:8–9)

TAKE *a moment to ask the Lord for the grace to grow in godly character.*

YEAR 2
DAY 90

OT 2 Chronicles 6:1–42

6 Then Solomon said, "The LORD has said that he would dwell in a dark cloud; 2I have built a magnificent temple for you, a place for you to dwell forever."

3While the whole assembly of Israel was standing there, the king turned around and blessed them. 4Then he said:

> "Praise be to the LORD, the God of Israel, who with his hands has fulfilled what he promised with his mouth to my father David. For he said, 5'Since the day I brought my people out of Egypt, I have not chosen a city in any tribe of Israel to have a temple built for my Name to be there, nor have I chosen anyone to be the leader over my people Israel. 6But now I have chosen Jerusalem for my Name to be there, and I have chosen David to rule my people Israel.'
>
> 7"My father David had it in his heart to build a temple for the Name of the LORD, the God of Israel. 8But the LORD said to my father David, 'Because it was in your heart to build a temple for my Name, you did well to have this in your heart. 9Nevertheless, you are not the one to build the temple, but your son, who is your own flesh and blood—he is the one who will build the temple for my Name.'
>
> 10"The LORD has kept the promise he made. I have succeeded David my father and now I sit on the throne of Israel, just as the LORD promised, and I have built the temple for the Name of the LORD, the God of Israel. 11There I have placed the ark, in which is the covenant of the LORD that he made with the people of Israel."

Solomon's Prayer of Dedication

12Then Solomon stood before the altar of the LORD in front of the whole assembly of Israel and spread out his hands. 13Now he had made a bronze platform, five cubits[a] long, five cubits wide and three cubits[b] high, and had placed it in the center of the outer court. He stood on the platform and then knelt down before

[a] 13 That is, about 7 1/2 feet (about 2.3 meters)
[b] 13 That is, about 4 1/2 feet (about 1.3 meters)

the whole assembly of Israel and spread
out his hands toward heaven. [14]He said:

"O LORD, God of Israel, there is no
God like you in heaven or on earth—
you who keep your covenant of love
with your servants who continue
wholeheartedly in your way. [15]You
have kept your promise to your servant David my father; with your
mouth you have promised and with
your hand you have fulfilled it—as it
is today.

[16]"Now LORD, God of Israel, keep
for your servant David my father the
promises you made to him when you
said, 'You shall never fail to have a
man to sit before me on the throne
of Israel, if only your sons are careful
in all they do to walk before me according to my law, as you have done.'
[17]And now, O LORD, God of Israel, let
your word that you promised your
servant David come true.

[18]"But will God really dwell on
earth with men? The heavens, even
the highest heavens, cannot contain
you. How much less this temple I
have built! [19]Yet give attention to
your servant's prayer and his plea for
mercy, O LORD my God. Hear the cry
and the prayer that your servant is
praying in your presence. [20]May your
eyes be open toward this temple day
and night, this place of which you
said you would put your Name there.
May you hear the prayer your servant
prays toward this place. [21]Hear the
supplications of your servant and of
your people Israel when they pray toward this place. Hear from heaven,
your dwelling place; and when you
hear, forgive.

[22]"When a man wrongs his neighbor and is required to take an oath
and he comes and swears the oath
before your altar in this temple,
[23]then hear from heaven and act.
Judge between your servants, repaying the guilty by bringing down on
his own head what he has done. Declare the innocent not guilty and so
establish his innocence.

[24]"When your people Israel have
been defeated by an enemy because
they have sinned against you and
when they turn back and confess
your name, praying and making supplication before you in this temple,
[25]then hear from heaven and forgive
the sin of your people Israel and
bring them back to the land you gave
to them and their fathers.

[26]"When the heavens are shut up
and there is no rain because your
people have sinned against you, and
when they pray toward this place and
confess your name and turn from
their sin because you have afflicted
them, [27]then hear from heaven and
forgive the sin of your servants, your
people Israel. Teach them the right
way to live, and send rain on the land
you gave your people for an inheritance.

[28]"When famine or plague comes
to the land, or blight or mildew, locusts or grasshoppers, or when enemies besiege them in any of their cities, whatever disaster or disease may
come, [29]and when a prayer or plea is
made by any of your people Israel—
each one aware of his afflictions and
pains, and spreading out his hands
toward this temple— [30]then hear
from heaven, your dwelling place.
Forgive, and deal with each man according to all he does, since you
know his heart (for you alone know
the hearts of men), [31]so that they will
fear you and walk in your ways all the
time they live in the land you gave
our fathers.

[32]"As for the foreigner who does
not belong to your people Israel but
has come from a distant land because
of your great name and your mighty
hand and your outstretched arm—
when he comes and prays toward this
temple, [33]then hear from heaven,
your dwelling place, and do whatever the foreigner asks of you, so that
all the peoples of the earth may know
your name and fear you, as do your
own people Israel, and may know
that this house I have built bears your
Name.

[34]"When your people go to war
against their enemies, wherever you
send them, and when they pray to
you toward this city you have chosen
and the temple I have built for your
Name, [35]then hear from heaven their

prayer and their plea, and uphold their cause.

36 "When they sin against you—for there is no one who does not sin—and you become angry with them and give them over to the enemy, who takes them captive to a land far away or near; 37 and if they have a change of heart in the land where they are held captive, and repent and plead with you in the land of their captivity and say, 'We have sinned, we have done wrong and acted wickedly'; 38 and if they turn back to you with all their heart and soul in the land of their captivity where they were taken, and pray toward the land you gave their fathers, toward the city you have chosen and toward the temple I have built for your Name; 39 then from heaven, your dwelling place, hear their prayer and their pleas, and uphold their cause. And forgive your people, who have sinned against you.

40 "Now, my God, may your eyes be open and your ears attentive to the prayers offered in this place.

41 "Now arise, O LORD God, and
come to your resting place,
you and the ark of your might.
May your priests, O LORD God, be
clothed with salvation,
may your saints rejoice in your
goodness.
42 O LORD God, do not reject your
anointed one.
Remember the great love
promised to David your
servant."

PRAYER: THANKSGIVING

I BLESS You, Lord, for You have heard the voice of my prayers. You are my strength and my shield; my heart trusts in You, and I am helped. My heart greatly rejoices, and I will give thanks to You in song.
(Psalm 28:6–7)

***PAUSE** to offer your own expressions of thanksgiving.*

NT Romans 8:18–39

Future Glory

18 I consider that our present sufferings are not worth comparing with the glory that will be revealed in us. 19 The creation waits in eager expectation for the sons of God to be revealed. 20 For the creation was subjected to frustration, not by its own choice, but by the will of the one who subjected it, in hope 21 that[a] the creation itself will be liberated from its bondage to decay and brought into the glorious freedom of the children of God.

22 We know that the whole creation has been groaning as in the pains of childbirth right up to the present time. 23 Not only so, but we ourselves, who have the firstfruits of the Spirit, groan inwardly as we wait eagerly for our adoption as sons, the redemption of our bodies. 24 For in this hope we were saved. But hope that is seen is no hope at all. Who hopes for what he already has? 25 But if we hope for what we do not yet have, we wait for it patiently.

26 In the same way, the Spirit helps us in our weakness. We do not know what we ought to pray for, but the Spirit himself intercedes for us with groans that words cannot express. 27 And he who searches our hearts knows the mind of the Spirit, because the Spirit intercedes for the saints in accordance with God's will.

More Than Conquerors

28 And we know that in all things God works for the good of those who love him,[b] who[c] have been called according to his purpose. 29 For those God foreknew he also predestined to be conformed to the likeness of his Son, that he might be the firstborn among many brothers. 30 And those he predestined, he also called; those

[a] 20,21 Or *subjected it in hope. 21 For* [b] 28 Some manuscripts *And we know that all things work together for good to those who love God* [c] 28 Or *works together with those who love him to bring about what is good—with those who*

he called, he also justified; those he justified, he also glorified.

[31]What, then, shall we say in response to this? If God is for us, who can be against us? [32]He who did not spare his own Son, but gave him up for us all—how will he not also, along with him, graciously give us all things? [33]Who will bring any charge against those whom God has chosen? It is God who justifies. [34]Who is he that condemns? Christ Jesus, who died—more than that, who was raised to life—is at the right hand of God and is also interceding for us. [35]Who shall separate us from the love of Christ? Shall trouble or hardship or persecution or famine or nakedness or danger or sword? [36]As it is written:

"For your sake we face death all day
long;
we are considered as sheep to be
slaughtered."[d]

[37]No, in all these things we are more than conquerors through him who loved us. [38]For I am convinced that neither death nor life, neither angels nor demons,[e] neither the present nor the future, nor any powers, [39]neither height nor depth, nor anything else in all creation, will be able to separate us from the love of God that is in Christ Jesus our Lord.

[d] 36 Psalm 44:22 [e] 38 Or *nor heavenly rulers*

PRAYER: MY RELATIONSHIP TO OTHERS

I WILL lay up Your words in my heart and in my soul and teach them to my children, talking about them when I sit in my house and when I walk along the way and when I lie down and when I rise up. (Deuteronomy 11:18–19) . . . Those who are foolish despise their father's discipline, but those who heed correction are prudent. (Proverbs 15:5)

PAUSE *to review your relationships with others and to commit them to the Lord.*

YEAR 2 DAY 91

OT Psalm 89

Psalm 89

A *maskil*[a] of Ethan the Ezrahite.

[1]I will sing of the LORD's great love
forever;
with my mouth I will make your
faithfulness known through all
generations.
[2]I will declare that your love stands
firm forever,
that you established your
faithfulness in heaven itself.

[3]You said, "I have made a covenant
with my chosen one,
I have sworn to David my servant,
[4]'I will establish your line forever
and make your throne firm through
all generations.' " *Selah*

[5]The heavens praise your wonders,
O LORD,
your faithfulness too, in the
assembly of the holy ones.
[6]For who in the skies above can
compare with the LORD?
Who is like the LORD among the
heavenly beings?
[7]In the council of the holy ones God is
greatly feared;
he is more awesome than all who
surround him.
[8]O LORD God Almighty, who is like you?
You are mighty, O LORD, and your
faithfulness surrounds you.

[9]You rule over the surging sea;
when its waves mount up, you still
them.
[10]You crushed Rahab like one of the
slain;
with your strong arm you scattered
your enemies.

[a] Title: Probably a literary or musical term

[11]The heavens are yours, and yours also
the earth;
you founded the world and all that
is in it.
[12]You created the north and the south;
Tabor and Hermon sing for joy at
your name.
[13]Your arm is endued with power;
your hand is strong, your right hand
exalted.

[14]Righteousness and justice are the
foundation of your throne;
love and faithfulness go before you.
[15]Blessed are those who have learned to
acclaim you,
who walk in the light of your
presence, O LORD.
[16]They rejoice in your name all day
long;
they exult in your righteousness.
[17]For you are their glory and strength,
and by your favor you exalt our
horn.[b]
[18]Indeed, our shield[c] belongs to the
LORD,
our king to the Holy One of Israel.

[19]Once you spoke in a vision,
to your faithful people you said:
"I have bestowed strength on a
warrior;
I have exalted a young man from
among the people.
[20]I have found David my servant;
with my sacred oil I have anointed
him.
[21]My hand will sustain him;
surely my arm will strengthen him.
[22]No enemy will subject him to tribute;
no wicked man will oppress him.
[23]I will crush his foes before him
and strike down his adversaries.
[24]My faithful love will be with him,
and through my name his horn[d]
will be exalted.
[25]I will set his hand over the sea,
his right hand over the rivers.
[26]He will call out to me, 'You are my
Father,
my God, the Rock my Savior.'
[27]I will also appoint him my firstborn,
the most exalted of the kings of the
earth.
[28]I will maintain my love to him
forever,
and my covenant with him will
never fail.
[29]I will establish his line forever,
his throne as long as the heavens
endure.

[30]"If his sons forsake my law
and do not follow my statutes,
[31]if they violate my decrees
and fail to keep my commands,
[32]I will punish their sin with the rod,
their iniquity with flogging;
[33]but I will not take my love from him,
nor will I ever betray my
faithfulness.
[34]I will not violate my covenant
or alter what my lips have uttered.
[35]Once for all, I have sworn by my
holiness—
and I will not lie to David—
[36]that his line will continue forever
and his throne endure before me
like the sun;
[37]it will be established forever like the
moon,
the faithful witness in the sky." *Selah*

[38]But you have rejected, you have
spurned,
you have been very angry with your
anointed one.
[39]You have renounced the covenant
with your servant
and have defiled his crown in the
dust.
[40]You have broken through all his walls
and reduced his strongholds to
ruins.
[41]All who pass by have plundered him;
he has become the scorn of his
neighbors.
[42]You have exalted the right hand of his
foes;
you have made all his enemies
rejoice.
[43]You have turned back the edge of his
sword
and have not supported him in
battle.
[44]You have put an end to his splendor
and cast his throne to the ground.
[45]You have cut short the days of his
youth;
you have covered him with a
mantle of shame. *Selah*

[46]How long, O LORD? Will you hide
yourself forever?

[b] *17 Horn* here symbolizes strong one. [c] *18* Or *sovereign* [d] *24 Horn* here symbolizes strength.

How long will your wrath burn like
fire?
47 Remember how fleeting is my life.
For what futility you have created
all men!
48 What man can live and not see death,
or save himself from the power of
the grave[e]? *Selah*
49 O Lord, where is your former great
love,
which in your faithfulness you
swore to David?
50 Remember, Lord, how your servant
has[f] been mocked,
how I bear in my heart the taunts of
all the nations,
51 the taunts with which your enemies
have mocked, O LORD,
with which they have mocked every
step of your anointed one.

52 Praise be to the LORD forever!
Amen and Amen.

[e] 48 Hebrew *Sheol* [f] 50 Or *your servants have*

PRAYER: ADORATION

YOU, O Lord, are the One who stretches out the heavens, lays the foundation of the earth, and forms the spirits of all people within them. (Zechariah 12:1) . . . Nothing is too difficult for You, Lord. (Genesis 18:14)

PAUSE *to express your thoughts of praise and worship.*

NT Romans 9:1-33

God's Sovereign Choice

9 I speak the truth in Christ—I am not
lying, my conscience confirms it in the
Holy Spirit— 2I have great sorrow and unceasing anguish in my heart. 3For I could
wish that I myself were cursed and cut off
from Christ for the sake of my brothers,
those of my own race, 4the people of Israel. Theirs is the adoption as sons; theirs
the divine glory, the covenants, the receiving of the law, the temple worship and
the promises. 5Theirs are the patriarchs,
and from them is traced the human ancestry of Christ, who is God over all, forever praised![a] Amen.
6It is not as though God's word had
failed. For not all who are descended from
Israel are Israel. 7Nor because they are his
descendants are they all Abraham's children. On the contrary, "It is through Isaac
that your offspring will be reckoned."[b] 8In
other words, it is not the natural children
who are God's children, but it is the children of the promise who are regarded as
Abraham's offspring. 9For this was how
the promise was stated: "At the appointed
time I will return, and Sarah will have a
son."[c]
10Not only that, but Rebekah's children
had one and the same father, our father
Isaac. 11Yet, before the twins were born or
had done anything good or bad—in order
that God's purpose in election might
stand: 12not by works but by him who
calls—she was told, "The older will serve
the younger."[d] 13Just as it is written: "Jacob I loved, but Esau I hated."[e]
14What then shall we say? Is God unjust? Not at all! 15For he says to Moses,

"I will have mercy on whom I have
mercy,
and I will have compassion on
whom I have compassion."[f]

16It does not, therefore, depend on man's
desire or effort, but on God's mercy. 17For
the Scripture says to Pharaoh: "I raised
you up for this very purpose, that I might
display my power in you and that my
name might be proclaimed in all the
earth."[g] 18Therefore God has mercy on
whom he wants to have mercy, and he
hardens whom he wants to harden.
19One of you will say to me: "Then why
does God still blame us? For who resists
his will?" 20But who are you, O man, to

[a] 5 Or *Christ, who is over all. God be forever praised!* Or *Christ. God who is over all be forever praised!*
[b] 7 Gen. 21:12 [c] 9 Gen. 18:10,14
[d] 12 Gen. 25:23 [e] 13 Mal. 1:2,3
[f] 15 Exodus 33:19 [g] 17 Exodus 9:16

talk back to God? "Shall what is formed
say to him who formed it, 'Why did you
make me like this?' "[h] 21Does not the potter have the right to make out of the same
lump of clay some pottery for noble purposes and some for common use?
22What if God, choosing to show his
wrath and make his power known, bore
with great patience the objects of his
wrath—prepared for destruction? 23What
if he did this to make the riches of his glory known to the objects of his mercy,
whom he prepared in advance for glory—
24even us, whom he also called, not only
from the Jews but also from the Gentiles?
25As he says in Hosea:

"I will call them 'my people' who are
not my people;
and I will call her 'my loved one'
who is not my loved one,"[i]

26and,

"It will happen that in the very place
where it was said to them,
'You are not my people,'
they will be called 'sons of the living
God.' "[j]

27Isaiah cries out concerning Israel:

"Though the number of the Israelites
be like the sand by the sea,
only the remnant will be saved.
28For the Lord will carry out
his sentence on earth with speed
and finality."[k]

29It is just as Isaiah said previously:

"Unless the Lord Almighty
had left us descendants,
we would have become like Sodom,
we would have been like
Gomorrah."[l]

Israel's Unbelief

30What then shall we say? That the Gentiles, who did not pursue righteousness,
have obtained it, a righteousness that is by
faith; 31but Israel, who pursued a law of
righteousness, has not attained it. 32Why
not? Because they pursued it not by faith
but as if it were by works. They stumbled
over the "stumbling stone." 33As it is written:

"See, I lay in Zion a stone that causes
men to stumble
and a rock that makes them fall,
and the one who trusts in him will
never be put to shame."[m]

[h] *20* Isaiah 29:16; 45:9 [i] *25* Hosea 2:23
[j] *26* Hosea 1:10 [k] *28* Isaiah 10:22,23
[l] *29* Isaiah 1:9 [m] *33* Isaiah 8:14; 28:16

PRAYER: THE ATTRIBUTES OF GOD

BEFORE You formed me in the womb, You knew me, O Lord; before I was born, You set me apart. (Jeremiah 1:5) . . .
O God, You number even the very hairs of my head. (Matthew 10:30; Luke 12:7)

***PAUSE** to reflect on these affirmations about the person, powers and perfection of God.*

YEAR 2 DAY 92

OT **2 Chronicles 7:1–8:18**

The Dedication of the Temple

7 When Solomon finished praying, fire
came down from heaven and consumed the burnt offering and the sacrifices, and the glory of the LORD filled the
temple. 2The priests could not enter the
temple of the LORD because the glory of
the LORD filled it. 3When all the Israelites
saw the fire coming down and the glory
of the LORD above the temple, they knelt
on the pavement with their faces to the
ground, and they worshiped and gave
thanks to the LORD, saying,

"He is good;
his love endures forever."

4Then the king and all the people offered
sacrifices before the LORD. 5And King Solomon offered a sacrifice of twenty-two

thousand head of cattle and a hundred and twenty thousand sheep and goats. So the king and all the people dedicated the temple of God. 6The priests took their positions, as did the Levites with the LORD's musical instruments, which King David had made for praising the LORD and which were used when he gave thanks, saying, "His love endures forever." Opposite the Levites, the priests blew their trumpets, and all the Israelites were standing.

7Solomon consecrated the middle part of the courtyard in front of the temple of the LORD, and there he offered burnt offerings and the fat of the fellowship offerings,[a] because the bronze altar he had made could not hold the burnt offerings, the grain offerings and the fat portions.

8So Solomon observed the festival at that time for seven days, and all Israel with him—a vast assembly, people from Lebo[b] Hamath to the Wadi of Egypt. 9On the eighth day they held an assembly, for they had celebrated the dedication of the altar for seven days and the festival for seven days more. 10On the twenty-third day of the seventh month he sent the people to their homes, joyful and glad in heart for the good things the LORD had done for David and Solomon and for his people Israel.

The LORD Appears to Solomon

11When Solomon had finished the temple of the LORD and the royal palace, and had succeeded in carrying out all he had in mind to do in the temple of the LORD and in his own palace, 12the LORD appeared to him at night and said:

> "I have heard your prayer and have chosen this place for myself as a temple for sacrifices.
>
> 13"When I shut up the heavens so that there is no rain, or command locusts to devour the land or send a plague among my people, 14if my people, who are called by my name, will humble themselves and pray and seek my face and turn from their wicked ways, then will I hear from heaven and will forgive their sin and will heal their land. 15Now my eyes will be open and my ears attentive to the prayers offered in this place. 16I have chosen and consecrated this temple so that my Name may be there forever. My eyes and my heart will always be there.
>
> 17"As for you, if you walk before me as David your father did, and do all I command, and observe my decrees and laws, 18I will establish your royal throne, as I covenanted with David your father when I said, 'You shall never fail to have a man to rule over Israel.'
>
> 19"But if you[c] turn away and forsake the decrees and commands I have given you[c] and go off to serve other gods and worship them, 20then I will uproot Israel from my land, which I have given them, and will reject this temple I have consecrated for my Name. I will make it a byword and an object of ridicule among all peoples. 21And though this temple is now so imposing, all who pass by will be appalled and say, 'Why has the LORD done such a thing to this land and to this temple?' 22People will answer, 'Because they have forsaken the LORD, the God of their fathers, who brought them out of Egypt, and have embraced other gods, worshiping and serving them—that is why he brought all this disaster on them.' "

Solomon's Other Activities

8 At the end of twenty years, during which Solomon built the temple of the LORD and his own palace, 2Solomon rebuilt the villages that Hiram[d] had given him, and settled Israelites in them. 3Solomon then went to Hamath Zobah and captured it. 4He also built up Tadmor in the desert and all the store cities he had built in Hamath. 5He rebuilt Upper Beth Horon and Lower Beth Horon as fortified cities, with walls and with gates and bars, 6as well as Baalath and all his store cities, and all the cities for his chariots and for his horses[e]—whatever he desired to build in Jerusalem, in Lebanon and throughout all the territory he ruled.

7All the people left from the Hittites, Amorites, Perizzites, Hivites and Jebusites (these peoples were not Israelites), 8that is, their descendants remaining in the land, whom the Israelites had not de-

[a] 7 Traditionally *peace offerings* [b] 8 Or *from the entrance to* [c] 19 The Hebrew is plural.
[d] 2 Hebrew *Huram,* a variant of *Hiram;* also in verse 18 [e] 6 Or *charioteers*

stroyed—these Solomon conscripted for
his slave labor force, as it is to this day.
9But Solomon did not make slaves of the
Israelites for his work; they were his fighting men, commanders of his captains,
and commanders of his chariots and charioteers. 10They were also King Solomon's
chief officials—two hundred and fifty officials supervising the men.

11Solomon brought Pharaoh's daughter
up from the City of David to the palace
he had built for her, for he said, "My wife
must not live in the palace of David king
of Israel, because the places the ark of the
LORD has entered are holy."

12On the altar of the LORD that he had
built in front of the portico, Solomon sacrificed burnt offerings to the LORD, 13ac-
cording to the daily requirement for offerings commanded by Moses for
Sabbaths, New Moons and the three annual feasts—the Feast of Unleavened
Bread, the Feast of Weeks and the Feast of
Tabernacles. 14In keeping with the ordinance of his father David, he appointed
the divisions of the priests for their duties,
and the Levites to lead the praise and to
assist the priests according to each day's
requirement. He also appointed the gatekeepers by divisions for the various gates,
because this was what David the man of
God had ordered. 15They did not deviate
from the king's commands to the priests
or to the Levites in any matter, including
that of the treasuries.

16All Solomon's work was carried out,
from the day the foundation of the temple of the LORD was laid until its completion. So the temple of the LORD was finished.

17Then Solomon went to Ezion Geber
and Elath on the coast of Edom. 18And Hiram sent him ships commanded by his
own officers, men who knew the sea.
These, with Solomon's men, sailed to
Ophir and brought back four hundred
and fifty talents[f] of gold, which they delivered to King Solomon.

[f] 18 That is, about 17 tons (about 16 metric tons)

PRAYER: CONFESSION

DEATH and Destruction lie open before You, O Lord; how much more do human hearts! (Proverbs 15:11)

__ASK__ the Spirit to search your heart and reveal any areas of unconfessed sin. Acknowledge these to the Lord and thank Him for His forgiveness.

NT Romans 10:1-21

10 Brothers, my heart's desire and prayer
to God for the Israelites is that they
may be saved. 2For I can testify about
them that they are zealous for God, but
their zeal is not based on knowledge.
3Since they did not know the righteousness that comes from God and sought to
establish their own, they did not submit
to God's righteousness. 4Christ is the end
of the law so that there may be righteousness for everyone who believes.

5Moses describes in this way the righteousness that is by the law: "The man who
does these things will live by them."[a] 6But
the righteousness that is by faith says: "Do
not say in your heart, 'Who will ascend into
heaven?'[b]" (that is, to bring Christ down)
7"or 'Who will descend into the deep?'[c]"
(that is, to bring Christ up from the dead).
8But what does it say? "The word is near you;
it is in your mouth and in your heart,"[d] that
is, the word of faith we are proclaiming:
9That if you confess with your mouth, "Jesus
is Lord," and believe in your heart that God
raised him from the dead, you will be saved.
10For it is with your heart that you believe
and are justified, and it is with your mouth
that you confess and are saved. 11As the Scripture says, "Anyone who trusts in him will
never be put to shame."[e] 12For there is no difference between Jew and Gentile—the same
Lord is Lord of all and richly blesses all who
call on him, 13for, "Everyone who calls on
the name of the Lord will be saved."[f]

14How, then, can they call on the one
they have not believed in? And how can
they believe in the one of whom they have
not heard? And how can they hear with-

[a] 5 Lev. 18:5 [b] 6 Deut. 30:12 [c] 7 Deut. 30:13
[d] 8 Deut. 30:14 [e] 11 Isaiah 28:16 [f] 13 Joel 2:32

out someone preaching to them? 15 And how can they preach unless they are sent? As it is written, "How beautiful are the feet of those who bring good news!"[g]

16 But not all the Israelites accepted the good news. For Isaiah says, "Lord, who has believed our message?"[h] 17 Consequently, faith comes from hearing the message, and the message is heard through the word of Christ. 18 But I ask: Did they not hear? Of course they did:

> "Their voice has gone out into all the
> earth,
> their words to the ends of the
> world."[i]

19 Again I ask: Did Israel not understand? First, Moses says,

> "I will make you envious by those
> who are not a nation;
> I will make you angry by a nation
> that has no understanding."[j]

20 And Isaiah boldly says,

> "I was found by those who did not
> seek me;
> I revealed myself to those who did
> not ask for me."[k]

21 But concerning Israel he says,

> "All day long I have held out my hands
> to a disobedient and obstinate
> people."[l]

[g] 15 Isaiah 52:7 [h] 16 Isaiah 53:1
[i] 18 Psalm 19:4 [j] 19 Deut. 32:21
[k] 20 Isaiah 65:1 [l] 21 Isaiah 65:2

PRAYER: THE WORKS OF GOD

BY the will of God, we have been sanctified through the offering of Your body, O Jesus Christ, once for all. And every priest stands daily ministering and offering again and again the same sacrifices, which can never take away sins. But when You had offered for all time one sacrifice for sins, You sat down at the right hand of God, waiting from that time for Your enemies to be made a footstool for Your feet. For by one offering, You have made perfect forever those who are being sanctified. (Hebrews 10:10–14)

***TAKE** a moment to consider the greatness of God's wonderful works.*

YEAR 2 DAY 93

OT 2 Chronicles 9:1–31

The Queen of Sheba Visits Solomon

9 When the queen of Sheba heard of Solomon's fame, she came to Jerusalem to test him with hard questions. Arriving with a very great caravan—with camels carrying spices, large quantities of gold, and precious stones—she came to Solomon and talked with him about all she had on her mind. 2 Solomon answered all her questions; nothing was too hard for him to explain to her. 3 When the queen of Sheba saw the wisdom of Solomon, as well as the palace he had built, 4 the food on his table, the seating of his officials, the attending servants in their robes, the cupbearers in their robes and the burnt offerings he made at[a] the temple of the LORD, she was overwhelmed.

5 She said to the king, "The report I heard in my own country about your achievements and your wisdom is true. 6 But I did not believe what they said until I came and saw with my own eyes. Indeed, not even half the greatness of your wisdom was told me; you have far exceeded the report I heard. 7 How happy your men must be! How happy your officials, who continually stand before you and hear your wisdom! 8 Praise be to the LORD your God, who has delighted in you and placed you on his throne as king to rule for the LORD your God. Because of the love of your God for Israel and his desire to uphold them forever, he has made you king over them, to maintain justice and righteousness."

9 Then she gave the king 120 talents[b] of

[a] 4 Or *the ascent by which he went up to*
[b] 9 That is, about 4 1/2 tons (about 4 metric tons)

gold, large quantities of spices, and precious stones. There had never been such spices as those the queen of Sheba gave to King Solomon.

10 (The men of Hiram and the men of Solomon brought gold from Ophir; they also brought algumwood[c] and precious stones. 11 The king used the algumwood to make steps for the temple of the LORD and for the royal palace, and to make harps and lyres for the musicians. Nothing like them had ever been seen in Judah.)

12 King Solomon gave the queen of Sheba all she desired and asked for; he gave her more than she had brought to him. Then she left and returned with her retinue to her own country.

Solomon's Splendor

13 The weight of the gold that Solomon received yearly was 666 talents,[d] 14 not including the revenues brought in by merchants and traders. Also all the kings of Arabia and the governors of the land brought gold and silver to Solomon.

15 King Solomon made two hundred large shields of hammered gold; six hundred bekas[e] of hammered gold went into each shield. 16 He also made three hundred small shields of hammered gold, with three hundred bekas[f] of gold in each shield. The king put them in the Palace of the Forest of Lebanon.

17 Then the king made a great throne inlaid with ivory and overlaid with pure gold. 18 The throne had six steps, and a footstool of gold was attached to it. On both sides of the seat were armrests, with a lion standing beside each of them. 19 Twelve lions stood on the six steps, one at either end of each step. Nothing like it had ever been made for any other kingdom. 20 All King Solomon's goblets were gold, and all the household articles in the Palace of the Forest of Lebanon were pure gold. Nothing was made of silver, because silver was considered of little value in Solomon's day. 21 The king had a fleet of trading ships[g] manned by Hiram's[h] men. Once every three years it returned, carrying gold, silver and ivory, and apes and baboons.

22 King Solomon was greater in riches and wisdom than all the other kings of the earth. 23 All the kings of the earth sought audience with Solomon to hear the wisdom God had put in his heart. 24 Year after year, everyone who came brought a gift—articles of silver and gold, and robes, weapons and spices, and horses and mules.

25 Solomon had four thousand stalls for horses and chariots, and twelve thousand horses,[i] which he kept in the chariot cities and also with him in Jerusalem. 26 He ruled over all the kings from the River[j] to the land of the Philistines, as far as the border of Egypt. 27 The king made silver as common in Jerusalem as stones, and cedar as plentiful as sycamore-fig trees in the foothills. 28 Solomon's horses were imported from Egypt[k] and from all other countries.

Solomon's Death

29 As for the other events of Solomon's reign, from beginning to end, are they not written in the records of Nathan the prophet, in the prophecy of Ahijah the Shilonite and in the visions of Iddo the seer concerning Jeroboam son of Nebat? 30 Solomon reigned in Jerusalem over all Israel forty years. 31 Then he rested with his fathers and was buried in the city of David his father. And Rehoboam his son succeeded him as king.

[c] 10 Probably a variant of *almugwood* [d] 13 That is, about 25 tons (about 23 metric tons) [e] 15 That is, about 7 1/2 pounds (about 3.5 kilograms) [f] 16 That is, about 3 3/4 pounds (about 1.7 kilograms) [g] 21 Hebrew *of ships that could go to Tarshish* [h] 21 Hebrew *Huram*, a variant of *Hiram* [i] 25 Or *charioteers* [j] 26 That is, the Euphrates [k] 28 Or possibly *Muzur*, a region in Cilicia

PRAYER: RENEWAL

MAY I observe all Your statutes and all Your judgments and follow them; You are the Lord. (Leviticus 19:37) . . .

May I not show partiality in judgment, but hear both small and great alike. May I not be afraid of anyone, for judgment belongs to You, O God. (Deuteronomy 1:17)

***PAUSE** to add your own prayers for personal renewal.*

NT Romans 11:1-24

The Remnant of Israel

11 I ask then: Did God reject his people?
By no means! I am an Israelite myself,
a descendant of Abraham, from the tribe
of Benjamin. 2 God did not reject his people, whom he foreknew. Don't you know
what the Scripture says in the passage
about Elijah—how he appealed to God
against Israel: 3 "Lord, they have killed
your prophets and torn down your altars;
I am the only one left, and they are trying
to kill me"[a]? 4 And what was God's answer
to him? "I have reserved for myself seven
thousand who have not bowed the knee
to Baal."[b] 5 So too, at the present time
there is a remnant chosen by grace. 6 And
if by grace, then it is no longer by works;
if it were, grace would no longer be grace.[c]

7 What then? What Israel sought so
earnestly it did not obtain, but the elect
did. The others were hardened, 8 as it is
written:

"God gave them a spirit of stupor,
eyes so that they could not see
and ears so that they could not
hear,
to this very day."[d]

9 And David says:

"May their table become a snare and a
trap,
a stumbling block and a retribution
for them.
10 May their eyes be darkened so they
cannot see,
and their backs be bent forever."[e]

Ingrafted Branches

11 Again I ask: Did they stumble so as to
fall beyond recovery? Not at all! Rather,
because of their transgression, salvation
has come to the Gentiles to make Israel
envious. 12 But if their transgression means
riches for the world, and their loss means
riches for the Gentiles, how much greater
riches will their fullness bring!

13 I am talking to you Gentiles. Inas-
much as I am the apostle to the Gentiles,
I make much of my ministry 14 in the hope
that I may somehow arouse my own people to envy and save some of them. 15 For
if their rejection is the reconciliation of
the world, what will their acceptance be
but life from the dead? 16 If the part of the
dough offered as firstfruits is holy, then
the whole batch is holy; if the root is holy,
so are the branches.

17 If some of the branches have been
broken off, and you, though a wild olive
shoot, have been grafted in among the
others and now share in the nourishing
sap from the olive root, 18 do not boast
over those branches. If you do, consider
this: You do not support the root, but the
root supports you. 19 You will say then,
"Branches were broken off so that I could
be grafted in." 20 Granted. But they were
broken off because of unbelief, and you
stand by faith. Do not be arrogant, but be
afraid. 21 For if God did not spare the natural branches, he will not spare you either.

22 Consider therefore the kindness and
sternness of God: sternness to those who
fell, but kindness to you, provided that
you continue in his kindness. Otherwise,
you also will be cut off. 23 And if they do
not persist in unbelief, they will be grafted in, for God is able to graft them in
again. 24 After all, if you were cut out of an
olive tree that is wild by nature, and contrary to nature were grafted into a cultivated olive tree, how much more readily
will these, the natural branches, be grafted into their own olive tree!

[a] *3* 1 Kings 19:10,14 [b] *4* 1 Kings 19:18
[c] *6* Some manuscripts *by grace. But if by works, then it is no longer grace; if it were, work would no longer be work.* [d] *8* Deut. 29:4; Isaiah 29:10
[e] *10* Psalm 69:22,23

PRAYER: MY RELATIONSHIP TO GOD

GOD of my Lord Jesus Christ, the Father of glory, may You give me a spirit of wisdom and of revelation in the full knowledge of You, and may the eyes of my heart be enlightened, in order that I may know

the hope to which You have called me, the riches of Your glorious inheritance in the saints, and the incomparable greatness of Your power toward us who believe. (Ephesians 1:17–19)

***PAUSE** to thank God for the relationship that you enjoy with Him in Jesus Christ.*

YEAR 2 DAY 94

OT 2 Chronicles 10:1–19

Israel Rebels Against Rehoboam

10 Rehoboam went to Shechem, for all the Israelites had gone there to make
him king. [2]When Jeroboam son of Nebat heard this (he was in Egypt, where he had fled from King Solomon), he returned from Egypt. [3]So they sent for Jeroboam, and he and all Israel went to Rehoboam and said to him: [4]"Your father put a heavy yoke on us, but now lighten the harsh labor and the heavy yoke he put on us, and we will serve you."

[5]Rehoboam answered, "Come back to me in three days." So the people went away.

[6]Then King Rehoboam consulted the elders who had served his father Solomon during his lifetime. "How would you advise me to answer these people?" he asked.

[7]They replied, "If you will be kind to these people and please them and give them a favorable answer, they will always be your servants."

[8]But Rehoboam rejected the advice the elders gave him and consulted the young men who had grown up with him and were serving him. [9]He asked them, "What is your advice? How should we answer these people who say to me, 'Lighten the yoke your father put on us'?"

[10]The young men who had grown up with him replied, "Tell the people who have said to you, 'Your father put a heavy yoke on us, but make our yoke lighter'—tell them, 'My little finger is thicker than my father's waist. [11]My father laid on you a heavy yoke; I will make it even heavier. My father scourged you with whips; I will scourge you with scorpions.' "

[12]Three days later Jeroboam and all the people returned to Rehoboam, as the king had said, "Come back to me in three days." [13]The king answered them harshly. Rejecting the advice of the elders, [14]he followed the advice of the young men and said, "My father made your yoke heavy; I will make it even heavier. My father scourged you with whips; I will scourge you with scorpions." [15]So the king did not listen to the people, for this turn of events was from God, to fulfill the word the LORD had spoken to Jeroboam son of Nebat through Ahijah the Shilonite.

[16]When all Israel saw that the king refused to listen to them, they answered the king:

> "What share do we have in David,
> what part in Jesse's son?
> To your tents, O Israel!
> Look after your own house,
> O David!"

So all the Israelites went home. [17]But as for the Israelites who were living in the towns of Judah, Rehoboam still ruled over them.

[18]King Rehoboam sent out Adoniram,[a] who was in charge of forced labor, but the Israelites stoned him to death. King Rehoboam, however, managed to get into his chariot and escape to Jerusalem. [19]So Israel has been in rebellion against the house of David to this day.

[a] 18 Hebrew *Hadoram,* a variant of *Adoniram*

PRAYER: PETITION

NO one who waits for You will be ashamed, but those who are treacherous without cause will be ashamed.
Show me Your ways, O Lord, teach me Your paths; lead me in

Your truth and teach me, for You are the God of my salvation, and my hope is in You all day long.
(Psalm 25:3–5)

PAUSE *here to petition God for spiritual insight so that you might have understanding of His Word. Ask for insight into your identity in Jesus Christ: that you might know who you are, what direction your life should take and what His purpose for your life is. Offer prayers regarding your activities for this day and any special concerns you may have.*

NT Romans 11:25–36

All Israel Will Be Saved

25 I do not want you to be ignorant of
this mystery, brothers, so that you may
not be conceited: Israel has experienced a
hardening in part until the full number of
the Gentiles has come in. 26 And so all Israel will be saved, as it is written:

"The deliverer will come from Zion;
he will turn godlessness away from Jacob.
27 And this is[a] my covenant with them
when I take away their sins."[b]

28 As far as the gospel is concerned, they
are enemies on your account; but as far as
election is concerned, they are loved on
account of the patriarchs, 29 for God's gifts
and his call are irrevocable. 30 Just as you
who were at one time disobedient to God
have now received mercy as a result of
their disobedience, 31 so they too have now
become disobedient in order that they too
may now[c] receive mercy as a result of
God's mercy to you. 32 For God has bound
all men over to disobedience so that he
may have mercy on them all.

Doxology

33 Oh, the depth of the riches of the wisdom and[d] knowledge of God!
How unsearchable his judgments,
and his paths beyond tracing out!
34 "Who has known the mind of the Lord?
Or who has been his counselor?"[e]
35 "Who has ever given to God,
that God should repay him?"[f]
36 For from him and through him and to him are all things.
To him be the glory forever! Amen.

[a] 27 Or *will be* [b] 27 Isaiah 59:20,21; 27:9; Jer. 31:33,34 [c] 31 Some manuscripts do not have *now.* [d] 33 Or *riches and the wisdom and the* [e] 34 Isaiah 40:13 [f] 35 Job 41:11

PRAYER: THE CHARACTER I WANT TO CULTIVATE

SINCE Your day, O Lord, will come like a thief, I ought to conduct my life with holiness and godliness as I look forward to the coming of Your day. According to Your promise I am looking for a new heaven and a new earth, in which righteousness dwells. Therefore, since I am looking for these things, I will be diligent to be found at peace with You—pure and blameless before You. (2 Peter 3:10–14)

TAKE *a moment to ask the Lord for the grace to grow in godly character.*

YEAR 2 DAY 95

OT Proverbs 20

20 Wine is a mocker and beer a brawler;
whoever is led astray by them is not wise.

2 A king's wrath is like the roar of a lion;
he who angers him forfeits his life.

3 It is to a man's honor to avoid strife,
but every fool is quick to quarrel.

[4] A sluggard does not plow in season;
so at harvest time he looks but finds nothing.

[5] The purposes of a man's heart are deep waters,
but a man of understanding draws them out.

[6] Many a man claims to have unfailing love,
but a faithful man who can find?

[7] The righteous man leads a blameless life;
blessed are his children after him.

[8] When a king sits on his throne to judge,
he winnows out all evil with his eyes.

[9] Who can say, "I have kept my heart pure;
I am clean and without sin"?

[10] Differing weights and differing measures—
the LORD detests them both.

[11] Even a child is known by his actions,
by whether his conduct is pure and right.

[12] Ears that hear and eyes that see—
the LORD has made them both.

[13] Do not love sleep or you will grow poor;
stay awake and you will have food to spare.

[14] "It's no good, it's no good!" says the buyer;
then off he goes and boasts about his purchase.

[15] Gold there is, and rubies in abundance,
but lips that speak knowledge are a rare jewel.

[16] Take the garment of one who puts up security for a stranger;
hold it in pledge if he does it for a wayward woman.

[17] Food gained by fraud tastes sweet to a man,
but he ends up with a mouth full of gravel.

[18] Make plans by seeking advice;
if you wage war, obtain guidance.

[19] A gossip betrays a confidence;
so avoid a man who talks too much.

[20] If a man curses his father or mother,
his lamp will be snuffed out in pitch darkness.

[21] An inheritance quickly gained at the beginning
will not be blessed at the end.

[22] Do not say, "I'll pay you back for this wrong!"
Wait for the LORD, and he will deliver you.

[23] The LORD detests differing weights,
and dishonest scales do not please him.

[24] A man's steps are directed by the LORD.
How then can anyone understand his own way?

[25] It is a trap for a man to dedicate something rashly
and only later to consider his vows.

[26] A wise king winnows out the wicked;
he drives the threshing wheel over them.

[27] The lamp of the LORD searches the spirit of a man[a];
it searches out his inmost being.

[28] Love and faithfulness keep a king safe;
through love his throne is made secure.

[29] The glory of young men is their strength,
gray hair the splendor of the old.

[30] Blows and wounds cleanse away evil,
and beatings purge the inmost being.

[a] 27 Or *The spirit of man is the LORD's lamp*

PRAYER: INTERCESSION

WE want to serve You, O God, in every way: in great endurance, in afflictions, in needs, in distresses, in beatings, in imprisonment, in tumult, in labor, in sleeplessness, in hunger, in purity, in knowledge, in patience, in kindness, in the Holy Spirit, in sincere love, in the

word of truth, in Your power, O God—through the weapons of righteousness in the right hand and in the left, through glory and dishonor, through bad report and good report—as deceivers, and yet true; as unknown, and yet well-known; as dying, and yet living; as beaten, and yet not killed; as sorrowful, yet always rejoicing; as poor, yet making many rich; as having nothing, and yet possessing everything. (2 Corinthians 6:4–10)

***TAKE** a few moments to intercede on behalf of other believers, such as your personal friends, those in ministry and those who are oppressed and in need.*

NT Romans 12:1-8

Living Sacrifices

12 Therefore, I urge you, brothers, in
view of God's mercy, to offer your
bodies as living sacrifices, holy and pleasing to God—this is your spiritual[a] act of
worship. 2Do not conform any longer to
the pattern of this world, but be transformed by the renewing of your mind.
Then you will be able to test and approve
what God's will is—his good, pleasing
and perfect will.
3For by the grace given me I say to every
one of you: Do not think of yourself more
highly than you ought, but rather think of
yourself with sober judgment, in accordance with the measure of faith God has
given you. 4Just as each of us has one
body with many members, and these
members do not all have the same function, 5so in Christ we who are many form
one body, and each member belongs to
all the others. 6We have different gifts, according to the grace given us. If a man's
gift is prophesying, let him use it in proportion to his[b] faith. 7If it is serving, let
him serve; if it is teaching, let him teach;
8if it is encouraging, let him encourage; if
it is contributing to the needs of others,
let him give generously; if it is leadership,
let him govern diligently; if it is showing
mercy, let him do it cheerfully.

[a] 1 Or *reasonable* [b] 6 Or *in agreement with the*

PRAYER: MY RELATIONSHIP TO OTHERS

BETTER a meal of vegetables where there is love than a fattened calf with hatred. (Proverbs 15:17) . . . If we erase a sin by forgiving it, we show love. But if we repeat the matter, we come between close friends. (Proverbs 17:9)

***PAUSE** to review your relationships with others and to commit them to the Lord.*

YEAR 2
DAY 96

OT 2 Chronicles 11:1-23

11 When Rehoboam arrived in Jerusalem,
he mustered the house of Judah and
Benjamin—a hundred and eighty thousand fighting men—to make war against
Israel and to regain the kingdom for Rehoboam.
2But this word of the LORD came to Shemaiah the man of God: 3"Say to Rehoboam
son of Solomon king of Judah and to all the
Israelites in Judah and Benjamin, 4'This is
what the LORD says: Do not go up to fight
against your brothers. Go home, every one
of you, for this is my doing.' " So they
obeyed the words of the LORD and turned
back from marching against Jeroboam.

Rehoboam Fortifies Judah

5Rehoboam lived in Jerusalem and
built up towns for defense in Judah:
6Bethlehem, Etam, Tekoa, 7Beth Zur, Soco,

Adullam, 8Gath, Mareshah, Ziph, 9Adora-
im, Lachish, Azekah, 10Zorah, Aijalon and
Hebron. These were fortified cities in Judah and Benjamin. 11He strengthened
their defenses and put commanders in
them, with supplies of food, olive oil and
wine. 12He put shields and spears in all
the cities, and made them very strong. So
Judah and Benjamin were his.

13The priests and Levites from all their
districts throughout Israel sided with him.
14The Levites even abandoned their pasturelands and property, and came to Judah and Jerusalem because Jeroboam and
his sons had rejected them as priests of
the LORD. 15And he appointed his own
priests for the high places and for the goat
and calf idols he had made. 16Those from
every tribe of Israel who set their hearts on
seeking the LORD, the God of Israel, followed the Levites to Jerusalem to offer
sacrifices to the LORD, the God of their fathers. 17They strengthened the kingdom of
Judah and supported Rehoboam son of
Solomon three years, walking in the ways
of David and Solomon during this time.

Rehoboam's Family

18Rehoboam married Mahalath, who
was the daughter of David's son Jerimoth
and of Abihail, the daughter of Jesse's son
Eliab. 19She bore him sons: Jeush, Shemariah and Zaham. 20Then he married
Maacah daughter of Absalom, who bore
him Abijah, Attai, Ziza and Shelomith.
21Rehoboam loved Maacah daughter of
Absalom more than any of his other wives
and concubines. In all, he had eighteen
wives and sixty concubines, twenty-eight
sons and sixty daughters.

22Rehoboam appointed Abijah son of
Maacah to be the chief prince among his
brothers, in order to make him king. 23He
acted wisely, dispersing some of his sons
throughout the districts of Judah and Benjamin, and to all the fortified cities. He
gave them abundant provisions and took
many wives for them.

PRAYER: AFFIRMATION

O LORD, what are human beings that You take care of them, or people that You think of them? They are like breaths; their days are like passing shadows. (Psalm 144:3–4) . . . Those who seek to keep their life will lose it, and those who lose their life will preserve it. (Luke 17:33)

***PAUSE** to reflect on these Biblical affirmations.*

NT Romans 12:9–21

Love

9Love must be sincere. Hate what is evil;
cling to what is good. 10Be devoted to one
another in brotherly love. Honor one another above yourselves. 11Never be lacking
in zeal, but keep your spiritual fervor,
serving the Lord. 12Be joyful in hope, patient in affliction, faithful in prayer.
13Share with God's people who are in
need. Practice hospitality.

14Bless those who persecute you; bless
and do not curse. 15Rejoice with those
who rejoice; mourn with those who
mourn. 16Live in harmony with one another. Do not be proud, but be willing to
associate with people of low position.[a]
Do not be conceited.

17Do not repay anyone evil for evil. Be
careful to do what is right in the eyes of
everybody. 18If it is possible, as far as it depends on you, live at peace with everyone.
19Do not take revenge, my friends, but
leave room for God's wrath, for it is written: "It is mine to avenge; I will repay,"[b]
says the Lord. 20On the contrary:

"If your enemy is hungry, feed him;
if he is thirsty, give him something
to drink.
In doing this, you will heap burning
coals on his head."[c]

21Do not be overcome by evil, but overcome evil with good.

[a] *16* Or *willing to do menial work* [b] *19* Deut. 32:35
[c] *20* Prov. 25:21,22

PRAYER: THE ATTRIBUTES OF GOD

LONG ago You ordained Your plan, O Lord, and now You are bringing it to pass. (2 Kings 19:25; Isaiah 37:26) . . . With You, Lord, one day is like a thousand years, and a thousand years are like one day. (2 Peter 3:8)

***PAUSE** to reflect on these affirmations about the person, powers and perfection of God.*

YEAR 2 DAY 97

OT 2 Chronicles 12:1–16

Shishak Attacks Jerusalem

12 After Rehoboam's position as king was
established and he had become strong,
he and all Israel[a] with him abandoned the
law of the LORD. 2Because they had been
unfaithful to the LORD, Shishak king of
Egypt attacked Jerusalem in the fifth year
of King Rehoboam. 3With twelve hundred
chariots and sixty thousand horsemen and
the innumerable troops of Libyans, Suk-
kites and Cushites[b] that came with him
from Egypt, 4he captured the fortified cities of Judah and came as far as Jerusalem.

5Then the prophet Shemaiah came to Rehoboam and to the leaders of Judah who
had assembled in Jerusalem for fear of Shishak, and he said to them, "This is what the
LORD says, 'You have abandoned me; therefore, I now abandon you to Shishak.' "

6The leaders of Israel and the king humbled themselves and said, "The LORD is
just."

7When the LORD saw that they humbled
themselves, this word of the LORD came to
Shemaiah: "Since they have humbled
themselves, I will not destroy them but
will soon give them deliverance. My wrath
will not be poured out on Jerusalem
through Shishak. 8They will, however, become subject to him, so that they may
learn the difference between serving me
and serving the kings of other lands."

9When Shishak king of Egypt attacked
Jerusalem, he carried off the treasures of
the temple of the LORD and the treasures
of the royal palace. He took everything,
including the gold shields Solomon had
made. 10So King Rehoboam made bronze
shields to replace them and assigned these
to the commanders of the guard on duty
at the entrance to the royal palace.
11Whenever the king went to the LORD's
temple, the guards went with him, bearing the shields, and afterward they returned them to the guardroom.

12Because Rehoboam humbled himself,
the LORD's anger turned from him, and he
was not totally destroyed. Indeed, there
was some good in Judah.

13King Rehoboam established himself
firmly in Jerusalem and continued as
king. He was forty-one years old when he
became king, and he reigned seventeen
years in Jerusalem, the city the LORD had
chosen out of all the tribes of Israel in
which to put his Name. His mother's
name was Naamah; she was an Ammonite. 14He did evil because he had not set
his heart on seeking the LORD.

15As for the events of Rehoboam's reign,
from beginning to end, are they not written in the records of Shemaiah the prophet and of Iddo the seer that deal with genealogies? There was continual warfare
between Rehoboam and Jeroboam. 16Re-
hoboam rested with his fathers and was
buried in the City of David. And Abijah
his son succeeded him as king.

[a] *1* That is, Judah, as frequently in 2 Chronicles
[b] *3* That is, people from the upper Nile region

PRAYER: THANKSGIVING

I WILL declare Your name to my brothers and sisters; in the midst of the congregation I will praise You. All who fear You, praise You, O Lord! All the descendants of Jacob glorify You! All the descendants

of Israel stand in awe of You! For You have not despised or disdained the suffering of the afflicted one; You have not hidden Your face from him, but You have listened to his cry for help. (Psalm 22:22–24)

PAUSE *to offer your own expressions of thanksgiving.*

NT Romans 13:1–14

Submission to the Authorities

13 Everyone must submit himself to the governing authorities, for there is no authority except that which God has established. The authorities that exist have been established by God. [2]Consequently, he who rebels against the authority is rebelling against what God has instituted, and those who do so will bring judgment on themselves. [3]For rulers hold no terror for those who do right, but for those who do wrong. Do you want to be free from fear of the one in authority? Then do what is right and he will commend you.
[4]For he is God's servant to do you good. But if you do wrong, be afraid, for he does not bear the sword for nothing. He is God's servant, an agent of wrath to bring punishment on the wrongdoer.
[5]Therefore, it is necessary to submit to the authorities, not only because of possible punishment but also because of conscience.

[6]This is also why you pay taxes, for the authorities are God's servants, who give their full time to governing. [7]Give everyone what you owe him: If you owe taxes, pay taxes; if revenue, then revenue; if respect, then respect; if honor, then honor.

Love, for the Day Is Near

[8]Let no debt remain outstanding, except the continuing debt to love one another, for he who loves his fellowman has fulfilled the law. [9]The commandments, "Do not commit adultery," "Do not murder," "Do not steal," "Do not covet,"[a] and whatever other commandment there may be, are summed up in this one rule: "Love your neighbor as yourself."[b] [10]Love does no harm to its neighbor. Therefore love is the fulfillment of the law.

[11]And do this, understanding the present time. The hour has come for you to wake up from your slumber, because our salvation is nearer now than when we first believed. [12]The night is nearly over; the day is almost here. So let us put aside the deeds of darkness and put on the armor of light. [13]Let us behave decently, as in the daytime, not in orgies and drunkenness, not in sexual immorality and debauchery, not in dissension and jealousy. [14]Rather, clothe yourselves with the Lord Jesus Christ, and do not think about how to gratify the desires of the sinful nature.[c]

[a] 9 Exodus 20:13–15,17; Deut. 5:17–19,21
[b] 9 Lev. 19:18 [c] 14 Or *the flesh*

PRAYER: THE WORKS OF GOD

EVERY good and perfect gift is from above, coming down from You, the Father of lights, with whom there is no variation or shifting shadow. Of Your own will You brought us forth by the word of truth, that we might be a kind of firstfruits of Your creatures. (James 1:17–18)

TAKE *a moment to consider the greatness of God's wonderful works.*

YEAR 2 DAY 98

OT Psalm 90

Psalm 90

A prayer of Moses the man of God.

1 Lord, you have been our dwelling place
throughout all generations.
2 Before the mountains were born
or you brought forth the earth and the world,
from everlasting to everlasting you are God.

3 You turn men back to dust,
saying, "Return to dust, O sons of men."
4 For a thousand years in your sight
are like a day that has just gone by,
or like a watch in the night.
5 You sweep men away in the sleep of death;
they are like the new grass of the morning—
6 though in the morning it springs up new,
by evening it is dry and withered.

7 We are consumed by your anger
and terrified by your indignation.
8 You have set our iniquities before you,
our secret sins in the light of your presence.
9 All our days pass away under your wrath;
we finish our years with a moan.
10 The length of our days is seventy years—
or eighty, if we have the strength;
yet their span[a] is but trouble and sorrow,
for they quickly pass, and we fly away.

11 Who knows the power of your anger?
For your wrath is as great as the fear that is due you.
12 Teach us to number our days aright,
that we may gain a heart of wisdom.

13 Relent, O LORD! How long will it be?
Have compassion on your servants.
14 Satisfy us in the morning with your unfailing love,
that we may sing for joy and be glad all our days.
15 Make us glad for as many days as you have afflicted us,
for as many years as we have seen trouble.
16 May your deeds be shown to your servants,
your splendor to their children.

17 May the favor[b] of the Lord our God rest upon us;
establish the work of our hands for us—
yes, establish the work of our hands.

[a] 10 Or *yet the best of them* [b] 17 Or *beauty*

PRAYER: ADORATION

WHERE does wisdom come from? Where does understanding dwell? It is hidden from the eyes of every living thing and concealed from the birds of the air. Destruction and Death say, "Only a rumor of it has reached our ears." You understand its way, O God, and You know its place. For You look to the ends of the earth and see everything under the heavens. (Job 28:20–24) . . . We fear You, O God, because You care about those who are wise. (Job 37:24)

PAUSE *to express your thoughts of praise and worship.*

NT Romans 14:1-23

The Weak and the Strong

14 Accept him whose faith is weak, without passing judgment on disputable matters. [2]One man's faith allows him to eat everything, but another man, whose faith is weak, eats only vegetables. [3]The man who eats everything must not look down on him who does not, and the man who does not eat everything must not condemn the man who does, for God has accepted him. [4]Who are you to judge someone else's servant? To his own master he stands or falls. And he will stand, for the Lord is able to make him stand.

[5]One man considers one day more sacred than another; another man considers every day alike. Each one should be fully convinced in his own mind. [6]He who regards one day as special, does so to the Lord. He who eats meat, eats to the Lord, for he gives thanks to God; and he who abstains, does so to the Lord and gives thanks to God. [7]For none of us lives to himself alone and none of us dies to himself alone. [8]If we live, we live to the Lord; and if we die, we die to the Lord. So, whether we live or die, we belong to the Lord.

[9]For this very reason, Christ died and returned to life so that he might be the Lord of both the dead and the living. [10]You, then, why do you judge your brother? Or why do you look down on your brother? For we will all stand before God's judgment seat. [11]It is written:

" 'As surely as I live,' says the Lord,
'every knee will bow before me;
every tongue will confess to God.' "[a]

[12]So then, each of us will give an account of himself to God.

[13]Therefore let us stop passing judgment on one another. Instead, make up your mind not to put any stumbling block or obstacle in your brother's way. [14]As one who is in the Lord Jesus, I am fully convinced that no food[b] is unclean in itself. But if anyone regards something as unclean, then for him it is unclean. [15]If your brother is distressed because of what you eat, you are no longer acting in love. Do not by your eating destroy your brother for whom Christ died. [16]Do not allow what you consider good to be spoken of as evil. [17]For the kingdom of God is not a matter of eating and drinking, but of righteousness, peace and joy in the Holy Spirit, [18]because anyone who serves Christ in this way is pleasing to God and approved by men.

[19]Let us therefore make every effort to do what leads to peace and to mutual edification. [20]Do not destroy the work of God for the sake of food. All food is clean, but it is wrong for a man to eat anything that causes someone else to stumble. [21]It is better not to eat meat or drink wine or to do anything else that will cause your brother to fall.

[22]So whatever you believe about these things keep between yourself and God. Blessed is the man who does not condemn himself by what he approves. [23]But the man who has doubts is condemned if he eats, because his eating is not from faith; and everything that does not come from faith is sin.

[a] 11 Isaiah 45:23 [b] 14 Or *that nothing*

PRAYER: MY RELATIONSHIP TO GOD

I TRUSTED in You, O Christ, when I heard the word of truth, the gospel of my salvation. Having believed, I was sealed in You with the Holy Spirit of promise, who is a deposit guaranteeing my inheritance until the redemption of those who are God's possession—to the praise of Your glory. (Ephesians 1:13–14)

PAUSE *to thank God for the relationship that you enjoy with Him in Jesus Christ.*

YEAR 2 DAY 99

OT **2 Chronicles 13:1–22**

Abijah King of Judah

13 In the eighteenth year of the reign of
Jeroboam, Abijah became king of Judah, 2and he reigned in Jerusalem three
years. His mother's name was Maacah,[a] a
daughter[b] of Uriel of Gibeah.

There was war between Abijah and Jeroboam. 3Abijah went into battle with a
force of four hundred thousand able
fighting men, and Jeroboam drew up a
battle line against him with eight hundred thousand able troops.

4Abijah stood on Mount Zemaraim, in
the hill country of Ephraim, and said,
"Jeroboam and all Israel, listen to me!
5Don't you know that the LORD, the God
of Israel, has given the kingship of Israel
to David and his descendants forever by
a covenant of salt? 6Yet Jeroboam son of
Nebat, an official of Solomon son of David, rebelled against his master. 7Some
worthless scoundrels gathered around
him and opposed Rehoboam son of
Solomon when he was young and inde-
cisive and not strong enough to resist
them.

8"And now you plan to resist the kingdom of the LORD, which is in the hands
of David's descendants. You are indeed a
vast army and have with you the golden
calves that Jeroboam made to be your
gods. 9But didn't you drive out the priests
of the LORD, the sons of Aaron, and the
Levites, and make priests of your own as
the peoples of other lands do? Whoever
comes to consecrate himself with a
young bull and seven rams may become
a priest of what are not gods.

10"As for us, the LORD is our God, and
we have not forsaken him. The priests
who serve the LORD are sons of Aaron,
and the Levites assist them. 11Every
morning and evening they present burnt
offerings and fragrant incense to the
LORD. They set out the bread on the ceremonially clean table and light the
lamps on the gold lampstand every
evening. We are observing the requirements of the LORD our God. But you have
forsaken him. 12God is with us; he is our
leader. His priests with their trumpets
will sound the battle cry against you.
Men of Israel, do not fight against the
LORD, the God of your fathers, for you
will not succeed."

13Now Jeroboam had sent troops
around to the rear, so that while he was
in front of Judah the ambush was behind
them. 14Judah turned and saw that they
were being attacked at both front and
rear. Then they cried out to the LORD. The
priests blew their trumpets 15and the
men of Judah raised the battle cry. At the
sound of their battle cry, God routed Jeroboam and all Israel before Abijah and
Judah. 16The Israelites fled before Judah,
and God delivered them into their
hands. 17Abijah and his men inflicted
heavy losses on them, so that there were
five hundred thousand casualties among
Israel's able men. 18The men of Israel
were subdued on that occasion, and the
men of Judah were victorious because
they relied on the LORD, the God of their
fathers.

19Abijah pursued Jeroboam and took
from him the towns of Bethel, Jeshanah
and Ephron, with their surrounding villages. 20Jeroboam did not regain power
during the time of Abijah. And the LORD
struck him down and he died.

21But Abijah grew in strength. He married fourteen wives and had twenty-two
sons and sixteen daughters.

22The other events of Abijah's reign,
what he did and what he said, are written in the annotations of the prophet
Iddo.

[a] 2 Most Septuagint manuscripts and Syriac (see also 2 Chron. 11:20 and 1 Kings 15:2); Hebrew *Micaiah* [b] 2 Or *granddaughter*

PRAYER: CONFESSION

***O GOD, You know my foolishness, and my guilt is not hidden from You.
May those who hope in You not be ashamed because of me,
O Lord God of hosts; may those who seek You not be dishonored because of me,
O God of Israel. (Psalm 69:5–6)***

***ASK** the Spirit to search your heart and reveal any areas of unconfessed sin. Acknowledge these to the Lord and thank Him for His forgiveness.*

NT Romans 15:1-13

15 We who are strong ought to bear with
the failings of the weak and not to
please ourselves. 2 Each of us should
please his neighbor for his good, to build
him up. 3 For even Christ did not please
himself but, as it is written: "The insults
of those who insult you have fallen on
me."[a] 4 For everything that was written in
the past was written to teach us, so that
through endurance and the encouragement of the Scriptures we might have
hope.
5 May the God who gives endurance and
encouragement give you a spirit of unity
among yourselves as you follow Christ
Jesus, 6 so that with one heart and mouth
you may glorify the God and Father of our
Lord Jesus Christ.
7 Accept one another, then, just as Christ
accepted you, in order to bring praise to
God. 8 For I tell you that Christ has become a servant of the Jews[b] on behalf of
God's truth, to confirm the promises
made to the patriarchs 9 so that the Gentiles may glorify God for his mercy, as it
is written:

"Therefore I will praise you among the
Gentiles;
I will sing hymns to your name."[c]

10 Again, it says,

"Rejoice, O Gentiles, with his
people."[d]

11 And again,

"Praise the Lord, all you Gentiles,
and sing praises to him, all you
peoples."[e]

12 And again, Isaiah says,

"The Root of Jesse will spring up,
one who will arise to rule over the
nations;
the Gentiles will hope in him."[f]

13 May the God of hope fill you with all
joy and peace as you trust in him, so that
you may overflow with hope by the power of the Holy Spirit.

[a] *3* Psalm 69:9 [b] *8* Greek *circumcision*
[c] *9* 2 Samuel 22:50; Psalm 18:49 [d] *10* Deut. 32:43
[e] *11* Psalm 117:1 [f] *12* Isaiah 11:10

PRAYER: THE CHARACTER I WANT TO CULTIVATE

***I WILL work out my salvation with fear and trembling, for it is You,
O God, who works in me to will and to act according to
Your good purpose. (Philippians 2:12–13) . . . Whatever I do, whether in word or
in deed, I will do all in Your name, Lord Jesus, giving thanks
to God the Father through You.
(Colossians 3:17)***

***TAKE** a moment to ask the Lord for the grace to grow in godly character.*

YEAR 2 DAY 100

OT 2 Chronicles 14:1–15:19

14 And Abijah rested with his fathers and was buried in the City of David. Asa his son succeeded him as king, and in his days the country was at peace for ten years.

Asa King of Judah

[2]Asa did what was good and right in the eyes of the LORD his God. [3]He removed the foreign altars and the high places, smashed the sacred stones and cut down the Asherah poles.[a] [4]He commanded Judah to seek the LORD, the God of their fathers, and to obey his laws and commands. [5]He removed the high places and incense altars in every town in Judah, and the kingdom was at peace under him. [6]He built up the fortified cities of Judah, since the land was at peace. No one was at war with him during those years, for the LORD gave him rest.

[7]"Let us build up these towns," he said to Judah, "and put walls around them, with towers, gates and bars. The land is still ours, because we have sought the LORD our God; we sought him and he has given us rest on every side." So they built and prospered.

[8]Asa had an army of three hundred thousand men from Judah, equipped with large shields and with spears, and two hundred and eighty thousand from Benjamin, armed with small shields and with bows. All these were brave fighting men.

[9]Zerah the Cushite marched out against them with a vast army[b] and three hundred chariots, and came as far as Mareshah. [10]Asa went out to meet him, and they took up battle positions in the Valley of Zephathah near Mareshah.

[11]Then Asa called to the LORD his God and said, "LORD, there is no one like you to help the powerless against the mighty. Help us, O LORD our God, for we rely on you, and in your name we have come against this vast army. O LORD, you are our God; do not let man prevail against you."

[12]The LORD struck down the Cushites before Asa and Judah. The Cushites fled, [13]and Asa and his army pursued them as far as Gerar. Such a great number of Cushites fell that they could not recover; they were crushed before the LORD and his forces. The men of Judah carried off a large amount of plunder. [14]They destroyed all the villages around Gerar, for the terror of the LORD had fallen upon them. They plundered all these villages, since there was much booty there. [15]They also attacked the camps of the herdsmen and carried off droves of sheep and goats and camels. Then they returned to Jerusalem.

Asa's Reform

15 The Spirit of God came upon Azariah son of Oded. [2]He went out to meet Asa and said to him, "Listen to me, Asa and all Judah and Benjamin. The LORD is with you when you are with him. If you seek him, he will be found by you, but if you forsake him, he will forsake you. [3]For a long time Israel was without the true God, without a priest to teach and without the law. [4]But in their distress they turned to the LORD, the God of Israel, and sought him, and he was found by them. [5]In those days it was not safe to travel about, for all the inhabitants of the lands were in great turmoil. [6]One nation was being crushed by another and one city by another, because God was troubling them with every kind of distress. [7]But as for you, be strong and do not give up, for your work will be rewarded."

[8]When Asa heard these words and the prophecy of Azariah son of[c] Oded the prophet, he took courage. He removed the detestable idols from the whole land of Judah and Benjamin and from the towns he had captured in the hills of Ephraim. He repaired the altar of the LORD that was in front of the portico of the LORD's temple.

[9]Then he assembled all Judah and Benjamin and the people from Ephraim, Manasseh and Simeon who had settled among them, for large numbers had come over to him from Israel when they saw that the LORD his God was with him.

[10]They assembled at Jerusalem in the third month of the fifteenth year of Asa's reign. [11]At that time they sacrificed to the LORD seven hundred head of cattle and

[a] 3 That is, symbols of the goddess Asherah; here and elsewhere in 2 Chronicles [b] 9 Hebrew *with an army of a thousand thousands* or *with an army of thousands upon thousands* [c] 8 Vulgate and Syriac (see also Septuagint and verse 1); Hebrew does not have *Azariah son of.*

seven thousand sheep and goats from the plunder they had brought back. [12]They entered into a covenant to seek the LORD, the God of their fathers, with all their heart and soul. [13]All who would not seek the LORD, the God of Israel, were to be put to death, whether small or great, man or woman. [14]They took an oath to the LORD with loud acclamation, with shouting and with trumpets and horns. [15]All Judah rejoiced about the oath because they had sworn it wholeheartedly. They sought God eagerly, and he was found by them. So the LORD gave them rest on every side.

[16]King Asa also deposed his grandmother Maacah from her position as queen mother, because she had made a repulsive Asherah pole. Asa cut the pole down, broke it up and burned it in the Kidron Valley. [17]Although he did not remove the high places from Israel, Asa's heart was fully committed ⌊to the LORD⌋ all his life. [18]He brought into the temple of God the silver and gold and the articles that he and his father had dedicated.

[19]There was no more war until the thirty-fifth year of Asa's reign.

PRAYER: RENEWAL

MAY I be like Solomon, O Lord, who asked You, "Give me wisdom and knowledge, that I may lead this people, for who is able to judge this great people of Yours?" You answered Solomon saying, "Because this was in your heart and you have not asked for riches, wealth or honor, nor for the life of your enemies, and since you have not asked for a long life but for wisdom and knowledge to judge My people over whom I have made you king, wisdom and knowledge will be given you. And I will also give you riches and wealth and honor, such as no king who was before you ever had and none after you will have." (2 Chronicles 1:10–12)

***PAUSE** to add your own prayers for personal renewal.*

NT Romans 15:14–33

Paul the Minister to the Gentiles

[14]I myself am convinced, my brothers, that you yourselves are full of goodness, complete in knowledge and competent to instruct one another. [15]I have written you quite boldly on some points, as if to remind you of them again, because of the grace God gave me [16]to be a minister of Christ Jesus to the Gentiles with the priestly duty of proclaiming the gospel of God, so that the Gentiles might become an offering acceptable to God, sanctified by the Holy Spirit.

[17]Therefore I glory in Christ Jesus in my service to God. [18]I will not venture to speak of anything except what Christ has accomplished through me in leading the Gentiles to obey God by what I have said and done— [19]by the power of signs and miracles, through the power of the Spirit. So from Jerusalem all the way around to Illyricum, I have fully proclaimed the gospel of Christ. [20]It has always been my ambition to preach the gospel where Christ was not known, so that I would not be building on someone else's foundation. [21]Rather, as it is written:

"Those who were not told about him
will see,
and those who have not heard will
understand."[a]

[22]This is why I have often been hindered from coming to you.

Paul's Plan to Visit Rome

[23]But now that there is no more place for me to work in these regions, and since I have been longing for many years to see you, [24]I plan to do so when I go to Spain. I hope to visit you while passing through and to have you assist me on my journey there, after I have enjoyed your company for a while. [25]Now, however, I am on my way to Jerusalem in the service of the

[a] 21 Isaiah 52:15

saints there. [26]For Macedonia and Achaia were pleased to make a contribution for the poor among the saints in Jerusalem.
[27]They were pleased to do it, and indeed they owe it to them. For if the Gentiles have shared in the Jews' spiritual blessings, they owe it to the Jews to share with them their material blessings. [28]So after I have completed this task and have made sure that they have received this fruit, I will go to Spain and visit you on the way.
[29]I know that when I come to you, I will come in the full measure of the blessing of Christ.

[30]I urge you, brothers, by our Lord Jesus Christ and by the love of the Spirit, to join me in my struggle by praying to God for me. [31]Pray that I may be rescued from the unbelievers in Judea and that my service in Jerusalem may be acceptable to the saints there, [32]so that by God's will I may come to you with joy and together with you be refreshed. [33]The God of peace be with you all. Amen.

PRAYER: MY RELATIONSHIP TO OTHERS

***I WILL** offer petitions, prayers, intercession and thanksgiving on behalf of all people, for kings and all those who are in authority, that I may live a peaceful and quiet life in all godliness and reverence. This is good and acceptable in Your sight, O God our Savior, for You desire all people to be saved and to come to the knowledge of the truth. (1 Timothy 2:1–4)*

***PAUSE** to review your relationships with others and to commit them to the Lord.*

YEAR 2 DAY 101

OT 2 Chronicles 16:1–17:19

Asa's Last Years

16 In the thirty-sixth year of Asa's reign Baasha king of Israel went up against Judah and fortified Ramah to prevent anyone from leaving or entering the territory of Asa king of Judah.

[2]Asa then took the silver and gold out of the treasuries of the LORD's temple and of his own palace and sent it to Ben-Hadad king of Aram, who was ruling in Damascus. [3]"Let there be a treaty between me and you," he said, "as there was between my father and your father. See, I am sending you silver and gold. Now break your treaty with Baasha king of Israel so he will withdraw from me."

[4]Ben-Hadad agreed with King Asa and sent the commanders of his forces against the towns of Israel. They conquered Ijon, Dan, Abel Maim[a] and all the store cities of Naphtali. [5]When Baasha heard this, he stopped building Ramah and abandoned his work. [6]Then King Asa brought all the men of Judah, and they carried away from Ramah the stones and timber Baasha had been using. With them he built up Geba and Mizpah.

[7]At that time Hanani the seer came to Asa king of Judah and said to him: "Because you relied on the king of Aram and not on the LORD your God, the army of the king of Aram has escaped from your hand. [8]Were not the Cushites[b] and Libyans a mighty army with great numbers of chariots and horsemen[c]? Yet when you relied on the LORD, he delivered them into your hand. [9]For the eyes of the LORD range throughout the earth to strengthen those whose hearts are fully committed to him. You have done a foolish thing, and from now on you will be at war."

[10]Asa was angry with the seer because of this; he was so enraged that he put him in prison. At the same time Asa brutally oppressed some of the people.

[11]The events of Asa's reign, from beginning to end, are written in the book of the kings of Judah and Israel. [12]In the thirty-ninth year of his reign Asa was afflicted

[a] 4 Also known as *Abel Beth Maacah* [b] 8 That is, people from the upper Nile region [c] 8 Or *charioteers*

with a disease in his feet. Though his disease was severe, even in his illness he did
not seek help from the LORD, but only
from the physicians. [13]Then in the forty-
first year of his reign Asa died and rested
with his fathers. [14]They buried him in the
tomb that he had cut out for himself in
the City of David. They laid him on a bier
covered with spices and various blended
perfumes, and they made a huge fire in
his honor.

Jehoshaphat King of Judah

17 Jehoshaphat his son succeeded him as
king and strengthened himself against
Israel. [2]He stationed troops in all the fortified cities of Judah and put garrisons in
Judah and in the towns of Ephraim that
his father Asa had captured.

[3]The LORD was with Jehoshaphat because
in his early years he walked in the ways his
father David had followed. He did not consult the Baals [4]but sought the God of his father and followed his commands rather
than the practices of Israel. [5]The LORD established the kingdom under his control;
and all Judah brought gifts to Jehoshaphat,
so that he had great wealth and honor. [6]His
heart was devoted to the ways of the LORD;
furthermore, he removed the high places
and the Asherah poles from Judah.

[7]In the third year of his reign he sent his
officials Ben-Hail, Obadiah, Zechariah,
Nethanel and Micaiah to teach in the
towns of Judah. [8]With them were certain
Levites—Shemaiah, Nethaniah, Zebadiah, Asahel, Shemiramoth, Jehonathan,
Adonijah, Tobijah and Tob-Adonijah—
and the priests Elishama and Jehoram.
[9]They taught throughout Judah, taking
with them the Book of the Law of the
LORD; they went around to all the towns
of Judah and taught the people.

[10]The fear of the LORD fell on all the
kingdoms of the lands surrounding Judah, so that they did not make war with
Jehoshaphat. [11]Some Philistines brought
Jehoshaphat gifts and silver as tribute, and
the Arabs brought him flocks: seven thousand seven hundred rams and seven thousand seven hundred goats.

[12]Jehoshaphat became more and more
powerful; he built forts and store cities in
Judah [13]and had large supplies in the
towns of Judah. He also kept experienced
fighting men in Jerusalem. [14]Their enroll-
ment by families was as follows:

From Judah, commanders of units of 1,000:
Adnah the commander, with 300,000 fighting men;
[15]next, Jehohanan the commander, with 280,000;
[16]next, Amasiah son of Zicri, who volunteered himself for the service of the LORD, with 200,000.
[17]From Benjamin:
Eliada, a valiant soldier, with 200,000 men armed with bows and shields;
[18]next, Jehozabad, with 180,000 men armed for battle.

[19]These were the men who served the
king, besides those he stationed in the fortified cities throughout Judah.

PRAYER: PETITION

MAY everything I do be done in love.
(1 Corinthians 16:14)

***PAUSE** here to petition God for growth in love and compassion toward others. Offer prayers for your loved ones, for those who do not know Jesus and for those in need. Offer prayers regarding your activities for this day and any special concerns you may have.*

NT Romans 16:1-27

Personal Greetings

16 I commend to you our sister Phoebe, a
servant[a] of the church in Cenchrea. [2]I
ask you to receive her in the Lord in a way
worthy of the saints and to give her any help
she may need from you, for she has been a
great help to many people, including me.

[a] 1 Or *deaconess*

[3]Greet Priscilla[b] and Aquila, my fellow workers in Christ Jesus. [4]They risked their lives for me. Not only I but all the churches of the Gentiles are grateful to them.
[5]Greet also the church that meets at their house.
Greet my dear friend Epenetus, who was the first convert to Christ in the province of Asia.
[6]Greet Mary, who worked very hard for you.
[7]Greet Andronicus and Junias, my relatives who have been in prison with me. They are outstanding among the apostles, and they were in Christ before I was.
[8]Greet Ampliatus, whom I love in the Lord.
[9]Greet Urbanus, our fellow worker in Christ, and my dear friend Stachys.
[10]Greet Apelles, tested and approved in Christ.
Greet those who belong to the household of Aristobulus.
[11]Greet Herodion, my relative.
Greet those in the household of Narcissus who are in the Lord.
[12]Greet Tryphena and Tryphosa, those women who work hard in the Lord.
Greet my dear friend Persis, another woman who has worked very hard in the Lord.
[13]Greet Rufus, chosen in the Lord, and his mother, who has been a mother to me, too.
[14]Greet Asyncritus, Phlegon, Hermes, Patrobas, Hermas and the brothers with them.
[15]Greet Philologus, Julia, Nereus and his sister, and Olympas and all the saints with them.
[16]Greet one another with a holy kiss.
All the churches of Christ send greetings.

[17]I urge you, brothers, to watch out for
those who cause divisions and put obstacles in your way that are contrary to the
teaching you have learned. Keep away
from them. [18]For such people are not serv-
ing our Lord Christ, but their own appetites. By smooth talk and flattery they deceive the minds of naive people.
[19]Everyone has heard about your obedience, so I am full of joy over you; but I want you to be wise about what is good, and innocent about what is evil.
[20]The God of peace will soon crush Satan under your feet.
The grace of our Lord Jesus be with you.
[21]Timothy, my fellow worker, sends his greetings to you, as do Lucius, Jason and Sosipater, my relatives.
[22]I, Tertius, who wrote down this letter, greet you in the Lord.
[23]Gaius, whose hospitality I and the whole church here enjoy, sends you his greetings.
Erastus, who is the city's director of public works, and our brother Quartus send you their greetings.[c]
[25]Now to him who is able to establish you by my gospel and the proclamation of Jesus Christ, according to the revelation of the mystery hidden for long ages past,
[26]but now revealed and made known through the prophetic writings by the command of the eternal God, so that all nations might believe and obey him—
[27]to the only wise God be glory forever through Jesus Christ! Amen.

[b] 3 Greek *Prisca,* a variant of *Priscilla* [c] 23 Some manuscripts *their greetings. [24]May the grace of our Lord Jesus Christ be with all of you. Amen.*

PRAYER: THE ATTRIBUTES OF GOD

O LORD, I know that You will maintain the cause of the afflicted and justice for the poor. (Psalm 140:12) . . . Good and upright are You, Lord; therefore You instruct sinners in Your ways. (Psalm 25:8)

PAUSE *to reflect on these affirmations about the person, powers and perfection of God.*

YEAR 2
DAY 102

OT 2 Chronicles 18:1–34

Micaiah Prophesies Against Ahab

18 Now Jehoshaphat had great wealth
and honor, and he allied himself with
Ahab by marriage. [2]Some years later he
went down to visit Ahab in Samaria. Ahab
slaughtered many sheep and cattle for
him and the people with him and urged
him to attack Ramoth Gilead. [3]Ahab king
of Israel asked Jehoshaphat king of Judah,
"Will you go with me against Ramoth Gilead?"
Jehoshaphat replied, "I am as you are,
and my people as your people; we will
join you in the war." [4]But Jehoshaphat
also said to the king of Israel, "First seek
the counsel of the LORD."
[5]So the king of Israel brought together
the prophets—four hundred men—and
asked them, "Shall we go to war against
Ramoth Gilead, or shall I refrain?"
"Go," they answered, "for God will give
it into the king's hand."
[6]But Jehoshaphat asked, "Is there not a
prophet of the LORD here whom we can
inquire of?"
[7]The king of Israel answered Jehoshaphat, "There is still one man through
whom we can inquire of the LORD, but I
hate him because he never prophesies
anything good about me, but always bad.
He is Micaiah son of Imlah."
"The king should not say that," Jehoshaphat replied.
[8]So the king of Israel called one of his
officials and said, "Bring Micaiah son of
Imlah at once."
[9]Dressed in their royal robes, the king
of Israel and Jehoshaphat king of Judah
were sitting on their thrones at the threshing floor by the entrance to the gate of
Samaria, with all the prophets prophesying before them. [10]Now Zedekiah son of
Kenaanah had made iron horns, and he
declared, "This is what the LORD says:
'With these you will gore the Arameans
until they are destroyed.' "
[11]All the other prophets were prophesying the same thing. "Attack Ramoth Gile
ad and be victorious," they said, "for the
LORD will give it into the king's hand."
[12]The messenger who had gone to summon Micaiah said to him, "Look, as one
man the other prophets are predicting
success for the king. Let your word agree
with theirs, and speak favorably."
[13]But Micaiah said, "As surely as the
LORD lives, I can tell him only what my
God says."
[14]When he arrived, the king asked him,
"Micaiah, shall we go to war against Ramoth Gilead, or shall I refrain?"
"Attack and be victorious," he answered, "for they will be given into your
hand."
[15]The king said to him, "How many
times must I make you swear to tell me
nothing but the truth in the name of the
LORD?"
[16]Then Micaiah answered, "I saw all Israel scattered on the hills like sheep without a shepherd, and the LORD said, 'These
people have no master. Let each one go
home in peace.' "
[17]The king of Israel said to Jehoshaphat,
"Didn't I tell you that he never prophesies
anything good about me, but only bad?"
[18]Micaiah continued, "Therefore hear
the word of the LORD: I saw the LORD sitting on his throne with all the host of
heaven standing on his right and on his
left. [19]And the LORD said, 'Who will entice
Ahab king of Israel into attacking Ramoth
Gilead and going to his death there?'
"One suggested this, and another that.
[20]Finally, a spirit came forward, stood before the LORD and said, 'I will entice him.'
" 'By what means?' the LORD asked.
[21]" 'I will go and be a lying spirit in the
mouths of all his prophets,' he said.
" 'You will succeed in enticing him,' said
the LORD. 'Go and do it.'
[22]"So now the LORD has put a lying spirit in the mouths of these prophets of
yours. The LORD has decreed disaster for
you."
[23]Then Zedekiah son of Kenaanah went
up and slapped Micaiah in the face.
"Which way did the spirit from[a] the LORD
go when he went from me to speak to
you?" he asked.
[24]Micaiah replied, "You will find out on
the day you go to hide in an inner room."
[25]The king of Israel then ordered, "Take
Micaiah and send him back to Amon the
ruler of the city and to Joash the king's

[a] 23 Or *Spirit of*

son, 26and say, 'This is what the king says:
Put this fellow in prison and give him
nothing but bread and water until I return
safely.' "
27Micaiah declared, "If you ever return
safely, the LORD has not spoken through
me." Then he added, "Mark my words, all
you people!"

Ahab Killed at Ramoth Gilead

28So the king of Israel and Jehoshaphat
king of Judah went up to Ramoth Gilead.
29The king of Israel said to Jehoshaphat, "I
will enter the battle in disguise, but you
wear your royal robes." So the king of Israel disguised himself and went into battle.
30Now the king of Aram had ordered
his chariot commanders, "Do not fight
with anyone, small or great, except the
king of Israel." 31When the chariot commanders saw Jehoshaphat, they thought,
"This is the king of Israel." So they turned
to attack him, but Jehoshaphat cried out,
and the LORD helped him. God drew them
away from him, 32for when the chariot
commanders saw that he was not the king
of Israel, they stopped pursuing him.
33But someone drew his bow at random
and hit the king of Israel between the sections of his armor. The king told the chariot driver, "Wheel around and get me out
of the fighting. I've been wounded." 34All
day long the battle raged, and the king of
Israel propped himself up in his chariot
facing the Arameans until evening. Then
at sunset he died.

PRAYER: INTERCESSION

I PRAY that words may be given to me, that I may open my mouth boldly to make known the mystery of the gospel.
(Ephesians 6:19)

TAKE *a few moments to intercede on behalf of friends, relatives, neighbors and coworkers who do not yet know salvation in Jesus Christ.*

NT Mark 1:1–39

John the Baptist Prepares the Way

1 The beginning of the gospel about Jesus
Christ, the Son of God.[a]

2It is written in Isaiah the prophet:

"I will send my messenger ahead of
you,
who will prepare your way"[b]—
3 "a voice of one calling in the desert,
'Prepare the way for the Lord,
make straight paths for him.' "[c]

4And so John came, baptizing in the
desert region and preaching a baptism of
repentance for the forgiveness of sins.
5The whole Judean countryside and all the
people of Jerusalem went out to him.
Confessing their sins, they were baptized
by him in the Jordan River. 6John wore
clothing made of camel's hair, with a
leather belt around his waist, and he ate
locusts and wild honey. 7And this was his
message: "After me will come one more
powerful than I, the thongs of whose sandals I am not worthy to stoop down and
untie. 8I baptize you with[d] water, but he
will baptize you with the Holy Spirit."

The Baptism and Temptation of Jesus

9At that time Jesus came from Nazareth
in Galilee and was baptized by John in the
Jordan. 10As Jesus was coming up out of
the water, he saw heaven being torn open
and the Spirit descending on him like a
dove. 11And a voice came from heaven:
"You are my Son, whom I love; with you
I am well pleased."
12At once the Spirit sent him out into the
desert, 13and he was in the desert forty days,
being tempted by Satan. He was with the
wild animals, and angels attended him.

The Calling of the First Disciples

14After John was put in prison, Jesus
went into Galilee, proclaiming the good
news of God. 15"The time has come," he
said. "The kingdom of God is near. Repent
and believe the good news!"

[a] *1* Some manuscripts do not have *the Son of God.*
[b] *2* Mal. 3:1 [c] *3* Isaiah 40:3 [d] *8* Or *in*

16 As Jesus walked beside the Sea of Galilee, he saw Simon and his brother Andrew casting a net into the lake, for they
were fishermen. 17 "Come, follow me,"
Jesus said, "and I will make you fishers of
men." 18 At once they left their nets and
followed him.
19 When he had gone a little farther, he
saw James son of Zebedee and his brother John in a boat, preparing their nets.
20 Without delay he called them, and they
left their father Zebedee in the boat with
the hired men and followed him.

Jesus Drives Out an Evil Spirit

21 They went to Capernaum, and when
the Sabbath came, Jesus went into the synagogue and began to teach. 22 The people
were amazed at his teaching, because he
taught them as one who had authority,
not as the teachers of the law. 23 Just then
a man in their synagogue who was possessed by an evil[e] spirit cried out, 24 "What
do you want with us, Jesus of Nazareth?
Have you come to destroy us? I know who
you are—the Holy One of God!"
25 "Be quiet!" said Jesus sternly. "Come
out of him!" 26 The evil spirit shook the
man violently and came out of him with
a shriek.
27 The people were all so amazed that
they asked each other, "What is this? A
new teaching—and with authority! He
even gives orders to evil spirits and they
obey him." 28 News about him spread
quickly over the whole region of Galilee.

Jesus Heals Many

29 As soon as they left the synagogue, they
went with James and John to the home of
Simon and Andrew. 30 Simon's mother-in-
law was in bed with a fever, and they told
Jesus about her. 31 So he went to her, took
her hand and helped her up. The fever left
her and she began to wait on them.
32 That evening after sunset the people
brought to Jesus all the sick and demon-
possessed. 33 The whole town gathered at
the door, 34 and Jesus healed many who had
various diseases. He also drove out many
demons, but he would not let the demons
speak because they knew who he was.

Jesus Prays in a Solitary Place

35 Very early in the morning, while it was
still dark, Jesus got up, left the house and
went off to a solitary place, where he
prayed. 36 Simon and his companions
went to look for him, 37 and when they
found him, they exclaimed: "Everyone is
looking for you!"
38 Jesus replied, "Let us go somewhere
else—to the nearby villages—so I can
preach there also. That is why I have
come." 39 So he traveled throughout Galilee, preaching in their synagogues and
driving out demons.

[e] 23 Greek *unclean;* also in verses 26 and 27

PRAYER: THE WORKS OF GOD

YOU will punish the world for its evil, the wicked for their iniquity. You will put an end to the arrogance of the haughty and will humble the pride of the ruthless. (Isaiah 13:11) . . . You, O God will judge our secret thoughts through Jesus Christ, according to the gospel. (Romans 2:16)

***TAKE** a moment to consider the greatness of God's wonderful works.*

YEAR 2 DAY 103

OT 2 Chronicles 19:1–20:37

19 When Jehoshaphat king of Judah returned safely to his palace in Jerusalem, 2 Jehu the seer, the son of Hanani,
went out to meet him and said to the
king, "Should you help the wicked and
love[a] those who hate the LORD? Because
of this, the wrath of the LORD is upon you.
3 There is, however, some good in you, for
you have rid the land of the Asherah poles
and have set your heart on seeking God."

[a] 2 Or *and make alliances with*

Jehoshaphat Appoints Judges

4 Jehoshaphat lived in Jerusalem, and he went out again among the people from Beersheba to the hill country of Ephraim and turned them back to the LORD, the God of their fathers. 5 He appointed judges in the land, in each of the fortified cities of Judah. 6 He told them, "Consider carefully what you do, because you are not judging for man but for the LORD, who is with you whenever you give a verdict. 7 Now let the fear of the LORD be upon you. Judge carefully, for with the LORD our God there is no injustice or partiality or bribery."

8 In Jerusalem also, Jehoshaphat appointed some of the Levites, priests and heads of Israelite families to administer the law of the LORD and to settle disputes. And they lived in Jerusalem. 9 He gave them these orders: "You must serve faithfully and wholeheartedly in the fear of the LORD. 10 In every case that comes before you from your fellow countrymen who live in the cities—whether bloodshed or other concerns of the law, commands, decrees or ordinances—you are to warn them not to sin against the LORD; otherwise his wrath will come on you and your brothers. Do this, and you will not sin.

11 "Amariah the chief priest will be over you in any matter concerning the LORD, and Zebadiah son of Ishmael, the leader of the tribe of Judah, will be over you in any matter concerning the king, and the Levites will serve as officials before you. Act with courage, and may the LORD be with those who do well."

Jehoshaphat Defeats Moab and Ammon

20 After this, the Moabites and Ammonites with some of the Meunites[b] came to make war on Jehoshaphat.

2 Some men came and told Jehoshaphat, "A vast army is coming against you from Edom,[c] from the other side of the Sea.[d] It is already in Hazazon Tamar" (that is, En Gedi). 3 Alarmed, Jehoshaphat resolved to inquire of the LORD, and he proclaimed a fast for all Judah. 4 The people of Judah came together to seek help from the LORD; indeed, they came from every town in Judah to seek him.

5 Then Jehoshaphat stood up in the assembly of Judah and Jerusalem at the temple of the LORD in the front of the new courtyard 6 and said:

"O LORD, God of our fathers, are you not the God who is in heaven? You rule over all the kingdoms of the nations. Power and might are in your hand, and no one can withstand you. 7 O our God, did you not drive out the inhabitants of this land before your people Israel and give it forever to the descendants of Abraham your friend? 8 They have lived in it and have built in it a sanctuary for your Name, saying, 9 'If calamity comes upon us, whether the sword of judgment, or plague or famine, we will stand in your presence before this temple that bears your Name and will cry out to you in our distress, and you will hear us and save us.'

10 "But now here are men from Ammon, Moab and Mount Seir, whose territory you would not allow Israel to invade when they came from Egypt; so they turned away from them and did not destroy them. 11 See how they are repaying us by coming to drive us out of the possession you gave us as an inheritance. 12 O our God, will you not judge them? For we have no power to face this vast army that is attacking us. We do not know what to do, but our eyes are upon you."

13 All the men of Judah, with their wives and children and little ones, stood there before the LORD.

14 Then the Spirit of the LORD came upon Jahaziel son of Zechariah, the son of Benaiah, the son of Jeiel, the son of Mattaniah, a Levite and descendant of Asaph, as he stood in the assembly.

15 He said: "Listen, King Jehoshaphat and all who live in Judah and Jerusalem! This is what the LORD says to you: 'Do not be afraid or discouraged because of this vast army. For the battle is not yours, but God's. 16 Tomorrow march down against them. They will be climbing up by the Pass of Ziz, and you will find them at the end of the gorge in the Desert of Jeruel. 17 You will not have to fight this battle. Take up your positions; stand firm and see the deliverance the LORD will give you, O Judah and Jerusalem. Do not be afraid; do not

[b] *1* Some Septuagint manuscripts; Hebrew *Ammonites* [c] *2* One Hebrew manuscript; most Hebrew manuscripts, Septuagint and Vulgate *Aram*
[d] *2* That is, the Dead Sea

be discouraged. Go out to face them tomorrow, and the LORD will be with you.' "
18Jehoshaphat bowed with his face to
the ground, and all the people of Judah
and Jerusalem fell down in worship before the LORD. 19Then some Levites from
the Kohathites and Korahites stood up
and praised the LORD, the God of Israel,
with very loud voice.
20Early in the morning they left for the
Desert of Tekoa. As they set out, Jehoshaphat stood and said, "Listen to me, Judah
and people of Jerusalem! Have faith in the
LORD your God and you will be upheld;
have faith in his prophets and you will be
successful." 21After consulting the people,
Jehoshaphat appointed men to sing to the
LORD and to praise him for the splendor
of his[e] holiness as they went out at the
head of the army, saying:

"Give thanks to the LORD,
for his love endures forever."

22As they began to sing and praise, the
LORD set ambushes against the men of
Ammon and Moab and Mount Seir who
were invading Judah, and they were defeated. 23The men of Ammon and Moab
rose up against the men from Mount Seir
to destroy and annihilate them. After they
finished slaughtering the men from Seir,
they helped to destroy one another.
24When the men of Judah came to the
place that overlooks the desert and looked
toward the vast army, they saw only dead
bodies lying on the ground; no one had escaped. 25So Jehoshaphat and his men went
to carry off their plunder, and they found
among them a great amount of equipment
and clothing[f] and also articles of value—
more than they could take away. There was
so much plunder that it took three days to
collect it. 26On the fourth day they assembled in the Valley of Beracah, where they
praised the LORD. This is why it is called the
Valley of Beracah[g] to this day.
27Then, led by Jehoshaphat, all the men
of Judah and Jerusalem returned joyfully
to Jerusalem, for the LORD had given them
cause to rejoice over their enemies. 28They
entered Jerusalem and went to the temple
of the LORD with harps and lutes and
trumpets.
29The fear of God came upon all the
kingdoms of the countries when they
heard how the LORD had fought against
the enemies of Israel. 30And the kingdom
of Jehoshaphat was at peace, for his God
had given him rest on every side.

The End of Jehoshaphat's Reign

31So Jehoshaphat reigned over Judah.
He was thirty-five years old when he became king of Judah, and he reigned in
Jerusalem twenty-five years. His mother's
name was Azubah daughter of Shilhi.
32He walked in the ways of his father Asa
and did not stray from them; he did what
was right in the eyes of the LORD. 33The
high places, however, were not removed,
and the people still had not set their
hearts on the God of their fathers.
34The other events of Jehoshaphat's reign,
from beginning to end, are written in the
annals of Jehu son of Hanani, which are
recorded in the book of the kings of Israel.
35Later, Jehoshaphat king of Judah made
an alliance with Ahaziah king of Israel,
who was guilty of wickedness. 36He agreed
with him to construct a fleet of trading
ships.[h] After these were built at Ezion Geber, 37Eliezer son of Dodavahu of Mareshah prophesied against Jehoshaphat, saying, "Because you have made an alliance
with Ahaziah, the LORD will destroy what
you have made." The ships were wrecked
and were not able to set sail to trade.[i]

[e] 21 Or *him with the splendor of* [f] 25 Some Hebrew manuscripts and Vulgate; most Hebrew manuscripts *corpses* [g] 26 *Beracah* means *praise.* [h] 36 Hebrew *of ships that could go to Tarshish* [i] 37 Hebrew *sail for Tarshish*

PRAYER: AFFIRMATION

The mouths of the righteous speak wisdom, and their tongues speak what is just. Your law is in their hearts, O God; their steps do not slide. (Psalm 37:30–31) . . . We should be quick to hear, slow to speak and slow to anger, for our anger does not produce Your righteousness, O God. (James 1:19–20)

PAUSE *to reflect on these Biblical affirmations.*

NT Mark 1:40–2:17

A Man With Leprosy

40 A man with leprosy[a] came to him and begged him on his knees, "If you are willing, you can make me clean."

41 Filled with compassion, Jesus reached out his hand and touched the man. "I am willing," he said. "Be clean!" 42 Immediately the leprosy left him and he was cured.

43 Jesus sent him away at once with a strong warning: 44 "See that you don't tell this to anyone. But go, show yourself to the priest and offer the sacrifices that Moses commanded for your cleansing, as a testimony to them." 45 Instead he went out and began to talk freely, spreading the news. As a result, Jesus could no longer enter a town openly but stayed outside in lonely places. Yet the people still came to him from everywhere.

Jesus Heals a Paralytic

2 A few days later, when Jesus again entered Capernaum, the people heard that he had come home. 2 So many gathered that there was no room left, not even outside the door, and he preached the word to them. 3 Some men came, bringing to him a paralytic, carried by four of them. 4 Since they could not get him to Jesus because of the crowd, they made an opening in the roof above Jesus and, after digging through it, lowered the mat the paralyzed man was lying on. 5 When Jesus saw their faith, he said to the paralytic, "Son, your sins are forgiven."

6 Now some teachers of the law were sitting there, thinking to themselves, 7 "Why does this fellow talk like that? He's blaspheming! Who can forgive sins but God alone?"

8 Immediately Jesus knew in his spirit that this was what they were thinking in their hearts, and he said to them, "Why are you thinking these things? 9 Which is easier: to say to the paralytic, 'Your sins are forgiven,' or to say, 'Get up, take your mat and walk'? 10 But that you may know that the Son of Man has authority on earth to forgive sins . . . ." He said to the paralytic, 11 "I tell you, get up, take your mat and go home." 12 He got up, took his mat and walked out in full view of them all. This amazed everyone and they praised God, saying, "We have never seen anything like this!"

The Calling of Levi

13 Once again Jesus went out beside the lake. A large crowd came to him, and he began to teach them. 14 As he walked along, he saw Levi son of Alphaeus sitting at the tax collector's booth. "Follow me," Jesus told him, and Levi got up and followed him.

15 While Jesus was having dinner at Levi's house, many tax collectors and "sinners" were eating with him and his disciples, for there were many who followed him. 16 When the teachers of the law who were Pharisees saw him eating with the "sinners" and tax collectors, they asked his disciples: "Why does he eat with tax collectors and 'sinners'?"

17 On hearing this, Jesus said to them, "It is not the healthy who need a doctor, but the sick. I have not come to call the righteous, but sinners."

[a] *40* The Greek word was used for various diseases affecting the skin—not necessarily leprosy.

PRAYER: MY RELATIONSHIP TO GOD

IF a man dies, will he live again? All the days of my hard service I will wait for my renewal to come. (Job 14:14) . . . As for me, I will see Your face in righteousness; when I awake, I will be satisfied with Your likeness. (Psalm 17:15)

PAUSE *to thank God for the relationship that you enjoy with Him in Jesus Christ.*

OT 2 Chronicles 21:1-20

21 Then Jehoshaphat rested with his fathers and was buried with them in the
City of David. And Jehoram his son succeeded him as king. 2Jehoram's brothers,
the sons of Jehoshaphat, were Azariah, Jehiel, Zechariah, Azariahu, Michael and
Shephatiah. All these were sons of Jehoshaphat king of Israel.[a] 3Their father
had given them many gifts of silver and
gold and articles of value, as well as fortified cities in Judah, but he had given the
kingdom to Jehoram because he was his
firstborn son.

Jehoram King of Judah

4When Jehoram established himself
firmly over his father's kingdom, he put
all his brothers to the sword along with
some of the princes of Israel. 5Jehoram
was thirty-two years old when he became
king, and he reigned in Jerusalem eight
years. 6He walked in the ways of the kings
of Israel, as the house of Ahab had done,
for he married a daughter of Ahab. He did
evil in the eyes of the LORD. 7Nevertheless,
because of the covenant the LORD had
made with David, the LORD was not willing to destroy the house of David. He had
promised to maintain a lamp for him and
his descendants forever.

8In the time of Jehoram, Edom rebelled
against Judah and set up its own king. 9So
Jehoram went there with his officers and
all his chariots. The Edomites surrounded
him and his chariot commanders, but he
rose up and broke through by night. 10To
this day Edom has been in rebellion
against Judah.

Libnah revolted at the same time, because Jehoram had forsaken the LORD, the
God of his fathers. 11He had also built
high places on the hills of Judah and had
caused the people of Jerusalem to prostitute themselves and had led Judah astray.

12Jehoram received a letter from Elijah
the prophet, which said:

"This is what the LORD, the God of
your father David, says: 'You have not
walked in the ways of your father Jehoshaphat or of Asa king of Judah.
13But you have walked in the ways of
the kings of Israel, and you have led
Judah and the people of Jerusalem to
prostitute themselves, just as the
house of Ahab did. You have also
murdered your own brothers, members of your father's house, men who
were better than you. 14So now the
LORD is about to strike your people,
your sons, your wives and everything
that is yours, with a heavy blow.
15You yourself will be very ill with a
lingering disease of the bowels, until
the disease causes your bowels to
come out.' "

16The LORD aroused against Jehoram the
hostility of the Philistines and of the
Arabs who lived near the Cushites. 17They
attacked Judah, invaded it and carried off
all the goods found in the king's palace,
together with his sons and wives. Not a
son was left to him except Ahaziah,[b] the
youngest.

18After all this, the LORD afflicted Jehoram with an incurable disease of the bowels. 19In the course of time, at the end of
the second year, his bowels came out because of the disease, and he died in great
pain. His people made no fire in his hon-
or, as they had for his fathers.

20Jehoram was thirty-two years old when
he became king, and he reigned in Jerusalem eight years. He passed away, to no
one's regret, and was buried in the City of
David, but not in the tombs of the kings.

[a] 2 That is, Judah, as frequently in 2 Chronicles
[b] 17 Hebrew *Jehoahaz,* a variant of *Ahaziah*

PRAYER: THANKSGIVING

I WILL exalt You, O Lord, for You lifted me up and did not let my enemies rejoice over me. O Lord my God, I cried to You for help and You healed me. (Psalm 30:1–2)

PAUSE *to offer your own expressions of thanksgiving.*

NT Mark 2:18–3:19

Jesus Questioned About Fasting

18 Now John's disciples and the Pharisees were fasting. Some people came and asked Jesus, "How is it that John's disciples and the disciples of the Pharisees are fasting, but yours are not?"

19 Jesus answered, "How can the guests of the bridegroom fast while he is with them? They cannot, so long as they have him with them. 20 But the time will come when the bridegroom will be taken from them, and on that day they will fast.

21 "No one sews a patch of unshrunk cloth on an old garment. If he does, the new piece will pull away from the old, making the tear worse. 22 And no one pours new wine into old wineskins. If he does, the wine will burst the skins, and both the wine and the wineskins will be ruined. No, he pours new wine into new wineskins."

Lord of the Sabbath

23 One Sabbath Jesus was going through the grainfields, and as his disciples walked along, they began to pick some heads of grain. 24 The Pharisees said to him, "Look, why are they doing what is unlawful on the Sabbath?"

25 He answered, "Have you never read what David did when he and his companions were hungry and in need? 26 In the days of Abiathar the high priest, he entered the house of God and ate the consecrated bread, which is lawful only for priests to eat. And he also gave some to his companions."

27 Then he said to them, "The Sabbath was made for man, not man for the Sabbath. 28 So the Son of Man is Lord even of the Sabbath."

3 Another time he went into the synagogue, and a man with a shriveled hand was there. 2 Some of them were looking for a reason to accuse Jesus, so they watched him closely to see if he would heal him on the Sabbath. 3 Jesus said to the man with the shriveled hand, "Stand up in front of everyone."

4 Then Jesus asked them, "Which is lawful on the Sabbath: to do good or to do evil, to save life or to kill?" But they remained silent.

5 He looked around at them in anger and, deeply distressed at their stubborn hearts, said to the man, "Stretch out your hand." He stretched it out, and his hand was completely restored. 6 Then the Pharisees went out and began to plot with the Herodians how they might kill Jesus.

Crowds Follow Jesus

7 Jesus withdrew with his disciples to the lake, and a large crowd from Galilee followed. 8 When they heard all he was doing, many people came to him from Judea, Jerusalem, Idumea, and the regions across the Jordan and around Tyre and Sidon. 9 Because of the crowd he told his disciples to have a small boat ready for him, to keep the people from crowding him. 10 For he had healed many, so that those with diseases were pushing forward to touch him. 11 Whenever the evil[a] spirits saw him, they fell down before him and cried out, "You are the Son of God." 12 But he gave them strict orders not to tell who he was.

The Appointing of the Twelve Apostles

13 Jesus went up on a mountainside and called to him those he wanted, and they came to him. 14 He appointed twelve—designating them apostles[b]—that they might be with him and that he might send them out to preach 15 and to have authority to drive out demons. 16 These are the twelve he appointed: Simon (to whom he gave the name Peter); 17 James son of Zebedee and his brother John (to them he gave the name Boanerges, which means Sons of Thunder); 18 Andrew, Philip, Bartholomew, Matthew, Thomas, James son of Alphaeus, Thaddaeus, Simon the Zealot 19 and Judas Iscariot, who betrayed him.

[a] *11* Greek *unclean;* also in verse 30 [b] *14* Some manuscripts do not have *designating them apostles.*

PRAYER: THE CHARACTER I WANT TO CULTIVATE

I WILL humble myself under Your mighty hand, O God, that You may exalt me in due time; I will cast all my anxiety upon You, because You care for me. (1 Peter 5:6–7)

***TAKE** a moment to ask the Lord for the grace to grow in godly character.*

YEAR 2 DAY 105

OT **Psalms 91–92**

Psalm 91

1 He who dwells in the shelter of the Most High
will rest in the shadow of the Almighty.[a]
2 I will say[b] of the LORD, "He is my refuge and my fortress,
my God, in whom I trust."

3 Surely he will save you from the fowler's snare
and from the deadly pestilence.
4 He will cover you with his feathers,
and under his wings you will find refuge;
his faithfulness will be your shield and rampart.
5 You will not fear the terror of night,
nor the arrow that flies by day,
6 nor the pestilence that stalks in the darkness,
nor the plague that destroys at midday.
7 A thousand may fall at your side,
ten thousand at your right hand,
but it will not come near you.
8 You will only observe with your eyes
and see the punishment of the wicked.

9 If you make the Most High your dwelling—
even the LORD, who is my refuge—
10 then no harm will befall you,
no disaster will come near your tent.
11 For he will command his angels concerning you
to guard you in all your ways;
12 they will lift you up in their hands,
so that you will not strike your foot against a stone.
13 You will tread upon the lion and the cobra;
you will trample the great lion and the serpent.

14 "Because he loves me," says the LORD,
"I will rescue him;
I will protect him, for he acknowledges my name.
15 He will call upon me, and I will answer him;
I will be with him in trouble,
I will deliver him and honor him.
16 With long life will I satisfy him
and show him my salvation."

Psalm 92

A psalm. A song. For the Sabbath day.

1 It is good to praise the LORD
and make music to your name, O Most High,
2 to proclaim your love in the morning
and your faithfulness at night,
3 to the music of the ten-stringed lyre
and the melody of the harp.

4 For you make me glad by your deeds, O LORD;
I sing for joy at the works of your hands.
5 How great are your works, O LORD,
how profound your thoughts!
6 The senseless man does not know,
fools do not understand,
7 that though the wicked spring up like grass
and all evildoers flourish,
they will be forever destroyed.

8 But you, O LORD, are exalted forever.

9 For surely your enemies, O LORD,
surely your enemies will perish;
all evildoers will be scattered.

[a] 1 Hebrew *Shaddai* [b] 2 Or *He says*

[10]You have exalted my horn[c] like that of
a wild ox;
fine oils have been poured upon me.
[11]My eyes have seen the defeat of my
adversaries;
my ears have heard the rout of my
wicked foes.

[12]The righteous will flourish like a palm
tree,
they will grow like a cedar of
Lebanon;
[13]planted in the house of the LORD,
they will flourish in the courts of
our God.
[14]They will still bear fruit in old age,
they will stay fresh and green,
[15]proclaiming, "The LORD is upright;
he is my Rock, and there is no
wickedness in him."

[c] 10 *Horn* here symbolizes strength.

PRAYER: ADORATION

YOU have chosen me as Your witness and servant so that I may know and believe You and understand that You are the Lord. Before You no god was formed nor will there be one after You. (Isaiah 43:10) . . . You are the Lord, Israel's King and Redeemer, the Lord of hosts; You have said, "I am the first and I am the last; apart from Me there is no God." (Isaiah 44:6)

***PAUSE** to express your thoughts of praise and worship.*

NT Mark 3:20–4:20

Jesus and Beelzebub

[20]Then Jesus entered a house, and again
a crowd gathered, so that he and his disciples were not even able to eat. [21]When
his family heard about this, they went to
take charge of him, for they said, "He is
out of his mind."

[22]And the teachers of the law who came
down from Jerusalem said, "He is possessed by Beelzebub[a]! By the prince of
demons he is driving out demons."

[23]So Jesus called them and spoke to
them in parables: "How can Satan drive
out Satan? [24]If a kingdom is divided
against itself, that kingdom cannot stand.
[25]If a house is divided against itself, that
house cannot stand. [26]And if Satan opposes himself and is divided, he cannot
stand; his end has come. [27]In fact, no one
can enter a strong man's house and carry
off his possessions unless he first ties up
the strong man. Then he can rob his
house. [28]I tell you the truth, all the sins
and blasphemies of men will be forgiven
them. [29]But whoever blasphemes against
the Holy Spirit will never be forgiven; he
is guilty of an eternal sin."

[30]He said this because they were saying,
"He has an evil spirit."

Jesus' Mother and Brothers

[31]Then Jesus' mother and brothers arrived. Standing outside, they sent someone in to call him. [32]A crowd was sitting
around him, and they told him, "Your
mother and brothers are outside looking
for you."

[33]"Who are my mother and my brothers?" he asked.

[34]Then he looked at those seated in a
circle around him and said, "Here are my
mother and my brothers! [35]Whoever does
God's will is my brother and sister and
mother."

The Parable of the Sower

4 Again Jesus began to teach by the lake.
The crowd that gathered around him
was so large that he got into a boat and
sat in it out on the lake, while all the people were along the shore at the water's
edge. [2]He taught them many things by
parables, and in his teaching said: [3]"Listen! A farmer went out to sow his seed.
[4]As he was scattering the seed, some fell
along the path, and the birds came and
ate it up. [5]Some fell on rocky places,
where it did not have much soil. It sprang
up quickly, because the soil was shallow.

[a] 22 Greek *Beezeboul* or *Beelzeboul*

6But when the sun came up, the plants
were scorched, and they withered because
they had no root. 7Other seed fell among
thorns, which grew up and choked the
plants, so that they did not bear grain.
8Still other seed fell on good soil. It came
up, grew and produced a crop, multiply-
ing thirty, sixty, or even a hundred times."
9Then Jesus said, "He who has ears to
hear, let him hear."
10When he was alone, the Twelve and
the others around him asked him about
the parables. 11He told them, "The secret
of the kingdom of God has been given to
you. But to those on the outside everything is said in parables 12so that,

" 'they may be ever seeing but never
perceiving,
and ever hearing but never
understanding;
otherwise they might turn and be
forgiven!'[b]"

13Then Jesus said to them, "Don't you
understand this parable? How then will
you understand any parable? 14The farmer
sows the word. 15Some people are like
seed along the path, where the word is
sown. As soon as they hear it, Satan comes
and takes away the word that was sown in
them. 16Others, like seed sown on rocky
places, hear the word and at once receive
it with joy. 17But since they have no root,
they last only a short time. When trouble
or persecution comes because of the
word, they quickly fall away. 18Still others,
like seed sown among thorns, hear the
word; 19but the worries of this life, the deceitfulness of wealth and the desires for
other things come in and choke the word,
making it unfruitful. 20Others, like seed
sown on good soil, hear the word, accept
it, and produce a crop—thirty, sixty or
even a hundred times what was sown."

[b] *12* Isaiah 6:9,10

PRAYER: MY RELATIONSHIP TO OTHERS

I WILL not judge, so that I will not be judged. For in the same way I judge others, I will be judged; and with the measure I use, it will be measured to me. (Matthew 7:1–2) . . . If I do not judge, I will not be judged; if I do not condemn, I will not be condemned; if I forgive, I will be forgiven. (Luke 6:37)

***PAUSE** to review your relationships with others and to commit them to the Lord.*

YEAR 2 DAY 106

OT 2 Chronicles 22:1-12

Ahaziah King of Judah

22 The people of Jerusalem made Ahaziah, Jehoram's youngest son, king in
his place, since the raiders, who came
with the Arabs into the camp, had killed
all the older sons. So Ahaziah son of Jehoram king of Judah began to reign.
2Ahaziah was twenty-two[a] years old
when he became king, and he reigned in
Jerusalem one year. His mother's name
was Athaliah, a granddaughter of Omri.
3He too walked in the ways of the
house of Ahab, for his mother encouraged
him in doing wrong. 4He did evil in the
eyes of the LORD, as the house of Ahab
had done, for after his father's death they
became his advisers, to his undoing. 5He
also followed their counsel when he went
with Joram[b] son of Ahab king of Israel to
war against Hazael king of Aram at Ramoth Gilead. The Arameans wounded Joram; 6so he returned to Jezreel to recover
from the wounds they had inflicted on
him at Ramoth[c] in his battle with Hazael
king of Aram.
Then Ahaziah[d] son of Jehoram king of

[a] *2* Some Septuagint manuscripts and Syriac (see also 2 Kings 8:26); Hebrew *forty-two* [b] *5* Hebrew *Jehoram,* a variant of *Joram;* also in verses 6 and 7 [c] *6* Hebrew *Ramah,* a variant of *Ramoth* [d] *6* Some Hebrew manuscripts, Septuagint, Vulgate and Syriac (see also 2 Kings 8:29); most Hebrew manuscripts *Azariah*

Judah went down to Jezreel to see Joram
son of Ahab because he had been wounded.
7 Through Ahaziah's visit to Joram, God
brought about Ahaziah's downfall. When
Ahaziah arrived, he went out with Joram
to meet Jehu son of Nimshi, whom the
LORD had anointed to destroy the house
of Ahab. 8 While Jehu was executing judgment on the house of Ahab, he found the
princes of Judah and the sons of Ahaziah's relatives, who had been attending
Ahaziah, and he killed them. 9 He then
went in search of Ahaziah, and his men
captured him while he was hiding in
Samaria. He was brought to Jehu and put
to death. They buried him, for they said,
"He was a son of Jehoshaphat, who
sought the LORD with all his heart." So
there was no one in the house of Ahaziah powerful enough to retain the kingdom.

Athaliah and Joash

10 When Athaliah the mother of Ahaziah saw that her son was dead, she proceeded to destroy the whole royal family
of the house of Judah. 11 But Jehosheba,[e]
the daughter of King Jehoram, took Joash
son of Ahaziah and stole him away from
among the royal princes who were about
to be murdered and put him and his
nurse in a bedroom. Because Jehosheba,[e]
the daughter of King Jehoram and wife of
the priest Jehoiada, was Ahaziah's sister,
she hid the child from Athaliah so she
could not kill him. 12 He remained hidden
with them at the temple of God for six
years while Athaliah ruled the land.

[e] 11 Hebrew *Jehoshabeath,* a variant of *Jehosheba*

PRAYER: CONFESSION

CAN human beings be more righteous than You, O God? Can we be more pure than our Maker? (Job 4:17)

***ASK** the Spirit to search your heart and reveal any areas of unconfessed sin. Acknowledge these to the Lord and thank Him for His forgiveness.*

NT Mark 4:21-41

A Lamp on a Stand

21 He said to them, "Do you bring in a
lamp to put it under a bowl or a bed? Instead, don't you put it on its stand? 22 For
whatever is hidden is meant to be disclosed, and whatever is concealed is
meant to be brought out into the open.
23 If anyone has ears to hear, let him hear."
24 "Consider carefully what you hear,"
he continued. "With the measure you use,
it will be measured to you—and even
more. 25 Whoever has will be given more;
whoever does not have, even what he has
will be taken from him."

The Parable of the Growing Seed

26 He also said, "This is what the kingdom of God is like. A man scatters seed
on the ground. 27 Night and day, whether
he sleeps or gets up, the seed sprouts and
grows, though he does not know how.
28 All by itself the soil produces grain—first
the stalk, then the head, then the full kernel in the head. 29 As soon as the grain is
ripe, he puts the sickle to it, because the
harvest has come."

The Parable of the Mustard Seed

30 Again he said, "What shall we say the
kingdom of God is like, or what parable
shall we use to describe it? 31 It is like a
mustard seed, which is the smallest seed
you plant in the ground. 32 Yet when
planted, it grows and becomes the largest
of all garden plants, with such big
branches that the birds of the air can
perch in its shade."
33 With many similar parables Jesus
spoke the word to them, as much as they
could understand. 34 He did not say anything to them without using a parable.
But when he was alone with his own disciples, he explained everything.

Jesus Calms the Storm

35 That day when evening came, he said
to his disciples, "Let us go over to the oth-

er side." [36]Leaving the crowd behind, they took him along, just as he was, in the boat. There were also other boats with him. [37]A furious squall came up, and the waves broke over the boat, so that it was nearly swamped. [38]Jesus was in the stern, sleeping on a cushion. The disciples woke him and said to him, "Teacher, don't you care if we drown?"

[39]He got up, rebuked the wind and said to the waves, "Quiet! Be still!" Then the wind died down and it was completely calm.

[40]He said to his disciples, "Why are you so afraid? Do you still have no faith?"

[41]They were terrified and asked each other, "Who is this? Even the wind and the waves obey him!"

PRAYER: THE ATTRIBUTES OF GOD

THE Lord is a jealous God, punishing the children for the sin of the fathers to the third and fourth generation of those who hate Him, but showing loving-kindness to a thousand generations of those who love Him and keep His commandments.

(Exodus 20:5–6; Deuteronomy 5:9–10)

***PAUSE** to reflect on these affirmations about the person, powers and perfection of God.*

YEAR 2 DAY 107

OT 2 Chronicles 23:1–21

23 In the seventh year Jehoiada showed his strength. He made a covenant with the commanders of units of a hundred: Azariah son of Jeroham, Ishmael son of Jehohanan, Azariah son of Obed, Maaseiah son of Adaiah, and Elishaphat son of Zicri. [2]They went throughout Judah and gathered the Levites and the heads of Israelite families from all the towns. When they came to Jerusalem, [3]the whole assembly made a covenant with the king at the temple of God.

Jehoiada said to them, "The king's son shall reign, as the LORD promised concerning the descendants of David. [4]Now this is what you are to do: A third of you priests and Levites who are going on duty on the Sabbath are to keep watch at the doors, [5]a third of you at the royal palace and a third at the Foundation Gate, and all the other men are to be in the courtyards of the temple of the LORD. [6]No one is to enter the temple of the LORD except the priests and Levites on duty; they may enter because they are consecrated, but all the other men are to guard what the LORD has assigned to them.[a] [7]The Levites are to station themselves around the king, each man with his weapons in his hand. Anyone who enters the temple must be put to death. Stay close to the king wherever he goes."

[8]The Levites and all the men of Judah did just as Jehoiada the priest ordered. Each one took his men—those who were going on duty on the Sabbath and those who were going off duty—for Jehoiada the priest had not released any of the divisions. [9]Then he gave the commanders of units of a hundred the spears and the large and small shields that had belonged to King David and that were in the temple of God. [10]He stationed all the men, each with his weapon in his hand, around the king—near the altar and the temple, from the south side to the north side of the temple.

[11]Jehoiada and his sons brought out the king's son and put the crown on him; they presented him with a copy of the covenant and proclaimed him king. They anointed him and shouted, "Long live the king!"

[12]When Athaliah heard the noise of the people running and cheering the king, she went to them at the temple of the LORD. [13]She looked, and there was the king, standing by his pillar at the entrance. The officers and the trumpeters were beside

[a] 6 Or *to observe the* LORD*'s command ⌊not to enter⌋*

the king, and all the people of the land
were rejoicing and blowing trumpets, and
singers with musical instruments were
leading the praises. Then Athaliah tore her
robes and shouted, "Treason! Treason!"
14 Jehoiada the priest sent out the commanders of units of a hundred, who were
in charge of the troops, and said to them:
"Bring her out between the ranks[b] and put
to the sword anyone who follows her."
For the priest had said, "Do not put her
to death at the temple of the LORD." 15 So
they seized her as she reached the entrance of the Horse Gate on the palace
grounds, and there they put her to death.
16 Jehoiada then made a covenant that
he and the people and the king[c] would be
the LORD's people. 17 All the people went
to the temple of Baal and tore it down.
They smashed the altars and idols and
killed Mattan the priest of Baal in front of
the altars.
18 Then Jehoiada placed the oversight of
the temple of the LORD in the hands of the
priests, who were Levites, to whom David
had made assignments in the temple, to
present the burnt offerings of the LORD as
written in the Law of Moses, with rejoicing and singing, as David had ordered.
19 He also stationed doorkeepers at the
gates of the LORD's temple so that no one
who was in any way unclean might enter.
20 He took with him the commanders of
hundreds, the nobles, the rulers of the
people and all the people of the land and
brought the king down from the temple
of the LORD. They went into the palace
through the Upper Gate and seated the
king on the royal throne, 21 and all the
people of the land rejoiced. And the city
was quiet, because Athaliah had been
slain with the sword.

[b] 14 Or *out from the precincts* [c] 16 Or *covenant between ˻the LORD˼ and the people and the king that they* (see 2 Kings 11:17)

PRAYER: RENEWAL

WHEN I have done all the things You have commanded me, let me realize that I am an unworthy servant; I have only done what I ought to have done. (Luke 17:10) . . . May I do Your work, O God, while it is day; night is coming, when no one can work. (John 9:4)

PAUSE *to add your own prayers for personal renewal.*

NT Mark 5:1–20

The Healing of a Demon-possessed Man

5 They went across the lake to the region
of the Gerasenes.[a] 2 When Jesus got out
of the boat, a man with an evil[b] spirit
came from the tombs to meet him. 3 This
man lived in the tombs, and no one could
bind him any more, not even with a
chain. 4 For he had often been chained
hand and foot, but he tore the chains
apart and broke the irons on his feet. No
one was strong enough to subdue him.
5 Night and day among the tombs and in
the hills he would cry out and cut himself
with stones.
6 When he saw Jesus from a distance, he
ran and fell on his knees in front of him.
7 He shouted at the top of his voice, "What
do you want with me, Jesus, Son of the
Most High God? Swear to God that you
won't torture me!" 8 For Jesus had said to
him, "Come out of this man, you evil
spirit!"
9 Then Jesus asked him, "What is your
name?"
"My name is Legion," he replied, "for
we are many." 10 And he begged Jesus again
and again not to send them out of the
area.
11 A large herd of pigs was feeding on the
nearby hillside. 12 The demons begged
Jesus, "Send us among the pigs; allow us
to go into them." 13 He gave them permission, and the evil spirits came out and
went into the pigs. The herd, about two
thousand in number, rushed down the
steep bank into the lake and were
drowned.

[a] 1 Some manuscripts *Gadarenes;* other manuscripts *Gergesenes* [b] 2 Greek *unclean;* also in verses 8 and 13

14Those tending the pigs ran off and reported this in the town and countryside, and the people went out to see what had happened. 15When they came to Jesus, they saw the man who had been possessed by the legion of demons, sitting there, dressed and in his right mind; and they were afraid. 16Those who had seen it told the people what had happened to the demon-possessed man—and told about the pigs as well. 17Then the people began to plead with Jesus to leave their region.

18As Jesus was getting into the boat, the man who had been demon-possessed begged to go with him. 19Jesus did not let him, but said, "Go home to your family and tell them how much the Lord has done for you, and how he has had mercy on you." 20So the man went away and began to tell in the Decapolis[c] how much Jesus had done for him. And all the people were amazed.

[c] *20* That is, the Ten Cities

PRAYER: THE WORKS OF GOD

***WHEN** You, O Christ, came as high priest of the good things that have come, You went through a greater and more perfect tabernacle—one not made with hands, that is to say, not a part of this creation. You did not enter through the blood of goats and calves; but through Your own blood, You entered the Most Holy Place once for all, having obtained eternal redemption. (Hebrews 9:11–12)*

***TAKE** a moment to consider the greatness of God's wonderful works.*

YEAR 2 DAY 108

OT 2 Chronicles 24:1–27

Joash Repairs the Temple

24 Joash was seven years old when he became king, and he reigned in Jerusalem forty years. His mother's name was Zibiah; she was from Beersheba. 2Joash did what was right in the eyes of the LORD all the years of Jehoiada the priest. 3Jehoiada chose two wives for him, and he had sons and daughters.

4Some time later Joash decided to restore the temple of the LORD. 5He called together the priests and Levites and said to them, "Go to the towns of Judah and collect the money due annually from all Israel, to repair the temple of your God. Do it now." But the Levites did not act at once.

6Therefore the king summoned Jehoiada the chief priest and said to him, "Why haven't you required the Levites to bring in from Judah and Jerusalem the tax imposed by Moses the servant of the LORD and by the assembly of Israel for the Tent of the Testimony?"

7Now the sons of that wicked woman Athaliah had broken into the temple of God and had used even its sacred objects for the Baals.

8At the king's command, a chest was made and placed outside, at the gate of the temple of the LORD. 9A proclamation was then issued in Judah and Jerusalem that they should bring to the LORD the tax that Moses the servant of God had required of Israel in the desert. 10All the officials and all the people brought their contributions gladly, dropping them into the chest until it was full. 11Whenever the chest was brought in by the Levites to the king's officials and they saw that there was a large amount of money, the royal secretary and the officer of the chief priest would come and empty the chest and carry it back to its place. They did this regularly and collected a great amount of money. 12The king and Jehoiada gave it to the men who carried out the work required for the temple of the LORD. They hired masons and carpenters to restore the LORD's temple, and also workers in iron and bronze to repair the temple.

13The men in charge of the work were

diligent, and the repairs progressed under them. They rebuilt the temple of God according to its original design and reinforced it. 14 When they had finished, they brought the rest of the money to the king and Jehoiada, and with it were made articles for the LORD's temple: articles for the service and for the burnt offerings, and also dishes and other objects of gold and silver. As long as Jehoiada lived, burnt offerings were presented continually in the temple of the LORD.

15 Now Jehoiada was old and full of years, and he died at the age of a hundred and thirty. 16 He was buried with the kings in the City of David, because of the good he had done in Israel for God and his temple.

The Wickedness of Joash

17 After the death of Jehoiada, the officials of Judah came and paid homage to the king, and he listened to them. 18 They abandoned the temple of the LORD, the God of their fathers, and worshiped Asherah poles and idols. Because of their guilt, God's anger came upon Judah and Jerusalem. 19 Although the LORD sent prophets to the people to bring them back to him, and though they testified against them, they would not listen.

20 Then the Spirit of God came upon Zechariah son of Jehoiada the priest. He stood before the people and said, "This is what God says: 'Why do you disobey the LORD's commands? You will not prosper. Because you have forsaken the LORD, he has forsaken you.' "

21 But they plotted against him, and by order of the king they stoned him to death in the courtyard of the LORD's temple. 22 King Joash did not remember the kindness Zechariah's father Jehoiada had shown him but killed his son, who said as he lay dying, "May the LORD see this and call you to account."

23 At the turn of the year,[a] the army of Aram marched against Joash; it invaded Judah and Jerusalem and killed all the leaders of the people. They sent all the plunder to their king in Damascus. 24 Although the Aramean army had come with only a few men, the LORD delivered into their hands a much larger army. Because Judah had forsaken the LORD, the God of their fathers, judgment was executed on Joash. 25 When the Arameans withdrew, they left Joash severely wounded. His officials conspired against him for murdering the son of Jehoiada the priest, and they killed him in his bed. So he died and was buried in the City of David, but not in the tombs of the kings.

26 Those who conspired against him were Zabad,[b] son of Shimeath an Ammonite woman, and Jehozabad, son of Shimrith[c] a Moabite woman. 27 The account of his sons, the many prophecies about him, and the record of the restoration of the temple of God are written in the annotations on the book of the kings. And Amaziah his son succeeded him as king.

[a] 23 Probably in the spring [b] 26 A variant of *Jozabad* [c] 26 A variant of *Shomer*

PRAYER: PETITION

MAY I be a person who fears You, O God, who loves truth and who hates dishonest gain. (Exodus 18:21)

PAUSE *here to petition God to help you be a faithful steward of your time, talents, possessions and relationships. Offer prayers of petition regarding your activities for this day and any special concerns you may have.*

NT Mark 5:21-43

A Dead Girl and a Sick Woman

21 When Jesus had again crossed over by boat to the other side of the lake, a large crowd gathered around him while he was by the lake. 22 Then one of the synagogue rulers, named Jairus, came there. Seeing Jesus, he fell at his feet 23 and pleaded earnestly with him, "My little daughter is dying. Please come and put your hands on her so that she will be healed and live." 24 So Jesus went with him.

A large crowd followed and pressed around him. 25And a woman was there who had been subject to bleeding for twelve years. 26She had suffered a great deal under the care of many doctors and had spent all she had, yet instead of getting better she grew worse. 27When she heard about Jesus, she came up behind him in the crowd and touched his cloak, 28because she thought, "If I just touch his clothes, I will be healed." 29Immediately her bleeding stopped and she felt in her body that she was freed from her suffering.

30At once Jesus realized that power had gone out from him. He turned around in the crowd and asked, "Who touched my clothes?"

31"You see the people crowding against you," his disciples answered, "and yet you can ask, 'Who touched me?' "

32But Jesus kept looking around to see who had done it. 33Then the woman, knowing what had happened to her, came and fell at his feet and, trembling with fear, told him the whole truth. 34He said to her, "Daughter, your faith has healed you. Go in peace and be freed from your suffering."

35While Jesus was still speaking, some men came from the house of Jairus, the synagogue ruler. "Your daughter is dead," they said. "Why bother the teacher any more?"

36Ignoring what they said, Jesus told the synagogue ruler, "Don't be afraid; just believe."

37He did not let anyone follow him except Peter, James and John the brother of James. 38When they came to the home of the synagogue ruler, Jesus saw a commotion, with people crying and wailing loudly. 39He went in and said to them, "Why all this commotion and wailing? The child is not dead but asleep." 40But they laughed at him.

After he put them all out, he took the child's father and mother and the disciples who were with him, and went in where the child was. 41He took her by the hand and said to her, *"Talitha koum!"* (which means, "Little girl, I say to you, get up!"). 42Immediately the girl stood up and walked around (she was twelve years old). At this they were completely astonished. 43He gave strict orders not to let anyone know about this, and told them to give her something to eat.

PRAYER: MY RELATIONSHIP TO GOD

I AM unworthy of all the loving-kindness and faithfulness You have shown Your servant. (Genesis 32:10) . . . You, O Lord, are a shield around me; You bestow glory on me and lift up my head. (Psalm 3:3)

***PAUSE** to thank God for the relationship that you enjoy with Him in Jesus Christ.*

OT **2 Chronicles 25:1–28** YEAR 2 DAY 109

Amaziah King of Judah

25 Amaziah was twenty-five years old when he became king, and he reigned in Jerusalem twenty-nine years. His mother's name was Jehoaddin[a]; she was from Jerusalem. 2He did what was right in the eyes of the LORD, but not wholeheartedly. 3After the kingdom was firmly in his control, he executed the officials who had murdered his father the king. 4Yet he did not put their sons to death, but acted in accordance with what is written in the Law, in the Book of Moses, where the LORD commanded: "Fathers shall not be put to death for their children, nor children put to death for their fathers; each is to die for his own sins."[b]

5Amaziah called the people of Judah together and assigned them according to their families to commanders of thousands and commanders of hundreds for all Judah and Benjamin. He then mus-

[a] *1* Hebrew *Jehoaddan,* a variant of *Jehoaddin*
[b] *4* Deut. 24:16

tered those twenty years old or more and found that there were three hundred thousand men ready for military service, able to handle the spear and shield. 6He also hired a hundred thousand fighting men from Israel for a hundred talents[c] of silver.

7But a man of God came to him and said, "O king, these troops from Israel must not march with you, for the LORD is not with Israel—not with any of the people of Ephraim. 8Even if you go and fight courageously in battle, God will overthrow you before the enemy, for God has the power to help or to overthrow."

9Amaziah asked the man of God, "But what about the hundred talents I paid for these Israelite troops?"

The man of God replied, "The LORD can give you much more than that."

10So Amaziah dismissed the troops who had come to him from Ephraim and sent them home. They were furious with Judah and left for home in a great rage.

11Amaziah then marshaled his strength and led his army to the Valley of Salt, where he killed ten thousand men of Seir. 12The army of Judah also captured ten thousand men alive, took them to the top of a cliff and threw them down so that all were dashed to pieces.

13Meanwhile the troops that Amaziah had sent back and had not allowed to take part in the war raided Judean towns from Samaria to Beth Horon. They killed three thousand people and carried off great quantities of plunder.

14When Amaziah returned from slaughtering the Edomites, he brought back the gods of the people of Seir. He set them up as his own gods, bowed down to them and burned sacrifices to them. 15The anger of the LORD burned against Amaziah, and he sent a prophet to him, who said, "Why do you consult this people's gods, which could not save their own people from your hand?"

16While he was still speaking, the king said to him, "Have we appointed you an adviser to the king? Stop! Why be struck down?"

So the prophet stopped but said, "I know that God has determined to destroy you, because you have done this and have not listened to my counsel."

17After Amaziah king of Judah consulted his advisers, he sent this challenge to Jehoash[d] son of Jehoahaz, the son of Jehu, king of Israel: "Come, meet me face to face."

18But Jehoash king of Israel replied to Amaziah king of Judah: "A thistle in Lebanon sent a message to a cedar in Lebanon, 'Give your daughter to my son in marriage.' Then a wild beast in Lebanon came along and trampled the thistle underfoot. 19You say to yourself that you have defeated Edom, and now you are arrogant and proud. But stay at home! Why ask for trouble and cause your own downfall and that of Judah also?"

20Amaziah, however, would not listen, for God so worked that he might hand them over to ⌊Jehoash⌋, because they sought the gods of Edom. 21So Jehoash king of Israel attacked. He and Amaziah king of Judah faced each other at Beth Shemesh in Judah. 22Judah was routed by Israel, and every man fled to his home. 23Jehoash king of Israel captured Amaziah king of Judah, the son of Joash, the son of Ahaziah,[e] at Beth Shemesh. Then Jehoash brought him to Jerusalem and broke down the wall of Jerusalem from the Ephraim Gate to the Corner Gate—a section about six hundred feet[f] long. 24He took all the gold and silver and all the articles found in the temple of God that had been in the care of Obed-Edom, together with the palace treasures and the hostages, and returned to Samaria.

25Amaziah son of Joash king of Judah lived for fifteen years after the death of Jehoash son of Jehoahaz king of Israel. 26As for the other events of Amaziah's reign, from beginning to end, are they not written in the book of the kings of Judah and Israel? 27From the time that Amaziah turned away from following the LORD, they conspired against him in Jerusalem and he fled to Lachish, but they sent men after him to Lachish and killed him there. 28He was brought back by horse and was buried with his fathers in the City of Judah.

[c] 6 That is, about 3 3/4 tons (about 3.4 metric tons); also in verse 9 [d] 17 Hebrew *Joash,* a variant of *Jehoash;* also in verses 18, 21, 23 and 25
[e] 23 Hebrew *Jehoahaz,* a variant of *Ahaziah*
[f] 23 Hebrew *four hundred cubits* (about 180 meters)

PRAYER: INTERCESSION

***RIGHTEOUSNESS** exalts a nation, but sin is a disgrace to any people.*
(Proverbs 14:34)

***TAKE** a few moments to intercede on behalf of your local, state or provincial, and national governments. Pray for spiritual revival in the nation and offer prayers regarding current events and concerns.*

NT Mark 6:1–29

A Prophet Without Honor

6 Jesus left there and went to his hometown, accompanied by his disciples.
2When the Sabbath came, he began to
teach in the synagogue, and many who
heard him were amazed.
"Where did this man get these things?"
they asked. "What's this wisdom that has
been given him, that he even does miracles! 3Isn't this the carpenter? Isn't this
Mary's son and the brother of James, Joseph,[a] Judas and Simon? Aren't his sisters
here with us?" And they took offense at
him.
4Jesus said to them, "Only in his hometown, among his relatives and in his own
house is a prophet without honor." 5He
could not do any miracles there, except
lay his hands on a few sick people and
heal them. 6And he was amazed at their
lack of faith.

Jesus Sends Out the Twelve

Then Jesus went around teaching from
village to village. 7Calling the Twelve to
him, he sent them out two by two and
gave them authority over evil[b] spirits.
8These were his instructions: "Take
nothing for the journey except a staff—no
bread, no bag, no money in your belts.
9Wear sandals but not an extra tunic.
10Whenever you enter a house, stay there
until you leave that town. 11And if any
place will not welcome you or listen to
you, shake the dust off your feet when you
leave, as a testimony against them."
12They went out and preached that people should repent. 13They drove out many
demons and anointed many sick people
with oil and healed them.

John the Baptist Beheaded

14King Herod heard about this, for
Jesus' name had become well known.
Some were saying,[c] "John the Baptist has
been raised from the dead, and that is
why miraculous powers are at work in
him."
15Others said, "He is Elijah."
And still others claimed, "He is a
prophet, like one of the prophets of long
ago."
16But when Herod heard this, he said,
"John, the man I beheaded, has been
raised from the dead!"
17For Herod himself had given orders to
have John arrested, and he had him
bound and put in prison. He did this because of Herodias, his brother Philip's
wife, whom he had married. 18For John
had been saying to Herod, "It is not lawful for you to have your brother's wife."
19So Herodias nursed a grudge against
John and wanted to kill him. But she was
not able to, 20because Herod feared John
and protected him, knowing him to be a
righteous and holy man. When Herod
heard John, he was greatly puzzled[d]; yet
he liked to listen to him.
21Finally the opportune time came. On
his birthday Herod gave a banquet for his
high officials and military commanders
and the leading men of Galilee. 22When
the daughter of Herodias came in and
danced, she pleased Herod and his dinner
guests.
The king said to the girl, "Ask me for
anything you want, and I'll give it to you."
23And he promised her with an oath,
"Whatever you ask I will give you, up to
half my kingdom."
24She went out and said to her mother,
"What shall I ask for?"
"The head of John the Baptist," she answered.

[a] 3 Greek *Joses,* a variant of *Joseph* [b] 7 Greek *unclean* [c] 14 Some early manuscripts *He was saying* [d] 20 Some early manuscripts *he did many things*

[25]At once the girl hurried in to the king with the request: "I want you to give me right now the head of John the Baptist on a platter."

[26]The king was greatly distressed, but because of his oaths and his dinner guests, he did not want to refuse her. [27]So he immediately sent an executioner with orders to bring John's head. The man went, beheaded John in the prison, [28]and brought back his head on a platter. He presented it to the girl, and she gave it to her mother. [29]On hearing of this, John's disciples came and took his body and laid it in a tomb.

PRAYER: THE CHARACTER I WANT TO CULTIVATE

I WILL not be like those who do not make You their strength, O God, but trust in the abundance of their wealth and strengthen themselves in evil desires. (Psalm 52:7) . . . I have sought You with my whole heart, O Lord; do not let me stray from Your commands. (Psalm 119:10)

TAKE *a moment to ask the Lord for the grace to grow in godly character.*

YEAR 2 DAY 110

OT 2 Chronicles 26:1–23

Uzziah King of Judah

26 Then all the people of Judah took Uzziah,[a] who was sixteen years old, and made him king in place of his father Amaziah. [2]He was the one who rebuilt Elath and restored it to Judah after Amaziah rested with his fathers.

[3]Uzziah was sixteen years old when he became king, and he reigned in Jerusalem fifty-two years. His mother's name was Jecoliah; she was from Jerusalem. [4]He did what was right in the eyes of the LORD, just as his father Amaziah had done. [5]He sought God during the days of Zechariah, who instructed him in the fear[b] of God. As long as he sought the LORD, God gave him success.

[6]He went to war against the Philistines and broke down the walls of Gath, Jabneh and Ashdod. He then rebuilt towns near Ashdod and elsewhere among the Philistines. [7]God helped him against the Philistines and against the Arabs who lived in Gur Baal and against the Meunites. [8]The Ammonites brought tribute to Uzziah, and his fame spread as far as the border of Egypt, because he had become very powerful.

[9]Uzziah built towers in Jerusalem at the Corner Gate, at the Valley Gate and at the angle of the wall, and he fortified them. [10]He also built towers in the desert and dug many cisterns, because he had much livestock in the foothills and in the plain. He had people working his fields and vineyards in the hills and in the fertile lands, for he loved the soil.

[11]Uzziah had a well-trained army, ready to go out by divisions according to their numbers as mustered by Jeiel the secretary and Maaseiah the officer under the direction of Hananiah, one of the royal officials. [12]The total number of family leaders over the fighting men was 2,600. [13]Under their command was an army of 307,500 men trained for war, a powerful force to support the king against his enemies. [14]Uzziah provided shields, spears, helmets, coats of armor, bows and slingstones for the entire army. [15]In Jerusalem he made machines designed by skillful men for use on the towers and on the corner defenses to shoot arrows and hurl large stones. His fame spread far and wide, for he was greatly helped until he became powerful.

[16]But after Uzziah became powerful, his pride led to his downfall. He was unfaithful to the LORD his God, and entered the temple of the LORD to burn incense on the altar of incense. [17]Azariah the priest with eighty other courageous priests of the LORD followed him in. [18]They confronted him and said, "It is not right for

[a] *1* Also called *Azariah* [b] *5* Many Hebrew manuscripts, Septuagint and Syriac; other Hebrew manuscripts *vision*

you, Uzziah, to burn incense to the LORD. That is for the priests, the descendants of Aaron, who have been consecrated to burn incense. Leave the sanctuary, for you have been unfaithful; and you will not be honored by the LORD God."

19Uzziah, who had a censer in his hand ready to burn incense, became angry. While he was raging at the priests in their presence before the incense altar in the LORD's temple, leprosy[c] broke out on his forehead. 20When Azariah the chief priest and all the other priests looked at him, they saw that he had leprosy on his forehead, so they hurried him out. Indeed, he himself was eager to leave, because the LORD had afflicted him.

21King Uzziah had leprosy until the day he died. He lived in a separate house[d]—leprous, and excluded from the temple of the LORD. Jotham his son had charge of the palace and governed the people of the land.

22The other events of Uzziah's reign, from beginning to end, are recorded by the prophet Isaiah son of Amoz. 23Uzziah rested with his fathers and was buried near them in a field for burial that belonged to the kings, for people said, "He had leprosy." And Jotham his son succeeded him as king.

[c] *19* The Hebrew word was used for various diseases affecting the skin—not necessarily leprosy; also in verses 20, 21 and 23. [d] *21* Or *in a house where he was relieved of responsibilities*

PRAYER: AFFIRMATION

LORD, teach me humility: You save the humble but bring low those whose eyes are haughty. (Psalm 18:27) . . . When pride comes, then comes dishonor, but with humility comes wisdom. (Proverbs 11:2) . . . Pride breeds nothing but strife, but wisdom is found in those who take advice. (Proverbs 13:10)

PAUSE *to reflect on these Biblical affirmations.*

NT Mark 6:30–56

Jesus Feeds the Five Thousand

30The apostles gathered around Jesus and reported to him all they had done and taught. 31Then, because so many people were coming and going that they did not even have a chance to eat, he said to them, "Come with me by yourselves to a quiet place and get some rest."

32So they went away by themselves in a boat to a solitary place. 33But many who saw them leaving recognized them and ran on foot from all the towns and got there ahead of them. 34When Jesus landed and saw a large crowd, he had compassion on them, because they were like sheep without a shepherd. So he began teaching them many things.

35By this time it was late in the day, so his disciples came to him. "This is a remote place," they said, "and it's already very late. 36Send the people away so they can go to the surrounding countryside and villages and buy themselves something to eat."

37But he answered, "You give them something to eat."

They said to him, "That would take eight months of a man's wages[a]! Are we to go and spend that much on bread and give it to them to eat?"

38"How many loaves do you have?" he asked. "Go and see."

When they found out, they said, "Five—and two fish."

39Then Jesus directed them to have all the people sit down in groups on the green grass. 40So they sat down in groups of hundreds and fifties. 41Taking the five loaves and the two fish and looking up to heaven, he gave thanks and broke the loaves. Then he gave them to his disciples to set before the people. He also divided the two fish among them all. 42They all ate and were satisfied, 43and the disciples picked up twelve basketfuls of broken pieces of bread and fish. 44The number of the men who had eaten was five thousand.

[a] *37* Greek *take two hundred denarii*

Jesus Walks on the Water

[45]Immediately Jesus made his disciples
get into the boat and go on ahead of him
to Bethsaida, while he dismissed the
crowd. [46]After leaving them, he went up
on a mountainside to pray.

[47]When evening came, the boat was in
the middle of the lake, and he was alone
on land. [48]He saw the disciples straining
at the oars, because the wind was against
them. About the fourth watch of the night
he went out to them, walking on the lake.
He was about to pass by them, [49]but when
they saw him walking on the lake, they
thought he was a ghost. They cried out,
[50]because they all saw him and were terrified.

Immediately he spoke to them and
said, "Take courage! It is I. Don't be
afraid." [51]Then he climbed into the boat
with them, and the wind died down. They
were completely amazed, [52]for they had
not understood about the loaves; their
hearts were hardened.

[53]When they had crossed over, they landed at Gennesaret and anchored there. [54]As
soon as they got out of the boat, people
recognized Jesus. [55]They ran throughout
that whole region and carried the sick on
mats to wherever they heard he was. [56]And
wherever he went—into villages, towns or
countryside—they placed the sick in the
marketplaces. They begged him to let them
touch even the edge of his cloak, and all
who touched him were healed.

PRAYER: MY RELATIONSHIP TO OTHERS

IF I give another a cup of water in Your name, O Christ, I will by no means lose my reward. (Mark 9:41) . . .

I will not forget to show hospitality to strangers, for by so doing some have entertained angels without knowing it. (Hebrews 13:2)

***PAUSE** to review your relationships with others and to commit them to the Lord.*

OT **2 Chronicles 27:1–28:27** **YEAR 2 DAY 111**

Jotham King of Judah

27 Jotham was twenty-five years old when
he became king, and he reigned in
Jerusalem sixteen years. His mother's name
was Jerusha daughter of Zadok. [2]He did
what was right in the eyes of the LORD, just
as his father Uzziah had done, but unlike
him he did not enter the temple of the
LORD. The people, however, continued their
corrupt practices. [3]Jotham rebuilt the Upper Gate of the temple of the LORD and did
extensive work on the wall at the hill of
Ophel. [4]He built towns in the Judean hills
and forts and towers in the wooded areas.

[5]Jotham made war on the king of the
Ammonites and conquered them. That
year the Ammonites paid him a hundred
talents[a] of silver, ten thousand cors[b] of
wheat and ten thousand cors of barley.
The Ammonites brought him the same
amount also in the second and third years.

[6]Jotham grew powerful because he
walked steadfastly before the LORD his
God.

[7]The other events in Jotham's reign, including all his wars and the other things
he did, are written in the book of the
kings of Israel and Judah. [8]He was twenty-five years old when he became king,
and he reigned in Jerusalem sixteen years.
[9]Jotham rested with his fathers and was
buried in the City of David. And Ahaz his
son succeeded him as king.

Ahaz King of Judah

28 Ahaz was twenty years old when he
became king, and he reigned in Jerusalem sixteen years. Unlike David his father, he did not do what was right in the
eyes of the LORD. [2]He walked in the ways
of the kings of Israel and also made cast

[a] 5 That is, about 3 3/4 tons (about 3.4 metric tons)
[b] 5 That is, probably about 62,000 bushels (about 2,200 kiloliters)

idols for worshiping the Baals. 3He
burned sacrifices in the Valley of Ben Hinnom and sacrificed his sons in the fire,
following the detestable ways of the nations the LORD had driven out before the
Israelites. 4He offered sacrifices and
burned incense at the high places, on the
hilltops and under every spreading tree.
5Therefore the LORD his God handed
him over to the king of Aram. The Arameans defeated him and took many of his
people as prisoners and brought them to
Damascus.
He was also given into the hands of the
king of Israel, who inflicted heavy casualties on him. 6In one day Pekah son of
Remaliah killed a hundred and twenty
thousand soldiers in Judah—because Judah had forsaken the LORD, the God of
their fathers. 7Zicri, an Ephraimite warrior,
killed Maaseiah the king's son, Azrikam
the officer in charge of the palace, and Elkanah, second to the king. 8The Israelites
took captive from their kinsmen two hundred thousand wives, sons and daughters.
They also took a great deal of plunder,
which they carried back to Samaria.
9But a prophet of the LORD named
Oded was there, and he went out to meet
the army when it returned to Samaria. He
said to them, "Because the LORD, the God
of your fathers, was angry with Judah, he
gave them into your hand. But you have
slaughtered them in a rage that reaches to
heaven. 10And now you intend to make
the men and women of Judah and Jerusalem your slaves. But aren't you also
guilty of sins against the LORD your God?
11Now listen to me! Send back your fellow
countrymen you have taken as prisoners,
for the LORD's fierce anger rests on you."
12Then some of the leaders in Ephraim—Azariah son of Jehohanan, Berekiah
son of Meshillemoth, Jehizkiah son of
Shallum, and Amasa son of Hadlai—confronted those who were arriving from the
war. 13"You must not bring those prisoners here," they said, "or we will be guilty
before the LORD. Do you intend to add to
our sin and guilt? For our guilt is already
great, and his fierce anger rests on Israel."
14So the soldiers gave up the prisoners
and plunder in the presence of the officials and all the assembly. 15The men designated by name took the prisoners, and
from the plunder they clothed all who
were naked. They provided them with
clothes and sandals, food and drink, and
healing balm. All those who were weak
they put on donkeys. So they took them
back to their fellow countrymen at Jericho, the City of Palms, and returned to
Samaria.
16At that time King Ahaz sent to the
king[c] of Assyria for help. 17The Edomites
had again come and attacked Judah and
carried away prisoners, 18while the Philistines had raided towns in the foothills
and in the Negev of Judah. They captured
and occupied Beth Shemesh, Aijalon and
Gederoth, as well as Soco, Timnah and
Gimzo, with their surrounding villages.
19The LORD had humbled Judah because
of Ahaz king of Israel,[d] for he had promoted wickedness in Judah and had been
most unfaithful to the LORD. 20Tiglath-Pi-
leser[e] king of Assyria came to him, but he
gave him trouble instead of help. 21Ahaz
took some of the things from the temple
of the LORD and from the royal palace and
from the princes and presented them to
the king of Assyria, but that did not help
him.
22In his time of trouble King Ahaz became even more unfaithful to the LORD.
23He offered sacrifices to the gods of Damascus, who had defeated him; for he
thought, "Since the gods of the kings of
Aram have helped them, I will sacrifice
to them so they will help me." But they
were his downfall and the downfall of all
Israel.
24Ahaz gathered together the furnishings from the temple of God and took
them away.[f] He shut the doors of the
LORD's temple and set up altars at every
street corner in Jerusalem. 25In every town
in Judah he built high places to burn sacrifices to other gods and provoked the
LORD, the God of his fathers, to anger.
26The other events of his reign and all
his ways, from beginning to end, are written in the book of the kings of Judah and
Israel. 27Ahaz rested with his fathers and
was buried in the city of Jerusalem, but he
was not placed in the tombs of the kings
of Israel. And Hezekiah his son succeeded him as king.

[c] *16* One Hebrew manuscript, Septuagint and Vulgate (see also 2 Kings 16:7); most Hebrew manuscripts *kings* [d] *19* That is, Judah, as frequently in 2 Chronicles [e] *20* Hebrew *Tilgath-Pilneser,* a variant of *Tiglath-Pileser* [f] *24* Or *and cut them up*

PRAYER: THANKSGIVING

HOW great is Your goodness, which You have stored up for those who fear You, which You have prepared for those who take refuge in You in the sight of others! (Psalm 31:19) . . . Surely You are my helper, O God; You sustain my soul. (Psalm 54:4)

PAUSE *to offer your own expressions of thanksgiving.*

NT Mark 7:1-23

Clean and Unclean

7 The Pharisees and some of the teachers of the law who had come from Jerusalem gathered around Jesus and [2]saw some of his disciples eating food with hands that were "unclean," that is, unwashed. [3](The Pharisees and all the Jews do not eat unless they give their hands a ceremonial washing, holding to the tradition of the elders. [4]When they come from the marketplace they do not eat unless they wash. And they observe many other traditions, such as the washing of cups, pitchers and kettles.[a])

[5]So the Pharisees and teachers of the law asked Jesus, "Why don't your disciples live according to the tradition of the elders instead of eating their food with 'unclean' hands?"

[6]He replied, "Isaiah was right when he prophesied about you hypocrites; as it is written:

" 'These people honor me with their lips,
but their hearts are far from me.
[7]They worship me in vain;
their teachings are but rules taught by men.'[b]

[8]You have let go of the commands of God and are holding on to the traditions of men."

[9]And he said to them: "You have a fine way of setting aside the commands of God in order to observe[c] your own traditions! [10]For Moses said, 'Honor your father and your mother,'[d] and, 'Anyone who curses his father or mother must be put to death.'[e] [11]But you say that if a man says to his father or mother: 'Whatever help you might otherwise have received from me is Corban' (that is, a gift devoted to God), [12]then you no longer let him do anything for his father or mother. [13]Thus you nullify the word of God by your tradition that you have handed down. And you do many things like that."

[14]Again Jesus called the crowd to him and said, "Listen to me, everyone, and understand this. [15]Nothing outside a man can make him 'unclean' by going into him. Rather, it is what comes out of a man that makes him 'unclean.'[f]"

[17]After he had left the crowd and entered the house, his disciples asked him about this parable. [18]"Are you so dull?" he asked. "Don't you see that nothing that enters a man from the outside can make him 'unclean'? [19]For it doesn't go into his heart but into his stomach, and then out of his body." (In saying this, Jesus declared all foods "clean.")

[20]He went on: "What comes out of a man is what makes him 'unclean.' [21]For from within, out of men's hearts, come evil thoughts, sexual immorality, theft, murder, adultery, [22]greed, malice, deceit, lewdness, envy, slander, arrogance and folly. [23]All these evils come from inside and make a man 'unclean.' "

[a] 4 Some early manuscripts *pitchers, kettles and dining couches* [b] 6,7 Isaiah 29:13 [c] 9 Some manuscripts *set up* [d] 10 Exodus 20:12; Deut. 5:16 [e] 10 Exodus 21:17; Lev. 20:9 [f] 15 Some early manuscripts *'unclean.'* [16]*If anyone has ears to hear, let him hear.*

PRAYER: THE ATTRIBUTES OF GOD

I KNOW that whatever You do, O God, will remain forever; nothing can be added to it and nothing taken from it. You do it so that people will revere You. (Ecclesiastes 3:14) . . . You, O God, will bring every work into judgment, including every hidden thing, whether it is good or evil. (Ecclesiastes 12:14)

***PAUSE** to reflect on these affirmations about the person, powers and perfection of God.*

YEAR 2
DAY 112

OT Psalm 93

Psalm 93

1The LORD reigns, he is robed in
majesty;
the LORD is robed in majesty
and is armed with strength.
The world is firmly established;
it cannot be moved.
2Your throne was established long ago;
you are from all eternity.

3The seas have lifted up, O LORD,
the seas have lifted up their voice;
the seas have lifted up their
pounding waves.
4Mightier than the thunder of the great
waters,
mightier than the breakers of the
sea—
the LORD on high is mighty.

5Your statutes stand firm;
holiness adorns your house
for endless days, O LORD.

PRAYER: ADORATION

WE see you, Jesus—the One who was made a little lower than the angels—now crowned with glory and honor because You suffered death, so that by the grace of God You might taste death for everyone. In bringing many of us to glory, it was fitting that God, for whom and through whom everything exists, should make You—the author of our salvation—perfect through suffering. (Hebrews 2:9–10)

***PAUSE** to express your thoughts of praise and worship.*

NT Mark 7:24–8:13

The Faith of a Syrophoenician Woman

24Jesus left that place and went to the
vicinity of Tyre.[a] He entered a house and
did not want anyone to know it; yet he
could not keep his presence secret. 25In
fact, as soon as she heard about him, a
woman whose little daughter was possessed by an evil[b] spirit came and fell at
his feet. 26The woman was a Greek, born
in Syrian Phoenicia. She begged Jesus to
drive the demon out of her daughter.
27"First let the children eat all they
want," he told her, "for it is not right to
take the children's bread and toss it to
their dogs."
28"Yes, Lord," she replied, "but even the
dogs under the table eat the children's
crumbs."
29Then he told her, "For such a reply,
you may go; the demon has left your
daughter."
30She went home and found her child
lying on the bed, and the demon gone.

[a] 24 Many early manuscripts *Tyre and Sidon*
[b] 25 Greek *unclean*

The Healing of a Deaf and Mute Man

31 Then Jesus left the vicinity of Tyre and went through Sidon, down to the Sea of Galilee and into the region of the Decapolis.[c] 32 There some people brought to him a man who was deaf and could hardly talk, and they begged him to place his hand on the man.

33 After he took him aside, away from the crowd, Jesus put his fingers into the man's ears. Then he spit and touched the man's tongue. 34 He looked up to heaven and with a deep sigh said to him, *"Ephphatha!"* (which means, "Be opened!"). 35 At this, the man's ears were opened, his tongue was loosened and he began to speak plainly.

36 Jesus commanded them not to tell anyone. But the more he did so, the more they kept talking about it. 37 People were overwhelmed with amazement. "He has done everything well," they said. "He even makes the deaf hear and the mute speak."

Jesus Feeds the Four Thousand

8 During those days another large crowd gathered. Since they had nothing to eat, Jesus called his disciples to him and said, 2 "I have compassion for these people; they have already been with me three days and have nothing to eat. 3 If I send them home hungry, they will collapse on the way, because some of them have come a long distance."

4 His disciples answered, "But where in this remote place can anyone get enough bread to feed them?"

5 "How many loaves do you have?" Jesus asked.

"Seven," they replied.

6 He told the crowd to sit down on the ground. When he had taken the seven loaves and given thanks, he broke them and gave them to his disciples to set before the people, and they did so. 7 They had a few small fish as well; he gave thanks for them also and told the disciples to distribute them. 8 The people ate and were satisfied. Afterward the disciples picked up seven basketfuls of broken pieces that were left over. 9 About four thousand men were present. And having sent them away, 10 he got into the boat with his disciples and went to the region of Dalmanutha.

11 The Pharisees came and began to question Jesus. To test him, they asked him for a sign from heaven. 12 He sighed deeply and said, "Why does this generation ask for a miraculous sign? I tell you the truth, no sign will be given to it." 13 Then he left them, got back into the boat and crossed to the other side.

[c] *31* That is, the Ten Cities

PRAYER: THE WORKS OF GOD

WHERE is the wise person? Where is the scholar? Where is the disputer of this age? O God, have You not made foolish the wisdom of the world? But to those whom You have called, both Jews and Greeks, Christ is Your power and Your wisdom. (1 Corinthians 1:20, 24) . . . The god of this age has blinded the minds of unbelievers, so that they cannot see the light of the gospel of Your glory, O Christ, who are the image of God. (2 Corinthians 4:4)

***TAKE** a moment to consider the greatness of God's wonderful works.*

YEAR 2 DAY 113

OT 2 Chronicles 29:1-36

Hezekiah Purifies the Temple

29 Hezekiah was twenty-five years old when he became king, and he reigned in Jerusalem twenty-nine years. His mother's name was Abijah daughter of Zechariah. 2 He did what was right in the eyes of the LORD, just as his father David had done.

3 In the first month of the first year of
his reign, he opened the doors of the temple of the LORD and repaired them. 4 He
brought in the priests and the Levites, assembled them in the square on the east
side 5 and said: "Listen to me, Levites!
Consecrate yourselves now and consecrate
the temple of the LORD, the God of your
fathers. Remove all defilement from the
sanctuary. 6 Our fathers were unfaithful;
they did evil in the eyes of the LORD our
God and forsook him. They turned their
faces away from the LORD's dwelling place
and turned their backs on him. 7 They also
shut the doors of the portico and put out
the lamps. They did not burn incense or
present any burnt offerings at the sanctuary to the God of Israel. 8 Therefore, the
anger of the LORD has fallen on Judah and
Jerusalem; he has made them an object of
dread and horror and scorn, as you can
see with your own eyes. 9 This is why our
fathers have fallen by the sword and why
our sons and daughters and our wives are
in captivity. 10 Now I intend to make a covenant with the LORD, the God of Israel, so
that his fierce anger will turn away from
us. 11 My sons, do not be negligent now,
for the LORD has chosen you to stand before him and serve him, to minister before him and to burn incense."

12 Then these Levites set to work:
from the Kohathites,
Mahath son of Amasai and Joel son of Azariah;
from the Merarites,
Kish son of Abdi and Azariah son of Jehallelel;
from the Gershonites,
Joah son of Zimmah and Eden son of Joah;
13 from the descendants of Elizaphan,
Shimri and Jeiel;
from the descendants of Asaph,
Zechariah and Mattaniah;
14 from the descendants of Heman,
Jehiel and Shimei;
from the descendants of Jeduthun,
Shemaiah and Uzziel.

15 When they had assembled their
brothers and consecrated themselves, they
went in to purify the temple of the LORD,
as the king had ordered, following the
word of the LORD. 16 The priests went into
the sanctuary of the LORD to purify it.
They brought out to the courtyard of the
LORD's temple everything unclean that
they found in the temple of the LORD. The
Levites took it and carried it out to the
Kidron Valley. 17 They began the consecration on the first day of the first month,
and by the eighth day of the month they
reached the portico of the LORD. For eight
more days they consecrated the temple of
the LORD itself, finishing on the sixteenth
day of the first month.

18 Then they went in to King Hezekiah
and reported: "We have purified the entire
temple of the LORD, the altar of burnt offering with all its utensils, and the table
for setting out the consecrated bread, with
all its articles. 19 We have prepared and
consecrated all the articles that King Ahaz
removed in his unfaithfulness while he
was king. They are now in front of the
LORD's altar."

20 Early the next morning King Hezekiah gathered the city officials together and
went up to the temple of the LORD. 21 They
brought seven bulls, seven rams, seven
male lambs and seven male goats as a sin
offering for the kingdom, for the sanctuary and for Judah. The king commanded
the priests, the descendants of Aaron, to
offer these on the altar of the LORD. 22 So
they slaughtered the bulls, and the priests
took the blood and sprinkled it on the altar; next they slaughtered the rams and
sprinkled their blood on the altar; then
they slaughtered the lambs and sprinkled
their blood on the altar. 23 The goats for
the sin offering were brought before the
king and the assembly, and they laid their
hands on them. 24 The priests then slaughtered the goats and presented their blood
on the altar for a sin offering to atone for
all Israel, because the king had ordered
the burnt offering and the sin offering for
all Israel.

25 He stationed the Levites in the temple
of the LORD with cymbals, harps and lyres
in the way prescribed by David and Gad
the king's seer and Nathan the prophet;
this was commanded by the LORD through
his prophets. 26 So the Levites stood ready
with David's instruments, and the priests
with their trumpets.

27 Hezekiah gave the order to sacrifice
the burnt offering on the altar. As the offering began, singing to the LORD began
also, accompanied by trumpets and the
instruments of David king of Israel. 28 The
whole assembly bowed in worship, while
the singers sang and the trumpeters

played. All this continued until the sacrifice of the burnt offering was completed.
[29]When the offerings were finished, the
king and everyone present with him knelt
down and worshiped. [30]King Hezekiah
and his officials ordered the Levites to
praise the LORD with the words of David
and of Asaph the seer. So they sang praises
with gladness and bowed their heads and
worshiped.
[31]Then Hezekiah said, "You have now
dedicated yourselves to the LORD. Come
and bring sacrifices and thank offerings to
the temple of the LORD." So the assembly
brought sacrifices and thank offerings,
and all whose hearts were willing brought
burnt offerings.
[32]The number of burnt offerings the assembly brought was seventy bulls, a hundred rams and two hundred male
lambs—all of them for burnt offerings to
the LORD. [33]The animals consecrated as
sacrifices amounted to six hundred bulls
and three thousand sheep and goats.
[34]The priests, however, were too few to
skin all the burnt offerings; so their kinsmen the Levites helped them until the
task was finished and until other priests
had been consecrated, for the Levites had
been more conscientious in consecrating
themselves than the priests had been.
[35]There were burnt offerings in abundance, together with the fat of the fellowship offerings[a] and the drink offerings
that accompanied the burnt offerings.
So the service of the temple of the LORD
was reestablished. [36]Hezekiah and all the
people rejoiced at what God had brought
about for his people, because it was done
so quickly.

[a] 35 Traditionally *peace offerings*

PRAYER: CONFESSION

I WILL endure discipline, for You are treating me as Your child. For what child is not disciplined by its father? If I am without discipline, of which all have become partakers, then I am an illegitimate child and not a true child. Moreover, we have all had human fathers who disciplined us, and we respected them; how much more should I be disciplined by You, the Father of my spirit, and live? (Hebrews 12:7–9)

***ASK** the Spirit to search your heart and reveal any areas of unconfessed sin. Acknowledge these to the Lord and thank Him for His forgiveness.*

NT Mark 8:14–38

The Yeast of the Pharisees and Herod

[14]The disciples had forgotten to bring
bread, except for one loaf they had with
them in the boat. [15]"Be careful," Jesus
warned them. "Watch out for the yeast of
the Pharisees and that of Herod."
[16]They discussed this with one another
and said, "It is because we have no bread."
[17]Aware of their discussion, Jesus asked
them: "Why are you talking about having
no bread? Do you still not see or understand? Are your hearts hardened? [18]Do
you have eyes but fail to see, and ears but
fail to hear? And don't you remember?
[19]When I broke the five loaves for the five
thousand, how many basketfuls of pieces
did you pick up?"
"Twelve," they replied.
[20]"And when I broke the seven loaves
for the four thousand, how many basketfuls of pieces did you pick up?"
They answered, "Seven."
[21]He said to them, "Do you still not understand?"

The Healing of a Blind Man at Bethsaida

[22]They came to Bethsaida, and some
people brought a blind man and begged
Jesus to touch him. [23]He took the blind
man by the hand and led him outside the
village. When he had spit on the man's
eyes and put his hands on him, Jesus
asked, "Do you see anything?"
[24]He looked up and said, "I see people;
they look like trees walking around."
[25]Once more Jesus put his hands on the
man's eyes. Then his eyes were opened,

his sight was restored, and he saw everything clearly. 26Jesus sent him home, saying, "Don't go into the village.[a]"

Peter's Confession of Christ

27Jesus and his disciples went on to the villages around Caesarea Philippi. On the way he asked them, "Who do people say I am?"

28They replied, "Some say John the Baptist; others say Elijah; and still others, one of the prophets."

29"But what about you?" he asked. "Who do you say I am?"

Peter answered, "You are the Christ.[b]"

30Jesus warned them not to tell anyone about him.

Jesus Predicts His Death

31He then began to teach them that the Son of Man must suffer many things and be rejected by the elders, chief priests and teachers of the law, and that he must be killed and after three days rise again. 32He spoke plainly about this, and Peter took him aside and began to rebuke him.

33But when Jesus turned and looked at his disciples, he rebuked Peter. "Get behind me, Satan!" he said. "You do not have in mind the things of God, but the things of men."

34Then he called the crowd to him along with his disciples and said: "If anyone would come after me, he must deny himself and take up his cross and follow me. 35For whoever wants to save his life[c] will lose it, but whoever loses his life for me and for the gospel will save it. 36What good is it for a man to gain the whole world, yet forfeit his soul? 37Or what can a man give in exchange for his soul? 38If anyone is ashamed of me and my words in this adulterous and sinful generation, the Son of Man will be ashamed of him when he comes in his Father's glory with the holy angels."

[a] 26 Some manuscripts *Don't go and tell anyone in the village* [b] 29 Or *Messiah.* "The Christ" (Greek) and "the Messiah" (Hebrew) both mean "the Anointed One." [c] 35 The Greek word means either *life* or *soul;* also in verse 36.

PRAYER: MY RELATIONSHIP TO GOD

MANY are the sorrows of the wicked, but loving-kindness shall surround the one who trusts in You, O Lord. (Psalm 32:10) . . . Your eye, O Lord, is on those who fear You, on those whose hope is in Your unfailing love. (Psalm 33:18)

***PAUSE** to thank God for the relationship that you enjoy with Him in Jesus Christ.*

OT 2 Chronicles 30:1–27 YEAR 2 DAY 114

Hezekiah Celebrates the Passover

30 Hezekiah sent word to all Israel and Judah and also wrote letters to Ephraim and Manasseh, inviting them to come to the temple of the LORD in Jerusalem and celebrate the Passover to the LORD, the God of Israel. 2The king and his officials and the whole assembly in Jerusalem decided to celebrate the Passover in the second month. 3They had not been able to celebrate it at the regular time because not enough priests had consecrated themselves and the people had not assembled in Jerusalem. 4The plan seemed right both to the king and to the whole assembly. 5They decided to send a proclamation throughout Israel, from Beersheba to Dan, calling the people to come to Jerusalem and celebrate the Passover to the LORD, the God of Israel. It had not been celebrated in large numbers according to what was written.

6At the king's command, couriers went throughout Israel and Judah with letters from the king and from his officials, which read:

"People of Israel, return to the

LORD, the God of Abraham, Isaac and
Israel, that he may return to you who
are left, who have escaped from the
hand of the kings of Assyria. [7]Do not
be like your fathers and brothers,
who were unfaithful to the LORD, the
God of their fathers, so that he made
them an object of horror, as you see.
[8]Do not be stiff-necked, as your fathers were; submit to the LORD. Come
to the sanctuary, which he has consecrated forever. Serve the LORD your
God, so that his fierce anger will turn
away from you. [9]If you return to the
LORD, then your brothers and your
children will be shown compassion
by their captors and will come back
to this land, for the LORD your God is
gracious and compassionate. He will
not turn his face from you if you return to him."

[10]The couriers went from town to town
in Ephraim and Manasseh, as far as Zebulun, but the people scorned and ridiculed
them. [11]Nevertheless, some men of Asher,
Manasseh and Zebulun humbled themselves and went to Jerusalem. [12]Also in Judah the hand of God was on the people to
give them unity of mind to carry out what
the king and his officials had ordered, following the word of the LORD.

[13]A very large crowd of people assembled in Jerusalem to celebrate the Feast of
Unleavened Bread in the second month.
[14]They removed the altars in Jerusalem
and cleared away the incense altars and
threw them into the Kidron Valley.

[15]They slaughtered the Passover lamb
on the fourteenth day of the second
month. The priests and the Levites were
ashamed and consecrated themselves and
brought burnt offerings to the temple of
the LORD. [16]Then they took up their regular positions as prescribed in the Law of
Moses the man of God. The priests sprinkled the blood handed to them by the Levites. [17]Since many in the crowd had not
consecrated themselves, the Levites had to
kill the Passover lambs for all those who
were not ceremonially clean and could
not consecrate ⌞their lambs⌟ to the LORD.
[18]Although most of the many people who
came from Ephraim, Manasseh, Issachar
and Zebulun had not purified themselves,
yet they ate the Passover, contrary to what
was written. But Hezekiah prayed for
them, saying, "May the LORD, who is
good, pardon everyone [19]who sets his
heart on seeking God—the LORD, the God
of his fathers—even if he is not clean according to the rules of the sanctuary."
[20]And the LORD heard Hezekiah and
healed the people.

[21]The Israelites who were present in
Jerusalem celebrated the Feast of Unleavened Bread for seven days with great rejoicing, while the Levites and priests sang
to the LORD every day, accompanied by
the LORD's instruments of praise.[a]

[22]Hezekiah spoke encouragingly to all
the Levites, who showed good understanding of the service of the LORD. For
the seven days they ate their assigned portion and offered fellowship offerings[b] and
praised the LORD, the God of their fathers.

[23]The whole assembly then agreed to
celebrate the festival seven more days; so
for another seven days they celebrated
joyfully. [24]Hezekiah king of Judah provided a thousand bulls and seven thousand
sheep and goats for the assembly, and the
officials provided them with a thousand
bulls and ten thousand sheep and goats.
A great number of priests consecrated
themselves. [25]The entire assembly of Judah rejoiced, along with the priests and
Levites and all who had assembled from
Israel, including the aliens who had come
from Israel and those who lived in Judah.
[26]There was great joy in Jerusalem, for
since the days of Solomon son of David
king of Israel there had been nothing like
this in Jerusalem. [27]The priests and the Levites stood to bless the people, and God
heard them, for their prayer reached heav-
en, his holy dwelling place.

[a] 21 Or *priests praised the LORD every day with resounding instruments belonging to the LORD*
[b] 22 Traditionally *peace offerings*

PRAYER: RENEWAL

MAY I not receive Your grace, O God, in vain. For You have said, "In the acceptable time I heard you, and in the day of salvation I helped you." Now is the time of Your favor; now is the day

of salvation. (2 Corinthians 6:1–2) . . . Lord, may You establish my heart as blameless and holy in Your presence at the coming of our Lord Jesus with all His saints. (1 Thessalonians 3:13)

***PAUSE** to add your own prayers for personal renewal.*

NT Mark 9:1–32

9 And he said to them, "I tell you the
truth, some who are standing here will
not taste death before they see the kingdom of God come with power."

The Transfiguration

2 After six days Jesus took Peter, James
and John with him and led them up a
high mountain, where they were all alone.
There he was transfigured before them.
3 His clothes became dazzling white,
whiter than anyone in the world could
bleach them. 4 And there appeared before
them Elijah and Moses, who were talking
with Jesus.
5 Peter said to Jesus, "Rabbi, it is good
for us to be here. Let us put up three shelters—one for you, one for Moses and one
for Elijah." 6 (He did not know what to
say, they were so frightened.)
7 Then a cloud appeared and enveloped
them, and a voice came from the cloud:
"This is my Son, whom I love. Listen to
him!"
8 Suddenly, when they looked around,
they no longer saw anyone with them except Jesus.
9 As they were coming down the mountain, Jesus gave them orders not to tell
anyone what they had seen until the Son
of Man had risen from the dead. 10 They
kept the matter to themselves, discussing
what "rising from the dead" meant.
11 And they asked him, "Why do the
teachers of the law say that Elijah must
come first?"
12 Jesus replied, "To be sure, Elijah does
come first, and restores all things. Why
then is it written that the Son of Man
must suffer much and be rejected? 13 But I
tell you, Elijah has come, and they have
done to him everything they wished, just
as it is written about him."

The Healing of a Boy With an Evil Spirit

14 When they came to the other disciples, they saw a large crowd around them
and the teachers of the law arguing with
them. 15 As soon as all the people saw
Jesus, they were overwhelmed with wonder and ran to greet him.
16 "What are you arguing with them
about?" he asked.
17 A man in the crowd answered,
"Teacher, I brought you my son, who is
possessed by a spirit that has robbed him
of speech. 18 Whenever it seizes him, it
throws him to the ground. He foams at
the mouth, gnashes his teeth and becomes rigid. I asked your disciples to drive
out the spirit, but they could not."
19 "O unbelieving generation," Jesus
replied, "how long shall I stay with you?
How long shall I put up with you? Bring
the boy to me."
20 So they brought him. When the spirit
saw Jesus, it immediately threw the boy
into a convulsion. He fell to the ground
and rolled around, foaming at the mouth.
21 Jesus asked the boy's father, "How
long has he been like this?"
"From childhood," he answered. 22 "It
has often thrown him into fire or water to
kill him. But if you can do anything, take
pity on us and help us."
23 " 'If you can'?" said Jesus. "Everything
is possible for him who believes."
24 Immediately the boy's father exclaimed, "I do believe; help me overcome
my unbelief!"
25 When Jesus saw that a crowd was running to the scene, he rebuked the evil[a]
spirit. "You deaf and mute spirit," he said,
"I command you, come out of him and
never enter him again."
26 The spirit shrieked, convulsed him violently and came out. The boy looked so
much like a corpse that many said, "He's
dead." 27 But Jesus took him by the hand
and lifted him to his feet, and he
stood up.
28 After Jesus had gone indoors, his disciples asked him privately, "Why couldn't
we drive it out?"

[a] 25 Greek *unclean*

29He replied, "This kind can come out
only by prayer.[b]"
30They left that place and passed
through Galilee. Jesus did not want anyone to know where they were, 31because he
was teaching his disciples. He said to
them, "The Son of Man is going to be betrayed into the hands of men. They will
kill him, and after three days he will rise."
32But they did not understand what he
meant and were afraid to ask him about it.

[b] 29 Some manuscripts *prayer and fasting*

PRAYER: THE CHARACTER I WANT TO CULTIVATE

BLESSED am I if I fear You, O God, but if I harden my heart I will fall into trouble. (Proverbs 28:14) . . . Who among us fears You, Lord, and obeys the word of Your Servant? Let those who walk in darkness and have no light trust in Your name, O Lord, and rely upon You, their God. (Isaiah 50:10)

***TAKE** a moment to ask the Lord for the grace to grow in godly character.*

OT 2 Chronicles 31:1–21

YEAR 2
DAY 115

31 When all this had ended, the Israelites
who were there went out to the towns
of Judah, smashed the sacred stones and
cut down the Asherah poles. They destroyed the high places and the altars
throughout Judah and Benjamin and in
Ephraim and Manasseh. After they had
destroyed all of them, the Israelites returned to their own towns and to their
own property.

Contributions for Worship

2Hezekiah assigned the priests and Levites to divisions—each of them according to their duties as priests or Levites—
to offer burnt offerings and fellowship
offerings,[a] to minister, to give thanks and
to sing praises at the gates of the LORD's
dwelling. 3The king contributed from his
own possessions for the morning and
evening burnt offerings and for the burnt
offerings on the Sabbaths, New Moons
and appointed feasts as written in the Law
of the LORD. 4He ordered the people living in Jerusalem to give the portion due
the priests and Levites so they could devote themselves to the Law of the LORD.
5As soon as the order went out, the Israelites generously gave the firstfruits of
their grain, new wine, oil and honey and
all that the fields produced. They brought
a great amount, a tithe of everything. 6The
men of Israel and Judah who lived in the
towns of Judah also brought a tithe of
their herds and flocks and a tithe of the
holy things dedicated to the LORD their
God, and they piled them in heaps. 7They
began doing this in the third month and
finished in the seventh month. 8When
Hezekiah and his officials came and saw
the heaps, they praised the LORD and
blessed his people Israel.
9Hezekiah asked the priests and Levites
about the heaps; 10and Azariah the chief
priest, from the family of Zadok, answered, "Since the people began to bring
their contributions to the temple of the
LORD, we have had enough to eat and
plenty to spare, because the LORD has
blessed his people, and this great amount
is left over."
11Hezekiah gave orders to prepare storerooms in the temple of the LORD, and this
was done. 12Then they faithfully brought
in the contributions, tithes and dedicated
gifts. Conaniah, a Levite, was in charge of
these things, and his brother Shimei was
next in rank. 13Jehiel, Azaziah, Nahath,
Asahel, Jerimoth, Jozabad, Eliel, Ismaki-
ah, Mahath and Benaiah were supervisors
under Conaniah and Shimei his brother,
by appointment of King Hezekiah and Azariah the official in charge of the temple
of God.
14Kore son of Imnah the Levite, keeper

[a] 2 Traditionally *peace offerings*

of the East Gate, was in charge of the freewill offerings given to God, distributing the contributions made to the LORD and also the consecrated gifts. [15]Eden, Miniamin, Jeshua, Shemaiah, Amariah and Shecaniah assisted him faithfully in the towns of the priests, distributing to their fellow priests according to their divisions, old and young alike.

[16]In addition, they distributed to the males three years old or more whose names were in the genealogical records—all who would enter the temple of the LORD to perform the daily duties of their various tasks, according to their responsibilities and their divisions. [17]And they distributed to the priests enrolled by their families in the genealogical records and likewise to the Levites twenty years old or more, according to their responsibilities and their divisions. [18]They included all the little ones, the wives, and the sons and daughters of the whole community listed in these genealogical records. For they were faithful in consecrating themselves.

[19]As for the priests, the descendants of Aaron, who lived on the farm lands around their towns or in any other towns, men were designated by name to distribute portions to every male among them and to all who were recorded in the genealogies of the Levites.

[20]This is what Hezekiah did throughout Judah, doing what was good and right and faithful before the LORD his God. [21]In everything that he undertook in the service of God's temple and in obedience to the law and the commands, he sought his God and worked wholeheartedly. And so he prospered.

PRAYER: PETITION

MAY I obey those who are in authority over me in all things, not with external service as one who pleases people, but with sincerity of heart, fearing You, Lord. Whatever I do, may I work at it with all my heart, as working for You and not for people, knowing that I will receive the reward of the inheritance from You. It is the Lord Christ I am serving. (Colossians 3:22–24)

__PAUSE__ here to offer prayers of petition regarding your family and your ministry. Ask for help and guidance in sharing Jesus with others and helping others grow in Him. Ask for guidance in your vocation and your avocations. Offer prayers of petition regarding your activities for this day and any special concerns you may have.

NT Mark 9:33–10:12

Who Is the Greatest?

[33]They came to Capernaum. When he was in the house, he asked them, "What were you arguing about on the road?" [34]But they kept quiet because on the way they had argued about who was the greatest.

[35]Sitting down, Jesus called the Twelve and said, "If anyone wants to be first, he must be the very last, and the servant of all."

[36]He took a little child and had him stand among them. Taking him in his arms, he said to them, [37]"Whoever welcomes one of these little children in my name welcomes me; and whoever welcomes me does not welcome me but the one who sent me."

Whoever Is Not Against Us Is for Us

[38]"Teacher," said John, "we saw a man driving out demons in your name and we told him to stop, because he was not one of us."

[39]"Do not stop him," Jesus said. "No one who does a miracle in my name can in the next moment say anything bad about me, [40]for whoever is not against us is for us. [41]I tell you the truth, anyone who gives you a cup of water in my name because you belong to Christ will certainly not lose his reward.

Causing to Sin

[42]"And if anyone causes one of these lit-

tle ones who believe in me to sin, it would
be better for him to be thrown into the
sea with a large millstone tied around his
neck. 43If your hand causes you to sin, cut
it off. It is better for you to enter life
maimed than with two hands to go into
hell, where the fire never goes out.[a] 45And
if your foot causes you to sin, cut it off. It
is better for you to enter life crippled than
to have two feet and be thrown into hell.[b]
47And if your eye causes you to sin, pluck
it out. It is better for you to enter the kingdom of God with one eye than to have
two eyes and be thrown into hell, 48where

" 'their worm does not die,
  and the fire is not quenched.'[c]

49Everyone will be salted with fire.
50"Salt is good, but if it loses its saltiness, how can you make it salty again?
Have salt in yourselves, and be at peace
with each other."

Divorce

10 Jesus then left that place and went
into the region of Judea and across
the Jordan. Again crowds of people came
to him, and as was his custom, he taught
them.
2Some Pharisees came and tested him
by asking, "Is it lawful for a man to divorce his wife?"
3"What did Moses command you?" he
replied.
4They said, "Moses permitted a man to
write a certificate of divorce and send her
away."
5"It was because your hearts were hard
that Moses wrote you this law," Jesus
replied. 6"But at the beginning of creation
God 'made them male and female.'[d] 7'For
this reason a man will leave his father and
mother and be united to his wife,[e] 8and
the two will become one flesh.'[f] So they
are no longer two, but one. 9Therefore
what God has joined together, let man
not separate."
10When they were in the house again,
the disciples asked Jesus about this. 11He
answered, "Anyone who divorces his wife
and marries another woman commits
adultery against her. 12And if she divorces
her husband and marries another man,
she commits adultery."

[a] 43 Some manuscripts *out, 44where / " 'their worm does not die, / and the fire is not quenched.'*
[b] 45 Some manuscripts *hell, 46where / " 'their worm does not die, / and the fire is not quenched.'*
[c] 48 Isaiah 66:24 [d] 6 Gen. 1:27 [e] 7 Some early manuscripts do not have *and be united to his wife.*
[f] 8 Gen. 2:24

PRAYER: MY RELATIONSHIP TO OTHERS

O GOD, because in our ministry we supply the needs of the saints, they will glorify You, for the obedience that accompanies our confession of the gospel of Christ, and for our liberality of sharing with them and with everyone else. (2 Corinthians 9:13)

PAUSE *to review your relationships with others and to commit them to the Lord.*

YEAR 2 DAY 116

OT Proverbs 21

21 The king's heart is in the hand of the LORD;
  he directs it like a watercourse
    wherever he pleases.

2All a man's ways seem right to him,
  but the LORD weighs the heart.

3To do what is right and just
  is more acceptable to the LORD than
    sacrifice.

4Haughty eyes and a proud heart,
  the lamp of the wicked, are sin!

5The plans of the diligent lead to profit
  as surely as haste leads to poverty.

6A fortune made by a lying tongue
  is a fleeting vapor and a deadly
    snare.[a]

[a] 6 Some Hebrew manuscripts, Septuagint and Vulgate; most Hebrew manuscripts *vapor for those who seek death*

[7] The violence of the wicked will drag them away,
for they refuse to do what is right.

[8] The way of the guilty is devious,
but the conduct of the innocent is upright.

[9] Better to live on a corner of the roof
than share a house with a quarrelsome wife.

[10] The wicked man craves evil;
his neighbor gets no mercy from him.

[11] When a mocker is punished, the simple gain wisdom;
when a wise man is instructed, he gets knowledge.

[12] The Righteous One[b] takes note of the house of the wicked
and brings the wicked to ruin.

[13] If a man shuts his ears to the cry of the poor,
he too will cry out and not be answered.

[14] A gift given in secret soothes anger,
and a bribe concealed in the cloak pacifies great wrath.

[15] When justice is done, it brings joy to the righteous
but terror to evildoers.

[16] A man who strays from the path of understanding
comes to rest in the company of the dead.

[17] He who loves pleasure will become poor;
whoever loves wine and oil will never be rich.

[18] The wicked become a ransom for the righteous,
and the unfaithful for the upright.

[19] Better to live in a desert
than with a quarrelsome and ill-tempered wife.

[20] In the house of the wise are stores of choice food and oil,
but a foolish man devours all he has.

[21] He who pursues righteousness and love
finds life, prosperity[c] and honor.

[22] A wise man attacks the city of the mighty
and pulls down the stronghold in which they trust.

[23] He who guards his mouth and his tongue
keeps himself from calamity.

[24] The proud and arrogant man—"Mocker" is his name;
he behaves with overweening pride.

[25] The sluggard's craving will be the death of him,
because his hands refuse to work.

[26] All day long he craves for more,
but the righteous give without sparing.

[27] The sacrifice of the wicked is detestable—
how much more so when brought with evil intent!

[28] A false witness will perish,
and whoever listens to him will be destroyed forever.[d]

[29] A wicked man puts up a bold front,
but an upright man gives thought to his ways.

[30] There is no wisdom, no insight, no plan
that can succeed against the LORD.

[31] The horse is made ready for the day of battle,
but victory rests with the LORD.

[b] 12 Or *The righteous man* [c] 21 Or *righteousness* [d] 28 Or / *but the words of an obedient man will live on*

PRAYER: INTERCESSION

O GOD, in the past You overlooked the times of ignorance, but now You command all people everywhere to repent. For You have set a day when You will judge the world with justice by the Man You have

appointed. You have given assurance of this to all people by raising Him from the dead.
(Acts 17:30–31)

***TAKE** a few moments to intercede on behalf of local, national and world missions. Pray that the Great Commission would be fulfilled and for any special concerns you may have for missions.*

NT Mark 10:13–52

The Little Children and Jesus

13 People were bringing little children to Jesus to have him touch them, but the disciples rebuked them. 14 When Jesus saw this, he was indignant. He said to them, "Let the little children come to me, and do not hinder them, for the kingdom of God belongs to such as these. 15 I tell you the truth, anyone who will not receive the kingdom of God like a little child will never enter it." 16 And he took the children in his arms, put his hands on them and blessed them.

The Rich Young Man

17 As Jesus started on his way, a man ran up to him and fell on his knees before him. "Good teacher," he asked, "what must I do to inherit eternal life?"

18 "Why do you call me good?" Jesus answered. "No one is good—except God alone. 19 You know the commandments: 'Do not murder, do not commit adultery, do not steal, do not give false testimony, do not defraud, honor your father and mother.'[a]"

20 "Teacher," he declared, "all these I have kept since I was a boy."

21 Jesus looked at him and loved him. "One thing you lack," he said. "Go, sell everything you have and give to the poor, and you will have treasure in heaven. Then come, follow me."

22 At this the man's face fell. He went away sad, because he had great wealth.

23 Jesus looked around and said to his disciples, "How hard it is for the rich to enter the kingdom of God!"

24 The disciples were amazed at his words. But Jesus said again, "Children, how hard it is[b] to enter the kingdom of God! 25 It is easier for a camel to go through the eye of a needle than for a rich man to enter the kingdom of God."

26 The disciples were even more amazed, and said to each other, "Who then can be saved?"

27 Jesus looked at them and said, "With man this is impossible, but not with God; all things are possible with God."

28 Peter said to him, "We have left everything to follow you!"

29 "I tell you the truth," Jesus replied, "no one who has left home or brothers or sisters or mother or father or children or fields for me and the gospel 30 will fail to receive a hundred times as much in this present age (homes, brothers, sisters, mothers, children and fields—and with them, persecutions) and in the age to come, eternal life. 31 But many who are first will be last, and the last first."

Jesus Again Predicts His Death

32 They were on their way up to Jerusalem, with Jesus leading the way, and the disciples were astonished, while those who followed were afraid. Again he took the Twelve aside and told them what was going to happen to him. 33 "We are going up to Jerusalem," he said, "and the Son of Man will be betrayed to the chief priests and teachers of the law. They will condemn him to death and will hand him over to the Gentiles, 34 who will mock him and spit on him, flog him and kill him. Three days later he will rise."

The Request of James and John

35 Then James and John, the sons of Zebedee, came to him. "Teacher," they said, "we want you to do for us whatever we ask."

36 "What do you want me to do for you?" he asked.

37 They replied, "Let one of us sit at your right and the other at your left in your glory."

38 "You don't know what you are asking," Jesus said. "Can you drink the cup I

[a] *19* Exodus 20:12–16; Deut. 5:16–20 [b] *24* Some manuscripts *is for those who trust in riches*

drink or be baptized with the baptism I am baptized with?"

[39] "We can," they answered.

Jesus said to them, "You will drink the cup I drink and be baptized with the baptism I am baptized with, [40] but to sit at my right or left is not for me to grant. These places belong to those for whom they have been prepared."

[41] When the ten heard about this, they became indignant with James and John. [42] Jesus called them together and said, "You know that those who are regarded as rulers of the Gentiles lord it over them, and their high officials exercise authority over them. [43] Not so with you. Instead, whoever wants to become great among you must be your servant, [44] and whoever wants to be first must be slave of all. [45] For even the Son of Man did not come to be served, but to serve, and to give his life as a ransom for many."

Blind Bartimaeus Receives His Sight

[46] Then they came to Jericho. As Jesus and his disciples, together with a large crowd, were leaving the city, a blind man, Bartimaeus (that is, the Son of Timaeus), was sitting by the roadside begging. [47] When he heard that it was Jesus of Nazareth, he began to shout, "Jesus, Son of David, have mercy on me!"

[48] Many rebuked him and told him to be quiet, but he shouted all the more, "Son of David, have mercy on me!"

[49] Jesus stopped and said, "Call him."

So they called to the blind man, "Cheer up! On your feet! He's calling you." [50] Throwing his cloak aside, he jumped to his feet and came to Jesus.

[51] "What do you want me to do for you?" Jesus asked him.

The blind man said, "Rabbi, I want to see."

[52] "Go," said Jesus, "your faith has healed you." Immediately he received his sight and followed Jesus along the road.

PRAYER: THE ATTRIBUTES OF GOD

YOU are the Lord, the God of our fathers—the God of Abraham, the God of Isaac and the God of Jacob. This is Your name forever, the name by which You are to be remembered from generation to generation.

(Exodus 3:15)

PAUSE *to reflect on these affirmations about the person, powers and perfection of God.*

YEAR 2 DAY 117

OT 2 Chronicles 32:1-33

Sennacherib Threatens Jerusalem

32 After all that Hezekiah had so faithfully done, Sennacherib king of Assyria came and invaded Judah. He laid siege to the fortified cities, thinking to conquer them for himself. [2] When Hezekiah saw that Sennacherib had come and that he intended to make war on Jerusalem, [3] he consulted with his officials and military staff about blocking off the water from the springs outside the city, and they helped him. [4] A large force of men assembled, and they blocked all the springs and the stream that flowed through the land. "Why should the kings[a] of Assyria come and find plenty of water?" they said. [5] Then he worked hard repairing all the broken sections of the wall and building towers on it. He built another wall outside that one and reinforced the supporting terraces[b] of the City of David. He also made large numbers of weapons and shields.

[6] He appointed military officers over the people and assembled them before him in the square at the city gate and encouraged them with these words: [7] "Be strong and courageous. Do not be afraid or discouraged because of the king of Assyria

[a] 4 Hebrew; Septuagint and Syriac *king* [b] 5 Or *the Millo*

and the vast army with him, for there is a
greater power with us than with him.
8With him is only the arm of flesh, but
with us is the LORD our God to help us
and to fight our battles." And the people
gained confidence from what Hezekiah
the king of Judah said.
9Later, when Sennacherib king of Assyria and all his forces were laying siege to
Lachish, he sent his officers to Jerusalem
with this message for Hezekiah king of Judah and for all the people of Judah who
were there:

> 10"This is what Sennacherib king of
> Assyria says: On what are you basing
> your confidence, that you remain in
> Jerusalem under siege? 11When Hez-
> ekiah says, 'The LORD our God will
> save us from the hand of the king of
> Assyria,' he is misleading you, to let
> you die of hunger and thirst. 12Did
> not Hezekiah himself remove this
> god's high places and altars, saying to
> Judah and Jerusalem, 'You must wor-
> ship before one altar and burn sacri-
> fices on it'?
> 13"Do you not know what I and my
> fathers have done to all the peoples
> of the other lands? Were the gods of
> those nations ever able to deliver
> their land from my hand? 14Who of
> all the gods of these nations that my
> fathers destroyed has been able to
> save his people from me? How then
> can your god deliver you from my
> hand? 15Now do not let Hezekiah de-
> ceive you and mislead you like this.
> Do not believe him, for no god of
> any nation or kingdom has been able
> to deliver his people from my hand
> or the hand of my fathers. How
> much less will your god deliver you
> from my hand!"

16Sennacherib's officers spoke further
against the LORD God and against his servant Hezekiah. 17The king also wrote letters
insulting the LORD, the God of Israel, and
saying this against him: "Just as the gods of
the peoples of the other lands did not rescue their people from my hand, so the god
of Hezekiah will not rescue his people from
my hand." 18Then they called out in Hebrew to the people of Jerusalem who were
on the wall, to terrify them and make them
afraid in order to capture the city. 19They
spoke about the God of Jerusalem as they
did about the gods of the other peoples of
the world—the work of men's hands.
20King Hezekiah and the prophet Isaiah
son of Amoz cried out in prayer to heav-
en about this. 21And the LORD sent an angel, who annihilated all the fighting men
and the leaders and officers in the camp
of the Assyrian king. So he withdrew to
his own land in disgrace. And when he
went into the temple of his god, some of
his sons cut him down with the sword.
22So the LORD saved Hezekiah and the
people of Jerusalem from the hand of
Sennacherib king of Assyria and from the
hand of all others. He took care of them[c]
on every side. 23Many brought offerings to
Jerusalem for the LORD and valuable gifts
for Hezekiah king of Judah. From then on
he was highly regarded by all the nations.

Hezekiah's Pride, Success and Death

24In those days Hezekiah became ill and
was at the point of death. He prayed to the
LORD, who answered him and gave him a
miraculous sign. 25But Hezekiah's heart was
proud and he did not respond to the kindness shown him; therefore the LORD's wrath
was on him and on Judah and Jerusalem.
26Then Hezekiah repented of the pride of
his heart, as did the people of Jerusalem;
therefore the LORD's wrath did not come
upon them during the days of Hezekiah.
27Hezekiah had very great riches and
honor, and he made treasuries for his silver
and gold and for his precious stones, spices,
shields and all kinds of valuables. 28He also
made buildings to store the harvest of
grain, new wine and oil; and he made stalls
for various kinds of cattle, and pens for the
flocks. 29He built villages and acquired great
numbers of flocks and herds, for God had
given him very great riches.
30It was Hezekiah who blocked the upper outlet of the Gihon spring and chan-
neled the water down to the west side of
the City of David. He succeeded in everything he undertook. 31But when envoys
were sent by the rulers of Babylon to ask
him about the miraculous sign that had
occurred in the land, God left him to test
him and to know everything that was in
his heart.
32The other events of Hezekiah's reign
and his acts of devotion are written in the

[c] 22 Hebrew; Septuagint and Vulgate *He gave them rest*

vision of the prophet Isaiah son of Amoz in the book of the kings of Judah and Israel. 33Hezekiah rested with his fathers and was buried on the hill where the tombs of David's descendants are. All Judah and the people of Jerusalem honored him when he died. And Manasseh his son succeeded him as king.

PRAYER: AFFIRMATION

O GOD, You who made the world and everything in it are Lord of heaven and earth, and You do not dwell in temples built by hands. You are not served by human hands, as though You needed anything, because You Yourself give all people life and breath and everything else. (Acts 17:24–25)

***PAUSE** to reflect on these Biblical affirmations.*

NT Mark 11:1–33

The Triumphal Entry

11 As they approached Jerusalem and came to Bethphage and Bethany at the Mount of Olives, Jesus sent two of his disciples, 2saying to them, "Go to the village ahead of you, and just as you enter it, you will find a colt tied there, which no one has ever ridden. Untie it and bring it here. 3If anyone asks you, 'Why are you doing this?' tell him, 'The Lord needs it and will send it back here shortly.' "

4They went and found a colt outside in the street, tied at a doorway. As they untied it, 5some people standing there asked, "What are you doing, untying that colt?" 6They answered as Jesus had told them to, and the people let them go. 7When they brought the colt to Jesus and threw their cloaks over it, he sat on it. 8Many people spread their cloaks on the road, while others spread branches they had cut in the fields. 9Those who went ahead and those who followed shouted,

"Hosanna![a]"

"Blessed is he who comes in the name
of the Lord!"[b]

10"Blessed is the coming kingdom of
our father David!"

"Hosanna in the highest!"

11Jesus entered Jerusalem and went to the temple. He looked around at everything, but since it was already late, he went out to Bethany with the Twelve.

Jesus Clears the Temple

12The next day as they were leaving Bethany, Jesus was hungry. 13Seeing in the distance a fig tree in leaf, he went to find out if it had any fruit. When he reached it, he found nothing but leaves, because it was not the season for figs. 14Then he said to the tree, "May no one ever eat fruit from you again." And his disciples heard him say it.

15On reaching Jerusalem, Jesus entered the temple area and began driving out those who were buying and selling there. He overturned the tables of the money changers and the benches of those selling doves, 16and would not allow anyone to carry merchandise through the temple courts. 17And as he taught them, he said, "Is it not written:

" 'My house will be called
a house of prayer for all nations'[c]?

But you have made it 'a den of robbers.'[d]"

18The chief priests and the teachers of the law heard this and began looking for a way to kill him, for they feared him, because the whole crowd was amazed at his teaching.

19When evening came, they[e] went out of the city.

The Withered Fig Tree

20In the morning, as they went along, they saw the fig tree withered from the roots. 21Peter remembered and said to Jesus, "Rabbi, look! The fig tree you cursed has withered!"

22"Have[f] faith in God," Jesus answered. 23"I tell you the truth, if anyone says to

[a] *9* A Hebrew expression meaning "Save!" which became an exclamation of praise; also in verse 10
[b] *9* Psalm 118:25,26
[c] *17* Isaiah 56:7
[d] *17* Jer. 7:11
[e] *19* Some early manuscripts *he*
[f] *22* Some early manuscripts *If you have*

this mountain, 'Go, throw yourself into the sea,' and does not doubt in his heart but believes that what he says will happen, it will be done for him. [24]Therefore I tell you, whatever you ask for in prayer, believe that you have received it, and it will be yours. [25]And when you stand praying, if you hold anything against anyone, forgive him, so that your Father in heaven may forgive you your sins.[g]"

The Authority of Jesus Questioned

[27]They arrived again in Jerusalem, and while Jesus was walking in the temple courts, the chief priests, the teachers of the law and the elders came to him. [28]"By what authority are you doing these things?" they asked. "And who gave you authority to do this?"

[29]Jesus replied, "I will ask you one question. Answer me, and I will tell you by what authority I am doing these things. [30]John's baptism—was it from heaven, or from men? Tell me!"

[31]They discussed it among themselves and said, "If we say, 'From heaven,' he will ask, 'Then why didn't you believe him?' [32]But if we say, 'From men' . . . ." (They feared the people, for everyone held that John really was a prophet.)

[33]So they answered Jesus, "We don't know."

Jesus said, "Neither will I tell you by what authority I am doing these things."

[g] 25 Some manuscripts *sins.* [26]*But if you do not forgive, neither will your Father who is in heaven forgive your sins.*

PRAYER: THE WORKS OF GOD

WHILE You were in the world, Jesus, You were the light of the world. For judgment You came into this world, that those who do not see may see, and that those who see may become blind. (John 9:5, 39) . . . You, Jesus, told Your opponents, "You are from below; I am from above. You are of this world; I am not of this world. I told you, therefore, that you would die in your sins, for if you do not believe that I AM, you will die in your sins." (John 8:23–24)

***TAKE** a moment to consider the greatness of God's wonderful works.*

OT 2 Chronicles 33:1-25

YEAR 2 DAY 118

Manasseh King of Judah

33 Manasseh was twelve years old when he became king, and he reigned in Jerusalem fifty-five years. [2]He did evil in the eyes of the LORD, following the detestable practices of the nations the LORD had driven out before the Israelites. [3]He rebuilt the high places his father Hezekiah had demolished; he also erected altars to the Baals and made Asherah poles. He bowed down to all the starry hosts and worshiped them. [4]He built altars in the temple of the LORD, of which the LORD had said, "My Name will remain in Jerusalem forever." [5]In both courts of the temple of the LORD, he built altars to all the starry hosts. [6]He sacrificed his sons in[a] the fire in the Valley of Ben Hinnom, practiced sorcery, divination and witchcraft, and consulted mediums and spiritists. He did much evil in the eyes of the LORD, provoking him to anger.

[7]He took the carved image he had made and put it in God's temple, of which God had said to David and to his son Solomon, "In this temple and in Jerusalem, which I have chosen out of all the tribes of Israel, I will put my Name forever. [8]I will not again make the feet of the Israelites leave the land I assigned to your forefathers, if only they will be careful to do everything I commanded them concerning all the laws, decrees and ordinances given through Moses." [9]But Manasseh led Judah and the people of Jerusalem astray,

[a] 6 Or *He made his sons pass through*

so that they did more evil than the nations the LORD had destroyed before the
Israelites.
10 The LORD spoke to Manasseh and his
people, but they paid no attention. 11 So the
LORD brought against them the army commanders of the king of Assyria, who took
Manasseh prisoner, put a hook in his nose,
bound him with bronze shackles and took
him to Babylon. 12 In his distress he sought
the favor of the LORD his God and humbled himself greatly before the God of his
fathers. 13 And when he prayed to him, the
LORD was moved by his entreaty and listened to his plea; so he brought him back
to Jerusalem and to his kingdom. Then
Manasseh knew that the LORD is God.
14 Afterward he rebuilt the outer wall of
the City of David, west of the Gihon
spring in the valley, as far as the entrance
of the Fish Gate and encircling the hill of
Ophel; he also made it much higher. He
stationed military commanders in all the
fortified cities in Judah.
15 He got rid of the foreign gods and removed the image from the temple of the
LORD, as well as all the altars he had built
on the temple hill and in Jerusalem; and
he threw them out of the city. 16 Then he
restored the altar of the LORD and sacrificed fellowship offerings[b] and thank offerings on it, and told Judah to serve the
LORD, the God of Israel. 17 The people,
however, continued to sacrifice at the high
places, but only to the LORD their God.
18 The other events of Manasseh's reign,
including his prayer to his God and the
words the seers spoke to him in the name
of the LORD, the God of Israel, are written
in the annals of the kings of Israel.[c] 19 His
prayer and how God was moved by his
entreaty, as well as all his sins and unfaithfulness, and the sites where he built
high places and set up Asherah poles and
idols before he humbled himself—all are
written in the records of the seers.[d] 20 Manasseh rested with his fathers and was
buried in his palace. And Amon his son
succeeded him as king.

Amon King of Judah

21 Amon was twenty-two years old when
he became king, and he reigned in Jerusalem two years. 22 He did evil in the eyes
of the LORD, as his father Manasseh had
done. Amon worshiped and offered sacrifices to all the idols Manasseh had made.
23 But unlike his father Manasseh, he did
not humble himself before the LORD;
Amon increased his guilt.
24 Amon's officials conspired against
him and assassinated him in his palace.
25 Then the people of the land killed all
who had plotted against King Amon, and
they made Josiah his son king in his
place.

[b] *16* Traditionally *peace offerings* [c] *18* That is, Judah, as frequently in 2 Chronicles [d] *19* One Hebrew manuscript and Septuagint; most Hebrew manuscripts *of Hozai*

PRAYER: THANKSGIVING

I WILL sing of Your strength; Yes, I will sing of Your mercy in the morning, for You have been my stronghold, my refuge in times of trouble. To You, O my strength, I will sing praises, for You are my fortress, my loving God. (Psalm 59:16–17)

PAUSE *to offer your own expressions of thanksgiving.*

NT Mark 12:1–27

The Parable of the Tenants

12 He then began to speak to them in
parables: "A man planted a vineyard.
He put a wall around it, dug a pit for the
winepress and built a watchtower. Then he
rented the vineyard to some farmers and
went away on a journey. 2 At harvest time
he sent a servant to the tenants to collect
from them some of the fruit of the vineyard. 3 But they seized him, beat him and
sent him away empty-handed. 4 Then he
sent another servant to them; they struck
this man on the head and treated him
shamefully. 5 He sent still another, and that
one they killed. He sent many others;
some of them they beat, others they killed.

6 "He had one left to send, a son, whom
he loved. He sent him last of all, saying,
'They will respect my son.'
7 "But the tenants said to one another,
'This is the heir. Come, let's kill him, and
the inheritance will be ours.' 8 So they took
him and killed him, and threw him out
of the vineyard.
9 "What then will the owner of the vineyard do? He will come and kill those tenants and give the vineyard to others.
10 Haven't you read this scripture:

" 'The stone the builders rejected
has become the capstone[a];
11 the Lord has done this,
and it is marvelous in our eyes'[b]?"

12 Then they looked for a way to arrest
him because they knew he had spoken the
parable against them. But they were afraid
of the crowd; so they left him and went
away.

Paying Taxes to Caesar

13 Later they sent some of the Pharisees
and Herodians to Jesus to catch him in
his words. 14 They came to him and said,
"Teacher, we know you are a man of integrity. You aren't swayed by men, because you pay no attention to who they
are; but you teach the way of God in accordance with the truth. Is it right to pay
taxes to Caesar or not? 15 Should we pay
or shouldn't we?"
But Jesus knew their hypocrisy. "Why
are you trying to trap me?" he asked.
"Bring me a denarius and let me look at
it." 16 They brought the coin, and he asked
them, "Whose portrait is this? And whose
inscription?"
"Caesar's," they replied.
17 Then Jesus said to them, "Give to Caesar what is Caesar's and to God what is
God's."
And they were amazed at him.

Marriage at the Resurrection

18 Then the Sadducees, who say there is
no resurrection, came to him with a question. 19 "Teacher," they said, "Moses wrote
for us that if a man's brother dies and
leaves a wife but no children, the man
must marry the widow and have children
for his brother. 20 Now there were seven
brothers. The first one married and died
without leaving any children. 21 The second one married the widow, but he also
died, leaving no child. It was the same
with the third. 22 In fact, none of the sev-
en left any children. Last of all, the
woman died too. 23 At the resurrection[c]
whose wife will she be, since the seven
were married to her?"
24 Jesus replied, "Are you not in error because you do not know the Scriptures or
the power of God? 25 When the dead rise,
they will neither marry nor be given in
marriage; they will be like the angels in
heaven. 26 Now about the dead rising—
have you not read in the book of Moses,
in the account of the bush, how God said
to him, 'I am the God of Abraham, the
God of Isaac, and the God of Jacob'[d]? 27 He
is not the God of the dead, but of the living. You are badly mistaken!"

[a] 10 Or *cornerstone* [b] 11 Psalm 118:22,23
[c] 23 Some manuscripts *resurrection, when men rise from the dead,* [d] 26 Exodus 3:6

PRAYER: MY RELATIONSHIP TO GOD

YOU, O Lord, are close to the brokenhearted and save those who are crushed in spirit. (Psalm 34:18) . . . Your sacrifices, O God, are a broken spirit; a broken and contrite heart, O God, You will not despise. (Psalm 51:17)

***PAUSE** to thank God for the relationship that you enjoy with Him in Jesus Christ.*

OT Psalm 94

Psalm 94

1 O LORD, the God who avenges,
O God who avenges, shine forth.
2 Rise up, O Judge of the earth;
pay back to the proud what they deserve.
3 How long will the wicked, O LORD,
how long will the wicked be jubilant?

4 They pour out arrogant words;
all the evildoers are full of boasting.
5 They crush your people, O LORD;
they oppress your inheritance.
6 They slay the widow and the alien;
they murder the fatherless.
7 They say, "The LORD does not see;
the God of Jacob pays no heed."

8 Take heed, you senseless ones among the people;
you fools, when will you become wise?
9 Does he who implanted the ear not hear?
Does he who formed the eye not see?
10 Does he who disciplines nations not punish?
Does he who teaches man lack knowledge?
11 The LORD knows the thoughts of man;
he knows that they are futile.

12 Blessed is the man you discipline, O LORD,
the man you teach from your law;
13 you grant him relief from days of trouble,
till a pit is dug for the wicked.
14 For the LORD will not reject his people;
he will never forsake his inheritance.
15 Judgment will again be founded on righteousness,
and all the upright in heart will follow it.

16 Who will rise up for me against the wicked?
Who will take a stand for me against evildoers?
17 Unless the LORD had given me help,
I would soon have dwelt in the silence of death.
18 When I said, "My foot is slipping,"
your love, O LORD, supported me.
19 When anxiety was great within me,
your consolation brought joy to my soul.

20 Can a corrupt throne be allied with you—
one that brings on misery by its decrees?
21 They band together against the righteous
and condemn the innocent to death.
22 But the LORD has become my fortress,
and my God the rock in whom I take refuge.
23 He will repay them for their sins
and destroy them for their wickedness;
the LORD our God will destroy them.

PRAYER: ADORATION

YOU, O Lord of hosts, will be exalted in judgment, and You, holy God, will show Yourself holy in righteousness. (Isaiah 5:16) . . . You long to be gracious and rise to show compassion, for You are a God of justice; blessed are all those who wait for You! (Isaiah 30:18)

***PAUSE** to express your thoughts of praise and worship.*

NT Mark 12:28-44

The Greatest Commandment

28 One of the teachers of the law came
and heard them debating. Noticing that
Jesus had given them a good answer, he
asked him, "Of all the commandments,
which is the most important?"
29 "The most important one," answered
Jesus, "is this: 'Hear, O Israel, the Lord our

God, the Lord is one.[a] 30 Love the Lord your God with all your heart and with all your soul and with all your mind and with all your strength.'[b] 31 The second is this: 'Love your neighbor as yourself.'[c] There is no commandment greater than these."

32 "Well said, teacher," the man replied. "You are right in saying that God is one and there is no other but him. 33 To love him with all your heart, with all your understanding and with all your strength, and to love your neighbor as yourself is more important than all burnt offerings and sacrifices."

34 When Jesus saw that he had answered wisely, he said to him, "You are not far from the kingdom of God." And from then on no one dared ask him any more questions.

Whose Son Is the Christ?

35 While Jesus was teaching in the temple courts, he asked, "How is it that the teachers of the law say that the Christ[d] is the son of David? 36 David himself, speaking by the Holy Spirit, declared:

" 'The Lord said to my Lord:
"Sit at my right hand
until I put your enemies
under your feet." '[e]

37 David himself calls him 'Lord.' How then can he be his son?"

The large crowd listened to him with delight.

38 As he taught, Jesus said, "Watch out for the teachers of the law. They like to walk around in flowing robes and be greeted in the marketplaces, 39 and have the most important seats in the synagogues and the places of honor at banquets. 40 They devour widows' houses and for a show make lengthy prayers. Such men will be punished most severely."

The Widow's Offering

41 Jesus sat down opposite the place where the offerings were put and watched the crowd putting their money into the temple treasury. Many rich people threw in large amounts. 42 But a poor widow came and put in two very small copper coins,[f] worth only a fraction of a penny.[g]

43 Calling his disciples to him, Jesus said, "I tell you the truth, this poor widow has put more into the treasury than all the others. 44 They all gave out of their wealth; but she, out of her poverty, put in everything—all she had to live on."

[a] 29 Or *the Lord our God is one Lord* [b] 30 Deut. 6:4,5 [c] 31 Lev. 19:18 [d] 35 Or *Messiah* [e] 36 Psalm 110:1 [f] 42 Greek *two lepta* [g] 42 Greek *kodrantes*

PRAYER: THE CHARACTER I WANT TO CULTIVATE

DISCIPLES are not above their teacher, nor servants above their master. It is enough for the disciples to be like their teacher, and the servants like their master. (Matthew 10:24–25)

***TAKE** a moment to ask the Lord for the grace to grow in godly character.*

OT 2 Chronicles 34:1–33 — YEAR 2 DAY 120

Josiah's Reforms

34 Josiah was eight years old when he became king, and he reigned in Jerusalem thirty-one years. 2 He did what was right in the eyes of the LORD and walked in the ways of his father David, not turning aside to the right or to the left.

3 In the eighth year of his reign, while he was still young, he began to seek the God of his father David. In his twelfth year he began to purge Judah and Jerusalem of high places, Asherah poles, carved idols and cast images. 4 Under his direction the altars of the Baals were torn down; he cut to pieces the incense altars that were above them, and smashed the Asherah poles, the idols and the images. These he broke to pieces and scattered over the graves of those who had sacrificed to them. 5 He burned the bones of the priests on their altars, and so he purged Judah

and Jerusalem. 6In the towns of Manasseh, Ephraim and Simeon, as far as Naphtali, and in the ruins around them, 7he
tore down the altars and the Asherah
poles and crushed the idols to powder
and cut to pieces all the incense altars
throughout Israel. Then he went back to
Jerusalem.

8In the eighteenth year of Josiah's reign,
to purify the land and the temple, he sent
Shaphan son of Azaliah and Maaseiah the
ruler of the city, with Joah son of Joahaz,
the recorder, to repair the temple of the
LORD his God.

9They went to Hilkiah the high priest
and gave him the money that had been
brought into the temple of God, which
the Levites who were the doorkeepers had
collected from the people of Manasseh,
Ephraim and the entire remnant of Israel
and from all the people of Judah and Benjamin and the inhabitants of Jerusalem.
10Then they entrusted it to the men appointed to supervise the work on the
LORD's temple. These men paid the workers who repaired and restored the temple.
11They also gave money to the carpenters
and builders to purchase dressed stone,
and timber for joists and beams for the
buildings that the kings of Judah had allowed to fall into ruin.

12The men did the work faithfully. Over
them to direct them were Jahath and Obadiah, Levites descended from Merari, and
Zechariah and Meshullam, descended
from Kohath. The Levites—all who were
skilled in playing musical instruments—
13had charge of the laborers and super-
vised all the workers from job to job.
Some of the Levites were secretaries,
scribes and doorkeepers.

The Book of the Law Found

14While they were bringing out the
money that had been taken into the temple of the LORD, Hilkiah the priest found
the Book of the Law of the LORD that had
been given through Moses. 15Hilkiah said
to Shaphan the secretary, "I have found
the Book of the Law in the temple of the
LORD." He gave it to Shaphan.

16Then Shaphan took the book to the
king and reported to him: "Your officials
are doing everything that has been committed to them. 17They have paid out the
money that was in the temple of the LORD
and have entrusted it to the supervisors
and workers." 18Then Shaphan the secretary informed the king, "Hilkiah the
priest has given me a book." And Shaphan read from it in the presence of the
king.

19When the king heard the words of the
Law, he tore his robes. 20He gave these orders to Hilkiah, Ahikam son of Shaphan,
Abdon son of Micah,[a] Shaphan the secretary and Asaiah the king's attendant:
21"Go and inquire of the LORD for me and
for the remnant in Israel and Judah about
what is written in this book that has been
found. Great is the LORD's anger that is
poured out on us because our fathers have
not kept the word of the LORD; they have
not acted in accordance with all that is
written in this book."

22Hilkiah and those the king had sent
with him[b] went to speak to the prophetess Huldah, who was the wife of Shallum
son of Tokhath,[c] the son of Hasrah,[d] keeper of the wardrobe. She lived in Jerusalem,
in the Second District.

23She said to them, "This is what the
LORD, the God of Israel, says: Tell the man
who sent you to me, 24'This is what the
LORD says: I am going to bring disaster on
this place and its people—all the curses
written in the book that has been read in
the presence of the king of Judah. 25Be-
cause they have forsaken me and burned
incense to other gods and provoked me to
anger by all that their hands have made,[e]
my anger will be poured out on this place
and will not be quenched.' 26Tell the king
of Judah, who sent you to inquire of the
LORD, 'This is what the LORD, the God of
Israel, says concerning the words you
heard: 27Because your heart was responsive and you humbled yourself before
God when you heard what he spoke
against this place and its people, and because you humbled yourself before me
and tore your robes and wept in my presence, I have heard you, declares the LORD.
28Now I will gather you to your fathers,
and you will be buried in peace. Your eyes
will not see all the disaster I am going to
bring on this place and on those who live
here.' "

[a] 20 Also called *Acbor son of Micaiah* [b] 22 One Hebrew manuscript, Vulgate and Syriac; most Hebrew manuscripts do not have *had sent with him.* [c] 22 Also called *Tikvah* [d] 22 Also called *Harhas* [e] 25 Or *by everything they have done*

So they took her answer back to the
king.
29 Then the king called together all the
elders of Judah and Jerusalem. 30 He went
up to the temple of the LORD with the
men of Judah, the people of Jerusalem,
the priests and the Levites—all the people
from the least to the greatest. He read in
their hearing all the words of the Book of
the Covenant, which had been found in
the temple of the LORD. 31 The king stood
by his pillar and renewed the covenant in
the presence of the LORD—to follow the
LORD and keep his commands, regulations and decrees with all his heart and all
his soul, and to obey the words of the covenant written in this book.
32 Then he had everyone in Jerusalem
and Benjamin pledge themselves to it; the
people of Jerusalem did this in accordance with the covenant of God, the God
of their fathers.
33 Josiah removed all the detestable
idols from all the territory belonging to
the Israelites, and he had all who were
present in Israel serve the LORD their God.
As long as he lived, they did not fail to follow the LORD, the God of their fathers.

PRAYER: CONFESSION

LORD, there are six things You hate, seven that are detestable to You: haughty eyes, a lying tongue, hands that shed innocent blood, a heart that devises wicked plans, feet that run swiftly to evil, a false witness who breathes lies, and one who causes strife among brothers and sisters. (Proverbs 6:16–19)

__ASK__ the Spirit to search your heart and reveal any areas of unconfessed sin. Acknowledge these to the Lord and thank Him for His forgiveness.

NT Mark 13:1–37

Signs of the End of the Age

13 As he was leaving the temple, one of
his disciples said to him, "Look,
Teacher! What massive stones! What magnificent buildings!"
2 "Do you see all these great buildings?"
replied Jesus. "Not one stone here will be
left on another; every one will be thrown
down."
3 As Jesus was sitting on the Mount of
Olives opposite the temple, Peter, James,
John and Andrew asked him privately,
4 "Tell us, when will these things happen?
And what will be the sign that they are all
about to be fulfilled?"
5 Jesus said to them: "Watch out that no
one deceives you. 6 Many will come in my
name, claiming, 'I am he,' and will deceive
many. 7 When you hear of wars and rumors of wars, do not be alarmed. Such
things must happen, but the end is still to
come. 8 Nation will rise against nation,
and kingdom against kingdom. There will
be earthquakes in various places, and
famines. These are the beginning of birth
pains.
9 "You must be on your guard. You will
be handed over to the local councils and
flogged in the synagogues. On account of
me you will stand before governors and
kings as witnesses to them. 10 And the
gospel must first be preached to all nations. 11 Whenever you are arrested and
brought to trial, do not worry beforehand
about what to say. Just say whatever is giv-
en you at the time, for it is not you speaking, but the Holy Spirit.
12 "Brother will betray brother to death,
and a father his child. Children will rebel
against their parents and have them put
to death. 13 All men will hate you because
of me, but he who stands firm to the end
will be saved.
14 "When you see 'the abomination that
causes desolation'[a] standing where it[b]
does not belong—let the reader understand—then let those who are in Judea
flee to the mountains. 15 Let no one on the
roof of his house go down or enter the
house to take anything out. 16 Let no one
in the field go back to get his cloak. 17 How
dreadful it will be in those days for preg-

[a] *14* Daniel 9:27; 11:31; 12:11 [b] *14* Or *he*; also in verse 29

nant women and nursing mothers! 18 Pray
that this will not take place in winter,
19 because those will be days of distress unequaled from the beginning, when God
created the world, until now—and never
to be equaled again. 20 If the Lord had not
cut short those days, no one would survive. But for the sake of the elect, whom
he has chosen, he has shortened them.
21 At that time if anyone says to you, 'Look,
here is the Christ[c]!' or, 'Look, there he is!'
do not believe it. 22 For false Christs and
false prophets will appear and perform
signs and miracles to deceive the elect—if
that were possible. 23 So be on your guard;
I have told you everything ahead of time.
24 "But in those days, following that distress,

" 'the sun will be darkened,
and the moon will not give its light;
25 the stars will fall from the sky,
and the heavenly bodies will be
shaken.'[d]

26 "At that time men will see the Son of
Man coming in clouds with great power
and glory. 27 And he will send his angels
and gather his elect from the four winds,
from the ends of the earth to the ends of
the heavens.

28 "Now learn this lesson from the fig
tree: As soon as its twigs get tender and its
leaves come out, you know that summer
is near. 29 Even so, when you see these
things happening, you know that it is
near, right at the door. 30 I tell you the
truth, this generation[e] will certainly not
pass away until all these things have happened. 31 Heaven and earth will pass away,
but my words will never pass away.

The Day and Hour Unknown

32 "No one knows about that day or
hour, not even the angels in heaven, nor
the Son, but only the Father. 33 Be on
guard! Be alert[f]! You do not know when
that time will come. 34 It's like a man going away: He leaves his house and puts his
servants in charge, each with his assigned
task, and tells the one at the door to keep
watch.
35 "Therefore keep watch because you do
not know when the owner of the house
will come back—whether in the evening,
or at midnight, or when the rooster crows,
or at dawn. 36 If he comes suddenly, do not
let him find you sleeping. 37 What I say to
you, I say to everyone: 'Watch!' "

[c] 21 Or *Messiah* [d] 25 Isaiah 13:10; 34:4
[e] 30 Or *race* [f] 33 Some manuscripts *alert and pray*

PRAYER: MY RELATIONSHIP TO OTHERS

I WILL not hate my brothers or sisters in my heart, but I will reprove my neighbors frankly and not incur sin because of them. (Leviticus 19:17) . . . I will not plan evil against my neighbors, since they live trustfully by me. (Proverbs 3:29)

PAUSE *to review your relationships with others and to commit them to the Lord.*

YEAR 2 DAY 121

OT 2 Chronicles 35:1–36:1

Josiah Celebrates the Passover

35 Josiah celebrated the Passover to the
LORD in Jerusalem, and the Passover
lamb was slaughtered on the fourteenth
day of the first month. 2 He appointed the
priests to their duties and encouraged
them in the service of the LORD's temple.
3 He said to the Levites, who instructed all
Israel and who had been consecrated to
the LORD: "Put the sacred ark in the temple that Solomon son of David king of Israel built. It is not to be carried about on
your shoulders. Now serve the LORD your
God and his people Israel. 4 Prepare yourselves by families in your divisions, according to the directions written by David
king of Israel and by his son Solomon.
5 "Stand in the holy place with a group

of Levites for each subdivision of the families of your fellow countrymen, the lay
people. 6Slaughter the Passover lambs,
consecrate yourselves and prepare ⌊the
lambs⌋ for your fellow countrymen, doing
what the LORD commanded through Moses."
7Josiah provided for all the lay people
who were there a total of thirty thousand
sheep and goats for the Passover offerings,
and also three thousand cattle—all from
the king's own possessions.
8His officials also contributed voluntarily to the people and the priests and Levites. Hilkiah, Zechariah and Jehiel, the
administrators of God's temple, gave the
priests twenty-six hundred Passover offerings and three hundred cattle. 9Also Conaniah along with Shemaiah and Nethanel, his brothers, and Hashabiah, Jeiel and
Jozabad, the leaders of the Levites, provided five thousand Passover offerings
and five hundred head of cattle for the Levites.
10The service was arranged and the
priests stood in their places with the
Levites in their divisions as the king had
ordered. 11The Passover lambs were
slaughtered, and the priests sprinkled the
blood handed to them, while the Levites
skinned the animals. 12They set aside the
burnt offerings to give them to the sub-
divisions of the families of the people to
offer to the LORD, as is written in the Book
of Moses. They did the same with the cattle. 13They roasted the Passover animals
over the fire as prescribed, and boiled the
holy offerings in pots, caldrons and pans
and served them quickly to all the people. 14After this, they made preparations
for themselves and for the priests, because the priests, the descendants of Aaron, were sacrificing the burnt offerings
and the fat portions until nightfall. So the
Levites made preparations for themselves
and for the Aaronic priests.
15The musicians, the descendants of
Asaph, were in the places prescribed by
David, Asaph, Heman and Jeduthun the
king's seer. The gatekeepers at each gate
did not need to leave their posts, because
their fellow Levites made the preparations
for them.
16So at that time the entire service of the
LORD was carried out for the celebration
of the Passover and the offering of burnt
offerings on the altar of the LORD, as King
Josiah had ordered. 17The Israelites who
were present celebrated the Passover at
that time and observed the Feast of Unleavened Bread for seven days. 18The
Passover had not been observed like this
in Israel since the days of the prophet
Samuel; and none of the kings of Israel
had ever celebrated such a Passover as did
Josiah, with the priests, the Levites and all
Judah and Israel who were there with the
people of Jerusalem. 19This Passover was
celebrated in the eighteenth year of Josiah's reign.

The Death of Josiah

20After all this, when Josiah had set the
temple in order, Neco king of Egypt went
up to fight at Carchemish on the Euphrates, and Josiah marched out to meet him
in battle. 21But Neco sent messengers to
him, saying, "What quarrel is there between you and me, O king of Judah? It is
not you I am attacking at this time, but
the house with which I am at war. God
has told me to hurry; so stop opposing
God, who is with me, or he will destroy
you."
22Josiah, however, would not turn away
from him, but disguised himself to engage him in battle. He would not listen to
what Neco had said at God's command
but went to fight him on the plain of Megiddo.
23Archers shot King Josiah, and he told
his officers, "Take me away; I am badly
wounded." 24So they took him out of his
chariot, put him in the other chariot he
had and brought him to Jerusalem, where
he died. He was buried in the tombs of
his fathers, and all Judah and Jerusalem
mourned for him.
25Jeremiah composed laments for Josiah, and to this day all the men and
women singers commemorate Josiah in
the laments. These became a tradition in
Israel and are written in the Laments.
26The other events of Josiah's reign and
his acts of devotion, according to what is
written in the Law of the LORD— 27all the
events, from beginning to end, are written
in the book of the kings of Israel and
Judah.
36 1And the people of the land
took Jehoahaz son of Josiah and
made him king in Jerusalem in place of
his father.

PRAYER: RENEWAL

I GREATLY rejoice in my salvation, even though now, for a little while, I grieve because of various trials. They come so that my faith, though much more precious than gold that perishes, even though it is refined by fire, may be proved genuine and that it may result in praise, glory and honor when You are revealed, O Jesus Christ. (1 Peter 1:6–7)

__PAUSE__ to add your own prayers for personal renewal.

NT Mark 14:1–42

Jesus Anointed at Bethany

14 Now the Passover and the Feast of Unleavened Bread were only two days
away, and the chief priests and the teachers of the law were looking for some sly
way to arrest Jesus and kill him. 2“But not
during the Feast,” they said, “or the people may riot.”
3While he was in Bethany, reclining at
the table in the home of a man known as
Simon the Leper, a woman came with an
alabaster jar of very expensive perfume,
made of pure nard. She broke the jar and
poured the perfume on his head.
4Some of those present were saying in-
dignantly to one another, “Why this waste
of perfume? 5It could have been sold for
more than a year's wages[a] and the money
given to the poor.” And they rebuked her
harshly.
6“Leave her alone,” said Jesus. “Why
are you bothering her? She has done a
beautiful thing to me. 7The poor you will
always have with you, and you can help
them any time you want. But you will
not always have me. 8She did what she
could. She poured perfume on my body
beforehand to prepare for my burial. 9I
tell you the truth, wherever the gospel is
preached throughout the world, what
she has done will also be told, in memory of her.”
10Then Judas Iscariot, one of the Twelve,
went to the chief priests to betray Jesus to
them. 11They were delighted to hear this
and promised to give him money. So he
watched for an opportunity to hand him
over.

The Lord's Supper

12On the first day of the Feast of Unleavened Bread, when it was customary to
sacrifice the Passover lamb, Jesus' disciples
asked him, “Where do you want us to go
and make preparations for you to eat the
Passover?”
13So he sent two of his disciples, telling
them, “Go into the city, and a man carrying a jar of water will meet you. Follow
him. 14Say to the owner of the house he
enters, 'The Teacher asks: Where is my
guest room, where I may eat the Passover
with my disciples?' 15He will show you a
large upper room, furnished and ready.
Make preparations for us there.”
16The disciples left, went into the city
and found things just as Jesus had told
them. So they prepared the Passover.
17When evening came, Jesus arrived
with the Twelve. 18While they were reclining at the table eating, he said, “I tell you
the truth, one of you will betray me—one
who is eating with me.”
19They were saddened, and one by one
they said to him, “Surely not I?”
20“It is one of the Twelve,” he replied,
“one who dips bread into the bowl with
me. 21The Son of Man will go just as it is
written about him. But woe to that man
who betrays the Son of Man! It would be
better for him if he had not been born.”
22While they were eating, Jesus took
bread, gave thanks and broke it, and gave
it to his disciples, saying, “Take it; this is
my body.”
23Then he took the cup, gave thanks and
offered it to them, and they all drank
from it.
24“This is my blood of the[b] covenant,
which is poured out for many,” he said to
them. 25“I tell you the truth, I will not
drink again of the fruit of the vine until
that day when I drink it anew in the kingdom of God.”

[a] 5 Greek *than three hundred denarii* [b] 24 Some manuscripts *the new*

[26]When they had sung a hymn, they went out to the Mount of Olives.

Jesus Predicts Peter's Denial

[27]"You will all fall away," Jesus told them, "for it is written:

" 'I will strike the shepherd,
and the sheep will be scattered.'[c]

[28]But after I have risen, I will go ahead of you into Galilee."

[29]Peter declared, "Even if all fall away, I will not."

[30]"I tell you the truth," Jesus answered, "today—yes, tonight—before the rooster crows twice[d] you yourself will disown me three times."

[31]But Peter insisted emphatically, "Even if I have to die with you, I will never disown you." And all the others said the same.

Gethsemane

[32]They went to a place called Gethsemane, and Jesus said to his disciples, "Sit here while I pray." [33]He took Peter, James and John along with him, and he began to be deeply distressed and troubled. [34]"My soul is overwhelmed with sorrow to the point of death," he said to them. "Stay here and keep watch."

[35]Going a little farther, he fell to the ground and prayed that if possible the hour might pass from him. [36]"*Abba*,[e] Father," he said, "everything is possible for you. Take this cup from me. Yet not what I will, but what you will."

[37]Then he returned to his disciples and found them sleeping. "Simon," he said to Peter, "are you asleep? Could you not keep watch for one hour? [38]Watch and pray so that you will not fall into temptation. The spirit is willing, but the body is weak."

[39]Once more he went away and prayed the same thing. [40]When he came back, he again found them sleeping, because their eyes were heavy. They did not know what to say to him.

[41]Returning the third time, he said to them, "Are you still sleeping and resting? Enough! The hour has come. Look, the Son of Man is betrayed into the hands of sinners. [42]Rise! Let us go! Here comes my betrayer!"

[c] *27* Zech. 13:7 [d] *30* Some early manuscripts do not have *twice.* [e] *36* Aramaic for *Father*

PRAYER: THE ATTRIBUTES OF GOD

BLESSED are You, Lord, the God of Israel, from everlasting to everlasting. I praise You, O Lord. (Psalm 106:48) . . . Who can express Your mighty acts, O Lord, or fully declare Your praise? (Psalm 106:2)

PAUSE *to reflect on these affirmations about the person, powers and perfection of God.*

OT 2 Chronicles 36:2–23

YEAR 2 DAY 122

Jehoahaz King of Judah

[2]Jehoahaz[a] was twenty-three years old when he became king, and he reigned in Jerusalem three months. [3]The king of Egypt dethroned him in Jerusalem and imposed on Judah a levy of a hundred talents[b] of silver and a talent[c] of gold. [4]The king of Egypt made Eliakim, a brother of Jehoahaz, king over Judah and Jerusalem and changed Eliakim's name to Jehoiakim. But Neco took Eliakim's brother Jehoahaz and carried him off to Egypt.

Jehoiakim King of Judah

[5]Jehoiakim was twenty-five years old when he became king, and he reigned in Jerusalem eleven years. He did evil in the

[a] *2* Hebrew *Joahaz,* a variant of *Jehoahaz;* also in verse 4 [b] *3* That is, about 3 3/4 tons (about 3.4 metric tons) [c] *3* That is, about 75 pounds (about 34 kilograms)

eyes of the LORD his God. 6 Nebuchadnezzar king of Babylon attacked him and
bound him with bronze shackles to take
him to Babylon. 7 Nebuchadnezzar also
took to Babylon articles from the temple
of the LORD and put them in his temple[d]
there.
8 The other events of Jehoiakim's reign,
the detestable things he did and all that
was found against him, are written in the
book of the kings of Israel and Judah. And
Jehoiachin his son succeeded him as king.

Jehoiachin King of Judah

9 Jehoiachin was eighteen[e] years old
when he became king, and he reigned in
Jerusalem three months and ten days. He
did evil in the eyes of the LORD. 10 In the
spring, King Nebuchadnezzar sent for
him and brought him to Babylon, together with articles of value from the temple of the LORD, and he made Jehoiachin's
uncle,[f] Zedekiah, king over Judah and
Jerusalem.

Zedekiah King of Judah

11 Zedekiah was twenty-one years old
when he became king, and he reigned in
Jerusalem eleven years. 12 He did evil in the
eyes of the LORD his God and did not
humble himself before Jeremiah the
prophet, who spoke the word of the LORD.
13 He also rebelled against King Nebuchadnezzar, who had made him take an
oath in God's name. He became stiff-
necked and hardened his heart and would
not turn to the LORD, the God of Israel.
14 Furthermore, all the leaders of the
priests and the people became more and
more unfaithful, following all the detestable practices of the nations and defiling the temple of the LORD, which he
had consecrated in Jerusalem.

The Fall of Jerusalem

15 The LORD, the God of their fathers,
sent word to them through his messengers again and again, because he had pity
on his people and on his dwelling place.
16 But they mocked God's messengers, despised his words and scoffed at his prophets until the wrath of the LORD was
aroused against his people and there was
no remedy. 17 He brought up against them
the king of the Babylonians,[g] who killed
their young men with the sword in the
sanctuary, and spared neither young man
nor young woman, old man or aged. God
handed all of them over to Nebuchadnezzar. 18 He carried to Babylon all the articles from the temple of God, both large
and small, and the treasures of the LORD's
temple and the treasures of the king and
his officials. 19 They set fire to God's temple and broke down the wall of Jerusalem;
they burned all the palaces and destroyed
everything of value there.
20 He carried into exile to Babylon the
remnant, who escaped from the sword,
and they became servants to him and his
sons until the kingdom of Persia came to
power. 21 The land enjoyed its sabbath
rests; all the time of its desolation it rested, until the seventy years were completed in fulfillment of the word of the LORD
spoken by Jeremiah.
22 In the first year of Cyrus king of Persia, in order to fulfill the word of the LORD
spoken by Jeremiah, the LORD moved the
heart of Cyrus king of Persia to make a
proclamation throughout his realm and
to put it in writing:

23 "This is what Cyrus king of Persia says:
" 'The LORD, the God of heaven,
has given me all the kingdoms of the
earth and he has appointed me to
build a temple for him at Jerusalem
in Judah. Anyone of his people
among you—may the LORD his God
be with him, and let him go up.' "

[d] 7 Or *palace* [e] 9 One Hebrew manuscript, some Septuagint manuscripts and Syriac (see also 2 Kings 24:8); most Hebrew manuscripts *eight* [f] 10 Hebrew *brother,* that is, relative (see 2 Kings 24:17) [g] 17 Or *Chaldeans*

PRAYER: PETITION

THE people of this world are more shrewd in dealing with their own kind than are the people of light. May I use worldly wealth to help others, making friends for myself, so that when it is gone, they may welcome me into Your eternal dwellings. (Luke 16:8–9)

***PAUSE** here to petition God for growth in your character and personal discipline, and for physical health and strength. Ask that He empower you for spiritual warfare against the temptations of the world, the flesh and the devil. Offer prayers regarding your activities for this day and any special concerns you may have.*

NT Mark 14:43–72

Jesus Arrested

43 Just as he was speaking, Judas, one of
the Twelve, appeared. With him was a
crowd armed with swords and clubs, sent
from the chief priests, the teachers of the
law, and the elders.
44 Now the betrayer had arranged a signal with them: "The one I kiss is the man;
arrest him and lead him away under
guard." 45 Going at once to Jesus, Judas
said, "Rabbi!" and kissed him. 46 The men
seized Jesus and arrested him. 47 Then one
of those standing near drew his sword and
struck the servant of the high priest, cutting off his ear.
48 "Am I leading a rebellion," said Jesus,
"that you have come out with swords and
clubs to capture me? 49 Every day I was
with you, teaching in the temple courts,
and you did not arrest me. But the Scriptures must be fulfilled." 50 Then everyone
deserted him and fled.
51 A young man, wearing nothing but a
linen garment, was following Jesus. When
they seized him, 52 he fled naked, leaving
his garment behind.

Before the Sanhedrin

53 They took Jesus to the high priest, and
all the chief priests, elders and teachers of
the law came together. 54 Peter followed
him at a distance, right into the courtyard
of the high priest. There he sat with the
guards and warmed himself at the fire.
55 The chief priests and the whole Sanhedrin were looking for evidence against
Jesus so that they could put him to death,
but they did not find any. 56 Many testified
falsely against him, but their statements
did not agree.
57 Then some stood up and gave this
false testimony against him: 58 "We heard
him say, 'I will destroy this man-made
temple and in three days will build another, not made by man.' " 59 Yet even then
their testimony did not agree.
60 Then the high priest stood up before
them and asked Jesus, "Are you not going
to answer? What is this testimony that
these men are bringing against you?" 61 But
Jesus remained silent and gave no answer.
Again the high priest asked him, "Are you
the Christ,[a] the Son of the Blessed One?"
62 "I am," said Jesus. "And you will see
the Son of Man sitting at the right hand
of the Mighty One and coming on the
clouds of heaven."
63 The high priest tore his clothes. "Why
do we need any more witnesses?" he
asked. 64 "You have heard the blasphemy.
What do you think?"
They all condemned him as worthy of
death. 65 Then some began to spit at him;
they blindfolded him, struck him with
their fists, and said, "Prophesy!" And the
guards took him and beat him.

Peter Disowns Jesus

66 While Peter was below in the courtyard, one of the servant girls of the high
priest came by. 67 When she saw Peter
warming himself, she looked closely at
him.
"You also were with that Nazarene,
Jesus," she said.
68 But he denied it. "I don't know or understand what you're talking about," he
said, and went out into the entryway.[b]

[a] 61 Or *Messiah* [b] 68 Some early manuscripts *entryway and the rooster crowed*

[69]When the servant girl saw him there,
she said again to those standing around,
"This fellow is one of them." [70]Again he
denied it.
After a little while, those standing near
said to Peter, "Surely you are one of them,
for you are a Galilean."
[71]He began to call down curses on himself, and he swore to them, "I don't know
this man you're talking about."
[72]Immediately the rooster crowed the
second time.[c] Then Peter remembered the
word Jesus had spoken to him: "Before
the rooster crows twice[d] you will disown
me three times." And he broke down and
wept.

[c] 72 Some early manuscripts do not have *the second time.* [d] 72 Some early manuscripts do not have *twice.*

PRAYER: THE WORKS OF GOD

YOU, O Son of Man, have authority on earth to forgive sins. (Matthew 9:6) . . . Jesus, when you said to the paralytic, "My son, your sins are forgiven," the scribes were sitting there and reasoned in their hearts, "Why does this man speak blasphemies like this? Who can forgive sins but God alone?" (Mark 2:5–7)

***TAKE** a moment to consider the greatness of God's wonderful works.*

YEAR 2 DAY 123

OT Isaiah 1:1–31

1 The vision concerning Judah and Jerusalem that Isaiah son of Amoz saw during the reigns of Uzziah, Jotham, Ahaz
and Hezekiah, kings of Judah.

A Rebellious Nation

[2]Hear, O heavens! Listen, O earth!
For the LORD has spoken:
"I reared children and brought them up,
but they have rebelled against me.
[3]The ox knows his master,
the donkey his owner's manger,
but Israel does not know,
my people do not understand."

[4]Ah, sinful nation,
a people loaded with guilt,
a brood of evildoers,
children given to corruption!
They have forsaken the LORD;
they have spurned the Holy One of Israel
and turned their backs on him.

[5]Why should you be beaten anymore?
Why do you persist in rebellion?
Your whole head is injured,
your whole heart afflicted.
[6]From the sole of your foot to the top of your head
there is no soundness—
only wounds and welts
and open sores,
not cleansed or bandaged
or soothed with oil.

[7]Your country is desolate,
your cities burned with fire;
your fields are being stripped by foreigners
right before you,
laid waste as when overthrown by strangers.
[8]The Daughter of Zion is left
like a shelter in a vineyard,
like a hut in a field of melons,
like a city under siege.
[9]Unless the LORD Almighty
had left us some survivors,
we would have become like Sodom,
we would have been like Gomorrah.

[10]Hear the word of the LORD,
you rulers of Sodom;
listen to the law of our God,
you people of Gomorrah!
[11]"The multitude of your sacrifices—
what are they to me?" says the LORD.

"I have more than enough of burnt
offerings,
of rams and the fat of fattened
animals;
I have no pleasure
in the blood of bulls and lambs and
goats.
12 When you come to appear before me,
who has asked this of you,
this trampling of my courts?
13 Stop bringing meaningless offerings!
Your incense is detestable to me.
New Moons, Sabbaths and
convocations—
I cannot bear your evil assemblies.
14 Your New Moon festivals and your
appointed feasts
my soul hates.
They have become a burden to me;
I am weary of bearing them.
15 When you spread out your hands in
prayer,
I will hide my eyes from you;
even if you offer many prayers,
I will not listen.
Your hands are full of blood;
16 wash and make yourselves clean.
Take your evil deeds
out of my sight!
Stop doing wrong,
17 learn to do right!
Seek justice,
encourage the oppressed.[a]
Defend the cause of the fatherless,
plead the case of the widow.

18 "Come now, let us reason together,"
says the LORD.
"Though your sins are like scarlet,
they shall be as white as snow;
though they are red as crimson,
they shall be like wool.
19 If you are willing and obedient,
you will eat the best from the land;
20 but if you resist and rebel,
you will be devoured by the sword."
For the mouth of the LORD
has spoken.

21 See how the faithful city
has become a harlot!
She once was full of justice;
righteousness used to dwell in
her—
but now murderers!
22 Your silver has become dross,
your choice wine is diluted with
water.
23 Your rulers are rebels,
companions of thieves;
they all love bribes
and chase after gifts.
They do not defend the cause of the
fatherless;
the widow's case does not come
before them.
24 Therefore the Lord, the LORD
Almighty,
the Mighty One of Israel, declares:
"Ah, I will get relief from my foes
and avenge myself on my enemies.
25 I will turn my hand against you;
I will thoroughly purge away your
dross
and remove all your impurities.
26 I will restore your judges as in days of
old,
your counselors as at the beginning.
Afterward you will be called
the City of Righteousness,
the Faithful City."

27 Zion will be redeemed with justice,
her penitent ones with
righteousness.
28 But rebels and sinners will both be
broken,
and those who forsake the LORD
will perish.

29 "You will be ashamed because of the
sacred oaks
in which you have delighted;
you will be disgraced because of the
gardens
that you have chosen.
30 You will be like an oak with fading
leaves,
like a garden without water.
31 The mighty man will become tinder
and his work a spark;
both will burn together,
with no one to quench the fire."

[a] 17 Or / *rebuke the oppressor*

PRAYER: INTERCESSION

THE end of all things is near; therefore, I should be clear minded and self-controlled so that I can pray. (1 Peter 4:7)

__TAKE__ a few moments to intercede on behalf of the poor and hungry, the oppressed and persecuted, and those in control of world and national resources. Offer prayers for peace among nations and regarding current events and concerns.

NT Mark 15:1–47

Jesus Before Pilate

15 Very early in the morning, the chief
priests, with the elders, the teachers of
the law and the whole Sanhedrin, reached
a decision. They bound Jesus, led him
away and handed him over to Pilate.
2 "Are you the king of the Jews?" asked
Pilate.
"Yes, it is as you say," Jesus replied.
3 The chief priests accused him of many
things. 4 So again Pilate asked him, "Aren't
you going to answer? See how many
things they are accusing you of."
5 But Jesus still made no reply, and Pilate was amazed.
6 Now it was the custom at the Feast to
release a prisoner whom the people requested. 7 A man called Barabbas was in
prison with the insurrectionists who had
committed murder in the uprising. 8 The
crowd came up and asked Pilate to do for
them what he usually did.
9 "Do you want me to release to you the
king of the Jews?" asked Pilate, 10 knowing
it was out of envy that the chief priests
had handed Jesus over to him. 11 But the
chief priests stirred up the crowd to have
Pilate release Barabbas instead.
12 "What shall I do, then, with the one
you call the king of the Jews?" Pilate asked
them.
13 "Crucify him!" they shouted.
14 "Why? What crime has he committed?" asked Pilate.
But they shouted all the louder, "Crucify him!"
15 Wanting to satisfy the crowd, Pilate released Barabbas to them. He had Jesus
flogged, and handed him over to be crucified.

The Soldiers Mock Jesus

16 The soldiers led Jesus away into the
palace (that is, the Praetorium) and called
together the whole company of soldiers.
17 They put a purple robe on him, then
twisted together a crown of thorns and set
it on him. 18 And they began to call out to
him, "Hail, king of the Jews!" 19 Again and
again they struck him on the head with a
staff and spit on him. Falling on their
knees, they paid homage to him. 20 And
when they had mocked him, they took off
the purple robe and put his own clothes
on him. Then they led him out to crucify
him.

The Crucifixion

21 A certain man from Cyrene, Simon,
the father of Alexander and Rufus, was
passing by on his way in from the country, and they forced him to carry the cross.
22 They brought Jesus to the place called
Golgotha (which means The Place of the
Skull). 23 Then they offered him wine
mixed with myrrh, but he did not take it.
24 And they crucified him. Dividing up his
clothes, they cast lots to see what each
would get.
25 It was the third hour when they crucified him. 26 The written notice of the
charge against him read: THE KING OF THE
JEWS. 27 They crucified two robbers with
him, one on his right and one on his left.[a]
29 Those who passed by hurled insults at
him, shaking their heads and saying, "So!
You who are going to destroy the temple
and build it in three days, 30 come down
from the cross and save yourself!"
31 In the same way the chief priests and
the teachers of the law mocked him
among themselves. "He saved others,"
they said, "but he can't save himself! 32 Let
this Christ,[b] this King of Israel, come

[a] 27 Some manuscripts *left,* [28]*and the scripture was fulfilled which says, "He was counted with the lawless ones"* (Isaiah 53:12) [b] 32 Or *Messiah*

down now from the cross, that we may see
and believe." Those crucified with him
also heaped insults on him.

The Death of Jesus

33 At the sixth hour darkness came over
the whole land until the ninth hour. 34 And
at the ninth hour Jesus cried out in a loud
voice, *"Eloi, Eloi, lama sabachthani?"*—
which means, "My God, my God, why
have you forsaken me?"[c]
35 When some of those standing near
heard this, they said, "Listen, he's calling
Elijah."
36 One man ran, filled a sponge with
wine vinegar, put it on a stick, and offered
it to Jesus to drink. "Now leave him alone.
Let's see if Elijah comes to take him
down," he said.
37 With a loud cry, Jesus breathed his
last.
38 The curtain of the temple was torn in
two from top to bottom. 39 And when the
centurion, who stood there in front of
Jesus, heard his cry and[d] saw how he died,
he said, "Surely this man was the Son[e] of
God!"
40 Some women were watching from a
distance. Among them were Mary Magdalene, Mary the mother of James the
younger and of Joses, and Salome. 41 In
Galilee these women had followed him
and cared for his needs. Many other
women who had come up with him to
Jerusalem were also there.

The Burial of Jesus

42 It was Preparation Day (that is, the
day before the Sabbath). So as evening
approached, 43 Joseph of Arimathea, a
prominent member of the Council, who
was himself waiting for the kingdom of
God, went boldly to Pilate and asked for
Jesus' body. 44 Pilate was surprised to hear
that he was already dead. Summoning the
centurion, he asked him if Jesus had already died. 45 When he learned from the
centurion that it was so, he gave the body
to Joseph. 46 So Joseph bought some linen
cloth, took down the body, wrapped it in
the linen, and placed it in a tomb cut out
of rock. Then he rolled a stone against the
entrance of the tomb. 47 Mary Magdalene
and Mary the mother of Joses saw where
he was laid.

[c] *34* Psalm 22:1 [d] *39* Some manuscripts do not have *heard his cry and* [e] *39* Or *a son*

PRAYER: MY RELATIONSHIP TO GOD

WHY should any of us complain when punished for our sins? Let us search out and examine our ways, and let us return to You, Lord. (Lamentations 3:39–40)

***PAUSE** to thank God for the relationship that you enjoy with Him in Jesus Christ.*

YEAR 2 DAY 124

OT Isaiah 2:1–22

The Mountain of the LORD

2 This is what Isaiah son of Amoz saw concerning Judah and Jerusalem:

2 In the last days

the mountain of the LORD's temple
will be established
as chief among the mountains;
it will be raised above the hills,
and all nations will stream to it.

3 Many peoples will come and say,

"Come, let us go up to the mountain
of the LORD,
to the house of the God of Jacob.
He will teach us his ways,
so that we may walk in his paths."
The law will go out from Zion,
the word of the LORD from
Jerusalem.
4 He will judge between the nations
and will settle disputes for many
peoples.

They will beat their swords into
plowshares
and their spears into pruning
hooks.
Nation will not take up sword against
nation,
nor will they train for war anymore.

5 Come, O house of Jacob,
let us walk in the light of the LORD.

The Day of the LORD

6 You have abandoned your people,
the house of Jacob.
They are full of superstitions from the
East;
they practice divination like the
Philistines
and clasp hands with pagans.
7 Their land is full of silver and gold;
there is no end to their treasures.
Their land is full of horses;
there is no end to their chariots.
8 Their land is full of idols;
they bow down to the work of their
hands,
to what their fingers have made.
9 So man will be brought low
and mankind humbled—
do not forgive them.[a]

10 Go into the rocks,
hide in the ground
from dread of the LORD
and the splendor of his majesty!
11 The eyes of the arrogant man will be
humbled
and the pride of men brought low;
the LORD alone will be exalted in that
day.

12 The LORD Almighty has a day in store
for all the proud and lofty,
for all that is exalted
(and they will be humbled),
13 for all the cedars of Lebanon, tall and
lofty,
and all the oaks of Bashan,
14 for all the towering mountains
and all the high hills,
15 for every lofty tower
and every fortified wall,
16 for every trading ship[b]
and every stately vessel.
17 The arrogance of man will be brought
low
and the pride of men humbled;
the LORD alone will be exalted in that
day,
18 and the idols will totally disappear.

19 Men will flee to caves in the rocks
and to holes in the ground
from dread of the LORD
and the splendor of his majesty,
when he rises to shake the earth.
20 In that day men will throw away
to the rodents and bats
their idols of silver and idols of gold,
which they made to worship.
21 They will flee to caverns in the rocks
and to the overhanging crags
from dread of the LORD
and the splendor of his majesty,
when he rises to shake the earth.

22 Stop trusting in man,
who has but a breath in his nostrils.
Of what account is he?

[a] 9 Or *not raise them up* [b] 16 Hebrew *every ship of Tarshish*

PRAYER: AFFIRMATION

YOUR eyes are too pure to look at evil; You cannot look on wickedness. (Habakkuk 1:13) . . . Far be it from You to kill the righteous along with the wicked, treating the righteous and the wicked alike. Far be it from You! Won't You, the Judge of all the earth, do right? (Genesis 18:25)

***PAUSE** to reflect on these Biblical affirmations.*

NT Mark 16:1–20

The Resurrection

16 When the Sabbath was over, Mary
Magdalene, Mary the mother of
James, and Salome bought spices so that
they might go to anoint Jesus' body. 2 Very
early on the first day of the week, just after sunrise, they were on their way to the
tomb 3 and they asked each other, "Who

will roll the stone away from the entrance of the tomb?"

[4]But when they looked up, they saw that the stone, which was very large, had been rolled away. [5]As they entered the tomb, they saw a young man dressed in a white robe sitting on the right side, and they were alarmed.

[6]"Don't be alarmed," he said. "You are looking for Jesus the Nazarene, who was crucified. He has risen! He is not here. See the place where they laid him. [7]But go, tell his disciples and Peter, 'He is going ahead of you into Galilee. There you will see him, just as he told you.' "

[8]Trembling and bewildered, the women went out and fled from the tomb. They said nothing to anyone, because they were afraid.

[The earliest manuscripts and some other ancient witnesses do not have Mark 16:9–20.]

[9]When Jesus rose early on the first day of the week, he appeared first to Mary Magdalene, out of whom he had driven seven demons. [10]She went and told those who had been with him and who were mourning and weeping. [11]When they heard that Jesus was alive and that she had seen him, they did not believe it.

[12]Afterward Jesus appeared in a different form to two of them while they were walking in the country. [13]These returned and reported it to the rest; but they did not believe them either.

[14]Later Jesus appeared to the Eleven as they were eating; he rebuked them for their lack of faith and their stubborn refusal to believe those who had seen him after he had risen.

[15]He said to them, "Go into all the world and preach the good news to all creation. [16]Whoever believes and is baptized will be saved, but whoever does not believe will be condemned. [17]And these signs will accompany those who believe: In my name they will drive out demons; they will speak in new tongues; [18]they will pick up snakes with their hands; and when they drink deadly poison, it will not hurt them at all; they will place their hands on sick people, and they will get well."

[19]After the Lord Jesus had spoken to them, he was taken up into heaven and he sat at the right hand of God. [20]Then the disciples went out and preached everywhere, and the Lord worked with them and confirmed his word by the signs that accompanied it.

PRAYER: THE CHARACTER I WANT TO CULTIVATE

YOU, O God, are not mocked, for whatever we sow, this we will also reap. The one who sows to please the flesh will reap corruption; the one who sows to please the Spirit will, from the Spirit, reap eternal life. (Galatians 6:7–8)

***TAKE** a moment to ask the Lord for the grace to grow in godly character.*

YEAR 2 DAY 125

OT Isaiah 3:1–4:6

Judgment on Jerusalem and Judah

3 See now, the Lord,
the LORD Almighty,
is about to take from Jerusalem and Judah
both supply and support:
all supplies of food and all supplies of water,
2 the hero and warrior,
the judge and prophet,
the soothsayer and elder,
3 the captain of fifty and man of rank,
the counselor, skilled craftsman and clever enchanter.

4 I will make boys their officials;
mere children will govern them.
5 People will oppress each other—
man against man, neighbor against neighbor.

The young will rise up against the old,
the base against the honorable.

6 A man will seize one of his brothers
at his father's home, and say,
"You have a cloak, you be our leader;
take charge of this heap of ruins!"
7 But in that day he will cry out,
"I have no remedy.
I have no food or clothing in my house;
do not make me the leader of the
people."

8 Jerusalem staggers,
Judah is falling;
their words and deeds are against the
LORD,
defying his glorious presence.
9 The look on their faces testifies against
them;
they parade their sin like Sodom;
they do not hide it.
Woe to them!
They have brought disaster upon
themselves.

10 Tell the righteous it will be well with
them,
for they will enjoy the fruit of their
deeds.
11 Woe to the wicked! Disaster is upon
them!
They will be paid back for what their
hands have done.

12 Youths oppress my people,
women rule over them.
O my people, your guides lead you
astray;
they turn you from the path.

13 The LORD takes his place in court;
he rises to judge the people.
14 The LORD enters into judgment
against the elders and leaders of his
people:
"It is you who have ruined my
vineyard;
the plunder from the poor is in
your houses.
15 What do you mean by crushing my
people
and grinding the faces of the poor?"
declares the Lord,
the LORD Almighty.

16 The LORD says,
"The women of Zion are haughty,
walking along with outstretched
necks,
flirting with their eyes,
tripping along with mincing steps,
with ornaments jingling on their
ankles.
17 Therefore the Lord will bring sores on
the heads of the women of
Zion;
the LORD will make their scalps bald."

18 In that day the Lord will snatch away
their finery: the bangles and headbands
and crescent necklaces, 19 the earrings and
bracelets and veils, 20 the headdresses and
ankle chains and sashes, the perfume bot-
tles and charms, 21 the signet rings and
nose rings, 22 the fine robes and the capes
and cloaks, the purses 23 and mirrors, and
the linen garments and tiaras and shawls.

24 Instead of fragrance there will be a
stench;
instead of a sash, a rope;
instead of well-dressed hair, baldness;
instead of fine clothing, sackcloth;
instead of beauty, branding.
25 Your men will fall by the sword,
your warriors in battle.
26 The gates of Zion will lament and
mourn;
destitute, she will sit on the ground.

4 In that day seven women
will take hold of one man
and say, "We will eat our own food
and provide our own clothes;
only let us be called by your name.
Take away our disgrace!"

The Branch of the LORD

2 In that day the Branch of the LORD will
be beautiful and glorious, and the fruit of
the land will be the pride and glory of the
survivors in Israel. 3 Those who are left in
Zion, who remain in Jerusalem, will be
called holy, all who are recorded among
the living in Jerusalem. 4 The Lord will
wash away the filth of the women of Zion;
he will cleanse the bloodstains from Jerusalem by a spirit[a] of judgment and a
spirit[a] of fire. 5 Then the LORD will create
over all of Mount Zion and over those
who assemble there a cloud of smoke by
day and a glow of flaming fire by night;
over all the glory will be a canopy. 6 It will
be a shelter and shade from the heat of
the day, and a refuge and hiding place
from the storm and rain.

[a] 4 Or *the Spirit*

PRAYER: THANKSGIVING

I AM continually with You; You hold me by my right hand. You guide me with Your counsel, and afterward You will take me to glory. (Psalm 73:23–24)

***PAUSE** to offer your own expressions of thanksgiving.*

NT 1 Corinthians 1:1–17

1 Paul, called to be an apostle of Christ Jesus by the will of God, and our brother Sosthenes,

[2]To the church of God in Corinth, to those sanctified in Christ Jesus and called to be holy, together with all those everywhere who call on the name of our Lord Jesus Christ—their Lord and ours:

[3]Grace and peace to you from God our Father and the Lord Jesus Christ.

Thanksgiving

[4]I always thank God for you because of his grace given you in Christ Jesus. [5]For in
him you have been enriched in every way—in all your speaking and in all your knowledge— [6]because our testimony
about Christ was confirmed in you.
[7]Therefore you do not lack any spiritual gift as you eagerly wait for our Lord Jesus
Christ to be revealed. [8]He will keep you
strong to the end, so that you will be blameless on the day of our Lord Jesus
Christ. [9]God, who has called you into fellowship with his Son Jesus Christ our Lord, is faithful.

Divisions in the Church

[10]I appeal to you, brothers, in the name of our Lord Jesus Christ, that all of you agree with one another so that there may be no divisions among you and that you may be perfectly united in mind and
thought. [11]My brothers, some from Chloe's household have informed me that
there are quarrels among you. [12]What I
mean is this: One of you says, "I follow Paul"; another, "I follow Apollos"; another, "I follow Cephas[a]"; still another, "I follow Christ."

[13]Is Christ divided? Was Paul crucified for you? Were you baptized into[b] the
name of Paul? [14]I am thankful that I did not baptize any of you except Crispus and
Gaius, [15]so no one can say that you were
baptized into my name. [16](Yes, I also baptized the household of Stephanas; beyond that, I don't remember if I baptized anyone else.)
[17]For Christ did not send me to baptize, but to preach the gospel—not with words of human wisdom, lest the cross of Christ be emptied of its power.

[a] *12* That is, Peter [b] *13* Or *in;* also in verse 15

PRAYER: MY RELATIONSHIP TO OTHERS

I WILL hold firmly to the faithful word as I have been taught, so that I can exhort others by sound doctrine and refute those who oppose it. (Titus 1:9) . . . We must take heed to ourselves and to all the flock of which the Holy Spirit has made us overseers to shepherd Your church, O God, which You purchased with Your own blood. (Acts 20:28)

***PAUSE** to review your relationships with others and to commit them to the Lord.*

YEAR 2 DAY 126

OT Psalms 95–96

Psalm 95

[1]Come, let us sing for joy to the LORD;
let us shout aloud to the Rock of our salvation.
[2]Let us come before him with thanksgiving
and extol him with music and song.

[3]For the LORD is the great God,
the great King above all gods.
[4]In his hand are the depths of the earth,
and the mountain peaks belong to him.
[5]The sea is his, for he made it,
and his hands formed the dry land.

[6]Come, let us bow down in worship,
let us kneel before the LORD our Maker;
[7]for he is our God
and we are the people of his pasture,
the flock under his care.

Today, if you hear his voice,
[8] do not harden your hearts as you did at Meribah,[a]
as you did that day at Massah[b] in the desert,
[9]where your fathers tested and tried me,
though they had seen what I did.
[10]For forty years I was angry with that generation;
I said, "They are a people whose hearts go astray,
and they have not known my ways."
[11]So I declared on oath in my anger,
"They shall never enter my rest."

Psalm 96

[1]Sing to the LORD a new song;
sing to the LORD, all the earth.
[2]Sing to the LORD, praise his name;
proclaim his salvation day after day.
[3]Declare his glory among the nations,
his marvelous deeds among all peoples.

[4]For great is the LORD and most worthy of praise;
he is to be feared above all gods.
[5]For all the gods of the nations are idols,
but the LORD made the heavens.
[6]Splendor and majesty are before him;
strength and glory are in his sanctuary.

[7]Ascribe to the LORD, O families of nations,
ascribe to the LORD glory and strength.
[8]Ascribe to the LORD the glory due his name;
bring an offering and come into his courts.
[9]Worship the LORD in the splendor of his[c] holiness;
tremble before him, all the earth.

[10]Say among the nations, "The LORD reigns."
The world is firmly established, it cannot be moved;
he will judge the peoples with equity.
[11]Let the heavens rejoice, let the earth be glad;
let the sea resound, and all that is in it;
[12] let the fields be jubilant, and everything in them.
Then all the trees of the forest will sing for joy;
[13] they will sing before the LORD, for he comes,
he comes to judge the earth.
He will judge the world in righteousness
and the peoples in his truth.

[a] 8 *Meribah* means *quarreling.* [b] 8 *Massah* means *testing.* [c] 9 Or *LORD with the splendor of*

PRAYER: ADORATION

YOU are seated on Your throne with all the host of heaven standing by You on Your right and on Your left. (1 Kings 22:19) . . . The heavens, even the highest heavens, cannot contain You, O Lord. (2 Chronicles 2:6; 6:18)

***PAUSE** to express your thoughts of praise and worship.*

NT 1 Corinthians 1:18–2:5

Christ the Wisdom and Power of God

18For the message of the cross is foolishness to those who are perishing, but to
us who are being saved it is the power of
God. 19For it is written:

"I will destroy the wisdom of the wise;
the intelligence of the intelligent I
will frustrate."[a]

20Where is the wise man? Where is the
scholar? Where is the philosopher of this
age? Has not God made foolish the wisdom of the world? 21For since in the wisdom of God the world through its wisdom did not know him, God was pleased
through the foolishness of what was
preached to save those who believe. 22Jews
demand miraculous signs and Greeks
look for wisdom, 23but we preach Christ
crucified: a stumbling block to Jews and
foolishness to Gentiles, 24but to those
whom God has called, both Jews and
Greeks, Christ the power of God and the
wisdom of God. 25For the foolishness of
God is wiser than man's wisdom, and the
weakness of God is stronger than man's
strength.

26Brothers, think of what you were
when you were called. Not many of you
were wise by human standards; not many
were influential; not many were of noble
birth. 27But God chose the foolish things
of the world to shame the wise; God
chose the weak things of the world to
shame the strong. 28He chose the lowly
things of this world and the despised
things—and the things that are not—to
nullify the things that are, 29so that no one
may boast before him. 30It is because of
him that you are in Christ Jesus, who has
become for us wisdom from God—that is,
our righteousness, holiness and redemption. 31Therefore, as it is written: "Let him
who boasts boast in the Lord."[b]

2 When I came to you, brothers, I did not
come with eloquence or superior wisdom as I proclaimed to you the testimony
about God.[c] 2For I resolved to know nothing while I was with you except Jesus
Christ and him crucified. 3I came to you
in weakness and fear, and with much
trembling. 4My message and my preaching
were not with wise and persuasive words,
but with a demonstration of the Spirit's
power, 5so that your faith might not rest
on men's wisdom, but on God's power.

[a] *19* Isaiah 29:14 [b] *31* Jer. 9:24 [c] *1* Some manuscripts *as I proclaimed to you God's mystery*

PRAYER: THE ATTRIBUTES OF GOD

YOU are the Lord; that is Your name. You will not give Your glory to another, or Your praise to idols. (Isaiah 42:8) . . .

Your name, O Lord, endures forever, Your renown, O Lord, through all generations. (Psalm 135:13)

***PAUSE** to reflect on these affirmations about the person, powers and perfection of God.*

YEAR 2 DAY 127

OT Isaiah 5:1–30

The Song of the Vineyard

5 I will sing for the one I love
a song about his vineyard:
My loved one had a vineyard
on a fertile hillside.
2He dug it up and cleared it of stones
and planted it with the choicest
vines.
He built a watchtower in it
and cut out a winepress as well.
Then he looked for a crop of good
grapes,
but it yielded only bad fruit.

3"Now you dwellers in Jerusalem and
men of Judah,
judge between me and my vineyard.

[4]What more could have been done for
my vineyard
than I have done for it?
When I looked for good grapes,
why did it yield only bad?
[5]Now I will tell you
what I am going to do to my
vineyard:
I will take away its hedge,
and it will be destroyed;
I will break down its wall,
and it will be trampled.
[6]I will make it a wasteland,
neither pruned nor cultivated,
and briers and thorns will grow
there.
I will command the clouds
not to rain on it."

[7]The vineyard of the LORD Almighty
is the house of Israel,
and the men of Judah
are the garden of his delight.
And he looked for justice, but saw
bloodshed;
for righteousness, but heard cries of
distress.

Woes and Judgments

[8]Woe to you who add house to house
and join field to field
till no space is left
and you live alone in the land.

[9]The LORD Almighty has declared in my
hearing:

"Surely the great houses will become
desolate,
the fine mansions left without
occupants.
[10]A ten-acre[a] vineyard will produce only
a bath[b] of wine,
a homer[c] of seed only an ephah[d] of
grain."

[11]Woe to those who rise early in the
morning
to run after their drinks,
who stay up late at night
till they are inflamed with wine.
[12]They have harps and lyres at their
banquets,
tambourines and flutes and wine,
but they have no regard for the deeds
of the LORD,
no respect for the work of his
hands.
[13]Therefore my people will go into exile
for lack of understanding;
their men of rank will die of hunger
and their masses will be parched
with thirst.
[14]Therefore the grave[e] enlarges its
appetite
and opens its mouth without limit;
into it will descend their nobles and
masses
with all their brawlers and revelers.
[15]So man will be brought low
and mankind humbled,
the eyes of the arrogant humbled.
[16]But the LORD Almighty will be exalted
by his justice,
and the holy God will show himself
holy by his righteousness.
[17]Then sheep will graze as in their own
pasture;
lambs will feed[f] among the ruins of
the rich.

[18]Woe to those who draw sin along
with cords of deceit,
and wickedness as with cart ropes,
[19]to those who say, "Let God hurry,
let him hasten his work
so we may see it.
Let it approach,
let the plan of the Holy One of
Israel come,
so we may know it."

[20]Woe to those who call evil good
and good evil,
who put darkness for light
and light for darkness,
who put bitter for sweet
and sweet for bitter.

[21]Woe to those who are wise in their
own eyes
and clever in their own sight.

[22]Woe to those who are heroes at
drinking wine
and champions at mixing drinks,
[23]who acquit the guilty for a bribe,
but deny justice to the innocent.
[24]Therefore, as tongues of fire lick up
straw

[a] *10* Hebrew *ten-yoke,* that is, the land plowed by 10 yoke of oxen in one day [b] *10* That is, probably about 6 gallons (about 22 liters) [c] *10* That is, probably about 6 bushels (about 220 liters) [d] *10* That is, probably about 3/5 bushel (about 22 liters) [e] *14* Hebrew *Sheol* [f] *17* Septuagint; Hebrew / *strangers will eat*

and as dry grass sinks down in the flames,
so their roots will decay
and their flowers blow away like dust;
for they have rejected the law of the LORD Almighty
and spurned the word of the Holy One of Israel.
25 Therefore the LORD's anger burns against his people;
his hand is raised and he strikes them down.
The mountains shake,
and the dead bodies are like refuse in the streets.

Yet for all this, his anger is not turned away,
his hand is still upraised.

26 He lifts up a banner for the distant nations,
he whistles for those at the ends of the earth.
Here they come,
swiftly and speedily!
27 Not one of them grows tired or stumbles,
not one slumbers or sleeps;
not a belt is loosened at the waist,
not a sandal thong is broken.
28 Their arrows are sharp,
all their bows are strung;
their horses' hoofs seem like flint,
their chariot wheels like a whirlwind.
29 Their roar is like that of the lion,
they roar like young lions;
they growl as they seize their prey
and carry it off with no one to rescue.
30 In that day they will roar over it
like the roaring of the sea.
And if one looks at the land,
he will see darkness and distress;
even the light will be darkened by the clouds.

PRAYER: CONFESSION

THIS is what You, the Lord God, the Holy One of Israel, have said: "In repentance and rest is your salvation; in quietness and trust is your strength." (Isaiah 30:15)

***ASK** the Spirit to search your heart and reveal any areas of unconfessed sin. Acknowledge these to the Lord and thank Him for His forgiveness.*

NT 1 Corinthians 2:6–16

Wisdom From the Spirit

6 We do, however, speak a message of
wisdom among the mature, but not the
wisdom of this age or of the rulers of this
age, who are coming to nothing. 7 No, we
speak of God's secret wisdom, a wisdom
that has been hidden and that God destined for our glory before time began.
8 None of the rulers of this age understood
it, for if they had, they would not have crucified the Lord of glory. 9 However, as it is
written:

"No eye has seen,
no ear has heard,
no mind has conceived
what God has prepared for those who love him"[a]—

10 but God has revealed it to us by his Spirit.

The Spirit searches all things, even the
deep things of God. 11 For who among
men knows the thoughts of a man except
the man's spirit within him? In the same
way no one knows the thoughts of God
except the Spirit of God. 12 We have not
received the spirit of the world but the
Spirit who is from God, that we may understand what God has freely given us.
13 This is what we speak, not in words
taught us by human wisdom but in
words taught by the Spirit, expressing
spiritual truths in spiritual words.[b] 14 The
man without the Spirit does not accept
the things that come from the Spirit of

[a] 9 Isaiah 64:4 [b] 13 Or *Spirit, interpreting spiritual truths to spiritual men*

God, for they are foolishness to him, and he cannot understand them, because they are spiritually discerned. [15]The spiritual man makes judgments about all things, but he himself is not subject to any man's judgment:

[16]"For who has known the mind of the
 Lord
 that he may instruct him?"[c]

But we have the mind of Christ.

[c] 16 Isaiah 40:13

PRAYER: THE WORKS OF GOD

O GOD, You completed the heavens and the earth in all their vast array. By the seventh day You finished the work that You had done, and You rested on the seventh day from all Your creative work. And You blessed the seventh day and sanctified it, because on it You rested from all the work of creating that You had done. (Genesis 2:1–3)

__TAKE__ a moment to consider the greatness of God's wonderful works.

YEAR 2 DAY 128

OT Isaiah 6:1–7:25

Isaiah's Commission

6 In the year that King Uzziah died, I
saw the Lord seated on a throne, high
and exalted, and the train of his robe
filled the temple. [2]Above him were seraphs, each with six wings: With two
wings they covered their faces, with two
they covered their feet, and with two they
were flying. [3]And they were calling to one
another:

"Holy, holy, holy is the LORD
 Almighty;
 the whole earth is full of his glory."

[4]At the sound of their voices the doorposts and thresholds shook and the temple was filled with smoke.
[5]"Woe to me!" I cried. "I am ruined! For
I am a man of unclean lips, and I live
among a people of unclean lips, and my
eyes have seen the King, the LORD
Almighty."
[6]Then one of the seraphs flew to me
with a live coal in his hand, which he had
taken with tongs from the altar. [7]With it
he touched my mouth and said, "See, this
has touched your lips; your guilt is taken
away and your sin atoned for."
[8]Then I heard the voice of the Lord saying, "Whom shall I send? And who will
go for us?"
And I said, "Here am I. Send me!"
[9]He said, "Go and tell this people:

" 'Be ever hearing, but never
 understanding;
 be ever seeing, but never perceiving.'
[10]Make the heart of this people calloused;
 make their ears dull
 and close their eyes.[a]
Otherwise they might see with their
 eyes,
 hear with their ears,
 understand with their hearts,
and turn and be healed."

[11]Then I said, "For how long, O Lord?"
And he answered:

"Until the cities lie ruined
 and without inhabitant,
until the houses are left deserted
 and the fields ruined and ravaged,
[12]until the LORD has sent everyone far
 away
 and the land is utterly forsaken.
[13]And though a tenth remains in the
 land,
 it will again be laid waste.
But as the terebinth and oak
 leave stumps when they are cut
 down,
 so the holy seed will be the stump
 in the land."

[a] 9,10 Hebrew; Septuagint *'You will be ever hearing, but never understanding; / you will be ever seeing, but never perceiving.' / [10]This people's heart has become calloused; / they hardly hear with their ears, / and they have closed their eyes*

The Sign of Immanuel

7 When Ahaz son of Jotham, the son of
Uzziah, was king of Judah, King Rezin
of Aram and Pekah son of Remaliah king
of Israel marched up to fight against Jerusalem, but they could not overpower it.
2Now the house of David was told,
"Aram has allied itself with[b] Ephraim"; so
the hearts of Ahaz and his people were
shaken, as the trees of the forest are shak-
en by the wind.
3Then the LORD said to Isaiah, "Go out,
you and your son Shear-Jashub,[c] to meet
Ahaz at the end of the aqueduct of the
Upper Pool, on the road to the Washerman's Field. 4Say to him, 'Be careful, keep
calm and don't be afraid. Do not lose
heart because of these two smoldering
stubs of firewood—because of the fierce
anger of Rezin and Aram and of the son
of Remaliah. 5Aram, Ephraim and Remaliah's son have plotted your ruin, saying,
6"Let us invade Judah; let us tear it apart
and divide it among ourselves, and make
the son of Tabeel king over it." 7Yet this is
what the Sovereign LORD says:

" 'It will not take place,
it will not happen,
8for the head of Aram is Damascus,
and the head of Damascus is only
Rezin.
Within sixty-five years
Ephraim will be too shattered to be
a people.
9The head of Ephraim is Samaria,
and the head of Samaria is only
Remaliah's son.
If you do not stand firm in your faith,
you will not stand at all.' "

10Again the LORD spoke to Ahaz, 11"Ask
the LORD your God for a sign, whether in
the deepest depths or in the highest
heights."
12But Ahaz said, "I will not ask; I will
not put the LORD to the test."
13Then Isaiah said, "Hear now, you
house of David! Is it not enough to try the
patience of men? Will you try the patience
of my God also? 14Therefore the Lord
himself will give you[d] a sign: The virgin
will be with child and will give birth to a
son, and[e] will call him Immanuel.[f] 15He
will eat curds and honey when he knows
enough to reject the wrong and choose
the right. 16But before the boy knows
enough to reject the wrong and choose
the right, the land of the two kings you
dread will be laid waste. 17The LORD will
bring on you and on your people and on
the house of your father a time unlike any
since Ephraim broke away from Judah—
he will bring the king of Assyria."
18In that day the LORD will whistle for
flies from the distant streams of Egypt
and for bees from the land of Assyria.
19They will all come and settle in the
steep ravines and in the crevices in the
rocks, on all the thornbushes and at all
the water holes. 20In that day the Lord will
use a razor hired from beyond the River[g]—the king of Assyria—to shave your
head and the hair of your legs, and to
take off your beards also. 21In that day, a
man will keep alive a young cow and two
goats. 22And because of the abundance of
the milk they give, he will have curds to
eat. All who remain in the land will eat
curds and honey. 23In that day, in every
place where there were a thousand vines
worth a thousand silver shekels,[h] there
will be only briers and thorns. 24Men will
go there with bow and arrow, for the land
will be covered with briers and thorns.
25As for all the hills once cultivated by the
hoe, you will no longer go there for fear
of the briers and thorns; they will become
places where cattle are turned loose and
where sheep run.

[b] 2 Or *has set up camp in* [c] 3 *Shear-Jashub* means *a remnant will return.* [d] 14 The Hebrew is plural. [e] 14 Masoretic Text; Dead Sea Scrolls *and he* or *and they* [f] 14 *Immanuel* means *God with us.* [g] 20 That is, the Euphrates [h] 23 That is, about 25 pounds (about 11.5 kilograms)

PRAYER: RENEWAL

MAY I do what is good and right in Your sight, O Lord my God. (2 Chronicles 14:2) . . . May my heart take delight in Your ways, O Lord, and may I remove the places of idolatry from my life. (2 Chronicles 17:6)

***PAUSE** to add your own prayers for personal renewal.*

NT 1 Corinthians 3:1–23

On Divisions in the Church

3 Brothers, I could not address you as spiritual but as worldly—mere infants in Christ. [2]I gave you milk, not solid food, for you were not yet ready for it. Indeed, you are still not ready. [3]You are still worldly. For since there is jealousy and quarreling among you, are you not worldly? Are you not acting like mere men? [4]For when one says, "I follow Paul," and another, "I follow Apollos," are you not mere men?

[5]What, after all, is Apollos? And what is Paul? Only servants, through whom you came to believe—as the Lord has assigned to each his task. [6]I planted the seed, Apollos watered it, but God made it grow. [7]So neither he who plants nor he who waters is anything, but only God, who makes things grow. [8]The man who plants and the man who waters have one purpose, and each will be rewarded according to his own labor. [9]For we are God's fellow workers; you are God's field, God's building.

[10]By the grace God has given me, I laid a foundation as an expert builder, and someone else is building on it. But each one should be careful how he builds. [11]For no one can lay any foundation other than the one already laid, which is Jesus Christ. [12]If any man builds on this foundation using gold, silver, costly stones, wood, hay or straw, [13]his work will be shown for what it is, because the Day will bring it to light. It will be revealed with fire, and the fire will test the quality of each man's work. [14]If what he has built survives, he will receive his reward. [15]If it is burned up, he will suffer loss; he himself will be saved, but only as one escaping through the flames.

[16]Don't you know that you yourselves are God's temple and that God's Spirit lives in you? [17]If anyone destroys God's temple, God will destroy him; for God's temple is sacred, and you are that temple.

[18]Do not deceive yourselves. If any one of you thinks he is wise by the standards of this age, he should become a "fool" so that he may become wise. [19]For the wisdom of this world is foolishness in God's sight. As it is written: "He catches the wise in their craftiness"[a]; [20]and again, "The Lord knows that the thoughts of the wise are futile."[b] [21]So then, no more boasting about men! All things are yours, [22]whether Paul or Apollos or Cephas[c] or the world or life or death or the present or the future—all are yours, [23]and you are of Christ, and Christ is of God.

[a] 19 Job 5:13 [b] 20 Psalm 94:11 [c] 22 That is, Peter

PRAYER: MY RELATIONSHIP TO GOD

I AM no longer a stranger and alien, but a fellow citizen with Your people, O God, and a member of Your household, built on the foundation of the apostles and prophets, with Christ Jesus Himself as the chief cornerstone. (Ephesians 2:19–20)

***PAUSE** to thank God for the relationship that you enjoy with Him in Jesus Christ.*

YEAR 2 DAY 129

OT Isaiah 8:1–9:21

Assyria, the LORD's Instrument

8 The LORD said to me, "Take a large scroll and write on it with an ordinary pen: Maher-Shalal-Hash-Baz.[a] [2]And I will call in Uriah the priest and Zechariah son of Jeberekiah as reliable witnesses for me."

[3]Then I went to the prophetess, and she conceived and gave birth to a son. And the LORD said to me, "Name him Maher-Shalal-Hash-Baz. [4]Before the boy knows how

[a] 1 *Maher-Shalal-Hash-Baz* means *quick to the plunder, swift to the spoil;* also in verse 3.

to say 'My father' or 'My mother,' the wealth of Damascus and the plunder of Samaria will be carried off by the king of Assyria."

5 The LORD spoke to me again:

6 "Because this people has rejected
the gently flowing waters of Shiloah
and rejoices over Rezin
and the son of Remaliah,
7 therefore the Lord is about to bring against them
the mighty floodwaters of the River[b]—
the king of Assyria with all his pomp.
It will overflow all its channels,
run over all its banks
8 and sweep on into Judah, swirling over it,
passing through it and reaching up to the neck.
Its outspread wings will cover the breadth of your land,
O Immanuel[c]!"

9 Raise the war cry,[d] you nations, and be shattered!
Listen, all you distant lands.
Prepare for battle, and be shattered!
Prepare for battle, and be shattered!
10 Devise your strategy, but it will be thwarted;
propose your plan, but it will not stand,
for God is with us.[e]

Fear God

11 The LORD spoke to me with his strong hand upon me, warning me not to follow the way of this people. He said:

12 "Do not call conspiracy
everything that these people call conspiracy[f];
do not fear what they fear,
and do not dread it.
13 The LORD Almighty is the one you are to regard as holy,
he is the one you are to fear,
he is the one you are to dread,
14 and he will be a sanctuary;
but for both houses of Israel he will be
a stone that causes men to stumble
and a rock that makes them fall.
And for the people of Jerusalem he will be
a trap and a snare.
15 Many of them will stumble;
they will fall and be broken,
they will be snared and captured."

16 Bind up the testimony
and seal up the law among my disciples.
17 I will wait for the LORD,
who is hiding his face from the house of Jacob.
I will put my trust in him.

18 Here am I, and the children the LORD
has given me. We are signs and symbols
in Israel from the LORD Almighty, who
dwells on Mount Zion.
19 When men tell you to consult mediums and spiritists, who whisper and mutter, should not a people inquire of their
God? Why consult the dead on behalf of
the living? 20 To the law and to the testimony! If they do not speak according to
this word, they have no light of dawn.
21 Distressed and hungry, they will roam
through the land; when they are famished, they will become enraged and,
looking upward, will curse their king and
their God. 22 Then they will look toward
the earth and see only distress and darkness and fearful gloom, and they will be
thrust into utter darkness.

To Us a Child Is Born

9 Nevertheless, there will be no more gloom for those who were in distress. In the past he humbled the land of Zebulun and the land of Naphtali, but in the future he will honor Galilee of the Gentiles, by the way of the sea, along the Jordan—

2 The people walking in darkness
have seen a great light;
on those living in the land of the shadow of death[g]
a light has dawned.
3 You have enlarged the nation
and increased their joy;
they rejoice before you
as people rejoice at the harvest,
as men rejoice
when dividing the plunder.

[b] 7 That is, the Euphrates [c] 8 *Immanuel* means *God with us.* [d] 9 Or *Do your worst* [e] 10 Hebrew *Immanuel* [f] 12 Or *Do not call for a treaty / every time these people call for a treaty* [g] 2 Or *land of darkness*

[4] For as in the day of Midian's defeat,
you have shattered
the yoke that burdens them,
the bar across their shoulders,
the rod of their oppressor.
[5] Every warrior's boot used in battle
and every garment rolled in blood
will be destined for burning,
will be fuel for the fire.
[6] For to us a child is born,
to us a son is given,
and the government will be on his shoulders.
And he will be called
Wonderful Counselor,[h] Mighty God,
Everlasting Father, Prince of Peace.
[7] Of the increase of his government and peace
there will be no end.
He will reign on David's throne
and over his kingdom,
establishing and upholding it
with justice and righteousness
from that time on and forever.
The zeal of the LORD Almighty
will accomplish this.

The LORD's Anger Against Israel

[8] The Lord has sent a message against Jacob;
it will fall on Israel.
[9] All the people will know it—
Ephraim and the inhabitants of Samaria—
who say with pride
and arrogance of heart,
[10] "The bricks have fallen down,
but we will rebuild with dressed stone;
the fig trees have been felled,
but we will replace them with cedars."
[11] But the LORD has strengthened Rezin's foes against them
and has spurred their enemies on.
[12] Arameans from the east and Philistines from the west
have devoured Israel with open mouth.

Yet for all this, his anger is not turned away,
his hand is still upraised.
[13] But the people have not returned to him who struck them,
nor have they sought the LORD Almighty.
[14] So the LORD will cut off from Israel both head and tail,
both palm branch and reed in a single day;
[15] the elders and prominent men are the head,
the prophets who teach lies are the tail.
[16] Those who guide this people mislead them,
and those who are guided are led astray.
[17] Therefore the Lord will take no pleasure in the young men,
nor will he pity the fatherless and widows,
for everyone is ungodly and wicked,
every mouth speaks vileness.

Yet for all this, his anger is not turned away,
his hand is still upraised.

[18] Surely wickedness burns like a fire;
it consumes briers and thorns,
it sets the forest thickets ablaze,
so that it rolls upward in a column of smoke.
[19] By the wrath of the LORD Almighty
the land will be scorched
and the people will be fuel for the fire;
no one will spare his brother.
[20] On the right they will devour,
but still be hungry;
on the left they will eat,
but not be satisfied.
Each will feed on the flesh of his own offspring[i]:
[21] Manasseh will feed on Ephraim,
and Ephraim on Manasseh;
together they will turn against Judah.

Yet for all this, his anger is not turned away,
his hand is still upraised.

[h] 6 Or *Wonderful, Counselor* [i] 20 Or *arm*

PRAYER: PETITION

***MAY** I put away perversity from my mouth and keep corrupt talk far from my lips. (Proverbs 4:24)*

***PAUSE** here to petition God for growth in your desire to know and please Jesus Christ. Pray for a greater love and commitment to Him, for the grace to practice His presence and for the grace to glorify Him in your life. Offer prayers regarding your activities for this day and any special concerns you may have.*

NT 1 Corinthians 4:1–21

Apostles of Christ

4 So then, men ought to regard us as servants of Christ and as those entrusted
with the secret things of God. [2]Now it is
required that those who have been given
a trust must prove faithful. [3]I care very little if I am judged by you or by any human
court; indeed, I do not even judge myself.
[4]My conscience is clear, but that does not
make me innocent. It is the Lord who
judges me. [5]Therefore judge nothing before the appointed time; wait till the Lord
comes. He will bring to light what is hidden in darkness and will expose the motives of men's hearts. At that time each
will receive his praise from God.
[6]Now, brothers, I have applied these
things to myself and Apollos for your benefit, so that you may learn from us the
meaning of the saying, "Do not go beyond what is written." Then you will not
take pride in one man over against another. [7]For who makes you different from
anyone else? What do you have that you
did not receive? And if you did receive it,
why do you boast as though you did not?
[8]Already you have all you want! Already
you have become rich! You have become
kings—and that without us! How I wish
that you really had become kings so that
we might be kings with you! [9]For it seems
to me that God has put us apostles on display at the end of the procession, like men
condemned to die in the arena. We have
been made a spectacle to the whole universe, to angels as well as to men. [10]We are
fools for Christ, but you are so wise in
Christ! We are weak, but you are strong!
You are honored, we are dishonored! [11]To
this very hour we go hungry and thirsty,
we are in rags, we are brutally treated, we
are homeless. [12]We work hard with our
own hands. When we are cursed, we bless;
when we are persecuted, we endure it;
[13]when we are slandered, we answer kindly. Up to this moment we have become the
scum of the earth, the refuse of the world.
[14]I am not writing this to shame you,
but to warn you, as my dear children.
[15]Even though you have ten thousand
guardians in Christ, you do not have
many fathers, for in Christ Jesus I became
your father through the gospel. [16]There-
fore I urge you to imitate me. [17]For this
reason I am sending to you Timothy, my
son whom I love, who is faithful in the
Lord. He will remind you of my way of
life in Christ Jesus, which agrees with
what I teach everywhere in every church.
[18]Some of you have become arrogant, as
if I were not coming to you. [19]But I will
come to you very soon, if the Lord is willing, and then I will find out not only how
these arrogant people are talking, but what
power they have. [20]For the kingdom of God
is not a matter of talk but of power. [21]What
do you prefer? Shall I come to you with a
whip, or in love and with a gentle spirit?

PRAYER: THE CHARACTER I WANT TO CULTIVATE

***I WILL** flee youthful lusts and pursue righteousness, faith, love, and peace, with those who call on You, O Lord, out of a pure heart. (2 Timothy 2:22)*

***TAKE** a moment to ask the Lord for the grace to grow in godly character.*

OT Isaiah 10:1–34

10 Woe to those who make unjust laws,
to those who issue oppressive decrees,
2 to deprive the poor of their rights
and withhold justice from the oppressed of my people,
making widows their prey
and robbing the fatherless.
3 What will you do on the day of reckoning,
when disaster comes from afar?
To whom will you run for help?
Where will you leave your riches?
4 Nothing will remain but to cringe among the captives
or fall among the slain.

Yet for all this, his anger is not turned away,
his hand is still upraised.

God's Judgment on Assyria

5 "Woe to the Assyrian, the rod of my anger,
in whose hand is the club of my wrath!
6 I send him against a godless nation,
I dispatch him against a people who anger me,
to seize loot and snatch plunder,
and to trample them down like mud in the streets.
7 But this is not what he intends,
this is not what he has in mind;
his purpose is to destroy,
to put an end to many nations.
8 'Are not my commanders all kings?'
he says.
9 'Has not Calno fared like Carchemish?
Is not Hamath like Arpad,
and Samaria like Damascus?
10 As my hand seized the kingdoms of the idols,
kingdoms whose images excelled those of Jerusalem and Samaria—
11 shall I not deal with Jerusalem and her images
as I dealt with Samaria and her idols?' "

12 When the Lord has finished all his
work against Mount Zion and Jerusalem,
he will say, "I will punish the king of Assyria for the willful pride of his heart and
the haughty look in his eyes. 13 For he says:

" 'By the strength of my hand I have done this,
and by my wisdom, because I have understanding.
I removed the boundaries of nations,
I plundered their treasures;
like a mighty one I subdued[a] their kings.
14 As one reaches into a nest,
so my hand reached for the wealth of the nations;
as men gather abandoned eggs,
so I gathered all the countries;
not one flapped a wing,
or opened its mouth to chirp.' "

15 Does the ax raise itself above him who swings it,
or the saw boast against him who uses it?
As if a rod were to wield him who lifts it up,
or a club brandish him who is not wood!
16 Therefore, the Lord, the LORD Almighty,
will send a wasting disease upon his sturdy warriors;
under his pomp a fire will be kindled
like a blazing flame.
17 The Light of Israel will become a fire,
their Holy One a flame;
in a single day it will burn and consume
his thorns and his briers.
18 The splendor of his forests and fertile fields
it will completely destroy,
as when a sick man wastes away.
19 And the remaining trees of his forests will be so few
that a child could write them down.

The Remnant of Israel

20 In that day the remnant of Israel,
the survivors of the house of Jacob,
will no longer rely on him
who struck them down

[a] 13 Or / *I subdued the mighty,*

but will truly rely on the LORD,
the Holy One of Israel.
21 A remnant will return,[b] a remnant of Jacob
will return to the Mighty God.
22 Though your people, O Israel, be like the sand by the sea,
only a remnant will return.
Destruction has been decreed,
overwhelming and righteous.
23 The Lord, the LORD Almighty, will carry out
the destruction decreed upon the whole land.

24 Therefore, this is what the Lord, the LORD Almighty, says:

"O my people who live in Zion,
do not be afraid of the Assyrians,
who beat you with a rod
and lift up a club against you, as Egypt did.
25 Very soon my anger against you will end
and my wrath will be directed to their destruction."

26 The LORD Almighty will lash them with a whip,
as when he struck down Midian at the rock of Oreb;
and he will raise his staff over the waters,
as he did in Egypt.
27 In that day their burden will be lifted from your shoulders,
their yoke from your neck;
the yoke will be broken
because you have grown so fat.[c]

28 They enter Aiath;
they pass through Migron;
they store supplies at Micmash.
29 They go over the pass, and say,
"We will camp overnight at Geba."
Ramah trembles;
Gibeah of Saul flees.
30 Cry out, O Daughter of Gallim!
Listen, O Laishah!
Poor Anathoth!
31 Madmenah is in flight;
the people of Gebim take cover.
32 This day they will halt at Nob;
they will shake their fist
at the mount of the Daughter of Zion,
at the hill of Jerusalem.

33 See, the Lord, the LORD Almighty,
will lop off the boughs with great power.
The lofty trees will be felled,
the tall ones will be brought low.
34 He will cut down the forest thickets with an ax;
Lebanon will fall before the Mighty One.

[b] 21 Hebrew *shear-jashub;* also in verse 22
[c] 27 Hebrew; Septuagint *broken / from your shoulders*

PRAYER: INTERCESSION

AS living stones, we are being built into a spiritual house to be a holy priesthood, offering spiritual sacrifices acceptable to You, O God, through Jesus Christ. We are a chosen people, a royal priesthood, a holy nation, a people for Your own possession, that we may declare Your praises—You who called us out of darkness into Your marvelous light. (1 Peter 2:5, 9)

__TAKE__ a few moments to intercede on behalf of your local church, other churches, evangelism and discipleship ministries, educational ministries and any other special concerns you may have.

NT 1 Corinthians 5:1–13

Expel the Immoral Brother!

5 It is actually reported that there is sexual immorality among you, and of a kind that does not occur even among pagans: A man has his father's wife. 2 And you are proud! Shouldn't you rather have been filled with grief and have put out of your fellowship the man who did this?
3 Even though I am not physically present, I am with you in spirit. And I have already

passed judgment on the one who did this,
just as if I were present. 4When you are assembled in the name of our Lord Jesus
and I am with you in spirit, and the power of our Lord Jesus is present, 5hand this
man over to Satan, so that the sinful nature[a] may be destroyed and his spirit
saved on the day of the Lord.

6Your boasting is not good. Don't you
know that a little yeast works through the
whole batch of dough? 7Get rid of the old
yeast that you may be a new batch without yeast—as you really are. For Christ,
our Passover lamb, has been sacrificed.
8Therefore let us keep the Festival, not
with the old yeast, the yeast of malice and
wickedness, but with bread without yeast,
the bread of sincerity and truth.

9I have written you in my letter not to
associate with sexually immoral people—
10not at all meaning the people of this
world who are immoral, or the greedy
and swindlers, or idolaters. In that case
you would have to leave this world. 11But
now I am writing you that you must not
associate with anyone who calls himself a
brother but is sexually immoral or greedy,
an idolater or a slanderer, a drunkard or a
swindler. With such a man do not even
eat.

12What business is it of mine to judge
those outside the church? Are you not to
judge those inside? 13God will judge those
outside. "Expel the wicked man from
among you."[b]

[a] 5 Or *that his body;* or *that the flesh* [b] *13* Deut. 17:7; 19:19; 21:21; 22:21,24; 24:7

PRAYER: MY RELATIONSHIP TO OTHERS

YOUR commandments will be upon my heart, and I will teach them diligently to my children and talk about them when I sit in my house and when I walk along the way and when I lie down and when I rise up. (Deuteronomy 6:6–7)

***PAUSE** to review your relationships with others and to commit them to the Lord.*

YEAR 2 DAY 131

OT Isaiah 11:1–12:6

The Branch From Jesse

11 A shoot will come up from the
stump of Jesse;
from his roots a Branch will bear
fruit.
2The Spirit of the LORD will rest on
him—
the Spirit of wisdom and of
understanding,
the Spirit of counsel and of power,
the Spirit of knowledge and of the
fear of the LORD—
3and he will delight in the fear of the
LORD.

He will not judge by what he sees
with his eyes,
or decide by what he hears with his
ears;
4but with righteousness he will judge
the needy,
with justice he will give decisions
for the poor of the earth.
He will strike the earth with the rod of
his mouth;
with the breath of his lips he will
slay the wicked.
5Righteousness will be his belt
and faithfulness the sash around his
waist.

6The wolf will live with the lamb,
the leopard will lie down with the
goat,
the calf and the lion and the yearling[a]
together;
and a little child will lead them.
7The cow will feed with the bear,
their young will lie down together,
and the lion will eat straw like the
ox.

[a] 6 Hebrew; Septuagint *lion will feed*

[8]The infant will play near the hole of
the cobra,
and the young child put his hand
into the viper's nest.
[9]They will neither harm nor destroy
on all my holy mountain,
for the earth will be full of the
knowledge of the LORD
as the waters cover the sea.

[10]In that day the Root of Jesse will stand
as a banner for the peoples; the nations
will rally to him, and his place of rest will
be glorious. [11]In that day the Lord will
reach out his hand a second time to re-
claim the remnant that is left of his people from Assyria, from Lower Egypt, from
Upper Egypt,[b] from Cush,[c] from Elam,
from Babylonia,[d] from Hamath and from
the islands of the sea.

[12]He will raise a banner for the nations
and gather the exiles of Israel;
he will assemble the scattered people
of Judah
from the four quarters of the earth.
[13]Ephraim's jealousy will vanish,
and Judah's enemies[e] will be cut off;
Ephraim will not be jealous of Judah,
nor Judah hostile toward Ephraim.
[14]They will swoop down on the slopes
of Philistia to the west;
together they will plunder the
people to the east.
They will lay hands on Edom and
Moab,
and the Ammonites will be subject
to them.
[15]The LORD will dry up
the gulf of the Egyptian sea;
with a scorching wind he will sweep
his hand
over the Euphrates River.[f]
He will break it up into seven streams
so that men can cross over in
sandals.
[16]There will be a highway for the
remnant of his people
that is left from Assyria,
as there was for Israel
when they came up from Egypt.

Songs of Praise

12 In that day you will say:

"I will praise you, O LORD.
Although you were angry with me,
your anger has turned away
and you have comforted me.
[2]Surely God is my salvation;
I will trust and not be afraid.
The LORD, the LORD, is my strength
and my song;
he has become my salvation."
[3]With joy you will draw water
from the wells of salvation.

[4]In that day you will say:

"Give thanks to the LORD, call on his
name;
make known among the nations
what he has done,
and proclaim that his name is
exalted.
[5]Sing to the LORD, for he has done
glorious things;
let this be known to all the world.
[6]Shout aloud and sing for joy, people
of Zion,
for great is the Holy One of Israel
among you."

[b] 11 Hebrew *from Pathros* [c] 11 That is, the upper Nile region [d] 11 Hebrew *Shinar* [e] 13 Or *hostility* [f] 15 Hebrew *the River*

PRAYER: AFFIRMATION

THE faith of Your chosen people, and the knowledge of the truth that leads to godliness, is faith and knowledge resting in the hope of eternal life. It is an eternal life that You promised before the beginning of time—and You do not lie. At the appointed time, You manifested Your word through the preaching entrusted to the apostles by Your command, O God our Savior. (Titus 1:1–3)

PAUSE *to reflect on these Biblical affirmations.*

NT 1 Corinthians 6:1–11

Lawsuits Among Believers

6 If any of you has a dispute with another, dare he take it before the ungodly for judgment instead of before the
saints? 2Do you not know that the saints
will judge the world? And if you are to
judge the world, are you not competent to
judge trivial cases? 3Do you not know that
we will judge angels? How much more
the things of this life! 4Therefore, if you
have disputes about such matters, appoint
as judges even men of little account in the
church![a] 5I say this to shame you. Is it
possible that there is nobody among you
wise enough to judge a dispute between
believers? 6But instead, one brother goes
to law against another—and this in front
of unbelievers!
7The very fact that you have lawsuits
among you means you have been completely defeated already. Why not rather
be wronged? Why not rather be cheated?
8Instead, you yourselves cheat and do
wrong, and you do this to your brothers.
9Do you not know that the wicked will
not inherit the kingdom of God? Do not
be deceived: Neither the sexually immoral
nor idolaters nor adulterers nor male
prostitutes nor homosexual offenders
10nor thieves nor the greedy nor drunkards nor slanderers nor swindlers will inherit the kingdom of God. 11And that is
what some of you were. But you were
washed, you were sanctified, you were justified in the name of the Lord Jesus Christ
and by the Spirit of our God.

[a] 4 Or *matters, do you appoint as judges men of little account in the church?*

PRAYER: THE ATTRIBUTES OF GOD

GREAT are You, Lord, and most worthy of praise in Your city, O God, Your holy mountain. As is Your name, O God, so is Your praise to the ends of the earth; Your right hand is filled with righteousness.

(Psalm 48:1, 10)

***PAUSE** to reflect on these affirmations about the person, powers and perfection of God.*

YEAR 2
DAY 132

OT Isaiah 13:1–22

A Prophecy Against Babylon

13 An oracle concerning Babylon that
Isaiah son of Amoz saw:

2Raise a banner on a bare hilltop,
shout to them;
beckon to them
to enter the gates of the nobles.
3I have commanded my holy ones;
I have summoned my warriors to
carry out my wrath—
those who rejoice in my triumph.

4Listen, a noise on the mountains,
like that of a great multitude!
Listen, an uproar among the
kingdoms,
like nations massing together!
The LORD Almighty is mustering
an army for war.
5They come from faraway lands,
from the ends of the heavens—
the LORD and the weapons of his
wrath—
to destroy the whole country.

6Wail, for the day of the LORD is near;
it will come like destruction from
the Almighty.[a]
7Because of this, all hands will go
limp,
every man's heart will melt.
8Terror will seize them,
pain and anguish will grip them;
they will writhe like a woman in
labor.

[a] 6 Hebrew *Shaddai*

They will look aghast at each other,
their faces aflame.

9 See, the day of the LORD is coming
—a cruel day, with wrath and fierce anger—
to make the land desolate
and destroy the sinners within it.
10 The stars of heaven and their constellations
will not show their light.
The rising sun will be darkened
and the moon will not give its light.
11 I will punish the world for its evil,
the wicked for their sins.
I will put an end to the arrogance of the haughty
and will humble the pride of the ruthless.
12 I will make man scarcer than pure gold,
more rare than the gold of Ophir.
13 Therefore I will make the heavens tremble;
and the earth will shake from its place
at the wrath of the LORD Almighty,
in the day of his burning anger.

14 Like a hunted gazelle,
like sheep without a shepherd,
each will return to his own people,
each will flee to his native land.
15 Whoever is captured will be thrust through;
all who are caught will fall by the sword.
16 Their infants will be dashed to pieces before their eyes;
their houses will be looted and their wives ravished.

17 See, I will stir up against them the Medes,
who do not care for silver
and have no delight in gold.
18 Their bows will strike down the young men;
they will have no mercy on infants
nor will they look with compassion on children.
19 Babylon, the jewel of kingdoms,
the glory of the Babylonians'[b] pride,
will be overthrown by God
like Sodom and Gomorrah.
20 She will never be inhabited
or lived in through all generations;
no Arab will pitch his tent there,
no shepherd will rest his flocks there.
21 But desert creatures will lie there,
jackals will fill her houses;
there the owls will dwell,
and there the wild goats will leap about.
22 Hyenas will howl in her strongholds,
jackals in her luxurious palaces.
Her time is at hand,
and her days will not be prolonged.

[b] 19 Or *Chaldeans'*

PRAYER: THANKSGIVING

YOUR word is settled in heaven forever, O Lord. Your faithfulness continues through all generations; You established the earth, and it stands. Your laws continue to this day according to Your purposes, for all things serve You. (Psalm 119:89–91)

***PAUSE** to offer your own expressions of thanksgiving.*

NT 1 Corinthians 6:12–20

Sexual Immorality

12 "Everything is permissible for me"—
but not everything is beneficial. "Everything is permissible for me"—but I will
not be mastered by anything. 13 "Food for
the stomach and the stomach for food"—
but God will destroy them both. The
body is not meant for sexual immorality,
but for the Lord, and the Lord for the
body. 14 By his power God raised the Lord
from the dead, and he will raise us also.
15 Do you not know that your bodies are
members of Christ himself? Shall I then
take the members of Christ and unite
them with a prostitute? Never! 16 Do you
not know that he who unites himself
with a prostitute is one with her in body?
For it is said, "The two will become one

flesh."[a] [17]But he who unites himself with
the Lord is one with him in spirit.
[18]Flee from sexual immorality. All other sins a man commits are outside his body, but he who sins sexually sins against his own body. [19]Do you not know
that your body is a temple of the Holy Spirit, who is in you, whom you have received from God? You are not your own;
[20]you were bought at a price. Therefore honor God with your body.

[a] *16* Gen. 2:24

PRAYER: THE WORKS OF GOD

THE mystery that has been kept hidden for ages and generations is now disclosed to the saints. You, Lord God, have chosen to make known among the Gentiles the glorious riches of this mystery, which is Christ in us, the hope of glory. (Colossians 1:26–27)

***TAKE** a moment to consider the greatness of God's wonderful works.*

YEAR 2 DAY 133

OT Psalms 97–98

Psalm 97

[1]The LORD reigns, let the earth be glad;
let the distant shores rejoice.

[2]Clouds and thick darkness surround him;
righteousness and justice are the foundation of his throne.
[3]Fire goes before him
and consumes his foes on every side.
[4]His lightning lights up the world;
the earth sees and trembles.
[5]The mountains melt like wax before the LORD,
before the Lord of all the earth.
[6]The heavens proclaim his righteousness,
and all the peoples see his glory.

[7]All who worship images are put to shame,
those who boast in idols—
worship him, all you gods!

[8]Zion hears and rejoices
and the villages of Judah are glad
because of your judgments, O LORD.
[9]For you, O LORD, are the Most High over all the earth;
you are exalted far above all gods.

[10]Let those who love the LORD hate evil,
for he guards the lives of his faithful ones
and delivers them from the hand of the wicked.
[11]Light is shed upon the righteous
and joy on the upright in heart.
[12]Rejoice in the LORD, you who are righteous,
and praise his holy name.

Psalm 98

A psalm.

[1]Sing to the LORD a new song,
for he has done marvelous things;
his right hand and his holy arm
have worked salvation for him.
[2]The LORD has made his salvation known
and revealed his righteousness to the nations.
[3]He has remembered his love
and his faithfulness to the house of Israel;
all the ends of the earth have seen
the salvation of our God.

[4]Shout for joy to the LORD, all the earth,
burst into jubilant song with music;
[5]make music to the LORD with the harp,
with the harp and the sound of singing,
[6]with trumpets and the blast of the ram's horn—

shout for joy before the LORD, the
King.

7 Let the sea resound, and everything in
it,
the world, and all who live in it.
8 Let the rivers clap their hands,
let the mountains sing together for
joy;
9 let them sing before the LORD,
for he comes to judge the earth.
He will judge the world in
righteousness
and the peoples with equity.

PRAYER: ADORATION

O GOD, You are my God; earnestly I seek You; my soul thirsts for You, my body longs for You, in a dry and weary land where there is no water. (Psalm 63:1)

***PAUSE** to express your thoughts of praise and worship.*

NT 1 Corinthians 7:1-40

Marriage

7 Now for the matters you wrote about: It is good for a man not to marry.[a] 2 But since there is so much immorality, each man should have his own wife, and each woman her own husband. 3 The husband should fulfill his marital duty to his wife, and likewise the wife to her husband. 4 The wife's body does not belong to her alone but also to her husband. In the same way, the husband's body does not belong to him alone but also to his wife. 5 Do not deprive each other except by mutual consent and for a time, so that you may devote yourselves to prayer. Then come together again so that Satan will not tempt you because of your lack of self-control. 6 I say this as a concession, not as a command. 7 I wish that all men were as I am. But each man has his own gift from God; one has this gift, another has that.

8 Now to the unmarried and the widows I say: It is good for them to stay unmarried, as I am. 9 But if they cannot control themselves, they should marry, for it is better to marry than to burn with passion.

10 To the married I give this command (not I, but the Lord): A wife must not separate from her husband. 11 But if she does, she must remain unmarried or else be reconciled to her husband. And a husband must not divorce his wife.

12 To the rest I say this (I, not the Lord): If any brother has a wife who is not a believer and she is willing to live with him, he must not divorce her. 13 And if a woman has a husband who is not a believer and he is willing to live with her, she must not divorce him. 14 For the unbelieving husband has been sanctified through his wife, and the unbelieving wife has been sanctified through her believing husband. Otherwise your children would be unclean, but as it is, they are holy.

15 But if the unbeliever leaves, let him do so. A believing man or woman is not bound in such circumstances; God has called us to live in peace. 16 How do you know, wife, whether you will save your husband? Or, how do you know, husband, whether you will save your wife?

17 Nevertheless, each one should retain the place in life that the Lord assigned to him and to which God has called him. This is the rule I lay down in all the churches. 18 Was a man already circumcised when he was called? He should not become uncircumcised. Was a man uncircumcised when he was called? He should not be circumcised. 19 Circumcision is nothing and uncircumcision is nothing. Keeping God's commands is what counts. 20 Each one should remain in the situation which he was in when God called him. 21 Were you a slave when you were called? Don't let it trouble you—although if you can gain your freedom, do so. 22 For he who was a slave when he was called by the Lord is the Lord's freedman; similarly, he who was a free man when he was called is Christ's slave. 23 You were bought at a price; do not become slaves of men.

[a] 1 Or *"It is good for a man not to have sexual relations with a woman."*

[24]Brothers, each man, as responsible to God, should remain in the situation God called him to.

[25]Now about virgins: I have no command from the Lord, but I give a judgment as one who by the Lord's mercy is trustworthy. [26]Because of the present crisis, I think that it is good for you to remain as you are. [27]Are you married? Do not seek a divorce. Are you unmarried? Do not look for a wife. [28]But if you do marry, you have not sinned; and if a virgin marries, she has not sinned. But those who marry will face many troubles in this life, and I want to spare you this.

[29]What I mean, brothers, is that the time is short. From now on those who have wives should live as if they had none; [30]those who mourn, as if they did not; those who are happy, as if they were not; those who buy something, as if it were not theirs to keep; [31]those who use the things of the world, as if not engrossed in them. For this world in its present form is passing away.

[32]I would like you to be free from concern. An unmarried man is concerned about the Lord's affairs—how he can please the Lord. [33]But a married man is concerned about the affairs of this world—how he can please his wife—[34]and his interests are divided. An unmarried woman or virgin is concerned about the Lord's affairs: Her aim is to be devoted to the Lord in both body and spirit. But a married woman is concerned about the affairs of this world—how she can please her husband. [35]I am saying this for your own good, not to restrict you, but that you may live in a right way in undivided devotion to the Lord.

[36]If anyone thinks he is acting improperly toward the virgin he is engaged to, and if she is getting along in years and he feels he ought to marry, he should do as he wants. He is not sinning. They should get married. [37]But the man who has settled the matter in his own mind, who is under no compulsion but has control over his own will, and who has made up his mind not to marry the virgin—this man also does the right thing. [38]So then, he who marries the virgin does right, but he who does not marry her does even better.[b]

[39]A woman is bound to her husband as long as he lives. But if her husband dies, she is free to marry anyone she wishes, but he must belong to the Lord. [40]In my judgment, she is happier if she stays as she is—and I think that I too have the Spirit of God.

[b] 36–38 Or [36]*If anyone thinks he is not treating his daughter properly, and if she is getting along in years, and he feels she ought to marry, he should do as he wants. He is not sinning. He should let her get married.* [37]*But the man who has settled the matter in his own mind, who is under no compulsion but has control over his own will, and who has made up his mind to keep the virgin unmarried—this man also does the right thing.* [38]*So then, he who gives his virgin in marriage does right, but he who does not give her in marriage does even better.*

PRAYER: MY RELATIONSHIP TO GOD

O LORD, You Yourself go before me and will be with me; You will never leave me nor forsake me. I will not be afraid or be dismayed. (Deuteronomy 31:8)

PAUSE *to thank God for the relationship that you enjoy with Him in Jesus Christ.*

YEAR 2 DAY 134

OT Isaiah 14:1-32

14 The LORD will have compassion on
 Jacob;
once again he will choose Israel
 and will settle them in their own
  land.
Aliens will join them
 and unite with the house of Jacob.
[2]Nations will take them
 and bring them to their own
  place.
And the house of Israel will possess
  the nations
 as menservants and maidservants in
  the LORD's land.

They will make captives of their captors
and rule over their oppressors.

[3]On the day the LORD gives you relief
from suffering and turmoil and cruel
bondage, [4]you will take up this taunt
against the king of Babylon:

How the oppressor has come to an end!
How his fury[a] has ended!
[5]The LORD has broken the rod of the wicked,
the scepter of the rulers,
[6]which in anger struck down peoples
with unceasing blows,
and in fury subdued nations
with relentless aggression.
[7]All the lands are at rest and at peace;
they break into singing.
[8]Even the pine trees and the cedars of Lebanon
exult over you and say,
"Now that you have been laid low,
no woodsman comes to cut us down."

[9]The grave[b] below is all astir
to meet you at your coming;
it rouses the spirits of the departed to greet you—
all those who were leaders in the world;
it makes them rise from their thrones—
all those who were kings over the nations.
[10]They will all respond,
they will say to you,
"You also have become weak, as we are;
you have become like us."
[11]All your pomp has been brought down to the grave,
along with the noise of your harps;
maggots are spread out beneath you
and worms cover you.

[12]How you have fallen from heaven,
O morning star, son of the dawn!
You have been cast down to the earth,
you who once laid low the nations!
[13]You said in your heart,
"I will ascend to heaven;
I will raise my throne
above the stars of God;
I will sit enthroned on the mount of assembly,
on the utmost heights of the sacred mountain.[c]
[14]I will ascend above the tops of the clouds;
I will make myself like the Most High."
[15]But you are brought down to the grave,
to the depths of the pit.

[16]Those who see you stare at you,
they ponder your fate:
"Is this the man who shook the earth
and made kingdoms tremble,
[17]the man who made the world a desert,
who overthrew its cities
and would not let his captives go home?"

[18]All the kings of the nations lie in state,
each in his own tomb.
[19]But you are cast out of your tomb
like a rejected branch;
you are covered with the slain,
with those pierced by the sword,
those who descend to the stones of the pit.
Like a corpse trampled underfoot,
[20]you will not join them in burial,
for you have destroyed your land
and killed your people.

The offspring of the wicked
will never be mentioned again.
[21]Prepare a place to slaughter his sons
for the sins of their forefathers;
they are not to rise to inherit the land
and cover the earth with their cities.

[22]"I will rise up against them,"
declares the LORD Almighty.
"I will cut off from Babylon her name and survivors,
her offspring and descendants,"
declares the LORD.
[23]"I will turn her into a place for owls
and into swampland;
I will sweep her with the broom of destruction,"
declares the LORD Almighty.

[a] *4* Dead Sea Scrolls, Septuagint and Syriac; the meaning of the word in the Masoretic Text is uncertain. [b] *9* Hebrew *Sheol;* also in verses 11 and 15 [c] *13* Or *the north;* Hebrew *Zaphon*

A Prophecy Against Assyria

[24]The LORD Almighty has sworn,

"Surely, as I have planned, so it will be,
and as I have purposed, so it will stand.
[25]I will crush the Assyrian in my land;
on my mountains I will trample him down.
His yoke will be taken from my people,
and his burden removed from their shoulders."

[26]This is the plan determined for the whole world;
this is the hand stretched out over all nations.
[27]For the LORD Almighty has purposed,
and who can thwart him?
His hand is stretched out, and who can turn it back?

A Prophecy Against the Philistines

[28]This oracle came in the year King Ahaz died:

[29]Do not rejoice, all you Philistines,
that the rod that struck you is broken;
from the root of that snake will spring up a viper,
its fruit will be a darting, venomous serpent.
[30]The poorest of the poor will find pasture,
and the needy will lie down in safety.
But your root I will destroy by famine;
it will slay your survivors.

[31]Wail, O gate! Howl, O city!
Melt away, all you Philistines!
A cloud of smoke comes from the north,
and there is not a straggler in its ranks.
[32]What answer shall be given
to the envoys of that nation?
"The LORD has established Zion,
and in her his afflicted people will find refuge."

PRAYER: CONFESSION

WHO is a God like You, who pardons iniquity and forgives the transgression of the remnant of Your inheritance? You do not stay angry forever but delight to show mercy. You will have compassion on Your people; You will tread their iniquities underfoot and hurl all their sins into the depths of the sea. (Micah 7:18–19)

***ASK** the Spirit to search your heart and reveal any areas of unconfessed sin. Acknowledge these to the Lord and thank Him for His forgiveness.*

NT 1 Corinthians 8:1–13

Food Sacrificed to Idols

8 Now about food sacrificed to idols: We
know that we all possess knowledge.[a]
Knowledge puffs up, but love builds up.
[2]The man who thinks he knows something does not yet know as he ought to
know. [3]But the man who loves God is
known by God.
[4]So then, about eating food sacrificed
to idols: We know that an idol is nothing
at all in the world and that there is no
God but one. [5]For even if there are so-
called gods, whether in heaven or on
earth (as indeed there are many "gods"
and many "lords"), [6]yet for us there is but
one God, the Father, from whom all
things came and for whom we live; and
there is but one Lord, Jesus Christ,
through whom all things came and
through whom we live.
[7]But not everyone knows this. Some
people are still so accustomed to idols
that when they eat such food they think
of it as having been sacrificed to an idol,
and since their conscience is weak, it is defiled. [8]But food does not bring us near to

[a] 1 Or *"We all possess knowledge," as you say*

God; we are no worse if we do not eat,
and no better if we do.
[9]Be careful, however, that the exercise of
your freedom does not become a stumbling block to the weak.
[10]For if anyone
with a weak conscience sees you who have this knowledge eating in an idol's temple, won't he be emboldened to eat what has been sacrificed to idols?
[11]So this weak
brother, for whom Christ died, is destroyed
by your knowledge.
[12]When you sin against
your brothers in this way and wound their weak conscience, you sin against Christ.
[13]Therefore, if what I eat causes my brother to fall into sin, I will never eat meat again, so that I will not cause him to fall.

PRAYER: THE CHARACTER I WANT TO CULTIVATE

IF I would love life and see good days, I must keep my tongue from evil and my lips from speaking guile. I must turn from evil and do good; I must seek peace and pursue it. For Your eyes, O Lord, are on the righteous, and Your ears attend to their prayer, but Your face is against those who do evil. (1 Peter 3:10–12)

***TAKE** a moment to ask the Lord for the grace to grow in godly character.*

OT Isaiah 15:1–16:14

YEAR 2 DAY 135

A Prophecy Against Moab

15 An oracle concerning Moab:

Ar in Moab is ruined,
destroyed in a night!
Kir in Moab is ruined,
destroyed in a night!
2 Dibon goes up to its temple,
to its high places to weep;
Moab wails over Nebo and Medeba.
Every head is shaved
and every beard cut off.
3 In the streets they wear sackcloth;
on the roofs and in the public squares
they all wail,
prostrate with weeping.
4 Heshbon and Elealeh cry out,
their voices are heard all the way to Jahaz.
Therefore the armed men of Moab cry out,
and their hearts are faint.

5 My heart cries out over Moab;
her fugitives flee as far as Zoar,
as far as Eglath Shelishiyah.
They go up the way to Luhith,
weeping as they go;
on the road to Horonaim
they lament their destruction.
6 The waters of Nimrim are dried up
and the grass is withered;
the vegetation is gone
and nothing green is left.
7 So the wealth they have acquired and stored up
they carry away over the Ravine of the Poplars.
8 Their outcry echoes along the border of Moab;
their wailing reaches as far as Eglaim,
their lamentation as far as Beer Elim.
9 Dimon's[a] waters are full of blood,
but I will bring still more upon Dimon[a]—
a lion upon the fugitives of Moab
and upon those who remain in the land.

16 Send lambs as tribute
to the ruler of the land,
from Sela, across the desert,
to the mount of the Daughter of Zion.
2 Like fluttering birds
pushed from the nest,
so are the women of Moab
at the fords of the Arnon.

3 "Give us counsel,
render a decision.
Make your shadow like night—

[a] 9 Masoretic Text; Dead Sea Scrolls, some Septuagint manuscripts and Vulgate *Dibon*

at high noon.
Hide the fugitives,
do not betray the refugees.
4 Let the Moabite fugitives stay with you;
be their shelter from the destroyer."

The oppressor will come to an end,
and destruction will cease;
the aggressor will vanish from the land.
5 In love a throne will be established;
in faithfulness a man will sit on it—
one from the house[b] of David—
one who in judging seeks justice
and speeds the cause of righteousness.

6 We have heard of Moab's pride—
her overweening pride and conceit,
her pride and her insolence—
but her boasts are empty.
7 Therefore the Moabites wail,
they wail together for Moab.
Lament and grieve
for the men[c] of Kir Hareseth.
8 The fields of Heshbon wither,
the vines of Sibmah also.
The rulers of the nations
have trampled down the choicest vines,
which once reached Jazer
and spread toward the desert.
Their shoots spread out
and went as far as the sea.
9 So I weep, as Jazer weeps,
for the vines of Sibmah.
O Heshbon, O Elealeh,
I drench you with tears!
The shouts of joy over your ripened fruit
and over your harvests have been stilled.
10 Joy and gladness are taken away from the orchards;
no one sings or shouts in the vineyards;
no one treads out wine at the presses,
for I have put an end to the shouting.
11 My heart laments for Moab like a harp,
my inmost being for Kir Hareseth.
12 When Moab appears at her high place,
she only wears herself out;
when she goes to her shrine to pray,
it is to no avail.

13 This is the word the LORD has already
spoken concerning Moab. 14 But now the
LORD says: "Within three years, as a servant bound by contract would count them, Moab's splendor and all her many people will be despised, and her survivors will be very few and feeble."

[b] 5 Hebrew *tent* [c] 7 Or *"raisin cakes,"* a wordplay

PRAYER: RENEWAL

MAY I be on my guard against all covetousness, for my life does not consist in the abundance of my possessions. (Luke 12:15) . . . May I keep my life free from the love of money and be content with what I have, for You have said, "I will never leave you, nor will I forsake you." (Hebrews 13:5)

PAUSE *to add your own prayers for personal renewal.*

NT 1 Corinthians 9:1–27

The Rights of an Apostle

9 Am I not free? Am I not an apostle?
Have I not seen Jesus our Lord? Are you
not the result of my work in the Lord?
2 Even though I may not be an apostle to
others, surely I am to you! For you are the
seal of my apostleship in the Lord.
3 This is my defense to those who sit in
judgment on me. 4 Don't we have the right
to food and drink? 5 Don't we have the
right to take a believing wife along with
us, as do the other apostles and the Lord's
brothers and Cephas[a]? 6 Or is it only I and
Barnabas who must work for a living?
7 Who serves as a soldier at his own expense? Who plants a vineyard and does
not eat of its grapes? Who tends a flock and
does not drink of the milk? 8 Do I say this
merely from a human point of view?
Doesn't the Law say the same thing? 9 For
it is written in the Law of Moses: "Do not

[a] 5 That is, Peter

muzzle an ox while it is treading out the
grain."[b] Is it about oxen that God is concerned? 10 Surely he says this for us, doesn't
he? Yes, this was written for us, because
when the plowman plows and the thresher threshes, they ought to do so in the hope
of sharing in the harvest. 11 If we have sown
spiritual seed among you, is it too much if
we reap a material harvest from you? 12 If
others have this right of support from you,
shouldn't we have it all the more?

But we did not use this right. On the
contrary, we put up with anything rather
than hinder the gospel of Christ. 13 Don't
you know that those who work in the
temple get their food from the temple,
and those who serve at the altar share in
what is offered on the altar? 14 In the same
way, the Lord has commanded that those
who preach the gospel should receive
their living from the gospel.

15 But I have not used any of these rights.
And I am not writing this in the hope that
you will do such things for me. I would
rather die than have anyone deprive me of
this boast. 16 Yet when I preach the gospel, I
cannot boast, for I am compelled to preach.
Woe to me if I do not preach the gospel!
17 If I preach voluntarily, I have a reward; if
not voluntarily, I am simply discharging the
trust committed to me. 18 What then is my
reward? Just this: that in preaching the
gospel I may offer it free of charge, and so
not make use of my rights in preaching it.

19 Though I am free and belong to no
man, I make myself a slave to everyone, to
win as many as possible. 20 To the Jews I became like a Jew, to win the Jews. To those
under the law I became like one under the
law (though I myself am not under the
law), so as to win those under the law. 21 To
those not having the law I became like one
not having the law (though I am not free
from God's law but am under Christ's
law), so as to win those not having the
law. 22 To the weak I became weak, to win
the weak. I have become all things to all
men so that by all possible means I might
save some. 23 I do all this for the sake of the
gospel, that I may share in its blessings.

24 Do you not know that in a race all the
runners run, but only one gets the prize?
Run in such a way as to get the prize.
25 Everyone who competes in the games
goes into strict training. They do it to get a
crown that will not last; but we do it to get
a crown that will last forever. 26 Therefore I
do not run like a man running aimlessly; I
do not fight like a man beating the air.
27 No, I beat my body and make it my slave
so that after I have preached to others, I myself will not be disqualified for the prize.

[b] 9 Deut. 25:4

PRAYER: MY RELATIONSHIP TO OTHERS

O GOD, You are the One who gives endurance and encouragement; grant that we be of the same mind toward one another, according to Christ Jesus, so that with one accord and one mouth we may glorify You, the God and Father of our Lord Jesus Christ. (Romans 15:5–6)

***PAUSE** to review your relationships with others and to commit them to the Lord.*

YEAR 2 DAY 136

OT Isaiah 17:1–18:7

An Oracle Against Damascus

17 An oracle concerning Damascus:

"See, Damascus will no longer be a city
but will become a heap of ruins.
2 The cities of Aroer will be deserted
and left to flocks, which will lie
down,
with no one to make them
afraid.
3 The fortified city will disappear from
Ephraim,
and royal power from Damascus;
the remnant of Aram will be
like the glory of the Israelites,"
declares the LORD Almighty.

[4] "In that day the glory of Jacob will fade;
the fat of his body will waste away.
[5] It will be as when a reaper gathers the standing grain
and harvests the grain with his arm—
as when a man gleans heads of grain
in the Valley of Rephaim.
[6] Yet some gleanings will remain,
as when an olive tree is beaten,
leaving two or three olives on the topmost branches,
four or five on the fruitful boughs,"
declares the LORD, the God of Israel.

[7] In that day men will look to their Maker
and turn their eyes to the Holy One of Israel.
[8] They will not look to the altars,
the work of their hands,
and they will have no regard for the Asherah poles[a]
and the incense altars their fingers have made.

[9] In that day their strong cities, which they
left because of the Israelites, will be like
places abandoned to thickets and undergrowth. And all will be desolation.

[10] You have forgotten God your Savior;
you have not remembered the Rock,
your fortress.
Therefore, though you set out the finest plants
and plant imported vines,
[11] though on the day you set them out,
you make them grow,
and on the morning when you plant them, you bring them to bud,
yet the harvest will be as nothing
in the day of disease and incurable pain.

[12] Oh, the raging of many nations—
they rage like the raging sea!
Oh, the uproar of the peoples—
they roar like the roaring of great waters!
[13] Although the peoples roar like the roar of surging waters,
when he rebukes them they flee far away,
driven before the wind like chaff on the hills,
like tumbleweed before a gale.
[14] In the evening, sudden terror!
Before the morning, they are gone!
This is the portion of those who loot us,
the lot of those who plunder us.

A Prophecy Against Cush

18 Woe to the land of whirring wings[b]
along the rivers of Cush,[c]
[2] which sends envoys by sea
in papyrus boats over the water.

Go, swift messengers,
to a people tall and smooth-skinned,
to a people feared far and wide,
an aggressive nation of strange speech,
whose land is divided by rivers.

[3] All you people of the world,
you who live on the earth,
when a banner is raised on the mountains,
you will see it,
and when a trumpet sounds,
you will hear it.
[4] This is what the LORD says to me:
"I will remain quiet and will look on from my dwelling place,
like shimmering heat in the sunshine,
like a cloud of dew in the heat of harvest."
[5] For, before the harvest, when the blossom is gone
and the flower becomes a ripening grape,
he will cut off the shoots with pruning knives,
and cut down and take away the spreading branches.
[6] They will all be left to the mountain birds of prey
and to the wild animals;
the birds will feed on them all summer,
the wild animals all winter.

[7] At that time gifts will be brought to the
LORD Almighty

from a people tall and smooth-skinned,
from a people feared far and wide,
an aggressive nation of strange speech,
whose land is divided by rivers—

the gifts will be brought to Mount Zion, the
place of the Name of the LORD Almighty.

[a] *8* That is, symbols of the goddess Asherah
[b] *1* Or *of locusts* [c] *1* That is, the upper Nile region

PRAYER: PETITION

MY eyes are upon You, O Sovereign Lord; in You I take refuge; You will not leave my soul destitute. (Psalm 141:8)

***PAUSE** here to petition God for wisdom. Ask Him to develop your eternal perspective, to renew your mind with truth and to help you develop greater skill in each area of your life. Offer prayers regarding your activities for this day and any special concerns you may have.*

NT 1 Corinthians 10:1–22

Warnings From Israel's History

10 For I do not want you to be ignorant of the fact, brothers, that our forefathers were all under the cloud and that they all passed through the sea. [2]They were all baptized into Moses in the cloud and in the sea. [3]They all ate the same spiritual food [4]and drank the same spiritual drink; for they drank from the spiritual rock that accompanied them, and that rock was Christ. [5]Nevertheless, God was not pleased with most of them; their bodies were scattered over the desert.

[6]Now these things occurred as examples[a] to keep us from setting our hearts on evil things as they did. [7]Do not be idolaters, as some of them were; as it is written: "The people sat down to eat and drink and got up to indulge in pagan revelry."[b] [8]We should not commit sexual immorality, as some of them did—and in one day twenty-three thousand of them died. [9]We should not test the Lord, as some of them did—and were killed by snakes. [10]And do not grumble, as some of them did—and were killed by the destroying angel.

[11]These things happened to them as examples and were written down as warnings for us, on whom the fulfillment of the ages has come. [12]So, if you think you are standing firm, be careful that you don't fall! [13]No temptation has seized you except what is common to man. And God is faithful; he will not let you be tempted beyond what you can bear. But when you are tempted, he will also provide a way out so that you can stand up under it.

Idol Feasts and the Lord's Supper

[14]Therefore, my dear friends, flee from idolatry. [15]I speak to sensible people; judge for yourselves what I say. [16]Is not the cup of thanksgiving for which we give thanks a participation in the blood of Christ? And is not the bread that we break a participation in the body of Christ? [17]Because there is one loaf, we, who are many, are one body, for we all partake of the one loaf.

[18]Consider the people of Israel: Do not those who eat the sacrifices participate in the altar? [19]Do I mean then that a sacrifice offered to an idol is anything, or that an idol is anything? [20]No, but the sacrifices of pagans are offered to demons, not to God, and I do not want you to be participants with demons. [21]You cannot drink the cup of the Lord and the cup of demons too; you cannot have a part in both the Lord's table and the table of demons. [22]Are we trying to arouse the Lord's jealousy? Are we stronger than he?

[a] 6 Or *types;* also in verse 11 [b] 7 Exodus 32:6

PRAYER: THE ATTRIBUTES OF GOD

ARE You a God nearby, and not a God far away? Who can hide in secret places so that You cannot see them? Do You not fill heaven and earth? (Jeremiah 23:23–24)

***PAUSE** to reflect on these affirmations about the person, powers and perfection of God.*

OT Proverbs 22

YEAR 2 DAY 137

22 A good name is more desirable than
great riches;
to be esteemed is better than silver
or gold.

2 Rich and poor have this in common:
The LORD is the Maker of them all.

3 A prudent man sees danger and takes
refuge,
but the simple keep going and
suffer for it.

4 Humility and the fear of the LORD
bring wealth and honor and life.

5 In the paths of the wicked lie thorns
and snares,
but he who guards his soul stays far
from them.

6 Train[a] a child in the way he should go,
and when he is old he will not turn
from it.

7 The rich rule over the poor,
and the borrower is servant to the
lender.

8 He who sows wickedness reaps trouble,
and the rod of his fury will be
destroyed.

9 A generous man will himself be blessed,
for he shares his food with the poor.

10 Drive out the mocker, and out goes
strife;
quarrels and insults are ended.

11 He who loves a pure heart and whose
speech is gracious
will have the king for his friend.

12 The eyes of the LORD keep watch over
knowledge,
but he frustrates the words of the
unfaithful.

13 The sluggard says, "There is a lion
outside!"
or, "I will be murdered in the streets!"

14 The mouth of an adulteress is a deep
pit;
he who is under the LORD's wrath
will fall into it.

15 Folly is bound up in the heart of a
child,
but the rod of discipline will drive
it far from him.

16 He who oppresses the poor to
increase his wealth
and he who gives gifts to the rich—
both come to poverty.

Sayings of the Wise

17 Pay attention and listen to the sayings
of the wise;
apply your heart to what I teach,
18 for it is pleasing when you keep them
in your heart
and have all of them ready on your
lips.
19 So that your trust may be in the LORD,
I teach you today, even you.
20 Have I not written thirty[b] sayings for
you,
sayings of counsel and knowledge,
21 teaching you true and reliable words,
so that you can give sound answers
to him who sent you?

22 Do not exploit the poor because they
are poor
and do not crush the needy in court,
23 for the LORD will take up their case
and will plunder those who plunder
them.

24 Do not make friends with a hot-
tempered man,
do not associate with one easily
angered,
25 or you may learn his ways
and get yourself ensnared.

26 Do not be a man who strikes hands in
pledge
or puts up security for debts;
27 if you lack the means to pay,
your very bed will be snatched from
under you.

28 Do not move an ancient boundary
stone
set up by your forefathers.

29 Do you see a man skilled in his work?
He will serve before kings;
he will not serve before obscure men.

[a] 6 Or *Start* [b] 20 Or *not formerly written;* or *not written excellent*

PRAYER: INTERCESSION

OUT of the riches of Your glory, Father, strengthen Your children with power through Your Spirit in their inner being, so that Christ may dwell in their hearts through faith. And may they, being rooted and grounded in love, be able to comprehend with all the saints the width and length and height and depth of the love of Christ. And may they know this love that surpasses knowledge, that they may be filled to the measure of all Your fullness.

(Ephesians 3:16–19)

***TAKE** a few moments to intercede on behalf of your immediate family and other relatives. Offer prayers for their spiritual, emotional and physical concerns.*

NT 1 Corinthians 10:23–11:1

The Believer's Freedom

23 "Everything is permissible"—but not everything is beneficial. "Everything is permissible"—but not everything is constructive. 24 Nobody should seek his own good, but the good of others.

25 Eat anything sold in the meat market without raising questions of conscience, 26 for, "The earth is the Lord's, and everything in it."[a]

27 If some unbeliever invites you to a meal and you want to go, eat whatever is put before you without raising questions of conscience. 28 But if anyone says to you, "This has been offered in sacrifice," then do not eat it, both for the sake of the man who told you and for conscience' sake[b]— 29 the other man's conscience, I mean, not yours. For why should my freedom be judged by another's conscience? 30 If I take part in the meal with thankfulness, why am I denounced because of something I thank God for?

31 So whether you eat or drink or whatever you do, do it all for the glory of God. 32 Do not cause anyone to stumble, whether Jews, Greeks or the church of God— 33 even as I try to please everybody in every way. For I am not seeking my own good but the good of many, so that they may be saved. **11** 1 Follow my example, as I follow the example of Christ.

[a] 26 Psalm 24:1 [b] 28 Some manuscripts *conscience' sake, for "the earth is the Lord's and everything in it"*

PRAYER: THE WORKS OF GOD

BY this Your love, O God, was manifested to us, that You have sent Your only begotten Son into the world that we might live through Him. In this is love, not that we loved You, O God, but that You loved us and sent Your Son to be the propitiation for our sins.

(1 John 4:9–10)

***TAKE** a moment to consider the greatness of God's wonderful works.*

YEAR 2 DAY 138

OT Isaiah 19:1–25

A Prophecy About Egypt

19 An oracle concerning Egypt:

See, the LORD rides on a swift cloud
and is coming to Egypt.
The idols of Egypt tremble before him,
and the hearts of the Egyptians melt within them.

2 "I will stir up Egyptian against
Egyptian—

brother will fight against brother,
neighbor against neighbor,
city against city,
kingdom against kingdom.
3 The Egyptians will lose heart,
and I will bring their plans to nothing;
they will consult the idols and the spirits of the dead,
the mediums and the spiritists.
4 I will hand the Egyptians over
to the power of a cruel master,
and a fierce king will rule over them,"
declares the Lord, the LORD Almighty.

5 The waters of the river will dry up,
and the riverbed will be parched and dry.
6 The canals will stink;
the streams of Egypt will dwindle and dry up.
The reeds and rushes will wither,
7 also the plants along the Nile,
at the mouth of the river.
Every sown field along the Nile
will become parched, will blow away and be no more.
8 The fishermen will groan and lament,
all who cast hooks into the Nile;
those who throw nets on the water
will pine away.
9 Those who work with combed flax will despair,
the weavers of fine linen will lose hope.
10 The workers in cloth will be dejected,
and all the wage earners will be sick at heart.

11 The officials of Zoan are nothing but fools;
the wise counselors of Pharaoh give senseless advice.
How can you say to Pharaoh,
"I am one of the wise men,
a disciple of the ancient kings"?

12 Where are your wise men now?
Let them show you and make known
what the LORD Almighty
has planned against Egypt.
13 The officials of Zoan have become fools,
the leaders of Memphis[a] are deceived;
the cornerstones of her peoples
have led Egypt astray.
14 The LORD has poured into them
a spirit of dizziness;
they make Egypt stagger in all that she does,
as a drunkard staggers around in his vomit.
15 There is nothing Egypt can do—
head or tail, palm branch or reed.

16 In that day the Egyptians will be like
women. They will shudder with fear at the
uplifted hand that the LORD Almighty
raises against them. 17 And the land of Judah will bring terror to the Egyptians;
everyone to whom Judah is mentioned
will be terrified, because of what the LORD
Almighty is planning against them.
18 In that day five cities in Egypt will
speak the language of Canaan and swear
allegiance to the LORD Almighty. One of
them will be called the City of Destruction.[b]
19 In that day there will be an altar to the
LORD in the heart of Egypt, and a monument to the LORD at its border. 20 It will be
a sign and witness to the LORD Almighty
in the land of Egypt. When they cry out to
the LORD because of their oppressors, he
will send them a savior and defender, and
he will rescue them. 21 So the LORD will
make himself known to the Egyptians,
and in that day they will acknowledge the
LORD. They will worship with sacrifices
and grain offerings; they will make vows
to the LORD and keep them. 22 The LORD
will strike Egypt with a plague; he will
strike them and heal them. They will turn
to the LORD, and he will respond to their
pleas and heal them.
23 In that day there will be a highway
from Egypt to Assyria. The Assyrians will
go to Egypt and the Egyptians to Assyria.
The Egyptians and Assyrians will worship
together. 24 In that day Israel will be the
third, along with Egypt and Assyria, a
blessing on the earth. 25 The LORD
Almighty will bless them, saying, "Blessed
be Egypt my people, Assyria my handi-
work, and Israel my inheritance."

[a] 13 Hebrew *Noph* [b] 18 Most manuscripts of the Masoretic Text; some manuscripts of the Masoretic Text, Dead Sea Scrolls and Vulgate *City of the Sun* (that is, Heliopolis)

PRAYER: AFFIRMATION

FAITH is the certainty of things hoped for and the conviction of things not seen. Without faith it is impossible to please You, O God, for the one who comes to You must believe that You exist, and that You reward those who earnestly seek You. (Hebrews 11:1, 6)

***PAUSE** to reflect on these Biblical affirmations.*

NT 1 Corinthians 11:2–16

Propriety in Worship

[2]I praise you for remembering me in everything and for holding to the teachings,[a] just as I passed them on to you.
[3]Now I want you to realize that the head of every man is Christ, and the head of the woman is man, and the head of Christ is God.
[4]Every man who prays or prophesies with his head covered dishonors his head.
[5]And every woman who prays or prophesies with her head uncovered dishonors her head—it is just as though her head were shaved.
[6]If a woman does not cover her head, she should have her hair cut off; and if it is a disgrace for a woman to have her hair cut or shaved off, she should cover her head.
[7]A man ought not to cover his head,[b] since he is the image and glory of God; but the woman is the glory of man.
[8]For man did not come from woman, but woman from man;
[9]neither was man created for woman, but woman for man.
[10]For this reason, and because of the angels, the woman ought to have a sign of authority on her head.
[11]In the Lord, however, woman is not independent of man, nor is man independent of woman.
[12]For as woman came from man, so also man is born of woman. But everything comes from God.
[13]Judge for yourselves: Is it proper for a woman to pray to God with her head uncovered?
[14]Does not the very nature of things teach you that if a man has long hair, it is a disgrace to him,
[15]but that if a woman has long hair, it is her glory? For long hair is given to her as a covering.
[16]If anyone wants to be contentious about this, we have no other practice—nor do the churches of God.

[a] 2 Or *traditions* [b] 4–7 Or [4]*Every man who prays or prophesies with long hair dishonors his head.* [5]*And every woman who prays or prophesies with no covering* ⌞*of hair*⌟ *on her head dishonors her head—she is just like one of the "shorn women."* [6]*If a woman has no covering, let her be for now with short hair, but since it is a disgrace for a woman to have her hair shorn or shaved, she should grow it again.* [7]*A man ought not to have long hair*

PRAYER: MY RELATIONSHIP TO GOD

IF I have found grace in Your sight, teach me Your ways, so I may know You and continue to find favor with You. (Exodus 33:13)

***PAUSE** to thank God for the relationship that you enjoy with Him in Jesus Christ.*

YEAR 2 DAY 139

OT Isaiah 20:1–21:17

A Prophecy Against Egypt and Cush

20 In the year that the supreme commander, sent by Sargon king of Assyria, came to Ashdod and attacked and captured it—
[2]at that time the LORD spoke through Isaiah son of Amoz. He said to him, "Take off the sackcloth from your body and the sandals from your feet." And he did so, going around stripped and barefoot.
[3]Then the LORD said, "Just as my servant

Isaiah has gone stripped and barefoot for
three years, as a sign and portent against
Egypt and Cush,[a] 4so the king of Assyria
will lead away stripped and barefoot the
Egyptian captives and Cushite exiles,
young and old, with buttocks bared—to
Egypt's shame. 5Those who trusted in
Cush and boasted in Egypt will be afraid
and put to shame. 6In that day the people
who live on this coast will say, 'See what
has happened to those we relied on, those
we fled to for help and deliverance from
the king of Assyria! How then can we escape?' "

A Prophecy Against Babylon

21 An oracle concerning the Desert by the Sea:

Like whirlwinds sweeping through the
southland,
an invader comes from the desert,
from a land of terror.

2A dire vision has been shown to me:
The traitor betrays, the looter takes
loot.
Elam, attack! Media, lay siege!
I will bring to an end all the
groaning she caused.

3At this my body is racked with pain,
pangs seize me, like those of a
woman in labor;
I am staggered by what I hear,
I am bewildered by what I see.
4My heart falters,
fear makes me tremble;
the twilight I longed for
has become a horror to me.

5They set the tables,
they spread the rugs,
they eat, they drink!
Get up, you officers,
oil the shields!

6This is what the Lord says to me:

"Go, post a lookout
and have him report what he sees.
7When he sees chariots
with teams of horses,
riders on donkeys
or riders on camels,
let him be alert,
fully alert."

8And the lookout[b] shouted,

"Day after day, my lord, I stand on the
watchtower;
every night I stay at my post.
9Look, here comes a man in a chariot
with a team of horses.
And he gives back the answer:
'Babylon has fallen, has fallen!
All the images of its gods
lie shattered on the ground!' "

10O my people, crushed on the
threshing floor,
I tell you what I have heard
from the LORD Almighty,
from the God of Israel.

A Prophecy Against Edom

11An oracle concerning Dumah[c]:

Someone calls to me from Seir,
"Watchman, what is left of the
night?
Watchman, what is left of the
night?"
12The watchman replies,
"Morning is coming, but also the
night.
If you would ask, then ask;
and come back yet again."

A Prophecy Against Arabia

13An oracle concerning Arabia:

You caravans of Dedanites,
who camp in the thickets of Arabia,
14 bring water for the thirsty;
you who live in Tema,
bring food for the fugitives.
15They flee from the sword,
from the drawn sword,
from the bent bow
and from the heat of battle.

16This is what the Lord says to me:
"Within one year, as a servant bound by
contract would count it, all the pomp of
Kedar will come to an end. 17The survivors
of the bowmen, the warriors of Kedar, will
be few." The LORD, the God of Israel, has
spoken.

[a] *3* That is, the upper Nile region; also in verse 5
[b] *8* Dead Sea Scrolls and Syriac; Masoretic Text *A lion*
[c] *11* *Dumah* means *silence* or *stillness,* a wordplay on *Edom.*

PRAYER: THANKSGIVING

EVEN to my old age, You are the same, and even when my hair is gray, You will carry me. You have made me, and You will bear me; You will sustain me, and You will deliver me. (Isaiah 46:4)

PAUSE *to offer your own expressions of thanksgiving.*

NT 1 Corinthians 11:17–34

The Lord's Supper

[17]In the following directives I have no
praise for you, for your meetings do more
harm than good. [18]In the first place, I hear
that when you come together as a church,
there are divisions among you, and to
some extent I believe it. [19]No doubt there
have to be differences among you to show
which of you have God's approval. [20]When
you come together, it is not the Lord's Supper you eat, [21]for as you eat, each of you
goes ahead without waiting for anybody
else. One remains hungry, another gets
drunk. [22]Don't you have homes to eat and
drink in? Or do you despise the church of
God and humiliate those who have nothing? What shall I say to you? Shall I praise
you for this? Certainly not!

[23]For I received from the Lord what I also
passed on to you: The Lord Jesus, on the
night he was betrayed, took bread, [24]and
when he had given thanks, he broke it and
said, "This is my body, which is for you; do
this in remembrance of me." [25]In the same
way, after supper he took the cup, saying,
"This cup is the new covenant in my blood;
do this, whenever you drink it, in remembrance of me." [26]For whenever you eat this
bread and drink this cup, you proclaim the
Lord's death until he comes.

[27]Therefore, whoever eats the bread or
drinks the cup of the Lord in an unworthy
manner will be guilty of sinning against
the body and blood of the Lord. [28]A man
ought to examine himself before he eats
of the bread and drinks of the cup. [29]For
anyone who eats and drinks without rec-
ognizing the body of the Lord eats and
drinks judgment on himself. [30]That is why
many among you are weak and sick, and
a number of you have fallen asleep. [31]But
if we judged ourselves, we would not come
under judgment. [32]When we are judged by
the Lord, we are being disciplined so that
we will not be condemned with the world.

[33]So then, my brothers, when you come
together to eat, wait for each other. [34]If
anyone is hungry, he should eat at home,
so that when you meet together it may not
result in judgment.

And when I come I will give further directions.

PRAYER: THE CHARACTER I WANT TO CULTIVATE

IF I say that I have fellowship with You, O Christ, and yet walk in the darkness, I lie and do not practice the truth. But if I walk in the light, as You are in the light, I have fellowship with others, and Your blood, O Jesus, purifies me from all sin. (1 John 1:6–7) . . . My desire is to continue to walk in the truth and to take pleasure when others do the same. (3 John 3–4)

TAKE *a moment to ask the Lord for the grace to grow in godly character.*

OT Psalms 99–100

YEAR 2 DAY 140

Psalm 99

[1]The LORD reigns,
let the nations tremble;
he sits enthroned between the cherubim,
let the earth shake.
[2]Great is the LORD in Zion;

he is exalted over all the nations.
3 Let them praise your great and awesome name—
he is holy.

4 The King is mighty, he loves justice—
you have established equity;
in Jacob you have done
what is just and right.
5 Exalt the LORD our God
and worship at his footstool;
he is holy.

6 Moses and Aaron were among his priests,
Samuel was among those who called on his name;
they called on the LORD
and he answered them.
7 He spoke to them from the pillar of cloud;
they kept his statutes and the decrees he gave them.

8 O LORD our God,
you answered them;
you were to Israel[a] a forgiving God,
though you punished their misdeeds.[b]
9 Exalt the LORD our God
and worship at his holy mountain,
for the LORD our God is holy.

Psalm 100

A psalm. For giving thanks.

1 Shout for joy to the LORD, all the earth.
2 Worship the LORD with gladness;
come before him with joyful songs.
3 Know that the LORD is God.
It is he who made us, and we are his[c];
we are his people, the sheep of his pasture.

4 Enter his gates with thanksgiving
and his courts with praise;
give thanks to him and praise his name.
5 For the LORD is good and his love endures forever;
his faithfulness continues through all generations.

[a] 8 Hebrew *them* [b] 8 Or / *an avenger of the wrongs done to them* [c] 3 Or *and not we ourselves*

PRAYER: ADORATION

ALL the earth sings joyfully to You, O God! The earth sings the glory of Your name, making Your praise glorious. We say to You, "How awesome are Your works! Through the greatness of Your power Your enemies submit themselves to You. All the earth will worship You and sing praises to You; they will sing praise to Your name." (Psalm 66:1–4)

__PAUSE__ to express your thoughts of praise and worship.

NT 1 Corinthians 12:1–31

Spiritual Gifts

12 Now about spiritual gifts, brothers, I
do not want you to be ignorant. 2You
know that when you were pagans, somehow or other you were influenced and led
astray to mute idols. 3Therefore I tell you
that no one who is speaking by the Spirit
of God says, "Jesus be cursed," and no one
can say, "Jesus is Lord," except by the Holy
Spirit.
4There are different kinds of gifts, but
the same Spirit. 5There are different kinds
of service, but the same Lord. 6There are
different kinds of working, but the same
God works all of them in all men.
7Now to each one the manifestation of
the Spirit is given for the common good.
8To one there is given through the Spirit
the message of wisdom, to another the
message of knowledge by means of the
same Spirit, 9to another faith by the same
Spirit, to another gifts of healing by that
one Spirit, 10to another miraculous powers, to another prophecy, to another distinguishing between spirits, to another
speaking in different kinds of tongues,[a]

[a] 10 Or *languages;* also in verse 28

and to still another the interpretation of
tongues.[b] 11 All these are the work of one
and the same Spirit, and he gives them to
each one, just as he determines.

One Body, Many Parts

12 The body is a unit, though it is made
up of many parts; and though all its parts
are many, they form one body. So it is
with Christ. 13 For we were all baptized by[c]
one Spirit into one body—whether Jews
or Greeks, slave or free—and we were all
given the one Spirit to drink.
14 Now the body is not made up of one
part but of many. 15 If the foot should say,
"Because I am not a hand, I do not belong
to the body," it would not for that reason
cease to be part of the body. 16 And if the
ear should say, "Because I am not an eye,
I do not belong to the body," it would not
for that reason cease to be part of the
body. 17 If the whole body were an eye,
where would the sense of hearing be? If
the whole body were an ear, where would
the sense of smell be? 18 But in fact God
has arranged the parts in the body, every
one of them, just as he wanted them to
be. 19 If they were all one part, where
would the body be? 20 As it is, there are
many parts, but one body.
21 The eye cannot say to the hand, "I
don't need you!" And the head cannot say
to the feet, "I don't need you!" 22 On the
contrary, those parts of the body that
seem to be weaker are indispensable,
23 and the parts that we think are less honorable we treat with special honor. And
the parts that are unpresentable are treated with special modesty, 24 while our presentable parts need no special treatment.
But God has combined the members of
the body and has given greater honor to
the parts that lacked it, 25 so that there
should be no division in the body, but
that its parts should have equal concern
for each other. 26 If one part suffers, every
part suffers with it; if one part is honored,
every part rejoices with it.
27 Now you are the body of Christ, and
each one of you is a part of it. 28 And in the
church God has appointed first of all
apostles, second prophets, third teachers,
then workers of miracles, also those having gifts of healing, those able to help others, those with gifts of administration,
and those speaking in different kinds of
tongues. 29 Are all apostles? Are all prophets? Are all teachers? Do all work miracles? 30 Do all have gifts of healing? Do all
speak in tongues[d]? Do all interpret? 31 But
eagerly desire[e] the greater gifts.

Love

And now I will show you the most excellent way.

[b] 10 Or *languages;* also in verse 28 [c] 13 Or *with;* or *in* [d] 30 Or *other languages* [e] 31 Or *But you are eagerly desiring*

PRAYER: MY RELATIONSHIP TO OTHERS

THE harvest is plentiful, but the workers are few. Therefore, I pray that You, Lord of the harvest, will send out workers into Your harvest. (Matthew 9:37–38; Luke 10:2) . . . You say to me, O Lord, "Behold, lift up your eyes and look at the fields, for they are white for harvest. Even now the reaper draws his wages and gathers fruit for eternal life, that those who sow and those who reap may rejoice together." (John 4:35–36)

PAUSE *to review your relationships with others and to commit them to the Lord.*

YEAR 2 DAY 141

OT Isaiah 22:1–25

A Prophecy About Jerusalem

22 An oracle concerning the Valley of Vision:

What troubles you now,
that you have all gone up on the
roofs,
2 O town full of commotion,
O city of tumult and revelry?
Your slain were not killed by the sword,

nor did they die in battle.
[3] All your leaders have fled together;
they have been captured without using the bow.
All you who were caught were taken prisoner together,
having fled while the enemy was still far away.
[4] Therefore I said, "Turn away from me;
let me weep bitterly.
Do not try to console me
over the destruction of my people."

[5] The Lord, the LORD Almighty, has a day
of tumult and trampling and terror
in the Valley of Vision,
a day of battering down walls
and of crying out to the mountains.
[6] Elam takes up the quiver,
with her charioteers and horses;
Kir uncovers the shield.
[7] Your choicest valleys are full of chariots,
and horsemen are posted at the city gates;
[8] the defenses of Judah are stripped away.

And you looked in that day
to the weapons in the Palace of the Forest;
[9] you saw that the City of David
had many breaches in its defenses;
you stored up water
in the Lower Pool.
[10] You counted the buildings in Jerusalem
and tore down houses to strengthen the wall.
[11] You built a reservoir between the two walls
for the water of the Old Pool,
but you did not look to the One who made it,
or have regard for the One who planned it long ago.

[12] The Lord, the LORD Almighty,
called you on that day
to weep and to wail,
to tear out your hair and put on sackcloth.
[13] But see, there is joy and revelry,
slaughtering of cattle and killing of sheep,
eating of meat and drinking of wine!
"Let us eat and drink," you say,
"for tomorrow we die!"

[14] The LORD Almighty has revealed this
in my hearing: "Till your dying day this
sin will not be atoned for," says the Lord,
the LORD Almighty.

[15] This is what the Lord, the LORD
Almighty, says:

"Go, say to this steward,
to Shebna, who is in charge of the palace:
[16] What are you doing here and who gave you permission
to cut out a grave for yourself here,
hewing your grave on the height
and chiseling your resting place in the rock?

[17] "Beware, the LORD is about to take firm hold of you
and hurl you away, O you mighty man.
[18] He will roll you up tightly like a ball
and throw you into a large country.
There you will die
and there your splendid chariots will remain—
you disgrace to your master's house!
[19] I will depose you from your office,
and you will be ousted from your position.

[20] "In that day I will summon my servant, Eliakim son of Hilkiah. [21] I will
clothe him with your robe and fasten your
sash around him and hand your authority over to him. He will be a father to those
who live in Jerusalem and to the house of
Judah. [22] I will place on his shoulder the
key to the house of David; what he opens
no one can shut, and what he shuts no
one can open. [23] I will drive him like a peg
into a firm place; he will be a seat[a] of hon-
or for the house of his father. [24] All the glory of his family will hang on him: its offspring and offshoots—all its lesser vessels,
from the bowls to all the jars.

[25] "In that day," declares the LORD Almighty, "the peg driven into the firm
place will give way; it will be sheared off
and will fall, and the load hanging on it
will be cut down." The LORD has spoken.

[a] 23 Or *throne*

PRAYER: CONFESSION

BEFORE my downfall, my heart is haughty, but I must have humility before I have honor. (Proverbs 18:12)

***ASK** the Spirit to search your heart and reveal any areas of unconfessed sin. Acknowledge these to the Lord and thank Him for His forgiveness.*

NT 1 Corinthians 13:1-13

13 If I speak in the tongues[a] of men and
of angels, but have not love, I am only
a resounding gong or a clanging cymbal.
[2]If I have the gift of prophecy and can
fathom all mysteries and all knowledge,
and if I have a faith that can move mountains, but have not love, I am nothing. [3]If
I give all I possess to the poor and surrender my body to the flames,[b] but have
not love, I gain nothing.

[4]Love is patient, love is kind. It does not
envy, it does not boast, it is not proud. [5]It
is not rude, it is not self-seeking, it is not
easily angered, it keeps no record of
wrongs. [6]Love does not delight in evil but
rejoices with the truth. [7]It always protects,
always trusts, always hopes, always perseveres.

[8]Love never fails. But where there are
prophecies, they will cease; where there
are tongues, they will be stilled; where
there is knowledge, it will pass away. [9]For
we know in part and we prophesy in part,
[10]but when perfection comes, the imperfect disappears. [11]When I was a child, I
talked like a child, I thought like a child,
I reasoned like a child. When I became a
man, I put childish ways behind me.
[12]Now we see but a poor reflection as in a
mirror; then we shall see face to face. Now
I know in part; then I shall know fully,
even as I am fully known.

[13]And now these three remain: faith,
hope and love. But the greatest of these is
love.

[a] 1 Or *languages* [b] 3 Some early manuscripts *body that I may boast*

PRAYER: THE ATTRIBUTES OF GOD

YOU are not a God who takes pleasure in wickedness; evil cannot dwell with You. (Psalm 5:4) . . . I will exalt You, Lord my God, and worship You, for You, Lord God, are holy. (Psalm 99:9)

***PAUSE** to reflect on these affirmations about the person, powers and perfection of God.*

YEAR 2 DAY 142

OT Isaiah 23:1-18

A Prophecy About Tyre

23 An oracle concerning Tyre:

Wail, O ships of Tarshish!
  For Tyre is destroyed
  and left without house or harbor.
From the land of Cyprus[a]
  word has come to them.

[2]Be silent, you people of the island
  and you merchants of Sidon,
  whom the seafarers have enriched.
[3]On the great waters
  came the grain of the Shihor;
the harvest of the Nile[b] was the
    revenue of Tyre,
  and she became the marketplace of
    the nations.

[4]Be ashamed, O Sidon, and you,
    O fortress of the sea,

[a] 1 Hebrew *Kittim* [b] 2,3 Masoretic Text; one Dead Sea Scroll *Sidon, / who cross over the sea; / your envoys* [3]*are on the great waters. / The grain of the Shihor, / the harvest of the Nile,*

for the sea has spoken:
"I have neither been in labor nor
given birth;
I have neither reared sons nor
brought up daughters."
5 When word comes to Egypt,
they will be in anguish at the report
from Tyre.

6 Cross over to Tarshish;
wail, you people of the island.
7 Is this your city of revelry,
the old, old city,
whose feet have taken her
to settle in far-off lands?
8 Who planned this against Tyre,
the bestower of crowns,
whose merchants are princes,
whose traders are renowned in the
earth?
9 The LORD Almighty planned it,
to bring low the pride of all glory
and to humble all who are
renowned on the earth.

10 Till[c] your land as along the Nile,
O Daughter of Tarshish,
for you no longer have a harbor.
11 The LORD has stretched out his hand
over the sea
and made its kingdoms tremble.
He has given an order concerning
Phoenicia[d]
that her fortresses be destroyed.
12 He said, "No more of your reveling,
O Virgin Daughter of Sidon, now
crushed!
"Up, cross over to Cyprus[e];
even there you will find no rest."
13 Look at the land of the Babylonians,[f]
this people that is now of no
account!
The Assyrians have made it
a place for desert creatures;
they raised up their siege towers,
they stripped its fortresses bare
and turned it into a ruin.

14 Wail, you ships of Tarshish;
your fortress is destroyed!

15 At that time Tyre will be forgotten for
seventy years, the span of a king's life. But
at the end of these seventy years, it will
happen to Tyre as in the song of the prostitute:

16 "Take up a harp, walk through the
city,
O prostitute forgotten;
play the harp well, sing many a song,
so that you will be remembered."

17 At the end of seventy years, the LORD
will deal with Tyre. She will return to her
hire as a prostitute and will ply her trade
with all the kingdoms on the face of the
earth. 18 Yet her profit and her earnings
will be set apart for the LORD; they will not
be stored up or hoarded. Her profits will
go to those who live before the LORD, for
abundant food and fine clothes.

[c] 10 Dead Sea Scrolls and some Septuagint manuscripts; Masoretic Text *Go through*
[d] 11 Hebrew *Canaan* [e] 12 Hebrew *Kittim*
[f] 13 Or *Chaldeans*

PRAYER: RENEWAL

MAY I not turn my heart away from You, O God of Israel, but do what You have commanded. (1 Kings 11:9–10) . . . May I do what is good and right and true before You, O Lord my God, by seeking You with all my heart. (2 Chronicles 31:20–21)

***PAUSE** to add your own prayers for personal renewal.*

NT 1 Corinthians 14:1–25

Gifts of Prophecy and Tongues

14 Follow the way of love and eagerly desire spiritual gifts, especially the gift of
prophecy. 2 For anyone who speaks in a
tongue[a] does not speak to men but to
God. Indeed, no one understands him;
he utters mysteries with his spirit.[b] 3 But
everyone who prophesies speaks to men
for their strengthening, encouragement
and comfort. 4 He who speaks in a tongue

[a] 2 Or *another language;* also in verses 4, 13, 14, 19, 26 and 27 [b] 2 Or *by the Spirit*

edifies himself, but he who prophesies edifies the church. 5I would like every one of
you to speak in tongues,[c] but I would
rather have you prophesy. He who prophesies is greater than one who speaks in
tongues,[c] unless he interprets, so that the
church may be edified.
6Now, brothers, if I come to you and
speak in tongues, what good will I be to
you, unless I bring you some revelation or
knowledge or prophecy or word of instruction? 7Even in the case of lifeless
things that make sounds, such as the flute
or harp, how will anyone know what tune
is being played unless there is a distinction
in the notes? 8Again, if the trumpet does
not sound a clear call, who will get ready
for battle? 9So it is with you. Unless you
speak intelligible words with your tongue,
how will anyone know what you are saying? You will just be speaking into the air.
10Undoubtedly there are all sorts of languages in the world, yet none of them is
without meaning. 11If then I do not grasp
the meaning of what someone is saying, I
am a foreigner to the speaker, and he is a
foreigner to me. 12So it is with you. Since
you are eager to have spiritual gifts, try to
excel in gifts that build up the church.
13For this reason anyone who speaks in
a tongue should pray that he may interpret
what he says. 14For if I pray in a tongue, my
spirit prays, but my mind is unfruitful. 15So
what shall I do? I will pray with my spirit,
but I will also pray with my mind; I will
sing with my spirit, but I will also sing with
my mind. 16If you are praising God with
your spirit, how can one who finds himself among those who do not understand[d]
say "Amen" to your thanksgiving, since he
does not know what you are saying? 17You
may be giving thanks well enough, but the
other man is not edified.
18I thank God that I speak in tongues
more than all of you. 19But in the church
I would rather speak five intelligible
words to instruct others than ten thousand words in a tongue.
20Brothers, stop thinking like children.
In regard to evil be infants, but in your
thinking be adults. 21In the Law it is written:

"Through men of strange tongues
  and through the lips of foreigners
I will speak to this people,
  but even then they will not listen to
    me,"[e]
says the Lord.

22Tongues, then, are a sign, not for believers but for unbelievers; prophecy, however, is for believers, not for unbelievers.
23So if the whole church comes together
and everyone speaks in tongues, and some
who do not understand[f] or some unbelievers come in, will they not say that you
are out of your mind? 24But if an unbeliever or someone who does not understand[g] comes in while everybody is prophesying, he will be convinced by all that he
is a sinner and will be judged by all, 25and
the secrets of his heart will be laid bare. So
he will fall down and worship God, exclaiming, "God is really among you!"

[c] 5 Or *other languages;* also in verses 6, 18, 22, 23 and 39 [d] 16 Or *among the inquirers*
[e] 21 Isaiah 28:11,12 [f] 23 Or *some inquirers*
[g] 24 Or *or some inquirer*

PRAYER: THE WORKS OF GOD

YOU form the light and create darkness; You bring prosperity and create disaster; You, the Lord, do all these things.
(Isaiah 45:7)

***TAKE** a moment to consider the greatness of God's wonderful works.*

OT **Isaiah 24:1-23** YEAR 2 DAY 143

The LORD's Devastation of the Earth

24 See, the LORD is going to lay waste
    the earth
  and devastate it;
  he will ruin its face
    and scatter its inhabitants—
2it will be the same
    for priest as for people,

for master as for servant,
for mistress as for maid,
for seller as for buyer,
for borrower as for lender,
for debtor as for creditor.
3 The earth will be completely laid waste
and totally plundered.
The LORD has spoken this word.

4 The earth dries up and withers,
the world languishes and withers,
the exalted of the earth languish.
5 The earth is defiled by its people;
they have disobeyed the laws,
violated the statutes
and broken the everlasting covenant.
6 Therefore a curse consumes the earth;
its people must bear their guilt.
Therefore earth's inhabitants are burned up,
and very few are left.
7 The new wine dries up and the vine withers;
all the merrymakers groan.
8 The gaiety of the tambourines is stilled,
the noise of the revelers has stopped,
the joyful harp is silent.
9 No longer do they drink wine with a song;
the beer is bitter to its drinkers.
10 The ruined city lies desolate;
the entrance to every house is barred.
11 In the streets they cry out for wine;
all joy turns to gloom,
all gaiety is banished from the earth.
12 The city is left in ruins,
its gate is battered to pieces.
13 So will it be on the earth
and among the nations,
as when an olive tree is beaten,
or as when gleanings are left after the grape harvest.

14 They raise their voices, they shout for joy;
from the west they acclaim the LORD's majesty.
15 Therefore in the east give glory to the LORD;
exalt the name of the LORD, the God of Israel,
in the islands of the sea.
16 From the ends of the earth we hear singing:
"Glory to the Righteous One."

But I said, "I waste away, I waste away!
Woe to me!
The treacherous betray!
With treachery the treacherous betray!"
17 Terror and pit and snare await you,
O people of the earth.
18 Whoever flees at the sound of terror
will fall into a pit;
whoever climbs out of the pit
will be caught in a snare.

The floodgates of the heavens are opened,
the foundations of the earth shake.
19 The earth is broken up,
the earth is split asunder,
the earth is thoroughly shaken.
20 The earth reels like a drunkard,
it sways like a hut in the wind;
so heavy upon it is the guilt of its rebellion
that it falls—never to rise again.

21 In that day the LORD will punish
the powers in the heavens above
and the kings on the earth below.
22 They will be herded together
like prisoners bound in a dungeon;
they will be shut up in prison
and be punished[a] after many days.
23 The moon will be abashed, the sun ashamed;
for the LORD Almighty will reign
on Mount Zion and in Jerusalem,
and before its elders, gloriously.

[a] 22 Or *released*

PRAYER: PETITION

PRESERVE me, O God, for I take refuge in You. I say to You, "You are my Lord; I have no goodness apart from You." (Psalm 16:1–2)

***PAUSE** here to petition God for spiritual insight so that you might have understanding of His Word. Ask for insight into your identity in Jesus Christ: that you might know who you are, what direction your life should take and what His purpose for your life is. Offer prayers regarding your activities for this day and any special concerns you may have.*

NT 1 Corinthians 14:26–40

Orderly Worship

26What then shall we say, brothers?
When you come together, everyone has a
hymn, or a word of instruction, a revelation, a tongue or an interpretation. All of
these must be done for the strengthening
of the church. 27If anyone speaks in a
tongue, two—or at the most three—
should speak, one at a time, and someone
must interpret. 28If there is no interpreter,
the speaker should keep quiet in the
church and speak to himself and God.
29Two or three prophets should speak,
and the others should weigh carefully
what is said. 30And if a revelation comes
to someone who is sitting down, the first
speaker should stop. 31For you can all
prophesy in turn so that everyone may be
instructed and encouraged. 32The spirits of
prophets are subject to the control of
prophets. 33For God is not a God of disorder but of peace.
As in all the congregations of the saints,
34women should remain silent in the
churches. They are not allowed to speak,
but must be in submission, as the Law
says. 35If they want to inquire about something, they should ask their own husbands at home; for it is disgraceful for a
woman to speak in the church.
36Did the word of God originate with
you? Or are you the only people it has
reached? 37If anybody thinks he is a
prophet or spiritually gifted, let him acknowledge that what I am writing to you
is the Lord's command. 38If he ignores
this, he himself will be ignored.[a]
39Therefore, my brothers, be eager to
prophesy, and do not forbid speaking in
tongues. 40But everything should be done
in a fitting and orderly way.

[a] 38 Some manuscripts *If he is ignorant of this, let him be ignorant*

PRAYER: MY RELATIONSHIP TO GOD

I WANT to love You, Lord my God, and to serve You with all my heart and with all my soul. (Deuteronomy 11:13)

***PAUSE** to thank God for the relationship that you enjoy with Him in Jesus Christ.*

YEAR 2
DAY 144

OT Isaiah 25:1–26:21

Praise to the L*ORD*

25 O LORD, you are my God;
I will exalt you and praise your
name,
for in perfect faithfulness
you have done marvelous things,
things planned long ago.
2You have made the city a heap of
rubble,
the fortified town a ruin,
the foreigners' stronghold a city no
more;
it will never be rebuilt.

[3]Therefore strong peoples will honor
you;
cities of ruthless nations will revere
you.
[4]You have been a refuge for the poor,
a refuge for the needy in his
distress,
a shelter from the storm
and a shade from the heat.
For the breath of the ruthless
is like a storm driving against a wall
[5] and like the heat of the desert.
You silence the uproar of foreigners;
as heat is reduced by the shadow of
a cloud,
so the song of the ruthless is stilled.

[6]On this mountain the LORD Almighty
will prepare
a feast of rich food for all peoples,
a banquet of aged wine—
the best of meats and the finest of
wines.
[7]On this mountain he will destroy
the shroud that enfolds all peoples,
the sheet that covers all nations;
[8] he will swallow up death forever.
The Sovereign LORD will wipe away
the tears
from all faces;
he will remove the disgrace of his
people
from all the earth.
The LORD has spoken.

[9]In that day they will say,

"Surely this is our God;
we trusted in him, and he saved us.
This is the LORD, we trusted in him;
let us rejoice and be glad in his
salvation."

[10]The hand of the LORD will rest on this
mountain;
but Moab will be trampled under
him
as straw is trampled down in the
manure.
[11]They will spread out their hands in it,
as a swimmer spreads out his hands
to swim.
God will bring down their pride
despite the cleverness[a] of their
hands.
[12]He will bring down your high fortified
walls
and lay them low;
he will bring them down to the
ground,
to the very dust.

A Song of Praise

26 In that day this song will be sung in
the land of Judah:

We have a strong city;
God makes salvation
its walls and ramparts.
[2]Open the gates
that the righteous nation may enter,
the nation that keeps faith.
[3]You will keep in perfect peace
him whose mind is steadfast,
because he trusts in you.
[4]Trust in the LORD forever,
for the LORD, the LORD, is the Rock
eternal.
[5]He humbles those who dwell on high,
he lays the lofty city low;
he levels it to the ground
and casts it down to the dust.
[6]Feet trample it down—
the feet of the oppressed,
the footsteps of the poor.

[7]The path of the righteous is level;
O upright One, you make the way
of the righteous smooth.
[8]Yes, LORD, walking in the way of your
laws,[b]
we wait for you;
your name and renown
are the desire of our hearts.
[9]My soul yearns for you in the night;
in the morning my spirit longs for
you.
When your judgments come upon the
earth,
the people of the world learn
righteousness.
[10]Though grace is shown to the wicked,
they do not learn righteousness;
even in a land of uprightness they go
on doing evil
and regard not the majesty of the
LORD.
[11]O LORD, your hand is lifted high,
but they do not see it.
Let them see your zeal for your people
and be put to shame;
let the fire reserved for your
enemies consume them.

[a] *11* The meaning of the Hebrew for this word is uncertain. [b] *8* Or *judgments*

12 LORD, you establish peace for us;
all that we have accomplished you have done for us.
13 O LORD, our God, other lords besides you have ruled over us,
but your name alone do we honor.
14 They are now dead, they live no more;
those departed spirits do not rise.
You punished them and brought them to ruin;
you wiped out all memory of them.
15 You have enlarged the nation, O LORD;
you have enlarged the nation.
You have gained glory for yourself;
you have extended all the borders of the land.

16 LORD, they came to you in their distress;
when you disciplined them,
they could barely whisper a prayer.[c]
17 As a woman with child and about to give birth
writhes and cries out in her pain,
so were we in your presence, O LORD.
18 We were with child, we writhed in pain,
but we gave birth to wind.
We have not brought salvation to the earth;
we have not given birth to people of the world.

19 But your dead will live;
their bodies will rise.
You who dwell in the dust,
wake up and shout for joy.
Your dew is like the dew of the morning;
the earth will give birth to her dead.

20 Go, my people, enter your rooms
and shut the doors behind you;
hide yourselves for a little while
until his wrath has passed by.
21 See, the LORD is coming out of his dwelling
to punish the people of the earth for their sins.
The earth will disclose the blood shed upon her;
she will conceal her slain no longer.

[c] 16 The meaning of the Hebrew for this clause is uncertain.

PRAYER: INTERCESSION

LORD Jesus Christ, grant that as Your body, we might reach unity in the faith and knowledge of You, the Son of God, so that we will become mature and attain to the whole measure of Your fullness. Then we will no longer be infants, being blown and carried by every wind of doctrine and by the cunning and craftiness of people who scheme deceitfully. Instead, we will speak the truth in love; we will grow up in every way in You, our Head. (Ephesians 4:13–15)

***TAKE** a few moments to intercede on behalf of other believers, such as your personal friends, those in ministry and those who are oppressed and in need.*

NT 1 Corinthians 15:1–11

The Resurrection of Christ

15 Now, brothers, I want to remind you of the gospel I preached to you, which you received and on which you have taken your stand.
2 By this gospel you are saved, if you hold firmly to the word I preached to you. Otherwise, you have believed in vain.
3 For what I received I passed on to you
as of first importance[a]: that Christ died for
our sins according to the Scriptures,
4 that he was buried, that he was raised on the
third day according to the Scriptures,
5 and that he appeared to Peter,[b] and then to the
Twelve.
6 After that, he appeared to more than five hundred of the brothers at the same time, most of whom are still living,
though some have fallen asleep.
7 Then he appeared to James, then to all the apos-

[a] 3 Or *you at the first* [b] 5 Greek *Cephas*

tles, [8]and last of all he appeared to me
also, as to one abnormally born.
[9]For I am the least of the apostles and
do not even deserve to be called an apostle, because I persecuted the church of
God. [10]But by the grace of God I am what
I am, and his grace to me was not without effect. No, I worked harder than all of
them—yet not I, but the grace of God that
was with me. [11]Whether, then, it was I or
they, this is what we preach, and this is
what you believed.

PRAYER: THE CHARACTER I WANT TO CULTIVATE

THROUGH love and truth iniquity is atoned for; in the fear of You, O Lord, we turn aside from evil. When our ways are pleasing to You, Lord, You make even our enemies live at peace with us. (Proverbs 16:6–7)

***TAKE** a moment to ask the Lord for the grace to grow in godly character.*

YEAR 2 DAY 145

OT Isaiah 27:1–13

Deliverance of Israel

27 In that day,

the LORD will punish with his sword,
his fierce, great and powerful sword,
Leviathan the gliding serpent,
Leviathan the coiling serpent;
he will slay the monster of the sea.

[2]In that day—

"Sing about a fruitful vineyard:
[3] I, the LORD, watch over it;
I water it continually.
I guard it day and night
so that no one may harm it.
[4] I am not angry.
If only there were briers and thorns
confronting me!
I would march against them in
battle;
I would set them all on fire.
[5]Or else let them come to me for
refuge;
let them make peace with me,
yes, let them make peace with me."

[6]In days to come Jacob will take root,
Israel will bud and blossom
and fill all the world with fruit.

[7]Has ⌊the LORD⌋ struck her
as he struck down those who struck
her?
Has she been killed
as those were killed who killed her?
[8]By warfare[a] and exile you contend
with her—
with his fierce blast he drives her
out,
as on a day the east wind blows.
[9]By this, then, will Jacob's guilt be
atoned for,
and this will be the full fruitage of
the removal of his sin:
When he makes all the altar stones
to be like chalk stones crushed to
pieces,
no Asherah poles[b] or incense altars
will be left standing.
[10]The fortified city stands desolate,
an abandoned settlement, forsaken
like the desert;
there the calves graze,
there they lie down;
they strip its branches bare.
[11]When its twigs are dry, they are
broken off
and women come and make fires
with them.
For this is a people without
understanding;
so their Maker has no compassion
on them,
and their Creator shows them no
favor.

[12]In that day the LORD will thresh from
the flowing Euphrates[c] to the Wadi of

[a] *8* See Septuagint; the meaning of the Hebrew for this word is uncertain. [b] *9* That is, symbols of the goddess Asherah [c] *12* Hebrew *River*

Egypt, and you, O Israelites, will be gathered up one by one. [13]And in that day a great trumpet will sound. Those who were perishing in Assyria and those who were exiled in Egypt will come and worship the LORD on the holy mountain in Jerusalem.

PRAYER: AFFIRMATION

THOSE who overcome will be clothed in white garments, and You, Jesus, will not blot out their names from the book of life, but You will confess their names before Your Father and before His angels. (Revelation 3:5)

***PAUSE** to reflect on these Biblical affirmations.*

NT 1 Corinthians 15:12–34

The Resurrection of the Dead

[12]But if it is preached that Christ has
been raised from the dead, how can some
of you say that there is no resurrection of
the dead? [13]If there is no resurrection of
the dead, then not even Christ has been
raised. [14]And if Christ has not been raised,
our preaching is useless and so is your
faith. [15]More than that, we are then found
to be false witnesses about God, for we
have testified about God that he raised
Christ from the dead. But he did not raise
him if in fact the dead are not raised. [16]For
if the dead are not raised, then Christ has
not been raised either. [17]And if Christ has
not been raised, your faith is futile; you
are still in your sins. [18]Then those also
who have fallen asleep in Christ are lost.
[19]If only for this life we have hope in
Christ, we are to be pitied more than all
men.

[20]But Christ has indeed been raised
from the dead, the firstfruits of those who
have fallen asleep. [21]For since death came
through a man, the resurrection of the
dead comes also through a man. [22]For as
in Adam all die, so in Christ all will be
made alive. [23]But each in his own turn:
Christ, the firstfruits; then, when he
comes, those who belong to him. [24]Then
the end will come, when he hands over
the kingdom to God the Father after he
has destroyed all dominion, authority and
power. [25]For he must reign until he has
put all his enemies under his feet. [26]The
last enemy to be destroyed is death. [27]For
he "has put everything under his feet."[a]
Now when it says that "everything" has
been put under him, it is clear that this
does not include God himself, who put
everything under Christ. [28]When he has
done this, then the Son himself will be
made subject to him who put everything
under him, so that God may be all in all.

[29]Now if there is no resurrection, what
will those do who are baptized for the
dead? If the dead are not raised at all, why
are people baptized for them? [30]And as for
us, why do we endanger ourselves every
hour? [31]I die every day—I mean that,
brothers—just as surely as I glory over you
in Christ Jesus our Lord. [32]If I fought wild
beasts in Ephesus for merely human reasons, what have I gained? If the dead are
not raised,

"Let us eat and drink,
for tomorrow we die."[b]

[33]Do not be misled: "Bad company corrupts good character." [34]Come back to
your senses as you ought, and stop sinning; for there are some who are ignorant
of God—I say this to your shame.

[a] 27 Psalm 8:6 [b] 32 Isaiah 22:13

PRAYER: MY RELATIONSHIP TO OTHERS

I WILL owe nothing to anyone except to love them, for those who love their neighbor have fulfilled the law. For the commandments, "You shall not commit adultery," "You shall not murder," "You shall not steal," "You shall not covet," and any other commandments there may

***be are summed up in this saying: "You shall love your neighbor as yourself." Love does no harm to a neighbor; therefore love is the fulfillment of the law.* (Romans 13:8–10)**

***PAUSE** to review your relationships with others and to commit them to the Lord.*

YEAR 2
DAY 146

OT Isaiah 28:1–29

Woe to Ephraim

28 Woe to that wreath, the pride of
Ephraim's drunkards,
to the fading flower, his glorious
beauty,
set on the head of a fertile valley—
to that city, the pride of those laid
low by wine!
2 See, the Lord has one who is powerful
and strong.
Like a hailstorm and a destructive
wind,
like a driving rain and a flooding
downpour,
he will throw it forcefully to the
ground.
3 That wreath, the pride of Ephraim's
drunkards,
will be trampled underfoot.
4 That fading flower, his glorious
beauty,
set on the head of a fertile valley,
will be like a fig ripe before harvest—
as soon as someone sees it and
takes it in his hand,
he swallows it.

5 In that day the LORD Almighty
will be a glorious crown,
a beautiful wreath
for the remnant of his people.
6 He will be a spirit of justice
to him who sits in judgment,
a source of strength
to those who turn back the battle at
the gate.

7 And these also stagger from wine
and reel from beer:
Priests and prophets stagger from beer
and are befuddled with wine;
they reel from beer,
they stagger when seeing visions,
they stumble when rendering
decisions.
8 All the tables are covered with vomit
and there is not a spot without
filth.

9 "Who is it he is trying to teach?
To whom is he explaining his
message?
To children weaned from their milk,
to those just taken from the breast?
10 For it is:
Do and do, do and do,
rule on rule, rule on rule[a];
a little here, a little there."

11 Very well then, with foreign lips and
strange tongues
God will speak to this people,
12 to whom he said,
"This is the resting place, let the
weary rest";
and, "This is the place of repose"—
but they would not listen.
13 So then, the word of the LORD to them
will become:
Do and do, do and do,
rule on rule, rule on rule;
a little here, a little there—
so that they will go and fall backward,
be injured and snared and captured.

14 Therefore hear the word of the LORD,
you scoffers
who rule this people in Jerusalem.
15 You boast, "We have entered into a
covenant with death,
with the grave[b] we have made an
agreement.
When an overwhelming scourge
sweeps by,
it cannot touch us,
for we have made a lie our refuge
and falsehood[c] our hiding place."

[a] *10* Hebrew / *sav lasav sav lasav* / *kav lakav kav lakav* (possibly meaningless sounds; perhaps a mimicking of the prophet's words); also in verse 13
[b] *15* Hebrew *Sheol;* also in verse 18
[c] *15* Or *false gods*

16 So this is what the Sovereign LORD says:

"See, I lay a stone in Zion,
a tested stone,
a precious cornerstone for a sure foundation;
the one who trusts will never be dismayed.
17 I will make justice the measuring line
and righteousness the plumb line;
hail will sweep away your refuge, the lie,
and water will overflow your hiding place.
18 Your covenant with death will be annulled;
your agreement with the grave will not stand.
When the overwhelming scourge sweeps by,
you will be beaten down by it.
19 As often as it comes it will carry you away;
morning after morning, by day and by night,
it will sweep through."

The understanding of this message
will bring sheer terror.
20 The bed is too short to stretch out on,
the blanket too narrow to wrap around you.
21 The LORD will rise up as he did at Mount Perazim,
he will rouse himself as in the Valley of Gibeon—
to do his work, his strange work,
and perform his task, his alien task.
22 Now stop your mocking,
or your chains will become heavier;
the Lord, the LORD Almighty, has told me
of the destruction decreed against the whole land.

23 Listen and hear my voice;
pay attention and hear what I say.
24 When a farmer plows for planting,
does he plow continually?
Does he keep on breaking up and harrowing the soil?
25 When he has leveled the surface,
does he not sow caraway and scatter cummin?
Does he not plant wheat in its place,[d]
barley in its plot,[d]
and spelt in its field?
26 His God instructs him
and teaches him the right way.

27 Caraway is not threshed with a sledge,
nor is a cartwheel rolled over cummin;
caraway is beaten out with a rod,
and cummin with a stick.
28 Grain must be ground to make bread;
so one does not go on threshing it forever.
Though he drives the wheels of his threshing cart over it,
his horses do not grind it.
29 All this also comes from the LORD Almighty,
wonderful in counsel and
magnificent in wisdom.

[d] 25 The meaning of the Hebrew for this word is uncertain.

PRAYER: THANKSGIVING

HAVING been justified by faith, I have peace with You, O God, through the Lord Jesus Christ, through whom I have gained access by faith into this grace in which I stand; and I rejoice in the hope of Your glory. (Romans 5:1–2)

***PAUSE** to offer your own expressions of thanksgiving.*

NT 1 Corinthians 15:35–58

The Resurrection Body

35 But someone may ask, "How are the
dead raised? With what kind of body will
they come?" 36 How foolish! What you
sow does not come to life unless it dies.
37 When you sow, you do not plant the
body that will be, but just a seed, perhaps
of wheat or of something else. 38 But God
gives it a body as he has determined, and
to each kind of seed he gives its own body.

39 All flesh is not the same: Men have one
kind of flesh, animals have another, birds
another and fish another. 40 There are also
heavenly bodies and there are earthly
bodies; but the splendor of the heavenly
bodies is one kind, and the splendor of
the earthly bodies is another. 41 The sun
has one kind of splendor, the moon another and the stars another; and star dif-
fers from star in splendor.

42 So will it be with the resurrection of
the dead. The body that is sown is perishable, it is raised imperishable; 43 it is
sown in dishonor, it is raised in glory; it
is sown in weakness, it is raised in power;
44 it is sown a natural body, it is raised a
spiritual body.

If there is a natural body, there is also a
spiritual body. 45 So it is written: "The first
man Adam became a living being"[a]; the
last Adam, a life-giving spirit. 46 The spiritual did not come first, but the natural,
and after that the spiritual. 47 The first man
was of the dust of the earth, the second
man from heaven. 48 As was the earthly
man, so are those who are of the earth;
and as is the man from heaven, so also are
those who are of heaven. 49 And just as we
have borne the likeness of the earthly
man, so shall we[b] bear the likeness of the
man from heaven.

50 I declare to you, brothers, that flesh
and blood cannot inherit the kingdom of
God, nor does the perishable inherit the
imperishable. 51 Listen, I tell you a mystery:
We will not all sleep, but we will all be
changed— 52 in a flash, in the twinkling of
an eye, at the last trumpet. For the trumpet will sound, the dead will be raised imperishable, and we will be changed. 53 For
the perishable must clothe itself with the
imperishable, and the mortal with immortality. 54 When the perishable has been
clothed with the imperishable, and the
mortal with immortality, then the saying
that is written will come true: "Death has
been swallowed up in victory."[c]

55 "Where, O death, is your victory?
Where, O death, is your sting?"[d]

56 The sting of death is sin, and the power
of sin is the law. 57 But thanks be to God!
He gives us the victory through our Lord
Jesus Christ.

58 Therefore, my dear brothers, stand
firm. Let nothing move you. Always give
yourselves fully to the work of the Lord,
because you know that your labor in the
Lord is not in vain.

[a] *45* Gen. 2:7 [b] *49* Some early manuscripts *so let us* [c] *54* Isaiah 25:8 [d] *55* Hosea 13:14

PRAYER: THE ATTRIBUTES OF GOD

I WILL not worship any other god, for You Lord, whose name is Jealous, are a jealous God. (Exodus 34:14) . . . O Lord my God, You are a consuming fire, a jealous God. (Deuteronomy 4:24)

PAUSE *to reflect on these affirmations about the person, powers and perfection of God.*

YEAR 2 DAY 147

OT Psalms 101–102

Psalm 101

Of David. A psalm.

1 I will sing of your love and justice;
to you, O LORD, I will sing praise.
2 I will be careful to lead a blameless
life—
when will you come to me?

I will walk in my house
with blameless heart.
3 I will set before my eyes
no vile thing.

The deeds of faithless men I hate;
they will not cling to me.
4 Men of perverse heart shall be far
from me;
I will have nothing to do with evil.

5 Whoever slanders his neighbor in
secret,

him will I put to silence;
whoever has haughty eyes and a proud heart,
him will I not endure.

6 My eyes will be on the faithful in the land,
that they may dwell with me;
he whose walk is blameless
will minister to me.

7 No one who practices deceit
will dwell in my house;
no one who speaks falsely
will stand in my presence.

8 Every morning I will put to silence
all the wicked in the land;
I will cut off every evildoer
from the city of the LORD.

Psalm 102

A prayer of an afflicted man. When he is faint and pours out his lament before the LORD.

1 Hear my prayer, O LORD;
let my cry for help come to you.
2 Do not hide your face from me
when I am in distress.
Turn your ear to me;
when I call, answer me quickly.

3 For my days vanish like smoke;
my bones burn like glowing embers.
4 My heart is blighted and withered like grass;
I forget to eat my food.
5 Because of my loud groaning
I am reduced to skin and bones.
6 I am like a desert owl,
like an owl among the ruins.
7 I lie awake; I have become
like a bird alone on a roof.
8 All day long my enemies taunt me;
those who rail against me use my name as a curse.
9 For I eat ashes as my food
and mingle my drink with tears
10 because of your great wrath,
for you have taken me up and thrown me aside.
11 My days are like the evening shadow;
I wither away like grass.

12 But you, O LORD, sit enthroned forever;
your renown endures through all generations.
13 You will arise and have compassion on Zion,
for it is time to show favor to her;
the appointed time has come.
14 For her stones are dear to your servants;
her very dust moves them to pity.
15 The nations will fear the name of the LORD,
all the kings of the earth will revere your glory.
16 For the LORD will rebuild Zion
and appear in his glory.
17 He will respond to the prayer of the destitute;
he will not despise their plea.

18 Let this be written for a future generation,
that a people not yet created may praise the LORD:
19 "The LORD looked down from his sanctuary on high,
from heaven he viewed the earth,
20 to hear the groans of the prisoners
and release those condemned to death."
21 So the name of the LORD will be declared in Zion
and his praise in Jerusalem
22 when the peoples and the kingdoms
assemble to worship the LORD.

23 In the course of my life[a] he broke my strength;
he cut short my days.
24 So I said:
"Do not take me away, O my God,
in the midst of my days;
your years go on through all generations.
25 In the beginning you laid the foundations of the earth,
and the heavens are the work of your hands.
26 They will perish, but you remain;
they will all wear out like a garment.
Like clothing you will change them
and they will be discarded.
27 But you remain the same,
and your years will never end.
28 The children of your servants will live in your presence;
their descendants will be established before you."

[a] 23 Or *By his power*

PRAYER: ADORATION

I HAVE tasted and seen that You, O Lord, are good; blessed is the one who takes refuge in You! All Your saints fear You, for those who fear You lack nothing. (Psalm 34:8–9)

PAUSE *to express your thoughts of praise and worship.*

NT 1 Corinthians 16:1–24

The Collection for God's People

16 Now about the collection for God's
people: Do what I told the Galatian
churches to do. 2On the first day of every
week, each one of you should set aside a
sum of money in keeping with his income, saving it up, so that when I come
no collections will have to be made.
3Then, when I arrive, I will give letters of
introduction to the men you approve and
send them with your gift to Jerusalem. 4If
it seems advisable for me to go also, they
will accompany me.

Personal Requests

5After I go through Macedonia, I will
come to you—for I will be going through
Macedonia. 6Perhaps I will stay with you
awhile, or even spend the winter, so that
you can help me on my journey, wherever I go. 7I do not want to see you now and
make only a passing visit; I hope to spend
some time with you, if the Lord permits.
8But I will stay on at Ephesus until Pentecost, 9because a great door for effective
work has opened to me, and there are
many who oppose me.
10If Timothy comes, see to it that he has
nothing to fear while he is with you, for
he is carrying on the work of the Lord, just
as I am. 11No one, then, should refuse to
accept him. Send him on his way in peace
so that he may return to me. I am expecting him along with the brothers.
12Now about our brother Apollos: I
strongly urged him to go to you with the
brothers. He was quite unwilling to go
now, but he will go when he has the opportunity.
13Be on your guard; stand firm in the
faith; be men of courage; be strong. 14Do
everything in love.
15You know that the household of
Stephanas were the first converts in Achaia, and they have devoted themselves to
the service of the saints. I urge you, brothers, 16to submit to such as these and to
everyone who joins in the work, and
labors at it. 17I was glad when Stephanas,
Fortunatus and Achaicus arrived, because
they have supplied what was lacking from
you. 18For they refreshed my spirit and
yours also. Such men deserve recognition.

Final Greetings

19The churches in the province of Asia
send you greetings. Aquila and Priscilla[a]
greet you warmly in the Lord, and so does
the church that meets at their house. 20All
the brothers here send you greetings.
Greet one another with a holy kiss.
21I, Paul, write this greeting in my own
hand.
22If anyone does not love the Lord—a
curse be on him. Come, O Lord[b]!
23The grace of the Lord Jesus be with
you.
24My love to all of you in Christ Jesus.
Amen.[c]

[a] *19* Greek *Prisca,* a variant of *Priscilla* [b] *22* In Aramaic the expression *Come, O Lord* is *Marana tha.* [c] *24* Some manuscripts do not have *Amen.*

PRAYER: THE WORKS OF GOD

O LORD, You made the earth by Your power; You established the world by Your wisdom and stretched out the heavens by Your understanding. (Jeremiah 51:15) . . . Your hands made me and fashioned me. (Psalm 119:73)

TAKE *a moment to consider the greatness of God's wonderful works.*

YEAR 2 DAY 148

OT Isaiah 29:1-24

Woe to David's City

29 Woe to you, Ariel, Ariel,
the city where David settled!
Add year to year
and let your cycle of festivals go on.
2 Yet I will besiege Ariel;
she will mourn and lament,
she will be to me like an altar hearth.[a]
3 I will encamp against you all around;
I will encircle you with towers
and set up my siege works against you.
4 Brought low, you will speak from the ground;
your speech will mumble out of the dust.
Your voice will come ghostlike from the earth;
out of the dust your speech will whisper.

5 But your many enemies will become like fine dust,
the ruthless hordes like blown chaff.
Suddenly, in an instant,
6 the LORD Almighty will come
with thunder and earthquake and great noise,
with windstorm and tempest and flames of a devouring fire.
7 Then the hordes of all the nations that fight against Ariel,
that attack her and her fortress and besiege her,
will be as it is with a dream,
with a vision in the night—
8 as when a hungry man dreams that he is eating,
but he awakens, and his hunger remains;
as when a thirsty man dreams that he is drinking,
but he awakens faint, with his thirst unquenched.
So will it be with the hordes of all the nations
that fight against Mount Zion.

9 Be stunned and amazed,
blind yourselves and be sightless;
be drunk, but not from wine,
stagger, but not from beer.
10 The LORD has brought over you a deep sleep:
He has sealed your eyes (the prophets);
he has covered your heads (the seers).

11 For you this whole vision is nothing
but words sealed in a scroll. And if you
give the scroll to someone who can read,
and say to him, "Read this, please," he will
answer, "I can't; it is sealed." 12 Or if you
give the scroll to someone who cannot
read, and say, "Read this, please," he will
answer, "I don't know how to read."

13 The Lord says:

"These people come near to me with their mouth
and honor me with their lips,
but their hearts are far from me.
Their worship of me
is made up only of rules taught by men.[b]
14 Therefore once more I will astound these people
with wonder upon wonder;
the wisdom of the wise will perish,
the intelligence of the intelligent will vanish."
15 Woe to those who go to great depths
to hide their plans from the LORD,
who do their work in darkness and think,
"Who sees us? Who will know?"
16 You turn things upside down,
as if the potter were thought to be like the clay!
Shall what is formed say to him who formed it,
"He did not make me"?
Can the pot say of the potter,
"He knows nothing"?

17 In a very short time, will not Lebanon be turned into a fertile field
and the fertile field seem like a forest?
18 In that day the deaf will hear the words of the scroll,

[a] 2 The Hebrew for *altar hearth* sounds like the Hebrew for *Ariel.* [b] 13 Hebrew; Septuagint *They worship me in vain; / their teachings are but rules taught by men*

and out of gloom and darkness
the eyes of the blind will see.
19 Once more the humble will rejoice in the LORD;
the needy will rejoice in the Holy One of Israel.
20 The ruthless will vanish,
the mockers will disappear,
and all who have an eye for evil will be cut down—
21 those who with a word make a man out to be guilty,
who ensnare the defender in court
and with false testimony deprive the innocent of justice.

22 Therefore this is what the LORD, who redeemed Abraham, says to the house of Jacob:

"No longer will Jacob be ashamed;
no longer will their faces grow pale.
23 When they see among them their children,
the work of my hands,
they will keep my name holy;
they will acknowledge the holiness of the Holy One of Jacob,
and will stand in awe of the God of Israel.
24 Those who are wayward in spirit will gain understanding;
those who complain will accept instruction."

PRAYER: CONFESSION

***MAY we not sin against You, Father. But if anyone sins, we have an Advocate with You; He is Jesus Christ, the Righteous. And He is the propitiation for our sins, and not for ours only but also for the whole world.* (1 John 2:1–2)**

***ASK** the Spirit to search your heart and reveal any areas of unconfessed sin. Acknowledge these to the Lord and thank Him for His forgiveness.*

NT 2 Corinthians 1:1–11

1 Paul, an apostle of Christ Jesus by the
will of God, and Timothy our brother,

To the church of God in Corinth, together with all the saints throughout Achaia:

2 Grace and peace to you from God our Father and the Lord Jesus Christ.

The God of All Comfort

3 Praise be to the God and Father of our
Lord Jesus Christ, the Father of compassion and the God of all comfort, 4 who
comforts us in all our troubles, so that we
can comfort those in any trouble with the
comfort we ourselves have received from
God. 5 For just as the sufferings of Christ
flow over into our lives, so also through
Christ our comfort overflows. 6 If we are
distressed, it is for your comfort and salvation; if we are comforted, it is for your
comfort, which produces in you patient
endurance of the same sufferings we suffer. 7 And our hope for you is firm, because
we know that just as you share in our sufferings, so also you share in our comfort.
8 We do not want you to be uninformed,
brothers, about the hardships we suffered
in the province of Asia. We were under
great pressure, far beyond our ability to
endure, so that we despaired even of life.
9 Indeed, in our hearts we felt the sentence
of death. But this happened that we might
not rely on ourselves but on God, who
raises the dead. 10 He has delivered us from
such a deadly peril, and he will deliver us.
On him we have set our hope that he will
continue to deliver us, 11 as you help us by
your prayers. Then many will give thanks
on our[a] behalf for the gracious favor granted us in answer to the prayers of many.

[a] 11 Many manuscripts *your*

PRAYER: MY RELATIONSHIP TO GOD

I WILL seek You, Lord while You may be found and call upon You while You are near. (Isaiah 55:6) . . . I will call upon You and come and pray to You, and You will listen to me. I will seek You and find You when I search for You with all my heart. (Jeremiah 29:12–13)

***PAUSE** to thank God for the relationship that you enjoy with Him in Jesus Christ.*

OT **Isaiah 30:1–33** — YEAR 2 DAY 149

Woe to the Obstinate Nation

30 "Woe to the obstinate children,"
declares the LORD,
"to those who carry out plans that are not mine,
forming an alliance, but not by my Spirit,
heaping sin upon sin;
2 who go down to Egypt
without consulting me;
who look for help to Pharaoh's protection,
to Egypt's shade for refuge.
3 But Pharaoh's protection will be to your shame,
Egypt's shade will bring you disgrace.
4 Though they have officials in Zoan
and their envoys have arrived in Hanes,
5 everyone will be put to shame
because of a people useless to them,
who bring neither help nor advantage,
but only shame and disgrace."

6 An oracle concerning the animals of the Negev:

Through a land of hardship and distress,
of lions and lionesses,
of adders and darting snakes,
the envoys carry their riches on donkeys' backs,
their treasures on the humps of camels,
to that unprofitable nation,
7 to Egypt, whose help is utterly useless.
Therefore I call her
Rahab the Do-Nothing.

8 Go now, write it on a tablet for them,
inscribe it on a scroll,
that for the days to come
it may be an everlasting witness.
9 These are rebellious people, deceitful children,
children unwilling to listen to the LORD's instruction.
10 They say to the seers,
"See no more visions!"
and to the prophets,
"Give us no more visions of what is right!
Tell us pleasant things,
prophesy illusions.
11 Leave this way,
get off this path,
and stop confronting us
with the Holy One of Israel!"

12 Therefore, this is what the Holy One of Israel says:

"Because you have rejected this message,
relied on oppression
and depended on deceit,
13 this sin will become for you
like a high wall, cracked and bulging,
that collapses suddenly, in an instant.
14 It will break in pieces like pottery,
shattered so mercilessly
that among its pieces not a fragment will be found
for taking coals from a hearth
or scooping water out of a cistern."

15 This is what the Sovereign LORD, the Holy One of Israel, says:

"In repentance and rest is your salvation,

in quietness and trust is your
strength,
but you would have none of it.
16 You said, 'No, we will flee on horses.'
Therefore you will flee!
You said, 'We will ride off on swift
horses.'
Therefore your pursuers will be
swift!
17 A thousand will flee
at the threat of one;
at the threat of five
you will all flee away,
till you are left
like a flagstaff on a mountaintop,
like a banner on a hill."

18 Yet the LORD longs to be gracious to
you;
he rises to show you compassion.
For the LORD is a God of justice.
Blessed are all who wait for him!

19 O people of Zion, who live in Jerusalem, you will weep no more. How gracious he will be when you cry for help! As
soon as he hears, he will answer you. 20 Although the Lord gives you the bread of
adversity and the water of affliction, your
teachers will be hidden no more; with
your own eyes you will see them.
21 Whether you turn to the right or to the
left, your ears will hear a voice behind
you, saying, "This is the way, walk in it."
22 Then you will defile your idols overlaid
with silver and your images covered with
gold; you will throw them away like a
menstrual cloth and say to them, "Away
with you!"

23 He will also send you rain for the seed
you sow in the ground, and the food that
comes from the land will be rich and
plentiful. In that day your cattle will graze
in broad meadows. 24 The oxen and donkeys that work the soil will eat fodder and
mash, spread out with fork and shovel.
25 In the day of great slaughter, when the
towers fall, streams of water will flow on
every high mountain and every lofty hill.
26 The moon will shine like the sun, and
the sunlight will be seven times brighter,
like the light of seven full days, when the
LORD binds up the bruises of his people
and heals the wounds he inflicted.

27 See, the Name of the LORD comes
from afar,
with burning anger and dense
clouds of smoke;
his lips are full of wrath,
and his tongue is a consuming fire.
28 His breath is like a rushing torrent,
rising up to the neck.
He shakes the nations in the sieve of
destruction;
he places in the jaws of the peoples
a bit that leads them astray.
29 And you will sing
as on the night you celebrate a holy
festival;
your hearts will rejoice
as when people go up with flutes
to the mountain of the LORD,
to the Rock of Israel.
30 The LORD will cause men to hear his
majestic voice
and will make them see his arm
coming down
with raging anger and consuming fire,
with cloudburst, thunderstorm and
hail.
31 The voice of the LORD will shatter
Assyria;
with his scepter he will strike them
down.
32 Every stroke the LORD lays on them
with his punishing rod
will be to the music of tambourines
and harps,
as he fights them in battle with the
blows of his arm.
33 Topheth has long been prepared;
it has been made ready for the king.
Its fire pit has been made deep and
wide,
with an abundance of fire and
wood;
the breath of the LORD,
like a stream of burning sulfur,
sets it ablaze.

PRAYER: RENEWAL

MAY I not let my heart be troubled; let me trust in You, O God, and trust also in Christ. (John 14:1) . . . Jesus, as the Father has loved You, You also have loved me. May I abide in Your love. If I

keep Your commandments, I will abide in Your love, just as You kept Your Father's commandments and abide in His love. You have told me this so that Your joy may be in me and that my joy may be full. (John 15:9–11)

***PAUSE** to add your own prayers for personal renewal.*

NT 2 Corinthians 1:12–2:4

Paul's Change of Plans

[12]Now this is our boast: Our conscience testifies that we have conducted ourselves in the world, and especially in our relations with you, in the holiness and sincerity that are from God. We have done so not according to worldly wisdom but according to God's grace. [13]For we do not write you anything you cannot read or understand. And I hope that, [14]as you have understood us in part, you will come to understand fully that you can boast of us just as we will boast of you in the day of the Lord Jesus.

[15]Because I was confident of this, I planned to visit you first so that you might benefit twice. [16]I planned to visit you on my way to Macedonia and to come back to you from Macedonia, and then to have you send me on my way to Judea. [17]When I planned this, did I do it lightly? Or do I make my plans in a worldly manner so that in the same breath I say, "Yes, yes" and "No, no"?

[18]But as surely as God is faithful, our message to you is not "Yes" and "No." [19]For the Son of God, Jesus Christ, who was preached among you by me and Silas[a] and Timothy, was not "Yes" and "No," but in him it has always been "Yes." [20]For no matter how many promises God has made, they are "Yes" in Christ. And so through him the "Amen" is spoken by us to the glory of God. [21]Now it is God who makes both us and you stand firm in Christ. He anointed us, [22]set his seal of ownership on us, and put his Spirit in our hearts as a deposit, guaranteeing what is to come.

[23]I call God as my witness that it was in order to spare you that I did not return to Corinth. [24]Not that we lord it over your faith, but we work with you for your joy, because it is by faith you stand firm.

2 [1]So I made up my mind that I would not make another painful visit to you. [2]For if I grieve you, who is left to make me glad but you whom I have grieved? [3]I wrote as I did so that when I came I should not be distressed by those who ought to make me rejoice. I had confidence in all of you, that you would all share my joy. [4]For I wrote you out of great distress and anguish of heart and with many tears, not to grieve you but to let you know the depth of my love for you.

[a] 19 Greek *Silvanus,* a variant of *Silas*

PRAYER: THE CHARACTER I WANT TO CULTIVATE

O LORD, I ask for a wise and understanding heart to discern between good and evil. (1 Kings 3:9, 12) . . . The entrance of Your words gives light; it gives understanding to the simple. (Psalm 119:130)

***TAKE** a moment to ask the Lord for the grace to grow in godly character.*

YEAR 2 DAY 150

OT Isaiah 31:1–32:20

Woe to Those Who Rely on Egypt

31 Woe to those who go down to Egypt
for help,
who rely on horses,
who trust in the multitude of their
chariots
and in the great strength of their
horsemen,

but do not look to the Holy One of
Israel,
or seek help from the LORD.
[2] Yet he too is wise and can bring
disaster;
he does not take back his words.
He will rise up against the house of
the wicked,
against those who help evildoers.
[3] But the Egyptians are men and not
God;
their horses are flesh and not spirit.
When the LORD stretches out his hand,
he who helps will stumble,
he who is helped will fall;
both will perish together.

[4] This is what the LORD says to me:

"As a lion growls,
a great lion over his prey—
and though a whole band of shepherds
is called together against him,
he is not frightened by their shouts
or disturbed by their clamor—
so the LORD Almighty will come down
to do battle on Mount Zion and on
its heights.
[5] Like birds hovering overhead,
the LORD Almighty will shield
Jerusalem;
he will shield it and deliver it,
he will 'pass over' it and will rescue
it."

[6] Return to him you have so greatly revolted against, O Israelites. [7] For in that day
every one of you will reject the idols of silver and gold your sinful hands have made.

[8] "Assyria will fall by a sword that is not
of man;
a sword, not of mortals, will devour
them.
They will flee before the sword
and their young men will be put to
forced labor.
[9] Their stronghold will fall because of
terror;
at sight of the battle standard their
commanders will panic,"
declares the LORD,
whose fire is in Zion,
whose furnace is in Jerusalem.

The Kingdom of Righteousness

32 See, a king will reign in
righteousness
and rulers will rule with justice.
[2] Each man will be like a shelter from
the wind
and a refuge from the storm,
like streams of water in the desert
and the shadow of a great rock in a
thirsty land.

[3] Then the eyes of those who see will
no longer be closed,
and the ears of those who hear will
listen.
[4] The mind of the rash will know and
understand,
and the stammering tongue will be
fluent and clear.
[5] No longer will the fool be called
noble
nor the scoundrel be highly
respected.
[6] For the fool speaks folly,
his mind is busy with evil:
He practices ungodliness
and spreads error concerning the
LORD;
the hungry he leaves empty
and from the thirsty he withholds
water.
[7] The scoundrel's methods are wicked,
he makes up evil schemes
to destroy the poor with lies,
even when the plea of the needy is
just.
[8] But the noble man makes noble
plans,
and by noble deeds he stands.

The Women of Jerusalem

[9] You women who are so complacent,
rise up and listen to me;
you daughters who feel secure,
hear what I have to say!
[10] In little more than a year
you who feel secure will tremble;
the grape harvest will fail,
and the harvest of fruit will not
come.
[11] Tremble, you complacent women;
shudder, you daughters who feel
secure!
Strip off your clothes,
put sackcloth around your waists.
[12] Beat your breasts for the pleasant
fields,
for the fruitful vines
[13] and for the land of my people,

a land overgrown with thorns and
briers—
yes, mourn for all houses of
merriment
and for this city of revelry.
14 The fortress will be abandoned,
the noisy city deserted;
citadel and watchtower will become a
wasteland forever,
the delight of donkeys, a pasture for
flocks,
15 till the Spirit is poured upon us from
on high,
and the desert becomes a fertile field,
and the fertile field seems like a
forest.
16 Justice will dwell in the desert
and righteousness live in the fertile
field.
17 The fruit of righteousness will be peace;
the effect of righteousness will be
quietness and confidence forever.
18 My people will live in peaceful
dwelling places,
in secure homes,
in undisturbed places of rest.
19 Though hail flattens the forest
and the city is leveled completely,
20 how blessed you will be,
sowing your seed by every stream,
and letting your cattle and donkeys
range free.

PRAYER: PETITION

MAY I walk in wisdom toward outsiders, making the most of every opportunity. My speech should always be graceful, seasoned with salt, so that I may know how to answer each person.
(Colossians 4:5–6)

__PAUSE__ here to petition God for growth in love and compassion toward others. Offer prayers for your loved ones, for those who do not know Jesus and for those in need. Offer prayers regarding your activities for this day and any special concerns you may have.

NT 2 Corinthians 2:5–3:6

Forgiveness for the Sinner

5 If anyone has caused grief, he has not
so much grieved me as he has grieved all
of you, to some extent—not to put it too
severely. 6 The punishment inflicted on
him by the majority is sufficient for him.
7 Now instead, you ought to forgive and
comfort him, so that he will not be overwhelmed by excessive sorrow. 8 I urge you,
therefore, to reaffirm your love for him.
9 The reason I wrote you was to see if you
would stand the test and be obedient in
everything. 10 If you forgive anyone, I also
forgive him. And what I have forgiven—if
there was anything to forgive—I have forgiven in the sight of Christ for your sake,
11 in order that Satan might not outwit us.
For we are not unaware of his schemes.

Ministers of the New Covenant

12 Now when I went to Troas to preach
the gospel of Christ and found that the
Lord had opened a door for me, 13 I still
had no peace of mind, because I did not
find my brother Titus there. So I said good-
by to them and went on to Macedonia.
14 But thanks be to God, who always
leads us in triumphal procession in Christ
and through us spreads everywhere the
fragrance of the knowledge of him. 15 For
we are to God the aroma of Christ among
those who are being saved and those who
are perishing. 16 To the one we are the
smell of death; to the other, the fragrance
of life. And who is equal to such a task?
17 Unlike so many, we do not peddle the
word of God for profit. On the contrary,
in Christ we speak before God with sincerity, like men sent from God.
3 Are we beginning to commend ourselves again? Or do we need, like some
people, letters of recommendation to you
or from you? 2 You yourselves are our letter, written on our hearts, known and read
by everybody. 3 You show that you are a
letter from Christ, the result of our ministry, written not with ink but with the

Spirit of the living God, not on tablets of stone but on tablets of human hearts.
[4]Such confidence as this is ours through Christ before God. [5]Not that we are competent in ourselves to claim anything for ourselves, but our competence comes from God. [6]He has made us competent as ministers of a new covenant—not of the letter but of the Spirit; for the letter kills, but the Spirit gives life.

PRAYER: MY RELATIONSHIP TO OTHERS

IF I am generous, I will prosper; if I water others, I will myself be refreshed. (Proverbs 11:25) . . . Those who are generous will be blessed, for they share their food with the poor. (Proverbs 22:9)

__PAUSE__ to review your relationships with others and to commit them to the Lord.

YEAR 2 DAY 151

OT **Isaiah 33:1-24**

Distress and Help

33 Woe to you, O destroyer,
you who have not been destroyed!
Woe to you, O traitor,
you who have not been betrayed!
When you stop destroying,
you will be destroyed;
when you stop betraying,
you will be betrayed.

[2]O LORD, be gracious to us;
we long for you.
Be our strength every morning,
our salvation in time of distress.
[3]At the thunder of your voice, the peoples flee;
when you rise up, the nations scatter.
[4]Your plunder, O nations, is harvested as by young locusts;
like a swarm of locusts men pounce on it.

[5]The LORD is exalted, for he dwells on high;
he will fill Zion with justice and righteousness.
[6]He will be the sure foundation for your times,
a rich store of salvation and wisdom and knowledge;
the fear of the LORD is the key to this treasure.[a]

[7]Look, their brave men cry aloud in the streets;
the envoys of peace weep bitterly.
[8]The highways are deserted,
no travelers are on the roads.
The treaty is broken,
its witnesses[b] are despised,
no one is respected.
[9]The land mourns[c] and wastes away,
Lebanon is ashamed and withers;
Sharon is like the Arabah,
and Bashan and Carmel drop their leaves.

[10]"Now will I arise," says the LORD.
"Now will I be exalted;
now will I be lifted up.
[11]You conceive chaff,
you give birth to straw;
your breath is a fire that consumes you.
[12]The peoples will be burned as if to lime;
like cut thornbushes they will be set ablaze."

[13]You who are far away, hear what I have done;
you who are near, acknowledge my power!
[14]The sinners in Zion are terrified;
trembling grips the godless:
"Who of us can dwell with the consuming fire?
Who of us can dwell with everlasting burning?"
[15]He who walks righteously
and speaks what is right,
who rejects gain from extortion

[a]6 Or *is a treasure from him* [b]8 Dead Sea Scrolls; Masoretic Text / *the cities* [c]9 Or *dries up*

and keeps his hand from accepting bribes,
who stops his ears against plots of murder
and shuts his eyes against contemplating evil—
16 this is the man who will dwell on the heights,
whose refuge will be the mountain fortress.
His bread will be supplied,
and water will not fail him.

17 Your eyes will see the king in his beauty
and view a land that stretches afar.
18 In your thoughts you will ponder the former terror:
"Where is that chief officer?
Where is the one who took the revenue?
Where is the officer in charge of the towers?"
19 You will see those arrogant people no more,
those people of an obscure speech,
with their strange, incomprehensible tongue.
20 Look upon Zion, the city of our festivals;
your eyes will see Jerusalem,
a peaceful abode, a tent that will not be moved;
its stakes will never be pulled up,
nor any of its ropes broken.
21 There the LORD will be our Mighty One.
It will be like a place of broad rivers and streams.
No galley with oars will ride them,
no mighty ship will sail them.
22 For the LORD is our judge,
the LORD is our lawgiver,
the LORD is our king;
it is he who will save us.

23 Your rigging hangs loose:
The mast is not held secure,
the sail is not spread.
Then an abundance of spoils will be divided
and even the lame will carry off plunder.
24 No one living in Zion will say, "I am ill";
and the sins of those who dwell there will be forgiven.

PRAYER: INTERCESSION

O GOD, open to me a door for the word, so that I may speak the mystery of Christ and proclaim it clearly, as I ought. (Colossians 4:3–4)

***TAKE** a few moments to intercede on behalf of friends, relatives, neighbors and coworkers who do not yet know salvation in Jesus Christ.*

NT 2 Corinthians 3:7–18

The Glory of the New Covenant

7 Now if the ministry that brought death,
which was engraved in letters on stone,
came with glory, so that the Israelites
could not look steadily at the face of Moses because of its glory, fading though it
was, 8 will not the ministry of the Spirit be
even more glorious? 9 If the ministry that
condemns men is glorious, how much
more glorious is the ministry that brings
righteousness! 10 For what was glorious has
no glory now in comparison with the surpassing glory. 11 And if what was fading
away came with glory, how much greater
is the glory of that which lasts!
12 Therefore, since we have such a hope,
we are very bold. 13 We are not like Moses,
who would put a veil over his face to keep
the Israelites from gazing at it while the radiance was fading away. 14 But their minds
were made dull, for to this day the same
veil remains when the old covenant is read.
It has not been removed, because only in
Christ is it taken away. 15 Even to this day
when Moses is read, a veil covers their
hearts. 16 But whenever anyone turns to the
Lord, the veil is taken away. 17 Now the Lord
is the Spirit, and where the Spirit of the
Lord is, there is freedom. 18 And we, who
with unveiled faces all reflect[a] the Lord's
glory, are being transformed into his likeness with ever-increasing glory, which
comes from the Lord, who is the Spirit.

[a] 18 Or *contemplate*

PRAYER: THE ATTRIBUTES OF GOD

THE Father loves You, Jesus the Son, and has given all things into Your hand. (John 3:35) . . . Where two or three come together in Your name, Jesus, You are there in our midst. (Matthew 18:20)

***PAUSE** to reflect on these affirmations about the person, powers and perfection of God.*

YEAR 2 DAY 152

OT **Isaiah 34:1–17**

Judgment Against the Nations

34 Come near, you nations, and listen;
pay attention, you peoples!
Let the earth hear, and all that is in it,
the world, and all that comes out of it!
2 The LORD is angry with all nations;
his wrath is upon all their armies.
He will totally destroy[a] them,
he will give them over to slaughter.
3 Their slain will be thrown out,
their dead bodies will send up a stench;
the mountains will be soaked with their blood.
4 All the stars of the heavens will be dissolved
and the sky rolled up like a scroll;
all the starry host will fall
like withered leaves from the vine,
like shriveled figs from the fig tree.

5 My sword has drunk its fill in the heavens;
see, it descends in judgment on Edom,
the people I have totally destroyed.
6 The sword of the LORD is bathed in blood,
it is covered with fat—
the blood of lambs and goats,
fat from the kidneys of rams.
For the LORD has a sacrifice in Bozrah
and a great slaughter in Edom.
7 And the wild oxen will fall with them,
the bull calves and the great bulls.
Their land will be drenched with blood,
and the dust will be soaked with fat.

8 For the LORD has a day of vengeance,
a year of retribution, to uphold Zion's cause.
9 Edom's streams will be turned into pitch,
her dust into burning sulfur;
her land will become blazing pitch!
10 It will not be quenched night and day;
its smoke will rise forever.
From generation to generation it will lie desolate;
no one will ever pass through it again.
11 The desert owl[b] and screech owl[b] will possess it;
the great owl[b] and the raven will nest there.
God will stretch out over Edom
the measuring line of chaos
and the plumb line of desolation.
12 Her nobles will have nothing there to be called a kingdom,
all her princes will vanish away.
13 Thorns will overrun her citadels,
nettles and brambles her strongholds.
She will become a haunt for jackals,
a home for owls.
14 Desert creatures will meet with hyenas,
and wild goats will bleat to each other;
there the night creatures will also repose
and find for themselves places of rest.
15 The owl will nest there and lay eggs,
she will hatch them, and care for her young under the shadow of her wings;
there also the falcons will gather,
each with its mate.

[a] *2* The Hebrew term refers to the irrevocable giving over of things or persons to the LORD, often by totally destroying them; also in verse 5. [b] *11* The precise identification of these birds is uncertain.

[16]Look in the scroll of the LORD and read:

None of these will be missing,
not one will lack her mate.
For it is his mouth that has given the order,
and his Spirit will gather them together.
[17]He allots their portions;
his hand distributes them by measure.
They will possess it forever
and dwell there from generation to generation.

PRAYER: AFFIRMATION

***SURELY** Your salvation is near to those who fear You. (Psalm 85:9) . . . Your secrets are with those who fear You, O Lord, and You will make them know Your covenant. (Psalm 25:14)*

***PAUSE** to reflect on these Biblical affirmations.*

NT 2 Corinthians 4:1–18

Treasures in Jars of Clay

4 Therefore, since through God's mercy we have this ministry, we do not lose heart. [2]Rather, we have renounced secret and shameful ways; we do not use deception, nor do we distort the word of God. On the contrary, by setting forth the truth plainly we commend ourselves to every man's conscience in the sight of God. [3]And even if our gospel is veiled, it is veiled to those who are perishing. [4]The god of this age has blinded the minds of unbelievers, so that they cannot see the light of the gospel of the glory of Christ, who is the image of God. [5]For we do not preach ourselves, but Jesus Christ as Lord, and ourselves as your servants for Jesus' sake. [6]For God, who said, "Let light shine out of darkness,"[a] made his light shine in our hearts to give us the light of the knowledge of the glory of God in the face of Christ.

[7]But we have this treasure in jars of clay to show that this all-surpassing power is from God and not from us. [8]We are hard pressed on every side, but not crushed; perplexed, but not in despair; [9]persecuted, but not abandoned; struck down, but not destroyed. [10]We always carry around in our body the death of Jesus, so that the life of Jesus may also be revealed in our body. [11]For we who are alive are always being given over to death for Jesus' sake, so that his life may be revealed in our mortal body. [12]So then, death is at work in us, but life is at work in you.

[13]It is written: "I believed; therefore I have spoken."[b] With that same spirit of faith we also believe and therefore speak, [14]because we know that the one who raised the Lord Jesus from the dead will also raise us with Jesus and present us with you in his presence. [15]All this is for your benefit, so that the grace that is reaching more and more people may cause thanksgiving to overflow to the glory of God.

[16]Therefore we do not lose heart. Though outwardly we are wasting away, yet inwardly we are being renewed day by day. [17]For our light and momentary troubles are achieving for us an eternal glory that far outweighs them all. [18]So we fix our eyes not on what is seen, but on what is unseen. For what is seen is temporary, but what is unseen is eternal.

[a] *6* Gen. 1:3 [b] *13* Psalm 116:10

PRAYER: THE WORKS OF GOD

***O LORD**, You said to Abraham, "By Myself I have sworn, that because you have not withheld your son, your only son, I will surely bless you and make your descendants as numerous as the stars in the sky and*

as the sand on the seashore. Your descendants will take possession of the cities of their enemies, and through your offspring all nations on earth will be blessed, because you have obeyed My voice." (Genesis 22:16–18)

***TAKE** a moment to consider the greatness of God's wonderful works.*

YEAR 2
DAY 153

OT Isaiah 35:1–36:22

Joy of the Redeemed

35 The desert and the parched land will
be glad;
the wilderness will rejoice and
blossom.
Like the crocus, [2]it will burst into
bloom;
it will rejoice greatly and shout for
joy.
The glory of Lebanon will be given to
it,
the splendor of Carmel and Sharon;
they will see the glory of the LORD,
the splendor of our God.

[3]Strengthen the feeble hands,
steady the knees that give way;
[4]say to those with fearful hearts,
"Be strong, do not fear;
your God will come,
he will come with vengeance;
with divine retribution
he will come to save you."

[5]Then will the eyes of the blind be
opened
and the ears of the deaf unstopped.
[6]Then will the lame leap like a deer,
and the mute tongue shout for joy.
Water will gush forth in the
wilderness
and streams in the desert.
[7]The burning sand will become a pool,
the thirsty ground bubbling springs.
In the haunts where jackals once lay,
grass and reeds and papyrus will
grow.

[8]And a highway will be there;
it will be called the Way of
Holiness.
The unclean will not journey on it;
it will be for those who walk in that
Way;
wicked fools will not go about on
it.[a]
[9]No lion will be there,
nor will any ferocious beast get up
on it;
they will not be found there.
But only the redeemed will walk there,
10 and the ransomed of the LORD will
return.
They will enter Zion with singing;
everlasting joy will crown their
heads.
Gladness and joy will overtake them,
and sorrow and sighing will flee
away.

Sennacherib Threatens Jerusalem

36 In the fourteenth year of King Hezekiah's reign, Sennacherib king of Assyria attacked all the fortified cities of Judah and captured them. [2]Then the king of
Assyria sent his field commander with a
large army from Lachish to King Hezekiah at Jerusalem. When the commander
stopped at the aqueduct of the Upper
Pool, on the road to the Washerman's
Field, [3]Eliakim son of Hilkiah the palace
administrator, Shebna the secretary, and
Joah son of Asaph the recorder went out
to him.

[4]The field commander said to them,
"Tell Hezekiah,

" 'This is what the great king, the
king of Assyria, says: On what are you
basing this confidence of yours? [5]You
say you have strategy and military
strength—but you speak only empty
words. On whom are you depending,
that you rebel against me? [6]Look
now, you are depending on Egypt,
that splintered reed of a staff, which
pierces a man's hand and wounds
him if he leans on it! Such is Pharaoh king of Egypt to all who depend
on him. [7]And if you say to me, "We
are depending on the LORD our
God"—isn't he the one whose high

[a] 8 Or / *the simple will not stray from it*

places and altars Hezekiah removed,
saying to Judah and Jerusalem, "You
must worship before this altar"?
8 " 'Come now, make a bargain
with my master, the king of Assyria: I
will give you two thousand horses—
if you can put riders on them! 9 How
then can you repulse one officer of
the least of my master's officials, even
though you are depending on Egypt
for chariots and horsemen? 10 Furthermore, have I come to attack and
destroy this land without the LORD?
The LORD himself told me to march
against this country and destroy it.' "

11 Then Eliakim, Shebna and Joah said
to the field commander, "Please speak to
your servants in Aramaic, since we understand it. Don't speak to us in Hebrew in
the hearing of the people on the wall."
12 But the commander replied, "Was it
only to your master and you that my master sent me to say these things, and not to
the men sitting on the wall—who, like
you, will have to eat their own filth and
drink their own urine?"
13 Then the commander stood and
called out in Hebrew, "Hear the words of
the great king, the king of Assyria! 14 This
is what the king says: Do not let Hezekiah deceive you. He cannot deliver you!
15 Do not let Hezekiah persuade you to
trust in the LORD when he says, 'The LORD
will surely deliver us; this city will not
be given into the hand of the king of Assyria.'
16 "Do not listen to Hezekiah. This is
what the king of Assyria says: Make peace
with me and come out to me. Then every
one of you will eat from his own vine and
fig tree and drink water from his own cistern, 17 until I come and take you to a land
like your own—a land of grain and new
wine, a land of bread and vineyards.
18 "Do not let Hezekiah mislead you
when he says, 'The LORD will deliver us.'
Has the god of any nation ever delivered
his land from the hand of the king of Assyria? 19 Where are the gods of Hamath
and Arpad? Where are the gods of Sepharvaim? Have they rescued Samaria from
my hand? 20 Who of all the gods of these
countries has been able to save his land
from me? How then can the LORD deliver
Jerusalem from my hand?"
21 But the people remained silent and
said nothing in reply, because the king
had commanded, "Do not answer him."
22 Then Eliakim son of Hilkiah the palace
administrator, Shebna the secretary, and
Joah son of Asaph the recorder went to
Hezekiah, with their clothes torn, and told
him what the field commander had said.

PRAYER: THANKSGIVING

LORD Jesus Christ, if I have been united with You in the likeness of Your death, I will certainly also be united with You in the likeness of Your resurrection. (Romans 6:5) . . . I thank You, God, because of Your grace in Christ Jesus. In Him we have been enriched in every way, in all speech and in all knowledge. We do not lack any spiritual gift, as we eagerly wait for the revelation of our Lord Jesus Christ. (1 Corinthians 1:4–5, 7)

PAUSE *to offer your own expressions of thanksgiving.*

NT 2 Corinthians 5:1–21

Our Heavenly Dwelling

5 Now we know that if the earthly tent
we live in is destroyed, we have a building from God, an eternal house in heav-
en, not built by human hands. 2 Meanwhile we groan, longing to be clothed
with our heavenly dwelling, 3 because
when we are clothed, we will not be
found naked. 4 For while we are in this
tent, we groan and are burdened, because
we do not wish to be unclothed but to be
clothed with our heavenly dwelling, so
that what is mortal may be swallowed up
by life. 5 Now it is God who has made us
for this very purpose and has given us the
Spirit as a deposit, guaranteeing what is to
come.
6 Therefore we are always confident and

know that as long as we are at home in
the body we are away from the Lord. [7]We
live by faith, not by sight. [8]We are confident, I say, and would prefer to be away
from the body and at home with the Lord.
[9]So we make it our goal to please him,
whether we are at home in the body or
away from it. [10]For we must all appear before the judgment seat of Christ, that each
one may receive what is due him for the
things done while in the body, whether
good or bad.

The Ministry of Reconciliation

[11]Since, then, we know what it is to fear
the Lord, we try to persuade men. What
we are is plain to God, and I hope it is
also plain to your conscience. [12]We are not
trying to commend ourselves to you
again, but are giving you an opportunity
to take pride in us, so that you can answer
those who take pride in what is seen
rather than in what is in the heart. [13]If we
are out of our mind, it is for the sake of
God; if we are in our right mind, it is for
you. [14]For Christ's love compels us, because we are convinced that one died for
all, and therefore all died. [15]And he died
for all, that those who live should no
longer live for themselves but for him
who died for them and was raised again.

[16]So from now on we regard no one
from a worldly point of view. Though we
once regarded Christ in this way, we do so
no longer. [17]Therefore, if anyone is in
Christ, he is a new creation; the old has
gone, the new has come! [18]All this is from
God, who reconciled us to himself
through Christ and gave us the ministry
of reconciliation: [19]that God was reconciling the world to himself in Christ, not
counting men's sins against them. And he
has committed to us the message of reconciliation. [20]We are therefore Christ's
ambassadors, as though God were making his appeal through us. We implore
you on Christ's behalf: Be reconciled to
God. [21]God made him who had no sin to
be sin[a] for us, so that in him we might become the righteousness of God.

[a] 21 Or *be a sin offering*

PRAYER: MY RELATIONSHIP TO GOD

I WANT to walk in Your steps, Lord Jesus; You often withdrew to lonely places and prayed. (Mark 1:35; Luke 5:16) . . . As one who shares in the heavenly calling, I am to fix my thoughts on You, Jesus, the Apostle and High Priest of my confession. (Hebrews 3:1)

PAUSE *to thank God for the relationship that you enjoy with Him in Jesus Christ.*

YEAR 2 DAY 154

OT Psalm 103

Psalm 103

Of David.

[1]Praise the LORD, O my soul;
all my inmost being, praise his holy
name.
[2]Praise the LORD, O my soul,
and forget not all his benefits—
[3]who forgives all your sins
and heals all your diseases,
[4]who redeems your life from the pit
and crowns you with love and
compassion,
[5]who satisfies your desires with good
things
so that your youth is renewed like
the eagle's.

[6]The LORD works righteousness
and justice for all the oppressed.

[7]He made known his ways to Moses,
his deeds to the people of Israel:
[8]The LORD is compassionate and
gracious,
slow to anger, abounding in love.
[9]He will not always accuse,
nor will he harbor his anger forever;

[10]he does not treat us as our sins
deserve
or repay us according to our
iniquities.
[11]For as high as the heavens are above
the earth,
so great is his love for those who
fear him;
[12]as far as the east is from the west,
so far has he removed our
transgressions from us.
[13]As a father has compassion on his
children,
so the LORD has compassion on
those who fear him;
[14]for he knows how we are formed,
he remembers that we are dust.
[15]As for man, his days are like grass,
he flourishes like a flower of the
field;
[16]the wind blows over it and it is gone,
and its place remembers it no more.
[17]But from everlasting to everlasting
the LORD's love is with those who
fear him,
and his righteousness with their
children's children—
[18]with those who keep his covenant
and remember to obey his precepts.

[19]The LORD has established his throne
in heaven,
and his kingdom rules over all.

[20]Praise the LORD, you his angels,
you mighty ones who do his
bidding,
who obey his word.
[21]Praise the LORD, all his heavenly hosts,
you his servants who do his will.
[22]Praise the LORD, all his works
everywhere in his dominion.

Praise the LORD, O my soul.

PRAYER: ADORATION

YOU, O Lord, execute righteousness and justice for all who are oppressed. You are compassionate and gracious, slow to anger and abounding in loving-kindness. (Psalm 103:6, 8) . . . Righteousness and justice are the foundation of Your throne; loving-kindness and truth go before You. (Psalm 89:14)

PAUSE *to express your thoughts of praise and worship.*

NT 2 Corinthians 6:1-13

6 As God's fellow workers we urge you
not to receive God's grace in vain. [2]For
he says,

"In the time of my favor I heard you,
and in the day of salvation I helped
you."[a]

I tell you, now is the time of God's favor,
now is the day of salvation.

Paul's Hardships

[3]We put no stumbling block in anyone's path, so that our ministry will not
be discredited. [4]Rather, as servants of God
we commend ourselves in every way: in
great endurance; in troubles, hardships
and distresses; [5]in beatings, imprisonments and riots; in hard work, sleepless
nights and hunger; [6]in purity, understanding, patience and kindness; in the
Holy Spirit and in sincere love; [7]in truthful speech and in the power of God; with
weapons of righteousness in the right
hand and in the left; [8]through glory and
dishonor, bad report and good report;
genuine, yet regarded as impostors;
[9]known, yet regarded as unknown; dying,
and yet we live on; beaten, and yet not
killed; [10]sorrowful, yet always rejoicing;
poor, yet making many rich; having nothing, and yet possessing everything.
[11]We have spoken freely to you, Corinthians, and opened wide our hearts to
you. [12]We are not withholding our affection from you, but you are withholding
yours from us. [13]As a fair exchange—I
speak as to my children—open wide your
hearts also.

[a] 2 Isaiah 49:8

PRAYER: THE CHARACTER I WANT TO CULTIVATE

THE teaching of the wise is a fountain of life to turn me away from the snares of death. (Proverbs 13:14) . . . The words of the wise are like goads and like nails driven by the masters who collect them; You, the one Shepherd, have given them (Ecclesiastes 12:11).

***TAKE** a moment to ask the Lord for the grace to grow in godly character.*

YEAR 2
DAY 155

OT Isaiah 37:1-38

Jerusalem's Deliverance Foretold

37 When King Hezekiah heard this, he tore his clothes and put on sackcloth and went into the temple of the LORD. 2He sent Eliakim the palace administrator, Shebna the secretary, and the leading priests, all wearing sackcloth, to the prophet Isaiah son of Amoz. 3They told him, "This is what Hezekiah says: This day is a day of distress and rebuke and disgrace, as when children come to the point of birth and there is no strength to deliver them. 4It may be that the LORD your God will hear the words of the field commander, whom his master, the king of Assyria, has sent to ridicule the living God, and that he will rebuke him for the words the LORD your God has heard. Therefore pray for the remnant that still survives."

5When King Hezekiah's officials came to Isaiah, 6Isaiah said to them, "Tell your master, 'This is what the LORD says: Do not be afraid of what you have heard—those words with which the underlings of the king of Assyria have blasphemed me. 7Listen! I am going to put a spirit in him so that when he hears a certain report, he will return to his own country, and there I will have him cut down with the sword.' "

8When the field commander heard that the king of Assyria had left Lachish, he withdrew and found the king fighting against Libnah.

9Now Sennacherib received a report that Tirhakah, the Cushite[a] king ⌞of Egypt⌟, was marching out to fight against him. When he heard it, he sent messengers to Hezekiah with this word: 10"Say to Hezekiah king of Judah: Do not let the god you depend on deceive you when he says, 'Jerusalem will not be handed over to the king of Assyria.' 11Surely you have heard what the kings of Assyria have done to all the countries, destroying them completely. And will you be delivered? 12Did the gods of the nations that were destroyed by my forefathers deliver them—the gods of Gozan, Haran, Rezeph and the people of Eden who were in Tel Assar? 13Where is the king of Hamath, the king of Arpad, the king of the city of Sepharvaim, or of Hena or Ivvah?"

Hezekiah's Prayer

14Hezekiah received the letter from the messengers and read it. Then he went up to the temple of the LORD and spread it out before the LORD. 15And Hezekiah prayed to the LORD: 16"O LORD Almighty, God of Israel, enthroned between the cherubim, you alone are God over all the kingdoms of the earth. You have made heaven and earth. 17Give ear, O LORD, and hear; open your eyes, O LORD, and see; listen to all the words Sennacherib has sent to insult the living God.

18"It is true, O LORD, that the Assyrian kings have laid waste all these peoples and their lands. 19They have thrown their gods into the fire and destroyed them, for they were not gods but only wood and stone, fashioned by human hands. 20Now, O LORD our God, deliver us from his hand, so that all kingdoms on earth may know that you alone, O LORD, are God.[b]"

Sennacherib's Fall

21Then Isaiah son of Amoz sent a message to Hezekiah: "This is what the LORD, the God of Israel, says: Because you have

[a] 9 That is, from the upper Nile region [b] 20 Dead Sea Scrolls (see also 2 Kings 19:19); Masoretic Text *alone are the LORD*

prayed to me concerning Sennacherib
king of Assyria, 22 this is the word the LORD
has spoken against him:

"The Virgin Daughter of Zion
despises and mocks you.
The Daughter of Jerusalem
tosses her head as you flee.
23 Who is it you have insulted and
blasphemed?
Against whom have you raised your
voice
and lifted your eyes in pride?
Against the Holy One of Israel!
24 By your messengers
you have heaped insults on the
Lord.
And you have said,
'With my many chariots
I have ascended the heights of the
mountains,
the utmost heights of Lebanon.
I have cut down its tallest cedars,
the choicest of its pines.
I have reached its remotest heights,
the finest of its forests.
25 I have dug wells in foreign lands[c]
and drunk the water there.
With the soles of my feet
I have dried up all the streams of
Egypt.'

26 "Have you not heard?
Long ago I ordained it.
In days of old I planned it;
now I have brought it to pass,
that you have turned fortified cities
into piles of stone.
27 Their people, drained of power,
are dismayed and put to shame.
They are like plants in the field,
like tender green shoots,
like grass sprouting on the roof,
scorched[d] before it grows up.

28 "But I know where you stay
and when you come and go
and how you rage against me.
29 Because you rage against me
and because your insolence has
reached my ears,
I will put my hook in your nose
and my bit in your mouth,
and I will make you return
by the way you came.

30 "This will be the sign for you, O Hezekiah:

"This year you will eat what grows by
itself,
and the second year what springs
from that.
But in the third year sow and reap,
plant vineyards and eat their fruit.
31 Once more a remnant of the house of
Judah
will take root below and bear fruit
above.
32 For out of Jerusalem will come a
remnant,
and out of Mount Zion a band of
survivors.
The zeal of the LORD Almighty
will accomplish this.

33 "Therefore this is what the LORD says
concerning the king of Assyria:

"He will not enter this city
or shoot an arrow here.
He will not come before it with shield
or build a siege ramp against it.
34 By the way that he came he will
return;
he will not enter this city,"
declares the LORD.
35 "I will defend this city and save it,
for my sake and for the sake of
David my servant!"

36 Then the angel of the LORD went out
and put to death a hundred and eighty-
five thousand men in the Assyrian camp.
When the people got up the next morning—there were all the dead bodies! 37 So
Sennacherib king of Assyria broke camp
and withdrew. He returned to Nineveh
and stayed there.

38 One day, while he was worshiping in
the temple of his god Nisroch, his sons
Adrammelech and Sharezer cut him down
with the sword, and they escaped to the
land of Ararat. And Esarhaddon his son
succeeded him as king.

[c] *25* Dead Sea Scrolls (see also 2 Kings 19:24); Masoretic Text does not have *in foreign lands.*
[d] *27* Some manuscripts of the Masoretic Text, Dead Sea Scrolls and some Septuagint manuscripts (see also 2 Kings 19:26); most manuscripts of the Masoretic Text *roof / and terraced fields*

PRAYER: CONFESSION

WHAT can I say to You? What can I speak? How can I justify myself? You have uncovered the iniquity of Your servant. (Genesis 44:16)

***ASK** the Spirit to search your heart and reveal any areas of unconfessed sin. Acknowledge these to the Lord and thank Him for His forgiveness.*

NT 2 Corinthians 6:14–7:1

Do Not Be Yoked With Unbelievers

14Do not be yoked together with unbelievers. For what do righteousness and
wickedness have in common? Or what fellowship can light have with darkness?
15What harmony is there between Christ
and Belial[a]? What does a believer have in
common with an unbeliever? 16What agreement is there between the temple of God
and idols? For we are the temple of the living God. As God has said: "I will live with
them and walk among them, and I will be
their God, and they will be my people."[b]

17 "Therefore come out from them
and be separate,
says the Lord.
Touch no unclean thing,
and I will receive you."[c]
18 "I will be a Father to you,
and you will be my sons and
daughters,
says the Lord Almighty."[d]

7 Since we have these promises, dear friends, let us purify ourselves from everything that contaminates body and spirit, perfecting holiness out of reverence for God.

[a] *15* Greek *Beliar*, a variant of *Belial*
[b] *16* Lev. 26:12; Jer. 32:38; Ezek. 37:27
[c] *17* Isaiah 52:11; Ezek. 20:34,41
[d] *18* 2 Samuel 7:14; 7:8

PRAYER: MY RELATIONSHIP TO OTHERS

I WILL not defraud my neighbors or rob them. (Leviticus 19:13) . . . I will not mistreat my neighbors, but I will fear You, God; for You are the Lord my God. (Leviticus 25:17)

***PAUSE** to review your relationships with others and to commit them to the Lord.*

YEAR 2 DAY 156

OT Isaiah 38:1–39:8

Hezekiah's Illness

38 In those days Hezekiah became ill and was at the point of death. The prophet Isaiah son of Amoz went to him and said, "This is what the LORD says: Put your house in order, because you are going to die; you will not recover."
2Hezekiah turned his face to the wall
and prayed to the LORD, 3"Remember,
O LORD, how I have walked before you
faithfully and with wholehearted devotion and have done what is good in your
eyes." And Hezekiah wept bitterly.
4Then the word of the LORD came to Isaiah: 5"Go and tell Hezekiah, 'This is what
the LORD, the God of your father David,
says: I have heard your prayer and seen
your tears; I will add fifteen years to your
life. 6And I will deliver you and this city
from the hand of the king of Assyria. I will
defend this city.
7" 'This is the LORD's sign to you that
the LORD will do what he has promised:
8I will make the shadow cast by the sun
go back the ten steps it has gone down
on the stairway of Ahaz.' " So the sun-

light went back the ten steps it had gone down.

[9]A writing of Hezekiah king of Judah after his illness and recovery:

[10]I said, "In the prime of my life
must I go through the gates of death[a]
and be robbed of the rest of my years?"
[11]I said, "I will not again see the LORD,
the LORD, in the land of the living;
no longer will I look on mankind,
or be with those who now dwell in this world.[b]
[12]Like a shepherd's tent my house
has been pulled down and taken from me.
Like a weaver I have rolled up my life,
and he has cut me off from the loom;
day and night you made an end of me.
[13]I waited patiently till dawn,
but like a lion he broke all my bones;
day and night you made an end of me.
[14]I cried like a swift or thrush,
I moaned like a mourning dove.
My eyes grew weak as I looked to the heavens.
I am troubled; O Lord, come to my aid!"

[15]But what can I say?
He has spoken to me, and he himself has done this.
I will walk humbly all my years
because of this anguish of my soul.
[16]Lord, by such things men live;
and my spirit finds life in them too.
You restored me to health
and let me live.
[17]Surely it was for my benefit
that I suffered such anguish.
In your love you kept me
from the pit of destruction;
you have put all my sins
behind your back.
[18]For the grave[a] cannot praise you,
death cannot sing your praise;
those who go down to the pit
cannot hope for your faithfulness.
[19]The living, the living—they praise you,
as I am doing today;
fathers tell their children
about your faithfulness.

[20]The LORD will save me,
and we will sing with stringed instruments
all the days of our lives
in the temple of the LORD.

[21]Isaiah had said, "Prepare a poultice of
figs and apply it to the boil, and he will
recover."
[22]Hezekiah had asked, "What will be
the sign that I will go up to the temple of
the LORD?"

Envoys From Babylon

39 At that time Merodach-Baladan son
of Baladan king of Babylon sent Hezekiah letters and a gift, because he had
heard of his illness and recovery. [2]Hezeki-
ah received the envoys gladly and showed
them what was in his storehouses—the
silver, the gold, the spices, the fine oil, his
entire armory and everything found
among his treasures. There was nothing in
his palace or in all his kingdom that Hezekiah did not show them.
[3]Then Isaiah the prophet went to King
Hezekiah and asked, "What did those
men say, and where did they come from?"
"From a distant land," Hezekiah replied. "They came to me from Babylon."
[4]The prophet asked, "What did they see
in your palace?"
"They saw everything in my palace,"
Hezekiah said. "There is nothing among
my treasures that I did not show them."
[5]Then Isaiah said to Hezekiah, "Hear
the word of the LORD Almighty: [6]The time
will surely come when everything in your
palace, and all that your fathers have
stored up until this day, will be carried off
to Babylon. Nothing will be left, says the
LORD. [7]And some of your descendants,
your own flesh and blood who will be
born to you, will be taken away, and they
will become eunuchs in the palace of the
king of Babylon."
[8]"The word of the LORD you have spoken is good," Hezekiah replied. For he
thought, "There will be peace and security in my lifetime."

[a] *10,18* Hebrew *Sheol* [b] *11* A few Hebrew manuscripts; most Hebrew manuscripts *in the place of cessation*

PRAYER: RENEWAL

MAY I walk properly as in the daytime, not in partying and drunkenness, not in sexual immorality and evil conduct, not in dissension and jealousy. Rather, may I put You on like clothing, Lord Jesus Christ, rather than thinking about how to satisfy my fleshly lusts. (Romans 13:13–14) . . . Since I have Your promises, O God, may I cleanse myself from all pollution of body and spirit, perfecting holiness in the fear of You. (2 Corinthians 7:1)

PAUSE *to add your own prayers for personal renewal.*

NT 2 Corinthians 7:2–16

Paul's Joy

[2]Make room for us in your hearts. We have wronged no one, we have corrupted no one, we have exploited no one. [3]I do not say this to condemn you; I have said before that you have such a place in our hearts that we would live or die with you. [4]I have great confidence in you; I take great pride in you. I am greatly encouraged; in all our troubles my joy knows no bounds.

[5]For when we came into Macedonia, this body of ours had no rest, but we were harassed at every turn—conflicts on the outside, fears within. [6]But God, who comforts the downcast, comforted us by the coming of Titus, [7]and not only by his coming but also by the comfort you had given him. He told us about your longing for me, your deep sorrow, your ardent concern for me, so that my joy was greater than ever.

[8]Even if I caused you sorrow by my letter, I do not regret it. Though I did regret it—I see that my letter hurt you, but only for a little while— [9]yet now I am happy, not because you were made sorry, but because your sorrow led you to repentance. For you became sorrowful as God intended and so were not harmed in any way by us. [10]Godly sorrow brings repentance that leads to salvation and leaves no regret, but worldly sorrow brings death. [11]See what this godly sorrow has produced in you: what earnestness, what eagerness to clear yourselves, what indignation, what alarm, what longing, what concern, what readiness to see justice done. At every point you have proved yourselves to be innocent in this matter. [12]So even though I wrote to you, it was not on account of the one who did the wrong or of the injured party, but rather that before God you could see for yourselves how devoted to us you are. [13]By all this we are encouraged.

In addition to our own encouragement, we were especially delighted to see how happy Titus was, because his spirit has been refreshed by all of you. [14]I had boasted to him about you, and you have not embarrassed me. But just as everything we said to you was true, so our boasting about you to Titus has proved to be true as well. [15]And his affection for you is all the greater when he remembers that you were all obedient, receiving him with fear and trembling. [16]I am glad I can have complete confidence in you.

PRAYER: THE ATTRIBUTES OF GOD

THE refining pot is for silver and the furnace for gold, but You, O Lord, test hearts. (Proverbs 17:3) . . . Your lamp, O Lord, searches my spirit; it searches the inward depths of my being. (Proverbs 20:27)

PAUSE *to reflect on these affirmations about the person, powers and perfection of God.*

YEAR 2 DAY 157

OT **Isaiah 40:1-31**

Comfort for God's People

40 Comfort, comfort my people,
says your God.
2 Speak tenderly to Jerusalem,
and proclaim to her
that her hard service has been completed,
that her sin has been paid for,
that she has received from the LORD's hand
double for all her sins.

3 A voice of one calling:
"In the desert prepare
the way for the LORD[a];
make straight in the wilderness
a highway for our God.[b]
4 Every valley shall be raised up,
every mountain and hill made low;
the rough ground shall become level,
the rugged places a plain.
5 And the glory of the LORD will be revealed,
and all mankind together will see it.
For the mouth of the LORD
has spoken."

6 A voice says, "Cry out."
And I said, "What shall I cry?"

"All men are like grass,
and all their glory is like the flowers of the field.
7 The grass withers and the flowers fall,
because the breath of the LORD blows on them.
Surely the people are grass.
8 The grass withers and the flowers fall,
but the word of our God stands forever."

9 You who bring good tidings to Zion,
go up on a high mountain.
You who bring good tidings to Jerusalem,[c]
lift up your voice with a shout,
lift it up, do not be afraid;
say to the towns of Judah,
"Here is your God!"
10 See, the Sovereign LORD comes with power,
and his arm rules for him.
See, his reward is with him,
and his recompense accompanies him.
11 He tends his flock like a shepherd:
He gathers the lambs in his arms
and carries them close to his heart;
he gently leads those that have young.

12 Who has measured the waters in the hollow of his hand,
or with the breadth of his hand marked off the heavens?
Who has held the dust of the earth in a basket,
or weighed the mountains on the scales
and the hills in a balance?
13 Who has understood the mind[d] of the LORD,
or instructed him as his counselor?
14 Whom did the LORD consult to enlighten him,
and who taught him the right way?
Who was it that taught him knowledge
or showed him the path of understanding?

15 Surely the nations are like a drop in a bucket;
they are regarded as dust on the scales;
he weighs the islands as though they were fine dust.
16 Lebanon is not sufficient for altar fires,
nor its animals enough for burnt offerings.
17 Before him all the nations are as nothing;
they are regarded by him as worthless
and less than nothing.

18 To whom, then, will you compare God?
What image will you compare him to?
19 As for an idol, a craftsman casts it,
and a goldsmith overlays it with gold

[a] 3 Or *A voice of one calling in the desert: / "Prepare the way for the* LORD [b] 3 Hebrew; Septuagint *make straight the paths of our God* [c] 9 Or *O Zion, bringer of good tidings, / go up on a high mountain. / O Jerusalem, bringer of good tidings* [d] 13 Or *Spirit;* or *spirit*

and fashions silver chains for it.
[20]A man too poor to present such an offering
selects wood that will not rot.
He looks for a skilled craftsman
to set up an idol that will not topple.

[21]Do you not know?
Have you not heard?
Has it not been told you from the beginning?
Have you not understood since the earth was founded?
[22]He sits enthroned above the circle of the earth,
and its people are like grasshoppers.
He stretches out the heavens like a canopy,
and spreads them out like a tent to live in.
[23]He brings princes to naught
and reduces the rulers of this world to nothing.
[24]No sooner are they planted,
no sooner are they sown,
no sooner do they take root in the ground,
than he blows on them and they wither,
and a whirlwind sweeps them away like chaff.

[25]"To whom will you compare me?
Or who is my equal?" says the Holy One.
[26]Lift your eyes and look to the heavens:
Who created all these?
He who brings out the starry host one by one,
and calls them each by name.
Because of his great power and mighty strength,
not one of them is missing.

[27]Why do you say, O Jacob,
and complain, O Israel,
"My way is hidden from the LORD;
my cause is disregarded by my God"?
[28]Do you not know?
Have you not heard?
The LORD is the everlasting God,
the Creator of the ends of the earth.
He will not grow tired or weary,
and his understanding no one can fathom.
[29]He gives strength to the weary
and increases the power of the weak.
[30]Even youths grow tired and weary,
and young men stumble and fall;
[31]but those who hope in the LORD
will renew their strength.
They will soar on wings like eagles;
they will run and not grow weary,
they will walk and not be faint.

PRAYER: PETITION

WE are all children of the light and children of the day. We do not belong to the night or to the darkness. So then, let us not be like others who are asleep, but let us be alert and self-controlled.

(1 Thessalonians 5:5–6)

PAUSE *here to petition God to help you be a faithful steward of your time, talents, possessions and relationships. Offer prayers of petition regarding your activities for this day and any special concerns you may have.*

NT 2 Corinthians 8:1-15

Generosity Encouraged

8 And now, brothers, we want you to know about the grace that God has given the Macedonian churches. [2]Out of the most severe trial, their overflowing joy and their extreme poverty welled up in rich generosity. [3]For I testify that they gave as much as they were able, and even beyond their ability. Entirely on their own, [4]they urgently pleaded with us for the privilege of sharing in this service to the saints. [5]And they did not do as we expected, but they gave themselves first to the Lord and then to us in keeping with God's will. [6]So we urged Titus, since he

had earlier made a beginning, to bring
also to completion this act of grace on
your part. [7]But just as you excel in everything—in faith, in speech, in knowledge,
in complete earnestness and in your love
for us[a]—see that you also excel in this
grace of giving.

[8]I am not commanding you, but I want
to test the sincerity of your love by comparing it with the earnestness of others.
[9]For you know the grace of our Lord Jesus
Christ, that though he was rich, yet for
your sakes he became poor, so that you
through his poverty might become rich.

[10]And here is my advice about what is
best for you in this matter: Last year you
were the first not only to give but also to
have the desire to do so. [11]Now finish the
work, so that your eager willingness to do
it may be matched by your completion of
it, according to your means. [12]For if the
willingness is there, the gift is acceptable
according to what one has, not according
to what he does not have.

[13]Our desire is not that others might be
relieved while you are hard pressed, but
that there might be equality. [14]At the
present time your plenty will supply what
they need, so that in turn their plenty will
supply what you need. Then there will be
equality, [15]as it is written: "He who gathered much did not have too much, and he
who gathered little did not have too little."[b]

[a] 7 Some manuscripts *in our love for you*
[b] 15 Exodus 16:18

PRAYER: THE WORKS OF GOD

HAS any other people heard Your voice, O God, speaking out of the midst of the fire, as the children of Israel have, and lived? Has any god ever tried to take for himself one nation from the midst of another nation, by trials, by miraculous signs and wonders, by war, by a mighty hand and an outstretched arm and by great and awesome deeds, like all the things You, Lord God, did for Israel in Egypt before their very eyes? The Israelites were shown these things so that they might know that You, the Lord, are God; there is no other besides You. (Deuteronomy 4:33–35)

***TAKE** a moment to consider the greatness of God's wonderful works.*

YEAR 2 DAY 158

OT Proverbs 23

23 When you sit to dine with a ruler,
note well what[a] is before you,
[2]and put a knife to your throat
if you are given to gluttony.
[3]Do not crave his delicacies,
for that food is deceptive.

[4]Do not wear yourself out to get rich;
have the wisdom to show restraint.
[5]Cast but a glance at riches, and they
are gone,
for they will surely sprout wings
and fly off to the sky like an eagle.

[6]Do not eat the food of a stingy man,
do not crave his delicacies;
[7]for he is the kind of man
who is always thinking about the
cost.[b]
"Eat and drink," he says to you,
but his heart is not with you.
[8]You will vomit up the little you have
eaten
and will have wasted your
compliments.

[9]Do not speak to a fool,
for he will scorn the wisdom of
your words.

[10]Do not move an ancient boundary
stone
or encroach on the fields of the
fatherless,
[11]for their Defender is strong;
he will take up their case against you.

[a] 1 Or *who* [b] 7 Or *for as he thinks within himself, / so he is;* or *for as he puts on a feast, / so he is*

[12] Apply your heart to instruction
and your ears to words of knowledge.

[13] Do not withhold discipline from a child;
if you punish him with the rod, he will not die.
[14] Punish him with the rod
and save his soul from death.[c]

[15] My son, if your heart is wise,
then my heart will be glad;
[16] my inmost being will rejoice
when your lips speak what is right.

[17] Do not let your heart envy sinners,
but always be zealous for the fear of the LORD.
[18] There is surely a future hope for you,
and your hope will not be cut off.

[19] Listen, my son, and be wise,
and keep your heart on the right path.
[20] Do not join those who drink too much wine
or gorge themselves on meat,
[21] for drunkards and gluttons become poor,
and drowsiness clothes them in rags.

[22] Listen to your father, who gave you life,
and do not despise your mother when she is old.
[23] Buy the truth and do not sell it;
get wisdom, discipline and understanding.
[24] The father of a righteous man has great joy;
he who has a wise son delights in him.
[25] May your father and mother be glad;
may she who gave you birth rejoice!

[26] My son, give me your heart
and let your eyes keep to my ways,
[27] for a prostitute is a deep pit
and a wayward wife is a narrow well.
[28] Like a bandit she lies in wait,
and multiplies the unfaithful among men.

[29] Who has woe? Who has sorrow?
Who has strife? Who has complaints?
Who has needless bruises? Who has bloodshot eyes?
[30] Those who linger over wine,
who go to sample bowls of mixed wine.
[31] Do not gaze at wine when it is red,
when it sparkles in the cup,
when it goes down smoothly!
[32] In the end it bites like a snake
and poisons like a viper.
[33] Your eyes will see strange sights
and your mind imagine confusing things.
[34] You will be like one sleeping on the high seas,
lying on top of the rigging.
[35] "They hit me," you will say, "but I'm not hurt!
They beat me, but I don't feel it!
When will I wake up
so I can find another drink?"

[c] 14 Hebrew *Sheol*

PRAYER: INTERCESSION

IF we trust in You, the Lord our God, we will be established; if we believe in Your prophets we will prosper.
(2 Chronicles 20:20)

***TAKE** a few moments to intercede on behalf of your local, state or provincial, and national governments. Pray for spiritual revival in the nation and offer prayers regarding current events and concerns.*

NT 2 Corinthians 8:16–9:5

Titus Sent to Corinth

[16] I thank God, who put into the heart of Titus the same concern I have for you. [17] For Titus not only welcomed our appeal, but he is coming to you with much enthusiasm and on his own initiative. [18] And we are sending along with him the brother who is praised by all the churches for his service to the gospel. [19] What is more, he was chosen by the churches to accompany us as we carry the offering, which we administer in order to honor the Lord

himself and to show our eagerness to
help. [20]We want to avoid any criticism of
the way we administer this liberal gift.
[21]For we are taking pains to do what is
right, not only in the eyes of the Lord but
also in the eyes of men.
[22]In addition, we are sending with them
our brother who has often proved to us in
many ways that he is zealous, and now
even more so because of his great confidence in you. [23]As for Titus, he is my partner and fellow worker among you; as for
our brothers, they are representatives of
the churches and an honor to Christ.
[24]Therefore show these men the proof of
your love and the reason for our pride in
you, so that the churches can see it.

9 There is no need for me to write to
you about this service to the saints.
[2]For I know your eagerness to help, and
I have been boasting about it to the
Macedonians, telling them that since last
year you in Achaia were ready to give;
and your enthusiasm has stirred most of
them to action. [3]But I am sending the
brothers in order that our boasting about
you in this matter should not prove hollow, but that you may be ready, as I said
you would be. [4]For if any Macedonians
come with me and find you unprepared,
we—not to say anything about you—
would be ashamed of having been so
confident. [5]So I thought it necessary to
urge the brothers to visit you in advance
and finish the arrangements for the generous gift you had promised. Then it will
be ready as a generous gift, not as one
grudgingly given.

PRAYER: MY RELATIONSHIP TO GOD

MY heart rejoices in You, O Lord; my horn is exalted in You. My mouth boasts over my enemies, for I delight in Your salvation. (1 Samuel 2:1) . . . I will bless You, Lord, at all times; Your praise will always be in my mouth. (Psalm 34:1)

__PAUSE__ to thank God for the relationship that you enjoy with Him in Jesus Christ.

OT Isaiah 41:1–29 — YEAR 2 DAY 159

The Helper of Israel

41 "Be silent before me, you islands!
Let the nations renew their strength!
Let them come forward and speak;
let us meet together at the place of judgment.

[2]"Who has stirred up one from the east,
calling him in righteousness to his service[a]?
He hands nations over to him
and subdues kings before him.
He turns them to dust with his sword,
to windblown chaff with his bow.
[3]He pursues them and moves on unscathed,
by a path his feet have not traveled before.
[4]Who has done this and carried it through,
calling forth the generations from the beginning?
I, the LORD—with the first of them
and with the last—I am he."

[5]The islands have seen it and fear;
the ends of the earth tremble.
They approach and come forward;
[6]each helps the other
and says to his brother, "Be strong!"
[7]The craftsman encourages the goldsmith,
and he who smooths with the hammer
spurs on him who strikes the anvil.
He says of the welding, "It is good."
He nails down the idol so it will not topple.

[8]"But you, O Israel, my servant,
Jacob, whom I have chosen,

[a] 2 Or / *whom victory meets at every step*

you descendants of Abraham my
friend,
[9] I took you from the ends of the earth,
from its farthest corners I called
you.
I said, 'You are my servant';
I have chosen you and have not
rejected you.
[10] So do not fear, for I am with you;
do not be dismayed, for I am your
God.
I will strengthen you and help you;
I will uphold you with my righteous
right hand.

[11] "All who rage against you
will surely be ashamed and disgraced;
those who oppose you
will be as nothing and perish.
[12] Though you search for your enemies,
you will not find them.
Those who wage war against you
will be as nothing at all.
[13] For I am the LORD, your God,
who takes hold of your right hand
and says to you, Do not fear;
I will help you.
[14] Do not be afraid, O worm Jacob,
O little Israel,
for I myself will help you," declares
the LORD,
your Redeemer, the Holy One of
Israel.
[15] "See, I will make you into a threshing
sledge,
new and sharp, with many teeth.
You will thresh the mountains and
crush them,
and reduce the hills to chaff.
[16] You will winnow them, the wind will
pick them up,
and a gale will blow them away.
But you will rejoice in the LORD
and glory in the Holy One of Israel.

[17] "The poor and needy search for water,
but there is none;
their tongues are parched with thirst.
But I the LORD will answer them;
I, the God of Israel, will not forsake
them.
[18] I will make rivers flow on barren
heights,
and springs within the valleys.
I will turn the desert into pools of
water,
and the parched ground into
springs.
[19] I will put in the desert
the cedar and the acacia, the myrtle
and the olive.
I will set pines in the wasteland,
the fir and the cypress together,
[20] so that people may see and know,
may consider and understand,
that the hand of the LORD has done
this,
that the Holy One of Israel has
created it.

[21] "Present your case," says the LORD.
"Set forth your arguments," says
Jacob's King.
[22] "Bring in ⌊your idols⌋ to tell us
what is going to happen.
Tell us what the former things were,
so that we may consider them
and know their final outcome.
Or declare to us the things to come,
[23] tell us what the future holds,
so we may know that you are gods.
Do something, whether good or bad,
so that we will be dismayed and
filled with fear.
[24] But you are less than nothing
and your works are utterly worthless;
he who chooses you is detestable.

[25] "I have stirred up one from the north,
and he comes—
one from the rising sun who calls
on my name.
He treads on rulers as if they were
mortar,
as if he were a potter treading the
clay.
[26] Who told of this from the beginning,
so we could know,
or beforehand, so we could say, 'He
was right'?
No one told of this,
no one foretold it,
no one heard any words from you.
[27] I was the first to tell Zion, 'Look, here
they are!'
I gave to Jerusalem a messenger of
good tidings.
[28] I look but there is no one—
no one among them to give
counsel,
no one to give answer when I ask
them.
[29] See, they are all false!
Their deeds amount to nothing;
their images are but wind and
confusion.

PRAYER: AFFIRMATION

O SON of Man, You are going to come in the glory of Your Father with Your angels, and then You will reward people according to their works. (Matthew 16:27) . . . If anyone is ashamed of You and Your words in this adulterous and sinful generation, then You, the Son of Man, will be ashamed of that person when You come in the glory of Your Father with the holy angels. (Mark 8:38; Luke 9:26)

***PAUSE** to reflect on these Biblical affirmations.*

NT 2 Corinthians 9:6–15

Sowing Generously

6Remember this: Whoever sows sparingly will also reap sparingly, and whoever sows generously will also reap generously. 7Each man should give what he has
decided in his heart to give, not reluctantly or under compulsion, for God loves
a cheerful giver. 8And God is able to make
all grace abound to you, so that in all
things at all times, having all that you
need, you will abound in every good
work. 9As it is written:

"He has scattered abroad his gifts to the poor;
his righteousness endures forever."[a]

10Now he who supplies seed to the sower
and bread for food will also supply and
increase your store of seed and will enlarge the harvest of your righteousness.
11You will be made rich in every way so
that you can be generous on every occasion, and through us your generosity will
result in thanksgiving to God.
12This service that you perform is not
only supplying the needs of God's people
but is also overflowing in many expressions of thanks to God. 13Because of the
service by which you have proved yourselves, men will praise God for the obedience that accompanies your confession
of the gospel of Christ, and for your generosity in sharing with them and with
everyone else. 14And in their prayers for
you their hearts will go out to you, because of the surpassing grace God has giv-
en you. 15Thanks be to God for his indescribable gift!

[a] 9 Psalm 112:9

PRAYER: THE CHARACTER I WANT TO CULTIVATE

I WILL watch carefully how I walk, not as unwise but as wise, making the most of every opportunity, because the days are evil. I will not be foolish, but understand what Your will is. (Ephesians 5:15–17) . . . If I lack wisdom, I will ask of You, O God, who gives generously to all without reproach, and You will give it to me. (James 1:5)

***TAKE** a moment to ask the Lord for the grace to grow in godly character.*

YEAR 2 DAY 160

OT Isaiah 42:1–25

The Servant of the LORD

42 "Here is my servant, whom I uphold,
my chosen one in whom I delight;
I will put my Spirit on him
and he will bring justice to the nations.
2He will not shout or cry out,
or raise his voice in the streets.
3A bruised reed he will not break,

and a smoldering wick he will not snuff out.
In faithfulness he will bring forth justice;
4 he will not falter or be discouraged
till he establishes justice on earth.
In his law the islands will put their hope."

5 This is what God the LORD says—
he who created the heavens and stretched them out,
who spread out the earth and all that comes out of it,
who gives breath to its people,
and life to those who walk on it:
6 "I, the LORD, have called you in righteousness;
I will take hold of your hand.
I will keep you and will make you
to be a covenant for the people
and a light for the Gentiles,
7 to open eyes that are blind,
to free captives from prison
and to release from the dungeon
those who sit in darkness.

8 "I am the LORD; that is my name!
I will not give my glory to another
or my praise to idols.
9 See, the former things have taken place,
and new things I declare;
before they spring into being
I announce them to you."

Song of Praise to the LORD

10 Sing to the LORD a new song,
his praise from the ends of the earth,
you who go down to the sea, and all that is in it,
you islands, and all who live in them.
11 Let the desert and its towns raise their voices;
let the settlements where Kedar lives rejoice.
Let the people of Sela sing for joy;
let them shout from the mountaintops.
12 Let them give glory to the LORD
and proclaim his praise in the islands.
13 The LORD will march out like a mighty man,
like a warrior he will stir up his zeal;
with a shout he will raise the battle cry
and will triumph over his enemies.

14 "For a long time I have kept silent,
I have been quiet and held myself back.
But now, like a woman in childbirth,
I cry out, I gasp and pant.
15 I will lay waste the mountains and hills
and dry up all their vegetation;
I will turn rivers into islands
and dry up the pools.
16 I will lead the blind by ways they have not known,
along unfamiliar paths I will guide them;
I will turn the darkness into light before them
and make the rough places smooth.
These are the things I will do;
I will not forsake them.
17 But those who trust in idols,
who say to images, 'You are our gods,'
will be turned back in utter shame.

Israel Blind and Deaf

18 "Hear, you deaf;
look, you blind, and see!
19 Who is blind but my servant,
and deaf like the messenger I send?
Who is blind like the one committed to me,
blind like the servant of the LORD?
20 You have seen many things, but have paid no attention;
your ears are open, but you hear nothing."
21 It pleased the LORD
for the sake of his righteousness
to make his law great and glorious.
22 But this is a people plundered and looted,
all of them trapped in pits
or hidden away in prisons.
They have become plunder,
with no one to rescue them;
they have been made loot,
with no one to say, "Send them back."

23 Which of you will listen to this
or pay close attention in time to come?

24 Who handed Jacob over to become
loot,
and Israel to the plunderers?
Was it not the LORD,
against whom we have sinned?
For they would not follow his ways;
they did not obey his law.
25 So he poured out on them his
burning anger,
the violence of war.
It enveloped them in flames, yet they
did not understand;
it consumed them, but they did not
take it to heart.

PRAYER: THANKSGIVING

THANKS be to God, the One who gives us the victory through You, our Lord Jesus Christ. Therefore let us be steadfast, immovable, abounding in Your work, knowing that our labor in You is not in vain. (1 Corinthians 15:57–58)

***PAUSE** to offer your own expressions of thanksgiving.*

NT 2 Corinthians 10:1–18

Paul's Defense of His Ministry

10 By the meekness and gentleness of
Christ, I appeal to you—I, Paul, who
am "timid" when face to face with you,
but "bold" when away!
2 I beg you that
when I come I may not have to be as bold
as I expect to be toward some people who
think that we live by the standards of this
world.
3 For though we live in the world,
we do not wage war as the world does.
4 The weapons we fight with are not the
weapons of the world. On the contrary,
they have divine power to demolish
strongholds.
5 We demolish arguments
and every pretension that sets itself up
against the knowledge of God, and we
take captive every thought to make it obedient to Christ.
6 And we will be ready to
punish every act of disobedience, once
your obedience is complete.
7 You are looking only on the surface of
things.[a] If anyone is confident that he belongs to Christ, he should consider again
that we belong to Christ just as much as
he.
8 For even if I boast somewhat freely
about the authority the Lord gave us for
building you up rather than pulling you
down, I will not be ashamed of it.
9 I do
not want to seem to be trying to frighten
you with my letters.
10 For some say, "His
letters are weighty and forceful, but in person he is unimpressive and his speaking
amounts to nothing."
11 Such people
should realize that what we are in our letters when we are absent, we will be in our
actions when we are present.
12 We do not dare to classify or compare
ourselves with some who commend
themselves. When they measure themselves by themselves and compare themselves with themselves, they are not wise.
13 We, however, will not boast beyond
proper limits, but will confine our boasting to the field God has assigned to us, a
field that reaches even to you.
14 We are
not going too far in our boasting, as
would be the case if we had not come to
you, for we did get as far as you with the
gospel of Christ.
15 Neither do we go be-
yond our limits by boasting of work done
by others.[b] Our hope is that, as your faith
continues to grow, our area of activity
among you will greatly expand,
16 so that
we can preach the gospel in the regions
beyond you. For we do not want to boast
about work already done in another
man's territory.
17 But, "Let him who
boasts boast in the Lord."[c]
18 For it is not
the one who commends himself who is
approved, but the one whom the Lord
commends.

[a] 7 Or *Look at the obvious facts* [b] 13–15 Or *[13]We, however, will not boast about things that cannot be measured, but we will boast according to the standard of measurement that the God of measure has assigned us—a measurement that relates even to you. [14] . . . . [15]Neither do we boast about things that cannot be measured in regard to the work done by others.* [c] 17 Jer. 9:24

PRAYER: MY RELATIONSHIP TO OTHERS

HOUSES and wealth are inherited from fathers, but a prudent wife is from You, Lord. (Proverbs 19:14) . . . Charm is deceptive, and beauty is fleeting; but a woman who fears You, Lord, shall be praised. (Proverbs 31:30)

__PAUSE__ to review your relationships with others and to commit them to the Lord.

YEAR 2 DAY 161

OT Psalm 104

Psalm 104

[1] Praise the LORD, O my soul.

O LORD my God, you are very great;
you are clothed with splendor and majesty.
[2] He wraps himself in light as with a garment;
he stretches out the heavens like a tent
[3] and lays the beams of his upper chambers on their waters.
He makes the clouds his chariot
and rides on the wings of the wind.
[4] He makes winds his messengers,[a]
flames of fire his servants.

[5] He set the earth on its foundations;
it can never be moved.
[6] You covered it with the deep as with a garment;
the waters stood above the mountains.
[7] But at your rebuke the waters fled,
at the sound of your thunder they took to flight;
[8] they flowed over the mountains,
they went down into the valleys,
to the place you assigned for them.
[9] You set a boundary they cannot cross;
never again will they cover the earth.

[10] He makes springs pour water into the ravines;
it flows between the mountains.
[11] They give water to all the beasts of the field;
the wild donkeys quench their thirst.
[12] The birds of the air nest by the waters;
they sing among the branches.
[13] He waters the mountains from his upper chambers;
the earth is satisfied by the fruit of his work.
[14] He makes grass grow for the cattle,
and plants for man to cultivate—
bringing forth food from the earth:
[15] wine that gladdens the heart of man,
oil to make his face shine,
and bread that sustains his heart.
[16] The trees of the LORD are well watered,
the cedars of Lebanon that he planted.
[17] There the birds make their nests;
the stork has its home in the pine trees.
[18] The high mountains belong to the wild goats;
the crags are a refuge for the coneys.[b]

[19] The moon marks off the seasons,
and the sun knows when to go down.
[20] You bring darkness, it becomes night,
and all the beasts of the forest prowl.
[21] The lions roar for their prey
and seek their food from God.
[22] The sun rises, and they steal away;
they return and lie down in their dens.
[23] Then man goes out to his work,
to his labor until evening.

[24] How many are your works, O LORD!
In wisdom you made them all;
the earth is full of your creatures.
[25] There is the sea, vast and spacious,

[a] 4 Or *angels* [b] 18 That is, the hyrax or rock badger

teeming with creatures beyond number—
living things both large and small.
26 There the ships go to and fro,
and the leviathan, which you formed to frolic there.

27 These all look to you
to give them their food at the proper time.
28 When you give it to them,
they gather it up;
when you open your hand,
they are satisfied with good things.
29 When you hide your face,
they are terrified;
when you take away their breath,
they die and return to the dust.
30 When you send your Spirit,
they are created,
and you renew the face of the earth.

31 May the glory of the LORD endure forever;
may the LORD rejoice in his works—
32 he who looks at the earth, and it trembles,
who touches the mountains, and they smoke.

33 I will sing to the LORD all my life;
I will sing praise to my God as long as I live.
34 May my meditation be pleasing to him,
as I rejoice in the LORD.
35 But may sinners vanish from the earth
and the wicked be no more.

Praise the LORD, O my soul.

Praise the LORD.[c]

[c] 35 Hebrew *Hallelu Yah;* in the Septuagint this line stands at the beginning of Psalm 105.

PRAYER: ADORATION

YOUR loving-kindness, O Lord, reaches to the heavens, Your faithfulness to the skies. Your righteousness is like Your mighty mountains; Your judgments are like the great deep. O Lord, You preserve people and beasts. How priceless is Your loving-kindness, O God! Your children find refuge in the shadow of Your wings. For with You is the fountain of life; in Your light we see light. (Psalm 36:5–7, 9)

PAUSE *to express your thoughts of praise and worship.*

NT 2 Corinthians 11:1–15

Paul and the False Apostles

11 I hope you will put up with a little of my foolishness; but you are already
doing that. 2 I am jealous for you with a
godly jealousy. I promised you to one
husband, to Christ, so that I might
present you as a pure virgin to him. 3 But
I am afraid that just as Eve was deceived
by the serpent's cunning, your minds may
somehow be led astray from your sincere
and pure devotion to Christ. 4 For if someone comes to you and preaches a Jesus
other than the Jesus we preached, or if you
receive a different spirit from the one you
received, or a different gospel from the
one you accepted, you put up with it easily enough. 5 But I do not think I am in the
least inferior to those "super-apostles." 6 I
may not be a trained speaker, but I do
have knowledge. We have made this perfectly clear to you in every way.
7 Was it a sin for me to lower myself in
order to elevate you by preaching the
gospel of God to you free of charge? 8 I
robbed other churches by receiving support from them so as to serve you. 9 And
when I was with you and needed something, I was not a burden to anyone, for
the brothers who came from Macedonia
supplied what I needed. I have kept myself from being a burden to you in any
way, and will continue to do so. 10 As surely as the truth of Christ is in me, nobody
in the regions of Achaia will stop this
boasting of mine. 11 Why? Because I do not
love you? God knows I do! 12 And I will
keep on doing what I am doing in order
to cut the ground from under those who
want an opportunity to be considered

equal with us in the things they boast about.
[13]For such men are false apostles, deceitful workmen, masquerading as apostles of Christ. [14]And no wonder, for Satan himself masquerades as an angel of light. [15]It is not surprising, then, if his servants masquerade as servants of righteousness. Their end will be what their actions deserve.

PRAYER: THE ATTRIBUTES OF GOD

YOU, O Lord, are the God of knowledge, and by You actions are weighed. (1 Samuel 2:3) . . . You have set our iniquities before You, our secret sins in the light of Your presence. (Psalm 90:8)

***PAUSE** to reflect on these affirmations about the person, powers and perfection of God.*

YEAR 2 DAY 162

OT Isaiah 43:1-28

Israel's Only Savior

43 But now, this is what the LORD says—
he who created you, O Jacob,
he who formed you, O Israel:
"Fear not, for I have redeemed you;
I have summoned you by name;
you are mine.
[2]When you pass through the waters,
I will be with you;
and when you pass through the rivers,
they will not sweep over you.
When you walk through the fire,
you will not be burned;
the flames will not set you ablaze.
[3]For I am the LORD, your God,
the Holy One of Israel, your Savior;
I give Egypt for your ransom,
Cush[a] and Seba in your stead.
[4]Since you are precious and honored in my sight,
and because I love you,
I will give men in exchange for you,
and people in exchange for your life.
[5]Do not be afraid, for I am with you;
I will bring your children from the east
and gather you from the west.
[6]I will say to the north, 'Give them up!'
and to the south, 'Do not hold them back.'
Bring my sons from afar
and my daughters from the ends of the earth—
[7]everyone who is called by my name,
whom I created for my glory,
whom I formed and made."
[8]Lead out those who have eyes but are blind,
who have ears but are deaf.
[9]All the nations gather together
and the peoples assemble.
Which of them foretold this
and proclaimed to us the former things?
Let them bring in their witnesses to prove they were right,
so that others may hear and say, "It is true."
[10]"You are my witnesses," declares the LORD,
"and my servant whom I have chosen,
so that you may know and believe me
and understand that I am he.
Before me no god was formed,
nor will there be one after me.
[11]I, even I, am the LORD,
and apart from me there is no savior.
[12]I have revealed and saved and proclaimed—
I, and not some foreign god among you.
You are my witnesses," declares the LORD, "that I am God.
[13] Yes, and from ancient days I am he.
No one can deliver out of my hand.
When I act, who can reverse it?"

[a] 3 That is, the upper Nile region

God's Mercy and Israel's Unfaithfulness

14 This is what the LORD says—
your Redeemer, the Holy One of Israel:
"For your sake I will send to Babylon
and bring down as fugitives all the Babylonians,[b]
in the ships in which they took pride.
15 I am the LORD, your Holy One,
Israel's Creator, your King."

16 This is what the LORD says—
he who made a way through the sea,
a path through the mighty waters,
17 who drew out the chariots and horses,
the army and reinforcements together,
and they lay there, never to rise again,
extinguished, snuffed out like a wick:
18 "Forget the former things;
do not dwell on the past.
19 See, I am doing a new thing!
Now it springs up; do you not perceive it?
I am making a way in the desert
and streams in the wasteland.
20 The wild animals honor me,
the jackals and the owls,
because I provide water in the desert
and streams in the wasteland,
to give drink to my people, my chosen,
21 the people I formed for myself
that they may proclaim my praise.

22 "Yet you have not called upon me, O Jacob,
you have not wearied yourselves for me, O Israel.
23 You have not brought me sheep for burnt offerings,
nor honored me with your sacrifices.
I have not burdened you with grain offerings
nor wearied you with demands for incense.
24 You have not bought any fragrant calamus for me,
or lavished on me the fat of your sacrifices.
But you have burdened me with your sins
and wearied me with your offenses.

25 "I, even I, am he who blots out
your transgressions, for my own sake,
and remembers your sins no more.
26 Review the past for me,
let us argue the matter together;
state the case for your innocence.
27 Your first father sinned;
your spokesmen rebelled against me.
28 So I will disgrace the dignitaries of your temple,
and I will consign Jacob to destruction[c]
and Israel to scorn.

[b] 14 Or *Chaldeans* [c] 28 The Hebrew term refers to the irrevocable giving over of things or persons to the LORD, often by totally destroying them.

PRAYER: CONFESSION

ALL Your paths are mercy and truth, O Lord, for those who keep Your covenant and Your testimonies. For Your name's sake, O Lord, pardon my iniquity, for it is great. (Psalm 25:10–11)

***ASK** the Spirit to search your heart and reveal any areas of unconfessed sin. Acknowledge these to the Lord and thank Him for His forgiveness.*

NT 2 Corinthians 11:16–33

Paul Boasts About His Sufferings

16 I repeat: Let no one take me for a fool.
But if you do, then receive me just as you
would a fool, so that I may do a little
boasting. 17 In this self-confident boasting
I am not talking as the Lord would, but as
a fool. 18 Since many are boasting in the
way the world does, I too will boast. 19 You
gladly put up with fools since you are so
wise! 20 In fact, you even put up with anyone who enslaves you or exploits you or
takes advantage of you or pushes himself

forward or slaps you in the face. [21]To my
shame I admit that we were too weak for
that!
What anyone else dares to boast
about—I am speaking as a fool—I also
dare to boast about. [22]Are they Hebrews?
So am I. Are they Israelites? So am I. Are
they Abraham's descendants? So am I.
[23]Are they servants of Christ? (I am out of
my mind to talk like this.) I am more. I
have worked much harder, been in prison
more frequently, been flogged more severely, and been exposed to death again
and again. [24]Five times I received from the
Jews the forty lashes minus one. [25]Three
times I was beaten with rods, once I was
stoned, three times I was shipwrecked, I
spent a night and a day in the open sea,
[26]I have been constantly on the move. I
have been in danger from rivers, in danger from bandits, in danger from my own
countrymen, in danger from Gentiles; in
danger in the city, in danger in the country, in danger at sea; and in danger from
false brothers. [27]I have labored and toiled
and have often gone without sleep; I have
known hunger and thirst and have often
gone without food; I have been cold and
naked. [28]Besides everything else, I face daily the pressure of my concern for all the
churches. [29]Who is weak, and I do not feel
weak? Who is led into sin, and I do not
inwardly burn?
[30]If I must boast, I will boast of the
things that show my weakness. [31]The God
and Father of the Lord Jesus, who is to be
praised forever, knows that I am not lying.
[32]In Damascus the governor under King
Aretas had the city of the Damascenes
guarded in order to arrest me. [33]But I was
lowered in a basket from a window in the
wall and slipped through his hands.

PRAYER: THE WORKS OF GOD

IN Your unfailing love, O Lord, You have led the people You have redeemed. In Your strength You have guided them to Your holy dwelling. You brought them in and planted them in the mountain of Your inheritance—the place, O Lord, You made for Your dwelling; the sanctuary, O Lord, Your hands have established. (Exodus 15:13, 17)

TAKE *a moment to consider the greatness of God's wonderful works.*

YEAR 2 DAY 163

OT Isaiah 44:1–28

Israel the Chosen

44 "But now listen, O Jacob, my servant,
Israel, whom I have chosen.
[2]This is what the LORD says—
he who made you, who formed you in the womb,
and who will help you:
Do not be afraid, O Jacob, my servant,
Jeshurun, whom I have chosen.
[3]For I will pour water on the thirsty land,
and streams on the dry ground;
I will pour out my Spirit on your offspring,
and my blessing on your descendants.
[4]They will spring up like grass in a meadow,
like poplar trees by flowing streams.
[5]One will say, 'I belong to the LORD';
another will call himself by the name of Jacob;
still another will write on his hand, 'The LORD's,'
and will take the name Israel.

The LORD, Not Idols

[6]"This is what the LORD says—
Israel's King and Redeemer, the LORD Almighty:
I am the first and I am the last;
apart from me there is no God.
[7]Who then is like me? Let him proclaim it.
Let him declare and lay out before me

what has happened since I established
my ancient people,
and what is yet to come—
yes, let him foretell what will come.
8 Do not tremble, do not be afraid.
Did I not proclaim this and foretell
it long ago?
You are my witnesses. Is there any
God besides me?
No, there is no other Rock; I know
not one."

9 All who make idols are nothing,
and the things they treasure are
worthless.
Those who would speak up for them
are blind;
they are ignorant, to their own
shame.
10 Who shapes a god and casts an idol,
which can profit him nothing?
11 He and his kind will be put to shame;
craftsmen are nothing but men.
Let them all come together and take
their stand;
they will be brought down to terror
and infamy.

12 The blacksmith takes a tool
and works with it in the coals;
he shapes an idol with hammers,
he forges it with the might of his
arm.
He gets hungry and loses his strength;
he drinks no water and grows faint.
13 The carpenter measures with a line
and makes an outline with a
marker;
he roughs it out with chisels
and marks it with compasses.
He shapes it in the form of man,
of man in all his glory,
that it may dwell in a shrine.
14 He cut down cedars,
or perhaps took a cypress or oak.
He let it grow among the trees of the
forest,
or planted a pine, and the rain
made it grow.
15 It is man's fuel for burning;
some of it he takes and warms
himself,
he kindles a fire and bakes bread.
But he also fashions a god and
worships it;
he makes an idol and bows down
to it.
16 Half of the wood he burns in the fire;
over it he prepares his meal,
he roasts his meat and eats his fill.
He also warms himself and says,
"Ah! I am warm; I see the fire."
17 From the rest he makes a god, his
idol;
he bows down to it and worships.
He prays to it and says,
"Save me; you are my god."
18 They know nothing, they understand
nothing;
their eyes are plastered over so they
cannot see,
and their minds closed so they
cannot understand.
19 No one stops to think,
no one has the knowledge or
understanding to say,
"Half of it I used for fuel;
I even baked bread over its coals,
I roasted meat and I ate.
Shall I make a detestable thing from
what is left?
Shall I bow down to a block of
wood?"
20 He feeds on ashes, a deluded heart
misleads him;
he cannot save himself, or say,
"Is not this thing in my right hand
a lie?"

21 "Remember these things, O Jacob,
for you are my servant, O Israel.
I have made you, you are my servant;
O Israel, I will not forget you.
22 I have swept away your offenses like a
cloud,
your sins like the morning mist.
Return to me,
for I have redeemed you."

23 Sing for joy, O heavens, for the LORD
has done this;
shout aloud, O earth beneath.
Burst into song, you mountains,
you forests and all your trees,
for the LORD has redeemed Jacob,
he displays his glory in Israel.

Jerusalem to Be Inhabited

24 "This is what the LORD says—
your Redeemer, who formed you in
the womb:

I am the LORD,
who has made all things,
who alone stretched out the heavens,
who spread out the earth by myself,

[25]who foils the signs of false prophets
and makes fools of diviners,
who overthrows the learning of the wise
and turns it into nonsense,
[26]who carries out the words of his servants
and fulfills the predictions of his messengers,

who says of Jerusalem, 'It shall be inhabited,'
of the towns of Judah, 'They shall be built,'
and of their ruins, 'I will restore them,'
[27]who says to the watery deep, 'Be dry,
and I will dry up your streams,'
[28]who says of Cyrus, 'He is my shepherd
and will accomplish all that I please;
he will say of Jerusalem, "Let it be rebuilt,"
and of the temple, "Let its foundations be laid." '

PRAYER: RENEWAL

MY struggle is not against flesh and blood, but against the rulers, against the authorities, against the powers of this dark world and against the spiritual forces of evil in the heavenly realms. Therefore, I will put on Your full armor, O God, so that I may be able to resist in the day of evil, and having done all, to stand. (Ephesians 6:12–13)

***PAUSE** to add your own prayers for personal renewal.*

NT 2 Corinthians 12:1-10

Paul's Vision and His Thorn

12 I must go on boasting. Although there
is nothing to be gained, I will go on
to visions and revelations from the Lord.
[2]I know a man in Christ who fourteen
years ago was caught up to the third heav-
en. Whether it was in the body or out of
the body I do not know—God knows.
[3]And I know that this man—whether in
the body or apart from the body I do not
know, but God knows— [4]was caught up
to paradise. He heard inexpressible things,
things that man is not permitted to tell. [5]I
will boast about a man like that, but I will
not boast about myself, except about my
weaknesses. [6]Even if I should choose to
boast, I would not be a fool, because I
would be speaking the truth. But I refrain,
so no one will think more of me than is
warranted by what I do or say.
[7]To keep me from becoming conceited
because of these surpassingly great revelations, there was given me a thorn in my
flesh, a messenger of Satan, to torment
me. [8]Three times I pleaded with the Lord
to take it away from me. [9]But he said to
me, "My grace is sufficient for you, for my
power is made perfect in weakness."
Therefore I will boast all the more gladly
about my weaknesses, so that Christ's
power may rest on me. [10]That is why, for
Christ's sake, I delight in weaknesses, in
insults, in hardships, in persecutions, in
difficulties. For when I am weak, then I
am strong.

PRAYER: MY RELATIONSHIP TO GOD

BECAUSE Your loving-kindness is better than life, O Lord, my lips will praise You. So I will bless You as long as I live; I will lift up my hands in Your name. (Psalm 63:3–4) . . . I will praise Your name in song, O God, and magnify You with thanksgiving. (Psalm 69:30)

***PAUSE** to thank God for the relationship that you enjoy with Him in Jesus Christ.*

YEAR 2 DAY 164

OT Isaiah 45:1-25

45 "This is what the LORD says to his anointed,
to Cyrus, whose right hand I take hold of
to subdue nations before him
and to strip kings of their armor,
to open doors before him
so that gates will not be shut:
2 I will go before you
and will level the mountains[a];
I will break down gates of bronze
and cut through bars of iron.
3 I will give you the treasures of darkness,
riches stored in secret places,
so that you may know that I am the LORD,
the God of Israel, who summons you by name.
4 For the sake of Jacob my servant,
of Israel my chosen,
I summon you by name
and bestow on you a title of honor,
though you do not acknowledge me.
5 I am the LORD, and there is no other;
apart from me there is no God.
I will strengthen you,
though you have not acknowledged me,
6 so that from the rising of the sun
to the place of its setting
men may know there is none besides me.
I am the LORD, and there is no other.
7 I form the light and create darkness,
I bring prosperity and create disaster;
I, the LORD, do all these things.

8 "You heavens above, rain down righteousness;
let the clouds shower it down.
Let the earth open wide,
let salvation spring up,
let righteousness grow with it;
I, the LORD, have created it.

9 "Woe to him who quarrels with his Maker,
to him who is but a potsherd
among the potsherds on the ground.
Does the clay say to the potter,
'What are you making?'
Does your work say,
'He has no hands'?
10 Woe to him who says to his father,
'What have you begotten?'
or to his mother,
'What have you brought to birth?'

11 "This is what the LORD says—
the Holy One of Israel, and its Maker:
Concerning things to come,
do you question me about my children,
or give me orders about the work of my hands?
12 It is I who made the earth
and created mankind upon it.
My own hands stretched out the heavens;
I marshaled their starry hosts.
13 I will raise up Cyrus[b] in my righteousness:
I will make all his ways straight.
He will rebuild my city
and set my exiles free,
but not for a price or reward,
says the LORD Almighty."

14 This is what the LORD says:

"The products of Egypt and the merchandise of Cush,[c]
and those tall Sabeans—
they will come over to you
and will be yours;
they will trudge behind you,
coming over to you in chains.
They will bow down before you
and plead with you, saying,
'Surely God is with you, and there is no other;
there is no other god.' "

15 Truly you are a God who hides himself,
O God and Savior of Israel.
16 All the makers of idols will be put to shame and disgraced;
they will go off into disgrace together.

[a] *2* Dead Sea Scrolls and Septuagint; the meaning of the word in the Masoretic Text is uncertain.
[b] *13* Hebrew *him* [c] *14* That is, the upper Nile region

[17]But Israel will be saved by the LORD
with an everlasting salvation;
you will never be put to shame or
disgraced,
to ages everlasting.

[18]For this is what the LORD says—
he who created the heavens,
he is God;
he who fashioned and made the
earth,
he founded it;
he did not create it to be empty,
but formed it to be inhabited—
he says:
"I am the LORD,
and there is no other.
[19]I have not spoken in secret,
from somewhere in a land of
darkness;
I have not said to Jacob's descendants,
'Seek me in vain.'
I, the LORD, speak the truth;
I declare what is right.

[20]"Gather together and come;
assemble, you fugitives from the
nations.
Ignorant are those who carry about
idols of wood,
who pray to gods that cannot save.
[21]Declare what is to be, present it—
let them take counsel together.
Who foretold this long ago,
who declared it from the distant
past?
Was it not I, the LORD?
And there is no God apart from me,
a righteous God and a Savior;
there is none but me.

[22]"Turn to me and be saved,
all you ends of the earth;
for I am God, and there is no other.
[23]By myself I have sworn,
my mouth has uttered in all
integrity
a word that will not be revoked:
Before me every knee will bow;
by me every tongue will swear.
[24]They will say of me, 'In the LORD
alone
are righteousness and strength.' "
All who have raged against him
will come to him and be put to
shame.
[25]But in the LORD all the descendants of
Israel
will be found righteous and will
exult.

PRAYER: PETITION

IN my distress may I seek Your favor, O Lord my God, and humble myself greatly before You, the God of my fathers, for I know that You are God. (2 Chronicles 33:12–13)

***PAUSE** here to offer prayers of petition regarding your family and your ministry. Ask for help and guidance in sharing Jesus with others and helping others grow in Him. Ask for guidance in your vocation and your avocations. Offer prayers of petition regarding your activities for this day and any special concerns you may have.*

NT 2 Corinthians 12:11–21

Paul's Concern for the Corinthians

[11]I have made a fool of myself, but you
drove me to it. I ought to have been commended by you, for I am not in the least
inferior to the "super-apostles," even
though I am nothing. [12]The things that
mark an apostle—signs, wonders and miracles—were done among you with great
perseverance. [13]How were you inferior to
the other churches, except that I was never a burden to you? Forgive me this wrong!

[14]Now I am ready to visit you for the
third time, and I will not be a burden to
you, because what I want is not your possessions but you. After all, children
should not have to save up for their parents, but parents for their children. [15]So I
will very gladly spend for you everything
I have and expend myself as well. If I love
you more, will you love me less? [16]Be that
as it may, I have not been a burden to you.
Yet, crafty fellow that I am, I caught you

by trickery! [17]Did I exploit you through
any of the men I sent you? [18]I urged Titus
to go to you and I sent our brother with
him. Titus did not exploit you, did he?
Did we not act in the same spirit and follow the same course?
[19]Have you been thinking all along that
we have been defending ourselves to you?
We have been speaking in the sight of God
as those in Christ; and everything we do,
dear friends, is for your strengthening. [20]For
I am afraid that when I come I may not find
you as I want you to be, and you may not
find me as you want me to be. I fear that
there may be quarreling, jealousy, outbursts
of anger, factions, slander, gossip, arrogance
and disorder. [21]I am afraid that when I
come again my God will humble me before
you, and I will be grieved over many who
have sinned earlier and have not repented
of the impurity, sexual sin and debauchery
in which they have indulged.

PRAYER: THE CHARACTER I WANT TO CULTIVATE

THOSE who partake only of milk are not accustomed to the word of righteousness, for they are infants. But solid food is for the mature, who because of use have their senses trained to distinguish good from evil. Therefore I will leave the elementary teachings about You, Jesus Christ, and go on to maturity. (Hebrews 5:13–6:1)

***TAKE** a moment to ask the Lord for the grace to grow in godly character.*

YEAR 2 DAY 165

OT Isaiah 46:1-13

Gods of Babylon

46 Bel bows down, Nebo stoops low;
their idols are borne by beasts of burden.[a]
The images that are carried about are burdensome,
a burden for the weary.
[2]They stoop and bow down together;
unable to rescue the burden,
they themselves go off into captivity.

[3]"Listen to me, O house of Jacob,
all you who remain of the house of Israel,
you whom I have upheld since you were conceived,
and have carried since your birth.
[4]Even to your old age and gray hairs
I am he, I am he who will sustain you.
I have made you and I will carry you;
I will sustain you and I will rescue you.

[5]"To whom will you compare me or count me equal?
To whom will you liken me that we may be compared?
[6]Some pour out gold from their bags
and weigh out silver on the scales;
they hire a goldsmith to make it into a god,
and they bow down and worship it.
[7]They lift it to their shoulders and carry it;
they set it up in its place, and there it stands.
From that spot it cannot move.
Though one cries out to it, it does not answer;
it cannot save him from his troubles.

[8]"Remember this, fix it in mind,
take it to heart, you rebels.
[9]Remember the former things, those of long ago;
I am God, and there is no other;
I am God, and there is none like me.
[10]I make known the end from the beginning,
from ancient times, what is still to come.
I say: My purpose will stand,
and I will do all that I please.

[a] 1 Or *are but beasts and cattle*

11 From the east I summon a bird of prey;
from a far-off land, a man to fulfill
my purpose.
What I have said, that will I bring
about;
what I have planned, that will I do.
12 Listen to me, you stubborn-hearted,
you who are far from righteousness.
13 I am bringing my righteousness near,
it is not far away;
and my salvation will not be
delayed.
I will grant salvation to Zion,
my splendor to Israel.

PRAYER: INTERCESSION

AS the Father has sent You, You also send us, Lord Jesus. (John 20:21)

***TAKE** a few moments to intercede on behalf of local, national and world missions. Pray that the Great Commission would be fulfilled and for any special concerns you may have for missions.*

NT 2 Corinthians 13:1-14

Final Warnings

13 This will be my third visit to you. "Every
matter must be established by the testimony of two or three witnesses."[a] 2I already
gave you a warning when I was with you
the second time. I now repeat it while absent: On my return I will not spare those
who sinned earlier or any of the others,
3since you are demanding proof that Christ
is speaking through me. He is not weak in
dealing with you, but is powerful among
you. 4For to be sure, he was crucified in
weakness, yet he lives by God's power. Likewise, we are weak in him, yet by God's power we will live with him to serve you.
5Examine yourselves to see whether you
are in the faith; test yourselves. Do you
not realize that Christ Jesus is in you—unless, of course, you fail the test? 6And I
trust that you will discover that we have
not failed the test. 7Now we pray to God
that you will not do anything wrong. Not
that people will see that we have stood the
test but that you will do what is right even
though we may seem to have failed. 8For
we cannot do anything against the truth,
but only for the truth. 9We are glad whenever we are weak but you are strong; and
our prayer is for your perfection. 10This is
why I write these things when I am absent, that when I come I may not have to
be harsh in my use of authority—the authority the Lord gave me for building you
up, not for tearing you down.

Final Greetings

11Finally, brothers, good-by. Aim for
perfection, listen to my appeal, be of one
mind, live in peace. And the God of love
and peace will be with you.
12Greet one another with a holy kiss.
13All the saints send their greetings.
14May the grace of the Lord Jesus Christ,
and the love of God, and the fellowship
of the Holy Spirit be with you all.

[a] *1* Deut. 19:15

PRAYER: MY RELATIONSHIP TO OTHERS

I WILL discipline my children while there is hope and not be a willing party to their death. (Proverbs 19:18) . . . The rod and reproof impart wisdom, but children left to themselves bring shame to their mother. (Proverbs 29:15)

***PAUSE** to review your relationships with others and to commit them to the Lord.*

YEAR 2 DAY 166

OT Isaiah 47:1–15

The Fall of Babylon

47 "Go down, sit in the dust,
Virgin Daughter of Babylon;
sit on the ground without a throne,
Daughter of the Babylonians.[a]
No more will you be called
tender or delicate.
2 Take millstones and grind flour;
take off your veil.
Lift up your skirts, bare your legs,
and wade through the streams.
3 Your nakedness will be exposed
and your shame uncovered.
I will take vengeance;
I will spare no one."

4 Our Redeemer—the LORD Almighty is his name—
is the Holy One of Israel.

5 "Sit in silence, go into darkness,
Daughter of the Babylonians;
no more will you be called
queen of kingdoms.
6 I was angry with my people
and desecrated my inheritance;
I gave them into your hand,
and you showed them no mercy.
Even on the aged
you laid a very heavy yoke.
7 You said, 'I will continue forever—
the eternal queen!'
But you did not consider these things
or reflect on what might happen.

8 "Now then, listen, you wanton creature,
lounging in your security
and saying to yourself,
'I am, and there is none besides me.
I will never be a widow
or suffer the loss of children.'
9 Both of these will overtake you
in a moment, on a single day:
loss of children and widowhood.
They will come upon you in full measure,
in spite of your many sorceries
and all your potent spells.
10 You have trusted in your wickedness
and have said, 'No one sees me.'
Your wisdom and knowledge mislead you
when you say to yourself,
'I am, and there is none besides me.'
11 Disaster will come upon you,
and you will not know how to conjure it away.
A calamity will fall upon you
that you cannot ward off with a ransom;
a catastrophe you cannot foresee
will suddenly come upon you.

12 "Keep on, then, with your magic spells
and with your many sorceries,
which you have labored at since childhood.
Perhaps you will succeed,
perhaps you will cause terror.
13 All the counsel you have received has only worn you out!
Let your astrologers come forward,
those stargazers who make predictions month by month,
let them save you from what is coming upon you.
14 Surely they are like stubble;
the fire will burn them up.
They cannot even save themselves
from the power of the flame.
Here are no coals to warm anyone;
here is no fire to sit by.
15 That is all they can do for you—
these you have labored with
and trafficked with since childhood.
Each of them goes on in his error;
there is not one that can save you.

[a] *1* Or *Chaldeans;* also in verse 5

PRAYER: AFFIRMATION

IN their hearts people plan their ways, but You, Lord, determine their steps. (Proverbs 16:9) . . . There is no wisdom or understanding or counsel that can succeed against You, Lord. (Proverbs 21:30)

***PAUSE** to reflect on these Biblical affirmations.*

NT Galatians 1:1–10

1 Paul, an apostle—sent not from men
nor by man, but by Jesus Christ and
God the Father, who raised him from the
dead— 2and all the brothers with me,

To the churches in Galatia:

3Grace and peace to you from God our
Father and the Lord Jesus Christ, 4who
gave himself for our sins to rescue us from
the present evil age, according to the will
of our God and Father, 5to whom be glory for ever and ever. Amen.

No Other Gospel

6I am astonished that you are so quickly deserting the one who called you by the
grace of Christ and are turning to a different gospel— 7which is really no gospel
at all. Evidently some people are throwing you into confusion and are trying to
pervert the gospel of Christ. 8But even if
we or an angel from heaven should
preach a gospel other than the one we
preached to you, let him be eternally condemned! 9As we have already said, so now
I say again: If anybody is preaching to you
a gospel other than what you accepted, let
him be eternally condemned!
10Am I now trying to win the approval
of men, or of God? Or am I trying to
please men? If I were still trying to please
men, I would not be a servant of Christ.

PRAYER: THE ATTRIBUTES OF GOD

NO one can see You, Lord, and live. (Exodus 33:20) . . . No one has seen the Father except You, the One who is from God; only You have seen the Father. (John 6:46)

***PAUSE** to reflect on these affirmations about the person, powers and perfection of God.*

YEAR 2 DAY 167

OT Isaiah 48:1–22

Stubborn Israel

48 "Listen to this, O house of Jacob,
you who are called by the name
of Israel
and come from the line of Judah,
you who take oaths in the name of
the LORD
and invoke the God of Israel—
but not in truth or righteousness—
2you who call yourselves citizens of the
holy city
and rely on the God of Israel—
the LORD Almighty is his name:
3I foretold the former things long ago,
my mouth announced them and I
made them known;
then suddenly I acted, and they
came to pass.
4For I knew how stubborn you were;
the sinews of your neck were iron,
your forehead was bronze.
5Therefore I told you these things long
ago;
before they happened I announced
them to you
so that you could not say,
'My idols did them;
my wooden image and metal god
ordained them.'
6You have heard these things; look at
them all.
Will you not admit them?

"From now on I will tell you of new
things,
of hidden things unknown to you.
7They are created now, and not long
ago;
you have not heard of them before
today.
So you cannot say,
'Yes, I knew of them.'
8You have neither heard nor
understood;

from of old your ear has not been open.
Well do I know how treacherous you are;
you were called a rebel from birth.
9 For my own name's sake I delay my wrath;
for the sake of my praise I hold it back from you,
so as not to cut you off.
10 See, I have refined you, though not as silver;
I have tested you in the furnace of affliction.
11 For my own sake, for my own sake, I do this.
How can I let myself be defamed?
I will not yield my glory to another.

Israel Freed

12 "Listen to me, O Jacob,
Israel, whom I have called:
I am he;
I am the first and I am the last.
13 My own hand laid the foundations of the earth,
and my right hand spread out the heavens;
when I summon them,
they all stand up together.

14 "Come together, all of you, and listen:
Which of ⌊the idols⌋ has foretold these things?
The LORD's chosen ally
will carry out his purpose against Babylon;
his arm will be against the Babylonians.[a]
15 I, even I, have spoken;
yes, I have called him.
I will bring him,
and he will succeed in his mission.

16 "Come near me and listen to this:
"From the first announcement I have not spoken in secret;
at the time it happens, I am there."

And now the Sovereign LORD has sent me,
with his Spirit.

17 This is what the LORD says—
your Redeemer, the Holy One of Israel:
"I am the LORD your God,
who teaches you what is best for you,
who directs you in the way you should go.
18 If only you had paid attention to my commands,
your peace would have been like a river,
your righteousness like the waves of the sea.
19 Your descendants would have been like the sand,
your children like its numberless grains;
their name would never be cut off
nor destroyed from before me."

20 Leave Babylon,
flee from the Babylonians!
Announce this with shouts of joy
and proclaim it.
Send it out to the ends of the earth;
say, "The LORD has redeemed his servant Jacob."
21 They did not thirst when he led them through the deserts;
he made water flow for them from the rock;
he split the rock
and water gushed out.

22 "There is no peace," says the LORD,
"for the wicked."

[a] 14 Or *Chaldeans;* also in verse 20

PRAYER: THANKSGIVING

FATHER, You are the One who makes me stand firm in Christ and You anointed me. You also sealed me and gave me Your Spirit in my heart as a deposit. (2 Corinthians 1:21–22) . . . Thanks be to You, Father, for You always lead us in triumph in Christ; and through us You spread everywhere the fragrance of the knowledge of Him. (2 Corinthians 2:14)

PAUSE *to offer your own expressions of thanksgiving.*

NT Galatians 1:11–24

Paul Called by God

11 I want you to know, brothers, that the
gospel I preached is not something that
man made up. 12 I did not receive it from
any man, nor was I taught it; rather, I received it by revelation from Jesus Christ.
13 For you have heard of my previous
way of life in Judaism, how intensely I
persecuted the church of God and tried to
destroy it. 14 I was advancing in Judaism
beyond many Jews of my own age and
was extremely zealous for the traditions of
my fathers. 15 But when God, who set me
apart from birth[a] and called me by his
grace, was pleased 16 to reveal his Son in
me so that I might preach him among the
Gentiles, I did not consult any man, 17 nor
did I go up to Jerusalem to see those who
were apostles before I was, but I went immediately into Arabia and later returned
to Damascus.
18 Then after three years, I went up to
Jerusalem to get acquainted with Peter[b]
and stayed with him fifteen days. 19 I saw
none of the other apostles—only James,
the Lord's brother. 20 I assure you before
God that what I am writing you is no lie.
21 Later I went to Syria and Cilicia. 22 I was
personally unknown to the churches of
Judea that are in Christ. 23 They only heard
the report: "The man who formerly persecuted us is now preaching the faith he
once tried to destroy." 24 And they praised
God because of me.

[a] 15 Or *from my mother's womb* [b] 18 Greek *Cephas*

PRAYER: THE WORKS OF GOD

O GOD, our Father, You presented Christ as a sacrifice of atonement through faith in His blood. You did this to demonstrate Your righteousness at the present time, because in Your mercy, You passed over the sins committed before Jesus died. You did it to demonstrate Your righteousness in the present time, that You might be just and the justifier of those who have faith in Jesus. (Romans 3:25–26)

***TAKE** a moment to consider the greatness of God's wonderful works.*

YEAR 2 DAY 168

OT Psalm 105

Psalm 105

1 Give thanks to the LORD, call on his
name;
make known among the nations
what he has done.
2 Sing to him, sing praise to him;
tell of all his wonderful acts.
3 Glory in his holy name;
let the hearts of those who seek the
LORD rejoice.
4 Look to the LORD and his strength;
seek his face always.

5 Remember the wonders he has done,
his miracles, and the judgments he
pronounced,
6 O descendants of Abraham his
servant,
O sons of Jacob, his chosen ones.
7 He is the LORD our God;
his judgments are in all the earth.

8 He remembers his covenant forever,
the word he commanded, for a
thousand generations,
9 the covenant he made with Abraham,
the oath he swore to Isaac.
10 He confirmed it to Jacob as a decree,
to Israel as an everlasting covenant:
11 "To you I will give the land of Canaan
as the portion you will inherit."

12 When they were but few in number,
few indeed, and strangers in it,
13 they wandered from nation to nation,
from one kingdom to another.
14 He allowed no one to oppress them;

for their sake he rebuked kings:
15 "Do not touch my anointed ones;
do my prophets no harm."

16 He called down famine on the land
and destroyed all their supplies of food;
17 and he sent a man before them—
Joseph, sold as a slave.
18 They bruised his feet with shackles,
his neck was put in irons,
19 till what he foretold came to pass,
till the word of the LORD proved him true.
20 The king sent and released him,
the ruler of peoples set him free.
21 He made him master of his household,
ruler over all he possessed,
22 to instruct his princes as he pleased
and teach his elders wisdom.

23 Then Israel entered Egypt;
Jacob lived as an alien in the land of Ham.
24 The LORD made his people very fruitful;
he made them too numerous for their foes,
25 whose hearts he turned to hate his people,
to conspire against his servants.
26 He sent Moses his servant,
and Aaron, whom he had chosen.
27 They performed his miraculous signs among them,
his wonders in the land of Ham.
28 He sent darkness and made the land dark—
for had they not rebelled against his words?
29 He turned their waters into blood,
causing their fish to die.
30 Their land teemed with frogs,
which went up into the bedrooms of their rulers.
31 He spoke, and there came swarms of flies,
and gnats throughout their country.
32 He turned their rain into hail,
with lightning throughout their land;
33 he struck down their vines and fig trees
and shattered the trees of their country.
34 He spoke, and the locusts came,
grasshoppers without number;
35 they ate up every green thing in their land,
ate up the produce of their soil.
36 Then he struck down all the firstborn in their land,
the firstfruits of all their manhood.

37 He brought out Israel, laden with silver and gold,
and from among their tribes no one faltered.
38 Egypt was glad when they left,
because dread of Israel had fallen on them.
39 He spread out a cloud as a covering,
and a fire to give light at night.
40 They asked, and he brought them quail
and satisfied them with the bread of heaven.
41 He opened the rock, and water gushed out;
like a river it flowed in the desert.

42 For he remembered his holy promise
given to his servant Abraham.
43 He brought out his people with rejoicing,
his chosen ones with shouts of joy;
44 he gave them the lands of the nations,
and they fell heir to what others had toiled for—
45 that they might keep his precepts
and observe his laws.

Praise the LORD.[a]

[a] 45 Hebrew *Hallelu Yah*

PRAYER: ADORATION

YOU, O Lord, are upright; You are my Rock, and there is no unrighteousness in You. (Psalm 92:15) . . .
I will seek You, Lord, and Your strength; I will seek Your face continually. I will remember the wonders You have done, Your miracles, and the judgments of Your mouth. (Psalm 105:4–5)

PAUSE *to express your thoughts of praise and worship.*

NT Galatians 2:1-10

Paul Accepted by the Apostles

2 Fourteen years later I went up again to
Jerusalem, this time with Barnabas. I
took Titus along also. 2I went in response
to a revelation and set before them the
gospel that I preach among the Gentiles.
But I did this privately to those who
seemed to be leaders, for fear that I was
running or had run my race in vain.
3Yet not even Titus, who was with me,
was compelled to be circumcised, even
though he was a Greek. 4⌊This matter
arose⌋ because some false brothers had in-
filtrated our ranks to spy on the freedom
we have in Christ Jesus and to make us
slaves. 5We did not give in to them for a
moment, so that the truth of the gospel
might remain with you.
6As for those who seemed to be important—whatever they were makes no difference to me; God does not judge by external appearance—those men added nothing to my message. 7On the contrary, they
saw that I had been entrusted with the task
of preaching the gospel to the Gentiles,[a]
just as Peter had been to the Jews.[b] 8For
God, who was at work in the ministry of
Peter as an apostle to the Jews, was also at
work in my ministry as an apostle to the
Gentiles. 9James, Peter[c] and John, those re-
puted to be pillars, gave me and Barnabas
the right hand of fellowship when they
recognized the grace given to me. They
agreed that we should go to the Gentiles,
and they to the Jews. 10All they asked was
that we should continue to remember the
poor, the very thing I was eager to do.

[a] 7 Greek *uncircumcised* [b] 7 Greek *circumcised*; also in verses 8 and 9 [c] 9 Greek *Cephas*; also in verses 11 and 14

PRAYER: MY RELATIONSHIP TO GOD

I DIED to sin; how can I live in it any longer? (Romans 6:2) . . . I delight in Your law, O God, in my inner being. (Romans 7:22)

PAUSE *to thank God for the relationship that you enjoy with Him in Jesus Christ.*

YEAR 2 DAY 169

OT Isaiah 49:1-26

The Servant of the Lord

49 Listen to me, you islands;
hear this, you distant nations:
Before I was born the Lord called me;
from my birth he has made
mention of my name.
2He made my mouth like a sharpened
sword,
in the shadow of his hand he hid
me;
he made me into a polished arrow
and concealed me in his quiver.
3He said to me, "You are my servant,
Israel, in whom I will display my
splendor."
4But I said, "I have labored to no
purpose;
I have spent my strength in vain
and for nothing.
Yet what is due me is in the Lord's
hand,
and my reward is with my God."

5And now the Lord says—
he who formed me in the womb to
be his servant
to bring Jacob back to him
and gather Israel to himself,
for I am honored in the eyes of the
Lord
and my God has been my
strength—
6he says:
"It is too small a thing for you to be
my servant
to restore the tribes of Jacob
and bring back those of Israel I have
kept.

I will also make you a light for the
Gentiles,
that you may bring my salvation to
the ends of the earth."

7 This is what the LORD says—
the Redeemer and Holy One of
Israel—
to him who was despised and
abhorred by the nation,
to the servant of rulers:
"Kings will see you and rise up,
princes will see and bow down,
because of the LORD, who is faithful,
the Holy One of Israel, who has
chosen you."

Restoration of Israel

8 This is what the LORD says:

"In the time of my favor I will answer
you,
and in the day of salvation I will
help you;
I will keep you and will make you
to be a covenant for the people,
to restore the land
and to reassign its desolate
inheritances,
9 to say to the captives, 'Come out,'
and to those in darkness, 'Be free!'

"They will feed beside the roads
and find pasture on every barren hill.
10 They will neither hunger nor thirst,
nor will the desert heat or the sun
beat upon them.
He who has compassion on them will
guide them
and lead them beside springs of
water.
11 I will turn all my mountains into
roads,
and my highways will be raised up.
12 See, they will come from afar—
some from the north, some from
the west,
some from the region of Aswan.[a]"

13 Shout for joy, O heavens;
rejoice, O earth;
burst into song, O mountains!
For the LORD comforts his people
and will have compassion on his
afflicted ones.

14 But Zion said, "The LORD has forsaken
me,
the Lord has forgotten me."

15 "Can a mother forget the baby at her
breast
and have no compassion on the
child she has borne?
Though she may forget,
I will not forget you!
16 See, I have engraved you on the palms
of my hands;
your walls are ever before me.
17 Your sons hasten back,
and those who laid you waste
depart from you.
18 Lift up your eyes and look around;
all your sons gather and come to
you.
As surely as I live," declares the LORD,
"you will wear them all as
ornaments;
you will put them on, like a bride.

19 "Though you were ruined and made
desolate
and your land laid waste,
now you will be too small for your
people,
and those who devoured you will
be far away.
20 The children born during your
bereavement
will yet say in your hearing,
'This place is too small for us;
give us more space to live in.'
21 Then you will say in your heart,
'Who bore me these?
I was bereaved and barren;
I was exiled and rejected.
Who brought these up?
I was left all alone,
but these—where have they come
from?' "

22 This is what the Sovereign LORD says:

"See, I will beckon to the Gentiles,
I will lift up my banner to the
peoples;
they will bring your sons in their arms
and carry your daughters on their
shoulders.
23 Kings will be your foster fathers,
and their queens your nursing
mothers.
They will bow down before you with
their faces to the ground;
they will lick the dust at your feet.

[a] *12* Dead Sea Scrolls; Masoretic Text *Sinim*

Then you will know that I am the
 LORD;
 those who hope in me will not be
 disappointed."

24 Can plunder be taken from warriors,
 or captives rescued from the
 fierce[b]?

25 But this is what the LORD says:

"Yes, captives will be taken from
 warriors,
 and plunder retrieved from the
 fierce;
I will contend with those who
 contend with you,
 and your children I will save.
26 I will make your oppressors eat their
 own flesh;
 they will be drunk on their own
 blood, as with wine.
Then all mankind will know
 that I, the LORD, am your Savior,
 your Redeemer, the Mighty One of
 Jacob."

[b] *24* Dead Sea Scrolls, Vulgate and Syriac (see also Septuagint and verse 25); Masoretic Text *righteous*

PRAYER: CONFESSION

***IF I am proud, I will be destroyed; if I have a haughty spirit, I will fall.* (Proverbs 16:18)**

***ASK** the Spirit to search your heart and reveal any areas of unconfessed sin. Acknowledge these to the Lord and thank Him for His forgiveness.*

NT Galatians 2:11–21

Paul Opposes Peter

11 When Peter came to Antioch, I opposed
him to his face, because he was clearly in
the wrong.
12 Before certain men came from
James, he used to eat with the Gentiles. But
when they arrived, he began to draw back
and separate himself from the Gentiles because he was afraid of those who belonged
to the circumcision group.
13 The other Jews
joined him in his hypocrisy, so that by their
hypocrisy even Barnabas was led astray.
14 When I saw that they were not acting
in line with the truth of the gospel, I said
to Peter in front of them all, "You are a
Jew, yet you live like a Gentile and not like
a Jew. How is it, then, that you force Gentiles to follow Jewish customs?
15 "We who are Jews by birth and not
'Gentile sinners'
16 know that a man is not
justified by observing the law, but by faith
in Jesus Christ. So we, too, have put our
faith in Christ Jesus that we may be justified by faith in Christ and not by observing the law, because by observing the law
no one will be justified.
17 "If, while we seek to be justified in
Christ, it becomes evident that we ourselves are sinners, does that mean that
Christ promotes sin? Absolutely not!
18 If I
rebuild what I destroyed, I prove that I am
a lawbreaker.
19 For through the law I died
to the law so that I might live for God.
20 I
have been crucified with Christ and I no
longer live, but Christ lives in me. The life
I live in the body, I live by faith in the Son
of God, who loved me and gave himself
for me.
21 I do not set aside the grace of
God, for if righteousness could be gained
through the law, Christ died for nothing!"[a]

[a] *21* Some interpreters end the quotation after verse 14.

PRAYER: THE CHARACTER I WANT TO CULTIVATE

***I WILL not accept a bribe, for a bribe blinds those who see and perverts the words of the righteous.* (Exodus 23:8) . . . *I will be careful that no one entices me by riches; I will not let a large bribe turn me aside.* (Job 36:18)**

***TAKE** a moment to ask the Lord for the grace to grow in godly character.*

YEAR 2
DAY 170

OT **Isaiah 50:1-11**

Israel's Sin and the Servant's Obedience

50 This is what the LORD says:

"Where is your mother's certificate of
divorce
with which I sent her away?
Or to which of my creditors
did I sell you?
Because of your sins you were sold;
because of your transgressions your
mother was sent away.
2 When I came, why was there no one?
When I called, why was there no
one to answer?
Was my arm too short to ransom you?
Do I lack the strength to rescue you?
By a mere rebuke I dry up the sea,
I turn rivers into a desert;
their fish rot for lack of water
and die of thirst.
3 I clothe the sky with darkness
and make sackcloth its covering."

4 The Sovereign LORD has given me an
instructed tongue,
to know the word that sustains the
weary.
He wakens me morning by morning,
wakens my ear to listen like one
being taught.
5 The Sovereign LORD has opened my
ears,
and I have not been rebellious;
I have not drawn back.
6 I offered my back to those who beat
me,
my cheeks to those who pulled out
my beard;
I did not hide my face
from mocking and spitting.
7 Because the Sovereign LORD helps me,
I will not be disgraced.
Therefore have I set my face like flint,
and I know I will not be put to
shame.
8 He who vindicates me is near.
Who then will bring charges against
me?
Let us face each other!
Who is my accuser?
Let him confront me!
9 It is the Sovereign LORD who helps
me.
Who is he that will condemn me?
They will all wear out like a garment;
the moths will eat them up.

10 Who among you fears the LORD
and obeys the word of his servant?
Let him who walks in the dark,
who has no light,
trust in the name of the LORD
and rely on his God.
11 But now, all you who light fires
and provide yourselves with flaming
torches,
go, walk in the light of your fires
and of the torches you have set
ablaze.
This is what you shall receive from my
hand:
You will lie down in torment.

PRAYER: RENEWAL

WHEN I am blessed with abundance, may I beware lest my heart become proud, so that I forget You, the Lord my God, who provides all good things, and lest I think that it was my power and the strength of my hand that brought this wealth. (Deuteronomy 8:12–14, 17)

***PAUSE** to add your own prayers for personal renewal.*

NT **Galatians 3:1-14**

Faith or Observance of the Law

3 You foolish Galatians! Who has bewitched you? Before your very eyes
Jesus Christ was clearly portrayed as crucified. 2 I would like to learn just one thing
from you: Did you receive the Spirit by
observing the law, or by believing what
you heard? 3 Are you so foolish? After be-

ginning with the Spirit, are you now trying to attain your goal by human effort?
4 Have you suffered so much for nothing—if it really was for nothing? 5 Does
God give you his Spirit and work miracles
among you because you observe the law,
or because you believe what you heard?
6 Consider Abraham: "He believed God,
and it was credited to him as righteousness."[a] 7 Understand, then, that those who
believe are children of Abraham. 8 The
Scripture foresaw that God would justify
the Gentiles by faith, and announced the
gospel in advance to Abraham: "All nations will be blessed through you."[b] 9 So
those who have faith are blessed along
with Abraham, the man of faith.
10 All who rely on observing the law are
under a curse, for it is written: "Cursed is
everyone who does not continue to do
everything written in the Book of the
Law."[c] 11 Clearly no one is justified before
God by the law, because, "The righteous
will live by faith."[d] 12 The law is not based
on faith; on the contrary, "The man who
does these things will live by them."[e]
13 Christ redeemed us from the curse of the
law by becoming a curse for us, for it is
written: "Cursed is everyone who is hung
on a tree."[f] 14 He redeemed us in order that
the blessing given to Abraham might
come to the Gentiles through Christ Jesus,
so that by faith we might receive the
promise of the Spirit.

[a] *6* Gen. 15:6 [b] *8* Gen. 12:3; 18:18; 22:18
[c] *10* Deut. 27:26 [d] *11* Hab. 2:4 [e] *12* Lev. 18:5
[f] *13* Deut. 21:23

PRAYER: MY RELATIONSHIP TO OTHERS

I WILL pursue the things that lead to peace and to mutual edification. (Romans 14:19) . . . We should bear with one another in love and make every effort to keep the unity of Your Spirit in the bond of peace. (Ephesians 4:2–3)

__PAUSE__ to review your relationships with others and to commit them to the Lord.

OT Isaiah 51:1–23

YEAR 2 DAY 171

Everlasting Salvation for Zion

51 "Listen to me, you who pursue
righteousness
and who seek the LORD:
Look to the rock from which you were
cut
and to the quarry from which you
were hewn;
2 look to Abraham, your father,
and to Sarah, who gave you birth.
When I called him he was but one,
and I blessed him and made him
many.
3 The LORD will surely comfort Zion
and will look with compassion on
all her ruins;
he will make her deserts like Eden,
her wastelands like the garden of
the LORD.
Joy and gladness will be found in her,
thanksgiving and the sound of
singing.
4 "Listen to me, my people;
hear me, my nation:
The law will go out from me;
my justice will become a light to
the nations.
5 My righteousness draws near speedily,
my salvation is on the way,
and my arm will bring justice to the
nations.
The islands will look to me
and wait in hope for my arm.
6 Lift up your eyes to the heavens,
look at the earth beneath;
the heavens will vanish like smoke,
the earth will wear out like a
garment
and its inhabitants die like flies.
But my salvation will last forever,
my righteousness will never fail.

7 "Hear me, you who know what is right,
you people who have my law in your hearts:
Do not fear the reproach of men
or be terrified by their insults.
8 For the moth will eat them up like a garment;
the worm will devour them like wool.
But my righteousness will last forever,
my salvation through all generations."

9 Awake, awake! Clothe yourself with strength,
O arm of the LORD;
awake, as in days gone by,
as in generations of old.
Was it not you who cut Rahab to pieces,
who pierced that monster through?
10 Was it not you who dried up the sea,
the waters of the great deep,
who made a road in the depths of the sea
so that the redeemed might cross over?
11 The ransomed of the LORD will return.
They will enter Zion with singing;
everlasting joy will crown their heads.
Gladness and joy will overtake them,
and sorrow and sighing will flee away.

12 "I, even I, am he who comforts you.
Who are you that you fear mortal men,
the sons of men, who are but grass,
13 that you forget the LORD your Maker,
who stretched out the heavens
and laid the foundations of the earth,
that you live in constant terror every day
because of the wrath of the oppressor,
who is bent on destruction?
For where is the wrath of the oppressor?
14 The cowering prisoners will soon be set free;
they will not die in their dungeon,
nor will they lack bread.
15 For I am the LORD your God,
who churns up the sea so that its waves roar—
the LORD Almighty is his name.
16 I have put my words in your mouth
and covered you with the shadow of my hand—
I who set the heavens in place,
who laid the foundations of the earth,
and who say to Zion, 'You are my people.' "

The Cup of the LORD's Wrath

17 Awake, awake!
Rise up, O Jerusalem,
you who have drunk from the hand of the LORD
the cup of his wrath,
you who have drained to its dregs
the goblet that makes men stagger.
18 Of all the sons she bore
there was none to guide her;
of all the sons she reared
there was none to take her by the hand.
19 These double calamities have come upon you—
who can comfort you?—
ruin and destruction, famine and sword—
who can[a] console you?
20 Your sons have fainted;
they lie at the head of every street,
like antelope caught in a net.
They are filled with the wrath of the LORD
and the rebuke of your God.

21 Therefore hear this, you afflicted one,
made drunk, but not with wine.
22 This is what your Sovereign LORD says,
your God, who defends his people:
"See, I have taken out of your hand
the cup that made you stagger;
from that cup, the goblet of my wrath,
you will never drink again.
23 I will put it into the hands of your tormentors,
who said to you,
'Fall prostrate that we may walk over you.'
And you made your back like the ground,
like a street to be walked over."

[a] *19* Dead Sea Scrolls, Septuagint, Vulgate and Syriac; Masoretic Text / *how can I*

PRAYER: PETITION

ANSWER me when I call to You, O my righteous God! You have relieved me from my distress; be merciful to me and hear my prayer. (Psalm 4:1)

PAUSE *here to petition God for growth in your character and personal discipline, and for physical health and strength. Ask that He empower you for spiritual warfare against the temptations of the world, the flesh and the devil. Offer prayers regarding your activities for this day and any special concerns you may have.*

NT Galatians 3:15–4:7

The Law and the Promise

15 Brothers, let me take an example from everyday life. Just as no one can set aside or add to a human covenant that has been duly established, so it is in this case. 16 The promises were spoken to Abraham and to his seed. The Scripture does not say "and to seeds," meaning many people, but "and to your seed,"[a] meaning one person, who is Christ. 17 What I mean is this: The law, introduced 430 years later, does not set aside the covenant previously established by God and thus do away with the promise. 18 For if the inheritance depends on the law, then it no longer depends on a promise; but God in his grace gave it to Abraham through a promise.

19 What, then, was the purpose of the law? It was added because of transgressions until the Seed to whom the promise referred had come. The law was put into effect through angels by a mediator. 20 A mediator, however, does not represent just one party; but God is one.

21 Is the law, therefore, opposed to the promises of God? Absolutely not! For if a law had been given that could impart life, then righteousness would certainly have come by the law. 22 But the Scripture declares that the whole world is a prisoner of sin, so that what was promised, being given through faith in Jesus Christ, might be given to those who believe.

23 Before this faith came, we were held prisoners by the law, locked up until faith should be revealed. 24 So the law was put in charge to lead us to Christ[b] that we might be justified by faith. 25 Now that faith has come, we are no longer under the supervision of the law.

Sons of God

26 You are all sons of God through faith in Christ Jesus, 27 for all of you who were baptized into Christ have clothed yourselves with Christ. 28 There is neither Jew nor Greek, slave nor free, male nor female, for you are all one in Christ Jesus. 29 If you belong to Christ, then you are Abraham's seed, and heirs according to the promise.

4 What I am saying is that as long as the heir is a child, he is no different from a slave, although he owns the whole estate. 2 He is subject to guardians and trustees until the time set by his father. 3 So also, when we were children, we were in slavery under the basic principles of the world. 4 But when the time had fully come, God sent his Son, born of a woman, born under law, 5 to redeem those under law, that we might receive the full rights of sons. 6 Because you are sons, God sent the Spirit of his Son into our hearts, the Spirit who calls out, "*Abba*,[c] Father." 7 So you are no longer a slave, but a son; and since you are a son, God has made you also an heir.

[a] *16* Gen. 12:7; 13:15; 24:7 [b] *24* Or *charge until Christ came* [c] *6* Aramaic for *Father*

PRAYER: THE ATTRIBUTES OF GOD

MY flesh trembles for fear of You; I stand in awe of Your judgments. (Psalm 119:120) . . .
I will recall to mind the former things, those of long ago; You are God, and there is no other; You are God, and there is none like You. (Isaiah 46:9)

***PAUSE** to reflect on these affirmations about the person, powers and perfection of God.*

YEAR 2 DAY 172

OT Isaiah 52:1–53:12

52 Awake, awake, O Zion,
clothe yourself with strength.
Put on your garments of splendor,
O Jerusalem, the holy city.
The uncircumcised and defiled
will not enter you again.
2 Shake off your dust;
rise up, sit enthroned, O Jerusalem.
Free yourself from the chains on your neck,
O captive Daughter of Zion.

3 For this is what the LORD says:

"You were sold for nothing,
and without money you will be redeemed."

4 For this is what the Sovereign LORD says:

"At first my people went down to Egypt to live;
lately, Assyria has oppressed them.

5 "And now what do I have here?" declares the LORD.

"For my people have been taken away for nothing,
and those who rule them mock,[a]"
declares the LORD.
"And all day long
my name is constantly blasphemed.
6 Therefore my people will know my name;
therefore in that day they will know
that it is I who foretold it.
Yes, it is I."

7 How beautiful on the mountains
are the feet of those who bring good news,
who proclaim peace,
who bring good tidings,
who proclaim salvation,
who say to Zion,
"Your God reigns!"
8 Listen! Your watchmen lift up their voices;
together they shout for joy.
When the LORD returns to Zion,
they will see it with their own eyes.
9 Burst into songs of joy together,
you ruins of Jerusalem,
for the LORD has comforted his people,
he has redeemed Jerusalem.
10 The LORD will lay bare his holy arm
in the sight of all the nations,
and all the ends of the earth will see
the salvation of our God.

11 Depart, depart, go out from there!
Touch no unclean thing!
Come out from it and be pure,
you who carry the vessels of the LORD.
12 But you will not leave in haste
or go in flight;
for the LORD will go before you,
the God of Israel will be your rear guard.

The Suffering and Glory of the Servant

13 See, my servant will act wisely[b];
he will be raised and lifted up and highly exalted.
14 Just as there were many who were appalled at him[c]—
his appearance was so disfigured beyond that of any man
and his form marred beyond human likeness—
15 so will he sprinkle many nations,[d]
and kings will shut their mouths because of him.

[a] 5 Dead Sea Scrolls and Vulgate; Masoretic Text *wail* [b] 13 Or *will prosper* [c] 14 Hebrew *you* [d] 15 Hebrew; Septuagint *so will many nations marvel at him*

For what they were not told, they will see,
and what they have not heard, they will understand.

53 Who has believed our message
and to whom has the arm of the LORD been revealed?
2 He grew up before him like a tender shoot,
and like a root out of dry ground.
He had no beauty or majesty to attract us to him,
nothing in his appearance that we should desire him.
3 He was despised and rejected by men,
a man of sorrows, and familiar with suffering.
Like one from whom men hide their faces
he was despised, and we esteemed him not.

4 Surely he took up our infirmities
and carried our sorrows,
yet we considered him stricken by God,
smitten by him, and afflicted.
5 But he was pierced for our transgressions,
he was crushed for our iniquities;
the punishment that brought us peace was upon him,
and by his wounds we are healed.
6 We all, like sheep, have gone astray,
each of us has turned to his own way;
and the LORD has laid on him
the iniquity of us all.

7 He was oppressed and afflicted,
yet he did not open his mouth;
he was led like a lamb to the slaughter,
and as a sheep before her shearers is silent,
so he did not open his mouth.
8 By oppression[e] and judgment he was taken away.
And who can speak of his descendants?
For he was cut off from the land of the living;
for the transgression of my people he was stricken.[f]
9 He was assigned a grave with the wicked,
and with the rich in his death,
though he had done no violence,
nor was any deceit in his mouth.

10 Yet it was the LORD's will to crush him
and cause him to suffer,
and though the LORD makes[g] his life a guilt offering,
he will see his offspring and prolong his days,
and the will of the LORD will prosper in his hand.
11 After the suffering of his soul,
he will see the light ⌊of life⌋[h] and be satisfied[i];
by his knowledge[j] my righteous servant will justify many,
and he will bear their iniquities.
12 Therefore I will give him a portion among the great,[k]
and he will divide the spoils with the strong,[l]
because he poured out his life unto death,
and was numbered with the transgressors.
For he bore the sin of many,
and made intercession for the transgressors.

[e] 8 Or *From arrest* [f] 8 Or *away. / Yet who of his generation considered / that he was cut off from the land of the living / for the transgression of my people, / to whom the blow was due?* [g] 10 Hebrew *though you make* [h] 11 Dead Sea Scrolls (see also Septuagint); Masoretic Text does not have *the light ⌊of life⌋.* [i] 11 Or (with Masoretic Text) [11] *He will see the result of the suffering of his soul / and be satisfied* [j] 11 Or *by knowledge of him* [k] 12 Or *many* [l] 12 Or *numerous*

PRAYER: INTERCESSION

MAY I help the weak and remember Your words, Lord Jesus, for You said, "It is more blessed to give than to receive." (Acts 20:35)

***TAKE** a few moments to intercede on behalf of the poor and hungry, the oppressed and persecuted, and those in control of world and national resources. Offer prayers for peace among nations and regarding current events and concerns.*

NT Galatians 4:8–31

Paul's Concern for the Galatians

[8]Formerly, when you did not know God,
you were slaves to those who by nature are
not gods. [9]But now that you know God—
or rather are known by God—how is it that
you are turning back to those weak and
miserable principles? Do you wish to be
enslaved by them all over again? [10]You are
observing special days and months and
seasons and years! [11]I fear for you, that
somehow I have wasted my efforts on you.
[12]I plead with you, brothers, become
like me, for I became like you. You have
done me no wrong. [13]As you know, it was
because of an illness that I first preached
the gospel to you. [14]Even though my illness was a trial to you, you did not treat
me with contempt or scorn. Instead, you
welcomed me as if I were an angel of God,
as if I were Christ Jesus himself. [15]What
has happened to all your joy? I can testify that, if you could have done so, you
would have torn out your eyes and given
them to me. [16]Have I now become your
enemy by telling you the truth?
[17]Those people are zealous to win you
over, but for no good. What they want is
to alienate you ⌊from us⌋, so that you may
be zealous for them. [18]It is fine to be zealous, provided the purpose is good, and to
be so always and not just when I am with
you. [19]My dear children, for whom I am
again in the pains of childbirth until
Christ is formed in you, [20]how I wish I
could be with you now and change my
tone, because I am perplexed about you!

Hagar and Sarah

[21]Tell me, you who want to be under the
law, are you not aware of what the law
says? [22]For it is written that Abraham had
two sons, one by the slave woman and the
other by the free woman. [23]His son by the
slave woman was born in the ordinary
way; but his son by the free woman was
born as the result of a promise.
[24]These things may be taken figuratively, for the women represent two covenants. One covenant is from Mount Sinai and bears children who are to be
slaves: This is Hagar. [25]Now Hagar stands
for Mount Sinai in Arabia and corre-
sponds to the present city of Jerusalem,
because she is in slavery with her children. [26]But the Jerusalem that is above is
free, and she is our mother. [27]For it is
written:

"Be glad, O barren woman,
who bears no children;
break forth and cry aloud,
you who have no labor pains;
because more are the children of the
desolate woman
than of her who has a husband."[a]

[28]Now you, brothers, like Isaac, are children of promise. [29]At that time the son
born in the ordinary way persecuted the
son born by the power of the Spirit. It is
the same now. [30]But what does the Scripture say? "Get rid of the slave woman and
her son, for the slave woman's son will
never share in the inheritance with the
free woman's son."[b] [31]Therefore, brothers,
we are not children of the slave woman,
but of the free woman.

[a] *27* Isaiah 54:1 [b] *30* Gen. 21:10

PRAYER: THE WORKS OF GOD

YOU, O Lord, relieve the humble, but You cast the wicked to the ground. (Psalm 147:6) . . . You, O Lord, humble those who dwell on high and You lay the lofty city low; You level it to the ground and cast it down to the dust. (Isaiah 26:5)

***TAKE** a moment to consider the greatness of God's wonderful works.*

YEAR 2 DAY 173

OT Isaiah 54:1-17

The Future Glory of Zion

54 "Sing, O barren woman,
you who never bore a child;
burst into song, shout for joy,
you who were never in labor;
because more are the children of the desolate woman
than of her who has a husband,"
says the LORD.
2 "Enlarge the place of your tent,
stretch your tent curtains wide,
do not hold back;
lengthen your cords,
strengthen your stakes.
3 For you will spread out to the right and to the left;
your descendants will dispossess nations
and settle in their desolate cities.

4 "Do not be afraid; you will not suffer shame.
Do not fear disgrace; you will not be humiliated.
You will forget the shame of your youth
and remember no more the reproach of your widowhood.
5 For your Maker is your husband—
the LORD Almighty is his name—
the Holy One of Israel is your Redeemer;
he is called the God of all the earth.
6 The LORD will call you back
as if you were a wife deserted and distressed in spirit—
a wife who married young,
only to be rejected," says your God.
7 "For a brief moment I abandoned you,
but with deep compassion I will bring you back.
8 In a surge of anger
I hid my face from you for a moment,
but with everlasting kindness
I will have compassion on you,"
says the LORD your Redeemer.

9 "To me this is like the days of Noah,
when I swore that the waters of Noah would never again cover the earth.
So now I have sworn not to be angry with you,
never to rebuke you again.
10 Though the mountains be shaken
and the hills be removed,
yet my unfailing love for you will not be shaken
nor my covenant of peace be removed,"
says the LORD, who has compassion on you.

11 "O afflicted city, lashed by storms and not comforted,
I will build you with stones of turquoise,[a]
your foundations with sapphires.[b]
12 I will make your battlements of rubies,
your gates of sparkling jewels,
and all your walls of precious stones.
13 All your sons will be taught by the LORD,
and great will be your children's peace.
14 In righteousness you will be established:
Tyranny will be far from you;
you will have nothing to fear.
Terror will be far removed;
it will not come near you.
15 If anyone does attack you, it will not be my doing;
whoever attacks you will surrender to you.

16 "See, it is I who created the blacksmith
who fans the coals into flame
and forges a weapon fit for its work.
And it is I who have created the destroyer to work havoc;
17 no weapon forged against you will prevail,
and you will refute every tongue that accuses you.
This is the heritage of the servants of the LORD,
and this is their vindication from me,"
declares the LORD.

[a] *11* The meaning of the Hebrew for this word is uncertain. [b] *11* Or *lapis lazuli*

PRAYER: AFFIRMATION

YOUR hands made me and fashioned me. (Psalm 119:73) . . . Before You formed me in the womb, You knew me; before I was born, You set me apart. (Jeremiah 1:5) . . . You know me, O Lord; You see me and test my thoughts about You. (Jeremiah 12:3)

***PAUSE** to reflect on these Biblical affirmations.*

NT Galatians 5:1–26

Freedom in Christ

5 It is for freedom that Christ has set us
free. Stand firm, then, and do not let
yourselves be burdened again by a yoke of
slavery.

2 Mark my words! I, Paul, tell you that if
you let yourselves be circumcised, Christ
will be of no value to you at all. 3 Again I
declare to every man who lets himself be
circumcised that he is obligated to obey
the whole law. 4 You who are trying to be
justified by law have been alienated from
Christ; you have fallen away from grace.
5 But by faith we eagerly await through the
Spirit the righteousness for which we
hope. 6 For in Christ Jesus neither circumcision nor uncircumcision has any value.
The only thing that counts is faith expressing itself through love.

7 You were running a good race. Who
cut in on you and kept you from obeying
the truth? 8 That kind of persuasion does
not come from the one who calls you. 9 "A
little yeast works through the whole batch
of dough." 10 I am confident in the Lord
that you will take no other view. The one
who is throwing you into confusion will
pay the penalty, whoever he may be.
11 Brothers, if I am still preaching circumcision, why am I still being persecuted? In
that case the offense of the cross has been
abolished. 12 As for those agitators, I wish
they would go the whole way and emasculate themselves!

13 You, my brothers, were called to be
free. But do not use your freedom to indulge the sinful nature[a]; rather, serve one
another in love. 14 The entire law is
summed up in a single command: "Love
your neighbor as yourself."[b] 15 If you keep
on biting and devouring each other,
watch out or you will be destroyed by
each other.

Life by the Spirit

16 So I say, live by the Spirit, and you will
not gratify the desires of the sinful nature.
17 For the sinful nature desires what is contrary to the Spirit, and the Spirit what is
contrary to the sinful nature. They are in
conflict with each other, so that you do
not do what you want. 18 But if you are led
by the Spirit, you are not under law.

19 The acts of the sinful nature are obvious: sexual immorality, impurity and debauchery; 20 idolatry and witchcraft; hatred, discord, jealousy, fits of rage, selfish
ambition, dissensions, factions 21 and
envy; drunkenness, orgies, and the like. I
warn you, as I did before, that those who
live like this will not inherit the kingdom
of God.

22 But the fruit of the Spirit is love, joy,
peace, patience, kindness, goodness, faithfulness, 23 gentleness and self-control.
Against such things there is no law.
24 Those who belong to Christ Jesus have
crucified the sinful nature with its passions and desires. 25 Since we live by the
Spirit, let us keep in step with the Spirit.
26 Let us not become conceited, provoking
and envying each other.

[a] *13* Or *the flesh;* also in verses 16, 17, 19 and 24
[b] *14* Lev. 19:18

PRAYER: MY RELATIONSHIP TO GOD

IF You, O Christ, are in me, my body is dead because of sin, yet my spirit is alive because of righteousness. And if the Spirit of Him who raised You, Jesus, from the dead is living in me,

He who raised You, Christ, from the dead will also give life to my mortal body through His Spirit, who lives in me.
(Romans 8:10–11)

***PAUSE** to thank God for the relationship that you enjoy with Him in Jesus Christ.*

YEAR 2
DAY 174

OT Isaiah 55:1–56:12

Invitation to the Thirsty

55 "Come, all you who are thirsty,
come to the waters;
and you who have no money,
come, buy and eat!
Come, buy wine and milk
without money and without cost.
2 Why spend money on what is not bread,
and your labor on what does not satisfy?
Listen, listen to me, and eat what is good,
and your soul will delight in the richest of fare.
3 Give ear and come to me;
hear me, that your soul may live.
I will make an everlasting covenant with you,
my faithful love promised to David.
4 See, I have made him a witness to the peoples,
a leader and commander of the peoples.
5 Surely you will summon nations you know not,
and nations that do not know you will hasten to you,
because of the LORD your God,
the Holy One of Israel,
for he has endowed you with splendor."

6 Seek the LORD while he may be found;
call on him while he is near.
7 Let the wicked forsake his way
and the evil man his thoughts.
Let him turn to the LORD, and he will have mercy on him,
and to our God, for he will freely pardon.

8 "For my thoughts are not your thoughts,
neither are your ways my ways,"
declares the LORD.
9 "As the heavens are higher than the earth,
so are my ways higher than your ways
and my thoughts than your thoughts.
10 As the rain and the snow
come down from heaven,
and do not return to it
without watering the earth
and making it bud and flourish,
so that it yields seed for the sower
and bread for the eater,
11 so is my word that goes out from my mouth:
It will not return to me empty,
but will accomplish what I desire
and achieve the purpose for which I sent it.
12 You will go out in joy
and be led forth in peace;
the mountains and hills
will burst into song before you,
and all the trees of the field
will clap their hands.
13 Instead of the thornbush will grow the pine tree,
and instead of briers the myrtle will grow.
This will be for the LORD's renown,
for an everlasting sign,
which will not be destroyed."

Salvation for Others

56 This is what the LORD says:

"Maintain justice
and do what is right,
for my salvation is close at hand
and my righteousness will soon be revealed.
2 Blessed is the man who does this,
the man who holds it fast,
who keeps the Sabbath without desecrating it,

and keeps his hand from doing any
evil."

3 Let no foreigner who has bound
himself to the LORD say,
"The LORD will surely exclude me
from his people."
And let not any eunuch complain,
"I am only a dry tree."

4 For this is what the LORD says:

"To the eunuchs who keep my
Sabbaths,
who choose what pleases me
and hold fast to my covenant—
5 to them I will give within my temple
and its walls
a memorial and a name
better than sons and daughters;
I will give them an everlasting name
that will not be cut off.
6 And foreigners who bind themselves
to the LORD
to serve him,
to love the name of the LORD,
and to worship him,
all who keep the Sabbath without
desecrating it
and who hold fast to my
covenant—
7 these I will bring to my holy
mountain
and give them joy in my house of
prayer.
Their burnt offerings and sacrifices
will be accepted on my altar;
for my house will be called
a house of prayer for all nations."
8 The Sovereign LORD declares—
he who gathers the exiles of Israel:
"I will gather still others to them
besides those already gathered."

God's Accusation Against the Wicked

9 Come, all you beasts of the field,
come and devour, all you beasts of
the forest!
10 Israel's watchmen are blind,
they all lack knowledge;
they are all mute dogs,
they cannot bark;
they lie around and dream,
they love to sleep.
11 They are dogs with mighty appetites;
they never have enough.
They are shepherds who lack
understanding;
they all turn to their own way,
each seeks his own gain.
12 "Come," each one cries, "let me get
wine!
Let us drink our fill of beer!
And tomorrow will be like today,
or even far better."

PRAYER: THANKSGIVING

YOU, O God, chose me in Christ, before the foundation of the world, to be holy and blameless in Your sight. In love You predestined me to be adopted as Your child through Jesus Christ, according to the good pleasure of Your will, to the praise of the glory of Your grace, which You bestowed upon me in the One You love. (Ephesians 1:4–6)

PAUSE *to offer your own expressions of thanksgiving.*

NT Galatians 6:1–18

Doing Good to All

6 Brothers, if someone is caught in a sin,
you who are spiritual should restore
him gently. But watch yourself, or you
also may be tempted. 2 Carry each other's
burdens, and in this way you will fulfill
the law of Christ. 3 If anyone thinks he is
something when he is nothing, he deceives himself. 4 Each one should test his
own actions. Then he can take pride in
himself, without comparing himself to
somebody else, 5 for each one should carry his own load.

6 Anyone who receives instruction in the
word must share all good things with his
instructor.

7 Do not be deceived: God cannot be
mocked. A man reaps what he sows. 8 The
one who sows to please his sinful nature,

from that nature[a] will reap destruction;
the one who sows to please the Spirit,
from the Spirit will reap eternal life. 9Let
us not become weary in doing good, for
at the proper time we will reap a harvest
if we do not give up. 10Therefore, as we
have opportunity, let us do good to all
people, especially to those who belong to
the family of believers.

Not Circumcision but a New Creation

11See what large letters I use as I write to
you with my own hand!
12Those who want to make a good im-
pression outwardly are trying to compel
you to be circumcised. The only reason
they do this is to avoid being persecuted
for the cross of Christ. 13Not even those
who are circumcised obey the law, yet
they want you to be circumcised that they
may boast about your flesh. 14May I never boast except in the cross of our Lord
Jesus Christ, through which[b] the world
has been crucified to me, and I to the
world. 15Neither circumcision nor uncircumcision means anything; what counts
is a new creation. 16Peace and mercy to all
who follow this rule, even to the Israel of
God.
17Finally, let no one cause me trouble,
for I bear on my body the marks of Jesus.
18The grace of our Lord Jesus Christ be
with your spirit, brothers. Amen.

[a] 8 Or *his flesh, from the flesh* [b] 14 Or *whom*

PRAYER: THE CHARACTER I WANT TO CULTIVATE

BLESSED are they who maintain justice, who do righteousness at all times. (Psalm 106:3) . . . Those who walk in uprightness fear You, Lord, but those who are devious in their ways despise You. (Proverbs 14:2)

TAKE *a moment to ask the Lord for the grace to grow in godly character.*

OT **Psalm 106** — YEAR 2 DAY 175

Psalm 106

1Praise the LORD.[a]

Give thanks to the LORD, for he is good;
his love endures forever.
2Who can proclaim the mighty acts of the LORD
or fully declare his praise?
3Blessed are they who maintain justice,
who constantly do what is right.
4Remember me, O LORD, when you show favor to your people,
come to my aid when you save them,
5that I may enjoy the prosperity of your chosen ones,
that I may share in the joy of your nation
and join your inheritance in giving praise.

6We have sinned, even as our fathers did;
we have done wrong and acted wickedly.
7When our fathers were in Egypt,
they gave no thought to your miracles;
they did not remember your many kindnesses,
and they rebelled by the sea, the Red Sea.[b]
8Yet he saved them for his name's sake,
to make his mighty power known.
9He rebuked the Red Sea, and it dried up;
he led them through the depths as through a desert.
10He saved them from the hand of the foe;
from the hand of the enemy he redeemed them.
11The waters covered their adversaries;
not one of them survived.

[a] 1 Hebrew *Hallelu Yah*; also in verse 48
[b] 7 Hebrew *Yam Suph*; that is, Sea of Reeds; also in verses 9 and 22

[12] Then they believed his promises
and sang his praise.

[13] But they soon forgot what he had done
and did not wait for his counsel.
[14] In the desert they gave in to their craving;
in the wasteland they put God to the test.
[15] So he gave them what they asked for,
but sent a wasting disease upon them.

[16] In the camp they grew envious of Moses
and of Aaron, who was consecrated to the LORD.
[17] The earth opened up and swallowed Dathan;
it buried the company of Abiram.
[18] Fire blazed among their followers;
a flame consumed the wicked.

[19] At Horeb they made a calf
and worshiped an idol cast from metal.
[20] They exchanged their Glory
for an image of a bull, which eats grass.
[21] They forgot the God who saved them,
who had done great things in Egypt,
[22] miracles in the land of Ham
and awesome deeds by the Red Sea.
[23] So he said he would destroy them—
had not Moses, his chosen one,
stood in the breach before him
to keep his wrath from destroying them.

[24] Then they despised the pleasant land;
they did not believe his promise.
[25] They grumbled in their tents
and did not obey the LORD.
[26] So he swore to them with uplifted hand
that he would make them fall in the desert,
[27] make their descendants fall among the nations
and scatter them throughout the lands.

[28] They yoked themselves to the Baal of Peor
and ate sacrifices offered to lifeless gods;
[29] they provoked the LORD to anger by their wicked deeds,
and a plague broke out among them.
[30] But Phinehas stood up and intervened,
and the plague was checked.
[31] This was credited to him as righteousness
for endless generations to come.

[32] By the waters of Meribah they angered the LORD,
and trouble came to Moses because of them;
[33] for they rebelled against the Spirit of God,
and rash words came from Moses' lips.[c]

[34] They did not destroy the peoples
as the LORD had commanded them,
[35] but they mingled with the nations
and adopted their customs.
[36] They worshiped their idols,
which became a snare to them.
[37] They sacrificed their sons
and their daughters to demons.
[38] They shed innocent blood,
the blood of their sons and daughters,
whom they sacrificed to the idols of Canaan,
and the land was desecrated by their blood.
[39] They defiled themselves by what they did;
by their deeds they prostituted themselves.

[40] Therefore the LORD was angry with his people
and abhorred his inheritance.
[41] He handed them over to the nations,
and their foes ruled over them.
[42] Their enemies oppressed them
and subjected them to their power.
[43] Many times he delivered them,
but they were bent on rebellion
and they wasted away in their sin.

[44] But he took note of their distress
when he heard their cry;
[45] for their sake he remembered his covenant
and out of his great love he relented.
[46] He caused them to be pitied
by all who held them captive.

[c] 33 Or *against his spirit, / and rash words came from his lips*

[47]Save us, O LORD our God,
and gather us from the nations,
that we may give thanks to your holy name
and glory in your praise.

[48]Praise be to the LORD, the God of Israel,
from everlasting to everlasting.
Let all the people say, "Amen!"

Praise the LORD.

PRAYER: ADORATION

O LORD of hosts, God of Israel, enthroned between the cherubim, You alone are God over all the kingdoms of the earth. You have made heaven and earth. (Isaiah 37:16) . . . Mighty One, God, the Lord, You have spoken and summoned the earth from the rising of the sun to the place where it sets. (Psalm 50:1)

***PAUSE** to express your thoughts of praise and worship.*

NT Ephesians 1:1–14

1 Paul, an apostle of Christ Jesus by the
will of God,

To the saints in Ephesus,[a] the faithful[b] in Christ Jesus:

[2]Grace and peace to you from God our Father and the Lord Jesus Christ.

Spiritual Blessings in Christ

[3]Praise be to the God and Father of our
Lord Jesus Christ, who has blessed us in
the heavenly realms with every spiritual
blessing in Christ. [4]For he chose us in him
before the creation of the world to be holy
and blameless in his sight. In love [5]he[c]
predestined us to be adopted as his sons
through Jesus Christ, in accordance with
his pleasure and will— [6]to the praise of
his glorious grace, which he has freely giv-
en us in the One he loves. [7]In him we
have redemption through his blood, the
forgiveness of sins, in accordance with the
riches of God's grace [8]that he lavished on
us with all wisdom and understanding.
[9]And he[d] made known to us the mystery
of his will according to his good pleasure,
which he purposed in Christ, [10]to be put
into effect when the times will have
reached their fulfillment—to bring all
things in heaven and on earth together
under one head, even Christ.
[11]In him we were also chosen,[e] having
been predestined according to the plan of
him who works out everything in conformity with the purpose of his will, [12]in order that we, who were the first to hope in
Christ, might be for the praise of his glory. [13]And you also were included in Christ
when you heard the word of truth, the
gospel of your salvation. Having believed,
you were marked in him with a seal, the
promised Holy Spirit, [14]who is a deposit
guaranteeing our inheritance until the redemption of those who are God's possession—to the praise of his glory.

[a] 1 Some early manuscripts do not have *in Ephesus.*
[b] 1 Or *believers who are*
[c] 4,5 Or *sight in love.* [5]*He*
[d] 8,9 Or *us. With all wisdom and understanding,* [9]*he*
[e] 11 Or *were made heirs*

PRAYER: MY RELATIONSHIP TO OTHERS

YOU have called us to go and make disciples of all nations, baptizing them in the name of the Father and of You, the Son, and of the Holy Spirit, teaching them to observe everything You have commanded us. And surely You are with us always, even to the end of the age. (Matthew 28:19–20)

***PAUSE** to review your relationships with others and to commit them to the Lord.*

YEAR 2 DAY 176

OT Isaiah 57:1-21

57 The righteous perish,
and no one ponders it in his heart;
devout men are taken away,
and no one understands
that the righteous are taken away
to be spared from evil.
2 Those who walk uprightly
enter into peace;
they find rest as they lie in death.

3 "But you—come here, you sons of a sorceress,
you offspring of adulterers and prostitutes!
4 Whom are you mocking?
At whom do you sneer
and stick out your tongue?
Are you not a brood of rebels,
the offspring of liars?
5 You burn with lust among the oaks
and under every spreading tree;
you sacrifice your children in the ravines
and under the overhanging crags.
6 ⌊The idols⌋ among the smooth stones
of the ravines are your portion;
they, they are your lot.
Yes, to them you have poured out drink offerings
and offered grain offerings.
In the light of these things, should I relent?
7 You have made your bed on a high and lofty hill;
there you went up to offer your sacrifices.
8 Behind your doors and your doorposts
you have put your pagan symbols.
Forsaking me, you uncovered your bed,
you climbed into it and opened it wide;
you made a pact with those whose beds you love,
and you looked on their nakedness.
9 You went to Molech[a] with olive oil
and increased your perfumes.
You sent your ambassadors[b] far away;
you descended to the grave[c] itself!
10 You were wearied by all your ways,
but you would not say, 'It is hopeless.'
You found renewal of your strength,
and so you did not faint.

11 "Whom have you so dreaded and feared
that you have been false to me,
and have neither remembered me
nor pondered this in your hearts?
Is it not because I have long been silent
that you do not fear me?
12 I will expose your righteousness and your works,
and they will not benefit you.
13 When you cry out for help,
let your collection ⌊of idols⌋ save you!
The wind will carry all of them off,
a mere breath will blow them away.
But the man who makes me his refuge
will inherit the land
and possess my holy mountain."

Comfort for the Contrite

14 And it will be said:

"Build up, build up, prepare the road!
Remove the obstacles out of the way of my people."
15 For this is what the high and lofty One says—
he who lives forever, whose name is holy:
"I live in a high and holy place,
but also with him who is contrite and lowly in spirit,
to revive the spirit of the lowly
and to revive the heart of the contrite.
16 I will not accuse forever,
nor will I always be angry,
for then the spirit of man would grow faint before me—
the breath of man that I have created.
17 I was enraged by his sinful greed;
I punished him, and hid my face in anger,
yet he kept on in his willful ways.
18 I have seen his ways, but I will heal him;
I will guide him and restore comfort to him,

[a] 9 Or *to the king* [b] 9 Or *idols* [c] 9 Hebrew *Sheol*

[19] creating praise on the lips of the
mourners in Israel.
Peace, peace, to those far and near,"
says the LORD. "And I will heal
them."
[20] But the wicked are like the tossing sea,
which cannot rest,
whose waves cast up mire and mud.
[21] "There is no peace," says my God, "for
the wicked."

PRAYER: CONFESSION

O GOD, there is no one on earth who continually does good and never sins. (Ecclesiastes 7:20)

***ASK** the Spirit to search your heart and reveal any areas of unconfessed sin. Acknowledge these to the Lord and thank Him for His forgiveness.*

NT Ephesians 1:15–2:10

Thanksgiving and Prayer

[15] For this reason, ever since I heard
about your faith in the Lord Jesus and
your love for all the saints, [16] I have not
stopped giving thanks for you, remembering you in my prayers. [17] I keep asking
that the God of our Lord Jesus Christ, the
glorious Father, may give you the Spirit[a]
of wisdom and revelation, so that you
may know him better. [18] I pray also that
the eyes of your heart may be enlightened in order that you may know the
hope to which he has called you, the
riches of his glorious inheritance in the
saints, [19] and his incomparably great
power for us who believe. That power is
like the working of his mighty strength,
[20] which he exerted in Christ when he
raised him from the dead and seated him
at his right hand in the heavenly realms,
[21] far above all rule and authority, power
and dominion, and every title that can be
given, not only in the present age but
also in the one to come. [22] And God
placed all things under his feet and appointed him to be head over everything
for the church, [23] which is his body, the
fullness of him who fills everything in
every way.

Made Alive in Christ

2 As for you, you were dead in your transgressions and sins, [2] in which you used
to live when you followed the ways of this
world and of the ruler of the kingdom of
the air, the spirit who is now at work in
those who are disobedient. [3] All of us also
lived among them at one time, gratifying
the cravings of our sinful nature[b] and following its desires and thoughts. Like the
rest, we were by nature objects of wrath.
[4] But because of his great love for us, God,
who is rich in mercy, [5] made us alive with
Christ even when we were dead in transgressions—it is by grace you have been
saved. [6] And God raised us up with Christ
and seated us with him in the heavenly
realms in Christ Jesus, [7] in order that in the
coming ages he might show the incomparable riches of his grace, expressed in
his kindness to us in Christ Jesus. [8] For it
is by grace you have been saved, through
faith—and this not from yourselves, it is
the gift of God— [9] not by works, so that
no one can boast. [10] For we are God's
workmanship, created in Christ Jesus to
do good works, which God prepared in
advance for us to do.

[a] 17 Or *a spirit* [b] 3 Or *our flesh*

PRAYER: THE ATTRIBUTES OF GOD

YOU are the Lord; You do not change. (Malachi 3:6) . . . Lord Jesus Christ, You are the same yesterday, today, and forever. (Hebrews 13:8)

***PAUSE** to reflect on these affirmations about the person, powers and perfection of God.*

OT **Isaiah 58:1-14**

YEAR 2
DAY 177

True Fasting

58 "Shout it aloud, do not hold back.
Raise your voice like a trumpet.
Declare to my people their rebellion
and to the house of Jacob their sins.
2 For day after day they seek me out;
they seem eager to know my ways,
as if they were a nation that does what is right
and has not forsaken the commands of its God.
They ask me for just decisions
and seem eager for God to come near them.
3 'Why have we fasted,' they say,
'and you have not seen it?
Why have we humbled ourselves,
and you have not noticed?'

"Yet on the day of your fasting, you do as you please
and exploit all your workers.
4 Your fasting ends in quarreling and strife,
and in striking each other with wicked fists.
You cannot fast as you do today
and expect your voice to be heard on high.
5 Is this the kind of fast I have chosen,
only a day for a man to humble himself?
Is it only for bowing one's head like a reed
and for lying on sackcloth and ashes?
Is that what you call a fast,
a day acceptable to the LORD?

6 "Is not this the kind of fasting I have chosen:
to loose the chains of injustice
and untie the cords of the yoke,
to set the oppressed free
and break every yoke?
7 Is it not to share your food with the hungry
and to provide the poor wanderer with shelter—
when you see the naked, to clothe him,
and not to turn away from your own flesh and blood?
8 Then your light will break forth like the dawn,
and your healing will quickly appear;
then your righteousness[a] will go before you,
and the glory of the LORD will be your rear guard.
9 Then you will call, and the LORD will answer;
you will cry for help, and he will say: Here am I.

"If you do away with the yoke of oppression,
with the pointing finger and malicious talk,
10 and if you spend yourselves in behalf of the hungry
and satisfy the needs of the oppressed,
then your light will rise in the darkness,
and your night will become like the noonday.
11 The LORD will guide you always;
he will satisfy your needs in a sun-scorched land
and will strengthen your frame.
You will be like a well-watered garden,
like a spring whose waters never fail.
12 Your people will rebuild the ancient ruins
and will raise up the age-old foundations;
you will be called Repairer of Broken Walls,
Restorer of Streets with Dwellings.

13 "If you keep your feet from breaking the Sabbath
and from doing as you please on my holy day,
if you call the Sabbath a delight
and the LORD's holy day honorable,
and if you honor it by not going your own way
and not doing as you please or speaking idle words,
14 then you will find your joy in the LORD,
and I will cause you to ride on the heights of the land
and to feast on the inheritance of your father Jacob."
The mouth of the LORD has spoken.

[a] 8 Or *your righteous One*

PRAYER: RENEWAL

WHATEVER I do, whether in word or in deed, may I do all in Your name, Lord Jesus, giving thanks to God the Father through You. (Colossians 3:17) . . . May I abide in You, O Christ, so that when You appear, I will have confidence and not be ashamed before You at Your coming. (1 John 2:28)

PAUSE *to add your own prayers for personal renewal.*

NT Ephesians 2:11-22

One in Christ

[11]Therefore, remember that formerly
you who are Gentiles by birth and called
"uncircumcised" by those who call themselves "the circumcision" (that done in
the body by the hands of men)— [12]re-
member that at that time you were separate from Christ, excluded from citizenship in Israel and foreigners to the
covenants of the promise, without hope
and without God in the world. [13]But now
in Christ Jesus you who once were far
away have been brought near through the
blood of Christ.
[14]For he himself is our peace, who has
made the two one and has destroyed the
barrier, the dividing wall of hostility, [15]by
abolishing in his flesh the law with its
commandments and regulations. His purpose was to create in himself one new
man out of the two, thus making peace,
[16]and in this one body to reconcile both
of them to God through the cross, by
which he put to death their hostility. [17]He
came and preached peace to you who
were far away and peace to those who
were near. [18]For through him we both
have access to the Father by one Spirit.
[19]Consequently, you are no longer foreigners and aliens, but fellow citizens
with God's people and members of God's
household, [20]built on the foundation of
the apostles and prophets, with Christ
Jesus himself as the chief cornerstone. [21]In
him the whole building is joined together and rises to become a holy temple in
the Lord. [22]And in him you too are being
built together to become a dwelling in
which God lives by his Spirit.

PRAYER: THE WORKS OF GOD

WAS it not You who dried up the sea, the waters of the great deep; who made the depths of the sea a road so that the redeemed might cross over? (Isaiah 51:10) . . . Lord, I have heard of Your fame, and I stand in awe of Your deeds. O Lord, revive Your work in the midst of the years, in our time make them known; in wrath remember mercy. (Habakkuk 3:2)

TAKE *a moment to consider the greatness of God's wonderful works.*

YEAR 2
DAY 178

OT Isaiah 59:1-21

Sin, Confession and Redemption

59 Surely the arm of the LORD is not
too short to save,
nor his ear too dull to hear.
[2]But your iniquities have separated
you from your God;
your sins have hidden his face from
you,
so that he will not hear.
[3]For your hands are stained with
blood,

your fingers with guilt.
Your lips have spoken lies,
and your tongue mutters wicked things.
4 No one calls for justice;
no one pleads his case with integrity.
They rely on empty arguments and speak lies;
they conceive trouble and give birth to evil.
5 They hatch the eggs of vipers
and spin a spider's web.
Whoever eats their eggs will die,
and when one is broken, an adder is hatched.
6 Their cobwebs are useless for clothing;
they cannot cover themselves with what they make.
Their deeds are evil deeds,
and acts of violence are in their hands.
7 Their feet rush into sin;
they are swift to shed innocent blood.
Their thoughts are evil thoughts;
ruin and destruction mark their ways.
8 The way of peace they do not know;
there is no justice in their paths.
They have turned them into crooked roads;
no one who walks in them will know peace.

9 So justice is far from us,
and righteousness does not reach us.
We look for light, but all is darkness;
for brightness, but we walk in deep shadows.
10 Like the blind we grope along the wall,
feeling our way like men without eyes.
At midday we stumble as if it were twilight;
among the strong, we are like the dead.
11 We all growl like bears;
we moan mournfully like doves.
We look for justice, but find none;
for deliverance, but it is far away.

12 For our offenses are many in your sight,
and our sins testify against us.
Our offenses are ever with us,
and we acknowledge our iniquities:
13 rebellion and treachery against the LORD,
turning our backs on our God,
fomenting oppression and revolt,
uttering lies our hearts have conceived.
14 So justice is driven back,
and righteousness stands at a distance;
truth has stumbled in the streets,
honesty cannot enter.
15 Truth is nowhere to be found,
and whoever shuns evil becomes a prey.

The LORD looked and was displeased
that there was no justice.
16 He saw that there was no one,
he was appalled that there was no one to intervene;
so his own arm worked salvation for him,
and his own righteousness sustained him.
17 He put on righteousness as his breastplate,
and the helmet of salvation on his head;
he put on the garments of vengeance
and wrapped himself in zeal as in a cloak.
18 According to what they have done,
so will he repay
wrath to his enemies
and retribution to his foes;
he will repay the islands their due.
19 From the west, men will fear the name of the LORD,
and from the rising of the sun, they will revere his glory.
For he will come like a pent-up flood
that the breath of the LORD drives along.[a]

20 "The Redeemer will come to Zion,
to those in Jacob who repent of their sins,"
declares the LORD.

21 "As for me, this is my covenant with
them," says the LORD. "My Spirit, who is on
you, and my words that I have put in your
mouth will not depart from your mouth,
or from the mouths of your children, or
from the mouths of their descendants from
this time on and forever," says the LORD.

[a] 19 Or *When the enemy comes in like a flood, / the Spirit of the LORD will put him to flight*

PRAYER: PETITION

WHEN I am afraid, I will trust in You, O God, whose word I praise. In You I have put my trust. I will not fear; what can mortals do to me? (Psalm 56:3–4)

***PAUSE** here to petition God for growth in your desire to know and please Jesus Christ. Pray for a greater love and commitment to Him, for the grace to practice His presence and for the grace to glorify Him in your life. Offer prayers regarding your activities for this day and any special concerns you may have.*

NT Ephesians 3:1–13

Paul the Preacher to the Gentiles

3 For this reason I, Paul, the prisoner of
Christ Jesus for the sake of you Gentiles—
[2]Surely you have heard about the administration of God's grace that was given
to me for you, [3]that is, the mystery made
known to me by revelation, as I have already written briefly. [4]In reading this, then,
you will be able to understand my insight
into the mystery of Christ, [5]which was not
made known to men in other generations
as it has now been revealed by the Spirit
to God's holy apostles and prophets. [6]This
mystery is that through the gospel the
Gentiles are heirs together with Israel,
members together of one body, and sharers together in the promise in Christ Jesus.
[7]I became a servant of this gospel by the
gift of God's grace given me through the
working of his power. [8]Although I am less
than the least of all God's people, this
grace was given me: to preach to the Gentiles the unsearchable riches of Christ,
[9]and to make plain to everyone the administration of this mystery, which for
ages past was kept hidden in God, who
created all things. [10]His intent was that
now, through the church, the manifold
wisdom of God should be made known
to the rulers and authorities in the heavenly realms, [11]according to his eternal purpose which he accomplished in Christ
Jesus our Lord. [12]In him and through faith
in him we may approach God with freedom and confidence. [13]I ask you, therefore, not to be discouraged because of my
sufferings for you, which are your glory.

PRAYER: MY RELATIONSHIP TO GOD

I HAVE been sanctified in You, Christ Jesus, and called to be a saint, together with all those everywhere who call on Your name, O Lord Jesus Christ—their Lord and mine. (1 Corinthians 1:2) . . . We do not live for ourselves alone, nor do we die for ourselves alone. If we live, we live to You, Lord; and if we die, we die to You, Lord. So, whether we live or die, we belong to You, Lord. (Romans 14:7–8)

***PAUSE** to thank God for the relationship that you enjoy with Him in Jesus Christ.*

YEAR 2
DAY 179

OT Isaiah 60:1–22

The Glory of Zion

60 "Arise, shine, for your light has come,
and the glory of the LORD rises
upon you.
[2]See, darkness covers the earth
and thick darkness is over the
peoples,
but the LORD rises upon you

and his glory appears over you.
[3] Nations will come to your light,
and kings to the brightness of your dawn.

[4] "Lift up your eyes and look about you:
All assemble and come to you;
your sons come from afar,
and your daughters are carried on the arm.
[5] Then you will look and be radiant,
your heart will throb and swell with joy;
the wealth on the seas will be brought to you,
to you the riches of the nations will come.
[6] Herds of camels will cover your land,
young camels of Midian and Ephah.
And all from Sheba will come,
bearing gold and incense
and proclaiming the praise of the LORD.
[7] All Kedar's flocks will be gathered to you,
the rams of Nebaioth will serve you;
they will be accepted as offerings on my altar,
and I will adorn my glorious temple.

[8] "Who are these that fly along like clouds,
like doves to their nests?
[9] Surely the islands look to me;
in the lead are the ships of Tarshish,[a]
bringing your sons from afar,
with their silver and gold,
to the honor of the LORD your God,
the Holy One of Israel,
for he has endowed you with splendor.

[10] "Foreigners will rebuild your walls,
and their kings will serve you.
Though in anger I struck you,
in favor I will show you compassion.
[11] Your gates will always stand open,
they will never be shut, day or night,
so that men may bring you the wealth of the nations—
their kings led in triumphal procession.
[12] For the nation or kingdom that will not serve you will perish;
it will be utterly ruined.

[13] "The glory of Lebanon will come to you,
the pine, the fir and the cypress together,
to adorn the place of my sanctuary;
and I will glorify the place of my feet.
[14] The sons of your oppressors will come bowing before you;
all who despise you will bow down at your feet
and will call you the City of the LORD,
Zion of the Holy One of Israel.

[15] "Although you have been forsaken and hated,
with no one traveling through,
I will make you the everlasting pride
and the joy of all generations.
[16] You will drink the milk of nations
and be nursed at royal breasts.
Then you will know that I, the LORD, am your Savior,
your Redeemer, the Mighty One of Jacob.
[17] Instead of bronze I will bring you gold,
and silver in place of iron.
Instead of wood I will bring you bronze,
and iron in place of stones.
I will make peace your governor
and righteousness your ruler.
[18] No longer will violence be heard in your land,
nor ruin or destruction within your borders,
but you will call your walls Salvation
and your gates Praise.
[19] The sun will no more be your light by day,
nor will the brightness of the moon shine on you,
for the LORD will be your everlasting light,
and your God will be your glory.
[20] Your sun will never set again,
and your moon will wane no more;
the LORD will be your everlasting light,
and your days of sorrow will end.
[21] Then will all your people be righteous

[a] 9 Or *the trading ships*

and they will possess the land
forever.
They are the shoot I have planted,
the work of my hands,
for the display of my splendor.
[22]The least of you will become a
thousand,
the smallest a mighty nation.
I am the LORD;
in its time I will do this swiftly."

PRAYER: INTERCESSION

THERE is neither Jew nor Greek, there is neither slave nor free, there is neither male nor female, for we are all one in You, Christ Jesus. (Galatians 3:28)

***TAKE** a few moments to intercede on behalf of your local church, other churches, evangelism and discipleship ministries, educational ministries and any other special concerns you may have.*

NT Ephesians 3:14–4:16

A Prayer for the Ephesians

[14]For this reason I kneel before the Father,
[15]from whom his whole family[a] in
heaven and on earth derives its name. [16]I
pray that out of his glorious riches he may
strengthen you with power through his
Spirit in your inner being, [17]so that Christ
may dwell in your hearts through faith.
And I pray that you, being rooted and established in love,
[18]may have power, together with all the saints, to grasp how wide
and long and high and deep is the love of
Christ, [19]and to know this love that surpasses knowledge—that you may be filled
to the measure of all the fullness of God.
[20]Now to him who is able to do immeasurably more than all we ask or imagine, according to his power that is at work
within us, [21]to him be glory in the church
and in Christ Jesus throughout all generations, for ever and ever! Amen.

Unity in the Body of Christ

4 As a prisoner for the Lord, then, I urge
you to live a life worthy of the calling
you have received. [2]Be completely humble
and gentle; be patient, bearing with one
another in love. [3]Make every effort to keep
the unity of the Spirit through the bond of
peace. [4]There is one body and one Spirit—
just as you were called to one hope when
you were called— [5]one Lord, one faith,
one baptism; [6]one God and Father of all,
who is over all and through all and in all.

[7]But to each one of us grace has been
given as Christ apportioned it. [8]This is
why it[b] says:

"When he ascended on high,
he led captives in his train
and gave gifts to men."[c]

[9](What does "he ascended" mean except
that he also descended to the lower, earthly regions[d]?
[10]He who descended is the very
one who ascended higher than all the heavens, in order to fill the whole universe.)
[11]It
was he who gave some to be apostles, some
to be prophets, some to be evangelists, and
some to be pastors and teachers, [12]to prepare God's people for works of service, so
that the body of Christ may be built up
[13]until we all reach unity in the faith and in
the knowledge of the Son of God and become mature, attaining to the whole measure of the fullness of Christ.
[14]Then we will no longer be infants,
tossed back and forth by the waves, and
blown here and there by every wind of
teaching and by the cunning and craftiness
of men in their deceitful scheming. [15]Instead, speaking the truth in love, we will in
all things grow up into him who is the
Head, that is, Christ. [16]From him the whole
body, joined and held together by every
supporting ligament, grows and builds itself up in love, as each part does its work.

[a] 15 Or *whom all fatherhood* [b] 8 Or God
[c] 8 Psalm 68:18 [d] 9 Or *the depths of the earth*

PRAYER: THE CHARACTER I WANT TO CULTIVATE

I WILL keep Your feast, O Christ my Passover, not with old leaven, or with the leaven of malice and wickedness, but with the unleavened bread of sincerity and truth. (1 Corinthians 5:8) . . . I desire to have a clear conscience and to live honorably in all things. (Hebrews 13:18)

__TAKE__ a moment to ask the Lord for the grace to grow in godly character.

YEAR 2
DAY 180

OT Isaiah 61:1–11

The Year of the LORD's Favor

61 The Spirit of the Sovereign LORD is on me,
because the LORD has anointed me
to preach good news to the poor.
He has sent me to bind up the brokenhearted,
to proclaim freedom for the captives
and release from darkness for the prisoners,[a]
2 to proclaim the year of the LORD's favor
and the day of vengeance of our God,
to comfort all who mourn,
3 and provide for those who grieve in Zion—
to bestow on them a crown of beauty
instead of ashes,
the oil of gladness
instead of mourning,
and a garment of praise
instead of a spirit of despair.
They will be called oaks of righteousness,
a planting of the LORD
for the display of his splendor.

4 They will rebuild the ancient ruins
and restore the places long devastated;
they will renew the ruined cities
that have been devastated for generations.
5 Aliens will shepherd your flocks;
foreigners will work your fields and vineyards.
6 And you will be called priests of the LORD,
you will be named ministers of our God.
You will feed on the wealth of nations,
and in their riches you will boast.

7 Instead of their shame
my people will receive a double portion,
and instead of disgrace
they will rejoice in their inheritance;
and so they will inherit a double portion in their land,
and everlasting joy will be theirs.

8 "For I, the LORD, love justice;
I hate robbery and iniquity.
In my faithfulness I will reward them
and make an everlasting covenant with them.
9 Their descendants will be known among the nations
and their offspring among the peoples.
All who see them will acknowledge
that they are a people the LORD has blessed."

10 I delight greatly in the LORD;
my soul rejoices in my God.
For he has clothed me with garments of salvation
and arrayed me in a robe of righteousness,
as a bridegroom adorns his head like a priest,
and as a bride adorns herself with her jewels.
11 For as the soil makes the sprout come up
and a garden causes seeds to grow,
so the Sovereign LORD will make righteousness and praise
spring up before all nations.

[a] *1* Hebrew; Septuagint *the blind*

PRAYER: AFFIRMATION

THOSE who love their father or mother more than You are not worthy of You; those who love their son or daughter more than You are not worthy of You. Those who do not take up the cross and follow after You are not worthy of You. Those who find their life will lose it, and those who lose their life for Your sake will find it. (Matthew 10:37–39)

PAUSE *to reflect on these Biblical affirmations.*

NT Ephesians 4:17-32

Living as Children of Light

17So I tell you this, and insist on it in
the Lord, that you must no longer live as
the Gentiles do, in the futility of their
thinking. 18They are darkened in their understanding and separated from the life of
God because of the ignorance that is in
them due to the hardening of their hearts.
19Having lost all sensitivity, they have giv-
en themselves over to sensuality so as to
indulge in every kind of impurity, with a
continual lust for more.

20You, however, did not come to know
Christ that way. 21Surely you heard of him
and were taught in him in accordance
with the truth that is in Jesus. 22You were
taught, with regard to your former way of
life, to put off your old self, which is being corrupted by its deceitful desires; 23to
be made new in the attitude of your
minds; 24and to put on the new self, created to be like God in true righteousness
and holiness.

25Therefore each of you must put off
falsehood and speak truthfully to his
neighbor, for we are all members of one
body. 26"In your anger do not sin"[a]: Do
not let the sun go down while you are still
angry, 27and do not give the devil a
foothold. 28He who has been stealing
must steal no longer, but must work, doing something useful with his own hands,
that he may have something to share with
those in need.

29Do not let any unwholesome talk
come out of your mouths, but only what
is helpful for building others up according to their needs, that it may benefit
those who listen. 30And do not grieve the
Holy Spirit of God, with whom you were
sealed for the day of redemption. 31Get rid
of all bitterness, rage and anger, brawling
and slander, along with every form of
malice. 32Be kind and compassionate to
one another, forgiving each other, just as
in Christ God forgave you.

[a] *26* Psalm 4:4

PRAYER: MY RELATIONSHIP TO OTHERS

MAY I learn the importance of forgiveness from You, Lord Jesus, who were asked by Peter: "Lord, how often shall my brother sin against me, and I forgive him? Up to seven times?" You said to him, "I tell you, not seven times, but up to seventy times seven." (Matthew 18:21–22) . . . I will love my enemies, do good to them, and lend to them, expecting nothing in return. Then my reward will be great, and I will be Your child, O Most High; for You are kind to the ungrateful and evil. I will be merciful just as You, Father, are merciful. (Luke 6:35–36)

PAUSE *to review your relationships with others and to commit them to the Lord.*

YEAR 2 DAY 181

OT Isaiah 62:1-12

Zion's New Name

62 For Zion's sake I will not keep silent,
for Jerusalem's sake I will not remain quiet,
till her righteousness shines out like the dawn,
her salvation like a blazing torch.
2 The nations will see your righteousness,
and all kings your glory;
you will be called by a new name
that the mouth of the LORD will bestow.
3 You will be a crown of splendor in the LORD's hand,
a royal diadem in the hand of your God.
4 No longer will they call you Deserted,
or name your land Desolate.
But you will be called Hephzibah,[a]
and your land Beulah[b];
for the LORD will take delight in you,
and your land will be married.
5 As a young man marries a maiden,
so will your sons[c] marry you;
as a bridegroom rejoices over his bride,
so will your God rejoice over you.

6 I have posted watchmen on your walls, O Jerusalem;
they will never be silent day or night.
You who call on the LORD,
give yourselves no rest,
7 and give him no rest till he establishes Jerusalem
and makes her the praise of the earth.

8 The LORD has sworn by his right hand
and by his mighty arm:
"Never again will I give your grain
as food for your enemies,
and never again will foreigners drink the new wine
for which you have toiled;
9 but those who harvest it will eat it
and praise the LORD,
and those who gather the grapes will drink it
in the courts of my sanctuary."

10 Pass through, pass through the gates!
Prepare the way for the people.
Build up, build up the highway!
Remove the stones.
Raise a banner for the nations.

11 The LORD has made proclamation
to the ends of the earth:
"Say to the Daughter of Zion,
'See, your Savior comes!
See, his reward is with him,
and his recompense accompanies him.' "
12 They will be called the Holy People,
the Redeemed of the LORD;
and you will be called Sought After,
the City No Longer Deserted.

[a] 4 *Hephzibah* means *my delight is in her.*
[b] 4 *Beulah* means *married.* [c] 5 Or *Builder*

PRAYER: THANKSGIVING

O GOD, in Christ I have redemption through His blood, the forgiveness of sins, in accordance with the riches of Your grace, which You lavished on me with all wisdom and understanding. (Ephesians 1:7–8)

***PAUSE** to offer your own expressions of thanksgiving.*

NT Ephesians 5:1-21

5 Be imitators of God, therefore, as dearly loved children 2 and live a life of love,
just as Christ loved us and gave himself
up for us as a fragrant offering and sacrifice to God.

3 But among you there must not be even
a hint of sexual immorality, or of any kind
of impurity, or of greed, because these are
improper for God's holy people. 4 Nor
should there be obscenity, foolish talk or

coarse joking, which are out of place, but
rather thanksgiving. [5]For of this you can
be sure: No immoral, impure or greedy
person—such a man is an idolater—has
any inheritance in the kingdom of Christ
and of God.[a] [6]Let no one deceive you with
empty words, for because of such things
God's wrath comes on those who are disobedient. [7]Therefore do not be partners
with them.

[8]For you were once darkness, but now
you are light in the Lord. Live as children
of light [9](for the fruit of the light consists
in all goodness, righteousness and truth)
[10]and find out what pleases the Lord.
[11]Have nothing to do with the fruitless
deeds of darkness, but rather expose
them. [12]For it is shameful even to mention
what the disobedient do in secret. [13]But
everything exposed by the light becomes
visible, [14]for it is light that makes everything visible. This is why it is said:

"Wake up, O sleeper,
rise from the dead,
and Christ will shine on you."

[15]Be very careful, then, how you live—
not as unwise but as wise, [16]making the
most of every opportunity, because the
days are evil. [17]Therefore do not be foolish, but understand what the Lord's will
is. [18]Do not get drunk on wine, which
leads to debauchery. Instead, be filled
with the Spirit. [19]Speak to one another
with psalms, hymns and spiritual songs.
Sing and make music in your heart to the
Lord, [20]always giving thanks to God the
Father for everything, in the name of our
Lord Jesus Christ.

[21]Submit to one another out of reverence for Christ.

[a] 5 Or *kingdom of the Christ and God*

PRAYER: THE ATTRIBUTES OF GOD

JESUS of Nazareth, the son of Joseph, You are the Messiah (that is, the Christ). You are the One Moses wrote about in the Law, and about whom the prophets also wrote. (John 1:41, 45) . . . It is easier for heaven and earth to disappear than for a stroke of a letter of Your law to fail, O God. (Luke 16:17)

PAUSE to reflect on these affirmations about the person, powers and perfection of God.

OT Psalm 107 — YEAR 2 DAY 182

Psalm 107

[1]Give thanks to the LORD, for he is
good;
his love endures forever.
[2]Let the redeemed of the LORD say
this—
those he redeemed from the hand
of the foe,
[3]those he gathered from the lands,
from east and west, from north and
south.[a]

[4]Some wandered in desert wastelands,
finding no way to a city where they
could settle.
[5]They were hungry and thirsty,
and their lives ebbed away.
[6]Then they cried out to the LORD in
their trouble,
and he delivered them from their
distress.
[7]He led them by a straight way
to a city where they could settle.
[8]Let them give thanks to the LORD for
his unfailing love
and his wonderful deeds for men,
[9]for he satisfies the thirsty
and fills the hungry with good
things.

[10]Some sat in darkness and the deepest
gloom,

[a] 3 Hebrew *north and the sea*

prisoners suffering in iron chains,
11 for they had rebelled against the words of God
and despised the counsel of the Most High.
12 So he subjected them to bitter labor;
they stumbled, and there was no one to help.
13 Then they cried to the LORD in their trouble,
and he saved them from their distress.
14 He brought them out of darkness and the deepest gloom
and broke away their chains.
15 Let them give thanks to the LORD for his unfailing love
and his wonderful deeds for men,
16 for he breaks down gates of bronze
and cuts through bars of iron.

17 Some became fools through their rebellious ways
and suffered affliction because of their iniquities.
18 They loathed all food
and drew near the gates of death.
19 Then they cried to the LORD in their trouble,
and he saved them from their distress.
20 He sent forth his word and healed them;
he rescued them from the grave.
21 Let them give thanks to the LORD for his unfailing love
and his wonderful deeds for men.
22 Let them sacrifice thank offerings
and tell of his works with songs of joy.

23 Others went out on the sea in ships;
they were merchants on the mighty waters.
24 They saw the works of the LORD,
his wonderful deeds in the deep.
25 For he spoke and stirred up a tempest
that lifted high the waves.
26 They mounted up to the heavens and went down to the depths;
in their peril their courage melted away.
27 They reeled and staggered like drunken men;
they were at their wits' end.
28 Then they cried out to the LORD in their trouble,
and he brought them out of their distress.
29 He stilled the storm to a whisper;
the waves of the sea were hushed.
30 They were glad when it grew calm,
and he guided them to their desired haven.
31 Let them give thanks to the LORD for his unfailing love
and his wonderful deeds for men.
32 Let them exalt him in the assembly of the people
and praise him in the council of the elders.

33 He turned rivers into a desert,
flowing springs into thirsty ground,
34 and fruitful land into a salt waste,
because of the wickedness of those who lived there.
35 He turned the desert into pools of water
and the parched ground into flowing springs;
36 there he brought the hungry to live,
and they founded a city where they could settle.
37 They sowed fields and planted vineyards
that yielded a fruitful harvest;
38 he blessed them, and their numbers greatly increased,
and he did not let their herds diminish.

39 Then their numbers decreased, and they were humbled
by oppression, calamity and sorrow;
40 he who pours contempt on nobles
made them wander in a trackless waste.
41 But he lifted the needy out of their affliction
and increased their families like flocks.
42 The upright see and rejoice,
but all the wicked shut their mouths.

43 Whoever is wise, let him heed these things
and consider the great love of the LORD.

PRAYER: ADORATION

WHOEVER is wise will consider Your loving-kindness, O Lord. (Psalm 107:43) . . . The sum of Your words is truth, and all of Your righteous judgments are eternal. (Psalm 119:160)

***PAUSE** to express your thoughts of praise and worship.*

NT Ephesians 5:22–6:9

Wives and Husbands

22Wives, submit to your husbands as to
the Lord. 23For the husband is the head of
the wife as Christ is the head of the
church, his body, of which he is the Savior. 24Now as the church submits to
Christ, so also wives should submit to
their husbands in everything.
25Husbands, love your wives, just as
Christ loved the church and gave himself
up for her 26to make her holy, cleansing[a]
her by the washing with water through the
word, 27and to present her to himself as a
radiant church, without stain or wrinkle
or any other blemish, but holy and
blameless. 28In this same way, husbands
ought to love their wives as their own
bodies. He who loves his wife loves himself. 29After all, no one ever hated his own
body, but he feeds and cares for it, just as
Christ does the church— 30for we are
members of his body. 31"For this reason a
man will leave his father and mother and
be united to his wife, and the two will become one flesh."[b] 32This is a profound
mystery—but I am talking about Christ
and the church. 33However, each one of
you also must love his wife as he loves
himself, and the wife must respect her
husband.

Children and Parents

6 Children, obey your parents in the
Lord, for this is right. 2"Honor your father and mother"—which is the first commandment with a promise— 3"that it may
go well with you and that you may enjoy
long life on the earth."[c]
4Fathers, do not exasperate your children; instead, bring them up in the training and instruction of the Lord.

Slaves and Masters

5Slaves, obey your earthly masters with
respect and fear, and with sincerity of
heart, just as you would obey Christ.
6Obey them not only to win their favor
when their eye is on you, but like slaves
of Christ, doing the will of God from your
heart. 7Serve wholeheartedly, as if you
were serving the Lord, not men, 8because
you know that the Lord will reward everyone for whatever good he does, whether
he is slave or free.
9And masters, treat your slaves in the
same way. Do not threaten them, since
you know that he who is both their Master and yours is in heaven, and there is no
favoritism with him.

[a] 26 Or *having cleansed* [b] 31 Gen. 2:24
[c] 3 Deut. 5:16

PRAYER: THE WORKS OF GOD

EVERYTHING You created is good, O God, and I am to reject nothing but receive it with thanksgiving, because it is sanctified by Your word, O God, and prayer. (1 Timothy 4:4–5)

***TAKE** a moment to consider the greatness of God's wonderful works.*

YEAR 2 DAY 183

OT Isaiah 63:1-19

God's Day of Vengeance and Redemption

63 Who is this coming from Edom,
from Bozrah, with his garments
stained crimson?
Who is this, robed in splendor,
striding forward in the greatness of
his strength?

"It is I, speaking in righteousness,
mighty to save."

2 Why are your garments red,
like those of one treading the
winepress?

3 "I have trodden the winepress alone;
from the nations no one was with
me.
I trampled them in my anger
and trod them down in my wrath;
their blood spattered my garments,
and I stained all my clothing.
4 For the day of vengeance was in my
heart,
and the year of my redemption has
come.
5 I looked, but there was no one to
help,
I was appalled that no one gave
support;
so my own arm worked salvation for
me,
and my own wrath sustained me.
6 I trampled the nations in my anger;
in my wrath I made them drunk
and poured their blood on the
ground."

Praise and Prayer

7 I will tell of the kindnesses of the
LORD,
the deeds for which he is to be
praised,
according to all the LORD has done
for us—
yes, the many good things he has
done
for the house of Israel,
according to his compassion and
many kindnesses.
8 He said, "Surely they are my people,
sons who will not be false to me";
and so he became their Savior.
9 In all their distress he too was
distressed,
and the angel of his presence saved
them.
In his love and mercy he redeemed
them;
he lifted them up and carried them
all the days of old.
10 Yet they rebelled
and grieved his Holy Spirit.
So he turned and became their enemy
and he himself fought against them.

11 Then his people recalled[a] the days of
old,
the days of Moses and his people—
where is he who brought them
through the sea,
with the shepherd of his flock?
Where is he who set
his Holy Spirit among them,
12 who sent his glorious arm of power
to be at Moses' right hand,
who divided the waters before them,
to gain for himself everlasting
renown,
13 who led them through the depths?
Like a horse in open country,
they did not stumble;
14 like cattle that go down to the plain,
they were given rest by the Spirit of
the LORD.
This is how you guided your people
to make for yourself a glorious
name.

15 Look down from heaven and see
from your lofty throne, holy and
glorious.
Where are your zeal and your might?
Your tenderness and compassion
are withheld from us.
16 But you are our Father,
though Abraham does not know us
or Israel acknowledge us;
you, O LORD, are our Father,
our Redeemer from of old is your
name.
17 Why, O LORD, do you make us wander
from your ways
and harden our hearts so we do not
revere you?
Return for the sake of your servants,

[a] 11 Or *But may he recall*

the tribes that are your inheritance.
[18]For a little while your people
possessed your holy place,
but now our enemies have trampled
down your sanctuary.
[19]We are yours from of old;
but you have not ruled over them,
they have not been called by your
name.[b]

[b] 19 Or *We are like those you have never ruled, / like those never called by your name*

PRAYER: CONFESSION

YOU have blotted out my transgressions like a thick cloud and my sins like the morning mist. I will return to You, for You have redeemed me. (Isaiah 44:22)

***ASK** the Spirit to search your heart and reveal any areas of unconfessed sin. Acknowledge these to the Lord and thank Him for His forgiveness.*

NT Ephesians 6:10–24

The Armor of God

[10]Finally, be strong in the Lord and in
his mighty power. [11]Put on the full armor
of God so that you can take your stand
against the devil's schemes. [12]For our
struggle is not against flesh and blood,
but against the rulers, against the authorities, against the powers of this dark world
and against the spiritual forces of evil in
the heavenly realms. [13]Therefore put on
the full armor of God, so that when the
day of evil comes, you may be able to
stand your ground, and after you have
done everything, to stand. [14]Stand firm
then, with the belt of truth buckled
around your waist, with the breastplate of
righteousness in place, [15]and with your
feet fitted with the readiness that comes
from the gospel of peace. [16]In addition to
all this, take up the shield of faith, with
which you can extinguish all the flaming
arrows of the evil one. [17]Take the helmet
of salvation and the sword of the Spirit,
which is the word of God. [18]And pray in
the Spirit on all occasions with all kinds
of prayers and requests. With this in
mind, be alert and always keep on praying for all the saints.
[19]Pray also for me, that whenever I open
my mouth, words may be given me so
that I will fearlessly make known the mystery of the gospel, [20]for which I am an
ambassador in chains. Pray that I may declare it fearlessly, as I should.

Final Greetings

[21]Tychicus, the dear brother and faithful
servant in the Lord, will tell you everything, so that you also may know how I
am and what I am doing. [22]I am sending
him to you for this very purpose, that you
may know how we are, and that he may
encourage you.
[23]Peace to the brothers, and love with
faith from God the Father and the Lord
Jesus Christ. [24]Grace to all who love our
Lord Jesus Christ with an undying love.

PRAYER: MY RELATIONSHIP TO GOD

I HAVE been chosen according to Your foreknowledge, O God my Father, in sanctification of the Spirit, for obedience to Jesus Christ and sprinkling of His blood; grace and peace are mine in abundance. (1 Peter 1:2)

***PAUSE** to thank God for the relationship that you enjoy with Him in Jesus Christ.*

YEAR 2
DAY 184

OT Isaiah 64:1-12

64 Oh, that you would rend the
heavens and come down,
that the mountains would tremble
before you!
[2]As when fire sets twigs ablaze
and causes water to boil,
come down to make your name
known to your enemies
and cause the nations to quake
before you!
[3]For when you did awesome things
that we did not expect,
you came down, and the mountains
trembled before you.
[4]Since ancient times no one has heard,
no ear has perceived,
no eye has seen any God besides you,
who acts on behalf of those who
wait for him.
[5]You come to the help of those who
gladly do right,
who remember your ways.
But when we continued to sin against
them,
you were angry.
How then can we be saved?
[6]All of us have become like one who is
unclean,
and all our righteous acts are like
filthy rags;
we all shrivel up like a leaf,
and like the wind our sins sweep us
away.
[7]No one calls on your name
or strives to lay hold of you;
for you have hidden your face from us
and made us waste away because of
our sins.

[8]Yet, O LORD, you are our Father.
We are the clay, you are the potter;
we are all the work of your hand.
[9]Do not be angry beyond measure,
O LORD;
do not remember our sins forever.
Oh, look upon us, we pray,
for we are all your people.
[10]Your sacred cities have become a
desert;
even Zion is a desert, Jerusalem a
desolation.
[11]Our holy and glorious temple, where
our fathers praised you,
has been burned with fire,
and all that we treasured lies in
ruins.
[12]After all this, O LORD, will you hold
yourself back?
Will you keep silent and punish us
beyond measure?

PRAYER: RENEWAL

LET me stop trusting in human beings, who only live for a little while. For of what account are they? (Isaiah 2:22) . . . May I trust in You enough to honor You as holy in the sight of others. (Numbers 20:12)

__PAUSE__ to add your own prayers for personal renewal.

NT Philippians 1:1-11

1 Paul and Timothy, servants of Christ Jesus,

To all the saints in Christ Jesus at Philippi, together with the overseers[a] and deacons:

[2]Grace and peace to you from God our Father and the Lord Jesus Christ.

Thanksgiving and Prayer

[3]I thank my God every time I remember you. [4]In all my prayers for all of you,
I always pray with joy [5]because of your
partnership in the gospel from the first
day until now, [6]being confident of this,
that he who began a good work in you
will carry it on to completion until the
day of Christ Jesus.
[7]It is right for me to feel this way about
all of you, since I have you in my heart;
for whether I am in chains or defending

[a] 1 Traditionally *bishops*

and confirming the gospel, all of you
share in God's grace with me. 8God can
testify how I long for all of you with the
affection of Christ Jesus.
9And this is my prayer: that your love
may abound more and more in knowledge and depth of insight, 10so that you
may be able to discern what is best and
may be pure and blameless until the day
of Christ, 11filled with the fruit of righteousness that comes through Jesus
Christ—to the glory and praise of God.

PRAYER: THE CHARACTER I WANT TO CULTIVATE

I WILL put away all filthiness and the overflow of wickedness, and in meekness I will accept the word planted in me, which is able to save my soul. (James 1:21) . . . I have been born again, not of perishable seed, but of imperishable, through Your living and abiding word, O God. Therefore, I will put away all malice and all guile and hypocrisy and envy and all slander. (1 Peter 1:23; 2:1)

***TAKE** a moment to ask the Lord for the grace to grow in godly character.*

YEAR 2
DAY 185

OT Isaiah 65:1–25

Judgment and Salvation

65 "I revealed myself to those who did
not ask for me;
I was found by those who did not
seek me.
To a nation that did not call on my
name,
I said, 'Here am I, here am I.'
2All day long I have held out my hands
to an obstinate people,
who walk in ways not good,
pursuing their own imaginations—
3a people who continually provoke me
to my very face,
offering sacrifices in gardens
and burning incense on altars of
brick;
4who sit among the graves
and spend their nights keeping
secret vigil;
who eat the flesh of pigs,
and whose pots hold broth of
unclean meat;
5who say, 'Keep away; don't come near
me,
for I am too sacred for you!'
Such people are smoke in my nostrils,
a fire that keeps burning all day.

6"See, it stands written before me:
I will not keep silent but will pay
back in full;
I will pay it back into their laps—
7both your sins and the sins of your
fathers,"
says the LORD.
"Because they burned sacrifices on the
mountains
and defied me on the hills,
I will measure into their laps
the full payment for their former
deeds."

8This is what the LORD says:

"As when juice is still found in a
cluster of grapes
and men say, 'Don't destroy it,
there is yet some good in it,'
so will I do in behalf of my servants;
I will not destroy them all.
9I will bring forth descendants from
Jacob,
and from Judah those who will
possess my mountains;
my chosen people will inherit them,
and there will my servants live.
10Sharon will become a pasture for
flocks,
and the Valley of Achor a resting
place for herds,
for my people who seek me.

11"But as for you who forsake the LORD
and forget my holy mountain,
who spread a table for Fortune

and fill bowls of mixed wine for
Destiny,
12 I will destine you for the sword,
and you will all bend down for the
slaughter;
for I called but you did not answer,
I spoke but you did not listen.
You did evil in my sight
and chose what displeases me."

13 Therefore this is what the Sovereign
LORD says:

"My servants will eat,
but you will go hungry;
my servants will drink,
but you will go thirsty;
my servants will rejoice,
but you will be put to shame.
14 My servants will sing
out of the joy of their hearts,
but you will cry out
from anguish of heart
and wail in brokenness of spirit.
15 You will leave your name
to my chosen ones as a curse;
the Sovereign LORD will put you to
death,
but to his servants he will give
another name.
16 Whoever invokes a blessing in the land
will do so by the God of truth;
he who takes an oath in the land
will swear by the God of truth.
For the past troubles will be forgotten
and hidden from my eyes.

New Heavens and a New Earth

17 "Behold, I will create
new heavens and a new earth.
The former things will not be
remembered,
nor will they come to mind.
18 But be glad and rejoice forever
in what I will create,
for I will create Jerusalem to be a delight
and its people a joy.
19 I will rejoice over Jerusalem
and take delight in my people;
the sound of weeping and of crying
will be heard in it no more.

20 "Never again will there be in it
an infant who lives but a few days,
or an old man who does not live
out his years;
he who dies at a hundred
will be thought a mere youth;
he who fails to reach[a] a hundred
will be considered accursed.
21 They will build houses and dwell in
them;
they will plant vineyards and eat
their fruit.
22 No longer will they build houses and
others live in them,
or plant and others eat.
For as the days of a tree,
so will be the days of my people;
my chosen ones will long enjoy
the works of their hands.
23 They will not toil in vain
or bear children doomed to
misfortune;
for they will be a people blessed by
the LORD,
they and their descendants with
them.
24 Before they call I will answer;
while they are still speaking I will
hear.
25 The wolf and the lamb will feed
together,
and the lion will eat straw like the ox,
but dust will be the serpent's food.
They will neither harm nor destroy
on all my holy mountain,"
says the LORD.

[a] 20 Or / *the sinner who reaches*

PRAYER: PETITION

KEEP falsehood and lies far from me; give me neither poverty nor riches; Give me only my daily bread, lest I be full and deny You and say, "Who is the Lord?" or lest I become poor and steal and profane Your name, my God. (Proverbs 30:8–9)

***PAUSE** here to petition God for wisdom. Ask Him to develop your eternal perspective, to renew your mind with truth and to help you develop greater skill in each area of your life. Offer prayers regarding your activities for this day and any special concerns you may have.*

NT Philippians 1:12–30

Paul's Chains Advance the Gospel

12Now I want you to know, brothers,
that what has happened to me has really
served to advance the gospel. 13As a result,
it has become clear throughout the whole
palace guard[a] and to everyone else that I
am in chains for Christ. 14Because of my
chains, most of the brothers in the Lord
have been encouraged to speak the word
of God more courageously and fearlessly.
15It is true that some preach Christ out
of envy and rivalry, but others out of goodwill. 16The latter do so in love, knowing
that I am put here for the defense of the
gospel. 17The former preach Christ out of
selfish ambition, not sincerely, supposing
that they can stir up trouble for me while
I am in chains.[b] 18But what does it matter?
The important thing is that in every way,
whether from false motives or true, Christ
is preached. And because of this I rejoice.
Yes, and I will continue to rejoice, 19for I
know that through your prayers and the
help given by the Spirit of Jesus Christ, what
has happened to me will turn out for my
deliverance.[c] 20I eagerly expect and hope that
I will in no way be ashamed, but will have
sufficient courage so that now as always
Christ will be exalted in my body, whether
by life or by death. 21For to me, to live is
Christ and to die is gain. 22If I am to go on
living in the body, this will mean fruitful labor for me. Yet what shall I choose? I do not
know! 23I am torn between the two: I desire
to depart and be with Christ, which is better by far; 24but it is more necessary for you
that I remain in the body. 25Convinced of
this, I know that I will remain, and I will
continue with all of you for your progress
and joy in the faith, 26so that through my
being with you again your joy in Christ
Jesus will overflow on account of me.
27Whatever happens, conduct yourselves
in a manner worthy of the gospel of
Christ. Then, whether I come and see you
or only hear about you in my absence, I
will know that you stand firm in one spirit, contending as one man for the faith of
the gospel 28without being frightened in
any way by those who oppose you. This is
a sign to them that they will be destroyed,
but that you will be saved—and that by
God. 29For it has been granted to you on
behalf of Christ not only to believe on
him, but also to suffer for him, 30since you
are going through the same struggle you
saw I had, and now hear that I still have.

[a] 13 Or *whole palace* [b] 16,17 Some late manuscripts have verses 16 and 17 in reverse order. [c] 19 Or *salvation*

PRAYER: MY RELATIONSHIP TO OTHERS

I WILL contribute to the needs of the saints and practice hospitality. (Romans 12:13) . . . I will not forget to do good and to share with others, for with such sacrifices You, my God, are well pleased. (Hebrews 13:16)

***PAUSE** to review your relationships with others and to commit them to the Lord.*

OT Proverbs 24

24 Do not envy wicked men,
do not desire their company;
2for their hearts plot violence,
and their lips talk about making
trouble.

3By wisdom a house is built,
and through understanding it is
established;
4through knowledge its rooms are filled
with rare and beautiful treasures.

5A wise man has great power,
and a man of knowledge increases
strength;
6for waging war you need guidance,
and for victory many advisers.

[7]Wisdom is too high for a fool;
in the assembly at the gate he has nothing to say.

[8]He who plots evil
will be known as a schemer.
[9]The schemes of folly are sin,
and men detest a mocker.

[10]If you falter in times of trouble,
how small is your strength!

[11]Rescue those being led away to death;
hold back those staggering toward slaughter.
[12]If you say, "But we knew nothing about this,"
does not he who weighs the heart perceive it?
Does not he who guards your life know it?
Will he not repay each person according to what he has done?

[13]Eat honey, my son, for it is good;
honey from the comb is sweet to your taste.
[14]Know also that wisdom is sweet to your soul;
if you find it, there is a future hope for you,
and your hope will not be cut off.

[15]Do not lie in wait like an outlaw against a righteous man's house,
do not raid his dwelling place;
[16]for though a righteous man falls seven times, he rises again,
but the wicked are brought down by calamity.

[17]Do not gloat when your enemy falls;
when he stumbles, do not let your heart rejoice,
[18]or the LORD will see and disapprove
and turn his wrath away from him.

[19]Do not fret because of evil men
or be envious of the wicked,
[20]for the evil man has no future hope,
and the lamp of the wicked will be snuffed out.

[21]Fear the LORD and the king, my son,
and do not join with the rebellious,
[22]for those two will send sudden destruction upon them,
and who knows what calamities they can bring?

Further Sayings of the Wise

[23]These also are sayings of the wise:

To show partiality in judging is not good:
[24]Whoever says to the guilty, "You are innocent"—
peoples will curse him and nations denounce him.
[25]But it will go well with those who convict the guilty,
and rich blessing will come upon them.

[26]An honest answer
is like a kiss on the lips.

[27]Finish your outdoor work
and get your fields ready;
after that, build your house.

[28]Do not testify against your neighbor without cause,
or use your lips to deceive.
[29]Do not say, "I'll do to him as he has done to me;
I'll pay that man back for what he did."

[30]I went past the field of the sluggard,
past the vineyard of the man who lacks judgment;
[31]thorns had come up everywhere,
the ground was covered with weeds,
and the stone wall was in ruins.
[32]I applied my heart to what I observed
and learned a lesson from what I saw:
[33]A little sleep, a little slumber,
a little folding of the hands to rest—
[34]and poverty will come on you like a bandit
and scarcity like an armed man.[a]

[a] 34 Or *like a vagrant / and scarcity like a beggar*

PRAYER: INTERCESSION

FATHER, this is my prayer for Your people: May their love abound more and more in full knowledge and depth of insight, so that they may be able to approve the things that are excellent,

in order to be sincere and blameless until the day of Christ—having been filled with the fruit of righteousness that comes through Jesus Christ, to Your glory and praise. (Philippians 1:9–11)

TAKE *a few moments to intercede on behalf of your immediate family and other relatives. Offer prayers for their spiritual, emotional and physical concerns.*

NT Philippians 2:1–18

Imitating Christ's Humility

2 If you have any encouragement from
being united with Christ, if any comfort from his love, if any fellowship with
the Spirit, if any tenderness and compassion, 2 then make my joy complete by being like-minded, having the same love,
being one in spirit and purpose. 3 Do
nothing out of selfish ambition or vain
conceit, but in humility consider others
better than yourselves. 4 Each of you
should look not only to your own interests, but also to the interests of others.
5 Your attitude should be the same as
that of Christ Jesus:

6 Who, being in very nature[a] God,
did not consider equality with God
something to be grasped,
7 but made himself nothing,
taking the very nature[b] of a servant,
being made in human likeness.
8 And being found in appearance as a
man,
he humbled himself
and became obedient to death—
even death on a cross!
9 Therefore God exalted him to the
highest place
and gave him the name that is
above every name,
10 that at the name of Jesus every knee
should bow,
in heaven and on earth and under
the earth,
11 and every tongue confess that Jesus
Christ is Lord,
to the glory of God the Father.

Shining as Stars

12 Therefore, my dear friends, as you
have always obeyed—not only in my presence, but now much more in my absence—continue to work out your salvation with fear and trembling, 13 for it is
God who works in you to will and to act
according to his good purpose.
14 Do everything without complaining or
arguing, 15 so that you may become blameless and pure, children of God without
fault in a crooked and depraved generation, in which you shine like stars in the
universe 16 as you hold out[c] the word of
life—in order that I may boast on the day
of Christ that I did not run or labor for
nothing. 17 But even if I am being poured
out like a drink offering on the sacrifice
and service coming from your faith, I am
glad and rejoice with all of you. 18 So you
too should be glad and rejoice with me.

[a] 6 Or *in the form of* [b] 7 Or *the form* [c] 16 Or *hold on to*

PRAYER: THE ATTRIBUTES OF GOD

O LORD, You shall reign for ever and ever. (Exodus 15:18) . . . O Lord God, You have shown Your servants Your greatness and Your strong hand, for what god is there in heaven or on earth who can do the works and mighty deeds You do? (Deuteronomy 3:24)

PAUSE *to reflect on these affirmations about the person, powers and perfection of God.*

YEAR 2 DAY 187

OT Isaiah 66:1–24

Judgment and Hope

66 This is what the LORD says:

"Heaven is my throne,
and the earth is my footstool.
Where is the house you will build for me?
Where will my resting place be?
2 Has not my hand made all these things,
and so they came into being?"
declares the LORD.

"This is the one I esteem:
he who is humble and contrite in spirit,
and trembles at my word.
3 But whoever sacrifices a bull
is like one who kills a man,
and whoever offers a lamb,
like one who breaks a dog's neck;
whoever makes a grain offering
is like one who presents pig's blood,
and whoever burns memorial incense,
like one who worships an idol.
They have chosen their own ways,
and their souls delight in their abominations;
4 so I also will choose harsh treatment for them
and will bring upon them what they dread.
For when I called, no one answered,
when I spoke, no one listened.
They did evil in my sight
and chose what displeases me."

5 Hear the word of the LORD,
you who tremble at his word:
"Your brothers who hate you,
and exclude you because of my name, have said,
'Let the LORD be glorified,
that we may see your joy!'
Yet they will be put to shame.
6 Hear that uproar from the city,
hear that noise from the temple!
It is the sound of the LORD
repaying his enemies all they deserve.

7 "Before she goes into labor,
she gives birth;
before the pains come upon her,
she delivers a son.
8 Who has ever heard of such a thing?
Who has ever seen such things?
Can a country be born in a day
or a nation be brought forth in a moment?
Yet no sooner is Zion in labor
than she gives birth to her children.
9 Do I bring to the moment of birth
and not give delivery?" says the LORD.
"Do I close up the womb
when I bring to delivery?" says your God.
10 "Rejoice with Jerusalem and be glad for her,
all you who love her;
rejoice greatly with her,
all you who mourn over her.
11 For you will nurse and be satisfied
at her comforting breasts;
you will drink deeply
and delight in her overflowing abundance."

12 For this is what the LORD says:

"I will extend peace to her like a river,
and the wealth of nations like a flooding stream;
you will nurse and be carried on her arm
and dandled on her knees.
13 As a mother comforts her child,
so will I comfort you;
and you will be comforted over Jerusalem."

14 When you see this, your heart will rejoice
and you will flourish like grass;
the hand of the LORD will be made known to his servants,
but his fury will be shown to his foes.
15 See, the LORD is coming with fire,
and his chariots are like a whirlwind;
he will bring down his anger with fury,
and his rebuke with flames of fire.
16 For with fire and with his sword
the LORD will execute judgment
upon all men,

and many will be those slain by the
LORD.

[17] "Those who consecrate and purify themselves to go into the gardens, following the one in the midst of[a] those who eat the flesh of pigs and rats and other abominable things—they will meet their end together," declares the LORD.

[18] "And I, because of their actions and their imaginations, am about to come[b] and gather all nations and tongues, and they will come and see my glory.

[19] "I will set a sign among them, and I will send some of those who survive to the nations—to Tarshish, to the Libyans[c] and Lydians (famous as archers), to Tubal and Greece, and to the distant islands that have not heard of my fame or seen my glory. They will proclaim my glory among
the nations. [20] And they will bring all your brothers, from all the nations, to my holy mountain in Jerusalem as an offering to the LORD—on horses, in chariots and wagons, and on mules and camels," says the LORD. "They will bring them, as the Israelites bring their grain offerings, to the temple of the LORD in ceremonially clean
vessels. [21] And I will select some of them also to be priests and Levites," says the LORD.

[22] "As the new heavens and the new earth that I make will endure before me," declares the LORD, "so will your name and
descendants endure. [23] From one New Moon to another and from one Sabbath to another, all mankind will come and bow down before me," says the LORD.
[24] "And they will go out and look upon the dead bodies of those who rebelled against me; their worm will not die, nor will their fire be quenched, and they will be loathsome to all mankind."

[a] 17 Or *gardens behind one of your temples, and*
[b] 18 The meaning of the Hebrew for this clause is uncertain.
[c] 19 Some Septuagint manuscripts *Put* (Libyans); Hebrew *Pul*

PRAYER: AFFIRMATION

YOU have called me to go and proclaim Your kingdom. (Luke 9:60) . . .
As I follow You, You will make me a fisher of people.
(Matthew 4:19; Mark 1:17)

***PAUSE** to reflect on these Biblical affirmations.*

NT Philippians 2:19–3:11

Timothy and Epaphroditus

[19] I hope in the Lord Jesus to send Timothy to you soon, that I also may be cheered when I receive news about you.
[20] I have no one else like him, who takes a genuine interest in your welfare. [21] For everyone looks out for his own interests, not those of Jesus Christ. [22] But you know that Timothy has proved himself, because as a son with his father he has served with me in the work of the gospel. [23] I hope, therefore, to send him as soon as I see how things go with me. [24] And I am confident in the Lord that I myself will come soon.

[25] But I think it is necessary to send back to you Epaphroditus, my brother, fellow worker and fellow soldier, who is also your messenger, whom you sent to take care of my needs. [26] For he longs for all of you and is distressed because you heard he was ill. [27] Indeed he was ill, and almost died. But God had mercy on him, and not on him only but also on me, to spare me sorrow upon sorrow. [28] Therefore I am all the more eager to send him, so that when you see him again you may be glad and I may have less anxiety. [29] Welcome him in the Lord with great joy, and honor men like him, [30] because he almost died for the work of Christ, risking his life to make up for the help you could not give me.

No Confidence in the Flesh

3 Finally, my brothers, rejoice in the Lord! It is no trouble for me to write the same things to you again, and it is a safeguard for you.

[2] Watch out for those dogs, those men who do evil, those mutilators of the flesh.
[3] For it is we who are the circumcision, we who worship by the Spirit of God, who

glory in Christ Jesus, and who put no confidence in the flesh— 4though I myself
have reasons for such confidence.
If anyone else thinks he has reasons to
put confidence in the flesh, I have more:
5circumcised on the eighth day, of the
people of Israel, of the tribe of Benjamin,
a Hebrew of Hebrews; in regard to the
law, a Pharisee; 6as for zeal, persecuting
the church; as for legalistic righteousness,
faultless.
7But whatever was to my profit I now
consider loss for the sake of Christ. 8What
is more, I consider everything a loss compared to the surpassing greatness of
knowing Christ Jesus my Lord, for whose
sake I have lost all things. I consider them
rubbish, that I may gain Christ 9and be
found in him, not having a righteousness
of my own that comes from the law, but
that which is through faith in Christ—the
righteousness that comes from God and
is by faith. 10I want to know Christ and the
power of his resurrection and the fellowship of sharing in his sufferings, becoming like him in his death, 11and so, somehow, to attain to the resurrection from the
dead.

PRAYER: THE WORKS OF GOD

IN Gethsemane, Jesus, You prayed, "Abba, Father, all things are possible for You; take this cup from Me. Yet not what I will, but what You will." (Mark 14:36)

***TAKE** a moment to consider the greatness of God's wonderful works.*

YEAR 2 DAY 188

OT Jeremiah 1:1–19

1 The words of Jeremiah son of Hilkiah,
one of the priests at Anathoth in the territory of Benjamin. 2The word of the LORD
came to him in the thirteenth year of the
reign of Josiah son of Amon king of Judah, 3and through the reign of Jehoiakim
son of Josiah king of Judah, down to the
fifth month of the eleventh year of Zedekiah son of Josiah king of Judah, when
the people of Jerusalem went into exile.

The Call of Jeremiah

4The word of the LORD came to me, saying,

5"Before I formed you in the womb I
knew[a] you,
before you were born I set you apart;
I appointed you as a prophet to the
nations."

6"Ah, Sovereign LORD," I said, "I do not
know how to speak; I am only a child."
7But the LORD said to me, "Do not say,
'I am only a child.' You must go to everyone I send you to and say whatever I command you. 8Do not be afraid of them, for
I am with you and will rescue you," declares the LORD.
9Then the LORD reached out his hand
and touched my mouth and said to me,
"Now, I have put my words in your mouth.
10See, today I appoint you over nations and
kingdoms to uproot and tear down, to destroy and overthrow, to build and to
plant."
11The word of the LORD came to me:
"What do you see, Jeremiah?"
"I see the branch of an almond tree," I
replied.
12The LORD said to me, "You have seen
correctly, for I am watching[b] to see that
my word is fulfilled."
13The word of the LORD came to me
again: "What do you see?"
"I see a boiling pot, tilting away from
the north," I answered.
14The LORD said to me, "From the north
disaster will be poured out on all who live
in the land. 15I am about to summon all
the peoples of the northern kingdoms,"
declares the LORD.

"Their kings will come and set up
their thrones

[a] 5 Or *chose* [b] 12 The Hebrew for *watching* sounds like the Hebrew for *almond tree.*

in the entrance of the gates of
Jerusalem;
they will come against all her
surrounding walls
and against all the towns of Judah.
16 I will pronounce my judgments on
my people
because of their wickedness in
forsaking me,
in burning incense to other gods
and in worshiping what their hands
have made.

17 "Get yourself ready! Stand up and say
to them whatever I command you. Do not
be terrified by them, or I will terrify you
before them. 18 Today I have made you a
fortified city, an iron pillar and a bronze
wall to stand against the whole land—
against the kings of Judah, its officials, its
priests and the people of the land. 19 They
will fight against you but will not overcome you, for I am with you and will rescue you," declares the LORD.

PRAYER: THANKSGIVING

I WILL not forget You, the God of my salvation; I will remember the Rock of my refuge. (Isaiah 17:10) . . . O Lord, You are my God; I will exalt You and praise Your name, for You have done wonderful things, things planned long ago in perfect faithfulness. (Isaiah 25:1)

PAUSE *to offer your own expressions of thanksgiving.*

NT Philippians 3:12–4:1

Pressing on Toward the Goal

12 Not that I have already obtained all
this, or have already been made perfect,
but I press on to take hold of that for
which Christ Jesus took hold of me.
13 Brothers, I do not consider myself yet to
have taken hold of it. But one thing I do:
Forgetting what is behind and straining
toward what is ahead, 14 I press on toward
the goal to win the prize for which God
has called me heavenward in Christ Jesus.
15 All of us who are mature should take
such a view of things. And if on some
point you think differently, that too God
will make clear to you. 16 Only let us live
up to what we have already attained.
17 Join with others in following my example, brothers, and take note of those
who live according to the pattern we gave
you. 18 For, as I have often told you before
and now say again even with tears, many
live as enemies of the cross of Christ.
19 Their destiny is destruction, their god is
their stomach, and their glory is in their
shame. Their mind is on earthly things.
20 But our citizenship is in heaven. And we
eagerly await a Savior from there, the
Lord Jesus Christ, 21 who, by the power
that enables him to bring everything under his control, will transform our lowly
bodies so that they will be like his glorious body.
4 Therefore, my brothers, you whom I
love and long for, my joy and crown,
that is how you should stand firm in the
Lord, dear friends!

PRAYER: MY RELATIONSHIP TO GOD

SURELY You are my salvation; I will trust and not be afraid. You, the Lord God, are my strength and my song, and You have become my salvation. (Isaiah 12:2) . . . Some trust in chariots and some in horses, but I will remember the name of the Lord my God. (Psalm 20:7)

PAUSE *to thank God for the relationship that you enjoy with Him in Jesus Christ.*

OT **Psalms 108–109** YEAR 2 DAY 189

Psalm 108

A song. A psalm of David.

1 My heart is steadfast, O God;
I will sing and make music with all my soul.
2 Awake, harp and lyre!
I will awaken the dawn.
3 I will praise you, O LORD, among the nations;
I will sing of you among the peoples.
4 For great is your love, higher than the heavens;
your faithfulness reaches to the skies.
5 Be exalted, O God, above the heavens,
and let your glory be over all the earth.

6 Save us and help us with your right hand,
that those you love may be delivered.
7 God has spoken from his sanctuary:
"In triumph I will parcel out Shechem
and measure off the Valley of Succoth.
8 Gilead is mine, Manasseh is mine;
Ephraim is my helmet,
Judah my scepter.
9 Moab is my washbasin,
upon Edom I toss my sandal;
over Philistia I shout in triumph."

10 Who will bring me to the fortified city?
Who will lead me to Edom?
11 Is it not you, O God, you who have rejected us
and no longer go out with our armies?
12 Give us aid against the enemy,
for the help of man is worthless.
13 With God we will gain the victory,
and he will trample down our enemies.

Psalm 109

For the director of music. Of David. A psalm.

1 O God, whom I praise,
do not remain silent,
2 for wicked and deceitful men
have opened their mouths against me;
they have spoken against me with lying tongues.
3 With words of hatred they surround me;
they attack me without cause.
4 In return for my friendship they accuse me,
but I am a man of prayer.
5 They repay me evil for good,
and hatred for my friendship.

6 Appoint[a] an evil man[b] to oppose him;
let an accuser[c] stand at his right hand.
7 When he is tried, let him be found guilty,
and may his prayers condemn him.
8 May his days be few;
may another take his place of leadership.
9 May his children be fatherless
and his wife a widow.
10 May his children be wandering beggars;
may they be driven[d] from their ruined homes.
11 May a creditor seize all he has;
may strangers plunder the fruits of his labor.
12 May no one extend kindness to him
or take pity on his fatherless children.
13 May his descendants be cut off,
their names blotted out from the next generation.
14 May the iniquity of his fathers be remembered before the LORD;
may the sin of his mother never be blotted out.
15 May their sins always remain before the LORD,
that he may cut off the memory of them from the earth.

16 For he never thought of doing a kindness,
but hounded to death the poor

[a] 6 Or ⌞*They say:*⌟ "*Appoint* (with quotation marks at the end of verse 19) [b] 6 Or *the Evil One* [c] 6 Or *let Satan* [d] 10 Septuagint; Hebrew *sought*

and the needy and the
brokenhearted.
17 He loved to pronounce a curse—
may it[e] come on him;
he found no pleasure in blessing—
may it be[f] far from him.
18 He wore cursing as his garment;
it entered into his body like water,
into his bones like oil.
19 May it be like a cloak wrapped about
him,
like a belt tied forever around him.
20 May this be the LORD's payment to my
accusers,
to those who speak evil of me.

21 But you, O Sovereign LORD,
deal well with me for your name's
sake;
out of the goodness of your love,
deliver me.
22 For I am poor and needy,
and my heart is wounded within me.
23 I fade away like an evening shadow;
I am shaken off like a locust.
24 My knees give way from fasting;
my body is thin and gaunt.
25 I am an object of scorn to my
accusers;
when they see me, they shake their
heads.

26 Help me, O LORD my God;
save me in accordance with your
love.
27 Let them know that it is your hand,
that you, O LORD, have done it.
28 They may curse, but you will bless;
when they attack they will be put to
shame,
but your servant will rejoice.
29 My accusers will be clothed with
disgrace
and wrapped in shame as in a
cloak.

30 With my mouth I will greatly extol the
LORD;
in the great throng I will praise him.
31 For he stands at the right hand of the
needy one,
to save his life from those who
condemn him.

[e] 17 Or *curse, / and it has* [f] 17 Or *blessing, / and it is*

PRAYER: ADORATION

O SOVEREIGN Lord, You are God! Your words are true, and You have promised good things to Your servant. (2 Samuel 7:28)
. . . I will sing of Your loving-kindness and justice; to You, O Lord, I will sing praises. (Psalm 101:1)

***PAUSE** to express your thoughts of praise and worship.*

NT Philippians 4:2–23

Exhortations

2 I plead with Euodia and I plead with
Syntyche to agree with each other in the
Lord. 3 Yes, and I ask you, loyal yokefel-
low,[a] help these women who have contended at my side in the cause of the
gospel, along with Clement and the rest
of my fellow workers, whose names are in
the book of life.
4 Rejoice in the Lord always. I will say it
again: Rejoice! 5 Let your gentleness be evident to all. The Lord is near. 6 Do not be
anxious about anything, but in everything, by prayer and petition, with thanksgiving, present your requests to God. 7 And
the peace of God, which transcends all
understanding, will guard your hearts and
your minds in Christ Jesus.
8 Finally, brothers, whatever is true, whatever is noble, whatever is right, whatever is
pure, whatever is lovely, whatever is admirable—if anything is excellent or praiseworthy—think about such things. 9 Whatever you have learned or received or heard
from me, or seen in me—put it into practice. And the God of peace will be with you.

Thanks for Their Gifts

10 I rejoice greatly in the Lord that at last
you have renewed your concern for me.

[a] 3 Or *loyal Syzygus*

Indeed, you have been concerned, but
you had no opportunity to show it. 11 I am
not saying this because I am in need, for
I have learned to be content whatever the
circumstances. 12 I know what it is to be in
need, and I know what it is to have plenty. I have learned the secret of being content in any and every situation, whether
well fed or hungry, whether living in plenty or in want. 13 I can do everything
through him who gives me strength.
14 Yet it was good of you to share in my
troubles. 15 Moreover, as you Philippians
know, in the early days of your acquain-
tance with the gospel, when I set out from
Macedonia, not one church shared with
me in the matter of giving and receiving,
except you only; 16 for even when I was in
Thessalonica, you sent me aid again and
again when I was in need. 17 Not that I am
looking for a gift, but I am looking for
what may be credited to your account. 18 I
have received full payment and even more;
I am amply supplied, now that I have received from Epaphroditus the gifts you
sent. They are a fragrant offering, an acceptable sacrifice, pleasing to God. 19 And
my God will meet all your needs according to his glorious riches in Christ Jesus.
20 To our God and Father be glory for
ever and ever. Amen.

Final Greetings

21 Greet all the saints in Christ Jesus. The
brothers who are with me send greetings.
22 All the saints send you greetings, especially those who belong to Caesar's household.
23 The grace of the Lord Jesus Christ be
with your spirit. Amen.[b]

[b] 23 Some manuscripts do not have *Amen.*

PRAYER: THE CHARACTER I WANT TO CULTIVATE

I WILL be satisfied with good from the fruit of my mouth, and the deeds of my hands will return to me. (Proverbs 12:14) . . . The tongue that brings healing is a tree of life, but perverseness in it crushes the spirit. (Proverbs 15:4)

***TAKE** a moment to ask the Lord for the grace to grow in godly character.*

YEAR 2 DAY 190

OT Jeremiah 2:1–37

Israel Forsakes God

2 The word of the LORD came to me: 2 "Go
and proclaim in the hearing of Jerusalem:

" 'I remember the devotion of your youth,
how as a bride you loved me
and followed me through the desert,
through a land not sown.
3 Israel was holy to the LORD,
the firstfruits of his harvest;
all who devoured her were held guilty,
and disaster overtook them,' "
declares the LORD.

4 Hear the word of the LORD, O house of Jacob,
all you clans of the house of Israel.

5 This is what the LORD says:

"What fault did your fathers find in me,
that they strayed so far from me?
They followed worthless idols
and became worthless themselves.
6 They did not ask, 'Where is the LORD,
who brought us up out of Egypt
and led us through the barren wilderness,
through a land of deserts and rifts,
a land of drought and darkness,[a]
a land where no one travels and no one lives?'
7 I brought you into a fertile land
to eat its fruit and rich produce.
But you came and defiled my land
and made my inheritance detestable.
8 The priests did not ask,
'Where is the LORD?'

[a] 6 Or *and the shadow of death*

Those who deal with the law did not
know me;
the leaders rebelled against me.
The prophets prophesied by Baal,
following worthless idols.

9 "Therefore I bring charges against you
again,"
declares the LORD.
"And I will bring charges against
your children's children.
10 Cross over to the coasts of Kittim[b] and
look,
send to Kedar[c] and observe closely;
see if there has ever been anything
like this:
11 Has a nation ever changed its gods?
(Yet they are not gods at all.)
But my people have exchanged their[d]
Glory
for worthless idols.
12 Be appalled at this, O heavens,
and shudder with great horror,"
declares the LORD.
13 "My people have committed two sins:
They have forsaken me,
the spring of living water,
and have dug their own cisterns,
broken cisterns that cannot hold
water.
14 Is Israel a servant, a slave by birth?
Why then has he become plunder?
15 Lions have roared;
they have growled at him.
They have laid waste his land;
his towns are burned and deserted.
16 Also, the men of Memphis[e] and
Tahpanhes
have shaved the crown of your head.[f]
17 Have you not brought this on
yourselves
by forsaking the LORD your God
when he led you in the way?
18 Now why go to Egypt
to drink water from the Shihor[g]?
And why go to Assyria
to drink water from the River[h]?
19 Your wickedness will punish you;
your backsliding will rebuke you.
Consider then and realize
how evil and bitter it is for you
when you forsake the LORD your God
and have no awe of me,"
declares the Lord,
the LORD Almighty.

20 "Long ago you broke off your yoke
and tore off your bonds;
you said, 'I will not serve you!'
Indeed, on every high hill
and under every spreading tree
you lay down as a prostitute.
21 I had planted you like a choice vine
of sound and reliable stock.
How then did you turn against me
into a corrupt, wild vine?
22 Although you wash yourself with soda
and use an abundance of soap,
the stain of your guilt is still before
me,"
declares the Sovereign LORD.
23 "How can you say, 'I am not defiled;
I have not run after the Baals'?
See how you behaved in the valley;
consider what you have done.
You are a swift she-camel
running here and there,
24 a wild donkey accustomed to the
desert,
sniffing the wind in her craving—
in her heat who can restrain her?
Any males that pursue her need not
tire themselves;
at mating time they will find her.
25 Do not run until your feet are bare
and your throat is dry.
But you said, 'It's no use!
I love foreign gods,
and I must go after them.'

26 "As a thief is disgraced when he is
caught,
so the house of Israel is disgraced—
they, their kings and their officials,
their priests and their prophets.
27 They say to wood, 'You are my father,'
and to stone, 'You gave me birth.'
They have turned their backs to me
and not their faces;
yet when they are in trouble, they say,
'Come and save us!'
28 Where then are the gods you made for
yourselves?
Let them come if they can save you
when you are in trouble!
For you have as many gods
as you have towns, O Judah.

29 "Why do you bring charges against
me?

[b] *10* That is, Cyprus and western coastlands
[c] *10* The home of Bedouin tribes in the Syro-Arabian desert
[d] *11* Masoretic Text; an ancient Hebrew scribal tradition *my*
[e] *16* Hebrew *Noph*
[f] *16* Or *have cracked your skull*
[g] *18* That is, a branch of the Nile
[h] *18* That is, the Euphrates

You have all rebelled against me,"
declares the LORD.
30 "In vain I punished your people;
they did not respond to correction.
Your sword has devoured your prophets
like a ravening lion.

31 "You of this generation, consider the word of the LORD:

"Have I been a desert to Israel
or a land of great darkness?
Why do my people say, 'We are free to roam;
we will come to you no more'?
32 Does a maiden forget her jewelry,
a bride her wedding ornaments?
Yet my people have forgotten me,
days without number.
33 How skilled you are at pursuing love!
Even the worst of women can learn from your ways.
34 On your clothes men find
the lifeblood of the innocent poor,
though you did not catch them breaking in.
Yet in spite of all this
35 you say, 'I am innocent;
he is not angry with me.'
But I will pass judgment on you
because you say, 'I have not sinned.'
36 Why do you go about so much,
changing your ways?
You will be disappointed by Egypt
as you were by Assyria.
37 You will also leave that place
with your hands on your head,
for the LORD has rejected those you trust;
you will not be helped by them.

PRAYER: CONFESSION

THE one You esteem is humble and contrite of spirit and trembles at Your word. (Isaiah 66:2)

***ASK** the Spirit to search your heart and reveal any areas of unconfessed sin. Acknowledge these to the Lord and thank Him for His forgiveness.*

NT Colossians 1:1-14

1 Paul, an apostle of Christ Jesus by the will of God, and Timothy our brother,

2 To the holy and faithful[a] brothers in Christ at Colosse:

Grace and peace to you from God our Father.[b]

Thanksgiving and Prayer

3 We always thank God, the Father of
our Lord Jesus Christ, when we pray for
you, 4 because we have heard of your faith
in Christ Jesus and of the love you have
for all the saints— 5 the faith and love that
spring from the hope that is stored up for
you in heaven and that you have already
heard about in the word of truth, the
gospel 6 that has come to you. All over the
world this gospel is bearing fruit and
growing, just as it has been doing among
you since the day you heard it and understood God's grace in all its truth. 7 You
learned it from Epaphras, our dear fellow
servant, who is a faithful minister of
Christ on our[c] behalf, 8 and who also told
us of your love in the Spirit.
9 For this reason, since the day we heard
about you, we have not stopped praying for
you and asking God to fill you with the
knowledge of his will through all spiritual
wisdom and understanding. 10 And we pray
this in order that you may live a life worthy
of the Lord and may please him in every
way: bearing fruit in every good work,
growing in the knowledge of God, 11 being
strengthened with all power according to
his glorious might so that you may have
great endurance and patience, and joyfully
12 giving thanks to the Father, who has qualified you[d] to share in the inheritance of the
saints in the kingdom of light. 13 For he has
rescued us from the dominion of darkness
and brought us into the kingdom of the
Son he loves, 14 in whom we have redemption,[e] the forgiveness of sins.

[a] 2 Or *believing* [b] 2 Some manuscripts *Father and the Lord Jesus Christ* [c] 7 Some manuscripts *your* [d] 12 Some manuscripts *us* [e] 14 A few late manuscripts *redemption through his blood*

PRAYER: MY RELATIONSHIP TO OTHERS

WHAT is my hope or joy or crown of rejoicing in Your presence, Lord Jesus, at Your coming? My glory and joy is the people in whose lives I have been privileged to have a ministry.
(1 Thessalonians 2:19–20)

__PAUSE__ to review your relationships with others and to commit them to the Lord.

YEAR 2
DAY 191

OT Jeremiah 3:1-25

3 "If a man divorces his wife
and she leaves him and marries
another man,
should he return to her again?
Would not the land be completely
defiled?
But you have lived as a prostitute with
many lovers—
would you now return to me?"
declares the LORD.
2 "Look up to the barren heights and see.
Is there any place where you have
not been ravished?
By the roadside you sat waiting for
lovers,
sat like a nomad[a] in the desert.
You have defiled the land
with your prostitution and
wickedness.
3 Therefore the showers have been
withheld,
and no spring rains have fallen.
Yet you have the brazen look of a
prostitute;
you refuse to blush with shame.
4 Have you not just called to me:
'My Father, my friend from my
youth,
5 will you always be angry?
Will your wrath continue forever?'
This is how you talk,
but you do all the evil you can."

Unfaithful Israel

6 During the reign of King Josiah, the
LORD said to me, "Have you seen what
faithless Israel has done? She has gone up
on every high hill and under every spreading tree and has committed adultery
there. 7 I thought that after she had done
all this she would return to me but she
did not, and her unfaithful sister Judah
saw it. 8 I gave faithless Israel her certificate
of divorce and sent her away because of
all her adulteries. Yet I saw that her unfaithful sister Judah had no fear; she also
went out and committed adultery. 9 Because Israel's immorality mattered so little to her, she defiled the land and committed adultery with stone and wood. 10 In
spite of all this, her unfaithful sister Judah
did not return to me with all her heart,
but only in pretense," declares the LORD.

11 The LORD said to me, "Faithless Israel
is more righteous than unfaithful Judah.
12 Go, proclaim this message toward the
north:

" 'Return, faithless Israel,' declares the
LORD,
'I will frown on you no longer,
for I am merciful,' declares the LORD,
'I will not be angry forever.
13 Only acknowledge your guilt—
you have rebelled against the LORD
your God,
you have scattered your favors to
foreign gods
under every spreading tree,
and have not obeyed me,' "
declares the LORD.

14 "Return, faithless people," declares
the LORD, "for I am your husband. I will
choose you—one from a town and two
from a clan—and bring you to Zion.
15 Then I will give you shepherds after my
own heart, who will lead you with knowledge and understanding. 16 In those days,
when your numbers have increased greatly in the land," declares the LORD, "men
will no longer say, 'The ark of the cov-

[a] 2 Or *an Arab*

enant of the LORD.' It will never enter their
minds or be remembered; it will not be
missed, nor will another one be made.
17 At that time they will call Jerusalem The
Throne of the LORD, and all nations will
gather in Jerusalem to honor the name of
the LORD. No longer will they follow the
stubbornness of their evil hearts. 18 In
those days the house of Judah will join
the house of Israel, and together they will
come from a northern land to the land I
gave your forefathers as an inheritance.

19 "I myself said,

" 'How gladly would I treat you like sons
and give you a desirable land,
the most beautiful inheritance of any nation.'
I thought you would call me 'Father'
and not turn away from following me.
20 But like a woman unfaithful to her husband,
so you have been unfaithful to me,
O house of Israel,"
declares the LORD.

21 A cry is heard on the barren heights,
the weeping and pleading of the people of Israel,
because they have perverted their ways
and have forgotten the LORD their God.

22 "Return, faithless people;
I will cure you of backsliding."

"Yes, we will come to you,
for you are the LORD our God.
23 Surely the ⌞idolatrous⌟ commotion on the hills
and mountains is a deception;
surely in the LORD our God
is the salvation of Israel.
24 From our youth shameful gods have consumed
the fruits of our fathers' labor—
their flocks and herds,
their sons and daughters.
25 Let us lie down in our shame,
and let our disgrace cover us.
We have sinned against the LORD our God,
both we and our fathers;
from our youth till this day
we have not obeyed the LORD our God."

PRAYER: RENEWAL

MAY I love You, Lord my God, and serve You with all my heart and with all my soul. (Deuteronomy 11:13) . . .
May I worship You, Lord my God, and serve You only. (Matthew 4:10)

PAUSE *to add your own prayers for personal renewal.*

NT Colossians 1:15–23

The Supremacy of Christ

15 He is the image of the invisible God,
the firstborn over all creation. 16 For by him
all things were created: things in heaven
and on earth, visible and invisible,
whether thrones or powers or rulers or authorities; all things were created by him
and for him. 17 He is before all things, and
in him all things hold together. 18 And he
is the head of the body, the church; he is
the beginning and the firstborn from
among the dead, so that in everything he
might have the supremacy. 19 For God was
pleased to have all his fullness dwell in
him, 20 and through him to reconcile to
himself all things, whether things on earth
or things in heaven, by making peace
through his blood, shed on the cross.
21 Once you were alienated from God
and were enemies in your minds because
of[a] your evil behavior. 22 But now he has
reconciled you by Christ's physical body
through death to present you holy in his
sight, without blemish and free from accusation— 23 if you continue in your faith,
established and firm, not moved from the
hope held out in the gospel. This is the
gospel that you heard and that has been
proclaimed to every creature under heav-
en, and of which I, Paul, have become a
servant.

[a] 21 Or *minds, as shown by*

PRAYER: THE ATTRIBUTES OF GOD

THE heavens and the highest heavens cannot contain You, O Lord. (2 Chronicles 2:6; 6:18) . . . O God, You alone stretch out the heavens and tread on the waves of the sea. (Job 9:8)

***PAUSE** to reflect on these affirmations about the person, powers and perfection of God.*

YEAR 2
DAY 192

OT Jeremiah 4:1-31

4 "If you will return, O Israel,
return to me,"
declares the LORD.
"If you put your detestable idols out
of my sight
and no longer go astray,
2 and if in a truthful, just and righteous
way
you swear, 'As surely as the LORD
lives,'
then the nations will be blessed by
him
and in him they will glory."

3 This is what the LORD says to the men
of Judah and to Jerusalem:

"Break up your unplowed ground
and do not sow among thorns.
4 Circumcise yourselves to the LORD,
circumcise your hearts,
you men of Judah and people of
Jerusalem,
or my wrath will break out and burn
like fire
because of the evil you have done—
burn with no one to quench it.

Disaster From the North

5 "Announce in Judah and proclaim in
Jerusalem and say:
'Sound the trumpet throughout the
land!'
Cry aloud and say:
'Gather together!
Let us flee to the fortified cities!'
6 Raise the signal to go to Zion!
Flee for safety without delay!
For I am bringing disaster from the
north,
even terrible destruction."

7 A lion has come out of his lair;
a destroyer of nations has set out.
He has left his place
to lay waste your land.
Your towns will lie in ruins
without inhabitant.
8 So put on sackcloth,
lament and wail,
for the fierce anger of the LORD
has not turned away from us.

9 "In that day," declares the LORD,
"the king and the officials will lose
heart,
the priests will be horrified,
and the prophets will be appalled."

10 Then I said, "Ah, Sovereign LORD, how
completely you have deceived this people
and Jerusalem by saying, 'You will have
peace,' when the sword is at our throats."
11 At that time this people and Jerusalem
will be told, "A scorching wind from the
barren heights in the desert blows toward
my people, but not to winnow or cleanse;
12 a wind too strong for that comes from
me.[a] Now I pronounce my judgments
against them."

13 Look! He advances like the clouds,
his chariots come like a whirlwind,
his horses are swifter than eagles.
Woe to us! We are ruined!
14 O Jerusalem, wash the evil from your
heart and be saved.
How long will you harbor wicked
thoughts?
15 A voice is announcing from Dan,
proclaiming disaster from the hills
of Ephraim.
16 "Tell this to the nations,
proclaim it to Jerusalem:
'A besieging army is coming from a
distant land,

[a] 12 Or *comes at my command*

raising a war cry against the cities of
Judah.
[17] They surround her like men guarding
a field,
because she has rebelled against
me,' "
declares the LORD.
[18] "Your own conduct and actions
have brought this upon you.
This is your punishment.
How bitter it is!
How it pierces to the heart!"

[19] Oh, my anguish, my anguish!
I writhe in pain.
Oh, the agony of my heart!
My heart pounds within me,
I cannot keep silent.
For I have heard the sound of the
trumpet;
I have heard the battle cry.
[20] Disaster follows disaster;
the whole land lies in ruins.
In an instant my tents are destroyed,
my shelter in a moment.
[21] How long must I see the battle
standard
and hear the sound of the trumpet?

[22] "My people are fools;
they do not know me.
They are senseless children;
they have no understanding.
They are skilled in doing evil;
they know not how to do good."

[23] I looked at the earth,
and it was formless and empty;
and at the heavens,
and their light was gone.
[24] I looked at the mountains,
and they were quaking;
all the hills were swaying.
[25] I looked, and there were no people;
every bird in the sky had flown
away.
[26] I looked, and the fruitful land was a
desert;
all its towns lay in ruins
before the LORD, before his fierce
anger.

[27] This is what the LORD says:

"The whole land will be ruined,
though I will not destroy it
completely.
[28] Therefore the earth will mourn
and the heavens above grow dark,
because I have spoken and will not
relent,
I have decided and will not turn
back."

[29] At the sound of horsemen and archers
every town takes to flight.
Some go into the thickets;
some climb up among the rocks.
All the towns are deserted;
no one lives in them.

[30] What are you doing, O devastated one?
Why dress yourself in scarlet
and put on jewels of gold?
Why shade your eyes with paint?
You adorn yourself in vain.
Your lovers despise you;
they seek your life.

[31] I hear a cry as of a woman in labor,
a groan as of one bearing her first
child—
the cry of the Daughter of Zion
gasping for breath,
stretching out her hands and saying,
"Alas! I am fainting;
my life is given over to murderers."

PRAYER: PETITION

MAY I take courage and not be afraid, for You, Lord Jesus, are with me. (Mark 6:50)

PAUSE *here to petition God for spiritual insight so that you might have understanding of His Word. Ask for insight into your identity in Jesus Christ: that you might know who you are, what direction your life should take and what His purpose for your life is. Offer prayers regarding your activities for this day and any special concerns you may have.*

NT Colossians 1:24–2:5

Paul's Labor for the Church

[24]Now I rejoice in what was suffered for
you, and I fill up in my flesh what is still
lacking in regard to Christ's afflictions, for
the sake of his body, which is the church.
[25]I have become its servant by the commission God gave me to present to you
the word of God in its fullness— [26]the
mystery that has been kept hidden for
ages and generations, but is now disclosed
to the saints. [27]To them God has chosen
to make known among the Gentiles the
glorious riches of this mystery, which is
Christ in you, the hope of glory.
[28]We proclaim him, admonishing and
teaching everyone with all wisdom, so
that we may present everyone perfect in
Christ. [29]To this end I labor, struggling
with all his energy, which so powerfully
works in me.
2 I want you to know how much I am
struggling for you and for those at Laodicea, and for all who have not met me
personally. [2]My purpose is that they may
be encouraged in heart and united in love,
so that they may have the full riches of
complete understanding, in order that
they may know the mystery of God,
namely, Christ, [3]in whom are hidden all
the treasures of wisdom and knowledge.
[4]I tell you this so that no one may deceive
you by fine-sounding arguments. [5]For
though I am absent from you in body, I
am present with you in spirit and delight
to see how orderly you are and how firm
your faith in Christ is.

PRAYER: THE WORKS OF GOD

O LORD, You have performed mighty deeds with Your arm; You have scattered those who are proud in the thoughts of their heart. You have brought down rulers from their thrones and lifted up the humble. (Luke 1:51–52)

***TAKE** a moment to consider the greatness of God's wonderful works.*

YEAR 2 DAY 193

OT Jeremiah 5:1-31

Not One Is Upright

5 "Go up and down the streets of Jerusalem,
look around and consider,
search through her squares.
If you can find but one person
who deals honestly and seeks the truth,
I will forgive this city.
[2]Although they say, 'As surely as the LORD lives,'
still they are swearing falsely."
[3]O LORD, do not your eyes look for truth?
You struck them, but they felt no pain;
you crushed them, but they refused correction.
They made their faces harder than stone
and refused to repent.
[4]I thought, "These are only the poor;
they are foolish,
for they do not know the way of the LORD,
the requirements of their God.
[5]So I will go to the leaders
and speak to them;
surely they know the way of the LORD,
the requirements of their God."
But with one accord they too had broken off the yoke
and torn off the bonds.
[6]Therefore a lion from the forest will attack them,
a wolf from the desert will ravage them,

a leopard will lie in wait near their towns
to tear to pieces any who venture out,
for their rebellion is great
and their backslidings many.

7 "Why should I forgive you?
Your children have forsaken me
and sworn by gods that are not gods.
I supplied all their needs,
yet they committed adultery
and thronged to the houses of prostitutes.
8 They are well-fed, lusty stallions,
each neighing for another man's wife.
9 Should I not punish them for this?"
declares the LORD.
"Should I not avenge myself
on such a nation as this?

10 "Go through her vineyards and ravage them,
but do not destroy them completely.
Strip off her branches,
for these people do not belong to the LORD.
11 The house of Israel and the house of Judah
have been utterly unfaithful to me,"
declares the LORD.

12 They have lied about the LORD;
they said, "He will do nothing!
No harm will come to us;
we will never see sword or famine.
13 The prophets are but wind
and the word is not in them;
so let what they say be done to them."

14 Therefore this is what the LORD God Almighty says:

"Because the people have spoken these words,
I will make my words in your mouth a fire
and these people the wood it consumes.
15 O house of Israel," declares the LORD,
"I am bringing a distant nation against you—
an ancient and enduring nation,
a people whose language you do not know,
whose speech you do not understand.
16 Their quivers are like an open grave;
all of them are mighty warriors.
17 They will devour your harvests and food,
devour your sons and daughters;
they will devour your flocks and herds,
devour your vines and fig trees.
With the sword they will destroy
the fortified cities in which you trust.

18 "Yet even in those days," declares the
LORD, "I will not destroy you completely.
19 And when the people ask, 'Why has the
LORD our God done all this to us?' you
will tell them, 'As you have forsaken me
and served foreign gods in your own land,
so now you will serve foreigners in a land
not your own.'

20 "Announce this to the house of Jacob
and proclaim it in Judah:
21 Hear this, you foolish and senseless people,
who have eyes but do not see,
who have ears but do not hear:
22 Should you not fear me?" declares the LORD.
"Should you not tremble in my presence?
I made the sand a boundary for the sea,
an everlasting barrier it cannot cross.
The waves may roll, but they cannot prevail;
they may roar, but they cannot cross it.
23 But these people have stubborn and rebellious hearts;
they have turned aside and gone away.
24 They do not say to themselves,
'Let us fear the LORD our God,
who gives autumn and spring rains in season,
who assures us of the regular weeks of harvest.'
25 Your wrongdoings have kept these away;
your sins have deprived you of good.

26 "Among my people are wicked men
who lie in wait like men who snare birds
and like those who set traps to catch men.
27 Like cages full of birds,
their houses are full of deceit;
they have become rich and powerful
28 and have grown fat and sleek.

Their evil deeds have no limit;
they do not plead the case of the
fatherless to win it,
they do not defend the rights of the
poor.
29 Should I not punish them for this?"
declares the LORD.
"Should I not avenge myself
on such a nation as this?
30 "A horrible and shocking thing
has happened in the land:
31 The prophets prophesy lies,
the priests rule by their own
authority,
and my people love it this way.
But what will you do in the end?

PRAYER: INTERCESSION

THOSE who love their brothers and sisters abide in the light, and there is no cause for stumbling in them. But those who hate their brothers and sisters are in the darkness and walk in the darkness and do not know where they are going, because the darkness has blinded their eyes.
(1 John 2:10–11)

***TAKE** a few moments to intercede on behalf of other believers, such as your personal friends, those in ministry and those who are oppressed and in need.*

NT Colossians 2:6–23

Freedom From Human Regulations Through Life With Christ

6 So then, just as you received Christ
Jesus as Lord, continue to live in him,
7 rooted and built up in him, strengthened
in the faith as you were taught, and overflowing with thankfulness.
8 See to it that no one takes you captive
through hollow and deceptive philosophy, which depends on human tradition
and the basic principles of this world
rather than on Christ.
9 For in Christ all the fullness of the Deity lives in bodily form, 10 and you have
been given fullness in Christ, who is the
head over every power and authority. 11 In
him you were also circumcised, in the
putting off of the sinful nature,[a] not with
a circumcision done by the hands of men
but with the circumcision done by Christ,
12 having been buried with him in baptism
and raised with him through your faith in
the power of God, who raised him from
the dead.
13 When you were dead in your sins and
in the uncircumcision of your sinful nature,[b] God made you[c] alive with Christ. He
forgave us all our sins, 14 having canceled
the written code, with its regulations, that
was against us and that stood opposed to
us; he took it away, nailing it to the cross.
15 And having disarmed the powers and authorities, he made a public spectacle of
them, triumphing over them by the cross.[d]
16 Therefore do not let anyone judge you
by what you eat or drink, or with regard to
a religious festival, a New Moon celebration or a Sabbath day. 17 These are a shadow of the things that were to come; the reality, however, is found in Christ. 18 Do not
let anyone who delights in false humility
and the worship of angels disqualify you
for the prize. Such a person goes into great
detail about what he has seen, and his unspiritual mind puffs him up with idle notions. 19 He has lost connection with the
Head, from whom the whole body, supported and held together by its ligaments
and sinews, grows as God causes it to grow.
20 Since you died with Christ to the basic principles of this world, why, as though
you still belonged to it, do you submit to
its rules: 21 "Do not handle! Do not taste!
Do not touch!"? 22 These are all destined to
perish with use, because they are based on
human commands and teachings. 23 Such
regulations indeed have an appearance of
wisdom, with their self-imposed worship,
their false humility and their harsh treatment of the body, but they lack any value
in restraining sensual indulgence.

[a] 11 Or *the flesh* [b] 13 Or *your flesh* [c] 13 Some manuscripts *us* [d] 15 Or *them in him*

PRAYER: MY RELATIONSHIP TO GOD

I HAVE tasted and seen that You are good, O Lord; blessed is the one who takes refuge in You! (Psalm 34:8) . . . Blessed are those who make the Lord their trust, who do not look to the proud or those who turn aside to lies. (Psalm 40:4)

***PAUSE** to thank God for the relationship that you enjoy with Him in Jesus Christ.*

YEAR 2 DAY 194

OT Jeremiah 6:1–30

Jerusalem Under Siege

6 "Flee for safety, people of Benjamin!
Flee from Jerusalem!
Sound the trumpet in Tekoa!
Raise the signal over Beth Hakkerem!
For disaster looms out of the north,
even terrible destruction.
2 I will destroy the Daughter of Zion,
so beautiful and delicate.
3 Shepherds with their flocks will come against her;
they will pitch their tents around her,
each tending his own portion."

4 "Prepare for battle against her!
Arise, let us attack at noon!
But, alas, the daylight is fading,
and the shadows of evening grow long.
5 So arise, let us attack at night
and destroy her fortresses!"

6 This is what the LORD Almighty says:

"Cut down the trees
and build siege ramps against Jerusalem.
This city must be punished;
it is filled with oppression.
7 As a well pours out its water,
so she pours out her wickedness.
Violence and destruction resound in her;
her sickness and wounds are ever before me.
8 Take warning, O Jerusalem,
or I will turn away from you
and make your land desolate
so no one can live in it."

9 This is what the LORD Almighty says:

"Let them glean the remnant of Israel
as thoroughly as a vine;
pass your hand over the branches again,
like one gathering grapes."

10 To whom can I speak and give warning?
Who will listen to me?
Their ears are closed[a]
so they cannot hear.
The word of the LORD is offensive to them;
they find no pleasure in it.
11 But I am full of the wrath of the LORD,
and I cannot hold it in.

"Pour it out on the children in the street
and on the young men gathered together;
both husband and wife will be caught in it,
and the old, those weighed down with years.
12 Their houses will be turned over to others,
together with their fields and their wives,
when I stretch out my hand
against those who live in the land,"
declares the LORD.
13 "From the least to the greatest,
all are greedy for gain;
prophets and priests alike,
all practice deceit.
14 They dress the wound of my people
as though it were not serious.
'Peace, peace,' they say,
when there is no peace.
15 Are they ashamed of their loathsome conduct?

[a] 10 Hebrew *uncircumcised*

No, they have no shame at all;
they do not even know how to blush.
So they will fall among the fallen;
they will be brought down when I punish them,"
says the LORD.

16 This is what the LORD says:

"Stand at the crossroads and look;
ask for the ancient paths,
ask where the good way is, and walk in it,
and you will find rest for your souls.
But you said, 'We will not walk in it.'
17 I appointed watchmen over you and said,
'Listen to the sound of the trumpet!'
But you said, 'We will not listen.'
18 Therefore hear, O nations;
observe, O witnesses,
what will happen to them.
19 Hear, O earth:
I am bringing disaster on this people,
the fruit of their schemes,
because they have not listened to my words
and have rejected my law.
20 What do I care about incense from Sheba
or sweet calamus from a distant land?
Your burnt offerings are not acceptable;
your sacrifices do not please me."

21 Therefore this is what the LORD says:

"I will put obstacles before this people.
Fathers and sons alike will stumble over them;
neighbors and friends will perish."

22 This is what the LORD says:

"Look, an army is coming
from the land of the north;
a great nation is being stirred up
from the ends of the earth.
23 They are armed with bow and spear;
they are cruel and show no mercy.
They sound like the roaring sea
as they ride on their horses;
they come like men in battle formation
to attack you, O Daughter of Zion."

24 We have heard reports about them,
and our hands hang limp.
Anguish has gripped us,
pain like that of a woman in labor.
25 Do not go out to the fields
or walk on the roads,
for the enemy has a sword,
and there is terror on every side.
26 O my people, put on sackcloth
and roll in ashes;
mourn with bitter wailing
as for an only son,
for suddenly the destroyer
will come upon us.

27 "I have made you a tester of metals
and my people the ore,
that you may observe
and test their ways.
28 They are all hardened rebels,
going about to slander.
They are bronze and iron;
they all act corruptly.
29 The bellows blow fiercely
to burn away the lead with fire,
but the refining goes on in vain;
the wicked are not purged out.
30 They are called rejected silver,
because the LORD has rejected them."

PRAYER: AFFIRMATION

THE greatest among us should be like the youngest, and the one who rules like the one who serves. For who is greater, the one who is at the table or the one who serves? Is it not the one who is at the table? But You, Jesus, came among us as the One who serves. (Luke 22:26–27) . . . Those who want to be first must be last of all and the servants of all. (Mark 9:35)

PAUSE *to reflect on these Biblical affirmations.*

NT Colossians 3:1–25

Rules for Holy Living

3 Since, then, you have been raised with
Christ, set your hearts on things above,
where Christ is seated at the right hand of
God. 2Set your minds on things above,
not on earthly things. 3For you died, and
your life is now hidden with Christ in
God. 4When Christ, who is your[a] life, appears, then you also will appear with him
in glory.
5Put to death, therefore, whatever belongs
to your earthly nature: sexual immorality,
impurity, lust, evil desires and greed, which
is idolatry. 6Because of these, the wrath of
God is coming.[b] 7You used to walk in these
ways, in the life you once lived. 8But now
you must rid yourselves of all such things as
these: anger, rage, malice, slander, and filthy
language from your lips. 9Do not lie to each
other, since you have taken off your old self
with its practices 10and have put on the new
self, which is being renewed in knowledge
in the image of its Creator. 11Here there is
no Greek or Jew, circumcised or uncircumcised, barbarian, Scythian, slave or free, but
Christ is all, and is in all.
12Therefore, as God's chosen people,
holy and dearly loved, clothe yourselves
with compassion, kindness, humility,
gentleness and patience. 13Bear with each
other and forgive whatever grievances you
may have against one another. Forgive as
the Lord forgave you. 14And over all these
virtues put on love, which binds them all
together in perfect unity.
15Let the peace of Christ rule in your
hearts, since as members of one body you
were called to peace. And be thankful. 16Let
the word of Christ dwell in you richly as
you teach and admonish one another with
all wisdom, and as you sing psalms, hymns
and spiritual songs with gratitude in your
hearts to God. 17And whatever you do,
whether in word or deed, do it all in the
name of the Lord Jesus, giving thanks to
God the Father through him.

Rules for Christian Households

18Wives, submit to your husbands, as is
fitting in the Lord.
19Husbands, love your wives and do not
be harsh with them.
20Children, obey your parents in everything, for this pleases the Lord.
21Fathers, do not embitter your children, or they will become discouraged.
22Slaves, obey your earthly masters in
everything; and do it, not only when their
eye is on you and to win their favor, but
with sincerity of heart and reverence for the
Lord. 23Whatever you do, work at it with all
your heart, as working for the Lord, not for
men, 24since you know that you will receive
an inheritance from the Lord as a reward.
It is the Lord Christ you are serving. 25Any-
one who does wrong will be repaid for his
wrong, and there is no favoritism.

[a] 4 Some manuscripts *our* [b] 6 Some early manuscripts *coming on those who are disobedient*

PRAYER: THE CHARACTER I WANT TO CULTIVATE

IT is better that I have a humble spirit with the lowly than to divide the spoil with the proud. (Proverbs 16:19) . . . If I am proud, I will be brought low, but with a humble spirit I will gain honor. (Proverbs 29:23)

***TAKE** a moment to ask the Lord for the grace to grow in godly character.*

YEAR 2 DAY 195

OT Jeremiah 7:1–34

False Religion Worthless

7 This is the word that came to Jeremiah
from the LORD: 2"Stand at the gate of
the LORD's house and there proclaim this
message:
" 'Hear the word of the LORD, all you
people of Judah who come through these
gates to worship the LORD. 3This is what the
LORD Almighty, the God of Israel, says: Reform your ways and your actions, and I will

let you live in this place. 4Do not trust in deceptive words and say, "This is the temple of the LORD, the temple of the LORD, the temple of the LORD!" 5If you really change your ways and your actions and deal with each other justly, 6if you do not oppress the alien, the fatherless or the widow and do not shed innocent blood in this place, and if you do not follow other gods to your own harm, 7then I will let you live in this place, in the land I gave your forefathers for ever and ever. 8But look, you are trusting in deceptive words that are worthless.

9" 'Will you steal and murder, commit adultery and perjury,[a] burn incense to Baal and follow other gods you have not known, 10and then come and stand before me in this house, which bears my Name, and say, "We are safe"—safe to do all these detestable things? 11Has this house, which bears my Name, become a den of robbers to you? But I have been watching! declares the LORD.

12" 'Go now to the place in Shiloh where I first made a dwelling for my Name, and see what I did to it because of the wickedness of my people Israel. 13While you were doing all these things, declares the LORD, I spoke to you again and again, but you did not listen; I called you, but you did not answer. 14Therefore, what I did to Shiloh I will now do to the house that bears my Name, the temple you trust in, the place I gave to you and your fathers. 15I will thrust you from my presence, just as I did all your brothers, the people of Ephraim.'

16"So do not pray for this people nor offer any plea or petition for them; do not plead with me, for I will not listen to you. 17Do you not see what they are doing in the towns of Judah and in the streets of Jerusalem? 18The children gather wood, the fathers light the fire, and the women knead the dough and make cakes of bread for the Queen of Heaven. They pour out drink offerings to other gods to provoke me to anger. 19But am I the one they are provoking? declares the LORD. Are they not rather harming themselves, to their own shame?

20" 'Therefore this is what the Sovereign LORD says: My anger and my wrath will be poured out on this place, on man and beast, on the trees of the field and on the fruit of the ground, and it will burn and not be quenched.

21" 'This is what the LORD Almighty, the God of Israel, says: Go ahead, add your burnt offerings to your other sacrifices and eat the meat yourselves! 22For when I brought your forefathers out of Egypt and spoke to them, I did not just give them commands about burnt offerings and sacrifices, 23but I gave them this command: Obey me, and I will be your God and you will be my people. Walk in all the ways I command you, that it may go well with you. 24But they did not listen or pay attention; instead, they followed the stubborn inclinations of their evil hearts. They went backward and not forward. 25From the time your forefathers left Egypt until now, day after day, again and again I sent you my servants the prophets. 26But they did not listen to me or pay attention. They were stiff-necked and did more evil than their forefathers.'

27"When you tell them all this, they will not listen to you; when you call to them, they will not answer. 28Therefore say to them, 'This is the nation that has not obeyed the LORD its God or responded to correction. Truth has perished; it has vanished from their lips. 29Cut off your hair and throw it away; take up a lament on the barren heights, for the LORD has rejected and abandoned this generation that is under his wrath.

The Valley of Slaughter

30" 'The people of Judah have done evil in my eyes, declares the LORD. They have set up their detestable idols in the house that bears my Name and have defiled it. 31They have built the high places of Topheth in the Valley of Ben Hinnom to burn their sons and daughters in the fire—something I did not command, nor did it enter my mind. 32So beware, the days are coming, declares the LORD, when people will no longer call it Topheth or the Valley of Ben Hinnom, but the Valley of Slaughter, for they will bury the dead in Topheth until there is no more room. 33Then the carcasses of this people will become food for the birds of the air and the beasts of the earth, and there will be no one to frighten them away. 34I will bring an end to the sounds of joy and gladness and to the voices of bride and bridegroom in the towns of Judah and the streets of Jerusalem, for the land will become desolate.

[a] 9 Or *and swear by false gods*

PRAYER: THANKSGIVING

YOU raised up Pharaoh for this purpose, that You might show him Your power and that Your name might be proclaimed through all the earth. (Exodus 9:16) . . . Others may intend evil, but You can use it for good to accomplish Your loving purposes. (Genesis 50:20)

***PAUSE** to offer your own expressions of thanksgiving.*

NT Colossians 4:1-18

4 Masters, provide your slaves with what
is right and fair, because you know that
you also have a Master in heaven.

Further Instructions

[2]Devote yourselves to prayer, being
watchful and thankful. [3]And pray for us,
too, that God may open a door for our
message, so that we may proclaim the
mystery of Christ, for which I am in
chains. [4]Pray that I may proclaim it clearly, as I should. [5]Be wise in the way you act
toward outsiders; make the most of every
opportunity. [6]Let your conversation be always full of grace, seasoned with salt, so
that you may know how to answer everyone.

Final Greetings

[7]Tychicus will tell you all the news
about me. He is a dear brother, a faithful
minister and fellow servant in the Lord. [8]I
am sending him to you for the express
purpose that you may know about our[a]
circumstances and that he may encourage
your hearts. [9]He is coming with Onesimus, our faithful and dear brother, who is
one of you. They will tell you everything
that is happening here.
[10]My fellow prisoner Aristarchus sends
you his greetings, as does Mark, the
cousin of Barnabas. (You have received instructions about him; if he comes to you,
welcome him.) [11]Jesus, who is called Justus, also sends greetings. These are the
only Jews among my fellow workers for
the kingdom of God, and they have
proved a comfort to me. [12]Epaphras, who
is one of you and a servant of Christ Jesus,
sends greetings. He is always wrestling in
prayer for you, that you may stand firm in
all the will of God, mature and fully assured. [13]I vouch for him that he is working hard for you and for those at Laodicea and Hierapolis. [14]Our dear friend
Luke, the doctor, and Demas send greetings. [15]Give my greetings to the brothers
at Laodicea, and to Nympha and the
church in her house.
[16]After this letter has been read to you,
see that it is also read in the church of the
Laodiceans and that you in turn read the
letter from Laodicea.
[17]Tell Archippus: "See to it that you
complete the work you have received in
the Lord."
[18]I, Paul, write this greeting in my own
hand. Remember my chains. Grace be
with you.

[a] 8 Some manuscripts *that he may know about your*

PRAYER: MY RELATIONSHIP TO OTHERS

THE husband should fulfill his marital duty to his wife, and likewise the wife to her husband. The wife's body does not belong to her alone, but also to her husband. In the same way, the husband's body does not belong to him alone, but also to his wife. (1 Corinthians 7:3–4) . . . Each husband must love his own wife as he loves himself, and each wife must respect her husband. (Ephesians 5:33)

***PAUSE** to review your relationships with others and to commit them to the Lord.*

Psalm 110

Of David. A psalm.

1 The LORD says to my Lord:
"Sit at my right hand
until I make your enemies
a footstool for your feet."

2 The LORD will extend your mighty scepter from Zion;
you will rule in the midst of your enemies.
3 Your troops will be willing
on your day of battle.
Arrayed in holy majesty,
from the womb of the dawn
you will receive the dew of your youth.[a]

4 The LORD has sworn
and will not change his mind:
"You are a priest forever,
in the order of Melchizedek."

5 The Lord is at your right hand;
he will crush kings on the day of his wrath.
6 He will judge the nations, heaping up the dead
and crushing the rulers of the whole earth.
7 He will drink from a brook beside the way[b];
therefore he will lift up his head.

Psalm 111[c]

1 Praise the LORD.[d]

I will extol the LORD with all my heart
in the council of the upright and in the assembly.

2 Great are the works of the LORD;
they are pondered by all who delight in them.
3 Glorious and majestic are his deeds,
and his righteousness endures forever.
4 He has caused his wonders to be remembered;
the LORD is gracious and compassionate.
5 He provides food for those who fear him;
he remembers his covenant forever.
6 He has shown his people the power of his works,
giving them the lands of other nations.
7 The works of his hands are faithful and just;
all his precepts are trustworthy.
8 They are steadfast for ever and ever,
done in faithfulness and uprightness.
9 He provided redemption for his people;
he ordained his covenant forever—
holy and awesome is his name.

10 The fear of the LORD is the beginning of wisdom;
all who follow his precepts have good understanding.
To him belongs eternal praise.

[a] 3 Or / *your young men will come to you like the dew* [b] 7 Or / *The One who grants succession will set him in authority* [c] This psalm is an acrostic poem, the lines of which begin with the successive letters of the Hebrew alphabet. [d] 1 Hebrew *Hallelu Yah*

PRAYER: ADORATION

YOU, O Lord of hosts, are wonderful in counsel and great in wisdom. (Isaiah 28:29) . . . You are the Lord, and there is no savior besides You. From ancient days You are He, and no one can deliver out of Your hand; You act, and who can reverse it? (Isaiah 43:11, 13)

PAUSE *to express your thoughts of praise and worship.*

NT Luke 1:1-56

Introduction

1 Many have undertaken to draw up an account of the things that have been fulfilled[a] among us, [2]just as they were handed down to us by those who from the first were eyewitnesses and servants of the word. [3]Therefore, since I myself have carefully investigated everything from the beginning, it seemed good also to me to write an orderly account for you, most excellent Theophilus, [4]so that you may know the certainty of the things you have been taught.

The Birth of John the Baptist Foretold

[5]In the time of Herod king of Judea there was a priest named Zechariah, who belonged to the priestly division of Abijah; his wife Elizabeth was also a descendant of Aaron. [6]Both of them were upright in the sight of God, observing all the Lord's commandments and regulations blamelessly. [7]But they had no children, because Elizabeth was barren; and they were both well along in years.

[8]Once when Zechariah's division was on duty and he was serving as priest before God, [9]he was chosen by lot, according to the custom of the priesthood, to go into the temple of the Lord and burn incense. [10]And when the time for the burning of incense came, all the assembled worshipers were praying outside.

[11]Then an angel of the Lord appeared to him, standing at the right side of the altar of incense. [12]When Zechariah saw him, he was startled and was gripped with fear. [13]But the angel said to him: "Do not be afraid, Zechariah; your prayer has been heard. Your wife Elizabeth will bear you a son, and you are to give him the name John. [14]He will be a joy and delight to you, and many will rejoice because of his birth, [15]for he will be great in the sight of the Lord. He is never to take wine or other fermented drink, and he will be filled with the Holy Spirit even from birth.[b] [16]Many of the people of Israel will he bring back to the Lord their God. [17]And he will go on before the Lord, in the spirit and power of Elijah, to turn the hearts of the fathers to their children and the disobedient to the wisdom of the righteous—to make ready a people prepared for the Lord."

[18]Zechariah asked the angel, "How can I be sure of this? I am an old man and my wife is well along in years."

[19]The angel answered, "I am Gabriel. I stand in the presence of God, and I have been sent to speak to you and to tell you this good news. [20]And now you will be silent and not able to speak until the day this happens, because you did not believe my words, which will come true at their proper time."

[21]Meanwhile, the people were waiting for Zechariah and wondering why he stayed so long in the temple. [22]When he came out, he could not speak to them. They realized he had seen a vision in the temple, for he kept making signs to them but remained unable to speak.

[23]When his time of service was completed, he returned home. [24]After this his wife Elizabeth became pregnant and for five months remained in seclusion. [25]"The Lord has done this for me," she said. "In these days he has shown his favor and taken away my disgrace among the people."

The Birth of Jesus Foretold

[26]In the sixth month, God sent the angel Gabriel to Nazareth, a town in Galilee, [27]to a virgin pledged to be married to a man named Joseph, a descendant of David. The virgin's name was Mary. [28]The angel went to her and said, "Greetings, you who are highly favored! The Lord is with you."

[29]Mary was greatly troubled at his words and wondered what kind of greeting this might be. [30]But the angel said to her, "Do not be afraid, Mary, you have found favor with God. [31]You will be with child and give birth to a son, and you are to give him the name Jesus. [32]He will be great and will be called the Son of the Most High. The Lord God will give him the throne of his father David, [33]and he will reign over the house of Jacob forever; his kingdom will never end."

[34]"How will this be," Mary asked the angel, "since I am a virgin?"

[35]The angel answered, "The Holy Spirit will come upon you, and the power of the Most High will overshadow you. So the holy one to be born will be called[c] the

[a] 1 Or *been surely believed* [b] 15 Or *from his mother's womb* [c] 35 Or *So the child to be born will be called holy,*

Son of God. 36 Even Elizabeth your relative
is going to have a child in her old age, and
she who was said to be barren is in her
sixth month. 37 For nothing is impossible
with God."
38 "I am the Lord's servant," Mary answered. "May it be to me as you have
said." Then the angel left her.

Mary Visits Elizabeth

39 At that time Mary got ready and hurried
to a town in the hill country of Judea,
40 where she entered Zechariah's home and
greeted Elizabeth. 41 When Elizabeth heard
Mary's greeting, the baby leaped in her
womb, and Elizabeth was filled with the
Holy Spirit. 42 In a loud voice she exclaimed:
"Blessed are you among women, and
blessed is the child you will bear! 43 But why
am I so favored, that the mother of my Lord
should come to me? 44 As soon as the sound
of your greeting reached my ears, the baby
in my womb leaped for joy. 45 Blessed is she
who has believed that what the Lord has
said to her will be accomplished!"

Mary's Song

46 And Mary said:

"My soul glorifies the Lord
47 and my spirit rejoices in God my
Savior,
48 for he has been mindful
of the humble state of his servant.
From now on all generations will call
me blessed,
49 for the Mighty One has done great
things for me—
holy is his name.
50 His mercy extends to those who fear
him,
from generation to generation.
51 He has performed mighty deeds with
his arm;
he has scattered those who are
proud in their inmost thoughts.
52 He has brought down rulers from
their thrones
but has lifted up the humble.
53 He has filled the hungry with good
things
but has sent the rich away empty.
54 He has helped his servant Israel,
remembering to be merciful
55 to Abraham and his descendants
forever,
even as he said to our fathers."

56 Mary stayed with Elizabeth for about
three months and then returned home.

PRAYER: THE ATTRIBUTES OF GOD

YOUR voice, O God, thunders in marvelous ways; You do great things which we cannot comprehend. (Job 37:5) . . .
Your counsel, O Lord, stands firm forever, the plans of Your heart through all generations. (Psalm 33:11)

***PAUSE** to reflect on these affirmations about the person, powers and perfection of God.*

YEAR 2
DAY 197

OT Jeremiah 8:1–9:26

8 " 'At that time, declares the LORD, the
bones of the kings and officials of Judah, the bones of the priests and prophets, and the bones of the people of Jerusalem will be removed from their graves.
2 They will be exposed to the sun and the
moon and all the stars of the heavens,
which they have loved and served and
which they have followed and consulted
and worshiped. They will not be gathered
up or buried, but will be like refuse lying
on the ground. 3 Wherever I banish them,
all the survivors of this evil nation will
prefer death to life, declares the LORD
Almighty.'

Sin and Punishment

4 "Say to them, 'This is what the LORD
says:

" 'When men fall down, do they not get up?
When a man turns away, does he not return?
5 Why then have these people turned away?
Why does Jerusalem always turn away?
They cling to deceit;
they refuse to return.
6 I have listened attentively,
but they do not say what is right.
No one repents of his wickedness,
saying, "What have I done?"
Each pursues his own course
like a horse charging into battle.
7 Even the stork in the sky
knows her appointed seasons,
and the dove, the swift and the thrush
observe the time of their migration.
But my people do not know
the requirements of the LORD.

8 " 'How can you say, "We are wise,
for we have the law of the LORD,"
when actually the lying pen of the scribes
has handled it falsely?
9 The wise will be put to shame;
they will be dismayed and trapped.
Since they have rejected the word of the LORD,
what kind of wisdom do they have?
10 Therefore I will give their wives to other men
and their fields to new owners.
From the least to the greatest,
all are greedy for gain;
prophets and priests alike,
all practice deceit.
11 They dress the wound of my people
as though it were not serious.
"Peace, peace," they say,
when there is no peace.
12 Are they ashamed of their loathsome conduct?
No, they have no shame at all;
they do not even know how to blush.
So they will fall among the fallen;
they will be brought down when they are punished,
says the LORD.

13 " 'I will take away their harvest,
declares the LORD.
There will be no grapes on the vine.
There will be no figs on the tree,
and their leaves will wither.
What I have given them
will be taken from them.[a]' "

14 "Why are we sitting here?
Gather together!
Let us flee to the fortified cities
and perish there!
For the LORD our God has doomed us to perish
and given us poisoned water to drink,
because we have sinned against him.
15 We hoped for peace
but no good has come,
for a time of healing
but there was only terror.
16 The snorting of the enemy's horses
is heard from Dan;
at the neighing of their stallions
the whole land trembles.
They have come to devour
the land and everything in it,
the city and all who live there."

17 "See, I will send venomous snakes among you,
vipers that cannot be charmed,
and they will bite you,"
declares the LORD.

18 O my Comforter[b] in sorrow,
my heart is faint within me.
19 Listen to the cry of my people
from a land far away:
"Is the LORD not in Zion?
Is her King no longer there?"

"Why have they provoked me to anger with their images,
with their worthless foreign idols?"

20 "The harvest is past,
the summer has ended,
and we are not saved."

21 Since my people are crushed, I am crushed;
I mourn, and horror grips me.
22 Is there no balm in Gilead?
Is there no physician there?
Why then is there no healing
for the wound of my people?

9 1 Oh, that my head were a spring of water
and my eyes a fountain of tears!
I would weep day and night

[a] *13* The meaning of the Hebrew for this sentence is uncertain. [b] *18* The meaning of the Hebrew for this word is uncertain.

for the slain of my people.
[2]Oh, that I had in the desert
a lodging place for travelers,
so that I might leave my people
and go away from them;
for they are all adulterers,
a crowd of unfaithful people.

[3]"They make ready their tongue
like a bow, to shoot lies;
it is not by truth
that they triumph[c] in the land.
They go from one sin to another;
they do not acknowledge me,"
declares the LORD.
[4]"Beware of your friends;
do not trust your brothers.
For every brother is a deceiver,[d]
and every friend a slanderer.
[5]Friend deceives friend,
and no one speaks the truth.
They have taught their tongues to lie;
they weary themselves with sinning.
[6]You[e] live in the midst of deception;
in their deceit they refuse to
acknowledge me,"
declares the LORD.

[7]Therefore this is what the LORD Almighty says:

"See, I will refine and test them,
for what else can I do
because of the sin of my people?
[8]Their tongue is a deadly arrow,
it speaks with deceit.
With his mouth each speaks cordially
to his neighbor,
but in his heart he sets a trap for
him.
[9]Should I not punish them for this?"
declares the LORD.
"Should I not avenge myself
on such a nation as this?"

[10]I will weep and wail for the
mountains
and take up a lament concerning
the desert pastures.
They are desolate and untraveled,
and the lowing of cattle is not
heard.
The birds of the air have fled
and the animals are gone.

[11]"I will make Jerusalem a heap of
ruins,
a haunt of jackals;
and I will lay waste the towns of Judah
so no one can live there."

[12]What man is wise enough to understand this? Who has been instructed by
the LORD and can explain it? Why has the
land been ruined and laid waste like a
desert that no one can cross?
[13]The LORD said, "It is because they have
forsaken my law, which I set before them;
they have not obeyed me or followed my
law. [14]Instead, they have followed the
stubbornness of their hearts; they have
followed the Baals, as their fathers taught
them." [15]Therefore, this is what the LORD
Almighty, the God of Israel, says: "See, I
will make this people eat bitter food and
drink poisoned water. [16]I will scatter them
among nations that neither they nor their
fathers have known, and I will pursue
them with the sword until I have destroyed them."

[17]This is what the LORD Almighty says:

"Consider now! Call for the wailing
women to come;
send for the most skillful of them.
[18]Let them come quickly
and wail over us
till our eyes overflow with tears
and water streams from our eyelids.
[19]The sound of wailing is heard from
Zion:
'How ruined we are!
How great is our shame!
We must leave our land
because our houses are in ruins.' "

[20]Now, O women, hear the word of the
LORD;
open your ears to the words of his
mouth.
Teach your daughters how to wail;
teach one another a lament.
[21]Death has climbed in through our
windows
and has entered our fortresses;
it has cut off the children from the
streets
and the young men from the public
squares.

[22]Say, "This is what the LORD declares:

" 'The dead bodies of men will lie
like refuse on the open field,
like cut grain behind the reaper,

[c]3 Or *lies; / they are not valiant for truth* [d]4 Or *a deceiving Jacob* [e]6 That is, Jeremiah (the Hebrew is singular)

with no one to gather them.' "

[23]This is what the LORD says:

"Let not the wise man boast of his
wisdom
or the strong man boast of his
strength
or the rich man boast of his riches,
[24]but let him who boasts boast about
this:
that he understands and knows me,
that I am the LORD, who exercises
kindness,
justice and righteousness on earth,
for in these I delight,"
declares the LORD.

[25]"The days are coming," declares the
LORD, "when I will punish all who are circumcised only in the flesh— [26]Egypt, Judah, Edom, Ammon, Moab and all who
live in the desert in distant places.[f] For all
these nations are really uncircumcised,
and even the whole house of Israel is uncircumcised in heart."

[f]26 Or *desert and who clip the hair by their foreheads*

PRAYER: CONFESSION

O SERVANT of God, people despised and rejected You; You were a man of sorrows, and acquainted with grief. And like one from whom others hide their faces, You were despised, and we did not esteem You. Surely You have borne our infirmities and carried our sorrows; yet we considered You stricken, smitten by God, and afflicted. But You were pierced for our transgressions, You were crushed for our iniquities; the punishment that brought us peace was upon You, and by Your wounds we are healed. All of us like sheep have gone astray, all of us have turned to our own way, and the Lord has laid on You the iniquity of us all. (Isaiah 53:3–6)

***ASK** the Spirit to search your heart and reveal any areas of unconfessed sin. Acknowledge these to the Lord and thank Him for His forgiveness.*

NT Luke 1:57-80

The Birth of John the Baptist

[57]When it was time for Elizabeth to
have her baby, she gave birth to a son.
[58]Her neighbors and relatives heard that
the Lord had shown her great mercy, and
they shared her joy.
[59]On the eighth day they came to circumcise the child, and they were going to
name him after his father Zechariah, [60]but
his mother spoke up and said, "No! He is
to be called John."
[61]They said to her, "There is no one
among your relatives who has that name."
[62]Then they made signs to his father, to
find out what he would like to name the
child. [63]He asked for a writing tablet, and
to everyone's astonishment he wrote, "His
name is John." [64]Immediately his mouth
was opened and his tongue was loosed,
and he began to speak, praising God. [65]The
neighbors were all filled with awe, and
throughout the hill country of Judea people were talking about all these things.
[66]Everyone who heard this wondered about
it, asking, "What then is this child going to
be?" For the Lord's hand was with him.

Zechariah's Song

[67]His father Zechariah was filled with
the Holy Spirit and prophesied:

[68]"Praise be to the Lord, the God of
Israel,
because he has come and has
redeemed his people.
[69]He has raised up a horn[a] of salvation
for us
in the house of his servant David
[70](as he said through his holy prophets
of long ago),
[71]salvation from our enemies
and from the hand of all who hate
us—
[72]to show mercy to our fathers
and to remember his holy covenant,

[a]69 *Horn* here symbolizes strength.

73 the oath he swore to our father
Abraham:
74 to rescue us from the hand of our
enemies,
and to enable us to serve him
without fear
75 in holiness and righteousness
before him all our days.

76 And you, my child, will be called a
prophet of the Most High;
for you will go on before the Lord
to prepare the way for him,
77 to give his people the knowledge of
salvation
through the forgiveness of their
sins,
78 because of the tender mercy of our
God,
by which the rising sun will come
to us from heaven
79 to shine on those living in darkness
and in the shadow of death,
to guide our feet into the path of
peace."

80 And the child grew and became strong
in spirit; and he lived in the desert until
he appeared publicly to Israel.

PRAYER: THE WORKS OF GOD

FROM Your fullness, O Jesus Christ, we have all received grace upon grace. For the law was given through Moses; grace and truth came through You. (John 1:16–17) . . . It is the Spirit who gives life; the flesh counts for nothing. The words You spoke, Jesus, are spirit and life. (John 6:63)

***TAKE** a moment to consider the greatness of God's wonderful works.*

YEAR 2 DAY 198

OT Jeremiah 10:1-25

God and Idols

10 Hear what the LORD says to you,
O house of Israel. 2 This is what the
LORD says:

"Do not learn the ways of the nations
or be terrified by signs in the sky,
though the nations are terrified by
them.
3 For the customs of the peoples are
worthless;
they cut a tree out of the forest,
and a craftsman shapes it with his
chisel.
4 They adorn it with silver and gold;
they fasten it with hammer and
nails
so it will not totter.
5 Like a scarecrow in a melon patch,
their idols cannot speak;
they must be carried
because they cannot walk.
Do not fear them;
they can do no harm
nor can they do any good."
6 No one is like you, O LORD;
you are great,
and your name is mighty in
power.
7 Who should not revere you,
O King of the nations?
This is your due.
Among all the wise men of the
nations
and in all their kingdoms,
there is no one like you.
8 They are all senseless and foolish;
they are taught by worthless
wooden idols.
9 Hammered silver is brought from
Tarshish
and gold from Uphaz.
What the craftsman and goldsmith
have made
is then dressed in blue and
purple—
all made by skilled workers.
10 But the LORD is the true God;
he is the living God, the eternal
King.

When he is angry, the earth trembles;
the nations cannot endure his wrath.

[11] "Tell them this: 'These gods, who did not make the heavens and the earth, will perish from the earth and from under the heavens.' "[a]

[12] But God made the earth by his power;
he founded the world by his wisdom
and stretched out the heavens by his understanding.
[13] When he thunders, the waters in the heavens roar;
he makes clouds rise from the ends of the earth.
He sends lightning with the rain
and brings out the wind from his storehouses.

[14] Everyone is senseless and without knowledge;
every goldsmith is shamed by his idols.
His images are a fraud;
they have no breath in them.
[15] They are worthless, the objects of mockery;
when their judgment comes, they will perish.
[16] He who is the Portion of Jacob is not like these,
for he is the Maker of all things,
including Israel, the tribe of his inheritance—
the LORD Almighty is his name.

Coming Destruction

[17] Gather up your belongings to leave the land,
you who live under siege.
[18] For this is what the LORD says:
"At this time I will hurl out
those who live in this land;
I will bring distress on them
so that they may be captured."

[19] Woe to me because of my injury!
My wound is incurable!
Yet I said to myself,
"This is my sickness, and I must endure it."
[20] My tent is destroyed;
all its ropes are snapped.
My sons are gone from me and are no more;
no one is left now to pitch my tent
or to set up my shelter.
[21] The shepherds are senseless
and do not inquire of the LORD;
so they do not prosper
and all their flock is scattered.
[22] Listen! The report is coming—
a great commotion from the land of the north!
It will make the towns of Judah desolate,
a haunt of jackals.

Jeremiah's Prayer

[23] I know, O LORD, that a man's life is not his own;
it is not for man to direct his steps.
[24] Correct me, LORD, but only with justice—
not in your anger,
lest you reduce me to nothing.
[25] Pour out your wrath on the nations
that do not acknowledge you,
on the peoples who do not call on your name.
For they have devoured Jacob;
they have devoured him completely
and destroyed his homeland.

[a] *11* The text of this verse is in Aramaic.

PRAYER: RENEWAL

MAY I not become weary in doing good, for at the proper time I will reap a harvest if I do not give up. (Galatians 6:9) . . . May I work out my salvation with fear and trembling, for it is You, O God, who work in me to will and to act according to Your good purpose. (Philippians 2:12–13)

PAUSE *to add your own prayers for personal renewal.*

NT **Luke 2:1-40**

The Birth of Jesus

2 In those days Caesar Augustus issued a decree that a census should be taken of the entire Roman world. 2(This was the first census that took place while Quirinius was governor of Syria.) 3And everyone went to his own town to register.

4So Joseph also went up from the town of Nazareth in Galilee to Judea, to Bethlehem the town of David, because he belonged to the house and line of David. 5He went there to register with Mary, who was pledged to be married to him and was expecting a child. 6While they were there, the time came for the baby to be born, 7and she gave birth to her firstborn, a son. She wrapped him in cloths and placed him in a manger, because there was no room for them in the inn.

The Shepherds and the Angels

8And there were shepherds living out in the fields nearby, keeping watch over their flocks at night. 9An angel of the Lord appeared to them, and the glory of the Lord shone around them, and they were terrified. 10But the angel said to them, "Do not be afraid. I bring you good news of great joy that will be for all the people. 11Today in the town of David a Savior has been born to you; he is Christ[a] the Lord. 12This will be a sign to you: You will find a baby wrapped in cloths and lying in a manger."

13Suddenly a great company of the heavenly host appeared with the angel, praising God and saying,

14"Glory to God in the highest,
and on earth peace to men on
whom his favor rests."

15When the angels had left them and gone into heaven, the shepherds said to one another, "Let's go to Bethlehem and see this thing that has happened, which the Lord has told us about."

16So they hurried off and found Mary and Joseph, and the baby, who was lying in the manger. 17When they had seen him, they spread the word concerning what had been told them about this child, 18and all who heard it were amazed at what the shepherds said to them. 19But Mary treasured up all these things and pondered them in her heart. 20The shepherds returned, glorifying and praising God for all the things they had heard and seen, which were just as they had been told.

Jesus Presented in the Temple

21On the eighth day, when it was time to circumcise him, he was named Jesus, the name the angel had given him before he had been conceived.

22When the time of their purification according to the Law of Moses had been completed, Joseph and Mary took him to Jerusalem to present him to the Lord 23(as it is written in the Law of the Lord, "Every firstborn male is to be consecrated to the Lord"[b]), 24and to offer a sacrifice in keeping with what is said in the Law of the Lord: "a pair of doves or two young pigeons."[c]

25Now there was a man in Jerusalem called Simeon, who was righteous and devout. He was waiting for the consolation of Israel, and the Holy Spirit was upon him. 26It had been revealed to him by the Holy Spirit that he would not die before he had seen the Lord's Christ. 27Moved by the Spirit, he went into the temple courts. When the parents brought in the child Jesus to do for him what the custom of the Law required, 28Simeon took him in his arms and praised God, saying:

29"Sovereign Lord, as you have
promised,
you now dismiss[d] your servant in
peace.
30For my eyes have seen your salvation,
31 which you have prepared in the
sight of all people,
32a light for revelation to the Gentiles
and for glory to your people Israel."

33The child's father and mother marveled at what was said about him. 34Then Simeon blessed them and said to Mary, his mother: "This child is destined to cause the falling and rising of many in Israel, and to be a sign that will be spoken against, 35so that the thoughts of many

[a] 11 Or *Messiah.* "The Christ" (Greek) and "the Messiah" (Hebrew) both mean "the Anointed One"; also in verse 26. [b] 23 Exodus 13:2,12 [c] 24 Lev. 12:8 [d] 29 Or *promised, / now dismiss*

hearts will be revealed. And a sword will pierce your own soul too."

[36]There was also a prophetess, Anna, the daughter of Phanuel, of the tribe of Asher. She was very old; she had lived with her husband seven years after her marriage, [37]and then was a widow until she was eighty-four.[e] She never left the temple but worshiped night and day, fasting and praying. [38]Coming up to them at that very moment, she gave thanks to God and spoke about the child to all who were looking forward to the redemption of Jerusalem.

[39]When Joseph and Mary had done everything required by the Law of the Lord, they returned to Galilee to their own town of Nazareth. [40]And the child grew and became strong; he was filled with wisdom, and the grace of God was upon him.

[e] 37 Or *widow for eighty-four years*

PRAYER: MY RELATIONSHIP TO GOD

I SHALL not live on bread alone, O God, but on every word that comes from Your mouth. (Matthew 4:4) . . . You are the bread of God; You come down from heaven and give life to the world. You are the bread of life. The one who comes to You will never hunger, and the one who believes in You will never thirst. (John 6:33, 35)

***PAUSE** to thank God for the relationship that you enjoy with Him in Jesus Christ.*

YEAR 2 DAY 199

OT Jeremiah 11:1–12:17

The Covenant Is Broken

11 This is the word that came to Jeremiah from the LORD: [2]"Listen to the terms of this covenant and tell them to the people of Judah and to those who live in Jerusalem. [3]Tell them that this is what the LORD, the God of Israel, says: 'Cursed is the man who does not obey the terms of this covenant— [4]the terms I commanded your forefathers when I brought them out of Egypt, out of the iron-smelting furnace.' I said, 'Obey me and do everything I command you, and you will be my people, and I will be your God. [5]Then I will fulfill the oath I swore to your forefathers, to give them a land flowing with milk and honey'—the land you possess today."

I answered, "Amen, LORD."

[6]The LORD said to me, "Proclaim all these words in the towns of Judah and in the streets of Jerusalem: 'Listen to the terms of this covenant and follow them. [7]From the time I brought your forefathers up from Egypt until today, I warned them again and again, saying, "Obey me." [8]But they did not listen or pay attention; instead, they followed the stubbornness of their evil hearts. So I brought on them all the curses of the covenant I had commanded them to follow but that they did not keep.' "

[9]Then the LORD said to me, "There is a conspiracy among the people of Judah and those who live in Jerusalem. [10]They have returned to the sins of their forefathers, who refused to listen to my words. They have followed other gods to serve them. Both the house of Israel and the house of Judah have broken the covenant I made with their forefathers. [11]Therefore this is what the LORD says: 'I will bring on them a disaster they cannot escape. Although they cry out to me, I will not listen to them. [12]The towns of Judah and the people of Jerusalem will go and cry out to the gods to whom they burn incense, but they will not help them at all when disaster strikes. [13]You have as many gods as you have towns, O Judah; and the altars you have set up to burn incense to that shameful god Baal are as many as the streets of Jerusalem.'

[14]"Do not pray for this people nor offer any plea or petition for them, because I

will not listen when they call to me in the time of their distress.

[15]"What is my beloved doing in my temple
as she works out her evil schemes with many?
Can consecrated meat avert ⌞your punishment⌟?
When you engage in your wickedness,
then you rejoice.[a]"

[16]The LORD called you a thriving olive tree
with fruit beautiful in form.
But with the roar of a mighty storm
he will set it on fire,
and its branches will be broken.

[17]The LORD Almighty, who planted you, has decreed disaster for you, because the house of Israel and the house of Judah have done evil and provoked me to anger by burning incense to Baal.

Plot Against Jeremiah

[18]Because the LORD revealed their plot
to me, I knew it, for at that time he
showed me what they were doing. [19]I had
been like a gentle lamb led to the slaughter; I did not realize that they had plotted against me, saying,

"Let us destroy the tree and its fruit;
let us cut him off from the land of the living,
that his name be remembered no more."
[20]But, O LORD Almighty, you who judge righteously
and test the heart and mind,
let me see your vengeance upon them,
for to you I have committed my cause.

[21]"Therefore this is what the LORD says
about the men of Anathoth who are seeking your life and saying, 'Do not prophesy in the name of the LORD or you will die
by our hands'— [22]therefore this is what
the LORD Almighty says: 'I will punish them. Their young men will die by the sword, their sons and daughters by
famine. [23]Not even a remnant will be left
to them, because I will bring disaster on the men of Anathoth in the year of their punishment.' "

Jeremiah's Complaint

12 You are always righteous, O LORD,
when I bring a case before you.
Yet I would speak with you about your justice:
Why does the way of the wicked prosper?
Why do all the faithless live at ease?
[2]You have planted them, and they have taken root;
they grow and bear fruit.
You are always on their lips
but far from their hearts.
[3]Yet you know me, O LORD;
you see me and test my thoughts about you.
Drag them off like sheep to be butchered!
Set them apart for the day of slaughter!
[4]How long will the land lie parched[b]
and the grass in every field be withered?
Because those who live in it are wicked,
the animals and birds have perished.
Moreover, the people are saying,
"He will not see what happens to us."

God's Answer

[5]"If you have raced with men on foot
and they have worn you out,
how can you compete with horses?
If you stumble in safe country,[c]
how will you manage in the thickets by[d] the Jordan?
[6]Your brothers, your own family—
even they have betrayed you;
they have raised a loud cry against you.
Do not trust them,
though they speak well of you.

[7]"I will forsake my house,
abandon my inheritance;
I will give the one I love
into the hands of her enemies.
[8]My inheritance has become to me
like a lion in the forest.
She roars at me;

[a] 15 Or *Could consecrated meat avert your punishment? / Then you would rejoice* [b] 4 Or *land mourn* [c] 5 Or *If you put your trust in a land of safety* [d] 5 Or *the flooding of*

therefore I hate her.
[9]Has not my inheritance become to me
like a speckled bird of prey
that other birds of prey surround
and attack?
Go and gather all the wild beasts;
bring them to devour.
[10]Many shepherds will ruin my vineyard
and trample down my field;
they will turn my pleasant field
into a desolate wasteland.
[11]It will be made a wasteland,
parched and desolate before me;
the whole land will be laid waste
because there is no one who cares.
[12]Over all the barren heights in the
desert
destroyers will swarm,
for the sword of the LORD will devour
from one end of the land to the
other;
no one will be safe.
[13]They will sow wheat but reap thorns;
they will wear themselves out but
gain nothing.
So bear the shame of your harvest
because of the LORD's fierce anger."

[14]This is what the LORD says: "As for all
my wicked neighbors who seize the inheritance I gave my people Israel, I will
uproot them from their lands and I will
uproot the house of Judah from among
them. [15]But after I uproot them, I will
again have compassion and will bring
each of them back to his own inheritance
and his own country. [16]And if they learn
well the ways of my people and swear by
my name, saying, 'As surely as the LORD
lives'—even as they once taught my people to swear by Baal—then they will be established among my people. [17]But if any
nation does not listen, I will completely
uproot and destroy it," declares the LORD.

PRAYER: PETITION

MAY I obey those who are in authority over me with fear and trembling and with sincerity of heart, as I would obey Christ—not with external service as one who wants to please people, but as a slave of Christ, doing Your will, O God, from my heart. With good will may I serve, as if I were serving You and not people, knowing that I will receive back from You whatever good I do. (Ephesians 6:5–8)

***PAUSE** here to petition God for growth in love and compassion toward others. Offer prayers for your loved ones, for those who do not know Jesus and for those in need. Offer prayers regarding your activities for this day and any special concerns you may have.*

NT Luke 2:41–3:20

The Boy Jesus at the Temple

[41]Every year his parents went to Jerusalem for the Feast of the Passover.
[42]When he was twelve years old, they went
up to the Feast, according to the custom.
[43]After the Feast was over, while his parents were returning home, the boy Jesus
stayed behind in Jerusalem, but they were
unaware of it. [44]Thinking he was in their
company, they traveled on for a day. Then
they began looking for him among their
relatives and friends. [45]When they did not
find him, they went back to Jerusalem to
look for him. [46]After three days they
found him in the temple courts, sitting
among the teachers, listening to them and
asking them questions. [47]Everyone who
heard him was amazed at his understanding and his answers. [48]When his parents saw him, they were astonished. His
mother said to him, "Son, why have you
treated us like this? Your father and I have
been anxiously searching for you."

[49]"Why were you searching for me?" he
asked. "Didn't you know I had to be in
my Father's house?" [50]But they did not understand what he was saying to them.

[51]Then he went down to Nazareth with
them and was obedient to them. But his
mother treasured all these things in her
heart. [52]And Jesus grew in wisdom and
stature, and in favor with God and men.

John the Baptist Prepares the Way

3 In the fifteenth year of the reign of Tiberius Caesar—when Pontius Pilate was governor of Judea, Herod tetrarch of Galilee, his brother Philip tetrarch of Iturea and Traconitis, and Lysanias tetrarch of Abilene— [2]during the high priesthood of Annas and Caiaphas, the word of God came to John son of Zechariah in the desert. [3]He went into all the country around the Jordan, preaching a baptism of repentance for the forgiveness of sins. [4]As is written in the book of the words of Isaiah the prophet:

"A voice of one calling in the desert,
'Prepare the way for the Lord,
make straight paths for him.
[5]Every valley shall be filled in,
every mountain and hill made low.
The crooked roads shall become straight,
the rough ways smooth.
[6]And all mankind will see God's salvation.' "[a]

[7]John said to the crowds coming out to be baptized by him, "You brood of vipers! Who warned you to flee from the coming wrath? [8]Produce fruit in keeping with repentance. And do not begin to say to yourselves, 'We have Abraham as our father.' For I tell you that out of these stones God can raise up children for Abraham. [9]The ax is already at the root of the trees, and every tree that does not produce good fruit will be cut down and thrown into the fire."

[10]"What should we do then?" the crowd asked.

[11]John answered, "The man with two tunics should share with him who has none, and the one who has food should do the same."

[12]Tax collectors also came to be baptized. "Teacher," they asked, "what should we do?"

[13]"Don't collect any more than you are required to," he told them.

[14]Then some soldiers asked him, "And what should we do?"

He replied, "Don't extort money and don't accuse people falsely—be content with your pay."

[15]The people were waiting expectantly and were all wondering in their hearts if John might possibly be the Christ.[b] [16]John answered them all, "I baptize you with[c] water. But one more powerful than I will come, the thongs of whose sandals I am not worthy to untie. He will baptize you with the Holy Spirit and with fire. [17]His winnowing fork is in his hand to clear his threshing floor and to gather the wheat into his barn, but he will burn up the chaff with unquenchable fire." [18]And with many other words John exhorted the people and preached the good news to them.

[19]But when John rebuked Herod the tetrarch because of Herodias, his brother's wife, and all the other evil things he had done, [20]Herod added this to them all: He locked John up in prison.

[a] 6 Isaiah 40:3–5 [b] 15 Or *Messiah* [c] 16 Or *in*

PRAYER: THE CHARACTER I WANT TO CULTIVATE

IF I think I am something when I am nothing, I deceive myself. (Galatians 6:3) . . . Those in humble circumstances should glory in their high position, and those who are rich should glory in their humiliation, because they will pass away like flowers of the field. (James 1:9–10)

***TAKE** a moment to ask the Lord for the grace to grow in godly character.*

OT Jeremiah 13:1–27

A Linen Belt

13 This is what the LORD said to me: "Go and buy a linen belt and put it around your waist, but do not let it touch water."

[2]So I bought a belt, as the LORD directed, and put it around my waist.

[3]Then the word of the LORD came to me a second time: [4]"Take the belt you bought

and are wearing around your waist, and
go now to Perath[a] and hide it there in a
crevice in the rocks." 5So I went and hid
it at Perath, as the LORD told me.

6Many days later the LORD said to me,
"Go now to Perath and get the belt I told
you to hide there." 7So I went to Perath
and dug up the belt and took it from the
place where I had hidden it, but now it
was ruined and completely useless.

8Then the word of the LORD came to
me: 9"This is what the LORD says: 'In the
same way I will ruin the pride of Judah
and the great pride of Jerusalem. 10These
wicked people, who refuse to listen to my
words, who follow the stubbornness of
their hearts and go after other gods to
serve and worship them, will be like this
belt—completely useless! 11For as a belt is
bound around a man's waist, so I bound
the whole house of Israel and the whole
house of Judah to me,' declares the LORD,
'to be my people for my renown and
praise and honor. But they have not listened.'

Wineskins

12"Say to them: 'This is what the LORD,
the God of Israel, says: Every wineskin
should be filled with wine.' And if they say
to you, 'Don't we know that every wineskin
should be filled with wine?' 13then
tell them, 'This is what the LORD says: I am
going to fill with drunkenness all who live
in this land, including the kings who sit
on David's throne, the priests, the prophets
and all those living in Jerusalem. 14I
will smash them one against the other, fathers
and sons alike, declares the LORD. I
will allow no pity or mercy or compassion
to keep me from destroying them.' "

Threat of Captivity

15Hear and pay attention,
do not be arrogant,
for the LORD has spoken.
16Give glory to the LORD your God
before he brings the darkness,
before your feet stumble
on the darkening hills.
You hope for light,
but he will turn it to thick darkness
and change it to deep gloom.
17But if you do not listen,
I will weep in secret
because of your pride;
my eyes will weep bitterly,
overflowing with tears,
because the LORD's flock will be taken captive.

18Say to the king and to the queen mother,
"Come down from your thrones,
for your glorious crowns
will fall from your heads."
19The cities in the Negev will be shut up,
and there will be no one to open them.
All Judah will be carried into exile,
carried completely away.

20Lift up your eyes and see
those who are coming from the north.
Where is the flock that was entrusted to you,
the sheep of which you boasted?
21What will you say when ⌊the LORD⌋ sets over you
those you cultivated as your special allies?
Will not pain grip you
like that of a woman in labor?
22And if you ask yourself,
"Why has this happened to me?"—
it is because of your many sins
that your skirts have been torn off
and your body mistreated.
23Can the Ethiopian[b] change his skin
or the leopard its spots?
Neither can you do good
who are accustomed to doing evil.

24"I will scatter you like chaff
driven by the desert wind.
25This is your lot,
the portion I have decreed for you,"
declares the LORD,
"because you have forgotten me
and trusted in false gods.
26I will pull up your skirts over your face
that your shame may be seen—
27your adulteries and lustful neighings,
your shameless prostitution!
I have seen your detestable acts
on the hills and in the fields.
Woe to you, O Jerusalem!
How long will you be unclean?"

[a] 4 Or possibly *the Euphrates;* also in verses 5–7
[b] 23 Hebrew *Cushite* (probably a person from the upper Nile region)

PRAYER: INTERCESSION

LORD, make me increase and abound in my love for believers and for unbelievers. (1 Thessalonians 3:12)

***TAKE** a few moments to intercede on behalf of friends, relatives, neighbors and coworkers who do not yet know salvation in Jesus Christ.*

NT Luke 3:21–4:12

The Baptism and Genealogy of Jesus

21 When all the people were being baptized, Jesus was baptized too. And as he
was praying, heaven was opened 22 and the
Holy Spirit descended on him in bodily
form like a dove. And a voice came from
heaven: "You are my Son, whom I love;
with you I am well pleased."
23 Now Jesus himself was about thirty
years old when he began his ministry. He
was the son, so it was thought, of Joseph,

the son of Heli, 24 the son of Matthat,
the son of Levi, the son of Melki,
the son of Jannai, the son of Joseph,
25 the son of Mattathias, the son of Amos,
the son of Nahum, the son of Esli,
the son of Naggai, 26 the son of Maath,
the son of Mattathias, the son of Semein,
the son of Josech, the son of Joda,
27 the son of Joanan, the son of Rhesa,
the son of Zerubbabel, the son of Shealtiel,
the son of Neri, 28 the son of Melki,
the son of Addi, the son of Cosam,
the son of Elmadam, the son of Er,
29 the son of Joshua, the son of Eliezer,
the son of Jorim, the son of Matthat,
the son of Levi, 30 the son of Simeon,
the son of Judah, the son of Joseph,
the son of Jonam, the son of Eliakim,
31 the son of Melea, the son of Menna,
the son of Mattatha, the son of Nathan,
the son of David, 32 the son of Jesse,
the son of Obed, the son of Boaz,
the son of Salmon,[a] the son of Nahshon,
33 the son of Amminadab, the son of Ram,[b]
the son of Hezron, the son of Perez,
the son of Judah, 34 the son of Jacob,
the son of Isaac, the son of Abraham,
the son of Terah, the son of Nahor,
35 the son of Serug, the son of Reu,
the son of Peleg, the son of Eber,
the son of Shelah, 36 the son of Cainan,
the son of Arphaxad, the son of Shem,
the son of Noah, the son of Lamech,
37 the son of Methuselah, the son of Enoch,
the son of Jared, the son of Mahalalel,
the son of Kenan, 38 the son of Enosh,
the son of Seth, the son of Adam,
the son of God.

The Temptation of Jesus

4 Jesus, full of the Holy Spirit, returned
from the Jordan and was led by the
Spirit in the desert, 2 where for forty days
he was tempted by the devil. He ate nothing during those days, and at the end of
them he was hungry.
3 The devil said to him, "If you are the
Son of God, tell this stone to become
bread."
4 Jesus answered, "It is written: 'Man
does not live on bread alone.'[c]"
5 The devil led him up to a high place
and showed him in an instant all the
kingdoms of the world. 6 And he said to
him, "I will give you all their authority
and splendor, for it has been given to me,
and I can give it to anyone I want to. 7 So
if you worship me, it will all be yours."
8 Jesus answered, "It is written: 'Worship
the Lord your God and serve him only.'[d]"
9 The devil led him to Jerusalem and
had him stand on the highest point of the
temple. "If you are the Son of God," he
said, "throw yourself down from here.
10 For it is written:

" 'He will command his angels
concerning you

[a] 32 Some early manuscripts *Sala* [b] 33 Some manuscripts *Amminadab, the son of Admin, the son of Arni;* other manuscripts vary widely. [c] 4 Deut. 8:3 [d] 8 Deut. 6:13

to guard you carefully;
[11] they will lift you up in their hands,
so that you will not strike your foot
against a stone.'[e]"

[12] Jesus answered, "It says: 'Do not put
the Lord your God to the test.'[f]"

[e] *11* Psalm 91:11,12 [f] *12* Deut. 6:16

PRAYER: MY RELATIONSHIP TO OTHERS

GRACE has been given to each one of us according to the measure of Your gift, Christ Jesus. And You gave some to be apostles, some to be prophets, some to be evangelists, and some to be pastors and teachers, to equip the saints for the work of ministry so that Your body will be built up. (Ephesians 4:7, 11–12)

***PAUSE** to review your relationships with others and to commit them to the Lord.*

YEAR 2 DAY 201

OT Jeremiah 14:1–22

Drought, Famine, Sword

14 This is the word of the LORD to Jeremiah concerning the drought:

[2] "Judah mourns,
her cities languish;
they wail for the land,
and a cry goes up from Jerusalem.
[3] The nobles send their servants for water;
they go to the cisterns
but find no water.
They return with their jars unfilled;
dismayed and despairing,
they cover their heads.
[4] The ground is cracked
because there is no rain in the land;
the farmers are dismayed
and cover their heads.
[5] Even the doe in the field
deserts her newborn fawn
because there is no grass.
[6] Wild donkeys stand on the barren
heights
and pant like jackals;
their eyesight fails
for lack of pasture."

[7] Although our sins testify against us,
O LORD, do something for the sake
of your name.
For our backsliding is great;
we have sinned against you.
[8] O Hope of Israel,
its Savior in times of distress,
why are you like a stranger in the land,
like a traveler who stays only a night?
[9] Why are you like a man taken by
surprise,
like a warrior powerless to save?
You are among us, O LORD,
and we bear your name;
do not forsake us!

[10] This is what the LORD says about this
people:

"They greatly love to wander;
they do not restrain their feet.
So the LORD does not accept them;
he will now remember their
wickedness
and punish them for their sins."

[11] Then the LORD said to me, "Do not
pray for the well-being of this people.
[12] Although they fast, I will not listen to
their cry; though they offer burnt offerings
and grain offerings, I will not accept them.
Instead, I will destroy them with the
sword, famine and plague."
[13] But I said, "Ah, Sovereign LORD, the
prophets keep telling them, 'You will not
see the sword or suffer famine. Indeed, I
will give you lasting peace in this place.' "
[14] Then the LORD said to me, "The prophets are prophesying lies in my name. I have
not sent them or appointed them or spoken to them. They are prophesying to you
false visions, divinations, idolatries[a] and
the delusions of their own minds. [15] There-

[a] *14* Or *visions, worthless divinations*

fore, this is what the LORD says about the
prophets who are prophesying in my
name: I did not send them, yet they are
saying, 'No sword or famine will touch
this land.' Those same prophets will perish
by sword and famine. [16]And the people
they are prophesying to will be thrown out
into the streets of Jerusalem because of the
famine and sword. There will be no one to
bury them or their wives, their sons or
their daughters. I will pour out on them
the calamity they deserve.

[17]"Speak this word to them:

" 'Let my eyes overflow with tears
night and day without ceasing;
for my virgin daughter—my people—
has suffered a grievous wound,
a crushing blow.
[18]If I go into the country,
I see those slain by the sword;
if I go into the city,
I see the ravages of famine.
Both prophet and priest
have gone to a land they know
not.' "

[19]Have you rejected Judah completely?
Do you despise Zion?
Why have you afflicted us
so that we cannot be healed?
We hoped for peace
but no good has come,
for a time of healing
but there is only terror.
[20]O LORD, we acknowledge our
wickedness
and the guilt of our fathers;
we have indeed sinned against you.
[21]For the sake of your name do not
despise us;
do not dishonor your glorious
throne.
Remember your covenant with us
and do not break it.
[22]Do any of the worthless idols of the
nations bring rain?
Do the skies themselves send down
showers?
No, it is you, O LORD our God.
Therefore our hope is in you,
for you are the one who does all
this.

PRAYER: AFFIRMATION

LORD Jesus, You are God's beloved Son, in whom He is well pleased. (Matthew 3:17; Mark 1:11; Luke 3:22) . . . Your Father loves You and has given all things into Your hand. (John 3:35)

***PAUSE** to reflect on these Biblical affirmations.*

NT Luke 4:13-44

[13]When the devil had finished all this
tempting, he left him until an opportune
time.

Jesus Rejected at Nazareth

[14]Jesus returned to Galilee in the power
of the Spirit, and news about him spread
through the whole countryside. [15]He
taught in their synagogues, and everyone
praised him.

[16]He went to Nazareth, where he had
been brought up, and on the Sabbath day
he went into the synagogue, as was his
custom. And he stood up to read. [17]The
scroll of the prophet Isaiah was handed to
him. Unrolling it, he found the place
where it is written:

[18]"The Spirit of the Lord is on me,
because he has anointed me
to preach good news to the poor.
He has sent me to proclaim freedom
for the prisoners
and recovery of sight for the blind,
to release the oppressed,
[19] to proclaim the year of the Lord's
favor."[a]

[20]Then he rolled up the scroll, gave it
back to the attendant and sat down. The
eyes of everyone in the synagogue were
fastened on him, [21]and he began by saying to them, "Today this scripture is fulfilled in your hearing."

[22]All spoke well of him and were
amazed at the gracious words that came

[a] *19* Isaiah 61:1,2

from his lips. "Isn't this Joseph's son?"
they asked.
23 Jesus said to them, "Surely you will
quote this proverb to me: 'Physician, heal
yourself! Do here in your hometown what
we have heard that you did in Capernaum.' "
24 "I tell you the truth," he continued,
"no prophet is accepted in his hometown.
25 I assure you that there were many widows in Israel in Elijah's time, when the sky
was shut for three and a half years and
there was a severe famine throughout the
land. 26 Yet Elijah was not sent to any of
them, but to a widow in Zarephath in the
region of Sidon. 27 And there were many in
Israel with leprosy[b] in the time of Elisha
the prophet, yet not one of them was
cleansed—only Naaman the Syrian."
28 All the people in the synagogue were
furious when they heard this. 29 They got
up, drove him out of the town, and took
him to the brow of the hill on which the
town was built, in order to throw him
down the cliff. 30 But he walked right
through the crowd and went on his way.

Jesus Drives Out an Evil Spirit

31 Then he went down to Capernaum, a
town in Galilee, and on the Sabbath began to teach the people. 32 They were
amazed at his teaching, because his message had authority.
33 In the synagogue there was a man
possessed by a demon, an evil[c] spirit. He
cried out at the top of his voice, 34 "Ha!
What do you want with us, Jesus of Nazareth? Have you come to destroy us? I
know who you are—the Holy One of
God!"
35 "Be quiet!" Jesus said sternly. "Come
out of him!" Then the demon threw the
man down before them all and came out
without injuring him.
36 All the people were amazed and said
to each other, "What is this teaching?
With authority and power he gives orders
to evil spirits and they come out!" 37 And
the news about him spread throughout
the surrounding area.

Jesus Heals Many

38 Jesus left the synagogue and went to
the home of Simon. Now Simon's mother-in-law was suffering from a high fever,
and they asked Jesus to help her. 39 So he
bent over her and rebuked the fever, and
it left her. She got up at once and began
to wait on them.
40 When the sun was setting, the people
brought to Jesus all who had various
kinds of sickness, and laying his hands on
each one, he healed them. 41 Moreover,
demons came out of many people, shouting, "You are the Son of God!" But he rebuked them and would not allow them to
speak, because they knew he was the
Christ.[d]
42 At daybreak Jesus went out to a solitary place. The people were looking for
him and when they came to where he
was, they tried to keep him from leaving
them. 43 But he said, "I must preach the
good news of the kingdom of God to the
other towns also, because that is why I
was sent." 44 And he kept on preaching in
the synagogues of Judea.[e]

[b] *27* The Greek word was used for various diseases affecting the skin—not necessarily leprosy.
[c] *33* Greek *unclean;* also in verse 36
[d] *41* Or *Messiah* [e] *44* Or *the land of the Jews;* some manuscripts *Galilee*

PRAYER: THE ATTRIBUTES OF GOD

YOU have established Your throne in heaven, O Lord, and Your kingdom rules over all. (Psalm 103:19) . . . Nothing is impossible with You, O God. (Luke 1:37)

PAUSE *to reflect on these affirmations about the person, powers and perfection of God.*

YEAR 2 DAY 202

OT **Jeremiah 15:1–21**

15 Then the LORD said to me: "Even if
Moses and Samuel were to stand before me, my heart would not go out to this
people. Send them away from my presence! Let them go! 2And if they ask you,
'Where shall we go?' tell them, 'This is
what the LORD says:

" 'Those destined for death, to death;
those for the sword, to the sword;
those for starvation, to starvation;
those for captivity, to captivity.'

3"I will send four kinds of destroyers
against them," declares the LORD, "the
sword to kill and the dogs to drag away and
the birds of the air and the beasts of the
earth to devour and destroy. 4I will make
them abhorrent to all the kingdoms of the
earth because of what Manasseh son of
Hezekiah king of Judah did in Jerusalem.

5"Who will have pity on you,
O Jerusalem?
Who will mourn for you?
Who will stop to ask how you are?
6You have rejected me," declares the
LORD.
"You keep on backsliding.
So I will lay hands on you and destroy
you;
I can no longer show compassion.
7I will winnow them with a winnowing
fork
at the city gates of the land.
I will bring bereavement and
destruction on my people,
for they have not changed their ways.
8I will make their widows more
numerous
than the sand of the sea.
At midday I will bring a destroyer
against the mothers of their young
men;
suddenly I will bring down on them
anguish and terror.
9The mother of seven will grow faint
and breathe her last.
Her sun will set while it is still day;
she will be disgraced and
humiliated.
I will put the survivors to the sword
before their enemies,"
declares the LORD.

10Alas, my mother, that you gave me
birth,
a man with whom the whole land
strives and contends!
I have neither lent nor borrowed,
yet everyone curses me.

11The LORD said,

"Surely I will deliver you for a good
purpose;
surely I will make your enemies
plead with you
in times of disaster and times of
distress.

12"Can a man break iron—
iron from the north—or bronze?
13Your wealth and your treasures
I will give as plunder, without
charge,
because of all your sins
throughout your country.
14I will enslave you to your enemies
in[a] a land you do not know,
for my anger will kindle a fire
that will burn against you."

15You understand, O LORD;
remember me and care for me.
Avenge me on my persecutors.
You are long-suffering—do not take
me away;
think of how I suffer reproach for
your sake.
16When your words came, I ate them;
they were my joy and my heart's
delight,
for I bear your name,
O LORD God Almighty.
17I never sat in the company of revelers,
never made merry with them;
I sat alone because your hand was on
me
and you had filled me with
indignation.
18Why is my pain unending
and my wound grievous and
incurable?
Will you be to me like a deceptive
brook,
like a spring that fails?

[a] *14* Some Hebrew manuscripts, Septuagint and Syriac (see also Jer. 17:4); most Hebrew manuscripts *I will cause your enemies to bring you / into*

19 Therefore this is what the LORD says:

"If you repent, I will restore you
that you may serve me;
if you utter worthy, not worthless,
words,
you will be my spokesman.
Let this people turn to you,
but you must not turn to them.
20 I will make you a wall to this people,
a fortified wall of bronze;
they will fight against you
but will not overcome you,
for I am with you
to rescue and save you,"
declares the LORD.
21 "I will save you from the hands of the
wicked
and redeem you from the grasp of
the cruel."

PRAYER: THANKSGIVING

IN my distress I called to You, Lord, and cried to You, my God, for help. You heard my voice from Your temple, and my cry came before You, into Your ears. You brought me out into a broad place; You rescued me because You delighted in me. (Psalm 18:6, 19)

***PAUSE** to offer your own expressions of thanksgiving.*

NT Luke 5:1–26

The Calling of the First Disciples

5 One day as Jesus was standing by the
Lake of Gennesaret,[a] with the people
crowding around him and listening to the
word of God, 2 he saw at the water's edge
two boats, left there by the fishermen,
who were washing their nets. 3 He got into
one of the boats, the one belonging to Simon, and asked him to put out a little
from shore. Then he sat down and taught
the people from the boat.
4 When he had finished speaking, he
said to Simon, "Put out into deep water,
and let down[b] the nets for a catch."
5 Simon answered, "Master, we've
worked hard all night and haven't caught
anything. But because you say so, I will let
down the nets."
6 When they had done so, they caught
such a large number of fish that their nets
began to break. 7 So they signaled their
partners in the other boat to come and
help them, and they came and filled both
boats so full that they began to sink.
8 When Simon Peter saw this, he fell at
Jesus' knees and said, "Go away from me,
Lord; I am a sinful man!" 9 For he and all
his companions were astonished at the
catch of fish they had taken, 10 and so were
James and John, the sons of Zebedee, Simon's partners.
Then Jesus said to Simon, "Don't be
afraid; from now on you will catch men."
11 So they pulled their boats up on shore,
left everything and followed him.

The Man With Leprosy

12 While Jesus was in one of the towns,
a man came along who was covered with
leprosy.[c] When he saw Jesus, he fell with
his face to the ground and begged him,
"Lord, if you are willing, you can make
me clean."
13 Jesus reached out his hand and
touched the man. "I am willing," he said.
"Be clean!" And immediately the leprosy
left him.
14 Then Jesus ordered him, "Don't tell
anyone, but go, show yourself to the priest
and offer the sacrifices that Moses commanded for your cleansing, as a testimony to them."
15 Yet the news about him spread all the
more, so that crowds of people came to
hear him and to be healed of their sicknesses. 16 But Jesus often withdrew to lonely places and prayed.

Jesus Heals a Paralytic

17 One day as he was teaching, Pharisees
and teachers of the law, who had come
from every village of Galilee and from Judea and Jerusalem, were sitting there. And

[a] *1* That is, Sea of Galilee [b] *4* The Greek verb is plural. [c] *12* The Greek word was used for various diseases affecting the skin—not necessarily leprosy.

the power of the Lord was present for him
to heal the sick. [18]Some men came carrying a paralytic on a mat and tried to take
him into the house to lay him before
Jesus. [19]When they could not find a way
to do this because of the crowd, they went
up on the roof and lowered him on his
mat through the tiles into the middle of
the crowd, right in front of Jesus.
[20]When Jesus saw their faith, he said,
"Friend, your sins are forgiven."
[21]The Pharisees and the teachers of the
law began thinking to themselves, "Who
is this fellow who speaks blasphemy?
Who can forgive sins but God alone?"
[22]Jesus knew what they were thinking
and asked, "Why are you thinking these
things in your hearts? [23]Which is easier: to
say, 'Your sins are forgiven,' or to say, 'Get
up and walk'? [24]But that you may know
that the Son of Man has authority on
earth to forgive sins. . . ." He said to the
paralyzed man, "I tell you, get up, take
your mat and go home." [25]Immediately
he stood up in front of them, took what
he had been lying on and went home
praising God. [26]Everyone was amazed and
gave praise to God. They were filled with
awe and said, "We have seen remarkable
things today."

PRAYER: THE WORKS OF GOD

MY body is a temple of the Holy Spirit, who is in me, whom I have from You, O God, and I am not my own. For I was bought at a price; therefore I will glorify You, O God, in my body. (1 Corinthians 6:19–20)

***TAKE** a moment to consider the greatness of God's wonderful works.*

YEAR 2 DAY 203

OT Psalms 112–113

Psalm 112[a]

[1]Praise the LORD.[b]

Blessed is the man who fears the LORD,
who finds great delight in his commands.

[2]His children will be mighty in the land;
the generation of the upright will be blessed.
[3]Wealth and riches are in his house,
and his righteousness endures forever.
[4]Even in darkness light dawns for the upright,
for the gracious and compassionate and righteous man.[c]
[5]Good will come to him who is generous and lends freely,
who conducts his affairs with justice.
[6]Surely he will never be shaken;
a righteous man will be remembered forever.
[7]He will have no fear of bad news;
his heart is steadfast, trusting in the LORD.
[8]His heart is secure, he will have no fear;
in the end he will look in triumph on his foes.
[9]He has scattered abroad his gifts to the poor,
his righteousness endures forever;
his horn[d] will be lifted high in honor.

[10]The wicked man will see and be vexed,
he will gnash his teeth and waste away;
the longings of the wicked will come to nothing.

Psalm 113

[1]Praise the LORD.[e]

Praise, O servants of the LORD,
praise the name of the LORD.

[a]This psalm is an acrostic poem, the lines of which begin with the successive letters of the Hebrew alphabet. [b]*1* Hebrew *Hallelu Yah* [c]*4* Or / *for* ⌞*the LORD*⌟ *is gracious and compassionate and righteous* [d]*9* *Horn* here symbolizes dignity. [e]*1* Hebrew *Hallelu Yah;* also in verse 9

2 Let the name of the LORD be praised,
both now and forevermore.
3 From the rising of the sun to the place where it sets,
the name of the LORD is to be praised.

4 The LORD is exalted over all the nations,
his glory above the heavens.
5 Who is like the LORD our God,
the One who sits enthroned on high,
6 who stoops down to look
on the heavens and the earth?

7 He raises the poor from the dust
and lifts the needy from the ash heap;
8 he seats them with princes,
with the princes of their people.
9 He settles the barren woman in her home
as a happy mother of children.

Praise the LORD.

PRAYER: ADORATION

YOU are the Lord, my Redeemer, who formed me in the womb. You have said, "I am the Lord, who made all things, who alone stretches out the heavens, who spread out the earth by Myself." (Isaiah 44:24) . . . Blessing and glory and wisdom and thanksgiving and honor and power and strength be to You, our God, for ever and ever. Amen. (Revelation 7:12)

PAUSE *to express your thoughts of praise and worship.*

NT Luke 5:27–6:16

The Calling of Levi

27 After this, Jesus went out and saw a tax
collector by the name of Levi sitting at his
tax booth. "Follow me," Jesus said to him,
28 and Levi got up, left everything and followed him.
29 Then Levi held a great banquet for
Jesus at his house, and a large crowd of tax
collectors and others were eating with
them. 30 But the Pharisees and the teachers
of the law who belonged to their sect
complained to his disciples, "Why do you
eat and drink with tax collectors and 'sinners'?"
31 Jesus answered them, "It is not the
healthy who need a doctor, but the sick.
32 I have not come to call the righteous,
but sinners to repentance."

Jesus Questioned About Fasting

33 They said to him, "John's disciples often fast and pray, and so do the disciples
of the Pharisees, but yours go on eating
and drinking."
34 Jesus answered, "Can you make the
guests of the bridegroom fast while he is
with them? 35 But the time will come when
the bridegroom will be taken from them;
in those days they will fast."
36 He told them this parable: "No one
tears a patch from a new garment and
sews it on an old one. If he does, he will
have torn the new garment, and the patch
from the new will not match the old.
37 And no one pours new wine into old
wineskins. If he does, the new wine will
burst the skins, the wine will run out and
the wineskins will be ruined. 38 No, new
wine must be poured into new wineskins.
39 And no one after drinking old wine
wants the new, for he says, 'The old is better.' "

Lord of the Sabbath

6 One Sabbath Jesus was going through
the grainfields, and his disciples began
to pick some heads of grain, rub them in
their hands and eat the kernels. 2 Some of
the Pharisees asked, "Why are you doing
what is unlawful on the Sabbath?"
3 Jesus answered them, "Have you never
read what David did when he and his
companions were hungry? 4 He entered
the house of God, and taking the consecrated bread, he ate what is lawful only

for priests to eat. And he also gave some
to his companions." 5Then Jesus said to
them, "The Son of Man is Lord of the Sabbath."
6On another Sabbath he went into the
synagogue and was teaching, and a man
was there whose right hand was shriveled.
7The Pharisees and the teachers of the law
were looking for a reason to accuse Jesus,
so they watched him closely to see if he
would heal on the Sabbath. 8But Jesus
knew what they were thinking and said to
the man with the shriveled hand, "Get up
and stand in front of everyone." So he got
up and stood there.
9Then Jesus said to them, "I ask you,
which is lawful on the Sabbath: to do
good or to do evil, to save life or to destroy it?"
10He looked around at them all, and
then said to the man, "Stretch out your
hand." He did so, and his hand was completely restored. 11But they were furious
and began to discuss with one another
what they might do to Jesus.

The Twelve Apostles

12One of those days Jesus went out to a
mountainside to pray, and spent the night
praying to God. 13When morning came,
he called his disciples to him and chose
twelve of them, whom he also designated
apostles: 14Simon (whom he named Peter), his brother Andrew, James, John,
Philip, Bartholomew, 15Matthew, Thomas,
James son of Alphaeus, Simon who was
called the Zealot, 16Judas son of James,
and Judas Iscariot, who became a traitor.

PRAYER: MY RELATIONSHIP TO GOD

YOU are the vine; I am a branch; if I abide in You, and You in me, I will bear much fruit; for apart from You, I can do nothing. (John 15:5) . . . If I abide in You, and Your words abide in me, I can ask whatever I wish, and it will be done for me. As I ask in Your name, I will receive, that my joy may be full. (John 15:7; 16:24)

***PAUSE** to thank God for the relationship that you enjoy with Him in Jesus Christ.*

YEAR 2 DAY 204

OT Jeremiah 16:1–17:27

Day of Disaster

16 Then the word of the LORD came to
me: 2"You must not marry and have
sons or daughters in this place." 3For this
is what the LORD says about the sons and
daughters born in this land and about the
women who are their mothers and the
men who are their fathers: 4"They will die
of deadly diseases. They will not be
mourned or buried but will be like refuse
lying on the ground. They will perish by
sword and famine, and their dead bodies
will become food for the birds of the air
and the beasts of the earth."
5For this is what the LORD says: "Do not
enter a house where there is a funeral
meal; do not go to mourn or show sympathy, because I have withdrawn my
blessing, my love and my pity from this
people," declares the LORD. 6"Both high
and low will die in this land. They will not
be buried or mourned, and no one will
cut himself or shave his head for them.
7No one will offer food to comfort those
who mourn for the dead—not even for a
father or a mother—nor will anyone give
them a drink to console them.
8"And do not enter a house where
there is feasting and sit down to eat and
drink. 9For this is what the LORD
Almighty, the God of Israel, says: Before
your eyes and in your days I will bring an
end to the sounds of joy and gladness
and to the voices of bride and bridegroom in this place.
10"When you tell these people all this
and they ask you, 'Why has the LORD
decreed such a great disaster against us?
What wrong have we done? What sin have

we committed against the LORD our God?'
11 then say to them, 'It is because your fathers forsook me,' declares the LORD, 'and
followed other gods and served and worshiped them. They forsook me and did
not keep my law. 12 But you have behaved
more wickedly than your fathers. See how
each of you is following the stubbornness
of his evil heart instead of obeying me.
13 So I will throw you out of this land into
a land neither you nor your fathers have
known, and there you will serve other
gods day and night, for I will show you no
favor.'

14 "However, the days are coming," declares the LORD, "when men will no
longer say, 'As surely as the LORD lives,
who brought the Israelites up out of
Egypt,' 15 but they will say, 'As surely as the
LORD lives, who brought the Israelites up
out of the land of the north and out of all
the countries where he had banished
them.' For I will restore them to the land
I gave their forefathers.

16 "But now I will send for many fishermen," declares the LORD, "and they will
catch them. After that I will send for many
hunters, and they will hunt them down
on every mountain and hill and from the
crevices of the rocks. 17 My eyes are on all
their ways; they are not hidden from me,
nor is their sin concealed from my eyes.
18 I will repay them double for their
wickedness and their sin, because they
have defiled my land with the lifeless
forms of their vile images and have filled
my inheritance with their detestable
idols."

19 O LORD, my strength and my fortress,
my refuge in time of distress,
to you the nations will come
from the ends of the earth and say,
"Our fathers possessed nothing but
false gods,
worthless idols that did them no
good.
20 Do men make their own gods?
Yes, but they are not gods!"

21 "Therefore I will teach them—
this time I will teach them
my power and might.
Then they will know
that my name is the LORD.

17 "Judah's sin is engraved with an iron
tool,
inscribed with a flint point,
on the tablets of their hearts
and on the horns of their altars.
2 Even their children remember
their altars and Asherah poles[a]
beside the spreading trees
and on the high hills.
3 My mountain in the land
and your[b] wealth and all your
treasures
I will give away as plunder,
together with your high places,
because of sin throughout your
country.
4 Through your own fault you will lose
the inheritance I gave you.
I will enslave you to your enemies
in a land you do not know,
for you have kindled my anger,
and it will burn forever."

5 This is what the LORD says:

"Cursed is the one who trusts in man,
who depends on flesh for his
strength
and whose heart turns away from
the LORD.
6 He will be like a bush in the
wastelands;
he will not see prosperity when it
comes.
He will dwell in the parched places of
the desert,
in a salt land where no one lives.

7 "But blessed is the man who trusts in
the LORD,
whose confidence is in him.
8 He will be like a tree planted by the
water
that sends out its roots by the stream.
It does not fear when heat comes;
its leaves are always green.
It has no worries in a year of drought
and never fails to bear fruit."

9 The heart is deceitful above all things
and beyond cure.
Who can understand it?

10 "I the LORD search the heart
and examine the mind,
to reward a man according to his
conduct,
according to what his deeds
deserve."

[a] 2 That is, symbols of the goddess Asherah
[b] 2,3 Or *hills / 3and the mountains of the land. / Your*

[11] Like a partridge that hatches eggs it did not lay
is the man who gains riches by unjust means.
When his life is half gone, they will desert him,
and in the end he will prove to be a fool.

[12] A glorious throne, exalted from the beginning,
is the place of our sanctuary.
[13] O LORD, the hope of Israel,
all who forsake you will be put to shame.
Those who turn away from you will be written in the dust
because they have forsaken the LORD,
the spring of living water.

[14] Heal me, O LORD, and I will be healed;
save me and I will be saved,
for you are the one I praise.
[15] They keep saying to me,
"Where is the word of the LORD?
Let it now be fulfilled!"
[16] I have not run away from being your shepherd;
you know I have not desired the day of despair.
What passes my lips is open before you.
[17] Do not be a terror to me;
you are my refuge in the day of disaster.
[18] Let my persecutors be put to shame,
but keep me from shame;
let them be terrified,
but keep me from terror.
Bring on them the day of disaster;
destroy them with double destruction.

Keeping the Sabbath Holy

[19] This is what the LORD said to me: "Go
and stand at the gate of the people,
through which the kings of Judah go in
and out; stand also at all the other gates
of Jerusalem. [20] Say to them, 'Hear the
word of the LORD, O kings of Judah and
all people of Judah and everyone living in
Jerusalem who come through these gates.
[21] This is what the LORD says: Be careful not
to carry a load on the Sabbath day or
bring it through the gates of Jerusalem.
[22] Do not bring a load out of your houses
or do any work on the Sabbath, but keep
the Sabbath day holy, as I commanded
your forefathers. [23] Yet they did not listen
or pay attention; they were stiff-necked
and would not listen or respond to discipline. [24] But if you are careful to obey me,
declares the LORD, and bring no load
through the gates of this city on the Sabbath, but keep the Sabbath day holy by
not doing any work on it, [25] then kings
who sit on David's throne will come
through the gates of this city with their officials. They and their officials will come
riding in chariots and on horses, accompanied by the men of Judah and those living in Jerusalem, and this city will be inhabited forever. [26] People will come from
the towns of Judah and the villages
around Jerusalem, from the territory of
Benjamin and the western foothills, from
the hill country and the Negev, bringing
burnt offerings and sacrifices, grain offerings, incense and thank offerings to the
house of the LORD. [27] But if you do not
obey me to keep the Sabbath day holy by
not carrying any load as you come
through the gates of Jerusalem on the Sabbath day, then I will kindle an unquenchable fire in the gates of Jerusalem that will
consume her fortresses.' "

PRAYER: CONFESSION

ALL my ways are pure in my own eyes, but You, O Lord, weigh my motives. (Proverbs 16:2)

***ASK** the Spirit to search your heart and reveal any areas of unconfessed sin. Acknowledge these to the Lord and thank Him for His forgiveness.*

NT **Luke 6:17–49**

Blessings and Woes

[17]He went down with them and stood
on a level place. A large crowd of his disciples was there and a great number of
people from all over Judea, from Jerusalem, and from the coast of Tyre and Sidon, [18]who had come to hear him and to
be healed of their diseases. Those troubled by evil[a] spirits were cured, [19]and the
people all tried to touch him, because
power was coming from him and healing
them all.

[20]Looking at his disciples, he said:

"Blessed are you who are poor,
for yours is the kingdom of God.
[21]Blessed are you who hunger now,
for you will be satisfied.
Blessed are you who weep now,
for you will laugh.
[22]Blessed are you when men hate you,
when they exclude you and insult
you
and reject your name as evil,
because of the Son of Man.

[23]"Rejoice in that day and leap for joy,
because great is your reward in heaven.
For that is how their fathers treated the
prophets.

[24]"But woe to you who are rich,
for you have already received your
comfort.
[25]Woe to you who are well fed now,
for you will go hungry.
Woe to you who laugh now,
for you will mourn and weep.
[26]Woe to you when all men speak well
of you,
for that is how their fathers treated
the false prophets.

Love for Enemies

[27]"But I tell you who hear me: Love your
enemies, do good to those who hate you,
[28]bless those who curse you, pray for
those who mistreat you. [29]If someone
strikes you on one cheek, turn to him the
other also. If someone takes your cloak,
do not stop him from taking your tunic.
[30]Give to everyone who asks you, and if
anyone takes what belongs to you, do not
demand it back. [31]Do to others as you
would have them do to you.

[32]"If you love those who love you, what
credit is that to you? Even 'sinners' love
those who love them. [33]And if you do
good to those who are good to you, what
credit is that to you? Even 'sinners' do
that. [34]And if you lend to those from
whom you expect repayment, what credit
is that to you? Even 'sinners' lend to 'sinners,' expecting to be repaid in full. [35]But
love your enemies, do good to them, and
lend to them without expecting to get
anything back. Then your reward will be
great, and you will be sons of the Most
High, because he is kind to the ungrateful
and wicked. [36]Be merciful, just as your Father is merciful.

Judging Others

[37]"Do not judge, and you will not be
judged. Do not condemn, and you will
not be condemned. Forgive, and you will
be forgiven. [38]Give, and it will be given
to you. A good measure, pressed down,
shaken together and running over, will
be poured into your lap. For with the
measure you use, it will be measured to
you."

[39]He also told them this parable: "Can
a blind man lead a blind man? Will they
not both fall into a pit? [40]A student is not
above his teacher, but everyone who is fully trained will be like his teacher.

[41]"Why do you look at the speck of saw-
dust in your brother's eye and pay no attention to the plank in your own eye?
[42]How can you say to your brother, 'Brother, let me take the speck out of your eye,'
when you yourself fail to see the plank in
your own eye? You hypocrite, first take the
plank out of your eye, and then you will
see clearly to remove the speck from your
brother's eye.

A Tree and Its Fruit

[43]"No good tree bears bad fruit, nor
does a bad tree bear good fruit. [44]Each tree
is recognized by its own fruit. People do
not pick figs from thornbushes, or grapes
from briers. [45]The good man brings good
things out of the good stored up in his
heart, and the evil man brings evil things
out of the evil stored up in his heart. For

[a] *18* Greek *unclean*

out of the overflow of his heart his mouth speaks.

The Wise and Foolish Builders

46“Why do you call me, ‘Lord, Lord,’ and do not do what I say? 47I will show you what he is like who comes to me and hears my words and puts them into practice. 48He is like a man building a house, who dug down deep and laid the foundation on rock. When a flood came, the torrent struck that house but could not shake it, because it was well built. 49But the one who hears my words and does not put them into practice is like a man who built a house on the ground without a foundation. The moment the torrent struck that house, it collapsed and its destruction was complete.”

PRAYER: THE CHARACTER I WANT TO CULTIVATE

THE wise in heart accept commands, but a chattering fool will be thrown down. (Proverbs 10:8) . . . The heart of the prudent acquires knowledge, and the ear of the wise seeks knowledge. (Proverbs 18:15)

***TAKE** a moment to ask the Lord for the grace to grow in godly character.*

YEAR 2
DAY 205

OT Jeremiah 18:1–19:15

At the Potter’s House

18 This is the word that came to Jeremiah from the LORD: 2“Go down to the potter’s house, and there I will give you my message.” 3So I went down to the potter’s house, and I saw him working at the wheel. 4But the pot he was shaping from the clay was marred in his hands; so the potter formed it into another pot, shaping it as seemed best to him.

5Then the word of the LORD came to me: 6“O house of Israel, can I not do with you as this potter does?” declares the LORD. “Like clay in the hand of the potter, so are you in my hand, O house of Israel. 7If at any time I announce that a nation or kingdom is to be uprooted, torn down and destroyed, 8and if that nation I warned repents of its evil, then I will relent and not inflict on it the disaster I had planned. 9And if at another time I announce that a nation or kingdom is to be built up and planted, 10and if it does evil in my sight and does not obey me, then I will reconsider the good I had intended to do for it.

11“Now therefore say to the people of Judah and those living in Jerusalem, ‘This is what the LORD says: Look! I am preparing a disaster for you and devising a plan against you. So turn from your evil ways, each one of you, and reform your ways and your actions.’ 12But they will reply, ‘It’s no use. We will continue with our own plans; each of us will follow the stubbornness of his evil heart.’ ”

13Therefore this is what the LORD says:

“Inquire among the nations:
Who has ever heard anything like this?
A most horrible thing has been done
by Virgin Israel.
14Does the snow of Lebanon
ever vanish from its rocky slopes?
Do its cool waters from distant sources
ever cease to flow?[a]
15Yet my people have forgotten me;
they burn incense to worthless idols,
which made them stumble in their ways
and in the ancient paths.
They made them walk in bypaths
and on roads not built up.
16Their land will be laid waste,
an object of lasting scorn;
all who pass by will be appalled
and will shake their heads.
17Like a wind from the east,

[a] *14* The meaning of the Hebrew for this sentence is uncertain.

I will scatter them before their
enemies;
I will show them my back and not my
face
in the day of their disaster."

18They said, "Come, let's make plans
against Jeremiah; for the teaching of the
law by the priest will not be lost, nor will
counsel from the wise, nor the word from
the prophets. So come, let's attack him
with our tongues and pay no attention to
anything he says."

19 Listen to me, O LORD;
hear what my accusers are saying!
20 Should good be repaid with evil?
Yet they have dug a pit for me.
Remember that I stood before you
and spoke in their behalf
to turn your wrath away from them.
21 So give their children over to famine;
hand them over to the power of the
sword.
Let their wives be made childless and
widows;
let their men be put to death,
their young men slain by the sword
in battle.
22 Let a cry be heard from their houses
when you suddenly bring invaders
against them,
for they have dug a pit to capture me
and have hidden snares for my feet.
23 But you know, O LORD,
all their plots to kill me.
Do not forgive their crimes
or blot out their sins from your
sight.
Let them be overthrown before you;
deal with them in the time of your
anger.

19 This is what the LORD says: "Go and
buy a clay jar from a potter. Take
along some of the elders of the people
and of the priests 2and go out to the Valley of Ben Hinnom, near the entrance of
the Potsherd Gate. There proclaim the
words I tell you, 3and say, 'Hear the word
of the LORD, O kings of Judah and people
of Jerusalem. This is what the LORD
Almighty, the God of Israel, says: Listen! I
am going to bring a disaster on this place
that will make the ears of everyone who
hears of it tingle. 4For they have forsaken
me and made this a place of foreign gods;
they have burned sacrifices in it to gods
that neither they nor their fathers nor the
kings of Judah ever knew, and they have
filled this place with the blood of the innocent. 5They have built the high places
of Baal to burn their sons in the fire as offerings to Baal—something I did not command or mention, nor did it enter my
mind. 6So beware, the days are coming,
declares the LORD, when people will no
longer call this place Topheth or the Valley of Ben Hinnom, but the Valley of
Slaughter.

7" 'In this place I will ruin[b] the plans of
Judah and Jerusalem. I will make them
fall by the sword before their enemies, at
the hands of those who seek their lives,
and I will give their carcasses as food to
the birds of the air and the beasts of the
earth. 8I will devastate this city and make
it an object of scorn; all who pass by will
be appalled and will scoff because of all
its wounds. 9I will make them eat the flesh
of their sons and daughters, and they will
eat one another's flesh during the stress of
the siege imposed on them by the enemies who seek their lives.'

10"Then break the jar while those who
go with you are watching, 11and say to
them, 'This is what the LORD Almighty
says: I will smash this nation and this city
just as this potter's jar is smashed and cannot be repaired. They will bury the dead
in Topheth until there is no more room.
12This is what I will do to this place and
to those who live here, declares the LORD.
I will make this city like Topheth. 13The
houses in Jerusalem and those of the
kings of Judah will be defiled like this
place, Topheth—all the houses where they
burned incense on the roofs to all the starry hosts and poured out drink offerings to
other gods.' "

14Jeremiah then returned from Topheth,
where the LORD had sent him to prophesy, and stood in the court of the LORD's
temple and said to all the people, 15"This
is what the LORD Almighty, the God of Israel, says: 'Listen! I am going to bring on
this city and the villages around it every
disaster I pronounced against them, because they were stiff-necked and would
not listen to my words.' "

[b] 7 The Hebrew for *ruin* sounds like the Hebrew for *jar* (see verses 1 and 10).

PRAYER: RENEWAL

MAY I revere Your glorious and awesome name—Lord my God. (Deuteronomy 28:58) . . . May I serve You, Lord, with fear and rejoice with trembling. (Psalm 2:11) . . . May I give You my heart and may my eyes delight in Your ways. (Proverbs 23:26)

***PAUSE** to add your own prayers for personal renewal.*

NT Luke 7:1–35

The Faith of the Centurion

7 When Jesus had finished saying all this
in the hearing of the people, he entered
Capernaum. 2There a centurion's servant,
whom his master valued highly, was sick
and about to die. 3The centurion heard of
Jesus and sent some elders of the Jews to
him, asking him to come and heal his servant. 4When they came to Jesus, they
pleaded earnestly with him, "This man
deserves to have you do this, 5because he
loves our nation and has built our synagogue." 6So Jesus went with them.
He was not far from the house when
the centurion sent friends to say to him:
"Lord, don't trouble yourself, for I do not
deserve to have you come under my roof.
7That is why I did not even consider myself worthy to come to you. But say the
word, and my servant will be healed. 8For
I myself am a man under authority, with
soldiers under me. I tell this one, 'Go,' and
he goes; and that one, 'Come,' and he
comes. I say to my servant, 'Do this,' and
he does it."
9When Jesus heard this, he was amazed
at him, and turning to the crowd following him, he said, "I tell you, I have not
found such great faith even in Israel."
10Then the men who had been sent returned to the house and found the servant
well.

Jesus Raises a Widow's Son

11Soon afterward, Jesus went to a town
called Nain, and his disciples and a large
crowd went along with him. 12As he approached the town gate, a dead person
was being carried out—the only son of his
mother, and she was a widow. And a large
crowd from the town was with her.
13When the Lord saw her, his heart went
out to her and he said, "Don't cry."
14Then he went up and touched the coffin, and those carrying it stood still. He
said, "Young man, I say to you, get up!"
15The dead man sat up and began to talk,
and Jesus gave him back to his mother.
16They were all filled with awe and
praised God. "A great prophet has appeared among us," they said. "God has
come to help his people." 17This news
about Jesus spread throughout Judea[a] and
the surrounding country.

Jesus and John the Baptist

18John's disciples told him about all
these things. Calling two of them, 19he
sent them to the Lord to ask, "Are you the
one who was to come, or should we expect someone else?"
20When the men came to Jesus, they
said, "John the Baptist sent us to you to
ask, 'Are you the one who was to come, or
should we expect someone else?' "
21At that very time Jesus cured many
who had diseases, sicknesses and evil spirits, and gave sight to many who were
blind. 22So he replied to the messengers,
"Go back and report to John what you
have seen and heard: The blind receive
sight, the lame walk, those who have leprosy[b] are cured, the deaf hear, the dead are
raised, and the good news is preached to
the poor. 23Blessed is the man who does
not fall away on account of me."
24After John's messengers left, Jesus began to speak to the crowd about John:
"What did you go out into the desert to
see? A reed swayed by the wind? 25If not,
what did you go out to see? A man
dressed in fine clothes? No, those who
wear expensive clothes and indulge in luxury are in palaces. 26But what did you go
out to see? A prophet? Yes, I tell you, and

[a] 17 Or *the land of the Jews* [b] 22 The Greek word was used for various diseases affecting the skin—not necessarily leprosy.

more than a prophet. [27]This is the one about whom it is written:

" 'I will send my messenger ahead of you,
who will prepare your way before you.'[c]

[28]I tell you, among those born of women there is no one greater than John; yet the one who is least in the kingdom of God is greater than he."

[29](All the people, even the tax collectors, when they heard Jesus' words, acknowledged that God's way was right, because they had been baptized by John. [30]But the Pharisees and experts in the law rejected God's purpose for themselves, because they had not been baptized by John.)

[31]"To what, then, can I compare the people of this generation? What are they like? [32]They are like children sitting in the marketplace and calling out to each other:

" 'We played the flute for you,
and you did not dance;
we sang a dirge,
and you did not cry.'

[33]For John the Baptist came neither eating bread nor drinking wine, and you say, 'He has a demon.' [34]The Son of Man came eating and drinking, and you say, 'Here is a glutton and a drunkard, a friend of tax collectors and "sinners." ' [35]But wisdom is proved right by all her children."

[c] 27 Mal. 3:1

PRAYER: MY RELATIONSHIP TO OTHERS

I WANT to speak words of encouragement to other believers. (Acts 20:2) . . . We should encourage one another and build each other up in You, Christ Jesus. (1 Thessalonians 5:11)

PAUSE *to review your relationships with others and to commit them to the Lord.*

YEAR 2 DAY 206

OT Jeremiah 20:1–21:14

Jeremiah and Pashhur

20 When the priest Pashhur son of Immer, the chief officer in the temple of the LORD, heard Jeremiah prophesying these things, [2]he had Jeremiah the prophet beaten and put in the stocks at the Upper Gate of Benjamin at the LORD's temple. [3]The next day, when Pashhur released him from the stocks, Jeremiah said to him, "The LORD's name for you is not Pashhur, but Magor-Missabib.[a] [4]For this is what the LORD says: 'I will make you a terror to yourself and to all your friends; with your own eyes you will see them fall by the sword of their enemies. I will hand all Judah over to the king of Babylon, who will carry them away to Babylon or put them to the sword. [5]I will hand over to their enemies all the wealth of this city—all its products, all its valuables and all the treasures of the kings of Judah. They will take it away as plunder and carry it off to Babylon. [6]And you, Pashhur, and all who live in your house will go into exile to Babylon. There you will die and be buried, you and all your friends to whom you have prophesied lies.' "

Jeremiah's Complaint

[7]O LORD, you deceived[b] me, and I was deceived[b];
you overpowered me and prevailed.
I am ridiculed all day long;
everyone mocks me.
[8]Whenever I speak, I cry out
proclaiming violence and destruction.
So the word of the LORD has brought me
insult and reproach all day long.
[9]But if I say, "I will not mention him
or speak any more in his name,"

[a] 3 *Magor-Missabib* means *terror on every side.*
[b] 7 Or *persuaded*

his word is in my heart like a fire,
a fire shut up in my bones.
I am weary of holding it in;
indeed, I cannot.
10 I hear many whispering,
"Terror on every side!
Report him! Let's report him!"
All my friends
are waiting for me to slip, saying,
"Perhaps he will be deceived;
then we will prevail over him
and take our revenge on him."

11 But the LORD is with me like a mighty warrior;
so my persecutors will stumble and not prevail.
They will fail and be thoroughly disgraced;
their dishonor will never be forgotten.
12 O LORD Almighty, you who examine the righteous
and probe the heart and mind,
let me see your vengeance upon them,
for to you I have committed my cause.

13 Sing to the LORD!
Give praise to the LORD!
He rescues the life of the needy
from the hands of the wicked.

14 Cursed be the day I was born!
May the day my mother bore me not be blessed!
15 Cursed be the man who brought my father the news,
who made him very glad, saying,
"A child is born to you—a son!"
16 May that man be like the towns
the LORD overthrew without pity.
May he hear wailing in the morning,
a battle cry at noon.
17 For he did not kill me in the womb,
with my mother as my grave,
her womb enlarged forever.
18 Why did I ever come out of the womb
to see trouble and sorrow
and to end my days in shame?

God Rejects Zedekiah's Request

21 The word came to Jeremiah from the
LORD when King Zedekiah sent to him
Pashhur son of Malkijah and the priest
Zephaniah son of Maaseiah. They said:
2 "Inquire now of the LORD for us because
Nebuchadnezzar[c] king of Babylon is attacking us. Perhaps the LORD will perform
wonders for us as in times past so that he
will withdraw from us."
3 But Jeremiah answered them, "Tell
Zedekiah, 4 'This is what the LORD, the God
of Israel, says: I am about to turn against
you the weapons of war that are in your
hands, which you are using to fight the
king of Babylon and the Babylonians[d]
who are outside the wall besieging you.
And I will gather them inside this city. 5 I
myself will fight against you with an outstretched hand and a mighty arm in anger
and fury and great wrath. 6 I will strike
down those who live in this city—both
men and animals—and they will die of a
terrible plague. 7 After that, declares the
LORD, I will hand over Zedekiah king of Judah, his officials and the people in this city
who survive the plague, sword and famine,
to Nebuchadnezzar king of Babylon and
to their enemies who seek their lives. He
will put them to the sword; he will show
them no mercy or pity or compassion.'
8 "Furthermore, tell the people, 'This is
what the LORD says: See, I am setting before you the way of life and the way of
death. 9 Whoever stays in this city will die
by the sword, famine or plague. But whoever goes out and surrenders to the Babylonians who are besieging you will live;
he will escape with his life. 10 I have determined to do this city harm and not good,
declares the LORD. It will be given into the
hands of the king of Babylon, and he will
destroy it with fire.'
11 "Moreover, say to the royal house of Judah, 'Hear the word of the LORD; 12 O house
of David, this is what the LORD says:

" 'Administer justice every morning;
rescue from the hand of his oppressor
the one who has been robbed,
or my wrath will break out and burn like fire
because of the evil you have done—
burn with no one to quench it.
13 I am against you, ⌞Jerusalem,⌟
you who live above this valley
on the rocky plateau,
declares the LORD—
you who say, "Who can come against us?

[c] 2 Hebrew *Nebuchadrezzar,* of which *Nebuchadnezzar* is a variant; here and often in Jeremiah and Ezekiel
[d] 4 Or *Chaldeans;* also in verse 9

Who can enter our refuge?"
[14] I will punish you as your deeds deserve,
declares the LORD.
I will kindle a fire in your forests
that will consume everything
around you.' "

PRAYER: PETITION

MAY I learn to be content in whatever circumstances I find myself. Whether I am in need or in abundance, whether I am filled or hungry, let me learn the secret of being content in any and every situation. I can do all things through You, the One who strengthens me. (Philippians 4:11–13)

__PAUSE__ here to petition God to help you be a faithful steward of your time, talents, possessions and relationships. Offer prayers of petition regarding your activities for this day and any special concerns you may have.

NT Luke 7:36–8:15

Jesus Anointed by a Sinful Woman

[36] Now one of the Pharisees invited
Jesus to have dinner with him, so he went
to the Pharisee's house and reclined at the
table. [37] When a woman who had lived a
sinful life in that town learned that Jesus
was eating at the Pharisee's house, she
brought an alabaster jar of perfume, [38] and
as she stood behind him at his feet weeping,
she began to wet his feet with her
tears. Then she wiped them with her hair,
kissed them and poured perfume on
them.

[39] When the Pharisee who had invited
him saw this, he said to himself, "If this
man were a prophet, he would know who
is touching him and what kind of woman
she is—that she is a sinner."

[40] Jesus answered him, "Simon, I have
something to tell you."

"Tell me, teacher," he said.

[41] "Two men owed money to a certain
moneylender. One owed him five hundred
denarii,[a] and the other fifty. [42] Neither
of them had the money to pay him
back, so he canceled the debts of both.
Now which of them will love him more?"

[43] Simon replied, "I suppose the one
who had the bigger debt canceled."

"You have judged correctly," Jesus said.

[44] Then he turned toward the woman
and said to Simon, "Do you see this
woman? I came into your house. You did
not give me any water for my feet, but she
wet my feet with her tears and wiped
them with her hair. [45] You did not give me
a kiss, but this woman, from the time I entered,
has not stopped kissing my feet.
[46] You did not put oil on my head, but she
has poured perfume on my feet. [47] Therefore,
I tell you, her many sins have been
forgiven—for she loved much. But he
who has been forgiven little loves little."

[48] Then Jesus said to her, "Your sins are
forgiven."

[49] The other guests began to say among
themselves, "Who is this who even forgives
sins?"

[50] Jesus said to the woman, "Your faith
has saved you; go in peace."

The Parable of the Sower

8 After this, Jesus traveled about from
one town and village to another, proclaiming
the good news of the kingdom
of God. The Twelve were with him, [2] and
also some women who had been cured of
evil spirits and diseases: Mary (called
Magdalene) from whom seven demons
had come out; [3] Joanna the wife of Cuza,
the manager of Herod's household; Susanna;
and many others. These women
were helping to support them out of their
own means.

[4] While a large crowd was gathering and
people were coming to Jesus from town
after town, he told this parable: [5] "A farmer
went out to sow his seed. As he was scat-

[a] *41* A denarius was a coin worth about a day's wages.

tering the seed, some fell along the path;
it was trampled on, and the birds of the
air ate it up. 6Some fell on rock, and when
it came up, the plants withered because
they had no moisture. 7Other seed fell
among thorns, which grew up with it and
choked the plants. 8Still other seed fell on
good soil. It came up and yielded a crop,
a hundred times more than was sown."
When he said this, he called out, "He
who has ears to hear, let him hear."
9His disciples asked him what this parable meant. 10He said, "The knowledge of
the secrets of the kingdom of God has
been given to you, but to others I speak in
parables, so that,

" 'though seeing, they may not see;
though hearing, they may not
understand.'[b]

11"This is the meaning of the parable:
The seed is the word of God. 12Those
along the path are the ones who hear, and
then the devil comes and takes away the
word from their hearts, so that they may
not believe and be saved. 13Those on the
rock are the ones who receive the word
with joy when they hear it, but they have
no root. They believe for a while, but in
the time of testing they fall away. 14The
seed that fell among thorns stands for
those who hear, but as they go on their
way they are choked by life's worries,
riches and pleasures, and they do not mature. 15But the seed on good soil stands for
those with a noble and good heart, who
hear the word, retain it, and by persever-
ing produce a crop.

[b] *10* Isaiah 6:9

PRAYER: THE ATTRIBUTES OF GOD

YOU have been just in all that has happened to us; You have acted faithfully, while we did wrong. (Nehemiah 9:33) . . . You, Lord, love justice; You hate robbery and iniquity. (Isaiah 61:8)

***PAUSE** to reflect on these affirmations about the person, powers and perfection of God.*

YEAR 2 DAY 207

OT Proverbs 25

More Proverbs of Solomon

25 These are more proverbs of Solomon, copied by the men of Hezekiah king of Judah:

2It is the glory of God to conceal a
matter;
to search out a matter is the glory of
kings.

3As the heavens are high and the earth
is deep,
so the hearts of kings are
unsearchable.

4Remove the dross from the silver,
and out comes material for[a] the
silversmith;
5remove the wicked from the king's
presence,
and his throne will be established
through righteousness.

6Do not exalt yourself in the king's
presence,
and do not claim a place among
great men;
7it is better for him to say to you,
"Come up here,"
than for him to humiliate you
before a nobleman.

What you have seen with your eyes
8 do not bring[b] hastily to court,
for what will you do in the end
if your neighbor puts you to shame?

9If you argue your case with a
neighbor,
do not betray another man's
confidence,
10or he who hears it may shame you

[a] *4* Or *comes a vessel from* [b] *7,8* Or *nobleman / on whom you had set your eyes. / 8Do not go*

and you will never lose your bad
reputation.

11 A word aptly spoken
is like apples of gold in settings of
silver.

12 Like an earring of gold or an
ornament of fine gold
is a wise man's rebuke to a listening
ear.

13 Like the coolness of snow at harvest
time
is a trustworthy messenger to those
who send him;
he refreshes the spirit of his
masters.

14 Like clouds and wind without rain
is a man who boasts of gifts he does
not give.

15 Through patience a ruler can be
persuaded,
and a gentle tongue can break a
bone.

16 If you find honey, eat just enough—
too much of it, and you will vomit.

17 Seldom set foot in your neighbor's
house—
too much of you, and he will hate
you.

18 Like a club or a sword or a sharp
arrow
is the man who gives false
testimony against his neighbor.

19 Like a bad tooth or a lame foot
is reliance on the unfaithful in
times of trouble.

20 Like one who takes away a garment
on a cold day,
or like vinegar poured on soda,
is one who sings songs to a heavy
heart.

21 If your enemy is hungry, give him
food to eat;
if he is thirsty, give him water to
drink.

22 In doing this, you will heap burning
coals on his head,
and the LORD will reward you.

23 As a north wind brings rain,
so a sly tongue brings angry looks.

24 Better to live on a corner of the roof
than share a house with a
quarrelsome wife.

25 Like cold water to a weary soul
is good news from a distant land.

26 Like a muddied spring or a polluted
well
is a righteous man who gives way to
the wicked.

27 It is not good to eat too much honey,
nor is it honorable to seek one's
own honor.

28 Like a city whose walls are broken
down
is a man who lacks self-control.

PRAYER: INTERCESSION

WE have acted very wickedly toward You. We have not obeyed the commandments, statutes, and ordinances that You gave Your servant Moses. (Nehemiah 1:7)

***TAKE** a few moments to intercede on behalf of your local, state or provincial, and national governments. Pray for spiritual revival in the nation and offer prayers regarding current events and concerns.*

NT Luke 8:16–39

A Lamp on a Stand

16 "No one lights a lamp and hides it in
a jar or puts it under a bed. Instead, he
puts it on a stand, so that those who come
in can see the light. 17 For there is nothing
hidden that will not be disclosed, and
nothing concealed that will not be known
or brought out into the open. 18 Therefore
consider carefully how you listen. Whoever has will be given more; whoever does
not have, even what he thinks he has will
be taken from him."

Jesus' Mother and Brothers

19 Now Jesus' mother and brothers came
to see him, but they were not able to get
near him because of the crowd. 20 Someone told him, "Your mother and brothers
are standing outside, wanting to see you."
21 He replied, "My mother and brothers
are those who hear God's word and put it
into practice."

Jesus Calms the Storm

22 One day Jesus said to his disciples,
"Let's go over to the other side of the
lake." So they got into a boat and set out.
23 As they sailed, he fell asleep. A squall
came down on the lake, so that the boat
was being swamped, and they were in
great danger.
24 The disciples went and woke him, saying, "Master, Master, we're going to
drown!"
He got up and rebuked the wind and
the raging waters; the storm subsided, and
all was calm. 25 "Where is your faith?" he
asked his disciples.
In fear and amazement they asked one
another, "Who is this? He commands
even the winds and the water, and they
obey him."

The Healing of a Demon-possessed Man

26 They sailed to the region of the Gerasenes,[a] which is across the lake from Galilee. 27 When Jesus stepped ashore, he was
met by a demon-possessed man from the
town. For a long time this man had not
worn clothes or lived in a house, but had
lived in the tombs. 28 When he saw Jesus,
he cried out and fell at his feet, shouting
at the top of his voice, "What do you want
with me, Jesus, Son of the Most High
God? I beg you, don't torture me!" 29 For
Jesus had commanded the evil[b] spirit to
come out of the man. Many times it had
seized him, and though he was chained
hand and foot and kept under guard, he
had broken his chains and had been driven by the demon into solitary places.
30 Jesus asked him, "What is your
name?"
"Legion," he replied, because many
demons had gone into him. 31 And they
begged him repeatedly not to order them
to go into the Abyss.
32 A large herd of pigs was feeding there
on the hillside. The demons begged Jesus
to let them go into them, and he gave
them permission. 33 When the demons
came out of the man, they went into the
pigs, and the herd rushed down the steep
bank into the lake and was drowned.
34 When those tending the pigs saw what
had happened, they ran off and reported
this in the town and countryside, 35 and
the people went out to see what had happened. When they came to Jesus, they
found the man from whom the demons
had gone out, sitting at Jesus' feet, dressed
and in his right mind; and they were
afraid. 36 Those who had seen it told the
people how the demon-possessed man
had been cured. 37 Then all the people of
the region of the Gerasenes asked Jesus to
leave them, because they were overcome
with fear. So he got into the boat and left.
38 The man from whom the demons had
gone out begged to go with him, but Jesus
sent him away, saying, 39 "Return home and
tell how much God has done for you." So
the man went away and told all over town
how much Jesus had done for him.

[a] 26 Some manuscripts *Gadarenes*; other manuscripts *Gergesenes*; also in verse 37
[b] 29 Greek *unclean*

PRAYER: THE WORKS OF GOD

YOU, Father, granted the Son authority over all people that He might give eternal life to as many as You have given Him.

As You, Father, sent Your Son into the world, Your Son also has sent us into the world. And He has prayed for those who will believe in You through our message. (John 17:2, 18, 20)

***TAKE** a moment to consider the greatness of God's wonderful works.*

YEAR 2 DAY 208

OT Jeremiah 22:1-30

Judgment Against Evil Kings

22 This is what the LORD says: "Go down
to the palace of the king of Judah and
proclaim this message there: [2]'Hear the
word of the LORD, O king of Judah, you
who sit on David's throne—you, your officials and your people who come
through these gates. [3]This is what the
LORD says: Do what is just and right. Rescue from the hand of his oppressor the
one who has been robbed. Do no wrong
or violence to the alien, the fatherless or
the widow, and do not shed innocent
blood in this place. [4]For if you are careful
to carry out these commands, then kings
who sit on David's throne will come
through the gates of this palace, riding in
chariots and on horses, accompanied by
their officials and their people. [5]But if you
do not obey these commands, declares
the LORD, I swear by myself that this
palace will become a ruin.' "

[6]For this is what the LORD says about
the palace of the king of Judah:

"Though you are like Gilead to me,
like the summit of Lebanon,
I will surely make you like a desert,
like towns not inhabited.
[7]I will send destroyers against you,
each man with his weapons,
and they will cut up your fine cedar
beams
and throw them into the fire.

[8]"People from many nations will pass
by this city and will ask one another, 'Why
has the LORD done such a thing to this
great city?' [9]And the answer will be: 'Because they have forsaken the covenant of
the LORD their God and have worshiped
and served other gods.' "

[10]Do not weep for the dead ⌊king⌋ or
mourn his loss;
rather, weep bitterly for him who is
exiled,
because he will never return
nor see his native land again.

[11]For this is what the LORD says about
Shallum[a] son of Josiah, who succeeded
his father as king of Judah but has gone
from this place: "He will never return.
[12]He will die in the place where they have
led him captive; he will not see this land
again."

[13]"Woe to him who builds his palace by
unrighteousness,
his upper rooms by injustice,
making his countrymen work for
nothing,
not paying them for their labor.
[14]He says, 'I will build myself a great
palace
with spacious upper rooms.'
So he makes large windows in it,
panels it with cedar
and decorates it in red.

[15]"Does it make you a king
to have more and more cedar?
Did not your father have food and
drink?
He did what was right and just,
so all went well with him.
[16]He defended the cause of the poor
and needy,
and so all went well.
Is that not what it means to know
me?"
declares the LORD.
[17]"But your eyes and your heart
are set only on dishonest gain,
on shedding innocent blood
and on oppression and extortion."

[18]Therefore this is what the LORD says
about Jehoiakim son of Josiah king of Judah:

"They will not mourn for him:
'Alas, my brother! Alas, my sister!'
They will not mourn for him:
'Alas, my master! Alas, his
splendor!'
[19]He will have the burial of a donkey—
dragged away and thrown
outside the gates of Jerusalem."

[20]"Go up to Lebanon and cry out,
let your voice be heard in Bashan,
cry out from Abarim,
for all your allies are crushed.
[21]I warned you when you felt secure,
but you said, 'I will not listen!'
This has been your way from your
youth;

[a] *11* Also called *Jehoahaz*

you have not obeyed me.
[22]The wind will drive all your shepherds away,
and your allies will go into exile.
Then you will be ashamed and disgraced
because of all your wickedness.
[23]You who live in 'Lebanon,[b]'
who are nestled in cedar buildings,
how you will groan when pangs come upon you,
pain like that of a woman in labor!

[24]"As surely as I live," declares the LORD,
"even if you, Jehoiachin[c] son of Jehoiakim
king of Judah, were a signet ring on my
right hand, I would still pull you off. [25]I
will hand you over to those who seek your
life, those you fear—to Nebuchadnezzar
king of Babylon and to the Babylonians.[d]
[26]I will hurl you and the mother who gave
you birth into another country, where neither of you was born, and there you both
will die. [27]You will never come back to the
land you long to return to."

[28]Is this man Jehoiachin a despised, broken pot,
an object no one wants?
Why will he and his children be hurled out,
cast into a land they do not know?
[29]O land, land, land,
hear the word of the LORD!
[30]This is what the LORD says:
"Record this man as if childless,
a man who will not prosper in his lifetime,
for none of his offspring will prosper,
none will sit on the throne of David
or rule anymore in Judah."

[b] 23 That is, the palace in Jerusalem (see 1 Kings 7:2) [c] 24 Hebrew *Coniah,* a variant of *Jehoiachin;* also in verse 28 [d] 25 Or *Chaldeans*

PRAYER: AFFIRMATION

O CHRIST, You were in the world, and the world was made through You, and the world did not know You. You came to Your own, but Your own did not receive You. O God, no one has ever seen You, but Your only begotten Son, who is in Your bosom, has made You known. (John 1:10–11, 18)

PAUSE *to reflect on these Biblical affirmations.*

NT Luke 8:40–9:17

A Dead Girl and a Sick Woman

[40]Now when Jesus returned, a crowd
welcomed him, for they were all expecting him. [41]Then a man named Jairus, a
ruler of the synagogue, came and fell at
Jesus' feet, pleading with him to come to
his house [42]because his only daughter, a
girl of about twelve, was dying.

As Jesus was on his way, the crowds almost crushed him. [43]And a woman was
there who had been subject to bleeding
for twelve years,[a] but no one could heal
her. [44]She came up behind him and
touched the edge of his cloak, and immediately her bleeding stopped.

[45]"Who touched me?" Jesus asked.

When they all denied it, Peter said,
"Master, the people are crowding and
pressing against you."

[46]But Jesus said, "Someone touched me;
I know that power has gone out from me."
[47]Then the woman, seeing that she
could not go unnoticed, came trembling
and fell at his feet. In the presence of all
the people, she told why she had touched
him and how she had been instantly
healed. [48]Then he said to her, "Daughter,
your faith has healed you. Go in peace."
[49]While Jesus was still speaking, someone came from the house of Jairus, the synagogue ruler. "Your daughter is dead," he
said. "Don't bother the teacher any more."
[50]Hearing this, Jesus said to Jairus,
"Don't be afraid; just believe, and she will
be healed."
[51]When he arrived at the house of Jairus, he did not let anyone go in with him

[a] 43 Many manuscripts *years, and she had spent all she had on doctors*

except Peter, John and James, and the
child's father and mother. 52 Meanwhile,
all the people were wailing and mourning
for her. "Stop wailing," Jesus said. "She is
not dead but asleep."
53 They laughed at him, knowing that
she was dead. 54 But he took her by the
hand and said, "My child, get up!" 55 Her
spirit returned, and at once she stood up.
Then Jesus told them to give her something to eat. 56 Her parents were astonished, but he ordered them not to tell anyone what had happened.

Jesus Sends Out the Twelve

9 When Jesus had called the Twelve together, he gave them power and authority to drive out all demons and to cure diseases, 2 and he sent them out to preach the
kingdom of God and to heal the sick. 3 He
told them: "Take nothing for the journey—
no staff, no bag, no bread, no money, no
extra tunic. 4 Whatever house you enter, stay
there until you leave that town. 5 If people
do not welcome you, shake the dust off
your feet when you leave their town, as a
testimony against them." 6 So they set out
and went from village to village, preaching
the gospel and healing people everywhere.
7 Now Herod the tetrarch heard about all
that was going on. And he was perplexed,
because some were saying that John had
been raised from the dead, 8 others that Elijah had appeared, and still others that one
of the prophets of long ago had come back
to life. 9 But Herod said, "I beheaded John.
Who, then, is this I hear such things
about?" And he tried to see him.

Jesus Feeds the Five Thousand

10 When the apostles returned, they reported to Jesus what they had done. Then
he took them with him and they withdrew
by themselves to a town called Bethsaida,
11 but the crowds learned about it and followed him. He welcomed them and spoke
to them about the kingdom of God, and
healed those who needed healing.
12 Late in the afternoon the Twelve came
to him and said, "Send the crowd away so
they can go to the surrounding villages
and countryside and find food and lodging, because we are in a remote place
here."
13 He replied, "You give them something
to eat."
They answered, "We have only five
loaves of bread and two fish—unless we
go and buy food for all this crowd."
14 (About five thousand men were there.)
But he said to his disciples, "Have them
sit down in groups of about fifty each."
15 The disciples did so, and everybody sat
down. 16 Taking the five loaves and the two
fish and looking up to heaven, he gave
thanks and broke them. Then he gave
them to the disciples to set before the people. 17 They all ate and were satisfied, and
the disciples picked up twelve basketfuls
of broken pieces that were left over.

PRAYER: MY RELATIONSHIP TO GOD

I AM not ashamed of the gospel, for it is Your power, O God, for salvation to everyone who believes, to the Jew first, and also to the Gentile. For in it Your righteousness, O God, is revealed from faith to faith, just as it is written: "The righteous will live by faith." (Romans 1:16–17)

__PAUSE__ to thank God for the relationship that you enjoy with Him in Jesus Christ.

YEAR 2 DAY 209

OT Jeremiah 23:1–40

The Righteous Branch

23 "Woe to the shepherds who are destroying and scattering the sheep of
my pasture!" declares the LORD. 2 Therefore this is what the LORD, the God of Israel, says to the shepherds who tend my
people: "Because you have scattered my
flock and driven them away and have not

bestowed care on them, I will bestow
punishment on you for the evil you have
done," declares the LORD. [3]"I myself will
gather the remnant of my flock out of all
the countries where I have driven them
and will bring them back to their pasture,
where they will be fruitful and increase in
number. [4]I will place shepherds over them
who will tend them, and they will no
longer be afraid or terrified, nor will any
be missing," declares the LORD.

[5]"The days are coming," declares the
 LORD,
 "when I will raise up to David[a] a
 righteous Branch,
 a King who will reign wisely
 and do what is just and right in the
 land.
[6]In his days Judah will be saved
 and Israel will live in safety.
 This is the name by which he will be
 called:
 The LORD Our Righteousness.

[7]"So then, the days are coming," declares
the LORD, "when people will no longer say,
'As surely as the LORD lives, who brought
the Israelites up out of Egypt,' [8]but they
will say, 'As surely as the LORD lives, who
brought the descendants of Israel up out
of the land of the north and out of all the
countries where he had banished them.'
Then they will live in their own land."

Lying Prophets

[9]Concerning the prophets:

My heart is broken within me;
 all my bones tremble.
I am like a drunken man,
 like a man overcome by wine,
because of the LORD
 and his holy words.
[10]The land is full of adulterers;
 because of the curse[b] the land lies
 parched[c]
 and the pastures in the desert are
 withered.
The ⌊prophets⌋ follow an evil course
 and use their power unjustly.

[11]"Both prophet and priest are godless;
 even in my temple I find their
 wickedness,"
 declares the LORD.
[12]"Therefore their path will become
 slippery;
 they will be banished to darkness
 and there they will fall.
I will bring disaster on them
 in the year they are punished,"
 declares the LORD.

[13]"Among the prophets of Samaria
 I saw this repulsive thing:
They prophesied by Baal
 and led my people Israel astray.
[14]And among the prophets of Jerusalem
 I have seen something horrible:
 They commit adultery and live a lie.
They strengthen the hands of
 evildoers,
 so that no one turns from his
 wickedness.
They are all like Sodom to me;
 the people of Jerusalem are like
 Gomorrah."

[15]Therefore, this is what the LORD
Almighty says concerning the prophets:

"I will make them eat bitter food
 and drink poisoned water,
because from the prophets of
 Jerusalem
 ungodliness has spread throughout
 the land."

[16]This is what the LORD Almighty says:

"Do not listen to what the prophets
 are prophesying to you;
 they fill you with false hopes.
They speak visions from their own
 minds,
 not from the mouth of the LORD.
[17]They keep saying to those who despise
 me,
 'The LORD says: You will have peace.'
And to all who follow the
 stubbornness of their hearts
 they say, 'No harm will come to
 you.'
[18]But which of them has stood in the
 council of the LORD
 to see or to hear his word?
 Who has listened and heard his
 word?
[19]See, the storm of the LORD
 will burst out in wrath,
a whirlwind swirling down
 on the heads of the wicked.
[20]The anger of the LORD will not turn
 back

[a]5 Or *up from David's line* [b]10 Or *because of these things* [c]10 Or *land mourns*

until he fully accomplishes
the purposes of his heart.
In days to come
you will understand it clearly.
21 I did not send these prophets,
yet they have run with their
message;
I did not speak to them,
yet they have prophesied.
22 But if they had stood in my council,
they would have proclaimed my
words to my people
and would have turned them from
their evil ways
and from their evil deeds.

23 "Am I only a God nearby,"
declares the LORD,
"and not a God far away?
24 Can anyone hide in secret places
so that I cannot see him?"
declares the LORD.
"Do not I fill heaven and earth?"
declares the LORD.

25 "I have heard what the prophets say
who prophesy lies in my name. They say,
'I had a dream! I had a dream!' 26 How
long will this continue in the hearts of
these lying prophets, who prophesy the
delusions of their own minds? 27 They
think the dreams they tell one another
will make my people forget my name, just
as their fathers forgot my name through
Baal worship. 28 Let the prophet who has
a dream tell his dream, but let the one
who has my word speak it faithfully. For
what has straw to do with grain?" declares
the LORD. 29 "Is not my word like fire," declares the LORD, "and like a hammer that
breaks a rock in pieces?

30 "Therefore," declares the LORD, "I am
against the prophets who steal from one
another words supposedly from me.
31 Yes," declares the LORD, "I am against the
prophets who wag their own tongues and
yet declare, 'The LORD declares.' 32 Indeed,
I am against those who prophesy false
dreams," declares the LORD. "They tell
them and lead my people astray with their
reckless lies, yet I did not send or appoint
them. They do not benefit these people in
the least," declares the LORD.

False Oracles and False Prophets

33 "When these people, or a prophet or
a priest, ask you, 'What is the oracle[d] of
the LORD?' say to them, 'What oracle?[e] I
will forsake you, declares the LORD.' 34 If a
prophet or a priest or anyone else claims,
'This is the oracle of the LORD,' I will punish that man and his household. 35 This is
what each of you keeps on saying to his
friend or relative: 'What is the LORD's answer?' or 'What has the LORD spoken?'
36 But you must not mention 'the oracle of
the LORD' again, because every man's own
word becomes his oracle and so you distort the words of the living God, the LORD
Almighty, our God. 37 This is what you
keep saying to a prophet: 'What is the
LORD's answer to you?' or 'What has the
LORD spoken?' 38 Although you claim, 'This
is the oracle of the LORD,' this is what the
LORD says: You used the words, 'This is the
oracle of the LORD,' even though I told you
that you must not claim, 'This is the oracle of the LORD.' 39 Therefore, I will surely
forget you and cast you out of my presence along with the city I gave to you and
your fathers. 40 I will bring upon you everlasting disgrace—everlasting shame that
will not be forgotten."

[d] 33 Or *burden* (see Septuagint and Vulgate)
[e] 33 Hebrew; Septuagint and Vulgate *'You are the burden.* (The Hebrew for *oracle* and *burden* is the same.)

PRAYER: THANKSGIVING

YOUR power, O God, toward those who believe, is according to the working of Your mighty strength, which You exerted in Christ when You raised Him from the dead and seated Him at Your right hand in the heavenly realms, far above all rule and authority, power and dominion, and every title that can be given, not only in the present age but also in the one to come. (Ephesians 1:19–21)

PAUSE *to offer your own expressions of thanksgiving.*

NT Luke 9:18–62

Peter's Confession of Christ

18 Once when Jesus was praying in private and his disciples were with him, he asked them, "Who do the crowds say I am?"

19 They replied, "Some say John the Baptist; others say Elijah; and still others, that one of the prophets of long ago has come back to life."

20 "But what about you?" he asked. "Who do you say I am?"

Peter answered, "The Christ[a] of God."

21 Jesus strictly warned them not to tell this to anyone. 22 And he said, "The Son of Man must suffer many things and be rejected by the elders, chief priests and teachers of the law, and he must be killed and on the third day be raised to life."

23 Then he said to them all: "If anyone would come after me, he must deny himself and take up his cross daily and follow me. 24 For whoever wants to save his life will lose it, but whoever loses his life for me will save it. 25 What good is it for a man to gain the whole world, and yet lose or forfeit his very self? 26 If anyone is ashamed of me and my words, the Son of Man will be ashamed of him when he comes in his glory and in the glory of the Father and of the holy angels. 27 I tell you the truth, some who are standing here will not taste death before they see the kingdom of God."

The Transfiguration

28 About eight days after Jesus said this, he took Peter, John and James with him and went up onto a mountain to pray. 29 As he was praying, the appearance of his face changed, and his clothes became as bright as a flash of lightning. 30 Two men, Moses and Elijah, 31 appeared in glorious splendor, talking with Jesus. They spoke about his departure, which he was about to bring to fulfillment at Jerusalem. 32 Peter and his companions were very sleepy, but when they became fully awake, they saw his glory and the two men standing with him. 33 As the men were leaving Jesus, Peter said to him, "Master, it is good for us to be here. Let us put up three shelters—one for you, one for Moses and one for Elijah." (He did not know what he was saying.)

34 While he was speaking, a cloud appeared and enveloped them, and they were afraid as they entered the cloud. 35 A voice came from the cloud, saying, "This is my Son, whom I have chosen; listen to him." 36 When the voice had spoken, they found that Jesus was alone. The disciples kept this to themselves, and told no one at that time what they had seen.

The Healing of a Boy With an Evil Spirit

37 The next day, when they came down from the mountain, a large crowd met him. 38 A man in the crowd called out, "Teacher, I beg you to look at my son, for he is my only child. 39 A spirit seizes him and he suddenly screams; it throws him into convulsions so that he foams at the mouth. It scarcely ever leaves him and is destroying him. 40 I begged your disciples to drive it out, but they could not."

41 "O unbelieving and perverse generation," Jesus replied, "how long shall I stay with you and put up with you? Bring your son here."

42 Even while the boy was coming, the demon threw him to the ground in a convulsion. But Jesus rebuked the evil[b] spirit, healed the boy and gave him back to his father. 43 And they were all amazed at the greatness of God.

While everyone was marveling at all that Jesus did, he said to his disciples, 44 "Listen carefully to what I am about to tell you: The Son of Man is going to be betrayed into the hands of men." 45 But they did not understand what this meant. It was hidden from them, so that they did not grasp it, and they were afraid to ask him about it.

Who Will Be the Greatest?

46 An argument started among the disciples as to which of them would be the greatest. 47 Jesus, knowing their thoughts, took a little child and had him stand beside him. 48 Then he said to them, "Whoever welcomes this little child in my name welcomes me; and whoever welcomes me welcomes the one who sent me. For he

[a] 20 Or *Messiah* [b] 42 Greek *unclean*

who is least among you all—he is the
greatest."
49 "Master," said John, "we saw a man
driving out demons in your name and we
tried to stop him, because he is not one
of us."
50 "Do not stop him," Jesus said, "for
whoever is not against you is for you."

Samaritan Opposition

51 As the time approached for him to be
taken up to heaven, Jesus resolutely set
out for Jerusalem. 52 And he sent messengers on ahead, who went into a Samaritan village to get things ready for him;
53 but the people there did not welcome
him, because he was heading for Jerusalem. 54 When the disciples James and
John saw this, they asked, "Lord, do you
want us to call fire down from heaven to
destroy them[c]?" 55 But Jesus turned and rebuked them, 56 and[d] they went to another
village.

The Cost of Following Jesus

57 As they were walking along the road,
a man said to him, "I will follow you
wherever you go."
58 Jesus replied, "Foxes have holes and
birds of the air have nests, but the Son of
Man has no place to lay his head."
59 He said to another man, "Follow me."
But the man replied, "Lord, first let me
go and bury my father."
60 Jesus said to him, "Let the dead bury
their own dead, but you go and proclaim
the kingdom of God."
61 Still another said, "I will follow you,
Lord; but first let me go back and say
good-by to my family."
62 Jesus replied, "No one who puts his
hand to the plow and looks back is fit for
service in the kingdom of God."

[c] 54 Some manuscripts *them, even as Elijah did*
[d] 55,56 Some manuscripts *them. And he said, "You do not know what kind of spirit you are of, for the Son of Man did not come to destroy men's lives, but to save them."* [56]*And*

PRAYER: THE CHARACTER I WANT TO CULTIVATE

IT is better to have a little with the fear of You, Lord, than great wealth with turmoil. (Proverbs 15:16) . . . It is better to have a little with righteousness than great income with injustice. (Proverbs 16:8)

TAKE *a moment to ask the Lord for the grace to grow in godly character.*

OT Psalms 114–115

YEAR 2 DAY 210

Psalm 114

1 When Israel came out of Egypt,
the house of Jacob from a people of
foreign tongue,
2 Judah became God's sanctuary,
Israel his dominion.

3 The sea looked and fled,
the Jordan turned back;
4 the mountains skipped like rams,
the hills like lambs.

5 Why was it, O sea, that you fled,
O Jordan, that you turned back,
6 you mountains, that you skipped like
rams,
you hills, like lambs?

7 Tremble, O earth, at the presence of
the Lord,
at the presence of the God of Jacob,
8 who turned the rock into a pool,
the hard rock into springs of water.

Psalm 115

1 Not to us, O LORD, not to us
but to your name be the glory,
because of your love and
faithfulness.

2 Why do the nations say,
"Where is their God?"
3 Our God is in heaven;
he does whatever pleases him.
4 But their idols are silver and gold,
made by the hands of men.
5 They have mouths, but cannot speak,
eyes, but they cannot see;

6 they have ears, but cannot hear,
noses, but they cannot smell;
7 they have hands, but cannot feel,
feet, but they cannot walk;
nor can they utter a sound with
their throats.
8 Those who make them will be like
them,
and so will all who trust in them.

9 O house of Israel, trust in the LORD—
he is their help and shield.
10 O house of Aaron, trust in the LORD—
he is their help and shield.
11 You who fear him, trust in the LORD—
he is their help and shield.

12 The LORD remembers us and will bless
us:
He will bless the house of Israel,
he will bless the house of Aaron,
13 he will bless those who fear the
LORD—
small and great alike.

14 May the LORD make you increase,
both you and your children.
15 May you be blessed by the LORD,
the Maker of heaven and earth.

16 The highest heavens belong to the
LORD,
but the earth he has given to man.
17 It is not the dead who praise the
LORD,
those who go down to silence;
18 it is we who extol the LORD,
both now and forevermore.

Praise the LORD.[a]

[a] 18 Hebrew *Hallelu Yah*

PRAYER: ADORATION

I WILL express the memory of Your abundant goodness and joyfully sing of Your righteousness. O Lord, You are gracious and compassionate, slow to anger and great in loving-kindness. You are good to all, and Your tender mercies are over all Your works. (Psalm 145:7–9)

PAUSE *to express your thoughts of praise and worship.*

NT Luke 10:1–42

Jesus Sends Out the Seventy-two

10 After this the Lord appointed seventy-
two[a] others and sent them two by two
ahead of him to every town and place where
he was about to go. 2 He told them, "The
harvest is plentiful, but the workers are few.
Ask the Lord of the harvest, therefore, to
send out workers into his harvest field. 3 Go!
I am sending you out like lambs among
wolves. 4 Do not take a purse or bag or sandals; and do not greet anyone on the road.
5 "When you enter a house, first say,
'Peace to this house.' 6 If a man of peace is
there, your peace will rest on him; if not,
it will return to you. 7 Stay in that house,
eating and drinking whatever they give
you, for the worker deserves his wages. Do
not move around from house to house.
8 "When you enter a town and are welcomed, eat what is set before you. 9 Heal
the sick who are there and tell them, 'The
kingdom of God is near you.' 10 But when
you enter a town and are not welcomed,
go into its streets and say, 11 'Even the dust
of your town that sticks to our feet we
wipe off against you. Yet be sure of this:
The kingdom of God is near.' 12 I tell you,
it will be more bearable on that day for
Sodom than for that town.
13 "Woe to you, Korazin! Woe to you,
Bethsaida! For if the miracles that were performed in you had been performed in Tyre
and Sidon, they would have repented long
ago, sitting in sackcloth and ashes. 14 But it
will be more bearable for Tyre and Sidon
at the judgment than for you. 15 And you,
Capernaum, will you be lifted up to the
skies? No, you will go down to the depths.[b]
16 "He who listens to you listens to me;
he who rejects you rejects me; but he who
rejects me rejects him who sent me."
17 The seventy-two returned with joy and
said, "Lord, even the demons submit to us
in your name."

[a] 1 Some manuscripts *seventy;* also in verse 17
[b] 15 Greek *Hades*

18He replied, "I saw Satan fall like lightning from heaven. 19I have given you authority to trample on snakes and scorpions and to overcome all the power of the
enemy; nothing will harm you. 20Howev-
er, do not rejoice that the spirits submit to
you, but rejoice that your names are written in heaven."

21At that time Jesus, full of joy through
the Holy Spirit, said, "I praise you, Father,
Lord of heaven and earth, because you
have hidden these things from the wise
and learned, and revealed them to little
children. Yes, Father, for this was your
good pleasure.

22"All things have been committed to me
by my Father. No one knows who the Son
is except the Father, and no one knows
who the Father is except the Son and those
to whom the Son chooses to reveal him."

23Then he turned to his disciples and
said privately, "Blessed are the eyes that
see what you see. 24For I tell you that
many prophets and kings wanted to see
what you see but did not see it, and to
hear what you hear but did not hear it."

The Parable of the Good Samaritan

25On one occasion an expert in the law
stood up to test Jesus. "Teacher," he asked,
"what must I do to inherit eternal life?"

26"What is written in the Law?" he
replied. "How do you read it?"

27He answered: " 'Love the Lord your
God with all your heart and with all your
soul and with all your strength and with
all your mind'[c]; and, 'Love your neighbor
as yourself.'[d]"

28"You have answered correctly," Jesus
replied. "Do this and you will live."

29But he wanted to justify himself, so he
asked Jesus, "And who is my neighbor?"

30In reply Jesus said: "A man was going
down from Jerusalem to Jericho, when he
fell into the hands of robbers. They stripped
him of his clothes, beat him and went away,
leaving him half dead. 31A priest happened
to be going down the same road, and when
he saw the man, he passed by on the other
side. 32So too, a Levite, when he came to the
place and saw him, passed by on the other
side. 33But a Samaritan, as he traveled, came
where the man was; and when he saw him,
he took pity on him. 34He went to him and
bandaged his wounds, pouring on oil and
wine. Then he put the man on his own
donkey, took him to an inn and took care
of him. 35The next day he took out two silver coins[e] and gave them to the innkeeper.
'Look after him,' he said, 'and when I return, I will reimburse you for any extra expense you may have.'

36"Which of these three do you think
was a neighbor to the man who fell into
the hands of robbers?"

37The expert in the law replied, "The
one who had mercy on him."

Jesus told him, "Go and do likewise."

At the Home of Martha and Mary

38As Jesus and his disciples were on
their way, he came to a village where a
woman named Martha opened her home
to him. 39She had a sister called Mary,
who sat at the Lord's feet listening to what
he said. 40But Martha was distracted by all
the preparations that had to be made. She
came to him and asked, "Lord, don't you
care that my sister has left me to do the
work by myself? Tell her to help me!"

41"Martha, Martha," the Lord answered,
"you are worried and upset about many
things, 42but only one thing is needed.[f]
Mary has chosen what is better, and it will
not be taken away from her."

[c] 27 Deut. 6:5 [d] 27 Lev. 19:18 [e] 35 Greek *two denarii* [f] 42 Some manuscripts *but few things are needed—or only one*

PRAYER: MY RELATIONSHIP TO OTHERS

WE love because You, O God, first loved us. Those who say, "I love God," and hate their neighbors are liars; for those who do not love their neighbors whom they have seen cannot love You whom they have not seen. And we have this commandment from You: that those who love You must also love their neighbors. (1 John 4:19–21)

***PAUSE** to review your relationships with others and to commit them to the Lord.*

YEAR 2 DAY 211

OT Jeremiah 24:1–25:38

Two Baskets of Figs

24 After Jehoiachin[a] son of Jehoiakim
king of Judah and the officials, the
craftsmen and the artisans of Judah were
carried into exile from Jerusalem to Babylon by Nebuchadnezzar king of Babylon,
the LORD showed me two baskets of figs
placed in front of the temple of the LORD.
2One basket had very good figs, like those
that ripen early; the other basket had very
poor figs, so bad they could not be eaten.
3Then the LORD asked me, "What do
you see, Jeremiah?"
"Figs," I answered. "The good ones are
very good, but the poor ones are so bad
they cannot be eaten."
4Then the word of the LORD came to me:
5"This is what the LORD, the God of Israel,
says: 'Like these good figs, I regard as good
the exiles from Judah, whom I sent away
from this place to the land of the Babylonians.[b] 6My eyes will watch over them for
their good, and I will bring them back to
this land. I will build them up and not tear
them down; I will plant them and not uproot them. 7I will give them a heart to
know me, that I am the LORD. They will be
my people, and I will be their God, for
they will return to me with all their heart.
8" 'But like the poor figs, which are so
bad they cannot be eaten,' says the LORD,
'so will I deal with Zedekiah king of Judah, his officials and the survivors from
Jerusalem, whether they remain in this
land or live in Egypt. 9I will make them
abhorrent and an offense to all the kingdoms of the earth, a reproach and a byword, an object of ridicule and cursing,
wherever I banish them. 10I will send the
sword, famine and plague against them
until they are destroyed from the land I
gave to them and their fathers.' "

Seventy Years of Captivity

25 The word came to Jeremiah concerning all the people of Judah in the
fourth year of Jehoiakim son of Josiah
king of Judah, which was the first year of
Nebuchadnezzar king of Babylon. 2So Jeremiah the prophet said to all the people
of Judah and to all those living in Jerusalem: 3For twenty-three years—from the
thirteenth year of Josiah son of Amon
king of Judah until this very day—the
word of the LORD has come to me and I
have spoken to you again and again, but
you have not listened.
4And though the LORD has sent all his
servants the prophets to you again and
again, you have not listened or paid any
attention. 5They said, "Turn now, each of
you, from your evil ways and your evil
practices, and you can stay in the land the
LORD gave to you and your fathers for ever
and ever. 6Do not follow other gods to
serve and worship them; do not provoke
me to anger with what your hands have
made. Then I will not harm you."
7"But you did not listen to me," declares the LORD, "and you have provoked
me with what your hands have made, and
you have brought harm to yourselves."
8Therefore the LORD Almighty says this:
"Because you have not listened to my
words, 9I will summon all the peoples of
the north and my servant Nebuchadnezzar king of Babylon," declares the LORD,
"and I will bring them against this land
and its inhabitants and against all the surrounding nations. I will completely destroy[c] them and make them an object of
horror and scorn, and an everlasting ruin.
10I will banish from them the sounds of
joy and gladness, the voices of bride and
bridegroom, the sound of millstones and
the light of the lamp. 11This whole country will become a desolate wasteland, and
these nations will serve the king of Babylon seventy years.
12"But when the seventy years are fulfilled, I will punish the king of Babylon
and his nation, the land of the Babylonians,[b] for their guilt," declares the LORD,
"and will make it desolate forever. 13I will
bring upon that land all the things I have
spoken against it, all that are written in
this book and prophesied by Jeremiah
against all the nations. 14They themselves
will be enslaved by many nations and
great kings; I will repay them according to
their deeds and the work of their hands."

[a] 1 Hebrew *Jeconiah,* a variant of *Jehoiachin*
[b] 5,12 Or *Chaldeans* [c] 9 The Hebrew term refers to the irrevocable giving over of things or persons to the LORD, often by totally destroying them.

The Cup of God's Wrath

15This is what the LORD, the God of Israel, said to me: "Take from my hand this
cup filled with the wine of my wrath and
make all the nations to whom I send you
drink it. 16When they drink it, they will
stagger and go mad because of the sword
I will send among them."

17So I took the cup from the LORD's
hand and made all the nations to whom
he sent me drink it: 18Jerusalem and the
towns of Judah, its kings and officials, to
make them a ruin and an object of horror
and scorn and cursing, as they are today;
19Pharaoh king of Egypt, his attendants,
his officials and all his people, 20and all
the foreign people there; all the kings of
Uz; all the kings of the Philistines (those
of Ashkelon, Gaza, Ekron, and the people
left at Ashdod); 21Edom, Moab and Ammon; 22all the kings of Tyre and Sidon; the
kings of the coastlands across the sea;
23Dedan, Tema, Buz and all who are in
distant places[d]; 24all the kings of Arabia
and all the kings of the foreign people
who live in the desert; 25all the kings of
Zimri, Elam and Media; 26and all the
kings of the north, near and far, one after
the other—all the kingdoms on the face
of the earth. And after all of them, the
king of Sheshach[e] will drink it too.

27"Then tell them, 'This is what the LORD
Almighty, the God of Israel, says: Drink, get
drunk and vomit, and fall to rise no more
because of the sword I will send among
you.' 28But if they refuse to take the cup
from your hand and drink, tell them, 'This
is what the LORD Almighty says: You must
drink it! 29See, I am beginning to bring disaster on the city that bears my Name, and
will you indeed go unpunished? You will
not go unpunished, for I am calling down
a sword upon all who live on the earth, declares the LORD Almighty.'

30"Now prophesy all these words
against them and say to them:

" 'The LORD will roar from on high;
he will thunder from his holy
dwelling
and roar mightily against his land.
He will shout like those who tread the
grapes,
shout against all who live on the
earth.
31The tumult will resound to the ends
of the earth,
for the LORD will bring charges
against the nations;
he will bring judgment on all
mankind
and put the wicked to the sword,' "
declares the LORD.

32This is what the LORD Almighty says:

"Look! Disaster is spreading
from nation to nation;
a mighty storm is rising
from the ends of the earth."

33At that time those slain by the LORD will
be everywhere—from one end of the earth
to the other. They will not be mourned or
gathered up or buried, but will be like
refuse lying on the ground.

34Weep and wail, you shepherds;
roll in the dust, you leaders of the
flock.
For your time to be slaughtered has
come;
you will fall and be shattered like
fine pottery.
35The shepherds will have nowhere to
flee,
the leaders of the flock no place to
escape.
36Hear the cry of the shepherds,
the wailing of the leaders of the
flock,
for the LORD is destroying their
pasture.
37The peaceful meadows will be laid
waste
because of the fierce anger of the
LORD.
38Like a lion he will leave his lair,
and their land will become desolate
because of the sword[f] of the oppressor
and because of the LORD's fierce
anger.

[d] 23 Or *who clip the hair by their foreheads*
[e] 26 *Sheshach* is a cryptogram for Babylon.
[f] 38 Some Hebrew manuscripts and Septuagint (see also Jer. 46:16 and 50:16); most Hebrew manuscripts *anger*

PRAYER: CONFESSION

OUT of the depths I call to You, O Lord. O Lord, hear my voice, and let Your ears be attentive to the voice of my supplications. If You should mark iniquities, O Lord, who could stand? But there is forgiveness with You; therefore You are feared. (Psalm 130:1–4)

__ASK__ the Spirit to search your heart and reveal any areas of unconfessed sin. Acknowledge these to the Lord and thank Him for His forgiveness.

NT Luke 11:1–54

Jesus' Teaching on Prayer

11 One day Jesus was praying in a certain place. When he finished, one of his disciples said to him, "Lord, teach us to pray, just as John taught his disciples."

2He said to them, "When you pray, say:

" 'Father,[a]
hallowed be your name,
your kingdom come.[b]
3Give us each day our daily bread.
4Forgive us our sins,
for we also forgive everyone who
sins against us.[c]
And lead us not into temptation.[d]' "

5Then he said to them, "Suppose one of you has a friend, and he goes to him at midnight and says, 'Friend, lend me three loaves of bread, 6because a friend of mine on a journey has come to me, and I have nothing to set before him.'

7"Then the one inside answers, 'Don't bother me. The door is already locked, and my children are with me in bed. I can't get up and give you anything.' 8I tell you, though he will not get up and give him the bread because he is his friend, yet because of the man's boldness[e] he will get up and give him as much as he needs.

9"So I say to you: Ask and it will be given to you; seek and you will find; knock and the door will be opened to you. 10For everyone who asks receives; he who seeks finds; and to him who knocks, the door will be opened.

11"Which of you fathers, if your son asks for[f] a fish, will give him a snake instead? 12Or if he asks for an egg, will give him a scorpion? 13If you then, though you are evil, know how to give good gifts to your children, how much more will your Father in heaven give the Holy Spirit to those who ask him!"

Jesus and Beelzebub

14Jesus was driving out a demon that was mute. When the demon left, the man who had been mute spoke, and the crowd was amazed. 15But some of them said, "By Beelzebub,[g] the prince of demons, he is driving out demons." 16Others tested him by asking for a sign from heaven.

17Jesus knew their thoughts and said to them: "Any kingdom divided against itself will be ruined, and a house divided against itself will fall. 18If Satan is divided against himself, how can his kingdom stand? I say this because you claim that I drive out demons by Beelzebub. 19Now if I drive out demons by Beelzebub, by whom do your followers drive them out? So then, they will be your judges. 20But if I drive out demons by the finger of God, then the kingdom of God has come to you.

21"When a strong man, fully armed, guards his own house, his possessions are safe. 22But when someone stronger attacks and overpowers him, he takes away the armor in which the man trusted and divides up the spoils.

23"He who is not with me is against me, and he who does not gather with me, scatters.

24"When an evil[h] spirit comes out of a man, it goes through arid places seeking rest and does not find it. Then it says, 'I will return to the house I left.' 25When it arrives, it finds the house swept clean and put in order. 26Then it goes and takes sev-

[a] 2 Some manuscripts *Our Father in heaven*
[b] 2 Some manuscripts *come. May your will be done on earth as it is in heaven.*
[c] 4 Greek *everyone who is indebted to us*
[d] 4 Some manuscripts *temptation but deliver us from the evil one*
[e] 8 Or *persistence*
[f] 11 Some manuscripts *for bread, will give him a stone; or if he asks for*
[g] 15 Greek *Beezeboul* or *Beelzeboul;* also in verses 18 and 19
[h] 24 Greek *unclean*

en other spirits more wicked than itself, and they go in and live there. And the final condition of that man is worse than the first."

[27]As Jesus was saying these things, a woman in the crowd called out, "Blessed is the mother who gave you birth and nursed you."

[28]He replied, "Blessed rather are those who hear the word of God and obey it."

The Sign of Jonah

[29]As the crowds increased, Jesus said, "This is a wicked generation. It asks for a miraculous sign, but none will be given it except the sign of Jonah. [30]For as Jonah was a sign to the Ninevites, so also will the Son of Man be to this generation. [31]The Queen of the South will rise at the judgment with the men of this generation and condemn them; for she came from the ends of the earth to listen to Solomon's wisdom, and now one[i] greater than Solomon is here. [32]The men of Nineveh will stand up at the judgment with this generation and condemn it; for they repented at the preaching of Jonah, and now one greater than Jonah is here.

The Lamp of the Body

[33]"No one lights a lamp and puts it in a place where it will be hidden, or under a bowl. Instead he puts it on its stand, so that those who come in may see the light. [34]Your eye is the lamp of your body. When your eyes are good, your whole body also is full of light. But when they are bad, your body also is full of darkness. [35]See to it, then, that the light within you is not darkness. [36]Therefore, if your whole body is full of light, and no part of it dark, it will be completely lighted, as when the light of a lamp shines on you."

Six Woes

[37]When Jesus had finished speaking, a Pharisee invited him to eat with him; so he went in and reclined at the table. [38]But the Pharisee, noticing that Jesus did not first wash before the meal, was surprised.

[39]Then the Lord said to him, "Now then, you Pharisees clean the outside of the cup and dish, but inside you are full of greed and wickedness. [40]You foolish people! Did not the one who made the outside make the inside also? [41]But give what is inside ⌊the dish⌋[j] to the poor, and everything will be clean for you.

[42]"Woe to you Pharisees, because you give God a tenth of your mint, rue and all other kinds of garden herbs, but you neglect justice and the love of God. You should have practiced the latter without leaving the former undone.

[43]"Woe to you Pharisees, because you love the most important seats in the synagogues and greetings in the marketplaces.

[44]"Woe to you, because you are like unmarked graves, which men walk over without knowing it."

[45]One of the experts in the law answered him, "Teacher, when you say these things, you insult us also."

[46]Jesus replied, "And you experts in the law, woe to you, because you load people down with burdens they can hardly carry, and you yourselves will not lift one finger to help them.

[47]"Woe to you, because you build tombs for the prophets, and it was your forefathers who killed them. [48]So you testify that you approve of what your forefathers did; they killed the prophets, and you build their tombs. [49]Because of this, God in his wisdom said, 'I will send them prophets and apostles, some of whom they will kill and others they will persecute.' [50]Therefore this generation will be held responsible for the blood of all the prophets that has been shed since the beginning of the world, [51]from the blood of Abel to the blood of Zechariah, who was killed between the altar and the sanctuary. Yes, I tell you, this generation will be held responsible for it all.

[52]"Woe to you experts in the law, because you have taken away the key to knowledge. You yourselves have not entered, and you have hindered those who were entering."

[53]When Jesus left there, the Pharisees and the teachers of the law began to oppose him fiercely and to besiege him with questions, [54]waiting to catch him in something he might say.

[i] *31* Or *something;* also in verse 32 [j] *41* Or *what you have*

PRAYER: THE ATTRIBUTES OF GOD

IT pleased You, Lord, for the sake of Your righteousness to make Your law great and glorious. (Isaiah 42:21) . . . Only in You, Lord, are righteousness and strength. (Isaiah 45:24)

***PAUSE** to reflect on these affirmations about the person, powers and perfection of God.*

YEAR 2
DAY 212

OT Jeremiah 26:1–27:22

Jeremiah Threatened With Death

26 Early in the reign of Jehoiakim son of Josiah king of Judah, this word came from the LORD: 2 "This is what the LORD says: Stand in the courtyard of the LORD's house and speak to all the people of the towns of Judah who come to worship in the house of the LORD. Tell them everything I command you; do not omit a word. 3 Perhaps they will listen and each will turn from his evil way. Then I will relent and not bring on them the disaster I was planning because of the evil they have done. 4 Say to them, 'This is what the LORD says: If you do not listen to me and follow my law, which I have set before you, 5 and if you do not listen to the words of my servants the prophets, whom I have sent to you again and again (though you have not listened), 6 then I will make this house like Shiloh and this city an object of cursing among all the nations of the earth.' "

7 The priests, the prophets and all the people heard Jeremiah speak these words in the house of the LORD. 8 But as soon as Jeremiah finished telling all the people everything the LORD had commanded him to say, the priests, the prophets and all the people seized him and said, "You must die! 9 Why do you prophesy in the LORD's name that this house will be like Shiloh and this city will be desolate and deserted?" And all the people crowded around Jeremiah in the house of the LORD.

10 When the officials of Judah heard about these things, they went up from the royal palace to the house of the LORD and took their places at the entrance of the New Gate of the LORD's house. 11 Then the priests and the prophets said to the officials and all the people, "This man should be sentenced to death because he has prophesied against this city. You have heard it with your own ears!"

12 Then Jeremiah said to all the officials and all the people: "The LORD sent me to prophesy against this house and this city all the things you have heard. 13 Now reform your ways and your actions and obey the LORD your God. Then the LORD will relent and not bring the disaster he has pronounced against you. 14 As for me, I am in your hands; do with me whatever you think is good and right. 15 Be assured, however, that if you put me to death, you will bring the guilt of innocent blood on yourselves and on this city and on those who live in it, for in truth the LORD has sent me to you to speak all these words in your hearing."

16 Then the officials and all the people said to the priests and the prophets, "This man should not be sentenced to death! He has spoken to us in the name of the LORD our God."

17 Some of the elders of the land stepped forward and said to the entire assembly of people, 18 "Micah of Moresheth prophesied in the days of Hezekiah king of Judah. He told all the people of Judah, 'This is what the LORD Almighty says:

" 'Zion will be plowed like a field,
Jerusalem will become a heap of rubble,
the temple hill a mound overgrown with thickets.'[a]

19 "Did Hezekiah king of Judah or anyone else in Judah put him to death? Did not Hezekiah fear the LORD and seek his favor? And did not the LORD relent, so that he did not bring the disaster he pronounced against them? We are about to bring a terrible disaster on ourselves!"

[a] *18* Micah 3:12

20(Now Uriah son of Shemaiah from Kiriath Jearim was another man who prophesied in the name of the LORD; he prophesied the same things against this city and
this land as Jeremiah did. 21When King Jehoiakim and all his officers and officials
heard his words, the king sought to put him
to death. But Uriah heard of it and fled in
fear to Egypt. 22King Jehoiakim, however,
sent Elnathan son of Acbor to Egypt, along
with some other men. 23They brought Uriah out of Egypt and took him to King Jehoiakim, who had him struck down with a
sword and his body thrown into the burial
place of the common people.)
24Furthermore, Ahikam son of Shaphan
supported Jeremiah, and so he was not
handed over to the people to be put to
death.

Judah to Serve Nebuchadnezzar

27 Early in the reign of Zedekiah[b] son of
Josiah king of Judah, this word came
to Jeremiah from the LORD: 2This is what
the LORD said to me: "Make a yoke out of
straps and crossbars and put it on your
neck. 3Then send word to the kings of
Edom, Moab, Ammon, Tyre and Sidon
through the envoys who have come to Jerusalem to Zedekiah king of Judah. 4Give
them a message for their masters and say,
'This is what the LORD Almighty, the God of
Israel, says: "Tell this to your masters: 5With
my great power and outstretched arm I
made the earth and its people and the animals that are on it, and I give it to anyone
I please. 6Now I will hand all your countries
over to my servant Nebuchadnezzar king of
Babylon; I will make even the wild animals
subject to him. 7All nations will serve him
and his son and his grandson until the time
for his land comes; then many nations and
great kings will subjugate him.
8" ' "If, however, any nation or kingdom
will not serve Nebuchadnezzar king of
Babylon or bow its neck under his yoke, I
will punish that nation with the sword,
famine and plague, declares the LORD, until I destroy it by his hand. 9So do not listen to your prophets, your diviners, your
interpreters of dreams, your mediums or
your sorcerers who tell you, 'You will not
serve the king of Babylon.' 10They prophesy lies to you that will only serve to remove
you far from your lands; I will banish you
and you will perish. 11But if any nation will
bow its neck under the yoke of the king of
Babylon and serve him, I will let that nation remain in its own land to till it and
to live there, declares the LORD." ' "
12I gave the same message to Zedekiah
king of Judah. I said, "Bow your neck under the yoke of the king of Babylon; serve
him and his people, and you will live.
13Why will you and your people die by the
sword, famine and plague with which the
LORD has threatened any nation that will
not serve the king of Babylon? 14Do not
listen to the words of the prophets who
say to you, 'You will not serve the king of
Babylon,' for they are prophesying lies to
you. 15'I have not sent them,' declares the
LORD. 'They are prophesying lies in my
name. Therefore, I will banish you and
you will perish, both you and the prophets who prophesy to you.' "
16Then I said to the priests and all these
people, "This is what the LORD says: Do
not listen to the prophets who say, 'Very
soon now the articles from the LORD's
house will be brought back from Babylon.'
They are prophesying lies to you. 17Do not
listen to them. Serve the king of Babylon,
and you will live. Why should this city become a ruin? 18If they are prophets and
have the word of the LORD, let them plead
with the LORD Almighty that the furnishings remaining in the house of the LORD
and in the palace of the king of Judah and
in Jerusalem not be taken to Babylon.
19For this is what the LORD Almighty says
about the pillars, the Sea, the movable
stands and the other furnishings that are
left in this city, 20which Nebuchadnezzar
king of Babylon did not take away when
he carried Jehoiachin[c] son of Jehoiakim
king of Judah into exile from Jerusalem to
Babylon, along with all the nobles of Judah and Jerusalem— 21yes, this is what the
LORD Almighty, the God of Israel, says
about the things that are left in the house
of the LORD and in the palace of the king
of Judah and in Jerusalem: 22'They will be
taken to Babylon and there they will remain until the day I come for them,' declares the LORD. 'Then I will bring them
back and restore them to this place.' "

[b] *1* A few Hebrew manuscripts and Syriac (see also Jer. 27:3, 12 and 28:1); most Hebrew manuscripts *Jehoiakim* (Most Septuagint manuscripts do not have this verse.) [c] *20* Hebrew *Jeconiah,* a variant of *Jehoiachin*

PRAYER: RENEWAL

If I died with You, I believe that I will also live with You, knowing that You, Jesus Christ, having been raised from the dead, cannot die again; death no longer has dominion over You. For the death that You died, You died to sin once for all; but the life that You live, You live to God. In the same way, may I consider myself to be dead to sin, but alive to God in You. (Romans 6:8–11)

PAUSE *to add your own prayers for personal renewal.*

NT Luke 12:1–34

Warnings and Encouragements

12 Meanwhile, when a crowd of many thousands had gathered, so that they were trampling on one another, Jesus began to speak first to his disciples, saying: "Be on your guard against the yeast of the Pharisees, which is hypocrisy. 2 There is nothing concealed that will not be disclosed, or hidden that will not be made known. 3 What you have said in the dark will be heard in the daylight, and what you have whispered in the ear in the inner rooms will be proclaimed from the roofs.

4 "I tell you, my friends, do not be afraid of those who kill the body and after that can do no more. 5 But I will show you whom you should fear: Fear him who, after the killing of the body, has power to throw you into hell. Yes, I tell you, fear him. 6 Are not five sparrows sold for two pennies[a]? Yet not one of them is forgotten by God. 7 Indeed, the very hairs of your head are all numbered. Don't be afraid; you are worth more than many sparrows.

8 "I tell you, whoever acknowledges me before men, the Son of Man will also acknowledge him before the angels of God. 9 But he who disowns me before men will be disowned before the angels of God. 10 And everyone who speaks a word against the Son of Man will be forgiven, but anyone who blasphemes against the Holy Spirit will not be forgiven.

11 "When you are brought before synagogues, rulers and authorities, do not worry about how you will defend yourselves or what you will say, 12 for the Holy Spirit will teach you at that time what you should say."

The Parable of the Rich Fool

13 Someone in the crowd said to him, "Teacher, tell my brother to divide the inheritance with me."

14 Jesus replied, "Man, who appointed me a judge or an arbiter between you?" 15 Then he said to them, "Watch out! Be on your guard against all kinds of greed; a man's life does not consist in the abundance of his possessions."

16 And he told them this parable: "The ground of a certain rich man produced a good crop. 17 He thought to himself, 'What shall I do? I have no place to store my crops.'

18 "Then he said, 'This is what I'll do. I will tear down my barns and build bigger ones, and there I will store all my grain and my goods. 19 And I'll say to myself, "You have plenty of good things laid up for many years. Take life easy; eat, drink and be merry." '

20 "But God said to him, 'You fool! This very night your life will be demanded from you. Then who will get what you have prepared for yourself?'

21 "This is how it will be with anyone who stores up things for himself but is not rich toward God."

Do Not Worry

22 Then Jesus said to his disciples: "Therefore I tell you, do not worry about your life, what you will eat; or about your body, what you will wear. 23 Life is more than food, and the body more than clothes. 24 Consider the ravens: They do not sow or reap, they have no storeroom or barn; yet God feeds them. And how much more valuable you are than birds!

[a] 6 Greek *two assaria*

25Who of you by worrying can add a single hour to his life[b]? 26Since you cannot
do this very little thing, why do you worry about the rest?

27"Consider how the lilies grow. They
do not labor or spin. Yet I tell you, not
even Solomon in all his splendor was
dressed like one of these. 28If that is how
God clothes the grass of the field, which
is here today, and tomorrow is thrown
into the fire, how much more will he
clothe you, O you of little faith! 29And do
not set your heart on what you will eat or
drink; do not worry about it. 30For the pagan world runs after all such things, and
your Father knows that you need them.
31But seek his kingdom, and these things
will be given to you as well.

32"Do not be afraid, little flock, for your
Father has been pleased to give you the
kingdom. 33Sell your possessions and give
to the poor. Provide purses for yourselves
that will not wear out, a treasure in heav-
en that will not be exhausted, where no
thief comes near and no moth destroys.
34For where your treasure is, there your
heart will be also.

[b] 25 Or *single cubit to his height*

PRAYER: THE WORKS OF GOD

THOSE who show contempt, O God, for the riches of Your kindness, forbearance, and patience do not realize that Your kindness leads toward repentance. (Romans 2:4)

TAKE *a moment to consider the greatness of God's wonderful works.*

YEAR 2 DAY 213

OT **Jeremiah 28:1–29:32**

The False Prophet Hananiah

28 In the fifth month of that same year,
the fourth year, early in the reign of
Zedekiah king of Judah, the prophet Hananiah son of Azzur, who was from Gibeon, said to me in the house of the LORD
in the presence of the priests and all the
people: 2"This is what the LORD Almighty,
the God of Israel, says: 'I will break the
yoke of the king of Babylon. 3Within two
years I will bring back to this place all the
articles of the LORD's house that Nebuchadnezzar king of Babylon removed
from here and took to Babylon. 4I will
also bring back to this place Jehoiachin[a]
son of Jehoiakim king of Judah and all the
other exiles from Judah who went to Babylon,' declares the LORD, 'for I will break
the yoke of the king of Babylon.' "

5Then the prophet Jeremiah replied to
the prophet Hananiah before the priests
and all the people who were standing in
the house of the LORD. 6He said, "Amen!
May the LORD do so! May the LORD fulfill
the words you have prophesied by bringing the articles of the LORD's house and all
the exiles back to this place from Babylon.
7Nevertheless, listen to what I have to say
in your hearing and in the hearing of all
the people: 8From early times the prophets who preceded you and me have
prophesied war, disaster and plague
against many countries and great kingdoms. 9But the prophet who prophesies
peace will be recognized as one truly sent
by the LORD only if his prediction comes
true."

10Then the prophet Hananiah took the
yoke off the neck of the prophet Jeremiah
and broke it, 11and he said before all the
people, "This is what the LORD says: 'In the
same way will I break the yoke of Nebuchadnezzar king of Babylon off the neck
of all the nations within two years.' " At
this, the prophet Jeremiah went on his
way.

12Shortly after the prophet Hananiah
had broken the yoke off the neck of the
prophet Jeremiah, the word of the LORD
came to Jeremiah: 13"Go and tell Hananiah, 'This is what the LORD says: You have
broken a wooden yoke, but in its place
you will get a yoke of iron. 14This is what

[a] 4 Hebrew *Jeconiah,* a variant of *Jehoiachin*

the LORD Almighty, the God of Israel, says: I will put an iron yoke on the necks of all these nations to make them serve Nebuchadnezzar king of Babylon, and they will serve him. I will even give him control over the wild animals.' "

15 Then the prophet Jeremiah said to Hananiah the prophet, "Listen, Hananiah! The LORD has not sent you, yet you have persuaded this nation to trust in lies. 16 Therefore, this is what the LORD says: 'I am about to remove you from the face of the earth. This very year you are going to die, because you have preached rebellion against the LORD.' "

17 In the seventh month of that same year, Hananiah the prophet died.

A Letter to the Exiles

29 This is the text of the letter that the prophet Jeremiah sent from Jerusalem to the surviving elders among the exiles and to the priests, the prophets and all the other people Nebuchadnezzar had carried into exile from Jerusalem to Babylon. 2 (This was after King Jehoiachin[b] and the queen mother, the court officials and the leaders of Judah and Jerusalem, the craftsmen and the artisans had gone into exile from Jerusalem.) 3 He entrusted the letter to Elasah son of Shaphan and to Gemariah son of Hilkiah, whom Zedekiah king of Judah sent to King Nebuchadnezzar in Babylon. It said:

> 4 This is what the LORD Almighty, the God of Israel, says to all those I carried into exile from Jerusalem to Babylon: 5 "Build houses and settle down; plant gardens and eat what they produce. 6 Marry and have sons and daughters; find wives for your sons and give your daughters in marriage, so that they too may have sons and daughters. Increase in number there; do not decrease. 7 Also, seek the peace and prosperity of the city to which I have carried you into exile. Pray to the LORD for it, because if it prospers, you too will prosper." 8 Yes, this is what the LORD Almighty, the God of Israel, says: "Do not let the prophets and diviners among you deceive you. Do not listen to the dreams you encourage them to have. 9 They are prophesying lies to you in my name. I have not sent them," declares the LORD.
>
> 10 This is what the LORD says: "When seventy years are completed for Babylon, I will come to you and fulfill my gracious promise to bring you back to this place. 11 For I know the plans I have for you," declares the LORD, "plans to prosper you and not to harm you, plans to give you hope and a future. 12 Then you will call upon me and come and pray to me, and I will listen to you. 13 You will seek me and find me when you seek me with all your heart. 14 I will be found by you," declares the LORD, "and will bring you back from captivity.[c] I will gather you from all the nations and places where I have banished you," declares the LORD, "and will bring you back to the place from which I carried you into exile."
>
> 15 You may say, "The LORD has raised up prophets for us in Babylon," 16 but this is what the LORD says about the king who sits on David's throne and all the people who remain in this city, your countrymen who did not go with you into exile— 17 yes, this is what the LORD Almighty says: "I will send the sword, famine and plague against them and I will make them like poor figs that are so bad they cannot be eaten. 18 I will pursue them with the sword, famine and plague and will make them abhorrent to all the kingdoms of the earth and an object of cursing and horror, of scorn and reproach, among all the nations where I drive them. 19 For they have not listened to my words," declares the LORD, "words that I sent to them again and again by my servants the prophets. And you exiles have not listened either," declares the LORD.
>
> 20 Therefore, hear the word of the LORD, all you exiles whom I have sent away from Jerusalem to Babylon. 21 This is what the LORD Almighty, the God of Israel, says about Ahab son of Kolaiah and Zedekiah son of Maaseiah, who are prophesying lies to you in my name: "I will hand them over

[b] 2 Hebrew *Jeconiah,* a variant of *Jehoiachin*
[c] 14 Or *will restore your fortunes*

to Nebuchadnezzar king of Babylon, and he will put them to death before your very eyes. 22Because of them, all the exiles from Judah who are in Babylon will use this curse: 'The LORD treat you like Zedekiah and Ahab, whom the king of Babylon burned in the fire.' 23For they have done outrageous things in Israel; they have committed adultery with their neighbors' wives and in my name have spoken lies, which I did not tell them to do. I know it and am a witness to it," declares the LORD.

Message to Shemaiah

24Tell Shemaiah the Nehelamite, 25"This is what the LORD Almighty, the God of Israel, says: You sent letters in your own name to all the people in Jerusalem, to Zephaniah son of Maaseiah the priest, and to all the other priests. You said to Zephaniah, 26'The LORD has appointed you priest in place of Jehoiada to be in charge of the house of the LORD; you should put any madman who acts like a prophet into the stocks and neck-irons. 27So why have you not reprimanded Jeremiah from Anathoth, who poses as a prophet among you? 28He has sent this message to us in Babylon: It will be a long time. Therefore build houses and settle down; plant gardens and eat what they produce.' "

29Zephaniah the priest, however, read the letter to Jeremiah the prophet. 30Then the word of the LORD came to Jeremiah: 31"Send this message to all the exiles: 'This is what the LORD says about Shemaiah the Nehelamite: Because Shemaiah has prophesied to you, even though I did not send him, and has led you to believe a lie, 32this is what the LORD says: I will surely punish Shemaiah the Nehelamite and his descendants. He will have no one left among this people, nor will he see the good things I will do for my people, declares the LORD, because he has preached rebellion against me.' "

PRAYER: PETITION

MAY I not hate my brothers and sisters in my heart, but reprove my neighbors frankly and not incur sin because of them. May I not take vengeance or bear a grudge against others, but may I love my neighbor as myself. (Leviticus 19:17–18)

***PAUSE** here to offer prayers of petition regarding your family and your ministry. Ask for help and guidance in sharing Jesus with others and helping others grow in Him. Ask for guidance in your vocation and your avocations. Offer prayers of petition regarding your activities for this day and any special concerns you may have.*

NT Luke 12:35–59

Watchfulness

35"Be dressed ready for service and keep your lamps burning, 36like men waiting for their master to return from a wedding banquet, so that when he comes and knocks they can immediately open the door for him. 37It will be good for those servants whose master finds them watching when he comes. I tell you the truth, he will dress himself to serve, will have them recline at the table and will come and wait on them. 38It will be good for those servants whose master finds them ready, even if he comes in the second or third watch of the night. 39But understand this: If the owner of the house had known at what hour the thief was coming, he would not have let his house be broken into. 40You also must be ready, because the Son of Man will come at an hour when you do not expect him."

41Peter asked, "Lord, are you telling this parable to us, or to everyone?"

42The Lord answered, "Who then is the faithful and wise manager, whom the master puts in charge of his servants to give them their food allowance at the proper time? 43It will be good for that ser-

vant whom the master finds doing so
when he returns. 44 I tell you the truth, he
will put him in charge of all his possessions. 45 But suppose the servant says to
himself, 'My master is taking a long time
in coming,' and he then begins to beat the
menservants and maidservants and to eat
and drink and get drunk. 46 The master of
that servant will come on a day when he
does not expect him and at an hour he is
not aware of. He will cut him to pieces
and assign him a place with the unbelievers.
47 "That servant who knows his master's
will and does not get ready or does not do
what his master wants will be beaten with
many blows. 48 But the one who does not
know and does things deserving punishment will be beaten with few blows. From
everyone who has been given much,
much will be demanded; and from the
one who has been entrusted with much,
much more will be asked.

Not Peace but Division

49 "I have come to bring fire on the
earth, and how I wish it were already kindled! 50 But I have a baptism to undergo,
and how distressed I am until it is completed! 51 Do you think I came to bring
peace on earth? No, I tell you, but division. 52 From now on there will be five in
one family divided against each other,
three against two and two against three.
53 They will be divided, father against son
and son against father, mother against
daughter and daughter against mother,
mother-in-law against daughter-in-law
and daughter-in-law against mother-in-
law."

Interpreting the Times

54 He said to the crowd: "When you see
a cloud rising in the west, immediately
you say, 'It's going to rain,' and it does.
55 And when the south wind blows, you
say, 'It's going to be hot,' and it is. 56 Hypocrites! You know how to interpret the
appearance of the earth and the sky. How
is it that you don't know how to interpret
this present time?
57 "Why don't you judge for yourselves
what is right? 58 As you are going with your
adversary to the magistrate, try hard to be
reconciled to him on the way, or he may
drag you off to the judge, and the judge
turn you over to the officer, and the officer throw you into prison. 59 I tell you, you
will not get out until you have paid the
last penny.[a]"

[a] 59 Greek *lepton*

PRAYER: MY RELATIONSHIP TO GOD

THOSE who live according to the flesh set their minds on the things of the flesh; but those who live according to You, Holy Spirit, set their minds on the things that You, O Spirit, desire. The mind of the flesh is death, but Your mind, O Spirit, is life and peace. If I live according to the flesh, I will die; but if by You, Holy Spirit, I put to death the deeds of the body, I will live. For those who are led by You, the Spirit of God, are children of God.

(Romans 8:5–6, 13–14)

PAUSE *to thank God for the relationship that you enjoy with Him in Jesus Christ.*

YEAR 2 DAY 214

OT Jeremiah 30:1-24

Restoration of Israel

30 This is the word that came to Jeremiah from the LORD: 2 "This is what the
LORD, the God of Israel, says: 'Write in a
book all the words I have spoken to you.
3 The days are coming,' declares the LORD,
'when I will bring my people Israel and
Judah back from captivity[a] and restore

[a] 3 Or *will restore the fortunes of my people Israel and Judah*

them to the land I gave their forefathers
to possess,' says the LORD."
4These are the words the LORD spoke
concerning Israel and Judah: 5"This is
what the LORD says:

" 'Cries of fear are heard—
terror, not peace.
6Ask and see:
Can a man bear children?
Then why do I see every strong man
with his hands on his stomach like
a woman in labor,
every face turned deathly pale?
7How awful that day will be!
None will be like it.
It will be a time of trouble for Jacob,
but he will be saved out of it.

8" 'In that day,' declares the LORD
Almighty,
'I will break the yoke off their necks
and will tear off their bonds;
no longer will foreigners enslave
them.
9Instead, they will serve the LORD their
God
and David their king,
whom I will raise up for them.

10" 'So do not fear, O Jacob my servant;
do not be dismayed, O Israel,'
declares the LORD.
'I will surely save you out of a distant
place,
your descendants from the land of
their exile.
Jacob will again have peace and
security,
and no one will make him afraid.
11I am with you and will save you,'
declares the LORD.
'Though I completely destroy all the
nations
among which I scatter you,
I will not completely destroy you.
I will discipline you but only with
justice;
I will not let you go entirely
unpunished.'

12"This is what the LORD says:

" 'Your wound is incurable,
your injury beyond healing.
13There is no one to plead your cause,
no remedy for your sore,
no healing for you.
14All your allies have forgotten you;
they care nothing for you.
I have struck you as an enemy would
and punished you as would the
cruel,
because your guilt is so great
and your sins so many.
15Why do you cry out over your wound,
your pain that has no cure?
Because of your great guilt and many
sins
I have done these things to you.

16" 'But all who devour you will be
devoured;
all your enemies will go into exile.
Those who plunder you will be
plundered;
all who make spoil of you I will
despoil.
17But I will restore you to health
and heal your wounds,'
declares the LORD,
'because you are called an outcast,
Zion for whom no one cares.'

18"This is what the LORD says:

" 'I will restore the fortunes of Jacob's
tents
and have compassion on his
dwellings;
the city will be rebuilt on her ruins,
and the palace will stand in its
proper place.
19From them will come songs of
thanksgiving
and the sound of rejoicing.
I will add to their numbers,
and they will not be decreased;
I will bring them honor,
and they will not be disdained.
20Their children will be as in days of old,
and their community will be
established before me;
I will punish all who oppress them.
21Their leader will be one of their own;
their ruler will arise from among
them.
I will bring him near and he will
come close to me,
for who is he who will devote
himself
to be close to me?'
declares the LORD.
22" 'So you will be my people,
and I will be your God.' "

23See, the storm of the LORD
will burst out in wrath,

a driving wind swirling down
on the heads of the wicked.
[24]The fierce anger of the LORD will not
turn back
until he fully accomplishes
the purposes of his heart.
In days to come
you will understand this.

PRAYER: INTERCESSION

I PRAY that Your Word, O Lord, may spread rapidly and be glorified, and that Your people may be delivered from perverse and evil men, for not all have faith. (2 Thessalonians 3:1–2)

***TAKE** a few moments to intercede on behalf of local, national and world missions. Pray that the Great Commission would be fulfilled and for any special concerns you may have for missions.*

NT Luke 13:1-35

Repent or Perish

13 Now there were some present at that
time who told Jesus about the Galileans whose blood Pilate had mixed with
their sacrifices. [2]Jesus answered, "Do you
think that these Galileans were worse sinners than all the other Galileans because
they suffered this way? [3]I tell you, no! But
unless you repent, you too will all perish.
[4]Or those eighteen who died when the
tower in Siloam fell on them—do you
think they were more guilty than all the
others living in Jerusalem? [5]I tell you, no!
But unless you repent, you too will all perish."
[6]Then he told this parable: "A man had
a fig tree, planted in his vineyard, and he
went to look for fruit on it, but did not
find any. [7]So he said to the man who took
care of the vineyard, 'For three years now
I've been coming to look for fruit on this
fig tree and haven't found any. Cut it
down! Why should it use up the soil?'
[8]" 'Sir,' the man replied, 'leave it alone
for one more year, and I'll dig around it
and fertilize it. [9]If it bears fruit next year,
fine! If not, then cut it down.' "

A Crippled Woman Healed on the Sabbath

[10]On a Sabbath Jesus was teaching in
one of the synagogues, [11]and a woman
was there who had been crippled by a
spirit for eighteen years. She was bent over
and could not straighten up at all. [12]When
Jesus saw her, he called her forward and
said to her, "Woman, you are set free from
your infirmity." [13]Then he put his hands
on her, and immediately she straightened
up and praised God.
[14]Indignant because Jesus had healed
on the Sabbath, the synagogue ruler said
to the people, "There are six days for work.
So come and be healed on those days, not
on the Sabbath."
[15]The Lord answered him, "You hypocrites! Doesn't each of you on the Sabbath
untie his ox or donkey from the stall and
lead it out to give it water? [16]Then should
not this woman, a daughter of Abraham,
whom Satan has kept bound for eighteen
long years, be set free on the Sabbath day
from what bound her?"
[17]When he said this, all his opponents
were humiliated, but the people were delighted with all the wonderful things he
was doing.

The Parables of the Mustard Seed and the Yeast

[18]Then Jesus asked, "What is the kingdom of God like? What shall I compare it
to? [19]It is like a mustard seed, which a
man took and planted in his garden. It
grew and became a tree, and the birds of
the air perched in its branches."
[20]Again he asked, "What shall I compare the kingdom of God to? [21]It is like
yeast that a woman took and mixed into
a large amount[a] of flour until it worked
all through the dough."

The Narrow Door

[22]Then Jesus went through the towns

[a] 21 Greek *three satas* (probably about 1/2 bushel or 22 liters)

and villages, teaching as he made his way
to Jerusalem. 23 Someone asked him,
"Lord, are only a few people going to be
saved?"
He said to them, 24 "Make every effort to
enter through the narrow door, because
many, I tell you, will try to enter and will
not be able to. 25 Once the owner of the
house gets up and closes the door, you
will stand outside knocking and pleading,
'Sir, open the door for us.'
"But he will answer, 'I don't know you
or where you come from.'
26 "Then you will say, 'We ate and drank
with you, and you taught in our streets.'
27 "But he will reply, 'I don't know you
or where you come from. Away from me,
all you evildoers!'
28 "There will be weeping there, and
gnashing of teeth, when you see Abraham, Isaac and Jacob and all the prophets in the kingdom of God, but you yourselves thrown out. 29 People will come
from east and west and north and south,
and will take their places at the feast in
the kingdom of God. 30 Indeed there are
those who are last who will be first, and
first who will be last."

Jesus' Sorrow for Jerusalem

31 At that time some Pharisees came to
Jesus and said to him, "Leave this place
and go somewhere else. Herod wants to
kill you."
32 He replied, "Go tell that fox, 'I will
drive out demons and heal people today
and tomorrow, and on the third day I will
reach my goal.' 33 In any case, I must keep
going today and tomorrow and the next
day—for surely no prophet can die outside Jerusalem!
34 "O Jerusalem, Jerusalem, you who kill
the prophets and stone those sent to you,
how often I have longed to gather your
children together, as a hen gathers her
chicks under her wings, but you were not
willing! 35 Look, your house is left to you
desolate. I tell you, you will not see me
again until you say, 'Blessed is he who
comes in the name of the Lord.'[b]"

[b] 35 Psalm 118:26

PRAYER: THE CHARACTER I WANT TO CULTIVATE

I WANT to be a person of faith, who does not doubt Your promises, O God, and not one who is double-minded and unstable in my ways. (James 1:6, 8)

***TAKE** a moment to ask the Lord for the grace to grow in godly character.*

YEAR 2
DAY 215

OT Jeremiah 31:1-40

31 "At that time," declares the LORD, "I
will be the God of all the clans of Israel, and they will be my people."
2 This is what the LORD says:

"The people who survive the sword
will find favor in the desert;
I will come to give rest to Israel."

3 The LORD appeared to us in the past,[a]
saying:

"I have loved you with an everlasting
love;
I have drawn you with loving-
kindness.
4 I will build you up again
and you will be rebuilt, O Virgin
Israel.
Again you will take up your
tambourines
and go out to dance with the joyful.
5 Again you will plant vineyards
on the hills of Samaria;
the farmers will plant them
and enjoy their fruit.
6 There will be a day when watchmen
cry out
on the hills of Ephraim,
'Come, let us go up to Zion,
to the LORD our God.' "

7 This is what the LORD says:

[a] 3 Or *LORD has appeared to us from afar*

"Sing with joy for Jacob;
shout for the foremost of the nations.
Make your praises heard, and say,
'O LORD, save your people,
the remnant of Israel.'
8 See, I will bring them from the land of the north
and gather them from the ends of the earth.
Among them will be the blind and the lame,
expectant mothers and women in labor;
a great throng will return.
9 They will come with weeping;
they will pray as I bring them back.
I will lead them beside streams of water
on a level path where they will not stumble,
because I am Israel's father,
and Ephraim is my firstborn son.

10 "Hear the word of the LORD, O nations;
proclaim it in distant coastlands:
'He who scattered Israel will gather them
and will watch over his flock like a shepherd.'
11 For the LORD will ransom Jacob
and redeem them from the hand of those stronger than they.
12 They will come and shout for joy on the heights of Zion;
they will rejoice in the bounty of the LORD—
the grain, the new wine and the oil,
the young of the flocks and herds.
They will be like a well-watered garden,
and they will sorrow no more.
13 Then maidens will dance and be glad,
young men and old as well.
I will turn their mourning into gladness;
I will give them comfort and joy instead of sorrow.
14 I will satisfy the priests with abundance,
and my people will be filled with my bounty,"
declares the LORD.

15 This is what the LORD says:

"A voice is heard in Ramah,
mourning and great weeping,
Rachel weeping for her children
and refusing to be comforted,
because her children are no more."

16 This is what the LORD says:

"Restrain your voice from weeping
and your eyes from tears,
for your work will be rewarded,"
declares the LORD.
"They will return from the land of the enemy.
17 So there is hope for your future,"
declares the LORD.
"Your children will return to their own land.

18 "I have surely heard Ephraim's moaning:
'You disciplined me like an unruly calf,
and I have been disciplined.
Restore me, and I will return,
because you are the LORD my God.
19 After I strayed,
I repented;
after I came to understand,
I beat my breast.
I was ashamed and humiliated
because I bore the disgrace of my youth.'
20 Is not Ephraim my dear son,
the child in whom I delight?
Though I often speak against him,
I still remember him.
Therefore my heart yearns for him;
I have great compassion for him,"
declares the LORD.

21 "Set up road signs;
put up guideposts.
Take note of the highway,
the road that you take.
Return, O Virgin Israel,
return to your towns.
22 How long will you wander,
O unfaithful daughter?
The LORD will create a new thing on earth—
a woman will surround[b] a man."

23 This is what the LORD Almighty, the
God of Israel, says: "When I bring them
back from captivity,[c] the people in the land
of Judah and in its towns will once again
use these words: 'The LORD bless you,
O righteous dwelling, O sacred mountain.'
24 People will live together in Judah and all
its towns—farmers and those who move

[b] 22 Or *will go about ⌞seeking⌟*; or *will protect*
[c] 23 Or *I restore their fortunes*

about with their flocks. [25]I will refresh the
weary and satisfy the faint."
[26]At this I awoke and looked around.
My sleep had been pleasant to me.
[27]"The days are coming," declares the
LORD, "when I will plant the house of Israel and the house of Judah with the offspring of men and of animals. [28]Just as I
watched over them to uproot and tear
down, and to overthrow, destroy and
bring disaster, so I will watch over them
to build and to plant," declares the LORD.
[29]"In those days people will no longer say,

'The fathers have eaten sour grapes,
and the children's teeth are set on edge.'

[30]Instead, everyone will die for his own
sin; whoever eats sour grapes—his own
teeth will be set on edge.

[31]"The time is coming," declares the LORD,
"when I will make a new covenant
with the house of Israel
and with the house of Judah.
[32]It will not be like the covenant
I made with their forefathers
when I took them by the hand
to lead them out of Egypt,
because they broke my covenant,
though I was a husband to[d] them,[e]"
declares the LORD.
[33]"This is the covenant I will make with the house of Israel
after that time," declares the LORD.
"I will put my law in their minds
and write it on their hearts.
I will be their God,
and they will be my people.
[34]No longer will a man teach his neighbor,
or a man his brother, saying, 'Know the LORD,'
because they will all know me,
from the least of them to the greatest,"
declares the LORD.
"For I will forgive their wickedness
and will remember their sins no more."

[35]This is what the LORD says,

he who appoints the sun
to shine by day,
who decrees the moon and stars
to shine by night,
who stirs up the sea
so that its waves roar—
the LORD Almighty is his name:
[36]"Only if these decrees vanish from my sight,"
declares the LORD,
"will the descendants of Israel ever cease
to be a nation before me."

[37]This is what the LORD says:

"Only if the heavens above can be measured
and the foundations of the earth below be searched out
will I reject all the descendants of Israel
because of all they have done,"
declares the LORD.

[38]"The days are coming," declares the
LORD, "when this city will be rebuilt for me
from the Tower of Hananel to the Corner
Gate. [39]The measuring line will stretch from
there straight to the hill of Gareb and then
turn to Goah. [40]The whole valley where
dead bodies and ashes are thrown, and all
the terraces out to the Kidron Valley on the
east as far as the corner of the Horse Gate,
will be holy to the LORD. The city will never again be uprooted or demolished."

[d] 32 Hebrew; Septuagint and Syriac / *and I turned away from* [e] 32 Or *was their master*

PRAYER: AFFIRMATION

If the many died by the trespass of one man, Adam, how much more did Your grace, O God, and the gift that came by the grace of the one Man, Jesus Christ, overflow to the many. And Your gift is not like the result of the one man's sin, for the judgment followed one sin and brought condemnation, but the gift followed many trespasses and brought justification.

(Romans 5:15–16)

***PAUSE** to reflect on these Biblical affirmations.*

NT Luke 14:1-35

Jesus at a Pharisee's House

14 One Sabbath, when Jesus went to eat in the house of a prominent Pharisee, he was being carefully watched. 2There in front of him was a man suffering from dropsy. 3Jesus asked the Pharisees and experts in the law, "Is it lawful to heal on the Sabbath or not?" 4But they remained silent. So taking hold of the man, he healed him and sent him away.

5Then he asked them, "If one of you has a son[a] or an ox that falls into a well on the Sabbath day, will you not immediately pull him out?" 6And they had nothing to say.

7When he noticed how the guests picked the places of honor at the table, he told them this parable: 8"When someone invites you to a wedding feast, do not take the place of honor, for a person more distinguished than you may have been invited. 9If so, the host who invited both of you will come and say to you, 'Give this man your seat.' Then, humiliated, you will have to take the least important place. 10But when you are invited, take the lowest place, so that when your host comes, he will say to you, 'Friend, move up to a better place.' Then you will be honored in the presence of all your fellow guests. 11For everyone who exalts himself will be humbled, and he who humbles himself will be exalted."

12Then Jesus said to his host, "When you give a luncheon or dinner, do not invite your friends, your brothers or relatives, or your rich neighbors; if you do, they may invite you back and so you will be repaid. 13But when you give a banquet, invite the poor, the crippled, the lame, the blind, 14and you will be blessed. Although they cannot repay you, you will be repaid at the resurrection of the righteous."

The Parable of the Great Banquet

15When one of those at the table with him heard this, he said to Jesus, "Blessed is the man who will eat at the feast in the kingdom of God."

16Jesus replied: "A certain man was preparing a great banquet and invited many guests. 17At the time of the banquet he sent his servant to tell those who had been invited, 'Come, for everything is now ready.'

18"But they all alike began to make excuses. The first said, 'I have just bought a field, and I must go and see it. Please excuse me.'

19"Another said, 'I have just bought five yoke of oxen, and I'm on my way to try them out. Please excuse me.'

20"Still another said, 'I just got married, so I can't come.'

21"The servant came back and reported this to his master. Then the owner of the house became angry and ordered his servant, 'Go out quickly into the streets and alleys of the town and bring in the poor, the crippled, the blind and the lame.'

22" 'Sir,' the servant said, 'what you ordered has been done, but there is still room.'

23"Then the master told his servant, 'Go out to the roads and country lanes and make them come in, so that my house will be full. 24I tell you, not one of those men who were invited will get a taste of my banquet.' "

The Cost of Being a Disciple

25Large crowds were traveling with Jesus, and turning to them he said: 26"If anyone comes to me and does not hate his father and mother, his wife and children, his brothers and sisters—yes, even his own life—he cannot be my disciple. 27And anyone who does not carry his cross and follow me cannot be my disciple.

28"Suppose one of you wants to build a tower. Will he not first sit down and estimate the cost to see if he has enough money to complete it? 29For if he lays the foundation and is not able to finish it, everyone who sees it will ridicule him, 30saying, 'This fellow began to build and was not able to finish.'

31"Or suppose a king is about to go to war against another king. Will he not first sit down and consider whether he is able with ten thousand men to oppose the one coming against him with twenty thousand? 32If he is not able, he will send a delegation while the other is still a long way off and will ask for terms of peace. 33In the

[a] 5 Some manuscripts *donkey*

same way, any of you who does not give up everything he has cannot be my disciple.

34"Salt is good, but if it loses its saltiness, how can it be made salty again? 35It is fit neither for the soil nor for the manure pile; it is thrown out.

"He who has ears to hear, let him hear."

PRAYER: MY RELATIONSHIP TO OTHERS

O LORD, You have given us a new commandment: to love one another even as You have loved us. By this all people will know that we are Your disciples, if we have love for one another. (John 13:34–35) . . . This is Your commandment, that we love one another as You have loved us. (John 15:12)

PAUSE *to review your relationships with others and to commit them to the Lord.*

YEAR 2 DAY 216

OT Jeremiah 32:1-44

Jeremiah Buys a Field

32 This is the word that came to Jeremiah from the LORD in the tenth year of Zedekiah king of Judah, which was the eighteenth year of Nebuchadnezzar. 2The army of the king of Babylon was then besieging Jerusalem, and Jeremiah the prophet was confined in the courtyard of the guard in the royal palace of Judah.

3Now Zedekiah king of Judah had imprisoned him there, saying, "Why do you prophesy as you do? You say, 'This is what the LORD says: I am about to hand this city over to the king of Babylon, and he will capture it. 4Zedekiah king of Judah will not escape out of the hands of the Babylonians[a] but will certainly be handed over to the king of Babylon, and will speak with him face to face and see him with his own eyes. 5He will take Zedekiah to Babylon, where he will remain until I deal with him, declares the LORD. If you fight against the Babylonians, you will not succeed.' "

6Jeremiah said, "The word of the LORD came to me: 7Hanamel son of Shallum your uncle is going to come to you and say, 'Buy my field at Anathoth, because as nearest relative it is your right and duty to buy it.'

8"Then, just as the LORD had said, my cousin Hanamel came to me in the courtyard of the guard and said, 'Buy my field at Anathoth in the territory of Benjamin. Since it is your right to redeem it and possess it, buy it for yourself.'

"I knew that this was the word of the LORD; 9so I bought the field at Anathoth from my cousin Hanamel and weighed out for him seventeen shekels[b] of silver. 10I signed and sealed the deed, had it witnessed, and weighed out the silver on the scales. 11I took the deed of purchase—the sealed copy containing the terms and conditions, as well as the unsealed copy—12and I gave this deed to Baruch son of Neriah, the son of Mahseiah, in the presence of my cousin Hanamel and of the witnesses who had signed the deed and of all the Jews sitting in the courtyard of the guard.

13"In their presence I gave Baruch these instructions: 14'This is what the LORD Almighty, the God of Israel, says: Take these documents, both the sealed and unsealed copies of the deed of purchase, and put them in a clay jar so they will last a long time. 15For this is what the LORD Almighty, the God of Israel, says: Houses, fields and vineyards will again be bought in this land.'

16"After I had given the deed of purchase to Baruch son of Neriah, I prayed to the LORD:

> 17"Ah, Sovereign LORD, you have made the heavens and the earth by your great power and outstretched arm. Nothing is too hard for you.

[a] 4 Or *Chaldeans;* also in verses 5, 24, 25, 28, 29 and 43 [b] 9 That is, about 7 ounces (about 200 grams)

[18]You show love to thousands but
bring the punishment for the fathers'
sins into the laps of their children after them. O great and powerful God,
whose name is the LORD Almighty,
[19]great are your purposes and mighty
are your deeds. Your eyes are open to
all the ways of men; you reward
everyone according to his conduct
and as his deeds deserve. [20]You performed miraculous signs and wonders in Egypt and have continued
them to this day, both in Israel and
among all mankind, and have gained
the renown that is still yours. [21]You
brought your people Israel out of
Egypt with signs and wonders, by a
mighty hand and an outstretched
arm and with great terror. [22]You gave
them this land you had sworn to give
their forefathers, a land flowing with
milk and honey. [23]They came in and
took possession of it, but they did
not obey you or follow your law; they
did not do what you commanded
them to do. So you brought all this
disaster upon them.

[24]"See how the siege ramps are
built up to take the city. Because of
the sword, famine and plague, the
city will be handed over to the Babylonians who are attacking it. What
you said has happened, as you now
see. [25]And though the city will be
handed over to the Babylonians, you,
O Sovereign LORD, say to me, 'Buy the
field with silver and have the trans-
action witnessed.' "

[26]Then the word of the LORD came to Jeremiah: [27]"I am the LORD, the God of all
mankind. Is anything too hard for me?
[28]Therefore, this is what the LORD says: I am
about to hand this city over to the Babylonians and to Nebuchadnezzar king of Babylon, who will capture it. [29]The Babylonians who are attacking this city will come in
and set it on fire; they will burn it down,
along with the houses where the people
provoked me to anger by burning incense
on the roofs to Baal and by pouring out
drink offerings to other gods.

[30]"The people of Israel and Judah have
done nothing but evil in my sight from
their youth; indeed, the people of Israel
have done nothing but provoke me with
what their hands have made, declares the
LORD. [31]From the day it was built until
now, this city has so aroused my anger
and wrath that I must remove it from my
sight. [32]The people of Israel and Judah
have provoked me by all the evil they have
done—they, their kings and officials, their
priests and prophets, the men of Judah
and the people of Jerusalem. [33]They
turned their backs to me and not their
faces; though I taught them again and
again, they would not listen or respond to
discipline. [34]They set up their abominable
idols in the house that bears my Name
and defiled it. [35]They built high places for
Baal in the Valley of Ben Hinnom to sacrifice their sons and daughters[c] to Molech,
though I never commanded, nor did it enter my mind, that they should do such a
detestable thing and so make Judah sin.

[36]"You are saying about this city, 'By the
sword, famine and plague it will be handed over to the king of Babylon'; but this is
what the LORD, the God of Israel, says: [37]I
will surely gather them from all the lands
where I banish them in my furious anger
and great wrath; I will bring them back to
this place and let them live in safety. [38]They
will be my people, and I will be their God.
[39]I will give them singleness of heart and action, so that they will always fear me for
their own good and the good of their children after them. [40]I will make an everlasting covenant with them. I will never stop
doing good to them, and I will inspire
them to fear me, so that they will never turn
away from me. [41]I will rejoice in doing them
good and will assuredly plant them in this
land with all my heart and soul.

[42]"This is what the LORD says: As I have
brought all this great calamity on this
people, so I will give them all the prosperity I have promised them. [43]Once more
fields will be bought in this land of which
you say, 'It is a desolate waste, without
men or animals, for it has been handed
over to the Babylonians.' [44]Fields will be
bought for silver, and deeds will be
signed, sealed and witnessed in the territory of Benjamin, in the villages around
Jerusalem, in the towns of Judah and in
the towns of the hill country, of the western foothills and of the Negev, because I
will restore their fortunes,[d] declares the
LORD."

[c] 35 Or *to make their sons and daughters pass through* ⌞*the fire*⌟ [d] 44 Or *will bring them back from captivity*

PRAYER: THANKSGIVING

MY citizenship is in heaven; from there I also eagerly await You, my Savior, Lord Jesus Christ. You will transform my lowly body and conform it to Your glorious body by the power that enables You to subject all things to Yourself. (Philippians 3:20–21)

***PAUSE** to offer your own expressions of thanksgiving.*

NT Luke 15:1–32

The Parable of the Lost Sheep

15 Now the tax collectors and "sinners" were all gathering around to hear him. [2]But the Pharisees and the teachers of the law muttered, "This man welcomes sinners and eats with them."

[3]Then Jesus told them this parable: [4]"Suppose one of you has a hundred sheep and loses one of them. Does he not leave the ninety-nine in the open country and go after the lost sheep until he finds it? [5]And when he finds it, he joyfully puts it on his shoulders [6]and goes home. Then he calls his friends and neighbors together and says, 'Rejoice with me; I have found my lost sheep.' [7]I tell you that in the same way there will be more rejoicing in heaven over one sinner who repents than over ninety-nine righteous persons who do not need to repent.

The Parable of the Lost Coin

[8]"Or suppose a woman has ten silver coins[a] and loses one. Does she not light a lamp, sweep the house and search carefully until she finds it? [9]And when she finds it, she calls her friends and neighbors together and says, 'Rejoice with me; I have found my lost coin.' [10]In the same way, I tell you, there is rejoicing in the presence of the angels of God over one sinner who repents."

The Parable of the Lost Son

[11]Jesus continued: "There was a man who had two sons. [12]The younger one said to his father, 'Father, give me my share of the estate.' So he divided his property between them.

[13]"Not long after that, the younger son got together all he had, set off for a distant country and there squandered his wealth in wild living. [14]After he had spent everything, there was a severe famine in that whole country, and he began to be in need. [15]So he went and hired himself out to a citizen of that country, who sent him to his fields to feed pigs. [16]He longed to fill his stomach with the pods that the pigs were eating, but no one gave him anything.

[17]"When he came to his senses, he said, 'How many of my father's hired men have food to spare, and here I am starving to death! [18]I will set out and go back to my father and say to him: Father, I have sinned against heaven and against you. [19]I am no longer worthy to be called your son; make me like one of your hired men.' [20]So he got up and went to his father.

"But while he was still a long way off, his father saw him and was filled with compassion for him; he ran to his son, threw his arms around him and kissed him.

[21]"The son said to him, 'Father, I have sinned against heaven and against you. I am no longer worthy to be called your son.[b]'

[22]"But the father said to his servants, 'Quick! Bring the best robe and put it on him. Put a ring on his finger and sandals on his feet. [23]Bring the fattened calf and kill it. Let's have a feast and celebrate. [24]For this son of mine was dead and is alive again; he was lost and is found.' So they began to celebrate.

[25]"Meanwhile, the older son was in the field. When he came near the house, he heard music and dancing. [26]So he called one of the servants and asked him what was going on. [27]'Your brother has come,' he replied, 'and your father has killed the fattened calf because he has him back safe and sound.'

[28]"The older brother became angry and

[a] 8 Greek *ten drachmas,* each worth about a day's wages [b] 21 Some early manuscripts *son. Make me like one of your hired men.*

refused to go in. So his father went out
and pleaded with him. [29]But he answered
his father, 'Look! All these years I've been
slaving for you and never disobeyed your
orders. Yet you never gave me even a
young goat so I could celebrate with my
friends. [30]But when this son of yours who
has squandered your property with prostitutes comes home, you kill the fattened
calf for him!'

[31]" 'My son,' the father said, 'you are always with me, and everything I have is
yours. [32]But we had to celebrate and be
glad, because this brother of yours was
dead and is alive again; he was lost and is
found.' "

PRAYER: THE ATTRIBUTES OF GOD

WHERE can I go from Your Spirit? Or where can I flee from Your presence? If I ascend to heaven, You are there. If I make my bed in Sheol, You are there. If I take the wings of the dawn, if I dwell in the depths of the sea, even there Your hand will lead me. Your right hand will lay hold of me. If I say, "Surely the darkness will cover me," even the night will be light around me. The darkness is not dark to You, and the night shines as the day; darkness and light are alike to You. (Psalm 139:7–12)

__PAUSE__ to reflect on these affirmations about the person, powers and perfection of God.

YEAR 2
DAY 217

OT **Psalms 116–117**

Psalm 116

[1]I love the LORD, for he heard my voice;
he heard my cry for mercy.
[2]Because he turned his ear to me,
I will call on him as long as I live.

[3]The cords of death entangled me,
the anguish of the grave[a] came upon me;
I was overcome by trouble and sorrow.
[4]Then I called on the name of the LORD:
"O LORD, save me!"

[5]The LORD is gracious and righteous;
our God is full of compassion.
[6]The LORD protects the simplehearted;
when I was in great need, he saved me.

[7]Be at rest once more, O my soul,
for the LORD has been good to you.

[8]For you, O LORD, have delivered my soul from death,
my eyes from tears,
my feet from stumbling,
[9]that I may walk before the LORD
in the land of the living.
[10]I believed; therefore[b] I said,
"I am greatly afflicted."
[11]And in my dismay I said,
"All men are liars."

[12]How can I repay the LORD
for all his goodness to me?
[13]I will lift up the cup of salvation
and call on the name of the LORD.
[14]I will fulfill my vows to the LORD
in the presence of all his people.

[15]Precious in the sight of the LORD
is the death of his saints.
[16]O LORD, truly I am your servant;
I am your servant, the son of your maidservant[c];
you have freed me from my chains.

[17]I will sacrifice a thank offering to you
and call on the name of the LORD.
[18]I will fulfill my vows to the LORD
in the presence of all his people,
[19]in the courts of the house of the LORD—
in your midst, O Jerusalem.

Praise the LORD.[d]

[a] 3 Hebrew *Sheol* [b] 10 Or *believed even when* [c] 16 Or *servant, your faithful son* [d] 19 Hebrew *Hallelu Yah*

Psalm 117

1 Praise the LORD, all you nations;
extol him, all you peoples.
2 For great is his love toward us,
and the faithfulness of the LORD
endures forever.

Praise the LORD.[a]

[a] 2 Hebrew *Hallelu Yah*

PRAYER: ADORATION

YOU are the Lord; You do not change. (Malachi 3:6) . . . I fear You, O God, and give You glory, because the hour of Your judgment has come. I worship You, the One who made the heavens and the earth, the sea and the springs of water. (Revelation 14:7)

PAUSE *to express your thoughts of praise and worship.*

NT Luke 16:1–31

The Parable of the Shrewd Manager

16 Jesus told his disciples: "There was a rich man whose manager was accused of wasting his possessions. 2So he called him in and asked him, 'What is this I hear about you? Give an account of your management, because you cannot be manager any longer.'

3"The manager said to himself, 'What shall I do now? My master is taking away my job. I'm not strong enough to dig, and I'm ashamed to beg— 4I know what I'll do so that, when I lose my job here, people will welcome me into their houses.'

5"So he called in each one of his master's debtors. He asked the first, 'How much do you owe my master?'

6" 'Eight hundred gallons[a] of olive oil,' he replied.

"The manager told him, 'Take your bill, sit down quickly, and make it four hundred.'

7"Then he asked the second, 'And how much do you owe?'

" 'A thousand bushels[b] of wheat,' he replied.

"He told him, 'Take your bill and make it eight hundred.'

8"The master commended the dishonest manager because he had acted shrewdly. For the people of this world are more shrewd in dealing with their own kind than are the people of the light. 9I tell you, use worldly wealth to gain friends for yourselves, so that when it is gone, you will be welcomed into eternal dwellings.

10"Whoever can be trusted with very little can also be trusted with much, and whoever is dishonest with very little will also be dishonest with much. 11So if you have not been trustworthy in handling worldly wealth, who will trust you with true riches? 12And if you have not been trustworthy with someone else's property, who will give you property of your own?

13"No servant can serve two masters. Either he will hate the one and love the other, or he will be devoted to the one and despise the other. You cannot serve both God and Money."

14The Pharisees, who loved money, heard all this and were sneering at Jesus. 15He said to them, "You are the ones who justify yourselves in the eyes of men, but God knows your hearts. What is highly valued among men is detestable in God's sight.

Additional Teachings

16"The Law and the Prophets were proclaimed until John. Since that time, the good news of the kingdom of God is being preached, and everyone is forcing his way into it. 17It is easier for heaven and earth to disappear than for the least stroke of a pen to drop out of the Law.

18"Anyone who divorces his wife and marries another woman commits adultery, and the man who marries a divorced woman commits adultery.

The Rich Man and Lazarus

19"There was a rich man who was dressed in purple and fine linen and lived

[a] 6 Greek *one hundred batous* (probably about 3 kiloliters) [b] 7 Greek *one hundred korous* (probably about 35 kiloliters)

in luxury every day. 20At his gate was laid
a beggar named Lazarus, covered with
sores 21and longing to eat what fell from
the rich man's table. Even the dogs came
and licked his sores.
22"The time came when the beggar died
and the angels carried him to Abraham's
side. The rich man also died and was
buried. 23In hell,[c] where he was in torment, he looked up and saw Abraham far
away, with Lazarus by his side. 24So he
called to him, 'Father Abraham, have pity
on me and send Lazarus to dip the tip of
his finger in water and cool my tongue,
because I am in agony in this fire.'
25"But Abraham replied, 'Son, remember that in your lifetime you received your
good things, while Lazarus received bad
things, but now he is comforted here and
you are in agony. 26And besides all this,
between us and you a great chasm has
been fixed, so that those who want to go
from here to you cannot, nor can anyone
cross over from there to us.'
27"He answered, 'Then I beg you, father,
send Lazarus to my father's house, 28for I
have five brothers. Let him warn them, so
that they will not also come to this place
of torment.'
29"Abraham replied, 'They have Moses
and the Prophets; let them listen to them.'
30" 'No, father Abraham,' he said, 'but if
someone from the dead goes to them,
they will repent.'
31"He said to him, 'If they do not listen
to Moses and the Prophets, they will not
be convinced even if someone rises from
the dead.' "

[c] 23 Greek *Hades*

PRAYER: THE WORKS OF GOD

YOUR wrath, O God, is revealed from heaven against all the godlessness and unrighteousness of those who suppress the truth by their unrighteousness, since what may be known about You, God, is evident to them, because You have shown it to them. People exchanged Your truth, O God, for a lie and worshiped and served the creation rather than You, the Creator, who are blessed forever. (Romans 1:18–19, 25)

***TAKE** a moment to consider the greatness of God's wonderful works.*

OT Jeremiah 33:1–26

YEAR 2 DAY 218

Promise of Restoration

33 While Jeremiah was still confined in
the courtyard of the guard, the word
of the LORD came to him a second time:
2"This is what the LORD says, he who made
the earth, the LORD who formed it and established it—the LORD is his name: 3'Call
to me and I will answer you and tell you
great and unsearchable things you do not
know.' 4For this is what the LORD, the God
of Israel, says about the houses in this city
and the royal palaces of Judah that have
been torn down to be used against the
siege ramps and the sword 5in the fight
with the Babylonians[a]: 'They will be filled
with the dead bodies of the men I will slay
in my anger and wrath. I will hide my face
from this city because of all its wickedness.
6" 'Nevertheless, I will bring health and
healing to it; I will heal my people and
will let them enjoy abundant peace and
security. 7I will bring Judah and Israel back
from captivity[b] and will rebuild them as
they were before. 8I will cleanse them from
all the sin they have committed against me
and will forgive all their sins of rebellion
against me. 9Then this city will bring me
renown, joy, praise and honor before all
nations on earth that hear of all the good
things I do for it; and they will be in awe
and will tremble at the abundant prosperity and peace I provide for it.'
10"This is what the LORD says: 'You say
about this place, "It is a desolate waste,

[a] 5 Or *Chaldeans* [b] 7 Or *will restore the fortunes of Judah and Israel*

without men or animals." Yet in the
towns of Judah and the streets of Jerusalem that are deserted, inhabited by neither men nor animals, there will be heard
once more 11the sounds of joy and gladness, the voices of bride and bridegroom,
and the voices of those who bring thank
offerings to the house of the LORD, saying,

"Give thanks to the LORD Almighty,
for the LORD is good;
his love endures forever."

For I will restore the fortunes of the land
as they were before,' says the LORD.
12"This is what the LORD Almighty says:
'In this place, desolate and without men or
animals—in all its towns there will again
be pastures for shepherds to rest their
flocks. 13In the towns of the hill country, of
the western foothills and of the Negev, in
the territory of Benjamin, in the villages
around Jerusalem and in the towns of Judah, flocks will again pass under the hand
of the one who counts them,' says the LORD.
14" 'The days are coming,' declares the
LORD, 'when I will fulfill the gracious
promise I made to the house of Israel and
to the house of Judah.

15" 'In those days and at that time
I will make a righteous Branch
sprout from David's line;
he will do what is just and right in
the land.
16In those days Judah will be saved
and Jerusalem will live in safety.
This is the name by which it[c] will be
called:
The LORD Our Righteousness.'

17For this is what the LORD says: 'David
will never fail to have a man to sit on the
throne of the house of Israel, 18nor will
the priests, who are Levites, ever fail to
have a man to stand before me continually to offer burnt offerings, to burn grain
offerings and to present sacrifices.' "
19The word of the LORD came to Jeremiah: 20"This is what the LORD says: 'If you can
break my covenant with the day and my
covenant with the night, so that day and
night no longer come at their appointed
time, 21then my covenant with David my
servant—and my covenant with the Levites
who are priests ministering before me—can
be broken and David will no longer have a
descendant to reign on his throne. 22I will
make the descendants of David my servant
and the Levites who minister before me as
countless as the stars of the sky and as measureless as the sand on the seashore.' "
23The word of the LORD came to Jeremiah: 24"Have you not noticed that these
people are saying, 'The LORD has rejected
the two kingdoms[d] he chose'? So they despise my people and no longer regard
them as a nation. 25This is what the LORD
says: 'If I have not established my covenant
with day and night and the fixed laws of
heaven and earth, 26then I will reject the
descendants of Jacob and David my servant and will not choose one of his sons
to rule over the descendants of Abraham,
Isaac and Jacob. For I will restore their fortunes[e] and have compassion on them.' "

[c] 16 Or *he* [d] 24 Or *families* [e] 26 Or *will bring them back from captivity*

PRAYER: CONFESSION

MY ears had heard of You but now my eyes have seen You. Therefore I despise myself and repent in dust and ashes. (Job 42:5–6)

***ASK** the Spirit to search your heart and reveal any areas of unconfessed sin. Acknowledge these to the Lord and thank Him for His forgiveness.*

NT Luke 17:1–37

Sin, Faith, Duty

17 Jesus said to his disciples: "Things that
cause people to sin are bound to
come, but woe to that person through
whom they come. 2It would be better for
him to be thrown into the sea with a millstone tied around his neck than for him
to cause one of these little ones to sin. 3So
watch yourselves.
"If your brother sins, rebuke him, and

if he repents, forgive him. [4]If he sins
against you seven times in a day, and sev-
en times comes back to you and says, 'I repent,' forgive him."
[5]The apostles said to the Lord, "Increase
our faith!"
[6]He replied, "If you have faith as small
as a mustard seed, you can say to this mulberry tree, 'Be uprooted and planted in the
sea,' and it will obey you.
[7]"Suppose one of you had a servant
plowing or looking after the sheep. Would
he say to the servant when he comes in
from the field, 'Come along now and sit
down to eat'? [8]Would he not rather say,
'Prepare my supper, get yourself ready and
wait on me while I eat and drink; after
that you may eat and drink'? [9]Would he
thank the servant because he did what he
was told to do? [10]So you also, when you
have done everything you were told to do,
should say, 'We are unworthy servants; we
have only done our duty.' "

Ten Healed of Leprosy

[11]Now on his way to Jerusalem, Jesus
traveled along the border between
Samaria and Galilee. [12]As he was going
into a village, ten men who had leprosy[a]
met him. They stood at a distance [13]and
called out in a loud voice, "Jesus, Master,
have pity on us!"
[14]When he saw them, he said, "Go,
show yourselves to the priests." And as
they went, they were cleansed.
[15]One of them, when he saw he was
healed, came back, praising God in a loud
voice. [16]He threw himself at Jesus' feet and
thanked him—and he was a Samaritan.
[17]Jesus asked, "Were not all ten cleansed?
Where are the other nine? [18]Was no one
found to return and give praise to God except this foreigner?" [19]Then he said to him,
"Rise and go; your faith has made you well."

The Coming of the Kingdom of God

[20]Once, having been asked by the Pharisees when the kingdom of God would
come, Jesus replied, "The kingdom of God
does not come with your careful observation, [21]nor will people say, 'Here it is,' or
'There it is,' because the kingdom of God
is within[b] you."
[22]Then he said to his disciples, "The time
is coming when you will long to see one
of the days of the Son of Man, but you will
not see it. [23]Men will tell you, 'There he is!'
or 'Here he is!' Do not go running off after them. [24]For the Son of Man in his day[c]
will be like the lightning, which flashes
and lights up the sky from one end to the
other. [25]But first he must suffer many
things and be rejected by this generation.
[26]"Just as it was in the days of Noah, so
also will it be in the days of the Son of
Man. [27]People were eating, drinking, marrying and being given in marriage up to
the day Noah entered the ark. Then the
flood came and destroyed them all.
[28]"It was the same in the days of Lot. People were eating and drinking, buying and
selling, planting and building. [29]But the day
Lot left Sodom, fire and sulfur rained down
from heaven and destroyed them all.
[30]"It will be just like this on the day the
Son of Man is revealed. [31]On that day no
one who is on the roof of his house, with
his goods inside, should go down to get
them. Likewise, no one in the field should
go back for anything. [32]Remember Lot's
wife! [33]Whoever tries to keep his life will
lose it, and whoever loses his life will preserve it. [34]I tell you, on that night two people will be in one bed; one will be taken
and the other left. [35]Two women will be
grinding grain together; one will be taken
and the other left.[d]"
[37]"Where, Lord?" they asked.
He replied, "Where there is a dead
body, there the vultures will gather."

[a] *12* The Greek word was used for various diseases affecting the skin—not necessarily leprosy.
[b] *21* Or *among*
[c] *24* Some manuscripts do not have *in his day.*
[d] *35* Some manuscripts *left.* [36]*Two men will be in the field; one will be taken and the other left.*

PRAYER: MY RELATIONSHIP TO GOD

KNOWING that I am not justified by the works of the law, but through faith in You, Christ Jesus, I have believed in You, that I may be justified through faith in You, O Christ, and not by the works of

the law; for by the works of the law, no flesh will be justified. (Galatians 2:16) . . . Christ Jesus my Lord, I have boldness and confident access through faith in You. (Ephesians 3:12)

***PAUSE** to thank God for the relationship that you enjoy with Him in Jesus Christ.*

YEAR 2
DAY 219

OT Jeremiah 34:1–22

Warning to Zedekiah

34 While Nebuchadnezzar king of Babylon and all his army and all the
kingdoms and peoples in the empire he
ruled were fighting against Jerusalem and
all its surrounding towns, this word came
to Jeremiah from the LORD: 2"This is what
the LORD, the God of Israel, says: Go to
Zedekiah king of Judah and tell him, 'This
is what the LORD says: I am about to hand
this city over to the king of Babylon, and
he will burn it down. 3You will not escape
from his grasp but will surely be captured
and handed over to him. You will see the
king of Babylon with your own eyes, and
he will speak with you face to face. And
you will go to Babylon.
4" 'Yet hear the promise of the LORD,
O Zedekiah king of Judah. This is what
the LORD says concerning you: You will
not die by the sword; 5you will die peacefully. As people made a funeral fire in
honor of your fathers, the former kings
who preceded you, so they will make a
fire in your honor and lament, "Alas,
O master!" I myself make this promise,
declares the LORD.' "
6Then Jeremiah the prophet told all this
to Zedekiah king of Judah, in Jerusalem,
7while the army of the king of Babylon
was fighting against Jerusalem and the
other cities of Judah that were still holding out—Lachish and Azekah. These were
the only fortified cities left in Judah.

Freedom for Slaves

8The word came to Jeremiah from the
LORD after King Zedekiah had made a covenant with all the people in Jerusalem to
proclaim freedom for the slaves. 9Everyone
was to free his Hebrew slaves, both male
and female; no one was to hold a fellow
Jew in bondage. 10So all the officials and
people who entered into this covenant
agreed that they would free their male and
female slaves and no longer hold them in
bondage. They agreed, and set them free.
11But afterward they changed their minds
and took back the slaves they had freed
and enslaved them again.
12Then the word of the LORD came to
Jeremiah: 13"This is what the LORD, the
God of Israel, says: I made a covenant
with your forefathers when I brought
them out of Egypt, out of the land of slavery. I said, 14'Every seventh year each of
you must free any fellow Hebrew who has
sold himself to you. After he has served
you six years, you must let him go free.'[a]
Your fathers, however, did not listen to me
or pay attention to me. 15Recently you repented and did what is right in my sight:
Each of you proclaimed freedom to his
countrymen. You even made a covenant
before me in the house that bears my
Name. 16But now you have turned around
and profaned my name; each of you has
taken back the male and female slaves you
had set free to go where they wished. You
have forced them to become your slaves
again.
17"Therefore, this is what the LORD says:
You have not obeyed me; you have not
proclaimed freedom for your fellow countrymen. So I now proclaim 'freedom' for
you, declares the LORD—'freedom' to fall
by the sword, plague and famine. I will
make you abhorrent to all the kingdoms
of the earth. 18The men who have violated my covenant and have not fulfilled the
terms of the covenant they made before
me, I will treat like the calf they cut in two
and then walked between its pieces. 19The
leaders of Judah and Jerusalem, the court
officials, the priests and all the people of
the land who walked between the pieces
of the calf, 20I will hand over to their en-

[a] *14* Deut. 15:12

emies who seek their lives. Their dead
bodies will become food for the birds of
the air and the beasts of the earth.
21 "I will hand Zedekiah king of Judah
and his officials over to their enemies who
seek their lives, to the army of the king of
Babylon, which has withdrawn from you.
22 I am going to give the order, declares the
LORD, and I will bring them back to this
city. They will fight against it, take it and
burn it down. And I will lay waste the
towns of Judah so no one can live there."

PRAYER: RENEWAL

MAY I not let any corrupt word come out of my mouth, but only what is helpful for building others up according to their needs, that it may impart grace to those who hear. (Ephesians 4:29) . . . I have been born again, not of perishable seed, but of imperishable seed, through Your living and abiding word, O God. Therefore, may I put away all malice and all guile and hypocrisy and envy and all slander. (1 Peter 1:23; 2:1)

PAUSE *to add your own prayers for personal renewal.*

NT Luke 18:1-17

The Parable of the Persistent Widow

18 Then Jesus told his disciples a parable
to show them that they should always
pray and not give up. 2 He said: "In a certain town there was a judge who neither
feared God nor cared about men. 3 And
there was a widow in that town who kept
coming to him with the plea, 'Grant me
justice against my adversary.'
4 "For some time he refused. But finally
he said to himself, 'Even though I don't
fear God or care about men, 5 yet because
this widow keeps bothering me, I will see
that she gets justice, so that she won't
eventually wear me out with her coming!' "
6 And the Lord said, "Listen to what the
unjust judge says. 7 And will not God bring
about justice for his chosen ones, who cry
out to him day and night? Will he keep
putting them off? 8 I tell you, he will see
that they get justice, and quickly. However, when the Son of Man comes, will he
find faith on the earth?"

The Parable of the Pharisee and the Tax Collector

9 To some who were confident of their
own righteousness and looked down on
everybody else, Jesus told this parable:
10 "Two men went up to the temple to pray,
one a Pharisee and the other a tax collector. 11 The Pharisee stood up and prayed
about[a] himself: 'God, I thank you that I
am not like other men—robbers, evildoers, adulterers—or even like this tax collector. 12 I fast twice a week and give a
tenth of all I get.'
13 "But the tax collector stood at a distance. He would not even look up to heav-
en, but beat his breast and said, 'God,
have mercy on me, a sinner.'
14 "I tell you that this man, rather than
the other, went home justified before
God. For everyone who exalts himself will
be humbled, and he who humbles himself will be exalted."

The Little Children and Jesus

15 People were also bringing babies to
Jesus to have him touch them. When the
disciples saw this, they rebuked them.
16 But Jesus called the children to him and
said, "Let the little children come to me,
and do not hinder them, for the kingdom
of God belongs to such as these. 17 I tell
you the truth, anyone who will not receive
the kingdom of God like a little child will
never enter it."

[a] *11* Or *to*

PRAYER: THE CHARACTER I WANT TO CULTIVATE

***LIKE** Ezra, I want to set my heart to study Your word, O Lord, and to do it, and to teach it to others. (Ezra 7:10) . . . I have hidden Your word in my heart that I might not sin against You. (Psalm 119:11)*

***TAKE** a moment to ask the Lord for the grace to grow in godly character.*

YEAR 2
DAY 220

OT Jeremiah 35:1–19

The Recabites

35 This is the word that came to Jeremiah from the LORD during the reign of Jehoiakim son of Josiah king of Judah: 2 "Go to the Recabite family and invite them to come to one of the side rooms of the house of the LORD and give them wine to drink."

3 So I went to get Jaazaniah son of Jeremiah, the son of Habazziniah, and his brothers and all his sons—the whole family of the Recabites. 4 I brought them into the house of the LORD, into the room of the sons of Hanan son of Igdaliah the man of God. It was next to the room of the officials, which was over that of Maaseiah son of Shallum the doorkeeper. 5 Then I set bowls full of wine and some cups before the men of the Recabite family and said to them, "Drink some wine."

6 But they replied, "We do not drink wine, because our forefather Jonadab son of Recab gave us this command: 'Neither you nor your descendants must ever drink wine. 7 Also you must never build houses, sow seed or plant vineyards; you must never have any of these things, but must always live in tents. Then you will live a long time in the land where you are nomads.' 8 We have obeyed everything our forefather Jonadab son of Recab commanded us. Neither we nor our wives nor our sons and daughters have ever drunk wine 9 or built houses to live in or had vineyards, fields or crops. 10 We have lived in tents and have fully obeyed everything our forefather Jonadab commanded us. 11 But when Nebuchadnezzar king of Babylon invaded this land, we said, 'Come, we must go to Jerusalem to escape the Babylonian[a] and Aramean armies.' So we have remained in Jerusalem."

12 Then the word of the LORD came to Jeremiah, saying: 13 "This is what the LORD Almighty, the God of Israel, says: Go and tell the men of Judah and the people of Jerusalem, 'Will you not learn a lesson and obey my words?' declares the LORD. 14 'Jonadab son of Recab ordered his sons not to drink wine and this command has been kept. To this day they do not drink wine, because they obey their forefather's command. But I have spoken to you again and again, yet you have not obeyed me. 15 Again and again I sent all my servants the prophets to you. They said, "Each of you must turn from your wicked ways and reform your actions; do not follow other gods to serve them. Then you will live in the land I have given to you and your fathers." But you have not paid attention or listened to me. 16 The descendants of Jonadab son of Recab have carried out the command their forefather gave them, but these people have not obeyed me.'

17 "Therefore, this is what the LORD God Almighty, the God of Israel, says: 'Listen! I am going to bring on Judah and on everyone living in Jerusalem every disaster I pronounced against them. I spoke to them, but they did not listen; I called to them, but they did not answer.' "

18 Then Jeremiah said to the family of the Recabites, "This is what the LORD Almighty, the God of Israel, says: 'You have obeyed the command of your forefather Jonadab and have followed all his instructions and have done everything he ordered.' 19 Therefore, this is what the LORD Almighty, the God of Israel, says: 'Jonadab son of Recab will never fail to have a man to serve me.' "

[a] 11 Or *Chaldean*

PRAYER: PETITION

MAY I not follow the crowd in doing wrong. May I not accept a bribe, for a bribe blinds those who see and perverts the words of the righteous. (Exodus 23:2, 8)

***PAUSE** here to petition God for growth in your character and personal discipline, and for physical health and strength. Ask that He empower you for spiritual warfare against the temptations of the world, the flesh and the devil. Offer prayers regarding your activities for this day and any special concerns you may have.*

NT Luke 18:18–43

The Rich Ruler

18A certain ruler asked him, "Good
teacher, what must I do to inherit eternal
life?"
19"Why do you call me good?" Jesus answered. "No one is good—except God
alone. 20You know the commandments:
'Do not commit adultery, do not murder,
do not steal, do not give false testimony,
honor your father and mother.'[a]"
21"All these I have kept since I was a
boy," he said.
22When Jesus heard this, he said to him,
"You still lack one thing. Sell everything
you have and give to the poor, and you
will have treasure in heaven. Then come,
follow me."
23When he heard this, he became very
sad, because he was a man of great wealth.
24Jesus looked at him and said, "How
hard it is for the rich to enter the kingdom
of God! 25Indeed, it is easier for a camel
to go through the eye of a needle than for
a rich man to enter the kingdom of God."
26Those who heard this asked, "Who
then can be saved?"
27Jesus replied, "What is impossible
with men is possible with God."
28Peter said to him, "We have left all we
had to follow you!"
29"I tell you the truth," Jesus said to
them, "no one who has left home or wife
or brothers or parents or children for the
sake of the kingdom of God 30will fail to
receive many times as much in this age
and, in the age to come, eternal life."

Jesus Again Predicts His Death

31Jesus took the Twelve aside and told
them, "We are going up to Jerusalem, and
everything that is written by the prophets
about the Son of Man will be fulfilled.
32He will be handed over to the Gentiles.
They will mock him, insult him, spit on
him, flog him and kill him. 33On the third
day he will rise again."
34The disciples did not understand any
of this. Its meaning was hidden from
them, and they did not know what he was
talking about.

A Blind Beggar Receives His Sight

35As Jesus approached Jericho, a blind
man was sitting by the roadside begging.
36When he heard the crowd going by, he
asked what was happening. 37They told
him, "Jesus of Nazareth is passing by."
38He called out, "Jesus, Son of David,
have mercy on me!"
39Those who led the way rebuked him
and told him to be quiet, but he shouted
all the more, "Son of David, have mercy
on me!"
40Jesus stopped and ordered the man to
be brought to him. When he came near,
Jesus asked him, 41"What do you want me
to do for you?"
"Lord, I want to see," he replied.
42Jesus said to him, "Receive your sight;
your faith has healed you." 43Immediate-
ly he received his sight and followed Jesus,
praising God. When all the people saw it,
they also praised God.

[a] *20* Exodus 20:12–16; Deut. 5:16–20

PRAYER: MY RELATIONSHIP TO OTHERS

THOSE who oppress the poor reproach You, our Maker, but whoever is kind to the needy honors You. (Proverbs 14:31) . . . Those who are kind to the poor lend to You, Lord, and You will reward them for what they have done. (Proverbs 19:17)

***PAUSE** to review your relationships with others and to commit them to the Lord.*

YEAR 2 DAY 221

OT Jeremiah 36:1–32

Jehoiakim Burns Jeremiah's Scroll

36 In the fourth year of Jehoiakim son
of Josiah king of Judah, this word
came to Jeremiah from the LORD: 2 "Take a
scroll and write on it all the words I have
spoken to you concerning Israel, Judah
and all the other nations from the time I
began speaking to you in the reign of Josiah till now. 3 Perhaps when the people of
Judah hear about every disaster I plan to
inflict on them, each of them will turn
from his wicked way; then I will forgive
their wickedness and their sin."
4 So Jeremiah called Baruch son of Neriah, and while Jeremiah dictated all the
words the LORD had spoken to him, Baruch wrote them on the scroll. 5 Then Jeremiah told Baruch, "I am restricted; I cannot go to the LORD's temple. 6 So you go to
the house of the LORD on a day of fasting
and read to the people from the scroll the
words of the LORD that you wrote as I dictated. Read them to all the people of Judah who come in from their towns. 7 Perhaps they will bring their petition before
the LORD, and each will turn from his
wicked ways, for the anger and wrath pronounced against this people by the LORD
are great."
8 Baruch son of Neriah did everything
Jeremiah the prophet told him to do; at
the LORD's temple he read the words of
the LORD from the scroll. 9 In the ninth
month of the fifth year of Jehoiakim son
of Josiah king of Judah, a time of fasting
before the LORD was proclaimed for all the
people in Jerusalem and those who had
come from the towns of Judah. 10 From the
room of Gemariah son of Shaphan the
secretary, which was in the upper courtyard at the entrance of the New Gate of
the temple, Baruch read to all the people
at the LORD's temple the words of Jeremiah from the scroll.
11 When Micaiah son of Gemariah, the
son of Shaphan, heard all the words of
the LORD from the scroll, 12 he went down
to the secretary's room in the royal palace,
where all the officials were sitting: Elishama the secretary, Delaiah son of Shemaiah, Elnathan son of Acbor, Gemariah son
of Shaphan, Zedekiah son of Hananiah,
and all the other officials. 13 After Micaiah
told them everything he had heard Baruch
read to the people from the scroll, 14 all the
officials sent Jehudi son of Nethaniah, the
son of Shelemiah, the son of Cushi, to say
to Baruch, "Bring the scroll from which
you have read to the people and come."
So Baruch son of Neriah went to them
with the scroll in his hand. 15 They said to
him, "Sit down, please, and read it to us."
So Baruch read it to them. 16 When they
heard all these words, they looked at each
other in fear and said to Baruch, "We must
report all these words to the king." 17 Then
they asked Baruch, "Tell us, how did you
come to write all this? Did Jeremiah dictate it?"
18 "Yes," Baruch replied, "he dictated all
these words to me, and I wrote them in
ink on the scroll."
19 Then the officials said to Baruch, "You
and Jeremiah, go and hide. Don't let anyone know where you are."
20 After they put the scroll in the room
of Elishama the secretary, they went to the
king in the courtyard and reported everything to him. 21 The king sent Jehudi to get
the scroll, and Jehudi brought it from the
room of Elishama the secretary and read
it to the king and all the officials standing

beside him. 22It was the ninth month and the king was sitting in the winter apartment, with a fire burning in the firepot in front of him. 23Whenever Jehudi had read three or four columns of the scroll, the king cut them off with a scribe's knife and threw them into the firepot, until the entire scroll was burned in the fire. 24The king and all his attendants who heard all these words showed no fear, nor did they tear their clothes. 25Even though Elnathan, Delaiah and Gemariah urged the king not to burn the scroll, he would not listen to them. 26Instead, the king commanded Jerahmeel, a son of the king, Seraiah son of Azriel and Shelemiah son of Abdeel to arrest Baruch the scribe and Jeremiah the prophet. But the LORD had hidden them.

27After the king burned the scroll containing the words that Baruch had written at Jeremiah's dictation, the word of the LORD came to Jeremiah: 28"Take another scroll and write on it all the words that were on the first scroll, which Jehoiakim king of Judah burned up. 29Also tell Jehoiakim king of Judah, 'This is what the LORD says: You burned that scroll and said, "Why did you write on it that the king of Babylon would certainly come and destroy this land and cut off both men and animals from it?" 30Therefore, this is what the LORD says about Jehoiakim king of Judah: He will have no one to sit on the throne of David; his body will be thrown out and exposed to the heat by day and the frost by night. 31I will punish him and his children and his attendants for their wickedness; I will bring on them and those living in Jerusalem and the people of Judah every disaster I pronounced against them, because they have not listened.' "

32So Jeremiah took another scroll and gave it to the scribe Baruch son of Neriah, and as Jeremiah dictated, Baruch wrote on it all the words of the scroll that Jehoiakim king of Judah had burned in the fire. And many similar words were added to them.

PRAYER: INTERCESSION

***SALVATION** belongs to You, Lord. May Your blessing be on Your people. (Psalm 3:8)*

***TAKE** a few moments to intercede on behalf of the poor and hungry, the oppressed and persecuted, and those in control of world and national resources. Offer prayers for peace among nations and regarding current events and concerns.*

NT Luke 19:1–27

Zacchaeus the Tax Collector

19 Jesus entered Jericho and was passing through. 2A man was there by the name of Zacchaeus; he was a chief tax collector and was wealthy. 3He wanted to see who Jesus was, but being a short man he could not, because of the crowd. 4So he ran ahead and climbed a sycamore-fig tree to see him, since Jesus was coming that way.

5When Jesus reached the spot, he looked up and said to him, "Zacchaeus, come down immediately. I must stay at your house today." 6So he came down at once and welcomed him gladly.

7All the people saw this and began to mutter, "He has gone to be the guest of a 'sinner.' "

8But Zacchaeus stood up and said to the Lord, "Look, Lord! Here and now I give half of my possessions to the poor, and if I have cheated anybody out of anything, I will pay back four times the amount."

9Jesus said to him, "Today salvation has come to this house, because this man, too, is a son of Abraham. 10For the Son of Man came to seek and to save what was lost."

The Parable of the Ten Minas

11While they were listening to this, he went on to tell them a parable, because he was near Jerusalem and the people thought that the kingdom of God was going to appear at once. 12He said: "A man of noble birth went to a distant country to have himself appointed king and then to return. 13So he called ten of his servants and gave them ten minas.[a] 'Put this money to work,' he said, 'until I come back.'

14 "But his subjects hated him and sent a delegation after him to say, 'We don't want this man to be our king.'

15 "He was made king, however, and returned home. Then he sent for the servants to whom he had given the money, in order to find out what they had gained with it.

16 "The first one came and said, 'Sir, your mina has earned ten more.'

17 " 'Well done, my good servant!' his master replied. 'Because you have been trustworthy in a very small matter, take charge of ten cities.'

18 "The second came and said, 'Sir, your mina has earned five more.'

19 "His master answered, 'You take charge of five cities.'

20 "Then another servant came and said, 'Sir, here is your mina; I have kept it laid away in a piece of cloth. 21 I was afraid of you, because you are a hard man. You take out what you did not put in and reap what you did not sow.'

22 "His master replied, 'I will judge you by your own words, you wicked servant! You knew, did you, that I am a hard man, taking out what I did not put in, and reaping what I did not sow? 23 Why then didn't you put my money on deposit, so that when I came back, I could have collected it with interest?'

24 "Then he said to those standing by, 'Take his mina away from him and give it to the one who has ten minas.'

25 " 'Sir,' they said, 'he already has ten!'

26 "He replied, 'I tell you that to everyone who has, more will be given, but as for the one who has nothing, even what he has will be taken away. 27 But those enemies of mine who did not want me to be king over them—bring them here and kill them in front of me.' "

[a] 13 A mina was about three months' wages.

PRAYER: THE ATTRIBUTES OF GOD

YOUR law, O Lord, is perfect, restoring the soul. Your testimony, O Lord, is sure, making wise the simple. Your precepts, O Lord, are right, rejoicing the heart. Your commandment, O Lord, is pure, enlightening the eyes. The fear of You, O Lord, is clean, enduring forever. Your judgments, O Lord, are true and altogether righteous. They are more desirable than gold, than much pure gold. They are sweeter than honey, than honey from the comb. Moreover, by them is Your servant warned—in keeping them there is great reward. (Psalm 19:7–11)

***PAUSE** to reflect on these affirmations about the person, powers and perfection of God.*

OT Jeremiah 37:1–21

YEAR 2 DAY 222

Jeremiah in Prison

37 Zedekiah son of Josiah was made king of Judah by Nebuchadnezzar king of Babylon; he reigned in place of Jehoiachin[a] son of Jehoiakim. 2 Neither he nor his attendants nor the people of the land paid any attention to the words the LORD had spoken through Jeremiah the prophet.

3 King Zedekiah, however, sent Jehucal son of Shelemiah with the priest Zephaniah son of Maaseiah to Jeremiah the prophet with this message: "Please pray to the LORD our God for us."

4 Now Jeremiah was free to come and go among the people, for he had not yet been put in prison. 5 Pharaoh's army had marched out of Egypt, and when the Babylonians[b] who were besieging Jerusalem heard the report about them, they withdrew from Jerusalem.

[a] 1 Hebrew *Coniah,* a variant of *Jehoiachin*
[b] 5 Or *Chaldeans;* also in verses 8, 9, 13 and 14

6Then the word of the LORD came to Jeremiah the prophet: 7"This is what the
LORD, the God of Israel, says: Tell the king
of Judah, who sent you to inquire of me,
'Pharaoh's army, which has marched out
to support you, will go back to its own
land, to Egypt. 8Then the Babylonians will
return and attack this city; they will capture it and burn it down.'
9"This is what the LORD says: Do not deceive yourselves, thinking, 'The Babylonians will surely leave us.' They will not!
10Even if you were to defeat the entire
Babylonian[c] army that is attacking you
and only wounded men were left in their
tents, they would come out and burn this
city down."
11After the Babylonian army had withdrawn from Jerusalem because of Pharaoh's army, 12Jeremiah started to leave the
city to go to the territory of Benjamin to
get his share of the property among the
people there. 13But when he reached the
Benjamin Gate, the captain of the guard,
whose name was Irijah son of Shelemiah,
the son of Hananiah, arrested him and
said, "You are deserting to the Babylonians!"
14"That's not true!" Jeremiah said. "I am
not deserting to the Babylonians." But Irijah would not listen to him; instead, he
arrested Jeremiah and brought him to the
officials. 15They were angry with Jeremiah
and had him beaten and imprisoned in
the house of Jonathan the secretary, which
they had made into a prison.
16Jeremiah was put into a vaulted cell in
a dungeon, where he remained a long
time. 17Then King Zedekiah sent for him
and had him brought to the palace, where
he asked him privately, "Is there any word
from the LORD?"
"Yes," Jeremiah replied, "you will be
handed over to the king of Babylon."
18Then Jeremiah said to King Zedekiah,
"What crime have I committed against you
or your officials or this people, that you
have put me in prison? 19Where are your
prophets who prophesied to you, 'The
king of Babylon will not attack you or this
land'? 20But now, my lord the king, please
listen. Let me bring my petition before
you: Do not send me back to the house of
Jonathan the secretary, or I will die there."
21King Zedekiah then gave orders for
Jeremiah to be placed in the courtyard of
the guard and given bread from the street
of the bakers each day until all the bread
in the city was gone. So Jeremiah remained in the courtyard of the guard.

c 10 Or *Chaldean;* also in verse 11

PRAYER: AFFIRMATION

O GOD, You set me apart from the time I was born and called me through Your grace. (Galatians 1:15) . . . I am joined to You, Jesus Christ; I am one with You in spirit. (1 Corinthians 6:17)

PAUSE *to reflect on these Biblical affirmations.*

NT Luke 19:28–20:8

The Triumphal Entry

28After Jesus had said this, he went on
ahead, going up to Jerusalem. 29As he approached Bethphage and Bethany at the
hill called the Mount of Olives, he sent
two of his disciples, saying to them, 30"Go
to the village ahead of you, and as you
enter it, you will find a colt tied there,
which no one has ever ridden. Untie it
and bring it here. 31If anyone asks you,
'Why are you untying it?' tell him, 'The
Lord needs it.' "
32Those who were sent ahead went and
found it just as he had told them. 33As they
were untying the colt, its owners asked
them, "Why are you untying the colt?"
34They replied, "The Lord needs it."
35They brought it to Jesus, threw their
cloaks on the colt and put Jesus on it. 36As
he went along, people spread their cloaks
on the road.
37When he came near the place where
the road goes down the Mount of Olives,
the whole crowd of disciples began joyfully to praise God in loud voices for all
the miracles they had seen:

38 "Blessed is the king who comes in the
name of the Lord!"[a]

"Peace in heaven and glory in the
highest!"

39 Some of the Pharisees in the crowd
said to Jesus, "Teacher, rebuke your disciples!"
40 "I tell you," he replied, "if they keep
quiet, the stones will cry out."
41 As he approached Jerusalem and saw
the city, he wept over it 42 and said, "If you,
even you, had only known on this day
what would bring you peace—but now it
is hidden from your eyes. 43 The days will
come upon you when your enemies will
build an embankment against you and
encircle you and hem you in on every
side. 44 They will dash you to the ground,
you and the children within your walls.
They will not leave one stone on another,
because you did not recognize the time of
God's coming to you."

Jesus at the Temple

45 Then he entered the temple area and
began driving out those who were selling.
46 "It is written," he said to them, " 'My
house will be a house of prayer'[b]; but you
have made it 'a den of robbers.'[c]"

47 Every day he was teaching at the temple. But the chief priests, the teachers of
the law and the leaders among the people
were trying to kill him. 48 Yet they could
not find any way to do it, because all the
people hung on his words.

The Authority of Jesus Questioned

20 One day as he was teaching the people in the temple courts and preaching the gospel, the chief priests and the
teachers of the law, together with the elders, came up to him. 2 "Tell us by what
authority you are doing these things,"
they said. "Who gave you this authority?"
3 He replied, "I will also ask you a question. Tell me, 4 John's baptism—was it
from heaven, or from men?"
5 They discussed it among themselves
and said, "If we say, 'From heaven,' he will
ask, 'Why didn't you believe him?' 6 But if
we say, 'From men,' all the people will
stone us, because they are persuaded that
John was a prophet."
7 So they answered, "We don't know
where it was from."
8 Jesus said, "Neither will I tell you by
what authority I am doing these things."

[a] *38* Psalm 118:26 [b] *46* Isaiah 56:7
[c] *46* Jer. 7:11

PRAYER: THE WORKS OF GOD

IF by the trespass of the one man, death reigned through that one man, much more will those who receive the abundance of grace and the gift of righteousness reign in life through You, the one Man, Jesus Christ. Consequently, just as the result of one trespass was condemnation for all, so also the result of one act of righteousness was justification that brings life for all. For just as through the disobedience of the one man the many were made sinners, so also through the obedience of the one Man the many will be made righteous. (Romans 5:17–19)

***TAKE** a moment to consider the greatness of God's wonderful works.*

YEAR 2
DAY 223

OT Jeremiah 38:1–28a

Jeremiah Thrown Into a Cistern

38 Shephatiah son of Mattan, Gedaliah
son of Pashhur, Jehucal[a] son of
Shelemiah, and Pashhur son of Malkijah
heard what Jeremiah was telling all the
people when he said, 2 "This is what the
LORD says: 'Whoever stays in this city will
die by the sword, famine or plague, but
whoever goes over to the Babylonians[b]

[a] *1* Hebrew *Jucal,* a variant of *Jehucal* [b] *2* Or *Chaldeans;* also in verses 18, 19 and 23

will live. He will escape with his life; he
will live.' 3 And this is what the LORD says:
'This city will certainly be handed over to
the army of the king of Babylon, who will
capture it.' "
4 Then the officials said to the king,
"This man should be put to death. He is
discouraging the soldiers who are left in
this city, as well as all the people, by the
things he is saying to them. This man is
not seeking the good of these people but
their ruin."
5 "He is in your hands," King Zedekiah
answered. "The king can do nothing to
oppose you."
6 So they took Jeremiah and put him
into the cistern of Malkijah, the king's son,
which was in the courtyard of the guard.
They lowered Jeremiah by ropes into the
cistern; it had no water in it, only mud,
and Jeremiah sank down into the mud.
7 But Ebed-Melech, a Cushite,[c] an official[d] in the royal palace, heard that they
had put Jeremiah into the cistern. While
the king was sitting in the Benjamin Gate,
8 Ebed-Melech went out of the palace and
said to him, 9 "My lord the king, these
men have acted wickedly in all they have
done to Jeremiah the prophet. They have
thrown him into a cistern, where he will
starve to death when there is no longer
any bread in the city."
10 Then the king commanded Ebed-Melech the Cushite, "Take thirty men from
here with you and lift Jeremiah the prophet out of the cistern before he dies."
11 So Ebed-Melech took the men with
him and went to a room under the treasury in the palace. He took some old rags
and worn-out clothes from there and let
them down with ropes to Jeremiah in the
cistern. 12 Ebed-Melech the Cushite said to
Jeremiah, "Put these old rags and worn-
out clothes under your arms to pad the
ropes." Jeremiah did so, 13 and they pulled
him up with the ropes and lifted him out
of the cistern. And Jeremiah remained in
the courtyard of the guard.

Zedekiah Questions Jeremiah Again

14 Then King Zedekiah sent for Jeremiah
the prophet and had him brought to the
third entrance to the temple of the LORD.
"I am going to ask you something," the
king said to Jeremiah. "Do not hide anything from me."
15 Jeremiah said to Zedekiah, "If I give
you an answer, will you not kill me? Even
if I did give you counsel, you would not
listen to me."
16 But King Zedekiah swore this oath secretly to Jeremiah: "As surely as the LORD
lives, who has given us breath, I will neither kill you nor hand you over to those
who are seeking your life."
17 Then Jeremiah said to Zedekiah, "This
is what the LORD God Almighty, the God
of Israel, says: 'If you surrender to the officers of the king of Babylon, your life will
be spared and this city will not be burned
down; you and your family will live. 18 But
if you will not surrender to the officers of
the king of Babylon, this city will be
handed over to the Babylonians and they
will burn it down; you yourself will not
escape from their hands.' "
19 King Zedekiah said to Jeremiah, "I am
afraid of the Jews who have gone over to
the Babylonians, for the Babylonians may
hand me over to them and they will mistreat me."
20 "They will not hand you over," Jeremiah replied. "Obey the LORD by doing
what I tell you. Then it will go well with
you, and your life will be spared. 21 But if
you refuse to surrender, this is what the
LORD has revealed to me: 22 All the
women left in the palace of the king of
Judah will be brought out to the officials
of the king of Babylon. Those women
will say to you:

" 'They misled you and overcame
you—
those trusted friends of yours.
Your feet are sunk in the mud;
your friends have deserted you.'

23 "All your wives and children will be
brought out to the Babylonians. You yourself will not escape from their hands but
will be captured by the king of Babylon;
and this city will[e] be burned down."
24 Then Zedekiah said to Jeremiah, "Do
not let anyone know about this conversation, or you may die. 25 If the officials hear
that I talked with you, and they come to
you and say, 'Tell us what you said to the
king and what the king said to you; do not
hide it from us or we will kill you,' 26 then
tell them, 'I was pleading with the king

[c] 7 Probably from the upper Nile region [d] 7 Or *a eunuch* [e] 23 Or *and you will cause this city to*

not to send me back to Jonathan's house
to die there.' "
27 All the officials did come to Jeremiah
and question him, and he told them everything the king had ordered him to say. So
they said no more to him, for no one had
heard his conversation with the king.
28 And Jeremiah remained in the courtyard of the guard until the day Jerusalem
was captured.

PRAYER: THANKSGIVING

WHEN I was dead in my trespasses and in the uncircumcision of my flesh, O God, You made me alive with Christ. You forgave me all my trespasses, having canceled the written code, with its regulations, that was against me and was contrary to me; You took it away, nailing it to the cross. And having disarmed the powers and authorities, You made a public spectacle of them, triumphing over them by the cross.

(Colossians 2:13–15)

PAUSE *to offer your own expressions of thanksgiving.*

NT Luke 20:9–47

The Parable of the Tenants

9 He went on to tell the people this parable: "A man planted a vineyard, rented it
to some farmers and went away for a long
time. 10 At harvest time he sent a servant to
the tenants so they would give him some
of the fruit of the vineyard. But the tenants beat him and sent him away empty-
handed. 11 He sent another servant, but
that one also they beat and treated shamefully and sent away empty-handed. 12 He
sent still a third, and they wounded him
and threw him out.
13 "Then the owner of the vineyard said,
'What shall I do? I will send my son, whom
I love; perhaps they will respect him.'
14 "But when the tenants saw him, they
talked the matter over. 'This is the heir,'
they said. 'Let's kill him, and the inheritance will be ours.' 15 So they threw him
out of the vineyard and killed him.
"What then will the owner of the vineyard do to them? 16 He will come and kill
those tenants and give the vineyard to
others."
When the people heard this, they said,
"May this never be!"
17 Jesus looked directly at them and
asked, "Then what is the meaning of that
which is written:

" 'The stone the builders rejected
has become the capstone[a,b]'?

18 Everyone who falls on that stone will be
broken to pieces, but he on whom it falls
will be crushed."
19 The teachers of the law and the chief
priests looked for a way to arrest him immediately, because they knew he had spoken this parable against them. But they
were afraid of the people.

Paying Taxes to Caesar

20 Keeping a close watch on him, they
sent spies, who pretended to be honest.
They hoped to catch Jesus in something
he said so that they might hand him over
to the power and authority of the governor. 21 So the spies questioned him:
"Teacher, we know that you speak and
teach what is right, and that you do not
show partiality but teach the way of God
in accordance with the truth. 22 Is it right
for us to pay taxes to Caesar or not?"
23 He saw through their duplicity and
said to them, 24 "Show me a denarius.
Whose portrait and inscription are on it?"
25 "Caesar's," they replied.
He said to them, "Then give to Caesar
what is Caesar's, and to God what is God's."
26 They were unable to trap him in what
he had said there in public. And astonished by his answer, they became silent.

The Resurrection and Marriage

27 Some of the Sadducees, who say there
is no resurrection, came to Jesus with a

[a] 17 Or *cornerstone* [b] 17 Psalm 118:22

question. 28"Teacher," they said, "Moses
wrote for us that if a man's brother dies
and leaves a wife but no children, the man
must marry the widow and have children
for his brother. 29Now there were seven
brothers. The first one married a woman
and died childless. 30The second 31and
then the third married her, and in the
same way the seven died, leaving no children. 32Finally, the woman died too.
33Now then, at the resurrection whose
wife will she be, since the seven were married to her?"

34Jesus replied, "The people of this age
marry and are given in marriage. 35But
those who are considered worthy of taking part in that age and in the resurrection
from the dead will neither marry nor be
given in marriage, 36and they can no
longer die; for they are like the angels.
They are God's children, since they are
children of the resurrection. 37But in the
account of the bush, even Moses showed
that the dead rise, for he calls the Lord 'the
God of Abraham, and the God of Isaac,
and the God of Jacob.'[c] 38He is not the
God of the dead, but of the living, for to
him all are alive."

39Some of the teachers of the law responded, "Well said, teacher!" 40And no
one dared to ask him any more questions.

Whose Son Is the Christ?

41Then Jesus said to them, "How is it
that they say the Christ[d] is the Son of David? 42David himself declares in the Book
of Psalms:

> " 'The Lord said to my Lord:
> "Sit at my right hand
> 43until I make your enemies
> a footstool for your feet." '[e]

44David calls him 'Lord.' How then can he
be his son?"

45While all the people were listening,
Jesus said to his disciples, 46"Beware of the
teachers of the law. They like to walk
around in flowing robes and love to be
greeted in the marketplaces and have the
most important seats in the synagogues
and the places of honor at banquets.
47They devour widows' houses and for a
show make lengthy prayers. Such men
will be punished most severely."

[c] 37 Exodus 3:6 [d] 41 Or *Messiah*
[e] 43 Psalm 110:1

PRAYER: MY RELATIONSHIP TO GOD

HAVING begun in You, Holy Spirit, I will not seek to be perfected by the flesh. (Galatians 3:3)

***PAUSE** to thank God for the relationship that you enjoy with Him in Jesus Christ.*

OT Psalm 118

Psalm 118

1Give thanks to the LORD, for he is
good;
his love endures forever.

2Let Israel say:
"His love endures forever."
3Let the house of Aaron say:
"His love endures forever."
4Let those who fear the LORD say:
"His love endures forever."

5In my anguish I cried to the LORD,
and he answered by setting me free.
6The LORD is with me; I will not be
afraid.
What can man do to me?
7The LORD is with me; he is my helper.
I will look in triumph on my
enemies.

8It is better to take refuge in the LORD
than to trust in man.
9It is better to take refuge in the LORD
than to trust in princes.

10All the nations surrounded me,
but in the name of the LORD I cut
them off.

11 They surrounded me on every side,
but in the name of the LORD I cut them off.
12 They swarmed around me like bees,
but they died out as quickly as burning thorns;
in the name of the LORD I cut them off.

13 I was pushed back and about to fall,
but the LORD helped me.
14 The LORD is my strength and my song;
he has become my salvation.

15 Shouts of joy and victory
resound in the tents of the righteous:
"The LORD's right hand has done mighty things!
16 The LORD's right hand is lifted high;
the LORD's right hand has done mighty things!"

17 I will not die but live,
and will proclaim what the LORD has done.
18 The LORD has chastened me severely,
but he has not given me over to death.

19 Open for me the gates of righteousness;
I will enter and give thanks to the LORD.
20 This is the gate of the LORD
through which the righteous may enter.
21 I will give you thanks, for you answered me;
you have become my salvation.

22 The stone the builders rejected
has become the capstone;
23 the LORD has done this,
and it is marvelous in our eyes.
24 This is the day the LORD has made;
let us rejoice and be glad in it.

25 O LORD, save us;
O LORD, grant us success.
26 Blessed is he who comes in the name of the LORD.
From the house of the LORD we bless you.[a]
27 The LORD is God,
and he has made his light shine upon us.
With boughs in hand, join in the festal procession
up[b] to the horns of the altar.

28 You are my God, and I will give you thanks;
you are my God, and I will exalt you.

29 Give thanks to the LORD, for he is good;
his love endures forever.

[a] 26 The Hebrew is plural. [b] 27 Or *Bind the festal sacrifice with ropes / and take it*

PRAYER: ADORATION

O GOD, will You indeed dwell on earth? Heaven and the highest heaven cannot contain You. (1 Kings 8:27) . . . Your voice, O God, thunders in marvelous ways; You do great things that we cannot comprehend. (Job 37:5)

PAUSE *to express your thoughts of praise and worship.*

NT Luke 21:1-38

The Widow's Offering

21 As he looked up, Jesus saw the rich
putting their gifts into the temple treasury. 2He also saw a poor widow put in
two very small copper coins.[a] 3"I tell you
the truth," he said, "this poor widow has
put in more than all the others. 4All these
people gave their gifts out of their wealth;
but she out of her poverty put in all she
had to live on."

Signs of the End of the Age

5Some of his disciples were remarking
about how the temple was adorned with
beautiful stones and with gifts dedicated
to God. But Jesus said, 6"As for what you
see here, the time will come when not one
stone will be left on another; every one of
them will be thrown down."

[a] 2 Greek *two lepta*

7“Teacher,” they asked, “when will these
things happen? And what will be the sign
that they are about to take place?”
8He replied: “Watch out that you are
not deceived. For many will come in my
name, claiming, ‘I am he,’ and, ‘The time
is near.’ Do not follow them. 9When you
hear of wars and revolutions, do not be
frightened. These things must happen
first, but the end will not come right
away.”
10Then he said to them: “Nation will
rise against nation, and kingdom against
kingdom. 11There will be great earthquakes, famines and pestilences in various places, and fearful events and great
signs from heaven.
12“But before all this, they will lay
hands on you and persecute you. They
will deliver you to synagogues and prisons, and you will be brought before kings
and governors, and all on account of my
name. 13This will result in your being witnesses to them. 14But make up your mind
not to worry beforehand how you will defend yourselves. 15For I will give you
words and wisdom that none of your adversaries will be able to resist or contradict. 16You will be betrayed even by parents, brothers, relatives and friends, and
they will put some of you to death. 17All
men will hate you because of me. 18But
not a hair of your head will perish. 19By
standing firm you will gain life.
20“When you see Jerusalem being surrounded by armies, you will know that its
desolation is near. 21Then let those who
are in Judea flee to the mountains, let
those in the city get out, and let those in
the country not enter the city. 22For this is
the time of punishment in fulfillment of
all that has been written. 23How dreadful
it will be in those days for pregnant
women and nursing mothers! There will
be great distress in the land and wrath
against this people. 24They will fall by the
sword and will be taken as prisoners to all
the nations. Jerusalem will be trampled
on by the Gentiles until the times of the
Gentiles are fulfilled.
25“There will be signs in the sun, moon
and stars. On the earth, nations will be in
anguish and perplexity at the roaring and
tossing of the sea. 26Men will faint from
terror, apprehensive of what is coming on
the world, for the heavenly bodies will be
shaken. 27At that time they will see the
Son of Man coming in a cloud with power and great glory. 28When these things begin to take place, stand up and lift up your
heads, because your redemption is drawing near.”
29He told them this parable: “Look at
the fig tree and all the trees. 30When they
sprout leaves, you can see for yourselves
and know that summer is near. 31Even so,
when you see these things happening, you
know that the kingdom of God is near.
32“I tell you the truth, this generation[b]
will certainly not pass away until all these
things have happened. 33Heaven and
earth will pass away, but my words will
never pass away.
34“Be careful, or your hearts will be
weighed down with dissipation, drunkenness and the anxieties of life, and that
day will close on you unexpectedly like a
trap. 35For it will come upon all those who
live on the face of the whole earth. 36Be always on the watch, and pray that you may
be able to escape all that is about to happen, and that you may be able to stand
before the Son of Man.”
37Each day Jesus was teaching at the
temple, and each evening he went out to
spend the night on the hill called the
Mount of Olives, 38and all the people
came early in the morning to hear him at
the temple.

[b] 32 Or *race*

PRAYER: THE CHARACTER I WANT TO CULTIVATE

THE wise fear and depart from evil, but fools are arrogant and bold. Those who are quick-tempered act foolishly, and those who plot evil are hated. (Proverbs 14:16–17) . . . The one who burns with wrath must pay the penalty; if I rescue such a person, I will have to do it again. (Proverbs 19:19)

TAKE *a moment to ask the Lord for the grace to grow in godly character.*

YEAR 2 DAY 225

OT **Jeremiah 38:28b–39:18**

The Fall of Jerusalem

39 This is how Jerusalem was taken: 1In the ninth year of Zedekiah king of Judah, in the tenth month, Nebuchadnezzar king of Babylon marched against Jerusalem with his whole army and laid siege to it. 2And on the ninth day of the fourth month of Zedekiah's eleventh year, the city wall was broken through. 3Then all the officials of the king of Babylon came and took seats in the Middle Gate: Nergal-Sharezer of Samgar, Nebo-Sarsekim[a] a chief officer, Nergal-Sharezer a high official and all the other officials of the king of Babylon. 4When Zedekiah king of Judah and all the soldiers saw them, they fled; they left the city at night by way of the king's garden, through the gate between the two walls, and headed toward the Arabah.[b]

5But the Babylonian[c] army pursued them and overtook Zedekiah in the plains of Jericho. They captured him and took him to Nebuchadnezzar king of Babylon at Riblah in the land of Hamath, where he pronounced sentence on him. 6There at Riblah the king of Babylon slaughtered the sons of Zedekiah before his eyes and also killed all the nobles of Judah. 7Then he put out Zedekiah's eyes and bound him with bronze shackles to take him to Babylon.

8The Babylonians[d] set fire to the royal palace and the houses of the people and broke down the walls of Jerusalem. 9Nebuzaradan commander of the imperial guard carried into exile to Babylon the people who remained in the city, along with those who had gone over to him, and the rest of the people. 10But Nebuzaradan the commander of the guard left behind in the land of Judah some of the poor people, who owned nothing; and at that time he gave them vineyards and fields.

11Now Nebuchadnezzar king of Babylon had given these orders about Jeremiah through Nebuzaradan commander of the imperial guard: 12"Take him and look after him; don't harm him but do for him whatever he asks." 13So Nebuzaradan the commander of the guard, Nebushazban a chief officer, Nergal-Sharezer a high official and all the other officers of the king of Babylon 14sent and had Jeremiah taken out of the courtyard of the guard. They turned him over to Gedaliah son of Ahikam, the son of Shaphan, to take him back to his home. So he remained among his own people.

15While Jeremiah had been confined in the courtyard of the guard, the word of the LORD came to him: 16"Go and tell Ebed-Melech the Cushite, 'This is what the LORD Almighty, the God of Israel, says: I am about to fulfill my words against this city through disaster, not prosperity. At that time they will be fulfilled before your eyes. 17But I will rescue you on that day, declares the LORD; you will not be handed over to those you fear. 18I will save you; you will not fall by the sword but will escape with your life, because you trust in me, declares the LORD.' "

[a] 3 Or *Nergal-Sharezer, Samgar-Nebo, Sarsekim*
[b] 4 Or *the Jordan Valley* [c] 5 Or *Chaldean*
[d] 8 Or *Chaldeans*

PRAYER: CONFESSION

O LORD, do not rebuke me in Your anger or chasten me in Your wrath. Be merciful to me, Lord, for I am weak; O Lord, heal me, for my bones are in distress. My soul also is greatly troubled. How long, O Lord, how long? (Psalm 6:1–3)

***ASK** the Spirit to search your heart and reveal any areas of unconfessed sin. Acknowledge these to the Lord and thank Him for His forgiveness.*

NT Luke 22:1-38

Judas Agrees to Betray Jesus

22 Now the Feast of Unleavened Bread,
called the Passover, was approaching,
2and the chief priests and the teachers of
the law were looking for some way to get
rid of Jesus, for they were afraid of the
people. 3Then Satan entered Judas, called
Iscariot, one of the Twelve. 4And Judas
went to the chief priests and the officers
of the temple guard and discussed with
them how he might betray Jesus. 5They
were delighted and agreed to give him
money. 6He consented, and watched for
an opportunity to hand Jesus over to
them when no crowd was present.

The Last Supper

7Then came the day of Unleavened
Bread on which the Passover lamb had to
be sacrificed. 8Jesus sent Peter and John,
saying, "Go and make preparations for us
to eat the Passover."

9"Where do you want us to prepare for
it?" they asked.

10He replied, "As you enter the city, a
man carrying a jar of water will meet you.
Follow him to the house that he enters,
11and say to the owner of the house, 'The
Teacher asks: Where is the guest room,
where I may eat the Passover with my disciples?' 12He will show you a large upper
room, all furnished. Make preparations
there."

13They left and found things just as
Jesus had told them. So they prepared the
Passover.

14When the hour came, Jesus and his
apostles reclined at the table. 15And he
said to them, "I have eagerly desired to eat
this Passover with you before I suffer.
16For I tell you, I will not eat it again until it finds fulfillment in the kingdom of
God."

17After taking the cup, he gave thanks
and said, "Take this and divide it among
you. 18For I tell you I will not drink again
of the fruit of the vine until the kingdom
of God comes."

19And he took bread, gave thanks and
broke it, and gave it to them, saying, "This
is my body given for you; do this in remembrance of me."

20In the same way, after the supper he
took the cup, saying, "This cup is the new
covenant in my blood, which is poured
out for you. 21But the hand of him who is
going to betray me is with mine on the
table. 22The Son of Man will go as it has
been decreed, but woe to that man who
betrays him." 23They began to question
among themselves which of them it might
be who would do this.

24Also a dispute arose among them as
to which of them was considered to be
greatest. 25Jesus said to them, "The kings
of the Gentiles lord it over them; and
those who exercise authority over them
call themselves Benefactors. 26But you are
not to be like that. Instead, the greatest
among you should be like the youngest,
and the one who rules like the one who
serves. 27For who is greater, the one who
is at the table or the one who serves? Is it
not the one who is at the table? But I am
among you as one who serves. 28You are
those who have stood by me in my trials.
29And I confer on you a kingdom, just as
my Father conferred one on me, 30so that
you may eat and drink at my table in my
kingdom and sit on thrones, judging the
twelve tribes of Israel.

31"Simon, Simon, Satan has asked to
sift you[a] as wheat. 32But I have prayed for
you, Simon, that your faith may not fail.
And when you have turned back, strength-
en your brothers."

33But he replied, "Lord, I am ready to go
with you to prison and to death."

34Jesus answered, "I tell you, Peter, before the rooster crows today, you will deny
three times that you know me."

35Then Jesus asked them, "When I sent
you without purse, bag or sandals, did
you lack anything?"

"Nothing," they answered.

36He said to them, "But now if you have
a purse, take it, and also a bag; and if you
don't have a sword, sell your cloak and
buy one. 37It is written: 'And he was numbered with the transgressors'[b]; and I tell
you that this must be fulfilled in me. Yes,
what is written about me is reaching its
fulfillment."

38The disciples said, "See, Lord, here are
two swords."

"That is enough," he replied.

[a] *31* The Greek is plural. [b] *37* Isaiah 53:12

PRAYER: MY RELATIONSHIP TO OTHERS

I WILL do no injustice in judgment, nor show partiality to the poor or favoritism to the great, but I will judge my neighbor fairly. (Leviticus 19:15) . . . In my faith in You, my glorious Lord Jesus Christ, I will not show partiality to some people above others. (James 2:1)

***PAUSE** to review your relationships with others and to commit them to the Lord.*

YEAR 2 DAY 226

OT Jeremiah 40:1–16

Jeremiah Freed

40 The word came to Jeremiah from the LORD after Nebuzaradan commander of the imperial guard had released him at Ramah. He had found Jeremiah bound in chains among all the captives from Jerusalem and Judah who were being carried into exile to Babylon. 2When the commander of the guard found Jeremiah, he said to him, "The LORD your God decreed this disaster for this place. 3And now the LORD has brought it about; he has done just as he said he would. All this happened because you people sinned against the LORD and did not obey him. 4But today I am freeing you from the chains on your wrists. Come with me to Babylon, if you like, and I will look after you; but if you do not want to, then don't come. Look, the whole country lies before you; go wherever you please." 5However, before Jeremiah turned to go,[a] Nebuzaradan added, "Go back to Gedaliah son of Ahikam, the son of Shaphan, whom the king of Babylon has appointed over the towns of Judah, and live with him among the people, or go anywhere else you please."

Then the commander gave him provisions and a present and let him go. 6So Jeremiah went to Gedaliah son of Ahikam at Mizpah and stayed with him among the people who were left behind in the land.

Gedaliah Assassinated

7When all the army officers and their men who were still in the open country heard that the king of Babylon had appointed Gedaliah son of Ahikam as governor over the land and had put him in charge of the men, women and children who were the poorest in the land and who had not been carried into exile to Babylon, 8they came to Gedaliah at Mizpah—Ishmael son of Nethaniah, Johanan and Jonathan the sons of Kareah, Seraiah son of Tanhumeth, the sons of Ephai the Netophathite, and Jaazaniah[b] the son of the Maacathite, and their men. 9Gedaliah son of Ahikam, the son of Shaphan, took an oath to reassure them and their men. "Do not be afraid to serve the Babylonians,[c]" he said. "Settle down in the land and serve the king of Babylon, and it will go well with you. 10I myself will stay at Mizpah to represent you before the Babylonians who come to us, but you are to harvest the wine, summer fruit and oil, and put them in your storage jars, and live in the towns you have taken over."

11When all the Jews in Moab, Ammon, Edom and all the other countries heard that the king of Babylon had left a remnant in Judah and had appointed Gedaliah son of Ahikam, the son of Shaphan, as governor over them, 12they all came back to the land of Judah, to Gedaliah at Mizpah, from all the countries where they had been scattered. And they harvested an abundance of wine and summer fruit.

13Johanan son of Kareah and all the army officers still in the open country came to Gedaliah at Mizpah 14and said to him, "Don't you know that Baalis king of the Ammonites has sent Ishmael son of Nethaniah to take your life?" But Gedaliah son of Ahikam did not believe them.

15Then Johanan son of Kareah said privately to Gedaliah in Mizpah, "Let me go and kill Ishmael son of Nethaniah, and

[a] 5 Or *Jeremiah answered* [b] 8 Hebrew *Jezaniah,* a variant of *Jaazaniah* [c] 9 Or *Chaldeans;* also in verse 10

no one will know it. Why should he take
your life and cause all the Jews who are
gathered around you to be scattered and
the remnant of Judah to perish?"

[16]But Gedaliah son of Ahikam said to
Johanan son of Kareah, "Don't do such a
thing! What you are saying about Ishmael is not true."

PRAYER: RENEWAL

I WILL stand firm. I will gird my waist with truth, put on the breastplate of righteousness, fit my feet with the readiness of the gospel of peace and take up the shield of faith with which I will be able to quench all the fiery darts of the evil one. I will take the helmet of salvation and the sword of the Spirit, which is Your word, O God. With all prayer and petition, I will pray always in the Spirit, and to this end I will be watchful with all perseverance and petition for all the saints. (Ephesians 6:14–18)

***PAUSE** to add your own prayers for personal renewal.*

NT Luke 22:39–71

Jesus Prays on the Mount of Olives

[39]Jesus went out as usual to the Mount
of Olives, and his disciples followed him.
[40]On reaching the place, he said to them,
"Pray that you will not fall into temptation." [41]He withdrew about a stone's
throw beyond them, knelt down and
prayed, [42]"Father, if you are willing, take
this cup from me; yet not my will, but
yours be done." [43]An angel from heaven
appeared to him and strengthened him.
[44]And being in anguish, he prayed more
earnestly, and his sweat was like drops of
blood falling to the ground.[a]
[45]When he rose from prayer and went
back to the disciples, he found them asleep,
exhausted from sorrow. [46]"Why are you
sleeping?" he asked them. "Get up and pray
so that you will not fall into temptation."

Jesus Arrested

[47]While he was still speaking a crowd
came up, and the man who was called Judas, one of the Twelve, was leading them.
He approached Jesus to kiss him, [48]but
Jesus asked him, "Judas, are you betraying
the Son of Man with a kiss?"
[49]When Jesus' followers saw what was
going to happen, they said, "Lord, should
we strike with our swords?" [50]And one of
them struck the servant of the high priest,
cutting off his right ear.
[51]But Jesus answered, "No more of
this!" And he touched the man's ear and
healed him.
[52]Then Jesus said to the chief priests, the
officers of the temple guard, and the elders, who had come for him, "Am I leading a rebellion, that you have come with
swords and clubs? [53]Every day I was with
you in the temple courts, and you did not
lay a hand on me. But this is your hour—
when darkness reigns."

Peter Disowns Jesus

[54]Then seizing him, they led him away
and took him into the house of the high
priest. Peter followed at a distance. [55]But
when they had kindled a fire in the middle of the courtyard and had sat down together, Peter sat down with them. [56]A servant girl saw him seated there in the
firelight. She looked closely at him and
said, "This man was with him."
[57]But he denied it. "Woman, I don't
know him," he said.
[58]A little later someone else saw him
and said, "You also are one of them."
"Man, I am not!" Peter replied.
[59]About an hour later another asserted,
"Certainly this fellow was with him, for
he is a Galilean."
[60]Peter replied, "Man, I don't know
what you're talking about!" Just as he was
speaking, the rooster crowed. [61]The Lord
turned and looked straight at Peter. Then
Peter remembered the word the Lord had
spoken to him: "Before the rooster crows

[a] *44* Some early manuscripts do not have verses 43 and 44.

today, you will disown me three times."
62And he went outside and wept bitterly.

The Guards Mock Jesus

63The men who were guarding Jesus began mocking and beating him. 64They
blindfolded him and demanded, "Prophesy! Who hit you?" 65And they said many
other insulting things to him.

Jesus Before Pilate and Herod

66At daybreak the council of the elders
of the people, both the chief priests and
teachers of the law, met together, and
Jesus was led before them. 67"If you are
the Christ,[b]" they said, "tell us."

Jesus answered, "If I tell you, you will
not believe me, 68and if I asked you, you
would not answer. 69But from now on, the
Son of Man will be seated at the right
hand of the mighty God."

70They all asked, "Are you then the Son
of God?"

He replied, "You are right in saying
I am."

71Then they said, "Why do we need any
more testimony? We have heard it from
his own lips."

[b]67 Or *Messiah*

PRAYER: THE ATTRIBUTES OF GOD

YOU, O Lord, are the true God; You are the living God and the everlasting King. At Your wrath the earth trembles, and the nations cannot endure Your indignation. (Jeremiah 10:10) . . . You, Lord Jesus, are the first and the last and the Living One; You were dead, and behold, You are alive forevermore and hold the keys of death and of Hades. (Revelation 1:17–18)

PAUSE *to reflect on these affirmations about the person, powers and perfection of God.*

YEAR 2
DAY 227

OT Jeremiah 41:1–18

41 In the seventh month Ishmael son of
Nethaniah, the son of Elishama, who
was of royal blood and had been one of
the king's officers, came with ten men to
Gedaliah son of Ahikam at Mizpah. While
they were eating together there, 2Ishmael
son of Nethaniah and the ten men who
were with him got up and struck down
Gedaliah son of Ahikam, the son of Shaphan, with the sword, killing the one
whom the king of Babylon had appointed as governor over the land. 3Ishmael
also killed all the Jews who were with
Gedaliah at Mizpah, as well as the Babylonian[a] soldiers who were there.

4The day after Gedaliah's assassination,
before anyone knew about it, 5eighty men
who had shaved off their beards, torn their
clothes and cut themselves came from Shechem, Shiloh and Samaria, bringing grain
offerings and incense with them to the
house of the LORD. 6Ishmael son of Nethaniah went out from Mizpah to meet
them, weeping as he went. When he met
them, he said, "Come to Gedaliah son of
Ahikam." 7When they went into the city,
Ishmael son of Nethaniah and the men
who were with him slaughtered them and
threw them into a cistern. 8But ten of them
said to Ishmael, "Don't kill us! We have
wheat and barley, oil and honey, hidden in
a field." So he let them alone and did not
kill them with the others. 9Now the cistern
where he threw all the bodies of the men
he had killed along with Gedaliah was the
one King Asa had made as part of his defense against Baasha king of Israel. Ishmael son of Nethaniah filled it with the dead.

10Ishmael made captives of all the rest of
the people who were in Mizpah—the king's
daughters along with all the others who
were left there, over whom Nebuzaradan
commander of the imperial guard had ap-

[a]3 Or *Chaldean*

pointed Gedaliah son of Ahikam. Ishmael son of Nethaniah took them captive and set out to cross over to the Ammonites.

[11]When Johanan son of Kareah and all the army officers who were with him heard about all the crimes Ishmael son of Nethaniah had committed, [12]they took all their men and went to fight Ishmael son of Nethaniah. They caught up with him near the great pool in Gibeon. [13]When all the people Ishmael had with him saw Johanan son of Kareah and the army officers who were with him, they were glad. [14]All the people Ishmael had taken captive at Mizpah turned and went over to Johanan son of Kareah. [15]But Ishmael son of Nethaniah and eight of his men escaped from Johanan and fled to the Ammonites.

Flight to Egypt

[16]Then Johanan son of Kareah and all the army officers who were with him led away all the survivors from Mizpah whom he had recovered from Ishmael son of Nethaniah after he had assassinated Gedaliah son of Ahikam: the soldiers, women, children and court officials he had brought from Gibeon. [17]And they went on, stopping at Geruth Kimham near Bethlehem on their way to Egypt [18]to escape the Babylonians.[b] They were afraid of them because Ishmael son of Nethaniah had killed Gedaliah son of Ahikam, whom the king of Babylon had appointed as governor over the land.

[b] 18 Or *Chaldeans*

PRAYER: PETITION

O LORD, that You would bless me and enlarge my territory! Let Your hand be with me and keep me from evil, so it may not grieve me. (1 Chronicles 4:10)

PAUSE *here to petition God for growth in your desire to know and please Jesus Christ. Pray for a greater love and commitment to Him, for the grace to practice His presence and for the grace to glorify Him in your life. Offer prayers regarding your activities for this day and any special concerns you may have.*

NT Luke 23:1-43

23 Then the whole assembly rose and led him off to Pilate. [2]And they began to accuse him, saying, "We have found this man subverting our nation. He opposes payment of taxes to Caesar and claims to be Christ,[a] a king."

[3]So Pilate asked Jesus, "Are you the king of the Jews?"

"Yes, it is as you say," Jesus replied.

[4]Then Pilate announced to the chief priests and the crowd, "I find no basis for a charge against this man."

[5]But they insisted, "He stirs up the people all over Judea[b] by his teaching. He started in Galilee and has come all the way here."

[6]On hearing this, Pilate asked if the man was a Galilean. [7]When he learned that Jesus was under Herod's jurisdiction, he sent him to Herod, who was also in Jerusalem at that time.

[8]When Herod saw Jesus, he was greatly pleased, because for a long time he had been wanting to see him. From what he had heard about him, he hoped to see him perform some miracle. [9]He plied him with many questions, but Jesus gave him no answer. [10]The chief priests and the teachers of the law were standing there, vehemently accusing him. [11]Then Herod and his soldiers ridiculed and mocked him. Dressing him in an elegant robe, they sent him back to Pilate. [12]That day Herod and Pilate became friends—before this they had been enemies.

[13]Pilate called together the chief priests, the rulers and the people, [14]and said to them, "You brought me this man as one who was inciting the people to rebellion. I have examined him in your presence and have found no basis for your charges against him. [15]Neither has Herod, for he sent him back to us; as you can see, he has

[a] 2 Or *Messiah;* also in verses 35 and 39 [b] 5 Or *over the land of the Jews*

done nothing to deserve death. 16There-
fore, I will punish him and then release
him.[c]"
18With one voice they cried out, "Away
with this man! Release Barabbas to us!"
19(Barabbas had been thrown into prison
for an insurrection in the city, and for
murder.)
20Wanting to release Jesus, Pilate appealed to them again. 21But they kept
shouting, "Crucify him! Crucify him!"
22For the third time he spoke to them:
"Why? What crime has this man committed? I have found in him no grounds for
the death penalty. Therefore I will have
him punished and then release him."
23But with loud shouts they insistently
demanded that he be crucified, and their
shouts prevailed. 24So Pilate decided to
grant their demand. 25He released the
man who had been thrown into prison
for insurrection and murder, the one they
asked for, and surrendered Jesus to their
will.

The Crucifixion

26As they led him away, they seized Simon from Cyrene, who was on his way in
from the country, and put the cross on
him and made him carry it behind Jesus.
27A large number of people followed him,
including women who mourned and
wailed for him. 28Jesus turned and said to
them, "Daughters of Jerusalem, do not
weep for me; weep for yourselves and for
your children. 29For the time will come
when you will say, 'Blessed are the barren
women, the wombs that never bore and
the breasts that never nursed!' 30Then

" 'they will say to the mountains, "Fall
on us!"
and to the hills, "Cover us!" '[d]

31For if men do these things when the tree
is green, what will happen when it is dry?"
32Two other men, both criminals, were
also led out with him to be executed.
33When they came to the place called the
Skull, there they crucified him, along with
the criminals—one on his right, the other on his left. 34Jesus said, "Father, forgive
them, for they do not know what they are
doing."[e] And they divided up his clothes
by casting lots.
35The people stood watching, and the
rulers even sneered at him. They said, "He
saved others; let him save himself if he is
the Christ of God, the Chosen One."
36The soldiers also came up and
mocked him. They offered him wine vinegar 37and said, "If you are the king of the
Jews, save yourself."
38There was a written notice above him,
which read: THIS IS THE KING OF THE JEWS.
39One of the criminals who hung there
hurled insults at him: "Aren't you the
Christ? Save yourself and us!"
40But the other criminal rebuked him.
"Don't you fear God," he said, "since you
are under the same sentence? 41We are
punished justly, for we are getting what
our deeds deserve. But this man has done
nothing wrong."
42Then he said, "Jesus, remember me
when you come into your kingdom.[f]"
43Jesus answered him, "I tell you the
truth, today you will be with me in paradise."

[c] 16 Some manuscripts *him." 17Now he was obliged to release one man to them at the Feast.* [d] 30 Hosea 10:8 [e] 34 Some early manuscripts do not have this sentence. [f] 42 Some manuscripts *come with your kingly power*

PRAYER: THE WORKS OF GOD

YOU, O God, will have mercy on whom You have mercy, and You will have compassion on whom You have compassion. It does not depend on human desire or effort, but on Your mercy.

(Romans 9:15–16)

TAKE *a moment to consider the greatness of God's wonderful works.*

OT Proverbs 26

26 Like snow in summer or rain in harvest,
honor is not fitting for a fool.

[2] Like a fluttering sparrow or a darting swallow,
an undeserved curse does not come to rest.

[3] A whip for the horse, a halter for the donkey,
and a rod for the backs of fools!

[4] Do not answer a fool according to his folly,
or you will be like him yourself.

[5] Answer a fool according to his folly,
or he will be wise in his own eyes.

[6] Like cutting off one's feet or drinking violence
is the sending of a message by the hand of a fool.

[7] Like a lame man's legs that hang limp
is a proverb in the mouth of a fool.

[8] Like tying a stone in a sling
is the giving of honor to a fool.

[9] Like a thornbush in a drunkard's hand
is a proverb in the mouth of a fool.

[10] Like an archer who wounds at random
is he who hires a fool or any passer-by.

[11] As a dog returns to its vomit,
so a fool repeats his folly.

[12] Do you see a man wise in his own eyes?
There is more hope for a fool than for him.

[13] The sluggard says, "There is a lion in the road,
a fierce lion roaming the streets!"

[14] As a door turns on its hinges,
so a sluggard turns on his bed.

[15] The sluggard buries his hand in the dish;
he is too lazy to bring it back to his mouth.

[16] The sluggard is wiser in his own eyes
than seven men who answer discreetly.

[17] Like one who seizes a dog by the ears
is a passer-by who meddles in a quarrel not his own.

[18] Like a madman shooting firebrands or deadly arrows
[19] is a man who deceives his neighbor
and says, "I was only joking!"

[20] Without wood a fire goes out;
without gossip a quarrel dies down.

[21] As charcoal to embers and as wood to fire,
so is a quarrelsome man for kindling strife.

[22] The words of a gossip are like choice morsels;
they go down to a man's inmost parts.

[23] Like a coating of glaze[a] over earthenware
are fervent lips with an evil heart.

[24] A malicious man disguises himself with his lips,
but in his heart he harbors deceit.
[25] Though his speech is charming, do not believe him,
for seven abominations fill his heart.
[26] His malice may be concealed by deception,
but his wickedness will be exposed in the assembly.

[27] If a man digs a pit, he will fall into it;
if a man rolls a stone, it will roll back on him.

[28] A lying tongue hates those it hurts,
and a flattering mouth works ruin.

[a] 23 With a different word division of the Hebrew; Masoretic Text *of silver dross*

PRAYER: INTERCESSION

LORD Jesus, grace has been given to each one of us according to the measure of Your gift. And You gave some to be apostles, some to be prophets, some to be evangelists and some to be pastors and teachers, to equip the saints for the work of ministry so that Your body will be built up, O Christ. (Ephesians 4:7, 11–12)

__TAKE__ a few moments to intercede on behalf of your local church, other churches, evangelism and discipleship ministries, educational ministries and any other special concerns you may have.

NT Luke 23:44–24:12

Jesus' Death

44 It was now about the sixth hour, and darkness came over the whole land until the ninth hour, 45 for the sun stopped shining. And the curtain of the temple was torn in two. 46 Jesus called out with a loud voice, "Father, into your hands I commit my spirit." When he had said this, he breathed his last.

47 The centurion, seeing what had happened, praised God and said, "Surely this was a righteous man." 48 When all the people who had gathered to witness this sight saw what took place, they beat their breasts and went away. 49 But all those who knew him, including the women who had followed him from Galilee, stood at a distance, watching these things.

Jesus' Burial

50 Now there was a man named Joseph, a member of the Council, a good and upright man, 51 who had not consented to their decision and action. He came from the Judean town of Arimathea and he was waiting for the kingdom of God. 52 Going to Pilate, he asked for Jesus' body. 53 Then he took it down, wrapped it in linen cloth and placed it in a tomb cut in the rock, one in which no one had yet been laid. 54 It was Preparation Day, and the Sabbath was about to begin.

55 The women who had come with Jesus from Galilee followed Joseph and saw the tomb and how his body was laid in it. 56 Then they went home and prepared spices and perfumes. But they rested on the Sabbath in obedience to the commandment.

The Resurrection

24 On the first day of the week, very early in the morning, the women took the spices they had prepared and went to the tomb. 2 They found the stone rolled away from the tomb, 3 but when they entered, they did not find the body of the Lord Jesus. 4 While they were wondering about this, suddenly two men in clothes that gleamed like lightning stood beside them. 5 In their fright the women bowed down with their faces to the ground, but the men said to them, "Why do you look for the living among the dead? 6 He is not here; he has risen! Remember how he told you, while he was still with you in Galilee: 7 'The Son of Man must be delivered into the hands of sinful men, be crucified and on the third day be raised again.' " 8 Then they remembered his words.

9 When they came back from the tomb, they told all these things to the Eleven and to all the others. 10 It was Mary Magdalene, Joanna, Mary the mother of James, and the others with them who told this to the apostles. 11 But they did not believe the women, because their words seemed to them like nonsense. 12 Peter, however, got up and ran to the tomb. Bending over, he saw the strips of linen lying by themselves, and he went away, wondering to himself what had happened.

PRAYER: MY RELATIONSHIP TO GOD

WITHOUT faith it is impossible to please You, O God, for those who come to You must believe that You exist, and that You reward those who earnestly seek You. (Hebrews 11:6) . . . Through faith I am guarded by Your power, O God, for salvation that is ready to be revealed in the last time. (1 Peter 1:5)

__PAUSE__ to thank God for the relationship that you enjoy with Him in Jesus Christ.

YEAR 2 DAY 229

OT Jeremiah 42:1–43:13

42 Then all the army officers, including
Johanan son of Kareah and Jezaniah[a]
son of Hoshaiah, and all the people from
the least to the greatest approached [2]Jere-
miah the prophet and said to him, "Please
hear our petition and pray to the LORD
your God for this entire remnant. For as
you now see, though we were once many,
now only a few are left. [3]Pray that the
LORD your God will tell us where we
should go and what we should do."
[4]"I have heard you," replied Jeremiah
the prophet. "I will certainly pray to the
LORD your God as you have requested; I
will tell you everything the LORD says and
will keep nothing back from you."
[5]Then they said to Jeremiah, "May the
LORD be a true and faithful witness against
us if we do not act in accordance with
everything the LORD your God sends you
to tell us. [6]Whether it is favorable or un-
favorable, we will obey the LORD our God,
to whom we are sending you, so that it
will go well with us, for we will obey the
LORD our God."
[7]Ten days later the word of the LORD
came to Jeremiah. [8]So he called together
Johanan son of Kareah and all the army
officers who were with him and all the
people from the least to the greatest. [9]He
said to them, "This is what the LORD, the
God of Israel, to whom you sent me to
present your petition, says: [10]'If you stay in
this land, I will build you up and not tear
you down; I will plant you and not uproot
you, for I am grieved over the disaster I
have inflicted on you. [11]Do not be afraid
of the king of Babylon, whom you now
fear. Do not be afraid of him, declares the
LORD, for I am with you and will save you
and deliver you from his hands. [12]I will
show you compassion so that he will have
compassion on you and restore you to
your land.'
[13]"However, if you say, 'We will not stay
in this land,' and so disobey the LORD your
God, [14]and if you say, 'No, we will go and
live in Egypt, where we will not see war or
hear the trumpet or be hungry for bread,'
[15]then hear the word of the LORD, O remnant of Judah. This is what the LORD
Almighty, the God of Israel, says: 'If you
are determined to go to Egypt and you do
go to settle there, [16]then the sword you
fear will overtake you there, and the
famine you dread will follow you into
Egypt, and there you will die. [17]Indeed, all
who are determined to go to Egypt to settle there will die by the sword, famine and
plague; not one of them will survive or escape the disaster I will bring on them.'
[18]This is what the LORD Almighty, the God
of Israel, says: 'As my anger and wrath
have been poured out on those who lived
in Jerusalem, so will my wrath be poured
out on you when you go to Egypt. You
will be an object of cursing and horror, of
condemnation and reproach; you will
never see this place again.'
[19]"O remnant of Judah, the LORD has
told you, 'Do not go to Egypt.' Be sure of
this: I warn you today [20]that you made a
fatal mistake[b] when you sent me to the
LORD your God and said, 'Pray to the LORD
our God for us; tell us everything he says
and we will do it.' [21]I have told you today,
but you still have not obeyed the LORD
your God in all he sent me to tell you. [22]So

[a] 1 Hebrew; Septuagint (see also 43:2) *Azariah*
[b] 20 Or *you erred in your hearts*

now, be sure of this: You will die by the
sword, famine and plague in the place
where you want to go to settle."

43 When Jeremiah finished telling the
people all the words of the LORD their
God—everything the LORD had sent him
to tell them— 2Azariah son of Hoshaiah
and Johanan son of Kareah and all the arrogant men said to Jeremiah, "You are lying! The LORD our God has not sent you
to say, 'You must not go to Egypt to settle
there.' 3But Baruch son of Neriah is inciting you against us to hand us over to the
Babylonians,[c] so they may kill us or carry
us into exile to Babylon."

4So Johanan son of Kareah and all the
army officers and all the people disobeyed
the LORD's command to stay in the land
of Judah. 5Instead, Johanan son of Kareah and all the army officers led away all
the remnant of Judah who had come back
to live in the land of Judah from all the
nations where they had been scattered.
6They also led away all the men, women
and children and the king's daughters
whom Nebuzaradan commander of the
imperial guard had left with Gedaliah son
of Ahikam, the son of Shaphan, and Jeremiah the prophet and Baruch son of Neriah. 7So they entered Egypt in disobedience to the LORD and went as far as Tahpanhes.

8In Tahpanhes the word of the LORD
came to Jeremiah: 9"While the Jews are
watching, take some large stones with you
and bury them in clay in the brick pavement at the entrance to Pharaoh's palace
in Tahpanhes. 10Then say to them, 'This is
what the LORD Almighty, the God of Israel, says: I will send for my servant Nebuchadnezzar king of Babylon, and I will set
his throne over these stones I have buried
here; he will spread his royal canopy above
them. 11He will come and attack Egypt,
bringing death to those destined for death,
captivity to those destined for captivity,
and the sword to those destined for the
sword. 12He[d] will set fire to the temples of
the gods of Egypt; he will burn their temples and take their gods captive. As a shepherd wraps his garment around him, so
will he wrap Egypt around himself and depart from there unscathed. 13There in the
temple of the sun[e] in Egypt he will demolish the sacred pillars and will burn
down the temples of the gods of Egypt.' "

[c] 3 Or *Chaldeans* [d] 12 Or *I* [e] 13 Or *in Heliopolis*

PRAYER: AFFIRMATION

AS Moses lifted up the snake in the desert, so You, Son of Man, had to be lifted up so that everyone who believes in You may have eternal life. Those who believe in You, Jesus, are not condemned, but those who do not believe are condemned already, because they have not believed in Your name—You who are the only begotten Son of God.

(John 3:14–15, 18)

PAUSE *to reflect on these Biblical affirmations.*

NT Luke 24:13–53

On the Road to Emmaus

13Now that same day two of them were
going to a village called Emmaus, about
seven miles[a] from Jerusalem. 14They were
talking with each other about everything
that had happened. 15As they talked and
discussed these things with each other,
Jesus himself came up and walked along
with them; 16but they were kept from rec-
ognizing him.

17He asked them, "What are you discussing together as you walk along?"
They stood still, their faces downcast.
18One of them, named Cleopas, asked
him, "Are you only a visitor to Jerusalem
and do not know the things that have
happened there in these days?"

19"What things?" he asked.

"About Jesus of Nazareth," they replied.
"He was a prophet, powerful in word and
deed before God and all the people. 20The
chief priests and our rulers handed him
over to be sentenced to death, and they cru-

[a] 13 Greek *sixty stadia* (about 11 kilometers)

cified him; 21but we had hoped that he was
the one who was going to redeem Israel.
And what is more, it is the third day since
all this took place. 22In addition, some of
our women amazed us. They went to the
tomb early this morning 23but didn't find
his body. They came and told us that they
had seen a vision of angels, who said he
was alive. 24Then some of our companions
went to the tomb and found it just as the
women had said, but him they did not see."

25He said to them, "How foolish you
are, and how slow of heart to believe all
that the prophets have spoken! 26Did not
the Christ[b] have to suffer these things and
then enter his glory?" 27And beginning
with Moses and all the Prophets, he explained to them what was said in all the
Scriptures concerning himself.

28As they approached the village to
which they were going, Jesus acted as if he
were going farther. 29But they urged him
strongly, "Stay with us, for it is nearly
evening; the day is almost over." So he
went in to stay with them.

30When he was at the table with them, he
took bread, gave thanks, broke it and began
to give it to them. 31Then their eyes were
opened and they recognized him, and he
disappeared from their sight. 32They asked
each other, "Were not our hearts burning
within us while he talked with us on the
road and opened the Scriptures to us?"

33They got up and returned at once to
Jerusalem. There they found the Eleven
and those with them, assembled together
34and saying, "It is true! The Lord has risen
and has appeared to Simon." 35Then the
two told what had happened on the way,
and how Jesus was recognized by them
when he broke the bread.

Jesus Appears to the Disciples

36While they were still talking about
this, Jesus himself stood among them and
said to them, "Peace be with you."

37They were startled and frightened,
thinking they saw a ghost. 38He said to
them, "Why are you troubled, and why do
doubts rise in your minds? 39Look at my
hands and my feet. It is I myself! Touch
me and see; a ghost does not have flesh
and bones, as you see I have."

40When he had said this, he showed
them his hands and feet. 41And while they
still did not believe it because of joy and
amazement, he asked them, "Do you have
anything here to eat?" 42They gave him a
piece of broiled fish, 43and he took it and
ate it in their presence.

44He said to them, "This is what I told
you while I was still with you: Everything
must be fulfilled that is written about me
in the Law of Moses, the Prophets and the
Psalms."

45Then he opened their minds so they
could understand the Scriptures. 46He told
them, "This is what is written: The Christ
will suffer and rise from the dead on the
third day, 47and repentance and forgiveness of sins will be preached in his name
to all nations, beginning at Jerusalem.
48You are witnesses of these things. 49I am
going to send you what my Father has
promised; but stay in the city until you
have been clothed with power from on
high."

The Ascension

50When he had led them out to the
vicinity of Bethany, he lifted up his hands
and blessed them. 51While he was blessing
them, he left them and was taken up into
heaven. 52Then they worshiped him and
returned to Jerusalem with great joy.
53And they stayed continually at the temple, praising God.

[b] 26 Or *Messiah;* also in verse 46

PRAYER: THE CHARACTER I WANT TO CULTIVATE

O LORD, I will make it my ambition to lead a quiet life, to mind my own business, and to work with my own hands, so that I may walk properly toward those who are outside and lack nothing.

(1 Thessalonians 4:11–12)

***TAKE** a moment to ask the Lord for the grace to grow in godly character.*

OT **Jeremiah 44:1–45:5** YEAR 2 DAY 230

Disaster Because of Idolatry

44 This word came to Jeremiah concerning all the Jews living in Lower Egypt—in Migdol, Tahpanhes and Memphis[a]—and in Upper Egypt[b]: 2 "This is what the LORD Almighty, the God of Israel, says: You saw the great disaster I brought on Jerusalem and on all the towns of Judah. Today they lie deserted and in ruins 3 because of the evil they have done. They provoked me to anger by burning incense and by worshiping other gods that neither they nor you nor your fathers ever knew. 4 Again and again I sent my servants the prophets, who said, 'Do not do this detestable thing that I hate!' 5 But they did not listen or pay attention; they did not turn from their wickedness or stop burning incense to other gods. 6 Therefore, my fierce anger was poured out; it raged against the towns of Judah and the streets of Jerusalem and made them the desolate ruins they are today.

7 "Now this is what the LORD God Almighty, the God of Israel, says: Why bring such great disaster on yourselves by cutting off from Judah the men and women, the children and infants, and so leave yourselves without a remnant? 8 Why provoke me to anger with what your hands have made, burning incense to other gods in Egypt, where you have come to live? You will destroy yourselves and make yourselves an object of cursing and reproach among all the nations on earth. 9 Have you forgotten the wickedness committed by your fathers and by the kings and queens of Judah and the wickedness committed by you and your wives in the land of Judah and the streets of Jerusalem? 10 To this day they have not humbled themselves or shown reverence, nor have they followed my law and the decrees I set before you and your fathers.

11 "Therefore, this is what the LORD Almighty, the God of Israel, says: I am determined to bring disaster on you and to destroy all Judah. 12 I will take away the remnant of Judah who were determined to go to Egypt to settle there. They will all perish in Egypt; they will fall by the sword or die from famine. From the least to the greatest, they will die by sword or famine. They will become an object of cursing and horror, of condemnation and reproach. 13 I will punish those who live in Egypt with the sword, famine and plague, as I punished Jerusalem. 14 None of the remnant of Judah who have gone to live in Egypt will escape or survive to return to the land of Judah, to which they long to return and live; none will return except a few fugitives."

15 Then all the men who knew that their wives were burning incense to other gods, along with all the women who were present—a large assembly—and all the people living in Lower and Upper Egypt,[c] said to Jeremiah, 16 "We will not listen to the message you have spoken to us in the name of the LORD! 17 We will certainly do everything we said we would: We will burn incense to the Queen of Heaven and will pour out drink offerings to her just as we and our fathers, our kings and our officials did in the towns of Judah and in the streets of Jerusalem. At that time we had plenty of food and were well off and suffered no harm. 18 But ever since we stopped burning incense to the Queen of Heaven and pouring out drink offerings to her, we have had nothing and have been perishing by sword and famine."

19 The women added, "When we burned incense to the Queen of Heaven and poured out drink offerings to her, did not our husbands know that we were making cakes like her image and pouring out drink offerings to her?"

20 Then Jeremiah said to all the people, both men and women, who were answering him, 21 "Did not the LORD remember and think about the incense burned in the towns of Judah and the streets of Jerusalem by you and your fathers, your kings and your officials and the people of the land? 22 When the LORD could no longer endure your wicked actions and the detestable things you did, your land became an object of cursing and a desolate waste without inhabitants, as it is today. 23 Because you have burned incense and have sinned against the LORD and have not obeyed him or followed his law or his de-

[a] 1 Hebrew *Noph* [b] 1 Hebrew *in Pathros*
[c] 15 Hebrew *in Egypt and Pathros*

crees or his stipulations, this disaster has come upon you, as you now see."

24Then Jeremiah said to all the people, including the women, "Hear the word of the LORD, all you people of Judah in Egypt. 25This is what the LORD Almighty, the God of Israel, says: You and your wives have shown by your actions what you promised when you said, 'We will certainly carry out the vows we made to burn incense and pour out drink offerings to the Queen of Heaven.'

"Go ahead then, do what you promised! Keep your vows! 26But hear the word of the LORD, all Jews living in Egypt: 'I swear by my great name,' says the LORD, 'that no one from Judah living anywhere in Egypt will ever again invoke my name or swear, "As surely as the Sovereign LORD lives." 27For I am watching over them for harm, not for good; the Jews in Egypt will perish by sword and famine until they are all destroyed. 28Those who escape the sword and return to the land of Judah from Egypt will be very few. Then the whole remnant of Judah who came to live in Egypt will know whose word will stand—mine or theirs.

29" 'This will be the sign to you that I will punish you in this place,' declares the LORD, 'so that you will know that my threats of harm against you will surely stand.' 30This is what the LORD says: 'I am going to hand Pharaoh Hophra king of Egypt over to his enemies who seek his life, just as I handed Zedekiah king of Judah over to Nebuchadnezzar king of Babylon, the enemy who was seeking his life.' "

A Message to Baruch

45 This is what Jeremiah the prophet told Baruch son of Neriah in the fourth year of Jehoiakim son of Josiah king of Judah, after Baruch had written on a scroll the words Jeremiah was then dictating: 2"This is what the LORD, the God of Israel, says to you, Baruch: 3You said, 'Woe to me! The LORD has added sorrow to my pain; I am worn out with groaning and find no rest.' "

4⌊The LORD said,⌋ "Say this to him: 'This is what the LORD says: I will overthrow what I have built and uproot what I have planted, throughout the land. 5Should you then seek great things for yourself? Seek them not. For I will bring disaster on all people, declares the LORD, but wherever you go I will let you escape with your life.' "

PRAYER: THANKSGIVING

WE are not to be ignorant about those who fall asleep or grieve like other people who have no hope. For if we believe that You, Jesus, died and rose again, even so the Father will bring with You those who have fallen asleep in You. According to Your own word, we who are alive and remain until Your coming will not precede those who have fallen asleep. For You Yourself will come down from heaven with a loud command, with the voice of the archangel, and with the trumpet of God, and the dead in You will rise first. Then we who are alive and remain will be caught up together with them in the clouds to meet You in the air. And so we will be with You forever.

(1 Thessalonians 4:13–17)

PAUSE *to offer your own expressions of thanksgiving.*

NT 1 Thessalonians 1:1–10

1 Paul, Silas[a] and Timothy,

To the church of the Thessalonians in God the Father and the Lord Jesus Christ:

Grace and peace to you.[b]

Thanksgiving for the Thessalonians' Faith

2We always thank God for all of you,

[a] 1 Greek *Silvanus*, a variant of *Silas* [b] 1 Some early manuscripts *you from God our Father and the Lord Jesus Christ*

mentioning you in our prayers. 3We continually remember before our God and
Father your work produced by faith, your
labor prompted by love, and your endurance inspired by hope in our Lord
Jesus Christ.
4For we know, brothers loved by God,
that he has chosen you, 5because our
gospel came to you not simply with
words, but also with power, with the Holy
Spirit and with deep conviction. You know
how we lived among you for your sake.
6You became imitators of us and of the
Lord; in spite of severe suffering, you welcomed the message with the joy given by
the Holy Spirit. 7And so you became a
model to all the believers in Macedonia
and Achaia. 8The Lord's message rang out
from you not only in Macedonia and
Achaia—your faith in God has become
known everywhere. Therefore we do not
need to say anything about it, 9for they
themselves report what kind of reception
you gave us. They tell how you turned to
God from idols to serve the living and true
God, 10and to wait for his Son from heav-
en, whom he raised from the dead—Jesus,
who rescues us from the coming wrath.

PRAYER: MY RELATIONSHIP TO OTHERS

WIVES should be submissive to their own husbands, so that if any of them do not believe the word, they may be won without a word by the behavior of their wives, when they see their purity and reverence. Husbands should be considerate as they live with their wives and treat them with respect as the weaker vessel and as co-heirs of the grace of life.

(1 Peter 3:1–2, 7)

***PAUSE** to review your relationships with others and to commit them to the Lord.*

OT Psalm 119:1-40

YEAR 2 DAY 231

Psalm 119[a]

א Aleph

1Blessed are they whose ways are
blameless,
who walk according to the law of
the LORD.
2Blessed are they who keep his statutes
and seek him with all their heart.
3They do nothing wrong;
they walk in his ways.
4You have laid down precepts
that are to be fully obeyed.
5Oh, that my ways were steadfast
in obeying your decrees!
6Then I would not be put to shame
when I consider all your
commands.
7I will praise you with an upright heart
as I learn your righteous laws.
8I will obey your decrees;
do not utterly forsake me.

ב Beth

9How can a young man keep his way
pure?
By living according to your word.
10I seek you with all my heart;
do not let me stray from your
commands.
11I have hidden your word in my heart
that I might not sin against you.
12Praise be to you, O LORD;
teach me your decrees.
13With my lips I recount
all the laws that come from your
mouth.
14I rejoice in following your statutes
as one rejoices in great riches.
15I meditate on your precepts
and consider your ways.
16I delight in your decrees;
I will not neglect your word.

[a] This psalm is an acrostic poem; the verses of each stanza begin with the same letter of the Hebrew alphabet.

ג Gimel

[17] Do good to your servant, and I will live;
I will obey your word.
[18] Open my eyes that I may see
wonderful things in your law.
[19] I am a stranger on earth;
do not hide your commands from me.
[20] My soul is consumed with longing
for your laws at all times.
[21] You rebuke the arrogant, who are cursed
and who stray from your commands.
[22] Remove from me scorn and contempt,
for I keep your statutes.
[23] Though rulers sit together and slander me,
your servant will meditate on your decrees.
[24] Your statutes are my delight;
they are my counselors.

ד Daleth

[25] I am laid low in the dust;
preserve my life according to your word.
[26] I recounted my ways and you answered me;
teach me your decrees.
[27] Let me understand the teaching of your precepts;
then I will meditate on your wonders.
[28] My soul is weary with sorrow;
strengthen me according to your word.
[29] Keep me from deceitful ways;
be gracious to me through your law.
[30] I have chosen the way of truth;
I have set my heart on your laws.
[31] I hold fast to your statutes, O LORD;
do not let me be put to shame.
[32] I run in the path of your commands,
for you have set my heart free.

ה He

[33] Teach me, O LORD, to follow your decrees;
then I will keep them to the end.
[34] Give me understanding, and I will keep your law
and obey it with all my heart.
[35] Direct me in the path of your commands,
for there I find delight.
[36] Turn my heart toward your statutes
and not toward selfish gain.
[37] Turn my eyes away from worthless things;
preserve my life according to your word.[b]
[38] Fulfill your promise to your servant,
so that you may be feared.
[39] Take away the disgrace I dread,
for your laws are good.
[40] How I long for your precepts!
Preserve my life in your righteousness.

[b] 37 Two manuscripts of the Masoretic Text and Dead Sea Scrolls; most manuscripts of the Masoretic Text *life in your way*

PRAYER: ADORATION

I PRAISE You, Lord! My soul praises You! I will praise You while I live; I will sing praises to You while I have my being. (Psalm 146:1–2) . . . My mouth will speak Your praise, O Lord, and all flesh will bless Your holy name for ever and ever. (Psalm 145:21)

__PAUSE__ to express your thoughts of praise and worship.

NT 1 Thessalonians 2:1–16

Paul's Ministry in Thessalonica

2 You know, brothers, that our visit to
you was not a failure. [2]We had previously suffered and been insulted in Philippi, as you know, but with the help of
our God we dared to tell you his gospel in
spite of strong opposition. [3]For the appeal
we make does not spring from error or
impure motives, nor are we trying to trick
you. [4]On the contrary, we speak as men
approved by God to be entrusted with the
gospel. We are not trying to please men

but God, who tests our hearts. 5You know we never used flattery, nor did we put on a mask to cover up greed—God is our witness. 6We were not looking for praise from men, not from you or anyone else.

As apostles of Christ we could have been a burden to you, 7but we were gentle among you, like a mother caring for her little children. 8We loved you so much that we were delighted to share with you not only the gospel of God but our lives as well, because you had become so dear to us. 9Surely you remember, brothers, our toil and hardship; we worked night and day in order not to be a burden to anyone while we preached the gospel of God to you.

10You are witnesses, and so is God, of how holy, righteous and blameless we were among you who believed. 11For you know that we dealt with each of you as a father deals with his own children, 12encouraging, comforting and urging you to live lives worthy of God, who calls you into his kingdom and glory.

13And we also thank God continually because, when you received the word of God, which you heard from us, you accepted it not as the word of men, but as it actually is, the word of God, which is at work in you who believe. 14For you, brothers, became imitators of God's churches in Judea, which are in Christ Jesus: You suffered from your own countrymen the same things those churches suffered from the Jews, 15who killed the Lord Jesus and the prophets and also drove us out. They displease God and are hostile to all men 16in their effort to keep us from speaking to the Gentiles so that they may be saved. In this way they always heap up their sins to the limit. The wrath of God has come upon them at last.[a]

[a] 16 Or *them fully*

PRAYER: THE ATTRIBUTES OF GOD

I KNOW that You can do all things and that no purpose of Yours can be thwarted. (Job 42:2) . . . From the rising of the sun to its setting, Your name, O Lord, is to be praised. You are high above all nations; Your glory is above the heavens. Who is like You, O Lord our God, the One who is enthroned on high, You who humble Yourself to behold the things that are in the heavens and in the earth? (Psalm 113:3–6)

PAUSE *to reflect on these affirmations about the person, powers and perfection of God.*

OT Jeremiah 46:1–28

YEAR 2 DAY 232

A Message About Egypt

46 This is the word of the LORD that came to Jeremiah the prophet concerning the nations:

2Concerning Egypt:

This is the message against the army of Pharaoh Neco king of Egypt, which was defeated at Carchemish on the Euphrates River by Nebuchadnezzar king of Babylon in the fourth year of Jehoiakim son of Josiah king of Judah:

3 "Prepare your shields, both large and small,
and march out for battle!
4 Harness the horses,
mount the steeds!
Take your positions
with helmets on!
Polish your spears,
put on your armor!
5 What do I see?
They are terrified,
they are retreating,
their warriors are defeated.
They flee in haste
without looking back,
and there is terror on every side,"
declares the LORD.
6 "The swift cannot flee
nor the strong escape.

In the north by the River Euphrates
they stumble and fall.

7 "Who is this that rises like the Nile,
like rivers of surging waters?
8 Egypt rises like the Nile,
like rivers of surging waters.
She says, 'I will rise and cover the earth;
I will destroy cities and their people.'
9 Charge, O horses!
Drive furiously, O charioteers!
March on, O warriors—
men of Cush[a] and Put who carry shields,
men of Lydia who draw the bow.
10 But that day belongs to the Lord, the LORD Almighty—
a day of vengeance, for vengeance on his foes.
The sword will devour till it is satisfied,
till it has quenched its thirst with blood.
For the Lord, the LORD Almighty, will offer sacrifice
in the land of the north by the River Euphrates.

11 "Go up to Gilead and get balm,
O Virgin Daughter of Egypt.
But you multiply remedies in vain;
there is no healing for you.
12 The nations will hear of your shame;
your cries will fill the earth.
One warrior will stumble over another;
both will fall down together."

13 This is the message the LORD spoke to
Jeremiah the prophet about the coming of
Nebuchadnezzar king of Babylon to at-
tack Egypt:

14 "Announce this in Egypt, and proclaim it in Migdol;
proclaim it also in Memphis[b] and Tahpanhes:
'Take your positions and get ready,
for the sword devours those around you.'
15 Why will your warriors be laid low?
They cannot stand, for the LORD will push them down.
16 They will stumble repeatedly;
they will fall over each other.
They will say, 'Get up, let us go back
to our own people and our native lands,
away from the sword of the oppressor.'
17 There they will exclaim,
'Pharaoh king of Egypt is only a loud noise;
he has missed his opportunity.'

18 "As surely as I live," declares the King,
whose name is the LORD Almighty,
"one will come who is like Tabor among the mountains,
like Carmel by the sea.
19 Pack your belongings for exile,
you who live in Egypt,
for Memphis will be laid waste
and lie in ruins without inhabitant.

20 "Egypt is a beautiful heifer,
but a gadfly is coming
against her from the north.
21 The mercenaries in her ranks
are like fattened calves.
They too will turn and flee together,
they will not stand their ground,
for the day of disaster is coming upon them,
the time for them to be punished.
22 Egypt will hiss like a fleeing serpent
as the enemy advances in force;
they will come against her with axes,
like men who cut down trees.
23 They will chop down her forest,"
declares the LORD,
"dense though it be.
They are more numerous than locusts,
they cannot be counted.
24 The Daughter of Egypt will be put to shame,
handed over to the people of the north."

25 The LORD Almighty, the God of Israel,
says: "I am about to bring punishment on
Amon god of Thebes,[c] on Pharaoh, on
Egypt and her gods and her kings, and on
those who rely on Pharaoh. 26 I will hand
them over to those who seek their lives, to
Nebuchadnezzar king of Babylon and his
officers. Later, however, Egypt will be inhabited as in times past," declares the LORD.

27 "Do not fear, O Jacob my servant;
do not be dismayed, O Israel.
I will surely save you out of a distant place,
your descendants from the land of their exile.
Jacob will again have peace and security,
and no one will make him afraid.

[a] 9 That is, the upper Nile region [b] 14 Hebrew *Noph*; also in verse 19 [c] 25 Hebrew *No*

[28]Do not fear, O Jacob my servant,
for I am with you," declares the LORD.
"Though I completely destroy all the nations
among which I scatter you,
I will not completely destroy you.
I will discipline you but only with justice;
I will not let you go entirely unpunished."

PRAYER: CONFESSION

O MY God, I am too ashamed and disgraced to lift up my face to You, because my sins have risen higher than my head and my guilt has reached to the heavens. (Ezra 9:6)

***ASK** the Spirit to search your heart and reveal any areas of unconfessed sin. Acknowledge these to the Lord and thank Him for His forgiveness.*

NT 1 Thessalonians 2:17–3:5

Paul's Longing to See the Thessalonians

[17]But, brothers, when we were torn
away from you for a short time (in person, not in thought), out of our intense
longing we made every effort to see you.
[18]For we wanted to come to you—certainly I, Paul, did, again and again—but Satan stopped us. [19]For what is our hope,
our joy, or the crown in which we will glory in the presence of our Lord Jesus when
he comes? Is it not you? [20]Indeed, you are
our glory and joy.
3 So when we could stand it no longer, we
thought it best to be left by ourselves in
Athens. [2]We sent Timothy, who is our
brother and God's fellow worker[a] in
spreading the gospel of Christ, to strength-
en and encourage you in your faith, [3]so that
no one would be unsettled by these trials.
You know quite well that we were destined
for them. [4]In fact, when we were with you,
we kept telling you that we would be persecuted. And it turned out that way, as you
well know. [5]For this reason, when I could
stand it no longer, I sent to find out about
your faith. I was afraid that in some way the
tempter might have tempted you and our
efforts might have been useless.

[a] 2 Some manuscripts *brother and fellow worker;* other manuscripts *brother and God's servant*

PRAYER: THE WORKS OF GOD

HOW shall we escape if we ignore Your great salvation? This salvation, which was first announced by the Lord Jesus, was confirmed by those who heard Him. You, O God, also bore witness to it by signs and wonders and various miracles and gifts of the Holy Spirit distributed according to Your will. (Hebrews 2:3–4)

***TAKE** a moment to consider the greatness of God's wonderful works.*

OT Jeremiah 47:1–7

YEAR 2 DAY 233

A Message About the Philistines

47 This is the word of the LORD that came to Jeremiah the prophet concerning the Philistines before Pharaoh attacked Gaza:

[2]This is what the LORD says:

"See how the waters are rising in the north;
they will become an overflowing torrent.
They will overflow the land and everything in it,

the towns and those who live in
them.
The people will cry out;
all who dwell in the land will wail
3 at the sound of the hoofs of galloping
steeds,
at the noise of enemy chariots
and the rumble of their wheels.
Fathers will not turn to help their
children;
their hands will hang limp.
4 For the day has come
to destroy all the Philistines
and to cut off all survivors
who could help Tyre and Sidon.
The LORD is about to destroy the
Philistines,
the remnant from the coasts of
Caphtor.[a]
5 Gaza will shave her head in mourning;
Ashkelon will be silenced.
O remnant on the plain,
how long will you cut yourselves?

6 " 'Ah, sword of the LORD,' ⌊you cry,⌋
'how long till you rest?
Return to your scabbard;
cease and be still.'
7 But how can it rest
when the LORD has commanded it,
when he has ordered it
to attack Ashkelon and the coast?"

[a] 4 That is, Crete

PRAYER: RENEWAL

MAY my attitude be the same as Yours, Christ Jesus; though You were in Your very nature God, You did not consider equality with Him something to be grasped, but emptied Yourself, becoming like a servant and being made in human form. And appearing as a human being, You humbled Yourself and became obedient to death, even death on a cross. May I seek Your interests, Christ Jesus, rather than my own. (Philippians 2:5–8, 21)

PAUSE *to add your own prayers for personal renewal.*

NT 1 Thessalonians 3:6–13

Timothy's Encouraging Report

6 But Timothy has just now come to us
from you and has brought good news
about your faith and love. He has told us
that you always have pleasant memories
of us and that you long to see us, just as
we also long to see you. 7 Therefore, brothers, in all our distress and persecution we
were encouraged about you because of
your faith. 8 For now we really live, since
you are standing firm in the Lord. 9 How
can we thank God enough for you in return for all the joy we have in the presence
of our God because of you? 10 Night and
day we pray most earnestly that we may
see you again and supply what is lacking
in your faith.

11 Now may our God and Father himself
and our Lord Jesus clear the way for us to
come to you. 12 May the Lord make your
love increase and overflow for each other
and for everyone else, just as ours does for
you. 13 May he strengthen your hearts so
that you will be blameless and holy in the
presence of our God and Father when our
Lord Jesus comes with all his holy ones.

PRAYER: MY RELATIONSHIP TO GOD

THOUGH You slay me, O God, yet will I hope in You. (Job 13:15) . . . If I seek to keep my life, I will lose it, and if I lose my life, I will preserve it. (Luke 17:33)

PAUSE *to thank God for the relationship that you enjoy with Him in Jesus Christ.*

OT Jeremiah 48:1-47

YEAR 2 DAY 234

A Message About Moab

48 Concerning Moab:

This is what the LORD Almighty, the God of Israel, says:

"Woe to Nebo, for it will be ruined.
Kiriathaim will be disgraced and captured;
the stronghold[a] will be disgraced and shattered.
2 Moab will be praised no more;
in Heshbon[b] men will plot her downfall:
'Come, let us put an end to that nation.'
You too, O Madmen,[c] will be silenced;
the sword will pursue you.
3 Listen to the cries from Horonaim,
cries of great havoc and destruction.
4 Moab will be broken;
her little ones will cry out.[d]
5 They go up the way to Luhith,
weeping bitterly as they go;
on the road down to Horonaim
anguished cries over the destruction are heard.
6 Flee! Run for your lives;
become like a bush[e] in the desert.
7 Since you trust in your deeds and riches,
you too will be taken captive,
and Chemosh will go into exile,
together with his priests and officials.
8 The destroyer will come against every town,
and not a town will escape.
The valley will be ruined
and the plateau destroyed,
because the LORD has spoken.
9 Put salt on Moab,
for she will be laid waste[f];
her towns will become desolate,
with no one to live in them.

10 "A curse on him who is lax in doing the LORD's work!
A curse on him who keeps his sword from bloodshed!

11 "Moab has been at rest from youth,
like wine left on its dregs,
not poured from one jar to another—
she has not gone into exile.
So she tastes as she did,
and her aroma is unchanged.
12 But days are coming,"
declares the LORD,
"when I will send men who pour from jars,
and they will pour her out;
they will empty her jars
and smash her jugs.
13 Then Moab will be ashamed of Chemosh,
as the house of Israel was ashamed
when they trusted in Bethel.

14 "How can you say, 'We are warriors,
men valiant in battle'?
15 Moab will be destroyed and her towns invaded;
her finest young men will go down in the slaughter,"
declares the King, whose name is the LORD Almighty.
16 "The fall of Moab is at hand;
her calamity will come quickly.
17 Mourn for her, all who live around her,
all who know her fame;
say, 'How broken is the mighty scepter,
how broken the glorious staff!'

18 "Come down from your glory
and sit on the parched ground,
O inhabitants of the Daughter of Dibon,
for he who destroys Moab
will come up against you
and ruin your fortified cities.
19 Stand by the road and watch,
you who live in Aroer.
Ask the man fleeing and the woman escaping,
ask them, 'What has happened?'
20 Moab is disgraced, for she is shattered.
Wail and cry out!
Announce by the Arnon
that Moab is destroyed.
21 Judgment has come to the plateau—
to Holon, Jahzah and Mephaath,
22 to Dibon, Nebo and Beth Diblathaim,

[a] 1 Or / *Misgab* [b] 2 The Hebrew for *Heshbon* sounds like the Hebrew for *plot.* [c] 2 The name of the Moabite town Madmen sounds like the Hebrew for *be silenced.* [d] 4 Hebrew; Septuagint / *proclaim it to Zoar* [e] 6 Or *like Aroer* [f] 9 Or *Give wings to Moab, / for she will fly away*

23 to Kiriathaim, Beth Gamul and Beth Meon,
24 to Kerioth and Bozrah—
to all the towns of Moab, far and near.
25 Moab's horn[g] is cut off;
her arm is broken,"
declares the LORD.

26 "Make her drunk,
for she has defied the LORD.
Let Moab wallow in her vomit;
let her be an object of ridicule.
27 Was not Israel the object of your ridicule?
Was she caught among thieves,
that you shake your head in scorn
whenever you speak of her?
28 Abandon your towns and dwell among the rocks,
you who live in Moab.
Be like a dove that makes its nest
at the mouth of a cave.

29 "We have heard of Moab's pride—
her overweening pride and conceit,
her pride and arrogance
and the haughtiness of her heart.
30 I know her insolence but it is futile,"
declares the LORD,
"and her boasts accomplish nothing.
31 Therefore I wail over Moab,
for all Moab I cry out,
I moan for the men of Kir Hareseth.
32 I weep for you, as Jazer weeps,
O vines of Sibmah.
Your branches spread as far as the sea;
they reached as far as the sea of Jazer.
The destroyer has fallen
on your ripened fruit and grapes.
33 Joy and gladness are gone
from the orchards and fields of Moab.
I have stopped the flow of wine from the presses;
no one treads them with shouts of joy.
Although there are shouts,
they are not shouts of joy.

34 "The sound of their cry rises
from Heshbon to Elealeh and Jahaz,
from Zoar as far as Horonaim and Eglath Shelishiyah,
for even the waters of Nimrim are dried up.
35 In Moab I will put an end
to those who make offerings on the high places
and burn incense to their gods,"
declares the LORD.
36 "So my heart laments for Moab like a flute;
it laments like a flute for the men of Kir Hareseth.
The wealth they acquired is gone.
37 Every head is shaved
and every beard cut off;
every hand is slashed
and every waist is covered with sackcloth.
38 On all the roofs in Moab
and in the public squares
there is nothing but mourning,
for I have broken Moab
like a jar that no one wants,"
declares the LORD.
39 "How shattered she is! How they wail!
How Moab turns her back in shame!
Moab has become an object of ridicule,
an object of horror to all those around her."

40 This is what the LORD says:

"Look! An eagle is swooping down,
spreading its wings over Moab.
41 Kerioth[h] will be captured
and the strongholds taken.
In that day the hearts of Moab's warriors
will be like the heart of a woman in labor.
42 Moab will be destroyed as a nation
because she defied the LORD.
43 Terror and pit and snare await you,
O people of Moab,"
declares the LORD.
44 "Whoever flees from the terror
will fall into a pit,
whoever climbs out of the pit
will be caught in a snare;
for I will bring upon Moab
the year of her punishment,"
declares the LORD.

45 "In the shadow of Heshbon
the fugitives stand helpless,
for a fire has gone out from Heshbon,
a blaze from the midst of Sihon;
it burns the foreheads of Moab,
the skulls of the noisy boasters.

[g] 25 *Horn* here symbolizes strength. [h] 41 Or *The cities*

[46]Woe to you, O Moab!
The people of Chemosh are destroyed;
your sons are taken into exile
and your daughters into captivity.

[47]"Yet I will restore the fortunes of Moab
in days to come,"
declares the LORD.

Here ends the judgment on Moab.

PRAYER: PETITION

MAY I be strong and not lose courage, for my work will be rewarded. (2 Chronicles 15:7)

PAUSE here to petition God for wisdom. Ask Him to develop your eternal perspective, to renew your mind with truth and to help you develop greater skill in each area of your life. Offer prayers regarding your activities for this day and any special concerns you may have.

NT 1 Thessalonians 4:1–12

Living to Please God

4 Finally, brothers, we instructed you how
to live in order to please God, as in fact
you are living. Now we ask you and urge
you in the Lord Jesus to do this more and
more. [2]For you know what instructions we
gave you by the authority of the Lord Jesus.
[3]It is God's will that you should be
sanctified: that you should avoid sexual
immorality; [4]that each of you should
learn to control his own body[a] in a way
that is holy and honorable, [5]not in passionate lust like the heathen, who do not
know God; [6]and that in this matter no
one should wrong his brother or take advantage of him. The Lord will punish men
for all such sins, as we have already told
you and warned you. [7]For God did not
call us to be impure, but to live a holy life.
[8]Therefore, he who rejects this instruction
does not reject man but God, who gives
you his Holy Spirit.
[9]Now about brotherly love we do not
need to write to you, for you yourselves
have been taught by God to love each other. [10]And in fact, you do love all the brothers throughout Macedonia. Yet we urge
you, brothers, to do so more and more.
[11]Make it your ambition to lead a quiet
life, to mind your own business and to
work with your hands, just as we told you,
[12]so that your daily life may win the respect of outsiders and so that you will not
be dependent on anybody.

[a] 4 Or *learn to live with his own wife;* or *learn to acquire a wife*

PRAYER: THE CHARACTER I WANT TO CULTIVATE

I WILL not neglect my spiritual gifts, O Lord. (1 Timothy 4:14) . . . O God, You have not given me a spirit of timidity, but a spirit of power, of love and of self-control. (2 Timothy 1:7)

TAKE a moment to ask the Lord for the grace to grow in godly character.

YEAR 2 DAY 235

OT Jeremiah 49:1–39

A Message About Ammon

49 Concerning the Ammonites:

This is what the LORD says:

"Has Israel no sons?
Has she no heirs?
Why then has Molech[a] taken
possession of Gad?
Why do his people live in its towns?

[a] 1 Or *their king;* Hebrew *malcam;* also in verse 3

2 But the days are coming,"
declares the LORD,
"when I will sound the battle cry
against Rabbah of the Ammonites;
it will become a mound of ruins,
and its surrounding villages will be set on fire.
Then Israel will drive out
those who drove her out,"
says the LORD.
3 "Wail, O Heshbon, for Ai is destroyed!
Cry out, O inhabitants of Rabbah!
Put on sackcloth and mourn;
rush here and there inside the walls,
for Molech will go into exile,
together with his priests and officials.
4 Why do you boast of your valleys,
boast of your valleys so fruitful?
O unfaithful daughter,
you trust in your riches and say,
'Who will attack me?'
5 I will bring terror on you
from all those around you,"
declares the Lord,
the LORD Almighty.
"Every one of you will be driven away,
and no one will gather the fugitives.

6 "Yet afterward, I will restore the fortunes of the Ammonites,"
declares the LORD.

A Message About Edom

7 Concerning Edom:

This is what the LORD Almighty says:

"Is there no longer wisdom in Teman?
Has counsel perished from the prudent?
Has their wisdom decayed?
8 Turn and flee, hide in deep caves,
you who live in Dedan,
for I will bring disaster on Esau
at the time I punish him.
9 If grape pickers came to you,
would they not leave a few grapes?
If thieves came during the night,
would they not steal only as much as they wanted?
10 But I will strip Esau bare;
I will uncover his hiding places,
so that he cannot conceal himself.
His children, relatives and neighbors will perish,
and he will be no more.
11 Leave your orphans; I will protect their lives.
Your widows too can trust in me."

12 This is what the LORD says: "If those
who do not deserve to drink the cup must
drink it, why should you go unpunished?
You will not go unpunished, but must
drink it. 13 I swear by myself," declares the
LORD, "that Bozrah will become a ruin
and an object of horror, of reproach and
of cursing; and all its towns will be in ruins forever."

14 I have heard a message from the LORD:
An envoy was sent to the nations to say,
"Assemble yourselves to attack it!
Rise up for battle!"

15 "Now I will make you small among the nations,
despised among men.
16 The terror you inspire
and the pride of your heart have deceived you,
you who live in the clefts of the rocks,
who occupy the heights of the hill.
Though you build your nest as high as the eagle's,
from there I will bring you down,"
declares the LORD.
17 "Edom will become an object of horror;
all who pass by will be appalled
and will scoff
because of all its wounds.
18 As Sodom and Gomorrah were overthrown,
along with their neighboring towns,"
says the LORD,
"so no one will live there;
no man will dwell in it.

19 "Like a lion coming up from Jordan's thickets
to a rich pastureland,
I will chase Edom from its land in an instant.
Who is the chosen one I will appoint for this?
Who is like me and who can challenge me?
And what shepherd can stand against me?"
20 Therefore, hear what the LORD has planned against Edom,
what he has purposed against those who live in Teman:

The young of the flock will be dragged away;
he will completely destroy their pasture because of them.
21 At the sound of their fall the earth will tremble;
their cry will resound to the Red Sea.[b]
22 Look! An eagle will soar and swoop down,
spreading its wings over Bozrah.
In that day the hearts of Edom's warriors
will be like the heart of a woman in labor.

A Message About Damascus

23 Concerning Damascus:

"Hamath and Arpad are dismayed,
for they have heard bad news.
They are disheartened,
troubled like[c] the restless sea.
24 Damascus has become feeble,
she has turned to flee
and panic has gripped her;
anguish and pain have seized her,
pain like that of a woman in labor.
25 Why has the city of renown not been abandoned,
the town in which I delight?
26 Surely, her young men will fall in the streets;
all her soldiers will be silenced in that day,"
declares the LORD Almighty.
27 "I will set fire to the walls of Damascus;
it will consume the fortresses of Ben-Hadad."

A Message About Kedar and Hazor

28 Concerning Kedar and the kingdoms of Hazor, which Nebuchadnezzar king of Babylon attacked:

This is what the LORD says:

"Arise, and attack Kedar
and destroy the people of the East.
29 Their tents and their flocks will be taken;
their shelters will be carried off
with all their goods and camels.
Men will shout to them,
'Terror on every side!'

30 "Flee quickly away!
Stay in deep caves, you who live in Hazor,"
declares the LORD.
"Nebuchadnezzar king of Babylon has plotted against you;
he has devised a plan against you.

31 "Arise and attack a nation at ease,
which lives in confidence,"
declares the LORD,
"a nation that has neither gates nor bars;
its people live alone.
32 Their camels will become plunder,
and their large herds will be booty.
I will scatter to the winds those who are in distant places[d]
and will bring disaster on them from every side,"
declares the LORD.
33 "Hazor will become a haunt of jackals,
a desolate place forever.
No one will live there;
no man will dwell in it."

A Message About Elam

34 This is the word of the LORD that came to Jeremiah the prophet concerning Elam, early in the reign of Zedekiah king of Judah:

35 This is what the LORD Almighty says:

"See, I will break the bow of Elam,
the mainstay of their might.
36 I will bring against Elam the four winds
from the four quarters of the heavens;
I will scatter them to the four winds,
and there will not be a nation
where Elam's exiles do not go.
37 I will shatter Elam before their foes,
before those who seek their lives;
I will bring disaster upon them,
even my fierce anger,"
declares the LORD.
"I will pursue them with the sword
until I have made an end of them.
38 I will set my throne in Elam
and destroy her king and officials,"
declares the LORD.

39 "Yet I will restore the fortunes of Elam
in days to come,"
declares the LORD.

[b] 21 Hebrew *Yam Suph;* that is, Sea of Reeds
[c] 23 Hebrew *on* or *by*
[d] 32 Or *who clip the hair by their foreheads*

PRAYER: INTERCESSION

***MAY** we encourage one another daily, as long as it is still called "Today," lest any of us be hardened by the deceitfulness of sin. (Hebrews 3:13)*

***TAKE** a few moments to intercede on behalf of your immediate family and other relatives. Offer prayers for their spiritual, emotional and physical concerns.*

NT 1 Thessalonians 4:13–5:11

The Coming of the Lord

13Brothers, we do not want you to be ignorant about those who fall asleep, or to grieve like the rest of men, who have no hope. 14We believe that Jesus died and rose again and so we believe that God will bring with Jesus those who have fallen asleep in him. 15According to the Lord's own word, we tell you that we who are still alive, who are left till the coming of the Lord, will certainly not precede those who have fallen asleep. 16For the Lord himself will come down from heaven, with a loud command, with the voice of the archangel and with the trumpet call of God, and the dead in Christ will rise first. 17After that, we who are still alive and are left will be caught up together with them in the clouds to meet the Lord in the air. And so we will be with the Lord forever. 18Therefore encourage each other with these words.

5 Now, brothers, about times and dates we do not need to write to you, 2for you know very well that the day of the Lord will come like a thief in the night. 3While people are saying, "Peace and safety," destruction will come on them suddenly, as labor pains on a pregnant woman, and they will not escape.

4But you, brothers, are not in darkness so that this day should surprise you like a thief. 5You are all sons of the light and sons of the day. We do not belong to the night or to the darkness. 6So then, let us not be like others, who are asleep, but let us be alert and self-controlled. 7For those who sleep, sleep at night, and those who get drunk, get drunk at night. 8But since we belong to the day, let us be self-controlled, putting on faith and love as a breastplate, and the hope of salvation as a helmet. 9For God did not appoint us to suffer wrath but to receive salvation through our Lord Jesus Christ. 10He died for us so that, whether we are awake or asleep, we may live together with him. 11Therefore encourage one another and build each other up, just as in fact you are doing.

PRAYER: MY RELATIONSHIP TO OTHERS

***I WILL** train up my children in the way they should go; even when they are old they will not depart from it. (Proverbs 22:6) . . .*
I will correct my children, and they will give me rest; they will bring delight to my soul. (Proverbs 29:17)

***PAUSE** to review your relationships with others and to commit them to the Lord.*

YEAR 2
DAY 236

OT Jeremiah 50:1–46

A Message About Babylon

50 This is the word the LORD spoke through Jeremiah the prophet concerning Babylon and the land of the Babylonians[a]:

[a] 1 Or *Chaldeans;* also in verses 8, 25, 35 and 45

2 "Announce and proclaim among the nations,
lift up a banner and proclaim it;
keep nothing back, but say,
'Babylon will be captured;
Bel will be put to shame,
Marduk filled with terror.
Her images will be put to shame
and her idols filled with terror.'
3 A nation from the north will attack her
and lay waste her land.
No one will live in it;
both men and animals will flee away.

4 "In those days, at that time,"
declares the LORD,
"the people of Israel and the people of Judah together
will go in tears to seek the LORD their God.
5 They will ask the way to Zion
and turn their faces toward it.
They will come and bind themselves to the LORD
in an everlasting covenant
that will not be forgotten.

6 "My people have been lost sheep;
their shepherds have led them astray
and caused them to roam on the mountains.
They wandered over mountain and hill
and forgot their own resting place.
7 Whoever found them devoured them;
their enemies said, 'We are not guilty,
for they sinned against the LORD, their true pasture,
the LORD, the hope of their fathers.'

8 "Flee out of Babylon;
leave the land of the Babylonians,
and be like the goats that lead the flock.
9 For I will stir up and bring against Babylon
an alliance of great nations from the land of the north.
They will take up their positions against her,
and from the north she will be captured.
Their arrows will be like skilled warriors
who do not return empty-handed.
10 So Babylonia[b] will be plundered;
all who plunder her will have their fill,"
declares the LORD.

11 "Because you rejoice and are glad,
you who pillage my inheritance,
because you frolic like a heifer threshing grain
and neigh like stallions,
12 your mother will be greatly ashamed;
she who gave you birth will be disgraced.
She will be the least of the nations—
a wilderness, a dry land, a desert.
13 Because of the LORD's anger she will not be inhabited
but will be completely desolate.
All who pass Babylon will be horrified and scoff
because of all her wounds.

14 "Take up your positions around Babylon,
all you who draw the bow.
Shoot at her! Spare no arrows,
for she has sinned against the LORD.
15 Shout against her on every side!
She surrenders, her towers fall,
her walls are torn down.
Since this is the vengeance of the LORD,
take vengeance on her;
do to her as she has done to others.
16 Cut off from Babylon the sower,
and the reaper with his sickle at harvest.
Because of the sword of the oppressor
let everyone return to his own people,
let everyone flee to his own land.

17 "Israel is a scattered flock
that lions have chased away.
The first to devour him
was the king of Assyria;
the last to crush his bones
was Nebuchadnezzar king of Babylon."

18 Therefore this is what the LORD Almighty, the God of Israel, says:

"I will punish the king of Babylon and his land
as I punished the king of Assyria.

[b] 10 Or *Chaldea*

[19]But I will bring Israel back to his own
pasture
and he will graze on Carmel and
Bashan;
his appetite will be satisfied
on the hills of Ephraim and Gilead.
[20]In those days, at that time,"
declares the LORD,
"search will be made for Israel's guilt,
but there will be none,
and for the sins of Judah,
but none will be found,
for I will forgive the remnant I
spare.

[21]"Attack the land of Merathaim
and those who live in Pekod.
Pursue, kill and completely destroy[c]
them,"
declares the LORD.
"Do everything I have commanded
you.
[22]The noise of battle is in the land,
the noise of great destruction!
[23]How broken and shattered
is the hammer of the whole earth!
How desolate is Babylon
among the nations!
[24]I set a trap for you, O Babylon,
and you were caught before you
knew it;
you were found and captured
because you opposed the LORD.
[25]The LORD has opened his arsenal
and brought out the weapons of his
wrath,
for the Sovereign LORD Almighty has
work to do
in the land of the Babylonians.
[26]Come against her from afar.
Break open her granaries;
pile her up like heaps of grain.
Completely destroy her
and leave her no remnant.
[27]Kill all her young bulls;
let them go down to the slaughter!
Woe to them! For their day has come,
the time for them to be punished.
[28]Listen to the fugitives and refugees
from Babylon
declaring in Zion
how the LORD our God has taken
vengeance,
vengeance for his temple.

[29]"Summon archers against Babylon,
all those who draw the bow.
Encamp all around her;
let no one escape.
Repay her for her deeds;
do to her as she has done.
For she has defied the LORD,
the Holy One of Israel.
[30]Therefore, her young men will fall in
the streets;
all her soldiers will be silenced in
that day,"
declares the LORD.
[31]"See, I am against you, O arrogant
one,"
declares the Lord, the LORD
Almighty,
"for your day has come,
the time for you to be punished.
[32]The arrogant one will stumble and fall
and no one will help her up;
I will kindle a fire in her towns
that will consume all who are
around her."

[33]This is what the LORD Almighty says:

"The people of Israel are oppressed,
and the people of Judah as well.
All their captors hold them fast,
refusing to let them go.
[34]Yet their Redeemer is strong;
the LORD Almighty is his name.
He will vigorously defend their cause
so that he may bring rest to their
land,
but unrest to those who live in
Babylon.

[35]"A sword against the Babylonians!"
declares the LORD—
"against those who live in Babylon
and against her officials and wise
men!
[36]A sword against her false prophets!
They will become fools.
A sword against her warriors!
They will be filled with terror.
[37]A sword against her horses and
chariots
and all the foreigners in her ranks!
They will become women.
A sword against her treasures!
They will be plundered.
[38]A drought on[d] her waters!
They will dry up.
For it is a land of idols,

[c] *21* The Hebrew term refers to the irrevocable giving over of things or persons to the LORD, often by totally destroying them; also in verse 26. [d] *38* Or *A sword against*

idols that will go mad with terror.

39 "So desert creatures and hyenas will live there,
and there the owl will dwell.
It will never again be inhabited
or lived in from generation to generation.
40 As God overthrew Sodom and Gomorrah
along with their neighboring towns,"
declares the LORD,
"so no one will live there;
no man will dwell in it.

41 "Look! An army is coming from the north;
a great nation and many kings
are being stirred up from the ends of the earth.
42 They are armed with bows and spears;
they are cruel and without mercy.
They sound like the roaring sea
as they ride on their horses;
they come like men in battle formation
to attack you, O Daughter of Babylon.
43 The king of Babylon has heard reports about them,
and his hands hang limp.
Anguish has gripped him,
pain like that of a woman in labor.
44 Like a lion coming up from Jordan's thickets
to a rich pastureland,
I will chase Babylon from its land in an instant.
Who is the chosen one I will appoint for this?
Who is like me and who can challenge me?
And what shepherd can stand against me?"
45 Therefore, hear what the LORD has planned against Babylon,
what he has purposed against the land of the Babylonians:
The young of the flock will be dragged away;
he will completely destroy their pasture because of them.
46 At the sound of Babylon's capture the earth will tremble;
its cry will resound among the nations.

PRAYER: AFFIRMATION

CHRIST, You have completed the law so that there may be righteousness to everyone who believes. (Romans 10:4) . . . My faith does not rest on human wisdom, but on Your power, O God. (1 Corinthians 2:5)

__PAUSE__ to reflect on these Biblical affirmations.

NT 1 Thessalonians 5:12–28

Final Instructions

12 Now we ask you, brothers, to respect
those who work hard among you, who
are over you in the Lord and who admonish you. 13 Hold them in the highest
regard in love because of their work. Live
in peace with each other. 14 And we urge
you, brothers, warn those who are idle,
encourage the timid, help the weak, be
patient with everyone. 15 Make sure that
nobody pays back wrong for wrong, but
always try to be kind to each other and to
everyone else.
16 Be joyful always; 17 pray continually;
18 give thanks in all circumstances, for this
is God's will for you in Christ Jesus.
19 Do not put out the Spirit's fire; 20 do
not treat prophecies with contempt. 21 Test
everything. Hold on to the good. 22 Avoid
every kind of evil.
23 May God himself, the God of peace,
sanctify you through and through. May
your whole spirit, soul and body be kept
blameless at the coming of our Lord Jesus
Christ. 24 The one who calls you is faithful
and he will do it.

25 Brothers, pray for us. 26 Greet all the
brothers with a holy kiss. 27 I charge you
before the Lord to have this letter read to
all the brothers.
28 The grace of our Lord Jesus Christ be
with you.

PRAYER: THE ATTRIBUTES OF GOD

GREAT and marvelous are Your works, Lord God Almighty! Righteous and true are Your ways, King of the nations! Who will not fear You, O Lord, and glorify Your name? For You alone are holy. All nations will come and worship before You, for Your righteous acts have been revealed. (Revelation 15:3–4)

***PAUSE** to reflect on these affirmations about the person, powers and perfection of God.*

YEAR 2 DAY 237

OT Jeremiah 51:1–64

51 This is what the LORD says:

"See, I will stir up the spirit of a destroyer
against Babylon and the people of Leb Kamai.[a]
2 I will send foreigners to Babylon
to winnow her and to devastate her land;
they will oppose her on every side
in the day of her disaster.
3 Let not the archer string his bow,
nor let him put on his armor.
Do not spare her young men;
completely destroy[b] her army.
4 They will fall down slain in Babylon,[c]
fatally wounded in her streets.
5 For Israel and Judah have not been forsaken
by their God, the LORD Almighty,
though their land[d] is full of guilt
before the Holy One of Israel.

6 "Flee from Babylon!
Run for your lives!
Do not be destroyed because of her sins.
It is time for the LORD's vengeance;
he will pay her what she deserves.
7 Babylon was a gold cup in the LORD's hand;
she made the whole earth drunk.
The nations drank her wine;
therefore they have now gone mad.
8 Babylon will suddenly fall and be broken.
Wail over her!
Get balm for her pain;
perhaps she can be healed.

9 " 'We would have healed Babylon,
but she cannot be healed;
let us leave her and each go to his own land,
for her judgment reaches to the skies,
it rises as high as the clouds.'

10 " 'The LORD has vindicated us;
come, let us tell in Zion
what the LORD our God has done.'

11 "Sharpen the arrows,
take up the shields!
The LORD has stirred up the kings of the Medes,
because his purpose is to destroy Babylon.
The LORD will take vengeance,
vengeance for his temple.
12 Lift up a banner against the walls of Babylon!
Reinforce the guard,
station the watchmen,
prepare an ambush!
The LORD will carry out his purpose,
his decree against the people of Babylon.
13 You who live by many waters
and are rich in treasures,
your end has come,
the time for you to be cut off.
14 The LORD Almighty has sworn by himself:
I will surely fill you with men, as with a swarm of locusts,

[a] 1 *Leb Kamai* is a cryptogram for Chaldea, that is, Babylonia. [b] 3 The Hebrew term refers to the irrevocable giving over of things or persons to the LORD, often by totally destroying them. [c] 4 Or *Chaldea* [d] 5 Or / *and the land ⌊of the Babylonians⌋*

and they will shout in triumph over
you.

[15] "He made the earth by his power;
he founded the world by his wisdom
and stretched out the heavens by
his understanding.
[16] When he thunders, the waters in the
heavens roar;
he makes clouds rise from the ends
of the earth.
He sends lightning with the rain
and brings out the wind from his
storehouses.

[17] "Every man is senseless and without
knowledge;
every goldsmith is shamed by his
idols.
His images are a fraud;
they have no breath in them.
[18] They are worthless, the objects of
mockery;
when their judgment comes, they
will perish.
[19] He who is the Portion of Jacob is not
like these,
for he is the Maker of all things,
including the tribe of his inheritance—
the LORD Almighty is his name.

[20] "You are my war club,
my weapon for battle—
with you I shatter nations,
with you I destroy kingdoms,
[21] with you I shatter horse and rider,
with you I shatter chariot and driver,
[22] with you I shatter man and woman,
with you I shatter old man and
youth,
with you I shatter young man and
maiden,
[23] with you I shatter shepherd and flock,
with you I shatter farmer and oxen,
with you I shatter governors and
officials.

[24] "Before your eyes I will repay Babylon
and all who live in Babylonia[e] for all the
wrong they have done in Zion," declares
the LORD.

[25] "I am against you, O destroying
mountain,
you who destroy the whole earth,"
declares the LORD.
"I will stretch out my hand against you,
roll you off the cliffs,
and make you a burned-out
mountain.
[26] No rock will be taken from you for a
cornerstone,
nor any stone for a foundation,
for you will be desolate forever,"
declares the LORD.

[27] "Lift up a banner in the land!
Blow the trumpet among the
nations!
Prepare the nations for battle against
her;
summon against her these kingdoms:
Ararat, Minni and Ashkenaz.
Appoint a commander against her;
send up horses like a swarm of
locusts.
[28] Prepare the nations for battle against
her—
the kings of the Medes,
their governors and all their officials,
and all the countries they rule.
[29] The land trembles and writhes,
for the LORD's purposes against
Babylon stand—
to lay waste the land of Babylon
so that no one will live there.
[30] Babylon's warriors have stopped
fighting;
they remain in their strongholds.
Their strength is exhausted;
they have become like women.
Her dwellings are set on fire;
the bars of her gates are broken.
[31] One courier follows another
and messenger follows messenger
to announce to the king of Babylon
that his entire city is captured,
[32] the river crossings seized,
the marshes set on fire,
and the soldiers terrified."

[33] This is what the LORD Almighty, the
God of Israel, says:

"The Daughter of Babylon is like a
threshing floor
at the time it is trampled;
the time to harvest her will soon
come."

[34] "Nebuchadnezzar king of Babylon has
devoured us,
he has thrown us into confusion,
he has made us an empty jar.
Like a serpent he has swallowed us

[e] 24 Or *Chaldea*; also in verse 35

and filled his stomach with our
delicacies,
and then has spewed us out.
35 May the violence done to our flesh[f] be
upon Babylon,"
say the inhabitants of Zion.
"May our blood be on those who live
in Babylonia,"
says Jerusalem.

36 Therefore, this is what the LORD says:

"See, I will defend your cause
and avenge you;
I will dry up her sea
and make her springs dry.
37 Babylon will be a heap of ruins,
a haunt of jackals,
an object of horror and scorn,
a place where no one lives.
38 Her people all roar like young lions,
they growl like lion cubs.
39 But while they are aroused,
I will set out a feast for them
and make them drunk,
so that they shout with laughter—
then sleep forever and not awake,"
declares the LORD.
40 "I will bring them down
like lambs to the slaughter,
like rams and goats.

41 "How Sheshach[g] will be captured,
the boast of the whole earth seized!
What a horror Babylon will be
among the nations!
42 The sea will rise over Babylon;
its roaring waves will cover her.
43 Her towns will be desolate,
a dry and desert land,
a land where no one lives,
through which no man travels.
44 I will punish Bel in Babylon
and make him spew out what he
has swallowed.
The nations will no longer stream to
him.
And the wall of Babylon will fall.

45 "Come out of her, my people!
Run for your lives!
Run from the fierce anger of the
LORD.
46 Do not lose heart or be afraid
when rumors are heard in the land;
one rumor comes this year, another
the next,
rumors of violence in the land
and of ruler against ruler.
47 For the time will surely come
when I will punish the idols of
Babylon;
her whole land will be disgraced
and her slain will all lie fallen
within her.
48 Then heaven and earth and all that is
in them
will shout for joy over Babylon,
for out of the north
destroyers will attack her,"
declares the LORD.

49 "Babylon must fall because of Israel's
slain,
just as the slain in all the earth
have fallen because of Babylon.
50 You who have escaped the sword,
leave and do not linger!
Remember the LORD in a distant land,
and think on Jerusalem."

51 "We are disgraced,
for we have been insulted
and shame covers our faces,
because foreigners have entered
the holy places of the LORD's
house."

52 "But days are coming," declares the
LORD,
"when I will punish her idols,
and throughout her land
the wounded will groan.
53 Even if Babylon reaches the sky
and fortifies her lofty stronghold,
I will send destroyers against her,"
declares the LORD.

54 "The sound of a cry comes from
Babylon,
the sound of great destruction
from the land of the Babylonians.[h]
55 The LORD will destroy Babylon;
he will silence her noisy din.
Waves ⌞of enemies⌟ will rage like great
waters;
the roar of their voices will resound.
56 A destroyer will come against
Babylon;
her warriors will be captured,
and their bows will be broken.
For the LORD is a God of retribution;
he will repay in full.
57 I will make her officials and wise men
drunk,

[f] 35 Or *done to us and to our children* [g] 41 *Sheshach* is a cryptogram for Babylon. [h] 54 Or *Chaldeans*

her governors, officers and warriors
as well;
they will sleep forever and not awake,"
declares the King, whose name is
the LORD Almighty.

58This is what the LORD Almighty says:

"Babylon's thick wall will be leveled
and her high gates set on fire;
the peoples exhaust themselves for
nothing,
the nations' labor is only fuel for
the flames."

59This is the message Jeremiah gave to
the staff officer Seraiah son of Neriah, the
son of Mahseiah, when he went to Babylon
with Zedekiah king of Judah in the fourth
year of his reign. 60Jeremiah had written on
a scroll about all the disasters that would
come upon Babylon—all that had been
recorded concerning Babylon. 61He said to
Seraiah, "When you get to Babylon, see
that you read all these words aloud. 62Then
say, 'O LORD, you have said you will destroy
this place, so that neither man nor animal
will live in it; it will be desolate forever.'
63When you finish reading this scroll, tie a
stone to it and throw it into the Euphrates.
64Then say, 'So will Babylon sink to rise no
more because of the disaster I will bring
upon her. And her people will fall.' "

The words of Jeremiah end here.

PRAYER: THANKSGIVING

IT is a trustworthy saying that deserves full acceptance—You, Christ Jesus, came into the world to save sinners. I obtained mercy as the worst of sinners, so that You might display Your unlimited patience as an example for those who would believe in You for eternal life. (1 Timothy 1:15–16) . . . O God, You have saved me and called me with a holy calling, not according to my works but according to Your own purpose and grace. (2 Timothy 1:9)

PAUSE *to offer your own expressions of thanksgiving.*

NT 2 Thessalonians 1:1–12

1 Paul, Silas[a] and Timothy,

To the church of the Thessalonians in God our Father and the Lord Jesus Christ:

2Grace and peace to you from God the
Father and the Lord Jesus Christ.

Thanksgiving and Prayer

3We ought always to thank God for you,
brothers, and rightly so, because your
faith is growing more and more, and the
love every one of you has for each other
is increasing. 4Therefore, among God's
churches we boast about your perseverance and faith in all the persecutions and
trials you are enduring.
5All this is evidence that God's judgment is right, and as a result you will be
counted worthy of the kingdom of God,
for which you are suffering. 6God is just:
He will pay back trouble to those who
trouble you 7and give relief to you who are
troubled, and to us as well. This will happen when the Lord Jesus is revealed from
heaven in blazing fire with his powerful
angels. 8He will punish those who do not
know God and do not obey the gospel of
our Lord Jesus. 9They will be punished
with everlasting destruction and shut out
from the presence of the Lord and from
the majesty of his power 10on the day he
comes to be glorified in his holy people
and to be marveled at among all those
who have believed. This includes you, because you believed our testimony to you.
11With this in mind, we constantly pray
for you, that our God may count you worthy of his calling, and that by his power
he may fulfill every good purpose of yours
and every act prompted by your faith.
12We pray this so that the name of our
Lord Jesus may be glorified in you, and
you in him, according to the grace of our
God and the Lord Jesus Christ.[b]

[a] 1 Greek *Silvanus,* a variant of *Silas* [b] 12 Or *God and Lord, Jesus Christ*

PRAYER: THE WORKS OF GOD

O GOD, as living stones, we are being built into a spiritual house to be a holy priesthood, offering spiritual sacrifices acceptable to You through Jesus Christ. We are a chosen people, a royal priesthood, a holy nation, a people for Your own possession, O God, that we may declare Your praises; You called us out of darkness into Your marvelous light. (1 Peter 2:5, 9)

***TAKE** a moment to consider the greatness of God's wonderful works.*

YEAR 2 DAY 238

OT Psalm 119:41–88

ו Waw

41 May your unfailing love come to me, O LORD,
your salvation according to your promise;
42 then I will answer the one who taunts me,
for I trust in your word.
43 Do not snatch the word of truth from my mouth,
for I have put my hope in your laws.
44 I will always obey your law,
for ever and ever.
45 I will walk about in freedom,
for I have sought out your precepts.
46 I will speak of your statutes before kings
and will not be put to shame,
47 for I delight in your commands
because I love them.
48 I lift up my hands to[a] your commands, which I love,
and I meditate on your decrees.

ז Zayin

49 Remember your word to your servant,
for you have given me hope.
50 My comfort in my suffering is this:
Your promise preserves my life.
51 The arrogant mock me without restraint,
but I do not turn from your law.
52 I remember your ancient laws, O LORD,
and I find comfort in them
53 Indignation grips me because of the wicked,
who have forsaken your law.
54 Your decrees are the theme of my song
wherever I lodge.
55 In the night I remember your name, O LORD,
and I will keep your law.
56 This has been my practice:
I obey your precepts.

ח Heth

57 You are my portion, O LORD;
I have promised to obey your words.
58 I have sought your face with all my heart;
be gracious to me according to your promise.
59 I have considered my ways
and have turned my steps to your statutes.
60 I will hasten and not delay
to obey your commands.
61 Though the wicked bind me with ropes,
I will not forget your law.
62 At midnight I rise to give you thanks
for your righteous laws.
63 I am a friend to all who fear you,
to all who follow your precepts.
64 The earth is filled with your love, O LORD;
teach me your decrees.

ט Teth

65 Do good to your servant
according to your word, O LORD.
66 Teach me knowledge and good judgment,
for I believe in your commands.
67 Before I was afflicted I went astray,
but now I obey your word.

[a] 48 Or *for*

[68]You are good, and what you do is good;
teach me your decrees.
[69]Though the arrogant have smeared me with lies,
I keep your precepts with all my heart.
[70]Their hearts are callous and unfeeling,
but I delight in your law.
[71]It was good for me to be afflicted
so that I might learn your decrees.
[72]The law from your mouth is more precious to me
than thousands of pieces of silver and gold.

י Yodh

[73]Your hands made me and formed me;
give me understanding to learn your commands.
[74]May those who fear you rejoice when they see me,
for I have put my hope in your word.
[75]I know, O LORD, that your laws are righteous,
and in faithfulness you have afflicted me.
[76]May your unfailing love be my comfort,
according to your promise to your servant.
[77]Let your compassion come to me that I may live,
for your law is my delight.
[78]May the arrogant be put to shame for wronging me without cause;
but I will meditate on your precepts.
[79]May those who fear you turn to me,
those who understand your statutes.
[80]May my heart be blameless toward your decrees,
that I may not be put to shame.

כ Kaph

[81]My soul faints with longing for your salvation,
but I have put my hope in your word.
[82]My eyes fail, looking for your promise;
I say, "When will you comfort me?"
[83]Though I am like a wineskin in the smoke,
I do not forget your decrees.
[84]How long must your servant wait?
When will you punish my persecutors?
[85]The arrogant dig pitfalls for me,
contrary to your law.
[86]All your commands are trustworthy;
help me, for men persecute me without cause.
[87]They almost wiped me from the earth,
but I have not forsaken your precepts.
[88]Preserve my life according to your love,
and I will obey the statutes of your mouth.

PRAYER: ADORATION

TO You, O God, belong wisdom and power; counsel and understanding are Yours. (Job 12:13) . . . You are holy; You are enthroned on the praise of Israel. (Psalm 22:3)

***PAUSE** to express your thoughts of praise and worship.*

NT 2 Thessalonians 2:1–12

The Man of Lawlessness

2 Concerning the coming of our Lord
Jesus Christ and our being gathered to
him, we ask you, brothers, [2]not to become
easily unsettled or alarmed by some
prophecy, report or letter supposed to
have come from us, saying that the day of
the Lord has already come. [3]Don't let anyone deceive you in any way, for ⌞that day
will not come⌟ until the rebellion occurs
and the man of lawlessness[a] is revealed,
the man doomed to destruction. [4]He will
oppose and will exalt himself over everything that is called God or is worshiped,
so that he sets himself up in God's temple, proclaiming himself to be God.
[5]Don't you remember that when I was

[a] 3 Some manuscripts *sin*

with you I used to tell you these things? [6]And now you know what is holding him back, so that he may be revealed at the proper time. [7]For the secret power of lawlessness is already at work; but the one who now holds it back will continue to do so till he is taken out of the way. [8]And then the lawless one will be revealed, whom the Lord Jesus will overthrow with the breath of his mouth and destroy by the splendor of his coming. [9]The coming of the lawless one will be in accordance with the work of Satan displayed in all kinds of counterfeit miracles, signs and wonders, [10]and in every sort of evil that deceives those who are perishing. They perish because they refused to love the truth and so be saved. [11]For this reason God sends them a powerful delusion so that they will believe the lie [12]and so that all will be condemned who have not believed the truth but have delighted in wickedness.

PRAYER: MY RELATIONSHIP TO GOD

O GOD, Your kingdom of heaven is like treasure hidden in a field, which a man found and hid; and from his joy, he went and sold all he had and bought that field. Again, the kingdom of heaven is like a merchant looking for fine pearls; and finding one pearl of great value, he went away and sold all that he had and bought it. (Matthew 13:44–46) . . . Those who do not count the cost and renounce all their possessions cannot be Your disciples. (Luke 14:28, 33)

***PAUSE** to thank God for the relationship that you enjoy with Him in Jesus Christ.*

YEAR 2 DAY 239

OT Jeremiah 52:1–34

The Fall of Jerusalem

52 Zedekiah was twenty-one years old when he became king, and he reigned in Jerusalem eleven years. His mother's name was Hamutal daughter of Jeremiah; she was from Libnah. [2]He did evil in the eyes of the LORD, just as Jehoiakim had done. [3]It was because of the LORD's anger that all this happened to Jerusalem and Judah, and in the end he thrust them from his presence.

Now Zedekiah rebelled against the king of Babylon.

[4]So in the ninth year of Zedekiah's reign, on the tenth day of the tenth month, Nebuchadnezzar king of Babylon marched against Jerusalem with his whole army. They camped outside the city and built siege works all around it. [5]The city was kept under siege until the eleventh year of King Zedekiah.

[6]By the ninth day of the fourth month the famine in the city had become so severe that there was no food for the people to eat. [7]Then the city wall was broken through, and the whole army fled. They left the city at night through the gate between the two walls near the king's garden, though the Babylonians[a] were surrounding the city. They fled toward the Arabah,[b] [8]but the Babylonian[c] army pursued King Zedekiah and overtook him in the plains of Jericho. All his soldiers were separated from him and scattered, [9]and he was captured.

He was taken to the king of Babylon at Riblah in the land of Hamath, where he pronounced sentence on him. [10]There at Riblah the king of Babylon slaughtered the sons of Zedekiah before his eyes; he also killed all the officials of Judah. [11]Then he put out Zedekiah's eyes, bound him with bronze shackles and took him to Babylon, where he put him in prison till the day of his death.

[12]On the tenth day of the fifth month, in the nineteenth year of Nebuchadnezzar king of Babylon, Nebuzaradan command-

[a] 7 Or *Chaldeans;* also in verse 17 [b] 7 Or *the Jordan Valley* [c] 8 Or *Chaldean;* also in verse 14

er of the imperial guard, who served the
king of Babylon, came to Jerusalem. 13He
set fire to the temple of the LORD, the royal palace and all the houses of Jerusalem.
Every important building he burned
down. 14The whole Babylonian army under the commander of the imperial guard
broke down all the walls around Jerusalem. 15Nebuzaradan the commander of
the guard carried into exile some of the
poorest people and those who remained
in the city, along with the rest of the craftsmen[d] and those who had gone over to the
king of Babylon. 16But Nebuzaradan left
behind the rest of the poorest people of
the land to work the vineyards and fields.
17The Babylonians broke up the bronze
pillars, the movable stands and the
bronze Sea that were at the temple of the
LORD and they carried all the bronze to
Babylon. 18They also took away the pots,
shovels, wick trimmers, sprinkling bowls,
dishes and all the bronze articles used in
the temple service. 19The commander of
the imperial guard took away the basins,
censers, sprinkling bowls, pots, lampstands, dishes and bowls used for drink
offerings—all that were made of pure gold
or silver.
20The bronze from the two pillars, the
Sea and the twelve bronze bulls under it,
and the movable stands, which King Solomon had made for the temple of the
LORD, was more than could be weighed.
21Each of the pillars was eighteen cubits
high and twelve cubits in circumference[e];
each was four fingers thick, and hollow.
22The bronze capital on top of the one pillar was five cubits[f] high and was decorated with a network and pomegranates of
bronze all around. The other pillar, with
its pomegranates, was similar. 23There
were ninety-six pomegranates on the
sides; the total number of pomegranates
above the surrounding network was a
hundred.
24The commander of the guard took as
prisoners Seraiah the chief priest, Zephaniah the priest next in rank and the three
doorkeepers. 25Of those still in the city, he
took the officer in charge of the fighting
men, and seven royal advisers. He also
took the secretary who was chief officer in
charge of conscripting the people of the
land and sixty of his men who were found
in the city. 26Nebuzaradan the commander took them all and brought them to the
king of Babylon at Riblah. 27There at Riblah, in the land of Hamath, the king had
them executed.
So Judah went into captivity, away from
her land. 28This is the number of the people Nebuchadnezzar carried into exile:

in the seventh year, 3,023 Jews;
29 in Nebuchadnezzar's eighteenth year,
832 people from Jerusalem;
30 in his twenty-third year,
745 Jews taken into exile by Nebuzaradan the commander of the
imperial guard.
There were 4,600 people in all.

Jehoiachin Released

31In the thirty-seventh year of the exile
of Jehoiachin king of Judah, in the year
Evil-Merodach[g] became king of Babylon,
he released Jehoiachin king of Judah and
freed him from prison on the twenty-fifth
day of the twelfth month. 32He spoke
kindly to him and gave him a seat of hon-
or higher than those of the other kings
who were with him in Babylon. 33So Jehoiachin put aside his prison clothes and
for the rest of his life ate regularly at the
king's table. 34Day by day the king of Babylon gave Jehoiachin a regular allowance
as long as he lived, till the day of his death.

[d] *15* Or *populace* [e] *21* That is, about 27 feet (about 8.1 meters) high and 18 feet (about 5.4 meters) in circumference [f] *22* That is, about 7 1/2 feet (about 2.3 meters) [g] *31* Also called *Amel-Marduk*

PRAYER: CONFESSION

WHAT are people that You should magnify them, that You should set Your heart on them, that You examine them every morning and test them every moment? (Job 7:17–18)

ASK *the Spirit to search your heart and reveal any areas of unconfessed sin. Acknowledge these to the Lord and thank Him for His forgiveness.*

NT 2 Thessalonians 2:13–3:5

Stand Firm

[13]But we ought always to thank God for you, brothers loved by the Lord, because from the beginning God chose you[a] to be saved through the sanctifying work of the Spirit and through belief in the truth. [14]He called you to this through our gospel, that you might share in the glory of our Lord Jesus Christ. [15]So then, brothers, stand firm and hold to the teachings[b] we passed on to you, whether by word of mouth or by letter.

[16]May our Lord Jesus Christ himself and God our Father, who loved us and by his grace gave us eternal encouragement and good hope, [17]encourage your hearts and strengthen you in every good deed and word.

Request for Prayer

3 Finally, brothers, pray for us that the message of the Lord may spread rapidly and be honored, just as it was with you. [2]And pray that we may be delivered from wicked and evil men, for not everyone has faith. [3]But the Lord is faithful, and he will strengthen and protect you from the evil one. [4]We have confidence in the Lord that you are doing and will continue to do the things we command. [5]May the Lord direct your hearts into God's love and Christ's perseverance.

[a] 13 Some manuscripts *because God chose you as his firstfruits* [b] 15 Or *traditions*

PRAYER: THE CHARACTER I WANT TO CULTIVATE

O LORD, may I not become weary in doing good, for at the proper time I will reap a harvest if I do not give up. (Galatians 6:9)

***TAKE** a moment to ask the Lord for the grace to grow in godly character.*

YEAR 2 DAY 240

OT Lamentations 1:1–22

1[a] How deserted lies the city,
once so full of people!
How like a widow is she,
who once was great among the nations!
She who was queen among the provinces
has now become a slave.

[2]Bitterly she weeps at night,
tears are upon her cheeks.
Among all her lovers
there is none to comfort her.
All her friends have betrayed her;
they have become her enemies.

[3]After affliction and harsh labor,
Judah has gone into exile.
She dwells among the nations;
she finds no resting place.
All who pursue her have overtaken her
in the midst of her distress.

[4]The roads to Zion mourn,
for no one comes to her appointed feasts.
All her gateways are desolate,
her priests groan,
her maidens grieve,
and she is in bitter anguish.

[5]Her foes have become her masters;
her enemies are at ease.
The LORD has brought her grief
because of her many sins.
Her children have gone into exile,
captive before the foe.

[6]All the splendor has departed
from the Daughter of Zion.
Her princes are like deer
that find no pasture;
in weakness they have fled
before the pursuer.

[a]This chapter is an acrostic poem, the verses of which begin with the successive letters of the Hebrew alphabet.

7 In the days of her affliction and wandering
Jerusalem remembers all the treasures
that were hers in days of old.
When her people fell into enemy hands,
there was no one to help her.
Her enemies looked at her
and laughed at her destruction.

8 Jerusalem has sinned greatly
and so has become unclean.
All who honored her despise her,
for they have seen her nakedness;
she herself groans
and turns away.

9 Her filthiness clung to her skirts;
she did not consider her future.
Her fall was astounding;
there was none to comfort her.
"Look, O LORD, on my affliction,
for the enemy has triumphed."

10 The enemy laid hands
on all her treasures;
she saw pagan nations
enter her sanctuary—
those you had forbidden
to enter your assembly.

11 All her people groan
as they search for bread;
they barter their treasures for food
to keep themselves alive.
"Look, O LORD, and consider,
for I am despised."

12 "Is it nothing to you, all you who pass by?
Look around and see.
Is any suffering like my suffering
that was inflicted on me,
that the LORD brought on me
in the day of his fierce anger?

13 "From on high he sent fire,
sent it down into my bones.
He spread a net for my feet
and turned me back.
He made me desolate,
faint all the day long.

14 "My sins have been bound into a yoke[b];
by his hands they were woven together.
They have come upon my neck
and the Lord has sapped my strength.
He has handed me over
to those I cannot withstand.

15 "The Lord has rejected
all the warriors in my midst;
he has summoned an army against me
to[c] crush my young men.
In his winepress the Lord has trampled
the Virgin Daughter of Judah.

16 "This is why I weep
and my eyes overflow with tears.
No one is near to comfort me,
no one to restore my spirit.
My children are destitute
because the enemy has prevailed."

17 Zion stretches out her hands,
but there is no one to comfort her.
The LORD has decreed for Jacob
that his neighbors become his foes;
Jerusalem has become
an unclean thing among them.

18 "The LORD is righteous,
yet I rebelled against his command.
Listen, all you peoples;
look upon my suffering.
My young men and maidens
have gone into exile.

19 "I called to my allies
but they betrayed me.
My priests and my elders
perished in the city
while they searched for food
to keep themselves alive.

20 "See, O LORD, how distressed I am!
I am in torment within,
and in my heart I am disturbed,
for I have been most rebellious.
Outside, the sword bereaves;
inside, there is only death.

21 "People have heard my groaning,
but there is no one to comfort me.
All my enemies have heard of my distress;
they rejoice at what you have done.
May you bring the day you have announced

[b] 14 Most Hebrew manuscripts; Septuagint *He kept watch over my sins* [c] 15 Or *has set a time for me* / *when he will*

so they may become like me.
[22] "Let all their wickedness come before you;
deal with them
as you have dealt with me
because of all my sins.
My groans are many
and my heart is faint."

PRAYER: RENEWAL

MAY I flee youthful lusts and pursue righteousness, faith, love and peace with those who call on You, Lord, out of a pure heart. May I avoid foolish and ignorant disputes, knowing that they produce quarrels. As Your servant, O Lord, I must not quarrel, but be gentle toward all, able to teach and patient. (2 Timothy 2:22–24)

PAUSE *to add your own prayers for personal renewal.*

NT 2 Thessalonians 3:6–18

Warning Against Idleness

[6]In the name of the Lord Jesus Christ,
we command you, brothers, to keep away
from every brother who is idle and does
not live according to the teaching[a] you received from us. [7]For you yourselves know
how you ought to follow our example. We
were not idle when we were with you,
[8]nor did we eat anyone's food without
paying for it. On the contrary, we worked
night and day, laboring and toiling so that
we would not be a burden to any of you.
[9]We did this, not because we do not have
the right to such help, but in order to
make ourselves a model for you to follow.
[10]For even when we were with you, we
gave you this rule: "If a man will not
work, he shall not eat."
[11]We hear that some among you are
idle. They are not busy; they are busybodies. [12]Such people we command and
urge in the Lord Jesus Christ to settle
down and earn the bread they eat. [13]And
as for you, brothers, never tire of doing
what is right.
[14]If anyone does not obey our instruction in this letter, take special note of him.
Do not associate with him, in order that
he may feel ashamed. [15]Yet do not regard
him as an enemy, but warn him as a
brother.

Final Greetings

[16]Now may the Lord of peace himself
give you peace at all times and in every
way. The Lord be with all of you.
[17]I, Paul, write this greeting in my own
hand, which is the distinguishing mark in
all my letters. This is how I write.
[18]The grace of our Lord Jesus Christ be
with you all.

[a] 6 Or *tradition*

PRAYER: MY RELATIONSHIP TO OTHERS

YOUR whole building, O God, is joined together in Christ Jesus, and growing into a holy temple in You, in whom we also are being built together into Your dwelling in the Spirit. (Ephesians 2:21–22)

PAUSE *to review your relationships with others and to commit them to the Lord.*

YEAR 2 DAY 241

OT Lamentations 2:1–22

2[a] How the Lord has covered the
Daughter of Zion
with the cloud of his anger[b]!
He has hurled down the splendor of
Israel
from heaven to earth;
he has not remembered his footstool
in the day of his anger.

2 Without pity the Lord has swallowed
up
all the dwellings of Jacob;
in his wrath he has torn down
the strongholds of the Daughter of
Judah.
He has brought her kingdom and its
princes
down to the ground in dishonor.

3 In fierce anger he has cut off
every horn[c] of Israel.
He has withdrawn his right hand
at the approach of the enemy.
He has burned in Jacob like a flaming
fire
that consumes everything around it.

4 Like an enemy he has strung his bow;
his right hand is ready.
Like a foe he has slain
all who were pleasing to the eye;
he has poured out his wrath like fire
on the tent of the Daughter of Zion.

5 The Lord is like an enemy;
he has swallowed up Israel.
He has swallowed up all her palaces
and destroyed her strongholds.
He has multiplied mourning and
lamentation
for the Daughter of Judah.

6 He has laid waste his dwelling like a
garden;
he has destroyed his place of
meeting.
The LORD has made Zion forget
her appointed feasts and her
Sabbaths;
in his fierce anger he has spurned
both king and priest.

7 The Lord has rejected his altar
and abandoned his sanctuary.
He has handed over to the enemy
the walls of her palaces;
they have raised a shout in the house
of the LORD
as on the day of an appointed feast.

8 The LORD determined to tear down
the wall around the Daughter of
Zion.
He stretched out a measuring line
and did not withhold his hand
from destroying.
He made ramparts and walls lament;
together they wasted away.

9 Her gates have sunk into the ground;
their bars he has broken and
destroyed.
Her king and her princes are exiled
among the nations,
the law is no more,
and her prophets no longer find
visions from the LORD.

10 The elders of the Daughter of Zion
sit on the ground in silence;
they have sprinkled dust on their
heads
and put on sackcloth.
The young women of Jerusalem
have bowed their heads to the
ground.

11 My eyes fail from weeping,
I am in torment within,
my heart is poured out on the ground
because my people are destroyed,
because children and infants faint
in the streets of the city.

12 They say to their mothers,
"Where is bread and wine?"
as they faint like wounded men
in the streets of the city,
as their lives ebb away
in their mothers' arms.

13 What can I say for you?
With what can I compare you,
O Daughter of Jerusalem?
To what can I liken you,
that I may comfort you,
O Virgin Daughter of Zion?

[a] This chapter is an acrostic poem, the verses of which begin with the successive letters of the Hebrew alphabet. [b] 1 Or *How the Lord in his anger / has treated the Daughter of Zion with contempt* [c] 3 Or / *all the strength;* or *every king; horn* here symbolizes strength.

Your wound is as deep as the sea.
  Who can heal you?

14 The visions of your prophets
  were false and worthless;
they did not expose your sin
  to ward off your captivity.
The oracles they gave you
  were false and misleading.

15 All who pass your way
  clap their hands at you;
they scoff and shake their heads
  at the Daughter of Jerusalem:
"Is this the city that was called
  the perfection of beauty,
  the joy of the whole earth?"

16 All your enemies open their mouths
  wide against you;
they scoff and gnash their teeth
  and say, "We have swallowed her up.
This is the day we have waited for;
  we have lived to see it."

17 The LORD has done what he planned;
  he has fulfilled his word,
  which he decreed long ago.
He has overthrown you without pity,
  he has let the enemy gloat over you,
  he has exalted the horn[d] of your foes.

18 The hearts of the people
  cry out to the Lord.
O wall of the Daughter of Zion,
  let your tears flow like a river
  day and night;
give yourself no relief,
  your eyes no rest.

19 Arise, cry out in the night,
  as the watches of the night begin;
pour out your heart like water
  in the presence of the Lord.
Lift up your hands to him
  for the lives of your children,
who faint from hunger
  at the head of every street.

20 "Look, O LORD, and consider:
  Whom have you ever treated like this?
Should women eat their offspring,
  the children they have cared for?
Should priest and prophet be killed
  in the sanctuary of the Lord?

21 "Young and old lie together
  in the dust of the streets;
my young men and maidens
  have fallen by the sword.
You have slain them in the day of your anger;
  you have slaughtered them without pity.

22 "As you summon to a feast day,
  so you summoned against me
  terrors on every side.
In the day of the LORD's anger
  no one escaped or survived;
those I cared for and reared,
  my enemy has destroyed."

[d] 17 *Horn* here symbolizes strength.

PRAYER: PETITION

IT is Your will, O God, that I be sanctified, that I abstain from immorality and learn to be in control of my own body in holiness and honor. For You did not call me to be impure, but to live a holy life. (1 Thessalonians 4:3–4, 7)

***PAUSE** here to petition God for spiritual insight so that you might have understanding of His Word. Ask for insight into your identity in Jesus Christ: that you might know who you are, what direction your life should take and what His purpose for your life is. Offer prayers regarding your activities for this day and any special concerns you may have.*

NT 1 Timothy 1:1–11

1 Paul, an apostle of Christ Jesus by the command of God our Savior and of Christ Jesus our hope,

2 To Timothy my true son in the faith:

Grace, mercy and peace from God the Father and Christ Jesus our Lord.

Warning Against False Teachers of the Law

[3]As I urged you when I went into Macedonia, stay there in Ephesus so that you
may command certain men not to teach
false doctrines any longer [4]nor to devote
themselves to myths and endless genealogies. These promote controversies
rather than God's work—which is by
faith. [5]The goal of this command is love,
which comes from a pure heart and a
good conscience and a sincere faith.
[6]Some have wandered away from these
and turned to meaningless talk. [7]They
want to be teachers of the law, but they do
not know what they are talking about or
what they so confidently affirm.
[8]We know that the law is good if one
uses it properly. [9]We also know that law[a]
is made not for the righteous but for lawbreakers and rebels, the ungodly and sinful, the unholy and irreligious; for those
who kill their fathers or mothers, for murderers, [10]for adulterers and perverts, for
slave traders and liars and perjurers—and
for whatever else is contrary to the sound
doctrine [11]that conforms to the glorious
gospel of the blessed God, which he entrusted to me.

[a] 9 Or *that the law*

PRAYER: THE ATTRIBUTES OF GOD

I WILL regard You as holy, Lord of hosts. You shall be my fear, and You shall be my dread. (Isaiah 8:13) . . . You, O Lord, are in Your holy temple; let all the earth be silent before You. (Habakkuk 2:20)

***PAUSE** to reflect on these affirmations about the person, powers and perfection of God.*

YEAR 2 DAY 242

OT Lamentations 3:1–66

3[a] I am the man who has seen affliction
by the rod of his wrath.
[2]He has driven me away and made me walk
in darkness rather than light;
[3]indeed, he has turned his hand against me
again and again, all day long.

[4]He has made my skin and my flesh grow old
and has broken my bones.
[5]He has besieged me and surrounded me
with bitterness and hardship.
[6]He has made me dwell in darkness
like those long dead.

[7]He has walled me in so I cannot escape;
he has weighed me down with chains.
[8]Even when I call out or cry for help,
he shuts out my prayer.
[9]He has barred my way with blocks of stone;
he has made my paths crooked.

[10]Like a bear lying in wait,
like a lion in hiding,
[11]he dragged me from the path and mangled me
and left me without help.
[12]He drew his bow
and made me the target for his arrows.

[13]He pierced my heart
with arrows from his quiver.
[14]I became the laughingstock of all my people;
they mock me in song all day long.
[15]He has filled me with bitter herbs
and sated me with gall.

[16]He has broken my teeth with gravel;
he has trampled me in the dust.
[17]I have been deprived of peace;
I have forgotten what prosperity is.

[a] This chapter is an acrostic poem; the verses of each stanza begin with the successive letters of the Hebrew alphabet, and the verses within each stanza begin with the same letter.

[18]So I say, "My splendor is gone
and all that I had hoped from the
LORD."

[19]I remember my affliction and my
wandering,
the bitterness and the gall.
[20]I well remember them,
and my soul is downcast within me.
[21]Yet this I call to mind
and therefore I have hope:

[22]Because of the LORD's great love we are
not consumed,
for his compassions never fail.
[23]They are new every morning;
great is your faithfulness.
[24]I say to myself, "The LORD is my
portion;
therefore I will wait for him."

[25]The LORD is good to those whose
hope is in him,
to the one who seeks him;
[26]it is good to wait quietly
for the salvation of the LORD.
[27]It is good for a man to bear the yoke
while he is young.

[28]Let him sit alone in silence,
for the LORD has laid it on him.
[29]Let him bury his face in the dust—
there may yet be hope.
[30]Let him offer his cheek to one who
would strike him,
and let him be filled with disgrace.

[31]For men are not cast off
by the Lord forever.
[32]Though he brings grief, he will show
compassion,
so great is his unfailing love.
[33]For he does not willingly bring
affliction
or grief to the children of men.

[34]To crush underfoot
all prisoners in the land,
[35]to deny a man his rights
before the Most High,
[36]to deprive a man of justice—
would not the Lord see such things?

[37]Who can speak and have it happen
if the Lord has not decreed it?
[38]Is it not from the mouth of the Most
High
that both calamities and good
things come?
[39]Why should any living man complain
when punished for his sins?

[40]Let us examine our ways and test
them,
and let us return to the LORD.
[41]Let us lift up our hearts and our hands
to God in heaven, and say:
[42]"We have sinned and rebelled
and you have not forgiven.

[43]"You have covered yourself with anger
and pursued us;
you have slain without pity.
[44]You have covered yourself with a
cloud
so that no prayer can get through.
[45]You have made us scum and refuse
among the nations.

[46]"All our enemies have opened their
mouths
wide against us.
[47]We have suffered terror and pitfalls,
ruin and destruction."
[48]Streams of tears flow from my eyes
because my people are destroyed.

[49]My eyes will flow unceasingly,
without relief,
[50]until the LORD looks down
from heaven and sees.
[51]What I see brings grief to my soul
because of all the women of my
city.

[52]Those who were my enemies without
cause
hunted me like a bird.
[53]They tried to end my life in a pit
and threw stones at me;
[54]the waters closed over my head,
and I thought I was about to be cut
off.

[55]I called on your name, O LORD,
from the depths of the pit.
[56]You heard my plea: "Do not close
your ears
to my cry for relief."
[57]You came near when I called you,
and you said, "Do not fear."

[58]O Lord, you took up my case;
you redeemed my life.
[59]You have seen, O LORD, the wrong
done to me.
Uphold my cause!
[60]You have seen the depth of their
vengeance,
all their plots against me.

[61]O LORD, you have heard their insults,
all their plots against me—
[62]what my enemies whisper and mutter
against me all day long.
[63]Look at them! Sitting or standing,
they mock me in their songs.
[64]Pay them back what they deserve, O LORD,
for what their hands have done.
[65]Put a veil over their hearts,
and may your curse be on them!
[66]Pursue them in anger and destroy them
from under the heavens of the LORD.

PRAYER: INTERCESSION

MAY I owe nothing to anyone except to love them, for those who love their neighbor have fulfilled the law. For the commandments, "You shall not commit adultery," "You shall not murder," "You shall not steal," "You shall not covet," and any other commandments there may be are summed up in this saying: "You shall love your neighbor as yourself." Love does no harm to a neighbor; therefore love is the fulfillment of the law. (Romans 13:8–10)

TAKE *a few moments to intercede on behalf of other believers, such as your personal friends, those in ministry and those who are oppressed and in need.*

NT 1 Timothy 1:12–20

The Lord's Grace to Paul

[12]I thank Christ Jesus our Lord, who has
given me strength, that he considered me
faithful, appointing me to his service.
[13]Even though I was once a blasphemer
and a persecutor and a violent man, I was
shown mercy because I acted in ignorance
and unbelief. [14]The grace of our Lord was
poured out on me abundantly, along with
the faith and love that are in Christ Jesus.
[15]Here is a trustworthy saying that deserves full acceptance: Christ Jesus came
into the world to save sinners—of whom
I am the worst. [16]But for that very reason
I was shown mercy so that in me, the
worst of sinners, Christ Jesus might display his unlimited patience as an example
for those who would believe on him and
receive eternal life. [17]Now to the King
eternal, immortal, invisible, the only God,
be honor and glory for ever and ever.
Amen.
[18]Timothy, my son, I give you this instruction in keeping with the prophecies
once made about you, so that by following them you may fight the good fight,
[19]holding on to faith and a good conscience. Some have rejected these and so
have shipwrecked their faith. [20]Among
them are Hymenaeus and Alexander,
whom I have handed over to Satan to be
taught not to blaspheme.

PRAYER: THE WORKS OF GOD

THERE is no one righteous, not even one; there is no one who understands, no one who seeks You, O God. All have turned away; they have together become useless; there is no one who does good, not even one. (Romans 3:10–12)

TAKE *a moment to consider the greatness of God's wonderful works.*

YEAR 2 DAY 243

OT **Lamentations 4:1–5:22**

4 [a] How the gold has lost its luster,
the fine gold become dull!
The sacred gems are scattered
at the head of every street.

2 How the precious sons of Zion,
once worth their weight in gold,
are now considered as pots of clay,
the work of a potter's hands!

3 Even jackals offer their breasts
to nurse their young,
but my people have become heartless
like ostriches in the desert.

4 Because of thirst the infant's tongue
sticks to the roof of its mouth;
the children beg for bread,
but no one gives it to them.

5 Those who once ate delicacies
are destitute in the streets.
Those nurtured in purple
now lie on ash heaps.

6 The punishment of my people
is greater than that of Sodom,
which was overthrown in a moment
without a hand turned to help her.

7 Their princes were brighter than snow
and whiter than milk,
their bodies more ruddy than rubies,
their appearance like sapphires.[b]

8 But now they are blacker than soot;
they are not recognized in the
streets.
Their skin has shriveled on their
bones;
it has become as dry as a stick.

9 Those killed by the sword are better
off
than those who die of famine;
racked with hunger, they waste away
for lack of food from the field.

10 With their own hands compassionate
women
have cooked their own children,
who became their food
when my people were destroyed.

11 The LORD has given full vent to his
wrath;
he has poured out his fierce anger.
He kindled a fire in Zion
that consumed her foundations.

12 The kings of the earth did not believe,
nor did any of the world's people,
that enemies and foes could enter
the gates of Jerusalem.

13 But it happened because of the sins of
her prophets
and the iniquities of her priests,
who shed within her
the blood of the righteous.

14 Now they grope through the streets
like men who are blind.
They are so defiled with blood
that no one dares to touch their
garments.

15 "Go away! You are unclean!" men cry
to them.
"Away! Away! Don't touch us!"
When they flee and wander about,
people among the nations say,
"They can stay here no longer."

16 The LORD himself has scattered them;
he no longer watches over them.
The priests are shown no honor,
the elders no favor.

17 Moreover, our eyes failed,
looking in vain for help;
from our towers we watched
for a nation that could not save us.

18 Men stalked us at every step,
so we could not walk in our streets.
Our end was near, our days were
numbered,
for our end had come.

19 Our pursuers were swifter
than eagles in the sky;
they chased us over the mountains
and lay in wait for us in the desert.

20 The LORD's anointed, our very life
breath,
was caught in their traps.
We thought that under his shadow
we would live among the nations.

21 Rejoice and be glad, O Daughter of
Edom,

[a] This chapter is an acrostic poem, the verses of which begin with the successive letters of the Hebrew alphabet. [b] 7 Or *lapis lazuli*

you who live in the land of Uz.
But to you also the cup will be passed;
you will be drunk and stripped naked.

22 O Daughter of Zion, your punishment will end;
he will not prolong your exile.
But, O Daughter of Edom, he will punish your sin
and expose your wickedness.

5 Remember, O LORD, what has happened to us;
look, and see our disgrace.
2 Our inheritance has been turned over to aliens,
our homes to foreigners.
3 We have become orphans and fatherless,
our mothers like widows.
4 We must buy the water we drink;
our wood can be had only at a price.
5 Those who pursue us are at our heels;
we are weary and find no rest.
6 We submitted to Egypt and Assyria
to get enough bread.
7 Our fathers sinned and are no more,
and we bear their punishment.
8 Slaves rule over us,
and there is none to free us from their hands.
9 We get our bread at the risk of our lives
because of the sword in the desert.
10 Our skin is hot as an oven,
feverish from hunger.
11 Women have been ravished in Zion,
and virgins in the towns of Judah.
12 Princes have been hung up by their hands;
elders are shown no respect.
13 Young men toil at the millstones;
boys stagger under loads of wood.
14 The elders are gone from the city gate;
the young men have stopped their music.
15 Joy is gone from our hearts;
our dancing has turned to mourning.
16 The crown has fallen from our head.
Woe to us, for we have sinned!
17 Because of this our hearts are faint,
because of these things our eyes grow dim
18 for Mount Zion, which lies desolate,
with jackals prowling over it.

19 You, O LORD, reign forever;
your throne endures from generation to generation.
20 Why do you always forget us?
Why do you forsake us so long?
21 Restore us to yourself, O LORD, that we may return;
renew our days as of old
22 unless you have utterly rejected us
and are angry with us beyond measure.

PRAYER: AFFIRMATION

IN You, O Christ, are hidden all the treasures of wisdom and knowledge. In You, O Christ, all the fullness of the Godhead lives in bodily form. (Colossians 2:3, 9)

***PAUSE** to reflect on these Biblical affirmations.*

NT 1 Timothy 2:1-15

Instructions on Worship

2 I urge, then, first of all, that requests,
prayers, intercession and thanksgiving
be made for everyone— 2for kings and all
those in authority, that we may live peaceful and quiet lives in all godliness and holiness. 3This is good, and pleases God our
Savior, 4who wants all men to be saved
and to come to a knowledge of the truth.
5For there is one God and one mediator
between God and men, the man Christ
Jesus, 6who gave himself as a ransom for
all men—the testimony given in its proper time. 7And for this purpose I was appointed a herald and an apostle—I am
telling the truth, I am not lying—and a
teacher of the true faith to the Gentiles.
8I want men everywhere to lift up holy
hands in prayer, without anger or disputing.

[9]I also want women to dress modestly, with decency and propriety, not with braided hair or gold or pearls or expensive clothes, [10]but with good deeds, appropriate for women who profess to worship God.

[11]A woman should learn in quietness and full submission. [12]I do not permit a woman to teach or to have authority over a man; she must be silent. [13]For Adam was formed first, then Eve. [14]And Adam was not the one deceived; it was the woman who was deceived and became a sinner. [15]But women[a] will be saved[b] through childbearing—if they continue in faith, love and holiness with propriety.

[a] 15 Greek *she* [b] 15 Or *restored*

PRAYER: MY RELATIONSHIP TO GOD

I DO not consider my life dear to me, if only I may finish my course and the ministry which I received from You, Lord Jesus—to testify to the gospel of the grace of God. (Acts 20:24) . . . I want Your name, Lord Jesus, to be magnified in my life. (Acts 19:17)

***PAUSE** to thank God for the relationship that you enjoy with Him in Jesus Christ.*

YEAR 2 DAY 244

OT Ezekiel 1:1–2:10

The Living Creatures and the Glory of the Lord

1 In the[a] thirtieth year, in the fourth month on the fifth day, while I was among the exiles by the Kebar River, the heavens were opened and I saw visions of God.

[2]On the fifth of the month—it was the fifth year of the exile of King Jehoiachin—[3]the word of the Lord came to Ezekiel the priest, the son of Buzi,[b] by the Kebar River in the land of the Babylonians.[c] There the hand of the Lord was upon him.

[4]I looked, and I saw a windstorm coming out of the north—an immense cloud with flashing lightning and surrounded by brilliant light. The center of the fire looked like glowing metal, [5]and in the fire was what looked like four living creatures. In appearance their form was that of a man, [6]but each of them had four faces and four wings. [7]Their legs were straight; their feet were like those of a calf and gleamed like burnished bronze. [8]Under their wings on their four sides they had the hands of a man. All four of them had faces and wings, [9]and their wings touched one another. Each one went straight ahead; they did not turn as they moved.

[10]Their faces looked like this: Each of the four had the face of a man, and on the right side each had the face of a lion, and on the left the face of an ox; each also had the face of an eagle. [11]Such were their faces. Their wings were spread out upward; each had two wings, one touching the wing of another creature on either side, and two wings covering its body. [12]Each one went straight ahead. Wherever the spirit would go, they would go, without turning as they went. [13]The appearance of the living creatures was like burning coals of fire or like torches. Fire moved back and forth among the creatures; it was bright, and lightning flashed out of it. [14]The creatures sped back and forth like flashes of lightning.

[15]As I looked at the living creatures, I saw a wheel on the ground beside each creature with its four faces. [16]This was the appearance and structure of the wheels: They sparkled like chrysolite, and all four looked alike. Each appeared to be made like a wheel intersecting a wheel. [17]As they moved, they would go in any one of the four directions the creatures faced; the wheels did not turn about[d] as the creatures went. [18]Their rims were high and awesome, and all four rims were full of eyes all around.

[a] 1 Or ⌊my⌋ [b] 3 Or *Ezekiel son of Buzi the priest* [c] 3 Or *Chaldeans* [d] 17 Or *aside*

19When the living creatures moved, the wheels beside them moved; and when the living creatures rose from the ground, the wheels also rose. 20Wherever the spirit would go, they would go, and the wheels would rise along with them, because the spirit of the living creatures was in the wheels. 21When the creatures moved, they also moved; when the creatures stood still, they also stood still; and when the creatures rose from the ground, the wheels rose along with them, because the spirit of the living creatures was in the wheels.

22Spread out above the heads of the living creatures was what looked like an expanse, sparkling like ice, and awesome. 23Under the expanse their wings were stretched out one toward the other, and each had two wings covering its body. 24When the creatures moved, I heard the sound of their wings, like the roar of rushing waters, like the voice of the Almighty,[e] like the tumult of an army. When they stood still, they lowered their wings.

25Then there came a voice from above the expanse over their heads as they stood with lowered wings. 26Above the expanse over their heads was what looked like a throne of sapphire,[f] and high above on the throne was a figure like that of a man. 27I saw that from what appeared to be his waist up he looked like glowing metal, as if full of fire, and that from there down he looked like fire; and brilliant light surrounded him. 28Like the appearance of a rainbow in the clouds on a rainy day, so was the radiance around him.

This was the appearance of the likeness of the glory of the LORD. When I saw it, I fell facedown, and I heard the voice of one speaking.

Ezekiel's Call

2 He said to me, "Son of man, stand up on your feet and I will speak to you." 2As he spoke, the Spirit came into me and raised me to my feet, and I heard him speaking to me.

3He said: "Son of man, I am sending you to the Israelites, to a rebellious nation that has rebelled against me; they and their fathers have been in revolt against me to this very day. 4The people to whom I am sending you are obstinate and stubborn. Say to them, 'This is what the Sovereign LORD says.' 5And whether they listen or fail to listen—for they are a rebellious house—they will know that a prophet has been among them. 6And you, son of man, do not be afraid of them or their words. Do not be afraid, though briers and thorns are all around you and you live among scorpions. Do not be afraid of what they say or terrified by them, though they are a rebellious house. 7You must speak my words to them, whether they listen or fail to listen, for they are rebellious. 8But you, son of man, listen to what I say to you. Do not rebel like that rebellious house; open your mouth and eat what I give you."

9Then I looked, and I saw a hand stretched out to me. In it was a scroll, 10which he unrolled before me. On both sides of it were written words of lament and mourning and woe.

[e] 24 Hebrew *Shaddai* [f] 26 Or *lapis lazuli*

PRAYER: THANKSGIVING

GOD, Your grace was given to us in Christ Jesus before the beginning of time and has now been revealed through the appearing of our Savior, Christ Jesus, who abolished death and brought life and immortality to light through the gospel. (2 Timothy 1:9–10)

***PAUSE** to offer your own expressions of thanksgiving.*

NT 1 Timothy 3:1–16

Overseers and Deacons

3 Here is a trustworthy saying: If anyone sets his heart on being an overseer,[a] he desires a noble task. 2Now the overseer must be above reproach, the husband of but one wife, temperate, self-controlled, respectable, hospitable, able to teach, 3not

[a] 1 Traditionally *bishop*; also in verse 2

given to drunkenness, not violent but gentle, not quarrelsome, not a lover of money.
4 He must manage his own family well and
see that his children obey him with proper respect. 5 (If anyone does not know how
to manage his own family, how can he take
care of God's church?) 6 He must not be a
recent convert, or he may become conceited and fall under the same judgment as the
devil. 7 He must also have a good reputation with outsiders, so that he will not fall
into disgrace and into the devil's trap.

8 Deacons, likewise, are to be men worthy of respect, sincere, not indulging in
much wine, and not pursuing dishonest
gain. 9 They must keep hold of the deep
truths of the faith with a clear conscience.
10 They must first be tested; and then if
there is nothing against them, let them
serve as deacons.

11 In the same way, their wives[b] are to be
women worthy of respect, not malicious
talkers but temperate and trustworthy in
everything.

12 A deacon must be the husband of but
one wife and must manage his children
and his household well. 13 Those who have
served well gain an excellent standing and
great assurance in their faith in Christ
Jesus.

14 Although I hope to come to you soon,
I am writing you these instructions so
that, 15 if I am delayed, you will know how
people ought to conduct themselves in
God's household, which is the church of
the living God, the pillar and foundation
of the truth. 16 Beyond all question, the
mystery of godliness is great:

He[c] appeared in a body,[d]
  was vindicated by the Spirit,
was seen by angels,
  was preached among the nations,
was believed on in the world,
  was taken up in glory.

[b] 11 Or *way, deaconesses* [c] 16 Some manuscripts *God* [d] 16 Or *in the flesh*

PRAYER: THE CHARACTER I WANT TO CULTIVATE

THOSE of us who suffer according to Your will, O God, should commit ourselves to You, our faithful Creator, in doing good. (1 Peter 4:19) . . . Who is going to harm me if I am eager to do good? But even if I should suffer for what is right, I am blessed, and I will not fear what they fear or be intimidated. (1 Peter 3:13–14)

TAKE *a moment to ask the Lord for the grace to grow in godly character.*

YEAR 2 DAY 245

OT Psalm 119:89-128

ל Lamedh

89 Your word, O LORD, is eternal;
  it stands firm in the heavens.
90 Your faithfulness continues through
    all generations;
  you established the earth, and it
    endures.
91 Your laws endure to this day,
  for all things serve you.
92 If your law had not been my delight,
  I would have perished in my
    affliction.
93 I will never forget your precepts,
  for by them you have preserved my
    life.
94 Save me, for I am yours;
  I have sought out your precepts.
95 The wicked are waiting to destroy me,
  but I will ponder your statutes.
96 To all perfection I see a limit;
  but your commands are boundless.

מ Mem

97 Oh, how I love your law!
  I meditate on it all day long.
98 Your commands make me wiser than
    my enemies,
  for they are ever with me.
99 I have more insight than all my
    teachers,
  for I meditate on your statutes.

100 I have more understanding than the
elders,
for I obey your precepts.
101 I have kept my feet from every evil
path
so that I might obey your word.
102 I have not departed from your laws,
for you yourself have taught me.
103 How sweet are your words to my
taste,
sweeter than honey to my mouth!
104 I gain understanding from your
precepts;
therefore I hate every wrong path.

נ Nun

105 Your word is a lamp to my feet
and a light for my path.
106 I have taken an oath and
confirmed it,
that I will follow your righteous
laws.
107 I have suffered much;
preserve my life, O LORD, according
to your word.
108 Accept, O LORD, the willing praise of
my mouth,
and teach me your laws.
109 Though I constantly take my life in
my hands,
I will not forget your law.
110 The wicked have set a snare for me,
but I have not strayed from your
precepts.
111 Your statutes are my heritage forever;
they are the joy of my heart.
112 My heart is set on keeping your
decrees
to the very end.

ס Samekh

113 I hate double-minded men,
but I love your law.
114 You are my refuge and my shield;
I have put my hope in your word.
115 Away from me, you evildoers,
that I may keep the commands of
my God!
116 Sustain me according to your
promise, and I will live;
do not let my hopes be dashed.
117 Uphold me, and I will be delivered;
I will always have regard for your
decrees.
118 You reject all who stray from your
decrees,
for their deceitfulness is in vain.
119 All the wicked of the earth you
discard like dross;
therefore I love your statutes.
120 My flesh trembles in fear of you;
I stand in awe of your laws.

ע Ayin

121 I have done what is righteous and
just;
do not leave me to my oppressors.
122 Ensure your servant's well-being;
let not the arrogant oppress me.
123 My eyes fail, looking for your
salvation,
looking for your righteous promise.
124 Deal with your servant according to
your love
and teach me your decrees.
125 I am your servant; give me
discernment
that I may understand your statutes.
126 It is time for you to act, O LORD;
your law is being broken.
127 Because I love your commands
more than gold, more than pure
gold,
128 and because I consider all your
precepts right,
I hate every wrong path.

PRAYER: ADORATION

YOU, O Lord, are a compassionate and gracious God, slow to anger and abounding in loving-kindness and truth. (Psalm 86:15) . . . My flesh trembles in fear of You; I stand in awe of Your judgments. (Psalm 119:120)

***PAUSE** to express your thoughts of praise and worship.*

NT 1 Timothy 4:1-16

Instructions to Timothy

4 The Spirit clearly says that in later times
some will abandon the faith and follow deceiving spirits and things taught by
demons. [2]Such teachings come through
hypocritical liars, whose consciences have
been seared as with a hot iron. [3]They forbid people to marry and order them to
abstain from certain foods, which God
created to be received with thanksgiving
by those who believe and who know the
truth. [4]For everything God created is
good, and nothing is to be rejected if it is
received with thanksgiving, [5]because it is
consecrated by the word of God and
prayer.

[6]If you point these things out to the
brothers, you will be a good minister of
Christ Jesus, brought up in the truths of
the faith and of the good teaching that
you have followed. [7]Have nothing to do
with godless myths and old wives' tales;
rather, train yourself to be godly. [8]For
physical training is of some value, but
godliness has value for all things, holding
promise for both the present life and the
life to come.

[9]This is a trustworthy saying that deserves full acceptance [10](and for this we labor and strive), that we have put our hope
in the living God, who is the Savior of all
men, and especially of those who believe.

[11]Command and teach these things.
[12]Don't let anyone look down on you because you are young, but set an example
for the believers in speech, in life, in love,
in faith and in purity. [13]Until I come, devote yourself to the public reading of
Scripture, to preaching and to teaching.
[14]Do not neglect your gift, which was giv-
en you through a prophetic message
when the body of elders laid their hands
on you.

[15]Be diligent in these matters; give yourself wholly to them, so that everyone may
see your progress. [16]Watch your life and
doctrine closely. Persevere in them, because if you do, you will save both yourself and your hearers.

PRAYER: MY RELATIONSHIP TO OTHERS

I WILL sanctify You, O Christ, as Lord in my heart, always being ready to give an answer, but with gentleness and respect, to everyone who asks me to give the reason for the hope that is in me.

(1 Peter 3:15)

***PAUSE** to review your relationships with others and to commit them to the Lord.*

YEAR 2 DAY 246

OT Ezekiel 3:1-27

3 And he said to me, "Son of man, eat
what is before you, eat this scroll; then
go and speak to the house of Israel." [2]So
I opened my mouth, and he gave me the
scroll to eat.

[3]Then he said to me, "Son of man, eat
this scroll I am giving you and fill your
stomach with it." So I ate it, and it tasted
as sweet as honey in my mouth.

[4]He then said to me: "Son of man, go
now to the house of Israel and speak my
words to them. [5]You are not being sent to
a people of obscure speech and difficult
language, but to the house of Israel— [6]not
to many peoples of obscure speech and
difficult language, whose words you cannot understand. Surely if I had sent you
to them, they would have listened to you.
[7]But the house of Israel is not willing to
listen to you because they are not willing
to listen to me, for the whole house of Israel is hardened and obstinate. [8]But I will
make you as unyielding and hardened as
they are. [9]I will make your forehead like
the hardest stone, harder than flint. Do

not be afraid of them or terrified by them,
though they are a rebellious house."
10 And he said to me, "Son of man, listen carefully and take to heart all the
words I speak to you. 11 Go now to your
countrymen in exile and speak to them.
Say to them, 'This is what the Sovereign
LORD says,' whether they listen or fail to
listen."
12 Then the Spirit lifted me up, and I
heard behind me a loud rumbling
sound—May the glory of the LORD be
praised in his dwelling place!— 13 the
sound of the wings of the living creatures
brushing against each other and the
sound of the wheels beside them, a loud
rumbling sound. 14 The Spirit then lifted
me up and took me away, and I went in
bitterness and in the anger of my spirit,
with the strong hand of the LORD upon
me. 15 I came to the exiles who lived at Tel
Abib near the Kebar River. And there,
where they were living, I sat among them
for seven days—overwhelmed.

Warning to Israel

16 At the end of seven days the word of the
LORD came to me: 17 "Son of man, I have
made you a watchman for the house of Israel; so hear the word I speak and give them
warning from me. 18 When I say to a wicked
man, 'You will surely die,' and you do not
warn him or speak out to dissuade him
from his evil ways in order to save his life,
that wicked man will die for[a] his sin, and I
will hold you accountable for his blood.
19 But if you do warn the wicked man and
he does not turn from his wickedness or
from his evil ways, he will die for his sin;
but you will have saved yourself.
20 "Again, when a righteous man turns
from his righteousness and does evil, and
I put a stumbling block before him, he
will die. Since you did not warn him, he
will die for his sin. The righteous things
he did will not be remembered, and I will
hold you accountable for his blood. 21 But
if you do warn the righteous man not to
sin and he does not sin, he will surely live
because he took warning, and you will
have saved yourself."
22 The hand of the LORD was upon me
there, and he said to me, "Get up and go
out to the plain, and there I will speak to
you." 23 So I got up and went out to the
plain. And the glory of the LORD was
standing there, like the glory I had seen by
the Kebar River, and I fell facedown.
24 Then the Spirit came into me and
raised me to my feet. He spoke to me and
said: "Go, shut yourself inside your house.
25 And you, son of man, they will tie with
ropes; you will be bound so that you cannot go out among the people. 26 I will
make your tongue stick to the roof of your
mouth so that you will be silent and unable to rebuke them, though they are a rebellious house. 27 But when I speak to you,
I will open your mouth and you shall say
to them, 'This is what the Sovereign LORD
says.' Whoever will listen let him listen,
and whoever will refuse let him refuse; for
they are a rebellious house.

[a] *18* Or *in;* also in verses 19 and 20

PRAYER: CONFESSION

YOU are good and upright, O Lord; therefore You instruct sinners in Your ways. You guide the humble in what is right and teach the humble Your way. (Psalm 25:8–9)

***ASK** the Spirit to search your heart and reveal any areas of unconfessed sin. Acknowledge these to the Lord and thank Him for His forgiveness.*

NT 1 Timothy 5:1–25

Advice About Widows, Elders and Slaves

5 Do not rebuke an older man harshly,
but exhort him as if he were your father. Treat younger men as brothers, 2 older women as mothers, and younger
women as sisters, with absolute purity.
3 Give proper recognition to those widows who are really in need. 4 But if a widow has children or grandchildren, these
should learn first of all to put their religion into practice by caring for their own
family and so repaying their parents and

grandparents, for this is pleasing to God.
5The widow who is really in need and left
all alone puts her hope in God and continues night and day to pray and to ask
God for help. 6But the widow who lives
for pleasure is dead even while she lives.
7Give the people these instructions, too,
so that no one may be open to blame. 8If
anyone does not provide for his relatives,
and especially for his immediate family,
he has denied the faith and is worse than
an unbeliever.

9No widow may be put on the list of
widows unless she is over sixty, has been
faithful to her husband,[a] 10and is well
known for her good deeds, such as bringing up children, showing hospitality,
washing the feet of the saints, helping
those in trouble and devoting herself to
all kinds of good deeds.

11As for younger widows, do not put
them on such a list. For when their sensual desires overcome their dedication to
Christ, they want to marry. 12Thus they
bring judgment on themselves, because
they have broken their first pledge. 13Be-
sides, they get into the habit of being idle
and going about from house to house. And
not only do they become idlers, but also
gossips and busybodies, saying things they
ought not to. 14So I counsel younger widows to marry, to have children, to manage
their homes and to give the enemy no opportunity for slander. 15Some have in fact
already turned away to follow Satan.

16If any woman who is a believer has
widows in her family, she should help
them and not let the church be burdened
with them, so that the church can help
those widows who are really in need.

17The elders who direct the affairs of the
church well are worthy of double honor,
especially those whose work is preaching
and teaching. 18For the Scripture says, "Do
not muzzle the ox while it is treading out
the grain,"[b] and "The worker deserves his
wages."[c] 19Do not entertain an accusation
against an elder unless it is brought by
two or three witnesses. 20Those who sin
are to be rebuked publicly, so that the others may take warning.

21I charge you, in the sight of God and
Christ Jesus and the elect angels, to keep
these instructions without partiality, and
to do nothing out of favoritism.

22Do not be hasty in the laying on of
hands, and do not share in the sins of others. Keep yourself pure.

23Stop drinking only water, and use a
little wine because of your stomach and
your frequent illnesses.

24The sins of some men are obvious,
reaching the place of judgment ahead of
them; the sins of others trail behind them.
25In the same way, good deeds are obvious, and even those that are not cannot
be hidden.

[a] 9 Or *has had but one husband* [b] 18 Deut. 25:4
[c] 18 Luke 10:7

PRAYER: THE ATTRIBUTES OF GOD

YOU reign, O Lord; You are clothed with majesty; You are robed in majesty and armed with strength. Indeed, the world is firmly established; it cannot be moved. Your throne is established from of old; You are from everlasting. Your testimonies stand firm; holiness adorns Your house, O Lord, forever. (Psalm 93:1–2, 5)

PAUSE *to reflect on these affirmations about the person, powers and perfection of God.*

YEAR 2 DAY 247

OT Ezekiel 4:1–5:17

Siege of Jerusalem Symbolized

4 "Now, son of man, take a clay tablet,
put it in front of you and draw the city
of Jerusalem on it. 2Then lay siege to it:
Erect siege works against it, build a ramp
up to it, set up camps against it and put
battering rams around it. 3Then take an
iron pan, place it as an iron wall between

you and the city and turn your face toward
it. It will be under siege, and you shall besiege it. This will be a sign to the house of
Israel.
4 "Then lie on your left side and put the
sin of the house of Israel upon yourself.[a]
You are to bear their sin for the number
of days you lie on your side. 5 I have assigned you the same number of days as
the years of their sin. So for 390 days you
will bear the sin of the house of Israel.
6 "After you have finished this, lie down
again, this time on your right side, and
bear the sin of the house of Judah. I have
assigned you 40 days, a day for each year.
7 Turn your face toward the siege of Jerusalem and with bared arm prophesy
against her. 8 I will tie you up with ropes
so that you cannot turn from one side to
the other until you have finished the days
of your siege.
9 "Take wheat and barley, beans and
lentils, millet and spelt; put them in a
storage jar and use them to make bread
for yourself. You are to eat it during the
390 days you lie on your side. 10 Weigh out
twenty shekels[b] of food to eat each day
and eat it at set times. 11 Also measure out
a sixth of a hin[c] of water and drink it at
set times. 12 Eat the food as you would a
barley cake; bake it in the sight of the people, using human excrement for fuel."
13 The LORD said, "In this way the people
of Israel will eat defiled food among the
nations where I will drive them."
14 Then I said, "Not so, Sovereign LORD!
I have never defiled myself. From my
youth until now I have never eaten anything found dead or torn by wild animals.
No unclean meat has ever entered my
mouth."
15 "Very well," he said, "I will let you
bake your bread over cow manure instead
of human excrement."
16 He then said to me: "Son of man, I
will cut off the supply of food in Jerusalem. The people will eat rationed food
in anxiety and drink rationed water in despair, 17 for food and water will be scarce.
They will be appalled at the sight of each
other and will waste away because of[d]
their sin.
5 "Now, son of man, take a sharp sword
and use it as a barber's razor to shave
your head and your beard. Then take a set
of scales and divide up the hair. 2 When
the days of your siege come to an end,
burn a third of the hair with fire inside the
city. Take a third and strike it with the
sword all around the city. And scatter a
third to the wind. For I will pursue them
with drawn sword. 3 But take a few strands
of hair and tuck them away in the folds of
your garment. 4 Again, take a few of these
and throw them into the fire and burn
them up. A fire will spread from there to
the whole house of Israel.
5 "This is what the Sovereign LORD says:
This is Jerusalem, which I have set in the
center of the nations, with countries all
around her. 6 Yet in her wickedness she has
rebelled against my laws and decrees
more than the nations and countries
around her. She has rejected my laws and
has not followed my decrees.
7 "Therefore this is what the Sovereign
LORD says: You have been more unruly
than the nations around you and have not
followed my decrees or kept my laws. You
have not even[e] conformed to the standards of the nations around you.
8 "Therefore this is what the Sovereign
LORD says: I myself am against you, Jerusalem, and I will inflict punishment on
you in the sight of the nations. 9 Because
of all your detestable idols, I will do to
you what I have never done before and
will never do again. 10 Therefore in your
midst fathers will eat their children, and
children will eat their fathers. I will inflict
punishment on you and will scatter all
your survivors to the winds. 11 Therefore as
surely as I live, declares the Sovereign
LORD, because you have defiled my sanctuary with all your vile images and detestable practices, I myself will withdraw
my favor; I will not look on you with pity
or spare you. 12 A third of your people will
die of the plague or perish by famine inside you; a third will fall by the sword outside your walls; and a third I will scatter
to the winds and pursue with drawn
sword.
13 "Then my anger will cease and my
wrath against them will subside, and I will
be avenged. And when I have spent my
wrath upon them, they will know that I
the LORD have spoken in my zeal.
14 "I will make you a ruin and a reproach

[a] 4 Or *your side* [b] 10 That is, about 8 ounces (about 0.2 kilogram) [c] 11 That is, about 2/3 quart (about 0.6 liter) [d] 17 Or *away in* [e] 7 Most Hebrew manuscripts; some Hebrew manuscripts and Syriac *You have*

among the nations around you, in the sight of all who pass by. [15]You will be a reproach and a taunt, a warning and an object of horror to the nations around you when I inflict punishment on you in anger and in wrath and with stinging rebuke. I the LORD have spoken. [16]When I shoot at you with my deadly and destructive arrows of famine, I will shoot to destroy you. I will bring more and more famine upon you and cut off your supply of food. [17]I will send famine and wild beasts against you, and they will leave you childless. Plague and bloodshed will sweep through you, and I will bring the sword against you. I the LORD have spoken."

PRAYER: RENEWAL

MAY I keep Your words and store up Your commands within me. May I keep Your commands and live, and may Your law be the apple of my eye. May I bind them on my fingers; may I write them on the tablet of my heart. May I say to wisdom, "You are my sister," and call understanding my kinsman. (Proverbs 7:1–4)

***PAUSE** to add your own prayers for personal renewal.*

NT 1 Timothy 6:1–10

6 All who are under the yoke of slavery should consider their masters worthy of full respect, so that God's name and our teaching may not be slandered. [2]Those who have believing masters are not to show less respect for them because they are brothers. Instead, they are to serve them even better, because those who benefit from their service are believers, and dear to them. These are the things you are to teach and urge on them.

Love of Money

[3]If anyone teaches false doctrines and does not agree to the sound instruction of our Lord Jesus Christ and to godly teaching, [4]he is conceited and understands nothing. He has an unhealthy interest in controversies and quarrels about words that result in envy, strife, malicious talk, evil suspicions [5]and constant friction between men of corrupt mind, who have been robbed of the truth and who think that godliness is a means to financial gain.

[6]But godliness with contentment is great gain. [7]For we brought nothing into the world, and we can take nothing out of it. [8]But if we have food and clothing, we will be content with that. [9]People who want to get rich fall into temptation and a trap and into many foolish and harmful desires that plunge men into ruin and destruction. [10]For the love of money is a root of all kinds of evil. Some people, eager for money, have wandered from the faith and pierced themselves with many griefs.

PRAYER: THE WORKS OF GOD

MY days are like a lengthened shadow, and I wither away like grass. But You, O Lord, will endure forever, and the remembrance of Your name to all generations. In the beginning You laid the foundations of the earth, and the heavens are the work of Your hands. They will perish, but You will endure. They will all wear out like a garment; like clothing You will change them, and they will be discarded. But You are the same, and Your years will have no end. (Psalm 102:11–12, 25–27)

***TAKE** a moment to consider the greatness of God's wonderful works.*

OT Ezekiel 6:1–7:27

YEAR 2 DAY 248

A Prophecy Against the Mountains of Israel

6 The word of the LORD came to me: 2"Son of man, set your face against the mountains of Israel; prophesy against them 3and say: 'O mountains of Israel, hear the word of the Sovereign LORD. This is what the Sovereign LORD says to the mountains and hills, to the ravines and valleys: I am about to bring a sword against you, and I will destroy your high places. 4Your altars will be demolished and your incense altars will be smashed; and I will slay your people in front of your idols. 5I will lay the dead bodies of the Israelites in front of their idols, and I will scatter your bones around your altars. 6Wherever you live, the towns will be laid waste and the high places demolished, so that your altars will be laid waste and devastated, your idols smashed and ruined, your incense altars broken down, and what you have made wiped out. 7Your people will fall slain among you, and you will know that I am the LORD.

8" 'But I will spare some, for some of you will escape the sword when you are scattered among the lands and nations. 9Then in the nations where they have been carried captive, those who escape will remember me—how I have been grieved by their adulterous hearts, which have turned away from me, and by their eyes, which have lusted after their idols. They will loathe themselves for the evil they have done and for all their detestable practices. 10And they will know that I am the LORD; I did not threaten in vain to bring this calamity on them.

11" 'This is what the Sovereign LORD says: Strike your hands together and stamp your feet and cry out "Alas!" because of all the wicked and detestable practices of the house of Israel, for they will fall by the sword, famine and plague. 12He that is far away will die of the plague, and he that is near will fall by the sword, and he that survives and is spared will die of famine. So will I spend my wrath upon them. 13And they will know that I am the LORD, when their people lie slain among their idols around their altars, on every high hill and on all the mountaintops, under every spreading tree and every leafy oak—places where they offered fragrant incense to all their idols. 14And I will stretch out my hand against them and make the land a desolate waste from the desert to Diblah[a]—wherever they live. Then they will know that I am the LORD.' "

The End Has Come

7 The word of the LORD came to me: 2"Son of man, this is what the Sovereign LORD says to the land of Israel: The end! The end has come upon the four corners of the land. 3The end is now upon you and I will unleash my anger against you. I will judge you according to your conduct and repay you for all your detestable practices. 4I will not look on you with pity or spare you; I will surely repay you for your conduct and the detestable practices among you. Then you will know that I am the LORD.

5"This is what the Sovereign LORD says: Disaster! An unheard-of[b] disaster is coming. 6The end has come! The end has come! It has roused itself against you. It has come! 7Doom has come upon you—you who dwell in the land. The time has come, the day is near; there is panic, not joy, upon the mountains. 8I am about to pour out my wrath on you and spend my anger against you; I will judge you according to your conduct and repay you for all your detestable practices. 9I will not look on you with pity or spare you; I will repay you in accordance with your conduct and the detestable practices among you. Then you will know that it is I the LORD who strikes the blow.

10"The day is here! It has come! Doom has burst forth, the rod has budded, arrogance has blossomed! 11Violence has grown into[c] a rod to punish wickedness; none of the people will be left, none of that crowd—no wealth, nothing of value. 12The time has come, the day has arrived. Let not the buyer rejoice nor the seller grieve, for wrath is upon the whole crowd. 13The seller will not recover the land he

[a] *14* Most Hebrew manuscripts; a few Hebrew manuscripts *Riblah* [b] *5* Most Hebrew manuscripts; some Hebrew manuscripts and Syriac *Disaster after* [c] *11* Or *The violent one has become*

has sold as long as both of them live, for the vision concerning the whole crowd will not be reversed. Because of their sins, not one of them will preserve his life. 14Though they blow the trumpet and get everything ready, no one will go into battle, for my wrath is upon the whole crowd.

15"Outside is the sword, inside are plague and famine; those in the country will die by the sword, and those in the city will be devoured by famine and plague. 16All who survive and escape will be in the mountains, moaning like doves of the valleys, each because of his sins. 17Every hand will go limp, and every knee will become as weak as water. 18They will put on sackcloth and be clothed with terror. Their faces will be covered with shame and their heads will be shaved. 19They will throw their silver into the streets, and their gold will be an unclean thing. Their silver and gold will not be able to save them in the day of the LORD's wrath. They will not satisfy their hunger or fill their stomachs with it, for it has made them stumble into sin. 20They were proud of their beautiful jewelry and used it to make their detestable idols and vile images. Therefore I will turn these into an unclean thing for them. 21I will hand it all over as plunder to foreigners and as loot to the wicked of the earth, and they will defile it. 22I will turn my face away from them, and they will desecrate my treasured place; robbers will enter it and desecrate it.

23"Prepare chains, because the land is full of bloodshed and the city is full of violence. 24I will bring the most wicked of the nations to take possession of their houses; I will put an end to the pride of the mighty, and their sanctuaries will be desecrated. 25When terror comes, they will seek peace, but there will be none. 26Calamity upon calamity will come, and rumor upon rumor. They will try to get a vision from the prophet; the teaching of the law by the priest will be lost, as will the counsel of the elders. 27The king will mourn, the prince will be clothed with despair, and the hands of the people of the land will tremble. I will deal with them according to their conduct, and by their own standards I will judge them. Then they will know that I am the LORD."

PRAYER: PETITION

MAY I be an example for other believers in speech, in behavior, in love, in faith and in purity. (1 Timothy 4:12)

***PAUSE** here to petition God for growth in love and compassion toward others. Offer prayers for your loved ones, for those who do not know Jesus and for those in need. Offer prayers regarding your activities for this day and any special concerns you may have.*

NT 1 Timothy 6:11-21

Paul's Charge to Timothy

11But you, man of God, flee from all this, and pursue righteousness, godliness, faith, love, endurance and gentleness. 12Fight the good fight of the faith. Take hold of the eternal life to which you were called when you made your good confession in the presence of many witnesses. 13In the sight of God, who gives life to everything, and of Christ Jesus, who while testifying before Pontius Pilate made the good confession, I charge you 14to keep this command without spot or blame until the appearing of our Lord Jesus Christ, 15which God will bring about in his own time—God, the blessed and only Ruler, the King of kings and Lord of lords, 16who alone is immortal and who lives in unapproachable light, whom no one has seen or can see. To him be honor and might forever. Amen.

17Command those who are rich in this present world not to be arrogant nor to put their hope in wealth, which is so uncertain, but to put their hope in God, who richly provides us with everything for our enjoyment. 18Command them to do good, to be rich in good deeds, and to be

generous and willing to share. [19]In this
way they will lay up treasure for themselves as a firm foundation for the coming age, so that they may take hold of the life that is truly life.
[20]Timothy, guard what has been entrusted to your care. Turn away from godless chatter and the opposing ideas of what is falsely called knowledge, [21]which
some have professed and in so doing have wandered from the faith.

Grace be with you.

PRAYER: MY RELATIONSHIP TO GOD

I DO not want to transgress Your commandments, O Lord, for I cannot prosper in disobedience. I will not forsake You, the Lord. (2 Chronicles 24:20) . . . When I have done all the things which are commanded me, O Lord, I should realize that I am an unworthy servant; I have only done what I ought to have done. (Luke 17:10)

PAUSE *to thank God for the relationship that you enjoy with Him in Jesus Christ.*

YEAR 2 DAY 249

OT Proverbs 27

27 Do not boast about tomorrow,
for you do not know what a day may bring forth.

[2] Let another praise you, and not your own mouth;
someone else, and not your own lips.

[3] Stone is heavy and sand a burden,
but provocation by a fool is heavier than both.

[4] Anger is cruel and fury overwhelming,
but who can stand before jealousy?

[5] Better is open rebuke
than hidden love.

[6] Wounds from a friend can be trusted,
but an enemy multiplies kisses.

[7] He who is full loathes honey,
but to the hungry even what is bitter tastes sweet.

[8] Like a bird that strays from its nest
is a man who strays from his home.

[9] Perfume and incense bring joy to the heart,
and the pleasantness of one's friend springs from his earnest counsel.

[10] Do not forsake your friend and the friend of your father,
and do not go to your brother's house when disaster strikes you—
better a neighbor nearby than a brother far away.

[11] Be wise, my son, and bring joy to my heart;
then I can answer anyone who treats me with contempt.

[12] The prudent see danger and take refuge,
but the simple keep going and suffer for it.

[13] Take the garment of one who puts up security for a stranger;
hold it in pledge if he does it for a wayward woman.

[14] If a man loudly blesses his neighbor early in the morning,
it will be taken as a curse.

[15] A quarrelsome wife is like
a constant dripping on a rainy day;
[16] restraining her is like restraining the wind
or grasping oil with the hand.

[17] As iron sharpens iron,
so one man sharpens another.

[18] He who tends a fig tree will eat its fruit,

and he who looks after his master
will be honored.

19 As water reflects a face,
so a man's heart reflects the man.

20 Death and Destruction[a] are never
satisfied,
and neither are the eyes of man.

21 The crucible for silver and the furnace
for gold,
but man is tested by the praise he
receives.

22 Though you grind a fool in a mortar,
grinding him like grain with a
pestle,
you will not remove his folly from
him.

23 Be sure you know the condition of
your flocks,
give careful attention to your herds;
24 for riches do not endure forever,
and a crown is not secure for all
generations.
25 When the hay is removed and new
growth appears
and the grass from the hills is
gathered in,
26 the lambs will provide you with
clothing,
and the goats with the price of a
field.
27 You will have plenty of goats' milk
to feed you and your family
and to nourish your servant girls.

[a] 20 Hebrew *Sheol and Abaddon*

PRAYER: INTERCESSION

MAY I have mercy on those who are doubting.
(Jude 22)

***TAKE** a few moments to intercede on behalf of friends, relatives, neighbors and coworkers who do not yet know salvation in Jesus Christ.*

NT 2 Timothy 1:1-18

1 Paul, an apostle of Christ Jesus by the will of God, according to the promise of life that is in Christ Jesus,

2 To Timothy, my dear son:

Grace, mercy and peace from God the Father and Christ Jesus our Lord.

Encouragement to Be Faithful

3 I thank God, whom I serve, as my forefathers did, with a clear conscience, as
night and day I constantly remember you
in my prayers. 4 Recalling your tears, I long
to see you, so that I may be filled with joy.
5 I have been reminded of your sincere
faith, which first lived in your grandmother Lois and in your mother Eunice and, I
am persuaded, now lives in you also. 6 For
this reason I remind you to fan into flame
the gift of God, which is in you through the
laying on of my hands. 7 For God did not
give us a spirit of timidity, but a spirit of
power, of love and of self-discipline.
8 So do not be ashamed to testify about
our Lord, or ashamed of me his prisoner.
But join with me in suffering for the
gospel, by the power of God, 9 who has
saved us and called us to a holy life—not
because of anything we have done but because of his own purpose and grace. This
grace was given us in Christ Jesus before
the beginning of time, 10 but it has now
been revealed through the appearing of
our Savior, Christ Jesus, who has destroyed
death and has brought life and immortality to light through the gospel. 11 And of this
gospel I was appointed a herald and an
apostle and a teacher. 12 That is why I am
suffering as I am. Yet I am not ashamed,
because I know whom I have believed, and
am convinced that he is able to guard what
I have entrusted to him for that day.
13 What you heard from me, keep as the
pattern of sound teaching, with faith and
love in Christ Jesus. 14 Guard the good deposit that was entrusted to you—guard it
with the help of the Holy Spirit who lives
in us.
15 You know that everyone in the province of Asia has deserted me, including
Phygelus and Hermogenes.
16 May the Lord show mercy to the

household of Onesiphorus, because he often refreshed me and was not ashamed of my chains. [17]On the contrary, when he was in Rome, he searched hard for me until he found me. [18]May the Lord grant that he will find mercy from the Lord on that day! You know very well in how many ways he helped me in Ephesus.

PRAYER: THE CHARACTER I WANT TO CULTIVATE

I AM hard pressed on every side, but not crushed; perplexed, but not in despair; persecuted, but not forsaken; struck down, but not destroyed; always carrying about in my body Your death, O Jesus, so that Your life may also be revealed in my body. For we who live are always being delivered over to death for Your sake, Jesus, so that Your life may be revealed in our mortal body. (2 Corinthians 4:8–11)

__TAKE__ a moment to ask the Lord for the grace to grow in godly character.

OT Ezekiel 8:1–9:11

YEAR 2 DAY 250

Idolatry in the Temple

8 In the sixth year, in the sixth month on the fifth day, while I was sitting in my house and the elders of Judah were sitting before me, the hand of the Sovereign LORD came upon me there. [2]I looked, and I saw a figure like that of a man.[a] From what appeared to be his waist down he was like fire, and from there up his appearance was as bright as glowing metal. [3]He stretched out what looked like a hand and took me by the hair of my head. The Spirit lifted me up between earth and heaven and in visions of God he took me to Jerusalem, to the entrance to the north gate of the inner court, where the idol that provokes to jealousy stood. [4]And there before me was the glory of the God of Israel, as in the vision I had seen in the plain.

[5]Then he said to me, "Son of man, look toward the north." So I looked, and in the entrance north of the gate of the altar I saw this idol of jealousy.

[6]And he said to me, "Son of man, do you see what they are doing—the utterly detestable things the house of Israel is doing here, things that will drive me far from my sanctuary? But you will see things that are even more detestable."

[7]Then he brought me to the entrance to the court. I looked, and I saw a hole in the wall. [8]He said to me, "Son of man, now dig into the wall." So I dug into the wall and saw a doorway there.

[9]And he said to me, "Go in and see the wicked and detestable things they are doing here." [10]So I went in and looked, and I saw portrayed all over the walls all kinds of crawling things and detestable animals and all the idols of the house of Israel. [11]In front of them stood seventy elders of the house of Israel, and Jaazaniah son of Shaphan was standing among them. Each had a censer in his hand, and a fragrant cloud of incense was rising.

[12]He said to me, "Son of man, have you seen what the elders of the house of Israel are doing in the darkness, each at the shrine of his own idol? They say, 'The LORD does not see us; the LORD has forsaken the land.' " [13]Again, he said, "You will see them doing things that are even more detestable."

[14]Then he brought me to the entrance to the north gate of the house of the LORD, and I saw women sitting there, mourning for Tammuz. [15]He said to me, "Do you see this, son of man? You will see things that are even more detestable than this."

[16]He then brought me into the inner court of the house of the LORD, and there at the entrance to the temple, between the portico and the altar, were about twenty-five men. With their backs toward the temple of the LORD and their faces toward the east, they were bowing down to the sun in the east.

[a] 2 Or *saw a fiery figure*

17He said to me, "Have you seen this,
son of man? Is it a trivial matter for the
house of Judah to do the detestable things
they are doing here? Must they also fill the
land with violence and continually provoke me to anger? Look at them putting
the branch to their nose! 18Therefore I will
deal with them in anger; I will not look
on them with pity or spare them. Although they shout in my ears, I will not
listen to them."

Idolaters Killed

9 Then I heard him call out in a loud
voice, "Bring the guards of the city
here, each with a weapon in his hand."
2And I saw six men coming from the direction of the upper gate, which faces
north, each with a deadly weapon in his
hand. With them was a man clothed in
linen who had a writing kit at his side.
They came in and stood beside the bronze
altar.
3Now the glory of the God of Israel
went up from above the cherubim, where
it had been, and moved to the threshold
of the temple. Then the LORD called to the
man clothed in linen who had the writing
kit at his side 4and said to him, "Go
throughout the city of Jerusalem and put
a mark on the foreheads of those who
grieve and lament over all the detestable
things that are done in it."
5As I listened, he said to the others,
"Follow him through the city and kill,
without showing pity or compassion.
6Slaughter old men, young men and
maidens, women and children, but do
not touch anyone who has the mark. Begin at my sanctuary." So they began with
the elders who were in front of the temple.
7Then he said to them, "Defile the temple and fill the courts with the slain. Go!"
So they went out and began killing
throughout the city. 8While they were
killing and I was left alone, I fell facedown, crying out, "Ah, Sovereign LORD!
Are you going to destroy the entire remnant of Israel in this outpouring of your
wrath on Jerusalem?"
9He answered me, "The sin of the house
of Israel and Judah is exceedingly great;
the land is full of bloodshed and the city
is full of injustice. They say, 'The LORD has
forsaken the land; the LORD does not see.'
10So I will not look on them with pity or
spare them, but I will bring down on their
own heads what they have done."
11Then the man in linen with the writing kit at his side brought back word, saying, "I have done as you commanded."

PRAYER: AFFIRMATION

JESUS Christ, during the days You lived on earth, You offered up prayers and petitions with loud cries and tears to the One who could save You from death, and You were heard because of Your reverent submission. Although You were a Son, You learned obedience by the things You suffered; and being perfected, You became the source of eternal salvation for all who obey You, being designated by God as a high priest according to the order of Melchizedek. (Hebrews 5:7–10)

***PAUSE** to reflect on these Biblical affirmations.*

NT 2 Timothy 2:1–13

2 You then, my son, be strong in the
grace that is in Christ Jesus. 2And the
things you have heard me say in the presence of many witnesses entrust to reliable
men who will also be qualified to teach
others. 3Endure hardship with us like a
good soldier of Christ Jesus. 4No one serving as a soldier gets involved in civilian affairs—he wants to please his commanding officer. 5Similarly, if anyone competes
as an athlete, he does not receive the victor's crown unless he competes according
to the rules. 6The hardworking farmer
should be the first to receive a share of the
crops. 7Reflect on what I am saying, for
the Lord will give you insight into all this.
8Remember Jesus Christ, raised from the
dead, descended from David. This is my

gospel, [9]for which I am suffering even to the point of being chained like a criminal. But God's word is not chained. [10]Therefore I endure everything for the sake of the elect, that they too may obtain the salvation that is in Christ Jesus, with eternal glory.

[11]Here is a trustworthy saying:

If we died with him,
we will also live with him;
[12]if we endure,
we will also reign with him.
If we disown him,
he will also disown us;
[13]if we are faithless,
he will remain faithful,
for he cannot disown himself.

PRAYER: MY RELATIONSHIP TO OTHERS

THIS is the message we heard from the beginning: that we should love one another. We know that we have passed out of death into life, because we love our brothers and sisters. The one who does not love abides in death. By this we know love, that You, O Jesus Christ, laid down Your life for us, and we ought to lay down our lives for our brothers and sisters. (1 John 3:11, 14, 16) . . . In obedience to the truth I will purify my soul for a sincere love of my brothers and sisters and love others fervently from the heart. (1 Peter 1:22)

__PAUSE__ to review your relationships with others and to commit them to the Lord.

YEAR 2 DAY 251

OT Ezekiel 10:1-22

The Glory Departs From the Temple

10 I looked, and I saw the likeness of a
throne of sapphire[a] above the expanse that was over the heads of the cherubim.
[2]The LORD said to the man clothed
in linen, "Go in among the wheels beneath the cherubim. Fill your hands with burning coals from among the cherubim and scatter them over the city." And as I watched, he went in.

[3]Now the cherubim were standing on
the south side of the temple when the man went in, and a cloud filled the inner court.
[4]Then the glory of the LORD rose
from above the cherubim and moved to the threshold of the temple. The cloud filled the temple, and the court was full of the radiance of the glory of the LORD.
[5]The
sound of the wings of the cherubim could be heard as far away as the outer court, like the voice of God Almighty[b] when he speaks.

[6]When the LORD commanded the man
in linen, "Take fire from among the wheels, from among the cherubim," the man went in and stood beside a wheel.
[7]Then one of the cherubim reached out
his hand to the fire that was among them. He took up some of it and put it into the hands of the man in linen, who took it and went out.
[8](Under the wings of the
cherubim could be seen what looked like the hands of a man.)

[9]I looked, and I saw beside the cherubim four wheels, one beside each of the cherubim; the wheels sparkled like chrysolite.
[10]As for their appearance, the
four of them looked alike; each was like a wheel intersecting a wheel.
[11]As they
moved, they would go in any one of the four directions the cherubim faced; the wheels did not turn about[c] as the cherubim went. The cherubim went in whatever direction the head faced, without turning as they went.
[12]Their entire bodies,
including their backs, their hands and their wings, were completely full of eyes, as were their four wheels.
[13]I heard the
wheels being called "the whirling wheels."
[14]Each of the cherubim had four
faces: One face was that of a cherub, the

[a] 1 Or *lapis lazuli* [b] 5 Hebrew *El-Shaddai*
[c] 11 Or *aside*

second the face of a man, the third the face of a lion, and the fourth the face of an eagle.

15Then the cherubim rose upward. These were the living creatures I had seen by the Kebar River. 16When the cherubim moved, the wheels beside them moved; and when the cherubim spread their wings to rise from the ground, the wheels did not leave their side. 17When the cherubim stood still, they also stood still; and when the cherubim rose, they rose with them, because the spirit of the living creatures was in them.

18Then the glory of the LORD departed from over the threshold of the temple and stopped above the cherubim. 19While I watched, the cherubim spread their wings and rose from the ground, and as they went, the wheels went with them. They stopped at the entrance to the east gate of the LORD's house, and the glory of the God of Israel was above them.

20These were the living creatures I had seen beneath the God of Israel by the Kebar River, and I realized that they were cherubim. 21Each had four faces and four wings, and under their wings was what looked like the hands of a man. 22Their faces had the same appearance as those I had seen by the Kebar River. Each one went straight ahead.

PRAYER: THANKSGIVING

WE are looking for Your blessed hope and Your glorious appearing, Christ Jesus, our great God and Savior; You gave Yourself for us to redeem us from all iniquity and to purify for Yourself a people for Your own possession, a people zealous for good works. (Titus 2:13–14) . . . You, O Lord, will deliver me from every evil work and will bring me safely to Your heavenly kingdom. To You be glory for ever and ever. (2 Timothy 4:18)

***PAUSE** to offer your own expressions of thanksgiving.*

NT 2 Timothy 2:14–26

A Workman Approved by God

14Keep reminding them of these things. Warn them before God against quarreling about words; it is of no value, and only ruins those who listen. 15Do your best to present yourself to God as one approved, a workman who does not need to be ashamed and who correctly handles the word of truth. 16Avoid godless chatter, because those who indulge in it will become more and more ungodly. 17Their teaching will spread like gangrene. Among them are Hymenaeus and Philetus, 18who have wandered away from the truth. They say that the resurrection has already taken place, and they destroy the faith of some. 19Nevertheless, God's solid foundation stands firm, sealed with this inscription: "The Lord knows those who are his,"[a] and, "Everyone who confesses the name of the Lord must turn away from wickedness."

20In a large house there are articles not only of gold and silver, but also of wood and clay; some are for noble purposes and some for ignoble. 21If a man cleanses himself from the latter, he will be an instrument for noble purposes, made holy, useful to the Master and prepared to do any good work.

22Flee the evil desires of youth, and pursue righteousness, faith, love and peace, along with those who call on the Lord out of a pure heart. 23Don't have anything to do with foolish and stupid arguments, because you know they produce quarrels. 24And the Lord's servant must not quarrel; instead, he must be kind to everyone, able to teach, not resentful. 25Those who oppose him he must gently instruct, in the hope that God will grant them repentance leading them to a knowledge of the truth, 26and that they will come to their senses and escape from the trap of the devil, who has taken them captive to do his will.

[a] *19* Num. 16:5 (see Septuagint)

PRAYER: THE ATTRIBUTES OF GOD

ONE thing You have spoken, O Lord, two things I have heard: That You, O God, are strong and that You, O Lord, are loving. For You reward each of us according to what we have done. (Psalm 62:11–12)

***PAUSE** to reflect on these affirmations about the person, powers and perfection of God.*

YEAR 2 DAY 252

OT **Psalm 119:129–176**

פ Pe

129 Your statutes are wonderful;
therefore I obey them.
130 The unfolding of your words gives light;
it gives understanding to the simple.
131 I open my mouth and pant,
longing for your commands.
132 Turn to me and have mercy on me,
as you always do to those who love your name.
133 Direct my footsteps according to your word;
let no sin rule over me.
134 Redeem me from the oppression of men,
that I may obey your precepts.
135 Make your face shine upon your servant
and teach me your decrees.
136 Streams of tears flow from my eyes,
for your law is not obeyed.

צ Tsadhe

137 Righteous are you, O LORD,
and your laws are right.
138 The statutes you have laid down are righteous;
they are fully trustworthy.
139 My zeal wears me out,
for my enemies ignore your words.
140 Your promises have been thoroughly tested,
and your servant loves them.
141 Though I am lowly and despised,
I do not forget your precepts.
142 Your righteousness is everlasting
and your law is true.
143 Trouble and distress have come upon me,
but your commands are my delight.
144 Your statutes are forever right;
give me understanding that I may live.

ק Qoph

145 I call with all my heart; answer me, O LORD,
and I will obey your decrees.
146 I call out to you; save me
and I will keep your statutes.
147 I rise before dawn and cry for help;
I have put my hope in your word.
148 My eyes stay open through the watches of the night,
that I may meditate on your promises.
149 Hear my voice in accordance with your love;
preserve my life, O LORD, according to your laws.
150 Those who devise wicked schemes are near,
but they are far from your law.
151 Yet you are near, O LORD,
and all your commands are true.
152 Long ago I learned from your statutes
that you established them to last forever.

ר Resh

153 Look upon my suffering and deliver me,
for I have not forgotten your law.
154 Defend my cause and redeem me;
preserve my life according to your promise.
155 Salvation is far from the wicked,
for they do not seek out your decrees.
156 Your compassion is great, O LORD;
preserve my life according to your laws.
157 Many are the foes who persecute me,

but I have not turned from your
statutes.
158 I look on the faithless with loathing,
for they do not obey your word.
159 See how I love your precepts;
preserve my life, O LORD, according
to your love.
160 All your words are true;
all your righteous laws are eternal.

ש Sin and Shin

161 Rulers persecute me without cause,
but my heart trembles at your word.
162 I rejoice in your promise
like one who finds great spoil.
163 I hate and abhor falsehood
but I love your law.
164 Seven times a day I praise you
for your righteous laws.
165 Great peace have they who love your
law,
and nothing can make them
stumble.
166 I wait for your salvation, O LORD,
and I follow your commands.
167 I obey your statutes,
for I love them greatly.
168 I obey your precepts and your
statutes,
for all my ways are known to you.

ת Taw

169 May my cry come before you,
O LORD;
give me understanding according to
your word.
170 May my supplication come before
you;
deliver me according to your
promise.
171 May my lips overflow with praise,
for you teach me your decrees.
172 May my tongue sing of your word,
for all your commands are righteous.
173 May your hand be ready to help me,
for I have chosen your precepts.
174 I long for your salvation, O LORD,
and your law is my delight.
175 Let me live that I may praise you,
and may your laws sustain me.
176 I have strayed like a lost sheep.
Seek your servant,
for I have not forgotten your
commands.

PRAYER: ADORATION

YOU are righteous in all Your ways and gracious in all Your works. (Psalm 145:17) . . . You declare the end from the beginning, and from ancient times, what is still to come, saying, "My purpose will stand, and I will do all My pleasure." (Isaiah 46:10)

***PAUSE** to express your thoughts of praise and worship.*

NT 2 Timothy 3:1–9

Godlessness in the Last Days

3 But mark this: There will be terrible
times in the last days. 2 People will be
lovers of themselves, lovers of money,
boastful, proud, abusive, disobedient to
their parents, ungrateful, unholy, 3 without
love, unforgiving, slanderous, without
self-control, brutal, not lovers of the good,
4 treacherous, rash, conceited, lovers of
pleasure rather than lovers of God— 5 having a form of godliness but denying its
power. Have nothing to do with them.

6 They are the kind who worm their way
into homes and gain control over weak-
willed women, who are loaded down
with sins and are swayed by all kinds of
evil desires, 7 always learning but never
able to acknowledge the truth. 8 Just as
Jannes and Jambres opposed Moses, so
also these men oppose the truth—men of
depraved minds, who, as far as the faith is
concerned, are rejected. 9 But they will not
get very far because, as in the case of those
men, their folly will be clear to everyone.

PRAYER: THE WORKS OF GOD

WHEN the fullness of time had come, You, O God, sent forth Your Son, born of a woman, born under law, to redeem those under law, that we might receive the adoption as children. (Galatians 4:4–5)

***TAKE** a moment to consider the greatness of God's wonderful works.*

YEAR 2 DAY 253

OT Ezekiel 11:1-25

Judgment on Israel's Leaders

11 Then the Spirit lifted me up and
brought me to the gate of the house of
the LORD that faces east. There at the entrance to the gate were twenty-five men,
and I saw among them Jaazaniah son of
Azzur and Pelatiah son of Benaiah, leaders of the people. 2The LORD said to me,
"Son of man, these are the men who are
plotting evil and giving wicked advice in
this city. 3They say, 'Will it not soon be
time to build houses?[a] This city is a cooking pot, and we are the meat.' 4Therefore
prophesy against them; prophesy, son of
man."
5Then the Spirit of the LORD came upon
me, and he told me to say: "This is what
the LORD says: That is what you are saying,
O house of Israel, but I know what is going through your mind. 6You have killed
many people in this city and filled its
streets with the dead.
7"Therefore this is what the Sovereign
LORD says: The bodies you have thrown
there are the meat and this city is the pot,
but I will drive you out of it. 8You fear the
sword, and the sword is what I will bring
against you, declares the Sovereign LORD.
9I will drive you out of the city and hand
you over to foreigners and inflict punishment on you. 10You will fall by the sword,
and I will execute judgment on you at the
borders of Israel. Then you will know that
I am the LORD. 11This city will not be a pot
for you, nor will you be the meat in it; I
will execute judgment on you at the borders of Israel. 12And you will know that I
am the LORD, for you have not followed
my decrees or kept my laws but have conformed to the standards of the nations
around you."
13Now as I was prophesying, Pelatiah
son of Benaiah died. Then I fell facedown
and cried out in a loud voice, "Ah, Sovereign LORD! Will you completely destroy
the remnant of Israel?"
14The word of the LORD came to me:
15"Son of man, your brothers—your
brothers who are your blood relatives[b]
and the whole house of Israel—are those
of whom the people of Jerusalem have
said, 'They are[c] far away from the LORD;
this land was given to us as our possession.'

Promised Return of Israel

16"Therefore say: 'This is what the Sovereign LORD says: Although I sent them far
away among the nations and scattered
them among the countries, yet for a little
while I have been a sanctuary for them in
the countries where they have gone.'
17"Therefore say: 'This is what the Sovereign LORD says: I will gather you from
the nations and bring you back from the
countries where you have been scattered,
and I will give you back the land of Israel again.'
18"They will return to it and remove all
its vile images and detestable idols. 19I will
give them an undivided heart and put a
new spirit in them; I will remove from
them their heart of stone and give them a
heart of flesh. 20Then they will follow my
decrees and be careful to keep my laws.
They will be my people, and I will be their
God. 21But as for those whose hearts are
devoted to their vile images and detestable idols, I will bring down on their
own heads what they have done, declares
the Sovereign LORD."
22Then the cherubim, with the wheels

[a] 3 Or *This is not the time to build houses.* [b] 15 Or *are in exile with you* (see Septuagint and Syriac) [c] 15 Or *those to whom the people of Jerusalem have said, 'Stay*

beside them, spread their wings, and the
glory of the God of Israel was above them.
23The glory of the LORD went up from
within the city and stopped above the
mountain east of it. 24The Spirit lifted me
up and brought me to the exiles in Babylonia[d] in the vision given by the Spirit of
God.

Then the vision I had seen went up
from me, 25and I told the exiles everything
the LORD had shown me.

[d] 24 Or *Chaldea*

PRAYER: CONFESSION

I HAVE sinned greatly in what I have done. But now, O Lord, take away the iniquity of Your servant, for I have acted very foolishly. (2 Samuel 24:10)

***ASK** the Spirit to search your heart and reveal any areas of unconfessed sin. Acknowledge these to the Lord and thank Him for His forgiveness.*

NT 2 Timothy 3:10–4:8

Paul's Charge to Timothy

10You, however, know all about my
teaching, my way of life, my purpose, faith,
patience, love, endurance, 11persecutions,
sufferings—what kinds of things happened
to me in Antioch, Iconium and Lystra, the
persecutions I endured. Yet the Lord rescued me from all of them. 12In fact, everyone who wants to live a godly life in Christ
Jesus will be persecuted, 13while evil men
and impostors will go from bad to worse,
deceiving and being deceived. 14But as for
you, continue in what you have learned
and have become convinced of, because
you know those from whom you learned
it, 15and how from infancy you have
known the holy Scriptures, which are able
to make you wise for salvation through
faith in Christ Jesus. 16All Scripture is God-
breathed and is useful for teaching, rebuking, correcting and training in righteousness, 17so that the man of God may be
thoroughly equipped for every good work.

4 In the presence of God and of Christ
Jesus, who will judge the living and the
dead, and in view of his appearing and his
kingdom, I give you this charge: 2Preach
the Word; be prepared in season and out
of season; correct, rebuke and encourage—with great patience and careful instruction. 3For the time will come when
men will not put up with sound doctrine.
Instead, to suit their own desires, they will
gather around them a great number of
teachers to say what their itching ears
want to hear. 4They will turn their ears
away from the truth and turn aside to
myths. 5But you, keep your head in all sit-
uations, endure hardship, do the work of
an evangelist, discharge all the duties of
your ministry.

6For I am already being poured out like
a drink offering, and the time has come
for my departure. 7I have fought the good
fight, I have finished the race, I have kept
the faith. 8Now there is in store for me the
crown of righteousness, which the Lord,
the righteous Judge, will award to me on
that day—and not only to me, but also to
all who have longed for his appearing.

PRAYER: MY RELATIONSHIP TO GOD

IF I love You, Jesus, I will keep Your word; and Your Father will love me, and You and Your Father will come to me and make Your home with me. (John 14:23)

***PAUSE** to thank God for the relationship that you enjoy with Him in Jesus Christ.*

YEAR 2
DAY 254

OT Ezekiel 12:1-28

The Exile Symbolized

12 The word of the LORD came to me:
2"Son of man, you are living among a
rebellious people. They have eyes to see
but do not see and ears to hear but do not
hear, for they are a rebellious people.
3"Therefore, son of man, pack your belongings for exile and in the daytime, as
they watch, set out and go from where
you are to another place. Perhaps they will
understand, though they are a rebellious
house. 4During the daytime, while they
watch, bring out your belongings packed
for exile. Then in the evening, while they
are watching, go out like those who go
into exile. 5While they watch, dig through
the wall and take your belongings out
through it. 6Put them on your shoulder as
they are watching and carry them out at
dusk. Cover your face so that you cannot
see the land, for I have made you a sign
to the house of Israel."
7So I did as I was commanded. During
the day I brought out my things packed
for exile. Then in the evening I dug
through the wall with my hands. I took
my belongings out at dusk, carrying them
on my shoulders while they watched.
8In the morning the word of the LORD
came to me: 9"Son of man, did not that
rebellious house of Israel ask you, 'What
are you doing?'
10"Say to them, 'This is what the Sovereign LORD says: This oracle concerns the
prince in Jerusalem and the whole house
of Israel who are there.' 11Say to them, 'I
am a sign to you.'

"As I have done, so it will be done to
them. They will go into exile as captives.
12"The prince among them will put his
things on his shoulder at dusk and leave,
and a hole will be dug in the wall for him
to go through. He will cover his face so
that he cannot see the land. 13I will spread
my net for him, and he will be caught in
my snare; I will bring him to Babylonia,
the land of the Chaldeans, but he will not
see it, and there he will die. 14I will scatter to the winds all those around him—
his staff and all his troops—and I will pursue them with drawn sword.
15"They will know that I am the LORD,
when I disperse them among the nations
and scatter them through the countries.
16But I will spare a few of them from the
sword, famine and plague, so that in the
nations where they go they may acknowledge all their detestable practices. Then
they will know that I am the LORD."
17The word of the LORD came to me:
18"Son of man, tremble as you eat your
food, and shudder in fear as you drink
your water. 19Say to the people of the land:
'This is what the Sovereign LORD says
about those living in Jerusalem and in the
land of Israel: They will eat their food in
anxiety and drink their water in despair,
for their land will be stripped of everything in it because of the violence of all
who live there. 20The inhabited towns will
be laid waste and the land will be desolate. Then you will know that I am the
LORD.' "
21The word of the LORD came to me:
22"Son of man, what is this proverb you
have in the land of Israel: 'The days go by
and every vision comes to nothing'? 23Say
to them, 'This is what the Sovereign LORD
says: I am going to put an end to this
proverb, and they will no longer quote it
in Israel.' Say to them, 'The days are near
when every vision will be fulfilled. 24For
there will be no more false visions or flattering divinations among the people of Israel. 25But I the LORD will speak what I
will, and it shall be fulfilled without delay. For in your days, you rebellious house,
I will fulfill whatever I say, declares the
Sovereign LORD.' "
26The word of the LORD came to me:
27"Son of man, the house of Israel is saying, 'The vision he sees is for many years
from now, and he prophesies about the
distant future.'
28"Therefore say to them, 'This is what
the Sovereign LORD says: None of my
words will be delayed any longer; whatever I say will be fulfilled, declares the
Sovereign LORD.' "

PRAYER: RENEWAL

MAY I return to You, my God, maintain mercy and justice, and wait on You continually. (Hosea 12:6) . . . May I not live on bread alone, but on every word that comes from Your mouth, O God. (Matthew 4:4)

***PAUSE** to add your own prayers for personal renewal.*

NT 2 Timothy 4:9–22

Personal Remarks

9 Do your best to come to me quickly,
10 for Demas, because he loved this world,
has deserted me and has gone to Thessalonica. Crescens has gone to Galatia, and
Titus to Dalmatia. 11 Only Luke is with me.
Get Mark and bring him with you, because he is helpful to me in my ministry.
12 I sent Tychicus to Ephesus. 13 When you
come, bring the cloak that I left with Car-
pus at Troas, and my scrolls, especially the
parchments.
14 Alexander the metalworker did me a
great deal of harm. The Lord will repay
him for what he has done. 15 You too
should be on your guard against him, because he strongly opposed our message.
16 At my first defense, no one came to
my support, but everyone deserted me.
May it not be held against them. 17 But the
Lord stood at my side and gave me
strength, so that through me the message
might be fully proclaimed and all the
Gentiles might hear it. And I was delivered from the lion's mouth. 18 The Lord
will rescue me from every evil attack and
will bring me safely to his heavenly kingdom. To him be glory for ever and ever.
Amen.

Final Greetings

19 Greet Priscilla[a] and Aquila and the
household of Onesiphorus. 20 Erastus stayed
in Corinth, and I left Trophimus sick in Miletus. 21 Do your best to get here before winter. Eubulus greets you, and so do Pudens,
Linus, Claudia and all the brothers.
22 The Lord be with your spirit. Grace be
with you.

[a] 19 Greek *Prisca*, a variant of *Priscilla*

PRAYER: THE CHARACTER I WANT TO CULTIVATE

O GOD, I desire to be righteous before You in my generation. (Genesis 7:1) . . . O Lord, You reward each of us for righteousness and faithfulness. (1 Samuel 26:23)

***TAKE** a moment to ask the Lord for the grace to grow in godly character.*

YEAR 2
DAY 255

OT Ezekiel 13:1–23

False Prophets Condemned

13 The word of the LORD came to me:
2 "Son of man, prophesy against the
prophets of Israel who are now prophesying. Say to those who prophesy out of
their own imagination: 'Hear the word of
the LORD! 3 This is what the Sovereign LORD
says: Woe to the foolish[a] prophets who
follow their own spirit and have seen
nothing! 4 Your prophets, O Israel, are like
jackals among ruins. 5 You have not gone
up to the breaks in the wall to repair it for
the house of Israel so that it will stand firm
in the battle on the day of the LORD. 6 Their
visions are false and their divinations a lie.
They say, "The LORD declares," when the
LORD has not sent them; yet they expect
their words to be fulfilled. 7 Have you not
seen false visions and uttered lying div-

[a] 3 Or *wicked*

inations when you say, "The LORD declares," though I have not spoken?

8 " 'Therefore this is what the Sovereign LORD says: Because of your false words and lying visions, I am against you, declares the Sovereign LORD. 9 My hand will be against the prophets who see false visions and utter lying divinations. They will not belong to the council of my people or be listed in the records of the house of Israel, nor will they enter the land of Israel. Then you will know that I am the Sovereign LORD.

10 " 'Because they lead my people astray, saying, "Peace," when there is no peace, and because, when a flimsy wall is built, they cover it with whitewash, 11 therefore tell those who cover it with whitewash that it is going to fall. Rain will come in torrents, and I will send hailstones hurtling down, and violent winds will burst forth. 12 When the wall collapses, will people not ask you, "Where is the whitewash you covered it with?"

13 " 'Therefore this is what the Sovereign LORD says: In my wrath I will unleash a violent wind, and in my anger hailstones and torrents of rain will fall with destructive fury. 14 I will tear down the wall you have covered with whitewash and will level it to the ground so that its foundation will be laid bare. When it[b] falls, you will be destroyed in it; and you will know that I am the LORD. 15 So I will spend my wrath against the wall and against those who covered it with whitewash. I will say to you, "The wall is gone and so are those who whitewashed it, 16 those prophets of Israel who prophesied to Jerusalem and saw visions of peace for her when there was no peace, declares the Sovereign LORD." '

17 "Now, son of man, set your face against the daughters of your people who prophesy out of their own imagination. Prophesy against them 18 and say, 'This is what the Sovereign LORD says: Woe to the women who sew magic charms on all their wrists and make veils of various lengths for their heads in order to ensnare people. Will you ensnare the lives of my people but preserve your own? 19 You have profaned me among my people for a few handfuls of barley and scraps of bread. By lying to my people, who listen to lies, you have killed those who should not have died and have spared those who should not live.

20 " 'Therefore this is what the Sovereign LORD says: I am against your magic charms with which you ensnare people like birds and I will tear them from your arms; I will set free the people that you ensnare like birds. 21 I will tear off your veils and save my people from your hands, and they will no longer fall prey to your power. Then you will know that I am the LORD. 22 Because you disheartened the righteous with your lies, when I had brought them no grief, and because you encouraged the wicked not to turn from their evil ways and so save their lives, 23 therefore you will no longer see false visions or practice divination. I will save my people from your hands. And then you will know that I am the LORD.' "

[b] 14 Or *the city*

PRAYER: PETITION

MAY I be above reproach and blameless as Your steward, O God—not self-willed, not quick-tempered, not given to wine, not violent, not fond of dishonest gain, but hospitable, a lover of what is good, sensible, just, holy and self-controlled. (Titus 1:6–8)

__PAUSE__ here to petition God to help you be a faithful steward of your time, talents, possessions and relationships. Offer prayers of petition regarding your activities for this day and any special concerns you may have.

NT Titus 1:1–16

1 Paul, a servant of God and an apostle of Jesus Christ for the faith of God's elect and the knowledge of the truth that leads to godliness— 2 a faith and knowledge resting on the hope of eternal life, which God, who does not lie, promised before

the beginning of time, 3 and at his appointed season he brought his word to light through the preaching entrusted to me by the command of God our Savior,

4 To Titus, my true son in our common faith:

Grace and peace from God the Father and Christ Jesus our Savior.

Titus' Task on Crete

5 The reason I left you in Crete was that you might straighten out what was left unfinished and appoint[a] elders in every town, as I directed you. 6 An elder must be blameless, the husband of but one wife, a man whose children believe and are not open to the charge of being wild and disobedient. 7 Since an overseer[b] is entrusted with God's work, he must be blameless—not overbearing, not quick-tempered, not given to drunkenness, not violent, not pursuing dishonest gain. 8 Rather he must be hospitable, one who loves what is good, who is self-controlled, upright, holy and disciplined. 9 He must hold firmly to the trustworthy message as it has been taught, so that he can encourage others by sound doctrine and refute those who oppose it.

10 For there are many rebellious people, mere talkers and deceivers, especially those of the circumcision group. 11 They must be silenced, because they are ruining whole households by teaching things they ought not to teach—and that for the sake of dishonest gain. 12 Even one of their own prophets has said, "Cretans are always liars, evil brutes, lazy gluttons." 13 This testimony is true. Therefore, rebuke them sharply, so that they will be sound in the faith 14 and will pay no attention to Jewish myths or to the commands of those who reject the truth. 15 To the pure, all things are pure, but to those who are corrupted and do not believe, nothing is pure. In fact, both their minds and consciences are corrupted. 16 They claim to know God, but by their actions they deny him. They are detestable, disobedient and unfit for doing anything good.

[a] 5 Or *ordain* [b] 7 Traditionally *bishop*

PRAYER: MY RELATIONSHIP TO OTHERS

I WILL remember those in prison as though bound with them, and those who are mistreated, as though suffering with them. (Hebrews 13:3) . . . This is pure and undefiled religion before You, my God and Father: to visit orphans and widows in their affliction and to keep oneself unspotted from the world. (James 1:27)

***PAUSE** to review your relationships with others and to commit them to the Lord.*

YEAR 2 DAY 256

OT Ezekiel 14:1–15:8

Idolaters Condemned

14 Some of the elders of Israel came to me and sat down in front of me. 2 Then the word of the LORD came to me: 3 "Son of man, these men have set up idols in their hearts and put wicked stumbling blocks before their faces. Should I let them inquire of me at all? 4 Therefore speak to them and tell them, 'This is what the Sovereign LORD says: When any Israelite sets up idols in his heart and puts a wicked stumbling block before his face and then goes to a prophet, I the LORD will answer him myself in keeping with his great idolatry. 5 I will do this to recapture the hearts of the people of Israel, who have all deserted me for their idols.'

6 "Therefore say to the house of Israel, 'This is what the Sovereign LORD says: Repent! Turn from your idols and renounce all your detestable practices!

7 " 'When any Israelite or any alien living in Israel separates himself from me and sets up idols in his heart and puts a

wicked stumbling block before his face
and then goes to a prophet to inquire of
me, I the LORD will answer him myself. 8I
will set my face against that man and
make him an example and a byword. I
will cut him off from my people. Then
you will know that I am the LORD.
9" 'And if the prophet is enticed to utter
a prophecy, I the LORD have enticed that
prophet, and I will stretch out my hand
against him and destroy him from among
my people Israel. 10They will bear their
guilt—the prophet will be as guilty as the
one who consults him. 11Then the people
of Israel will no longer stray from me, nor
will they defile themselves anymore with
all their sins. They will be my people, and
I will be their God, declares the Sovereign
LORD.' "

Judgment Inescapable

12The word of the LORD came to me:
13"Son of man, if a country sins against
me by being unfaithful and I stretch out
my hand against it to cut off its food supply and send famine upon it and kill its
men and their animals, 14even if these
three men—Noah, Daniel[a] and Job—
were in it, they could save only themselves
by their righteousness, declares the Sovereign LORD.
15"Or if I send wild beasts through that
country and they leave it childless and it
becomes desolate so that no one can pass
through it because of the beasts, 16as surely as I live, declares the Sovereign LORD,
even if these three men were in it, they
could not save their own sons or daughters. They alone would be saved, but the
land would be desolate.
17"Or if I bring a sword against that
country and say, 'Let the sword pass
throughout the land,' and I kill its men
and their animals, 18as surely as I live, declares the Sovereign LORD, even if these
three men were in it, they could not save
their own sons or daughters. They alone
would be saved.
19"Or if I send a plague into that land
and pour out my wrath upon it through
bloodshed, killing its men and their animals, 20as surely as I live, declares the Sovereign LORD, even if Noah, Daniel and
Job were in it, they could save neither son
nor daughter. They would save only themselves by their righteousness.
21"For this is what the Sovereign LORD
says: How much worse will it be when I
send against Jerusalem my four dreadful
judgments—sword and famine and wild
beasts and plague—to kill its men and
their animals! 22Yet there will be some
survivors—sons and daughters who will
be brought out of it. They will come to
you, and when you see their conduct and
their actions, you will be consoled regarding the disaster I have brought upon
Jerusalem—every disaster I have brought
upon it. 23You will be consoled when you
see their conduct and their actions, for
you will know that I have done nothing
in it without cause, declares the Sovereign
LORD."

Jerusalem, A Useless Vine

15 The word of the LORD came to me:
2"Son of man, how is the wood of a
vine better than that of a branch on any
of the trees in the forest? 3Is wood ever
taken from it to make anything useful?
Do they make pegs from it to hang things
on? 4And after it is thrown on the fire as
fuel and the fire burns both ends and
chars the middle, is it then useful for anything? 5If it was not useful for anything
when it was whole, how much less can it
be made into something useful when the
fire has burned it and it is charred?
6"Therefore this is what the Sovereign
LORD says: As I have given the wood of the
vine among the trees of the forest as fuel
for the fire, so will I treat the people living in Jerusalem. 7I will set my face against
them. Although they have come out of the
fire, the fire will yet consume them. And
when I set my face against them, you will
know that I am the LORD. 8I will make the
land desolate because they have been unfaithful, declares the Sovereign LORD."

[a] 14 Or *Danel;* the Hebrew spelling may suggest a person other than the prophet Daniel; also in verse 20.

PRAYER: INTERCESSION

***WHEN the children of Judah were victorious, it was because they relied on You, the God of their fathers.* (2 Chronicles 13:18)**

***TAKE** a few moments to intercede on behalf of your local, state or provincial, and national governments. Pray for spiritual revival in the nation and offer prayers regarding current events and concerns.*

NT Titus 2:1-10

What Must Be Taught to Various Groups

2 You must teach what is in accord with sound doctrine. 2Teach the older men to be temperate, worthy of respect, self-controlled, and sound in faith, in love and in endurance.
3Likewise, teach the older women to be reverent in the way they live, not to be slanderers or addicted to much wine, but to teach what is good. 4Then they can train the younger women to love their husbands and children, 5to be self-controlled and pure, to be busy at home, to be kind, and to be subject to their husbands, so that no one will malign the word of God.
6Similarly, encourage the young men to be self-controlled. 7In everything set them an example by doing what is good. In your teaching show integrity, seriousness 8and soundness of speech that cannot be condemned, so that those who oppose you may be ashamed because they have nothing bad to say about us.
9Teach slaves to be subject to their masters in everything, to try to please them, not to talk back to them, 10and not to steal from them, but to show that they can be fully trusted, so that in every way they will make the teaching about God our Savior attractive.

PRAYER: THE ATTRIBUTES OF GOD

IN the beginning was the Word, and the Word was with You, O God, and the Word was You. The Word was in the beginning with You. (John 1:1–2) . . . The Word became flesh and dwelt among us. We have seen His glory, the glory of Your only begotten, O Father, full of grace and truth. (John 1:14)

***PAUSE** to reflect on these affirmations about the person, powers and perfection of God.*

YEAR 2
DAY 257

OT Ezekiel 16:1-63

An Allegory of Unfaithful Jerusalem

16 The word of the LORD came to me: 2"Son of man, confront Jerusalem with her detestable practices 3and say, 'This is what the Sovereign LORD says to Jerusalem: Your ancestry and birth were in the land of the Canaanites; your father was an Amorite and your mother a Hittite. 4On the day you were born your cord was not cut, nor were you washed with water to make you clean, nor were you rubbed with salt or wrapped in cloths. 5No one looked on you with pity or had compassion enough to do any of these things for you. Rather, you were thrown out into the open field, for on the day you were born you were despised.
6" 'Then I passed by and saw you kick-

ing about in your blood, and as you lay
there in your blood I said to you, "Live!"[a]
[7]I made you grow like a plant of the field.
You grew up and developed and became
the most beautiful of jewels.[b] Your breasts
were formed and your hair grew, you who
were naked and bare.
[8]" 'Later I passed by, and when I looked
at you and saw that you were old enough
for love, I spread the corner of my garment over you and covered your nakedness. I gave you my solemn oath and entered into a covenant with you, declares
the Sovereign LORD, and you became
mine.
[9]" 'I bathed[c] you with water and washed
the blood from you and put ointments on
you. [10]I clothed you with an embroidered
dress and put leather sandals on you. I
dressed you in fine linen and covered you
with costly garments. [11]I adorned you with
jewelry: I put bracelets on your arms and a
necklace around your neck, [12]and I put a
ring on your nose, earrings on your ears
and a beautiful crown on your head. [13]So
you were adorned with gold and silver;
your clothes were of fine linen and costly
fabric and embroidered cloth. Your food
was fine flour, honey and olive oil. You became very beautiful and rose to be a queen.
[14]And your fame spread among the nations
on account of your beauty, because the
splendor I had given you made your beauty perfect, declares the Sovereign LORD.
[15]" 'But you trusted in your beauty and
used your fame to become a prostitute.
You lavished your favors on anyone who
passed by and your beauty became his.[d]
[16]You took some of your garments to
make gaudy high places, where you carried on your prostitution. Such things
should not happen, nor should they ever
occur. [17]You also took the fine jewelry I
gave you, the jewelry made of my gold
and silver, and you made for yourself
male idols and engaged in prostitution
with them. [18]And you took your embroidered clothes to put on them, and you offered my oil and incense before them.
[19]Also the food I provided for you—the
fine flour, olive oil and honey I gave you
to eat—you offered as fragrant incense before them. That is what happened, declares the Sovereign LORD.
[20]" 'And you took your sons and daughters whom you bore to me and sacrificed
them as food to the idols. Was your prostitution not enough? [21]You slaughtered
my children and sacrificed them[e] to the
idols. [22]In all your detestable practices and
your prostitution you did not remember
the days of your youth, when you were
naked and bare, kicking about in your
blood.
[23]" 'Woe! Woe to you, declares the Sovereign LORD. In addition to all your other
wickedness, [24]you built a mound for yourself and made a lofty shrine in every public square. [25]At the head of every street you
built your lofty shrines and degraded your
beauty, offering your body with increasing
promiscuity to anyone who passed by.
[26]You engaged in prostitution with the
Egyptians, your lustful neighbors, and provoked me to anger with your increasing
promiscuity. [27]So I stretched out my hand
against you and reduced your territory; I
gave you over to the greed of your enemies, the daughters of the Philistines, who
were shocked by your lewd conduct. [28]You
engaged in prostitution with the Assyrians
too, because you were insatiable; and even
after that, you still were not satisfied.
[29]Then you increased your promiscuity to
include Babylonia,[f] a land of merchants,
but even with this you were not satisfied.
[30]" 'How weak-willed you are, declares
the Sovereign LORD, when you do all these
things, acting like a brazen prostitute!
[31]When you built your mounds at the head
of every street and made your lofty shrines
in every public square, you were unlike a
prostitute, because you scorned payment.
[32]" 'You adulterous wife! You prefer
strangers to your own husband! [33]Every
prostitute receives a fee, but you give gifts
to all your lovers, bribing them to come to
you from everywhere for your illicit favors.
[34]So in your prostitution you are the opposite of others; no one runs after you for
your favors. You are the very opposite, for
you give payment and none is given to you.
[35]" 'Therefore, you prostitute, hear the
word of the LORD! [36]This is what the Sovereign LORD says: Because you poured out
your wealth[g] and exposed your nakedness
in your promiscuity with your lovers, and

[a] 6 A few Hebrew manuscripts, Septuagint and Syriac; most Hebrew manuscripts *"Live!" And as you lay there in your blood I said to you, "Live!"* [b] 7 Or *became mature* [c] 9 Or *I had bathed* [d] 15 Most Hebrew manuscripts; one Hebrew manuscript (see some Septuagint manuscripts) *by. Such a thing should not happen* [e] 21 Or *and made them pass through* ⌊*the fire*⌋ [f] 29 Or *Chaldea* [g] 36 Or *lust*

because of all your detestable idols, and because you gave them your children's blood, [37]therefore I am going to gather all your lovers, with whom you found pleasure, those you loved as well as those you hated. I will gather them against you from all around and will strip you in front of them, and they will see all your nakedness. [38]I will sentence you to the punishment of women who commit adultery and who shed blood; I will bring upon you the blood vengeance of my wrath and jealous anger. [39]Then I will hand you over to your lovers, and they will tear down your mounds and destroy your lofty shrines. They will strip you of your clothes and take your fine jewelry and leave you naked and bare. [40]They will bring a mob against you, who will stone you and hack you to pieces with their swords. [41]They will burn down your houses and inflict punishment on you in the sight of many women. I will put a stop to your prostitution, and you will no longer pay your lovers. [42]Then my wrath against you will subside and my jealous anger will turn away from you; I will be calm and no longer angry.

[43]" 'Because you did not remember the days of your youth but enraged me with all these things, I will surely bring down on your head what you have done, declares the Sovereign LORD. Did you not add lewdness to all your other detestable practices?

[44]" 'Everyone who quotes proverbs will quote this proverb about you: "Like mother, like daughter." [45]You are a true daughter of your mother, who despised her husband and her children; and you are a true sister of your sisters, who despised their husbands and their children. Your mother was a Hittite and your father an Amorite. [46]Your older sister was Samaria, who lived to the north of you with her daughters; and your younger sister, who lived to the south of you with her daughters, was Sodom. [47]You not only walked in their ways and copied their detestable practices, but in all your ways you soon became more depraved than they. [48]As surely as I live, declares the Sovereign LORD, your sister Sodom and her daughters never did what you and your daughters have done.

[49]" 'Now this was the sin of your sister Sodom: She and her daughters were arrogant, overfed and unconcerned; they did not help the poor and needy. [50]They were haughty and did detestable things before me. Therefore I did away with them as you have seen. [51]Samaria did not commit half the sins you did. You have done more detestable things than they, and have made your sisters seem righteous by all these things you have done. [52]Bear your disgrace, for you have furnished some justification for your sisters. Because your sins were more vile than theirs, they appear more righteous than you. So then, be ashamed and bear your disgrace, for you have made your sisters appear righteous.

[53]" 'However, I will restore the fortunes of Sodom and her daughters and of Samaria and her daughters, and your fortunes along with them, [54]so that you may bear your disgrace and be ashamed of all you have done in giving them comfort. [55]And your sisters, Sodom with her daughters and Samaria with her daughters, will return to what they were before; and you and your daughters will return to what you were before. [56]You would not even mention your sister Sodom in the day of your pride, [57]before your wickedness was uncovered. Even so, you are now scorned by the daughters of Edom[h] and all her neighbors and the daughters of the Philistines—all those around you who despise you. [58]You will bear the consequences of your lewdness and your detestable practices, declares the LORD.

[59]" 'This is what the Sovereign LORD says: I will deal with you as you deserve, because you have despised my oath by breaking the covenant. [60]Yet I will remember the covenant I made with you in the days of your youth, and I will establish an everlasting covenant with you. [61]Then you will remember your ways and be ashamed when you receive your sisters, both those who are older than you and those who are younger. I will give them to you as daughters, but not on the basis of my covenant with you. [62]So I will establish my covenant with you, and you will know that I am the LORD. [63]Then, when I make atonement for you for all you have done, you will remember and be ashamed and never again open your mouth because of your humiliation, declares the Sovereign LORD.' "

[h] 57 Many Hebrew manuscripts and Syriac; most Hebrew manuscripts, Septuagint and Vulgate *Aram*

PRAYER: AFFIRMATION

O GOD, to do Your work I must believe in Christ Jesus whom You have sent. (John 6:28–29) . . . Father, You have sent Your Son to be the Savior of the world. If we confess that Jesus is Your Son, You abide in us and we abide in You. (1 John 4:14–15)

***PAUSE** to reflect on these Biblical affirmations.*

NT Titus 2:11–3:8

[11]For the grace of God that brings salvation has appeared to all men. [12]It teaches us to say "No" to ungodliness and worldly passions, and to live self-controlled, upright and godly lives in this present age, [13]while we wait for the blessed hope—the glorious appearing of our great God and Savior, Jesus Christ, [14]who gave himself for us to redeem us from all wickedness and to purify for himself a people that are his very own, eager to do what is good.

[15]These, then, are the things you should teach. Encourage and rebuke with all authority. Do not let anyone despise you.

Doing What Is Good

3 Remind the people to be subject to rulers and authorities, to be obedient, to be ready to do whatever is good, [2]to slander no one, to be peaceable and considerate, and to show true humility toward all men.

[3]At one time we too were foolish, disobedient, deceived and enslaved by all kinds of passions and pleasures. We lived in malice and envy, being hated and hating one another. [4]But when the kindness and love of God our Savior appeared, [5]he saved us, not because of righteous things we had done, but because of his mercy. He saved us through the washing of rebirth and renewal by the Holy Spirit, [6]whom he poured out on us generously through Jesus Christ our Savior, [7]so that, having been justified by his grace, we might become heirs having the hope of eternal life. [8]This is a trustworthy saying. And I want you to stress these things, so that those who have trusted in God may be careful to devote themselves to doing what is good. These things are excellent and profitable for everyone.

PRAYER: THE WORKS OF GOD

BEFORE faith in You, O Christ, came, we were guarded by the law, confined for the faith which was later to be revealed. So the law has become our tutor to lead us to You, Jesus, that we might be justified by faith. Now that faith has come, we are no longer under a tutor. (Galatians 3:23–25) . . . If righteousness could be gained through the law, You, O Christ, died for nothing. (Galatians 2:21)

***TAKE** a moment to consider the greatness of God's wonderful works.*

YEAR 2
DAY 258

OT Ezekiel 17:1–24

Two Eagles and a Vine

17 The word of the LORD came to me: [2]"Son of man, set forth an allegory and tell the house of Israel a parable. [3]Say to them, 'This is what the Sovereign LORD says: A great eagle with powerful wings, long feathers and full plumage of varied colors came to Lebanon. Taking hold of the top of a cedar, [4]he broke off its top-

most shoot and carried it away to a land of merchants, where he planted it in a city of traders.

5 " 'He took some of the seed of your land and put it in fertile soil. He planted it like a willow by abundant water, 6 and it sprouted and became a low, spreading vine. Its branches turned toward him, but its roots remained under it. So it became a vine and produced branches and put out leafy boughs.

7 " 'But there was another great eagle with powerful wings and full plumage. The vine now sent out its roots toward him from the plot where it was planted and stretched out its branches to him for water. 8 It had been planted in good soil by abundant water so that it would produce branches, bear fruit and become a splendid vine.'

9 "Say to them, 'This is what the Sovereign LORD says: Will it thrive? Will it not be uprooted and stripped of its fruit so that it withers? All its new growth will wither. It will not take a strong arm or many people to pull it up by the roots. 10 Even if it is transplanted, will it thrive? Will it not wither completely when the east wind strikes it—wither away in the plot where it grew?' "

11 Then the word of the LORD came to me: 12 "Say to this rebellious house, 'Do you not know what these things mean?' Say to them: 'The king of Babylon went to Jerusalem and carried off her king and her nobles, bringing them back with him to Babylon. 13 Then he took a member of the royal family and made a treaty with him, putting him under oath. He also carried away the leading men of the land, 14 so that the kingdom would be brought low, unable to rise again, surviving only by keeping his treaty. 15 But the king rebelled against him by sending his envoys to Egypt to get horses and a large army. Will he succeed? Will he who does such things escape? Will he break the treaty and yet escape?

16 " 'As surely as I live, declares the Sovereign LORD, he shall die in Babylon, in the land of the king who put him on the throne, whose oath he despised and whose treaty he broke. 17 Pharaoh with his mighty army and great horde will be of no help to him in war, when ramps are built and siege works erected to destroy many lives. 18 He despised the oath by breaking the covenant. Because he had given his hand in pledge and yet did all these things, he shall not escape.

19 " 'Therefore this is what the Sovereign LORD says: As surely as I live, I will bring down on his head my oath that he despised and my covenant that he broke. 20 I will spread my net for him, and he will be caught in my snare. I will bring him to Babylon and execute judgment upon him there because he was unfaithful to me. 21 All his fleeing troops will fall by the sword, and the survivors will be scattered to the winds. Then you will know that I the LORD have spoken.

22 " 'This is what the Sovereign LORD says: I myself will take a shoot from the very top of a cedar and plant it; I will break off a tender sprig from its topmost shoots and plant it on a high and lofty mountain. 23 On the mountain heights of Israel I will plant it; it will produce branches and bear fruit and become a splendid cedar. Birds of every kind will nest in it; they will find shelter in the shade of its branches. 24 All the trees of the field will know that I the LORD bring down the tall tree and make the low tree grow tall. I dry up the green tree and make the dry tree flourish.

" 'I the LORD have spoken, and I will do it.' "

PRAYER: THANKSGIVING

MY hope in You, Father God, is an anchor for my soul, both sure and steadfast, and it enters the inner sanctuary behind the veil, where Jesus the forerunner has entered on my behalf, having become a high priest forever, according to the order of Melchizedek.

(Hebrews 6:19–20)

***PAUSE** to offer your own expressions of thanksgiving.*

NT Titus 3:9–15

9But avoid foolish controversies and genealogies and arguments and quarrels
about the law, because these are unprofitable and useless. 10Warn a divisive person once, and then warn him a second
time. After that, have nothing to do with
him. 11You may be sure that such a man
is warped and sinful; he is self-con-
demned.

Final Remarks

12As soon as I send Artemas or Tychicus
to you, do your best to come to me at Ni-
copolis, because I have decided to winter
there. 13Do everything you can to help Ze-
nas the lawyer and Apollos on their way
and see that they have everything they
need. 14Our people must learn to devote
themselves to doing what is good, in order that they may provide for daily neces-
sities and not live unproductive lives.
15Everyone with me sends you greetings. Greet those who love us in the faith.
Grace be with you all.

PRAYER: MY RELATIONSHIP TO GOD

YOU are my hope, O Lord God; You are my trust from my youth. As for me, I will always have hope; I will praise You more and more. (Psalm 71:5, 14)

***PAUSE** to thank God for the relationship that you enjoy with Him in Jesus Christ.*

YEAR 2
DAY 259

OT Psalms 120–121

Psalm 120

A song of ascents.

1I call on the LORD in my distress,
and he answers me.
2Save me, O LORD, from lying lips
and from deceitful tongues.

3What will he do to you,
and what more besides, O deceitful
tongue?
4He will punish you with a warrior's
sharp arrows,
with burning coals of the broom
tree.

5Woe to me that I dwell in Meshech,
that I live among the tents of
Kedar!
6Too long have I lived
among those who hate peace.
7I am a man of peace;
but when I speak, they are for
war.

Psalm 121

A song of ascents.

1I lift up my eyes to the hills—
where does my help come from?
2My help comes from the LORD,
the Maker of heaven and earth.

3He will not let your foot slip—
he who watches over you will not
slumber;
4indeed, he who watches over Israel
will neither slumber nor sleep.

5The LORD watches over you—
the LORD is your shade at your right
hand;
6the sun will not harm you by day,
nor the moon by night.

7The LORD will keep you from all harm—
he will watch over your life;
8the LORD will watch over your coming
and going
both now and forevermore.

PRAYER: ADORATION

O LORD, our Lord, we join Your heavenly host in praising You: And the four living creatures, each having six wings, were full of eyes around and within; and they do not rest day or night, saying, "Holy, holy, holy is the Lord God Almighty, who was, and is, and is to come." (Revelation 4:8) . . . Then a voice came from the throne, saying: "Praise our God, all you his servants, you who fear Him, both small and great!" (Revelation 19:5)

PAUSE *to express your thoughts of praise and worship.*

NT Philemon 1–25

1 Paul, a prisoner of Christ Jesus, and Timothy our brother,

To Philemon our dear friend and fellow worker, 2 to Apphia our sister, to Archippus our fellow soldier and to the church that meets in your home:

3 Grace to you and peace from God our Father and the Lord Jesus Christ.

Thanksgiving and Prayer

4 I always thank my God as I remember you in my prayers, 5 because I hear about your faith in the Lord Jesus and your love for all the saints. 6 I pray that you may be active in sharing your faith, so that you will have a full understanding of every good thing we have in Christ. 7 Your love has given me great joy and encouragement, because you, brother, have refreshed the hearts of the saints.

Paul's Plea for Onesimus

8 Therefore, although in Christ I could be bold and order you to do what you ought to do, 9 yet I appeal to you on the basis of love. I then, as Paul—an old man and now also a prisoner of Christ Jesus— 10 I appeal to you for my son Onesimus,[a] who became my son while I was in chains. 11 Formerly he was useless to you, but now he has become useful both to you and to me.

12 I am sending him—who is my very heart—back to you. 13 I would have liked to keep him with me so that he could take your place in helping me while I am in chains for the gospel. 14 But I did not want to do anything without your consent, so that any favor you do will be spontaneous and not forced. 15 Perhaps the reason he was separated from you for a little while was that you might have him back for good— 16 no longer as a slave, but better than a slave, as a dear brother. He is very dear to me but even dearer to you, both as a man and as a brother in the Lord.

17 So if you consider me a partner, welcome him as you would welcome me. 18 If he has done you any wrong or owes you anything, charge it to me. 19 I, Paul, am writing this with my own hand. I will pay it back—not to mention that you owe me your very self. 20 I do wish, brother, that I may have some benefit from you in the Lord; refresh my heart in Christ. 21 Confident of your obedience, I write to you, knowing that you will do even more than I ask.

22 And one thing more: Prepare a guest room for me, because I hope to be restored to you in answer to your prayers.

23 Epaphras, my fellow prisoner in Christ Jesus, sends you greetings. 24 And so do Mark, Aristarchus, Demas and Luke, my fellow workers.

25 The grace of the Lord Jesus Christ be with your spirit.

[a] *10 Onesimus* means *useful.*

PRAYER: THE CHARACTER I WANT TO CULTIVATE

I WILL be careful to lead a blameless life. I will walk in the integrity of my heart in the midst of my house. I will set no wicked thing before my eyes. I hate the work of those who fall away; it will not cling to

me. A perverse heart shall depart from me; I will not know evil. Those who slander a neighbor in secret, I will silence; I will not endure those who have haughty eyes and proud hearts. My eyes will be on the faithful in the land, that they may dwell with me; the one whose walk is blameless will minister to me. No one who practices deceit will dwell in my house; no one who speaks falsely will stand in my presence. (Psalm 101:2–7)

TAKE *a moment to ask the Lord for the grace to grow in godly character.*

YEAR 2 DAY 260

OT Ezekiel 18:1-32

The Soul Who Sins Will Die

18 The word of the LORD came to me:
2 "What do you people mean by quot-
ing this proverb about the land of Israel:

" 'The fathers eat sour grapes,
and the children's teeth are set on edge'?

3 "As surely as I live, declares the Sovereign LORD, you will no longer quote this
proverb in Israel. 4 For every living soul belongs to me, the father as well as the
son—both alike belong to me. The soul
who sins is the one who will die.

5 "Suppose there is a righteous man
who does what is just and right.
6 He does not eat at the mountain shrines
or look to the idols of the house of Israel.
He does not defile his neighbor's wife
or lie with a woman during her period.
7 He does not oppress anyone,
but returns what he took in pledge for a loan.
He does not commit robbery
but gives his food to the hungry
and provides clothing for the naked.
8 He does not lend at usury
or take excessive interest.[a]
He withholds his hand from doing wrong
and judges fairly between man and man.
9 He follows my decrees
and faithfully keeps my laws.
That man is righteous;
he will surely live,
declares the Sovereign LORD.

10 "Suppose he has a violent son, who
sheds blood or does any of these other
things[b] 11 (though the father has done
none of them):

"He eats at the mountain shrines.
He defiles his neighbor's wife.
12 He oppresses the poor and needy.
He commits robbery.
He does not return what he took in pledge.
He looks to the idols.
He does detestable things.
13 He lends at usury and takes excessive interest.

Will such a man live? He will not! Because
he has done all these detestable things, he
will surely be put to death and his blood
will be on his own head.
14 "But suppose this son has a son who
sees all the sins his father commits, and
though he sees them, he does not do such
things:

15 "He does not eat at the mountain shrines
or look to the idols of the house of Israel.
He does not defile his neighbor's wife.
16 He does not oppress anyone
or require a pledge for a loan.
He does not commit robbery
but gives his food to the hungry
and provides clothing for the naked.
17 He withholds his hand from sin[c]
and takes no usury or excessive interest.
He keeps my laws and follows my decrees.

[a] 8 Or *take interest;* similarly in verses 13 and 17
[b] 10 Or *things to a brother*
[c] 17 Septuagint (see also verse 8); Hebrew *from the poor*

He will not die for his father's sin; he will surely live. 18But his father will die for his own sin, because he practiced extortion, robbed his brother and did what was wrong among his people.

19"Yet you ask, 'Why does the son not share the guilt of his father?' Since the son has done what is just and right and has been careful to keep all my decrees, he will surely live. 20The soul who sins is the one who will die. The son will not share the guilt of the father, nor will the father share the guilt of the son. The righteousness of the righteous man will be credited to him, and the wickedness of the wicked will be charged against him.

21"But if a wicked man turns away from all the sins he has committed and keeps all my decrees and does what is just and right, he will surely live; he will not die. 22None of the offenses he has committed will be remembered against him. Because of the righteous things he has done, he will live. 23Do I take any pleasure in the death of the wicked? declares the Sovereign LORD. Rather, am I not pleased when they turn from their ways and live?

24"But if a righteous man turns from his righteousness and commits sin and does the same detestable things the wicked man does, will he live? None of the righteous things he has done will be remembered. Because of the unfaithfulness he is guilty of and because of the sins he has committed, he will die.

25"Yet you say, 'The way of the Lord is not just.' Hear, O house of Israel: Is my way unjust? Is it not your ways that are unjust? 26If a righteous man turns from his righteousness and commits sin, he will die for it; because of the sin he has committed he will die. 27But if a wicked man turns away from the wickedness he has committed and does what is just and right, he will save his life. 28Because he considers all the offenses he has committed and turns away from them, he will surely live; he will not die. 29Yet the house of Israel says, 'The way of the Lord is not just.' Are my ways unjust, O house of Israel? Is it not your ways that are unjust?

30"Therefore, O house of Israel, I will judge you, each one according to his ways, declares the Sovereign LORD. Repent! Turn away from all your offenses; then sin will not be your downfall. 31Rid yourselves of all the offenses you have committed, and get a new heart and a new spirit. Why will you die, O house of Israel? 32For I take no pleasure in the death of anyone, declares the Sovereign LORD. Repent and live!

PRAYER: CONFESSION

TRULY I have sinned against You, the Lord, the God of Israel.
(Joshua 7:20)

***ASK** the Spirit to search your heart and reveal any areas of unconfessed sin. Acknowledge these to the Lord and thank Him for His forgiveness.*

NT Hebrews 1:1-14

The Son Superior to Angels

1 In the past God spoke to our forefathers through the prophets at many times and in various ways, 2but in these last days he has spoken to us by his Son, whom he appointed heir of all things, and through whom he made the universe. 3The Son is the radiance of God's glory and the exact representation of his being, sustaining all things by his powerful word. After he had provided purification for sins, he sat down at the right hand of the Majesty in heaven. 4So he became as much superior to the angels as the name he has inherited is superior to theirs.

5For to which of the angels did God ever say,

"You are my Son;
today I have become your Father[a]"[b]?

Or again,

"I will be his Father,
and he will be my Son"[c]?

[a] 5 Or *have begotten you* [b] 5 Psalm 2:7
[c] 5 2 Samuel 7:14; 1 Chron. 17:13

[6]And again, when God brings his firstborn into the world, he says,

"Let all God's angels worship him."[d]

[7]In speaking of the angels he says,

"He makes his angels winds,
his servants flames of fire."[e]

[8]But about the Son he says,

"Your throne, O God, will last for ever and ever,
and righteousness will be the scepter of your kingdom.
[9]You have loved righteousness and hated wickedness;
therefore God, your God, has set you above your companions
by anointing you with the oil of joy."[f]

[10]He also says,

"In the beginning, O Lord, you laid the foundations of the earth,
and the heavens are the work of your hands.
[11]They will perish, but you remain;
they will all wear out like a garment.
[12]You will roll them up like a robe;
like a garment they will be changed.
But you remain the same,
and your years will never end."[g]

[13]To which of the angels did God ever say,

"Sit at my right hand
until I make your enemies
a footstool for your feet"[h]?

[14]Are not all angels ministering spirits sent to serve those who will inherit salvation?

[d] 6 Deut. 32:43 (see Dead Sea Scrolls and Septuagint) [e] 7 Psalm 104:4 [f] 9 Psalm 45:6,7 [g] 12 Psalm 102:25–27 [h] 13 Psalm 110:1

PRAYER: MY RELATIONSHIP TO OTHERS

WE love because You, O God, first loved us. Those who say, "I love God," and hate their neighbors are liars; for those who do not love their neighbors whom they have seen cannot love You whom they have not seen. And we have this commandment from You: that those who love You must also love their neighbors. (1 John 4:19–21)

***PAUSE** to review your relationships with others and to commit them to the Lord.*

OT Ezekiel 19:1–14 — YEAR 2 DAY 261

A Lament for Israel's Princes

19 "Take up a lament concerning the princes of Israel [2]and say:

" 'What a lioness was your mother
among the lions!
She lay down among the young lions
and reared her cubs.
[3]She brought up one of her cubs,
and he became a strong lion.
He learned to tear the prey
and he devoured men.
[4]The nations heard about him,
and he was trapped in their pit.
They led him with hooks
to the land of Egypt.

[5]" 'When she saw her hope unfulfilled,
her expectation gone,
she took another of her cubs
and made him a strong lion.
[6]He prowled among the lions,
for he was now a strong lion.
He learned to tear the prey
and he devoured men.
[7]He broke down[a] their strongholds
and devastated their towns.
The land and all who were in it
were terrified by his roaring.
[8]Then the nations came against him,
those from regions round about.
They spread their net for him,
and he was trapped in their pit.

[a] 7 Targum (see Septuagint); Hebrew *He knew*

[9]With hooks they pulled him into a
cage
and brought him to the king of
Babylon.
They put him in prison,
so his roar was heard no longer
on the mountains of Israel.

[10]" 'Your mother was like a vine in your
vineyard[b]
planted by the water;
it was fruitful and full of branches
because of abundant water.
[11]Its branches were strong,
fit for a ruler's scepter.
It towered high
above the thick foliage,
conspicuous for its height
and for its many branches.
[12]But it was uprooted in fury
and thrown to the ground.
The east wind made it shrivel,
it was stripped of its fruit;
its strong branches withered
and fire consumed them.
[13]Now it is planted in the desert,
in a dry and thirsty land.
[14]Fire spread from one of its main[c]
branches
and consumed its fruit.
No strong branch is left on it
fit for a ruler's scepter.'

This is a lament and is to be used as a lament."

[b] *10* Two Hebrew manuscripts; most Hebrew manuscripts *your blood* [c] *14* Or *from under its*

PRAYER: RENEWAL

MAY I love my enemies and pray for those who persecute me. (Matthew 5:44) . . . Whatever I want others to do to me, may I also do to them, for this sums up the Law and the Prophets. (Matthew 7:12)

***PAUSE** to add your own prayers for personal renewal.*

NT Hebrews 2:1-18

Warning to Pay Attention

2 We must pay more careful attention,
therefore, to what we have heard, so
that we do not drift away. [2]For if the message spoken by angels was binding, and
every violation and disobedience received
its just punishment, [3]how shall we escape
if we ignore such a great salvation? This
salvation, which was first announced by
the Lord, was confirmed to us by those
who heard him. [4]God also testified to it
by signs, wonders and various miracles,
and gifts of the Holy Spirit distributed according to his will.

Jesus Made Like His Brothers

[5]It is not to angels that he has subjected the world to come, about which we are
speaking. [6]But there is a place where
someone has testified:

"What is man that you are mindful of
him,
the son of man that you care for
him?
[7]You made him a little[a] lower than the
angels;
you crowned him with glory and
honor
[8] and put everything under his feet."[b]

In putting everything under him, God left nothing that is not subject to him. Yet at present we do not see everything subject
to him. [9]But we see Jesus, who was made
a little lower than the angels, now crowned with glory and honor because he suffered death, so that by the grace of God he might taste death for everyone.
[10]In bringing many sons to glory, it was
fitting that God, for whom and through whom everything exists, should make the author of their salvation perfect through
suffering. [11]Both the one who makes men
holy and those who are made holy are of

[a] *7* Or *him for a little while*; also in verse 9
[b] *8* Psalm 8:4–6

the same family. So Jesus is not ashamed to call them brothers. [12]He says,

"I will declare your name to my
brothers;
in the presence of the congregation
I will sing your praises."[c]

[13]And again,

"I will put my trust in him."[d]

And again he says,

"Here am I, and the children God has
given me."[e]

[14]Since the children have flesh and blood, he too shared in their humanity so that by his death he might destroy him who holds the power of death—that is, the devil— [15]and free those who all their lives were held in slavery by their fear of death. [16]For surely it is not angels he helps, but Abraham's descendants. [17]For this reason he had to be made like his brothers in every way, in order that he might become a merciful and faithful high priest in service to God, and that he might make atonement for[f] the sins of the people. [18]Because he himself suffered when he was tempted, he is able to help those who are being tempted.

[c] 12 Psalm 22:22 [d] 13 Isaiah 8:17
[e] 13 Isaiah 8:18 [f] 17 Or *and that he might turn aside God's wrath, taking away*

PRAYER: THE ATTRIBUTES OF GOD

ALL Your works will praise you, O Lord, and Your saints will bless You. They will speak of the glory of Your kingdom and talk of Your power, so that all people may know of Your mighty acts and the glorious majesty of Your kingdom. Your kingdom is an everlasting kingdom, and Your dominion endures through all generations.

(Psalm 145:10–13)

PAUSE *to reflect on these affirmations about the person, powers and perfection of God.*

OT Ezekiel 20:1–49

YEAR 2 DAY 262

Rebellious Israel

20 In the seventh year, in the fifth month on the tenth day, some of the elders of Israel came to inquire of the LORD, and they sat down in front of me.

[2]Then the word of the LORD came to me: [3]"Son of man, speak to the elders of Israel and say to them, 'This is what the Sovereign LORD says: Have you come to inquire of me? As surely as I live, I will not let you inquire of me, declares the Sovereign LORD.'

[4]"Will you judge them? Will you judge them, son of man? Then confront them with the detestable practices of their fathers [5]and say to them: 'This is what the Sovereign LORD says: On the day I chose Israel, I swore with uplifted hand to the descendants of the house of Jacob and revealed myself to them in Egypt. With uplifted hand I said to them, "I am the LORD your God." [6]On that day I swore to them that I would bring them out of Egypt into a land I had searched out for them, a land flowing with milk and honey, the most beautiful of all lands. [7]And I said to them, "Each of you, get rid of the vile images you have set your eyes on, and do not defile yourselves with the idols of Egypt. I am the LORD your God."

[8]" 'But they rebelled against me and would not listen to me; they did not get rid of the vile images they had set their eyes on, nor did they forsake the idols of Egypt. So I said I would pour out my wrath on them and spend my anger against them in Egypt. [9]But for the sake of my name I did what would keep it from being profaned in the eyes of the nations they lived among and in whose sight I had revealed myself to the Israelites by

bringing them out of Egypt. 10Therefore I
led them out of Egypt and brought them
into the desert. 11I gave them my decrees
and made known to them my laws, for
the man who obeys them will live by
them. 12Also I gave them my Sabbaths as
a sign between us, so they would know
that I the LORD made them holy.
13" 'Yet the people of Israel rebelled
against me in the desert. They did not follow my decrees but rejected my laws—although the man who obeys them will live
by them—and they utterly desecrated my
Sabbaths. So I said I would pour out my
wrath on them and destroy them in the
desert. 14But for the sake of my name I did
what would keep it from being profaned
in the eyes of the nations in whose sight
I had brought them out. 15Also with uplifted hand I swore to them in the desert
that I would not bring them into the land
I had given them—a land flowing with
milk and honey, most beautiful of all
lands— 16because they rejected my laws
and did not follow my decrees and desecrated my Sabbaths. For their hearts were
devoted to their idols. 17Yet I looked on
them with pity and did not destroy them
or put an end to them in the desert. 18I
said to their children in the desert, "Do
not follow the statutes of your fathers or
keep their laws or defile yourselves with
their idols. 19I am the LORD your God; follow my decrees and be careful to keep my
laws. 20Keep my Sabbaths holy, that they
may be a sign between us. Then you will
know that I am the LORD your God."
21" 'But the children rebelled against
me: They did not follow my decrees, they
were not careful to keep my laws—although the man who obeys them will live
by them—and they desecrated my Sabbaths. So I said I would pour out my
wrath on them and spend my anger
against them in the desert. 22But I withheld my hand, and for the sake of my
name I did what would keep it from being profaned in the eyes of the nations in
whose sight I had brought them out.
23Also with uplifted hand I swore to them
in the desert that I would disperse them
among the nations and scatter them
through the countries, 24because they had
not obeyed my laws but had rejected my
decrees and desecrated my Sabbaths, and
their eyes ⌊lusted⌋ after their fathers' idols.
25I also gave them over to statutes that
were not good and laws they could not
live by; 26I let them become defiled
through their gifts—the sacrifice of every
firstborn[a]—that I might fill them with
horror so they would know that I am the
LORD.'
27"Therefore, son of man, speak to the
people of Israel and say to them, 'This is
what the Sovereign LORD says: In this also
your fathers blasphemed me by forsaking
me: 28When I brought them into the land
I had sworn to give them and they saw
any high hill or any leafy tree, there they
offered their sacrifices, made offerings
that provoked me to anger, presented
their fragrant incense and poured out
their drink offerings. 29Then I said to
them: What is this high place you go to?' "
(It is called Bamah[b] to this day.)

Judgment and Restoration

30"Therefore say to the house of Israel:
'This is what the Sovereign LORD says: Will
you defile yourselves the way your fathers
did and lust after their vile images?
31When you offer your gifts—the sacrifice
of your sons in[c] the fire—you continue to
defile yourselves with all your idols to this
day. Am I to let you inquire of me,
O house of Israel? As surely as I live, declares the Sovereign LORD, I will not let
you inquire of me.
32" 'You say, "We want to be like the nations, like the peoples of the world, who
serve wood and stone." But what you have
in mind will never happen. 33As surely as
I live, declares the Sovereign LORD, I will
rule over you with a mighty hand and an
outstretched arm and with outpoured
wrath. 34I will bring you from the nations
and gather you from the countries where
you have been scattered—with a mighty
hand and an outstretched arm and with
outpoured wrath. 35I will bring you into
the desert of the nations and there, face to
face, I will execute judgment upon you.
36As I judged your fathers in the desert of
the land of Egypt, so I will judge you, declares the Sovereign LORD. 37I will take
note of you as you pass under my rod,
and I will bring you into the bond of the
covenant. 38I will purge you of those who
revolt and rebel against me. Although I

[a] 26 Or —*making every firstborn pass through ⌊the fire⌋*
[b] 29 *Bamah* means *high place.* [c] 31 Or —*making your sons pass through*

will bring them out of the land where
they are living, yet they will not enter the
land of Israel. Then you will know that I
am the LORD.
39 " 'As for you, O house of Israel, this is
what the Sovereign LORD says: Go and
serve your idols, every one of you! But afterward you will surely listen to me and
no longer profane my holy name with
your gifts and idols. 40 For on my holy
mountain, the high mountain of Israel,
declares the Sovereign LORD, there in the
land the entire house of Israel will serve
me, and there I will accept them. There I
will require your offerings and your
choice gifts,[d] along with all your holy sacrifices. 41 I will accept you as fragrant incense when I bring you out from the nations and gather you from the countries
where you have been scattered, and I will
show myself holy among you in the sight
of the nations. 42 Then you will know that
I am the LORD, when I bring you into the
land of Israel, the land I had sworn with
uplifted hand to give to your fathers.
43 There you will remember your conduct
and all the actions by which you have defiled yourselves, and you will loathe yourselves for all the evil you have done. 44 You
will know that I am the LORD, when I deal
with you for my name's sake and not according to your evil ways and your corrupt
practices, O house of Israel, declares the
Sovereign LORD.' "

Prophecy Against the South

45 The word of the LORD came to me:
46 "Son of man, set your face toward the
south; preach against the south and
prophesy against the forest of the southland. 47 Say to the southern forest: 'Hear
the word of the LORD. This is what the
Sovereign LORD says: I am about to set fire
to you, and it will consume all your trees,
both green and dry. The blazing flame will
not be quenched, and every face from
south to north will be scorched by it.
48 Everyone will see that I the LORD have
kindled it; it will not be quenched.' "
49 Then I said, "Ah, Sovereign LORD!
They are saying of me, 'Isn't he just telling
parables?' "

[d] 40 Or *and the gifts of your firstfruits*

PRAYER: PETITION

SINCE I have in You a great high priest who has passed through the heavens, O Jesus, I will hold firmly to the faith I confess. For in You I do not have a high priest who is unable to sympathize with my weaknesses, but one who has been tempted in every way, just as I am, yet one who is without sin. Therefore, I will approach the throne of grace with confidence, so that I may receive mercy and find grace to help me in my time of need. (Hebrews 4:14–16)

PAUSE *here to offer prayers of petition regarding your family and your ministry. Ask for help and guidance in sharing Jesus with others and helping others grow in Him. Ask for guidance in your vocation and your avocations. Offer prayers of petition regarding your activities for this day and any special concerns you may have.*

NT Hebrews 3:1–19

Jesus Greater Than Moses

3 Therefore, holy brothers, who share in
the heavenly calling, fix your thoughts
on Jesus, the apostle and high priest
whom we confess. 2 He was faithful to the
one who appointed him, just as Moses
was faithful in all God's house. 3 Jesus has
been found worthy of greater honor than
Moses, just as the builder of a house has
greater honor than the house itself. 4 For
every house is built by someone, but God
is the builder of everything. 5 Moses was
faithful as a servant in all God's house,
testifying to what would be said in the future. 6 But Christ is faithful as a son over
God's house. And we are his house, if we

hold on to our courage and the hope of
which we boast.

Warning Against Unbelief

7 So, as the Holy Spirit says:

"Today, if you hear his voice,
8 do not harden your hearts
as you did in the rebellion,
during the time of testing in the desert,
9 where your fathers tested and tried me
and for forty years saw what I did.
10 That is why I was angry with that generation,
and I said, 'Their hearts are always going astray,
and they have not known my ways.'
11 So I declared on oath in my anger,
'They shall never enter my rest.' "[a]

12 See to it, brothers, that none of you
has a sinful, unbelieving heart that turns
away from the living God. 13 But encourage one another daily, as long as it is
called Today, so that none of you may be
hardened by sin's deceitfulness. 14 We have
come to share in Christ if we hold firmly
till the end the confidence we had at first.
15 As has just been said:

"Today, if you hear his voice,
do not harden your hearts
as you did in the rebellion."[b]

16 Who were they who heard and rebelled? Were they not all those Moses led
out of Egypt? 17 And with whom was he
angry for forty years? Was it not with
those who sinned, whose bodies fell in
the desert? 18 And to whom did God swear
that they would never enter his rest if not
to those who disobeyed[c]? 19 So we see that
they were not able to enter, because of
their unbelief.

[a] *11* Psalm 95:7–11 [b] *15* Psalm 95:7,8 [c] *18* Or *disbelieved*

PRAYER: THE WORKS OF GOD

YOU, O Christ, our Passover lamb, have been sacrificed for us. (1 Corinthians 5:7) . . . Thanks be to You, O God, for Your indescribable gift! (2 Corinthians 9:15)

TAKE *a moment to consider the greatness of God's wonderful works.*

YEAR 2 DAY 263

OT Ezekiel 21:1-32

Babylon, God's Sword of Judgment

21 The word of the LORD came to me:
2 "Son of man, set your face against
Jerusalem and preach against the sanctuary. Prophesy against the land of Israel
3 and say to her: 'This is what the LORD
says: I am against you. I will draw my
sword from its scabbard and cut off from
you both the righteous and the wicked.
4 Because I am going to cut off the righteous and the wicked, my sword will be
unsheathed against everyone from south
to north. 5 Then all people will know that
I the LORD have drawn my sword from its
scabbard; it will not return again.'
6 "Therefore groan, son of man! Groan
before them with broken heart and bitter
grief. 7 And when they ask you, 'Why are
you groaning?' you shall say, 'Because of
the news that is coming. Every heart will
melt and every hand go limp; every spirit
will become faint and every knee become
as weak as water.' It is coming! It will surely take place, declares the Sovereign LORD."
8 The word of the LORD came to me:
9 "Son of man, prophesy and say, 'This is
what the Lord says:

" 'A sword, a sword,
sharpened and polished—
10 sharpened for the slaughter,
polished to flash like lightning!

" 'Shall we rejoice in the scepter of my
son ⌊Judah⌋? The sword despises every
such stick.

11 " 'The sword is appointed to be polished,

to be grasped with the hand;
it is sharpened and polished,
made ready for the hand of the slayer.
12 Cry out and wail, son of man,
for it is against my people;
it is against all the princes of Israel.
They are thrown to the sword
along with my people.
Therefore beat your breast.

13 " 'Testing will surely come. And what
if the scepter ⌊of Judah⌋, which the sword
despises, does not continue? declares the
Sovereign LORD.'

14 "So then, son of man, prophesy
and strike your hands together.
Let the sword strike twice,
even three times.
It is a sword for slaughter—
a sword for great slaughter,
closing in on them from every side.
15 So that hearts may melt
and the fallen be many,
I have stationed the sword for slaughter[a]
at all their gates.
Oh! It is made to flash like lightning,
it is grasped for slaughter.
16 O sword, slash to the right,
then to the left,
wherever your blade is turned.
17 I too will strike my hands together,
and my wrath will subside.
I the LORD have spoken."

18 The word of the LORD came to me:
19 "Son of man, mark out two roads for the
sword of the king of Babylon to take, both
starting from the same country. Make a
signpost where the road branches off to
the city. 20 Mark out one road for the sword
to come against Rabbah of the Ammonites and another against Judah and
fortified Jerusalem. 21 For the king of Babylon will stop at the fork in the road, at
the junction of the two roads, to seek an
omen: He will cast lots with arrows, he
will consult his idols, he will examine the
liver. 22 Into his right hand will come the
lot for Jerusalem, where he is to set up
battering rams, to give the command to
slaughter, to sound the battle cry, to set
battering rams against the gates, to build
a ramp and to erect siege works. 23 It will
seem like a false omen to those who have
sworn allegiance to him, but he will remind them of their guilt and take them
captive.
24 "Therefore this is what the Sovereign
LORD says: 'Because you people have
brought to mind your guilt by your open
rebellion, revealing your sins in all that
you do—because you have done this, you
will be taken captive.
25 " 'O profane and wicked prince of Israel, whose day has come, whose time of
punishment has reached its climax, 26 this
is what the Sovereign LORD says: Take off
the turban, remove the crown. It will not
be as it was: The lowly will be exalted and
the exalted will be brought low. 27 A ruin!
A ruin! I will make it a ruin! It will not be
restored until he comes to whom it right-
fully belongs; to him I will give it.'
28 "And you, son of man, prophesy and
say, 'This is what the Sovereign LORD says
about the Ammonites and their insults:

" 'A sword, a sword,
drawn for the slaughter,
polished to consume
and to flash like lightning!
29 Despite false visions concerning you
and lying divinations about you,
it will be laid on the necks
of the wicked who are to be slain,
whose day has come,
whose time of punishment has reached its climax.
30 Return the sword to its scabbard.
In the place where you were created,
in the land of your ancestry,
I will judge you.
31 I will pour out my wrath upon you
and breathe out my fiery anger against you;
I will hand you over to brutal men,
men skilled in destruction.
32 You will be fuel for the fire,
your blood will be shed in your land,
you will be remembered no more;
for I the LORD have spoken.' "

[a] *15* Septuagint; the meaning of the Hebrew for this word is uncertain.

PRAYER: INTERCESSION

MAY I not forget to do good and to share with others, for with such sacrifices You are well pleased.
(Hebrews 13:16)

TAKE *a few moments to intercede on behalf of local, national and world missions. Pray that the Great Commission would be fulfilled and for any special concerns you may have for missions.*

NT Hebrews 4:1-13

A Sabbath-Rest for the People of God

4 Therefore, since the promise of entering his rest still stands, let us be careful
that none of you be found to have fallen
short of it. 2For we also have had the
gospel preached to us, just as they did; but
the message they heard was of no value to
them, because those who heard did not
combine it with faith.[a] 3Now we who
have believed enter that rest, just as God
has said,

"So I declared on oath in my anger,
'They shall never enter my rest.' "[b]

And yet his work has been finished since
the creation of the world. 4For somewhere
he has spoken about the seventh day in
these words: "And on the seventh day God
rested from all his work."[c] 5And again in
the passage above he says, "They shall
never enter my rest."

6It still remains that some will enter
that rest, and those who formerly had the
gospel preached to them did not go in,
because of their disobedience. 7Therefore
God again set a certain day, calling it Today, when a long time later he spoke
through David, as was said before:

"Today, if you hear his voice,
do not harden your hearts."[d]

8For if Joshua had given them rest, God
would not have spoken later about another day. 9There remains, then, a Sabbath-rest for the people of God; 10for anyone who enters God's rest also rests from
his own work, just as God did from his.
11Let us, therefore, make every effort to enter that rest, so that no one will fall by following their example of disobedience.

12For the word of God is living and active. Sharper than any double-edged
sword, it penetrates even to dividing soul
and spirit, joints and marrow; it judges
the thoughts and attitudes of the heart.
13Nothing in all creation is hidden from
God's sight. Everything is uncovered and
laid bare before the eyes of him to whom
we must give account.

[a] 2 Many manuscripts *because they did not share in the faith of those who obeyed* [b] 3 Psalm 95:11; also in verse 5 [c] 4 Gen. 2:2 [d] 7 Psalm 95:7,8

PRAYER: MY RELATIONSHIP TO GOD

YOU, O Lord, take pleasure in those who fear You, who put their hope in Your unfailing love. (Psalm 147:11) . . . I will watch in hope for You, O Lord; I will wait for You, O God of my salvation; my God, You will hear me.
(Micah 7:7)

PAUSE *to thank God for the relationship that you enjoy with Him in Jesus Christ.*

OT Ezekiel 22:1-31

YEAR 2 DAY 264

Jerusalem's Sins

22 The word of the LORD came to me:
2 "Son of man, will you judge her?
Will you judge this city of bloodshed?
Then confront her with all her detestable
practices 3 and say: 'This is what the Sovereign LORD says: O city that brings on
herself doom by shedding blood in her
midst and defiles herself by making idols,
4 you have become guilty because of the
blood you have shed and have become
defiled by the idols you have made. You
have brought your days to a close, and the
end of your years has come. Therefore I
will make you an object of scorn to the
nations and a laughingstock to all the
countries. 5 Those who are near and those
who are far away will mock you, O infa-
mous city, full of turmoil.

6 " 'See how each of the princes of Israel who are in you uses his power to shed
blood. 7 In you they have treated father
and mother with contempt; in you they
have oppressed the alien and mistreated
the fatherless and the widow. 8 You have
despised my holy things and desecrated
my Sabbaths. 9 In you are slanderous men
bent on shedding blood; in you are those
who eat at the mountain shrines and
commit lewd acts. 10 In you are those who
dishonor their fathers' bed; in you are
those who violate women during their period, when they are ceremonially unclean.
11 In you one man commits a detestable offense with his neighbor's wife, another
shamefully defiles his daughter-in-law,
and another violates his sister, his own father's daughter. 12 In you men accept
bribes to shed blood; you take usury and
excessive interest[a] and make unjust gain
from your neighbors by extortion. And
you have forgotten me, declares the Sovereign LORD.

13 " 'I will surely strike my hands together at the unjust gain you have made
and at the blood you have shed in your
midst. 14 Will your courage endure or your
hands be strong in the day I deal with
you? I the LORD have spoken, and I will
do it. 15 I will disperse you among the nations and scatter you through the countries; and I will put an end to your uncleanness. 16 When you have been defiled[b]
in the eyes of the nations, you will know
that I am the LORD.' "

17 Then the word of the LORD came to
me: 18 "Son of man, the house of Israel has
become dross to me; all of them are the
copper, tin, iron and lead left inside a furnace. They are but the dross of silver.
19 Therefore this is what the Sovereign LORD
says: 'Because you have all become dross,
I will gather you into Jerusalem. 20 As men
gather silver, copper, iron, lead and tin
into a furnace to melt it with a fiery blast,
so will I gather you in my anger and my
wrath and put you inside the city and melt
you. 21 I will gather you and I will blow on
you with my fiery wrath, and you will be
melted inside her. 22 As silver is melted in
a furnace, so you will be melted inside her,
and you will know that I the LORD have
poured out my wrath upon you.' "

23 Again the word of the LORD came to
me: 24 "Son of man, say to the land, 'You
are a land that has had no rain or showers[c] in the day of wrath.' 25 There is a conspiracy of her princes[d] within her like a
roaring lion tearing its prey; they devour
people, take treasures and precious things
and make many widows within her. 26 Her
priests do violence to my law and profane
my holy things; they do not distinguish
between the holy and the common; they
teach that there is no difference between
the unclean and the clean; and they shut
their eyes to the keeping of my Sabbaths,
so that I am profaned among them. 27 Her
officials within her are like wolves tearing
their prey; they shed blood and kill people to make unjust gain. 28 Her prophets
whitewash these deeds for them by false
visions and lying divinations. They say,
'This is what the Sovereign LORD says'—
when the LORD has not spoken. 29 The people of the land practice extortion and
commit robbery; they oppress the poor
and needy and mistreat the alien, denying
them justice.

30 "I looked for a man among them who
would build up the wall and stand before
me in the gap on behalf of the land so I

[a] *12* Or *usury and interest* [b] *16* Or *When I have allotted you your inheritance* [c] *24* Septuagint; Hebrew *has not been cleansed or rained on* [d] *25* Septuagint; Hebrew *prophets*

would not have to destroy it, but I found none. [31]So I will pour out my wrath on them and consume them with my fiery anger, bringing down on their own heads all they have done, declares the Sovereign LORD."

PRAYER: AFFIRMATION

THANK You, Lord Jesus, that You expressed Your willingness to die for us when You said, "My Father loves Me because I lay down My life that I may take it up again. No one takes it from Me, but I lay it down of My own accord. I have authority to lay it down and authority to take it up again. This command I received from My Father." (John 10:17–18)

PAUSE *to reflect on these Biblical affirmations.*

NT Hebrews 4:14–5:10

Jesus the Great High Priest

[14]Therefore, since we have a great high priest who has gone through the heavens,[a] Jesus the Son of God, let us hold firmly to the faith we profess. [15]For we do not have a high priest who is unable to sympathize with our weaknesses, but we have one who has been tempted in every way, just as we are—yet was without sin. [16]Let us then approach the throne of grace with confidence, so that we may receive mercy and find grace to help us in our time of need.

5 Every high priest is selected from among men and is appointed to represent them in matters related to God, to offer gifts and sacrifices for sins. [2]He is able to deal gently with those who are ignorant and are going astray, since he himself is subject to weakness. [3]This is why he has to offer sacrifices for his own sins, as well as for the sins of the people.

[4]No one takes this honor upon himself; he must be called by God, just as Aaron was. [5]So Christ also did not take upon himself the glory of becoming a high priest. But God said to him,

"You are my Son;
today I have become your Father.[b]"[c]

[6]And he says in another place,

"You are a priest forever,
in the order of Melchizedek."[d]

[7]During the days of Jesus' life on earth, he offered up prayers and petitions with loud cries and tears to the one who could save him from death, and he was heard because of his reverent submission. [8]Although he was a son, he learned obedience from what he suffered [9]and, once made perfect, he became the source of eternal salvation for all who obey him [10]and was designated by God to be high priest in the order of Melchizedek.

[a] 14 Or *gone into heaven* [b] 5 Or *have begotten you*
[c] 5 Psalm 2:7 [d] 6 Psalm 110:4

PRAYER: THE CHARACTER I WANT TO CULTIVATE

IT is better to take refuge in You, O Lord, than to trust in people. (Psalm 118:8) . . . Let me stop trusting in human beings, who only live for a little while. For of what account are they? (Isaiah 2:22)

TAKE *a moment to ask the Lord for the grace to grow in godly character.*

YEAR 2 DAY 265

OT Ezekiel 23:1–49

Two Adulterous Sisters

23 The word of the LORD came to me:
2 "Son of man, there were two women,
daughters of the same mother. 3 They became prostitutes in Egypt, engaging in
prostitution from their youth. In that land
their breasts were fondled and their virgin
bosoms caressed. 4 The older was named
Oholah, and her sister was Oholibah.
They were mine and gave birth to sons
and daughters. Oholah is Samaria, and
Oholibah is Jerusalem.

5 "Oholah engaged in prostitution while
she was still mine; and she lusted after her
lovers, the Assyrians—warriors 6 clothed in
blue, governors and commanders, all of
them handsome young men, and mounted horsemen. 7 She gave herself as a prostitute to all the elite of the Assyrians and
defiled herself with all the idols of everyone she lusted after. 8 She did not give up
the prostitution she began in Egypt, when
during her youth men slept with her, caressed her virgin bosom and poured out
their lust upon her.

9 "Therefore I handed her over to her
lovers, the Assyrians, for whom she lusted. 10 They stripped her naked, took away
her sons and daughters and killed her
with the sword. She became a byword
among women, and punishment was inflicted on her.

11 "Her sister Oholibah saw this, yet in
her lust and prostitution she was more
depraved than her sister. 12 She too lusted
after the Assyrians—governors and commanders, warriors in full dress, mounted
horsemen, all handsome young men. 13 I
saw that she too defiled herself; both of
them went the same way.

14 "But she carried her prostitution still
further. She saw men portrayed on a wall,
figures of Chaldeans[a] portrayed in red,
15 with belts around their waists and flowing turbans on their heads; all of them
looked like Babylonian chariot officers, na-
tives of Chaldea.[b] 16 As soon as she saw
them, she lusted after them and sent messengers to them in Chaldea. 17 Then the
Babylonians came to her, to the bed of love,
and in their lust they defiled her. After she
had been defiled by them, she turned away
from them in disgust. 18 When she carried
on her prostitution openly and exposed her
nakedness, I turned away from her in disgust, just as I had turned away from her sister. 19 Yet she became more and more
promiscuous as she recalled the days of her
youth, when she was a prostitute in Egypt.
20 There she lusted after her lovers, whose
genitals were like those of donkeys and
whose emission was like that of horses. 21 So
you longed for the lewdness of your youth,
when in Egypt your bosom was caressed
and your young breasts fondled.[c]

22 "Therefore, Oholibah, this is what the
Sovereign LORD says: I will stir up your
lovers against you, those you turned away
from in disgust, and I will bring them
against you from every side— 23 the Babylonians and all the Chaldeans, the men of Pekod and Shoa and Koa, and all the Assyrians with them, handsome young men, all
of them governors and commanders, chariot officers and men of high rank, all
mounted on horses. 24 They will come
against you with weapons,[d] chariots and
wagons and with a throng of people; they
will take up positions against you on every
side with large and small shields and with
helmets. I will turn you over to them for
punishment, and they will punish you according to their standards. 25 I will direct my
jealous anger against you, and they will deal
with you in fury. They will cut off your noses
and your ears, and those of you who are left
will fall by the sword. They will take away
your sons and daughters, and those of you
who are left will be consumed by fire. 26 They
will also strip you of your clothes and take
your fine jewelry. 27 So I will put a stop to the
lewdness and prostitution you began in
Egypt. You will not look on these things
with longing or remember Egypt anymore.

28 "For this is what the Sovereign LORD
says: I am about to hand you over to those
you hate, to those you turned away from
in disgust. 29 They will deal with you in hatred and take away everything you have
worked for. They will leave you naked and
bare, and the shame of your prostitution
will be exposed. Your lewdness and

[a] 14 Or *Babylonians* [b] 15 Or *Babylonia;* also in verse 16 [c] 21 Syriac (see also verse 3); Hebrew *caressed because of your young breasts* [d] 24 The meaning of the Hebrew for this word is uncertain.

promiscuity [30]have brought this upon
you, because you lusted after the nations
and defiled yourself with their idols. [31]You
have gone the way of your sister; so I will
put her cup into your hand.
[32]"This is what the Sovereign LORD says:

"You will drink your sister's cup,
a cup large and deep;
it will bring scorn and derision,
for it holds so much.
[33]You will be filled with drunkenness
and sorrow,
the cup of ruin and desolation,
the cup of your sister Samaria.
[34]You will drink it and drain it dry;
you will dash it to pieces
and tear your breasts.

I have spoken, declares the Sovereign
LORD.

[35]"Therefore this is what the Sovereign
LORD says: Since you have forgotten me
and thrust me behind your back, you
must bear the consequences of your lewdness and prostitution."
[36]The LORD said to me: "Son of man,
will you judge Oholah and Oholibah?
Then confront them with their detestable
practices, [37]for they have committed adultery and blood is on their hands. They
committed adultery with their idols; they
even sacrificed their children, whom they
bore to me,[e] as food for them. [38]They have
also done this to me: At that same time
they defiled my sanctuary and desecrated
my Sabbaths. [39]On the very day they sacrificed their children to their idols, they
entered my sanctuary and desecrated it.
That is what they did in my house.
[40]"They even sent messengers for men
who came from far away, and when they
arrived you bathed yourself for them,
painted your eyes and put on your jewelry.
[41]You sat on an elegant couch, with a table
spread before it on which you had placed
the incense and oil that belonged to me.
[42]"The noise of a carefree crowd was
around her; Sabeans[f] were brought from
the desert along with men from the rabble,
and they put bracelets on the arms of the
woman and her sister and beautiful crowns
on their heads. [43]Then I said about the one
worn out by adultery, 'Now let them use
her as a prostitute, for that is all she is.'
[44]And they slept with her. As men sleep
with a prostitute, so they slept with those
lewd women, Oholah and Oholibah. [45]But
righteous men will sentence them to the
punishment of women who commit adultery and shed blood, because they are adulterous and blood is on their hands.
[46]"This is what the Sovereign LORD says:
Bring a mob against them and give them
over to terror and plunder. [47]The mob will
stone them and cut them down with their
swords; they will kill their sons and
daughters and burn down their houses.
[48]"So I will put an end to lewdness in the
land, that all women may take warning and
not imitate you. [49]You will suffer the penalty for your lewdness and bear the consequences of your sins of idolatry. Then you
will know that I am the Sovereign LORD."

[e] 37 Or *even made the children they bore to me pass through ⌞the fire⌟* [f] 42 Or *drunkards*

PRAYER: THANKSGIVING

I HAVE been chosen according to Your foreknowledge, Father, through sanctification of Your Spirit, for obedience to Jesus Christ and sprinkling of His blood; grace and peace are mine in abundance. (1 Peter 1:2) . . . Through Jesus I will continually offer to You, O God, a sacrifice of praise, that is, the fruit of lips that give thanks to Your name. (Hebrews 13:15)

PAUSE *to offer your own expressions of thanksgiving.*

NT Hebrews 5:11–6:12

Warning Against Falling Away

[11]We have much to say about this, but
it is hard to explain because you are slow
to learn. [12]In fact, though by this time you
ought to be teachers, you need someone
to teach you the elementary truths of
God's word all over again. You need milk,
not solid food! [13]Anyone who lives on

milk, being still an infant, is not acquainted with the teaching about righteousness. 14 But solid food is for the mature, who by constant use have trained
themselves to distinguish good from evil.
6 Therefore let us leave the elementary
teachings about Christ and go on to maturity, not laying again the foundation of
repentance from acts that lead to death,[a]
and of faith in God, 2 instruction about
baptisms, the laying on of hands, the resurrection of the dead, and eternal judgment. 3 And God permitting, we will do so.
4 It is impossible for those who have once
been enlightened, who have tasted the
heavenly gift, who have shared in the Holy
Spirit, 5 who have tasted the goodness of the
word of God and the powers of the coming
age, 6 if they fall away, to be brought back to
repentance, because[b] to their loss they are
crucifying the Son of God all over again and
subjecting him to public disgrace.
7 Land that drinks in the rain often
falling on it and that produces a crop useful to those for whom it is farmed receives
the blessing of God. 8 But land that produces thorns and thistles is worthless and
is in danger of being cursed. In the end it
will be burned.
9 Even though we speak like this, dear
friends, we are confident of better things
in your case—things that accompany salvation. 10 God is not unjust; he will not
forget your work and the love you have
shown him as you have helped his people
and continue to help them. 11 We want
each of you to show this same diligence
to the very end, in order to make your
hope sure. 12 We do not want you to become lazy, but to imitate those who
through faith and patience inherit what
has been promised.

[a] 1 Or *from useless rituals* [b] 6 Or *repentance while*

PRAYER: MY RELATIONSHIP TO OTHERS

WE must not forsake meeting together, as some are in the habit of doing, but encourage one another all the more as we see the day approaching. (Hebrews 10:25)

PAUSE *to review your relationships with others and to commit them to the Lord.*

YEAR 2 DAY 266

OT **Psalms 122–123**

Psalm 122

A song of ascents. Of David.

1 I rejoiced with those who said to me,
"Let us go to the house of the LORD."
2 Our feet are standing
in your gates, O Jerusalem.

3 Jerusalem is built like a city
that is closely compacted together.
4 That is where the tribes go up,
the tribes of the LORD,
to praise the name of the LORD
according to the statute given to Israel.
5 There the thrones for judgment stand,
the thrones of the house of David.

6 Pray for the peace of Jerusalem:
"May those who love you be secure.
7 May there be peace within your walls
and security within your citadels."
8 For the sake of my brothers and friends,
I will say, "Peace be within you."
9 For the sake of the house of the LORD our God,
I will seek your prosperity.

Psalm 123

A song of ascents.

1 I lift up my eyes to you,
to you whose throne is in heaven.
2 As the eyes of slaves look to the hand of their master,
as the eyes of a maid look to the hand of her mistress,

so our eyes look to the LORD our God,
till he shows us his mercy.
3 Have mercy on us, O LORD, have
mercy on us,
for we have endured much contempt.
4 We have endured much ridicule from
the proud,
much contempt from the arrogant.

PRAYER: ADORATION

YOU reign, O Lord; You are clothed with majesty; You are robed in majesty and are armed with strength. Indeed, the world is firmly established; it cannot be moved. Your throne is established from of old; You are from everlasting. Your testimonies stand firm; holiness adorns Your house, O Lord, forever. (Psalm 93:1–2, 5)

PAUSE *to express your thoughts of praise and worship.*

NT Hebrews 6:13–7:10

The Certainty of God's Promise

13 When God made his promise to Abraham, since there was no one greater for
him to swear by, he swore by himself,
14 saying, "I will surely bless you and give
you many descendants."[a] 15 And so after
waiting patiently, Abraham received what
was promised.
16 Men swear by someone greater than
themselves, and the oath confirms what is
said and puts an end to all argument. 17 Because God wanted to make the unchanging
nature of his purpose very clear to the heirs
of what was promised, he confirmed it with
an oath. 18 God did this so that, by two unchangeable things in which it is impossible
for God to lie, we who have fled to take
hold of the hope offered to us may be greatly encouraged. 19 We have this hope as an
anchor for the soul, firm and secure. It enters the inner sanctuary behind the curtain,
20 where Jesus, who went before us, has entered on our behalf. He has become a high
priest forever, in the order of Melchizedek.

Melchizedek the Priest

7 This Melchizedek was king of Salem and
priest of God Most High. He met Abraham returning from the defeat of the kings
and blessed him, 2 and Abraham gave him
a tenth of everything. First, his name means
"king of righteousness"; then also, "king of
Salem" means "king of peace." 3 Without father or mother, without genealogy, without
beginning of days or end of life, like the
Son of God he remains a priest forever.
4 Just think how great he was: Even the
patriarch Abraham gave him a tenth of
the plunder! 5 Now the law requires the
descendants of Levi who become priests
to collect a tenth from the people—that
is, their brothers—even though their
brothers are descended from Abraham.
6 This man, however, did not trace his descent from Levi, yet he collected a tenth
from Abraham and blessed him who had
the promises. 7 And without doubt the
lesser person is blessed by the greater. 8 In
the one case, the tenth is collected by men
who die; but in the other case, by him
who is declared to be living. 9 One might
even say that Levi, who collects the tenth,
paid the tenth through Abraham, 10 because when Melchizedek met Abraham,
Levi was still in the body of his ancestor.

[a] *14* Gen. 22:17

PRAYER: THE ATTRIBUTES OF GOD

YOU, O Lord, are a compassionate and gracious God, slow to anger and abounding in loving-kindness and truth. (Psalm 86:15)

PAUSE *to reflect on these affirmations about the person, powers and perfection of God.*

OT Ezekiel 24:1–27

YEAR 2
DAY 267

The Cooking Pot

24 In the ninth year, in the tenth month
on the tenth day, the word of the LORD
came to me: [2]"Son of man, record this date,
this very date, because the king of Babylon
has laid siege to Jerusalem this very day. [3]Tell
this rebellious house a parable and say to
them: 'This is what the Sovereign LORD says:

" 'Put on the cooking pot; put it on
and pour water into it.
[4]Put into it the pieces of meat,
all the choice pieces—the leg and
the shoulder.
Fill it with the best of these bones;
[5] take the pick of the flock.
Pile wood beneath it for the bones;
bring it to a boil
and cook the bones in it.

[6]" 'For this is what the Sovereign LORD says:

" 'Woe to the city of bloodshed,
to the pot now encrusted,
whose deposit will not go away!
Empty it piece by piece
without casting lots for them.

[7]" 'For the blood she shed is in her
midst:
She poured it on the bare rock;
she did not pour it on the ground,
where the dust would cover it.
[8]To stir up wrath and take revenge
I put her blood on the bare rock,
so that it would not be covered.

[9]" 'Therefore this is what the Sovereign
LORD says:

" 'Woe to the city of bloodshed!
I, too, will pile the wood high.
[10]So heap on the wood
and kindle the fire.
Cook the meat well,
mixing in the spices;
and let the bones be charred.
[11]Then set the empty pot on the coals
till it becomes hot and its copper
glows
so its impurities may be melted
and its deposit burned away.
[12]It has frustrated all efforts;
its heavy deposit has not been
removed,
not even by fire.

[13]" 'Now your impurity is lewdness. Because I tried to cleanse you but you would
not be cleansed from your impurity, you
will not be clean again until my wrath
against you has subsided.

[14]" 'I the LORD have spoken. The time
has come for me to act. I will not hold
back; I will not have pity, nor will I relent.
You will be judged according to your conduct and your actions, declares the Sovereign LORD.' "

Ezekiel's Wife Dies

[15]The word of the LORD came to me:
[16]"Son of man, with one blow I am about
to take away from you the delight of your
eyes. Yet do not lament or weep or shed
any tears. [17]Groan quietly; do not mourn
for the dead. Keep your turban fastened
and your sandals on your feet; do not
cover the lower part of your face or eat the
customary food ⌞of mourners⌟."

[18]So I spoke to the people in the morning, and in the evening my wife died. The
next morning I did as I had been commanded.

[19]Then the people asked me, "Won't
you tell us what these things have to do
with us?"

[20]So I said to them, "The word of the
LORD came to me: [21]Say to the house of Israel, 'This is what the Sovereign LORD says:
I am about to desecrate my sanctuary—
the stronghold in which you take pride,
the delight of your eyes, the object of your
affection. The sons and daughters you left
behind will fall by the sword. [22]And you
will do as I have done. You will not cover
the lower part of your face or eat the customary food ⌞of mourners⌟. [23]You will
keep your turbans on your heads and your
sandals on your feet. You will not mourn
or weep but will waste away because of[a]
your sins and groan among yourselves.
[24]Ezekiel will be a sign to you; you will do
just as he has done. When this happens,
you will know that I am the Sovereign
LORD.'

[25]"And you, son of man, on the day I
take away their stronghold, their joy and

[a] 23 Or *away in*

glory, the delight of their eyes, their heart's desire, and their sons and daughters as well— [26]on that day a fugitive will come to tell you the news. [27]At that time your mouth will be opened; you will speak with him and will no longer be silent. So you will be a sign to them, and they will know that I am the LORD."

PRAYER: CONFESSION

FORGIVE me when I desert You, the Rock who begot me, and forget You, the God who gave me birth.
(Deuteronomy 32:18)

***ASK** the Spirit to search your heart and reveal any areas of unconfessed sin. Acknowledge these to the Lord and thank Him for His forgiveness.*

NT Hebrews 7:11–28

Jesus Like Melchizedek

[11]If perfection could have been attained through the Levitical priesthood (for on the basis of it the law was given to the people), why was there still need for another priest to come—one in the order of Melchizedek, not in the order of Aaron? [12]For when there is a change of the priesthood, there must also be a change of the law. [13]He of whom these things are said belonged to a different tribe, and no one from that tribe has ever served at the altar. [14]For it is clear that our Lord descended from Judah, and in regard to that tribe Moses said nothing about priests. [15]And what we have said is even more clear if another priest like Melchizedek appears, [16]one who has become a priest not on the basis of a regulation as to his ancestry but on the basis of the power of an indestructible life. [17]For it is declared:

"You are a priest forever,
in the order of Melchizedek."[a]

[18]The former regulation is set aside because it was weak and useless [19](for the law made nothing perfect), and a better hope is introduced, by which we draw near to God.

[20]And it was not without an oath! Others became priests without any oath, [21]but he became a priest with an oath when God said to him:

"The Lord has sworn
and will not change his mind:
'You are a priest forever.' "[a]

[22]Because of this oath, Jesus has become the guarantee of a better covenant.

[23]Now there have been many of those priests, since death prevented them from continuing in office; [24]but because Jesus lives forever, he has a permanent priesthood. [25]Therefore he is able to save completely[b] those who come to God through him, because he always lives to intercede for them.

[26]Such a high priest meets our need—one who is holy, blameless, pure, set apart from sinners, exalted above the heavens. [27]Unlike the other high priests, he does not need to offer sacrifices day after day, first for his own sins, and then for the sins of the people. He sacrificed for their sins once for all when he offered himself. [28]For the law appoints as high priests men who are weak; but the oath, which came after the law, appointed the Son, who has been made perfect forever.

[a] *17,21* Psalm 110:4 [b] *25* Or *forever*

PRAYER: THE WORKS OF GOD

O GOD, You raised Jesus from the dead, freeing Him from the agony of death, because it was impossible for Him to be held by it.
(Acts 2:24) . . . You, O Lord Jesus, were taken up to heaven, after You gave instructions through the Holy Spirit to the apostles You had chosen. (Acts 1:2)

***TAKE** a moment to consider the greatness of God's wonderful works.*

YEAR 2 DAY 268

OT Ezekiel 25:1–26:21

A Prophecy Against Ammon

25 The word of the LORD came to me: [2]"Son of man, set your face against the Ammonites and prophesy against them. [3]Say to them, 'Hear the word of the Sovereign LORD. This is what the Sovereign LORD says: Because you said "Aha!" over my sanctuary when it was desecrated and over the land of Israel when it was laid waste and over the people of Judah when they went into exile, [4]therefore I am going to give you to the people of the East as a possession. They will set up their camps and pitch their tents among you; they will eat your fruit and drink your milk. [5]I will turn Rabbah into a pasture for camels and Ammon into a resting place for sheep. Then you will know that I am the LORD. [6]For this is what the Sovereign LORD says: Because you have clapped your hands and stamped your feet, rejoicing with all the malice of your heart against the land of Israel, [7]therefore I will stretch out my hand against you and give you as plunder to the nations. I will cut you off from the nations and exterminate you from the countries. I will destroy you, and you will know that I am the LORD.' "

A Prophecy Against Moab

[8]"This is what the Sovereign LORD says: 'Because Moab and Seir said, "Look, the house of Judah has become like all the other nations," [9]therefore I will expose the flank of Moab, beginning at its frontier towns—Beth Jeshimoth, Baal Meon and Kiriathaim—the glory of that land. [10]I will give Moab along with the Ammonites to the people of the East as a possession, so that the Ammonites will not be remembered among the nations; [11]and I will inflict punishment on Moab. Then they will know that I am the LORD.' "

A Prophecy Against Edom

[12]"This is what the Sovereign LORD says: 'Because Edom took revenge on the house of Judah and became very guilty by doing so, [13]therefore this is what the Sovereign LORD says: I will stretch out my hand against Edom and kill its men and their animals. I will lay it waste, and from Teman to Dedan they will fall by the sword. [14]I will take vengeance on Edom by the hand of my people Israel, and they will deal with Edom in accordance with my anger and my wrath; they will know my vengeance, declares the Sovereign LORD.' "

A Prophecy Against Philistia

[15]"This is what the Sovereign LORD says: 'Because the Philistines acted in vengeance and took revenge with malice in their hearts, and with ancient hostility sought to destroy Judah, [16]therefore this is what the Sovereign LORD says: I am about to stretch out my hand against the Philistines, and I will cut off the Kerethites and destroy those remaining along the coast. [17]I will carry out great vengeance on them and punish them in my wrath. Then they will know that I am the LORD, when I take vengeance on them.' "

A Prophecy Against Tyre

26 In the eleventh year, on the first day of the month, the word of the LORD came to me: [2]"Son of man, because Tyre has said of Jerusalem, 'Aha! The gate to the nations is broken, and its doors have swung open to me; now that she lies in ruins I will prosper,' [3]therefore this is what the Sovereign LORD says: I am against you, O Tyre, and I will bring many nations against you, like the sea casting up its waves. [4]They will destroy the walls of Tyre and pull down her towers; I will scrape away her rubble and make her a bare rock. [5]Out in the sea she will become a place to spread fishnets, for I have spoken, declares the Sovereign LORD. She will become plunder for the nations, [6]and her settlements on the mainland will be ravaged by the sword. Then they will know that I am the LORD.

[7]"For this is what the Sovereign LORD says: From the north I am going to bring against Tyre Nebuchadnezzar[a] king of Babylon, king of kings, with horses and chariots, with horsemen and a great army. [8]He will ravage your settlements on the mainland with the sword; he will set up siege works against you, build a ramp up

[a] 7 Hebrew *Nebuchadrezzar,* of which *Nebuchadnezzar* is a variant; here and often in Ezekiel and Jeremiah

to your walls and raise his shields against
you. 9He will direct the blows of his battering rams against your walls and demolish your towers with his weapons.
10His horses will be so many that they will
cover you with dust. Your walls will tremble at the noise of the war horses, wagons
and chariots when he enters your gates as
men enter a city whose walls have been
broken through. 11The hoofs of his horses
will trample all your streets; he will kill
your people with the sword, and your
strong pillars will fall to the ground.
12They will plunder your wealth and loot
your merchandise; they will break down
your walls and demolish your fine houses
and throw your stones, timber and rubble
into the sea. 13I will put an end to your
noisy songs, and the music of your harps
will be heard no more. 14I will make you
a bare rock, and you will become a place
to spread fishnets. You will never be rebuilt, for I the LORD have spoken, declares
the Sovereign LORD.

15"This is what the Sovereign LORD says
to Tyre: Will not the coastlands tremble at
the sound of your fall, when the wounded groan and the slaughter takes place in
you? 16Then all the princes of the coast
will step down from their thrones and lay
aside their robes and take off their embroidered garments. Clothed with terror,
they will sit on the ground, trembling
every moment, appalled at you. 17Then
they will take up a lament concerning you
and say to you:

" 'How you are destroyed, O city of
renown,
peopled by men of the sea!
You were a power on the seas,
you and your citizens;
you put your terror
on all who lived there.
18Now the coastlands tremble
on the day of your fall;
the islands in the sea
are terrified at your collapse.'

19"This is what the Sovereign LORD says:
When I make you a desolate city, like cities no longer inhabited, and when I bring
the ocean depths over you and its vast waters cover you, 20then I will bring you down
with those who go down to the pit, to the
people of long ago. I will make you dwell
in the earth below, as in ancient ruins, with
those who go down to the pit, and you will
not return or take your place[b] in the land
of the living. 21I will bring you to a horrible end and you will be no more. You will
be sought, but you will never again be
found, declares the Sovereign LORD."

[b] 20 Septuagint; Hebrew *return, and I will give glory*

PRAYER: RENEWAL

LORD, by Your grace I want to hear the words, "Well done, good and faithful servant; you have been faithful with a few things; I will put you in charge of many things. Enter into My joy." (Matthew 25:21) . . . May I not love praise from people more than praise from You, O God. (John 12:43)

***PAUSE** to add your own prayers for personal renewal.*

NT Hebrews 8:1–13

The High Priest of a New Covenant

8 The point of what we are saying is this:
We do have such a high priest, who sat
down at the right hand of the throne of
the Majesty in heaven, 2and who serves in
the sanctuary, the true tabernacle set up by
the Lord, not by man.

3Every high priest is appointed to offer
both gifts and sacrifices, and so it was necessary for this one also to have something
to offer. 4If he were on earth, he would
not be a priest, for there are already men
who offer the gifts prescribed by the law.
5They serve at a sanctuary that is a copy
and shadow of what is in heaven. This is
why Moses was warned when he was
about to build the tabernacle: "See to it
that you make everything according to the
pattern shown you on the mountain."[a]

[a] 5 Exodus 25:40

[6]But the ministry Jesus has received is as superior to theirs as the covenant of which he is mediator is superior to the old one, and it is founded on better promises.
[7]For if there had been nothing wrong with that first covenant, no place would have been sought for another. [8]But God
found fault with the people and said[b]:

"The time is coming, declares the Lord,
when I will make a new covenant
with the house of Israel
and with the house of Judah.
[9]It will not be like the covenant
I made with their forefathers
when I took them by the hand
to lead them out of Egypt,
because they did not remain faithful
to my covenant,
and I turned away from them,
declares the Lord.
[10]This is the covenant I will make with
the house of Israel
after that time, declares the Lord.
I will put my laws in their minds
and write them on their hearts.
I will be their God,
and they will be my people.
[11]No longer will a man teach his
neighbor,
or a man his brother, saying, 'Know
the Lord,'
because they will all know me,
from the least of them to the
greatest.
[12]For I will forgive their wickedness
and will remember their sins no
more."[c]

[13]By calling this covenant "new," he has made the first one obsolete; and what is obsolete and aging will soon disappear.

[b] 8 Some manuscripts may be translated *fault and said to the people.* [c] 12 Jer. 31:31–34

PRAYER: MY RELATIONSHIP TO GOD

I WILL judge nothing before the time, until You come, O Lord Jesus; You who will bring to light what is hidden in darkness and will expose the motives of people's hearts; and then each one's praise, Lord, will come from You. (1 Corinthians 4:5)

PAUSE *to thank God for the relationship that you enjoy with Him in Jesus Christ.*

YEAR 2 DAY 269

OT Ezekiel 27:1-36

A Lament for Tyre

27 The word of the LORD came to me:
[2]"Son of man, take up a lament concerning Tyre. [3]Say to Tyre, situated at the gateway to the sea, merchant of peoples on many coasts, 'This is what the Sovereign LORD says:

" 'You say, O Tyre,
"I am perfect in beauty."
[4]Your domain was on the high seas;
your builders brought your beauty
to perfection.
[5]They made all your timbers
of pine trees from Senir[a];
they took a cedar from Lebanon
to make a mast for you.
[6]Of oaks from Bashan
they made your oars;
of cypress wood[b] from the coasts of
Cyprus[c]
they made your deck, inlaid with
ivory.
[7]Fine embroidered linen from Egypt
was your sail
and served as your banner;
your awnings were of blue and
purple
from the coasts of Elishah.
[8]Men of Sidon and Arvad were your
oarsmen;

[a] 5 That is, Hermon [b] 6 Targum; the Masoretic Text has a different division of the consonants.
[c] 6 Hebrew *Kittim*

your skilled men, O Tyre, were
aboard as your seamen.
9 Veteran craftsmen of Gebal[d] were on
board
as shipwrights to caulk your seams.
All the ships of the sea and their
sailors
came alongside to trade for your
wares.

10 " 'Men of Persia, Lydia and Put
served as soldiers in your army.
They hung their shields and helmets
on your walls,
bringing you splendor.
11 Men of Arvad and Helech
manned your walls on every side;
men of Gammad
were in your towers.
They hung their shields around your
walls;
they brought your beauty to
perfection.

12 " 'Tarshish did business with you because of your great wealth of goods; they
exchanged silver, iron, tin and lead for
your merchandise.
13 " 'Greece, Tubal and Meshech traded
with you; they exchanged slaves and articles of bronze for your wares.
14 " 'Men of Beth Togarmah exchanged
work horses, war horses and mules for
your merchandise.
15 " 'The men of Rhodes[e] traded with
you, and many coastlands were your customers; they paid you with ivory tusks
and ebony.
16 " 'Aram[f] did business with you because of your many products; they exchanged turquoise, purple fabric, embroidered work, fine linen, coral and rubies
for your merchandise.
17 " 'Judah and Israel traded with you;
they exchanged wheat from Minnith and
confections,[g] honey, oil and balm for your
wares.
18 " 'Damascus, because of your many
products and great wealth of goods, did
business with you in wine from Helbon
and wool from Zahar.
19 " 'Danites and Greeks from Uzal
bought your merchandise; they exchanged wrought iron, cassia and calamus
for your wares.
20 " 'Dedan traded in saddle blankets
with you.
21 " 'Arabia and all the princes of Kedar
were your customers; they did business
with you in lambs, rams and goats.
22 " 'The merchants of Sheba and Raamah traded with you; for your merchandise they exchanged the finest of all kinds
of spices and precious stones, and gold.
23 " 'Haran, Canneh and Eden and merchants of Sheba, Asshur and Kilmad traded with you. 24 In your marketplace they
traded with you beautiful garments, blue
fabric, embroidered work and multicol-
ored rugs with cords twisted and tightly
knotted.

25 " 'The ships of Tarshish serve
as carriers for your wares.
You are filled with heavy cargo
in the heart of the sea.
26 Your oarsmen take you
out to the high seas.
But the east wind will break you to
pieces
in the heart of the sea.
27 Your wealth, merchandise and wares,
your mariners, seamen and
shipwrights,
your merchants and all your soldiers,
and everyone else on board
will sink into the heart of the sea
on the day of your shipwreck.
28 The shorelands will quake
when your seamen cry out.
29 All who handle the oars
will abandon their ships;
the mariners and all the seamen
will stand on the shore.
30 They will raise their voice
and cry bitterly over you;
they will sprinkle dust on their heads
and roll in ashes.
31 They will shave their heads because of
you
and will put on sackcloth.
They will weep over you with anguish
of soul
and with bitter mourning.
32 As they wail and mourn over you,
they will take up a lament
concerning you:
"Who was ever silenced like Tyre,
surrounded by the sea?"
33 When your merchandise went out on
the seas,

[d] 9 That is, Byblos [e] 15 Septuagint; Hebrew *Dedan* [f] 16 Most Hebrew manuscripts; some Hebrew manuscripts and Syriac *Edom* [g] 17 The meaning of the Hebrew for this word is uncertain.

you satisfied many nations;
with your great wealth and your wares
you enriched the kings of the earth.
34 Now you are shattered by the sea
in the depths of the waters;
your wares and all your company
have gone down with you.
35 All who live in the coastlands
are appalled at you;
their kings shudder with horror
and their faces are distorted with
fear.
36 The merchants among the nations hiss
at you;
you have come to a horrible end
and will be no more.' "

PRAYER: PETITION

MAY I not throw away my confidence; it will be richly rewarded. Let me persevere so that when I have done Your will, O God, I will receive what You have promised. (Hebrews 10:35–36)

__PAUSE__ here to petition God for growth in your character and personal discipline, and for physical health and strength. Ask that He empower you for spiritual warfare against the temptations of the world, the flesh and the devil. Offer prayers regarding your activities for this day and any special concerns you may have.

NT Hebrews 9:1-10

Worship in the Earthly Tabernacle

9 Now the first covenant had regulations for worship and also an earthly sanctuary.
2 A tabernacle was set up. In its first room were the lampstand, the table and the consecrated bread; this was called the Holy Place.
3 Behind the second curtain was a room called the Most Holy Place,
4 which had the golden altar of incense and the gold-covered ark of the covenant. This ark contained the gold jar of manna, Aaron's staff that had budded, and the stone tablets of the covenant.
5 Above the ark were the cherubim of the Glory, overshadowing the atonement cover.[a] But we cannot discuss these things in detail now.
6 When everything had been arranged like this, the priests entered regularly into the outer room to carry on their ministry.
7 But only the high priest entered the inner room, and that only once a year, and never without blood, which he offered for himself and for the sins the people had committed in ignorance.
8 The Holy Spirit was showing by this that the way into the Most Holy Place had not yet been disclosed as long as the first tabernacle was still standing.
9 This is an illustration for the present time, indicating that the gifts and sacrifices being offered were not able to clear the conscience of the worshiper.
10 They are only a matter of food and drink and various ceremonial washings—external regulations applying until the time of the new order.

[a] 5 Traditionally *the mercy seat*

PRAYER: THE CHARACTER I WANT TO CULTIVATE

AS one who knows righteousness, who has Your law in my heart, I will not fear when people reproach me or be terrified when they revile me. (Isaiah 51:7) . . . Lord, I will not fear those who kill the body but cannot kill the soul, but rather, I will fear You, the One who is able to destroy both soul and body in hell. (Matthew 10:28)

__TAKE__ a moment to ask the Lord for the grace to grow in godly character.

YEAR 2 DAY 270

OT Ezekiel 28:1-26

A Prophecy Against the King of Tyre

28 The word of the LORD came to me:
[2] "Son of man, say to the ruler of Tyre,
'This is what the Sovereign LORD says:

" 'In the pride of your heart
you say, "I am a god;
I sit on the throne of a god
in the heart of the seas."
But you are a man and not a god,
though you think you are as wise as
a god.
3 Are you wiser than Daniel[a]?
Is no secret hidden from you?
4 By your wisdom and understanding
you have gained wealth for yourself
and amassed gold and silver
in your treasuries.
5 By your great skill in trading
you have increased your wealth,
and because of your wealth
your heart has grown proud.

6 " 'Therefore this is what the Sovereign
LORD says:

" 'Because you think you are wise,
as wise as a god,
7 I am going to bring foreigners against
you,
the most ruthless of nations;
they will draw their swords against
your beauty and wisdom
and pierce your shining splendor.
8 They will bring you down to the pit,
and you will die a violent death
in the heart of the seas.
9 Will you then say, "I am a god,"
in the presence of those who kill
you?
You will be but a man, not a god,
in the hands of those who slay you.
10 You will die the death of the
uncircumcised
at the hands of foreigners.

I have spoken, declares the Sovereign
LORD.' "

11 The word of the LORD came to me:
12 "Son of man, take up a lament concerning the king of Tyre and say to him: 'This
is what the Sovereign LORD says:

" 'You were the model of perfection,
full of wisdom and perfect in
beauty.
13 You were in Eden,
the garden of God;
every precious stone adorned you:
ruby, topaz and emerald,
chrysolite, onyx and jasper,
sapphire,[b] turquoise and beryl.[c]
Your settings and mountings[d] were
made of gold;
on the day you were created they
were prepared.
14 You were anointed as a guardian
cherub,
for so I ordained you.
You were on the holy mount of God;
you walked among the fiery stones.
15 You were blameless in your ways
from the day you were created
till wickedness was found in you.
16 Through your widespread trade
you were filled with violence,
and you sinned.
So I drove you in disgrace from the
mount of God,
and I expelled you, O guardian
cherub,
from among the fiery stones.
17 Your heart became proud
on account of your beauty,
and you corrupted your wisdom
because of your splendor.
So I threw you to the earth;
I made a spectacle of you before
kings.
18 By your many sins and dishonest
trade
you have desecrated your
sanctuaries.
So I made a fire come out from you,
and it consumed you,
and I reduced you to ashes on the
ground
in the sight of all who were
watching.
19 All the nations who knew you
are appalled at you;
you have come to a horrible end
and will be no more.' "

[a] 3 Or *Danel;* the Hebrew spelling may suggest a person other than the prophet Daniel. [b] 13 Or *lapis lazuli* [c] 13 The precise identification of some of these precious stones is uncertain. [d] 13 The meaning of the Hebrew for this phrase is uncertain.

A Prophecy Against Sidon

[20]The word of the LORD came to me:
[21]"Son of man, set your face against Sidon;
prophesy against her [22]and say: 'This is
what the Sovereign LORD says:

" 'I am against you, O Sidon,
and I will gain glory within you.
They will know that I am the LORD,
when I inflict punishment on her
and show myself holy within her.
[23]I will send a plague upon her
and make blood flow in her streets.
The slain will fall within her,
with the sword against her on every side.
Then they will know that I am the LORD.

[24]" 'No longer will the people of Israel
have malicious neighbors who are painful
briers and sharp thorns. Then they will
know that I am the Sovereign LORD.

[25]" 'This is what the Sovereign LORD
says: When I gather the people of Israel
from the nations where they have been
scattered, I will show myself holy among
them in the sight of the nations. Then
they will live in their own land, which I
gave to my servant Jacob. [26]They will live
there in safety and will build houses and
plant vineyards; they will live in safety
when I inflict punishment on all their
neighbors who maligned them. Then
they will know that I am the LORD their
God.' "

PRAYER: INTERCESSION

MANY are asking, "Who will show us any good?" O Lord, lift up the light of Your countenance upon us.
(Psalm 4:6)

***TAKE** a few moments to intercede on behalf of the poor and hungry, the oppressed and persecuted, and those in control of world and national resources. Offer prayers for peace among nations and regarding current events and concerns.*

NT Hebrews 9:11–28

The Blood of Christ

[11]When Christ came as high priest of
the good things that are already here,[a] he
went through the greater and more perfect
tabernacle that is not man-made, that is
to say, not a part of this creation. [12]He did
not enter by means of the blood of goats
and calves; but he entered the Most Holy
Place once for all by his own blood, having
obtained eternal redemption. [13]The
blood of goats and bulls and the ashes of
a heifer sprinkled on those who are ceremonially
unclean sanctify them so that
they are outwardly clean. [14]How much
more, then, will the blood of Christ, who
through the eternal Spirit offered himself
unblemished to God, cleanse our consciences
from acts that lead to death,[b] so
that we may serve the living God!

[15]For this reason Christ is the mediator
of a new covenant, that those who are
called may receive the promised eternal
inheritance—now that he has died as a
ransom to set them free from the sins
committed under the first covenant.

[16]In the case of a will,[c] it is necessary to
prove the death of the one who made it,
[17]because a will is in force only when
somebody has died; it never takes effect
while the one who made it is living. [18]This
is why even the first covenant was not put
into effect without blood. [19]When Moses
had proclaimed every commandment of
the law to all the people, he took the
blood of calves, together with water, scarlet
wool and branches of hyssop, and
sprinkled the scroll and all the people.
[20]He said, "This is the blood of the covenant,
which God has commanded you to
keep."[d] [21]In the same way, he sprinkled
with the blood both the tabernacle and
everything used in its ceremonies. [22]In
fact, the law requires that nearly everything
be cleansed with blood, and with-

[a] 11 Some early manuscripts *are to come* [b] 14 Or *from useless rituals* [c] 16 Same Greek word as *covenant;* also in verse 17 [d] 20 Exodus 24:8

out the shedding of blood there is no forgiveness.

[23]It was necessary, then, for the copies of the heavenly things to be purified with these sacrifices, but the heavenly things themselves with better sacrifices than these. [24]For Christ did not enter a man-made sanctuary that was only a copy of the true one; he entered heaven itself, now to appear for us in God's presence. [25]Nor did he enter heaven to offer himself again and again, the way the high priest enters the Most Holy Place every year with blood that is not his own. [26]Then Christ would have had to suffer many times since the creation of the world. But now he has appeared once for all at the end of the ages to do away with sin by the sacrifice of himself. [27]Just as man is destined to die once, and after that to face judgment, [28]so Christ was sacrificed once to take away the sins of many people; and he will appear a second time, not to bear sin, but to bring salvation to those who are waiting for him.

PRAYER: MY RELATIONSHIP TO OTHERS

I PRAY that I may share my faith effectively through the knowledge of every good thing I have in You, Christ Jesus. (Philemon 6)

***PAUSE** to review your relationships with others and to commit them to the Lord.*

YEAR 2 DAY 271

OT Ezekiel 29:1–21

A Prophecy Against Egypt

29 In the tenth year, in the tenth month on the twelfth day, the word of the LORD came to me: [2]"Son of man, set your face against Pharaoh king of Egypt and prophesy against him and against all Egypt. [3]Speak to him and say: 'This is what the Sovereign LORD says:

" 'I am against you, Pharaoh king of
Egypt,
you great monster lying among
your streams.
You say, "The Nile is mine;
I made it for myself."
[4]But I will put hooks in your jaws
and make the fish of your streams
stick to your scales.
I will pull you out from among your
streams,
with all the fish sticking to your
scales.
[5]I will leave you in the desert,
you and all the fish of your streams.
You will fall on the open field
and not be gathered or picked up.
I will give you as food
to the beasts of the earth and the
birds of the air.

[6]Then all who live in Egypt will know that I am the LORD.

" 'You have been a staff of reed for the house of Israel. [7]When they grasped you with their hands, you splintered and you tore open their shoulders; when they leaned on you, you broke and their backs were wrenched.[a]

[8]" 'Therefore this is what the Sovereign LORD says: I will bring a sword against you and kill your men and their animals. [9]Egypt will become a desolate wasteland. Then they will know that I am the LORD.

" 'Because you said, "The Nile is mine; I made it," [10]therefore I am against you and against your streams, and I will make the land of Egypt a ruin and a desolate waste from Migdol to Aswan, as far as the border of Cush.[b] [11]No foot of man or animal will pass through it; no one will live there for forty years. [12]I will make the land of Egypt desolate among devastated lands, and her cities will lie desolate forty years among ruined cities. And I will disperse the Egyptians among the nations and scatter them through the countries.

[13]" 'Yet this is what the Sovereign LORD says: At the end of forty years I will gather the Egyptians from the nations where they were scattered. [14]I will bring them

[a] *7* Syriac (see also Septuagint and Vulgate); Hebrew *and you caused their backs to stand* [b] *10* That is, the upper Nile region

back from captivity and return them to Upper Egypt,[c] the land of their ancestry. There they will be a lowly kingdom. [15]It will be the lowliest of kingdoms and will never again exalt itself above the other nations. I will make it so weak that it will never again rule over the nations. [16]Egypt will no longer be a source of confidence for the people of Israel but will be a reminder of their sin in turning to her for help. Then they will know that I am the Sovereign LORD.' "

[17]In the twenty-seventh year, in the first month on the first day, the word of the LORD came to me: [18]"Son of man, Nebuchadnezzar king of Babylon drove his army in a hard campaign against Tyre; every head was rubbed bare and every shoulder made raw. Yet he and his army got no reward from the campaign he led against Tyre. [19]Therefore this is what the Sovereign LORD says: I am going to give Egypt to Nebuchadnezzar king of Babylon, and he will carry off its wealth. He will loot and plunder the land as pay for his army. [20]I have given him Egypt as a reward for his efforts because he and his army did it for me, declares the Sovereign LORD.

[21]"On that day I will make a horn[d] grow for the house of Israel, and I will open your mouth among them. Then they will know that I am the LORD."

[c] 14 Hebrew *to Pathros* [d] 21 *Horn* here symbolizes strength.

PRAYER: AFFIRMATION

O GOD, You raised Jesus from the dead, freeing Him from the agony of death, because it was impossible for Him to be held by it. (Acts 2:24) . . . Just as You, Father, raise the dead and give them life, even so Your Son gives life to whom He wishes. (John 5:21)

***PAUSE** to reflect on these Biblical affirmations.*

NT Hebrews 10:1-18

Christ's Sacrifice Once for All

10 The law is only a shadow of the good things that are coming—not the realities themselves. For this reason it can never, by the same sacrifices repeated endlessly year after year, make perfect those who draw near to worship. [2]If it could, would they not have stopped being offered? For the worshipers would have been cleansed once for all, and would no longer have felt guilty for their sins. [3]But those sacrifices are an annual reminder of sins, [4]because it is impossible for the blood of bulls and goats to take away sins.

[5]Therefore, when Christ came into the world, he said:

"Sacrifice and offering you did not
desire,
but a body you prepared for me;
[6]with burnt offerings and sin offerings
you were not pleased.
[7]Then I said, 'Here I am—it is written
about me in the scroll—
I have come to do your will,
O God.' "[a]

[8]First he said, "Sacrifices and offerings, burnt offerings and sin offerings you did not desire, nor were you pleased with them" (although the law required them to be made). [9]Then he said, "Here I am, I have come to do your will." He sets aside the first to establish the second. [10]And by that will, we have been made holy through the sacrifice of the body of Jesus Christ once for all.

[11]Day after day every priest stands and performs his religious duties; again and again he offers the same sacrifices, which can never take away sins. [12]But when this priest had offered for all time one sacrifice for sins, he sat down at the right hand of God. [13]Since that time he waits for his enemies to be made his footstool, [14]because by one sacrifice he has made perfect forever those who are being made holy.

[15]The Holy Spirit also testifies to us about this. First he says:

[16]"This is the covenant I will make with
them

[a] 7 Psalm 40:6-8 (see Septuagint)

after that time, says the Lord.
I will put my laws in their hearts,
and I will write them on their
minds."[b]

17 Then he adds:

"Their sins and lawless acts
I will remember no more."[c]

18 And where these have been forgiven, there is no longer any sacrifice for sin.

[b] 16 Jer. 31:33 [c] 17 Jer. 31:34

PRAYER: THE ATTRIBUTES OF GOD

JESUS is Your beloved Son, O God, in whom You are well pleased. (Matthew 3:17; Mark 1:11; Luke 3:22) . . . No one has ever seen You, O God, but the One and Only God who is at your side; He has made You known. (John 1:18)

***PAUSE** to reflect on these affirmations about the person, powers and perfection of God.*

YEAR 21
DAY 272

OT **Ezekiel 30:1–31:18**

A Lament for Egypt

30 The word of the LORD came to me:
2 "Son of man, prophesy and say:
'This is what the Sovereign LORD says:

" 'Wail and say,
"Alas for that day!"
3 For the day is near,
the day of the LORD is near—
a day of clouds,
a time of doom for the nations.
4 A sword will come against Egypt,
and anguish will come upon Cush.[a]
When the slain fall in Egypt,
her wealth will be carried away
and her foundations torn down.

5 Cush and Put, Lydia and all Arabia, Libya[b] and the people of the covenant land
will fall by the sword along with Egypt.
6 " 'This is what the LORD says:

" 'The allies of Egypt will fall
and her proud strength will fail.
From Migdol to Aswan
they will fall by the sword within her,
declares the Sovereign LORD.
7 " 'They will be desolate
among desolate lands,
and their cities will lie
among ruined cities.
8 Then they will know that I am the
LORD,
when I set fire to Egypt
and all her helpers are crushed.

9 " 'On that day messengers will go out
from me in ships to frighten Cush out of
her complacency. Anguish will take hold
of them on the day of Egypt's doom, for
it is sure to come.

10 " 'This is what the Sovereign LORD
says:

" 'I will put an end to the hordes of
Egypt
by the hand of Nebuchadnezzar
king of Babylon.
11 He and his army—the most ruthless
of nations—
will be brought in to destroy the
land.
They will draw their swords against
Egypt
and fill the land with the slain.
12 I will dry up the streams of the Nile
and sell the land to evil men;
by the hand of foreigners
I will lay waste the land and
everything in it.

I the LORD have spoken.

13 " 'This is what the Sovereign LORD
says:

" 'I will destroy the idols
and put an end to the images in
Memphis.[c]

[a] 4 That is, the upper Nile region; also in verses 5 and 9 [b] 5 Hebrew *Cub* [c] 13 Hebrew *Noph*; also in verse 16

No longer will there be a prince in Egypt,
and I will spread fear throughout the land.
14 I will lay waste Upper Egypt,[d]
set fire to Zoan
and inflict punishment on Thebes.[e]
15 I will pour out my wrath on Pelusium,[f]
the stronghold of Egypt,
and cut off the hordes of Thebes.
16 I will set fire to Egypt;
Pelusium will writhe in agony.
Thebes will be taken by storm;
Memphis will be in constant distress.
17 The young men of Heliopolis[g] and Bubastis[h]
will fall by the sword,
and the cities themselves will go into captivity.
18 Dark will be the day at Tahpanhes
when I break the yoke of Egypt;
there her proud strength will come to an end.
She will be covered with clouds,
and her villages will go into captivity.
19 So I will inflict punishment on Egypt,
and they will know that I am the LORD.' "

20 In the eleventh year, in the first month
on the seventh day, the word of the LORD
came to me: 21 "Son of man, I have broken
the arm of Pharaoh king of Egypt. It has
not been bound up for healing or put in
a splint so as to become strong enough to
hold a sword. 22 Therefore this is what the
Sovereign LORD says: I am against Pharaoh
king of Egypt. I will break both his arms,
the good arm as well as the broken one,
and make the sword fall from his hand.
23 I will disperse the Egyptians among the
nations and scatter them through the
countries. 24 I will strengthen the arms of
the king of Babylon and put my sword in
his hand, but I will break the arms of
Pharaoh, and he will groan before him
like a mortally wounded man. 25 I will
strengthen the arms of the king of Babylon,
but the arms of Pharaoh will fall
limp. Then they will know that I am the
LORD, when I put my sword into the hand
of the king of Babylon and he brandishes
it against Egypt. 26 I will disperse the Egyptians
among the nations and scatter them
through the countries. Then they will
know that I am the LORD."

A Cedar in Lebanon

31 In the eleventh year, in the third
month on the first day, the word of
the LORD came to me: 2 "Son of man, say
to Pharaoh king of Egypt and to his
hordes:

" 'Who can be compared with you in majesty?
3 Consider Assyria, once a cedar in Lebanon,
with beautiful branches overshadowing the forest;
it towered on high,
its top above the thick foliage.
4 The waters nourished it,
deep springs made it grow tall;
their streams flowed
all around its base
and sent their channels
to all the trees of the field.
5 So it towered higher
than all the trees of the field;
its boughs increased
and its branches grew long,
spreading because of abundant waters.
6 All the birds of the air
nested in its boughs,
all the beasts of the field
gave birth under its branches;
all the great nations
lived in its shade.
7 It was majestic in beauty,
with its spreading boughs,
for its roots went down
to abundant waters.
8 The cedars in the garden of God
could not rival it,
nor could the pine trees
equal its boughs,
nor could the plane trees
compare with its branches—
no tree in the garden of God
could match its beauty.
9 I made it beautiful
with abundant branches,
the envy of all the trees of Eden
in the garden of God.

10 " 'Therefore this is what the Sovereign

[d] 14 Hebrew *waste Pathros* [e] 14 Hebrew *No*; also in verses 15 and 16 [f] 15 Hebrew *Sin*; also in verse 16 [g] 17 Hebrew *Awen* (or *On*) [h] 17 Hebrew *Pi Beseth*

LORD says: Because it towered on high, lifting its top above the thick foliage, and because it was proud of its height, 11 I handed it over to the ruler of the nations, for him to deal with according to its wickedness. I cast it aside, 12 and the most ruthless of foreign nations cut it down and left it. Its boughs fell on the mountains and in all the valleys; its branches lay broken in all the ravines of the land. All the nations of the earth came out from under its shade and left it. 13 All the birds of the air settled on the fallen tree, and all the beasts of the field were among its branches. 14 Therefore no other trees by the waters are ever to tower proudly on high, lifting their tops above the thick foliage. No other trees so well-watered are ever to reach such a height; they are all destined for death, for the earth below, among mortal men, with those who go down to the pit.

15 " 'This is what the Sovereign LORD says: On the day it was brought down to the grave[i] I covered the deep springs with mourning for it; I held back its streams, and its abundant waters were restrained. Because of it I clothed Lebanon with gloom, and all the trees of the field withered away. 16 I made the nations tremble at the sound of its fall when I brought it down to the grave with those who go down to the pit. Then all the trees of Eden, the choicest and best of Lebanon, all the trees that were well-watered, were consoled in the earth below. 17 Those who lived in its shade, its allies among the nations, had also gone down to the grave with it, joining those killed by the sword.

18 " 'Which of the trees of Eden can be compared with you in splendor and majesty? Yet you, too, will be brought down with the trees of Eden to the earth below; you will lie among the uncircumcised, with those killed by the sword.

" 'This is Pharaoh and all his hordes, declares the Sovereign LORD.' "

[i] 15 Hebrew *Sheol;* also in verses 16 and 17

PRAYER: THANKSGIVING

THOUGH I have not seen You, Jesus, I love You; and though I do not see You now, I believe in You; I rejoice with joy that is inexpressible and full of glory, for I am receiving the end of my faith, the salvation of my soul. (1 Peter 1:8–9) . . . Since I am receiving a kingdom that cannot be shaken, may I be thankful and so worship You acceptably with reverence and awe, for You are a consuming fire. (Hebrews 12:28–29)

PAUSE *to offer your own expressions of thanksgiving.*

NT Hebrews 10:19–39

A Call to Persevere

19 Therefore, brothers, since we have confidence to enter the Most Holy Place by the blood of Jesus, 20 by a new and living way opened for us through the curtain, that is, his body, 21 and since we have a great priest over the house of God, 22 let us draw near to God with a sincere heart in full assurance of faith, having our hearts sprinkled to cleanse us from a guilty conscience and having our bodies washed with pure water. 23 Let us hold unswervingly to the hope we profess, for he who promised is faithful. 24 And let us consider how we may spur one another on toward love and good deeds. 25 Let us not give up meeting together, as some are in the habit of doing, but let us encourage one another—and all the more as you see the Day approaching.

26 If we deliberately keep on sinning after we have received the knowledge of the truth, no sacrifice for sins is left, 27 but only a fearful expectation of judgment and of raging fire that will consume the enemies of God. 28 Anyone who rejected the law of Moses died without mercy on the testimony of two or three witnesses. 29 How much more severely do you think a man deserves to be punished who has trampled the Son of God under foot, who has treated as an unholy thing the blood of the covenant that sanctified him, and who has insulted the Spirit of grace? 30 For

we know him who said, "It is mine to
avenge; I will repay,"[a] and again, "The
Lord will judge his people."[b] 31It is a
dreadful thing to fall into the hands of the
living God.

32Remember those earlier days after you
had received the light, when you stood
your ground in a great contest in the face
of suffering. 33Sometimes you were publicly exposed to insult and persecution; at
other times you stood side by side with
those who were so treated. 34You sympa-
thized with those in prison and joyfully
accepted the confiscation of your property, because you knew that you yourselves
had better and lasting possessions.

35So do not throw away your confidence; it will be richly rewarded. 36You
need to persevere so that when you have
done the will of God, you will receive
what he has promised. 37For in just a very
little while,

"He who is coming will come and
will not delay.
38 But my righteous one[c] will live by
faith.
And if he shrinks back,
I will not be pleased with him."[d]

39But we are not of those who shrink back
and are destroyed, but of those who believe and are saved.

[a] *30* Deut. 32:35 [b] *30* Deut. 32:36; Psalm 135:14
[c] *38* One early manuscript *But the righteous*
[d] *38* Hab. 2:3,4

PRAYER: THE WORKS OF GOD

JESUS, You told Your disciples, "I came from the Father and entered the world; now I am leaving the world and going back to the Father." (John 16:28) . . . O Lord Jesus, You prayed, "I glorified You on the earth by completing the work You gave Me to do. And now, Father, glorify Me in Your presence with the glory I had with You before the world began." (John 17:4–5)

TAKE *a moment to consider the greatness of God's wonderful works.*

OT Psalms 124–125

YEAR 2 DAY 273

Psalm 124

A song of ascents. Of David.

1If the LORD had not been on our
side—
let Israel say—
2if the LORD had not been on our side
when men attacked us,
3when their anger flared against us,
they would have swallowed us alive;
4the flood would have engulfed us,
the torrent would have swept over us,
5the raging waters
would have swept us away.

6Praise be to the LORD,
who has not let us be torn by their
teeth.
7We have escaped like a bird
out of the fowler's snare;
the snare has been broken,
and we have escaped.
8Our help is in the name of the LORD,
the Maker of heaven and earth.

Psalm 125

A song of ascents.

1Those who trust in the LORD are like
Mount Zion,
which cannot be shaken but
endures forever.
2As the mountains surround Jerusalem,
so the LORD surrounds his people
both now and forevermore.

3The scepter of the wicked will not
remain
over the land allotted to the
righteous,

for then the righteous might use
their hands to do evil.

4 Do good, O LORD, to those who are
good,
to those who are upright in heart.

5 But those who turn to crooked
ways
the LORD will banish with the
evildoers.

Peace be upon Israel.

PRAYER: ADORATION

JESUS, You are the radiance of God's glory and the exact representation of His being, upholding all things by Your powerful word. After You cleansed our sins, You sat down at the right hand of the Majesty on high, having become as much superior to angels as the name You have inherited is superior to theirs. (Hebrews 1:3–4)

PAUSE *to express your thoughts of praise and worship.*

NT Hebrews 11:1–19

By Faith

11 Now faith is being sure of what we
hope for and certain of what we do
not see. 2 This is what the ancients were
commended for.
3 By faith we understand that the universe was formed at God's command, so
that what is seen was not made out of
what was visible.
4 By faith Abel offered God a better sacrifice than Cain did. By faith he was commended as a righteous man, when God
spoke well of his offerings. And by faith
he still speaks, even though he is dead.
5 By faith Enoch was taken from this life,
so that he did not experience death; he
could not be found, because God had tak-
en him away. For before he was taken, he
was commended as one who pleased God.
6 And without faith it is impossible to
please God, because anyone who comes to
him must believe that he exists and that
he rewards those who earnestly seek him.
7 By faith Noah, when warned about
things not yet seen, in holy fear built an
ark to save his family. By his faith he condemned the world and became heir of the
righteousness that comes by faith.
8 By faith Abraham, when called to go
to a place he would later receive as his inheritance, obeyed and went, even though
he did not know where he was going. 9 By
faith he made his home in the promised
land like a stranger in a foreign country;
he lived in tents, as did Isaac and Jacob,
who were heirs with him of the same
promise. 10 For he was looking forward to
the city with foundations, whose architect
and builder is God.
11 By faith Abraham, even though he was
past age—and Sarah herself was barren—
was enabled to become a father because
he[a] considered him faithful who had made
the promise. 12 And so from this one man,
and he as good as dead, came descendants
as numerous as the stars in the sky and as
countless as the sand on the seashore.
13 All these people were still living by
faith when they died. They did not receive
the things promised; they only saw them
and welcomed them from a distance. And
they admitted that they were aliens and
strangers on earth. 14 People who say such
things show that they are looking for a
country of their own. 15 If they had been
thinking of the country they had left, they
would have had opportunity to return.
16 Instead, they were longing for a better
country—a heavenly one. Therefore God
is not ashamed to be called their God, for
he has prepared a city for them.
17 By faith Abraham, when God tested
him, offered Isaac as a sacrifice. He who
had received the promises was about to sacrifice his one and only son, 18 even though
God had said to him, "It is through Isaac
that your offspring[b] will be reckoned."[c]
19 Abraham reasoned that God could raise
the dead, and figuratively speaking, he did
receive Isaac back from death.

[a] 11 Or *By faith even Sarah, who was past age, was enabled to bear children because she* [b] 18 Greek *seed* [c] 18 Gen. 21:12

PRAYER: MY RELATIONSHIP TO GOD

YOU, O Lord, will deliver me from every evil work and will bring me safely to Your heavenly kingdom. To You be glory forever and ever. (2 Timothy 4:18)

***PAUSE** to thank God for the relationship that you enjoy with Him in Jesus Christ.*

OT **Ezekiel 32:1-32** YEAR 2 DAY 274

A Lament for Pharaoh

32 In the twelfth year, in the twelfth
month on the first day, the word of
the LORD came to me: 2 "Son of man, take
up a lament concerning Pharaoh king of
Egypt and say to him:

" 'You are like a lion among the nations;
you are like a monster in the seas
thrashing about in your streams,
churning the water with your feet
and muddying the streams.

3 " 'This is what the Sovereign LORD says:

" 'With a great throng of people
I will cast my net over you,
and they will haul you up in my net.
4 I will throw you on the land
and hurl you on the open field.
I will let all the birds of the air settle on you
and all the beasts of the earth gorge themselves on you.
5 I will spread your flesh on the mountains
and fill the valleys with your remains.
6 I will drench the land with your flowing blood
all the way to the mountains,
and the ravines will be filled with your flesh.
7 When I snuff you out, I will cover the heavens
and darken their stars;
I will cover the sun with a cloud,
and the moon will not give its light.
8 All the shining lights in the heavens
I will darken over you;
I will bring darkness over your land,
declares the Sovereign LORD.
9 I will trouble the hearts of many peoples
when I bring about your destruction among the nations,
among[a] lands you have not known.
10 I will cause many peoples to be appalled at you,
and their kings will shudder with horror because of you
when I brandish my sword before them.
On the day of your downfall
each of them will tremble
every moment for his life.

11 " 'For this is what the Sovereign LORD
says:

" 'The sword of the king of Babylon
will come against you.
12 I will cause your hordes to fall
by the swords of mighty men—
the most ruthless of all nations.
They will shatter the pride of Egypt,
and all her hordes will be overthrown.
13 I will destroy all her cattle
from beside abundant waters
no longer to be stirred by the foot of man
or muddied by the hoofs of cattle.
14 Then I will let her waters settle
and make her streams flow like oil,
declares the Sovereign LORD.
15 When I make Egypt desolate
and strip the land of everything in it,
when I strike down all who live there,
then they will know that I am the LORD.'

16 "This is the lament they will chant for
her. The daughters of the nations will

[a] 9 Hebrew; Septuagint *bring you into captivity among the nations, / to*

chant it; for Egypt and all her hordes they
will chant it, declares the Sovereign
LORD."

17 In the twelfth year, on the fifteenth day
of the month, the word of the LORD came
to me: 18 "Son of man, wail for the hordes of
Egypt and consign to the earth below both
her and the daughters of mighty nations,
with those who go down to the pit. 19 Say to
them, 'Are you more favored than others?
Go down and be laid among the uncircumcised.' 20 They will fall among those
killed by the sword. The sword is drawn; let
her be dragged off with all her hordes.
21 From within the grave[b] the mighty leaders
will say of Egypt and her allies, 'They have
come down and they lie with the uncircumcised, with those killed by the sword.'

22 "Assyria is there with her whole army;
she is surrounded by the graves of all her
slain, all who have fallen by the sword.
23 Their graves are in the depths of the pit
and her army lies around her grave. All
who had spread terror in the land of the
living are slain, fallen by the sword.

24 "Elam is there, with all her hordes
around her grave. All of them are slain,
fallen by the sword. All who had spread
terror in the land of the living went down
uncircumcised to the earth below. They
bear their shame with those who go down
to the pit. 25 A bed is made for her among
the slain, with all her hordes around her
grave. All of them are uncircumcised,
killed by the sword. Because their terror
had spread in the land of the living, they
bear their shame with those who go down
to the pit; they are laid among the slain.

26 "Meshech and Tubal are there, with all
their hordes around their graves. All of
them are uncircumcised, killed by the
sword because they spread their terror in
the land of the living. 27 Do they not lie
with the other uncircumcised warriors
who have fallen, who went down to the
grave with their weapons of war, whose
swords were placed under their heads? The
punishment for their sins rested on their
bones, though the terror of these warriors
had stalked through the land of the living.

28 "You too, O Pharaoh, will be broken
and will lie among the uncircumcised,
with those killed by the sword.

29 "Edom is there, her kings and all her
princes; despite their power, they are laid
with those killed by the sword. They lie
with the uncircumcised, with those who
go down to the pit.

30 "All the princes of the north and all
the Sidonians are there; they went down
with the slain in disgrace despite the terror caused by their power. They lie uncircumcised with those killed by the sword
and bear their shame with those who go
down to the pit.

31 "Pharaoh—he and all his army—will
see them and he will be consoled for all
his hordes that were killed by the sword,
declares the Sovereign LORD. 32 Although I
had him spread terror in the land of the
living, Pharaoh and all his hordes will be
laid among the uncircumcised, with those
killed by the sword, declares the Sovereign
LORD."

[b] 21 Hebrew *Sheol;* also in verse 27

PRAYER: CONFESSION

YOU, Lord, do not see as people see. People look at my outward appearance, but You look at my heart.
(1 Samuel 16:7)

ASK *the Spirit to search your heart and reveal any areas of unconfessed sin. Acknowledge these to the Lord and thank Him for His forgiveness.*

NT Hebrews 11:20–40

20 By faith Isaac blessed Jacob and Esau
in regard to their future.

21 By faith Jacob, when he was dying,
blessed each of Joseph's sons, and worshiped as he leaned on the top of his staff.

22 By faith Joseph, when his end was
near, spoke about the exodus of the Israelites from Egypt and gave instructions
about his bones.

23 By faith Moses' parents hid him for

three months after he was born, because
they saw he was no ordinary child, and
they were not afraid of the king's edict.
24By faith Moses, when he had grown up,
refused to be known as the son of Pharaoh's daughter. 25He chose to be mistreated along with the people of God rather
than to enjoy the pleasures of sin for a short
time. 26He regarded disgrace for the sake of
Christ as of greater value than the treasures
of Egypt, because he was looking ahead to
his reward. 27By faith he left Egypt, not fearing the king's anger; he persevered because
he saw him who is invisible. 28By faith he
kept the Passover and the sprinkling of
blood, so that the destroyer of the firstborn
would not touch the firstborn of Israel.
29By faith the people passed through
the Red Sea[a] as on dry land; but when the
Egyptians tried to do so, they were
drowned.
30By faith the walls of Jericho fell, after
the people had marched around them for
seven days.
31By faith the prostitute Rahab, because
she welcomed the spies, was not killed
with those who were disobedient.[b]
32And what more shall I say? I do not
have time to tell about Gideon, Barak, Samson, Jephthah, David, Samuel and the
prophets, 33who through faith conquered
kingdoms, administered justice, and gained
what was promised; who shut the mouths
of lions, 34quenched the fury of the flames,
and escaped the edge of the sword; whose
weakness was turned to strength; and who
became powerful in battle and routed foreign armies. 35Women received back their
dead, raised to life again. Others were tortured and refused to be released, so that
they might gain a better resurrection.
36Some faced jeers and flogging, while still
others were chained and put in prison.
37They were stoned[c]; they were sawed in
two; they were put to death by the sword.
They went about in sheepskins and
goatskins, destitute, persecuted and mistreated— 38the world was not worthy of
them. They wandered in deserts and mountains, and in caves and holes in the ground.
39These were all commended for their
faith, yet none of them received what had
been promised. 40God had planned something better for us so that only together
with us would they be made perfect.

[a] *29* That is, Sea of Reeds [b] *31* Or *unbelieving*
[c] *37* Some early manuscripts *stoned; they were put to the test;*

PRAYER: THE CHARACTER I WANT TO CULTIVATE

I WANT to let justice roll down like a river, O God, and righteousness like an ever-flowing stream. (Amos 5:24) . . . May I be righteous, O God, that my mouth will speak wisdom, and my tongue speak what is just. May Your law, O God, be in my heart so my steps do not slide. (Psalm 37:30–31)

***TAKE** a moment to ask the Lord for the grace to grow in godly character.*

YEAR 2 DAY 275

OT Ezekiel 33:1–33

Ezekiel a Watchman

33 The word of the LORD came to me:
2"Son of man, speak to your countrymen and say to them: 'When I bring the
sword against a land, and the people of the
land choose one of their men and make
him their watchman, 3and he sees the
sword coming against the land and blows
the trumpet to warn the people, 4then if
anyone hears the trumpet but does not take
warning and the sword comes and takes his
life, his blood will be on his own head.
5Since he heard the sound of the trumpet
but did not take warning, his blood will be
on his own head. If he had taken warning,
he would have saved himself. 6But if the
watchman sees the sword coming and does
not blow the trumpet to warn the people
and the sword comes and takes the life of
one of them, that man will be taken away
because of his sin, but I will hold the watchman accountable for his blood.'

7 "Son of man, I have made you a watchman for the house of Israel; so hear the word I speak and give them warning from me. 8 When I say to the wicked, 'O wicked man, you will surely die,' and you do not speak out to dissuade him from his ways, that wicked man will die for[a] his sin, and I will hold you accountable for his blood. 9 But if you do warn the wicked man to turn from his ways and he does not do so, he will die for his sin, but you will have saved yourself.

10 "Son of man, say to the house of Israel, 'This is what you are saying: "Our offenses and sins weigh us down, and we are wasting away because of[b] them. How then can we live?" ' 11 Say to them, 'As surely as I live, declares the Sovereign LORD, I take no pleasure in the death of the wicked, but rather that they turn from their ways and live. Turn! Turn from your evil ways! Why will you die, O house of Israel?'

12 "Therefore, son of man, say to your countrymen, 'The righteousness of the righteous man will not save him when he disobeys, and the wickedness of the wicked man will not cause him to fall when he turns from it. The righteous man, if he sins, will not be allowed to live because of his former righteousness.' 13 If I tell the righteous man that he will surely live, but then he trusts in his righteousness and does evil, none of the righteous things he has done will be remembered; he will die for the evil he has done. 14 And if I say to the wicked man, 'You will surely die,' but he then turns away from his sin and does what is just and right— 15 if he gives back what he took in pledge for a loan, returns what he has stolen, follows the decrees that give life, and does no evil, he will surely live; he will not die. 16 None of the sins he has committed will be remembered against him. He has done what is just and right; he will surely live.

17 "Yet your countrymen say, 'The way of the Lord is not just.' But it is their way that is not just. 18 If a righteous man turns from his righteousness and does evil, he will die for it. 19 And if a wicked man turns away from his wickedness and does what is just and right, he will live by doing so. 20 Yet, O house of Israel, you say, 'The way of the Lord is not just.' But I will judge each of you according to his own ways."

Jerusalem's Fall Explained

21 In the twelfth year of our exile, in the tenth month on the fifth day, a man who had escaped from Jerusalem came to me and said, "The city has fallen!" 22 Now the evening before the man arrived, the hand of the LORD was upon me, and he opened my mouth before the man came to me in the morning. So my mouth was opened and I was no longer silent.

23 Then the word of the LORD came to me: 24 "Son of man, the people living in those ruins in the land of Israel are saying, 'Abraham was only one man, yet he possessed the land. But we are many; surely the land has been given to us as our possession.' 25 Therefore say to them, 'This is what the Sovereign LORD says: Since you eat meat with the blood still in it and look to your idols and shed blood, should you then possess the land? 26 You rely on your sword, you do detestable things, and each of you defiles his neighbor's wife. Should you then possess the land?'

27 "Say this to them: 'This is what the Sovereign LORD says: As surely as I live, those who are left in the ruins will fall by the sword, those out in the country I will give to the wild animals to be devoured, and those in strongholds and caves will die of a plague. 28 I will make the land a desolate waste, and her proud strength will come to an end, and the mountains of Israel will become desolate so that no one will cross them. 29 Then they will know that I am the LORD, when I have made the land a desolate waste because of all the detestable things they have done.'

30 "As for you, son of man, your countrymen are talking together about you by the walls and at the doors of the houses, saying to each other, 'Come and hear the message that has come from the LORD.' 31 My people come to you, as they usually do, and sit before you to listen to your words, but they do not put them into practice. With their mouths they express devotion, but their hearts are greedy for unjust gain. 32 Indeed, to them you are nothing more than one who sings love songs with a beautiful voice and plays an instrument well, for they hear your words but do not put them into practice.

33 "When all this comes true—and it surely will—then they will know that a prophet has been among them."

[a] *8* Or *in;* also in verse 9 [b] *10* Or *away in*

PRAYER: RENEWAL

MAY I be faithful, not doubting Your promises, O God, and not double-minded and unstable in all my ways. (James 1:6, 8) . . . If I live according to the flesh, I will die; but if by Your Spirit I put to death the deeds of the body, I will live. For those who are led by Your Spirit are Your children. (Romans 8:13–14)

***PAUSE** to add your own prayers for personal renewal.*

NT Hebrews 12:1-13

God Disciplines His Sons

12 Therefore, since we are surrounded by such a great cloud of witnesses, let us throw off everything that hinders and the sin that so easily entangles, and let us run with perseverance the race marked out for us. 2Let us fix our eyes on Jesus, the author and perfecter of our faith, who for the joy set before him endured the cross, scorning its shame, and sat down at the right hand of the throne of God. 3Consider him who endured such opposition from sinful men, so that you will not grow weary and lose heart.

4In your struggle against sin, you have not yet resisted to the point of shedding your blood. 5And you have forgotten that word of encouragement that addresses you as sons:

"My son, do not make light of the
 Lord's discipline,
and do not lose heart when he
 rebukes you,
6because the Lord disciplines those he
 loves,
and he punishes everyone he
 accepts as a son."[a]

7Endure hardship as discipline; God is treating you as sons. For what son is not disciplined by his father? 8If you are not disciplined (and everyone undergoes discipline), then you are illegitimate children and not true sons. 9Moreover, we have all had human fathers who disciplined us and we respected them for it. How much more should we submit to the Father of our spirits and live! 10Our fathers disciplined us for a little while as they thought best; but God disciplines us for our good, that we may share in his holiness. 11No discipline seems pleasant at the time, but painful. Later on, however, it produces a harvest of righteousness and peace for those who have been trained by it.

12Therefore, strengthen your feeble arms and weak knees. 13"Make level paths for your feet,"[b] so that the lame may not be disabled, but rather healed.

[a] *6* Prov. 3:11,12 [b] *13* Prov. 4:26

PRAYER: MY RELATIONSHIP TO OTHERS

I WILL bless those who persecute me; I will bless and not curse. (Romans 12:14) . . . I will bear with others and forgive whatever complaints I have against them; I will forgive just as You, Lord, forgave me. (Colossians 3:13)

***PAUSE** to review your relationships with others and to commit them to the Lord.*

OT **Ezekiel 34:1–35:15**

YEAR 2 DAY 276

Shepherds and Sheep

34 The word of the LORD came to me: [2]"Son of man, prophesy against the shepherds of Israel; prophesy and say to them: 'This is what the Sovereign LORD says: Woe to the shepherds of Israel who only take care of themselves! Should not shepherds take care of the flock? [3]You eat the curds, clothe yourselves with the wool and slaughter the choice animals, but you do not take care of the flock. [4]You have not strengthened the weak or healed the sick or bound up the injured. You have not brought back the strays or searched for the lost. You have ruled them harshly and brutally. [5]So they were scattered because there was no shepherd, and when they were scattered they became food for all the wild animals. [6]My sheep wandered over all the mountains and on every high hill. They were scattered over the whole earth, and no one searched or looked for them.

[7]" 'Therefore, you shepherds, hear the word of the LORD: [8]As surely as I live, declares the Sovereign LORD, because my flock lacks a shepherd and so has been plundered and has become food for all the wild animals, and because my shepherds did not search for my flock but cared for themselves rather than for my flock, [9]therefore, O shepherds, hear the word of the LORD: [10]This is what the Sovereign LORD says: I am against the shepherds and will hold them accountable for my flock. I will remove them from tending the flock so that the shepherds can no longer feed themselves. I will rescue my flock from their mouths, and it will no longer be food for them.

[11]" 'For this is what the Sovereign LORD says: I myself will search for my sheep and look after them. [12]As a shepherd looks after his scattered flock when he is with them, so will I look after my sheep. I will rescue them from all the places where they were scattered on a day of clouds and darkness. [13]I will bring them out from the nations and gather them from the countries, and I will bring them into their own land. I will pasture them on the mountains of Israel, in the ravines and in all the settlements in the land. [14]I will tend them in a good pasture, and the mountain heights of Israel will be their grazing land. There they will lie down in good grazing land, and there they will feed in a rich pasture on the mountains of Israel. [15]I myself will tend my sheep and have them lie down, declares the Sovereign LORD. [16]I will search for the lost and bring back the strays. I will bind up the injured and strengthen the weak, but the sleek and the strong I will destroy. I will shepherd the flock with justice.

[17]" 'As for you, my flock, this is what the Sovereign LORD says: I will judge between one sheep and another, and between rams and goats. [18]Is it not enough for you to feed on the good pasture? Must you also trample the rest of your pasture with your feet? Is it not enough for you to drink clear water? Must you also muddy the rest with your feet? [19]Must my flock feed on what you have trampled and drink what you have muddied with your feet?

[20]" 'Therefore this is what the Sovereign LORD says to them: See, I myself will judge between the fat sheep and the lean sheep. [21]Because you shove with flank and shoulder, butting all the weak sheep with your horns until you have driven them away, [22]I will save my flock, and they will no longer be plundered. I will judge between one sheep and another. [23]I will place over them one shepherd, my servant David, and he will tend them; he will tend them and be their shepherd. [24]I the LORD will be their God, and my servant David will be prince among them. I the LORD have spoken.

[25]" 'I will make a covenant of peace with them and rid the land of wild beasts so that they may live in the desert and sleep in the forests in safety. [26]I will bless them and the places surrounding my hill.[a] I will send down showers in season; there will be showers of blessing. [27]The trees of the field will yield their fruit and the ground will yield its crops; the people will be secure in their land. They will know that I am the LORD, when I break the bars of their yoke and rescue them from the hands of those who enslaved them. [28]They will no longer be plundered by the

[a] 26 Or *I will make them and the places surrounding my hill a blessing*

nations, nor will wild animals devour them.
They will live in safety, and no one will make
them afraid. 29I will provide for them a land
renowned for its crops, and they will no
longer be victims of famine in the land or
bear the scorn of the nations. 30Then they
will know that I, the LORD their God, am
with them and that they, the house of Israel, are my people, declares the Sovereign
LORD. 31You my sheep, the sheep of my pasture, are people, and I am your God, declares
the Sovereign LORD.' "

A Prophecy Against Edom

35 The word of the LORD came to me:
2"Son of man, set your face against
Mount Seir; prophesy against it 3and say:
'This is what the Sovereign LORD says: I am
against you, Mount Seir, and I will stretch
out my hand against you and make you a
desolate waste. 4I will turn your towns
into ruins and you will be desolate. Then
you will know that I am the LORD.
5" 'Because you harbored an ancient hostility and delivered the Israelites over to the
sword at the time of their calamity, the time
their punishment reached its climax, 6there-
fore as surely as I live, declares the Sovereign LORD, I will give you over to bloodshed
and it will pursue you. Since you did not
hate bloodshed, bloodshed will pursue
you. 7I will make Mount Seir a desolate
waste and cut off from it all who come and
go. 8I will fill your mountains with the
slain; those killed by the sword will fall on
your hills and in your valleys and in all your
ravines. 9I will make you desolate forever;
your towns will not be inhabited. Then you
will know that I am the LORD.
10" 'Because you have said, "These two
nations and countries will be ours and we
will take possession of them," even though
I the LORD was there, 11therefore as surely
as I live, declares the Sovereign LORD, I will
treat you in accordance with the anger and
jealousy you showed in your hatred of
them and I will make myself known
among them when I judge you. 12Then you
will know that I the LORD have heard all
the contemptible things you have said
against the mountains of Israel. You said,
"They have been laid waste and have been
given over to us to devour." 13You boasted
against me and spoke against me without
restraint, and I heard it. 14This is what the
Sovereign LORD says: While the whole earth
rejoices, I will make you desolate. 15Be-
cause you rejoiced when the inheritance of
the house of Israel became desolate, that is
how I will treat you. You will be desolate,
O Mount Seir, you and all of Edom. Then
they will know that I am the LORD.' "

PRAYER: PETITION

SINCE I have a great cloud of witnesses surrounding me, may I lay aside every impediment and the sin that so easily entangles, and run with endurance the race that is set before me, fixing my eyes on You, Jesus, the author and perfecter of my faith, who for the joy set before You endured the cross, despising the shame, and sat down at the right hand of the throne of God. May I consider You who endured such hostility from sinners, so that I will not grow weary and lose heart. (Hebrews 12:1–3)

__PAUSE__ here to petition God for growth in your desire to know and please Jesus Christ. Pray for a greater love and commitment to Him, for the grace to practice His presence and for the grace to glorify Him in your life. Offer prayers regarding your activities for this day and any special concerns you may have.

NT Hebrews 12:14–29

Warning Against Refusing God

14Make every effort to live in peace with
all men and to be holy; without holiness
no one will see the Lord. 15See to it that
no one misses the grace of God and that
no bitter root grows up to cause trouble
and defile many. 16See that no one is sexually immoral, or is godless like Esau,
who for a single meal sold his inheritance

rights as the oldest son. 17Afterward, as
you know, when he wanted to inherit this
blessing, he was rejected. He could bring
about no change of mind, though he
sought the blessing with tears.
18You have not come to a mountain
that can be touched and that is burning
with fire; to darkness, gloom and storm;
19to a trumpet blast or to such a voice
speaking words that those who heard it
begged that no further word be spoken
to them, 20because they could not bear
what was commanded: "If even an animal
touches the mountain, it must be
stoned."[a] 21The sight was so terrifying that
Moses said, "I am trembling with fear."[b]
22But you have come to Mount Zion, to
the heavenly Jerusalem, the city of the living
God. You have come to thousands
upon thousands of angels in joyful assembly,
23to the church of the firstborn, whose
names are written in heaven. You have
come to God, the judge of all men, to the
spirits of righteous men made perfect, 24to
Jesus the mediator of a new covenant, and
to the sprinkled blood that speaks a better
word than the blood of Abel.
25See to it that you do not refuse him
who speaks. If they did not escape when
they refused him who warned them on
earth, how much less will we, if we turn
away from him who warns us from heaven?
26At that time his voice shook the
earth, but now he has promised, "Once
more I will shake not only the earth but
also the heavens."[c] 27The words "once
more" indicate the removing of what can
be shaken—that is, created things—so
that what cannot be shaken may remain.
28Therefore, since we are receiving a
kingdom that cannot be shaken, let us be
thankful, and so worship God acceptably
with reverence and awe, 29for our "God is
a consuming fire."[d]

[a] *20* Exodus 19:12,13 [b] *21* Deut. 9:19
[c] *26* Haggai 2:6 [d] *29* Deut. 4:24

PRAYER: THE ATTRIBUTES OF GOD

WHO has understood what is in Your mind, O Lord, or instructed You as Your counselor? Whom did You consult to enlighten You, and who taught You the path of justice? Who taught You knowledge or showed You the way of understanding? Surely the nations are like a drop in a bucket; they are regarded as dust on the scales; You weigh the islands as though they were fine dust. Before You all the nations are as nothing; You regard them as less than nothing and worthless. To whom, then, will I compare You, O God? Or what likeness will I compare with You?

(Isaiah 40:13–15, 17–18)

***PAUSE** to reflect on these affirmations about the person, powers and perfection of God.*

YEAR 2 DAY 277

OT Proverbs 28

28 The wicked man flees though no one pursues,
but the righteous are as bold as a lion.

2 When a country is rebellious, it has many rulers,
but a man of understanding and knowledge maintains order.

3 A ruler[a] who oppresses the poor
is like a driving rain that leaves no crops.

4 Those who forsake the law praise the wicked,
but those who keep the law resist them.

5 Evil men do not understand justice,
but those who seek the LORD understand it fully.

[a] *3* Or *A poor man*

[6] Better a poor man whose walk is blameless
than a rich man whose ways are perverse.

[7] He who keeps the law is a discerning son,
but a companion of gluttons disgraces his father.

[8] He who increases his wealth by exorbitant interest
amasses it for another, who will be kind to the poor.

[9] If anyone turns a deaf ear to the law,
even his prayers are detestable.

[10] He who leads the upright along an evil path
will fall into his own trap,
but the blameless will receive a good inheritance.

[11] A rich man may be wise in his own eyes,
but a poor man who has discernment sees through him.

[12] When the righteous triumph, there is great elation;
but when the wicked rise to power, men go into hiding.

[13] He who conceals his sins does not prosper,
but whoever confesses and renounces them finds mercy.

[14] Blessed is the man who always fears the LORD,
but he who hardens his heart falls into trouble.

[15] Like a roaring lion or a charging bear
is a wicked man ruling over a helpless people.

[16] A tyrannical ruler lacks judgment,
but he who hates ill-gotten gain will enjoy a long life.

[17] A man tormented by the guilt of murder
will be a fugitive till death;
let no one support him.

[18] He whose walk is blameless is kept safe,
but he whose ways are perverse will suddenly fall.

[19] He who works his land will have abundant food,
but the one who chases fantasies will have his fill of poverty.

[20] A faithful man will be richly blessed,
but one eager to get rich will not go unpunished.

[21] To show partiality is not good—
yet a man will do wrong for a piece of bread.

[22] A stingy man is eager to get rich
and is unaware that poverty awaits him.

[23] He who rebukes a man will in the end gain more favor
than he who has a flattering tongue.

[24] He who robs his father or mother
and says, "It's not wrong"—
he is partner to him who destroys.

[25] A greedy man stirs up dissension,
but he who trusts in the LORD will prosper.

[26] He who trusts in himself is a fool,
but he who walks in wisdom is kept safe.

[27] He who gives to the poor will lack nothing,
but he who closes his eyes to them receives many curses.

[28] When the wicked rise to power,
people go into hiding;
but when the wicked perish, the righteous thrive.

PRAYER: INTERCESSION

JUST as the body is one, but has many parts, and all the parts of the body, being many, are one body; so also are You, O Christ. (1 Corinthians 12:12)

***TAKE** a few moments to intercede on behalf of your local church, other churches, evangelism and discipleship ministries, educational ministries and any other special concerns you may have.*

NT Hebrews 13:1-25

Concluding Exhortations

13 Keep on loving each other as brothers. 2 Do not forget to entertain strangers, for by so doing some people have entertained angels without knowing it. 3 Remember those in prison as if you were their fellow prisoners, and those who are mistreated as if you yourselves were suffering.

4 Marriage should be honored by all, and the marriage bed kept pure, for God will judge the adulterer and all the sexually immoral. 5 Keep your lives free from the love of money and be content with what you have, because God has said,

> "Never will I leave you;
> never will I forsake you."[a]

6 So we say with confidence,

> "The Lord is my helper; I will not be afraid.
> What can man do to me?"[b]

7 Remember your leaders, who spoke the word of God to you. Consider the outcome of their way of life and imitate their faith. 8 Jesus Christ is the same yesterday and today and forever.

9 Do not be carried away by all kinds of strange teachings. It is good for our hearts to be strengthened by grace, not by ceremonial foods, which are of no value to those who eat them. 10 We have an altar from which those who minister at the tabernacle have no right to eat.

11 The high priest carries the blood of animals into the Most Holy Place as a sin offering, but the bodies are burned outside the camp. 12 And so Jesus also suffered outside the city gate to make the people holy through his own blood. 13 Let us, then, go to him outside the camp, bearing the disgrace he bore. 14 For here we do not have an enduring city, but we are looking for the city that is to come.

15 Through Jesus, therefore, let us continually offer to God a sacrifice of praise—the fruit of lips that confess his name. 16 And do not forget to do good and to share with others, for with such sacrifices God is pleased.

17 Obey your leaders and submit to their authority. They keep watch over you as men who must give an account. Obey them so that their work will be a joy, not a burden, for that would be of no advantage to you.

18 Pray for us. We are sure that we have a clear conscience and desire to live honorably in every way. 19 I particularly urge you to pray so that I may be restored to you soon.

20 May the God of peace, who through the blood of the eternal covenant brought back from the dead our Lord Jesus, that great Shepherd of the sheep, 21 equip you with everything good for doing his will, and may he work in us what is pleasing to him, through Jesus Christ, to whom be glory for ever and ever. Amen.

22 Brothers, I urge you to bear with my word of exhortation, for I have written you only a short letter.

23 I want you to know that our brother Timothy has been released. If he arrives soon, I will come with him to see you.

24 Greet all your leaders and all God's people. Those from Italy send you their greetings.

25 Grace be with you all.

[a] 5 Deut. 31:6 [b] 6 Psalm 118:6,7

PRAYER: THE WORKS OF GOD

ALL these testified that You, O Jesus, are the Son of God: John the Baptist, the works that You did, the Father, and the Scriptures. (John 5:31–39) . . . Never did anyone speak the way You did, O Jesus Christ. (John 7:46)

__TAKE__ a moment to consider the greatness of God's wonderful works.

OT Ezekiel 36:1-38 — YEAR 2 DAY 278

A Prophecy to the Mountains of Israel

36 "Son of man, prophesy to the mountains of Israel and say, 'O mountains of Israel, hear the word of the LORD. 2This is what the Sovereign LORD says: The enemy said of you, "Aha! The ancient heights have become our possession." ' 3Therefore prophesy and say, 'This is what the Sovereign LORD says: Because they ravaged and hounded you from every side so that you became the possession of the rest of the nations and the object of people's malicious talk and slander, 4therefore, O mountains of Israel, hear the word of the Sovereign LORD: This is what the Sovereign LORD says to the mountains and hills, to the ravines and valleys, to the desolate ruins and the deserted towns that have been plundered and ridiculed by the rest of the nations around you— 5this is what the Sovereign LORD says: In my burning zeal I have spoken against the rest of the nations, and against all Edom, for with glee and with malice in their hearts they made my land their own possession so that they might plunder its pastureland.' 6Therefore prophesy concerning the land of Israel and say to the mountains and hills, to the ravines and valleys: 'This is what the Sovereign LORD says: I speak in my jealous wrath because you have suffered the scorn of the nations. 7Therefore this is what the Sovereign LORD says: I swear with uplifted hand that the nations around you will also suffer scorn.

8" 'But you, O mountains of Israel, will produce branches and fruit for my people Israel, for they will soon come home. 9I am concerned for you and will look on you with favor; you will be plowed and sown, 10and I will multiply the number of people upon you, even the whole house of Israel. The towns will be inhabited and the ruins rebuilt. 11I will increase the number of men and animals upon you, and they will be fruitful and become numerous. I will settle people on you as in the past and will make you prosper more than before. Then you will know that I am the LORD. 12I will cause people, my people Israel, to walk upon you. They will possess you, and you will be their inheritance; you will never again deprive them of their children.

13" 'This is what the Sovereign LORD says: Because people say to you, "You devour men and deprive your nation of its children," 14therefore you will no longer devour men or make your nation childless, declares the Sovereign LORD. 15No longer will I make you hear the taunts of the nations, and no longer will you suffer the scorn of the peoples or cause your nation to fall, declares the Sovereign LORD.' "

16Again the word of the LORD came to me: 17"Son of man, when the people of Israel were living in their own land, they defiled it by their conduct and their actions. Their conduct was like a woman's monthly uncleanness in my sight. 18So I poured out my wrath on them because they had shed blood in the land and because they had defiled it with their idols. 19I dispersed them among the nations, and they were scattered through the countries; I judged them according to their conduct and their actions. 20And wherever they went among the nations they profaned my holy name, for it was said of them, 'These are the LORD's people, and yet they had to leave his land.' 21I had concern for my holy name, which the house of Israel profaned among the nations where they had gone.

22"Therefore say to the house of Israel, 'This is what the Sovereign LORD says: It is not for your sake, O house of Israel, that I am going to do these things, but for the sake of my holy name, which you have profaned among the nations where you have gone. 23I will show the holiness of my great name, which has been profaned among the nations, the name you have profaned among them. Then the nations will know that I am the LORD, declares the Sovereign LORD, when I show myself holy through you before their eyes.

24" 'For I will take you out of the nations; I will gather you from all the countries and bring you back into your own land. 25I will sprinkle clean water on you, and you will be clean; I will cleanse you from all your impurities and from all your idols. 26I will give you a new heart and put a new spirit in you; I will remove from you your heart of stone and give you a heart of flesh. 27And I will put my Spirit in you and move you to follow my decrees and be careful to keep my laws. 28You will live in the land I gave your forefathers; you will be my people, and I will be your God. 29I will save you from all your uncleanness. I will call for the grain and make it plentiful and will not bring famine upon you. 30I will increase the fruit of the trees and the crops of the field, so that you will no longer suffer disgrace among the nations because of famine. 31Then you will remember your evil ways and wicked deeds, and you will loathe yourselves for your sins and detestable practices. 32I want you to know that I am not doing this for your sake, declares the Sovereign LORD. Be ashamed and disgraced for your conduct, O house of Israel!

33" 'This is what the Sovereign LORD says: On the day I cleanse you from all your sins, I will resettle your towns, and the ruins will be rebuilt. 34The desolate land will be cultivated instead of lying desolate in the sight of all who pass through it. 35They will say, "This land that was laid waste has become like the garden of Eden; the cities that were lying in ruins, desolate and destroyed, are now fortified and inhabited." 36Then the nations around you that remain will know that I the LORD have rebuilt what was destroyed and have replanted what was desolate. I the LORD have spoken, and I will do it.'

37"This is what the Sovereign LORD says: Once again I will yield to the plea of the house of Israel and do this for them: I will make their people as numerous as sheep, 38as numerous as the flocks for offerings at Jerusalem during her appointed feasts. So will the ruined cities be filled with flocks of people. Then they will know that I am the LORD."

PRAYER: AFFIRMATION

LORD, You are my portion and my inheritance. (Numbers 18:20) . . . As for me and my household, we will serve You, Lord. (Joshua 24:15)

PAUSE *to reflect on these Biblical affirmations.*

NT James 1:1–18

1 James, a servant of God and of the Lord Jesus Christ,

To the twelve tribes scattered among the nations:

Greetings.

Trials and Temptations

2Consider it pure joy, my brothers, whenever you face trials of many kinds, 3because you know that the testing of your faith develops perseverance. 4Perseverance must finish its work so that you may be mature and complete, not lacking anything. 5If any of you lacks wisdom, he should ask God, who gives generously to all without finding fault, and it will be given to him. 6But when he asks, he must believe and not doubt, because he who doubts is like a wave of the sea, blown and tossed by the wind. 7That man should not think he will receive anything from the Lord; 8he is a double-minded man, unstable in all he does.

9The brother in humble circumstances ought to take pride in his high position. 10But the one who is rich should take pride in his low position, because he will pass away like a wild flower. 11For the sun rises with scorching heat and withers the plant; its blossom falls and its beauty is destroyed. In the same way, the rich man will fade away even while he goes about his business.

12Blessed is the man who perseveres under trial, because when he has stood the test, he will receive the crown of life that God has promised to those who love him.

13When tempted, no one should say, "God is tempting me." For God cannot be tempted by evil, nor does he tempt anyone; 14but each one is tempted when, by his own evil desire, he is dragged away and enticed. 15Then, after desire has conceived, it gives birth to sin; and sin, when it is full-grown, gives birth to death.

16Don't be deceived, my dear brothers.
17Every good and perfect gift is from
above, coming down from the Father of
the heavenly lights, who does not change
like shifting shadows. 18He chose to give
us birth through the word of truth, that
we might be a kind of firstfruits of all he
created.

PRAYER: MY RELATIONSHIP TO GOD

I WILL hold fast the confession of my hope, for You who promised are faithful. (Hebrews 10:23) . . . Like Abraham, I am looking for a city which has foundations, whose architect and builder is You, O God. (Hebrews 11:10)

***PAUSE** to thank God for the relationship that you enjoy with Him in Jesus Christ.*

YEAR 2
DAY 279

OT Ezekiel 37:1–28

The Valley of Dry Bones

37 The hand of the LORD was upon me,
and he brought me out by the Spirit
of the LORD and set me in the middle of a
valley; it was full of bones. 2He led me
back and forth among them, and I saw a
great many bones on the floor of the valley, bones that were very dry. 3He asked
me, "Son of man, can these bones live?"
I said, "O Sovereign LORD, you alone
know."
4Then he said to me, "Prophesy to these
bones and say to them, 'Dry bones, hear
the word of the LORD! 5This is what the
Sovereign LORD says to these bones: I will
make breath[a] enter you, and you will
come to life. 6I will attach tendons to you
and make flesh come upon you and cover you with skin; I will put breath in you,
and you will come to life. Then you will
know that I am the LORD.' "
7So I prophesied as I was commanded.
And as I was prophesying, there was a
noise, a rattling sound, and the bones
came together, bone to bone. 8I looked,
and tendons and flesh appeared on them
and skin covered them, but there was no
breath in them.
9Then he said to me, "Prophesy to the
breath; prophesy, son of man, and say to
it, 'This is what the Sovereign LORD says:
Come from the four winds, O breath, and
breathe into these slain, that they may
live.' " 10So I prophesied as he commanded me, and breath entered them; they
came to life and stood up on their feet—
a vast army.
11Then he said to me: "Son of man, these
bones are the whole house of Israel. They
say, 'Our bones are dried up and our hope
is gone; we are cut off.' 12Therefore prophesy and say to them: 'This is what the Sovereign LORD says: O my people, I am going
to open your graves and bring you up from
them; I will bring you back to the land of
Israel. 13Then you, my people, will know
that I am the LORD, when I open your
graves and bring you up from them. 14I will
put my Spirit in you and you will live, and
I will settle you in your own land. Then
you will know that I the LORD have spoken,
and I have done it, declares the LORD.' "

One Nation Under One King

15The word of the LORD came to me:
16"Son of man, take a stick of wood and
write on it, 'Belonging to Judah and the Israelites associated with him.' Then take another stick of wood, and write on it,
'Ephraim's stick, belonging to Joseph and
all the house of Israel associated with him.'
17Join them together into one stick so that
they will become one in your hand.
18"When your countrymen ask you,
'Won't you tell us what you mean by this?'
19say to them, 'This is what the Sovereign
LORD says: I am going to take the stick of
Joseph—which is in Ephraim's hand—
and of the Israelite tribes associated with

[a] 5 The Hebrew for this word can also mean *wind* or *spirit* (see verses 6–14).

him, and join it to Judah's stick, making them a single stick of wood, and they will become one in my hand.' 20 Hold before their eyes the sticks you have written on 21 and say to them, 'This is what the Sovereign LORD says: I will take the Israelites out of the nations where they have gone. I will gather them from all around and bring them back into their own land. 22 I will make them one nation in the land, on the mountains of Israel. There will be one king over all of them and they will never again be two nations or be divided into two kingdoms. 23 They will no longer defile themselves with their idols and vile images or with any of their offenses, for I will save them from all their sinful backsliding,[b] and I will cleanse them. They will be my people, and I will be their God.

24 " 'My servant David will be king over them, and they will all have one shepherd. They will follow my laws and be careful to keep my decrees. 25 They will live in the land I gave to my servant Jacob, the land where your fathers lived. They and their children and their children's children will live there forever, and David my servant will be their prince forever. 26 I will make a covenant of peace with them; it will be an everlasting covenant. I will establish them and increase their numbers, and I will put my sanctuary among them forever. 27 My dwelling place will be with them; I will be their God, and they will be my people. 28 Then the nations will know that I the LORD make Israel holy, when my sanctuary is among them forever.' "

[b] 23 Many Hebrew manuscripts (see also Septuagint); most Hebrew manuscripts *all their dwelling places where they sinned*

PRAYER: THANKSGIVING

YOU did not redeem me from an aimless way of life, O Christ, with perishable things such as silver or gold, but with Your precious blood, as of a lamb without blemish or defect. (1 Peter 1:18–19) . . . How great is Your love, O Father, that You have lavished on me, that I should be called Your child—and I am! Therefore the world does not know me, because it did not know You. (1 John 3:1)

***PAUSE** to offer your own expressions of thanksgiving.*

NT James 1:19–27

Listening and Doing

19 My dear brothers, take note of this: Everyone should be quick to listen, slow to speak and slow to become angry, 20 for man's anger does not bring about the righteous life that God desires. 21 Therefore, get rid of all moral filth and the evil that is so prevalent and humbly accept the word planted in you, which can save you.

22 Do not merely listen to the word, and so deceive yourselves. Do what it says. 23 Anyone who listens to the word but does not do what it says is like a man who looks at his face in a mirror 24 and, after looking at himself, goes away and immediately forgets what he looks like. 25 But the man who looks intently into the perfect law that gives freedom, and continues to do this, not forgetting what he has heard, but doing it—he will be blessed in what he does.

26 If anyone considers himself religious and yet does not keep a tight rein on his tongue, he deceives himself and his religion is worthless. 27 Religion that God our Father accepts as pure and faultless is this: to look after orphans and widows in their distress and to keep oneself from being polluted by the world.

PRAYER: THE CHARACTER I WANT TO CULTIVATE

I REJOICE, O my Lord, at Your word as one who finds great spoil. I hate and abhor falsehood, but I love Your law. Great peace have they who love Your law, and nothing causes them to stumble. O Lord, I hope for

Your salvation, and I follow Your commands. My soul keeps Your testimonies, for I love them greatly. I keep Your precepts and Your testimonies, for all my ways are known to You. (Psalm 119:162–163, 165–168)

***TAKE** a moment to ask the Lord for the grace to grow in godly character.*

YEAR 2 DAY 280

OT Psalms 126–127

Psalm 126

A song of ascents.

[1]When the LORD brought back the captives to[a] Zion,
we were like men who dreamed.[b]
[2]Our mouths were filled with laughter,
our tongues with songs of joy.
Then it was said among the nations,
"The LORD has done great things for them."
[3]The LORD has done great things for us,
and we are filled with joy.

[4]Restore our fortunes,[c] O LORD,
like streams in the Negev.
[5]Those who sow in tears
will reap with songs of joy.
[6]He who goes out weeping,
carrying seed to sow,
will return with songs of joy,
carrying sheaves with him.

Psalm 127

A song of ascents. Of Solomon.

[1]Unless the LORD builds the house,
its builders labor in vain.
Unless the LORD watches over the city,
the watchmen stand guard in vain.
[2]In vain you rise early
and stay up late,
toiling for food to eat—
for he grants sleep to[d] those he loves.

[3]Sons are a heritage from the LORD,
children a reward from him.
[4]Like arrows in the hands of a warrior
are sons born in one's youth.
[5]Blessed is the man
whose quiver is full of them.
They will not be put to shame
when they contend with their enemies in the gate.

[a] 1 Or *LORD restored the fortunes of* [b] 1 Or *men restored to health* [c] 4 Or *Bring back our captives* [d] 2 Or *eat— / for while they sleep he provides for*

PRAYER: ADORATION

YOU are He; You are the first, and You are the last. (Isaiah 48:12) . . . We confess that in the beginning was the Word, and the Word was with You, and the Word was You, O God. The Word was in the beginning with You. (John 1:1–2)

***PAUSE** to express your thoughts of praise and worship.*

NT James 2:1–13

Favoritism Forbidden

2 My brothers, as believers in our glorious Lord Jesus Christ, don't show favoritism. [2]Suppose a man comes into
your meeting wearing a gold ring and fine
clothes, and a poor man in shabby clothes
also comes in. [3]If you show special attention to the man wearing fine clothes and
say, "Here's a good seat for you," but say
to the poor man, "You stand there" or "Sit
on the floor by my feet," [4]have you not
discriminated among yourselves and become judges with evil thoughts?

[5]Listen, my dear brothers: Has not God
chosen those who are poor in the eyes of
the world to be rich in faith and to inher-

it the kingdom he promised those who love him? 6But you have insulted the poor. Is it not the rich who are exploiting you? Are they not the ones who are dragging you into court? 7Are they not the ones who are slandering the noble name of him to whom you belong?

8If you really keep the royal law found in Scripture, "Love your neighbor as yourself,"[a] you are doing right. 9But if you show favoritism, you sin and are convicted by the law as lawbreakers. 10For whoever keeps the whole law and yet stumbles at just one point is guilty of breaking all of it. 11For he who said, "Do not commit adultery,"[b] also said, "Do not murder."[c] If you do not commit adultery but do commit murder, you have become a lawbreaker.

12Speak and act as those who are going to be judged by the law that gives freedom, 13because judgment without mercy will be shown to anyone who has not been merciful. Mercy triumphs over judgment!

[a] *8* Lev. 19:18 [b] *11* Exodus 20:14; Deut. 5:18
[c] *11* Exodus 20:13; Deut. 5:17

PRAYER: MY RELATIONSHIP TO OTHERS

I WILL submit myself for Your sake, O Lord, to every human authority, whether to a king as being supreme, or to the governors he sends to punish evildoers and to praise those who do right; for it is Your will, O God, that by doing good I may silence the ignorance of foolish people.

(1 Peter 2:13–15)

PAUSE *to review your relationships with others and to commit them to the Lord.*

YEAR 2
DAY 281

OT Ezekiel 38:1-23

A Prophecy Against Gog

38 The word of the LORD came to me: 2"Son of man, set your face against Gog, of the land of Magog, the chief prince of[a] Meshech and Tubal; prophesy against him 3and say: 'This is what the Sovereign LORD says: I am against you, O Gog, chief prince of[b] Meshech and Tubal. 4I will turn you around, put hooks in your jaws and bring you out with your whole army—your horses, your horsemen fully armed, and a great horde with large and small shields, all of them brandishing their swords. 5Persia, Cush[c] and Put will be with them, all with shields and helmets, 6also Gomer with all its troops, and Beth Togarmah from the far north with all its troops—the many nations with you.

7" 'Get ready; be prepared, you and all the hordes gathered about you, and take command of them. 8After many days you will be called to arms. In future years you will invade a land that has recovered from war, whose people were gathered from many nations to the mountains of Israel, which had long been desolate. They had been brought out from the nations, and now all of them live in safety. 9You and all your troops and the many nations with you will go up, advancing like a storm; you will be like a cloud covering the land.

10" 'This is what the Sovereign LORD says: On that day thoughts will come into your mind and you will devise an evil scheme. 11You will say, "I will invade a land of unwalled villages; I will attack a peaceful and unsuspecting people—all of them living without walls and without gates and bars. 12I will plunder and loot and turn my hand against the resettled ruins and the people gathered from the nations, rich in livestock and goods, living at the center of the land." 13Sheba and Dedan and the merchants of Tarshish and all her villages[d] will say to you, "Have you come to plunder? Have you gathered your

[a] *2* Or *the prince of Rosh,* [b] *3* Or *Gog, prince of Rosh,* [c] *5* That is, the upper Nile region [d] *13* Or *her strong lions*

hordes to loot, to carry off silver and gold,
to take away livestock and goods and to
seize much plunder?" '

14 "Therefore, son of man, prophesy and
say to Gog: 'This is what the Sovereign
LORD says: In that day, when my people Israel are living in safety, will you not take
notice of it? 15 You will come from your
place in the far north, you and many nations with you, all of them riding on
horses, a great horde, a mighty army.
16 You will advance against my people Israel like a cloud that covers the land. In
days to come, O Gog, I will bring you
against my land, so that the nations may
know me when I show myself holy
through you before their eyes.

17 " 'This is what the Sovereign LORD
says: Are you not the one I spoke of in
former days by my servants the prophets
of Israel? At that time they prophesied
for years that I would bring you against
them. 18 This is what will happen in that
day: When Gog attacks the land of Israel, my hot anger will be aroused, declares
the Sovereign LORD. 19 In my zeal and
fiery wrath I declare that at that time
there shall be a great earthquake in the
land of Israel. 20 The fish of the sea, the
birds of the air, the beasts of the field,
every creature that moves along the
ground, and all the people on the face of
the earth will tremble at my presence.
The mountains will be overturned, the
cliffs will crumble and every wall will fall
to the ground. 21 I will summon a sword
against Gog on all my mountains, declares the Sovereign LORD. Every man's
sword will be against his brother. 22 I will
execute judgment upon him with plague
and bloodshed; I will pour down torrents of rain, hailstones and burning sulfur on him and on his troops and on the
many nations with him. 23 And so I will
show my greatness and my holiness, and
I will make myself known in the sight of
many nations. Then they will know that
I am the LORD.'

PRAYER: CONFESSION

O MY Lord, please do not hold against me the sin that I have foolishly committed. (Numbers 12:11)

ASK *the Spirit to search your heart and reveal any areas of unconfessed sin. Acknowledge these to the Lord and thank Him for His forgiveness.*

NT James 2:14-26

Faith and Deeds

14 What good is it, my brothers, if a man
claims to have faith but has no deeds?
Can such faith save him? 15 Suppose a
brother or sister is without clothes and
daily food. 16 If one of you says to him,
"Go, I wish you well; keep warm and well
fed," but does nothing about his physical
needs, what good is it? 17 In the same way,
faith by itself, if it is not accompanied by
action, is dead.

18 But someone will say, "You have faith;
I have deeds."

Show me your faith without deeds, and
I will show you my faith by what I do. 19 You
believe that there is one God. Good! Even
the demons believe that—and shudder.

20 You foolish man, do you want evidence that faith without deeds is useless[a]?
21 Was not our ancestor Abraham considered righteous for what he did when he
offered his son Isaac on the altar? 22 You
see that his faith and his actions were
working together, and his faith was made
complete by what he did. 23 And the scripture was fulfilled that says, "Abraham believed God, and it was credited to him as
righteousness,"[b] and he was called God's
friend. 24 You see that a person is justified
by what he does and not by faith alone.

25 In the same way, was not even Rahab
the prostitute considered righteous for
what she did when she gave lodging to the
spies and sent them off in a different direction? 26 As the body without the spirit
is dead, so faith without deeds is dead.

[a] *20* Some early manuscripts *dead* [b] *23* Gen. 15:6

PRAYER: THE ATTRIBUTES OF GOD

YOUR word is settled in heaven forever, O Lord. Your faithfulness continues through all generations. You established the earth, and it stands. Your laws continue to this day according to Your purposes, for all things serve You. (Psalm 119:89–91)

***PAUSE** to reflect on these affirmations about the person, powers and perfection of God.*

YEAR 2
DAY 282

OT Ezekiel 39:1–29

39 "Son of man, prophesy against Gog
and say: 'This is what the Sovereign
LORD says: I am against you, O Gog, chief
prince of[a] Meshech and Tubal. 2I will turn
you around and drag you along. I will bring
you from the far north and send you
against the mountains of Israel. 3Then I will
strike your bow from your left hand and
make your arrows drop from your right
hand. 4On the mountains of Israel you will
fall, you and all your troops and the nations with you. I will give you as food to all
kinds of carrion birds and to the wild animals. 5You will fall in the open field, for I
have spoken, declares the Sovereign LORD.
6I will send fire on Magog and on those
who live in safety in the coastlands, and
they will know that I am the LORD.
7" 'I will make known my holy name
among my people Israel. I will no longer
let my holy name be profaned, and the
nations will know that I the LORD am the
Holy One in Israel. 8It is coming! It will
surely take place, declares the Sovereign
LORD. This is the day I have spoken of.
9" 'Then those who live in the towns of
Israel will go out and use the weapons for
fuel and burn them up—the small and
large shields, the bows and arrows, the
war clubs and spears. For seven years they
will use them for fuel. 10They will not
need to gather wood from the fields or cut
it from the forests, because they will use
the weapons for fuel. And they will plunder those who plundered them and loot
those who looted them, declares the Sovereign LORD.
11" 'On that day I will give Gog a burial
place in Israel, in the valley of those who
travel east toward[b] the Sea.[c] It will block
the way of travelers, because Gog and all
his hordes will be buried there. So it will
be called the Valley of Hamon Gog.[d]
12" 'For seven months the house of Israel will be burying them in order to
cleanse the land. 13All the people of the
land will bury them, and the day I am glorified will be a memorable day for them,
declares the Sovereign LORD.
14" 'Men will be regularly employed to
cleanse the land. Some will go throughout the land and, in addition to them,
others will bury those that remain on the
ground. At the end of the seven months
they will begin their search. 15As they go
through the land and one of them sees a
human bone, he will set up a marker beside it until the gravediggers have buried
it in the Valley of Hamon Gog. 16(Also a
town called Hamonah[e] will be there.)
And so they will cleanse the land.'
17"Son of man, this is what the Sovereign LORD says: Call out to every kind of
bird and all the wild animals: 'Assemble
and come together from all around to the
sacrifice I am preparing for you, the great
sacrifice on the mountains of Israel. There
you will eat flesh and drink blood. 18You
will eat the flesh of mighty men and drink
the blood of the princes of the earth as if
they were rams and lambs, goats and
bulls—all of them fattened animals from
Bashan. 19At the sacrifice I am preparing
for you, you will eat fat till you are glut-
ted and drink blood till you are drunk.
20At my table you will eat your fill of
horses and riders, mighty men and soldiers of every kind,' declares the Sovereign
LORD.

[a] *1* Or *Gog, prince of Rosh,* [b] *11* Or *of* [c] *11* That is, the Dead Sea [d] *11* *Hamon Gog* means *hordes of Gog.* [e] *16* *Hamonah* means *horde.*

21 "I will display my glory among the nations, and all the nations will see the punishment I inflict and the hand I lay upon them. 22 From that day forward the house of Israel will know that I am the LORD their God. 23 And the nations will know that the people of Israel went into exile for their sin, because they were unfaithful to me. So I hid my face from them and handed them over to their enemies, and they all fell by the sword. 24 I dealt with them according to their uncleanness and their offenses, and I hid my face from them.

25 "Therefore this is what the Sovereign LORD says: I will now bring Jacob back from captivity[f] and will have compassion on all the people of Israel, and I will be zealous for my holy name. 26 They will forget their shame and all the unfaithfulness they showed toward me when they lived in safety in their land with no one to make them afraid. 27 When I have brought them back from the nations and have gathered them from the countries of their enemies, I will show myself holy through them in the sight of many nations. 28 Then they will know that I am the LORD their God, for though I sent them into exile among the nations, I will gather them to their own land, not leaving any behind. 29 I will no longer hide my face from them, for I will pour out my Spirit on the house of Israel, declares the Sovereign LORD."

[f] 25 Or *now restore the fortunes of Jacob*

PRAYER: RENEWAL

MAY I guard my heart with all diligence, for out of it flow the issues of life. (Proverbs 4:23) . . . May I be ready, for You, O Son of Man, will come at an hour when I do not expect You. (Matthew 24:44; Luke 12:40)

***PAUSE** to add your own prayers for personal renewal.*

NT James 3:1-18

Taming the Tongue

3 Not many of you should presume to be teachers, my brothers, because you know that we who teach will be judged more strictly. 2 We all stumble in many ways. If anyone is never at fault in what he says, he is a perfect man, able to keep his whole body in check.

3 When we put bits into the mouths of horses to make them obey us, we can turn the whole animal. 4 Or take ships as an example. Although they are so large and are driven by strong winds, they are steered by a very small rudder wherever the pilot wants to go. 5 Likewise the tongue is a small part of the body, but it makes great boasts. Consider what a great forest is set on fire by a small spark. 6 The tongue also is a fire, a world of evil among the parts of the body. It corrupts the whole person, sets the whole course of his life on fire, and is itself set on fire by hell.

7 All kinds of animals, birds, reptiles and creatures of the sea are being tamed and have been tamed by man, 8 but no man can tame the tongue. It is a restless evil, full of deadly poison.

9 With the tongue we praise our Lord and Father, and with it we curse men, who have been made in God's likeness. 10 Out of the same mouth come praise and cursing. My brothers, this should not be. 11 Can both fresh water and salt[a] water flow from the same spring? 12 My brothers, can a fig tree bear olives, or a grapevine bear figs? Neither can a salt spring produce fresh water.

Two Kinds of Wisdom

13 Who is wise and understanding among you? Let him show it by his good life, by deeds done in the humility that comes from wisdom. 14 But if you harbor bitter envy and selfish ambition in your hearts, do not boast about it or deny the truth. 15 Such "wisdom" does not come down from heaven but is earthly, unspiritual, of the devil. 16 For where you have envy and selfish ambition, there you find disorder and every evil practice.

[a] 11 Greek *bitter* (see also verse 14)

17But the wisdom that comes from heaven is first of all pure; then peace-loving, considerate, submissive, full of mercy and good fruit, impartial and sincere.
18Peacemakers who sow in peace raise a harvest of righteousness.

PRAYER: THE WORKS OF GOD

YOU, O God, so loved the world that You gave Your only begotten Son, that whoever believes in Him should not perish but have eternal life. For You did not send Him into the world to condemn the world, but to save the world through Him. (John 3:16–17)

***TAKE** a moment to consider the greatness of God's wonderful works.*

YEAR 2 DAY 283

OT Ezekiel 40:1–49

The New Temple Area

40 In the twenty-fifth year of our exile, at the beginning of the year, on the tenth of the month, in the fourteenth year after the fall of the city—on that very day the hand of the LORD was upon me and he took me there.
2In visions of God he took me to the land of Israel and set me on a very high mountain, on whose south side were some buildings that looked like a city.
3He took me there, and I saw a man whose appearance was like bronze; he was standing in the gateway with a linen cord and a measuring rod in his hand.
4The man said to me, "Son of man, look with your eyes and hear with your ears and pay attention to everything I am going to show you, for that is why you have been brought here. Tell the house of Israel everything you see."

The East Gate to the Outer Court

5I saw a wall completely surrounding the temple area. The length of the measuring rod in the man's hand was six long cubits, each of which was a cubit[a] and a handbreadth.[b] He measured the wall; it was one measuring rod thick and one rod high.

6Then he went to the gate facing east. He climbed its steps and measured the threshold of the gate; it was one rod deep.[c]
7The alcoves for the guards were one rod long and one rod wide, and the projecting walls between the alcoves were five cubits thick. And the threshold of the gate next to the portico facing the temple was one rod deep.

8Then he measured the portico of the gateway;
9it[d] was eight cubits deep and its jambs were two cubits thick. The portico of the gateway faced the temple.

10Inside the east gate were three alcoves on each side; the three had the same measurements, and the faces of the projecting walls on each side had the same measurements.
11Then he measured the width of the entrance to the gateway; it was ten cubits and its length was thirteen cubits.
12In front of each alcove was a wall one cubit high, and the alcoves were six cubits square.
13Then he measured the gateway from the top of the rear wall of one alcove to the top of the opposite one; the distance was twenty-five cubits from one parapet opening to the opposite one.
14He measured along the faces of the projecting walls all around the inside of the gateway—sixty cubits. The measurement was up to the portico[e] facing the courtyard.[f]
15The distance from the entrance of the gateway to the far end of its portico was fifty cubits.
16The alcoves and the projecting walls inside the gateway were surmounted by narrow parapet openings all around, as was the portico; the openings all around faced inward. The faces of the

[a] 5 The common cubit was about 1 1/2 feet (about 0.5 meter). [b] 5 That is, about 3 inches (about 8 centimeters) [c] 6 Septuagint; Hebrew *deep, the first threshold, one rod deep* [d] 8,9 Many Hebrew manuscripts, Septuagint, Vulgate and Syriac; most Hebrew manuscripts *gateway facing the temple; it was one rod deep. 9Then he measured the portico of the gateway; it* [e] 14 Septuagint; Hebrew *projecting wall* [f] 14 The meaning of the Hebrew for this verse is uncertain.

projecting walls were decorated with palm trees.

The Outer Court

[17]Then he brought me into the outer court. There I saw some rooms and a pavement that had been constructed all around the court; there were thirty rooms along the pavement. [18]It abutted the sides of the gateways and was as wide as they were long; this was the lower pavement. [19]Then he measured the distance from the inside of the lower gateway to the outside of the inner court; it was a hundred cubits on the east side as well as on the north.

The North Gate

[20]Then he measured the length and width of the gate facing north, leading into the outer court. [21]Its alcoves—three on each side—its projecting walls and its portico had the same measurements as those of the first gateway. It was fifty cubits long and twenty-five cubits wide. [22]Its openings, its portico and its palm tree decorations had the same measurements as those of the gate facing east. Seven steps led up to it, with its portico opposite them. [23]There was a gate to the inner court facing the north gate, just as there was on the east. He measured from one gate to the opposite one; it was a hundred cubits.

The South Gate

[24]Then he led me to the south side and I saw a gate facing south. He measured its jambs and its portico, and they had the same measurements as the others. [25]The gateway and its portico had narrow openings all around, like the openings of the others. It was fifty cubits long and twenty-five cubits wide. [26]Seven steps led up to it, with its portico opposite them; it had palm tree decorations on the faces of the projecting walls on each side. [27]The inner court also had a gate facing south, and he measured from this gate to the outer gate on the south side; it was a hundred cubits.

Gates to the Inner Court

[28]Then he brought me into the inner court through the south gate, and he measured the south gate; it had the same measurements as the others. [29]Its alcoves, its projecting walls and its portico had the same measurements as the others. The gateway and its portico had openings all around. It was fifty cubits long and twenty-five cubits wide. [30](The porticoes of the gateways around the inner court were twenty-five cubits wide and five cubits deep.) [31]Its portico faced the outer court; palm trees decorated its jambs, and eight steps led up to it.

[32]Then he brought me to the inner court on the east side, and he measured the gateway; it had the same measurements as the others. [33]Its alcoves, its projecting walls and its portico had the same measurements as the others. The gateway and its portico had openings all around. It was fifty cubits long and twenty-five cubits wide. [34]Its portico faced the outer court; palm trees decorated the jambs on either side, and eight steps led up to it.

[35]Then he brought me to the north gate and measured it. It had the same measurements as the others, [36]as did its alcoves, its projecting walls and its portico, and it had openings all around. It was fifty cubits long and twenty-five cubits wide. [37]Its portico[g] faced the outer court; palm trees decorated the jambs on either side, and eight steps led up to it.

The Rooms for Preparing Sacrifices

[38]A room with a doorway was by the portico in each of the inner gateways, where the burnt offerings were washed. [39]In the portico of the gateway were two tables on each side, on which the burnt offerings, sin offerings and guilt offerings were slaughtered. [40]By the outside wall of the portico of the gateway, near the steps at the entrance to the north gateway were two tables, and on the other side of the steps were two tables. [41]So there were four tables on one side of the gateway and four on the other—eight tables in all—on which the sacrifices were slaughtered. [42]There were also four tables of dressed stone for the burnt offerings, each a cubit and a half long, a cubit and a half wide and a cubit high. On them were placed the utensils for slaughtering the burnt offerings and the other sacrifices. [43]And double-pronged hooks, each a handbreadth long, were attached to the wall all around. The tables were for the flesh of the offerings.

[g] 37 Septuagint (see also verses 31 and 34); Hebrew *jambs*

Rooms for the Priests

44 Outside the inner gate, within the inner court, were two rooms, one[h] at the side of the north gate and facing south, and another at the side of the south[i] gate and facing north. 45 He said to me, "The room facing south is for the priests who have charge of the temple, 46 and the room facing north is for the priests who have charge of the altar. These are the sons of Zadok, who are the only Levites who may draw near to the LORD to minister before him."

47 Then he measured the court: It was square—a hundred cubits long and a hundred cubits wide. And the altar was in front of the temple.

The Temple

48 He brought me to the portico of the temple and measured the jambs of the portico; they were five cubits wide on either side. The width of the entrance was fourteen cubits and its projecting walls were[j] three cubits wide on either side. 49 The portico was twenty cubits wide, and twelve[k] cubits from front to back. It was reached by a flight of stairs,[l] and there were pillars on each side of the jambs.

[h] 44 Septuagint; Hebrew *were rooms for singers, which were* [i] 44 Septuagint; Hebrew *east*
[j] 48 Septuagint; Hebrew *entrance was*
[k] 49 Septuagint; Hebrew *eleven* [l] 49 Hebrew; Septuagint *Ten steps led up to it*

PRAYER: PETITION

MAY I not live the rest of my time on earth for my human desires, but for Your will, O God. For I have spent enough time in the past doing the will of those apart from You, when I participated in licentiousness, lust, drunkenness, carousals, drinking parties and detestable idolatries. (1 Peter 4:2–3)

PAUSE *here to petition God for wisdom. Ask Him to develop your eternal perspective, to renew your mind with truth, and to help you develop greater skill in each area of your life. Offer prayers regarding your activities for this day and any special concerns you may have.*

NT James 4:1–17

Submit Yourselves to God

4 What causes fights and quarrels among you? Don't they come from your desires that battle within you? 2 You want something but don't get it. You kill and covet, but you cannot have what you want. You quarrel and fight. You do not have, because you do not ask God. 3 When you ask, you do not receive, because you ask with wrong motives, that you may spend what you get on your pleasures.

4 You adulterous people, don't you know that friendship with the world is hatred toward God? Anyone who chooses to be a friend of the world becomes an enemy of God. 5 Or do you think Scripture says without reason that the spirit he caused to live in us envies intensely?[a] 6 But he gives us more grace. That is why Scripture says:

"God opposes the proud
but gives grace to the humble."[b]

7 Submit yourselves, then, to God. Resist the devil, and he will flee from you. 8 Come near to God and he will come near to you. Wash your hands, you sinners, and purify your hearts, you double-minded. 9 Grieve, mourn and wail. Change your laughter to mourning and your joy to gloom. 10 Humble yourselves before the Lord, and he will lift you up.

11 Brothers, do not slander one another. Anyone who speaks against his brother or judges him speaks against the law and judges it. When you judge the law, you are not keeping it, but sitting in judgment on it. 12 There is only one Lawgiver and Judge, the one who is able to save and destroy. But you—who are you to judge your neighbor?

[a] 5 Or *that God jealously longs for the spirit that he made to live in us;* or *that the Spirit he caused to live in us longs jealously* [b] 6 Prov. 3:34

Boasting About Tomorrow

13 Now listen, you who say, "Today or tomorrow we will go to this or that city, spend a year there, carry on business and make money." 14 Why, you do not even know what will happen tomorrow. What is your life? You are a mist that appears for a little while and then vanishes. 15 Instead, you ought to say, "If it is the Lord's will, we will live and do this or that." 16 As it is, you boast and brag. All such boasting is evil. 17 Anyone, then, who knows the good he ought to do and doesn't do it, sins.

PRAYER: MY RELATIONSHIP TO GOD

BLESSED are You, the God and Father of my Lord Jesus Christ; according to Your great mercy You have given me new birth into a living hope through the resurrection of Jesus Christ from the dead, and into an inheritance that is incorruptible and undefiled and unfading, reserved in heaven for me. (1 Peter 1:3–4)

PAUSE *to thank God for the relationship that you enjoy with Him in Jesus Christ.*

YEAR 2 DAY 284

OT Ezekiel 41:1–42:20

41 Then the man brought me to the outer sanctuary and measured the jambs; the width of the jambs was six cubits[a] on each side.[b] 2 The entrance was ten cubits wide, and the projecting walls on each side of it were five cubits wide. He also measured the outer sanctuary; it was forty cubits long and twenty cubits wide.

3 Then he went into the inner sanctuary and measured the jambs of the entrance; each was two cubits wide. The entrance was six cubits wide, and the projecting walls on each side of it were seven cubits wide. 4 And he measured the length of the inner sanctuary; it was twenty cubits, and its width was twenty cubits across the end of the outer sanctuary. He said to me, "This is the Most Holy Place."

5 Then he measured the wall of the temple; it was six cubits thick, and each side room around the temple was four cubits wide. 6 The side rooms were on three levels, one above another, thirty on each level. There were ledges all around the wall of the temple to serve as supports for the side rooms, so that the supports were not inserted into the wall of the temple. 7 The side rooms all around the temple were wider at each successive level. The structure surrounding the temple was built in ascending stages, so that the rooms widened as one went upward. A stairway went up from the lowest floor to the top floor through the middle floor.

8 I saw that the temple had a raised base all around it, forming the foundation of the side rooms. It was the length of the rod, six long cubits. 9 The outer wall of the side rooms was five cubits thick. The open area between the side rooms of the temple 10 and the ⌊priests'⌋ rooms was twenty cubits wide all around the temple. 11 There were entrances to the side rooms from the open area, one on the north and another on the south; and the base adjoining the open area was five cubits wide all around.

12 The building facing the temple courtyard on the west side was seventy cubits wide. The wall of the building was five cubits thick all around, and its length was ninety cubits.

13 Then he measured the temple; it was a hundred cubits long, and the temple courtyard and the building with its walls were also a hundred cubits long. 14 The width of the temple courtyard on the east, including the front of the temple, was a hundred cubits.

15 Then he measured the length of the building facing the courtyard at the rear

[a] *1* The common cubit was about 1 1/2 feet (about 0.5 meter). [b] *1* One Hebrew manuscript and Septuagint; most Hebrew manuscripts *side, the width of the tent*

of the temple, including its galleries on
each side; it was a hundred cubits.

The outer sanctuary, the inner sanctuary and the portico facing the court, 16 as
well as the thresholds and the narrow
windows and galleries around the three of
them—everything beyond and including
the threshold was covered with wood. The
floor, the wall up to the windows, and the
windows were covered. 17 In the space
above the outside of the entrance to the
inner sanctuary and on the walls at regular intervals all around the inner and outer sanctuary 18 were carved cherubim and
palm trees. Palm trees alternated with
cherubim. Each cherub had two faces:
19 the face of a man toward the palm tree
on one side and the face of a lion toward
the palm tree on the other. They were
carved all around the whole temple.
20 From the floor to the area above the entrance, cherubim and palm trees were
carved on the wall of the outer sanctuary.

21 The outer sanctuary had a rectangular
doorframe, and the one at the front of the
Most Holy Place was similar. 22 There was
a wooden altar three cubits high and two
cubits square[c]; its corners, its base[d] and its
sides were of wood. The man said to me,
"This is the table that is before the LORD."
23 Both the outer sanctuary and the Most
Holy Place had double doors. 24 Each door
had two leaves—two hinged leaves for
each door. 25 And on the doors of the outer sanctuary were carved cherubim and
palm trees like those carved on the walls,
and there was a wooden overhang on the
front of the portico. 26 On the sidewalls of
the portico were narrow windows with
palm trees carved on each side. The side
rooms of the temple also had overhangs.

Rooms for the Priests

42 Then the man led me northward into
the outer court and brought me to the
rooms opposite the temple courtyard and
opposite the outer wall on the north side.
2 The building whose door faced north was
a hundred cubits[e] long and fifty cubits
wide. 3 Both in the section twenty cubits
from the inner court and in the section opposite the pavement of the outer court,
gallery faced gallery at the three levels. 4 In
front of the rooms was an inner passageway ten cubits wide and a hundred cubits[f]
long. Their doors were on the north. 5 Now
the upper rooms were narrower, for the
galleries took more space from them than
from the rooms on the lower and middle
floors of the building. 6 The rooms on the
third floor had no pillars, as the courts
had; so they were smaller in floor space
than those on the lower and middle floors.
7 There was an outer wall parallel to the
rooms and the outer court; it extended in
front of the rooms for fifty cubits. 8 While
the row of rooms on the side next to the
outer court was fifty cubits long, the row
on the side nearest the sanctuary was a
hundred cubits long. 9 The lower rooms
had an entrance on the east side as one enters them from the outer court.

10 On the south side[g] along the length of
the wall of the outer court, adjoining the
temple courtyard and opposite the outer
wall, were rooms 11 with a passageway in
front of them. These were like the rooms
on the north; they had the same length
and width, with similar exits and dimensions. Similar to the doorways on the
north 12 were the doorways of the rooms
on the south. There was a doorway at the
beginning of the passageway that was parallel to the corresponding wall extending
eastward, by which one enters the rooms.

13 Then he said to me, "The north and
south rooms facing the temple courtyard
are the priests' rooms, where the priests
who approach the LORD will eat the most
holy offerings. There they will put the
most holy offerings—the grain offerings,
the sin offerings and the guilt offerings—
for the place is holy. 14 Once the priests enter the holy precincts, they are not to go
into the outer court until they leave behind the garments in which they minister,
for these are holy. They are to put on other clothes before they go near the places
that are for the people."

15 When he had finished measuring
what was inside the temple area, he led
me out by the east gate and measured the
area all around: 16 He measured the east
side with the measuring rod; it was five
hundred cubits.[h] 17 He measured the
north side; it was five hundred cubits[i] by

[c] *22* Septuagint; Hebrew *long* [d] *22* Septuagint; Hebrew *length* [e] *2* The common cubit was about 1 1/2 feet (about 0.5 meter). [f] *4* Septuagint and Syriac; Hebrew *and one cubit* [g] *10* Septuagint; Hebrew *Eastward* [h] *16* See Septuagint of verse 17; Hebrew *rods*; also in verses 18 and 19. [i] *17* Septuagint; Hebrew *rods*

the measuring rod. [18]He measured the south side; it was five hundred cubits by the measuring rod. [19]Then he turned to the west side and measured; it was five hundred cubits by the measuring rod. [20]So he measured the area on all four sides. It had a wall around it, five hundred cubits long and five hundred cubits wide, to separate the holy from the common.

PRAYER: INTERCESSION

O LORD God, may I lay up Your words in my heart and in my soul and teach them to my children, talking about them when I sit in my house and when I walk along the way and when I lie down and when I rise up. (Deuteronomy 11:18–19)

TAKE *a few moments to intercede on behalf of your immediate family and other relatives. Offer prayers for their spiritual, emotional and physical concerns.*

NT James 5:1–20

Warning to Rich Oppressors

5 Now listen, you rich people, weep and wail because of the misery that is coming upon you. [2]Your wealth has rotted, and moths have eaten your clothes. [3]Your gold and silver are corroded. Their corrosion will testify against you and eat your flesh like fire. You have hoarded wealth in the last days. [4]Look! The wages you failed to pay the workmen who mowed your fields are crying out against you. The cries of the harvesters have reached the ears of the Lord Almighty. [5]You have lived on earth in luxury and self-indulgence. You have fattened yourselves in the day of slaughter.[a] [6]You have condemned and murdered innocent men, who were not opposing you.

Patience in Suffering

[7]Be patient, then, brothers, until the Lord's coming. See how the farmer waits for the land to yield its valuable crop and how patient he is for the autumn and spring rains. [8]You too, be patient and stand firm, because the Lord's coming is near. [9]Don't grumble against each other, brothers, or you will be judged. The Judge is standing at the door!

[10]Brothers, as an example of patience in the face of suffering, take the prophets who spoke in the name of the Lord. [11]As you know, we consider blessed those who have persevered. You have heard of Job's perseverance and have seen what the Lord finally brought about. The Lord is full of compassion and mercy.

[12]Above all, my brothers, do not swear—not by heaven or by earth or by anything else. Let your "Yes" be yes, and your "No," no, or you will be condemned.

The Prayer of Faith

[13]Is any one of you in trouble? He should pray. Is anyone happy? Let him sing songs of praise. [14]Is any one of you sick? He should call the elders of the church to pray over him and anoint him with oil in the name of the Lord. [15]And the prayer offered in faith will make the sick person well; the Lord will raise him up. If he has sinned, he will be forgiven. [16]Therefore confess your sins to each other and pray for each other so that you may be healed. The prayer of a righteous man is powerful and effective.

[17]Elijah was a man just like us. He prayed earnestly that it would not rain, and it did not rain on the land for three and a half years. [18]Again he prayed, and the heavens gave rain, and the earth produced its crops.

[19]My brothers, if one of you should wander from the truth and someone should bring him back, [20]remember this: Whoever turns a sinner from the error of his way will save him from death and cover over a multitude of sins.

[a] 5 Or *yourselves as in a day of feasting*

PRAYER: THE CHARACTER I WANT TO CULTIVATE

IN the way of righteousness there is life, Lord God, and in that pathway there is no death. (Proverbs 12:28) . . . Your name, O Lord, is a strong tower; the righteous run to it and are safe. (Proverbs 18:10)

***TAKE** a moment to ask the Lord for the grace to grow in godly character.*

YEAR 2 DAY 285

OT **Ezekiel 43:1–27**

The Glory Returns to the Temple

43 Then the man brought me to the gate
facing east, [2]and I saw the glory of the
God of Israel coming from the east. His
voice was like the roar of rushing waters,
and the land was radiant with his glory.
[3]The vision I saw was like the vision I had
seen when he[a] came to destroy the city
and like the visions I had seen by the Kebar River, and I fell facedown. [4]The glory
of the LORD entered the temple through
the gate facing east. [5]Then the Spirit lifted
me up and brought me into the inner
court, and the glory of the LORD filled the
temple.
[6]While the man was standing beside
me, I heard someone speaking to me from
inside the temple. [7]He said: "Son of man,
this is the place of my throne and the
place for the soles of my feet. This is
where I will live among the Israelites forever. The house of Israel will never again
defile my holy name—neither they nor
their kings—by their prostitution[b] and the
lifeless idols[c] of their kings at their high
places. [8]When they placed their threshold
next to my threshold and their doorposts
beside my doorposts, with only a wall between me and them, they defiled my holy
name by their detestable practices. So I
destroyed them in my anger. [9]Now let
them put away from me their prostitution
and the lifeless idols of their kings, and I
will live among them forever.
[10]"Son of man, describe the temple to
the people of Israel, that they may be
ashamed of their sins. Let them consider
the plan, [11]and if they are ashamed of all
they have done, make known to them the
design of the temple—its arrangement, its
exits and entrances—its whole design and
all its regulations[d] and laws. Write these
down before them so that they may be
faithful to its design and follow all its regulations.
[12]"This is the law of the temple: All the
surrounding area on top of the mountain
will be most holy. Such is the law of the
temple.

The Altar

[13]"These are the measurements of the
altar in long cubits, that cubit being a cubit[e] and a handbreadth[f]: Its gutter is a cubit deep and a cubit wide, with a rim of
one span[g] around the edge. And this is the
height of the altar: [14]From the gutter on
the ground up to the lower ledge it is two
cubits high and a cubit wide, and from the
smaller ledge up to the larger ledge it is
four cubits high and a cubit wide. [15]The
altar hearth is four cubits high, and four
horns project upward from the hearth.
[16]The altar hearth is square, twelve cubits
long and twelve cubits wide. [17]The upper
ledge also is square, fourteen cubits long
and fourteen cubits wide, with a rim of
half a cubit and a gutter of a cubit all
around. The steps of the altar face east."
[18]Then he said to me, "Son of man, this
is what the Sovereign LORD says: These
will be the regulations for sacrificing
burnt offerings and sprinkling blood
upon the altar when it is built: [19]You are
to give a young bull as a sin offering to the
priests, who are Levites, of the family of
Zadok, who come near to minister before
me, declares the Sovereign LORD. [20]You are

[a] *3* Some Hebrew manuscripts and Vulgate; most Hebrew manuscripts *I* [b] *7* Or *their spiritual adultery*; also in verse 9 [c] *7* Or *the corpses*; also in verse 9 [d] *11* Some Hebrew manuscripts and Septuagint; most Hebrew manuscripts *regulations and its whole design* [e] *13* The common cubit was about 1 1/2 feet (about 0.5 meter). [f] *13* That is, about 3 inches (about 8 centimeters) [g] *13* That is, about 9 inches (about 22 centimeters)

to take some of its blood and put it on the four horns of the altar and on the four corners of the upper ledge and all around the rim, and so purify the altar and make atonement for it. [21]You are to take the bull for the sin offering and burn it in the designated part of the temple area outside the sanctuary.

[22]"On the second day you are to offer a male goat without defect for a sin offering, and the altar is to be purified as it was purified with the bull. [23]When you have finished purifying it, you are to offer a young bull and a ram from the flock, both without defect. [24]You are to offer them before the LORD, and the priests are to sprinkle salt on them and sacrifice them as a burnt offering to the LORD.

[25]"For seven days you are to provide a male goat daily for a sin offering; you are also to provide a young bull and a ram from the flock, both without defect. [26]For seven days they are to make atonement for the altar and cleanse it; thus they will dedicate it. [27]At the end of these days, from the eighth day on, the priests are to present your burnt offerings and fellowship offerings[h] on the altar. Then I will accept you, declares the Sovereign LORD."

[h] 27 Traditionally *peace offerings*

PRAYER: AFFIRMATION

YOU order my steps, O Lord, and You will delight in my way; though I stumble, I will not be cast down, for You uphold me with Your hand. (Psalm 37:23–24) . . . Lord, I have made You my refuge, even You, Most High, my habitation. (Psalm 91:9)

PAUSE *to reflect on these Biblical affirmations.*

NT 1 Peter 1:1–12

1 Peter, an apostle of Jesus Christ,

To God's elect, strangers in the world, scattered throughout Pontus, Galatia, Cappadocia, Asia and Bithynia, [2]who have been chosen according to the foreknowledge of God the Father, through the sanctifying work of the Spirit, for obedience to Jesus Christ and sprinkling by his blood:

Grace and peace be yours in abundance.

Praise to God for a Living Hope

[3]Praise be to the God and Father of our Lord Jesus Christ! In his great mercy he has given us new birth into a living hope through the resurrection of Jesus Christ from the dead, [4]and into an inheritance that can never perish, spoil or fade—kept in heaven for you, [5]who through faith are shielded by God's power until the coming of the salvation that is ready to be revealed in the last time. [6]In this you greatly rejoice, though now for a little while you may have had to suffer grief in all kinds of trials. [7]These have come so that your faith—of greater worth than gold, which perishes even though refined by fire—may be proved genuine and may result in praise, glory and honor when Jesus Christ is revealed. [8]Though you have not seen him, you love him; and even though you do not see him now, you believe in him and are filled with an inexpressible and glorious joy, [9]for you are receiving the goal of your faith, the salvation of your souls.

[10]Concerning this salvation, the prophets, who spoke of the grace that was to come to you, searched intently and with the greatest care, [11]trying to find out the time and circumstances to which the Spirit of Christ in them was pointing when he predicted the sufferings of Christ and the glories that would follow. [12]It was revealed to them that they were not serving themselves but you, when they spoke of the things that have now been told you by those who have preached the gospel to you by the Holy Spirit sent from heaven. Even angels long to look into these things.

PRAYER: MY RELATIONSHIP TO OTHERS

WE are always to thank You, God, for other believers, mentioning them in our prayers. (1 Thessalonians 1:2) . . . We should ask for one another's prayers. (1 Thessalonians 5:25)

***PAUSE** to review your relationships with others and to commit them to the Lord.*

YEAR 2
DAY 286

OT Ezekiel 44:1-31

The Prince, the Levites, the Priests

44 Then the man brought me back to
the outer gate of the sanctuary, the
one facing east, and it was shut. 2The LORD
said to me, "This gate is to remain shut. It
must not be opened; no one may enter
through it. It is to remain shut because the
LORD, the God of Israel, has entered
through it. 3The prince himself is the only
one who may sit inside the gateway to eat
in the presence of the LORD. He is to enter by way of the portico of the gateway
and go out the same way."
4Then the man brought me by way of
the north gate to the front of the temple.
I looked and saw the glory of the LORD filling the temple of the LORD, and I fell facedown.
5The LORD said to me, "Son of man,
look carefully, listen closely and give attention to everything I tell you concerning all the regulations regarding the temple of the LORD. Give attention to the
entrance of the temple and all the exits of
the sanctuary. 6Say to the rebellious house
of Israel, 'This is what the Sovereign LORD
says: Enough of your detestable practices,
O house of Israel! 7In addition to all your
other detestable practices, you brought
foreigners uncircumcised in heart and
flesh into my sanctuary, desecrating my
temple while you offered me food, fat and
blood, and you broke my covenant. 8In-
stead of carrying out your duty in regard
to my holy things, you put others in
charge of my sanctuary. 9This is what the
Sovereign LORD says: No foreigner uncircumcised in heart and flesh is to enter my
sanctuary, not even the foreigners who
live among the Israelites.
10" 'The Levites who went far from me
when Israel went astray and who wandered from me after their idols must bear
the consequences of their sin. 11They may
serve in my sanctuary, having charge of
the gates of the temple and serving in it;
they may slaughter the burnt offerings
and sacrifices for the people and stand before the people and serve them. 12But because they served them in the presence of
their idols and made the house of Israel
fall into sin, therefore I have sworn with
uplifted hand that they must bear the consequences of their sin, declares the Sovereign LORD. 13They are not to come near to
serve me as priests or come near any of
my holy things or my most holy offerings;
they must bear the shame of their detestable practices. 14Yet I will put them in
charge of the duties of the temple and all
the work that is to be done in it.
15" 'But the priests, who are Levites and
descendants of Zadok and who faithfully
carried out the duties of my sanctuary
when the Israelites went astray from me,
are to come near to minister before me;
they are to stand before me to offer sacrifices of fat and blood, declares the Sovereign LORD. 16They alone are to enter my
sanctuary; they alone are to come near my
table to minister before me and perform
my service.
17" 'When they enter the gates of the inner court, they are to wear linen clothes;
they must not wear any woolen garment
while ministering at the gates of the inner
court or inside the temple. 18They are to
wear linen turbans on their heads and
linen undergarments around their waists.
They must not wear anything that makes
them perspire. 19When they go out into
the outer court where the people are, they
are to take off the clothes they have been
ministering in and are to leave them in

the sacred rooms, and put on other clothes, so that they do not consecrate the people by means of their garments.

20 " 'They must not shave their heads or let their hair grow long, but they are to keep the hair of their heads trimmed. 21 No priest is to drink wine when he enters the inner court. 22 They must not marry widows or divorced women; they may marry only virgins of Israelite descent or widows of priests. 23 They are to teach my people the difference between the holy and the common and show them how to distinguish between the unclean and the clean.

24 " 'In any dispute, the priests are to serve as judges and decide it according to my ordinances. They are to keep my laws and my decrees for all my appointed feasts, and they are to keep my Sabbaths holy.

25 " 'A priest must not defile himself by going near a dead person; however, if the dead person was his father or mother, son or daughter, brother or unmarried sister, then he may defile himself. 26 After he is cleansed, he must wait seven days. 27 On the day he goes into the inner court of the sanctuary to minister in the sanctuary, he is to offer a sin offering for himself, declares the Sovereign LORD.

28 " 'I am to be the only inheritance the priests have. You are to give them no possession in Israel; I will be their possession. 29 They will eat the grain offerings, the sin offerings and the guilt offerings; and everything in Israel devoted[a] to the LORD will belong to them. 30 The best of all the firstfruits and of all your special gifts will belong to the priests. You are to give them the first portion of your ground meal so that a blessing may rest on your household. 31 The priests must not eat anything, bird or animal, found dead or torn by wild animals.

[a] *29* The Hebrew term refers to the irrevocable giving over of things or persons to the LORD.

PRAYER: THANKSGIVING

YOU have given me life and shown me favor, and Your care has preserved my spirit. (Job 10:12) . . . You are my shield, God Most High; You save the upright in heart. (Psalm 7:10) . . . I will be glad and rejoice in Your love, for You saw my affliction and knew the anguish of my soul. (Psalm 31:7)

PAUSE *to offer your own expressions of thanksgiving.*

NT 1 Peter 1:13–2:3

Be Holy

13 Therefore, prepare your minds for action; be self-controlled; set your hope fully on the grace to be given you when Jesus Christ is revealed. 14 As obedient children, do not conform to the evil desires you had when you lived in ignorance. 15 But just as he who called you is holy, so be holy in all you do; 16 for it is written: "Be holy, because I am holy."[a]

17 Since you call on a Father who judges each man's work impartially, live your lives as strangers here in reverent fear. 18 For you know that it was not with perishable things such as silver or gold that you were redeemed from the empty way of life handed down to you from your forefathers, 19 but with the precious blood of Christ, a lamb without blemish or defect. 20 He was chosen before the creation of the world, but was revealed in these last times for your sake. 21 Through him you believe in God, who raised him from the dead and glorified him, and so your faith and hope are in God.

22 Now that you have purified yourselves by obeying the truth so that you have sincere love for your brothers, love one another deeply, from the heart.[b] 23 For you have been born again, not of perishable seed, but of imperishable, through the living and enduring word of God. 24 For,

"All men are like grass,
    and all their glory is like the flowers
        of the field;
the grass withers and the flowers fall,

[a] *16* Lev. 11:44,45; 19:2; 20:7 [b] *22* Some early manuscripts *from a pure heart*

[25] but the word of the Lord stands
forever."[c]

And this is the word that was preached to you.

2 Therefore, rid yourselves of all malice
and all deceit, hypocrisy, envy, and
slander of every kind. [2]Like newborn babies, crave pure spiritual milk, so that by
it you may grow up in your salvation,
[3]now that you have tasted that the Lord
is good.

[c] 25 Isaiah 40:6–8

PRAYER: THE ATTRIBUTES OF GOD

O SOVEREIGN Lord, You are God! Your words are true, and You have promised good things to Your servant. (2 Samuel 7:28)
. . . You, O Lord, are the Spirit, and where the Spirit of the Lord is, there is freedom. (2 Corinthians 3:17)

***PAUSE** to reflect on these affirmations about the person, powers and perfection of God.*

YEAR 2 DAY 287

OT Psalms 128–129

Psalm 128

A song of ascents.

[1]Blessed are all who fear the LORD,
who walk in his ways.
[2]You will eat the fruit of your labor;
blessings and prosperity will be
yours.
[3]Your wife will be like a fruitful
vine
within your house;
your sons will be like olive shoots
around your table.
[4]Thus is the man blessed
who fears the LORD.

[5]May the LORD bless you from
Zion
all the days of your life;
may you see the prosperity of
Jerusalem,
[6] and may you live to see your
children's children.

Peace be upon Israel.

Psalm 129

A song of ascents.

[1]They have greatly oppressed me from
my youth—
let Israel say—
[2]they have greatly oppressed me from
my youth,
but they have not gained the victory
over me.
[3]Plowmen have plowed my back
and made their furrows long.
[4]But the LORD is righteous;
he has cut me free from the cords of
the wicked.

[5]May all who hate Zion
be turned back in shame.
[6]May they be like grass on the roof,
which withers before it can grow;
[7]with it the reaper cannot fill his hands,
nor the one who gathers fill his arms.
[8]May those who pass by not say,
"The blessing of the LORD be upon
you;
we bless you in the name of the
LORD."

PRAYER: ADORATION

BLESSED be Your name, O God, for ever and ever, for wisdom and power belong to You. You change the times and the seasons; You raise up kings and depose them. You give wisdom to the wise

and knowledge to those who have understanding. You reveal deep and hidden things; You know what is in the darkness, and light dwells with You. (Daniel 2:20–22)

***PAUSE** to express your thoughts of praise and worship.*

NT 1 Peter 2:4–12

The Living Stone and a Chosen People

[4]As you come to him, the living Stone—
rejected by men but chosen by God and
precious to him— [5]you also, like living
stones, are being built into a spiritual house
to be a holy priesthood, offering spiritual
sacrifices acceptable to God through Jesus
Christ. [6]For in Scripture it says:

"See, I lay a stone in Zion,
a chosen and precious cornerstone,
and the one who trusts in him
will never be put to shame."[a]

[7]Now to you who believe, this stone is
precious. But to those who do not believe,

"The stone the builders rejected
has become the capstone,[b]"[c]

[8]and,

"A stone that causes men to stumble
and a rock that makes them fall."[d]

They stumble because they disobey the message—which is also what they were destined for.

[9]But you are a chosen people, a royal
priesthood, a holy nation, a people belonging to God, that you may declare the
praises of him who called you out of darkness into his wonderful light. [10]Once you
were not a people, but now you are the
people of God; once you had not received
mercy, but now you have received mercy.
[11]Dear friends, I urge you, as aliens and
strangers in the world, to abstain from
sinful desires, which war against your
soul. [12]Live such good lives among the pagans that, though they accuse you of doing wrong, they may see your good deeds
and glorify God on the day he visits us.

[a] 6 Isaiah 28:16 [b] 7 Or *cornerstone*
[c] 7 Psalm 118:22 [d] 8 Isaiah 8:14

PRAYER: THE WORKS OF GOD

CHRIST Jesus, You cured many who had diseases, sicknesses, and evil spirits, and gave sight to many who were blind.
So You replied to the messengers sent from John the Baptist, "Go back and report to John what you have seen and heard: The blind receive sight, the lame walk, the lepers are cured, the deaf hear, the dead are raised and the good news is preached to the poor. And blessed is the one who does not fall away on account of Me." (Luke 7:21–23)

***TAKE** a moment to consider the greatness of God's wonderful works.*

YEAR 2 DAY 288

OT Ezekiel 45:1–46:24

Division of the Land

45 " 'When you allot the land as an inheritance, you are to present to the
LORD a portion of the land as a sacred district, 25,000 cubits long and 20,000[a] cubits wide; the entire area will be holy. [2]Of
this, a section 500 cubits square is to be
for the sanctuary, with 50 cubits around it
for open land. [3]In the sacred district, measure off a section 25,000 cubits[b] long and
10,000 cubits[c] wide. In it will be the sanc-

[a] 1 Septuagint (see also verses 3 and 5 and 48:9); Hebrew *10,000* [b] 3 That is, about 7 miles (about 12 kilometers) [c] 3 That is, about 3 miles (about 5 kilometers)

tuary, the Most Holy Place. 4 It will be the sacred portion of the land for the priests, who minister in the sanctuary and who draw near to minister before the LORD. It will be a place for their houses as well as a holy place for the sanctuary. 5 An area 25,000 cubits long and 10,000 cubits wide will belong to the Levites, who serve in the temple, as their possession for towns to live in.[d]

6 " 'You are to give the city as its property an area 5,000 cubits wide and 25,000 cubits long, adjoining the sacred portion; it will belong to the whole house of Israel.

7 " 'The prince will have the land bordering each side of the area formed by the sacred district and the property of the city. It will extend westward from the west side and eastward from the east side, running lengthwise from the western to the eastern border parallel to one of the tribal portions. 8 This land will be his possession in Israel. And my princes will no longer oppress my people but will allow the house of Israel to possess the land according to their tribes.

9 " 'This is what the Sovereign LORD says: You have gone far enough, O princes of Israel! Give up your violence and oppression and do what is just and right. Stop dispossessing my people, declares the Sovereign LORD. 10 You are to use accurate scales, an accurate ephah[e] and an accurate bath.[f] 11 The ephah and the bath are to be the same size, the bath containing a tenth of a homer[g] and the ephah a tenth of a homer; the homer is to be the standard measure for both. 12 The shekel[h] is to consist of twenty gerahs. Twenty shekels plus twenty-five shekels plus fifteen shekels equal one mina.[i]

Offerings and Holy Days

13 " 'This is the special gift you are to offer: a sixth of an ephah from each homer of wheat and a sixth of an ephah from each homer of barley. 14 The prescribed portion of oil, measured by the bath, is a tenth of a bath from each cor (which consists of ten baths or one homer, for ten baths are equivalent to a homer). 15 Also one sheep is to be taken from every flock of two hundred from the well-watered pastures of Israel. These will be used for the grain offerings, burnt offerings and fellowship offerings[j] to make atonement for the people, declares the Sovereign LORD. 16 All the people of the land will participate in this special gift for the use of the prince in Israel. 17 It will be the duty of the prince to provide the burnt offerings, grain offerings and drink offerings at the festivals, the New Moons and the Sabbaths—at all the appointed feasts of the house of Israel. He will provide the sin offerings, grain offerings, burnt offerings and fellowship offerings to make atonement for the house of Israel.

18 " 'This is what the Sovereign LORD says: In the first month on the first day you are to take a young bull without defect and purify the sanctuary. 19 The priest is to take some of the blood of the sin offering and put it on the doorposts of the temple, on the four corners of the upper ledge of the altar and on the gateposts of the inner court. 20 You are to do the same on the seventh day of the month for anyone who sins unintentionally or through ignorance; so you are to make atonement for the temple.

21 " 'In the first month on the fourteenth day you are to observe the Passover, a feast lasting seven days, during which you shall eat bread made without yeast. 22 On that day the prince is to provide a bull as a sin offering for himself and for all the people of the land. 23 Every day during the seven days of the Feast he is to provide seven bulls and seven rams without defect as a burnt offering to the LORD, and a male goat for a sin offering. 24 He is to provide as a grain offering an ephah for each bull and an ephah for each ram, along with a hin[k] of oil for each ephah.

25 " 'During the seven days of the Feast, which begins in the seventh month on the fifteenth day, he is to make the same provision for sin offerings, burnt offerings, grain offerings and oil.

46 " 'This is what the Sovereign LORD says: The gate of the inner court facing east is to be shut on the six working days, but on the Sabbath day and on the day of the New Moon it is to be opened.

[d] 5 Septuagint; Hebrew *temple; they will have as their possession 20 rooms* [e] 10 An ephah was a dry measure. [f] 10 A bath was a liquid measure. [g] 11 A homer was a dry measure. [h] 12 A shekel weighed about 2/5 ounce (about 11.5 grams). [i] 12 That is, 60 shekels; the common mina was 50 shekels. [j] 15 Traditionally *peace offerings;* also in verse 17 [k] 24 That is, probably about 4 quarts (about 4 liters)

[2]The prince is to enter from the outside through the portico of the gateway and stand by the gatepost. The priests are to sacrifice his burnt offering and his fellowship offerings.[l] He is to worship at the threshold of the gateway and then go out, but the gate will not be shut until evening. [3]On the Sabbaths and New Moons the people of the land are to worship in the presence of the LORD at the entrance to that gateway. [4]The burnt offering the prince brings to the LORD on the Sabbath day is to be six male lambs and a ram, all without defect. [5]The grain offering given with the ram is to be an ephah,[m] and the grain offering with the lambs is to be as much as he pleases, along with a hin[n] of oil for each ephah. [6]On the day of the New Moon he is to offer a young bull, six lambs and a ram, all without defect. [7]He is to provide as a grain offering one ephah with the bull, one ephah with the ram, and with the lambs as much as he wants to give, along with a hin of oil with each ephah. [8]When the prince enters, he is to go in through the portico of the gateway, and he is to come out the same way.

[9]" 'When the people of the land come before the LORD at the appointed feasts, whoever enters by the north gate to worship is to go out the south gate; and whoever enters by the south gate is to go out the north gate. No one is to return through the gate by which he entered, but each is to go out the opposite gate. [10]The prince is to be among them, going in when they go in and going out when they go out.

[11]" 'At the festivals and the appointed feasts, the grain offering is to be an ephah with a bull, an ephah with a ram, and with the lambs as much as one pleases, along with a hin of oil for each ephah. [12]When the prince provides a freewill offering to the LORD—whether a burnt offering or fellowship offerings—the gate facing east is to be opened for him. He shall offer his burnt offering or his fellowship offerings as he does on the Sabbath day. Then he shall go out, and after he has gone out, the gate will be shut.

[13]" 'Every day you are to provide a year-old lamb without defect for a burnt offering to the LORD; morning by morning you shall provide it. [14]You are also to provide with it morning by morning a grain offering, consisting of a sixth of an ephah with a third of a hin of oil to moisten the flour. The presenting of this grain offering to the LORD is a lasting ordinance. [15]So the lamb and the grain offering and the oil shall be provided morning by morning for a regular burnt offering.

[16]" 'This is what the Sovereign LORD says: If the prince makes a gift from his inheritance to one of his sons, it will also belong to his descendants; it is to be their property by inheritance. [17]If, however, he makes a gift from his inheritance to one of his servants, the servant may keep it until the year of freedom; then it will revert to the prince. His inheritance belongs to his sons only; it is theirs. [18]The prince must not take any of the inheritance of the people, driving them off their property. He is to give his sons their inheritance out of his own property, so that none of my people will be separated from his property.' "

[19]Then the man brought me through the entrance at the side of the gate to the sacred rooms facing north, which belonged to the priests, and showed me a place at the western end. [20]He said to me, "This is the place where the priests will cook the guilt offering and the sin offering and bake the grain offering, to avoid bringing them into the outer court and consecrating the people."

[21]He then brought me to the outer court and led me around to its four corners, and I saw in each corner another court. [22]In the four corners of the outer court were enclosed[o] courts, forty cubits long and thirty cubits wide; each of the courts in the four corners was the same size. [23]Around the inside of each of the four courts was a ledge of stone, with places for fire built all around under the ledge. [24]He said to me, "These are the kitchens where those who minister at the temple will cook the sacrifices of the people."

[l] *2* Traditionally *peace offerings;* also in verse 12
[m] *5* That is, probably about 3/5 bushel (about 22 liters) [n] *5* That is, probably about 4 quarts (about 4 liters) [o] *22* The meaning of the Hebrew for this word is uncertain.

PRAYER: CONFESSION

BLESSED is the one You discipline, O Lord, the one You teach from Your word. (Psalm 94:12)

***ASK** the Spirit to search your heart and reveal any areas of unconfessed sin. Acknowledge these to the Lord and thank Him for His forgiveness.*

NT 1 Peter 2:13–25

Submission to Rulers and Masters

[13]Submit yourselves for the Lord's sake to every authority instituted among men: whether to the king, as the supreme authority, [14]or to governors, who are sent by him to punish those who do wrong and to commend those who do right. [15]For it is God's will that by doing good you should silence the ignorant talk of foolish men. [16]Live as free men, but do not use your freedom as a cover-up for evil; live as servants of God. [17]Show proper respect to everyone: Love the brotherhood of believers, fear God, honor the king.

[18]Slaves, submit yourselves to your masters with all respect, not only to those who are good and considerate, but also to those who are harsh. [19]For it is commendable if a man bears up under the pain of unjust suffering because he is conscious of God. [20]But how is it to your credit if you receive a beating for doing wrong and endure it? But if you suffer for doing good and you endure it, this is commendable before God. [21]To this you were called, because Christ suffered for you, leaving you an example, that you should follow in his steps.

[22]"He committed no sin,
and no deceit was found in his
mouth."[a]

[23]When they hurled their insults at him, he did not retaliate; when he suffered, he made no threats. Instead, he entrusted himself to him who judges justly. [24]He himself bore our sins in his body on the tree, so that we might die to sins and live for righteousness; by his wounds you have been healed. [25]For you were like sheep going astray, but now you have returned to the Shepherd and Overseer of your souls.

[a] 22 Isaiah 53:9

PRAYER: MY RELATIONSHIP TO GOD

I THANK You, O God, because of Your grace in Christ Jesus. In Him we have been enriched in every way, in all speech and in all knowledge. We do not lack any spiritual gift, as we eagerly wait for the revelation of our Lord Jesus Christ. (1 Corinthians 1:4–5, 7)

***PAUSE** to thank God for the relationship that you enjoy with Him in Jesus Christ.*

YEAR 2
DAY 289

OT Ezekiel 47:1–23

The River From the Temple

47 The man brought me back to the entrance of the temple, and I saw water coming out from under the threshold of the temple toward the east (for the temple faced east). The water was coming down from under the south side of the temple, south of the altar. [2]He then brought me out through the north gate and led me around the outside to the outer gate facing east, and the water was flowing from the south side.

[3]As the man went eastward with a measuring line in his hand, he measured off a

thousand cubits[a] and then led me
through water that was ankle-deep. 4He
measured off another thousand cubits
and led me through water that was knee-
deep. He measured off another thousand
and led me through water that was up to
the waist. 5He measured off another thousand, but now it was a river that I could
not cross, because the water had risen and
was deep enough to swim in—a river that
no one could cross. 6He asked me, "Son
of man, do you see this?"

Then he led me back to the bank of the
river. 7When I arrived there, I saw a great
number of trees on each side of the river.
8He said to me, "This water flows toward
the eastern region and goes down into the
Arabah,[b] where it enters the Sea.[c] When it
empties into the Sea,[c] the water there becomes fresh. 9Swarms of living creatures
will live wherever the river flows. There will
be large numbers of fish, because this water flows there and makes the salt water
fresh; so where the river flows everything
will live. 10Fishermen will stand along the
shore; from En Gedi to En Eglaim there will
be places for spreading nets. The fish will
be of many kinds—like the fish of the Great
Sea.[d] 11But the swamps and marshes will
not become fresh; they will be left for salt.
12Fruit trees of all kinds will grow on both
banks of the river. Their leaves will not
wither, nor will their fruit fail. Every month
they will bear, because the water from the
sanctuary flows to them. Their fruit will
serve for food and their leaves for healing."

The Boundaries of the Land

13This is what the Sovereign LORD says:
"These are the boundaries by which you
are to divide the land for an inheritance
among the twelve tribes of Israel, with two
portions for Joseph. 14You are to divide it
equally among them. Because I swore with
uplifted hand to give it to your forefathers,
this land will become your inheritance.

15"This is to be the boundary of the
land:

"On the north side it will run from the
Great Sea by the Hethlon road past
Lebo[e] Hamath to Zedad, 16Berothah[f]
and Sibraim (which lies on the border between Damascus and Hamath), as far as Hazer Hatticon,
which is on the border of Hauran.
17The boundary will extend from the
sea to Hazar Enan,[g] along the northern border of Damascus, with the
border of Hamath to the north. This
will be the north boundary.

18"On the east side the boundary will run
between Hauran and Damascus,
along the Jordan between Gilead and
the land of Israel, to the eastern sea
and as far as Tamar.[h] This will be the
east boundary.

19"On the south side it will run from Tamar as far as the waters of Meribah
Kadesh, then along the Wadi ⌊of
Egypt⌋ to the Great Sea. This will be
the south boundary.

20"On the west side, the Great Sea will be
the boundary to a point opposite
Lebo[i] Hamath. This will be the west
boundary.

21"You are to distribute this land among
yourselves according to the tribes of Israel. 22You are to allot it as an inheritance
for yourselves and for the aliens who have
settled among you and who have children. You are to consider them as native-
born Israelites; along with you they are to
be allotted an inheritance among the
tribes of Israel. 23In whatever tribe the
alien settles, there you are to give him his
inheritance," declares the Sovereign LORD.

[a] *3* That is, about 1,500 feet (about 450 meters)
[b] *8* Or *the Jordan Valley* [c] *8* That is, the Dead Sea
[d] *10* That is, the Mediterranean; also in verses 15, 19 and 20
[e] *15* Or *past the entrance to*
[f] *15,16* See Septuagint and Ezekiel 48:1; Hebrew *road to go into Zedad, 16Hamath, Berothah*
[g] *17* Hebrew *Enon,* a variant of *Enan*
[h] *18* Septuagint and Syriac; Hebrew *Israel. You will measure to the eastern sea*
[i] *20* Or *opposite the entrance to*

PRAYER: RENEWAL

LIKE Noah, may I do everything just as You, O God, command me. (Genesis 6:22) . . . May I be righteous before You in my generation. (Genesis 7:1)

PAUSE *to add your own prayers for personal renewal.*

NT **1 Peter 3:1–22**

Wives and Husbands

3 Wives, in the same way be submissive
to your husbands so that, if any of
them do not believe the word, they may
be won over without words by the behavior of their wives, 2 when they see the purity and reverence of your lives. 3 Your
beauty should not come from outward
adornment, such as braided hair and the
wearing of gold jewelry and fine clothes.
4 Instead, it should be that of your inner
self, the unfading beauty of a gentle and
quiet spirit, which is of great worth in
God's sight. 5 For this is the way the holy
women of the past who put their hope in
God used to make themselves beautiful.
They were submissive to their own husbands, 6 like Sarah, who obeyed Abraham
and called him her master. You are her
daughters if you do what is right and do
not give way to fear.
7 Husbands, in the same way be considerate as you live with your wives, and treat
them with respect as the weaker partner
and as heirs with you of the gracious gift
of life, so that nothing will hinder your
prayers.

Suffering for Doing Good

8 Finally, all of you, live in harmony
with one another; be sympathetic, love as
brothers, be compassionate and humble.
9 Do not repay evil with evil or insult with
insult, but with blessing, because to this
you were called so that you may inherit a
blessing. 10 For,

"Whoever would love life
and see good days
must keep his tongue from evil
and his lips from deceitful speech.
11 He must turn from evil and do good;
he must seek peace and pursue it.
12 For the eyes of the Lord are on the
righteous
and his ears are attentive to their
prayer,
but the face of the Lord is against
those who do evil."[a]

13 Who is going to harm you if you are
eager to do good? 14 But even if you
should suffer for what is right, you are
blessed. "Do not fear what they fear[b]; do
not be frightened."[c] 15 But in your hearts
set apart Christ as Lord. Always be prepared to give an answer to everyone who
asks you to give the reason for the hope
that you have. But do this with gentleness
and respect, 16 keeping a clear conscience,
so that those who speak maliciously
against your good behavior in Christ may
be ashamed of their slander. 17 It is better,
if it is God's will, to suffer for doing good
than for doing evil. 18 For Christ died for
sins once for all, the righteous for the unrighteous, to bring you to God. He was
put to death in the body but made alive
by the Spirit, 19 through whom[d] also he
went and preached to the spirits in prison
20 who disobeyed long ago when God
waited patiently in the days of Noah
while the ark was being built. In it only a
few people, eight in all, were saved
through water, 21 and this water symbolizes baptism that now saves you also—
not the removal of dirt from the body but
the pledge[e] of a good conscience toward
God. It saves you by the resurrection of
Jesus Christ, 22 who has gone into heaven
and is at God's right hand—with angels,
authorities and powers in submission to
him.

[a] 12 Psalm 34:12–16 [b] 14 Or *not fear their threats* [c] 14 Isaiah 8:12 [d] 18,19 Or *alive in the spirit, 19through which* [e] 21 Or *response*

PRAYER: THE CHARACTER I WANT TO CULTIVATE

I WILL take heed not to practice my righteousness before others to be seen by them. Otherwise, I will have no reward from You, my Father in heaven. (Matthew 6:1) . . . I want to be more concerned about the things of You, O God, than human things. (Mark 8:33)

***TAKE** a moment to ask the Lord for the grace to grow in godly character.*

OT **Ezekiel 48:1-35** YEAR 2 DAY 290

The Division of the Land

48 "These are the tribes, listed by name:
At the northern frontier, Dan will
have one portion; it will follow the Hethlon road to Lebo[a] Hamath; Hazar Enan
and the northern border of Damascus
next to Hamath will be part of its border
from the east side to the west side.
2 "Asher will have one portion; it will
border the territory of Dan from east to
west.
3 "Naphtali will have one portion; it will
border the territory of Asher from east to
west.
4 "Manasseh will have one portion; it
will border the territory of Naphtali from
east to west.
5 "Ephraim will have one portion; it will
border the territory of Manasseh from east
to west.
6 "Reuben will have one portion; it will
border the territory of Ephraim from east
to west.
7 "Judah will have one portion; it will
border the territory of Reuben from east
to west.
8 "Bordering the territory of Judah from
east to west will be the portion you are to
present as a special gift. It will be 25,000
cubits[b] wide, and its length from east to
west will equal one of the tribal portions;
the sanctuary will be in the center of it.
9 "The special portion you are to offer to
the LORD will be 25,000 cubits long and
10,000 cubits[c] wide. 10 This will be the
sacred portion for the priests. It will
be 25,000 cubits long on the north side,
10,000 cubits wide on the west side,
10,000 cubits wide on the east side and
25,000 cubits long on the south side. In
the center of it will be the sanctuary of the
LORD. 11 This will be for the consecrated
priests, the Zadokites, who were faithful
in serving me and did not go astray as the
Levites did when the Israelites went astray.
12 It will be a special gift to them from the
sacred portion of the land, a most holy
portion, bordering the territory of the Levites.
13 "Alongside the territory of the priests,
the Levites will have an allotment 25,000
cubits long and 10,000 cubits wide. Its total length will be 25,000 cubits and its
width 10,000 cubits. 14 They must not sell
or exchange any of it. This is the best of
the land and must not pass into other
hands, because it is holy to the LORD.
15 "The remaining area, 5,000 cubits
wide and 25,000 cubits long, will be for
the common use of the city, for houses
and for pastureland. The city will be in the
center of it 16 and will have these measurements: the north side 4,500 cubits,
the south side 4,500 cubits, the east side
4,500 cubits, and the west side 4,500 cubits. 17 The pastureland for the city will be
250 cubits on the north, 250 cubits on the
south, 250 cubits on the east, and 250 cubits on the west. 18 What remains of the
area, bordering on the sacred portion and
running the length of it, will be 10,000 cubits on the east side and 10,000 cubits on
the west side. Its produce will supply food
for the workers of the city. 19 The workers
from the city who farm it will come from
all the tribes of Israel. 20 The entire portion
will be a square, 25,000 cubits on each
side. As a special gift you will set aside the
sacred portion, along with the property of
the city.
21 "What remains on both sides of the
area formed by the sacred portion and the
city property will belong to the prince. It
will extend eastward from the 25,000 cubits of the sacred portion to the eastern
border, and westward from the 25,000 cubits to the western border. Both these areas running the length of the tribal portions will belong to the prince, and the
sacred portion with the temple sanctuary
will be in the center of them. 22 So the
property of the Levites and the property
of the city will lie in the center of the area
that belongs to the prince. The area belonging to the prince will lie between the
border of Judah and the border of Benjamin.
23 "As for the rest of the tribes: Benjamin
will have one portion; it will extend from
the east side to the west side.
24 "Simeon will have one portion; it will
border the territory of Benjamin from east
to west.

[a] *1* Or *to the entrance to* (about 12 kilometers) [b] *8* That is, about 7 miles (about 12 kilometers) [c] *9* That is, about 3 miles (about 5 kilometers)

25 "Issachar will have one portion; it will
border the territory of Simeon from east
to west.
26 "Zebulun will have one portion; it
will border the territory of Issachar from
east to west.
27 "Gad will have one portion; it will
border the territory of Zebulun from east
to west.
28 "The southern boundary of Gad will
run south from Tamar to the waters of
Meribah Kadesh, then along the Wadi ⌊of
Egypt⌋ to the Great Sea.[d]
29 "This is the land you are to allot as an
inheritance to the tribes of Israel, and
these will be their portions," declares the
Sovereign LORD.

The Gates of the City

30 "These will be the exits of the city: Beginning on the north side, which is 4,500
cubits long, 31 the gates of the city will be
named after the tribes of Israel. The three
gates on the north side will be the gate of
Reuben, the gate of Judah and the gate of
Levi.
32 "On the east side, which is 4,500 cubits long, will be three gates: the gate of
Joseph, the gate of Benjamin and the gate
of Dan.
33 "On the south side, which measures
4,500 cubits, will be three gates: the gate
of Simeon, the gate of Issachar and the
gate of Zebulun.
34 "On the west side, which is 4,500 cubits long, will be three gates: the gate of
Gad, the gate of Asher and the gate of
Naphtali.
35 "The distance all around will be
18,000 cubits.

"And the name of the city from that
time on will be:

THE LORD IS THERE."

[d] 28 That is, the Mediterranean

PRAYER: PETITION

BY Your grace, O God, may I not despise my birthright for the things of this world. (Genesis 25:33–34)

PAUSE *here to petition God for spiritual insight so that you might have understanding of His Word. Ask for insight into your identity in Jesus Christ; that you might know who you are, what direction your life should take and what His purpose for your life is. Offer prayers regarding your activities for this day and any special concerns you may have.*

NT 1 Peter 4:1-19

Living for God

4 Therefore, since Christ suffered in his
body, arm yourselves also with the
same attitude, because he who has suffered in his body is done with sin. 2 As a
result, he does not live the rest of his
earthly life for evil human desires, but
rather for the will of God. 3 For you have
spent enough time in the past doing what
pagans choose to do—living in debauchery, lust, drunkenness, orgies, carousing
and detestable idolatry. 4 They think it
strange that you do not plunge with them
into the same flood of dissipation, and
they heap abuse on you. 5 But they will
have to give account to him who is ready
to judge the living and the dead. 6 For this
is the reason the gospel was preached
even to those who are now dead, so that
they might be judged according to men in
regard to the body, but live according to
God in regard to the spirit.
7 The end of all things is near. Therefore
be clear minded and self-controlled so
that you can pray. 8 Above all, love each
other deeply, because love covers over a
multitude of sins. 9 Offer hospitality to
one another without grumbling. 10 Each
one should use whatever gift he has received to serve others, faithfully administering God's grace in its various forms. 11 If
anyone speaks, he should do it as one
speaking the very words of God. If anyone
serves, he should do it with the strength
God provides, so that in all things God
may be praised through Jesus Christ. To

him be the glory and the power for ever and ever. Amen.

Suffering for Being a Christian

[12]Dear friends, do not be surprised at the painful trial you are suffering, as though something strange were happening to you. [13]But rejoice that you participate in the sufferings of Christ, so that you may be overjoyed when his glory is revealed. [14]If you are insulted because of the name of Christ, you are blessed, for the Spirit of glory and of God rests on you. [15]If you suffer, it should not be as a murderer or thief or any other kind of criminal, or even as a meddler. [16]However, if you suffer as a Christian, do not be ashamed, but praise God that you bear that name. [17]For it is time for judgment to begin with the family of God; and if it begins with us, what will the outcome be for those who do not obey the gospel of God? [18]And,

"If it is hard for the righteous to be
saved,
what will become of the ungodly
and the sinner?"[a]

[19]So then, those who suffer according to God's will should commit themselves to their faithful Creator and continue to do good.

[a] *18* Prov. 11:31

PRAYER: MY RELATIONSHIP TO OTHERS

I PRAY that words may be given to me, that I may open my mouth boldly to make known the mystery of the gospel. (Ephesians 6:19) . . . I pray that You, O God, may open to me a door for the word, so that I may speak the mystery of Christ and proclaim it clearly, as I ought. (Colossians 4:3–4)

***PAUSE** to review your relationships with others and to commit them to the Lord.*

YEAR 2
DAY 291

OT Daniel 1:1–2:49

Daniel's Training in Babylon

1 In the third year of the reign of Jehoiakim king of Judah, Nebuchadnezzar king of Babylon came to Jerusalem and besieged it. [2]And the Lord delivered Jehoiakim king of Judah into his hand, along with some of the articles from the temple of God. These he carried off to the temple of his god in Babylonia[a] and put in the treasure house of his god.

[3]Then the king ordered Ashpenaz, chief of his court officials, to bring in some of the Israelites from the royal family and the nobility— [4]young men without any physical defect, handsome, showing aptitude for every kind of learning, well informed, quick to understand, and qualified to serve in the king's palace. He was to teach them the language and literature of the Babylonians.[b] [5]The king assigned them a daily amount of food and wine from the king's table. They were to be trained for three years, and after that they were to enter the king's service.

[6]Among these were some from Judah: Daniel, Hananiah, Mishael and Azariah. [7]The chief official gave them new names: to Daniel, the name Belteshazzar; to Hananiah, Shadrach; to Mishael, Meshach; and to Azariah, Abednego.

[8]But Daniel resolved not to defile himself with the royal food and wine, and he asked the chief official for permission not to defile himself this way. [9]Now God had caused the official to show favor and sympathy to Daniel, [10]but the official told Daniel, "I am afraid of my lord the king, who has assigned your[c] food and drink. Why should he see you looking worse than the other young men your age? The

[a] *2* Hebrew *Shinar* [b] *4* Or *Chaldeans* [c] *10* The Hebrew for *your* and *you* in this verse is plural.

king would then have my head because of you."

[11]Daniel then said to the guard whom the chief official had appointed over Daniel, Hananiah, Mishael and Azariah, [12]"Please test your servants for ten days: Give us nothing but vegetables to eat and water to drink. [13]Then compare our appearance with that of the young men who eat the royal food, and treat your servants in accordance with what you see." [14]So he agreed to this and tested them for ten days.

[15]At the end of the ten days they looked healthier and better nourished than any of the young men who ate the royal food. [16]So the guard took away their choice food and the wine they were to drink and gave them vegetables instead.

[17]To these four young men God gave knowledge and understanding of all kinds of literature and learning. And Daniel could understand visions and dreams of all kinds.

[18]At the end of the time set by the king to bring them in, the chief official presented them to Nebuchadnezzar. [19]The king talked with them, and he found none equal to Daniel, Hananiah, Mishael and Azariah; so they entered the king's service. [20]In every matter of wisdom and understanding about which the king questioned them, he found them ten times better than all the magicians and enchanters in his whole kingdom.

[21]And Daniel remained there until the first year of King Cyrus.

Nebuchadnezzar's Dream

2 In the second year of his reign, Nebuchadnezzar had dreams; his mind was troubled and he could not sleep. [2]So the king summoned the magicians, enchanters, sorcerers and astrologers[d] to tell him what he had dreamed. When they came in and stood before the king, [3]he said to them, "I have had a dream that troubles me and I want to know what it means.[e]"

[4]Then the astrologers answered the king in Aramaic,[f] "O king, live forever! Tell your servants the dream, and we will interpret it."

[5]The king replied to the astrologers, "This is what I have firmly decided: If you do not tell me what my dream was and interpret it, I will have you cut into pieces and your houses turned into piles of rubble. [6]But if you tell me the dream and explain it, you will receive from me gifts and rewards and great honor. So tell me the dream and interpret it for me."

[7]Once more they replied, "Let the king tell his servants the dream, and we will interpret it."

[8]Then the king answered, "I am certain that you are trying to gain time, because you realize that this is what I have firmly decided: [9]If you do not tell me the dream, there is just one penalty for you. You have conspired to tell me misleading and wicked things, hoping the situation will change. So then, tell me the dream, and I will know that you can interpret it for me."

[10]The astrologers answered the king, "There is not a man on earth who can do what the king asks! No king, however great and mighty, has ever asked such a thing of any magician or enchanter or astrologer. [11]What the king asks is too difficult. No one can reveal it to the king except the gods, and they do not live among men."

[12]This made the king so angry and furious that he ordered the execution of all the wise men of Babylon. [13]So the decree was issued to put the wise men to death, and men were sent to look for Daniel and his friends to put them to death.

[14]When Arioch, the commander of the king's guard, had gone out to put to death the wise men of Babylon, Daniel spoke to him with wisdom and tact. [15]He asked the king's officer, "Why did the king issue such a harsh decree?" Arioch then explained the matter to Daniel. [16]At this, Daniel went in to the king and asked for time, so that he might interpret the dream for him.

[17]Then Daniel returned to his house and explained the matter to his friends Hananiah, Mishael and Azariah. [18]He urged them to plead for mercy from the God of heaven concerning this mystery, so that he and his friends might not be executed with the rest of the wise men of Babylon. [19]During the night the mystery was revealed to Daniel in a vision. Then

[d] 2 Or *Chaldeans;* also in verses 4, 5 and 10 [e] 3 Or *was* [f] 4 The text from here through chapter 7 is in Aramaic.

Daniel praised the God of heaven 20and
said:

"Praise be to the name of God for ever
and ever;
wisdom and power are his.
21He changes times and seasons;
he sets up kings and deposes them.
He gives wisdom to the wise
and knowledge to the discerning.
22He reveals deep and hidden things;
he knows what lies in darkness,
and light dwells with him.
23I thank and praise you, O God of my
fathers:
You have given me wisdom and
power,
you have made known to me what we
asked of you,
you have made known to us the
dream of the king."

Daniel Interprets the Dream

24Then Daniel went to Arioch, whom
the king had appointed to execute the
wise men of Babylon, and said to him,
"Do not execute the wise men of Babylon.
Take me to the king, and I will interpret
his dream for him."
25Arioch took Daniel to the king at once
and said, "I have found a man among the
exiles from Judah who can tell the king
what his dream means."
26The king asked Daniel (also called
Belteshazzar), "Are you able to tell me
what I saw in my dream and interpret it?"
27Daniel replied, "No wise man, enchanter, magician or diviner can explain
to the king the mystery he has asked
about, 28but there is a God in heaven who
reveals mysteries. He has shown King
Nebuchadnezzar what will happen in
days to come. Your dream and the visions
that passed through your mind as you lay
on your bed are these:
29"As you were lying there, O king, your
mind turned to things to come, and the
revealer of mysteries showed you what is
going to happen. 30As for me, this mystery
has been revealed to me, not because I
have greater wisdom than other living
men, but so that you, O king, may know
the interpretation and that you may understand what went through your mind.
31"You looked, O king, and there before
you stood a large statue—an enormous,
dazzling statue, awesome in appearance.
32The head of the statue was made of pure
gold, its chest and arms of silver, its belly
and thighs of bronze, 33its legs of iron, its
feet partly of iron and partly of baked clay.
34While you were watching, a rock was cut
out, but not by human hands. It struck
the statue on its feet of iron and clay and
smashed them. 35Then the iron, the clay,
the bronze, the silver and the gold were
broken to pieces at the same time and became like chaff on a threshing floor in the
summer. The wind swept them away without leaving a trace. But the rock that struck
the statue became a huge mountain and
filled the whole earth.
36"This was the dream, and now we will
interpret it to the king. 37You, O king, are
the king of kings. The God of heaven has
given you dominion and power and
might and glory; 38in your hands he has
placed mankind and the beasts of the
field and the birds of the air. Wherever
they live, he has made you ruler over them
all. You are that head of gold.
39"After you, another kingdom will rise,
inferior to yours. Next, a third kingdom,
one of bronze, will rule over the whole
earth. 40Finally, there will be a fourth kingdom, strong as iron—for iron breaks and
smashes everything—and as iron breaks
things to pieces, so it will crush and break
all the others. 41Just as you saw that the
feet and toes were partly of baked clay and
partly of iron, so this will be a divided
kingdom; yet it will have some of the
strength of iron in it, even as you saw iron
mixed with clay. 42As the toes were partly
iron and partly clay, so this kingdom will
be partly strong and partly brittle. 43And
just as you saw the iron mixed with baked
clay, so the people will be a mixture and
will not remain united, any more than
iron mixes with clay.
44"In the time of those kings, the God
of heaven will set up a kingdom that will
never be destroyed, nor will it be left to
another people. It will crush all those
kingdoms and bring them to an end, but
it will itself endure forever. 45This is the
meaning of the vision of the rock cut out
of a mountain, but not by human
hands—a rock that broke the iron, the
bronze, the clay, the silver and the gold to
pieces.
"The great God has shown the king
what will take place in the future. The

dream is true and the interpretation is
trustworthy."
46 Then King Nebuchadnezzar fell prostrate before Daniel and paid him honor
and ordered that an offering and incense
be presented to him. 47 The king said to
Daniel, "Surely your God is the God of
gods and the Lord of kings and a revealer
of mysteries, for you were able to reveal
this mystery."
48 Then the king placed Daniel in a
high position and lavished many gifts on
him. He made him ruler over the entire
province of Babylon and placed him in
charge of all its wise men. 49 Moreover, at
Daniel's request the king appointed Shadrach, Meshach and Abednego administrators over the province of Babylon,
while Daniel himself remained at the
royal court.

PRAYER: INTERCESSION

MY soul waits silently for You alone, O God, for my hope comes from You. You alone are my rock and my salvation; You are my fortress, I will not be shaken. In You are my salvation and my glory; my rock of strength, my refuge is in You. O, that others, too, will trust in You at all times and pour out their hearts before You; You are our refuge.

(Psalm 62:5–8)

TAKE *a few moments to intercede on behalf of other believers, such as your personal friends, those in ministry and those who are oppressed and in need.*

NT 1 Peter 5:1–14

To Elders and Young Men

5 To the elders among you, I appeal as a
fellow elder, a witness of Christ's sufferings and one who also will share in the
glory to be revealed: 2 Be shepherds of
God's flock that is under your care, serving as overseers—not because you must,
but because you are willing, as God wants
you to be; not greedy for money, but eager to serve; 3 not lording it over those entrusted to you, but being examples to the
flock. 4 And when the Chief Shepherd appears, you will receive the crown of glory
that will never fade away.
5 Young men, in the same way be submissive to those who are older. All of you,
clothe yourselves with humility toward
one another, because,

"God opposes the proud
but gives grace to the humble."[a]

6 Humble yourselves, therefore, under
God's mighty hand, that he may lift you
up in due time. 7 Cast all your anxiety on
him because he cares for you.
8 Be self-controlled and alert. Your enemy the devil prowls around like a roaring
lion looking for someone to devour. 9 Resist him, standing firm in the faith, because you know that your brothers
throughout the world are undergoing the
same kind of sufferings.
10 And the God of all grace, who called
you to his eternal glory in Christ, after you
have suffered a little while, will himself restore you and make you strong, firm and
steadfast. 11 To him be the power for ever
and ever. Amen.

Final Greetings

12 With the help of Silas,[b] whom I regard
as a faithful brother, I have written to you
briefly, encouraging you and testifying
that this is the true grace of God. Stand
fast in it.
13 She who is in Babylon, chosen together with you, sends you her greetings,
and so does my son Mark. 14 Greet one another with a kiss of love.
Peace to all of you who are in Christ.

[a] 5 Prov. 3:34 [b] 12 Greek *Silvanus,* a variant of *Silas*

PRAYER: THE ATTRIBUTES OF GOD

YOU are the righteous God, who searches my heart and secret thoughts. (Psalm 7:9) . . . What I do may seem right to me, but You, Lord, know what I am thinking. (Proverbs 21:2)

***PAUSE** to reflect on these affirmations about the person, powers and perfection of God.*

YEAR 2 DAY 292

OT Daniel 3:1-30

The Image of Gold and the Fiery Furnace

3 King Nebuchadnezzar made an image of gold, ninety feet high and nine feet[a] wide, and set it up on the plain of Dura in the province of Babylon. 2He then summoned the satraps, prefects, governors, advisers, treasurers, judges, magistrates and all the other provincial officials to come to the dedication of the image he had set up. 3So the satraps, prefects, governors, advisers, treasurers, judges, magistrates and all the other provincial officials assembled for the dedication of the image that King Nebuchadnezzar had set up, and they stood before it.

4Then the herald loudly proclaimed, "This is what you are commanded to do, O peoples, nations and men of every language: 5As soon as you hear the sound of the horn, flute, zither, lyre, harp, pipes and all kinds of music, you must fall down and worship the image of gold that King Nebuchadnezzar has set up. 6Whoever does not fall down and worship will immediately be thrown into a blazing furnace."

7Therefore, as soon as they heard the sound of the horn, flute, zither, lyre, harp and all kinds of music, all the peoples, nations and men of every language fell down and worshiped the image of gold that King Nebuchadnezzar had set up.

8At this time some astrologers[b] came forward and denounced the Jews. 9They said to King Nebuchadnezzar, "O king, live forever! 10You have issued a decree, O king, that everyone who hears the sound of the horn, flute, zither, lyre, harp, pipes and all kinds of music must fall down and worship the image of gold, 11and that whoever does not fall down and worship will be thrown into a blazing furnace. 12But there are some Jews whom you have set over the affairs of the province of Babylon—Shadrach, Meshach and Abednego—who pay no attention to you, O king. They neither serve your gods nor worship the image of gold you have set up."

13Furious with rage, Nebuchadnezzar summoned Shadrach, Meshach and Abednego. So these men were brought before the king, 14and Nebuchadnezzar said to them, "Is it true, Shadrach, Meshach and Abednego, that you do not serve my gods or worship the image of gold I have set up? 15Now when you hear the sound of the horn, flute, zither, lyre, harp, pipes and all kinds of music, if you are ready to fall down and worship the image I made, very good. But if you do not worship it, you will be thrown immediately into a blazing furnace. Then what god will be able to rescue you from my hand?"

16Shadrach, Meshach and Abednego replied to the king, "O Nebuchadnezzar, we do not need to defend ourselves before you in this matter. 17If we are thrown into the blazing furnace, the God we serve is able to save us from it, and he will rescue us from your hand, O king. 18But even if he does not, we want you to know, O king, that we will not serve your gods or worship the image of gold you have set up."

19Then Nebuchadnezzar was furious with Shadrach, Meshach and Abednego, and his attitude toward them changed. He ordered the furnace heated seven times hotter than usual 20and commanded some of the strongest soldiers in his army to tie up Shadrach, Meshach and Abednego and throw them into the blazing furnace. 21So these men, wearing their robes, trousers, turbans and other clothes, were bound and thrown into the blazing fur-

[a] *1* Aramaic *sixty cubits high and six cubits wide* (about 27 meters high and 2.7 meters wide)
[b] *8* Or *Chaldeans*

nace. 22The king's command was so urgent and the furnace so hot that the flames of the fire killed the soldiers who took up Shadrach, Meshach and Abednego, 23and these three men, firmly tied, fell into the blazing furnace.

24Then King Nebuchadnezzar leaped to his feet in amazement and asked his advisers, "Weren't there three men that we tied up and threw into the fire?"

They replied, "Certainly, O king."

25He said, "Look! I see four men walking around in the fire, unbound and unharmed, and the fourth looks like a son of the gods."

26Nebuchadnezzar then approached the opening of the blazing furnace and shouted, "Shadrach, Meshach and Abednego, servants of the Most High God, come out! Come here!"

So Shadrach, Meshach and Abednego came out of the fire, 27and the satraps, prefects, governors and royal advisers crowded around them. They saw that the fire had not harmed their bodies, nor was a hair of their heads singed; their robes were not scorched, and there was no smell of fire on them.

28Then Nebuchadnezzar said, "Praise be to the God of Shadrach, Meshach and Abednego, who has sent his angel and rescued his servants! They trusted in him and defied the king's command and were willing to give up their lives rather than serve or worship any god except their own God. 29Therefore I decree that the people of any nation or language who say anything against the God of Shadrach, Meshach and Abednego be cut into pieces and their houses be turned into piles of rubble, for no other god can save in this way."

30Then the king promoted Shadrach, Meshach and Abednego in the province of Babylon.

PRAYER: AFFIRMATION

THE word is very near me; it is in my mouth and in my heart, so that I may obey it. Your words are not just idle words for me—they are my life. (Deuteronomy 30:14; 32:47) How can a young man keep his way pure? By keeping it according to Your word. (Psalm 119:9)

***PAUSE** to reflect on these Biblical affirmations.*

NT 2 Peter 1:1-11

1 Simon Peter, a servant and apostle of Jesus Christ,

To those who through the righteousness of our God and Savior Jesus Christ have received a faith as precious as ours:

2Grace and peace be yours in abundance through the knowledge of God and of Jesus our Lord.

Making One's Calling and Election Sure

3His divine power has given us everything we need for life and godliness through our knowledge of him who called us by his own glory and goodness. 4Through these he has given us his very great and precious promises, so that through them you may participate in the divine nature and escape the corruption in the world caused by evil desires.

5For this very reason, make every effort to add to your faith goodness; and to goodness, knowledge; 6and to knowledge, self-control; and to self-control, perseverance; and to perseverance, godliness; 7and to godliness, brotherly kindness; and to brotherly kindness, love. 8For if you possess these qualities in increasing measure, they will keep you from being ineffective and unproductive in your knowledge of our Lord Jesus Christ. 9But if anyone does not have them, he is nearsighted and blind, and has forgotten that he has been cleansed from his past sins.

10Therefore, my brothers, be all the more eager to make your calling and election sure. For if you do these things, you will never fall, 11and you will receive a rich welcome into the eternal kingdom of our Lord and Savior Jesus Christ.

PRAYER: THE WORKS OF GOD

LORD, You confirmed that Abraham would surely become a great and powerful nation, and all nations on earth would be blessed through him. (Genesis 18:18) . . . Lord, You said to Abraham, "By Myself I have sworn, that because you have not withheld your son, your only son, I will surely bless you and make your descendants as numerous as the stars in the sky and as the sand on the seashore. Your descendants will take possession of the cities of their enemies, and through your offspring all nations on earth will be blessed, because you have obeyed My voice." (Genesis 22:16–18)

TAKE *a moment to consider the greatness of God's wonderful works.*

YEAR 2 DAY 293

OT Daniel 4:1–37

Nebuchadnezzar's Dream of a Tree

4 King Nebuchadnezzar,

To the peoples, nations and men of every language, who live in all the world:

May you prosper greatly!

2 It is my pleasure to tell you about the miraculous signs and wonders that the Most High God has performed for me.

3 How great are his signs,
how mighty his wonders!
His kingdom is an eternal kingdom;
his dominion endures from generation to generation.

4 I, Nebuchadnezzar, was at home in my palace, contented and prosperous. 5 I had a dream that made me afraid. As I was lying in my bed, the images and visions that passed through my mind terrified me. 6 So I commanded that all the wise men of Babylon be brought before me to interpret the dream for me. 7 When the magicians, enchanters, astrologers[a] and diviners came, I told them the dream, but they could not interpret it for me. 8 Finally, Daniel came into my presence and I told him the dream. (He is called Belteshazzar, after the name of my god, and the spirit of the holy gods is in him.)

9 I said, "Belteshazzar, chief of the magicians, I know that the spirit of the holy gods is in you, and no mystery is too difficult for you. Here is my dream; interpret it for me. 10 These are the visions I saw while lying in my bed: I looked, and there before me stood a tree in the middle of the land. Its height was enormous. 11 The tree grew large and strong and its top touched the sky; it was visible to the ends of the earth. 12 Its leaves were beautiful, its fruit abundant, and on it was food for all. Under it the beasts of the field found shelter, and the birds of the air lived in its branches; from it every creature was fed.

13 "In the visions I saw while lying in my bed, I looked, and there before me was a messenger,[b] a holy one, coming down from heaven. 14 He called in a loud voice: 'Cut down the tree and trim off its branches; strip off its leaves and scatter its fruit. Let the animals flee from under it and the birds from its branches. 15 But let the stump and its roots, bound with iron and bronze, remain in the ground, in the grass of the field.

" 'Let him be drenched with the dew of heaven, and let him live with the animals among the plants of the earth. 16 Let his mind be changed from that of a man and let him be given the mind of an animal, till seven times[c] pass by for him.

17 " 'The decision is announced by

[a] 7 Or *Chaldeans* [b] 13 Or *watchman;* also in verses 17 and 23 [c] 16 Or *years;* also in verses 23, 25 and 32

messengers, the holy ones declare the
verdict, so that the living may know
that the Most High is sovereign over
the kingdoms of men and gives them
to anyone he wishes and sets over
them the lowliest of men.'
18 "This is the dream that I, King
Nebuchadnezzar, had. Now, Belteshazzar, tell me what it means, for
none of the wise men in my kingdom can interpret it for me. But you
can, because the spirit of the holy
gods is in you."

Daniel Interprets the Dream

19 Then Daniel (also called Belteshazzar) was greatly perplexed for a
time, and his thoughts terrified him.
So the king said, "Belteshazzar, do
not let the dream or its meaning
alarm you."
Belteshazzar answered, "My lord, if
only the dream applied to your enemies and its meaning to your adversaries! 20 The tree you saw, which grew
large and strong, with its top touching the sky, visible to the whole earth,
21 with beautiful leaves and abundant
fruit, providing food for all, giving
shelter to the beasts of the field, and
having nesting places in its branches
for the birds of the air — 22 you,
O king, are that tree! You have become great and strong; your greatness
has grown until it reaches the sky,
and your dominion extends to distant parts of the earth.
23 "You, O king, saw a messenger, a
holy one, coming down from heaven
and saying, 'Cut down the tree and
destroy it, but leave the stump,
bound with iron and bronze, in the
grass of the field, while its roots remain in the ground. Let him be
drenched with the dew of heaven; let
him live like the wild animals, until
seven times pass by for him.'
24 "This is the interpretation, O king,
and this is the decree the Most High has
issued against my lord the king: 25 You
will be driven away from people and
will live with the wild animals; you will
eat grass like cattle and be drenched
with the dew of heaven. Seven times
will pass by for you until you acknowledge that the Most High is sovereign
over the kingdoms of men and gives
them to anyone he wishes. 26 The command to leave the stump of the tree
with its roots means that your kingdom
will be restored to you when you acknowledge that Heaven rules. 27 Therefore, O king, be pleased to accept my advice: Renounce your sins by doing what
is right, and your wickedness by being
kind to the oppressed. It may be that
then your prosperity will continue."

The Dream Is Fulfilled

28 All this happened to King Nebuchadnezzar. 29 Twelve months later, as
the king was walking on the roof of
the royal palace of Babylon, 30 he said,
"Is not this the great Babylon I have
built as the royal residence, by my
mighty power and for the glory of my
majesty?"
31 The words were still on his lips
when a voice came from heaven,
"This is what is decreed for you, King
Nebuchadnezzar: Your royal authority has been taken from you. 32 You will
be driven away from people and will
live with the wild animals; you
will eat grass like cattle. Seven times
will pass by for you until you acknowledge that the Most High is sovereign over the kingdoms of men and
gives them to anyone he wishes."
33 Immediately what had been said
about Nebuchadnezzar was fulfilled.
He was driven away from people and
ate grass like cattle. His body was
drenched with the dew of heaven until his hair grew like the feathers of an
eagle and his nails like the claws of a
bird.

34 At the end of that time, I, Nebuchadnezzar, raised my eyes toward
heaven, and my sanity was restored.
Then I praised the Most High; I honored and glorified him who lives forever.

His dominion is an eternal dominion;
his kingdom endures from
generation to generation.
35 All the peoples of the earth
are regarded as nothing.
He does as he pleases
with the powers of heaven
and the peoples of the earth.

No one can hold back his hand
or say to him: "What have you
done?"

[36]At the same time that my sanity
was restored, my honor and splendor
were returned to me for the glory of
my kingdom. My advisers and nobles
sought me out, and I was restored to
my throne and became even greater
than before. [37]Now I, Nebuchadnezzar, praise and exalt and glorify the
King of heaven, because everything
he does is right and all his ways are
just. And those who walk in pride he
is able to humble.

PRAYER: THANKSGIVING

THE righteous shall rejoice in You, O Lord, and trust in You, and all the upright in heart shall glory. (Psalm 64:10) . . . You, O Lord, will judge Your people and have compassion on Your servants. (Psalm 135:14)

PAUSE *to offer your own expressions of thanksgiving.*

NT 2 Peter 1:12–21

Prophecy of Scripture

[12]So I will always remind you of these
things, even though you know them and
are firmly established in the truth you now
have. [13]I think it is right to refresh your
memory as long as I live in the tent of this
body, [14]because I know that I will soon put
it aside, as our Lord Jesus Christ has made
clear to me. [15]And I will make every effort
to see that after my departure you will always be able to remember these things.
[16]We did not follow cleverly invented
stories when we told you about the power and coming of our Lord Jesus Christ,
but we were eyewitnesses of his majesty.
[17]For he received honor and glory from
God the Father when the voice came to
him from the Majestic Glory, saying, "This
is my Son, whom I love; with him I am
well pleased."[a] [18]We ourselves heard this
voice that came from heaven when we
were with him on the sacred mountain.
[19]And we have the word of the prophets made more certain, and you will do
well to pay attention to it, as to a light
shining in a dark place, until the day
dawns and the morning star rises in your
hearts. [20]Above all, you must understand
that no prophecy of Scripture came about
by the prophet's own interpretation. [21]For
prophecy never had its origin in the will
of man, but men spoke from God as they
were carried along by the Holy Spirit.

[a] *17* Matt. 17:5; Mark 9:7; Luke 9:35

PRAYER: MY RELATIONSHIP TO GOD

WE have known and have believed the love You, O God, have for us. O God, You are love, and those who abide in love abide in You, and You in them. In this way, love has been perfected among us so that we may have confidence in the day of judgment; because as You are, so are we in this world. There is no fear in love, but perfect love casts out fear, because fear involves punishment, and the one who fears has not been perfected in love. (1 John 4:16–18)

PAUSE *to thank God for the relationship that you enjoy with Him in Jesus Christ.*

YEAR 2 DAY 294

OT Psalms 130–131

Psalm 130

A song of ascents.

[1]Out of the depths I cry to you, O LORD;
[2] O Lord, hear my voice.
Let your ears be attentive
to my cry for mercy.

[3]If you, O LORD, kept a record of sins,
O Lord, who could stand?
[4]But with you there is forgiveness;
therefore you are feared.

[5]I wait for the LORD, my soul waits,
and in his word I put my hope.
[6]My soul waits for the Lord
more than watchmen wait for the morning,
more than watchmen wait for the morning.

[7]O Israel, put your hope in the LORD,
for with the LORD is unfailing love
and with him is full redemption.
[8]He himself will redeem Israel
from all their sins.

Psalm 131

A song of ascents. Of David.

[1]My heart is not proud, O LORD,
my eyes are not haughty;
I do not concern myself with great matters
or things too wonderful for me.
[2]But I have stilled and quieted my soul;
like a weaned child with its mother,
like a weaned child is my soul within me.

[3]O Israel, put your hope in the LORD
both now and forevermore.

PRAYER: ADORATION

WE sing to You a new song; let all the earth sing to You. We sing to You, Lord, and bless Your name; we proclaim the good news of Your salvation day after day. We declare Your glory among the nations, Your marvelous works among all people. (Psalm 96:1–3)

***PAUSE** to express your thoughts of praise and worship.*

NT 2 Peter 2:1–22

False Teachers and Their Destruction

2 But there were also false prophets
among the people, just as there will be
false teachers among you. They will secretly introduce destructive heresies, even
denying the sovereign Lord who bought
them—bringing swift destruction on
themselves. [2]Many will follow their
shameful ways and will bring the way of
truth into disrepute. [3]In their greed these
teachers will exploit you with stories they
have made up. Their condemnation has
long been hanging over them, and their
destruction has not been sleeping.
[4]For if God did not spare angels when
they sinned, but sent them to hell,[a] putting
them into gloomy dungeons[b] to be held for
judgment; [5]if he did not spare the ancient
world when he brought the flood on its ungodly people, but protected Noah, a
preacher of righteousness, and seven others; [6]if he condemned the cities of Sodom
and Gomorrah by burning them to ashes,
and made them an example of what is going to happen to the ungodly; [7]and if he
rescued Lot, a righteous man, who was distressed by the filthy lives of lawless men
[8](for that righteous man, living among
them day after day, was tormented in his
righteous soul by the lawless deeds he saw
and heard)— [9]if this is so, then the Lord
knows how to rescue godly men from trials and to hold the unrighteous for the day
of judgment, while continuing their pun-

[a] 4 Greek *Tartarus* [b] 4 Some manuscripts *into chains of darkness*

ishment.[c] [10]This is especially true of those who follow the corrupt desire of the sinful nature[d] and despise authority.

Bold and arrogant, these men are not afraid to slander celestial beings; [11]yet even angels, although they are stronger and more powerful, do not bring slanderous accusations against such beings in the presence of the Lord. [12]But these men blaspheme in matters they do not understand. They are like brute beasts, creatures of instinct, born only to be caught and destroyed, and like beasts they too will perish.

[13]They will be paid back with harm for the harm they have done. Their idea of pleasure is to carouse in broad daylight. They are blots and blemishes, reveling in their pleasures while they feast with you.[e] [14]With eyes full of adultery, they never stop sinning; they seduce the unstable; they are experts in greed—an accursed brood! [15]They have left the straight way and wandered off to follow the way of Balaam son of Beor, who loved the wages of wickedness. [16]But he was rebuked for his wrongdoing by a donkey—a beast without speech—who spoke with a man's voice and restrained the prophet's madness.

[17]These men are springs without water and mists driven by a storm. Blackest darkness is reserved for them. [18]For they mouth empty, boastful words and, by appealing to the lustful desires of sinful human nature, they entice people who are just escaping from those who live in error. [19]They promise them freedom, while they themselves are slaves of depravity—for a man is a slave to whatever has mastered him. [20]If they have escaped the corruption of the world by knowing our Lord and Savior Jesus Christ and are again entangled in it and overcome, they are worse off at the end than they were at the beginning. [21]It would have been better for them not to have known the way of righteousness, than to have known it and then to turn their backs on the sacred command that was passed on to them. [22]Of them the proverbs are true: "A dog returns to its vomit,"[f] and, "A sow that is washed goes back to her wallowing in the mud."

[c] 9 Or *unrighteous for punishment until the day of judgment* [d] 10 Or *the flesh* [e] 13 Some manuscripts *in their love feasts* [f] 22 Prov. 26:11

PRAYER: THE CHARACTER I WANT TO CULTIVATE

LIKE Barnabas, I want to be a good person, full of You, O Holy Spirit, and of faith. (Acts 11:24) . . . I will not be lacking in zeal, but I will keep fervent in spirit, serving You, Lord. (Romans 12:11)

__TAKE__ a moment to ask the Lord for the grace to grow in godly character.

YEAR 2 DAY 295

OT Daniel 5:1-31

The Writing on the Wall

5 King Belshazzar gave a great banquet for a thousand of his nobles and drank wine with them. [2]While Belshazzar was drinking his wine, he gave orders to bring in the gold and silver goblets that Nebuchadnezzar his father[a] had taken from the temple in Jerusalem, so that the king and his nobles, his wives and his concubines might drink from them. [3]So they brought in the gold goblets that had been taken from the temple of God in Jerusalem, and the king and his nobles, his wives and his concubines drank from them. [4]As they drank the wine, they praised the gods of gold and silver, of bronze, iron, wood and stone.

[5]Suddenly the fingers of a human hand appeared and wrote on the plaster of the wall, near the lampstand in the royal palace. The king watched the hand as it wrote. [6]His face turned pale and he was so frightened that his knees knocked together and his legs gave way.

[7]The king called out for the enchanters, astrologers[b] and diviners to be brought and said to these wise men of Babylon,

[a] 2 Or *ancestor;* or *predecessor;* also in verses 11, 13 and 18 [b] 7 Or *Chaldeans;* also in verse 11

"Whoever reads this writing and tells me what it means will be clothed in purple and have a gold chain placed around his neck, and he will be made the third highest ruler in the kingdom."

8 Then all the king's wise men came in, but they could not read the writing or tell the king what it meant. 9 So King Belshazzar became even more terrified and his face grew more pale. His nobles were baffled.

10 The queen,[c] hearing the voices of the king and his nobles, came into the banquet hall. "O king, live forever!" she said. "Don't be alarmed! Don't look so pale! 11 There is a man in your kingdom who has the spirit of the holy gods in him. In the time of your father he was found to have insight and intelligence and wisdom like that of the gods. King Nebuchadnezzar your father—your father the king, I say—appointed him chief of the magicians, enchanters, astrologers and diviners. 12 This man Daniel, whom the king called Belteshazzar, was found to have a keen mind and knowledge and understanding, and also the ability to interpret dreams, explain riddles and solve difficult problems. Call for Daniel, and he will tell you what the writing means."

13 So Daniel was brought before the king, and the king said to him, "Are you Daniel, one of the exiles my father the king brought from Judah? 14 I have heard that the spirit of the gods is in you and that you have insight, intelligence and outstanding wisdom. 15 The wise men and enchanters were brought before me to read this writing and tell me what it means, but they could not explain it. 16 Now I have heard that you are able to give interpretations and to solve difficult problems. If you can read this writing and tell me what it means, you will be clothed in purple and have a gold chain placed around your neck, and you will be made the third highest ruler in the kingdom."

17 Then Daniel answered the king, "You may keep your gifts for yourself and give your rewards to someone else. Nevertheless, I will read the writing for the king and tell him what it means.

18 "O king, the Most High God gave your father Nebuchadnezzar sovereignty and greatness and glory and splendor. 19 Because of the high position he gave him, all the peoples and nations and men of every language dreaded and feared him. Those the king wanted to put to death, he put to death; those he wanted to spare, he spared; those he wanted to promote, he promoted; and those he wanted to humble, he humbled. 20 But when his heart became arrogant and hardened with pride, he was deposed from his royal throne and stripped of his glory. 21 He was driven away from people and given the mind of an animal; he lived with the wild donkeys and ate grass like cattle; and his body was drenched with the dew of heaven, until he acknowledged that the Most High God is sovereign over the kingdoms of men and sets over them anyone he wishes.

22 "But you his son,[d] O Belshazzar, have not humbled yourself, though you knew all this. 23 Instead, you have set yourself up against the Lord of heaven. You had the goblets from his temple brought to you, and you and your nobles, your wives and your concubines drank wine from them. You praised the gods of silver and gold, of bronze, iron, wood and stone, which cannot see or hear or understand. But you did not honor the God who holds in his hand your life and all your ways. 24 Therefore he sent the hand that wrote the inscription.

25 "This is the inscription that was written:

MENE, MENE, TEKEL, PARSIN[e]

26 "This is what these words mean:

Mene[f]: God has numbered the days of your reign and brought it to an end.
27 *Tekel*[g]: You have been weighed on the scales and found wanting.
28 *Peres*[h]: Your kingdom is divided and given to the Medes and Persians."

29 Then at Belshazzar's command, Daniel was clothed in purple, a gold chain was placed around his neck, and he was proclaimed the third highest ruler in the kingdom.

30 That very night Belshazzar, king of the Babylonians,[i] was slain, 31 and Darius the Mede took over the kingdom, at the age of sixty-two.

[c] 10 Or *queen mother* [d] 22 Or *descendant*; or *successor* [e] 25 Aramaic *UPARSIN* (that is, *AND PARSIN*) [f] 26 *Mene* can mean *numbered* or *mina* (a unit of money). [g] 27 *Tekel* can mean *weighed* or *shekel*. [h] 28 *Peres* (the singular of *Parsin*) can mean *divided* or *Persia* or *a half mina* or *a half shekel*. [i] 30 Or *Chaldeans*

PRAYER: CONFESSION

O LORD, how can I discern my errors? Cleanse me from hidden faults. Keep Your servant also from presumptuous sins; let them not rule over me. Then will I be blameless, and innocent of great transgression. (Psalm 19:12–13)

***ASK** the Spirit to search your heart and reveal any areas of unconfessed sin. Acknowledge these to the Lord and thank Him for His forgiveness.*

NT 2 Peter 3:1-18

The Day of the Lord

3 Dear friends, this is now my second letter to you. I have written both of them
as reminders to stimulate you to wholesome thinking. 2I want you to recall the
words spoken in the past by the holy
prophets and the command given by our
Lord and Savior through your apostles.
3First of all, you must understand that
in the last days scoffers will come, scoffing and following their own evil desires.
4They will say, "Where is this 'coming' he
promised? Ever since our fathers died,
everything goes on as it has since the beginning of creation." 5But they deliberately forget that long ago by God's word the
heavens existed and the earth was formed
out of water and by water. 6By these waters also the world of that time was deluged and destroyed. 7By the same word
the present heavens and earth are reserved
for fire, being kept for the day of judgment and destruction of ungodly men.
8But do not forget this one thing, dear
friends: With the Lord a day is like a thousand years, and a thousand years are like a
day. 9The Lord is not slow in keeping his
promise, as some understand slowness. He
is patient with you, not wanting anyone to
perish, but everyone to come to repentance.
10But the day of the Lord will come like
a thief. The heavens will disappear with a
roar; the elements will be destroyed by
fire, and the earth and everything in it will
be laid bare.[a]
11Since everything will be destroyed in
this way, what kind of people ought you
to be? You ought to live holy and godly
lives 12as you look forward to the day of
God and speed its coming.[b] That day will
bring about the destruction of the heavens
by fire, and the elements will melt in the
heat. 13But in keeping with his promise we
are looking forward to a new heaven and
a new earth, the home of righteousness.
14So then, dear friends, since you are
looking forward to this, make every effort
to be found spotless, blameless and at
peace with him. 15Bear in mind that our
Lord's patience means salvation, just as
our dear brother Paul also wrote you with
the wisdom that God gave him. 16He
writes the same way in all his letters,
speaking in them of these matters. His letters contain some things that are hard to
understand, which ignorant and unstable
people distort, as they do the other Scriptures, to their own destruction.
17Therefore, dear friends, since you already know this, be on your guard so that
you may not be carried away by the error
of lawless men and fall from your secure
position. 18But grow in the grace and
knowledge of our Lord and Savior Jesus
Christ. To him be glory both now and forever! Amen.

[a] 10 Some manuscripts *be burned up* [b] 12 Or *as you wait eagerly for the day of God to come*

PRAYER: MY RELATIONSHIP TO OTHERS

ABOVE all, I will love others fervently, because love covers a multitude of sins. (1 Peter 4:8) . . . In this is love, not that we loved You, O God, but that You loved us and sent Your Son to be the propitiation for our sins. Since You so loved us, we also ought to love

one another. No one has ever seen You; but if we love one another, You abide in us, and Your love is perfected in us.
(1 John 4:10–12)

PAUSE *to review your relationships with others and to commit them to the Lord.*

YEAR 2
DAY 296

OT **Daniel 6:1–28**

Daniel in the Den of Lions

6 It pleased Darius to appoint 120 satraps to rule throughout the kingdom, 2with three administrators over them, one of whom was Daniel. The satraps were made accountable to them so that the king might not suffer loss. 3Now Daniel so distinguished himself among the administrators and the satraps by his exceptional qualities that the king planned to set him over the whole kingdom. 4At this, the administrators and the satraps tried to find grounds for charges against Daniel in his conduct of government affairs, but they were unable to do so. They could find no corruption in him, because he was trustworthy and neither corrupt nor negligent. 5Finally these men said, "We will never find any basis for charges against this man Daniel unless it has something to do with the law of his God."

6So the administrators and the satraps went as a group to the king and said: "O King Darius, live forever! 7The royal administrators, prefects, satraps, advisers and governors have all agreed that the king should issue an edict and enforce the decree that anyone who prays to any god or man during the next thirty days, except to you, O king, shall be thrown into the lions' den. 8Now, O king, issue the decree and put it in writing so that it cannot be altered—in accordance with the laws of the Medes and Persians, which cannot be repealed." 9So King Darius put the decree in writing.

10Now when Daniel learned that the decree had been published, he went home to his upstairs room where the windows opened toward Jerusalem. Three times a day he got down on his knees and prayed, giving thanks to his God, just as he had done before. 11Then these men went as a group and found Daniel praying and asking God for help. 12So they went to the king and spoke to him about his royal decree: "Did you not publish a decree that during the next thirty days anyone who prays to any god or man except to you, O king, would be thrown into the lions' den?"

The king answered, "The decree stands—in accordance with the laws of the Medes and Persians, which cannot be repealed."

13Then they said to the king, "Daniel, who is one of the exiles from Judah, pays no attention to you, O king, or to the decree you put in writing. He still prays three times a day." 14When the king heard this, he was greatly distressed; he was determined to rescue Daniel and made every effort until sundown to save him.

15Then the men went as a group to the king and said to him, "Remember, O king, that according to the law of the Medes and Persians no decree or edict that the king issues can be changed."

16So the king gave the order, and they brought Daniel and threw him into the lions' den. The king said to Daniel, "May your God, whom you serve continually, rescue you!"

17A stone was brought and placed over the mouth of the den, and the king sealed it with his own signet ring and with the rings of his nobles, so that Daniel's situation might not be changed. 18Then the king returned to his palace and spent the night without eating and without any entertainment being brought to him. And he could not sleep.

19At the first light of dawn, the king got up and hurried to the lions' den. 20When he came near the den, he called to Daniel in an anguished voice, "Daniel, servant of the living God, has your God, whom you serve continually, been able to rescue you from the lions?"

21Daniel answered, "O king, live forev-

er! 22My God sent his angel, and he shut
the mouths of the lions. They have not
hurt me, because I was found innocent in
his sight. Nor have I ever done any wrong
before you, O king."
23The king was overjoyed and gave orders to lift Daniel out of the den. And
when Daniel was lifted from the den, no
wound was found on him, because he
had trusted in his God.
24At the king's command, the men who
had falsely accused Daniel were brought
in and thrown into the lions' den, along
with their wives and children. And before
they reached the floor of the den, the lions overpowered them and crushed all
their bones.
25Then King Darius wrote to all the peoples, nations and men of every language
throughout the land:

"May you prosper greatly!

26"I issue a decree that in every part
of my kingdom people must fear and
reverence the God of Daniel.

"For he is the living God
and he endures forever;
his kingdom will not be destroyed,
his dominion will never end.
27He rescues and he saves;
he performs signs and wonders
in the heavens and on the earth.
He has rescued Daniel
from the power of the lions."

28So Daniel prospered during the reign
of Darius and the reign of Cyrus[a] the Persian.

[a] 28 Or *Darius, that is, the reign of Cyrus*

PRAYER: RENEWAL

MAY I honor You with my wealth, O Lord, and with the firstfruits of all my increase. (Proverbs 3:9) . . . I will not lay up treasure for myself without being rich toward You, O God. (Luke 12:21)

***PAUSE** to add your own prayers for personal renewal.*

NT John 1:1-42

The Word Became Flesh

1 In the beginning was the Word, and the
Word was with God, and the Word was
God. 2He was with God in the beginning.
3Through him all things were made;
without him nothing was made that has
been made. 4In him was life, and that life
was the light of men. 5The light shines in
the darkness, but the darkness has not understood[a] it.
6There came a man who was sent from
God; his name was John. 7He came as a
witness to testify concerning that light, so
that through him all men might believe.
8He himself was not the light; he came
only as a witness to the light. 9The true
light that gives light to every man was
coming into the world.[b]
10He was in the world, and though the
world was made through him, the world
did not recognize him. 11He came to that
which was his own, but his own did not
receive him. 12Yet to all who received him,
to those who believed in his name, he
gave the right to become children of
God— 13children born not of natural descent,[c] nor of human decision or a husband's will, but born of God.
14The Word became flesh and made his
dwelling among us. We have seen his glory, the glory of the One and Only,[d] who
came from the Father, full of grace and
truth.
15John testifies concerning him. He
cries out, saying, "This was he of whom I
said, 'He who comes after me has surpassed me because he was before me.' "
16From the fullness of his grace we have
all received one blessing after another.
17For the law was given through Moses;
grace and truth came through Jesus
Christ. 18No one has ever seen God, but

[a] 5 Or *darkness, and the darkness has not overcome*
[b] 9 Or *This was the true light that gives light to every man who comes into the world*
[c] 13 Greek *of bloods*
[d] 14 Or *the Only Begotten*

God the One and Only,[e,f] who is at the Father's side, has made him known.

John the Baptist Denies Being the Christ

19 Now this was John's testimony when
the Jews of Jerusalem sent priests and Levites to ask him who he was. 20 He did not
fail to confess, but confessed freely, "I am
not the Christ.[g]"
21 They asked him, "Then who are you?
Are you Elijah?"
He said, "I am not."
"Are you the Prophet?"
He answered, "No."
22 Finally they said, "Who are you? Give
us an answer to take back to those who
sent us. What do you say about yourself?"
23 John replied in the words of Isaiah the
prophet, "I am the voice of one calling in
the desert, 'Make straight the way for the
Lord.' "[h]
24 Now some Pharisees who had been
sent 25 questioned him, "Why then do you
baptize if you are not the Christ, nor Elijah, nor the Prophet?"
26 "I baptize with[i] water," John replied,
"but among you stands one you do not
know. 27 He is the one who comes after
me, the thongs of whose sandals I am not
worthy to untie."
28 This all happened at Bethany on the
other side of the Jordan, where John was
baptizing.

Jesus the Lamb of God

29 The next day John saw Jesus coming
toward him and said, "Look, the Lamb of
God, who takes away the sin of the world!
30 This is the one I meant when I said, 'A
man who comes after me has surpassed
me because he was before me.' 31 I myself
did not know him, but the reason I came
baptizing with water was that he might be
revealed to Israel."
32 Then John gave this testimony: "I saw
the Spirit come down from heaven as a
dove and remain on him. 33 I would not
have known him, except that the one
who sent me to baptize with water told
me, 'The man on whom you see the Spirit come down and remain is he who will
baptize with the Holy Spirit.' 34 I have
seen and I testify that this is the Son of
God."

Jesus' First Disciples

35 The next day John was there again
with two of his disciples. 36 When he saw
Jesus passing by, he said, "Look, the Lamb
of God!"
37 When the two disciples heard him say
this, they followed Jesus. 38 Turning
around, Jesus saw them following and
asked, "What do you want?"
They said, "Rabbi" (which means
Teacher), "where are you staying?"
39 "Come," he replied, "and you will
see."
So they went and saw where he was
staying, and spent that day with him. It
was about the tenth hour.
40 Andrew, Simon Peter's brother, was
one of the two who heard what John had
said and who had followed Jesus. 41 The
first thing Andrew did was to find his
brother Simon and tell him, "We have
found the Messiah" (that is, the Christ).
42 And he brought him to Jesus.
Jesus looked at him and said, "You are
Simon son of John. You will be called Cephas" (which, when translated, is Peter[j]).

[e] *18* Or *the Only Begotten* [f] *18* Some manuscripts *but the only* (or *only begotten*) *Son* [g] *20* Or *Messiah.* "The Christ" (Greek) and "the Messiah" (Hebrew) both mean "the Anointed One"; also in verse 25. [h] *23* Isaiah 40:3 [i] *26* Or *in;* also in verses 31 and 33 [j] *42* Both *Cephas* (Aramaic) and *Peter* (Greek) mean *rock.*

PRAYER: THE ATTRIBUTES OF GOD

YOU, O Lord, are righteous; You love righteousness; the upright will see Your face. (Psalm 11:7) . . . Your eyes are too pure to look at evil; You cannot look on wickedness, my holy God. (Habakkuk 1:13)

PAUSE *to reflect on these affirmations about the person, powers and perfection of God.*

OT **Daniel 7:1–28** YEAR 2 DAY 297

Daniel's Dream of Four Beasts

7 In the first year of Belshazzar king of
Babylon, Daniel had a dream, and visions passed through his mind as he was
lying on his bed. He wrote down the sub-
stance of his dream.
2 Daniel said: "In my vision at night I
looked, and there before me were the four
winds of heaven churning up the great
sea. 3 Four great beasts, each different from
the others, came up out of the sea.
4 "The first was like a lion, and it had the
wings of an eagle. I watched until its
wings were torn off and it was lifted from
the ground so that it stood on two feet
like a man, and the heart of a man was
given to it.
5 "And there before me was a second
beast, which looked like a bear. It was
raised up on one of its sides, and it had
three ribs in its mouth between its teeth.
It was told, 'Get up and eat your fill of
flesh!'
6 "After that, I looked, and there before
me was another beast, one that looked
like a leopard. And on its back it had four
wings like those of a bird. This beast had
four heads, and it was given authority to
rule.
7 "After that, in my vision at night I
looked, and there before me was a fourth
beast—terrifying and frightening and very
powerful. It had large iron teeth; it
crushed and devoured its victims and
trampled underfoot whatever was left. It
was different from all the former beasts,
and it had ten horns.
8 "While I was thinking about the
horns, there before me was another horn,
a little one, which came up among them;
and three of the first horns were uprooted before it. This horn had eyes like the
eyes of a man and a mouth that spoke
boastfully.
9 "As I looked,

"thrones were set in place,
  and the Ancient of Days took his
    seat.
His clothing was as white as snow;
  the hair of his head was white like
    wool.
His throne was flaming with fire,
  and its wheels were all ablaze.
10 A river of fire was flowing,
  coming out from before him.
Thousands upon thousands attended
    him;
  ten thousand times ten thousand
    stood before him.
The court was seated,
  and the books were opened.

11 "Then I continued to watch because of
the boastful words the horn was speaking.
I kept looking until the beast was slain
and its body destroyed and thrown into
the blazing fire. 12 (The other beasts had
been stripped of their authority, but were
allowed to live for a period of time.)
13 "In my vision at night I looked, and
there before me was one like a son of
man, coming with the clouds of heaven.
He approached the Ancient of Days and
was led into his presence. 14 He was given
authority, glory and sovereign power; all
peoples, nations and men of every language worshiped him. His dominion is an
everlasting dominion that will not pass
away, and his kingdom is one that will
never be destroyed.

The Interpretation of the Dream

15 "I, Daniel, was troubled in spirit, and
the visions that passed through my mind
disturbed me. 16 I approached one of those
standing there and asked him the true
meaning of all this.
"So he told me and gave me the interpretation of these things: 17 'The four great
beasts are four kingdoms that will rise
from the earth. 18 But the saints of the
Most High will receive the kingdom and
will possess it forever—yes, for ever and
ever.'
19 "Then I wanted to know the true
meaning of the fourth beast, which was
different from all the others and most terrifying, with its iron teeth and bronze
claws—the beast that crushed and devoured its victims and trampled underfoot whatever was left. 20 I also wanted to
know about the ten horns on its head and
about the other horn that came up, before
which three of them fell—the horn that
looked more imposing than the others

and that had eyes and a mouth that spoke
boastfully. [21]As I watched, this horn was
waging war against the saints and defeating them, [22]until the Ancient of Days
came and pronounced judgment in favor
of the saints of the Most High, and the
time came when they possessed the kingdom.
[23]"He gave me this explanation: 'The
fourth beast is a fourth kingdom that will
appear on earth. It will be different from
all the other kingdoms and will devour
the whole earth, trampling it down and
crushing it. [24]The ten horns are ten kings
who will come from this kingdom. After
them another king will arise, different
from the earlier ones; he will subdue three
kings. [25]He will speak against the Most
High and oppress his saints and try to
change the set times and the laws. The
saints will be handed over to him for a
time, times and half a time.[a]
[26]" 'But the court will sit, and his power will be taken away and completely destroyed forever. [27]Then the sovereignty,
power and greatness of the kingdoms under the whole heaven will be handed over
to the saints, the people of the Most High.
His kingdom will be an everlasting kingdom, and all rulers will worship and obey
him.'
[28]"This is the end of the matter. I, Daniel, was deeply troubled by my thoughts,
and my face turned pale, but I kept the
matter to myself."

[a] 25 Or *for a year, two years and half a year*

PRAYER: PETITION

MAY I not go about spreading slander among people, nor do anything that endangers the life of my neighbor. May I not mistreat my neighbor, but fear You, my God, for You are the Lord my God. (Leviticus 19:16; 25:17)

***PAUSE** here to petition God for growth in love and compassion toward others. Offer prayers for your loved ones, for those who do not know Jesus and for those in need. Offer prayers regarding your activities for this day and any special concerns you may have.*

NT John 1:43–2:11

Jesus Calls Philip and Nathanael

[43]The next day Jesus decided to leave for
Galilee. Finding Philip, he said to him,
"Follow me."
[44]Philip, like Andrew and Peter, was
from the town of Bethsaida. [45]Philip found
Nathanael and told him, "We have found
the one Moses wrote about in the Law, and
about whom the prophets also wrote—
Jesus of Nazareth, the son of Joseph."
[46]"Nazareth! Can anything good come
from there?" Nathanael asked.
"Come and see," said Philip.
[47]When Jesus saw Nathanael approaching, he said of him, "Here is a true Israelite, in whom there is nothing false."
[48]"How do you know me?" Nathanael
asked.
Jesus answered, "I saw you while you
were still under the fig tree before Philip
called you."
[49]Then Nathanael declared, "Rabbi, you
are the Son of God; you are the King of Israel."
[50]Jesus said, "You believe[a] because I told
you I saw you under the fig tree. You shall
see greater things than that." [51]He then
added, "I tell you[b] the truth, you[b] shall see
heaven open, and the angels of God ascending and descending on the Son of
Man."

Jesus Changes Water to Wine

2 On the third day a wedding took place
at Cana in Galilee. Jesus' mother was
there, [2]and Jesus and his disciples had
also been invited to the wedding. [3]When
the wine was gone, Jesus' mother said to
him, "They have no more wine."
[4]"Dear woman, why do you involve
me?" Jesus replied. "My time has not yet
come."

[a] 50 Or *Do you believe . . . ?* [b] 51 The Greek is plural.

[5]His mother said to the servants, "Do
whatever he tells you."
[6]Nearby stood six stone water jars, the
kind used by the Jews for ceremonial
washing, each holding from twenty to
thirty gallons.[c]
[7]Jesus said to the servants, "Fill the jars
with water"; so they filled them to the
brim.
[8]Then he told them, "Now draw some
out and take it to the master of the banquet."
They did so, [9]and the master of the banquet tasted the water that had been turned
into wine. He did not realize where it had
come from, though the servants who had
drawn the water knew. Then he called the
bridegroom aside [10]and said, "Everyone
brings out the choice wine first and then
the cheaper wine after the guests have had
too much to drink; but you have saved the
best till now."
[11]This, the first of his miraculous signs,
Jesus performed at Cana in Galilee. He
thus revealed his glory, and his disciples
put their faith in him.

[c]6 Greek *two to three metretes* (probably about 75 to 115 liters)

PRAYER: THE WORKS OF GOD

IN Your Father's house are many dwellings, Lord Jesus; if it were not so, You would have told us. You went there to prepare a place for us. And as You went to prepare a place for us, You will come again and receive us to Yourself, that we also may be where You are. (John 14:2–3)

***TAKE** a moment to consider the greatness of God's wonderful works.*

YEAR 2 DAY 298

OT Proverbs 29

29 A man who remains stiff-necked
after many rebukes
will suddenly be destroyed—
without remedy.

[2]When the righteous thrive, the people
rejoice;
when the wicked rule, the people
groan.

[3]A man who loves wisdom brings joy
to his father,
but a companion of prostitutes
squanders his wealth.

[4]By justice a king gives a country
stability,
but one who is greedy for bribes
tears it down.

[5]Whoever flatters his neighbor
is spreading a net for his feet.

[6]An evil man is snared by his own sin,
but a righteous one can sing and be
glad.

[7]The righteous care about justice for
the poor,
but the wicked have no such
concern.

[8]Mockers stir up a city,
but wise men turn away anger.

[9]If a wise man goes to court with a
fool,
the fool rages and scoffs, and there
is no peace.

[10]Bloodthirsty men hate a man of
integrity
and seek to kill the upright.

[11]A fool gives full vent to his anger,
but a wise man keeps himself under
control.

[12]If a ruler listens to lies,
all his officials become wicked.

[13]The poor man and the oppressor have
this in common:
The LORD gives sight to the eyes of
both.

[14]If a king judges the poor with fairness,
his throne will always be secure.

[15]The rod of correction imparts wisdom,

but a child left to himself disgraces
his mother.

16 When the wicked thrive, so does sin,
but the righteous will see their
downfall.

17 Discipline your son, and he will give
you peace;
he will bring delight to your soul.

18 Where there is no revelation, the
people cast off restraint;
but blessed is he who keeps the law.

19 A servant cannot be corrected by mere
words;
though he understands, he will not
respond.

20 Do you see a man who speaks in
haste?
There is more hope for a fool than
for him.

21 If a man pampers his servant from
youth,
he will bring grief[a] in the end.

22 An angry man stirs up dissension,
and a hot-tempered one commits
many sins.

23 A man's pride brings him low,
but a man of lowly spirit gains
honor.

24 The accomplice of a thief is his own
enemy;
he is put under oath and dare not
testify.

25 Fear of man will prove to be a snare,
but whoever trusts in the LORD is
kept safe.

26 Many seek an audience with a ruler,
but it is from the LORD that man
gets justice.

27 The righteous detest the dishonest;
the wicked detest the upright.

[a] *21* The meaning of the Hebrew for this word is uncertain.

PRAYER: INTERCESSION

HELP us, O God of our salvation, for the glory of Your name; deliver us and forgive our sins for Your name's sake.
(Psalm 79:9)

TAKE *a few moments to intercede on behalf of friends, relatives, neighbors and coworkers who do not yet know salvation in Jesus Christ.*

NT John 2:12–3:21

Jesus Clears the Temple

12 After this he went down to Capernaum with his mother and brothers and
his disciples. There they stayed for a few
days.
13 When it was almost time for the Jewish Passover, Jesus went up to Jerusalem.
14 In the temple courts he found men selling cattle, sheep and doves, and others sitting at tables exchanging money. 15 So he
made a whip out of cords, and drove all
from the temple area, both sheep and cattle; he scattered the coins of the money
changers and overturned their tables. 16 To
those who sold doves he said, "Get these
out of here! How dare you turn my Father's house into a market!"
17 His disciples remembered that it is
written: "Zeal for your house will consume me."[a]
18 Then the Jews demanded of him,
"What miraculous sign can you show us
to prove your authority to do all this?"
19 Jesus answered them, "Destroy this
temple, and I will raise it again in three
days."
20 The Jews replied, "It has taken forty-
six years to build this temple, and you are
going to raise it in three days?" 21 But the
temple he had spoken of was his body.
22 After he was raised from the dead, his
disciples recalled what he had said. Then
they believed the Scripture and the words
that Jesus had spoken.
23 Now while he was in Jerusalem at the
Passover Feast, many people saw the

[a] *17* Psalm 69:9

miraculous signs he was doing and believed in his name.[b] 24 But Jesus would not entrust himself to them, for he knew all men. 25 He did not need man's testimony about man, for he knew what was in a man.

Jesus Teaches Nicodemus

3 Now there was a man of the Pharisees named Nicodemus, a member of the Jewish ruling council. 2 He came to Jesus at night and said, "Rabbi, we know you are a teacher who has come from God. For no one could perform the miraculous signs you are doing if God were not with him."

3 In reply Jesus declared, "I tell you the truth, no one can see the kingdom of God unless he is born again.[c]"

4 "How can a man be born when he is old?" Nicodemus asked. "Surely he cannot enter a second time into his mother's womb to be born!"

5 Jesus answered, "I tell you the truth, no one can enter the kingdom of God unless he is born of water and the Spirit. 6 Flesh gives birth to flesh, but the Spirit[d] gives birth to spirit. 7 You should not be surprised at my saying, 'You[e] must be born again.' 8 The wind blows wherever it pleases. You hear its sound, but you cannot tell where it comes from or where it is going. So it is with everyone born of the Spirit."

9 "How can this be?" Nicodemus asked.

10 "You are Israel's teacher," said Jesus, "and do you not understand these things? 11 I tell you the truth, we speak of what we know, and we testify to what we have seen, but still you people do not accept our testimony. 12 I have spoken to you of earthly things and you do not believe; how then will you believe if I speak of heavenly things? 13 No one has ever gone into heaven except the one who came from heaven—the Son of Man.[f] 14 Just as Moses lifted up the snake in the desert, so the Son of Man must be lifted up, 15 that everyone who believes in him may have eternal life.[g]

16 "For God so loved the world that he gave his one and only Son,[h] that whoever believes in him shall not perish but have eternal life. 17 For God did not send his Son into the world to condemn the world, but to save the world through him. 18 Whoever believes in him is not condemned, but whoever does not believe stands condemned already because he has not believed in the name of God's one and only Son.[i] 19 This is the verdict: Light has come into the world, but men loved darkness instead of light because their deeds were evil. 20 Everyone who does evil hates the light, and will not come into the light for fear that his deeds will be exposed. 21 But whoever lives by the truth comes into the light, so that it may be seen plainly that what he has done has been done through God."[j]

[b] 23 Or *and believed in him* [c] 3 Or *born from above;* also in verse 7 [d] 6 Or *but spirit* [e] 7 The Greek is plural. [f] 13 Some manuscripts *Man, who is in heaven* [g] 15 Or *believes may have eternal life in him* [h] 16 Or *his only begotten Son* [i] 18 Or *God's only begotten Son* [j] 21 Some interpreters end the quotation after verse 15.

PRAYER: MY RELATIONSHIP TO GOD

THE salvation of the righteous comes from You, the Lord; You are their stronghold in time of trouble. You, O Lord, help them and deliver them; You deliver them from the wicked and save them, because they take refuge in You. (Psalm 37:39–40) . . . My soul silently waits, O God, for You alone; my salvation comes from You. You alone are my rock and my salvation; You are my stronghold. I will never be shaken. (Psalm 62:1–2)

PAUSE *to thank God for the relationship that you enjoy with Him in Jesus Christ.*

OT **Daniel 8:1–27**

YEAR 2 DAY 299

Daniel's Vision of a Ram and a Goat

8 In the third year of King Belshazzar's
reign, I, Daniel, had a vision, after the
one that had already appeared to me. 2In
my vision I saw myself in the citadel of
Susa in the province of Elam; in the vision
I was beside the Ulai Canal. 3I looked up,
and there before me was a ram with two
horns, standing beside the canal, and the
horns were long. One of the horns was
longer than the other but grew up later. 4I
watched the ram as he charged toward the
west and the north and the south. No animal could stand against him, and none
could rescue from his power. He did as he
pleased and became great.
5As I was thinking about this, suddenly
a goat with a prominent horn between his
eyes came from the west, crossing the
whole earth without touching the ground.
6He came toward the two-horned ram I
had seen standing beside the canal and
charged at him in great rage. 7I saw him
attack the ram furiously, striking the ram
and shattering his two horns. The ram was
powerless to stand against him; the goat
knocked him to the ground and trampled
on him, and none could rescue the ram
from his power. 8The goat became very
great, but at the height of his power his
large horn was broken off, and in its place
four prominent horns grew up toward the
four winds of heaven.
9Out of one of them came another
horn, which started small but grew in
power to the south and to the east and toward the Beautiful Land. 10It grew until it
reached the host of the heavens, and it
threw some of the starry host down to the
earth and trampled on them. 11It set itself
up to be as great as the Prince of the host;
it took away the daily sacrifice from him,
and the place of his sanctuary was
brought low. 12Because of rebellion, the
host ⌞of the saints⌟[a] and the daily sacrifice
were given over to it. It prospered in everything it did, and truth was thrown to the
ground.
13Then I heard a holy one speaking, and
another holy one said to him, "How long
will it take for the vision to be fulfilled—
the vision concerning the daily sacrifice,
the rebellion that causes desolation, and
the surrender of the sanctuary and of the
host that will be trampled underfoot?"
14He said to me, "It will take 2,300
evenings and mornings; then the sanctuary will be reconsecrated."

The Interpretation of the Vision

15While I, Daniel, was watching the vision and trying to understand it, there before me stood one who looked like a
man. 16And I heard a man's voice from the
Ulai calling, "Gabriel, tell this man the
meaning of the vision."
17As he came near the place where I was
standing, I was terrified and fell prostrate.
"Son of man," he said to me, "understand
that the vision concerns the time of the
end."
18While he was speaking to me, I was in
a deep sleep, with my face to the ground.
Then he touched me and raised me to my
feet.
19He said: "I am going to tell you what
will happen later in the time of wrath, because the vision concerns the appointed
time of the end.[b] 20The two-horned ram
that you saw represents the kings of Media and Persia. 21The shaggy goat is the
king of Greece, and the large horn between his eyes is the first king. 22The four
horns that replaced the one that was broken off represent four kingdoms that will
emerge from his nation but will not have
the same power.
23"In the latter part of their reign, when
rebels have become completely wicked, a
stern-faced king, a master of intrigue, will
arise. 24He will become very strong, but
not by his own power. He will cause astounding devastation and will succeed in
whatever he does. He will destroy the
mighty men and the holy people. 25He
will cause deceit to prosper, and he will
consider himself superior. When they feel
secure, he will destroy many and take
his stand against the Prince of princes. Yet
he will be destroyed, but not by human
power.
26"The vision of the evenings and mornings that has been given you is true, but

[a] 12 Or *rebellion, the armies* [b] 19 Or *because the end will be at the appointed time*

seal up the vision, for it concerns the distant future."
27I, Daniel, was exhausted and lay ill for
several days. Then I got up and went about
the king's business. I was appalled by the
vision; it was beyond understanding.

PRAYER: AFFIRMATION

UNLESS You build the house, O Lord, its builders labor in vain. Unless You guard the city, the watchmen stay awake in vain.

(Psalm 127:1)

***PAUSE** to reflect on these Biblical affirmations.*

NT John 3:22–4:26

John the Baptist's Testimony About Jesus

22After this, Jesus and his disciples went
out into the Judean countryside, where he
spent some time with them, and baptized.
23Now John also was baptizing at Aenon
near Salim, because there was plenty of water, and people were constantly coming to
be baptized. 24(This was before John was
put in prison.) 25An argument developed
between some of John's disciples and a certain Jew[a] over the matter of ceremonial
washing. 26They came to John and said to
him, "Rabbi, that man who was with you
on the other side of the Jordan—the one
you testified about—well, he is baptizing,
and everyone is going to him."
27To this John replied, "A man can receive only what is given him from heaven.
28You yourselves can testify that I said, 'I am
not the Christ[b] but am sent ahead of him.'
29The bride belongs to the bridegroom. The
friend who attends the bridegroom waits
and listens for him, and is full of joy when
he hears the bridegroom's voice. That joy
is mine, and it is now complete. 30He must
become greater; I must become less.
31"The one who comes from above is
above all; the one who is from the earth
belongs to the earth, and speaks as one
from the earth. The one who comes from
heaven is above all. 32He testifies to what
he has seen and heard, but no one accepts
his testimony. 33The man who has accepted it has certified that God is truthful.
34For the one whom God has sent speaks
the words of God, for God[c] gives the Spirit without limit. 35The Father loves the Son
and has placed everything in his hands.
36Whoever believes in the Son has eternal
life, but whoever rejects the Son will not
see life, for God's wrath remains on him."[d]

Jesus Talks With a Samaritan Woman

4 The Pharisees heard that Jesus was
gaining and baptizing more disciples
than John, 2although in fact it was not
Jesus who baptized, but his disciples.
3When the Lord learned of this, he left
Judea and went back once more to Galilee.
4Now he had to go through Samaria.
5So he came to a town in Samaria called
Sychar, near the plot of ground Jacob had
given to his son Joseph. 6Jacob's well was
there, and Jesus, tired as he was from the
journey, sat down by the well. It was
about the sixth hour.
7When a Samaritan woman came to
draw water, Jesus said to her, "Will you
give me a drink?" 8(His disciples had gone
into the town to buy food.)
9The Samaritan woman said to him,
"You are a Jew and I am a Samaritan
woman. How can you ask me for a
drink?" (For Jews do not associate with
Samaritans.[e])
10Jesus answered her, "If you knew the
gift of God and who it is that asks you for
a drink, you would have asked him and
he would have given you living water."
11"Sir," the woman said, "you have
nothing to draw with and the well is deep.
Where can you get this living water? 12Are
you greater than our father Jacob, who
gave us the well and drank from it himself, as did also his sons and his flocks
and herds?"
13Jesus answered, "Everyone who drinks
this water will be thirsty again, 14but who-

[a] 25 Some manuscripts *and certain Jews* [b] 28 Or *Messiah* [c] 34 Greek *he* [d] 36 Some interpreters end the quotation after verse 30. [e] 9 Or *do not use dishes Samaritans have used*

ever drinks the water I give him will never thirst. Indeed, the water I give him will become in him a spring of water welling up to eternal life."

[15]The woman said to him, "Sir, give me this water so that I won't get thirsty and have to keep coming here to draw water."

[16]He told her, "Go, call your husband and come back."

[17]"I have no husband," she replied.

Jesus said to her, "You are right when you say you have no husband. [18]The fact is, you have had five husbands, and the man you now have is not your husband. What you have just said is quite true."

[19]"Sir," the woman said, "I can see that you are a prophet. [20]Our fathers worshiped on this mountain, but you Jews claim that the place where we must worship is in Jerusalem."

[21]Jesus declared, "Believe me, woman, a time is coming when you will worship the Father neither on this mountain nor in Jerusalem. [22]You Samaritans worship what you do not know; we worship what we do know, for salvation is from the Jews. [23]Yet a time is coming and has now come when the true worshipers will worship the Father in spirit and truth, for they are the kind of worshipers the Father seeks. [24]God is spirit, and his worshipers must worship in spirit and in truth."

[25]The woman said, "I know that Messiah" (called Christ) "is coming. When he comes, he will explain everything to us."

[26]Then Jesus declared, "I who speak to you am he."

PRAYER: THE CHARACTER I WANT TO CULTIVATE

SINCE I have Your promises, O God, I will cleanse myself from all pollution of body and spirit, perfecting holiness in the fear of You, God. (2 Corinthians 7:1) . . . I will conduct myself in a manner worthy of Your gospel, O Christ, standing firm in one spirit with other believers, with one mind striving together for the faith of the gospel. (Philippians 1:27)

TAKE *a moment to ask the Lord for the grace to grow in godly character.*

OT Daniel 9:1–11:1

YEAR 2 DAY 300

Daniel's Prayer

9 In the first year of Darius son of Xerxes[a] (a Mede by descent), who was made ruler over the Babylonian[b] kingdom— [2]in the first year of his reign, I, Daniel, understood from the Scriptures, according to the word of the LORD given to Jeremiah the prophet, that the desolation of Jerusalem would last seventy years. [3]So I turned to the Lord God and pleaded with him in prayer and petition, in fasting, and in sackcloth and ashes.

[4]I prayed to the LORD my God and confessed:

"O Lord, the great and awesome God, who keeps his covenant of love with all who love him and obey his commands, [5]we have sinned and done wrong. We have been wicked and have rebelled; we have turned away from your commands and laws. [6]We have not listened to your servants the prophets, who spoke in your name to our kings, our princes and our fathers, and to all the people of the land.

[7]"Lord, you are righteous, but this day we are covered with shame—the men of Judah and people of Jerusalem and all Israel, both near and far, in all the countries where you have scattered us because of our unfaithfulness to you. [8]O LORD, we and our kings, our princes and our fathers are covered with shame because we have sinned against you. [9]The Lord our God is merciful and forgiving, even though we have rebelled against him; [10]we have not obeyed the LORD

[a] 1 Hebrew *Ahasuerus* [b] 1 Or *Chaldean*

our God or kept the laws he gave us through his servants the prophets. 11All Israel has transgressed your law and turned away, refusing to obey you.

"Therefore the curses and sworn judgments written in the Law of Moses, the servant of God, have been poured out on us, because we have sinned against you. 12You have fulfilled the words spoken against us and against our rulers by bringing upon us great disaster. Under the whole heaven nothing has ever been done like what has been done to Jerusalem. 13Just as it is written in the Law of Moses, all this disaster has come upon us, yet we have not sought the favor of the LORD our God by turning from our sins and giving attention to your truth. 14The LORD did not hesitate to bring the disaster upon us, for the LORD our God is righteous in everything he does; yet we have not obeyed him.

15"Now, O Lord our God, who brought your people out of Egypt with a mighty hand and who made for yourself a name that endures to this day, we have sinned, we have done wrong. 16O Lord, in keeping with all your righteous acts, turn away your anger and your wrath from Jerusalem, your city, your holy hill. Our sins and the iniquities of our fathers have made Jerusalem and your people an object of scorn to all those around us.

17"Now, our God, hear the prayers and petitions of your servant. For your sake, O Lord, look with favor on your desolate sanctuary. 18Give ear, O God, and hear; open your eyes and see the desolation of the city that bears your Name. We do not make requests of you because we are righteous, but because of your great mercy. 19O Lord, listen! O Lord, forgive! O Lord, hear and act! For your sake, O my God, do not delay, because your city and your people bear your Name."

The Seventy "Sevens"

20While I was speaking and praying, confessing my sin and the sin of my people Israel and making my request to the LORD my God for his holy hill— 21while I was still in prayer, Gabriel, the man I had seen in the earlier vision, came to me in swift flight about the time of the evening sacrifice. 22He instructed me and said to me, "Daniel, I have now come to give you insight and understanding. 23As soon as you began to pray, an answer was given, which I have come to tell you, for you are highly esteemed. Therefore, consider the message and understand the vision:

24"Seventy 'sevens'[c] are decreed for your people and your holy city to finish[d] transgression, to put an end to sin, to atone for wickedness, to bring in everlasting righteousness, to seal up vision and prophecy and to anoint the most holy.[e]

25"Know and understand this: From the issuing of the decree[f] to restore and rebuild Jerusalem until the Anointed One,[g] the ruler, comes, there will be seven 'sevens,' and sixty-two 'sevens.' It will be rebuilt with streets and a trench, but in times of trouble. 26After the sixty-two 'sevens,' the Anointed One will be cut off and will have nothing.[h] The people of the ruler who will come will destroy the city and the sanctuary. The end will come like a flood: War will continue until the end, and desolations have been decreed. 27He will confirm a covenant with many for one 'seven.'[i] In the middle of the 'seven'[i] he will put an end to sacrifice and offering. And on a wing ⌞of the temple⌟ he will set up an abomination that causes desolation, until the end that is decreed is poured out on him.[j]"[k]

Daniel's Vision of a Man

10 In the third year of Cyrus king of Persia, a revelation was given to Daniel (who was called Belteshazzar). Its message was true and it concerned a great war.[l] The understanding of the message came to him in a vision.

2At that time I, Daniel, mourned for three weeks. 3I ate no choice food; no meat or wine touched my lips; and I used

[c] 24 Or *'weeks'*; also in verses 25 and 26 [d] 24 Or *restrain* [e] 24 Or *Most Holy Place*; or *most holy One* [f] 25 Or *word* [g] 25 Or *an anointed one*; also in verse 26 [h] 26 Or *off and will have no one*; or *off, but not for himself* [i] 27 Or *'week'* [j] 27 Or *it* [k] 27 Or *And one who causes desolation will come upon the pinnacle of the abominable ⌞temple⌟, until the end that is decreed is poured out on the desolated ⌞city⌟* [l] 1 Or *true and burdensome*

no lotions at all until the three weeks were
over.
4 On the twenty-fourth day of the first
month, as I was standing on the bank of
the great river, the Tigris, 5 I looked up and
there before me was a man dressed in
linen, with a belt of the finest gold around
his waist. 6 His body was like chrysolite,
his face like lightning, his eyes like flaming torches, his arms and legs like the
gleam of burnished bronze, and his voice
like the sound of a multitude.
7 I, Daniel, was the only one who saw
the vision; the men with me did not see
it, but such terror overwhelmed them that
they fled and hid themselves. 8 So I was
left alone, gazing at this great vision; I had
no strength left, my face turned deathly
pale and I was helpless. 9 Then I heard him
speaking, and as I listened to him, I fell
into a deep sleep, my face to the ground.
10 A hand touched me and set me trembling on my hands and knees. 11 He said,
"Daniel, you who are highly esteemed,
consider carefully the words I am about
to speak to you, and stand up, for I have
now been sent to you." And when he said
this to me, I stood up trembling.
12 Then he continued, "Do not be afraid,
Daniel. Since the first day that you set
your mind to gain understanding and to
humble yourself before your God, your
words were heard, and I have come in response to them. 13 But the prince of the
Persian kingdom resisted me twenty-one
days. Then Michael, one of the chief
princes, came to help me, because I was
detained there with the king of Persia.
14 Now I have come to explain to you what
will happen to your people in the future,
for the vision concerns a time yet to
come."
15 While he was saying this to me, I
bowed with my face toward the ground
and was speechless. 16 Then one who
looked like a man[m] touched my lips, and
I opened my mouth and began to speak.
I said to the one standing before me, "I
am overcome with anguish because of the
vision, my lord, and I am helpless. 17 How
can I, your servant, talk with you, my
lord? My strength is gone and I can hardly breathe."
18 Again the one who looked like a man
touched me and gave me strength. 19 "Do
not be afraid, O man highly esteemed,"
he said. "Peace! Be strong now; be
strong."
When he spoke to me, I was strengthened and said, "Speak, my lord, since you
have given me strength."
20 So he said, "Do you know why I have
come to you? Soon I will return to fight
against the prince of Persia, and when I
go, the prince of Greece will come; 21 but
first I will tell you what is written in the
Book of Truth. (No one supports me
against them except Michael, your prince.
11 1 And in the first year of Darius the
Mede, I took my stand to support and
protect him.)

[m] *16* Most manuscripts of the Masoretic Text; one manuscript of the Masoretic Text, Dead Sea Scrolls and Septuagint *Then something that looked like a man's hand*

PRAYER: THANKSGIVING

YOU, O Son of Man, did not come to be served, but to serve, and to give Your life as a ransom for many. (Mark 10:45)

. . . While You were eating Your last Passover meal with Your disciples, Jesus, You took bread, blessed it, and broke it, and gave it to Your disciples, saying, "Take it; this is My body." Then You took the cup, and when You had given thanks You gave it to them, and they all drank from it. And You said to them, "This is My blood of the covenant, which is poured out for many." (Mark 14:22–24)

PAUSE *to offer your own expressions of thanksgiving.*

NT John 4:27-54

The Disciples Rejoin Jesus

27 Just then his disciples returned and
were surprised to find him talking with a
woman. But no one asked, "What do you
want?" or "Why are you talking with her?"
28 Then, leaving her water jar, the
woman went back to the town and said to
the people, 29 "Come, see a man who told
me everything I ever did. Could this be
the Christ[a]?" 30 They came out of the town
and made their way toward him.
31 Meanwhile his disciples urged him,
"Rabbi, eat something."
32 But he said to them, "I have food to
eat that you know nothing about."
33 Then his disciples said to each other,
"Could someone have brought him
food?"
34 "My food," said Jesus, "is to do the will
of him who sent me and to finish his work.
35 Do you not say, 'Four months more and
then the harvest'? I tell you, open your eyes
and look at the fields! They are ripe for harvest. 36 Even now the reaper draws his wages,
even now he harvests the crop for eternal
life, so that the sower and the reaper may
be glad together. 37 Thus the saying 'One
sows and another reaps' is true. 38 I sent you
to reap what you have not worked for. Others have done the hard work, and you have
reaped the benefits of their labor."

Many Samaritans Believe

39 Many of the Samaritans from that town
believed in him because of the woman's
testimony, "He told me everything I ever
did." 40 So when the Samaritans came to
him, they urged him to stay with them, and
he stayed two days. 41 And because of his
words many more became believers.
42 They said to the woman, "We no
longer believe just because of what you
said; now we have heard for ourselves,
and we know that this man really is the
Savior of the world."

Jesus Heals the Official's Son

43 After the two days he left for Galilee.
44 (Now Jesus himself had pointed out that
a prophet has no honor in his own country.) 45 When he arrived in Galilee, the Galileans welcomed him. They had seen all
that he had done in Jerusalem at the
Passover Feast, for they also had been there.
46 Once more he visited Cana in Galilee,
where he had turned the water into wine.
And there was a certain royal official
whose son lay sick at Capernaum. 47 When
this man heard that Jesus had arrived in
Galilee from Judea, he went to him and
begged him to come and heal his son,
who was close to death.
48 "Unless you people see miraculous
signs and wonders," Jesus told him, "you
will never believe."
49 The royal official said, "Sir, come
down before my child dies."
50 Jesus replied, "You may go. Your son
will live."
The man took Jesus at his word and departed. 51 While he was still on the way, his
servants met him with the news that his
boy was living. 52 When he inquired as to
the time when his son got better, they said
to him, "The fever left him yesterday at
the seventh hour."
53 Then the father realized that this was
the exact time at which Jesus had said to
him, "Your son will live." So he and all his
household believed.
54 This was the second miraculous sign
that Jesus performed, having come from
Judea to Galilee.

[a] 29 Or *Messiah*

PRAYER: MY RELATIONSHIP TO OTHERS

LORD, we know that there should be no division in the body, but its members should have concern for each other. If one member suffers, all the members suffer with it; if one member is honored, all the members rejoice with it. Now we are Your body, O Christ, and each one of us is a member of it. (1 Corinthians 12:25–27)

***PAUSE** to review your relationships with others and to commit them to the Lord.*

Psalm 132

A song of ascents.

1 O LORD, remember David
and all the hardships he endured.

2 He swore an oath to the LORD
and made a vow to the Mighty One of Jacob:
3 "I will not enter my house
or go to my bed—
4 I will allow no sleep to my eyes,
no slumber to my eyelids,
5 till I find a place for the LORD,
a dwelling for the Mighty One of Jacob."

6 We heard it in Ephrathah,
we came upon it in the fields of Jaar[a]:[b]
7 "Let us go to his dwelling place;
let us worship at his footstool—
8 arise, O LORD, and come to your resting place,
you and the ark of your might.
9 May your priests be clothed with righteousness;
may your saints sing for joy."

10 For the sake of David your servant,
do not reject your anointed one.

11 The LORD swore an oath to David,
a sure oath that he will not revoke:
"One of your own descendants
I will place on your throne—
12 if your sons keep my covenant
and the statutes I teach them,
then their sons will sit
on your throne for ever and ever."

13 For the LORD has chosen Zion,
he has desired it for his dwelling:
14 "This is my resting place for ever and ever;
here I will sit enthroned, for I have desired it—
15 I will bless her with abundant provisions;
her poor will I satisfy with food.
16 I will clothe her priests with salvation,
and her saints will ever sing for joy.

17 "Here I will make a horn[c] grow for David
and set up a lamp for my anointed one.
18 I will clothe his enemies with shame,
but the crown on his head will be resplendent."

Psalm 133

A song of ascents. Of David.

1 How good and pleasant it is
when brothers live together in unity!
2 It is like precious oil poured on the head,
running down on the beard,
running down on Aaron's beard,
down upon the collar of his robes.
3 It is as if the dew of Hermon
were falling on Mount Zion.
For there the LORD bestows his blessing,
even life forevermore.

[a] 6 That is, Kiriath Jearim [b] 6 Or *heard of it in Ephrathah, / we found it in the fields of Jaar.* (And no quotes around verses 7–9) [c] 17 *Horn* here symbolizes strong one, that is, king.

PRAYER: ADORATION

YOU are the Lord, the God of our fathers—the God of Abraham, the God of Isaac and the God of Jacob. This is Your name forever, the name by which You are to be remembered from generation to generation. (Exodus 3:15) . . . I will sing to You, Lord, for You are highly exalted. You are my strength and my song; You have become my salvation. You are my God, and I will praise You, my father's God, and I will exalt You. (Exodus 15:1–2)

PAUSE *to express your thoughts of praise and worship.*

NT John 5:1-30

The Healing at the Pool

5 Some time later, Jesus went up to Jerusalem for a feast of the Jews. 2Now there is in Jerusalem near the Sheep Gate a pool, which in Aramaic is called Bethesda[a] and which is surrounded by five covered colonnades. 3Here a great number of disabled people used to lie—the blind, the lame, the paralyzed.[b] 5One who was there had been an invalid for thirty-eight years. 6When Jesus saw him lying there and learned that he had been in this condition for a long time, he asked him, "Do you want to get well?"

7"Sir," the invalid replied, "I have no one to help me into the pool when the water is stirred. While I am trying to get in, someone else goes down ahead of me."

8Then Jesus said to him, "Get up! Pick up your mat and walk." 9At once the man was cured; he picked up his mat and walked.

The day on which this took place was a Sabbath, 10and so the Jews said to the man who had been healed, "It is the Sabbath; the law forbids you to carry your mat."

11But he replied, "The man who made me well said to me, 'Pick up your mat and walk.' "

12So they asked him, "Who is this fellow who told you to pick it up and walk?"

13The man who was healed had no idea who it was, for Jesus had slipped away into the crowd that was there.

14Later Jesus found him at the temple and said to him, "See, you are well again. Stop sinning or something worse may happen to you." 15The man went away and told the Jews that it was Jesus who had made him well.

Life Through the Son

16So, because Jesus was doing these things on the Sabbath, the Jews persecuted him. 17Jesus said to them, "My Father is always at his work to this very day, and I, too, am working." 18For this reason the Jews tried all the harder to kill him; not only was he breaking the Sabbath, but he was even calling God his own Father, making himself equal with God.

19Jesus gave them this answer: "I tell you the truth, the Son can do nothing by himself; he can do only what he sees his Father doing, because whatever the Father does the Son also does. 20For the Father loves the Son and shows him all he does. Yes, to your amazement he will show him even greater things than these. 21For just as the Father raises the dead and gives them life, even so the Son gives life to whom he is pleased to give it. 22Moreover, the Father judges no one, but has entrusted all judgment to the Son, 23that all may honor the Son just as they honor the Father. He who does not honor the Son does not honor the Father, who sent him.

24"I tell you the truth, whoever hears my word and believes him who sent me has eternal life and will not be condemned; he has crossed over from death to life. 25I tell you the truth, a time is coming and has now come when the dead will hear the voice of the Son of God and those who hear will live. 26For as the Father has life in himself, so he has granted the Son to have life in himself. 27And he has given him authority to judge because he is the Son of Man.

28"Do not be amazed at this, for a time is coming when all who are in their graves will hear his voice 29and come out—those who have done good will rise to live, and those who have done evil will rise to be condemned. 30By myself I can do nothing; I judge only as I hear, and my judgment is just, for I seek not to please myself but him who sent me.

[a] 2 Some manuscripts *Bethzatha;* other manuscripts *Bethsaida* [b] 3 Some less important manuscripts *paralyzed—and they waited for the moving of the waters. 4From time to time an angel of the Lord would come down and stir up the waters. The first one into the pool after each such disturbance would be cured of whatever disease he had.*

PRAYER: THE ATTRIBUTES OF GOD

I WILL proclaim Your name, O Lord, and praise Your greatness, O my God. (Deuteronomy 32:3) . . . Your name is the Lord: I know that You alone are the Most High over all the earth. (Psalm 83:18)

***PAUSE** to reflect on these affirmations about the person, powers and perfection of God.*

YEAR 2 DAY 302

OT Daniel 11:2-45

The Kings of the South and the North

2 "Now then, I tell you the truth: Three
more kings will appear in Persia, and then
a fourth, who will be far richer than all
the others. When he has gained power by
his wealth, he will stir up everyone against
the kingdom of Greece. 3 Then a mighty
king will appear, who will rule with great
power and do as he pleases. 4 After he has
appeared, his empire will be broken up
and parceled out toward the four winds of
heaven. It will not go to his descendants,
nor will it have the power he exercised,
because his empire will be uprooted and
given to others.
5 "The king of the South will become
strong, but one of his commanders will
become even stronger than he and will
rule his own kingdom with great power.
6 After some years, they will become allies.
The daughter of the king of the South will
go to the king of the North to make an alliance, but she will not retain her power,
and he and his power[a] will not last. In
those days she will be handed over, together with her royal escort and her father[b] and the one who supported her.
7 "One from her family line will arise to
take her place. He will attack the forces of
the king of the North and enter his
fortress; he will fight against them and be
victorious. 8 He will also seize their gods,
their metal images and their valuable articles of silver and gold and carry them off
to Egypt. For some years he will leave the
king of the North alone. 9 Then the king of
the North will invade the realm of the
king of the South but will retreat to his
own country. 10 His sons will prepare for
war and assemble a great army, which will
sweep on like an irresistible flood and carry the battle as far as his fortress.
11 "Then the king of the South will
march out in a rage and fight against the
king of the North, who will raise a large
army, but it will be defeated. 12 When the
army is carried off, the king of the South
will be filled with pride and will slaughter many thousands, yet he will not remain triumphant. 13 For the king of the
North will muster another army, larger
than the first; and after several years, he
will advance with a huge army fully
equipped.
14 "In those times many will rise against
the king of the South. The violent men
among your own people will rebel in fulfillment of the vision, but without success. 15 Then the king of the North will
come and build up siege ramps and will
capture a fortified city. The forces of the
South will be powerless to resist; even
their best troops will not have the strength
to stand. 16 The invader will do as he
pleases; no one will be able to stand
against him. He will establish himself in
the Beautiful Land and will have the power to destroy it. 17 He will determine to
come with the might of his entire kingdom and will make an alliance with the
king of the South. And he will give him a
daughter in marriage in order to overthrow the kingdom, but his plans[c] will
not succeed or help him. 18 Then he will
turn his attention to the coastlands and
will take many of them, but a commander will put an end to his insolence and
will turn his insolence back upon him.
19 After this, he will turn back toward the
fortresses of his own country but will
stumble and fall, to be seen no more.
20 "His successor will send out a tax col-

[a] *6* Or *offspring* [b] *6* Or *child* (see Vulgate and Syriac) [c] *17* Or *but she*

lector to maintain the royal splendor. In a
few years, however, he will be destroyed,
yet not in anger or in battle.
21 "He will be succeeded by a contemptible person who has not been given
the honor of royalty. He will invade the
kingdom when its people feel secure, and
he will seize it through intrigue. 22 Then an
overwhelming army will be swept away
before him; both it and a prince of the
covenant will be destroyed. 23 After coming to an agreement with him, he will act
deceitfully, and with only a few people he
will rise to power. 24 When the richest
provinces feel secure, he will invade them
and will achieve what neither his fathers
nor his forefathers did. He will distribute
plunder, loot and wealth among his followers. He will plot the overthrow of
fortresses—but only for a time.
25 "With a large army he will stir up his
strength and courage against the king of
the South. The king of the South will wage
war with a large and very powerful army,
but he will not be able to stand because
of the plots devised against him. 26 Those
who eat from the king's provisions will try
to destroy him; his army will be swept
away, and many will fall in battle. 27 The
two kings, with their hearts bent on evil,
will sit at the same table and lie to each
other, but to no avail, because an end will
still come at the appointed time. 28 The
king of the North will return to his own
country with great wealth, but his heart
will be set against the holy covenant. He
will take action against it and then return
to his own country.
29 "At the appointed time he will invade
the South again, but this time the outcome will be different from what it was
before. 30 Ships of the western coastlands[d]
will oppose him, and he will lose heart.
Then he will turn back and vent his fury
against the holy covenant. He will return
and show favor to those who forsake the
holy covenant.
31 "His armed forces will rise up to desecrate the temple fortress and will abolish
the daily sacrifice. Then they will set up
the abomination that causes desolation.
32 With flattery he will corrupt those who
have violated the covenant, but the people who know their God will firmly resist
him.
33 "Those who are wise will instruct
many, though for a time they will fall by
the sword or be burned or captured or
plundered. 34 When they fall, they will receive a little help, and many who are not
sincere will join them. 35 Some of the wise
will stumble, so that they may be refined,
purified and made spotless until the time
of the end, for it will still come at the appointed time.

The King Who Exalts Himself

36 "The king will do as he pleases. He
will exalt and magnify himself above
every god and will say unheard-of things
against the God of gods. He will be successful until the time of wrath is completed, for what has been determined
must take place. 37 He will show no regard
for the gods of his fathers or for the one
desired by women, nor will he regard any
god, but will exalt himself above them all.
38 Instead of them, he will honor a god of
fortresses; a god unknown to his fathers
he will honor with gold and silver, with
precious stones and costly gifts. 39 He will
attack the mightiest fortresses with the
help of a foreign god and will greatly hon-
or those who acknowledge him. He will
make them rulers over many people and
will distribute the land at a price.[e]
40 "At the time of the end the king of the
South will engage him in battle, and the
king of the North will storm out against
him with chariots and cavalry and a great
fleet of ships. He will invade many countries and sweep through them like a flood.
41 He will also invade the Beautiful Land.
Many countries will fall, but Edom, Moab
and the leaders of Ammon will be delivered from his hand. 42 He will extend his
power over many countries; Egypt will not
escape. 43 He will gain control of the treasures of gold and silver and all the riches
of Egypt, with the Libyans and Nubians in
submission. 44 But reports from the east
and the north will alarm him, and he will
set out in a great rage to destroy and annihilate many. 45 He will pitch his royal
tents between the seas at[f] the beautiful
holy mountain. Yet he will come to his
end, and no one will help him.

[d] 30 Hebrew *of Kittim* [e] 39 Or *land for a reward*
[f] 45 Or *the sea and*

PRAYER: CONFESSION

HAVE mercy on me, O God, according to Your loyal love; according to the greatness of Your compassion blot out my transgressions. Wash me completely from my iniquity and cleanse me from my sin. For I know my transgressions, and my sin is ever before me. Against You, You only, have I sinned and done what is evil in Your sight, so that You are justified when You speak and blameless when You judge.

(Psalm 51:1–4)

***ASK** the Spirit to search your heart and reveal any areas of unconfessed sin. Acknowledge these to the Lord and thank Him for His forgiveness.*

NT John 5:31–47

Testimonies About Jesus

31 "If I testify about myself, my testimony is not valid. 32 There is another who testifies in my favor, and I know that his testimony about me is valid.

33 "You have sent to John and he has testified to the truth. 34 Not that I accept human testimony; but I mention it that you
may be saved. 35 John was a lamp that
burned and gave light, and you chose for
a time to enjoy his light.

36 "I have testimony weightier than that
of John. For the very work that the Father
has given me to finish, and which I am
doing, testifies that the Father has sent
me. 37 And the Father who sent me has
himself testified concerning me. You have
never heard his voice nor seen his form,
38 nor does his word dwell in you, for you
do not believe the one he sent. 39 You diligently study[a] the Scriptures because you
think that by them you possess eternal
life. These are the Scriptures that testify
about me, 40 yet you refuse to come to me
to have life.

41 "I do not accept praise from men,
42 but I know you. I know that you do not
have the love of God in your hearts. 43 I
have come in my Father's name, and you
do not accept me; but if someone else
comes in his own name, you will accept
him. 44 How can you believe if you accept
praise from one another, yet make no effort to obtain the praise that comes from
the only God[b]?

45 "But do not think I will accuse you before the Father. Your accuser is Moses, on
whom your hopes are set. 46 If you believed Moses, you would believe me, for
he wrote about me. 47 But since you do not
believe what he wrote, how are you going
to believe what I say?"

[a] 39 Or *Study diligently* (the imperative)
[b] 44 Some early manuscripts *the Only One*

PRAYER: THE WORKS OF GOD

JESUS, You had compassion on the crowds, because they were like sheep without a shepherd. So You began to teach them many things. (Mark 6:34) . . . Those who were sick with various kinds of disease were brought to You, Lord Jesus; and, laying Your hands on each one, You healed them.

(Luke 4:40)

***TAKE** a moment to consider the greatness of God's wonderful works.*

YEAR 2
DAY 303

OT Daniel 12:1-13

The End Times

12 "At that time Michael, the great prince
who protects your people, will arise.
There will be a time of distress such as has
not happened from the beginning of nations until then. But at that time your people—everyone whose name is found written in the book—will be delivered.
2Multitudes who sleep in the dust of the
earth will awake: some to everlasting life,
others to shame and everlasting contempt. 3Those who are wise[a] will shine
like the brightness of the heavens, and
those who lead many to righteousness,
like the stars for ever and ever. 4But you,
Daniel, close up and seal the words of the
scroll until the time of the end. Many will
go here and there to increase knowledge."

5Then I, Daniel, looked, and there before me stood two others, one on this
bank of the river and one on the opposite
bank. 6One of them said to the man
clothed in linen, who was above the waters of the river, "How long will it be before these astonishing things are fulfilled?"
7The man clothed in linen, who was
above the waters of the river, lifted his
right hand and his left hand toward heav-
en, and I heard him swear by him who
lives forever, saying, "It will be for a time,
times and half a time.[b] When the power
of the holy people has been finally broken, all these things will be completed."
8I heard, but I did not understand. So I
asked, "My lord, what will the outcome of
all this be?"
9He replied, "Go your way, Daniel, because the words are closed up and sealed
until the time of the end. 10Many will be
purified, made spotless and refined, but
the wicked will continue to be wicked.
None of the wicked will understand, but
those who are wise will understand.
11"From the time that the daily sacrifice
is abolished and the abomination that
causes desolation is set up, there will
be 1,290 days. 12Blessed is the one who
waits for and reaches the end of the 1,335
days.
13"As for you, go your way till the end.
You will rest, and then at the end of the
days you will rise to receive your allotted
inheritance."

[a] 3 Or *who impart wisdom* [b] 7 Or *a year, two years and half a year*

PRAYER: RENEWAL

JESUS, You are the vine; I am a branch. If I abide in You, and You in me, I will bear much fruit; for apart from You, I can do nothing. By this is Your Father glorified, that I bear much fruit, showing myself to be Your disciple. (John 15:5, 8)

***PAUSE** to add your own prayers for personal renewal.*

NT John 6:1-24

Jesus Feeds the Five Thousand

6 Some time after this, Jesus crossed to
the far shore of the Sea of Galilee (that
is, the Sea of Tiberias), 2and a great crowd
of people followed him because they saw
the miraculous signs he had performed on
the sick. 3Then Jesus went up on a mountainside and sat down with his disciples.
4The Jewish Passover Feast was near.
5When Jesus looked up and saw a great
crowd coming toward him, he said to
Philip, "Where shall we buy bread for
these people to eat?" 6He asked this only
to test him, for he already had in mind
what he was going to do.
7Philip answered him, "Eight months'
wages[a] would not buy enough bread for
each one to have a bite!"
8Another of his disciples, Andrew, Si-

[a] 7 Greek *two hundred denarii*

mon Peter's brother, spoke up, 9“Here is a
boy with five small barley loaves and two
small fish, but how far will they go among
so many?”
10Jesus said, “Have the people sit
down.” There was plenty of grass in that
place, and the men sat down, about five
thousand of them. 11Jesus then took the
loaves, gave thanks, and distributed to
those who were seated as much as they
wanted. He did the same with the fish.
12When they had all had enough to eat,
he said to his disciples, “Gather the pieces
that are left over. Let nothing be wasted.”
13So they gathered them and filled twelve
baskets with the pieces of the five barley
loaves left over by those who had eaten.
14After the people saw the miraculous
sign that Jesus did, they began to say,
“Surely this is the Prophet who is to come
into the world.” 15Jesus, knowing that they
intended to come and make him king by
force, withdrew again to a mountain by
himself.

Jesus Walks on the Water

16When evening came, his disciples
went down to the lake, 17where they got
into a boat and set off across the lake for
Capernaum. By now it was dark, and Jesus
had not yet joined them. 18A strong wind
was blowing and the waters grew rough.
19When they had rowed three or three and
a half miles,[b] they saw Jesus approaching
the boat, walking on the water; and they
were terrified. 20But he said to them, “It is
I; don't be afraid.” 21Then they were willing to take him into the boat, and immediately the boat reached the shore where
they were heading.
22The next day the crowd that had
stayed on the opposite shore of the lake
realized that only one boat had been
there, and that Jesus had not entered it
with his disciples, but that they had gone
away alone. 23Then some boats from Tiberias landed near the place where the
people had eaten the bread after the Lord
had given thanks. 24Once the crowd realized that neither Jesus nor his disciples
were there, they got into the boats and
went to Capernaum in search of Jesus.

[b] *19* Greek *rowed twenty-five or thirty stadia* (about 5 or 6 kilometers)

PRAYER: MY RELATIONSHIP TO GOD

THOSE who believe in You, the Son, have eternal life, but those who reject You, the Son, will not see life, for the wrath of God remains on them. (John 3:36) . . . Blessed are those who have not seen You, Jesus, and yet have believed in You. (John 20:29)

PAUSE *to thank God for the relationship that you enjoy with Him in Jesus Christ.*

YEAR 2 DAY 304

OT Hosea 1:1–2:23

1 The word of the LORD that came to Hosea son of Beeri during the reigns of Uzziah, Jotham, Ahaz and Hezekiah, kings
of Judah, and during the reign of Jeroboam son of Jehoash[a] king of Israel:

Hosea's Wife and Children

2When the LORD began to speak
through Hosea, the LORD said to him,
“Go, take to yourself an adulterous wife
and children of unfaithfulness, because
the land is guilty of the vilest adultery in
departing from the LORD.” 3So he married
Gomer daughter of Diblaim, and she conceived and bore him a son.
4Then the LORD said to Hosea, “Call
him Jezreel, because I will soon punish
the house of Jehu for the massacre at Jezreel, and I will put an end to the kingdom
of Israel. 5In that day I will break Israel's
bow in the Valley of Jezreel.”
6Gomer conceived again and gave birth
to a daughter. Then the LORD said to Hosea, “Call her Lo-Ruhamah,[b] for I will no

[a] *1* Hebrew *Joash,* a variant of *Jehoash*
[b] *6* *Lo-Ruhamah* means *not loved.*

longer show love to the house of Israel,
that I should at all forgive them. 7 Yet I will
show love to the house of Judah; and I
will save them—not by bow, sword or battle, or by horses and horsemen, but by the
LORD their God."

8 After she had weaned Lo-Ruhamah,
Gomer had another son. 9 Then the LORD
said, "Call him Lo-Ammi,[c] for you are not
my people, and I am not your God.

10 "Yet the Israelites will be like the sand
on the seashore, which cannot be measured or counted. In the place where it
was said to them, 'You are not my people,'
they will be called 'sons of the living God.'
11 The people of Judah and the people of
Israel will be reunited, and they will appoint one leader and will come up out of
the land, for great will be the day of Jezreel.

2 "Say of your brothers, 'My people,' and
of your sisters, 'My loved one.'

Israel Punished and Restored

2 "Rebuke your mother, rebuke her,
for she is not my wife,
and I am not her husband.
Let her remove the adulterous look
from her face
and the unfaithfulness from
between her breasts.
3 Otherwise I will strip her naked
and make her as bare as on the day
she was born;
I will make her like a desert,
turn her into a parched land,
and slay her with thirst.
4 I will not show my love to her
children,
because they are the children of
adultery.
5 Their mother has been unfaithful
and has conceived them in disgrace.
She said, 'I will go after my lovers,
who give me my food and my
water,
my wool and my linen, my oil and
my drink.'
6 Therefore I will block her path with
thornbushes;
I will wall her in so that she cannot
find her way.
7 She will chase after her lovers but not
catch them;
she will look for them but not find
them.
Then she will say,
'I will go back to my husband as at
first,
for then I was better off than now.'
8 She has not acknowledged that I was
the one
who gave her the grain, the new
wine and oil,
who lavished on her the silver and
gold—
which they used for Baal.

9 "Therefore I will take away my grain
when it ripens,
and my new wine when it is ready.
I will take back my wool and my
linen,
intended to cover her nakedness.
10 So now I will expose her lewdness
before the eyes of her lovers;
no one will take her out of my
hands.
11 I will stop all her celebrations:
her yearly festivals, her New Moons,
her Sabbath days—all her
appointed feasts.
12 I will ruin her vines and her fig trees,
which she said were her pay from
her lovers;
I will make them a thicket,
and wild animals will devour them.
13 I will punish her for the days
she burned incense to the Baals;
she decked herself with rings and
jewelry,
and went after her lovers,
but me she forgot,"
declares the LORD.

14 "Therefore I am now going to allure
her;
I will lead her into the desert
and speak tenderly to her.
15 There I will give her back her
vineyards,
and will make the Valley of Achor[d]
a door of hope.
There she will sing[e] as in the days of
her youth,
as in the day she came up out of
Egypt.

16 "In that day," declares the LORD,
"you will call me 'my husband';
you will no longer call me 'my
master.[f]'

[c] 9 *Lo-Ammi* means *not my people.* [d] 15 *Achor* means *trouble.* [e] 15 Or *respond* [f] 16 Hebrew *baal*

[17]I will remove the names of the Baals
from her lips;
no longer will their names be
invoked.
[18]In that day I will make a covenant for
them
with the beasts of the field and the
birds of the air
and the creatures that move along
the ground.
Bow and sword and battle
I will abolish from the land,
so that all may lie down in safety.
[19]I will betroth you to me forever;
I will betroth you in[g] righteousness
and justice,
in[h] love and compassion.
[20]I will betroth you in faithfulness,
and you will acknowledge the LORD.

[21]"In that day I will respond,"
declares the LORD—
"I will respond to the skies,
and they will respond to the earth;
[22]and the earth will respond to the
grain,
the new wine and oil,
and they will respond to Jezreel.[i]
[23]I will plant her for myself in the land;
I will show my love to the one I
called 'Not my loved one.[j]'
I will say to those called 'Not my
people,[k]' 'You are my people';
and they will say, 'You are my
God.' "

[g] 19 Or *with;* also in verse 20 [h] 19 Or *with* [i] 22 *Jezreel* means *God plants.* [j] 23 Hebrew *Lo-Ruhamah* [k] 23 Hebrew *Lo-Ammi*

PRAYER: PETITION

LISTEN to my cry for help, my King and my God, for to You I pray. In the morning, O Lord, You will hear my voice; in the morning I will set my prayers before You and I will look to You. (Psalm 5:2–3)

PAUSE *here to petition God to help you be a faithful steward of your time, talents, possessions and relationships. Offer prayers of petition regarding your activities for this day and any special concerns you may have.*

NT John 6:25–59

Jesus the Bread of Life

[25]When they found him on the other
side of the lake, they asked him, "Rabbi,
when did you get here?"
[26]Jesus answered, "I tell you the truth,
you are looking for me, not because you
saw miraculous signs but because you ate
the loaves and had your fill. [27]Do not
work for food that spoils, but for food
that endures to eternal life, which the Son
of Man will give you. On him God the Father has placed his seal of approval."
[28]Then they asked him, "What must we
do to do the works God requires?"
[29]Jesus answered, "The work of God is
this: to believe in the one he has sent."
[30]So they asked him, "What miraculous
sign then will you give that we may see it
and believe you? What will you do? [31]Our
forefathers ate the manna in the desert; as
it is written: 'He gave them bread from
heaven to eat.'[a]"
[32]Jesus said to them, "I tell you the
truth, it is not Moses who has given you
the bread from heaven, but it is my Father
who gives you the true bread from heav-
en. [33]For the bread of God is he who
comes down from heaven and gives life to
the world."
[34]"Sir," they said, "from now on give us
this bread."
[35]Then Jesus declared, "I am the bread
of life. He who comes to me will never go
hungry, and he who believes in me will
never be thirsty. [36]But as I told you, you
have seen me and still you do not believe.
[37]All that the Father gives me will come to
me, and whoever comes to me I will never drive away. [38]For I have come down
from heaven not to do my will but to do
the will of him who sent me. [39]And this is
the will of him who sent me, that I shall
lose none of all that he has given me, but

[a] 31 Exodus 16:4; Neh. 9:15; Psalm 78:24,25

raise them up at the last day. [40]For my Father's will is that everyone who looks to the Son and believes in him shall have eternal life, and I will raise him up at the last day."

[41]At this the Jews began to grumble about him because he said, "I am the bread that came down from heaven." [42]They said, "Is this not Jesus, the son of Joseph, whose father and mother we know? How can he now say, 'I came down from heaven'?"

[43]"Stop grumbling among yourselves," Jesus answered. [44]"No one can come to me unless the Father who sent me draws him, and I will raise him up at the last day. [45]It is written in the Prophets: 'They will all be taught by God.'[b] Everyone who listens to the Father and learns from him comes to me. [46]No one has seen the Father except the one who is from God; only he has seen the Father. [47]I tell you the truth, he who believes has everlasting life. [48]I am the bread of life. [49]Your forefathers ate the manna in the desert, yet they died. [50]But here is the bread that comes down from heaven, which a man may eat and not die. [51]I am the living bread that came down from heaven. If anyone eats of this bread, he will live forever. This bread is my flesh, which I will give for the life of the world."

[52]Then the Jews began to argue sharply among themselves, "How can this man give us his flesh to eat?"

[53]Jesus said to them, "I tell you the truth, unless you eat the flesh of the Son of Man and drink his blood, you have no life in you. [54]Whoever eats my flesh and drinks my blood has eternal life, and I will raise him up at the last day. [55]For my flesh is real food and my blood is real drink. [56]Whoever eats my flesh and drinks my blood remains in me, and I in him. [57]Just as the living Father sent me and I live because of the Father, so the one who feeds on me will live because of me. [58]This is the bread that came down from heaven. Your forefathers ate manna and died, but he who feeds on this bread will live forever." [59]He said this while teaching in the synagogue in Capernaum.

[b] *45* Isaiah 54:13

PRAYER: THE CHARACTER I WANT TO CULTIVATE

I WANT to be an example, Lord, for other believers—in speech, in behavior, in love, in faith and in purity. (1 Timothy 4:12) . . . As one who has believed in You, O God, I want to be careful to devote myself to doing what is good. These things are good and profitable for everyone. (Titus 3:8)

***TAKE** a moment to ask the Lord for the grace to grow in godly character.*

YEAR 2 DAY 305

OT Hosea 3:1–4:19

Hosea's Reconciliation With His Wife

3 The LORD said to me, "Go, show your love to your wife again, though she is loved by another and is an adulteress. Love her as the LORD loves the Israelites, though they turn to other gods and love the sacred raisin cakes."

[2]So I bought her for fifteen shekels[a] of silver and about a homer and a lethek[b] of barley. [3]Then I told her, "You are to live with[c] me many days; you must not be a prostitute or be intimate with any man, and I will live with[c] you."

[4]For the Israelites will live many days without king or prince, without sacrifice or sacred stones, without ephod or idol. [5]Afterward the Israelites will return and seek the LORD their God and David their king. They will come trembling to the LORD and to his blessings in the last days.

[a] *2* That is, about 6 ounces (about 170 grams)
[b] *2* That is, probably about 10 bushels (about 330 liters) [c] *3* Or *wait for*

The Charge Against Israel

4 Hear the word of the LORD, you Israelites,
because the LORD has a charge to bring
against you who live in the land:
"There is no faithfulness, no love,
no acknowledgment of God in the land.
2 There is only cursing,[d] lying and murder,
stealing and adultery;
they break all bounds,
and bloodshed follows bloodshed.
3 Because of this the land mourns,[e]
and all who live in it waste away;
the beasts of the field and the birds of the air
and the fish of the sea are dying.

4 "But let no man bring a charge,
let no man accuse another,
for your people are like those
who bring charges against a priest.
5 You stumble day and night,
and the prophets stumble with you.
So I will destroy your mother—
6 my people are destroyed from lack of knowledge.

"Because you have rejected knowledge,
I also reject you as my priests;
because you have ignored the law of your God,
I also will ignore your children.
7 The more the priests increased,
the more they sinned against me;
they exchanged[f] their[g] Glory for something disgraceful.
8 They feed on the sins of my people
and relish their wickedness.
9 And it will be: Like people, like priests.
I will punish both of them for their ways
and repay them for their deeds.

10 "They will eat but not have enough;
they will engage in prostitution but not increase,
because they have deserted the LORD
to give themselves 11 to prostitution,
to old wine and new,
which take away the understanding
12 of my people.
They consult a wooden idol
and are answered by a stick of wood.
A spirit of prostitution leads them astray;
they are unfaithful to their God.
13 They sacrifice on the mountaintops
and burn offerings on the hills,
under oak, poplar and terebinth,
where the shade is pleasant.
Therefore your daughters turn to prostitution
and your daughters-in-law to adultery.

14 "I will not punish your daughters
when they turn to prostitution,
nor your daughters-in-law
when they commit adultery,
because the men themselves consort with harlots
and sacrifice with shrine prostitutes—
a people without understanding
will come to ruin!

15 "Though you commit adultery, O Israel,
let not Judah become guilty.

"Do not go to Gilgal;
do not go up to Beth Aven.[h]
And do not swear, 'As surely as the LORD lives!'
16 The Israelites are stubborn,
like a stubborn heifer.
How then can the LORD pasture them
like lambs in a meadow?
17 Ephraim is joined to idols;
leave him alone!
18 Even when their drinks are gone,
they continue their prostitution;
their rulers dearly love shameful ways.
19 A whirlwind will sweep them away,
and their sacrifices will bring them shame.

[d] 2 That is, to pronounce a curse upon [e] 3 Or *dries up* [f] 7 Syriac and an ancient Hebrew scribal tradition; Masoretic Text *I will exchange* [g] 7 Masoretic Text; an ancient Hebrew scribal tradition *my* [h] 15 *Beth Aven* means *house of wickedness* (a name for Bethel, which means *house of God*).

PRAYER: INTERCESSION

LORD Jesus, You have promised that if two of us agree on earth about anything we may ask, it will be done for us by Your Father in heaven. Where two or three come together in Your name, You are here in our midst. (Matthew 18:19–20)

__TAKE__ a few moments to intercede on behalf of your local, state or provincial, and national governments. Pray for spiritual revival in the nation and offer prayers regarding current events and concerns.

NT John 6:60–7:24

Many Disciples Desert Jesus

60 On hearing it, many of his disciples said, "This is a hard teaching. Who can accept it?"

61 Aware that his disciples were grumbling about this, Jesus said to them, "Does this offend you? 62 What if you see the Son of Man ascend to where he was before! 63 The Spirit gives life; the flesh counts for nothing. The words I have spoken to you are spirit[a] and they are life. 64 Yet there are some of you who do not believe." For Jesus had known from the beginning which of them did not believe and who would betray him. 65 He went on to say, "This is why I told you that no one can come to me unless the Father has enabled him."

66 From this time many of his disciples turned back and no longer followed him.

67 "You do not want to leave too, do you?" Jesus asked the Twelve.

68 Simon Peter answered him, "Lord, to whom shall we go? You have the words of eternal life. 69 We believe and know that you are the Holy One of God."

70 Then Jesus replied, "Have I not chosen you, the Twelve? Yet one of you is a devil!" 71 (He meant Judas, the son of Simon Iscariot, who, though one of the Twelve, was later to betray him.)

Jesus Goes to the Feast of Tabernacles

7 After this, Jesus went around in Galilee, purposely staying away from Judea because the Jews there were waiting to take his life. 2 But when the Jewish Feast of Tabernacles was near, 3 Jesus' brothers said to him, "You ought to leave here and go to Judea, so that your disciples may see the miracles you do. 4 No one who wants to become a public figure acts in secret. Since you are doing these things, show yourself to the world." 5 For even his own brothers did not believe in him.

6 Therefore Jesus told them, "The right time for me has not yet come; for you any time is right. 7 The world cannot hate you, but it hates me because I testify that what it does is evil. 8 You go to the Feast. I am not yet[b] going up to this Feast, because for me the right time has not yet come." 9 Having said this, he stayed in Galilee.

10 However, after his brothers had left for the Feast, he went also, not publicly, but in secret. 11 Now at the Feast the Jews were watching for him and asking, "Where is that man?"

12 Among the crowds there was widespread whispering about him. Some said, "He is a good man."

Others replied, "No, he deceives the people." 13 But no one would say anything publicly about him for fear of the Jews.

Jesus Teaches at the Feast

14 Not until halfway through the Feast did Jesus go up to the temple courts and begin to teach. 15 The Jews were amazed and asked, "How did this man get such learning without having studied?"

16 Jesus answered, "My teaching is not my own. It comes from him who sent me. 17 If anyone chooses to do God's will, he will find out whether my teaching comes from God or whether I speak on my own. 18 He who speaks on his own does so to gain honor for himself, but he who works for the honor of the one who sent him is a man of truth; there is nothing false about him. 19 Has not Moses given you the

[a] 63 Or *Spirit* [b] 8 Some early manuscripts do not have *yet.*

law? Yet not one of you keeps the law. Why are you trying to kill me?"
[20]"You are demon-possessed," the crowd answered. "Who is trying to kill you?"
[21]Jesus said to them, "I did one miracle, and you are all astonished. [22]Yet, because Moses gave you circumcision (though actually it did not come from Moses, but from the patriarchs), you circumcise a child on the Sabbath. [23]Now if a child can be circumcised on the Sabbath so that the law of Moses may not be broken, why are you angry with me for healing the whole man on the Sabbath? [24]Stop judging by mere appearances, and make a right judgment."

PRAYER: MY RELATIONSHIP TO OTHERS

JUST as the body is one, but has many parts, and all the parts of the body, being many, are one body, so also are You, O Christ Jesus. (1 Corinthians 12:12)

***PAUSE** to review your relationships with others and to commit them to the Lord.*

YEAR 2 DAY 306

OT Hosea 5:1-15

Judgment Against Israel

5 "Hear this, you priests!
Pay attention, you Israelites!
Listen, O royal house!
This judgment is against you:
You have been a snare at Mizpah,
a net spread out on Tabor.
[2]The rebels are deep in slaughter.
I will discipline all of them.
[3]I know all about Ephraim;
Israel is not hidden from me.
Ephraim, you have now turned to prostitution;
Israel is corrupt.

[4]"Their deeds do not permit them
to return to their God.
A spirit of prostitution is in their heart;
they do not acknowledge the LORD.
[5]Israel's arrogance testifies against them;
the Israelites, even Ephraim,
stumble in their sin;
Judah also stumbles with them.
[6]When they go with their flocks and herds
to seek the LORD,
they will not find him;
he has withdrawn himself from them.
[7]They are unfaithful to the LORD;
they give birth to illegitimate children.
Now their New Moon festivals
will devour them and their fields.

[8]"Sound the trumpet in Gibeah,
the horn in Ramah.
Raise the battle cry in Beth Aven[a];
lead on, O Benjamin.
[9]Ephraim will be laid waste
on the day of reckoning.
Among the tribes of Israel
I proclaim what is certain.
[10]Judah's leaders are like those
who move boundary stones.
I will pour out my wrath on them
like a flood of water.
[11]Ephraim is oppressed,
trampled in judgment,
intent on pursuing idols.[b]
[12]I am like a moth to Ephraim,
like rot to the people of Judah.

[13]"When Ephraim saw his sickness,
and Judah his sores,
then Ephraim turned to Assyria,
and sent to the great king for help.
But he is not able to cure you,
not able to heal your sores.
[14]For I will be like a lion to Ephraim,
like a great lion to Judah.

[a] *8 Beth Aven* means *house of wickedness* (a name for Bethel, which means *house of God*). [b] *11* The meaning of the Hebrew for this word is uncertain.

I will tear them to pieces and go away;
I will carry them off, with no one to rescue them.
15 Then I will go back to my place
until they admit their guilt.
And they will seek my face;
in their misery they will earnestly seek me."

PRAYER: AFFIRMATION

WHOEVER loves instruction loves knowledge, but those who hate correction are stupid. O Lord, there is a way that seems right to us, but its end is the way of death. (Proverbs 12:1, 28) . . . In the way of righteousness there is life, and in that pathway there is no death. (Proverbs 14:12)

***PAUSE** to reflect on these Biblical affirmations.*

NT John 7:25–53

Is Jesus the Christ?

25 At that point some of the people of
Jerusalem began to ask, "Isn't this the
man they are trying to kill? 26 Here he is,
speaking publicly, and they are not saying
a word to him. Have the authorities really
concluded that he is the Christ[a]? 27 But we
know where this man is from; when the
Christ comes, no one will know where he
is from."
28 Then Jesus, still teaching in the temple courts, cried out, "Yes, you know me,
and you know where I am from. I am not
here on my own, but he who sent me is
true. You do not know him, 29 but I know
him because I am from him and he
sent me."
30 At this they tried to seize him, but no
one laid a hand on him, because his time
had not yet come. 31 Still, many in the
crowd put their faith in him. They said,
"When the Christ comes, will he do more
miraculous signs than this man?"
32 The Pharisees heard the crowd whispering such things about him. Then the
chief priests and the Pharisees sent temple guards to arrest him.
33 Jesus said, "I am with you for only a
short time, and then I go to the one who
sent me. 34 You will look for me, but you
will not find me; and where I am, you
cannot come."
35 The Jews said to one another, "Where
does this man intend to go that we cannot find him? Will he go where our people live scattered among the Greeks, and
teach the Greeks? 36 What did he mean
when he said, 'You will look for me, but
you will not find me,' and 'Where I am,
you cannot come'?"
37 On the last and greatest day of the
Feast, Jesus stood and said in a loud
voice, "If anyone is thirsty, let him come
to me and drink. 38 Whoever believes in
me, as[b] the Scripture has said, streams of
living water will flow from within him."
39 By this he meant the Spirit, whom those
who believed in him were later to receive.
Up to that time the Spirit had not been
given, since Jesus had not yet been glorified.
40 On hearing his words, some of the
people said, "Surely this man is the
Prophet."
41 Others said, "He is the Christ."
Still others asked, "How can the Christ
come from Galilee? 42 Does not the Scripture say that the Christ will come from
David's family[c] and from Bethlehem, the
town where David lived?" 43 Thus the people were divided because of Jesus. 44 Some
wanted to seize him, but no one laid a
hand on him.

Unbelief of the Jewish Leaders

45 Finally the temple guards went back
to the chief priests and Pharisees, who
asked them, "Why didn't you bring
him in?"
46 "No one ever spoke the way this man
does," the guards declared.
47 "You mean he has deceived you also?"

[a] 26 Or *Messiah*; also in verses 27, 31, 41 and 42
[b] 37,38 Or / *If anyone is thirsty, let him come to me. / And let him drink, 38 who believes in me. / As*
[c] 42 Greek *seed*

the Pharisees retorted. [48]"Has any of the
rulers or of the Pharisees believed in him?
[49]No! But this mob that knows nothing of
the law—there is a curse on them."
[50]Nicodemus, who had gone to Jesus
earlier and who was one of their own
number, asked, [51]"Does our law condemn
anyone without first hearing him to find
out what he is doing?"
[52]They replied, "Are you from Galilee,
too? Look into it, and you will find that
a prophet[d] does not come out of Galilee."

[The earliest manuscripts and many other ancient witnesses do not have John 7:53–8:11.]

[53]Then each went to his own home.

[d] 52 Two early manuscripts *the Prophet*

PRAYER: THE ATTRIBUTES OF GOD

ALL people are like grass, and all their glory is like the flower of the field. The grass withers and the flower fades, because Your breath, O Lord, blows on it. Surely the people are like grass. The grass withers and the flower fades, but Your word, O God, stands forever.
(Isaiah 40:6–8)

PAUSE *to reflect on these affirmations about the person, powers and perfection of God.*

YEAR 2 DAY 307

OT Hosea 6:1–11a

Israel Unrepentant

6 "Come, let us return to the LORD.
He has torn us to pieces
but he will heal us;
he has injured us
but he will bind up our wounds.
[2]After two days he will revive us;
on the third day he will restore us,
that we may live in his presence.
[3]Let us acknowledge the LORD;
let us press on to acknowledge him.
As surely as the sun rises,
he will appear;
he will come to us like the winter rains,
like the spring rains that water the earth."

[4]"What can I do with you, Ephraim?
What can I do with you, Judah?
Your love is like the morning mist,
like the early dew that disappears.
[5]Therefore I cut you in pieces with my prophets,
I killed you with the words of my mouth;
my judgments flashed like lightning upon you.
[6]For I desire mercy, not sacrifice,
and acknowledgment of God rather than burnt offerings.
[7]Like Adam,[a] they have broken the covenant—
they were unfaithful to me there.
[8]Gilead is a city of wicked men,
stained with footprints of blood.
[9]As marauders lie in ambush for a man,
so do bands of priests;
they murder on the road to Shechem,
committing shameful crimes.
[10]I have seen a horrible thing
in the house of Israel.
There Ephraim is given to prostitution
and Israel is defiled.

[11]"Also for you, Judah,
a harvest is appointed.

[a] 7 Or *As at Adam;* or *Like men*

PRAYER: THANKSGIVING

IF I believe in You, as the Scripture has said, rivers of living water will flow from within me, because Your Spirit indwells me.
(John 7:38–39)

PAUSE *to offer your own expressions of thankfulness.*

NT John 8:1–30

8 But Jesus went to the Mount of Olives. 2At dawn he appeared again in the temple courts, where all the people gathered around him, and he sat down to teach them. 3The teachers of the law and the Pharisees brought in a woman caught in adultery. They made her stand before the group 4and said to Jesus, "Teacher, this woman was caught in the act of adultery. 5In the Law Moses commanded us to stone such women. Now what do you say?" 6They were using this question as a trap, in order to have a basis for accusing him.

But Jesus bent down and started to write on the ground with his finger. 7When they kept on questioning him, he straightened up and said to them, "If any one of you is without sin, let him be the first to throw a stone at her." 8Again he stooped down and wrote on the ground.

9At this, those who heard began to go away one at a time, the older ones first, until only Jesus was left, with the woman still standing there. 10Jesus straightened up and asked her, "Woman, where are they? Has no one condemned you?"

11"No one, sir," she said.

"Then neither do I condemn you," Jesus declared. "Go now and leave your life of sin."

The Validity of Jesus' Testimony

12When Jesus spoke again to the people, he said, "I am the light of the world. Whoever follows me will never walk in darkness, but will have the light of life."

13The Pharisees challenged him, "Here you are, appearing as your own witness; your testimony is not valid."

14Jesus answered, "Even if I testify on my own behalf, my testimony is valid, for I know where I came from and where I am going. But you have no idea where I come from or where I am going. 15You judge by human standards; I pass judgment on no one. 16But if I do judge, my decisions are right, because I am not alone. I stand with the Father, who sent me. 17In your own Law it is written that the testimony of two men is valid. 18I am one who testifies for myself; my other witness is the Father, who sent me."

19Then they asked him, "Where is your father?"

"You do not know me or my Father," Jesus replied. "If you knew me, you would know my Father also." 20He spoke these words while teaching in the temple area near the place where the offerings were put. Yet no one seized him, because his time had not yet come.

21Once more Jesus said to them, "I am going away, and you will look for me, and you will die in your sin. Where I go, you cannot come."

22This made the Jews ask, "Will he kill himself? Is that why he says, 'Where I go, you cannot come'?"

23But he continued, "You are from below; I am from above. You are of this world; I am not of this world. 24I told you that you would die in your sins; if you do not believe that I am ⌞the one I claim to be⌟,[a] you will indeed die in your sins."

25"Who are you?" they asked.

"Just what I have been claiming all along," Jesus replied. 26"I have much to say in judgment of you. But he who sent me is reliable, and what I have heard from him I tell the world."

27They did not understand that he was telling them about his Father. 28So Jesus said, "When you have lifted up the Son of Man, then you will know that I am ⌞the one I claim to be⌟ and that I do nothing on my own but speak just what the Father has taught me. 29The one who sent me is with me; he has not left me alone, for I always do what pleases him." 30Even as he spoke, many put their faith in him.

[a] 24 Or *I am he;* also in verse 28

PRAYER: THE WORKS OF GOD

YOU, Lord God, promised to gather the children of Israel from the nations and bring them back from the countries where they were scattered: "And I will give them the land of Israel. They will return to it and remove all its detestable images and abominations. I will give them one heart and put a new spirit within them, and I will remove the stony heart out of their flesh and give them a heart of flesh, that they may walk in My statutes and keep My ordinances. They shall be My people, and I will be their God." (Ezekiel 11:17–20)

***TAKE** a moment to consider the greatness of God's wonderful works.*

YEAR 2 DAY 308

OT Psalms 134–135

Psalm 134

A song of ascents.

[1]Praise the LORD, all you servants of the LORD
who minister by night in the house of the LORD.
[2]Lift up your hands in the sanctuary
and praise the LORD.

[3]May the LORD, the Maker of heaven and earth,
bless you from Zion.

Psalm 135

[1]Praise the LORD.[a]

Praise the name of the LORD;
praise him, you servants of the LORD,
[2]you who minister in the house of the LORD,
in the courts of the house of our God.

[3]Praise the LORD, for the LORD is good;
sing praise to his name, for that is pleasant.
[4]For the LORD has chosen Jacob to be his own,
Israel to be his treasured possession.

[5]I know that the LORD is great,
that our Lord is greater than all gods.
[6]The LORD does whatever pleases him,
in the heavens and on the earth,
in the seas and all their depths.
[7]He makes clouds rise from the ends of the earth;
he sends lightning with the rain
and brings out the wind from his storehouses.

[8]He struck down the firstborn of Egypt,
the firstborn of men and animals.
[9]He sent his signs and wonders into your midst, O Egypt,
against Pharaoh and all his servants.
[10]He struck down many nations
and killed mighty kings—
[11]Sihon king of the Amorites,
Og king of Bashan
and all the kings of Canaan—
[12]and he gave their land as an inheritance,
an inheritance to his people Israel.

[13]Your name, O LORD, endures forever,
your renown, O LORD, through all generations.
[14]For the LORD will vindicate his people
and have compassion on his servants.

[15]The idols of the nations are silver and gold,
made by the hands of men.
[16]They have mouths, but cannot speak,
eyes, but they cannot see;
[17]they have ears, but cannot hear,
nor is there breath in their mouths.
[18]Those who make them will be like them,
and so will all who trust in them.

[a] 1 Hebrew *Hallelu Yah*; also in verses 3 and 21

19 O house of Israel, praise the LORD;
O house of Aaron, praise the LORD;
20 O house of Levi, praise the LORD;
you who fear him, praise the LORD.

21 Praise be to the LORD from Zion,
to him who dwells in Jerusalem.

Praise the LORD.

PRAYER: ADORATION

I WILL not fear, for You are with me; I will not be dismayed, for You are my God. You will strengthen me and help me; You will uphold me with Your righteous right hand. For You are the Lord my God, who takes hold of my right hand and says to me, "Do not fear; I will help you." (Isaiah 41:10, 13) . . . I call this to mind, and therefore I have hope: Your mercies never cease, for Your compassions never fail. They are new every morning; great is Your faithfulness. (Lamentations 3:21–23)

PAUSE *to express your thoughts of praise and worship.*

NT John 8:31–59

The Children of Abraham

31 To the Jews who had believed him,
Jesus said, "If you hold to my teaching,
you are really my disciples. 32 Then you
will know the truth, and the truth will set
you free."
33 They answered him, "We are Abraham's descendants[a] and have never been
slaves of anyone. How can you say that we
shall be set free?"
34 Jesus replied, "I tell you the truth,
everyone who sins is a slave to sin. 35 Now
a slave has no permanent place in the
family, but a son belongs to it forever. 36 So
if the Son sets you free, you will be free
indeed. 37 I know you are Abraham's descendants. Yet you are ready to kill me, because you have no room for my word. 38 I
am telling you what I have seen in the Father's presence, and you do what you have
heard from your father.[b]"
39 "Abraham is our father," they answered.
"If you were Abraham's children," said
Jesus, "then you would[c] do the things
Abraham did. 40 As it is, you are determined to kill me, a man who has told you
the truth that I heard from God. Abraham
did not do such things. 41 You are doing
the things your own father does."
"We are not illegitimate children," they
protested. "The only Father we have is
God himself."

The Children of the Devil

42 Jesus said to them, "If God were your
Father, you would love me, for I came
from God and now am here. I have not
come on my own; but he sent me. 43 Why
is my language not clear to you? Because
you are unable to hear what I say. 44 You
belong to your father, the devil, and you
want to carry out your father's desire. He
was a murderer from the beginning, not
holding to the truth, for there is no truth
in him. When he lies, he speaks his native
language, for he is a liar and the father of
lies. 45 Yet because I tell the truth, you do
not believe me! 46 Can any of you prove
me guilty of sin? If I am telling the truth,
why don't you believe me? 47 He who belongs to God hears what God says. The
reason you do not hear is that you do not
belong to God."

The Claims of Jesus About Himself

48 The Jews answered him, "Aren't we
right in saying that you are a Samaritan
and demon-possessed?"
49 "I am not possessed by a demon,"
said Jesus, "but I honor my Father and
you dishonor me. 50 I am not seeking glory for myself; but there is one who seeks
it, and he is the judge. 51 I tell you the

[a] 33 Greek *seed;* also in verse 37 [b] 38 Or *presence. Therefore do what you have heard from the Father.* [c] 39 Some early manuscripts *"If you are Abraham's children," said Jesus, "then*

truth, if anyone keeps my word, he will never see death."
[52]At this the Jews exclaimed, "Now we know that you are demon-possessed! Abraham died and so did the prophets, yet you say that if anyone keeps your word, he will never taste death. [53]Are you greater than our father Abraham? He died, and so did the prophets. Who do you think you are?"
[54]Jesus replied, "If I glorify myself, my glory means nothing. My Father, whom you claim as your God, is the one who glorifies me. [55]Though you do not know him, I know him. If I said I did not, I would be a liar like you, but I do know him and keep his word. [56]Your father Abraham rejoiced at the thought of seeing my day; he saw it and was glad."
[57]"You are not yet fifty years old," the Jews said to him, "and you have seen Abraham!"
[58]"I tell you the truth," Jesus answered, "before Abraham was born, I am!" [59]At this, they picked up stones to stone him, but Jesus hid himself, slipping away from the temple grounds.

PRAYER: MY RELATIONSHIP TO GOD

FROM the beginning, O God, You chose me for salvation through sanctification by the Spirit and through belief in the truth. You called me to this through the gospel, that I might obtain the glory of my Lord Jesus Christ. (2 Thessalonians 2:13–14) . . . I was washed, I was sanctified, I was justified in Your name, Lord Jesus Christ, and by Your Spirit. (1 Corinthians 6:11)

***PAUSE** to thank God for the relationship that you enjoy with Him in Jesus Christ.*

OT Hosea 6:11b–7:16

"Whenever I would restore the
fortunes of my people,
7 [1]whenever I would heal Israel,
the sins of Ephraim are exposed
and the crimes of Samaria revealed.
They practice deceit,
thieves break into houses,
bandits rob in the streets;
[2]but they do not realize
that I remember all their evil deeds.
Their sins engulf them;
they are always before me.

[3]"They delight the king with their
wickedness,
the princes with their lies.
[4]They are all adulterers,
burning like an oven
whose fire the baker need not stir
from the kneading of the dough till
it rises.
[5]On the day of the festival of our king
the princes become inflamed with
wine,
and he joins hands with the mockers.
[6]Their hearts are like an oven;
they approach him with intrigue.
Their passion smolders all night;
in the morning it blazes like a
flaming fire.
[7]All of them are hot as an oven;
they devour their rulers.
All their kings fall,
and none of them calls on me.

[8]"Ephraim mixes with the nations;
Ephraim is a flat cake not turned
over.
[9]Foreigners sap his strength,
but he does not realize it.
His hair is sprinkled with gray,
but he does not notice.
[10]Israel's arrogance testifies against him,
but despite all this
he does not return to the LORD his God
or search for him.

[11]"Ephraim is like a dove,
easily deceived and senseless—

now calling to Egypt,
now turning to Assyria.
[12]When they go, I will throw my net over them;
I will pull them down like birds of the air.
When I hear them flocking together,
I will catch them.
[13]Woe to them,
because they have strayed from me!
Destruction to them,
because they have rebelled against me!
I long to redeem them
but they speak lies against me.
[14]They do not cry out to me from their hearts
but wail upon their beds.
They gather together[a] for grain and new wine
but turn away from me.
[15]I trained them and strengthened them,
but they plot evil against me.
[16]They do not turn to the Most High;
they are like a faulty bow.
Their leaders will fall by the sword
because of their insolent words.
For this they will be ridiculed
in the land of Egypt.

[a] 14 Most Hebrew manuscripts; some Hebrew manuscripts and Septuagint *They slash themselves*

PRAYER: CONFESSION

O GOD, if I claim to be without sin, I deceive myself and the truth is not in me. If I confess my sins, You are faithful and just and will forgive me my sins and purify me from all unrighteousness. If I claim I have not sinned, I make You out to be a liar and Your word is not in me. (1 John 1:8–10)

***ASK** the Spirit to search your heart and reveal any areas of unconfessed sin. Acknowledge these to the Lord and thank Him for His forgiveness.*

NT John 9:1–41

Jesus Heals a Man Born Blind

9 As he went along, he saw a man blind
from birth. [2]His disciples asked him,
"Rabbi, who sinned, this man or his parents, that he was born blind?"
[3]"Neither this man nor his parents
sinned," said Jesus, "but this happened so
that the work of God might be displayed
in his life. [4]As long as it is day, we must
do the work of him who sent me. Night
is coming, when no one can work. [5]While
I am in the world, I am the light of the world."
[6]Having said this, he spit on the
ground, made some mud with the saliva,
and put it on the man's eyes. [7]"Go," he
told him, "wash in the Pool of Siloam"
(this word means Sent). So the man went
and washed, and came home seeing.
[8]His neighbors and those who had formerly seen him begging asked, "Isn't this
the same man who used to sit and beg?"
[9]Some claimed that he was.

Others said, "No, he only looks like him."

But he himself insisted, "I am the man."

[10]"How then were your eyes opened?"
they demanded.
[11]He replied, "The man they call Jesus
made some mud and put it on my eyes.
He told me to go to Siloam and wash. So
I went and washed, and then I could see."
[12]"Where is this man?" they asked him.

"I don't know," he said.

The Pharisees Investigate the Healing

[13]They brought to the Pharisees the
man who had been blind. [14]Now the day
on which Jesus had made the mud and
opened the man's eyes was a Sabbath.
[15]Therefore the Pharisees also asked him
how he had received his sight. "He put
mud on my eyes," the man replied, "and
I washed, and now I see."
[16]Some of the Pharisees said, "This man
is not from God, for he does not keep the Sabbath."

But others asked, "How can a sinner do

such miraculous signs?" So they were divided.
17 Finally they turned again to the blind
man, "What have you to say about him?
It was your eyes he opened."
The man replied, "He is a prophet."
18 The Jews still did not believe that he
had been blind and had received his sight
until they sent for the man's parents. 19 "Is
this your son?" they asked. "Is this the one
you say was born blind? How is it that
now he can see?"
20 "We know he is our son," the parents
answered, "and we know he was born
blind. 21 But how he can see now, or who
opened his eyes, we don't know. Ask
him. He is of age; he will speak for himself." 22 His parents said this because they
were afraid of the Jews, for already the
Jews had decided that anyone who acknowledged that Jesus was the Christ[a]
would be put out of the synagogue.
23 That was why his parents said, "He is of
age; ask him."
24 A second time they summoned the
man who had been blind. "Give glory to
God,[b]" they said. "We know this man is a
sinner."
25 He replied, "Whether he is a sinner or
not, I don't know. One thing I do know. I
was blind but now I see!"
26 Then they asked him, "What did he
do to you? How did he open your eyes?"
27 He answered, "I have told you already
and you did not listen. Why do you want
to hear it again? Do you want to become
his disciples, too?"
28 Then they hurled insults at him and
said, "You are this fellow's disciple! We
are disciples of Moses! 29 We know that
God spoke to Moses, but as for this fellow, we don't even know where he comes
from."
30 The man answered, "Now that is remarkable! You don't know where he
comes from, yet he opened my eyes. 31 We
know that God does not listen to sinners.
He listens to the godly man who does his
will. 32 Nobody has ever heard of opening
the eyes of a man born blind. 33 If this man
were not from God, he could do nothing."
34 To this they replied, "You were
steeped in sin at birth; how dare you lecture us!" And they threw him out.

Spiritual Blindness

35 Jesus heard that they had thrown him
out, and when he found him, he said,
"Do you believe in the Son of Man?"
36 "Who is he, sir?" the man asked. "Tell
me so that I may believe in him."
37 Jesus said, "You have now seen him;
in fact, he is the one speaking with you."
38 Then the man said, "Lord, I believe,"
and he worshiped him.
39 Jesus said, "For judgment I have come
into this world, so that the blind will see
and those who see will become blind."
40 Some Pharisees who were with him
heard him say this and asked, "What? Are
we blind too?"
41 Jesus said, "If you were blind, you
would not be guilty of sin; but now that
you claim you can see, your guilt remains.

[a] 22 Or *Messiah* [b] 24 A solemn charge to tell the truth (see Joshua 7:19)

PRAYER: THE CHARACTER I WANT TO CULTIVATE

I SHOULD live as one who is free, but without using my freedom as a cloak for evil, but as Your servant, O God. (1 Peter 2:16)

. . . I will not imitate what is evil but what is good. The one who does good is You, O God; the one who does evil has not seen You.

(3 John 11)

***TAKE** a moment to ask the Lord for the grace to grow in godly character.*

YEAR 2
DAY 310

OT Hosea 8:1-14

Israel to Reap the Whirlwind

8 "Put the trumpet to your lips!
An eagle is over the house of the LORD
because the people have broken my covenant
and rebelled against my law.
2 Israel cries out to me,
'O our God, we acknowledge you!'
3 But Israel has rejected what is good;
an enemy will pursue him.
4 They set up kings without my consent;
they choose princes without my approval.
With their silver and gold
they make idols for themselves
to their own destruction.
5 Throw out your calf-idol, O Samaria!
My anger burns against them.
How long will they be incapable of purity?
6 They are from Israel!
This calf—a craftsman has made it;
it is not God.
It will be broken in pieces,
that calf of Samaria.

7 "They sow the wind
and reap the whirlwind.
The stalk has no head;
it will produce no flour.
Were it to yield grain,
foreigners would swallow it up.
8 Israel is swallowed up;
now she is among the nations
like a worthless thing.
9 For they have gone up to Assyria
like a wild donkey wandering alone.
Ephraim has sold herself to lovers.
10 Although they have sold themselves among the nations,
I will now gather them together.
They will begin to waste away
under the oppression of the mighty king.

11 "Though Ephraim built many altars for sin offerings,
these have become altars for sinning.
12 I wrote for them the many things of my law,
but they regarded them as something alien.
13 They offer sacrifices given to me
and they eat the meat,
but the LORD is not pleased with them.
Now he will remember their wickedness
and punish their sins:
They will return to Egypt.
14 Israel has forgotten his Maker
and built palaces;
Judah has fortified many towns.
But I will send fire upon their cities
that will consume their fortresses."

PRAYER: RENEWAL

LIKE the Bereans, give me the nobility of mind to receive the word with great eagerness and to examine the Scriptures daily.
(Acts 17:11)

***PAUSE** to add your own prayers for personal renewal.*

NT John 10:1-42

The Shepherd and His Flock

10 "I tell you the truth, the man who
does not enter the sheep pen by the
gate, but climbs in by some other way, is
a thief and a robber. 2The man who enters
by the gate is the shepherd of his sheep.
3The watchman opens the gate for him,
and the sheep listen to his voice. He calls
his own sheep by name and leads them
out. 4When he has brought out all his
own, he goes on ahead of them, and his
sheep follow him because they know his
voice. 5But they will never follow a
stranger; in fact, they will run away from
him because they do not recognize a

stranger's voice." 6Jesus used this figure of speech, but they did not understand what he was telling them.

7Therefore Jesus said again, "I tell you the truth, I am the gate for the sheep. 8All who ever came before me were thieves and robbers, but the sheep did not listen to them. 9I am the gate; whoever enters through me will be saved.[a] He will come in and go out, and find pasture. 10The thief comes only to steal and kill and destroy; I have come that they may have life, and have it to the full.

11"I am the good shepherd. The good shepherd lays down his life for the sheep. 12The hired hand is not the shepherd who owns the sheep. So when he sees the wolf coming, he abandons the sheep and runs away. Then the wolf attacks the flock and scatters it. 13The man runs away because he is a hired hand and cares nothing for the sheep.

14"I am the good shepherd; I know my sheep and my sheep know me— 15just as the Father knows me and I know the Father—and I lay down my life for the sheep. 16I have other sheep that are not of this sheep pen. I must bring them also. They too will listen to my voice, and there shall be one flock and one shepherd. 17The reason my Father loves me is that I lay down my life—only to take it up again. 18No one takes it from me, but I lay it down of my own accord. I have authority to lay it down and authority to take it up again. This command I received from my Father."

19At these words the Jews were again divided. 20Many of them said, "He is demon-possessed and raving mad. Why listen to him?"

21But others said, "These are not the sayings of a man possessed by a demon. Can a demon open the eyes of the blind?"

The Unbelief of the Jews

22Then came the Feast of Dedication[b] at Jerusalem. It was winter, 23and Jesus was in the temple area walking in Solomon's Colonnade. 24The Jews gathered around him, saying, "How long will you keep us in suspense? If you are the Christ,[c] tell us plainly."

25Jesus answered, "I did tell you, but you do not believe. The miracles I do in my Father's name speak for me, 26but you do not believe because you are not my sheep. 27My sheep listen to my voice; I know them, and they follow me. 28I give them eternal life, and they shall never perish; no one can snatch them out of my hand. 29My Father, who has given them to me, is greater than all[d]; no one can snatch them out of my Father's hand. 30I and the Father are one."

31Again the Jews picked up stones to stone him, 32but Jesus said to them, "I have shown you many great miracles from the Father. For which of these do you stone me?"

33"We are not stoning you for any of these," replied the Jews, "but for blasphemy, because you, a mere man, claim to be God."

34Jesus answered them, "Is it not written in your Law, 'I have said you are gods'[e]? 35If he called them 'gods,' to whom the word of God came—and the Scripture cannot be broken— 36what about the one whom the Father set apart as his very own and sent into the world? Why then do you accuse me of blasphemy because I said, 'I am God's Son'? 37Do not believe me unless I do what my Father does. 38But if I do it, even though you do not believe me, believe the miracles, that you may know and understand that the Father is in me, and I in the Father." 39Again they tried to seize him, but he escaped their grasp.

40Then Jesus went back across the Jordan to the place where John had been baptizing in the early days. Here he stayed 41and many people came to him. They said, "Though John never performed a miraculous sign, all that John said about this man was true." 42And in that place many believed in Jesus.

[a] 9 Or *kept safe* [b] 22 That is, Hanukkah [c] 24 Or *Messiah* [d] 29 Many early manuscripts *What my Father has given me is greater than all* [e] 34 Psalm 82:6

PRAYER: MY RELATIONSHIP TO OTHERS

ALL things are from You, O God, who reconciled us to Yourself through Christ and gave us the ministry of reconciliation: namely, that You were reconciling the world to Yourself in Christ,

not counting our trespasses against us. And You have committed to us the message of reconciliation. Therefore we are ambassadors for Christ, as though You, O God, were appealing to others through us—we implore them on Christ's behalf to be reconciled to You. (2 Corinthians 5:18–20)

***PAUSE** to review your relationships with others and to commit them to the Lord.*

YEAR 2 DAY 311

OT Hosea 9:1–17

Punishment for Israel

9 Do not rejoice, O Israel;
do not be jubilant like the other nations.
For you have been unfaithful to your God;
you love the wages of a prostitute
at every threshing floor.
2 Threshing floors and winepresses will not feed the people;
the new wine will fail them.
3 They will not remain in the LORD's land;
Ephraim will return to Egypt
and eat unclean[a] food in Assyria.
4 They will not pour out wine offerings to the LORD,
nor will their sacrifices please him.
Such sacrifices will be to them like the bread of mourners;
all who eat them will be unclean.
This food will be for themselves;
it will not come into the temple of the LORD.

5 What will you do on the day of your appointed feasts,
on the festival days of the LORD?
6 Even if they escape from destruction,
Egypt will gather them,
and Memphis will bury them.
Their treasures of silver will be taken over by briers,
and thorns will overrun their tents.
7 The days of punishment are coming,
the days of reckoning are at hand.
Let Israel know this.
Because your sins are so many
and your hostility so great,
the prophet is considered a fool,
the inspired man a maniac.
8 The prophet, along with my God,
is the watchman over Ephraim,[b]
yet snares await him on all his paths,
and hostility in the house of his God.
9 They have sunk deep into corruption,
as in the days of Gibeah.
God will remember their wickedness
and punish them for their sins.

10 "When I found Israel,
it was like finding grapes in the desert;
when I saw your fathers,
it was like seeing the early fruit on the fig tree.
But when they came to Baal Peor,
they consecrated themselves to that shameful idol
and became as vile as the thing they loved.
11 Ephraim's glory will fly away like a bird—
no birth, no pregnancy, no conception.
12 Even if they rear children,
I will bereave them of every one.
Woe to them
when I turn away from them!
13 I have seen Ephraim, like Tyre,
planted in a pleasant place.
But Ephraim will bring out
their children to the slayer."

14 Give them, O LORD—
what will you give them?
Give them wombs that miscarry
and breasts that are dry.

15 "Because of all their wickedness in Gilgal,
I hated them there.
Because of their sinful deeds,
I will drive them out of my house.
I will no longer love them;

[a] 3 That is, ceremonially unclean [b] 8 Or *The prophet is the watchman over Ephraim, / the people of my God*

all their leaders are rebellious.
[16] Ephraim is blighted,
their root is withered,
they yield no fruit.
Even if they bear children,
I will slay their cherished offspring."
[17] My God will reject them
because they have not obeyed him;
they will be wanderers among the nations.

PRAYER: PETITION

O LORD, continue Your loving-kindness to those who know You, and Your righteousness to the upright in heart. Do not let the foot of pride come against me, and let not the hand of the wicked drive me away. (Psalm 36:10–11)

***PAUSE** here to offer prayers of petition regarding your family and your ministry. Ask for help and guidance in sharing Jesus with others and helping others grow in Him. Ask for guidance in your vocation and your avocations. Offer prayers of petition regarding your activities for this day and any special concerns you may have.*

NT John 11:1-44

The Death of Lazarus

11 Now a man named Lazarus was sick.
He was from Bethany, the village of
Mary and her sister Martha. [2]This Mary,
whose brother Lazarus now lay sick, was
the same one who poured perfume on the
Lord and wiped his feet with her hair. [3]So
the sisters sent word to Jesus, "Lord, the
one you love is sick."
[4]When he heard this, Jesus said, "This
sickness will not end in death. No, it is for
God's glory so that God's Son may be glorified through it." [5]Jesus loved Martha and
her sister and Lazarus. [6]Yet when he heard
that Lazarus was sick, he stayed where he
was two more days.
[7]Then he said to his disciples, "Let us go
back to Judea."
[8]"But Rabbi," they said, "a short while
ago the Jews tried to stone you, and yet
you are going back there?"
[9]Jesus answered, "Are there not twelve
hours of daylight? A man who walks by
day will not stumble, for he sees by this
world's light. [10]It is when he walks by
night that he stumbles, for he has no
light."
[11]After he had said this, he went on to
tell them, "Our friend Lazarus has fallen
asleep; but I am going there to wake
him up."
[12]His disciples replied, "Lord, if he
sleeps, he will get better." [13]Jesus had been
speaking of his death, but his disciples
thought he meant natural sleep.
[14]So then he told them plainly, "Lazarus is dead, [15]and for your sake I am glad
I was not there, so that you may believe.
But let us go to him."
[16]Then Thomas (called Didymus) said
to the rest of the disciples, "Let us also go,
that we may die with him."

Jesus Comforts the Sisters

[17]On his arrival, Jesus found that Lazarus had already been in the tomb for four
days. [18]Bethany was less than two miles[a]
from Jerusalem, [19]and many Jews had
come to Martha and Mary to comfort them
in the loss of their brother. [20]When Martha
heard that Jesus was coming, she went out
to meet him, but Mary stayed at home.
[21]"Lord," Martha said to Jesus, "if you
had been here, my brother would not
have died. [22]But I know that even now
God will give you whatever you ask."
[23]Jesus said to her, "Your brother will
rise again."
[24]Martha answered, "I know he will rise
again in the resurrection at the last day."
[25]Jesus said to her, "I am the resurrection and the life. He who believes in me
will live, even though he dies; [26]and whoever lives and believes in me will never
die. Do you believe this?"

[a] 18 Greek *fifteen stadia* (about 3 kilometers)

[27]"Yes, Lord," she told him, "I believe
that you are the Christ,[b] the Son of God,
who was to come into the world."
[28]And after she had said this, she went
back and called her sister Mary aside. "The
Teacher is here," she said, "and is asking
for you." [29]When Mary heard this, she got
up quickly and went to him. [30]Now Jesus
had not yet entered the village, but was
still at the place where Martha had met
him. [31]When the Jews who had been with
Mary in the house, comforting her, noticed how quickly she got up and went
out, they followed her, supposing she was
going to the tomb to mourn there.
[32]When Mary reached the place where
Jesus was and saw him, she fell at his feet
and said, "Lord, if you had been here, my
brother would not have died."
[33]When Jesus saw her weeping, and the
Jews who had come along with her also
weeping, he was deeply moved in spirit
and troubled. [34]"Where have you laid
him?" he asked.
"Come and see, Lord," they replied.
[35]Jesus wept.
[36]Then the Jews said, "See how he loved
him!"
[37]But some of them said, "Could not he
who opened the eyes of the blind man
have kept this man from dying?"

Jesus Raises Lazarus From the Dead

[38]Jesus, once more deeply moved, came
to the tomb. It was a cave with a stone laid
across the entrance. [39]"Take away the
stone," he said.
"But, Lord," said Martha, the sister of
the dead man, "by this time there is a bad
odor, for he has been there four days."
[40]Then Jesus said, "Did I not tell you
that if you believed, you would see the
glory of God?"
[41]So they took away the stone. Then
Jesus looked up and said, "Father, I thank
you that you have heard me. [42]I knew that
you always hear me, but I said this for the
benefit of the people standing here, that
they may believe that you sent me."
[43]When he had said this, Jesus called in
a loud voice, "Lazarus, come out!" [44]The
dead man came out, his hands and feet
wrapped with strips of linen, and a cloth
around his face.
Jesus said to them, "Take off the grave
clothes and let him go."

[b] 27 Or *Messiah*

PRAYER: THE ATTRIBUTES OF GOD

I WILL sing of Your mercies forever, O Lord. With my mouth I will make Your faithfulness known through all generations. I will declare that Your loving-kindness will be built up forever, that You will establish Your faithfulness in the heavens. The heavens will praise Your wonders, O Lord, and Your faithfulness in the assembly of the holy ones. For who in the heavens can be compared with You, Lord? Who is like You among the children of the mighty? You, O God, are greatly feared in the council of the holy ones and You are more awesome than all who surround You. O Lord God of hosts, who is like You? O mighty Lord, Your faithfulness surrounds You. (Psalm 89:1–2, 5–8)

***PAUSE** to reflect on these affirmations about the person, powers and perfection of God.*

YEAR 2
DAY 312

OT Hosea 10:1–15

10 Israel was a spreading vine;
he brought forth fruit for himself.
As his fruit increased,
he built more altars;
as his land prospered,
he adorned his sacred stones.
[2]Their heart is deceitful,
and now they must bear their guilt.
The LORD will demolish their altars
and destroy their sacred stones.

[3]Then they will say, "We have no king
because we did not revere the LORD.
But even if we had a king,
what could he do for us?"
[4]They make many promises,
take false oaths
and make agreements;
therefore lawsuits spring up
like poisonous weeds in a plowed field.
[5]The people who live in Samaria fear
for the calf-idol of Beth Aven.[a]
Its people will mourn over it,
and so will its idolatrous priests,
those who had rejoiced over its splendor,
because it is taken from them into exile.
[6]It will be carried to Assyria
as tribute for the great king.
Ephraim will be disgraced;
Israel will be ashamed of its wooden idols.[b]
[7]Samaria and its king will float away
like a twig on the surface of the waters.
[8]The high places of wickedness[c] will be destroyed—
it is the sin of Israel.
Thorns and thistles will grow up
and cover their altars.
Then they will say to the mountains,
"Cover us!"
and to the hills, "Fall on us!"

[9]"Since the days of Gibeah, you have sinned, O Israel,
and there you have remained.[d]
Did not war overtake
the evildoers in Gibeah?
[10]When I please, I will punish them;
nations will be gathered against them
to put them in bonds for their double sin.
[11]Ephraim is a trained heifer
that loves to thresh;
so I will put a yoke
on her fair neck.
I will drive Ephraim,
Judah must plow,
and Jacob must break up the ground.
[12]Sow for yourselves righteousness,
reap the fruit of unfailing love,
and break up your unplowed ground;
for it is time to seek the LORD,
until he comes
and showers righteousness on you.
[13]But you have planted wickedness,
you have reaped evil,
you have eaten the fruit of deception.
Because you have depended on your own strength
and on your many warriors,
[14]the roar of battle will rise against your people,
so that all your fortresses will be devastated—
as Shalman devastated Beth Arbel on the day of battle,
when mothers were dashed to the ground with their children.
[15]Thus will it happen to you, O Bethel,
because your wickedness is great.
When that day dawns,
the king of Israel will be completely destroyed.

[a]5 *Beth Aven* means *house of wickedness* (a name for Bethel, which means *house of God*). [b]6 Or *its counsel* [c]8 Hebrew *aven,* a reference to Beth Aven (a derogatory name for Bethel) [d]9 Or *there a stand was taken*

PRAYER: INTERCESSION

THIS is Your commandment, Lord Jesus, that we love one another as You have loved us. Greater love has no one than this, that he lay down his life for his friends. (John 15:12–13)

***TAKE** a few moments to intercede on behalf of local, national and world missions. Pray that the Great Commission would be fulfilled and for any special concerns you may have for missions.*

NT John 11:45–12:11

The Plot to Kill Jesus

45 Therefore many of the Jews who had
come to visit Mary, and had seen what
Jesus did, put their faith in him. 46 But
some of them went to the Pharisees and
told them what Jesus had done. 47 Then
the chief priests and the Pharisees called
a meeting of the Sanhedrin.

"What are we accomplishing?" they
asked. "Here is this man performing
many miraculous signs. 48 If we let him go
on like this, everyone will believe in him,
and then the Romans will come and take
away both our place[a] and our nation."

49 Then one of them, named Caiaphas,
who was high priest that year, spoke up,
"You know nothing at all! 50 You do not realize that it is better for you that one man
die for the people than that the whole nation perish."

51 He did not say this on his own, but as
high priest that year he prophesied that
Jesus would die for the Jewish nation,
52 and not only for that nation but also for
the scattered children of God, to bring
them together and make them one. 53 So
from that day on they plotted to take his
life.

54 Therefore Jesus no longer moved
about publicly among the Jews. Instead
he withdrew to a region near the desert,
to a village called Ephraim, where he
stayed with his disciples.

55 When it was almost time for the Jewish Passover, many went up from the
country to Jerusalem for their ceremonial
cleansing before the Passover. 56 They kept
looking for Jesus, and as they stood in the
temple area they asked one another,
"What do you think? Isn't he coming to
the Feast at all?" 57 But the chief priests and
Pharisees had given orders that if anyone
found out where Jesus was, he should report it so that they might arrest him.

Jesus Anointed at Bethany

12 Six days before the Passover, Jesus arrived at Bethany, where Lazarus lived,
whom Jesus had raised from the dead.
2 Here a dinner was given in Jesus' honor.
Martha served, while Lazarus was among
those reclining at the table with him.
3 Then Mary took about a pint[b] of pure
nard, an expensive perfume; she poured it
on Jesus' feet and wiped his feet with her
hair. And the house was filled with the fragrance of the perfume.

4 But one of his disciples, Judas Iscariot,
who was later to betray him, objected,
5 "Why wasn't this perfume sold and the
money given to the poor? It was worth a
year's wages.[c]" 6 He did not say this because he cared about the poor but because
he was a thief; as keeper of the money
bag, he used to help himself to what was
put into it.

7 "Leave her alone," Jesus replied. "⌊It
was intended⌋ that she should save this
perfume for the day of my burial. 8 You
will always have the poor among you, but
you will not always have me."

9 Meanwhile a large crowd of Jews
found out that Jesus was there and came,
not only because of him but also to see
Lazarus, whom he had raised from the
dead. 10 So the chief priests made plans to
kill Lazarus as well, 11 for on account of
him many of the Jews were going over to
Jesus and putting their faith in him.

[a] 48 Or *temple* [b] 3 Greek *a litra* (probably about 0.5 liter) [c] 5 Greek *three hundred denarii*

PRAYER: THE WORKS OF GOD

O LORD, You have bared Your holy arm in the sight of all the nations, and all the ends of the earth will see Your salvation, O God. Nations will come to Your light and kings to the brightness of your dawning. (Isaiah 52:10; 60:3)

***TAKE** a moment to consider the greatness of God's wonderful works.*

YEAR 2 DAY 313

OT **Hosea 11:1–12:14**

God's Love for Israel

11 "When Israel was a child, I loved
him,
and out of Egypt I called my son.
2 But the more I[a] called Israel,
the further they went from me.[b]
They sacrificed to the Baals
and they burned incense to images.
3 It was I who taught Ephraim to walk,
taking them by the arms;
but they did not realize
it was I who healed them.
4 I led them with cords of human
kindness,
with ties of love;
I lifted the yoke from their neck
and bent down to feed them.

5 "Will they not return to Egypt
and will not Assyria rule over them
because they refuse to repent?
6 Swords will flash in their cities,
will destroy the bars of their gates
and put an end to their plans.
7 My people are determined to turn
from me.
Even if they call to the Most High,
he will by no means exalt them.

8 "How can I give you up, Ephraim?
How can I hand you over, Israel?
How can I treat you like Admah?
How can I make you like Zeboiim?
My heart is changed within me;
all my compassion is aroused.
9 I will not carry out my fierce anger,
nor will I turn and devastate
Ephraim.
For I am God, and not man—
the Holy One among you.
I will not come in wrath.[c]
10 They will follow the LORD;
he will roar like a lion.
When he roars,
his children will come trembling
from the west.
11 They will come trembling
like birds from Egypt,
like doves from Assyria.
I will settle them in their homes,"
declares the LORD.

Israel's Sin

12 Ephraim has surrounded me with lies,
the house of Israel with deceit.
And Judah is unruly against God,
even against the faithful Holy One.

12 1 Ephraim feeds on the wind;
he pursues the east wind all day
and multiplies lies and violence.
He makes a treaty with Assyria
and sends olive oil to Egypt.
2 The LORD has a charge to bring against
Judah;
he will punish Jacob[d] according to
his ways
and repay him according to his
deeds.
3 In the womb he grasped his brother's
heel;
as a man he struggled with God.
4 He struggled with the angel and
overcame him;
he wept and begged for his favor.
He found him at Bethel
and talked with him there—
5 the LORD God Almighty,
the LORD is his name of renown!
6 But you must return to your God;
maintain love and justice,
and wait for your God always.

7 The merchant uses dishonest scales;
he loves to defraud.
8 Ephraim boasts,
"I am very rich; I have become
wealthy.
With all my wealth they will not find
in me
any iniquity or sin."

9 "I am the LORD your God,
⌊who brought you⌋ out of[e] Egypt;
I will make you live in tents again,
as in the days of your appointed
feasts.
10 I spoke to the prophets,
gave them many visions
and told parables through them."

11 Is Gilead wicked?
Its people are worthless!

[a] 2 Some Septuagint manuscripts; Hebrew *they*
[b] 2 Septuagint; Hebrew *them* [c] 9 Or *come against any city* [d] 2 *Jacob* means *he grasps the heel* (figuratively, *he deceives*). [e] 9 Or *God / ever since you were in*

Do they sacrifice bulls in Gilgal?
Their altars will be like piles of stones
on a plowed field.
12 Jacob fled to the country of Aram[f];
Israel served to get a wife,
and to pay for her he tended sheep.
13 The LORD used a prophet to bring
Israel up from Egypt,
by a prophet he cared for him.
14 But Ephraim has bitterly provoked him to anger;
his Lord will leave upon him the guilt of his bloodshed
and will repay him for his contempt.

[f] 12 That is, Northwest Mesopotamia

PRAYER: AFFIRMATION

FROM everyone who has been given much, much will be required, and from the one who has been entrusted with much, much more will be asked. (Luke 12:48) . . . Those who do not count the cost and renounce all their possessions cannot be Your disciples. (Luke 14:28, 33)

***PAUSE** to reflect on these Biblical affirmations.*

NT John 12:12–36

The Triumphal Entry

12 The next day the great crowd that had come for the Feast heard that Jesus was on his way to Jerusalem. 13 They took palm branches and went out to meet him, shouting,

"Hosanna![a]"

"Blessed is he who comes in the name of the Lord!"[b]

"Blessed is the King of Israel!"

14 Jesus found a young donkey and sat upon it, as it is written,

15 "Do not be afraid, O Daughter of Zion;
see, your king is coming,
seated on a donkey's colt."[c]

16 At first his disciples did not understand all this. Only after Jesus was glorified did they realize that these things had been written about him and that they had done these things to him.
17 Now the crowd that was with him when he called Lazarus from the tomb and raised him from the dead continued to spread the word. 18 Many people, because they had heard that he had given this miraculous sign, went out to meet him. 19 So the Pharisees said to one another, "See, this is getting us nowhere. Look how the whole world has gone after him!"

Jesus Predicts His Death

20 Now there were some Greeks among those who went up to worship at the Feast. 21 They came to Philip, who was from Bethsaida in Galilee, with a request. "Sir," they said, "we would like to see Jesus." 22 Philip went to tell Andrew; Andrew and Philip in turn told Jesus.
23 Jesus replied, "The hour has come for the Son of Man to be glorified. 24 I tell you the truth, unless a kernel of wheat falls to the ground and dies, it remains only a single seed. But if it dies, it produces many seeds. 25 The man who loves his life will lose it, while the man who hates his life in this world will keep it for eternal life. 26 Whoever serves me must follow me; and where I am, my servant also will be. My Father will honor the one who serves me.
27 "Now my heart is troubled, and what shall I say? 'Father, save me from this hour'? No, it was for this very reason I came to this hour. 28 Father, glorify your name!"
Then a voice came from heaven, "I have glorified it, and will glorify it again." 29 The crowd that was there and heard it said it

[a] 13 A Hebrew expression meaning "Save!" which became an exclamation of praise [b] 13 Psalm 118:25,26 [c] 15 Zech. 9:9

had thundered; others said an angel had
spoken to him.
30 Jesus said, "This voice was for your
benefit, not mine. 31 Now is the time for
judgment on this world; now the prince
of this world will be driven out. 32 But I,
when I am lifted up from the earth, will
draw all men to myself." 33 He said this to
show the kind of death he was going to
die.
34 The crowd spoke up, "We have heard
from the Law that the Christ[d] will remain
forever, so how can you say, 'The Son of
Man must be lifted up'? Who is this 'Son
of Man'?"
35 Then Jesus told them, "You are going
to have the light just a little while longer.
Walk while you have the light, before
darkness overtakes you. The man who
walks in the dark does not know where he
is going. 36 Put your trust in the light while
you have it, so that you may become sons
of light." When he had finished speaking,
Jesus left and hid himself from them.

[d] 34 Or *Messiah*

PRAYER: MY RELATIONSHIP TO GOD

OTHERS may intend evil, but You, God, can use it for good to accomplish Your loving purposes. (Genesis 50:20) . . . The secret things belong to You, Lord our God, but the things revealed belong to us and to our children forever, that we may observe Your words. (Deuteronomy 29:29)

***PAUSE** to thank God for the relationship that you enjoy with Him in Jesus Christ.*

YEAR 2 DAY 314

OT Hosea 13:1-16

The LORD's Anger Against Israel

13 When Ephraim spoke, men
trembled;
he was exalted in Israel.
But he became guilty of Baal
worship and died.
2 Now they sin more and more;
they make idols for themselves
from their silver,
cleverly fashioned images,
all of them the work of craftsmen.
It is said of these people,
"They offer human sacrifice
and kiss[a] the calf-idols."
3 Therefore they will be like the
morning mist,
like the early dew that disappears,
like chaff swirling from a threshing
floor,
like smoke escaping through a
window.

4 "But I am the LORD your God,
⌊who brought you⌋ out of[b] Egypt.
You shall acknowledge no God but
me,
no Savior except me.
5 I cared for you in the desert,
in the land of burning heat.
6 When I fed them, they were satisfied;
when they were satisfied, they
became proud;
then they forgot me.
7 So I will come upon them like a lion,
like a leopard I will lurk by the
path.
8 Like a bear robbed of her cubs,
I will attack them and rip them
open.
Like a lion I will devour them;
a wild animal will tear them apart.

9 "You are destroyed, O Israel,
because you are against me, against
your helper.
10 Where is your king, that he may save
you?
Where are your rulers in all your
towns,
of whom you said,
'Give me a king and princes'?
11 So in my anger I gave you a king,

[a] 2 Or *"Men who sacrifice / kiss* [b] 4 Or *God / ever since you were in*

and in my wrath I took him away.
[12]The guilt of Ephraim is stored up,
his sins are kept on record.
[13]Pains as of a woman in childbirth
come to him,
but he is a child without wisdom;
when the time arrives,
he does not come to the opening of
the womb.

[14]"I will ransom them from the power
of the grave[c];
I will redeem them from death.
Where, O death, are your plagues?
Where, O grave,[c] is your
destruction?

"I will have no compassion,
15 even though he thrives among his
brothers.
An east wind from the LORD will
come,
blowing in from the desert;
his spring will fail
and his well dry up.
His storehouse will be plundered
of all its treasures.
[16]The people of Samaria must bear their
guilt,
because they have rebelled against
their God.
They will fall by the sword;
their little ones will be dashed to
the ground,
their pregnant women ripped
open."

[c]14 Hebrew *Sheol*

PRAYER: THANKSGIVING

JESUS, IN Your Father's house are many dwellings, Lord Jesus; if it were not so, You would have told us. You went there to prepare a place for us. And as You went to prepare a place for us, You will come again and receive us to Yourself, that we also may be where You are. Lord Jesus, You are in Your Father, and I am in You, and You are in me. (John 14:2–3, 20)

PAUSE *to offer your own expressions of thanksgiving.*

NT John 12:37–13:17

The Jews Continue in Their Unbelief

[37]Even after Jesus had done all these
miraculous signs in their presence, they
still would not believe in him. [38]This was
to fulfill the word of Isaiah the prophet:

"Lord, who has believed our message
and to whom has the arm of the
Lord been revealed?"[a]

[39]For this reason they could not believe,
because, as Isaiah says elsewhere:

[40]"He has blinded their eyes
and deadened their hearts,
so they can neither see with their eyes,
nor understand with their hearts,
nor turn—and I would heal them."[b]

[41]Isaiah said this because he saw Jesus'
glory and spoke about him.
[42]Yet at the same time many even
among the leaders believed in him. But
because of the Pharisees they would not
confess their faith for fear they would be
put out of the synagogue; [43]for they loved
praise from men more than praise from
God.
[44]Then Jesus cried out, "When a man
believes in me, he does not believe in me
only, but in the one who sent me. [45]When
he looks at me, he sees the one who sent
me. [46]I have come into the world as a
light, so that no one who believes in me
should stay in darkness.
[47]"As for the person who hears my
words but does not keep them, I do not
judge him. For I did not come to judge the
world, but to save it. [48]There is a judge for
the one who rejects me and does not accept my words; that very word which I
spoke will condemn him at the last day.
[49]For I did not speak of my own accord,
but the Father who sent me commanded
me what to say and how to say it. [50]I know
that his command leads to eternal life. So

[a]38 Isaiah 53:1 [b]40 Isaiah 6:10

whatever I say is just what the Father has
told me to say."

Jesus Washes His Disciples' Feet

13 It was just before the Passover Feast.
Jesus knew that the time had come for
him to leave this world and go to the Father. Having loved his own who were in
the world, he now showed them the full
extent of his love.[c]
2The evening meal was being served,
and the devil had already prompted Judas
Iscariot, son of Simon, to betray Jesus.
3Jesus knew that the Father had put all
things under his power, and that he had
come from God and was returning to
God; 4so he got up from the meal, took
off his outer clothing, and wrapped a towel around his waist. 5After that, he poured
water into a basin and began to wash his
disciples' feet, drying them with the towel that was wrapped around him.
6He came to Simon Peter, who said to
him, "Lord, are you going to wash my
feet?"
7Jesus replied, "You do not realize now
what I am doing, but later you will understand."
8"No," said Peter, "you shall never wash
my feet."
Jesus answered, "Unless I wash you,
you have no part with me."
9"Then, Lord," Simon Peter replied,
"not just my feet but my hands and my
head as well!"
10Jesus answered, "A person who has had
a bath needs only to wash his feet; his
whole body is clean. And you are clean,
though not every one of you." 11For he knew
who was going to betray him, and that was
why he said not every one was clean.
12When he had finished washing their
feet, he put on his clothes and returned to
his place. "Do you understand what I have
done for you?" he asked them. 13"You call
me 'Teacher' and 'Lord,' and rightly so, for
that is what I am. 14Now that I, your Lord
and Teacher, have washed your feet, you
also should wash one another's feet. 15I
have set you an example that you should
do as I have done for you. 16I tell you the
truth, no servant is greater than his master, nor is a messenger greater than the one
who sent him. 17Now that you know these
things, you will be blessed if you do them.

[c] 1 Or *he loved them to the last*

PRAYER: THE CHARACTER I WANT TO CULTIVATE

SURELY You desire truth in the inner parts, and in the hidden part You make me know wisdom. (Psalm 51:6) . . . Lord God, I will preserve sound wisdom and discretion, not letting them out of my sight; they will be life to my soul. (Proverbs 3:21–22)

***TAKE** a moment to ask the Lord for the grace to grow in godly character.*

YEAR 2 DAY 315

OT Psalms 136–137

Psalm 136

1Give thanks to the LORD, for he is
good.
His love endures forever.
2Give thanks to the God of gods.
His love endures forever.
3Give thanks to the Lord of lords:
His love endures forever.

4to him who alone does great wonders,
His love endures forever.
5who by his understanding made the
heavens,
His love endures forever.
6who spread out the earth upon the
waters,
His love endures forever.
7who made the great lights—
His love endures forever.
8the sun to govern the day,
His love endures forever.
9the moon and stars to govern the night;
His love endures forever.

[10] to him who struck down the firstborn
of Egypt
His love endures forever.
[11] and brought Israel out from among
them
His love endures forever.
[12] with a mighty hand and outstretched
arm;
His love endures forever.

[13] to him who divided the Red Sea[a]
asunder
His love endures forever.
[14] and brought Israel through the midst
of it,
His love endures forever.
[15] but swept Pharaoh and his army into
the Red Sea;
His love endures forever.

[16] to him who led his people through
the desert,
His love endures forever.
[17] who struck down great kings,
His love endures forever.
[18] and killed mighty kings—
His love endures forever.
[19] Sihon king of the Amorites
His love endures forever.
[20] and Og king of Bashan—
His love endures forever.
[21] and gave their land as an inheritance,
His love endures forever.
[22] an inheritance to his servant Israel;
His love endures forever.

[23] to the One who remembered us in
our low estate
His love endures forever.
[24] and freed us from our enemies,
His love endures forever.
[25] and who gives food to every creature.
His love endures forever.

[26] Give thanks to the God of heaven.
His love endures forever.

Psalm 137

[1] By the rivers of Babylon we sat and
wept
when we remembered Zion.
[2] There on the poplars
we hung our harps,
[3] for there our captors asked us for
songs,
our tormentors demanded songs of
joy;
they said, "Sing us one of the songs
of Zion!"

[4] How can we sing the songs of the
LORD
while in a foreign land?
[5] If I forget you, O Jerusalem,
may my right hand forget ⌊its skill⌋.
[6] May my tongue cling to the roof of
my mouth
if I do not remember you,
if I do not consider Jerusalem
my highest joy.

[7] Remember, O LORD, what the
Edomites did
on the day Jerusalem fell.
"Tear it down," they cried,
"tear it down to its foundations!"

[8] O Daughter of Babylon, doomed to
destruction,
happy is he who repays you
for what you have done to us—
[9] he who seizes your infants
and dashes them against the rocks.

[a] 13 Hebrew *Yam Suph*; that is, Sea of Reeds; also in verse 15

PRAYER: ADORATION

I WILL arise and bless You, Lord, my God; You are from everlasting to everlasting. Blessed be Your glorious name, which is exalted above all blessing and praise! (Nehemiah 9:5) . . . As for me, O Lord, I will see Your face in righteousness; when I awake, I will be satisfied with Your likeness. (Psalm 17:15)

***PAUSE** to express your thoughts of praise and worship.*

NT John 13:18-38

Jesus Predicts His Betrayal

[18] "I am not referring to all of you; I know those I have chosen. But this is to fulfill the scripture: 'He who shares my bread has lifted up his heel against me.'[a]

[19] "I am telling you now before it happens, so that when it does happen you will believe that I am He. [20] I tell you the truth, whoever accepts anyone I send accepts me; and whoever accepts me accepts the one who sent me."

[21] After he had said this, Jesus was troubled in spirit and testified, "I tell you the truth, one of you is going to betray me."

[22] His disciples stared at one another, at a loss to know which of them he meant. [23] One of them, the disciple whom Jesus loved, was reclining next to him. [24] Simon Peter motioned to this disciple and said, "Ask him which one he means."

[25] Leaning back against Jesus, he asked him, "Lord, who is it?"

[26] Jesus answered, "It is the one to whom I will give this piece of bread when I have dipped it in the dish." Then, dipping the piece of bread, he gave it to Judas Iscariot, son of Simon. [27] As soon as Judas took the bread, Satan entered into him.

"What you are about to do, do quickly," Jesus told him, [28] but no one at the meal understood why Jesus said this to him. [29] Since Judas had charge of the money, some thought Jesus was telling him to buy what was needed for the Feast, or to give something to the poor. [30] As soon as Judas had taken the bread, he went out. And it was night.

Jesus Predicts Peter's Denial

[31] When he was gone, Jesus said, "Now is the Son of Man glorified and God is glorified in him. [32] If God is glorified in him,[b] God will glorify the Son in himself, and will glorify him at once.

[33] "My children, I will be with you only a little longer. You will look for me, and just as I told the Jews, so I tell you now: Where I am going, you cannot come.

[34] "A new command I give you: Love one another. As I have loved you, so you must love one another. [35] By this all men will know that you are my disciples, if you love one another."

[36] Simon Peter asked him, "Lord, where are you going?"

Jesus replied, "Where I am going, you cannot follow now, but you will follow later."

[37] Peter asked, "Lord, why can't I follow you now? I will lay down my life for you."

[38] Then Jesus answered, "Will you really lay down your life for me? I tell you the truth, before the rooster crows, you will disown me three times!

[a] 18 Psalm 41:9 [b] 32 Many early manuscripts do not have *If God is glorified in him.*

PRAYER: MY RELATIONSHIP TO OTHERS

I WILL not judge my brothers and sisters or regard them with contempt. Instead of judging them, I will resolve not to put a stumbling block or obstacle in their way. (Romans 14:10, 13) . . . I will accept others just as You, O Jesus Christ, accepted me to the glory of God. (Romans 15:7)

PAUSE *to review your relationships with others and to commit them to the Lord.*

YEAR 2 DAY 316

OT Hosea 14:1-9

Repentance to Bring Blessing

14 Return, O Israel, to the LORD your
God.
Your sins have been your downfall!
[2] Take words with you
and return to the LORD.
Say to him:

"Forgive all our sins
and receive us graciously,
that we may offer the fruit of our lips.[a]
3 Assyria cannot save us;
we will not mount war-horses.
We will never again say 'Our gods'
to what our own hands have made,
for in you the fatherless find compassion."

4 "I will heal their waywardness
and love them freely,
for my anger has turned away from them.
5 I will be like the dew to Israel;
he will blossom like a lily.
Like a cedar of Lebanon
he will send down his roots;
6 his young shoots will grow.
His splendor will be like an olive tree,
his fragrance like a cedar of Lebanon.
7 Men will dwell again in his shade.
He will flourish like the grain.
He will blossom like a vine,
and his fame will be like the wine from Lebanon.
8 O Ephraim, what more have I[b] to do with idols?
I will answer him and care for him.
I am like a green pine tree;
your fruitfulness comes from me."

9 Who is wise? He will realize these things.
Who is discerning? He will understand them.
The ways of the LORD are right;
the righteous walk in them,
but the rebellious stumble in them.

[a] 2 Or *offer our lips as sacrifices of bulls* [b] 8 Or *What more has Ephraim*

PRAYER: CONFESSION

NO temptation has overtaken me except what is common to all people. And You, O God, are faithful; You will not let me be tempted beyond what I am able, but with the temptation You will also provide a way out, so that I may be able to endure it. (1 Corinthians 10:13)

***ASK** the Spirit to search your heart and reveal any areas of unconfessed sin. Acknowledge these to the Lord and thank Him for His forgiveness.*

NT John 14:1-31

Jesus Comforts His Disciples

14 "Do not let your hearts be troubled.
Trust in God[a]; trust also in me. 2 In my
Father's house are many rooms; if it were
not so, I would have told you. I am going
there to prepare a place for you. 3 And if I
go and prepare a place for you, I will
come back and take you to be with me
that you also may be where I am. 4 You
know the way to the place where I am going."

Jesus the Way to the Father

5 Thomas said to him, "Lord, we don't
know where you are going, so how can we
know the way?"
6 Jesus answered, "I am the way and the
truth and the life. No one comes to the Father
except through me. 7 If you really
knew me, you would know[b] my Father as
well. From now on, you do know him and
have seen him."
8 Philip said, "Lord, show us the Father
and that will be enough for us."
9 Jesus answered: "Don't you know me,
Philip, even after I have been among you
such a long time? Anyone who has seen
me has seen the Father. How can you say,
'Show us the Father'? 10 Don't you believe
that I am in the Father, and that the Father
is in me? The words I say to you are
not just my own. Rather, it is the Father,
living in me, who is doing his work. 11 Believe
me when I say that I am in the Father
and the Father is in me; or at least believe
on the evidence of the miracles
themselves. 12 I tell you the truth, anyone
who has faith in me will do what I have

[a] 1 Or *You trust in God* [b] 7 Some early manuscripts *If you really have known me, you will know*

been doing. He will do even greater things
than these, because I am going to the Father. 13 And I will do whatever you ask in
my name, so that the Son may bring glory to the Father. 14 You may ask me for anything in my name, and I will do it.

Jesus Promises the Holy Spirit

15 "If you love me, you will obey what I
command. 16 And I will ask the Father, and
he will give you another Counselor to be
with you forever— 17 the Spirit of truth.
The world cannot accept him, because it
neither sees him nor knows him. But you
know him, for he lives with you and will
be[c] in you. 18 I will not leave you as orphans; I will come to you. 19 Before long,
the world will not see me anymore, but
you will see me. Because I live, you also
will live. 20 On that day you will realize
that I am in my Father, and you are in me,
and I am in you. 21 Whoever has my commands and obeys them, he is the one who
loves me. He who loves me will be loved
by my Father, and I too will love him and
show myself to him."

22 Then Judas (not Judas Iscariot) said,
"But, Lord, why do you intend to show
yourself to us and not to the world?"

23 Jesus replied, "If anyone loves me, he
will obey my teaching. My Father will love
him, and we will come to him and make
our home with him. 24 He who does not
love me will not obey my teaching. These
words you hear are not my own; they belong to the Father who sent me.

25 "All this I have spoken while still with
you. 26 But the Counselor, the Holy Spirit,
whom the Father will send in my name,
will teach you all things and will remind
you of everything I have said to you.
27 Peace I leave with you; my peace I give
you. I do not give to you as the world
gives. Do not let your hearts be troubled
and do not be afraid.

28 "You heard me say, 'I am going away
and I am coming back to you.' If you loved
me, you would be glad that I am going to
the Father, for the Father is greater than I.
29 I have told you now before it happens,
so that when it does happen you will believe. 30 I will not speak with you much
longer, for the prince of this world is coming. He has no hold on me, 31 but the
world must learn that I love the Father
and that I do exactly what my Father has
commanded me.

"Come now; let us leave.

[c] 17 Some early manuscripts *and is*

PRAYER: THE ATTRIBUTES OF GOD

YOU live, O Lord! Blessed are You, my Rock! You are exalted, O God, Rock of my salvation! (2 Samuel 22:47) . . . I will trust in You forever, for in You, Yahweh, the Lord, I have an everlasting Rock. (Isaiah 26:4)

***PAUSE** to reflect on these affirmations about the person, powers and perfection of God.*

YEAR 2
DAY 317

OT Joel 1:1–2:17

1 The word of the LORD that came to Joel
son of Pethuel.

An Invasion of Locusts

2 Hear this, you elders;
listen, all who live in the land.
Has anything like this ever happened
in your days
or in the days of your forefathers?
3 Tell it to your children,
and let your children tell it to their
children,
and their children to the next
generation.
4 What the locust swarm has left
the great locusts have eaten;
what the great locusts have left
the young locusts have eaten;
what the young locusts have left

other locusts[a] have eaten.

5 Wake up, you drunkards, and weep!
Wail, all you drinkers of wine;
wail because of the new wine,
for it has been snatched from your lips.
6 A nation has invaded my land,
powerful and without number;
it has the teeth of a lion,
the fangs of a lioness.
7 It has laid waste my vines
and ruined my fig trees.
It has stripped off their bark
and thrown it away,
leaving their branches white.

8 Mourn like a virgin[b] in sackcloth
grieving for the husband[c] of her youth.
9 Grain offerings and drink offerings
are cut off from the house of the LORD.
The priests are in mourning,
those who minister before the LORD.
10 The fields are ruined,
the ground is dried up[d];
the grain is destroyed,
the new wine is dried up,
the oil fails.
11 Despair, you farmers,
wail, you vine growers;
grieve for the wheat and the barley,
because the harvest of the field is destroyed.
12 The vine is dried up
and the fig tree is withered;
the pomegranate, the palm and the apple tree—
all the trees of the field—are dried up.
Surely the joy of mankind
is withered away.

A Call to Repentance

13 Put on sackcloth, O priests, and mourn;
wail, you who minister before the altar.
Come, spend the night in sackcloth,
you who minister before my God;
for the grain offerings and drink offerings
are withheld from the house of your God.
14 Declare a holy fast;
call a sacred assembly.
Summon the elders
and all who live in the land
to the house of the LORD your God,
and cry out to the LORD.

15 Alas for that day!
For the day of the LORD is near;
it will come like destruction from the Almighty.[e]

16 Has not the food been cut off
before our very eyes—
joy and gladness
from the house of our God?
17 The seeds are shriveled
beneath the clods.[f]
The storehouses are in ruins,
the granaries have been broken down,
for the grain has dried up.
18 How the cattle moan!
The herds mill about
because they have no pasture;
even the flocks of sheep are suffering.

19 To you, O LORD, I call,
for fire has devoured the open pastures
and flames have burned up all the trees of the field.
20 Even the wild animals pant for you;
the streams of water have dried up
and fire has devoured the open pastures.

An Army of Locusts

2 Blow the trumpet in Zion;
sound the alarm on my holy hill.
Let all who live in the land tremble,
for the day of the LORD is coming.
It is close at hand—
2 a day of darkness and gloom,
a day of clouds and blackness.
Like dawn spreading across the mountains
a large and mighty army comes,
such as never was of old
nor ever will be in ages to come.

3 Before them fire devours,
behind them a flame blazes.
Before them the land is like the garden of Eden,
behind them, a desert waste—

[a] 4 The precise meaning of the four Hebrew words used here for locusts is uncertain. [b] 8 Or *young woman* [c] 8 Or *betrothed* [d] 10 Or *ground mourns* [e] 15 Hebrew *Shaddai* [f] 17 The meaning of the Hebrew for this word is uncertain.

nothing escapes them.
[4]They have the appearance of horses;
they gallop along like cavalry.
[5]With a noise like that of chariots
they leap over the mountaintops,
like a crackling fire consuming stubble,
like a mighty army drawn up for
battle.

[6]At the sight of them, nations are in
anguish;
every face turns pale.
[7]They charge like warriors;
they scale walls like soldiers.
They all march in line,
not swerving from their course.
[8]They do not jostle each other;
each marches straight ahead.
They plunge through defenses
without breaking ranks.
[9]They rush upon the city;
they run along the wall.
They climb into the houses;
like thieves they enter through the
windows.

[10]Before them the earth shakes,
the sky trembles,
the sun and moon are darkened,
and the stars no longer shine.
[11]The LORD thunders
at the head of his army;
his forces are beyond number,
and mighty are those who obey his
command.
The day of the LORD is great;
it is dreadful.
Who can endure it?

Rend Your Heart

[12]"Even now," declares the LORD,
"return to me with all your heart,
with fasting and weeping and
mourning."

[13]Rend your heart
and not your garments.
Return to the LORD your God,
for he is gracious and
compassionate,
slow to anger and abounding in love,
and he relents from sending
calamity.
[14]Who knows? He may turn and have
pity
and leave behind a blessing—
grain offerings and drink offerings
for the LORD your God.

[15]Blow the trumpet in Zion,
declare a holy fast,
call a sacred assembly.
[16]Gather the people,
consecrate the assembly;
bring together the elders,
gather the children,
those nursing at the breast.
Let the bridegroom leave his room
and the bride her chamber.
[17]Let the priests, who minister before
the LORD,
weep between the temple porch and
the altar.
Let them say, "Spare your people,
O LORD.
Do not make your inheritance an
object of scorn,
a byword among the nations.
Why should they say among the
peoples,
'Where is their God?' "

PRAYER: RENEWAL

MAY I not be quickly provoked in my spirit, for anger rests in the hearts of the foolish. (Ecclesiastes 7:9) . . .
May I not return evil for evil or insult for insult, but blessing instead, because to this I was called, that I may inherit a blessing. (1 Peter 3:9)

***PAUSE** to add your own prayers for personal renewal.*

NT John 15:1–16:4

The Vine and the Branches

15 "I am the true vine, and my Father is the gardener. [2]He cuts off every branch in me that bears no fruit, while every branch that does bear fruit he prunes[a] so

[a] 2 The Greek for *prunes* also means *cleans.*

that it will be even more fruitful. 3You are already clean because of the word I have spoken to you. 4Remain in me, and I will remain in you. No branch can bear fruit by itself; it must remain in the vine. Neither can you bear fruit unless you remain in me.

5"I am the vine; you are the branches. If a man remains in me and I in him, he will bear much fruit; apart from me you can do nothing. 6If anyone does not remain in me, he is like a branch that is thrown away and withers; such branches are picked up, thrown into the fire and burned. 7If you remain in me and my words remain in you, ask whatever you wish, and it will be given you. 8This is to my Father's glory, that you bear much fruit, showing yourselves to be my disciples.

9"As the Father has loved me, so have I loved you. Now remain in my love. 10If you obey my commands, you will remain in my love, just as I have obeyed my Father's commands and remain in his love. 11I have told you this so that my joy may be in you and that your joy may be complete. 12My command is this: Love each other as I have loved you. 13Greater love has no one than this, that he lay down his life for his friends. 14You are my friends if you do what I command. 15I no longer call you servants, because a servant does not know his master's business. Instead, I have called you friends, for everything that I learned from my Father I have made known to you. 16You did not choose me, but I chose you and appointed you to go and bear fruit—fruit that will last. Then the Father will give you whatever you ask in my name. 17This is my command: Love each other.

The World Hates the Disciples

18"If the world hates you, keep in mind that it hated me first. 19If you belonged to the world, it would love you as its own. As it is, you do not belong to the world, but I have chosen you out of the world. That is why the world hates you. 20Remember the words I spoke to you: 'No servant is greater than his master.'[b] If they persecuted me, they will persecute you also. If they obeyed my teaching, they will obey yours also. 21They will treat you this way because of my name, for they do not know the One who sent me. 22If I had not come and spoken to them, they would not be guilty of sin. Now, however, they have no excuse for their sin. 23He who hates me hates my Father as well. 24If I had not done among them what no one else did, they would not be guilty of sin. But now they have seen these miracles, and yet they have hated both me and my Father. 25But this is to fulfill what is written in their Law: 'They hated me without reason.'[c]

26"When the Counselor comes, whom I will send to you from the Father, the Spirit of truth who goes out from the Father, he will testify about me. 27And you also must testify, for you have been with me from the beginning.

16 "All this I have told you so that you will not go astray. 2They will put you out of the synagogue; in fact, a time is coming when anyone who kills you will think he is offering a service to God. 3They will do such things because they have not known the Father or me. 4I have told you this, so that when the time comes you will remember that I warned you. I did not tell you this at first because I was with you.

[b] *20* John 13:16 [c] *25* Psalms 35:19; 69:4

PRAYER: THE WORKS OF GOD

THE children of Israel were a people holy to You, O Lord, their God. Out of all the peoples on the face of the earth, You chose them to be Your treasured possession. You, O Lord, are the One who went with Israel to fight for them against their enemies, to save them.

(Deuteronomy 14:2; 20:4)

TAKE *a moment to consider the greatness of God's wonderful works.*

OT Joel 2:18–3:21

The LORD's Answer

18 Then the LORD will be jealous for his land
and take pity on his people.

19 The LORD will reply[a] to them:

"I am sending you grain, new wine and oil,
enough to satisfy you fully;
never again will I make you
an object of scorn to the nations.

20 "I will drive the northern army far from you,
pushing it into a parched and barren land,
with its front columns going into the eastern sea[b]
and those in the rear into the western sea.[c]
And its stench will go up;
its smell will rise."

Surely he has done great things.[d]
21 Be not afraid, O land;
be glad and rejoice.
Surely the LORD has done great things.
22 Be not afraid, O wild animals,
for the open pastures are becoming green.
The trees are bearing their fruit;
the fig tree and the vine yield their riches.
23 Be glad, O people of Zion,
rejoice in the LORD your God,
for he has given you
the autumn rains in righteousness.[e]
He sends you abundant showers,
both autumn and spring rains, as before.
24 The threshing floors will be filled with grain;
the vats will overflow with new wine and oil.

25 "I will repay you for the years the locusts have eaten—
the great locust and the young locust,
the other locusts and the locust swarm[f]—
my great army that I sent among you.
26 You will have plenty to eat, until you are full,
and you will praise the name of the LORD your God,
who has worked wonders for you;
never again will my people be shamed.
27 Then you will know that I am in Israel,
that I am the LORD your God,
and that there is no other;
never again will my people be shamed.

The Day of the LORD

28 "And afterward,
I will pour out my Spirit on all people.
Your sons and daughters will prophesy,
your old men will dream dreams,
your young men will see visions.
29 Even on my servants, both men and women,
I will pour out my Spirit in those days.
30 I will show wonders in the heavens
and on the earth,
blood and fire and billows of smoke.
31 The sun will be turned to darkness
and the moon to blood
before the coming of the great and dreadful day of the LORD.
32 And everyone who calls
on the name of the LORD will be saved;
for on Mount Zion and in Jerusalem
there will be deliverance,
as the LORD has said,
among the survivors
whom the LORD calls.

The Nations Judged

3 "In those days and at that time,
when I restore the fortunes of Judah and Jerusalem,
2 I will gather all nations

[a] 18,19 Or *LORD was jealous . . . / and took pity . . . / 19The LORD replied* [b] 20 That is, the Dead Sea [c] 20 That is, the Mediterranean [d] 20 Or *rise. / Surely it has done great things."* [e] 23 Or */ the teacher for righteousness:* [f] 25 The precise meaning of the four Hebrew words used here for locusts is uncertain.

and bring them down to the Valley
of Jehoshaphat.[g]
There I will enter into judgment
against them
concerning my inheritance, my
people Israel,
for they scattered my people among
the nations
and divided up my land.
3 They cast lots for my people
and traded boys for prostitutes;
they sold girls for wine
that they might drink.

4 "Now what have you against me,
O Tyre and Sidon and all you regions of
Philistia? Are you repaying me for something I have done? If you are paying me
back, I will swiftly and speedily return on
your own heads what you have done. 5 For
you took my silver and my gold and carried off my finest treasures to your temples. 6 You sold the people of Judah and
Jerusalem to the Greeks, that you might
send them far from their homeland.
7 "See, I am going to rouse them out of
the places to which you sold them, and I
will return on your own heads what you
have done. 8 I will sell your sons and
daughters to the people of Judah, and
they will sell them to the Sabeans, a nation far away." The LORD has spoken.

9 Proclaim this among the nations:
Prepare for war!
Rouse the warriors!
Let all the fighting men draw near
and attack.
10 Beat your plowshares into swords
and your pruning hooks into spears.
Let the weakling say,
"I am strong!"
11 Come quickly, all you nations from
every side,
and assemble there.

Bring down your warriors, O LORD!

12 "Let the nations be roused;
let them advance into the Valley of
Jehoshaphat,
for there I will sit
to judge all the nations on every
side.
13 Swing the sickle,
for the harvest is ripe.
Come, trample the grapes,
for the winepress is full
and the vats overflow—
so great is their wickedness!"

14 Multitudes, multitudes
in the valley of decision!
For the day of the LORD is near
in the valley of decision.
15 The sun and moon will be darkened,
and the stars no longer shine.
16 The LORD will roar from Zion
and thunder from Jerusalem;
the earth and the sky will tremble.
But the LORD will be a refuge for his
people,
a stronghold for the people of
Israel.

Blessings for God's People

17 "Then you will know that I, the LORD
your God,
dwell in Zion, my holy hill.
Jerusalem will be holy;
never again will foreigners invade
her.

18 "In that day the mountains will drip
new wine,
and the hills will flow with milk;
all the ravines of Judah will run
with water.
A fountain will flow out of the LORD's
house
and will water the valley of acacias.[h]
19 But Egypt will be desolate,
Edom a desert waste,
because of violence done to the
people of Judah,
in whose land they shed innocent
blood.
20 Judah will be inhabited forever
and Jerusalem through all
generations.
21 Their bloodguilt, which I have not
pardoned,
I will pardon."

The LORD dwells in Zion!

[g] 2 *Jehoshaphat* means *the LORD judges;* also in verse 12.
[h] 18 Or *Valley of Shittim*

PRAYER: PETITION

I HAVE hidden Your word in my heart that I might not sin against You. Blessed are You, O Lord; teach me Your statutes. (Psalm 119:11–12)

***PAUSE** here to petition God for growth in your character and personal discipline, and for physical health and strength. Ask that He empower you for spiritual warfare against the temptations of the world, the flesh and the devil. Offer prayers regarding your activities for this day and any special concerns you may have.*

NT John 16:5–33

The Work of the Holy Spirit

5 "Now I am going to him who sent me,
yet none of you asks me, 'Where are you
going?' 6 Because I have said these things,
you are filled with grief. 7 But I tell you the
truth: It is for your good that I am going
away. Unless I go away, the Counselor will
not come to you; but if I go, I will send
him to you. 8 When he comes, he will convict the world of guilt[a] in regard to sin and
righteousness and judgment: 9 in regard to
sin, because men do not believe in me;
10 in regard to righteousness, because I am
going to the Father, where you can see me
no longer; 11 and in regard to judgment,
because the prince of this world now
stands condemned.

12 "I have much more to say to you, more
than you can now bear. 13 But when he, the
Spirit of truth, comes, he will guide you
into all truth. He will not speak on his
own; he will speak only what he hears,
and he will tell you what is yet to come.
14 He will bring glory to me by taking from
what is mine and making it known to you.
15 All that belongs to the Father is mine.
That is why I said the Spirit will take from
what is mine and make it known to you.

16 "In a little while you will see me no
more, and then after a little while you will
see me."

The Disciples' Grief Will Turn to Joy

17 Some of his disciples said to one another, "What does he mean by saying, 'In
a little while you will see me no more, and
then after a little while you will see me,'
and 'Because I am going to the Father'?"
18 They kept asking, "What does he mean
by 'a little while'? We don't understand
what he is saying."

19 Jesus saw that they wanted to ask him
about this, so he said to them, "Are you
asking one another what I meant when I
said, 'In a little while you will see me no
more, and then after a little while you will
see me'? 20 I tell you the truth, you will
weep and mourn while the world rejoices.
You will grieve, but your grief will turn to
joy. 21 A woman giving birth to a child has
pain because her time has come; but
when her baby is born she forgets the anguish because of her joy that a child is
born into the world. 22 So with you: Now
is your time of grief, but I will see you
again and you will rejoice, and no one
will take away your joy. 23 In that day you
will no longer ask me anything. I tell you
the truth, my Father will give you whatever you ask in my name. 24 Until now you
have not asked for anything in my name.
Ask and you will receive, and your joy will
be complete.

25 "Though I have been speaking figuratively, a time is coming when I will no
longer use this kind of language but will
tell you plainly about my Father. 26 In that
day you will ask in my name. I am not
saying that I will ask the Father on your
behalf. 27 No, the Father himself loves you
because you have loved me and have believed that I came from God. 28 I came
from the Father and entered the world;
now I am leaving the world and going
back to the Father."

29 Then Jesus' disciples said, "Now you
are speaking clearly and without figures of
speech. 30 Now we can see that you know
all things and that you do not even need
to have anyone ask you questions. This
makes us believe that you came from
God."

[a] 8 Or *will expose the guilt of the world*

[31] "You believe at last!"[b] Jesus answered.
[32] "But a time is coming, and has come,
when you will be scattered, each to his
own home. You will leave me all alone.
Yet I am not alone, for my Father is
with me.

[33] "I have told you these things, so that
in me you may have peace. In this world
you will have trouble. But take heart! I
have overcome the world."

[b] 31 Or *"Do you now believe?"*

PRAYER: MY RELATIONSHIP TO GOD

LORD, there is no one besides You to help the powerless against the mighty. Help us, O Lord our God, for we rest in You. O Lord, You are our God; do not let people prevail against You. (2 Chronicles 14:11) . . . You are my lamp, O Lord; You turn my darkness into light. (2 Samuel 22:29–30)

PAUSE *to thank God for the relationship that you enjoy with Him in Jesus Christ.*

OT Proverbs 30

YEAR 2
DAY 319

Sayings of Agur

30 The sayings of Agur son of Jakeh—an oracle[a]:

This man declared to Ithiel,
to Ithiel and to Ucal:[b]

[2] "I am the most ignorant of men;
I do not have a man's
understanding.
[3] I have not learned wisdom,
nor have I knowledge of the Holy
One.
[4] Who has gone up to heaven and come
down?
Who has gathered up the wind in
the hollow of his hands?
Who has wrapped up the waters in his
cloak?
Who has established all the ends of
the earth?
What is his name, and the name of
his son?
Tell me if you know!

[5] "Every word of God is flawless;
he is a shield to those who take
refuge in him.
[6] Do not add to his words,
or he will rebuke you and prove
you a liar.

[7] "Two things I ask of you, O LORD;
do not refuse me before I die:
[8] Keep falsehood and lies far from me;
give me neither poverty nor riches,
but give me only my daily bread.
[9] Otherwise, I may have too much and
disown you
and say, 'Who is the LORD?'
Or I may become poor and steal,
and so dishonor the name of my
God.

[10] "Do not slander a servant to his
master,
or he will curse you, and you will
pay for it.

[11] "There are those who curse their
fathers
and do not bless their mothers;
[12] those who are pure in their own eyes
and yet are not cleansed of their
filth;
[13] those whose eyes are ever so haughty,
whose glances are so disdainful;
[14] those whose teeth are swords
and whose jaws are set with knives
to devour the poor from the earth,
the needy from among mankind.

[15] "The leech has two daughters.
'Give! Give!' they cry.

"There are three things that are never
satisfied,
four that never say, 'Enough!':

[a] 1 Or *Jakeh of Massa* [b] 1 Masoretic Text; with a different word division of the Hebrew *declared, "I am weary, O God; / I am weary, O God, and faint.*

[16]the grave,[c] the barren womb,
land, which is never satisfied with water,
and fire, which never says, 'Enough!'

[17]"The eye that mocks a father,
that scorns obedience to a mother,
will be pecked out by the ravens of the valley,
will be eaten by the vultures.

[18]"There are three things that are too amazing for me,
four that I do not understand:
[19]the way of an eagle in the sky,
the way of a snake on a rock,
the way of a ship on the high seas,
and the way of a man with a maiden.

[20]"This is the way of an adulteress:
She eats and wipes her mouth
and says, 'I've done nothing wrong.'

[21]"Under three things the earth trembles,
under four it cannot bear up:
[22]a servant who becomes king,
a fool who is full of food,
[23]an unloved woman who is married,
and a maidservant who displaces her mistress.

[24]"Four things on earth are small,
yet they are extremely wise:
[25]Ants are creatures of little strength,
yet they store up their food in the summer;
[26]coneys[d] are creatures of little power,
yet they make their home in the crags;
[27]locusts have no king,
yet they advance together in ranks;
[28]a lizard can be caught with the hand,
yet it is found in kings' palaces.

[29]"There are three things that are stately in their stride,
four that move with stately bearing:
[30]a lion, mighty among beasts,
who retreats before nothing;
[31]a strutting rooster, a he-goat,
and a king with his army around him.[e]

[32]"If you have played the fool and exalted yourself,
or if you have planned evil,
clap your hand over your mouth!
[33]For as churning the milk produces butter,
and as twisting the nose produces blood,
so stirring up anger produces strife."

[c] *16* Hebrew *Sheol* [d] *26* That is, the hyrax or rock badger [e] *31* Or *king secure against revolt*

PRAYER: INTERCESSION

O LORD, may I not repay anyone evil for evil, but seek to do what is right in the sight of all people. If it is possible, as far as it depends on me, let me live at peace with everyone. (Romans 12:17–18)

***TAKE** a few moments to intercede on behalf of the poor and hungry, the oppressed and persecuted, and those in control of world and national resources. Offer prayers for peace among nations and regarding current events and concerns.*

NT John 17:1–26

Jesus Prays for Himself

17 After Jesus said this, he looked toward heaven and prayed:

"Father, the time has come. Glorify your Son, that your Son may glorify you. [2]For you granted him authority over all people that he might give eternal life to all those you have
given him. [3]Now this is eternal life:
that they may know you, the only true God, and Jesus Christ, whom
you have sent. [4]I have brought you
glory on earth by completing the
work you gave me to do. [5]And now,
Father, glorify me in your presence with the glory I had with you before the world began.

Jesus Prays for His Disciples

6 "I have revealed you[a] to those whom you gave me out of the world. They were yours; you gave them to me and they have obeyed your word. 7 Now they know that everything you have given me comes from you. 8 For I gave them the words you gave me and they accepted them. They knew with certainty that I came from you, and they believed that you sent me. 9 I pray for them. I am not praying for the world, but for those you have given me, for they are yours. 10 All I have is yours, and all you have is mine. And glory has come to me through them. 11 I will remain in the world no longer, but they are still in the world, and I am coming to you. Holy Father, protect them by the power of your name—the name you gave me—so that they may be one as we are one. 12 While I was with them, I protected them and kept them safe by that name you gave me. None has been lost except the one doomed to destruction so that Scripture would be fulfilled.

13 "I am coming to you now, but I say these things while I am still in the world, so that they may have the full measure of my joy within them. 14 I have given them your word and the world has hated them, for they are not of the world any more than I am of the world. 15 My prayer is not that you take them out of the world but that you protect them from the evil one. 16 They are not of the world, even as I am not of it. 17 Sanctify[b] them by the truth; your word is truth. 18 As you sent me into the world, I have sent them into the world. 19 For them I sanctify myself, that they too may be truly sanctified.

Jesus Prays for All Believers

20 "My prayer is not for them alone. I pray also for those who will believe in me through their message, 21 that all of them may be one, Father, just as you are in me and I am in you. May they also be in us so that the world may believe that you have sent me. 22 I have given them the glory that you gave me, that they may be one as we are one: 23 I in them and you in me. May they be brought to complete unity to let the world know that you sent me and have loved them even as you have loved me.

24 "Father, I want those you have given me to be with me where I am, and to see my glory, the glory you have given me because you loved me before the creation of the world.

25 "Righteous Father, though the world does not know you, I know you, and they know that you have sent me. 26 I have made you known to them, and will continue to make you known in order that the love you have for me may be in them and that I myself may be in them."

[a] 6 Greek *your name;* also in verse 26 [b] 17 Greek *hagiazo (set apart for sacred use* or *make holy);* also in verse 19

PRAYER: THE CHARACTER I WANT TO CULTIVATE

THE fruit of the righteous, O God, is a tree of life, and those who win souls are wise. (Proverbs 11:30) . . . Fear of You, O Lord, is a fountain of life, turning me away from the snares of death. (Proverbs 14:27)

***TAKE** a moment to ask the Lord for the grace to grow in godly character.*

OT Amos 1:1-15 — YEAR 2 DAY 320

1 The words of Amos, one of the shepherds of Tekoa—what he saw concerning Israel two years before the earthquake, when Uzziah was king of Judah and Jeroboam son of Jehoash[a] was king of Israel.

[a] 1 Hebrew *Joash,* a variant of *Jehoash*

2 He said:

"The LORD roars from Zion
and thunders from Jerusalem;
the pastures of the shepherds dry up,[b]
and the top of Carmel withers."

Judgment on Israel's Neighbors

3 This is what the LORD says:

"For three sins of Damascus,
even for four, I will not turn back
⌊my wrath⌋.
Because she threshed Gilead
with sledges having iron teeth,
4 I will send fire upon the house of
Hazael
that will consume the fortresses of
Ben-Hadad.
5 I will break down the gate of
Damascus;
I will destroy the king who is in[c]
the Valley of Aven[d]
and the one who holds the scepter in
Beth Eden.
The people of Aram will go into
exile to Kir,"
says the LORD.

6 This is what the LORD says:

"For three sins of Gaza,
even for four, I will not turn back
⌊my wrath⌋.
Because she took captive whole
communities
and sold them to Edom,
7 I will send fire upon the walls of Gaza
that will consume her fortresses.
8 I will destroy the king[e] of Ashdod
and the one who holds the scepter
in Ashkelon.
I will turn my hand against Ekron,
till the last of the Philistines is dead,"
says the Sovereign LORD.

9 This is what the LORD says:

"For three sins of Tyre,
even for four, I will not turn back
⌊my wrath⌋.
Because she sold whole communities
of captives to Edom,
disregarding a treaty of
brotherhood,
10 I will send fire upon the walls of Tyre
that will consume her fortresses."

11 This is what the LORD says:

"For three sins of Edom,
even for four, I will not turn back
⌊my wrath⌋.
Because he pursued his brother with a
sword,
stifling all compassion,[f]
because his anger raged continually
and his fury flamed unchecked,
12 I will send fire upon Teman
that will consume the fortresses of
Bozrah."

13 This is what the LORD says:

"For three sins of Ammon,
even for four, I will not turn back
⌊my wrath⌋.
Because he ripped open the pregnant
women of Gilead
in order to extend his borders,
14 I will set fire to the walls of Rabbah
that will consume her fortresses
amid war cries on the day of battle,
amid violent winds on a stormy day.
15 Her king[g] will go into exile,
he and his officials together,"
says the LORD.

[b] 2 Or *shepherds mourn* [c] 5 Or *the inhabitants of* [d] 5 *Aven* means *wickedness.* [e] 8 Or *inhabitants* [f] 11 Or *sword / and destroyed his allies* [g] 15 Or / *Molech;* Hebrew *malcam*

PRAYER: AFFIRMATION

YOU, Father, judge no one, but have given all judgment to the Son, that all may honor Him just as they honor You. The one who does not honor the Son does not honor You, Father, who sent Him. (John 5:22–23) . . . Lord Jesus, whoever acknowledges You before others, You will also acknowledge before the angels of God and Your Father in heaven. But whoever denies You before others, You will also deny before the angels of God and Your Father in heaven. (Matthew 10:32–33; Luke 12:8–9)

***PAUSE** to reflect on these Biblical affirmations.*

NT **John 18:1-27**

Jesus Arrested

18 When he had finished praying, Jesus
left with his disciples and crossed the
Kidron Valley. On the other side there was
an olive grove, and he and his disciples
went into it.
2Now Judas, who betrayed him, knew
the place, because Jesus had often met
there with his disciples. 3So Judas came to
the grove, guiding a detachment of soldiers and some officials from the chief
priests and Pharisees. They were carrying
torches, lanterns and weapons.
4Jesus, knowing all that was going to
happen to him, went out and asked them,
"Who is it you want?"
5"Jesus of Nazareth," they replied.
"I am he," Jesus said. (And Judas the
traitor was standing there with them.)
6When Jesus said, "I am he," they drew
back and fell to the ground.
7Again he asked them, "Who is it you
want?"
And they said, "Jesus of Nazareth."
8"I told you that I am he," Jesus answered. "If you are looking for me, then
let these men go." 9This happened so that
the words he had spoken would be fulfilled: "I have not lost one of those you
gave me."[a]
10Then Simon Peter, who had a sword,
drew it and struck the high priest's servant, cutting off his right ear. (The servant's name was Malchus.)
11Jesus commanded Peter, "Put your
sword away! Shall I not drink the cup the
Father has given me?"

Jesus Taken to Annas

12Then the detachment of soldiers with
its commander and the Jewish officials arrested Jesus. They bound him 13and
brought him first to Annas, who was the
father-in-law of Caiaphas, the high priest
that year. 14Caiaphas was the one who had
advised the Jews that it would be good if
one man died for the people.

Peter's First Denial

15Simon Peter and another disciple
were following Jesus. Because this disciple
was known to the high priest, he went
with Jesus into the high priest's courtyard,
16but Peter had to wait outside at the door.
The other disciple, who was known to the
high priest, came back, spoke to the girl
on duty there and brought Peter in.
17"You are not one of his disciples, are
you?" the girl at the door asked Peter.
He replied, "I am not."
18It was cold, and the servants and officials stood around a fire they had made
to keep warm. Peter also was standing
with them, warming himself.

The High Priest Questions Jesus

19Meanwhile, the high priest questioned Jesus about his disciples and his
teaching.
20"I have spoken openly to the world,"
Jesus replied. "I always taught in synagogues or at the temple, where all the Jews
come together. I said nothing in secret.
21Why question me? Ask those who heard
me. Surely they know what I said."
22When Jesus said this, one of the officials nearby struck him in the face. "Is this
the way you answer the high priest?" he
demanded.
23"If I said something wrong," Jesus
replied, "testify as to what is wrong. But if
I spoke the truth, why did you strike me?"
24Then Annas sent him, still bound, to Caiaphas the high priest.[b]

Peter's Second and Third Denials

25As Simon Peter stood warming himself, he was asked, "You are not one of his
disciples, are you?"
He denied it, saying, "I am not."
26One of the high priest's servants, a relative of the man whose ear Peter had cut
off, challenged him, "Didn't I see you
with him in the olive grove?" 27Again Peter denied it, and at that moment a rooster began to crow.

[a] 9 John 6:39 [b] 24 Or *(Now Annas had sent him, still bound, to Caiaphas the high priest.)*

PRAYER: MY RELATIONSHIP TO OTHERS

I WILL do all things without complaining or arguing, so that I may become blameless and pure—Your child, O God, without fault in the midst of a crooked and perverse generation, among whom I shine as a light in the world, holding out the word of life. (Philippians 2:14–16)

__PAUSE__ to review your relationships with others and to commit them to the Lord.

YEAR 2 DAY 321

OT Amos 2:1-16

2 This is what the LORD says:

"For three sins of Moab,
even for four, I will not turn back
⌞my wrath⌟.
Because he burned, as if to lime,
the bones of Edom's king,
2 I will send fire upon Moab
that will consume the fortresses of
Kerioth.[a]
Moab will go down in great tumult
amid war cries and the blast of the
trumpet.
3 I will destroy her ruler
and kill all her officials with him,"
says the LORD.

4 This is what the LORD says:

"For three sins of Judah,
even for four, I will not turn back
⌞my wrath⌟.
Because they have rejected the law of
the LORD
and have not kept his decrees,
because they have been led astray by
false gods,[b]
the gods[c] their ancestors followed,
5 I will send fire upon Judah
that will consume the fortresses of
Jerusalem."

Judgment on Israel

6 This is what the LORD says:

"For three sins of Israel,
even for four, I will not turn back
⌞my wrath⌟.
They sell the righteous for silver,
and the needy for a pair of sandals.
7 They trample on the heads of the poor
as upon the dust of the ground
and deny justice to the oppressed.
Father and son use the same girl
and so profane my holy name.
8 They lie down beside every altar
on garments taken in pledge.
In the house of their god
they drink wine taken as fines.

9 "I destroyed the Amorite before them,
though he was tall as the cedars
and strong as the oaks.
I destroyed his fruit above
and his roots below.

10 "I brought you up out of Egypt,
and I led you forty years in the desert
to give you the land of the Amorites.
11 I also raised up prophets from among
your sons
and Nazirites from among your
young men.
Is this not true, people of Israel?"
declares the LORD.
12 "But you made the Nazirites drink wine
and commanded the prophets not
to prophesy.

13 "Now then, I will crush you
as a cart crushes when loaded with
grain.
14 The swift will not escape,
the strong will not muster their
strength,
and the warrior will not save his life.
15 The archer will not stand his ground,
the fleet-footed soldier will not get
away,
and the horseman will not save his
life.
16 Even the bravest warriors
will flee naked on that day,"
declares the LORD.

[a] 2 Or *of her cities* [b] 4 Or *by lies* [c] 4 Or *lies*

PRAYER: THANKSGIVING

I HAVE died to the law through Your body, O Christ, that I might belong to You who were raised from the dead, in order that I might bear fruit to God. But now, by dying to what once bound me, I have been released from the law, so that I serve in newness of the Spirit and not in the old way of the letter. (Romans 7:4, 6)

PAUSE *to offer your own expressions of thanksgiving.*

NT John 18:28–19:16a

Jesus Before Pilate

28Then the Jews led Jesus from Caiaphas
to the palace of the Roman governor. By
now it was early morning, and to avoid
ceremonial uncleanness the Jews did not
enter the palace; they wanted to be able
to eat the Passover. 29So Pilate came out
to them and asked, "What charges are you
bringing against this man?"
30"If he were not a criminal," they
replied, "we would not have handed him
over to you."
31Pilate said, "Take him yourselves and
judge him by your own law."
"But we have no right to execute anyone," the Jews objected. 32This happened
so that the words Jesus had spoken indicating the kind of death he was going to
die would be fulfilled.
33Pilate then went back inside the
palace, summoned Jesus and asked him,
"Are you the king of the Jews?"
34"Is that your own idea," Jesus asked,
"or did others talk to you about me?"
35"Am I a Jew?" Pilate replied. "It was
your people and your chief priests who
handed you over to me. What is it you
have done?"
36Jesus said, "My kingdom is not of this
world. If it were, my servants would fight
to prevent my arrest by the Jews. But now
my kingdom is from another place."
37"You are a king, then!" said Pilate.
Jesus answered, "You are right in saying
I am a king. In fact, for this reason I was
born, and for this I came into the world,
to testify to the truth. Everyone on the
side of truth listens to me."
38"What is truth?" Pilate asked. With
this he went out again to the Jews and
said, "I find no basis for a charge against
him. 39But it is your custom for me to release to you one prisoner at the time of
the Passover. Do you want me to release
'the king of the Jews'?"
40They shouted back, "No, not him!
Give us Barabbas!" Now Barabbas had
taken part in a rebellion.

Jesus Sentenced to be Crucified

19 Then Pilate took Jesus and had him
flogged. 2The soldiers twisted together a crown of thorns and put it on his
head. They clothed him in a purple robe
3and went up to him again and again, saying, "Hail, king of the Jews!" And they
struck him in the face.
4Once more Pilate came out and said to
the Jews, "Look, I am bringing him out to
you to let you know that I find no basis
for a charge against him." 5When Jesus
came out wearing the crown of thorns and
the purple robe, Pilate said to them, "Here
is the man!"
6As soon as the chief priests and their
officials saw him, they shouted, "Crucify!
Crucify!"
But Pilate answered, "You take him and
crucify him. As for me, I find no basis for
a charge against him."
7The Jews insisted, "We have a law, and
according to that law he must die, because
he claimed to be the Son of God."
8When Pilate heard this, he was even
more afraid, 9and he went back inside the
palace. "Where do you come from?" he
asked Jesus, but Jesus gave him no answer.
10"Do you refuse to speak to me?" Pilate
said. "Don't you realize I have power either to free you or to crucify you?"
11Jesus answered, "You would have no
power over me if it were not given to you
from above. Therefore the one who handed me over to you is guilty of a greater sin."
12From then on, Pilate tried to set Jesus
free, but the Jews kept shouting, "If you

let this man go, you are no friend of Caesar. Anyone who claims to be a king opposes Caesar."
13 When Pilate heard this, he brought
Jesus out and sat down on the judge's seat
at a place known as the Stone Pavement
(which in Aramaic is Gabbatha). 14 It was
the day of Preparation of Passover Week,
about the sixth hour.

"Here is your king," Pilate said to the Jews.

15 But they shouted, "Take him away! Take him away! Crucify him!"

"Shall I crucify your king?" Pilate asked.

"We have no king but Caesar," the chief priests answered.

16 Finally Pilate handed him over to them to be crucified.

PRAYER: THE ATTRIBUTES OF GOD

YOU, Almighty God, are beyond our reach; You are exalted in power, and in Your justice and great righteousness You do not oppress. (Job 37:23) . . . Great are You, Lord, and mighty in power; Your understanding is infinite. (Psalm 147:5)

***PAUSE** to reflect on these affirmations about the person, powers and perfection of God.*

YEAR 2 DAY 322

OT Psalms 138–139

Psalm 138

Of David.

1 I will praise you, O LORD, with all my heart;
before the "gods" I will sing your praise.
2 I will bow down toward your holy temple
and will praise your name
for your love and your faithfulness,
for you have exalted above all things
your name and your word.
3 When I called, you answered me;
you made me bold and stouthearted.

4 May all the kings of the earth praise you, O LORD,
when they hear the words of your mouth.
5 May they sing of the ways of the LORD,
for the glory of the LORD is great.

6 Though the LORD is on high, he looks upon the lowly,
but the proud he knows from afar.
7 Though I walk in the midst of trouble,
you preserve my life;
you stretch out your hand against the anger of my foes,
with your right hand you save me.
8 The LORD will fulfill ⌊his purpose⌋ for me;
your love, O LORD, endures forever—
do not abandon the works of your hands.

Psalm 139

For the director of music. Of David. A psalm.

1 O LORD, you have searched me
and you know me.
2 You know when I sit and when I rise;
you perceive my thoughts from afar.
3 You discern my going out and my lying down;
you are familiar with all my ways.
4 Before a word is on my tongue
you know it completely, O LORD.

5 You hem me in—behind and before;
you have laid your hand upon me.
6 Such knowledge is too wonderful for me,
too lofty for me to attain.

7 Where can I go from your Spirit?

Where can I flee from your
presence?
[8]If I go up to the heavens, you are
there;
if I make my bed in the depths,[a]
you are there.
[9]If I rise on the wings of the dawn,
if I settle on the far side of the sea,
[10]even there your hand will guide me,
your right hand will hold me fast.

[11]If I say, "Surely the darkness will hide
me
and the light become night around
me,"
[12]even the darkness will not be dark to
you;
the night will shine like the day,
for darkness is as light to you.

[13]For you created my inmost being;
you knit me together in my
mother's womb.
[14]I praise you because I am fearfully and
wonderfully made;
your works are wonderful,
I know that full well.
[15]My frame was not hidden from you
when I was made in the secret
place.
When I was woven together in the
depths of the earth,
[16] your eyes saw my unformed body.
All the days ordained for me
were written in your book
before one of them came to be.

[17]How precious to[b] me are your
thoughts, O God!
How vast is the sum of them!
[18]Were I to count them,
they would outnumber the grains of
sand.
When I awake,
I am still with you.

[19]If only you would slay the wicked,
O God!
Away from me, you bloodthirsty
men!
[20]They speak of you with evil intent;
your adversaries misuse your name.
[21]Do I not hate those who hate you,
O LORD,
and abhor those who rise up
against you?
[22]I have nothing but hatred for them;
I count them my enemies.

[23]Search me, O God, and know my
heart;
test me and know my anxious
thoughts.
[24]See if there is any offensive way in me,
and lead me in the way everlasting.

[a] 8 Hebrew *Sheol* [b] 17 Or *concerning*

PRAYER: ADORATION

YOU are the great God, the great King above all gods. In Your hand are the depths of the earth, and the summits of the mountains are Yours also. The sea is Yours, for You made it, and Your hands formed the dry land. You are our God and we are the people of Your pasture and the sheep under Your care. (Psalm 95:3–5, 7)

***PAUSE** to express your thoughts of praise and worship.*

NT John 19:16b–42

The Crucifixion

So the soldiers took charge of Jesus.
[17]Carrying his own cross, he went out to
the place of the Skull (which in Aramaic
is called Golgotha). [18]Here they crucified
him, and with him two others—one on
each side and Jesus in the middle.
[19]Pilate had a notice prepared and fastened to the cross. It read: JESUS OF NAZARETH, THE KING OF THE JEWS. [20]Many of the
Jews read this sign, for the place where
Jesus was crucified was near the city, and
the sign was written in Aramaic, Latin and
Greek. [21]The chief priests of the Jews
protested to Pilate, "Do not write 'The
King of the Jews,' but that this man
claimed to be king of the Jews."
[22]Pilate answered, "What I have written,
I have written."

23 When the soldiers crucified Jesus, they
took his clothes, dividing them into four
shares, one for each of them, with the undergarment remaining. This garment was
seamless, woven in one piece from top to
bottom.
24 "Let's not tear it," they said to one another. "Let's decide by lot who will get it."
This happened that the scripture might
be fulfilled which said,

"They divided my garments among
them
and cast lots for my clothing."[a]

So this is what the soldiers did.
25 Near the cross of Jesus stood his
mother, his mother's sister, Mary the wife
of Clopas, and Mary Magdalene. 26 When
Jesus saw his mother there, and the disciple whom he loved standing nearby, he
said to his mother, "Dear woman, here is
your son," 27 and to the disciple, "Here is
your mother." From that time on, this disciple took her into his home.

The Death of Jesus

28 Later, knowing that all was now completed, and so that the Scripture would be
fulfilled, Jesus said, "I am thirsty." 29 A jar
of wine vinegar was there, so they soaked
a sponge in it, put the sponge on a stalk
of the hyssop plant, and lifted it to Jesus'
lips. 30 When he had received the drink,
Jesus said, "It is finished." With that, he
bowed his head and gave up his spirit.
31 Now it was the day of Preparation,
and the next day was to be a special Sabbath. Because the Jews did not want the
bodies left on the crosses during the Sabbath, they asked Pilate to have the legs
broken and the bodies taken down. 32 The
soldiers therefore came and broke the legs
of the first man who had been crucified
with Jesus, and then those of the other.
33 But when they came to Jesus and found
that he was already dead, they did not
break his legs. 34 Instead, one of the soldiers pierced Jesus' side with a spear,
bringing a sudden flow of blood and water. 35 The man who saw it has given testimony, and his testimony is true. He
knows that he tells the truth, and he testifies so that you also may believe. 36 These
things happened so that the scripture
would be fulfilled: "Not one of his bones
will be broken,"[b] 37 and, as another scripture says, "They will look on the one they
have pierced."[c]

The Burial of Jesus

38 Later, Joseph of Arimathea asked Pilate for the body of Jesus. Now Joseph was
a disciple of Jesus, but secretly because he
feared the Jews. With Pilate's permission,
he came and took the body away. 39 He
was accompanied by Nicodemus, the man
who earlier had visited Jesus at night. Nicodemus brought a mixture of myrrh and
aloes, about seventy-five pounds.[d] 40 Taking Jesus' body, the two of them wrapped
it, with the spices, in strips of linen. This
was in accordance with Jewish burial customs. 41 At the place where Jesus was crucified, there was a garden, and in the garden a new tomb, in which no one had
ever been laid. 42 Because it was the Jewish
day of Preparation and since the tomb
was nearby, they laid Jesus there.

[a] *24* Psalm 22:18 [b] *36* Exodus 12:46; Num. 9:12; Psalm 34:20 [c] *37* Zech. 12:10 [d] *39* Greek *a hundred litrai* (about 34 kilograms)

PRAYER: THE WORKS OF GOD

LORD, You led Your people all the way in the wilderness for forty years, to humble them and to test them in order to know what was in their heart, whether or not they would keep Your commands. You humbled them, allowing them to hunger and then feeding them with manna, which neither they nor their fathers had known, to teach them that man does not live on bread alone; but man lives by every word that proceeds from Your mouth, O Lord. (Deuteronomy 8:2–3)

***TAKE** a moment to consider the greatness of God's wonderful works.*

Witnesses Summoned Against Israel

3 Hear this word the LORD has spoken against you, O people of Israel—against the whole family I brought up out of Egypt:

[2] "You only have I chosen
of all the families of the earth;
therefore I will punish you
for all your sins."

[3] Do two walk together
unless they have agreed to do so?
[4] Does a lion roar in the thicket
when he has no prey?
Does he growl in his den
when he has caught nothing?
[5] Does a bird fall into a trap on the ground
where no snare has been set?
Does a trap spring up from the earth
when there is nothing to catch?
[6] When a trumpet sounds in a city,
do not the people tremble?
When disaster comes to a city,
has not the LORD caused it?

[7] Surely the Sovereign LORD does nothing
without revealing his plan
to his servants the prophets.

[8] The lion has roared—
who will not fear?
The Sovereign LORD has spoken—
who can but prophesy?

[9] Proclaim to the fortresses of Ashdod
and to the fortresses of Egypt:
"Assemble yourselves on the mountains of Samaria;
see the great unrest within her
and the oppression among her people."

[10] "They do not know how to do right,"
declares the LORD,
"who hoard plunder and loot in their fortresses."

[11] Therefore this is what the Sovereign LORD says:

"An enemy will overrun the land;
he will pull down your strongholds
and plunder your fortresses."

[12] This is what the LORD says:

"As a shepherd saves from the lion's mouth
only two leg bones or a piece of an ear,
so will the Israelites be saved,
those who sit in Samaria
on the edge of their beds
and in Damascus on their couches.[a]"

[13] "Hear this and testify against the house of Jacob," declares the Lord, the LORD God Almighty.

[14] "On the day I punish Israel for her sins,
I will destroy the altars of Bethel;
the horns of the altar will be cut off
and fall to the ground.
[15] I will tear down the winter house
along with the summer house;
the houses adorned with ivory will be destroyed
and the mansions will be demolished,"
declares the LORD.

Israel Has Not Returned to God

4 Hear this word, you cows of Bashan on Mount Samaria,
you women who oppress the poor
and crush the needy
and say to your husbands, "Bring us some drinks!"
[2] The Sovereign LORD has sworn by his holiness:
"The time will surely come
when you will be taken away with hooks,
the last of you with fishhooks.
[3] You will each go straight out
through breaks in the wall,
and you will be cast out toward Harmon,[b]"
declares the LORD.

[4] "Go to Bethel and sin;
go to Gilgal and sin yet more.
Bring your sacrifices every morning,
your tithes every three years.[c]
[5] Burn leavened bread as a thank offering

[a] *12* The meaning of the Hebrew for this line is uncertain. [b] *3* Masoretic Text; with a different word division of the Hebrew (see Septuagint) *out, O mountain of oppression* [c] *4* Or *tithes on the third day*

and brag about your freewill
offerings—
boast about them, you Israelites,
for this is what you love to do,"
declares the Sovereign LORD.

6 "I gave you empty stomachs[d] in every
city
and lack of bread in every town,
yet you have not returned to me,"
declares the LORD.

7 "I also withheld rain from you
when the harvest was still three
months away.
I sent rain on one town,
but withheld it from another.
One field had rain;
another had none and dried up.
8 People staggered from town to town
for water
but did not get enough to drink,
yet you have not returned to me,"
declares the LORD.

9 "Many times I struck your gardens and
vineyards,
I struck them with blight and
mildew.
Locusts devoured your fig and olive
trees,
yet you have not returned to me,"
declares the LORD.

10 "I sent plagues among you
as I did to Egypt.
I killed your young men with the
sword,
along with your captured horses.
I filled your nostrils with the stench of
your camps,
yet you have not returned to me,"
declares the LORD.

11 "I overthrew some of you
as I[e] overthrew Sodom and
Gomorrah.
You were like a burning stick snatched
from the fire,
yet you have not returned to me,"
declares the LORD.

12 "Therefore this is what I will do to
you, Israel,
and because I will do this to you,
prepare to meet your God,
O Israel."

13 He who forms the mountains,
creates the wind,
and reveals his thoughts to man,
he who turns dawn to darkness,
and treads the high places of the
earth—
the LORD God Almighty is his name.

[d]6 Hebrew *you cleanness of teeth* [e]11 Hebrew *God*

PRAYER: CONFESSION

YOU, Lord God, declared this assurance to Jeremiah: "I will cleanse them from all of the sin they have committed against Me, and I will forgive all of the sin they committed when they turned away from Me." (Jeremiah 33:8)

***ASK** the Spirit to search your heart and reveal any areas of unconfessed sin. Acknowledge these to the Lord and thank Him for His forgiveness.*

NT John 20:1-31

The Empty Tomb

20 Early on the first day of the week,
while it was still dark, Mary Magdalene went to the tomb and saw that the
stone had been removed from the entrance. 2 So she came running to Simon
Peter and the other disciple, the one Jesus
loved, and said, "They have taken the Lord
out of the tomb, and we don't know
where they have put him!"

3 So Peter and the other disciple started
for the tomb. 4 Both were running, but the
other disciple outran Peter and reached
the tomb first. 5 He bent over and looked
in at the strips of linen lying there but did
not go in. 6 Then Simon Peter, who was behind him, arrived and went into the
tomb. He saw the strips of linen lying
there, 7 as well as the burial cloth that had
been around Jesus' head. The cloth was
folded up by itself, separate from the

linen. [8]Finally the other disciple, who had reached the tomb first, also went inside. He saw and believed. [9](They still did not understand from Scripture that Jesus had to rise from the dead.)

Jesus Appears to Mary Magdalene

[10]Then the disciples went back to their homes, [11]but Mary stood outside the tomb crying. As she wept, she bent over to look into the tomb [12]and saw two angels in white, seated where Jesus' body had been, one at the head and the other at the foot.

[13]They asked her, "Woman, why are you crying?"

"They have taken my Lord away," she said, "and I don't know where they have put him." [14]At this, she turned around and saw Jesus standing there, but she did not realize that it was Jesus.

[15]"Woman," he said, "why are you crying? Who is it you are looking for?"

Thinking he was the gardener, she said, "Sir, if you have carried him away, tell me where you have put him, and I will get him."

[16]Jesus said to her, "Mary."

She turned toward him and cried out in Aramaic, "Rabboni!" (which means Teacher).

[17]Jesus said, "Do not hold on to me, for I have not yet returned to the Father. Go instead to my brothers and tell them, 'I am returning to my Father and your Father, to my God and your God.' "

[18]Mary Magdalene went to the disciples with the news: "I have seen the Lord!" And she told them that he had said these things to her.

Jesus Appears to His Disciples

[19]On the evening of that first day of the week, when the disciples were together, with the doors locked for fear of the Jews, Jesus came and stood among them and said, "Peace be with you!" [20]After he said this, he showed them his hands and side. The disciples were overjoyed when they saw the Lord.

[21]Again Jesus said, "Peace be with you! As the Father has sent me, I am sending you." [22]And with that he breathed on them and said, "Receive the Holy Spirit. [23]If you forgive anyone his sins, they are forgiven; if you do not forgive them, they are not forgiven."

Jesus Appears to Thomas

[24]Now Thomas (called Didymus), one of the Twelve, was not with the disciples when Jesus came. [25]So the other disciples told him, "We have seen the Lord!"

But he said to them, "Unless I see the nail marks in his hands and put my finger where the nails were, and put my hand into his side, I will not believe it."

[26]A week later his disciples were in the house again, and Thomas was with them. Though the doors were locked, Jesus came and stood among them and said, "Peace be with you!" [27]Then he said to Thomas, "Put your finger here; see my hands. Reach out your hand and put it into my side. Stop doubting and believe."

[28]Thomas said to him, "My Lord and my God!"

[29]Then Jesus told him, "Because you have seen me, you have believed; blessed are those who have not seen and yet have believed."

[30]Jesus did many other miraculous signs in the presence of his disciples, which are not recorded in this book. [31]But these are written that you may[a] believe that Jesus is the Christ, the Son of God, and that by believing you may have life in his name.

[a] *31* Some manuscripts *may continue to*

PRAYER: MY RELATIONSHIP TO GOD

O LORD, my Redeemer, the Holy One of Israel, You are the Lord my God; You teach me to profit; You lead me in the way I should go. (Isaiah 48:17) . . . By Your grace I will not forsake You, the fountain of living waters, to dig my own cisterns, broken cisterns that can hold no water. (Jeremiah 2:13)

***PAUSE** to thank God for the relationship that you enjoy with Him in Jesus Christ.*

A Lament and Call to Repentance

5 Hear this word, O house of Israel, this
lament I take up concerning you:

2 "Fallen is Virgin Israel,
never to rise again,
deserted in her own land,
with no one to lift her up."

3 This is what the Sovereign LORD says:

"The city that marches out a thousand strong for Israel
will have only a hundred left;
the town that marches out a hundred strong
will have only ten left."

4 This is what the LORD says to the house of Israel:

"Seek me and live;
5 do not seek Bethel,
do not go to Gilgal,
do not journey to Beersheba.
For Gilgal will surely go into exile,
and Bethel will be reduced to nothing.[a]"
6 Seek the LORD and live,
or he will sweep through the house of Joseph like a fire;
it will devour,
and Bethel will have no one to quench it.

7 You who turn justice into bitterness
and cast righteousness to the ground
8 (he who made the Pleiades and Orion,
who turns blackness into dawn
and darkens day into night,
who calls for the waters of the sea
and pours them out over the face of the land—
the LORD is his name—
9 he flashes destruction on the stronghold
and brings the fortified city to ruin),
10 you hate the one who reproves in court
and despise him who tells the truth.

11 You trample on the poor
and force him to give you grain.
Therefore, though you have built stone mansions,
you will not live in them;
though you have planted lush vineyards,
you will not drink their wine.
12 For I know how many are your offenses
and how great your sins.

You oppress the righteous and take bribes
and you deprive the poor of justice in the courts.
13 Therefore the prudent man keeps quiet in such times,
for the times are evil.

14 Seek good, not evil,
that you may live.
Then the LORD God Almighty will be with you,
just as you say he is.
15 Hate evil, love good;
maintain justice in the courts.
Perhaps the LORD God Almighty will have mercy
on the remnant of Joseph.

16 Therefore this is what the Lord, the LORD God Almighty, says:

"There will be wailing in all the streets
and cries of anguish in every public square.
The farmers will be summoned to weep
and the mourners to wail.
17 There will be wailing in all the vineyards,
for I will pass through your midst,"
says the LORD.

The Day of the LORD

18 Woe to you who long
for the day of the LORD!
Why do you long for the day of the LORD?
That day will be darkness, not light.
19 It will be as though a man fled from a lion
only to meet a bear,
as though he entered his house
and rested his hand on the wall
only to have a snake bite him.
20 Will not the day of the LORD be
darkness, not light—

[a] 5 Or *grief;* or *wickedness;* Hebrew *aven,* a reference to Beth Aven (a derogatory name for Bethel)

pitch-dark, without a ray of
brightness?

21 "I hate, I despise your religious feasts;
I cannot stand your assemblies.
22 Even though you bring me burnt
offerings and grain offerings,
I will not accept them.
Though you bring choice fellowship
offerings,[b]
I will have no regard for them.
23 Away with the noise of your songs!
I will not listen to the music of your
harps.
24 But let justice roll on like a river,
righteousness like a never-failing
stream!

25 "Did you bring me sacrifices and
offerings
forty years in the desert, O house of
Israel?
26 You have lifted up the shrine of your
king,
the pedestal of your idols,
the star of your god[c]—
which you made for yourselves.
27 Therefore I will send you into exile
beyond Damascus,"
says the LORD, whose name is God
Almighty.

[b] 22 Traditionally *peace offerings* [c] 26 Or *lifted up Sakkuth your king / and Kaiwan your idols, / your star-gods;* Septuagint *lifted up the shrine of Molech / and the star of your god Rephan, / their idols*

PRAYER: RENEWAL

MAY I not become conceited, provoking others and envying others. (Galatians 5:26) . . . May I submit myself to You, O God, and resist the devil, and he will flee from me. May I humble myself before You, O Lord, and You will exalt me. (James 4:7, 10)

***PAUSE** to add your own prayers for personal renewal.*

NT John 21:1-25

Jesus and the Miraculous Catch of Fish

21 Afterward Jesus appeared again to his
disciples, by the Sea of Tiberias.[a] It
happened this way: 2 Simon Peter, Thomas (called Didymus), Nathanael from
Cana in Galilee, the sons of Zebedee, and
two other disciples were together. 3 "I'm
going out to fish," Simon Peter told them,
and they said, "We'll go with you." So
they went out and got into the boat, but
that night they caught nothing.
4 Early in the morning, Jesus stood on
the shore, but the disciples did not realize
that it was Jesus.
5 He called out to them, "Friends,
haven't you any fish?"
"No," they answered.
6 He said, "Throw your net on the right
side of the boat and you will find some."
When they did, they were unable to haul
the net in because of the large number of
fish.
7 Then the disciple whom Jesus loved
said to Peter, "It is the Lord!" As soon as
Simon Peter heard him say, "It is the
Lord," he wrapped his outer garment
around him (for he had taken it off) and
jumped into the water. 8 The other disciples followed in the boat, towing the net
full of fish, for they were not far from
shore, about a hundred yards.[b] 9 When
they landed, they saw a fire of burning
coals there with fish on it, and some
bread.
10 Jesus said to them, "Bring some of the
fish you have just caught."
11 Simon Peter climbed aboard and
dragged the net ashore. It was full of large
fish, 153, but even with so many the net
was not torn. 12 Jesus said to them, "Come
and have breakfast." None of the disciples
dared ask him, "Who are you?" They
knew it was the Lord. 13 Jesus came, took
the bread and gave it to them, and did the
same with the fish. 14 This was now the
third time Jesus appeared to his disciples
after he was raised from the dead.

Jesus Reinstates Peter

15 When they had finished eating, Jesus

[a] 1 That is, Sea of Galilee [b] 8 Greek *about two hundred cubits* (about 90 meters)

said to Simon Peter, "Simon son of John, do you truly love me more than these?"

"Yes, Lord," he said, "you know that I love you."

Jesus said, "Feed my lambs."

[16]Again Jesus said, "Simon son of John, do you truly love me?"

He answered, "Yes, Lord, you know that I love you."

Jesus said, "Take care of my sheep."

[17]The third time he said to him, "Simon son of John, do you love me?"

Peter was hurt because Jesus asked him the third time, "Do you love me?" He said, "Lord, you know all things; you know that I love you."

Jesus said, "Feed my sheep.
[18]I tell you the truth, when you were younger you dressed yourself and went where you wanted; but when you are old you will stretch out your hands, and someone else will dress you and lead you where you do not want to go."
[19]Jesus said this to indicate the kind of death by which Peter would glorify God. Then he said to him, "Follow me!"

[20]Peter turned and saw that the disciple whom Jesus loved was following them. (This was the one who had leaned back against Jesus at the supper and had said, "Lord, who is going to betray you?")
[21]When Peter saw him, he asked, "Lord, what about him?"

[22]Jesus answered, "If I want him to remain alive until I return, what is that to you? You must follow me."
[23]Because of this, the rumor spread among the brothers that this disciple would not die. But Jesus did not say that he would not die; he only said, "If I want him to remain alive until I return, what is that to you?"

[24]This is the disciple who testifies to these things and who wrote them down. We know that his testimony is true.

[25]Jesus did many other things as well. If every one of them were written down, I suppose that even the whole world would not have room for the books that would be written.

PRAYER: THE CHARACTER I WANT TO CULTIVATE

THERE is no wisdom or understanding or counsel that can succeed against You, O Lord. (Proverbs 21:30) . . . I will go to the law and to the testimony! If I do not speak according to Your word, I have no light of dawn. (Isaiah 8:20)

***TAKE** a moment to ask the Lord for the grace to grow in godly character.*

YEAR 2 DAY 325

OT Amos 6:1-14

Woe to the Complacent

6 Woe to you who are complacent in Zion,
and to you who feel secure on Mount Samaria,
you notable men of the foremost nation,
to whom the people of Israel come!
[2]Go to Calneh and look at it;
go from there to great Hamath,
and then go down to Gath in Philistia.
Are they better off than your two kingdoms?
Is their land larger than yours?
[3]You put off the evil day
and bring near a reign of terror.
[4]You lie on beds inlaid with ivory
and lounge on your couches.
You dine on choice lambs
and fattened calves.
[5]You strum away on your harps like David
and improvise on musical instruments.
[6]You drink wine by the bowlful
and use the finest lotions,
but you do not grieve over the ruin of Joseph.
[7]Therefore you will be among the first to go into exile;
your feasting and lounging will end.

The LORD *Abhors the Pride of Israel*

[8]The Sovereign LORD has sworn by himself—the LORD God Almighty declares:

"I abhor the pride of Jacob
and detest his fortresses;
I will deliver up the city
and everything in it."

[9]If ten men are left in one house, they too will die. [10]And if a relative who is to burn the bodies comes to carry them out of the house and asks anyone still hiding there, "Is anyone with you?" and he says, "No," then he will say, "Hush! We must not mention the name of the LORD."

[11]For the LORD has given the command,
and he will smash the great house
into pieces
and the small house into bits.
[12]Do horses run on the rocky crags?
Does one plow there with oxen?
But you have turned justice into
poison
and the fruit of righteousness into
bitterness—
[13]you who rejoice in the conquest of Lo
Debar[a]
and say, "Did we not take Karnaim[b]
by our own strength?"

[14]For the LORD God Almighty declares,
"I will stir up a nation against you,
O house of Israel,
that will oppress you all the way
from Lebo[c] Hamath to the valley of
the Arabah."

[a] 13 *Lo Debar* means *nothing.* [b] 13 *Karnaim* means *horns; horn* here symbolizes strength. [c] 14 Or *from the entrance to*

PRAYER: PETITION

MAY I keep the pattern of sound teaching that I have heard, in faith and love which are in You, Christ Jesus. (2 Timothy 1:13) . . . May I hold firmly to the faithful word as I have been taught, so that I can exhort others by sound doctrine and refute those who oppose it. (Titus 1:9)

PAUSE *here to petition God for growth in your desire to know and please Jesus Christ. Pray for a greater love and commitment to Him, for the grace to practice His presence and for the grace to glorify Him in your life. Offer prayers regarding your activities for this day and any special concerns you may have.*

NT 1 John 1:1-10

The Word of Life

1 That which was from the beginning, which we have heard, which we have seen with our eyes, which we have looked at and our hands have touched—this we proclaim concerning the Word of life.
[2]The life appeared; we have seen it and testify to it, and we proclaim to you the eternal life, which was with the Father and has appeared to us. [3]We proclaim to you what we have seen and heard, so that you also may have fellowship with us. And our fellowship is with the Father and with his Son, Jesus Christ. [4]We write this to make our[a] joy complete.

Walking in the Light

[5]This is the message we have heard from him and declare to you: God is light; in him there is no darkness at all. [6]If we claim to have fellowship with him yet walk in the darkness, we lie and do not live by the truth. [7]But if we walk in the light, as he is in the light, we have fellowship with one another, and the blood of Jesus, his Son, purifies us from all[b] sin.

[8]If we claim to be without sin, we deceive ourselves and the truth is not in us.
[9]If we confess our sins, he is faithful and just and will forgive us our sins and purify us from all unrighteousness. [10]If we claim we have not sinned, we make him out to be a liar and his word has no place in our lives.

[a] 4 Some manuscripts *your* [b] 7 Or *every*

PRAYER: MY RELATIONSHIP TO OTHERS

WE should bear one another's burdens and so fulfill Your law, O Christ. (Galatians 6:2) . . . We should submit to one another out of reverence for You, O Christ. (Ephesians 5:21)

***PAUSE** to review your relationships with others and to commit them to the Lord.*

YEAR 2 DAY 326

OT Amos 7:1–8:14

Locusts, Fire and a Plumb Line

7 This is what the Sovereign LORD showed me: He was preparing swarms of locusts after the king's share had been harvested and just as the second crop was coming up. 2When they had stripped the land clean, I cried out, "Sovereign LORD, forgive! How can Jacob survive? He is so small!"

3So the LORD relented.

"This will not happen," the LORD said.

4This is what the Sovereign LORD showed me: The Sovereign LORD was calling for judgment by fire; it dried up the great deep and devoured the land. 5Then I cried out, "Sovereign LORD, I beg you, stop! How can Jacob survive? He is so small!"

6So the LORD relented.

"This will not happen either," the Sovereign LORD said.

7This is what he showed me: The Lord was standing by a wall that had been built true to plumb, with a plumb line in his hand. 8And the LORD asked me, "What do you see, Amos?"

"A plumb line," I replied.

Then the Lord said, "Look, I am setting a plumb line among my people Israel; I will spare them no longer.

9"The high places of Isaac will be destroyed
and the sanctuaries of Israel will be ruined;
with my sword I will rise against the house of Jeroboam."

Amos and Amaziah

10Then Amaziah the priest of Bethel sent a message to Jeroboam king of Israel: "Amos is raising a conspiracy against you in the very heart of Israel. The land cannot bear all his words. 11For this is what Amos is saying:

" 'Jeroboam will die by the sword,
and Israel will surely go into exile,
away from their native land.' "

12Then Amaziah said to Amos, "Get out, you seer! Go back to the land of Judah. Earn your bread there and do your prophesying there. 13Don't prophesy anymore at Bethel, because this is the king's sanctuary and the temple of the kingdom."

14Amos answered Amaziah, "I was neither a prophet nor a prophet's son, but I was a shepherd, and I also took care of sycamore-fig trees. 15But the LORD took me from tending the flock and said to me, 'Go, prophesy to my people Israel.' 16Now then, hear the word of the LORD. You say,

" 'Do not prophesy against Israel,
and stop preaching against the house of Isaac.'

17"Therefore this is what the LORD says:

" 'Your wife will become a prostitute in the city,
and your sons and daughters will fall by the sword.
Your land will be measured and divided up,
and you yourself will die in a pagan[a] country.
And Israel will certainly go into exile,
away from their native land.' "

A Basket of Ripe Fruit

8 This is what the Sovereign LORD showed me: a basket of ripe fruit. 2"What do you see, Amos?" he asked.

[a] 17 Hebrew *an unclean*

"A basket of ripe fruit," I answered.
Then the LORD said to me, "The time is ripe for my people Israel; I will spare them no longer.
3 "In that day," declares the Sovereign LORD, "the songs in the temple will turn to wailing.[b] Many, many bodies—flung everywhere! Silence!"

4 Hear this, you who trample the needy
and do away with the poor of the land,

5 saying,

"When will the New Moon be over
that we may sell grain,
and the Sabbath be ended
that we may market wheat?"—
skimping the measure,
boosting the price
and cheating with dishonest scales,
6 buying the poor with silver
and the needy for a pair of sandals,
selling even the sweepings with the wheat.

7 The LORD has sworn by the Pride of Jacob: "I will never forget anything they have done.

8 "Will not the land tremble for this,
and all who live in it mourn?
The whole land will rise like the Nile;
it will be stirred up and then sink
like the river of Egypt.

9 "In that day," declares the Sovereign LORD,

"I will make the sun go down at noon
and darken the earth in broad daylight.
10 I will turn your religious feasts into mourning
and all your singing into weeping.
I will make all of you wear sackcloth
and shave your heads.
I will make that time like mourning for an only son
and the end of it like a bitter day.

11 "The days are coming," declares the Sovereign LORD,
"when I will send a famine through the land—
not a famine of food or a thirst for water,
but a famine of hearing the words of the LORD.
12 Men will stagger from sea to sea
and wander from north to east,
searching for the word of the LORD,
but they will not find it.

13 "In that day

"the lovely young women and strong young men
will faint because of thirst.
14 They who swear by the shame[c] of Samaria,
or say, 'As surely as your god lives, O Dan,'
or, 'As surely as the god[d] of Beersheba lives'—
they will fall,
never to rise again."

[b] 3 Or *"the temple singers will wail* [c] 14 Or *by Ashima;* or *by the idol* [d] 14 Or *power*

PRAYER: INTERCESSION

LORD, help us who are strong to bear the weaknesses of those who are not strong, and not to please ourselves. We should please our neighbors for their good, to build them up. (Romans 15:1–2)

***TAKE** a few moments to intercede on behalf of your local church, other churches, evangelism and discipleship ministries, educational ministries and any other special concerns you may have.*

NT 1 John 2:1-14

2 My dear children, I write this to you so that you will not sin. But if anybody does sin, we have one who speaks to the Father in our defense—Jesus Christ, the Righteous One. 2 He is the atoning sacrifice for our sins, and not only for ours but also for[a] the sins of the whole world.
3 We know that we have come to know

[a] 2 Or *He is the one who turns aside God's wrath, taking away our sins, and not only ours but also*

him if we obey his commands. [4]The man who says, "I know him," but does not do what he commands is a liar, and the truth is not in him. [5]But if anyone obeys his word, God's love[b] is truly made complete in him. This is how we know we are in him: [6]Whoever claims to live in him must walk as Jesus did.

[7]Dear friends, I am not writing you a new command but an old one, which you have had since the beginning. This old command is the message you have heard. [8]Yet I am writing you a new command; its truth is seen in him and you, because the darkness is passing and the true light is already shining.

[9]Anyone who claims to be in the light but hates his brother is still in the darkness. [10]Whoever loves his brother lives in the light, and there is nothing in him[c] to make him stumble. [11]But whoever hates his brother is in the darkness and walks around in the darkness; he does not know where he is going, because the darkness has blinded him.

[12]I write to you, dear children,
because your sins have been
forgiven on account of his
name.
[13]I write to you, fathers,
because you have known him who
is from the beginning.
I write to you, young men,
because you have overcome the evil
one.
I write to you, dear children,
because you have known the Father.
[14]I write to you, fathers,
because you have known him who
is from the beginning.
I write to you, young men,
because you are strong,
and the word of God lives in you,
and you have overcome the evil one.

[b] 5 Or *word, love for God* [c] 10 Or *it*

PRAYER: THE ATTRIBUTES OF GOD

IT is good to give thanks to You, Lord, to sing praises to Your name, O Most High, to declare Your loving-kindness in the morning and Your faithfulness at night. (Psalm 92:1–2) . . . How precious are Your thoughts to me, O God! How vast is the sum of them! If I should count them, they would outnumber the grains of sand. When I awake, I am still with You. (Psalm 139:17–18)

***PAUSE** to reflect on these affirmations about the person, powers and perfection of God.*

OT Amos 9:1–15

YEAR 2 DAY 327

Israel to Be Destroyed

9 I saw the Lord standing by the altar, and he said:

"Strike the tops of the pillars
so that the thresholds shake.
Bring them down on the heads of all
the people;
those who are left I will kill with
the sword.
Not one will get away,
none will escape.
[2]Though they dig down to the depths
of the grave,[a]
from there my hand will take them.
Though they climb up to the heavens,
from there I will bring them down.
[3]Though they hide themselves on the
top of Carmel,
there I will hunt them down and
seize them.
Though they hide from me at the
bottom of the sea,
there I will command the serpent to
bite them.
[4]Though they are driven into exile by
their enemies,

[a] 2 Hebrew *to Sheol*

there I will command the sword to
slay them.
I will fix my eyes upon them
for evil and not for good."

5 The Lord, the LORD Almighty,
he who touches the earth and it
melts,
and all who live in it mourn—
the whole land rises like the Nile,
then sinks like the river of Egypt—
6 he who builds his lofty palace[b] in the
heavens
and sets its foundation[c] on the earth,
who calls for the waters of the sea
and pours them out over the face of
the land—
the LORD is his name.

7 "Are not you Israelites
the same to me as the Cushites[d]?"
declares the LORD.
"Did I not bring Israel up from Egypt,
the Philistines from Caphtor[e]
and the Arameans from Kir?

8 "Surely the eyes of the Sovereign LORD
are on the sinful kingdom.
I will destroy it
from the face of the earth—
yet I will not totally destroy
the house of Jacob,"
declares the LORD.
9 "For I will give the command,
and I will shake the house of Israel
among all the nations
as grain is shaken in a sieve,
and not a pebble will reach the
ground.
10 All the sinners among my people
will die by the sword,
all those who say,
'Disaster will not overtake or meet
us.'

Israel's Restoration

11 "In that day I will restore
David's fallen tent.
I will repair its broken places,
restore its ruins,
and build it as it used to be,
12 so that they may possess the remnant
of Edom
and all the nations that bear my
name,[f]"
declares the LORD,
who will do these things.

13 "The days are coming," declares the
LORD,

"when the reaper will be overtaken by
the plowman
and the planter by the one treading
grapes.
New wine will drip from the
mountains
and flow from all the hills.
14 I will bring back my exiled[g] people
Israel;
they will rebuild the ruined cities
and live in them.
They will plant vineyards and drink
their wine;
they will make gardens and eat their
fruit.
15 I will plant Israel in their own land,
never again to be uprooted
from the land I have given them,"

says the LORD your God.

[b] 6 The meaning of the Hebrew for this phrase is uncertain. [c] 6 The meaning of the Hebrew for this word is uncertain. [d] 7 That is, people from the upper Nile region [e] 7 That is, Crete [f] 12 Hebrew; Septuagint *so that the remnant of men / and all the nations that bear my name may seek ⌊the Lord⌋* [g] 14 Or *will restore the fortunes of my*

PRAYER: AFFIRMATION

JESUS, we are Your friends if we do what You command. No longer do You call us servants, because a servant does not know what his master is doing. Instead, You have called us friends, for everything that You learned from Your Father, You have made known to us. We did not choose You, but You chose us and appointed us to go and bear fruit, and that our fruit should remain, that whatever we ask the Father in Your name, He may give to us. (John 15:14–16).

PAUSE *to reflect on these Biblical affirmations.*

NT 1 John 2:15-27

Do Not Love the World

[15]Do not love the world or anything in the world. If anyone loves the world, the love of the Father is not in him. [16]For everything in the world—the cravings of sinful man, the lust of his eyes and the boasting of what he has and does—comes not from the Father but from the world.
[17]The world and its desires pass away, but the man who does the will of God lives forever.

Warning Against Antichrists

[18]Dear children, this is the last hour; and as you have heard that the antichrist is coming, even now many antichrists have come. This is how we know it is the last hour. [19]They went out from us, but they did not really belong to us. For if they had belonged to us, they would have remained with us; but their going showed that none of them belonged to us.
[20]But you have an anointing from the Holy One, and all of you know the truth.[a]
[21]I do not write to you because you do not know the truth, but because you do know it and because no lie comes from the truth. [22]Who is the liar? It is the man who denies that Jesus is the Christ. Such a man is the antichrist—he denies the Father and the Son. [23]No one who denies the Son has the Father; whoever acknowledges the Son has the Father also.
[24]See that what you have heard from the beginning remains in you. If it does, you also will remain in the Son and in the Father. [25]And this is what he promised us—even eternal life.
[26]I am writing these things to you about those who are trying to lead you astray.
[27]As for you, the anointing you received from him remains in you, and you do not need anyone to teach you. But as his anointing teaches you about all things and as that anointing is real, not counterfeit—just as it has taught you, remain in him.

[a] 20 Some manuscripts *and you know all things*

PRAYER: THE WORKS OF GOD

I WILL praise You forever for what You have done; I will hope in Your name, for it is good. I will praise You in the presence of Your saints. (Psalm 52:9) . . . Blessed are You, Lord God, God of Israel, who alone does wonderful things. (Psalm 72:18)

***TAKE** a moment to consider the greatness of God's wonderful works.*

YEAR 2 DAY 328

OT Obadiah 1-21

[1]The vision of Obadiah.

This is what the Sovereign LORD says about Edom—

We have heard a message from the LORD:
An envoy was sent to the nations to say,
"Rise, and let us go against her for battle"—
[2]"See, I will make you small among the nations;
you will be utterly despised.
[3]The pride of your heart has deceived you,
you who live in the clefts of the rocks[a]
and make your home on the heights,
you who say to yourself,
'Who can bring me down to the ground?'
[4]Though you soar like the eagle
and make your nest among the stars,

[a] 3 Or *of Sela*

from there I will bring you down,"
declares the LORD.
5 "If thieves came to you,
if robbers in the night—
Oh, what a disaster awaits you—
would they not steal only as much
as they wanted?
If grape pickers came to you,
would they not leave a few grapes?
6 But how Esau will be ransacked,
his hidden treasures pillaged!
7 All your allies will force you to the
border;
your friends will deceive and
overpower you;
those who eat your bread will set a
trap for you,[b]
but you will not detect it.

8 "In that day," declares the LORD,
"will I not destroy the wise men of
Edom,
men of understanding in the
mountains of Esau?
9 Your warriors, O Teman, will be
terrified,
and everyone in Esau's mountains
will be cut down in the slaughter.
10 Because of the violence against your
brother Jacob,
you will be covered with shame;
you will be destroyed forever.
11 On the day you stood aloof
while strangers carried off his
wealth
and foreigners entered his gates
and cast lots for Jerusalem,
you were like one of them.
12 You should not look down on your
brother
in the day of his misfortune,
nor rejoice over the people of Judah
in the day of their destruction,
nor boast so much
in the day of their trouble.
13 You should not march through the
gates of my people
in the day of their disaster,
nor look down on them in their
calamity
in the day of their disaster,
nor seize their wealth
in the day of their disaster.
14 You should not wait at the crossroads
to cut down their fugitives,
nor hand over their survivors
in the day of their trouble.

15 "The day of the LORD is near
for all nations.
As you have done, it will be done to
you;
your deeds will return upon your
own head.
16 Just as you drank on my holy hill,
so all the nations will drink
continually;
they will drink and drink
and be as if they had never been.
17 But on Mount Zion will be
deliverance;
it will be holy,
and the house of Jacob
will possess its inheritance.
18 The house of Jacob will be a fire
and the house of Joseph a flame;
the house of Esau will be stubble,
and they will set it on fire and
consume it.
There will be no survivors
from the house of Esau."
The LORD has spoken.

19 People from the Negev will occupy
the mountains of Esau,
and people from the foothills will
possess
the land of the Philistines.
They will occupy the fields of Ephraim
and Samaria,
and Benjamin will possess Gilead.
20 This company of Israelite exiles who
are in Canaan
will possess ⌊the land⌋ as far as
Zarephath;
the exiles from Jerusalem who are in
Sepharad
will possess the towns of the Negev.
21 Deliverers will go up on[c] Mount Zion
to govern the mountains of Esau.
And the kingdom will be the
LORD's.

[b] 7 The meaning of the Hebrew for this clause is uncertain. [c] 21 Or *from*

PRAYER: THANKSGIVING

O GOD, in the past You spoke to the fathers through the prophets at many times and in various ways, but in these last days You have spoken to us by Your Son, whom You appointed heir of all things, and through whom You made the universe. (Hebrews 1:1–2) . . . You placed all things under Christ's feet and gave Him to be head over all things to the church, which is His body, the fullness of Him who fills all in all.

(Ephesians 1:22–23)

PAUSE *to offer your own expressions of thanksgiving.*

NT 1 John 2:28–3:10

Children of God

28 And now, dear children, continue in him, so that when he appears we may be confident and unashamed before him at his coming.

29 If you know that he is righteous, you know that everyone who does what is right has been born of him.

3 How great is the love the Father has lavished on us, that we should be called children of God! And that is what we are! The reason the world does not know us is that it did not know him. 2 Dear friends, now we are children of God, and what we will be has not yet been made known. But we know that when he appears,[a] we shall be like him, for we shall see him as he is. 3 Everyone who has this hope in him purifies himself, just as he is pure.

4 Everyone who sins breaks the law; in fact, sin is lawlessness. 5 But you know that he appeared so that he might take away our sins. And in him is no sin. 6 No one who lives in him keeps on sinning. No one who continues to sin has either seen him or known him.

7 Dear children, do not let anyone lead you astray. He who does what is right is righteous, just as he is righteous. 8 He who does what is sinful is of the devil, because the devil has been sinning from the beginning. The reason the Son of God appeared was to destroy the devil's work. 9 No one who is born of God will continue to sin, because God's seed remains in him; he cannot go on sinning, because he has been born of God. 10 This is how we know who the children of God are and who the children of the devil are: Anyone who does not do what is right is not a child of God; nor is anyone who does not love his brother.

[a] 2 Or *when it is made known*

PRAYER: MY RELATIONSHIP TO GOD

O GOD, You made known to us the mystery of Your will according to Your good pleasure, which You purposed in Yourself, that in the fullness of the times You might gather together all things in Christ, things in the heavens and things upon the earth. (Ephesians 1:9–10) . . . May I grow in the grace and knowledge of You, my Lord and Savior Jesus Christ. To You be glory both now and forever.

(2 Peter 3:18)

PAUSE *to thank God for the relationship that you enjoy with Him in Jesus Christ.*

OT Psalms 140–141

YEAR 2 DAY 329

Psalm 140

For the director of music. A psalm of David.

1 Rescue me, O LORD, from evil men;
protect me from men of violence,
2 who devise evil plans in their hearts
and stir up war every day.
3 They make their tongues as sharp as a serpent's;
the poison of vipers is on their lips. *Selah*

4 Keep me, O LORD, from the hands of the wicked;
protect me from men of violence
who plan to trip my feet.
5 Proud men have hidden a snare for me;
they have spread out the cords of their net
and have set traps for me along my path. *Selah*

6 O LORD, I say to you, "You are my God."
Hear, O LORD, my cry for mercy.
7 O Sovereign LORD, my strong deliverer,
who shields my head in the day of battle—
8 do not grant the wicked their desires, O LORD;
do not let their plans succeed,
or they will become proud. *Selah*

9 Let the heads of those who surround me
be covered with the trouble their lips have caused.
10 Let burning coals fall upon them;
may they be thrown into the fire,
into miry pits, never to rise.
11 Let slanderers not be established in the land;
may disaster hunt down men of violence.

12 I know that the LORD secures justice for the poor
and upholds the cause of the needy.
13 Surely the righteous will praise your name
and the upright will live before you.

Psalm 141

A psalm of David.

1 O LORD, I call to you; come quickly to me.
Hear my voice when I call to you.
2 May my prayer be set before you like incense;
may the lifting up of my hands be like the evening sacrifice.

3 Set a guard over my mouth, O LORD;
keep watch over the door of my lips.
4 Let not my heart be drawn to what is evil,
to take part in wicked deeds
with men who are evildoers;
let me not eat of their delicacies.

5 Let a righteous man[a] strike me—it is a kindness;
let him rebuke me—it is oil on my head.
My head will not refuse it.

Yet my prayer is ever against the deeds of evildoers;
6 their rulers will be thrown down from the cliffs,
and the wicked will learn that my words were well spoken.
7 ⌊They will say,⌋ "As one plows and breaks up the earth,
so our bones have been scattered at the mouth of the grave.[b]"

8 But my eyes are fixed on you, O Sovereign LORD;
in you I take refuge—do not give me over to death.
9 Keep me from the snares they have laid for me,
from the traps set by evildoers.
10 Let the wicked fall into their own nets,
while I pass by in safety.

[a] 5 Or *Let the Righteous One* [b] 7 Hebrew *Sheol*

PRAYER: ADORATION

WHO is like You, O Lord? Who is like You—majestic in holiness, awesome in praises, working wonders? (Exodus 15:11) . . . Lord, there is no one holy like You; there is no one besides You; nor is there any Rock like You, our God. (1 Samuel 2:2)

***PAUSE** to express your thoughts of praise and worship.*

NT 1 John 3:11–4:6

Love One Another

[11]This is the message you heard from the beginning: We should love one another. [12]Do not be like Cain, who belonged to the evil one and murdered his brother. And why did he murder him? Because his own actions were evil and his brother's were righteous. [13]Do not be surprised, my brothers, if the world hates you. [14]We know that we have passed from death to life, because we love our brothers. Anyone who does not love remains in death. [15]Anyone who hates his brother is a murderer, and you know that no murderer has eternal life in him.

[16]This is how we know what love is: Jesus Christ laid down his life for us. And we ought to lay down our lives for our brothers. [17]If anyone has material possessions and sees his brother in need but has no pity on him, how can the love of God be in him? [18]Dear children, let us not love with words or tongue but with actions and in truth. [19]This then is how we know that we belong to the truth, and how we set our hearts at rest in his presence [20]whenever our hearts condemn us. For God is greater than our hearts, and he knows everything.

[21]Dear friends, if our hearts do not condemn us, we have confidence before God [22]and receive from him anything we ask, because we obey his commands and do what pleases him. [23]And this is his command: to believe in the name of his Son, Jesus Christ, and to love one another as he commanded us. [24]Those who obey his commands live in him, and he in them. And this is how we know that he lives in us: We know it by the Spirit he gave us.

Test the Spirits

4 Dear friends, do not believe every spirit, but test the spirits to see whether they are from God, because many false prophets have gone out into the world. [2]This is how you can recognize the Spirit of God: Every spirit that acknowledges that Jesus Christ has come in the flesh is from God, [3]but every spirit that does not acknowledge Jesus is not from God. This is the spirit of the antichrist, which you have heard is coming and even now is already in the world.

[4]You, dear children, are from God and have overcome them, because the one who is in you is greater than the one who is in the world. [5]They are from the world and therefore speak from the viewpoint of the world, and the world listens to them. [6]We are from God, and whoever knows God listens to us; but whoever is not from God does not listen to us. This is how we recognize the Spirit[a] of truth and the spirit of falsehood.

[a] 6 Or *spirit*

PRAYER: THE CHARACTER I WANT TO CULTIVATE

IF I am wise, I will understand these things; if I am discerning, I know them. Your ways, O Lord, are right; the righteous will walk in them, but transgressors will stumble in them. (Hosea 14:9) . . . I will see to it that no one takes me captive through philosophy and empty deceit, according to the human tradition, according to the basic principles of this world, and not according to You, O Christ. (Colossians 2:8)

***TAKE** a moment to ask the Lord for the grace to grow in godly character.*

YEAR 2
DAY 330

OT Jonah 1:1-17

Jonah Flees From the LORD

1 The word of the LORD came to Jonah
son of Amittai: 2 "Go to the great city of
Nineveh and preach against it, because its
wickedness has come up before me."
3 But Jonah ran away from the LORD and
headed for Tarshish. He went down to
Joppa, where he found a ship bound for
that port. After paying the fare, he went
aboard and sailed for Tarshish to flee
from the LORD.
4 Then the LORD sent a great wind on the
sea, and such a violent storm arose that
the ship threatened to break up. 5 All the
sailors were afraid and each cried out to
his own god. And they threw the cargo
into the sea to lighten the ship.
But Jonah had gone below deck, where
he lay down and fell into a deep sleep.
6 The captain went to him and said, "How
can you sleep? Get up and call on your
god! Maybe he will take notice of us, and
we will not perish."
7 Then the sailors said to each other,
"Come, let us cast lots to find out who is
responsible for this calamity." They cast
lots and the lot fell on Jonah.
8 So they asked him, "Tell us, who is responsible for making all this trouble for
us? What do you do? Where do you come
from? What is your country? From what
people are you?"
9 He answered, "I am a Hebrew and I
worship the LORD, the God of heaven,
who made the sea and the land."
10 This terrified them and they asked,
"What have you done?" (They knew he
was running away from the LORD, because
he had already told them so.)
11 The sea was getting rougher and
rougher. So they asked him, "What
should we do to you to make the sea calm
down for us?"
12 "Pick me up and throw me into the
sea," he replied, "and it will become calm.
I know that it is my fault that this great
storm has come upon you."
13 Instead, the men did their best to row
back to land. But they could not, for the
sea grew even wilder than before. 14 Then
they cried to the LORD, "O LORD, please
do not let us die for taking this man's life.
Do not hold us accountable for killing an
innocent man, for you, O LORD, have
done as you pleased." 15 Then they took
Jonah and threw him overboard, and the
raging sea grew calm. 16 At this the men
greatly feared the LORD, and they offered
a sacrifice to the LORD and made vows to
him.
17 But the LORD provided a great fish to
swallow Jonah, and Jonah was inside the
fish three days and three nights.

PRAYER: CONFESSION

LET the wicked forsake their ways and the unrighteous their thoughts. Let us return to You, Lord, and You will have mercy on us; let us return to You, our God, for You will abundantly pardon. (Isaiah 55:7)

***ASK** the Spirit to search your heart and reveal any areas of unconfessed sin. Acknowledge these to the Lord and thank Him for His forgiveness.*

NT 1 John 4:7-21

God's Love and Ours

7 Dear friends, let us love one another,
for love comes from God. Everyone who
loves has been born of God and knows
God. 8 Whoever does not love does not
know God, because God is love. 9 This is
how God showed his love among us: He
sent his one and only Son[a] into the world
that we might live through him. 10 This is
love: not that we loved God, but that he
loved us and sent his Son as an atoning
sacrifice for[b] our sins. 11 Dear friends, since
God so loved us, we also ought to love

[a] 9 Or *his only begotten Son* [b] 10 Or *as the one who would turn aside his wrath, taking away*

one another. [12]No one has ever seen God; but if we love one another, God lives in us and his love is made complete in us.

[13]We know that we live in him and he in us, because he has given us of his Spirit. [14]And we have seen and testify that the Father has sent his Son to be the Savior of the world. [15]If anyone acknowledges that Jesus is the Son of God, God lives in him and he in God. [16]And so we know and rely on the love God has for us.

God is love. Whoever lives in love lives in God, and God in him. [17]In this way, love is made complete among us so that we will have confidence on the day of judgment, because in this world we are like him. [18]There is no fear in love. But perfect love drives out fear, because fear has to do with punishment. The one who fears is not made perfect in love.

[19]We love because he first loved us. [20]If anyone says, "I love God," yet hates his brother, he is a liar. For anyone who does not love his brother, whom he has seen, cannot love God, whom he has not seen. [21]And he has given us this command: Whoever loves God must also love his brother.

PRAYER: MY RELATIONSHIP TO OTHERS

MY love must be sincere. I will hate what is evil and cling to what is good. (Romans 12:9) . . . I will rejoice with those who rejoice and weep with those who weep. (Romans 12:15)

***PAUSE** to review your relationships with others and to commit them to the Lord.*

YEAR 2 DAY 331

OT Jonah 2:1-10

Jonah's Prayer

2 From inside the fish Jonah prayed to the LORD his God. [2]He said:

"In my distress I called to the LORD,
and he answered me.
From the depths of the grave[a] I called for help,
and you listened to my cry.
[3]You hurled me into the deep,
into the very heart of the seas,
and the currents swirled about me;
all your waves and breakers
swept over me.
[4]I said, 'I have been banished
from your sight;
yet I will look again
toward your holy temple.'
[5]The engulfing waters threatened me,[b]
the deep surrounded me;
seaweed was wrapped around my head.
[6]To the roots of the mountains I sank down;
the earth beneath barred me in forever.
But you brought my life up from the pit,
O LORD my God.

[7]"When my life was ebbing away,
I remembered you, LORD,
and my prayer rose to you,
to your holy temple.

[8]"Those who cling to worthless idols
forfeit the grace that could be theirs.
[9]But I, with a song of thanksgiving,
will sacrifice to you.
What I have vowed I will make good.
Salvation comes from the LORD."

[10]And the LORD commanded the fish, and it vomited Jonah onto dry land.

[a] 2 Hebrew *Sheol* [b] 5 Or *waters were at my throat*

PRAYER: RENEWAL

MAY I be self-controlled in all things, endure hardship, do the work of an evangelist and fulfill my ministry. (2 Timothy 4:5) . . . May I abound in love and faith toward You, Lord Jesus, and toward all the saints. (Philemon 5)

***PAUSE** to add your own prayers for personal renewal.*

NT 1 John 5:1–21

Faith in the Son of God

5 Everyone who believes that Jesus is the Christ is born of God, and everyone who loves the father loves his child as well. [2]This is how we know that we love the children of God: by loving God and carrying out his commands. [3]This is love for God: to obey his commands. And his commands are not burdensome, [4]for everyone born of God overcomes the world. This is the victory that has overcome the world, even our faith. [5]Who is it that overcomes the world? Only he who believes that Jesus is the Son of God.

[6]This is the one who came by water and blood—Jesus Christ. He did not come by water only, but by water and blood. And it is the Spirit who testifies, because the Spirit is the truth. [7]For there are three that testify: [8]the[a] Spirit, the water and the blood; and the three are in agreement. [9]We accept man's testimony, but God's testimony is greater because it is the testimony of God, which he has given about his Son. [10]Anyone who believes in the Son of God has this testimony in his heart. Anyone who does not believe God has made him out to be a liar, because he has not believed the testimony God has given about his Son. [11]And this is the testimony: God has given us eternal life, and this life is in his Son. [12]He who has the Son has life; he who does not have the Son of God does not have life.

Concluding Remarks

[13]I write these things to you who believe in the name of the Son of God so that you may know that you have eternal life. [14]This is the confidence we have in approaching God: that if we ask anything according to his will, he hears us. [15]And if we know that he hears us—whatever we ask—we know that we have what we asked of him.

[16]If anyone sees his brother commit a sin that does not lead to death, he should pray and God will give him life. I refer to those whose sin does not lead to death. There is a sin that leads to death. I am not saying that he should pray about that. [17]All wrongdoing is sin, and there is sin that does not lead to death.

[18]We know that anyone born of God does not continue to sin; the one who was born of God keeps him safe, and the evil one cannot harm him. [19]We know that we are children of God, and that the whole world is under the control of the evil one. [20]We know also that the Son of God has come and has given us understanding, so that we may know him who is true. And we are in him who is true—even in his Son Jesus Christ. He is the true God and eternal life.

[21]Dear children, keep yourselves from idols.

[a] 7,8 Late manuscripts of the Vulgate *testify in heaven: the Father, the Word and the Holy Spirit, and these three are one.* [8]*And there are three that testify on earth: the* (not found in any Greek manuscript before the sixteenth century)

PRAYER: THE ATTRIBUTES OF GOD

JESUS, You are the Christ, the Son of the living God. (Matthew 16:16) . . . Jesus, You are the way and the truth and the life. No one comes to the Father except through You. (John 14:6)

***PAUSE** to reflect on these affirmations about the person, powers and perfection of God.*

YEAR 2 DAY 332

OT Jonah 3:1–4:11

Jonah Goes to Nineveh

3 Then the word of the LORD came to Jonah a second time: 2 "Go to the great city of Nineveh and proclaim to it the message I give you."

3 Jonah obeyed the word of the LORD and went to Nineveh. Now Nineveh was a very important city—a visit required three days. 4 On the first day, Jonah started into the city. He proclaimed: "Forty more days and Nineveh will be overturned." 5 The Ninevites believed God. They declared a fast, and all of them, from the greatest to the least, put on sackcloth.

6 When the news reached the king of Nineveh, he rose from his throne, took off his royal robes, covered himself with sackcloth and sat down in the dust. 7 Then he issued a proclamation in Nineveh:

"By the decree of the king and his nobles:

> Do not let any man or beast, herd or flock, taste anything; do not let them eat or drink. 8 But let man and beast be covered with sackcloth. Let everyone call urgently on God. Let them give up their evil ways and their violence. 9 Who knows? God may yet relent and with compassion turn from his fierce anger so that we will not perish."

10 When God saw what they did and how they turned from their evil ways, he had compassion and did not bring upon them the destruction he had threatened.

Jonah's Anger at the LORD's Compassion

4 But Jonah was greatly displeased and became angry. 2 He prayed to the LORD, "O LORD, is this not what I said when I was still at home? That is why I was so quick to flee to Tarshish. I knew that you are a gracious and compassionate God, slow to anger and abounding in love, a God who relents from sending calamity. 3 Now, O LORD, take away my life, for it is better for me to die than to live."

4 But the LORD replied, "Have you any right to be angry?"

5 Jonah went out and sat down at a place east of the city. There he made himself a shelter, sat in its shade and waited to see what would happen to the city. 6 Then the LORD God provided a vine and made it grow up over Jonah to give shade for his head to ease his discomfort, and Jonah was very happy about the vine. 7 But at dawn the next day God provided a worm, which chewed the vine so that it withered. 8 When the sun rose, God provided a scorching east wind, and the sun blazed on Jonah's head so that he grew faint. He wanted to die, and said, "It would be better for me to die than to live."

9 But God said to Jonah, "Do you have a right to be angry about the vine?"

"I do," he said. "I am angry enough to die."

10 But the LORD said, "You have been concerned about this vine, though you did not tend it or make it grow. It sprang up overnight and died overnight. 11 But Nineveh has more than a hundred and twenty thousand people who cannot tell their right hand from their left, and many cattle as well. Should I not be concerned about that great city?"

PRAYER: PETITION

O LORD, may I be diligent to realize the full assurance of hope to the end. Do not let me become sluggish, but may I imitate those who through faith and patience inherit the promises. (Hebrews 6:11–12)

__PAUSE__ here to petition God for wisdom. Ask Him to develop your eternal perspective, to renew your mind with truth, and to help you develop greater skill in each area of your life. Offer prayers regarding your activities for this day and any special concerns you may have.

NT 2 John 1-13

1 The elder,

To the chosen lady and her children,
whom I love in the truth—and not I only,
but also all who know the truth— 2 because of the truth, which lives in us and
will be with us forever:

3 Grace, mercy and peace from God the
Father and from Jesus Christ, the Father's
Son, will be with us in truth and love.

4 It has given me great joy to find some
of your children walking in the truth, just
as the Father commanded us. 5 And now,
dear lady, I am not writing you a new
command but one we have had from the
beginning. I ask that we love one another. 6 And this is love: that we walk in obedience to his commands. As you have
heard from the beginning, his command
is that you walk in love.
7 Many deceivers, who do not acknowledge Jesus Christ as coming in the flesh,
have gone out into the world. Any such
person is the deceiver and the antichrist.
8 Watch out that you do not lose what you
have worked for, but that you may be rewarded fully. 9 Anyone who runs ahead
and does not continue in the teaching of
Christ does not have God; whoever continues in the teaching has both the Father
and the Son. 10 If anyone comes to you and
does not bring this teaching, do not take
him into your house or welcome him.
11 Anyone who welcomes him shares in his
wicked work.
12 I have much to write to you, but I do
not want to use paper and ink. Instead, I
hope to visit you and talk with you face
to face, so that our joy may be complete.

13 The children of your chosen sister
send their greetings.

PRAYER: THE WORKS OF GOD

MAY the heavens shout for joy! May the earth rejoice! May the mountains break out into singing! For You, Lord, have comforted Your people and will have compassion on Your afflicted. (Isaiah 49:13)

***TAKE** a moment to consider the greatness of God's wonderful works.*

YEAR 2 DAY 333

OT Micah 1:1-16

1 The word of the LORD that came to Micah of Moresheth during the reigns of
Jotham, Ahaz and Hezekiah, kings of Judah—the vision he saw concerning
Samaria and Jerusalem.

2 Hear, O peoples, all of you,
listen, O earth and all who are in it,
that the Sovereign LORD may witness against you,
the Lord from his holy temple.

Judgment Against Samaria and Jerusalem

3 Look! The LORD is coming from his dwelling place;
he comes down and treads the high places of the earth.
4 The mountains melt beneath him
and the valleys split apart,
like wax before the fire,
like water rushing down a slope.
5 All this is because of Jacob's transgression,
because of the sins of the house of Israel.
What is Jacob's transgression?
Is it not Samaria?
What is Judah's high place?
Is it not Jerusalem?

6 "Therefore I will make Samaria a heap of rubble,
a place for planting vineyards.
I will pour her stones into the valley

and lay bare her foundations.
[7]All her idols will be broken to pieces;
all her temple gifts will be burned with fire;
I will destroy all her images.
Since she gathered her gifts from the wages of prostitutes,
as the wages of prostitutes they will again be used."

Weeping and Mourning

[8]Because of this I will weep and wail;
I will go about barefoot and naked.
I will howl like a jackal
and moan like an owl.
[9]For her wound is incurable;
it has come to Judah.
It[a] has reached the very gate of my people,
even to Jerusalem itself.
[10]Tell it not in Gath[b];
weep not at all.[c]
In Beth Ophrah[d]
roll in the dust.
[11]Pass on in nakedness and shame,
you who live in Shaphir.[e]
Those who live in Zaanan[f]
will not come out.
Beth Ezel is in mourning;
its protection is taken from you.
[12]Those who live in Maroth[g] writhe in pain,
waiting for relief,
because disaster has come from the LORD,
even to the gate of Jerusalem.
[13]You who live in Lachish,[h]
harness the team to the chariot.
You were the beginning of sin
to the Daughter of Zion,
for the transgressions of Israel
were found in you.
[14]Therefore you will give parting gifts
to Moresheth Gath.
The town of Aczib[i] will prove deceptive
to the kings of Israel.
[15]I will bring a conqueror against you
who live in Mareshah.[j]
He who is the glory of Israel
will come to Adullam.
[16]Shave your heads in mourning
for the children in whom you delight;
make yourselves as bald as the vulture,
for they will go from you into exile.

[a] 9 Or *He* [b] 10 *Gath* sounds like the Hebrew for *tell.* [c] 10 Hebrew; Septuagint may suggest *not in Acco.* The Hebrew for *in Acco* sounds like the Hebrew for *weep.* [d] 10 *Beth Ophrah* means *house of dust.* [e] 11 *Shaphir* means *pleasant.* [f] 11 *Zaanan* sounds like the Hebrew for *come out.* [g] 12 *Maroth* sounds like the Hebrew for *bitter.* [h] 13 *Lachish* sounds like the Hebrew for *team.* [i] 14 *Aczib* means *deception.* [j] 15 *Mareshah* sounds like the Hebrew for *conqueror.*

PRAYER: INTERCESSION

O CHRIST, let Your word dwell in us richly as we teach and admonish one another with all wisdom, and as we sing psalms, hymns and spiritual songs with gratitude in our hearts to God. (Colossians 3:16)

***TAKE** a few moments to intercede on behalf of your immediate family and other relatives. Offer prayers for their spiritual, emotional and physical concerns.*

NT 3 John 1-14

[1]The elder,

To my dear friend Gaius, whom I love in the truth.

[2]Dear friend, I pray that you may enjoy good health and that all may go well with you, even as your soul is getting along well. [3]It gave me great joy to have some brothers come and tell about your faithfulness to the truth and how you continue to walk in the truth. [4]I have no greater joy than to hear that my children are walking in the truth.

[5]Dear friend, you are faithful in what you are doing for the brothers, even though they are strangers to you. [6]They have told the church about your love. You will do well to send them on their way in a manner worthy of God. [7]It was for the sake of the Name that they went out, re-

ceiving no help from the pagans. [8]We
ought therefore to show hospitality to
such men so that we may work together
for the truth.
[9]I wrote to the church, but Diotrephes,
who loves to be first, will have nothing to
do with us. [10]So if I come, I will call attention to what he is doing, gossiping maliciously about us. Not satisfied with that,
he refuses to welcome the brothers. He
also stops those who want to do so and
puts them out of the church.
[11]Dear friend, do not imitate what is
evil but what is good. Anyone who does
what is good is from God. Anyone who
does what is evil has not seen God.
[12]Demetrius is well spoken of by everyone—and even by the truth itself. We also
speak well of him, and you know that our
testimony is true.
[13]I have much to write you, but I do not
want to do so with pen and ink. [14]I hope
to see you soon, and we will talk face to
face.

Peace to you. The friends here send their greetings. Greet the friends there by name.

PRAYER: MY RELATIONSHIP TO GOD

THOSE who obey Your commandments, O Christ, abide in You, and You in them. And this is how I know that You abide in me: by the Spirit whom You have given me. I know that I abide in You, O Christ, and You in me, because You have given me of Your Spirit. (1 John 3:24; 4:13)

***PAUSE** to thank God for the relationship that you enjoy with Him in Jesus Christ.*

YEAR 2
DAY 334

OT Micah 2:1-13

Man's Plans and God's

2 Woe to those who plan iniquity,
to those who plot evil on their beds!
At morning's light they carry it out
because it is in their power to do it.
[2]They covet fields and seize them,
and houses, and take them.
They defraud a man of his home,
a fellowman of his inheritance.

[3]Therefore, the LORD says:

"I am planning disaster against this people,
from which you cannot save yourselves.
You will no longer walk proudly,
for it will be a time of calamity.
[4]In that day men will ridicule you;
they will taunt you with this mournful song:
'We are utterly ruined;
my people's possession is divided up.
He takes it from me!
He assigns our fields to traitors.' "
[5]Therefore you will have no one in the assembly of the LORD
to divide the land by lot.

False Prophets

[6]"Do not prophesy," their prophets say.
"Do not prophesy about these things;
disgrace will not overtake us."
[7]Should it be said, O house of Jacob:
"Is the Spirit of the LORD angry?
Does he do such things?"

"Do not my words do good
to him whose ways are upright?
[8]Lately my people have risen up
like an enemy.
You strip off the rich robe
from those who pass by without a care,
like men returning from battle.
[9]You drive the women of my people
from their pleasant homes.
You take away my blessing
from their children forever.
[10]Get up, go away!

For this is not your resting place,
because it is defiled,
it is ruined, beyond all remedy.
[11] If a liar and deceiver comes and says,
'I will prophesy for you plenty of wine and beer,'
he would be just the prophet for this people!

Deliverance Promised

[12] "I will surely gather all of you, O Jacob;
I will surely bring together the remnant of Israel.
I will bring them together like sheep in a pen,
like a flock in its pasture;
the place will throng with people.
[13] One who breaks open the way will go up before them;
they will break through the gate and go out.
Their king will pass through before them,
the LORD at their head."

PRAYER: AFFIRMATION

HAVING the firstfruits of the Spirit, O God, I groan inwardly as I wait eagerly for my adoption, the redemption of my body. For in hope I have been saved, but hope that is seen is not hope; for who hopes for what he sees? But if I hope for what I do not yet see, I eagerly wait for it with perseverance. (Romans 8:23–25) . . . I know that You who raised the Lord Jesus will also raise me with Him and present me in Your presence. (2 Corinthians 4:14)

PAUSE *to reflect on these Biblical affirmations.*

NT Jude 1–25

[1]Jude, a servant of Jesus Christ and a brother of James,

To those who have been called, who are loved by God the Father and kept by[a] Jesus Christ:

[2]Mercy, peace and love be yours in abundance.

The Sin and Doom of Godless Men

[3]Dear friends, although I was very eager to write to you about the salvation we share, I felt I had to write and urge you to contend for the faith that was once for all entrusted to the saints. [4]For certain men whose condemnation was written about[b] long ago have secretly slipped in among you. They are godless men, who change the grace of our God into a license for immorality and deny Jesus Christ our only Sovereign and Lord.

[5]Though you already know all this, I want to remind you that the Lord[c] delivered his people out of Egypt, but later destroyed those who did not believe. [6]And the angels who did not keep their positions of authority but abandoned their own home—these he has kept in darkness, bound with everlasting chains for judgment on the great Day. [7]In a similar way, Sodom and Gomorrah and the surrounding towns gave themselves up to sexual immorality and perversion. They serve as an example of those who suffer the punishment of eternal fire.

[8]In the very same way, these dreamers pollute their own bodies, reject authority and slander celestial beings. [9]But even the archangel Michael, when he was disputing with the devil about the body of Moses, did not dare to bring a slanderous accusation against him, but said, "The Lord rebuke you!" [10]Yet these men speak abusively against whatever they do not understand; and what things they do understand by instinct, like unreasoning animals—these are the very things that destroy them.

[11]Woe to them! They have taken the way of Cain; they have rushed for profit into Balaam's error; they have been destroyed in Korah's rebellion.

[a] 1 Or *for;* or *in for condemnation* [b] 4 Or *men who were marked out* [c] 5 Some early manuscripts *Jesus*

12These men are blemishes at your love
feasts, eating with you without the slight-
est qualm—shepherds who feed only
themselves. They are clouds without rain,
blown along by the wind; autumn trees,
without fruit and uprooted—twice dead.
13They are wild waves of the sea, foaming
up their shame; wandering stars, for
whom blackest darkness has been reserved forever.

14Enoch, the seventh from Adam,
prophesied about these men: "See, the
Lord is coming with thousands upon
thousands of his holy ones 15to judge
everyone, and to convict all the ungodly
of all the ungodly acts they have done in
the ungodly way, and of all the harsh
words ungodly sinners have spoken
against him." 16These men are grumblers
and faultfinders; they follow their own
evil desires; they boast about themselves
and flatter others for their own advantage.

A Call to Persevere

17But, dear friends, remember what the
apostles of our Lord Jesus Christ foretold.
18They said to you, "In the last times there
will be scoffers who will follow their own
ungodly desires." 19These are the men
who divide you, who follow mere natural instincts and do not have the Spirit.

20But you, dear friends, build yourselves
up in your most holy faith and pray in the
Holy Spirit. 21Keep yourselves in God's
love as you wait for the mercy of our Lord
Jesus Christ to bring you to eternal life.

22Be merciful to those who doubt;
23snatch others from the fire and save
them; to others show mercy, mixed with
fear—hating even the clothing stained by
corrupted flesh.

Doxology

24To him who is able to keep you from
falling and to present you before his glorious presence without fault and with
great joy— 25to the only God our Savior
be glory, majesty, power and authority,
through Jesus Christ our Lord, before all
ages, now and forevermore! Amen.

PRAYER: THE CHARACTER I WANT TO CULTIVATE

WHOEVER is wise and understanding, O Lord, will show it by good conduct and works done in the humility that comes from wisdom. If I harbor bitter envy and selfish ambition in my heart, I should not boast and lie against the truth. This wisdom does not come down from above, but is earthly, natural, demonic. For where there is envy and selfish ambition, Lord, there is disorder and every evil practice. (James 3:13–16)

***TAKE** a moment to ask the Lord for the grace to grow in godly character.*

YEAR 2 DAY 335

OT Micah 3:1–4:13

Leaders and Prophets Rebuked

3 Then I said,

"Listen, you leaders of Jacob,
you rulers of the house of Israel.
Should you not know justice,
2 you who hate good and love evil;
who tear the skin from my people
and the flesh from their bones;
3 who eat my people's flesh,
strip off their skin
and break their bones in pieces;
who chop them up like meat for the pan,
like flesh for the pot?"

4 Then they will cry out to the LORD,
but he will not answer them.
At that time he will hide his face from them
because of the evil they have done.

5 This is what the LORD says:

"As for the prophets
who lead my people astray,
if one feeds them,

they proclaim 'peace';
if he does not,
they prepare to wage war against him.
6 Therefore night will come over you, without visions,
and darkness, without divination.
The sun will set for the prophets,
and the day will go dark for them.
7 The seers will be ashamed
and the diviners disgraced.
They will all cover their faces
because there is no answer from God."

8 But as for me, I am filled with power,
with the Spirit of the LORD,
and with justice and might,
to declare to Jacob his transgression,
to Israel his sin.
9 Hear this, you leaders of the house of Jacob,
you rulers of the house of Israel,
who despise justice
and distort all that is right;
10 who build Zion with bloodshed,
and Jerusalem with wickedness.
11 Her leaders judge for a bribe,
her priests teach for a price,
and her prophets tell fortunes for money.
Yet they lean upon the LORD and say,
"Is not the LORD among us?
No disaster will come upon us."
12 Therefore because of you,
Zion will be plowed like a field,
Jerusalem will become a heap of rubble,
the temple hill a mound overgrown with thickets.

The Mountain of the LORD

4 In the last days

the mountain of the LORD's temple will be established
as chief among the mountains;
it will be raised above the hills,
and peoples will stream to it.

2 Many nations will come and say,

"Come, let us go up to the mountain of the LORD,
to the house of the God of Jacob.
He will teach us his ways,
so that we may walk in his paths."
The law will go out from Zion,
the word of the LORD from Jerusalem.
3 He will judge between many peoples
and will settle disputes for strong nations far and wide.
They will beat their swords into plowshares
and their spears into pruning hooks.
Nation will not take up sword against nation,
nor will they train for war anymore.
4 Every man will sit under his own vine
and under his own fig tree,
and no one will make them afraid,
for the LORD Almighty has spoken.
5 All the nations may walk
in the name of their gods;
we will walk in the name of the LORD
our God for ever and ever.

The LORD's Plan

6 "In that day," declares the LORD,

"I will gather the lame;
I will assemble the exiles
and those I have brought to grief.
7 I will make the lame a remnant,
those driven away a strong nation.
The LORD will rule over them in Mount Zion
from that day and forever.
8 As for you, O watchtower of the flock,
O stronghold[a] of the Daughter of Zion,
the former dominion will be restored to you;
kingship will come to the Daughter of Jerusalem."

9 Why do you now cry aloud—
have you no king?
Has your counselor perished,
that pain seizes you like that of a woman in labor?
10 Writhe in agony, O Daughter of Zion,
like a woman in labor,
for now you must leave the city
to camp in the open field.
You will go to Babylon;
there you will be rescued.
There the LORD will redeem you
out of the hand of your enemies.

11 But now many nations
are gathered against you.

[a] 8 Or *hill*

They say, "Let her be defiled,
let our eyes gloat over Zion!"
12 But they do not know
the thoughts of the LORD;
they do not understand his plan,
he who gathers them like sheaves to the threshing floor.

13 "Rise and thresh, O Daughter of Zion,
for I will give you horns of iron;
I will give you hoofs of bronze
and you will break to pieces many nations."

You will devote their ill-gotten gains to the LORD,
their wealth to the Lord of all the earth.

PRAYER: THANKSGIVING

THERE will be no temple in the new Jerusalem, because You, O Lord God Almighty, and the Lamb will be its temple. The city will not need the sun or the moon to shine on it, for the glory of God gives it light, and the Lamb is its lamp. The nations will walk by its light, and the kings of the earth will bring their splendor into it. And its gates will never be shut by day, for there will be no night there. (Revelation 21:22–25)

***PAUSE** to offer your own expressions of thanksgiving.*

NT Revelation 1:1-8

Prologue

1 The revelation of Jesus Christ, which God gave him to show his servants what must soon take place. He made it known by sending his angel to his servant John,
2 who testifies to everything he saw—that is, the word of God and the testimony of Jesus Christ.
3 Blessed is the one who reads the words of this prophecy, and blessed are those who hear it and take to heart what is written in it, because the time is near.

Greetings and Doxology

4 John,

To the seven churches in the province of Asia:

Grace and peace to you from him who is, and who was, and who is to come, and from the seven spirits[a] before his throne,
5 and from Jesus Christ, who is the faithful witness, the firstborn from the dead, and the ruler of the kings of the earth.

To him who loves us and has freed us from our sins by his blood,
6 and has made us to be a kingdom and priests to serve his God and Father—to him be glory and power for ever and ever! Amen.

7 "Look, he is coming with the clouds,
and every eye will see him,
even those who pierced him;
and all the peoples of the earth will mourn because of him.
So shall it be! Amen.

8 "I am the Alpha and the Omega," says the Lord God, "who is, and who was, and who is to come, the Almighty."

[a] 4 Or *the sevenfold Spirit*

PRAYER: MY RELATIONSHIP TO OTHERS

I WILL not repay anyone evil for evil, but I will seek to do what is right in the sight of all people. (Romans 12:17) . . . I will not repay evil for evil to anyone, but I will pursue what is good for others. (1 Thessalonians 5:15)

***PAUSE** to review your relationships with others and to commit them to the Lord.*

OT **Psalms 142–143**

Psalm 142

A *maskil*[a] of David. When he was in the cave. A prayer.

[1]I cry aloud to the LORD;
I lift up my voice to the LORD for mercy.
[2]I pour out my complaint before him;
before him I tell my trouble.

[3]When my spirit grows faint within me,
it is you who know my way.
In the path where I walk
men have hidden a snare for me.
[4]Look to my right and see;
no one is concerned for me.
I have no refuge;
no one cares for my life.

[5]I cry to you, O LORD;
I say, "You are my refuge,
my portion in the land of the living."
[6]Listen to my cry,
for I am in desperate need;
rescue me from those who pursue me,
for they are too strong for me.
[7]Set me free from my prison,
that I may praise your name.

Then the righteous will gather about me
because of your goodness to me.

Psalm 143

A psalm of David.

[1]O LORD, hear my prayer,
listen to my cry for mercy;
in your faithfulness and righteousness
come to my relief.
[2]Do not bring your servant into judgment,
for no one living is righteous before you.

[3]The enemy pursues me,
he crushes me to the ground;
he makes me dwell in darkness
like those long dead.
[4]So my spirit grows faint within me;
my heart within me is dismayed.

[5]I remember the days of long ago;
I meditate on all your works
and consider what your hands have done.
[6]I spread out my hands to you;
my soul thirsts for you like a parched land. *Selah*

[7]Answer me quickly, O LORD;
my spirit fails.
Do not hide your face from me
or I will be like those who go down to the pit.
[8]Let the morning bring me word of your unfailing love,
for I have put my trust in you.
Show me the way I should go,
for to you I lift up my soul.
[9]Rescue me from my enemies, O LORD,
for I hide myself in you.
[10]Teach me to do your will,
for you are my God;
may your good Spirit
lead me on level ground.

[11]For your name's sake, O LORD,
preserve my life;
in your righteousness, bring me out of trouble.
[12]In your unfailing love, silence my enemies;
destroy all my foes,
for I am your servant.

[a]Title: Probably a literary or musical term

PRAYER: ADORATION

YOU will command Your loving-kindness by day; in the night Your song is with me—a prayer to You, the God of my life. (Psalm 42:8) . . . Blessed are You, Lord God, the God of Israel; You alone do wonderful things. Blessed be Your glorious name forever; may the whole earth be filled with Your glory. Amen and Amen. (Psalm 72:18–19)

PAUSE *to express your thoughts of praise and worship.*

NT Revelation 1:9-20

One Like a Son of Man

9 I, John, your brother and companion
in the suffering and kingdom and patient
endurance that are ours in Jesus, was on
the island of Patmos because of the word
of God and the testimony of Jesus. 10 On
the Lord's Day I was in the Spirit, and I
heard behind me a loud voice like a trumpet, 11 which said: "Write on a scroll what
you see and send it to the seven churches:
to Ephesus, Smyrna, Pergamum, Thyatira,
Sardis, Philadelphia and Laodicea."

12 I turned around to see the voice that
was speaking to me. And when I turned I
saw seven golden lampstands, 13 and
among the lampstands was someone "like
a son of man,"[a] dressed in a robe reaching down to his feet and with a golden
sash around his chest. 14 His head and hair
were white like wool, as white as snow,
and his eyes were like blazing fire. 15 His
feet were like bronze glowing in a furnace,
and his voice was like the sound of rushing waters. 16 In his right hand he held sev-
en stars, and out of his mouth came a
sharp double-edged sword. His face was
like the sun shining in all its brilliance.

17 When I saw him, I fell at his feet as
though dead. Then he placed his right
hand on me and said: "Do not be afraid.
I am the First and the Last. 18 I am the Living One; I was dead, and behold I am
alive for ever and ever! And I hold the
keys of death and Hades.

19 "Write, therefore, what you have seen,
what is now and what will take place later. 20 The mystery of the seven stars that
you saw in my right hand and of the sev-
en golden lampstands is this: The seven
stars are the angels[b] of the seven churches,
and the seven lampstands are the seven
churches.

[a] 13 Daniel 7:13 [b] 20 Or *messengers*

PRAYER: THE ATTRIBUTES OF GOD

YOU are in Your holy temple, O Lord; You are on Your heavenly throne.
You observe all people; Your eyes examine them.
(Psalm 11:4)

***PAUSE** to reflect on these affirmations about the person, powers and perfection of God.*

YEAR 2 DAY 337

OT Micah 5:1-15

A Promised Ruler From Bethlehem

5 Marshal your troops, O city of
troops,[a]
for a siege is laid against us.
They will strike Israel's ruler
on the cheek with a rod.

2 "But you, Bethlehem Ephrathah,
though you are small among the
clans[b] of Judah,
out of you will come for me
one who will be ruler over Israel,
whose origins[c] are from of old,
from ancient times.[d]"

3 Therefore Israel will be abandoned
until the time when she who is in
labor gives birth
and the rest of his brothers return
to join the Israelites.

4 He will stand and shepherd his flock
in the strength of the LORD,
in the majesty of the name of the
LORD his God.
And they will live securely, for then
his greatness
will reach to the ends of the earth.
5 And he will be their peace.

[a] 1 Or *Strengthen your walls, O walled city* [b] 2 Or *rulers* [c] 2 Hebrew *goings out* [d] 2 Or *from days of eternity*

Deliverance and Destruction

When the Assyrian invades our land
and marches through our fortresses,
we will raise against him seven
shepherds,
even eight leaders of men.
6 They will rule[e] the land of Assyria
with the sword,
the land of Nimrod with drawn
sword.[f]
He will deliver us from the Assyrian
when he invades our land
and marches into our borders.

7 The remnant of Jacob will be
in the midst of many peoples
like dew from the LORD,
like showers on the grass,
which do not wait for man
or linger for mankind.
8 The remnant of Jacob will be among
the nations,
in the midst of many peoples,
like a lion among the beasts of the
forest,
like a young lion among flocks of
sheep,
which mauls and mangles as it goes,
and no one can rescue.
9 Your hand will be lifted up in triumph
over your enemies,
and all your foes will be destroyed.

10 "In that day," declares the LORD,

"I will destroy your horses from
among you
and demolish your chariots.
11 I will destroy the cities of your land
and tear down all your strongholds.
12 I will destroy your witchcraft
and you will no longer cast spells.
13 I will destroy your carved images
and your sacred stones from among
you;
you will no longer bow down
to the work of your hands.
14 I will uproot from among you your
Asherah poles[g]
and demolish your cities.
15 I will take vengeance in anger and
wrath
upon the nations that have not
obeyed me."

[e] 6 Or *crush* [f] 6 Or *Nimrod in its gates* [g] 14 That is, symbols of the goddess Asherah

PRAYER: CONFESSION

SEARCH me, O God, and know my heart; try me and know my anxious thoughts. See if there is any wicked way in me, and lead me in the way everlasting. (Psalm 139:23–24)

***ASK** the Spirit to search your heart and reveal any areas of unconfessed sin. Acknowledge these to the Lord and thank Him for His forgiveness.*

NT Revelation 2:1-11

To the Church in Ephesus

2 "To the angel[a] of the church in Ephesus
write:

These are the words of him who
holds the seven stars in his right
hand and walks among the seven
golden lampstands: 2 I know your
deeds, your hard work and your perseverance. I know that you cannot
tolerate wicked men, that you have
tested those who claim to be apostles
but are not, and have found them
false. 3 You have persevered and have
endured hardships for my name, and
have not grown weary.
4 Yet I hold this against you: You
have forsaken your first love. 5 Remember the height from which you have
fallen! Repent and do the things you
did at first. If you do not repent, I will
come to you and remove your lampstand from its place. 6 But you have this
in your favor: You hate the practices of
the Nicolaitans, which I also hate.
7 He who has an ear, let him hear
what the Spirit says to the churches.
To him who overcomes, I will give
the right to eat from the tree of life,
which is in the paradise of God.

[a] 1 Or *messenger;* also in verses 8, 12 and 18

To the Church in Smyrna

[8] "To the angel of the church in Smyrna write:

These are the words of him who is the First and the Last, who died and came to life again. [9] I know your afflictions and your poverty—yet you are rich! I know the slander of those who say they are Jews and are not, but are a synagogue of Satan. [10] Do
not be afraid of what you are about to suffer. I tell you, the devil will put some of you in prison to test you, and you will suffer persecution for ten days. Be faithful, even to the point of death, and I will give you the crown of life.

[11] He who has an ear, let him hear what the Spirit says to the churches. He who overcomes will not be hurt at all by the second death.

PRAYER: THE WORKS OF GOD

I GIVE honor and praise to You, O Christ, for You are the head of the body, the church; You are the beginning and the firstborn from among the dead, so that in everything You might have supremacy.

(Colossians 1:18)

***TAKE** a moment to consider the greatness of God's wonderful works.*

YEAR 2 DAY 338

OT Micah 6:1–16

The LORD's Case Against Israel

6 Listen to what the LORD says:

"Stand up, plead your case before the mountains;
let the hills hear what you have to say.
[2] Hear, O mountains, the LORD's accusation;
listen, you everlasting foundations of the earth.
For the LORD has a case against his people;
he is lodging a charge against Israel.

[3] "My people, what have I done to you?
How have I burdened you? Answer me.
[4] I brought you up out of Egypt
and redeemed you from the land of slavery.
I sent Moses to lead you,
also Aaron and Miriam.
[5] My people, remember
what Balak king of Moab counseled
and what Balaam son of Beor answered.
Remember ⌞your journey⌟ from Shittim to Gilgal,
that you may know the righteous acts of the LORD."

[6] With what shall I come before the LORD
and bow down before the exalted God?
Shall I come before him with burnt offerings,
with calves a year old?
[7] Will the LORD be pleased with thousands of rams,
with ten thousand rivers of oil?
Shall I offer my firstborn for my transgression,
the fruit of my body for the sin of my soul?
[8] He has showed you, O man, what is good.
And what does the LORD require of you?
To act justly and to love mercy
and to walk humbly with your God.

Israel's Guilt and Punishment

[9] Listen! The LORD is calling to the city—
and to fear your name is wisdom—
"Heed the rod and the One who appointed it.[a]

[a] 9 The meaning of the Hebrew for this line is uncertain.

[10]Am I still to forget, O wicked house,
your ill-gotten treasures
and the short ephah,[b] which is
accursed?
[11]Shall I acquit a man with dishonest
scales,
with a bag of false weights?
[12]Her rich men are violent;
her people are liars
and their tongues speak deceitfully.
[13]Therefore, I have begun to destroy you,
to ruin you because of your sins.
[14]You will eat but not be satisfied;
your stomach will still be empty.[c]
You will store up but save nothing,
because what you save I will give to
the sword.
[15]You will plant but not harvest;
you will press olives but not use the
oil on yourselves,
you will crush grapes but not drink
the wine.
[16]You have observed the statutes of Omri
and all the practices of Ahab's house,
and you have followed their
traditions.
Therefore I will give you over to ruin
and your people to derision;
you will bear the scorn of the
nations.[d]"

[b] *10* An ephah was a dry measure. [c] *14* The meaning of the Hebrew for this word is uncertain. [d] *16* Septuagint; Hebrew *scorn due my people*

PRAYER: RENEWAL

MAY I continue in Your grace, O God. I do not consider my life dear to me, if only I may finish my course and the ministry which I received from the Lord Jesus, to testify to the gospel of Your grace. (Acts 13:43; 20:24)

***PAUSE** to add your own prayers for personal renewal.*

NT Revelation 2:12–17

To the Church in Pergamum

[12]"To the angel of the church in Pergamum write:

These are the words of him who
has the sharp, double-edged sword.
[13]I know where you live—where Satan has his throne. Yet you remain
true to my name. You did not renounce your faith in me, even in the
days of Antipas, my faithful witness,
who was put to death in your city—
where Satan lives.
[14]Nevertheless, I have a few things
against you: You have people there
who hold to the teaching of Balaam,
who taught Balak to entice the Israelites to sin by eating food sacrificed
to idols and by committing sexual
immorality.
[15]Likewise you also have
those who hold to the teaching of the
Nicolaitans.
[16]Repent therefore! Otherwise, I will soon come to you and
will fight against them with the
sword of my mouth.
[17]He who has an ear, let him hear
what the Spirit says to the churches.
To him who overcomes, I will give
some of the hidden manna. I will
also give him a white stone with a
new name written on it, known only
to him who receives it.

PRAYER: MY RELATIONSHIP TO GOD

YOU who make me stand firm in Christ and anointed me are God; You also sealed me and gave me the Spirit in my heart as a deposit. (2 Corinthians 1:21–22)

***PAUSE** to thank God for the relationship that you enjoy with Him in Jesus Christ.*

OT Micah 7:1-20 — YEAR 2 DAY 339

Israel's Misery

7 What misery is mine!
I am like one who gathers summer fruit
at the gleaning of the vineyard;
there is no cluster of grapes to eat,
none of the early figs that I crave.
2 The godly have been swept from the land;
not one upright man remains.
All men lie in wait to shed blood;
each hunts his brother with a net.
3 Both hands are skilled in doing evil;
the ruler demands gifts,
the judge accepts bribes,
the powerful dictate what they desire—
they all conspire together.
4 The best of them is like a brier,
the most upright worse than a thorn hedge.
The day of your watchmen has come,
the day God visits you.
Now is the time of their confusion.
5 Do not trust a neighbor;
put no confidence in a friend.
Even with her who lies in your embrace
be careful of your words.
6 For a son dishonors his father,
a daughter rises up against her mother,
a daughter-in-law against her mother-in-law—
a man's enemies are the members of his own household.

7 But as for me, I watch in hope for the LORD,
I wait for God my Savior;
my God will hear me.

Israel Will Rise

8 Do not gloat over me, my enemy!
Though I have fallen, I will rise.
Though I sit in darkness,
the LORD will be my light.
9 Because I have sinned against him,
I will bear the LORD's wrath,
until he pleads my case
and establishes my right.
He will bring me out into the light;
I will see his righteousness.
10 Then my enemy will see it
and will be covered with shame,
she who said to me,
"Where is the LORD your God?"
My eyes will see her downfall;
even now she will be trampled underfoot
like mire in the streets.

11 The day for building your walls will come,
the day for extending your boundaries.
12 In that day people will come to you
from Assyria and the cities of Egypt,
even from Egypt to the Euphrates
and from sea to sea
and from mountain to mountain.
13 The earth will become desolate
because of its inhabitants,
as the result of their deeds.

Prayer and Praise

14 Shepherd your people with your staff,
the flock of your inheritance,
which lives by itself in a forest,
in fertile pasturelands.[a]
Let them feed in Bashan and Gilead
as in days long ago.

15 "As in the days when you came out of Egypt,
I will show them my wonders."

16 Nations will see and be ashamed,
deprived of all their power.
They will lay their hands on their mouths
and their ears will become deaf.
17 They will lick dust like a snake,
like creatures that crawl on the ground.
They will come trembling out of their dens;
they will turn in fear to the LORD our God
and will be afraid of you.
18 Who is a God like you,
who pardons sin and forgives the transgression
of the remnant of his inheritance?
You do not stay angry forever
but delight to show mercy.

[a] 14 Or *in the middle of Carmel*

[19]You will again have compassion on us;
you will tread our sins underfoot
and hurl all our iniquities into the
depths of the sea.

[20]You will be true to Jacob,
and show mercy to Abraham,
as you pledged on oath to our fathers
in days long ago.

PRAYER: PETITION

IN my faith in You, our glorious Lord Jesus Christ, may I not show partiality to some people above others. (James 2:1) . . . Above all, give me a fervent love for others, because love covers a multitude of sins. (1 Peter 4:8)

***PAUSE** here to petition God for spiritual insight so that you might have understanding of His Word. Ask for insight into your identity in Jesus Christ: that you might know who you are, what direction your life should take and what His purpose for your life is. Offer prayers regarding your activities for this day and any special concerns you may have.*

NT Revelation 2:18–29

To the Church in Thyatira

[18]"To the angel of the church in Thyatira write:

These are the words of the Son of
God, whose eyes are like blazing fire
and whose feet are like burnished
bronze. [19]I know your deeds, your
love and faith, your service and perseverance, and that you are now doing more than you did at first.
[20]Nevertheless, I have this against
you: You tolerate that woman Jezebel, who calls herself a prophetess.
By her teaching she misleads my servants into sexual immorality and the
eating of food sacrificed to idols. [21]I
have given her time to repent of her
immorality, but she is unwilling. [22]So
I will cast her on a bed of suffering,
and I will make those who commit
adultery with her suffer intensely, unless they repent of her ways. [23]I will
strike her children dead. Then all the
churches will know that I am he who
searches hearts and minds, and I will
repay each of you according to your
deeds. [24]Now I say to the rest of you
in Thyatira, to you who do not hold
to her teaching and have not learned
Satan's so-called deep secrets (I will
not impose any other burden on
you): [25]Only hold on to what you
have until I come.
[26]To him who overcomes and does
my will to the end, I will give authority over the nations—

[27]'He will rule them with an iron
scepter;
he will dash them to pieces
like pottery'[a]—

just as I have received authority from
my Father. [28]I will also give him the
morning star. [29]He who has an ear, let
him hear what the Spirit says to the
churches.

[a] 27 Psalm 2:9

PRAYER: THE CHARACTER I WANT TO CULTIVATE

THOUGH I walk in the flesh, O God, I do not war according to the flesh. The weapons of my warfare are not fleshly, but divinely powerful to overthrow strongholds, casting down arguments and every pretension that sets itself up against the knowledge of You, O God, and taking every thought captive to the obedience of Christ. (2 Corinthians 10:3–5)

***TAKE** a moment to ask the Lord for the grace to grow in godly character.*

YEAR 2 DAY 340

OT Proverbs 31

Sayings of King Lemuel

31 The sayings of King Lemuel—an oracle[a] his mother taught him:

2 "O my son, O son of my womb,
O son of my vows,[b]
3 do not spend your strength on women,
your vigor on those who ruin kings.

4 "It is not for kings, O Lemuel—
not for kings to drink wine,
not for rulers to crave beer,
5 lest they drink and forget what the law decrees,
and deprive all the oppressed of their rights.
6 Give beer to those who are perishing,
wine to those who are in anguish;
7 let them drink and forget their poverty
and remember their misery no more.

8 "Speak up for those who cannot speak for themselves,
for the rights of all who are destitute.
9 Speak up and judge fairly;
defend the rights of the poor and needy."

Epilogue: The Wife of Noble Character

10[c] A wife of noble character who can find?
She is worth far more than rubies.
11 Her husband has full confidence in her
and lacks nothing of value.
12 She brings him good, not harm,
all the days of her life.
13 She selects wool and flax
and works with eager hands.
14 She is like the merchant ships,
bringing her food from afar.
15 She gets up while it is still dark;
she provides food for her family
and portions for her servant girls.
16 She considers a field and buys it;
out of her earnings she plants a vineyard.
17 She sets about her work vigorously;
her arms are strong for her tasks.
18 She sees that her trading is profitable,
and her lamp does not go out at night.
19 In her hand she holds the distaff
and grasps the spindle with her fingers.
20 She opens her arms to the poor
and extends her hands to the needy.
21 When it snows, she has no fear for her household;
for all of them are clothed in scarlet.
22 She makes coverings for her bed;
she is clothed in fine linen and purple.
23 Her husband is respected at the city gate,
where he takes his seat among the elders of the land.
24 She makes linen garments and sells them,
and supplies the merchants with sashes.
25 She is clothed with strength and dignity;
she can laugh at the days to come.
26 She speaks with wisdom,
and faithful instruction is on her tongue.
27 She watches over the affairs of her household
and does not eat the bread of idleness.
28 Her children arise and call her blessed;
her husband also, and he praises her:
29 "Many women do noble things,
but you surpass them all."
30 Charm is deceptive, and beauty is fleeting;
but a woman who fears the LORD is to be praised.
31 Give her the reward she has earned,
and let her works bring her praise at the city gate.

[a] *1* Or *of Lemuel king of Massa, which* [b] *2* Or / *the answer to my prayers* [c] *10* Verses 10–31 are an acrostic, each verse beginning with a successive letter of the Hebrew alphabet.

PRAYER: INTERCESSION

WE should always thank You, O God, for other believers, mentioning them in our prayers. (1 Thessalonians 1:2)

***TAKE** a few moments to intercede on behalf of other believers, such as your personal friends, those in ministry and those who are oppressed and in need.*

NT Revelation 3:1-13

To the Church in Sardis

3 "To the angel[a] of the church in Sardis write:

These are the words of him who holds the seven spirits[b] of God and the seven stars. I know your deeds; you have a reputation of being alive, but you are dead. 2Wake up! Strengthen what remains and is about to die, for I have not found your deeds complete in the sight of my God. 3Remember, therefore, what you have received and heard; obey it, and repent. But if you do not wake up, I will come like a thief, and you will not know at what time I will come to you.

4Yet you have a few people in Sardis who have not soiled their clothes. They will walk with me, dressed in white, for they are worthy. 5He who overcomes will, like them, be dressed in white. I will never blot out his name from the book of life, but will acknowledge his name before my Father and his angels. 6He who has an ear, let him hear what the Spirit says to the churches.

To the Church in Philadelphia

7"To the angel of the church in Philadelphia write:

These are the words of him who is holy and true, who holds the key of David. What he opens no one can shut, and what he shuts no one can open. 8I know your deeds. See, I have placed before you an open door that no one can shut. I know that you have little strength, yet you have kept my word and have not denied my name. 9I will make those who are of the synagogue of Satan, who claim to be Jews though they are not, but are liars—I will make them come and fall down at your feet and acknowledge that I have loved you. 10Since you have kept my command to endure patiently, I will also keep you from the hour of trial that is going to come upon the whole world to test those who live on the earth.

11I am coming soon. Hold on to what you have, so that no one will take your crown. 12Him who overcomes I will make a pillar in the temple of my God. Never again will he leave it. I will write on him the name of my God and the name of the city of my God, the new Jerusalem, which is coming down out of heaven from my God; and I will also write on him my new name. 13He who has an ear, let him hear what the Spirit says to the churches.

[a] *1* Or *messenger;* also in verses 7 and 14 [b] *1* Or *the sevenfold Spirit*

PRAYER: MY RELATIONSHIP TO OTHERS

WE should consider how to stir up one another to love and to do good works. (Hebrews 10:24) . . . We should all be of one mind and be sympathetic, loving as brothers and sisters, compassionate and humble. (1 Peter 3:8)

***PAUSE** to review your relationships with others and to commit them to the Lord.*

YEAR 2 DAY 341

OT Nahum 1:1–2:13

1 An oracle concerning Nineveh. The book of the vision of Nahum the Elkoshite.

The LORD's Anger Against Nineveh

2 The LORD is a jealous and avenging
God;
the LORD takes vengeance and is
filled with wrath.
The LORD takes vengeance on his foes
and maintains his wrath against his
enemies.
3 The LORD is slow to anger and great in
power;
the LORD will not leave the guilty
unpunished.
His way is in the whirlwind and the
storm,
and clouds are the dust of his feet.
4 He rebukes the sea and dries it up;
he makes all the rivers run dry.
Bashan and Carmel wither
and the blossoms of Lebanon fade.
5 The mountains quake before him
and the hills melt away.
The earth trembles at his presence,
the world and all who live in it.
6 Who can withstand his indignation?
Who can endure his fierce anger?
His wrath is poured out like fire;
the rocks are shattered before him.

7 The LORD is good,
a refuge in times of trouble.
He cares for those who trust in him,
8 but with an overwhelming flood
he will make an end of ⌊Nineveh⌋;
he will pursue his foes into
darkness.

9 Whatever they plot against the LORD
he[a] will bring to an end;
trouble will not come a second
time.
10 They will be entangled among thorns
and drunk from their wine;
they will be consumed like dry
stubble.[b]
11 From you, ⌊O Nineveh,⌋ has one come
forth
who plots evil against the LORD
and counsels wickedness.

12 This is what the LORD says:

"Although they have allies and are
numerous,
they will be cut off and pass away.
Although I have afflicted you,
⌊O Judah,⌋
I will afflict you no more.
13 Now I will break their yoke from your
neck
and tear your shackles away."

14 The LORD has given a command
concerning you, ⌊Nineveh⌋:
"You will have no descendants to
bear your name.
I will destroy the carved images and
cast idols
that are in the temple of your gods.
I will prepare your grave,
for you are vile."

15 Look, there on the mountains,
the feet of one who brings good
news,
who proclaims peace!
Celebrate your festivals, O Judah,
and fulfill your vows.
No more will the wicked invade you;
they will be completely destroyed.

Nineveh to Fall

2 An attacker advances against you,
⌊Nineveh⌋.
Guard the fortress,
watch the road,
brace yourselves,
marshal all your strength!

2 The LORD will restore the splendor of
Jacob
like the splendor of Israel,
though destroyers have laid them
waste
and have ruined their vines.

3 The shields of his soldiers are red;
the warriors are clad in scarlet.
The metal on the chariots flashes
on the day they are made ready;
the spears of pine are brandished.[c]
4 The chariots storm through the streets,

[a] 9 Or *What do you foes plot against the LORD? / He*
[b] 10 The meaning of the Hebrew for this verse is uncertain. [c] 3 Hebrew; Septuagint and Syriac / *the horsemen rush to and fro*

rushing back and forth through the
squares.
They look like flaming torches;
they dart about like lightning.

5 He summons his picked troops,
yet they stumble on their way.
They dash to the city wall;
the protective shield is put in place.
6 The river gates are thrown open
and the palace collapses.
7 It is decreed[d] that ⌞the city⌟
be exiled and carried away.
Its slave girls moan like doves
and beat upon their breasts.
8 Nineveh is like a pool,
and its water is draining away.
"Stop! Stop!" they cry,
but no one turns back.
9 Plunder the silver!
Plunder the gold!
The supply is endless,
the wealth from all its treasures!
10 She is pillaged, plundered, stripped!
Hearts melt, knees give way,
bodies tremble, every face grows
pale.

11 Where now is the lions' den,
the place where they fed their
young,
where the lion and lioness went,
and the cubs, with nothing to fear?
12 The lion killed enough for his cubs
and strangled the prey for his mate,
filling his lairs with the kill
and his dens with the prey.

13 "I am against you,"
declares the LORD Almighty.
"I will burn up your chariots in
smoke,
and the sword will devour your
young lions.
I will leave you no prey on the
earth.
The voices of your messengers
will no longer be heard."

[d] 7 The meaning of the Hebrew for this word is uncertain.

PRAYER: AFFIRMATION

O GOD, You made known to us the mystery of Your will according to Your good pleasure, which You purposed in Yourself, that in the fullness of the times, You might gather together all things in Christ, things in the heavens and things upon the earth. (Ephesians 1:9–10)

***PAUSE** to reflect on these Biblical affirmations.*

NT Revelation 3:14–22

To the Church in Laodicea

14 "To the angel of the church in Laodicea write:

These are the words of the Amen, the faithful and true witness, the ruler of God's creation. 15 I know your deeds, that you are neither cold nor hot. I wish you were either one or the other! 16 So, because you are lukewarm—neither hot nor cold—I am about to spit you out of my mouth. 17 You say, 'I am rich; I have acquired wealth and do not need a thing.' But you do not realize that you are wretched, pitiful, poor, blind and naked. 18 I counsel you to buy from me gold refined in the fire, so you can become rich; and white clothes to wear, so you can cover your shameful nakedness; and salve to put on your eyes, so you can see.

19 Those whom I love I rebuke and discipline. So be earnest, and repent.
20 Here I am! I stand at the door and knock. If anyone hears my voice and opens the door, I will come in and eat with him, and he with me.
21 To him who overcomes, I will give the right to sit with me on my throne, just as I overcame and sat down with my Father on his throne.
22 He who has an ear, let him hear what the Spirit says to the churches."

PRAYER: THE ATTRIBUTES OF GOD

I WILL give thanks to You, O Lord, because of Your righteousness. I will sing praise to Your name, O Lord Most High. (Psalm 7:17) . . . My soul magnifies You, O Lord, and my spirit rejoices in You, God my Savior, for You, Mighty One, have done great things for me, and holy is Your name. Your mercy is on those who fear You, from generation to generation. (Luke 1:46–47, 49–50)

***PAUSE** to reflect on these affirmations about the person, powers and perfection of God.*

YEAR 2 DAY 342

OT Nahum 3:1–19

Woe to Nineveh

3 Woe to the city of blood,
full of lies,
full of plunder,
never without victims!
2 The crack of whips,
the clatter of wheels,
galloping horses
and jolting chariots!
3 Charging cavalry,
flashing swords
and glittering spears!
Many casualties,
piles of dead,
bodies without number,
people stumbling over the corpses—
4 all because of the wanton lust of a harlot,
alluring, the mistress of sorceries,
who enslaved nations by her prostitution
and peoples by her witchcraft.

5 "I am against you," declares the LORD Almighty.
"I will lift your skirts over your face.
I will show the nations your nakedness
and the kingdoms your shame.
6 I will pelt you with filth,
I will treat you with contempt
and make you a spectacle.
7 All who see you will flee from you and say,
'Nineveh is in ruins—who will mourn for her?'
Where can I find anyone to comfort you?"

8 Are you better than Thebes,[a]
situated on the Nile,
with water around her?
The river was her defense,
the waters her wall.
9 Cush[b] and Egypt were her boundless strength;
Put and Libya were among her allies.
10 Yet she was taken captive
and went into exile.
Her infants were dashed to pieces
at the head of every street.
Lots were cast for her nobles,
and all her great men were put in chains.
11 You too will become drunk;
you will go into hiding
and seek refuge from the enemy.

12 All your fortresses are like fig trees
with their first ripe fruit;
when they are shaken,
the figs fall into the mouth of the eater.
13 Look at your troops—
they are all women!
The gates of your land
are wide open to your enemies;
fire has consumed their bars.

14 Draw water for the siege,
strengthen your defenses!
Work the clay,
tread the mortar,
repair the brickwork!
15 There the fire will devour you;
the sword will cut you down

[a] 8 Hebrew *No Amon* [b] 9 That is, the upper Nile region

and, like grasshoppers, consume
you.
Multiply like grasshoppers,
multiply like locusts!
16 You have increased the number of
your merchants
till they are more than the stars of
the sky,
but like locusts they strip the land
and then fly away.
17 Your guards are like locusts,
your officials like swarms of locusts
that settle in the walls on a cold
day—
but when the sun appears they fly
away,
and no one knows where.

18 O king of Assyria, your shepherds[c]
slumber;
your nobles lie down to rest.
Your people are scattered on the
mountains
with no one to gather them.
19 Nothing can heal your wound;
your injury is fatal.
Everyone who hears the news about
you
claps his hands at your fall,
for who has not felt
your endless cruelty?

[c] 18 Or *rulers*

PRAYER: THANKSGIVING

BECAUSE You live forever, Jesus, You have a permanent priesthood. Therefore You are also able to save completely those who come to God through You, since You always live to intercede for them. (Hebrews 7:24–25) . . . I can say with confidence, "You, O Lord, are my helper; I will not be afraid. What can anyone do to me?" (Hebrews 13:6)

***PAUSE** to offer your own expressions of thanksgiving.*

NT Revelation 4:1–11

The Throne in Heaven

4 After this I looked, and there before me
was a door standing open in heaven.
And the voice I had first heard speaking to
me like a trumpet said, "Come up here,
and I will show you what must take place
after this." 2 At once I was in the Spirit, and
there before me was a throne in heaven
with someone sitting on it. 3 And the one
who sat there had the appearance of jasper
and carnelian. A rainbow, resembling an
emerald, encircled the throne. 4 Surrounding the throne were twenty-four other
thrones, and seated on them were twenty-
four elders. They were dressed in white
and had crowns of gold on their heads.
5 From the throne came flashes of lightning, rumblings and peals of thunder. Before the throne, seven lamps were blazing.
These are the seven spirits[a] of God. 6 Also
before the throne there was what looked
like a sea of glass, clear as crystal.

In the center, around the throne, were
four living creatures, and they were covered with eyes, in front and in back. 7 The
first living creature was like a lion, the second was like an ox, the third had a face
like a man, the fourth was like a flying eagle. 8 Each of the four living creatures had
six wings and was covered with eyes all
around, even under his wings. Day and
night they never stop saying:

"Holy, holy, holy
is the Lord God Almighty,
who was, and is, and is to come."

9 Whenever the living creatures give glory,
honor and thanks to him who sits on the
throne and who lives for ever and ever,
10 the twenty-four elders fall down before
him who sits on the throne, and worship
him who lives for ever and ever. They lay
their crowns before the throne and say:

11 "You are worthy, our Lord and God,
to receive glory and honor and
power,
for you created all things,
and by your will they were created
and have their being."

[a] 5 Or *the sevenfold Spirit*

PRAYER: THE WORKS OF GOD

O SERVANT of God, people despised and rejected You; You were a man of sorrows, and acquainted with grief. And like one from whom others hide their faces, You were despised, and we did not esteem You. Surely You have borne our infirmities and carried our sorrows; yet we considered You stricken, smitten by God, and afflicted. But You were pierced for our transgressions, You were crushed for our iniquities; the punishment that brought us peace was upon You, and by Your wounds we are healed. All of us like sheep have gone astray, all of us have turned to our own way, and the Lord has laid on You the iniquity of us all. (Isaiah 53:3–6)

***TAKE** a moment to consider the greatness of God's wonderful works.*

YEAR 2 DAY 343

OT Psalms 144–145

Psalm 144

Of David.

1 Praise be to the LORD my Rock,
who trains my hands for war,
my fingers for battle.
2 He is my loving God and my fortress,
my stronghold and my deliverer,
my shield, in whom I take refuge,
who subdues peoples[a] under me.

3 O LORD, what is man that you care for him,
the son of man that you think of him?
4 Man is like a breath;
his days are like a fleeting shadow.

5 Part your heavens, O LORD, and come down;
touch the mountains, so that they smoke.
6 Send forth lightning and scatter ⌊the enemies⌋;
shoot your arrows and rout them.
7 Reach down your hand from on high;
deliver me and rescue me
from the mighty waters,
from the hands of foreigners
8 whose mouths are full of lies,
whose right hands are deceitful.

9 I will sing a new song to you, O God;
on the ten-stringed lyre I will make music to you,
10 to the One who gives victory to kings,
who delivers his servant David from the deadly sword.
11 Deliver me and rescue me
from the hands of foreigners
whose mouths are full of lies,
whose right hands are deceitful.

12 Then our sons in their youth
will be like well-nurtured plants,
and our daughters will be like pillars
carved to adorn a palace.
13 Our barns will be filled
with every kind of provision.
Our sheep will increase by thousands,
by tens of thousands in our fields;
14 our oxen will draw heavy loads.[b]
There will be no breaching of walls,
no going into captivity,
no cry of distress in our streets.

15 Blessed are the people of whom this is true;
blessed are the people whose God is the LORD.

Psalm 145[c]

A psalm of praise. Of David.

1 I will exalt you, my God the King;

[a] 2 Many manuscripts of the Masoretic Text, Dead Sea Scrolls, Aquila, Jerome and Syriac; most manuscripts of the Masoretic Text *subdues my people*
[b] 14 Or *our chieftains will be firmly established*
[c] This psalm is an acrostic poem, the verses of which (including verse 13b) begin with the successive letters of the Hebrew alphabet.

I will praise your name for ever and
ever.
[2] Every day I will praise you
and extol your name for ever and
ever.

[3] Great is the LORD and most worthy of
praise;
his greatness no one can fathom.
[4] One generation will commend your
works to another;
they will tell of your mighty acts.
[5] They will speak of the glorious
splendor of your majesty,
and I will meditate on your
wonderful works.[d]
[6] They will tell of the power of your
awesome works,
and I will proclaim your great
deeds.
[7] They will celebrate your abundant
goodness
and joyfully sing of your
righteousness.

[8] The LORD is gracious and
compassionate,
slow to anger and rich in love.
[9] The LORD is good to all;
he has compassion on all he has
made.
[10] All you have made will praise you,
O LORD;
your saints will extol you.
[11] They will tell of the glory of your
kingdom
and speak of your might,
[12] so that all men may know of your
mighty acts
and the glorious splendor of your
kingdom.
[13] Your kingdom is an everlasting
kingdom,
and your dominion endures
through all generations.

The LORD is faithful to all his promises
and loving toward all he has made.[e]
[14] The LORD upholds all those who fall
and lifts up all who are bowed
down.
[15] The eyes of all look to you,
and you give them their food at the
proper time.
[16] You open your hand
and satisfy the desires of every
living thing.

[17] The LORD is righteous in all his ways
and loving toward all he has made.
[18] The LORD is near to all who call on
him,
to all who call on him in truth.
[19] He fulfills the desires of those who
fear him;
he hears their cry and saves them.
[20] The LORD watches over all who love
him,
but all the wicked he will destroy.

[21] My mouth will speak in praise of the
LORD.
Let every creature praise his holy
name
for ever and ever.

[d] 5 Dead Sea Scrolls and Syriac (see also Septuagint); Masoretic Text *On the glorious splendor of your majesty / and on your wonderful works I will meditate* [e] 13 One manuscript of the Masoretic Text, Dead Sea Scrolls and Syriac (see also Septuagint); most manuscripts of the Masoretic Text do not have the last two lines of verse 13.

PRAYER: ADORATION

I WILL enter Your gates with thanksgiving, O Lord, and Your courts with praise; I will give thanks to You and bless Your name. For You are good and Your loving-kindness endures forever; Your faithfulness continues through all generations. (Psalm 100:4–5)

***PAUSE** to express your thoughts of praise and worship.*

NT Revelation 5:1-14

The Scroll and the Lamb

5 Then I saw in the right hand of him
who sat on the throne a scroll with
writing on both sides and sealed with sev-
en seals. [2] And I saw a mighty angel proclaiming in a loud voice, "Who is worthy

to break the seals and open the scroll?"
[3]But no one in heaven or on earth or under the earth could open the scroll or even look inside it. [4]I wept and wept because no one was found who was worthy to open the scroll or look inside. [5]Then one of the elders said to me, "Do not weep! See, the Lion of the tribe of Judah, the Root of David, has triumphed. He is able to open the scroll and its seven seals."

[6]Then I saw a Lamb, looking as if it had been slain, standing in the center of the throne, encircled by the four living creatures and the elders. He had seven horns and seven eyes, which are the seven spirits[a] of God sent out into all the earth. [7]He came and took the scroll from the right hand of him who sat on the throne. [8]And when he had taken it, the four living creatures and the twenty-four elders fell down before the Lamb. Each one had a harp and they were holding golden bowls full of incense, which are the prayers of the saints. [9]And they sang a new song:

"You are worthy to take the scroll
and to open its seals,
because you were slain,
and with your blood you purchased
men for God
from every tribe and language and
people and nation.
[10]You have made them to be a kingdom
and priests to serve our God,
and they will reign on the earth."

[11]Then I looked and heard the voice of many angels, numbering thousands upon thousands, and ten thousand times ten thousand. They encircled the throne and the living creatures and the elders. [12]In a loud voice they sang:

"Worthy is the Lamb, who was slain,
to receive power and wealth and
wisdom and strength
and honor and glory and praise!"

[13]Then I heard every creature in heaven and on earth and under the earth and on the sea, and all that is in them, singing:

"To him who sits on the throne and
to the Lamb
be praise and honor and glory and
power,
for ever and ever!"

[14]The four living creatures said, "Amen," and the elders fell down and worshiped.

[a] 6 Or *the sevenfold Spirit*

PRAYER: MY RELATIONSHIP TO GOD

O GOD, You said, "Let light shine out of darkness"; You made Your light shine in my heart to give me the light of the knowledge of Your glory in the face of Christ. But I have this treasure in an earthen vessel to show that this all-surpassing power is from You, O God, and not from me. (2 Corinthians 4:6–7)

***PAUSE** to thank God for the relationship that you enjoy with Him in Jesus Christ.*

YEAR 2 DAY 344

OT Habakkuk 1:1–2:20

1 The oracle that Habakkuk the prophet received.

Habakkuk's Complaint

[2]How long, O LORD, must I call for
help,
but you do not listen?
Or cry out to you, "Violence!"
but you do not save?
[3]Why do you make me look at
injustice?
Why do you tolerate wrong?
Destruction and violence are before
me;
there is strife, and conflict abounds.
[4]Therefore the law is paralyzed,
and justice never prevails.
The wicked hem in the righteous,

so that justice is perverted.

The LORD's Answer

[5] "Look at the nations and watch—
and be utterly amazed.
For I am going to do something in your days
that you would not believe,
even if you were told.
[6] I am raising up the Babylonians,[a]
that ruthless and impetuous people,
who sweep across the whole earth
to seize dwelling places not their own.
[7] They are a feared and dreaded people;
they are a law to themselves
and promote their own honor.
[8] Their horses are swifter than leopards,
fiercer than wolves at dusk.
Their cavalry gallops headlong;
their horsemen come from afar.
They fly like a vulture swooping to devour;
[9] they all come bent on violence.
Their hordes[b] advance like a desert wind
and gather prisoners like sand.
[10] They deride kings
and scoff at rulers.
They laugh at all fortified cities;
they build earthen ramps and capture them.
[11] Then they sweep past like the wind and go on—
guilty men, whose own strength is their god."

Habakkuk's Second Complaint

[12] O LORD, are you not from everlasting?
My God, my Holy One, we will not die.
O LORD, you have appointed them to execute judgment;
O Rock, you have ordained them to punish.
[13] Your eyes are too pure to look on evil;
you cannot tolerate wrong.
Why then do you tolerate the treacherous?
Why are you silent while the wicked
swallow up those more righteous than themselves?
[14] You have made men like fish in the sea,
like sea creatures that have no ruler.
[15] The wicked foe pulls all of them up with hooks,
he catches them in his net,
he gathers them up in his dragnet;
and so he rejoices and is glad.
[16] Therefore he sacrifices to his net
and burns incense to his dragnet,
for by his net he lives in luxury
and enjoys the choicest food.
[17] Is he to keep on emptying his net,
destroying nations without mercy?

2 I will stand at my watch
and station myself on the ramparts;
I will look to see what he will say to me,
and what answer I am to give to this complaint.[c]

The LORD's Answer

[2] Then the LORD replied:

"Write down the revelation
and make it plain on tablets
so that a herald[d] may run with it.
[3] For the revelation awaits an appointed time;
it speaks of the end
and will not prove false.
Though it linger, wait for it;
it[e] will certainly come and will not delay.

[4] "See, he is puffed up;
his desires are not upright—
but the righteous will live by his faith[f]—
[5] indeed, wine betrays him;
he is arrogant and never at rest.
Because he is as greedy as the grave[g]
and like death is never satisfied,
he gathers to himself all the nations
and takes captive all the peoples.

[6] "Will not all of them taunt him with ridicule and scorn, saying,

" 'Woe to him who piles up stolen goods
and makes himself wealthy by extortion!
How long must this go on?'
[7] Will not your debtors[h] suddenly arise?

[a] 6 Or *Chaldeans* [b] 9 The meaning of the Hebrew for this word is uncertain. [c] 1 Or *and what to answer when I am rebuked* [d] 2 Or *so that whoever reads it* [e] 3 Or *Though he linger, wait for him; / he* [f] 4 Or *faithfulness* [g] 5 Hebrew *Sheol* [h] 7 Or *creditors*

Will they not wake up and make
you tremble?
Then you will become their victim.
[8] Because you have plundered many
nations,
the peoples who are left will
plunder you.
For you have shed man's blood;
you have destroyed lands and cities
and everyone in them.

[9] "Woe to him who builds his realm by
unjust gain
to set his nest on high,
to escape the clutches of ruin!
[10] You have plotted the ruin of many
peoples,
shaming your own house and
forfeiting your life.
[11] The stones of the wall will cry out,
and the beams of the woodwork
will echo it.

[12] "Woe to him who builds a city with
bloodshed
and establishes a town by crime!
[13] Has not the LORD Almighty determined
that the people's labor is only fuel
for the fire,
that the nations exhaust themselves
for nothing?
[14] For the earth will be filled with the
knowledge of the glory of the
LORD,
as the waters cover the sea.

[15] "Woe to him who gives drink to his
neighbors,
pouring it from the wineskin till
they are drunk,
so that he can gaze on their naked
bodies.
[16] You will be filled with shame instead
of glory.
Now it is your turn! Drink and be
exposed[i]!
The cup from the LORD's right hand is
coming around to you,
and disgrace will cover your glory.
[17] The violence you have done to
Lebanon will overwhelm you,
and your destruction of animals
will terrify you.
For you have shed man's blood;
you have destroyed lands and cities
and everyone in them.

[18] "Of what value is an idol, since a man
has carved it?
Or an image that teaches lies?
For he who makes it trusts in his own
creation;
he makes idols that cannot speak.
[19] Woe to him who says to wood, 'Come
to life!'
Or to lifeless stone, 'Wake up!'
Can it give guidance?
It is covered with gold and silver;
there is no breath in it.
[20] But the LORD is in his holy temple;
let all the earth be silent before
him."

[i] *16* Masoretic Text; Dead Sea Scrolls, Aquila, Vulgate and Syriac (see also Septuagint) *and stagger*

PRAYER: CONFESSION

SAVE me from bloodguilt, O God, the God of my salvation, and my tongue will sing aloud of Your righteousness. O Lord, open my lips, and my mouth will declare Your praise. For You do not desire sacrifice, or I would bring it; You do not delight in burnt offerings. The sacrifices You desire are a broken spirit; a broken and contrite heart, O God, You will not despise. (Psalm 51:14–17)

***ASK** the Spirit to search your heart and reveal any areas of unconfessed sin. Acknowledge these to the Lord and thank Him for His forgiveness.*

NT Revelation 6:1–17

The Seals

6 I watched as the Lamb opened the first
of the seven seals. Then I heard one of
the four living creatures say in a voice like
thunder, "Come!" [2] I looked, and there before me was a white horse! Its rider held

a bow, and he was given a crown, and he
rode out as a conqueror bent on conquest.
3When the Lamb opened the second
seal, I heard the second living creature say,
"Come!" 4Then another horse came out,
a fiery red one. Its rider was given power
to take peace from the earth and to make
men slay each other. To him was given a
large sword.
5When the Lamb opened the third seal,
I heard the third living creature say,
"Come!" I looked, and there before me
was a black horse! Its rider was holding a
pair of scales in his hand. 6Then I heard
what sounded like a voice among the four
living creatures, saying, "A quart[a] of wheat
for a day's wages,[b] and three quarts of barley for a day's wages,[b] and do not damage
the oil and the wine!"
7When the Lamb opened the fourth
seal, I heard the voice of the fourth living
creature say, "Come!" 8I looked, and there
before me was a pale horse! Its rider was
named Death, and Hades was following
close behind him. They were given power
over a fourth of the earth to kill by sword,
famine and plague, and by the wild beasts
of the earth.
9When he opened the fifth seal, I saw
under the altar the souls of those who had
been slain because of the word of God
and the testimony they had maintained.
10They called out in a loud voice, "How
long, Sovereign Lord, holy and true, until
you judge the inhabitants of the earth and
avenge our blood?" 11Then each of them
was given a white robe, and they were told
to wait a little longer, until the number of
their fellow servants and brothers who
were to be killed as they had been was
completed.
12I watched as he opened the sixth seal.
There was a great earthquake. The sun
turned black like sackcloth made of goat
hair, the whole moon turned blood red,
13and the stars in the sky fell to earth, as
late figs drop from a fig tree when shaken
by a strong wind. 14The sky receded like a
scroll, rolling up, and every mountain and
island was removed from its place.
15Then the kings of the earth, the
princes, the generals, the rich, the mighty,
and every slave and every free man hid in
caves and among the rocks of the mountains. 16They called to the mountains and
the rocks, "Fall on us and hide us from the
face of him who sits on the throne and
from the wrath of the Lamb! 17For the
great day of their wrath has come, and
who can stand?"

[a] 6 Greek *a choinix* (probably about a liter)
[b] 6 Greek *a denarius*

PRAYER: THE CHARACTER I WANT TO CULTIVATE

I WILL not say when I am tempted, "I am being tempted by God"; for You, O God, cannot be tempted by evil, nor do You tempt anyone. But each one of us is tempted when we are drawn away and enticed by our own lust. Then, after lust has conceived, it gives birth to sin; and sin, when it is full-grown, gives birth to death. (James 1:13–15) . . . Lord Jesus, as an alien and a stranger in the world, I will abstain from fleshly lusts, which war against my soul. (1 Peter 2:11)

TAKE *a moment to ask the Lord for the grace to grow in godly character.*

YEAR 2 DAY 345

OT Habakkuk 3:1–19

Habakkuk's Prayer

3 A prayer of Habakkuk the prophet. On *shigionoth*.[a]

2LORD, I have heard of your fame;
I stand in awe of your deeds,
O LORD.
Renew them in our day,
in our time make them known;

[a] 1 Probably a literary or musical term

in wrath remember mercy.

[3]God came from Teman,
the Holy One from Mount Paran. *Selah*[b]
His glory covered the heavens
and his praise filled the earth.
[4]His splendor was like the sunrise;
rays flashed from his hand,
where his power was hidden.
[5]Plague went before him;
pestilence followed his steps.
[6]He stood, and shook the earth;
he looked, and made the nations tremble.
The ancient mountains crumbled
and the age-old hills collapsed.
His ways are eternal.
[7]I saw the tents of Cushan in distress,
the dwellings of Midian in anguish.

[8]Were you angry with the rivers, O LORD?
Was your wrath against the streams?
Did you rage against the sea
when you rode with your horses
and your victorious chariots?
[9]You uncovered your bow,
you called for many arrows. *Selah*
You split the earth with rivers;
[10] the mountains saw you and writhed.
Torrents of water swept by;
the deep roared
and lifted its waves on high.

[11]Sun and moon stood still in the heavens
at the glint of your flying arrows,
at the lightning of your flashing spear.
[12]In wrath you strode through the earth
and in anger you threshed the nations.
[13]You came out to deliver your people,
to save your anointed one.
You crushed the leader of the land of wickedness,
you stripped him from head to foot. *Selah*
[14]With his own spear you pierced his head
when his warriors stormed out to scatter us,
gloating as though about to devour
the wretched who were in hiding.
[15]You trampled the sea with your horses,
churning the great waters.

[16]I heard and my heart pounded,
my lips quivered at the sound;
decay crept into my bones,
and my legs trembled.
Yet I will wait patiently for the day of calamity
to come on the nation invading us.
[17]Though the fig tree does not bud
and there are no grapes on the vines,
though the olive crop fails
and the fields produce no food,
though there are no sheep in the pen
and no cattle in the stalls,
[18]yet I will rejoice in the LORD,
I will be joyful in God my Savior.

[19]The Sovereign LORD is my strength;
he makes my feet like the feet of a deer,
he enables me to go on the heights.

For the director of music. On my stringed instruments.

[b] 3 A word of uncertain meaning; possibly a musical term; also in verses 9 and 13

PRAYER: RENEWAL

I DIED to sin; how can I live in it any longer? All of us who were baptized into You, Christ Jesus, were baptized into Your death. We are therefore buried with You through baptism into death, in order that, just as You were raised from the dead through the glory of the Father, so we too may walk in newness of life.

(Romans 6:2–4)

PAUSE *to add your own prayers for personal renewal.*

NT Revelation 7:1-8

144,000 Sealed

7 After this I saw four angels standing at
the four corners of the earth, holding
back the four winds of the earth to prevent any wind from blowing on the land
or on the sea or on any tree. 2 Then I saw
another angel coming up from the east,
having the seal of the living God. He
called out in a loud voice to the four angels who had been given power to harm
the land and the sea: 3 "Do not harm the
land or the sea or the trees until we put a
seal on the foreheads of the servants of
our God." 4 Then I heard the number of
those who were sealed: 144,000 from all
the tribes of Israel.

5 From the tribe of Judah 12,000 were sealed,
from the tribe of Reuben 12,000,
from the tribe of Gad 12,000,
6 from the tribe of Asher 12,000,
from the tribe of Naphtali 12,000,
from the tribe of Manasseh 12,000,
7 from the tribe of Simeon 12,000,
from the tribe of Levi 12,000,
from the tribe of Issachar 12,000,
8 from the tribe of Zebulun 12,000,
from the tribe of Joseph 12,000,
from the tribe of Benjamin 12,000.

PRAYER: MY RELATIONSHIP TO OTHERS

I WILL accept those whose faith is weak, without passing judgment on their opinions. Who am I to judge another's servant? Whether they stand or fall is their own master's concern. And they will stand, for You, O Lord, are able to make them stand. (Romans 14:1, 4) . . . Knowledge puffs up, but love builds up. (1 Corinthians 8:1)

***PAUSE** to review your relationships with others and to commit them to the Lord.*

YEAR 2 DAY 346

OT Zephaniah 1:1–2:15

1 The word of the LORD that came to
Zephaniah son of Cushi, the son of
Gedaliah, the son of Amariah, the son of
Hezekiah, during the reign of Josiah son
of Amon king of Judah:

Warning of Coming Destruction

2 "I will sweep away everything
from the face of the earth,"
declares the LORD.
3 "I will sweep away both men and animals;
I will sweep away the birds of the air
and the fish of the sea.
The wicked will have only heaps of rubble[a]
when I cut off man from the face of the earth,"
declares the LORD.

Against Judah

4 "I will stretch out my hand against Judah
and against all who live in Jerusalem.
I will cut off from this place every remnant of Baal,
the names of the pagan and the idolatrous priests—
5 those who bow down on the roofs
to worship the starry host,
those who bow down and swear by the LORD
and who also swear by Molech,[b]
6 those who turn back from following the LORD
and neither seek the LORD nor inquire of him.

[a] 3 The meaning of the Hebrew for this line is uncertain. [b] 5 Hebrew *Malcam,* that is, Milcom

[7]Be silent before the Sovereign LORD,
for the day of the LORD is near.
The LORD has prepared a sacrifice;
he has consecrated those he has invited.
[8]On the day of the LORD's sacrifice
I will punish the princes
and the king's sons
and all those clad
in foreign clothes.
[9]On that day I will punish
all who avoid stepping on the threshold,[c]
who fill the temple of their gods
with violence and deceit.

[10]"On that day," declares the LORD,
"a cry will go up from the Fish Gate,
wailing from the New Quarter,
and a loud crash from the hills.
[11]Wail, you who live in the market district[d];
all your merchants will be wiped out,
all who trade with[e] silver will be ruined.
[12]At that time I will search Jerusalem with lamps
and punish those who are complacent,
who are like wine left on its dregs,
who think, 'The LORD will do nothing,
either good or bad.'
[13]Their wealth will be plundered,
their houses demolished.
They will build houses
but not live in them;
they will plant vineyards
but not drink the wine.

The Great Day of the LORD

[14]"The great day of the LORD is near—
near and coming quickly.
Listen! The cry on the day of the LORD will be bitter,
the shouting of the warrior there.
[15]That day will be a day of wrath,
a day of distress and anguish,
a day of trouble and ruin,
a day of darkness and gloom,
a day of clouds and blackness,
[16]a day of trumpet and battle cry
against the fortified cities
and against the corner towers.
[17]I will bring distress on the people
and they will walk like blind men,
because they have sinned against the LORD.
Their blood will be poured out like dust
and their entrails like filth.
[18]Neither their silver nor their gold
will be able to save them
on the day of the LORD's wrath.
In the fire of his jealousy
the whole world will be consumed,
for he will make a sudden end
of all who live in the earth."

2 Gather together, gather together,
O shameful nation,
[2]before the appointed time arrives
and that day sweeps on like chaff,
before the fierce anger of the LORD comes upon you,
before the day of the LORD's wrath comes upon you.
[3]Seek the LORD, all you humble of the land,
you who do what he commands.
Seek righteousness, seek humility;
perhaps you will be sheltered
on the day of the LORD's anger.

Against Philistia

[4]Gaza will be abandoned
and Ashkelon left in ruins.
At midday Ashdod will be emptied
and Ekron uprooted.
[5]Woe to you who live by the sea,
O Kerethite people;
the word of the LORD is against you,
O Canaan, land of the Philistines.

"I will destroy you,
and none will be left."

[6]The land by the sea, where the Kerethites[f] dwell,
will be a place for shepherds and sheep pens.
[7]It will belong to the remnant of the house of Judah;
there they will find pasture.
In the evening they will lie down
in the houses of Ashkelon.
The LORD their God will care for them;
he will restore their fortunes.[g]

Against Moab and Ammon

[8]"I have heard the insults of Moab
and the taunts of the Ammonites,
who insulted my people

[c] 9 See 1 Samuel 5:5. [d] 11 Or *the Mortar* [e] 11 Or *in* [f] 6 The meaning of the Hebrew for this word is uncertain. [g] 7 Or *will bring back their captives*

and made threats against their land.
[9]Therefore, as surely as I live,"
declares the LORD Almighty, the
God of Israel,
"surely Moab will become like Sodom,
the Ammonites like Gomorrah—
a place of weeds and salt pits,
a wasteland forever.
The remnant of my people will
plunder them;
the survivors of my nation will
inherit their land."

[10]This is what they will get in return for
their pride,
for insulting and mocking the
people of the LORD Almighty.
[11]The LORD will be awesome to them
when he destroys all the gods of the
land.
The nations on every shore will
worship him,
every one in its own land.

Against Cush

[12]"You too, O Cushites,[h]
will be slain by my sword."

Against Assyria

[13]He will stretch out his hand against
the north
and destroy Assyria,
leaving Nineveh utterly desolate
and dry as the desert.
[14]Flocks and herds will lie down there,
creatures of every kind.
The desert owl and the screech owl
will roost on her columns.
Their calls will echo through the
windows,
rubble will be in the doorways,
the beams of cedar will be exposed.
[15]This is the carefree city
that lived in safety.
She said to herself,
"I am, and there is none besides me."
What a ruin she has become,
a lair for wild beasts!
All who pass by her scoff
and shake their fists.

[h] *12* That is, people from the upper Nile region

PRAYER: PETITION

AS I have been instructed how I ought to walk and to please You, O God, may I follow Paul's exhortation in the name of the Lord Jesus to do this more and more. (1 Thessalonians 4:1) . . . May I never leave You, my first love. (Revelation 2:4)

PAUSE *here to petition God for growth in love and compassion toward others. Offer prayers for your loved ones, for those who do not know Jesus and for those in need. Offer prayers regarding your activities for this day and any special concerns you may have.*

NT Revelation 7:9-17

The Great Multitude in White Robes

[9]After this I looked and there before me
was a great multitude that no one could
count, from every nation, tribe, people
and language, standing before the throne
and in front of the Lamb. They were wearing white robes and were holding palm
branches in their hands. [10]And they cried
out in a loud voice:

"Salvation belongs to our God,
who sits on the throne,
and to the Lamb."

[11]All the angels were standing around the
throne and around the elders and the four
living creatures. They fell down on their
faces before the throne and worshiped
God, [12]saying:

"Amen!
Praise and glory
and wisdom and thanks and honor
and power and strength
be to our God for ever and ever.
Amen!"

[13]Then one of the elders asked me,
"These in white robes—who are they, and
where did they come from?"
[14]I answered, "Sir, you know."
And he said, "These are they who have

come out of the great tribulation; they have
washed their robes and made them white
in the blood of the Lamb. [15]Therefore,

"they are before the throne of God
and serve him day and night in his temple;
and he who sits on the throne will
spread his tent over them.
[16]Never again will they hunger;
never again will they thirst.
The sun will not beat upon them,
nor any scorching heat.
[17]For the Lamb at the center of the throne will be their shepherd;
he will lead them to springs of living water.
And God will wipe away every tear from their eyes."

PRAYER: THE ATTRIBUTES OF GOD

BEFORE Abraham was born, You always existed, Jesus Christ. (John 8:58) . . . In You, O Christ, all the fullness of the Godhead lives in bodily form. (Colossians 2:9)

***PAUSE** to reflect on these affirmations about the person, powers and perfection of God.*

OT Zephaniah 3:1-20

YEAR 2 DAY 347

The Future of Jerusalem

3 Woe to the city of oppressors,
rebellious and defiled!
[2]She obeys no one,
she accepts no correction.
She does not trust in the LORD,
she does not draw near to her God.
[3]Her officials are roaring lions,
her rulers are evening wolves,
who leave nothing for the morning.
[4]Her prophets are arrogant;
they are treacherous men.
Her priests profane the sanctuary
and do violence to the law.
[5]The LORD within her is righteous;
he does no wrong.
Morning by morning he dispenses his justice,
and every new day he does not fail,
yet the unrighteous know no shame.

[6]"I have cut off nations;
their strongholds are demolished.
I have left their streets deserted,
with no one passing through.
Their cities are destroyed;
no one will be left—no one at all.
[7]I said to the city,
'Surely you will fear me
and accept correction!'
Then her dwelling would not be cut off,
nor all my punishments come upon her.
But they were still eager
to act corruptly in all they did.
[8]Therefore wait for me," declares the LORD,
"for the day I will stand up to testify.[a]
I have decided to assemble the nations,
to gather the kingdoms
and to pour out my wrath on them—
all my fierce anger.
The whole world will be consumed
by the fire of my jealous anger.

[9]"Then will I purify the lips of the peoples,
that all of them may call on the name of the LORD
and serve him shoulder to shoulder.
[10]From beyond the rivers of Cush[b]
my worshipers, my scattered people,
will bring me offerings.
[11]On that day you will not be put to shame
for all the wrongs you have done to me,

[a] 8 Septuagint and Syriac; Hebrew *will rise up to plunder* [b] 10 That is, the upper Nile region

because I will remove from this city
those who rejoice in their pride.
Never again will you be haughty
on my holy hill.
12 But I will leave within you
the meek and humble,
who trust in the name of the LORD.
13 The remnant of Israel will do no
wrong;
they will speak no lies,
nor will deceit be found in their
mouths.
They will eat and lie down
and no one will make them afraid."

14 Sing, O Daughter of Zion;
shout aloud, O Israel!
Be glad and rejoice with all your heart,
O Daughter of Jerusalem!
15 The LORD has taken away your
punishment,
he has turned back your enemy.
The LORD, the King of Israel, is with
you;
never again will you fear any harm.
16 On that day they will say to
Jerusalem,
"Do not fear, O Zion;
do not let your hands hang limp.
17 The LORD your God is with you,
he is mighty to save.
He will take great delight in you,
he will quiet you with his love,
he will rejoice over you with
singing."

18 "The sorrows for the appointed feasts
I will remove from you;
they are a burden and a reproach to
you.[c]
19 At that time I will deal
with all who oppressed you;
I will rescue the lame
and gather those who have been
scattered.
I will give them praise and honor
in every land where they were put
to shame.
20 At that time I will gather you;
at that time I will bring you home.
I will give you honor and praise
among all the peoples of the earth
when I restore your fortunes[d]
before your very eyes,"
says the LORD.

[c] 18 Or *"I will gather you who mourn for the appointed feasts; / your reproach is a burden to you* [d] 20 Or *I bring back your captives*

PRAYER: INTERCESSION

O LORD, may I be of the same mind with others; instead of being haughty in mind or wise in my own estimation, let me associate with the humble. (Romans 12:16) . . . From now on, may I regard no one only according to the flesh. (2 Corinthians 5:16)

***TAKE** a few moments to intercede on behalf of friends, relatives, neighbors and coworkers who do not yet know salvation in Jesus Christ.*

NT Revelation 8:1-13

The Seventh Seal and the Golden Censer

8 When he opened the seventh seal,
there was silence in heaven for about
half an hour.
2 And I saw the seven angels who stand
before God, and to them were given sev-
en trumpets.
3 Another angel, who had a golden
censer, came and stood at the altar. He
was given much incense to offer, with the
prayers of all the saints, on the golden altar before the throne. 4 The smoke of the
incense, together with the prayers of the
saints, went up before God from the angel's hand. 5 Then the angel took the
censer, filled it with fire from the altar,
and hurled it on the earth; and there came
peals of thunder, rumblings, flashes of
lightning and an earthquake.

The Trumpets

6 Then the seven angels who had the
seven trumpets prepared to sound them.
7 The first angel sounded his trumpet,
and there came hail and fire mixed with
blood, and it was hurled down upon the

earth. A third of the earth was burned up, a third of the trees were burned up, and all the green grass was burned up.

[8]The second angel sounded his trumpet, and something like a huge mountain, all ablaze, was thrown into the sea. A third of the sea turned into blood, [9]a third of the living creatures in the sea died, and a third of the ships were destroyed.

[10]The third angel sounded his trumpet, and a great star, blazing like a torch, fell from the sky on a third of the rivers and on the springs of water— [11]the name of the star is Wormwood.[a] A third of the waters turned bitter, and many people died from the waters that had become bitter.

[12]The fourth angel sounded his trumpet, and a third of the sun was struck, a third of the moon, and a third of the stars, so that a third of them turned dark. A third of the day was without light, and also a third of the night.

[13]As I watched, I heard an eagle that was flying in midair call out in a loud voice: "Woe! Woe! Woe to the inhabitants of the earth, because of the trumpet blasts about to be sounded by the other three angels!"

[a] *11* That is, Bitterness

PRAYER: THE WORKS OF GOD

LORD, You are our praise, and You are our God, who performed for the children of Israel those great and awesome wonders which they saw with their own eyes. (Deuteronomy 10:21) . . . O Lord, the things that happened to the Israelites in the wilderness were examples and were written for our admonition, upon whom the fulfillment of the ages has come. (1 Corinthians 10:11)

TAKE *a moment to consider the greatness of God's wonderful works.*

YEAR 2 DAY 348

OT Haggai 1:1–15

A Call to Build the House of the LORD

1 In the second year of King Darius, on the first day of the sixth month, the word of the LORD came through the prophet Haggai to Zerubbabel son of Shealtiel, governor of Judah, and to Joshua[a] son of Jehozadak, the high priest:

[2]This is what the LORD Almighty says: "These people say, 'The time has not yet come for the LORD's house to be built.' "

[3]Then the word of the LORD came through the prophet Haggai: [4]"Is it a time for you yourselves to be living in your paneled houses, while this house remains a ruin?"

[5]Now this is what the LORD Almighty says: "Give careful thought to your ways. [6]You have planted much, but have harvested little. You eat, but never have enough. You drink, but never have your fill. You put on clothes, but are not warm. You earn wages, only to put them in a purse with holes in it."

[7]This is what the LORD Almighty says: "Give careful thought to your ways. [8]Go up into the mountains and bring down timber and build the house, so that I may take pleasure in it and be honored," says the LORD. [9]"You expected much, but see, it turned out to be little. What you brought home, I blew away. Why?" declares the LORD Almighty. "Because of my house, which remains a ruin, while each of you is busy with his own house. [10]Therefore, because of you the heavens have withheld their dew and the earth its crops. [11]I called for a drought on the fields and the mountains, on the grain, the new wine, the oil and whatever the ground produces, on men and cattle, and on the labor of your hands."

[12]Then Zerubbabel son of Shealtiel, Joshua son of Jehozadak, the high priest, and the whole remnant of the people obeyed the voice of the LORD their God and the message of the prophet Haggai,

[a] *1* A variant of *Jeshua;* here and elsewhere in Haggai

because the LORD their God had sent him.
And the people feared the LORD.
[13]Then Haggai, the LORD's messenger,
gave this message of the LORD to the people: "I am with you," declares the LORD.
[14]So the LORD stirred up the spirit of Zerubbabel son of Shealtiel, governor of Judah, and the spirit of Joshua son of Jehozadak, the high priest, and the spirit of
the whole remnant of the people. They
came and began to work on the house of
the LORD Almighty, their God, [15]on the
twenty-fourth day of the sixth month in
the second year of King Darius.

PRAYER: AFFIRMATION

YOUR kingdom, O God, is not a matter of eating and drinking, but of righteousness and peace and joy in the Holy Spirit. (Romans 14:17) . . . The goal of our instruction is love, which comes from a pure heart and a good conscience and a sincere faith. (1 Timothy 1:5)

***PAUSE** to reflect on these Biblical affirmations.*

NT Revelation 9:1-21

9 The fifth angel sounded his trumpet,
and I saw a star that had fallen from the
sky to the earth. The star was given the key
to the shaft of the Abyss. [2]When he opened
the Abyss, smoke rose from it like the
smoke from a gigantic furnace. The sun and
sky were darkened by the smoke from the
Abyss. [3]And out of the smoke locusts came
down upon the earth and were given power like that of scorpions of the earth. [4]They
were told not to harm the grass of the earth
or any plant or tree, but only those people
who did not have the seal of God on their
foreheads. [5]They were not given power to
kill them, but only to torture them for five
months. And the agony they suffered was
like that of the sting of a scorpion when it
strikes a man. [6]During those days men will
seek death, but will not find it; they will
long to die, but death will elude them.
[7]The locusts looked like horses prepared for battle. On their heads they wore
something like crowns of gold, and their
faces resembled human faces. [8]Their hair
was like women's hair, and their teeth
were like lions' teeth. [9]They had breastplates like breastplates of iron, and the
sound of their wings was like the thun-
dering of many horses and chariots rushing into battle. [10]They had tails and stings
like scorpions, and in their tails they had
power to torment people for five months.
[11]They had as king over them the angel of
the Abyss, whose name in Hebrew is
Abaddon, and in Greek, Apollyon.[a]
[12]The first woe is past; two other woes
are yet to come.
[13]The sixth angel sounded his trumpet,
and I heard a voice coming from the
horns[b] of the golden altar that is before
God. [14]It said to the sixth angel who had
the trumpet, "Release the four angels who
are bound at the great river Euphrates."
[15]And the four angels who had been kept
ready for this very hour and day and
month and year were released to kill a
third of mankind. [16]The number of the
mounted troops was two hundred million. I heard their number.
[17]The horses and riders I saw in my vision looked like this: Their breastplates
were fiery red, dark blue, and yellow as sulfur. The heads of the horses resembled the
heads of lions, and out of their mouths
came fire, smoke and sulfur. [18]A third of
mankind was killed by the three plagues
of fire, smoke and sulfur that came out of
their mouths. [19]The power of the horses
was in their mouths and in their tails; for
their tails were like snakes, having heads
with which they inflict injury.
[20]The rest of mankind that were not
killed by these plagues still did not repent
of the work of their hands; they did not
stop worshiping demons, and idols of gold,
silver, bronze, stone and wood—idols that
cannot see or hear or walk. [21]Nor did they
repent of their murders, their magic arts,
their sexual immorality or their thefts.

[a] *11* *Abaddon* and *Apollyon* mean *Destroyer.*
[b] *13* That is, projections

PRAYER: MY RELATIONSHIP TO GOD

O CHRIST, You are not weak in dealing with us but powerful among us. For though You were crucified in weakness, yet You live by the power of God. For we are weak in You, yet by the power of God we will live with You to serve others. (2 Corinthians 13:3–4)

***PAUSE** to thank God for the relationship that you enjoy with Him in Jesus Christ.*

OT Haggai 2:1–23

The Promised Glory of the New House

2 On the twenty-first day of the seventh month, the word of the LORD came through the prophet Haggai: 2"Speak to Zerubbabel son of Shealtiel, governor of Judah, to Joshua son of Jehozadak, the high priest, and to the remnant of the people. Ask them, 3'Who of you is left who saw this house in its former glory? How does it look to you now? Does it not seem to you like nothing? 4But now be strong, O Zerubbabel,' declares the LORD. 'Be strong, O Joshua son of Jehozadak, the high priest. Be strong, all you people of the land,' declares the LORD, 'and work. For I am with you,' declares the LORD Almighty. 5'This is what I covenanted with you when you came out of Egypt. And my Spirit remains among you. Do not fear.'

6"This is what the LORD Almighty says: 'In a little while I will once more shake the heavens and the earth, the sea and the dry land. 7I will shake all nations, and the desired of all nations will come, and I will fill this house with glory,' says the LORD Almighty. 8'The silver is mine and the gold is mine,' declares the LORD Almighty. 9'The glory of this present house will be greater than the glory of the former house,' says the LORD Almighty. 'And in this place I will grant peace,' declares the LORD Almighty."

Blessings for a Defiled People

10On the twenty-fourth day of the ninth month, in the second year of Darius, the word of the LORD came to the prophet Haggai: 11"This is what the LORD Almighty says: 'Ask the priests what the law says: 12If a person carries consecrated meat in the fold of his garment, and that fold touches some bread or stew, some wine, oil or other food, does it become consecrated?' "

The priests answered, "No."

13Then Haggai said, "If a person defiled by contact with a dead body touches one of these things, does it become defiled?"

"Yes," the priests replied, "it becomes defiled."

14Then Haggai said, " 'So it is with this people and this nation in my sight,' declares the LORD. 'Whatever they do and whatever they offer there is defiled.

15" 'Now give careful thought to this from this day on[a]—consider how things were before one stone was laid on another in the LORD's temple. 16When anyone came to a heap of twenty measures, there were only ten. When anyone went to a wine vat to draw fifty measures, there were only twenty. 17I struck all the work of your hands with blight, mildew and hail, yet you did not turn to me,' declares the LORD. 18'From this day on, from this twenty-fourth day of the ninth month, give careful thought to the day when the foundation of the LORD's temple was laid. Give careful thought: 19Is there yet any seed left in the barn? Until now, the vine and the fig tree, the pomegranate and the olive tree have not borne fruit.

" 'From this day on I will bless you.' "

Zerubbabel the LORD's Signet Ring

20The word of the LORD came to Haggai a second time on the twenty-fourth day of the month: 21"Tell Zerubbabel governor of Judah that I will shake the heavens and the earth. 22I will overturn royal thrones and shatter the power of the foreign kingdoms. I will overthrow chariots and their

[a] 15 *Or to the days past*

drivers; horses and their riders will fall,
each by the sword of his brother.
23" 'On that day,' declares the LORD
Almighty, 'I will take you, my servant Zerubbabel son of Shealtiel,' declares the
LORD, 'and I will make you like my signet
ring, for I have chosen you,' declares the
LORD Almighty."

PRAYER: THANKSGIVING

THIS is the confidence I have in You, O Son of God, that if I ask anything according to Your will, You hear me. And if I know that You hear me, whatever I ask, I know that I have what I have asked from You. (1 John 5:14–15) . . . You, O God, supply all my needs according to Your glorious riches in Christ Jesus. To You, my God and Father, be glory for ever and ever. (Philippians 4:19–20)

***PAUSE** to offer your own expressions of thanksgiving.*

NT Revelation 10:1-11

The Angel and the Little Scroll

10 Then I saw another mighty angel coming down from heaven. He was robed
in a cloud, with a rainbow above his head;
his face was like the sun, and his legs were
like fiery pillars. 2He was holding a little
scroll, which lay open in his hand. He
planted his right foot on the sea and his left
foot on the land, 3and he gave a loud shout
like the roar of a lion. When he shouted,
the voices of the seven thunders spoke.
4And when the seven thunders spoke, I was
about to write; but I heard a voice from
heaven say, "Seal up what the seven thunders have said and do not write it down."
5Then the angel I had seen standing on
the sea and on the land raised his right
hand to heaven. 6And he swore by him
who lives for ever and ever, who created
the heavens and all that is in them, the
earth and all that is in it, and the sea and
all that is in it, and said, "There will be no
more delay! 7But in the days when the
seventh angel is about to sound his trumpet, the mystery of God will be accomplished, just as he announced to his servants the prophets."
8Then the voice that I had heard from
heaven spoke to me once more: "Go, take
the scroll that lies open in the hand of the
angel who is standing on the sea and on
the land."
9So I went to the angel and asked him
to give me the little scroll. He said to me,
"Take it and eat it. It will turn your stomach sour, but in your mouth it will be as
sweet as honey." 10I took the little scroll
from the angel's hand and ate it. It tasted
as sweet as honey in my mouth, but when
I had eaten it, my stomach turned sour.
11Then I was told, "You must prophesy
again about many peoples, nations, languages and kings."

PRAYER: THE CHARACTER I WANT TO CULTIVATE

THE tongue, Lord Jesus, is a small part of the body, but it makes great boasts. I will consider, therefore, what a great forest is set on fire by a small spark. The tongue also is a fire, a world of evil set among the parts of the body, that corrupts the whole body, and sets the whole course of our life on fire and is set on fire by hell. (James 3:5–6) . . . Lord God, the tongue has the power of death and life, and those who love it will eat its fruit. (Proverbs 18:21)

***TAKE** a moment to ask the Lord for the grace to grow in godly character.*

OT Psalms 146–147 YEAR 2 DAY 350

Psalm 146

[1] Praise the LORD.[a]

Praise the LORD, O my soul.
[2] I will praise the LORD all my life;
I will sing praise to my God as long as I live.

[3] Do not put your trust in princes,
in mortal men, who cannot save.
[4] When their spirit departs, they return to the ground;
on that very day their plans come to nothing.

[5] Blessed is he whose help is the God of Jacob,
whose hope is in the LORD his God,
[6] the Maker of heaven and earth,
the sea, and everything in them—
the LORD, who remains faithful forever.
[7] He upholds the cause of the oppressed
and gives food to the hungry.
The LORD sets prisoners free,
[8] the LORD gives sight to the blind,
the LORD lifts up those who are bowed down,
the LORD loves the righteous.
[9] The LORD watches over the alien
and sustains the fatherless and the widow,
but he frustrates the ways of the wicked.

[10] The LORD reigns forever,
your God, O Zion, for all generations.

Praise the LORD.

Psalm 147

[1] Praise the LORD.[a]

How good it is to sing praises to our God,
how pleasant and fitting to praise him!

[2] The LORD builds up Jerusalem;
he gathers the exiles of Israel.
[3] He heals the brokenhearted
and binds up their wounds.
[4] He determines the number of the stars
and calls them each by name.
[5] Great is our Lord and mighty in power;
his understanding has no limit.
[6] The LORD sustains the humble
but casts the wicked to the ground.

[7] Sing to the LORD with thanksgiving;
make music to our God on the harp.
[8] He covers the sky with clouds;
he supplies the earth with rain
and makes grass grow on the hills.
[9] He provides food for the cattle
and for the young ravens when they call.

[10] His pleasure is not in the strength of the horse,
nor his delight in the legs of a man;
[11] the LORD delights in those who fear him,
who put their hope in his unfailing love.

[12] Extol the LORD, O Jerusalem;
praise your God, O Zion,
[13] for he strengthens the bars of your gates
and blesses your people within you.
[14] He grants peace to your borders
and satisfies you with the finest of wheat.

[15] He sends his command to the earth;
his word runs swiftly.
[16] He spreads the snow like wool
and scatters the frost like ashes.
[17] He hurls down his hail like pebbles.
Who can withstand his icy blast?
[18] He sends his word and melts them;
he stirs up his breezes, and the waters flow.

[19] He has revealed his word to Jacob,
his laws and decrees to Israel.
[20] He has done this for no other nation;
they do not know his laws.

Praise the LORD.

[a] 1 Hebrew *Hallelu Yah;* also in verse 10

PRAYER: ADORATION

MAY we glory in Your holy name, O Lord. Let the hearts of those who seek You rejoice. May we seek You and Your strength; may we seek Your face always. May we remember the wonderful works You have done, the miracles and the judgments You have pronounced. (1 Chronicles 16:10–12)

***PAUSE** to express your thoughts of praise and worship.*

NT Revelation 11:1–14

The Two Witnesses

11 I was given a reed like a measuring rod and was told, "Go and measure the temple of God and the altar, and count the worshipers there. 2But exclude the outer court; do not measure it, because it has been given to the Gentiles. They will trample on the holy city for 42 months. 3And I will give power to my two witnesses, and they will prophesy for 1,260 days, clothed in sackcloth." 4These are the two olive trees and the two lampstands that stand before the Lord of the earth. 5If anyone tries to harm them, fire comes from their mouths and devours their enemies. This is how anyone who wants to harm them must die. 6These men have power to shut up the sky so that it will not rain during the time they are prophesying; and they have power to turn the waters into blood and to strike the earth with every kind of plague as often as they want.

7Now when they have finished their testimony, the beast that comes up from the Abyss will attack them, and overpower and kill them. 8Their bodies will lie in the street of the great city, which is figuratively called Sodom and Egypt, where also their Lord was crucified. 9For three and a half days men from every people, tribe, language and nation will gaze on their bodies and refuse them burial. 10The inhabitants of the earth will gloat over them and will celebrate by sending each other gifts, because these two prophets had tormented those who live on the earth.

11But after the three and a half days a breath of life from God entered them, and they stood on their feet, and terror struck those who saw them. 12Then they heard a loud voice from heaven saying to them, "Come up here." And they went up to heaven in a cloud, while their enemies looked on.

13At that very hour there was a severe earthquake and a tenth of the city collapsed. Seven thousand people were killed in the earthquake, and the survivors were terrified and gave glory to the God of heaven.

14The second woe has passed; the third woe is coming soon.

PRAYER: MY RELATIONSHIP TO OTHERS

IF I am righteous, I will be cautious about the friends I choose, but the ways of the wicked will lead me astray. (Proverbs 12:26) . . . I will not give cause for offense in anything, so that my ministry will not be discredited. (2 Corinthians 6:3)

***PAUSE** to review your relationships with others and to commit them to the Lord.*

OT **Zechariah 1:1–2:13** YEAR 2 DAY 351

A Call to Return to the LORD

1 In the eighth month of the second year
of Darius, the word of the LORD came to
the prophet Zechariah son of Berekiah,
the son of Iddo:
2 "The LORD was very angry with your
forefathers. 3Therefore tell the people: This
is what the LORD Almighty says: 'Return to
me,' declares the LORD Almighty, 'and I will
return to you,' says the LORD Almighty. 4Do
not be like your forefathers, to whom the
earlier prophets proclaimed: This is what
the LORD Almighty says: 'Turn from your
evil ways and your evil practices.' But they
would not listen or pay attention to me,
declares the LORD. 5Where are your forefathers now? And the prophets, do they live
forever? 6But did not my words and my decrees, which I commanded my servants
the prophets, overtake your forefathers?
"Then they repented and said, 'The
LORD Almighty has done to us what our
ways and practices deserve, just as he determined to do.' "

The Man Among the Myrtle Trees

7On the twenty-fourth day of the
eleventh month, the month of Shebat, in
the second year of Darius, the word of the
LORD came to the prophet Zechariah son
of Berekiah, the son of Iddo.
8During the night I had a vision—and
there before me was a man riding a red
horse! He was standing among the myrtle
trees in a ravine. Behind him were red,
brown and white horses.
9I asked, "What are these, my lord?"
The angel who was talking with me answered, "I will show you what they are."
10Then the man standing among the myrtle trees explained, "They are the ones the
LORD has sent to go throughout the earth."
11And they reported to the angel of the
LORD, who was standing among the myrtle trees, "We have gone throughout the
earth and found the whole world at rest
and in peace."
12Then the angel of the LORD said,
"LORD Almighty, how long will you withhold mercy from Jerusalem and from the
towns of Judah, which you have been angry with these seventy years?" 13So the
LORD spoke kind and comforting words to
the angel who talked with me.
14Then the angel who was speaking to
me said, "Proclaim this word: This is what
the LORD Almighty says: 'I am very jealous
for Jerusalem and Zion, 15but I am very
angry with the nations that feel secure. I
was only a little angry, but they added to
the calamity.'
16 "Therefore, this is what the LORD says:
'I will return to Jerusalem with mercy, and
there my house will be rebuilt. And the
measuring line will be stretched out over
Jerusalem,' declares the LORD Almighty.
17 "Proclaim further: This is what the
LORD Almighty says: 'My towns will again
overflow with prosperity, and the LORD
will again comfort Zion and choose Jerusalem.' "

Four Horns and Four Craftsmen

18Then I looked up—and there before
me were four horns! 19I asked the angel
who was speaking to me, "What are these?"
He answered me, "These are the horns
that scattered Judah, Israel and Jerusalem."
20Then the LORD showed me four craftsmen. 21I asked, "What are these coming
to do?"
He answered, "These are the horns that
scattered Judah so that no one could raise
his head, but the craftsmen have come to
terrify them and throw down these horns
of the nations who lifted up their horns
against the land of Judah to scatter its
people."

A Man With a Measuring Line

2 Then I looked up—and there before me
was a man with a measuring line in his
hand! 2I asked, "Where are you going?"
He answered me, "To measure Jerusalem, to find out how wide and how
long it is."
3Then the angel who was speaking to
me left, and another angel came to meet
him 4and said to him: "Run, tell that
young man, 'Jerusalem will be a city without walls because of the great number of
men and livestock in it. 5And I myself will
be a wall of fire around it,' declares the
LORD, 'and I will be its glory within.'

[6]"Come! Come! Flee from the land of
the north," declares the LORD, "for I have
scattered you to the four winds of heav-
en," declares the LORD.
[7]"Come, O Zion! Escape, you who live
in the Daughter of Babylon!" [8]For this is
what the LORD Almighty says: "After he
has honored me and has sent me against
the nations that have plundered you—for
whoever touches you touches the apple of
his eye— [9]I will surely raise my hand
against them so that their slaves will plunder them.[a] Then you will know that the
LORD Almighty has sent me.
[10]"Shout and be glad, O Daughter of
Zion. For I am coming, and I will live
among you," declares the LORD. [11]"Many
nations will be joined with the LORD in
that day and will become my people. I
will live among you and you will know
that the LORD Almighty has sent me to
you. [12]The LORD will inherit Judah as his
portion in the holy land and will again
choose Jerusalem. [13]Be still before the
LORD, all mankind, because he has roused
himself from his holy dwelling."

[a] 8,9 Or *says after . . . eye: 9"I . . . plunder them."*

PRAYER: CONFESSION

I WILL sing praises to You, O Lord, and give thanks at the remembrance of Your holy name. For Your anger lasts only a moment, but Your favor is for a lifetime; weeping may endure for a night, but joy comes in the morning. (Psalm 30:4–5)

ASK *the Spirit to search your heart and reveal any areas of unconfessed sin. Acknowledge these to the Lord and thank Him for His forgiveness.*

NT Revelation 11:15–19

The Seventh Trumpet

[15]The seventh angel sounded his trumpet, and there were loud voices in heaven,
which said:

"The kingdom of the world has
become the kingdom of our
Lord and of his Christ,
and he will reign for ever and ever."

[16]And the twenty-four elders, who were
seated on their thrones before God, fell on
their faces and worshiped God, [17]saying:

"We give thanks to you, Lord God
Almighty,
the One who is and who was,
because you have taken your great
power
and have begun to reign.
[18]The nations were angry;
and your wrath has come.
The time has come for judging the
dead,
and for rewarding your servants the
prophets
and your saints and those who
reverence your name,
both small and great—
and for destroying those who destroy
the earth."

[19]Then God's temple in heaven was
opened, and within his temple was seen the
ark of his covenant. And there came flashes
of lightning, rumblings, peals of thunder,
an earthquake and a great hailstorm.

PRAYER: THE ATTRIBUTES OF GOD

THERE is none like You, O Lord; You are great, and Your name is mighty in power. Who should not revere You, O King of the nations? It is Your rightful due. For among all the wise of the nations and in all their kingdoms, there is no one like You. (Jeremiah 10:6–7)

PAUSE *to reflect on these affirmations about the person, powers and perfection of God.*

YEAR 2 DAY 352

OT Zechariah 3:1–4:14

Clean Garments for the High Priest

3 Then he showed me Joshua[a] the high
priest standing before the angel of the
LORD, and Satan[b] standing at his right side
to accuse him. 2The LORD said to Satan,
"The LORD rebuke you, Satan! The LORD,
who has chosen Jerusalem, rebuke you! Is
not this man a burning stick snatched
from the fire?"
3Now Joshua was dressed in filthy
clothes as he stood before the angel. 4The
angel said to those who were standing before him, "Take off his filthy clothes."
Then he said to Joshua, "See, I have tak-
en away your sin, and I will put rich garments on you."
5Then I said, "Put a clean turban on his
head." So they put a clean turban on his
head and clothed him, while the angel of
the LORD stood by.
6The angel of the LORD gave this charge
to Joshua: 7"This is what the LORD
Almighty says: 'If you will walk in my
ways and keep my requirements, then you
will govern my house and have charge of
my courts, and I will give you a place
among these standing here.
8" 'Listen, O high priest Joshua and
your associates seated before you, who are
men symbolic of things to come: I am going to bring my servant, the Branch. 9See,
the stone I have set in front of Joshua!
There are seven eyes[c] on that one stone,
and I will engrave an inscription on it,'
says the LORD Almighty, 'and I will remove
the sin of this land in a single day.
10" 'In that day each of you will invite
his neighbor to sit under his vine and fig
tree,' declares the LORD Almighty."

The Gold Lampstand and the Two Olive Trees

4 Then the angel who talked with me returned and wakened me, as a man is
wakened from his sleep. 2He asked me,
"What do you see?"
I answered, "I see a solid gold lampstand
with a bowl at the top and seven lights on
it, with seven channels to the lights. 3Also
there are two olive trees by it, one on the
right of the bowl and the other on its left."
4I asked the angel who talked with me,
"What are these, my lord?"
5He answered, "Do you not know what
these are?"
"No, my lord," I replied.
6So he said to me, "This is the word of
the LORD to Zerubbabel: 'Not by might
nor by power, but by my Spirit,' says the
LORD Almighty.
7"What[d] are you, O mighty mountain?
Before Zerubbabel you will become level
ground. Then he will bring out the capstone to shouts of 'God bless it! God
bless it!' "
8Then the word of the LORD came to me:
9"The hands of Zerubbabel have laid the
foundation of this temple; his hands will
also complete it. Then you will know that
the LORD Almighty has sent me to you.
10"Who despises the day of small
things? Men will rejoice when they see the
plumb line in the hand of Zerubbabel.
"(These seven are the eyes of the LORD,
which range throughout the earth.)"
11Then I asked the angel, "What are
these two olive trees on the right and the
left of the lampstand?"
12Again I asked him, "What are these
two olive branches beside the two gold
pipes that pour out golden oil?"
13He replied, "Do you not know what
these are?"
"No, my lord," I said.
14So he said, "These are the two who are
anointed to[e] serve the Lord of all the
earth."

[a] *1* A variant of *Jeshua;* here and elsewhere in Zechariah [b] *1* *Satan* means *accuser.* [c] *9* Or *facets* [d] *7* Or *Who* [e] *14* Or *two who bring oil and*

PRAYER: RENEWAL

SINCE Your day, O Lord, will come like a thief, what kind of person should I be? In holy conduct and godliness I am to look forward to Your coming day. According to Your promise, I am looking for a new

heaven and a new earth where righteousness will dwell. Therefore, since I am looking for these things, may I be diligent to be found at peace with You, pure and blameless before You. (2 Peter 3:10–14)

***PAUSE** to add your own prayers for personal renewal.*

NT Revelation 12:1–13:1a

The Woman and the Dragon

12 A great and wondrous sign appeared
in heaven: a woman clothed with the
sun, with the moon under her feet and a
crown of twelve stars on her head. 2She
was pregnant and cried out in pain as she
was about to give birth. 3Then another
sign appeared in heaven: an enormous
red dragon with seven heads and ten
horns and seven crowns on his heads.
4His tail swept a third of the stars out of
the sky and flung them to the earth. The
dragon stood in front of the woman who
was about to give birth, so that he might
devour her child the moment it was born.
5She gave birth to a son, a male child, who
will rule all the nations with an iron
scepter. And her child was snatched up to
God and to his throne. 6The woman fled
into the desert to a place prepared for her
by God, where she might be taken care of
for 1,260 days.
7And there was war in heaven. Michael
and his angels fought against the dragon,
and the dragon and his angels fought back.
8But he was not strong enough, and they
lost their place in heaven. 9The great dragon was hurled down—that ancient serpent
called the devil, or Satan, who leads the
whole world astray. He was hurled to the
earth, and his angels with him.
10Then I heard a loud voice in heaven
say:

"Now have come the salvation and
the power and the kingdom of
our God,
and the authority of his Christ.
For the accuser of our brothers,
who accuses them before our God
day and night,
has been hurled down.
11They overcame him
by the blood of the Lamb
and by the word of their testimony;
they did not love their lives so much
as to shrink from death.
12Therefore rejoice, you heavens
and you who dwell in them!
But woe to the earth and the sea,
because the devil has gone down to
you!
He is filled with fury,
because he knows that his time is
short."

13When the dragon saw that he had
been hurled to the earth, he pursued the
woman who had given birth to the male
child. 14The woman was given the two
wings of a great eagle, so that she might fly
to the place prepared for her in the desert,
where she would be taken care of for a
time, times and half a time, out of the serpent's reach. 15Then from his mouth the
serpent spewed water like a river, to overtake the woman and sweep her away with
the torrent. 16But the earth helped the
woman by opening its mouth and swallowing the river that the dragon had
spewed out of his mouth. 17Then the dragon was enraged at the woman and went
off to make war against the rest of her offspring—those who obey God's commandments and hold to the testimony of
13 Jesus. 1And the dragon[a] stood on the
shore of the sea.

[a] *1* Some late manuscripts *And I*

PRAYER: THE WORKS OF GOD

WE know with all our hearts and souls that not one of all the good promises You, O Lord our God, gave us will fail. Every promise will be fulfilled; not one will fail. (Joshua 23:14) . . . Is the law opposed to Your promises, O God? Certainly not! For if a law had been given that

could impart life, then righteousness would indeed have been by the law. But the Scripture has confined all under sin, so that the promise by faith in Jesus Christ might be given to those who believe. (Galatians 3:21–22)

***TAKE** a moment to consider the greatness of God's wonderful works.*

YEAR 2 DAY 353

OT Zechariah 5:1–6:15

The Flying Scroll

5 I looked again—and there before me was a flying scroll!

[2]He asked me, "What do you see?"

I answered, "I see a flying scroll, thirty feet long and fifteen feet wide.[a]"

[3]And he said to me, "This is the curse that is going out over the whole land; for according to what it says on one side, every thief will be banished, and according to what it says on the other, everyone who swears falsely will be banished. [4]The LORD Almighty declares, 'I will send it out, and it will enter the house of the thief and the house of him who swears falsely by my name. It will remain in his house and destroy it, both its timbers and its stones.' "

The Woman in a Basket

[5]Then the angel who was speaking to me came forward and said to me, "Look up and see what this is that is appearing."

[6]I asked, "What is it?"

He replied, "It is a measuring basket.[b]" And he added, "This is the iniquity[c] of the people throughout the land."

[7]Then the cover of lead was raised, and there in the basket sat a woman! [8]He said, "This is wickedness," and he pushed her back into the basket and pushed the lead cover down over its mouth.

[9]Then I looked up—and there before me were two women, with the wind in their wings! They had wings like those of a stork, and they lifted up the basket between heaven and earth.

[10]"Where are they taking the basket?" I asked the angel who was speaking to me.

[11]He replied, "To the country of Babylonia[d] to build a house for it. When it is ready, the basket will be set there in its place."

Four Chariots

6 I looked up again—and there before me were four chariots coming out from between two mountains—mountains of bronze! [2]The first chariot had red horses, the second black, [3]the third white, and the fourth dappled—all of them powerful. [4]I asked the angel who was speaking to me, "What are these, my lord?"

[5]The angel answered me, "These are the four spirits[e] of heaven, going out from standing in the presence of the Lord of the whole world. [6]The one with the black horses is going toward the north country, the one with the white horses toward the west,[f] and the one with the dappled horses toward the south."

[7]When the powerful horses went out, they were straining to go throughout the earth. And he said, "Go throughout the earth!" So they went throughout the earth.

[8]Then he called to me, "Look, those going toward the north country have given my Spirit[g] rest in the land of the north."

A Crown for Joshua

[9]The word of the LORD came to me: [10]"Take ⌊silver and gold⌋ from the exiles Heldai, Tobijah and Jedaiah, who have arrived from Babylon. Go the same day to the house of Josiah son of Zephaniah. [11]Take the silver and gold and make a crown, and set it on the head of the high priest, Joshua son of Jehozadak. [12]Tell him this is what the LORD Almighty says: 'Here is the man whose name is the Branch, and he will branch out from his place and build the temple of the LORD. [13]It is he who will build the temple of the LORD, and he will be clothed with majesty and will sit and rule on his throne. And he will be a priest on his throne. And there will be harmony between the two.' [14]The crown will be given to Heldai,[h] Tobijah,

[a] 2 Hebrew *twenty cubits long and ten cubits wide* (about 9 meters long and 4.5 meters wide)
[b] 6 Hebrew *an ephah*; also in verses 7–11
[c] 6 Or *appearance*
[d] 11 Hebrew *Shinar*
[e] 5 Or *winds*
[f] 6 Or *horses after them*
[g] 8 Or *spirit*
[h] 14 Syriac; Hebrew *Helem*

Jedaiah and Hen[i] son of Zephaniah as a memorial in the temple of the LORD.
[15]Those who are far away will come and help to build the temple of the LORD, and you will know that the LORD Almighty has sent me to you. This will happen if you diligently obey the LORD your God."

[i] 14 Or *and the gracious one, the*

PRAYER: PETITION

O LORD, set a guard over my mouth; keep watch over the door of my lips. Do not let my heart turn aside to any evil thing to practice wicked deeds with those who work iniquity, and do not let me eat of their delicacies. (Psalm 141:3–4)

***PAUSE** here to petition God to help you be a faithful steward of your time, talents, possessions and relationships. Offer prayers of petition regarding your activities for this day and any special concerns you may have.*

NT Revelation 13:1b–10

The Beast out of the Sea

And I saw a beast coming out of the sea. He had ten horns and seven heads, with ten crowns on his horns, and on each head a blasphemous name.
[2]The beast I saw resembled a leopard, but had feet like those of a bear and a mouth like that of a lion. The dragon gave the beast his power and his throne and great authority.
[3]One of the heads of the beast seemed to have had a fatal wound, but the fatal wound had been healed. The whole world was astonished and followed the beast.
[4]Men worshiped the dragon because he had given authority to the beast, and they also worshiped the beast and asked, "Who is like the beast? Who can make war against him?"
[5]The beast was given a mouth to utter proud words and blasphemies and to exercise his authority for forty-two months.
[6]He opened his mouth to blaspheme God, and to slander his name and his dwelling place and those who live in heaven.
[7]He was given power to make war against the saints and to conquer them. And he was given authority over every tribe, people, language and nation.
[8]All inhabitants of the earth will worship the beast—all whose names have not been written in the book of life belonging to the Lamb that was slain from the creation of the world.[a]

[9]He who has an ear, let him hear.

[10]If anyone is to go into captivity,
into captivity he will go.
If anyone is to be killed[b] with the sword,
with the sword he will be killed.

This calls for patient endurance and faithfulness on the part of the saints.

[a] 8 Or *written from the creation of the world in the book of life belonging to the Lamb that was slain*
[b] 10 Some manuscripts *anyone kills*

PRAYER: MY RELATIONSHIP TO GOD

BLESSED are You, O God and Father of our Lord Jesus Christ; You have blessed me with every spiritual blessing in the heavenly realms in Christ. (Ephesians 1:3) . . . May I never boast except in Your cross, O Lord Jesus Christ, through which the world has been crucified to me and I to the world. (Galatians 6:14)

***PAUSE** to thank God for the relationship that you enjoy with Him in Jesus Christ.*

YEAR 2 DAY 354

OT Zechariah 7:1-14

Justice and Mercy, Not Fasting

7 In the fourth year of King Darius, the
word of the LORD came to Zechariah on
the fourth day of the ninth month, the
month of Kislev. 2The people of Bethel
had sent Sharezer and Regem-Melech, together with their men, to entreat the LORD
3by asking the priests of the house of the
LORD Almighty and the prophets, "Should
I mourn and fast in the fifth month, as I
have done for so many years?"
4Then the word of the LORD Almighty
came to me: 5"Ask all the people of the
land and the priests, 'When you fasted
and mourned in the fifth and seventh
months for the past seventy years, was it
really for me that you fasted? 6And when
you were eating and drinking, were you
not just feasting for yourselves? 7Are these
not the words the LORD proclaimed
through the earlier prophets when Jerusalem and its surrounding towns were at
rest and prosperous, and the Negev and
the western foothills were settled?' "
8And the word of the LORD came again
to Zechariah: 9"This is what the LORD
Almighty says: 'Administer true justice;
show mercy and compassion to one another. 10Do not oppress the widow or the
fatherless, the alien or the poor. In your
hearts do not think evil of each other.'
11"But they refused to pay attention;
stubbornly they turned their backs and
stopped up their ears. 12They made their
hearts as hard as flint and would not listen to the law or to the words that the
LORD Almighty had sent by his Spirit
through the earlier prophets. So the LORD
Almighty was very angry.
13" 'When I called, they did not listen;
so when they called, I would not listen,'
says the LORD Almighty. 14'I scattered them
with a whirlwind among all the nations,
where they were strangers. The land was
left so desolate behind them that no one
could come or go. This is how they made
the pleasant land desolate.' "

PRAYER: INTERCESSION

I WILL conduct myself in a manner worthy of Your gospel, O Christ, standing firm in one spirit with other believers, with one mind striving together for the faith of the gospel. (Philippians 1:27)

__TAKE__ a few moments to intercede on behalf of your local, state or provincial, and national governments. Pray for spiritual revival in the nation and offer prayers regarding current events and concerns.

NT Revelation 13:11–14:5

The Beast out of the Earth

11Then I saw another beast, coming out
of the earth. He had two horns like a
lamb, but he spoke like a dragon. 12He exercised all the authority of the first beast
on his behalf, and made the earth and its
inhabitants worship the first beast, whose
fatal wound had been healed. 13And he
performed great and miraculous signs,
even causing fire to come down from
heaven to earth in full view of men. 14Be-
cause of the signs he was given power to
do on behalf of the first beast, he deceived
the inhabitants of the earth. He ordered
them to set up an image in honor of the
beast who was wounded by the sword and
yet lived. 15He was given power to give
breath to the image of the first beast, so
that it could speak and cause all who refused to worship the image to be killed.
16He also forced everyone, small and
great, rich and poor, free and slave, to receive a mark on his right hand or on his
forehead, 17so that no one could buy or
sell unless he had the mark, which is the
name of the beast or the number of his
name.
18This calls for wisdom. If anyone has
insight, let him calculate the number of

the beast, for it is man's number. His number is 666.

The Lamb and the 144,000

14 Then I looked, and there before me was the Lamb, standing on Mount Zion, and with him 144,000 who had his name and his Father's name written on their foreheads. 2And I heard a sound from heaven like the roar of rushing waters and like a loud peal of thunder. The sound I heard was like that of harpists playing their harps. 3And they sang a new song before the throne and before the four living creatures and the elders. No one could learn the song except the 144,000 who had been redeemed from the earth. 4These are those who did not defile themselves with women, for they kept themselves pure. They follow the Lamb wherever he goes. They were purchased from among men and offered as firstfruits to God and the Lamb. 5No lie was found in their mouths; they are blameless.

PRAYER: THE CHARACTER I WANT TO CULTIVATE

O GOD, I will let another praise me, and not my own mouth; someone else, and not my own lips. (Proverbs 27:2) . . . Woe to those, O God, who are wise in their own eyes and clever in their own sight! (Isaiah 5:21)

***TAKE** a moment to ask the Lord for the grace to grow in godly character.*

YEAR 2 DAY 355

OT **Zechariah 8:1-23**

The LORD Promises to Bless Jerusalem

8 Again the word of the LORD Almighty came to me. 2This is what the LORD Almighty says: "I am very jealous for Zion; I am burning with jealousy for her."

3This is what the LORD says: "I will return to Zion and dwell in Jerusalem. Then Jerusalem will be called the City of Truth, and the mountain of the LORD Almighty will be called the Holy Mountain."

4This is what the LORD Almighty says: "Once again men and women of ripe old age will sit in the streets of Jerusalem, each with cane in hand because of his age. 5The city streets will be filled with boys and girls playing there."

6This is what the LORD Almighty says: "It may seem marvelous to the remnant of this people at that time, but will it seem marvelous to me?" declares the LORD Almighty.

7This is what the LORD Almighty says: "I will save my people from the countries of the east and the west. 8I will bring them back to live in Jerusalem; they will be my people, and I will be faithful and righteous to them as their God."

9This is what the LORD Almighty says: "You who now hear these words spoken by the prophets who were there when the foundation was laid for the house of the LORD Almighty, let your hands be strong so that the temple may be built. 10Before that time there were no wages for man or beast. No one could go about his business safely because of his enemy, for I had turned every man against his neighbor. 11But now I will not deal with the remnant of this people as I did in the past," declares the LORD Almighty.

12"The seed will grow well, the vine will yield its fruit, the ground will produce its crops, and the heavens will drop their dew. I will give all these things as an inheritance to the remnant of this people. 13As you have been an object of cursing among the nations, O Judah and Israel, so will I save you, and you will be a blessing. Do not be afraid, but let your hands be strong."

14This is what the LORD Almighty says: "Just as I had determined to bring disaster upon you and showed no pity when your fathers angered me," says the LORD Almighty, 15"so now I have determined to do good again to Jerusalem and Judah. Do not be afraid. 16These are the things

you are to do: Speak the truth to each other, and render true and sound judgment
in your courts; 17do not plot evil against
your neighbor, and do not love to swear
falsely. I hate all this," declares the LORD.
18Again the word of the LORD Almighty
came to me. 19This is what the LORD
Almighty says: "The fasts of the fourth,
fifth, seventh and tenth months will become joyful and glad occasions and happy festivals for Judah. Therefore love truth
and peace."
20This is what the LORD Almighty says:
"Many peoples and the inhabitants of
many cities will yet come, 21and the inhabitants of one city will go to another
and say, 'Let us go at once to entreat the
LORD and seek the LORD Almighty. I myself am going.' 22And many peoples and
powerful nations will come to Jerusalem
to seek the LORD Almighty and to entreat
him."
23This is what the LORD Almighty says:
"In those days ten men from all languages
and nations will take firm hold of one Jew
by the hem of his robe and say, 'Let us go
with you, because we have heard that God
is with you.' "

PRAYER: AFFIRMATION

O GOD, You give life to the dead and call into being things that do not exist. (Romans 4:17) . . . Anyone who believes in Your Son, O God, has everlasting life. (John 6:47) . . . You raised Jesus Christ and will also raise me up through Your power. (1 Corinthians 6:14)

***PAUSE** to reflect on these Biblical affirmations.*

NT Revelation 14:6-20

The Three Angels

6Then I saw another angel flying in
midair, and he had the eternal gospel to
proclaim to those who live on the earth—
to every nation, tribe, language and people. 7He said in a loud voice, "Fear God
and give him glory, because the hour of
his judgment has come. Worship him
who made the heavens, the earth, the sea
and the springs of water."
8A second angel followed and said,
"Fallen! Fallen is Babylon the Great,
which made all the nations drink the
maddening wine of her adulteries."
9A third angel followed them and said
in a loud voice: "If anyone worships the
beast and his image and receives his mark
on the forehead or on the hand, 10he, too,
will drink of the wine of God's fury, which
has been poured full strength into the cup
of his wrath. He will be tormented with
burning sulfur in the presence of the holy
angels and of the Lamb. 11And the smoke
of their torment rises for ever and ever.
There is no rest day or night for those who
worship the beast and his image, or for
anyone who receives the mark of his
name." 12This calls for patient endurance
on the part of the saints who obey God's
commandments and remain faithful to
Jesus.
13Then I heard a voice from heaven say,
"Write: Blessed are the dead who die in
the Lord from now on."
"Yes," says the Spirit, "they will rest
from their labor, for their deeds will follow them."

The Harvest of the Earth

14I looked, and there before me was a
white cloud, and seated on the cloud was
one "like a son of man"[a] with a crown of
gold on his head and a sharp sickle in his
hand. 15Then another angel came out of
the temple and called in a loud voice to
him who was sitting on the cloud, "Take
your sickle and reap, because the time to
reap has come, for the harvest of the earth
is ripe." 16So he who was seated on the
cloud swung his sickle over the earth, and
the earth was harvested.
17Another angel came out of the temple in heaven, and he too had a sharp
sickle. 18Still another angel, who had
charge of the fire, came from the altar
and called in a loud voice to him who
had the sharp sickle, "Take your sharp

[a] *14* Daniel 7:13

sickle and gather the clusters of grapes from the earth's vine, because its grapes are ripe." [19]The angel swung his sickle on the earth, gathered its grapes and threw them into the great winepress of God's wrath. [20]They were trampled in the winepress outside the city, and blood flowed out of the press, rising as high as the horses' bridles for a distance of 1,600 stadia.[b]

[b] *20* That is, about 180 miles (about 300 kilometers)

PRAYER: MY RELATIONSHIP TO OTHERS

If someone is caught in a trespass, we who are spiritual should restore that person in a spirit of gentleness, taking care lest we ourselves should be tempted. (Galatians 6:1)

***PAUSE** to review your relationships with others and to commit them to the Lord.*

YEAR 2 DAY 356

OT Zechariah 9:1–17

Judgment on Israel's Enemies

An Oracle

9 The word of the LORD is against the
land of Hadrach
and will rest upon Damascus—
for the eyes of men and all the tribes
of Israel
are on the LORD—[a]
2 and upon Hamath too, which borders
on it,
and upon Tyre and Sidon, though
they are very skillful.
3 Tyre has built herself a stronghold;
she has heaped up silver like dust,
and gold like the dirt of the streets.
4 But the Lord will take away her
possessions
and destroy her power on the sea,
and she will be consumed by fire.
5 Ashkelon will see it and fear;
Gaza will writhe in agony,
and Ekron too, for her hope will
wither.
Gaza will lose her king
and Ashkelon will be deserted.
6 Foreigners will occupy Ashdod,
and I will cut off the pride of the
Philistines.
7 I will take the blood from their
mouths,
the forbidden food from between
their teeth.
Those who are left will belong to our
God
and become leaders in Judah,
and Ekron will be like the Jebusites.
8 But I will defend my house
against marauding forces.
Never again will an oppressor overrun
my people,
for now I am keeping watch.

The Coming of Zion's King

9 Rejoice greatly, O Daughter of Zion!
Shout, Daughter of Jerusalem!
See, your king[b] comes to you,
righteous and having salvation,
gentle and riding on a donkey,
on a colt, the foal of a donkey.
10 I will take away the chariots from
Ephraim
and the war-horses from Jerusalem,
and the battle bow will be broken.
He will proclaim peace to the nations.
His rule will extend from sea to sea
and from the River[c] to the ends of
the earth.[d]
11 As for you, because of the blood of
my covenant with you,
I will free your prisoners from the
waterless pit.
12 Return to your fortress, O prisoners of
hope;
even now I announce that I will
restore twice as much to you.

[a] *1* Or *Damascus. / For the eye of the LORD is on all mankind, / as well as on the tribes of Israel,* [b] *9* Or *King* [c] *10* That is, the Euphrates [d] *10* Or *the end of the land*

[13] I will bend Judah as I bend my bow
and fill it with Ephraim.
I will rouse your sons, O Zion,
against your sons, O Greece,
and make you like a warrior's
sword.

The Lord Will Appear

[14] Then the Lord will appear over them;
his arrow will flash like lightning.
The Sovereign Lord will sound the
trumpet;
he will march in the storms of the
south,
[15] and the Lord Almighty will shield
them.
They will destroy
and overcome with slingstones.
They will drink and roar as with wine;
they will be full like a bowl
used for sprinkling[e] the corners of
the altar.
[16] The Lord their God will save them on
that day
as the flock of his people.
They will sparkle in his land
like jewels in a crown.
[17] How attractive and beautiful they will
be!
Grain will make the young men
thrive,
and new wine the young women.

[e] 15 Or *bowl, / like*

PRAYER: THANKSGIVING

YOU, O Christ, our Passover lamb, have been sacrificed for us. (1 Corinthians 5:7) . . . You died for our sins according to the Scriptures; You were buried, and You were raised on the third day according to the Scriptures. (1 Corinthians 15:3–4) . . . You died and returned to life, that You might be the Lord of both the dead and the living. (Romans 14:9)

PAUSE *to offer your own expressions of thanksgiving.*

NT Revelation 15:1-8

Seven Angels With Seven Plagues

15 I saw in heaven another great and marvelous sign: seven angels with the seven last plagues—last, because with them God's wrath is completed. [2] And I saw what looked like a sea of glass mixed with fire and, standing beside the sea, those who had been victorious over the beast and his image and over the number of his name. They held harps given them by God [3] and sang the song of Moses the servant of God and the song of the Lamb:

"Great and marvelous are your deeds,
Lord God Almighty.
Just and true are your ways,
King of the ages.
[4] Who will not fear you, O Lord,
and bring glory to your name?
For you alone are holy.
All nations will come
and worship before you,
for your righteous acts have been
revealed."

[5] After this I looked and in heaven the temple, that is, the tabernacle of the Testimony, was opened. [6] Out of the temple came the seven angels with the seven plagues. They were dressed in clean, shining linen and wore golden sashes around their chests. [7] Then one of the four living creatures gave to the seven angels seven golden bowls filled with the wrath of God, who lives for ever and ever. [8] And the temple was filled with smoke from the glory of God and from his power, and no one could enter the temple until the seven plagues of the seven angels were completed.

PRAYER: THE ATTRIBUTES OF GOD

I WILL give thanks to You, O Lord, for You are good; Your loving-kindness endures forever. I will give thanks to You, Lord, for Your unfailing love and Your wonderful acts to Your people, for You satisfy the thirsty soul and fill the hungry soul with good things. (Psalm 107:1, 8–9)

PAUSE *to reflect on these affirmations about the person, powers and perfection of God.*

YEAR 2 DAY 357

OT Psalm 148

Psalm 148

1 Praise the LORD.[a]

Praise the LORD from the heavens,
praise him in the heights above.
2 Praise him, all his angels,
praise him, all his heavenly hosts.
3 Praise him, sun and moon,
praise him, all you shining stars.
4 Praise him, you highest heavens
and you waters above the skies.
5 Let them praise the name of the LORD,
for he commanded and they were created.
6 He set them in place for ever and ever;
he gave a decree that will never pass away.

7 Praise the LORD from the earth,
you great sea creatures and all ocean depths,
8 lightning and hail, snow and clouds,
stormy winds that do his bidding,
9 you mountains and all hills,
fruit trees and all cedars,
10 wild animals and all cattle,
small creatures and flying birds,
11 kings of the earth and all nations,
you princes and all rulers on earth,
12 young men and maidens,
old men and children.

13 Let them praise the name of the LORD,
for his name alone is exalted;
his splendor is above the earth and the heavens.
14 He has raised up for his people a horn,[b]
the praise of all his saints,
of Israel, the people close to his heart.

Praise the LORD.

[a] 1 Hebrew *Hallelu Yah;* also in verse 14
[b] 14 *Horn* here symbolizes strong one, that is, king.

PRAYER: ADORATION

WE praise You, O Lord! We praise You from the heavens; we praise You in the heights. You are praised by all Your angels; You are praised by all Your heavenly hosts. The sun and moon praise You; All the shining stars praise You; the highest heavens praise You and the waters above the heavens. Everything praises Your name, O Lord, for You commanded and they were created. You established them for ever and ever; You gave a decree that will not pass away. (Psalm 148:1–6)

PAUSE *to express your thoughts of praise and worship.*

NT Revelation 16:1–21

The Seven Bowls of God's Wrath

16 Then I heard a loud voice from the temple saying to the seven angels, "Go, pour out the seven bowls of God's wrath on the earth."

2The first angel went and poured out his bowl on the land, and ugly and painful sores broke out on the people who had the mark of the beast and worshiped his image.

3The second angel poured out his bowl on the sea, and it turned into blood like that of a dead man, and every living thing in the sea died.

4The third angel poured out his bowl on the rivers and springs of water, and they became blood. 5Then I heard the angel in charge of the waters say:

"You are just in these judgments,
you who are and who were, the Holy One,
because you have so judged;
6for they have shed the blood of your saints and prophets,
and you have given them blood to drink as they deserve."

7And I heard the altar respond:

"Yes, Lord God Almighty,
true and just are your judgments."

8The fourth angel poured out his bowl on the sun, and the sun was given power to scorch people with fire. 9They were seared by the intense heat and they cursed the name of God, who had control over these plagues, but they refused to repent and glorify him.

10The fifth angel poured out his bowl on the throne of the beast, and his kingdom was plunged into darkness. Men gnawed their tongues in agony 11and cursed the God of heaven because of their pains and their sores, but they refused to repent of what they had done.

12The sixth angel poured out his bowl on the great river Euphrates, and its water was dried up to prepare the way for the kings from the East. 13Then I saw three evil[a] spirits that looked like frogs; they came out of the mouth of the dragon, out of the mouth of the beast and out of the mouth of the false prophet. 14They are spirits of demons performing miraculous signs, and they go out to the kings of the whole world, to gather them for the battle on the great day of God Almighty.

15"Behold, I come like a thief! Blessed is he who stays awake and keeps his clothes with him, so that he may not go naked and be shamefully exposed."

16Then they gathered the kings together to the place that in Hebrew is called Armageddon.

17The seventh angel poured out his bowl into the air, and out of the temple came a loud voice from the throne, saying, "It is done!" 18Then there came flashes of lightning, rumblings, peals of thunder and a severe earthquake. No earthquake like it has ever occurred since man has been on earth, so tremendous was the quake. 19The great city split into three parts, and the cities of the nations collapsed. God remembered Babylon the Great and gave her the cup filled with the wine of the fury of his wrath. 20Every island fled away and the mountains could not be found. 21From the sky huge hailstones of about a hundred pounds each fell upon men. And they cursed God on account of the plague of hail, because the plague was so terrible.

[a] *13* Greek *unclean*

PRAYER: THE WORKS OF GOD

O GOD, You have made everything beautiful in its time. You have also set eternity in our hearts; yet we cannot fathom what You have done from beginning to end. (Ecclesiastes 3:11)

***TAKE** a moment to consider the greatness of God's wonderful works.*

YEAR 2 DAY 358

OT **Zechariah 10:1-12**

The Lord *Will Care for Judah*

10 Ask the Lord for rain in the springtime;
it is the Lord who makes the storm clouds.
He gives showers of rain to men,
and plants of the field to everyone.
2 The idols speak deceit,
diviners see visions that lie;
they tell dreams that are false,
they give comfort in vain.
Therefore the people wander like sheep
oppressed for lack of a shepherd.

3 "My anger burns against the shepherds,
and I will punish the leaders;
for the Lord Almighty will care
for his flock, the house of Judah,
and make them like a proud horse in battle.
4 From Judah will come the cornerstone,
from him the tent peg,
from him the battle bow,
from him every ruler.
5 Together they[a] will be like mighty men
trampling the muddy streets in battle.
Because the Lord is with them,
they will fight and overthrow the horsemen.

6 "I will strengthen the house of Judah
and save the house of Joseph.
I will restore them
because I have compassion on them.
They will be as though
I had not rejected them,
for I am the Lord their God
and I will answer them.
7 The Ephraimites will become like mighty men,
and their hearts will be glad as with wine.
Their children will see it and be joyful;
their hearts will rejoice in the Lord.
8 I will signal for them
and gather them in.
Surely I will redeem them;
they will be as numerous as before.
9 Though I scatter them among the peoples,
yet in distant lands they will remember me.
They and their children will survive,
and they will return.
10 I will bring them back from Egypt
and gather them from Assyria.
I will bring them to Gilead and Lebanon,
and there will not be room enough for them.
11 They will pass through the sea of trouble;
the surging sea will be subdued
and all the depths of the Nile will dry up.
Assyria's pride will be brought down
and Egypt's scepter will pass away.
12 I will strengthen them in the Lord
and in his name they will walk,"
declares the Lord.

[a] 4,5 Or *ruler, all of them together.* / [5]*They*

PRAYER: CONFESSION

O LORD, God of heaven, You are the great and awesome God, keeping Your covenant of loyal love with those who love You and obey Your commands. Let Your ear be attentive and Your eyes open so that You may hear the prayer Your servant is praying before You day and night. I confess the sins I have committed against You. (Nehemiah 1:5–6)

ASK *the Spirit to search your heart and reveal any areas of unconfessed sin. Acknowledge these to the Lord and thank Him for His forgiveness.*

NT Revelation 17:1–18

The Woman on the Beast

17 One of the seven angels who had the
seven bowls came and said to me,
"Come, I will show you the punishment
of the great prostitute, who sits on many
waters. [2]With her the kings of the earth
committed adultery and the inhabitants
of the earth were intoxicated with the
wine of her adulteries."

[3]Then the angel carried me away in the
Spirit into a desert. There I saw a woman
sitting on a scarlet beast that was covered
with blasphemous names and had seven
heads and ten horns. [4]The woman was
dressed in purple and scarlet, and was glittering with gold, precious stones and
pearls. She held a golden cup in her hand,
filled with abominable things and the
filth of her adulteries. [5]This title was written on her forehead:

MYSTERY
BABYLON THE GREAT
THE MOTHER OF PROSTITUTES
AND OF THE ABOMINATIONS OF THE EARTH.

[6]I saw that the woman was drunk with the
blood of the saints, the blood of those
who bore testimony to Jesus.

When I saw her, I was greatly astonished. [7]Then the angel said to me: "Why
are you astonished? I will explain to you
the mystery of the woman and of the
beast she rides, which has the seven heads
and ten horns. [8]The beast, which you saw,
once was, now is not, and will come up
out of the Abyss and go to his destruction.
The inhabitants of the earth whose names
have not been written in the book of life
from the creation of the world will be astonished when they see the beast, because
he once was, now is not, and yet will
come.

[9]"This calls for a mind with wisdom.
The seven heads are seven hills on which
the woman sits. [10]They are also seven
kings. Five have fallen, one is, the other
has not yet come; but when he does come,
he must remain for a little while. [11]The
beast who once was, and now is not, is an
eighth king. He belongs to the seven and
is going to his destruction.

[12]"The ten horns you saw are ten kings
who have not yet received a kingdom, but
who for one hour will receive authority as
kings along with the beast. [13]They have
one purpose and will give their power and
authority to the beast. [14]They will make
war against the Lamb, but the Lamb will
overcome them because he is Lord of
lords and King of kings—and with him
will be his called, chosen and faithful followers."

[15]Then the angel said to me, "The waters you saw, where the prostitute sits, are
peoples, multitudes, nations and languages. [16]The beast and the ten horns you
saw will hate the prostitute. They will
bring her to ruin and leave her naked;
they will eat her flesh and burn her with
fire. [17]For God has put it into their hearts
to accomplish his purpose by agreeing to
give the beast their power to rule, until
God's words are fulfilled. [18]The woman
you saw is the great city that rules over the
kings of the earth."

PRAYER: MY RELATIONSHIP TO GOD

I HAVE put off the old self with its practices and have put on the new self, which is being renewed in full knowledge according to Your image, for You are its Creator. (Colossians 3:9–10) . . . You, O God, have given me eternal life, and this life is in Your Son. Those who have the Son have life; those who do not have the Son of God do not have life. Since I believe in the name of Your Son, O God, I know that I have eternal life. (1 John 5:11–13)

***PAUSE** to thank God for the relationship that you enjoy with Him in Jesus Christ.*

YEAR 2 DAY 359

OT Zechariah 11:1-17

11 Open your doors, O Lebanon,
so that fire may devour your cedars!
2 Wail, O pine tree, for the cedar has fallen;
the stately trees are ruined!
Wail, oaks of Bashan;
the dense forest has been cut down!
3 Listen to the wail of the shepherds;
their rich pastures are destroyed!
Listen to the roar of the lions;
the lush thicket of the Jordan is ruined!

Two Shepherds

4 This is what the LORD my God says:
"Pasture the flock marked for slaughter.
5 Their buyers slaughter them and go unpunished. Those who sell them say,
'Praise the LORD, I am rich!' Their own
shepherds do not spare them. 6 For I will
no longer have pity on the people of the
land," declares the LORD. "I will hand
everyone over to his neighbor and his
king. They will oppress the land, and I
will not rescue them from their hands."
7 So I pastured the flock marked for
slaughter, particularly the oppressed of
the flock. Then I took two staffs and called
one Favor and the other Union, and I pastured the flock. 8 In one month I got rid of
the three shepherds.
The flock detested me, and I grew weary
of them 9 and said, "I will not be your
shepherd. Let the dying die, and the perishing perish. Let those who are left eat
one another's flesh."
10 Then I took my staff called Favor and
broke it, revoking the covenant I had
made with all the nations. 11 It was revoked
on that day, and so the afflicted of the
flock who were watching me knew it was
the word of the LORD.
12 I told them, "If you think it best, give
me my pay; but if not, keep it." So they
paid me thirty pieces of silver.
13 And the LORD said to me, "Throw it to
the potter"—the handsome price at which
they priced me! So I took the thirty pieces
of silver and threw them into the house
of the LORD to the potter.
14 Then I broke my second staff called
Union, breaking the brotherhood between Judah and Israel.
15 Then the LORD said to me, "Take again
the equipment of a foolish shepherd. 16 For
I am going to raise up a shepherd over the
land who will not care for the lost, or seek
the young, or heal the injured, or feed the
healthy, but will eat the meat of the choice
sheep, tearing off their hoofs.

17 "Woe to the worthless shepherd,
who deserts the flock!
May the sword strike his arm and his right eye!
May his arm be completely withered,
his right eye totally blinded!"

PRAYER: RENEWAL

MAY I draw near to You, O God, with a sincere heart in full assurance of faith, having my heart sprinkled to cleanse me from an evil conscience and my body washed with pure water. (Hebrews 10:22) . . . You, O God, have made me adequate as a minister of the new covenant; as I have received Your mercy, may I not lose heart. (2 Corinthians 3:6, 4:1)

PAUSE *to add your own prayers for personal renewal.*

NT Revelation 18:1-10

The Fall of Babylon

18 After this I saw another angel coming
down from heaven. He had great authority, and the earth was illuminated by
his splendor. 2 With a mighty voice he
shouted:

"Fallen! Fallen is Babylon the Great!
She has become a home for demons
and a haunt for every evil[a] spirit,
a haunt for every unclean and detestable bird.
3 For all the nations have drunk
the maddening wine of her adulteries.
The kings of the earth committed adultery with her,
and the merchants of the earth grew rich from her excessive luxuries."

4 Then I heard another voice from heaven say:

"Come out of her, my people,
so that you will not share in her sins,
so that you will not receive any of her plagues;
5 for her sins are piled up to heaven,
and God has remembered her crimes.
6 Give back to her as she has given;
pay her back double for what she has done.
Mix her a double portion from her own cup.
7 Give her as much torture and grief
as the glory and luxury she gave herself.
In her heart she boasts,
'I sit as queen; I am not a widow,
and I will never mourn.'
8 Therefore in one day her plagues will overtake her:
death, mourning and famine.
She will be consumed by fire,
for mighty is the Lord God who judges her.

9 "When the kings of the earth who
committed adultery with her and shared
her luxury see the smoke of her burning,
they will weep and mourn over her. 10 Terrified at her torment, they will stand far
off and cry:

" 'Woe! Woe, O great city,
O Babylon, city of power!
In one hour your doom has come!'

[a] 2 Greek *unclean*

PRAYER: THE CHARACTER I WANT TO CULTIVATE

YOU have called the humble of the earth, those who have upheld Your justice, to seek You, O Lord—to seek righteousness and to seek humility. (Zephaniah 2:3) . . . Let those who boast, boast in You, O Lord. (1 Corinthians 1:31)

TAKE *a moment to ask the Lord for the grace to grow in godly character.*

YEAR 2 DAY 360

OT Zechariah 12:1–13:9

Jerusalem's Enemies to Be Destroyed

An Oracle

12 This is the word of the LORD concerning Israel. The LORD, who stretches out
the heavens, who lays the foundation of
the earth, and who forms the spirit of
man within him, declares: 2 "I am going to
make Jerusalem a cup that sends all the
surrounding peoples reeling. Judah will
be besieged as well as Jerusalem. 3 On that
day, when all the nations of the earth are
gathered against her, I will make Jerusalem an immovable rock for all the nations. All who try to move it will injure
themselves. 4 On that day I will strike every
horse with panic and its rider with madness," declares the LORD. "I will keep a
watchful eye over the house of Judah, but
I will blind all the horses of the nations.
5 Then the leaders of Judah will say in their
hearts, 'The people of Jerusalem are
strong, because the LORD Almighty is their
God.'
6 "On that day I will make the leaders of
Judah like a firepot in a woodpile, like a
flaming torch among sheaves. They will
consume right and left all the surround-

ing peoples, but Jerusalem will remain intact in her place.
7 "The LORD will save the dwellings of
Judah first, so that the honor of the house
of David and of Jerusalem's inhabitants
may not be greater than that of Judah.
8 On that day the LORD will shield those
who live in Jerusalem, so that the feeblest
among them will be like David, and the
house of David will be like God, like the
Angel of the LORD going before them. 9 On
that day I will set out to destroy all the nations that attack Jerusalem.

Mourning for the One They Pierced

10 "And I will pour out on the house of
David and the inhabitants of Jerusalem a
spirit[a] of grace and supplication. They will
look on[b] me, the one they have pierced,
and they will mourn for him as one
mourns for an only child, and grieve bitterly for him as one grieves for a firstborn
son. 11 On that day the weeping in Jerusalem will be great, like the weeping of
Hadad Rimmon in the plain of Megiddo.
12 The land will mourn, each clan by itself,
with their wives by themselves: the clan of
the house of David and their wives, the
clan of the house of Nathan and their
wives, 13 the clan of the house of Levi and
their wives, the clan of Shimei and their
wives, 14 and all the rest of the clans and
their wives.

Cleansing From Sin

13 "On that day a fountain will be
opened to the house of David and the
inhabitants of Jerusalem, to cleanse them
from sin and impurity.
2 "On that day, I will banish the names
of the idols from the land, and they will
be remembered no more," declares the
LORD Almighty. "I will remove both the
prophets and the spirit of impurity from
the land. 3 And if anyone still prophesies,
his father and mother, to whom he was
born, will say to him, 'You must die, because you have told lies in the LORD's
name.' When he prophesies, his own parents will stab him.
4 "On that day every prophet will be
ashamed of his prophetic vision. He will
not put on a prophet's garment of hair in
order to deceive. 5 He will say, 'I am not a
prophet. I am a farmer; the land has been
my livelihood since my youth.[c]' 6 If someone asks him, 'What are these wounds on
your body[d]?' he will answer, 'The wounds
I was given at the house of my friends.'

The Shepherd Struck, the Sheep Scattered

7 "Awake, O sword, against my
shepherd,
against the man who is close to
me!"
declares the LORD Almighty.
"Strike the shepherd,
and the sheep will be scattered,
and I will turn my hand against the
little ones.
8 In the whole land," declares the LORD,
"two-thirds will be struck down and
perish;
yet one-third will be left in it.
9 This third I will bring into the fire;
I will refine them like silver
and test them like gold.
They will call on my name
and I will answer them;
I will say, 'They are my people,'
and they will say, 'The LORD is our
God.' "

[a] 10 Or *the Spirit* [b] 10 Or *to* [c] 5 Or *farmer; a man sold me in my youth* [d] 6 Or *wounds between your hands*

PRAYER: PETITION

MAY I humble myself under Your mighty hand, O God, that You may exalt me in due time; I will cast all my anxiety upon You, because You care for me. (1 Peter 5:6–7)

PAUSE *here to offer prayers of petition regarding your family and your ministry. Ask for help and guidance in sharing Jesus with others and helping others grow in Him. Ask for guidance in your vocation and your avocations. Offer prayers of petition regarding your activities for this day and any special concerns you may have.*

NT Revelation 18:11–24

11 "The merchants of the earth will weep
and mourn over her because no one buys
their cargoes any more— 12 cargoes of gold,
silver, precious stones and pearls; fine
linen, purple, silk and scarlet cloth; every
sort of citron wood, and articles of every
kind made of ivory, costly wood, bronze,
iron and marble; 13 cargoes of cinnamon
and spice, of incense, myrrh and frankincense, of wine and olive oil, of fine flour
and wheat; cattle and sheep; horses and
carriages; and bodies and souls of men.
14 "They will say, 'The fruit you longed
for is gone from you. All your riches and
splendor have vanished, never to be recovered.' 15 The merchants who sold these
things and gained their wealth from her
will stand far off, terrified at her torment.
They will weep and mourn 16 and cry out:

" 'Woe! Woe, O great city,
dressed in fine linen, purple and scarlet,
and glittering with gold, precious stones and pearls!
17 In one hour such great wealth has been brought to ruin!'

"Every sea captain, and all who travel
by ship, the sailors, and all who earn their
living from the sea, will stand far off.
18 When they see the smoke of her burning, they will exclaim, 'Was there ever a
city like this great city?' 19 They will throw
dust on their heads, and with weeping
and mourning cry out:

" 'Woe! Woe, O great city,
where all who had ships on the sea
became rich through her wealth!
In one hour she has been brought to ruin!
20 Rejoice over her, O heaven!
Rejoice, saints and apostles and prophets!
God has judged her for the way she treated you.' "

21 Then a mighty angel picked up a boul-
der the size of a large millstone and threw
it into the sea, and said:

"With such violence
the great city of Babylon will be thrown down,
never to be found again.
22 The music of harpists and musicians,
flute players and trumpeters,
will never be heard in you again.
No workman of any trade
will ever be found in you again.
The sound of a millstone
will never be heard in you again.
23 The light of a lamp
will never shine in you again.
The voice of bridegroom and bride
will never be heard in you again.
Your merchants were the world's great men.
By your magic spell all the nations were led astray.
24 In her was found the blood of prophets and of the saints,
and of all who have been killed on the earth."

PRAYER: MY RELATIONSHIP TO OTHERS

I WAS called to freedom, but I will not use my freedom to indulge the flesh, but through love I will serve others. For the whole law is summed up in this Your word, O God: "You shall love your neighbor as yourself." (Galatians 5:13–14)

***PAUSE** to review your relationships with others and to commit them to the Lord.*

YEAR 2 DAY 361

OT **Zechariah 14:1-21**

The Lord Comes and Reigns

14 A day of the LORD is coming when your plunder will be divided among you.

2 I will gather all the nations to Jerusalem to fight against it; the city will be captured, the houses ransacked, and the women raped. Half of the city will go into exile, but the rest of the people will not be taken from the city.

3 Then the LORD will go out and fight against those nations, as he fights in the day of battle. 4 On that day his feet will stand on the Mount of Olives, east of Jerusalem, and the Mount of Olives will be split in two from east to west, forming a great valley, with half of the mountain moving north and half moving south. 5 You will flee by my mountain valley, for it will extend to Azel. You will flee as you fled from the earthquake[a] in the days of Uzziah king of Judah. Then the LORD my God will come, and all the holy ones with him.

6 On that day there will be no light, no cold or frost. 7 It will be a unique day, without daytime or nighttime—a day known to the LORD. When evening comes, there will be light.

8 On that day living water will flow out from Jerusalem, half to the eastern sea[b] and half to the western sea,[c] in summer and in winter.

9 The LORD will be king over the whole earth. On that day there will be one LORD, and his name the only name.

10 The whole land, from Geba to Rimmon, south of Jerusalem, will become like the Arabah. But Jerusalem will be raised up and remain in its place, from the Benjamin Gate to the site of the First Gate, to the Corner Gate, and from the Tower of Hananel to the royal winepresses. 11 It will be inhabited; never again will it be destroyed. Jerusalem will be secure.

12 This is the plague with which the LORD will strike all the nations that fought against Jerusalem: Their flesh will rot while they are still standing on their feet, their eyes will rot in their sockets, and their tongues will rot in their mouths. 13 On that day men will be stricken by the LORD with great panic. Each man will seize the hand of another, and they will attack each other. 14 Judah too will fight at Jerusalem. The wealth of all the surrounding nations will be collected—great quantities of gold and silver and clothing. 15 A similar plague will strike the horses and mules, the camels and donkeys, and all the animals in those camps.

16 Then the survivors from all the nations that have attacked Jerusalem will go up year after year to worship the King, the LORD Almighty, and to celebrate the Feast of Tabernacles. 17 If any of the peoples of the earth do not go up to Jerusalem to worship the King, the LORD Almighty, they will have no rain. 18 If the Egyptian people do not go up and take part, they will have no rain. The LORD[d] will bring on them the plague he inflicts on the nations that do not go up to celebrate the Feast of Tabernacles. 19 This will be the punishment of Egypt and the punishment of all the nations that do not go up to celebrate the Feast of Tabernacles.

20 On that day HOLY TO THE LORD will be inscribed on the bells of the horses, and the cooking pots in the LORD's house will be like the sacred bowls in front of the altar. 21 Every pot in Jerusalem and Judah will be holy to the LORD Almighty, and all who come to sacrifice will take some of the pots and cook in them. And on that day there will no longer be a Canaanite[e] in the house of the LORD Almighty.

[a] 5 Or *5 My mountain valley will be blocked and will extend to Azel. It will be blocked as it was blocked because of the earthquake* [b] 8 That is, the Dead Sea [c] 8 That is, the Mediterranean [d] 18 Or *part, then the LORD* [e] 21 Or *merchant*

PRAYER: INTERCESSION

THE harvest is plentiful, but the workers are few. Therefore, I pray that You, Lord of the harvest, will send out workers into Your harvest. (Matthew 9:37–38; Luke 10:2)

TAKE *a few moments to intercede on behalf of local, national and world missions. Pray that the Great Commission would be fulfilled and for any special concerns you may have for missions.*

NT Revelation 19:1–10

Hallelujah!

19 After this I heard what sounded like
the roar of a great multitude in heav-
en shouting:

"Hallelujah!
Salvation and glory and power belong
to our God,
2 for true and just are his judgments.
He has condemned the great
prostitute
who corrupted the earth by her
adulteries.
He has avenged on her the blood of
his servants."

3 And again they shouted:

"Hallelujah!
The smoke from her goes up for ever
and ever."

4 The twenty-four elders and the four living creatures fell down and worshiped
God, who was seated on the throne. And
they cried:

"Amen, Hallelujah!"

5 Then a voice came from the throne,
saying:

"Praise our God,
all you his servants,
you who fear him,
both small and great!"

6 Then I heard what sounded like a great
multitude, like the roar of rushing waters
and like loud peals of thunder, shouting:

"Hallelujah!
For our Lord God Almighty reigns.
7 Let us rejoice and be glad
and give him glory!
For the wedding of the Lamb has
come,
and his bride has made herself ready.
8 Fine linen, bright and clean,
was given her to wear."
(Fine linen stands for the righteous acts
of the saints.)

9 Then the angel said to me, "Write:
'Blessed are those who are invited to the
wedding supper of the Lamb!' " And he
added, "These are the true words of God."
10 At this I fell at his feet to worship him.
But he said to me, "Do not do it! I am a
fellow servant with you and with your
brothers who hold to the testimony of
Jesus. Worship God! For the testimony of
Jesus is the spirit of prophecy."

PRAYER: THE ATTRIBUTES OF GOD

LORD Jesus Christ, Your works have proved that the Father is in You, and that You are in the Father. (John 10:38) . . . You knew, Jesus, that the Father had given all things into Your hands and that You had come from God and were returning to God. (John 13:3)

PAUSE *to reflect on these affirmations about the person, powers and perfection of God.*

YEAR 2 DAY 362

OT **Malachi 1:1–14**

1 An oracle: The word of the LORD to Israel through Malachi.[a]

Jacob Loved, Esau Hated

2 "I have loved you," says the LORD.

"But you ask, 'How have you loved us?'

"Was not Esau Jacob's brother?" the LORD says. "Yet I have loved Jacob, 3 but Esau I have hated, and I have turned his mountains into a wasteland and left his inheritance to the desert jackals."

4 Edom may say, "Though we have been crushed, we will rebuild the ruins."

But this is what the LORD Almighty says: "They may build, but I will demolish. They will be called the Wicked Land, a people always under the wrath of the LORD. 5 You will see it with your own eyes and say, 'Great is the LORD—even beyond the borders of Israel!'

Blemished Sacrifices

6 "A son honors his father, and a servant his master. If I am a father, where is the honor due me? If I am a master, where is the respect due me?" says the LORD Almighty. "It is you, O priests, who show contempt for my name.

"But you ask, 'How have we shown contempt for your name?'

7 "You place defiled food on my altar.

"But you ask, 'How have we defiled you?'

"By saying that the LORD's table is contemptible. 8 When you bring blind animals for sacrifice, is that not wrong? When you sacrifice crippled or diseased animals, is that not wrong? Try offering them to your governor! Would he be pleased with you? Would he accept you?" says the LORD Almighty.

9 "Now implore God to be gracious to us. With such offerings from your hands, will he accept you?"—says the LORD Almighty.

10 "Oh, that one of you would shut the temple doors, so that you would not light useless fires on my altar! I am not pleased with you," says the LORD Almighty, "and I will accept no offering from your hands. 11 My name will be great among the nations, from the rising to the setting of the sun. In every place incense and pure offerings will be brought to my name, because my name will be great among the nations," says the LORD Almighty.

12 "But you profane it by saying of the Lord's table, 'It is defiled,' and of its food, 'It is contemptible.' 13 And you say, 'What a burden!' and you sniff at it contemptuously," says the LORD Almighty.

"When you bring injured, crippled or diseased animals and offer them as sacrifices, should I accept them from your hands?" says the LORD. 14 "Cursed is the cheat who has an acceptable male in his flock and vows to give it, but then sacrifices a blemished animal to the Lord. For I am a great king," says the LORD Almighty, "and my name is to be feared among the nations.

[a] 1 *Malachi* means *my messenger.*

PRAYER: AFFIRMATION

O LORD, by wisdom You founded the earth; by understanding You established the heavens; by Your knowledge the deeps were divided, and the clouds drop down the dew. (Proverbs 3:19–20) . . . You will create new heavens and a new earth. The former things will not be remembered, nor will they come to mind. (Isaiah 65:17)

PAUSE *to reflect on these Biblical affirmations.*

NT Revelation 19:11–20:6

The Rider on the White Horse

[11]I saw heaven standing open and there before me was a white horse, whose rider is called Faithful and True. With justice he judges and makes war. [12]His eyes are like blazing fire, and on his head are many crowns. He has a name written on him that no one knows but he himself. [13]He is dressed in a robe dipped in blood, and his name is the Word of God. [14]The armies of heaven were following him, riding on white horses and dressed in fine linen, white and clean. [15]Out of his mouth comes a sharp sword with which to strike down the nations. "He will rule them with an iron scepter."[a] He treads the winepress of the fury of the wrath of God Almighty. [16]On his robe and on his thigh he has this name written:

KING OF KINGS AND LORD OF LORDS.

[17]And I saw an angel standing in the sun, who cried in a loud voice to all the birds flying in midair, "Come, gather together for the great supper of God, [18]so that you may eat the flesh of kings, generals, and mighty men, of horses and their riders, and the flesh of all people, free and slave, small and great."

[19]Then I saw the beast and the kings of the earth and their armies gathered together to make war against the rider on the horse and his army. [20]But the beast was captured, and with him the false prophet who had performed the miraculous signs on his behalf. With these signs he had deluded those who had received the mark of the beast and worshiped his image. The two of them were thrown alive into the fiery lake of burning sulfur. [21]The rest of them were killed with the sword that came out of the mouth of the rider on the horse, and all the birds gorged themselves on their flesh.

The Thousand Years

20 And I saw an angel coming down out of heaven, having the key to the Abyss and holding in his hand a great chain. [2]He seized the dragon, that ancient serpent, who is the devil, or Satan, and bound him for a thousand years. [3]He threw him into the Abyss, and locked and sealed it over him, to keep him from deceiving the nations anymore until the thousand years were ended. After that, he must be set free for a short time.

[4]I saw thrones on which were seated those who had been given authority to judge. And I saw the souls of those who had been beheaded because of their testimony for Jesus and because of the word of God. They had not worshiped the beast or his image and had not received his mark on their foreheads or their hands. They came to life and reigned with Christ a thousand years. [5](The rest of the dead did not come to life until the thousand years were ended.) This is the first resurrection. [6]Blessed and holy are those who have part in the first resurrection. The second death has no power over them, but they will be priests of God and of Christ and will reign with him for a thousand years.

[a] *15* Psalm 2:9

PRAYER: THE WORKS OF GOD

GOD placed all things under Your feet, O Christ, and gave You to be head over all things to the church, which is Your body, Your fullness—You who fill all in all. (Ephesians 1:22–23) . . . In You, O Christ, there is neither Greek or Jew, circumcised or uncircumcised, barbarian, Scythian, slave or free, but You are all and in all. (Colossians 3:11)

TAKE *a moment to consider the greatness of God's wonderful works.*

Admonition for the Priests

2 "And now this admonition is for you, O priests. [2]If you do not listen, and if you do not set your heart to honor my name," says the LORD Almighty, "I will send a curse upon you, and I will curse your blessings. Yes, I have already cursed them, because you have not set your heart to honor me.

[3]"Because of you I will rebuke[a] your descendants[b]; I will spread on your faces the offal from your festival sacrifices, and you will be carried off with it. [4]And you will know that I have sent you this admonition so that my covenant with Levi may continue," says the LORD Almighty. [5]"My covenant was with him, a covenant of life and peace, and I gave them to him; this called for reverence and he revered me and stood in awe of my name. [6]True instruction was in his mouth and nothing false was found on his lips. He walked with me in peace and uprightness, and turned many from sin.

[7]"For the lips of a priest ought to preserve knowledge, and from his mouth men should seek instruction—because he is the messenger of the LORD Almighty. [8]But you have turned from the way and by your teaching have caused many to stumble; you have violated the covenant with Levi," says the LORD Almighty. [9]"So I have caused you to be despised and humiliated before all the people, because you have not followed my ways but have shown partiality in matters of the law."

Judah Unfaithful

[10]Have we not all one Father[c]? Did not one God create us? Why do we profane the covenant of our fathers by breaking faith with one another?

[11]Judah has broken faith. A detestable thing has been committed in Israel and in Jerusalem: Judah has desecrated the sanctuary the LORD loves, by marrying the daughter of a foreign god. [12]As for the man who does this, whoever he may be, may the LORD cut him off from the tents of Jacob[d]—even though he brings offerings to the LORD Almighty.

[13]Another thing you do: You flood the LORD's altar with tears. You weep and wail because he no longer pays attention to your offerings or accepts them with pleasure from your hands. [14]You ask, "Why?" It is because the LORD is acting as the witness between you and the wife of your youth, because you have broken faith with her, though she is your partner, the wife of your marriage covenant.

[15]Has not ⌞the LORD⌟ made them one? In flesh and spirit they are his. And why one? Because he was seeking godly offspring.[e] So guard yourself in your spirit, and do not break faith with the wife of your youth.

[16]"I hate divorce," says the LORD God of Israel, "and I hate a man's covering himself[f] with violence as well as with his garment," says the LORD Almighty.

So guard yourself in your spirit, and do not break faith.

The Day of Judgment

[17]You have wearied the LORD with your words.

"How have we wearied him?" you ask.

By saying, "All who do evil are good in the eyes of the LORD, and he is pleased with them" or "Where is the God of justice?"

[a] 3 Or *cut off* (see Septuagint) [b] 3 Or *will blight your grain* [c] 10 Or *father* [d] 12 Or [12]*May the LORD cut off from the tents of Jacob anyone who gives testimony in behalf of the man who does this* [e] 15 Or [15]*But the one ⌞who is our father⌟ did not do this, not as long as life remained in him. And what was he seeking? An offspring from God* [f] 16 Or *his wife*

PRAYER: THANKSGIVING

WE will not all sleep, but we will all be changed in a moment, in the twinkling of an eye, at the last trumpet. For the trumpet will sound, and the dead will be raised imperishable, and we shall be changed. For this perishable must clothe itself with the imperishable and this mortal with immortality. (1 Corinthians 15:51–53)

***PAUSE** to offer your own expressions of thanksgiving.*

NT Revelation 20:7-15

Satan's Doom

[7]When the thousand years are over, Satan
will be released from his prison [8]and will go
out to deceive the nations in the four corners of the earth—Gog and Magog—to
gather them for battle. In number they are
like the sand on the seashore. [9]They
marched across the breadth of the earth and
surrounded the camp of God's people, the
city he loves. But fire came down from heav-
en and devoured them. [10]And the devil, who
deceived them, was thrown into the lake of
burning sulfur, where the beast and the false
prophet had been thrown. They will be tormented day and night for ever and ever.

The Dead Are Judged

[11]Then I saw a great white throne and
him who was seated on it. Earth and sky
fled from his presence, and there was no
place for them. [12]And I saw the dead,
great and small, standing before the
throne, and books were opened. Another book was opened, which is the book
of life. The dead were judged according
to what they had done as recorded in the
books. [13]The sea gave up the dead that
were in it, and death and Hades gave up
the dead that were in them, and each person was judged according to what he had
done. [14]Then death and Hades were
thrown into the lake of fire. The lake of
fire is the second death. [15]If anyone's
name was not found written in the book
of life, he was thrown into the lake of
fire.

PRAYER: MY RELATIONSHIP TO GOD

I AM not ashamed, because I know whom I have believed and am convinced that You, Christ Jesus, are able to guard what I have entrusted to You until that day. (2 Timothy 1:12) . . . This is a trustworthy saying: If we died with You, we will also live with You; if we endure, we will also reign with You. If we deny You, You will also deny us; if we are faithless, You will remain faithful, for You cannot deny Yourself. (2 Timothy 2:11–13)

***PAUSE** to thank God for the relationship that you enjoy with Him in Jesus Christ.*

YEAR 2 DAY 364

OT Psalms 149–150

Psalm 149

[1]Praise the LORD.[a]

Sing to the LORD a new song,
his praise in the assembly of the saints.

[2]Let Israel rejoice in their Maker;

[a] 1 Hebrew *Hallelu Yah;* also in verse 9

let the people of Zion be glad in
their King.
[3] Let them praise his name with
dancing
and make music to him with
tambourine and harp.
[4] For the LORD takes delight in his
people;
he crowns the humble with
salvation.
[5] Let the saints rejoice in this honor
and sing for joy on their beds.

[6] May the praise of God be in their
mouths
and a double-edged sword in their
hands,
[7] to inflict vengeance on the nations
and punishment on the peoples,
[8] to bind their kings with fetters,
their nobles with shackles of iron,
[9] to carry out the sentence written
against them.
This is the glory of all his saints.

Praise the LORD.

Psalm 150

[1] Praise the LORD.[b]

Praise God in his sanctuary;
praise him in his mighty heavens.
[2] Praise him for his acts of power;
praise him for his surpassing
greatness.
[3] Praise him with the sounding of the
trumpet,
praise him with the harp and lyre,
[4] praise him with tambourine and
dancing,
praise him with the strings and
flute,
[5] praise him with the clash of cymbals,
praise him with resounding
cymbals.

[6] Let everything that has breath praise
the LORD.

Praise the LORD.

[b] 1 Hebrew *Hallelu Yah;* also in verse 6

PRAYER: ADORATION

ALL Your works will praise you, O Lord, and Your saints will bless You. They will speak of the glory of Your kingdom and talk of Your power, so that all people may know of Your mighty acts and the glorious majesty of Your kingdom. Your kingdom is an everlasting kingdom, and Your dominion endures through all generations. (Psalm 145:10–13)

***PAUSE** to express your thoughts of praise and worship.*

NT Revelation 21:1–27

The New Jerusalem

21 Then I saw a new heaven and a new
earth, for the first heaven and the first
earth had passed away, and there was no
longer any sea. [2]I saw the Holy City, the
new Jerusalem, coming down out of heav-
en from God, prepared as a bride beauti-
fully dressed for her husband. [3]And I
heard a loud voice from the throne saying, "Now the dwelling of God is with
men, and he will live with them. They will
be his people, and God himself will be
with them and be their God. [4]He will
wipe every tear from their eyes. There will
be no more death or mourning or crying
or pain, for the old order of things has
passed away."
[5]He who was seated on the throne said,
"I am making everything new!" Then he
said, "Write this down, for these words are
trustworthy and true."
[6]He said to me: "It is done. I am the Alpha and the Omega, the Beginning and
the End. To him who is thirsty I will give
to drink without cost from the spring of
the water of life. [7]He who overcomes will
inherit all this, and I will be his God and
he will be my son. [8]But the cowardly, the
unbelieving, the vile, the murderers, the
sexually immoral, those who practice
magic arts, the idolaters and all liars—
their place will be in the fiery lake of
burning sulfur. This is the second death."
[9]One of the seven angels who had the

seven bowls full of the seven last plagues
came and said to me, "Come, I will show
you the bride, the wife of the Lamb."
10And he carried me away in the Spirit to
a mountain great and high, and showed
me the Holy City, Jerusalem, coming
down out of heaven from God. 11It shone
with the glory of God, and its brilliance
was like that of a very precious jewel, like
a jasper, clear as crystal. 12It had a great,
high wall with twelve gates, and with
twelve angels at the gates. On the gates
were written the names of the twelve
tribes of Israel. 13There were three gates on
the east, three on the north, three on the
south and three on the west. 14The wall of
the city had twelve foundations, and on
them were the names of the twelve apostles of the Lamb.

15The angel who talked with me had a
measuring rod of gold to measure the city,
its gates and its walls. 16The city was laid
out like a square, as long as it was wide.
He measured the city with the rod and
found it to be 12,000 stadia[a] in length,
and as wide and high as it is long. 17He
measured its wall and it was 144 cubits[b]
thick,[c] by man's measurement, which the
angel was using. 18The wall was made of
jasper, and the city of pure gold, as pure
as glass. 19The foundations of the city
walls were decorated with every kind of
precious stone. The first foundation was
jasper, the second sapphire, the third chalcedony, the fourth emerald, 20the fifth sardonyx, the sixth carnelian, the seventh
chrysolite, the eighth beryl, the ninth topaz, the tenth chrysoprase, the eleventh
jacinth, and the twelfth amethyst.[d] 21The
twelve gates were twelve pearls, each gate
made of a single pearl. The great street of
the city was of pure gold, like transparent
glass.

22I did not see a temple in the city, because the Lord God Almighty and the
Lamb are its temple. 23The city does not
need the sun or the moon to shine on it,
for the glory of God gives it light, and the
Lamb is its lamp. 24The nations will walk
by its light, and the kings of the earth will
bring their splendor into it. 25On no day
will its gates ever be shut, for there will be
no night there. 26The glory and honor of
the nations will be brought into it.
27Nothing impure will ever enter it, nor
will anyone who does what is shameful or
deceitful, but only those whose names are
written in the Lamb's book of life.

[a] *16* That is, about 1,400 miles (about 2,200 kilometers) [b] *17* That is, about 200 feet (about 65 meters) [c] *17* Or *high* [d] *20* The precise identification of some of these precious stones is uncertain.

PRAYER: THE CHARACTER I WANT TO CULTIVATE

I KNOW that friendship with the world is enmity toward You, O God. Those who want to be friends of the world make themselves Your enemies. (James 4:4) . . . The end of all things is near, Lord; therefore I will be clear-minded and self-controlled for prayer. (1 Peter 4:7)

***TAKE** a moment to ask the Lord for the grace to grow in godly character.*

YEAR 2 DAY 365

OT Malachi 3:1–4:6

3 "See, I will send my messenger, who
will prepare the way before me. Then
suddenly the Lord you are seeking will
come to his temple; the messenger of the
covenant, whom you desire, will come,"
says the LORD Almighty.

2But who can endure the day of his
coming? Who can stand when he appears? For he will be like a refiner's fire or
a launderer's soap. 3He will sit as a refiner and purifier of silver; he will purify the
Levites and refine them like gold and silver. Then the LORD will have men who
will bring offerings in righteousness, 4and
the offerings of Judah and Jerusalem will
be acceptable to the LORD, as in days gone
by, as in former years.

5"So I will come near to you for judg-

ment. I will be quick to testify against sorcerers, adulterers and perjurers, against
those who defraud laborers of their wages,
who oppress the widows and the fatherless, and deprive aliens of justice, but do
not fear me," says the LORD Almighty.

Robbing God

6 "I the LORD do not change. So you,
O descendants of Jacob, are not destroyed.
7 Ever since the time of your forefathers
you have turned away from my decrees
and have not kept them. Return to me,
and I will return to you," says the LORD
Almighty.

"But you ask, 'How are we to return?'

8 "Will a man rob God? Yet you rob me.

"But you ask, 'How do we rob you?'

"In tithes and offerings. 9 You are under
a curse—the whole nation of you—because you are robbing me. 10 Bring the
whole tithe into the storehouse, that there
may be food in my house. Test me in
this," says the LORD Almighty, "and see if
I will not throw open the floodgates of
heaven and pour out so much blessing
that you will not have room enough for
it. 11 I will prevent pests from devouring
your crops, and the vines in your fields
will not cast their fruit," says the LORD
Almighty. 12 "Then all the nations will call
you blessed, for yours will be a delightful
land," says the LORD Almighty.

13 "You have said harsh things against
me," says the LORD.

"Yet you ask, 'What have we said against
you?'

14 "You have said, 'It is futile to serve
God. What did we gain by carrying out his
requirements and going about like
mourners before the LORD Almighty?
15 But now we call the arrogant blessed.
Certainly the evildoers prosper, and even
those who challenge God escape.' "

16 Then those who feared the LORD
talked with each other, and the LORD listened and heard. A scroll of remembrance
was written in his presence concerning
those who feared the LORD and honored
his name.

17 "They will be mine," says the LORD
Almighty, "in the day when I make up my
treasured possession.[a] I will spare them,
just as in compassion a man spares his
son who serves him. 18 And you will again
see the distinction between the righteous
and the wicked, between those who serve
God and those who do not.

The Day of the LORD

4 "Surely the day is coming; it will burn
like a furnace. All the arrogant and
every evildoer will be stubble, and that
day that is coming will set them on fire,"
says the LORD Almighty. "Not a root or a
branch will be left to them. 2 But for you
who revere my name, the sun of righteousness will rise with healing in its
wings. And you will go out and leap like
calves released from the stall. 3 Then you
will trample down the wicked; they will
be ashes under the soles of your feet on
the day when I do these things," says the
LORD Almighty.

4 "Remember the law of my servant Moses, the decrees and laws I gave him at Horeb for all Israel.

5 "See, I will send you the prophet Elijah before that great and dreadful day of
the LORD comes. 6 He will turn the hearts
of the fathers to their children, and the
hearts of the children to their fathers; or
else I will come and strike the land with
a curse."

[a] 17 Or *Almighty, "my treasured possession, in the day when I act*

PRAYER: CONFESSION

HAVE You as much delight in burnt offerings and sacrifices, O Lord, as in obedience to Your voice? To obey is better than sacrifice, and to heed is better than the fat of rams. For rebellion is like the sin of divination, and stubbornness is as iniquity and idolatry.

(1 Samuel 15:22–23)

ASK *the Spirit to search your heart and reveal any areas of unconfessed sin. Acknowledge these to the Lord and thank Him for His forgiveness.*

NT Revelation 22:1–21

The River of Life

22 Then the angel showed me the river of
the water of life, as clear as crystal,
flowing from the throne of God and of the
Lamb 2down the middle of the great street
of the city. On each side of the river stood
the tree of life, bearing twelve crops of
fruit, yielding its fruit every month. And
the leaves of the tree are for the healing of
the nations. 3No longer will there be any
curse. The throne of God and of the Lamb
will be in the city, and his servants will
serve him. 4They will see his face, and his
name will be on their foreheads. 5There
will be no more night. They will not need
the light of a lamp or the light of the sun,
for the Lord God will give them light. And
they will reign for ever and ever.
6The angel said to me, "These words are
trustworthy and true. The Lord, the God
of the spirits of the prophets, sent his angel to show his servants the things that
must soon take place."

Jesus Is Coming

7"Behold, I am coming soon! Blessed is
he who keeps the words of the prophecy
in this book."

8I, John, am the one who heard and saw
these things. And when I had heard and
seen them, I fell down to worship at the feet
of the angel who had been showing them
to me. 9But he said to me, "Do not do it! I
am a fellow servant with you and with your
brothers the prophets and of all who keep
the words of this book. Worship God!"
10Then he told me, "Do not seal up the
words of the prophecy of this book, because the time is near. 11Let him who does
wrong continue to do wrong; let him who
is vile continue to be vile; let him who
does right continue to do right; and let
him who is holy continue to be holy."

12"Behold, I am coming soon! My reward is with me, and I will give to everyone according to what he has done. 13I am
the Alpha and the Omega, the First and
the Last, the Beginning and the End.
14"Blessed are those who wash their
robes, that they may have the right to the
tree of life and may go through the gates
into the city. 15Outside are the dogs, those
who practice magic arts, the sexually immoral, the murderers, the idolaters and
everyone who loves and practices falsehood.
16"I, Jesus, have sent my angel to give
you[a] this testimony for the churches. I am
the Root and the Offspring of David, and
the bright Morning Star."

17The Spirit and the bride say, "Come!"
And let him who hears say, "Come!"
Whoever is thirsty, let him come; and
whoever wishes, let him take the free gift
of the water of life.

18I warn everyone who hears the words
of the prophecy of this book: If anyone
adds anything to them, God will add to
him the plagues described in this book.
19And if anyone takes words away from
this book of prophecy, God will take away
from him his share in the tree of life and
in the holy city, which are described in
this book.
20He who testifies to these things says,
"Yes, I am coming soon."
Amen. Come, Lord Jesus.
21The grace of the Lord Jesus be with
God's people. Amen.

[a] *16* The Greek is plural.

PRAYER: MY RELATIONSHIP TO OTHERS

I WILL avoid foolish and ignorant disputes, knowing that they produce quarrels. As Your servant, O Lord, I must not quarrel but be gentle toward all, able to teach and patient. (2 Timothy 2:23–24) . . . I will not return evil for evil or insult for insult, but I will give blessing instead, because to this You called me, Lord, that I may inherit a blessing. (1 Peter 3:9)

***PAUSE** to review your relationships with others and to commit them to the Lord.*

Weights and Measures

THE FIGURES of the table are calculated on the basis of a shekel equaling 11.5 grams, a cubit equaling 18 inches and an ephah equaling 22 liters. The quart referred to is either a dry quart (slightly smaller than a liter) or a liquid quart (slightly larger than a liter), whichever is applicable. The ton referred to in the footnotes is the American ton of 2,000 pounds.

This table is based upon the best available information, but it is not intended to be mathematically precise; like the measurement equivalents in the footnotes, it merely gives approximate amounts and distances. Weights and measures differed somewhat at various times and places in the ancient world. There is uncertainty particularly about the ephah and the bath; further discoveries may shed more light on these units of capacity.

		BIBLICAL UNIT	APPROXIMATE AMERICAN EQUIVALENT	APPROXIMATE METRIC EQUIVALENT
WEIGHTS	talent	*(60* minas*)*	75 pounds	34 kilograms
	mina	*(50* shekels*)*	1 1/4 pounds	0.6 kilogram
	shekel	*(2* bekas*)*	2/5 ounce	11.5 grams
	pim	*(2/3* shekel*)*	1/3 ounce	7.6 grams
	beka	*(10* gerahs*)*	1/5 ounce	5.5 grams
	gerah		1/50 ounce	0.6 gram
LENGTH	cubit		18 inches	0.5 meter
	span		9 inches	23 centimeters
	handbreadth		3 inches	8 centimeters
CAPACITY				
Dry Measure	cor [homer]	*(10* ephahs*)*	6 bushels	220 liters
	lethek	*(5* ephahs*)*	3 bushels	110 liters
	ephah	*(10* omers*)*	3/5 bushel	22 liters
	seah	*(1/3* ephah*)*	7 quarts	7.3 liters
	omer	*(1/10* ephah*)*	2 quarts	2 liters
	cab	*(1/18* ephah*)*	1 quart	1 liter
Liquid Measure	bath	*(1* ephah*)*	6 gallons	22 liters
	hin	*(1/6* bath*)*	4 quarts	4 liters
	log	*(1/72* bath*)*	1/3 quart	0.3 liter

Index of Bible Readings

*T*HIS INDEX of the daily Bible readings in the Daily Reading & Prayer Bible is to help you locate specific passages of Scripture. The readings are listed in traditional Biblical order followed by the year and day of the reading, and the number of the page on which the passage can be found.

OT Years One and Two

GENESIS

EXODUS

LEVITICUS

NUMBERS

DEUTERONOMY

JOSHUA

JUDGES

RUTH

1 SAMUEL

2 SAMUEL

1 KINGS

2 KINGS

1 CHRONICLES

2 CHRONICLES

EZRA

NEHEMIAH

ESTHER

JOB

PSALMS

PROVERBS

ECCLESIASTES

SONG OF SONGS

ISAIAH

JEREMIAH

LAMENTATIONS

EZEKIEL

DANIEL

HOSEA

JOEL

AMOS

OBADIAH

JONAH

MICAH

NAHUM

HABAKKUK

ZEPHANIAH

HAGGAI

ZECHARIAH

MALACHI

NT Year One

MATTHEW

MARK

LUKE

JOHN

ACTS

ROMANS

1 CORINTHIANS

2 CORINTHIANS

GALATIANS

EPHESIANS

PHILIPPIANS

COLOSSIANS

1 THESSALONIANS

2 THESSALONIANS

1 TIMOTHY

2 TIMOTHY

TITUS

PHILEMON

HEBREWS

JAMES

1 PETER

2 PETER

1 JOHN

2 JOHN

3 JOHN

JUDE

REVELATION

NT Year Two

MATTHEW

MARK

LUKE

JOHN

ACTS

Daily Reading & Prayer Bible

Scripture prayers translated and adapted by
Kenneth Boa

Daily readings arranged by
Kenneth Boa

Literary agency by
Wolgemuth and Hyatt, Brentwood, TN

Project management and editorial by
Ruth DeJager

Interior design by
Sharon Wright, Belmont, MI

Interior typesetting by
Multnomah Graphics, Troutdale, OR

Interior proofreadng by
Peachtree Editorial and Proofreading Service,
Peachtree City, GA

Cover design by
Chris Tobias

Cover art by
Don Demers

Printed
by R.R. Donnelley, Crawfordsville, IN

Guarantee

Zondervan Publishing House guarantees leather Bibles unconditionally against manufacturing defects for a lifetime and hardcover and softcover Bibles for four years. This guarantee does not apply to normal wear. Contact Zondervan Customer Service, 800-727-1309, for replacement instructions.

Care

We suggest loosening the binding of your new Bible by gently pressing on a small section of pages at a time from the center. To ensure against breakage of the spine, it is best not to bend the cover backward around the spine or to carry study notes, church bulletins, pens, and the like, inside the cover. Because a felt-tipped marker will "bleed" through the pages, we recommend use of a ball-point pen or pencil to underline favorite passages. Your Bible should not be exposed to excessive heat, cold or humidity. Protecting the gold or silver edges of the paper from moisture will avoid spotting, streaking or fading.

Definitions

Bonded leather: no less than 90% leather fibers with latex base.
Top-Grain leather: 100% pigskin
Cowhide: 100% cowhide